MUSIC LOVERS' ENCYCLOPEDIA

MUSIC LOVERS' ENCYCLOPEDIA

Containing a pronouncing and defining
DICTIONARY OF TERMS, INSTRUMENTS, *etc., including*
a KEY TO THE PRONUNCIATION *of sixteen Lan-*
guages, many CHARTS; *an* EXPLANATION OF THE
CONSTRUCTION OF MUSIC *for the* UNINITIATED;
a pronouncing BIOGRAPHICAL DICTIONARY;
the STORIES OF THE OPERAS; *and numer-*
ous BIOGRAPHICAL *and* CRITICAL ESSAYS
by distinguished AUTHORITIES.

Compiled by
RUPERT HUGHES
Completely Revised and Newly Edited by
DEEMS TAYLOR
and
RUSSELL KERR

GARDEN CITY BOOKS
Garden City, New York

PUBLISHER'S PREFACE
TO THE REVISED EDITION

WHEN THE MUSIC LOVERS' ENCYCLOPEDIA was first compiled it was Rupert Hughes' effort to make it the most nearly complete desk reference work of its kind. In this he succeeded admirably. Time has, however, changed the whole world gallery of musicians and music lovers and we have therefore invited the outstanding authority in the field, Mr. Deems Taylor, to work with Mr. Russell Kerr, of *Musical America,* in the present complete revision of the book which has been the standard desk reference book on Music for nearly fifty years.

We wish to make particular acknowledgment to Simon and Schuster for permission to reprint THE MONSTER by Deems Taylor, an excerpt from OF MEN AND MUSIC, and to acknowledge that RECOLLECTIONS OF MY LAZY CHILDHOOD by Maurice Ravel is copyrighted by Opera Mundi, Paris. For permission to reprint a short passage from THE MAGIC MOUNTAIN by Thomas Mann we make acknowledgment to Alfred A. Knopf, Inc., New York, and Martin Secker and Warburg, Ltd., London. For the permission to quote from THE STORY OF MUSIC by W. J. Henderson we make acknowledgment to Longmans, Green & Co.

We have included the synopses of ninety operas. These, because of exigencies of space, represent the barest outline of plot. We therefore encourage the reader to refer to the complete librettos (in English) available from the following music publishers:

Chas. E. Burden for *Carmen, Lucia di Lammermoor, Hérodiade, The Tales of Hoffmann;* Oliver Ditson for *Mefistofele, La Gioconda, Lakmé, Romeo and Juliet, Les Huguenots, The Tales of Hoffmann, Don Giovanni, The Marriage of Figaro, Mignon, The Flying Dutchman, Der Meistersinger, Martha, La Juive, Tristan und Isolde, Tannhäuser, Das Rheingold, Die Walküre, Götterdämmerung, Parsifal;* J. Fischer, *The King's Henchman, Peter Ibbetson;* Ricordi for *La Bohème, Tosca, Madame Butterfly, The Girl of the Golden West, Gianni Schicchi, La Rondine, Turandot, L'Amore dei Tre Re, Falstaff, Manon Lescaut;* F. Rullman for *Fidelio, Norma, La Sonnambula, Ariadne and Bluebeard,*

Orfeo ed Euridice, Faust, Hänsel und Gretel, Königskinder, Cavalleria Rusticana, Manon, L'Africaine, Le Prophète, The Magic Flute, The Barber of Seville, William Tell, The Bartered Bride, Salome, Aïda, Otello, Rigoletto, La Traviata, Il Trovatore, Lohengrin, Siegfried, Der Freischütz, Werther, Prince Igor, Emperor Jones, La Juive, Boris Godunoff, Cosi Fan Tutte, L'Heure Espagnole, Sadko, Simon Boccanegra, Schwanda, The Snow Maiden, Le Coq d'Or, Le Rossignol; G. Schirmer for *The Jewels of the Madonna, Le Donne Curiose, I Pagliacci, Secret of Suzanne, The Man Without a Country, Cyrano, Natoma, Marouf;* Steinway & Sons for *Louise, Pelléas et Mélisande, Le Jongleur de Notre Dame, Thaïs, Elektra, The Tales of Hoffmann.*

For the use of the Bach Family Tree facing page 482, we make acknowledgment to the Macmillan Company, publishers of *Dictionary of Music and Musicians,* by Sir George Grove, edited by J. A. Fuller Maitland.

INTRODUCTION

By Deems Taylor

O NE OF MY EARLY recollections is that of poring delightedly over the pages of my father's encyclopaedia. It was entitled, as I recall, *Chambers' Library of Universal Knowledge,* and had been published, in several volumes, some time in the early seventies. My father had acquired it as a young man. I mention it here because of a phrase from it that still sticks in my memory. It occurred in the course of the article on appendicitis, conveying the information that the only remedy for this malady was "the application of leeches to the abdomen."

Which statement is, I think, a fairly vivid illustration of the reason why it is advisable, from time to time, to issue revised editions of reference works. Not, I hasten to add, that the earlier editions of the *Music Lovers' Encyclopedia* contained such howlers as the one I have quoted. Music is a vaguer and at the same time more exact science than medicine. Its laws may be more intuitive than rational, but they are less liable to repeal. An elder generation of musicologists seldom needs to blush in the presence of its juniors.

None the less this work has needed revision in order to repair, not its mistakes, but its omissions. Lamentable as these omissions were, they are pardonable, in view of the fact that the events that should have been chronicled had not yet occurred. Musical history has moved fast during the past fifty years. In 1903, the year the first edition of this book appeared, Verdi had been dead just two years. Giacomo Puccini had finished his sixth opera, based on John Luther Long's play, *"Madame Butterfly,"* and was arranging for its production at La Scala in Milan; Richard Strauss had started work on an operatic version of Oscar Wilde's *Salome;* and Claude Debussy had just written to his publishers that he was busy with a trio of symphonic sketches to be called *La Mer.* Arnold Schönberg, who was later to horrify the conventional musical world with his harmonic theories, had not yet composed his pleasant but innocuous *"Verklärte Nacht";* Jan Sibelius had published his first symphony two years before; and

vii

a young Russian named Igor Stravinsky was studying orchestration with Rimsky-Korsakov.

Even in 1912, when the second edition appeared, Strauss's *"Der Rosenkavalier"* existed only as a mass of sketches; Montemezzi's *"L'Amore Dei Tre Re"* was promised for the following year, but no one had heard it. Maurice Ravel's *"Daphnis et Chloë"* had just had its first performance, in Paris, by the Diaghileff Ballet Russe. The young Russian, Stravinsky, was putting the finishing touches to another ballet for Diaghileff, *"Le Sacre du Printemps,"* that was destined to make musical history. Jan Sibelius had just published his fourth symphony. Phonographs were using a mechanical pickup; the sound-film was unthought-of, and radio was a dream.

Hence the need for this new edition of a work that has been proving its usefulness for many years. As in the earlier editions, it is divided into two main sections: a dictionary of musical terms, and a biographical dictionary of musicians. This seems to me to be a sensible and convenient differentiation. One is not likely to be anxious for information concerning "Mendelssohn" and "metronome" at the same instant. The bulk of the revision, naturally, has been done in the biographical section; and in this department the revised edition of the *Music Lovers' Encyclopedia* may venture to claim to be the most completely up-to-date work in this or any other country. Eight hundred new names have been added, making the chronology and necrology complete up to 1954, and encompassing a completely new "Supplementary List of Modern Composers."

As a rule, biographical dictionaries grade musicians according to their purely academic importance. This practice results in the inclusion and over-emphasising of many persons whose work is no actual, important contribution to music as a living art. In this edition we have attempted to include new personalities that are playing an important part in the modern world of music, not only in the field of composition, but also in that of production and performance.

I say "we." As a matter of fact, the merits of the revised biographical dictionary are almost entirely due to the extraordinarily conscientious and expert labours of Mr. Russell Kerr, of the staff of the New York *Musical America,* and whose share in the production of this work is hereby gratefully acknowledged.

The charts and tables of the earlier editions have been retained and revised. They should be useful, particularly the table showing the pronunciation of the various letters of the alphabet as they occur in sixteen modern languages. There may be a similar chart published elsewhere; if there is, I am unfamiliar with it. Likewise retained, verbatim, is the prefatory *An Introduction to Music*, by this book's first editor, Rupert Hughes. Mr. Hughes, who is chiefly known to the world as a novelist, is a musical amateur in the finest sense of the word, a music-lover who has studied and practiced the art of music all his life, purely for the fun of it. To realise that profound scholarship can be coexistent with an amateur standing, you have only to read his chapter. Naturally the science of music has progressed. The past quarter of a century has seen the development of theories concerning harmony, counterpoint, melody, and rhythm that were unthinkable in 1903. Nevertheless the *fundamentals* of music remain constant, and almost any literate and intelligent lay music-lover should be able to obtain the foundation of a musical education by reading this *Introduction to Music*. Written nearly fifty years ago, it remains a sound and useful little treatise.

The section entitled *Stories of the Operas* originally contained synopses of the plots of sixty operas in the standard repertoire. Since the last edition of this book was published, a few have so definitely joined the limbo of forgotten things that there seemed to be no further use in including them. They have, accordingly, been dropped from the present roster. "In revenge," as the French say, we have added the stories of thirty-four additional operas that have been either added or restored to the repertoire during the past twenty years.

One of the most admired features of the *Music Lovers' Encyclopedia* has been its series of contributed essays by eminent musical authorities, discussing various branches of music and the lives of famous composers. The best of these have been retained, and many more added. Moreover, instead of being scattered alphabetically through the dictionary sections of the book, they have been brought together in two special sections of their own, to the great enhancement of their readability and accessibility.

"The marriage of completeness with conciseness," writes Rupert Hughes in his preface to the first edition of this book, "is a hard knot to tie." That statement has lost none of its truth. It is manifestly hopeless, in a single volume, to cover every phase of music in the detail that is offered by the great musical encyclopaedias and the countless biographies of individual composers that have appeared within the past decade. On the other hand, we offer discussions of more subjects, biographies of more musicians, than any other single volume that I know. Our definitions and biographical sketches may be brief, but they present the main facts; and they are, so far as is humanly possible to make them so, accurate. It is our hope that this new edition of the *Music Lovers' Encyclopedia* may continue to be what it has always been, a storehouse of information to the layman, and a useful reminder to the expert.

DEEMS TAYLOR

CONTENTS

CONTENTS

SYNOPSES OF NINETY OPERAS CURRENT IN PRESENT-DAY REPERTOIRES

CONTENTS

CONTENTS

LIST OF CHARTS

PHONETIC MEANING
OF THE LETTERS AND SYMBOLS USED
IN THE PRONUNCIATION OF NAMES

ä as in father; *ā* as in fate; *ă* as in fat; *än* and *ăn* as in French *élan* and *fin*.

b as in bob.

c used only in *ch*, as in church. The Scotch and German guttural as in *loch* and *ich* is indicated by *kh*.

d as in deed; *dh* as *th* in these; *dj* as in adjoin.

ē as in bean; *ĕ* as in pet—at the end of words it is almost like *ŭ*.

f as in fife.

g as in gig.

h as in hate.

ī as in fight; *ĭ* as in pin.

j as in jug.

k as in kick; *kh* is used here to indicate the German or Scotch *ch* or *g*.

m as in mum.

n as in nun; *ṅ* indicates the French nasal *n* or *m*.

ō as in note; *oi* as in noise; *oo* as in moon or foot; *ô* as in wrong; *ow* as in cow; *ôṅ* as in French *bon*.

p as in pop.

r as in roar.

s as in sense.

t as in tot; *th* as in think; the sound of *th* in these is indicated by *dh*.

ū always with the sound of you; the French *u* and the German long *ü* are both indicated by *ü*.

v as in revive.

w as in will.

x as in fix.

y as in yoke.

z as in zone.

PRONOUNCING DICTIONARY OF
GIVEN NAMES, TITLES, EPITHETS, ETC.

abbate (äb′-bä-tĕ), *I.* **abbé** (äbbā), *F.* Abbot (often honorary).

l'ainé (lĕn-ā), *F.* The elder. **cadet** (kă-dā), *F.* The younger. Usually of brothers.

camerlingo (kä-mĕr-lēn′-gō), *I.* Chamberlain.

cantab(rigiensis). Of Cambridge University.

cavaliere (kä-väl-yā′-rĕ), *I.* Knight, sir.

chevalier (shŭ-văl-yā), *F.* Knight.

cie, *F.* Company; et cie (ä sē). & Co.

comte (kôṅt), *F.*

conte (kōn′-tĕ), *I.* Count.

detto or **-a** (dĕt′-tō). "Called."

duc (dük), *F.* **duca** (doo′-kä), *I.* Duke.

Edler von (āt′-ler fōn). Nobleman of.

fils (fēs), *F.* Son.

Frau (frow), *G.* Mrs. **Fräulein** (frī′-lin). Miss.

Freiherr (frī′-hăr), *G.* Baron.

Geheimrath (gĕ-hīm′-rät), *G.* Privy counsellor.

Gesellschaft (gĕ-zĕl′-shäft), *G.* Association, society.

Graf (gräf), *G.* Count. **Gräfin** (grä-fĭn). Countess.

Herr (hăr), *G.* Mr.

Hauptkirche (howpt-kēr′-khĕ), *G.* Chief church.

Hofkapellmeister (mī-shtĕr). Court-conductor. **Hofmusik′intendant** (moo-zek′), *G.* Supt. of court-music.

le jeune (lŭ zhŭn), *F.* The younger.

Justizrath (yoos′-tēts-rät), *G.* Counsellor of justice; often honorary.

Kammersänger (zĕngk-ĕr), *G.* Chamber-singer (to the court).

maestro (ᴍä-äs′-tro), *I.* Master.

il maggiore (ēl mäd-jō′-rĕ), *I.* The greater.

maistre (old French), or **maître** (mĕtr), *F.* Master.

marchesa (mär-kä′-zä), *I.* Marchioness.

il minore (ēl-mē-nō′-rĕ), *I.* The lesser.

mus. bach(elor) and **mus.** doc(tor). Vide the D. D.

oxon(ensis). Of Oxford University.

père (păr), *F.* Father.

Reichsfreiherr (rīkhs′-frī-hăr), *G.* Baron of the empire.

Ritter (rĭt′-tĕr), *G.* Knight, chevalier.

sieur (s'yŭr), *F.* Sir, Mr.

und Sohn (oont zōn), *G.* & Son. **und Söhne** (oont zā′-nĕ), *G.* & Sons.

van (vän), *Dutch.* **von** (fōn), *G.* de (dŭ), *F.* **di** (dē), *I.* and *Sp.* From, of.

vicomtesse (vē-kôn-tĕs). Viscountess.

le vieux (lŭ v'yŭ), *F.* The elder.

y (ē), *Sp.* "And," used in joining two proper names somewhat as we use a hyphen; the Spaniard keeping his mother's as well as his father's name.

zu (tsoo), *G.* To.

(Others will be found in the D. D.)

NOTE.—In the Biographical Dictionary, given names are regularly abbreviated as in the following list, the same abbreviation serving for one name in its different forms in different languages.

Abramo (ä′-brä-mō), *I.*

Adam (ä′-däm), *G.*

Adalbert (ä′-däl-bĕrt), *G.*

Adelaide (ä-dā-lä-ē′-dĕ), *I.* and *G.*

(Ad.) Adolf (ä′-dôlf), *G.*

(Ad.) Adolph, *G.*

(Ad.) Adolphe (ăd-ôlf), *F.*

(Adr.) Adriano (ä-drī-ä′-nō), *I.*

Adrien (ăd′-rĭ-äṅ), *F.*

Agathon (ä′-gä-tōn), *G.*

(Ag.) Agostino (ä-gôs-tē′-nō), *I.*

Aimable (ĕm-äb″l), *F.*

(Alb.) Albrecht (äl′-brĕkht), *G.*

(Ales.) Alessandro (ä-lĕs-sän′-drō), *I.*

(Alex.) Alexan′der.

(Alex.) Alexandre (ăl-ĕx-äṅdr′), *F.*

Alexis (ăl-ĕx-ēs), *F.*

Aloys (ä-lois).

Aloysia (ä-loi′-zĭ-ä), *G.*

Amadeo (äm-ä-dā′-ō), *I.* **-deus** (dä′-oos), *G.*

Amalie (ä′-mäl-ē), *G.*

Ambroise (äṅ-bwäz), *F.*

Amédée (ăm′-ā-dā), *F.*

Amélie (ăm′-ä-lē), *F.*

Anatole (ăn-ä-tôl), *F.*

André (äṅ-drā), *F.*

(And.) Andrea (än′-drä-ä), *I.*

(Ands) Andreas (än′-drä-äs), *G.*

Ange (äṅzh), *F.*

Angelica (än-jä′-lē-kä), *I.*

(Ang.) Angelo (än′-jä-lō), *I.*

(A. or Ant.) Antoine (äṅ-twän), *F.*

(Ant.) Anton (än′-tōn), *G.*

(A. or Ant.) Anto′nio, *I.*
(Ap.) Apollon (ăp-ŏl-lóṅ), *F.*
Aristide (är-ĭs-tēd), *F.*
Armin (är′-mēn), *G.*
Arnaud (ăr-nō), *F.*
Arrigo (är′-rē-gō), *I.*
Arsène (är-sĕn), *F.*
Arthur (ăr-tür), *F.*
Attilio (ät-tē′-lĭ-ō), *I.*
(Aug.) August (ow′-goost), *G.*
Auguste (ō-güst), *F.*
Augustin (ow′-goos-ten, *G.*) (ō-güs-täṅ, *F.*).
(Aug.) Augusto (ä-oo-goost′-ō), *I.*

Baldassare (bäl-däs-sä′-rĕ), *I.*
(Bal.) Balthasar (bäl-tă-zăr′), *F.*
(Bap.) Baptiste (bă-tēst), *F.*
(Bart.) Bartolommeo (bär-tō-lóm-mä′-ō), *I.*
(Bat.) Battista (bät-tē′-stä), *I.*
Benedikt (bā′-nĕ-dēkt), *G.*
Beniamino (bän-yĕ-mē′-nō), *I.*
(Bv.) Benvenuto (bän-vĕ-noo′-tŏ), *I.*
(Bdo.) Bernardo (bĕr-när′-dō), *I.*
(Bd.) Bernhard (bärn′-härt), *G.*
Bertrand (bĕr-träṅ), *F.*
Bianca (bē-än′-kä), *I.*
Blasius (blä′-zĭ-oos), *G.*
Bonaventure (bón-ăv-äṅ-tür′), *F.*
Bonifacio (bō-nē-fä′-chō), *I.*
Bonafazio (bōn-ē-fä′-tsĭ-ō), *I.*
Brigida (brē′-jē-dä), *I.*

Camille (kăm-ē′-yŭ), *F.*
Carlo (kär′-lō), *I.*
Casimir (kăs-ĭ-mēr), *F.*
Catherino (kät-tĕr-rē′-nō), *I.*
Caytan (kä′-ē-tän), *Sp.*
César (sā-zăr), *F.*
Cesare (chā-zä′-rĕ), *I.*
(Chas.) Charles (shärl), *F.*
Chrisostomus (krē-sós′-tō-moos), *G.*
(Chr.) Christian (krēst′-ĭ-än), *G.*
(Chp.) Christoph (krĕs′-tóph), *G.*
Cinthie (săṅ-tē), *F.*
Claude (klōd), *F.*
Clément (klā-mäṅ), *F.*
Clotilde (klō-tēl′-dĕ), *G.*
Colin (kó-läṅ), *F.*
Constanze (kón-stän′-tsĕ), *G.*
Cornelius (kŏr-nā′-lĭ-oos), *G.*
Costanzo (kō-stän′-tsō), *I.*

Damaso (dä-mä′-sō), *Sp.*
(D.) David (dä-vēd), *F.*
(D.) David (dä′-fēt), *G.*
Delphin (dĕl-făṅ), *F.*
Dietrich (dēt′-rĭkh), *G.*
Dieudonné (d′yŭ-dŭn-nā), *F.*
Diogenio (dē-ō-jä-nē′-ō), *I.*
Dioma (dē-ō′-mä), *I.*

(Dion.) Dionisio (dĕ-ᴜ-nè′-sĭ-ō), *Sp.*
Dionys (dē′-o-nēs), *G.*
(Dom.) Domenico (dō-mä′-nĭ-kō), *I.*
(Dom.) Dominique (dŏm-ĭ-nēk), *F.*
Dufrèsne (dü-frĕn), *F.*

(Edm.) Edmond (ĕd-móṅ), *F.*
(Edm.) Edmund (ät′-moont), *G.*
(Edw.) Edward (äd-văr), *F.*
Egidio (ä-jē′-dĭ-ō), *I.*
Eleonore (ä-lä-ō-nō′-rĕ), *G.*
Eléonore (ä-lä-ō-nór), *F.* Also a masculine name.
Elias (ä-lē′-äs), *G.*
Eligio (ä-lē′-jō), *I.*
Eliodoro (ä-lĭ-ō-dō′-rō), *I.*
Eliseo (ä-lē′-zä-ō), *I.*
Eliza (ä-lē′-zä), *I.*
(Em.) Emanuel (ä-män-wĕl), *F.*
Emil (ä-mēl), *G.*
Emilie (ä′-mĭ-lē), *F.*
(Em.) Emilio (ä-mēl′-yō), *I.*
(Emm.) Emmanuele (ĕm-mäṅ-oo-ä′-lĕ), *I.*
(Eng.) Engelbert (ĕng′-ĕl-bĕrt), *G.*
Enrico (ĕn-rē′-kō), *I.*
Erasmo (ä-räs′-mō), *I.*
Ercole (är′-kō-lä′), *I.*
(Erh.) Erhard (ăr′-härt), *G.*
Ernst (ärnst), *G.*
Errico (ĕr′-rĭ-kō), *I.*
(Et.) Etienne (ät′-yĕn), *F.*
(Eug.) Eugen (oi-gän), *G.*
(Eug.) Eugène (ŭ-zhĕn′), *F.*
(Eug.) Eugenio (ä-oo-jä′-nĕ-ō), *I.*
Eustache (ŭs-täsh), *F.*
Evarista (ä-vä-rē′-stä), *I.*

Fabio (fäb′-yō), *I.*
(F.) Felice (fä-lē′-chĕ).
Félicien (fā-lĕs-yäṅ), *F.*
(F.) Félix (fä′-lēx), *F.*
(F.) Felix (fä-lēx), *G.*
(Fd.) Ferdinand (făr′-dĭ-nänt, *G.*) (fär-dĭ-näṅ, *F.*).
(Fdo.) Ferdinando (fĕr-dē-nän′-dō), *I.*
Ferencz (fĕr′-ĕns), *Hung.*
Féréol (fā-rā-ól), *F.*
Fernandez (fĕr-nän′-dĕth), *Sp.*
Fernando (fĕr-nän′-dō), *I.*
Ferruccio (fĕr-root′-chō), *I.*
Firmin (fĕr-mäṅ), *F.*
Florence (flór-äṅs), *F.* Commonly a masculine name.
Florian (flór-yäṅ, *F.*) (flór′-ĭ-än, *G.*).
(Ft.) Fortunato (fór-too-nä′-tō), *I.*
(Fran.) Francesco (frän-chäs′-kō), *I.*
Francesco (frän-thäs′-kō), *Sp.*
Francisco (frän-thēs′-kō), *Sp.*
(Fran.) François (fräṅ-swä), *F.*
Frantisek (frän′-tĭ-shĕk), *Bohemian.*

PRONOUNCING DICTIONARY

(Fz.) **Franz** (fränts), *G.*
(Fr.) **Frédéric** (frä-dä-rēk), *F.*
Fridolin (frē'-dō-lēn), *G.*
(Fr.) **Friedrich** (frēt'-rĭkh), *G.*

Gabriele (gä-brĭ-ā'-lĕ), *G.*
(Gaet.) **Gaetano** (gä-ä-tä'-nō), *I.*
(Gasp.) **Gasparo** (gäs-pä'-rō), *I.*
Gellio (jĕl'-lĭ-ō), *I.*
Geminiano (jĕm-ēn-ĭ-ä'-nō), *I.*
Gennaro (gĕn-nä'-rō), *I.*
(G.) **Georg** (gä-ôrkh'), *G.*
(G.) **George**, *E.*
(G.) **Georges** (zhôrzh), *F.*
(Ger.) **Gerolamo** (jĕ-rō'-lä-mō), *I.*
(Geron.) **Geronimo** (jĕ-rō'-nĭ-mō), *I.*
Gervais (zhĕr-vĕ'), *F.*
Gesu (hä'-zoo), *Sp.*
Ghislein (ges-lăṅ), *F.*
Giacinto (jä-chēn'-tō), *I.*
Giacomo (jäk'-ō-mō), *I.*
Gialdino (jäl-dē'-nō), *I.*
Gioacchino (jō-ä-kē'-nō), *I.*
Giordano (jôr-dä-nō), *I.*
Gioseffo (jō-sĕf'-fō), *I.*
(Giov.) **Giovanne** (jō-vän'-nĕ), *I.*
Giuditta (joo-dĭt'-tä), *I.*
Giulia (jool'-yä), *I.*
Giulio (jool'-yō), *I.*
(Gius.) **Giuseppe** (joo-sĕp'-pĕ), *I.*
Gjula (gū'-lä), *Hung.*
Gotifredo (gō-tē-frä'-dō), *I.*
(Gf.) **Gottfried** (gôt'-frēt), *G.*
Gotthard (gôt'-härt), *G.*
(Gh.) **Gotthilf** (gôt'-hĭlf), *G.*
(Gl.) **Gottlieb** (gôt'-lēp), *G.*
Gottlob (gôt'-lōp), *G.*
Gregorio (grä-gō'-rĭ-ō), *I.*
Guido (goo-ē'-dō), *I.*
(Guil.) **Guillaume** (gē-yōm), *F.*
(Gv.) **Gustav** (goos'-täf), *G.*
(Gve.) **Gustave** (güs-täv), *F.*

Hamish (hä'-mēsh), *Gaelic.*
Hans (häns), *G.*
(H.) **Heinrich** (hĭn'-rĭkh).
(H.) **Henri** (äṅ-rē), *F.*
(H.) **Hen'ry.**
(Hn.) **Hermann** (hăr'-män), *G.*
Hieronymus (hē-ĕr-ōn'-ē-moos), *G.*
(Hip.) **Hippolyte** (ēp-ō-lēt), *F.*
Hugo (hoo'-gō, *G.*) (ü-gō, *F.*).

(Ign.) **Ignace** (ēn-yăs), *F.*
(Ign.) **Ignazio** (ēn-yät'-sĭ-ō), *I.*
(I.) **Igraz** (ēkh'-räts), *G.*
Ilitch (ē'-lĭtsh), *Rus.*
Ilja (ēl'-jä), *Rus.*
Ingeborg (ĭng'-ĕ-bôrkh), *G.*
(Ipp.) **Ippolito** (ēp-pō-lē'-tō), *I.*
Isidore (ē-zē-dôr), *F.*
Italo (ēt'-ä-lō). *I.*

Jacob (yäk'-ōp), *G.*
Jacopo (yäk'-ō-pō), *I.*
(Jac.) **Jacques** (zhăk), *F.*
Jan (yän), *Dutch.*
Jan (yän), *Polish.*
Javier (häv-yăr), *Sp.*
(J.) **Jean** (zhäṅ), *F.*
Jefte (yĕf'-tĕ), *I.*
Jérome (zhä-rôm), *F.*
(Joa.) **Joachim** (yö'-ä-khēm), *G.*
Joaquin (wä'-kēn), *Sp.*
(Jn.) **Johann** (yō'-hän), *G.*
(Jns.) **Johannes** (yō-hän'-nĕs), *G.*
(J.) **John.**
José (hō-zā'), *Sp.*
(Jos.) **Josef**, or **Joseph** (yō'-zĕf, G ';
 (zhō-zĕf, *F.*).
Josquin (zhôs-kăṅ), *F.*
Juan (hoo-än'), *Sp.*
Jules (zhül), *F.*
Julie (zhü-lē), *F.*
Julien (zhül-yăṅ), *F.*
Juliette (zhül-yĕt), *F.*
Julius (yoo'-lĭ-oos), *G.*
Juste (zhüst), *F.*
Justin (zhüs-tăṅ), *F.*

Karl (kärl), *G.*
Karoline (kä-rō-lē'-nĕ), *G.*
Kasper (käs'-pĕr), *G.*
(Kd.) **Konrad** (kôn'-rät), *G.*
(Konst.) **Konstantin** (kōn-stän-tēn), *G.*

Ladislaw (lăd'-ĭs-lăf), *Pol.*
Laure (lōr), *F.*
Laurent (lō-räṅ), *F.*
Leberecht (lä'-bĕ-rĕkht), *G.*
Léon (lä'-ôṅ), *F.*
Léonard (lä-ō-năr), *F.*
Léonce (lä-ôṅs), *F.*
Leone (lä-ō'-nĕ), *I.*
(Ld.) **Léopold** (lä-ŭ-pôld), *F.*
(Ld.) **Leopold** (lä-ō-pōlt), *G.*
Lopez (lō'-pĕth), *Sp.*
(Lor.) **Lorenz** (lō'-rĕnts), *G.*
(L.) **Louis** (loo-ē), *F.*
Louise (loo-ēz), *F.*
Luca (loo'-kä), *I.*
Lucien (lüs-yäṅ), *F.*
Lucrezia (loo-krä'-tsē-ä), *I.*
(Lud.) **Ludovico** (loo-dō-vē'-kŏ), *I.*
(L.) **Ludwig** (loot'-vĭkh), *G.*
(L.) **Luigi** (loo-ē'-jē), *I.*
Luigia (loo-ē'-jä), *I.*
Luise (loo-ē'-zĕ), *G.*

Manfredo (män-frä'-dō), *I.*
Manuel (män'-oo-ĕl), *G.*
Marcello (mär-chĕl'-lō), *I.*
Marco (mär'-kō), *I.*
Marguerite (măr-gŭ-rēt'), *F.*
(M.) **Maria** (mä-rē'-ä), *G., I.* and *Sp.*
 Commonly a masculine name.

Marie (mă-rē), *F.* Commonly a masculine name.
Mathias (mä-tē'-ăs), *F.* and *G.*
Mathieu (măt-yŭ), *F.*
(Mat.) Matteo (mät-tä'-ō), *I.*
Matthäus (mät-tä'-oos), *G.*
Mattia (mät-tē'-ä), *I.*
Maturin (măt-ŭ-răṅ), *F.*
Maurice (mō-rēs), *F.*
Max (mäx), *G.*
Maximilian (mäx-ĭ-mēl'-ĭ-än), *G.*
Melchior (mĕl-shĭ-ôr), *F.*
Melchiore (mĕl-kĭ-ō'-rĕ), *I.*
Michael (mē'-kä-ĕl), *I.*
Michel (mē-shĕl), *F.*
Michele (mē-kä'-lĕ), *I.*
Miroslaw (mē'-rō-släf), *Russian.*
Modeste (mō-dĕst), *F.*
Moritz (mō'-rēts), *G.*
Muzio (moo'-tsĭ-ō), *I.*

Napoléon (nă-pō'-lä-ȯṅ), *F.*
Natale (nä-tä'-lĕ), *I.*
Nepomuk (nä'-pō-mook), *G.*
Niccola (nēk'-kō-lä), *I.*
(N.) Nich'olas, *E.*
(N.) Nicolas (nē-kō-lăs), *F.*
(N.) Nicolò (nē-kō-lō'), *I.*
Nikolai (nē'-kō-lä'), *G.*
(N.) Nikolaus (ne'-kō-lows), *G.*

Octave (ȯk-tăv), *F.*
Orazio (ō-rä·-tsĭ'-ō), *I.*
Otto (ȯt'-tō), *G.*
Ottokar (ȯt'-tō-kär), *Pol.*

Pantaléon (pän-tä-lä-ȯṅ), *F.*
Paolo (pä'-ō-lō), *I.*
Pascal (păs-kăl), *F.*
Pasquale (päs-kwä'-lĕ), *I.*
Paul (pōl), *F.*
Pedro (pä'-dhrō), *Sp.*
Peregrino (pä-rä-grē··nō), *I.*
(P.) Peter.
(P.) Peter (pä'-tĕr), *G.*
Philibert (fē-lĭ-băr), *F.*
(Ph.) Philipp (fē'-lĭp), *G.*
(Ph.) Philippe (fē-lēp), *F.*
Pierluigi (pē-är-loo-ē'-jē), *I.*
(P.) Pierre (pĭ-är'), *F.*
(P.) Pietro (pĭ-ā'-trō), *I.*
Polibio (pō-lē'-bē-ō), *I.*
Pompeo (pȯm-pä'-ō), *I.*
Primo (prē'-mō), *I.*
Prosper (prȯs'-pär), *F.*
Prudent (prü-däṅ), *F.*

Rafael (rä'-fä-ĕl), *I.* and *Sp.*
Regnault (rĕn-yō), *F.*
Reichardt (rīkh'-ärt), *G.*
Reinhold (rīn'-hōlt), *G.*

Réné (rä-nä), *F.*
(R.) Rob'ert, *E.* (in *F.* rō'-băr, in *G.* rō'-bärt).
Roberte (rō-bärt), *F.*
(R.) Rober'to, *I.*
Romano, *I.*
Romualdo (rōm-oo-äl'-dō), *I.*
Rose (rōz), *F.*
(Rud.) Rudolf (roo'-dôlf), *G.*
Ruggiero (rood-jä'-rō), *I.*
Ruprecht (roo'-prĕkht), *G.*

Sabine (zä-bē'-nĕ), *G.*
(S.) Salvatore (säl-vä-tō'-rĕ), *I.*
(Sml.) Samuel (zäm'-oo-ĕl), *G.*
Scipione (shē-pĭ-ō'-nĕ), *I.*
Sebald (zä'-bält), *G.*
(Séb.) Sébastian (sä-băst-yäṅ), *F.*
(Seb.) Sebastiano (sä-bäs-tĭ'-ä'-nō), *I.* and *Sp.*
Siegfried (zēkh'-frēt), *G.*
Siegmund (zēkh'-moont), *G.*
Simon (zē'-mōn), *G.*
(Sim.) Simone (sē'-mō-nĕ), *I.*
Spiro (spē'-rō).
Steffano (stĕf-fä'-nō), *I.*
Sylvain (sēl-văṅ), *F.*

Teodulo (tä-ō-doo'-lo), *I.*
Teresa (tä-rä'-sä), *I.*
Theobald (tä'-ō-bält), *G.*
Theodor (tä'-ō-dôr), *G.*
(The.) Théodore (tä-ŭ-dȯr), *F.*
(T.) Thomas.
Thueskon (too-ĕs'-kōn), *G.*
(Tim.) Timothée (tē-mō-tä'), *F.*
(T.) Tommasso (tȯm-mäs'-sō), *I*
Traugott (trow'-gȯt), *G.*
Turlogh (toor'-lȯkh), *G.*

(Val.) Valentin (văl-äṅ-tăṅ), *F.*
Venanzio (vä-nän'-tsĭ-ō), *I.*
(V.) Vincent (văn-säṅ), *F.*
(V.) Vincent (fēn'-tsĕnt), *G.*
(V.) Vincenzo (vēn-chän'-tsō), *I.*
Vincesleo (vēn-chĕs-lä'-ō), *I.*
Violante (vē-ō-län'-tĕ), *I.*

Wendela (vĕn'-dĕ-lä), *G.*
Wenzel (vĕn'-tsĕl), *G.*
Werner (văr'-nĕr), *G.*
(Wm.) Wilhelm (vĕl'-hĕlm), *G.*
Wilhelmine (vēl-hĕl-mē'-nĕ), *G.*
Wilibald (vē'-lĭ-bält), *G.*
Willem (wĭl'-lĕm), *Dutch.*
(Wm.) William, *E.*
Woldemar (vōl'-dĕ-mär), *G.*
(Wg.) Wolfgang (vȯlf-gäng), *G.*
Wulf (voolf), *G.*

(X.) Xavier (ksăv-yä), *F.*
(X.) Xavier (zä-fēr'), *G.*

A LIST OF ABBREVIATIONS, TITLES, DIGNITIES, INSTITUTIONS, ETC.

Acad., Academy.
a capp. (*I.,* *a cappella*), unaccompanied.
acc., according(ly).
accomp., accompaniment.
allg., allgem. (*G.,* *allgemein*), universal, general.
app., appointed.
apt., appointment.
Arab., Arabian.
Archbp., Archbishop.
arr., arranged, arrangement.
asst., assistant.

b., born.
bandm., bandmaster.
bar., barytone.
B. D., used of the Biographical Dictionary in this volume.
biog., biography, biographical.

c., composed.
ca circa (*L.*), about.
cath., cathedral.
Cav. (*I., Cavaliere*), Chevalier.
cent., century, as *18th cent.*
cf. (*L., confer*), compare.
ch., church, chorus, choir.
chapelle (*F.*), chapel, choir.
Chev., Chevalier.
choirm., choirmaster.
clar., clarinet.
coll., collected, collection, collector, college.
collab., collaborated, collaboration.
comp(s)., composition(s).
cond., conducted, conductor (this abbreviation is here used for the equivalents in various languages, *Kapellmeister, maestro di cappella, maître de chapelle,* etc.).
Cons., Conservatory (Conservatoire, Conservatorio, Conservatorium).
cpt., counterpoint.
cptist., contrapuntist (used of an early composer of highly contrapuntal works).
ct., court; **ct.-cond.,** court-conductor; **ct.-Th.,** court-theatre; **ct.-opera,** court-opera.

d., died.
D. D., used of the Dictionary of Definitions in this volume.
dict., dictionary.

dir., director.
do., ditto.
dram., dramatic.
Dr. jur. (*L., doctor juris*), Doctor of Law(s).
Dr. phil. (*L., doctor philosophiæ*), Doctor of Philosophy. *h. c.* (*L. honoris causa,* i.e., honorarily.)

eccl., ecclesiastical.
ed., edited, editor, edition.
e. g. (*L., exempli gratia*), for example.
eng., engaged.
Engl., England, English.
est., establ., established.
et seq. (*L., et sequentes, sequentia*) and the following.

F., Fr., French.
Fest., Festival.
fl., flute.
fragm., fragmentary; fragment(s).
F. (R.) C. O., Fellow of the (Royal) College of Organists, London.
Frl. (*G., Fräulein*), Miss.

G., Ger., German.
gen., general.
Govt., Government.
Gr., Greek.
gr., grand.
grossherzöglich (grôs-hăr-tsäkh-lĭkh, *G.*), Grandducal.
Gym., Gymnasium.

harm., harmony.
harps., harpsichord.
h. c. (*L., honoris causa*), used of honorary titles.
Heb., Hebrew.
herzöglich (*G.*), Ducal.
H. M.'s Th., Her Majesty's Theatre, London.
Hochschule (hôkh'-shoo-lĕ, *G.*), "High School," college, university.
Hof (hôf, *G.*), court; a frequent prefix, as in *Hof-kapelle,* court-chapel, or court-orchestra; *Hof Kapellmeister,* court-conductor; *Hofmusikintendant,* superintendent of the court-music, etc.
hon., honorary.
Hun., Hungarian.

I., It., Ital., Italian.
ib., ibid. (*L.*, *ibidem*), in the same place.
id. (*L.*, *idem*), the same.
i. e. (*L.*, *id est*), that is.
Imp., Imperial.
Incid. music, incidental music (to a
    drama).
incl., including.
inst., institute, institution.
instr(s)., instrument(s), instrumental.
introd., introduction, introduced.
inv., invented, inventor.

Jap., Japanese.

L., Latin.
libr., librarian.
lit., literally.
lyr., lyric.

m., married.
M(aestro) (*I.*), teacher, conductor;
    m. al cembalo, the conductor, who
    formerly sat at the harpsichord; *m.
    dei putti*, Master of the choir-boys.
m. de chap. (*F.*, *maître de chappelle*),
    conductor.
m. di capp. (*I.*, *maestro di cappella*)
    conductor.
M. E., Methodist Episcopal.
melodr., melodrama.
Met. Op., Metropolitan Opera House,
    New York.
mfr., manufacturer.
mgr., manager.
mid., middle.
min., minor.
mod., moderately.
m.-sopr., mezzo-soprano.
M. T. (N.) A., Music Teachers' (Na-
    tional) Association.
mus., music, musical, musician.
Mus. Antiq. Soc., Musical Antiqua-
    rian Society, London.
Mus. Bac. (Doc.), Bachelor (Doctor)
    of Music. Vide D. D.

n., near.
Nat. Cons., National Conservatory,
    New York.
N. E. Cons., New England Conserva-
    tory, Boston.
n. s., new style (referring to the use of
    our calendar in place of the Russian
    or old style).
N. Y., New York, U. S. A.

O., Ohio, U. S. A.
Obbl., obbligato.
obs., obsolete.

op., opus, opera.
Op. com., opéra-comique; or the Opéra
    Comique at Paris.
Oper (*G.*), opera.
Opéra, used of the Grand Opéra at
    Paris.
orch., orchl., orchestra, orchestral.
org., organ, organist.
o. s., old style, see n. s. above.
Oxon. (*L.*, *Oxoniae*), of Oxford.

p., part.
pcs., pieces.
P. E., Protestant Episcopal.
perf., performed.
pf., pianoforte.
Philh., Philharm., Philharmonic.
Pol., Polish.
pop., popular.
Port., Portuguese.
pres., president.
Presb., Presbyterian.
prod., produced.
Prof., Professor (a special title of great
    distinction in Germany).
pseud., pseudonym.
pt., pianist.
pub., published, publisher.

R., Royal.
R. A. M., Royal Academy of Music,
    London.
R. C., Roman Catholic.
R. C. M., Royal College of Music,
    London.
Regius musicus, Royal musician.
ret., retired, retiring, returned.
rev., revised.
Rev., Reverend.
Rus., Russian.

sch., school.
sec., secretary.
soc., society.
sopr., soprano.
Sp., Spanish.
st., studied, studying, student.
succ., successfully, success.
supt., superintendent.
symph., symphonic, symphony.

t., teacher, taught.
th., theatre.
th., theorist (writer of treatises).
th.-cond., conductor of theatre-orches-
    tra.
transcr., transcribed, transcription.
transl., translated, translation, trans-
    lator.
Tur., Turkish.

Unit., Unitarian.
U. S., United States.
U., Univ., university.

v., 1. (*L.*, *vide*) see; as *v.* B. D., see the Biographical part of this volume. *v.* D. D., see the Defining Dictionary. 2. very, as *v. succ.*, very successful(ly).

var.(s), variation(s).
vla., viola.
vln., violin.
vt., violinist.

w., with.
Wis., Wisconsin, U. S. A.

Ztg. (*G.*, *Zeitung*), Gazette.

AN INTRODUCTION TO MUSIC
FOR THE UNINITIATED

A Free Translation of its Technicalities into Untechnical Language
(especially for those who do not Read Music and
do not Care to Study it).

By Rupert Hughes

THERE is almost as much humbug about the mysteries of music as there was about the oracles of Delphi. And the vast majority of music-lovers have as meek and uninquiring a dread of the inner art and science of composition as the old pagans had of priestcraft.

There is no deeper mystery about the tools and the trade of music than about those of any other carpentry and joinery. It is far easier for some people to write a melody than to drive a nail straight. But anybody who will earnestly try, can learn to do the one as easily as the other. And there are thousands of professional composers who ought to be earning honest livings driving nails home instead of starving to death dishonestly driving audiences home.

The one mystery of music is the one mystery of all art and all other human intercourse—personality. Everybody can write a novel or a play. Almost everybody does. So everyone can write a sonata or a string-quartet. But the number of those who possess the spark (divine, prenatal, accidental or howsoever secured)—the spark of magnetism, felicity, and eloquence, that number is small and is no more superabundant than on the day when little Hermes found the old tortoise-shell and made the first harp out of it.

The reason the Editor is desirous of taking the veil from certain of the arcana of music is not that he wishes to increase the number of composers—Heaven forbid! The one object is to increase the number of those who will listen to music intelligently and know just what they are hearing, and pretty well why they like this and dislike that. For like and dislike by pure instinct are relics of mere animalism.

The open highway to the enjoyment of so-called classic music is the hearing of it in large quantities. There is a short cut for those who lack the time or the inclination for this long training— and it is by way of learning the elements of musical form. For it

is the crystallisation of human passion into some graceful and powerful form that gives music long life.   Many wretched pedants think
that the number of forms is limited; but this is a fallacy that is dis-
proved every day.

Some form, however, is as necessary in music as in sculpture.
And though the number and variety of forms available are as
infinite and illimitable in music as in sculpture, still some definite
shape must be in the artist's mind and must be discoverable by an
unprejudiced, attentive, and educated audience.

If you do not already know the skeleton that underlies the
shapely contours and full, fair flesh of melody and harmony, you
can find some enlightenment in the anatomical lecture that follows,
provided you will use your own scalpel, and carry out the suggestions
made.   It is not easy to avoid asking the reader to master the
language and symbols of music, but much that is important can
be learned from the following, without this long special study, if
an occasional general truth will be allowed to stand without stating
its exceptions, and if permission be granted to arrive at certain facts
in a homely and button-hole manner.

I

FIRST, turn to a piano or organ—either of these is more
convenient for illustration than a bow or wind-instrument.
The highly-organized instrument before you is the result of
centuries of blind groping in the dark, of unnumbered great failures
for every little triumph.   This is true not only of the mechanism
of strings, hammers, keys, shape, size and materials of wood and
metal, but of the very music the instrument is intended to send
out upon the air.

If you will simply glide your finger-nail along the white keys
you will produce a scale which in itself is the result not only of
ages of experiment but of the bitterest conflict between scholarly
musicians,—a conflict still raging.   But this cannot be discussed
here.   Let us for the present take the instrument as we find it.

On page 877 of this book will be found a chart of the middle
portion of the key-board, with the letter-names that have been,
for convenience' sake, given to the tones marked on it.   They are
easily recognisable by the alternation of the black keys in groups
of twos and threes.   For convenience it might be well to transfer

the letter-names to the white keys with ink, which will be easily washed off with a wet cloth.

The first thing noteworthy about the diagram is that this series of letter-names is made of only seven letters and begins over again at every eighth tone. This is because the eighth tone (or octave) is produced by a string or a column of air making just twice as many vibrations as the original tone; the 15th tone by 4 times as many, etc., and because each group of seven steps plus the octave or 8th step, is built on a uniform model of ratios. The series from one letter-name to its reappearance, as from c to c', is subdivided into 12 half-steps or semitones.

This extended series of tones thus divided into octaves is the material from which all European and American music is made. Save for a few changes and choices made for convenience, this scale is based on human nature and physical law, and is not likely to be materially altered in our generation. Other fundamental facts will be discovered on studying this array of *whole-steps* (white keys —except e to f and b to c) and *half-steps* (from a black key to the next white—also from b to c and e to f).

You will observe that the black keys carry the same names as the white keys they interpose between, except that the letter-name carries the symbol ♭ ("flat") for the key next below or the symbol ♯ ("sharp") for the key next above. The same black key represents two white keys. If you are advancing from f to g, for instance, the black key between is a half-step above f; it is said to "sharpen" the note, by a half-step (or a "chromatic" degree); if, however, you are moving down the scale from g to f the black key is said to "flatten" the note g by a half-step (or a "chromatic" degree). The same black key serves conveniently then both as f♯ (f "sharp") and g♭ (g "flat") in our system of music. Tones not thus "chromatically altered" by a sharp or flat are said to be "natural." If you have struck g♭ or f♯ and wish to reassert the white key, the tone is now called g♮ (g "natural") or f natural.

The signs, ♯'s, ♭'s and ♮'s are called "sharps, flats and naturals," or in general "chromatics."

Put your finger at random on any of the white keys and move downwards on the white keys in strict succession. You will find (if you have a normal ear) that, whatever the tone you sounded first, you do not feel a willingness to stop till you reach a certain tone or one of its octaves. That tone will invariably be one of the notes lettered C.

If now you begin at random on any note and move upward keeping to the white keys except in the case of f, for which you substitute f♯, you will find that the letter c no longer gives a sense of repose, but that you unconsciously desire and demand one of the letters marked g.

If you run a scale on all the white keys except b, and substitute for this note the b♭, you will find no resting-place except upon one of the letters marked f.

It is a physical fact, then, that a scale with neither sharps nor flats finds its end on the note c; a scale with one sharp (which is always f) is based on the note g; a scale with one flat (b flat) is based on the note f. Hence one speaks of the scale of C, or of G, or of F.

If you try the substitution of some other single sharp or flat for the f sharp or b flat, you will get no satisfactory point of repose at all. But by keeping b flat and adding e flat you will find b flat a comfortable pausing-place; by adding a flat to the b♭ and e♭, you will find a pleasant scale ending on e♭. By adding flats in the following order (and only in the following order), b, e, a, d, g, c, you will construct symmetrical scales reposing always on the next to the last flat added.

By substituting sharps for the natural tones of the original scale of C, you build scales satisfactorily only by heaping up sharps in the following order, f, c, g, d, a, e, which scales are based respectively on the notes g, d, a, e, b, f, the point of repose being in each case a half-tone above the last sharp added.

The scales take their names from the note of repose. A scale together with all the chords that can be built upon its notes is called a *key*. The word "key" is often loosely used (and has been used in this essay thus far) to indicate a finger-lever which causes a string to sound; this is better called a "digital." From now on the word "key" will be used only to designate a group of harmonies and a scale belonging to some series of progressions ending on a certain note, as the "key of C," the "key of G" (which contains f sharp), the "key of D" (which contains f sharp and c sharp), the "key of E flat" (which contains b flat, e flat and a flat), and the others.

Since practically every musical composition has some principal key to which it harks back as its home, however far or often it may wander away, so you will find at the beginning of every new line of a composition a list of the sharps or flats in that key which predominates, and these sharps or flats affect every tone not otherwise marked throughout the composition. This group is called the *key-signature*.

A convenient trick of deciding the key from the number of sharps or flats is as follows: where there are flats the key is next to the last flat; where there are sharps the key is always the next letter-name above the last sharp. This is true of every key except three which are easily remembered, F with one flat, G with one sharp, C with neither flats nor sharps.

Before studying chords, it will be necessary to have another look at the diagram of the key-board. We have spoken of half-steps and whole steps. But it is possible also (and often desirable) to desert the monotonous progression of whole and half-steps and skip several steps, as one does in singing a tune. The space covered by a skip is called an *interval.* As geography has its imaginary equator, and as geometry has its imaginary lines without breadth and its planes without depth, so music has one imaginary interval which is no interval at all, but identity. The distance from a note to the very same note is called a *prime.* (This is sometimes useful when speaking, for instance, of a♭ and a♯, which are a prime apart, and are called *primes* of each other.) The interval from one white digital to the next white digital is called a *second*, the skip to the next but one is called a *third* (the original note being always numbered one), the skip to the third white digital is called a *fourth*, and so on; the interval of an eighth being called an *octave*. Also the tones separated by an interval may be called by the names of the interval as c and g, or d and a are called *fifths;* f and d, or g and e are called *sixths*, etc.

It will greatly clear the belt of fog we are now going through if you will pick out the examples on the key-board.

The skip from a white to a black digital results in an interval which is either greater or less than the nearest interval on the white digitals alone. The normal or greater of two similarly named intervals as c to e is called a *major* third, while c to e♭ is called a lesser or *minor* third. C to e♯ is greater even than the major and is called an *augmented* third, while c to e♭♭ ("double flat") is a *diminished* third.

Owing to the elasticity of the letter-names of the notes, an interval may be expressed or *spelled* in different ways, thus c to e♭ is called a *minor* third, but the very same tones may be called c to d♯, an *augmented* second, c–f♭♭ a *diminished* fourth, b♯–d♯ a *minor* third, etc. The name of the interval depends upon the key we happen to have most in mind at the time.

It is a curious fact that all major scales are made up of exactly the same intervals in the same order. Try over any of the scales you wish, and you will find that you move upward by the following degrees, in the following order: (1) a whole step, (2) a whole step, (3) a half-step, (4) a whole step, (5) a whole step, (6) a whole step, (7) a half-step; this last bringing you to the octave of the note you started from.

As earnestly as the soul demands that in the last act of a play we shall see the villain sent to prison and the hero and heroine locked in each other's arms, so our nature demands this arrangement of tones, and when it says half-step or whole step we must move so, or leave the key we started in and take up another.

This explains why there is no black digital between the notes, b–c, and e–f: the scale of C, which has no sharps or flats, must still have its two half-steps at these points; there is accordingly no sharp or flat to be put there.

II

WE HAVE now had a bird's-eye view of the natural arrangement of tones, one at a time. But we grow tired of one note at a time. Four men singing along a midnight street or a picnic group riding home in a moonstruck mood fall to singing favourite melodies and naturally avoid singing in unison. They spontaneously sing in chords. These chords are formed individually and succeed one another according to certain fundamental demands of the ear just as noticeably as the tones of the scale followed a rigid pattern.

First, let us combine various tones. Take the middle c' and strike this tone with the right thumb while another finger strikes another tone above. c' and c'$\sharp$ do not sound well together, nor yet c' and d'; c' and d'$\sharp$ (or e'$\flat$) is not unpleasant, but rather sombre (it is indeed a minor harmony, the interval c'–e'$\flat$ being a minor third); c' and e' make a pure, sweet concord, however. Let us keep c' and e' and see if we can add another tone, c' + e' + f' is very bad; c' + e' + f'$\sharp$ is also rough; c' + e' + g' is very comfortable. We have now a three-tone chord, which we may call a *triad;* it happens to be based on the 1st, 3d and 5th degrees of the scale.

Let us see if we can build triads on other tones of the C scale. We find by trying all the combinations on the note d', that while the triad d′–f′–a′ is pleasant but sombre (it is minor), the only clear harmony is d′–f′♯–a′; but as f♯ does not belong to the scale of C, we cannot include it. On the note e′ we find e′–g′–b′, minor, and e′–g′♯–b′ pleasant; this again is outlawed by the g♯. On f′, however, we can form a triad f′–a′–c′, which has no foreign chromatics and is yet satisfying. On g′ we find another triad, g′–b′–d″, which is native to the C scale and which impels us strongly to substitute the e″ above for the d″, and c″ for the b′; when we have done this we find we have the chord c′–e′–g′ again, only now arranged differently, as g′–c″–e″.

If we rearrange the chord on g′ differently, as b′–d″–g″, we shall be impelled to move on to c″–e″–g″, which is again our old friend the original triad on c′ in its original form.

This hankering after the original triad on the key-note whenever we form a triad on the fifth tone of the scale, is one of the most noteworthy and inescapable factors of the chord-world.

But let us proceed with our triads; on a′ we find a′–c″–e″ to be minor; the major chord b′–d♯″–f♯″ is doubly ruled out; while b′–d″–f″ is doubly minor, the fifth (b′–f″) being imperfect and the third (b′–d″) being minor.

It may be well to state here a handy way of telling the majority or minority of intervals; imagine the lower note to be the key-note; if the upper note would occur in a major scale on that key-note its interval is major or diatonic. Thus on b: the key of B has 5 sharps, f, c, g, d, and a; both d and f are sharp, therefore b–d♮–f♮ has neither interval major.

Looking back over the chords of the scale of C, we find the only major triads to be those on c′, f′ and g′. Since that on g′ is so urgent in demanding the main triad on C, it is called the *dominant* triad, and the tone g is called the *dominant* of the scale of C. f′ being beneath it is called *subdominant*, and its chord the *subdominant chord;* the note c being the foundation note of the whole scale and key is called the *tonic* (*tonus* being an old name for scale).

The principal chord-material of any scale is, then, made up of the triads on the tonic (or 1st), the dominant (or 5th) and the subdominant (or 4th).

Try another Key, F for instance, which has b♭. After testing all the combinations on the key-note or tonic f′ we find only f′–a″–c″; on g′ the triad, to be in the key, must be g′–b′♭–d″ (since b♭ is a characteristic of the key of F), and this is a minor chord; a′–c″–e″ is also minor, but b′♭–d″–f″ is a major triad; it is indeed a chord on the *subdominant*. We should expect also to find a major triad on the dominant (which, in the key of F, is the tone c), and so we find c″–e″–g″, which we recognise as the tonic chord of the scale of C. But strange to say it offers no repose in its new environment with the other chords of the key of F; on the contrary, we have an irresistible desire to move on from it to c″–f″–a″ (the same as the key-chord or tonic chord, f′–a′–c″, where we feel at home). The two remaining tones of the scale of F offer no satisfactory chords.

Let us try a key with one sharp in it, that is to say, the key of G. Beginning on g′ we find after groping about that the only chord endurable is g′–b′–d″. Building triads on all the other tones, a, b, c, d, e and f♯, we find all of them outlawed as unpleasant or at least minor, except two, which again are on the *subdominant* and the *dominant* tones of the key of G, and are c″–e″–g″, and d″–f″♯–a″.

Taking the sum-total of the chords of these three keys, c, f, and g, we have the following chords: (C) c–e–g, f–a–c, g–b–d; (F) f–a–c, b♭–d–f, c–e–g; (G) g–b–d, c–e–g, d–f♯–a. You will see that each of the two subordinate keys has two of the chords of the key of C. This will be found the case with any group of three keys similarly differing only by one sharp or flat, that is to say, having their tonics a fifth above or below. On this account the keys based on the dominant and subdominant tones of the scale of any given key are said to be closely *related* in the first degree of relationship.

Add another flat and another sharp, that is, take the key of B♭ and the key of D, and we find the following principal chords: (B♭) b♭–d–f, e♭–g–b♭ and f–a–c; (D) d–f♯–a, g–b–d, a–c♯–e. Each of these keys has only one of the chords belonging to the key of C. These keys are then *related*, but only in the *second* degree.

If we add three flats or three sharps and study the keys of E♭ and A we find the chords (E♭) e♭–g–b♭, a♭–c–e♭, b♭–d–f; (A) a–c♯–e, d–f♯–a, e–g♯–b♭. None of these chords occur in C, and these keys are said to be *remote* from it. On the other hand comparing E♭ with the key which had only 2 flats (B♭), we find that E♭ has two chords belonging to B♭. We also find that A has two of the chords belonging to the key with one sharp less, viz., D. We may generalise, then, by saying that the most closely related keys are those that differ by one flat or one sharp; the next nearest relations are those differing by two flats or sharps.

III

WHILE we are on the subject of heredity take another point of view of this family-tree:

The tone f′, which is four steps above c′, is called its subdominant; on looking below the note c, we find another f, but where it was four tones above, it is five tones below. The key of F has added one flat to the key of C. Counting five more whole steps down (always counting the note you began on as first) we find the note B♭. The scale on that tone has yet another flat, two more than C. The tone a full fifth below (E♭) has three flats. So we find that moving downward by fifths we add one flat every step. A♭ has 4, D♭ has 5, and G♭ has 6 flats.

Now counting upwards from our starting point on c′, we find that the key based on the fifth (g′) adds one sharp; a fifth above G is D, a key with two sharps; a fifth above is A with three sharps, a fifth further is E with four sharps, and, as we continue, B with five sharps and F♯ with six sharps.

But the key of F♯ on our piano or organ passes over the very same digitals as the key of G♭, is identical with it in fact. We have therefore been personally conducted through the grand tour of keys by way of the *circle of fifths*, twelve in all.

We see therefore that all keys are related, and by careful procedure in chords a player can move through them all in succession with the greatest smoothness. The more modern the composition the more widely does it rove from key to key until in some works, Wagner's for instance, it is sometimes hard to say just what key we are driving at. Instead of keeping to the iron rails of one key as earlier music aimed to do, and only leaving the main line at certain definite set switches, the art has recently left the hard and fast railroad and taken to the pathless waters where, to use Wagner's words, it "swims in a sea of tone."

Some very formal minds grow speedily sea-sick and prefer the rigid grooves of the older school. Each one to his tastes. But the broadest mind will find pleasure both in land-travel and sea-change, insisting only that the composer shall have a plan and know what he is about, and not send his locomotives slashing and sinking in the buxom waves, nor drag his yacht gratingly along the hard ground. Live and let live is the best art motto.

One more point is worth noting in this increasingly important subject of key-relationships. Reverting for a moment to the key of C with its first cousins f and g, we find if we take the tonic triads of the three keys and arrange them as follows:

tonic,

f–a–c–e–g–b–d.

subdominant dominant

These tones include the complete scale of C. So it will be found of every key-scale that it contains within itself the tonic triads of itself, of its subdominant and its dominant keys.

This scale and key principle is further justified by a study of the mathematics and physics of music. And the Relationship of Keys is given a still greater importance in the more recent writers on the theory of music, especially in Riemann's beautiful theory of clang-kevs (see this word in the Dictionary of Definitions).

IV

NOW that we have laboriously picked out our triads, they will be found more elastic than they look. Take the triad c′–e′–g′, the tonic triad of the key of C, which is now said to be in the root or first position, c′ being the root or generator of the triad. We can place the c′ uppermost and have e′–g′–c″, which is in effect the same chord, though a chord is said to be *inverted* when any note except its root is in the bass. The second *inversion* places the fifth in the bass, as g′–c″–e″ or g–c′–e′–g′ or g–e′–g′–c″. These 3 *positions* are all we have for a 3-tone chord or triad. They can be sounded anywhere on the key-board, however.

Still another possibility is to repeat some of these letter-names, as to sound the triad c′–e′–g′ with the right hand and touch the tone c an octave below with the left hand; or the tones c–g with the left hand and e′–g′–c″ with the right. This process called *doubling* may be carried on indefinitely. In a piano-duet, sometimes twenty notes or more are struck, all of them repetitions of the inner kernel or triad of three notes.

Strike the left-hand note c first, then the right-hand triad c′–e′–g′ twice; then strike the note f with the left hand and the subdominant triad c′–f′–a′ twice, now c and the tonic triad again; then strike g with the left hand and the dominant triad b–d′–g′ twice; and return

finally to C and the tonic triad.   This little plot in three instalments
constitutes the whole harmonic accompaniment of many a modern
popular song and many an old work of classic reputation.

You can usually tell the key of a song by humming it and picking
out on the piano or organ its very last note; nine times in ten this
will be the *tonic* or homenote of the composition.   Suppose this
to be B♭.   How shall one find chords to accompany it?   Build a
major triad on b′♭; it will be b′♭–d′–f′; build a triad on the dominant
or fifth (f), f′–a′–c″; build another on the subdominant or fourth
(e♭), e′♭–g′–b′♭.   Play these three notes (B♭, f, e♭) with the left
hand, and use triads with the right, rearranging the three notes in
any of the inversions as they run most smoothly into one another.
Your ear will help you find the right order of the chords.   This will
serve as a recipe for easy accompaniments.

More elaborate songs rove through so many keys with so little
warning that only trained ears and hands can pick out their accompaniment; but it will clear up a deal of the construction of music
if you will take some simple tune and study out its accompaniment
on these lines, however painful the operation may be to yourself
and your neighbors.   (Familiar songs requiring only these three
chords are "The Star Spangled Banner," "God Save the King,"
"Home Sweet Home," "Suwanee River," "Dixie," etc., and most
of the hymn-tunes.)

V

BUT the simple triads grow monotonous, and it is desirable,
if possible, to enrich them.   Take the all important dominant triad of the key of C (namely, g′–b′–d″) and see if we
can lay another third on top of it like a musical brick.   The next
major third above d″ is f″♯.   But f♯ does not belong to the key
of C.   The minor third f″♮ does beautifully, however, and we have
a warm rich chord which more than ever goads us on to the tonic
triad; the g′ holding over, the b′ and the d″ both merging into c″,
and the f″ subsiding blissfully into e″.

A chord of 4 tones is called a *chord of the seventh* or *seventh chord*,
because the interval between the first and last tones is a *seventh*
(g′–f″).   This chord, g′–b′–d″–f″, is a *dominant* 7th, then.   If we
wish, we can add another third, a″, and make a chord g–b–d–f–a,
called a *ninth chord*.   The dominant 7th, however, is far the more
useful.   In fact it is the most energetic chord in all music, and

whatever key you may be in, if you stray into the dominant seventh of a foreign key, it drags you along eagerly and hales you into that foreign key to which it belongs and for which it is a most eager usher.

This seventh chord, pleasant as it is, is only a go-between, it offers no point of repose, but requires an almost immediate dissolution into another chord. The musical term for one of these restless chords is *dissonance;* the musical term for the necessity and process of merging it into another is called *resolution*. The word *dissonant* does not necessarily mean "ugly" or "harsh" in music, but merely implies lack of stability.

This dominant 7th chord has magical powers for transition. Take the tonic triad of the key of C major in the second inversion, that is, touch g with the left hand and e′–g′–c″ with the right. Now lift the finger off the upper g′ and place it on b′♭. Instantly you find it undesirable to go back to the c′–e′–g′ triad and you are impelled to lower that b′♭ to a′, bring the e′ up to f′, keep the c″ where it is and lower the g in the left hand to f. Now you feel at rest; if you will pause and look, you will find that the b′♭, which is characteristic of the key of F, has led you into the triad f′–a′–c″, which is the tonic triad of the key of F. If you revert to the state of affairs existing when that foreigner b′♭ entered the peaceful key of C, you will find that the chord formed by its entrance could be arranged to read c′–e′–g′–b′♭. This is a 7th chord on the tone c. But while the tone c′ is tonic of the key of C, it is the fifth or dominant of the key of F. Yet, though this 7th chord was built on the tonic of C, as it happened to be the dominant of F, it forced the key over into the tonality of F. This is the case with every dominant 7th chord.

It is possible by a slight diversion to throw the resolution of the chord into other keys, but this always comes as a surprise to the hearer. It may be justified and it may be pleasurable, but it is a surprise, and in a sense abnormal.

Going back to the first formation of the 7th chord, it will be found that the 7th chord, on other tones than the dominant, are rather murky or even distressing. These are called *secondary* 7ths and must be handled in gingerly manner.

VI

NOW if we take our dominant 7th of the key of C, that is, g′–b′–d″–f″, and raise the g′ a half-step so that the chord reads g′♯–b′–d″–f″, it will most naturally *resolve* itself into this chord, a′–c″–e″, a sombre chord which is minor because its third from a–c is minor (the major third being a–c♯, as c♯ would be characteristic of the key of A). This chord, a′–c″–c″, has the look of a chord in the key of C, but it seems to offer a sense of dejected repose and makes no demand for progress to the tonic chord, c′–e′–g′. We arrived at this chord by way of a curious chord with f♮ but g♯. The chord g′–b′–d″–f″ had been a minor 7th (the interval from g′ to f″ being less than the major interval, which would be g′ to f″♯), but this chord, g′♯–b′–d″–f″, is even narrower than minor. It is hence called a *diminished 7th chord*.

We have been led to believe that the first sharp of a major key was f, and that c followed, then g. This is true of a major key, but here we are under a different flag. You can construct a scale out of these two chords, the diminished 7th and its resolution, and g♯–b–d–f; a–c–e gives us a–b–c–d–e–f–g♯–a as an octave scale. This scale, which is closely related to the C major scale, is founded on a′, which is a minor third below c″. So it will be found that every major key has one of these disappointed relative keys a minor third below and differing from it, for harmonic purposes, only in the fact that the 7th tone of this minor scale is raised a half-step above the tone of the same name in the major scale (in the scale of A minor, the 7th tone, g♯, is the only tone foreign to the scale of C major, and it is a half-tone higher than the tone g; the key of C minor corresponds exactly with the major key a minor third above, that is E♭, except that where b is flattened in the key of E♭ major, it is made natural in the scale of C minor). This is the case with every major and minor key; the related minor key is a minor third below and raises the 7th tone of its major scale a half-step (as g to g♯; e♭ to e♮). Thus far we have concerned ourselves only with major scales, keys and intervals. But life would be very monotonous if it were all sunshine, blue sky and laughter. Music could not represent or stimulate human emotion, as it does, without a large armoury of sombre colours, bitter dissonances and, in place of a sense of cheerful repose, a feeling of resigned despair. These purposes are subserved by the minor key.

In looking at scales and intervals we find that certain of the intervals were to be distinguished as "greater" and "lesser." The Latin words meaning greater and lesser are *major* and *minor*. (And as the mediæval Latinity of the Catholic Church was the fountain-head of modern music, many of its terms persist.) On the major scale there were indeed four minor triads to only three major. There is abundance of minor material then in music. Its arrangement into scales and keys cannot be so easily explained as that of the major mode; indeed upon this subject scientists are mutually discordant and commonly as "troubled" (*betrübt*) as the great musical scientist Helmholtz found the minor scale itself.

Where doctors disagree, the layman would do best to pass by on the other side. Let us take the minor keys as we find them and thank Heaven for their existence as mirrors to the chillier, grayer moods of the mind. Music has indeed laid up something for a rainy day.

To go any further into the construction of chords would be to write a text-book on Harmony.

Those who wish to pursue the subject of chord construction and progression will find further information in such articles as Chord, Harmony, Thorough-bass, Parallel, Covered, Anticipation, Suspension, Interval, Altered, etc., in the Dictionary of Definitions.

VII

GIVEN the scales for melody and the chords for harmony, with an unlimited variety of progressions, the subject of rhythm enters. There was a time when the music of the scholars was all in notes of equal length; such music was well called plain-song (*planus* meaning literally "smooth"). But popular instinct and popular music still had drum-rhythms and dances and finally forced the music of the scholars to return to humanity; and so-called mensurable (i.e., measurable) music began.

The definition of rhythm is so native and instinctive in everyone that it would be impertinence to foist it on the reader. It is to be noted, however, that in music it depends on the relative accent and duration of notes following a pattern more or less closely. The rhythm of a composition can be expressed by thumping it on a table with your fingers, for rhythm is independent of height or lowness of the tone and the volume of sound. Strum out in this way such tunes as "Comin' Thro' the Rye," "Yankee Doodle," "We

Won't Go Home Until Morning," or the like, or airs of more dignity. If you mark the accents forcefully, the regularity of the rhythmical pattern becomes evident, and almost as monotonous as certain styles of wall-paper. If you tap with the left hand a regular beat like a clock's, only faster, the rhythm of the air will assume new vividness.

Take "Comin' Thro' the Rye" for example, the rhythm could be expressed by underlining with the right hand a series of numbers to be ticked off by the left hand:

If a bod-y meet a bod - y com - in' thro' the rye————
1–2, 3, 4–5, 6, 7–8, 9, 10–11, 12, 13–14, 15, 16–17, 18, 19, 20, 21, 22, 23, 24,

If a bod-y   kiss a bod-y   need a bod-y   cry————
25–26, 27, 28–29, 30, 31–32, 33, 34–35, 36, 37–38, 39, 40–41, 42, 43, 44, 45, 46, 47, 48

This covers two lines of the song, the rest of which follows the same model. We find 48 beats in the two lines of verse, 24 to each line. The rhythm is almost exactly stencilled all the way through; it begins over again, after every sixth count, each 7th count having a marked accent, the 4th of each group of 6 having a lighter accent. If, since the rhythm is the same, we simply repeat the first 6 numerals and cut off with a line every group of 6, we shall have the song pictured in as simple a pattern as that of the maid's own print gown.

If   a body meet a body   com-in' thro' the rye————
/1–2, 3, 4, 5, 6/1–2, 3, 4–5, 6/1–2, 3, 4–5, 6/1, 2, 3, 4, 5, 6/

Call each of these groups a *measure*, the slanted line a *bar*, take a certain time or *note*-value as the unit in place of these numbers and you will have the musical terminology. As the notes are short the quick eighth note (one-eighth of a whole note) may be taken as the unit; there are 6 of these in each measure, and the *time* of the song is said to be *six-eighths* or 6–8 time. This is a combination of triple and duple rhythm, for, while each measure contains 6 counts, these counts are divided into two groups of three each and there are two accents to each measure, consequently 6–8 time is sometimes used for marches.

But the typical march time for marches (as well as for many other moods, as "Auld lang syne," etc.) is, as you will find, divisible into measures of 4 counts each, with two accents to each measure. As the whole note is taken as the whole extent of each measure, the presence of four beats to the measure gives each beat a fourth or quarter-note value. It is therefore called *4–4 time*, or simply *common-time.* Very quick marches are sometimes written in 2–4 time with one beat to the measure. Waltzes are written with 3 beats and only one accent to the measure. This time is called 3–4 time. Other rhythms are 3–2, a slow time (with 3 half-notes and 3 accents to the measure); 3–8 time (a light quick time with 3 eighth notes and one accent to the measure); 6–4 time (a slower form of 6–8 measure, differing from 3–2 only in having two accents to the measure); 9–8 (with 9 eighth notes and 3 accents), &c. (v. article on Time).

VIII

NO WAY of submitting music to the all-devouring decimal system has yet been brought into play. The measure-notes are all multiples of 2 and 4: whole notes, half, quarter, 8th, 16th, 32d, and 64th notes.

The larger divisions of music also fail to follow the decimal system. In the analysis of "Comin' Thro' the Rye" the measures themselves can be collected into groups of 2, 4 and 8. There is a slight pause after every other measure, a perceptible pause at the end of the 4th measure, a longer pause at the end of the 8th. The next group of 8 measures is likewise divisible into groups of 2 and 4.

This quality of divisibility into 4 and 8 measures is a fundamental law of musical structure. Because it is such a law many composers strive to hide its nakedness or re-shape it to special purposes, but these are exceptions which by their very sense of novelty and oddity prove and emphasise the general rule.

A group of eight measures is called a *period;* this period contains two *phrases* of four measures each; each *phrase* contains two *sections*, of 2 measures; and each section is generally divisible into its melodic or rhythmic *motive* or *subject.* The song "Comin' Thro' the Rye" is especially clean-cut in its divisions. They correspond in spirit to the comma, semicolon, colon and period of ordinary prose, but occur with far more regularity. Frequently the periods themselves can be collected into larger groups or *compound periods* corresponding to paragraphs. The first accent of a measure has a stronger accent than the second or third. So the first accent of the first measure of a period should receive a greater stress than the first accent of the first measure of a phrase, and so on. In the proper distribution of accents lies the larger part of musical punctuation, or, as it is called, *phrasing.*

IX

IN THE first group of 8 measures of "Comin' Thro' the Rye"
there is a general upward tendency to the melody.   The second
period begins on a high note (at the words "Ilka body") and has
a downward tendency.   This desire for a contrast is at the root of
all musical form.   This song is condensed even beyond the usual
popular form, partly because of the stanza-form of its poetry.
"The Last Rose of Summer" fulfils the typical *song-form* which
contains a *theme* of one or more periods, followed by a contrasting or
subsidiary theme of one or more periods, the song concluding with a
repetition of the first or principal theme.   Practically the same idea
governs the typical dance-form though the themes are likely to be
more elaborate and the second theme is still stupidly called a *trio*
(from the fact that it was actually in old times given to a trio of
instruments in order to contrast its simple song-like manner with
the more ornate and broken progress of the principal theme).

It would naturally occur to composers seeking variety, to put this
subsidiary theme into a different key, to emphasise the contrast.
The key naturally chosen would be a closely related key.   This is
usually the case, and the contrast of keys is a most important part
of classic forms.

The elaboration or variation of the themes in a way to show off
the composer's scholarship and cleverness, was also as inevitable as
human pride in skill.

The word *variations* has, in the general mind, a thought of "The
Old Oaken Bucket" and "Nearer, My God, to Thee" "with variations." "*Variations*" is an incorrect word here; the proper term for
these cheap and gaudy works being *embellishments*, for the air is
simply made a trellis for all manner of running vines and frippery.

The true variation of a theme is its genuine manipulation.   Take
the first 2 measures of "Comin' Thro' the Rye" as a theme; i.e.,
the notes to the words "Gin a body meet a body," sit down again
before the piano and play this theme, picking out the notes as indicated from their letter-names as shown in the Chart.

Suppose the notes to be placed—

/c' c' c' e'/ d' c' d' e'/g g a g/c'.

If with the right hand you play the theme as indicated, and shortly
after follow in with the left hand (as you would follow the leading

voice in singing such a round as "Three Blind Mice"), you will use the frequent device called for evident reasons *imitation*, as here:

Right hand /c' c' c' e' / d' c' d' e'/g g a g/c' --- /&c.
Left hand /- - - - - /-----------/c c c e/d c d e/&c.

This is imitation *at the octave* and at two measures' *distance;* imitation may be at a different interval and distance, *at the fifth,* for instance:

Right hand/ c' c' c' e / d' c' d' e' / &c.
Left hand / ——— / f f f a / &c.

Imitation need not be so *strict* as this; it may be *free*, the intervals being slightly changed to enrich the harmony, for it is not every air that can be treated smoothly and strictly at the same time. Here, for instance, the a in the left hand might be reduced to a g. Imitation in the orchestra has vast scope. The trombones may proclaim a splendid phrase which the oboes will cackle over ludicrously, the flutes whistle gaily, the clarinets echo gurgingly, the 'cellos bemoan nasally, and the violins murmur deliciously.

But in piano or organ composition, imitation is more restricted. Sometimes a composer in mathematical mood will set an elaborate air jogging, and when it has gone a few spaces along, will start after it its very double. The two will race like twin snakes.

When the imitation is exact, whole step by whole step, skip by skip, whole note by whole note, and half-note by half-note, the composition is said to be a *canon*. The canon may set more than two snakes wriggling swiftly along at always the same distance from head to head. Fugue is only a special form of composition in which the canon plays a large part, the word *"fuga"* meaning "flight."

X

THE devices for varying a theme are infinite. It can be played in longer notes while another theme chosen from another part of the song ripples about it; or the duration of the notes can be shortened. The new treatment of a theme by lengthening its notes is called *augmentation;* the shortening of the notes is *diminution*.

The upper of two themes can be made the lower at different intervals than the octave; this is called *inversion*. Another form of inversion is the turning of a theme upside down, so that whenever it went up before, it goes down now, and *vice versa;* this is *imitation by contrary motion.*

A theme can be picked to pieces and different fragments of it tossed to and fro with the skill of a juggler (and about as much importance).   The first 4 notes of "Comin' Thro' the Rye" could be taken as a figure and repeated.   Thus:

$$c'\ c'\ c'\ e',\ e'\ e'\ e'\ g'\sharp,\ g'\sharp\ g'\sharp\ g'\sharp\ b',\ \text{etc.}$$

This would be called a *sequence.*   The themes could be played in octaves, or in varied and key-changing chords as:

It could be ornamented as:

$$\begin{array}{cccc} \text{If} & \text{a} & \text{bod} & \text{-y} \\ c',\ c',\ d', & c',\ b',\ c', & d',\ c',\ e', & e',\ e',\ e'. \end{array}$$

In fact, there is no hinting here the dissection and reconstruction of which a theme is capable.   As opposed to a melodious or lyric treatment, this method is called *thematic.*   Common names for this sort of treatment are "development, elaboration, variation, working-out, free fantasy," &c., &c., the Germans calling it Durchführung, "going through."

XI

THE highest and noblest form of strictly academic and formal composition is the *sonata,* for the symphony is only a sonata for orchestra.   We have now arrived hastily at a point where a rough explanation of this form is possible.

This is the way you should set about writing a sonata, or rather, one of the ways, for the sonata is elastic and has some room for individual tastes.

First you select a melody, one with an elocutionary and sententious manner, and containing many good texts to develop.   You write it out plainly and emphatically in the key that suits it best. As a sidelight and a foil you select some more lyrical and song-like air, and for contrast you put it in another key, naturally one of the related keys, most naturally the nearest related key, or the dominant.   Or you might put the second melody in the relative minor. Having stated your two subjects, you may choose to repeat them word for word, or note for note, so that there shall be no mistaking them; you may then add a concluding reflection more or less elaborate. This is the first section of the sonata.

Having stated the two texts, the *principal* and the *subsidiary*, you now propose to show their true profoundness, and your own true skill as an orator. You employ the devices of elaboration mentioned above, and you play battledore and shuttlecock with the two themes in all the keys you wish till they fly to pieces; then you juggle the pieces; you modulate from grave to gay; from cold to tropical, from whisper to shriek, from insinuation to fervid appeal, from metaphor to homely paraphrase; in fact, you invoke every art and artifice you can borrow from the schools or can find in the promptings of your own emotions. When you have exhausted all the devices propriety or your knowledge permits, you have finished the second section of the sonata, the so-called Working-out, or Development, or Free Fantasy, or Elaboration.

The third section consists of a re-statement of the first theme in the original or tonic key, followed by the second theme, not in its related key, but now *in the same key as the first theme*, in order that a definite key may be left in the mind to give an effect of unity. A short peroration or coda ends the sermon like a welcome benediction.

This is what is strictly called the sonata form. It is reasonable and based on a natural and artistic arrangement of ideas and their development.

The sonata is not complete in this one composition, or *movement* as it is called. Three or usually four contrasted movements are strung together. They usually have some faint suggestion of similarity of theme, but variety of mood and key is the chief endeavor. A slow movement (called from its slowness by one of the Italian words meaning "slow"—Andante, lento, largo), marked by deep pathos or tragedy, usually follows the passionate outburst. Then comes a lighter mood in one or two movements in the form of (a) an optimistic and prettily braided Rondo with one chief theme and two attendant themes; (b) a gallant Minuet; or (c) a witty and jocose scherzo.

The sonata ends with a Finale of stormy and brilliant character generally built on the same scheme as the first movement and written in the same key.

The whole group of three or four movements makes up a sonata. The first movement of the sonata is often also called the "sonata-form."

AN INTRODUCTION TO MUSIC   21

An *overture* (excepting one that is a medley of airs) is merely the first movement of a sonata, written out for an orchestra. A *symphony* is merely a whole sonata written to take advantage of the enlarged opportunities of a great orchestra of from 50 to 120 instruments. The sonata-formula is also the basis of the *string-quartet*, -quintet, etc., and of *concertos* for solo instruments with orchestra.

A *symphonic poem* is a symphony only in the breadth of its orches tration and its high demands. Like many smaller forms it forsakes the somewhat rigid arrangement of the sonata and other classical forms and lets the moods or the story it tells furnish the programme of musical events. A composition which has some programme other than the classic arrangement of keys and sections;—a programme for instance representing musically a storm or the tragedy of "Romeo and Juliet"—such a composition is said to be *programme music*. In its worst form, when programme music descends to cheap and unconvincing imitations of natural sounds instead of contenting itself with an artistic suggestion of them to the hearers' imagination, such music, if music it can be called, becomes quite as hopeless trash as that school of music which stoops to cheap and unconvincing imitations of classical masters and parrots devices which only the original spontaneity of the old master himself can keep alive. But generalisations are vain. What is poison as one man serves it up, is meat from another's hands. One failure or one triumph no more makes a rule than one bluebird brings the spring.

This hasty and incomplete sketch will have failed in its purpose if it leads its reader to the delusion that he need investigate no further the real mysteries of the art of music; if it lead to the delusion that because the art is founded on certain physical laws of inner and outer nature, the artistic imagination is to be hobbled to them; or if it lead to the delusion that any one form, symmetrical or natural soever, can suffice for all generations or all moods, or that any school of masters can hope to embody all that is good and solid in the art.

The classic masters were once living, breathing, passionate young artists, impatient of precedent and breaking rules for sheer pleasure as wanton boys smash windows. He who approaches them with intelligence and sympathy will find them still made of bone and blood, sinew and spirit. But once he has had the inestimable delight of their acquaintance, he must, above all things, avoid the belief that art and glory died with them. He should approach every new work, howsoever startling, with a readiness to be convinced that the new trumpeter, standing on the outer hilltop which we thought was the rim of the art, may, after all, be looking into a further world and be proclaiming to us new fields and streams, and a new horizon. And though his music may seem strange, blatant and incoherent to us at first, perhaps the fault is not with him, nor with us, but only with the great new wonder-land he sees beyond.

Music, like any other living speech, is always growing and must always be newly studied. If we would not have it a dead language we must be prepared for change, and be willing to learn.

BIOGRAPHICAL DICTIONARY
OF MUSICIANS

N.B. The German modified vowels ä, ö, ü, are often spelled ae, oe, ue. For convenience they will here be arranged alphabetically as if a, o, u. For the system on which given names are abbreviated, and for their pronunciation, see the pages devoted to them. The word "Gerbert," or "Coussemaker" in a parenthesis means that some of the composer's works are in the great collections of Gerbert or Coussemaker (q. v.). Where not otherwise stated the man is a composer.

A

Aaron (ä'-rōn), (1) d. Cologne, 1052; abbot and theorist. (2) (or **Aron**), **Pietro,** Florence, 1480 or '90—bet. 1545–62; theorist.

Abaco (děl ä'-bä-kō), **E. Fel. dall',** Verona, July 12, 1675—Munich, July 12, 1742; court-conductor and composer.

Abbà-Cornaglia (äb-ba' kôr-näl'-yä), Alessandria, Piedmont, 1851—1894; composed operas and church-music.

Abbadia (äb-bä-dē'-ä), (1) **Natale,** Genoa, 1792—Milan, ca. 1875; dram. and ch. composer. (2) **Luigia,** daughter of above, b. Genoa, 1821; mezzosoprano.

Abbatini (äb-bä-tē'-nē), **A. M.,** Castello, ca. 1595—1677; composer.

Abbé (äb-bā), (1) **Philippe P. de St. Sevin,** lived 18th cent.; 'cellist. (2) **Pierre de St. Sevin,** bro. of above; 'cellist.

Ab'bey, (1) **J.,** Northamptonshire, 1785—Versailles, 1859; organbuilder. (2) **Henry Eugene,** Akron, O., 1846—New York, 1896; impresario; manager of Met. Op., N. Y., 1883–4, 1891–2, and 1894–6.

Ab'bott, (1) **Emma,** Chicago, 1850—Salt Lake City, 1891; operatic soprano; toured America with great popular success. (2) **Bessie** (Ab'ott), Riverdale, N. Y., 1878—New York, 1919; soprano; pupil of Mrs. Ashford, N. Y., and of Koenig, Paris; début 1902 at the Opéra there, after singing in ballad concerts in England; 1906, U. S.

Abeille (ä-bī'-lě), **Jn. Chr. L.,** Bayreuth, 1761—Stuttgart, 1838; composer and court-conductor.

Abel (ä'-běl), (1) **Clamor H.,** b. Westphalia 17th cent.; court-mus. (2) **Chr. Fd.,** gambist at Köthen, 1720–37. (3) **Ld. Aug.,** b. Köthen, 1717, son of above; court-violinist. (4) **K. Fr.,** Köthen, 1725—London, 1787; bro. of above and the last virtuoso on the gambà. (5) **L.,** Eckartsberga, Thuringia, Jan. 14, 1834—Neu-Pasing, Aug. 13, 1895; violinist.

Abell', J., London, ca. 1660—Cambridge (?) ca. 1724; alto (musico) and lutenist; collector and composer.

Abendroth (ä'-běnd-rōt), **Hermann,** b. Frankfort, Jan. 19, 1883; conductor; pupil of Thuille; cond. in Munich, 1903–4; Lübeck, 1905–11; Essen, 1911; after 1915, civic music dir. and head of Cons. at Cologne; in 1922–3 also led concerts of Berlin State Op. and as guest in London and other European cities; cond. Gewandhaus Orch., Leipzig, after 1934.

Abenheim (ä'-běn-hīm), **Jos.,** Worms, 1804—Stuttgart, 1891; conductor and violinist.

Abert (ä'-běrt), (1) **Jn. Jos.,** Kochowitz, Bohemia, Sept. 21, 1832—Stuttgart, April 1, 1915; double-bass virtuoso and important composer for the instr.; also composed operas, etc. (2) **Hermann,** Stuttgart, March 25, 1871—Aug. 13, 1927; son of (1); noted musical historian; Ph. D., Tübingen Univ.; 1902, docent in mus. science, Halle Univ.; 1909, prof.; 1919, do., Heidelberg Univ.; 1920, Leipzig Univ. (*vice* Riemann); 1923, Berlin Univ.; author of biog. of Schumann and large number of important historical and scientific works on music; after 1914 ed. the "*Gluck-Jahrbuch.*"

Aborn (ä'-bōrn), (1) **Milton,** Marysville, Cal., May 18, 1864—New York, Nov. 13, 1933; impresario; early in life an actor; after 1902 managed Aborn Op. Co., in productions in English; 1913–15, seasons at Century

Theat., N. Y.; later Gilbert and Sullivan productions. (2) **Sargent,** b. Boston, 1866; brother of Milton, assoc. in his work as impresario and in Aborn Op. Sch., N. Y.

Abos (ä'bōs) (or **Avos, Avos'sa**), **Gir.,** Malta, ca. 1708—Naples, 1786 (?); composer of operas, etc.

A'braham, Gerald, b. 1904; Eng. writer; wrote "*Studies of Russian Music,*" etc.

Abrányi, (1) **Kornel,** d. Budapest, Dec. 20, 1903; nobleman; editor and composer. His son (2) **Emil,** b. Budapest, Sept. 22, 1882; c. operas.

Abra'vanel, Maurice, conductor; mus. dir., Utah Symph. Orch., after 1947.

Abt (äpt), **Franz,** Eilenburg, Dec. 22, 1819—Wiesbaden, March 31, 1885; court-conductor at Bernburg, Zurich and Brunswick; visited America, 1872; immensely popular as a writer in the folk-song spirit, of such simple and pure songs as "*When the Swallows Homeward Fly,*" etc.; c. 500 works comprising over 3,000 numbers (the largest are 7 secular cantatas) and numerous choruses and other cantatas.

Ab'yngdon, Henry, d. Wells, England, 1497; composer.

Achenbach. Vide ALVARY.

Achron (äkh'-rŏn), **Joseph,** b. Losdseye, Russia, May 1, 1886; composer; studied Petrograd Cons., violin with Auer (grad. gold medal), harmony with Liadoff, orchestration with Steinberg. Toured Russia at age of 11; head of vln. and chamber music, Kharkov Cons., 1913–16; later toured widely, Russia, Palestine and Europe. Since 1925, res. in New York. C. chamber music and vln. works, d. Calif., 1943.

Achscharumov (äsh-tshä'-roo-mŏf), **Demetrius Vladimirovitsch,** b. Odessa, Sept. 20, 1864; violinist and c.; pupil of Auer.

Ack'ermann, A. J., Rotterdam, April 2, 1836—The Hague, April 22, 1914; composer.

Ackté (äk'-tä), **Aïno,** b. Helsingfors, Finland, April 23, 1876; soprano; sang at Paris Opéra; 1904–5, Met. Op., N. Y.; d. Helsinki, 1944.

Ac'ton, J. B., b. Manchester (?), 1863; singing-teacher and composer.

Adalid y Gurréa (ä-dhä'-lēd h-ē-goo-rä'-ä), **Marcel del.,** Coruna, Aug. 26, 1826—Longara, Dec. 16, 1881; pianist; pupil of Moscheles and Chopin; c. opera, etc.

Adam (äd-äṅ), (1) **Louis,** Muttersholtz, Alsatia, 1758—Paris, 1848; teacher and composer. (2) **Adolphe Charles,** Paris, July 24, 1803—May 3, 1856; son of above; c. many successful operas; *Pierre et Catherine* (1829), *Le Châlet* (1834), *Postillon de Longjumeau* (1836), *Le Fidèle Berger, Le Brasseur de Preston* (1838), *Le Roi d' Yvetot* (1842), *La Poupée de Nuremberg, Cagliostro,* and *Richard en Palestine* (1844), the ballets *Giselle, Le Corsaire, Faust,* etc.; in 1847 he founded the Théâtre National, but was made bankrupt by the revolution of 1848, and entered the Conservatoire as prof. of composition to succeed his father.

Adam (ät'-äm) **K. F.,** Constappel, Saxony, Dec. 22, 1806—Leisnig, 1867; cantor and composer.

Adam de la Hale (or **Halle**) (äd-äṅ dŭ lä äl), Arras, ca. 1240—Naples, 1287; called "Le bossu d'Arras" (Hunchback of Arras); a picturesque trouvère of great historical importance; c. chansons, jeux (operettas) and motets; his works were pub. 1872.

Adamberger (ät'-äm-bĕrkh-ĕr), **Valentin** (not **Joseph**), Munich, 1743—Vienna, 1804; dram. tenor; assumed name "Adamonti"; Mozart wrote the rôle of Belmonte, etc., for him.

Adami da Bolsena (or **da Volterra**) (ä'-dä-mē dä bŏl-sä'-nä), **And.,** Bologna, 1663—Rome, 1742; theorist.

Adamon'ti. Vide ADAMBERGER.

Adamowski (äd-ä-mŏf'-shkĬ), (1) **Timothée,** Warsaw, March 24, 1858 —Boston, Apr. 18, 1943; vln. pupil of Kontchi, Warsaw Cons. and Massart, Paris Cons.; 1879 travelled to America as soloist with Clara Louise Kellogg, and later with a company of his own 1885–86; teacher, New Engl. Cons., Boston; organised the Adamowski String-quartet (1888). (2) **Joseph,** Warsaw, 1862—Boston, May 8, 1930; bro. of above.; 'cellist; member of the same quartet; married Szumowska; 1903, New Engl. Cons. teacher.

Ad'ams, (1) **Th.,** London, 1785—1858; organist. (2) **Charles R.,** Charleston, Mass., ca. 1834—July 3, 1900; tenor. (3) **Suzanne,** b. Cambridge, Mass., 1873; soprano; studied with Bouhy in Paris; sang at the Op. there, 1894–7; then in Nice; from 1898 to 1906 at Covent Garden; 1898,

Chicago; 1899 at Met. Op. House; m. Leo Stern, 'cellist; lived in England, 1903; d. London, 1953.

Ad'cock, Jas., Fton, England, 1778— Cambridge, 1860; choir-master and composer.

Ad'dison, J., London, ca. 1766—1844; double-bass player, dram. composer.

Adelburg (fōn ä'-dĕl-boorkh), **Aug., Ritter von**, Constantinople, 1830— (insane) Vienna, 1873; violinist.

Adler (ät'-lĕr), **Guido**, Eibenschütz, Moravia, Nov. 1, 1855—Vienna, February, 1941; pupil at Academic Gym. in Vienna, and Vienna Cons.; ('78) Dr. jur., and ('80) Ph. D.; 1885 prof. of mus. science Prague Univ.; ('95) prof. of mus. history, Univ. of Vienna (vice Hanslick); from 1894, ed.-in-chief, *"Denkmäler d. Tonkunst in Oesterreich"*; after 1913, ed. *"Studien zur Musikwissenschaft"*; author of many valuable essays on music.

Ad!gasser (ät'-'l-gäs-sĕr), **Anton Cajotan**, Innzell, Bavaria, 1728—1777; organist.

Adlung (ät'-loongk), or **A'delung, Jakob**, Bindersleben, near Erfurt, 1699—1762; organist, teacher and writer.

Adolfati (ä-dōl-fä'-tē), **And.**, Venice, 1711—Genoa (?) 1760; composer.

Adriano di Bologna. Vide BANCHIERI.

Ad'riansen (or **Hadrianus**), **Emanuel;** lived Antwerp 16th cent.; lutenist and collector.

Adrien (ăd-rĭ-äṅ) or **Andrien. Martin Joseph** (called **la Neuville**, or **l'Ainé**), Liége, 1767—Paris, 1824; bass and composer.

Ægid'ius de Muri'no, 15th cent.; theorist. (Coussemaker.)

Ælsters (ĕl'-stĕrs), **Georges Jacques**, Ghent, 1770—1849.

Ærts (ĕrts), **Egide**, Boom, Antwerp, 1822—Brussels, 1853.

Afanassiev (ä-fä-näs'-sĭ-ĕv), **Nikolai Jakovlevich**, Tobolsk, 1821—St. Petersburg, June 3, 1898; violinist and c.

Affer'ni, Ugo, b. Florence, Jan. 1, 1871; pianist and cond.; studied at Frankfort and Leipzig; m. the violinist Mary Brammer, 1872; c. operas, etc.

Affilard (läf'-fē-lär'), **Michel l'**, 1683—1708; singer to Louis XIV.

Afranio (ä-frä'-nĭ-ō), b. Pavia, end of 15th cent.; canon at Ferrara; inv. the bassoon.

Afzelius (äf-tsä'-lĭ-oos), **Arvid A..**

Enköping, Sweden, 1785—1871; collector.

Agazza'ri (ä-gäd-zä'-rē), **Ag.**, Siena, 1578—1640; church-conductor.

Agnelli (än-yĕl'-lē), **Salv.**, Palermo, 1817—1874; pupil of Naples Cons.; lived Marseilles and c. operas, cantata *"Apothéose de Napoléon I.,"* etc.

Agnesi (dän-yä'-sē), (1) **M. Theresia d'**, Milan, 1724—1780; pianist and dram. composer. (2) **Luigi** (rightly **F. L. Agniez**), Erpent, Namur, 1833 —London, 1875; bass.

Agniez (än-yĕz). Vide AGNESI (2).

Agostini (äg-ôs-tē'-nē), (1) **Paolo**, Vallerano, 1593—Rome, 1629; wonderful contrapuntist, some of his works being in 48 parts. (2) **P. Simone**, b. Rome, ca. 1650. c. an opera, etc.

Agrel (ä'-grĕl), **J.**, Loth, Sweden, 1701 —Nürnberg, 1765; court-violinist and conductor.

Agric'ola, (1) **Alex.**, Germany (?) ca. 1446—Valladolid, Spain, 1506; court-singer and church-composer. (2) **Martin**, Sorau, Saxony, 1486— Magdeburg, June 10, 1556; eminent writer and theorist. (3) **Jn.**, b. Nürnberg ca. 1570; prof. and composer. (4) **Wolfgang Chp.**, German composer (1651); (5) **G. L.**, Grossfurra, 1643—Gotha, 1676; conductor. (6) **Jn. Fr.**, Dobitschen, 1720— Berlin, 1774; court-cond.

Agthe (äkh'-tĕ), **K. Ch.**, (1) Hettstadt, 1762—Ballenstedt, 1797; composer. (2) **W. Jos. Albrecht**, Ballenstedt, 1790—Berlin, 1873; son of above, teacher. (3) **Fr. W.**, Sangershausen, 1796—(insane) Sonnenstein, ca. 1830; cantor.

Aguado (ä-gwä'-dhō), **Dionisio**, Madrid, 1784—1849; performer and composer for guitar.

Aguiari, Lucrezia. Vide AGUJARI.

Aguilar (à'-gē-lär), (1) **Emanuel Abraham**, London, Aug. 23, 1824— London, Feb. 18, 1904; pianist of Spanish origin; c. 2 operas, 3 symph. (2) **Elisa**, (3) **Ezequiel**, (4) **Francisco**, (5) **José**, lute players, comprising Aguilar Lute Quartet; toured widely in Europe and America, New York début 1929-30.

Aguilera de Heredia (ä-gwĭ-lä'-rä dä ä-rä'-dhē-ä), **Seb.**, b. Sargossa, 17th cent.; monk and composer.

Agujari (ä-goo-hä'-rē), **Lucrezia** (calle·d **La Bastardina**, or **Bastardella**, being the natural daughter of a nobleman), Ferrara, 1743—Parma, May 18, 1783; a phenomenal singer; Mozart remarked her "lovely voice, flexible throat, and incredibly high range," which reached from middle C three octaves up; she could shake on f''' (vide CHART OF PITCH); she m. Colla, 1780, and retired from the stage.

Ahle (ä'-lĕ), (1) **Jn. Rud.**, Mülhausen, 1625—1673; theorist and church-composer. (2) **Jn. G.**, Mülhausen, 1651—1706; son of above; organist, poet and theorist.

Ahlström (äl'-shträm), (1) **Olof**, Stockholm, Aug. 14, 1756—Aug. 11, 1835; organist. (2) **Jakob Niklas**, Wisby, Sweden, June 5, 1805—Stockholm, May 14, 1859; son of above; dram. composer.

Ahna. Vide DE AHNA.

Aibl (ī'-bl), **Jos.**, founded publishing firm, Munich, 1824; later heads were Eduard Spitzweg (1836) and his sons, Eugen and Otto.

Aiblinger (ī'-blĭng-ĕr), **Jn. Kasper**, Wasserburg, Bavaria, 1779—Munich, 1867; court-conductor, collector and composer.

Aichinger (ī'-khĭng-ĕr), **Gregor**, Regensburg ca. 1564—Augsburg, 1628; canon and composer.

Aigner (īkh'-nĕr), **Engelbert**, Vienna, 1798—1851; dram. composer.

Aimo (ä'-ē-ĭnō). Vide HAYM, N. F.

Aimon (ĕm-ôṅ), **Pamphile Ld. Fran.**, b. L'Isle, near Avignon, 1779; 'cellist, conductor, theorist.

Ajolla. Vide LAYOLLE.

À Kem'pis, Nicholas, organist and c., at Brussels, ca. 1628.

Akimen'ko, Theodore, composer; b. Kharkov, Russia, Feb. 8, 1876; studied St. Petersburg Cons., 1895—1900, harmony with Rimsky-Korsakoff and Liadoff, piano with Balakireff. C. two symphonies, orchestral poems, chamber music works, opera "*Rudy.*" Resident in France.

Ala (ä'-lä), **Giov. Bat.**, Monza, 1580—1612 (?); organist and composer.

Alabieff (ä-lä-bĭ-ĕf), **Alex.**, Moscow, Aug. 16, 1787—March 6, 1851; composer.

Alaleona (äl-äl-ä'-ō-nä) **Domenico**, composer, musicologist; Montegiorgio, Italy, Nov. 16, 1881—Dec. 29, 1928; grad. St. Cecilia Acad., Rome, 1906; studied piano with Bustini, composition with De Sanctis and

Renzi; cond., Augusteo concerts, Rome, and prof., Rome Conservatory, after 1910. C. opera, "*Mirra,*" choral works, chamber music, songs; author articles on Cavalieri and other early Italian composers.

Alard (äl-är), **J. Delphin**, Bayonne, March 8, 1815—Paris, Feb. 22, 1888; violinist, teacher and composer.

Albanese (äl-bä-nä'-zē), **Licia**, soprano; studied in Milan; Met. Op. after 1939.

Albanesi (äl-bä'-nä'-zē), **Luigi**, Rome, March 3, 1821—Naples, Dec. 4, 1897; pianist and composer.

Albani (äl-bä'-nĭ) (stage name of **Marie Louise Cecilia Emma La Jeunesse**), Chambly, near Montreal, Nov. 1, 1852—London, April 3, 1930; operatic soprano; sang in Cathedral, Albany, N. Y., whence her name was mistakenly supposed to have been taken; pupil of Duprez, and of Lamperti; début at Messina in 1870; sang much in England, at Covent Garden and a favourite in concert; 1878, m. Ernest Gye, impresario; retired from stage, 1906.

Albani, Mathias, Bozen, 1621—1673; famous father of more famous son of same name and trade, violin-making; the younger A.'s violins (1702-9) rival Amati's.

Albeniz (äl-bā'-nĕth), (1) **Pedro**, Logroño, 1795—Madrid, 1855; court-organist. (2) **Pedro**, b. Biscay, San Sebastian, 1755; monk, church-cond. and composer. (3) **Isaac**, Camprodon (Gerona), Spain, May 29, 1860—Cambo-les-Bains, June 16, 1909; eminent composer; a leading representative of the "New Spanish" school of nationalistic composers. He was markedly precocious as a child and appeared as a pianist at the age of 4 in Madrid. At 6 he was taken to Paris, where he studied with Marmontel, and from 11 to 15 appeared as a concert player in North and South America. He attended the Leipzig Cons. for a short time, and later the Brussels Cons. with the aid of funds provided by Alfonso XII. He studied at various times with Brassin and Jadassohn, and also with Liszt at Weimar and Rome. His life was one of continuous uncertainties. As a composer he was prolific, his compositions falling into two separate groups, the first extending from 1883 to about 1890, during which time he composed over 200 piano works including concertos and sonatas and many smaller pieces; after 1890 he undertook the study of composition in Paris with d'Indy and composed the operas "*Pepita Jiminez*," "*Henry Clifford*," a trilogy "*King Arthur*," and the orch. suite "*Catalonia*." Among other compositions are "*Iberia*" suite for piano (several numbers orch. by Arbos), an oratorio "*Cristo*," and many songs. His piano music carries on the traditions of Chopin and Liszt, but is endowed with quite individual folk-colour and intensity of feeling, and also has many impressionistic influences. His trilogy "*King Arthur*" was left unfinished at his death. In 1923 his "*Pepita Jiminez*" was restored with success at the Paris Op.-Comique.

Albergati (däl-bĕr-gà'-tē), (1) **Pirro Capacelli, Conte d'**. Lived in Bologna, 17th cent.; composer. (2) **Aldobrandini**, lived in Bologna, 17th cent.; dram. composer.

Al'bert, Prinz von **Sachsen-Coburg Gotha**, Schloss Rosenau, 1819—1861; consort of Queen Victoria, patron of music and composer of an opera, "*Jean le Fol*" (Bagnières de Bigorre, 1865), an operetta, masses, etc.

Albert (äl'-bĕrt), (1) **H.**, Lobenstein, Saxony, 1604—Königsberg, 1651; poet, organist and composer, called the father of the German *Lied*, and, as he alludes to a "Comödien-musik" (1644), he must have been, with Schültz, one of the founders of German opera. (2) **Charles L. N. d'**, Nienstetten, near Hamburg, 1809—London, 1886; dancing master and composer. (3) **Eugen d'**, rightly **Eugène** (**Francis Charles**) (däl-bär, or däl'-bĕrt), Glasgow, April 10, 1864—Riga, March 3, 1932; son and pupil of above; pianist; Newcastle scholar in the London Nat. Training School, 1876; pupil of Pauer (pf.) and Stainer, Prout and Sullivan (harm. and comp.); 1881, Mendelssohn scholar and pupil of Richter and Liszt, who called him "the young Tausig"; 1881, he played the Schumann concerto at the Crystal Palace, London; Oct. 24, a concerto of his own, at a Richter concert; he performed 5 Beethoven sonatas (op. 31, 53, 90, 109, 110) at a Gewandhaus recital, 1893; he married the pianist Carreño in 1892 (divorced 1895); first

conductor at Weimar, vice Lassen, but soon resigned; composed a symphony, 2 overtures ("*Hyperion*" and "*Esther*"), 2 pf.-concertos, libretto and music of the operas "*Der Rubin*" (Carlsruhe, Oct. 12, 1893), "*Ghismonda*" (Dresden, 1895), "*Gernot*" (Mannheim, 1897), 1-act mus. comedy "*Die Abreise*" (Frankfort, 1898); operas "*Kain*" and "*Der Improvisator*" (both Berlin, 1900), "*Tiefland*" (Prague, 1903), "*Flauto solo*" (Prague, 1905), "*Tragaldabas*" (Hamburg, 1907), "*Die Verschenkte Frau*" or "*The Bartered Wife*" (1912, Munich). His opera "*Tiefland*" (based on Guimera's play, "*Marta of the Lowlands*") has had immense success; in Berlin alone (prod. 1907) it reached its 400th performance in Feb., 1912; it was sung at the Met. Op., 1908, and throughout Europe; also c. the operas "*Liebesketten*," "*Izeil*," "*Die Toten Augen*" (1917); perf. also in N. Y. by German Op. Co., 1924); "*Der Stier von Oliveira*" (Leipzig, 1918); "*Revolutionshochzeit*" (do, 1919); "*Scirocco*" (Darmstadt, 1921); "*Mareike von Nymwegen*" (1923); "*Der Golem*"; "*Die Schwarze Orchidee*" (musical detective drama, using jazz effects); and a posth. work, "*Mr. Wu*," (prod. 1932); string quartets, violin con certo; pf. pieces, etc. His later marriages were to Hermine Finck, singer (1895-1910); Ida Theumann (1910-12); he is esp. remembered for his piano transcriptions of Bach organ works; his revision of the "*Well-Tempered Clavichord*"; his editions of various Liszt works and of the sonatas of Beethoven.

Albertazzi (äl-bĕr-täd'-zē), **Emma** (née **Howson**), London, 1814—1847; operatic contralto.

Alberti (äl-bĕr'-tē), (1) **Jn. Fr.**, Tonning, 1642—Merseburg, 1710; organist. (2) **Giusi Matteo**, Bologna, 1685—1746; violinist and composer. (3) **Domenico**, Venice, ca. 1717—Formio, 1740; singer then pianist; in his piano music he made use of the since-called "Alberti bass" (vide D. D.).

Alberti'ni (äl-bĕr-ιē'-nē), (1) **Gioacchino**, b. 1751—Warsaw, April, 1812; conductor and dram. composer.

Albicas'tro, Henrico (rightly, **Weissenburg**), b. Switzerland, 17th cent.; court-violinist.

DICTIONARY OF MUSICIANS

Albino'ni, Tommaso, Venice, 1674—1745; violinist.

Albo'ni, Marietta, Cesena, Romagna, March 10, 1823—Ville d'Avray, near Paris, June 23, 1894; eminent dram. contralto, compass g–g″ (vide PITCH, D. D.); pupil of Rossini; début La Scala, Milan, 1843; m. Count Pepoli, 1854.

Albrechtsberger (äl-brĕkhts-bĕrkh-ĕr), **Jn. G.,** Klosternenburg, near Vienna, Feb. 3, 1736—Vienna, March 7, 1809; eminent composer, court-organist, theorist and teacher (Beethoven was his unappreciated pupil).

Albri'ci (äl-brē'-chē), **V.,** Rome, 1631—Prague, 1696; court-conductor.

Alcarrot'ti, Giov. Fran., lived in Italy 16th cent.; organist, 1740–91.

Al'cock, (1) **John,** London, 1715—Lichfield, 1806, organist. (2) **J.,** son of above; organist.

Alda, Frances (rightly **Davis**), b. Christchurch, New Zealand, May 31, 1883; soprano; studied with Mathilde Marchesi; début as Manon (Massenet), Paris Op.-Comique, 1905; sang in Brussels, London, Warsaw, Milan, and Buenos Aires; début with Met. Op. Co., New York, 1908, as Gilda; sang more than 30 rôles with this company. Retired from opera, 1929; also active in concert and radio; m. Giulio Gatti-Casazza, 1910; divorced 1929; (2) Ray VirDen; d. Venice, 1952.

Aldovrandini (äl-dō-vrän-dē'-nē), **Gius. A. V.,** b. Bologna, 1665; court-conductor and dram. composer.

Al'drich, (1) **H.,** Westminster, 1647—Oxford, 1710, theorist and composer. (2) **Richard,** Providence, R. I., July 31, 1863—Rome, June 2, 1937; graduated Harvard, 1885, won scholarships and honours; studied music under J. K. Paine; 1885 he went on the staff of the *Providence Journal*, soon reaching an editorial position, and being put in charge of the musical and other critical departments of the paper; 1888 he spent in study abroad, chiefly of music; 1889 to 1891, private secretary to U. S. Senator N. F. Dixon; 1891—1902 joined the staff of the *New York Tribune* as associate musical critic with H. E. Krehbiel, and as collaborator in their "*History of the Philharmonic Society*"; 1902–24, music critic, *N. Y. Times*; author of various magazine articles, and editor of a series of musical biographies; also guides to

Wagner music-dramas, etc. (3) **Mariska,** b. Boston, 1881; soprano; pupil of Giraudet and Henschel; début, New York, 1908; sang with Met. Op. Co., 1909–13; Brünnhilde at Bayreuth, 1914. (4) **Perley Dunn,** Blackstone, Mass., 1863—New York, Nov. 21, 1933; singer and teacher; pupil of Shakespeare, Trabadello and Sbriglia; taught at Univ. of Kansas, 1885–7; Utica Cons., 1889–91; after 1903 in Philadelphia.

Alembert (däl-äṅ-bär), **J. Le Rond d',** Paris, 1717—1783; theorist.

Alessan'dri, (1) **Giulio,** c. an oratorio (ca. 1690). (2) **Felice,** Rome, 1747—Casalbino, 1798; pianist and conductor.

Alessan'dro Merlo (or **Aless. Romano**), called **Della Viola,** b. Rome (?) ca. 1530; monk, singer and composer.

Alfano (äl-fä'-nō), **Franco,** composer; b. Naples, March 8, 1877; studied at Naples and Leipzig Cons.; succeeded Busoni as dir. Bologna Liceo, 1917; later, at Liceo Verdi, Turin. Toured as pianist. C. (operas), "*Miranda,*" Leipzig, 1897; "*La Fonte d'Enshir,*" Breslau, 1898; "*Risurrezione*" (based on Tolstoy's work), Turin, 1904, Chicago, 1925, with Mary Garden as Katiusha; "*Il Principe Zilah,*" Genoa, 1909; "*L'Ombra di Don Giovanni,*" 1913; "*La Leggenda di Sakuntala,*" 1921; "*Madonna Imperia,*" 1925 (Met. Op., New York, 1927–8); "*Il Piccolo Lord,*" comic opera (based on "*Little Lord Fauntleroy*"); "*Cyrano de Bergerac*" (based on Rostand drama), 1935–6. Chosen to complete final act of Puccini's posth. opera, "*Turandot.*" Also c. symphony, suites, ballet and piano works.

Alfarâbi (äl-fä-rä'-bē), or **Alphara'bius,** properly **El Farâbi** (abbr. **Farâbi**) Farâb (now Othrax), 900 (?)—Damascus, 950; Arabian theorist who vainly advocated Greek theories.

Alfieri (äl-fē-ā'-rē), **Abbate Pietro,** Rome, 1801—1863; Camadulian monk; teacher and theorist.

Alfvén (älf'-vĕn), **Hugo,** b. Stockholm, May 1, 1872; violinist; studied at the Cons. and with César Thomson; 1900 received Jenny Lind scholarship for 3 years foreign study; from 1904 prof. of comp. Stockholm University; from 1910 mus. dir. Upsala Univ., in 1912 conducting a concert of Upsala students in Berlin; c. 3 symphonies; symph. poem *"Aus den Schären"*: cantata *"The Bells," "The Lord's Prayer,"* for chorus; scene with orch., male choruses, etc.

Algarot'ti, Count **Fran.,** Venice, 1712—Pisa, 1764; writer.

Alipran'di, (1) **Bdo.,** b. Tuscany, Bavaria, ca. 1730; his son (2) **Bdo.,** 'cellist at Munich, 1780.

Alkan (äl-käṅ), (1) **Chas. H. Val.** (*l'ainé*), Paris, Nov. 30, 1813—March 29, 1888; pianist, teacher, and brilliant composer for piano.

Allacci (äl-lät'chē), **Leone** (or **Leo Allatius**), Chios, 1586—Rome, 1669; writer.

All'chin; conductor Oxford Music Society, 1869–81.

Allegran'ti, Maddalena; dram. soprano; début, Venice, 1771.

Allegri (äl-lā'-grē), (1) **Gregorio,** Rome, 1584—Feb. 18, 1652; pupil of Nanini; composed a celebrated Miserere in 9 parts, sung during Holy Week at the Sistine Chapel; its publication was forbidden on pain of excommunication; but Mozart after twice hearit, wrote it out, and it has since been frequently published. (2) **Dom.;** lived 1610–29 at Rome; one of the first to write instrumental accompaniments not in mere unison with the voices.

Al'len, (1) **H. R.,** Cork, 1809—London, 1876; bass. (2) **G. B.,** London, 1822 —Brisbane, Queensland, 1897; singer, organist, conductor, manager, and composer. (3) **Nathan H.,** Marion, Mass., 1848—1925; pupil of Haupt, Berlin; organist, teacher in Hartford, Conn.; composer of cantatas, etc. (4) **Sir Hugh Percy,** b. Reading, Engl., 1869—Oxford, Feb. 20, 1946; 1887, org. Chichester Cathedral; 1901 at Oxford, where he was made Mus. Doc. 1898, and University Choregus 1909; 1908, mus. dir. Reading University College; 1909, mus. dir., Oxford; 1918–38, dir. R. C. M., London.

Allihn (äl-lēn'), **H. Max.,** b. Halle-on-Saale, Aug. 31, 1851—Nov. 15, 1910; writer on organ-building.

Al'lison, (1) **Richard,** teacher at London, 1592. (2) **Robt.,** member of Chapel Royal till 1609. (3) **Horton Claridge,** b. London, July 25, 1846; pianist; pupil R. A. M. and Leipzig Cons.; Mus. Doc. (Dublin), c. piano and organ music, songs; d. (?).

Almeida (däl-mä'-ē-dhä), **Fernando d',** Lisbon, ca. 1618—1660; monk and church-composer.

Almenräder (äl'-měn-rä-děr), **Karl,** Ronsdorf, 1786—Nassau, 1843; virtuoso and manufacturer of the bassoon.

Alois (ä'-lō-ês), **Ladislaus,** Prague, 1860—Russia, 1917; 'cellist; pupil Paris Cons.; soloist Royal orch., St. Petersburg; c. concertos, etc.

Al'paerts, Flor, b. Antwerp, Sept. 12, 1876; composer; pupil of Cons. in native city, and after 1902 its dir.; also active as orch. cond.; c. operas, orch., chamber and choral works, piano pieces.

Al'sager, Thos. Massa, Cheshire, 1779 —1846; English amateur and patron.

Al'sen, Elsa, b. Germany; early sang as contralto, later dram. soprano; début as Fidelio, sang rôle in several German op. houses, also Isolde; came to U. S. 1923 with German Op. Co., singing leading Wagner rôles with succ.; Chicago Op., 1926–8; also widely in concert.

Alsleben (äls'-lā-běn), **Julius,** Berlin, 1832—1894; editor and writer.

Alsted(t) (äl'-shtät), **Jn. H.,** Herborn, Nassau, 1588—Weissenburg, 1638; writer.

Altenburg (äl'-těn-boorkh), (1) **Michael,** Alach, near Erfurt, 1584—Erfurt, 1640; pastor and composer. (2) **Jn. Ernst,** Weissenfels, 1736—Bitterfield, 1801; trumpet-virtuoso; son of (3) **Jn. Kasper,** do.

Altès (äl-tês), (1) **Jos. H.,** Rouen, 1826 —Paris, 1895; flutist. (2) **Ernest-Eugène,** Paris, March 28, 1830—St. Dye, July 8, 1899; bro. of above; pupil Paris Cons.; violinist and conductor; 1871 deputy conductor of the Opéra; 1879–87, conductor.

Alt'house, Paul, tenor; b. Reading, Pa., Dec. 2, 1889; grad. Bucknell University; début, Met. Op. Co., 1913, as Dmitri in *"Boris Godounoff"*; sang Berlin State Op., Stockholm Royal Op., Landestheatre, Stuttgart; Philadelphia Civic Op., Chicago Civic Op. (1930–31), returned to Met. Op. Co., as singer of Wagner rôles, 1934. Also heard widely in concert, oratorio, festivals; d. N. Y., Feb. 6, 1954.

Alt'mann, Wilhelm, b. Adelnau, Germany, April 4, 1862; editor and musical historian; from 1900, chief librarian of Berlin Royal Library; after 1914, chief of mus. section,

Prussian State Library; 1906, dir. of Deutsche Musiksammlung; 1904, critic, "*National-Zeitung*"; a prolific and scholarly writer on a great number of musical subjects; ed. letters of Wagner and Brahms, etc.

Altnikol (ält'-nē-kôl), **Jn. Chp.,** d. Naumberg, 1759; son-in-law and pupil of J. S. Bach; organist and composer.

Altschuler (ält'-shōōl-ĕr), **Modeste,** conductor; b. Mohilev, Russia, Feb. 15, 1873; studied Moscow Cons., 'cello, orch., with Arensky, Safonoff, Taneieff; European tour with Moscow Trio; came to America as 'cellist and teacher, 1900; founded Russian Symph. Orch., New York, 1903; cond. many first perf. of Russian works with this group, now disbanded. Res. Los Angeles.

Alvarez (ăl-vä'-rĕth), (1) **Fermin Maria,** b. Saragossa; d. Barcelona, 1898; c. popular songs, etc. (2) (ăl-vä-rĕz), stage name of **Albert Raymond Gourron;** Bordeaux, 1861 —Nice, Feb. 1, 1933; tenor; pupil of A. de Martini; début at Ghent, later at Paris Opéra as leading tenor for many years; 1898 Met. Op. House, New York.

Alvary (ăl-vä'-rē), **Max** (rightly **Achenbach**), Düsseldorf, 1856—Datenberg, Thuringia, Nov. 8, 1898; eminent Wagnerian tenor; début at Weimar.

Alvsleben, Melitta. Vide OTTO-ALVSLEBEN.

Amadé (äm-ä-dā), (1) **Ladislaw,** Baron von. Kaschau, Hungary, 1703—Felbar, 1764; poet and composer. (2) **Thaddäus,** Graf von Pressburg, 1782—Vienna, 1845; pianist.

Amadei (äm-ä-dā'-ē), **R.,** Loreto, Italy, Nov. 29, 1840—Dec. 13, 1913; succeeded his father as organist and conductor.

Amati (ä-mä'-tē), a family of famous violin-makers at Cremona, Italy. (1) **Andrea,** 1530 (?)—1611 (?), evolved the violin from the viol; his younger bro., (2) **Niccolò,** made fine bass-viols 1568–86. A.'s 2 sons, (3) **Antonio,** 1555—1638, and (4) **Geronimo,** d. 1630, produced violins of the same style. The most famous was Geronimo's son, (5) **Niccolò,** Sept. 3, 1596—Aug. 12, 1684, who built the 'Grand' Amatis," large violins of powerful tone; his label is "Nicolaus Amati Cremonens. Hieronimi filius Antonii nepos. Fecit anno 16—";

he trained Andrea **Guarneri** and Antonio **Stradivari.** (6) His son **Giralomo,** the last of the family, was inferior. (7) **Giuseppe A.,** b. 17th cent., Bologna, a violin-maker, may have been of the same family. (8) **V.** (called **Amatus**), Cimmina, Sicily, 1629—Palermo, 1670, conductor and composer. (9) **Antonio** and (10) **Angelo,** brothers, and organ-builders at Pavia, ca. 1830.

Amato (ä-mä'-to), **Pasquale,** Naples, Mar. 21, 1878—N. Y., Aug. 1942: barytone; deb. Naples, 1900; sang Milan, then at Trieste, etc.; 1909, Manhattan Opera; from 1911 Met. Op., singing leading rôles in variety of operas for a decade; heard widely in concerts and opera in U. S. and Europe; taught Louisiana Univ.

Ambrogetti (äm-brō-jĕt'-tē), **G.,** sang 1807—1838, basso-buffo.

Ambros (äm'-brôs), **Aug. W.,** Mauth, near Prague, Nov. 17, 1816—Vienna, June 28, 1876, eminent historian and critic.

Ambrose (Ambro'sius), Trèves A. D. 333—Milan April 4, 397; Bishop of Milan, regulated (384) and developed Western church-music by introducing ritual as practised in the Eastern Church; the adoption of the four authentic church-modes was probably due to him; he has been called "The Father of Christian Hymnology," though his authorship of the so-called Ambrosian Hymn is discredited further than the translation of the text into the "*Te Deum*"; it is improbable that he was acquainted with the use of letters for notation.

Am(m)erbach (äm'-ĕr-bäkh), **Elias Nikolaus,** ca. 1530—Leipzig, 1597 organist, theorist and composer.

Amfitheátrov, Daniele, b. Russia, 1901; assoc. cond. Minneapolis Symph. 1937.

Amiot (äm-yō), **Father,** b. Toulon, 1718; Jesuit missionary and writer on Chinese music.

Am(m)on (äm-mōn), (1) **Blasius,** b. in the Tyrol—d. Vienna, June 1590, court-sopranist, later Franciscan friar, composer. (2) **Jn. Ands.,** Bamberg, 1763—Ottingen, 1825; virtuoso on the Waldhorn.

Am'ner, (1) **John,** b. late 16th cent.— d. 1641; organist. (2) His son **Ralph,** bass at Windsor, 1623—1663.

Amorevoli (ä-mō-rä'-vō-lē), **Angelo,** Venice, 1716—Dresden, 1798; singer.
Anacker (ä'-näk-ĕr), **Aug. Fd.,** Freiberg, Saxony, 1790—1854; cantor and composer.
Ancot (äṅ-kō), a family of pianists and composers at Bruges. (1) **Jean** (*père*), 1779—1848. His two sons, (2) **Jean** (*fils*), 1799—Boulogne, 1829, (3) **Louis,** 1803—Bruges, 1836.
Ander (än'-dĕr), **Aloys,** Liebititz, Bohemia, 1824—Bad Wartenberg, 1864; tenor.
An'ders, Gf. Eng., Bonn, 1795—Paris, 1866; writer.
Andersen (1) **Joachim,** Copenhagen, April 29, 1847—May 7, 1909. Soloist at 13. Toured widely; court musician, Copenhagen, Petersburg and Berlin; for 8 years solo flutist and assistant conductor of Berlin Phil. Orch., of which he was one of the founders; 1895—1909, the ruling musical force in Copenhagen, as conductor of the Palace concerts, the Tivoli Orchestra, the Municipal Summer concerts, his orchestral school, and Inspector (with rank of Captain) of all the military music of Denmark. Made Knight of Dannebrog Order by King Charles IX; received the "Palms" of the Acad. from the Pres. of France, and was made "Prof." by King Frederik of Denmark. (2) **Vigo,** Copenhagen, April 21, 1852—Chicago, Jan. 29, 1895; solo flutist with Thomas orch.; brother of (1).
An'derson, (1) **Lucy,** née **Philpot,** Bath, 1790—London, 1878; pianist. (2) **Geo. Fr.,** King's bandmaster in England, 1848. (3) **Thomas,** Birmingham, England, April 15, 1836—Sept. 18, 1903; critic, organist and c. (4) **Marian,** b. Philadelphia; eminent Negro contralto; studied with Giuseppe Boghetti; first gained prominence as soloist with Philadelphia Phil. Symph., and in New York recital début; winner of contest to appear with N. Y. Phil. at Stadium concerts, 1925; European appearances, 1930-5, incl. Berlin, Vienna, Paris, where she gained remarkable triumphs and returned to U. S. in latter year, giving several N. Y. recitals with outstanding succ. Chosen to sing in Brahms' alto rhapsody with Vienna Phil. under Bruno Walter during festival there in 1936.
Andrade (dän-drä-dhĕ) **Fran. d',** Lis-

bon, 1859—Berlin, Feb. 8, 1921; barytone; studied with Miraglia and Ronconi; sang leading rôles in many European cities.
André (äṅ-drä), a musical family of Offenbach. (1) **Jn.,** 1741—1799, publisher and pianist; he originated in 1783 the *durchkomponirte Ballade* (vide D. D.). (2) **Jn. Ant.,** 1775—1842; third son of above; pianist, publisher, theorist. (3) **Karl Aug.,** 1806—Frankfort, 1887; publisher and writer. (4) **Julius,** 1808—Frankfort, 1880; organist. (5) **Jn. Aug.,** 1817—1887; publisher; his 2 sons, (6) **Karl** (b. 1853) and (7) **Adolf** (b. 1885), were later the proprietors. (8) **Jean Baptiste** (de St. Gilles), 1823—Frankfort, 1882; pianist and composer.
An'dreae, Volkmar, b. Berne, July 5, 1879; conductor and composer; studied Cologne Cons.; led choruses in Winterthur and Zurich; after 1906, led symph. concerts of the Tonhalle Soc.; 1914, dir. of Zurich Cons.; president of the Swiss Composers' Soc. after 1920; has appeared as guest cond. in other European cities; c. (operas) *"Ratcliff"* and *"Abenteuer des Casanova"*; also orch. and chamber music.
Andreoli (än-drä-ō'-lē), (1) **Evangalista,** 1810—1875; organist at Mirandola; his two sons, (2) **Guglielmo** (Modena, 1835—Nice, 1860) and (3) **Carlo** (Mirandola, 1840—Regio Emilia, 1910 ?), were pianists, the latter also organist and composer. (4) **Giuseppe,** Milan, 1757—1832; double-bassist and harpist.
Andreozzi (än-drä-ôd'-zē), **Gaetano,** Naples, 1763—Paris, 1826; dram. composer.
Andrésen (än-drä'-zĕn), **Ivar,** b. 1895; bass; sang Dresden Op., 1925-33; Bayreuth, 1927; Met. Op., 1930; Berlin Op., 1931.
Andreva (än-drä'-vä), **Stella,** b. London, of Scotch-German ancestry; coloratura soprano; studied singing at R. A. M.; sang in operettas, then engaged for three years at Stockholm R. Op.; 1934-5; Covent Garden; Met. Op., N. Y., 1936-37.
Andrevi (än-drä'-vē), **Fran.,** Sanabuya, near Lerida, 1786—Barcelona, 1853; critic and writer.
Andrien. Vide ADRIEN.
An'dries, Jean, Ghent, 1798—1872; teacher and writer.

Androt (äṅ-drō), **Albert Auguste,** Paris, 1781—Aug. 9, 1804; c. opera, requiem, etc.

Anerio (ä-nä'-rē-ō), (1) **Felice,** Rome, 1560—Sept. 26, 1614; successor to Palestrina. (2) **Giovanni Fran.,** Rome, ca. 1567—1621 (?), bro. of above; conductor and church-composer.

Anfos'si, **Pasquale,** Taggia, near Naples, 1727—Rome, 1797; pupil and rival of Piccinni; composed 54 operas, etc.

Angelet (äṅ'-zhŭ-lä), **Chas. Fran.,** Ghent, 1797—Brussels, 1832.

Angeli (dän-jä'-lē), **Andrea d',** b. Padua, Nov. 9, 1868; historian; c. opera "*L'Innocente*" (Bologna), etc.

Angelini (än-jä-lē'-nĭ), **Bontempi Giov. And.,** Perugia, ca. 1624—1705; court-singer and dram. composer.

Angeloni (än-jä-lō'-nĭ), **Luigi,** Frosinone, Papal States, 1758—London, 1842; writer.

An'gerer, **Gottfried,** Waldsee, Feb. 3, 1851—Zurich, Aug. 19, 1909; c. male choruses.

Anglebert (däṅ-glŭ-băr), **J. Bapt. H. d',** 1628 (?)—Paris, 1691; court-clavicembalist to Louis XIV.

Animuccia (än-ē-moot'-chä), (1) **Giov.,** Florence, ca. 1500—Rome, March, 1571; wrote the first *Laudi spirituali* for the lectures of Neri in the oratory of S. Philippo, has hence been called "Father of Oratorio"; he was Palestrina's predecessor as conductor at the Vatican. (2) **Paolo,** d. Rome, 1563, bro. of above.

Ankerts, **D'.** Vide DANKERS, GHISELIN.

Annibale (än-nĭ-bä'-lĕ), (1) (called **Il Padova'no,** or **Patavi'nus,** from Padua, where he was born 1527) d. Groz 1575; organist and composer. (2) **Domenico,** Italian sopranist in London, 1756.

An'rooy, **Peter van,** b. Zalt-Bommel, Holland, Oct. 13, 1879; conductor; composer; pupil of Joh. Wagenaar and Taneiev; cond. orchestras in Amsterdam, Groningen, Arnhem, and after 1917 of the Residentie Orch. in The Hague; hon. doctorate from Univ. of Gronigen; c. chamber, orch., and choral works.

Ansani (än-sä'-nē) **Giovanni,** b. Rome, 18th cent.; dram. tenor.

Anschütz (än'-shüts), **K.,** Coblenz,

1815—New York, 1870; cond. and composer.

Ansermet (än-sĕr-mä'), **Ernest,** b. Vevey, Switzerland, Nov. 11, 1883; conductor; studied with Denéreaz, Gédalge, Barblan, Bloch; after 1912, cond. of concerts at Montreux Kursaal; cond. Geneva subscription concerts, 1915–18; founder, Orchestre de la Suisse-Romande, Geneva, 1918; conductor after 1915 with Diaghileff Ballet Russe, in Paris, London, Italy, Spain, America. Made guest tours of other countries, also America. C. symphonic poem "*Feuilles au printemps*" and other works.

Ansorge (än-sŏr'-gĕ), (1) **Max,** b Striegau, Silesia, Oct. 1, 1862; organist; son of a cantor; studied at Berlin; c. songs, motets, etc. (2) **Konrad (Eduard Reinhold),** Buchwald, Silesia, Oct. 15, 1862—Berlin, Feb. 13, 1930; pianist; pupil Leipzig Cons and of Liszt; toured America; c for orchestra, and piano.

Ant'cliffe, **Herbert,** b. Sheffield, Engl. July 30, 1875; writer on music; au thor of studies of Schubert, Brahms, etc.

Antegnati (än-tän-yä'-tĭ), **Costanzo,** Brescia, 1557—ca. 1620; organ-builder, etc.

Antheil (än'-tīl), **George,** b. Trenton, N. J., July 8, 1900; composer; studied Sternberg Cons., Philadelphia; res. in Europe for some years; c. (opera) "*Transatlantic*", based on modern American "jazz age" theme (Frankfort State Op., 1930); Symphony in F (Paris, 1926); Piano Concerto in A (Paris, 1927); music to Sophocles' "*Oedipus*" (Berlin State Theat., 1929); (ballet) "*Fighting the Waves*" (text by W. B. Yeats), Abbey Theatre, Dublin; (opera) "*Helen Retires*" (book by Erskine), N. Y., 1934; two string quartets, orchestral, chamber music. Earlier manner radical to extent of introducing noise-making instruments as in "*Ballet Mécanique,*" c. opera, *Volpone* (N. Y., 1954).

An'tipov, **Constantin,** b. Russia, Jan. 18, 1859; c. symph. allegro for orch., and piano pieces; d. (?).

Antoine (änt-wän'), **Josephine,** b. Boulder, Colo.; soprano; studied Juilliard Sch.; Met. Op. after 1935.

Apel (ä'pĕl), **Jn. Aug.,** Leipzig, 1771—1816; writer.

Apél, Willi, b. Könitz; Ph.D., Berlin Univ.; ed. *"Harvard Dict. of Music."*

Apell (ä-pĕl'), **Jn. D.** von, Cassel, 1754—1833; conductor and dram. composer.

Appel (äp' pĕl), **K.,** Dessau, 1812—Dec. 9, 1895; violinist, court-leader, composed opera *"Die Rauberbraut"* (Dessau, 1840), and humorous male quartets.

Appun (äp-poon'), **G. A. I.,** Hanau, 1816—1885; versatile performer on nearly every instr.; writer on and experimenter in acoustics; made an harmonium of 53 degrees to the octave.

Aprile (ä-prē'-lĕ), **Gius,** Bisceglia, 1738—Martina, 1814; celebrated contralto musico and vocal teacher; writer and composer.

Ap'thorp, W. Foster, Boston, Mass., Oct. 24, 1848—Vevey, Feb. 19, 1913; Harvard, '69, studied piano, harmony, cpt. with J. K. Paine and B. J. Lang; teacher of theory, and for many years distinguished critic and writer on music; author of *"Hector Berlioz"*; *"Musicians and Music-Lovers, and other Essays"*; *"By the Way, About Music and Musicians"*; *"Opera and Opera Singers"*, etc.

Aptom'mas, (1) **John,** (2) **Thomas,** brothers; b. Bridgend, England, 1826, and 1829; harp-players and teachers.

Ar'a, Ugo, Venice, 1876—Lausanne, 1936; pupil of Tirindelli, Thomson and Fuchs; 1903-17, viola player in Flonzaley Quartet.

Araja (ä-rä'-yä), **Fran.,** Naples, 1700—Bologna, ca. 1767; dram. composer; composed the first opera written in Russian.

Arauxo (ä-rä-ooks'-ō) (or **Araujo** (ä-rä-oo'-hō)), **Francisco Correa de,** ca. 1581—Segovia, 1663; bishop, theorist.

Arbeau, Thoinot (twä-nō är-bō). Vide TABOUROT.

Arbós (är'-vōs), **E. Fernandez,** b. Madrid, 1863—San Sebastian, 1939; violinist; grandfather & father were bandmasters in army; pupil Madrid Cons.; took prizes at 12; then studied with Vieuxtemps, Gevaërt and Joachim; cond. Berlin Phil. Society; taught at Hamburg, Madrid, and Royal College, London; c. comic opera, *"El Cientro de la Tierra,"* Madrid, 1895; also for violin and orch.; after 1908, cond. Madrid

Orquesta Sinfonica; guest cond. in Europe and U. S.

Ar'cadelt, Jacob (or **Jachet Arkadelt, Archadet, Arcadet, Harcadelt**), ca. 1514—after 1557; distinguished Flemish composer and teacher; 1540, singer in Paris; 1557, *Regius musicus;* composed masses, etc.

Archadet (är-chä-dä'). Vide ARCADELT.

Archambeau (är'-shän-bō), **Iwan d',** b. Liége, 1879; 'cellist; pupil of his father, Massau and Jacobs; after 1903 mem. of Flonzaley Quartet.

Archangel'ski, Alexander A., Pensa, Russia, Oct. 23, 1846—Prague, 1924; organist and cond.; c. masses, a requiem, much church music.

Ar'cher, Fredk., Oxford, England, June 16, 1838—Pittsburgh, Pa. Oct. 22, 1901; pupil of his father; studied in London and Leipzig; organist and opera-director in London; 1881, organist of Plymouth Church, Brooklyn, later in New York; 1887, conductor of Boston Oratorio Soc.; 1895-98, Pittsburgh (Pa.) Orchestra; composed cantata, organ-pieces, etc.

Arditi (är-dē'-tē), (1) **Michele,** Marchese, Naples, 1745—1838; composer. (2) **Luigi,** Crescentino, Piedmont, July 16, 1822—Hove, England May 1, 1903; pupil of Milan Cons.; violinist, then director of opera, 1843, Milan, Turin, and Havana. He visited New York with the Havana opera company, 1847, and at intervals thereafter until 1856. Composed 3 operas, vocal waltzes, *"Il Bacio,"* etc.; wrote *"My Reminiscences"* (London, 1896).

Arens (ä'-rĕns), **Fz. Xaver,** Neef, Germany, Oct. 28, 1856—Los Angeles, Jan. 28, 1932; came to America early in youth; pupil of his father, and of Rheinberg, etc.; conductor, organist; composer of symphonic fantasia, etc.

Arensky (ä-rĕn'-shkĭ), **Anton Stepanovitch,** Novgorod, Russia, July 31, 1861—Tarioki, Finland, Feb. 25, 1906; composer and pianist; pupil of Johanssen and Rimsky-Korsakov; Prof. Imp. Cons. Moscow, and conductor Imperial Court Choir; composed a symphony, 4 suites for orch., 1-act opera *"Rafaello,"* string quartets, concerto for piano, etc., including *"Essais sur des rythmes oubliés,"* f. pf. 4 hands.

Aretino. Vide GUIDO D'AREZZO.

Argentina (ärkh-ĕn-tē'-nä), **La** (stage name of **Antonia Mercè**) Buenos Aires—Bayonne, France, July 18, 1936; noted dancer, esp. famed for her perf. of Spanish dances and remarkable skill in playing on castanets; her parents were members of the R. Op. ballet, Madrid, of which she became *prima ballerina* at 19; later made world tours with great succ., incl. United States

Aria (ä'-rĭ-ä), **Cesare**, Bologna, 1820—1894; singing-teacher.

Aribo (ä-rē'-bō), **Scholas'ticus**, d. ca. 1078; probably from the Netherlands; writer. (Gerbert.)

Arien'zo (där-ĭ-ĕn'-tsō), **Nicolà d',** Naples, Dec. 24, 1842—April 25, 1915; composed 5 operas in Neapolitan dialect, "*Monzu Gnazio*" (Naples, 1860), and "*I Due Mariti*" (Naples, 1866), the most successful, realistic and original; also an oratorio, a "*Pensiero Sinfonico*," overtures, etc.; wrote a treatise advocating pure intonation in-tead of temperament, and a third mode (the Minor Second), besides the usual major and minor.

A'rion, partly traditional Greek singer and lyrist (7th cent., B. C.), hence, the name of a vocal society.

Arios'ti, **Attilio**, Bologna, 1660—ca. 1740; composed 15 operas; 1716 a rival of Buononcini, and of Händel; in London in 1720, the three composed the opera "*Muzio Scaevola*."

Aristi'des Quintilia'nus, Greek teacher and writer on music, ca. 160.

Ar'istotle, (1) Stagyra, 384 B.C.—322 B. C.; Greek philosopher, whose works include valuable information concerning Greek music. (2) Pseudonym of a writer on mensurable music, 12th—13th cent.

Aristox'enos, b. Tarentum, ca. 354 B.C.; one of the first Greek writers on music.

Arl'berg, **Georg Ephraim, F.,** Leksand, Sweden, 1830—Christiania, Feb. 21, 1896; barytone.

Armbrust (ärm'-broost), **K. F.,** Hamburg, 1849—Hanover, 1896; teacher and critic.

Armbruster (ärm'-broo-stĕr), **K.,** Andernach-on-Rhine, July 13, 1846—London, June 10, 1917; pupil of Hompesch; pianist and lecturer: Hans Richter's assistant conductor at the Wagner concerts, 1882–84;

later conducted at va.ious London theatres.

Armes, Philip, b. Norwich, England, 1836; Mus. Doc. Oxon, 1864; organ composer; d. Durham, Feb. 10, 1908.

Armingaud (ăr-măṅ-gō), **Jules,** Bayonne, May 3, 1820—Paris, Feb. 27, 1900; was refused admission to the Paris Cons. at 19 since he was "too far advanced"; leader of a string quartet enlarged to the *Société Classique;* said to have introduced Beethoven's quartets into Paris.

Arms'heimer, Ivan Ivanovitch, b. St. Petersburg, March 19, 1860; pupil at the cons.; c. 1-act opera "*Sous la feuillée*" (French text); 2-act opera "*Der Oberförster*" (German text). 3-act opera "*Jaegerliv*" (Danish text); cantatas, songs, etc.

Arnaud (ăr-nō), (1) Abbé **Fran.,** Aubignan, 1721—Paris, 1784; writer. (2) **J. Et. Guil.,** Marseilles, 1807—Jan., 1863; composer.

Arne (ärn), (1) Dr. **Thomas Augustine** London, March 12, 1710—March 5. 1778; by secret nightly practice he learned the spinet and violin, his father wishing him to study law: 1736, m. Cecilia Young, a favourite singer of Händel's; 1738, he was composer to the Drury Lane Th. and set Dalton's adaptation of Milton's "*Comus*"; in his masque "*Alfred*" (1740) is "Rule Britannia"; in Dublin (1742–44) he produced two operas, "*Britannia*" and "*Eliza*", and a musical farce "*Thomas and Sally*"; 1745, composer to Vauxhall Gardens, London; set to music the songs in "*As You Like It*," "*Where the Bee Sucks*," in "*The Tempest*," etc.; Mus. Doc. Oxon, 1759; he was the first to use female voices in oratorio-choruses ("*Judith*"); composed 2 oratorios, many masques, orch. overtures, vln.-sonatas, organ-music, harpsichord-sonatas, glees, catches, canons, etc. (2) **Michael,** London, 1741—Jan. 14, 1786 (not 1806); natural son of above; conductor and dram. composer.

Arneiro (där-nä'-ē-rō), **Jose Aug. Ferreira Veiga,** Viscount d', Macao, China, Nov. 22, 1838—San Remo, July, 1903; of Portuguese parents; composed 2 operas.

Arnold (är'-nōlt), (1) **G.,** b. Weldsberg, Tyrol, 17th cent.; organist. (2) **Samuel,** London, 1740–1802; organist Westminster Abbey. (3) **Jn. Gottf.,** near Oehringen, 1773—Frankfort, 18c6; 'cellist, etc. (4) **Ignaz ErnstFd.**, Erfurt, 1774—1812; writer. (5) **K.**, near Mergentheim, Würtemberg, 1794—Christiania, 1873; son of (3) **J. G.**; pianist and composer. (6) **K.**, b. St. Petersburg, 1820; son of (5); 'cellist in Royal Orch.; studied Stockholm. (7) **Fr. W.**, near Heilbronn, 1810—Elberfeld, 1864; collector and composer. (8) **Yourij von**, St. Petersburg, 1811—Simferopol, Crimea, 1898; singing-teacher and dram. composer. (9) **Richard,** Eilenburg, Jan. 10, 1845—New York, June 21, 1918; at 8 taken to U. S.; pupil of Fd. David, 1869–76; 1st violinist of Theo. Thomas' orch., 1878; leader New York Philh. Club, 1891; 1897, organised a sextet. (10) **Maurice** (real name Strothotte), b. St. Louis, Jan. 19, 1865—New York, 1937; pupil of the Cincinnati Coll., 1883; Vierling and Urban, Berlin; Cologne Cons. and Max Bruch, Breslau; lived St. Louis, then New York as teacher in the Nat. Cons. and pupil of Dvořák; composed notable *"Plantation Dances,"* a *"Dramatic Overture,"* 2 comic operas, etc. Wrote *"Some Points on Modern Orchestration."*

Ar'noldson, (1) **Oscar,** Stockholm, 1839—Carlsbad, 1881; tenor. (2) **Sigrid,** b. Stockholm, 1864; daughter of above; operatic soprano; pupil of Maurice Strakosch and Desirée Artot; début, Moscow, 1886; has sung in Europe and America (1894) with success; m. Alfred Fischof.

Arnould (är-noo), **Madeleine Sophie,** Paris, 1744—1802; soprano, created Gluck's *"Iphigénie."*

Ar'rau, **Claudio,** b. Chillan (Chile) Feb. 6, 1903; pianist; pupil of Paoli, Martin Krause; made first appearances as piano prodigy, winning international prize; later toured Europe and U. S., developing into mature artist of strong powers.

Arres'ti, **Giulio Cesare,** ca. 1630—ca 1695; organist and c. at Bologna.

Arriaga·y Balzola (där-rĭ-ä'-gä e bäl'-thō-lä), **Juan C. J. A. d'.** Bilboa, 1806—1826.

Arrieta (är-rĭ-ā'-tä), **J. Emilio,** Puenta la Reina, 1823—Madrid, 1894; dram. composer.

Arrigoni (är-rē-gō'-nĕ), **Carlo,** Florence, ca. 1705—Tuscany (?) ca. 1743; lutenist and composer, rival in London to Händel.

Arronge (lär-rônzh), **Adolf l',** Hamburg, March 8, 1838—Berlin, 1908; pupil of Genée, and at Leipzig Cons.; 1874, theatre-manager, Breslau; composed comic operas, *"Singspiele,"* etc.

Artaria (är-tä-rē'-ä), music publishing house in Vienna, founded by Carlo A., 1780.

Arteaga (är-tä-äg'-ä), **Stefano,** Madrid, 1730—Paris, 1799; Span.sh Jesuit; theorist.

Artot (är-tō), (1) **Maurice Montagney** (ancestor of a line of musicians named Montagney), Gray (Haute-Saône), 1772—Brussels, 1829; bandmaster. (2) **J. Désiré M.,** Paris, 1803—St. Josse ten Noode, 1887; son of above; horn-player and teacher. (3) **Alex. Jos.,** son of Maurice, Brussels, 1815—Ville-d'Avray, 1845; notable violinist and composer. (4) **Marguerite Josephine Désirée,** Paris, July 21, 1835; Vienna, April 3, 1907; daughter of (2) Jean-Désiré; dram.-soprano, pupil of Viardot-Garcia (1855–57); début Brussels, 1857; sang Grand Opera, Paris, 1858, e.c., m. the Spanish barytone, Padilla, in 1869. (5) **Lola** (A. de Padilla), Sèvres, 1885 —Berlin, 1933; daughter of the preceding, also a noted operatic soprano.

Artusi (är-too'-zē), **Giov. M.,** Bologna ca. 1545—1613; canon and theorist.

Asantchevski (Asantchewski, Assantchevski) (ä-sänt-shĕf'-shkĭ), **Michael Pavlovitch,** Moscoʍ, 1838—1881; composer.

Aschenbren'ner (ä'-shĕn-) **Chr. H.,** Altstettin, 1654—Jena, 1732; violinist and court-conductor.

Ash'ley, (1) **John,** d. 1805; bassoonist and manager; his three sons were (2) **General,** d. 1818, violinist. (3) **Chas. Jane,** 1773—1843, 'cellist and manager. (4) **J. Jas.,** 1771—1815, organist and singing teacher. (5) **J.,** "Ashley of Bath," 1780—1830, bassoonist. (6) **Richard,** 1775—1837, London viola-player.

Ash'ton, Algernon Bennet Langton, b. Durham, Dec. 9, 1859—London, April 11, 1937; pupil Leipzig Cons., pf. teacher, R. C. M., London: after 1913 at London and Trinity Colleges; composer.

Ash'well, Thos., 16th cent., organist and composer in England.

Asioli (äs-ē-ō'-lē), **Bonifacio,** Correggio.

1769—1832; at the age of 8 he had composed 3 masses, 20 other sacred works, a harpsichord-concerto, a vln. concerto, with orch., and 2 harp-sonatas for 4 hands; pupil of Morigi; successful cembalist, improviser; his first opera buffa, *"La Volubile"* (1785), was successful; his opera *"Cinna,"* favourably received in 1793; prof. of cpt. at Milan Cons.

Asola (or) **Asula** (ä'-sō-lä), **Giov. Mat.,** Verona ca. 1560—Venice, 1609; church-composer.

Aspa (äs'-pä), **Mario,** Messina, 1799—1868; composed 42 operas.

Assantsheffsky. Vide ASANTCHEVSKI.

Assmayer (äs'-mī-ĕr), **Ignaz,** Salzburg, 1790—Vienna, 1862; conductor.

Astarit'ta, Gennaro, Naples, ca. 1749—1803; composed 20 operas.

As'ton, Hugh, English organist and composer in reign of Henry VIII.

Astorga (däs-tôr'gä), **Emmanuele,** Baron d', Sicily, 1680—Madrid (?), 1736; church-composer.

Ath'erton, Percy Lee, Roxbury, Mass., Sept. 25, 1871—Atlantic City, Mar., 1944; grad. Harvard, 1893, studied music under Paine; studied two years in Munich with Rheinberger and Thuille, then a year in Berlin with O. B. Boise; 1900 studied with Sgambati and Widor; c. symph., tone poem for orch., *" Noon in the Forest,"* opera-comique *"The Maharaja,"* comic opera, and many songs.

At'kins, Sir Ivor Algernon, b. Cardiff, Nov. 29, 1889; organist and cond.; son and pupil of an organist; later pupil and assistant of C. L. Williams; since 1897, org. Worcester Cath.; cond. of three Choirs Festivals in that city, Mus. D., Oxford; knighted 1921; d. 1953.

Attaignant (ăt-tīn'-yän), **Pierre** (also **Attaingnant, Atteignant**), 16th cent. music-printer.

Attenhofer (ät'-tĕn-hôf-ĕr), **K.,** Wettingen, Switzerland, May 5, 1837—Zurich, May 22, 1914; pupil of Leipzig Cons.; cond., organist, and teacher; notable composer of male choruses.

At'terberg, Kurt; b. Gothenburg, Sweden, Dec. 12, 1887; composer, conductor; studied to be electrical engineer; also 'cello and composition; début with Gothenburg Symph. Orch., 1912; pres., Swedish Soc. of Composers; c. six symphonies, 2 operas, 2 ballets. violin and 'cello

concertos, chamber music works; winner, Intern. Prize, Schubert Centennial Contest, 1928.

Attrup (ät'-troop), **K.,** Copenhagen, March 4, 1848—Oct. 5, 1892; pupil of Gade, whom he succeeded as organ-teacher Copenhagen Cons.; composed studies for organ and songs.

Att'wood, Thos., London, Nov. 23, 1765—Chelsea, March 24, 1838; important English composer; chorister and court-organist; pupil of Mozart; 1796 organist St. Paul's Cathedral; composed 19 operas, anthems, sonatas for piano, etc.

Auber (ō-băr), **Daniel François Esprit,** Caen, Normandy, Jan. 29, 1782—Paris, May 12 (13?), 1871; notable opera-composer; his father an art-dealer in Paris, sent him to London to learn the trade; but in 1804 he returned to Paris; composed opera *"Julie,"* produced by amateurs in 1812 with an orch. of six stringed instrs.; Cherubini heard of it, recognised A.'s talent and taught him; 1842 dir. the Cons. of Music, Paris, as Cherubini's successor; 1857 imperial conductor to Napoleon III. A.'s first public productions were 2 unsuccessful operas; *'La Bergère Chatelaine'?* (1820) was a success; before 1869, he composed over forty operas; his one serious opera, *"Masaniello ou la Muette de Portici"* (1828), with Meyerbeer's *"Robert le Diable"* and Rossini's *"Guillaume Tell,"* established French grand opera; its vivid portrayal of popular fury caused riots in Brussels; his comic operas (to Scribe's librettos) are the best of France; his last opera, *"Rêves d'Amour,"* was produced when he was 87 years old. Other operas are: *"La Marquise de Brinvilliers"* (1831 with eight other composers), *"Le Domino Noir"* (1837), *"Zanetta"* (1840), *"Les Diamants de la Couronne"* (1841), *"La Sirène"* (1844), *"Haydée"* (1847), *"L'Enfant Prodigue"* (1850), *"Zerline,"* *"Manon Lescaut"* (1856).

Aubert (ō-băr), (1) **Jac.** ("le vieux"), b. 1678—Belleville, 1753; violinist. (2) **Louis,** 1720—after 1779; son of above; violinist, etc. (3) **T. Fran. Olivier,** b. Amiens, 1763; 'cellist and composer. (4) **Louis,** b. Paramé, France, Feb. 19, 1877; studied Paris Cons., mem. jury, Paris Cons., music critic; Chevalier, Legion of Honour; c. (opera) *"La Forêt Bleue"*, (Boston, 1913); (symphonic poem) *"Havanera"* (Paris, 1919); (ballet) *"La Nuit Ensorcelée"* (1922); chamber music works, songs, choruses, piano pieces.

Aubery du Boulley (ō-bā-rē′ dü bool-lĕ′), **Prudent-L.**, Verneuil, Eure, 1796—1870; teacher and composer.

Aubry (ō-brē), **Pierre**, Paris, Feb. 14, 1874—Dieppe, Aug. 31, 1910; historian of liturgical music.

Audran (ō-dräṅ), (1) **Marius-P.**, Aix, Provence, 1816—Marseilles, 1887; 1st tenor at the Paris Opéra-Comique. (2) **Edmond,** Lyons, April 11, 1842—Tierceville, n. Gisors, Aug. 17, 1901; son of above; pupil of École Niedermeyer, Paris; Marseilles, 1862, his first opera; produced 36 others, chiefly of a light character. Among his most pop. works are, *"Olivette," "La Mascotte"* (1880), given over 1700 times; *"Miss Hel-yett," "La Poupée,"* etc.

Auer (ow′-ĕr), (1) **Ld.,** Veszprem, Hungary, June 7, 1845—near Dresden July 16, 1930 (of pneumonia); vln.-virtuoso; pupil of Khonetol at Pesth, of Dont, Vienna, then of Joachim; soloist to the Czar, who conferred on him the order of St. Vladimir, carrying hereditary nobility; from 1868 violin-Prof. at the St. Petersburg Cons.; 1887–92, dir. Imp. Mus. Soc.; teacher of many eminent violinists; after 1918 he lived principally in New York, author book on vln.-playing (1921).

Au′gener & Co., London firm of music pub., founded by **G. A.,** 1853.

Aulin (ow′-lēn), **Tor,** Stockholm, Sept. 10, 1866—March 1, 1914; violinist; pupil of Sauret and Ph. Scharwenka; from 1889 Konzertmeister Stockholm, court-opera; 1887 organised the Aulin Quartet.

Auric (ō′-rēk), **Georges,** b. Lodève, France, Feb. 15, 1899; composer; pupil of Paris Cons., and of d'Indy; c. ballets, orchestral and chamber music works, piano pieces, songs; member of former Group of Six: his ballets *"Les Facheux"* and *"Les Matelots"* had particular succ. when given by Diaghileff.

Aus der Ohe (ows′-dĕr ō′-ĕ), **Adèle,** Hanover, Germany, Dec. 11, 1864—Berlin, Dec. 8, 1937; noted pianist; pupil of Kullak and Liszt; composed

2 piano suites, concert étude, etc.; toured widely with great success.

Aus′tin, (1) **Frederic,** b. London, Mar. 30, 1872—Apr. 10, 1952; org. at Liverpool for some years; then teacher at the College of Music, there till 1906; then studied voice with Lunn; début, 1902, favourite in oratorio and in Wagner operas; c. overture *"Richard II"* (Liverpool, 1900); rhapsody *"Spring"* (Queens Hall, 1907), symph. poem *"Isabella,"* also arr. music of *"Beggar's Opera"* by Gay and Pepusch, which had 1463 consecutive perfs. in London, 1920–3. His brother (2) **Ernest,** b. London, Dec. 31, 1874; on the Board of Trade till 33 years old, then studied comp. with J. Davenport; c. symph., idyll, march; *"Love Songs from Don Quixote,"* for voices and orch.; piano sonata, etc.

Aus′tral, Florence (rightly **Wilson**); b. Richmond near Melbourne, Australia, April 26, 1894; studied Melbourne Cons. and London; début in opera as Brünnhilde, London, 1922; toured with British Nat'l. Op. Co., and heard as soloist with orchestras and in oratorio, London; début, Covent Garden Op., 1929; concert tours, England, Australia, New Zealand, South Africa, and America. M. John Amadio, flutist.

Auteri-Manzocchi (ä-oo-tā′-rǐ män-tsôk′-kē), **Salv.,** Palermo, Dec. 25, 1845—Parma, Feb. 21, 1924; pupil of Platania at Palermo, and Mabellini at Florence; composed successful operas, among them *"Graziella"* (Milan, 1894).

Auvergne (dō-vĕrn), **A. d',** Clermont-Ferrand, Oct. 4, 1713—Lyons, Feb. 12, 1797; violinist and dram. composer.

A′verkamp, Anton, Willige Langerak, Holland, Feb. 18, 1861—Bussum, Holland, June 1, 1934; composer and conductor; pupil of Daniel de Lange, Kiel, Rheinberger, Messchaert; dir. of a singing school in Amsterdam and (1890–1914) of a famous *a cappella* choir with which he perf. old church music; c. orch., chamber music, choral works, songs, etc.

A′very, J., d. England, 1808; organ-builder.

Av′ison, Chas., Newcastle-on-Tyne, 1710—May 9, 1770; organist, writer and composer; vide Robert Browning's "PARLEYINGS."

Aylward (āl'-wärd), **Th.,** ca. 1730—
1801; teacher and composer.
Ayrton (ăr'-tŭn), (1) **Edm.,** Ripon,
Yorks, 1734—Westminster, 1808;
composer. (2) **W.,** London, 1777—
1858; son of above; writer and editor.
Azzopardi (äd-zō-pär'-dē), **Francesco,**
conductor and theorist at Malta,
1786.
Azevedo (äth-ā-vā'-dhō), **Alexis Jacob,**
Bordeaux, 1813—Paris, 1875; writer.

B

Babbi (bäb'-bē), **Christoph** (or **Cristo-
foro**), Cesena, 1748—Dresden, 1814;
violinist and composer.
Babbini (bä-bē'-nē), **Mat.,** Bologna,
1754—1816; tenor, début, 1780.
Ba'bell, Wm., ca. 1690—Canonbury,
England, 1723; organist, teacher and
composer; son of a bassoon-player.
Bacc̃loni (bäk-ä-lō'-nē), **Salvatóre,**
noted Ital. buffo-bass; Met. Op.,
1939.
Bac'fark (or **Bacfarre**), **Valentin** (rightly
Graew (gräv), Kronstadt, 1507
—Padua, 1576; lutenist and writer.
Bach (bäkh), the name of a Thuringian
family prominent for two centuries
in music and furnishing so many
organists, Kapellmeisters and cantors
that town musicians were called "the
Bachs," after them. Outstanding
were: (1) **Bach, Jn. Sebastian,** Eisenach, March 21, 1685—Leipzig,
July 28, 1750; youngest son of **Jn.
Ambrosius B.** and Elizabeth (née
Lammerhit) of Erfurt; early left an
orphan; both parents died when he
was 10, his father having begun
teaching him the violin. He went to
the home of his brother Jn. Christoph, who taught him the clavichord,
but forbade him inspection of a MS.
vol. of works by Frohberger, Buxtehude, etc., obtaining it secretly **B.**
copied it by moonlight for 6 months,
though near-sighted, with results
fatal to his eyes in later life. This
desire to study other men's work
characterised his whole career. At
15 his fine soprano voice secured him
free tuition at St. Michael's Ch. in
Lüneberg (he having already attended the Ohrdruff Lyceum). He
went on foot on holidays to Hamburg
to hear the great Dutch organist
Reinken, and at Celle he heard the
French instr. music used in the
Royal Chapel. He studied also the

work of Böhm, organist at Lüneberg,
and practised violin, clavichord and
org. often all night; 1703, in the
Weimar ct.-orch.; 1704, organist at
Arnstadt; 1705, walked 50 miles to
Lübeck to hear Buxtehude, and
stayed till a peremptory recall from
the Church at Arnstadt; 1707, organist at Mühlhausen. On Oct. 17, he
m. Maria Barbara Bach, his cousin,
who bore him 7 children, of whom 4
died, leaving a daughter, Wm.-
Friedemann, and K. P. E. (See below.) 1708, he played before the
Duke at Weimar, and was made ct.-
organist; 1714 Konzertmeister. In
his vacations he made clavichord and
org. tours. 1714, he furnished the
organ-music for a service conducted
in the Thomaskirche, Leipzig, and
produced a cantata. Dresden, 1717.
he challenged Marchand, a French
organist of high reputation, who was
afraid to compete. 1717 Kapellmeister to Prince Leopold of Anhalt,
at Köthen, and composed much
orch.- and chamber-music. In 1719
he revisited Halle, to meet Händel,
but he had just gone to England.
1720, his wife died. He applied for
the organ of the Jacobskirche, Hamburg. **B.** was now famous, but a
young rival offered to pay 4,000
marks for the place and got it. In
1721 he m. Anna Magdalene Wülken,
daughter of the ct.-trumpeter at
Weissenfels. She bore him 13 children, 9 of them sons, of whom only
2 survived him: Jn., Christoph, Fr.,
and Jn. Christian. His second wife
had a fine voice and musical taste,
and wrote out the parts of many of
his cantatas; for her he prepared
2 books of music. In May, 1723,
cantor at the Thomasschule, Leipzig,
vice Jn. Kuhnau; also organist and
dir. of mus. at the Thomaskirche and
the Nicolaikirche, continuing as
"Kapellmeister vom Haus aus." to
Prince Leopold. He was made,
1736, hon. cond. to the Duke of
Weissenfels, and court-composer to
the King of Poland, and Elector of
Saxony. He kept his place at Leipzig for twenty-seven years, and there
wrote most of his sacred music. He
often visited Dresden, where he could
hear the Italian opera, cond. by
Hasse. Frederick the Great having
asked to hear him, on May 7, 1747,
with his son Wilhelm Friedemann.

B. arrived at Potsdam. He improvised upon the various Silbermann pianos in the palace, followed from room to room by the king and his musicians. The next day he tried the principal organs in Potsdam, improvising a 6-part fugue on a theme proposed by the king. He afterward wrote a 3-part fugue on this theme, a Ricercare in 6 parts, several canons inscribed "Thematis regii elaborationes canonicae," and a trio for flute, violin, and bass, dedicating the *"Musikalisches Opfer"* to the king. 1749, two operations to restore his sight, weakened by copying his own and other men's works and engraving his *"Art of Fugue,"* left him totally blind and ruined his previous vigour. His sight was suddenly restored, July 10, 1750; but 10 days later he died of apoplexy. He dictated the choral *"Vor deinen Thron tret' ich hiemit,"* shortly before his death.

Among his distinguished pupils were Krebs, Homilius, Agricola, Kirnberger, Goldberg, Marpurg; J. Kasper Vogler; Altnikol, his son-in-law, and his sons for whom he wrote the *"Klavierbüchlein,"* and the *"Kunst der Fuge."* He engraved on copper; invented the "viola pomposa" and the "Lauten-Clavicembalum"; he advocated equal temperament (vide D. D.), tuning his own pianos and writing *"Das Wohltemperirte Klavier,"* to further the cause. This work (known in English as *"The welltempered Clavichord,"* or *"The 48-Fugues"*) is a set of 48 preludes and fugues, two of each to each key, major and minor. The works are very chromatic and use the keys enharmonically. Some of his improvements in fingering still survive. Bach was little known as a composer during his life, and few of his works were published then. He was not indeed established on his present pinnacle till Mendelssohn took up his cause, in 1829; Franz was also an important agent in preparing his scores for general use. In 1850, a hundred years after his death, the BACH-GESELLSCHAFT began to publish his complete works. Many other Bach societies now exist. **B's.** enormous list of works includes: VOCAL, 5 sets of church Cantatas for Sundays and feast-days, *"Gottes Zeit ist die*

beste Zeit," etc., various secular cantatas, 2 comic cantatas, the *"Bauern Cantate"* and *"Coffee-Cantate,"* a protest against the excessive use of the beverage, and *Trauerode*, on the death of the Electress of Saxony; 5 Passions, incl. the *St. Matthew*, the *St. John*, and the *St. Luke* (doubtful); a *Christmas Oratorio*, in 5 parts; 4 small masses and the Grand Mass in B min.; motets; 2 Magnificats; 5 Sanctus. INSTRUMENTAL, numerous pieces for clavichord: inventions in 2 and 3 parts; 6 "small" French suites; 6 "large" English suites; Preludes and Fugues, incl. *"Das Wohltemperirte Klavier"*; the remarkable *"Goldberg Variations"*; pf.-sonatas with instrs., incl. 6 famous sonatas for pf. and vln.; solo sonatas for vln. and 'cello; solos, trios, etc., for various combinations of instrs., concertos for 1 to 4 pfs. vln. and other instrs., concertos with orch.; 6 notable *"Brandenburg"* concertos; overtures and suites, and fantasias, toccatas, preludes, fugues, and chorale-arrangements for organ. The modern-minded musicians of the twentieth century have found new formal and harmonic interest in **B's.** works, and an entire school has used as its slogan, "Back to Bach," in an effort to throw off the influence of Romantic styles of thought and feeling. Such a work as his monumental *"Art of the Fugue"* has gained wide popularity in the concert-room, the latter arr. for orch. by W. Graeser, heard in Europe and U. S. often after 1926. The best biography of **B.** is by Spitta (Leipzig, 1873–80, 2 vols.; Eng. transl., London, 1884–85). Other memoirs by Forkel, Schweitzer, Parry, Pirro, C. S. Terry, Boughton, Buhrman and C. F. A. Williams. The Bach *"Jahrbücher,"* pub. by Breitkopf & Härtel, also hold much material of value. Books on **B's.** music have been issued in great numbers, incl. works by Fuller-Maitland, Grace, Iliffe, Prout, Riemann, Schweitzer, Whittaker and C. S. Terry. (See article, page 482.)

(2) **Karl Philipp Emanuel** ("the Berlin" or "Hamburg Bach"), Weimar, March (8?) 14, 1714—Hamburg (Sept. ?) Dec. 14, 1788. Son of above (Johann Sebastian Bach). Studied philosophy and law at Leip-

zig and Frankfort; cond. a singing society at Frankfort, for which he composed. 1737 (38?) in Berlin. Chamber-mus. and clavecinist to Frederick the Great, 1746–57 [or 1740–67?]. 1757 Hamburg as Ch. mus.-dir.; 1767 as Musik-director of the principal church there, vice Telemann, a position held till death. He was one of the chief virtuosos of the day. He was the founder of the modern school of piano-playing, and a pioneer of greatest importance in the sonata and symphony-forms and orchestration, his works having a graceful modernity not possessed even by most of his father's. He wrote *"Versuch über die wahre Art das Clavier zu spielen"* (2 parts, 1753–62), an important work containing detailed explanations concerning ornaments. His very numerous comps. include 210 solo pieces; 52 concertos with orch.; quartets, trios, duets, sonatas, sonatinas, minuets, polonaises, solfeggi, fugues, marches, etc., for clavier; 18 symphonies; 34 miscellaneous pieces for wind-instrs., trios; flute-, 'cello-, and oboe-concertos; soli for flute, viola di gamba, oboe, 'cello, and harp, etc., and 2 oratorios (*"Die Israeliten in der Wüste,"* and *"Die Auferstehung und Himmelfahrt Jesu"*), 22 Passions; cantatas, etc.

(3) **Johann Chr.** ("the London Bach"), Leipzig, Sept. 7 (?), 1735–London, Jan. 1, 1782; youngest son of J. S. Bach; pupil of his brother Emanuel and Martini in Bologna; 1760–2, org. Milan Cathedral; after 1762 lived in London as music master. C. over 15 operas, choral works, many symphonies or overtures, clavier concertos and sonatas. (4) **Wilhelm Friedemann**, Weimar, 1710–Berlin, 1784; eldest son of J. S. Bach; gifted but dissolute; 1733, org. in Dresden; 1747–64, Halle; c. 25 cantatas, many concertos, etc.

Bache (bäch), (1) **Francis Edw.**, Birmingham, 1833–1858; violinist. (2) **Walter**, Birmingham, 1842–London, 1888, bro. of above; pianist and teacher. (3) **Constance**, Edgbaston, March 11, 1846–Montreux, June 28, 1903; sister and pupil of above; pupil of Klindworth and Hartvigson; teacher, translator, and composer in London.

Bachelet (bäsh-lā), **Alfred**, b. Paris Feb. 26, 1864–194–; studied at Cons. in Paris; won Prix de Rome; from 1919 dir. of Nancy Cons.; after almost a quarter century of obscurity, he prod. several lyric dramas that placed him in front rank of contemporary French composers, esp. *"Quand la Cloche Sonnera"* (Paris Op.-Comique, 1922) and *"Scemo"* (Paris Op., 1914, later revived).

Bachmann (bäkh'-män), (1) **Anton**, 1716–1800; court-musician at Berlin, instr.-maker; inv. the machine-head. His son and successor, (2) **Karl L.**, 1743–1800, court-violinist, player, married the pianist and singer (3) **Charlotte Karoline Wilhelmine Stowe**, Berlin, 1757–1817. (4) Pater **Sixtus**, Kettershausen, Bavaria, July 18, 1754–Marchthal, near Vienna, 1818; organist and pianist of unusual precocity, and memory; said to have played by heart over 200 pieces at 9; at 12 equalled Mozart, then 10 years old, in organ-competition, at Biberach; became a Premonstrant monk, composed Masses, etc. (5) **G. Chr.**, Paderborn, 1804–Brussels, 1842; clarinet-maker, soloist and teacher. (6) **Georges**, ca. 1848–Paris, 1894. (7) **Gottlob**, Bornitz, Saxony, 1763–Zeitz, 1840, organist. (8) **Alberto** (rightly **Abraham**), b. Geneva, Switzerland, March 20, 1875; violin virtuoso; pupil of Thomson, Hubay and Petri; lived in Paris as teacher; made many tours of Europe and after 1916 in U. S.; ed. *"Encyclopedia of the Violin"* (1925).

Bachofen (bäkh'-ôf-ĕn), **Jn. Kaspar**, Zurich, 1697–1755; organist.

Bachrich (bäkh'-rĭkh), **Sigismund**, Zsambokreth, Hungary, Jan. 23, 1841–Vienna, July 16, 1913; violinist, pupil and then teacher at Vienna Cons.; composed 4 comic operas incl. *"Der Fuchs-Major"* (Prague, 1889), etc.

Ba(c)ker-Gröndahl (bäk'-ĕr grön'-däl), **Agathe**, Holmestrand, Norway, Dec. 1, 1847–Christiania, June 6, 1907; pianist and composer; pupil of Kjerulf, Bülow and Liszt; she married 1875, Gröndahl, singing-teacher in Christiania.

Back'ers, Americus. Vide BROADWOOD.

Bac(k)haus (bäk'-hows), **Wilhelm**, b. Leipzig, March 26, 1884; eminent pianist; pupil of Reckendorf and at the Cons., later of d'Albert; from

1900 toured; 1905, piano teacher R. C. M., Manchester, but won the Rubinstein prize and toured again; 1911 the U. S.; 1907 taught master-courses at Sondershausen Cons.

Back'ofen, Jn. G. H., Durlach, Baden, 1768—Darmstadt, 1839; virtuoso and manufacturer of wind-instrs. at Darmstadt; writer and composer.

Ba'con, (1) **Richard Mackenzie**, Norwich, Engl. 1776—1844; teacher and writer. (2 **Katherine,** b. Chesterfield, Engl., June 2, 1896; pupil of Arthur Newstead, whom she married 1916; toured United States and Canada, including series of Beethoven and Schubert sonatas, New York; member, faculty, Juilliard School of Music, New York.

Bader (bä'-dĕr), **K. Adam,** Bamberg, 1789—Berlin, 1870; cathedral-organist, Bamberg (1807); later first tenor Berlin court opera (1820-45).

Badia (bä-dē'-ä), (1) **Carlo Ag.,** Venice, 1672—Vienna, 1738; court-composer at Vienna. (2) **Luigi,** Tirano, Naples, 1819—Milan, 1899; composed 4 operas.

Badiali (bä-dĭ-ä'-lē), **Cesare,** Imola, 1810—Nov. 17, 1865; basso; début, Trieste, 1827; sang throughout Italy; 1859 in London.

Bagge (bäg'-gĕ), **Selmar,** Coburg, 1823 —Basel, 1896; editor and composer.

Bai (or **Baj**) (bä'-ē), **Tommaso,** Crevalcuore, near Bologna, ca. 1650—Rome, Dec. 22, 1714; tenor at the Vatican; conductor, 1713; composed a "*Miserere*," sung in the Papal Chapel, during Holy Week, alternately with those by Allegri and Baini.

Baif (bīf), **Jn. A. de,** Venice, 1532—Paris, 1589; composer.

Bai'ley Apfelbeck, Marie Louise, b. Nashville, Tenn., Oct. 24, 1876; Leipzig, Cons. Pupil of C. Reinecke, winning a scholarship, and with Leschetizky; début, 1893, Gewandhaus, Leipzig; former chamber-virtuoso to King Albert of Saxony; after 1900 toured Europe and U. S.

Bailly (bī'-yē), **Louis,** b. Valenciennes, France; violist; pupil of Paris Cons., first prize for viola; played with Capet, Geloso, Flonzaley, Elman and Curtis Quartets; soloist with leading Amer. orchestras; head of dept. of viola and chamber music, Curtis Inst., Philadelphia; cond. at

Pittsfield Fest., 1918, and also of chamber ensemble of Curtis school.

Baillot (bī'yō), (1) **P. M. Fran. de Sales,** Passy, Oct. 1, 1771—Paris, Sept. 15, 1842; eminent violinist, pupil of Polidori, Sainte, Marie, and Pollani; later prof. of vln. at the Paris Cons.; toured Europe; 1821, leader at the Grand Opera; 1825, solo violinist, Royal Orch.; wrote famous "*L'Art du Violon*" (1834) and "*Méthode du Violon*"; composed 10 vln. concertos, 3 string-quartets, 24 preludes in all keys, etc. (2) **Réné Paul,** Paris, 1813—1889; son of above, Prof. at Paris Cons.

Baini (bä-ē'-nē), **Abbate, Gins.,** Rome, 1775—1844; composer and conductor at St. Peter's; wrote famous life of Palestrina.

Bain'ton, Edgar Leslie, b. London, Feb. 14, 1880; composer; studied R. Coll. of Music, under Davies. Stanford and Wood, winning several state prizes; after 1912, dir. of Cons. at Newcastle-on-Tyne, and led Phil. Orch. there, retiring in 1918; appeared as guest cond. with Amsterdam Concertgebouw; c. symph., choral, piano works, etc.

Baj (bä'-ē). Vide BAI.

Bajetti (bä-yĕt'-tē), **Giov.,** Brescia, ca. 1815—Milan, 1876; violinist, conductor and dram. composer.

Ba'ker, (1) **G.,** Exeter, England, 1773 —Rugeley, 1847; organist, violinist, and composer. (2) **Benj. Franklin,** Wenham, Mass., July 10, 1811—Boston, 1889; singer, teacher, and editor. (3) **Theodore,** New York, June 3, 1851—Leipzig, Oct. 13, 1934; editor and author; Ph.D.; Leipzig Univ., 1882, with thesis on music of North American Indians; also studied with Oscar Paul there; after 1892, literary ed. for publishing house of G. Schirmer, N. Y.; ed. Baker's '*Dictionary of Musical Terms*" and "*Biographical Dictionary of Musicians*"; tr. many technical works on music.

Baklanoff (bäk-län'-ŏf), **Georges,** b. St. Petersburg, 1882—Basle, 1938; barytone; LL. B., Petersburg Univ., 1904; studied singing with Vittorio Vanzo; début in Rubinstein's "*Demon*," 1905; sang Covent Garden Op., Berlin Royal Op., Vienna Imp. Op., Moscow, Petrograd, Monte Carlo, Budapest, Stockholm, Munich; first visited U. S., 1909; member

Boston Op. Co., and after 1917 of Chicago Op. Co.

Balakirew (bä-lä-kē'-rĕf), **Mily Alexejevitch,** Nijni-Novgorod, Jan. 2, 1837 —St. Petersburg, May 28, 1910; eminent composer; member Group of Five; studied at Kasan Univ., as a musician, self-taught; début as pianist in St. Petersburg, 1855; founded the "Free Music School," 1862; 1866, opera-conductor Prague; 1867–70, conductor Imp. Music Society, St. Petersburg, retired 1872; composed symph. poems *"Russia"* and *"Tamara"*; music to *"King Lear"*; 4 overtures; an Oriental fantasia, *"Islamey,"* for pf., also symphonies in C and in D minor; piano concerto, many smaller works for the instrument and two collections of songs. His letters to and from Tschaikovsky were ed. by Liapunov (1912).

Balart (bä-lärt'), **Gabriel,** Barcelona, 1824—1893; studied in Paris; conductor, later director, Barcelona Cons.; composed zarzuelas (Vide D. D.).

Balat'ka, Hans, Hoffnungsthal, Moravia, 1827—Chicago, 1899; studied at Vienna; 1849, America; 1851, founded the Milwaukee Musikverein; 1860, conductor of Chicago Philh. Soc.; composed cantatas, etc.

Balbâtre or **Balbastre** (bäl-bätr), **Claude Louis,** Dijon, 1729—Paris, 1799; pupil and friend of Rameau; organist and composer.

Balbi (bäl'-bē), (1) **Ludovico,** composer and conductor at S. Antonio, Padua; d. 1604, Franciscan monastery, Venice. (2) (Cav.) **Melchiore,** Venice, 1796—Padua, 1879; church-conductor, theorist and composer.

Baldewin (bäl-dĕ-vēn). Vide BAULDEWIJN.

Bald'win, (1) **Ralph Lyman,** East-hampton, Mass., March 27, 1872; educator and composer; active as organist, choir director and music supervisor in Northampton, Mass., and Hartford, Conn; after 1900 faculty member of Inst. of Music Pedagogy at former city. (2) **Samuel Atkinson,** b. Lake City, Minn., Jan. 22, 1862; organist; studied at Dresden Cons.; active as org. in Chicago, St. Paul, Minneapolis, and after 1895 in New York, where he taught at City College and gave a memorable series of recitals during many years.

Balfe (bǎlf), **Michael Wm.,** Dublin, May 15, 1808—Rowney Abbey, Hertfordshire, Oct. 20, 1870; operatic composer; pupil of O'Rourke, Ireland, and C. F. Horn, London; 1824, violinist Drury Lane; also sang in London; went to Italy with his patron Count Mazzara, and studied comp. with Frederici at Rome, and singing with F. Galli at Milan; his ballet *"La Pérouse,"* prod. there (1826); pupil of Bordogni, and first barytone at the Ital. Opera, Paris (1828), and elsewhere till 1835; composed several Italian operas; m. the Hungarian singer **Lina Rosen** (1808 —London, 1888); he ret. to England 1835, and prod. *"The Siege of Rochelle"* (Drury Lane); failed as manager; went to Paris, returned 1843, and prod. *"The Bohemian Girl,"* very successful everywhere; prod. Paris, 1850, in 5-act version as *"La Bohémienne."* In 1857, his daughter **Victorie** made her début in Italian opera; 1864, he retired to his country-seat, Rowney Abbey; he composed 31 operas in all, including *"The Rose of Castile"* (1857); *"Satanella"* (1858); *"Il Talismano"* (1874); biog. by C. L. Kenny (London, 1878), and W. A. Barrett (do. 1882).

Bal'lantine, Edward, b. Oberlin, O., Aug. 8, 1886; pianist and composer; pupil of Schnabel and Ganz (piano); Spalding and Converse (comp.); after 1912 taught theory at Harvard; c. orch. works incl. *"The Eve of Saint Agnes"* (Boston Symph., 1917); chorus, piano, violin pieces, etc.

Ballard (bäl-lär'), a family of French music-printers; founded 1552 by **Robert B.,** with a patent, from Henri II., as "Seul imprimeur de la musique de la chambre, chapelle et menus plaisirs du roy." The patent expired 1776.

Bal'ling, Michael, Heidingsfeld, Bavaria, Aug. 28, 1866—Darmstadt, Sept. 1, 1925; noted conductor; pupil of Würzburg Mus. Sch.; at 18 played 'cello in Mainz City Orch.; and later in Schwerin and Bayreuth orcns.; founded mus. sch. in Nelson, Australia; later a viola virtuoso in England; 1896, assistant cond. at Bayreuth; choral dir. at Hamburg Op.; 1898, first cond. at Lübeck; after 1906, regularly cond. at Bayreuth; 1911–14, succeeded Richter as cond. in Manchester, Engl.; after 1919, gen. mus. dir. in Darmstadt; one of the leading Wagner conductors of his day and ed. that composer's works for the Breitkopf and Härtel complete edition.

Baltzell, Winton J., Shiremanstown, Penn., Dec. 18, 1864—New York, Jan. 10, 1928; graduated Lebanon Valley College: at 24 took up music, studied with Emery and Thayer; later in London with Bridge and Parker, later with H. A. Clarke, Philadelphia, as editor; taught musical history and theory at Ohio Wesleyan University one year, then returned to Philadelphia; edited a *"Dictionary of Musicians"* (1911).

Bamp'ton, Rose, b. Cleveland, O., 1910; soprano; studied at Curtis Inst. of Music, Philadelphia, with Horatio Connell and Queena Mario; sang with Chautauqua, N. Y., Op. Ass'n., 1929; with Philadelphia Grand Op. Co. for three seasons; with Philadelphia Orch., in Schönberg's *"Gurrelieder"; and* after 1933 with Met. Op. Co.; toured Europe with succ., 1937.

Banchieri (bän-kĭ-ā'-rē), **Adr.,** Bologna, 1565 (?)—1634; theorist and organist.

Banck (bänk), **K.,** Magdeburg, 1809—Dresden, 1889; critic and vocal teacher.

Banderali (bän-dä-rä'-lē), **Davidde,** Lodi, 1780—Paris, 1849, buffo tenor, then teacher at Paris Cons.

Bandini (bän-dē'-nē) (1) **Primo,** Parma, Nov. 29, 1857—Piacenza, May 3, 1928, where he was dir. of Cons. after 1886; pupil R. School of Music there; composed successful operas *"Eufemio di Messina"* (Parma, 1878), *"Fausta"* (Milan, 1886), *"Janko"* (Turin, 1897). (2) **Uberto Rieti,** Umbria, March 28, 1860—near Naples, Nov. 20, 1919; pupil of Giustiniani, Boldoni, Rossi Tergiani, and Sgambati; composed prize overture *"Eleonora,"* symphony, etc.

Bandrowski (bän-drôf'-shkĭ), **Alex. Ritter von,** Lubackzow, Galicia, April 22, 1860—Cracow, May 28, 1913; operatic tenor, studied Cracow University, then with Sangiovanni, Milan, and Salvi, Vienna; début Berlin, for some years leading tenor Cologne opera, also in Russia, and oratorio in England; sang Paderewski's *"Manru"* at Warsaw and in New York, 1902.

Ban'ester, Gilbert, 16th cent.: English composer of Flemish influences.

Bang, Maia, b. Norway. April 1877; N. Y. Oct. 1040: violinist. pedagogue: pupil of Leipzig Cons., Marteau and Auer; début in Oslo, 1900, where she founded a music school; 1919 taught in Auer's Academy in New York; has toured and lectured extensively and is author of methods for violin.

Ban'ister, (1) **J.,** London, 1630—1676 (79?); court-violinist and composer. (2) **J.** (Jr.), d. 1735, son of above; court-violinist. (3) **Chas. Wm.,** 1768 —1831; composer. (4) **Hy. Joshua,** London, 1803—1847. (5) **Hy. Chas.,** London, 1831—1897, son of (3); pianist, teacher, and writer, pub. *"Lectures on Musical Analysis,"* etc.

Banti-Giorgi (bän'-tē-jôr'-jē), **Brigida,** Crema, Lombardy, 1759—Bologna, Feb. 18, 1806; dram. soprano; first a *chanteuse* in a Paris café, later engaged at the Grand Opera; toured Europe with great success; her voice was remarkable in compass and evenness, but she was musically illiterate; m. the dancer Zaccaria Banti.

Ban'tock, Sir Granville, b. London, 1868—d. 1946; studied R. A. M., took 1st. Macfarren Prize for comp.; his first work, dram. cantata *"The Fire-Worshippers,"* successfully prod., 1889; successful 1-act romantic opera *"Caedmar"* (London, 1892), conductor of Gaiety Theatre Troupe; 1898 he founded the New Brighton Choral Society; 1900 Principal Birmingham and Midland Inst. School of Music and cond. various societies; 1908 succeeded Elgar in Peyton Chair of Music at Birmingham Univ.; 1898 he married Helena von Schweitzer. He c. *"Omar Khayyam"* for voices and orch. Part I (Birmingham Fest., 1906), Part II (Cardiff Fest., 1907), Part III (Birmingham Fest., 1909); comedy overture, *"The Pierrot of the Minute,"* overture to *"Oedipos at Kolonos"* (Worcester Fest., 1911); mass for male voices; chamber music; choral symphs., *"Atalanta in Calydon"* and *"Vanity of Vanities"*; festival symph., *"Christus"*; choral suite, *"Pageant of Human Life"*; tone-poems, *"Thalabra," "Dante," "Hudibras," "Witch of Atlas," "Lalla Rookh," "Great God Pan," "Dante and Beatrice," "Fifine at the Fair," "Hebridean"* Symph.; overtures *"Saul," "Cain," "Belshazzar," "Eugene Aram," "To a Greek Tragedy"*; suites, *"Russian Scenes," "English*

Scenes," "Dances and Scenes from Scottish Highlands," "Pagan" Symph.; ballets, songs, etc.; symph. overture "Saul"; dram. symphony in 24 parts, "The Curse of Kehama," etc.

Bap'tie, David, Edinburgh, Nov. 30, 1822—Glasgow, March 26, 1906; composed anthems, etc.; compiled hymn-books.

Barbaco'la. Vide BARBIREAU.

Barbaja (bär-bä'-yä), **Domenico,** Milan, 1778—Posilippo, 1841; impresario.

Barbarieu. Vide BARBIREAU.

Barbedette (bärb-dĕt) **H.,** Poitiers, 1827—Paris, 1901; writer and composer.

Barbel'la, Emanuele, d. Naples, 1773; violinist and composer.

Bar'ber, Samuel, b. West Chester, Pa., 1910; composer; nephew of Mme. Louise Homer; grad. Curtis Institute of Music; awarded fellowship at American Academy in Rome and Pulitzer Prize, 1935; c. (orch.) "Music for a Scene from Shelley" (N. Y. Phil., 1935); 'cello and piano sonata; "Dover Beach" for voice and string quartet; songs and piano works, etc.

Bar'bi, Alice, b. Brodena, 1862; mezzosopr.; pupil of Zamboni, Busi, and Vannucceni; début, Milan, 1882; toured Europe in concert; also a violinist and poet; (1) m. Baron Wolff-Stomersee; (2) Marchese della Torretta, Italian ambassador to London, 1920.

Barbier (bärb-yä), (1) **Fr. Ét.,** Metz, 1829—Paris, 1889; teacher and leader; composed over 30 operas. (2) **Jules Paul,** Paris, 1825—Jan., 1901. collaborator with Carré, in the libretti of many operas including "Les Noces de Jeannette" (Massé); "Le Pardon de Ploërmel" (Meyerbeer); "Faust" (Gounod); "Philemon et Baucis" (Gounod); "Roméo et Juliette" (Gounod); "Hamlet" (Ambr. Thomas).

Barbieri (bär-bĭ-ā'-rē), (1) **Carlo Emm. di,** b. Genoa, 1822—Pesth, 1867; conductor and diam. composer. (2) **Francisco Asenjo,** Madrid, 1823 —1894, very pop. composer of "Zarzuelas" (Vide D. D.).

Barbireau (bär-bĭ-rō) (or **Barbiriau, Barbarieu, Barbyria'nus, Barberau, Barbingaut** (bär-băn-gō), or **Bar-**

baco'la), d. Aug. 8, 1491; from 1448 choirmaster of Nôtre-Dame; notable cptist., composed masses, etc.

Barbirolli (bär-bē-rôl'-ē), **Sir John,** b. London, 1899; 'cellist and conductor; of Italian-French parentage; studied at R. Acad. of Music; début as 'cellist, Queen's Hall, 1911; member of Intern. String Quartet, with which toured Europe; founded Barbirolli Chamber Orch., 1925; cond. Brit. Nat'l. Op. Co., 1926; later appeared with London Symph. and Royal Phil.; cond. Scottish Orch. and Leeds Symph.; guest appearances in Russia; 1936–7, cond. N. Y. Phil. for 5 season term; conductor, Hallé Orch., Manchester, 1942; knighted, 1949.

Barbot (bär-bō), **Jos. Th. Désiré,** Toulouse, 1824—Paris, 1897, tenor; created "Faust," 1859; 1875, prof Paris Cons.

Barcewicz (bär'-tsĕ-vĭts), **Stanislaus,** Warsaw, April 16, 1858—Sept. 2, 1929; violinist; pupil of Moscow Cons.; opera cond. at Warsaw; from 1885 violin prof. at the Cons.; c. violin pieces.

Bardi (bär'-dē), **Giov.,** conte del Vernio, Florentine nobleman and patron of the 16th cent., under whose influence the attempted revival of the Greek lyric drama led to modern opera. At his house "Dafne" was performed. (Vide PERI.)

Barge (bär'-gĕ), **Jn. H. Wm.,** Wulfsahl, Hanover, Nov. 23, 1836—Hanover, July 16, 1925; self-taught flutist; 1867–95 first flute, Leipzig Gewandhaus Orch., retired on pension; teacher Leipzig Cons.; wrote "Method for Flute"; composed 4 orchestral flute-studies, etc.

Bargheer (bär'-khär), (1) **K. Louis,** Bückeburg, Dec. 31, 1831—Hamburg, May 19, 1902; violinist; pupil of Spohr, David, and Joachim; 1863, court-conductor at Detmold; made concert-tours; 1879–89, leader Hamburg Phil. Soc., teacher in the Cons.; later leader in Bülow orch. (2) **A.,** Bückeburg, Oct. 21, 1840—Basel, March 10, 1901; brother of above, pupil of Spohr; court-violinist Letmold; 1866, Prof. Basel Sch. of Music.

Bargiel (bär'-gēl), **Woldemar,** Berlin, Oct. 3, 1828—Feb. 23, 1897; composer; pupil, Leipzig Cons.; later Prof. in Cologne Cons.; 1865, dir. and cond. of the Mus. Sch., Amsterdam; 1874 Prof. R. Hochschule, Berlin; 1882, Pres. "Meisterschule für musikalische Komposition"; composed 3 overtures *"Zu einem Trauerspiel (Romeo and Juliet)"* *"Prometheus,"* *"Medea"*; a symphony; 2 psalms for chorus and orchestra; pf.-pcs. etc.

Bar'ker, Chas. Spackmann, b. Bath, 1806—Maidstone, 1879; organ-builder; invented the pneumatic lever.

Bar'low, Howard, b. Plain City, Ohio, May 1, 1892; conductor; grad. Reed College, Portland, Ore.; studied music with Lucien Becker, also with Frank E. Ward and Cornelius Rybner (at Columbia Univ., N. Y.); cond. Reed Coll. choral soc.; after 1915, Riverdale Choral Soc., N. Y.; then at Neighborhood Playhouse, N. Y., and in recent years active as a leading cond. of radio programmes.

Bärman (bär'-män), (1) **H. Jos.,** Potsdam, 1784—Munich, 1847; clarinet-virtuoso and composer. His brother (2) **K.,** 1782–1842, was a bassoonist; (3) **K. (Sr.),** (1811–1885), son of H. J. B., was a clarinettist; his son (4) **K. (Jr.),** Munich, July 9, 1839—Newton, Mass., Jan. 17, 1913; pupil of Liszt and Lachner; teacher at Munich Cons.; later lived in Boston, Mass., as pianist and teacher; composed piano pieces.

Bar'nard, Mrs. Chas. (née Alington), 1830—Dover, 1869; composed popular songs, etc., under name **"Claribel."**

Barn'by, (1) Rob., York, England, 1821—London, 1875; alto-singer, Chapel Royal. (2) **Sir Jos.,** York, Engl., Aug. 12, 1838—London, Jan. 28, 1896; choirboy at 7; at 10 taught other boys; at 12 organist; at 15 music-master; 1854 entered the R. A. M., London; then organist various churches and cond.; 1875, precentor and dir. at Eton; 1892 Principal of Guildhall Sch. of Mus.; knighted, July, 1892; composed, *"Rebekah,"* a sacred idyll; Psalm 97; Service in E, etc.

Bar'nekov, Christian, St. Sauveur, France, July 28, 1837—Copenhagen, March 20, 1913; musician; of Danish parentage; pianist and organist; pupil of Helfstedt, Copenhagen; c. women's choruses with orch.; chamber music and songs.

Barnes, Robt., (1) violin-maker, London, 1760—1800. (2) **Edward Shippen,** b. Seabright, N. J., Sept. 14, 1887; organist, composer; studied Yale Univ., with Parker and Jepson; ass't. org. there; later pupil of Paris Schola Cantorum with d'Indy, Vierne and Decaux; org. at various N. Y. churches; c. organ and choral works, songs.

Barnett, (1) **J.,** Bedford, England, July 1, 1802—Cheltenham, April 17, 1890, "The father of English opera"; pupil of C. E. Horn, Price, and Ries; brought out his first opera *"Before Breakfast,"* 1825; *"The Mountain Sylph"* (1834); the very succ. *"Fair Rosamond"* (1837), and *"Farinelli"* (London, 1838); 1841, singing teacher at Cheltenham; left 2 unfinished oratorios, a symphony, etc. (2) **Jos. Alfred,** London, 1810 (?), 1898; bro. of above; composer. (3) **J. Francis,** London, 1837—1916; nephew of above; studied with Dr. Wylde; and at R. A. M., and Leipzig Cons.; début as pianist, 1853; 1883, prof. at R. Coll. of Mus.; composed oratorio *"The Raising of Lazarus,"* symphony in A min., "Ouverture symphonique," overture to *"Winter's Tale,"* cantatas, etc.

Barome'o, Chase, b. Augusta, Ga., Aug. 19, 1893; bass; grad. school of music, Univ. of Michigan; studied singing in Italy; sang at La Scala, in Buenos Aires; with Chicago Op., and after 1935 with Met. Op. Co., N. Y.

Baron (bä'-rōn), **Ernst Gl.,** Breslau, 1696—Berlin, 1760; court-lutenist and theorist; writer and composer.

Barré (or **Barra**) (băr-rā or bär'-rä), (1) **Léonard,** b. Limoges; singer in Papal Chapel (1537) and special musical envoy to the Council of Trent (1545); composed madrigals and motets. (2) **A.,** printer, etc., Rome, 1555–70, later Milan.

Barrère (bär-âr'), **Georges,** b. Bordeaux, France, Oct. 31, 1876; flutist, conductor; studied Paris Cons., 1st prize, 1895; member orchestra, Paris Op., Colonne Orch.; teacher, Schola Cantorum, Paris; founder, Modern Society of Wind Instruments, Paris, 1895; member N. Y. Symph. Orch., 1905-1928; taught Inst. of Musical Art, New York, after 1910; founded Barrère Little Symphony Orchestra, 1914; member trio with Carlos Salzedo and Horace Britt; c. cham. wks., d. Kingston, N. Y., June, 1944.

46   DICTIONARY OF MUSICIANS

Barret (băr-rā), **A. M. Rose,** Paris, 1808
—London, 1879; oboist.
Bar'rett, (1) **J.,** 1674—London, 1735
(8 ?); organist. (2) **Thos.,** violin-
maker, London, 1710–30. (3) **Wm.
Alex.,** Hackney, Middlesex, 1836—
London, 1891; editor and writer; co-
editor with Sir John Stainer of a
"Dict. of Music. Terms."
Barrien'tos, Maria, b. Barcelona,
1885—d. 1946; coloratura soprano;
sang with success in Rome at 11
years; took two medals for violin-
playing; later heard in Madrid and
various Italian theatres as a singer;
at Met. Op., N. Y., for several seasons
after 1916; also in South America.
Bar'rington, Daines, London, 1727—
1800; lawyer and musical essayist.
Bar'ry, Chas. Ainslie, London, June 10,
1830—March 21, 1915, pupil of
Cologne Cons. and Leipzig Cons.;
editor and organist; composed a symphony, 2 overtures, etc.
Barsanti (bär-sän'-tē), **Fran.,** Lucca,
ca. 1690—1760; flutist, oboist, and
composer; 1750, viola-player at London.
Barsot'ti, Tommaso G. F., Florence,
1786—Marseilles, 1868; teacher and
composer.
Bartay (bär'-tä-ē), (1) **Andreas,** Szé-
plak, Hungary, 1798—Mayence,
1856; 1838 dir. Nat. Th., Pesth;
composed Hungarian operas, etc.
(2) **Ede,** Oct. 6, 1825—Sept., 1901,
son of above; pupil Nat. Mus. Academy, Pesth; founded pension-fund
for musicians; composed overture,
"*Pericles,*" etc.
Bartei (bär-tā'-ē), **Girolamo,** general of
Augustinan monks at Rome; pub-
lisher and composer (1607–18).
Barth (bärt), (1) **Chr. Samuel,** Glau-
cheau, Saxony, 1735—Copenhagen,
1809; oboist. (2) **F. Phil. K. Ant.,**
b. Cassel, ca 1775; son of above;
composer. (3) **Jos. Jn. Aug.,** b.
Grosslippen, Bohemia, 1781; 1810–
30, tenor, Vienna. (4) **Gustav,**
Vienna, 1800—Frankfort, 1897; son
of (3); pianist and conductor.
(5) **K. H.,** Pillau, Prussia, July 12,
1847—Berlin, Dec. 23, 1923; pianist,
pupil of Von Bülow, Bronsart, and
Tausig; 1871, teacher at R. Hoch-
schüle für Musik, conductor of the
Philh. concerts at Hamburg (vice
von Bülow). (6) **Richard,** Gros-
swanzleben, Saxony, June 5, 1850—
Hamburg, 1923: left-handed violin-

virtuoso; Univ. Mus. Dir. Marburg,
till 1894; then Dir. of Hamburg
Philh. Concerts; 1908. dir. Cons.
there; sonatas, string quartet, etc.
Barthe, Grat-Norbert (grä-nôr-bĕr-
bärt), Bayonne, 1828—Asniéres, Aug.
1898; pupil Paris Cons., 1854: won
the Grand Prix de Rome; wrote cantata "*Francesca da Rimini*"; composed operas "*Don Carlos*" and "*La
Fiancée d'Abydos*" (1865); oratorio,
"*Judith,*" etc.
Barthel (bär'-tĕl), **Jn. Chr.,** Plauen,
Saxony, 1776—Altenburg, 1831;
court-organist.
Barthélemon (bär-tā-lŭ-môn) (in English **Bar'tleman**), **Fran. Hip.,** Bordeaux, 1741—London, 1808: violinist and composer.
Barthol'omew, Wm., London, 1793—
1867; translator.
Bart'lett, (1) **J.,** 17th century English
composer. (2) **Homer Newton,**
Olive, N. Y., Dec. 28, 1846—Hobo-
ken, N. J., April 3, 1920; pupil of
S. B. Mills, Max Braun, Jacobson,
etc. From 14 organist New York
churches, including Madison Av
Bapt. Ch.; published a sextet, a cantata "*The Last Chieftain,*" many
songs, etc.; opera, "*La Vallière,*"
oratorio, "*Samuel,*" etc.
Bart'muss, Richard, Bitterfeld, Dec.
23, 1859—Dessau, Dec. 25, 1910;
organist; pupil of Grell, Haupt,
Löschhorn; 1896 royal music director;
1902, professor; c. oratorio "*Der
Tag des Pfingsten,*" 4 organ sonatas
and much sacred music.
Bartók, Béla (bä'-lä bär-tŏk'), b. Nagy
Szent Miklos, Hungary, March 25,
1881—d. N. Y., Sept. 26, 1945; noted
for researches in folk-music and for
compositions in original modern
idiom; studied with Koessler and
Erkel, and at Budapest Acad.; prof.
at latter school after 1906; his music
employs various ancient scales and
harmonies, abandoning traditional
diatonic and chromatic system, and
treating twelve tones of chromatic
scale as separate entities; the influence of archaic folk music was noted
in B's. turning, about 1907, to this
new style, which then sounded extremely formidable to listeners and
roused considerable opposition; for a
time he retired from active composition, visiting Biskra to collect
Arabian folk music; his first major
recognition came in 1917 when the

DICTIONARY OF MUSICIANS 47

dance-play *"Der Holzgeschnitzte Prinz"* was prod. at Budapest Op.; since that time his works have aroused keen interest among modern-minded musicians, his greatest succ. probably coming with the perf. of his *"Dance Suite"* for orch., based on folk airs, at Prague in 1925; **B.** has visited the U. S. as lecturer on music and for concerts of his chamber music; c. (opera) *"Ritter Blaubarts Burg"* (1918); (pantomime) *"Der wunderbare Mandarin"* (1924); orchestral and chamber music works, among which several string quartets have had international hearings; two violin sonatas, and many piano works, incl. collection, *"Mikrokosmos"*; 3 Piano Concertos; Concerto for Orch.; Concerto for Vln. and Orch.; Viola Concerto (posth.).

Bartoli (bär-tō′-lē), Padre **Erasmo,** Gaeta, 1606—Naples, 1656; church-composer under the name "Padre Raimo."

Barzin (bär-zăn′), **Léon,** b. Brussels; conductor and violist; brought to U. S. at age of two; had early lessons from his father, who was first violist in Met. Op. orchestra; later a pupil of Henrotte, Deru, Megerlin and Ysaye; harmony and counterpoint with Lilienthal; was mem. of Nat'l. Symph. Orch., N. Y., 1919; the next year, second violinist, N. Y. Phil. Orch.; first violist in same, and member of Phil. Quartet, 1925; after 1929 cond. American Orch. Soc., N. Y., which was reformed as the Nat'l. Orch. Ass'n., 1930.

Baselt (bä′zĕlt), **Fritz (Fr. Gv. O.),** Oels, Silesia, May 26, 1863—Nov. 12, 1931; pupil of Köhler and Bussler; music-dealer, teacher, and conductor Breslau, Essen and Nürnberg; 1894, director of Philh. Verein, and "Sängervereinigung" (ca. 1,200 voices), Frankfort-on-Main; composed 9 operettas, nearly 100 male choruses, etc.

Basevi (bä-sä′-vē), **Abramo,** Leghorn, 1818—Florence, 1885; journalist and composer.

Ba′sil (Saint), **The Great,** Caesarea, 329—Cappadocia, 379; bishop; reputed introducer of congregational (antiphonal) singing into the Eastern Ch.; preceding St. Ambrose in the Western.

Basili (bä-zē′-lē), (1) Dom. **Andrea,** 1720—Loreto, 1775; conductor and

composer; his son (2) **Fran.,** Loreto, 1767—Rome, 1850; prod. 11 operas, and several dram. oratorios in Rome; 1837, conductor at St. Peter's, Rome; composed also symphonies, etc.

Basiron (bä′-sĭ-rōn), **Giovanni,** developed the motet, ca. 1430—1480.

Bassani (bäs-sä′-nē), (1) **Giov.,** ca. 1600; conductor at St. Mark's, Venice. (2) (or **Bassiani**), **Giov. Bat.,** Padua, ca. 1657—Ferrara, 1716; violinist, conductor, and composer. (3) **Geron.,** b. Padua, 17th cent.; singer, teacher, and composer.

Bassevi (bäs-sä′-vē), **Giacomo.** Vide CERVETTO.

Bass′ford, Wm. Kipp, New York, April 23, 1839—Dec. 22, 1902; pupil of Samuel Jackson; toured the U. S. as pianist; later organist at East Orange, N. J.; also composer.

Bassi (bäs′-sē), **Luigi,** Pesaro, 1766—Dresden, 1825; barytone and director; Mozart wrote the rôle of "Don Giovanni" for him.

Bassiron (bäs-sĭ-rôn), **Ph.,** 15th cent.; Netherland contrapuntist; composed masses.

Bastardella. Vide AGUJARI.

Bastiaans (bäs′-tē-äns), (1) **J. G.,** Wilp, 1812—Haarlem, 1875; organist and teacher at Amsterdam and at St. Bavo's; his son and successor (2) **Jn.,** 1854—1885; teacher and composer.

Baston (bäs-tôn), **Josquin,** lived, 1556, Netherlands; contrapuntist.

Bates, (1) **Joah,** Halifax, 1741—London, 1799; conductor; promoter and conductor of the famous "Händel Commemoration" festivals in London (1784-91). (2) His wife was a singer. (3) **Wm.,** 1720—1790 (?); English opera composer.

Ba′teson, T., England, ca. 1575—after 1611; organist and composer of madrigals.

Bath, Hubert, Barnstaple, Eng., Nov. 6, 1883—1945; 1901, pupil of Beringer and Corder at R. A. M.; London; 1904, won Goring Thomas scholarship; c. 1-act opera, *"The Spanish Student"*; symph. poems; cantata *"The Wedding of Shon Maclean"*; also *"Cornish Rhapsody"* from film score.

Bathe (bäth), **Wm.,** Dublin, 1564—Madrid, 1614; writer.

Batiste (bă-tēst), **A. Éd.,** Paris, 1820—1876; organist, teacher, and composer.

Bat'ka, Richard, Prague, Dec. 14, 1868
—Vienna, April 24, 1922; critic, historian, and librettist.

Batta (bät'-tä), (1) **Pierre,** Maastricht,
Holland, 1795—Brussels, 1876;
'cellist and teacher. His sons were
(2) **Alex.,** Maastricht, July 9, 1816
—Versailles, Oct. 8, 1902; 'cellist and
composer. (3) **J. Laurent,** Maastricht, 1817—Nancy, 1880; pianist
and teacher.

Battaille (băt-tī'-yŭ), **Chas. Aimable,**
Nantes, 1822—Paris, 1872; dram.
bass.

Battanchon (băt-tän-shôn), **F.,** Paris,
1814—1893; 'cellist; inv. (1846) a
small 'cello, the "barytone."

Bat'ten, Adrian, ca. 1585—ca. 1637;
English organist.

Bat'tishill, Jonathan, London, 1738—
Islington, 1801; conductor and dram.
composer.

Battista (bät-tēs'-tä), **V.,** Naples, 1823
—1873; dram. composer.

Battistini (bät-tēs-tē'-nē), **Mattia,**
Rome, Feb. 27, 1857—Rieti, Nov. 7,
1928; dram. barytone; début, Rome,
1878; sang at Buenos Aires and
principal theatres in Europe; one of
most accomplished "*bel canto*" singers of his period; was often reported
to be contemplating tour of U. S.,
for which he received tempting offers,
but his terror of seasickness is said
to have caused him to refuse them;
he knew about eighty rôles, principally Italian; a notable "Don Giovanni," etc.

Batton (băt-tôn), **Désiré Alex.,** Paris,
1797—Versailles, 1855; teacher and
dram. composer.

Battu (băt-tü), **Pantaléon,** Paris, 1799
—1870; violinist and composer.

Baudiot (bōd-yō), **Chas. N.,** Nancy,
1773—Paris, 1849; 'cellist.

Baudoin (or **Baudouyn**) (bō-dwăn).
Vide BAULDEWIJN.

Bauer (bow'-ĕr), (1) **Harold,** b. London,
April 28, 1873, of English mother and
German father; eminent pianist;
played violin in public at 9; studied
with Gorski, Paris; then the piano,
in 1892, under Paderewski; début as
pianist, Paris, 1893; has toured Europe and, since 1900, America, with
great success; res. in New York for
many years; he has long been ranked
as one of leading solo and ensemble
players; pres., Beethoven Ass'n. of
New York; also active as master
teacher; d. Miami, Fla., Mar. 12, 1951.

(2) **Marion,** b. Walla Walla, Wash.,
Aug. 15, 1887; composer; incid. music
for "*Prometheus Bound*," string quartet, songs, etc.; asst. prof. of music,
N. Y. Univ., 1926; mem. bd. of dirs.,
League of Comps.

Bauldewijn (bōd-wăn) (or **Baulduin,
Baldewin, Balduin, Baudoin, Baudouyn), Noël (Natalis),** Antwerp,
1513 (or 1518?)—1529; conductor at
Nôtre Dame; and composer.

Baumfelder (bowm'-fĕlt-ĕr), **Fr.,** Dresden, May 28, 1836—Aug. 8, 1916;
pianist; pupil of J. Otto, and Leipzig
Cons.

Baumgarten (bowm'-gärt-ĕn), **K. Fr.,**
Germany, 1740 (?)—London, 1824;
violinist and dram. composer.

Baumgärtner (bowm'-gĕrt-nĕr), (1)
Aug., Munich, 1814—1862; writer on
"musical shorthand," etc. (2) **Wm.
(Guillaume),** 1820—Zurich, 1867;
composer and mus. dir. at St. Gallen.

Bäumker (bīm'-kĕr), **Wm.,** Elberfeld,
Oct. 25, 1842—Rurich, 1905; chaplain and school-inspector, Niederkrüchten; wrote biogs. of Palestrina,
Lassus, etc.

Bausch (bowsh), (1) **L. Chr. Aug.,**
Naumburg, 1805—Leipzig, 1871;
maker of violins and bows. His 2
sons were also vln.-makers: (2)
Ludwig (1829—Leipzig, 1871), lived
New York, then in Leipzig; and (3)
Otto, 1841–1874.

Bausznern (bows'-nĕrn), **Waldemar
von,** Berlin, Nov. 29, 1866—Potsdam, Aug. 20, 1931; studied at
Kronstadt, Budapest, Vienna, and
with Bargiel and Fr. Kiel at the
Berlin Hochschule; 1894 in Dresden,
as dir. Singakademie and Liedertafel; 1903, docent at Cologne Cons.
and dir. of Soc. of Musicians there;
1908, dir. of Weimar School of
Music; 1916, dir. of Hoch Cons.,
Frankfort; c. 4 symphonies; operas,
"*Dürer in Venedig*," "*Herbort und
Hilda*," "*Der Bundschuh*," "*Satyros*"; choral works, chamber music,
song cycles, etc.

Bax (băks), **Sir Arnold,** b. London,
Nov. 8, 1883—Cork, Oct. 3, 1953; pupil
R.A.M., studying piano with Matthay
and comp. with Frederick Corder;
one of leading contemporary British
creative figures, with Celtic, neo-
Romantic spirit and clarity of form
among his salient characteristics,
individual type of chromaticism and
reticence of expression; c. (orch.) five

symphonies; Festival Overture; Four Pieces; Symphonic Variations for piano and orch.; *"Tintagel," "Summer Music," "Mediterranean," "The Happy Forest,"* "The Garden of Fand," *"Overture to a Picaresque Comedy," "The Tale the Pine Trees Knew," "In the Faery Hills"; "Enchanted Summer"* for two sopranos, chorus and orch.; *"Christmas Eve in the Mountains," "Spring Fire," "In Memoriam," "November Woods,"* *"Moy Mell,"* (chamber music) trio; sonata for violin and piano; quintet; string quartet; quintet for strings and harp; quartet for piano and strings; quintet for oboe and strings; sonata for violin and piano; 'cello sonata; sonata for two pianos; sonata for viola and harp; (ballet scores) *"Between Dusk and Dawn," "The Frog-skin," "The Truth about the Russian Dancers,"* also piano music and songs. Knighted, 1937.

Bayer (bī'-ĕr), **Josef**, Vienna, Mar. 6, 1852—March 12, 1913; composer of ballets and operettas; studied at Vienna Cons.; cond. at Court Opera.

Bazin (bă-zăṅ), **Fran. Em. Jos.**, Marseilles, 1816—Paris, 1878; dram. composer.

Bazzini (bäd-zē'-nē), **A.**, Brescia, March 11, 1818—Milan, Feb. 10, 1897; violinist; pupil of Camisani; at 17 conductor Church of S. Filippo, where he prod. masses and vespers, and 6 oratorios with full orch., and gave successful concert-tours through Europe. 1873, prof. of comp., 1882, dir. of Milan Cons. In his compositions his native melodiousness gained unusual value from a German solidity of harmony.

Bé, Le. Vide LE BÉ.

Beach, Mrs. **H. H. A.** (née **Amy Marcy Cheney**), Henniker, N. H., Sept. 5, 1867—N. Y., Dec., 1944; pupil of E. Perabo and K. Baermann (pf.), and Junius W. Hill (harmony); self-taught in cpt., comp. and orchestration, having transl. Berlioz and Gevaert for her own use; Pres. Board of Councillors, N. E. Cons., Boston; composed *"Gaelic"* symphony, Mass with orch., piano quintet, piano concerto, choral works, a number of attractive songs, etc.

Beale, (1) **Wm.**, Landrake, Cornwall, 1784—London, 1854; famous glee-composer. (2) **J.**, London, ca. 1796; pianist.

Beard, **J.**, England, ca. 1717—Hampton, 1791; eminent tenor for whom Händel wrote the tenor rôles in his chief oratorios.

Beauchamps (bō-shäṅ), **P. Fran. Godard de**, Paris, ca. 1689—1761; writer.

Beaulieu (rightly **Martin**) (bōl-yŭ', or măr-tăṅ), **M. Désiré**, Paris, 1791—Niort, 1863; patron, writer, and composer.

Beauquier (bōk-yā), **Chas.**, 1833— ?; writer of "Philosophie de musique" (1865), and librettist.

Beauvarlet - Charpentier (bō-văr-lä-shăr-päṅt-yā), (1) **Jean Jacques**, Abbeyville, 1730—Paris, 1794; organist and comp. (2) **Jacques Marie**, Lyons, July 3, 1776—Paris, Nov., 1834; organist and comp., son of (1).

Becher (bĕkh'-ĕr), (1) **Alfred Julius**, Manchester, 1803—Vienna, 1848; editor. (2) **Jos.**, Neukirchen, Bavaria, Aug. 1, 1821—Sept. 23, 1888; composed over 60 masses, etc.

Bechstein (bĕkh'-shtīn), **Fr. Wm. K.**, Gotha, June 1, 1826—Berlin, March 6, 1900; 1856, worked in German factories, later established the well-known piano factory in Berlin.

Beck, (1) **David**, Germany, ca. 1590; organ-builder. (2) **Reichardt K.**, lived in Strassburg, ca. 1650; composer. (3) **Jn. Philip**, 1677; editor. (4) **Michael**, b. Ulm, 1653; writer. (5) **Gf. Jos.**, Podiebrad, Bohemia, 1723—Prague, 1787, Dominican (later Provincial) friar, organist. (6) **Chr. Fr.**, b. Kirchheim, ca. 1755; composer. (7) **Fz.**, Mannheim, 1730—Bordeaux, 1809; court-violinist. (8) **Fr. Ad.**, pub. at Berlin, *"Dr. M. Luther's Gedanken über die Musik,"* 1825. (9) **K.**, 1814—Vienna, 1879; tenor; created *"Lohengrin."* (10) **Jn. Nepomuk**, Pesth, 1827—Pressburg, 1904; dram. barytone. (11) **Jos.**, Mainz, June 11, 1850—Pressburg, Feb. 15, 1903; son of above, barytone, sang in Austria, Berlin (1876), and Frankfort (1880). (12) **Johann Heinrich**, Cleveland, Sept. 12, 1856—May 26, 1924; violinist; pupil Leipzig Cons.; founded the Cleveland "Schubert Quartet"; composed overtures to Byron's *"Lara,"* to *"Romeo and Juliet"*; cantata *"Deukalion"* (Bayard Taylor), etc. (13) **Conrad**, b. Schaffhausen, Switzerland, June 16, 1901; composer; studied with Andreae and at Zurich Cons.; res. in Berlin, later Paris, where studied with Honegger; c. in neo-classic manner, but modern harmonisation, cantata *"Death of Oedipus"*; four symphonies, concertino for piano and orch., concerto for string quartet and orch.; three string quartets, choral works, etc.

Beck'er, (1) **Dietrich** (1668), composer at Hamburg, 1668. (2) **Jn.,** Helsa, near Cassel, 1726—1803; court-organist. (3) **K. Fd.,** Leipzig, 1804 —1877; organist and writer. (4) **Konstantin Julius,** Freiberg, Saxony, 1811—Oberlössnitz, 1859; editor. (5) **Val. Ed.,** Würzburg, 1814— Vienna, 1890; dram. composer. (6) **Georg,** Frankenthal, Palatinate, June 24, 1834—Geneva, July 18, 1928; pianist and writer; lived in Geneva; pub. *"La Musique en Suisse,"* etc. (7) **Albert Ernst Ant.,** Quedlinburg, June 13, 1834—Berlin, Jan. 10, 1899, pupil of Bonicke and Dehn; 1881, teacher of comp. at Scharwenka's Cons.; also conductor Berlin cathedral choir; composed a noteworthy symphony, a Grand Mass in B♭ min. (1878), and oratorio *"Selig aus Gnade,"* etc. (8) **Jean,** Mannheim, May 11, 1833—Oct. 10, 1884; violinist, leader Mannheim orch.; after concert-tours, lived in Florence and founded the famous "Florentine Quartet"; toured with his children. (9) His daughter **Jeanne,** Mannheim, June 9, 1859— April 6, 1893; pianist, pupil of Reinecke and Bargiel. (10) **Hans.,** Strassburg, May 12, 1860—May 1, 1917; viola-player, pupil of Singer. (11) **Hugo,** b. Strassburg, Feb. 13, 1864; 'cellist; son of Jean B.; pupil of his father, Grützmacher, Piatti, etc.; 'cellist at the Opera Frankfort, 1884-86 and 1890-1906; 1896, Royal Prof.; succeeded Piatti as 'cellist at London Monday concerts; 1909-29, taught Berlin Hochschule; later lived in Switzerland; made many concert tours, including U. S., 1900. (12) **Rheinhold,** Adorf, Saxony, 1842— Dresden, Dec. 4, 1924; violinist; lived in Dresden; composed succ. operas *"Frauenlob"* (Dresden, 1892), and *"Ratbold"* (Mayence, 1896), 1-act; symph. poem *"Der Prinz von Homburg,"* etc. (13) **K.,** Kirrweiler, near Trier, June 5, 1853—Berlin, Aug. 31, 1928; teacher at Neuwied; pub. songbooks. (14) **Jakob,** founder (1841) of large Russian pf.-factory.

Beck'mann, Jn. Fr. Gl., 1737—Celle, 1792; organist, harpsichord-virtuoso, and dram. composer.

Beck'with, J. Christmas, Norwich, England, 1750–1809; organist and writer.

Becquié (běk-yā), (1) **A.** (?), Toulouse, ca. 1800—Paris, 1825; flutist. His brother (2) **("De Peyre Ville"), Jean Marie,** Toulouse, 1797—Paris, 1876; violinist.

Bečvařovsky (běch'-var-shôf'-shkǐ), **Ant. F.,** Jungbunzlau, Bohemia, 1754—Berlin, 1823; organist and composer.

Bed'ford, Herbert, b. London, Jan. 23, 1867; composer; lectured on un-accompanied vocal music and published an essay on this subject; c. (opera) *"Kit Marlowe,"* symph. cham., vocal mus., m. Liza Lehmann d. London. March 16, 1945.

Bedos de Celles (bŭ-dō du -sěl), Caux, near Bézières, 1706—St. Maur, 1779; Benedictine monk and writer.

Beech'am, (1) Sir **Thomas,** b. near Liverpool, Engl., April 29, 1879; eminent conductor; son of Sir Joseph Beecham; educated at Rossall Sch.; studied comp. with Dr. Sweeting, later with Varley Roberts at Oxford Univ.; from 1899 founder and leader of amateur orch. soc. at Huyton; also substituted for Richter in a concert given by his father; 1902, cond. of Kelson Truman's touring op. co.; studied comp. for a year and prod. three operas; 1905, led his first orch. concert in London; 1906-8 founded New Symph. Orch. there and in latter year formed Beecham Symph. Orch.; 1910 organised season of opera at Covent Garden, following this with others until 1915, in which a number of first perfs. in England were given, esp. Strauss operas, Wagner and works in English; later cond. of Royal Op. Syndicate and after 1915 of London Phil. Soc.; knighted 1916; in recent years artistic dir. of Covent Garden Op.; has appeared widely as guest cond. in other countries, incl. N. Y. Phil. Orch. and Philadelphia Orch. in U. S. (2) **Adrian,** b. London, Sept. 4, 1904; son of (1); composer of music to *"The Merchant of Venice,"* songs, etc.

Beecke (bā'-kě), **Ignaz von,** 1733 —Wallerstein, 1803; captain of dragoons, then "Musikintendant" to

Prince of Ottingen-Wallerstein; harpsichordist; composer of 7 operas, etc.

Beellaerts (bāl-lärts), **Jean.** Vide BELLERE.

Beer (bār), (1) **Jacob Liebmann.** Vide MEYERBEER. (2) **Josef,** Grünwald, Bohemia, 1744—Potsdam, 1811; player of the clarinet, for which he invented the fifth key. (3) **Max Josef,** Vienna, Aug. 25, 1851—Nov. 25, 1908; pianist; pupil of Dessoff; lived in Vienna; composed 4 operas, incl. the succ. *"Der Striek der Schmiede"* (Augsburg, 1897), etc.

Beer-Walbrunn, Anton, Kohlberg, June 29, 1864—Munich, March 22, 1929; studied with Rheinberger, leader in Regensburg orch., later lived in Munich; taught piano and theory at Akad. there after 1901; prof., 1908; c. operas, many orch., chamber, piano works, etc.

Beethoven (bāt'-hō-fĕn, not bā-tō'-vĕn), **Ludwig van,** b. Bonn-on-Rhine, Dec. 16 (baptised, Dec. 17, 1770) (Beethoven said Dec. 16, 1772), d. Vienna, March 26, 1827; grandson of **Ludwig van B.** (a native of Maestricht, bass singer, opera composer, and conductor to the Elector Clemens August, at Bonn), 2d child of **Jn. van B.** (a tenor singer in the Electoral choir), who had m. a widow, Magdelena Laym (née Keverich), a daughter of the chief cook at Ehrenbreitstein. **B.** studied at the public schools at Bonn till 14. From his fourth year, his father taught him music with great severity till 1779. He played the vln. well at 8; at 11 he knew Bach's *"Wohltemperirte Clavier."* Became pupil of Pfeiffer, a music-dir. and oboist; and Van der Eeden, court-organist, who predicted that he would be "a second Mozart"; 1785, studied vln. with Franz Ries; 1787, took a few lessons of Mozart; 1792, Haydn, passing through Bonn, praised a cantata of his (now lost). The Elector sent **B.** to Vienna, where he studied cpt. with Haydn, who seemed to neglect him, so that he secretly studied with Schenck; later he went to Albrechtsberger, who said "he has learnt nothing, and will never do anything in decent style"; he studied the vln. with Schuppanzigh and consulted Salieri and Aloys Förster; 1781, he is believed to have written a Funeral

Cantata in memory of the English *chargé d'affaires* at Bonn, who had advanced money to the family; 1781 (1782 ?), his first publication, 3 pf.-sonatas, 1782; deputy organist, 1783; cembalist for rehearsals of the opera-orch., without compensation 1784–92; asst. organist at an annual salary of 150 florins (about $63); from 1788 also 2d viola of the theatre orch. Visited Vienna, 1787, and made a sensation by extemporising, Mozart exclaiming "He will make a noise in the world some day." In July his tender-hearted mother died of consumption; his father lost his voice and became a sot. **B.**'s only home was in the family of the widow von Breuning, to whose daughter and son he gave lessons. Here he acquired his passion for English literature. He now made acquaintance of young Count Waldstein, who became his life-long patron, and in 1792 sent him to Vienna, where he henceforward lived. The decade 1782–92 does not show much fertility in composition, half a dozen songs, a rondo, a minuet, and 3 preludes for pf., 3 pf.-quartets, a pf.-trio, a string-trio, op. 3; 4 sets of pf. variations; a rondino for wind; the *"Ritter Ballet"* with orch. (pub. 1872); *"The Bagatelles,"* op. 33; 2 vln.-rondos, op. 51; the *"Serenade Trio"* op. 8; the lost cantata, a lost trio for pf., flute, and bassoon, and an Allegro and Minuet for 2 flutes. 1792, he was sent to Vienna by the Elector, who paid him his salary for 2 years; he had growing royalties from his comps., also 600 florins annually from Prince Lichnowsky, his warmest admirer. March 29, 1795, he played his C major pf.-concerto in the Burgtheater, his first public appearance; 1796, he played before King Fr. Wm. II.; 1798, at Prague, he gave 2 sensational concerts and met two piano virtuosi: Steibelt who challenged **B.** to extemporise and was sadly worsted, and Wölffl, who became his friend. 1800 ends what is called (after von Lenz's book *"B. et ses trois styles"*) his "first period" of composition; the "second period," extending to 1815; the "third" to 1827. This first period includes op. 1–18, pf. and string-trios, string-quartets, 9 pf.-sonatas, 7 variations on *"God Save the Queen,"* and 5 on *"Rule Britan-*

nia," the aria "*Ah perfido*," etc. Now a severe and early venereal trouble affected his liver, and began to ruin his hearing, which by 1822 was entirely gone. Though he had always been brusque (especially with the aristocracy, among whom he had an extraordinarily long list of friendships and love-affairs), his former generosity and geniality speedily developed into atrocious suspiciousness and violence toward his best friends. The wild life of a nephew whom he supported brought him great bitterness. Until the beginning of the "third period," however, he had large stores of joy in life, open-air Nature, and the details of his compositions which were worked up with utmost care from "sketch-books," always carried with him, and still extant as a unique example of genius at work. In the arbitrary but somewhat convenient von Lenz classification the 2d period includes the symphonies III—VIII; the opera "*Fidelio*"; the music to "*Egmont*"; the ballet "*Prometheus*"; the Mass in C, op. 86, the oratorio "*Christus am Oelberg*" (1803); the "*Coriolanus*" overture; 2 pf.-concertos, 1 vln.-concerto; 3 quartets; 4 pf.-trios and 14 pf.-sonatas (among them op. 27, op. 28, 31, No. 2, 53, 57, and 81); the "*Liederkreis*," etc. The "third period" incl. the five pf.-sonatas, op. 101, 111, the "*Missa solennis*," the Ninth Symphony, the overture "*Ruins of Athens*," the overtures op. 115, 124; the grand fugue for string-quartet, and the string-quartets op. 127, 130, 131, 132, 135 (F).

"*Fidelio*," first named "*Leonore*," was prod. Nov. 20, 1805, just a week after the French army entered Vienna. It was withdrawn after three consecutive performances; revised and prod. March 29, 1806, but withdrawn by B. after two performances. Once more revised, it was revived in 1814, very successfully; the present overture is the result of various versions known as the *Leonore* overtures 1, 2, and 3. The "*Eroica*" symphony (No. 3) was called "*Sinfonia grande Napoleon Bonaparte*" in honour of his advocacy of "liberty, equality, and fraternity." When Napoleon proclaimed himself emperor, B. tore up the title-page in wrath and changed the name to

"*Sinfonia eroica composta per festeggiare il sovvenire d'un gran uomo.*" (Heroic symphony, composed to celebrate the memory of a great man.) In the Ninth Symphony, a choral Finale is used as the final addition to the orchestral climax of ecstasy (the words from Schiller's "*Hymn to Joy*"). In 1809 Jerome Bonaparte invited **B**. to become conductor at Cassel with a salary of 600 ducats (about $1,500); but his Viennese patrons Archduke Rudolf and the Princes Lobkowitz and Kinsky, settled on him an annuity of 4,000 florins ($2,000). Dec., 1826, a violent cold resulted in pneumonia; dropsy followed, **B**. saying to the doctors who tapped him three times and drew out the water, "Better from my belly than from my pen." After an illness of 3 months he took the Roman Catholic sacraments, a two-days' agony of semi-consciousness followed and he died, just after shaking his clenched fist in the air, during a terrific thunderstorm, the evening of March 26, 1827. 20,000 persons attended his funeral.

His complete works comprise 138 opus-numbers and about 70 unnumbered comp. The following are those published. INSTRUMENTAL.— 9 Symphonies—No. 1, op. 21, in C; 2, op. 36, in D; 3, op. 55, in E♭ (the "*Eroica*"); 4, op. 60, in B♭; 5, op. 67, in C min.; 6, op. 68, in F ("*Pastoral*"); 7, op. 92, in A; 8, op. 93, in F; 9, op. 125, in D min. ("*Choral*"). "*The Battle of Vittoria*" (op. 91); music to the ballet "*Prometheus*" (op. 43), and to Goethe's "*Egmont*" (op. 84), both with overtures, besides, nine overtures—"*Coriolanus*"; "*Leonore*" (Nos. 1, 2, and 3); "*Fidelio*"; "*King Stephen*"; "*Ruins of Athens*"; "*Namensfeier*," op. 115; "*Weihe des Hauses*" (op. 124). Also for orch.; Allegretto in E♭; March from "*Tarpeia*," in C; "*Military March*," in D; "*Ritter-Ballet*"; 12, Minuets; 12, "deutsche Tänze"; 12, Contretänze; violin-concerto, op. 61. Five pf.-concertos, the last op. 73, in E ("*Emperor*"); also a pf.-concerto arranged from the violin-concerto. A triple-concerto, op. 56, for pf., vln., 'cello and orch.; a "*Choral Fantasia*" for pf., chorus and orch.; a Rondo in B, for pf. and orch.; cadences to the pf.-concertos.

Two Octets for wind, both in E♭. Septet for strings and wind. Sextet for strings and 2 horns. One sextet for wind, E♭. Two quintets for strings; fugue for string-quintet; also quintet arr. from pf.-trio in C min. Sixteen string-quartets; Op. 18, Nos. 1-6 in F, G, D, C min., A and B♭ (first period); op. 59, Nos. 1-3; op. 74, in E♭ (the "*Harfenquartett*"); op. 95 (second period); op. 127; op. 130; op. 131; op. 132; op. 135. A grand fugue for string-quartet, op. 133, in B♭ (third period). One pf.-quartet (arr. from the pf.-quintet); 3 juvenile pf.-quartets; five string-trios; eight pf.-trios, that in E♭ being juvenile; an arr. of the "*Eroica*" symphony. Grand trios for pf., clar. and 'cello op. 11; in B♭ and in E♭ (arr. from septet, op. 20); trio for 2 oboes and *cor anglais*, in C op. 87. Ten sonatas for pf. and violin, incl. op. 47 ("*Kreutzer*"); rondo for pf. and vln.; 12 variations for do. Five sonatas and 31 variations for pf. and 'cello. Sonata for pf. and horn. Sonata for pf., 4 hands. 38 Sonatas for piano, incl. op. 27. Nos. 1 and 2 ("*Quasi Fantasia*"), op. 28 ("*Pastorale*") in D; op. 53 ("*Waldstein*") in C; op. 57 ("*Appassionata*") in F min.; op. 81 ("*Caractéristique*"—"*Les adieux, l'absence, le retour*") in E♭. Also 6 easy sonatas, 3 of them composed at age of 10; 21 sets of variations for pf.; 3 sets of bagatelles; 4 rondos; fantasia in G min.; 3 preludes; polonaise; andante in F ("*Favori*"); 7 minuets; 13 Ländler, for 4 hands; 3 marches; 14 variations. VOCAL.—Opera "*Fidelio*," in 2 acts, op. 72. 2 Masses, in C and D ("*Solennis*"). Oratorio "*Christus am Oelberg*," op. 85. Cantata "*Der glorreiche Augenblick*," op. 136 (1814); also arr. as *Preis der Tonkunst. Meeresstille und Glückliche Fahrt*, op. 112 (poem by Goethe). Scena and aria for soprano, "*Ah Perfido*," with orch., op. 65. Trio for soprano, tenor, and bass, "*Tremate, Empt, Tremate*," op. 116. "*Opferlied*" for soprano solo, chorus, and orch. "*Bundeslied*" for 2 solo voices. 3-part chorus and wind. "*Elegischer Gesang*" for 4 voice-parts and strings; 66 songs with pf.-accomp.; one duet, "*Gesang der Mönche*"; 3 voice-parts *a capp.* 18 vocal canons. 7 books of English, Scotch, Irish, Welsh, and Italian songs, with pf., vln, and 'cello. A symphony supposed to be a youthful work of his was discovered 1911 in the library of the University of Jena, by Prof. Fritz Stein, was performed there Jan. 17, 1910, and published 1911; performed in Leipzig, Nov., 1911, and by Boston Symph., 1912. It is not generally accepted as Beethoven's but is found weak and uninteresting, of Haydnlike simplicity, with echoes of Mozart. The best biography is Alex. W. Thayer's. Partial collections of Beethoven's letters are pub. and his sketch-books are discussed in Ignaz von Seyfried's "*Ludwig van Beethoven's Studien im Generalbass, Kontrapunkt und in der Kompositionslehre*." Selections from these have been published; a complete edition projected (1935) in Germany. Biogs. also by Schindler, Nohl, Crowest, etc. Wagner wrote an estimate. The vast Beethoven literature includes studies of the composer by Bekker, Grace, Grove, Kalischer, Kerst, Herriot, Kullak, Mason, d'Indy, Mies, Newman, Rolland, Marion Scott, Sonneck, Specht, J. W. N. Sullivan, Ernest Walker, etc. Studies of his sonatas by Behrend, Elterlein, Harding, Marx, McEwen, Milne, Shedlock and Tovey; of the symphonies, by Berlioz, Edwin Evans, Sr., Grove, Tovey, and Weingartner; the string quartets by J. de Marliave (1928). A thematic index of his works was made by Nottebohm. (See article, page 485.)

Beffara (bĕf'-fä-rä), **Louis François,** Nonancourt, Eure, 1751—Paris, 1838; 1792-1816, commissaire de police, at Paris; musical historian.

Begnis (bān'-yēs), (1) **Gius or Wm. de,** Lugo, Papal States, 1793—Bath(?), England, 1849; buffo singer; in 1816, he m. (2) Signora **Ronzi,** Paris, 1800 (?)—Italy, 1853; comic soprano.

Behaim (bĕ-hīm'), **Michel,** Sulzbach, 1416—murdered there, 1474; soldier and minnesinger.

Behm (bām), **Eduard,** b. Stettin, April 8, 1862; studied with Paul, Weidenbach, Reinecke, Härtel, Raif and Kiel; pianist and teacher in various cities, then at Berlin as dir. (until 1901) Schwantzer Cons.; composed an opera, "*Schelm von Bergen*" (Dresden, 1899), a symphony, pf.-concerto, etc.

Behnke (bān'-kē), **Emil**, Stettin, 1836 —Ostend, 1892; teacher and writer.

Behr (bār), (1) **Fz.**, Lubtheen, Mecklenburg, July 22, 1837—Dresden, Feb. 15, 1898; composed pf.-pieces, under pseud. of "William Cooper," "Charles Morley," or "Francesco d'Orso." (2) **Therese**, b. Stuttgart, Sept. 14, 1876; alto; pupil of J. Stakhausen, of Schulz-Dornberg and of Etelka Gerster; m. Artur Schnabel, pianist.

Beier (bī'-ĕr), **Fz.**, Berlin, April 18, 1857—Cassel, June 25, 1914; son of a military band-master; pupil Stern and Kullak Cons.; cond. at the Royal Theatre; composed succ. opera *"Der Posaunist von Scherkingen"* (Cassel, 1889), a parody on Nessler's well-known *"Der Trompeter von Säkkingen"*; succ. comic operetta *"der Gaunerkönig"* (Cassel, 1890), etc.

Bek'ker, Paul, Berlin, Sept. 11, 1882— New York, Feb., 1937; writer; originally a violinist; pupil of Rehfeld, Sormann, and Horwitz; became critic of Berlin Neueste Nachrichten, 1906; Allgemeine Zeitung, 1909; Frankfurter Zeitung, 1911–23; intendant of Cassel Stadttheat., 1925–7; and of Wiesbaden Op., 1927–32; after 1934 critic of Staats-Zeitung, New York; author of many books on music, incl. *"Beethoven"* (1911); *"Das Deutsche Musikleben"* (1916); *"Die Symphonien Gustav Mahlers"* (1921); *"Richard Wagner"* (1925); *"Die Oper,"* etc.

Belaiev, (1) **Mitrofan**, St. Petersburg, Feb. 10, 1836—Jan. 10, 1904; noted music patron and eccentric millionaire, who sponsored the work of the Russian Nationalist group of composers, also establishing in 1885 the important pub. house in Leipzig for works by his countrymen. (2) **Victor Michailovitch**, b. Uralsk, Russia, Feb. 5, 1888; eminent musicologist and writer on music.

Belce. Vide REUSS-BELCE.

Belcke (bĕl'-kĕ), (1) **Fr. Aug.**, Lucka, Altenburg, 1795—1874; the first trombone virtuoso. (2) **Chr. Gl.**, Lucka, 1796—1875; bro. of above; flutist.

Beldoman'dis (or **Beldeman'dis, Beldeman'do**), **Prosdo'cimus de**, b. Padua, 15th cent.; prof. of philosophy. ca. 1422: theorist.

Beliczay (bā'-lǐ-chä-ĕ), **Julius von,** Komorn, Hungary, 1835—Pesth. 1893; violinist.

Belin (or **Bellin**) (bŭ-lăṅ), (1) **Guil.,** ca. 1547; tenor Chapelle Royale, Paris. (2) **Julien**, b. Le Mans, ca. 1530; lutenist.

Bell, William Henry, b. St. Albans, Aug. 20, 1873; pupil at the R. A. M.; won Goss scholarship, 1889; 1903, prof. of harmony there; c. symphonies *"Walt Whitman"* and *"The Open Road,"* 3 symph. poems to the *"Canterbury Tales"*; symph. poems, *"Love Among the Ruins"*; *"The Shepherd,"* etc. 1912, dir. of Cape Town Cons.

Bellaigue (bĕl-lĕg), **Camille**, Paris, May 24, 1858—Oct. 4, 1930; critic and essayist; pupil of Paladilhe and Marmontel.

Bellasio (bĕl-lä'-sǐ-ō), **Paolo**, 1579-95; pub. madrigals, etc., at Venice.

Bel'lasis, Edw., b. Jan. 28, 1852; English writer and composer; wrote biog. of Cherubini (1912).

Bell'avere (or **Bell'haver**) (bĕl-ä-vä'-rĕ), **V.**, Venice, 1530 (?)—1588 (?), organist and composer.

Bellazzi (bĕl-läd'-zē), **Fran. C.**, at Venice, 1618–28.

Bellère (bĕl-lär') (or **Belle'rus**, rightly **Beellaerts**) (bāl-lärts'), (1) **Jean**, d. Antwerp, ca. 1595; publisher. His son and successor was (2) **Balthasar.**

Bel'lermann, (1) **Konstantin**, Erfurt. 1696—Münden, 1758; rector and composer. (2) **Jn. Fr.**, Erfurt, 1795 —Berlin, 1874; writer on Greek music. His son (3), **Jn. Gf. H.**, Berlin, March 10, 1832—Potsdam, April 10, 1903; pupil R. Inst. for ch.-music, 1866; prof. of mus. Berlin U (vice Marx.); theorist and composer.

Bellet'ti, Giov. Bat., Sarzana, Feb. 17, 1813—Dec. 27, 1890; barytone; pupil of Pilotti at Bologna; début, 1838, Stockholm; sang with Jenny Lind on tour; retired, 1862.

Bellezza, Vincenzo (vǐn-chĕn'-tsō bĕl-lĕts'-ä), b. Bitonto, Italy, Feb. 17, 1888; operatic conductor; studied Naples Cons.; has conducted at Met. Op. House, N. Y.; Covent Garden Op., London; Teatro Colon, Buenos Aires; also in various opera houses of Italy, Spain, Portugal, and South America.

Bell'haver, V. Vide BELL'AVERE.

Belli (bĕl'-lē), (1) **Gir.**, pub., 1586-94.

madrigals, etc. (2) **Giulio**, b. Longiano, ca. 1560; ch.-composer and cond. (3) **Dom.**, 1616; court-musician at Parma.

Bellin, G. Vide BELIN.

Bellincioni (běl-lǐn-chō'-nē), **Gemma**, Monza, 1864—Naples, Apr. 23, 1950; Italian soprano; toured U. S. in opera, 1899; after 1911 taught in Berlin; and later at Academy of Sta. Cecilia, Rome; pub. a vocal method; she created Santuzza in "*Cavalleria Rusticana.*"

Bellini (běl-lē'-nē), (1) **Vincenzo**, Catania, Sicily, Nov. 3, 1801—Puteaux, near Paris, Sept. 23, 1835; opera composer; son and pupil of an organist; a nobleman sent him (1819) to the Cons. at Naples; studied under Furno, Tritto, and Zingarelli, until 1827; privately studied with Haydn and Mozart, and chiefly Pergolesi; as a student composed a symphony, 2 masses, several psalms, a cantata, etc.; his first opera, "*Adelson e Salvini*," was performed by Cons. pupils, 1825, whereupon the manager of La Scala, Milan, commissioned him to write an opera; 1826, "*Bianca e Fernando*" was prod. with succ.; 1827, "*Il Pirata*"; 1829, "*La Straniera.*" The librettist of the latter 2 was Felice Romani, who wrote the books of all B.'s operas, except "*I Puritani.*" "*Zaira*" (1829) was a failure; "*I Capuleti e Montecchi,*" written in forty days (1830), was a great succ.; "*La Sonnambula,*" and "*Norma*" (1831), with Malibran in the title-rôle, established his fame; "*Beatrice di Tenda*" (Venice. 1833) failed; "*I Puritani*" (libretto by Count Pepoli), written to order 1834, for the Théâtre Italien, Paris, was a great success, and his last finished work. B.'s work abounds in delightful, spontaneous melodies, though the lack of variety in his rhythmic scheme and orchestral accompaniments makes his scores today sound rather pale; Norma remains a great rôle for sopranos of a heroic vocal equipment. He died youngest of all prominent composers—at the age of 33, from dysentery due to overwork. Biog. by Scherillo (Milan, 1885), Pougin (Paris, 1868), etc. Other studies by Cicconetti, Amore, Voss, Lloyd and Parodi; collections of B.'s letters ed. by Scherillo and Salvioli. (2) **Carmelo**, Catania, 1802—1884;

brother of above; composed church-music.

Belloc (běl-lôk'), **Teresa** (G. Trombet'ta-Belloc), San Begnino, Canavese, 1784—S. Giorgio, 1855; mezzo-soprano; repertoire of 80 operas.

Belloli (běl-lō'-lē), (1) **Luigi**, Castelfranco, Bologna, 1770—Milan, 1817; horn-player and composer. (2) **Ag.**, b. Bologna; first horn (1819–29) at La Scala, Milan, and dram. composer.

Bemberg (bän-běrg), **Henri**, b. Paris, March 29, 1861; pupil of Dubois, Franck and Massenet, Paris Cons.; 1887 took Rossini prize; composed 1-act opera "*Le Baiser de Suzon*" (Paris, Op.-com., 1888), mod. succ.; opera "*Elaine*" (London, 1892: New York, 1894), cantata, "*Mort de Jeanne d'Arc,*" and songs.

Bemetzrieder (bā'-měts-rē-děr), **A.**, b. Alsatia, 1743; Benedictine monk; composer and writer.

Ben'da, (1) **Franz**, Alt-Benátek, Bohemia, Nov. 25, 1709—Potsdam, March 7, 1786; court-violinist to Frederick II., whom he accompanied for 40 years in flute-concertos; composed symphonies, etc. His 3 brothers (2) **Jn.**, Alt-Benátek, 1713—Potsdam, 1752; violinist. (3) **G.**, Jungbunzlau, Bohemia, 1722—Koestritz, Nov. 6, 1795; court-cond., 1748 (Gotha); 1764–66, Italy; prod. at Gotha 10 operas in which he originated the idea of spoken words with orchestral accompaniment, literal "melodrama." (4) **Jos.**, 1724—Berlin, 1804; violinist. His sister, (5) **Anna Frangiska**, 1726—Gotha, 1780; singer. (6) **Fr. Wm. H.**, Potsdam, 1745—1814; son and pupil of (1); composed operas, etc. (7) **Fr. L.**, Gotha, 1746—Königsberg, 1793; son of (3); cond. and composer. (8) **K. Hermann H.**, Potsdam, 1748—1836; son of rich father; court-violinist and composer.

Ben'del, Fz., Schönlinde, northern Bohemia, March 23, 1832—Berlin, July 3, 1874; pianist; composed symphonies, 4 masses, songs, and piano pieces.

Ben'deler, Jn. Ph., Riethnordhausen, near Erfurt, ca. 1660—Quedlinburg, ca. 1712; clavecinist, organist, and writer.

Ben'der, Paul, b. Driedorf, Germany, July 28, 1875; operatic bass; first studied medicine; singing with Luise

Ress and Baptist Hoffmann; member Breslau Op., after 1900; Munich Op. after 1903; sang at Bayreuth Festivals, beginning 1902; was member of Metropolitan Op., N. Y., in 1922–6.

Ben'dix, (1) Victor E., Copenhagen, May 7, 1851—Jan. 5, 1926; pianist, pupil and protégé of Gade; lived in Copenh. as pf.-teacher and cond.; composed 4 symphonies, incl. *"Zur Höhe,"* in C (also named *"Felsensteigung"*); and *"Sommerklänge aus Südrussland"* in D. **(2) Max,** b. Detroit, Mich., March 28, 1866; violinist; early played in orchestras; studied with Jacobsohn; 1886, concertm. at Met. Op. House; also of Thomas Orch., of which ass't. cond.; founded Bendix Quartet; cond. at Manhattan Op. House, 1906; at Met. Op., 1909–10; 1915, San Francisco Exp.; later teacher in New York.

Ben'dl (bĕnt'-'l), K., Prague, April 16, 1838—Sept. 20, 1897; important Czech composer; pupil of Blažok and Pitsch, at Prague; chorus-master, Amsterdam (1864); 1866, cond. Prague choral society, "Hlahol"; composed Czech operas incl. *"Dite Tábora"* (Child of the Camp), 1892 (3 acts); given at Prague; 3 masses, cantatas, an overture, a *"Dithyramb,"* *"Slavonic Rhapsody,"* for orch., etc.

Ben'edict, Sir Julius, Stuttgart, Nov. 27, 1804—London, June 5, 1885; son of a Jewish banker; pupil of Abeille, Hummel, and Weber, 1825 at Naples, where his first opera was prod. 1829, without success; his next (Stuttgart, 1830) was not a success; settled in London as pf.-teacher and concert-giver; 1836, cond. opera buffa; 1837 at Drury Lane, there his first English opera, *"The Gypsy's Warning,"* was prod. (1838); he accompanied Jenny Lind to America, then cond. at Her Majesty's Th., and Drury Lane; 1859 at Covent Garden, and "Monday Popular Concerts"; cond. also Norwich festivals, and (1876–80) the Liverpool Philharmonic; knighted in 1871; composed 11 operas; 2 oratorios, *"St. Cecilia"* (1866), and *"St. Peter"* (1870); 2 symphonies, 2 pf.-concertos, etc.; wrote a biog. of Weber.

Benedic'tus Appenzelders (äp'-pĕntsĕlt-ĕrs) (**B.** of **Appenzell**), b. Appenzell, Switzerland; choir-master in Brussels (1539–55) and composer;

often confused with Benedictu* Ducis.

Benel'li, (1) Alemanno. Vide BOT-TRIGARI. **(2) A. Peregrino,** Forli, Romagna, 1771—Bornichau, Saxony, 1830; tenor.

Benevoli (bā-nā'-vō-lē), **Orazio,** Rome, 1602—1672; natural son of Duke Albert of Lorraine, but lived in poverty; cond. at the Vatican (1646); remarkable contrapuntist; in writing chorals with instrs. he was a pioneer; his Salzburg mass being written on 54 staves.

Ben'jamin, Arthur, b. Sydney, pup. Stanford; res. Can.; comp.

Ben'net, (1) J., English composer (1599). **(2) Saunders,** d. 1809; English organist and composer. **(3) Theodore.** Vide TH. RITTER.

Ben'nett, (1) Wm., b. Teignmouth, ca. 1767; organist. **(2) Thos.,** ca. 1774–1848; organist. **(3) Alfred,** 1805—1830; English organist. **(4) Sir Wm. Sterndale,** Sheffield, April 13, 1816—London, Feb. 1, 1875; son of an organist (who died 1819); at 8 entered the choir of King's College Chapel; at 10 pupil of R. A. M.; at 17 played there an original pf.-concerto, later pub. by the Academy, sent 1837 by the Broadwoods to Leipzig for one year; friend of Schumann and Mendelssohn; 1844 m. Mary Anne Wood, founded the Bach Society, 1849; cond. Philh. Society, 1856–66; 1856, Mus. Doc. Cambridge and prof. of mus. there; 1866, Principal there; 1871, knighted; buried in Westminster Abbey; composed 1 symphony, an oratorio *"The Woman of Samaria,"* music to Sophokles' *"Ajax";* 5 overtures, *"Parisina,"* *"The Naiads,"* *"The Wood-nymph,"* *"Paradise and the Peri,"* *"Merry Wives of Windsor,"* sonatas, etc. **(5) Jos.,** Berkeley, Gloucestershire, Nov. 29, 1831—June 12, 1911; organist of Westminster Chapel; then music critic for various London newspapers; finally *The Telegraph;* wrote various libretti; pub. *"Letters from Bayreuth"* (1877); *"The Musical Year"* (1883), etc. **(6) Robert Russell,** b. Kansas City, Mo., 1894; composer; early pupil of Carl Busch; res. in New York after 1916, where active as orchestrator and arranger; won Guggenheim Fellowship; studied with Nadia Boulanger, Paris; c. (opera) *"Maria Malibran,"* text by

Robert A. Simon, prod. by Juilliard School, N. Y., 1935; (ballet) *"Endymion"* (orch.) symphony; *"Charleston Rhapsody,"* *"Sights and Sounds"* (won RCA-Victor Co. prize); *"Abraham Lincoln"*; concerto grosso; March for two pianos and orch.; Six Variations on a Theme of Jerome Kern; chamber music, incl. "Toy" Symphony and string quartet.

Bennewitz (bĕn'-nĕ-vēts), (1) **Wm.**, Berlin, 1832—1871; dram. composer. (2) **Anton**, Privat, Bohemia, March 26, 1833—Hirschberg near Leipzig, May 30, 1926; violinist; 1882–1901, dir. of Prague Cons.

Benoist (bŭn-wä), **François**, Nantes, 1794—Paris, 1878; organ-prof. Paris Cons.; composed operas, etc.

Benoît (bŭn-wä), (1) **Pierre Léonard Ld.**, Harlebecke, Belgium, Aug. 17, 1834—Antwerp, Mar. 4, 1901; Flemish composer and writer; pupil Brussels Cons., 1851–55; at same time prod. a small opera and wrote music for Flemish melodramas; 1856, cond. Park Th.; 1857, won the Prix de Rome, with the cantata *"Le Meurtre d'Abel"*; studied at Leipzig, Dresden, Munich, and Berlin, and wrote a thesis for the Brussels Academy *"L'école de musique flamande et son avenir."* In 1861 his opera *"Le Roi des Aulnes,"* was accepted by Théâtre Lyrique, Paris, but not given; cond. at the Bouffes-Parisiennes; from 1867, dir. Antwerp Cons.; 1882, member of the R. A., Berlin; composed *"Messe solennelle"* (1862); *"TeDeum"* (1863); *"Requiem"* (1863); 2 oratorios, *"Lucifer"* and *"De Schelde"*; 2 operas, *"Het Dorp int Gebergte"* and *"Isa"*; *"Drama Christi,"* a sacred drama in Flemish; a cantata *"De Oorlog War"*; *"Children's Oratorio"*; a choral symphony, *"De Maaiers"* (The Reapers); music to *"Charlotte Corday,"* and to *"Willem de Zwijger"* (1876); the "Rubens cantata" *"Flanderens kunstroem"*; *"Antwerpen,"* for triple male chorus (1877); vocal works with orch. incl. *"Joncfrou Kathelijne,"* scena for alto (1879); *"Muse der Geschiednis"* (1880); and "Hucbald," *"Triomfmarsch"* (1880); grand cantata *"De Rhyn"* (1889); a mass, etc. Wrote *"De vlaamsche Musiek-school van Antwerpen"* (1873), *"Verhandelung over de nationale Toonkunde"* (2 vols., 1877–79), etc. (2) **Camille**, Roanne,

Nov. 7, 1851—Paris, July 1, 1923; pupil of César Franck; 1888–1895, assistant conservator at the Louvre; 1895, conservator; c. overture, 1880; text and music of opera *"Cléopatre,"* etc.; author of *"Souvenirs,"* 1884, and *"Musiciens, poetes et philosophes,"* 1887; also translator.

Bentonel'li, Joseph (rightly **Benton**), b. Oklahoma; tenor; grad. Okla. State Univ.; studied with Jean de Reszke in France, coached operatic rôles in Italy for three years, and made début at Bologna as Alfredo; sang in Italian theatres, also in Austria, France, Belgium, and Holland; mem. Chicago Op. Co., 1934-5, singing with this company in latter year leading tenor rôle in Am. prem. of Respighi's *"La Fiamma,"* also with Philadelphia Orch. in its stage prod. of Gluck's *"Iphigénie en Aulide"*; concert tour in U. S.; audition with Met. Op. Co. was followed by sudden call two days later to take place of indisposed tenor as Des Grieux in *"Manon,"* 1936, which he sang with succ. and was engaged as regular mem. of company.

Benvenuti (bĕn-vä-noo'-tē), **Tommaso,** Venice, 1838—Rome, 1906; dram. composer.

Berardi (bä-rär'-dē), **Ang.**, b. Bologna, 1681; conductor and theorist.

Ber'ber, Felix, Jena, March 11, 1871—Nov. 2, 1930; violinist; pupil of Dresden Cons. and Leipzig Cons.; concertmaster in various cities; 1904-1907 prof. Royal Acad., London; 1907 at Frankfort-on-Main; 1908 at Geneva Cons.; toured widely; 1910, America; after 1912 in Munich; 1920, teaching at Cons. there.

Berbiguier (bĕr-bĭg-yä), **Benoît Tranquille**, Caderousse, Vaucluse, 1782—near Blois, 1838; flute-virtuoso and composer.

Berchem (or **Berghem**) (bĕrkh'-ĕm), **Jachet de** (also **Jaquet, Jacquet,** and **Giachetto di Mantova**), Berchem (?) near Antwerp, ca. 1500—1580; contrapuntist and conductor.

Berens (bä'-rĕns), (1) **Hermann,** Hamburg, 1826—Stockholm, 1880; son and pupil of (2) **K. B.** (1801–1857); court-conductor and composer.

Beret'ta, Giov. Batt, Verona, 1819—Milan, 1876; theorist, editor, and composer.

Berezowsky (bĕr-ē-sŏf'-skē), **Nicolai,** b. St. Petersburg, May 17, 1900;

d. N. Y., Aug. 26, 1953; entered Imp. Capella and grad. with honours; 1918, concertm. Saratov Nat'l. Op.; 1921, dir. Sch. of Mod. Art, Moscow; after 1922 in U. S.; studied with Josef Borisoff, then at Juilliard Sch. of Mus. with R. Goldmark and Kochanski; played in N. Y. Phil.; c. sextet for strings, piano, and clarinet (heard Washington Chamber Mus. Fest., 1926); four string quartets; quartet for soprano and strings; piano trio; quintet for wind instruments; (orch.) two symphonies (the first played by Boston Symph., as well as his 'cello concerto); "*Hebrew*" *Suite* (N. Y. Phil.); Sinfonietta; violin concerto (played by Flesch with Dresden Phil. under composer's baton); (opera) "*Prince Batrak*."

Berg (bĕrkh), (1) **Adam**, 1540—1599; music-printer, Munich. (2) **Jn. von**, 1550; music-printer, Ghent, Nürnberg. (3) **G.**, German composer in England, 1763-71. (4) **Kon. Mat.**, Colmar, Alsatia, 1785—Strassburg, 1852; violinist, pianist, and writer. (5) **Alban**, Vienna, Feb. 9, 1885—Dec. 24, 1935; eminent composer; studied with Schönberg, 1904-08, whose radical doctrines in harmony and tonality he combined in his work with an original capacity of expression that makes him the outstanding member of that composer's school; served as director of concerts given by Private Performing Society organized by Schörberg in Vienna; c. piano sonata (1908); string quartet (1910); songs with piano and orchestra (1908-09); four pieces for clarinet and orchestra (1913); three orchestral pieces (1914); chamber concerto for piano, violin, and 13 wind instruments (1924); the expressionistic music-drama "*Wozzeck*" (based on play by Georg Büchner, nineteenth-century German poet), which is written in novel style, partly atonal, and utilizing antique forms such as suite, passacaglia, etc., in its operatic texture (première after many rehearsals evoked sensational impression at Berlin State Op., Dec. 14, 1925); Lyric Suite for string quartet (1926); concert aria, "*Le Vin*," for soprano and orchestra (1929); partially completed music drama, "*Lulu*" (based on Wedekind dramas, "*Erdgeist*" and "*Pandora's Box*"), which after his death aroused wide interest when premiered, Zurich, 1937; also posth. violin concerto (Barcelona, 1936, Intern. Society for Contemp. Music Festival). One of the most original figures in early twentieth-century music, B. in his "*Wozzeck*," relates the heart-rending tragedy of an ignorant soldie: who, oppressed by his superiors, murders his sweetheart and drowns himself; this work made a definite contribution to post-Wagnerian music drama. The opera was given its American première by the Philadelphia Orch. and Grand Opera Co., under Stokowski, both in Phila. and N. Y., with impressive effect in 1931. B. also served as editor of the Vienna publication "*Musikblätter des Anbruch*," for a period after 1920.

Berger (bĕr'-gĕr), (1) **L.**, Berlin, 1777—1839; from 1815 pf.-teacher and composer. (2) **Francesco**, London, June 10, 1834—April 25, 1933; pupil of Ricci and Lickl (pf.), Hauptmann and Plaidy; from 1855 pf.-prof. R. A. M., and Guildhall Sch. of Mus.; for years dir., and 1884-1911, sec., Philh.; composed an opera, a mass (prod. in Italy), etc.; wrote "*First Steps at the Pianoforte*." (3) **Wm.**, Boston, Mass., Aug. 8, 1861—Jena Germany, Jan. 16, 1911; taken by parents to Bremen; pupil of Kiel, etc.; lived Berlin as teacher and composer; 1898 won a prize of 2,000 marks, with a setting of Goethe's "*Meine Göttin*" (op. 72); composed "*Gesang der Geister über den Wassern*," for mixed choir and orch. (4) **Erna**, b. Dresden, 1901; coloratura soprano; Dresden State Op. and after 1932 at Berlin; London, 1947; Met. Op. début, 1949, as Sophie (Strauss).

Berggreen (bĕrkh'-grän), **Andreas P.**, Copenhagen, 1801—1880; teacher.

Berghem. Vide BERCHEM.

Bergmann (bĕrkh'-män), **K.**, Ebersbach, Saxony, 1821—New York, Aug. 16, 1876; in America, 1850, with "Germania" Orch., later its cond. till 1854; cond. "Händel and Haydn" Soc., Boston, 1852-54; in 1855 alternate cond. Philh. Soc., New York; 1862-76, sole cond.; also cond. "Arion" Society; active in introducing Wagner, Liszt, etc., to America.

Bergner (bĕrkh'-nĕr), **Wm.**, Riga, Nov. 4, 1837—June 9, 1907; organist; founded a Bach Society and a cathedral choir.

Bergonzi (bĕr-gŏn'-tsē), (1) **Carlo**, d. 1747; vln.-maker at Cremona; best pupil of Stradivari. His son (2) **Michelangelo**, and his 2 nephews, (3) **Niccolo** and (4) **Carlo**, were less important. (5) **Benedetto**, Cremonu, 1790—1840; horn-player and inventor.

Bergson (bĕrkh'-zōn), **Michael**, Warsaw, May 20, 1820—London, March 9, 1898; pianist and composer; pupil of Schneider, Rungenhagen, and Taubert, Paris (1840); Italy, 1846, where his opera "*Louisa di Montfort*" was succ. (Florence, 1847); Paris, 1859, prod. a 1-act operetta; 1863, 1st pf.-teacher and for a time dir. Geneva Cons.; later in London as teacher.

Bergt (bĕrkht), **Chr. Gl. Aug.**, b. Oderan, Saxony, 1772—Bautzen, 1837; organist, violinist, and conductor.

Beringer (bā'-rĭng-ĕr), **Oscar**, Furtwangen, July 14, 1844—London, Feb. 21, 1922; pupil of Plaidy, Moscheles, Leipzig Cons., 1864–66; later of Tausig, Ehrlich, and Weitzmann, Berlin; teacher there, 1869; London, 1873–97; after 1885, pf.-prof. in R. A. M.; composed Technical Exercises, etc.

Bériot (dŭ bār-yō), (1) **Chas. Auguste de**, Louvain, Feb. 20, 1802—Brussels, April 8, 1870; vln.-virtuoso; pupil of Viotti and Baillot, but chiefly of his guardian, Tiby; at 9 he played a concerto; 1821, made a brilliant début, Paris; chamber-violinist to the King of France, solo-violinist to the King of the Netherlands (1826–30); 1830–35 toured Europe with Mme. Garcia-Malibran, whom he m. in 1836; from 1843–52, prof. at Brussels Cons.; became blind and paralysed in left arm; pub. method and 7 concertos, etc., for vln. (2) **Chas. Vilfride de**, Paris, Feb. 12, 1833—near Paris, 1914; son of above; pupil of Thalberg; prof. of pf., Paris Cons.; composed symphonies, etc.; wrote with his father a "*Methode d'accompagnement*."

Berlijn (or **Berlyn**) (băr'-lēn), **Anton** (or **Aron Wolf** ?), Amsterdam, 1817—1870; conductor.

Berlin', **Irving** (rightly **Baline**), b. Russia, May 11, 1888; composer of popular music; was largely responsible for start of "ragtime" craze with his "*Alexander's Ragtime Band*"

several years before the war; has since c. more elaborate scores for musical comedies and the radio; pres. of his own publishing firm, Irving Berlin Inc., New York; m. Ellin Mackay, daughter of Clarence H. Mackay.

Berlioz (bār-lĭ-ōs not bār-lĭ-ō), **Hector** (**Louis**), Côte-Saint-André, near Grenoble, France, Dec. 11, 1803—Paris, March 8, 1869; "Father of modern orchestration"; conductor, critic, writer of verse and electric prose; sent to Paris to study medicine, he accepted disinheritance and took up music, though he could never play any instr. save the guitar and flageolet; while pupil at the Cons., he earned a bare living; joined the chorus of the Gymnase Dramatique; left the Cons. in disgust with Reicha's formalism, and plunged with characteristic energy—or rather fury—into the cause of romanticism; 1825, an orchestral mass given at St. Roch brought the ridicule he usually had in France where he was little thought of as a composer though admired as a writer; 1828 saw the production of two overtures, "*Waverley*" and "*Les Frances-Juges*," and a Symphonie fantastique, "*Épisode de la vie d'un artiste*"; 1829, his "*Concerts des Sylphes*," publicly produced at 26, show him an ardent believer in programme-music (vide D. D.) and a marvellous virtuoso in instrumentation. He reëntered the Cons. under Lesueur, in spite of Cherubini, who fought his admission; 1830, he took the Prix de Rome with a cantata, "*Sardanapale*"; after 18 months in Italy he returned to Paris and took up journalism with marked success. His symphony "*Harold en Italie*" (1834), the "*Messe des Morts*" (1837), the dram. symphony "*Roméo et Juliette*," with vocal soli and chorus (1839), and the overture "*Carneval romain*," were well received, but the 2-act opera semi-seria "*Benvenuto Cellini*" failed both in Paris and in London, 1838. In 1839 he was made Conservator of the Cons.; librarian, 1852, but was never made professor as he desired. Concert tours through Germany and Russia, 1843–47, were very successful and are described in his book "*Voyage musical*." London (1852) he cond. the "New Philh. Concerts"; prod. comic opera "*Béat-*

rice et Bénédict (1862, Baden-Baden); 1865, member of the Académie, and decorated with cross of Legion of Honour. He m. Henrietta Smithson, an Irish actress who made a sensation in Paris in Shakespearian rôles, but later was hissed off, and became a peevish invalid. His opera, *"Les Troyens à Carthage,"* (1863) was a failure. His son Louis died 1867. *"Les Troyens,"* in two parts; *"La Prise de Troie,"* 3 acts, and *"Les Troyens à Carthage,"* in 5 acts was given complete for the first time, at Carlsruhe, 1897. His most succ. work was his "oratorio," *"La Damnation de Faust"* (1846). His *"Traité d'instrumentation"* is a classic in orchestration, though its then sensational modernity is lost. **B.** strangely despised Wagner, who, however, confessed his large indebtedness to **B.** Other books are *"Soirées d'orchestre"* (1853), *"Grotesques de la musique"* (1859), *"A travers chants"* (1862), and an autobiography, *"Mémoires,"* from 1803-65. In original verse are the text to the sacred trilogy *"L'Enfance du Christ"* (*Part I.*, *Le songe d' Hérode; II.*, *La fuite en Égypte; III.*, *L'Arrivée à Sais*); and his operas *"Les Troyens"* and *"Béatrice et Bénédict."* He composed also a *"Te Deum"* for 3 choirs, orch. and org.; a *"Grand symphonie funèbre et triomphale"* for full military band, with strings and chorus ad lib.; overture to *"Le Corsaire"*; *"Le Cinq Mai,"* for chorus and orch. (on the anniversary of Napoleon's death), etc. Recent studies of **B.** have been published in English by W. J. Turner (1934) and Tom S. Wotton (1935); coinciding with a resurgence of interest in this composer on the part of a modern-minded coterie of musicians in Britain. Revivals of Berlioz operas have also taken place, notably of *"Les Troyens,"* and *"Béatrice and Bénédict,"* at Glasgow. (See article, page 488.)

Berlyn, Anton. Vide BERLIJN.

Bermudo (bĕr-moo'-dhō), Juan, Astorga, ca. 1510; writer.

Bernabei (bĕr-nä-bā'-ē), (1) **Gius, Ercole,** Caprarola, ca. 1620—Munich, 1687; 1672 cond. at the Vatican; 1674 cond. at Munich; composed three operas (prod. in Munich), etc. (2) **Gius. A.,** Rome, 1649—Munich,

1732; son of above and his successor at Munich.

Bernacchi (bĕr-näk'-kē), A., Bologna, 1685—1756; soprano-musico, engaged by Händel for London, 1729, as the greatest living dram. singer; 1736 founded a singing-school at Bologna.

Bernard (bĕr-năr, in *F.*), **Émile,** Marseilles, Nov. 28, 1843—Paris, Sept. 11, 1902; until 1895 organist of Nôtre-Dame-des-Champs, Paris; composer of vln.-concerto; concert-stück for pf. with orch.; overture *"Beatrice"*; cantatas; much chamber-music, etc.

Bernardel. Vide LUPOT.

Bernar'di, (1) **Steffano,** ca. 1634; canon at Salzburg; theorist and composer. (2) **Francesco.** Vide SENESINO. (3) **Enrico,** Milan, 1838—1900; conductor and dram. composer.

Bernardini (bĕr-när-dē'-nē), **Marcello** (*"Marcello di Capua"*), b. Capua, ca. 1762; dram. composer.

Bernasco'ni, (1) **Andrea,** Marseilles, 1706—Munich, 1784; court-conductor. (2) **P.,** d. Varese, May 27, 1895; organ-builder.

Bern'eker, Constanz, Darkehmen, E. Prussia, Oct. 31, 1844—Königsberg, June 9, 1906; conductor and comp.

Ber'ner, Fr. Wm., Breslau, 1780—1827; organist.

Ber'ners, Lord (Gerald Tyrwhitt), b. Bridgnorth, Engl., Sept. 18, 1883; d. London, Apr. 19, 1950; studied in Dresden, London; self-taught in music, but orchestration with Stravinsky, some of whose modern musical devices are reflected in his work; entered diplomatic service, 1909; after 1912 connected with British Embassy in Rome; succeeded to British peerage, 1918; c. (opera in one act) *"Le Carrosse de Saint-Sacrement"*; (orchestra) *"Fantaisie Espagnole"* (1919); *"Funeral Marches for a Statesman, a Canary, and a Rich Aunt"* (for two pianos); *"Valse Bourgeoise"* (Salzburg Festival, 1923); Fugue for Orchestra (danced by Diaghileff Ballet, London, 1925); also an amusing nautical ballet, *"The Triumph of Neptune,"* suggested by Rowlandson prints, from which a succ. orch. suite has been drawn.

Bernhard (bĕrn'-härt), (1) der Deutsche (dĕr doit'-shĕ); organist, Venice, 1445-59; known as "Bernardo di Steffanino Murer": perhaps inv.,

DICTIONARY OF MUSICIANS 61

certainly introduced, into Italy, the organ-pedal. (2) **Chr.**, Danzig, 1627 —Dresden, 1692; court-conductor and notable contrapuntist.

Ber'no, Augien'sis, d. Riechenau, 1048; abbot and theorist.

Bernoulli (bǎr-noo'-yē), (1) **Jn.**, Basel, 1667—1747. His son (2) **Daniel**, Groningen, 1700—Basel, 1781, also was prof. and writer on acoustics.

Bern'stein,Leonard,b.Lawrence,Mass., 1918; studied Harvard, Curtis Inst.; ass't. to Koussevitzky, Berkshire Fest.; cond. as guest in Europe; c. symphs., *"Jeremiah," "Age of Anxiety."*

Bernuth (bǎr'-noot), **Julius von**, Rees, Rhine Province, Aug. 8, 1830— Hamburg, Dec. 24, 1902; studied law and music at Berlin, 1854; studied at Leipzig Cons. till 1857; founded the "Aufschwung Society," and 1859 "Dilettante's Orchestral Society"; also cond. 3 other societies; later cond. at Hamburg; 1873, dir. of a cons. there; 1878, "Royal Prussian Professor."

Berr (bĕr), **Fr.**, Mannheim, 1794— Paris, 1838; bandmaster; 1831, prof. of clar., Paris Cons.; 1836, dir. School of Military Music; composer.

Bertali (bĕr-tä'-lē), **Ant.**, Verona, 1605 —Vienna, 1669; court-conductor and dram. composer.

Ber'telsmann, K. Aug., Gütersloh, Westphalia,1811—Amsterdam,1861; director and composer.

Berthaume (bĕr-tōm), **Isidore**, Paris, 1752—St. Petersburg, 1802; violinist and conductor.

Berthold (bĕr'-tôlt), **K. Fr. Theodor**, Dresden, 1815—1882; court-organist.

Bertin (bĕr'-tǎṅ), **Louise Angélique**, Roches, near Paris, 1805—Paris, 1877; singer, pianist, and dram. composer.

Bertini (bĕr-tē'-nē), (1) **Abbate Gius.**, Palermo, 1756—1849 (?); court-cond. and lexicographer. (2) **Benoît Auguste**, b. Lyons, 1780; writer. (3) **H. Jérome**, London, 1798— Meylau, near Grenoble, 1876; bro. and pupil of above; pianist and composer; at 12, toured the Netherlands and Germany; retired, 1859; wrote technical studies. (4) **Dom.**, Lucca, 1829—Florence, 1890; teacher, critic, theorist, and director.

Bertinot'ti, Teresa, Piedmont, 1776— Bologna, 1854; operatic soprano; m.

Felix Radicati, a violinist and composer.

Bertolli (tôl'-lǐ), **Fran.**, Italian contralto in Händel's operas, London, 1729–37.

Berton (bĕr-tôṅ), (1) **P. Montan**, Paris, 1727—1780; conductor grand opera and dram. composer. (2) **H. Montan**, Paris, 1767—1844; son of above; composer. (3) **François**, Paris, 1784 —1832; natural son of (2); pupil, later prof. of singing, at Cons.; composed operas and songs.

Berto'ni, Fdo Giu., Venice, 1725— Desenzano, 1813; organist and dram. composer.

Bertrand (bĕr-träṅ), **J. Gv.**, Vaugirard, near Paris, 1834—Paris, 1880; writer and critic.

Berwald (bĕr'-vält), (1) **Jn. Fr.**, Stockholm, 1787—1861; precocious violinist, etc.; pupil of Abbé Vogler; composed a symphony at 9. (2) **Fz.**, Stockholm, 1796—1868; nephew of above; dram. composer.

Besekirsky (bā-zĕ-kēr'-shkǐ), (1) **Vasilly Vasilevitch**, Moscow, 1835— St. Petersburg, 1910; concert violinist and composer. (2) **Vasilly**, b. Moscow, 1879; son of (1); violinist; pupil of his father; 1910–13, prof. Odessa Cons.; after 1914 toured and taught in U. S.

Besler (bās'-lĕr), (1) **Samuel**, Brieg, Silesia, 1574—Breslau, 1625; rector and composer. (2) **Simon**, cantor at Breslau, and composer, 1615–28.

Besozzi (bā-sôd'-zē), the name of 4 brothers, all oboists except (3). (1) **Ales.**, Parma, 1700—Turin, 1775. (2) **Antonio**, Parma, 1707—Turin, 1781; (3) **Girolamo**, Parma, 1713 —1786, bassoonist. (4) **Gaetano**, b. Parma, 1727. (5) **Carlo**, b. Dresden, 1745; oboist, son of (2). (6) **Hieronimo**, d. 1785; son of (3); oboist. His son (7) **Henri** was a flutist, and father of (8) **Louis Désiré**, Versailles, 1814—Paris, 1879; teacher and composer.

Bessems (bĕs'-sāms), **A.**, Antwerp, 1809—1868; violinist and composer.

Besson (bŭs-sôṅ), **Gv. Aug.**, Paris, 1820—1875; improver of valves in wind-instruments.

Best, Wm. T., Carlisle, Engl., Aug. 13, 1826—Liverpool, May 10, 1897; org.-virtuoso; pupil of Young; organist at various ch., and the Philh. Society; in 1880, declined knighthood, but accepted Civil-List pension of £100 per annum; 1894, retired; 1890 went to Sydney, Australia, to inaugurate the organ in the new Town Hall; composed overtures, sonatas, preludes, etc., for organ, also 2 overtures and march for orch.; and pf.-pcs.; wrote "*The Art of Organ-playing*," etc.

Beständig (bĕ-stĕn'-dĭkh), **Otto**, Striegau, Silesia, Feb. 21, 1835—Wandsbeck, Feb., 1917; cond. and comp.; pupil of Mettner, etc., in Breslau; founded a conservatory in Hamburg; c. oratorio "*Der Tod Baldurs*" and "*Victoria Crucis*," etc.

Bet'ti, Adolfo, b. Bagni di Lucca, Italy, March 21, 1875; violinist; studied with César Thomson, Liége Cons., 1st prize, harmony and chamber music, 1895; gold medal in violin, 1896; début Vienna, 1897; toured in solo recitals in various European countries; assist. prof., Brussels Cons., 1900–03; first violinist, of Flonzaley Quartet, 1903–29, touring widely in Europe and U. S.; then made home in Italy; was Podestà of Bagni di Lucca, 1945; edited and arranged early Italian music for orchestra, including works of Geminiani; d. Bagni di Lucca, Dec. 2, 1950.

Betz (bĕts), **Fz.,** Mayence, March 19, 1835—Berlin, Aug. 12, 1900; barytone; created "Wotan," and "Hans Sachs."

Bev'an, Fr. Chas., b. London, July 3, 1856—Adelaide, 1939; pupil of Willing and Hoyte; organist; then studied singing with Schira, Deacon, and Walker; 1877 Gentleman of the Chapel Royal; composed pop. songs.

Bevignani (bā-vēn-yä'-nē), Cavaliere **Enrico,** Naples, Sept. 29, 1841—Aug. 29, 1903; pupil of Albanese, Lillo, etc., 1st opera, "*Caterina Bloom*," succ.; Czar made him Knight of the Order of St. Stanislas, and conferred a life-pension; noted as cond. in London, Moscow, and New York; after 1894 at Met. Op., N. Y.

Bev'in, Elway, Wales, 1560 (-70 ?)—1640 (?); Gentleman of the Chapel Royal; organist, writer, and composer.

Bex'field, Wm. Rd., Norwich, 1824—London, 1853; organist and composer.

Biaggi (bē-äd'-jē), **Gir. Ales.,** Milan, 1819—Florence, 1897; prof., dram. composer, writer under pseudonym "Ippolito d'Albano."

Bianchi (bē-än'-kē), (1) **Fran., Cremona**, 1752—London, 1810; organist; composed 47 operas. (2) **Valentine,** Wilna, 1839—Candau, Kurland, 1884; dram. soprano; début, 1855. (3) **Bianca** (rightly **Schwarz**), b. Heidelberg, Jan. 28, 1855; dram.-soprano; pupil of Wilczek and Viardot-Garcia; Pollini (whom she m., 1894) paid her tuition and then engaged her for 10 years; début Carlsruhe, 1873; taught Munich Akad., 1902–25; later at Salzburg Mozarteum. (4) **Eliodoro,** 1773—1848, a tenor singer who composed operas; "*Gara d'Amore*" (Bari, 1873); "*Sarah*"; "*Almanzor*." (5) **Renzo,** b. Maggianico, Italy, July 29, 1887; composer; grad. of Milan Cons.; c. (operas) "*Fausta*" (Florence), "*Ghismonda*" (La Scala, 1918), "*Ghibellina*" (Costanzi Theat., Rome, 1924), also orch. works.

Biber (bē'-bĕr), (1) **H. Jn. Fz. von,** Wartenberg, Bohemia, 1644—Salzburg, May 3, 1704; violinist, and one of the founders of the German school of vln.-playing; Leopold I. ennobled him. (2) **Aloys,** Ellingen, 1804—Munich, 1858; piano-maker.

Bibl (bēb-'l), (1) **Andreas,** Vienna, 1797—1878 organist and composer. His son and pupil (2) **Rudolf,** Vienna, Jan. 6, 1832—Aug. 2, 1902; pupil of Lechter; organist and composer of organ sonata, etc.

Bie (bē) **Oskar,** b. Breslau, Feb. 9, 1864; critic; pupil of Ph. Scharwenka; 1886, Dr. Phil.; 1890, Privat Docent at Technical High School, Berlin; author of books; also comp.

Biehr (bēr), **Oskar,** Dresden, 1851—Munich, March 7, 1922; violinist; pupil of David; for twenty-five years member of Munich court orchestra.

Bierey (bēr'-ī), **Gl. Benedikt,** Dresden, 1772—Breslau, 1840; conductor and dram. composer.

Biernacki (bē-ĕr-nät'-skē), **Michael Marian,** b. Lublin, Sept. 9, 1855; comp.; pupil of Warsaw Cons.; later director there; comp. 2 masses, *Prologue* for orch., etc.

Bignami (bēn-yä'-mē), (1) **Carlo,** Cremona, Dec. 6, 1808—Voghera, Aug. 2, 1848; cond., violinist and dir., Cremona; Paganini called him "the first violinist of Italy." (2) **Enrico,** 1836—Genoa, 1894; violinist, dram. composer.

Bigot (bē-gō), **M. (née Kiene),** Colmar,

Upper Alsatia, 1786—Paris, 1820; pianist.

Bilhon (or **Billon**) (bē-yôn), **J. de**, 16th cent.; composer and singer in the Papal Chapel.

Bil'lings, Wm., Boston, Mass., Oct. 7, 1746—Sept. 29, 1800; composed hymns; introduced the pitch-pipe and the 'cello into American church-choirs, and is said to have given the first concert in New England.

Bil'lington, (1) **Th.**, pianist, harpist, and composer, latter part of 18th cent. (2) **Elizabeth** (née **Weichsel**), London, ca. 1768—near Venice, Aug. 23, 1818; pupil of her father, a clarinet-tist; then of J. Chr. Bach; handsome operatic soprano, had a compass of 3 octaves, a-a''' (Vide PITCH, D. D.), 1784, Dublin; 1786, Covent Garden; retired, 1818.

Billrot(h) (bēl'-rōt), (1) **Jn. Gv. Fr.**, Halle, near Lübeck, 1808—Halle, 1836; composer and writer. (2) **Theodor**, Bergen, Isle of Rügen, 1829—Abbazia, 1894; surgeon and writer.

Bilse (bēl'-sĕ), **Benj.**, Liegnitz, Aug. 17, 1816—Berlin, July 13, 1902, where 1868-84 he cond. notable popular series of orch. concerts; originally "Stadtmusikus" at Lieg-nitz, and trained a remarkable orchestra; retired 1894 as "Hofmusikus."

Binchois (**Gilles de Binche**, called **Binchois**) (bǎnsh-wä), Binche, in Belgian Hainault, ca. 1400—Lille, 1460; one of the early Netherland composers; 3-part chanson, ron-deaux, etc., of his are extant.

Binder (bĭnt'-ĕr), (1) **K. Wm. Fd.**, b. Dresden, 1764; harp-maker at Weimar, ca. 1797. (2) **K.**, Vienna, 1816—1860; conductor and dram. composer.

Bini (bē'nē), **Pasqualino**, b. Pesaro, ca. 1720; violinist.

Bioni (bē-ō'-nē), **A.**, b. Venice, 1698; composed 26 operas.

Birch'all, Robt., d. 1819; music-pub-lisher, London.

Birckenstock (bĕr'-kĕn-shtôk), **Johann Adam**, Alsfeld, 1687—Eisenach, 1733; conductor.

Bird, (1) **Wm.** Vide BYRD. (2) **Arthur**, Cambridge, Mass., July 23, 1856—Berlin, Dec. 22, 1923; pupil of Haupt, Löschhorn, and Rohde, Berlin, 1875-77; organist and teacher at Halifax, N. S.; founded the first male chorus in N. S., 1881; studied comp.

and orchestration with Urban, Berlin; 1885-86 with Liszt at Weimar; 1886, gave a successful concert, and lived, later, in Berlin-Grünewald; composed symphony and 3 suites for orch.; various pieces for piano; comic opera "Daphne" (New York, 1897); and a ballet, "Rübezahl." (3) **Henry Richard**, Walthamstow, Nov. 14, 1842—London, 1915; organist; son of George B., an organist; at 9, be-came org.; pupil of Turle; since 1872 org. at St. Mary Abbots, London; conducted concerts, and won promi-nence as accompanist.

Birnbach (bērn'-bäkh), (1) **K. Jos.**, Köpernick, Silesia, 1751—Warsaw, 1805; conductor. (2) **Jos. Benj. H.**, Breslau, 1795—Berlin, 1879, pianist and composer; son and pupil of above.

Bischoff (bēsh'-ôf), (1) **G. Fr.**, Ellrich, Harz Mts., 1780—Hildesheim, 1841; conductor; founded the German mus. festivals. (2) **L. Fr. Ch.**, Dessau, 1794—Cologne, 1867; translator; son of (3) **K. B.**, court-mus., Dresden. (4) **Kasper Jakob**, Ansbach, 1823—Munich, 1893; teacher and composer. (5) **Hans**, Berlin, 1852—Nieder-schönhausen, near Berlin, 1889; pf.-teacher, conductor, and editor.

Bish'op, (1) **Sir H. Rowley**, London, Nov. 18, 1786—April 30, 1855; noted Engl. composer; pupil of Bianca; his first opera, "The Circassian Bride," was prod. Drury Lane, when he was 20; 1810-11 comp. and cond. at Co-vent Garden; 1813 alternate cond. Philh. Soc.; 1825 cond. at Drury Lane; 1830 musical dir. at Vauxhall; 1841-43, prof. music, Edinburgh; knighted, 1842; 1848 prof. of music at Oxford; 1853, Mus. Doc. (Oxon); prod. over 80 operas, farces, ballets, an oratorio, cantata, etc. (2) **J.**, b. Cheltenham, 1814; organist, editor, and composer. (3) **Ann**, or **Anna**, London, 1814—New York, March 18, 1884; soprano; daughter of Jules Rivière; married Sir Henry Bishop, 1831, deserted him for the harpist Bochsa, with whom she toured the world in concert; after his death, in 1856, she married a Mr. Schulz.

Bispham (bĭsp'-hăm), **David**, Philadel-phia, Jan. 5, 1857—New York, Oct. 2, 1921; dram. barytone; sang in church and oratorio; 1885-87 pupil of Vannuccini and Wm. Shakespeare; from 1891 in opera at Covent Garden, and America, with much success and versatility; and also in recitals, in both of which fields his high dramatic intelligence played an unusual part; brilliant in comic or tragic rôles; he had a huge repertoire, including 50 operatic rôles, more than 100 oratorio parts, and some 1500 recital numbers. After 1909 he withdrew from opera and sang in concerts. A brilliant teacher.

Bitt′ner, Julius, b. April, 1874, Vienna, d. there Jan. 9, 1939; composer and jurist; active for many years as a judge in Vienna, he was a pupil in music of Josef Labor and also for a time of Bruno Walter. He is best known for a series of popular operas many of which are written to his own texts, including *"Der Musikant"* (Vienna, 1910), *"Der Bergsee"* (Vienna, 1911), *"Der Abenteurer"* (Cologne, 1912), *"Das Höllisch Gold"* (Dresden, 1916), usually considered his most successful work; *"Die Kohlhaimerin"* (Vienna, 1921); and *"Das Rosengärtlein"* (Mannheim, 1923); also dance plays, piano works, songs, etc.

Bizet (bē-zā), **G. (Alex. César Léopold),** Paris, Oct. 25, 1838—Bougival, June 3, 1875; distinguished composer. At 9, pupil at Paris Cons. of Marmontel (pf.), Benoist (org.), Zimmerman (harm.), and Halévy (whose opera *"Noë"* he finished, and whose daughter Geneviéve he m.); 1857, too, Offenbach 1st prize for an opera buffa, *"Le Docteur Miracle,"* prod. at Bouffes Parisiens, 1863; also won the Grand Prix de Rome. In place of the Mass prescribed he sent from Rome a 2-act Ital. opera buffa *"Don Procopio"*; 2 movements of a symphony, *"La Chasse D'Ossian,"* an overture; and *"La Guzla de l'Emir,"* a comic opera, 1836, his grand opera, *"Les Pêcheurs de Perles,"* was prod. Paris (Th. Lyrique); it failed, as did *"La Jolie Fille de Perth"* (1867), and the 1-act *"Djamileh"* (1872). In all his music B. revealed a strong leaning toward Wagner, then so unpopular in France; but 1872 his overture *"Patrie,"* the 2 symphonic movements, and incidental music to Daudet's *"L'Arlésienne,"* brought him success; and *"Carmen"* (Opéra-Com., March 3, 1875) brought him a fame, which he hardly knew, as he

died three months later of heart disease; c. Symph. in C; 2 operas, *"Numa"* (1871) and *"Ivan le Terrible"*; 150 pf.-pcs., songs, etc.; collaborated with Délibes, Jonah and Legouix in opera *"Malbrough, s'en va-t-en-guerre."* Biog. by Pigot, 1886, and D. C. Parker, 1926. (See article, page 488.)

Björling, Jussi (Yōō′-sĭ byār′-ling), b. Dalarna, Sweden, February 2, 1910; eminent tenor; son of operatic singer; one of three brothers, all singers, who with father formed quartet and made American concert tour when **B.** was eight years old, singing in churches, etc.; on return to Sweden **B.** began vocal study with Julia Svedelius; in 1929 admitted to Royal Op. Sch., Stockholm, where in one year of intensive study under John Forsell, Opera director, he prepared for his début as Don Ottavio (Don Giovanni); won permanent contract there and sang some fifty rôles in less than decade; 1935, made guest appearances in Vienna, Prague and Dresden with sensational success; engaged for America; début N. Y. at soloist on General Motors Radio Hour, with symphony orchestra, 1937–8; same season sang in *"La Bohème"* and *"Rigoletto"* with Chicago Op. Co., and gave concerts; engaged for Met. Op., 1938–9.

Black, Frank, b. Philadelphia; conductor; studied to be chemical engineer, but after graduation decided on musical career; studied piano with Joseffy; active in radio programmes, esp. as cond.; appointed mus. dir. of Nat'l. Broadcasting Co., 1930, in which post has taken leading part in direction of musical programmes; he has appeared as guest cond. with other Amer. orchs.; hon. Mus. D., and Officer with Palms of the French Académie.

Blahag (blä′häkh) (or **Blahak**), Josef, Raggendorf, Hungary, 1779—Vienna, 1846; tenor, conductor, and composer.

Blahet′ka (or **Piahet′ka**), **Marie-Léopoldine,** Gumtramsdorf, near Vienna, 1811—Boulogne, 1887; pianist and dram. composer.

Blainville (blǎṅ-vē′-yŭ), **Chas. H.,** near Tours, 1711—Paris, 1769; 'cellist, writer, and composer.

Blanchet (blän-shā′), **Emile,** b. Lausanne, Switzerland, July 17, 1877;

pianist and composer; studied at Cologne Cons. and with Busoni; was for three years dir. of Cons. in native city and taught there afterward; c. piano works rich in colour and of refined harmonic style.

Blanckenburgh (blänk'-ĕn-boorkh), Gerbrandt van, organist at Gouda, 17th century.

Bland (blänt), (1) Maria Theresa (née Romanzini), 1769—1838; pop. Italian singer in England; married an actor, Bland, and had two sons. (2) Chas., tenor. (3) James, 1798—1861, bass.

Blangini (blän-jē'-nē), Giu. Marco, M. Felice, Turin, 1781—Paris, 1841; organist.

Blankenburg (blänk-ĕn-boorkh), (1) Quirin van, Gouda, Holland, 1654— The Hague, ca. 1740; probably son of GERBRANDT VAN BLANCKENBURGH (q. v.); organist and writer. (2) Chr. Fr. von, Kolberg, Pomerania, 1744—Leipzig, 1796; Prussian officer and composer.

Blaramberg (blä'-räm-bĕrkh), Paul I., Orenburg, Russia, Sept. 26, 1841— Nice, Feb. 28, 1907; pupil of Balakirew; lawyer, then editor; composed succ. operas, "Maria Tudor" (St. Petersburg, 1882); "The First Russian Comedian"; "Tuschinsky" (Moscow, 1895).

Blaser'na, Pietro, Fiumicello, Feb. 29, 1836—Rome, 1917; teacher and theorist.

Blasius (bläz'-yüs), Mathieu Fr., Lauterburg, Alsatia, 1758—Versailles, 1829; cond. Op. Comique, Paris; composer.

Blassmann (bläs'-män), Ad. Jos. M., Dresden, 1823—Bautzen, 1891; pianist, court-conductor, and writer.

Blauvelt (blou'-fĕlt), Lillian, b. Brooklyn, N. Y., March 16, 1873; soprano; studied Nat. Cons., N. Y., and in Paris; after years of success at home, toured Europe, 1900; decorated in Italy with the order of St. Cecilia; she made her début in opera in "Faust" at Covent Garden, 1903, with success; until 1914 sang much in Europe; d. Chicago, Aug. 31, 1947.

Blauwart (blow'-värt), Emil, St. Nicholas, Belgium, 1845—Brussels, 1891; barytone.

Blavet (blä-vä), Michel, Besançon, Mar. 13, 1700—Paris, Dec. 28, 1768; composer of comic operas, etc.

Blaze (bläz) (1) (Called Castil-Blaze), Fran. H. Jos., Cavaillon Vaucluse,

1784—Paris, 1857; "The father of modern French musical criticism"; son and pupil of Henri Sebastian B.; wrote scathing "L'Opéra en France" (1820); was made critic on "Journal des Débats," where his articles were signed "X X X"; transl. libretti of German and Italian operas; composed 3 operas, several "pastiches," etc. (2) H., Baron de Bury, Avignon, 1813—Paris, 1888; son of above; writer.

Blech (blākh), Leo, b. Aachen, April 22, 1871; conductor; pupil of Berlin Hochschule; 1893—1896, cond. at Municipal Theatre, Aachen, and pupil of Humperdinck; 1899—1906, cond. German Landestheatre at Prague; 1906, Royal Opera, Berlin; 1908, cond. first East-Prussian Festival at Königsberg; c. 3 symph. poems, successful 1-act opera, "Das War Ich" (Dresden, 1902); 3-act opera "Aschenbrödel" (Prague, 1905); "Versiegelt" (Hamburg, 1908; New York, 1912); operetta "Die Strohwitwe"; orch. works, etc.; 1925, cond. in Stockholm; after 1949 again at Berlin Opera.

Bleichmann (blīkh'-män), Julius Ivanovitch, St. Petersburg, Dec. 5, 1868—Jan. 10, 1909; conductor; pupil at the Cons., and of Reinecke and Jadassohn; cond. various orchs. at St. Petersburg; c. 2 operas, chamber music, etc.

Bleuer (bloi'-ĕr), L., Budapest, 1863 —Berlin, 1897; violinist; 1883-93, leader of Philh. orch., Berlin; 1894, of Philh. Club, Detroit (Michigan).

Blew'itt, (1) Jonathan, London, 1782— 1853; organist and director; son and pupil of (2) Jonas, organist and writer.

Bleyle (blī'-lĕ), Karl, b. Feldkirch, May 7, 1880; pupil of Wehrle and de Lange; later at Stuttgart Cons. and of Thuille; gave up violin on account of nervous affliction of the arm; lived in Munich; c. symph., "An den Mistral" (from Nietzsche), for mixed chorus and orch., "Lernt lachen" (from Nietzsche's "Zarathustra"); do.; symph. poem "Flagellantenzug," etc.

Bliss, Sir Arthur, b. London, Aug. 2, 1891; educated at Pembroke Coll.; Cambridge, and R. Coll. of Mus.; pupil of Stanford, Charles Wood and Vaughan Williams; his early string quartet in A and piano quartet in

A minor were perf. during his period of war service, but though pub., were later withdrawn by him; incid. mus. to "*As You Like It*" heard at Stratford, 1919; his rhapsody for soprano and tenor, flute, "*cor anglais*," string quartet, and bass (winning Carnegie Pub. Fund award and heard at Salzburg Fest., 1922) and his "*Rout*" (for soprano and chamber orch.) both date from 1920; also c. "*Colour Symphony*" (the movements portraying different colours), heard Three Choirs Fest., 1922; "*Melée Fantasque*" and "*Madame Noy*," Pastorale, string quartet; concerto for two pianos and orch.; (orch.) "*Two Studies*," "*Battle Variations*," "*Hymn to Apollo*"; Introduction and Allegro: Serenade (for barytone and orch.); songs, piano pieces, etc.; "*Morning Heroes*," for orator, chorus, orch. (1930); ballets, "*Checkmate*," "*Miracle in the Gorbals*" (both for Sadler's Wells Ballet, London); grand opera,"*The Olympians*" (Covent Garden, 1949), libretto by Priestley; mus. dir. of B. B. C. radio, England; lived in U. S., 1923-5; arr. suite by Purcell; knighted, 1950.

Blitzstein (blĭts'-stĭn), **Marc,** b. Philadelphia, March 2, 1905; composer; studied piano with Siloti; comp. with Scalero at Curtis Inst. of Mus.; Nadia Boulanger and Schönberg; composer of modern tendencies; c. (orch.) "*Romantic Piece*"; piano concerto; music for film "*Surf and Seaweed*"; (chamber works) "*Gods*" for mezzo-soprano and chamber orch.; "*Serenade*"; string quartet; (opera-farce) "*Triple-Sec*"; (short operas) "*Parabola and Circula*"; "*Harpies*"; "*The Condemned*" (latter written for four choruses); (ballet) "*Cain*"; (song cycle) "*Is Five*"; "*Percussion Music*" and other pieces for piano; mus. play, "*The Cradle Will Rock.*"

Bloch (blôkh) (1) **G.,** Breslau, Nov. 2, 1847—Berlin, Feb. 11, 1910; pupil of Hainsch, J. Schubert, Taubert, and F. Geyer; teacher in Breslau's Cons., Berlin; founded Opera Society, 1879; composer. (2) **Ernest,** b. Geneva, Switzerland, July 24, 1880; now American citizen; studied violin with Ysaye; composition with Dalcroze, Rasse, and Knorr; acted as lecturer at Geneva Cons.; conducted symphony concerts. Lausanne

and Neuchatel; made first America tour as conductor for Maud Allan dancer, 1916; has led own works with various American orchestras; direc tor of Cleveland Institute of Music 1920-25; also of San Francisco Cons., 1925-30; received fund with annual income of $5,000 for ten years, beginning 1930, from family of late Jacob and Rosa Stern, San Francisco, on agreement that he devote himself to creative work entirely; c. symphony in C sharp minor (1902); (Symphonic poems) "*Winter-Spring*" (1905); (opera) "*Macbeth*" (Paris Op. Comique, 1910); Prelude and Two Psalms, for sopr. or ten. and orch. (1914); "*Psalm 22*" for bar or alt. and orch. (1916); "*Israel*" Symphony with 5 solo voices (1915); "*Schelomo,*" Hebrew rhapsody for 'cello and orch. (1916); "*Trois Poèmes Juifs,*" for orchestra; Suite for viola and piano or orch. (Coolidge Prize, 1919); "*Baal Shem,*" for violin and piano (1923); Concerto Grosso for strings and piano (1925); "*America,*" epic rhapsody for orchestra (won Musical America $3,000 prize, 1927-28); string quartets, piano quintet, violin and piano works; also sacred service for barytone, mixed chorus and orchestra, a setting of Jewish liturgy (1935). B. combines a strong sense of modern orchestral colour, formal ingenuity, and emotional fervour. Racial colouring predominates in many of his works.

Blockx (blôx), **Jan.,** Antwerp, Jan. 25, 1851—May 22, 1912; pianist and composer; pupil, Flemish Mus. School; from 1886, teacher of harm. there; 1901 succeeded Benoît, at Antwerp Cons.; composed succ. operas, incl. "*Maître Martin,*" etc.

Blodek (blôd-ĕk), (1) **P. Aug. L.,** Paris, 1784—1856; viola-player and dram. composer. (2) **Wm.,** Prague, 1834—1874; prof. and dram. composer.

Blon (blôn), **Franz von,** b. Berlin, July 16, 1861; cond.; pupil of Stern's Cons.; 1898, c. operettas "*Sub rosa*" (Lübeck, 1887); "*Die Amazone*" (Magdeburg, 1903), etc.

Blondeau (blôn-dō), **Pierre Auguste Louis,** Paris, Aug. 15, 1784—1865; viola-player at the Opéra; pupil of the Cons., taking the Prix de Rome, 1808; c. opera, ballet, etc.

Bloomfield-Zeisler (tsīs'-lĕr), **Fanny,**

Bielitz, Austrian Silesia, July 16, 1863—Chicago, Aug. 21, 1927; pianist; at 2 was brought to Chicago, where she lived; played in public at 10; was pupil of Ziehn and Karl Wolfsohn, and 1876–81 of Leschetizky; from 1883 toured America with distinction; from 1893, Germany, Austria, England, and France with great success.

Blow, John (Mus. Doc. Oxon.), Collingham, Nottinghamshire, 1649—Westminster (London), Oct. 1, 1708; organist Westminster Abbey, 1680; was superseded by Purcell, whom he in turn succeeded; he is buried in the Abbey; 1674, organist and (1699) composer to the Chapel Royal; beginning to compose as a boy, he achieved a vast amount of church-music.

Blum (bloom), K. L., Berlin, 1786—July 2, 1844; actor, singer, poet, organist. 'cellist, cond., and composer: chamber-musician to the Prussian Ct., 1822; stage mgr.; prod. nearly 30 operas, ballets, songs, etc.; also vaudevilles, which he introduced to the German stage.

Blumenfeld (bloo'-měn-fělt), Felix M., Kovalevska, Russia, April 19, 1863—Moscow, Jan. 23, 1931; pianist, pupil of Th. Stein; took gold medal at St. Petersburg Cons.; composed "Allegro de Concert," with orchestra, etc.; many pf. works; 1898–1912 cond. Imperial Opera, St. Petersburg; also after 1885 prof. at Cons. there. His brothers (2), Stanislaus, Kiev, 1850–97, pianist and teacher; (3) Sigismund, Odessa, Dec. 27, 1852—St. Petersburg, 1920; song-composer.

Blumenthal (bloo'-měn-täl), (1) Jos. von, Brussels, 1782—Vienna, 1850, violinist and dram. composer. (2) Jacob (Jacques), Hamburg, Oct. 4, 1829—Chelsea, May 17, 1908; pupil of Grund, Bocklet, and Sechter (Vienna), and 1846 of Herz and Halévy; after 1848 in London; pianist to the Queen, and composer. (3) Paul, Steinau-on-Oder, Silesia, Aug. 13, 1843—Frankfort-on-Oder, May 9, 1930; pupil of R. A., Berlin, 1870; organist, Frankfort-on-Oder; from 1870, "R. mus. dir."; composed masses, motets, etc.

Blumner (bloom'-něr), Martin, Fürstenberg, Mecklenburg, Nov. 21, 1827—Berlin, Nov. 6, 19..; pupil of S. W. Dehn; 1876, cond. of Berlin Singakademie; titles "R. Musik-dir," and "Prof."; composed 2 oratorios, "Abraham" and "Der Fall Jerusalems"; cantata "Columbus"; "Te Deum," etc.

Blüthner (blüt'-něr), Julius Fd., Falkenhain, near Merseburg, March 11, 1824—Leipzig, April 13, 1910; piano-maker, Leipzig, from 1853.

Boccabadati (bŏk-kä-bä-dä'-tē), Luigia, Parma—Turin, 1850; soprano.

Boccherini (bŏk-kĕ-rē'-nē), Luigi, Lucca, Italy, Feb. 19, 1743—Madrid, May 28, 1805; 'cellist; toured with success; 1797, made chamber-composer to Friedrich Wilhelm II., of Prussia, in return for a dedication; after the king's death B.'s fortune left him, and he died in dire poverty. His prolific and of en fascinatingly graceful compositions include 2c symphonies, an opera, an orchestral suite, a 'cello-concerto, 2 octets 16 sextets, 125 string-quintets, 12 pf.-quintets, 18 quintets for strings and flute (o. oboe), 91 string-quartets, 54 string-trios, 42 trios, sonatas and duets for vln., etc.; biog. by Picquot (Paris, 1851), and Schletternd (Leipzig).

Bochsa (bŏkh'-sä), (1) K., Bohemia—Paris, 1821; oboist; music-seller. (2) Rob. Nic. Chas., Montmedy. Meuse, Aug. 9, 1789—Sydney, Australia, Jan. 6, 1856; son and pupil of above; composed a symphony at 9, an opera at 16; pupil of Fr. Beck; harpist to Napoleon and .o Louis XVIII.; he eloped with Sir Henry Bishop's wife, made tours in Europe and America, and finally to Australia; composed 9 French operas, prod. in Lyons (1804), and in Paris (1813–16); 4 ballets; an oratorio, etc.; wrote a standard method for harp.

Bock'elmann, Rudolf, b. Bodenteich, Germany, April 2, 1892; barytone; studied at Leipzig Univ.; voice with Oscar Lassner in that city; sang at Neues Theat. there, 1921–26; after latter year heroic rôles at Hamburg Stadtheat.; also guest engagements at Covent Garden, with Chicago Op., etc.; esp. noted for his Wotan and other Wagnerian portrayals.

Bockshorn (bŏks'-hôrn) ("Capricornus"), Samuel, Germany, 1629—Stuttgart, 1665; composer and conductor.

Bodanzky (bō-däntz'-shkǐ), **Artur**, b. Vienna, Dec. 1877—N. Y., Nov. 23, 1939; grad. Vienna Cons., 1896; début, Budweiss, Bohemia, 1900; from 1896 violinist at the Vienna Op.; in 1901, took up baton activities in native city; in 1903 assistant to Mahler at the Opéra; 1904, cond. Theater an der Wien, Vienna; 1905, at Lortzing Theatre, Berlin; 1906–09, orchestra and theatre cond., Prague; 1909–15, Grand Ducal Theatre, Mannheim, also appearing widely as guest conductor; 1912, Mahler Fest., in Mannheim; 1914, London première of *"Parsifal"*; engaged Met. Op., N. Y., in 1915, where he has since served as principal conductor and leader of German opera performances; in 1919 conducted National Symphony Orchestra (since merged with N. Y. Philharmonic); cond. New York Friends of Music Society in programmes of rare music by older composers, Bruckner, Mahler, etc.

Bodenschatz (bō'-d'n-shäts), **Erhard**, Lichtenberg, Saxony, 1576—Gross-Osterhausen, near Querfurt, 1636; publisher.

Boedecker (bā'-děk-ĕr), **Louis**, Hamburg, 1845—1899; teacher, critic, and composer.

Boehm, Boehme. Vide BÖHM (E).

Boekelman (bā'-kĕl-män), **Bernardus**, Utrecht, Holland, 1838—New York, Aug. 2, 1930; pupil and son of A. J. B.; director, studied with Moscheles, Richter and Hauptmann, at Leipzig Cons.; von Bülow, Kiel, and Weitzmann, at Berlin; from 1866, lived in New York; founded and cond. (till 1888) the N. Y. Trio Club; 1883–97, mus. dir. Miss Porter's School, Farmington, Conn.; later pianist and teacher in New York; composed orch.-pcs., etc.; ed. an analytical edition of Bach's *"Well-tempered Clavichord,"* in colours, etc.

Boëllmann (bwěl'-män), **Léon**, Ensisheim, Alsatia, 1862—Paris, 1897; composer and teacher.

Boëly (bwěl'-ē), **Alex. P. Fran.**, Versailles, 1785—Paris, 1858; pianist and composer.

Boers (boors), **Jos. Karel**, Nymwegen, Holland, 1812—Delft, 1896; cond. and writer.

Boesset (bwôs-sā), (1) **A.**, Sieur de Villedieu, ca. 1585—1643; intendant of music to Louis XIII. (2) **J. B.**,

1612—1685; son and successor of above; and in turn succeeded by his son. (3) **C. J. B.**, b. ca. 1636.

Boe'tius (or **Boethius**), **Ani'cius Man'lius Torqua'tus Severi'nus**, Rome ca. 475—executed 524 (?); eminent poet and writer on music.

Bohlmann (bōl'-man), **Th. H. Fr.**, Osterwieck am Harz, Germany, June 23, 1865—Memphis, Tenn., Feb., 1926; pianist; pupil of Dr. Stade, Barth, Klindworth, Tiersch, d'Albert, and Moszkowski; début Berlin, 1890; toured Germany 1890, pf.-prof. Cincinnati Cons.; later head of his own school in Memphis.

Bohm (bōm), **K.**, Berlin, Sept. 11, 1844 —April 4, 1920; pupil of Löschhorn, Reissmann, and Geyer; pianist and composer in Berlin.

Böhm (bām), (1) **G.**, Goldbach, Thuringia, 1661—Lüneburg, 1733; organist and clavichordist; composed important organ preludes and suites. (2) **Elizabeth Riga**, 1756—1797; soprano, m. the actor **B.** (3) **Theobald**, Munich, April 9, 1793 —Nov. 15, 1881; inv. the "Böhm flute" (vide D. D.); flutist and composer for flute; "Hofmusikus," and player in royal orch. (4) **Jos.**, Pesth, 1795—Vienna, 1876; son and pupil of above; violinist and prof. (5) **Heinrich**, Blatu, Bohemia, 1836— (?); composed 35 operas in Bohemian. (6) **Jos.**, Kühnitz, Moravia, 1841— Vienna, 1893; organist, cond., and director. (7) **Karl**, b. Graz, Aug. 28, 1894; cond. Munich, 1921; 1927, Darmstadt; 1933, dir. Dresden Op.

Böhme (bā'mě), (1) **Jn. Aug.**, 1794; founder of pub. house at Hamburg. His son, (2) **Justus Eduard**, succeeded him in 1839; and his grandson, (3) **August Eduard**, in 1885. (4) **Aug. Julius Fd.**, Ganderheim, Brunswick, 1815—1883; conductor. (5) **Fz. Magnus**, Wellerstedt, near Weimar, 1827—Dresden, 1898; teacher, Dresden, later prof.; composer, writer, and collector.

Böhmer (bā'-měr), **K.** (Hermann Ehrfried), The Hague, 1799—Berlin, 1884; dram. composer.

Bohn (bōn), **Emil**, Bielau, near Neisse, Jan. 14, 1839—Breslau, July 5, 1909; organist, 1884, founded the Bohn Choral Society, giving historical concerts; lecturer, writer, critic, and composer; R. Prof. of Music.

Bohnen, Michael (mē'-kěl bō'-něn).

b. Keulen, Germany, Jan. 23, 1888; opera bass; studied Cologne Cons., début in *"Der Freischütz,"* Düsseldorf; has sung in opera at Berlin, Bayreuth, London, Vienna, Barcelona, Stockholm, and New York (member of Met. Op. Co. for a number of years after 1923); also has appeared in motion pictures in Germany; m. Mary Lewis, soprano; divorced.

Böhner (bǎ'-nĕr), **Jn. L.**, Tôttelstedt, Gotha, 1787—near Gotha, 1860; composer; led a roving life of drunkenness and talent; said to be the original of Hofmann's *"Kreisler"* (vide SCHUMANN); composed opera, etc.

Bohrer (bō'-rer), (1) **Anton**, Munich, 1783—Hanover, 1852; violinist; composer for vln.; a co-member of the Bavarian Court-orch. and concertgiver with his brother, (2) **Max**, Mannheim, 1785—Stuttgart, 1867; 'cellist.

Boïeldieu (bō-ĕld-yŭ), (1) **Fran. Adrien**, Rouen, Dec. 16 (not 15), 1775—Jarcy, near Grosbois, Oct. 8, 1834; son of secretary of Archp. Larochefoucauld and a milliner; apprenticed to the intemperate, brutal cathedral organist Broche, he ran away, at 12, and walked to Paris, but was brought back. He is not known to have had other teaching. At 18, he prod. succ. *"La fille coupable"* (Rouen, 1793); 1795, *"Rosalie et Myrza,"* text of both by his father. Discouraged in a planned Cons. at Rouen, he again walked to Paris, and subsisted as teacher and piano-tuner to Erard. The tenor Garat sang his still pop. songs, in public, and won him a publisher. 1796, *"La Dot de Suzette,"* in one act, was prod. with succ. (Opéra-Com.); 1797, *"La famille Suisse"* (ran 30 nights at the Th. Feydeau); 1798, he pub. sonatas, and a pf.-concerto, etc.; 1800, prof. of piano, Paris Cons. *"Zoraime et Zulnare"* (1798), *"Beniowski,"* and *"Le Calife de Bagdad"* (1800) were succ. and ended his first period, one of light gracefulness. He now studied cpt. seriously, probably with Cherubini, who had criticised him. After 3 years' silence, he reappeared with enlarged powers, succ. in *"Ma Tante Aurore"* (Th. Feydeau, 1803). In 1802 he m. Clotilde Mafleuroy, a ballet-dancer; 1803, he went to St.

Petersburg, partially perhaps (but not surely) because of domestic unhappiness, and became cond. of the Imperial Opera, writing by contract 3 operas annually and a number of marches. He returned to Paris, 1811; had immense succ., particularly with *"Jean de Paris,"* 1812; 1817 prof. of comp. at the Cons. and member of Institut; 1821, Chévalier of the Legion of Honour; 1818, *"Le Petit Chaperon rouge"* was succ., followed, after 7 years' silence, by *"La Dame Blanche,"* his masterpiece. His last opera, *"Les Deux Nuits"* (1829), failed. His wife d. 1825, and 1827 he m. Mlle. Phillis, a singer, who was a devoted wife. The poverty of their last years was relieved by Thiers, minister of Louis Philippe, who made him an annuity of 6,000 francs. He died at his countryhome, of pulmonary trouble. **B.**'s work has great vivacity and vitality combined with musical sweetness, and rhythm without jingle. His large gifts in the construction of ensembles are seen in the septet and chorus at the end of the 2d act of *"La Dame Blanche,"* which up to 1875 had been performed 1340 times at the same theatre; its libretto is a combination of 2 of Scott's novels "The Monastery" and "Guy Mannering." He collaborated with Cherubini in *"La Prisonnière"* (1799); with Méhul, Kreutzer, and others, in *"Le Baiser et la Quittance"* (1802); with Cherubini, Catel, and Niccôlo Isouard, in *"Bayard à Mézières"*, with Kreutzer in *"Henri IV. en Voyage"* (1814); with Mme. Gail, in *"Angela"* (1814); with Hérold in *"Charles de France"*; with Cherubini, Berton, and others, in *"La Cour des Fées"* (1821) and *"Pharamond"*; with Auber, in *"Les Trois Genres"*; with Berton, and others, in *"La Marquise de Brinvilliers."* Biog. by A. Pougin, 1875. (2) **Adrien L. V.**, b. Paris, 1816—near Paris, 1883; son and pupil of above; dram. composer.

Boisdeffre (bwä-dĕfr), **Chas. H. Réné de**, Vesoul (Haute-Savoie), 1838—Vézelise, Dec., 1906; Chev. of Legion of Honour; composer of religious and chamber music, the latter taking Chartier prize, 1883.

Boise (bois), **Otis Bardwell**, Oberlin, Ohio, Aug. 13, 1844—Baltimore,

Md., Dec. 16, 1912; organist; 1861 pupil of Hauptmann, Richter, Moscheles, etc., Leipzig; 1864, of Kullak, at Berlin; 1864-70, organist and teacher in Cleveland; 1870-76, in New York; 1876-78, spent in Europe; for some years prominent in Berlin as a teacher; 1901, settled in Baltimore; composed symphonies, overtures, pf.-concertos, etc., wrote *"Music and Its Masters"* (1902), etc.

Boismortier (bwä-môrt-yä), **Josef Bodin De,** Perpignan, ca. 1691—Paris, ca. 1765; c. ballet operas, cantatas, etc.

Boisselot (bwäs-lō), (1) **J. Louis,** Montpellier, 1785—Marseilles, 1847; piano-maker at Marseilles; his eldest son (2) **Louis** (1809—1850) was the manager. His grandson, (3) **François,** was later the proprietor. (4) **Xavier,** Montpellier, 1811—Marseilles, 1893; second son of above; composer.

Boïto (bō-ē'-tō), **Arrigo,** Padua, Feb. 24, 1842—Milan, June 10, 1918; poet, soldier, novelist, editor, essayist, librettist, and composer; son of an Italian painter and a Polish woman. Pupil, 1853-62, of Milan Cons., almost dismissed for mus. incompetence (cf. VERDI); composed 2 cantatas, *"Il 4 di Giugno"* (1860), and *"Le Sorelle d'Italia"* (1862), in collab. with Faccio; they met with such great succ. that the Govt. gave F. and B. funds for 2 years in Paris and Germany. B. had already taken up Goethe's *"Faust,"* long before Gounod, at the suggestion of his bro. Camillo, an eminent architect. B. brought back from Germany a passion for Beethoven, then little heeded in Italy. 1867 at Paris, as journalist; then Poland, where he sketched out text and music of *"Mefistofele,"* which was prod. at Milan, 1868 (La Scala), after 52 rehearsals, and with great hopes; but it was then in a rather shapeless state, and Gounod's *"Faust"* having meanwhile been prod. at Milan with succ., B.'s work was hissed by some, and having provoked riots and duels was withdrawn by order of the police. It was remodelled with more attention to stage requirements and prod. with great succ. at Bologna, Oct. 4, 1875. An earlier opera, *"Ero e Leandro,"* was never prod., B. lending his own libretto to Botte-

sini, and later to Mancinelli. Other libretti of his are, Ponchielli's *"Gioconda,"* Verdi's *"Otello"* and *"Falstaff,"* Faccio's *"Amleto"* and Coronaro's *"Un Tramonto."* His opera, *"Nerone,"* on which he worked for many years and which was repeatedly announced for production, finally saw the stage posthumously when Toscanini cond. the work at La Scala, with great scenic splendour of production, May 1, 1924, before a distinguished international audience. Its succ. proved not to be lasting. B. translated 2 of Wagner's libretti into Italian, and wrote often under the pseud. "Tobia Gorrio." The King made him "Cavaliere" and "Commendatore"; 1892, Inspector-Gen. of Technical Instruction in the Italian Cons. and Lyceums; 1895 Chevalier of the Legion of Honour.

Bok, Mary Louise Curtis (Mrs. Edward Bok), b. Boston, Aug. 6, 1876; music patron; d. of Cyrus H. K. Curtis and Louisa (Knapp); founder (1923) and pres. Curtis Institute of Music, Philadelphia, est. in memory of her father, the prominent publisher; also active in many other musical and civic philanthropies.

Bolck (bôlk), **Oskar,** Hohenstein, 1839—Bremen, 1888; dram. composer.

Bolm, Adolph, b. St. Petersburg, Russia, Sept. 25, 1884; dancer and ballet director; educated Imp. Ballet School; début, Maryinsky Theatre, St. Petersburg, 1904; soloist, Diaghileff Ballet Russe, 1909-17; org. his own ballet company, 1917; has also directed ballets and appeared as soloist at Met. Op.; d. 1951.

Bölsche (bĕl'-shĕ), **Franz,** b. Wegenstedt, Aug. 20, 1869—Bad Oeynhausen, 1935; theorist; pupil Berlin Royal Hochschule; 1896, teacher Cologne Cons.; c. overture *Judith,* etc.

Bomtempo (bōm-täm'-pō), **João Domingos,** Lisbon, 1775—1842; pianist, director, and writer.

Bona (bō'-nä), **Giov.,** Mondovi, 1609—Rome, 1674; cardinal and composer.

Bonawitz (bō'-nä-vēts) (or **Bonewitz**), **Jn. H.,** Dürkheim-on-Rhine, Dec. 4, 1839—London, Aug. 15, 1917; pupil Liége Cons. till 1852, then brought to America; 1872-73 cond. "Popular Symphony Concerts," New York; 1873, toured U. S., prod. 2 operas in Philadelphia; 1876, ret. to Europe; lived in Vienna and London.

Bonci (bôn'chě), **Alessandro, b.** Cesena, Feb. 10, 1870—Milan, Aug. 10, 1940; lyric tenor; at 7 sang in choir, studied singing with Coen at Pesaro Lyceum for 5 years; then member of choir at Loreto; operatic début in "*Falstaff*"; sang with great success at Covent Garden, 1900, and in 1908 at Metropolitan Opera House; toured U. S., 1911–12; 1912–13, Chicago Op. Co.

Bond, Carrie Jacobs, b. Janesville, Wis.; composer; studied with Bischoff; c. many songs of ballad variety, usually with sentimental texts, among which wide popularity has been won by "*A Perfect Day*," "*Just A-Wearyin' For You*," and "*I Love You Truly*"; also composed scores for films; d. Los Angeles, Dec. 28, 1946.

Bonel'li, Richard, b. Port Byron, N. Y.; barytone; educated Syracuse Univ.; studied voice with Arthur Alexander and William Vilonat; début as Valentine, Brooklyn, N. Y., 1915; member San Carlo Opera, in America; later sang with Monte Carlo Op., La Scala Op., Milan and in Germany; member Chicago Civic Op., 1925–31; since 1933 with Met. Op. Co.; m. Pauline Cornelys, soprano.

Bönicke (bä'nĭ-kě), **Hermann,** Endorf, 1821—Hermannstadt, Transylvania, 1879; conductor, composer, and writer.

Bo'niforti, Carlo, Arona, Sept. 25, 1818—Trezzo d'Adda, Dec. 10, 1879; organist and comp.

Bonini (bō-nē'-nē), **Severo, b.** Florence, 17th century; Benedictine monk, one of the first writers in monodic style; c. madrigals, etc., 1607–13.

Boniventi (bō-nĭ-věn'-tē) (or **Boneventi**), **Gius, b.** Venice, ca. 1660; conductor and dram. composer.

Bonnet (bŭn-nä), (1) **Jacques,** Paris, 1644—1724; writer. (2) **J. Bap., b.** Montauban, 1763; organist and composer. (3) **Joseph, b.** Bordeaux, France, March 17, 1884; organist; studied with Tournemire, Gédalge, and Guilmant; 1st prize, organ playing and improvisation, Paris Cons., 1906; won competition in 1906 as organist at St. Eustache, Paris; organist Société des Concerts du Conservatoire, 1911–20; soloist with various European and American orchestras; made many tours of Can. and U. S., d. Can., Aug., 1944.

Bonno (bôn'-nō) (or **Bono**), **Jos.,** Vienna, 1710—1788; court-cond. and dram. composer.

Bononcini (bō-nôn-chē'-nē), (1) **Giov. M.,** Modena, 1640—Nov. 19, 1678; conductor, composer, and writer of Bologna. (2) Who usually wrote it **Buononcini** (boo-ō-nôn-chē'-nē), **Giov. Bat.,** Modena, 1660 (?)—Venice (?), 1750 (?); son and pupil of above; studied with Colonna and Buoni ('cello), at Bologna; 1685–91, pub. 7 vols. masses and instr. mus.; in 1690, court 'cellist of Vienna; 1694, Rome, prod. 2 operas, "*Tullo Ostilio*" and "*Serse*"; 1699–1701 prod. 2 operas at Vienna; 1703–05, at Berlin as court-composer; prod. "*Polifemo*" (1703); ret. to Vienna, where 6 new operas were prod. In 1716, invited to London as cond. and composer for the new King's Theatre, and to rival Händel; this provoked a famous and bitter war with some success for B., who prod. 8 operas, 1702–27; but in 1731 he was caught in a plagiarism from A. Lotti (a crime of which Händel was by no means guiltless himself); 1733 an alchemist swindled him from affluence to bankruptcy. Later he appeared in Paris and prod. a motet for the "Chapelle royale," playing the 'cello-accomp. before the King; 1737 his opera "*Alessandro in Sidone*," and an oratorio, "*Ezechia*," were prod. in Vienna; 1748, he was called to Vienna to write peace-festival music and later went to Venice as theatre-composer, a post retained at least till he was 90. (3) **Marc An.,** Modena, 1675 (?)—1726; bro. of above; court-cond. there; prod. 11 operas highly rated by Padre Martini; also composed an oratorio.

Bonporti (bôn-pôr'-tē), **F. A.,** Trent, ca. 1660; Imperial Counsellor and composer.

Bontemni (bôn-těm'-pē) (surnamed **Angeıini**), **Giov. Andrea,** Peruugia, ca. 1624—Bruso, near Perugia, 1705, dram. composer and writer.

Bonvin (bôṅ-văṅ), **L., b.** Siders, Feb. 17, 1850—Buffalo, Feb. 18, 1939; self-taught; studied medicine, Vienna; entered Jesuit novitiate in Holland; became organist and choirmaster; from 1887, mus. dir. Canisius College, Buffalo, N. Y.; pub. masses, etc.

Boom (bōm), (1) **Jan. E. G. van** (Senior), **b.** Rotterdam, April 17,

1783; flutist and composer for flute. (2) **Jan.** (Jns.) van, Utrecht, 1807— Stockholm, 1872; son of above; pianist, professor, and dram. composer. (3) **Hermann M.** van, Utrecht, 1809—1883; son and pupil of (1); flutist.

Boo'sey, Thos. (1825), founded the London pub. house of Boosey & Co.

Boott, Francis, Boston, Mass., June 21, 1813—Cambridge, Mass., March 2, 1904; pupil of L. Picchianti, in Florence; lived in Cambridge, Mass.; composed under pseud. "Telford."

Bopp, Wilhelm, Mannheim, Nov. 4, 1863—Bühler Höhe, June 11, 1931; pupil of Leipzig Cons., and of Emil Paur; 1884, dir. in Freiburg; 1886, assistant to Mottl at Bayreuth; 1889, teacher at Mannheim Cons.; 1900, opened a High School of Music; 1907-19, dir. Royal Cons., Vienna; cond. His wife, born Glaser, a court opera singer at Stuttgart.

Bordes (bôrd), **Charles,** Vouvray-sur-Loire, May 12, 1863—Toulon, Nov. 8, 1909; composer; important figure in the revival of French church music; pupil of César Franck; 1887, church-conductor at Nogent-sur-Marne; 1889 commissioned by the govt. to collect Basque folk music; from 1890 chapel-master at St. Gervais, Paris; founder of the *"Association of the Singers of St. Gervais"* and of the *"Schola Cantorum de St. G.,"* 1898 with d'Indy and Guilmant; 1905 retired to Montpellier and founded a *Schola* there; 1909 went to Nice to give a concert and died on his way home. He resuscitated many forgotten master works; and wrote many articles on them; c. *"Phantasie"* and *"Rapsodie Basque"* for orch.; opera *"Les trois Vagues,"* religious music, choruses, and songs and piano pieces.

Bordese (bôr-dä'-zĕ), **Luigi,** Naples, 1815—Paris, 1886; singing teacher and dram. composer.

Bordier (bôrd-yā), (1) **L. Chas.,** Paris, 1700—1764; abbé, conductor, composer, and writer. (2) **Jules,** 1846 (?) —Paris, 1896; dram. composer.

Bordogni (bôr-dōn'-yē), **Giulio Marco,** Gazzaniga, Bergamo, 1788—Paris, July 31, 1856; distinguished tenor and singing teacher; prof. Paris Cons.; pub. standard *"Vocalises."*

Bordo'ni, Faustina. Vide HASSE, FAUSTINA.

Borghi (bôr'-gē), **Luigi,** Italian violinist, came to London, ca. 1774; pub. symphonies, excellent music for vln., etc.

Borghi-Mamo (mä'-mō), (1) **Adelaide,** Bologna, 1826—1901; mezzo-soprano; début, 1846, at Urbino, where she was engaged; then in Vienna and Paris; later lived in Florence; her daughter (2) **Erminia,** soprano; début 1874, Bologna; sang in Italy and Paris.

Borgioli (bôr-jō'-lē), **Dino,** b. Florence. Italy; operatic tenor; became member of Dal Verme Op., Milan, 1918, following war service; has sung at Costanzi, Rome; San Carlo, Naples; Covent Garden, London; Monte Carlo, Lisbon, Madrid, and La Scala Op., Milan, also as assisting artist to Dame Nellie Melba in tour of Australia, 1924; came to America, 1928, making début in California; New York début, Dec., 1930, and sang with Met. Op. Co., N. Y., 1934.

Bori (bō'-rē), **Lucrezia** (rightly **Borgia**), b. Valencia, Spain, Dec. 24, 1888; noted soprano; pupil of Vidal; made début at Rome, in *"Carmen,"* 1908, singing rôle of Micaela; appeared in other leading opera theatres with succ., incl. Naples, Milan, Buenos Aires, and at Paris in 1910 when the Met. Op. Co. made a guest appearance there; 1912-13, made début with that company in *"Manon"* in the autumn at New York; quickly became one of most popular members of forces; owing to vocal indisposition, retired for brief period in 1915, but returned to New York several seasons later and resumed place as an important singer, esp. in lyric rôles; member of Met. Op. until 1935-36, portraying large variety of French, Italian, Spanish, and English parts; a distinguished actress and an exemplary vocalist; she took active part in assisting company to raise fund to cover deficit in 1933-34, and was elected a member of the Met. Op. board of directors.

Borodin (bō'-rō-dēn), **Alex. Porphyrjevitch,** St. Petersburg, Nov. 12, 1834—Feb. 29, 1887; composer of the neo-Russian school; Prof. at the St. P. Medico-surg. Institute; Counsellor of State; Knight; pres. Mus. Soc. of Amateurs; at Balakirev's suggestion studied music; composed opera, *"Prince Igor"* (finished after his death by Rimsky-Korsakov, and prod. succ. 1891); 3 symphonies, A flat, B minor, and A minor (last left incomplete, ed. by Glazounov), symphonic poem, *"On the Steppes of Central Asia"*; scherzo for orch., 2 string-quartets, piano quintet; string trio; pf. pcs., etc.; biog. by A. Habets, in English, London, 1895. Memoirs by Stassov and Gerald Abraham also published.

Boroni (bō-rō'-nē) (or **Buroni**), **A.**, Rome, 1738—1792; court-conductor.

Borovsky (bōr-ŏf'-skē), **Alexandre**, b. Libau, Russia, March 19, 1889; pianist; studied at Petersburg Cons. with Essipov.; studied to be lawyer; won gold medal and Rubinstein prize as pianist, 1912; taught at Moscow Cons. after 1915; following 1920 he made tours of France, England, Germany, and U. S.

Borowski (bōr-ŏf'-skē), **Felix**, b. Burton, Engl., March 10, 1872; studied Cologne Cons. and London; taught composition and history, Chicago Musical College, 1897; pres. of this school, 1916–24; music ed., Chic. *Eve. Post*, 1908, and Chic. *Herald*, 1909–17; ed. programme book, Chic. Symph. Orch.; c. orchestral and chamber music works, organ, piano, and other pieces; (ballet) *"Boudour"* (Chic. Op., 1919).

Bortnianski (bôrt-nyän'-shkĭ) (or **Bartñansky**) **Dimitry Stepanovitch**, Gluchov, Ukraine, 1751—St. Petersburg, Sept. 28 (Oct. 9), 1825; choir dir. and dram. composer, called "the Russian Palestrina"; pupil of Galuppi, under patronage of Empress Catherine, 1779–96 dir. of her choir; then of her orchestra.

Bor'wick, Leonard, Walthamstow, Essex, Engl., 1868—Le Mans, France, Sept. 17, 1925; pianist; pupil H. R. Bird, and Clara Schumann, B. Scholtz, and Ivan Knorr at Frankfort Cons.; début, at London Philh. Concert, 1890; toured Europe, 1895–96; 1914, U. S.

Bos (bōs), **Coenraad V.**, b. Leiden, Dec. 7, 1875; pianist; studied Amsterdam Cons.; played in Berlin, a member of the "Dutch Trio" with J. M. van Veen and J. van Lier; after 1908 toured U. S. as accompanist to noted singers; also active as vocal coach.

Boschetti (bôs-kĕt'-tē), **Viktor**, Frankfort-on-Main, Aug. 13, 1871—April 12, 1933; pupil of Prague Cons.; organist at Vienna (1896–1921), St. Stephen's Cath.); and Dir. Court Opera, 1900–03; c. 5 operas, church music, etc.

Bösendorfer (bā'-zĕn-dôrf-ĕr), firm of Vienna pf.-makers founded by (1) **Ignaz B.**, Vienna, 1796—1859, later managed by his son (2) **Ludwig**, b. Vienna, 1835.

Bosio (bō'-zĭ-ō), **Angiolina**, Turin, 1830—St. Petersburg, 1859; mezzo-soprano.

Bos'si, (bôs'-sē), (1) **Pietro B.**, Morbegno, 1834—1896; organist. (2) **Marco Enrico**, Salè, Brescia, Italy, April 25, 1861—Feb. 21, 1925, while returning from America; son and pupil of above, 1881–91, conductor and organist at Como Cath.; then till 1895, prof. of org. and harm. Naples; 1896, dir. and prof. Liceo Benedetto Marcello, Venice; 1902–12, dir. Bologna Liceo; after 1916, dir. Liceo of Santa Cecilia, Rome; member of the permanent govt. commission for musical art, Chevalier of the Italian Crown and of the Spanish order of Isabella la Catolica; composed 2 1-act operas, *"Paquita"* and *"Il Veggente"*; 4-act melodrama *"L'Angelo Della Notte"* (Como); symph. poem *"Il Cieco"* (1897), with tenor solo, and chorus; *"Westminster Abbey,"* Inno di Gloria, for chorus and organ, Requiem Masses, etc.; wrote important *"Metodo di Studio per l'Organo moderno,"* with G. Tebaldini (Milan, 1893). (3) **Renzo**, b. Como, Italy, April 9, 1883; composer, pianist; son of (2); active as conductor in Italy, Germany, and Austria; later prof. of organ and comp. at Parma Cons.; and then of comp. at Milan Cons.; appeared widely with the Polo and Bolognese Quartets; c. orch., chamber and vocal works, also stage music, incl. *"Volpino,"* which won a national lyric prize and was given at the Carcano Theat., Milan, 1924.

Bote und Bock (bō'-tĕ oont bôk), firm of mus. pubs., Berlin, est. 1838 by Eduard Bote and Gustav Bock.

Bott (bôt), **Jean Jos.**, Cassel, March 9, 1826—New York, April 30, 1895; violinist; son and pupil of a court-musician; 1852, court-conductor; 1878 pensioned; 1885 came to New York; composed 2 operas, etc.

Bot'ta, Luca, Italy, 1882—New York,

1917; tenor; sang with Pacific Coast Op. Co., 1912; after 1914 until his death, mem. of Met. Op. Co., also appearing in South America with success.

Bottée, de Toulmon (dŭ toomôṅ bôt-tä), **Aug.,** Paris, 1797—1850; 'cellist and writer.

Bottesini (bôt-tĕ-sē'-nē), **Giov.,** Crema, Lombardy, 1821—Parma, 1889; double-bass virtuoso; conductor and dram. composer.

Bottrigari (bôt-trē-gä'-rē), **Ercole,** Bologna, Aug. 1531—S. Alberto, Sept. 30, 1612; wrote 3 learned theoretical treatises, each called by the name of a friend (a) Patrizio, (b) Desiderio, and (c) Melone.

Boucher (boo-shā), **Alex J.,** Paris, April 11, 1778—Dec. 29, 1861; vln.-virtuoso; a charlatan but amazing in technic; played before the court at 6; composed vln.-concertos; his wife was a clever harpist, also eccentric, playing duets with one hand on harp and one on a piano.

Boughton (bow'-tŏn), **Rutland,** b. Aylesbury, England, Jan. 23, 1878; composer; educated, Royal College of Music, London; studied with Stanford and Walford Davies; teacher at Birmingham School of Music; founder, Glastonbury Festival, 1914, aim of which was to produce music dramas based on Arthurian legend; c. (operas) *"The Immortal Hour"* (London, 1922) which had a long run and subsequent revivals, also having brief New York production without pronounced success; *"Bethlehem"* (London, 1923); *"Alkestis"* (Covent Garden Op., 1924); also choral works *"The Birth of Arthur,"* *"The Skeleton in Armor,"* *"The Invincible Armada"*; in 1921-22 B. founded the Bristol Fest. School; he has also c. chamber music.

Bouhy (boo'-ē), **Jacques,** Pepinster, Belgium, 1848—Paris, 1929; barytone; pupil at Liège Cons., then Paris Cons.; 1871 the Opéra Paris; after 1872 at Opéra Comique creating the Toreador rôle in *"Carmen,"* etc.; 1885-89, director of New York Conservatory; returned to Paris Opéra; later a famous teacher; c. songs.

Bouichère (bwē-shăr), **Émile,** 1860 (?)—Paris, Sept. 4, 1895; pupil of G. Lefèvre's Acad.; est. a vocal acad. 1892; composed valuable sacred and chamber music.

Boulanger (boc-läṅ-zhā), (1) **Marie Julie** (née **Halliger**), 1786—1850; dram. singer. (2) **Henri Alex, André Ernest,** Paris, Dec. 16, 1815—April 14, 1900. Son of above. Pupil of Lesueur and Halévy at the Cons., taking Grand Prix de Rome, 1835; prof. there 1871. Composed many operettas for Opéra Comique. Legion of Honour, 1868. (3) **Nadia,** b. Paris, Sept. 16, 1887; studied Paris Cons., 1st prizes in harmony, organ and accompanying, fugue and counterpoint; third Rome Prix; teachers incl. Chapuis, Guilmant, Vierne, Vidal, Fauré and Widor; prof. of harmony, counterpoint, history of music, at École Normale, Paris; prof. history of music and harmony, American Cons., Fontainebleau; has had among her pupils many of the younger American composers. (4) **Lili,** Paris, Aug. 21, 1893—March 15, 1918; composer; sister of (3); trained at Paris Cons.; won Prix de Rome, 1913; composed various orch., chamber music, and vocal works of considerable promise and left incomplete at her early death the opera *"La Princesse Maleine."*

Boult (bōlt), **Sir Adrian,** b. Chester, Engl., April 8, 1889; ed. Westminster School, Christ Church, Oxford; studied Leipzig Cons.; Mus. D., Oxford; début as conductor, Covent Garden Op., 1914; led Birmingham Orch., 1923-36; London Bach Choir, after 1928; guest cond., Royal Philharmonic Soc., London Symphony and Queens Hall Orch.; prof. conducting at Royal College of Music since 1919; cond., Patron's Fund Concerts and of British Broadcasting Corp. Orch.; visited America as guest cond. of Boston Symph. Orch., 1935. Knighted, 1937.

Bouman (boo'-man), **Martin G.,** Herzogenbusch, Holland, Dec. 29, 1858—Gouda, May 11, 1901; pupil of Brée and Holl; city director at Gouda; c. operas, masses, etc.

Bourgault-Ducoudray (boor-gō-dü-koo-drē), **Louis-Albert,** Nantes, Feb. 2, 1840—Vernouillet, July 4, 1910; pupil of Thomas at Paris Cons., taking Grand Prix de Rome, 1862; prof. of mus. hist. at the Cons. 1878; wounded as volunteer at siege of Paris; later visited Greece and wrote on Oriental music.

Bourgeois (boor'-zhwä), (1) **Loys**

(Louis), Paris, ca. 1510—(?); disciple of Calvin; 1545-57, Geneva; one of the first to harmonise the French melodies; wrote "*Le droict chemin de musique*," proposing the naming the tones after solmisation-syllables, a system since prevalent in France. (2) Louis Thomas, Fontaine l'Évêque, 1676—Paris, 1750; tenor and composer; d. in poverty.

Bourges (boorzh), (1) Clémentine de, d. 1561; notable woman-composer. (2) J. Maurice, Bordeaux, 1812—Paris, 1881; critic and dram. composer.

Bousquet (boos-kā), G., Perpignan, 1818—St. Cloud, 1854; conductor at the Paris Opéra (1847); critic and dram. composer.

Bovéry (bō-vā-rē), Jules (rightly Bovy (bō'-vē), A. Nic. Jos.), Liége, 1808—Paris, 1868; self-taught violinist, conductor and dram. composer.

Bovy (bō'-vē), (1) Chas. Sml. (known under pseud. Lysberg), Lysberg, near Geneva, 1821—Geneva, 1873; composer. (2) Vina, b. Ghent; soprano; début Met. Op., 1936.

Bo'wen, York, b. London, Feb. 22, 1884; composer and pianist; 1898—1905, pupil of the R. A. M.; then piano teacher there; c. 3 pf.-concertos; symph. fantasia for orch., concerto and sonatas for the viola; Phantasy Trio; string quartet, pf.-pieces, etc.

Bow'man, Ed. Morris, Barnard, Vt., July 18, 1848—Brooklyn, N. Y., Aug. 27, 1913; pupil Wm. Mason, and J. P. Morgan, at New York, 1866; 1867-70, organist St. Louis, Mo.; studied in Berlin and Paris, 1873; 1874, St. Louis; 1881 studied under Bridge, Macfarren, Turpin, and Guilmant; was the first American to pass the examination of the London R. Coll. for Organists; 1884, one of the founders of Amer. Coll. of Musicians; organist, Brooklyn, N. Y.; 1891-95, prof. of music Vassar Coll.; 1895 founded the "Temple Choir," Brooklyn (200 voices); cond. also the Newark Harmonic Soc. and the Cecilian Choir.

Boyce (bois), Wm., London, 1710—Kensington, 1779; organist and composer.

Boyd, Chas. N., Pleasant Unity, Pa., Dec. 2, 1875—Pittsburgh, April 24, 1937; pupil of Fred K. Hodge, Leo Oehmler, and von Kunits; grad. Univ. of Pittsburgh: Mus. D., 1926;

beginning 1894 active in that city as conductor and organist; after 1903, instructor in church music, Western Theol. Sem.; 1915 appointed dir. Pittsburgh Mus. Inst.; after 1924, treasurer, Nat'l Ass'n. of Schools of Music; ass't. ed. Amer. vol., *Grove's Dictionary*; author of articles on music.

Boyle, Geo. Frdk, b. Sydney, Australia, June 29, 1886; pianist, composer and teacher; 1910, at Peabody Cons., Baltimore; later at Curtis Inst. of Music; then at Inst. of Musical Art, Juilliard School, N. Y.; c. piano concerto, which he cond. with success Feb. 1912 at New York Phil. concert; also chamber works, cantatas, etc.; d. Philadelphia, 1948.

Brade (brä'-dĕ), Wm., b. England, lived and died at Frankfort, 1630; player of the viol, etc.

Brad'ford, Jacob, London, June 3, 1842—April 19, 1897; organist; pupil of Goss and Steggal; Mus. Doc. Oxford, 1878; 1892 organist at St. Mary's, Newington; c. oratorio "*Judith*"; "*Sinfonia Ecclesiastica*" with double chorus; overtures, etc.

Bradsky (brät'-shkē), Wenzel Th., Rakovnik, Bohemia, 1833—1881; dram. composer.

Braga (brä'-gä), Gaetano, Giulianova, Abruzzi, June 9, 1829—Milan, Nov. 21, 1907; 'cellist, pupil of C. Gaetano (1841-52); lived at Florence, Vienna, Paris, and London and toured Europe; dram. composer; also wrote "*Metodo di Violoncello*."

Braham (rightly Abraham), J., London, 1774—Feb. 17, 1856; noted tenor; compass 3 octaves; composed pop. ballads.

Brahms (bräms), Johannes, Hamburg, May 7, 1833—Vienna, April 3, 1897; son and pupil of a double-bass player in the Hamburg City Theatre, later studied with Marxsen of Altona; début Hamburg, at 14, playing his own variations on a folk-song; 1853, toured with Remenyi. Joachim heard him and sent him to Schumann, at Düsseldorf. Schumann, with characteristic openness of mind and enthusiasm, pub. an article in the *Neue Zeitschrift für Musik*, greeting B. as the new Messiah of music, a welcome that was a mixture of blessing and bane, embarrassing the young Brahms with a mission that was a white elephant on his hands; for he forsook the romanticism which Schumann, and later Liszt expected of him, and took up a determined classicism in the matter of form, in which, however, he made many modifications to suit his enormous intellectuality and technical resource. This early welcome also gave him over to be bandied between believers like Hanslick who were frantic to find an opponent to the progress of Wagner, and sceptics who would not have him praised for any quality. Schumann's advocacy did not save B.'s publication and concert performance of his 3 pf.-sonatas and 3 books of songs from failure. After serving for a time as cond. to the Prince of Lippe-Detmold, he retired for study to Hamburg, 1858–62. 1862 Vienna; 1863–64 cond. of the *Singakademie* there; 1864–69 Hamburg, Zurich, Baden-Baden, etc., and made tours with Stockhausen; 1869, Vienna, which was afterward his headquarters. In 1871–74, cond. "Gesellschaft der Musikfreunde." In 1877 Cambridge University offered him the degree of Mus. Doc., which offer he ignored, accepting, 1881, Dr. Phil. from Breslau and writing in acknowledgment the "*Akademische Festouvertüre*"; 1886, a knight of the Prussian Ordre pour le Mérite, with voting privilege, and a member of the Berlin Acad. of Arts. 1889 presented with the freedom of Hamburg. His "*German Requiem*," op. 45 (the first 3 choruses given in Vienna, 1867), was given complete in the Bremen cathedral, April, 1868, and established him on a peak where he has since remained while the storms of debate rage below him. He wrote in almost every form but opera (he had considered that at one time) but admitted he "knew nothing about the theatre." He valued Wagner's scores, and owned several Wagner autographs; Wagner, however, said "Brahms is a composer whose importance lies in not wishing to create any striking effect." His first symphony, on which he had spent 10 years, made a sensation when prod. 1876. His vln.-concerto when first shown to Joachim was so impossible to the vln. that J. laughed at it till tears poured down his cheeks; he is said to have materially assisted in its

revision. **Brahms** was a brilliant pianist in his youth; in his 20th year, at a concert with Remenyi, the piano was discovered to be a semitone below concert-pitch; **B.**, playing without notes, transposed the accompaniment to Beethoven's "*Kreutzer Sonata*," a semitone higher throughout. (Beethoven similarly transposed his own concerto in C to C♯ at a rehearsal.)

COMPOSITIONS (exclusive of Songs for one voice with pf.). For orch. Symphonies, Op. 68, in C minor, Op. 73, D, op. 90, F, op. 98, E minor; overtures, op. 80, "*Akademische Festovertüre*"; op. 81, "*Pragische Ouvertüre*"; op. 11–16, serenades; op. 56, variations on a theme of Haydn's. CHAMBER MUSIC. Op. 8, trio for pf., vln., 'cello; 18, 36, sextet for strings; 40, trios, pf., vln., horn; 114, pf., clar. and 'cello; 51, two string-quartets; 67, string-quartet; 88, 111, string-quintet; 115, quintet for clar. and strings. For piano, op. 1, 2 and 5, sonatas, 4, scherzo; variations on a theme by Schumann; 10, four ballads; 15, 83, concertos; 21, 35, variations; 24, variations and fugue on theme by Händel; op. 76, 8 pcs.; 79, 2 Rhapsodies; 116, Fantasien; 117, 3 Intermezzi; 118, 6 Clavierstücke (3 Intermezzi, Ballades, Romanze); 119, 4 Clavierstücke (3 Intermezzi, Rhapsodie;—unnumbered—Gluck's gavotte, and 2 studies). For piano, 4 hands, op. 23, variations on a theme by Schumann; 34, sonata arr. from op. 34; 39, 16 waltzes; op. 25, 26, 60, pf.-quartets; 34, pf.-quintet; 87, 101, pf.-trios. For piano and 'cello, op. 38, and 99; sonatas; for vln., 77, concerto; 78, 100—108, sonatas pf. and vln.; for vln. and 'cello, op. 102, concerto; for clarinet (or viola) and pf., op. 120, 2 sonatas; for organ, Prelude and fugue, and fugue (unnumbered). For voices, op. 50, "*Rinaldo*" cantata (Goethe); 63, Rhapsodie (from Goethe's "*Harzreise*"), for alto solo, male chor. and orch.; 54, "*Schicksalslied*" (Song of Destiny), for chor. and orch.; 55, "*Triumphlied*" (Revelations, chap. XIX.), for 8-part chor. and orch.; 82, "*Nänie*" (Schiller), for chor. and orch.; 89. "*Gesang der parzer*" (Goethe), for 6-part chor. and orch.; op. 12, "*Ave Maria*," female chor-with orch. (or org.); 13, funeral hymn, 109. Deutsche Fest-und Gedenkspruche, for double chorus, also numerous works for choruses of all sorts accompanied or a cappella. Brahms' songs are generally admired even by those opposed to him; they are very numerous and are pub. in sets, op. 121 being his last published work, except for several posth. songs for Ophelia in Shakespeare's "Hamlet," which were pub. in 1936 by Schirmer.

Memoirs and studies of the composer's music have been written by Deiters, Köhler, Mesnard, Reimann, Dietrich, Widmann, Kalbeck (most imp. biography, in 8 vols.), Erb, Antcliffe, Jenner, Imbert, Henschel, Pauli, Leyen, Von Perger, Colles, Fuller-Maitland, Thomas-San Galli, Evans, Lee, Niemann, Friedländer, May, Murdoch, Parker, Pulver, Specht, and Eugenie Schumann. His letters pub. in part by the German B.—Gesellschaft; thematic catalogue of his works, by Simrock. (See article, page 489.)

Brailowsky (brä-ē-lŏf'skē), **Alexander,** b. Kiev, Russia; pianist; studied with nis father and after 1911 with Leschetizky, Vienna; res. in Switzerland 1914–18; thereafter in Paris, where made his début with striking succ.; toured Europe, South America, Australia, and after 1926 in U. S.; one of most brilliant younger virtuosi.

Brambach (bräm'-bäkh), (1) **Kaspar Jos.,** Bonn, July 14, 1833—June 19, 1902; pupil in comp. of A. zur Nieden, then of Cologne Cor 5.; won Mozart scholarship, and studied under Fd. Hiller, Frankfort; 1858–61, teacher Cologne Cons.; 1861–69, dir. at Bonn, where he composed important secular cantatas; also an opera "Ariadne"; concert-overture "Tasso"; pf.-concerto, etc. (2) **Wm.,** Bonn, Dec. 17, 1841—Carlsruhe, Feb. 26, 1932; where from 1872, librarian; writer.

Brambilla (bräm-bēl'-lä), (1) **Paolo,** Milan, 1786—1838; dram. composer. (2) **Marietta,** Cassano D'Adda, 1807 —Milan, 1875; singer, teacher, and composer; contralto and eldest of five singers. (3) **Teresa,** Cassano d'Adda, 1813—Milan, 1895; sister of above, soprano; she created "Gilda" in "Rigoletto," 1851.

Branca (brän'-kä), **Gugliẽlmo,** b. Bo-

logna, April 13, 1849; pupil of A. Busi, Bologna Cons., where he taught after 1890; composed succ. operas "La Catalana" (Florence, 1876); "Hermosa" (Florence, 1883); and "La Figlia di Jorio" (Cremona, 1897).

Brancaccio (brän-kät'-chō), **A.,** Naples, 1813—1846; dram. composer.

Brandeis (brän'-dīs), **Fr.,** Vienna, 1835 —New York, 1899; toured the U. S., then lived in N. Y., later Brooklyn, as organist and prolific composer.

Brandenburg (brän'-děn-boorkh), **Fd.,** b. Erfurt—d. Rudolstadt, 1850; violinist and dram. composer.

Brandl (bränt'-'l), (1) **Jn.,** Kloster Rohr, near Ratisbon, 1760—Carlsruhe, 1837; dir. and dram. composer. (2) **Johann,** Kirchenbirk, Bohemia, Aug. 30, 1835—Vienna, June 10, 1913; c. operettas.

Brandstetter. Vide GARBRECHT.

Brandt (bränt), **Marianne** (rightly **Marie Bischof**), Vienna, Sept. 12, 1842—July 9, 1921; dram. contralto; pupil Frau Marschner and of Viardot-Garcia; 1868–86 at Berlin Ct. Opera; created "Kundry" in "Parsifal" at Bayreuth, 1882; 1886–90, sang in New York, at Met. Op.; later active as teacher in Vienna.

Brandts-Buys (bränt-bois), (1) **Cornelius Alex.,** Zait-Bommel, April 3, 1812—Dordrecht, Nov. 18, 1890; from 1840 lived in Deventer as organist and cond. His sons are (2) **Marius Adrianus** (b. 1840); (3) **L. F.** (1847—1917) organist and conductor at Rotterdam; (4) **H.** (1851—1905), conductor at Amsterdam and dram. composer. (5) **Jan** (1868—1933), son of (2); composer of operas, songs, etc.; pupil of Frankfort Cons.; lived in Vienna and after 1910 at Bozen.

Bran'dukov, Anatol Andrejevitch, Moscow, Jan. 6, 1859—Oct., 1930; 'cellist; pupil Moscow Cons.; spent many years in Paris; founded a quartet there with Marsick; 1890 returned to Moscow; c. for 'cello and orch., etc.

Brant (bränt), **Jobst** (or **Jodocus**) **vom,** Junior, 16th cent. captain and gov. of Liebenstein; cptist.

Branzell, Karin (kär'-ĭn bränt-sěl), b. Stockholm, Sept. 24, 1891; mezzo-soprano; studied with Thekla Hofer and Louis Bachner (Berlin); début Stockholm; member Berlin State

Op., after 1919; Met. Op. Co., N. Y. after 1924; has also sung at Buenos Aires, and in various European cities; repertoire includes principal Wagner contralto rôles.

Braslau (bräs'-lä), **Sophie**, New York, Aug. 16, 1892—Dec. 22, 1935; contralto; studied piano with Alexander Lambert and voice with A. Buzzi-Peccia, Gabriele Sibella, and Dr. M. Marafioti; début Met. Op. Co., 1913, as Feodor in *"Boris Godounoff"*; member of company for seven years, singing title rôle in Cadman's opera *"Shanewis,"* 1918; sang in concerts and with leading orchestras; toured Scandinavia, Netherlands, and England, 1931.

Brassart, Johannes, priest, composer, and singer; in Papal Choir in 1431; probably same as **Johannes de Ludo;** c. sacred music.

Brassin (bräs-săn), (1) **Louis**, Aix-la-Chapelle, 1840—St. Petersburg, 1884; pianist. (2) **Ld.**, Strassburg, 1843—Constantinople, 1890; bro. and pupil of above; pianist. (3) **Gerhard**, Aix-la-Chapelle, June 10, 1844—Constantinople (?); leader; teacher at Stern Cons., Berlin; 1875-80, cond. of *Tonkünstlerverein* in Breslau; then, St. Petersburg and Constantinople.

Brauer (brow'ĕr, **Max**, Mannheim, May 9, 1855—Carlsruhe, Jan. 2, 1918; pupil of V. Lachner, Hiller, Jensen, and De Lange; 1880–88, dir. Kaiserslautern; 1888, dir. court-church at Carlsruhe; prod. *"Der Lotse,"* succ. 1-act opera, Carlsruhe, 1885.

Braun, (1) **Anton**, Cassel, Feb. 6, 1729—1785; violinist and c.; perhaps the son of (2) **Braun**, whose flute compositions were pub. in Paris, 1729–40. His brother (3) **Johann**, Cassel, 1753—Berlin, 1795, violinist and comp. (4) **Johann Fr.**, Cassel, 1759—Ludwigslust, 1824; oboist and comp.; father of (5) **Karl A. P.**, b. Ludwigslust, 1788; oboist; and of (6) **Wilhelm**, b. Ludwigslust, 1791; oboist, whose wife was his cousin (7) **Kathinka B.**, a singer.

Braunfels (brän'-fĕls), **Walter**, b. Frankfort, Dec. 19, 1882; composer of neo-Romantic tendency, with satiric elements and modern outlook; grad. Hoch Cons. in native city; also pupil of Kwast, Leschetizky, Navratil and Thuille; res. in Munich after 1903, but several years in war service; c. (operas) *"Prinzessin Brambilla"* (1919), *"Ulenspiegel"* (1913), *"Die Vögel"* (1920, a work portraying denizens of birdland and enjoying popularity when prod. in Munich), *"Don Gil von den grünen Hosen"* (1924), *"Galatea"*; (orch.) Variations on an Old Nursery Song; *"Ariel's Song"*; Serenade; Fantastic Variations on a Theme by Berlioz; *"Don Juan"* (variations on the champagne song from Mozart's opera); Praeludium and Fugue; Symphonic Suite; 'cello concerto; *"Funk"* (Radio) *Music;* (choral) *"Te Deum"*; Mass; *"Revelation of St. John"* (tenor solo and orch.); *"Neues Federspiel"* for voices and orch.; *"Die Ammen-Uhr"* for boys' chorus and orch.; orch. songs; music to *"As You Like It"* and *"Macbeth"*; *"Witches' Sabbath"* for piano and orch.; piano concerto and many pieces for this instrum.; songs, etc.; after 1925 dir. (with H. Abendroth) of Cologne Cons.

Bree (brā) **(Jn. Bernardus)**, **J. Bernard van**, Amsterdam, 1801—1857; violinist; 1840, founded the "Cecilia."

Breil (bríl), **Jos. Carl**, Pittsburgh, 1870—Los Angeles, Cal., Jan. 23, 1926; composer and tenor; studied in Leipzig and Milan; sang in Juch Op. Co., later at Pittsburgh; after 1897 theat. cond.; c. comic operas, also a one-act grand opera, *"The Legend,"* given by Met. Op. Co., 1919.

Breithaupt (brīt-howpt), **Rudolf Maria**, b. Braunschweig, Aug. 11, 1873; critic and teacher; pupil Leipzig Cons., 1897; after 1918 taught at Stern Cons., Berlin; author of influential works on piano technique, espousing a system of "weight"; c. songs.

Breitkopf und Härtel (brīt'-kôpf oont hĕrt''-l), mus.-publishers, founded (as a printing-office) 1719 by **B. C. Breitkopf**; Klausthal, Harz, 1695—1777. His son, **J. G. Immanuel Breitkopf** (1719—1794), succeeded and revived Petrucci's invention of movable types and took up music printing. 1795, **Gottfr. Chr. Härtel** (Schneeberg, 1763—1857) added a piano-factory, founded the "Allg. musikalische Zeitung" (1798); later heads were **Florenz Härtel** (1827-35), **Dr. Hermann Härtel** (d. 1875), and his bro. **Reimund** (d. 1888); two nephews, Wm. Volkmann (1837–1896 ?) and Dr. Oskar von Hase (b. 1846).

Brema (brä'-mä), Marie, London, Feb. 28, 1856—March 22, 1925; notable dramatic soprano; début in opera, Shaftesbury Theatre, 1891; sang in New York, 1895–96; 1897 at Bayreuth; long a favourite in oratorio perfs. in England; later prof., Manchester Coll. of Music.

Brem'mer, Robt., Scotland, 1720—Kensington, 1789; teacher.

Brendel (brĕnt'-'l), K. Fz., Stolberg, 1811—Leipzig, 1868; critic, prof., and writer.

Brenet (brŭ-nā), Michel, Luneville, France, April 11, 1858—Paris, Nov. 4, 1918; wrote "Histoire de la symphonie à orchestre depuis ses origines" (prize-essay), etc.

Brenner (brĕn'-nĕr), L., Ritter von, Leipzig, 1833—1902; pupil of the Cons.; toured the Continent; 15 years member of the Imp. orch.; 1872–76, cond. Berlin Symphony Orch.; 1897, cond. Meyder's Concert Orch., Breslau; composed 4 grand masses; symphonic poems.

Brent, Charlotte, d. 1802, Engl.; soprano; m. Pinto, a violinist, 1766.

Brescianello (brĕ'-shä-nĕl'-lō), Giuseppe Antonio, Mus. Director at Stuttgart, 1717–57; published violin concertos, etc.

Breslaur (bräs'-lowr), Emil, Kottbus, May 20, 1836—Berlin, July 26, 1899; pupil Stern Cons., Berlin; 1868–79, teacher Kullak's Acad.; 1883 choirm., Reformed Synagogue; founder and dir. Piano-Teachers' Seminary; ed. "Klavierlehrer"; wrote technical works, etc.

Bress'ler-Gianoli (jä-nō'-lē), Clotilde, b. Geneva, 1875; d. there after operation for appendicitis, May 12, 1912. Operatic mezzo-sopr.; studied Paris Cons., début Geneva, at 19; 1900, Paris Op. Com.; 1903 with New Orleans Op. Co.; from 1907 sang with success at Manhattan Opera, N. Y.; 1910 with Metropolitan Opera, N. Y.; her "Carmen" was famous.

Breton y Hernàndez (brä-tŏn ē ĕr-nän'-dĕth), Tomas, Salamanca, Dec. 23, 1850—Madrid, Dec. 10, 1923; leading Spanish composer of zarzuelas, an oratorio "Apocalypsia"; for orch.

"Andalusian Scenes"; funeral march for Alfonso XII., etc.

Breuer (broi'-ĕr), Hans, b. Cologne, 1869; tenor; studied at the Cons. at Stolzenberg. Sang "Mime" and "David" at Bayreuth; d. Vienna, 1929.

Breuning (broi'-nĭng), Fd., Brotterode, Thuringia, 1830 — Aix-la-Chapelle, 1883; pf. prof., Cologne Cons.; 1865, director.

Bréval (brä-văl), (1) J. Bap., Dept. of l'Aisne, France, 1756—Chamouille, 1825; 'cellist and teacher. (2) Lucienne, Berlin, Nov. 4, 1869—Paris, Aug. 15, 1935; pupil of Warot at Paris Cons.; notable dramatic soprano at Grand Opéra, Paris, for years; début there in "L'Africaine," 1892; created "Brünnhilde" in French; sang at Covent Garden, and 1900 in New York.

Bréville (brä-vĕl), Pierre Onfroy de, b. Bar-le-Duc, France, Feb. 21, 1861; d. Paris, Sept., 1949; had diplomatic career; then studied at Paris Cons. and with César Franck; teacher at the Schola Cantorum; c. masses, sacred chorus with orch., "Sainte Rose de Lima"; symph. poem, "Nuit de décembre"; overture, "Princesse Maleine," music for "Les sept Princesses," and "Sakuntala," etc., orch. fantasie "Portraits des Musiciens"; songs, etc.

Brew'er, (1) Thos., 1609—1676; viol.-player, "father of the glee." (2) J. Hyatt, Brooklyn, N. Y., 1856—Nov. 30, 1931; for 7 years boy-soprano; studied with Dudley Buck and others; 1871 organist various churches, 1881 at the Lafayette Av. Presby. Ch.; cond. various vocal societies; composed cantatas, etc.

Brick'en, Carl, b. Shelbyville, Ky., 1898; comp.; cond. U. of Chi. Symph., 1931; Seattle Symph. after 1944.

Bridge, (1) Sir J. Fr., Oldbury, Worcestershire, Engl., Dec. 5, 1844—London, March 16, 1924; son and pupil of J. Bridge, lay-clerk; pupil later of J. Hopkins and Sir J. Goss; organist 1869 Manchester cathedral; 1882 of Westminster Abbey; 1868 Mus. Bac. (Oxford), with the oratorio "Mount Moriah"; prof. of harm. and cpt. R. A. M.; cond. Western and the Madrigal Societies; 1897, knighted; composed cantatas, overtures, etc. 1902, made member of the Victorian Order; 1903, King Edward Prof. of Music, London

University and R. C. M. (2) **Frank,**
b. Brighton, 1879—London, Jan. 11,
1941; Viola pupil, R. A. M., gaining
a scholarship in composition; c.
prize quartet in E. Minor (Bologna
competition); string quartet "*Three
Idylls*"; rhapsody for orch. and
symp. poem, "*Isabella*"; "*Sea*" *Suite*;
"*Dance Rhapsody*"; "*Dance Poem*";
piano trio and many chamber works;
member of various quartets; cond.
Covent Garden, 1913.

Bridge'tower, G. A. P., Poland, 1779—
ca. 1845; son of an African father
and European mother; brilliant violinist.

Briegel (brē'gĕl), **Wg. K.,** Germany,
1626—Darmstadt, 1712; conductor
and composer.

Brighenti (or **Brighetti**) (brē-gĕt'-tē),
Maria (née Giorgi), b. Bologna, 1792;
soprano; created "Rosina" in "*Barbiere di Siviglia*."

Bright, Dora Estella, b. Sheffield,
Aug. 16, 1863; pianist; pupil R. A.
M., London; 1892 married Capt.
Knatchbull; c. 2 piano concertos;
variations with orch., etc.

Brink, Jules Ten (tān brĕnk), Amsterdam, 1838—Paris, 1889; director and
dram. composer.

Brins'mead, (1) **J.,** North Devon,
Oct. 13, 1814—London, Feb. 17,
1908; 1835, founded piano-factory,
London; inv. "Perfect Check Re-
peater Action"; in 1863 his sons
(2) **Thomas** and (3) **Edgar** were
taken in partnership.

Bris'tow, (1) **W. R.,** England, 1803
—N. Y., 1867; cond. in New York.
(2) **G. Fr.,** Brooklyn, N. Y., Dec. 19,
1825—New York, Dec. 13, 1898;
son of above; violinist N. Y. Philh.
Soc.; cond. of the Harmonic Soc.,
later of the Mendelssohn Union; organist various churches; composed
operas, oratorios, etc.

Britt, Horace, b. Antwerp; 'cellist;
studied Paris Cons. with Delsart and
Lavignac, 1st prize at 14; soloist
with Paris orchs.; U. S. tours.

Brit'ten, Benjamin, b. Lowestoft, Eng.,
1913; pupil, R. C. M.; c. operas,
"*Peter Grimes*" (Berkshire Fest., and
Met. Op.); "*Rape of Lucretia*"
(Glyndebourne Fest., 1946, also in
N. Y.); "*Albert Herring*" (Glynde-
bourne, 1947; Berkshire Fest.).
(See Composers' List)

Brit'ton, Thos., 1651—1714; called
"Musical Small-coal Man," because

he earned his living by hawking coal;
gave concerts in a room over his shop,
which were patronised by the aristocracy; Händel and Pepusch were performers at these concerts.

Brixi (brēx'-ē), **Fz. Xaver,** Prague,
1732—1771; conductor and com-
poser.

Broad'wood & Sons, firm of London
pf.-makers; est. 1730 by the Swiss
harpsichord-maker **Burkhard Tschudi** (or **Shudi**), succeeded by his son-
in-law **J. Broadwood** (1732—1812),
later by **James** and **Thos. Shudi;**
then by **H. Fowler Broadwood** (d.
London, 1893).

Brock'way, Howard A., b. Brooklyn,
N. Y., Nov. 22, 1870; studied pf.
with Kortheuer; 1890–95, Berlin;
pupil of Barth (pf.) and O. B. Boise
(comp.); since 1895, has lived in
N. Y. teaching and touring; his
symphony in D succ., prod. Berlin;
composed also cantata, Ballade and
Scherzo for orch.; d. 1951.

Brod (brō), **H.,** Paris, 1801—1839;
oboist and conductor.

Brode (brō'-dĕ), **Max,** Berlin, Feb. 25,
1850—Königsberg, Dec. 30, 1917;
studied with Paul Mendelssohn and
at Stern Cons., Leipzig Cons., and
Berlin Hochschule; début Frankfort-
on-Main; prof. and teacher at
Königsberg, violinist, conductor.

Brodsky (brôd'-shkĭ), **Adolf,** Taganrog,
Russia, March 21, 1851—Manches-
ter, Jan. 22, 1929; violinist; pupil of
J. Hellmesberger and Vienna Cons.;
member Hellmesberger Quartet;
1868–70 Imp. Opera orch.; pupil of
Laub, Moscow, later prof. at the
Cons.; 1879, cond. symphony concerts at Kiev; toured, 1881; 1883,
vln.-prof. at Leipzig Cons.; 1891–94,
N. Y.; 1894 in Berlin; 1895, prof. of
vln., later dir. R. C. M., Manchester,
England.

Bron'ner, Georg, Holstein, 1666—
Hamburg, 1724; organist; c. for the
Hamburg Opera "*Echo and Nar-
cissus*," "*Venus*," etc.

Bronsart (brôn'-zärt) (1) **von Schel-
lendorf, Hans (Hans von Bronsart),**
Berlin, Feb. 11, 1830—Munich,
Nov. 3, 1913; pupil, Dehn, Kullak,
Liszt; concerts in Paris; 1867, intendant R. Th. at Hanover; 1887–95,
"Hofmusikintendant," Weimar: composed opera, cantata, symphony "*In
den Alpen*," etc. (2) **Ingeborg, von**
(née Starck), St. Petersburg, Aug. 24,

1840—Munich, June 17, 1913; wife (since 1862) of above; pupil of Liszt; composed 3 operas, etc.

Bro'sa, Antonio, violinist; founder, 1925, in London of noted Brosa Quartet, with himself as 1st vln., David Wise, 2nd vln., Leonard Rubens, viola, and Livio Mannucci, 'cello; début, 1926, London; next year heard at Siena Fest. of I. S. C. M.; toured England, Germany, France, Holland, Italy; 1930, Amer. début at Coolidge Fest., Washington, D. C.

Brosig (brō'-zĭkh), **Moritz,** Fuchswinkel, Upper Silesia, 1815—Breslau, 1887; organist and theorist.

Brossard (dŭ brôs-săr), **Sébastien de,** 1654—Meux, France, 1730; conductor, lexicographer, and composer.

Brounoff (broo'-nôf), **Platon,** Elizabethgrad, Russia, 1869—New York, July 11, 1924; composer; pupil of Rubinstein and Rimsky-Korsakov, St. Petersburg Cons.; cantata *"The Angel,"* prod. at court; lived in New York as cond. of Russian choral society, etc.; c. operas, piano suites, and songs.

Broustet (broo-stā), **Ed.,** Toulouse, April 29, 1836—Louchon, Dec., 1901; pupil of Stamaty, Litolff, and Ravina; pianist and composer; toured Russia, etc.; lived in Toulouse; composer.

Brown, (1) Dr. **J.,** Northumberland, 1715—1766; writer. (2) **Eddy,** b. Chicago, July 15, 1895; violinist; studied with Hubay and Auer; début with London Philh. Orch., 1909; toured widely in Europe and America; active also in chamber music groups, particularly in radio programmes.

Brown'lee, John, b. Geelong, Australia, 1901; operatic barytone; studied with Gilly; discovered by Melba and came to England, sang at her Covent Garden Op. farewell, 1926; début Paris Op. 1927, of which he has been a member since; has also sung at Monte Carlo and Covent Garden, principally in Italian and French rôles; engaged for Met. Op. Co., 1936-37.

Bruch (brookh), **Max,** Cologne, Jan. 6, 1838—near Berlin, Oct. 2, 1920; noted pianist and composer; at first, pupil of his mother (née Almenrader), a singer; later with Breidenstein, Bonn; 1853 he gained the four-year scholarship of the Mozart Foundation at Frankfort, and stud-

ied with Hiller, Reinecke, and Breuning; at 14, prod. a symphony, Cologne; 1858, his first dram. work, Goethe's *Singspiel, "Scherz, List und Rache"* (op. 1); 1864, prod. opera *"Loreley,"* etc.; male chorus *"Frithjof"*; 1865-67, at Coblenz, composed his first pop. vln.-concerto (G minor); 1867-70, court-cond. at Sondershausen; in 1878 cond. Stern Choral Union, Berlin; in 1880, cond. Liverpool Philh. Soc.; 1883, dir. Breslau Orchestral Soc.; 1881, m. Frl. Tuczek, of Berlin, a singer; lived in Breslau till 1890; 1892-1910, at K. Hochschule in Berlin; he received in 1908 the Prussian order for merit in art and learning, and many honours from England, France, etc.; prod. 1872, *"Hermione,"* based on *"Winter's Tale"*; 1873-78, prod. the chorals *"Arminius"* and *"Lied von der Glocke,"* and the 2d vln.-concerto; 1883, came to U. S. and prod. his *"Arminius,"* Boston. The epic cantata is his special field; among his works of this sort are *"Odysseus," "Arminius," "Lied von der Glocke,"* and *"Achilleus"*; for male chorus, *"Frithjof," "Salamis," "Normannenzug"* and *"Leonidas"* (op. 66). He arranged the old Hebrew melody *Kol Nidre,* and composed a cantata *"Das Feuerkreuz"* (op. 52, 1888); three symphonies; oratorio, *"Moses"* (1895); 3 vln.-concertos, which have won great popularity; secular oratorio, *"Gustav Adolf"; "Nal und Damajant"; "Die Macht des Gesanges,"* for barytone, mixed chor. and orch., etc.

Brückler (brük'-lĕr), **Hugo,** Dresden, 1845—1871; composer.

Bruckner (brook'-nĕr), **Anton,** Ausfelden, Upper Austria, Sept. 4, 1824—Vienna, Oct. 11, 1896; eminent composer; mainly self-taught as organist; 1867, court-organist at Vienna; prof. of org., harm. and cpt. at Vienna Cons.; 1875, "Lektor" of music at Vienna Univ.; 1891, Dr. hon. causa; noted organ-virtuoso and a disciple of Wagner; he composed nine symphonies: 1, C minor (1868); 2, C minor (1873); 3, D minor (1877); 4, E flat, known as the *"Romantic"* (1881); 5, B flat (1894); 6, A (1899); 7, E (1884); 8, C minor (1892); 9, left incomplete but often played with his *"Te Deum"* as concluding choral movement.

In 1936 the publication of the

original version of Bruckner's symphonies by the Musikwissentschaftliche Verlag, Vienna, led to a controversy as to whether the previously known copies had been indefensibly altered and ed. by his pupils Ferdinand Loewe and the brothers Franz and Josef Schalk. But evidence was adduced to show that **B.** approved these changes.

His choral works include three Grand Masses, a "*Te Deum*," a Requiem, motets, psalms, and various church music, pcs. for male chorus. C. also a string quintet. The fame of **B.** has grown to great proportions since his death, not only in Germany and Austria, where he is considered a classic in the great line of Romantic composers, but also in other countries. An International Bruckner Soc. devotes itself to furthering perfs. of his music. The best passages in his works are undoubtedly of noble fervour and breadth, some even approaching sublimity, but other pages are clumsy, repetitious, and lacking in contrast. The influence of Wagner is evident in his scores, also of baroque organ style. Biog. by Fz. Brunner (Linz-on-Danube, 1895). Other memoirs by Louis, Funtek, Gräflinger, Morold, Halm, Krug, Grunsky and Göllerich.

Brückner (brük'-nĕr), **Oscar**, Erfurt, Jan. 2, 1857—Wiesbaden, June 8, 1930; 'cellist; pupil of Grützmacher and Draeseke; toured Germany, Russia, etc.; Ducal chamber-virtuoso at Strelitz; 1889 teacher in the Wiesbaden Cons., and composer.

Brugnoli (broōn-yō'-lē), **Attilio**, b. Rome, Sept. 7, 1880—Bolzano, July 10, 1937; won 1st prize in international Rubinstein contest, Paris, 1905; appointed prof. of piano at Parma Cons. in competition same year; 1907, Naples Cons.; 1916, at Rome Cons. and after 1921, Florence Cons.; has c. music for orch., piano, violin, also ed. complete works of Chopin.

Bruhns (broons), **Nikolaus**, Schwabstadt, Schleswig, 1665 — Husum, 1697; organist and violinist.

Brüll (brïl), **Ignaz**, Moravia, Nov. 7, 1846—Vienna, Sept. 17, 1907; pianist; pupil of Epstein, Rufinatscha and Dessoff; 1872–78, pf.-prof. Horak Institute, Vienna; his first opera

"*Die Bettler von Sammarkand*" (1864) was not succ., but "*Das Goldene Kreuz*" (Berlin) (1875) was very pop.; followed by 6 other operas and the succ. comic opera "*Der Husar*" (Vienna, March 2, 1898); composed also hunting overture "*Im Walde*," etc.

Brumel (broo'-mĕl), **Anton**, ca. 1480— ca. 1520; Flemish cptist.

Bruneau (brü-nō) (**Louis Chas. Bonaventure**), **Alfred**, Paris, March 3, 1857—June 15, 1934; pupil of Franchomme at the Cons.; took first 'cello prize, 1876; studied with Savart and Massenet; 1881, took first prize with cantata "*Sainte Geneviève*"; composed operas "*Kerim*" (Opéra-Populaire, 1887), "*Le Rêve*" (Paris, 1892), and the very succ. drame lyrique "*L'Attaque du Moulin*" (Opéra-Comique, Paris, 1893); unsucc. drame lyrique "*Messidor*" (Paris, Gr. Opera, Feb. 19, 1897); the last three are on texts from Zola, as are "*L'Ouragan*" (Op. Com., 1901); lyric comedy in 3 acts, "*L'Enfant Roi*" (Op. Com., 1905); 1-act lyric drama "*Lazare*" (1905); incid. music to "*La Faute de l'Abbé Mouret*" (Odéon, 1907); lyric drama "*Naïs Nicoulin*" (Monte Carlo, 1907); "*Le Roi Candaule*" (1920); "*Le Jardin du Paradis*" (1921); ballets, orch. and choral works; songs set to Catulle Mendès' "*Lieds en prose*"; 1893–95, critic of "*Gil Blas*," 1895 of "*Le Figaro*," officier of Legion of Honour.

Brunelli (broo-nĕl'-lē), **A.**, 17th cent.; conductor to Duke of Florence; writer and composer.

Brunetti (broo-nĕt'-tē), **Gaetano**, Pisa, 1740?—Madrid, 1808; composer.

Bruni (broo'-nē), **A. Bart.**, Coni, Piedmont, 1759—1823; violinist, cond. and dram. composer.

Brun'skill, **Muriel**, b. Kendall, England, Dec. 18, 1899; contralto; début, London, in recital, 1920; member British Nat'l. Op. Co., 1922–27; has sung with leading British orchs. and at festivals; also appeared in United States.

Bruyck (broik), **K. Debrois van**, Brünn, March 14, 1828—Waidhofen, Aug. 1, 1902; studied law, Vienna, 1850; and theory with Rufinatscha; writer on Bach, etc.

Bryen'nius, **Manuel**, lived ca. 1320; last Greek theorist.

Buchholz (bookh'-hŏlts), (1) **Jn. Simeon,** Schlosswippach, 1758—Berlin, 1825; founded firm of organ-builders; succeeded by his son (2) **K. Aug.** (1796—1884), whose son (3) **K. Fr.,** d. Feb. 17, 1885.

Buchner (bookh'-nĕr), **Philipp Fr.,** Wertheim, 1614—Würzburg, 1669; cond. and comp.

Büchner (bükh'-nĕr), **Emil,** Osterfield, near Naumburg, Dec. 25, 1826—Erfurt, June 9, 1908; pupil of Leipzig Cons.; 1865, court-conductor; composed 2 operas, etc.

Buck, (1) **Zechariah,** Norwich, England, 1798—Newport, Essex, 1879; organist Norwich Cathedral; teacher and composer. (2) **Dudley,** Hartford, Conn., March 10, 1839—Orange, N. J., Oct. 6, 1909; pupil W. J. Babcock (pf.), then of Plaidy and Moscheles (pf.); Hauptmann (comp.) and J. Reitz (instrumentation), Leipzig Cons.; later Dresden, under Reitz and Johann Schneider (organ); and 1861–62 in Paris; 1862, organist of the Park Ch., Hartford, U. S. A.; St. James, Chicago, 1872, St. Paul's and of the Music Hall Association, Boston; 1875, organist Cincinnati May Festival; then, asst. cond. to Th. Thomas, New York; organist of Holy Trinity Ch., Brooklyn; director Apollo Club; composed comic opera "*Deseret*" (prod. 1880); symphonic overture "*Marmion*" (1880), many cantatas; the 46th Psalm; "*The Christian Year*," a series of 5 cantatas; wrote 2 books of Pedal-phrasing Studies, and "*Illustrations on Choir-accompaniment, with Hints on Registration*"; pub. "*The Organist's Repertoire*" (with A. P. Warren); "*The Influence of the Organ in History*" (1882); and a "*Dictionary of Musical Terms.*" (3) **Percy Carter,** b. West Ham., March 25, 1871; pupil at R. A. M., London; won scholarship 1891–4, organist at Oxford; 1893, Mus. Doc.; 1896–9, organist Wells Cathedral, 1899–1901, Bristol Cathedral; 1910, prof. of music Dublin University, vice-pres.; 1927, prof. of music, Univ. of Sheffield; c. overture "*Coeur de Lion*"; chamber music, etc.

Buhl (bül), **Joseph David,** b. Amboise, 1781; famous trumpet-player at Paris; author of trumpet-method.

Bühler (bü'-lĕr), **Fz. P. Gregorius,** Schneidheim, 1760—Augsburg, 1824;

Benedictine monk, 1794, conductor at Botzen; dram. composer and theorist.

Buh'lig, Richard, b. Chicago, Dec. 21, 1880; pianist; studied in native city and with Leschetizky in Vienna; after 1901 taught in Berlin, and toured in Europe and U. S. as recitalist; Amer. début, 1907, with Phila. Orch.; 1918–20, taught at Inst. of Mus. Art, N. Y.; later lived on Pacific Coast; d. Los Angeles, 1952.

Bull, John, Dr., Somersetshire, England, 1563—Antwerp, March 12, 1628; 1582, organist; 1592, Mus. Doc. Oxon.; 1596, prof. of music at Gresham Coll. on Queen Elizabeth's recommendation; resigned on his marriage, 1607; 1617, organist Nôtre Dame, Antwerp; an early English composer whom Oscar Bie credits with remarkable originality in the midst of over-ornamentation.

Bull (bool), **Ole (Bornemann),** Bergen, Norway, Feb. 5, 1810—Lysoen, Aug. 17, 1880; enormously popular and brilliant violin-virtuoso, a whit charlatanic; pupil of Paulsen; then self-taught, using a bridge almost level and a flat fingerboard; studied theology, but failed in examinations; 1828, dir. Philh. and Dram. Soc., Bergen; 1829, studied with Spohr briefly; 1832, début, Paris, after living there a year observing Paganini's methods; toured Europe frequently, and North America 5 times (1843–79); he died at his country-seat. He played his own comps. almost altogether; wrote 2 concertos, and characteristic solos; biog. by Sara C. Bull, his second wife, Boston, 1883, and by Vlik (Bergen, 1890).

Bul'lard, Fred. F., Boston, Mass., Sept. 21, 1864—June 24, 1904; 1888–92, studied comp. under Rheinberger, Munich; teacher of comp., critic and composer, Boston; pub. many successful ballads and four-part songs for male voices, also sacred music.

Bülow (fōn bü'-lō), **Hans Guido von,** Dresden, Jan. 8, 1830—Cairo, Egypt, Feb. 12, 1894; versatile and influential musician; pianist and conductor of remarkable accuracy and memory, popularising the custom of conducting without score; often called the best interpreter of Beethoven, but rather cold as a pianist; at 9, studied pf. with Fr. Wieck; harmony with

Ebewein; 1848, entered Leipzig Univ. as law-student, but studied cpt. with Hauptmann; 1849, Wagner's *"Die Kunst und die Revolution"* stirred him deeply, and having heard *"Lohengrin"* at Weimar under Liszt's direction, he joined Wagner, then exiled at Zurich, 1850–51; studied conducting with him, and acted as cond. in theatres at Zurich and St. Gallen, and later with Liszt; 1853 and 1855 toured Germany and Austria, with success; 1855–64, first pf.-teacher Stern Cons., Berlin. 1857, m. Cosima, Liszt's natural daughter, whom he later surrendered to his friend Wagner (q. v.); 1858, court-pianist; 1863, Dr. Phil. *hon. causa*, Univ. of Jena; 1864, court-pianist, Munich; 1867–69, court-conductor and dir. School of Music; 1869–72, teacher and pianist in Florence; 1875–76, gave 139 concerts in America; 1878–80, court-conductor at Hanover; then till 1885, Hofmusikintendant, Saxe-Meiningen; 1882, m. Marie Schanzer; 1885–88, teacher Raff Cons., Frankfort, Klindworth Cons., Berlin, and dir. Berlin Philh. Concerts; in 1888, founded the succ. "Subscription Concerts." Composed music to *"Julius Cæsar"* (op. 10); a Ballade for orch., *"Des Sängers Fluch"* (op. 16); *"Nirwana,"* a symphonic Stimmungsbild (op. 20); 4 Charakterstücke for orch. (op. 23); a few pf.-pcs. and songs; also many piano arrangements. His critical ed. of Beethoven's sonatas, and Cramer's études, are standard; biog. by his 2d wife (Leipzig, 1895).

Bulss (bools), **Paul,** Birkholz Manor, Priegnitz, Dec. 19, 1847—Temesvar, Hungary, March 20, 1902; pupil of G. Engel; barytone at Dresden (1876–89), later at Berlin court opera.

Bulthaupt (boolt'-howpt), **H.,** Bremen, Oct. 26, 1849—Aug. 21, 1905; wrote a valuable *"Dramaturgie der Oper"* (Leipzig, 1887).

Bungert (boong'-ĕrt), **August,** Mühlheim-on-Ruhr, March 14, 1846—Leutesdorf-on-Rhine, Oct. 26, 1915; pupil of Kufferath (pf.), later at Cologne Cons.; for 4 years at Paris Cons.; then (1869) with Mathias; lived (1873–81) at Berlin, and studied cpt. with Kiel; lived near Genoa. C. *"Das Homerische Welt,"* in 2 Homeric opera-cycles, occupying 6

"evenings" (*Abende*), each with a "Vorspiel"; The Iliad (*"Die Ilias"*) is unfinished: (a) *Achilles;* (b) *Klytemnestra.* The Odyssey (*"Die Odyssee"*) consists of *Circe; Nausikaa; Odysseus' Heimkehr* (Berlin, March 31, 1898; succ.), and *Odysseus' Tod* (Dresden, 1902). Other comp. are (comic opera) *"Die Studenten von Salamanca"* (Leipzig, 1884); symph. poem, *"Auf der Wartburg"; "Hohes Lied der Liebe,"* with orch.; overture, *"Tasso,"* pf. quartet, op. 18; Florentine quartet (prize, 1878); *"Italienishe Reisebilder,"* etc., for pf.; songs to Carmen Sylva's *"Lieder einer Königin,"* etc.

Bun'nett, Edw., near Norwich, England, 1834—1923; articled to Dr. Buck, 1849; organist various churches, Mus. Doc. Oxon, 1869; 1871–92, cond. Norwich Mus. Union; 1872 organist of the Norwich Festivals; composed cantata, etc.

Bun'ning, Herbert, b. London, May 2, 1863—Thundersley, 1937; pupil of V. Ferroni; c. Italian scena, *"Ludovico il Moro"* (prod. with succ., 1892), also 2 symphonic poems, opera *"The Last Days of Pompeii"* (M.S.)

Bun'ting, Edw., Armagh, Feb., 1773—Belfast, 1843; historian and collector of Irish music.

Buonamente (boo-ō-nä-mĕn'-tĕ), **Giov. Bat.,** cond. Franciscan monastery at Assisi; early and important composer for violin, also cornetti (1623–36); confused by Fétis with Bonometti.

Buonamici (boo-ō-nä-mē'-chē) (1) **Giu.,** Florence, Feb. 12, 1846—March 18, 1914; pianist; pupil of his uncle Ceccherini, and of Bülow and Rheinberger at Munich; 1873, cond. Florentine Choral Society "Cherubini"; founded the Flor. "Trio Society"; pub. études, etc. (2) **Carlo,** Florence, June 20, 1875—Boston (?), 1920; pianist; son and pupil of Giuseppe (q. v.), later studied at Würzburg Royal Musicsch., with Van Zeyl, taking first prize; after year in the army, settled in Boston, 1896, as teacher and pianist with Boston Symph. Orch., etc.; 1908 toured Europe.

Buongiorno (boo-ōn-jôr'-nō), **Crescenzo,** Bonito, 1864—Dresden, Nov. 7, 1903; c. operas.

Buononcini. Vide BONONCINI.

Burbure de Wesembeck (bür-bür dŭ vä-zäṅ-bĕk), **Léon Ph. M.,** Chevalier de, Termonde, 1812—Antwerp, 1889; Flemish nobleman; writer and composer.

Bürde-Ney (bür'-dĕ-nī'), Jenny, Graz, 1826—Dresden, 1886; soprano; 1855, m. the actor E. Bürde.

Burette (bü-rĕt), P. J., Paris, 1665—1747; Prof. of Medicine, Paris Univ.; writer on Greek music.

Burgk (boorkh'), Joachim Moller (or Müller), called Joachim A. Burgk (or Burg, or Burck), Burg, near Magdeburg; ca. 1541—Mülhausen, Thuringia, May 24, 1610; organist and eminent composer of Protestant music.

Burgmein, J., pen-name of "Giulio Ricordi."

Burgmüller (boorkh'-mül-lĕr), Norbert, Düsseldorf, 1810—Aix-la-Chapelle, 1836; pianist and composer.

Burgstaller (boorkh'-shtäl-lĕr), Alois, b. Holzkirchen, Sept. 27, 1871; tenor; studied with Bellurth and Kniese; sang small rôles at Bayreuth from 1894, "Siegfried" (1897); "Siegmund" (1899); sang Met. Op., from 1903.

Bur'leigh, (1) Cecil, b. Wyoming, N. Y., April 17, 1885; violinist; studied in Berlin with Grünberg and Witek (vln.), Leichtentritt (comp.) and in Chicago with Sauret, Hugo Heermann and Felix Borowski; made concert tours, and taught after 1909 in Denver, Sioux City and Missoula; res. in N. Y., 1919-21; thereafter taught at Univ. of Wis. (vln.); c. violin works and songs. (2) Harry Thacker, b. Erie, Pa., Dec. 2, 1866; Negro barytone and composer; studied Nat'l. Cons. in N. Y., where he has lived since 1892; active as concert singer in U. S. and Europe; has c. or arr. more than 100 songs, esp. spirituals; d. Stamford, Conn., 1949.

Burmeister (boor'-mī-shtĕr), (1) Richard, Hamburg, 1860—Berlin, Feb. 9, 1944; pupil Liszt, accompanying him as he travelled; teacher Hamburg Cons.; for 12 years head of pf. dept., Peabody Inst., Baltimore; 1898, dir. N. Y. Scharwenka Cons.; 1903-06, Dresden Cons.; 1906-25, lived in Berlin; 1925-33 in Merano; c. pf.-concerto (op. 1), "The Chase after Fortune" ("Die Jagd nach dem Glück"), a symphonic fantasy in 3 movements; rescored Chopin's F minor concerto, and wrote orch. accomp. for Liszt's "Pathetic" concerto. (2) Dory (née Peterson), b.

Oldenburg, 1860; pianist; wife of above.

Burmester (boor'-mä-shtĕr), Willy, Hamburg, March 16, 1869—Jan. 16, 1933; violin-virtuoso; studied with his father and Joachim; toured with his sister, a concert-pianist. Von Bülow aided him and brought public attention to his abilities; toured Europe, and 1899, America. Long a leading virtuoso, but in later years also a serious interpreter; revisited America a few years before his death.

Bur'ney, Chas., Shrewsbury, England, 1726—Chelsea, 1814; toured Europe; Mus. Doc. Oxon, 1769; pub. very interesting and gossipy "The Present State of Music in France and Italy," etc. (1771); "do. in Germany, the Netherlands," etc. (1773); "General History of Music" (4 vols., 1776–89), etc.

Bur'rian, Carl (rightly Karel Burian), Rausinow near Rakonitz, Jan. 12, 1870—Senomat, Sept. 25, 1924; opera tenor; pupil of Pivoda in Prague; début, 1891, in Brünn; sang in Reval, Cologne, Hanover, Hamburg; 1898-1911 at the Dresden Op.; then several years in Vienna and Budapest; at Met. Op., N. Y., and at Bayreuth.

Bur'rowes, J. Freckleton, London, 1787—1852; organist, pianist and writer.

Bur'tius (or Burci (boor'-chē)) or Burzio (boor'-tsī-ō), Nicolaus, Parma, 1450—1518; wrote the earliest specimen of printed mensural music.

Bur'ton, Frederick R., Jonesville, Mich., 1861—Lake Hopatcong, N. J., 1909; graduated at Harvard; l. Yonkers, N. Y.; founded there, 1896, a choral society; c. pop. cantata "Hiawatha," etc.

Bus'by, Thos., Westminster, England, 1755—London, 1838; Mus. Doc.; composer and writer.

Busch, (1) Adolf, b. Siegen, Germany, Aug. 8, 1891—Guilford, Vt., June 9, 1952; studied at Cologne Cons.; first vln., Vienna Orch., 1912-18; toured as solo performer in European cities, 1918-22; in sonata recitals with Rudolf Serkin, pianist, and in trio with Serkin and H. Busch; succeeded Marteau as teacher at Berlin Hochsch., 1919, where formed string quartet; has toured in U. S., as soloist with leading orchs.; c. orchestral and chamber works, songs. (2) Carl,

Bjerre, Denmark, March 29, 1862—
Kan. City, Dec., 1943; pupil Brussels
Cons., with Gade, Svendsen, Godard
and others; res. in Kansas City, Mo.,
since 1887; org. and cond. Symph.
Orch. there for some years, beginning
1912; knighted by Danish Gov't.
same year; c. cantatas, orchestral
and chamber music works, anthems
and part-songs. (3) **Fritz,** b. Siegen,
Mar. 13, 1890—London, Sept. 14, 1951;
conductor; bro. of Adolf; studied at
Cologne Cons., conductor Riga Op.,
1909; summer concerts, Bad Pyrmont, 1910–12; choral director,
Gotha Musikverein, 1911–12; court
music director, Stuttgart, and cond.
Opera there, 1918; conductor Dresden Op. and Symph. Concerts, 1922
until 1933, during which time he
made guest tours to other countries
including U. S., where led N. Y.
Symph. Orch. as guest in 1925–26;
has conducted opera and concerts in
Buenos Aires, 1933 and subsequent
years; also led Mozart opera festivals
at Glyndebourne, Sussex, beginning
1934; with Met. Op., after 1946.

Busi (boo'-zē), (1) **Giu.,** Bologna, 1808
—1871; Prof. (2) **Alessandro,** Bologna, 1833—1895; son of above;
'cellist and conductor.

Busnois (bün-wä), **A.** (rightly **de Busne**
(dŭ bün)), d. 1481; Netherland contrapuntist.

Busoni (boo-sō'-nē), **Ferruccio Benvenuto,** Empoli, near Florence, April 1,
1866—Berlin, July 27, 1924; noted
comp. and pianist; pupil of his father
(**Fdo.**), clarinettist, and his mother
(*née* **Weiss**), a pianist; at 8, début
at Vienna; then studied with W. A.
Remy; 1881, toured Italy; at 15,
elected a member of the Reale Accademia Filarmonica, Bologna; 1886,
Leipzig, where he c. a fantastic opera,
a string-quartet (D min.), symphonic suite, etc.; 1888–89, Prof.
Helsingfors Cons.; 1890, won Rubinstein prizes for comp. and pf.-playing,
with a *Concertstück* for pf. and orch.,
op. 31a; sonata for pf. and vln.; pf.
arr. of Bach's Eb *Organ Prelude,* and
Fugue; and other pf. pcs. incl. 2
Cadenzas to Beethoven's *Concerto in
G;* 1890, Prof. in the Moscow Imp.
Cons.; 1891–93 at New England
Cons., Boston; in 1907 he succeeded
Sauer as teacher of the master class
at Vienna Cons.; 1911 toured
America; 1913–15, dir. Bologna

Liceo; 1915, took up residence in
Zurich; after 1920, taught master
class in comp. at Berlin Acad. of
Arts. He made notable transcriptions of Bach organ works for piano,
which have held a place in the
repertoire; also Liszt piano pieces;
mem. Legion of Honour, 1913. Wrote
treatise on notation (1910); edited
Bach's *"Well-tempered Clavichord"*
with études; other comps., *"Lustspiel Ouvertüre";* 4 choruses with
orch.; 2 suites for orch.; a *"Sym-
phonisches Tongedicht"* for orch.,
symph. tone-poem *"Pojohla's Tochter,"* festival overture, 1897; music
to *"Berceuse élégiaque,"* for orch.;
wrote *"Entwurf einer neuen Aesthe-
tik der Tonkunst."* His opera, *"Der
Brautwahl,"* was prod. Hamburg,
April 13, 1912, based on Hoffman's
"Serapeons' Brüder." His operas
"Turandot" and *"Arlecchino"* were
planned on old Italian *"Commedia
dell' Arte"* (latter, Zurich, 1918). He
left unfinished an opera, *"Doktor
Faust,"* on which he had worked for
many years; completed by Jarnach,
it was prod. with succ. (Dresden,
1925). Wrote memoirs.

Büsser (büs-sā), **Henri,** b. Toulouse,
Jan. 16, 1872; pupil of Guiraud and
Gounod; took first Grand Prix de
Rome, with cantata *"Antigone";*
1892, organist at St. Cloud; after
1902, cond. at Op.-Comique; c. succ.
1-act pastorale *"Daphnis et Chloe"*
(Paris, Op. Com.), 1897; cantata
"Amadis de Gaule," 1892 (taking 2d
Grand Prix de Rome); ballets
"Colomba" and *"Les Noces Corin-
thiennes";* *"Sommeil de l'Enfant
Jesus"* for vln. and orch.; also over-
tures, suites, organ works, harp and
orch. comp. Member, Institut de
France.

Bussler (boos'-lĕr), **L.,** Berlin, Nov. 26,
1838—Jan. 18, 1901; theorist; son of
the painter-author, Robert Bussler;
pupil of von Hertzberg, Dehn, Grell,
and Wieprecht; 1865, teacher of
theory, Ganz School of Music; from
1879, at the Stern Cons., Berlin;
critic and writer of various treatises.

Bussmeyer (boos'-mī-ĕr), (1) **Hugo,**
Brunswick, 1842—Rio de Janeiro, ?;
pianist; pupil of K. Richter, Litolff
(pf.), and Methfessel (comp.); 1860,
toured in South America; 1860, N.
Y.; settled in Rio de Janeiro; composer and writer. (2) **Hans,** Bruns-

wick, 1853—Poecking, Sept. 21, 1930; bro. of above; pianist; pupil of Royal School of Music at Munich, and teacher there, 1874; also studied with Liszt; toured S. America, 1872–74; 1879, founded Munich Choral Society.

Bustini (boos-tē'-nē), **Aless.; b.** Rome, Dec. 24, 1876; Italian composer, prod. succ. opera *"Maria Dulcis,"* Rome, 1902; libretto by Luigi Ilica.

Buths (boots), **Julius,** Wiesbaden, May 7, 1851—Düsseldorf, March 12, 1920; pianist; pupil of his father (an oboist), also of Gernsheim, Hiller and Kiel; 1871–72, cond. the "Cecilia," at Wiesbaden; 1873, won Meyerbeer Scholarship, and lived in Milan and Paris; 1875–79, cond. in Breslau; in Elberfeld, 1879–90; cond. Mus. Soc. at Elberfeld; 1890–1908, civic mus. dir., Düsseldorf and, 1902, head of Cons. there; c. concerto, etc., for pf.

Butt, Clara, Southwick, Sussex, Feb. 1, 1873—near Oxford, Jan. 23, 1936; eminent English contralto; won scholarship at London R. C. M.; pupil of Bouhy and Mme. Gerster; début, London, 1892; toured America several times after 1899; long a favourite soloist at festivals in Great Britain, and one of the most popular concert singers of her day; made world tour in 1913–14 with her husband, R. Kennerly Rumford, barytone; works esp. written for her included Elgar's *"Sea Pictures";* Dame Commander of the British Empire.

Butterworth, George, London, July 12, 1885—died in battle, at Pozières, Aug. 5, 1916; composer; grad. of Oxford Univ., studied music privately; a short time at R. College of Music; c. orch. works incl. *"A Shropshire Lad,"* chamber music and songs.

Buttstedt (boot'-shtĕt), **Jn. H.,** Bindersleben, 1666—Erfurt, 1727; writer of a famous defence of sol-mi-sa-tion; also organist and composer.

Buus (boos), **Jachet (Jacques) de,** Bruges (?), 1510—Vienna, 1565; Flemish cptist; 1541, asst. organist, San Marco.

Buxtehude (boox'-tĕ-hoo-dĕ), **Dietrich,** Helsingör (Elsinore), Denmark, 1637—Lübeck, 1707; organist; 1673, he established the "Abendmusiken," which J. S. Bach walked 50 miles to hear; great composer of fugues and suites.

Byrd (Byrde, Bird, or **Byred), Wm.;**

according to his will, discovered in 1897, he was born London, 1542, or 1543 (not 1538 or 1546, as stated); d. July 4, 1623; organist and notable English composer, in whose work there is much modernity; 1554, organist; 1563, choirmaster and organist Lincoln Cathedral; 1575, procured with Tallis, his former teacher, an exclusive patent for the privilege of printing music and selling music-paper; has been called "English Palestrina" for his supreme church choral music; also celebrated for his harpsichord comps.

C

Caballero (kä-bä-yä'-rō), **Manuel Fernandez,** Murcia, March 14, 1835—Madrid, Feb. 20, 1906; pupil of Fuertes (harm.) and Eslava (comp.), Madrid Cons.; c. pop. *Zarzuelas* (v. D. D.) and church-music.

Cabel (kǎ-bĕl), rightly **Cabu,** (1) **Ed.,** singer Op. Com., Paris. (2) **Marie Josephe** (née **Dreulette**), Liége, 1827—1885; sister-in-law, or perhaps mother, of above; soprano.

Cabezon (kǎ'-bä-thôn), (1) **(Felix), Antonio De,** Santander, March 30, 1510—May 26, 1566; composer; cembalist and organist to Philip II; called "The Spanish Bach"; blind from birth; c. harp and lute pieces, published in 1578 by his son (2) **Hernando,** who succeeded him.

Cabo (kä'-bō), **Francisco Javier,** Naguera, near Valencia, 1768—Valencia, 1832; organist, conductor and composer.

Caccini (kät-chē'-nē), **Giulio** (called **Romano**), Rome, ca. 1546—Florence, 1618; a revolutionary composer well called "The father of a new style of music"; studied singing and flute-playing with Scipione della Palla. Wrote and sang *"Musica in Stile Rappresentativo,"* and c. *"Il Raptimento di Cefalo"* (Oct. 9, 1600), the first opera ever publicly prod.; he had also set to music other works by Bardi (q. v.), and collaborated with Peri (q. v.) in *"Dafne,"* the first opera ever composed. He c. also a novel set of madrigals justly called *"Le nuove musiche,"* and other works of notable originality and importance to progress.

Cadman, Charles Wakefield, b. Johnstown, Pa., Dec. 24, 1881; at 13 began piano studies, at 19 composed a comic opera, prod. at Pittsburgh, but did not study composition till 20; pupil of W. K. Steiner (organ), Luigi von Kunits (orchestration), with critical advice from Emil Paur; took up Indian music, 1906 published *"Four Indian Songs";* 1909 spent summer among the Omaha Indians, taking phonograph records and transcribing them; gives lecture-recitals on Indian music. C. *"Three Moods"* for symph. orch.; chamber music; cantata for male voices *"The Vision of Sir Launfal,"* Japanese romance for two voices, *"Sayonara";* three *"Songs to Odysseus";* Indian songs, operas, *"Shanewis"* (Met. Op., 1918); *"Witch of Salem"* (Chicago Op., 1926); *"Sunset Trail"* (Denver, Col., 1922); *"Garden of Mystery"* (N. Y., 1925); song cycle, *"White Enchantment";* also *"Dark Dancers of the Mardi Gras"* for piano and orch., in which the comp. has played as soloist with orchs.; d. Los Angeles, Dec. 30, 1946.

Cafaro (kä-fä'-rō), **Pasq.** (called **Caffariel'lo**), San Pietro, Glatina, Italy, 1706—Naples, 1787; noted composer; c. operas, oratorios, a notable *"Stabat mater,"* etc.

Caffarelli (rightly **Gaetano Majorano**) (käf-fä-rĕl'-lĭ), Bari, April 16, 1703—Santo-Dorato, near Naples, Nov. 30, 1783; famous male soprano; discovered as a peasant boy, by Caffaro, a musician, he took the name Caffarelli out of gratitude; he studied 5 years with Porpora; was a skilful sight-reader and harpsichordist, a marvellous singer of florid music, and also gifted with pathos; had most successful début, Rome, 1724, in a female rôle, and sang with enormous success everywhere except London; made money enough to buy a dukedom.

Caffi (käf'-fē), **Fran.,** Venice, 1780—Padua, 1874; writer.

Cagnoni (kän-yō'-nĭ), **A.,** Godiasco, 1828—Bergamo, 1896; conductor and dram. composer.

Cahen (kä-än), (1) **Ernest,** Paris, 1828—1893; pianist and dram. composer. (2) **Albert,** Paris, Jan. 8, 1846—Cap d'Ail, March, 1903; pianist; pupil of Mme. Szarvady and César Franck; c. *"Jean le Précurseur,"* biblical poem (1874); com. opera *"Le Bois"* (1880, Op. Com.); fairy opera *"La Belle au Bois Dormant"* (Geneva, 1886); 4-

act opera *"Le Vénitien"* (Rouen, 1890); unsucc. opera *"La Femme de Claude"* (Paris, Op. Com., 1896), etc.

Cahier (kä-yā), **Mme. Charles** (née **Walker**), b. Nashville, Tenn., Jan. 6, 1875—Manhattan Beach, Cal., Apr. 15, 1951; sang in concerts, then studied with Jean de Reszke; début in opera as "Orfeo" (Nice, 1904); sang in other cities and from 1909 at Vienna Royal Opera. 1912 at Met. Op., N. Y.; also widely in concert; a noted contralto and teacher.

Caimo (kä'-ē-mö), **Joseffo,** b. Milan, ca. 1540; composer.

Caland (kä'-länt), **Elizabeth,** Rotterdam, Jan. 30, 1862—Berlin, Jan. 26, 1929; teacher and author of piano methods.

Caldara (käl-dä'-rä), **A.,** Venice, 1670—Vienna, Dec. 28, 1736; court-conductor and noted composer, Vienna; c. operas, 70 sacred dramas, etc.

Cal'dicott, Alfred Jas., Worcester, England, 1842 — near Gloucester, Oct. 24, 1897; organist of St. Stephen's Church, Worcester, and Corporation organist; 1883, prof. at R. C. M., London; from 1885, cond. at the Albert Palace; c. cantatas, 13 operettas, etc.

Calegari (käl-ā-gä'-rē), (1) (or **Callegari**) **Fran. A.,** d. Padua, 1740?; a Franciscan monk, 1702–24; conductor and writer at Venice, then Padua. (2) **A.,** Padua, 1757—1828; dram. composer and writer.

Cal'kin, J. Bapt., London, March 16, 1827—May 15, 1905; pianist, organist and composer; prof. Guildhall School of Mus.; pub. services, etc.

Callaerts (käl'-lärts), **Jos.,** Antwerp, Aug. 22, 1838—March 3, 1901; pupil of Lemmens at Brussels Cons.; organist at Antwerp Cathedral, and teacher at the Music School from 1867; c. a prize symphony and pf. trio, comic opera; *"Le Retour Imprévu"* (Antwerp, 1889), etc.

Call'cott, (1) **J. Wall,** Kensington, Nov. 20, 1766—May 15, 1821; mainly self-taught; organist; 1789 he won all the prizes offered by the "Catch Club"; 1790, pupil of Haydn; 1800, Mus. Doc. (Oxon); 1806, lectured at the Royal Institute; projected unfinished musical dictionary; mental disorder overtook him before it was concluded; his *"Grammar of Music"* (1806) is standard.

(2) **Wm. Hutchins**, Kensington, 1807 —London, 1882, son of above; organist and pianist.

Calliope (kăl-lī'-ō-pĕ or kăl-lē'-ō-pā), the Greek muse of heroic verse.

Calo'ri, Angiola, Milan, 1732—1790; soprano.

Calsabigi (kăl-sä-bē'-jē), **Raniero da**, Livorno, 1715 — Naples, 1795; Gluck's librettist and aide in opera-reformation.

Calvé (kăl-vä), **Emma (de Roquer)**, Décazeville, France, 1863 (1866?) —Millau, France, Jan. 6 (?) 1942; soprano; pupil of Marchesi and Pugets; 1882, début in Massenet's "*Hérodiade*," Th. de la Monnaie, Brussels; 1884, Paris Th. Italien; 1885, Op. Com.; also in London; after 1893 sang in New York, making great furore with her inimitable and rakish "Carmen"; also feted for her "Santuzza," "Juliette," etc., at Met. Op.; a concert singer of note; she was an Officier d'Académie and lived in Paris.

Calvis'ius, Sethus (rightly **Seth Kallwitz** (kăl'-vēts)), Feb. 21, 1556—Leipzig, Nov. 24, 1615; son of a peasant; singer for alms, then as a teacher obtained funds to study; (1581) mus. dir.; writer of important treatises and composer.

Calvocores'si, Michel D., b. Marseilles (of Greek parents), Oct. 2, 1877; critic and musicologist; studied Paris Cons.; writer and lecturer on French and especially Russian music; wrote biogs. of Liszt, Moussorgsky, Glinka, Schumann, and author of "*La Musique Russe*"; has contributed to many periodicals, and translated into French Rimsky-Korsakoff's treatise on orchestration, as well as mus. texts into various languages; lived London, where d. Feb. 1, 1944.

Calvör (kăl'-fär), **Kaspar**, Hildesheim, 1650—Clausthal, 1725; theorist.

Camar'go, (1) **Felix Antonio**, b. Guadalajara, 16th cent.; cathedral cond. at Valladolid; c. remarkable hymn to St. Iago, etc. (2) see CUPIS.

Cambert (kän-băr), **Rob.**, Paris, ca. 1628—London, 1677; first composer of French operas; organist at St. Honoré; 1659, "*La Pastorale*" was succ. prod. at the Château d'Issy; and followed by others on the texts of Perrin, who received letters patent for establishing the "Académie royale de musique" (now the Gr.

Opéra); with Perrin he also wrote the first genuine opera, "*Pomone*," prod. 1671, before Lully, who later took the patent for himself; he went to England where he died as Master of the Music to Charles II.

Cambini (käm-bē'-nē), **Giov. Giu.**, Leghorn, 1746—Bicêtre, 1825 (?); cond. at Paris, and prolific but cheap composer of over 60 symphonies, 144 string-quartets, several operas, etc.; he died in the almshouse.

Cam'eron, Basil, b. Reading, England, 1885; conductor; sang as choir boy; began vln. study at 8 with Otto Milani, harmony and comp. from Tertius Noble; 1902, studied with Joachim in Berlin, conducting with Hausmann; played in Queen's Hall Orch. as violinist, also studying with Auer; 1913 cond. Munic. Orch., Torquay, where gave a Wagner Fest.; after war in charge of music at Harrogate and Hastings; guest cond. R. Phil. Soc., London; 1930, cond. San Francisco Symph. with Dobrowen, re-engaged for 2nd season; after 1932, cond. Seattle Symph.; later again in England.

Camet'ti, Alberto, b. Rome, May 5, 1871—1935; pupil at Academy of St. Cecilia; organist of the French church of St. Louis at Rome; historian of music and comp.

Cam'idge, (1) **J.**, ca. 1735—Yorb Engl., 1803; organist York cath., 4 years; composer. (2) **Mat.**, York, 1764—1844; son and successor of above. (3) **J.**, York, 1790—1859; son and successor of (2).

Campagnoli (käm-pän-yō'-lē), **Bart.** Cento, 1751—Neustrelitz, 1827; vio linist and court-conductor.

Campana (käm-pä'-nä), **Fabio**, Leghorn, 1819—London, 1882; singing-teacher and dram. composer.

Campanari (käm-pä-nä'-rē), (1) **Leandro**, b. Rovigo, Italy, Oct. 20, 1857; pupil at Milan Cons.; toured Europe 2 years; America, 1879; lived in Boston; organised "C. String-quartet"; 1883 1st prof. of vln. in N. E. Cons.; 1890, 1st. prof. of vln. and head of orch. dept. Cincinnati Cons.; 1897-1905, conductor at Milan; 1906, at Manhattan Op. House, N. Y.; after 1907, taught in San Francisco; where d. April 23, 1939. (2) **Giuseppe**, Venice, Nov. 17, 1858—Milan, May 31, 1927; eminent dram. barytone; at first a 'cellist at Le

Scala; engaged to play in Boston Symph.; also in Adamowski Quartet; 1893, after vocal study, sang with Hinrichs Op. Co.; also with Juch and Grau companies; 1895–08, Met. Op.; later in Europe.

Campanini (käm-pä-nē'-nē), (1) **Italo,** Parma, 1846—Vigatto, near Parma, Nov. 22, 1896; operatic tenor, a blacksmith when discovered; début, 1869, at Odessa, without much success; then studied with Lamperti, and reappeared, Florence, 1871, as "Lohengrin," with great succ.; toured Europe and U. S. with Nilsson, Patti, etc. (2) **Cleofonte,** Parma, Sept. 1, 1860—Chicago, Dec. 19, 1919; conductor; pupil Milan Cons., later teacher there; cond. at La Scala, Covent Garden, and 1906–09, at Manhattan Opera House, New York; married Eva Tetrazzini, operatic soprano (sister and teacher of Luisa); from 1910 he was cond. and after 1913 artistic dir. of the Chicago Op. Co. He was instrumental in founding the Edith Rockefeller McCormick Prize for opera composers at the Milan Cons.

Campbell-Tipton, Louis, Chicago, Nov. 21, 1877—Paris, May 1, 1921; studied in Chicago, Boston and Leipzig; lived in Paris; his important compositions played abroad, notably his "*Heroic*" sonata for piano, piano suites, "*The Four Seasons,*" "*Suite Pastorale,*" for piano and violin; also c. striking songs.

Cam'pion, (1) **Thos.,** d. London, Feb., 1620; English physician, poet, dramatist and noteworthy writer and composer; pub. two books of Ayres, etc. (1610); 2 more (1612). (2) **Fran.,** 1703–19, theorbist, Paris Gr. Opéra.

Campio'ni, Carlo A., Leghorn, ca. 1720 —Florence, 1793; court-conductor.

Camporese (käm-pō-rä'-zĕ), **Violante,** b. Rome, 1785; operatic sopr. of Napoleon's private music; début, London, 1817; retired, 1829.

Campos (käm'pōs), **João Ribeiro de Almeida de,** b. Vizen, Portugal, ca. 1770; cond. and professor.

Campra (kän-prä), (1) **André,** Dec. 4, 1660—Versailles, July 29, 1744; cond. at Nôtre Dame; prod. 2 succ. operas under his bro.'s name and gave up church-mus.; cond. Royal Orch. and c. 18 operas. (2) **Jos.,** bro. of above; double-bass player.

Camps y Soler (kämps ē sō'-lär), **Oscar,** Alexandria, Nov. 21, 1837--Madrid, ?; Spanish pianist; pupil of Döhler and Mercadante; played in public at 13; lived in Madrid; writer and theorist.

Canal (kä'-näl), **Abbate Pietro,** Crespano, April 13, 1807—Dec. 15, 1883; historian and comp.

Canale (or **Canali**) (kä-nä'-lē), **Floriano,** organist at Brescia, 1585–1603; c. church-music.

Candeille (käṅ-dĕ'-yŭ), (1) **P. Jos.,** Estaires, 1744 — Chantilly, 1827; dram. composer. (2) (**Simons-Candeille**) **Amélie Julie,** Paris, 1767 —1834; operatic sopr., actress, and composer; daughter of above; lived in Paris as teacher; she wrote libretto and music of the succ. operetta "*La Belle Fermière*" (1792); she played the leading rôle and sang to her own accomp. on piano and harp.

Cange (dü känzh), **Chas.-Dufrêsne,** sieur du, Amiens, 1610—Paris, 1688; lawyer and lexicographer.

Cannabich (kän'-nä-bĭkh), (1) **Chr.,** Mannheim, 1731—Frankfort, 1798; noteworthy violinist and conductor, a pioneer in orchestral diminuendo; son of (2) **Mathias,** a flutist in the Electoral Orch. at Mannheim of which **Chr. C.** became leader in 1765, and cond. 1775. (3) **K.,** Mannheim, 1764—Munich, 1806; son of (1); court-conductor. (4) **Rose,** b. about 1762 according to Mozart, whose pupil she was; daughter of (2); pianist.

Canniciari (kän-nē-chä'-rē), **Don Pompeo,** d. Rome, 1744; conductor; comp.

Cantelli, Guido, b. Novara, 1920; guest cond., N. Y. Philh-Symphony, 1951.

Capet (kä-pā'), **Lucien,** Paris, Jan. 8, 1873—Dec. 19, 1928; violinist and chamber music performer; pupil of Paris Cons., where won 1st prize; taught at Bordeaux; after 1907 led chamber music classes at Paris Cons., and after 1924 artistic dir. of Paris Inst. de Violon; founded noted Capet Quartet in 1903, with which he appeared with succ. in many European cities.

Caplet (käp-lā), **André,** Havre, Nov. 25, 1878—Paris, April 24, 1925; eminent composer; pupil of Wollett; violinist at Havre Theatre, 1896; pupil of Leroux at Paris Cons., winning first harmony prize, 1898, and Prix de Rome, 1901; lived in Rome, then in Germany; acted as

DICTIONARY OF MUSICIANS 91

assistant to Colonne, 1898; 1900, was
the first to cond. Debussy's *"Martyre
de San Sebastien"*; 1911–12 cond. at
Boston Op.; also at Covent Garden,
London; c. piano quintet; *"Legend"*
for harp and orch. after Poe's
"Masque of the Red Death"; *"Suite
Persane"* for wood-winds; Septet for
three women's voices and strings;
Mass for three-part women's chorus;
Sonata for voice, 'cello and piano;
"Le Miroir de Jésus," 15 pieces for
soloists, chorus and orch., which has
been perf. frequently in France; a
number of songs and choruses.

Capocci (kä-pôt'-chē), (1) **Gaetano,**
Rome, Oct. 16, 1811—Jan. 11, 1898;
notable teacher; pub. much sacred
music. (2) **Filippo,** Rome, May 11,
1840—July 25, 1911; son of above;
Italian organist; 1875 organist of
San Giovanni at the Lateran; c.
works for organ.

Capoul (kä-pool) (**Jos. Amédée**), **Victor,** Toulouse, Feb. 27, 1839—Pujan-
dran-du-Gers, Feb. 18, 1924; tenor;
pupil of Révial and Mocker, Paris
Cons.; 1861–72 at the Op. Com.;
1892 prof. of operatic singing in Nat.
Cons., New York; 1897, stage manager, Paris Opéra.

Capuzzi (kä-pood'-zē), **Giuseppe Antonio,** Brescia, 1753–1818; c. 5 operas,
etc.

Caraccioli (kä-rät-chō-'lē), **Luigi,** Andria
(Bari), 1849—London, 1887; dram.
composer.

Carado'ri-Allan, Maria C. R. (née de
Munck), Milan, 1800 — London,
1865; soprano.

Carafa de Colobrano (kä-rä'-fä dä
kō-lō-brä'-nō), **Michele Enrico,** Naples, Nov. 17, 1787—Paris, July 26,
1872; son of Prince Colobrano; while
very young c. an opera, 2 cantatas,
etc., with much success; 1837, member of the Academy; 1840, prof. of
comp. at Cons.; c. also ballets, cantatas, and good church-music.

Cardon (kăr-dôṅ), (1) **Louis,** Paris,
1747—Russia, 1805; harpist. (2) **P.,**
b. Paris, 1751; 'cellist and singer.

Cardo'so, Manuel, Fronteira, 1569;
Spanish priest and composer.

Caresana (kär-ä-sä'-nä), **Cristoforo,** b.
Tarentum, 1655; lived in Naples as
composer.

Carestini (kä-räs-tē'-nē), **Giov.** (stage
name **Cusanino**), Mente Filatrano
(Ancona), ca. 1705—1760; male soprano (musico).

Ca'rey, (1) **Henry,** 1685 (?)—London,
Oct. 4, 1743; a reputed natural son of
Marquis of Halifax, and disputed
composer of *"God Save the King"*;
c. the song *"Sally in Our Alley"*;
ballad operas, etc. (2) **Bruce,** b.
Hamilton, Ontario, 1877; conductor;
studied at R. Coll. of Music, London,
also in Florence and Munich;
founded and cond. Hamilton Elgar
Choir for 17 years; later Phila.
Mendelssohn Club and music dir. at
Girard Coll. there; succeeded the
late Dr. J. Fred Wolle as cond. of
Bethlehem Bach Choir, 1933–8

Carissimi (kä-rĭs'-sē-mē), **Giacomo,**
Marino, near Rome, ca. 1604—
Rome, Jan. 12, 1674; ca. 1624,
church-conductor at Rome; important ch.-composer and writer; many
of his MSS. are lost; 5 oratorios and
other pieces remain.

Carl, Wm. Crane, Bloomfield, N. J.,
March 2, 1865—New York, Dec. 8,
1936; pupil of S. P. Warren, Mad
Schiller (pf.) and Guilmant, Paris;
after 1892, organist First Presby.
Ch., N. Y.; made tours as concert-
organist; 1899, founded Guilmant
Organ School, New York; had pub.
collections of organ music; active as
lecturer.

Car'michael, Mary Grant, Birkenhead,
Engl., 1851—London, March 17,
1935; pupil of O. Beringer, W. Bache,
and F. Hartvigson (pf.) and E.
Prout (comp.); accompanist; c. operetta, *"The Snow Queen"*; a pf.-suite;
and many pop. songs.

Carnicer (kär'-nē-thär), **Ramon,** Tar-
egga, Catalonia, Oct. 24, 1789—
Madrid, March 17, 1855; cond.
Royal Opera, Madrid, 1830–54, prof.
of comp. Madrid Cons.; one of the
creators of the *Zarzuela* (v. D. D.).

Caro (kä'rō), **Paul,** b. Breslau, Dec. 25,
1859; pupil of Schäffer and Scholz,
and Vienna Cons.; c. 2 operas, 5
symphs.; str-qts.; etc.; d. (?).

Caron (kä-rôṅ), (1) **Philippe,** 15th cent.,
cptist. (of Netherlands ?). (2) **Rose
Lucile** (née **Meuniez**), Monerville,
France, Nov. 17, 1857—Paris, April
9, 1930; soprano; after her marriage
entered Paris Cons., 1880, as pupil of
Tharset, later of Marie Sasse; début
Brussels, 1883; 1885–88, Opéra Paris;
1888–90, Brussels; from 1890, Opéra
Paris; also at the Op. Com., from
1902 prof. at the Cons. She created
many of the chief rôles in modern

French Opera and in French versions of Wagner. She sang "Salammbô" at the Opéra, 1908.

Carpani (kär-pä'-nē), **Giu. A., b.** Vilalbese (Como), 1752—Vienna, 1825; writer.

Car'penter, John Alden, b. Park Ridge, Ill., Feb. 28, 1876—May, 1951; grad. Harvard Univ.; studied with Bernard Ziehn and Seeboeck; a prominent business executive in Chicago, he has made much more than an avocation of music, taking his place among the most accomplished American comps.; his musical idiom is modern and his output fairly large. C. (ballets) *"The Birthday of the Infanta"* (Chicago Op., 1919-20); *"Krazy Kat"; "Skyscrapers"* (Met. Op., 1926); the orch. works, *"Adventures in a Perambulator"*; symphony (Norfolk Fest., 1917); concertino with piano; *"Sea Drift"* (N. Y. Philh., 1935); also a string quartet (Coolidge Fest., Washington); violin sonata; *"Water Colors"* for mezzo-soprano and chamber orch.; *"Improving Songs for Anxious Children"*; and many songs incl. the cycle *"Gitanjali."*

Carpentras (Il **Carpentras'so**). Vide ELEAZER GENET.

Carré (kär-rā), (1) **Louis,** Clofontaine Brie, 1663—Paris, 1711; writer. (2) **Albert, b.** Strassburg, June 22, 1852; 1898-1912, dir. Op. Com., Paris; librettist; d. Paris, Dec. 12, 1938.

Carreño (kär-rän'-yō), **Teresa,** Caracas, Venezuela, Dec. 22, 1853—New York, June 13, 1917; pupil of L. M. Gottschalk, and G. Mathias; notable pianist; played in public at 12; at 22 toured the U. S.; 1889-90 toured Germany with much success; for some years wife of E. Sauret; then of Giov. Tagliapietra; 1892-95, wife of Eugen d'Albert; 1902, m. Arturo Tagliapietra, bro. of Giov. T.; c. a string-quartet and pf. salon pieces. Her daughter **Teresita Tagliapietra,** also a pianist.

Carreras (kä-rä'-räs), **Maria, b.** Italy; pianist; at six awarded 1st prize at Acad. of Santa Cecilia, Rome, by Liszt, then hon. pres. of this school; studied with Sgambati, under whose baton at 15 she played his concerto with Rome Philh. with much succ.; immediately engaged for concerts in Russia with Imp. Music. Soc. under Safonoff; toured widely in Europe

and South America; later in U. S., where she has been res. for some years and has given master classes.

Carrillo (kär-ē'-yō), **Julian, b.** Mexico. 1875; composer who has embodied novel harmonic system in his orch., chamber music and choral works; also author of *"Synthetic Treatise of Harmony."*

Carro'dus, J. Tiplady, Keighley (Yorkshire), 1836—London, 1895; violinist.

Car'ron, Arthur (rightly **Cox**), **b.** England; tenor; pupil of Florence Easton; sang with Old Vic. Op. Co., London; début, Met. Op. Co., summer popular season, 1936, as Canio; engaged for regular roster of company following unusual succ. in this rôle.

Carse, Adam, b. Newcastle-on-Tyne, May 19, 1878; pupil R. A. M., with the Macfarren scholarship; made an associate there in 1902; c. symph. in C minor; symph. in G minor, symph. poem, *"In a Balcony"*; concert overture, etc.; writer on music.

Car'ter, (1) **Thos.,** Ireland, ca. 1735—London, 1804; composer. (2) **Ernest Trow, b.** Orange, N. J., 1866; organist, conductor, composer; studied New York and Berlin; org. of Amer. Ch. in latter city and 1899-1901 at Princeton Univ.; c. comic op., *"The Blonde Donna"*; opera, *"The White Bird"* (Chicago, 1924; Osnabrück, Germany, 1927); pantomime, *"Namba"*; d. Wallack's Pt., Conn., 1953.

Cartier (kärt-yā), **J. Bap.,** Avignon, 1765—Paris, 1841; violinist and dram. composer.

Carulli (kä-rool'-lē), (1) **Fdo.,** Naples, 1770—Paris, 1841; self-taught guitar-virtuoso and teacher; c. 400 concertos. (2) **Gustavo,** Leghorn, 1801—Bologna, 1876; son of above; teacher and dram. composer.

Caruso (kä-roo'-zō), **Luigi,** Naples, 1754—Perugia, 1821; conductor, c. 69 operas. (2) **Enrico,** Naples, Feb. 25, 1873—Aug. 2, 1921; famous Italian tenor; pupil of Vergine; début, 1895, winning gradual success in Italy (Naples, 1898; 1899 La Scala), and creating the tenor rôles in Giordano's *"Fedora,"* Cilea's *"Lécouvreur,"* and Franchetti's *"Germania"*; 1899-1903 sang in St. Petersburg and Buenos Aires; 1902, appeared with Melba at Monte Carlo, began his tremendous vogue;

1902 at Covent Garden; 1903–21, Met. Op. House, N. Y.; 1908, his voice was threatened, but an operation restored it. He created the tenor rôle in Puccini's "*Girl of the Golden West,*" in addition to a large number of first Amer. perfs. His repertoire incl. more than 50 rôles, chiefly in Italian and French works, both old and modern. In his later years the voice which was unique among singers of his period for robustness of timbre and fine cultivation, changed slightly from its earlier lyric quality to a darker dram. colour. His powers of characterisation developed also and he made a deep and poignant impression as Eleazar in "*La Juive,*" the rôle he last sang at the Met. Op., Christmas Eve, 1920, when stricken with a hemorrhage of the throat. An emergency operation later performed to relieve an abscessed condition of one lung resulted in a partial convalescence and he sailed for Naples, but passed away suddenly there during the summer. He was for long the most fêted vocalist throughout the world and sang for the highest fees in European capitals, but from 1903 made N. Y. his headquarters. A clever cartoonist, he pub. a book of his drawings and also c. several popular songs.

Carvalho (kär-văl'-ō) (rightly **Carvaille**), (1) **Léon**, in a French colony, 1825—Paris, 1897; from 1875 dir. Op. Com. (2) **Carvalho-Miolan** (mē-ô-läṅ), **Caroline M.-Félix**, Marseilles, 1827—Puys, near Dieppe, 1895; soprano; wife of above; début 1849.

Ca'ry, Annie Louise, Wayne, Kennebec County, Me., Oct. 22, 1842—Norwalk, Conn., April 13, 1921; noted operatic and concert contralto; studied in Boston and Milan, also with Viardot-Garcia, etc.; début 1868, at Hamburg; later Stockholm, Copenhagen, Brussels, London, New York (1870), St. Petersburg (1875); 1882, m. C. M. Raymond, Cincinnati.

Casadesus (cäs-ä-děs-üs'), (1) **Francis,** b. Paris, Dec. 2, 1870; conductor, composer; studied Paris Cons., with Lavignac and Franck (harmony prize); Tremont Prize, French Inst.; cond. symph. concerts, Trocadero, Paris, 1918–24; dir. American Cons., Fontainebleau, 1921–23; has cond. radio concerts and been active as

music critic; among his dram. works, "*Un Beau Jardin de France*" was given at Paris Op. Comique, 1918; also c. orchestral works and songs. (2) **Henri,** b. Paris, Sept. 30, 1879; violist; dir. Société des Instruments Anciens, which he founded in collaboration with Saint-Saëns, 1901; of which members are Henri, viole d'amour; Marius C., quinton; Maurice Devilliers, basse de viole; Lucette C., viole de gambe, and Regina C.-Patorni, clavecin; this group has toured widely in Europe, also visiting U. S., and presenting programmes of rare interest from historical standpoint; C. has also been a collector of old music and insts.; Chev. of the Legion of Honor; d. in Paris, May 31, 1947. (3) **Marius,** b. Paris, Oct. 24, 1892; violinist; studied Paris Cons., 1st prize, 1914; c. works for vln., orch., voice, 'cello, also chamber music; has appeared as vln. soloist with Boston Symph. Orch. (4) **Robert,** b. Paris, April 7, 1899; pianist; received early training from Mme. Marie Simon, an aunt; at 13 entered Paris Cons., winning 1st prize in piano; has appeared widely in concerts in France, Belgium, Holland, etc., after 1935–36 in U. S., where made début as soloist with N. Y. Philh.; dir. piano dept., Amer. Cons., Fontainebleau.

Casali (kä-sä'-lē), **Giov. Bat.,** d. 1792; conductor and dram. composer.

Casals', Pablo, b. Vendrell, Spain, Dec. 30, 1876; eminent 'cellist; pupil of Jose Garcia, Rodereda and Breton; 1897, prof. at Barcelona Cons.; toured widely; c. "*La Vision de Fray Martin,*" for chorus and orch.; 'cello pieces, etc.; after 1919 cond. of Orquesta Pau Casals, Barcelona, and made few concert appearances as 'cellist; member of noted trio including Cortot and Thibaud; m. Guilhermina Suggia, 'cellist, 1906; divorced, 1912; (2) Susan Metcalfe, singer; lived in France after 1938.

Casamorata (kä-sä-mō-rä'-tä), **Luigi Fdo.,** Würzburg, 1807—Florence, 1881; editor, writer, and composer.

Casati (kä-sä'-tē), **Gasparo,** d. Novara, 1643; cond. at Novara Cathedral; c. church music.

Casa'vola, Franco, b. Bari, Italy, July 13, 1892; composer; pupil of La Rotella, Mapelli and Respighi; his music has been called "futuristic" and includes various ballets and a comic opera, *"Il Gobbo del Califfo,"* which won 1st prize in a nat'l. contest and was given at the Rome R. Op., 1929.

Case, Anna, b. Clinton, N. J., Oct. 29, 1889; soprano; studied with Augusta Ohrstrom-Renard; mem. Met. Op. Co., 1909–16; has also sung in concerts and at festivals; m. Clarence H. Mackay, chm. board of directors, N. Y. Philh. Soc.

Casel'la, P., (1) Pieve (Umbria), 1769 —Naples, 1843; dram. composer. (2) Alfredo, b. Turin, Italy, July 25, 1883—Rome, March 3, 1947; composer; studied with Diémer, Leroux and Fauré, Paris Cons., 1st piano prize, 1899; début, Paris, 1911; cond. popular concerts, Trocadero, Paris, 1912; prof. advanced pf., Paris Cons., 1912–15; also at Liceo Musicale di S. Cecilia, Rome, 1915; has served as guest cond. of many orchs. in various Eur. and Amer. cities; leading spring concert series with Boston Symph. Orch., 1927–29; is best known as a versatile, somewhat eclectic but highly accomplished composer of works in modern idiom, incl. *"Italia,"* rhapsody for orch.; the ballet, *"La Giara"* (Met. Op. House production, 1926–27); 2 symphonies; *"Prologue pour une Tragedie,"* *"Notte di Maggio"* (with chorus), string-quartet, 'cello sonata, and other chamber music, songs, piano pieces; Serenata for small chamber ensemble, etc. C. in 1917 founded a Societa di Musica Moderna in Rome; he has lectured in America and also appeared here with the Trio Italiano; winner in 1928 of 1st prize of Philadelphia Musical Fund Soc. for composition. Has also c. an opera, *"La Donna Serpente"* after a fairy tale by Gozzi (1932); symph. suite, *"Le Couvent sur l'Eau"* from a ballet of the same name; *"Elegia Eroica"* and *"Pagine di Guerra"* for orch.; *"Pupazzetti,"* 5 pieces for marionettes; *"Concerto Romano"* for organ and orch.; *"Siciliana e Burlesca"* for vln., 'cello and pf.; *"Cinque Pezzi"* for string-quartet, etc. His earlier style was markedly dissonantal as shown in his *"A Notte Alta"*; later comps. show a reversion to a simpler manner based on pre-classic models. Author, *"The Evolution of Music,"* *"Stravinsky,"* etc.

Caser'ta, Philippe de, Neapolitan theorist, 15th century.

Casimiro (kă-sē-mē'-rō), da Silva Joaquim, Lisbon, May 30, 1808— Dec. 28, 1862; Portuguese comp. of church music.

Casini (kä-sē'-nē), G. M., b. 1670 (?); Florentine priest; he tried to revive Greek modes.

Cassado (cä-sä'-dō), Gaspar, b. Barcelona, 1898; 'cellist; pupil of Casals; has toured widely as outstanding virtuoso, incl. Spain, France, Germany, Austria, and in 1936 for first time in U. S.; also active as composer; his Rapsodia Catalana played by N. Y. Philh. under Mengelberg, 1928; c. 3 string quartets, trio for piano, vln. and 'cello; ed. works of Mozart, Weber and Schubert.

Castagna (käs-tän'-yä), Bruna; Ital. mezzo-soph.; sang Met. Op. after 1935.

Castel (kăs-tĕl), Louis Bertrand, Montpellier, 1688—Paris, 1757; a Jesuit writer who attempted without success to construct a "Clavecin oculaire," to prod. colour harmonies.

Castellan (kăs-tel-läṅ), Jeanne A., b. Beaujeu, Oct. 26, 1819; retired, 1859; singer.

Castel'li, (1) Ignaz Fz., Vienna, 1781 —1862; editor.

Castelmary (kăs-tĕl-mä-rē) (stage name of Comte Armand de Castan), Toulouse, Aug. 16, 1834—New York, Feb. 9, 1897; barytone; died on the stage of the Met. Op., N. Y., just after the first act of *"Martha."*

Castelnuovo-Tedesco (cäs-tĕl-nŏŏ-ō'-vō tĕ-dĕs'-kō), Mario, b. Florence, April 3, 1895; composer; studied Cherubini Cons., Florence; composition with Pizzetti; c. opera *"La Mandragola,"* which won national lyric prize in 1925 and had première at Venice, 1926; "Italian" Concerto for vln. and orch., concerto for piano and orch. (1926); Symphonic Variations for vln. and orch. (N. Y. Philh., under Toscanini, 1930); also many madrigals, part-songs, songs and piano works; in the last category are some 30 *"Poemetti"* and 3 *"Poemi Campestri"*; he is known for his *"Three Chorales on Hebrew Melodies"* for voice and piano; also about 100 settings of lyrics in various languages, incl. original series of *"Shakespeare Songs"*; a trio, a quartet; *"Cipressi,"* an orch. sonata; *"Tre Fioretti di*

Santo Francesco" for voice and orch.; and "*Bacco in Toscana*," a "dithyramb in one act" for soloists, chorus, orch. and dancers, to a poem by Redi; has written extensively on music.

Castil-Blaze. Vide BLAZE, F. H. J.

Castillon (käs-tē-yôn), **Alexis de, Vicomte de Saint Victor,** Chartres, Dec. 13, 1838—Paris, March 5, 1873; composer; pupil of Massé and César Franck; c. symphony; overture, *Torquato Tasso, Psalm 84* with orch.; piano concerto and important chamber music.

Cas'tro, (1) **Jean de,** played Lyons, 1570; composer and lutenist. (2) **Juan Jose,** b. Buenos Aires, March 7, 1895; composer; pupil of d'Indy at Paris Schola Cantorum; cond. of orch. at Colon Theatre, in native city, introd. many modern scores; c. of orch. works, incl. "*Biblical*" *Symphony.*

Castrucci (käs-troot'-chē), (1) P., Rome, 1679—Dublin, 1752; violinist; leader of Händel's opera-orch.; inv. and played the *violetta marina.* His bro. (2) **Prospero** (d. London, 1769); violinist and composer.

Catalani (kät-ä-lä'-nē), (1) **Angelica,** Sinigaglia, Oct., 1780—Paris, June 12, 1849; famous operatic soprano of great beauty; her voice was notably flexible and reached to g''' (v. CHART OF PITCH); in 1806, at London, she earned over £16,000 ($80,000) in one year; 1814-17, she took up management of the Th. Italien, Paris, without succ. After final appearance, York festival, in 1828, she retired to her country-seat, near Florence. (2) **Alfredo,** Lucca, June 19, 1854—Milan, Aug. 6, 1893; pupil of his father, an organist; at 14, c. a mass sung at the cathedral; pupil of Magi, and of Paris Cons. and Milan Cons.; c. operas "*La Falce*" (Milan, 1875); "*Elda*" (Turin, 1880; revised as "*Loreley,*" 1890); "*Dejanice*" (1883); "*Ero e Leandro*" (1885), "*Edmea*" (1886), "*La Wally*" (La Scala, 1892); symph. poem "*Ero e Leandro,*" etc.

Catel (kä-těl), **Chas. Simon,** L'Aigle, Orne, 1773—Paris, 1830; dram. composer and writer.

Catelani (kät-ä-lä'-nē), **Angelo,** Guastalla, 1811—S. Martino di Mugnano, 1866; dram. composer and writer.

Catoire (kät-wär), **Georg L.,** Moscow, April 27, 1861—May, 1926; pupil

of Klindworth, Willborg, and Liadov; c. symphony; symph. poem, "*Mzyri*"; cantata, "*Russalka*," piano concerto, quintet, quartet and trio for strings, "*Poème*" for vln., choruses, songs, etc.

Catrufo (kä-troo'-fō), **Giu.,** Naples, 1771—London, 1851; dram. composer.

Caurroy (kōr-wä), **Fran. Eustache du,** sieur de St.-Fremin, Gerberoy, 1549—Paris, 1609; singer and conductor.

Cavaccio (kä-vät'-chō), **Giovanni,** Bergamo, ca. 1556—Rome, 1626; conductor.

Cavaillé-Coll. (kä-vī'-yä-kôl'), **Aristide,** Montpellier, 1811—Paris, 1899; famous organ-builder; son of **Hyacinthe Cavaillé,** c. 1771—1862, org.-builder and inv. of separate windchests with different pressures, etc.

Cavalieri (děl kä-väl-yä'-rē), (1) **Emilio del,** Rome, ca. 1550—March 11, 1602; appointed "Inspector-Gen. of Art and Artists" to the Tuscan court; advocated non-polyphonic music; his "*Rappresentazione di Anima e di Corpo*" (Rome, 1600) is the first oratorio. (2) **Katherina,** Vienna, 1761—1801; singer, whom Mozart wrote for and praised. (3) **Lina,** b. Rome, Dec. 24, 1874; soprano; won notoriety as beauty and singer in cafés chantants; studied with Mme. Mariani-Maesi; succ. début in "*Pagliacci,*" Lisbon, 1900; sang Naples, Warsaw, and 1902, at Dal Verme Th., Milan; 1906, Met. Op.; 1908-9, Manhattan Op.; 1915-16, Chicago Op.; m. Lucien Muratore, tenor; d. (air raid) Italy, Feb. 8, 1944.

Caval'li, Fran., Crema, Feb. 14, 1602—Venice, Jan. 14, 1676 (rightly Pier Francesco, **Caletti-Bruni**), son of **Giambatt. Caletti,** called **Bruni,** Maestro at Crema. A Venetian nobleman, Federigo Cavalli, had him taught and he took his name. He sang at S. Marco, 1665; first organist there; 1668, conductor; he was a pupil of Monteverde and developed M.'s principles, composing 41 operas, the most succ. being "*Giasone*" (Venice, 1649); "*Serse*" (1654); "*Ercole Amante*" (Paris, 1662); he c. also a notable requiem, and other church-music.

Cavallini (lē'-nē), **Ernesto,** Milan, 1807—1874; clarinettist and composer.

Cavos (kä'-vōs), **Catterino,** Venice,

1776—St. Petersburg, 1840; 1799, court-conductor; c. 13 Russian operas; also others.

Cazzati (käd-zä'-tē), **Maurizio,** Mantua, ca. 1620—1677; composer and conductor.

Cecil'ia (Saint), d. Rome, A.D. 230, in Christian martyrdom; her feast-day is Nov. 22d; legendary inventor of the organ, and patron saint of Christian music.

Cellier (sĕl'-yĕr), **Alfred,** Hackney, London, Dec. 1, 1844—Dec. 28, 1891; conductor in London, etc.; c. 15 operettas, incl. the very succ. "*Dorothy*" (1886); "*The Mountebanks*" (London, 1892), etc.

Cerone (chā-rō'-nĕ), **Dom. P.,** b. Bergamo, ca. 1566; theorist.

Cerreto (chĕr-rā'-tō), **Scipione,** Naples, 1551—ca. 1632; lutist and theorist.

Certon (sĕr-tôn), **P.,** 16th cent., contrapuntist; choirm. Sainte Chapelle, Paris.

Cerù (chā-roo'), **Dom. Ag.,** b. Lucca, Aug. 28, 1817; engineer and writer.

Červeny (chär'-vä-nē), **V. F. (Wenzel Fz.),** Dubec, Bohemia, 1819—Königgrätz, Jan. 19, 1896; maker and improver of brass instrs. and inv. of the important "roller" cylinder mechanism, also of the contrabass (1845), metal contrafagotto ('56), althorn obbligato ('59), primhorn ('73), and the complete waldhorn quartet (primhorn, E♭ alto, waldhorn in F, tenor in B♭, basso, 11 in D♭), subcontrabass and subcontrafagotto; improved the family of cornets, the euphonion, the screwdrum, and the church-kettledrum, etc.

Cervetti. Vide GELINEK.

Cervetto (chĕr-vĕt'-tō), (1) **Giacomo** (rightly **Bassevi**), Italy, ca. 1682—London, Jan. 14, 1783; 'cellist. (2) **Giacomo,** London, 1749 (?)—Feb. 5, 1837; son of above; 'cellist and composer.

Cesi (chā'-zē), **Beniamino,** Naples, Nov. 6, 1845—Jan. 19, 1907; pupil of Naples Cons. under Mercadante and Pappalardo, pf.-pupil of Thalberg; 1866, prof. Naples Cons.; c. an opera, "*Vittor Pisani*" (not prod.), etc.

Cesti (chās'-tē), **Marc A.,** Arezzo, 1618—Venice, 1669; Franciscan monk; conductor and tenor singer; first opera, "*Orontea*," succ. at Venice, 1649; wrote 10 other operas

mainly succ., all lost now except "*La Dori*" (Venice, 1663); his cantatas are better preserved; he wrote them for the stage.

Chabran (shǎ-brän), or **Ciabrano** (cha-brä'-nō), **Francesco,** b. Piedmont, 1723; violinist and comp.; 1751, toured Europe with success.

Chabrier (shǎb-rǐ-ā), **Alexis Emm.,** Auvergne, Jan. 18, 1841—Paris, Sept. 13, 1894; studied law in Paris, then music; 1881, choirm., under Lamoureux; c. operettas, rhapsodie "*España*" for orch., etc. After his death in 1894 his unfinished opera, "*Briséis,*" was given at the Opéra Paris, 1899; his opera "*Gwendoline*" (text by Catulle Mendès), at the Op. Com., 1911. C. also opera "*Le Roi malgré lui*" (1887); scena, "*La Sulamite*"; choral, orch. and piano works. Memoirs pub. by Séré and Servières.

Chad'wick, George Whitefield, Lowell, Mass., Nov. 13, 1854—Boston, April 7, 1931; studied organ, etc., under Eugene Thayer at Boston; 1876 head of mus. dept. of Olivet Coll., Mich.; 1877–78 studied Leipzig Cons. (Reinecke, Jadassohn), his graduation piece being an overture to "*Rip Van Winkle*"; studied at Munich with Rheinberger; 1880, organist Boston and teacher of harm., comp. and instrumentation at the N. E. Cons.; 1897–1931, dir.; cond. the Worcester Mus. Festivals, resigned, 1902; c. 3 symphonies, overtures, "*Rip Van Winkle*" ('79), "*Thalia*" ('83), "*Melpomene*" ('87), "*The Miller's Daughter*" ('88); 3 symphonic sketches for orch.; comic opera "*Tabasco*" (New York, '94); many choral works; "*The Columbian Ode*" (Chicago, '93); overtures "*Adonais*" (1900); "*Euterpe*" (1904); "*Cleopatra*" (1906); symphonic sketches (1908); theme, variations and fugue for organ and orch. (1909); "*Sinfonietta*" (1910); "*Suite Symphonique*" for orch. winning $700 prize of Nat. Federation of Clubs (1910); c. also "*Noel*" (1909); "*Lochinvar*," ballad for barytone and orch., 1909. "*Judith*" lyric drama, Worcester Fest., 1900; incid. music to "*Everywoman*" (1911); symph. poem "*Aphrodite*" (Norfolk, 1912), "*Tam O'Shanter*" (1917); opera "*Love's Sacrifice*" (1915), 5 string quartets, trio, piano quintet, church music, songs, etc.; wrote a text-book on "Harmony" (Boston, 1898).

Chaliapine (shäl-yä'-pēn), **Fedor Ivanovich,** Kazan, Feb. 11, 1873— Paris, April 12, 1938. Eminent Russian bass; pupil of Oussatov, in Tiflis; sang in various cities, finally at Moscow, and with immense success in European capitals; 1908, New York, at Met. Op. in Italian rôles, but on his return in 1921 to U. S. he established his full artistic stature as a powerfully eloquent protagonist in *"Boris Godounoff,"* and as Mephistopheles, King Philip in *"Don Carlos,"* etc.; also a highly individual concert singer, mostly of Russian songs.

Challier (shäl'-lĭ-ĕr), **Ernst,** Berlin, July 9, 1843—Giessen, Sept. 19, 1914; music-publisher, Berlin.

Cham'berlain, Houston Stewart, Portsmouth, England, Sept. 9, 1855— Bayreuth, Jan. 9, 1927; son-in-law of Richard Wagner, whose daughter, Eva, he m. 1908; renounced British citizenship and became German subject; son of a British Admiral, took doctor's degree in Germany, and lived at Vienna because of his health; pub. famous book "Richard Wagner" (Leipzig, 1892), followed by others.

Chambonnières (shän-bŭn-yăr), **Jacques Champion** (called "Champion de Chamb."), d. ca. 1670; first chamber cembalist to Louis XIV.

Chaminade (shăm'-ĭ-năd'), **Cécile (Louise Stéphanie)**, Paris, Aug. 8, 1861—Monte Carlo, April 18, 1944; noted composer, pianist; pupil of Lecouppey, Savard, Marsick and Godard; c. the succ. "ballet-symphonie" *"Callirhoë"* (Marseilles, 1888); the "symphonie lyrique" *"Les Amazones"* (Anvers, 1888); 2 suites for orch.; "Concert-stück" for pf. with orch. and many pop. songs and pf.-pieces; opéra comique, *"La Sevillane,"* etc.

Cham'lee (chăm'-lē), **Mario,** b. Los Angeles, 1892; tenor; Mus. M., Univ. of Calif., 1924; studied with Achille Alberti and Riccardo Dellera; début Met. Op. Co., 1920, as Cavaradossi in *"Tosca"*; also sang with Scotti and Ravinia Op. Cos., and has made appearances in concerts and radio programmes; m. Ruth Miller, soprano.

Champein (shän-păṅ), **Stanislas,** Marseilles, 1753—Paris, 1830; dram. composer.

Champion (shänp-yôṅ), **Jacques.** Vide CHAMBONNIÈRES.

Chanot (shă-nō), **Fran.,** Mirecourt, 1787—Brest, 1823; retired as a naval engineer; designed a violin which the Academy pronounced equal to Stradivari's; his bro., a Paris luthier, manufactured it, but found it impracticable.

Chapi (y Lorente) (chă-pē' ē lō rĕn'-tĕ), **Ruperto,** Villena, March 27, 1851— Madrid, March 25, 1909; pupil Madrid Cons.; c. operas and 78 zarzuelas; also a symph.; oratorio, etc.

Chap'man, William Rogers, Hanover, Mass., Aug. 4, 1855—Palm Beach, Fla., March 27, 1935; composer, choral conductor; founded and led Apollo Club of New York; after 1897, the Maine Festivals in Bangor and Portland; and the Rubinstein Club, a N. Y. women's chorus, which had a continuous existence under his baton from 1887.

Chap'pell & Co., music-publishers, London; founded 1812 by (1) **Samuel C.,** the pianist, Cramer, and F. T. Latour (1809—1888). (2) **Wm. C.** became the head of the firm; in 1840 he founded the "Antiquarian Society," and pub. colls. of old Engl. music. His brothers, (3) **Thomas,** founded, and (4) **Arthur,** conducted, the Monday and Saturday Pop. Concerts.

Chap'ple, Samuel, Crediton (Devon), 1775—Ashburton, 1833; organist and pianist, blind from infancy; composer.

Chapuis (shäp-wē), **Aug. Paul J. Bap.,** Dampierre-sur-Saône, France, April 20, 1862—Paris, Dec., 1933; pupil of Dubois, Massenet, and César Franck, Paris Cons., took first prize in harm., 1st prize for org., and the Rossini prize; organist at Saint Roch.; from 1894, prof. of harm. at the Cons.; 1895, inspector-gen. of music instruction in Paris schools; c. unsucc. lyric drama *"Enguerrande"* (Op. Com., 1892); lyric drama *"Tancred"* (Op. Com., 1898 ?); an oratorio; a pf.-suite "on the oriental scale," etc.; pub. a treatise on harm.

Char (khär), **Fr. Ernst ("Fritz"),** Cleves-on-Rhein, May 5, 1865— Velden, Sept. 21, 1932; pupil of C. Kistler, Wüllner and Neitzel; cond. opera at Zwickau, Stettin, and

St. Gallen; later at Ulm; wrote book and music of succ. opera *"Der Schelm von Bergen"* (Zwickau, 1895); c. cantata *"Spielmann,"* etc.

Chard, G. W., ca. 1765—May 23, 1849; English organist and composer.

Charpentier (shär-pänt-yā), (1) **Marc A.,** Paris, 1634—March, 1704; conductor to the Dauphin; c. 16 operas for the stage and many "tragédies spirituelles" for the Jesuits, masses, etc. (2) **Gustave,** b. Dieuze, Lorraine, June 25, 1860; pupil of Massart, Pessard, and Massenet, Paris Cons.; 1887, took grand prix de Rome; c. orch. suite *"Impressions d'Italie"*; scène lyrique *"Didon"*; symphonic drama (or concert opera) *"La Vie du Poète"* (Grand Opera, 1892), and *"Italien"* (Hamburg, 1902); symph. poem *"Napoli"* (1891); book and music of succ. opera *"Louise,"* impressionistic study of poet life in Montmartre, première Op.-Comique, 1900, and heard at Manhattan Op., N. Y., 1907, with Mary Garden, and with Farrar at Met. Op., 1921; he wrote a sequel, *"Julien,"* Op.-Com., 1913, also at Met. Op., with Farrar and Caruso, but not succ.; also c. *"Marie," "Orphée,"* and *"Tête Rouge,"* unprod.; and songs, *"Les Fleurs du Mal," "Quinze poèmes,"* some of them with chorus and orchestra. He founded Cercle Mimi Pinson and Cons. of same name for working girls.

Chasins (chās'-ĭns), **Abram,** b. New York, Aug. 17, 1903; pianist, composer; studied piano with Hutcheson, Hofmann and others; composition with Rubin Goldmark; début as soloist with Phila. Orch., 1929, playing his own concerto; member of piano faculty, Curtis Inst., Phila.; has composed numerous piano pieces, some of which he has arranged for orch.; his *"Parade"* and *"In a Chinese Garden"* played by N. Y. Philh.

Chatterton, J. B., Norwich, 1805—London, 1871; court-harpist and composer.

Chaumet (shō-mā), **J. B. Wm.,** Bordeaux, April 26, 1842—Gajac, Gironde, Oct. 28, 1903; won the Prix Cressent, with the comic opera *"Bathyle"* (prod. 1877), also the Prix Rossini; c. comic operas; lyric drama *"Mauprat"* (MS.), etc.

Chausson (shōs-sôṅ), **Ernest, Paris,** June 21, 1855—(killed in bicycle accident), Limay n. Mantes, June 10, 1899; pupil of Massenet and César Franck; c. symph.; symph. poems *"Viviane"* and *"Les caprices de Marianne"*; operas *"Helene," "Le roi Arthus"* (Brussels, 1903; text by the composer); songs and piano pieces; *"Poème de l'Amour et de la Mer,"* and *"Chanson Perpetuelle,"* dram. scenas; lyric scene, *"Jeanne d'Arc"*; *"Un Soir de Fête"* and *"Solitude dans le Bois"* for orch.; piano and vln. concertos; string quartet; piano quartet; string trio; and popular *"Poème"* for vln. and orch. A highly individual genius. Memoir by Séré.

Chauvet (shō-vä), **Chas. Alexis,** Marnies, June 7, 1837—Argentan, Jan. 28, 1871; organist; c. noteworthy org.-music.

Chavanne (shä-vär.'-nĕ), **Irène von,** b. Gratz, 1868; contralto; pupil Vienna Cons., 1882–85; 1885 at the Dresden Court-opera.

Chavez (chä'-vĕth), **Carlos,** b. Mexico City, June 13, 1899; composer, conductor; studied with Manuel Ponce and Pedro Ogazon, also in Europe; founded and led Symph. Orch. of Mexico after 1928; same year appointed dir. of Nat'l. Cons. of Mexico, resigned 1934; guest cond. of Boston and Phila. Orchs., 1936; N. Y. Philh., 1937; c. modern style works of originality, incl. (ballet) *"H. P."* ("Horsepower"), staged by Stokowski in Phila., 1932; (orch.) *"Sinfonia de Antigona,"* sonatinas for various chamber combinations; piano sonata, etc.

Cheath'am, Kitty, b. Nashville, Tenn., mezzo-soprano; esp. known for her concerts of folk music and children's songs; ed. two collections of these works; res. in New York for some years; d. Greenwich, Conn., 1946.

Chelard (shŭ-lär) **Hippolyte André J. Bap.,** Paris, Feb. 1, 1789—Weimar, Feb. 12, 1861; 1815, prod. his first opera, *"La Casa a Vendere,"* Naples; entered the Paris Operatic orch. as violinist; in 1827 his opera *"Macbeth"* (text by Rouget de Lisle) was prod., but failed; he went to Munich, and 1828 prod. a revised version of *"Macbeth"* with such succ. that he was made court-conductor; he returned to Paris.

1829, and failed with 3 other operas; conducted the German Opera in London, which failed; returned to Munich, and prod. his best work, *"Die Hermannsschlacht,"* 1835; 1836, court-conductor at Weimar, where he prod. 2 comic operas.

Chelleri (kĕl'-lĕ-rē), **Fortunato** (rightly **Keller**), Parma, 1686—Cassel, 1757; court-conductor and dram. composer.

Chemin-Petit (shŭ-măn-pŭ-tē'), **Hans,** d. Potsdam, 1917; c. operas, including *"Der Liebe Augustin"* (Brandenburg, 1906).

Chéri (shā-rē), **Victor** (rightly **Cizos**), Auxerre, 1830—suicide, Paris, 1882; cond. and dram. composer.

Cherkass'ky, Shura, b. Odessa, Oct. 7, 1911; pianist; studied with Josef Hofmann; début as youthful pianist prodigy; developed into excellent performer of mature ability; has appeared with leading orchs. and as recitalist, in many Eur. and Amer. cities, also extensive tours of Russia and Far East.

Cherniav'sky, (1) **Jan,** b. Odessa, June 25, 1892; pianist; pupil of Leschetizky, Vienna; founded Cherniavsky Trio with his brothers, (2) **Leo** (b. Odessa, Aug. 30, 1890), violinist, who was pupil of Wilhelmj; and (3) **Michel** (b. Odessa, Nov. 2, 1893), 'cellist, pupil of Popper. Tours in U. S. and other countries.

Cherubini (kā-roo-bē'-nē) (**M.**) **Luigi** (**Carlo Zenobio Salvatore**), Florence, Sept. 14, 1760—Paris, March 15, 1842; one of the greatest masters of counterpoint; pupil of his father, (cembalist, at the Pergola Th.), then of B. and A. Felici, Bizarri and Castrucci; 1779 sent (under patronage of the future Emperor Leopold III.) to Milan, to study cpt. with Sarti; at 13, had c. a mass and an intermezzo for a society theatre; at 15, another intermezzo; 1780, *"Quinto Fabio"* was prod. without succ. though with better results in a revised version (1783); he had succ. with 6 other operas, and was in 1784 invited to London, where he prod. an opera buffa, with some success, and another with none; he was court composer for one year; 1788 he prod. *"Ifigenia in Aulide"* at Turin; and then lived in Paris, where his French opera *"Démophon"* (Grand Opéra, 1788) failed; he then cond. at a small opera

house, until 1792. His opera *"Lodoiska,"* 1791, showed a new style of emotional strength, powerful ensemble, and novel orchestral colour that founded a school of imitators. 7 other operas and a ballet followed, incl. his masterpiece (1800), *"Les deux journées"* (in Germany called *"Der Wasserträger"*; in England, "The Water-carrier"). 1795 he had been made one of the inspectors of the new Cons., Paris, but was not liked by Napoleon, whose musical opinion he had not flattered. On invitation he wrote for Vienna *"Faniska,"* a great succ. (1806); an invitation to write a mass for the Prince of Chimay resulted in the famous 3-part mass in F. He wrote 4 more operas, but found church-music more satisfactory. 1815, visited London; wrote a symphony, an overture, and a *Hymn to Spring,* for the Philh. Soc. After many vicissitudes he became in 1816 prof. of comp. at the Cons., Paris, and 1821-41 dir. His enormous list of works includes 15 Italian and 14 French operas, 17 cantatas, 11 solemn masses, 2 requiems, 1 oratorio; 1 symphony, 1 overture; 6 string quartets; 6 pf.-sonatas, and a mass of smaller works, mus. for pf., etc. The best biog. is by Bellasis (London, 1874).

Chessin (chĕs'-sēn), **Alexander Borissovich,** b. St. Petersburg Oct. 19, 1869; conductor; pupil of the Cons., and of Nikisch at Leipzig; 1901, cond. at St. Petersburg and 1903 of Philharmonic concerts at Moscow; c. cantata, etc.

Chevé (shŭ-vā), **Emile Jos. Maurice,** Douarnenez, Finistere, 1804—1864; a physician; wrote pamphlets attacking the methods at the Paris Cons. His wife (née **Manine,** Paris) collaborated with him.

Chevillard (shŭ-vē-yăr), **Camille,** Paris, Oct. 14, 1859—May 30, 1923; pupil of G. Mathias; took 2d pf. prize at Cons.; till 1886, asst.-cond. of the Lamoureux Concerts; 1897, cond.; after 1907, prof. at Paris Cons.; 1913 also concert master at the Opéra; 1903, won Prix Chartier for chamber music; pres., Chamber Mus. Soc.; Officier of Public Instruction and mem. of the Legion of Honour; c. a symph. ballade, *"Le chêne et le roseau"*; a symph. poem, a symph.

100 DICTIONARY OF MUSICIANS

fantasie; incid. mus. to *"La Rous-salka* (1903); allegro for horn and piano, 1905; piano pieces and songs; 2 string quartets, trio, piano quintet, sonatas for vln. and for 'cello, etc.

Chiaromonte (kē-är-ō-môn'-tĕ), **Fran.** Castrogofovanni, 1809—Brussels, 1886; tenor; prof. of singing and dram. composer.

Chick'ering & Sons, American firm of pf.-makers, est. 1823, by (1) **Jonas Chickering** (New Ipswich, N. H., 1798—Boston, 1853); and his sons (2) **Col. Thos. E. C.** (Boston, 1824—1871), (3) **Geo. H.** (1830-96), and (4) **C. Frank** (1827-91). Last was named Chev. of the Legion of Honour, and took first pf.-prize at the Paris Exposition, 1867. In 1908 the firm was merged with the Amer. Piano Co.

Child, Wm., Bristol, 1606—Windsor, 1697; organist.

Chilesotti (kē-lā-sôt'-tē), **Oscare,** Bassano, Italy, July 12, 1848—June 20, 1916; law graduate Padua Univ.; flutist and 'cellist; self-taught in harm.; lived in Milan; wrote important historical works.

Chipp, Edm. Thos. (Mus. Doc.), London, 1823—Nice, 1886; organist.

Chladni (khlät'-nē), **Ernst Florens Fr.,** Wittenberg, Nov. 30, 1756—Breslau, April 3, 1827; prof. of law and investigator in physics and acoustics; discovered the sound-figures which sand assumes on a vibrating plate, and which bear his name; inv. the euphonium and clavicylinder (v. D.D.).

Chollet (shôl-lā), **J. B. M.,** b. Paris, May, 1798; violinist and singer in opera.

Chop (khôp), **Max,** Greuszen, Thuringia, May 17, 1862—Berlin, Dec. 20, 1929; mus. writer, critic in Berlin, under the name "Monsieur Charles"; c. piano concerto, etc. Was ed. of the *"Signale,"* Berlin mus. publication. M. Celeste Groenvelt, pianist.

Chopin (shô-păň) **(François) Frédéric,** Zelazowa Wola (Jeliasovaya Volia), near Warsaw, Feb. 22, 1810—Paris, Oct. 17, 1849; eminent composer for the piano; son of Nicholas C. (a native of Nancy, France, who was at first bookkeeper in a cigar factory, then teacher in the Warsaw Gymnasium), and a Polish woman (née Justine Kryzanowska). **C.** studied at his father's private school, among young Polish noblemen; Albert Zwyny taught him pf. and Joseph Elsner, harm., etc. At 9 he played in public a pf.-concerto and improvisations; c. polonaises, mazurkas, and waltzes; in 1825, pub. as op. 1 a rondo; op. 2 a fantasie with orch. He played in German cities and had at 19 an individual style of comp., having written his 2 pf.-concertos, mazurkas, nocturnes, rondos, etc. He started for London, and played in Vienna, 1829, with such success that a critic called him "one of the most brilliant meteors blazing on the musical horizon": and at Paris he had such succ. in his first concert, 1831, that he settled there for life as a teacher of the pf. and occasional giver of concerts. His pupils were of the most aristocratic, and his friends included Liszt, Berlioz, Meyerbeer, Bellini, Balzac, and Heine. Schumann with typical spontaneity (cf. **BRAHMS**) was moved in 1831 by Chopin's op. 2 to say, "Hats off, gentlemen:—a genius"; and in 1839, in reviewing certain of his preludes, mazurkas, and valses, to say "He is and remains the keenest and staunchest poet-soul of the time." **C.**'s liaison with Mme. Dudevant ("George Sand"), begun in 1836 and ended in 1844, has caused endless controversy. In 1838 an attack of bronchitis drove him to Majorca, where she seems to have been a devoted nurse, but the peevishness and weakness due to his developing consumption caused bitter quarrels, and she is believed to have caricatured him as Prince Karol in her novel *"Lucrezia Floriani."* Concert tours and social life in England and Scotland in 1841-49 destroyed his strength.

His comps. include beside those mentioned (74, with opus-number 12 lacking): *"Don Giovanni,"* fantasia, op. 2; *"Krakoviak,"* rondo, op. 14; E♭ *Polonaise,* op. 22; and a fantasia on Polish airs for pf. with orch; duo concertant on themes from *"Robert le Diable";* an introd. et Polonaise, op. 3, and a sonata, op. 65 for pf. and 'cello; pf. trio, op. 8; and a rondo for 2pfs. op. 73. FOR PF. SOLO: *Allegro de concert;* 1 ballades; barcarolle, op. 60; berceuse, op. 57; bolero, op. 19; 3 écos-

saises, op. 72; 12 grandes études, op. 10; 12 études, op. 25; 3 études; 4 fantasies; 3 impromptus; marche funèbre, op. 72; 52 mazurkas. "*Morceau de concert sur la Marche des Puritains de Bellini*"; 19 nocturnes, 11 polonaises; 24 préludes, op. 28; prélude, op. 45; 3 rondos; 4 scherzos; 3 sonatas; tarantelle, op. 43; 13 valses; variations on "*Je vends des scapulaires*," op. 12; "*Variation dans l' Hexaméron*"; 16 Polish songs op. 74.
A collection of his letters was pub. (Dresden, 1877). A collection by Opienski was tr. into English by Voynich and pub. 1931. His many biographers include Liszt, M. Karasowski (Dresden, 1877), M. A. Audley, Fr. Niecks (Leipzig, 1889). Other studies by Huneker, Finck, Bidou, Dry, J. P. Dunn, Hadden, Jachimecki, Kelley, Kleczynski, Maine, Murdoch, Pourtalès, Tarnowski, Niggli, Schucht, Willeby, Hoesick (3 vols.), Leichtentritt, Opienski, Poirée, Redenbacher, Weissmann, Ganche, Scharlitt, etc. (See article, page 490.)

Chor'ley, H. Fothergill, Blackley Hurst, Lancashire, 1808—London, 1872; critic and widely travelled writer.

Choron (shô-rôn), **Alex. Ét.**, Caen, Oct. 21, 1772—Paris, June 29, 1834; an ardent student of musical theory and practice, historian and benefactor who devoted his fortune to the advance of the art.

Chotzinoff (khôt'-zē-nôf), **Samuel**, pianist, critic; toured as accompanist with Heifetz and Zimbalist; former mus. critic., N. Y. "*World*"; critic, N. Y. "*Post*" after 1934; author "*Eroica*," novel based on life of Beethoven.

Choudens (shoo-däns), **A.**, Paris, 1849 —1902; son of a music publisher; c. 2 operas, "*Graziella*" (Paris, 1877), and "*La Jeunesse de Don Juan*," etc.

Chouquet (shoo-kä), **Ad. Gv.**, Havre, 1819—Paris, 1886; teacher and writer of historical works.

Chris'tiansen, F. Melius, b. Eidsvold, Norway, April 1, 1871; choral conductor and composer; pupil of Oscar Hansen, in organ and conducting, at Larvik; came to America; 1888; later studied at Northwestern Cons. and at Leipzig Cons.; after 1903 dir. of mus. at St. Olaf Coll., Northfield, Minn., where he has led the notable

St. Olaf Choir; c. and arr. choral music; wrote books on theory.

Chris'tie, Winifred, Scottish pianist; studied R. Coll. of Music, London, winning Liszt scholarship; also studied in Leipzig; and with Harold Bauer; toured in Eur. countries; res. in America 1915–19; later returned here for tours; plays double-keyboard piano invented by Emanuel Moór (1863—1931), whom she married.

Christ'mann, Jn. Fr., Ludwigsburg, Würtemberg, 1752—Heutingsheim, 1817; composer and writer.

Chrysander (krē'-zänt-ĕr), **Fr.**, Lübtheen, Mecklenburg, July 8, 1826—Bergedorf, Sept. 3, 1901; editor and writer of the standard biography of Händel, and with Gervinus of the monumental H.-Gesellschaft edition of that master's works.

Chrysan'thos of Madyton; writer 19th century; teacher of church singing, Constantinople, later Archbishop of Durazzo in Albania.

Chva'la (shvä'-lä), **Emanuel**, Prague Jan. 1, 1851—Oct. 31, 1924; pupil of Förster and Fibich; historian and c. of chamber music, etc.

Chwatal (khwä'-täl), **Fz. Xaver**, Rumburg, Bohemia, 1808—Elmen (Soolbad), 1879; teacher and composer.

Chybinski (khe-bēn'-yĕ-shkĭ), **Adolf**, b. Cracow, March 29, 1880; historian of Polish music; after 1912 taught at Lemberg U.; d. Oct. 31, 1952.

Ciaja (chä'-yä), **Azzolino Bdo. della**, b. Siena, 1671; organist, amateur org.-builder, and composer.

Ciampi (chäm'-pē), **Legrenzio V.**, b. Piacenza, 1719; dram. composer.

Cianchettini (chän-kĕt-tē'-nē), (1) **Veronica** (née **Dussek**), Czaslau, Bohemia, 1779; composer and teacher. (2) **Pio**, London, 1799—1840; son of above; composer and pianist; first appearance at 5 years; at 10 performed an original concerto in public.

Cibber (sĭb'-bĕr), **Susanna M.** (née **Arne**), 1714—1766; great English actress and notable singer, sister of Dr. Arne.

Ciconia (chĭ-kōn'-yä), **Johannes**, canon at Padua about 1400; theorist and comp.

Cifra (chē'-frä), **A.**, Rome, 1584— Loreto, 1629; important composer of the Roman School; pupil of Palestrina and B. Nanini; court-conductor.

Cigna (chēn'-yä), **Gina**; dramatic soprano, of French-Italian ancestry; early studied piano, composition and theory at Paris Cons.; awarded gold medal; later instruction in singing; after 1928 active as vocalist; from 1930 mem. of La Scala; has also sung at Paris Op., Rome Teatro Reale and Augusteo, Budapest Op., Teatro Colon (Buenos Aires), Teatro Municipal (Rio de Janeiro), and in many Italian cities; created title role in Respighi's "*La Fiamma*" at Milan; sang Norma at centenary festival of Bellini in Catania; and Gioconda at La Scala on Ponchielli centenary; engaged for Met. Op., N. Y., 1936-37.

Cilèa (chē'-lĕ-ä), **Francesco**, b. Palmi, July 29, 1866—Varezze, Nov. 20, 1950; comp.; at 9 had c. a notturno and a mazurka; at 15 entered the Naples Cons.; while yet a student he had success with a suite for orch., and a 3-act opera "*Gina*" (1889); 1896-1904, professor at Royal Institute, Florence; 1913-16, dir. Palermo Cons.; from 1917 of Naples Cons.; c. operas "*La Tilda*" (1892); "*L'Arlesiana*" (Milan, 1896); "*Adrianna Lécouvreur*" (Milan, 1902, Covent Garden, 1904); "*Gloria*," (La Scala, Milan, 1907); also "*Poema Sinfonica*"; orch. suite, piano trio, 'cello sonata, etc.

Cimarosa (chē-mä-rō'-sä), **Domenico**, Aversa, near Naples, Dec. 17, 1749—Venice, Jan. 11, 1801; the orphan of a poor mason; studied at Minorite charity-school, his first teacher being Polcano, monastery organist; when 12 years old was given a scholarship in the Cons. di S. Maria di Loreto, where he studied singing with Manna and Sacchini, cpt. with Fenaroli, and comp. with Piccinni. 1770 his oratorio "*Giuditta*" was prod. in Rome; 1772, his first opera, "*Le Stravaganze del Conte*," at Naples, without succ., which was won, however, next year by "*La Finta Parigina*." Of phenomenal facility, he c. 76 operas in 29 years. He lived alternately in Rome and Naples. 1781, he prod. two operas in Naples, one in Rome, and two in Turin; invited 1789 to be court-composer at St. Petersburg (vice Paesiello), he spent 5 months of triumphal progress thither, being lionised at various courts; he stayed there 3 years, prod. 3 operas and wrote 500 pieces of

music for the court; but he could not tolerate the climate, and was reluctantly released, being engaged as cond. to Emperor Leopold at Vienna, with a salary of 12,000 florins. He prod. 3 operas incl. his masterpiece "*Il Matrimonio Segreto*" (1787), which won an all-effacing success. 1793, he returned to Naples. 1799, he took part in the Neapolitan revolutionary demonstration on the entrance of the French army, and was condemned to death by King Ferdinand, but banished instead; he died suddenly at Venice. It being everywhere claimed that he had been poisoned by order of Queen Caroline of Naples, the Pope's physician made an examination, and swore that he died of a gangrenous abdominal tumour. Particularly in comic, but at times also in serious opera, C. almost challenges comparison with Mozart for fluency of melody and orchestral richness. His best operas are "*La Finta*" (Naples, 1773), "*L'Italiana in Londra*" (Rome, 1774), "*Il Fanatico per gli Antichi Romani*" (Naples, 1777), in which were introduced dramatically vocal-trios and quartets, "*La Ballerina Amante*" (Naples, 1782), "*Le Trame Deluse*" (Naples, 1786), "*L'Impresario in Angustie*" (Naples, 1786), "*Giannina e Bernadone*" (Naples, 1788), "*La Vergine del Sole*" (St. Petersburg, 1791), "*Il Matrimonio Segreto*" (Vienna, 1792), "*Le Astuzie Femminile*" (Naples, 1794). He also prod. 2 oratorios, 7 symphonies, several cantatas; masses, etc.

Cimini (chī'-mī-nē), **Pietro**, b. Carpi (Modena), Italy, 1876; conductor; studied at the Bologna Liceo with Sarti, Dall'Olio and Martucci; early active as violinist; cond. opera in Italy, Warsaw (1910-14), also in Russia, at Madrid Reale, Chicago Auditorium, Manhattan Op. House, New York; later for some years on the Pacific Coast.

Cipollini (chē-pôl-lē'-nē), **Gaetano**, Tropea, Italy, Feb. 8, 1857—Milan, Oct. 2, 1935; pupil of Francesco Coppa; lived at Milan as dram. composer.

Cirri (chēr'-rē), (1) **Ignazio**, organist and comp.; his son (2) **Giovanni Baptista**, b. Forli, ca. 1740; 'cellist; spent many years in London, then

returned to Italy; c. important
'cello music.
Cisneros (sĭs-nä'-rŏs), **Eleanora de**
(née **Broadfoot**), New York, Nov. 1,
1880—Feb. 3, 1934; soprano; studied
with Mme. Murio-Celli, and made
début as Rossweise in "*Die Walküre*"
at Met. Op. House, 1900; later
studied with Jean de Reszke, Maurel,
Trabadello and Lombardi; after
1902, sang widely in Europe, South
and Central America, and Australia;
1906–08, Manhattan Op. House,
N. Y.; sang "Clytemnestra" in "*Elektra*" at Milan; after 1910 with Chicago Op.
Claassen (kläs'-sĕn), **Arthur**, Stargard,
Prussia, Feb. 19, 1859—San Fran-
cisco, March 16, 1920; graduated
from Danzig Gym.; 1875, studied
under Müller-Hartung, Gottschalk
and Sulze, Weimar Music School;
1880–84, cond. Göttingen and
Magdeburg; 1884, cond. "Arion"
and other societies of Brooklyn,
N. Y.; est. the "Claassen Mus.
Inst."; after 1910 active as choral
and orch. cond., San Antonio, Tex.;
c. choruses, incl. "*Der Kamerad*"
(prize), and symph. poem "*Hohen-
friedberg*," etc.
Clag'get, **Chas.**, London, 1755—1820;
violinist and inventor.
Clapisson (klä-pĭs-sôn), **Antoine L.**,
Naples, 1808—Paris, 1866; violinist,
professor and dram. composer.
Clapp, **Philip Greeley**, b. Boston, Aug.
4, 1888; composer, educator; grad.
Harvard Univ., *magna cum laude;*
cond. Pierian Sodality there; studied
in Europe as Sheldon Fellow of that
Univ.; Ph.D.; dir. of music, Dartmouth Coll., 1915–19; after latter
year prof. of mus., Univ. of Iowa;
for a time associated with Juilliard
Foundation, N. Y.; c. symph.,
choral works, etc., two of former
perf. Boston; d. Apr. 9, 1954.
Clari (klä'-rē), **Giov. M.**, Pisa, 1669—
Pistoia, ca. 1754; conductor and
composer.
Clar'ibel. Vide MRS. CHAS. BARNARD.
Clark(e), (1) **Jeremiah**, London, 1670
—(?), ca. 1707; organist and dram.
composer; a suicide for love. (2)
Richard, Datchet (Bucks), 1780—
London, 1856; composer and writer.
(3) Vide SCOTSON CLARK.
Clarke, (1) **Jas. Peyton**, Scotland,
1808—Toronto, Canada, 1877; organist and professor. (2) **Hugh**

Archibald, Toronto, Aug. 15, 1839—
Philadelphia, Dec. 16, 1927; son
of above; organist in Philadelphia
churches; 1875, prof. of music in the
Univ. of Pennsylv.; made Mus. Doc.
(1886) by the Univ. when his music
to Aristophanes' "*Acharnians*" was
prod.; also c. an oratorio, "*Jerusalem*" (Phila., 1891), etc. (3) **J.**
(**Whitfield-Clarke**), Gloucester, England, 1770—Holmer, 1836; organist,
professor and editor. (4) **James
Hamilton Smee**, Birmingham, England, Jan. 25, 1840—Banstead, July
9, 1912; at 12 organist; 1866 at
Queen's College, Oxford; Mus. Bac.,
1867; cond. various theatres; 1893,
cond. Carl Rosa Opera Co.; c.
operettas, 2 symphonies, etc. (5)
Wm. Horatio, Newton, Mass., March
8, 1840—Reading, Mass., 1913;
1878–87, organist at Tremont Temple, Boston, then retired to Reading,
Mass., where he had an estate and
a chapel of music, Clarigold Hall,
containing a large 4-manual organ
with 100 stops; wrote 15 instructive
works "*Outline of the Structure of the
Pipe-Organ*" (1877), etc. (6) **Maria
Victoria** (**Cowden-Clarke**). Vide
NOVELLO. (7) **Rebecca**, b. Harrow,
England, Aug. 27, 1886; composer
and 'cellist; studied with Stanford
at R. Coll. of Music; after 1916 she
visited New York as performer; c.
chamber music, her piano trio being
awarded a Coolidge Prize.
Clarus (klä'-roos), **Max.**, Mühlberg-
on-Elbe, March 31, 1852—Bruns-
wick, Dec. 12, 1916; pupil of his
father, the municipal mus. dir. there,
and of Haupt, Schneider, and
Löschorn, Berlin; cond. in various
German, Austrian and Hungarian
theatres; 1890, mus. dir. Brunswick court; from 1884 cond. the
"Orpheus," and from 1890 the
"Chorgesangverein"; c. "Patriotic
spectacular" opera, "*Des Grossen
Königs Rekrut*" (Brunswick, 1889);
succ. romantic opera "*Ilse*" (Brunswick, 1895); "*Der wunschpeter*"
(1910), "*Hans Däumling*" (1911),
"*Der Zwerg Nase*" (1912), choral
works, ballets, etc.
Clasing (klä'-zĭng), **Jn. H.**, Hamburg,
1779—1829; teacher and dram. composer.
Claudin (klō-dăn), (1). Vide SERMISY
(2) **Le Jeune**. Vide LEJEUNE.
Claus'sen, **Julia**, (née **Ohlson**), b

Stockholm, 1879–1941; contralto; studied R. Acad. in native city; début there at R. Op., 1903; mem. Chicago Op., 1912–17; after 1917 sang for some years with Met. Op. Co., N. Y., esp. in Wagnerian rôles.

Clausz-Szarvady (klows'-shär-vä'-dē), **Wilhelmine**, Prague, 1834—Paris, 1907; pianist.

Clavé (klă-vä'), **José Anselmo**, Barcelona, April 21, 1824—Feb., 1874; founder of male choral societies in Spain; c. very popular songs and choruses.

Clavijo Del Castillo (klă-vē'-hō dĕl kăs-tĕl'-yō), **Bernardo**, d. Madrid, Feb. 1626; Spanish organist and comp.

Clay, Fr. (of English parents), Paris, 1840—Great Marlow, near London, 1889; dram. composer.

Clegg, J., Ireland (probably), 1714—Nisane, 1742; remarkable violinist and composer.

Clem'ens, Jacob (called **"Cl. Non Papa"**) (i.e., "not the Pope" Clement VII.); d. ca. 1557 (?); played several instrs. and composed.

Clem'ens, Charles Edwin, b. Devenport, England, March 12, 1858—Cleveland, O., Dec. 27, 1933; organist; 1889—1895, organist at the English church, and to Empress Frederick in Berlin, and teacher at Scharwenka Cons.; then moved to Cleveland, Ohio; prof. Western Reserve Univ.; author of organ-methods.

Clement (klä'-mĕnt), **Fz.**, Vienna, 1780—1842; violinist and dram. composer.

Clément (klä-mäṅ), (1) **Félix**, Paris, 1822—1885; organist. (2) **Edmond**, France, 1867—Nice, Feb. 23, 1928; eminent lyric tenor; early made succ. at Paris Op.-Comique; 1909–10, sang at Met. Op. House; 1911–13, with Boston Op. Co.; after the war returned to U. S. for concert tour.

Clementi (klä-mĕn'-tē), **Muzio**, Rome, 1752—near Evesham, England, March 10, 1832; son of a goldsmith and musical amateur who had him taught by A. Buroni, then by the organist Condicelli. At 9 he was chosen as an organist in competition with older players; until 14, studied under G. Carpani (comp.) and Sartartelli (voice); 1766, an Englishman named Beckford secured permission 'o educate him in England, and till

1770 he lived and studied in Dorsetshire; then made a sensation as pianist in London. 1773, pub. pf.-sonatas dedicated to Haydn, and highly praised by Emmanuel Bach; 1777–80, cembalist at the Italian Opera; 1781 toured the continent, meeting Mozart in "friendly" rivalry. without victory for either; lived in London, 1782–1802; he amassed a fortune as a teacher, pianist and composer in spite of losses from the failure of Longman and Broderip, instr.-makers; he estab. a succ. piano-factory and pub. house (now Collard's). 1802, he made a brilliant tour with his pupil Field; he taught other famous pupils, incl. Moscheles, Kalkbrenner, Meyerbeer. His comps. incl. symphonies and overtures; 106 pf.-sonatas (46, with vln., 'cello, or flute); fugues, preludes, and exercises in canon form, toccatas, etc. His book of études, the *"Gradus ad Parnassum,"* 1817, is a standard; biog. by Giov. Froju (Milan, 1878); O. Chilesotti (Milan, 1882), and Clement (Paris, 1878).

Clérambault (klā-räṅ-bō), **Louis Nicolas**, Paris, 1676—1749; organist and comp.

Clérice (klā-rēs), **Justin**, Buenos Aires, Oct. 16, 1863—Toulouse, Sept, 1908; 1882, pupil of Délibes and Pessard, Paris Cons.; lived in Paris; prod. comic operas, etc.

Cleve (klĕv), (1) **Johannes De**, Cleve (?) 1529—Augsburg, 1582; court tenor at Vienna and Prague; c. church music; (2) **Halfdan**, b. Kongsberg, Norway, Oct. 5, 1879; pianist; pupil of his father and of Raif and the two Scharwenkas at Berlin; c. piano-concertos, etc.

Clicquot (klē-kō), **Fran. H.**, Paris, 1728 —1791; organ-builder.

Cliffe (klĭf), **Frederick**, Lowmoor, May 2, 1857—Dec., 1931; organist; pupil of Sullivan, Stainer, and at R. C. M.; toured Europe with success; after 1901, taught R. A. M.; c. 2 symph.; symph poem *"Clouds and Sunshine"*; alto solo with crch., *"The Triumph of Alcestis,"* etc.

Clif'ford, Rev. Jas., Oxford, 1622—London, 1698; composer.

Clif'ton, Chalmers, b. Jackson, Miss., April 30, 1889: conductor, composer, grad. Cincinnati Cons. and Harvard Univ.; studied with d'Indy and Gédalge; cond. Cecilia Soc., Boston

1915-17; Amer. Orch. Soc., N. Y., 1922-30; also guest cond. with orch. in Boston, New York, Cincinnati, Baltimore and Conservatoire Orch., Paris; c. orch., piano works and songs; orchestrated MacDowell piano works.

Clive, Catherine (née **Raftor**) (called "Kitty Clive"), London, 1711—Dec. 6, 1785; famous actress, also singer.

Clough-Leiter (klŭf-lī'-tĕr) **Henry,** b. Washington, D. C., May 13, 1874; composer and musical editor; pupil of his mother, Edw. Kimball, H. Xande, and Dr. J. H. Anger; org. at Washington and various churches at Providence, R. I. c. "*Lasca*" for tenor and orch.; 4 cantatas, "*A Day of Beauty*," for string quintet; 200 songs.

Clu'er, J., d. London, 1729, English publisher, reputed inventor of engraving on tin plates.

Coates, (1) **John,** b. Girlington, June 29, 1865—Northwood, Aug. 16, 1941; tenor; sang choir at 5; pupil of Burton and Bridge, later of Shakespeare; sang in light opera, London and America, as barytone, 1893-1899; decided he was a tenor; studied and made début, 1900, at Covent Garden; favourite festival tenor; also in opera in Germany and 1910 chief tenor at Beecham's season. (2) **Albert,** b. St. Petersburg, Russia, 1882—Capetown, Dec. 11, 1953; versatile conductor and composer; studied piano with Carreño, conducting with Nikisch; after baton experience in opera at Elberfeld, Dresden, Mannheim and Covent Garden (1914), he became dir. of the St. Petersburg Op., 1914-17, and continued in this post under the Soviets until 1918, subsequently returning to Russia for many engagements; has also appeared with Beecham and British Nat'l. Op. Cos., with Covent Garden Op. Syndicate, Royal Philh. and London Symph. Orchs.; in Paris, Berlin, Vienna, in Spain, Italy and Scandinavia; in U. S. with N. Y. Symph. (1921), Rochester Philh. (1921-22), N. Y. Stadium and Hollywood Bowl (1928-30); c. (operas) "*Sardanapolus*" (St. Petersburg, 1916), "*Samuel Pepys*" (Munich, 1930); "*Pickwick*"; also a "*Launcelot*" Symphony (N. Y. Philh. Stadium Concerts, 1930). (3) **Eric,** b. Hucknall, England, Aug. 27, 1886;

composer; studied at R. Coll. of Mus., viola with Tertis. comp. with Corder; played with Hamburg String Quartet and in Queen's Hall Orch.; after 1918 devoted himself increasingly to composition, esp. orch. music and songs.

Cobb, Gerard Francis, Nettlestead, Kent, Oct. 15, 1838—Cambridge, March 31, 1904; Fellow Trinity Coll., Cambridge, 1863; studied music, Dresden; 1877-92, chairman Board of Music Studies, Cambridge; c. Psalm 62, with orch., etc.

Cob'bett, Walter Willson, Blackheath, July 11, 1847—London, Jan. 22, 1937; music patron, violinist, author; organised first Cobbett Competition, 1905; had given many prizes, particularly for chamber music works; also annual prizes for chamber music performances at R. Coll. and Acad. of Mus.; particularly known as editor of monumental "*International Encyclopedia of Chamber Music*" (1929).

Cocchi (kôk'-kē), **Gioacchino,** Padua, 1715?—Venice, 1804; dram. composer.

Coccia (kôt'-chä), **Carlo,** Naple_, 1782—Novara, 1873; cond. and dram. composer.

Coccon (kôk-kōn), **Nicolò,** Venice, Aug. 10, 1826—Aug. 4, 1903; pupil of E. Fabio; 1856 organist, 1873 conductor at San Marco; c. over 450 numbers, an oratorio, "*Saul*," 8 requiem masses, 30 "messe da gloria," 2 operas, etc.

Cochläus (kôkh'-lĕ-oos), **Jns.** (rightly **Jns. Dobnek,** pseud. "**Wendelstein**"), 1479—Breslau, 1552; writer; opponent of Luther.

Cocks, Robt., & Co., firm of London mus. publishers, founded, 1827, by (1) **Robt. C.,** succeeded by his sons, (2) **Arthur Lincoln C.,** and (3) **Stroud Lincoln C.,** d. 1868; (4) **Robt. Macfarlane C.** in charge until 1908; on his retirement it was bought by Augener & Co.

Coclico (kō'-klē-ko) (**Co'clicus**), **Adrian Petit,** b. in the Hennegau (Hainaut), ca. 1500; singer and composer.

Coenen (koo'-nĕn), (1) **Jns. Meinardus,** The Hague, Jan. 28, 1824—Amsterdam, Jan. 9, 1899; bassoonist, pupil of Lübeck Cons. 1864, cond. at Amsterdam; later municipal mus. dir.; c. ballet-mus., 2 symphonies, cantatas, etc. (2) **Fz.,** Rotterdam,

Dec. 26, 1826—Leyden, Jan. 24, 1904; violinist; pupil of Vieuxtemps and Molique; lived in Amsterdam, 1895, dir. of the Cons. and prof. of vln. and comp.; solo violinist to the Queen; leader of a quartet; and composer of a notable symphony, cantatas, etc. (3) **Willem,** Rotterdam, Nov. 17, 1837—Lugano, March 18, 1918; bro. of above; pianist, toured S. America, and W. Indies; 1862, concert-giver in London; c. oratorio, *"Lazarus"* (1878), etc. (4) **Cornelius,** The Hague, 1838—Arnhem, March, 1913; violinist; 1859, cond. at Amsterdam; 1860 bandm. Garde Nationale, Utrecht; c. overtures, etc.

Coerne (kĕr′-nĕ), **Louis Adolphe,** Newark, N. J., 1870—New London, Conn., Sept. 11, 1922; 1876–80 studied at Stuttgart and Paris, then entered Harvard College and studied with Paine and Kneisel, Boston, U. S. A.; 1890 studied with Rheinberger and Hieber, Munich; 1893 organist at Boston, also at the Columbian Exposition; 1893–96 dir. Liedertafel, Buffalo; 1897, in Columbus, O.; 1902–03, taught Harvard; 1903–04, Smith Coll.; 1907–09, dir. of mus., Troy, N. Y.; 1909–10, dir. Olivet Coll.; 1910, prof. at Univ. of Wis.; 1915, Conn. Coll.; his opera, *"Zenobia"* was prod. at Bremen, 1905; author of *"The Evolution of Modern Orchestration"*; c. great variety of chamber, orch., vocal music; an opera *"The Maid of Marblehead,"* symph. poem *"Hiawatha,"* etc.

Co′gan, Phillip, b. Cork, 1750; organist, teacher and composer.

Cohen (kow′-ĕn or kō′-ĕn), (1) **H.,** Amsterdam, 1808—Brie-sur-Marne, 1880; writer. (2) **Jules Émile David,** Marseilles, Nov. 2, 1830—Paris, Jan. 14, 1901; pupil of Zimmerman, Marmontel, Benoist, and Halévy, Paris Cons.; won first prize for pf., organ, cpt. and fugue; 1870, teacher of ensemble singing at the Cons.; since 1877 *Chef de Chant,* and chorusmaster Gr. Opéra; prod. 4 operas; c. 3 cantatas, several symphonies, masses, oratorios, etc. (3) **K. Hubert,** b. Laurenzkirg (near Aix), Oct. 18, 1851; a priest, studied at Aix and Raliston, 1879–87 cond. Bamberg; 1887–1910 at Cologne Cath.; c. masses, etc. (4) **Harriet,** b. London, England; pianist; her

father a composer, mother a pianist; studied with them and with Matthay; won Ada Lewis Scholarship, R. Acad. of Mus.; début, London, at 13; has appeared widely in Bach programs and works of modern school, incl. Salzburg Fest.; soloist with orch., London, Vienna, Barcelona, Warsaw, New York; also in sonata recitals with Joseph Szigeti, Beatrice Harrison, Lionel Tertis; Amer. début, 1930. Dame Commander.

Colasse (kô-lăs), **Pascal,** Rheims, Jan. 22, 1649—Versailles, 1709; cond. and dram. composer.

Col′bran, (1) **Gianni,** court-musician to King of Spain, 18th century. (2) **Isabella A.,** Madrid, 1785—Bologne, 1845, daughter of above; singer and composer.

Cole, Rossetter G., b. near Clyde, Mich., Feb. 5, 1866—Chicago, May 18, 1952; grad. of Michigan Univ., taking musical courses also; at his graduation the Univ. Mus. Soc. performed his cantata with orch. *"The Passing of Summer"*; 1888–90, he taught English and Latin in high schools; 1890–92 in Berlin, winning competitive scholarship at Royal Master-school, and studying with Max Bruch; 1892–94, prof. of music Ripon College; 1894—1901, Iowa College; from 1902 in Chicago as teacher, and from 1908 also in charge of summer music classes of Columbia Univ., N. Y. c. *"King Robert of Sicily"* and *"Hiawatha's Wooing,"* as musical backgrounds for recitation, ballade for 'cello and orch.; sonata for violin, songs, etc.

Co′leridge-Taylor, Samuel, London, Aug. 15, 1875—Thornton Heath, Sept. 1, 1912 (of African descent; his father a native of Sierra Leone, his mother, English); composer; pupil (vln.) of the R. A. M., 1890; won composition-scholarship in 1893; until 1896 pupil of V. Stanford; 1892 pub. an anthem; c. a nonet for pf., strings, and wind (1894); a symphony (1896); a quintet for clar. and strings (1897), a string-quartet, and a Morning and Evening Service; pub. a ballade for viola and orch., operetta *"Dream Lovers,"* 4 waltzes for orch.; he was made cond. Handel Society, 1904; his *"Hiawatha"* was developed as a trilogy, *"Hiawatha's Wedding Feast,"* (R. C. M., London, 1898),

"The Death of Minnehaha" (North Staffordshire Fest., 1899); *"Hiawatha's Departure"* (London, 1900), the overture the same year; c. also for voices and orch., *"The Blind Girl of Castel-Cuillé"* (Leeds Fest., 1901), *"Meg Blane"* (Sheffield Fest., 1902), *"The Atonement"* (Hereford Fest., 1903), *"Kubla Khan"* (Handel Society, 1906); incid. music to Stephen Phillips's plays, *"Herod," "Ulysses," "Nero,"* and *"Faust"* (1908); concert march, *"Ethiopia Saluting the Colours"*; 5 ballads by Longfellow, with orch. (Norwich Fest., 1905); *"A Tale of Old Japan,"* voices and orch. (London, 1912), etc.

Colin (kȯ-lăṅ), **P. Gilbert** (Colinus, Colinaus, Chamault), singer and notable composer, Paris, 1532.

Col'la, Giuseppe, cond. at Parma, 1780, m. Agujari.

Collard (kȯl-lăr'), a London family of pf.-makers. (1) **Fr. W. Collard** (1772—1860), in partnership with Clementi, bought out Longman & Broderip, 1798, then **C.** bought out Clementi; he inv. various devices; the firm name now Collard & Collard, (2) **Chas. Lukey C.** being the head until his death, 1891; then (3) **J. C.** (Collard) was dir.

Colles (cȯl'-lĕs), **Henry Cope**, London, April 20, 1879—March 4, 1943; critic, editor; educated R. Coll. of Mus., Worcester Coll., Oxford; M.A. Oxon.; asst. music critic, *"London Times,"* after 1906, and critic since 1911; prof., R. Coll. of Mus.; ed. new edition Grove's Dictionary, 1928; served as guest critic, New York *"Times,"* 1923; author, *"Brahms," "The Growth of Music."*

Colombani (kȯ-lȯm-bä'-nē), **Orazio**, monk, conductor, and cptist. at Verona, 1576–92.

Colonna (kȯ-lȯn'-nä), **Giov. Paolo**, Bologna (or Brescia), 1637—Bologna, 1693; organist, conductor, and dram. composer.

Colonne (kȯ-lŭn'), **Edouard** (rightly **Judas**), Bordeaux, July 23, 1838—Paris, March 28, 1910; pupil of Girard and Sauzay (vln.), Elwart, and A. Thomas (comp.), Paris Cons.; 1874, founded the famous "Concerts du Chatelet"; 1878, cond. official Exposition concerts; 1892 cond. at the Gr. Opéra; cond. often in London, and 1902, Vienna and 1905, New York.

Colyns (kȯ-lăṅs), **Jean Baptiste**, Brussels, Nov. 25, 1834—Oct. 31, 1902; violinist and comp.

Combs, Gilbert Raynolds, Philadelphia, Jan. 5, 1863—Mt. Airy, Pa., June 14, 1934; son and pupil of a pianist, organist and composer; organist and conductor in Philadelphia; 1885 founded the Broad St. Cons. of Mus., of which he was for many years the enterprising dir.

Comes (kȯ'-mās), **Juan Baptista**, Valencia, ca. 1560; conductor and composer.

Comettant (kȯm-ĕt-täṅ), (**J. P.**) **Oscar**, Bordeaux, Gironde, 1819—Montvilliers, 1898; writer and composer.

Commer (kȯm'-měr), **Fz.**, Cologne, 1813—Berlin, 1887; editor and composer.

Compère (kȯṅ-păr), **Louis** (diminutive, Loyset), Flanders, 15th cent.—St. Quentin, Aug. 16, 1518; famous contrapuntist.

Concone (kȯn-kȯ'-nĕ), **Giu.**, Turin, 1810—June, 1861; organist, famous singing-teacher in Paris, 1832–48, later court-organist Turin; c. 2 operas and famous vocal exercises.

Co'ninck, **Jacques Félix de**, Antwerp, 1791—Schaerbeck-les-Bruxelles, 1866; conductor at Berlin, and composer.

Conradi (kȯn-rä'-dē), (1) **Jn. G.**, 17th cent.; conductor; one of the first composers of German opera, his works prod. at Hamburg. (2) **Johan G.**, Tönsberg, Norway, 1820—Christiania, 1896; composer. (3) **Aug.**, Berlin, 1821—1873; organist and dram. composer.

Conried (kän'-rēd), **He'nrich**, Bielitz, Silesia, Sept. 13, 1855—Meran, April 27, 1909; impresario; came to New York 1878; 1901, succeeded Grau as manager of the Metropolitan Opera House, where in 1903 he made the first production outside Bayreuth of *"Parsifal"*; 1905, Franz Leopold decorated him and gave him the privilege of the prefix "von"; ill health forced his retirement in 1908.

Con'solo, (1) **Frederigo**, Ancona, 1841—Florence, Dec. 14, 1906; violinist and comp. (2) **Ernesto**, London, Sept. 15, 1864—Florence, March 21, 1931; noted pianist; pupil of Sgambati and Reinecke; toured widely; 1906–09, taught Chicago Mus. Coll.; later at Geneva and Florence Cons.; ed. Beethoven sonatas for pf.

Constantin (kôn-stän-tăn), **Titus Chas.,** Marseilles, Jan. 7, 1835—Pau, Oct., 1891; pupil of Thomas, Paris Cons., 1860; cond. of the "Fantasies Parisiennes"; 1875, Op. Com.; c. a comic-opera, *"Dans la Forêt"* (1872), etc.

Conti (kôn'-tē), (1) **Fran. Bart.,** Florence, 1682—1732; court-theorbist and dram. composer. (2) ("**Contini**") **Ignazio,** Florence, 1699—Vienna, 1759; son and successor of above; composer. (3) **Gioacchino** (named Gizziello, after his teacher Dom. Gizzi), Arpino, Naples, 1714—Rome, 1761; famous male soprano; 1739, in London with Händel; retired to Arpino in 1753. (4) **Carlo,** Arpino, Naples, 1796—Naples, 1868; prof. and dram. composer.

Contino (kōn-tē'-no), **Giov.,** d. Mantua, 1565; conductor and contrapuntist.

Co'nus (or **Conius** or **Konius**), (1) **George Edwardovich,** composer; Moscow, Oct. 1, 1862—Aug., 1933; theorist; pupil of the Cons.; 1891-99 teacher of theory there; 1902 prof. at the Opera School; c. symph. poem *"From the Realm of Illusions,"* orch. suite, *"Child-Life,"* cantata, etc. His brother, (2) **Julius,** b. Moscow, 1869; gold medallist at the Cons. and later teacher of violin there; c. violin concerto, etc. (3) **Leo,** pianist; pupil at the Cons.; later founded a school; d. Cincinnati, Jan. 18, 1944.

Converse, Frederick Shepherd, b. Newton, Mass., Jan. 1, 1871—Westwood, Mass., June 8, 1940; grad. Harvard and studied music with Bährmann and G. W. Chadwick; 1896-98 with Rheinberger, then taught theory and comp. at the New England Cons.; 1901-07, Harvard Univ.; c. operas *"The Pipe of Desire"* (in concert form, Boston, 1906, as an opera, Met. Op., N. Y., 1910, Boston Op., 1911); symph. (1907); overtures, *"Youth"* and *"Euphrosyne"*; orch. romance, *"The Festival of Pan"*; orch. fantasie, *"The Mystic Trumpeter"*; symph. poem *"Ormazd,"* (Boston Symph. Orch., 1912); violin concerto and sonata, 2 string quartets, etc.

Conver'si, Girolamo, b. Correggio, 16th cent.; c. madrigals, etc.

Cooke, (1) **H.,** d. July 13, 1672; buried Westminster Abbey; court-composer and teacher. (2) **Nathaniel,** b. Bosham, 1773; organist. (3) **Benj.,** London, 1734—1793; conductor and composer. (4) **Thos. Simpson,** Dublin, 1782—London, 1848; conductor, later tenor, then prof. at the R. A. M.; prod. nearly 20 operas at Drury Lane. (5) **H. Angelo Michael** (called **Grattan**), son of above; oboist and bandmaster. (6) **James Francis,** b. Bay City, Mich., Nov. 14, 1875; pianist, composer, editor, teacher; studied in New York with W. H. Hall, Woodman, Eberhard and Medorn; also at Würzburg R. Cons. with Meyer-Olbersleben and Hermann Ritter; for some years active as piano teacher in New York, also org. and vocal teacher; beginning 1907 ed. *"The Etude"*; pres. Presser Foundation, Phila., after 1917; Mus. D., Ohio Northwestern Univ., 1919; c. piano pieces and songs; author, *"Great Pianists upon Piano Playing"*; *"Standard History of Music"*; *"Mastering the Scales and Arpeggios"*; *"Musical Playlets"*; *"Music-Masters Old and New,"* etc.

Coolidge, Elizabeth Sprague (Mrs. Frederick Shurtleff Coolidge), noted music patron, composer, pianist; founder and sponsor for many years of the Pittsfield, Mass., Music Fests., on her estate, where invited audiences attended these events; in recent years transferred to auditorium in Library of Congress, Washington, which she donated and endowed by means of trust fund; commissioned works from many leading contemporary composers; has established a Coolidge Chamber Music Prize for such awards, and has sponsored festivals in Chicago (1930) and in many European cities, in which eminent solo artists and chamber music groups have participated; c. chamber music; d. Cambridge, Mass., Nov. 4, 1953.

Coombs, Chas. Whitney, b. Bucksport, Me., Dec. 25, 1859—Montclair, N.J., Jan. 24, 1940; pupil of Speidel (pf.) and Max Seifriz, Draeseke (comp.), Hermann John, P. Janssen, and Lamperti; 1887-91, organist Amer. Ch., in Dresden; 1892, as organist Church of the Holy Communion, New York, 1908, St. Luke's; pub. *"The Vision of St. John,"* cantata with orch. and org., songs, etc.

Coo'per, (1) **G.,** Lambeth, London, 1820—London, 1876; organist and composer. (2) **Emil,** Russian conductor; pupil of Taneyeff; cond. at Moscow Imp. Op. and Imp. Mus.

Soc. of Cons. in that city before the world war; led 50th anniversary concerts of latter organization, presenting works of Scriabin, Taneyeff and Rachmaninoff in presence of composers; 1909-14, led seasons of Russian opera in London and Paris; after 1917 lived in Paris, cond. of opera in Champs-Elysées Theat.; also guest appearances in other European countries; cond. of Chicago Op. Co., 1929-31, presenting American premières of Moret's *"Lorenzaccio"* and Hamilton Forrest's *"Camille."*

Coperario (kō-pĕr-ä′-rĭ-ō) (rightly **J. Cooper**), famous English lutenist and viola-da-gambist, 17th century.

Copland (cōp′-lănd), **Aaron**, b. Brooklyn, N. Y., Nov. 14, 1900; composer; studied with Rubin Goldmark, also with Nadia Boulanger, Fontainebleau; piano with Victor Wittgenstein and Clarence Adler; lecturer on modern music, New School for Social Research, N. Y.; organized and promoted Copland-Sessions Concerts of Contemporary Music, N. Y. (with Roger Sessions); mem. board of directors, League of Composers; c. ballets, *"Billy the Kid," "Rodeo," "Appalachian Spring"; "A Lincoln Portrait"* (with speaker); *"Music for Theatre"*; orch., Piano Concerto; *"El Salon Mexico"*; opera, *"Tender Land."*

Coppet (kŏ-pā), **Edward J. de**, New York, May 28, 1855—April 30, 1916; of Swiss descent; music patron; founded series of chamber music programmes at his home, 1886, more than a thousand being given before his death; in 1902, the Flonzaley Quartet (Adolfo Betti, Alfred Pochon, Ugo Ara and Iwan d'Archambeau) was organised to play at these events, being named after his summer home in Switzerland; this group became one of world's leading ensembles and made many Amer. and Eur. tours, first under his patronage and later as a public concert-giving enterprise: after 1917 Ara being succeeded as violist by Louis Bailly.

Cop′pola, (1) **Giu.**, singer in London, 1777. (2) **P. A. (Pierantonio)**, Castrogiovanni, Sicily, 1793—Catania, 1877; dram. composer and conductor. (3) **Piero**, b. Milan, Oct. 11, 1888; conductor and composer; grad. Cons. Verdi, in native city; led appeared as cond. in Turin, Milan (La Scala), Modena, Florence, Bo-

logna, Brussels (La Monnaie), London, Oslo, Gothenberg, Copenhagen, Palermo, etc.; after 1923 res. in Paris as artistic dir. of French Gramophone Co. and as cond. of concerts; c. of stage and orch. music.

Coquard (kŏ-kăr), **Arthur**, Paris, May 26, 1846—Noirmoutier, Aug. 20, 1910; pupil of César Franck; mus. prof. Nat. Inst. of the Young Blind; critic for *"Le Monde"*; c. operas *"L' Epée du Roi"* (Angers, 1884); *"Le Mari d'un Jour"* (Paris, 1886); lyric dramas, *"L'oiseau bleu"* (Paris, 1894); *"La Jacquerie"* (Monte Carlo and Paris, 1895), *"Jahel"* (Lyons, 1900), *"La troupe Jolicoeur"* (1902), etc. Won prize from French Acad. for his study, *"De la Musique en France depuis Rameau"* (1892).

Cor′bett, Wm., 1669 (?)—London (?), 1748; Engl. violinist and composer.

Cordans (kŏr-däns), **Bart.**, Venice, 1700—Udine, 1757; Franciscan monk, then conductor and dram. composer.

Cordel′la, Giacomo, Naples, 1783—1847; dram. composer.

Cor′der, Fr., Hackney, London, Jan. 26, 1852—Sept. 21, 1932; pupil of R. A. M.; 1875, won the Mendelssohn Scholarship; 1875-78, pupil of Ferd. Hiller; 1880, cond. of Aquarium Concerts at Brighton where he lived as a transl. and critic, and composer of operas, cantatas, etc.; after 1886 prof. at R. A. M., London; 1889, curator there; wrote *"The Orchestra and How to Write for It,"* etc., ed. a musical encyclopedia (1915).

Corel′li, Arcangelo, Fusignano, near Imola, Italy, Feb. 17, 1653—Rome, Jan. 8, 1713; pupil of Bessani and Simonelli; toured Germany, then lived under patronage of Cardinal Ollobone; one of the founders of vln.-style, systematiser of bowing and shifting, introducer of chord-playing; a composer for the vln. whose works still hold favour. On invitation from the King of Naples he gave a succ. court-concert, but at a second made various blunders and returned to Rome, in chagrin, increased with fatal results on finding or imagining himself supplanted there by a poor violinist named Valentini. His masterpieces *"Concerti grossi,"* were pub. just before his death. Many spurious comps. were issued under his name.

Corfe, (1) **Jos.,** Salisbury, 1740—1820; organist and composer. (2) **Arthur T.,** Salisbury, 1773—1863; son of above; pianist, organist and writer. (3) **Chas. W.,** son of above; organist Christ Church, Oxford.

Cornelius (kôr-nā'-lǐ-oos), **Peter,** Mayence, Dec. 24, 1824—Oct. 26, 1874, unsucc. actor; then studied cpt. with Dehn at Berlin, and joined the Wagnerian coterie at Weimar. His opera *"Der Barbier von Bagdad"* was a failure through organised opposition which led Liszt to leave the town, but in 1886–87 it succeeded. C. wrote his own libretti and transl. others. 1886–87, at Dresden, and other cities; 1859, with Wagner at Vienna, and Munich, where he became reader to King Ludwig, and prof.; prod. the opera *"Der Cid,"* Weimar, 1865; he left *"Gunlöd"* unfinished; Lassen completed it, and it was prod., Strassburg, 1892; he pub. many songs. Biog. by Sandberger (Leipzig, 1887).

Cornell', J. H., New York, 1828—1894; organist, composer and writer.

Cornet (kôr'-nät), (1) **Julius,** S. Candido, Tyrol, 1793—Berlin, 1860; tenor and dir. His wife, (2) **Franziska** (1806—1870), was also a singer.

Coronaro (kō-rō-nä'-rō), (1) **Gaetano,** Vicenza, Italy, Dec. 18, 1852— Milan, April 5, 1908; violinist; till 1873, pupil, Milan Cons., then in Germany; prod. the succ. opera *"Un Tramonto"* (Milan Cons. Th., 1873); 3-act *"La Creola"* (Bologna, 1878); *"Il Malacarne"* (Brescia, 1894); for several years prof. of harm., and 1894, prof. of comp., Milan Cons. (2) **Antonio,** Vicenza, 1851—March 24, 1933; brother of **Gaetano C.,** and comp. of operas; his son was (3) **Arrigo,** Vicenza, 1880—October, 1906; c. opera *"Turiddu"* (Turin, 1905). (4) **Gellio Bv.,** Vicenza, Nov. 30, 1863—Milan, July 26, 1916; pianist (protégé of Sonzogno); début at 8; at 9, organist in Vicenza; at 13, th. cond., Marosteca; at 15, chorusm.; at 16, pupil Bologna Cons., graduating with first prizes; c. a symphony; opera, *"Jolanda"* (1889 ?); unsucc. *"Claudia"* (Milan, 1895).

Corri (kôr'-rē), **Dom.,** Rome, 1744— London, 1825; dram. composer and writer.

Cor'si, Jacopo, ca. 1560—1604; Florentine nobleman, in whose house and in Bardi's, Peri, Caccini, Emilio del Cavaliere, Galilei, Rinuccini, and others met and inaugurated modern opera (v. PERI); **C.** was a skilful gravicembalist.

Corteccia (kôr-tĕt'-chä), **Fran. Bdo. di,** Arezzo, 16th cent., Florence, 1571; organist, conductor and composer.

Cortellini (kôr-tĕl-lē'-nē), **Camillo,** called "Il violino" from his skill; at Bologna, 1583, as municipal musician and comp.

Cortesi (kôr-tā'-zē), **Francesco,** Florence, 1826—Jan. 3, 1904; conductor, composer of operas, and teacher of voice.

Cortot (kôr-tō'), **Alfred,** b. Nyon, Switzerland, Sept. 26, 1877; pianist; studied at Paris Cons., with Decombes and Diémer; début, Colonne Concerts, Paris, 1896; served as *répétiteur* at Bayreuth; founder and leader of Assoc. des Concerts Cortot in Paris (1902–04) and led performances of Wagnerian operas; prof., Paris Cons., 1907; after 1904 toured as pianist in many Eur. cities and in America with great succ.; also has been associated with Thibaud and Casals in trio of exemplary merit, and with these musicians has been leading factor in the École Normale de Musique, Paris; mem. of the Legion of Honor.

Coss'mann, B., Dessau, May 17, 1822 —Frankfort, May 7, 1910; 'cellist; pupil of Espenhahn, Drechsler, Theo. Müller and Kummer; 1840, member of Gr. Opéra Orch., Paris; 1847–48, solo 'cellist at Gewandhaus, Leipzig; then studied comp. under Hauptmann; 1850, at Weimar, with Liszt; 1866, prof. Moscow Cons.; 1870–78 at Baden-Baden; then prof. of 'cello, Frankfort Cons.; composer.

Cossoul (kôs'-sool), **Guilherme Antonio,** Lisbon, April 22, 1828— May 26, 1880; 'cellist and comp.

Cos'ta, (1) Sir **Michael** (rightly **Michele**), Naples, Feb. 4, 1808— Brighton, England, April 29, 1884; son and pupil of (2) **Pasquale C.** (composer ch.-mus.); pupil also of Tritto, Zingarelli (comp.), and Crescentini (singing) at the Naples Cons.; prod. 4 succ. operas at Naples, was sent to Birmingham, England, to cond. a psalm of Zingarelli's, but through a misunderstanding, had to sing the tenor part; he thereafter lived in England as dir. and cond.

of King's Th., London, where he prod. three ballets; 1846, cond. of the Philh. and the new Ital. Opera; 1848, Sacred Harmonic Society; from 1849, cond. Birmingham festivals; from 1857, the Handel festivals; knighted in 1869; 1871 dir. of the music and cond. at H. M.'s Opera; c. 3 oratorios, 6 operas, 3 symphonies, etc. (3) **Andrea,** b. Brescia, settled London, 1825; composer and teacher. (4) **Carlo,** Naples, 1826 — 1888; teacher Naples Cons. (5) **P. Mario,** Tarento, July 26, 1858—San Remo, Sept. 27, 1933; nephew of above; c. chamber-music and pop. songs in Neapolitan dialect; also 2 pantomimes, *"Le Modèle Rêve,"* and the succ. *"L'Histoire d'un Pierrot"* (Paris, 1894 ?).

Costantini (tē'-nē), **Fabio,** b. Rome ca. 1570; composer and teacher.

Costanzi (kō-stän'-tsĭ), **Juan** (or **Gioannino**), Rome, 1754—1778; conductor.

Cotes (kō'-tĕs), **Ambrosio de,** d. Seville, Sept. 9, 1603; Spanish composer and cond.

Cott'low, Augusta, b. Shelbyville, Ill., April 2, 1878; pianist; pupil in Chicago of Wolfsohn and Gleason; orch. début there, 1889; N. Y., under Seidl, 1891; later studied in Berlin with Busoni and Boise; toured Eur. countries and after 1900 in U. S.

Cot'to (**Cotto'nius**), **Jns.,** 11th to 12th cent.; writer.

Cottrau (kŏt-trō, or kŏt-trä'-oo), (1) **Guillaume** (**Guglielmo**), Paris, 1797 —Naples, 1847; composer. His sons (2) **Teodoro** (pen-name **Eutalindo Martelli**) (Naples, 1827—1879) and (3) **Giulio** (**Jules**), (Naples, 1831— Rome, 1916) also song-composers; the latter c. operas.

Coucy (dŭ koo-sē), **Regnault,** Chatelain, **de,** d. Palestine, 1192; troubadour to Richard Cœur de Lion; his songs are in MSS. in the Paris Library, and have been re-published.

Couperin (koo-pŭ-răn), a family of French musicians, famous for two centuries. The first known were three brothers: (1) **Louis,** 1626— 1661; organist of St. Gervais and composer. (2) **Fran.** (Sieur de Crouilly), 1631—1698; organist and composer. (3) **Chas.,** 1638—1669; organist; his son, (4) **Fran.** (called **Le Grand**), Paris, 1668—1733; the

composer of choral and chamber wks., much music for harpsichord (clavecin); pupil of Thomelin, and successor of his uncle François, at St. G., 1698; 1701, clavecinist and organist to the King; c. brilliant and fascinating music pub. at Paris, and wrote *"L'Art de toucher du Clavecin"* (1711). (5) His son **Nicholas,** Paris, 1680—1748, was organist. (6) **Armand Louis,** Paris, 1725—1789, son of (5), a remarkable org.-virtuoso. His wife (7) **Élisabeth Antoinette** (née **Blanchet**), b. 1721, was an organist and clavecinist, and played in public at 81. They had 2 sons (8) **P. Louis** (d. 1789), his father's asst. organist, and (9) **Gervais Fran.,** his father's successor.

Courboin (kōōr'-bwän), **Charles-Marie,** b. Antwerp, April 2, 1886; organist; pupil of Blockx at Cons. in native city; also at Brussels Cons. of Mailly, Gilson, Huberti and Tinel; won prizes in several fields, also internat'l. competition; after 1902, org. Antwerp Cathedral; appeared widely as recitalist; after 1904 in U. S., at Syracuse, Springfield, Mass., etc.; c. choral and organ music.

Courtois (koor-twä), **Jean,** 16th cent., French contrapuntist; conductor and composer.

Courvoisier (koor-vwäs-yā, or koor'-foi-sēr), (1) **K.,** Basel, Nov. 12, 1864 —1908; violinist; pupil of David, Röntgen and Joachim; 1871, a member of the Thalia Th., orch.; then, till 1875, cond. of singing with Gustav Barth; '76, cond. Düsseldorf Th., orch., and choral societies; 1885, singing-teacher at Liverpool; c. a symphony, 2 concert-overtures, a vln.-concerto (MS.), etc.; wrote *"Die Violintechnik"* (transl. by H. E. Krehbiel; N. Y., 1896); an *"École de la velocité"* and a *"Méthode"* (London, 1892). (2) **Walter,** near Basel, Feb. 7, 1875 —Locarno, Dec. 27, 1931; pupil of Bagge and Thuille; after 1910, prof. of theory, Munich Akad.

Coussemaker (koos-mă-kăr'), **Chas. Ed. H.,** Bailleul, Nord, April 19, 1805— Boubourg, Jan. 10, 1876; a remarkable sight-reader, studied cpt. with V. Lefèbvre; while serving as a judge he made musical research his avocation, and pub. important works on Hucbald and mediæval instruments, theory and composers, incl. his

"Scriptores de musica medii evi, nova series" (1864–76, 4 vols.), a great collection intended as supplement to Gerbert.

Cousser. Vide KUSSER.

Cow'ard, (1) **Jas.**, London, 1824—1880; organist, conductor, composer. (2) Sir **Henry**, Liverpool, Nov. 26, 1849—Sheffield, 1944; noted choral cond.; 1889 Mus. Bac.; 1894 Mus. Doc. Oxon; Univ.-teacher and cond. at Sheffield; after 1904, docent in music; knighted, 1919. (3) **Noel**, Engl. composer for stage; c. *"Bitter Sweet,"* etc.

Cow'ell, Henry, b. Menlo Park, Cal., March 11, 1897; composer, pianist; studied Univ. of Calif. and in Europe; début, Munich, 1923; toured in Europe and America; his compositions early attracted attention because of use of "tone-clusters," groups of notes which might be performed on the piano keyboard with forearm or fist; in recent years has also c. orchestral and chamber music; carried on research under Guggenheim Fellowship in European folk music; dir. New Mus. Soc. of Calif., which issued contemporary Amer. music in quarterly form and recordings.

Cow'en, Sir **Frederic Hymen,** Kingston, Jamaica, Jan. 29, 1852—London, Oct. 6, 1935; at 4 brought to London to study, pupil of Benedict and Goss, then of Hauptmann, Moscheles, Reinecke, Richter, and Plaidy, Leipzig; and Kiel, Berlin; 1882, dir. Edinburgh Acad. of Music; 1887, cond. London Philh.; 1888–89, mus.-dir. Melbourne Centennial Exhibition; 1896–1914, cond. Liverpool Phil., and the Manchester Concerts; 1900, of Scottish Orch.; knighted 1911; prod. four operas; two oratorios, *"The Deluge"* (1878), and *"Ruth"* (1887); 7 cantatas; 6 symphonies (No. 3 *"Scandinavian"* (1880), 4 *"Welsh,"* 6 *"Idyllic"*); four orchestral suites, *"The Language of Flowers," "In the Olden Time," "In Fairyland," "Suite de Ballet,"* Sinfonietta in A for orch.; 2 overtures; pf.-concerto; pf.-trio; pf.-quartet; pf.-pcs.; over 250 songs.

Crabbé (kräb-ä), **Armand,** b. Brussels, 1884; barytone; pupil of Cons. in native city; 1904–08, sang at La Monnaie, Brussels; 1908–10, Manhattan Op. House, New York; after 1910 for several seasons with Chicago

Op. Co., also at Covent Garden, Berlin; d. Buenos Aires, Jan., 1948.

Craft, Marcella, b. Indianapolis, Aug. 11, 1880; soprano; studied with Charles Adams, also 1901 in Milan with Guagni and Mottino; op. début, Morbegno, 1902; sang in Italy, at Mainz, Kiel, and at Munich Op., 1909–14; in America, 1917–18; after 1923 lived in Germany as singer and teacher.

Cramer (krä'-měr or krä'-měr), (1) **Wm.,** Mannheim, 1745 (1743 ?)—London, 1799 (1800?); violinist and conductor. (2) **K. Fr.,** Quedlinburg, 1752—Paris, Dec. 1807; professor. (3) **Jn. Bap.,** Mannheim, Feb. 24, 1771—London, April 16, 1858; eldest son and pupil of (1). Brought to London when a year old; pupil of Benser, Schroeter, then of Clementi; in comp., chiefly self-taught; toured as concert-pianist at 17; in 1828 est. a mus.-pub. firm (now Cramer & Co.) in partnership with Addison; managed it till 1842; 1832–45, lived in Paris, pub. "a Method for pf. (*"Grosse praktische Pfte.-Schule"*), in 5 parts," the last containing the celebrated *"84 Studies"* (op. 50), still a standard; c. 7 concertos, 105 sonatas, quartet, quintet, and many pf.-pcs.

Cranz (kränts), **August,** Hamburg, mus.-pub. firm, founded 1813 by **A. H. Cranz** (1789–1870). His son **Alwin** (b. 1834) succeeded him, and in 1896 his grandson **Oscar** became head.

Craywinckel (krī'-vĭnk-ĕl), **Fd. Manuel Martin Louis Barthélemy de,** Madrid, Aug. 24, 1820—?; pupil of Bellon; cond. St. Bruno, at Bordeaux, where he lived from 1825; c. excellent masses and other church-mus.

Cre(c)quillon (krěk-wē-yōn), **Thos.,** n. Ghent (?)—Béthune, 1557; ca. 1544–47 conductor and composer.

Crescentini (krā-shĕn-tē'-nē), **Girolamo,** Urbania, near Urbino, Feb. 2, 1766—Naples, April 24, 1846; famous male soprano and composer.

Cre'ser, William, York, Sept. 9, 1844—1933; organist, composer; pupil of Macfarren; 1880, Mus. Doc. Oxford; 1881, 1891–1902, org. Chapel Royal; St. James, and comp. to Chapel Royal; married Amelia Clarke mezzo-soprano; c. oratorio, *"Micaiah"*; cantatas *"Eudora"*

(Leeds, 1882); "*The Sacrifice of Freia*" (Leeds, 1889), etc.

Cressent (krĕs-sän), **Anatole**, Argenteuil, 1824—Paris, 1870; lawyer and founder of the triennial prize "prix Cressent," endowed with 120,000 francs, to be equally divided between the librettist and composer.

Creston, Paul, b. N. Y., 1906; comp.; 1938 Guggen. fellow; c. symph., etc.

Creyghton (krā'-tŭn), Rev. **Robt.**, b. ca. 1639; English composer.

Crist, Bainbridge, b. Lawrenceburg, Ind., 1883; composer; pupil of Juon, Emerich and Shakespeare; after 1914 was active as teacher in Boston; c. dance-drama, "*Le Pied de la Momie*," orch. and chamber music, and songs.

Cristofo'ri, Bart. (wrongly **Cristofali** and **Cristofani**), Padua, May 4, 1655 —Florence, Jan. 27, 1731; inv. the first practical hammer-action to which he gave the name "pianoforte" (v. D. D.); in 1711 he substituted for the plucking quills "a row of little hammers striking the strings from below," the principle adopted by Broadwood, and called the "English action."

Crivel'li, (1) **Arcangelo**, Bergamo, 1546 —1617; tenor and composer. (2) **Giov. Bat.**, Scandiano, Modena (?)— Modena, 1682; organist and conductor. (3) **Gaetano**, Bergamo, 1774 —Brescia, 1836; famous tenor. (4) **Dom.**, b. Brescia, 1793; son of above, dram. composer.

Croce (krō'-chĕ), **Giov. della** (called "Il Chiozzotto"), Chioggia, ca. 1557 —Venice, 1609; conductor and composer.

Croes (kroos), **H. Jas. de**, Antwerp, 1705—Brussels, 1786; violinist and conductor.

Croft(s), Wm., Nether-Eatington, Warwickshire, Engl., 1678—Bath, 1727 (buried Westm. Abbey); 1704, joint organist, 1707, sole organist Westm. Abbey; pub. "*Musica sacra*" (the first English church-music engraved in score on plates).

Crooks, Richard, b. Trenton, N. J.; tenor; sang as boy soprano in church choir at 8; pupil of Sydney H. Bourne; concert appearances at 12; following war service, was soloist at First Presbyterian Church, N. Y.; first came into prominence as soloist with N. Y. Symph., 1922; made U. S. concert tours, also of England,

Scandinavia and Central Europe, 1927; as Cavaradossi, Hamburg Op., same year; also at Berlin Op.; soloist with leading Amer. orchs.; mem. Met. Op. Co., after 1933, singing leading French and Italian rôles.

Cros'dill, J., London, 1751—Escrick, Yorkshire, 1825; 'cellist.

Cross, Michael Hurley, Philadelphia, 1833—1897; composer and director.

Cross'ley, Ada, near Bairnsdale, Australia, March 3, 1874—London, Oct. 17, 1929; noted mezzo-soprano; début, Melbourne as a girl; after 1894 lived in London; studied with Santley and later with Marchesi; sang at many English festivals; 1904 toured Australia; later also U. S.; m. F. E. Muecke.

Crotch, Wm., Norwich, Engl., July 5, 1775—Taunton, Dec. 29, 1847; at the age of 2½ he played on a small organ, built by his father, a mastercarpenter; at 10 played in public at London; at the age of 11 asst. organist of Trinity and King's Colleges Cambridge; at 14 c. on oratorio, "*The Captivity of Judah*" (perf. 1789), became organist of Christ Ch., Oxford; 1797, prof. of mus. Oxford; 1799, Mus. Doc. there; 1822 principal of the new R. A. M., c. 2 oratorios.

Crouch, (1) Mrs. **Anna M.** (née **Phillips**), 1763—Brighton, 1805; Engl. operatic singer. (2) Fr. **Nicholls**, London, July 31, 1808—Portland, Me., Aug. 18, 1896; basso, 'cellist and singing-teacher; c. 2 operas, and songs, incl. "*Kathleen Mavourneen*."

Cro'west, Fr. J., London, Nov. 30, 1850 —Birmingham, June 14, 1927; eminent organist, writer and composer.

Crüger (krü'-gĕr), **Jns.**, Gross-Breese, near Guben, 1598—Berlin, 1662; organist.

Crusell (kroos'-sĕl), **Bernhard**, Finland, 1775—Stockholm, 1838; composer.

Cruvel'li (rightly **Crüwell**) (krü'-vĕl), (1) **Friederike M.**, Bielefeld, Westphalia, 1824—1868; noted contralto in London, but lost her voice. (2) **Jne. Sophie Charlotte**, Bielefeld, Mar. 12, 1826—Nice, Nov. 6, 1907; sister of above; also contralto, illtrained, but had enormous success at Paris Gr. Opéra, 1854, at a salary of 100,000 francs; in 1856 m. Comte Vigier, and left the stage.

Cui (kwē), **César Antonovitch**, Vilna.

Russia, Jan. 18, 1835—d. at Vilna, September 14, 1918; one of the most important of Russian composers; pupil of Moniuszko and Balakirev; a military engineer; Prof. of fortification at the St. Petersburg Engineering Acad ; from 1864–68, critic of the St. P. *"Gazette"*; 1878–79, pub. articles in Paris, on *"La musique en Russie'* ; c. operas, *"William Ratcliffe"* (St. P., 1869); *"The Prisoner in the Caucasus"* (1873); *"Angelo"* (1876); *"The Mandarin's Son"* (1878); lyric comedy, *"Le Filibustier"* (Paris, 1894); the very succ. *"The Saracen"* (1899); *"A Feast in Time of Plague"* (1901); *"Mam'zelle Fifi"* (1903); *"Matteo Falcone"* (1908); *"The Captain's Daughter"*; some thirty mixed choruses; string quartet, many vln. works, 2 scherzos and a tarantella for orch.; suite for pf. and vln.; pf.-pcs.; some 200 songs. *"Esquisse critique"* on Cui and his works by the Comtesse de Mercy-Argenteau; also studies by Koptiaev, Weimarn, etc.

Cul'bertson, Sasha, b. Russia, Dec. 29, 1893; violinist; pupil of Suchorukoff; at 9 entered Cons. at Rostoff; in 1905 pupil of Sevcik, Prague; début, Vienna 1908; toured Europe and Amer.; d. N. Y., Apr. 16, 1944.

Culp (koolp), **Julia,** b. Groningen, Oct. 1, 1881; mezzo-soprano; wellknown Liedersinger; pupil of Amsterdam Cons. and of Etelka Gerster; has toured Europe with great success; after 1912, America.

Culwick (kŭl'-lĭk), **James C.,** West Bromwich, April 28, 1845—Dublin, Oct. 5, 1907; organist, theorist and comp. Prof. Alexandria College, Dublin; cond. Dublin Philharmonic Soc., etc. 1903, Mus. Doc. Univ. of Dublin.

Cum'mings, Wm. Hayman, Sudbury, Devon, Eng., Aug. 22, 1831—London, August, 1915; organist Waltham Abbey; prof. of singing R. Coll. for the Blind, Norwood; 1896, principal of Guildhall Sch. of Mus.; founded the Purcell Society, ed. its pubs.; wrote biog. of Purcell (London, 1882); had also pub. a music *"Primer,"* 1877; and a *"Biog. Dictionary of Musicians"* (1892); c. a cantata, *"The Fairy Ring,"* etc.

Curci (koor'-chē), **Giu.,** Barletta, 1808 —1877; singing teacher and dram. composer.

Cur'ry, Arthur Mansfield, b. Chelsea, Mass., Jan. 27, 1866; violin pupil of Franz Kneisel and Edward MacDowell in harmony; teacher and cond. in Boston; c. overture *"Blomidon"* (Worcester, Mass., Fest. 1902); symph. poem *"Atala"* (Boston Symph., 1911); *"The Winning of Amarac"*; Keltic legend for a reader, chorus and orch., etc.

Curschmann (koorsh'-män), **K. Fr.,** Berlin, 1805—Langfuhr, near Danzig, 1841; singer, dram. composer and pop. song-writer.

Curti (koor'-tē), **Fz.** (or **Francesco**), Cassel, 1854—Dresden, 1898; dram. composer.

Curtis, (1) H. Holbrook, New York, Dec. 15, 1856—1920; grad. Yale, 1877; 1880, M.D.; vice-pres. Am. Social Science Assn., prominent throat specialist and writer on the voice, pub. *"Voice Building and Tone Placing."* (2) **Natalie,** New York– Paris, Oct. 23, 1921; writer on Indian and Negro music; studied with Friedheim, Busoni, Giraudet, Wolff and Kniese; early active as pianist; made collection of 200 songs of Am. Indians, also Negro folk-songs; m. Paul Burlin, painter.

Cur'wen, (1) Rev. J., Heckmondwike, Yorkshire, Engl., 1816—near Manchester, 1880; 1862, resigned his pastorate, and founded a college, also a pub.-house, to exploit Tonic-sol-fa. (2) **J. Spencer,** Plaistow, 1847— London, 1916; son and pupil of above; pupil also of G. Oakey and R.A.M.; writer, and 1880 pres. Tonic-sol-fa Coll.

Cur'zon, Clifford, b. 1907; British pianist.

Cusins (kŭz'-ĭns), **Sir Wm. G.,** London, 1833 — Remonchamps (Ardennes), 1893; pf.-prof. R.A.M.; knighted 1892; conductor and composer.

Cuzzoni (kood-zō'-nē), **Fran.,** Parma, 1700—Bologna, 1770; début 1715; m. the pianist Sandoni; very successful contralto till her latter days, when it is said she earned a pittance by covering silk buttons.

Czernohorsky (chĕr-nō-hôr'-shkĭ), **Bohuslav,** Nimburg, Bohemia, Feb. 26, 1684—Graz, July 2, 1740. Franciscan monk, organist and comp.

Czerny (Cerny) (chār'-nē), **Karl,** Vienna, Feb. 20, 1791—July 15, 1857; pupil of his father **Wenzel C.,** later of Beethoven; and had advice from

Clementi and Hummel; made an early reputation as pianist and was an eminent teacher from his 16th year; Liszt, Döhler, and Thalberg were among his pupils; pub. over 1,000 works, his pf.-studies, still standard, incl. many such works as *"Die Schule der Geläufigkeit"* (School of Velocity) (op. 299); c. also masses, symphonies, overtures, etc.

Czersky (chär'-shkĭ). Vide TSCHIRCH.

Czerwonky (chĕr'-vŏn-kē), **Richard**, b. Birnbaum, Germany, May 23, 1886; violinist, conductor; studied at Klindworth-Scharwenka Cons. and Hochsch., Berlin; pupil of Zajic, Moser and Joachim; début with Berlin Philh., 1906; later concertm. of Boston and Minneapolis Symphs.; head of Bush Cons., Chicago, vln. dept., after 1919.

Czibulka (chē-bool'-kä), **Alphons**, Szepes-Várallya, Hungary, May 14, 1842—Vienna, Oct. 27, 1894; pianist and conductor; c. 5 operettas, incl. *"Der Bajazzo"* (Vienna, 1892), waltzes, etc.

D

Dachs (däkhs), **Jos.**, Ratisbon, 1825— Vienna, 1896; teacher and pianist.

Daff'ner, **Hugo**, b. Munich, May 2, 1882; author and comp.; pupil of Thuille, Schmid-Lindner and Max Reger; 1904, Ph.D.; c. symph., sonatas, etc.

Dalayrac (or **D'Alayrac**) (dăl-ĕ-răk), **Nicolas**, Muret, Haute-Garonne, June 13, 1753—Paris, Nov. 27, 1809; prod. about 60 operas.

Dalberg (däl'-bărkh), **Jn. Fr. Hugo**, Reichsfreiherr von, Herrnsheim, 1760 —1812; writer and composer.

D'Albert, **Eugen.** Vide ALBERT, d'.

Dalcroze (dăl-krôz), **Emile Jaques**, b. Vienna, July 6, 1865; of Swiss parentage—d. Geneva, July 2, 1950; founder system of rhythmic exercises known as "Eurhythmics"; 1910–15, founded school at Hellerau, near Dresden; pupil of Fuchs, Bruchner and Délibes; teacher, lecturer and critic at Geneva Cons.; c. lyric comedies *"Janie"* (Geneva, 1893), and *"Sancho Panza"* (1897); *"Poème Alpestre"* for voices and orch. (1896, London, 1897); a violin concerto played by Marteau on his tours, and Swiss songs of popularity and national feeling; his theories of bodily move-

ment have had deep influence on the internat'l. world of music and dance; author of many works on the subject.

Dale, **Benjamin James**, b. Crouch Hill, London, July 17, 1885; organist; prof. of R. A. M.; c. symph., 2 overtures, successful piano sonata in D Min., etc., d. London, July 30, 1943.

Dal'lam, Engl. family of organ-builders 17th cent. (also spelled **Dallans**, **Dallum, Dalham**).

Dalmores (dăl-mō'-rĕs), **Charles**, b. Nancy, France, Dec. 31, 1871; tenor; pupil Paris and Lyons Cons.; sang in France; 1896, at Manhattan Opera, N. Y.; 1910, Chicago Op.; also widely in Europe, incl. Bayreuth; later res. in Los Angeles as vocal teacher.

D'Alvarez (däl-vär'-ĕth), **Marguerite**, b. England; contralto; of Peruvian and French ancestry; daughter of nobleman and diplomat; studied at Brussels Cons., winning 1st prizes in singing and declamation, also Prix de la Reine; appointed Court Singer to King of Belgians; studied opera in Milan; début at Rouen; also with succ. at La Scala; Amer. début with Manhattan Op. Co., 1909; with Boston Op. Co., 1913; later at Covent Garden; 1920, Chicago Op.; d. Alassio, Italy, Oct. 18, 1953.

Dalvimare (dăl-vē-mä'-rĕ) or **d'Alvimare** (dăl-vĭ-măr), **Martin P.**, Dreux Eure-et-Loire, 1772—Paris, 1839; composer.

Dambois (däm-bwä'), **Maurice**, b. Liége, Belgium, 1889; 'cellist; pupil of Cons. in native city; 1st public appearance at 12; later toured extensively; dir. Liége Académie, 1910– 14; first visited the U. S. in 1917 in company with Ysaye, where he later lived; c. orch., chamber music, songs, etc.

Damcke (däm'-kĕ), **Berthold**, Hanover, 1812—Paris, 1875; conductor.

Damoreau (dăm-ō-rō), **Laure-Cinthie** (née **Montalant**, first known as "Mlle. Cinti"), Paris, 1801—Chantilly, 1863; soprano, later prof. of singing, Paris Cons.; wrote *"Méthode de chant."*

Da Mot'ta, **José Vianna**, b. Isle St. Thomas, April 22, 1868—Lisbon, June 1, 1948; noted pianist; studied Lisbon; début there 1881, then studied Scharwenka Cons., with Liszt and Von Bülow; toured widely; lived in

Berlin for some years; 1915–17, taught at Geneva Cons.; later in Lisbon as dir. of Cons. and cond. of symph. orch.; c. symph. *"An das Vaterland,"* 5 Portuguese rhapsodies on native melodies, etc.; also critic and author.

Damrosch (däm'-rôsh), (1) **Dr. Leopold**, Posen, Prussia, Oct. 22, 1832 —New York, Feb. 15, 1885; 1854, M.D.; took up music as solo-violinist; then as cond. at minor theatres; 1855, solo violinist Grand Ducal Orch., at Weimar; here he m. Helene von Heimburg, a singer; 1859–60 cond. Breslau Phil. Soc., etc.; 1871, invited to New York to conduct the Arion Society, made his first appearance as conductor and composer and violinist; 1873, founded the Oratorio Society, 1878 the Symphony Society; 1880 Mus. Doc. Columbia Coll.; 1884, cond. German opera at Met. Op.; c. 7 cantatas; symphony; music to Schiller's *"Joan of Arc,"* etc. (2) **Frank**, Breslau, June 22, 1859— New York, Oct. 21, 1937; son and pupil of above; pupil of Pruckner, Jean Vogt, and von Inten (pf.), Moszkowski (comp.); 1882–85, cond. Denver (Col.) Chorus Club; 1884–85 supervisor of music in public schools, also organist in various churches; 1885–91, chorusm. Met. Op.; till 1887 cond. the Newark Harmonic Society; 1892 organized the People's Singing Classes; 1897, supervisor of music, N. Y. City public schools; cond. 1898–1912, Oratorio Society, and 1893–1920, Mus. Art Soc. (N. Y.), Oratorio Soc., Bridgeport (Conn.), *"Orpheus"* and *"Eurydice"* Phila., etc.; for nearly 30 years from 1905 he was the first and sole dir. of the Inst. of Music. Art, noted New York school, which was later merged with the Juilliard School of Music but still functions; he wrote treatises; Mus. D., Yale Univ., 1904; pub. songs and choruses, and a method of sight-singing. (3) **Walter** Breslau, Jan. 30, 1862—N. Y., Dec. 22, 1950; son of (1); pupil of Rischbieter and Draeseke (harm.), von Inten, Boekelman, and Max Pinner, (pf.), von Bülow (conducting); 1885–99 cond. N. Y. Oratorio and Symphony Societies; 1892 founded the N. Y. Symphony Orch.; 1894, organized and cond. the Damrosch Opera Co.; 1899, cond. at

Philadelphia; 1902, cond. N. Y. Philh. (vice Paur); he toured Europe with the N. Y. Symphony, 1920, and remained its permanent cond. for more than 40 years; during this time he developed esp. popularity as a cond. and lecturer at children's orch. concerts; he resigned this post in 1926 to become musical counsel of the Nat'l. Broadcasting Co., and annually led a notable series of "music appreciation" concerts for the school children of the country over this radio chain. He is the recipient of many honours, incl. the Legion of Honour and a half-dozen doctorates from American univs. Pub. his memoirs, *"My Musical Life"* (1930); prod. opera, *"The Scarlet Letter"* (Boston, 1896), text by Geo. Parsons Lathrop; c. also *"The Dove of Peace"* (1912), *"Cyrano de Bergerac"* (text by W. J. Henderson after Rostand play, Met. Op., 1913); *"The Man Without a Country"* (libretto by Arthur Guiterman), Met. Op. 1937; choruses, songs, etc.

Da'na, Chas. Henshaw, West Newton, Mass., 1846—Worcester, 1883; pianist, organist and composer.

Danbé (dän-bä), **Jules**, Caen, France, Nov. 15, 1840—Vichy, Nov. 10, 1905; violinist; pupil of Paris Cons.; till 1892 2nd dir. of the Cons. Concerts; 1895, cond. Op. Com., Paris; composer.

Dan'by, J., 1757—London, May 16, 1798; English organist and composer.

Dancla (dän-klä), (1) **J. Bap. Chas.**, Bagnères-de-Bigorre, Dec. 19, 1818— Tunis, Nov. 9, 1907; 1828 pupil of Baillot, Halévy, and Berton, Paris Cons.; 1834, 2nd solo vln. Op.-Com.; 1857, prof. of vln. at the Cons., giving famous quartet soirées; c. four symphonies, over 130 works for vln., etc.; wrote 5 technical books, *"Les compositeurs chefs d'orchestre,"* etc. (2) **Arnaud**, Bagnères-de-Bigorre, 1820—1862, bro. of above; 'cellist and writer. (3) **Léopold**, Bagnères-de-Bigorre, 1823 — Paris, 1895, bro. of above; composer.

Dan'do, Jos. H. B., b. Somers Town, London, 1806; violinist.

Danhauser (dän-how'-zĕr or dän-ō-zä), **Ad. Ld.**, Paris, 1835—1896; prof. of solfeggio at Cons. and dram. composer.

Danican. V. PHILIDOR.

Daniel, Salvador, b. Bourges, 1830 (?); for a few days dir. Paris Cons., under the Commune; killed in battle, May 23, 1871; writer.

Danise (dä-ne'-zä), **Giuseppe,** b. Naples, Jan. 11, 1883; opera barytone; 1st studied law, then singing with Colonnese and Petillo; début, Naples, 1906; has sung in leading Italian theatres, also Russia, South and Central America and U. S.; Met. Op. Co., N. Y., for some years after 1920; also in America with Ravinia Op. Co.

Danjou (dän'-zhoo), **J. L. F.,** Paris, 1812—Montpellier, 1866; 1840, organist and erudite historian.

Dan'kers (or **Danckerts**), **Ghiselin,** b. Tholen, Zealand; chorister in Papal chapel, 1538–65; composer and writer.

Dann, Hollis, b. Canton, Pa., May 1, 1861—N. Y., Jan. 3, 1939; Mus. D., Alfred Univ., 1906; dir. public school music, Ithaca, N. Y., 1887–1903; 1906–21, headed dept. of music, Cornell Univ., leading Glee Club and Music Fest.; began work in training music supervisors which he continued at Penna. State Coll., 1921–25; head dept. of music education, N. Y. Univ., 1925–35; author of works on school music; ed. collections of school songs, hymns, etc.

Dannreuther (dän'-roi-tĕr), **(1) Edward,** Strassburg, Nov. 4, 1844—Pimlico, London, Feb. 12, 1905; at 5 taken to Cincinnati, where he studied with F. L. Ritter; later, pupil of Richter, Moscheles, Hauptmann, Leipzig Cons.; 1863, London, as pianist; 1872 founded and cond. London Wagner Society; wrote *"Richard Wagner, His Tendencies and Theories"* (London, 1873); also composer. **(2) Gustav,** Cincinnati, July 21, 1853—New York, Dec. 19, 1923; pupil of de Ahna and Joachim (vln.) and Heitel (theory), Berlin; lived in London till 1877; joined Mendelssohn Quintet Club of Boston, where in 1880 he settled as a member of the newly formed Symphony Orch.; 1882–84 dir. Philh. Soc., Buffalo, N. Y.; founded the "Beethoven String-Quartet" of N. Y. (called "Dannr. Q." from 1894); for 3 years leader Symphony and Oratorio Societies, N. Y.; 1907, taught Vassar Coll.; wrote musical treatises.

Danzi (dän'-tsē), **(1) Fz.,** Mannheim,

May 15, 1763—Carlsruhe, April 13, 1826; dram. composer.

Da Ponte (dä pôn'-tĕ), **Lorenzo,** Ceneda, near Venice, March 10, 1749—New York, Aug. 17, 1838; of Jewish race; poet-laureate to Joseph II. at Vienna, until 1792; wrote text of Mozart's *"Don Giovanni"* and *"Cosi Fan Tutte"*; London, 1803, teacher of Italian and poet to the Italian Opera; made a failure of different pursuits in the U. S. A., and was finally teacher of Italian at Columbia College, N. Y.; pub. *"Memorie"* (Memoirs). There is a sketch of his life in Krehbiel's *"Music and Manners"* (N. Y., 1890).

Daquin (dä-kän), **L. Claude,** Paris, 1694—1772; notable organist, clavecinist and composer.

D'Aranyi, Yelly (yĕl'-ē dä-rän'-yē), b. Budapest, May 30, 1895 (grandniece of Joachim); violinist; studied piano at 6; later vln. with Hubay; made début at 13; has toured Germany, Austria, France, Italy, England, U. S.; appeared in sonata recitals with Myra Hess; res. in London since 1913; among composers who have created works for her are Bartok, Ravel and Vaughan Williams.

Dargomyzsky (där-gō-mēsh'-shkē), **Alex. Sergievitch,** Toula, Feb. 14, 1813 —St. Petersburg, Jan. 17, 1869; pianist and composer; pupil of Schoberlechner; his opera *"Esmeralda"* (c. 1839) was prod. 1847 with succ.; his best opera *"Russalka"* followed in 1856; in 1867, at Moscow, an opera-ballet, *"The Triumph of Bacchus"* (written 1847), was instrumented; left an unfinished opera. *"Kammennoi Gost"* ("The Marble Guest") (finished by Rimsky-Korsakov). *"Rogdana,"* a fantasy-opera, was only sketched; c. also pop. orch. works.

Da(s)ser (dä'-sĕr), **(Dasserus) Ludwig,** until 1562 conductor and composer at Munich, predecessor of Lassus.

Daube (dow'-bĕ), **Fr.,** Cassel (Augsburg ?), 1730—Augsburg, 1797; composer and writer.

Dau'ney, Wm., Aberdeen, 1800—Demerara, 1843; writer.

Dauprat (dō-prä), **L. Fr.,** Paris, 1781 —July 16, 1868; notable horn-player and composer.

Daussoigne-Méhul (dōs'-swăn-mā'-ül), **L. Jos.,** Givet, Ardennes, 1790—Liége, 1875; dram. composer.

Dauvergne (dō-věrn), **Ant. C.**, Ferrand, 1713—Lyons, 1797; violinist and dram. composer.

Davaux (dă-vō), **Jean Baptiste**, Côte-St-André, 1737—Paris, Feb. 22, 1822; c. many symphonies, chamber music, etc.

Davenport, Francis W., Wilderslowe, near Derby, England, 1847—London, Nov., 1925; pupil of Macfarren, whose daughter he m.; 1879, prof. R. A. M., and 1882 Guildhall Sch. of Music; c. two symphonies (the 1st winning 1st prize at Alexandra Palace, 1876), and other comps.; wrote text-books.

Davico (dä-vē'-kō), **Vincenzo**, b. Monaco, Jan. 14, 1889; pupil of Reger; c. operas, orch., chamber music, songs, etc.

David (dä'-fēt), **Fd.**, Hamburg, June 19, 1810—near Klosters, Switzerland, July 19, 1873; pupil of Spohr and Hauptmann; at 15 played in the Gewandhaus, Leipzig; 1827, in Königstadt Th. orch., Berlin; at 19, 1st vln. in the private quartet of the wealthy Baron von Liphardt, at Dorpat, whose daughter he m.; gave concerts till 1835 in Russia; at 26 leader of the Gewandhaus Orch. at Mendelssohn's invitation; his rigorous precision of drill is still a terrifying tradition. In the composition of Mendelssohn's vln.-concerto he was almost a collaborator (cf. Joachim and Brahms). The Cons. was estab. in 1843, and **D.**'s unsurpassed gifts as a teacher had a large influence in making its reputation, among his pupils being Wilhelmj and Joachim; as a leader he had a wonderful faculty of inspiring the players with his own enthusiasm. His student editions of classical works embrace nearly all compositions of standard vln. literature; edited many classics, including the "*Hohe Schule des Violinspiels.*" His comp. include an opera, "*Hans Wacht*" (Leipzig, 1852); 2 symphonies; 5 vln.-concertos, etc.; wrote a standard meth. for vln.

David (dä-vēd), (1) **Félicien César**, Cadenet, Vaucluse, April 13, 1810—St. Germain-en-Laye, Aug. 29, 1876; at 7 a pupil and chorister in the maîtrise of Saint-Sauveur at Aix; c. hymns, motets, etc.; 1825–28 studied in the Jesuit college, but ran away to continue his music, and became asst.-cond. in the theatre at Aix, and at

19 cond. at Saint-Sauveur; 1830 Paris Cons., under Bénoist (org.), Reber and Millot (harm.), Fétis (cpt. and fugue). 1831, his rich uncle withdrew his allowance of 50 francs a month, and he took up Saint-Simonism, composing hymns for this socialistic sect, which coming under ban of the law in 1833, he went with other members on a tour through Turkey, Egypt, etc.; he returned in 1835 with a fund of Oriental musical impressions, resulting in an unsucc. volume of "*Mélodies Orientales.*" He retired to the country home of a friend and c. 2 symphonies, 24 string-quintets, etc. 1838 his first symphony was prod.; and 1844, his ode-symphonie "*Le Désert*" had a "delirious succ."; the oratorio, "*Moïse au Sinaï,*" 1846; a second symphonic-ode "*Christophe Colombe*" and "*L'Eden,*" a "mystery" in 2 parts (Grand Opéra, 1848) had no succ.; his opera "*La Perle du Brésil*" (Th. Lyrique, 1851) is still popular; the opera "*La Fin du Monde*" was rejected by the Gr. Opéra, and put in rehearsal, but not produced, by the Th. Lyrique, and in 1859 produced at the Gr. Opéra as "*Herculaneum,*" the great state prize of 20,000 francs being awarded it in 1867; "*Lalla Rookh*" (1862) was a decided succ., but "*Le Saphir,*" (1865) also at the Op. Com., failed, and he now abandoned dram. comp., withdrawing "*La Captive.*" 1869, Academician and librarian of the Cons. Biog. by Azevedo (Paris, 1863). (2) **Samuel**, Paris, 1836—1895; professor, director and dram. composer. (3) **Ad. Isaac**, Nantes, 1842—Paris, 1897; dram. composer. (4) **Ernst**, Nancy, 1824—Paris, 1886; writer.

Davide (dä-vē'-dĕ), (1) **Giacomo** (called le père), Presezzo, near Bergamo, 1750—Bergamo, 1830; famous tenor. (2) **Giovanni**, 1789, St. Petersburg, ca. 1851; son of above; tenor of remarkable range Bb–b''.

Davidov (dä'-vĭ-dôf), **Karl**, Goldingen, Kurland, 1838—Moscow, 1889; solo 'cellist to the Czar; 1876–87, dir. St. Petersburg Cons.; c. symph. poem, "*The Gifts of Perek,*" etc.

Davies (dä'-vĭs), (1) **Ben**, Pontardaroe, near Swansea, Wales, Jan. 6, 1858—Ashwick, Eng., Mar. 29, 1943; tenor; 1880–83 pupil of Randegger at R. A.

M.; won bronze, silver, and gold medals, and the Evill prize for declamatory Engl. singing; 3 years with Carl Rosa Opera-troupe; most prominent in oratorio; after 1893 often sang in U. S. (2) **David Ffrangcon**, Bethesda, Carnarvonshire, Dec. 11, 1860—Hampstead, April 5, 1918; barytone; M. A. Oxford; pupil of Shakespeare; début Manchester, 1890; sang with Carl Rosa Opera Co., then oratorio; toured U. S. (3) **Fanny**, Guernsey, July 27, 1861—London, Sept. 1, 1934; eminent pianist; pupil of Reinecke, Paul and Jadassohn, Leipzig Cons.; later of Frau Schumann and Dr. Scholz; début Crystal Palace, London, 1885; toured in England, Germany and Italy. (4) Sir **Henry Walford**, b. Oswestry, 1869—Wrington, March 11, 1941; pupil of Sir Walter Parratt; 1898, organist of the Temple Church; 1898, Mus. Doc., Cantab.; 1895, prof. of cpt. R. C. M.; knighted 1922; 1923, national mus. dir. for Wales; 1934 made Master of King's Music (vice Elgar). C. 2 symphonies, many notable oratorios and other choral works; 2 string quartets, 3 violin sonatas, part-songs, etc.

Da′vis, John David, Edgbaston, Oct. 22, 1869—June 21, 1926; pupil Raff and Brussels Cons.; 1889, teacher at Birmingham; c. opera *"The Cossacks"* (Antwerp, 1903), also symph. variations (London, 1905), symph. ballade *"The Cenci"*; symph. poem *"The Maid of Astolat"*; chamber music; prize *"Coronation March"* (1902), etc.

Da′vison, (1) **Arabella**. Vide GODDARD. (2) **J. W.**, London, 1813—Margate, 1885; pianist, critic and composer.

Da′vy, (1) **Richard**, Engl., comp. 16th century. (2) **John**, Upton-Helion, Exeter, 1763—London, 1824; violinist.

Day, Charles Russell, Horstead, Norfolk, 1860—killed Feb. 18, 1900, in the battle of Paardeberg; major in British army and writer of books on musical instruments.

Dayas (dī′-äs), **W. Humphries**, b. New York, Sept. 12, 1863—Manchester, May 3, 1903; pupil of S. Jackson, Warren, S. B. Mills and Joseffy; organist of various churches; then studied with Kullak, Haupt, Erlich, Urban, and Liszt; made concert-tour 1888; 1890 pf.-teacher Helsingfors

Cons.; in Düsseldorf (1894), Wiesbaden Cons., and Cologne Cons.; c. organ and piano sonatas, etc.

De Ahna (dā-ä′-nä), (1) **H. K. Hermann**, Vienna, 1835—Berlin, 1892; violinist, teacher and composer. His sister (2) **Eleonore**, Vienna, 1838—Berlin, 1865; mezzo-soprano.

De Angelis (dā än′-jā-lēs), **Girolamo**, Civita Vecchia, Jan. 1, 1858—Calolzio, Feb. 9, 1935; pupil of Bazzini, Milan Cons.; 1881, prof. there of vln. and vla.; 1879–97, solo violinist at La Scala; 1897 teacher Royal Irish Acad. of Music, Dublin; c. (text and music) *"L'Innocente"* (Novi Ligure, 1896).

Debain (dŭ-băṅ), **Alex. Fran.**, Paris, 1809—Dec. 3, 1877; 1834 made pianos and organs in Paris; inv. the harmonium 1840, also "antiphonel" and "harmonichorde"; improved the accordion.

Debefve (dŭ-bŭv′), **Jules**, b. Liége, Jan. 16, 1863; pianist; pupil and later teacher at the Cons.; c. opera, rhapsody for orch., etc.; d. Paris, 1932.

Debillemont (dŭ-bē′-yŭ-môṅ), **J. Jacques**, Dijon, 1824—Paris, 1879; dram. composer.

De Boeck (dĕ-book), **Auguste**, Merchtem, Belgium, May 9, 1865—Merchtem, Belgium, Oct. 9, 1937; organist, son of an organist; pupil of Brussels Cons., later a teacher there; c. symph., *Rhapsodie Dahomienne* for orch., organ music, etc.

Debussy (dŭ-bü′-sē), **Claude Achille**, St. Germain-en-Laye, Aug. 22, 1862—Paris, March 26, 1918; one of the most important composers of recent times, and the instigator of the entire "modern" movement in music; already acknowledged to be a classic, D. has had a profound influence on creative musicians of every country. He came from a family of tradespeople with no musical background. At 11 he entered the Paris Cons. where he won several prizes for piano and studied with Massenet, winning the Prix de Rome with his cantata, *"L'Enfant Prodigue."* During his sojourn in Italy, his originality began to assert itself, so much so that his orch. suite, *"Printemps,"* shocked the conservatives by its harmonic audacities; he also c. a work for two women soloists and female chorus, *"La Demoiselle Élue,"* at this time. Returning to Paris, he was attracted by the school of the poetic Symbolists and frequented their circle, composing meanwhile his *"Arabesques"* for piano, *"Suite Bergamasque"* (do.), *"Ariettes Oubliées,"* etc.

His early works were influenced by the French school of Massenet, Chabrier, Lalo, Fauré, and by Wagner, but he soon developed an original style which came to be known as "impressionism" and consisted in painting with brilliant but rare and elusive tonal colours, applied in little, independent units, as the painters of the *"pointillist"* school were doing. His Prelude to *"L'Après-midi d'un Faune,"* based on Mallarmé's cryptic nature poem, was completed 1894 and created a deep impression, entirely revising the possibilities contained in orchestral tone-colour. D's. use of distantly related overtones widened harmonic boundaries, and his use of chords not as a part of a continuous structure, but as individual entities introduced a new principle into modern music.

He carried on this revolutionary work with a string quartet (1893), *"Proses Lyriques"* for voice to his own text, the *"Chansons de Bilitis,"* and the 3 *"Nocturnes"* for orch. (*"Clouds," "Festivals"* and *"Sirens,"* the last employing a wordless women's chorus.)

D's. masterpiece is commonly acknowledged to be his music drama, *"Pelléas et Mélisande,"* a setting of Maeterlinck's symbolic play, which had its première at the Paris Op.-Comique in 1902 before a somewhat irreverent audience. Here, as in most of his works, D. creates an atmosphere of half-lights, mystery and poetry by the use of an original harmonic system in which dissonance takes the place of consonance; old church modes are used or suggested; as are the whole-tone scale and other exotic progressions. The voices employ a form of recitative; all climaxes are rigidly restrained. The popular following developed by this singular but highly artistic work came a few years later.

The most important productions of D's. final period include music for D'Annunzio's "mystery," *"The Martyrdom of St. Sebastian"*; the ballet *"Jeux,"* written for Diaghileff's company; and the notable orch. works,

"La Mer," "Rondes de Printemps"[1] and *"Iberia,"* in which his original art of novel form, orchestration and objectivity of impression reach their climax. His final period saw the production of many works for chamber combinations, piano, etc., but with a slight growth of austerity in his manner.

His compositions include also: (voice and orch.) *"Le Jet d'Eau"*; (vocal quartet) *"Trois Chansons"*; (orch.) *"Images"*; (Harp and orch.) *"Danse Sacrée et Danse Profane"*; (voice) *"Cinq Poèmes"*; *"Mandoline"*; *"Fêtes Galantes"*; *"Trois Chansons de France"*; *"Trois Ballades de François Villon"*; *"Le Promenoir des Deux Amants"*; *"Trois Poèmes"*; *"Noël des Enfants qui n'ont plus de Maison"*; (piano) *"L'Isle Joyeuse"*; *"Estampes"*; *"Masques"*; *"Images"* (2 series); *"Children's Corner"*; *"La Plus que Lente"*; 2 series of 12 preludes each; *"La Boîte à Joujoux"*; *"Berceuse Héroïque"*; 12 etudes; (piano, four hands) *"Marche Écossaise"*; *"Petite Suite"*; 6 *"Épigraphes Antiques"*; (2 pianos, 4 hands) *"En Blanc et noir."* Many of his piano works have been orchestrated.

The Debussy literature is a large one, with the composer's own critical writings appearing under the title *"M. Croche, Anti-Dilettante"* (1923). D.-studies have been pub. by Daly Liebig, Laurencie, Laloy, Sartoliquido, Caillard and De Bérys, Setaccioli, Rivière, Séré, Rolland, Chennevière, Paglia, Jean-Aubry, Cortot, Boucher, Dumesnil, Gilman, Shera, etc. Léon Vallas has issued a thematic catalogue, and countless magazine articles exist on his music. (See article, page 492.)

Dechert (děkh'-ěrt), **Hugo**, Potschappel near Dresden, Sept. 16, 1860—Nov. 28, 1923; 'cellist; studied with his father, then with H. Tiets, and at the Berlin Hochschule; toured; 1894 soloist court-chapel, Berlin; mem. of Halir and Hess Quartets.

Deck'er, Konst., Fürstenau, Brandenburg, 1810—Stolp, Pomerania, 1878; pianist and dram. composer.

Dedekind (dā'-dě-kǐnt), (1) **Henning,** ca. 1590 cantor, theorist and composer at Langensalza, Thuringia. (2) **Konst. Chr.,** Reinsdorf, Anhalt-Köthen, 1628—ca. 1697, comp.

Dedler (dāt'-lěr), **Rochus,** Oberammergau, Jan. 15, 1779—Munich, Oct. 15, 1822; c. music still used in the Passion-Play.

De(e)r'ing, Richard, b. Kent, d. London (?), 1630; studied in Italy; court-organist; pub. the oldest extant comp. with basso continuo, etc.

De Falla, Manuel (dä fä'-yä), Cadiz, Nov. 23, 1877—Alta Gracia, Argentina, Nov. 14, 1946; pupil of Trago, Pedrell, Dukas and Debussy; passed student years in Paris but retired to Granada, 1914, where he has made his home regularly since; one of most original and characteristic modern Spanish comps., esp. noted for his ballets and orchestral works in impressionistic style; c. (opera) "La Vida Breva" (Paris Op.-Comique, 1914, has also been given at Met. Op. House, N. Y.); (ballets) "El Amor Brujo" and "Sombrero de Tres Picos"; (puppet opera) "El Retablo de Maese Pedro"; 3 symphonic nocturnes, "Noches en los Jardines de España" (with piano), "En el Generalife" and "Danza Lejana" (the first esp. popular); concerto for harpsichord and small ensemble; "Don Quixote," fantasy for 3 voices and orch., and numerous songs and piano works; one of the outstanding modern comps., with folk-music ingredients especially prominent in his works; a master of orchestration, and influenced by the music of Debussy and atonalists such as Schönberg; a vivid imagination, colorful and passionate romantic subjects and an ingredient of mysticism are features of his work. He was reported in 1935 to be at work on "L'Atlantide," later in S. Amer. (Article, P. 495).

Defauw (dü-fō'), Désiré, b. Ghent, 1885; cond. Chicago Symphony, 1943.

Defesch (dä-fĕsh'), Wm., d. ca. 1758; Flemish organist and violinist.

Deffès (dŭf-fĕs'), L. P., Toulouse, July 25, 1819—June 10, 1900; pupil of Halévy and Barbereau, Paris Cons., took Grand prix de Rome for cantata "L'Ange et Tobie"; his 1-act com.-op. "l'Anneau d'argent" was prod. Paris, 1855; 14 others since, the last very succ., "Jessica" (Toulouse, 1898); dir. of the Toulouse branch of the Cons.; c. also masses, etc.

Degele (dä'-gĕ-lĕ), Eugen, Munich, 1834—Dresden, 1886; barytone and composer.

De Gogorza, Emilio (ä-mē'-yō dä gō-gōr'-thä), b. Brooklyn, N. Y., May 29, 1874; barytone; studied with Moderate and Agramonte, N. Y.; boy soloist in English churches; res. as youth in Spain and France; concert début with Sembrich, 1897; toured widely in concert incl. appearances with Emma Eames, whom he married in 1911; member of faculty, Curtis Inst., Phila., during later years; d. N. Y., May 10, 1949.

De Greef, Arthur, b. Löwen, Belgium, Oct. 10, 1862; composer and pianist; studied with Brassin at Brussels Cons. and with Liszt; taught piano at Brussels Cons., 1885; toured throughout Europe as virtuoso; has also cond., and c. chamber and piano works.

Degtarev (dĕkh'-tä-rĕv), Stepoan Ankiewitsch, 1766–1813; Russian director in St. Petersburg and Italy; c. 60 concertos, and church choral music.

De Haan, Willem, Rotterdam, Sept. 24, 1849—Berlin, Sept. 26, 1930; pupil of Nicolai, de Lange, and Bargiel, also at Leipzig Cons.; 1873 dir. at Bingen; cond. "Mozartverein" at Darmstadt, 1876; 1895 court-conductor there; c. 2 operas "Die Kaiserstochter" and the succ. "Die Inkasöhne" (Darmstadt, 1895); 3 cantatas.

Dehn (dän), Siegfried Wm., Altona, Feb. 25, 1799—Berlin, April 12, 1858; noteworthy theorist and teacher; among his pupils Rubinstein, Kullak, Glinka, Kiel, Hofmann, etc.

Deiters (dī'-tĕrs), Hermann, Bonn, June 27, 1833—Coblentz, May 11, 1907; 1858, Dr. jur., and Dr. Phil., at Bonn; dir. of gymnasia at Bonn, 1858, and other cities; 1885 of the "Provincial Schulrath" at Coblentz; writer and translator.

De Ko'ven, (Henry Louis) Reginald, Middletown, Conn., April 3, 1859—Chicago, Jan. 16, 1920; composer; educated in Europe, took degree at Oxford, Engl., 1879; pupil of W. Speidel (pf.) at Stuttgart, Lebert (pf.), and Pruckner (harm.), Dr. Hauff (comp.), Vanuccini (singing), Genée (operatic comp.); after 1889, critic in Chicago and 1891, New York, incl. period on the "World"; 1902–05, organised and cond. Philharmonic Orch. at Washington, D. C.: c. about a score of succ. comic operas, incl. "*Robin Hood*" (Chicago, 1890); "*The Fencing Master*" (Boston, 1892); "*The Highwayman*" (New Haven, 1897); "*Maid Marian*" (1901); and two grand operas, "*The Canterbury Pilgrims*" (Met. Op., 1917) and "*Rip Van Winkle*" (Chicago Op., 1920), neither a succ.; also many songs; an orch. suite, a pf.-sonata, etc.

Delaborde (dŭ-lä-bôrd), (1) **J. Benj.**, Paris, 1734—guillotined, 1794; dram. composer and writer. (2) **Élie Miriam**, Chaillot, France, Feb. 8, 1839 —Paris, Dec., 1913; pupil of Alkan, Liszt, and Moscheles; pf.-prof. at Paris Cons. and dram. composer.

DeLamar'ter, **Eric**, b. Lansing, Mich., Feb. 18, 1880; conductor, composer, organist; studied with Middelschulte, Widor and Guilmant; org. in various Chicago churches; asst. cond., Chicago Symph., 1918-1936; taught at Olivet Coll., Mich., and Chicago Mus. Coll.; d. Orlando, Fla., 1953.

De Lara. Vide LARA.

De Lange. Vide LANGE.

Delâtre (dŭ-lät′r), (1) **Olivier**, Belgian music-pub. Antwerp, (1539-55). (2) **Claude Petit Jan.**, conductor and composer at Liége, 1555.

Deldevez (dŭl-dŭ-věs), **Ed. Ernest**, Paris, 1817—1897; 1859, asst.-cond. Gr. Opéra and Paris Cons., dram. composer and writer.

Delezenne (dŭ-lŭ-zěn), **Chas. Ed. Jos.**, Lille, 1776—1866; writer.

Delhasse (děl-ăs), **Félix**, Spaa, Jan. 5, 1809—Brussels, 1898; founder and ed. of "*Guide Musicale*"; writer.

Delibes (dŭ-lēb′), **Clément Philibert Léo**, St. Germain-du-Val, Sarthe, Feb. 21, 1836—Paris, Jan. 16, 1891; composer of graceful and polished operatic and ballet scores; entered the Paris Cons. in 1848, Le Couppey, Bazin, Adam, and Bénoist being his chief teachers, 1853 organist at the Ch. of St.-Jean et St.-François; his first operetta, "*Deux Sacs de Charbon*," was followed by nearly a score more; 1865, 2nd chorus-master Gr. Opéra; his first ballet "*La Source*" was prod. here 1866 with striking succ., later in Vienna as "*Naila*"; the second, "*Coppelia*" (Gr. Opéra, 1870), is still popular, as is "*Sylvia*" (1876); 1881, prof. of comp. at the Cons.; c. also the succ. opera "*Lakmé*" (v. STORIES OF OPERAS).

"*Le Roi l'a dit*" (1873); "*Jean de Nivelle*" (1880) and an unfinished stage work, "*Kassya*," which was completed by Massenet and prod. 1893; also songs, etc.

Delioux (**De Savignac**) (dŭl-yoo dŭ säv-ēn-yăk), **Chas.**, Lorient, Morbihan, April, 1830—Paris, ca. 1880; self-taught as pianist; studied harmony with Halévy; 1846 took Grand Prix for cpt.; prod. 1-act comic opera "*Yvonne et Loie*" (Gymnase, 1854); c. pf.-pcs. and wrote technical works.

Delius (dā′-lē-ōōs), **Frederick**, Bradford, England, Jan. 29, 1863—Grez-sur-Loing, France, June 10, 1934; highly original and important composer; son of a naturalised German, a wool merchant; 1876-79 educated in Bradford schools and at Internat'l. Coll., Spring Grove; refusing to enter the family business, he was sent by his father to an orange plantation in Florida, where he had lessons in music from an Amer. musician, Thomas F. Ward; 1885, he taught music in Danville, Virginia, and the following year persuaded his parents to send him to Leipzig, where he made little progress at the Cons. but learned much from Grieg, who lived there; in 1888 he moved to Paris, where he worked as a solitary comp.; his first public perf. was in 1899, when a concert of his music was given in London at St. James's Hall; after an interval of 8 years his works began to have hearings in Germany; his "*Appalachia*" for orch. with choral finale given at the Lower Rhenish Fest., 1905; his "*Sea-Drift*" for orch., barytone and chorus at the fest. of the Allgemeine Deutscher Musikverein in 1906; in England his recognition was slower, but owing to the championship of Beecham, who gave many of works, and organised a fest. of 6 programmes in 1929, D. came into his own as one of the most important comps. of the day. After 1890 he lived on a small estate at Grez-sur-Loing; he m. Jelka Rosen, painter, in 1897; his latter years were clouded by the affliction of blindness and paralysis, but he continued his work in composition by dictating his music. His style is original, partaking somewhat of French impressionism, and also showing the influence of Scandinavian comps. His work is marked by an almost complete absence of polyphony, but achieved a markedly personal force and beauty through his sensitiveness to moods of Nature. His chief works include: fantasy overture, "*Over the Hills*" (Elberfeld, 1897); "*Norwegian Suite*" for orch.; piano concerto in C minor; the music dramas, "*Koanga*" (Elberfeld, 1904); "*Romeo und Julia auf dem Dorfe*" (Berlin, 1907); "*Margot la Rouge*"; "*Fennimore und Gerda*" (Frankfort, 1919); music for Flecker's "*Hassan*" (Darmstadt, 1923); "*Paris*," a Night Piece for orch.; "*Dance of Life*" for orch.; "*Legende*" for vln. and orch.; "*A Mass of Life*" for soloists, chorus and orch.; orch. rhapsody, "*Brigg Fair*," "*Songs of Sunset*" for soloists, chorus and orch.; "*Song of the High Hills*" for orch. with concluding chorus; the orch. works, "*In a Summer Garden*," "*Dance Rhapsody*," "*On Hearing the First Cuckoo in Spring*," "*North Country Sketches*," "*Eventyr*," "*Summer Night on the River*"; vln. concerto, 'cello concerto; double concerto for vln. and 'cello; songs and choral pieces. Studies of his music were pub. by Chop and Heseltine.

Della Maria (děl'-lä mä-rē'-ä), **Doménique**, Marseilles, 1769—Paris, March 9, 1800; son of an Italian mandolinist; played mandolin and 'cello; at 18 prod. a grand opera; studied comp. in Italy, and c. 7 operas, incl. the very succ. "*Le Prisonnier*" (1798).

Delle Sedie (děl-lě sād'-yě), **Enrico**, Leghorn, June 17, 1826—Paris, Nov. 28, 1907; pupil of Galeffi, Persanola, and Domeniconi; 1848, imprisoned as a Revolutionist; then studied singing; début, Florence, 1851; later prof. of singing Paris Cons.; lived in Paris as singing teacher.

Dellinger (děl'-lǐng-ěr), **Rudolf**, Graslitz, Bohemia, July 8, 1857—Dresden, Sept. 24, 1910; 1883, conductor at Hamburg; 1893, Dresden Ct. Opera; c. operettas, incl. succ. "*Capitän Fracasse*" (Hamburg, 1889), "*Don Cesar*," etc.

Deil' Orefice (děl ō-rä-fē'-chě), **Giu.**, Fara, Abruzzio, Chietino, 1848—Naples, 1889; cond. and dram. composer.

Delmas (děl-mǎs), **Jean Fr.**, Lyons, France, April 14, 1861—Paris, Sept. 29, 1933; bass; pupil Paris Cons.; 1886, joined the Opéra where he created many rôles with great success. (2) **Marc**, St. Quentin, March 28, 1885—Paris, Nov. 30, 1931; composer of operas, orch. and chamber music.

Delmotte (děl-môt), **Henri Florent**, Mons, Belgium, 1799—1836; writer.

Delprat (dŭl-prä'), **Chas.**, 1803—Pau, Pyrenees, 1888; singing-teacher and writer there.

Delsarte (dŭl-särt), **Fran. Alex. Nicholas Chéri**, Solesmes, Nord, 1811—Paris, 1871; tenor; teacher of a well-known physical culture; 1855 inv. the Guide-Accord, or Sonotype, to facilitate piano-tuning.

De Lu'ca, **Giuseppe**, b. Rome, Dec. 25, 1876—N. Y., Aug. 26, 1950; grad. St. Cecilia Acad.; début, Valentin, Piacenza, 1897; sang as regular mem. of La Scala, Milan, for 8 years, prior to engagement for Met. Op., N. Y., 1915; sang with latter company until 1935, in great variety of Italian and French barytone rôles; also prominent in concert; commander, Order of the Crown of Italy.

Delune (dŭ-lün), **Louis**, b. Charleroi, March 15, 1876—Jan. 1940; Belgian cond. and pupil at Brussels Cons., winning prize, 1900, and Prix de Rome, 1903; c. sonatas and songs.

Del Valle de Paz (děl väl'-lä dä pätz), **Edgardo**, Alexandria, Egypt, Oct. 18, 1861—Florence, April 5, 1920; pf.-pupil at Naples Cons., of Cesi (pf.), and Serrao (comp.); at 16 toured in Italy and Egypt, 1890, prof. in Florence Cons.; pub. pf.-method, etc.; c. orchestral suites, etc.; dir. of "*La Nuova Musica*," 1896-1914.

Demantius (dä-män'-tsǐ-oos), **Chr.**, Reichenberg, 1567—Freiburg, Saxony, 1643; prolific composer of church-music and songs; wrote a vocal method.

Demeur (dŭ-mŭr'), (1) **Anne Arsène** (née **Charton**), Sanjon, Charente, 1827—Paris, 1892; soprano; m. (2) **J. A. Demeur**, flutist and composer.

Demol (dŭ-môl), (1) **Pierre**, Brussels, 1825—Alost, Belgium, 1899; dir. and composer. (2) **Fran. M.**, Brussels, 1844—Ostend, 1883; nephew of above; cond., prof., and dram. composer.

Demunck', (1) **François**, Brussels, 1815
—1854; 'cellist and prof. (2) **Ernest**, Brussels, Dec. 21, 1840—London, Feb. 6, 1915; son and pupil of
above; pupil of Servais; 1870, 'cellist
Weimar Court orch.; 1879 m. Carlotta Patti; 1893, prof. R. A. M.,
London.

Denefve (dŭ-nŭf), **Jules**, Chimay,
1814—Mons, 1877; 'cellist and dram.
composer.

Dengremont (dän-grŭ-môṅ), **Maurice**,
b. of French parents, Rio de Janeiro,
1866—Buenos Aires, 1893; violinist;
at 11 played with succ. in Europe.

Dennée (děn-nā), **Chas.**, b. Oswego,
N. Y., Sept. 1, 1863; studied with
Emery, Boston; teacher and com-
poser; d. April 29, 1946.

Den'ner, Jn. Chp., Leipzig, 1655—
Nürnberg, 1707; maker of wind-
insts.; inv. 1690 or 1700 the clarinet,
perhaps also the Stockfagott and the
Rackettenfagott.

Dent, Edward Joseph, b. Ribston,
England, July, 18, 1876; educator
and writer on music; pupil of Wood
and Stanford at Cambridge Univ.,
fellow of King's Coll.; an ed. of
Encyclopedia Britannica; ed. second
edition of Grove's Musical Dictionary; pres. of Internat'l. Soc. for
Contemp. Music; after 1926 prof.
of musical science, Cambridge Univ.;
author of life of A. Scarlatti; "*A
Jesuit at the Opera in 1680*"; "*Italian
Chamber Cantatas*," "*Mozart's
Operas*," "*Foundations of English
Opera*," "*Busoni*," etc.; has also tr.
librettos of Mozart operas into
English.

Denza (děn'-tsä), **Luigi**, Castellam-
mare di Stabia, Feb. 24, 1846—
London, Feb. 13, 1922; pupil of
Naples Cons.; c. opera "*Wallenstein*"
(Naples, 1876), many pop. songs
(some in Neapolitan dialect), incl.
"*Funiculi-Funicula*"; after 1898,
prof. R. A. M., London.

Deppe (děp'-pě), **Ludwig**, Alverdissen,
Lippe, 1828—Pyrmont, Sept. 5–6,
1890; notable pf.-teacher and conductor.

Deprès (or **Després**) (dŭ-prě' or dā-
prä), **Jossé** (known as **Josquin**),
Condé (?) in Hainault, Burgundy,
ca. 1450—Condé, Aug. 27, 1521.
[His epitaph reads "Jossé Despres";
other spellings are Desprès, De(s)prez,
Depret, De(s)pret(s), Dupré, and by
the Italians, Del Prato, Latinised as

a Prato, a Pratis, Pratensis, etc.;
Josquin appears as Jossé, Jossien,
Jusquin, Giosquin, Josquinus, Jaco-
bo, Jodocus, Jodoculus, etc.] One
of the most eminent of musicians and
the chief contrapuntist of his day;
pupil of Okeghem; 1471–84 a singer
in the Sistine Chapel, and about
1488 in Ferrara; he was already now
accepted as "princeps musicorum,"
and had international vogue. He was
received with honour by various
princes, and was court-musician to
Louis XII., many amusing anecdotes
of his musical humour being told. He
finally returned to Condé as Provost
of the Cathedral Chapter. Burney
called him "the father of modern
harmony." The florid and restless
cpt. of his church-works and the secular *cantus firmus* (v. D. D.) that was
the basis of most of them, brought
his school into disfavour and disuse
when the revolutionary Palestrina appeared. But he was at least the culmination of his style, and his erudition
was moulded into suave and emotional effects, so that Ambros says
that he was the "first musician who
impresses us as being a genius." His
period coinciding with the use of
movable types for music, his works
are preserved in large quantities in
volumes and in the collections of Petrucci and Peutinger. His French
chansons were pub. by T. Susato,
1545, P. Attaignant, 1549, and Du
Chemin, 1553; excerpts in modern
notation are in the "*Bibliothek für
Kirchenmusik*," 1844; in Commer's
"*Collectio*," Rochlitz' "*Sammlung
vorzüglicher Gesangstücke*," 1838,
Choron's "*Collection*," and in the
histories of Ambros, Burney, Hawkins, etc.

De Reszké (dŭ rěsh'-kä), (1) **Jean**,
Warsaw, Jan. 14, 1850—Nice, April
3, 1925; perhaps the chief tenor of
his generation, great in opera of all
schools; pupil of Ciaffei, Cotogni,
etc.; 1874, début as barytone at
Venice, as Alfonso in "*La Favorita*,"
under the name "De Reschi"; after
singing in Italy and Paris and studying with Sbriglia, he made his début
as tenor in "*Robert le Diable*"
(Madrid, 1879); 1884, Th. des
Nations; 1885 at the Gr. Opéra,
Paris, creating Massenet's "*Le Cid*";
from 1887 he sang constantly in London, and 1891–1901 at the Met.

Op., N. Y., where he was an unforgettable "Tristan," etc.; retired from stage 1902 and taught singing in Paris. (2) **Édouard,** Warsaw, Dec. 23, 1855—near Piotrkow, May 25, 1917; bro. of above; pupil of his brother, of Ciaffei, Steller, and Coletti; début, Paris, April 22, 1876, as the King in "*Aïda*" (Th. des Italiens), sang there two seasons, then at Turin and Milan; 1880–84 at the Italian Opera, London; then in Paris, London, America; a magnificent basso of enormous repertory and astonishing versatility as an actor; a master in tragic, comic, or buffa opera. His sister, (3) **Josephine,** was a soprano of greatest promise, but left the stage on her marriage.

Dering, v. DEERING.

De Sabata (dä sä-bä'-tä), **Victor,** b. Trieste, 1892; composer, conductor; studied Milan Cons. (gold medal) with Orefice and Saladino; has led symph. concerts at La Scala, Augusteo (Rome), Turin, Bologna, Palermo, Trieste; guest cond., Cincinnati Symph., 1927–28; and with much succ. at Berlin and Vienna both as op. and symph. cond.; c. (opera) "*Il Macigno*" (La Scala, 1917); (orch.) "*Juventus,*" Andante and Scherzo; Orch. Suite; "*La Notte di Platon,*" "*Getsemane*" (N. Y. Philh. under Toscanini, 1926); chamber music, etc.

De Sanctis (dä sänk'-tēs), **Cesare,** b. Rome, 1830—ca. 1900; 1876, prof. of harm. in the Liceo; c. overture, Requiem Mass, "100 fugues," a cappella in strict style; pub. treatises.

Désaugiers (dä-sō-zhä), **Marc Ant.,** Fréjus, 1742—Paris, 1793; prod. numerous succ. short operas.

Deshayes (dŭz-ĕz), **Prosper Didier,** prod., 1780, oratorio "*Les Machabées*"; c. operettas and ballets, etc.

Deslandres (dē-läṅ'-drŭ), **Adolphe Eduard Marie,** Paris, Jan. 22, 1840—July 30, 1911; pupil Paris Cons.; organist at St. Marie at Batignolles, where his father was director; c. operettas and church music.

Desmarets (dä-mă-rā), **H.,** Paris, 1662—Luneville, 1741; dram. composer.

Dessau (dĕs'-sow), **Bd.,** Hamburg, March 1, 1861—Berlin, 1923; pupil of Schradieck, Joachim, and Wieniawski; leader at various theatres;

1898 Konzertmeister at the court-opera, Berlin, and teacher Stern Cons.

Dessauer (dĕs'-sow-ĕr), **Jos.,** Prague, May 28, 1798—Mödling, near Vienna, July 8, 1876; c. 5 operas and many pop. songs.

Dessoff (dĕs'-sôf), (1) **Felix Otto,** Leipzig, 1835—Frankfort, 1892; court-cond. at Carlsruhe. (2) **Margarete,** b. Vienna, June 11, 1874; conductor; daughter of (1); studied at Hoch Cons. in Frankfort; founded women's chorus which made début at Wiesbaden Brahms Fest. in 1912; later a madrigal chorus; was choral cond. at Hoch Cons., 1912–17; of Bach Soc., in Frankfort, 1917–20; after 1920 res. for fifteen years in N. Y., where she led the Adesdi Chorus and A Cappella Singers in programmes incl. rare old and mod. mus.; gave Amer. première of Vecchi's "*L'Amfiparnaso*"; d. Locarno, Nov. 27, 1944.

Destinn (dä'-shtĭn), **Emmy,** Prague, Feb. 26, 1878—Budweis, Bohemia, Jan. 28, 1930; soprano; studied with Loewe-Destinn; her real name was Kittl—she chose "Destinn" in honour of her teacher; she sang at Bayreuth, 1891; from 1908 she had great success at the Met. Op., N. Y., also at Covent Garden and Berlin Royal Op.; she created the rôle of "*Minnie*" in Puccini's "*Fanciulla del West*"; during the war she was interned in her estate in Bohemia on the ground of enemy sympathies; and after 1918 toured again in the U. S., and sang for one season at the Met. Op.; her voice was of rare purity; her repertoire embraced 80 rôles; also a poet and writer.

Destouches (dä-toosh), (1) **André Cardinal,** Paris, 1672—1749; dram. composer. (2) **Franz Seraph von,** Munich, 1772—1844; dram. composer.

Desvignes (dä-vēn'-yŭ), **Fran.,** Trier, 1805—Metz, 1853; violinist; founded conservatory at Metz; dram. composer.

Deswert (dä-vărt), (1) **J. Caspar Isidore,** Louvain, 1830—Schaerbeck, near Brussels, 1896; 'cellist; prof. Brussels Cons. (2) **Jules,** Louvain, 1843—Ostend, 1891; brother of above; conductor and dram. composer.

Dé'thier (dä'-tē-ā), (1) **Gaston Marie,** b. Liége, April 19, 1875; organist and teacher; pupil of Liége Cons., grad. at 17 with gold medals in piano, organ and 1st prize for fugue; early active as concert org.; after 1894 at St. Xavier's Ch., N. Y.; beginning 1907 excl. in concert work and as teacher at Inst. of Mus. Art. (2) **Edouard,** b. Liége, 1885; violinist; pupil of Liége and Brussels Cons.; taught at latter; début in concert, 1903; after 1906 taught at Inst. of Mus. Art, N. Y., and toured as soloist; with his bro. Gaston gave series of sonata recitals in N. Y.

Dett, Robert Nathaniel, b. Drummondsville, Quebec, Oct. 11, 1882; Negro composer; studied at Oberlin, Ohio and Columbia Univs.; taught at Lane Coll., Lincoln Inst., and after 1913 at the Hampton (Va.) Inst., where he led a choral group; won Bowdoin prize, Harvard Univ., for essay on *"The Emancipation of Negro Music"*; c. choral works, pf. music and spiritual settings; d. Battle Creek, Mich., Oct. 2, 1943.

Dett'mer, Wm., Breinum, near Hildesheim, 1808—Frankfort, 1876; operatic bass; 1842 engaged for leading rôles Dresden; retired 1874.

Deutz (doits). Vide MAGNUS.

Devienne (dŭv-yĕn), **Fran.,** Joinville, Haute-Marne, Jan. 31, 1759—(insane), Charenton, Sept. 5, 1803; flutist and bassoonist; important in improving wind instr.; prof., composer and writer.

Devries (dü-vrēz'), **Herman,** b. New York, Dec. 25, 1858; sang Paris Op. and Op.-Comique; Met. Op., Covent Garden, etc.; after 1900 in Chicago as teacher and critic of the *"American"*; d. Chicago, Aug. 23, 1949.

Diabelli (dē-ä-bĕl'-lē), **Antonio,** Mattsee, near Salzburg, Sept. 6, 1781—Vienna, April 7, 1858; pf.-and guitar-teacher; partner of Cappi, the music-publisher; c. opera and pop. sonatinas, etc.

Diaghileff (dē-ä'-gē-lyĕf), **Serge,** govt. of Novgorod, Russia, March 19, 1872—Venice, Aug. 19, 1929; ballet director; studied law in St. Petersburg, also music theory with Cotogni, Sokoloff and Liadoff; served as critic of the newspaper *"Les Nouvelles"*; in 1899 founded periodical and promoted art exhibitions; after 1907, arranged concerts of Russian music in Paris; prod. *"Boris Godounoff"* at the Op. there with Chaliapin

and chorus of Petersburg Imp. Op., in 1908; in 1909 the first season of the Russian ballets was organized by him in Paris, incl. Nijinsky, Pavlowa, Karsavina, Fokine, etc.; this group established world-wide fame, and toured in Europe and America with brilliant succ. (N. Y., 1916); **D.** gave the impetus to a notable renaissance of ballet art, and was responsible for the development of many composers who later became famous, incl. Stravinsky; the Diaghileff Ballet Russe commissioned and prod. new scores of more advanced creators than any other organisation of its period.

Diaz (de la Peña) (dē'-ăth dŭ-lä-pän'-yä), **Eugène Émile,** Paris, Feb. 27, 1837—Sept. 12, 1901; son of the painter; pupil of Paris Cons. (Halévy, Réber); prod. the com. opera *"Le Roi Candaule"* (1865, Th. Lyrique); 1867 won the prize for opera, *"La Coupe du Roi de Thule"* (Grand Opéra); 1890 prod. lyric drama *"Benvenuto"* (Op.-Com.); pub. many songs.

Dib'din, (1) **Chas.,** Dibdin, near Southampton, 1745—London, 1814; composer, singer, accompanist, actoi, manager and writer. (2) **Henry Edward,** Sadlers Wells, 1813—1866; harpist, organist, violinist and composer; youngest son of above.

Dick'inson, Clarence, b. Lafayette, Ind., May 7, 1873; organist and composer; studied with Singer, Reimann, Guilmant, Moszkowski, and Vierne; founded Mus. Art Ass'n., Chicago; res. in New York since 1909, where he is organist at Brick Presbyterian Church, teacher of church music at Gen'l. Theological Seminary; also active as composer and writer on music.

Didur (dē'-dŏŏr), **Adamo,** b. Sanok, Galicia, Dec. 24, 1874; bass; studied with Wysocki in Lemberg and Emerich in Milan; début, Rio de Janeiro, 1894; sang at La Scala, 1899–1903; also in England, Russia, Spain, South America, and for a number of years at the Met. Op. House, N. Y.; d. Katowice, Jan. 15, 1946.

Did'ymus, b. Alexandria, Egypt, 63 B. C.; wrote 4,000 works in all, incl. a treatise on harmony. Vide TETRA CHORDS and COMMA (D. D.).

Diémer (d'yä-mā), **Louis,** Paris, Feb.

14, 1843—Dec. 21, 1919; pianist; pupil at Cons. of Marmontel; took 1st pf.-prize at 13, later 1st harm., 2nd org. and 1st cpt.-prizes; pupil Ambr. Thomas and Bazin; after 1887 pf.-prof. at the Cons. (vice Marmontel); besides brilliant concerts of modern music, he presented programmes of old keyboard works played on ancient instrs.; c. pf.-concerto, chamber-music, etc., ed. collections.

Diener (dē'-nĕr), **Fz.**, Dessau, 1849—1879; tenor.

Diepenbrock (dē'-pĕn-brök), **A. J. M.**, Amsterdam, Sept. 2, 1862—April 5, 1921; teacher and comp. of church music.

Dierich (dē'-rĭkh), **Carl**, b. Heinrichau, March 31, 1852; tenor in concert, opera and oratorio; studied with Graben-Hoffman.

Diës (dē'-ĕs), **Albert K.**, Hanover, 1755—Vienna, 1822; writer.

Diet (dē-ā), **Edmond M.**, Paris, Sept. 25, 1854—Oct., 1924; pupil of César Franck, and Guiraud; officier of the Academy; prod. 3 comic operas, incl. *"Stratonice"* (1887), many ballets and pantomimes, etc.

Diet(t)er (dē'-tĕr), **Chr. L.**, Ludwigsburg, 1757—Stuttgart, 1822; dram. composer.

Dietrich (dē'-trĭkh) (or **Dieterich**), (1) **Sixtus**, Augsburg (?) 1490 (95)—St. Gallen, Switzerland, 1548; composer. (2) **Albert Hn.**, Golk, near Meissen, Aug. 28, 1829—Berlin, Nov. 20, 1908; composer; pupil of J. Otto, Moscheles, Reitz and Schumann; 1855-61, concert-cond., 1859, principal mus.-dir. at Bonn; 1861, court-cond. at Oldenburg; 1894 Leipzig; c. succ. opera *"Robin Hood"* (Frankfort, 1879); a symphony; overture, *"Normannenfahrt"*; cantatas with orch., 'cello- and vln.-concertos, etc.

Dietsch (dētsh), **Pierre L. Ph.**, Dijon, 1808—1865; composer and conductor.

Dieupart (d'yŭ-pär), **Chas.**, 18th cent.; violinist and harpsichordist.

Dil'liger, Jn., Eisfeld, 1593—Coburg, 1647, cantor and composer.

Dippel (dĭp'-pĕl), **Andreas**, Cassel, Nov. 30, 1866—Hollywood, Cal., May 12, 1932; notable tenor; studied with Hey, Leoni and Rau; 1887-92, Bremen opera, then in New York for several seasons, also in Breslau, Vienna; 1889 at Bayreuth, from 1897 at Covent Garden; associated with Gatti-Casazza in management of Met. Op. House, N. Y., 1908; then directed opera seasons in Chicago and Philadelphia, 1910-13; later organised his own Wagnerian op. company, with financial fiasco; taught singing on Pacific Coast in latter years.

Diruta (dē-roo'-tä), (1) **Gir.**, b. Perugia, ca. 1560; organist; pub. technical books on org., cpt., etc. (2) **Ag.**, b. Perugia, 1622; Augustine monk; composer.

Dit'son, (1) **Oliver**, 1811—1888; founder of the music-pub. firm O. Ditson Co., at Boston, Mass.; 1867, his eldest son, (2) **Chas.**, took charge of N. Y. branch (C. H. Ditson & Co.). After 1875 (3) **J. Edward** Ditson cond. Philadelphia branch (J. E. D. & Co.), but this was discontinued in 1910. A branch for the importation of instrs., etc., was est. at Boston in 1860 as John C. Haynes & Co.; and 1864 a Chicago branch, Lyon & Healy. In 1932 the publishing activities were taken over by the Theodore Presser Co.

Ditters (dĭt'-tĕrs) (**von Dittersdorf**), **Karl**, Vienna, Nov. 2, 1739—Neuhof, Bohemia, Oct. 24, 1799; noteworthy as forerunner of Mozart, and early writer of programme-music (v. D. D.); pupil of König and Ziegler, of Trani (vln.), and Bono (comp.); he played in the orch. of his patron Prince Joseph of Hildburghausen, 1759, and then in the ct.-Th. at Vienna (1761); toured Italy with Gluck, and made great succ. as violinist; 1764-69 conductor to the Bishop of Gross-Wardein, Hungary. Prod. his first opera, *"Amore in Musica,"* 1767; followed by various oratorios, and much orchestral and chamber-music. Later conductor to the Prince-Bishop of Breslau; built a small theatre and prod. several pieces. 1770 the Pope bestowed on him the Order of the Golden Spur; 1773 the Emperor ennobled him as "von Dittersdorf." Prod. 28 operas; *"Doktor und Apotheker"* (Vienna, 1786), still pop.; several oratorios and cantatas, 12 symphonies on Ovid's *"Metamorphoses"* (Vienna, 1785) (noteworthy as early attempts at programme-music); 41 other symphonies; a "Concerto grosso" for 11 concerted instrs. with orch.; 12

vln.-concertos, etc. Autobiography (Leipzig, 1801). Studies by Arnold, Krebs, Klob and Riedinger. Krebs also issued a thematic catalogue, with additions later by Istel.

Divitis (dē'-vĭ-tēs), **Antonius** (rightly **Antoine Le Riche**), French contrapuntist and singer, 16th century.

Dizi (dē-zē), **Fran. J.**, Namur, France, Jan. 14, 1780—Paris, Nov., 1847; composer and harpist.

Dlabacz (dlä'-bäch), **Gottf. J.**, Böhmisch-Brod, Bohemia, 1758—Prague, 1820; pub. a biog. dict., etc.

Dobrowen (dō-brō-věn'), **Issay**, b. Nishni-Novgorod, Russia, Feb. 27, 1893; conductor, composer; pupil of Moscow Cons., where won gold medal, 1911; also studied piano with Godowsky in Vienna; prof. at Moscow Philharmonie, 1917–21, and after 1919 cond. at the Great Theatre there; beginning 1923 he was cond. and scenic director at the Dresden Op.; 1924–25, Berlin Volksoper; 1931–32, Museum Concerts, Frankfort; until 1931 he was the regular cond. of the Oslo Philh. Orch., and the San Francisco Symph. Orch, 1931–33; c. chamber and orch. music and piano wks.; d. Oslo, Dec. 9, 1952.

Dobrzynski (dō-brŭ-tsēn'-shkĭ), **Ignacy Félix**, Romanoff, Volhynia, Feb. 25, 1807—Oct. 9, 1867; pupil of Elsner; pianist and dram. composer.

Doebber (děp'-běr), **Js.**, Berlin, March 28, 1866—Jan. 26, 1921; pupil of Radecke, Bussler and Agghazy, Stern Cons.; taught the 1st pf.-class in Kullak's Cons.; then conductor at Kroll's Th.; at Darmstadt ct.-Th.; 1895, cond. at the ct.-Th. in Coburg-Gotha, and tutor to Princess Beatrice; later in Hanover, and after 1908 in Berlin as critic and voice teacher; c. succ. operas, *"Die Strassensängerin"* (Gotha, 1890); *"Der Schmied von Gretna-Green"* (Berlin, 1893); burlesque-opera *"Dolcetta"* (Brandenburg, 1894); *"Die Rose von Genzanô"* (Gotha, 1895); *"Die Grille"* (Leipzig, 1897), a symphony, songs, etc.

Döhler (dä'-lěr), **Th.**, Naples, 1814—Florence, 1856; pianist and dram. composer.

Dohnanyi (dökh-nän'-yē), **Ernst von, b.** Pressburg, Hungary, July 27, 1877; notable pianist and composer; first lessons from his father, an amateur ʻcellist; later studied with Foerster,

Koessler, Thoman, and Eugen D'Albert; début, Vienna; 1898, won prize there with his pf.-concerto. 1900 and 1901 toured in America with great succ.; after 1907 taught at Berlin Hochsch.; 1919, dir. Budapest Acad. of Mus.; he cond. State Symph. in New York 1925–6 season; c. operas *"Tante Simona,"* *"The Tenor,"* *"The Voyevode's Tower"*; also pantomimes; 2 symphonies, 2 pf.-concertos, 4 rhapsodies, string sextet, piano quintet, 2 string quartets. 3 'cello sonatas, 2 piano sonatas, songs, etc.

Doles (dō'-lěs), **J. Fr.**, Steinbach, Saxe-Meiningen, 1715—Leipzig, 1797; director and composer.

Dol'metsch, Arnold, b. Le Mans, France, Feb. 24, 1858—London, Feb. 29, 1940; of mixed French and Swiss parentage; studied with Vieuxtemps in Brussels and at R. Coll. of Mus., London; taught at Dulwich Coll., in latter city; began collecting and playing ancient instruments; was active in Chickering's workshop, Boston, 1902–09; and in that of Gaveau, Paris, 1910–14; in latter year settled at Haslemere, Surrey, where he in 1925 began a series of notable annual chamber music fests., in which he has restored rare old music and dances, his entire family participating in programmes; also has constructed his own instruments for these events.

Domanievski (dō-män-yěf'-shkĭ), **Boleslaus,** b. Gronówek, Poland, 1857—1925; Polish piano teacher; pupil of Jos. Wieniawski and Rubinstein; 1890–1900, prof. at Cracow Cons., 1902, director Warsaw Music School; author of piano methods; from 1906, dir. of Warsaw Musikgesellschaft.

Dominiceti (dō-mē-nē-chä'-tē), **Cesare,** Desenzano, Lago di Garda, 1821—Sesto di Monza, 1888; prof. of comp. at Milan Cons., and dram. composer.

Dom'mer, Arrey von, Danzig, Feb. 9, 1828—Treysa, Feb. 18, 1905; pupil of Richter and Lobe (comp.), and Schallenburg (org.); 1863 Hamburg as a lecturer, critic, and (1873–79) sec. to the Town Library; 1892, Dr. phil. hon. causa (Marburg Univ.); writer and composer.

Domnich (dôm'-nĭkh), **Heinrich,** Würzburg, May 13, 1767—Paris, June 19, 1844; horn virtuoso; first teacher of the horn at Paris Cons., 1795; author of methods.

Donal'da, Pauline (rightly **Lightstone**), b. Montreal, March 5, 1884; soprano; studied at Victoria Cons., and with Duvernoy at Paris Cons.; début as Manon, Nice, 1904; sang at La Monnaie, Brussels, Covent Garden, Manhattan Op. House, N. Y. (1905); at Paris Op., 1907, etc.

Donati (dō-nä'-tē), (1) **Ignazio**, Casalmaggiore, near Cremona, 16th cent., composer and conductor. (2) **Baldassaro**, d. Venice, 1603; cond. and composer.

Donaudy (dō-nä'-oo-dē), **Stefano**, Palermo, Feb. 21, 1879—Naples, May 30, 1925; c. operas *"Folchetto"* (Palermo, 1892); *"Theodor Körner"* (Hamburg, 1902), and *"Sperduti nel Buio"* (Palermo, 1907), songs, etc.

Done (dōn), **Wm.**, Worcester, 1815—1895; Engl. organist and conductor.

Doni (dō'-nē), (1) **A. Fran.**, Florence, 1519—Monselice, near Padua, 1574; pub. a *"Dialogue on Music."* (2) **Giov. Bat.**, 1594—1647; Florentine nobleman of great learning and research in ancient music; inv. the Lyra Barberina or Amphichord.

Donizetti (dō-nē-tsĕt'-tē), (1) **Gaetano**, Bergamo, Nov. 25, 1797—April 8, 1848; son of a weaver; pupil of Salari (voice), Gonzales (pf. and accomp.), and Mayr (harm.); Pilotti and Padre Mattei (cpt.); his father opposing his making mus. a profession, he entered the army, was posted at Venice, where he c. and prod. with succ. *"Enrico di Borgogna"* (1819); *"Il Falegname di Livonia"* (Venice, 1820), first given as *"Pietro il Grande,"* also succeeded; *"Le Nozze in Villa"* (Mantua, 1820) failed; *"Zoraide di Granata"* (1822) succeeded and he left the army; 1823 he m. Virginie Vasselli (d. 1837); 1822–29 he c. 23 operas, none of them of great originality or importance. With *"Anna Bolena"* (Milan, 1830), he began a better period, incl. the great successes *"L'Elisir d'Amore"* (Milan, 1832), *"Lucrezia Borgia"* (La Scala, Milan, 1833), *"Lucia di Lammermoor"* (Naples, 1835). 1835 at Paris he prod. *"Marino Faliero."* 1837 dir. Naples Cons. The censor forbade his *"Poliuto"* (it was prod. at Naples after his death, 1848), and in wrath he left for Paris, where he prod. with much succ. *"La Fille du*

Régiment" (Op.-Com., 1840), *"Les Martyrs"* (a new version of *"Poliuto"*) (Opéra, 1840?) and *"La Favorita"* (Opéra, 1840). Returned to Italy, and succ. prod. *"Adelasia"* (Rome, 1841), and *"Maria Padilla"* (Milan, 1841). At Vienna, 1842, c. and prod. with great succ. *"Linda di Chamounix."* The Emperor made him Court Composer and Master of the Imperial Chapel; c. a Miserere and an Ave Maria in strict style. *"Don Pasquale"* was prod. in Paris, 1843. Violent headaches and mental depression now assailed him, but he continued to write and prod. *"Caterino Cornaro"* (Naples, 1844), his last work; he was found stricken with paralysis, never recovered, and died in 1848 at Bergamo. Besides 67 operas, all of them produced, he c. 6 masses, a requiem; cantatas; 12 string-quartets; pf.-pcs. and songs. Biog. by Cicconetti (Rome, 1864). (2) **Alfredo** (rightly **Ciummei**), b. Smyrna, Sept. 2, 1867—Rosario de Santa Fe, Argentina; Feb. 4, 1921; pupil of Ponchielli and Dominiceti, Milan Cons., graduating with a noteworthy "Stabat Mater" with orch.; lived at Milan as cond. and teacher of cpt.; c. 1-act operas *"Nana"* (Milan, 1889), and *"Dopo l'Ave Maria"* (Milan, 1897), *"La Locandiera,"* etc.

Dont (dônt), (1) **Jos. Val.**, Georgenthal, Bohemia,1776—Vienna,1833;'cellist. (2) **Jakob**, Vienna, 1815—1888; son of above; violinist and composer.

Donzelli (dôn-jĕl'-lē), **Dom.**, Bergamo, 1790—Bologna, 1873; tenor.

Door (dōr), **Anton**, Vienna, June 20, 1833—Nov. 7, 1919; pupil of Czerny and Sechter; court pianist at Stockholm; 1859 teacher at the Imp. Inst., Moscow; 1864 prof. at the Cons.; 1869 1st prof. Vienna Cons., resigned 1901; edited classical and pedagogic works.

Dopp'ler, (1) **Albert Fr.**, Lemberg, 1821—Baden, near Vienna, 1883; flutist, conductor, professor, and dram. composer. (2) **Karl**, Lemberg, 1825—Stuttgart, March 10, 1900; bro. of above; flutist, and conductor; c. operas, incl. *"Erzebeth"* in collab. with his bro. and Erkel. (3) **Arpad**, Pesth, June 5, 1857—Stuttgart, Aug. 13, 1927; son and pupil of (2); pupil of Stuttgart Cons., later pf.-teacher; 1880–83 New York;

returned to Stuttgart Cons., 1889.
Dorati (dō-rä'-tē), **Antal**, b. Budapest; studied Mus. Acad. there; cond. Ballet Russe on tours; Dallas Symph., 1945–9; mus. dir. Minneapolis Symph., 1949.

Doret (dō-rā), **Gustave**, b. Aigle, Switzerland, Sept. 20, 1866; studied violin with Joachim and Marsick, and composition at Paris Cons.; lived at Paris as cond.; c. operas "*Les Armailles*" (Op. Com., 1906), "*Le nain de Hassli*" (Geneva, 1908), etc.; d. Lausanne, April 19, 1944.

Dörffel (děrf'-fěl), **Alfred**, Waldenburg, Saxony, Jan. 24, 1821—Leipzig, Jan. 22, 1905; pupil at Leipzig of Fink, Muller, Mendelssohn, etc.; mus.-libr. Leipzig City Library; critic and editor; 1885 Dr. phil. h. c.

Do'ria, Clara, v. MRS. C. K. ROGERS.

Döring (dā'-rǐng), (1) **G.,** Pomerendorf, near Elbing, 1801—1869; cantor; pub. choral books and historical essays. (2) **Karl,** Dresden, July 4, 1834—March 26, 1916; pupil Leipzig Cons.; 1858, Dresden Cons.; 1875, prof.; c. suites for string-orch., Grand Mass., etc.

Dorn, (1) **H.** (**L. Edm.**), Königsberg, Nov. 14, 1804—Berlin, Jan. 10, 1892; pupil of Berger, Zelter, and Klein, Berlin; ct.-cond. at Königsberg; cond. Cologne; founded the "Rheinische Musikschule," which, 1850, became the Cologne Cons.; cond. Royal Opera, Berlin; teacher and critic; notable composer of 12 operas, symphonies, etc. (2) **Julius Paul,** Riga, June 8, 1833—Berlin, Nov. 27, 1901; son and pupil of above; pianist; teacher in Poland, Cairo, and Alexandria; 1865–68 cond. the Crefeld "Liedertafel"; then pf.-teacher at the R. Hochschule, Berlin, with title "Royal Prof."; c. over 400 works, incl. 3 masses with orch. (3) **Otto,** Cologne, Sept. 7, 1848—Wiesbaden, Nov. 8, 1931; son and pupil of (1); studied at Stern Cons., took the Meyerbeer scholarship (1st prize), 1873; lived in Wiesbaden; c. succ. opera "*Afraja*" (Gotha, 1891); symphony, "*Prometheus*"; overtures, "*Hermannsschlacht*," and "*Sappho*," etc. (4) **Edward,** Pen-name of **J. L. Röckel.**

Dorus-Gras (dō-rü-gräs), **Julie Aimée Josèphe** (rightly **Van Steenkiste**) (Dorus, stage-name); Valenciennes, 1805—Paris, 1896; operatic soprano; created important rôles.

Doss (dôs), **Adolf von,** Pfarrkirchen, Lower Bavaria, 1825—Rome, 1886; Jesuit priest and dram. composer.

Dotzauer (dôt'-tsow-ĕr), (1) **Justus J. Fr.,** Hasselrieth, near Hildburghausen, 1783—Dresden, 1860; 'cellist, and dram. composer. (2) **Justus B. Fr.,** Leipzig, 1808—Hamburg, 1874; son of above; teacher. (3) **K. L.** ("**Louis**"), Dresden, Dec. 7, 1811—1897; son and pupil of (1); 'cellist.

Dourlen (door-lǎn), **Victor Chas. Paul,** Dunkirk, 1780—Batignolles, near Paris, 1864; prof. and dram. composer.

Dow'land, (1) **John,** Westminster, London, 1562—London, April, 1626; famed for polyphonic vocal music; lutenist and composer to Christian IV. of Denmark. (2) **Robert,** 1641; son of above; lutenist and editor.

Downes, Olin, b. Evanston, Ill., Jan. 27, 1886; music critic, pianist; studied piano with Carl Baermann, harmony with Homer Norris and Clifford Heilman, mus. hist. and analysis with Dr. Louis Kelterborn and John P. Marshall; mus. critic, Boston "*Post*," 1906–24; music critic, New York "*Times*," after 1924; has appeared widely as a lecturer on music and has written works on symphonic analysis; also has participated as pianist in chamber music programmes.

Draeseke (drä'-zĕ-kĕ), **Felix Aug. Bhd.,** Coburg, Oct. 7, 1835—Dresden, Feb. 26, 1913; important composer; pupil of Rietz, Leipzig Cons., and of Liszt at Weimar; 1864–74 Lausanne Cons., except 1868–69, in the R. M. S. at Munich; 1875 Geneva, then Dresden as teacher; 1884 prof. of comp. at the Cons.; c. 4 operas: "*Sigura*," "*Gudrun*" (Hanover, 1884), "*Bertrana de Born*" (book and music), and the succ. "*Herrat*" (Dresden, 1892); 3 symphonies (op. 40 "*Tragica*," in C); Grand Mass with orch.; "*Akademische Festouvertüre*"; symphonic preludes to Calderon's "*Life a Dream*," Kleist's "*Penthesilea*" (both MS.), etc; wrote treatises and a "*Harmony*" in verse.

Draghi (drä'-gē), (1) **Antonio,** Rimini, 1635—Vienna, 1700; c. 87 operas, 87 festival plays, etc. (2) **Gio. Bat.,** 1667—1706, harpsichordist, organist and composer, London.

Dragonet'ti, Dom., Venice, April 7,

1763—London, April 16, 1846; called "the Paganini of the contra-basso"; composed, played and taught.

Drago'ni, Giovanni Andrea, Mendola, ca. 1540—Rome, 1598; composer; pupil of Palestrina; cond. at the Lateran.

Draud (drowt) (Drau'dius), Georg, Davernheim, Hesse, 1573—Butzbach, ca. 1636; pub. "Bibliotheca Classica," and other musical works of great informational value.

Drdla, Franz, Saar, Moravia, Nov. 28, 1868; violinist and composer; pupil of Prague and Vienna Cons.; c. over 200 smaller instrumental works, among which his "Souvenir" had world-wide popularity; also two stage works; 1923-25, lived in New York.

Drechsler (drĕkhs'-lĕr), (1) Jos., Wallisch-Birken (Vlachovo Brezi), Bohemia, 1782—Vienna, 1852; organist, conductor and dram. composer. (2) Karl, Kamenz, 1800—Dresden, 1873; 'cellist teacher.

Dregert (drä'-gĕrt), Alfred, Frankforton-Oder, 1836—Elberfeld, 1893; conductor, dir. and composer.

Drese (drä'-zĕ), Adam, Thüringen, Dec., 1620—Arnstadt, Feb. 15, 1701; director and comp.

Dresel (drä'-zĕl), Otto, Andernach, 1826—Beverly, Mass., 1890; composer.

Dreszer (drĕsh'-ĕr), Anastasius W., Kalisch, Poland, April 28, 1845—Halle, June 2, 1907; a brilliant pianist at 12; studied with Döring, Krebs, and Früh, Dresden Cons.; lived in Leipzig; 1868, Halle; founded a music-school of which he was dir.; c. 2 symphonies, opera "Valmoda," etc.

Dreyschock (drī'-shôk), (1) Alex., Zack, Bohemia, Oct. 15, 1818—Venice, April 1, 1869; one of the most dextrous of pf.-virtuosi; c. an opera, etc. (2) Raimund, Zack, 1824—Leipzig, 1869, br. of above; leader. His wife (3) Elisabeth (née Nose), Cologne, 1832, a contralto. (4) Felix, Leipzig, Dec. 27, 1860—Berlin, Aug. 1, 1906; son of (1); pianist; student under Grabau, Ehrlich, Taubert, and Kiel at the Berlin Royal Hochschule; prof. Stern Cons., Berlin; c. a vln.-sonata (op. 16), etc.

Drieberg (drē'-bĕrkh), Fr. J. von, Charlottenburg, 1780--1856; writer on Greek music; dram. composer.

Drigo (drē'-gō), Riccardo, Padua, 1846—Oct. 1, 1930; composer; active as conductor at St. Petersburg Imp. Op. and piano teacher there for many years; after 1919 again lived in Padua; c. operas, and ballets; among the latter "Il Flauto Magico" and "Les Millions d'Arlequin" have had wide popularity; also salon works for piano.

Drobisch (drō'-bĭsh), (1) Moritz W., Leipzig, Aug. 16, 1802—Sept. 30, 1896; from 1842 prof. of phil., Leipzig Univ.; pub. important treatises on the mathematical determination of relative pitches. (2) Karl L., Leipzig, 1803—Augsburg, 1854; bro. of above; c. 3 oratorios.

Drouet (droo-ā), L. Franç. Ph., Amsterdam, 1792—Bern, Sept. 30, 1873; flutist and composer.

Duben'sky, Arcady, b. Russia, 1890; composer, violinist; pupil of Moscow Cons.; played vln. in Phila. Orch.; guest cond. of his works in America; c. (opera) "Romance with Double Bass" (Moscow Imp. Op., 1916); "The Raven," a melo-declamation to text by Poe; orch. works, incl. symphony, "Russian Bells" (N. Y. Symph., 1927); Fugue for 18 violins, etc.

Dubois (dü-bwä) (1) (Clément Fran.) Th., Rosnay, Marne, Aug. 24, 1837—Paris, June 11, 1924; studied at Rheims, then under Marmontel, Bénoist, Bazin, and Thomas (fugue and cpt.) at Paris Cons.; took Grand prix de Rome with the cantata "Atala"; also first prizes in all departments; sent from Rome a Solemn Mass (perf. at the Madeleine in 1870), a dram. work, "La Prova d'un Opera Seria," and 2 overtures; returned to Paris as a teacher; cond. at Saint-Clotilde; organist at the Madeleine; 1871 prof. of harm. at the Cons.; 1891 prof. of comp.; 1894, elected to Acad.; 1896, dir. of the Cons., and officier of the Legion of Honour; c. operas; oratorios: "Les Septs Paroles du Christ" (1867), "Le Paradis Perdu" (1878) (city of Paris prize), and "Nôtre Dame de la Mer" (1897); cantatas; masses, etc.; 3 overtures, incl. "Frithiof." (2) Léon, Brussels, Jan. 9, 1859—1935; pupil of Cons., took Grand prix de Rome; 1890 second cond., Th. de la Monnaie, Brussels, 1912-25, dir. of Brussels Cons. (vice Tinel); c.

operas, ballet, symphonic poem, "*Atala*," etc.

Duburg, Matthew, London, 1703—1767; violinist and conductor.

Ducange. Vide CANGE, DU.

Ducasse (dü-käs), **Roger**, b. Bordeaux, April 18, 1873; pupil Paris Cons., with Gabriel Fauré, winning Prix de Rome, 1902; from 1909 inspector in elementary schools; c. *suite française* for orch. (Colonne concerts, 1909, twice. Boston Symph., 1910); "*Variations plaisantes sur un thème grave*" for harp and orch. (Colonne concerts, 1909), "*Sarabande*"; d. Bordeaux, July 20, 1954.

Ducis (dü-sē), **Benoît (Benedictus Ducis)**, b. Bruges, 1480; important composer; not to be confused with Benedictus of Appenzell.

Dufay (dü-fĕ), **Guill.**, ca. 1400—Cambrai, Nov. 27, 1474; a canon; said to have inv. white (open) notes.

Dufranne (dü-frän'), **Hector**, b. Belgium; tenor; sang at Brussels Op., 1896; then in London and after 1899 at Paris Op.-Comique; 1908, Manhattan Op. House, N. Y.; 1910–13 with Chicago Op.; sang in the premières of "*Griselidis*," "*Monna Vanna*" and "*Pelléas et Mélisande.*"

Dugazon (dü-gä-zôn), **Louise-Rosalie** (née **Lefèvre**), Berlin, 1753—Paris, 1821; untrained singer in light opera, so charming in both young and old rôles as to give rise to the descriptive terms "Jeunes Dugazon," and "Mères Dugazon."

Dug'gan, Jos. Francis, Dublin, July 10, 1817—London, 1900(?); opera-conductor and teacher in various cities in America, also Paris and London; c. succ. operas, "*Pierre*," and "*Léonie*," and 3 not produced; 2 symphonies, etc.

Duiffopruggar (rightly **Tieffenbrücker**) (dwĕf'-fō-proog'-gär or tĕf'-fĕn-brük-ĕr), (1) **Gaspar**, Freising, Bavaria, 1514—Lyons, 1571; long considered the first vln.-maker; went to Lyons in 1553, naturalised in 1559, and made violas da gamba and lutes. Other instr.-makers of the same surname were (2) **Wendelin**, (3) **Leonhard**, (4) **Leopold**, (5) **Ulrich**, and (6) **Magnus**. The latest made lutes at Venice, 1607.

Dukas (dü-käs), **Paul**, Paris, Oct. 1, 1865—May 17, 1935; one of the most original of French composers; pupil at the Cons. of Dubois, Mathias and Guiraud; won prize in counterpoint, 1888, second Prix de Rome with cantata "*Velleda*"; spent a year in Rome, then a year of military service; his overture "*Polyeucte*"; was played by Lamoureux in 1892; his symphony, 1896, and elsewhere; 1897 "*L'Apprenti-Sorcier*"; 1900, piano sonata; 1906, *Villanelle* for horn and piano; 1907, his opera "*Ariane et Barbe Bleue*" made a great stir and was played in Vienna, 1908, Met. Op., N. Y., 1911, etc.; had edited texts of Rameau, ar.d c. for piano "*Variations, Interlude et Final*," on a theme of Rameau's 1902; *Prelude élégiaque* on the name of Haydn, 1909; also a ballet "*La Péri*," dance-poem in one act (Paris 1911), etc.; after 1909 he was prof. at the Paris Cons. Studies by Séré and Samazeuilh.

Dukelsky (dōō-kĕl'-skē), **Vladimir**, b. Parifianova near Polotzk, Russia, Sept. 27, 1903; composer; studied in Moscow and Kiev; came into prominence through prod. of his ballet, "*Zephyr et Flore*" by Diaghileff at Monte Carlo, 1925; he has c. a large amount of chamber music, orch works, etc.; also popular stage revues and ballads under the pseudonym of "**Vernon Duke**"; res. in America, where he has appeared as pianist in concerts of his works.

Dulcken (dool'-kĕn), (1) **Louise** (née **David**), Hamburg, 1811—London 1850, a sister of Fd. David; pianist. (2) **Fd. Quentin**, London, June 1, 1837—Astoria, N. Y., 1902; son of above; pupil of Mendelssohn, Moscheles, Gade, Hauptmann, Becker and F. Hiller; prof. Warsaw Cons.; toured in Europe; lived for years in New York; c. an opera, "*Wieslav*"; a mass, etc.

Dulichius (dō-lĭkh'-ĭ-oos) also (**Deulich** or **Deilich**) **Philip**, Chemnitz (christened Dec. 19), 1562—March 25, 1631; teacher and comp.

Dülon (doo'-lōn), **Fr. L.**, Oranienburg, near Potsdam, 1769—Würzburg, 1826; a blind flutist and composer.

Dumont (dü-môn), **Henri**, Villers, near Liége, 1610—Paris, May 8, 1684; organist and comp.

Dunc'an, William Edmondstoune, Sale, Cheshire, 1866—June 26, 1920; organist; at 16 an associate of the Royal College of Organists: 1883, obtained scholarship at R. C. M., pupil of Parry, Stanford and Macfarren; critic for some years, then prof. at Oldham College; c. successful odes with orch., notably "*Ye Mariners of England*" (1890), etc.

Dun'ham, Henry Morton, Brockton, Mass., July 27, 1853—1929; grad. New England Cons., as pupil of G. E. Whiting (organ), J. C. D. Parker (piano), Emery and Paine (theory); held various church positions till 1911, and gave organ recitals on the Great Organ at Boston, at St. Louis Exposition; long prof. of organ at N. E. Cons.; author of an organ method; c. symph., poem "*Easter Morning*," a book of organ studies, Meditation for organ, harp and violin; 3 organ sonatas, etc.

Dun'hill, Thomas Frederick, b. Hampstead, London, Feb. 1, 1877; composer; studied at R. Coll. of Mus., after 1905 prof. there; also taught at Eton Coll., and toured colonies as examiner; 1907, founded concerts of British chamber music that have been influential in introducing new works and composers; c. large variety of orch. and esp. chamber works of tasteful quality and traditional form; opera, "*The Ice Queen*," etc.; d. Scunthorpe, March 13, 1946.

Duni (doo'-nē), **Egidio Romualdo,** Matera, near Otranto, Feb. 9, 1709 —Paris, June 11, 1775; pupil of Durante; his first opera, "*Nerone*," prod. Rome, 1735, with great succ., triumphing over Pergolesi's last opera "*Olimpiado*," which the generous Duni said was too good for the public, declaring himself "frenetico contre il pubblico Romano"; he c. French operettas with such succ. that he settled in Paris, where he is considered the founder of French opera-bouffe; c. 13 Italian operas and 20 French.

Dunk'ley, Fd. (Louis), b. London, England, July 16, 1869; pupil of G. A. Higgs, Bainbridge, J. Higgs (cpt.), and E. H. Turpin (comp.); and at R. A. M. (Scholarship), under Parry, Bridge, Martin, Gladstone, Sharpe and Barnet; 1893, dir. at St. Agnes' School, Albany, N. Y.; also organist 1897 at Trinity M. E. Ch.; pub. "*The Wreck of the Hesperus*," ballade for soli, chor., and orch., etc.; 1889 took prize of 50 guineas

with orch. suite; lived in various cities; after 1920 in Birmingham, Ala.

Dunoyer (dün-wä-yā'). Vide GAUCQUIER.

Dun'stable (Dunstaple), John, Dunstable, Bedfordshire, England, 1370 (?)—Walbrook, Dec. 24, 1453; called by Tinctor one of the "fathers" of counterpoint.

Duparc (dü-păr) **(Fouques Duparc), Henri,** Paris, Jan. 21, 1848—Mont de Marsan, Feb. 12, 1933; pupil of César Franck; soldier in war of 1870-71; ill health led to a life of seclusion to César Franck's great regret; c. symph. poem "*Lenore*," orch nocturne, "*Aux Étoiles*"; 6 pf.-pieces; vocal duet, "*La Fuite*"; other works destroyed by the comp., and some songs of the highest importance.

Dupont (dü-pôṅ), (1) **Pierre,** Rochetaillée, near Lyons, April 23, 1821—Saint-Étienne, July 25, 1870; c. the words and tunes of popular and political songs which Reyer wrote out; provoked such riots that Napoleon banished him, 1851. (2) **Joseph** (ainé), Liége, 1821—1861, violinist; prof. and dram. composer. (3) **J. Fran.,** Rotterdam, 1822—Nürnberg, 1875; violinist and dram. composer. (4) **Aug.,** Ensival, near Liége, 1827—Brussels, 1890; composer. (5) **Alex.,** Liége, 1833—1888; bro. of above; pub. a "*Répertoire dramatique Belge.*" (6) **Jos.** (le jeune), Ensival, near Liége, Jan. 3, 1838—Brussels, Dec. 21, 1899; bro. of (3), pupil at Liége and Brussels Cons., took Grand prix de Rome at Brussels; 1867 cond. at Warsaw; 1871, in Moscow; 1872, prof. of harm., Brussels Cons.; cond. Th. de la Monnaie, the Society of Musicians, and the Popular Concerts. (7) **Jos. D.,** d. The Hague, June 26, 1867; bro. of above; dir. German Op. at Amsterdam. (8) **Gabriel,** Caen, March 1, 1878—Vésinet, Aug. 3, 1914; composer, esp. known for his operas "*La Cabrera*" which won the Sonzogno prize, 1904; "*La Glu*" (1910); "*La Farce du Cuvier*" (1912) and "*Antar*" (prod. 1921), also orch. works, chamber music, etc.

Duport (dü-pôr), (1) **J. P.,** Paris, 1741—Berlin, 1818; 'cellist. (2) **J. L.,** Paris, 1749—1819; more famous bro. of above; also 'cellist; composer and writer.

Duprato (dü-prä′-tō), **Jules Laurent,** Nîmes, 1827—Paris, 1892; prof. of harm. and dram. composer.

Dupré (dü-prä′), **Marcel,** b. Rouen, May 3, 1886; organist; pupil of his father, Albert, Rouen organist, then of Guilmant, Diémer, and Widor; won many 1st prizes at Cons. in Paris; succeeded Widor as ᐟorg. at St.-Sulpice and played at Notre Dame; toured as recitalist in Europe and U. S.; noted for his ability at improvisation; c. org. and choral works.

Duprez (dü-prä′), **Gilbert L.,** Paris, 1806—1896; tenor and composer.

Dupuis (dü-pwē), (1) **Thomas Sanders,** London, Nov. 5, 1733—July 17, 1796; comp. and organist of Chapel Royal London; of French parentage, but lived in London, and is buried in Westminster Abbey. (2) **José** (**Joseph Lambert**), Liége, 1833—Nogent-sur-Marne, 1900; opera-bouffe singer. (3) **Sylvain,** Liége, Nov. 9, 1856—Bruges, Sept. 28, 1931; pupil Liége Cons., 1881 Prix de Rome; teacher of cpt. and cond. of a singing-society; 1900-11, cond. at La Monnaie, Brussels; and of Concerts Populaires; c. operas, incl. the succ. com. opera "*L'Idylle,*" 3 cantatas, symphonic poem, "*Macbeth,*" etc. (4) **Albert,** b. Verviers, France, March 1, 1877; prod. opera "*L'Idylle*" (Verviers, 1896); "*Bilitis*" (Verviers, 1899); won Prix de Rome at Brussels with opera "*Hans Michel,*" 1903; c. cantata, etc.

Dupuy (dü-pwē). Vide PUTEANUS.

Durand (rightly **Duranowski**) (dü-räṅ or doo-rän-ôf′-shkĭ), (1) **Auguste Frédéric,** b. Warsaw, 1770; violinist and cond., son of a court-mus. (2) **Émile,** St.-Brieue, Côtes du Nord, Feb. 16, 1830—Neuilly, May 6, 1903; while still a pupil at the Paris Cons. he was appointed teacher of an elementary singing-class; 1871 prof. of harm.; dram. composer and writer. (3) **Marie Auguste,** Paris, July 18, 1830—May 31, 1909; pupil of Benoist; 1849-74 organist at various churches; 1870 est. mus.-pub. business of "Durand et Schönewerk," later "Durand et Fils"; a critic and composer.

Durante (doo-rän′-tĕ), **Fran.,** Fratta Maggiore, Naples, March 15, 1684—Naples, Aug. 13, 1755; director and conductor; an important teacheɪ and composer of the "Neapolitan School"; c. 13 masses, etc.

Durey (dü′-rē), **Louis,** b. France. May 27, 1888; composer; mem. of former Group of Six; studied with Léon Saint-Requier; after 1914 c. various orch., chamber music and other works; also wrote critical study of Ravel's music and magazine articles.

Durutte (dü-rüt), **Fran. Camille Ant.,** Ypres, East Flanders, 1803—Paris, 1881; wrote a new but erroneous system of harm.; c. operas, etc.

Du(s)sek (**Dušek, Duschek**) (doos′-sĕk or better doo′-shĕk), (1) **Fz.,** Chotiborz, Bohemia, 1736—Prague, 1799; composer, pianist and teacher. (2) **Joséphine,** b. Prague, 1756; pianist, composer, singer. (3) **J. Ladislaus,** Caslav (Tschaslau), Bohemia, Feb. 12, 1760—Saint-Germain-en-Laye, March 20, 1812; a boy-soprano at Iglau, pupil of Father Spenar at the Jesuit College; organist Jesuit Church, Kuttenburg, for 2 years; studied theology at Prague Univ., also music; became organist of Saint-Rimbaut's, Mechlin; lived Bergenop-Zoom; Amsterdam; The Hague, 1783; studied with C. P. E. Bach, Hamburg; became famous pianist and performer on Hessel'ſ "Harmonica," Berlin and St. Petersburg; lived in Lithuania a year at Prince Radziwill's Court; lived Italy, Paris, London; 1792 m. (4) **Sofia Corri** (b. Edinburgh, 1775; a singer, harpist and composer). He entered a mus.-business with his father-in-law, 1800, failed and fled to Hamburg to escape creditors. He was in the service of various princes, and (1808) of Prince Talleyrand in Paris. A pioneer among Bohemian and Polish virtuosi and composers he disputed with Clementi the invention of the "singing-touch." Prod. 2 English operas in London with success, and pub. a Mass (comp. at the age of 13), oratorios and church-music; pub. nearly 100 works for pf., incl. 12 concertos, 80 sonatas with vln.; 53 sonatas for pf.-solo, etc.; pub. a "*Method.*"

Dushkin (dōōsh′-kēn), **Samuel,** b. Suwalki, Russian Poland, Dec. 13, 1898; violinist; studied with Auer, Kreisler, Remy; European début, 1918; 1st Amer. tour in 1924; has appeared widely in Europe, Egypt,

Palestine, and U. S., esp. in joint programmes with Igor Stravinsky.

Dustmann (doost'-män), **Marie Luise** (née **Meyer**), Aix-la-Chapelle, 1831 —1899; soprano.

Duvernoy (or **Duvernois**) (dü-věrn-wä), (1) **Ir.**, Montbéliard, 1765—Paris, 1838; prof. at the Cons.; composer. (2) **Charles**, Montbéliard, 1766—Paris, 1845; bro. of above; clarinettist; prof. and composer. (3) **Chas. Fran.**, Paris, 1796—1872; singer. (4) **H. L. Chas.**, Paris, Nov. 16, 1820—Jan., 1906; son of (3); pupil of Halévy and Zimmermann, Paris Cons.; 1839, assist.-prof.; 1848, prof. there of solfeggio; composer. (5) **Victor Alphonse**, Paris, Aug. 30, 1842—March 7, 1907; pupil of Bazin and Marmontel Paris Cons.; took first pf. prize; teacher of piano at the Cons.; a Chev. of the Legion of Honour, and officier of public instruction; 1892 prod. the succ. opera "*Sardanapale*" (Lyons), also opera "*Helle*" (Gr. Opéra, 1896); his symph. poem, "*La Tempête*," won the City of Paris prize.

Dux (dooks), **Claire**, b. Witkowicz, Poland, Aug. 2, 1885; soprano; studied voice with Teresa Arkel, also in Milan; début, Cologne, 1906; sang with Berlin Op., 1911–18; Stockholm Op., 1918–21; Chicago Op., 1921–23; also at Covent Garden, and widely as concert performer in Europe and U. S.; m. Charles H. Swift; res. in Chicago since 1926, with occasional appearances.

Dvořák (dvôr'-shäk), **Antonin**, Mühlhausen, Bohemia, Sept. 8, 1841—Prague, May 1, 1904; one of the most eminent Bohemian composers; son of an inn-keeper, who wished him to be a butcher, but he learned the vln. from the schoolmaster, and at 16 entered the Prague Org.-Sch. under Pitzsch, earning a livelihood as violinist in a small orchestra; graduated in 1862, became vla.-player at the Nat. Theatre. He was 33 before an important comp. was prod., a hymn for male chorus and orch., which attracted such attention that 1875 he received a government stipend and devoted himself to composition. 1891 Mus. Doc. Cambridge Univ.; 1892–95 dir. Nat. Cons., New York; later lived at Prague; 1901, director of the Prague Cons; 1902, prod.

opera "*Armida*," Pilsen Nat. Th. He was a disciple of nationalism in music, and provoked much controversy by advising American composers to found their school on the harmonic and melodic elements of plantation-music.   In his highly popular 5th symphony, op. 95, "*From the New World*," he made some use of such a manner. His other comp. are: Bohemian operas "*The King and the Charcoal-Burner*" (Prague, 1874); "*Wanda*" (1876); "*Selma Sedlák*" (1878); "*Turde Palice*" (1881); "*Dimitrije*" (1882); "*The Jacobins*" (1889); "*Rusalka, the Water Nixie*" (Nat. Th. Prague, 1901); "*Armida*" (1904); oratorio "*St. Ludmila*" (Leeds Mus. Fest., 1886); Requiem Mass, op. 89, with orch. (Birmingham Fest., 1891); cantatas "*The Spectre's Bride*," op. 69, with orch. (Birmingham Fest., 1885), and "*The American Flag*" (N. Y., 1895); Hymn of the Bohemian Peasants, for mixed ch.; hymn for mixed ch. and orch.; "*Stabat Mater*" with orch. (London, 1883); Psalm 149 with orch.; 5 symphonies; 3 orchestral ballades, "*Der Wassermann*," "*Die Mittagshexe*," and "*Das goldene Spinnrad*"; 2 sets of symphonic variations for orch.; overtures, "*Mein Heim*," "*Husitska*," "*In der Natur*," "*Othello*," "*Carneval*"; concertos for 'cello, pf., vln.; "*Slavische Tänze*," and "*Slavische Rhapsodien*"; scherzo capriccioso for orch.; string-sextet; 2 string-quintets; pf.-quintet; 6 string-quartets; 2 pf.-quartets; a string-trio; 2 pf.-trios; mazurek for vln. with orch., serenade for wind with 'cello and double-bass; notturno for string-orch.; pf. music, "*Legenden*," "*Dumka*" (Elegy), "*Furiante*" (Boh. natl. dances); "*Klänge aus Mahren*," and "*Silhouetten*" for pf. 4-hands; violin-sonata, op. 57; songs; etc.

Dwight, J. Sullivan, Boston, Mass., 1813—1893; editor and critic; one of the founders of the Harvard Musical Association; was a member of the Brook Farm Community; 1852–81, edited "*Dwight's Journal of Music*."

Dykema (dī'-kē-mä), **Peter W.**, b. Grand Rapids, Mich.. Nov. 25, 1873; educator; studied N. Y. and Berlin, with Arens, Frank Shephard and at Inst. of Music. Art; dir. of music,

Ethical Culture School, N. Y., 1901–13; prof. of music, Univ. of Wis., 1913–24; thereafter, prof. of music. education, Teachers College, Columbia Univ., author of *"School Music Handbook"* (with Cundiff), and ed.; d. Hastings, N. Y., 1951.

Dykes (Rev.), **J. Bacchus,** Kingston-upon-Hull, Eng., 1823—St. Leonard's, 1876; conductor.

Dy'son, **Sir George,** b. Halifax, England, May 28, 1883; composer and educator; pupil of R. Coll. of Mus., where won Mendelssohn Stipend; dir. of music at R. Naval Coll., Marlborough Coll., and Wellington Coll.; 1918, Mus. D., Oxford; has c. orch. and choral music; author of *"The New Music."* Dir., R. C. M., 1938; knighted, 1940.

E

Eames (āmz), **Emma,** b. (of American parents) at Shanghai, Aug. 13, 1865; noted soprano; at 5 went with her mother, her first teacher, to Bath, Maine; pupil of Miss Munger at Boston; 1886–88 at Paris, of Madame Marchesi (voice), and Pluque (acting, etc.); 1888, engaged at the Op.-Com., but made début with succ. at the Gr. Opéra, March 13, 1889, as "Juliette" in Gounod's *"Roméo et Juliette,"* a rôle previously sacred to Patti; sang at the Opera for 2 years, creating "Colombe" in St.-Saens' *"Ascanio"* and as "Zäire" in De La Nux's opera; 1891, Covent Garden in *"Faust"*; m. the painter Julian Story the same year, and in Oct. appeared in New York at Met. Op.; from then until 1909, when she retired from the stage, she sang regularly in N. Y. and London, except 1892–93, at Madrid, and 1895–96, during ill-health; "Sieglinde" was perhaps her best rôle. In 1911 she m. Emilio de Gogorza, barytone, and toured in concert with him, later separated. Lived in N. Y., where d. June 13, 1952.

Ear'hart, **Will,** b. Franklin, O., April 1, 1871; educator; after 1913 mus. dir. of School of Education, Univ. of Pittsburgh; author of works on school music; pres. Music Supervisors' Nat'l. Conference, 1915–16; Mus. D., Univ. of Pittsburgh, 1920.

East'man, **George,** Waterville, N. Y., July 12, 1854—Rochester, N. Y., March 14, 1932 (suicide); music

patron; in 1919 made gift of $3,500,-000 to found Eastman School of Music, as part of the Univ. of Rochester, and the next year added another million, the permanent endowment fund being about three millions; Rochester as a result has become an active centre of music, with the Eastman Theatre, Philh. Orch., and other enterprises incl. annual fests. of American music deriving their impetus from his generosity.

East'on, **Florence,** b. Middlesbrough, England, Oct. 25, 1884; soprano; studied R. Coll. of Mus., London, and with Elliott Haslam, Paris; made appearance as pianist at 8; opera début as Madame Butterfly with Moody-Manners Op. Co., London, 1903; toured U. S. with Savage Op. Co., 1904–05 and 1906–07; sang with Berlin Op., 1907–13; Covent Garden in *"Elektra,"* 1910; Hamburg Op., 1913–15; Met. Op., where she sang German and other rôles with marked versatility, 1917–28, and again in 1936; has also sung widely in concert, and as orchestral and festival soloist; a gifted lieder singer; m. Francis Maclennan, tenor; divorced.

Eaton, **Louis H.,** b. Taunton, Mass., May 9, 1861; organist; pupil of Guilmant; 1901, org. at San Francisco.

Eb'don, **Thos.,** Durham, 1738—1811; organist and composer.

Ebeling (ā'-bĕ-lĭng), (1) **J. G.,** Lüneburg, 1637—Stettin, 1676; prof. and composer. (2) **Chp. Daniel,** Garmissen, near Hildesheim, 1741—Hamburg, 1817; prof. and writer.

Ebell (ā'-bĕl), **H. K.,** Neuruppin, 1775—Oppeln, 1824; conductor and dram. composer.

Eberhard (1) **von Freisingen** (ā'-bĕr-härt fōn frī'-zĭng-ĕn), **Eberhar'dus Frisengen'sis,** Benedictine monk, 11th cent.; wrote on the scale of pipes and bell-founding. (2) **J. Aug.,** Halberstadt, 1739—Halle, 1809; professor.

Eberl (ā'-bĕrl), **Anton,** Vienna, June 13, 1766—March 11, 1807; famous pianist, conductor and dram. composer.

Eberlin (ā'-bĕr-lēn), (1) **Daniel,** Nürnberg, ca. 1630—Cassel, 1692; contrapuntist and violinist; famous as a composer in his day. (2) (or **Eberle**) **J. Ernst,** Jettenbach, Swabia, 1702

—Salzburg, 1762; conductor and composer.

Ebers (ā'-bĕrs), **K. Fr.**, Cassel, 1770 —Berlin, 1836; conductor and dram. composer.

Ebert (ā'-bĕrt), **Ludwig**, Kladrau, Bohemia, April 13, 1834—Coblenz, 1908; 'cellist; pupil Prague Cons.; 1854–74, first 'cellist at Oldenburg; 1875–88, teacher at Cologne Cons.; 1889, founded Cons. at Coblenz; c. 'cello pieces.

Eberwein (ā'-bĕr-vīn), (1) **Traugott Maximilian**, Weimar, 1775—Rudolstadt, 1831; dram. composer. (2) **Karl**, Weimar, 1786—1868, bro. of above; dram. composer.

Ebner (āp'-nĕr), **Wolfgang**, Augsburg, ca. 1610—Vienna, Feb., 1665; organist and comp.

Eccard (ĕk'-kärt), **J.**, Mühlhausen, Thuringia, 1553—Berlin, 1611; important composer of church-music.

Eccles (ĕk'-kĕls), (1) **John**, London (?), 1668—Kingston, Surrey, 1735; son and pupil of the violinist, (2) **Solomon E. C.** His brother (3) **Henry**, was violinist and composer. (4) **Solomon Thomas**, bro. of above, also violinist.

Eck (ĕk), (1) **J. Fr.**, Mannheim, 1766— Bamberg (?), 1809 (1810 ?); violinist and composer. (2) **Fz.**, Mannheim, 1774—insane, Strassburg, 1804; bro. and pupil of above; violinist.

Eckelt (ĕk'-ĕlt), **J. Val.**, Werningshausen, near Erfurt, 1673—Sondershausen, 1732; writer.

Eckert (ĕk'-ĕrt), **K. Ant. Florian**, Potsdam, 1820—Berlin, 1879; at 10 c. an opera, at 13 an oratorio; court-conductor and dram. composer.

Ed'dy, (1) **Clarence H.**, Greenfield, Mass., June 23, 1851—Chicago, Jan. 10, 1937; organist; pupil of J. G. Wilson and Dudley Buck; 1871 of Haupt and Löschhorn (pf.); toured in Germany, Austria, Switzerland, and Holland; 1874, organist, Chicago; 1876, dir. Hershey School of Musical Art; toured America and Europe, 1879 gave 100 recitals at Chicago without repeating a number; for some years cond. Chicago Philh. Vocal Soc.; after 1910 in San Francisco; c. organ and church music, etc.; pub. *"The Church and Concert Organist," "The Organ in Church"* and transl. Haupt's *"Cpt. and Fugue."* (2) **Nelson**, b. Providence, R. I., June 29, 1901; barytone;

sang as boy soprano in choir of Grace Church, New York; pupil of David Bispham and William Vilonat; début, in benefit perf., Phila., 1922; sang with Savoy Op. Co. and Phila. Civic Op., making New York début in *"Wozzeck,"* 1931; sang leading male rôle in Respighi's *"Maria Egiziaca"* with N. Y. Philh. under baton of composer; later won outstanding reputation as concert singer, in radio programmes and as featured performer in musical films.

Edelmann (ā'-dĕl-män), **Joh. Fr.**, Strassburg, May 6, 1749—Paris, July 17, 1794; c. opera, ballets, etc.

Ed'son, **Lewis**, Bridgewater, Mass., 1748—Woodstock, N. Y., 1820; pub. a coll. of hymns, etc.

Edwards, (1) **Henry Sutherland**, b. London, Sept. 5, 1829—Jan. 21, 1906; writer; historian and critic for many years of the *St. James Gazette*. (2) **Henry John**, b. Barnstaple, Feb. 24, 1854—April 8, 1933; of an organist, then pupil of Bennett, Macfarren; 1885, Mus. Doc. Oxford; c. oratorios, etc. (3) **Julian** (rightly **D. H. Barnard**), Manchester, England, Dec. 11, 1855—Yonkers, N. Y., Sept. 5, 1910; pupil Sir H. Oakley, Edinburgh, then of Macfarren, London; 1875, pianist to Carl Rosa Opera Co.; 1877, cond. Royal Eng. Opera Co. and prod. *"Victorian"* Covent Garden. 1880, prod. *"Corinne"* at St. James's Hall, London; cond. Engl. Opera at Covent Garden, and prod. 2 operas, *"Corinne"* and *"Victorian,"* at Sheffield, 1883; came to the U. S., 1889, and prod. with success various comic operas, incl. *"Madeleine or the Magic Kiss"* (Boston, 1894), and *"Brian Boru"* (N. Y., 1896); *"The Wedding Day,"* *"The Jolly Musketeer," "Princess Chic"* (1899), *"Dolly Varden"* (N. Y., 1902), and *"When Johnny Comes Marching Home"*; prod. also romantic opera *"King Réné's Daughter"*; c. gr. opera *"Elfinella"* (MS.), symphonies, overtures, etc.

Eeden (ā'-dĕn), **Jean Baptiste van den**, Ghent, Dec. 26, 1842—Mons, April 4, 1917; pupil of Ghent and Brussels Cons.; 1st prize for comp. (1869) with the cantata *"Faust's Laaste Nacht"*; 1878 dir. of Cons. at Mons; c. opera *"Numance"* (Antwerp, 1897), oratorios and the trilogy *"Judith,"* cantatas with orch., a

symph. poem, "*La Lutte au XVI.
Siècle*," etc.

Egenolff (or **Egenolph**) (ā'-gĕn-ôlf), 502—55; a slovenly and piratical German mus.-printer.

Egidi (ā'-khē-dē), **Arthur**, b. Berlin, Aug. 9, 1859; organist; pupil of Kiel and Taubert; 1885–92, teacher at the Hoch Cons., Frankfort-on-Main; then org. at Berlin, and Royal Prof.; comp.; d. 1943.

Egk, Werner, b. Auchsesheim, Bavaria, May 17, 1901; composer; studied in Germany and Italy; after 1929 lived in Munich; c. an opera, "*Zaubergeige*" (première, Frankfort, 1935) based on nursery tale and with South German peasant songs utilised, which had succ. on several German stages; also popular orch. work, "*Georgica*," etc.

Egli (āl'-yē or ā'-glē), **Johann Heinrich**, Seegräben, canton Zurich, 1742—1810; c. "*Oden*," etc.

Ehlert (ā'-lĕrt), **Louis**, Königsberg, 1825—Wiesbaden, 1884; teacher and critic; conductor and composer.

Ehnn-Sand (ān'-zänt), **Bertha**, Budapest, Nov. 30, 1847—Aschberg, March 2, 1932; dramatic soprano, pupil of Frau Andriessen.

Ehrlich (ār'-līkh), (1) **Fr. Chr.**, Magdeburg, 1807—1887; conductor, singing-teacher, and dram. composer. (2) **Alfred H.**, Vienna, Oct. 5, 1822—Berlin, Dec. 30, 1899; pupil of Henselt, Bocklet, Thalberg (pf.), and Sechter (comp.); court-pianist to King George V.; 1864–72 pf.-teacher Stern Cons., and 1866–98 critic in Berlin; composer and editor.

Eibenschütz (ī'-bĕn-shüts), (1) **Albert**, Berlin, April 15, 1857—Vienna, Nov. 15, 1930; pianist; pupil of Reinecke and Paul, Leipzig Cons., won the Diploma of Honour. 1876–80, prof. in Charkoff (Russia); 1880–84 at Leipzig Cons., then Cologne Cons.; 1893, dir. Cologne Liederkranz; 1896, 1st pf.-prof. Stern Cons., Berlin; c. pf.-sonatas, etc. (2) **Ilona**, Budapest, May 18, 1872; cousin of above; pianist; at 5 she played in a concert with Liszt; 1878–85, pupil of Hans Schmitt; 1885–89, studied with Frau Schumann; lived in Vienna and made tours.

Eichberg (īkh'-bĕrkh or īch'-bŭrg), (1) **Julius**, b. Düsseldorf, June 13, 1824—Boston, Mass., Jan. 18, 1893; violinist and notable teacher; c. 4

operettas, etc. (2) **Oskar, Berlin**, 1845—1898; singing-teacher, conductor, critic, editor, and composer.

Eichborn (īkh'-bôrn), **H. L.**, Breslau, Oct. 30, 1847—near Bozen, April 15, 1918; studied pf., flute, trumpet, horn, etc., at an early age; at 14 pupil of the trumpeter Ad. Scholz; studied theory with Dr. E. Bohn; became a Waldhorn virtuoso; 1882 inv. the Oktav (or soprano) Waldhorn; wrote musical essays, etc.; cond. at Gries, near Bozen; editor, writer and composer.

Eichheim (īkh'-hīm), **Henry**, Chicago, 1870—Santa Barbara, Aug. 22, 1942; grad. Chicago Music. Coll. with vln. prize; studied with Carl Becker, Jacobsohn and Lichtenberg; played 1st vln. in Boston Symph., 1890–1912; has toured as soloist in modern programmes, and cond. own works as guest in Eur. and Amer. cities; c. orch. works based on native folk material of the Orient, also chamber music, piano pieces and songs.

Eichner (īkh'-nĕr), **Ernst**, Mannheim, 1740—Potsdam, 1777; c. important symphonies, concertos, etc.

Eijken (ī'-kĕn) (or **Eyken**), **van** (1) **Jan Albert**, Amersfoort, Holland, April 25, 1822—Elberfeld, Sept. 24, 1868; organist and comp.; his son. (2) **Heinrich**, Elberfeld, July 19, 1861—Berlin, Aug. 28, 1908; composer; pupil of Leipzig Cons.; teacher of theory; c. songs with orch.

Ein'stein, Alfred, b. Munich, Dec. 30, 1880; critic and writer on music; studied with Sandberger and Beer-Walbrunn; after 1917, critic of Munich "*Post*"; later of Berlin "*Tageblatt*"; now res. in U. S. A.; after 1919 he ed. 9th edition of Riemann's Music Lexicon; ed. "*Neue Musik-Lexicon*" (1926), a revision of Eaglefield Hull's "*Dictionary of Modern Music and Musicians*"; until 1933 he was the ed. of the "*Zeitschrift für Musikwissentschaft*"; d. Feb. 13, 1952.

Eisfeld (īs'-fĕlt), **Th.**, Wolfenbüttel, April 11, 1816—Wiesbaden, Sept. 2, 1882; cond., N. Y. Philh. (with Bergmann), 1849–64; previously conductor at Wiesbaden; then of "Concerts Viviennes," Paris.

Eis'ler, Hanns, b. Leipzig, July 6, 1898; composer; pupil of Schönberg and Anton Webern; after 1925 taught at Klindworth-Scharwenka Cons., Berlin; visited America, 1935; esp. noted for his works written to revolutionary song texts, also chamber music.

Eitner (īt'-nĕr), **Rob.**, Breslau, Oct. 22, 1832—Templin, Jan. 22, 1905; pupil of Brosig; 1853, teacher at Berlin; est. a pf.-sch., 1863; from 1865 he was engaged in musicological work of the highest value, incl. the compilation of a *"Source Lexicon of Musicians and Musical Scientists"* (10 vols.), which has not been surpassed in its particular field; important for work in musical literature, and research in 16th and 17th centuries, Dutch music, etc.; c. "Biblical opera," *"Judith"*; overture to *"Der Cid"*; etc.

El'dering, Bram, Groningen, Holland, 1865—Cologne (air raid) 1943; pupil Poortmann, Hubay, and Joachim; Konzertmeister Berlin Philh.; then do. in Meiningen ct.-chapel; and 1899 in Gürzenich Orch.; after 1903 taught at Cologne Cons.

Elers (ā'-lĕrs) (called **El'erus**), **Fz.**, Uelzen, ca. 1500—1590, Hamburg; teacher, director, and composer.

Elewyck (vän ā'-lŭ-vĕk), **Xavier Victor** (Chevalier) **van,** Ixelles les Bruxelles, Belgium, 1825—in an insane asylum, Zickemont, 1888; writer.

El'gar, Sir Edward, Broadheath, Worcester, Engl., June 2, 1857—London, Feb. 23, 1934; important English composer; violinist; and organist; cond. Worcester Instrumental Soc., 1882–89; 1885–89, organist at St. George's; as part of his early training he was bandmaster 1879–1884 at the County Asylum with attendants as musicians; he retired to Malvern in 1891 discouraged with his prospects in London; lived as teacher and occasionally cond. His *" King Olaf"* (1896) brought his first real success, which his orch. variations (1899) increased and the *"Dream of Gerontius"* (1900) established; Cambridge made him Mus. Doc. that year; Strauss cond. *"Gerontius"* in Germany, 1902; 1904 an Elgar Festival was given for 3 days at Covent Garden, and the same year he was knighted. He c. Imperial March, 2 military marches, called *"Pomp and Circumstance," "Sea Pictures,"* contralto and orch.; Coronation Ode (1902), *"The Apostles"* (Birmingham Fest., 1903); Symphony No. 1 in A flat (1908); Symphony No. 2 in E flat *"To the*

Memory of Edward VII" (London Mus. Fest., 1911, and the same year by Cincinnati Symph., N. Y. Phil., Boston Symph., etc.). In 1906 he visited the U. S. and conducted his music at the Cincinnati Fest.; he served as prof. of music in Birmingham Univ., 1905–08; in 1924 he was created Master of the King's Musick. He lived at Hereford (after 1904), but in later years, though he maintained an estate there, he passed much of his time in London. Honorary degrees of Mus. D. were conferred upon him by Durham, Oxford and Yale Univs.; LL. D., by Leeds, Aberdeen and Pittsburgh Univs. His large output of compositions includes also a symph. study, *"Falstaff"* (1913), symph. poem; *"Polonia"* (1915), a much played vln. concerto in B minor (1910); Introduction and Allegro for strings (1905); incidental music for *"Grania and Diarmid,"* the notable *"Enigma"* Variations for orch. (1899) in which the identity of various of his friends is concealed; *"The Kingdom,"* oratorio (1906, Birmingham Fest.); *"The Music-Makers"* (1912) for chorus; *"The Crown of India"* (1912); *"The Spirit of England"* (1916), do.; 2 string quartets, oratorio, *"The Light of Life"* (1896); cantata, *"Caractacus"*; overtures, *"Froissart," "In the South," "Cockaigne"* (1901); 6 Scenes from the Bavarian Highlands, for chorus and orch. (1896); Spanish serenade for ch. and orch.; romance for vln. and orch.; church-music; pcs. for vln. and pf.; organ-sonata; songs, etc.

Elias (ā'-lĭ-äs), **Salomonis,** monk at Saint-Astère, Perigord, wrote in 1274 the oldest extant book of rules for improvised counterpoint.

El'kus, Albert, b. Sacramento, Cal., April 30, 1884; composer; studied with Oscar Weil, Robert Fuchs, Karl Prohaska, Georg Schumann, Harold Bauer and Lhevinne; c. orch., chamber music and choral works.

El'ler, Louis, Graz, 1820—Pau, 1862; vln.-virtuoso; c. *"Valse Diabolique,"* a *"Rhapsodie Hongroise,"* etc., for vln.

El'lerton, J. Lodge, Chester, 1807—London, 1873; dram. composer.

El'man, Mischa, b. Talnoe, Russia, Jan. 21, 1891; violinist; played at 5 in public; studied 16 months at

Odessa with Fidelmann, 1903 invited by Auer to become his pupil; début at St. Petersburg, 1904, and greeted as a great artist though only 12; toured widely; 1908, America; he has long ranked as one of the most eminent performers in his field. He has made his home in N. Y. for some years.

Elmblad (ĕlm'-blät), Jns., b. Stockholm, Aug. 22, 1853; bass; studied with Stockhausen and Garcia; 1876, Wagner chose him for "Donner" (Rheingold), but his father, a prof. of theology, objected; 1880, he went into opera and sang in various cities, as well as in London and America; 1896, sang "Fafner" at Bayreuth; 1897 at ct.-Th., Stockholm; d. 1911.

Elmendorff, Karl, b. Düsseldorf, Germany, Jan. 25, 1891; conductor; pupil of Steinbach and Abendroth at Cologne Cons.; active as cond. at native city, Mainz, Hagen, Aachen; 1925-32, first cond. of Munich State Op.; after 1932 in Wiesbaden; appeared at Bayreuth, beginning 1927.

Elsenheimer (ĕl'-zēn-hī-mĕr), Nicholas J., Wiesbaden, 1866—Limburg, Germany, July 12, 1935; pupil of his father and of Jakobsthal, Strassburg, LL.D., Heidelberg; 1890, America; 1891, prof. at Coll. of Music, Cincinnati; c. cantata "Valerian," with orch. "Belshazzar," etc.

Elsner (ĕls'-nĕr), Jos. Xavier, Grottkau, Silesia, 1769—Warsaw, 1854; writer and composer of 19 operas.

El'son, (1) Louis Chas., Boston, April 17, 1848—Feb. 14, 1920; writer and teacher; pupil of Kreissmann (singing), Boston, and Gloggner-Castelli (theory), Leipzig; edited the "Vox Humana"; then on the "Music Herald"; for years critic of the "Boston Courier," then of the "Advertiser"; 1881 prof. of theory and lecturer on the orch. and musical history at N. E. Cons.; lectured on music with much success; pub. "Curiosities of Music," "The History of German Song," "The Theory of Music," "The Realm of Music," "German Songs and Song-writers," "European Reminiscences," "Syllabus of Musical History," and "Great Composers and Their Work" (1899), "The National Music of America" (1900), "Home and School Songs"; c. operettas, songs, and instr.-works; transl. and arranged over 2,000 songs, operas, etc. (2)

Arthur B., b. Boston, Nov. 18, 1873; d. N. Y., Feb. 24, 1940; son and pupil of (1); grad. Harvard Univ.; and Mass. Inst. of Technology; author of books on music.

El'vey, (1) Stephen, Canterbury, 1805 —Oxford, 1860; organist. (2) Sir George (Job), Canterbury, 1816—Windlesham, Surrey, 1893; bro. of above; c. oratorios.

Elwart (ĕl'-värt), Antoine Aimable Elie, Paris, 1808—1877; violinist and dram. composer.

El'wes, Gervase Cary, Northampton, England, Nov. 15, 1866—Boston, Mass., 1921 (killed by locomotive while on American tour); tenor; studied Vienna, Paris, etc.; at first in diplomatic life; professional début, 1903; sang in Europe and America; excelled in Brahms songs.

Em'ery, Stephen Albert, Paris, Maine, Oct. 4, 1841—Boston, April 15, 1891; prof. of harm. and cpt.; asst.-ed. "Musical Herald"; graceful composer and pop. theorist.

Emman'uel, Maurice, b. Bar-sur-Aube, May 2, 1862—Paris, Dec. 14, 1938; writer on music; pupil of Paris Cons., and Gevaert in Brussels; also at Sorbonne, Paris; won Kastner-Boursault prize from French Acad. for his "Histoire de la Langue Musicale"; has also written treatises on Greek music and modal accompaniment to the psalms; 1909, appointed prof. of music. hist. at Paris Cons.; c. orch., chamber and choral music, org. pieces and songs.

Emmerich (ĕm'-mĕr-ĭkh), Robt., Hanau, 1836—Baden-Baden, 1891; composer.

Enckhausen (ĕnk'-how-zĕn), H. Fr., Celle, 1799—Hanover, 1885; court-organist, pianist and director.

Enesco (ā-nĕs'-koo), Georges, b. Cordaremi, Roumania, Aug. 7, 1882; violinist, conductor, composer: at 4 played and composed, at 7 was admitted to Vienna Cons., by Hellmesberger, in whose family he lived; at 11, took first prizes for violin and harmony; 1896, studied in Paris Cons. with Marsick and Fauré; in 1897, he took second accessit for counterpoint and fugue, and a concert of his works was given in Paris, including a violin sonata, a piano suite, quintet, 'cello pieces and songs;

1898, Colonne prod. his "*Poème Roumain*" for orch.; 1899, he took first violin prize at the Cons.; toured and became court violinist to the Roumanian queen; c. symph. (Colonne orch., 1906; N. Y. Phil., 1911) and symph. in E flat, op. 13 (Berlin, 1912) Pastoral fantasie for orch. (Colonne orch., 1899); Dixtuor, or symphony for wind instrs., do. for 'cello and orch. (Lamoureux orch., 1909); suite for orch. (Boston Symph., 1911); 3 Rhapsodies Roumaines, (1911), etc. He has appeared in the U. S. both as violinist and conductor, and was engaged for guest appearances in latter capacity with N. Y. Philh. Orch., 1936–37; his music drama "*Oedipe,*" on which he had worked for many years, was prod. at the Paris Op., 1936, creating a marked impression by its nobility and original form of expression.

Engel (ĕng'-ĕl), (1) **Jn.** Jakob, Parchim, Mecklenburg, 1741—1802; dir. and composer. (2) **David Hn.,** Neuruppin, 1816—Merseburg, 1877; organist, writer and dram. composer. (3) **K.,** Thiedewiese, near Hanover, 1818—suicide, London, 1882; organist and writer. (4) **Gv. Ed.,** Königsberg, 1823—Berlin, 1895; singing-teacher, composer and theorist. (5) **Carl,** Paris, July 21, 1883—N. Y., May 6, 1944; musicologist; studied Strasbourg and Munich Univ., studied composition with Thuille; res. U. S. since 1905, became Amer. citizen, 1917; chief of music division, Library of Congress, Washington, 1921–29; pres. publishing firm of G. Schirmer, Inc., N. Y., and ed. of "*Musical Quarterly*"; has written extensively on musical subjects.

En'na, Aug., Nakskov, Denmark, May 13, 1860—Copenhagen, Aug. 3, 1939; grandson of an Italian soldier in Napoleon's army; son of a shoemaker; self-taught in pf. and instrumentation, and had almost no teaching in vln. or theory; went with a small orch. to Finland (1880); played various insts., even a drum before a circus-tent; returned to Copenhagen; prod. the operetta "*A Village Tale*" (1880) in provincial theatres; played at dancing-lessons, and gave pf.-lessons at 12 cents an hour; 1883, cond. for a small provincial troupe, for which he wrote act-tunes, and 10 overtures; pub. songs,

pf.-pcs., an orchl. suite, and a symphony; this gained him, through Gade's interest, the Ancker scholarship, enabling him to study in Germany (1888–89). After producing an operetta "*Areta,*" he prod. with unequalled succ. for a Dane, the opera "*The Witch,*" 1892, at the R. Opera House, Copenhagen. The opera "*Cleopatra*" (Copenhagen, 1894) failed, but 1895, with new cast, was succ. as also "*Aucassin and Nicolette*" (Copenhagen, 1896; Hamburg, 1897). Opera "*Aglaia,*" in MS. Pub. a vln.-concerto, etc.

E'noch & Co., London music-pub. firm, est. 1869.

Épine (dĕ-lä-pē'-nĕ), **Francesca Margerita de l',** extremely popular Italian singer and harpsichordist in London, from ca. 1698—1718, when she m. Dr. Pepusch; her sister sang in London from 1703–1748 as Maria Gallia.

Epstein (ĕp'-shtĭn), (1) **Julius,** Agram, Aug. 7, 1832—Vienna, March 1, 1926; pupil of Lichtenegger, Halm (pf.), and Rufinatscha (comp.); 1867–1902, prof. of pf. Vienna Cons. Among his pupils were Mahler, Ignace Brüll, Ugo Reinhold, August Sturn, etc., and he is said to have discovered the voice of Marcella Sembrich, when she studied piano with him. His two daughters, (2) **Rudolfine** ('cellist), and (3) **Eugénie** (violinist), toured Austria and Germany, 1876–77. (4) **Richard** (1869–1919), his son, pianist; toured Europe, and 1914 in U. S.

Érard (ā'-răr), (1) **Sébastien,** Strassburg, April 5, 1752—near Paris, Aug. 5, 1831; notable piano-maker and inventor; inv. a "Clavecin Mécanique"; the "Piano organisé," finally the double-action mechanism, which made a new instr. of the harp (v. D. D.); perfected in 1811 his greatest achievement, the repetition action of the piano (v. D. D.). His successor as a piano-maker was his nephew, (2) **Pierre** (1796—1855), succeeded by Pierre Schaffer (d. 1878); he was succeeded by Count de Franqueville.

Erb (ĕrp), (1) **M. Jos.,** b. Strassburg, 1860—d. 1944; pupil of Saint-Saens, Gigout, and Loret, Paris; lived in Strassburg as teacher and organist at the Johanniskirche and the Synagogue; c. a symphony; a symphonic suite; sonatas and "dram.

episode" *"Der letzte Ruf"* (Strassburg, 1895), with some succ., etc.
(2) **Karl,** b. Ravensburg, July 13,
1877: tenor; sang as choir boy; later
entered chorus of Stuttgart Op. when
it was on guest tour in his native
town; 5 months later made début
at Stuttgart without formal vocal
study; 1913–25, member of Munich
Op.; also active as recital and oratorio singer. (3) **John Lawrence,**
b. Reading, Pa., 1877; organist;
studied Metropolitan Coll., N. Y.,
and Virgil School; headed mus. dept.
of Wooster Univ., later dir. school of
music, Univ. of Illinois; after 1922
dir. at Conn. Coll., New London;
wrote life of Brahms; c. organ, piano,
vocal mus.; d. Eugene, Ore., 1950.

Er'ba, Don Dionigi, nobleman and
composer at Milan, 1694; Händel
appropriated some of his best works.

Erbach (ĕr'-bäkh), **Chr.,** Algesheim,
Palatinate, 1570—Augsburg, 1635;
composer and organist.

Er'ben, Robert, Troppau, March 9,
1862—Berlin, Oct. 17, 1925; 1894,
conductor at Frankfort-on-M.; 1896,
at Mannheim; prod. the succ. 1-act
opera *"Enoch Arden"* (Frankfort-on-
M., 1895), and a "fairy comedy,"
"Die Heinzelmännchen" (Mayence,
1896).

Erdmannsdörffer (ĕrt'-mäns-dĕrf-fĕr),
(1) **Max,** Nürnberg, June 14, 1848—
Munich, Feb. 14, 1905; pupil Leipzig
Cons., and in Dresden of Rietz;
1871–80, ct.-cond., Sondershausen;
1882, dir. Imp. Mus. Soc. at Moscow,
and prof. at the Cons.; 1885, founded
a students' orch. society; returned to
Germany, cond. the Bremen Philh.
Concerts till 1895; 1896, cond. Symphony Concerts St. Petersburg; 1896,
cond. at the ct.-Th., Munich; c.
"Prinzessin Ilse," "a forest-legend";
and other works for soli, chor. and
orch.; overture to Brachvogel's
"Narciss," etc.; 1874 he m. (2) **Pauline Fichtner Oprawill,** b. Vienna,
June 28, 1847—Munich, Sept. 24,
1916; pupil of Pirkhert and Liszt;
court-pianist.

Erk (ĕrk), (1) **Adam Wm.,** Herpf, Saxe-
Meiningen, 1779—Darmstadt, 1820;
organist and composer. (2) **Ludwig**
(Chr.), Wetzlar, 1807—Berlin, 1883;
son of above; conductor. (3) **Fr.
Albrecht,** Wetzlar, 1809—Düsseldorf,
1879; bro. of above; pub. the
"Lehrer Commersbuch," etc.

Erkel (ĕr'-kĕl), (1) **Franz (or Ferencz)**,
Gyula, Hungary, Nov. 7, 1810—
Pesth, June 15, 1893; the father of
Hungarian opera; conductor and
prof., composer of operas incl.
"Hunyády Lázló" and *"Bank Ban."*
(2) **Alexander** (or Alexius), Pesth,
1846—1900, son of above; dir. of
Philh. Conc., Pesth, 1875–93; 1896,
dir. Royal Opera, Pesth; prod.
opera *"Tempeföi"* (Pesth, 1883).
(3) **Julius,** d. Budapest, March 22,
1909; son of (1), prof. at Acad. of
Mus., Pesth; conductor for many
years at R. Opera.

Erlanger (ĕr-läñ-zhā), (1) **Camille,**
Paris, May 25, 1863—April 24, 1919;
pupil of Délibes, Paris Cons.; 1888
took Grand prix de Rome with cantata *"Velleda"*; c. symphonic piece,
"La Chasse Fantastique"; dram. legend, *"Saint Julien L' Hospitalier"*
(Paris, 1896); the succ. lyric drama
"Kermaria" (Paris, Op.-Com., 1897),
"Aphrodite," (1906) etc. (2) Baron
Frédéric d' (pen-names **Fr. Regna¹**
or **Federico Ringel),** b. Paris, May
29, 1868; son of a banker; prod. succ.
opera *"Jehan de Saintre,"* Hamburg
(1894), and mod. succ. opera *"Inez
Mendo"* (London, 1897), *"Tess."*
"Noel," etc.; d. London, 1943.

Erlebach (ĕr'-lĕ-bäkh), **Ph. H.,** Essen,
July 25, 1657—Rudolstadt, April 17,
1714; court-cond.; c. overtures,
etc.

Er'ler, Hermann, Radeberg, near Dresden, June 3, 1844—Berlin, Dec. 13,
1918; 1873 est. a mus.-pub. business
(now Ries and Erler); editor and
critic.

Ernst, Heinrich Wilhelm, Brünn, Moravia, May 6, 1814—Nice, Oct. 8, 1865;
violinist; pupil Vienna Cons. and
with Böhm and Mayseder; followed
Paganini about to learn his methods;
1832–38 lived at Paris; 1838–44
toured Europe with greatest success;
c. violin-concerto, etc.

Errani (ĕr-rä'-nē), Achille, Italy, 1823
—New York, 1897; operatic tenor
and notable singing-teacher in N. Y.

Er'skine, John, b. New York, Oct. 5,
1879—N. Y., June 2, 1951; writer, musician; pres. Juilliard School of Music,
N. Y., until 1937; heard as lecturer,
and as piano soloist with leading
Amer. orchestras; prof. of English
lit., Columbia University; among
many academic degrees, hon. D.
Litt., Bordeaux Univ.; Chevalier of

the Legion of Honour; author of librettos to operas, *"Jack and the Beanstalk"* (Gruenberg) and *"Helen Retires"* (Antheil).

Er'tel, Jean Paul, Posen, Jan. 22, 1865 —Berlin, Feb. 11, 1933; critic and composer; pupil of Tauwitz, Brassin and Liszt; self-taught in instrumentation; teacher at Brandenburg Cons.; 1897–1905, edited the *"Deutsche Musiker Zeitung"*; c. symphony *"Harald"*; symph. poems *"Maria Stuart," "Der Mensch," "Belsazar," " Hero und Leander"* (1909); a double fugue for orchestra and organ, etc.

Ert'mann, Baroness, ca. 1778—Vienna, 1848; pianist; intimate friend of Beethoven.

Eschmann (ĕsh'-män), **Jn. K.,** Winterthur, Switzerland, 1826—Zurich, 1882; pianist, teacher and composer at Leipzig.

Escudier (ĕs-küd-yä), two brothers, of Castelnaudary, Aude, (1) **Marie,** 1819—1880, and (2) **Léon,** 1821— Paris, 1881; journalists.

Eslava (ĕs-lä'-vä), **Don Miguel Hilario,** Burlada, Navarra, 1807—Madrid, 1878; court-conductor, editor and theorist.

Espagne (ĕs-päkh'-nĕ), **Fz.,** Münster, Westphalia, 1828—Berlin, 1878; director and editor.

Esplá, Oscar, b. Alicante, Aug. 5, 1886; Spanish composer; one of the leading composers of his country, his works based on folk music of eastern Spain; utilises original musical scale drawn from folk music; forswears impressionism and romanticism for classical method; c. orch., chamber and other music of marked originality.

Espo'sito, Michele, Castellammare, near Naples, Sept. 29, 1855—Dublin, Nov. 19, 1929; pianist; pupil of Naples Cons., under Cesi; 1878–82, at Paris; from 1882, piano-prof., Royal Irish Acad. of Music, Dublin; 1899 organised and cond. an orchestra in Dublin; c. cantata *"Deirdre"* winning Feis Ceoil prize (1897); operetta, *"The Postbag," "Irish"* symph. (Feis Ceoil prize, 1902), etc.

Es'ser, H., Mannheim, 1818—Salzburg, 1872; court-conductor.

Es'sipoff (or **Essipova**) (ĕs-sĭ-pôf'-ä), **Annette,** St. Petersburg, Feb. 1, 1851 —Aug. 18, 1914; pianist; pupil of Wielhorski; of Leschetizky, whom she m. 1880; début, 1874, St. Petersburg; toured Europe with great succ.; toured America (1876); 1885, pianist to the Russian Court; 1893–1908, pf.-prof. St. Petersburg Cons.

Este (or **Est, East, Easte**), (1) **Thomas,** London music-printer, ca. 1550— ca. 1609. (2) **Michael,** son of above; 17th cent. composer.

Esterházy (esh'-tĕr-hä-zē), Count **Nicholas,** 1839—Castle Totis, Hungary, 1897; generous patron of music.

Ett (ĕt), **Kaspar,** Erringen, Bavaria, 1788—Munich, 1847; court-organist and composer.

Ett'inger, Max, b. Lemberg, Dec. 27, 1874; comp. of operas, *"Clavigo," "Judith,"* etc.

Eulenburg (tsoo oi'-lĕn-boorkh), (1) **Ph., Graf zu,** Königsberg, Feb. 12, 1847 —Liebenberg, Sept. 17, 1921; Royal Prussian Ambassador, Stuttgart; c. songs (words and music). (2) **Ernst,** Berlin, 1847—Leipzig, 1926; founder of Leipzig publishing house.

Ev'ans, (1) **Edwin,** 1844—London, Dec. 21, 1923; organist; writer; author, *"Beethoven's Nine Symphonies," "Record of Instrumentation,"* etc.; his son (2) **Edwin;** b. London, Sept. 1, 1874; music critic; educated at Lille, Echtemach, Luxembourg; self-taught in music; critic, *"Pall Mall Gazette,"* 1914–23; contributor to many periodicals; one of the founders of the Internat'l Soc. for Contemporary Music; wrote work on Tschaikowsky; d. 1945.

Evers (ā'-vĕrs), **K.,** Hamburg, 1819— Vienna, 1875; pianist and composer.

Ew'er & Co., London mus.-publishers; founded 1820 by J. J. Ewer, succeeded by E. Buxton; 1860, W. Witt; 1867, became Novello, Ewer & Co.

Eximeno (ĕx-ĭ-mä'-nō), **Ant.,** Valencia, 1729—Rome, 1808; Jesuit priest; had historical controversy with Padre Martini.

Expert (ĕx-pär), **Henri,** b. Bordeaux, May 12, 1863; pupil of César Franck and Gigout; authority on 15–16th century music and editor of many important texts; from 1909 librarian Paris Cons.; d. Alpes Maritimes, 1952.

Eybler (ī'-blĕr), **Jos.** (later, in 1834, **Edler von Eybler**), Schwechat, near Vienna, 1765—Schönbrunn, 1846; conductor and composer.

Eyken (ī'-kĕn), (1) **Simon van (or**

Eycken; du Chesne). Vide QUERCU.
(2) (Eijken), **Jan Albert van,** Amersfoort, Holland, 1822—Elberfeld, 1868; organist and composer; c. valuable chorals, etc.

Eymieu (ĕm'-yŭ), **Henri,** b. Saillans Drôme, France, May 7, 1860; a lawyer, but studied with E. Gazier (theory) and Widor (comp.); writer and critic for "*Le Ménestrel,*" etc.; c. a stage-piece, "*Un Mariage sous Néron*" (Paris, 1898), and an oratorio, "*Marthe et Marie*" (Asnières, 1898), etc.

Eysler (īs'-lĕr), or **Eisler, Edmund,** b. Vienna, Mar. 12, 1874; c. operettas "*The Feast of Lucullus*" (Vienna, 1901), and "*Brother Straubinger*" (1903), "*Vera Violetta,*" 1907, etc.; d. Vienna, Oct. 4, 1949.

F

Faber (fä'-bĕr), (1) **Nikolaus (Nicol),** priest at Halberstadt, 1359–61, built there what is considered the first organ made in Germany. (2) **Nikolaus (II.),** a native of Bozen, Tyrol; pub. "*Rudimenta musicae,*" Augsburg, 1516. (3) **Heinrich,** "Magister," b. Lichtenfels, d. Oelsnitz, Saxony, 1552; rector of a school, whence he was expelled for satirical songs against the Pope; then rector of Brunswick; pub. a pop. book of rudiments. (4) **Benedikt,** Hildburghausen, 1602—Coburg, 1631; composer.

Fabio. Vide URSILLO.

Fabri (fä'-brē), (1) **Stefano** (*il maggiore*), b. Rome, ca. 1550; 1599—1601, conductor. (2) **Stefano** (*il minore*), Rome, 1606—1658; conductor and composer. (3) **Annibale Pio** (called **Balino**), Bologna, 1697—Lisbon, 1760; tenor, etc.

Fabricius (fä-brē'-tsǐ-oos), (1) **Werner,** Itzehoe, 1633—Leipzig, 1679; composer. (2) **J. Albert,** Leipzig, 1668—Hamburg, 1736, son of above; professor.

Faccio (fät'-chō), **Franco,** Verona, March 8, 1840—Monza, July 21, 1891; an important composer; criticised as Wagnerite; notable cond.; prof. at Milan Cons. (harmony, later cpt.). Vide BOITO.

Faelten (fĕl'-tĕn), (1) **K.,** Ilmenau, Thuringia, Dec. 21, 1846—Readfield, Me., Jan. 5, 1928; studied as a school-boy with Montag; for 6 years orchestra-violinist; 1867 studied with J. Schoch, Frankfort, and was for 10 years friend of Raff; 1868–82, Frankfort; 1878, Hoch Cons.; 1882–85, Peabody Institute, Baltimore, U. S. A.; 1885–97, N. E. Cons., Boston; dir. 1890–97; 1897, founded the Faelten Pf.-School (Teachers' Seminary), at Boston; pub. text-books. (2) **Reinhold,** b. Ilmenau, Jan. 17, 1856; brother of (1); pupil of Klughardt and Gottschalg in Weimar; also for many years in the U. S., active in Baltimore and Boston as teacher, writer.

Fago (fä'-gō), **Nicola** (called "Il Tarentino"), Tarento, 1674—1745 (?); c. oratorio, masses; prod. several very succ. operas.

Fahrbach (fär'-bäkh), (1) **Jos.,** Vienna, 1804—1883; flutist, conductor, and composer. (2) **Ph. (Sr.),** Vienna, 1815—1885; conductor and dram. composer. (3) **Wm.,** Vienna, 1838—1866; conductor and composer. (4) **Ph. (Jr.),** Vienna, 1840—1894; son of (2); conductor.

Fährmann (fär'-män) **Ernst Hans,** b. Beicha, Dec. 17, 1860; organist; 1892, teacher at Dresden Cons.; c. organ sonatas, etc.

Faignient (fĭn-yän), **Noë,** b. Antwerp, ca. 1570, Flemish contrapuntist.

Fair'child, Blair, Belmont, Mass., June 23, 1877—Paris, April 23, 1933; composer; studied at Harvard Univ., with Paine and W. Spalding, also in Florence with Buonamici; entered diplomatic service in Constantinople and Persia; Oriental impressions notable in his music; after 1903 lived in Paris, studied with Widor and Ganaye; c. (pantomime) "*Dame Libellule*" (Paris Op.-Comique, 1921); also many orch., chamber music, vocal and piano works.

Faiszt (fīst), **Immanuel G. Fr.,** Essligen, Würtemberg, 1823—Stuttgart, 1894; organist.

Falcke (fälk), **Henri,** Paris, 1866—May, 1901; pupil of Saint-Saëns, Massenet, Dubois, and Mathias, Paris Cons.; won 1st prizes in pf. and harm.; studied in Germany; pub. a useful text-book on arpeggios.

Falcon (fäl-kôn), **M. Cornélie,** Paris, 1812—1897; soprano singer.

Falk Mehlig (fälk mā'-lǐkh), **Anna,** Stuttgart, July 11, 1846—Berlin, July 16, 1928; studied at the Cons., also with Liszt; toured as concert pianist throughout Germany, England, and America; court-pianist to the king of Würtemberg.

Fall, Leo, Olmütz, Feb. 2, 1873—Vienna, Sept. 15, 1925; composer of light operas; *"Irrlicht"* (Mannheim, 1905), *"Der Rebell"* (Vienna, 1905), *"Der fidele Bauer"* (Mannheim, 1907), *"Die Dollar Prinzessin,"* (Vienna, 1907, London and America as *"The Dollar Princess"*), etc.

Falla, De. Vide DE FALLA.

Faltin (fäl'-tēn), **R. Fr.,** Danzig, Jan. 5, 1835—Helsingfors, June 1, 1918; pupil of Markull, Schneider, and Leipzig Cons. Since 1869 lived at Helsingfors, Finland, as cond.; pub. *"Finnish Folk-Songs"* and a *"Finnish Song-Book."*

Faminzin (fä-mēn'-tsēn), **Alex. Sergievitch,** Kaluga, Russia, 1841—Ligovo, near St. Petersburg, 1896; critic and dram. composer.

Fanel'li, Ernest, Paris, 1860—1917; studied Paris Cons.; violinist; played in cafés, dance halls, acted as music copyist; in 1912 his symphony *"Tableaux Symphoniques,"* written in 1883, prod. by the Colonne orch., received with greatest approval. His works, in modern style of much originality, are prophetic of Debussy.

Fan'ing, Eaton, Helston, Cornwall, May 20, 1850—Brighton, Oct. 28, 1927; pupil of the R. A. M., took Mendelssohn Scholarship in 1873 and the Lucas Medal in 1876; 1894 Mus. Bac., Cantab.; 1885 dir. music at Harrow School; c. 3 operettas, cantata for female voices, symphony in C minor, overture, *"The Holiday,"* etc.

Farabi. Vide ALFARABI.

Farina (fä-rē'-nä), **Carlo,** b. Mantua; one of the earliest of violin virtuosos; 1625 court chamber musician at Vienna; c. violin pieces.

Farinel'li, (1) Carlo Broschi (brôs'-kē), Naples, June 24, 1705—Bologna, July 15, 1782; famous male soprano; début 1722 at Rome; he sang with the utmost brilliancy and success, being only once overcome by a rival (Bernacchi) from whom he immediately took lessons; he joined the opposition to Händel in London, and Händel went into bankruptcy and took to oratorio. He amassed great wealth and became the chief adviser of Philip V. of Spain; biog. by Sacchi (Venice, 1784). (2) **Giu.,** Este, 1769—Trieste, 1836; org.; c. 60 operas.

Far'jeon, Harry, b. Hohokus, N. J., May 6, 1878; composer; of English parentage, and taken to England in infancy; pupil of Landon Ronald, Storer, and 1895-1901, R. A. M.; prod. operetta *"Floretta,"* 1899; from 1903, prof. of theory at the R. A. M.; c. piano concerto, orch. suite *"Hans Andersen"*; symph. poems, *"Mowgli,"* and *"Summer Vision"*; chamber music, songs, etc.; d. Dec. 29, 1948.

Farkas (fär'-kǎsh), **Edmund** (Hung., Ödön), Puszta-Monostor (Heves), Hungary, 1852—Klausenburg, Sept. 1, 1912; important figure in national Hungarian music; of noble family, intended to be a civil engineer; but studied 3 years at the R. Mus. Acad., Pesth; next year became dir. at the Cons. at Klausenburg, Transylvania; was for a time op. cond. and wrote mus. articles; 1876, while still studying engineering, he prod. a 1-act opera *"Bayadér"* (Pesth); won the Haynald prize of 300 florins with a mass; c. also mixed choruses, and the orch. works *"Dawn"* (Virradat), *"Evensong"* (Estidal), *"Twilight"* (Alkony), and *"Dies iræ"*; a pop. symphony and 5 string-quartets; a prize *"Festouvertüre"*; and the operas *"Fairy fountain"* (Tünderhorrás), 1-act (Klausenburg, 1892); *"The Penitent"* (Veseklök) (Pesth, 1893); *"Balassa Balint,"* comic (Pesth, 1896); and *"The Blood-ordeal"* (Tetemre Hivás) (not prod.).

Far'mer, (1) John, important English composer of madrigals; author of a treatise pub. 1591, and madrigals, 1599-1602. (2) **Thomas,** d. 1694 (?); composer; graduated at Cambridge, 1684; published songs, stage music, etc., 1675-1695; Purcell wrote an elegy to Nahum Tate's words, on his death. (3) **H.,** Nottingham, England, 1819—1891; violinist and organist. (4) **J.,** Nottingham, Aug. 16, 1836—July, 1901; nephew of above; pupil of Leipzig Cons. and of Spath; teacher in Zurich for some years; 1862-85 mus.-master at Harrow School, then organist at Balliol Coll., Oxford, where he founded a mus. society; edited song-books, etc.; c. an oratorio; a fairy opera; comic cantata; a requiem, etc.

Far'naby, Giles, English composer, ca. 1565—1600 (?).

Far'rant, (1) John, English organist, ca. 1600. (2) **John,** English or-

ganist, Salisbury cath., ca. 1600.
(3) **Richard,** d. Nov. 30, 1580;
English organist and notable composer of church-music.

Farrar', Geraldine, b. Melrose, Mass.,
Feb. 28, 1882; soprano; at 12, pupil
of J. H. Long, Boston; later of
Trabadello and Lilli Lehmann; 1901,
début Berlin Royal Opera; also at
the Op. Com., Paris, and 1906-22,
at the Met. Op. House in N. Y.,
creating the rôle of the Goosegirl
in Humperdinck's "*Königskinder*"
(1910). Her striking dram. and
music. gifts, coupled with charm of
personality, placed her in the front
rank of Amer. singers, and she was
heard widely as a concert and fest.
soloist. She made several successful
silent motion pictures, and also
toured with her own company in a
version of "*Carmen,*" a rôle in which
she had enjoyed favour at the Metropolitan. After retiring from the
stage and later the concert field, she
sang in radio programmes and also
acted as commentator for the Met.
Op. broadcast performances, 1935.

Farrenc (făr-räṅk), (1) **Jacq. Hipp, Aristide,** Marseilles, 1794—Paris, 1865;
teacher and composer. (2) **Jeanne
Louise** (née **Dumont**), Paris, 1804-
1875; wife of above, pf.-professor.

Far'well, Arthur, b. St. Paul, Minn.,
April 23, 1872; American composer;
pupil of H. A. Norris, Boston, and of
Humperdinck; founded at Newton
Center, Mass., 1901, the "Wawan
Press" for the artistic pub. of comps.
by Americans, particularly music
based on Indian themes. In 1905 he
established the Amer. Music Soc.
From 1909-15 he was a member of
the staff of "*Musical America*" and
in 1910-13, dir. of municipal concerts
in New York; 1915-18, dir. of Music
School Settlement there; 1918-19,
acting prof., Univ. of Calif. His
comps. include for orch. "*Dawn,*"
"*The Domain of Hurakan,*" "*Navajo War-Dance*" (all on Indian
themes). "*Cornell*" overture, and
"*Love Song*"; for piano many pieces
of Indian theme, and numerous fine
songs; d. N. Y., Jan. 20, 1952.

Fasch (fäsh), (1) **Jn. Fr.,** Buttlestadt,
near Weimar, 1688—Zerbst, 1758;
court-conductor, composer. (2) **K.
Fr. Chr.,** Zerbst, 1736—Berlin, 1800;
cembalist; son of above; conductor.

Faugues, Vincent (or **Fauques, Fa'gus,**

La Fage) (fōg, fōk, lä fäzh), 15th
cent. contrapuntist.

Faure (fōr), **J. Bapt.,** Moulins, Allier,
Jan. 15, 1830—Paris, Nov. 9, 1914;
1841, Paris Cons.; choir-boy at the
Madeleine, and studied with Trevaux; took 1st prize for comic opera;
1852-76, at the Op. Com. as leading
barytone with great succ.; 1857,
teacher in the Cons.; after 1876 sang
in concert; pub. "*L'Art du Chant*";
c. songs, etc.

Fauré (fō-rā), **Gabriel Urbain,** Pamiers,
Ariège, May 13, 1845—Paris, Nov. 4,
1924; eminent French composer;
pupil of Niedermayer, Dietsch, and
Saint-Saëns; 1866, organist at Rennes,
then at St.-Sulpice and St.-Honoré;
1885 took Prix Chartier for chamber
music; 1896 organist at the Madeleine, and prof. of comp., cpt., and
fugue at the Cons. (vice Massenet);
1905-20, he became director; c.
music to "*Prométhée*" (Béziers, 1900),
"*Julius Cæsar*" (1905), "*Pelléas et
Mélisande,*" 1898; arranged as an
orch. suite, 1901; also much chamber
music, and religious choruses, piano
pieces and many highly important
songs; 1-act opera "*L'Organiste*"
(1887); "*La Naissance de Venus,*"
for soli, chorus, and orch.; "*Chœur
de Djinns*"; requiem; symphony;
vln.-concerto; orchestral suite; 2 pf.-
quartets; *Élégie,* for 'cello; *Berceuse
and Romance,* for vln. and orch., a
vln.-sonata, etc.; 1909, elected to
French Académie; 1910, commander,
Legion of Honour. Memoirs pub.
by Séré and Vuillemin.

Fayolle (fī-yôl), **Fran. Jos. M.,** Paris,
1774—1852; mus. biographer and
lexicographer.

Fayr'fax, Robt., Mus. Doc., Cantab.
and Oxon, 1504-11; organist and
composer.

Fechner (fĕkh'-nĕr), **Gv. Th.,** Gross-
Sarchen, Niederlausitz, 1801—Leipzig, 1887; writer.

Fedele (fā-dā'-lĕ). Vide TREU.

Federici (fā-dā-rē'-chē), **V.,** Pesaro,
1764—Milan, 1826; went to London,
where he became cembalist; returned
to Italy in 1803 and prod. many succ.
operas.

Federlein (fā'-dĕr-līn), **Gottfried,** b.
New York, 1883; organist; pupil of
his father, Goetschius and Saar;
church organist; former warden A.G.O.;
d. Flushing, N. Y., Feb. 26, 1952.

Fein'berg, Samuel Eugenievitch, b.

Odessa, May 26, 1890; composer; pupil of Jensen and Goldenweiser; grad. of Moscow Cons., as pianist; representative of the more advanced modern Russian school of composition; c. piano works and songs.

Felix (fā-lĕks), Dr. **Hugo**, Vienna, Nov. 19, 1866—Los Angeles, Aug. 24, 1934; c. operettas "*Husarenblut*," Vienna, 1894; "*Rhodope*," Berlin, 1900; "*Mme. Sherry*" (Berlin, 1902, with great success in America, 1910).

Fel'lowes, Edmund Horace, b. London, Nov. 11, 1870; author, lecturer, editor; specialist in Elizabethan madrigal; grad. Winchester Coll. and Oriel Coll., Oxford; hon. Mus. D., Trinity Coll., Dublin; dir. Choir of St. George's Chapel, Windsor Castle, 1923-27; has toured Canada as cond. of Westminster Abbey singers, and d. Windsor, Engl., Dec. 21, 1951.

Felstein (fĕl'-shtīn) (called **Felstinen'-sis**), **Sebastian von,** ca. 1530; church-conductor and composer, Cracow.

Fenaroli (fā-nä-rō'-lē), **Fedele,** Lanciano, Abruzzi, 1730—Naples, 1818; teacher and composer.

Feo (fā'-ō), **Francesco,** b. Naples, ca. 1685; composer and teacher.

Fer(r)abosco (fĕr-rä-bôs'-kō), (1) **Alfonso,** Italy, 1543—1588; c. madrigals. (2) **Dom. M.,** Rome, 16th cent., member Papal Choir; composer. (3) **Costantino,** court-musician and composer at Vienna, 1591. (4) **Alfonso,** Greenwich, England, ca. 1575—1628; probably son of (1); composer. (5) **John,** d. 1682, son of (4); organist Ely Cathedral.

Ferrari, (1) **Benedetto** (called **della Tiorba** "the theorbist") (fĕr-rä'-rē dĕl-la tē-ôr'-bä), Reggio d'Emilia, 1597 — Modena, 1681; court-conductor and dram. composer. (2) **Domenico,** Piacenza, (?)—Paris, 1780; violinist, conductor and composer. (3) **Carlo,** Piacenza, ca. 1730—Parma, 1789, bro. of above; 'cellist. (4) **Giacomo Gotifredo,** Roveredo, Tyrol, 1759—London, 1842; cembalist, writer, teacher, and composer. (5) **Francisca,** Christiania, ca. 1800—Gross-Salzbrunn, Silesia, 1828; harpist. (6) **Serafino Amadeo de',** Genoa, 1824—1885; pianist and dram. composer. (7) **Carlotta,** Lodi, Italy, Jan. 27, 1837—Bologna, 1907; pupil of Strepponi and Panzini (1844-50) of Mazzucato at Milan Cons.; wrote text and music of succ.

operas "*Ugo*" (Milan, 1857); "*Sofia*" (Lodi, 1866); "*Eleanora d'Arborea*" (Cagliari, 1871); also masses; a *Requiem for Turin,* 1868, etc. (8) **Gabrielle,** Paris, March 14, 1860 —July 4, 1921; pupil of Ketten, Duprato, later of Gounod and Leborne; at 12 début as pianist, Naples; c. opera "*Le Colzar*," given at Monte Carlo in one act, enlarged to two (Paris Opéra, 1912); also orch. suites and many popular songs.

Ferrari-Fontan'a, Edoardo, Rome, July 8, 1878—Toronto, Can., July 4, 1936; tenor; early in life entered medical career, later diplomatic service at Italian consulate in Montevideo and Rio de Janeiro; opera début, Turin, 1910, as "Kurwenal" in "*Tristan und Isolde*"; sang later in leading Italian theatres, South America, Paris, Boston and New York, with Met. Op. Co. after 1914; m. Margarete Matzenauer, contralto; divorced.

Ferreira (fĕr-rā'-ē-rä), **Da Costa, Rodrigo,** 1776—1825; Portuguese writer.

Fer(r)et'ti, Giov., b. Venice, ca. 1540; composer.

Ferri (fĕr'-rē), (1) **Baldassare,** Perugia, 1610—Sept. 8, 1680; one of the most gifted and successful of singers; a male soprano; possessed extraordinary endurance of breath, flexibility of voice, and depth of emotion; at 65 returned to Perugia; on his death left 600,000 crowns for charity.

Ferrier (fĕr-ē-ā'), **Kathleen,** b. Lancashire, 1912—d. London, Oct. 8, 1953; noted contralto; pupil of J. E. Hutchinson, Roy Henderson; sang Glyndebourne Opera; toured U. S.

Ferro'ni, V. Emidio Carmine, Tramutola, Italy, Feb. 17, 1858—Milan, Jan. 11, 1934; pupil Paris Cons.; 1st prize in harm. and comp., 1880-83; 1881, asst.-prof. of harm. at the Cons.; 1888 prof. of comp. at Milan Cons., and mus. dir. of the "Famiglia Artistica." 1897, Chevalier of the Ital. Crown; c. operas "*Rudello*" (Milan, 1892); and (text and mus. of) "*Ettore Fieramosca*" (Como, 1896).

Ferroud (fā-rōōd'), **Pierre-Octave,** Chesselay, France, 1900—near Debrecen, Hungary, Aug. 17, 1936 (motor accident); composer; had shown sensitive impressionistic manner in his works; studied with Florent Schmitt; served as critic on various periodicals; c. (orch.) "*Foules*," perf. with succ. by various

Amer. orchestras; *"Au Parc Monceau"*; Serenade; also a comic opera *"Chirurgie,"* given at Monte Carlo, 1928; ballet, *"Jeunesse,"* etc.

Fes'ca, (1) **Fr. Ernst,** Magdeburg, 1789 —Carlsruhe, 1826; violinist and composer. (2) **Alex. Ernst,** Carlsruhe, May 22, 1820—Brunswick, Feb. 22, 1849; son of above; brilliant pianist and dram. composer.

Fes'ta, (1) **Costanzo,** Rome, ca. 1490 —April 10, 1545; singer and contrapuntist. (2) **Giu. M.,** Trani, 1771— Naples, 1839; violinist, conductor and composer. (3) **Francesca,** Naples, 1778—St. Petersburg, 1836; operatic singer; m. Maffei.

Fest'ing, Michael Christian, London, ca. 1700—1752; son of a flutist, of same name; conductor, violinist, and composer.

Fétis (fā-tēs), (1) **François Joseph,** Mons, Belgium, March 25, 1784— Brussels, March 26, 1871; indefatigable scholar and historian; he worked 16–18 hours a day; his father, organist and conductor at the Cathedral, was his first teacher; he learned the vln., and c. a concerto for vln. and orch.; the same year became organist to the Noble Chapter of Saint Waudra; 1800–03 in the Paris Cons.; 1803, Vienna, for study of fugue, and master-work of German music; here began an investigation of Guido d'Arezzo's system and the history of notation. 1804 he started a short-lived mus. periodical. 1806 he began the 30 years' task (still unpub.) of revising the plain-song and entire ritual of the Roman Church. He m. a wealthy woman, and was enabled to pursue his studies comfortably till 1811, when her fortune was lost. He returned to the Ardennes and made researches into harmony, which led to his formulating the modern theory of tonality. 1813, organist and teacher at Douai; wrote *"La Science de l'Organist,"* and *"Méthode élémentaire d'harmonie et d'accompagnement."* 1818, Paris, where he prod. various operas with succ. 1821, prof. of comp. at the Cons., later librarian. 1827–35 founded and edited *"La Revue Musicale."* In 1832 began historical lectures and concerts. 1833, cond. to King Leopold I., Brussels, and for 39 years dir. of the Cons. there, and 1845 member of the Belgian

Academy. On his wedding-jubilee a Mass of his was sung, and his bust was unveiled. In 1806, he began collecting and preparing for his great *"Biographie universelle des musiciens et bibliographie générale de la musique"* in 8 volumes (1837–1844). This invaluable monument is, like everything else of its kind, bristling inevitably with error, bias, and excess; yet is a standard of highest repute. Pub. many treatises and c. 6 operas (1820–32); 2 symphonies, an overture for orch.; masses, a requiem, motets, etc. Biog. in his Dictionary by L. Alvin (Brussels, 1874); and Gollmick (Leipzig, 1852). (2) **Ed. L. Fran.,** Bouvignes, near Dinant, May 16, 1812—Brussels, Jan. 31, 1909; son of above; editor; for years libr. Brussels Library; pub. *"Les musiciens Belges"* (1848). (3) **Adolphe L. Eugène,** Paris, 1820— 1873; son and pupil of (1); pianist, teacher and dram. composer.

Feuermann (foi'-ĕr-män), **Emanuel,** Kolomea, Poland, Nov. 22, 1902— N. Y., May 25, 1942; cellist; pupil Anton Walter, Julius Klengel; concert début at 11; at 17 teacher at Cologne Cons., where he was active until 1923; solo 'cellist with Gürzenich Orch. and mem. Gürzenich Quartet; later res. in Vienna; taught Berlin Hochsch.; solo 'cellist in Philh. Orch. in that city; has made world tours with succ., incl. U. S., where made début in recital and as soloist with N. Y. Philh., 1935–36.

Feurich (foi'-rĭkh), **Julius,** Leipzig, 1821—1900; founded pf. factory, 1851.

Fevin (fū-văň), **Ant. (Antonius) de,** ca. 1473—1515 (?); Netherlandish (?) contrapuntist; contemporary with Josquin Després, and rated second only to him. (2) **Robert (Robertus),** Cambrai, 15th cent.; c. masses.

Février (fāv'-rē-ā), (1) **Henri Louis,** Abbeville—Paris, ca. 1780; composer of clavecin music, of which he pub. 2 collections in 1734 and 1755. (2) **Henry,** b. Paris, 1875; composer; pupil of H. Woollett and the Paris Cons., studying with Pugno, Leroux and Massenet; also privately with Messager; his first compositions were chamber music, incl. a piano trio and sonata for vln. and piano; he has also written pieces for the latter instrument, choruses and songs, but is chiefly known for his operas, among which are "*Le Roi aveugle*" (Paris, 1906), "*Monna Vanna*" after Maeterlinck (Paris, 1909), "*Gismonda*," taken from Sardou drama (Chicago, 1919), and a number of operettas.

Fiala (fē'-ä-lä), **Jos.**, Lobkowitz, Bohemia, 1749—Donauchingen, 1816; oboist, 'cellist, composer, and conductor.

Fibich (fē'bĭkh), **Zdenko**, Seborschitz, Bohemia, Dec. 21, 1850—Prague, Oct. 15, 1900; pupil at Prague, Leipzig Cons. (1865), and of Lachner; 1876 asst. cond. at the National Th., Prague; 1878, dir. Russian Church Choir; notable Czech dram. composer. Prod. at Prague 6 operas incl. "*Sarka*" (1898); c. the symphonic poems "*Othello*," "*Zaboj and Slavoj*," "*Toman and the Nymph*," and "*Vesna*"; "*Lustspiel Ouvertüre*," etc. "*A Night on Kaarlstein*," and other overtures.

Fiby (fē'-bē), **Heinrich**, Vienna, May 15, 1834—Znaim, Oct. 23, 1917; pupil of the Cons.; from 1857 city mus. dir., Znaim; founded a music-school and a society; c. 3 operettas; pop. male choruses, etc.

Fiebach (fē'-bäkh), **Otto**, b. Ohlau, Silesia, Feb. 9, 1851—Königsberg, 1937; mus. dir., Königsberg University; royal conductor; c. operas, and an oratorio; author of "*Die Physiologie der Tonkunst*" (1891).

Fiedler (fēt'-lĕr), (1) **August Max**, b. Zittau, Dec. 31, 1859; piano pupil of his father, and studied organ and theory with G. Albrecht; 1877-80 Leipzig Cons.; won the Holstein Scholarship; 1882 teacher, Hamburg Cons.; in 1903, became director of the Hamburg Cons.; 1904 cond. the Philharmonic concerts; 1908-12, cond. Boston Symphony Orchestra with great success during the leave of absence of Karl Muck (q. v.), c. 'cello sonata (Boston, 1909), chamber music, etc.; 1916-33, he was dir. of music in Essen. (2) **Arthur**, b. Boston, Dec. 17, 1894; studied Berlin R. Acad. of Mus.; after 1930, cond. Boston "Pop" Concerts; teacher Boston Univ.

Field (1) **John**, Dublin, July 26, 1782—Moscow, Jan. 11, 1837; a great though gentle revolutionist of music, to whom much of Chopin's glory belongs, for Field developed the more lyric manner of pf.-playing and carried it into his composition, in which he gave the piano-song or poem its first escape from the old stiff forms. He created the Nocturne, and many of his comps. in this form have practically every quality and mannerism characteristic of those of Chopin, who excelled him in passion, resource, and harmonic breadth. He was the son of a violinist, and grandson and pupil of an organist, who compelled him to practise so hard that he ran away, but was brought back and later was apprenticed to Clementi as a salesman. He also had lessons from C., and went with him to Paris in 1802, making a great stir with his interpretation of Bach's and Händel's fugues; he was kept at his salesman's tasks till 1804, when he settled at St. Petersburg as a teacher and pianist of great vogue. After touring Russia, in London, 1832, he played a concerto of his own at the Philh.; then to Paris; 1833 Belgium, Switzerland, Italy, where he was not a succ. Intemperance and fistula kept him nine months in a Naples hospital; whence he was rescued by a Russian family Raemanow and taken to Moscow, playing in Vienna with greatest succ.; but his health was lost and he died a few years later and was buried in Moscow. Besides 20 nocturnes (of which only 12 were so named by Field) he c. 7 concertos (No. 4 in E flat the most popular); 4 sonatas; "*Air russe*"; "*Air russe varié*" (4 hands); "*Chanson russe varié*," in D min.; polonaise, "*Reviens, reviens.*" Romanza and Cavatina in E; 4 romances; 7 rondeaux; rondeau with 2 vlns., viola, and bass; variation in C; 2 divertissements with 2 vlns., viola and bass; 2 fantasias; and pf.-exercises in all keys. (2) **Henry**, "Field of Bath," Dec. 6, 1797—May 19, 1848; pianist and teacher.

Fielitz (fōn fē'-lĭts), **Alexander von**, Leipzig, Dec. 28, 1860—Bad Salzungen, July 29, 1930; pupil in Dresden of J. Schulhoff (pf.) and Kretschmer (comp.); he became opera-cond. in Zürich, Lübeck, and Leipzig (City Th.); a nervous disorder compelled his retirement; lived in Italy as a composer of choruses, orch. pcs., songs, which attained popularity. 1906-08, cond. and teacher, Chicago;

taught Stern Cons., Berlin (dir. 1915).

Filippi (fē-lĭp'-pǐ) (1) **Giu. de,** Milan, 1825—Neuilly, near Paris, 1887; writer. (2) **Filippo,** Vicenza, 1830 —Milan, 1887; critic, writer, and composer.

Fil'ke, Max, Staubendorf-Leobschütz, Silesia, Oct. 5, 1855—Breslau, Oct. 8, 1911; organist and singing teacher; pupil of Brosig and Leipzig Cons.; 1891, cathedral cond. at Breslau, teacher 1893 at the Royal Inst. for Church music; 1899, Royal Music director; c. several masses with orch.; choruses, etc.

Fill'more, J. Comfort, Franklin, Conn., 1843—1898; studied at Oberlin (O.) Coll., and Leipzig Cons.; 1884-95 founder and dir. of Sch. of Mus. in Milwaukee; then mus. dir. Pomona Coll., Claremont, Cal.; pub. *"A Study of Omaha Indian Music"* (with Miss Fletcher and F. La Flesche; Peabody Museum, 1893); and other treatises; tr. Riemann's works.

Finck (fĭnk), (1) **Heinrich,** 1482, conductor to John Albert I., Cracow; eminent contrapuntist. (2) **Hermann,** Pirna, Saxony, 1527—Wittenburg, 1558, grand-nephew of above; composer and writer. (3) **Henry Theophilus,** Bethel, Missouri, Sept. 22, 1854—Rumford Falls, Minn., Sept. 29, 1926; prominent American critic and essayist; influential advocate of Wagner; lived in Oregon, then (1876) graduate of Harvard, having studied theory and hist. of mus. with J. K. Paine; 1876, attended the first Bayreuth festival, and studied at Munich; pub. the valuable *"Wagner and His Works"* (N. Y., 1893, 2 vols., Germ. transl., Breslau, 1897); 1877-78, studied anthropology at Harvard; received a Fellowship and spent 3 years at Berlin, Heidelberg, and Vienna, studying comparative psychology and sending mus. letters to N. Y. *"Nation"*; and for some 40 years was mus.-ed. of the N. Y. *"Evening Post"*; pub. *"Chopin, and other Mus. Essays," "Paderewski and His Art," "Songs and Song-Writers"* (1901); *"The Pictorial Wagner," "Anton Seidl," "Grieg and His Music," "Success in Music," "Massenet and His Operas," "Richard Strauss";* also four collections of songs; 3 books of

travel: *"Pacific Coast Scenic Tour," "Lotos-time in Japan," "Spain and Morocco"; "Romantic Love and Personal Beauty," "Primitive Love and Love Stories"* (1900), etc.

Findeisen (fĭnt'-ī-zĕn), **Otto,** b. Brünn, Dec. 23, 1862; theat. conductor in Magdeburg and Leipzig, prod. succ. operetta *"Der Alte Dessauer"* (Magdeburg, 1890); and the succ. folk-opera *"Henings von Treffenfeld"* (ib. 1891).

Finger (fĭng'-ĕr), **Gf.,** b. Olmütz, Bavaria; in England, 1685-1701; then chamber-mus. to queen of Prussia, till 1717.

Fink, (1) **Gf. Wm.,** Sulza, Thuringia, 1783—Halle, 1846; editor, writer, and composer. (2) **Chr.,** Dettingen, Würtemberg, Aug. 9, 1831—Esslingen, Sept. 5, 1911; pupil Esslingen Seminary; Leipzig Cons., and Schneider, Dresden; till 1860 lived as organist and teacher, Leipzig; then teacher and organist, Esslingen, and prof. in 1862; composer.

Fioravanti (fē-ôr-ä-vän'-tē), (1) **Valentino,** Rome, 1764—Capua, June 16, 1837; opera-cond. and composer. (2) **Vincenzo,** Rome, 1799—Naples, 1877, son of above; conductor and dram. composer.

Fiore (fĭ-ō'-rĕ), **Andrea Stefano,** Milan, 1675—Turin, 1739; composer of operas.

Fiorillo (fē-ô-rĭl'-lō), (1) **Ignazio,** Naples, 1715—Fritzlar, near Cassel, 1787; court-conductor and composer. (2) **Federigo,** b. Brunswick, 1753 (?): son and pupil of above; viola player and composer.

Fiqué (fē-kā), **Karl,** Bremen, 1861— Brooklyn, N. Y., Dec., 1930; pupil of Leipzig Cons.; lived in Brooklyn, N. Y.; pianist and composer.

Firkusny (fēr-kŭzh'-nē), **Rudolf,** b. 1912, Napajdla, Czechoslovakia; pianist; studied Brnö Cons. and with Schnabel, Janacek and Suk; début at 14, Vienna; toured Europe; res. in U. S. where appeared widely in concerts.

Fischer (fĭsh'-ĕr), (1) **Johann Kaspar Ferdinand,** ca. 1650—1746; important composer for organ and clavier; cond. to Markgraf Ludwig in Bohemia, 1688. (2) **Jn. Chr.,** Freiburg, Baden, 1733—London, 1800; oboist and composer. (3) **K. Aug.,** Ebersdorf, Saxony, 1828— Dresden, 1892; organist. (4) **Emil,** Brunswick, Germany, 1838—Hamburg, 1914; notable German basso in Wagnerian rôles; début 1849; sang at Met. Op., N. Y., 1885–98; 1899 m. Camille Seygard; divorced 1902. (5) **Edwin**, b. Basel, Oct. 6, 1886; pianist; pupil of Basel Cons., and Stern. Cons., Berlin, where he taught from 1905 to 1914; since then has toured as concert pianist, having esp. rank as performer of Bach and Beethoven; also has conducted and c. songs and piano works; ed. Bach's piano works.

Fischhof (físh′-ôf), **Jos.**, Butschowitz, Moravia, 1804—Vienna, 1857; prof., composer and writer.

Fish′er, (1) **John A.**, b. Dunstable, 1774, pf.- and organ-virtuoso; violinist and composer. (2) **Wm. Arms**, San Francisco, 1861—Boston, 1948; pupil of J. P. Morgan (org. and pf.), H. W. Parker, and Dvořák, New York; also studied singing in London; from 1897, ed. and mgr. Oliver Ditson Co., Boston; composer. (3) **Susanne**, b. West Virginia; soprano; grad. Cincinnati Cons.; studied at Juilliard Grad. School, N. Y.; heard with Little Theatre Op. Co. in New York; sang at Berlin State Op., début as "Butterfly"; later at Paris Op.-Comique; début, Met. Op. Co., N. Y., 1935.

Fissot (fís-sō) **Alexis Henri**, Airaines (Somme). 1843—Paris, 1896; pf.- and organ-virtuoso and composer.

Fitelberg (fē′-těl-běrkh), (1) **Georg**, b. Dünaburg, 1879—d. Stalinograd, 1953; Polish composer; pupil Warsaw Cons., taking Paderewski prize with a violin sonata, 1896, and 1901 the Zamoyski prize with a piano trio; concertmaster, and 1908 conductor Warsaw Philharmonic; 1912, engaged for 6 years to cond. Vienna Royal Opera; later cond. in England and Russia; c. 2 symphonies, orch.; chamber music, songs, etc. (2) **Jerzy**, b. Warsaw, May 20, 1903; composer; pupil of Schreker; won Coolidge Prize; d. N. Y., Apr. 25, 1953.

Flagstad (fläg′-shtät), **Kirsten**, b. Oslo, Norway; dramatic soprano; her father an orchestral conductor, her mother a well-known pianist and coach; received her training from the latter; early designed for medical career, but at 15 began voice study; made début at Oslo when 18; engaged for Gothenburg Op. Co.; for a time retired from singing on marriage to Henry Johansen, industrial-

ist; consented to sing at Oslo as substitute for indisposed artist, and her succ. led to permanent engagement at the Op. there; had sung entirely in Scandinavian countries before engagement at Bayreuth, 1933–34; was offered Berlin contract but declined it; engaged for Met. Op. and made début in 1934–35 season as "Sieglinde" with sensational effect, and at once became celebrated in New York for her "Isolde," "Brünnhilde," "Elsa," etc.; next season also sang in "Fidelio"; Covent Garden début, spring of 1936, as "Isolde," the three Brünnhildes; also a high-ranking concert singer.

Flecha (flě′-chä), (1) **Juan**, music teacher; Catalonia, 1483–1553; Carmelite monk and teacher; his nephew (2) **Fray Matheo**, 1520—Feb. 20, 1604, was an abbot and cond. to Charles V. at Prague; both were composers.

Flégier (flā-zhā), **Ange**, Marseilles, Feb. 25, 1846—Oct. 8, 1927; pupil of Marseilles Cons. and Paris Cons. 1870; returned to Marseilles; c. 1-act comic opera, "Fatima" (Mars. 1875), "Ossian" and "Françoise de Rimini," cantata, with orch., etc.

Fleischer (flī′-shěr), (1) **Reinhold**, Dabsau, Silesia, April 12, 1842—Görlitz, Feb. 1, 1904; pupil of the R. Inst. for Church-music, and R. Akademie, at Berlin; 1870, organist at Görlitz and dir. Singakademie; 1885, Royal Mus. Dir.; c. a cantata, "Holda," etc. (2) **Oskar**, Zörbig, Nov. 1, 1856—Berlin, Feb. 8, 1923; studied in Italy on govt. stipend; pupil and, since 1896, successor of Spitta as Prof. Extraordinary, at the Berlin Univ., also custodian of the Royal Coll. of Mus. Instrs., and teacher of history at the Hochschule für Musik; pub. a study of neumes, 1895, etc. (3) **Fleischer-Edel** (ā′-děl), **Katharina**, Mülheim, Sept. 27, 1873—Dresden, July 17, 1928; soprano; studied with Iffert; sang at court-opera, Dresden.

Flem′ming, Fr. Fd., Neuhausen, Saxony, 1778—Berlin, 1813; c. pop. "Integer vitæ," etc.

Flesch, Carl, Moson, Hungary, Oct. 9, 1873—Lausanne, Nov. 15, 1944; pupil Grün at Vienna, and Marsick at Paris Cons.; in 1897–1902 prof. at Bucharest Cons.; and chamber violinist to Roumanian queen; 1903-8, teacher at Amsterdam Cons.

1925 at Curtis Inst., Phila.; later taught in Baden-Baden, London, etc.; author of vln. method.

Fleta (flä'-tä), **Miguel**, Albalete, 1897—Corunna, 1938; Spanish tenor; studied Barcelona Cons.; sang Met. Op. 1923-4, also widely in Europe.

Floridia (flō-rēd'-yä), (**Baron Napolino**), Modica, Sicily, March 5, 1860—New York, Aug. 16, 1932; pianist, pupil of S. Pietro a Majello, Naples; while there he pub. succ. pf.-pcs.; prod. succ. comic opera *"Carlotta Clepier"* (Naples, 1882), retired for 3 years to Sicily; toured 1885-86; 1888-90, prof. of pf. Palermo Cons.; 1889, his symphony won 1st prize of the Soc. del Quartetto, Milan; w. text and music of succ. opera *"Maruzza"* (Venice, 1894). He came to America in 1904, was for a year piano-prof. at Cincinnati Cons., and was commissioned to write the opera *"Paoletta,"* for the Exposition of 1910; after 1913 he lived in N. Y. where he cond. Italian Symph.; c. (with Luigi Illica) *"La Colonia Libera," "Festouvertüre,"* opera *"The Scarlet Letter," "Madrigal"* for barytone and orch., songs, etc.

Florimo (flō'-rĭ-mō), **Fran.**, San Giorgio Morgeto, Calabria, 1800—Naples, 1888; writer, teacher, and composer.

Flo'rio, Caryl, pen-name of **Wm. Jas. Robjohn.**

Flotow (flō'-tō), **Friedrich**, Freiherr von, Teutendorf, Mecklenburg, April 27, 1812—Darmstadt, Jan. 24, 1883; composer of 2 extremely popular and melodious, also extremely light, operas; son of a landed nobleman; studied composition with Reicha, Paris; he fled from the July Revolution to Mecklenburg, where he c. 2 operettas; returning to Paris, he prod. *"Séraphine,"* 1836, *"Rob Roy,"* and the succ. *"Le Naufrage de la Méduse,"* 1839 (given Hamburg, 1845, as *"Die Matrosen"*), in which he collaborated with Paloti and Grisan; 3 later works failed, incl. the ballet *"Lady Harriet"* (Opéra, 1843); afterwards rewritten with great succ. as *"Martha"* (Vienna, 1847). *"Alessandro Stradella"* (Hamburg, 1844; rewritten from a "pièce lyrique," *"Stradella,"* Paris, 1837), made his name in Germany. He fled from the March Revolution (1848), and prod. *"Die Gross-fürstin"* (Berlin, 1853), and *"Indra"* (Berlin Opera,

1850); 3 later works failed. 1856-63, he was intendant of court-music, Schwerin, and c. a "Torch-Dance" and excellent music to Shakespeare's *"Winter's Tale";* 1863-68, he prod. 2 operettas, 2 operas, and 2 ballets, without succ.; 1868, he retired to one of his estates, near Vienna, made visits to Vienna, Paris, Italy; 1870, *"L'Ombre"* (Paris, Op. Com., 1870; prod. in London, 1878, as the *"Phantom"*) was very succ.; *"Naïda"* (Milan, 1873) and *"Il Fior d' Harlem"* (Turin, 1876) were revisions, and he rewrote *"Indra"* as *"l' Enchanteresse"* (Paris and London, 1878); Italy, *"Alma l'Incancatrice";* Germany *"Die Hexe";* after his death *"Rosellana," "Der Graf Saint-Mégrin"* (Cologne, 1884), and *"Die Musikanten"* (Hanover, 1887) were produced.

Flügel (flü'-gĕl), (1) **Gustav**, Nienburg-on-Saale, July 2, 1812—Stettin, 1900; cantor, organist, writer, and composer. (2) **Ernest Paul**, Stettin, Aug. 31, 1844—Breslau, Oct. 20, 1912; son and pupil of above; studied at the R. Inst. for Church-music, and the Akademie, Berlin; private pupil of von Bülow; 1867, organist and teacher at the Prenzlau Gymnasium; in 1879, cantor, Breslau, and founded a singing soc.; 1901, gained title of professor; writer and composer.

Fo'dor, (1) **Jos.**, Venloo, 1752—1828, violinist and composer. (2) **Josephine,** b. Paris, 1793; soprano; retired, 1833; daughter of above; m. the actor Mainvielle.

Foerster (fĕr'-shtĕr), **Ad. Martin,** Pittsburgh, Pa., Feb. 2, 1854—Aug. 10, 1927; American composer; pupil of his mother and of Leipzig Cons.; 1875-76, teacher at Ft. Wayne (Ind.), Cons., then Pittsburgh as a teacher of singing and pf.; c. orch., chamber music, choruses, songs, etc.

Fogg, Eric, b. Feb. 21, 1903 at Manchester—London, Sept. 4, 1941; studied with his father (a well-known organist) and Bantock; c. orch., chamber, piano music, songs, etc.

Foggia (fôd'-jä), **Fran.**, Rome, 1605-1688, composer and conductor.

Fogliani (fōl-yä'-nē), (1) **Ludovico,** Modena, ca. 1490—ca. 1559, theorist and composer. (2) **Giacomo,** Modena, 1473—April 4, 1548; brother of **Ludovico F.,** organist and comp.

Földesy (fŭl'-dĕ-shē), **Arnold**, b. Budapest, Dec. 20, 1882; 'cellist, succ. in London, 1902; son of a military bandman at Budapest; pupil of Popper.

Fo'ley ("Signor Foli"), **Allan Jas.**, Cahir, Tipperary, Ireland, 1835—Southport, England, Oct. 20, 1899; concert and operatic bass.

Folville (fôl-vē'-yŭ), **(Eugénie Émilie) Juliette**, b. Liége, Jan. 5, 1870; —d. 1946; pianist, violinist; teacher; conductor and composer; pupil of her father, a distinguished lawyer; studied vln. with Malherbes, Musin, and César Thomson; in 1879, début at Liége as concert-violinist; frequently directed her own orchestral works; annually conducted at Liége Cons. a concert of ancient music, and gave clavecin-recitals; prod. 1893, succ. opera *"Atala"* (Lille, 1892; Rouen, 1893); 1898, pf. prof. at Liége Cons.; c. orchestral suites: *"Scènes champêtres, de la mer, d'hiver,"* etc.

Fontana (fôn-tä'-nä), **Giov. Bat.**, d. Brescia, 1630; composer.

Foote, **Arthur Wm.**, Salem, Mass., March 5, 1853—Boston, April 9, 1937; composer; pupil of B. J. Lang (pf.), S. A. Emery, and J. K. Paine (comp.) 1875, A. M. Harvard (for mus.); 1878–1910, organist of the first Unitarian Ch., Boston; pub. overture, *"In the Mountains,"* symphonic prologue, *"Francesca da Rimini,"* 'cello concerto; orch. suite and choral works, *"Farewell of Hiawatha,"* *"The Wreck of the Hesperus,"* and *"The Skeleton in Armour"*; pf.-quintet, quartet in C; pf.-trio in C min.; sonata for pf., and vln.; 2 string-quartets; pcs. for vln. and 'cello; orch. suite in D minor (played in Boston, London, N. Y., etc.) Suite for strings (do.); 4 character pieces for orch. (Thomas Orch., Boston Symph., 1912, etc.) "Bedouin Song," male chorus sung very widely; organ suite in D (played by Guilmant on American tour); two piano suites, 5 poems from Omar Khayyám for piano, songs, etc.

Forchhammer (fôrkh'-häm-mĕr), **Th.**, Schiers, Gray Cantons, July 29, 1847—Magdeburg, Aug. 1, 1923; pupil of Stuttgart Cons.; 1885, organist at Magdeburg Cath.; 1888 Royal Mus. Dir.; writer and composer.

Ford, **Thos.**, England, ca. 1580—1648; composer and writer.

For'kel, **Jn. Nikolaus**, Meeder, near Coburg, 1749—Göttingen, 1818; historian, organist, harpist, and teacher. Wrote biography of Bach, 1803.

For'mes, (1) **K. Jos.**, Mülheim-on-Rhine, 1816—San Francisco, 1889; operabass. (2) **Theodor**, Mülheim, 1826—Endenich, near Bonn, 1874; tenor, bro. of above.

Fornari (fôr-nä'-rē), **V.**, Naples, May 11, 1848—Aug., 1900; pupil of Sira (pf.) and Battista (comp.); c. operas, *"Maria di Torre"* (Naples, 1872), *"Salammbo,"* *"Zuma"* (Naples, 1881), and 1-act opera-seria *"U Dramma in Vendemmia"* (Florence, 1896), succ.

Fornia, **Rita** (**P. Newman**), San Francisco, July 17, 1879—Paris, Oct. 27, 1922; soprano; pupil of Jean de Reszké and Frau Kempner; début, 1901, Hamburg Stadttheater; sang at Covent Garden and Met. Op., N. Y.

Forsell', **John**, b. Stockholm, Nov. 6, 1868—Sept. 4, 1941; barytone; studied at Cons. in native city with Günther; mem. R. Op. there, also guest appearances in Paris, Berlin, and (1909–10) at Met. Op., N. Y., a notable exponent of Mozart rôles; also known as concert singer; after 1913 he was dir. of the Stockholm Op.

Forster (fôr'-shtĕr), **G.**, (1) Amberg (?) —Nürnberg, 1568; editor and coll. (2) **G.** (II), d. Dresden, 1587; double-bass; conductor. (3) **Nikolaus** (called **Fortius**), 1499—1535; contrapuntist. (4) (or **Förster**) **Kaspar**, Danzig, 1617—1673; composer, theorist and conductor. (5) **Wm.** (Sr.), Brampton, Cumberland, 1739 —London, 1808; vln.-maker; his son and successor was (6), **Wm.**, London, 1764—1824.

För'ster (fĕr'-shtĕr), (1) v. FORSTER (4). (2) **Chr.**, Bebra, Thuringia, 1693—Rudolstadt, 1745; organist, conductor and composer. (3) **Emanuel Aloys**, Neurath, Austrian Silesia, 1748—Vienna, 1823; theorist and composer. (4) **Jos.**, Osojnitz, Bohemia, Feb. 22, 1833—Prague, Jan. 3, 1907; noted organist in various churches; since 1887, Prague Cath.; prof. of theory, Prague Cons.; c. masses and requiems, org.-pcs;

wrote a treatise on harmony. (5)
Vide FOERSTER. (6) **Alban,** Reichenbach, Saxony, Oct. 23, 1849—Neustrelitz, Jan. 18, 1916; violinist; pupil R. Blume, later of Dresden Cons.; leader at Carlsbad, Breslau, Stettin; 1871, court mus., and cond. Neustrelitz, 1881, teacher in Dresden. (7) **Josef B.,** b. Prague, Sept. 30, 1859; son of (4); pupil of Prague Cons.; c. 5 operas, 2 symphonies, chamber mus.; d. Prague, 1951.

Fortlage (fôrt'-lä-gě), **K.,** Osnabruck, 1806—Jena, 1881; writer.

Förtsch (fěrtsh), **Jn. Ph.,** Wertheim, Franconia, 1652—Eutin, 1732; conductor, singer, and dram. composer.

Fos'ter, (1) **Stephen Collins,** Lawrenceville (Pittsburgh), Pa., July 4, 1826—New York, Jan. 13, 1864; chiefly self-taught as flageolet-player and composer; a writer of words and music of genuine American folk-song; he enjoyed enormous vogue, receiving $500 for the privilege of singing "Old Folks at Home" (or "Suwanee River"); died poor in the Bowery; c. 160 songs, incl. "My Old Kentucky Home," "Nellie Was a Lady," and many war-songs; his melody, though simple, was rarely banal and has elements of immortality. (2) **(Myles) Birket,** London, Nov. 29, 1851—Dec. 18, 1922; organist and composer; pupil of Hamilton Clarke, and at R. A. M. of Sullivan, Prout, and Westlake; 1873–74, organist at Haweis' Church; 1880–92, at the Foundling Hospital; then mus.-ed. for Boosey & Co.; c. 2 Evening Services; symphony, "*Isle of Arran*"; overtures, etc. (3) **Muriel,** Sunderland, Nov. 22, 1877—London, Dec. 23, 1937; contralto of remarkable range, g to b' ' flat; pupil of Anna Williams at the R. A. M., winning a scholarship, 1897; début 1896 in oratorio; sang with her sister Hilda in 1899; and at festivals; also in Germany, Russia and America.

Foulds, John, b. Manchester, Nov. 2, 1880—Calcutta, April, 1939; conductor; early played in Hallé Orch.; after 1921, dir. of Univ. of London Mus. Soc.; c. stage music, orch. and piano works.

Fourdrain (foor'-drăn), **Félix,** Paris, Feb. 3, 1880—Oct. 23, 1923; composer; studied with Widor at Cons., organist in several Paris churches; made esp. succ. with his lighter

operatic works; c (stage **works)** "*La Grippe*"; "*Echo*" (1906); "*La Légende de Point d'Argentan*" (1907); also heard in America at Ravinia Op.; "*La Glaneuse*" (1909); "*Vercingétorix*" (1912); "*Madame Roland*" (1913); "*Les Contes de Perrault*" (1913); well known for his art-songs.

Fournier (foorn-yā), (1) **P. Simon,** Paris, 1712—1768; introducer of round-headed notes, and writer on history of music-types. (2) **Émile Eugène Alex.,** Paris, 1864—Joinville-le-Pont, 1897; pupil of Délibes and Dubois at Cons.; 1891 took 2d Grand prix de Rome, and 1892 Prix Cressent; for 1-act opera "*Stratonice*". (Gr. Opéra, Paris, 1892); c. opera "*Carloman*," etc.

Fox, Félix, b. Breslau, Germany, May 25, 1876; pianist, pedagogue; brought to Boston as a child; studied there, in N. Y., and after 1892 at Leipzig with Reinecke and Jadassohn, also with Philipp in Paris; début, Leipzig, 1896; Paris in 1897; same year returned to U. S., giving concerts; and in 1898 (with Carlo Buonamici) founded school of piano in Boston that continued under his own name for more than three decades; officier of French Académie; d. Boston, 1947.

Fox-Strang'ways, Arthur Henry, Norwich, England, Sept. 14, 1859; d. 1948; critic, writer on music; studied Wellington Coll., and Balliol, Oxford, also at Berlin Hochsch.; dir. of music, Wellington Coll., 1893–1901; visited India and wrote "*The Music of Hindustan*"; in 1920 he founded the quarterly periodical, "*Music and Letters*"; was critic of London "*Times*" after 1911 and co-editor of the London "*Mercury*."

Fragerolle (frä-zhě-růl), **Georges Auguste,** Paris, March 11, 1855—Feb. 21, 1920; pupil of Guiraud; c. patriotic songs, operettas, pantomimes, etc.

Framery (frăm-rē), **Nicolas Ét.,** 1745—Paris, 1810; writer.

Fran'çaix, Jean, b. Mans, May 23, 1912; composer.

Francescatti (frän-chĕs-kät'-tē), **Zino,** Fr., violinist; U. S. début, 1939.

Franchetti (frän-kĕt'-tē), (1) **Alberto** (Baron); b. Turin, 1860, pupil, Munich Cons.; 1926, dir. of Cherubini Cons., Florence; prod. "dram. legend" "*Asraële*" (Brescia, 1888); opera

"Cristoforo Colombo" (Genoa, 1892),
"Fior d'Alpe" (Milan, 1894), *"Il
Signor di Pourceaugnac"* (Milan,
1897), all succ.; his opera *"Germania"*
(prod. Milan, 1902) has been per-
formed widely, at Covent Garden
1907 and 1911 at the Metropolitan
Opera House, N. Y.; also *"La
Figlia di Jorio"* (1906), *"Notte di
Leggenda"* (1914); (with Giordano)
"Giove a Pompei" (1921); *"Glauco"*
(1922), etc.; d. Viareggio, 1942.

Franchinus (frän-kē'-noos). Vide
GAFORIO.

Franchi-Verney (frän'-kē-věr'-nā), **Giu.
Ip.,** Conte della Valetta; Turin,
Feb. 17, 1848—Rome, May 15, 1911;
1874 gave up law for music; 1875–77
under the pen-name "Ippolito Valetta" contributed to various papers;
1889, m. Teresina Tua; c. succ.
lyric sketch *"Il Valdese"* (Turin,
1885), and succ. ballet, *"Il Mulatto"*
(Naples, 1896).

Franchomme (frän-shŭm), **Auguste,**
Lille, April 10, 1808—Paris, Jan.
21, 1884; 'cellist; teacher at the
Cons. and composer.

Franck (fränk), (1) **Melchior,** Zittau,
ca. 1573—Coburg, June 1, 1639;
from 1603 court-cond. at Coburg;
a prolific and important c. of secular
and church-music, a pioneer in improving instrumental accompaniment; two of his chorales *"Jerusalem,
das hochgebaute Stadt,"* and *"Wenn
ich Todesnöthen bin,"* are still sung;
he is said to have written the text for
many hymns. (2) **Jn. W.,** Hamburg,
1641—London, ca. 1696; opera-
cond.; c. 14 operas. (3) (frän),
César Auguste, Liége, Dec. 10, 1822
—Paris, Nov. 8, 1890; important and
influential Belgian composer; pupil
Liége Cons., then of Paris Cons.,
where he took 1st prize for piano,
and 2d for comp., after succeeding
his organ-teacher, Benoist, as prof.
there in 1872, and as organist at
Ste. Clothilde; c. a notable symph.
poem with chorus *"Les béatitudes,"*
symph. poems *"Le chasseur mau-
dit," "Psyché"* and *"Les Eolides"*;
a universally popular symphony in
D minor, a succ. com. opera *"Hulda"*
(Monte Carlo, 1894), 2 oratorios, an
unfinished opera *"Ghisella,"* a sonata
for pf. and vln.; quintet for piano
and strings; pf.-pcs.; organ-music,
songs, etc.; biog. by Derepas (Paris,
'97), Destranges, the superb volume

of Vincent d'Indy, one of the best
estimates; and other studies by
Coquard, Meyer, Garnier, Balden-
sperger, Canudo, Van den Borren,
Séré, de Rudder, etc.
A peculiarly lovable figure in music,
F. has gained a great discipleship
since his death both among musicians
and the general public. His modesty and nobility of soul were allied
with a highly original musical equipment, in which the sensuous and
mystical elements are balanced by a
strong sense of form. He entirely
revolutionised the pattern of French
instrumental music by reviving the
polyphony which had long ceased
to be a prominent factor in it; his
harmonic modulations were also
much freer than those previously
in vogue in France. Through his
disciple, d'Indy, he set in motion a
whole school of "Franckists," who
were opposed in aim to the extreme
modernists who took their start from
Debussy. These two tendencies are
still warring in French music. (See
article, page 496.) (4) **Eduard,** Breslau, 1817—Berlin, 1893; professor
and composer. (5) **Jos.,** Liége, 1820
—Paris, 1891; bro. of (3); organist
and teacher, Paris; pub. *"Ode to
St. Cecilia"* (with orch.); cantatas,
etc.

Franck'enstein, Clemens, Freiherr
von, Wiesentheid, Lower Franconia,
July 14, 1875—Munich, Aug., 1942;
impresario; pupil of Thuille, also
of Knorr at Hoch Cons.; visited
America; cond. in London, 1902–07;
then in Wiesbaden and Berlin;
1912–18 and 1924–34, general intendant at Munich Op.; c. (operas)
*"Griseldis," "Rahab," "Fortunatus,"
"Li-Tai-Pe"* (the last with succ. in
Hamburg and Munich); also orch.,
chamber music, songs.

Fran'co, a name honoured in mensural
music and probably belonging to two,
perhaps three, men: (1) **F.** of **Paris**
(the *elder*), cond. at Nôtre-Dame,
Paris, ca. 1100 (?) A.D.; and (2) **F.**
of **Cologne,** Dortmund and prior of
the Benedictine Abbey at Cologne
in 1190, author of 2 treatises.

Francœur (frän-kŭr), (1) **François,**
Paris, 1698—1787; violinist and
dram. composer. (2) **Louis Jos.,**
Paris, 1738—1804; nephew of above;
violinist, conductor and dram. composer.

Frank (1) **Melchior.** Vide FRANCK.
(2) **Ernst,** Munich, 1847—(insane), Oberdöbling, near Vienna, 1889; court-organist and dram. composer.

Frankenberger (fränk'-ĕn-bĕrkh-ĕr), **H.**, Wümbach, Schwarzburg-Sondershausen, 1824—Sondershausen, 1885; conductor, violinist, and dram. composer.

Frank'lin, Benj., Boston, Mass., 1706—Philadelphia, 1790; the eminent philosopher; inv. the harmonica (v. D. D.), and wrote wittily on Scotch and contemporary music, etc.

Frank'o, (1) **Sam,** New Orleans, Jan. 20, 1857—New York, May 6, 1937; violinist; pupil of Wilhelmj, Joachim and Vieuxtemps; toured with Patti; cond. concerts of ancient music in New York; 1912, Berlin; arr. music for orch., etc. (2) **Nahan,** New Orleans, July 23, 1861—Amityville, L. I., June 7, 1930; violinist and cond.; at 8, toured the world with Patti; later studied with Rappoldi, De Ahna, Wilhelmj, and Joachim; member of Met. Op. orchestra, N. Y.; from 1883 concertmaster; 1905–07 conductor; later cond. his own orchestra.

Franz (fränts), (1) **K.,** Langenbielau, Silesia, 1738—Munich, 1802; virtuoso on the waldhorn, and the baryton. (2) **J. H.,** pen-name of Count B. von Hochberg. (3) **Robt.,** Halle, June 28, 1815—Oct. 24, 1892; 1847, changed his family-name **Knauth,** by royal permission; long opposed by his parents, he finished his musical studies 1835–37, under Fr. Schneider, Dessau; returned to Halle, and spent six years studying Bach, etc.; 1843, his first album of 12 songs appeared, and was cordially rec'd. by Liszt and Mendelssohn and by Schumann, who wrote about him in his periodical. He became organist at the Ulrichskirche, and later cond. of the Singakademie, and mus. dir. at Halle Univ., which made him Mus. Doc., 1861. In 1868, deafness attacked him, and nervous disorders prevented his writing further. His distress was relieved by the receipt of $25,000, from a series of concerts organised 1872, in Germany, by Helene Magnus, Joachim, Liszt, and in America, by Dresel, Schlesinger, and B. J. Lang. His wife (4) **Marie** (née **Hinrichs,** 1828–91) pub. many excellent songs.

His supplementing of the old musical shorthand of Bach and Händel, by full scores with modern instrumentation has been of invaluable service. He also pub. essays and "open letters" to Hanslick on Bach and Händel. He pub. 257 songs; the 117th Psalm, for double chorus a cappella; Kyrie for soli and 4-part chorus, a cappella, a liturgy for 6 chorals, 6 part-songs for mixed chorus, and 6 do. for male chorus. Biog. sketches, by Ambros, Liszt, Dr. W. Waldmann (Leipzig, 1895), Schuster, La Mara, Prochazka, Golther, Bethge, etc.

Fränzl (frĕnts'l), (1) **Ignaz,** Mannheim, 1736—1811; violinist, conductor and composer. (2) **Fd.,** Schwetzingen, Palatinate, 1770—Mannheim, 1833; son and pupil of above; conductor and dram. composer.

Fraschini (fräs-kē'-nē), **Gaetano,** Pavia, 1815—Naples, May 24, 1887; tenor in Italy and England.

Freccia (frā'-chǐ-ä), **Massimo,** b. Florence; cond. N. Orleans Symph., 1946.

Frederick II. (the Great), of Prussia; Berlin, 1712—Potsdam, 1786; flute-player and composer of remarkable skill—for a king.

Frédérix (frā-dā-rēx), **Gv.,** Liége, 1834 —Brussels, 1894; critic.

Freer, Eleanor Everest, b. Philadelphia, May 14, 1864; composer; pupil of Marchesi and Godard; theory with Ziehn; c. operas, incl. "The Court Jester" and "The Legend of the Piper" (Amer. Op. Co., 1928–29); d. Chi., Dec. 13, 1942.

Frege (frā'-gĕ), **Livia** (née **Gerhard),** Gera, June 13, 1818—Leipzig, Aug. 22, 1891; singer; pupil of Pohlenz; début at 15 with Clara Wieck, who was then 13, at the Gewandhaus, Leipzig.

Freiberg (frī'-bĕrkh), **Otto,** Naumburg, April 26, 1846—Göttingen, Nov. 2, 1926; studied, Leipzig Cons.; from 1865, violinist in court-orch., Carlsruhe; studied with V. Lachner; became mus. dir. Marburg Univ.; 1887, mus. dir. and prof. Göttingen.

Fremstad (frĕm'-stät), **Olive,** Stockholm, 1872—d. N. Y., April 21, 1951; dramatic soprano; at 9, a pianist; brought to America by her parents, at 12; 1890, soloist at St. Patrick's Cathedral, N. Y.; 1893–94, pupil of Lilli Lehmann at Berlin; 1895, début; 1896 sang at Bayreuth;

1897-1900, Vienna Royal Opera; later at Munich, Covent Garden and 1903-14 at Met. Op. House, N. Y.; officer of the French Academy, and 1907 of Public Instruction. One of the most notable Isoldes of her generation, and a fine dram. artist, whose powers were superbly schooled. She toured as a concert singer, but for some years has lived in retirement; 1906, m. Edson Sutphen; 1916, Harry L. Brainard.

Frère (frăr), **Marguerite Jeanne** (called **Hatto**), b. Lyons, Jan. 30, 1879; soprano; pupil of the Cons., took 2 opera prizes, 1899; début Opéra, 1899; created "Floria" in Saint-Saëns' *"Les Barbares"*; sang at Monte Carlo, etc.

Freschi (frĕs'-kē), **Giov. Dom.**, Vicenza, 1640—1690; conductor and dram. composer.

Frescobaldi (frĕs-kō-bäl'-dē), **Girolamo**, Ferrara, 1583—(buried) Rome, March 2, 1644; the greatest organist of his time, a revolutionist in harmony and important developer of fugue and notation; he was so famous that 30,000 people attended his first performance as organist of St. Peter's, Rome (1610, or -14); pupil of Luzzacchi; organist at Mechlin probably 1607; c. org.-pcs., fugues, double-choir church-music, etc.; biog. by Haberl.

Freudenberg (froi'-dĕn-bĕrkh), **Wm.**, Raubacher Hütte, Prussia, March 11, 1838—Schweidnitz, May 22, 1928; studied in Leipzig; th.-cond. in various places; 1865, cond. of the Cecilia Singing Society, and the Synagogenverein, Wiesbaden; 1870, founded a Cons., and till 1886, cond. the Singakademie; later opera-cond. at Augsburg and (1889) Ratisbon; 1895, choir dir. at Gedächtniskirche, Berlin; c. many operas, chiefly comic; symph. poem, etc.

Frezzolini (frĕd-zō-lē'-nē), **Erminia**, Orvieto, 1818—Paris, 1884; soprano; début, 1838.

Friberth (frī'bĕrt), **K.**, Wullersdorf, Lower Austria, 1736—Vienna, 1816, tenor; conductor.

Frick (or **Frike**) (frĭk, or frē'-kĕ), **Ph. Jos.**, near Würzburg, 1740—London, 1798; organist and composer.

Frick'er, Herbert Austin, b. Canterbury, England, Feb. 12, 1868; con-

ductor and organist; studied at Canterbury Cath. School, and lived in Leeds, 1898-1917, serving as civic org. and choral dir. at the fests. there; founded Leeds Orch. and led Mendelssohn Choir, Toronto, Canada, where d. Nov. 11, 1943.

Fricsay (frēk'-sī), **Ferenc**, Hungarian cond., RIAS Orch., Berlin; after 1954 of Houston, Tex., Symph.

Friderici (or **Friederich**), **Daniel,** Eisleben (?) before 1600—after 1654; cantor at Rostock; c. madrigals, etc.

Fried (frēt), **Oskar**, b. Berlin, Aug. 10, 1871; pupil of Humperdinck; since 1904 director Stern Gesangverein and the Gesellschaft der Musikfreunde; later guest cond. in England, Russia and of N. Y. Symph., 1926; c. choral works with orch., double fugue for strings; a work for 13 wind instruments and two harps, etc.; d. 1949.

Friedberg (frēd'-bĕrkh), **Carl**, b. Bingen-on-Rhine, Germany, Sept. 18, 1872; pianist; pupil of Clara Schumann and James Kwast; début with Vienna Philh. Orch., 1892; has appeared widely with leading orchestras in Europe and America, and as recitalist; has taught at Juilliard School of Music, N. Y., and as head of piano dept., Inst. of Music. Art.

Friedenthal (frē'-dĕn-täl), **Albert,** Bromberg, Sept. 25, 1862—Batavia, Jan. 17, 1921; pianist; pupil of Fr. and W. Steinbrunn, and of Kullak; toured the world.

Friedheim (frēt'-hīm), **Arthur**, St. Petersburg, Oct. 26, 1859—New York, Oct. 19, 1932; pianist and conductor; pupil of Rubinstein one year, and of Liszt, 8 years; spent many years in America as teacher and pianist; prof. at R. C. M., Manchester, England, till 1904; c. opera *"Die Tänzerin"* (Cologne, 1905); also pf. pieces and arrangements.

Friedländer (frēt'-lĕnt-ĕr), **Max.,** Brieg, Silesia, Oct. 12, 1852—Berlin, May 2, 1934; concert-bass and editor; pupil of Manuel Garcia and Stockhausen; début, 1880, London; 1881-83, Frankfort; since in Berlin; 1882, Dr. Phil. h. c. (Breslau); 1894, prof., Berlin Univ.; lectured at Harvard, 1911; LL.D., Univ. of Wis.; wrote works on Schubert, and discovered more than 100 of that composer's songs which were previously unknown; with Bolte and

Meier made valuable collection of German folk-songs.

Friedman (frēt'-män), Ignaz, b. Podgorze, near Cracow, Feb. 14, 1882, pianist, pupil of his father and of Leschetizky; toured with success; c. piano pieces and songs. One of most notable piano virtuosi, esp. in Chopin; d. Sydney, Jan. 26, 1948.

Frike. Vide FRICK.

Friml, Rudolf, b. Prague, Dec. 2, 1879; composer; studied Prague Cons.; in 1901–06 toured with Kubelik; since latter year has lived in N. Y.; best known for a number of tuneful and musicianly light operas, among which are *"The Firefly," "High Jinks," "Katinka," "Rose Marie," "The Vagabond King"* and others, some of which have had internat'l. popularity; also piano concerto, and pieces for orch., piano, vln., 'cello, songs.

Frimmel (frĭm'-mĕl), Th., Amstetten, Lower Austria, Dec. 15, 1853— Vienna, Dec. 27, 1928; M. D. (Vienna); writer.

Fris'kin, James, b. Glasgow, Mar. 3, 1886; pianist; pupil of London R. C. M., winning scholarship in 1900 and composition scholarship 1905; member of faculty Inst. of Musical Art, New York; active as recitalist; c. piano quintet in C minor, 'cello sonata, etc.

Fritzsch (frĭtsh), Ernst Wm., Lützen, Aug. 24, 1840—Leipzig, Aug. 14, 1902; pupil Leipzig Cons.; acquired the music-pub. business of Bomnitz in Leipzig; 1870, ed. the radical *"Musikalisches Wochenblatt,"* and 1875 started the *"Musikalische Hausblätter"*; a member of the Gewandhaus Orch.; pub. the works of Wagner, Grieg, etc.

Froberger (frō'-bĕrkh-ĕr), Jn. Jakob, 1605 (?)—Héricourt, France, May 7, 1667; chief German organist of the 17th cent.; son of a cantor at Halle; studied in Rome with Fresco-baldi; court organist at Vienna; travelled, and in England, being robbed, became a bellows-treader; he overblew during Chas. II's marriage and was beaten by the organist Gibbons; he fell to improvising shortly after, and was recognised by a pupil who presented him to the king.

Frö(h)lich (frā-lĭkh), (1) Jos., Würzburg, 1780—1862; musical director; writer and dram. composer. (2) The name of three sisters b. Vienna,

(a) Nanette (Anna), 1793—1880, pianist, teacher, and singer. (b) Barbara, 1797—1879; contralto and painter, m. F. Bogner. (c) Josephine, 1803—1878, notable singer and teacher.

Fromm (frôm), Emil, Spremberg, Niederlausitz, Jan. 29, 1835—Flensburg, Dec. 12, 1916; pupil of R. Inst. for Church-music, Berlin; 1866, Royal Mus. Dir.; 1869, organist and conductor at Flensburg; c. 2 Passion cantatas, an oratorio, etc.

Frontini (frôn-tē'-nē), F. Paolo, b. Catania, Aug. 6, 1860; pupil of P. Platania, and Lauro Rossi; dir. Catania Mus. Inst.; c. succ. opera *"Malia"* (Bologna, 1893); oratorio *"Sansone"* (1882), etc.

Frost, (1) Chas. Jos., Westbury-on-Tyne, Engl., June 20, 1848—London, 1918; son and pupil of an organist at Tewkesbury, also pupil of Cooper, Goss, and Steggall; organist various churches; 1882, Mus. Doc. Cantab.; 1880 prof. of organ Guildhall Sch. of Mus.; c. oratorio, *"Nathan's Parable"* (1878); a symphony, etc. (2) H. Fr., London, March 15, 1848—June, 1901; studied organ with Seb Hart; 1865–91, organist of the Chapel Royal, Savoy; 1880–88, pf.-prof. Guildhall Sch. of Mus.; from 1877 critic of *"The Academy,"* later of *"The Athenæum,"* and *"The Standard"*; pub. biog. of Schubert, and the *"Savoy Hymn-tunes and Chants."*

Frugatta (froo-gät'-tä), Giu., Bergamo, May 26, 1860—Milan, May 30, 1933; pianist; pupil of Bazzini (comp.) and Andreoli (pf.) at Milan Cons.; prof. there; also at the "Collegio reale delle Fanciulle"; composer.

Fruytiers (froi'-tĕrs), Jan., Flemish composer at Antwerp 16th century.

Fry, Wm. H., Philadelphia, 1813—Santa Cruz, 1864; dram. composer; critic N. Y. *Tribune.*

Fuchs (fookhs), (1) G. Fr., Mayence, 1752—Paris, 1821; clarinettist and bandm. (2) Aloys, Raase, Austrian Silesia, 1799—Vienna, 1853; collector and writer. (3) K. Dorius Jn., Potsdam, Oct. 22, 1838—Danzig, Aug. 24, 1922; pupil of his father and v. Bülow, Weitzmann and Kiel; Dr. phil., Greifswald; 1871–75, concert pianist, teacher and critic, Berlin; 1875–79, Hirschberg; 1879, Danzig; '86, organist at the Petrikirche, there. Pub. numerous valuable musical treatises. (4) **Jn. Nepomuk,** Frauenthal, Styria, May 5, 1842—Vienna, Oct. 5, 1899; from 1893, dir. of Vienna Cons.; dir. and dram. composer. (5) **Robt.,** Frauenthal, Feb. 15, 1847—Vienna, Feb. 19, 1927; bro. of above; 1875—1912, prof. theory at Vienna Cons.; pub. 3 symphonies, serenades, etc.; prod. succ. "Spieloper" "*Die Teufelsglocke*" (Leipzig, 1893) and the succ. com. opera "*Die Königsbraut*" (Vienna, 1889). (6) **Albert,** Basel, Aug. 6, 1858—Dresden, Feb. 15, 1910; pupil of Leipzig Cons.; 1880, mus. dir. at Trier; 1889, owner and manager Wiesbaden Cons.; comp.

Füchs (füks), **Fd. K.,** Vienna, 1811—1848; dram. composer.

Fuenllana (fwĕn-lĭ-än'-nä), **Miguel de,** flourished 1554 in Spain; lute-virtuoso and court composer; blind from birth.

Fuentes (foo-än'-tĕs), **Don Pasquale,** b. Albayda, Valencia, d. there 1768; conductor and composer.

Fuertes, M. S. Vide SORIANO.

Fugère (fü-zhăr), **Lucien,** Paris, March 3, 1848—July 15, 1935; barytone; pupil of Raguenau; début, 1870; sang for many years with notable succ. at Paris Op. and Op.-Comique; occasionally made operatic appearances when over 80.

Führer (fü'-rĕr), **Robt.,** Prague, 1807—Vienna, Nov., 1861; organ-composer.

Fuhrmann (foor'-män), (1) **G. Ld.,** wrote work on the lute, Nürnberg, 1615. (2) **Martin H.,** 1669—after 1740; theorist and writer.

Fuller-Maitland. Vide MAITLAND.

Fumagalli (foo-mä-gäl'-lē), name of four bros. b. at Inzago, Italy: (1) **Disma,** 1826—Milan, 1893; professor and composer. (2) **Adolfo,** 1828—Florence, May 3, 1856; pianist. (3) **Polibio,** Nov. 2, 1830—Milan, June 21. 1901; pianist and composer. (4) **Luca,** Inzago, May 29, 1837—Milan, June 5, 1908; pupil Milan Cons.; concert-pianist; prod. opera "*Luigi XI*" (Florence, 1875).

Fumi (foo'-mē), **Vinceslao,** Montepulciano, Tuscany, 1823—Florence, 1880; conductor, violinist, dram. composer and collector.

Furlanetto (foor-lä-nĕt'-tō), **Bonaventura** (called **Musin**), Venice, 1738—1817; singing-teacher, conductor and composer.

Furno (foor'-nō), **Giov.,** Capua, 1748

—Naples, 1837; professor and dram. composer.

Fursch-Madi (foorsh'-mä-dē), **Emmy,** Bayonne, France, 1847—Warrenville, N. J., Sept. 20, 1894; pupil of Paris Cons., début, Paris; came to America, 1874, with the New Orleans French Opera Company; 1879-81, Covent Garden, London; her final appearance was as "Ortrud," N. Y., 1894.

Fürstenau (fürsht'-ĕ-now), (1) **Kaspar,** Münster, Westphalia, 1772—Oldenburg, 1819; flute-virtuoso; composer. (2) **Anton B.,** Münster, 1792—Dresden, 1852; son and pupil of above; flutist and composer. (3) **Moritz,** Dresden, 1824—1889; son and pupil of (2); flutist and writer.

Fürstner (fürsht'-nĕr), **Ad.,** Berlin, 1833—Bad Nauheim, 1908; founded (1868) notable mus.-pub. house, Berlin.

Furtwängler (foort'-väng-lĕr), **Wilhelm,** b. Berlin, Jan. 25, 1886; conductor; pupil of Beer-Walbrunn, Rheinberger and Schillings; following early engagements as cond. in Zurich, Strasbourg, Lübeck, etc., succeeded Bodanzky at Mannheim Op., 1915; Vienna Tonkünstler Orch., 1919; Berlin Op. and symph. concerts, after 1920; cond. Museum Concerts, Frankfort; Leipzig Gewandhaus, after 1922; N. Y. Philh. Orch., 1925-26; Berlin Philh. Orch.. incl. tours to other countries with this organisation; Berlin State Op., also several seasons at Bayreuth; guest cond. at Vienna Op. and with Philh. Orch.; nominated to succeed Toscanini as cond. N. Y. Philh., 1936, but cancelled engagement owing to controversy among subscribers of this orch. as to his political and racial sympathies; has at times enjoyed the highest honours from the Nat'l. Socialist regime in Germany, incl. vice-presidency of Reich Music Chamber, as well as virtual dictator of music in Berlin, at other times has either resigned or been relieved of his posts; one of these instances occurred in 1934 following a stand which he took in championing the music of Paul Hindemith, outlawed by German Ministry of Culture and Propaganda as showing traits of "cultural Bolshevism"; later restored to his orchestral and operatic baton posts; appointed mus. dir. of Vienna Philh. Orchestra, 1950.

Fux (foox), **Jn. Jos.,** Hirtenfeld, Upper Styria, 1660—Vienna, Feb. 14, 1741; eminent theorist, organist, and court-conductor and writer; c. 405 works (few pub.), incl. 18 operas, 10 oratorios, 50 masses, incl. *missa canonica.* He wrote the famous treatise on cpt. *"Gradus ad Parnassum"* in dialogue form; it is based on the church-modes. Biogr. by Köchel (Vienna, 1872).

G

Gabler (gäp'-lĕr), **Jn.,** d. ca. 1784; organ builder at Ulm.

Gabriel (1) (gä'-brĭ-ĕl), **Mary Ann Virginia,** Banstead, Surrey, Engl., 1825—London, 1877; c. cantatas, operas, etc. (2) (gä'-brĭ-ĕl), **Max,** b. Elbing, 1861; 1890, cond. Residenz Th., Hanover; later in America, then at Rembrandt Theatre, Amsterdam; prod. succ. operettas.

Gabrieli (gä-brĭ-ä'-lē), (1) **Andrea,** Venice, ca. 1510—1586; eminent organist and teacher and composer of the first "real" fugues (v. D. D.). (2) **Giov.,** Venice, 1558—Aug. 12, 1613 (acc. to his monument); nephew and pupil of above, and equally famous; an extraordinary contrapuntist, his "symphoniæ sacræ" employing 3 simultaneous choirs independently handled; he has been called "the father of the chromatic style" because of his bold modulations. (3) **Dom.** (called "Menghino del violoncello"), Bologna, ca. 1640—ca. 1690; 'cellist, conductor, and composer.

Gabrielli (gä-brĭ-ĕl'-lē), (1) **Catterina,** Rome, Nov. 12, 1730—April, 1796; daughter of Prince G.'s cook (and hence called "La Cochetta," or "Cochettina"); one of the most beautiful and brilliant of singers; her extraordinarily flexible voice had a "thrilling quality" (Burney); her caprices and her high-handed treatment of the nobility and royalty enamoured of her make her a most picturesque figure; she sang with greatest succ. all over Europe and retired wealthy. Her sister (2) **Francesca** (called "La Gabriellina," or "La Ferrarese"), Ferrara, 1755—Venice, 1795, was a celebrated prima donna buffa. (3) Conte **Nicolo,** Naples, 1814—1891; prod. 22 operas and 60 ballets.

Gabriels'ki, (1) **Jn. Wm.,** Berlin, 1791—1846; flutist and composer. (2) **Julius,** Berlin, 1806—1878; bro. and pupil of above; flutist.

Gabrilowitsch (gä-brē-lō'-vĭtsh), **Ossip,** St. Petersburg, Jan. 26, 1878—Detroit, Mich., Sept. 14, 1936; eminent pianist and conductor; studied at the Cons. with Glazounoff, Liadoff and Rubinstein; at 16 took the Rubinstein prize; studied with Leschetizky at Vienna, 1894–96; 1896 began touring with success; 1900, America. He was resident in Munich for the most part between 1904 and 1914, and cond. the Konzertverein concerts there, 1910–14. From 1907 he also led orch. programmes in N. Y. Between 1912 and 1916 he gave a series of historical piano recitals in Eur. cities and U. S., illustrating growth of the concerto. He was appointed cond. of the Detroit Symph. Orch. in 1918, a post which he filled with distinction until 1935. He also served as one of the leaders of the Phila. Orch. for several seasons and appeared as guest with other orchs. in this country. A notable ensemble perf. as well as one of the most brilliant and scholarly soloists. He m. Clara Clemens, daughter of "Mark Twain," a mezzo-soprano. C. *"Overture-Rhapsody"* for orch.; *"Elegy"* for 'cello; piano pieces, songs, etc.

Gabussi (gä-bōos'-sē), **V.,** Bologna, 1800—London, 1846; teacher and composer.

Gade (gä'-dĕ), **Niels Wm.,** Copenhagen, Feb. 22, 1817—Dec. 21, 1890; son of an instr.-maker; at 15 refused to learn his father's trade, and became pupil of Wexschall (vln.) Berggreen (theory); at 16 a concert-violinist. His overture, *"Nachklänge von Ossian,"* took first prize at the Copenhagen Mus. Soc. competition (1841) and won for him a royal stipend. In 1842 the C min. symphony, and 1846 the cantata *"Comala,"* were prod. by Mendelssohn at the Gewandhaus. He travelled in Italy; then, 1844, lived in Leipzig as sub-cond. to Mendelssohn, and regular cond. at his death (1847); 1848, he returned to Copenhagen as cond. of the Mus. Soc. and as organist; 1861, court-cond., made Prof. by the King, and Dr. Phil. *h. c.* by the Univ.; 1886, Commander in the

Order of Danebrog; 1876 the govt. voted him a life-pension. Autobiog. *"Aufzeichnungen und Briefe"* (Basel, 1893). Pub. 7 symphonies (D minor, No. 5 with pf.); 4 overtures, *"Nachklänge von Ossian,"* *"Im Hochlande,"* *"Hamlet,"* *"Michelangelo,"* octet, sextet, and quartet for strings; 7 cantatas, *"Elverskind"* (Erl-King's Daughter),*"Frühlingsbotschaft,"* *"Die Heilige Nacht,"* *"Zion,"* *"Kalanus,"* *"Die Kreuzfahrer,"* *"Psyche,"* etc.; 2 vln.-concertos; pf. sonata and pcs., songs, etc.

Gads'by, H. Robt., Hackney, London, Dec. 15, 1842—Putney, Nov. 11, 1907; pupil of Wm. Bayley, but mainly self-taught; organist at St. Peter's, Brockley; 1884, prof. of harm. Queen's Coll., London; also at Guildhall Sch. of Mus.; c. *"Festival Service"*; 3 symphonies; 3 overtures, *"Andromeda,"* *"The Golden Legend,"* and *"The Witches' Frolic,"* etc.

Gad'ski, Johanna, Anclam, Prussia, June 15, 1871—Berlin, Feb. 23, 1932 (in automobile accident); notable soprano, educated at Stettin; 1892, m. H. Tauscher; sang in U. S. A. for many years, 1899 Covent Garden and as "Eva" (*Meistersinger*) at Bayreuth. She was a leading member of the Met. Op. Co., in Wagnerian rôles, from 1898 to 1917, also appearing widely in concerts. During the war she was accused of anti-American activities and retired to Berlin. She was again heard in the United States as leading singer with the Wagnerian Op. Co. in two tours, 1930 and 1931. A large and freely produced voice of striking dram. timbre and much dignity of stage deportment marked her interpretations of a great variety of rôles, including "Senta" and "Brünnhilde."

Gaforio (gä-fō'-rǐ-ō) (or **Gafori, Gafuri, Gaffurio**), **Franchino** (Latinised "Franchinus Gafurius," or "Franchinus"), Lodi, Jan. 14, 1451—Milan, June 24, 1522; priest, eminent theorist, choirmaster and singer.

Gagliano (gäl-yä'-nō), (1) **Marco di Zanobi da,** b. Florence; d. there, Feb. 24, 1642; conductor and composer. (2) A family of Naples vln.-makers, (a) **Alessandro,** pupil of Stradivari, worked ca. 1695—1725. His sons, (b) **Nicolò** (1700-40), and (c) **Gennaro** (1710-50), and his grandson, (d) **Ferdinando** (1736-81)

succeeded him; later descendants est. factory of strings, still famous.

Gährich (gä'-rǐkh), **Wenzel,** Zerchowitz, Bohemia, 1794—Berlin, 1864; violinist, ballet-master, and dram. composer.

Gaïl (gä-ēl), **Edmée Sophia** (née **Garre**), Paris, Aug. 28, 1775—July 24, 1819; singer and dram. composer.

Gailhard (gī'-yăr), **Pierre,** Toulouse, Aug. 1, 1848—Paris, Oct. 12, 1918; bass; pupil Paris Cons.; début, 1867, Op. Com., Paris; later at the Opéra, of which he was director 1899-1907.

Gál, Hans, b. Brünn, Austria, Aug. 5, 1890; composer; Ph.D., Univ. of Vienna; pupil of Mandyczewski and Robert; c. (operas) *"Der Arzt der Sobeide"* (Breslau, 1919); *"Die Heilige Ente"* (Düsseldorf, 1923); *"Das Lied der Nacht"* (Breslau, 1926); also orchestral and chamber music, choruses; won Austrian State Prize, 1915, for his 1st symphony; after 1918 lecturer in counterpoint, harmony and musical form at Univ. of Vienna.

Galeazzi (gä-lä-äd'-zē), **Fran.,** Turin, 1758—Rome, 1819; violinist.

Galeffi (gä-lä'-fē), **Carlo,** b. Rome; barytone; début in *"Aïda"* at Rome, 1907; created rôle of Gianni Schicchi in Puccini's opera at Costanzi Theat.; has also sung in other Eur. countries, and North and South America.

Gal'eotti, Cesare, b. Pietrasanta, June 5, 1872; c. operas *"Anton"* (La Scala, Milan, 1900) and *"La Dorise"* (1910), etc.; d. Paris, Feb. 19, 1929.

Galilei (gä-lǐ-lä'-ē), **V.,** Florence, ca. 1533—1591; lutenist, violinist and theorist; father of the astronomer.

Galin (gä-lăn), **P.,** Samatan Gers, France, 1786—Bordeaux, 1821; wrote pop. method *"Meloplaste"* (v. D. D.).

Galitzin (gä-lē'-tshēn), (1) **Nicolas Borissovitch,** 1794—1866; a Russian prince, to whom Beethoven dedicated an overture, and 3 quartets; he advanced Beethoven liberal sums for his dedications; a skilful 'cellist. (2) **G.** (Prince), St. Petersburg, 1823 —1872; son of above; composer and cond.; maintained in Moscow (1842) a choir of 70 boys; later an orchestra.

Gal'kin, Nikolai Vladimirovich, St. Petersburg, Dec. 6, 1856—May 21, 1906; violinist and composer for violin; pupil of Kaminsky, Auer, Joachim, Sauret and Wieniawski;

toured Europe and after 1877 was cond. in St. Petersburg and from 1880 teacher at the Cons.; from 1892, prof.

Gall, (1) **Jan,** Warsaw, Aug. 18, 1856 —Lemberg, Oct. 30, 1912; pupil of Krenn and Rheinberger 1886, teacher of song at Cracow Cons. then pupil of Mme. Lamperti, director of the Lemberg *"Echo"* society; composer of some 400 vocal numbers. (2) **Yvonne,** b. Paris, March 6, 1885; soprano; studied Paris Cons., début as "Marguerite," Paris Op.; has also sung with Op.-Comique, and widely in various Eur. countries and America; several seasons with Ravinia Op. Co., after 1927; also as recitalist in U. S.

Gallay (găl-lĕ), (1) **Jacques Fran.,** Perpignan, 1795—Paris, 1864; horn-virtuoso and composer. (2) **Jules,** Saint-Quentin, 1822—Paris, 1897; amateur 'cellist of wealth; made researches and pub. valuable treatises.

Gallenberg (găl'-lĕn-bĕrkh), **Wenzel Robt.,** Graf **von,** Vienna, 1783— Rome, 1839; c. ballets.

Gallet'ti-Gianoli (jä-nō'-lē), **Isabella,** Bologna, Nov. 11, 1835—Milan, Aug. 31, 1901; operatic soprano; later contralto.

Gal'li, Filippo, Rome, 1783—Paris, June 3, 1853; first most successful as a tenor; illness changed his voice, and he achieved great success as a bass.

Galli-Curci, Amelita (äm-ä-lē'-tä gäl-lĭ-kōōrt'-chē), b. Milan, Nov. 18, 1889; coloratura soprano; studied piano, Milan Cons., in voice largely self-taught; début as "Gilda," "Costanzi," Rome, 1910; sang in various Eur. theatres and in South America; American début with Chicago Op., with sensational success, as "Gilda," 1916; member of this company until 1924; Met. Op., N. Y., 1921–30; many concert tours in U. S., Great Britain, Australia and Orient; m. Homer Samuels, pianist-composer.

Gal'lia. Vide ÉPINE.

Galliard (găl'-lĭ-ärt), **Jn. Ernst,** Celle, Hanover, 1687—London, 1749; oboist and organist.

Gal'lico, Paolo, b. Trieste, May 13, 1868; at 15 gave a pf.-recital at Trieste; then studied Vienna Cons. with Julius Epstein; at 18 graduating with first prize and "Gesellschafts" medal: toured Europe; 1892

pianist and teacher, New York; his oratorio, *"The Apocalypse,"* won Nat'l. Fed. of Mus. Clubs prize, 1921; c. operettas, pf.-pieces, songs, etc.

Gallic'ulus, Jns., contrapuntist at Leipzig, 1520–48.

Galli-Marié (găl-lĭ măr-yä), **Celéstine** (née **Marie de l'Isle**), Paris, Nov., 1840—Nice, 1905; mezzo-soprano; daughter of an opera-singer; début Strassburg, 1859; sang Toulouse, 1860, Lisbon, 1861, Rouen, 1862; 1862–78, and 1883–85, Paris Opéra Comique; she created "Mignon" (1866), "Carmen" (1875), etc.

Gal'lus, (1) **Jacobus** (rightly **Jacob Händl, Handl** or **Hähnel**); Carniola, ca. 1550—Prague, 1591; composer and conductor. (2) **Jns. (Jean le Cocq, Maître Jean,** or **Mestre Jhan**), d. before 1543; a Dutch contrapuntist, conductor and composer. (3) Vide MEDERITSCH, JN.

Gal'ston, Gottfried, b. Vienna, Aug. 31, 1879—St. Louis, Apr. 2, 1950; studied Vienna Cons., piano with Leschetizky, theory with Jadassohn and Reinecke, Leipzig; toured Australia and (1913–14) U. S. as pianist; taught Stern Cons., Berlin, 1903–07, and again after 1921; also appeared in series of historical recitals and as orch. soloist in leading capitals, incl. Russia; later active as pedagogue in America; author of *"Studienbuch."*

Galuppi (gä-loop'-pĭ), **Baldassare** (called **Il Buranello**), Island of Burano, near Venice, Oct. 18, 1706— Venice, Jan. 3, 1785; harpsichord virtuoso; organist 1765–68; conductor; c. 54 comic operas.

Gambale (gäm-bä'-lĕ), **Emm.,** music-teacher, Milan; pub. *"La riforma musicale"* (1840), etc., advocating a scale of 12 semitones.

Gambini (gäm-bē'-nē), **Carlo Andrea,** Genoa, 1819—1865; c. operas, etc.

Gamucci (gä-moot'-chē), **Baldassare,** Florence, 1822—1892; pianist and writer.

Ganassi (gä-näs'-sē), **Silvestro,** b. Fontego, near Venice, ca. 1500 (called "del Fontego"); editor and writer on graces.

Gand (gän), **Ch. Nicolas Eugène,** ca. 1826—Boulogne-sur-Seine, 1892; vln.-maker. V. LUPOT.

Gandini (gän-dē'-nē), (1) **A.,** Modena, 1786—Formigine, 1842; conductor and dram. composer. (2) **Alessan-**

dro, Modena, ca. 1807—1871; son, pupil (1842) and successor of above; dram. composer and writer.

Ganne (găn), **L.** Gaston, Buxières-les-Mines, Allier, April 5, 1862—Paris, July 14, 1923; pupil of Dubois and Franck, Paris Cons.; cond. at Monte Carlo; c. comic opera *"Rabelais"* (1892), vaudeville, operetta, ballets, etc.

Gänsbacher (gĕns'-bäkh-ĕr), **Jn.**, Sterzing, Tyrol, 1778—Vienna, 1844; conductor and composer.

Ganz (gänts), (1) **Ad.**, Mayence, 1796 —London, 1870; violinist and cond.; his 2 brothers were, (2) **Moritz,** Mayence, 1806—Berlin, 1868; 'cellist; (3) **Ld.**, Mayence, 1810—Berlin, 1869; violinist and composer; Adolf's 2 sons were, (4) **Eduard,** Mayence, 1827—1869; pianist. (5) **Wilhelm,** Mayence, Nov. 6, 1833—London, Sept. 12, 1914; pianist, professor, conductor. (6) **Rudolph,** b. Zürich, Feb. 24, 1877; début at 10 as 'cellist, at 12 as pianist; then pupil of his uncle, Eschmann-Dumur, and later of Busoni; début as pianist and composer Berlin, 1899; 1901–05 succeeded Friedheim in Chicago; has toured widely; cond. St. Louis Symph., 1921–27; also guest cond. in New York Stadium series, Hollywood Bowl, in Los Angeles, San Francisco, Denver, etc.; after 1929, dir. of Chicago Mus. Coll. and of modern music soc. in that city; c. orch., piano music, songs; mem. Legion of Honour.

Garat (gä-rä), **P. J.,** Ustaritz, Basses-Pyrénées, April 25, 1764—Paris, March 1, 1823; most remarkable French singer of his time, a barytone of great compass and amazing memory and mimicry; professor and composer.

Garaudé (gär-ō-dä), **Alexis de,** Nancy, 1779—Paris, 1852; professor, composer and writer.

Garbou'sova, Raya, b. Tiflis, 1909; 'cellist; grad. State Cons. of Tiflis; pupil of Hugo Becker; début Moscow, 1923; has toured in European cities and America as orch. soloist and in recitals.

Garbrecht (gär'-brĕkht), **Fr. F. W.** (d. 1874), founded at Leipzig (1862) a music engraving establishment, owned since 1880 by Os. Brandstetter.

Garcia (gär-thē'-ä), a notable family of Spanish vocal teachers. (1) **Don Fran.** Saverio (Padre Garcia, called "lo Spagnoletto"), Nalda, Spain, 1731—Saragossa, 1809; conductor and composer. (2) **Manuel del Popolo Vicente,** Sevilla, Jan. 22, 1775 —Paris, June 2, 1832; eminent as tenor, teacher, and progenitor of singers; successful as manager, cond. and composer; took his family, his wife, son (3), and daughter (5) and others to America for a v. succ. opera season, 1825–26. Produced 43 operas and c. others. (3) **Manuel,** Madrid, March 17, 1805—London, July 1, 1906; son of above; bass (in Paris); he was a scientific investigator, and inv. the laryngoscope, receiving Dr. Phil. *h. c.* Königsberg Univ.; 1847, prof. at the Cons., 1850, London, R. A. M. Jenny Lind was one of his pupils; pub. *"Traité complet de l'art du chant,"* 1847. (4) **Eugènie** (née **Mayer**), Paris, 1818 —1880; wife and pupil of (3); soprano and teacher. (5) **M. Félicité,** v. MALIBRAN. (6) **Pauline,** v. VIARDOT GARCIA.

Garcin (gär-săṅ), **Jules Aug. Salomon,** Bourges, 1830—Paris, 1896; violinist, conductor and professor.

Gardano (gär-dä'-nō), (1) **A.** (till 1557 called himself **Gardane**), ca. 1500— Venice, 1571 (?); early Italian mus.-printer, succeeded by sons, (2) **Alessandro** and (3) **Angelo.**

Gar'den, Mary, b. Aberdeen, Feb. 20, 1877; notable soprano; as a child brought to America; pupil of Mrs. Duff; (1896) Paris with Trabadello and Fugère; début, 1900, Paris Op. Com.; has created various rôles there, including "Mélisande" in Debussy's *"Pelléas et Mélisande,"* 1902; sang at Covent Garden, 1902; leading singer with Manhattan Op. Co., N. Y., after 1907, in French rôles; 1910–30, one of the guiding artistic personalities in the Chicago Op. Co., of which she was also artistic dir., 1921–22. Sang in Amer. premières of many operas; an outstanding concert singer; in later years has taught, lectured.

Gar'diner, H. Balfour, b. London, Nov. 7, 1877—1950; pupil of Knorr, Frankfort; also studied with Uzielli, and 1895 at New Coll. Oxford; he was for a short time a singing teacher in Winchester, then for the most part devoting himself to composition; dir. of concert series in London, 1912–13, of modern English orch. and choral music; c. popular *"Shepherd Fennel's Dance"*; overture; Suite and Fantasy for orch.; Humoresque for small orch.; string quintet and quartet; piano pieces, songs, choral works, etc.

Gard'ner, Samuel, b. Elizabethgrad, Russia, 1892; violinist, composer; studied vln. with Winternitz and Kneisel, composition with Goetschius; début, N. Y., 1912; res. in U. S.; has appeared as soloist and guest cond. in his works with leading Amer. orchestras.

Gardo'ni, Italo, b. Parma, 1821; retired, 1874; operatic singer; d. 1882.

Garlan'dia, Johannes de, ca. 1210–32; French theorist.

Garnier (gărn-yā), **Fran. Jos.,** Lauris, Vaucluse, 1759–ca. 1825; oboist and composer.

Gar'rett, Geo. Mursell, Winchester, England, 1834—Cambridge, 1897; pianist, conductor, composer and lecturer.

Gar'rison, Mabel, b. Baltimore, Md.; coloratura soprano; studied Peabody Cons.; début as "Filina" in *"Mignon,"* Boston, 1912; sang with Met. Op. Co., N. Y., for 6 years after 1914; also as concert artist in U. S.; toured Orient; m. George Siemonn, conductor.

Gas'par van Weerbeke (vär'-bĕ-kĕ), b. Oudenarde, Flanders, ca. 1440; eminent contrapuntist and teacher.

Gaspari (gäs-pä'-rē), **Gaetano,** Bologna, 1807—1881; librarian, professor and composer.

Gasparini (or **Guasparini**) (gäs-pä-rē'-nĕ), (1) **Fran.,** Camaiore, near Lucca, 1668—Rome, 1727; director, conductor and theorist. (2) **Michelangelo,** Lucca, 1685—Venice, 1732; male contralto and dram. composer. (3) **Don Quirino,** 'cellist at Turin; 1749–70; conductor and composer.

Gasparo da Salo (gäs-pä'-rō dä sä'-lō) (family name **Bertolot'ti**), Salo, Brescia, Italy, ca. 1542—Brescia (?), 1609; famous maker of viols.

Gassier (gäs-yā), **L. Éd.,** France, 1822—Havana, 1871; barytone.

Gassmann (gäs'-män), **Florian L.,** Brux, Bohemia, 1723—Vienna, 1774; court-conductor and dram. composer.

Gass'ner, F. Simon, Vienna, 1798—Carlsruhe, 1851; violinist, teacher, editor and composer.

Gast, Peter. Vide KÖSELITZ.

Gastaldon (gäs-täl'-dōn), **Stanislas,** b. Turin, 1861—Florence, March, 1939; pub. nocturnes, *ballabili*, songs, etc., some of them v. pop.; c. succ. 1-act opera-seria, *"Il Pater"* (Milan, 1894).

Gastinel (gäs-tĭ-nĕl), **Léon G. Cyprien,** Villers, near Auxonne, Aug. 15, 1823—Paris, Nov., 1906; pupil of Halévy, Paris Cons.; took first Gr. prix de Rome with cantata *"Velasquez"*; prod. comic operas; ballet *"Le Rêve"* (Gr. Opera, 1890), etc.

Gastoldi (gäs-tōl'-dē), **Giov. Giacomo,** Caravaggio, ca. 1556—Milan (?), 1622; conductor, contrapuntist and composer.

Gastoué (gäs-too'ā), **Amadée,** b. Paris, March 13, 1873; writer; prof. of church music; d. Clamart, 1943.

Gatayes (gă-tĕz'), (1) **Guill. P. A.,** Paris, 1774—1846; guitar-player and composer. (2) **Jos. Léon,** Paris, 1805—1877; son of above; harpist, critic and composer. (3) **Félix,** b. Paris, 1809; bro. of above; pianist, chiefly self-taught; for 20 years toured Europe, America, Australia.

Gathy (gä-tē), **Aug.,** Liége, 1800—Paris, 1858; editor, teacher and composer.

Gat'ti, Guido M., b. Chieti, May 30, 1893; writer on music; ed. monthly pub., *"Il Pianoforte"* (Turin) which he founded 1920; also organized modern chamber music and orch. concerts in that city; author of many articles on music.

Gatti-Casazza (gät'-tĭ kä-sät'-sä), **Giulio,** Udine, Feb. 5, 1869—Ferrara, Sept. 2, 1940; operatic impresario; Naval engineer; 1894–08 dir. Municipal Theatre at Ferrara; 1898–1909, dir. La Scala, Milan; 1909 co-director with A. Dippel of the Metropolitan Opera House, N. Y.; 1910–35, in full charge; he gave a number of native American operas, and the first prods. anywhere of Humperdinck's *"Königskinder,"* and Puccini's *"Girl of the Golden West."*

Gat'ty, (1) **Sir Alfred Scott,** Ecclesfield, Yorks., April 25, 1847—London, 1919; 1880 Poursuivant of Arms, Heralds' Coll. London; c. operettas, many pop. songs, particularly in imitation of American Plantation songs, pf.-pieces. (2) **Nicholas Comyn,** b. Bradfield, Sept. 13, 1874; d. 1946; critic, organist and comp., pupil R. C. M., where he produced orch.-variations on *"Old King Cole"*; 1907-14, critic on *"Pall Mall Gazette"*; assistant at Covent Garden; c. 1-act operas *"Greysteel"* (Sheffield, 1906), and *"Duke or Devil"* (Manchester, 1909); Milton's *"Ode on Time,"* for chorus w. orch., (Sheffield Festival, 1905); operas *"Prince Ferelon"* (Old Vic, London, 1921); *"The Tempest"* (1920); *"Macbeth,"* etc.

Gaubert (gō-bär'), **Philippe,** b. Cahors, 1879; Paris, 1941; pupil at Paris Cons. of Taffanel; won 2 Rome prizes, 1905; 1919, chosen to succeed Messager as cond. of Société des Concerts du Conservatoire; after 1920, 1st cond. at Opéra; c. opera, ballets, chamber and orch. music.

Gaucquier (gōk-yā), **Alard** (rightly **Dunoyer** Latinized **Nuceus**), called du Gaucquier and **Insulanus** from Lille-l'isle, court-bandm. to Maximilian II.; famous 16th cent. contrapuntist.

Gaul (gôl), (1) **Alfred Robt.,** Norwich, England, April 30, 1837—Birmingham, Sept. 13, 1913; at 9 a cath. chorister articled to Dr. Buck; 1863, Mus. Bac. Contab.; 1887, cond. Walsall Philh.; later teacher and cond. at the Birmingham and Midland Inst., etc.; c. oratorio *"Hezekiah"*; cantatas, incl. *"Ruth"* and *"The Holy City,"* etc. (2) **Harvey Bartlett,** b. New York, April 11, 1881; organist and composer; pupil of LeJeune; later in Paris with Decaux and d'Indy at Schola Cantorum, with Widor and Guilmant; res. in Pittsburgh after 1910 as church org.; mem. faculty, Pittsburgh Inst.; critic on several newspapers of that city; c. choral, org. works; d. Dec. 1, 1945.

Gau(l)tier (gōt-yā), (1) **Jacques** (G. *d'Angleterre,* or *l'ancien*), Lyons, ca. 1600—Paris, ca. 1670; lutenist. (2) **Denis** (*le jeune,* or *l'illustré*), Marseilles, ca. 1610—Paris, 1672; cousin of above, and his partner in a lutenist school; famous lutenist and collector of lute-music.

Gaunt'lett, H. J., Wellington, Shropshire, 1805—London, 1876; organist and composer.

Gauthier (gōt-yā), (1) **Gabriel,** b. in Saône-et-Loire, France, 1808; became blind when 11 months old; was pupil and (1827-40) teacher Paris Inst. for the Blind, then organist of St. Étienne-du-Mont, Paris; pub. treatises. (2) **Eva,** b. Ottawa, Can.,

Sept. 20, 1886; soprano; studied with Bouhy, Shakespeare, Carigiani and Oxilla; début in Carmen, Pavia, Italy; sang rôle of "Yniold" in London première of *"Pelléas"*; best known as soloist and recitalist in programmes of modern music; active in U. S. for some years; made researches in Javanese and Malay folk-songs.

Gautier (gōt-yā), (1) V. GAULTIER. (2) **J. Fran. Eug.,** Vaugirard n. Paris, 1822—Paris, 1878; conductor and dram. composer.

Gaveaux (gă-vō), **P.,** Béziers, Hérault, Aug., 1761—insane, Paris, 1825; tenor; c. operas, incl. *"Leonore"* (1788), the same subject afterwards used in Beethoven's *"Fidelio."*

Gaviniès (gă-vēn-yĕs), **P.,** Bordeaux, 1726—Paris, 1800; violinist, professor and dram. composer.

Gavron'ski, Woitech, b. Seimony near Wilna, June 27, 1868; pupil Warsaw Mus. Inst.; toured Russia, taught in Orel and Warsaw; c. symph.; 2 operas and a string quartet (Paderewski prize, Leipzig, 1898); d. 1913.

Gay (gī), **Maria,** Barcelona, Sp., June 13, 1879—N. Y., July 29, 1943; contralto; 1st studied vln.; self-taught voice; sang at some of Pugno's concerts, and while in Brussels was heard by director of La Monnaie, where she made her début as "Carmen" in 1902 on five days' notice; studied with Madame Adiny in Paris; toured Europe; sang Covent Garden as "Carmen," 1906; Met. Op. Co. 1908-09; Boston Op. Co. 1910-12; 1913, Chicago Op. and later again Boston; m. Giovanni Zenatello, tenor.

Gayarré (gĕ-yär-rā'), **Julian,** Roncal, Jan. 9, 1844—Madrid, Jan. 2, 1890; operatic tenor, son of a blacksmith.

Gaztambide (gäth-täm-bē'-dhĕ), **Joaquin,** Tudela, Navarra, 1822—Madrid, 1870; composer, teacher and conductor.

Gazzaniga (gäd-zän-ē'-ga), **Giu.,** Verona, 1743—Crema, 1818; conductor and dram. composer.

Gear (gēr), **Geo. Fr.,** b. London, May 21, 1857; pianist; pupil of Dr. Wylde and J. F. Barnett; 1872 scholarship London Acad. of Mus., later prof. there; 1876-92 mus.-dir. German-Reed Company; composed scena for sopr. solo and orch.; d. (?).

Gebauer (zhŭ-bō-ā), (1) **Michel Jos.,** La Fère, Aisne, 1763—1812, on the retreat from Moscow; oboist, violinist and viol-player; also extraordinary virtuoso on the Jew's harp. He had 3 brothers, (2) **François Réné,** Versailles, 1773—Paris, 1844; bassoonist, prof., writer, and composer. (3) **P. Paul,** b. Versailles, 1775; died young, pub. 20 horn-duets. (4) **Et. Fran.,** Versailles, 1777 —Paris, 1823, flutist and composer. (5) (gĕ-bow'-ĕr), **Fz. X.,** Eckersdorf, near Glatz, 1784—Vienna, 1822; 'cellist, conductor, teacher and composer.

Gebel (gä'-bĕl), (1) **Georg** (Sr.), Breslau, 1685—1750; organist; inv. clavichord with quarter tones and clavicymbalum with pedal-keyboard; composer; he had 2 sons, (2) **Georg** (Jr.), Brieg, Silesia, 1709—Rudolstadt, 1753; son of above; conductor, organist and composer. (3) **Georg Sigismund,** d. 1775; organist and composer. (4) **Fz. X.,** Fürstenau, near Breslau, 1787—Moscow, 1843; conductor, pf.-teacher, and composer.

Gebhard (gĕp'-härt), **Heinrich,** b. Sobernheim, near Bingen, July 25, 1878; pianist; taken to America at 10; pupil of Clayton Johns, début, 1896, Boston, playing his violin and piano sonata, then studied with Leschetizky and Heuberger; 1899 reappeared Boston with symph. orch. 1900–04, pianist of Longy Club; c. quartet, piano pieces, etc.

Gebhar'di, **Ludwig Ernst,** Nottleben, Thuringia, 1787—Erfurt, 1862; organist, composer and teacher.

Gédalge (zhä-dälzh), **André,** Paris, Dec. 27, 1856—Feb. 26, 1926; pupil of Guiraud at the Cons.; took 2nd Grand prix de Rome, 1885; prof. of theory at Paris Cons. for many years, his pupils including Ravel, Milhaud, Honegger, Florent Schmitt and many others who attained eminence; wrote notable treatise on fugue; lyric drama "*Hélène*"; pantomime "*Le Petit Savoyard*" (Paris, 1891); a succ. 1-act opera-bouffe "*Pris au Piège*" (Paris, 1895); 2 symphonies, etc.

Gehring (gā'-rĭng), **F.,** 1838—Penzing, near Vienna, 1884; writer.

Gehr'kens, **Karl Wilson;** b. Kelleys Island, O., April 19, 1882; educator; A. M., Oberlin Coll. and Cons., prof. at this inst., author of many works on music; has served as pres. of Music Supervisors Nat'l. Conference and Music Teachers Nat'l. Ass'n.,

ed. of School Music, periodical ol latter organization.

Gehrmann (gär'-män), **Hermann,** Wernigerode, Dec. 22, 1861—Cassel, July 8, 1916; historian and theorist: pupil Stern Cons., Berlin; 1908, Royal Proi.; c. string-quartet and songs.

Geíringer, **Karl,** b. Vienna, 1899; musicologist; later in U. S.; biog. of Haydn, etc.

Geisler (gīs'-lĕr), (1) **Jn. G.,** d. Zittau, 1827; writer. (2) **Paul,** Stolp, Pomerania, Aug. 10, 1856—Posen, April 3, 1919; grandson and pupil of a mus.-dir. at Mecklenburg; studied also with K. Decker; 1881–82 chorusm. Leipzig City Th., then with Neumann's Wagner Co.; 1883–85 at Bremen (under Seidl); then lived in Leipzig; prod. 5 operas; c 12 symphonic poems, incl. "*Der Rattenfänger von Hameln,*" "*Till Eulenspiegel,*" etc.

Geistinger (gīs'-tĭng-ĕr), **Maria** ("**Marie**") **Charlotte Cäcilia,** Graz, Styria, July 26, 1836—Rastenfield, Sept. 29, 1903; soprano; sang at Vienna Op., 1865–75; in U. S., 1897–99.

Gelinek (gā'-lĭ-nĕk), (1) **Hn. Anton** (called **Cervetti**), Horzeniowecs, Bohemia, 1709—Milan, 1779; ex-priest, violinist and composer. (2) **Joseph,** Abbé; Selcz, Bohemia, 1758—Vienna, 1825; teacher and composer.

Geminiani (jĕm-ē-nĭ-ä'-nē), **Fran.,** Lucca, 1687—Dublin, Dec. 17, 1762; brilliant and original violinist of great importance in English progress, author of the first vln. method pub. (1740), c. concerti, sonatas, etc.

Gemünder (gĕ-münt'-ĕr), **Aug. Martin,** Würtemberg, March 22, 1814—New York, Sept. 7, 1895; a maker whose vlns. were of the very highest perfection; his sons succeeded him.

Genast (gĕ-näst'), **Ed.,** Weimar, 1797 —Wiesbaden, 1866; barytone and composer.

Genée (zhŭ-nā), **Franz Friedrich Richard,** Danzig, Feb. 7, 1823—Baden, near Vienna, June 15, 1895; pupil of Stalleknacht, Berlin; theatre conductor various cities; a student, then conductor and operatic composer; 1868–78 at Th. an der Wien, Vienna; wrote libretti for many of his own works and for Strauss and others; c. light operas with succ., incl. "*Der Geiger aus Tirol,*" "*Nanon,*" etc.

Generali (jä-nĕ-rä'-lē), **Pietro** (rightly

Mercandet'ti), Masserano, Piedmont, 1783—Novara, 1832; conductor and dram. composer.

Genet (zhŭ-nā), **Eleazar** (called **il Carpentras'so,** or **Carpentras** (kăr-pän-trăs)), Carpentras Vaucluse, ca. 1470 —Avignon, June 14, 1548; singer, then cond., then bishop; his admired masses, etc., were the first printed in round notes without ligature.

Genss (gĕns), **Hermann,** b. Tilsit, Jan. 6, 1856; pianist; pupil of the Royal Hochsch. für Mus., Berlin; teacher in various cities; 1893, co-dir. Scharwenka-Klindworth Cons., Berlin; after 1899 teacher in and 1905 dir. of Irving Inst., San Francisco, Cal.; c. orch. wks., etc.; d. (?).

Georges (zhôrzh), **Alex.,** Arras, France, Feb. 25, 1850—Paris, Jan. 19, 1938; pupil, later prof. of harm., Niedermeyer Sch., Paris; c. operas *"Le Printemps"* (1888) and *"Poèmes d'Amour"* (1892); *"Charlotte Corday"* (1901); 2 oratorios, a mystery *"La Passion"* (1902); symph. poem, songs, etc.

Gérard (zhā-răr), **H. P.,** Liége, 1763— Versailles, 1848; teacher and writer.

Gérardy (zhā-răr-dē), **Jean,** Spa, Belgium, Dec. 7, 1877—July 4, 1929; notable 'cellist; studied with Bellmann: a pupil of Grützmacher; played as a child in England; at 13 in Dresden; 1899, etc., toured America.

Ger'ber, (1) **H. Nikolaus,** Wenigen-Ehrich, near Sondershausen, 1702— Sondershausen, 1775; organist and composer. (2) **Ernst L.,** Sondershausen, 1746—1819; son, pupil and successor (1775) of above; 'cellist, organist, lexicographer and composer.

Gerbert (gĕr'-bĕrt), **(von Hornau) Martin,** Harb-on-Neckar, Aug. 12, 1720—St. Blaise, May 13, 1793; collector of the invaluable *"Scriptores ecclesiastici de musica sacra potissimum,"* noteworthy treatises of the Middle Ages, reproduced exactly (the compilation was continued by Coussemaker). The work is briefly referred to in this book as "Gerbert." He became in 1736 cond. at St. Blaise; when he died, the peasants erecting a statue to him; pub. also other very important works, and c. offertories, etc.

Ger'hardt, (1) **Paul,** b. Leipzig, Nov. 10. 1867; organ-virtuoso; pupil at the

Cons.; since 1898 org. at Zwickau; c. organ works, etc. (2) **Elena,** b. Leipzig, Nov. 11, 1883; soprano, esp. noted as a Lieder singer; pupil of cons. in native city, with Madame Hedmondt; after 1903 appeared in many recitals with Nikisch; sang at Leipzig Op., but gave up stage career for concert activity; has toured widely in Europe, England, and in America after 1912.

Gericke (gā'-rĭ-kĕ), **Wilhelm,** Graz, Styria, April 18, 1845—Vienna, Oct. 27, 1925; pupil of Dessoff, Vienna, Cons., then cond. at Linz; 1874, 2d. cond. Vienna ct.-opera (with Hans Richter); 1880, cond. of the "Gesellschaftsconcerte" (vice Brahms); also cond. the Singerverein; 1884–89, cond. Boston (Mass.) Symphony Orch., resuming the post 1898–1908, (vice Emil Paur) after being dir. "Gesellschaftsconcerte" at Vienna until 1895; pub. several choruses, pf.-pcs. and songs; also c. operetta *"Schön Hännchen"* (Linz, 1865); a Requiem; a concert-overture, etc.

Gerlach (gĕr'-läkh), (1) **Dietrich,** d. Nürnberg, 1574; music-printer, 1566– 1571. (2) **Theodor,** b. Dresden, June 25, 1861; pupil of Wüllner; at 22 prod. a notable cantata, *"Luther's Lob der Musica,"* 1884; Italy, 1885; cond. Sondershausen Th., then of German Opera in Posen; his *"Epic Symphony"* caused his appointment as ct.-cond. in Coburg, 1891; 1894, cond. at Cassel; then living in Dresden and Berlin; after 1904 dir. of a mus. school at Carlsruhe; c. succ. opera (book and music) *"Matteo Falcone"* (Hanover, '98, Berlin, 1902); orch. pieces, etc.

Gerle (gĕr'-lĕ), (1) **Konrad,** d. Nürnberg, 1521; lute-maker. (2) **Hans,** d. Nürnberg, 1570; probably son of above; violinist and vln.-maker.

Ger'man, Sir Edward (rightly **Jones),** Whitechurch, Feb. 17, 1862—London, Nov. 11, 1936; violin pupil of R. A. M.; 1889, dir. Globe Th., London; 1901 completed Arthur Sullivan's unfinished opera *"The Emerald Isle,"* prod. with succ. London, 1901; c. operas, 2 symphonies; various suites, including the "Gipsy" suite, chamber-music, songs, etc. His incidental music to Shakespeare's plays is especially notable, and much popularity has been won by his suites for *"Nell Gwynne"* and *"Henry VIII."* Knighted, 1928.

Germer (gĕr'-mĕr), **H.**, Sommersdorf, Province of Saxony, Dec. 30, 1837 —Dresden, Jan. 4, 1913; pupil Berlin Akademie; teacher, pianist and writer.

Gernsheim (gĕrns'-hīm), **Fr.**, Worms, July 17, 1839—Berlin, Sept. 11, 1916; of Hebrew parents; pupil of Rosenhain and Hauff, Frankfort, and Leipzig Cons.; 1865, teacher of comp. and pf. Cologne Cons.; 1872, Prof.; 1874, dir. of the Cons. at Rotterdam and cond. "Winter Concerts"; 1890 at Stern Cons., Berlin; c. 4 symphonies, overtures, etc.

Gero (gā'-rō), **Jhan** (**Johann**) (called **Maister Jan** or **Jehan**, or **Joannes Gallus**), conductor and composer at Orvieto Cath., 16th cent.

Gersh'win, George, Brooklyn, N. Y., Sept. 26, 1898—Hollywood, July 12, 1937; one of the most talented pioneers in the creation of music with jazz idiom as basis, incl. orchestral works on symph. scale; studied piano with Hambitzer, composition with Kilenyi and Rubin Goldmark; c. many pop. operettas and musical revues; came into internat'l. prominence with his *"Rhapsody in Blue,"* first heard at a Paul Whiteman concert in N. Y., a work written for piano and orchestra, exploiting jazz idiom treated in elaborate form; this work heard widely in U. S. and in Europe; also c. *"An American in Paris,"* symph. poem; piano concerto in F (latter commissioned by Walter Damrosch for N. Y. Symph. Orch.), and a Negro folk opera, *"Porgy and Bess,"* presented by N. Y. Theatre Guild, 1935. (See article, page 498.)

Gerster (gĕr'-shtĕr), **Etelka**, Kaschau, Hungary, June 16, 1857—near Bologna, Aug. 20, 1920; one of the most remarkable coloratura-sopranos of her time; 1874-75, a pupil of Marchesi, Vienna Cons.; v. succ. début Venice, Jan. 8, 1876; m. her impresario Dr. Carlo Gardini and toured Europe and America after 1878 until her retirement in 1890; lost her voice suddenly and opened (1896) a singing-school in Berlin.

Gervasoni (jĕr-vä-sō'-nē), **Carlo**, Milan, 1762-1819; writer and theorist.

Gerville-Réache (jĕr'-vēl-rä-äsh'), **Jeanne**, Orthez, France, 1882—New York, 1915; contralto; studied with Laborde, Madame Viardot-Garcia and Criticos; after 1900 sang at Paris Op.-Comique; 1902, Brussels; 1907-10, Manhattan Op. Co., New York; 1911-12, Chicago Op.; 1913-14, Gr. Op. of Canada.

Gervinus (gĕr-vē'-noos), **Georg Gf.**, Darmstadt, 1805—Heidelberg, 1871; professor and writer.

Geselschap (gĕ-zĕl'-shäp), **Marie, b.** Batavia, Java, Dec. 15, 1874; pianist; pupil of X. Scharwenka, Berlin; played in America, etc.; 1895 in London.

Gesius (rightly **Göss**) (gā'-sĭ-oos; gĕs), **Bartholomäus**, Müncheberg, ca. 1555 —Frankfort-on-Oder, 1613; cantor and composer.

Gesualdo (jä-zoo-äl'-dō), **Don Carlo,** Prince of Venosa, d. 1614; one of the most intellectual and progressive mus. of his time; wishing to revive the chromatic and enharmonic genera of the Greeks, he strayed out of the old church-modes and, becoming one of the "chromaticista," wrote almost in modern style.

Gevaërt (zhŭ-vărt'), **François Auguste**, Huysse, near Oudenarde, July 31, 1828—Brussels, Dec. 24, 1908; pupil of Sommère (pf.) and Mengal (comp.) at Ghent Cons., taking Gr. prix de Rome for comp.; 1843, organist at the Jesuit church; he prod. 2 operas; lived in Paris (1849-50); then went to Spain and c. *"Fantasia sobre motivos espanoles,"* still pop. there, for which he was given the order of Isabella la Catolica; he sent back reports on Spanish music (pub. by the Academy, 1851); he returned to Ghent 1852, prod. 9 operas, 2 of them, *"Georgette"* and *"Le billet de Marguerite,"* with much success; in 1857 his festival cantata *"De Nationale Verjaerdag"* brought him the Order of Leopold; 1867-70 chef de chant Gr. Opéra, Paris; 1871, dir. Brussels Cons. (vice Fétis); created a baron by Belgian Government, 1908; pub. colls. of Italian music, also the valuable fruits of much research in old plain-song. His *"Traité d'instrumentation"* (1863) revised as *"Nouveau traité,"* etc. (1885); he prod. also cantatas, *"Missa pro Defunctis"* and *"Super Flumina Babylonis"* for male chorus and orch.; overture *"Flandre au Lion,"* etc.

Geyer (gī-ĕr), **Flodoard**, Berlin, 1811
—1872; prof., critic, theorist and
dram. composer.

Gheyn (gĕn), **Matthias van den**, Tirle-
mont, Brabant, 1721 — Louvain,
1785; one of a Flemish family of bell
founders; organist. Of his 17 children his son **Jossé Thos.** (b. 1752)
was his successor as organist.

Ghione (gē-ō'-nä), **Franco**, Italian
cond., appointed to lead Detroit
Symph. Orch., 1937.

Ghiselin(g) (gē-zĕ-lŭng) (or **Ghiseli-
nus**), **Jean**, Netherlandish; contrapuntist 15–16th cent.

Ghislanzoni (gēs-län-tsō'-nē), **A.**, Lecca,
1824 — Caprino-Bergamasco, 1893;
barytone and writer; wrote more
than 60 opera librettos, incl. that of
"Aïda."

Ghizeghem. Vide HEYNE.

Ghizzolo (gēd'-zō-lō), **Gio.**, b. Brescia,
1560 (?); monk and composer.

Ghys (gēs), **Joseph**, Ghent, 1801—St.
Petersburg, 1848; violinist, teacher
and composer.

Giacomelli (jäk-ō-mĕl'lē), **Geminiano**,
Parma, 1686—Naples, 1743; dram.
composer.

Gianelli (jä-nĕl'-lē), **Pietro**, (Abbate)
Friuli, Italy, ca. 1770—Venice, 1822
(?); lexicographer.

Gianettini (jä-nĕt-tē'-nē) (or **Zanettini**), **A.**, Venice, 1649—Modena,
1721; dram. composer.

Giannini (1) **Dusolina** (dōōs-ō-lē'-nä
'jä-nē'-nē), b. Philadelphia, Dec. 19,
1902; soprano; studied with Marcella
Sembrich; début, New York, in concert, 1923; has appeared widely in
opera in Europe, including Hamburg,
Berlin, Paris, Budapest, also at
Covent Garden; Met. Op. Co., N. Y.,
début as "Aïda," 1935–36; has made
concert tours of U. S., Europe,
Australia, New Zealand; also sang in
opera at Salzburg Fest. (2) **Vittorio**, bro. of **Dusolina**; b. 1903,
Philadelphia; composer; studied composition with Rubin Goldmark; also
trained as violinist; c. (operas)
"Lucedia" (Munich, 1934), *"The
Scarlet Letter"*; *"Symphony in Memoriam T. Roosevelt"*; Requiem;
songs; awarded fellowship at Amer.
Acad. in Rome.

Gianotti (jä-nôt'-tē), **P.**, Lucca—Paris,
1765; double-bassist, composer and
writer.

Giarda (jär'-dä), **Luigi Stefano, b.**
Castelnuovo, Pavia, March 19, 1868;
'cellist; pupil Milan Cons.; teacher at
Padua, 1893–07; 1897–1920, at Royal
Cons., Naples; then at Santiago
Cons., vice-dir.; c. opera *"Reietto"*
(Naples, 1898), 'cello-music and
method.

Giardini (jär-dē'-nē), **Felice de**, Turin,
1716—Moscow, 1796; violinist and
dram. composer.

Gib'bons, (1) **Orlando**, Cambridge,
England, 1583—Canterbury, June 5,
1625; esteemed as one of the foremost of Engl. organists and composers; Mus. Doc. Oxon; 1604, organist Chapel Royal; 1623, organist
Westminster Abbey. (2) **Christopher**, London, 1615—Oct. 20, 1676;
son of (1), organist and composer.

Gibbs, **Cecil Armstrong**, b. Great
Baddow, Engl., Aug. 10, 1889; composer; studied at Winchester and
Trinity Coll., Cambridge, with Dent
and Wood; also with Vaughan Williams and Boult; teacher of composition and theory at R. Coll. of Mus.;
c. many orch., chamber music and
other works, in conservative style,
well constructed and imaginative.

Gibert (zhē-bär), **Paul César**, Versailles, 1717—Paris, 1787; dram.
composer.

Gibert (hē-bĕrt) (or **Gisbert, Gispert**),
Francisco Xavier, Granadella, Spain
—Madrid, 1848; priest. cond. and
composer.

Gide (zhēd), **Casimir**, Paris, 1804—
1868; composer.

Gieseking (gē-sĕ-kĕng), **Walter**, b.
Lyons, France, Nov. 5, 1895; German pianist; trained at Hanover
Cons., study with Karl Leimer;
début, 1920; has made many tours
of Germany, Switzerland and other
Eur. countries; Amer. début 1926;
a brilliant virtuoso, with reputation
as interpreter of modern music, particularly Debussy; c. quintet for
piano and wind instruments, piano
pieces, songs.

Gigli, **Beniamino** (bĕn-yä-mēn'-ō jēl-
yē), b. Recanati, Italy, March 20,
1890; operatic tenor; studied at
Rome Liceo di Santa Cecilia with
Cotogni and Enrico Rosati; début
as "Enzo," Rovigo, 1914; sang widely
in Italian opera houses, incl. Rome,
Naples, Milan, also in South America; Met. Op. Co., N. Y., début **in**

"Mefistofele," 1920; sang leading rôles with this co. until 1934; has also sung in London, Berlin and elsewhere, enjoying internat'l. reputation; concert tours in U. S. and Europe; Grand Ufficiale, Order of the Crown of Italy.

Gigout (zhē-goo). **Eugene,** Nancy, France, March 23, 1844—Paris, Dec. 9, 1925; organ-virtuoso, critic, etc.; pupil in the *maîtrise* of Nancy cath.; at 13 entered Niedermeyer Sch., Paris, and was later teacher there for over 20 years; studied also with Saint-Saëns; 1863, organist at the Ch. of St. Augustin; succ. concert organist throughout Europe; 1885, founded an organ-sch. subsidized by the govt.; commander of the order of Isabella la Catolica; 1885, officier of pub. instruction; 1895, Chev. of the Legion of Honour; pub. over 300 Gregorian and plain-song compositions.

Gil'bert (1) **Alfred,** Salisbury, Oct. 21, 1828—London, Feb. 6, 1902; organist and composer; his brother, (2) **Ernest Thos. Bennett,** Salisbury, Oct. 22, 1833—London, May 11, 1885; organist, teacher and composer. (3) **Walter Bond,** Exeter, April 21, 1829—Oxford, 1910; organist; pupil of Wesley and Bishop; 1886, Mus. Doc. Oxford; 1889, came to New York; c. oratorios, etc. (4) **Henry Franklin Belknap,** Somerville, Mass., Sept. 26, 1868—Cambridge, Mass., May 19, 1928; violin pupil of Mollenhauer; studied harmony with G. H. Howard and for 3 years with MacDowell; 1892–1901 in business, then took up composition. His work is full of originality and character; c. Comedy Overture on Negro Themes (Boston Symph., 1911); *Americanesque, Two Episodes, I, Legend; II, Negro Episode,* Boston (1896, and often elsewhere); *"Salammbo's Invocation to Tanith"* for soprano and orch. (1906); *"American Dances in Rag-Time"* for orch.; symph. poem, *"The Dance in Place Congo"*; for piano *"Indian Scenes," "Negro Episode,"* etc., many beautiful songs, including the well-known *"Pirate Song"*; also *"Negro Rhapsody"* (1913), and symph. prologue *"Riders to the Sea"* (1915). He lectured at Harvard and Columbia Univs.; his *"Place Congo"* was given as a ballet at Met. Op., 1918.

Gil'christ, W. Wallace, Jersey City, N. J., Jan. 8, 1846—Easton, Pa., Dec. 20, 1916; pupil of H. A. Clarke at the U. of Penn.; from 1877 organist and choirm. Christ Ch., Germantown; from 1882 teacher Phila. Mus. Acad.; cond. of orch. and choral societies; c. prize *Psalm xlvi.* for soli, chorus, orch. and org. (Cincinnati Festival, 1882), *"Song of Thanksgiving"* for chorus and orch.; a cantata *"The Rose,"* etc.

Giles (jīlz), **Nathaniel,** near Worcester, Engl., ca. 1550—Windsor, Jan. 24, 1633; organist; Mus. Doc. Oxon; writer and composer.

Gilibert (zhēl-ē-bār'), **Chas.,** Paris, 1866—New York, 1910; barytone; pupil of Paris Cons.; after about 1888 sang at Brussels; 1900–03, Met. Op Co.; 1906–10, Manhattan Op. Co.; was to have returned to Met. but died suddenly; an excellent song interpreter.

Gille (gĭl'-lĕ), **Karl,** Eldagsen, Hanover, Sept. 30, 1861—Hanover, June 14, 1917; pupil of J. Fischer, Bott and Metadorf; theatre-cond. in various cities; 1891–97 court cond., Schwerin; 1897 succeeded Mahler at Hamburg Stadttheater; 1906, first cond. Vienna Volksoper; after 1910 in Hanover.

Gilly (zhē-lē), **Dinh,** Algeria—London, May 19, 1940; barytone; Met. Op. 1909–14.

Gil'man, Lawrence, b. Flushing, N. Y., July 5, 1878—Franconia, N. H., Sept. 8, 1939; ed. Collins St. Classical School, Hartford, Conn.; self-trained in music; 1901–13, music critic for Harper's *Weekly*; after 1913, music and dram. critic, *The North American Review;* beginning 1923, music critic of N. Y. *Tribune* (later *Herald-Tribune*), succeeding the late H. E. Krehbiel; for some seasons he has written the annotations for the N. Y. Philh. Orch. programmes, in which he has shown distinguished literary and musical taste; author, *"Phases of Modern Music," "Edward MacDowell," "The Music of Tomorrow," "Guide to Strauss' Salome," "Stories of Symphonic Music," "Guide to Debussy's Pelléas et Mélisande"; "Aspects of Modern Music," "Life of Edward MacDowell," "Nature in Music,"* etc.; c. *"A Dream of Youth,"* etc.

Gil'more, Patrick Sarsfield, near Dublin, Dec. 25 1829—St. Louis, Mo.

DICTIONARY OF MUSICIANS 171

Sept. 24, 1892; an immensely popular conductor, some of whose influence went to the popularising of good music; on occasions he cond. an orch. of 1,000 and a chorus of 10,000, also an orch. of 2,000 and a chorus of 20,000, reinforced with cannon fired by electricity, an organ, anvils, chimes, etc. (cf. Sarti); he c. pop. military and dance music.

Gilson (zhēl-sōñ), **Paul,** b. Brussels, June 15, 1865; self-taught; his cantata *"Sinai"* won the Grand prix de Rome, 1892; 1896 prod. opera *"Alvar,"* Brussels; completed Ragghianti's opera *"Jean-Marie"*; 1904, teacher of harmony Antwerp Cons., and critic of the *"Soir"*; composed operas, *"Gens de mer,"* (based on Victor Hugo's novel, Brussels, 1902; Antwerp, 1904) and *"Prinses Zonnenschijn"* (Antwerp, 1903); ballet, *"La Captive,"* Brussels, 1902; symph. *"La Mer,"* 1892; orch. fantasy on Canadian folk-songs, symph. poems, etc.; d. Brussels, 1942.

Giner (hē-nār'), **Salvador,** Valencia, Jan. 17, 1832—Nov. 3, 1911; pupil of Gascons; dir. Valencia Cons.; c. a symph. *"The Four Seasons,"* operas, etc.

Ginguené (zhăñ-gŭ-nā), **P. L.,** Renne , 1748—Paris, 1816; writer.

Giordani (jôr-dä'-nē), name of a family, father, 3 sisters and 2 brothers, all singers in comic opera at Naples, till 1762 when they came to London (except Giuseppe); one of the brothers wrote the still pop. song *"Caro mio ben."* (1) **Tommaso** (rightly **Carmine**), Naples, ca. 1740—Dublin after 1816; dram. composer. (2) **Giuseppe** (called **Giordanel'lo**), Naples, 1744—Fermo, 1798; bro. of above; conductor; c. 30 operas.

Giordano (jôr-dä'-nō), **Umberto,** b. Foggia, Aug. 27, 1867; studied with Paolo Serrao at the Naples Cons.; c. operas; very succ. *"Andrea Chénier"* (La Scala, Milan, 1896; in Berlin, 1898, and U. S.); also *"Miranda,"* unsucc., *"Regina Diaz"* (Naples, 1894); and succ. 3-act melodrama *"Mala Vita"* (Rome, 1892, prod. as *"Il Voto,"* Milan, 1897); *"Fédora"* (Milan, 1898), *"Siberia,"* (do, 1903, Leipzig, 1907), and *"Marcella"* (Milan, 1907); *"Mme. Sans Gene"* (Met. Op., 1915); mus. comedy, *"Giove a Pompei"* (Rome, 1921); *"La Cena delle Beffe"* (La Scala,

1924, at Met. Op., 1926) and *"Il Re"* (1928); d. Milan, Nov. 12, 1948.

Giorgetti (jôr-jĕt-té), **Ferdinando,** Florence, 1796–1867; violinist, teacher and comp.

Giorgi (jôr'-jē). Vide BANTI.

Giorni (jôr'-nē), **Aurelio,** Perugia, Italy, Sept. 15, 1895, Pittsfield, Mass., Sept. 23, 1938; composer, pianist; studied St. Cecilia Acad., Rome, piano with Sgambati, composition with Humperdinck, piano with Busoni, Gabrilowitsch, Lhevinne and Da Motta; début as orch. soloist, Rome, 1912; appeared also in Berlin, London and U. S. (after 1914); mem. of Elshuco Trio; taught formerly at Inst. of Music. Art, N. Y., later at Phila. Cons.; composed orchestral, chamber music, choral and piano works.

Giornovichi. Vide JARNOVIC.

Giorza (jôr'-tsä), **Paolo,** Milan, Nov. 11, 1838—Seattle, Wash., May 4, 1914; son and pupil of an organist and dram. singer; studied cpt. with La Croix; lived New York some years, later London; prod. unsucc. opera *"Corrado"* (Milan, 1869), and many succ. ballets.

Giovanelli (jō-vä-nĕl'-lē), **Ruggiero,** Velletri, ca. 1560—Rome, 1625; 1599 successor of Palestrina as conductor at St. Peter's, Rome; an important composer.

Giraldoni (zhē-răl-dō'-nē), **Leone,** Paris, 1824—Moscow, 1897; barytone.

Girard (zhē-răr), **Narcisse,** Nantes, France, 1797—Paris, 1860; conductor and violin professor.

Girardeau (zhē-răr-dō), **Isabella,** called **la Isabella,** Italian singer in London, ca. 1700.

Gizziello (gǐd-zǐ-ĕl'-lō), **Gioacchino.** Vide CONTI.

Glad'stone, Francis Edw., Summertown, near Oxford, May 2, 1845—Hereford, Sept. 5, 1928; pupil of S. Wesley; organist various churches; 1879 Mus. Doc., Contab; 1881, prof. of cpt. Trinity Coll., London; prof. of harm. and cpt. R. C. M.; c. an overture, chamber-music, etc.

Glarea'nus, Henricus (rightly **Heinrich Lo'ris,** Latinized, **Lori'tus**), Glarus, 1488 — Freiburg, Baden, March 28, 1563; poet and important theorist.

Glasenapp (glä'-zĕ-näp), **Karl Fr.,**

Riga, October 3, 1847—April 14; 1915; studied philosophy at Dorpat, since 1875 head-master at Riga; wrote on Wagner, a biography in 3 vols., a lexicon, and a Wagner Encyclopædia, etc.

Gläser (glä'-zēr), (1) K. G., Weissenfels, 1784—Barmen, 1829; mus. dir. and later dealer, composer and writer. (2) Fz., Obergeorgenthal, Bohemia, 1798—Copenhagen, 1861; conductor, violinist, and dram. composer.

Glaz(o)unow (glä'-tsoo-nôf), Alex., St. Petersburg, Aug. 10, 1865—Paris, March 21, 1936; eminent Russian composer; studied till 1883 at Polytechnic Inst., then took up music; studied with Rimsky-Korsakov; 1881 his first symphony was produced, repeated under Liszt in 1884 at Weimar; he cond. his second symphony in Paris, 1889; his fourth symphony, London Phil.; 1896–97, with Rimsky-Korsakov and Liadov, cond. Russian Symphony Concerts at St. P.; from 1899 he was prof. of instrumentation, St. Petersburg Cons.; 1909–12 director; honoured by Soviets but lived Paris after 1930. He c. 8 symphs. 5 suites, ballets, 4 overtures, a symph. poem, "Stenka Rasin," a symphonic fantasy, "Through Night to Light," and a great number of other orch. works, chamber music in large quantity and high quality, cantatas, the "Memorial" (Leeds, Fest., 1901), ballets, violin concerto (1904), etc.

Gleason (glē'-sŭn), Fr. Grant, Middletown, Conn., Dec. 17, 1848—Chicago, June 12, 1903; pupil of Dudley Buck and at Leipzig Cons.; later at Berlin, of Loeschorn, Weitzmann and Haupt; later with Beringer (pf.) in London; 1875 organist Hartford; 1877, teacher Hershey Sch. of Music, Chicago; critic for years of Chicago Tribune; c. (text and music) grand operas "Otho Visconti" and "Montezuma"; cantata "The Culprit Fay," with orch.; "Praise-song to Harmony," symphonic cantata; "Auditorium Festival Ode," symph. cantata with orch.; op. 21, "Edris," symphonic poem (after the prologue to "Ardath" by Marie Corelli), etc.

Gleich (glīkh), Fd., Erfurt, 1816—Langebrück, near Dresden, 1898; critic and writer; c. symphonies.

Gleissner (glīs'-nĕr), Fz., Neustadt-on-the-Waldnab, 1760—Munich, after 1815; printed songs of his own by lithographic process, the first music so printed.

Gleitz (glīts), K., Hetzerode, near Cassel, Sept. 13, 1862—Torgau, June, 1920; studied Leipzig Cons. and Munich Music School, and in Berlin; c. symph.-poem "Fata Morgana" (played by Nikisch at the Berlin Philh. concerts, 1898); "Ahasuerus," "Venus and Bellona," etc., for orch.; "Hafbur and Signild," for chorus; "Inlichter," a pf.-fantasy with orch.; vln.-sonata, etc.

Glière (glē-ăr), Reinhold Moritzovich, composer; b. Kiev, Dec. 30, 1874 (O. S.), or Jan. 11, 1875, (N. S.); pupil of Moscow Cons., winning gold medal; in 1913, prof. Kiev Cons.; 1914, dir. of same; after 1920, prof. of comp., Moscow Cons. He has enjoyed honours under the Soviet regime, and has striven to embody revolutionary and proletarian ideals in his later productions. His ballet, "The Red Poppy," became for a time most popular on the stages of the U. S. S. R., and a lively "Sailor's Dance" from this work has been perf. widely in other countries, incl. U. S. His principal works include 2 symphonies, "Les Sirènes," "Ilya Mourometz"; and "Triana" for orch.; 3 string quartets, 3 string sextets, octet for strings; the ballet "Chrysis," etc.

Glinka (glĭnk'-ä), Michail Ivanovitch, Novospasköi, near Smolensk, Russia, June 1 (new style), 1804—Berlin, Feb. 15, 1857; piano-virtuoso and composer, father of the new nationalistic Russian Musical School; of noble birth; pupil of Bohm (vln.), Mayer (theory and pf.), John Field (pf.). Of very weak health, he studied vocal composition in Italy; 1834 with Dehn in Berlin; prod. at St. Petersburg, 1836, the first Russian national opera "A Life for the Czar" (Zarskaja Skisu or Ivan Sussanina), with succ. still lasting; the next opera "Russlan and Ludmilla" (St. P., 1842) was also succ. (book by Pushkin); 1844 in Paris he gave orch. concerts strongly praised by Berlioz; 1845–47, Madrid and Seville, where he c. "Jota Aragonese," a "Capriccio brillante" for orch., and "Souvenir d'une nuit d'été à Madrid,"

for orch.; 1851. Paris; 1854–55, near
St. Petersburg writing his autobiography, planning a never-attempted
opera; he visited Dehn at Berlin in
1856, and died there suddenly; Glinka's other comp. incl. 2 unfinished
symphonies; 2 polonaises for orch.; a
fantasia, "*La Kamarinskaja*"; a
septet; 2 string-quartets; trio for
pf., clar. and oboe; dramatic scenes;
vocal-quartets, songs and pf.-pcs.

Glöggl (glĕg'-gl), (1) **Fz. X.,** Linz-on-
Danube, 1764—July 16, 1839; con-
ductor, mus. dir.; writer. (2) **Fz.,**
Linz, 1797—Vienna, 1872; son of
above; est. music business, 1843;
writer and mus. director.

Glover (glŭv'-ĕr), (1) **Sarah Ann,** Norwich, Engl., 1785—Malvern, 1867;
inv. the Tonic Sol-fa system of notation and wrote about it. (2) **Chas.
W.,** Feb., 1806—London, 1863; violinist, etc. (3) **Stephen,** London,
1812—Dec. 7, 1870; teacher and
composer. (4) **W. Howard,** London,
1819—New York, 1875; violinist and
critic; sang in opera. (5) **John Wm.,**
Dublin, June 19, 1815—Jan. 15,
1900; violinist and choirmaster at
the Cathedral from 1860; c. opera
"*The Deserted Village*" (London,
1880), etc.

Gluck (glook), (1) **Christoph Wilibald**
(Ritter **von**), Weidenwang, near Neu-
markt, Upper Palatinate, July 2,
1714—Vienna, Nov. 15, 1787; son of
head-gamekeeper to Prince Lobkowitz; at twelve sent to the Jesuit
Coll. at Komotau (1726–32), where
he learnt the violin, clavecin, and
organ, and was chorister in the Ch.
of St. Ignaz; at eighteen he went to
Prague, earning a living by playing
at rural dances, giving concerts and
singing and playing in various
churches; under the tuition of Father
Czernohorsky he mastered singing
and the 'cello, his favourite instr.;
1736 entered the service of Prince
Melzi, Vienna, who took him to
Milan and had him study harm. and
cpt. with Sammartini. After four
years' study he prod. "*Artaserse*"
(La Scala, 1741) with great succ. and
was commissioned to c. for other
theatres; prod. 8 operas 1742–45.
On invitation he went to London
1745 as composer for the Haymarket,
in opposition to Händel. "*La Ca-
duca dei Giganti*" was given on the
defeat of the Pretender, 1746,

"*Artamene,*" followed by "*Piramo e
Tisbe,*" a pasticcio of his best arias,
had no succ. and led Händel to say
that the music was detestable, and
that Gluck knew no more counterpoint than his cook.   The operas G.
had written up to this time were
thoroughly Italian.   The influence
of Händel and Rameau's works heard
at Paris awakened him, and led him
to that gradual reform which made
him immortal, though it brought on
him the most ferocious opposition.
"*La Semiramide Riconosciuta*" (Vienna, 1748) began the change to
more serious power.   1750–62 he
prod. "*Telemaco*" (Rome, 1750),
"*La Clemenza di Tito*" (Naples,
1751), and 4 others.   1754–64 he
was dir. court-opera Vienna and
prod. 6 more works.   He made great
succ. in spite of opposition with
"*Orfeo ed Euridice*" (1762), "*Alceste*"
(1767), "*Paride ed Elena*" (1769),
libretti by Calzabigi.   2 other inferior works were performed by
members of the royal family (1765).
In the dedicatory prefaces to "*Alceste*" and "*Paride ed Elena,*" G.
expressed his protest against the
Italian school, and declared for
dramatic consistency unhampered by
rigid formulæ for arias, duets, etc.,
and interpolated cadenzas.   He had
such harsh criticism at home and
such encouragement from du Rollet
of the French Embassy at Vienna
in 1772 that he went to Paris.   But
here also he met such opposition
that all his diplomacy and all the
power of his former pupil, Queen
Marie Antoinette, hardly availed to
bring about the presentation of
"*Iphigénie en Aulide*" (1774); its
great succ. was repeated in "*Orphée*" (Aug., 1774), "*Alceste*" (1776),
and "*Armide*" (1777).   Piccinni was
brought to Paris as a rival, and prod.
"*Roland*" while Gluck was preparing
the same subject.   Gluck burned his
score and published a letter which
precipitated an unimaginably fierce
war of pamphlets.   Both men now
set to composing "*Iphigénie en Tauride*"; here Gluck forestalled his rival
by two years (1779), and Piccinni's
work on appearing was not a succ.,
while Gluck's succeeded enormously.
His last opera, "*Echo et Narcisse,*"
was not succ. (Sept. 21, 1779); 1780,
he retired to Vienna and lived on his

well-earned wealth, till apoplexy carried him off. He wrote a De profundis for chorus and orch., 6 overtures and an incomplete cantata, "*Das Jüngste Gericht,*" finished by Salieri, and 7 odes for solo voice and pf. Biog. by A. Schmidt (1854); Marx (1863); Desnoiresterres (1872); also studies of his operas by Berlioz and Newman. (2) **Alma** (née **Reba Fierson**), Bucharest, Roumania, May 11, 1866—New York, Oct. 26, 1938; pupil of Buzzi-Peccia; début New Theatre, N. Y., 1909; the same year at the Met. Op.; of which mem. until 1912; sang widely in concert; m. Efrem Zimbalist, violinist.

Gluth (gloot), **Victor**, Pilsen, May 6, 1852—Munich, Jan. 17, 1917; taught Akademie der Tonkunst, Munich; c. operas "*Zlatorog*" and "*Horand und Hilde.*"

Gmeiner (g'mī'nĕr), **Lula, Mysz-**, b. Kronstadt, Aug. 16, 1876; alto; studied vln. with Olga Grigorourcz; then studied voice with Gr. Walter and Emilie Herzog; noted Lieder singer.

Gnecchi (nyĕ'-kē), **Vittorio**, b. Milan, July 17, 1876; composer; private pupil of Saladino, Coronaro, Serafin and Gatti; c. (operas) "*Virtu d'Amore*" (1895); "*Cassandra*" (Bologna, 1905, also heard in Phila., 1914); "*La Rosiera*" (prod. in Germany); "*Judith*"; orch. works, songs; his "*Cassandra*" is asserted by Giovanni Tebaldini to have suggested certain details of Strauss's "*Elektra.*"

Gnecco (n'yĕk'-kō), **Francesco**, Genoa, 1769—Milan, 1810; dram. composer.

Gniessin (gnyĕs'-ĕn), **Michael**, b. Rostoff, Russia, Jan. 23, 1883; composer; studied at Moscow and Petrograd Cons.; since 1923 teacher at the State Cons. in Moscow; his music utilises Jewish folk themes and shows an impressionistic manner; c. (opera) "*The Youth of Abraham,*" symphonic, choral and chamber music, songs.

Gobbaerts (gŭb'-bărts), **Jean Louis**, Antwerp, 1835—Saint Gilles, near Brussels, 1886; pianist and composer.

Göbel (gā'-bĕl), **K. H.**, Berlin, 1815—Bromberg, 1879; pianist, conductor, and dram. composer.

Gockel (gŏk'ĕl), **Aug.**, Willibadessen, Westphalia, 1831—1861; pianist and composer.

Godard (gō-dăr). **Benjamin (Louis Paul)**, Paris, Aug. 18, 1849—Cannes, Jan. 11, 1895; studied vln. with Hammer and played in public at 9; then studied with Reber (comp.) and Vieuxtemps (vln.), Paris Cons.; 1865 pub. a vln.-sonata, later other chamber-compositions; rec'd the Prix Chartier from the Institut de France for merit in the department of chamber-music; prod. 5 operas, incl. "*Jocelyn*" (Brussels, 1888), and the very succ. posthumous "*La Vivandière*" (Paris Op.-Com., 1895), the last 2 acts orchestrated by Paul Vidal; 2 operas not prod.; he c. also incid. mus. and 6 symphonies; "*Le Tasse*" (Tasso), dram. symphony with soli and chorus took the city of Paris prize in 1878; concerto for vln.; a pf.-concerto, songs and pf.-pcs.

God'dard (**Davison**), **Arabella**, St Servan, near Saint Malo, Brittany, Jan. 12, 1836—Boulogne, April 6, 1922; pianist; at 4 played in public, at 6 studied with Kalkbrenner at Paris, at 8 played to Queen Victoria; pub. 6 waltzes and studied with Mrs. Anderson and Thalberg; at 12 played at the Grand National Concerts; 1850-53 pupil of J. W. Davison, whom she m. (1860); toured Germany and at 17 played at Leipzig Gewandhaus 1855; 1873-76 toured the world; retired 1880 and lived in Tunbridge Wells.

Godebrye. Vide JACOTIN.

Godefroid (gŏd-fwä), (1) **Jules Joseph**, Namur, Belgium, 1811—Paris, 1840, harpist and dram. composer. (2) **Dieudonné Jos. Guil. Félix**, Namur, 1818—Villers-sur-mer, 1897; bro. of above; harpist and dram. composer.

God'frey, (1) **Chas.**, Kingston, Surrey, 1790—1863; bassoonist and conductor. (2) **Daniel**, Westminster, Engl., Sept. 4, 1831—Beeston, near Nottingham, June 30, 1903; conductor; son of above; pupil R. A. M., later Fellow and Prof. of Military Mus.; 1856 bandm. of the Grenadier Guards; 1872 and 1898 toured the U. S. with his band, composer. (3) **Sir Daniel Eyers**, b. London, 1868; son of (2); noted conductor; after 1894 led symph. concerts at Bournemouth for more than 40 years, presenting series of eminent soloists and also organising fests. there; retired 1934; d. Bournemouth, July 20, 1939.

Godowsky (gō-dôf'-skē), **Leopold,** b. Wilna (Vilno), Russian Poland, Feb. 13, 1870—N. Y., Nov. 21, 1938; pianist; pupil of Rudorff; 1881–84 R. Hochschule, Berlin; 1887–90 studied with Saint-Saëns; 1890–91 toured America again; 1894 dir. pf.-dept., Broad St. Cons., Phila.; 1895–99 head of pf.-dept., Chicago Cons.; then toured Europe; 1902 lived in Berlin; succeeded Busoni in 1910, as head of the Master-School of the Vienna Imperial Academy; 1904, married Frieda Saxe; after 1912 made home in U. S.; c. symphonic Dance-pictures from Strauss *"Fledermaus"*; sonata E minor, for piano; left-hand transcriptions of Chopin Études, 50 études on Chopin's Études, and many brilliant piano works, incl. *"Java"* suite, etc.

Goedicke (gĕd'-ĕ-kē), **Aiex. Fedorovitch,** b. Moscow, March 3, 1877; composer, pianist and organist; pupil of Pabst and Safonoff at the Cons. in his native city; won Vienna Rubinstein prize in 1900 for his piano concerto; after 1907 taught at Moscow Cons.; c. orch., chamber and piano works of classical trend.

Goepfart (gĕp'-färt), (1) **Chr. H.,** Weimar, 1835—Baltimore, Md., 1890; organist and composer. (2) **Karl Eduard,** b. Weimar, March 8, 1859; son of above; 1891, cond. Baden-Baden Mus. Union; 1909–27, active in Potsdam; after 1928 in Weimar; c. *"Sarastro,"* a sequel to Mozart's *"Magic Flute,"* etc. (3) **Otto Ernst,** Weimar, July 31, 1864—Jan. 13, 1911; bro. of above; since 1888 Weimar town cantor and composer.

Goepp (gĕp), **Philip Henry,** New York, June 23, 1864—Philadelphia, Aug., 25, 1936; composer, writer; grad., Harvard Univ., studied comp. with Paine; 1892, founded Manuscript Soc.; after 1900 wrote programme notes for Phila. Orch.; prof. of theory, Temple Univ.; c. orch., chamber music, choral works, songs; author, *"Symphonies and Their Meaning."*

Goes (gō'-ĕs), **Damião de,** Alemquer, Portugal, 1501—Lisbon, 1572; ambassador, theorist and composer.

Goethe (gā'-tĕ), **Walther Wg. von,** Weimar, 1818—Leipzig, 1885; grandson of the poet; c. 3 operettas, etc.

Goetschius (gĕt'-shǐ-oos), **Percy,** Paterson, N. J., Aug. 30, 1853—N. Y., Oct. 29, 1943; pupil Stuttgart Cons.;

1885, Royal Prof.; critic for various German music papers; 1890–92, prof. Syracuse (N. Y.) Univ. and Mus. Doc.; 1892–96, taught comp. and lectured on mus., hist., etc., N. E. Cons., Boston; 1896, private teacher Boston, and essayist; 1897, organist First Parish Ch., Brookline, 1905–25, prof. at Inst. of Music. Art, N. Y.; pub. important and original treatises; ed. piano works of Mendelssohn; c. piano pieces and songs.

Goetz (gĕts), **Hn.,** Königsberg, Prussia, 1840—Hottingen, near Zurich, 1876; 1863, organist and conductor; c. operas, notably *"Taming of the Shrew"*; orch., chamber music, choruses, songs, etc.

Göhler (gā'-lĕr), **Karl Georg,** b. Zwickau, June 29, 1874; author and comp.; pupil of Vollhardt and Leipzig Cons.; 1896, Ph.D.; from 1898 director of the Riedelverein, also from 1903 court cond. at Altenburg; 1907–09 at Carlsruhe; 1909–13, Leipzig; 1913–14, Hamburg Op.; 1915–18, cond. Philh. Chorus and Orch., Lübeck; 1922–33, cond. Halle Philh. Orch.; c. 2 symphs.; orch. suite *"Indian Songs."*

Goldbeck (gōlt'-bĕk), **Robert,** Potsdam, April 19, 1839—St. Louis, May 16, 1908); pupil of Kohler and H. Litolff; gave succ. concerts in London and prod. operetta; 1857–67 in New York as teacher; 1868 founded a Cons. at Chicago; dir. till 1873; cond. St. Louis Harmonic Soc.

Goldberg (gōlt'-bĕrkh), (1) **Jn. G.** (Theophilus), Königsberg, ca. 1730—Dresden (?), 1760 (?); organ and clavichord player. (2) **Jos. Pasquale,** Vienna, 1825—1890; vln.-pupil of Mayseder and Seyfried, then operatic bass and teacher. His 2 sisters, (3) **Fanny G.-Marini** and (4) **Catherine G.-Strossi,** were singers.

Gold'man, Edwin Franko, Amer. bandmaster, composer; led Goldman Band in N. Y. park concerts after 1912.

Goldmark (gōlt'-märk), (1) **Karl,** Keszthely, Hungary, May 18, 1830—Vienna, Jan. 2, 1915; noted composer; violinist and pianist, pupil of Jansa (vln.), later of Bohm (theory) at the Vienna Cons., then mainly self-taught; début 1858 Vienna, with his own pf.-concerto; the popular overture *"Sakuntala"* (op. 13); and a Scherzo, Andante, and Finale for Orch. (op. 19) won him success strengthened by his opera *"Die Königin von Saba"* (Vienna, 1875); c. also operas *"Merlin"* (Vienna, 1886) v. succ.; *"Das Heimchen am Herd"* based on Dickens' "Cricket on the Hearth" (Vienna, 1896); *"Die Kriegsgefangene"* (Vienna Ct.-opera, 1899); *"Der Fremdling"* (not prod.) and *"Götz von Berlichingen"*; c. also 2 symphonies, incl. *"Landliche Hochzeit"*; overtures, *"Im Frühling,"* *"Prometheus Bound,"* and *"Sappho,"* also a pop. vln. concerto, suite for vln. and piano, choruses, songs, piano works; author, *"Reminiscences of My Life."* (2) **Rubin,** New York City, Aug. 15, 1872—March 6, 1936; composer; nephew of above; at 7 began to study with A. M. Livonius, with whom he went to Vienna, 1889; studied there also with Door and Fuchs; later in New York with Joseffy and Dvořák; 1892-1901, in Colorado Springs, Colorado; founder and dir. of a Coll. of Mus. there, *"Theme and Variations"* for orch. (performed by Seidl, 1895); c. a pf.-trio, cantata with orch. *"Pilgrimage to Kevlaar,"* overture *"Hiawatha"* (played by Boston Symph. Orch.), vln.-sonata, etc.; after 1902 lived again in N. Y. as teacher and comp.; 1924 until his death, head of comp. dept., Juilliard Grad. School; c. *"Gettysburg Requiem"* (N. Y. Philh., 1917); *"Negro Rhapsody"* (1922, played by many orchs.); founder and long pres., N. Y. Bohemians' Club.

Goldner (gŏlt'-nĕr), **Wm.,** Hamburg, June 30, 1839—Paris, Feb. 8, 1907; pupil Leipzig Cons.; lived in Paris as a pianist and composer.

Goldschmidt (gŏlt-shmĭt), (1) **Sigismund,** Prague, 1815—Vienna, 1877; pianist and composer. (2) **Otto,** Hamburg, Aug. 21, 1829—London, Feb. 24, 1907; pianist; pupil of Jakob Schmitt and F. W. Grund, Mendelssohn, and Chopin; 1849 London with Jenny Lind, whom he accompanied on her American tour and m. (Boston, 1852); 1852-55 Dresden; 1858-87 London; 1863 vice-principal of the R. A. M., 1875 founded Bach Choir, also cond. mus. festivals at Düsseldorf (1863) and Hamburg (1866); c. oratorio *"Ruth"* (Hereford, 1867); pf.-concerto and trio, etc. (3) **Adalbert von,** Vienna, May 5, 1848—Dec. 21, 1906; pupil

Vienna Cons.; amateur composer; prod. with great succ. cantata *"Die Sieben Todsünden"* (Berlin, 1875), and succ. opera *"Helianthus"* (Leipzig, 1884); prod. trilogy *"Gaea"* 1889. (4) **Hugo,** Breslau, Sept. 19, 1859—Wiesbaden, Dec. 26, 1920; 1884 Dr. jur.; studied singing with Stockhausen (1887-90); 1893-1905, co-dir Scharwenka-Klindworth Cons., Berlin; writer.

Gold'win, John, d. Nov., 1719; Engl. organist and composer.

Golinel'li, Stefano, Bologna, Oct. 26, 1818—July 3, 1891; pianist; pupil of B. Donelli and N. Vaccai; pf.-prof. Liceo Musicale till 1870; c. 5 pf.-sonatas, etc.

Gollmick (gŏl'-mĭk), (1) **Fr. K.,** Berlin, 1774—Frankfort-on-Main, 1852; tenor. (2) **Karl,** Dessau, 1796—Frankfort-on-Main, 1866; son of above; theorist and writer. (3) **Adolf,** Frankfort-on-M., 1825—London, 1883; pianist; son and pupil of (2); studied also with Riefstahl, 1844; c. comic operas, etc.

Golsch'mann, Vladimir, b. Paris, Dec. 16, 1893; conductor; studied vln. with Möller, Berthelier, piano with de Saunieres and Braud, comp. with Dumas, and Caussade; founded Golschmann Orch., Paris, 1919, and led this series until 1923; guest cond. in other European cities; came to America as musical dir. of Swedish Ballet, invited to lead N. Y. Symph. as guest by Damrosch; cond. St. Louis Symph. Orch. after 1934.

Goltermann (gŏl'-tĕr-män), (1) **G. Ed.,** Hanover, 1824 — Frankfort-on-M., 1898; 'cellist and composer. (2) **Jn. Aug. Julius,** Hamburg, 1825—Stuttgart, 1876; 'cellist. (3) **Aug.,** 1826—Schwerin, 1890; court pianist.

Gombert (gôm'-bĕrt), **Nicolas,** Bruges, ca. 1495—after 1570; a most important 16th cent. composer, one of the first to take up secular music seriously; a lover of Nature and a writer of descriptive and pastoral songs of much beauty; his motet *"Paster Noster"* was prod. at Paris by Fétis with impressive effect.

Gomes (or **Gomez**) (gō'-mäs), **Antonio Carlos,** Campinas, Brazil, July 11, 1839—Para, Sept. 16, 1896; pupil of Rossi, Milan Cons.; Dir. of Para Cons.; c. succ. operas *"Il Guarany,"* *"Salvator Rosa,"* *"Lo Schiavo,"* *"Maria Tudor,"* etc.

Gomiz (gō'-mĕth) Jose Melchior, Valencia, Jan. 6, 1791—Paris, July 26, 1836; military bandmaster and singing teacher at Paris; c. operas and patriotic songs.

Gom'pertz, Richard, Cologne, April 27, 1859—Dresden, 1921; violinist; pupil at the Cons., and of Joachim; toured, then invited to teach at Cambridge University; from 1883, teacher at R. C. M., 1895, prof.; from 1899 at Dresden; c. violin sonatas, etc.

Good'rich, (1) Alfred John, Chile, Ohio, May 8, 1847—Paris, April 25, 1920; eminent theorist; except for a year's instruction from his father, wholly self-taught; teacher theory Grand Cons., N. Y., 1876; voice, pf. and theory Fort Wayne Cons., Ind.; dir. vocal-dept. Beethoven Cons., St. Louis; 2 years at Martha Washington Coll., Va.; lived in Chicago, New York as teacher; pub. theoretical essays and books of radical and scholarly nature, the important products of research and individuality, incl. "Complete Musical Analysis" (1889), "Analytical Harmony" (1894), "Theory of Interpretation" (1898), "Counterpoint." (2) (John) Wallace, b. Newton, Mass., May 27, 1871—Boston, June 6, 1952; conductor; studied in Boston and Munich, and with Widor, Paris; taught New England Cons.; dean after 1907; became dir., succeeding Chadwick, 1931; 1897–1909, org. for Boston Symph., also in various churches in that city; 1902–08, cond. and founder, Boston Choral Art. Soc.; until 1907, dir. of choral work, Worcester Fest.; 1907–10, cond. Cecilia Soc.; in latter year also of orch. concerts; cond. with Boston Op. Co., 1907–12, when it disbanded; c. choral music; also author and translator of works on organ, etc.

Good'son, Katharine, b. Watford, England, June 18, 1872; pianist; at 12 pupil at the R. A. M., till 1892, then four years with Leschetizky—début, 1896, London Pop. Concerts; has toured widely; 1903, married Arthur Hinton (q.v.).

Goos'sens, (1) Eugene, b. London, May 26, 1893; conductor, composer; studied Bruges Cons. and Liverpool Coll. of Mus., later grad. R. Coll. of Mus., London; 1911–15, played in Queen's Hall Orch. and Philh. String Quartet; 1916, cond. Stanford's

opera, "The Critic"; 1915–20, cond. in association with enterprises of Beecham; 1921, founded own orch. in London for a season; later with Brit. Nat'l. Op. Co. and Carl Rosa Co., the Russian Ballet, and London Symph.; 1923–31, cond. Rochester Symph. Orch. in U. S.; founded chamber music concerts in London; after 1931 cond. Cincinnati Symph. until 1948; then dir. Sydney Cons., cond. Symph. there; c. op. "Judith," to libretto by Arnold Bennett, (Covent Garden, 1929); "Don Juan de Mañara"; (orch.) "Tam o' Shanter"; "Four Conceits"; "The Eternal Rhythm"; "Kaleidoscope"; "Rhythmic Dance"; Sinfonietta; Fantasy for 9 wind instruments; 3 Greek Dances; Concertino for double string orch.; Poem for viola and orch.; Rhapsody for 'cello and orch.; "By the Tarn" for strings and clarinet; "Silence" for chorus and orch.; (chamber music) Fantasy Quartet; Sextet (commissioned for Berkshire Fest., 1923); Spanish Serenade; String Quartet in C; sonata for piano and vln.; piano sonatas, songs, piano pieces; "Five Impressions of a Holiday" for piano, flute (or vln.) and 'cello; (ballet) "L'École en Crinoline." (2) Léon, bro. of Eugene; oboist; pupil of R. Coll. of Mus.; mem. Philh. Trio; soloist in Covent Garden, Philh. and Queen's Hall orchs.; later active as solo performer; gave N. Y. recital, 1927.

Goovaerts (gō'-värts), Alphonse, J. M. André, Antwerp, May 25, 1847—Brussels, Dec. 25, 1922; 1866, assist. librarian, Antwerp; founded an amateur cathedral choir to cultivate Palestrina and the Netherland cptists; 1887 royal archivist, Brussels; writer and composer.

Göpfert (gĕp'-fĕrt), (1) K. And., Rimpar, near Würzburg, 1768—Meiningen, 1818; clarinetist and dram. composer. (2) K. G., Weesenstein, near Dresden, 1733—Weimar, 1798; vln. virtuoso; conductor and composer.

Gordigiani (gôr-dēd-jä'-nē), (1) Giov. Bat., Mantua, 1795—Prague, 1871; son of a musician; dram. composer. (2) Antonio, a singer. (3) Luigi, Modena, 1806—Florence, 1860; bro. of (1); dram. composer.

Goria (gō-rē'-ä), Alex. Éd., Paris, 1823—1860; teacher and composer.

Go'ritz, Otto, Berlin, June 8, 1872—

Hamburg, April 11, 1929; barytone; studied with his mother; début, Neustrelitz, 1895; thereafter at Breslau and Hamburg Ops.; Met. Op. Co., N. Y., 1903–17; noted for Wagnerian character rôles.

Görner (gĕr'-nĕr), (1) **Jno. Gottlieb,** Penig, 1697—Leipzig, 1778; organist; his brother, (2) **J. N. Valentin,** b. Penig, 1702, cond. at Hamburg Cathedral: c. songs.

Gorno (gôr'-nō), **Albino,** Cassalmorano, Italy, 1859—Cincinnati, Oct. 29, 1944; pupil Milan Cons., graduating with 3 gold medals; pianist; accompanist Adelina Patti on Amer. tour 1881–1882; then pf.-prof. Cincinnati Coll. of Music; c. opera, cantata "*Garibaldi*," etc.

Göroldt (gā'-rôlt), **Jn. H.,** Stempeda near Stolberg (Harz), 1773—after 1835; mus. dir., writer and composer.

Gorria, Tobio. Vide BOITO, ARRIGO.

Gorter (gôr'-tĕr), **Albert,** Nürnberg, Nov. 23, 1862—March 14, 1936; studied medicine; then music at R. Mus. Sch., Munich; took 3 prizes for composition; studied a year in Italy; assist. cond. Bayreuth Festivals; cond. Breslau, etc.; 1894–99 assist. cond. Carlsruhe Ct.-Th., then cond. Leipzig City Th.; 1903, Strasbourg, 1910–25, munic. cond. in Mainz; c. (text and mus.) opera "*Harold*" and comic opera "*Der Schatz des Rhampsinnit*" (Mannheim, 1894); 2 symphonic poems, etc.

Goss, (1) **John Jeremiah,** Salisbury, 1770—1817; alto. (2) **Sir John,** Fareham, Hants, England; 1800—London, 1880; organist; knighted, 1872; composer and writer.

Gossec (gôs'sĕk) (rightly **Gossé, Gosset** or **Gossez**) (gôs-sā), **François Joseph,** Vergniers, Belgium, Jan. 17, 1734—Passy, near Paris, Feb. 16, 1829; 1741–49 chorister Antwerp cath.; for 2 years he then studied vln. and comp.; 1751 Paris, cond. private orch. of La Pouplinière; then *fermier-général;* 1754 he pub. his first symphonies (5 years before Haydn's); 1759 his first string-quartets which became pop.; 1769 his "*Messe des Morts*" made a sensation (the "*Tuba mirum*" being written for 2 orch., one for wind. instrs., concealed, a new effect he repeated in his first oratorio); 1762 cond. of Prince Conti's orch. at Chantilly; from 1764 prod. 3-act operas "*Le Faux Lord*,"

etc., incl. succ. "*Les Pêcheurs*" (Comédie It., 1766); 1770 founded Concerts des Amateurs; 1773 re-organised and cond. the Concerts Spirituels till 1777; 1780–82 assist. cond. Académie de Musique (later Gr. Opera); 1784 founded and dir. École Royale de Chant, the beginning of the Cons. of which (1795) he was an inspector and prof. of comp.; c. 26 symphonies, 3 symphonies for wind, "*Symphonie concertante*" for 11 insts., overtures, 3 oratorios, etc.; masses with orch.; string-quartets, etc.

Gottschalg (gôt'-shälkh), **Alex. W.,** Mechelrode, near Weimar, Feb. 14, 1827—Weimar, May 31, 1908; pupil Teachers' Seminary, Weimar; succeeding Göpfer there later; court organist, teacher, editor and writer.

Gottschalk (gôts'-chôlk), (1) **Louis Moreau,** New Orleans, La., May 8, 1829—Rio de Janeiro, Dec. 18, 1869; brilliant and original pianist and composer; studied in Paris; began c. at 10; c. operas, etc., and 90 pf.-pcs. of distinct and tropical charm. (2) **Gaston,** bro. of above, singer and for years teacher in Chicago.

Götze (gĕt'-zĕ), (1) **Jn. Nik. K.,** Weimar, 1791—1861; violinist and dram. composer. (2) **Fz.,** Neustadt-on-Orla, 1814—Leipzig, 1888; tenor, teacher and composer. (3) **Karl,** Weimar, 1836—Magdeburg, 1887; pianist and dram. composer. (4) **H.,** Wartha, Silesia, April 7, 1836—Breslau, Dec. 14, 1906; studied singing with (2); lost his voice; teacher in Russia and Breslau; 1885 Ziegenhals, Silesia; 1889 Royal Mus. Dir.; wrote 2 technical books; c. a mass with orch., etc. (5) **Auguste,** Weimar, Feb. 24, 1840—Leipzig, April 29, 1908; daughter of (2); teacher Cons., Dresden; founded a school there; 1891 taught at Leipzig Cons.; wrote under name "**Auguste Weimar.**" (6) **Emil,** Leipzig, July 19, 1856—Charlottenburg, Berlin, Sept. 28, 1901; pupil of Scharfe, Dresden; 1878–81, tenor Dresden Ct.-Th., then at Cologne Th., then toured as "star," 1900 lived in Berlin as court-singer. (7) **Otto,** 1886, conductor at Essen-on-Ruhr; prod. succ. opera "*Riscatto*" (Sondershausen, 1896). (8) **Fz.,** 1892, prod. Volksoper "*Utopia*" (Stettin, 1892) and 1-act opera "*Die Rose von Thiessow*,"

(Glogau, 1895). (9) **Marie,** Berlin, Nov. 2, 1865—Feb. 18, 1922; alto, studied Stern Cons. and with Jenny Meyer and Levysohn; sang Berlin opera, then at Hamburg City Th.; 2 years in America; 1892 Berlin ct.-opera.

Goudimel (goo-dĭ-mĕl), **Claude,** Vaison, near Avignon, ca. 1505—killed in St. Bartholomew massacre, Lyons, Aug. 24, 1572; pupil perhaps of Josquin Desprès; est. a school and formed Palestrina and other pupils, winning name "Father of the Roman School"; a music printer for a time; his important comp. incl. *"The Psalms of David,"* complete.

Gould, Nathaniel Duren, Chelmsford, Mass., 1781—Boston, 1864; conductor and writer.

Gounod (goo-nō), **Charles François,** Paris, June 17, 1818—Oct. 17, 1893; son of a talented painter and engraver; his mother taught him the pf. and he entered the Lycée Saint-Louis; 1836 studied at the Paris Cons. with Reicha (harm.), Halévy (cpt. and fugue), Lesueur and Paer (comp.); took 2nd Prix de Rome with cantata *"Marie Stuart et Rizzio"* in 1837; his cantata *"Fernanda"* won the Grand Prix de Rome in 1839, and he studied church music at Rome; 1841 his orch. mass was performed; in 1842 he cond. his *Requiem* at Vienna with great succ.; returned to Paris as precentor and organist of the Missions Étrangères; studied theology 2 years, intended to take orders and was called l'**Abbé Gounod** by a publisher in 1846; after 5 years of seclusion, parts of his *Messe Solennelle* were played with profound succ. in London; he prod. a symphony, but his opera *"Sappho"* failed (Gr.)péra, 1851); revised 1884, it failed again; a gr. opera, *"La Nonne Sanglante"* (1854), and a comic opera, *"Le Médecin Malgré Lui"* (played in London as "The Mock Doctor") (1858), both failed; 1852–5o cond. the "Orphéon," Paris, and c. choruses and 2 masses. The opera *"Faust"* (Th. Lyrique, 1859) was and still is a great succ. *"Philémon et Baucis"* (186o); *"La Reine de Sabä"* (in London as "Irene") (1862); *"Mireille"* (1864), *"La Colombe"* (1866), were not great works, but *"Romeo et Juliette"* (1867) still holds the stage; 1866 member of the Insti-

tut de France and commander of the Legion of Honour. In 1870, during the war he lived in London; founded Gounod's Choir. In 1871 he prod. *"Gallia,"* a cantata based on "Lamentations"; 1875 returned to Paris, prod. *"Cinq Mars"* (Opéra Comique, 1877), *"Polyeucte"* (Gr. Opéra, 1878), and *"Le Tribut de Zamora"* (1881), none succ. The sacred trilogy *"La Rédemption"* (Birmingham, 1882) (music and French words), and *"Mors et Vita"* (Birmingham, 1885) (Latin text arranged by Gounod) are standard. He also c. *"Messe Solennelle à Ste. Cecile"*; masses; *"Angeli custo des"* (1882); *"Jeanne d'Arc"* (1887); a Stabat Mater with orch.; the oratorios *"Tobie," "Les Sept Paroles de Jésus," "Jésus sur le Lac de Tibériade"*; the cantatas *"A la Frontière"* (1870, Gr. Opéra), *"Le Vin des Gaulois,"* and *"La Danse de l'Épée,"* the French and English songs, etc. He left 2 operas, *"Maître Pierre"* (incomplete) and *"Georges Dandin"* (said to be the first comic opera set to prose text, cf. Bruneau). He wrote *"Méthode de cor a pistons,"* essays, etc. Biog. by Jules Clarétie (Paris, 1875); Mme. Weldon (London, 1875); Paul Voss (Leipzig, 1895); *"Mémoires"* (Paris, 1895).

Gouvy (goo-vē), **Louis Théodore,** Goffontaine, Rhenish Prussia, 1819—Leipzig, 1898; pianist and composer.

Gow, (1) **Niel,** Strathband, 1727—Inver, Scotland, 1807; violinist and composer. (2) **Nathaniel,** 1763—1831; son of above, also violinist and composer. (3) **Donald,** brother of (1), was a 'cellist. And (4) **Niel, Jr.,** 1795-1823, son of (2), was violinist and composer. (5) **George Coleman,** b. Ayer Junction, Mass., Nov. 27, 1860—Jan. 12, 1938; pupil of Blodgett, Pittsfield and Story (Worcester); graduate Brown Univ., 1884, and Newton Theol. Seminary, 1889; then teacher of harm. and pf. Smith College; studied with Büssler in Berlin; 1895 prof. of music Vassar Coll.; composer and writer.

Graben-Hoffmann (grä'-bĕn hôf'-män), **Gustav** (rightly **Gustav Hoffmann**), Bnin, near Posen, March 7, 1820—Potsdam, May 21, 1900; singing teacher, writer and composer.

Grädener (grä'-dĕ-nĕr), (1) **K. G. P.,** Rostock, 1812—Hamburg. 1883; dir., conductor, writer, and dram. composer. (2) **Hermann** (Th. Otto), Kiel, May 8, 1844—Vienna, Sept. 18, 1929; son and pupil of above; later studied Vienna Cons.; 1873 teacher harmony Horak's Pf. Sch., later Vienna Cons.; from 1890 lecturer on harm. and cpt. Vienna Univ.; cond. Singakademie; c. Capriccietta and Sinfonietta for orch. (op. 14), etc.

Graen'er, Paul, Berlin, Jan. 11, 1872—Nov., 1944; studied Berlin Music. Acad.; mus. dir., Haymarket Theat. and teacher at Royal Acad., London, 1896-1904; principal, Mozarteum, Salzburg, 1910-14; taught master class in comp., Leipzig Cons., 1920-24; dir. of Stern Cons., Berlin, 1930-33; until 1935 mem. of the presiding council of the German Music Chamber; associate of the Berlin Acad. of Arts; c. (operas) *"Don Juans Letztes Abenteuer,"* *"Schirin und Gertraude,"* *"Friedemann Bach,"* *"Hanneles Himmelfahrt"* (after Hauptmann drama), *"Der Prinz von Homburg"*; also symphonic works, piano and 'cello concertos, chamber music, and many songs.

Graew (gräv). Vide BACFART.

Graf (gräf), (1) **Fr. Hartman,** Rudolfstadt, 1727—Augsburg, 1795; flutist and comp. (2) **Max,** b. Vienna, Oct. 1, 1873; music critic; grad. Vienna Univ.; critic of *Wiener Allgemeine Zeitung,* and prof. of mus. hist. and aesthetics, State Acad. of Mus.; author of books on Wagner, etc. His son (3) **Herbert,** b. Vienna, April 10, 1903; noted stage director; studied at State Acad. of Mus. and Vienna Univ., Ph.D.; filled early posts as operatic *régisseur* at Münster, Breslau and Frankfort-am-Main; 1933, stage manager, Munic. Theat., Basel; then with German Theat., Prague; staged opera perfs. of Phila. Orch., 1934-35; at Florentine Musical May Fest., 1935; Salzburg Fest., 1936; engaged for Met. Op., N. Y., 1936-37.

Graffigna (gräf-fēn'-yä), **Achille,** San Martino dell' Argine, Italy, 1816—Padua, 1896; conductor, teacher, and dram. composer.

Gra'ham, Geo. F., Edinburgh, 1789—1867; composer and writer.

Grahl (gräl), **Heinrich,** Stralsund, Nov. 30, 1860—Berlin, March 14, 1923; concert tenor in Berlin; pupil of Felix Schmidt.

Grainger (grān'-jĕr), **Percy,** b. Brighton, Australia, July 8, 1882; composer and pianist; pupil of Louis Pabst, Melbourne, and James Kwast, Frankfort; after 1900, appeared in London and other centres with succ.; 1907, chosen by Grieg to play his piano concerto at Leeds Fest.; 1909, made tour of Scandinavia and other parts of Europe; after 1915 made his home for the most part in the U. S., becoming an Amer. citizen in 1917; he was for a time dir. of the mus. dept., N. Y. Univ., but resigned in 1934 to engage in a world tour; his compositions include many arrangements of folk-song material; c. (orch.) *"Molly on the Shore"*; *"Shepherd's Hey"*; *"Colonial Song"*; *"Mock Morris"*; *"Irish Tune from County Derry"* for strings; *"Handel in the Strand"* for piano and orch.; (chorus) *"The Bride's Tragedy," "Father and Daughter," "Sir Eglamore," "Two Welsh War Songs"*; *"The Hunter in His Career"*; *"Marching Song of Democracy," "Brigg Fair," "The Warriors," "Hill-Songs"* Nos. 1 and 2; *"To a Nordic Princess"*; and many settings of British folk music; m. Ella Viola Strom, sculptress, 1928, the marriage ceremony taking place after a concert at the Hollywood Bowl in view of the audience.

Grammann (gräm'-män), **Karl,** Lübeck, 1844—Dresden, 1897; dram. composer and writer.

Granados y Campina (grä-nä'-dhōs ē käm-pē'-nä), **Enrique,** Lerida, July 27, 1867—March 24, 1916, perished on torpedoed ship, Sussex, when returning from a visit to the U. S.; Spanish composer of strong nationalistic leanings and marked individuality; son of a military officer, he had his first musical instruction from the army conductor Junceda; later studied piano with Jurnet and Pujol in Barcelona, also comp. with Felipe Pedrell, and had further piano work with de Beriot in Paris. He founded and dir. (after 1900) the Sociedad de Conciertos Clasicos; toured Spain and France as an excellent pianist. His opera, *"Goyescas,"* was composed in his latter years, using material from some of his pop. piano works, and was premièred at the Met. Op., N. Y., in the presence of the composer, 1915-16. His output included also the operas *"Petrarca," "Foilet,"*

"Maria del Carmen" as well as numerous *zarzuelas;* (orch.) *"Dante"*; *"Elisenda"* Suite; *"La Nit del Mort"*; *"Serenata"*; *Suites Gallega and Arabe;* *"Marcha de los Vencidos"*; *"Tres Danzas Espagnoles"*; piano trio; works for 'cello and piano, piano and orch., songs with piano acc.; but his princ. legacy remains his large collection of keyboard music, which has won a wide popularity with performers.

Grandi (grän'-dē), **Ales. de**, Venice (?) —Bergamo, 1630; singer and composer.

Grandval (grän-văl), Mme. **Marie Félicie Clémence de Reiset**, Vicomtesse de, Saint-Rémy-des-Monts (Sarthe), France, Jan. 20, 1830— Paris, Jan., 1907; pupil of Flotow and Saint-Saëns (comp.); prod. the operas *"Piccolini"* (Op.-Com., 1868), *"Les Fiances des Rosa"* (Th.-Lyr., 1863), *"Atala"* (Paris, 1888), *"Mazeppa"* (Bordeaux, 1892) and others; won the Prix Rossini with oratorio *"La Fille de Jaïre,"* *"drame sacré,"* *"Sainte-Agnès"* in MS.; had prod. symph. works and songs; sometimes wrote under pen names **"Tesier, Valgrand, Jasper, Banger,"** etc.

Gras (dorü-gräs), Mme. **Julia Aimée Dorus**, Valenciennes, 1807—retired, 1850; operatic singer Paris and London.

Grasse (gräs), **Edwin**, b. New York City, Aug. 13, 1884; blind violinist, pianist and composer; pupil of Carl Hauser, N. Y.; at 13, of César Thomson, Brussels, then at the Cons., taking 1st prize; 1901 took "Prix de Capacité"; début Berlin, Feb. 22, 1902, with succ. N. Y., 1903; has given many concerts in U. S., incl. his own works for piano, vln., org., etc.

Grasset (gräs-sä), **J. Jacques**, Paris, ca. 1767—1839; violinist, conductor, professor, etc.

Grassini (gräs-sē'-nē), **Josephina**, Varese, Lombardy, 1773—Milan, 1850; Italian soprano of remarkable talent and beauty.

Gratiani. Vide GRAZIANI.

Grau (grow), **Maurice**, Brünn, Austria, 1849—Paris, March 13, 1907; impresario of Met. Op., 1883, 1891–1903.

Graumann (grow'-män), **Mathilde.** Vide MARCHESI.

Graun (grown), (1) **Aug. Fr.**, 1727–71,

tenor, cantor. (2) **Jn. Gl.**, 1698— Berlin, 1771; bro. of above; violinist; pupil of Pisendel and Tartini; in service of Fredk. the Great and cond. of Royal band; c. 40 symphonies, etc. (3) **K. H.**, Wahrenbrück, Prussian Saxony, May 7, 1701—Berlin, Aug. 8, 1759; bro. of above; organist, singer, court-conductor, and composer.

Graupner (growp'-nĕr), **Chp.**, Kirchberg, Saxony, 1687 — Darmstadt, 1760; dram. composer.

Graveure (gräv-ĕr'), **Louis**, American tenor; originally sang as barytone; N. Y. début, 1915; has appeared widely as Lieder singer; formerly faculty member, Mich. State Inst. of Mus. and Allied Arts; held private classes in several Amer. cities; now res. in Europe; m. Eleanor Painter, soprano; divorced.

Gray, Alan, York, Dec. 23, 1855— Cambridge, England, Sept. 27, 1935; organist; studied law, then music under Dr. E. G. Monk; 1883–92, musical dir. Wellington College; then org. Trinity College, Cambridge, and cond. of the University Musical Society; c. cantatas *"Arethusa"* (Leeds Festival, 1892) and *"A Song of Redemption"* (do., 1898), 4 organ sonatas, string quartet, piano quartet, violin sonata, part-songs, etc.

Graziani (grä-tsē-ä'-nē), (1) (Padre) **Tommaso**, b. Bagnacavallo, Papal States; conductor and composer of 16th cent. (2) (or **Gratiani**) **Boniface**, Marino, Papal States, ca. 1606 —Rome, 1664; cond. and composer. (3) **Ludovico**, Fermo, Italy, 1823— 1885; tenor. (4) **Francesco**, Fermo, April 16, 1829—Fermo, June 30, 1901, bro. of above; barytone, sang in Italy, Paris, New York.

Grazzini (gräd-zē'-nē), **Reginaldo**, Florence, Oct. 15, 1848—Oct. 6, 1906; studied R. Cons. with T. Mabellini; op.-cond. in Florence, later prof. of mus. theory and artistic dir. Liceo Benedetto Marcello, Venice; c. symphonies; a mass with orch., etc.

Great'orex, Thos., North Wingfield, Derby, Engl., 1758—Hampton, near London, 1831; organist, teacher, and composer (1789–93); then conductor.

Green, Samuel, London, 1740—Isleworth, 1796; organ-builder.

Greene, (1) **Maurice**, London, 1696 (1695 ?)—1755; teacher and composer. (2) (**Harry**) **Plunket**, Old

Connaught House, Co. Wicklow, Ireland, June 24, 1865—London, Aug. 19, 1936; basso; studied with Hromada and Goetschius, Stuttgart, 1883–86, and 6 months with Vannuccini of Florence; later with J. B. Welch and Alf. Blume, London; début, Jan. 21, 1888, in "*Messiah*"; début in opera at Covent Garden, 1890; heard widely in recitals; sang frequently in America.

Grefinger (or **Gräfinger**) (grä'-fĭng-ĕr), Jn. W., Vienna, 16th cent. composer.

Gregh (grĕg), **Louis**, Paris, 1843—Dourdan, 1915; Paris music-publisher; 1894 prod. pantomime; vaudeville operettas, etc.

Gregoir (grŭg-wăr), (1) **Jacques Mathieu Joseph**, Antwerp, 1817—Brussels, 1876; teacher and dram. composer. (2) **Ed.**, Turnhout, near Antwerp, Nov. 7, 1822—Wyneghem, June 28, 1890; bro. and pupil of above; pianist, dram. composer and writer.

Gregoro'vitch, Charles, St. Petersburg, Oct. 25, 1867—(suicide) 1926 (?); violinist; pupil of Wieniawski, Dont and Joachim; 1896–97 toured Europe and America.

Greg'ory I. ("The Great"), Rome, 540–604; Pope from 590; reformer and reviser of Roman Catholic ritual. V. GREGORIAN and MODES (D D.).

Greith (grīt), **Karl**, Aarau, Feb. 21, ~828—Munich, Nov. 17, 1887; org. and comp. of church music.

Grell, Ed. Aug., Berlin, 1800—Steglitz, near Berlin, 1886; organist, conductor, prof. and composer.

Grenié (grŭn-yä) **Gabriel Jos.**, Bordeaux, 1756—Paris, 1837; inv. of the *orgue expressif* (v. HARMONIUM, D. D.), which Erard improved.

Gren'ville, Lillian, b. New York, Nov. 20, 1888; soprano; studied with Algier, Aramis, Rossi and Sebastiani; début as "Juliette," Nice, 1906; sang also in Milan, Brussels, Naples, Genoa and Lisbon; mem. Chicago Op., 1910–11; d. Paris, 1928.

Gresnich (grĕn-ĭsh), **Ant. Frédéric**, Liége, 1755—Paris, 1799; conductor and dram. composer.

Gretchaninoff (grä-chä'-nē-nôf), **Alex. Tikhonovich**, b. Moscow, Oct. 26, 1864; composer; pupil of Safonoff at the Cons.; later at St. Petersburg Cons., under Rachmaninoff; prof. of comp. Moscow Cons. until 1928;

visited U. S. 1930, and now resides in N. Y.; appeared in concerts of his works; c. succ. opera "*Dobringa Nikitich*" (Moscow, 1903); incidental music to Tolstoi's "*Feodor*," and "*Ivan*," and to Ostroski's "*Snow-Maiden*"; 2 symphonies; 3 string quartets; (opera) "*Sœur Beatrice*" after Maeterlinck play (prod. Moscow, 1912, but later withdrawn because appearance of the Virgin on stage considered sacrilegious); also sacred choruses and liturgies; "*At the Cross-roads*" for bass and orch.; vln. works, songs, chamber comps., etc.

Grétry (grä-trwē), (1) **André Ernest Modeste**, Liége, Feb. 9, 1741—Montmorency, near Paris, Sept. 24, 1813; dram. composer; son of a violinist. Chorister at 6, but dismissed for incapacity at 11, then pupil of Leclerc and Renekin. R. failing to keep him to the strict course of cpt. Moreau later tried with equal failure; 1758 he prod. 6 symphonies at Liége; 1759 a mass for which the Canon du Harlez sent him to study in Rome, to which he walked; he studied cpt. and comp. with Casali and Martini for 5 years, but was again dismissed as impossible; a dramatic intermezzo, "*Le Vendemmiatrice*," was succ. 1765, but reading Monsigny's "*Rose et Colas*," he decided that his restless dramatic longings were best adapted for French opéra comique. He was a long time finding a fit librettist (Voltaire declining his invitation). He reached Paris slowly *via* Geneva, where he taught singing a year and prod. the succ. 1-act "*Isabelle et Gertrude*." In Paris after 2 years' hardships his "*Les Mariages Samnites*" was rehearsed, and though not prod., won him a patron in Count Creutz, the Swedish Minister, who secured him as libretto Marmontel's comedy "*Le Huron*." This was prod. (Op.-com., 1768) with a great succ., enjoyed also in extraordinary degree by an astounding series of works, mostly comic and mostly successful, the best of which are "*Lucile*," "*Le Tableau Parlant*" (1769), "*Les Deux Avares*," "*Zémire et Azor*" (1771), "*Le Magnifique*" (1773); "*La Rosière de Salency*" (1774); "*La Fausse Magie*" (1775), "*Le Jugement de Midas*" (in which he satirised the old French music and its rendition at the Académie), and *"L'Amant Jaloux"* (1778); the grand opera *"Andromaque"* (1780) (in which the chief rôle is accompanied by 3 flutes throughout); *"La Double Épreuve"* (or *"Colinette à la cour"*) (1782); *"Théodore et Pauline"* (or *"L'Épreuve villageoise"*); and *"Richard Cœur de Lion"* (his best work, still played in Paris); the gr. opera *"La Caravane du Caïre"* (1785) performed 506 times; (libretto by the Comte de Provence, later Louis XVIII.); *"La Rosière Républicaine"* (1793); *"La Fête de la Raison"* (prod. 1794 during the Revolution); *"Lisbeth"*; *"Anacreon chez Polycrate"* (1797); c. 50 operas in all, remarkable for spontaneity, grace and fervour of melody, dramatic effect and general charm, but open to serious criticism as works of formal art. He was called "the Molière of music." Mozart and Beethoven wrote Variations on themes of his. Once launched, his progress was a triumph of honour of all kinds; in 1802 Napoleon made him Chevalier of the Legion of Honour with a pension of 4,000 francs. He bought Rousseau's former residence at Montmorency and retired there; wrote *Memoirs*, etc. He had several children, including the gifted Lucille (v. *infra*), all of whom he outlived. He left 6 unprod. operas and c. also 6 symphonies; 6 pf.-sonatas, 6 string-quartets, church-mus., etc. Biog. by his nephew, A. J. G. (1815); Grégoir (1883); Brunet (1884), etc. (2) **Lucille**, Paris, 1773–93; daughter of above, who instrumented her opera *"Le Mariage d'Antonio,"* written and prod. at the Op.-Com., with succ. when she was only 13; the next year her opera *"Toinette et Louis"* was not a success; she married unhappily and died at 20.

Greulich (groi'-lĭkh), (1) **K. W.,** Kunzendorf, Silesia, 1796—1837; teacher and composer. (2) **Ad.,** Posen, 1819—Moscow, 1868; teacher and composer. (3) **Ad.,** Schmiedeberg, Silesia, 1836—Breslau, 1890; conductor, bass., organist and composer.

Grey, Madeleine, b. Villaines, France, June 11, 1897; soprano; studied piano with Cortot, voice with Hettlich; début, Paris, 1921; appearances in recital and with orch. in many Eur. countries, South America,

Egypt, U. S.; specialist in modern French and Spanish music and folksongs.

Grieg (grēg), **Edvard Hagerup,** Bergen, June 15, 1843—Sept. 4, 1907; pupil of his mother, a pianist; at 15 entered Leipzig Cons.; pupil of Hauptmann and Richter (harm. and cpt.); Rietz and Reinecke (comp.); Wenzel and Moscheles (pf.); then with Gade, Copenhagen. With the young Norwegian composer Rikard Nordraak, he conspired, as he said, "Against the effeminate Mendelssohnian-Gade Scandinavianism, turning with enthusiasm into the new, well-defined path along which the Northern School is now travelling." 1867 Grieg founded a Musical Union in Christiania and was cond. till 1880; 1865 visited Ita y, again in 1870, meeting Liszt in Rome. 1879 he performed his pf.-concerto at the Gewandhaus, Leipzig. After 1880 lived chiefly in Bergen; cond. the Christiania Phil.; 1888 played his concerto and cond. his 2 melodies for string-orch. at London Phil. 1894 Mus. Doc. Cantab. C. concert-overture *"In Autumn"*; op. 20, *"Vor der Klosterpforte,"* for solo, female voices and orch.; *"Landerkennung"* for male chorus with orch.; *"Der Einsame"* for barytone, string orch. and 2 horns; op. 35, *"Norwegische Tänze,"* for orch.; op. 40, *"Aus Holzberg's Zeit,"* suite for string orch.; *"Bergliot,"* melodrama with orch.; *"Peer Gynt,"* suites 1 and 2 for orch.; op. 50, *"Olav Trygvason,"* for solo, chorus, and orch.; *"Sigurd Jorsalfar"* for orch., etc.; op. 22, 2 songs for male voices and orch.; various pcs. for string orch., string-quartet in G min.; pf.-concerto; pf.-sonatas, 3 vln.-sonatas, a 'cello-sonata, also for pf.-*"Poetische Tonbilder,"* Romanzen and Balladen; several sets of *"Lyrische Stücke,"* *"Symphonische Stücke"* (4 hands), *"Norwegische Volkslieder und Tänze,"* *"Bilder aüs dem Volksleben,"* *Peer Gynt* suite No. 1 (4 hands), and many songs, incl. song-cycle to Garborg's *"Haugtussa."* Biog. by Ernest Closson, Mason, Schelderup, Finck, Lee, La Mara.

Griepenkerl (grē'-pĕnk-ĕrl), (1) **F. K.,** Peine, Brunswick, 1782—Brunswick, 1849; Prof. (2) **W. Rob.,**

Holwyl, 1810—Brunswick, 1868; son of above; teacher and writer.

Griesbach (grēs'-bäkh), (1) John Hy., Windsor, 1798—London, 1875; son of the 'cellist. (2) J. C. G., pianist, 'cellist, dir. and writer.

Griesbacher (grēs'-bäkh-ĕr) Peter, Egglham, March 25, 1864—Regensburg, Jan. 29, 1933; priest and teacher at Regensburg; c. 40 masses, and other church music, also cantatas, etc.

Griesinger (grē'-zĭng-ĕr), G. Aug., d. Leipzig, 1828; writer.

Griffes (grĭf'-ĕs), Charles Tomlinson, Elmira, N. Y., Sept. 7, 1884—New York, April 8, 1920; composer; one of the most gifted and individual creators of Amer. impressionistic music, particularly for orch. and piano; studied with Jedliczka, Galston, Klatte, Loewengard and Humperdinck; taught in Berlin, later at Tarrytown, N. Y., and N. Y.; c. *"The Pleasure Dome of Kubla Khan"* for orch.; Poem for flute and orch.; (dance-drama) *"The Kairn of Koridwen"* for wind, harp, celesta and piano; Japanese mimeplay, *"Schojo"*; 2 pieces for string quartet; piano sonata, and many shorter works for this instrument, incl. *"Four Roman Sketches"* (among which *"The White Peacock"* is particularly pop. in its orchestrated version); and a quantity of original songs, incl. Japanese poems set in pentatonic scale; his early death was a deep loss to Amer. music.

Grif'fin, (1) Thos., English organ builder 18th cent. (2) George Eugene, 1781—London, 1863; Engl. pianist and composer.

Griffith, Frederick, Swansea, Nov. 12, 1867—London, May, 1917; at 14 won prize at a Welsh national Eisteddfod; pupil at R. A. M.; 1889–91 with Svendsen, later with Jaffanel, Paris; toured widely; flutist at Covent Garden, and prof. at R. A. M.

Grigny (grēn'-yē), Nicolas de, Reims, 1671—1703; organist and comp.

Grillet (grē-yā), Laurent, Sancoins, Cher, France, May 22, 1851—Paris, Nov. 5, 1901; pupil of A. Martin ('cello), E. Mangin (harm.), and Ratez (cpt. and fugue); cond. various theatres; 1886 Nouveau-Cirque, Paris; writer; c. comic opera *"Graciosa"* (Paris, 1892), ballets, etc.

Grill'parzer, Fz., Vienna, Jan. 15, 1791—Jan. 21, 1871; friend of Beethoven and Schubert. Comp.

Grimm, (1) Fr. Melchior, Baron von, Ratisbon, 1723—Gotha, 1807; one of the advocates and controversialists for the Ital. *opera buffa.* (2) Karl, Hildburghausen, 1819—Freiburg, Silesia, 1888; 'cellist and composer. (3) K. Konst., lived in Berlin, 1820—1882; harpist. (4) Julius Otto, Pernau, Livonia, March 6, 1827—Münster, Dec. 7, 1903; pianist; pupil of Leipzig Cons.; founded vocal society at Göttingen, then R. Mus. Dir. Münster Academy and cond.; c. a symphony, 2 suites in canon-form, etc.

Grim'mer, Chr. Fr., Mulda, Saxony, 1798—1850; composer.

Grisar (grē-zär), Albert, Antwerp, Dec. 26, 1808—Asnières, near Paris, June 15, 1869; prolific dram. composer; biog. by Pougin, Paris.

Grisart (grē-zär), Chas. J. Bapt., prod. light operas in minor theatres, the last *"Le Petit Bois"* (1893) and *"Voilà le Roi"* (1894).

Grisi (grē-zē), (1) Giuditta, Milan, July 28, 1805—near Cremona, May 1, 1840; famous mezzo-soprano; pupil of Milan Cons.; m. Count Barni, 1834. (2) Giulia, Milan, July 28, 1811—Berlin, Nov. 29, 1869; sister and pupil of above; famous dramatic soprano; pupil of Giacomelli, Pasta and Marliani; m. Count Melcy, later m. Mario.

Griswold, Putnam, Minneapolis, Dec. 23, 1875—New York, Feb. 2ɔ, 1914; bass; pupil of Randegger, Bouhy, Stockhausen and Emerich; début, Covent Garden, 1901; sang in Berlin and with Savage Op. Co. in *"Parsifal"*; Berlin R. Op., 1906–11; Met. Op. Co., after latter year, winning succ. in Wagnerian rôles.

Grofé (grō'-fā), Ferde (rightly Ferdinand Rudolph von Grofe), b. New York, 1892; conductor and composer; studied harmony and theory with his mother, Elsa von Grofe, a grad. of Leipzig Cons.; at 16 pub. first composition; following year mem. of Los Angeles Symph.; won increasing reputation as cond. of modern syncopated music; known as comp. particularly of picturesque descriptive suites, in which he has employed novel jazz scoring devices.

Groningen (grō'-nĭng-ĕn), Stefan van,

Deventer, Holland, June 23, 1851— Laren, March 25, 1926; pupil of Raif and Kiel, Berlin; pianist; teacher in Zwolle, The Hague, Leyden; composer.

Grosheim (grōs'-hīm), G. Chr., Cassel, 1764—1847; dram. composer.

Grosjean (grō-zhäṅ), J. Romary, Rochesson, Vosges, France, 1815— St. Dié, 1888; org. composer and writer.

Gross (grôs), Jn. Benj., Elbing, West Prussia, 1809—St. Petersburg, 1848; 'cellist and composer.

Grosz, Wilhelm, b. Vienna, Aug. 11, 1894—N. Y., 1939; pupil of Schreker and Guido Adler; Ph. D.; c. (opera) "Sganarell"; chamber and vocal music in modern, satiric style.

Gross'man, Ludwig, Kalisz, Poland, 1835—Warsaw, July 15, 1915; c. overtures "Lear" and "Marie," and succ. operas "Fisherman of Palermo" (Warsaw, 1866) and "Woyewoda's Ghost" (1872).

Grove, Sir George, Clapham, Surrey, Aug. 13, 1820—London, May 28, 1900; civil engineer; Sec. to the Society of Arts; 1852, Sec., and 1873 a member of the Board of Directors, Crystal Palace; edited Macmillan's Magazine; later dir. of the Royal Coll. of Mus.; 1883, knighted; 1875 D.C.L. Univ. of Durham; 1885 LL.D., Glasgow; wrote important book "Beethoven and His Nine Symphonies" (1896), etc., and was the editor-in-chief 1879-89 of the musical dictionary known by his name.

Grovlez (grôv'-lāz), Gabriel, Lille, April 4, 1879—Paris, Oct. 24, 1944; pianist; educated Paris Cons., 1st prize in piano; studied with Diémer, Lavignac, Fauré; cond. at Paris Op.-Comique, Chicago Op.; c. incidental music for plays, orchestral and piano works, songs, also a ballet, "La Fête à Robinson," given by Chicago Op., 1921.

Grua (groo'-ä), (1) C. L. P., court-conductor at Mannheim and composer, 1700—1755. (2) Paul, Mannheim, 1754—Munich, 1833; son of above; conductor and dram. composer.

Gruber (groo'-bĕr), Jn. Sigismund, Nürnberg, 1759—1805; lawyer and writer.

Gruen'berg, Louis, b. Russia, Aug. 3, 1883; composer, pianist; taken to America at age of 2; studied Vienna

Cons. and with Busoni and Friedrich Koch; c. (orch.) "The Hill of Dreams" (N. Y. Symph. Orch. prize, 1919); "The Enchanted Isle" (Worcester Fest.); "The Valley of Voices," "The Blue Castle," "Vagabondia" (Prague Philh., under comp.); "Jazz Suite" (Boston Symph.); symph. "Music to an Imaginary Ballet"; "Daniel Jazz" for tenor and 8 instruments (Internat'l. Soc. for Contemporary Music Fest.); "The Creation" for barytone and 8 instruments (N. Y. League of Comp.); 2 suites for vln. and piano, 2 vln. sonatas; "Indiscretions" and "Diversations" for string quartet; (operas) "Jack and the Beanstalk" (Juilliard Op. School, N. Y., and Chicago Op., 1936-37); "Emperor Jones" (after O'Neill drama), Met. Op. Co., 1932, one of the most graphic and stageworthy of Amer. operas, in impressionistic modern idiom; his music in general has many colourful elements, strikingly orchestrated and dissonantal in harmony; mem., board of directors, N. Y. League of Comp.; has taught at Chicago Musical College.

Grün (grün), Friederike, Mannheim, June 14, 1836—Jan., 1917; soprano, at first in the opera-chorus, then sang solo parts at Frankfort, later (1863) at Cassel and 1866-69 Berlin; 1869 m. Russian Baron von Sadler; studied with Lamperti at Milan and continued to sing with success.

Grünberger (grün'-bĕrkh-ĕr), Ludwig, Prague, 1839—1896; pianist and composer.

Grund (groont), Fr. Wm., Hamburg, 1791—1874; conductor and dram. composer.

Grünfeld (grün'-fĕlt), (1) Alfred, Prague, July 4, 1852—Vienna, Jan. 5, 1924; pianist and composer; pupil of Hoger and Krejci, later at Kullak's Academy, Berlin; 1873, chamber-virtuoso, Vienna; toured Europe and the U. S. (2) Heinrich, Prague, April 21, 1855—Berlin, Aug. 26, 1931; bro. of above; 'cellist; pupil of Prague Cons.; 1876, teacher in Kullak's Academy; 1886 'cellist to the Emperor; wrote memoirs, "In Dur und Moll" (1924).

Grützmacher (grüts'-mäkh-ĕr), (1) Fr. Wm. L., Dessau, March 1, 1832— Dresden, Feb. 23, 1903; eminent 'cellist; son and pupil of a chamber-musician at Dessau; later studied with Drechsler ('cello) and Schneider (theory); at 16 joined a small Leipzig orch.; was "discovered" by David, and at 17 made 1st 'cello, Gewandhaus orch. and teacher at the Cons.; 1869 Dresden, later Cologne; 1902 Philadelphia; c. concerto for 'cello, orch.-and chamber-music, pf.-pcs., songs, etc. (2) **Ld.**, Dessau, Sept. 4, 1835—Weimar, Feb. 27, 1900; bro. and pupil of above; studied with Drechsler ('cello) and Schneider (theory); played in the Gewandhaus orch., Leipzig; then 1st 'cello Schwerin court-orch.; 1876 chamber virtuoso at Weimar. (3) **Friedrich,** Meiningen, July 20, 1866—Cologne, July 25, 1919; son and pupil of (2); 1st 'cello Sondershausen court-orch., then Pesth (1890); 1892–94 prof. at the Cons., Pesth; 1894 in the Gürzenich Orch. and teacher at the Cons., Cologne.

Guadagni (goo-ä-dän'-yē), **Gaetano,** Lodi, 1725 (?)—1785 (97?); male contralto (later a soprano) of 18th cent.; Gluck wrote *"Telemaco"* for him.

Guadagnini (goo-ä-dän-yē'-nē), family of vln.-makers of the Cremona school. (1) **Lorenzo** and (2) **John Baptiste,** worked 1690–1740. (3) **J. B.,** the younger (son of Lorenzo), also made excellent violins.

Guarducci (goo-är-doot'-chē), Montefiascone, ca. 1720 (?); Italian singer in London, 1766–71.

Guarneri (goo-är-nä'-rē) (Latinized **Guarne'rius**), family of famous vln.-makers at Cremona. (1) **Pietro Andrea,** b. ca. 1626; worked 1650–95; pupil of N. Amati; his label *Andreas Guarnerius Cremonæ sub titolo Santæ Theresiæ* 16—. (2) **Giuseppe,** b. 1666; son of above; worked 1690–1730; his label *Joseph Guarnerius filius Andreas fecit Cremonæ sub titolo St. Theresiæ* 16—. (3) **P.,** b. ca. 1670; son of (1); worked 1690–1700. (4) **P.,** son of (2); worked 1725–40. (5) **Giuseppe Antonio** (known as **Guarneri del Gesù,** i.e., "the Jesus," from the "I H S" on his labels), Oct. 16, 1687—ca. 1745; the best of the family; nephew of (1); his label, *Joseph Guarnerius Andreæ Nepos Cremonæ* 17—, I H S.

Gudehus (goo'-dĕ-hoos), **H.,** Altenhagen, Hanover, March 30, 1845—Dresden, Oct. 9, 1909; tenor. son

of a village schoolmaster; pupil of Frau Schnorr von Karolsfeld at Brunswick; 1870–73 engaged for the court opera, Berlin; 1872, studied with Louise Ress. Dresden; re-appeared 1875; 1880–90 at Dresden ct.-opera, creating *"Parsifal"* at Bayreuth, 1882; in New York 1890–91, later at Berlin c'.-opera.

Guénin (gā-năn), **Marie Alex.,** Maubeuge (Nord), France, 1744—Paris, 1819; violinist and composer.

Guercia (goo-är-chē'-ä), **Alphonso,** b. Naples, Nov. 13, 1831—June, 1890; pupil of Mercadante; dram. barytone for a time; after 1859 vocal teacher, Naples; c. succ. opera *"Rita"* (Naples, 1875), etc.

Guérin (gā-răn), **Emmanuel,** b. Versailles, 1779; 'cellist.

Guerrero (gĕr-rā'-rō), **Francisco,** Sevilla, Spain, 1528—1599; conductor, singer and composer.

Gueymard (gĕ'-măr), **Louis,** Chapponay (Isère), France, 1822—Corbeil, near Paris, 1880; tenor, 1848–68 at the Gr. Opéra.

Guglielmi (gool-yĕl'-mē), (1) **Pietro** cond. to Duke of Modena. His son (2) **P.,** Massa di Carrara, Italy, Dec. 9, 1728—Rome, Nov. 19, 1804; conductor, teacher and composer of over 200 operas. (Perhaps the (3) **Signora G.** who sang in London 1770–72 was the wife he treated so shamefully.) Rival of Paisiello and Cimarosa; 1793 cond. at the Vatican, composed only church-music. (4) **Pietro Carlo** (called **Guglielmini**), Naples, ca. 1763—Massa di Carrara, 1827; son of above; dram. composer, teacher and conductor.

Gui (goo-ē'), **Vittorio,** b. Rome, Sept. 14, 1885; conductor, composer; pupil of Santa Cecilia Liceo, Rome, with Setaccioli and Falchi; début at Teatro Adriano in that city, 1907; later cond. in Parma, Turin, at Naples San Carlo Op., Bergamo, La Scala, at Augusteo (Rome), and at Lisbon; c. (lyric fable) *"Fata Malerba",* also orch. music, cantatas, song cycles.

Guicciardi (goo-ēt-chär'-dē) **Giulietta** (or *Julie*), Countess (or Gräfin), Nov. 24, 1784—March 22, 1855; pianist; pupil of Beethoven and his enamoured *inamorata;* a Viennese woman, m. Count Gallenberg, 1803.

Gui de Châlis (gē dŭ shäl-ēs) (**Guido**), end of the 12th cent.; writer.

Guidetti (goo-ē-dĕt'-tē), Giov., Bologna, 1530—Rome, 1592; pupil and
assistant of Palestrina; conductor
and composer.
Guido d'Arezzo (goo-ē'-dō där-rĕd'-zō)
(Latinized Areti'nus), (?) ca. 995—
Avellano (?), May 17 (?), 1050 (?);
eminent revolutionist in music; a
Benedictine monk at Pomposo, near
Ferrara, later perhaps at Arezzo;
some investigators identify him with
a Benedictine monk in the Monastery of St. Maur des Fosses, a
Frenchman who went to Italy, not
an Italian; his abilities as a singing-
teacher and musician led Pope John
XIX. to summon him to Rome; he
was later probably a Prior at Avellano; though he is being stripped of
many of his early honours, it seems
true that he introd. the 4-line staff,
and ledger-lines and Solmisation
(v. ARETINIAN; GAMUT and SOLMISA-
TION, D. D.).
Guido de Châlis. Vide GUI DE CHÂLIS.
Guignon (gēn-yôň), J. P., Turin, 1702
—Versailles, 1774; violinist and
composer.
Guilbert, Yvette (gĕl-bār, ē-vĕt'),
Paris, 1867—Aix-la-Provence, Feb.
2, 1944; début as actress, 1885, as
singer, 1890; especially noted for her
dram. gifts and as singer of chansons;
appeared in leading Eur. capitals,
also in America at various times
after 1906; estab. school for dram.
artists with branch in N. Y.
Guillemain (gē'-yŭ-măň), Gabriel,
Paris, Nov. 15, 1705—(suicide) Oct.
1, 1770; c. violin pieces.
Guilmant (gĕl-mäň), (1) Félix Alex.,
Boulogne, March 12, 1837—Meudon
near Paris, March 29, 1911; son
and pupil of the org. (2) Jean Baptiste G. (Boulogne, 1793—1800);
later pupil of Lemmens and G.
Carulli (harm.); at 12 substitute for
his father at the church of St. Nicolas; at 16 organist at St. Joseph; at
18 prod. a solemn mass; at 20 choirm.
at St. Nicholas, teacher in Boulogne
Cons. and cond. of a mus. soc.; 1871
organist of Ste. Trinité; 1893 chev.
of Legion of Honour; 1896 org.-
prof., Paris Cons.; 1893, 1897-98,
toured Europe and U. S. with much
succ.; 1901 resigned from Ste. Trinité; made concert tours of England,
Italy, Russia; one of the founders
of the Schola Cantorum; after 1906
prof. of org., Paris Cons.; c. "lyric

scene" "Belsazar" for soli, chorus
and orch.; "Christus Vincit," hymn
for chorus, orch., harps and org.;
org. sonatas, symphonies for organ
and orch., etc., wrote treatise on
instrumentation; ed. collection of
Gregorian music.
Guiraud (gē-rō), (1) Ernest, New
Orleans, June 23, 1837—Paris, May
6, 1892; son of (2) Jean Baptiste
G. (Prix de Rome, Paris Cons., 1827),
at 12 in Paris; at 15 prod. opera
"Le roi David" at New Orleans;
studied Paris Cons., and took Grand
Prix de Rome; later prof. of Paris
Cons. and dram. composer.
Gulbranson (gool'-brän-zōn), Ellen,
b. Stockholm, March 3, 1863; notable
soprano; studied with Marchesi, sang
in concert; 1889 entered opera, sing-
ing "Brünnhilde," 1899 "Kundry" at
Bayreuth and other rôles in other
cities; lived on her estate near
Christiania; d. Nov., 1948.
Gumbert (goom'-bĕrt), Fd., Berlin,
1818—1896; tenor and barytone;
also critic and dram. composer.
Gumpeltzhaimer (goom'-pĕlts-hī-mĕr),
Adam, Trostberg, Bavaria, 1559—
Augsburg, 1625; composer and theorist.
Gumpert (goom'-pĕrt), Fr. Ad.,
Lichtenau, Thuringia, April 27,
1841—Leipzig, Dec. 31, 1906; pupil
of Hammann; from 1864 1st horn
Gewandhaus Orch., Leipzig; writer
and composer.
Gumprecht (goom'-prĕkht), Otto, b.
Erfurt, April 4, 1823—Merano, 1900;
Dr. jur.; 1849 critic and writer.
Gungl (or Gung'l) (goong'-l), (1) Joseph, Zsámbék, Hungary, Dec. 1,
1810—Weimar, Jan. 31, 1889; oboist,
bandmaster and composer of pop.
dance-music. (2) Virginia, daughter
of above; opera-singer; début ct.-
opera, Berlin, 1871; later at Frankfort. (3) Jn., Zsámbék, 1828—Pecs,
Hungary, 1883; nephew of (1); composer.
Gunn, (1) Barnaby, 1730-53, organist.
(2) John, Edinburgh (?), 1765 (?)—
ca. 1824; Chelsea Hospital, 1730-53;
'cello-teacher and writer. (3) Glenn
Dillard, b. Topeka, Kans., Oct. 2,
1874; pianist, educator; studied in
Leipzig with Reinecke, Teichmüller,
Schreck; début as pianist, 1896;
toured Germany; taught Amer.
Cons., Chicago, 1900-01; Chicago
Mus. Coll. from latter year to 1906;

founded his own school of music, 1906; mus. ed., Chicago *Herald Examiner;* has appeared as soloist with leading orchs.

Günther (gün'-tĕr), (1) **Hermann**, Leipzig, 1834–71; a physician; c. opera under name "F. Hesther." (2) **Otto**, Leipzig, 1822—1897; bro. of above; dir. (3) **Günther-Bachmann, Karoline**, Düsseldorf, 1816— Leipzig, 1874; singer.

Gunz (goonts), **G.**, Gaunersdorf, Lower Austria, 1831—Frankfort, 1894; tenor.

Gura (goo'-rä), (1) **Eugen**, Pressern, n. Saatz, Bohemia, Nov. 8, 1842— Aufkirchen, Aug. 26, 1906; barytone; pupil of Polytechnic and the Akademie, Vienna; then Munich Cons., début 1865, Munich; 1867–70 Breslau; 1870–76 Leipzig with great succ.; 1876–83 Hamburg, Munich, 1883–95. His son (2) **Hermann** (b. Breslau, April 5, 1870) barytone; operatic stage director and after 1927 a singing teacher in Berlin.

Gurlitt (goor'-lĭt), **Cornelius**, Altona, near Hamburg, Feb. 10, 1820— Berlin, 1901; pupil of the elder Reinecke and Weyse; army mus. dir. in the Schleswig-Holstein campaign; prof. Hamburg Cons.; 1874 Royal Mus. Dir.; c. 3 operas, incl. *"Die römische Mauer"* (Altona, 1860), etc.

Gürrlich (gür'-lĭkh), **Jos. Augustin**, Munsterberg, Silesia, 1761—Berlin, 1817; organist, bass, court-conductor and dram. composer.

Gusikow (goo'-zĭ-kôf), **Michael Jos.**, Sklow, in Poland, Sept. 1806—Aix-la-Chapelle, Oct., 1837; remarkable virtuoso on the xylophone.

Gutheil-Schoder (goot'-hīl-shō'-dĕr), **Marie**, Weimar, Feb. 10, 1874— Ilmenau, Oct. 4, 1935; mezzo-soprano; pupil of Virginia Gungl, and Weimar Music School; 1891–1900 at Weimar court opera; later at Vienna opera; m. Gustav Gutheil, conductor at Vienna Volksoper.

Gyrowetz (gē'-rō-vēts), **Adalbert**, Budweis, Bohemia, Feb. 19, 1763— Vienna, March 19, 1850; son and pupil of a choirm.; c. symphonies, operettas, etc.; court-conductor.

H

Haack (häk), **Karl**, Potsdam, Feb. 18, 1751—Sept. 28, 1819; violinist and teacher; court cond. to Fr.

Wilhelm II. at Potsdam; c. violin pieces.

Haas (häz), **Jos.**, b. Maihingen, Bavaria, Mar. 19, 1879; composer; pupil of Reger; 1911, taught Stuttgart Cons.; 1921, Manich Akad.; c. oratorios, orch. and chamber works, songs, based on German folk-style.

Ha'ba (ä'-bä), (1) **Alois**, b. Wisowitz, Moravia, June 21, 1893; comp. esp. known for his researches and works in style of quarter-tone music; pupil of Vienna and Prague Cons., won Mendelssohn Prize, 1921; taught at Berlin Hochsch., 1921–23; c. of much chamber music in which he has used a quarter-tone scale, and in later works a sixth-tone system; has given concerts on specially constructed quarter-tone piano; author of *"The Theory of Quarter-tones,"* *"Treatise on the Foundations of Tonal Differentiation."* (2) **Karel**, his bro.. has also c. music in the same style.

Habeneck (äb'-ĕ-nĕk), **François Ant.**, Mézières (Ardennes), France, June 1 (Jan. 25 ?), 1781—Paris, Feb. 8, 1849; son and pupil of a German musician; studied Paris Cons.; later cond. of its concerts and vln.-prof.; introd. Beethoven's symphonies to the French public; composer.

Haberbier (hä'-bĕr-bēr), **Ernst**, Königsberg, Oct. 5, 1813—Bergen, Norway, March 12, 1869; son and pupil of an organist; court-pianist at St. Petersburg; later toured with great success; composer.

Haberl (hä'-bĕrl), **Fz. X.**, Oberellenbach, Lower Bavaria, April 12, 1840—Ratisbon, Sept. 7, 1910; took orders 1862; 1862–67 cath. cond. and mus. dir. Passau Seminary; 1867–70 organist, Rome; 1871–82 cath.-cond. at Ratisbon; 1875 founded famous sch. for church-music; edited Palestrina's works, etc.; 1889, Dr. Theol. *h. c.*, Univ. of Würzburg.

Habermann (hä'-bĕr-män), **Fz. Jn.**, Königswarth, Bohemia, 1706—Eger, 1783; conductor, teacher and composer.

Habert (hä'-bĕrt), **Jns. Evangelista**, Oberplan, Bohemia, 1833—Gmunden, 1896; editor and collector.

Hack'ett, (1) **Chas.**, Worcester, Mass., 1889—Jan. 1, 1942; tenor; pupil Arthur Hubbard and Lombardi; opera début in Mignon, Genoa, 1916; sang at Milan, Rome, London, Paris,

Madrid, and in South America; début Met. Op. as "Almaviva," 1919, sang with co. for 3 years, and again after 1935; was regular mem. of Chicago Op. from 1923 for more than a decade; also heard with Ravinia and Los Angeles Op. and in concert. (2) **Arthur,** b. Portland. Me., tenor; bro. of **Charles H.;** studied vln. in youth, also voice with Hubbard; appeared at Paris Op., recital tours in U. S. and Great Britain, well known as oratorio soloist; prof. of voice, Univ. of Mich. (3) **Karleton,** Brookline. Mass., Oct. 8, 1867—Chicago, Oct. 7, 1935; mus. critic, teacher of singing: grad. Harvard Univ., 1891; vice-pres. and head of vocal dept., Amer. Cons., Chicago; was critic of the Chicago *Evening Post* for a number of years; for a brief time before his death he had been pres. of the Chicago City Op. Co.

Hackh (häk). Otto (**Chp.**), Stuttgart, Sept. 30, 1852—Brooklyn, N. Y., 1917; pupil of Stuttgart Cons. and of A. de Kontski (pf.), at New York; 1872-75 teacher at the Cons.; 1877-78 toured; 1878 teacher in London; in 1880-89 Ger. Cons., New York; later private teacher and composer.

Hadley, Henry Kimball, b. Somerville, Mass., Dec. 20, 1871—New York, Sept. 6, 1937; showed early musical precocity; studied with Heindl, Emery and Chadwick; in 1893 toured with the Mapleson Opera Co. as violinist in its orch.; the next year went to Vienna for study under Mandyczewski; returned to U. S. and taught music (1896) at St. Paul's Episcopal School for Boys, Garden City, L. I.; made début as cond. in concert at Waldorf-Astoria, N. Y., 1900; again toured Europe, 1904-10, having further study with Thuille in Munich and acting as guest cond. of orchs. in Warsaw and Mainz; in the latter city his opera *"Safie"* was prod., 1909 (he had already had a symph., *" Youth and Life,"* perf. by Seidl in 1897). On his return from Europe, he became cond. of the Seattle Symph. Orch., 1909-11; and of the San Francisco Symph. Orch., 1911-15. He also appeared as guest leader in Europe, America and Japan. In later years he had been assoc. cond. of the N. Y. Philh. Orch., beginning 1920; cond.

Manhattan Symph. in N. Y., 1931-32; and of the Berkshire Fest., 1934-35. Among the very large number of his comps., the following are outstanding: (operas) *"Azora"* (Chicago, 1917); *"Bianca"* (one-act work winning award of Amer. Soc. of Singers, 1918, and perf. N. Y.); *"Cleopatra's Night"* (Met. Op. Co., 1920); also 4 symph., the 2nd of which, subtitled *"The Four Seasons,"* took two prizes simultaneously in 1901, the Paderewski and the New England Cons. His fourth symph. *" North, East, South and West"* he cond. himself with the London Philh., Boston Symph., and other orch.; c. overtures *"Hector and Andromache"* (Boston, 1901); *"In Bohemia"* (1903), *"Herod,"* symph. fantasie *"Salome"* (Boston Symph., 1907, Monte Carlo, 1907; Warsaw, 1908, Cassel, 1908); lyric drama *"Merlin and Vivien,"* piano quintet, (1907), etc. poetic rhapsody, *"The Culprit Fay"* (N. Y., 1912); a music drama, *"The Atonement of Pan"* (San Francisco, 1912); cantatas, *"In Music's Praise"* (winning Ditson Prize, 1899); *"A Legend of Granada," "The Nightingale and the Rose," "The Fate of Princess Kiyo," "The Golden Prince"* for women's voices; *"Mirtil in Arcadia,"* large-scale choral work; also the lyric drama, *"Ode to Music,"* for soloists, chorus and orch., a setting of a poem by Henry Van Dyke (Worcester, Mass., Fest., 1917); 7 Ballads for chorus and orch.; tone-poem, *"Lucifer"* (Norfolk Fest., 1915); Concertino for piano and orch.; 3 ballet suites for orch.; the descriptive suite, *"Streets of Pekin";* and a quantity of chamber music, incl. string quartet; vln. sonatas, and more than 150 songs; m. Inez Barbour, soprano.

Had'ow, Sir **William Henry,** b. Ehrington (Gloucester), England, Dec. 27, 1859—London, April 9, 1937; writer; grad. Oxford Univ., in 1885, a fellow, and 1888-1909, dean of Worcester Coll. at that Univ.; after 1909 principal of Armstrong Coll., New-castle-on-Tyne; he was knighted in 1918; 1919-30, vice-Chancellor of Sheffield Univ.; Mus. D., Oxford and Durham Univs.; author of *"William Byrd," "Studies in Modern Music,"* 2 series; *"Sonata Form"; "A Croatian Composer,"* a study of

Haydn; *"The Viennese Period"* comprising Vol. V of the Oxford Hist. of Music, of which he was the ed. (1901–05); also ed. *"Songs of the British Isles."*

Hadria'nus. Vide ADRIANSEN.

Häffner (hĕf'-nĕr), **Jn. Chr. Fr.**, Oberschönau, near Suhl, 1759—Upsala, Sweden, 1833; organist, court-conductor, dram. composer and collector.

Hageman (hä'-gĕ-män), (1) **Maurits Leonard,** Zutphen, Sept. 23, 1829—Dutch East Indies, 1900; violinist and pianist; pupil of Brussels Cons.; 1865–75 dir. Cons., Batavia; 1875 founder and dir. of a Cons., Leeuwarden; c. oratorio *"Daniel,"* etc. (2) **Richard,** b. Leeuwarden, Holland; composer, conductor; son of (1); studied with his father, and at Brussels under De Greef and Gevaert; asst. cond. Amsterdam Op., at 16; came to U. S. in 1906 as accompanist for Yvette Guilbert; asst. cond. Met. Op., N. Y., 1908–21; has also cond. at Chicago Op., Ravinia and Los Angeles Op.; and has appeared with Amer. orch.; c. opera *"Caponsacchi"* (based on Browning's *"Ring and the Book,"* libretto by Arthur Goodrich), première, Freiburg, Germany, 1931; later at Vienna, and was prod. by Met. Op. Co., in English, 1936–37; he again cond. with latter co. in 1936; known also as composer of many songs.

Hagen (hä'-gĕn), (1) **Fr. H. von der,** Schmiedeberg, Ukraine, 1780—Berlin, 1856; prof. and writer. (2) **Jn. Bapt.,** Mayence, 1818—Wiesbaden, 1870; conductor and composer. (3) **Ad.,** Bremen, Sept. 4, 1851—Dresden, June 6, 1926; son of above; violinist; 1879–82 cond. Hamburg Th.; 1883, court cond. Dresden, and 1884 manager of the Cons.; c. comic opera *"Zwei Komponisten,"* Hamburg, 1882, etc. (4) **Theodor,** Hamburg, 1823—New York, 1871; teacher, critic and composer.

Hahn (hän), (1) **Albert,** Thorn, West Prussia, 1828—Lindenau, near Leipzig, 1880; teacher. (2) **Reynaldo,** b. Caracas, Venezuela, Aug. 9, 1874; pupil of Massenet, Paris Cons.; lived in Paris; c. 3-act "idylle polynésienne" *"L'Ile du Rêve"* (Paris, Op.-com., 1898); opera, *"La Carme-*

lite," was prod. at the Opéra Comique, Paris, 1902; incidental music to C. Mendés' *"Scarron,"* Racine's *"Esther,"* and V. Hugo's *"Angelo"* (all in 1905); 2-act ballet *"La fête chez Thérèse"* (Opéra, 1910); *"Le Dieu Bleu"* (1912); *"Le Bois Sacré"* (1912); *"Nausicaa"* (Monte Carlo, 1919; Paris Op., 1923); music for Guitry's comedy *"Mozart"* (1925); also symph. poems, *"Nuit d'Amour,"* *"Bergamasque,"* *"Promethée Triomphant,"* etc.; songs of remarkable beauty and originality, etc.; d. Paris, Jan. 27, 1947.

Hähnel (hā'-nĕl). Vide GALLUS, J.

Haines, Napoleon J., London, 1824—New York, 1900; founder of Haines Bros. Piano Mfrs., N. Y.

Hainl (ăṅl), **Georges François,** Issoire, Puy-de-Dôme, 1807—Paris, 1873; 'cellist; conductor, writer and composer.

Haizinger (hī'-tsĭng-ĕr), **Anton,** Wilfersdorf, Lichtenstein, 1796—Vienna, 1869; tenor.

Hale (1), **Philip,** Norwich, Vt., March 5, 1854—Boston, Nov. 30, 1934; notable American critic and essayist; as a boy, organist Unit. Ch., Northampton, Mass.; 1876 grad. Yale Univ.; 1880 admitted to the Albany bar; pupil of D. Buck, 1876; 1882–87 studied organ and comp. with Haupt. Faiszt, Rheinberger and Guilmant, Urban, Bargiel, Raif and Scholz; 1879–82 organist St. Peter's, Albany; 1887–89 St. John's, Troy; 1889 of First Religious Soc., Roxbury, Mass.; 1887–89 also cond. of Schubert Club at Albany; 1889–91 critic successively of the Boston *Home Journal, Post;* 1891, *Journal;* 1897–1901 edited *Mus. Record;* 1901, ed. *Musical World;* lecturer on mus. subjects; critic, Boston *Herald,* 1903–34; wrote series of notable programme annotations for Boston Symph. (after 1901), extending over 3 decades; Mus. D., Dartmouth Coll.

Hale (or **Halle**). Vide ADAM DE LA HALE.

Halévy (ă-lā-vē), **Jac. Franç. Fromental Élie,** Paris, May 27, 1799—of consumption, Nice, March 17, 1862; of Jewish parentage; pupil of Cazot, Lambert (pf.), and Berton (harm.), Cherubini (cpt.); Paris Cons. winning 2nd harmony prize; 1816 and 1817, 2nd Prix de Rome; 1819 won Prix de Rome; 1827 prof.

of harmony and accomp. at the Cons.; 1833 prof. of cpt. and fugue; 1829 prod. 2 succ. operas; 1830 succ. ballet "*Manon Lescaut*"; 1830–46 *chef de chant* at the Opera; 1832 he completed Herold's "*Ludovic*" with succ.; 1835 he wrote and prod. 2 great successes, his masterpiece "*La Juive*" (Gr. Opéra) and a comic opera "*L'Eclair*"; Chevalier of the Legion of Honour; 1836 member of the Académie; 1854, secretary for life. In 1836 Meyerbeer appeared, and in efforts to rival his prestige H. wrote too much with inferior librettos, among his works being (1841) "*La Reine de Chypre*." He collaborated with Adam, Auber and Carafe in 4 operas; he left 2 unfinished operas, "*Vanina d'Ornano*" (completed by Bizet) and "*Le Déluge*." Biog. by his brother Léon (1862), etc.

Halff'ter, Ernesto, b. Madrid, Jan. 16, 1905; composer; studied with Esplá, Salazar and de Falla; cond. chamber orch. in Seville, 1924; c. Sinfonietta, "*Deux Esquisses*" and other works for orch., string quartets, piano music; won National State Prize, 1924–25; one of the most promising younger Spanish comps., whose style shows influences of Ravel and Stravinsky.

Halir (hä'-lĕr), (1) **Karl,** Hohenelbe, Bohemia, Feb. 1, 1859—Berlin, Dec. 21, 1909; violinist; pupil of Bennewitz, Prague Cons. and Joachim in Berlin; 1884 leader of the ct.-orch., Weimar; 1896 toured the U. S.

Hall, (1) **Henry,** Windsor, ca. 1655—1707; organist and composer. (2) **Henry, Jr.,** d. 1763; son of above; organist and composer. (3) **Wm.,** 17th cent. violinist and composer. (4) **Marie** (Mary Paulina), b. Newcastle-on-Tyne, April 8, 1884; violinist; as a child played in Bristol streets; pupil of her father and Hildegarde Werner; later of J. Kruse; at 15 won an exhibition at the R. A. M.; from 1901, pupil of Sevcik; toured widely. (5) **Walter Henry,** London, April 25, 1862—New York, Dec. 11, 1935; choral cond.; pupil of R. Coll. of Mus.; came to America, 1883; org. in various churches; 1893, founded Brooklyn Oratorio Soc., after 1901 taught at Columbia Univ., and, beginning 1913, was prof. of

church music and leader of Univ Chorus there.

Halle (äl). Vide ADAM DE LA H.

Hallé (äl-lā), Sir **Charles** (rightly **Karl Halle**), Hagen, Westphalia, April 11, 1819—Manchester, Oct. 25, 1895; pianist and conductor, Paris, 1836–48; later pop. cond. at Manchester and dir. of "Gentlemen's Concerts" there; also closely connected with London Popular Concerts; 1888 m. Mme. Neruda (q.v.); after his death appeared his autobiography, "*Life and Letters*" (1896).

Hallen (häl'-lĕn), **Anders,** Gotenburg, Dec. 22, 1846—Stockholm, March 11, 1925; pupil of Reinecke, Rheinberger, and Rietz: cond. of the Mus. Union, Gotenburg; 1892–97. cond. Royal Opera, Stockholm: 1902–07, cond. in Malmö; after 1907, taught comp., Stockholm Cons.; c. 3 operas, "*Herald der Viking*" (Leipzig, 1881; Stockholm, 1883). v. succ. "*Hexfallen*" ("*Der Hexenfang*") (Stockholm, 1896); "*Waldemar*" (Stockholm, 1899); 2 Swedish Rhapsodies; ballad cycles with orch.; symphonic poem "*Ein Sommermärchen*"; romance for vln. with orch.; German and Swedish songs, etc.

Haller (häl'-lĕr), **Michael,** Neusaat (Upper Palatinate), Jan. 13, 1840—Regensburg, Jan. 4, 1915; 1864 took orders; studied with Schrems; 1866 cond. "*Realinstitut*"; teacher of vocal comp. and cpt. at the Sch. of Church-music; writer and composer; completed the lost 3rd-choir parts of six 12-part comps. of Palestrina's.

Hallström (häl'-străm), **Ivar,** Stockholm, June 5, 1826—April 10, 1901; dram. composer; librarian to the Crown Prince, later King of Sweden; 1861 dir. of Sch. of Music. His first opera failed—having 20 numbers in minor keys; his 2d also; but others were succ., incl. "*Nyaga*" (1885; book by "Carmen Sylva").

Halm (hälm), **Anton,** Altenmarkt, Styria, 1789—Vienna, 1872; pianist and composer.

Halvor'sen, Johan, Drammen, Norway, March 15, 1864—Oslo, Dec. 4, 1935; composer, conductor; pupil of Stockholm Cons. also of Brodsky in Leipzig; toured as vln. virtuoso; taught Helsingfors Cons.; studied with Albert Becker and César Thomson; after 1899 cond. at the Nat'l. Theat.. Christiania. where he also led symph. concerts; c. 2 symphs., and much other orch., chamber and vln. music, incidental scores for plays, etc.; best known for his *"March of the Boyars"* and his arr. of a Handel Passacaglia.

Hambourg (häm'-boorg), (1) **Mark,** b. Gogutschar-Woronesch, Russia, May 31, 1879; notable piano-virtuoso; studied with his father (a teacher in London), and with Leschetizky; toured widely with brilliant success; 1900, America; lived in London. (2) **Boris,** b. Woronesch, S. Russia, Dec. 27, 1884; 'cellist; studied with Walenn, Hugo Becker and at Hoch Cons., Frankfort; début in Pyrmont, 1903; toured Australia, Belgium, Great Britain, U. S. (lived in Pittsburgh, 1910); with father and bro. opened a school in Toronto, 1911. (3) **Jan,** bro. of **Mark** and **Boris,** b. at Woronesch, Aug. 27, 1882; violinist; studied with Wilhelmj, Sauret, Heermann, Sevcik and Ysaye; début, 1905, in Berlin; toured widely in concerts.

Ham'boys. Vide HANBOYS.

Hamel (ä-mĕl), **M. P.,** Auneuil (Oise), France, 1786—Beauvais, after 1870; amateur expert in organ-building; writer.

Ham'erik, Asger, Copenhagen, April 8, 1843—July 13, 1923; pupil of Gade, Matthison-Hansen and Haberbier; 1862 of von Bülow; c. two operas; 1870 at Milan prod. an Ital. opera *"La Vendetta"*; 1871-98, dir. of the Cons. of the Peabody Institute and of the Peabody symphony concerts, Baltimore, Md.; 1890 knighted by the King of Denmark; c. 1866 a festival cantata to commemorate the new Swedish constitution, *"Der Wanderer"* (1872); 1883 *"Oper ohne Worte"*; a choral work *"Christliche Trilogie"* (a pendant to a *"Trilogie judaique"* brought out in Paris); 7 symphonies, etc.

Ham'ilton, (1) **Jas. Alex.,** London, 1785—1845; writer. (2) **Clarence Grant,** b. Providence, R. I., June 9, 1865; pianist, educator; grad. Brown Univ.; pupil of Dannreuther and Matthay; after 1904 prof. at Wellesley Coll.; author and ed. of books on mus. hist. and pedagogy.

Ham'lin, (1) **George John,** Elgin, Ill., 1868—New York, 1923; tenor; sang in concert after 1895, and from 1911 a mem. of Chicago Op. with notable succ. as recitalist and as soloist at fests. (2) **Anna,** b. Chicago, Sept. 10, 1902; daughter of preceding; soprano; début, Albenga, Italy, 1926; sang with Chicago Op., also in concerts.

Ham'merich, Angul, Copenhagen, Nov. 25, 1848—April 26, 1931; 'cellist; pupil of Rüdinger and Neruda; 1896 prof. of musical science Copenhagen University; brother of Asger Hamerik (q.v.)

Hammerschmidt (häm'-mĕr-shmĭt), **Ands.,** Brüx, Bohemia, 1611—Zittau, Oct. 29, 1675; organist, 1639, at Zittau; c. important and original concertos, motets, madrigals, etc.

Ham'merstein, (1) **Oscar,** Berlin, 1847 —New York, Aug. 1, 1919, impresario; came to America at 16; made a fortune by the invention of a cigar-making machine; wrote a comic opera in 24 hours on a wager, and produced it at his own theatre; built five theatres in N. Y. and the Manhattan Opera House; where he gave opposition to the Metropolitan, 1906-08; built also an opera house in Philadelphia; sold out his interests to the Metropolitan Co., and built opera house in London; opened, 1911, but it was a complete fiasco and closed after one season; he then built the Lexington Op. House in N. Y. and planned to open opera season there, but the Met. prevented it by legal measures; he died while in the midst of other plans. His son (2) **Arthur,** a leading producer of operettas and musical shows in N. Y.

Hammond, (1) **Richard,** b. Kent, England, Aug. 26, 1896; composer; grad. Yale Univ. where studied music, also with Mortimer Wilson and Nadia Boulanger; mem. board of dir., League of Comps., N. Y.; c. (ballet) *"Fiesta,"* also chamber and orch. works, piano pieces, songs. (2) **John Hays, Jr.,** his bro., invented novel contrivance known as "sustaining pedal" for piano, which makes tones on that instrument capable of being held or released at the player's will; this was demonstrated in concerts under the sponsorship of Stokowski and Phila. Orch. and promised to make possible technical innovations in comp. (3) **William Churchill,** b. Rockville, Conn., Nov. 25, 1860; organist, pupil of Allen and S. P. Warren; gave notable series of more than 1,000 recitals at Holyoke, Mass.; 1890, teacher of org., Smith Coll., Northampton, Mass.; after 1900 head of mus. dept., Mount Holyoke Coll.

Han'boys (or **Hamboys**), **John,** English theorist ca. 1470.

Hand (hänt), **F. G.,** b. Plauen, Saxony, 1786—Jena, 1851; writer.

Handel (or **Händel, Handl**). (1) Vide GALLUS. (2) Vide HÄNDEL.

Händel (hĕnt'-l) (**Hendel, Hendeler, Handeler** or **Hendtler**), **Georg Friedrich** (at first spelt **Hendel** in England; later he anglicised it to **George Frederic Handel** (hăn'-dĕl, the form now used in England), Halle, Feb. 23, 1685—London, April 14, 1759; son of a barber (afterwards surgeon and valet to the Prince of Saxe-Magdeburg) and his second wife Dorothea Taust. Intended for a lawyer; in spite of bitter opposition he secretly learned to play a dumb spinet. At 7 on a visit to his elder step-brother, valet at the court of Saxe-Weissenfels, Händel while playing the chapel-organ was heard by the Duke, who persuaded the father to give the boy lessons. Zachau, organist of Halle, taught him cpt., canon and fugue, and he practised the oboe, spinet, harpsichord and organ; he soon c. sonatas for 2 oboes and bass, became assist. organist, and for 3 years wrote a motet for every Sunday. In 1696 his skill on organ and harpsichord won him at Berlin the friendship of Ariosti and the jealousy of Bononcini. The Elector offered to send him to Italy; but his father took him back to Halle; the next year his father died, and he went to Halle Univ. (1702-03) to study law, at the same time serving as organist at the cathedral at a salary of $50 a year. 1703 he went to Hamburg as *violino di ripieno*. He fought a duel with Mattheson, later his friend and biographer, and was saved by a button. When Keiser the dir. fled from debt, H. was engaged as clavecinist. He c. a "Passion" and prod. 2 operas, *"Almira"* (succ.) and *"Nero"* (1705); he was also commissioned to write *"Florindo und Daphne"* (1708), an opera filling two evenings. In 1706, with 200 ducats earned by teaching, he went to Italy and made success and powerful acquaintances,

incl. the Scarlattis. In Florence (1707) he prod. with succ. *"Rodrigo"* (Venice, 1708), and *"Agrippina"* with great succ. In Rome he prod. 2 oratorios, and in Naples a serenata, *"Aci, Galatea e Polifemo,"* in which is a bass solo with a compass of 2 octaves and a fifth. 1709, in Germany as cond. to the Elector of Hanover; 1710 visited England on leave of absence. In 2 weeks he c. the opera *"Rinaldo,"* a pasticcio of his older songs. It was prod. at the Haymarket Th. with great succ.; 1712 he returned to London on leave; but stayed. His first two operas were not succ.; but an ode for the Queen's birthday, and a Te Deum and Jubilate in celebration of the Peace of Utrecht won him royal favour and an annuity of £200; 1714 his Hanover patron became George I. of England, and he was for a time out of that monarch's good graces, but had already been restored when, at the request of Baron Kilmanseck, he produced the delightful 25 pieces called the *"Water-Music,"* at a royal aquatic fête. 1716-18 he went to Hanover with the King. He there c. his only German oratorio, the *"Passion"*; 1718 cond. to the Duke of Chandos and c. the English oratorio *"Esther,"* the secular oratorio *"Acis and Galatea,"* and the Chandos Te Deums and Anthems. He taught the Prince of Wales' daughters, and c. for Princess Anne *"Suites de Pièces"* for harpsichord (*The Lessons*) including *"The Harmonious Blacksmith."*

He was dir. of new R. A. of M. 1720 prod. the succ. opera *"Radamisto"* (prod. 1721 in Hamburg as *"Zenobia"*). Now Bononcini and Ariosti appeared as rivals and a famous and lasting feud arose around the three after they had prod. one opera, *"Muzio Scaevola,"* in which each wrote an act. B. had rather the better of it, when he was caught in a plagiarism (a crime not unknown in Händel's works (v. LOTTI). B. left England without reply (1731). Up to this time H. had prod. 12 operas.

1726 he was naturalised. 1729-31 he was in partnership with Heidegger, proprietor of the King's Th., where he prod. *"Lotario,"* followed by 4 more operas. 1732 he prod. his two oratorios revised; 1733 the oratorios *"Deborah"* and *"Athaliah"* at Oxford, when he was made Mus. Doc. *h. c.* 1733 he began a stormy management of opera, quarrelled with the popular singer Senesino, and drove many of his subscribers to forming a rival troupe "The Opera of the Nobility," with Porpora and afterwards Hasse as composer and conductor; 1737 the companies failed, **H.** having prod. 5 operas; the ode *"Alexander's Feast"* (Dryden), and the revised *"Trionfo del Tempo e della Verita."* Overexertion brought on a stroke of paralysis in one of his hands and he went to Aix-la-Chapelle, returning to London with improved health. He now prod., under Heidegger, 5 operas, incl. *"Faramondo," "Serse"* (1738), and *"Deidamia"* (1741). Now he abandoned the stage and turned to oratorio, producing *"Saul,"* and *"Israel in Egypt"* (1739); the *"Ode for St. Cecilia's Day,"* and in 1740 *"L'Allegro and Il Penseroso"* (Milton), and a supplement *"Il Moderato,"* written by Chas. Jennens, who also wrote the text of the Messiah. 1741 he visited Dublin and prod. there his masterpiece the *"Messiah,"* April 13, 1742. This re-established him in English favour and raised him from bankruptcy. It was followed by *"Samson,"* the *"Dettingen Te Deum," "Semele," "Joseph"* (1743), *"Belshazzar,"* and *"Heracles"* (1744). His rivals worked against him still, and in 1745 he was again bankrupt, writing little for a year and a half, when he prod. with renewed success and fortune his *"Occasional Oratorio,"* and *"Judas Maccabaeus"* (1746); *"Joshua"* (1747), *"Solomon"* (1748), *"Susannah"* (1748); *"Theodora"* (1749); *"The Choice of Hercules"* (1750); and *"Jephthah"* (1752), his last. During the comp. of *"Jephthah"* he underwent three unsuccessful operations for cataract. He was practically blind the rest of his life, but continued to play org.-concertos and accompany his oratorios on the organ up to 1759. He was buried in Westminster Abbey. His other comp. incl. the *"Forest Musick"* (Dublin, 1742), etc., for harps.; the *"Fireworks Musick"* (1749) for strings; 6 organ-concertos; concertos for trumpets and horns; and for horns and side drums (MS.):

sonatas for vln., viola and oboe, **etc.** A complete edition of his works in 100 vols. was undertaken in 1856 for the German Händel Soc. by Dr. Chrysander as editor. Biog. by Mattheson (1740); Mainwaring (1760); Forstemann (1844); Schölcher (1857); Rockstro (1883); Chrysander (unfinished at his death), Leichtentritt and Müller-Blattau (in German). Various aspects of Händel's life and art are considered in studies in English by Benson, Davey, Flower, Marshall, Romain Rolland, Streatfeild, C. F. A. Williams. **Händel** as an opera composer has been rediscovered by the 20th cent., after the long dominance of his oratorios. Esp. in Germany there occurred a remarkable **"H.** Renaissance" from about the year 1920, centring in the Univ. of Göttingen, where German adaptations of such works as *"Rodelinda," "Ottone," "Giulio Cesare,"* etc., were staged in annual fests. Productions also took place in Berlin, and in America at Smith Coll., Northampton, Mass.

Hand'lo, Robert de, Engl. theorist of 14th century.

Hand'rock, Julius, Naumburg, 1830 —Halle, 1894; teacher and composer.

Hänel von Cronenthal (hä'-něl fōn krō'-něn-täl), **Julia,** Graz, 1839—Paris, March 9, 1896; wife of the Marquis d'Héricourt de Valincourt; studied in Paris; c. 4 symphonies. 22 pf.-sonatas, etc.

Hanff, J. Nicolaus, Wechmar, 1630—Schleswig, 1706; cathedral organist at Schleswig and important predecessor of Bach in choral-writing.

Hanfstängel (hänf'-shtěng-ěl), **Marie** (née **Schröder**), Breslau, April 30, 1848—Munich, 1917; soprano; pupil of Viardot-Garcia; début, 1867, Paris; studied 1878 with Vannucini; 1882–97 Stadt-theatre, Frankfort.

Hanisch (hä'-nĭsh) **Jos.,** Ratisbon, 1812—1892; organist, teacher and composer.

Hanke (hänk'-ě), **K.,** Rosswalde, Schleswig, 1754—Hamburg, 1835; conductor and composer.

Hansen (hän'-sĕn), **Cecilia,** b. Stanitza Kamenska, Russia, Feb. 17, 1898; violinist; studied with Auer; has appeared as orchestral soloist and recitalist in many Eur. centres, also in U. S. 1923–24: m. Boris Sacharoff, pianist.

Hanslick (häns'-lĭk), **Eduard,** Prague, Sept. 11, 1825—Baden near Vienna, Aug. 6, 1904; eminent critic and writer; Dr. Jur., 1849; studied piano under Tomaschek at Prague 1848–49; critic for the *Wiener Zeitung;* among his many books his first is most famous, *"Vom Musikalisch-Schönen"* (Leipzig, 1854); a somewhat biassed, yet impressive plea for absolute music as opposed to programme (v. D. D.) or fallaciously sentimental music; a bitter opponent of all Wagnerianism and an ardent Brahmsite; 1855–64 mus. editor *Presse;* then, of the *Neue freie Presse;* lecturer on mus. hist. and æsthetics Vienna Univ.; 1861 prof. extraordinary, 1870 full prof.; 1895 retired.

Han'son, Howard, b. Wahoo, Nebr., Oct. 28, 1896; composer, conductor, educator; grad. Luther Coll., Inst. of Music. Art, N. Y., hon. Mus.D., Northwestern Univ.; first to be awarded music fellowship at Amer. Acad. in Rome, 1921–24; dir. Eastman School of Music at Univ. of Rochester, N. Y., after latter year; has been active in nat'l. educational organisations in music field, and has carried on a unique series of several annual American Comps. Concerts at Rochester as well as fests. of native music there; has served as guest cond. of his works with many Amer. orchs.; c. (opera) *"Merry Mount"* (libretto by Richard Stokes), Met. Op. Co. (commissioned), 1933; two symphonies (*"Nordic"* and *"Romantic"*), also for orch. *"Before the Dawn," "Exaltation," "North and West," "Lux Aeterna," "Pan and the Priest,"* Symphonic Legend; (chorus and orch.) *"The Lament for Beowulf," "Heroic Elegy," "Drum Taps"* (after Walt Whitman); concerto for org. and orch., 2 quintets for piano and strings, string quartet.

Hanssens (häns'-sĕns), (1) **Chas. L. Jos.** (ainé), Ghent, 1777—Brussels, 1852; conductor and composer. (2) **Chas. L.** (cadet), Ghent, 1802—Brussels, 1871; conductor, professor, 'cellist and composer.

Harcourt (dăr-koor), **Eugene d',** Paris, 1855—March 8, 1918; composer; pupil Paris Cons., and of Schulze and Bargiel, in Berlin; 1890 gave concerts in his own Salle Harcourt; 1900 gave oratorios at St.

Eustache; c. mass (Brussels, 1876); opera *"Tasso"* (Monte Carlo, 1903); 3 symph., etc.

d'Hardelot (gĕ-dărd'-lō), **Guy (Mrs. Rhodes),** near Boulogne, France—London, Jan. 7, 1936; c. operetta *"Elle et Lui"* and many pop. songs.

Hark'nes. Vide SENKRAH.

Harling, W. Franke, b. London, Jan. 18, 1887; composer; studied Grace Church Choir School, N. Y., Acad. of Mus., London, and with Théophile Ysaye, Brussels; active as org. in Brussels and at West Point Mil. Acad.; c. (opera) *"A Light from St. Agnes"* (Chicago Op., 1925); (lyric drama) *"Deep River"* (N. Y., 1926); Jazz Concerto; *"Venetian Fantasy,"* cantatas and songs; also scores for motion pictures.

Harma'ti, Sandor, Budapest, July 9, 1892—Flemington, N. J., Apr. 4, 1936; composer, violinist, conductor; grad. Budapest Acad. of Mus.; concertm. State Orch., Budapest, 1912–14; People's Op. there, 1912–14; coming to America, led Lenox String Quartet; cond. N. Y. Women's String Orch., Omaha Symph. Orch.. 1924–28; Westchester, N. Y. Fest. also led orchs. as guest in Paris Berlin, Frankfort, St. Louis; c. symph. poem winning Pulitzer Prize, 1923; string quartet (Phila. Chamber Music Ass'n. Prize, 1925), other orch. works and songs.

Harp'er, (1) **Thos.,** Worcester, 1787—London, 1853; trumpet virtuoso. His 3 sons were (2) **Thomas, his** successor. (3) **Charles,** horn-player. (4) **Edward,** pianist.

Har'raden, Samuel, Cambridge, Engl., 1821 (?)—Hampstead, London, 1897; org.-professor.

Harriers-Wippern (här'-rĭ-ĕrs vĭp'-pĕrn), **Louise** (née **Wippern**), Hildesheim, 1837—Grobersdorf, Silesia, 1878; soprano.

Har'ris, (1) **Jos. M.,** London, 1799—Manchester, 1869; organist and composer. (2) **Augustus (Sir),** Paris, 1852—Folkestone, Engl., June 22, 1896; an actor, début as "Macbeth" in Manchester, 1873; then stage manager; 1879 leased Drury Lane Th. for spectacle; 1887 he took up opera and controlled successively H. M.'s Th., the Olympia, etc., finally Covent Garden. (3) **Victor, N. Y.,** April 27, 1869—Feb. 15, 1943; pupil of Charles Blum (pf.), Wm. Court-ney (voice), Fredk. Schilling (harm. and comp.), Anton Seidl (cond.); 1889–95 org. various churches; 1892–95 *répétiteur* and coach at Met. Op.; 1893–94 cond. Utica Choral Union; 1895–96 asst.-cond. to Seidl, Brighton Beach Concerts; vocal teacher and accompanist, N. Y.; long cond. of Cecilia Chorus; c. a pf.-suite, a cantata, an operetta *"Mlle. Mai et M. de Septembre,"* songs, etc. (4) **Roy,** b. Lincoln Co., Okla., Feb. 12, 1898; composer; educated Univ. of Calif.; studied with Fanny Dillon, Arthur Farwell, Modeste Altschuler, Arthur Bliss, Rosario Scalero and Nadia Boulanger; awarded Guggenheim Fellowship for study in Europe, 1927–28; Intercollegiate Fellowship for Comp., California; has lectured extensively and taught at Westminster Choir School, Princeton, N. J., where he organised fest. of modern Amer. music, 1936; c. symph.; andante for orch.; sextet for clarinet, strings and piano; suite for string quartet; symphonic poem, trio and chorus; suite for women's chorus and 2 pianos; *"A Song for Occupations"* for mixed chorus to Whitman's words; symph. for voices, etc.

Har′rison, (1) **Wm.,** London, 1813—London, 1868; tenor. (2) **Beatrice,** b. Roorkee, India, 1892; 'cellist; senior medal of Assoc. Board, London; exhibitor R. Coll. of Music at 11; won Mendelssohn Prize, Berlin Hochsch.; studied with Whitehouse and Hugo Becker; début, Berlin, 1910; has appeared in chief Eur. centres, also in U. S. after 1913. (3) **May,** b. Roorkee, India, 1890; sister of **Beatrice H.;** violinist; studied in London, also with Fernandez Arbos and Auer; has toured as soloist since 1907 and in joint recitals with her sister. (4) **Julius,** b. Stourport, England, March 26, 1885; composer and conductor; studied on stipend with Bantock; cond. of Beecham Op. Co., later the Scottish Orch., and the British Nat'l. Op. Co.; c. orch., chamber music, choral works; also an opera, *"The Canterbury Pilgrims."*

Har′rold, Orville, Muncie, Ind., 1878—Darien, Conn., Oct. 23, 1933; operatic tenor; reputed to have been discovered singing in vaudeville, by Oscar Hammerstein, N. Y.,

taught by Oscar Saenger, 1909–10; début Manhattan Op., N. Y., 1910; sang with Mme. Trentini in comic opera; 1911 at Hammerstein's London Opera; Met. Op. Co. after 1919.

Harsan′yi, Tibor, b. Ober-Kanizsa, Hungary, June 27, 1898; composer; pupil of the Budapest Acad. of Mus.; lives in Paris; c. 2 orch. suites; *"Les Invités,"* setting of text by Jean-Victor Pellerin; sonatina for piano and vln.; sonata for vln. and piano; piano trio; string quartet; pf. sonata and other works.

Har′shaw, Margaret, Amer. soprano, orig. contralto; Met. Op., 1942; sang also at Covent Garden.

Hart, (1) **James,** d. 1718; Engl. bass and composer. (2) **Philip,** d. ca. 1749; Gentleman of Chapel Royal; son of above (?); organist and composer; wrote music for *"The Morning Hymn"* from Book V. of Milton's *"Paradise Lost."* (3) **J. Thos.,** 1805—London, 1874; vln. maker. (4) **George,** London, 1839—1891; son of above; writer.

Härtel (hĕr′-tĕl), (1) Vide BREITKOPF UND HÄRTEL. (2) **G. Ad.,** Leipzig, 1836—Homburg, 1876; violinist, conductor and dram. composer. (3) **Benno,** Jauer, Silesia, May 1, 1846—Berlin, Aug. 4, 1909; pupil of Hoppe (pf.), Jappsen (vln.), Kiel (comp.); 1870 teacher of theory, Berlin Royal High Sch. for Music; c. an opera, over 300 canons, etc. (4) **Luise** (née **Hauffe),** Düben, 1837—Leipzig 1882; pianist; wife of (5) **Hermann H.** Vide BREITKOPF.

Hart′mann, (1) **Johan Peder Emilius,** Copenhagen, May 14, 1805—Copenhagen, March 10, 1900; organist and dram. composer; grandson of a German court-cond. (d. 1763); son of an organist at Copenhagen. (2) **Emil** (Jr.) Copenhagen, 1836—1898; son and pupil of above, and court-organist; composer. (3) **Ludwig,** Neuss-on-Rhine, 1836—Dresden, Feb. 14, 1910; pianist, composer and critic (son and pupil of (4) **Friedrich,** song-composer, b. 1805); also studied at Leipzig Cons. and with Liszt; lived in Dresden; prominent Wagnerian champion; c. an opera, etc. (5) **Arthur,** b. Maté Szalka, Hungary, July 23, 1881; taken to Philadelphia at the age of two months; violinist; all his schooling in America; has toured Europe and America with succ. (6) **Karl Amadeus,** b. Munich, 1905; composer; studied with Scherchen; dir., Musica Viva.

Har'tog, (1) **Edouard de,** Amsterdam, Aug. 15, 1829—The Hague, Nov. 8, 1909; pupil of Hoch, Bartelmann, Litolff, etc.; 1852 in Paris as teacher of pf., comp. and harm.; decorated with the orders of Leopold and the Oaken Crown; c. operas, the 43rd psalm with orch., etc. (2) **Jacques,** Zalt-Bommel, Holland, Oct. 24, 1837—Amsterdam, Oct. 3, 1917; pupil of Wilhelm and Fd. Hiller; prof. Amsterdam Sch. of Music.

Hartvigson (härt'-vĭkh-zōn), (1) **Frits,** Grenaa, Jutland, May 31, 1841—Copenhagen, 1919; pianist; pupil of Gade, Gebauer, Ree, and von Bülow; 1864, London; 1873 pianist to the Princess of Wales; 1875 prof. at the Norwood Coll. for the Blind; 1887 pf.-prof. Crystal Palace. (2) **Anton,** Aarhus, Oct. 16, 1845—Copenhagen, Dec. 29, 1911; bro. of above; pianist; pupil of Tausig and Neupert; lived in London.

Har'ty, Sir Hamilton, b. Hillsborough, Co. Down, Ireland, Dec. 4, 1879; d. Brighton, England, Feb. 19, 1941; pupil of his father, an organist; later studied in Dublin; début, London, as an accompanist; after 1920, cond. Hallé Orch. Soc., Manchester; guest cond., London and U. S.; c. setting of Keats's "Ode to a Nightingale," for soprano and orch.; "Irish Symphony"; vln. Concerto in D minor; "Wild Geese," symph. poem; "Comedy Overture"; Piano Quartet in F major; also 'cello pieces, chamber music and songs; m. Mme. Agnes Nicholls, singer.

Har'wood, Basil, b. Woodhouse, Gloucestershire, April 11, 1859; pianist, composer; pupil of Roeckel, Risley, Corfe, and at Leipzig Cons.; 1880, Mus. Bac., Oxford; 1896, Mus. Doc.; organist various churches; from 1892 at Christ Church, Oxford; retired in 1909 from his posts there as organist and *choragus;* c. church music; "Capriccio," "Three Cathedral Preludes," and Sonata No. 2, in F-sharp minor, for org.; Concerto in D for organ and orchestra; cantata, "Song on May Morning," psalm, "Inclina, Domine," voices and orch. (Gloucester Fest., 1898); ed.OxfordHymnBook;d.April3,1949.

Häsche (hĕsh'-ĕ), **William Edwin,** b. New Haven, April 11, 1867; pupil of Listemann, Perabo, and Parker; dir. New Haven Symph. Orch.; 1903 teacher of instrumentation at Yale; cond. N. H. Choral Union (250 voices); c. symph., symph. poems "Waldidylle," "Fridjof and Ingeborg"; cantata "The Haunted Oak," etc.; d. Roanoke, Va., Jan. 26, 1929.

Hase (Dr.), **Oskar von.** Vide BREITKOPF UND HÄRTEL.

Häser (hä'zĕr), (1) **Aug. Fd.,** Leipzig 1799—Weimar, 184? theorist, conductor, writer and composer. (2) **Charlotte Henriette,** Leipzig, 1784—1871; sister of above; singer; m. a lawyer Vera.

Has(s)ler (häs'-lĕr), (1) **Hans Leo von,** Nürnberg, 1564—Frankfort, June 5, 1612; the eldest of 3 sons of ((2) **Isaac H.,** town-mus., Nürnberg); pupil of his father; organist and composer. (3) **Jakob,** Nürnberg, 1566 —Hechingen (?), 1601; bro. of (1), conductor, organ virtuoso and composer. (4) **Kaspar,** Nürnberg, 1570 —1618; bro. of above; organist.

Haslinger (häs'-lĭng-ĕr), (1) **Tobias,** Zell, Upper Austria, 1787—Vienna, 1842; conductor and publisher. (2) **Karl,** Vienna, 1816—1868; son and successor of above; pianist; c. opera "Wanda," etc.

Hasse (häs'-sĕ), (1) **Nikolaus,** ca. 1650; organist and writer at Rostock. (2) **Jn. Ad.,** Bergedorf, near Hamburg, March 25, 1699—Venice, Dec. 16, 1783; famous tenor and v. succ. operatic cond.; rival of Porpora; c. over 100 operas, etc. (3) **Faustina** (née Bordoni), Venice, 1693 (1700?)—1781; of noble birth; one of the most cultivated mezzo-sopr.; m. the above 1730, a happy union, she collaborating in his success. (4) **Gustav,** Peitz, Brandenburg, Sept. 4, 1834—Berlin, Dec. 31, 1889; studied Leipzig Cons., afterward with Kiel and F. Kroll; settled in Berlin as teacher and composer.

Has'selbeck, Rosa. Vide SUCHER.

Has'selmans, (1) **Louis,** b. Paris, July 25, 1878; conductor; studied at Paris Cons. with Delsart, Lavignac, Godard and Massenet; 1st prize in 'cello; mem. Caplet Quartet; début as cond. at Lamoureux Concerts, Paris, 1905; founded and led Hasselmans Orch., after 1907; cond. at Op.-Comique, 1909–11; Montreal Op., 1911–13;

Marseilles Concerts Classiques, 1913–14; Chicago Op., 1918–20; also at Ravinia Op., and at Met. Op. House, N. Y., 1921–36; m. Minnie Egener, soprano. (2) Alph. J., Liége, 1845—Paris, 1912; harpist.

Hasselt-Barth (häs'-sĕlt-bärt), **Anna Maria Wilhelmine** (née van Hasselt), Amsterdam, July 15, 1813—Mannheim, Jan. 4, 1881; soprano; début Trieste (1831).

Hässler (hess'-lĕr), (1) **Jn. Wm.**, Erfurt, March 29, 1747—Moscow, March 29, 1822; organist and famous teacher; toured widely; 1792–94 royal cond. St. Petersburg; then teacher at Moscow; c. important piano and organ pieces; his wife, (2) **Sophie**, was a singer who travelled with him.

Hast'ings, Thos., Washington, Conn., 1787—New York, 1872; editor and composer.

Hastreiter (häst'rī-tĕr), **Helene**, b. Louisville, Ky., Nov. 14, 1858; operatic contralto, popular in Italy; pupil of Lamperti; m. Dr. Burgunzio; d. (?).

Hatto. Vide FRÈRE.

Hat'ton, J. Liptrott, Liverpool, Oct. 20, 1809—Margate, Sept. 20, 1886; cond. and dram. composer.

Hattstädt (hät'-shtĕt), **J. J.**, Monroe, Mich., Dec. 29, 1851—Chicago, Dec., 1931; studied in Germany; pf.-teacher and writer in Detroit, St. Louis, and for 11 years, Chicago Coll. of Mus.; 1886, dir. Amer. Cons., Chicago.

Haubiel (hō'-bĕl), **Charles**, b. Delta, Ohio, Jan. 31, 1894; composer, educator; studied with Ganz, Lhevinne (piano) and Scalero (comp.); toured with Kocian; taught at Oklahoma City Mus. Art Inst., later at N. Y. Univ.; has toured as pianist and lecturer; c. "Karma," symph. variations which won prize in Schubert Centenary contest; also other orch., chamber music and piano works, incid. music to plays, etc.

Hau(c)k (howk), **Minnie**, New York, Nov. 14, 1852—Villa Triebschen, Lucerne, Feb. 6, 1929; notable soprano; pupil of Errani and Moritz Strakosch; début 1866, N. Y., as "Norma"; 1868–72 Vienna ct.-opera; 1875, Berlin; sang with great succ. in Europe and America. She was court-singer in Prussia, Officier d'Académie, Paris, and member of the Roman Mus. Academy.

Hauer (how'-ĕr), **K. H. Ernst, Halber-**stadt, 1828—Berlin, 1892; organist and composer.

Hauff (howf), **Jn. Chr.**, Frankfort, 1811—1891; founder and prof., Frankfort School of Music; writer and composer.

Hauffe (howf'-fĕ), **Luise.** Vide HÄRTEL, LUISE.

Haupt (howpt), **K. Aug.**, b. Kunern, Silesia, Aug. 25, 1810—Berlin July 4, 1891; pupil of A. W. Bach, Klein, and Dehn; famous as organist and teacher at Berlin; composer.

Hauptmann (howpt'-män), **Moritz,** Dresden, Oct. 13, 1792—Leipzig, Jan. 3, 1868; violinist; pupil of Spohr; famous as theorist and teacher; from 1842 prof. of cpt. and comp. Leipzig Cons., and dir. Thomasschule. His canon was "unity of idea and perfection of form," exemplified in his comps., enforced upon his many eminent pupils and exploited in many essays and standard works, incl. *"Die Natur der Harmonik und Metrik"* (1833); the posthumous, *"Die Lehre von der Harmonik,"* 1868, etc.; c. opera, *"Mathilde"* (Cassel, 1826); quartets, masses, etc.

Hauptner (howpt'-nĕr), **Thuiskon,** Berlin, 1821—1889; conductor and composer.

Hauschka (howsh'-kä), **Vincenz,** Mies, Bohemia, 1766—Vienna, 1840; 'cellist and barytone player; composer.

Hause (how'-zĕ), **Wenzel,** b. Bohemia, ca. 1780; prof. of double-bass, Prague Cons.; writer.

Hausegger (hows'-ĕg-gĕr), (1) **Fr. von,** Vienna, April 26, 1837—Graz, Feb. 23, 1899; pupil of Salzmann and Dessoff; barrister at Graz; 1872 teacher of history and theory, Univ. of Graz; writer. (2) **Siegmund von,** b. Graz, Aug. 16, 1872; pupil of his father, of Degners and Pohlig; 1896 cond. at Graz; 1899 of the Kaim concerts at Munich; 1903–06 the Museum Concerts at Frankfort-on-Main; 1910, dir. of Hamburg Philh.; 1920–34, dir. Acad. der Tonkunst, Munich, and leader of orch. concerts there; c. mass, an opera *"Helfrid"* (Graz, 1893); *"Zinnober"* (Munich, 1898); *"Dionysian Fantasie"* for orch., symph. poems, *"Barbarossa,"* *"Wieland,"* choruses, etc.; d. 1948.

Hauser (how'-zĕr), (1) **Fz.**, b. Crasowitz, near Prague, 1794—Freiburg,

Baden, 1870; bass-barytone; teacher.
(2) **Miska** (**Michael**), Pressburg, Hungary, 1822—Vienna, 1887; vln.-virtuoso; composer.

Häuser (hi-zĕr), **Jn. Ernst**, b. Dittchenroda, near Quedlinburg, 1803; teacher, Q. Gymnasium; writer.

Haussmann (hows'-män), **Valentin**, the name of five generations, (1) **V. I.**, b. Nürnberg, 1484; a friend of Luther; composer and conductor. His son (2) **V. II.**, organist and composer. His son (3) **V. III.**, organist at Löbejün, expert in org.-building. His son (4) **V. IV.**, organist and court-conductor at Köthen; writer. His son (5) **V. V.** Vide BARTHOLOMAUS; Löbejün, 1678—Lauchstadt, after 1740; cath. organist and theorist. (6) **Robt.**, Rottleberode, Harz Mts., Aug. 13, 1852—Vienna, Jan. 19, 1909, while on a concert tour; 'cellist; pupil of Th. Müller, and Piatti in London; teacher, Berlin Royal "Hochschule"; 1879, member Joachim Quartet.

Hav'ergal, Rev. **Wm. H.**, Buckinghamshire, 1793—1870; composer.

Haweis (hôz), Rev. **H. R.**, Egham, Surrey, 1838—London, Jan. 30, 1901; amateur violinist and popular writer on music.

Hawes (hôz), **Wm.**, Engl., London, 1785—1846; conductor and composer.

Hawkins (Sir), **J.**, London, March 30, 1719—Spa, May 14, 1789; an attorney; eminent historian of music; knighted, 1772.

Haydn (hīd'-'n), (1) (**Fz.**) **Josef**, Rohrau-on-Leitha, Lower Austria, March 31, 1732—Vienna, May 31, 1809; second son of a wheelwright who was the sexton and organist of the village church, and a fine tenor, and whose wife, Maria Koler, had served as cook for Count Harrach. She sang in the choir. At 5, H. was taken to the home of a paternal cousin, Frankh, who taught him Latin, singing, the vln. and other instrs. He was engaged as a chorister for St. Stephen's, and taught by Reutter the cond., who gave him no encouragement and dismissed him in 1748. At 8, he went to Vienna, and studied singing, vln. and clavier, with Finsterbusch and Gegenbauer. He studied harmony chiefly from Fux' *"Gradus ad Parnassum"* and Mattheson's *"Volkommener Kappell-*

meister." At 13 he c. a mass. He obtained a few pupils, and a Viennese tradesman lent him 150 florins, with which he rented an attic-room and an old harpsichord. He practised C. P. E. Bach's first 6 sonatas and the vln.; Metastasio taught him Italian, and recommended him to a Spanish family as teacher for their daughter, who was studying with Porpora. From Porpora, in return for menial attentions, H. received some instruction in comp. and a recommendation to the Venetian ambassador for a stipend of 50 francs a month. At 20, he had c. 6 trios, sonatas, his first mass, and a comic opera *"Der neue krumme Teufel"* (Stadttheater, 1752), a satire on the lame baron Affligi the ct.-opera dir.; this work was suppressed but revived afterwards, and he received 24 ducats for it. He began to make powerful friends, and became Musikdirektor and Kammercompositeur to Count Fd. Maximilian Morzin. 1759 Prince Paul Anton Esterházy heard his 1st symph. and 1760 took him into his service as 2d (later 1st) conductor; the same year H. m. Maria Anna, the elder sister of the girl whom he loved and who had entered a convent. This marriage was as unhappy as one would expect. Prince Nikolaus Esterházy, who succeeded his bro. in 1762, retained H. as conductor and in his service H. c. 30 symphonies, 40 quartets, a concerto for French horn, 12 minuets, most of his operas, etc. He was soon very pop. through Europe, and royalty sent him gifts. 1785 commissioned to write a mass, *"The Seven Words on the Cross,"* for the Cath. of Cadiz; in 1790 Prince Nikolaus was succeeded by his son Anton, who kept H. as cond. and increased his stipend of 1,000 florins to 1,400. In 1791 on a pressing invitation brought by Salomon, he went to England and was for 18 months the lion of the season. Oxford made him Mus. Doc.; and he c. the so-called *"Salomon Symphonies,"* 1or his concerts. On his way home, he visited his native place to witness the unveiling of a monument erected in his honour by Count Harrach. In this year Beethoven became his pupil. 1794, he revisited London, with renewed triumph, the King urging him to stay, but, at the invitation of a new Prince Esterházy, he returned. 1797, he c. the Austrian national anthem. At 65, he prod. his great oratorio "*The Creation*" ("*Die Schöpfung*"); in 1801 "*The Seasons*" ("*Die Jahreszeiten*"). His health failing he went into retirement, appearing in public only once in 1808, when he was carried in a chair to hear a special performance of the "*Creation.*" His agitation was so great that he had to be taken away after the first half; the throng giving him a sad farewell, and Beethoven bending to kiss his hands and forehead. In 1809, his death was hastened by the shock of the bombardment of Vienna by the French. His astounding list of works includes besides those mentioned, 125 symphonies and overtures, incl. the "*Farewell*" ("*Abschiedssymphonie*," 1772), the "*Fire S.*" ("*Fuersymph.*, 1774), the "*Toy S.*" ("*Kindersymph.*), "*La Chasse*" (1870), the "*Oxford*" (1788), the "*Surprise*" ("*S. mit dem Paukenschlag*," 1791); "*S. with the drumroll*" ("*S. mit den Paukenwirbel*," 1795); 51 concertos for harpsichord, vln., 'cello, lyre, barytone, doublebass, flute and horn; 77 stringquartets; 175 numbers for barytone; 4 vln.-sonatas; 38 pf.-trios; 53 sonatas and divertimenti; an oratorio "*Il Ritorno di Tobia*"; 14 masses; 4 operas; 4 Italian comedies; 14 Ital. opere buffe, and 5 marionette-operas; music to plays; 22 arias; cantatas, incl. "*Ariana a Naxos*," "*Deutschlands Klage auf den Tod Friedrichs des Grossen*," "*The* 10 *Commandments*" in canon-form; 36 German songs; collections of Scotch and Welsh folk-songs, etc. Biog. by S. Mayr, 1809; K. F. Pohl (Leipzig, 1875, 1882; completed by E. von Mandyczewski). Haydn's diary is quoted from extensively in Krehbiel's "*Music and Manners*" (New York, 1898). Studies of Haydn have been published by Brenet, Hadden, Hadow and Runciman.

(2) **Jn. Michael**, Rohrau, Sept. 14, 1737—Salzburg, Aug. 10, 1806; bro. of above; soprano chorister, with compass of 3 octaves, at St. Stephen's, Vienna, replacing his brother Josef. Studied vln. and organ, and became asst.-organist; 1757, cond. at Grosswardein; 1762, dir. to Archbishop Sigismund, Salz-

burg; 1777, organist of the Cath. and St. Paul's Ch. He m. Maria Magdalena Lipp, an excellent soprano; 1880 he lost his property, by the French occupation, but was aided by his bro. and 2 others, and the Empress Maria Theresa rewarded him for a mass c. at her command, in which she sang the soprano solos. He founded a school of composition, and had many pupils, incl. Reicha and Weber. Prince Esterházy twice offered to make him vice-cond.; but **H.** refused, hoping to reorganise the Salzburg Chapel. His best works were sacred music, which his brother esteemed above his own. He declined publication, however; c. 360 church-comps., incl. oratorios, masses, etc., 30 symphonies; operas, etc. Biog. by Schinn and Otter (Salzburg, 1808).

Hayes (hāz), (1) **Wm.**, Hanbury, Worcestershire, Dec., 1706—Oxford, July 27, 1777; organist, conductor and writer. (2) **Philip**, Oxford, April, 1738—London, March 19, 1797; son and pupil of above, and his successor as Univ. Prof. of Mus. at Oxford; also organist there; c. oratorio; a masque; 6 concertos, etc. (3) **Roland**, b. Chattanooga, Tenn., June 3, 1887; Negro tenor; has made recital tours of Europe and U. S., with succ.; specialist in Lieder, classic and modern songs, spirituals.

Haym (hīm), (1) (or **Hennius**), **Gilles**, Belgian composer 16th cent. (2) Italian composer, **Aimo** (ä'-ē-mō), (3) **Niccolo Franc.**, Rome, ca. 1679— London, 1729; 'cellist and librettist.

Heap, Chas. Swinnerton, Birmingham, Engl., April 10, 1847—June 11, 1900; won the Mendelssohn scholarship and studied at Leipzig Cons.; also organ with Best; Mus. Doc. Cambridge, 1872; cond. Birmingham Phil. (1870–86) and other societies; c. an oratorio "*The Captivity*"; cantatas, etc.

Hebenstreit (hāb'-'n-shtrīt), **Pantaleon**, Eisleben, 1660 (9?)—Dresden, 1750; conductor; improved the dulcimer as the "Pantalon" (v. D. D.).

Hecht (hĕkht), **Ed.**, Dürkheim, Rhine Palatinate, 1832—Didsbury, near Manchester, 1887; pianist; prof. and composer.

Heckel (hĕk'-ĕl), **Wolf**, lutenist at Strassburg. 16th cent.

Heckmann (hĕk'-män), (1) G. Julius Robt., Mannheim, 1848—Glasgow, 1891; violinist. His wife (2) Marie (née Hartwig), Greiz, 1843—Cologne, 1890; pianist.

Hédouin (ād-wăñ), P., Boulogne, 1789—Paris, 1868; lawyer, writer, librettist and composer.

Heermann (hār'-män), Hugo, Heilbronn, March 3, 1844—Merano, Switz., Nov. 6, 1935; violinist; studied with J. Meerts, Brussels Cons. 1878, also with Joachim; in Frankfort as soloist and teacher at the Hoch Cons.; 1906–09, taught Chicago Mus. Coll.; 1910, Stern Cons., Berlin; 1911, Geneva Cons.; ed. de Bériot vln. method.

Heeringen (hā'-rǐng-ĕn), Ernst von, Grossmehlza, near Sondershausen, 1810—Washington, U. S. A., 1855; unsuccessful innovator in notation and scoring.

Hegar (hā'-gär), (1) Fr., Basel, Oct. 11, 1841—Zurich, June 2, 1927; studied Leipzig Cons., 1861; from 1863 cond. Subscription Concerts, and of the Choral Soc., Zürich; 1875 founded Cons. at Zürich; c. vln.-concerto in D; succ. dram. poem, "Manasse," for soli, chorus and orch.; "Festouvertüre," etc. (2) Emil, Basel, Jan. 3, 1843—June 13, 1921; bro. of above; pupil, later 'cello-teacher at Leipzig Cons., and 1st 'cello Gewandhaus Orch.; then studied singing; vocal-teacher Basel Sch. of Mus. (3) Julius, bro. of above; 'cellist at Zurich.

Hegedüs (hĕg-ĕ-düsh), Ferencz, b. Fünfkirchen, Feb. 26, 1881; violinist; succ. début, London, 1901; lived in Zurich; d. 1944.

Heger (hā'-gĕr), Robert, b. Strasbourg, Aug. 19, 1886; German conductor and composer; studied with Stockhausen in Strasbourg Cons., later in Zurich and with Schillings at Munich; cond. at Strasbourg, Ulm, Barmen, Nuremberg, Munich and after 1925 at Vienna State Op., also guest cond. at Covent Garden; c. operas, orch. works, chamber music, choruses.

Hegner (hākh'-nĕr), (1) Anton, b. Copenhagen, March 2, 1861—N. Y., Dec. 4, 1915; 'cellist; studied Copenh. Cons.; début at 14; later a teacher N. Y.; c. 4 quartets; 2 concertos for 'cello, etc. (2) Otto, Basel, Nov. 18, 1876—Hamburg, Feb. 22, 1907;

pianist; pupil of Fricker, Huber, and Glaus; made début very early at Basel (1888), England and America, at the Gewandhaus, Leipzig, 1890; c. pf.-pcs.

Hegyesi (hĕg'-yā-zē), Louis, Arpad, Hungary, 1853—Cologne, Feb., 1894; 'cellist.

Heide, von der. Vide VON DER H.

Heidingsfeld (hī'-dǐngs-fĕlt), L., Jauer, Prussia, March 24, 1854—Danzig, Sept. 14, 1920; pupil, later teacher Stern Cons., Berlin; composer.

Heifetz, Jascha (hī'-fĕtz yä'-shä), b. Vilna, Russia, Feb. 2, 1901; violinist; grad. Vilna School of Music at 8: studied with Auer at St. Petersburg Cons.; 1st appearance at 5; début, Berlin Philh. under Nikisch, 1912; toured Europe; Amer. début, N. Y., Oct. 27, 1917, in recital, with sensational succ.; at 15 estab. as one of foremost technicians of vln., a reputation he has subsequently enhanced with ripening of stylistic and interpretative powers; has made appearances around world, incl. Orient; became U. S. citizen, 1925; soloist with leading orchs. in the princ. cities of Europe and America; has arranged comps. for vln.; donor $1,000 prize for vln. concerto.

Hein (hīn), Carl, b. Rendsburg, 1864; 'cellist; pupil Hamburg Cons.; 1885–90 'cellist Hamburg Philharmonic Orch.; 1890 teacher in New York at German Cons.; 1903, joined with a fellow-pupil from the Hamburg Cons., August Fraemcke, in its direction; dir. N. Y. Coll. of Mus., 1906—1945; d. N. Y., Feb. 27, 1945.

Heinemeyer (hī'-nĕ-mī-ĕr), (1) Chr. H., 1796—1872; flutist at Hanover; composer. (2) Ernst Wm., Hanover, 1827—Vienna, 1869; son of above; flutist and composer.

Heinichen (hī'-nĭkh-ĕn), Jn. D., Krössuln, near Weissenfels, 1683—Dresden, 1729; dram. composer and writer.

Heinrich (hīn'-rĭkh), (1) Jn. G., Steinsdorf (Silesia), 1807—Sorau, 1882; organist, writer and composer. (2) Heinrich XXIV., Prince Reuss j. L., Dec. 8, 1855—Einstbrunn, Oct. 2, 1910; pianist; c. a symphony, a pf.-sonata, etc.

Heinroth (hīn'-rōt), (1) Chp. Gl., for 62 years organist at Nordhausen. (2) Jn. Aug. Günther, Nordhausen, 1780—Göttingen, 1846; son of above;

director and composer. (3) **Charles,** b. New York, Jan. 2, 1874; organist; studied piano with Friedheim and Spicker, org. with John White and comp. with Herbert; also in Munich with Hieber and Rheinberger; after 1893, org. in various N. Y. and Brooklyn churches and taught at Nat'l. Cons.; after 1907, org. and dir. of music at Carnegie Inst., Pittsburgh, Pa., where he has given notable series of weekly recitals; also heard in other cities.

Heintz (hīnts), **Albert,** Eberswalde, Prussia, March 21, 1882—Berlin, June 14, 1911; organist "Petri-kirche," Berlin; writer on Wagner; composer.

Heinze (hīnts'-ĕ), (1) **Wm. H. H.,** b. 1790; clarinettist in the Gewandhaus Orch. (2) **Gv. Ad.,** Leipzig, Oct. 1, 1820—near Amsterdam, Feb. 2, 1904; son and pupil of above; at 15 clarinettist in the Gewandhaus; 1844, 2d cond. Breslau Th., and prod. 2 operas (of which his wife wrote the libretti); 1850, Amsterdam as cond.; c. 5 oratorios, 3 masses, 3 overtures, etc. (3) **Sarah** (née **Magnus**), Stockholm, 1836—Dresden, Jan. 27, 1901; pianist; pupil of Kullak, Al. Dreyschock, and Liszt; lived in Dresden.

Heise (hī'-zĕ), **Peder Arnold,** Copenhagen, 1830—1879; teacher and dram. composer.

Heiser (hī'-zĕr), **Wm.,** Berlin, 1816—Friedenau, 1897; singer, bandmaster, and composer.

Hek'king, Anton, b. The Hague, Sept. 7, 1855—Nov. 18, 1935; noted 'cellist; teacher at the Stern Cons.; toured widely.

Hel'ler, Stephen, Pesth, May 15, 1813 —Paris, Jan. 14, 1888; notable composer who, like Chopin, confined his abilities to the pf. Lacking the breath, passion and colour of Chopin's, his music has a candour and vivacity and a fascinating quaintness that give it peculiar charm; his études, simpler than Chopin's, are as well imbued with art and personality. Studied piano with F. Bräuer; at 9 played in pub. with succ.; then studied with Czerny and Halm; at 12, gave concerts in Vienna, and toured; at Pesth studied a little harmony with Czibulka; at Augsburg, fell ill, and was adopted by a wealthy family, who aided his

studies; 1838, Paris. Schumann praised his first ccmp. highly. 1849, London, he played with succ. though infrequently because of nervousness; thereafter lived in Paris. C. several hundred pf.-pcs., incl. 4 sonatas and the famous Études. Biogr. by H. Barbadette (1876).

Hel'lin(k, Joannes Lupus (often called Lupus or Lupi), d. 1541; Flemish choir master at Cambrai and Bruges; c. many masses, influencing Palestrina; important motets, hymns and songs.

Hellmesberger (hĕl'-mĕs-bĕrkh-ĕr), (1) **G.** (Sr.), Vienna, 1800—Neuwaldegg, 1873; violinist, conductor and composer. (2) **G.** (Jr.), Vienna, 1830—Hanover, 1852; son and pupil of above; violinist and dram. composer. (3) **Rosa,** daughter of (2), was a singer, début 1883, ct.-opera, Vienna. (4) **Jos.** (Sr.), Vienna, 1828—1893; son of (1); conductor, violinist and professor. (5) **Jos.** (Jr.), Vienna, April 9, 1855—April 26, 1907; son of (4); violinist and composer of operettas, ballets, etc. 1902, cond. Vienna Philh. Orch. (6) **Fd.,** b. Vienna, Jan. 24, 1863; bro. of above; 'cellist in ct.-orch. from 1879; from 1883 with his father's quartet; 1885 teacher at the Cons.; 1886, solo 'cellist, ct.-opera; 1905-06, cond. at same; 1908-11, cond. in Abbazia.

Hellwig (hĕl'-vĭkh), **K. Fr. L.,** Künersdorf, 1773—Berlin, 1838; conductor and dram. composer.

Helm, Theodor, Vienna, April 9, 1843 —Dec. 23, 1920; studied law, entered govt. service; 1867 critic for various journals, and writer; 1874, teacher of mus. hist. and æsthetics, Horak's School of Music; author, studies of music of Beethoven and Mozart.

Helmholtz (hĕlm'-hôlts), **Hermann L. Fd.,** Potsdam, Aug. 31, 1821—Charlottenburg, Sept. 8, 1894; eminent scientist; pub. famous treatises such as "*Sensations of Tone as a Physiological Basis for the Theory of Music*" (*Lehre von den Tonempfindungen als physiologische Grundlage für die Theorie der Musik*) (Brunswick, 1863; English trans. by Ellis, 1875); this work, the result of much experiment, is the very foundation of modern acoustics, though Riemann, who was in some opposition to H., says his conclusions are not infallible.

H. inv. also a double harmonium with 24 vibrators to the octave; this lacks the dissonant 3rds and 6ths of equal temperament (v. D. D.) and permits the same modulation into all keys.

Hem'pel, Frieda, b. Leipzig, June 26, 1885; soprano; studied the piano at Leipzig Cons., 1903–05; then voice with Frau Lempner; début in Stettin; 1906, at Bayreuth; 1907 Covent Garden; has sung in Paris Opéra, Brussels, Vienna, etc.; from 1908 Berlin Royal Opera; engaged for Met. Op., N. Y., 1912; and sang with that co. for nearly a decade with distinction in wide variety of German and Italian rôles; thereafter prominent as a concert singer.

Henderson, William James, b. Newark N. J., Dec. 4, 1855—New York, June 5, 1937; noted critic; grad. Princeton Univ., 1876; Litt. D., 1922; from 1887–1902 critic, New York *Times*; 1902–1937, critic New York *Sun*; lectured, N. Y. Coll. of Music and Inst. of Music. Art; wrote librettos for Damrosch's operas *"The Scarlet Letter"* and *"Cyrano de Bergerac"*; author of *"The Story of Music," "Preludes and Studies," "What Is Good Music?", "How Music Developed," "The Orchestra and Orchestral Music," "Wagner, His Life and Dramas," "Modern Music Drift," "The Art of the Singer," "Some Forerunners of Italian Opera," "The Early History of Singing," "The Soul of a Tenor"* (novel), *"Pipes and Timbrels,"* poems. He long upheld a high standard of musical commentary, combined with a vast knowledge of musical hist. and an experience of actual concert and opera-going covering a half-cent.; his style, urbane, pithy and often marked by gentle satire, retaining its pungency, while he also saluted with an open mind some of the more advanced musical manifestations of latter days.

Henkel (hěnk'-ěl), (1) **Michael,** Fulda, 1780—1851; composer. (2) **G. Andreas,** Fulda, 1805—1871; organist and composer. (3) **H.,** Fulda, Feb. 16, 1822—Frankfort-on-Main, April 10, 1899; son and pupil of (1), also studied with Aloys Schmitt, and theory with Kessler and Anton Andre: 1849, teacher, etc.,

Frankfort. (4) **K.,** Brünn, May 28, 1867—near Vienna, Dec. 2, 1924; son of (3); studied in Berlin Hochschule; lived in London, as violinist.

Henneberg (hěn'-ně-běrkh), **Jn. Bapt.,** Vienna, 1768—1822; organist, conductor and composer.

Hennig (hěn'-nǐkh), (1) **K.,** Berlin, 1819—1873; organist, dir. and composer. (2) **K. Rafael,** Berlin, Jan. 4, 1845—Posen, Feb. 6, 1914; son of above; pupil of Richter and Kiel; 1869–75, organist Posen; 1873, founder of "Hennig" Vocal Soc.; 1883, Royal Mus. Dir.; 1892, R. Prof.; composer and writer.

Hen'nius. Vide HAYM, GILLES.

Henrion (äṅ-rǐ-ôṅ), **Paul,** Paris, July 20, 1819—Oct. 24, 1901; c. operettas and over a thousand popular songs.

Henriques (hěn-rē'-kěs), **Fini Baidemar,** b. Copenhagen, Dec. 20, 1867; violinist; pupil of Tofte, Svendsen, and Joachim; member of court orch. at Copenhagen; c. incidental mus. to *"Wieland der Schmied"*, piano wks., etc.; d. 1940.

Henschel (hěn'-shěl), (1) Sir **George,** Breslau, Feb. 18, 1850—Aletna-Criche, Scotland, Sept. 10, 1934; prominent barytone, pianist, and teacher; pupil of Wandelt and Schaeffer, Breslau; of Leipzig Cons. also Kiel and Ad. Schulze (singing); Berlin; 1877–80, lived in London; 1881–84, cond. Boston (U. S. A.) Symph. Orch.; 1885, London; founded the *"London Symphony Concerts";* 1886–88, prof. of singing R. C. Mus.; c. operas, *"Friedrich der Schöne"* and *"Nubia";* operetta, *"A Sea Change, or Love's Castaway";* an oratorio, etc. (2) **Lillian** (née **Bailey),** Columbus, Ohio, Jan., 1860 —London, Nov. 4, 1901; pupil and (1881) wife of above; also studied with C. Hayden and Viardot-Garcia; concert-soprano; she and her husband gave recitals with great art and success. (3) **Helen,** daughter of above, soprano; sang N. Y. 1902.

Hensel (hěn'-zěl), (1) **Fanny Cäcilia** (née **Mendelssohn),** Hamburg, Nov. 14, 1805—Berlin, May 14, 1847; eldest sister of FELIX M., whose devoted companion she was, and who died six months after her sudden death. He said she was a better pianist than he, and six of her songs are pub. under his name: viz., his op. 8 (Nos. 2, 3, 12), and op. 9 (7, 10,

12); she pub. under her own name "*Gartenlieder*," part-songs and songs; c. also pf.-trios and pcs. (2) **Octavia.** Vide FONDA.

Henselt (hĕn'-zĕlt), **Ad. von,** Schwabach, Bavaria, May 12, 1814—Warmbrunn, Silesia, Oct. 10, 1889; eminent pianist who played with remarkable sonority and emotion; to obtain his remarkable reach he c. and practised incessantly very difficult studies; he c. a famous pf.-concerto, études, etc.

Hentschel (hĕnt'-shĕl), **Theodor,** Schirgiswalde, Upper Lusatia, 1830 —Hamburg, 1892; conductor, pianist and dram. composer.

Herbart (hĕr'-bärt), **Jn. Fr.,** Oldenburg, 1776—Göttingen, 1841; writer.

Herbeck (hĕr'-bĕk), **Jn. Fz. von,** Vienna, Dec. 25, 1831—Oct. 28, 1877; important cond., mainly self-taught; dir. 1866, ct.-cond. at Vienna and prof. at the Cons.

Her'bert, Victor, Dublin, Ireland, Feb. 1, 1859—New York, May 26, 1924; a grandson of Samuel Lover, the novelist; at 7, sent to Germany to study music; 1st 'cello ct.-orch. Stuttgart, and elsewhere; 1886 solo 'cellist, Metropolitan Orch., New York; later Theodore Thomas' and Seidl's orchs. (also associate-cond.); 1894, bandm. 22d Regt., vice Gilmore; 1898—1904 cond. of Pittsburgh (Pa.) Orch. (70 performers); then founded and cond. the Victor Herbert Orch., with which he toured widely; c. pcs. for orch. and 'cello; 'cello-concerto; an oratorio, "*The Captive*" (Worcester Festival); and numerous comic operas, incl. "*Prince Ananias*," a failure, "*The Wizard of the Nile*," "*The Serenade*," "*The dol's Eye*," "*The Fortune Teller*," "*The Singing Girl*," "*Babes in Toyland*," "*The Red Mill*," "*Naughty Marietta*," "*The Enchantress*," "*Mlle. Modiste*," "*The Lady of the Slipper*," "*The Madcap Duchess*," "*Sweethearts*," "*The Debutante*," "*The Only Girl*," "*Princess Pat*," "*Eileen*," "*Her Regiment*," etc. He c. also the grand opera "*Natoma*," libretto by Jos. D. Redding, which was prod. by the Philadelphia Opera Co., 1911, in Philadelphia and at the Met. Op., N. Y., the same year; and a one-act lyric opera, "*Madeleine*" (book by Grant Stewart), Met. Op., Jan. 24, 1914. (See article, page 499.)

Heritte - Viardot (ŭr-ĕt-v'yăr-dō), **Louise Pauline Marie,** Paris, Dec. 14, 1841—Heidelberg, Jan. 17, 1918; daughter of Viardot-Garcia; vocal teacher St. Petersburg Cons.; later at Frankfort, and Berlin; m. Consul-General Heritte; c. opera "*Lindora*" (Weimar, 1879), and cantatas.

Hermann (hĕr'-män), (1) **Matthias,** called **Verrecoiensis,** or **Verrecorensis,** from his supposed birthplace, Warkenz or Warkoing, Holland; Netherland cptist. 16th cent. (2) **Jn. D.,** Germany, ca. 1760—Paris, 1846; pianist and composer. (3) **Jn. Gf. Jakob,** Leipzig, 1772—1848; writer. (4) **Fr.,** Frankfort, 1828—Leipzig, 1907; pupil Leipzig Cons.; 1846-75, viola-player, Gewandhaus and theatre orchs.; 1848, vln.-teacher at the Cons.; 1883 Royal Saxon Prof.; c. symphony, etc.; editor and collector. (5) **Rheinhold L.,** Prenzlau, Brandenburg, Sept. 21, 1849—1919; pupil of Stern Cons., Berlin; 1878-81 dir. of it; 1871-78 singing-teacher and cond. New York; 1884, cond. N. Y. "Liederkranz"; 1887, prof. of sacred history at the Theol. Seminary; 1898, cond. Handel and Haydn Soc., Boston; 1900 returned to Berlin; c. 4 operas incl. "*Vineta*" (Breslau, 1895), and "*Wulfrin*" (Cologne, 1896); 5 cantatas, overtures, etc. (6) **Robt.,** Bern, Switzerland, April 29, 1869—Ambach, Oct. 10, 1912; studied Frankfort Cons; previously self-taught in zither, pf., comp. and had c. works of much originality in which Grieg encouraged him; 1893, studied with Humperdinck, then went to Leipzig and Berlin, where (1895) his symphony and a concert-overture were prod. at the Philh., provoking much critical controversy; lived in Leipzig; c. also "*Petites variations pour rire*," for pf. and vln.; etc. (7) **Hans,** Leipzig, Aug. 17, 1870—Berlin, May 18, 1931; contrabassist and composer; studied with Rust, Kretschmer and von Herzogenberg; c. string-quartets, pf.-pcs., etc., and many songs. (8) **J. Z.** Vide ZENNER. (9) Vide HERRMANN.

Herman'nus (called **Contrac'tus** or "**der Lahme,**" for his lameness), Graf von Vehrihgen, Saulgau Swabia, July 18, 1013—Alshausen, near Biuerach, Sept. 24, 1054; important writer and theorist.

Hermesdorff (hĕr'-mĕs-dôrf), **Michael,** Trier (Trèves), 1833—1885; organist, composer and editor.

Hermstedt (hĕrm'-shtĕt), **Jn. Simon,** Langensalza, near Dresden, 1778—Sondershausen, 1846; composer.

Hernandez (ĕr-nän'-dĕth), **Pablo,** b. Saragossa, Jan. 25, 1834—187–; pupil Madrid Cons.; organist and (1863) auxiliary prof. there; c. *zarzuelas;* a mass, symphony, etc.

Hernando (ĕr-nän'-dō), **Rafael José M.,** Madrid, May 31, 1822—after 1867; pupil of R. Carnicer, Madrid Cons.; 1848-53, he prod. several succ. *zarzuelas,* some in collab.; later dir and composer to Th. des Variétés; 1852, secretary, later prof. of harm., Madrid Cons.; founded a Mutual Aid Mus. Soc.

Hérold (ā-rŏl), (1) **Louis Jos. Fd.,** Paris, Jan. 28, 1791—(of consumption) Thernes, near Paris, Jan. 19, 1833; son of (2) **Fran. Jos. H.** (d. 1802; pf.-teacher and composer, pupil of P. E. Bach), who opposed his studying music, though Fétis taught him solfège and L. Adam. pf. After his father's death (1802), he studied piano with Louis Adam, Paris Cons. (first prize, 1810); harmony with Catel and (from 1811) comp. with Méhul; 1812 won the Prix de Rome, with cantata "*Mlle. de la Vallière*"; studied at Rome and Naples, where he was pianist to Queen Caroline, and prod. opera "*La Gioventù di Enrico Quinto*" (1815); Paris, 1815, finished Boieldieu's "*Charles de France*" (prod. with succ. 1816, Op. Com.); "*Les Rosières*" and "*La Clochette*" followed 1817, both v. succ.; others followed; the last (1820) failing, he imitated Rossini in several operas, but recovered himself in the succ. "*Marie*" (1826); 1824, pianist, later chorusm. at the Ital. Opera, but soon relinquished. 1827 Chef du Chant at the Gr. Opéra, for which he wrote several succ. ballets, incl. "*La Somnambule*," which gave a suggestion to Bellini; 1828, Legion of Honour. "*Zampa*" (1831) gave him European rank and is considered his best work by all except the French, who prefer his last work "*Le Pre aux Clercs*" (1832); he prod. also "*L'Auberge d'Airey*" (1830) (with Carafa), "*La Marquise de Brinvilliers*" (1831), with Auber, Boïeldieu,

Cherubini, and 5 others; and "*La Médicine sans Médecin*" (1832); he left "*Ludovic*" unfinished, to be completed by Halévy with succ.; c. also much pf.-mus. Biogr. by Jouvin (Paris, 1868).

Herrmann (hĕr'-män), (1) **Gf.,** Sondershausen, 1808—Lübeck, 1878; violinist, pianist, organist and dram. composer. (2) **K.,** d. Stuttgart, 1894; 'cellist.

Herschel (hĕr-shĕl), **Fr. Wm.** (Anglicised, Sir William Herschel, K.C. H., D.C.L.), Hanover, 1738—Slough, near Windsor, 1822; oboist; organist at Bath; astronomy, in which he won such fame, was till 1781 only his diversion.

Hertel (hĕr'-t'l), (1) **Jn. Chr.,** Oettingen, Swabia, 1699—Strelitz, 1754; singer, viola da gambist, violinist and composer. (2) **Jn. Wm.,** Eisenach, 1727—Schwerin, 1789; son and pupil of above; violinist, conductor and composer. (3) **K.,** 1784-1868; violinist. (4) **Peter L.,** Berlin, 1817 —1899; son of above; composer.

Hertz (hĕrtz), **Alfred,** Frankfort-on-Main, July 15, 1872—San Francisco, Cal., April 17, 1942; studied Raff Cons.; from 1895 2d-cond. various cities; 1899 cond. city theatre Breslau; 1899, London; 1909-15, Met. Op., N. Y., 1915-30, cond. San Francisco Symph. Orch.

Hertzberg (hĕrts'-bĕrkh), **Rudolph von,** Berlin, 1818—1893; conductor and editor.

Hervé rightly **Florimond Ronger** (ĕr-vā or rôń-zhā), (1) Houdain, near Arras, June 30, 1825—Paris, Nov. 4, 1892; singer, then organist, conductor; in Paris acting as librettist, composer and actor, and producing flippant but ingenious little works in which French operetta finds a real origin; c. over 50 operettas, also heroic symphony "*The Ashantee War*," and ballets. (2) **Gardel,** son of above, prod. 1871 operetta "*Ni, ni, c'est fini.*"

Hervey (här'-vĭ), **Arthur,** of Irish parents, Paris, Jan. 26, 1855—London, March 10, 1922; pupil of B. Tours (harm.) and Ed. Marlois (instr.); intended for the diplomatic service, till 1880; critic of "*Vanity Fair*"; from 1892, London "*Post*"; c. a 1-act opera, a dram. overture "*Love and Fate*," etc.; author of biog. and other works.

Herz (hĕrts or ĕrs), (1) Jacques Simon, Frankfort, Dec. 31, 1794—Nice, Jan. 27, 1880; of Jewish parentage; studied at Paris Cons. with Pradher; pianist and teacher in Paris; then London; 1857, acting-prof. Paris Cons.; c. vln.-sonatas, etc. (2) Henri, Vienna, Jan. 6, 1806—Paris, Jan. 5, 1888; 1st prize pf.-pupil Paris Cons.; very popular as touring pianist; succ. as mfr. of pianos; obtained extravagant prices for his comps.; prof. at the Cons.; writer.

Herzog (hĕr'-tsōkh), (1) Jn. G., Schmolz, Bavaria, Sept. 6, 1822—Munich, Feb. 4, 1909; pupil of Bodenschatz, and at Altdorf Seminary; 1842, organist at Munich; 1848, cantor; 1850, organ-prof. at the Cons.; 1854, mus. dir. Erlangen Univ.; 1866, Dr. Phil.; later prof.; retired 1888; composer. (2) Emilie, Ermatingen, Switzerland, 1859—Aarburg, Sept. 16, 1923; soubrette coloratura-singer; pupil Zurich Sch. of Mus., then of Gloggner, and Ad. Schimon, Munich; début, Munich (1879); 1889-1916, Berlin ct.-opera; 1922 taught Zurich Cons.

Herzogenberg (hĕr'-tsōkh-ĕn-bĕrkh), (1) H. von, Graz, Styria, June 10, 1843—Wiesbaden, 1900; prof. at Berlin, etc.; director, professor and composer. (2) Elizabeth (née von Stockhausen) (?) 1848—San Remo, 1892; pianist, wife of above.

Hes'eltine, (1) Jas., d. 1763; English organist and composer. (2) Philip, London, Oct. 30, 1894—Dec. 17, 1930; composer and author, known under pseudonym of "Peter Warlock"; studied at Eton, and with Colin Taylor, Delius and van Dieren; founded and ed. periodical, "The Sackbut," 1920-21; wrote books on Delius, Gesualdo; also "The English Ayre"; c. chamber and orch. music, many songs.

Hess, (1) Joachim, organist, writer and carillonneur, Gouda, Holland, from 1766—1810. (2) Willy, b. Mannheim, July 14, 1859—Berlin, Feb. 17, 1939; pupil of Joachim; at 19 Konzertmeister at Frankfort, 1886 at Rotterdam, then England; 1895 1st vln.-prof. Cologne Cons., and 1st vln. Gürzenich Quartet. He was made Royal Prof., 1900; 1903-4 he was violin prof. R. A. M., London; resigned and became concertmaster Boston Symph. Orch., and leader of

the Quartet; 1908 co-founded the Hess-Schroeder Quartet; 1910-28, taught Berlin Hochsch. (3) Ludwig, b. Marburg, March 23, 1877; pupil Berlin Royal Hochsch. and Vidal in Milan; toured as concert singer; from 1907 succeeded Felix Mottl as dir. Munich Konzertgesellschaft; c. symphony "Hans Memling," an epic "Ariadne," and other works for voices and orch.; songs, etc.; 1912 engaged to tour America; 1925-34, prof. Berlin Acad. for Church and School Mus., d. 1944.

Myra, b. London, Feb. 25, 1890; pianist; studied R. Coll. of Mus. with Tobias Matthay; has toured France, Holland, Belgium, Canada, also U. S. annually after about 1920; one of pre-eminent pianists of her generation; has made arr. of Bach chorales for piano: created Dame Commander of British Empire, 1936.

Hesse (hĕs'-sĕ), (1) Ernst Chr., Grossen-Gottern, Thuringia, 1676—Darmstadt, 1762; viola-da-gambist. conductor. (2) Ad. (Fr.), Breslau, 1809—1863; org.-virtuoso and composer. (3) Julius, Hamburg, 1823—Berlin, 1881; introduced the present measurement for pf.-keys; and pub. a method. (4) Max, Sondershausen, Feb. 18, 1858—Leipzig, Nov. 24, 1907; 1880 founded mus. pub. house in Leipzig; in 1883, founded H. und Becker.

Hetsch (hĕtsh), K. Fr. L., Stuttgart, 1806—Mannheim, 1872; pianist, violinist and dram. composer.

Heuberger (hoi'-bĕrkh-ĕr), Richard Fz. Jos., Graz, Styria, June 18, 1850—Vienna, Oct. 28, 1914; a civil engineer; in 1876 took up music, which he had previously studied; chorusm., Vienna academical Gesangverein; 1878 cond. Singakademie; c. operas "Abenteuer einer Neujahrsnacht" (Leipzig, 1886); "Manuel Venegas" (do., 1889), remodelled as "Mirjam" (Vienna, '94); 2 operettas; critic, and teacher at Vienna Cons.

Heubner (hoip'-nĕr), Konrad, Dresden, 1860—Coblenz, June 6, 1905; pupil of the "Kreuzschule"; 1878-79, at Leipzig Cons. and writer; with Riemann, later Nottebohm, Vienna; Wüllner, Nicodé and Blassmann, Dresden; 1882, cond. Leipzig Singakademie; 1884, asst. cond. Berlin Singakademie; 1890, dir. Coblenz

Cons. and Mus. Soc.; c. a symphony, overtures, etc.

Heugel (ŭ-zhĕl), **Jacques Ld.**, La Rochelle, 1815—Paris, 1883; editor and publisher.

Hey (hī), **Julius**, Irmelshausen, Lower Franconia, April 29, 1832—Munich, April 22, 1909; studied with Lachner (harm. and cpt.), and F. Schmitt (singing); later with von Bülow at the Munich Sch. of Mus. (estab. by King Ludwig II. on Wagner's plans); attempted a reform in the cultivation of singing, but resigned at Wagner's death (1883), and pub. important vocal method, "*Deutscher Gesangsunterricht*" (4 parts, 1886), exploiting Wagner's views. Wagner called him "the chief of all singing-teachers." 1887, Berlin; later Munich; composer.

Heyden (hī'-d'n), (1) **Sebald**, Nürnberg, 1498 (1494 ?)—1561; cantor, writer. (2) **Hans**, Nürnberg, 1540—1613; son of above; organist; inv. the "Geigenclavicimbal."

Heydrich (hī'-drĭkh), **Bruno**, b. Leuben, Feb. 23, 1863—Halle, August, 1938; pupil of Dresden Cons.; 1879-82, took prizes as double-bass player, pianist and composer; for a year in von Bülow's Weimar orch.; 4 years Dresden ct.-orch.; also studied singing with Scharfe, Hey and v. Milde; succ. début as tenor at Sondershausen theatre; prod. 1-act opera-drama, with pantomimic prologue, "*Amen*," Cologne, 1895; c. songs; after 1909, dir. of a mus. school in Halle.

Hey'man, Katherine Ruth, Sacramento, Cal.—d. Sept. 28, 1944; pianist; studied in Europe; début, Boston, 1899, also heard in Europe; known particularly as an interpreter of Scriabin, for which she has won internat'l. reputation.

Heymann (hī'-män), (1) **Karl**, pianist, Filehna, Posen, Oct. 6, 1854—Haarlem, Nov., 1922. Son of (2) **Isaac H.** (cantor); pupil of Hiller, Gernsheim, Breunung and Cologne Cons. and of Kiel; ill-health ended his promising career as virtuoso; 1874, mus. dir. at Bingen; court-pianist to the Landgrave of Hesse; 1879-80, Hoch Cons., Frankfort; c. concerto "*Elfenspiel*," "*Mummenschanz*," "*Phantasiestücke*," etc., for piano.

Heymann-Rheineck (hī'-män-rī'-nĕk) (**K. Aug. Heymann**), b. Burg-

Rheineck on Rhine, Nov. 24, 1852; pianist; pupil Cologne Cons., and R. Hochschule, Berlin; 1875-1920, teacher there; composer.

Heyne Van Ghizeghem (also **Hayne**, or **Ayne**, "Henry"), Netherland contrapuntist and court-singer, ca. 1468.

Hiebsch (hēpsh), **Josef**, Tyssa, Bohemia, 1854—Carlsbad, 1897; teacher and writer in Vienna.

Hientzsch (hēntsh), **Jn. Gf.**, Mokrehna, near Torgau, 1787—Berlin, 1856; teacher, composer and writer.

Hig'ginson, Henry Lee, New York, Nov. 18, 1834—Boston, Nov. 15, 1919; music patron; banker; had studied music in Vienna; founded Boston Symph., 1881, with a million-dollar endowment; directed its policies until 1918, when gave control to a board of directors; also a trustee of N. E. Cons.

Hignard (ēn-yăr) (**J. L.**), **Aristide**, Nantes, 1822—Vernon, 1898; the preface to his "*Hamlet*," written 1868, not prod. till Nantes, 1888, shows him to have attempted a new and serious manner, but he found production only for comic operas which were usually succ.

Hildach (hĭl'-däkh), (1) **Eugen**, Wittenberg-on-the-Elbe, Nov. 20, 1849 —Berlin-Zehlendorf, July 28, 1924; barytone; pupil of Frau Prof. El. Dreyschock. (2) **Anna** (née **Schubert**), Königsberg, 1852—Nov. 18, 1935; wife of above; mezzo-soprano; teacher Dresden Cons., 1880–86.

Hildebrand (hēl'-dĕ-bränt), **Camillo**, b. Prague, 1879; conductor 1912–19, Berlin Philh.; 1921–24, Berlin Symph.; composer.

Hiles (hīlz), (1) **J.**, Shrewsbury, 1810 —London, 1882; organist, writer and composer. (2) **H.**, Shrewsbury, Dec. 31, 1826—Worthing near London, Oct. 20, 1904; bro. and pupil of above; organist various churches; 1867, Mus. Doc. Oxon; 1876, lecturer; later, prof. R. Manchester Coll. of Music; 1885, editor and writer; c. 2 oratorios, 3 cantatas, an historic opera, etc.

Hilf (hēlf), (1) **Arno**, Bad Elster, Saxony, March 14, 1858—Aug. 2, 1909; vln.-virtuoso; son and pupil of (2) **Wm. Chr. H.**; from 1872 he also studied with David, Röntgen, and Schradieck, Leipzig Cons.; second concertm., 1878, and teacher at Moscow Cons., (1888) Sonders-

hausen; 1889–91, concertm. Gewandhaus orch., Leipzig; after 1892, 1st
vln. prof. at the Conservatorium.
Hill, (1) **Wm.,** London, 1800—1870;
org.-builder. (2) **Wm. Ebsworth,**
London, 1817—Hanley, 1895; vln.-
maker. (3) **Thos. H. Weist,** London, 1828—1891; violinist, conductor
and composer. (4) **Ureli C.,** New
York, 1802 (?)—1875; violinist.
(5) **Wm.,** Fulda, March 28, 1838—
Homburg, June 6, 1902; pianist;
pupil of H. Henkel and Hauff; lived
in Frankfort; c. prize-opera "*Alona*";
vln.-sonatas, etc. (6) **Edward Bur-
lingame,** b. Cambridge, Mass., Sept.
9, 1872; composer; grad. Harvard,
1894, with highest honours in mus.;
pupil of Lang and Whiting, piano;
Widor, comp.; Bullard, theory;
Chadwick, instrumentation; 1887–
1902, taught piano and harmony in
Boston; instructor of mus., Harvard
Univ., after 1908; in recent years,
head of the mus. dept. there; a prolific comp.; among his works: fantastic pantomime for orch. "*Jack
Frost in Midsummer*" (Chicago
Orch. 1907, N. Y. Symph. 1908);
women's chorus with orch. "*Nuns
of the Perpetual Adoration*" (Musical
Art Soc., 1907, Birmingham Orch.,
etc.); Stevensonia Suite Nos. 1 and
2, symphonies, "*Sinfonietta*," "*Li-
lacs*"; Concertino, for orch.; chamber
music, 3 piano sonatas, songs.
Hille (hǐl′-lĕ), (1) **Ed.,** Wahlhausen,
Hanover, 1822—Göttingen, 1891;
cond. and teacher. (2) **Gv.,** b. Jeri-
chow-on-Elbe, near Berlin, May, 31,
1850; violinist; pupil of R. Wüerst
(theory), Kullak's Acad., 1869–74 w.
Joachim (vln.); lived in Berlin, as a
solo-player; 1879, invited to the
Mendelssohn Quintet Club, Boston,
Mass.; toured; then teacher at Mus.
Acad., Phila.; co.-dir. of Leefson-
Hille Cons. there; 1910, returned to
Germany; c. 5 vln.-concertos with
orch.; etc.; d. (?).
Hillemacher (hǐl′-lĕ-mäkh-er, or ēl-
mǎ-shä), two brothers. (1) **Paul
Jos. Wm.,** Paris, Nov. 25, 1852—
Versailles, Aug. 13, 1933. (2) **Lucien
Jos. Ed.,** Paris, June 10, 1860—
June 2, 1909; both studied at the
Cons., and took the first Grand Prix
de Rome, (1) in 1876; (2) in 1880.
For some years they wrote all their
scores in collaboration. C. symph.
legend "*Lorely*" (1882, City of Paris

prize); succ. opera "*St. Megrin*"
(Brussels, 1886), etc.; "*Orsola*" (Gr.
Opéra, Paris, 1902).
Hiller (Hüller) (hǐl′-lĕr), (1) **Jn. Adam,**
Wendisch-Ossig, near Görlitz, Dec.
25, 1728—Leipzig, June 16. 1804;
pupil of Homilius (Kreuzschule) and
U. of Leipzig; flutist in concerts, and
teacher; 1754 tutor to the son of
Count Brühl; 1758, accompanied him
to Leipzig, where he lived thereafter;
1763, revived, at his own expense,
the subscription concerts, which developed into the famous "Gewandhaus" concerts, of which he was
cond.; 1771, founded a singing-
school; 1789–1801, cantor and dir.
Thomasschule. He founded the
"*Singspiel*," from which German
"comedy-opera" developed, contem-
poraneously with *opera buffa* and
opéra comique. In his dram. works
the aristocratic personages sing arias,
while the peasants, etc., sing simple
ballads, etc. His *Singspiele*, all
prod. at Leipzig, had immense vogue,
some of the songs being still sung;
1766–70, he wrote, edited collections,
etc.; c. also a Passion cantata,
funeral music (in honour of Hasse),
symphonies and partitas, the 100th
Psalm, etc. Biog. by Carl Peiser
(Leipzig, 1895). (2) **Fr. Adam,**
Leipzig, 1768—Königsberg, Nov. 23,
1812; violinist and tenor; son and
pupil of above; mus. dir. of Schwerin
Th.; 1803, cond. of Königsberg Th.;
c. 4 operettas, etc. (3) **Fd. von,**
Frankfort, Oct. 24, 1811—Cologne,
May 12, 1885; of wealthy Jewish
parentage; a pupil of Hofmann
(vln.), Aloys Schmitt (pf.) and Vollweiler (harm. and cpt.); at 10 played
a Mozart concerto in public, at 12
began comp.; from 1825 pupil of
Hummel; at 16 his string-quartet
was pub. Vienna; at 15, he saw
Beethoven on his death-bed; 1828–
35, taught Choron's School, Paris;
then independently giving occasional
concerts; 1836, he returned to Frankfort, and cond. the Cäcilien-Verein;
1839, prod. succ. opera "*Romilda*,"
at Milan; oratorio, "*Die Zerstörung
Jerusalems*" (Gewandhaus, 1840);
1841, studied church-music with
Baini, Rome; 1843–44 he cond. the
Gewandhaus; prod. at Dresden, 2
operas; 1847, municipal cond. at
Düsseldorf; 1850 at Cologne, where
he organised the Cons.; cond. Gürze-

uich Concerts, and the Lower Rhine Festivals; 1852–53, cond. Opera Italien, Paris; 1868, Dr. Phil. *h. c.* Bonn Univ.; 1884 he retired. He was a classicist in ideal of the Mendelssohn type and his comp. are of precise form and great clarity. He was also a lecturer and writer on music. He c. 3 other operas, 2 oratorios, 6 cantatas, 3 overtures, 3 symphonies, a ballad "*Richard Löwenherz*," with orch. (1883), etc.

(4) **Paul**, Seifersdorf, near Liegnitz, Nov. 16, 1850—Breslau, Dec. 27, 1924; 1870, asst.-organist, and 1881 organist St. Maria-Magdalena, and dir. of a music school, Breslau; composer.

Hil'pert, W. Kasimir Fr., Nürnberg, 1841—Munich, 1896; 'cellist.

Hils'berg, (1) **Ignace**, b. Warsaw, July 8, 1894; pianist; pupil of St. Petersburg Cons., with Essipov and Sauer; soloist with orchs. in Europe and U. S., also Far East; mem. of faculty, Inst. of Musical Art, Juilliard School, N. Y. (2) **Alexander**, his bro.; b. Warsaw; violinist; mem. of faculty, Curtis Inst. of Mus., Phila.; also heard in concerts here and in Europe; later active as conductor.

Hilton, (1) **John**, d. before 1612; organist at Cambridge, 1594; perhaps the father of (2) **John**, 1599—1656-7; organist at Westminster; c. anthems, madrigals, etc.

Him'mel, Fr. H., Treuenbrietzen, Brandenburg, 1765—Berlin, 1814; court-cond. and dram. composer.

Hinck'ley, Allen Carter, b. Boston Oct. 11, 1877; bass; pupil of Carl Schachner and Oscar Saenger; début with Bostonian Light Op. Co., 1901; op. début, Hamburg as "King Henry" in "*Lohengrin*," 1903; sang at Covent Garden and Bayreuth; Met. Op. Co., 1908–11; later with Chicago Op. Co., also in other cities of Europe and U. S.; d. Yonkers, N. Y., 1954.

Hindemith (hĭn'-dĕ-mĭt), (1) **Paul**, b. Hanau, Germany, Nov. 16, 1895; composer, viola player; one of the most prolific, scholarly and original comps. among the younger German school, combining remarkable command of cpt. with original harmonic style, including use of atonality; there are both romantic and parodistic elements in his work; studied comp. with Arnold Mendelssohn and Sekles; played in Frankfort Op.

orch., 1915–23; after which he was active mainly as composer and as a member of the Amar String Quartet; taught at Berlin Hochsch., 1927–34; in latter year his music fell under ban in Germany as opposed to cultural policies then enforced by the state regime, although he had in his opera "*Mathis der Maler*" (1934) shown a return to orthodox tonality and romantic subject matter; c. (operas) "*Mörder, Hoffnung der Frauen*," "*Das Nusch-Nuschi*" and "*Sankta Johanna*," 3 one-act works (1920); "*Cardillac*" (1926); "*Neues vom Tag*"; "*Hin und Zurueck*" (short opera in which action reverses); orch., Konzertmusik for strings and brass; "*The 4 Temperaments*" (also str. quart., pf., double bass); Symphonia Serena; "*Metamorphoses on Themes of Weber*"; "*Nobilissima Visione*" (orch. suite from ballet); pantomime, "*Der Dämon*," an oratorio "*Das Unaufhörliche*," (cantata) "*Die Serenaden*"; (vocal works) "*Marienleben*," "*Junge Nonne*," and a large amount of ingenious chamber music, incl. 4 string quartets, sonatas for piano and vln., viola and 'cello, piano suite "*1912*," orchestral, piano, vln., 'cello, viola and viola d'amour concertos, various forms of writing known as "Kammermusik" with pieces for piano and 'cello, songs; Prof. of music, Yale Univ., 1941. (2) **Rudolf**, bro. of **Paul**, b. Jan. 9, 1900, in Hanau; 'cellist; pupil of Hoch Cons.; was solo 'cellist at Munich and Vienna State Op.; mem. of Amar Quartet and of Munich Trio; after 1927 taught at Carlsruhe Cons.

Hinrichs (hĭn'-rĭkhs), (1) **Fz.**, Halle-on-the-Saale, ca. 1820—Berlin, 1892; composer and writer on music. His sister (2) **Maria**. Vide FRANZ. (3) **Gustav**, Ludwigslust, Mecklenburg, 1850—Mountain Lakes, N. J., March 26, 1942; conductor; studied with his father, Marxsen and Reisland; early active as a violinist, after 1870 in San Francisco; cond. of Amer. Op. Co., assisting Theodore Thomas, 1885–86; 1886–96, manager of his own opera company; 1899–1906, dir. of music at Columbia Univ.; 1903–08, cond. at Met. Op.; c. operas, orch. works, choral pieces, songs, etc.

Hin'shaw, William Wade, b. Union, Iowa, Nov. 3, 1867; bass and impresario; studied with R. A. Heritage, L. G. Gottschalk and L. A. Phelps; early active as voice teacher and choir dir.; début at St. Louis with Savage Op. Co., 1899, as "Mephistopheles"; organised school of opera, Chicago, 1903; 1909 founded Internat'l Gr. Op. Co.; sang at Met. Op. House, 1910–13; after 1917, manager of Soc. of Amer. Singers, N. Y., and later of his own touring opera company which gave Mozart and other works; d. Washington, 1947.

Hin'ton, Arthur, Beckenham, 1869— Rottingdean, 1941; pupil R. A. M., later with Rheinberger at Munich Cons., where his first symph. was played; his second symph. was played in London, 1903; c. also opera "Tamara"; operettas for children, and piano pieces played by his wife, Katharine Goodson, whom he married in 1903.

Hip'kins, Alfred Jas., Westminster, June 17, 1826—London, June 3, 1903; writer; an authority on ancient instrs., etc.; was for a time in business with Broadwood; wrote many articles for the "Encyclopædia Britannica," and "Grove's Dictionary of Music," also books on old instr. and pitch.

Hirn (hērn), Gv. Ad., Logelbach, near Colmar (Alsatia), 1815—Colmar, 1890; writer.

Hirsch (hērsh), (1) Dr., Rudolf, Napagedl, Moravia, 1816—Vienna, 1872; critic, poet and composer. (2) Karl, Wemding, Bavaria, March 17, 1858 —Faulenbach, Nov. 3, 1918; studied in Munich; 1885–87, church mus.-dir., Munich; 1887–92, Mannheim; then Cologne; after 1893 lived in other cities as dir. various societies, etc.; c. numerous pop. a cappella choruses.

Hirschbach (hērsh'-bäkh), H., Berlin, 1812—Gohlis, 1888; editor and composer.

Hirschfeld (hērsh'-fĕlt), Robt., Moravia, Sept. 17, 1857—Salzburg, April 2, 1914, where he was dir. of Mozarteum; studied Vienna Cons.; later lecturer there; 1884 teacher of musical æsthetics; took Dr. Phil. with dissertation on "Johannes de Muris"; he wrote a pamphlet against Hanslick in defence of ancient a cappella music, and founded the "Renaissance-Abende" to cultivate it.

Hirsch'mann, Henri, b. St. Maudé, 1872; composer, under pen-name of V. H. Herblay, of operas, "L'Amour à la Bastille" (Paris, 1897), "Lovelace" (do., 1898), "Hermani" (do., 1909); operettas "Das Schwalbennest" (Berlin, 1904, in Paris, 1907, as Les hirondelles); "La petite Bohême" (Paris, 1905; in Berlin 1905, as "Musette"), etc.

Hobrecht (hō'-brĕkht) (or Obrecht, Obreht, Ober'tus, Hober'tus), Jakob, Utrecht, ca. 1430—Antwerp, 1505; church composer of great historical importance.

Hochberg (hôkh'-bĕrkh), Bolko, Graf von (pseud. J. H. Franz), Fürstenstein Castle, Silesia, Jan. 23, 1843— Bad Salzbrunn, Dec. 1, 1926; maintained the H. quartet at Dresden; 1876 founded the Silesian music festivals; 1886–1903, general intendant Prussian Ct. Th.; prod. 2 operas; c. symphonies, etc.

Hoffmann (hôf'-män), (1) Eucharius, b. Heldburg, Franconia, cantor at Stralsund; writer and composer, 1577–84. (2) Ernst Th. (Amadeus) Wm. (he added Amadeus from love of Mozart), Königsberg, 1776— Berlin, 1822; gifted poet, caricaturist, and dram. composer. (3) H. Aug. (called H. von Fallersleben), Fallersleben, Hanover, 1798—Castle Korvei, 1874; writer. (4) Richard, Manchester, Engl., May 24, 1831— Mt. Kisco, N. Y., Aug. 17, 1909; pianist and teacher; pupil of his father, and de Meyer, Pleyel, Moscheles, Rubinstein, Döhler, Thalberg, and Liszt; 1847, New York; solo pianist with Jenny Lind on tours, etc.; also with von Bülow, in N. Y. (1875); c. anthems, pf.-pcs., etc. (5) Karl, Prague, Dec. 12, 1872— 1936; violinist; studied Prague Cons.; founder and 1st vln. the famous "Bohemian String-quartet"; after 1922 taught master class at Prague Cons.

Hoffmeister (hôf'-mī-shtĕr), Fz. Anton, Rotenburg-on-Neckar, 1754—Vienna, 1812; conductor and dram. composer, etc.

Hofhaimer (hôf'-hī-mĕr) (Hoffheimer, Hoffhaimer, Hoffhaymer), Paulus von, Radstadt, Salzburg, 1459—Salzburg, 1537; eminent organist; lutenist, composer and teacher.

Hofmann (hôf'-män), (1) Chr., ca. 1668; cantor at Krossen: writer.

(2) **H. (K. Jn.)**, Berlin, Jan. 13, 1842 —July 19, 1902; pupil of Würst, Kullak's Academy; famous pf.-virtuoso and teacher; prod. succ. operas *"Cartouche"* (Berlin, 1869) and *"Donna Diana,"* and 4 others; and succ. orch. works, *"Hungarian Suite"* (1873) and *"Frithjof"* symph. (1874); was a Prof., and a member of the Berlin R. Acad. of Arts; c. 6 other operas, "secular oratorio" *"Prometheus"* (1896); cantatas; *"Schauspiel"* overture; *"Trauermarsch,"* etc., for orch.; a vln.-sonata, etc. (3) **Richard**, Delitzsch, Prussian Saxony, April 30, 1844—Leipzig, Nov. 11, 1918; son of municipal mus.-dir.; pupil of Dreyschock and Jadassohn; lived in Leipzig as teacher; pub. a valuable *"Praktische Instrumentationsschule"* (Leipzig, 1893), a catechism of instrs., etc. (4) **Casimir** (rightly **Wyszkowski**) (wěsh-kŏf'-shkǐ), Cracow, 1842—Berlin, 1911; pianist; prof. of harm. and comp. at Cons., and cond. of opera, Warsaw. (5) **Josef**, b. Cracow, Jan. 20, 1876. Son and (till 1892) pupil of (4); at 6 played in public; at 9 toured Europe; at 10 gave 52 concerts in America; then studied 2 years with Rubinstein and made new début in Dresden, 1894, and has toured Europe since and (beginning 1899) America; from being a sensational prodigy, he developed into a brilliant pianist of great power, virtuosity and charm; his technique is probably unsurpassed in his generation; after 1924 dir. of Curtis Inst. of Mus., Phila.; c. symph. work, *"The Haunted Castle"*; pf.-concerto, and numerous other pieces; author, *"Piano Playing,"* etc.

Hofmeister (hŏf'-mī-shtěr), (1) **Fr.**, 1782—1864; publisher; his son and successor (2) **Ad. H.**, ca. 1818—Leipzig, 1870; was succeeded by Albert **Rothing**, 1845—1907.

Ho'garth, G., Carfrae Mill, near Oxton, Berwickshire, 1783—London, 1870; 'cellist and composer; his daughter m. Charles Dickens.

Hohlfeld (hōl'-fělt), **Otto**, Zeulenroda, Voigtland, 1854—Darmstadt, 1895; vln.-virtuoso and composer.

Hohnstock (hōn'-shtŏk), **Carl**, Brunswick, 1828—1889; teacher, violinist, pianist and composer.

Hol, Richard, Amsterdam, July 23, 1825—Utrecht, May 14, 1904; pupil

Martens (org.) and of Bertelman (harm. and cpt.); teacher at Amsterdam; 1862, city mus.-dir., Utrecht; 1869, cath.-organist; 1875, dir. Sch. of Mus.; also cond. "Diligentia" Concerts at The Hague, Classical Concerts at Amsterdam; 1878, officer of the French Academy; c. oratorio *"David"* (op. 81); 2 operas; 2 symphonies, etc.

Hol'borne, Antony and **Wm.**, English composers, 1597.

Hol'brooke, Josef, b. Croyden, July 6, 1878; English composer; pupil of the R. A. M., till 1898; c. symph. poems *"The Raven"* (Crystal Palace, 1900); *"Ode to Victory,"* *"The Skeleton in Armour,"* *"Ulalume"* (London Symph., 1904), *"Queen Mab"* (Leeds Fest., 1904), *"The Masque of the Red Death,"* overture, *"The New Renaissance,"* etc. His opera *"The Children of Don"* (libretto by Lord Howard de Walden) was prod. at the London Op., June 15, 1912, with Nikisch conducting. Other works include: (operas) *"Pierrot and Pierrette,"* *"Dylan,"* *"Bronwen, Daughter of Llyr,"* *"The Wizard,"* *"The Stranger"*; chamber music, ballets, suites for orch., vln. concerto. Author, *"Contemporary British Composers"* (1931).

Hol'der, Rev. Wm., Nottinghamshire, 1616—Amen Corner, 1697; writer, editor and composer.

Holländer (hŏl'-lěnt-ěr), (1) **Alexis**, Ratibor, Silesia, Feb. 25, 1840—Berlin, Feb. 5, 1924; pianist; pupil of Schnabel and Hesse at Breslau; cond. of the Gymnasium Singing Society; 1858-61, studied with Grell and A. W. Bach, and K. Bohmer, Berlin, R. Akad.; 1861, teacher at Kullak's Acad.; 1864, cond.; 1870-1902, cond. the "Cäcilienverein"; 1888, professor; c. 6 pf. Intermezzi for left hand, etc. (2) **Gv.**, Leobschütz, Upper Silesia, Feb. 15, 1855 —Berlin, Dec. 4, 1915; played in public early; pupil of David, of Joachim (vln.), and Kiel (theory); 1874, principal teacher Kullak's Acad. and royal chamber-mus.; toured Austria with Carlotta Patti; 1881, teacher at the Cons., Cologne; 1884, leader at the Stadttheater; 1894, dir. Stern Cons., Berlin; c. vln. and pf.-pcs. (3) **Victor**, b. Leobschütz, April 20, 1866; pupil of Kullak; c. succ. comic operas and stage music, also for films; after 1934 comp. in Hollywood.

Hollander (hŏl'-lĕn-dĕr), **Benno, b.** Amsterdam, June 8, 1853; violinist; played as child, then studied with Massart and Saint-Saëns at Paris Cons., winning first violin prize, 1873; after 1876 toured, then settled in London as viola player; 1882, cond. German Opera season; 1887 violin prof. at the Guildhall; cond. London Symph. Concerts; 1903, organised the Benno H. Orchestral Society; c. symph. *"Roland"*; violin concertos, pastoral fantasia played by Ysaye; d. London, 1942.

Hollangue. Vide MOUTON.

Hol'lins, Alfred, Hull, Sept. 11, 1865 —Edinburgh, May 18, 1942; blind organist; pupil Hartvigson; played Beethoven concerto as boy; at 16 played for the Queen; pupil of Bülow, later at Raff Cons.; played for crowned heads, and toured America; 1884, org. at Redhill; 1888 at People's Palace; 1897 at Edinburgh, Free St. George's Church; c. 2. overtures, organ music, etc.

Hollmann (hŏl'-män), **Josef,** Maestricht, Holland, Oct. 16, 1852— Paris, Jan. 1, 1927; notable 'cellist; studied with Servais; toured Europe, England and America; court-mus., Holland, and many decorations.

Holmes (hōmz), (1) **Edw.,** near London, 1797—U. S., 1859; pf.-teacher, editor and critic. (2) **Wm. H.,** Sudbury, Derbyshire, 1812—London, 1885; pianist and professor. (3) **Alfred,** London, 1837—Paris, 1876; son of above; dram. composer. (4) **Hy.,** London, Nov. 7, 1839—San Francisco, Cal., Dec. 9, 1905; bro. of above; after 1866 was long vln.-prof. R. C. M.; c. 4 symphonies, etc.

Holmès (ŏl'-mĕs) (rightly **Holmes**), **Augusta Mary Anne,** (of Irish parents) Paris, Dec. 16, 1847—Jan. 28, 1903; at first a pianist; studied comp. with Lambert, Klosé and César Franck; 1873, prod. a psalm, *"In Exitu"*; 1874, a 1-act stage work *"Héro et Leandre"* (Chatelet); the symphonies *"Lutece"* and *"Les Argonautes,"* 1883; symph. *"Irlande,"* 1885; unsucc. drama *"La Montagne Noire"* (Gr. Opera), 1895; symphonic poems, *"Roland," "Pologne," "Au Pays Bleu";* 2 operas, etc.; she sometimes uses pseud. *"Hermann Zenta."*

Holst, Gustav, Cheltenham, England, Sept. 21, 1874—London, May 25, 1934; studied R. Coll. of Mus. with Stanford; fellow and prof. of comp., R. Coll. of Mus.; formerly dir. of music, Morley Coll.; lectured on music, Harvard Univ., one of the most accomplished of modern English comps., though of Teutonic ancestry; introduced British folk-song elements into some of his works, also arranged many traditional pieces in choral transcriptions; showed interest in and influence of Oriental themes; modern French school and Stravinsky among others contributed to his style; c. (operas) *"Savitri,"* one-act work with chamber ensemble (London, 1916); *"The Perfect Fool"* (a ballet-opera, said to satirise Wagner's *"Parsifal"*), Covent Garden, 1923; *"At the Boar's Head,"* based on Shakespeare's *"Henry IV"* and using actual folk melodies (British Nat'l. Op. Co., 1927); also *"Ave Maria"* for 8 women's voices; (masque) *"The Vision of Dame Christian"* (1909); *"The Mystic Trumpeter,"* scena for soprano and orch. (1905); Cotswolds Symphony (1900); *"The Planets"* (1915) and *"Beni-Mora"* suite (1910); *"Phantasies"* (1912), *"Indra"* (1903), *"Japanese"* suite (1916); *"A Somerset Rhapsody"* for orch. (1907); (choral works) *"King Estmere"* (1903), *"Choral Hymns from the Rig-Veda"* (1912), *"The Cloud-Messenger"* (1910), *"Hymn of Jesus"* and *"Ode to Death"* (Leeds Fest., 1921), Choral Symphony (do., 1924); Fugal Concerto, St. Paul's Suite, *"Songs without Words," "Songs of the West,"* and numerous choruses and part-songs, besides 2 wind quintets and other chamber works.

Holstein (hŏl'-shtīn), **Fz. (Fr.) von,** Brunswick, 1826 — Leipzig, 1878; dram. composer.

Holten (hŏl'-tĕn), **K. von,** Hamburg, July 26, 1836—Altona, Jan. 12, 1912; pianist; pupil of J. Schmitt, Ave-Lallemant and Grädener, and at Leipzig Cons.; after 1874, teacher Hamburg Cons.; c. a *Kindersymphonie,* etc.

Holy (ō'-lē), **Alfred, b.** Oporto, Aug. 5, 1866; harp-virtuoso; son and pupil of a cond. and teacher from Prague; studied at Prague Cons., and lived there till 1896, when he went to the

Berlin ct.-opera; after 1913, solo harpist, Boston Symph.; d. Vienna, 1948.

Holzbauer (hôlts'-bow-ĕr), **Ignaz,** Vienna, 1711—Mannheim, 1783; courtconductor and dram. composer; highly praised by Mozart.

Hölzl (hĕl'-ts'l), **Fz.** Severin, Malaczka, Hungary, 1808—Fünfkirchen, 1884; conductor and composer.

Ho'mer, (1) **Sidney,** b. Boston, Mass., Dec. 9, 1864—Winter Park, Fla., July 10, 1953; composer; pupil, G. W. Chadwick, then of Rheinberger, O. Hieter and Abel in Germany; 1888–96 teacher of theory in Boston; c. many important songs. In 1895 he married (2) **Louise (Dilworth Beatty),** b. Pittsburgh—d. Winter Park, Fla., 1947; contralto, pupil of Miss Whinnery and Miss Goff, W. L. Whitney, and of her husband in theory; then studied in Paris with Fidèle Koenig; début, 1898, at Vichy; 1899 at Covent Garden, also at La Monnaie, Brussels; 1900–19 sang regularly at Met. Op. House as a leading member of co. in Italian, German, French rôles; created title rôle in Parker's *"Mona,"* etc.; guest appearances with co. after the latter year; also an eminent concert singer. (3) **Louise (Homer-Stires),** their daughter, also active as a concert singer (soprano) in joint programmes with her mother.

Homeyer (hō'-mī-ĕr), name of a musical family. The most prom. of them is **Paul Joseph M.,** Osterode, Harz, Oct. 26, 1853—Leipzig, July 27, 1908; famous organist at the Gewandhaus, and teacher Leipzig Cons.

Homilius (hō-mē'-lǐ-oos), **Gf. Aug.,** Rosenthal, Saxony, 1714—Dresden, 1785; eminent organist and composer.

Honegger (ŏn'-ĕg-ĕr), **Arthur,** b. Le Havre, France, March 10, 1892, of Swiss ancestry; composer; studied with Martin, Gédalge, Widor and Capet; an exponent of Polytonality, but classic in form; one of most gifted members of former "Group of Six"; since 1913 active in Paris; c. (operas) *"Morte de Ste. Almeenne"; "Antigone," "Judith,"* produced by Chicago Op. with Mary Garden; (cantata with narrator) *"Le Roi David"* to text by Morax, widely performed (N. Y., 1925); music to Méral's *"Dit des Jeux du Monde";* (ballet) *"Verité Mensonge?",* Concertino for piano

and orch., and (orch.) *"Horace Victorieux," "Pastorale d'Été," "Pacific 231"* (literal depiction in sound of the journey of a locomotive), prelude to *"The Tempest,"* prelude to Act II of d'Annunzio's *"Phaedre," "Skating Rink," "Rugby"* (descriptive of a football game); Symph. for String Orch.; *"Jeanne au Bûcher,"* dramatic oratorio for woman reciter, vocal soloists, choruses and orch.

Hood, **Helen,** b. Chelsea, Mass., June 28, 1863; pupil of B. J. Lang (pf.) and Chadwick (comp.), Boston; and Moszkowski (pf.); composer.

Hook, **Jas.,** Norwich, 1746—Boulogne, 1827; organist and composer.

Hope'kirk, **Helen,** b. near Edinburgh, Scotland, May 20, 1856; studied with Lichtenstein and A. C. Mackenzie; for 2 years at Leipzig, later with Leschetizky; début as pianist at Gewandhaus, Leipzig, 1878; gave concerts in Great Britain and (1883–84) U. S.; 1897–1901, teacher N. E. Cons.; later private teacher, Boston, Mass.; c. Concertstück for pf. and orch.; 1894, orch. pcs.; a pf.-concerto; sonata for pf. and vln., and songs; d. Cambridge, Mass., 1945.

Hopffer (hŏp'-fĕr), **L. Bd.,** Berlin, 1840—Niederwald, near Rüdesheim, 1877; dram. composer.

Hop'kins, (1) **Edw. J.,** Westminster, June 30, 1818—London, Feb. 4, 1901; self-taught organist at various churches; 1843–1898, to the Temple Ch., London; wrote *"The Organ; Its History and Construction"* (Rimbault); contributed to *"Grove's Dict. of Mus.";* c. 3 prize anthems, hymntunes, chants and church-services. (2) **Edw. Jerome,** Burlington, Vt., 1836—Athenia, N. J., 1898; self-taught in harmony; began composing at 4; organist, editor and lecturer; (3) **Harry Patterson,** b. Baltimore, 1873; graduated Peabody Inst., 1896; studied with Dvořák in Bohemia; after 1899 active as organist and teacher, Baltimore; c. a symphony, songs, etc.

Hop'kinson, **Francis,** composer; 1737–91; one of the earliest American composers; inventor of the *"Bellarmonica."*

Hoplit. Vide **POHL, R.**

Horák (hō'-räk), (1) **Wenzel (Václav) Emanuel,** Mscheno-Lobes, Bohemia, 1800—Prague, 1871; organist, teacher and composer. (2) **Ed.,** Holitz,

Bohemia, 1839—Riva, Lake of Garda, 1892; teacher and writer. (3) **Ad.**, Jankovic, Bohemia, Feb. 15, 1850—Vienna (?); pianist; bro. of above and co-founder, "Horák". Pf.-School, Vienna; writer.

Horn, (1) **K. Fr.**, Nordhausen, Saxony, 1762—Windsor, Engl., 1830; organist, writer and theorist. (2) **Chas. Edw.**, London, 1786—Boston, Mass., 1849; son of above; singer, teacher, cond., and composer. (3) **Aug.**, Freiberg, Saxony, 1825—Leipzig, 1893; dram. composer.

Horneman (hôr'-nĕ-män), (1) **Johan Ole Emil**, Copenhagen, 1809—1870; composer. (2) **Emil Chr.**, Copenhagen, Dec. 17, 1841—June 9, 1906; son and pupil of above; studied at Leipzig Cons.; dir. of sch. of mus. in Copenhagen; c. overtures "*Aladdin*" and "*Heldenleben*," etc.

Hornstein (hôrn'-shtīn), **Robt. von,** Donaueschingen, 1833 — Munich, 1890; dram. composer.

Horowitz (hôr'-ō-vētz), **Vladimir,** b. Kiev, Russia, Oct. 1, 1904; pianist; grad. Kiev Cons. at 17; studied with Blumenfeld; début, Kharkov; since 1924 has made appearances in leading Eur. capitals with pronounced succ.; a brilliant virtuoso, he has appeared with the princ. orchs. in Germany, France, England, Italy and U. S. (Amer. début with N. Y. Philh., 1928); m. Wanda, daughter of Arturo Toscanini.

Hors'ley, (1) **Wm.**, London, 1774—1858; organist, theorist and composer. (2) **Chas. Edw.**, London, 1822—New York, 1876; son and pupil of above; organist, writer and composer.

Horszowski (hôr-shôf'-skē), **Miecio,** b. Lemberg, Poland, 1892; pianist; pupil of Leschetizky, Cyrill Kistler and Heuberger; after early successes went into retirement for several years, then reappeared in concerts 1913; toured widely in Europe, South America and also visited U. S.; lives in Paris.

Hor'vath, (1) **Cecile de** (née Ayres), b. Boston, 1889; pianist; studied with her father, Eugene Ayres, and with Safonoff and Gabrilowitsch; after 1910 active as concert artist in Europe and U. S., later taught in Chicago. (2) **Zoltan,** her husband, b. Chicago, 1886; also a pianist and teacher, was long active in Phila-

Horwitz (hôr'-vĭts), **Benno,** Berlin, March 17, 1855—Berlin, June 3, 1904; violinist and composer; pupil of the Rl. Hochschule, and of Kiel and Albert Becker; c. symph. poem "*Dionysos*," etc.

Hostinsky (hô-shtēn'-shkĭ), **Ottokar,** Martinoves, Bohemia, Jan. 2, 1847 —Prague, Jan. 19, 1910; Dr. Phil., Prague; writer.

Hoth'by (or **Hothobus, Otteby, Fra Ottobi**), **John** (or **Johannes**), d. London, Nov., 1487; English Carmelite monk; famous for science.

Hotteterre (ôt'-tăr), (1) **Henri,** d. 1683; instr.-maker, musette player, ct.-musician. (2) **Louis** (called "*Le Romain*," having lived in Rome); son of above; notable flutist and writer. (3) **Nicolas,** d. 1695; noted bassoonist and oboist; bro. of (2).

Ho'ven, J., pen-name of **V. von Puttlingen.**

How'ard, (1) **Samuel,** 1710—1782; English organist and composer. (2) **Kathleen,** b. Clifton, Canada; contralto; pupil of Saenger and Jean de Reszke; début, Metz, 1906; 1909-12, Darmstadt Op., Century Op. Co., N. Y., 1913-15; Met. Op. Co., 1916-28; also toured in Europe; author "*Confessions of an Opera Singer.*" (3) **John Tasker,** b. Brooklyn, N. Y., Nov. 30, 1890; composer and writer; educated Williams Coll.; studied comp. with Howard Brockway and Mortimer Wilson; c. orch., piano and vocal works; author, "*Studies of Contemporary American Composers,*" "*Our American Music,*" "*Stephen Foster,*" etc.

How'ell, Jas., b. Plymouth, England, d. 1879; singer and double-bass player.

How'ells, Herbert, b. Lydney, Australia, 1892; composer; pupil of Brewer and of R. Coll. of Mus., London, where has been prof. since 1920; c. piano concerto, orch. and chamber music, choral works, org. pieces and songs.

Hrimaly (h'rĭm'-ŭ-lē), **Adalbert,** Pilsen, Bohemia, July 30, 1842—Vienna, June 17, 1908; violinist; pupil of Mildner, Prague Cons., 1861; cond. Gothenburg orch., 1868; National Th., Prague; at the German Th., there in 1873, and at Czernowitz, Bukowina, in 1875; his succ. opera "*Der Verzauberte Prinz*" (1871) played at Prague.

Hubay (hoo'-bä-ĕ) (or **Huber**), (1) **K.**, Varjas, Hungary, 1828—Pesth, 1885; vln.-prof., Pesth Cons.; conductor and dram. composer. (2) **Jeno**, Budapest, Sept. 15, 1858—Vienna, March 12, 1937; son and pupil of above, and 1886 his successor as prof.; also studied with Joachim; gave succ. concerts in Hungary and at Paris; 1882 principal vln.-prof., Brussels Cons.; 1886, prof. and 1919–34, dir. Budapest Cons.; 1894, m. Countess Rosa Cebrian; c. succ. opera "*Der Geigenmacher von Cremona*" (Pesth, 1893); opera "*Alienor*" (Pesth, 1892); succ. Hungarian opera "*A Falu Rossza*" (The Townloafer) (Budapest, 1896); opera, "*Anna Karenina*"; 3 symphonies, many notable vln. works, incl. 4 concertos.

Huber (hoo'-bĕr), (1) **F.**, d. Berne, Feb. 23, 1810; poet and songcomposer. (2) **Fd.**, 1791—St. Gallen, 1863; Swiss song-writer. (3) **K.** Vide HUBAY. (4) **Jos.**, Sigmaringen, 1837—Stuttgart, 1886; violinist and lram. composer. (5) **Hans**, Schönewerd, Switzerland, June 28, 1852—Locarno, Dec. 25, 1921; pupil Leipzig Cons.; teacher at Wesserling for 2 years, then at Thann (Alsatia), later Basel Music School; 1892, Dr. Phil. *h. c.*, Basel Univ.; 1896, dir. of the Mus. Sch.; c. succ. operas "*Weltfrühling*" (Basel, 1894); and "*Gudrun*" (Basel, 1896); cantatas, sonatas, concertos, overtures "*Lustspiel*," symph. "*Tell*," etc. (6) **Eugen.** Vide HUBAY, JENO.

Huberdeau (ü'-bĕr-dō), **Gustave**, b. Paris, 1878 (?); notable operatic bass; studied at Paris Cons.; début, 1898; sang at Op.-Comique; 1908, Manhattan Op. Co., N. Y.; after 1910 with Chicago Op. Co. in French and Italian rôles.

Hu'berman, **Bronislaw**, b. Czenstochova near Warsaw, Dec. 19, 1882; d. Nant-sur-Corsier, Switz., June 6, 1947; violinist; made succ. début as prodigy; retired for five years' study; reappeared, Bucharest, 1902; had since won world-wide reputation as a leading virtuoso, and had toured continuously in Europe and at intervals in the U. S. (first Amer. tour, 1896–97); founded Palestine Orch., 1935.

Hubert (hoo'-bĕrt), **Nikolai Albertovitch**, 1840—1888; prof. and writer.

Huberti (ü-bĕr'-tē), **Gve. Léon**, Brussels, April 14, 1843—July 23, 1910;

pupil Brussels Cons.; 1865, won Prix de Rome; 1874–78, dir. of Mons. Cons.; 1880–89, Antwerp; then prof. at Brussels Cons., and dir. of the Mus.-School of St. Josse-ten-Noode-Schaerbeek; 1891, member of the Belgian Academy; 1893, Chevalier of the Legion of Honour. C. oratorios, the dram. poem "*Verlichting*" ("*Fiat lux*"), with orch.; symphonic poem "*Kinderlust en Leed*," chorus and orch., etc.; symphonie funèbre, festival marches, etc.

Hucbald (hook'-bält, or ük-băl) (**Hugbal'dus**, **Ubal'dus**, **Uchubal'dus**) de S. Amand(o), ca. 840—St. Amand, near Tournay, June 25 (or Oct. 21), 930 (or June 20, 932). He is perhaps credited with some works belonging to a monk of the same name living a century later; pupil of his uncle, Milo, a mus.-dir., whose jealousy drove him to Nevers, where he taught singing; 872 he succeeded his uncle; ca. 893, the Archbishop of Rheims invited him to reform the music of the diocese. His works (Gerbert) contain the first known notation showing difference of pitch on lines.

Hue (ü), **Georges Ad.**, b. Versailles, May 6, 1858; pupil of Paris Cons., took 1st Grand prix de Rome; later Prix Cressent; 1922 elected mem. of French Acad. to take place of late Camille Saint-Saëns; c. op. com. "*Les Pantins*" (Op.-Com., 1881); "*Rübezahl*," symphonic legend in 3 parts ("Concerts Colonne," 1886); succ. "Féerie dramatique" "*La Belle au Bois Dormant*" (Paris, 1894); "épisode sacré" "*Resurrection*"; a symphony, a symphonic overture; the operas "*Le roi de Paris*," 1901; "*Titania*," 1903; "*Le Miracle*," 1910; "*Dans l'Ombre de la Cathédrale*" (Op.-Comique, 1921), ballet "*Siang-Sin*" (Opera, 1922); d. 1948.

Hueffer (hüf'-fĕr), **Francis**, Münster, 1843—London, Jan. 19, 1889; 1869, lived in London; from 1878, critic of *The Times*; librettist and writer.

Hughes, (1) **Edwin**, b. Washington, D. C., Aug. 15, 1884; pianist, pedagogue; pupil of S. M. Fabian, Joseffy, and Leschetizky; appeared in concerts in Europe and U. S., active in Munich, 1912; taught at Inst. of Mus. Art, N. Y., 1916–22; later cond. many master classes in Amer. cities; ed. piano works. (2) **Herbert**, b. Belfast, March 16,

1882—Brighton, Engl., May 2, 1937; pupil of R. Coll. of Mus.; founder of Irish Folk-Song Soc. (1904); after 1911, music ed. on London *Daily Telegraph*; visited America in 1922; ed. Modern Festival Series; Irish Country Songs, Historical Songs and Ballads of Ireland; c. chamber music and songs. (3) **Rupert,** b. Lancaster, Mo., Jan. 21, 1872; Amer. writer on music; novelist, dramatist; grad. Adelbert Coll. (Western Reserve Univ.); A. M., Yale Univ.; studied comp. with Wilson Smith, Edgar Stillman Kelley, and C. W. Pearce; music critic and mem. of editorial board of various Amer. periodicals, incl. *Current Literature, The Criterion*; mem. of the N. Y. editorial board of the Encyclopedia Britannica; author *"Contemporary Amer. Composers," "Love Affairs of Great Musicians," "Music Lovers' Cyclopedia"*; ed. *"Songs by Thirty Americans."*

Huhn, Bruno (Siegfried), b. London, 1871—N. Y., May 13, 1950; pupil of Sophie Taunton, later in New York of S. B. Mills and L. Alberti; has toured Europe as pianist; prominent composer, choral conductor and accompanist in New York; c. *"Te Deum"* with orch., and many songs.

Hull, Arthur Eaglefield, Market Harborough, England, March 10, 1876—Huddersfield, Nov. 4, 1928; organist, teacher, composer, writer; pupil of Wood, Matthay and Pearce; Mus. D., Oxford; ed. *"The Music Lover's Library"*; c. oratorios, org. and piano pieces; ed. org. works of Bach and Mendelssohn; wrote books on Bach, Scriabin, Cyril Scott, also *"Modern Harmony"* and ed. *"Dictionary of Modern Music and Musicians."*

Hul'lah, John Pyke, Worcester, June 27, 1812—London, Feb. 21, 1884; professor, conductor, writer and dram. composer.

Hüller, J. A. Vide HILLER.

Hüllmandel (hĭl'-mänt-'l), **Nicholas Jos.,** Strassburg, 1751 — London, 1823; pianist and harmonica-player; c. 12 piano trios, 14 vln. sonatas, 6 piano sonatas, etc.

Hüllweck (hĭl'-vĕk), **Fd.,** Dessau, 1824 —Blasewitz, 1887; concert-violinist and composer.

Hulsteyn (hŭl'-shīn), **Joaі'n C. Van,** b. Amsterdam, 1869; violinist; pupil at Liége Cons. of César Thomson; won first prize; played in Lamoureux orch., Paris; prof. at Peabody Inst., Baltimore; d. there March 2, 1947.

Humbert (ŭṅ-bǎr), **Georges,** b. St. Croix, Switzerland, Aug. 10, 1870; organist; pupil Leipzig and Brussels Cons., and of Bargiel; teacher of mus. history at Geneva Cons. and org. at Nôtre Dame; from 1893 at Lausanne; after 1918 dir. of a mus. school at Neuchâtel, where he d. Jan. 1, 1936.

Hum'frey (Humphrey, Humphrys), Pelham, London, 1647—Windsor, July 14, 1674; English composer. Charles II. sent him to Paris to study with Lully; 1672 master Chapel Royal children and with Purcell ct.-composer.

Hu'miston, William Henry, Marietta, O., April 27, 1869—New York, Dec. 5, 1923; pianist, conductor, writer; grad. Lake Forest Coll., studied piano with Mathews and org. with Eddy; also later comp. with MacDowell; active as teacher, lecturer, and cond. with opera companies on tour; after 1912 ed. programme notes of N. Y. Philh.; following 1916 was asst. cond. of this orch.; 1914 led MacDowell Club perf. of Mozart's *"Bastien et Bastienne"* and Bach programmes in 1916 and 1918; c. orch. works and songs.

Hummel (hoom'-mĕl), (1) **Jos.,** music-master Wartberg Military Acad.; 1786, conductor at Vienna. (2) **Jn. Nepomuk,** Pressburg, Nov. 14, 1778 —Weimar, Oct. 17, 1837; son of above; a famous pianist and improviser, and a composer of cnce popular pieces in which ornament outweighs matter; and form, interest; protégé of Mozart; début 1787; toured Europe frequently; 1793 studied with Albrechtsberger; asst.-cond. to Haydn, 1804–11; 1830 and 1833 cond. German opera in London; c. operas, cantatas, ballets, 3 masses, sonatas; he pub. a notable pf.-method; c. dram. pcs., concertos, sonatas, septet in D minor, etc. (3) **Elisabeth** (née Röckl), 1783—Weimar, 1883; wife of above; opera-singer. (4) **Jos. Fr.,** Innsbruck, Aug. 14, 1841—Salzburg, Aug. 29, 1919; pupil Munich Cons., 1861–80; th.-cond. Vienna 1880–1907, dir. Mozarteum at Salzburg, and cond. *Liedertafel.* (5) **Fd.,** Berlin, Sept. 6, 1855—April 24, 1928; son and pupil of a musician; at 7 a harp virtuoso:

1864–67 toured Europe, and received a royal grant for study at Kullak's Akademie, Berlin; 1871–75, studied R. High Sch. of Mus., then at Akademie; for years active as cond. and comp. for the Berlin ct.-theatres. c. succ. operas, *"Mara"* (Berlin, 1893); *"Ein Treuer Schelm"* (Prague, 1894); *"Assarpai"* (Gotha, 1898); a symphony, sonatas, etc.

Humperdinck (hoom'-pĕr-dĭnk), **Engelbert**, Siegburg, near Bonn, Sept. 1, 1854—Neustrelitz, Sept. 27, 1921; studied architecture, Cologne, then mus. at the Cons.; won Mozart scholarship at Frankfort; studied 2 years with Franz Lachner, Munich, also with Rheinberger and Barmann at the Cons.; pub. Humoreske for orch. and *"Die Wallfahrt nach Kevelaar"* for chorus; 1878 won the Mendelssohn prize (3,000 marks), 1880 the Meyerbeer prize (7,600 marks); 1885–86, prof. Barcelona Cons.; 1881–82, a special protégé of R. Wagner in Bayreuth; made pf.-scores, and aided in the preparation of *"Parsifal."* Returned to Cologne, 1887, went to Mayence in the employ of Schott & Co.; 1890 teacher Hoch Cons., Frankfort, critic on the Frankfort *Zeitung;* later lived at Boppard-on-Rhine. In 1900–20, he was dir. of Master-School of the Berlin Royal Acad. of Arts. His first international succ. was the graceful 2-act fairy-opera *"Hänsel und Gretel,"* Munich, 1893 (prod. at Milan, 1897, as *"Nino e Rita"*), which has taken its place in the repertoire as an enduring little masterpiece. H. never again quite equalled this work, though he made an approach to it in *"Die Königskinder,"* originally conceived as incid. music to the spoken play but re-written as opera; prod. at Met. Op., N. Y., 1910; with success, later in Europe. *"Dornröschen"* was prod. Frankfort-on-Main (1902); com. op. *"Die Heirat wider Willen"* (Berlin, 1905); he also c. incid. music to Aristophanes' *"Lysistrata"* (do., 1908); Shakespeare's *"Winter's Tale"* and *"Tempest"* (do. 1906); to the pantomime, *"The Miracle"* by Vollmoeller (staged in U. S. by Max Reinhardt). His last 2 operas, *"Die Marketenderin"* (1914) and *"Gaudeamus,"* (1919) were not successful.

Huneker (hū'-nĕk-ĕr). **James Gibbons,** Philadelphia, Jan. 31, 1860—New York, Feb. 9, 1921; eminent critic and writer; pupil of Michael Cross, L. Damrosch and Joseffy, and for 10 years asst. to Joseffy at the Nat'l. Cons. in N. Y.; music and dram. critic of the *Commercial Advertiser* and *The Recorder,* transferring in 1901 to the New York *Sun;* after 1918 to the New York *Times;* and for a short period before his death, to the New York *World;* wrote for Philadelphia *Press,* and for many years for the *Musical Courier;* champion of Brahms and some moderns, an outstanding stylist; author of *"Mezzotints in Modern Music," "Chopin, the Man and His Music," "Melomaniacs," "Franz Liszt," "Overtones (in) Music and Literature," "Iconoclasts," "Visionaries," "Egoists," "Promenades of an Impressionist," "The Pathos of Distance," "Old Fogy," "New Cosmopolis," "Ivory Apes and Peacocks," "Unicorns," "The N. Y. Philharmonic Soc.," "Charles Baudelaire," "Steeplejack," "Bedouins," "Mary Garden,"* etc.

Hunke (hoon'-kē), **Jos.,** Josephstadt, Bohemia, 1801—St. Petersburg, 1883 choirm. Russian ct.-chapel; composer.

Hünten (hĭn'-tĕn), **Fz.,** Coblenz, 1793—1878; c. pop. pf.-pcs., etc.

Huré (ü-rā'), **Jean,** Gien, Loiret, Sept. 17, 1877—Paris, Jan. 27, 1930; studied in monastery at Angers; lived in Paris after 1895; active as pianist and comp.; founded Paris Normal School for pianists, organists; c. operas, symphonies, chamber and choral works; author, *"La Technique du Piano," "La Technique de l'Orgue"*; pub. periodical, *L'Orgue et les Organistes.*

Hurel de Lamare (ü'-rĕl-dŭ-lä-măr), **Jacques Michel,** Paris, 1772—Caen, 1823; 'cellist and composer; his friend Auber pub. some comp. under **H.**'s name.

Hurl'stone, Wm. Yeates, London, Jan. 7, 1876—May 30, 1906; composer; at 9 pub. 5 waltzes; at 18 held scholarship at R. A. M.; later prof. there of harmony and counterpoint; c. piano concerto, etc.

Huss (hoos), **Henry Holden,** b. Newark, N. J., June 21, 1862—N. Y., Sept. 17, 1953; composer; studied O. B. Boise (cpt. and comp.), also at

Munich Cons.; lived in N. Y. as teacher of pf., comp. and instr. He and his wife, the soprano, **Hildegard Hoffman,** have given joint recitals throughout America, and 1910 in London. His piano concerto in B major was played with the composer as soloist by the N. Y. Philh., Boston Symph., Pittsburgh and Cincinnati Symph. orch's. and by the Monte Carlo Symph., with Pugno as soloist; his violin sonata by Kneisel, Spiering, etc.; also c. *"Recessional"* for mixed chorus, organ, and orch. (Worcester, Mass., Festival, 1911); string quartet in E minor (Kneisel Quartet); 'cello sonata; songs, etc.

Hutch'eson, Ernest, b. Melbourne, July 20, 1871—d. N. Y., Feb. 9, 1951; pupil, Leipzig Cons., winning Mozart prize with a trio; toured Australia; studied with Stavenhagen; 1898 married Baroness von Pilsach; from 1900 teacher Peabody Cons., Baltimore; c. symph. poem *"Merlin and Vivien"* (Berlin, 1899); orch. suite (do.), piano concerto (1899); symphony; two-piano concerto; vln. concerto, etc.; 1912-14, toured Europe; after latter year in N. Y.; after 1911 taught Chautauqua Inst.; and had been dean of Juilliard Grad. School of Music, N. Y., since 1926; author, *"Guide to Strauss' Elektra."*

Hutschenruijter (hoot'-shĕn-roi-tĕr), (1) **Wouter,** Rotterdam, 1796—1878; horn- and trumpet-virtuoso; professor, conductor, director and dram. composer. (2) **Wouter,** Rotterdam, Aug. 15, 1859—1943; conductor; after 1890 asst. cond. of Concertgebouw, Amsterdam; then of Utrecht Orch.; 1917-25, dir. Rotterdam Munic. School of Music.

Hüttenbrenner (hĭt'-tĕn-brĕn-nĕr), **Anselm,** Graz, Styria, 1794—Ober-Andritz, 1868; pianist, conductor and dram. composer.

Huygens (hī'-gĕns), (1) **Constantin,** The Hague, Sept. 4, 1596—March 28, 1687; poet and military secretary to William II. and William III.; also skilful performer; c. over 700 airs for lute, theorbo, etc.; his son (2) **Christian,** The Hague, April 14, 1629—June 8, 1695; mathematician and musician.

Hyllested (hŭl'-lĕ-städh), **Aug.,** b. (of Danish parents) Stockholm, June 17, 1858; violinist; at 5 played in public;

studied with Holger Dahl till 1869, and then made succ. tour through Scandinavia; entered the Royal Cons. at Copenhagen; 1876, organist of the Cath. and dir. of a mus. soc.; 1879, studied with Kullak, Kiel, and later Liszt; 1885, toured U. S.; 1886-91, asst.-dir. Chicago Mus. Coll.; 1891-94, Gottschalk Lyric Sch.; 1894-97, toured Europe; prod. in London symph. poem *"Elizabeth,"* with double chorus; 1897, Chicago; c. romantic play *"Die Rheinnixe,"* orch. suites, etc.; d. (?).

I

Ibach (ē'-bäkh), (1) **Jns. Ad.,** 1766—1848; pf. and organ-builder. His son (2) **C. Rudolf** (d. 1862), and (3) **Richard,** joined the firm; a third son (4) **Gustav J.** founded another business 1869. (5) **Rudolf** (d. Herrenalb, Black Forest, July, 1892), son of (2), continued the pf.-factory, and **Richard,** the organ-factory.

Ibert (ē-bār'), **Jacques,** b. Paris, Aug. 15, 1890; composer; studied Paris Cons., Prix de Rome, 1919; an accomplished modern-style comp., especially known for his colourful orchestral compositions in which one finds the influence of Franck, Ravel and Debussy; *"Escales,"* a suite depicting marine ports, has had internat'l. hearings; also c. a light opera, *"Angélique,"* given with succ. in Paris; (opera) *"Le Roi d' Yvetot"*; the symph. poems, *"Noël en Picardie,"* *"The Ballad of Reading Gaol"* (after Wilde); *"Persée et Andromède,"* orchestral phantasy; lyric scene, *"La Poète et la Fée"*; wind quartet, vln. sonata, 'cello concerto, concerto for saxophone and orch.; org. and piano pieces; his ballet, *"Gold Standard,"* was prod. by Chicago Op. in 1934.

If'fert, August, Braunschweig, May 31, 1859—near Dresden, Aug. 13, 1930; singer and teacher in various cities; author of a vocal method.

Igumnoff (ē-goom'-noff), **Konstantin Nikolajavich,** b. Lebedjana, Tambouv, May 1, 1873; Russian pianist; pupil of Svereff, Siloti and Pabst; 1898, teacher in Tiflis; 1900 prof. at Moscow Cons.

Iliffe (ī'-lĭf), **Fr.,** Smeeton-Westerby, Leicester, Engl., Feb. 21, 1847—Oxford, Feb. 2, 1928; 1883, organist and choirm. St. John's Coll., Oxford; cond. of Queen's Coll. Mus. Soc., 1873, Mus. Bac. Oxon.; wrote *"Critical Analysis of Bach's Clavichord"* (London, 1896; 4 parts); c. oratorio, *"The Visions of St. John the Divine"*; cantata with orch. *"Lara,"* etc.

Ilinski (ĕ-lĭn'-shkĭ), Count **Jan Stanislaw**, b. Castle Romanov, 1795; composer.

Iljinski (ĕl-yēn'-shkĭ), **Alexander Alexandrovich**, Tsarkoe Selo, Jan. 24, 1859—Moscow, 1919?; composer; pupil of Kullak and Bargiel; 1885 prof. of theory at the Philharmonic Music School in Moscow; c. opera *"The Fountain of Bastchi-Sarai"*; symph.; symphonic scherzo; pf.-pcs., songs, etc.

Imbert (ĕn-bār), **Hugues**, Moulins-Engilbert 1842—Paris, 1905; noted writer of biogs., etc.

Inc'ledon, **Chas.**, Bery St. Kevern, Cornwall, 1763—1826; tenor, called "The Wandering Melodiste."

Indy (dăn-dē), (**Paul M. Th.**) **Vincent d'**, Paris, March 27, 1851—Dec. 3, 1931; pupil of César Franck (comp.) and at the Cons., 1875, chorusm. with Colonne; played drum-parts for 3 years to learn instrumentation; pres. of various concert-societies; mus.-inspector of Paris schools; Chev. of the Legion of Honour; 1896 he became prof. of composition at Paris Cons.; 1896 with Bordes and Guilmant founded the *Schola Cantorum*, and became director; c. a 3-part symph. poem *"Wallenstein"* (Part II., *"I Piccolomini,"* prod. 1874 by Pasdeloup); symphonies (1) *"On a French mountaineer-song,"* and (2) *"Jean Hunyadi,"* symphonic legend *"La forêt enchantée"*; overture to *"Antony and Cleopatra"*; *"La Chevauchée du Cid,"* for orch.; symphonic pf.-concerto; prod. 1-act comic opera, *"Attendez-moi sous l'Orme"* (Op.-com., 1882); c. text and mus.; succ. mus. drama, *"Fervaal"* (Brussels, 1897); *"L'Étranger"* (do. 1903); *"Le chant de la cloche,"* dramatic legend in seven pictures, with his own text, for soli, double chorus and orch. Festival cantata *"Pour l'inauguration d'une Statue"* for barytone, chorus and orch., *"Ode à Valence,"* do. symph. in B flat, 1902; *"Jour d'été à la montagne,"* 1905; *"Souvenirs"* for orch. 1906;

songs, piano pieces and choruses, author of a *"Cours de Composition Musicale,"* 1902, and a life of César Franck, 1906.

Infante (ēn-fän'-tä), **Manuel**, b. Osuna near Seville; composer; has c. many piano works of graceful sort and attractive folk colouring, first made pop. by the pianist Iturbi; res. in Paris.

Ingegneri (ēn-gān-yā'-rē), **Marco A.**, Verona, ca. 1545—Cremona, July 1, 1592; conductor, composer and publisher.

Inghelbrecht (ēn'-gĕl-brĕkht), **Desiré Emile**, b. Paris, Sept. 17, 1880; composer; pupil of Cons.; a friend of Debussy in the composer's latter days, whose works he excels in conducting; after 1908 active at various Paris theatres and following 1925 music. dir. at the Op.-Comique; c. ballet, *"Le Diable dans le beffroi"* (after Poe), and numerous orch., chamber music, and vocal works; arr. works of Couperin and Albeniz for orch.

In'gram, **Frances**, b. Liverpool, England, 1888; contralto; studied with Maurel; after 1911 sang for several years with Chicago Op. Co.; 1913, Montreal Op. Co., and also in concerts.

Insanguine (ēn-sän-gwē'-nä), **Giacomo** (called **Monopoli**), Monopili, ca. 1740—Naples, 1795; teacher and dram. composer.

Ippolitov-Ivanov (ēp-pō'-lē-tôf-ē'-vä-nôf), **Mikhail Mikhailovitch**, Gatchina, Nov. 19, 1859—Moscow, Jan. 26, 1935; added his mother's name to Ivanoff, to distinguish him from Ivanoff (2); pupil of Rimsky-Korsakov; at St. Petersburg Cons.; 1882 dir. of the Music School and cond. in Tiflis; 1884 cond. at the Imperial Theatre; from 1893 prof. of theory Moscow Cons.; dir., 1906–22; from 1899 cond. the Private Opera; c. operas *"Ruth"* (Tiflis, 1887), *"Asja"* (Moscow, 1900); and *"Sabava Putjatischna"* (St. Petersburg, 1901); overtures *"Jar Chmel,"* *"Spring,"* and *"Medea"*; orch. suite, *"Caucasian Sketches"*; violin-sonata (rearranged as a Sinfonietta); character-pictures for chorus and orch.; cantatas *"In Memory of Pushkin,"* of *"Gogol"* and *"Shukovski,"* and *"Legend of the White Swan of Novgorod,"* etc.; author of a book on Georgian folk-songs.

Ire'land, John, b. Bowdon, England, Aug. 13, 1879; composer; pupil of Stanford; one of the more able and original modern British creators; he destroyed his earlier comps. and 1st became known for his Phantasy Trio in A Minor (1908) and *"Songs of a Wayfarer"* (1910); his reputation grew after the prod. of his 2nd sonata for vln. and piano; c. many orch. and chamber works fairly simple in structure and of traditional form, among which are: the rhapsodies *"Mai-Dun"* and *"The Forgotten Rite"*; overtures *"Pelléas et Mélisande"* and *"Midsummer"*; symph. poem in A Minor; sextet for strings, clarinet and horn; 2 string quartets; 3 piano trios; 4 vln. sonatas; piano sonata; many piano works, incl. *"Decorations,"* *"London Pieces"* and *"Preludes,"* Mass in Dorian Mode; choral and org. pieces and songs.

Irgang (ēr'-gäng), Fr. Wm., Hirschberg, Schleswig, Feb. 23, 1836—Carlsruhe, 1918?; teacher in Proksch's Sch., Prague; 1863, founded sch. at Görlitz; also organ composer. (2) Irr'-gang, H. Bd., Krotoschin, 1869—Berlin, 1916; noted organist, teacher.

Isaak (ē'-zäk), H. (or Isaac, Izak, Yzac, Ysack; in Italy Arrigo Tedesco, Henry the German; Low; Lat. Arrighus, ca. 1450—ca. 1517; famous contrapuntist doubtless of Netherlandish birth; conductor and organist.

Iserlies (Is'-ĕr-léz), Julius, b. Kishinev, Russia, Nov. 8, 1888; noted pianist; 1907–9, toured U. S.; after 1913 taught Moscow Philh. Cons.

Isouard (ē-zoo-är), Niccolò (called Niccolo de Malte), Malta, 1775—Paris, March 23, 1818; pupil of Amendola, Sala, and Guglelmi; organist, conductor and prolific dram. composer.

Israel (ēs'-rä-ĕl), K., Heiligenrode, Electoral Hesse, 1841—Frankfort-on-M., 1881; critic and bibliographer.

Is'tel, Edgar, b. Mainz, Germany, Feb. 23, 1880; composer and writer on music; pupil of Thuille and Sandberger; Ph. D., Munich Univ., 1900; lecturer on music; c. operas, choral music and songs; author of many books on music.

Iturbi (ē-tōōr'-vē), (1) José, b. Valencia, Spain, Nov. 28, 1895; pianist and conductor; studied Valencia Cons., 1st prize in piano at 13; grad. Paris Cons. with highest honours at 17, pupil of Joaquin Malats, Barcelona; was head of piano faculty, Geneva Cons., 1919–23; began tours of chief Eur. countries and South America. establishing reputation as one of the pre-eminent piano virtuosi of the day; Amer. début, 1928; won marked popularity, esp. for his performance of Mozart and Beethoven works, to which he brings polished readings; began conducting activities in Mexico City, 1933, and estab. permanent orch. there to give summer series under his baton; has since led N. Y. Philh. Orch. (summer series at Lewisohn Stadium), Phila. Orch., Los Angeles Philh. at Hollywood Bowl, sometimes playing concertos and conducting from the piano; appointed permanent cond. Rochester, N. Y., Philh. Orch., 1936. (2) Amparo, his sister, also a skilled pianist.

I'vanov, (1) Nicholas Kusmich, Poltava, Oct. 22, 1810—Bologna, July 7, 1887; tenor; popular in London, 1834–37; accumulated a fortune in Italy and Paris and retired in 1845; (2) Michael Mikhailovich, Moscow, Sept. 23, 1849—Rome, Oct. 20, 1927; pupil of Tchaikovsky and Dubuque at the Cons.; critic and comp.; 1870–76 at Rome; then critic for the *Novoe Vremya*; c. symph. *"A Night in May"*; symph. prologue *"Savonarola"*; four operas including *"Potemkin's Feast"* (1888), and *"Sabava Putjatischna"* (Moscow, 1899); incidental music to *"Medea,"* etc. His opera *"Treachery"* (Moscow, Feb. 1911) made great success.

Ives, Charles Edward, b. Danbury, Conn., Oct. 20, 1874; composer; studied with Dudley Buck, H. R. Shelley and Parker; an original figure among Amer. comps., working in seclusion and with music as an avocation, Ives' scores when prod. by modernist organizations in N. Y. and elsewhere have created considerable interest; one of his theories being that several musical units of an ensemble may proceed independently of each other; also employs much freedom in tonality, rhythm and harmony; among his productions, the work of many years, are 4 symphonies, 3 orch. suites, 2 cantatas, 4 vln. sonatas, 2 piano sonatas, 2 overtures, works for chorus and orch., chamber music incl. a string quartet and quarter-tone pieces, and especially a collection of about 200 highly original songs; some of his subjects are drawn from New England; d. N. Y., May 19, 1954.

Ivogün, (1) Maria (ēf'-ō-gün mä-rē'-ä) (rightly **Inge von Günther**), b. Budapest, Nov. 11, 1891; coloratura soprano; studied Vienna Acad.; regular mem. Munich Op., 1913–25; Berlin Städtische Op., 1925–32; also sang in America with Chicago Op., and in concert; m. Karl Erb, tenor, 1921, (2) **Michael Raucheisen**, pianist, 1933.

Ivry (dēv-rē), **Paul Xavier Désiré**, Marquis **Richard d'**, Beaune, Côte D'Or, Feb. 4, 1829—Hyères, Dec. 18, 1903; pupil of A. Hignard and Leborne; c. operas, *"Fatma,"* *"Quentin Metzys"* (1854), *"La Maison du Docteur"* (Dijon, 1855), *"Omphale et Pénélopé,"* *"Les Amants de Vérone"* (1867), under the pen-name *"Richard Irvid"*; revised as *"Roméo et Juliette,"* 1878; *"Persévérance D'Amour"* (MS.); concert-overture, songs, etc.

Izac. Vide ISAAK.

J

Jacchia, Agide (yä-kē'-ä ä-jē'-dä), Lugo, Jan. 5, 1875—Siena, Nov. 29, 1932; conductor; studied at Parma and Pesaro Cons., pupil of Mascagni; after 1898 cond. at Brescia, Ferrara and La Fenice Op., Venice; 1902, visited America with Mascagni; 1903–06, at Milan, Leghorn and Siena; 1907–09, led Milan Op. Co. tour of Canada and U. S.; 1909–10, cond. op. season at Acad. of Mus., N. Y.; 1910–14, dir. Montreal and Nat'l. Op. Cos., Canada; 1914–15, chief cond., Century Op. Co., N. Y.; 1915–16, Boston Nat'l. Op. Co.; led "Pop" Concerts, Boston Symph., 1916–23; dir. music school in Boston after 1919; c. cantata and choral works.

Jachet. Vide BERCHEM.

Jachmann-Wagner (yäkh'-män). Vide WAGNER, JOHANNA.

Jack'son, (1) Wm., Exeter, 1730—1803; organist, writer, and dram. composer. (2) **Wm.,** Masham, Yorks, Engl., 1815—Bradford, 1866; organist, conductor, writer and composer. (3) **Samuel P.,** Manchester,

Engl., 1818—Brooklyn, N. Y., 1885; composer; son of (4) **James J.,** organ-builder.

Ja'cob, Gordon, b. London, 1895; comp.; pupil R. C. M.; c. oboe concerto, ballets, orch. works.

Jaco'bi, Frederick, b. San Francisco, May 4, 1891—N. Y., Oct. 24, 1952; pupil, R. Goldmark, Gallico, Joseffy, Juon and Ernest Bloch; asst. cond., Met. Op. Co., 1913–17; one of founders, Amer. Mus. Guild; mem. executive board, League of Comps., N. Y.; from 1936 teacher of comp., Juilliard School of Music; c. string quartet based on Amer. Indian themes (Zurich Fest., Internat'l. Soc. for Contemp. Music, 1926); (orch.) *"The Pied Piper," "California Suite," "The Eve of Saint Agnes," "Indian Dances"; "Two Assyrian Prayers"* for voice and orch., *"The Poet in the Desert,"* for barytone, chorus and orch.; piano concerto; 'cello concerto; *"Sacred Service"* for synagogue; vln. and piano works; m. Irene Schwarz, pianist.

Jacobs (zhǎ-kō), **Édouard,** b. Hal, Belgium, 1851; pupil of Servais, Brussels Cons.; 'cellist Weimar ct. orch. for some years; 1885 prof. Brussels Cons.; d. (?)

Ja'cobsen, Sascha, b. Finland (Russian parents); violinist; studied piano at 5, violin at 8; pupil of Kneisel, also of St. Petersburg Cons.; N. Y. début, 1915; has toured England, Germany, France, Spain and U. S.

Jacobsohn (yäk'-ōp-zōn), **Simon E.,** Mitau, Kurland, Dec. 24, 1839—Chicago, 1902; violinist; pupil Leipzig Cons.; 1860 leader Bremen orch.; 1872, of Theodore Thomas's orch., N. Y.; teacher Cincinnati Cons., then Chicago.

Jacobsthal (yäk'-ōps-täl), **Gv.,** Pyritz, Pomerania, March 14, 1845—Berlin, Nov. 9, 1912; 1872, lecturer on music Strassburg Univ.; 1875 professor extraordinary; writer.

Jacotin (rightly **Jacques Godebrye),** (zhäk-ō-tǎṅ) (or gōd-brē), ca. 1445—March 24, 1529; famous Flemish cptist.; singer and composer at Antwerp.

Jacquard (zhǎk-kǎr), **Léon J.,** Paris, 1826—1886; 'cellist; composer.

Jadassohn (yä'-däs-zōn), **Salomon,** Breslau, Aug. 13, 1831—Leipzig, Feb. 1, 1902; eminent theorist; pupil

of Hesse (pf.) Lüstner (vln.) and Brosig (harm.); later Leipzig Cons., then
with Liszt and Hauptmann (comp.);
from 1852 lived in Leipzig; 1866
cond. "Balterion" choral soc.; 1867-
69 cond. "Euterpe"; from 1871, prof.
of pf., harm., cpt., comp. and instrumentation at the Cons. 1877, Dr.
Phil., *h. c.;* 1893 Royal Prof. He m.
a singing-teacher. Wrote occasionally under name "Lübenau" (lü'-
bĕ-now). Pub. very succ. text-books
all trans. in English. *"Harmonielehre"* (Leipzig, 1883); *"Kontrapunkt"* (1884); *"Kanon und Fuge"*
(1884); *"Die Formen in den Werk-
en der Tonkunst"* (1889); *"Lehrbuch der Instrumentation"* (1889);
"Allgemeine Musiklehre" (1895).
His comps. are notable for form,
particularly his many works in canon
incl. serenade for orch. (op. 35), and
ballet-mus.; which have won him the
name **"Musical Krupp";** c. also
4 symphonies; 2 overtures; a pf.-
concerto; The 100th Psalm, for
double chorus with orchestration,
etc.

Jadin (zhă-dăn), (1) **Louis Emmanuel,**
Versailles, 1768—Paris, 1853; prof.,
conductor and dram. composer.
Son and pupil of Jean J., violinist.

Jadlowker (yäd'-lŏf-kĕr), **Hermann,**
Riga, 1879—Tel-Aviv, 1953; tenor;
sang Met. Op., 1910–12; Berlin, Vienna.

Jaell (yāl), (1) **Alfred,** Trieste, March
5, 1832—Paris, Feb. 27, 1882; noted
touring pianist and composer, son of
(2) **Eduard J.** (d. Vienna, 1849). (3)
Jaell-Trautmann, Marie, Steinseltz,
Alsatia, 1846—Paris, Feb. 7, 1925;
wife of (1); pianist, composer and
writer.

Jaffé (yäf'-fā), **Moritz,** Posen, Jan.
3, 1835—Berlin, May 7, 1925; violinist; pupil of Ries Bohmer (harm.),
of Maurin and Massard, Laub, Wuerst
and Bussler; c. operas, etc.

Ja'gel, Frederick, b. Brooklyn, N. Y.,
1897; tenor; studied with Portanova
and Castaldi; début in *"La Bohème,"*
Livorno, Italy; sang in that country
4 years, heard in Calif. opera seasons;
début, Met. Op. Co., as "Radames,"
1927; has sung leading rôles with
that co., also in concert.

Jahn (yän), (1) **Otto,** Kiel, June 16,
1813—Göttingen, Sept. 9, 1869;
prof. of archæology, Bonn Univ.;
wrote a model biog. of Mozart (1856–
59, 4 vols.), etc., also composed.

(2) **Wm.,** Hof, Moravia, Nov. 24,
1835—Vienna, April 14, 1900; 1854
conductor; dir. ct.-opera, Vienna,
etc.

Jähns (yäns), **Fr. Wm.,** Berlin, 1809
—1888; singer, composer and writer.

James, Philip, b. Jersey City, N. J.,
May 17, 1890; composer, conductor;
studied comp. with Norris and
Schenck, also at City College, N. Y.;
cond. New Jersey Orch., Brooklyn
Orch. Soc. and later the Bamberger
Little Symph. in weekly radio
programmes; taught at N. Y. Univ.
music dept., c. orch. music, including
prize-winning work, RCA-Victor
contest; also vln. sonata; appeared
as guest cond. of several major
Amer. orchestras.

Jan (yän), (1) **Maistre.** Vide GAL-
IUS, J. (2) **K. von,** Schweinfurt,
1836—Adelboden, Sept. 4, 1899;
Dr. Phil., Berlin, 1859; writer.

Jan'acek (yän-ä'-chĕk), **Leos,** Huk-
valdy, July 3, 1854—Möhr.-Ostrau,
Aug. 12, 1928; composer of original
style, studied at Prague Organ
School, Leipzig and Vienna Cons.,
but largely self-taught; evolved
manner of expression based on
natural accents and declamation of
human voice, also unconventional
in harmonic method; influenced by
folklore; late in life he was accepted
by the internat'l. music world as
in some measure a pioneer; founded
org. school in Brünn, 1881, where
he passed most of his life; after 1919,
taught comp. at the Cons. there; c.
(operas) *"Jenufa,"* story of Moravian peasant life, 1901, not
prod. until 1916 in Prague, but
thereafter pop. in German version
in Austria and Germany, heard also
at Met. Op. House, 1924; *" Katja
Kabanova"* (1922); *"Das Schlaue
Füchslein,"* an animal fable (1925);
"Die Sache Makropoulos" (1925)
and a posth. work, *"Aus einem
Totenhaus"* (after Dostoievsky
novel), with libretto by composer
(Brünn, 1930); also Fest. Mass,
Sinfonietta for orch., string quartet,
piano sonata, songs; orch. rhapsodie
"Taras Bulba," etc.

Janiewiecz (yän'-ē-vĕch), **Felix,** Wilna,
1762—Edinburgh, 1848; violinist and
composer.

Jankó (yäng'-kō), **Paul von,** Totis,
Hungary, June 2, 1856—Constantinople, March 17, 1919; pupil Poly-

technic, Vienna, and at the Cons. with Hans Schmitt, Krenn, and Bruckner; 1881-82, mathematics at Berlin Univ., pf. with Ehrlich; inv. in 1882 the admirable keyboard known by his name (v. D. D.); taught in Leipzig Cons., etc.

Jan(n)aconi (yän-nä-kō'-nē), **Gius.**, Rome, 1741—March 16, 1816; eminent church-composer; conductor at St. Peter's; pupil of Rinaldini and Carpani.

Jannequin (or **Janequin**, **Jennekin**) (zhän-kăn), **Clément**, a French (or Belgian) contrapuntist of the 16th cent.; nothing is known of him except that he lived to be old and poor; c. genuine "programme" music.

Janotha (yä-nō'-tä), **Nathalie**, Warsaw, June 8, 1856—The Hague, June 9, 1932; pupil of Joachim and Rudorff, Clara Schumann, Brahms, and Princess Czartoryska, F. Weber (harm.) and Bargiel; début at the Gewandhaus, Leipzig, 1874; 1885, ct.-pianist to the German Emperor, and decorated with many orders; pub. a trans. with additions of Kleczynski's "Chopin"; c. "*Ave Maria*" (dedicated to Pope Leo), "*Mountain Scenes*" (to Frau Schumann), gavottes, etc., for piano.

Janowka (yä-nôf'-kä), **Thos. Balthasar**, b. Kuttenberg, Bohemia; organist and writer at Prague ca. 1660.

Jansa (yän'-sä), **Ld.**, Wildenschwert, Bohemia, 1795—Vienna, 1875; violinist, teacher and composer.

Jansen (yän'-zĕn), **F. Gv.**, Jever, Hanover, Dec. 15, 1831—Hanover, May 3, 1910; pupil of Coccius and Riccius; teacher at Göttingen; 1855-1900, organist Verden Cath.; 1861, Royal Mus. Dir.; composer and writer.

Janssen (yäns'-zĕn), (1) **N. A.**, Carthusian monk; organist and writer at Louvain, 1845. (2) **Julius**, Venlo, Holland, June 4, 1852—Dortmund, Sept. 24, 1921; studied Cologne Cons.; 1876, cond. Mus. Soc., Minden; later cond. at Dortmund; 1890, city mus. dir.; cond. the 1st and 2d Westphalian Mus. Festivals; pub. songs. (3) **Werner**, b. New York, June 1, 1899; composer, conductor; grad. Dartmouth Coll.; studied with Converse, Stone, Friedheim and Chadwick; Mus. D., Univ. of Calif., 1923; began career as comp. of musical comedies and pop. songs;

won fellowship, Amer. Acad. in Rome, 1930; guest cond. of various Eur. and Amer. orchs., incl. Sibelius programmes in Helsingfors; engaged as one of conductors for N. Y. Philh. Orch., 1934; c. symphony, symph. poem "*New Year's Eve in New York*," given dance prod. by Neighborhood Playhouse, N. Y.; cond. Baltimore Symph., 1937-9; Janssen Symph., Los Angeles, 1940. (4) **Herbert**, German barytone; mem. Met. Op., after 1938, Wotan, etc.

Janssens (yäns'-zĕns), **Jean Fran. Jos.**, Antwerp, 1801—insane, 1835; dram. composer.

Januschowsky (yän-oo-shôf'-shkĭ), (Frau) **Georgine von**, b. Austria, ca. 1859—New York, 1914; 1875, soprano in operetta at Sigmaringen; 1877, soubrette, Th. an der Wien, Vienna; 1879-80, Leipzig; 1880, Germania Th., New York; 1892, at Mannheim and Wiesbaden; 1893-95, prima donna, Imp. Opera, Vienna; sang Wagner, etc.; comic operas and operettas; m. Ad. Neuendorff.

Japha (yä'-fä), (1) **G. Jos.**, Königsberg, 1835—Cologne, 1892; violinist. (2) **Louise**, Hamburg, Feb. 2, 1826—Wiesbaden, Oct. 13, 1910; pianist and composer; pupil of Warendorf (pf.), Gross and Grund (comp.) and Robt. and Clara Schumann; 1858, she m. W. Langhans, with whom she gave v. succ. concerts; after 1874, Wiesbaden; c. an opera, etc.

Jaques-Dalcroze. Vide DALCROZE.

Jarecki(yä-rēts'-kē),(1) **Henri**, Warsaw, Dec. 6, 1846—Lemberg, Dec. 18, 1918; dir. at Lemberg; c. operas, incl. "*Wanda*," etc. (2) **Tadeusz**, his son, b. Lemberg, 1889; composer; in New York, 1920.

Jarnach (yär'-näkh), **Philipp**, b. Noisy, France, July 26, 1892; composer (of Catalonian ancestry); largely self-trained but studied with Lavignac and Risler; taught at Zurich Cons., 1918-21; lived in Berlin 1921-27; prof. at Cologne Hochsch. after 1927; c. 2 symphonies, overtures, string quintet, piano works, songs, string quartet, sonata for vln. alone, vln. and piano sonata, sonatinas for flute and 'cello, exhibiting a modern style of interesting originality; completed Busoni's opera, "*Doktor Faust.*"

Järnefelt (yärn'-ĕ-fĕlt), **Armas**, b.

Wiborg, Finland, Aug. 14, 1869; composer, conductor; pupil of Helsingfors Cons., Busoni, Becker and Massenet; chorusmaster, Magdeburg Op., 1896; Düsseldorf Op., 1897; cond. Wiborg Orch., 1898–1903; won a gov't. award for study in other countries; in 1904–05, was dir. of Helsingfors Op.; in 1905–07, cond. Stockholm R. Orch.; in latter year cond. also of R. Op. in same city; dir., Helsingfors Cons., 1906–07; c. the orch. works, "Korsholm"; "Heimatklang" (latter a symph. fantasy); Serenade; 4 suites; 2 overtures; the choral comps., "Laula vuoksella," "Suomen synty," "Ago Slott," also many notable works for male chorus; songs, piano pieces, etc.; m. Maikki Parkarinnen, singer; divorced; (2) Liva Edström, singer.

Jarnowic (or **Giornovi(c)chi**) (yär′-nō-vĕk, or jôr-nō-vē′-kĕ), **Giov. M.**, Palermo, 1745—St. Petersburg, Nov. 21, 1804; violinist and composer; pupil of Lolli, whose intolerable eccentricities and immorality, as well as virtuosity, he adopted with disastrous results; J. B. Cramer challenged him, but he would not fight.

Jar′off, Serge, b. Russia, March 20, 1896; choral conductor; studied at Moscow Synodal Acad. for Church Choral Song; in 1920 founded the celebrated Don Cossack Russian Male Chorus, composed of former soldiers in the White Russian Armies; beginning 1923 began triumphal tours with this group in Europe; 1930, U. S.

Jar′vis, (1) **Stephen**, 1834 ?—London, 1880; composer. (2) **Chas. H.**, Philadelphia, 1837—1895; pianist and conductor.

Jaspar (zhăs-păr), **Maurice**, b. Liége, June 20, 1870; pianist; pupil and (1909-16) teacher at the Cons.; 1909, founded (with Lebefve) the Walloon Music Fests.; c. piano pieces and songs.

Jean-Aubry (zhän-ō′-brē), **G.**, b. Le Havre, France, 1885; writer on music; ed. of "The Chesterian," London, since 1918; author of "La Musique française d'aujourd'hui," etc.

Jean le Coq, or **Jehan.** Vide GALLUS, JOHANNES.

Jedliczka (yāt-lěch′-kä), **Ernest**, Poltawa, Russia, June 5, 1855—Berlin, Aug. 8, 1904; pianist; pupil of

Moscow Cons.; teacher there till 1888, then teacher Berlin, Stern Cons.

Jeff′ries, (1) **G.**, organist to Chas. I., 1643. Had a son (2) **Christopher**, organist and composer. (3) **Stephen**, 1660—1712; Engl. organist and composer.

Jéhin (zhā-ăṅ), **Léon**, Spa, Belgium, July 17, 1853—Monte Carlo, Feb. 15, 1928; violinist; pupil of Leonard, Brussels Cons.; cond. at Antwerp and Vauxhall, Brussels; 1879–89, asst.-prof. of theory, Brussels Cons.; cond. at Monaco; composer.

Jéhin (**Jéhin-Prume**) (zhā-ăṅ-prüm), **Fz. H.**, Spa, Belgium, April 18, 1839—Montreal, May 29, 1899; one of the most eminent violinists of Belgian sch.; composer.

Jelensperger (yā′-lĕn-shpĕrkh-ĕr), **Daniel**, near Mühlhausen, Alsatia, 1797—1831; writer.

Jelinek (yĕ′-lĭ-nĕk), **Fz. X.**, b. Kaurins, Bohemia, 1818—Salzburg, 1880; oboist and composer.

Jenk′ins, (1) **J.**, Maidstone, 1592—Kimberley, Norfolk, 1678; courtlutist and lyra-violist to Chas. I. and II.; composed. "12 Sonatas for 2 Vlns. and a Base, with a Thorough Base for the Organ or Theorbo," the first Engl. comp. of the sort; the pop. "The Lady Katherine Audley's Bells, or The Five Bell Consort," etc. (2) **David**, b. Trecastell, Brecon, Jan. 1, 1849—Aberystwith, Dec. 10, 1916; 1878; Mus. Bac. Contab.; 1885, cond. America; prof. Univ. Coll. of Wales; c. operetta, 2 oratorios, 3 cantatas, A Psalm of Life, etc. (3) **Cyril**, b. Dunvant near Swansea, South Wales, Oct. 9, 1885; comp. of symph. poems, chamber music, cantatas, some of which have won prizes at the nat'l. Eisteddfod.

Jennekin (zhĕn-kăṅ). Vide JANNEQUIN.

Jenner (yĕn′-něr), **Gustav**, Keitum, Island of Sylt, Dec. 3, 1865—Marburg, Aug. 29, 1920; pupil of Stange and Gänge in Kiel, of Brahms and Mandyczewski in Vienna; from 1895 director in Marburg; c. songs and quartets for women's voices.

Jensen (yĕn′-sĕn), (1) **Ad.**, Königsberg, Jan. 12, 1837—of consumption, Baden-Baden, Jan. 23, 1879; one of the most original and poetical of composers for piano and voice; his pf.-pcs. have an unexcelled lyricism, and marked melodiousness. Self-taught, but advised by L. Ehlert and

Fr. Marburg; before 20 had **c.** overtures, a string-quartet, sonatas and songs. 1856, teacher in Russia; then studied with Schumann; 1857, cond. Posen City Th.; 1858–60, studied with Gade; 1860, returned to Königsberg; 1866–68, teacher at Tausig's Sch. in Berlin; compelled by ill-health to retire to Dresden, 1870 to Graz, finally to Baden-Baden. C. opera *"Turandot"* (finished by Kienzl); *"Nonnengesang,"* and *"Brautlied"* for solo and chorus with 2 horns, harp and a piano, *"Jephtha's Tochter"* and *"Adonis-Feier,"* *"Donald Caird ist wieder da,"* and other vocal works with orch.; concert-overture; *"Geistlicher Tonstück"*; *"Hochzeitsmusik," "Abendmusik," "Lebensbilder,"* 6 *"Silhouetten,"* and *"Ländliche Festmusik,"* for pf. (4 hands); and *"Innere Stimmen," "Wanderbilder,"* a sonata; 6 German Suites, *"Idyllen,"* *"Erotikon"* (7 pcs.), a scherzo, *"Wald-Idylle,"* op. 47, *"Scenes carnavalesques,"* for pf.-solo; and 160 solo songs. Biog. by Niggli. (2) **Gustav,** Königsberg, 1843—Cologne, 1895; pupil of Dehn (comp.) and Laub and Joachim (vln.); violinist Königsberg Th.; 1872–75, prof. of cpt., Cologne Cons.; c. symphony, etc.

Jentsch (yĕntsh), **Max,** Ziesar, Saxony, Aug. 5, 1855—Stendal, Nov., 1918; pianist and teacher; pupil of Stern Cons.; toured the Orient; 1884–89 in Constantinople; later in Berlin; from 1894 in Vienna; c. symphony, *"Elysium"* for chorus and orch., 2 operas, etc.

Jep'son, (1) **Harry Benjamin,** b. New Haven, Conn., Aug. 16, 1870; educator; grad. Yale Univ.; studied with Stoeckel, Parker, Widor; after 1899 ass't. prof. of theory at Yale, and 1906 prof. and Univ. org.; c. vocal wks.; d. Groton, Conn., 1952. (2) **Helen,** b. Akron, O.; soprano; studied with Horatio Connell at Curtis Inst. of Mus., Phila.; also with Richard Hageman; sang with Chautauqua, N. Y., Op. Ass'n.; with Phila. Gr. Op. Co.; soloist with various orchs.; after 1935 with Met. Op. Co.; 1936, also Chicago Op. Co.

Jeritza (yĕr'-ĕt-sä), **Maria,** b. Brünn, Moravia, Oct. 6, 1887; soprano; family name Jedlitzka; studied singing with Auspitzer; first sang in operetta at Stadttheatre in native town; later in Olmütz; then in comic opera at Munich and Vienna; after 1912 a regular mem. of Vienna State Op., where became known as dram. actress of pronounced powers; Amer. début, Met. Op. Co. as "Marietta" in Korngold's *"Die Tote Stadt,"* 1921; sang leading rôles in Wagnerian and Italian works with this co. for more than a decade; a striking "Tosca"; "Turandot" and "Helena" in Strauss's opera (creations for America); in 1933 with Chicago Op., also appeared at Covent Garden and widely in concerts.

Jess'ner, Irene, b. Vienna; soprano; studied Cons. there; mem. Met. Op., 1936.

Jiménez (hǐ'-mǐ-nĕth), **Jeronimo,** Seville, 1854—Madrid, 1923; comp. of 50 zarzuelas.

Jimmerthal (yǐm'-mĕr-täl), **Hn.,** Lübeck, 1809—1886; organist, org.-builder and writer.

Jiránek (yē'-rä-nĕk), (1) **Anton,** ca. 1712—Dresden, Jan. 16, 1761; studied at Prague; later joined the royal chapel at Warsaw. (2) **Josef,** Ledec, March 24, 1855—d. 1940; pianist; pupil of Smetana, and of the organ school at Prague; studied the harp with Stanek, the violin with Hrimaly, and was a harpist at first; 1877–91 piano teacher at Charkov; 1891–1913, prof. at Prague Cons.; c. *"Ballade"* and *"Scherzo fantastique"* for orch., piano pieces; author of methods. His brother (3) **Aloys,** b. Ledec, Sept. 3, 1858; pupil of Prague Organ School, and in composition of Fibich; from 1881, piano teacher at Charkov; c. opera *"Dagmar,"* etc.

Joachim (yō'-ä-khēm), (1) **Jos.,** Kittsee, near Pressburg, June 28, 1831—Berlin, Aug. 15, 1907; eminent violinist; studied at 5 with Szervacinski, Pesth, with whom he appeared in public at 7; from 1841, at Vienna Cons. with Böhm; at 12, played in Leipzig, and soon after at the Gewandhaus, with much succ.; frequently leader of the Gewandhaus Orchestra; 1844, made his first of many appearances in London; 1849, *Concertmeister* of the Weimar orch.; 1854, cond. and solo violinist to the King of Hanover; 1863 m. Amalie Weiss (v. infra); 1868 head of the Hochschule, Berlin; 1877, Mus. Doc. *h. c.,* Cambridge Univ.; had many degrees from German universities, and various orders of knighthood; undisputed preeminence as a classicist and soloperformer; his famous J. Quartet included De Ahna, Wirth and Hausmann. He c. "Hungarian" concerto for violin, and 2 others, and variations with orch., also overture to "*Hamlet*"; 4 overtures incl. "*Dem Andenken Kleists*"; Hebrew Melodies, for vla. and pf.; Op. 14, "*Szene der Marfa*" (from Schiller's *Demetrius*), for contralto solo with orch.; three cadenzas to Beethoven's vln.-concerto, etc. (2) **Amalie** (née **Weiss**, rightly, **Schneeweiss**), Marburg, Styria, May 10, 1839—Berlin, Feb. 3, 1899; eminent concert and operatic soprano; then contralto and teacher; wife of above.

Jobin (zhô-băñ'), **Raoul**, French-Canadian tenor; sang Paris Op.; Met. Op., 1940.

Johns, Clayton, New Castle, Del., Nov. 24, 1857—Boston, March 7, 1932; pupil of J. K. Paine, and W. H. Sherwood, Boston; later with Kiel, Grabow, Raif, and Rummel (pf.) in Berlin; in Boston, Mass., as a concert-pianist and teacher; after 1912 taught N. E. Cons.; c. a Berceuse and Scherzino for stringorch. (played by Boston Symph. orch.); many songs, etc.

John's, (1) Edw., English composer, 1594. (2) **Robert**, Engl. 16th cent. ecclesiastic and church composer. (3) **Robert**, lutenist and prominent composer, 1573—1625. (4) **John**, d. 1594-95; musician to Queen Elizabeth; c. lute-music. (5) **Edward**, b. Guelph, Ontario, tenor and impresario; studied Univ. of Toronto; singing with Lombardi in Florence; early sang in concerts and in light operas in N. Y.; opera début at Padua; heard in several Italian theatres, incl. La Scala (1st Ital. perf. of Parsifal, 1914); sang Chicago Op. Co. 1920, also Ravinia Op.; Met. Op. Co., after 1921, interpreting romantic rôles such as "Pelléas" and in Italian works with succ.; created parts in 1st Amer. hearings of operas by Puccini, Pizzetti, Montemezzi, Zandonai and Deems Taylor ("*King's Henchman*" and "*Peter Ibbetson*"); chosen as asst. general manager, Met. Op. Co., 1935, and same year succeeded

to managership on death of Herbert Witherspoon; hon. LL. D., Univ of Western Ontario; Cav. Ufficiale, Order of the Crown of Italy; Commander of the British Empire. (6) **Horace**, b. Waltham, Mass., October 5, 1893; composer; studied comp. with Bainbridge Crist, org. and pf. with John P. Marshall; c. orch. suites, pf. pieces, songs, etc. (7) **Thor**, b. Wisc. Rapids, Wis., 1913; grad. Univ. of N. C.; studied with Walter, Malko and Weingartner; cond., Ann Arbor, Mich., Fest.; cond. Cincinnati Symph., after 1946.

Jommelli (yôm-měl'-lī), **Niccolò**, Aversa, near Naples, Sept. 11, 1714 —Naples, Aug. 28, 1774; eminent operatic and church-composer; pupil of Canon Mozzillo, Durante, Feo, Leo, Prato and Mancini. C. ballets and songs, then dram. cantatas; at 23 prod. opera "*L'Errore Amoroso*" (Naples, 1737), under the name "**Valentino**"; its succ. relieved his anxiety and removed his anonymity and he followed it with other succ. works in various cities under various patronage. He was made Dir. of the Cons. del Ospedaletto, Venice; 1748-54 asst. *Maestro* at St. Peter's, Rome, until 1754; cond. to the Duke of Würtemberg. Lived in Germany 15 years and made great succ. He profited artistically by German influence, but when the Stuttgart opera was disbanded and he retired to Italy his style was too serious and perhaps his best works "*Armida Abbandonata*" (1770), "*Demofoönte*" (1770), and "*Ifigenia in Tauride*" (1771), were failures when prod. at Naples. The humiliation after such long triumph brought on apoplexy (1773), from which he recovered only long enough to write a cantata on the birth of a prince, and his masterpiece, a "*Miserere*." The King of Portugal commissioned him to write 2 operas and a cantata; but he did not live to finish them; he c. over 50 known operas and divertissements, and equally fine sacred mus., incl. 4 oratorios, a magnificat, with echo, etc.

Jonás (zhō-năs), (1) **Émile**, Paris, March 5, 1827—St. Germain-en-Laye, Paris, May 21, 1905; pupil of Carafa at the Cons.; from 1847 teacher there also mus.-dir. Portuguese synagogue. (2) (hō'-näs).

Alberto, Madrid, June 8, 1868—
Phila., Nov. 9, 1943; pianist; pupil of
Madrid Cons.; at 18 with Gevaert,
Brussels Cons.; won 1st prize for pf.,
and later 2 first prizes in harm.;
début, Brussels, 1880; 1890, studied
St. Petersburg Cons. under Rubinstein's tuition; since toured Europe
and America; 1894 head of the pf.-
dep. Univ. of Michigan; since 1914
taught in N. Y. (2) **Maryla,** Polish
pianist; N. Y. début, 1946.

Joncières (zhôn-sǐ-ărs), **Victorin de,**
Paris, April 12, 1839—Oct. 26, 1903;
studied painting, then mus. with
Elwart at the Cons.; an ardent
Wagnerian, he left the Cons. because
of Elwart's adverse opinion; pres.
"Soc. des Compositeurs de musique,"
Chev. of the Legion of Honour, and
officer of public instruction; 1871
critic of *"La Liberté,"* etc.; prod. 4
operas, incl. *"Le Chevalier Jean"*
(Op.-com., 1885), a symph. ode,
"La Mer"; a *"Symphonie romantique"*; *"Li Tsin,"* a Chinese theme
for soli and orch., etc.

Jones, (1) **Robt.,** Engl. lutenist and
composer, 1601–16; one of his songs,
"Farewell deere love," is alluded to
in *"Twelfth Night."* (2) **Wm.** ("of
Nayland"), Lowick, Northamptonshire, 1736—Nayland, Suffolk, 1800;
writer and composer. (3) **J.,** 1728—
London, 1796; organist and composer. (4) (Sir) **Wm.,** London,
1746—Calcutta, 1794; writer. (5)
Edw. ("Brady Brenin"), Llander-
fel, Merionethshire, April 18, 1752—
London, April 18, 1824; Welsh
harpist, writer and composer. (6)
Griffith, British writer, pub. *"A
History of the Origin and Progress
of Theoretical and Practical Music,"*
1819. (7) **Sidney,** b. Leeds, 1869;
theater conductor and composer of
the succ. operetta *"The Gaiety Girl"*
(London, 1893); *"An Artist's Model"*
(Daly's Th., London, 1895); *"The
Geisha"* (1896); d. Kew, Eng., 1946.

Jongen (zhôn'-gĕn), (1) **Joseph,** b.
Liége, Dec. 14, 1873—Sart-les-Spa,
July 14, 1953; pupil Liége Cons., won
many prizes incl. Prix de Rome;
1903 prof. of harmony and cpt.
there; after 1904 res. in Brussels;
1920 taught at Cons. there; 1925,
dir.; with Lekeu and Vreuls, one
of leading Belgian comps., influenced
by Franck and Debussy; c. much
orch. and chamber music, 'cello

concerto, cantatas, piano and org.
music, and stage works. (2) **Léon,**
b. Liége, March 2, 1884; bro. of
Joseph; studied Liége Cons., won
Prix de Rome; c. dram. works.

Jorda (hör-dä'), **Enrique,** b. San Sebastian, 1911; cond., San Francisco
Symph., 1954–55.

Jor'dan, Jules, Willimantic, Conn.,
Nov. 10, 1850—Providence, R. I.,
March 5, 1927; studied singing with
Osgood, Boston, Shakespeare, London, and Sbriglia, Paris; for 13 years
choirm. of Grace Ch., Providence;
1880 cond. Arion Club; c. comedy-
opera *"Rip Van Winkle"* (pub.
1898); cantata with orch.; songs,
etc.

Jörn (yärn), **Karl,** b. Riga, Jan. 5,
1876; tenor; pupil of Lohse, Schutte,
Harmsen and Elis. Jacobs, also Mme.
Ress and Weiss; made début at
Freiburg, 1896; sang at Zurich, Ham-
burg, Berlin; also in London, 1905–08,
Met. Op., 1908–11; d. Denver, 1947.

Joseffy (yŏ-zĕf'-fĭ), **Rafael,** Miskolcz,
Hungary, July 3, 1853—New York,
June 25, 1915; eminent pianist; pupil
of Moscheles, Leipzig Cons., Liszt,
Tausig; toured Europe with succ.;
lived in Vienna; for many years at
New York; teacher Nat. Cons.; c.
pf.-pcs.

Josephson (yŏ'-zĕf-zōn), **Jacob Axel,**
Stockholm, March 27, 1818—Upsala,
March 29, 1880; Swedish cond. and
composer.

Josquin. Vide DESPRÈS.

Josten (yōs'-tĕn), **Werner,** b. Elberfeld, Germany, June 12, 1888; composer; since 1923 prof. of music,
Smith Coll., Northampton, Mass.;
also dir. music fests. there, incl.
perfs. of Händel operas, etc.; c.
"Jungle" for orch.; *"Concerto Sacro"*
for strings and piano; *"Hymnus to
the Quene of Paradys,"* for alto solo,
women's chorus, strings and org.;
"Crucifixion," for bass solo and
mixed chorus; *"Indian Serenade,"*
for tenor and orch., *"Ode for St.
Cecilia's Day"* for soprano, barytone,
mixed chorus, orch.; *"A Une
Madone"* for tenor and orch.; string
quartet; (ballet) *"Joseph and His
Brethren"* (Juilliard School of Music,
1936).

Jouret (zhoo-rä), (1) **Th.,** Ath, Belgium, 1821—Kissingen, 1887; critic
and dram. composer. (2) **Léon,**
Ath, Oct. 17, 1828—Brussels, June 6,

1905; bro. of above; pupil Brussels Cons. and after 1874 vocal teacher there; c. 2 operas, cantatas, etc.

Journet (zhoor'-nā), **Marcel,** Grasse, 1869—Vittel, Sept. 6, 1933; bass; pupil of the Cons.; début Th. de la Monnaie, Brussels; sang often at Covent Garden; 1900 at Met. Op., N. Y.; 1914, Chicago Op. Co.

Jousse (zhoos), **J.,** Orleans, France, 1760—1837; teacher and writer.

Juch (yookh), **Emma,** Vienna, July 4, 1865—N. Y., March 6, 1939; soprano; studied in New York with Mme. Murio-Celli; concert début, 1882; in opera at Her Majesty's Theat., London, the following year in *"Mignon"*; sang under Mapleson's mgt. there for 3 seasons in leading rôles; 1886–87 with Amer. Op. Co. under Thomas; 1889 founded her own co. and sang in U. S. and Mexico; also heard in concerts and with orchs. in U. S.

Judenkunig (yoo'-den-koo-nǐkh), **Hans,** b. Schwäbisch-Gmünd; lutenist, violist and composer at Vienna, 1523.

Jue (zhü), **Edouard,** b. Paris, 1794 (?); violinist and writer.

Jul(l)ien (zhül-yäṅ), (1) **Marcel Bd.,** Paris, 1798—1881; writer. (2) **Jean Lucien Ad.,** Paris, June 1, 1845—1932; son of above; prominent critic and writer. (3) **Louis Ant.,** Sisteron, Basses-Alpes, April 23, 1812—insane, Paris, March 14, 1860; pop. conductor and composer of dance music, etc. (4) **Paul,** Brest, France, Feb. 12, 1841—at sea, 1866; violinist; pupil Paris Cons., took 1st prize; toured America, 1853–66.

Jumilhac (zhü-mēl-yăk), **Dom P. Benoît de,** near Limoges, 1611—St. Germain-des-Pres, 1682; writer.

Junck (yoonk), **Benedetto,** Turin, Aug. 24, 1852—Vigilio (Bergamo), Oct. 3, 1903; pupil of Bazzini and Mazzucato; lived in Milan; c. string-quartet, etc.

Jüngst (yǐnkst), **Hugo,** Dresden, Feb. 26, 1853—Feb. 6, 1923; studied at Cons. there; founded the Julius Otto Soc.; and cond. Male Choral Soc.; 1898 made prof. by King of Saxony; c. male choruses.

Junker (yoonk'-ĕr), **K. L.,** Öhringen, ca. 1740—Kirchberg, 1797; writer and composer.

Juon (zhwôn), **Paul,** Moscow, Mar. 8, 1872—Vevey. Switz.. Aug. 21, 1940;

violinist; pupil Hrimaly, Taneiev and Arensky, later of Bargiel in Berlin, where he won the Mendelssohn Scholarship; 1896 taught theory at Baku; 1897 settled in Berlin; 1906–34, teacher of composition at the High School for Music; c. 2 symph., the second prod. with much interest at Meiningen, 1903, and in London, 1904 and 1905; fantasie for orch., *"Wächterweise,"* on Danish folk-themes, orch. suite, *"Aus meinem Tagebuch"*; chamber music, *"Satyrs and Nymphs,"* and other piano pieces, 3 vln. concerti, etc.

Jupin (zhü-păṅ), **Chas. Fran.,** Chambéry, 1805—Paris, 1839; violinist, professor, conductor, and dram. composer.

Jürgenson (yür'-gĕn-zōn), **Peter,** Reval, 1836—Moscow, Jan. 2, 1904; founded mus.-pub. house, Moscow, 1861.

K

Kaan (kän) (**"Albést-Kahn"**), **H. von,** Tarnopol, Galicia, May 29, 1852—Rudna, May, 1926; pianist; pupil of Blodek and Skuhersky, Prague; dir. Cons. there, 1907–18, comp.

Kabalev'sky, Dimitri, b. Leningd., 1904; pupil Mosc. Cons., c. opera *"Colas Breugnon,"* 2 symphs., etc.

Kade (kä'-dĕ), **Otto,** Dresden, 1825—Schwerin, 1900; ct.-conductor, writer and composer.

Kaempfert (kĕmp'-fĕrt), **Max,** b. Berlin, Jan. 3, 1871; studied in Paris and Munich; 1899—1923 cond. at Frankfort-on-Main; c. opera; 4 rhapsodies for orch., etc.

Kahl (käl), **H.,** Munich, 1840—Berlin, 1892; conductor.

Kahlert (kä'-lĕrt), **Aug. K. Timotheus,** Breslau, 1807—1864; writer and composer.

Kahn (kän), (1) **Robt.,** b. Mannheim, July 21, 1865; pianist; pupil of Ernst Frank and V. Lachner, Kiel, and Jos. Rheinberger (Munich, 1885;) 1891 founded Ladies' Choral Union, Leipzig; 1898—1930, prof. of comp., Berlin Hochschule für Musik; c. orch., chamber and choral music, songs, etc. His bro. (2) **Otto Hermann,** Mannheim, Germany, Feb. 21, 1867—New York, March 29, 1934; patron of music; 1908–31, chairman of board of directors, Met. Op. Co., and for some years dominated its artistic policies;

DICTIONARY OF MUSICIANS 229

possessing wide interests, he was also a generous supporter of many of the foreign musical and other productions brought to N. Y.; influential in sponsoring the Century Op. Co., Boston Op. Co., Chicago Op. Ass'n., the French-American Ass'n. for Mus. Art, and other projects; he was interested in promoting a plan for a new opera house in N. Y. and even bought up parcels of land for such a structure, but opposition in the Met. Op. directorate caused the matter to be shelved.

Kalint (känt), **Chr. Fr.**, 1823—Leipzig, 1897; mus.-publisher.

Kaiser (kī'-zĕr), (1) **K.**, Leipa, Bohemia, 1837—Vienna, 1890; founded sch. continued by his son (2) **Rudolf.** (3) **Fr. Emil**, Coburg, Feb. 7, 1853—Munich, 1929; regimental bandm. Prague; prod. 5 operas, incl. "*Der Trompeter von Säkkingen*" (Olmütz, 1882).

Kajanus (kä-jä'-noos), **Robert**, Helsingfors, Dec. 2, 1856—July 6, 1933; Finnish composer; pupil Leipzig Cons.; returned to Helsingfors, founded an orchestra school, and developed the Phil. orch.; 1897 mus. director of the University; c. 2 Finnish rhapsodies, symph. poems "*Aino*" and "*Kullervo*"; orch. suite "*Summer Memories*," cantata, etc.

Kal'beck, Max, Breslau, Jan. 4, 1850—Vienna, May 5, 1921; studied Munich Sch. of Mus.; 1875, writer, critic at Breslau; then on the "*Wiener Montags-Revue*," and the "*Neues Tageblatt.*"

Kalin'nikov, Vassili Sergeievich, Voina, Jan. 13, 1866—Jalta, Crimea, Jan. 11, 1901; pupil of Iljinski and Blaramberg at Moscow; 1893 assistant cond. at the Italian Opera there; compelled to retire because of pulmonary trouble and go south; c. 2 symph., the first in G minor, much played; 2 symph. poems, "*The Nymphs*" and "*Cedar and Palm*"; music to Tolstoi's "*Czar Boris,*" (Little Theatre, Moscow, 1899); "*Russalka*," ballade with orch., cantata, "*St. John of Damascus*," etc.

Kalisch (kä'-lĭsh), **Paul**, b. Berlin, Nov. 6, 1855; tenor; studied with Leoni; sang Berlin ct.-opera; m. Lilli Lehmann; sang at Cologne and six times in America; d. (?).

Kalischer (kä'-lĭsh-ĕr), **Alfred**, Thorn, March 4, 1842—Berlin, Oct. 8, 1909;

Dr. Phil., Leipzig U.; studied with Bürgel and Böhmer; lived in Berlin, as a writer and teacher; editor "*Neue Berliner Musikzeitung*"; pub. "*Lessing als Musikästhetiker*"; "*Musik und Moral,*" "*Beethoven und seine Zeitgenossen*"; ed. collection of Beethoven's letters.

Kalkbrenner (kälk'-brĕn-nĕr), (1) **Chr.**, Minden, Hanover, 1755—Paris, 1806; writer and dram. composer. (2) **Fr. Wm. Michael**, b. on a journey from Cassel to Berlin, 1788—d. of cholera Enghien-les-Bains, near Paris, June 10, 1849; son and pupil of above; very succ. pianist and teacher; developed modern octave-playing, left-hand technique and pedalling; wrote valuable études and other comps.; also studied Paris Cons. and with Clementi and Albrechtsberger. (3) **Arthur**, d. near Paris, 1869; son of (2); composer.

Kalliwoda (käl'-lĭ-vō-dä), (1) **Jn. Wenzel**, Prague, 1801—Carlsruhe, 1866; pianist, conductor and dram. composer. (2) **Wm.**, Donaueschingen, 1827—Carlsruhe, 1893; son and pupil of above; dir., ct.-conductor, pianist and composer.

Kallwitz, or **Kalwitz**. Vide CALVISIUS.

Kal'man, Emmerich, b. Siofok, Hungary, Oct. 24, 1882; composer of operettas, some of which have had world-wide popularity; pupil of Koessler; c. among other works "*Die Czardasfürstin*," "*Gräfin Maritza*," "*Die Zirkusprinzessin*"; lived U. S.; d. Paris, Oct. 30, 1953.

Kamienski (käm-ĭ-ĕn'-shkĭ), **Mathias**, Odenburg, Hungary, 1734—Warsaw, 1821; teacher and composer of the first Polish opera "*The Wretched Made Happy*" (1778), etc.

Kamin'ski, Heinrich, b. Tiengen, Baden, Germany, July 4, 1886; composer; studied at Heidelberg Univ., and with Klatte, Kaun and Juon; his works based on pre-Bach polyphonic style; c. (music drama) "*Jürg Jenatsch*" (prod. Dresden Op.), concerto grosso and suite for orch., chamber music, many choral works and motets, Magnificat, (widely sung, incl. Boston perf.); Psalms for chorus and orch.; Passion (mystery play); org. works, etc.; 1930-32, leader of master school in comp. at Berlin Akad. der Künste; also cond. of orch. concerts in Bielefeld, 1930-33; d. 1946.

Kam'mel, Anton, Hanna, Bohemia, 1740—London, before 1788; violinist and composer; pupil of Tartini; c. masses, violin duets, etc.

Kammerlander (käm'-měr-länt-ěr), **K.,** Weissenhorn, Swabia, 1828—Augsburg, 1892; conductor and composer.

Kandler (känt'-lěr), **Fz.** Sales, Klosterneuburg, Lower Austria, 1792—Baden, 1831; writer.

Kapp, Julius, b. Steinbach, Baden, Oct. 1, 1883; Ph. D.; editor; writer of biogs. of Wagner, Berlioz, Liszt, etc.

Kappel (kä'-pěl), **Gertrude;** b. Halle, Germany; studied piano and singing Leipzig Cons., with Nikisch and Nce; has appeared in opera at Hanover, Vienna, Munich, London, Madrid, Amsterdam, and after 1927 with Met. Op. Co., N. Y., singing leading Wagnerian rôles, also Strauss's "*Elektra.*"

Kapsberger (käps'-běrkh-ěr), **Jn.** Hieronymus von, b. of noble German family, d. Rome, ca. 1650; virtuoso on theorbo, chitarrone, lute, and trumpet; notable composer.

Karajan (kä'-rä-yän), Herbert von; cond.; 1935, Aachen; later, Vienna Symph.

Karasowski (kä-rä-shôf'-shkĭ), **Moritz,** Warsaw, 1823—Dresden, 1892; 'cellist, writer and composer.

Karg-Elert (kärkh-ä'-lěrt), **Sigfrid,** Oberndorf, Nov. 21, 1879—Leipzig, April 9, 1933; pupil Leipzig Cons.; teacher and composer; after 1919, taught at Leipzig Cons.; eminent concert organist; toured U. S. shortly before his death; c. a large variety of works for org., incl. sonatas, etc.

Karl, Tom, Dublin, Jan. 19, 1846—Rochester, N. Y., 1916; tenor; studied with H. Phillips, Sangiovanni and Trivulzi; sang in Italian opera for years, went to America with Parepa-Rosa, then with "The Bostonians" in comic opera many years; retired 1896; later vocal teacher, N. Y.

Karlovicz (kärl'-yō-vĭch), **Mieczyslav,** Wisznievo, Lithuania, Dec. 11, 1876—(in an avalanche), Zakopane, Galicia, Feb. 10, 1909; composer; studied in Warsaw and Berlin; c. symph., symphonic-trilogy "*Three Ancient Songs*" (1907), "*Lithuanian Rhapsody*" (1908), also published Chopin letters and documents (Warsaw and Paris, 1905).

Karpath (kär'-pät), **Ludwig,** Budapest, 1866—Vienna, 1936; singer and critic; pupil Budapest Cons.; sang with Nat'l. Op. Cc., N. Y., 1886–88; after 1894, critic "*Neues Wiener Tageblatt*"; 1910–17, ed., "*Merker*"; author of books on Wagner.

Kasan'li, Nicolai Ivanovich, Tiraspol, Dec. 17, 1869—St. Petersburg, 1913 (?); Russian composer; pupil Odessa Music School and St. Petersburg Cons.; had cond. Russian symph. concerts in Germany, Bohemia, etc.; c. symph., Sinfonietta, cantata "*Russalka*" (Munich, 1897), and "*Leonore*" (do.).

Kasatchen'ko, Nicolai Ivanovich, b. Russia, May 3, 1858; cond.; pupil St. Petersburg Cons.; 1883 chorus master at the Imperial Opera; cond "*Russian Concerts*" in Paris, 1898; after 1924 prof. of choral singing, Leningrad Cons.; c. symph., 2 oriental suites, 2 operas, "*Prince Serebrianni*" (St. Petersburg, 1892), and "*Pan Sothin*"; d. Leningrad (?).

Kasch'in, Daniel Nikitich, Moscow, 1773–1844; composer of Polish folk and patriotic songs; also three operas.

Kash'perov, Vladimir Nikitich, Simbirsk, 1827—Romanzevo, July 8, 1894; Russian composer; pupil of Voigt and Henselt; and comp. an opera in 1850, then went to Berlin to study with Dehn; thence with Glinka to Italy, where he produced various operas. "*Maria Tudor*" (Milan, 1859), "*Rienzi*" (Florence, 1863), "*Consuelo*" (Venice); 1866–72 he was singing teacher at Moscow Cons., and organised public chorus-classes; c. also operas "*The Weather*" (St. Petersburg, 1867), and "*Taras Bulba*" (Moscow, 1893).

Kaskel (käs'-kěl), **Freiherr K. von,** b. Dresden, Oct. 10, 1866; studied law at Leipzig, also mus. in the Cons. with Reinecke and Jadassohn (1886–87), and later with Wüllner and Jensen, Cologne; lived in Dresden; c. succ. 1-act opera "*Hochzeitsmorgen*" (Hamburg, 1893); v. succ. opera "*Sjula*" (Cologne, 1895), etc.

Kässmeyer (kěs'-mī-ěr), **Moritz,** Vienna, 1831—1884; violinist; c. 5 string-quartets, some of them humorous.

Kastal'sky, Alexander Dmitrievitch, Moscow, Nov. 28, 1856—Dec. 17, 1926; important Russian church composer; after 1887 teacher and conductor at the School of the Synodal Chorus, renamed the People's Choral Acad. in 1918 and

merged with Moscow Cons. in 1923;
also c. operas, etc.

Kastner (käst'-nĕr), (1) **Jn. G.**, Strassburg, March 9, 1810—Paris, Dec. 19,
1867; pupil of Maurer and Romer;
at 10, organist; at 20, bandm.; at
25 had prod. 4 operas, and was sent
ʰy the town council to Paris, to study
with Berton and Reicha; 1837,
pub. treatise *"On Instrumentation"*
among others; also methods adopted
at the Paris Cons.; lived thereafter
at Paris as teacher; wrote learned
essays and an *"Encyclopédie de la
musique."* C. 3 later operas incl.
"Le dernier roi de Juda," his masterpiece, also 3 symphonies, 5 overtures,
10 serenades for wind; *"Livres-
partitions"* (symphony-cantatas,
prefaced by brilliant historical essays, incl. *"Les danses des morts"*),
a vol. of 310 pages; *"La harpe
d'éole"* (1856); *"Les voix de Paris,"*
followed by *"Les cris de Paris,"*
grande symphonie humoristique voc.
et instr. (1857); *"Les Sirènes,"*
etc. Biog. by Jan (Leipzig, 1886).
(2) **G. Fr.** **Eugen**, Strassburg, 1852
—Bonn, 1882; son of above; inv.
the pyrophone (v. D. D.), and pub.
work on it. (3) **Emmerich**, Vienna,
March 29, 1847—1916; editor and
writer.

Kate (kä'-tĕ), **André Ten**, Amsterdam,
1796—Haarlem, 1858; 'cellist and
dram. composer.

Katims (kā'-tĭms), **Milton**, American
violist; cond. with NBC Symph.;
1954-55, cond. Seattle Symph.

Kauer (kow'-ĕr), **Fd.**, Klein-Thaya,
Moravia, Jan. 8, 1751—Vienna,
April 13, 1831; prolific c. of *Singspiele;* organist, conductor, 'cellist;
c. 200 operas and operettas.

Kauffmann (kowf'-män), (1) **Ernst
Fr.**, Ludwigsburg, 1803—Stuttgart,
1856; pianist and composer. (2)
Emil, Ludwigsburg, Nov. 23, 1836—
Tübingen, June 18, 1909; violinist;
son of above; pupil of Stuttgart
Cons.; musical dir. Tübingen Univ.;
Dr. Phil., 1885. (3) **Fritz**, Berlin,
June 17, 1855—Magdeburg, Sept.
29, 1934; a druggist, Leipzig and
Hamburg; took up music, 1878,
entered the Akademische Hochschule
at Berlin, won Mendelssohn prize for
comp. 1881; till 1889, lived in Berlin
as a teacher and then cond. of the
"Gesellschaftsconcerte" at Magdeburg; 1893, Royal Musik-Direktor;

c. comic opera, *"Die Herzkrankheit"*;
symphony, etc.

Kaun (kown), **Hugo**, Berlin, March
21, 1863—April 2, 1932; pupil at
Royal High School under Giabau
and Fr. Schulz; also with K. and O.
Raif, and Fr. Kiel; 1887 took up
residence in Milwaukee, Wis., as
teacher and cond.; 1900 returned to
Berlin; 1912, elected to Berlin Royal
Academy; c. symph. *"An Mein
Vaterland,"* symph. prolog *"Marie
Magdalene"*; symph. poems; festival
march *"The Star Spangled Banner,"*
chamber music with orch., *"Nor-
mannen Abschied"*; 1-act opera *"Der
Pietist"* or *"Oliver Brown,"* and
important songs and piano pieces.

Kazynski (kä-zēn'-shkĭ), **Victor**, Wilna,
Lithuania, Dec. 18, 1812—St. Petersburg, 1870; pupil of Elsner, Warsaw;
prod. 3 operas; 1843, cond. Imp. Th.
St. Petersburg.

Ke'fer, Paul, Rouen, 1875—Rochester,
N. Y., 1941; 'cellist; pupil Verviers
Mus. School and Paris Cons.; after
1900 played in Paris orchs., and 1908-
13 with N. Y. Symph., also heard as
soloist.

Keiser (kī'-zĕr), **Reinhard**, Teuchern,
near Weissenfels, Jan. 9, 1674—
Hamburg, Sept. 12, 1739; the father
of German opera, the first to employ
popular subjects and to leave the
Italian and French pattern; also noteworthy for his instrumentation and
dramatic force; pupil of his father; c.
116 operas at Hamburg from 1694;
mgr. the opera there, ct. cond. and
later canon and cantor; c. also oratorios, masses, etc.

Kel'berine, Alex, Kiev, 1903—N. Y.,
Jan. 30, 1940; pupil of Busoni and
Siloti; toured in Europe; N. Y.
début, 1928; head of piano dept.,
Sternberg Cons., Phila.; has appeared as soloist with leading Amer.
orchs.

Keler-Bela (rightly **Adabert von Keler**)
(kā'-lĕr bā'-lä), Bartfeld, Hungary,
Feb. 13, 1820—Wiesbaden, Nov. 20,
1882; violinist, conductor and composer.

Kel'ler, (1) **Gottfried** (called **Godfrey**),
b. in Germany; teacher and writer in
London, 1707. (2) **Max**, Trostberg,
Bavaria, 1770—Altötting, 1855;
organist and composer. (3) **K.**,
Dessau, 1784—Schaffhausen, 1855;
ct.-flutist, conductor and composer.
(4) **F. A. E.**, inv., 1835 the unsucc.

"pupître-improvisateur" (v. D. D.), and pub. a method.

Kel'lermann, (1) **Berthold,** Nürnberg, March 5, 1853—Munich, June 14, 1926; p'anist; pupil of his parents and of Liszt, 1878–81 Wagner's secretary; 1882, teacher Munich R. Mus. Sch.; conductor and ct.-pianist. (2) **Chr.,** Randers, Jutland, 1815— Copenhagen, 1866; 'cellist and composer.

Kel'ley, Edgar Stillman, Sparta, Wis., April 14, 1857—N. Y., Nov. 12, 1944; composer; pupil of F. W. Merriam, Clarence Eddy, and N. Ledochowski (Chicago), and 1876–80 of Seifriz (comp.), Krüger and Speidel (pf.) and Fr. Finck (org.), at Stuttgart; organist at Oakland and San Francisco, Cal.; cond. comic opera, 1890–91; teacher pf., org., and comp. in various schools, incl. N. Y. Coll. of Mus.; critic for the *"Examiner,"* San Francisco, 1893–95; and essayist for various periodicals; 1896 lecturer on music for the Univ. of New York; 1901–02 at Yale University; 1902–10, taught in Berlin; then head of comp. dept., Cincinnati Cons.; later held comp. fellowship, Western Coll., Oxford, Ohio; c. *"Gulliver,"* humorous symph.; Chinese suite, *"Aladdin,"* for orch.; comic opera, *"Puritania"* (Boston, 1892); succ. incid. music to *"Macbeth"* and to *"Ben Hur,"* both for chorus and orch.; string-quartet and quintet; *"Wedding-Ode,"* for tenor solo, male chorus and orch. (MS.); 6 songs, *"Phases of Love"*; notable songs, *"Eldorado"* and *"Israfel,"* and others.

Kell'ner, (1) **David,** dir. German ch. and Th. at Stockholm, 1732. (2) **Jn. Chp.,** Gräfenroda, 1736—Cassel, 1803; ct.-organist and dram. composer.

Kel'logg, Clara Louise, Sumterville, S. C., July, 1842—New Hartford, Conn., May 13, 1916; noted soprano; 1856–61, studied in New York; début Acad. of Mus. (1861); début, London, at H. M's. Th. (1867), as "Margherita," with great succ.; sang in many capitals.

Kel'ly, Michael, Dublin, 1764—Margate, 1826; tenor and dram. composer; friend of Mozart; wrote musical "Reminiscences."

Kelterborn, Louis, Boston, April 28, 1891—Neuchâtel, July 9, 1933; composer and conductor; of Swiss

parentage; studied at Basel and Geneva Cons.; 1917–19, teacher of theory at Wolff Cons., Basel; after 1919, org. in Burgdorf; 1927, taught Neuchâtel Cons.; c. symph., choral and org. music.

Kempff, Wilhelm, b. Jüterbog, Germany, Nov. 25, 1895; composer; pianist; studied at Berlin Hochsch., winning both Mendelssohn prizes, 1917; toured as piano and org. virtuoso; 1924–29, dir. Stuttgart Cons.; c. orch., chamber and choral music.

Kemp'ter, (1) **K.,** Limbach, Bavaria, 1819—Augsburg, 1871; conductor. (2) **Lothar,** Lauingen, Bavaria, Feb. 5, 1844—Vitznau, July 14, 1918; cond., professor, and dram. composer; son and pupil of (3) **Fr. K.** (music-teacher); studied Munich Univ., then with Rheinberger; chorus-dir.; 1886 prof. of mus. theory, Zurich Mus. Sch.

Ken'nedy, Daisy, b. Burra-Burra near Adelaide, Australia, 1893; violinist; studied at Adelaide Cons. and with Sevcik, in Vienna Master School; toured Great Britain, Austria and U. S.; m. Benno Moiseiwitsch, pianist; divorced; (2) John Drinkwater, dramatist.

Ken'nedy-Fra'ser, Marjory, Perth, Scotland, Oct. 1, 1857—Edinburgh, Nov. 21, 1930; composer, alto singer and pianist; esp. known for her *"Songs of the Hebrides."*

Ker'by, Paul, b. South Africa; conductor, composer; studied at London R. Coll. of Mus. (Associate); began baton career at Capitol Theat., N. Y.; 1926, foreign adviser to Salzburg Fest.; res. in Vienna 1926–33, appearing as cond. with Philh. and Symph. in that city, also as guest in Budapest, Frankfort, Wiesbaden; mus. dir. in Vienna for Columbia Phon. Co.; 1933 led Chicago Symph. in Viennese concert as official repr. of Austrian gov't.; cond. at Chicago Op., 1933–34, own English translation of *"Le Coq d'Or"*; 1936, cond. of part of summer season N. Y. Philh. at Lewisohn Stadium.

Kerekjar'to, Duci de (rightly **Julius**), b. Budapest, 1898; violinist; studied at Acad. of Mus. there, also with Hubay; toured in Europe and after 1922 in America.

Kerle (kĕrl), **Jacques de,** b. Ypres,

Flanders, 16th cent.; conductor and composer.

Kerl(l) (Kherl, Cherl), Jn. Caspar, Gaimersheim, near Ingolstadt, 1627 —Munich, Feb. 13, 1693; organist, ct.-conductor, teacher, and notable composer of the "Missa nigra" (all in black notes), etc.

Kern, Jerome David, b. New York, Jan. 27, 1885; composer of operettas and musical comedies; studied with Gallico, Lambert and Pierce, also at N. Y. Coll. of Mus.; has produced since 1915 many operetta scores marked by pleasing melody and tasteful style, among which some of the outstanding were: *"Sally,"* *"Sunny," "Show Boat," "Music in the Air," "The Cat and the Fiddle," "Roberta,"* etc. d. N.Y.,Nov.11,1945.

Ker'nochan, Marshall Rutgers, b. New York, Dec. 14, 1880; composer, editor; pupil of Wetzler, Knorr and Goetschius; musical editor of *The Outlook* for a period; later pres. of Galaxy Music Corp., N. Y. publishing firm; c. (cantata) *"The Foolish Virgins"; "The Sleep of Summer"* for women's chorus and orch.; and numerous songs.

Kes (käs), Willem, Dordrecht, Holland, Feb. 16, 1856—Munich, Feb. 21, 1934; violinist; pupil of Böhm, etc., then of David, and, under royal patronage, of Wieniawski, and Joachim; 1876, leader Park Orch. and Felix Meritis Soc., Amsterdam; then cond. "Society" concerts, Dordrecht; 1883–95 cond. at Amsterdam; 1895 Glasgow orch.; 1898 cond. Philh. and dir. Moscow Cons.; 1905–26, dir. Coblenz Musikverein.

Kess'ler, (1) Fr., preacher and writer, (2) Fd., Frankfort-on-Main, 1793—1856; violinist and composer. (3) (rightly Kötzler) (kĕts'-lĕr), Jos. Chp., Augsburg, 1800—Vienna, 1872; teacher, organist and composer.

Ketel'bey, Albert William, b. Birmingham, England; composer and conductor; studied Trinity Coll., London; cond. at theatres there; was music ed. and also dir. of Columbia Gramophone Co.; c. pop. orch. works, of which *"In a Monastery Garden"* has wide currency.

Ket'ten, H., Baja, Hungary, 1848—Paris, 1883; pianist and composer.

Kettenus (kĕt-tā'-noos) (or kĕt-nüs), Aloys, Verviers, 1823—London, 1896; violinist and dram. composer.

Ketterer (kĕt-tŭ-rā), Eugène, Rouen, 1831—Paris, 1870; pianist and composer.

Keurvels (kŭr'-vĕls), Edw. H. J., Antwerp, 1853—Eeckeren, Jan. 19, 1916; pupil of Benoît; till 1882, chorusm. Royal Th.; cond. Nat. Flemish Th., Antwerp, c. operas, cantatas, etc.

Keussler (kois'-lĕr), Gerhard von, b. Schwanenburg, Livonia, July 6, 1874; pupil Leipzig Cons.; cond. 2 singing societies in Prague; 1918–31, Hamburg; after 1931 in Melbourne; c. orch. wks.; d. n. Dresden, 1949.

Kewitsch (Kiewics) (kā'-vĭtsh or kē'-vēch), (Karl) Theodor, Posilge, W. Prussia, Feb. 3, 1834—Berlin, July 18, 1903; son and pupil of an organist; studied with Maslon.

Khachatur'ian, Aram, b. Tiflis, 1903; pupil of Moscow Cons.; c. symphs., pf. concerto, etc.

Kiefer (kē'-fĕr), Heinrich, Nuremberg, Feb. 16, 1867—Eisenach, Aug. 15, 1922; 'cellist; pupil of Royal Cons., 1883 at Munich, 1884, Stuttgart, 1887–90, Frankfort-on-Main with Cossmann; 1896, soloist of Leipzig, Phil.; 1898 do. of Berlin Phil.; 1900, teacher at Stern Cons.; from 1902, co-founder of the Munich string quartet; toured widely.

Kiel (kēl), Fr., Puderbach, near Siegen (Rh. Prussia), Oct. 7, 1821—Berlin, Sept. 13, 1885; notable teacher and composer of classic sch.; self-taught as pianist and composer; vln.-pupil of Prince Karl von Wittgenstein and later, on stipend from Fr. Wm. IV., studied with Dehn; lived in Berlin; 1868 "Royal Prof."; c. oratorios, etc.

Kiene (kē'-nĕ). Vide BIGOT.

Kienle (kēn'-lĕ), Ambrosius, b. Siegmaringen, May 8, 1852; Benedictine monk and writer, d. Einsiedeln Convent, June 18, 1905.

Kienzl (kĕnts'-'l), Wm., b. Waizenkirchen, Jan. 17, 1857—Vienna, Oct. 3, 1941; pupil of Buwa, Uhl, Remy, Mortier de Fontain, Jos. Krejci, and later, Liszt; 1879 Dr. Phil. at Vienna; 1880 lectured at Munich; 1881–82 toured as pianist; 1883–84 chief cond. of German Opera, Amsterdam; 1886 m. the concert-singer Lili Hoke; 1886–90 dir. Styrian Musikverein at Graz and cond.; 1890–92, 1st cond. Hamburg Opera; 1892–93, at Munich; 1899–1901 at Graz as composer. His first opera *" Urvasi"* (Dresden,

1886) was succ., as was "*Heilmar, der Narr*" (Munich, 1892), and still more so "*Der Evangelimann*"; his opera, "*Kuhreigen*" (Vienna Volksoper, Nov. 25, 1911) a succ. in Europe; c. also "*Don Quichote*," a "musical tragi-comedy"; he finished Jensen's "*Turandot*," and c. also songs, etc.; author of books on music, volumes of memoirs, etc.

Kiepura (kē-ä-pōō'-rä), **Jan**; Polish tenor; after 1924 sang at Vienna State Op. with sensational succ., while still in his twenties; also heard as guest artist in many other Eur. cities; with Chicago Op. Co., 1930; has sung in motion pictures in England and Hollywood. Met. Op., 1937–8.

Kiesewetter (kē'-zĕ-vĕt-tĕr), **Raphael G.** (Edler von Wiesenbrunn), Holleschau, Moravia, 1773—Baden, near Vienna, 1850; important coll. of mus. MSS. and historian of many obscure periods, etc.; later ennobled.

Kiewics. Vide KEWITSCH.

Kilen'yi, Edward, b. Hungary, Jan. 25, 1884; composer; pupil of Nat'l. Mus. School, Rome, and Cologne Cons.; 1913, Mosenthal Fellow at Columbia Univ.; studied with Mason and Rybner; c. opera, overture, string quartet, vln. pieces and songs.

Kilpinen (kĭl-pē'-nĕn), **Yrö,** b. Helsingfors, Feb. 4, 1892; studied in native city, Vienna and Berlin; comp. of Lieder in romantic style, incl. more than 400 works, some to German texts.

Kind (kĭnt), **J. F.,** Leipzig, 1768—Dresden, 1843; librettist of "*Der Freischütz*," afterwards composer.

Kindermann (kĭnt'-ĕr-män), (1) **Jn. Erasmus,** b. Nürnberg, 1616—Venice, 1655; organist and composer. (2) **Aug.,** Potsdam, 1817—Munich, 1891; barytone. (3) **Hedwig,** daughter of above. Vide REICHER, K.

Kind'ler, Hans, b. Rotterdam, Jan. 8, 1893—Watch Hill, R. I., Aug. 29, 1949; studied at Rotterdam Cons.; also later with Mossel, Casals and Gerardy; served as teacher of 'cello at Scharwenka Cons., Berlin, and chief 'cellist at Charlottenburg Op.; had toured widely in Eur. countries; also in U. S., where he had been resident for some years; organised and cond. Nat'l. Symph. Orch., Washington, D. C., after 1930; also in Paris, Brussels, Vienna, Prague, Rome, Milan, and world première

of Stravinsky's "*Apollon Musagète*" at Washington Fest.

King, (1) **Wm.,** 1624—1680; Engl. organist and composer. (2) **Robt.,** d. after 1711; Engl. composer. (3) **Chas.,** Bury St. Edmunds, 1687—London, 1748; composer. (4) **Matthew Peter,** London, 1773—1823; theorist and dram. composer. (5) **Oliver A.,** London, 1855—Sept., 1923; pianist; pupil of W. H. Holmes, and Reinecke, Leipzig Cons.; pianist to the Princess Louise, 1879; toured Canada and New York; 1899 pf.-prof. at R. A. M.; c. cantatas, 147th Psalm, with orch. (Chester Festival, 1888), a symphony, "*Night.*" (6) **Julie.** Vide RIVE-KING.

King'ston, Morgan, Nottinghamshire, 1875—England, 1936; operatic tenor; in early life a coal miner; after period of struggle secured mus. education and made début at Queen's Hall, London, with succ., 1909; Amer. début as "Radames" at Century Theat., N. Y., 1913; mem. of Met. Op Co., for several seasons after 1916; also sang with Chicago Op. Co., and at Covent Garden, 1924–25.

Kinkeldey (kēn'-kĕl-dī), **Otto,** b. New York, Nov. 27, 1878; musicologist; M. A., N. Y. Univ. and Columbia; Ph. D., Univ. of Berlin; studied with MacDowell, Radecke, Thiel, Fleischer, Kretzschmar, Egidi, Wolf and Friedländer; was choir dir. and teacher, N. Y., 1898–1902; prof. org. and theory, Univ. of Breslau, 1909; royal Prussian prof., 1910–14; chief of mus. div., N. Y. Public Library 1915–23; prof. of mus., Cornell Univ., 1923–27; wrote and ed. scientific works on music.

Kipke (kĭp'-kĕ), **K.,** Breslau, Nov. 20, 1850—Leipzig, Nov. 14, 1923; editor.

Kip'nis, Alexander, b. Schitomir, Ukrainia, Feb. 1, 1891; bass; grad. Warsaw Cons., also studied Klindworth-Scharwenka Cons., Berlin, with Ernst Grenzebach; début, Hamburg Op., 1915; 1916–18 in Wiesbaden; after latter year sang at Deutsche Opernhaus, Berlin; toured America with Wagnerian Op. Co., 1923; sang for several years with Chicago Op., also in Munich, London, Milan, Paris, Buenos Aires; after 1932 engaged at Berlin State Op., and in 1936 at Vienna State Op., has a wide following as a concert singer. Mem. Met. Op. Co.

Kip'per, Hn., Coblenz, Aug. 27, 1826—Cologne, Oct. 25, 1910; pupil of Anschütz and H. Dorn; teacher and critic at Cologne; c. operettas.

Kircher (kĕrkh'-ĕr), **Athanasius**, Geisa (Buchow?), near Fulda, 1602—Rome, 1680; Jesuit archæologist and coll. of airs, some of them supposed to have curative effects.

Kirchhoff (kĕrkh'-hŏf), **Walther**, b. Berlin, March 17, 1879; tenor; studied with Lilli Lehmann and in Milan; 1906-1920, a leading heroic tenor of the Berlin Op., thereafter appearing in Buenos Aires and for several seasons at the Met. Op. House in Wagnerian rôles.

Kirchner (kĕrkh'-nĕr), (1) **Fz.**, Potsdam, Nov. 3, 1840—Berlin, May 14, 1907; pianist; pupil Kullak's Acad., where he taught 1864-89, then in the Mädchenheim sch., Berlin; c. pf.-pcs., etc. (2) **Hn.**, Wolfis, Jan. 23, 1861—Breslau, Dec. 26, 1928; tenor, and composer at Berlin. (3) **Theodor**, Neukirchen, Saxony, Dec. 10, 1823—Hamburg, Sept. 18, 1903; pupil of J. Knorr (pf.), K. F. Becker (org.), Jn. Schneider, and at Leipzig Cons.; 1843-62, organist Winterthur; 1862-72, teacher Zurich Mus. Sch., and cond.; 1873-75, dir. Würzburg Cons., Leipzig; 1883, Dresden; 1890, Hamburg; c. pf.-pcs., etc.

Kirnberger (kĕrn'-bĕrkh-ĕr), **Jn. Ph.**, Saalfeld, Thuringia, 1721—Berlin, 1783; eminent theorist, conductor and composer.

Kir'sten, Dorothy, American soprano; studied with Astolfo Pescia; début in Italy; sang Met. Op. from 1945, Mimi, Louise, Fiora, etc.

Kistler, Cyrill, Grossaitingen, near Augsburg, March 12, 1848—Kissingen, Jan. 1, 1907; studied with Wüllner, Rheinberger, and Fr. Lachner; 1883 teacher Sondershausen Cons.; since 1885 lived in Bad Kissingen as principal of a sch., pub. of text-books, incl. *"A Harmony, based on Wagner,"* etc.; c. 2 operas; a succ. "musical comedy" *"Eulenspiegel"* (Würzburg, 1893); etc.

Kist'ner, (1) **Fr.**, Leipzig, 1797—1844; pub. His son (2) **Julius** succeeded him.

Kittel (kĭt'-tĕl), (1) **Jn. Chr.**, Erfurt, Feb. 18, 1732—May 18, 1809; J. S. Bach's last pupil; organist in Erfurt; famous but ill-paid virtuoso and teacher. (2) **Bruno**, b. Entenbruch,

Posen, May 26, 1870; conductor; studied with Sauret and others in Berlin; early played as violinist; founded chorus named after him in Berlin, 1902, which has played important rôle in that city's music; cond. at R. Theat. there, later founded and dir. Brandenburg Cons.; after 1935, dir. of Stern Cons., Berlin.

Kittl (kĭt'-'l), **Jn. Fr.**, b. Schloss, Worlik, Bohemia, 1806—Lissa, 1868; conductor and dram. composer.

Kitzler (kĭts'-lĕr), **Otto**, Dresden, March 16, 1834—Graz, Sept. 6, 1915; pupil of Schneider, Otto, and Kummer ('cello), later of Servais and Fétis, Brussels Cons.; 'cellist in opera-orchs. at Strassburg and Lyons; cond. at various theatres; 1868 dir. Brünn Mus. Soc. and Mus. Sch., also cond. of the Männergesangverein; he was Anton Bruckner's teacher; pub. orch.-mus., pf.-pcs., etc.

Kjerulf (k'yä'-roolf), **Halfdan**, Christiania, Sept. 15, 1815—Bad Grafsee, Aug. 11, 1868, composer; gave up theology for music; studied at Leipzig; settled in Christiania; c. songs and pf.-pcs.

Klafsky (Lohse-Klafsky) (kläf'-shkĭ), **Katharina**, St. Johann, Hungary, 1855—Hamburg, 1896; sopr.; pupil of Mme. Marchesi; sang in comic opera chorus, later leading Wagnerian rôles in Europe and America; m. Otto Lohse.

Klatte (klä'-tĕ), **Wilhelm**, b. Bremen, Feb. 13, 1870; author biog. of Schubert, etc.

Klauser (klow'-zĕr), (1) **K.** (of Swiss parents), St. Petersburg, Aug. 24, 1823—Farmington, Conn., Jan. 9, 1905; chiefly self-taught; 1850, New York; 1856, Mus.-Dir. Farmington Cons.; editor. (2) **Julius**, New York, July 5, 1854—Milwaukee, 1907; pupil of Wenzel, Leipzig Cons.; mus.-teacher, Milwaukee; pub. *"The Septonate and the Centralization of the Tonal System"* (1890).

Klauwell (klow'-vĕl), (1) **Ad.**, Langensalza, Thuringia, 1818 — Leipzig, 1879; teacher, writer, etc. (2) **Otto**, Langensalza, April 7, 1851—Cologne, May 12, 1917; nephew of above; pupil of Schulpforta, and at Leipzig Cons.; Dr. Phil.; 1875 prof. Cologne Cons.; 1885, dir. Teachers' Seminary; writer and dram. composer.

Klee (klā), **L.**, Schwerin, April 13, 1846

—Berlin, April 14, 1920; pupil of
Th. Kullak, and until 1875, teacher
Kullak's Acad., then dir. of his own
sch.; "Musik-Direktor," writer and
editor.

Kleeberg (klä-bǎr), **Clotilde**, Paris,
June 27, 1866—Brussels, Feb. 7,
1909; pianist; pupil of Mmes. Rety
and Massart at the Cons., won 1st
prize; début, at 12, with Pasdeloup
orch.; toured Europe with great
succ.; 1894, Officier de l'Académie.

Kleefeld (klä'-fĕlt), **Wilhelm**, b. Mayence, April 2, 1868; author and
comp.; pupil of Radecke, Härtel and
Spitta; 1891 cond. in Mayence, etc.;
1897 Ph. D., 1898-'01 teacher at the
Klindworth-Scharwenka Cons.; c.
opera "*Anarella*" (Königsberg, 1896),
string suite, etc.

Kleemann (klä'-män), **K.**, Rudolstadt,
Sept. 9, 1842—Gera, Feb. 18, 1923;
pupil of Müller, 1878, studied in
Italy; then 2nd opera cond. and ct.
mus.-dir. Dessau; c. 2 symphonies,
etc.

Kleffel (klĕf'-fĕl), **Arno**, Possneck,
Thuringia, Sept. 4, 1840—near Berlin, July 15, 1913; studied Leipzig
Cons., and with Hauptmann; 1863–
67, dir. Riga Mus. Soc.; then th.
cond. in Cologne; later teacher of
theory, Stern's Cons., Berlin; 1895,
professor; c. opera, Christmas legend,
overtures, etc.

Kleiber (klī'-bĕr), **Erich**, b. Vienna,
Aug. 5, 1890; conductor; served in
theatres at Darmstadt, 1912–19;
Barmen-Elberfeld, Düsseldorf and
Mannheim; general mus. director at
Berlin 1923–35, incl. chief conductorship of one of the city's State Op.
Houses and symph. concerts; also
cond. as guest in Rome, Paris, Barcelona, Budapest, Prague, Buenos
Aires, Copenhagen, Bucharest, Vienna, Leningrad; N. Y. Philh. Orch.,
1930–31; in Feb., 1935, he resigned
Berlin post as consequence of artistic
differences with Nat'l. Socialist regime and took up res. in Mondsee,
near Salzburg, Austria; in the
autumn of that year he was invited
to direct German opera at La Scala,
and later was active in Buenos Aires.

Klein (klīn), (1) **Jn. Jos.**, Arnstadt,
1740—Kahla, near Jena, 1823; writer.
(2) **Bd.**, Cologne, 1793—Berlin, 1832;
teacher and composer. (3) **Joseph**,
1801—1862, bro. of above; lived as
composer in Berlin and Cologne.

(4) **Bruno Oscar**, Osnabrück, Hanover, June 6, 1856—New York,
June 22, 1911; son and pupil of
(5) **Carl K.** (organist Osnabrück
Cath.); (4) studied at Munich Cons.,
1878, gave concerts in America; 1883,
New York; 1884, chief pf.-teacher
Convent of the Sacred Heart; also,
1884–94, organist St. Francis Xavier,
and 1887–92, prof. of cpt. and comp.
Nat. Cons.; 1894–95, gave concerts
in Germany; prod. succ. gr. opera,
"*Kenilworth*" (Hamburg, 1895), vln.-
sonata, etc. (6) **Hermann**, Norwich,
Eng., 1856—London, March 10,
1934; critic and teacher; studied law;
1874 singing with Manuel Garcia;
1881-1901, critic London *Sunday
Times;* 1887, prof. of singing at
Guildhall; 1896, dir. opera-class (vice
Weist Hill); 1901-09, taught N. Y.;
then again in London; author, "*30
Years of Musical Life in London,*"
"*The Reign of Patti,*" etc.

Kleinmichel (klīn'-mǐkh-'l), (1) **Hermann**; (?) 1816—Hamburg, 1894;
bandmaster. (2) **Richard**, Posen,
Dec. 31, 1846—Berlin, 1901; son and
pupil of above; studied also at Hamburg and at Leipzig Cons.; teacher,
Hamburg; 1876, Leipzig; 1882, mus.
dir. City Th.; c. 2 operas; 2 symphonies; chamber-music, valuable
études, etc.; m. a dramatic soprano,
(3) **Clara Monhaupt**.

Klem'perer, Otto, b. Breslau, May 15,
1885; conductor; studied Frankfort
Cons., with P. Scharwenka and
Pfitzner; after 1907 cond. at Prague
Op., on recommendation of Mahler;
Hamburg Op., 1909, also in Bremen,
Strasbourg and Cologne (1917–24);
general mus. director, Wiesbaden,
1924–27; similar post at State Op. on
Platz der Republik, Berlin, 1927–31,
and that on Unter den Linden,
1931–33, where he inst. a regime of
notable enterprise in the prod. of
modern works and novel scenic dress,
also cond. symph. concerts; resigned
Berlin posts on accession to political
power of Nat'l. Socialists; after 1935,
cond. Los Angeles Philh. Orch., also
led part of season with N. Y. Philh.
Orch., 1934 and 1935; c. opera,
choral works and songs.

Kle'nau, Paul von, b. Copenhagen,
Feb. 11, 1883; composer; pupil of
Bruch, Thuille and Schillings; theatre
cond., Freiburg, 1897–1908, and after
1920 of Copenhagen Philh.; c.

(operas) "*Sulamith*" (Munich, 1913); "*Kjartan und Gudrun*" (Mannheim, 1918); "*The School for Scandal*" (after Sheridan), prod. Frankfort; (dance-play) "*Klein Idas Blumen*" (Stuttgart, 1916); 4 symphonies, (orch.) "*Paolo and Francesca*"; "*Gespräch mit dem Tod*" for alto and orch.; "*Ebba Skammelsen,*" ballade for barytone and orch.; piano quintet, string quartet, songs.

Klengel (klĕng'-ĕl), (1) **Aug. Alex.** ("Kanon-Klengel"), Dresden, 1783—1852; organist and composer of an attempt to rival Bach's "Well-tempered Clavichord," etc. (2) **Paul,** b. Leipzig, May 13, 1854—April 24, 1935; violinist; Dr. Phil., Leipzig; 1881–86, cond., Leipzig, "Euterpe" concerts; 1888–93, 2nd ct.-cond., Stuttgart; cond. "Arion," Leipzig; 1898, New York. (3) **Julius,** Leipzig, Sept. 24, 1859—Oct. 26, 1933; bro. of above; 'cellist, pupil of Emil Hegar ('cello) and Jadassohn (comp.); 1st 'cello in Gewandhaus Orch., and teacher at the Cons.; composer.

Klenov'ski, Nicholas Semenovich, b. Odessa, 1857; pupil Moscow Cons.; leader of private concerts there 1883–93; when he became cond. at the Imperial Theatre, then a teacher at Tiflis till 1902, then assistant cond. of the Imperial Chapel at St. Petersburg; c. ballets, "*Hasheesh,*" Moscow, 1885; "*Salanga*" (St. Petersburg, 1900); orch. suites, cantatas; d. Petrograd, July 6, 1915.

Kliebert (klē'-bĕrt), **K.,** Prague, Dec. 13, 1849—Würzburg, May 23, 1907; Ph. D., Prague; pupil of Rheinberger and Wüllner, Munich; 1876, dir. R. Sch. of Mus., Würzburg.

Klindworth (klĭnt'-vôrt), **K.,** Hanover, Sept. 25, 1830—Oranienburg (Berlin), July 27, 1916; pianist, eminent teacher and editor; self-taught pianist; at 6 played in public; at 17, cond. of an opera-troupe; 1849, teacher at Hanover; 1852, a Jewish woman advanced him money to study with Liszt; 1854. music-début, London; Wagner admired him, and they became friends. 1854–68, he gave concerts and lessons, London; then pf.-prof. Imp. Cons., Moscow; while here he completed two monumental works, his pf.-scores of Wagner's "*Ring des Nibelungen,*" and a rev. ed. of Chopin. 1882–92, cond. at Berlin the Wagnerverein

and (with Joachim and Wüllner) the Philharm. Concerts. Est. a "Klavierschule" (Sch. of Pf.-playing), later united with the Scharwenka Cons., 1893, when he retired to Potsdam; composed piano-pieces.

Kling, H., Paris, Feb. 14, 1842—Geneva, May 2, 1918; prof. Geneva Cons. and teacher in city schools; writer and dram. composer.

Klitzsch (klĭtsh), **K. Emanuel,** Schönhaide, Saxony, 1812—Zwickau, 1889; writer and composer.

Klose (klō'-zĕ), **Friedrich,** b. Karlsruhe, Nov. 29, 1862; composer; pupil of Lachner, Ruthardt and Bruckner; 1907–19, teacher of comp. at the Akademie der Tonkunst, Munich; c. dramatic symph. "*Ilsebill,*" or "*The Fisher and His Wife*" (Karlsruhe, 1903); mass with orch.; symph. poem in three parts "*Das Leben ein Traum*" with organ and women's chorus, chamber, orch. and vocal music; d. n. Lugano, Dec. 24, 1942.

Klosé (klō-zā), **Hyacinthe Eléonore,** Isle of Corfu, 1808—Paris, 1880; clarinettist and prof., Paris Cons.; composer.

Klotz (klôts), family of Bavarian violinmakers at Mittenwald. The first (1) **Ægidius,** sen., the best; another, (2) **Matthias** (1653—1743). Matthias's sons were (3) **Sebastian** and (4) **Joseph,** and their sons (5) **Georg,** (6) **Karl,** (7) **Michael,** and (8) **Ægidius, Jr.**

Klughardt (klookh'-härt), **Aug.** (**Fr. Martin**), Köthen, Nov. 30, 1847—Dessau, Aug. 3, 1902; pupil of Blassmann and Reichel, Dresden; ct.-cond. at Neustrelitz and later at Dessau; prod. 4 operas, the symphonic poem, "*Leonore*"; 3 symph. (1. "*Waldweben*"), overtures "*Im Frühling*"; "*Sophonisbe,*" "*Siegesouvertüre,*" and "*Festouverture,*" etc.

Knabe (k'nä'-bĕ), (1) **Wm.,** Kreuzburg, Prussia, 1797—Baltimore, 1864; founder of pf.-factory at Baltimore, Md.; succeeded by his sons (2) **Wm.** (1841—89) and (3) **Ernest,** and they by (4) **Ernest J.** (b. July 5, 1869) and (5) **Wm.** (b. March 23, 1872). In 1908 the business was amalgamated with the Amer. Piano Co. of N. Y.

Knap'pertsbusch, Hans, b. Elberfeld, Germany, March 12, 1888; conductor; studied Bonn Univ. and Cologne Cons.; cond. in Elberfeld,

Leipzig, Dessau, and 1920–35 succeeded Bruno Walter as general music director of Munich Op.; he resigned this post following controversy with Nat'l. Socialist authorities as to his political views, and in 1936 was active as guest cond. at Vienna State Op.

Knecht (knĕkht), **Justin H.**, Biberach, Würtemberg, Sept. 30, 1752—Dec. 1, 1817; rival of Vogler as organist, and important theorist, conductor and composer.

Kneisel (knī'-zĕl), (1) **Fz.** (of German parents), Bucharest, Jan. 26, 1865—Boston, March 27, 1926; violinist; pupil of Grün and Hellmesberger, Vienna; *Konzertmeister*, Hofburg Th.-Orch.; then of Bilse's Orch., Berlin; 1885–1903, concertm. and soloist, Boston Symphony Orch.; 1887, founded the "Kneisel Quartet," which played with greatest succ. in America and Europe until 1917; 1902, cond. Worcester (Massachusetts) Festival; after 1905, prof. of vln., Inst. of Mus. Art, N. Y. (2) **Frank**, his son, and (3) **Marianne**, his daughter, both accomplished string players.

Kniese (knē'-zĕ), **Julius**, Roda, near Jena, Dec. 21, 1848—Dresden, April 22, 1905; pianist and organist; pupil of Stade, at Altenburg, Brendel and C. Riedel, Leipzig; 1884–89, mus.-dir. at Aix; 1882, chorusm. at Bayreuth, where he lived; 1889, dir. Preparatory Sch. for Stage-Singers; c. opera, "*König Wittichis*"; symphonic poem, "*Frithjof*," etc.

Knip'per, Lyof, b. Tiflis, Dec. 16, 1898; composer; studied in Russia, also with Jarnach in Berlin; c. works in modern style, some in satirical vein, incl. (operas) "*Til Eulenspiegel*," "*Cities and Years*"; (orch.) "*Legend of a Plaster God*" (Phila. Orch., 1930), symphonies; chamber music; (ballet) "*Santanella*."

Knoch (knôkh), **Ernst**, b. Carlsruhe, Aug. 1, 1875; conductor; pupil of Mottl; esp. known as interpreter of Wagner works; 1914, cond. for Century Op. Co.; 1916, Ravinia Park Op.; also with many other touring organisations in U. S.

Knorr (knôr), (1) **Julius**, Leipzig, 1807—1861; pf.-teacher and deviser of standard rudimentary exercises; pub. "*Methods*," etc. (2) **Ivan**, Mewe, West Prussia, Jan. 3, 1853—Frank-

fort-on-Main, Jan. 22, 1916; studied Leipzig Cons. with Richter, Reinecke; 1883, prof. of theory, Hoch Cons. Frankfort-on-Main; c. 2 suites, etc.

Knote, Heinrich, b. Munich, Nov. 20, 1870; tenor; studied with Kirschner in native city, where he was mem. of Op., 1892–1914; guest appearances in America, incl. Met. Op. Co., 1903; also at Charlottenburg Op., and after 1924 again in Munich; one of leading Wagner tenors; d. Garmisch, 1952.

Kny'vett, (1) **Chas.**, England, 1752—London, 1822; tenor and organist. (2) **Chas.**, 1773—1852; son of above; organist and teacher. (3) **Wm.**, 1779—Ryde, 1856; bro. of above; composer and conductor.

Kobbé (kôb-bā), **Gustav**, New York, March 4, 1857—Bay Shore, N. Y., July 27, 1918; studied pf. and comp. with Adolf Hagen, Wiesbaden; later with Jos. Mosenthal, New York; 1877, graduated Columbia Coll.; 1879, Sch. of Law; served as music critic on various N. Y. papers; wrote "*Wagner's Life and Works*" "*The Ring of the Nibelung*," etc.; teacher; pub. a few songs.

Kobelius (kō-bā'-lĭ-oos), **Jn. Augustin**, Wählitz, near Halle, 1674—Weisenfels, 1731; ct.-cond. and dram. composer.

Koch (kōkh), (1) **H. Chp.**, Rudolstadt, 1749—1816; violinist; writer and composer. (2) **Eduard Emil**, Schloss Solitude, near Stuttgart, 1809—Stuttgart, 1871; writer. (3) **Emma**, b. Mayence; pianist; pupil of Liszt, Moszkowski, etc.; 1898, teacher Stern Cons. (4) **Fr.**, Berlin, July 3, 1862—Jan. 30, 1927; pupil of the Hochschule; conductor, 'cellist and c. of operas, "*Die Halliger*" and "*Lea*" (Cologne, 1896), etc.; 1901, mem. of the Prussian Acad. of Arts; 1917, head of theory dept., Berlin Hochsch.

Kochanski (kō-hän'-skē), **Paul**, Odessa, 1887—New York, Jan. 12, 1934; violinist; studied with Mlynarski, and César Thomson, Brussels Cons., début with Musical Soc., Warsaw, 1898; toured Europe and U. S.; estab. high reputation as solo and chamber music player; was dir. of vln. dept., Juilliard School of Mus., N. Y., until his death.

Köchel (kĕkh'-'l), **L. Ritter von**, Stein-on-Danube, Lower Austria, 1800—Vienna, 1877; writer.

Kocher (kōkh'-ĕr), **Conrad**, Ditzingen,

near Stuttgart, 1786 — Stuttgart, 1872; mus.-dir. and dram. composer.

Kocian (kō'-tsĭ-ŭn), **Jaroslav**, b. Wildenschwert, Bohemia, Feb. 22, 1884; violinist, son and pupil of a school-teacher; studied violin at 3½ years; at 12, Prague Cons. under Sevcik (vln.), and Dvořák (comp.); début, 1901; toured Europe with much succ.; 1902, Amer.; d. Prague, 1950.

Koczalski (kō-chäl'-shkĭ), **Raoul (Armand G.)**, b. Warsaw, Jan. 3, 1885; studied pf. with his mother; then with Godowski at Warsaw; at 4 played in public with great succ.; at 7, played at Vienna, St. Petersburg, etc.; at one time ct.-pianist to the Shah of Persia; c. 1-act operas, "*Hagar*," "*Rymond*," etc.; d. 1949.

Kodaly (kō-dä'-ē), **Zoltan**, b. Kecskemet, Hungary, Dec. 16, 1882; composer; Ph. D., Budapest Univ., 1905; studied Budapest Acad., under Koessler; made researches in folk music of his country, incl. about 3500 melodies; prof. of comp. at Budapest Acad. since 1907; his works incl. modern harmonic treatment, with some elements of atonality, and abound in colourful folk inspiration and brilliant orchestration; c. (comic folk opera) "*Hary Janos*"; (Budapest, 1926); (opera) "*Szekely Spinning Room*"; a highly praised "*Psalmus Hungaricus*" for tenor solo, chorus and orch., heard widely in Europe, also in U. S.; "*Summer Evening*," tone poem; "*Dances of Marosszek*" for orch. (perf. by N. Y. Philh.); Serenade for 2 violins and viola; 2 string quartets, 'cello sonata; songs with orch., choruses, etc.

Koechlin (kĕsh'-lĕn), **Charles**, b. Paris, Nov. 27, 1867; studied Paris Cons., c. ballets, choral and chamber music, orch. works, suites for various instruments; choral, piano and org. pieces, songs; contrib. to Lavignac's Encycl.; d. Canaden, Dec. 31, 1950.

Koemmenich (kĕm'-mĕ-nĭkh), **Louis**, Elberfeld, Germany, Oct. 4, 1866— New York, 1922; pupil of Anton Krause, Barmen and at Kullak's Acad. 1890, New York, as conductor and teacher; since 1894, cond. Brooklyn Sängerbund; 1898, organised an Oratorio Soc.; 1912–17, cond. N. Y. Oratorio Soc.; 1913–19, Mendelssohn Glee Club; after 1917 New Beethoven Soc.; c. a cantata, choruses. etc.

Koenen (kā'-nĕn), (1) **Fr.**, Rheinbach, near Bonn, 1829—Cologne, 1887; conductor and composer. (2) (koo'-nĕn), **Tilly**, b. Java, Dec. 25, 1873, of Dutch parents, her father a cavalry general and Governor of the Province; pupil of the Amsterdam Cons. and with Cornelie van Zanten; 1899, sang in London, Berlin, etc.; toured U. S.; d. Amsterdam, 1941.

Koessler (kĕs'-lĕr), **Hans**, Waldeck, Jan. 1, 1853—Ansbach, May 23, 1926; organist; pupil Munich Cons.; 1877 teacher at Dresden Cons., and cond. of the Liedertafel; 1882–1908, teacher at Budapest Landesakad.; c. Psalm for 16 voices, winning a prize at Vienna; a symph., an opera "*Der Münzenfranz*" (Strassburg, 1902), etc.; a personal friend of Brahms and an eminent teacher, numbering among his pupils a whole generation of younger Hungarian comps.; after 1908 he was pensioned and lived in Berlin and other cities, but returned to Budapest to cond. a master class in comp., 1920–25.

Kofler (kôf'-lĕr), **Leo**, Brixen, Austrian Tyrol, March 13, 1837—New Orleans, 1908; from 1877, organist and choirm. of St. Paul's Chapel, New York; writer and composer.

Kogel (kō'-gĕl), **Gv.**, Leipzig, Jan. 16, 1849—Frankfort-on-Main, Nov. 13, 1921; pupil of the Cons.; th.-cond. various cities; 1891–1902, cond. Museum Concerts, Frankfort; editor and composer.

Köhler (kā'-lĕr), (1) **Ernst**, Langenbielau, Silesia, 1799—Breslau, 1847; organist and composer. (2) (**Chr.**) **Louis (H.)**, Brunswick, 1820—Königsberg, 1886; pianist, teacher and dramatic composer, also notable critic.

Kohut (kō-hoot'), **Ad.**, Mindszent, Hungary, Nov. 10, 1847—Berlin, Sept. 21, 1917; writer.

Kolachev'ski, Michail Nicolaievich, b. Oct. 2, 1851; pupil Leipzig Cons.; c. "*Ukranian*" symph. and church music; d. (?).

Ko'lar, Victor, b. Budapest, Feb. 12, 1888; composer, violinist, conductor; grad. Prague Cons., 1904; mem. N. Y. Symph., 1907–19; assoc. cond. Detroit Symph., after 1919; c. symphonic and chamber music.

Kolbe (kôl'-bĕ), **Oskar**, Berlin, 1836—1878; composer and writer.

Kol'berg, Oskar, near Radom, 1815—Warsaw, 1890; comp. of Polish dances and songs.

Ko'lisch, Rudolf, b. Klamm, Austria, June 20, 1896; violinist; pupil of Egghard, Grädener, Sevcik, Schreker and Schönberg; studied at Vienna Akad. für Musik and Univ.; after 1922 leader of the Kolisch String Quartet (with Felix Khuner, E. Lehner and B. Heifetz), which toured with succ. in Europe and after 1933 in U. S. (début Coolidge Fest., Washington, D. C.)

Kollmann (kŏl'-män), **Aug. Fr. K.,** Engelbostel, Hanover, 1756—London, 1829; organist, theorist and composer.

Kömpel (kĕm'-pĕl), **Aug.,** Brückenau, 1831—Weimar, 1891; violinist.

Kom'zak, (1) **Karl,** Prague, Nov. 8, 1850—Baden near Vienna, April 23, 1905; cond. of military bands; composer of many pop. dances, operettas, etc. His son (2) **Karl,** Jr., d. Vienna, Sept. 5, 1924, also a comp. of dance music.

Königslöw (kā'-nĭkhs-lāv), (1) **Jn. Wm. Cornelius von,** Hamburg, 1745—1833; organist and composer. (2) **Otto Fr. von,** b. Hamburg, Nov. 13, 1824—Bonn, Oct. 6, 1898; pupil of Fr. Pacius and K. Hafner, and at Leipzig Cons.; toured for 12 years; 1858–81, leader Gürzenich Orch., Cologne; vice-dir. and vln.-prof. at the Cons.; Royal Prof.; retired to Bonn.

Königsperger (kā'-nĭkhs-pĕrkh-ĕr), **Marianus,** Roding, Bavaria, Dec. 4, 1708 — Ratisbon, Oct. 9, 1769. Benedictine monk who devoted the proceeds of his very successful works to the Abbey; c. church music, also operas.

Koning (kō'-nĭng), **David,** Rotterdam, 1820—Amsterdam, 1876; pianist, conductor and composer.

Konradin (kŏn'-rät-ēn), **K. Fd.,** St. Helenenthal, near Baden, 1833—Vienna, 1884; dram. composer.

Kontski (kônt'-shkē), (1) **Antoine de,** Cracow, Oct. 27, 1817—Ivanitchi, Novgorod, Russia, Dec. 2, 1899; pianist; pupil of Markendorf and Field; made v. succ. tours; teacher, London; lived in Buffalo, N. Y.; at 80 toured round the world; c. an opera, an oratorio; symph.; pop. pf.-pcs., incl. "*Le Réveil du Lion,*" etc. (2) **Chas.,** 1815—Paris, 1867; com-

poser. (3) **Apollinaire de,** Warsaw, 1825—1879; violinist; bro. and pupil of (2). (4) **Stanislas,** Cracow, Oct. 8, 1820—?; bro. of above; vln.-teacher and composer, Paris.

Koptjajev (kŏpt'-yä-yĕf), **Alexander Petrovich,** b. St. Petersburg, Oct. 12, 1868; author and composer of "*Oriental Dances*" and "*Elégie,*" for orch., etc.

Kopylow (kō'-pē-lŏf), **Alex.,** St. Petersburg, July 14, 1854—Feb. 20, 1911; pupil of Liadoff and Rimsky-Korsakoff; teacher of singing at the Imp. Court Chapel; c. finale for chorus and orch. to "*The Bride of Messina*"; also orch. and chamber music, piano works, etc.

Korestchenko (kŏr-ĕsht-chĕn'-kō), **Arseni Nicholaievich,** Moscow, Dec. 18, 1870—1918; pupil Cons., winning a gold medal in 1891; later teacher there and in the School of the Synod; c. 1-act opera "*Belshazzar's Feast*" (Moscow, 1892), 2-act "*The Angel of Death,*" "*The Ice Palace*" (Moscow 1892); two "*Symphonic Pictures,*" "*Symphonie Lyrique*" (op. 23), chamber music, etc.

Kor'ganov, Gennari Ossipovich, Kwarelia, May 12, 1858—Rostov, April 12, 1890; pianist and composer; pupil of Leipzig and St. Petersburg Cons.; c. piano pieces, etc.

Kornauth (kŏr'-naut), **Egon,** b. Olmütz, Austria, May 14, 1891; composer; studied at Vienna Acad. of Mus.; with Fuchs, Schreker, Schmidt, also at Univ. there with Guido Adler; Ph. D.; toured America as accompanist, 1910; solo répetiteur at Vienna Op.; teacher and lecturer; c. many works in neo-Romantic style, esp. chamber, orch. and vocal music.

Körner (kĕr'-nĕr), **Gotthilf Wm.,** Teicha, near Halle, 1809—Erfurt, 1865; publisher.

Korn'gold, Erich Wolfgang, b. Brünn, May 29, 1897; composer and pianist; son of Julius K., Viennese mus. critic; at early age showed remarkable prowess as a comp.; at a concert in Berlin, March, 1911, his trio in D Major, op. I., composed at the age of 13, was played; also portions of two piano sonatas, and a series of "*Fairy Pictures*"; he c. a ballet given at the Royal Opera and elsewhere; trio (Rosé Quartet, Berlin); serenade and pantomime, "*The Snowman*" (London, 1912); his one-act operas,

"Violanta" and *"Der Ring des Polykrates,"* were given in Munich, 1916; the former work was sung at the Met. Op., 1928, and the latter prod. by the Phila. Civic Op. 1927–28; a marked succ. was won by his *"Die tote Stadt"* (Hamburg, 1920; Met. Op. Co., 1921, with Jeritza in chief rôle); this work showing a somewhat modernistic idiom; his opera *"Das Wunder der Heliane"* (1927) was sung on a number of Central Eur. stages; **K.** was a cond. in 1919–20 at the Hamburg Stadttheat.; and for a time after 1927 taught at the Vienna Akad. für Tonkunst; he modernised a number of Johann Strauss operettas and cond. them in Berlin and elsewhere; after 1934 he was active as comp. for motion pictures in Hollywood; c. also incid. music to *"Much Ado about Nothing"*; Sinfonietta; string sextet; 2 piano sonatas; piano trio; vln. sonata, etc.

Kort'schak, Hugo, b. Graz, Austria, Feb. 24, 1884; violinist, conductor; grad. Prague Cons., studied with Sevcik; début, Prague, 1904; mem. Berlin Philh., Frankfort Museum Quartet, Chicago Symph., founded Kortschak Quartet (later reorg. as Berkshire String Quartet), which played at Berkshire Fests., also appeared as soloist; prof. vln., Yale Univ. School of Mus.

Koschat (kō'-shät), **Thos.,** Viktring, near Klagenfurt, Aug. 8, 1845—Vienna, May 19, 1914; studied science at Vienna; joined the ct.-opera chorus, soon became leader; 1874, joined cath.-choir; 1878, the Hofkapelle. 1871, he began the pub. of original poems in Carinthian dialect, which he set to music for male quartets; these had great popularity; 1875, founded the "Kärnthner Quintett"; prod. 4-act "Volksstück mit Gesang," *"Die Rosenthaler Nachtigall,"* and succ. "Singspiel" *"Der Burgermeister von St. Anna,"* etc.

Köselitz (kā'-zĕ-lĭts), **H.,** Annaberg, Saxony, 1854—1918; pupil of Richter, Leipzig Cons. and Nietzsche, Basel, lived in Italy; under the name **"Peter Gast"** prod. opera, *"Die Heimliche Ehe"* (Danzig, 1891), etc.

Kosleck (kôs'-lĕk), **Julius,** Neugard, Pomerania, Dec. 1, 1825—Berlin, Nov. 5, 1905; trumpet- and cornet-virtuoso; member of the royal band, Berlin; teacher.

Kossmaly (kôs'-mä-lē), **Karl,** 1812—Stettin, 1893; teacher, conductor and writer.

Köstlin (kĕst'-lēn), (1) **K. Rheinhold,** Urach, Würtemberg, 1819—1894; prof. and writer. (2) **H. Ad.,** b. Tübingen, Sept. 4, 1846—Kannstadt, June 4, 1907; preacher; 1875 he united the choirs of three towns, which became in 1877 the Würtemberg Evangelical "Kirchengesangverein," and which he cond.; 1891, Darmstadt; writer.

Kotchetov, Nikolai, b. Oranienbaum, 1864; composer.

Kothe (kō'-tĕ), **Bd.,** Gröbnig, Silesia, 1821—Breslau, 1897; teacher and composer.

Köttlitz (kĕt'-lĭts), (1) **Ad.,** Trier, 1820—Siberia, 1860; dir. and composer. His wife (2) **Clothilde** (née **Ellendt**), 1822–67, was an excellent singing-teacher.

Ko(t)že'luch (kôt'-zĕ-lookh or kō'-zhĕ-lookh), (1) **Jn. A.** (rightly **Jan Antonin**), Wellwarn, Bohemia 1738—Prague, 1814; mus.-dir.; conductor and dram. composer. (2) **Ld. Anton,** Wellwarn, 1748—Vienna, 1818; pupil and cousin of above; conductor, teacher and composer.

Kotzolt (kôt'-tsôlt), **H.,** Schnellwalde, Upper Silesia, 1814—Berlin, 1881; conductor and composer.

Kotzschmar (kôtsh'-mär), **Hn.,** Finsterwalde, Germany, July 4, 1829—Portland, Me., 1909; his father taught him various instrs.; studied also with his uncle Hayne and Jul. Otto, Dresden; in the opera-orch.; 1848, America, with Saxonia Band; from 1849 lived Portland, Me.; cond. "Haydn Assoc.," and was long active as organist there; a memorial org. in his honour was presented to the city by Cyrus H. K. Curtis.

Koussevitzky (kōō-sĕ-vēt'-skē), **Serge,** b. Vishni Volochok, Russia, June 30, 1874—Boston, June 4, 1951; grad. Moscow Cons.; hon. Mus. D., Brown Univ., 1926; after 1900 prof. at the Philh. Mus. School, Moscow; began career as double-bass virtuoso in the Imp. Theat. orch. there; in 1910 founded his own symph. orch. which he led until 1918, making 3 tours of Russia with it on chartered steamer down the Volga; his reputation as a cond. grew rapidly when he led the Koussevitzky Concerts in Paris after 1920, winning rank as one of the most brilliant leaders of the day, and making guest appearances in Germany, Italy, England and Spain; since 1924, cond. of the Boston Symph.; where he had maintained an aggressive campaign for the introd. of outstanding modern compositions; founder publishing house for Russian music in Paris, 1909; French Legion of Honour, 1924; cond. Berkshire Fest., Stockbridge, Mass., after 1935.

Kovařovic (kō-vär'-zhō-vĭts), **Karl**, Prague, Dec. 9, 1862—Dec. 6, 1920; pupil of the Cons., and of Fibich; from 1899 cond. at the Bohemian Landestheater in Prague; where many of his operas given from 1884 to *"Fraquita"* (1902); c. ballet *"Hasheesh,"* piano concerto, etc.

Kowalski (kō-väl'-shkĭ), **H.,** b. Paris, 1841—Bordeaux, 1916; pianist; pupil of Marmontel (pf.) and Keber (comp.); composer.

Kozlovski (kôs-l'yôf'-ski), **Joseph Antonovich,** Warsaw, 1757—St. Petersburg, Feb. 11, 1831; teacher in the household of Pr'nce Oginski; went to the Turkish war, attracting the notice of Prince Potemkin, who took him to St. Petersburg, where he became director of the court balls, and c. a war song which was for a long time the Russian national anthem; c. also requiem to the Polish King Stanislas, and the Czar Alexander I, etc.

Kraft (kräft), (1) **Anton,** Rokitzan, 1752—Vienna, 1820; 'cellist and composer. (2) **Nicolaus,** Esterháza, Hungary, 1778—Stuttgart, 1853; 'cellist and composer; son and pupil of above; became a member of the famous "Schuppanzigh Quartett."

Kram'er, A. Walter, b. New York, Sept. 23, 1890; composer, editor; studied with father, Maximilian Kramer, also with Carl Hauser, Richard Arnold and James Abraham; mem. editorial staff, *Musical America*, 1916–21; ed.-in-chief 1929–36; vice-pres. and exec. dir., Galaxy Mus. Corp., N. Y., publishers; c. 2 Symph. Sketches; Symph. Rhapsody for vln. and orch., *"Rococo Romance,"* choral cycle; *"Interlude for a Drama,"* for wordless solo voice, oboe, viola, 'cello and piano; *"The Hour of Prayer"* for chorus; other choruses, vln. and piano works and many songs; transc. for orchestra.

Krantz (kränts), **Eugen,** Dresden, 1844—1898; pianist and critic, teacher and composer.

Kraus (krows), (1) **Joseph Martin,** Miltenberg, 1756—Stockholm, 1792; pupil of Abt Vogler; 1778 director and cond. at Stockholm opera; c. operas, symphs., etc. (2) **Ernst,** Erlangen, 1863—April 24, 1933; tenor; pupil of Galliera and Frau Schimon-Regan; 1893 sang at Mannheim; from 1896, Berlin Royal Opera; (3) **Felix von,** b. Vienna, Oct. 3, 1870—Munich, Nov., 1937; bass; pupil of Stockhausen but largely self-taught; sang Hagen and Gurnemanz at Bayreuth; from 1908 teacher at Royal Akad. der Tonkunst, Munich. His wife (4) **Adrienne, (Osborne)** b. Buffalo, N. Y., 1873; pupil of Marie Götze, also a prominent opera singer.

Krause (krow'-zĕ), (1) **Chr. Gf.,** Winzig, 1719—Berlin, 1770; writer. (2) **Karl Chr. Fr.,** Eisenberg, Altenburg, 1781—Munich, 1832; writer. (3) **Theodor,** Halle, 1833—Berlin, 1910; rector at Berlin; cond. Seiffert Soc.; R. Mus.-Dir., 1887; composer. (4) **Anton,** Geithain, 1834—Dresden, 1907; at 6 pupil of cantor Dietrich; then of Fr. Wieck, Reissiger, and Spindler, Dresden, later Leipzig Cons., début, as pianist, Geithain, 1846; 1853–59, teacher and cond. Leipzig *Liedertafel;* 1859–97, dir. *Singverein* and the *Concertgesellschaft* (retired); 1877 Royal Mus. Dir.; prof.; c. *"Prinzessin Ilse."* *"Rübezahl Legend."* (5) (Prof. Dr.) **Eduard,** Swinemünde, 1837—Berlin, 1892; pianist, teacher and composer. (6) (Dr.) **Emil,** Schassburg in Transylvania, 1840 — Hamburg, 1889; barytone. (7) **Emil,** Hamburg, July 30, 1840—Sept. 5, 1916; pupil of Leipzig Cons.; since 1860, teacher of pf. and theory at Hamburg; since 1885 at the Cons.; c. an Ave Maria at 6, etc. (8) **Martin,** Lobstädt, near Leipzig, June 17, 1853—Plattling, Bavaria, Aug. 2, 1918; pianist and teacher; son and pupil of a cantor, then studied with Fuchs, Borna Teachers' Sem., and at Leipzig Cons.; toured Holland and Germany; had the friendship and advice of Liszt for years; 1885, with Siloti and others, founded the Leipzig "Lisztverein"; 1892, professor; 1901 Munich Cons; 1904, Stern Cons., Berlin.

Kraushaar (krows'-här), **Otto**, Cassel, 1812—1866; writer and composer.

Krauss (krows), (1) **Marie Gabrielle**, Vienna, March 24, 1842—Paris, Jan. 6, 1906; soprano; pupil of Vienna Cons. and Marchesi; 1860–67, Vienna ct. opera; 1867 Th. des Italiens, Paris; 1875–86, Gr. Opéra, Paris; then a teacher at Paris and officier d'Académie. (2) **Clemens**, b. Vienna, March 31, 1893; conductor; sang as boy soprano in Imp. Chapel, Vienna; grad. Cons. there, 1912; cond. German Theatre, Riga, 1913–14; Nuremberg, 1915–16; Stettin, 1916–22; Graz, 1921–22; Vienna State Op., 1922; Tonkünstler Orch., there, 1923–27; Frankfort Op. and Museum Concerts, 1924–29; dir., Vienna State Op. from 1929 to 1934, when he was appointed to similar post at Berlin State Op.; dir. Munich Op. after 1936; has also cond. as guest at Munich Fest., Salzburg Fest., at Leipzig Gewandhaus, Budapest, Barcelona, Paris, Prague, Leningrad; visited America in 1929, as guest cond. of N. Y. Philh. and Phila. Orch.; d. Mexico City, May 6, 1954.

Krebs (kräps), (1) **Jn. L.**, Buttelstedt, Thuringia, 1713—Altenburg, 1780; organist and composer. (2) **Karl Aug.** (rightly, **Miedcke**, changed after adoption by his teacher the opera-singer **J. B. Krebs**), Nürnberg, 1804—Dresden, 1880; c. operas. (3) **Marie** (Frau Brenning), Dresden, Dec. 5, 1851—June 27, 1900; daughter of above; pianist and teacher. (4) **K.**, b. near Hanseberg, Würtemberg, Feb. 5, 1857; studied R. Hochschule, Berlin; lived in Berlin as critic and writer, where d. Feb. 9, 1937.

Krečman. Vide KRETSCHMANN.

Krehbiel (krä'-běl), **H. Edw.**, Ann Arbor, Mich., March 10, 1854—New York, March 20, 1923; prominent American critic; studied law at Cincinnati, but entered journalism; 1874–78, mus.-critic Cincinnati *Gazette;* later editor New York *Mus. Review*, and, 1880 to his death, critic of the *Tribune;* pub. many succ. books, incl. *"Studies in the Wagnerian Drama," "How to Listen to Music";* *"Annotated Bibliography of Fine Art,"* with R. Sturgis; *"Music and Manners in the 18th Century," "Chapters of Opera," "A Book of Operas," "The Pianoforte and Its Music," "Afro-American Folk Songs," "A*

Second Book of Operas," "More Chapters of Opera"; prepared English version of *"Parsifal";* was mem. of ed. committee for *"The Music of the Modern World"* (1895–97), Amer. ed. for 2nd edition of *"Grove's Dictionary,"* and translated, revised and completed Thayer's life of Beethoven; mem. French Legion of Honour

Krehl (krāl), **Stephan**, Leipzig, July 5, 1864—April 8, 1924; studied Leipzig Cons. and Dresden Cons., 1889; teacher of pf. and theory, Carlsruhe Cons.; 1902, Leipzig Cons.; composer; wrote 5 treatises on comp.

Krein (1), **Alexander**, b. Nizhny-Novgorod, Russia, Oct. 20, 1883; d. Moscow, Apr. 2, 1951; cellist in Moscow; noted for the employment of ancient Jewish melodies in his works; c. *"Salome,"* symph. poem; chamber music, piano pieces; *"Kadisch,"* a requiem; incid. music to Jewish plays, songs. (2) **Grigori**, bro. of (1); b. 1879; studied with Juon and Glière; lives in Moscow; c. chamber music, piano sonata, songs.

Kreisler (krīs'-lěr), (1) **Jns.** Vide E. T. A. HOFFMANN. (2) **Fritz**, b. Vienna, Feb. 2, 1875; violinist; pupil of Massart and Delibes; début Paris; has toured Europe and U. S. with eminent succ. for many years; he has long held a leading rank among the world's vln. artists, both for stylistic qualities and virtuosity; c. a string quartet, several operettas many pop. smaller pieces for his instrument and others, some of which are adaptations of Viennese folk music; the bulk of them he long attributed to little known composers of the past, whose works he was supposed to possess in MS.; but in 1935 he astounded the musical world by announcing that they were his own compositions.

Kreissle von Hellborn (krīs'-lě fōn hěl'-bôrn), **H.**, Vienna, 1812—1869; writer; wrote *"Biog. of Schubert."*

Krejči (krā'-chē), **Josef**, Milostin, Bohemia, 1822—Prague, 1881; organist and composer.

Krempelsetzer (krěm'-p'l-zěts-ěr), **G.**, Vilsbiburg, Bavaria, 1827—1871; cond. and dram. composer.

Kremser (krěm'-zěr), **Eduard**, Vienna, April 10, 1838—Nov. 26, 1914; from 1869, chorusm. the Vienna "Männergesangverein"; c. operettas, a cantata, with orch., famous *"Altnieu..."*

ländische Volkslieder," and other part-songs, etc.

Křenek (krzhĕn'-ĕk), **Ernst,** b. Vienna, Aug. 23, 1900 (of Czech ancestry); composer; studied with Schreker, but departed from that composer's manner in the direction of extreme modernity, his works embodying atonality; lived in Berlin 1920–24, the following year in Zurich; served as choral répétiteur at the Cassel and Wiesbaden Ops.; c. (operas) *"Die Zwingburg"* (Berlin State Op., 1924); *"Der Sprung über den Schatten"* (Frankfort, 1923); *"Orpheus und Eurydike"* (1926), *"Jonny Spielt Auf"* (Leipzig, 1927, the last making a sensational but brief effect because of its introd. of jazz motifs and story of modern "machine" age, sung on many German stages, also at Met. Op. House, in 1929); 3 one-act operas, 1928; *"Die Heimkehr des Orest"* (1929); *"Karl V,"* completed 1933, but not immediately performed, partly owing to ban upon his works by Nat'l. Socialist regime in Germany; also incid. music to Goethe's *"Triumph der Empfindsamkeit,"* ballets, symphonies, concerti grossi, piano concerto, vln. concerto, string quartet, piano sonatas, choruses and songs; m. a daughter of Mahler; prof. Vassar Coll., 1941.

Krenn (krĕn), **Fz.,** Dross, Lower Austria, 1816—St. Andrä vorm Hagenthal, 1897; organist, composer and conductor; prof. harmony, Vienna Cons.

Kretschmann (or **Krečman**) (krĕtch'-män), **Theobald,** b. Vinos, near Prague, 1850; solo 'cellist, Vienna ct.-opera; d. Vienna, Apr. 16, 1929.

Kretschmer (krĕtsh'-mĕr), (1) **Edmund,** Ostritz, Saxony, Aug. 31, 1830 —Dresden, Sept. 13, 1908; pupil of Otto and Schneider, Dresden; ct.-organist; founder and till 1897 cond. the Cäcilia Singing-Soc., etc.; teacher in the R. "Kapellknaben-Institut," where his son (2) **Fz.** succeeded him; **E. K.** c. text and music of 2 important operas, *"Die Folkunger"* (Dresden, 1874) and *"Heinrich der Löwe"* (Leipzig, 1877); operetta, *"Der Flüchtling"* (Ulm, 1881); a romantic opera *"Schön Rohtraut"* (Dresden, 1887); *"Geisterschlacht"* (prize, Dresden, 1865); 3-part mass for male chorus (Brussels Acad. prize, 1868); an orch. suite *"Hochzeitsmusik,"* etc.

Kretzschmar (krĕtsh'-mär) **(Aug. Fd.),** **Hermann,** Olbernhau, Saxony, Jan. 19, 1848—Berlin, May 11, 1924; organist and conductor; pupil of Otto at the Kreuzschule, Dresden, and at Leipzig Cons.; 1871 Dr. Phil. at Leipzig, with a thesis on notation prior to Guido d'Arezzo; then teacher of org. and harm. at the Cons. and cond. several societies; 1887, mus.-dir. of Leipzig Univ. and cond. "Paulus." 1888–97, cond. of the "Riedel-Verein," retired because of ill-health; 1890, prof., critic, lecturer and writer; 1904, prof. at Berlin Univ.; 1907–22, dir. R. Inst. for Church Music; 1909–22, of the "Hochschule für Musik.-Wissenschaft." Author, studies of Bach, Cornelius, and many pop. musical treatises; c. org.-pcs. and part-songs.

Kreubé (krŭ-bā), **Chas. Frédéric,** Luneville, 1777—at his villa, near St. Denis, 1846; cond. at Paris Op. Com.; c. 10 comic operas.

Kreu(t)zer (kroi'-tsĕr), (1) **Conradin,** Messkirch, Baden, Nov. 22, 1780— Riga, Dec. 14, 1849; pupil of Riegard, Weibrauch and Albrechtsberger; toured as pianist; ct.-cond.; c. 30 operas, incl. *"Das Nachtlager von Granada"* (1834) and *"Jery und Bätely,"* still played, etc. His daughter (2) **Cäcilie** was an operatic singer. (3) (pron. in France, krŭt-zăr), **Rodolphe,** Versailles, Nov. 16, 1766; —Geneva, Jan. 6, 1831; famous violinist to whom Beethoven dedicated the *"Kreutzer Sonata";* son and pupil of a German violinist and of Stawitz; prof. at the Cons.; ct.-violinist to Napoleon and to Louis XVIII., 1802–26; prod. at Paris over 40 operas, incl. *"Lodoiska,"* also collaborated with Rode and Baillot in a standard method and c. famous vln.-études, etc. (4) **Aug.,** Versailles, 1778—Paris, Aug. 31, 1832; bro. of above, and 1826, his successor as vln.-prof. at the Cons.; composer. (5) **(Chas.) Léon (Fran.),** Paris, 1817 —Vichy, 1868. Son of (3); writer and composer. (6) **Leonid,** b. St. Petersburg, March 13, 1884; pianist and conductor; studied Petersburg Cons., with Essipov and Glazounoff; prof. at Berlin Hochschule, 1920–33; since 1935 res. in Tokyo; c. (ballet) *"Der Gott und die Bajadere"* (Mannheim, 1921); author books on piano and ed. Chopin wks.; d. Tokyo, 1953.

Krička (kr°sh'-kä), Jaroslav, b. Kelč, Moravia, Aug. 27, 1882; choral dir. and after 1918 teacher at the Prague Cons., c. (opera) "*Spuk im Schloss*," which blends jazz and folk themes in lively manner and attained succ. on several German stages; also cantatas, overtures, chamber music, choruses and song cycles.

Krieger (krē'-gĕr), (1) Adam, Driesen, 1634—Dresden, 1666; ct.-organist and composer. (2) (Jn.) Phillip, Nürnberg, 1649—Weissenfels, 1725; ct.-organist, ct.-cond., and dram. composer. (3) Jn., Nürnberg, Dec. 28, 1651—Zittau, July 18, 1735; famous contrapuntist; bro. and pupil of above, and his succ. as ct.-cond.

Kriens, Christiaan, Amsterdam, April 29, 1881—West Hartford, Conn., Dec. 17, 1934; composer, conductor; studied at Hague Cons., winning gold medal; début 1895 with his father's orch. in Amsterdam, cond. own symph. and playing both vln. and piano concertos; toured France, Holland, Belgium; came to U. S. 1906 as cond. of French Op. Co., New Orleans; after 1907, active as teacher and cond. in New York, founding and leading there a Symph. Club to train young players.

Krips, Josef, b. Vienna, 1902; vlnst.; 1933, cond. Vienna Op.; 1954, cond. Buffalo Philharm. Orch.

Kroeger (krä'-gĕr), Ernest R., St. Louis, Mo., Aug. 10, 1862—April 7, 1934; composer, organist and teacher; active as recitalist (piano), dir. of mus. at Forest Park Univ. and after 1904 head of his own music school in St. Louis; mem. French Academie and Nat'l Inst. of Arts and Letters; c. overtures, orch. suite, "*Lalla Rookh*"; various types of chamber music, a piano sonata op. 33, concert studies for the piano, violin and piano sonata; and many other piano pieces, songs, etc.

Krogulski (krō-gool'-skĭ), Joseph, Tarnov, 1815—Warsaw, Jan. 9, 1842; composer; pupil of Elsner; c. 10 masses, an oratorio, etc.

Krohn (krōn), Ilmari Henrik Rheinhold, b. Helsingfors, Nov. 8, 1867; Finnish author and comp. of sacred songs, piano sonatas, etc.

Krommer (krôm'-mĕr), Fz., Kamenitz, Moravia, 1760—Vienna, 1831; violinist, organist and conductor.

Kronach. Vide KLITZSCH.

Kronke (krônk'-ĕ), Emil, b. Danzig, Nov. 29, 1865; pianist; pupil of Reinecke and Paul, Nicodé and Th. Kirchner, Dresden; 1886 won pf.-prize, Dresden Cons.; 1887, diploma of honour; ed. of Liszt's wks.; d. Dresden, Dec. 16, 1938.

Kroy'er. Theodor, b. Munich, Sept. 9, 1873; author, critic and comp. studied theology, then music at the Akademie der Tonkunst; 1897, Ph. D. Munich University; 1920, taught Heidelberg Univ.; 1922, Leipzig, where developed school for musical science; after 1933 at Cologne Univ. c. 2 symphonies with chorus and soli, chamber music, etc.

Krueger (krü'-gĕr), Karl, b. New York, 1894; conductor; studied with Fuchs, Schalk, Weingartner and Nikisch; early active as 'cello and organ virtuoso, touring in Europe and South America; asst. cond. Vienna Op.; 1926 –31, led Seattle Symph. Orch., following its reorganisation; also guest cond. Phila. Orch. and in Hollywood Bowl, Cal.; after 1933 cond. Kansas City Philh. Orch. and chamber opera perfs.; cond., Detroit Symph., 1943.

Krug (krookh), (1) Fr., Cassel, 1812—Carlsruhe, 1892; op. barytone and dram. composer. (2) Dietrich, Hamburg, 1821—1880; pianist and composer. (3) Arnold, Hamburg, Oct. 16, 1849—Aug. 4, 1904; son and pupil of above; studied also with Gurlitt and Reinecke; won Mozart scholarship, 1869; studied with Kiel and Ed. Franck, Berlin; 1872–77, pf.-teacher, Stern Cons.; won Meyerbeer scholarship, and studied in France and Italy; 1885, ct.-cond. at the Hamburg Cons.; pub. a symph., symph. prologue "*Otello*," and orch. suite; choral works, etc. (4) (Wenzel) Jos. (called Krug-Waldsee), Waldsee, Upper Swabia, Nov. 8, 1858 —Magdeburg, Oct. 8, 1915; chiefly self-taught until 1872, then studied vln., pf., singing and comp. with Faiszt, at Stuttgart Cons.; 1882–89, cond. at Stuttgart; 1889, chorusm., mus.-dir. Municipal Th., Hamburg; 1892, th.-cond. various cities; 1889, Munich; 1900, Nürnberg; 1901, Magdeburg; 1902, concert-cantatas, "*Dornröschen*," "*Hochzeitslied*," "*Geiger zu Gmund*" and "*Seebilder*"; succ. opera "*Astorre*" (Stuttgart, 1896); "secular oratorio" "*König Rother*," etc.

Krüger (krü'-gĕr), **Eduard,** Lüneburg, 1807—Göttingen, 1885; prof. and writer.

Kruis (krīs), **M. H.** van, Oudewater, Holland, March 8, 1861—Lausanne, Feb. 14, 1919; pupil of Nikolai at The Hague; 1884, organist, teacher and writer, Rotterdam; 1886, founded monthly "Het Orgel"; c. an opera "*De Bloem Van Island,*" 3 symph., 8 overtures, etc.

Krumpholtz (kroomp'-hŏlts), (1) **Jn. Bap.,** Zlonitz, near Prague, ca. 1745 —Paris, Feb. 19, 1790; harpist, composer; he m. his 16-year old pupil, Frl. Meyer, a brilliant harpist; they gave concerts together, until her elopement, when he drowned himself in the Seine. (2) **Wenzel,** 1750— Vienna, 1817; bro. of above; violinist and composer.

Kubelik (koo'-bĕ-lĭk), (1) **Jan,** b. Michle, July 5, 1880—Prague, Dec. 5, 1940; violinist; son and pupil of a Bohemian gardener; pupil for 6 years of Sevcik, Prague Cons.; studied later at Vienna; début there 1898; then toured Europe, 1900, with great success; 1901, U. S. (2) **Rafael,** b. Batchory, Czechoslovakia, 1914; son of (1); conductor; grad. Prague Cons.; cond. Czech Philh., 1936-1948; guest cond. London, Paris, etc.; 1950, mus. dir., Chicago Symph. Orch.

Kucharž (koo'-chärzh), **Jn. Bap.,** Chotecz, Bohemia, 1751—Prague, 1829; organist and conductor.

Kücken (kĭk'-'n), **Fr. Wm.,** Bleckede, Hanover, 1810 — Schwerin, 1882; composer of operas and pop. songs; for some time cond. at Stuttgart.

Kuczynski (koo-chēn'-shkĭ), **Paul,** Berlin, Nov. 10, 1846—Oct. 21, 1897; Polish composer; pupil of von Bülow; c. succ. cantata "*Ariadne.*"

Kudelski (koo-dĕl'-shkĭ), **K. Mat.,** Berlin, 1805—Baden-Baden, 1877; violinist, composer and conductor.

Kufferath (koof'-fĕr-ät), (1) **Jn. Hn.,** Mühlheim-on-the-Ruhr, 1797—Weisbaden, 1864; conductor. (2) **Louis,** Mühlheim, 1811 — near Brussels, 1882; pianist, teacher and composer. (3) **Maurice,** Brussels, Jan. 8, 1852— Dec. 8, 1919; studied with Servais (père and fils) 'cello; 1873-1900, editor "*Guide musicale*" later, proprietor; writer and translator; 1900, dir. Théâtre de la Monnaie, Brussels.

Küffner (kĭf'-nĕr), **Jos.,** Würzburg, 1776—1856; dram. composer.

Kugelmann (koo'-gĕl-män), **Hans,** d. Königsberg, 1542; trumpeter and composer.

Kuhe (koo'-ĕ), **Wm.,** Prague, Dec. 10, 1823—London, Oct. 9, 1912; pianist; pupil of Proksch, Tomaschek and Thalberg; 1845, London; from 1886 prof. the R. A. M.; composer.

Kuhlau (koo'-low), **Fr.,** Ülzen, Hanover, Sept. 11, 1786—Copenhagen, March 12, 1832; ct.-flutist, dram. composer, teacher and composer of important technical pf.-pcs., etc.

Kühmstedt (küm'-shtĕt), **Fr.,** Oldisleben, Saxe-Weimar, 1809—Eisenach, 1858; theorist, composer, writer and teacher.

Kuhnau (koo'-now), **Jn.,** Geysing, Saxony, April 6, 1660—Leipzig, June 5, 1722; pupil of Henry, Albrici and Edelmann; organist at the Thomaskirche, Leipzig, and 1700 cantor, before Bach; pub. the first sonata for harpsichord, of which he was a noted player; also famous Biblical sonatas; composer and writer.

Kulenkampff (koo'-l'n-kämpf), (1) **Gus.,** Bremen, Aug. 11, 1849—Berlin, Feb. 10, 1921: concert pianist and teacher; pupil of Reinthaler, Barth and Bargiel, Berlin Hochschule; organised the succ. "Kulenkampscher Frauenchor"; dir. Schwantzer Cons. at Berlin for a few years; c. succ. comic operas "*Der Page*" (Bremen, 1890) and "*Der Mohrenfürst*" (Magdeburg, 1892); "*Die Braut von Cypern*" (Schwerin, 1899); male choruses, etc. (2) **Georg,** b. Bremen, Jan. 23, 1888; noted violinist; pupil of Willy Hess; prof. Berlin Hochschule; d. Switz., 1948.

Kullak (kool'-läk), (1) **Theodor,** Krotoschin, Posen, Sept. 12, 1818—Berlin, March 1, 1882; eminent teacher; Prince Radziwill had him taught by the pianist Agthe; at 11 he played at a ct.-concert; studied with Dehn, Czerny, Sechter and Nicolai; then teacher to the royal family; 1845, ct.-pianist, Berlin; 1850. founded (with Julius Stern and Bern. Marx) the Berlin (later Stern) Cons.; 1855, resigned, established his famous "Neue Akademie der Tonkunst"; 1861, royal prof.; wrote standard works, "*Sch. of Octave-playing,*" "*Seven Studies in Octave-playing,*" etc.; c. a concerto, sonata and other brilliant

pf.-pcs., etc., incl. "*Kinderleben.*"
(2) **Ad.**, Meseritz, 1823—Berlin,
1862; bro. of above; writer and com-
poser. (3) **Fz.**, Berlin, 1844—1913;
son and pupil of (1); studied with
Wieprecht and Liszt; 1867, pf.-
teacher and dir. orch.-class in Acad.
of his father, on whose death he be-
came dir. in 1890; writer; c. an opera
"*Ines de Castro*" (Berlin, 1877), etc.
Kull'mann, Charles, b. New Haven,
Conn., Jan. 13, 1903; tenor; studied
Juilliard School of Music, also at
Fontainebleau, and with Francis
Rogers and Mme. Schoen-René;
toured Europe as soloist with Yale
Glee Club; op. début with Amer.
Op. Co., 1929; sang with Berlin
State Op. and at Vienna with succ.
for several years; also at Salzburg
Fest.; début, Met. Op., 1935–36.
Kummer (koom'-m'r), (1) **Kaspar,**
Erlau, 1795—Coburg, 1870; flute-
virtuoso. (2) **Fr. Aug.,** Meiningen,
Aug. 5, 1797—Dresden, Aug. 22,
1879; notable 'cellist and composer
for 'cello; wrote method.
Kümmerle (kïm'-měr-lě), **Salomon,**
Malmsheim, near Stuttgart, 1838—
Samaden, 1896; prof. and composer.
Kun'its, Luigi von, Vienna, July 30,
1870—Toronto, Oct., 1931; violinist,
conductor; grad. Univ. of Vienna;
studied vln. with Kral, Gruen and
Sevcik, comp. with Bruckner; led
string quartet of Tonkünstlerverein
there; came to America 1893 and
taught in Chicago; 1896–1910, concertm. of Pittsburgh Orch.; taught
at Cons. there; 1910–12 in Vienna;
after latter year in Toronto, where
prof. in Canadian Acad. of Music,
and leader of Symph. Band.
Kunwald (koon'-vält), **Ernst,** b. Vienna,
April 14, 1868—Dec. 12, 1939; stud-
ied music at Leipzig Cons.; became
correpetitor at the city theatre; 1895,
cond. operetta at Rostock, 1901–02
at Teatro Real, Madrid, where he
gave Wagner's Ring cycle complete
and was decorated by the Queen of
Spain; 1902, cond. at opera Frankfort. 1906 cond. at Nuremberg city
theatre; conducting two concerts of
the New York Phil. as guest, Feb.
1906; 1907 director of the Berlin
Phil. orch.; 1912 engaged to conduct
the Cincinnati Symph. Orch.; held
post till 1917; interned as enemy alien;
1922–27, gen. mus. dir., Königsberg;
1928–32, cond., Berlin Symphony.

Kunz (koonts), **Konrad Max,** Schwan-
dorf, Bav. Palatinate, 1812—Munich, 1875; conductor and composer.
Kunzen (koonts'-'n), (1) **Jn. Paul,** Leisnig, Saxony, 1696—Lübeck, 1757;
organist and composer. (2) **K. Ad.,**
Wittenberg, 1720—Lübeck, 1781;
organist, pianist and composer.
(3) **Fr. L. Æmilius,** Lübeck, 1761—
Copenhagen, 1817; ct.-conductor and
composer.
Kupfer-Berger (koop'-f'r-běrkh-'r),
Ludmilla, Vienna, 1850—May 12,
1905; pupil of the Cons.; début Linz-
on-Danube, 1868, then at the Berlin
Ct.-opera; m. the Berlin merchant
Kupfer; later at Vienna, ct.-opera as
alternate with Materna.
Kurenko (koōr-yěnk'-ō) **Maria,** b.
Tomsk, Siberia; law grad. Moscow
Univ., also Cons. there, with Masetti
and Gontzoff; début in op. at Khar-
kov; has sung with Moscow Op.;
in N. Y., Chicago and Los Angeles;
concert appearances Europe and
America.
Kurpinski (koor-pǐn'-shkǐ), **Karl** (**Ka-
simir**), Luschwitz, Posen, 1785—
Warsaw, 1857; conductor and dram.
composer.
Kurt, Melanie, b. Vienna, 1880—
N. Y., March 11, 1941; studied at
Vienna Cons. and as pianist with
Leschetizky; toured in that capacity,
then turned to singing, working with
Lilli Lehmann; sang Lübeck and
Leipzig, after 1905 at Brunswick
Op.; 1908–12, Berlin Op.; 1915–17,
pronounced succ. in début with Met.
Op. in Wagnerian rôles.
Kurtz (koorts), **Efrem,** b. Berlin, 1900;
conductor; début 1920 there; cond.
Ballet Russe; later of Houston Symph.
Küster (kǐs'-těr), **Hn.,** Templin, Bran-
denburg, 1817—Herford, Westpha-
lia, 1878; ct.-organist, theorist and
composer.
Küzdö, Victor, b. Budapest, 1869;
violinist; grad. of Cons. there at 13;
tours of Europe and after 1884 in
U. S.; further study with Lotto and
Auer; after 1887, lived as concert
artist and teacher in New York.
Kuzniet'zof, Maria, b. Odessa, 1884;
operatic soprano; has appeared
widely in Russia, Spain, France,
England, U. S. (after 1915) and in
South America.
Kwast (kwäst), **Jas.,** Nijkerk, Holland,
Nov. 23, 1852—Berlin, Oct. 31, 1927;
pianist; pupil of his father and Fd.

Böhme; Reinecke and Richter, Kullak and Wuerst, Brassin and Gevaert, Brussels; 1874 teacher Cologne Cons.; 1883–1903, Hoch Cons., Frankfort; then Stern Cons.; composer.

L

Labarre (lä-bär), **Th.**, Paris, 1805—1870; harpist and dram. composer.

Labey (lă-bĕ'), **Marcel**, b. Dept. Besinet, France, 1875; studied law in Paris, then with d'Indy at the *Schola Cantorum*, where until 1914 taught piano and orch. classes; c. symph., fantasie for orch., sonatas, songs, etc.

Labitzky (lä-bĭt'-shkĭ), (1) **Jos.**, Schönfeld, near Eger, 1802—Carlsbad, 1881; violinist. (2) **Aug.**, Petschau, Saxony, Oct. 22, 1832—Reichenhall, Aug. 28, 1903; pupil of Prague Cons., of David and Hauptmann, Leipzig; 1853, cond. and composer at Carlsbad.

Lablache (lä-bläsh), **Luigi**, son of French father and Irish mother, Naples, Dec. 6, 1794—Jan. 23, 1858; eminent bass, with powerful and flexible voice with compass (Eb-e'); pupil of Valesi, pupil Cons. della Pietà; début Naples as buffo; later in heroic rôles throughout Europe; wrote "Méthode de chant."

Labor (lä'-bôr), **Josef**, Horowitz, Bohemia, June 29, 1842—Vienna, April 26, 1924; a blind pianist and organist; pupil of Sechter and Pirkjer, Vienna Cons.; chamber-pianist and teacher of the Princess of Hanover; after 1866 taught in Vienna, his pupils incl. Schönberg and Julius Bittner; composer.

Laborde. Vide DELABORDE.

Labro'ca, Mario, b. Rome, Nov. 22, 1896; composer and music critic; studied with Respighi and Malipiero; c. ballets, chamber symph., piano concerto, chamber music and vocal works; 1936 appointed pres. of Florence Teatro Comunale.

Lachmund (läkh'-moont), **Carl V.**, b. Booneville, Mo., 1857—Yonkers, N. Y., Feb. 20, 1928; at 13 studied in Cologne with Heller, Jensen and Seiss; then Berlin, also 4 years with Liszt at Weimar; c. trio (played by Berlin Philh. orch.), "*Japanese*" overture (perf. by Thomas and Seidl), etc.; lived in New York as teacher, conductor and composer.

Lachner (läkh'-nĕr), (1) **Theodor**, b. 1798; son of a poor organist at **Rain**, Upper Bavaria; organist at Munich. (2) **Thekla**, b. 1803; sister of above, organist at Augsburg. (3) **Christiane**, b. 1805; sister of above; organist at Rain. (4) **Fz.**, Rain, April 2, 1803—Munich, Jan. 20, 1890; half-brother of above; studied with Eisenhofer (comp.), and with Ett; 1882, organist Protestant Church. Vienna, and studied with Stadler, Sechter, and Weigl; a friend of Schubert and Beethoven; 1826, cond. Kärthnerthor Th.; 1834, Mannheim; 1836, the production of his D minor symph. at Munich won him the appointment of ct.-cond.; from 1852, was gen. mus. dir.; 1868 retired with pension in protest against the growing Wagnerianism at court; his eight orch. suites are his best work, showing his contrapuntal gifts at their best; he prod. 4 operas, 2 oratorios, 8 symphs., incl. the "*Appassionata*," chamber-music, etc. (5) **Ignaz**, Rain, Sept. 11, 1807—Hanover, Feb 24, 1895. Bro. of (4) and his successor as organist, 1825. 2nd cond. of court-opera, later ct. mus.-dir., Stuttgart; 1858, ct.-cond., Stockholm; c. operas, pop. Singspiele, etc. (6) **Vincenz**, Rain, July 19, 1811—Carlsruhe, Jan. 22, 1893; bro. of above; his successor as organist and later successor of Fz., as ct.-cond.; teacher and composer.

Lachnith (läk'-nĭt), **L. Wenzel**, b. Prague, 1746; horn-player, and deranger of famous works.

Lack (läk), **Théodore**, Quimper, France, Sept. 3, 1846—Paris, Nov. 25, 1921; pupil of Marmontel (pf.) and Bazin (harm.) Paris Cons.; teacher at Paris; 1881 officier of the Académie; officier of public instruction; c. much light and graceful pf.-music.

Lackowitz (läk'-ō-vĭts), **Walter**, Trebbin, near Berlin, Jan. 13, 1837—Berlin, March 11, 1916; pupil of Erk, Kullak, and Dehn; editor.

Lacombe (lä-kôṅb), (1) **Louis (Brouillon-Lacombe)**, Bourges, France, Nov. 26, 1818—St. Vaast-la-Hougue, Sept. 30, 1884; pianist; pupil of Paris Cons.; writer and dram. composer. (2) **Paul**, Carcassonne, Oude, France, July 11, 1837—June 5, 1927; studied with Teysseyre, but mainly self-taught; 1880 won the Prix Chartier, for chamber-mus.; c. also 3 symph., a symph. overture, etc.

Lacome (lä-kŭm), **Paul (P. J. Jac. Lacome de L'Estaleux)**, Houga, Gers, France, March 4, 1838— Dec. 12, 1920; lived since 1860, Paris; essayist and composer of many light operas, incl. *"Jeanne, Jeannette et Jeanneton"*; orchestral suites; songs, incl. *"L'Estudiantina,"* etc.

La'cy, Michael Rophino, Bilbao, 1795 —Pentonville, 1867: English violinist and composer.

Ladegast (lä'-dĕ-gäst), **Fr.,** b. Hochhermsdorf, near Leipzig, Aug. 30, 1818; org.-builder; d. Weissenfels, 1905.

Ladmirault (lăd-mē-rō), **Paul Émile,** b. Nantes, Dec. 8, 1877; began to study at the Cons. piano, violin, organ, and harmony at 7, and to compose at 8; at 15 his 3-act opera *"Gilles de Retz,"* was given at Nantes (1893); the next year he refused to allow its repetition; he took first harmony prize at the Nantes Cons. and 1895 entered Paris Cons. under Faudou, winning first harmony prize 1899. After a year of military service, he entered the classes of Fauré and Gédalge; failing three times to win the Prix de Rome, he left the Cons. His comps. include *"Le Chœur des âmes de la Forêt"* (1903), *"Suite Bretonne"* for orch. (1904), a *"Tantum Ergo"* (1907) crowned by the Société des Compositeurs de Musique; prélude symphonique, *"Brocéliande au Matin,"* a portion of a dramatic work *"Myrdhin"*; a symphony in C major, 1910; songs, piano pieces, and pieces for military band; d. Brittany, 1944.

Laduchin (läd'-oo-chēn), **Nikolai Mikailovich,** b. St. Petersburg, Oct. 3, 1860; violinist and pianist; pupil of Taneiev at Moscow Cons.; c. symphonic variations; 100 children's songs, *"Liturgy of Johann Slatoust"* for chorus, etc.

Ladurner (lä-door'-nĕr), **Ignaz Ant. Fz.,** Aldein, Tyrol, 1766—Villain (Massy), 1839; pianist and composer.

Lafage (lä-făzh), **Juste Adrien Lenoir de,** Paris, 1801—Charenton Insane Asylum, 1862; singing-teacher, conductor, composer and writer.

Lafont (lä-fôn), **Chas. Philippe,** Paris, 1781—near Tarbes, 1839; violinist and composer.

La Forge, Frank, b. Rockford, Ill., Oct. 22, 1877; pupil of his sister-in-law, Mrs. Ruth La Forge, then of Harrison M. Wild of Chicago, 1900–04, Leschetizky, Vienna, and Josef Labor (theory); accompanist to Gadski and Sembrich on their tours; later had lived in N. Y. as voice teacher, coach of noted singers, and c. piano pieces and songs; d. while giving concert, N. Y., May 5, 1953.

La Grange (lä gränzh), **Mme. Anna (Caroline) de,** b. Paris, July 24, 1825 —April, 1905; colorature soprano of remarkable range and flexibility; pupil of Bordogni and Lamperti; début 1842, at Varese; m. the wealthy Russian Stankowich, lived in Paris as teacher.

La Harpe (lä-ärp), **J. Fran. de,** Paris, 1739—1803; critic.

Lahee', (1) **H.,** Chelsea, England, April 11, 1826—London, April 29, 1912; pupil of Bennett, Potter and J. Goss (comp.); concert-pianist; lived in Croydon as teacher; c. 5 cantatas, etc. His son (2) **H. Chas.,** b. London, 1856; writer; after about 1883 in U. S., and 1891–99 sec'y of N. E. Cons., Boston; author, *"Annals of Music in America"*; d. 1953.

Laid'law, Anna Robena (Mrs. **Thomson**), Bretton, Yorkshire, April 30, 1819—May, 1901; successful concert-pianist until her marriage, 1852.

Lajarte (lä-zhärt), **Th. Ed. Dufaure de,** Bordeaux, 1826—Paris, 1890; writer and dram. composer.

Lajeunesse, M. Vide ALBANI.

Lajtha (loi'-tä), **Ladislas,** b. Budapest, June 30, 1892; composer; c. chamber music, incl. four string quartets (No. 3 perf. at Coolidge Fest., Washington, 1930).

Lalande (lä-länd), (1) **Michel Richard de,** Paris, 1657—1726; organist, conductor and composer. (2) (**Méric-Lalande**) **Henriette Clémentine,** Dunkirk, 1798—Paris, 1867; brilliant soprano.

La Lau'rencie, Lionel de, Nantes, July 24, 1861—Paris, Nov. 21, 1934; eminent writer on music; ed. Lavignac's Encyclopedia of Music; wrote life of Rameau, etc.

Lalevicz (lä-lä'-vĭch), **Georg von,** b. St. Petersburg, Aug. 21, 1876; piano teacher; pupil of the Cons.; 1900, won the Rubinstein competition in Vienna; 1902–05 prof. in Odessa Cons., then Cracow, Vienna, Lemberg; Paris; lives Buenos Aires.

Lalo', (1) Edouard Victor Antoine, Lille, Jan. 27, 1823—Paris, Apr. 22, 1892; eminent French composer; studied at Paris Cons., winning the 2nd Prix de Rome in 1847; little known until 1872 when his orchestral works began to appear, and 1874 when Sarasate played his vln. concerto. C. (operas) "*Le Roi d' Ys*," "*Savonarola*" and "*La Jacquerie*" (latter 2 fragmentary, last completed by Coquard, 1895); 3 symphonies and many shorter orchestral works, a string quartet, piano trios, sonatas for vln. and for 'cello, vln. concertos; "*Symphonie Espagnole*," for vln. and orch.; choral church music and many songs. The popularity of his works, particularly the vln. concertos and the "*Symphonie Espagnole*," is owing to their genial melodic qualities. After early neglect he established his place among the more gifted French comps. of his time. "*Le Roi d' Ys*" has held the stage in France. He m. the contralto, Mlle. Bernier de Maligny. (2) **Pierre**, his son, critic in Paris.

Laloy', Louis, b. Graz, 1874; musicologist.

La Mara. Vide LIPSIUS, MARIE.

Lambert (läṅ-băr), (1) **Michel**, Vivonne, Poitou, 1610—Paris, 1696; conductor and composer. (2) **Lucien**, b. Paris, Jan., 1861; pupil of Paris Cons.; 1883, took Prix Rossini w. cantata "*Prométhée Enchainé*"; c. lyric dram. "*Le Spahi*" (Op.-com., 1897), "*Brocéliande*," "*Marseillaise*," etc.

Lambert (läm'-bĕrt), (1) **Jn. H.**, Mühlhausen, Alsatia, 1728—Berlin, 1777; writer. (2) **Geo.**, b. Beverley, 1795; organist there, succeeded by his son (3) **Geo. Jackson** in 1818; retired, 1874. (4) **Alex.**, Warsaw, Poland, Nov. 1, 1862—New York, Dec. 31, 1929 (killed by taxicab); pianist; son and pupil of (5) **Henry L.**; (4) studied at Vienna Cons.; graduated at 16; studied with Urban, Berlin; toured Germany and Russia; studied some months at Weimar with Liszt; 1884, America; 1888, dir. N. Y. Coll. of Mus.; long active as teacher in N. Y.; c. piano works. (6) **Constant**, b. London, 1905; composer; began piano study at early age; at 16 won gold medal award and entered R. Coll. of Music, studying with Vaughan Williams and R. O.

Morris; Adrian Boult and Malcolm Sargent (cond.); c. (ballets) "*Romeo and Juliet*" (1st work commissioned from an Englishman by Diaghileff); "*Pomona*"; also "*Music for Orch.*"; settings of 7 poems by Li Po; "*The Rio Grande*," for contralto, chorus, orch. and piano (setting of poem by Sacheverell Sitwell), with pungent use of barbaric rhythm and jazz, which had immense succ., and was given in U. S.; piano music, incl. sonata and "*Elegiac Blues*," etc.; wrote book, "*Music Ho!*" subtitled "A study of music in decline." Cond. for Sadler's Wells Ballet and c. many works for this medium; toured U. S.; d. London, Aug. 2, 1951.

Lamberti (läm-bĕr'-tē), **Gius.**, Cuneo, Italy, 1820 (?)—Turin, 1894; dram composer.

Lam'beth, H. A., b. Hardway, near Gosport, 1822; organist; d. Glasgow, 1895.

Lambillotte (läṅ-bĭ-yôt), **Père Louis**, Charleroi, Hainault, 1796—Vaugirard, 1855; organist, conductor and composer.

Lambrino (läm-brē'-nō), **Télémaque**, Odessa, Oct. 27. 1878 (of Greek parents)—Leipzig, Feb. 25, 1930; pianist; studied music at the Royal Akad. der Tonkunst, Munich, and with Teresa Carreño; from 1900 lived in Leipzig, from 1908 teacher at the Cons.

Lamond', (1) **Frederic**, b. Glasgow, Jan. 28, 1868; eminent pianist (pupil of his bro. (2) **David**); 1882 at Raff Cons., Frankfort; later with von Bülow and Liszt; début, Berlin, 1885; toured Europe; after 1902, America; c. symph., overture, etc.; d. Stirling, Scotland, Feb. 21, 1948.

Lamont', **Forrest**, Springfield, Mass., 1880—Chicago, Dec. 17, 1937; tenor; studied in U. S. and Europe; op. début, Rome; toured Italy, West Indies and South America; after 1917 sang for several years with Chicago Op. Co., also with Cincinnati and Phila. Operas.

Lamoureux (läm-oo-rŭ'), **Chas.**, Bordeaux, Sept. 28, 1834—Paris, Dec. 21, 1899; eminent conductor; pupil of Girard, Paris Cons.; later with Tolbecque, Leborne and Chauvet; co-founder of a soc. for chambermus.; 1872, organist "Société de musique sacrée;" 1876, assist.-cond. Paris Opéra; 1878, first cond.;

1872–78, also assist.-cond. the Cons. Concerts; resigned from the Opéra, 1881, and est. the celebrated "Concerts Lamoureux" (Nouveaux Concerts).

Lampadius (läm-pä'-dĭ-oos), **Wm. Ad.,** 1812—Leipzig, 1892; writer.

Lamperti (läm-pĕr'-tē)͵ (1) **Fran.,** Savona, Italy, March 11, 1813—Como, May 1, 1892; eminent singing-teacher; pupil of Milan Cons. and teacher there, 1850–76; pub. treatises. (2) **Giovanni Battista,** Italy, 1839—Berlin, March 19, 1910. Famous singing master; wrote "*The Technic of Bel Canto*," 1905.

Lampugnani (läm-poon-yä'-nē), **Giov. Bat.,** Milan, 1706—ca. 1780; dram. composer.

Land (länt), **Dr. Jan Pieter Nicolaas,** Delft, 1834—Arnhem, 1897; professor; pub. important results of research in Arabian and Javanese mus., etc.

Landi (län'-dē), (1) **Stefano,** Rome, ca. 1590—ca. 1655; conductor, composer and singer. (2) **Camilla,** b. Geneva 1866; mezzo-soprano, daughter and pupil of singers; début 1884 Florence; 1886–92 in Paris, then in London where her mother taught; toured widely and returned to Geneva.

Landino (län-dē'-nō), **Fran.** (called **Francesco Cieco** "the blind," or **Degli Organi**), Florence, ca. 1325—1397; notable organist and composer.

Landolfi (län-dôl'-fē) (or **Landul'-phus**), (1) **Carlo Fdo.,** l. Milan, 1750–60; maker of 'cellos, etc. (2) **Pietro,** instr.-maker at Milan ca. 1760, probably son or bro. of above.

Landormy (län-dôr-mē), **Paul Charles René,** b. Issy, near Paris, Jan. 3, 1869; studied singing with Sbriglia and Plançon; published philosophical wks.; biog. of Brahms; d. Paris, 1943.

Landowska (län-dôf'-skä), **Wanda,** b. Warsaw, July 5, 1877; harpsichordist and pianist; studied Warsaw Cons., and with Michalowski, Moszkowski and Urban; début at 11 in native city; teacher of piano, Schola Cantorum, Paris, 1900–13; of harpsichord (newly estab. class) at Berlin Hochsch., 1913–19; founded her own school of music at St. Leu-La-Forêt, France, 1927; has internat'l. reputation as performer of cembalo music, 17th and 18th cent. in particular; wrote "*Bach et ses Inter-*

prètes," "*La Musique Ancienne*," "*Les Allemandes et la Musique Française au XVIII Siècle*"; toured Europe and America as recitalist and orch. soloist; Amer. début with Phila. Orch., 1923.

Lang (läng), (1) **(Lang-Köstlin), Josephine,** Munich, 1815—Tübingen, 1880; composer. (2) **Benj. Johnson,** Salem, Mass., Dec. 28, 1837—Boston, April 3, 1909; prominent pf.-teacher and conductor, pupil of his father and of F. G. Hill at Boston, Jaell and Satter, later in Berlin, and with Liszt; organist various churches, Boston; for over 25 years organist Handel and Haydn Soc. and cond., 1895; also cond. the Apollo Club and the Cecilia, etc.; c. an oratorio "*David*"; symphs., etc. (3) **Margaret Ruthven,** b. Boston, Nov. 27, 1867; daughter and pupil of above; studied also with Schmidt of Boston, Drechsler and Abel (vln.) and Gluth (comp.) in Munich; pub. many songs and pf.-pcs.

Langbecker (läng'-bĕk-ĕr), **Emanuel Chr. Gl.,** Berlin, 1792—1843; writer.

Lange (läng'-ĕ), (1) **Otto,** Graudenz, 1815—Cassel, 1879; editor and writer. (2) **Gustav,** Schwerstedt, near Erfurt, 1830—Wernigerode, 1889; pianist and composer. (3) **Samuel de,** Rotterdam, Feb. 22, 1840—Stuttgart, July 7, 1911; son and pupil of the organist, (4) **Samuel de L.** (1811—1884); later studied with Winterberger, Vienna, and Damcke and Mikuli, Lemberg; 1863 organist and teacher Rotterdam Mus. Sch., often touring Europe; 1876 teacher Cologne Cons., also cond.; 1885–93, cond. at The Hague, later teacher and vice-dir. Stuttgart Cons., and 1895, dir.; c. oratorio "*Moses*," 8 organ sonatas, 3 symph., etc. (5) **Daniel de,** Rotterdam, July 11, 1841—Point Loma, Cal., Jan. 31, 1918; bro. of above; studied with Ganz and Servais ('cello), Verhulst and Damcke (comp.), at Lemberg Cons. 1860–63, then studied pf. with Mme. Dubois at Paris; chiefly self-taught as organist; 1895—1913, dir. Amsterdam Cons., and cond.; also critic; c. opera "*De Val Van Kuilenburg*"; two symphs.; overture, "*Willem van Holland*," etc. (6) **Aloysia.** Vide WEBER. (7) **Hieronymus Gregor,** Havelberg, Brandenburg—Breslau, 1587; in 1574 cantor at Frankfort-am-Oder; comp. of Latin motets and songs. (8) **Hans,** b. Constantinople, Feb. 14, 1884; pupil of Brassin and Wondra; then of Prague Cons.; début Berlin, 1903; 1910, concertm., Frankfort Op.; also led a string quartet there; came to America and played in the N. Y. Philh. Orch., after 1924 serving as concertm. and asst. cond.; his duties in the latter capacity were extended until in 1934–36, under Toscanini's régime, he led annually a number of concerts of the organisation, showing high musicianship and presenting a number of new works; in 1936 he presented in N. Y. the 1st of a series of historical concerts by the N. Y. Philh. Chamber Orch., composed of solo players in the larger ensemble; and he has also appeared as guest cond. in several other American cities; 1936–37, assoc. cond., Chicago Symph.; 1950. Albuquerque Symph.

Lange-Müller (läng'-ĕ-mǐl-lĕr), **Peter Erasmus,** Frederiksberg, Dec. 1, 1850—Feb. 25, 1926; Danish composer; pupil of Copenhagen Cons.; c. operas "*Tove*" (to his own libretto 1878); "*The Spanish Students,*" (1883); "*Frau Jeanna*" (1891) and "*Vikingeblod*" (Copenhagen and Stockholm, 1900); symph. "*Autumn*"; incid. music to "*Fulvia*" and "*Es war einmal*"; orch. suite "*Alhambra*" and songs of decidedly national feeling.

Langer (läng'-ĕr), (1) **Hn.,** Höckendorf, near Tharandt, Saxony, 1819—Dresden, 1889; organist, conductor and teacher. (2) **Fd.,** Leimen, near Heidelberg, Jan. 21, 1839—Kirneck, Aug. 25, 1905; 'cellist at Mannheim ct.-Th., and later 2nd cond.; prod. there 5 succ. operas. (3) **Victor,** Pesth, Oct. 14, 1842—March 19, 1902; pupil R. Volkmann, and Leipzig Cons.; teacher, th.-cond. and editor; pub. under the name of "Aladar Tisza" very pop. songs, etc.

Langert (läng'-ĕrt), (**Jn.**) **Aug.** (**Ad.**), Coburg, Nov. 26, 1836—Dec. 28, 1920; dram. composer; th.-cond. Coburg; 1872, teacher of comp. Geneva Cons.; 1873, ct.-cond., Gotha, reappointed 1893; prod. 7 operas.

Langhans (läng'-häns), (**Fr.**) **Wm.,** Hamburg, 1832—Berlin, 1892; writer.

Langlé (län'-lā), **Honoré Fran. M.,**

Monaco, 1741—Villiers-le-Bel, near Paris, 1807; mus.-dir., theorist and composer.

Lanière (**Lanier** or **Lanieri**) (län-yăr, län-ēr', or län-ĭ-ā'-rē), (1) **Nicholas,** London, Sept. 10, 1588—London, Feb., 1666; son of (2) **Jos.,** and nephew of (3) **Nicholas.** (2) and (3) came to England, were mus. to Queen Elizabeth. (1) was ct.-musician to Charles I; a prolific composer and singer who introduced the recitative style into England.

Lanner (län'-nĕr), (1) **Jos.** (**Fz. K.**), Oberdöbling, near Vienna, 1801—1843; violinist, composer and conductor. (2) **Aug.** (**Jos.**), 1834—1855; son of above; violinist, conductor and dance-composer of prominence.

Lanzetti (län-tsĕt'-tē), **Salvatore,** Naples, ca. 1710—Turin, ca. 1780; one of the earliest 'cello virtuosi; c. 'cello sonatas and a method.

Lapar'ra, Raoul, Bordeaux, France, 1876—(air raid) 1942; composer; pupil Paris Cons. with Godard, Lavignac, Diémer, Gédalge, Massenet and Fauré; Prix de Rome, 1903; Chevalier, Legion of Honour, 1923; Inspector of Musical Instruction for French govt., after 1930; c. (operas) "*La Habanera*" (Paris Op.-Comique, 1908; Boston, 1910; Met. Op., 1924); "*La Jota*" (Op.-Comique, 1911); "*Le Joueur de Viole*" (do., 1925); "*Las Toreras*" (Lille, 1929); "*Amphitryon,*" "*L'Aventure Pittoresque*"; also chamber and piano works, latter incl. two series for children "*Iberian Scenes*" and "*Book of the Dawn*"; wrote "*La Musique Populaire en Espagne.*"

Lapicida (lä-pǐ-chē'-dä), **Erasmus,** 16th cent. composer.

Laporte (lä-pôrt), **Jos. de,** Befort, 1713—Paris, 1779; Jesuit abbé; writer.

Lara (lä'-rä), **Isidore de** (rightly **Cohen**), London, Aug. 9, 1858—Paris, Sept. 2, 1935; of English father and Portuguese mother; studied at Milan Cons.; took 1st prize for comp. at age of 17; c. operas: "*La Luce dell' Asia,*" founded on Sir Edwin Arnold's poem (London, 1892); "*Amy Robsart*" (1893); "*Moina*" (1897); "*Messaline,*" Monte Carlo (1899), very successful; "*Le Réveil de Bouddha*" (1904), "*Sangä*" (1906), "*Solea*" (1907), "*Les Trois Masques*" (1912), etc.

DICTIONARY OF MUSICIANS 253

Laroche (lä-rôsh), **Hermann,** St. Petersburg, May 25, 1845—Oct. 18, 1904; critic and comp; pupil of the Cons. and of Tchaikovsky, whose friend and biographer he was; prof. at Moscow, later at St. Petersburg Cons.; c. overture, etc.

La Rue (lä-rü), **Pierre de** (Latinised **Petrus Platensis;** also called **Perisone, Pierchon, Pierson, Pierzon,** or **Pierazon de la Ruellien**), eminent 16th cent. Netherland contrapuntist and composer; fellow-pupil (with Desprès) of Okeghem; ct.-singer and favourite of Margaret of Austria.

Laruette (lä-rü-ĕt), **J. L.,** Toulouse, 1731—1792; composer.

Lashan'ska, Hulda, b. New York; soprano; studied with Frieda Ashforth and Mme. Sembrich; début as soloist with N. Y. Symph.; has made concert tours and fest. appearances.

Lassale (lăs-săl), **Jean,** Lyons, France, Dec. 14, 1847—Paris, Sept. 7, 1909; studied Paris Cons.; notable barytone; début, Brussels, 1871; sang at Paris Opéra, in America, etc.; after 1903, prof. Paris Cons.

Lassen (läs'-sĕn), **Eduard,** Copenhagen, April 13, 1830—Weimar, Jan. 15, 1904; at 2 was taken to Brussels and at 12 studied in the Cons. there; won first pf.-prize, 1844; harm. prize, 1847; 2nd prize in comp. and 1851 Prix de Rome; travelled in Germany and Italy and made a long stay in Rome; 1858, ct.-mus.-dir. at Weimar; Liszt procured the prod. of his opera "*Landgraf Ludwig's Brautfahrt*" (Weimar, 1857); 1861–95, Liszt's successor as ct.-cond. at Weimar; then pensioned; c. operas "*Frauenlob*" (Weimar, 1860); "*Le Captif*" (Brussels, 1865; in German, Weimar, 1868); 11 characteristic orch.-pcs.; Bible-scenes with orch.; cantatas, 2 symphs., pop. songs, etc.

Lasserre (läs-săr), **Jules,** Tarbes, July 29, 1838—Feb. 19, 1906; pupil Paris Cons.; took 1st and 2nd prize as 'cellist; lived for some time in Madrid and, after 1869, in London; composer.

Lasso (läs'-sō), (1) **Orlando di** (rightly **Roland de Lattre,** Lat. **Orlan'dus Las'sus**), Mons (Hainault), 1530—Munich, June 14, 1594; most eminent of Netherland and (except Palestrina) of 16th cent. composers

and conductors. Haberl claims that he was born in 1532, in spite of Vinchant's contemporary statement that 1520 was the date, and Quichelberg's that 1530 was the date. His family seems to have used the name Lassus for some time before him; he signed his own name variously. C. 2,500 compositions, still beautiful to modern ears, as his melodic suavity was not smothered by the erudition which gave him even among contemporaries the name "Prince of Music." Befriended by various noblemen and given much Italian travel, he became 1541–48 cond. at S. Giovanni in Laterano at Rome; then visited Mons and ca. 1554, England, settling in Antwerp the same year; 1557 joined on invitation the ct.-chapel of Albert V., Duke of Bavaria; from 1562 he was cond. there, full of honours. His complete works (in course of pub. by Breitkopf & Härtel) include his famous "*Psalmi Davidis poenitentiales*," masses, psalms, and secular compositions of occasionally humorous vein. Biogr. by Dehn (1837), Bäumkehr (1878), and Sandberger. (2) **Fd. di,** d. Munich, Aug. 27, 1609, eldest son of above; ct.-cond. (3) **Rudolf di,** d. Munich, 1625; second son of (1); organist and composer. (4) **Fd. di,** d. 1636; son of (2); conductor and composer.

Lászl'ó (läsh'-lō), **Alexander,** b. Budapest, Nov. 22, 1895; composer; studied at Acad., in native city; best known as inventor of a system of music synchronized with color.

Latilla (lä-tĭl'-lä), **Gaetano,** Bari, Naples, 1711—Naples, 1791; conductor, teacher and composer.

La Tombelle. Vide TOMBELLE.

Latrobe, (1) Rev. **Chr. I.,** Fulnes, Leeds, 1758—Fairfield, near Liverpool, 1836; composer. (2) **J. Antes,** London, 1799—Gloucester, 1878; son of above; organist and composer.

Lattre, de. Vide LASSO.

Lattuada (lät-ōō-ä'-dä), **Felice,** b. Casella di Morimondo, Italy, Feb. 5, 1882; composer; grad. in comp. of Verdi Cons., Milan; c. (operas) "*Sandha*," (Genoa, 1921); "*La Tempesta*," based on Shakespeare (Dal Verme, Milan, 1922); "*Le Preziose Ridicole*," after Molière (La Scala, 1929; Met. Op., 1930); "*Don Giovanni*" (Naples, 1929); also (orch.)

Sinfonia Romantica, and chamber music, songs; ed. *"Raccolta di canzoni populari."*

Laub (lowp), **Fd.**, Prague, 1832— Gries, Tyrol, 1875; vln.-virtuoso; teacher and composer.

Laubenthal (lä'-bĕn-täl), **Rudolf**; b. Düsseldorf; tenor; sang with Berlin Op. at Covent Garden, and for nearly a decade until 1932 with Met. Op., N. Y., in Wagnerian rôles, etc.

Laurencie, see LA LAURENCIE.

Laurencin (low'-rĕn-sēn), Graf **Fd. P.**, Kremsier, Moravia, 1819— Vienna, 1890; writer.

Lauri-Volpi (lä-ōō-rē-vôl'-pē), **Giacomo** (rightly **Volpi**), b. Lanuvio, Italy, Dec. 12, 1892; tenor; early studied law; served in the war, winning 3 decorations; début as singer at the Costanzi, Rome, 1920, as Des Grieux; has sung in leading theatres of Europe and was mem. of Met Op. Co. for several years after 1925.

Lauska (lä-oos'-kä), **Fz.** (Seraphinus Ignatius), Brünn, Moravia, 1764— Berlin, 1825; teacher, composer.

Lauterbach (low'-tĕr-bäkh), **Jn. Chr.**, Culmbach, Bavaria, July 24, 1832— Dresden, March 28, 1918; pupil Würzburg Mus. Sch., and of Fétis and de Bériot at Brussels (1850), won gold medal for vln.-playing, 1851; 1853 Munich Cons.; 1860–77 Dresden Cons.; 1889, pensioned; composer.

Lavallée (lä-väl-lä), **Calixa**, Verchères, Canada, 1842—Boston, Mass., 1891; concert-pianist; toured U. S., giving frequent concerts of American composers' works, 1886–87; c. 2 operas, an oratorio, a symph., etc.

Lavigna (lä-vēn'-yä), **V.**, Naples, 1777 —Milan, ca. 1837; teacher and dram. composer.

Lavignac (lä-vēn-yǎk), **Albert**, Paris, Jan. 21, 1846—May 28, 1916; pupil of the Cons., and from 1882 prof. there; author of many important works; ed. notable *"Encyclopédie de Musique,"* subsidized by French Gov't. (1903); new edition by Lionel de la Laurencie, 1929; pub. a *"Cours complet théorique et pratique de dictée musicale,"* 1882, which led to the general adoption in mus. schs. of courses in mus. dictation; also *"La musique et les musiciens."*

Lavigne (lä-vēn), (1) **Jacques Émile**, Pau, 1782—1855; tenor. (2) **A. Jos.**,

Besançon, France, March 23, 1816— Manchester, Aug. 1, 1886; oboist; pupil Paris Cons.; from 1841 in Drury Lane Promenade Concerts, later in Halle's Manchester orch.; he partially adapted Böhm's system to the oboe.

Lavoix (lä-vwä), **H. M. Fran.**, Paris, 1846—1897; writer and composer.

Lawes (lôz), (1) **Wm.**, Salisbury, Wiltshire, 1582—killed at the siege of Chester, 1645; composer. (2) **H.**, Dinton, near Salisbury, Dec., 1595— London, Oct. 21, 1662; bro. of above; one of the most original and important of song-writers, forestalling in his principles those of Franz, etc., in that he made his music respect the poetry he was setting; Milton, Herrick and others accordingly praised him. Pupil of Coperario. 1625 Epistler and Gentleman, Chapel Royal; on Charles I's execution he lost his places but re-found them in the Restoration in 1660; buried in Cloisters of Westminster Abbey; c. the music to Milton's *"Comus,"* etc.

Law'rence, Marjorie, b. Melbourne, Australia; dram. soprano; studied in Paris; début at Monte Carlo, 1932, as "Elisabeth"; sang heroic rôles with Paris Op., incl. "Brünnhilde", "La Juive", "Salome" and "Aïda"; début, Met. Op., N. Y., 1935–36.

Layol(l)e (or dell'Aiole, Ajolla) (lī-yôl', or ä-yō'-lĕ), **Fran.**, Florentine composer 16th cent.

Lazar (lä'-zär), **Filip**, b. Craiova, 1894; composer of orch., piano and vocal music; played his pf.-concerto with Boston Symph., 1936; d. Paris, 1936.

Lázaro (lä'-thär-ō), **Hipólito**; b. in Catalonia; tenor; noted for his virile timbre of voice; sang at Teatro Real, Madrid; at Barcelona, La Scala and at Met. Op. House, N. Y.

Laz'arus, (1) **H.**, London, 1815—1895; clarinettist. (2) **Gustav**, Cologne, 1861—Berlin, 1920; pianist, composer.

Lazzari (läd-zä'-rē), (1) **Silvio**, Bozen, 1858—Paris, June 15, 1944; pupil Franck, Paris Cons.; composer of operas "La Lépreuse" (Op. Com., Paris, 1912), "Moelenis," lyric drama "Armor" (prelude at Lamoureux concerts, 1895—prod. at opera Lyons 1903, revived 1912); "Le Sauteriot" (Chicago, 1917); "La Tour de Feu" (Paris Op., 1928), orch., chamber music, songs, etc. (2) **Carolina**,

1892—1946; contralto; sang with Chicago Op., 1918; (3) **Virgilio,** b. Assisi, Italy; bass; pupil of Cotogni; sang with Chicago Op. after 1918; Met. Op., after 1934; also widely in Europe; d. Castel Gandolfi, 1953.

Le Bé (lŭ-bā), **Guil.,** 16th cent. French type-founder.

Le Beau (lŭ-bō), **Louise Adolpha,** Rastatt, Baden, April 25, 1850—Baden-Baden, July 2, 1927; concert-pianist; pupil of Kalliwoda, Frau Schumann, Sachs, Rheinberger and Fr. Lachner; c. choral works, piano works, songs, etc.; pub. memoirs.

Lebègue (lŭ-bĕg), **Nicolas A.,** Laon, 1630—Paris, 1702; ct.-organist and composer.

Lebert (lā'-bĕrt) (rightly **Levy**), **Siegmund,** Ludwigsburg, near Stuttgart, 1822—Stuttgart, 1884; teacher, writer and composer; co-founder of Stuttgart Cons. (1856—57).

Lebeuf (lŭ-bŭf), Abbé **Jean,** Auxerre, 1687—1760; writer.

Leblanc (lŭ-bläṅ), **Georgette,** Rouen—Cannes, Oct. 26, 1941 ; pupil of Bax; début Op. Com., Paris, 1893, in "L'Attaque de Moulin." 1895, Th. de la Monnaie, Brussels ; then gave song recitals in costume with much effect.

Leborne (lŭ-bȯrn), (1) **Aimé Ambroise Simon,** Brussels, 1797-—Paris, 1866; teacher and writer. (2) (or **Le Borne**), **Fd.,** Charleroi, March 10, 1862—Paris, February, 1929; pupil of Massenet, Saint-Saëns, and Franck, Paris Cons.; lived in Paris as critic; c. operas; a symph. légende; symphs., etc.

Lebouc (lŭ-book), **Chas. Jos.,** Besançon, 1822—Hyères, 1893; 'cello-virtuoso.

Lebrun (lĕ-broon'), (1) **L. Aug.,** Mannheim, 1746—Berlin, 1790; greatest oboist of the 18th cent.; composer. (2) (née **Danzi**), **Franciska,** Mannheim, 1756—Berlin, 1791; wife of above; soprano. Their two daughters, (3) **Sophie** and (4) **Rosine,** were distinguished singers.

Lebrun (lŭ-brŭṅ), (1) **Jean,** Lyons, 1759—suicide, Paris, 1809; horn-virtuoso. (2) **Louis Sébastien,** Paris, 1764—1829; tenor and teacher. (3) **Paul H. Jos.,** Ghent, April 21, 1861—Louvain, Nov. 4, 1920; pupil of the Ghent Cons.; 1891 won the Prix de Rome for composition and the Belgian Academie 1st prize for a symphony; 1889, prof. of theory at

Ghent Cons., after 1913 dir. of a mus. school in Louvain.

Lechner (lĕkh'-nĕr), **Ld.,** ca. 1550, Etschthal, Switzerland (?)—Stuttgart, 1606; ct.-cond. and composer.

Léclair (lā-klăr), **J. M.,** Lyons, 1697 —assassinated, Paris, 1764; violinist; c. operas, 48 notable vln.-sonatas, etc.; his wife, a singer, engraved his compositions.

Lecocq (lŭ-kȯk), **(Alex.) Chas.,** Paris, June 3, 1832—Oct. 24, 1918; studied at the Cons., won 1st prize for harm., and 2d prize for fugue; his first work, "Le Docteur Miracle," in conjunction with Bizet (prod., 1857), won a prize offered by Offenbach for opera buffa; smaller succ. culminated in "Fleur de Thé" (1868); followed by the sensational succ. "La Fille de Mme. Angot" (Brussels, 1872; Paris, 1873), which ran uninterruptedly over a year; its succ. was equalled by "Giroflé-Girofla" (1874); 1894, chev. of the Legion of Honour; prod. over 40 operas-bouffes, comic operas and operettas, written with scholarship and brilliant instrumentation; sacred and other songs, etc.

Le Couppey (lŭ koop'-pĕ'), **Félix,** Paris, April 14, 1811—July 5, 1887; prof., pf.-teacher and composer.

Ledebur (lā'-dĕ-boor), **K. Freiherr von,** Schildesche, near Bielefeld, April 20, 1806—Stolp, Oct. 25, 1872; Prussian cavalry officer and lexicographer.

Leduc (lŭ-dük), **Alphonse,** Nantes, 1804—Paris, 1868; pianist, bassoonist and composer.

Lee (lā), **Louis,** Hamburg, Oct. 19, 1819—Lübeck, Aug. 26, 1896; 'cellist; pupil of J. N. Prell; at 12 gave concerts; 'cellist in the Hamburg Th.; lived several years in Paris; organist, chamber-mus. soirées, Hamburg; until 1884, teacher in the Cons. and 1st 'cello; c. symphonies, overtures, etc.

Lefébure-Wély (lŭ-fā-bür-vā-lē), **L. Jas. Alfred,** Paris, 1817—1869; noted organist; c. opera, masses, etc.

Lefèbvre (lŭ-fĕv'-r), **Chas. Édouard,** Paris, June 19, 1843—Aix-les-Bains, Sept. 8, 1917; pupil of Ambr. Thomas, Paris Cons.; 1870, Grand prix de Rome; 1873, after touring the Orient settled in Paris; after 1895, theory prof., Paris Cons.; c. succ. opera, "Djelma" (1894); "Zaïre" (1887), etc.

Lefèvre (lŭ-fĕv′-r), **J. X.**, Lausanne, 1763—Paris, 1829; clarinettist, composer and professor.

Le Flem (lŭ flŭm′), **Paul**, b. Lèzardieux (Côtes du Nord), France, March 18, 1881; composer; pupil of d'Indy; studied at Paris Cons. and Schola Cantorum; winner Laserre Prize, 1928; Chevalier, Legion of Honour; c. (lyric fable) "*Aucassin et Nicolette*"; (orch.) 1st symphony; "*La Voix du Large*" (symph. sketch); "*Pour les Morts,*" "*Danse*" and "*Invocation,*" comprising symph. in form of triptych; piano quintet; vln. sonata, fantasie for piano and orch., works for piano, for chorus, and songs.

Legiņska, Ethel (rightly **Liggins**), b. Hull, England, April 13, 1890; composer, pianist, conductor; studied Frankfort Cons. and with Leschetizky; toured Europe and U. S. as pianist, N. Y. début, 1913; cond. Boston Philh., Chicago Women's Symph., and similar orch. in Boston, also operatic prod. of Suppé's "*Boccaccio*"; c. orchestral and other works; also one-act opera "*Gale,*" prod. by Chicago Op., 1935; she later lived as pianist and teacher on the Pacific Coast.

Legouix (lŭ-gwēx), **Isidore Éd.**, Paris, April 1, 1834—Boulogne, Sept., 1916; pupil of Reber and Thomas at the Cons.; prod. 4 operas, etc.

Legrenzi (lā-grĕn′-tsē), **Giov.**, Clusone, near Bergamo, 1626—Venice, 1690; organist, conductor and dram. composer.

Lehár (lĕ-här′), **Franz**, b. Komorn, Hungary, April 30, 1870; composer of the world sweeping operetta "*Die Lustige Witwe*" (Vienna, 1905, in New York and London as "*The Merry Widow*"); lived in Vienna; c. also operas "*Kukuska,*" Leipzig, 1896, revised as "*Tatjana,*" Brünn, 1905; operettas "*Wiener Frauen*" (Vienna, 1902; revised as "*Der Schlüssel zum Paradiese,*" Leipzig, 1906); "*Mitislav*" (Vienna, 1907); "*Edelweiss und Rosenstock*" (1907); "*Peter and Paul reisen ins Schlaraffenland*" (Vienna, 1906); "*Der Mann mit den drei Frauen*" (1908); "*Das Fürstenkind,*" "*Der Graf von Luxemburg,*" "*Zigeunerliebe,*" "*Die blaue Mazur,*" "*Frasquita,*" "*Paganini,*" "*Friederike,*" "*Zarevitch,*" "*Das Land des Lächelns*" (revision of "*Die blaue Jacke*"), and the

grand opera, "*Giuditta*" (Vienna, 1934), etc.; d. Ischl, Oct. 24, 1948.

Lehmann (lā′-män), (1) **T. Marie**, (I.) prima donna at Cassel under Spohr; (2) **Lilli**, Würzburg, Nov. 24, 1842—Berlin, May 16, 1929; daughter and pupil of above; eminent soprano; début at Prague as "First Boy" in "*Die Zauberflöte*"; 1868, at Danzig, and Leipzig, 1870; in the same year obtained a life-engagement at the Royal Opera, Berlin, with the title (1876) of Imp. Chamber-singer; she sang "*Woglinde,*" "*Helmwige*" and the "*Bird,*" at their first performance, 1876; 1885, broke her contract, and sang in the U. S.; was as a result banned from German stages for several seasons but restored to favor by Emperor; sang at Met. Op. Co., N. Y., 1885–89 and 1891–92, revealing highest dram. and technical powers in such rôles as "Isolde" and even some Italian parts; she lived in Berlin after 1892, and also took active share in Salzburg Fests., devoting much of her time to teaching, but continuing to appear in opera occasionally as late as 1910; m. Paul Kalisch, tenor. (3) **Marie** (II.), Hamburg, May 15, 1851—Berlin, Dec. 9, 1931; daughter and pupil of (1); at 16 sang in Leipzig City Th.; for many years, till 1897, Vienna ct.-opera; lived in Berlin. (4) **Liza** (Mrs. Herbert Bedford), London, July 11, 1862—Sept. 19, 1918; concert-soprano; pupil of Randegger and Raunkilde at Rome (voice) and of Freudenberg (Wiesbaden), and Hamish MacCunn (comp.); début, Nov. 23, 1885, at a Monday Pop. Concert; 1887, sang at the Norwich Festival; 1894, m. and retired; c. many songs incl. the very pop. song-cycle from Omar Khayyám, "*In a Persian Garden,*" also "*In Memoriam,*" etc. (5) **Lotte**, b. Perleberg, Germany, July 2, 1885; soprano; studied Berlin R. Acad. of Music and with Mathilde Mallinger; début, Hamburg, 1910; won high rank as lyric-dram. soprano, being heard in Dresden, Berlin, and as a regular mem. of the Vienna State Op., where she has enjoyed much popularity for her perfs. in Wagner, Strauss and other works; created rôle of the composer in "*Ariadne auf Naxos*"; heard at Salzburg Fest.,

Covent Garden, Chicago Op., (début as "Sieglinde," 1930), and after 1934 at Met. Op., N. Y.; also holds distinguished place as Lieder singer; awarded decoration of Officer Public Instruction, France; Swedish Medal of Arts and Sciences.

Leibrock (līp'-rôk), **Jos. Ad.**, Brunswick, 1808—Berlin, 1886; writer and composer.

Leichtentritt (līkh'-tĕn-trĭt), **Hugo**, b. Pleschen, Posen, Jan. 1, 1874; at 15 taken to America, where he studied with J. K. Paine, Boston, then at the Royal Hochschule, Berlin; 1901, Ph. D.; wrote theoretical and historical works and c. chamber music and songs; 1902–24, taught Klindworth-Scharwenka Cons., Berlin; after 1933, at Harvard Univ., d. Cambridge, Mass., Nov. 13, 1951.

Leider (lī'-dĕr), **Frida**, b. Berlin, April 18, 1888; soprano; studied in Berlin and Milan; sang in many opera houses of her native country, incl. Rostock, Aachen and Hamburg; after 1924 with the Berlin State Op.; beginning 1928 at Bayreuth Fest. ("Brünnhilde," "Kundry"); also at Covent Garden; Chicago Civic Op., 1930; thereafter for several seasons at Met. Op., N. Y., in Wagnerian rôles.

Leighton (lā'-tŭn), **Sir Wm.**, Engl. composer, 1641.

Leins'dorf, **Erich**, b. 1912; cond. Met. Op., 1937–43; Cleveland Symph., 1943; Rochester Philh., 1946.

Leitert (lī'-tĕrt), **Jn. G.**, Dresden, Sept. 29, 1852—1901; pianist; pupil of Kragen and Reichel (pf.) and Rischbieter (harm.); début Dresden, 1865; studied with Liszt; 1879–81 teacher Horak Mus. Sch., Vienna; composer.

Le Jeune (lŭ-zhŭn), **Claudin**, Valenciennes, 1528—1602; highly original French contrapuntist and composer.

Lekeu (lŭ-kŭ), **Guillaume**, Heusy-les-Verviers, Jan. 20, 1870—Angers, Jan. 21, 1894; composer. His death at 24 left many unfinished works, but enough were complete to assure his fame, among them 3 études symphoniques (1889, 1890); adagio for quatuor and orch. (1891), epithalame, for string quintet, organ and 3 trombones; introduction and adagio for orch. with tuba solo; fantaisie symphonique sur deux airs populaires angévins, 1892; (unfin.) comedy, "Barberine"; cantata, "Andromède"

(2nd Prix de Rome at Brussels, 1891); chamber music, including sonata for piano and 'cello, finished by V. d'Indy, 1910, and a quatuor finished by the same; sonata for piano and violin (ded. to and played by Ysaye), etc.

Le Maistre (lŭ-mĕtr) (or **Le Maître**), **Mattheus**, d. 1577; Netherland contrapuntist; ct.-conductor and composer.

Lemare (lĕ-măr'), **Edwin Henry**, Ventnor, Isle of Wight, Sept. 9, 1865—March 19, 1929; organist; pupil R. A. M. London, with Goss Scholarship, then made an associate, later a fellow; 1884 fellow Royal College of Organists; occupied various church positions, and gave recitals; 1902–04, organist at Carnegie Hall, Pittsburgh, Pa.; 1905, again in London; c. symph., a pastorale and much organ music.

Lemmens (lĕm'-mĕns), **Nicolas Jacques**, Zoerle-Parwys, Belgium, 1823—Castle Linterport, near Malines, 1881; organist, professor and composer.

Lemoine (lŭm-wăn), (1) **Ant. Marcel**, Paris, 1763—1817; publisher, ct.-conductor and writer. (2) **H.**, Paris, 1786—1854; son of above and his successor in business; writer. (3) **Aimé**, b. 1795 (?); pub. "Méthode du Méloplaste"; teacher.

Lemoyne (lŭm-wăn) (rightly **Moyne**) (mwăn), **J. Bap.**, Eymet, Périgord, 1751—Paris, 1796; conductor and dram. composer.

Lenaerts (lŭ-nărts), **Constant**, b. Antwerp, March 9, 1852; pupil of Benoît; at 18 dir. Flemish National Th.; teacher Antwerp Cons.; founder, 1914, Société Royale de l'harmonie; d. (?).

Lendvai (lĕnd'-vī), **Erwin**, b. Budapest, June 4, 1882; composer; pupil of Koessler and Puccini; after 1901 lived in Germany, teaching at Dalcroze School, Hellerau, 1914; later prof. at Hoch Cons., Frankfort; 1919 at Klindworth-Scharwenka Cons., Berlin; also in Jena; 1923, choral dir. in Hamburg-Altona; 1926 at Coblentz; and since 1929 in Stockdorf and Erfurt; c. opera, "Elga" (1916), a symph. and other orch. works, chamber music, choral pieces, songs, etc., in modern style; a study of his work has been written by Leichtentritt.

Lenepveu (lŭ-nŭp'-vŭ), **Chas. Fd.,** Rouen, Oct. 4, 1840—Paris, Aug. 16, 1910; studied with Servais, in 1861 won 1st prize at Caen; studied with Thomas at the Cons., 1865 took Grand prix de Rome, rt. from Rome; won a prize with opera "*Le Florentin*" (Op.-com., 1874); prod. gr. opera "*Velleda*" (Covent Garden, 1882); 1891 harm.-prof. in the Cons. and 1893 prof. of comp.; 1896, Académie des Beaux-Arts; Chev. of the Legion of Honour, and officer of pub. instruction; c. lyric drama "*Jeanne d'Arc*" (Rouen Cath., 1886); "*Hymne funèbre et triomphal*" (V. Hugo) (Rouen, 1889), etc.

Léner, Jenö, b. Szabadka, Hungary, June 24, 1871; violinist; studied with Hubay, Budapest Acad. of Music; début in that city, 1913; solo player with Budapest Philh., until 1918; founded and led after 1920 the eminent string quartet named after him, with headquarters in London; N. Y., 1929; where d. Nov. 4, 1948.

Le'normand, René, Elbeuf, Aug. 5, 1846—Paris, Dec. 5, 1932; pianist, composer; c. many songs, orch. works, chamber music and stage pieces; author, study of modern harmony.

Len'ton, J., d. after 1711; band-musician and composer, London.

Lenz (lĕnts), **Wm. von,** Russia, 1808—St. Petersburg, Feb. 12, 1883; pianist; wrote genial and enthusiastic studies of musicians, "*Beethoven et ses trois styles*" (1852), etc., being the first so to divide B.'s art.

Leo (lä'-ō), **Leonardo,** Brindisi, 1694—Naples, 1744; eminent pioneer in the Neapolitan Sch. and noted teacher, conductor and organist; pupil of Aless. Scarlatti, Fago, and Pitoni; ct.-organist; c. 60 operas, also religious mus., incl. a noble 8-part "*Miserere*," a cappella.

Léonard (lä-ō-när), **Hubert,** Bellaire, near Liége, April 7, 1819—Paris, May 6, 1890; eminent violinist; pub. technical studies.

Leoncavallo (lä-ōn-kä-väl'-lō), **Ruggiero,** Naples, March 8, 1858—Montecatini near Florence, Aug. 9, 1919; noted opera composer; studied Naples Cons., and at 16 made a tour as pianist; his first opera "*Tommaso Chatterton*," failed at first but was succ. revived at Rome, 1896; a disciple whom Wagner per-

sonally encouraged, he spent 6 years in researches, resulting in an "historic" trilogy (uncompleted) "*Crepusculum*" ("Twilight"), I. *Medici,* II. *Girolamo Savonarola,* III. *Cezare Borgia;* toured as pianist through Egypt, Greece, Turkey, etc.; lived in Paris some years and had an opera "*Songe d'une Nuit d'Été*," privately performed, and many songs published; he prod. 2-act opera seria "*I Pagliacci*" (Milan Dal Verme Th., 1892, in Germany 1893, as "*Der Bajazzo*") of which he wrote the masterfully constructed libretto as well as the strenuous music that made it a universal succ. The first part of the trilogy, the 4-act "*I Medici,*" was not succ. (La Scala, Milan, 1893); the 4-act opera "*La Bohème*" (Venice) was a succ. but was overshadowed by that of Puccini and did not hold the repertoire; other of his works were moderate successes, notably "*Zaza*" (Milan, 1900), sung in other cities and revived at Met. Op. 1919-20 as an effective vehicle for Farrar; the Kaiser commissioned "*Roland,*" but it failed (Berlin R. Op., 1904). Other later works were "*La Jeunesse de Figaro*" (sung in America, 1906); "*Maja*" (Rome, 1910); "*Malbruck*" (operetta, do.); "*La Reginetta della Rose*" (operetta, Rome, 1912); "*I Zingari*" (London and Milan, 1912); "*La Candidata*" (operetta, Rome, 1915); "*Goffredo Mameli*" (Genoa, 1916); "*Edipo Re*" (one act, Chicago Op., 1920); and a number of other works that never saw the stage. L. also served as librettist for Machado and Pennachio, and his song texts were set, among others, by Tosti. He also c. a symph. poem, "*Nuit de Mai,*" ballets, choral works, and an unfinished operetta, "*La Maschera Nuda,*" orchestrated by S. Allegra and given at Naples, 1925. He visited the U. S., 1906 and 1913.

Leonhard (lä'-ōn-härt), **Julius Emil,** Lauban, 1810—Dresden, 1883; professor and composer.

Leoni (lä-ō'-nē), (1) **Leone,** cond. Vicenza Cath., 1588—1623, and composer. (2) **Carlo,** Italian composer; prod. 3-act operetta "*Per un Bacio*" (Siena, 1894), and text and music of succ. comic opera "*Urbano*" (Pienza, 1896). (3) **Franco,** b.

Milan, Oct. 24, 1865—London, 1949; pupil of Ponchielli; for 25 years res. in London; after 1914 in Milan; c. pop. realistic one-act opera "*L'Oracolo*," a melodrama of China-town, which gave striking rôle to Scotti at Met. Op.; also opera, "*Rip Van Winkle*" (London, 1897); can-tata "*Sardanapalus*," and many other stage works and pop. songs.

Leono'va, Daria Mikhailovna, in the Russian Govt. of Twer, 1825—St. Petersburg, Feb. 9, 1896; alto; début at 18 in Glinka's "*Life for the Czar*"; sang for many years at the National Opera, and toured around the world.

Leopo'lita (or **Lvovczyk**) (l'vôf'-chěk), **Martin**, Lemberg, ca. 1540—Cracow, 1589; from 1560 Polish court com-poser; c. masses, chorales, etc.

Ler'ner, Tina, b. Odessa, 1890; pianist; toured Europe; from 1908, toured America; m. Louis Bachner; (2) Vladimir Shavitch, conductor.

Le Roi (lür-wä), **Adrien**, 16th cent.; partner of Ballard (q. v.).

Leroux (lŭ-roo), **Xavier**, Velletri, Papal States, Oct. 11, 1863—Paris, Feb. 2, 1919; pupil of Paris Cons., took Grand Prix de Rome, 1885; c. opera "*Cléopatre*" (1890), lyric drama "*Evangeline*," a dramatic overture "*Harold*," and operas "*William Ratcliff*" and "*L'Epavo*" (not prod.); "*Astarté*" (Gr. Opéra, 1901), "*La Reine Fiammette*" (1902), "*Théodora*" (Monte Carlo, 1907); "*Le Chemineau*" (Paris Op.-Comique, 1907, also with succ. at Ravinia (Chicago)); "*Le Carilloneur*" (Op.-Comique, 1913); "*La Fille de Figaro*" (Paris, 1914); "*Les Cadeaux de Noël*" (do., 1916); "*18*—" (do., 1918); and the posthumous "*Nausi-thoe*" (Nice, 1920); also "*L'Ingénu*" (unpub.); and partially finished work, "*La Plus For*—" orch. by Büsser and prod. Op.-Comique. He was a prof. at the Paris Cons.

Lert, (1) **Ernst**, b. Vienna, May 12, 1883; theatre and opera director; Ph. D.; stage director, Breslau Op., 1909; Leipzig Op., 1912; Basel, 1919; Frankfort Op., 1920–23; also for a season at Met. Op., N. Y.; teacher at Curtis Inst., Phila. (2) **Richard**, b. Vienna, Sept. 19, 1885; conductor; bro. of Ernst; cond. at Düsseldorf, Darmstadt, Breslau, and (1929–32) at Berlin State Op., later res. in Los Angeles as orch. and choral

cond., including Hollywood Bowl appearances.

Lesage de Richée (lŭ-săzh-dŭ-rē-shä), **Philipp Fz.**, lutenist and composer.

Leschetizky (lě-shě-tĭt'-shkĭ), **Theodor**, Lancut, Austrian Poland, June 22, 1830—Dresden, Nov. 14, 1915; emi-nent pf. teacher; son and pupil of a prominent teacher in Vienna; studied with Czerny (pf.) and Sechter (comp.); at 15 began teaching; 1842 made succ. tours; 1852 teacher in the St. Petersburg Cons.; 1878 toured; 1880 m. his former pupil Annette Essipoff, and settled as a teacher in Vienna; c. succ. opera, "*Die Erste Falte*" (Prague, 1867), piano pieces, etc.

Les'lie, (1) **H. David**, London, 1822 —London, 1896; 'cellist, cond. and composer. (2) **Ernest**, pen-name of **Brown, O. B.**

Les'sel, Fz., Pulaivi, Poland, 1780— Petrikow, 1838; composer.

Less'man (**W. J.**), **Otto**, Rüdersdorf, near Berlin, Jan. 30, 1844—Jena, April 28, 1918; critic and composer; teacher at Stern's Cons.; then at Tausig's Acad. until 1871; organised a piano-sch. of his own; 1882 pro-prietor and ed. *Allgm. Musik-Zeitung*.

Le Sueur (lŭ-sür) (or **Lesueur**), **J.- Fran.**, Drucat-Plessiel, near Abbe-ville, France, Feb. 15, 1760—Paris, Oct. 6, 1837; chiefly self-taught; 1786 cond. at Notre Dame, Paris, where he drew crowds and criticism by his progammatic mus.; he pub. pamphlets defending "dramatic and descriptive" church-mus.; the oppo-sition prevailed, however, and he re-tired to the country for 4 years; 1793 he prod. succ. opera "*La Caverne*," followed by others; 1804 Napoleon raised him from distress to the post of ct.-cond.

Letz, Hans, b. Ittenheim, Alsace, March 18, 1887; violinist; studied Strasbourg Cons. and Berlin Hochsch. (with Joachim); recital début, N. Y., 1909; concertm. Thomas Orch., Chicago, 1910–12; mem. Kneisel Quartet, later org. Letz Quartet; taught Juilliard School of Music and N. Y. School of Music.

Leuckart (loik'-ärt), **F. Ernst Chp.**, founded mus. business at Breslau, 1782, bought 1856 by C. Sanders.

Leva (dě lā'-vä), **Enrico de**, b. Naples, Jan. 18, 1867; singing teacher, pupil

of Puzone and Arienzo; c. opera
"*La Camargo*," (Naples, 1898); sere-
nade "*A Capomonte*" and popular
Neapolitan canzonets.
Levadé (lŭ-vă-dā'), **Charles Gaston,**
b. Paris, Jan. 3, 1869; pupil of
Massenet at the Cons.; c. opera
"*Les Hérétiques*" (Béziers, 1905),
operetta "*L'Amour d'Héliodora*"
(Paris, 1903), pantomime, suites,
etc.
Levasseur (lŭ-văs-sŭr), (1) **P. Fran.,**
b. Abbeville, France, 1753; 'cellist,
Paris Grand Opéra; composer. (2)
J. H., Paris, 1765—1823; 'cellist.
(3) **Rosalie,** soprano, Paris Opéra,
1766–85. (4) **Nicholas Prosper,** b.
in Picardy, March 9, 1791; dram.-
bass and professor; d. Paris, Dec. 7,
1871.
Lev'ey, **Wm. Chas.,** Dublin, 1837—
London, 1894; dram. composer.
Levi (lā'-vē), (1) **Hermann,** Giessen,
Nov. 7, 1839—Munich, May 13,
1900; eminent conductor; pupil of
V. Lachner and of Leipzig Cons.;
1859–61, mus.-dir., Saarbrücken;
1861–64, cond. German Opera at
Rotterdam; 1864–72, ct.-cond. at
Carlsruhe; from 1872, ct.-cond. at
Munich; 1894, Gen. mus. dir.
Munich; 1896, pensioned. (2) **Levi**
(or Levy, Lewy). Vide LEBERT.
Levitzki (lĕ-vēt'-skē), **Mischa,** b.
Krementchug, Russia, May 25, 1898;
d. Avon, N. J., Jan. 2, 1941; studied
N. Y., and Berlin Hochsch. under
Dohnanyi; grad. with artist's
diploma; début, Berlin, 1914; has
toured widely in Europe, America
and Orient as recitalist and with
orchs. following N. Y. début, 1916;
a brilliant technician; has also c.
piano works.
Lewalter (lĕ-väl'-tĕr), **Johann,** b.
Cassel, Jan. 24, 1862; pupil Leipzig
Cons.; from 1886 music teacher and
writer; d. Cassel, 1941.
Lewinger (lā'-vǐng-ĕr), **Max,** Sulkov,
near Cracow, March 17, 1870—
Dresden, Aug. 31, 1908; violinist;
pupil of Cracow and Lemberg Cons.;
and with Grüns Scholarship, at the
Vienna Cons.; from 1892 toured;
teacher at Bucharest Cons.; thence
to Helsingfors as concertmaster;
1897, do. at the Gewandhaus Orch.,
Leipzig; 1898 Royal Court concert
master in Dresden.
Lewis, **Mary,** b. Hot Springs, Ark.,
1900—N. Y., Dec. 31, 1941; sang in

choir in native state, later entered
musical comedy in N. Y.; op. début
as "Marguerite," Vienna Volksop.,
1923; sang in Monte Carlo, London
and Paris, 1924–25; concert début
with State Sympl. Orch., N. Y.;
mem. Met. Op. Co., 1926–30, début as
"Mimi"; sang "Marguerite" at Berlin
Op., 1927; also appeared in recitals
in U. S.; m. Michael Bohnen, bass;
divorced; (2) Robert Hague.
Lewy (lā'-vē), (1) **Eduard Constantin,**
Saint-Avold, Moselle, 1796—Vienna,
1846; horn-virtuoso and prof. (2)
Jos. Rodolphe, Nancy, 1804—Ober-
lissnitz, near Dresden, 1881; bro. and
pupil of above; horn-virtuoso. (3)
Chas., Lausanne, 1823—Vienna,
1883; son of (1); pianist and composer. (4) **Richard Levy,** Vienna,
1827—1883; son of (1); horn-player,
singing-teacher. (5) Vide LEBERT.
Leybach (lī'-bäkh), **Ignace,** Gambs-
heim, Alsatia, 1817—Toulouse,
1891; pianist, teacher and composer.
L'Héritier (lā-rǐt-yā), (1) **Jean,**
flourished 1519–1588; French pupil
of Deprès; c. masses and songs. (2)
Antoine, court musician to Charles
V. at Toledo, 1520–1531; (3) **Isaac,**
probably the same as Jean.
Lhévinne (lā'-vēn), (1) **Josef,** Moscow,
Dec. 3, 1874—N. Y., Dec. 2, 1944;
noted pianist; pupil of his father
and of Chrysander; later also of
the noted pianist and conductor, W.
Safonoff at the Cons.; 1885, winning
highest honours; 1895 won Rubinstein prize; 1902–06 teacher at the
Cons., and toured Europe; 1905,
the U. S.; again, 1912; resided in
N. Y. and had toured widely, giving
two-piano programmes with his wife,
(2) **Rosina L.**; also a noted teacher.
Liadoff (or Liadow) (l'yä'-dôf), **Anatole,** St. Petersburg, May 12, 1885—
Novgorod, Aug. 28, 1914; pupil
Johansen (cpt. and fugue) and
Rimsky-Korsakov (form and instr.)
at St. P. Cons.; 1878, prof. of harmony there; also at the Imp. Chapel;
1894, cond. Mus. Soc.; in 1908 he
resigned on account of the expulsion
of Rimsky-Korsakov (q.v.) and was
later reinstated in the Cons.; c.
scherzos for orch.; the popular symphonic poems, "*The Enchanted Lake*"
and "*Kikimora*"; "*Baba-Yaga*" tone-
picture (1905, Boston Symph., 1910),
8 folk-songs for orch.; suite "*To
Maeterlinck*" for orch., choruses with

orch.; "*The Music Box*," and other piano pieces and songs.

Liapunov (or **Liapounow**) (lē-ä'-poonŏf), **Serge Michailovitch**, Jarslavi, Russia, Nov. 30, 1859—Paris, Nov. 9, 1924; pupil Klindworth and Pabst (pf.) and Hubert (comp.) Moscow Cons.; sub-dir. Imp. Choir, St. Petersburg, and a member of the Imp. Geographical Soc., which 1893 commissioned him to collect the folk-songs of Vologda, Viatna and Kostroma, which he pub. 1897; 1894, mus.-master to the Grand Duke; pub. concerto, a symph., pf.-pcs., etc.

Libon (lē'-bōn), **Felipe**, Cadiz, Aug. 17, 1775—Paris, Feb. 5, 1838; violinist and comp. for violin.

Lichey (lēkh'-ī), **Rheinhold**, b. Neumark, near Breslau, March 26, 1880; organist; pupil of Baumert and Rudnick, later at the Royal High School in Berlin; from 1907 org. Königsberg; c. organ pieces, choruses, etc.

Lichtenberg (lĭkh'-t'n-bĕrkh), **Leopold**, San Francisco, Nov. 22, 1861—Brooklyn, N. Y., May 16, 1935; vln.-virtuoso; pupil of Beaujardin; at 8 played in public; at 12 pupil of Wieniawski, and his aide on a U. S. tour; studied 6 months with Lambert in Paris, then studied again with Wieniawski 3 years; won first prize of honour at the "National concourse"; toured America and Europe; member of Boston Symph. Orch.; 1899, vln. prof. Nat. Cons., New York.

Lichtenstein (lĭkh'-t'n-shtīn), **K. Aug.**, Freiherr **von**, Lahm, Franconia, 1767—Berlin, 1845; c. operas.

Lichtenthal (lĭkh'-t'n-täl), **Peter**, Pressburg, 1780—Milan, 1853; dram. composer and writer on mus.

Lidon (lē'-thon), **José**, Bejar, Salamanca, 1752—Madrid, Feb. 11, 1827; organist; 1808, royal chapel organist and royal cond. at Madrid; c. operas, church music, etc.

Lie (lē), (1) **Erica** (Mme. **Nissen**), Kongsvinger, near Christiania, Jan. 17, 1845—Christiania, Oct. 27, 1903; pianist, pupil of Kjerulf, and of Th. Kullak; teacher at the Kullak's Acad., toured Germany, etc.; member R. Acad., Stockholm. (2) (l'yä), **Sigurd**, May 23, 1871—Sept. 29, 1904; important Norwegian conductor and composer; pupil Leipzig Cons.; 1894 cond. in Bergen, studied

again in Berlin; cond. of vocal society in Christiania; c. symph., Marche symphonique; orch. suite, "*Oriental-isk*," cantatas, chorals and songs.

Liebe (lē'-bĕ), **Ed. L.**, Magdeburg, Nov. 26, 1819—Coire, Switz., 1900; pianist, organist and dram. composer.

Liebig (lē'-bĭkh), **K.**, Schwedt, 1808—Berlin, 1872; staff oboist in a Regt.; 1843, est. Berlin "Symphoniekapelle"; 1860, R. Mus. Dir.

Liebling (lēp'-lĭng), (1) **Emil**, **Pless**, Silesia, April 12, 1851—Chicago, Jan. 20, 1914; concert-pianist; pf.-pupil of Ehrlich and Th. Kullak, Berlin; Dachs, Vienna, Liszt and Dorn; since 1867, America, and since 1872, Chicago, as reviewer and concert-pianist, teacher and writer. Co-ed. in a "*Dictionary of Terms*"; pub. pf.-pcs. and songs. (2) **G.**, b. Berlin, 1865—d. N. Y., 1945; pupil Th., and Fr. Kullak, and Liszt (pf.), H. Urban and H. Dorn (comp.); 1880-85, teacher in Kullak's Acad.; 1881-89 toured Germany and Austria, with success; 1890, ct.-pianist to Duke of Coburg; 1908-23, res. in Munich; more recently in Los Angeles. (3) **Leonard**, b. N. Y., 1880—d. N. Y., 1945; pianist, editor; grad. Coll. of the City of N. Y.; pupil of Kullak and Godowsky at Berlin Hochsch.; taught piano in Berlin and N. Y. for several years; after 1899, active as critic and librettist; joined staff of *Musical Courier*, 1902; and has regularly written "Variations" column in that paper; after 1911, ed.-in-chief; music critic of N. Y. *American* until 1936; wrote plays. (4) **Estelle**, b. New York, 1886; soprano and teacher; sang opera in Europe and U. S.; faculty mem., Curtis Inst.

Lienau (lē'-now), **Robt.**, Neustadt, Holstein, Dec. 28, 1838—July 22, 1920; mus.-pub., Berlin.

Lier (văn lēr), **Jacques Van**, b. The Hague, April 24, 1875; pupil of Hartog, Giese and Eberle; 1891 first 'cellist Amsterdam Palace Orch.; 1897 Berlin Phil. Orch.; teacher at Klindworth-Scharwenka Cons. until 1915; later in The Hague; 'cellist of the Dutch Trio and the Dutch String Quartet; author of methods.

Liliencron (lē'-lĭ-ĕn-krōn), **Rochus**, Freiherr **von**, Plön, Holstein, Dec. 8, 1820—Coblenz, March 5, 1912; prof.; commissioned by the Historical

Commission of Munich to collect the mediæval German folk-songs, and pub. them.

Lillo (lïl'-lō), **Gius.**, Galatina, Lecce, Italy, 1814—Naples, 1863; teacher and dram. composer.

Lim'bert, Frank L., b. New York, Nov. 15, 1866; at 8 taken to Germany; pupil of Hoch Cons. and of Rheinberger; 1894 Ph. D. Berlin; 1901 cond. of the Düsseldorf Singing Society, and teacher at the Cons. 1906, at Hanau; c. choral works with orch., etc.

Limnan'der de Nieuwenhove (nā'-věn-hō-vě), **Armand Marie Ghislain**, Ghent, 1814—Moignanville 1892; dram. composer.

Lincke (lïnk'-ě), (1) **Jos.**, Trachenberg, Silesia, 1783—Vienna, 1837; 'cellist. (2) **Paul,** b. Berlin, Nov. 7, 1866—d. Sept. 4, 1946; composer.

Lind (lïnt), **Jenny**, Stockholm, Oct. 6, 1820—at her villa, Wynds Point, Malvern Wells, Nov. 2, 1887; "The Swedish Nightingale," one of the most eminent and pop. of sopranos; had a remarkably sympathetic voice of great compass (d' –e''', v. CHART OF PITCH), remarkable purity, breath, endurance and flexibility; studied with Berg and Lindblad, at the court where she made her very succ. début, 1838, in *"Der Frei-schütz"*; 1841, studied with Manuel Garcia, in Paris, for nine months; 1842, sang at the Opéra, but was not engaged; 1844, studied German at Berlin, and sang with greatest succ. in Germany and Sweden; 1847, made a furore in London; 1849, she left the operatic stage, and created even greater sensations in concert; 1850–52, under the management of P. T. Barnum, she toured the U. S., earning $120,000; 1852, she m. Otto Gold-schmidt in Boston; lived in Dresden; 1856, London, appearing especially with the Bach Choir which her husband cond. Her last pub. appearance was in his oratorio *"Ruth,"* Düsseldorf, 1870. Her private life was unusually serene, impeccable, and generous. Her bust is in Westminster Abbey. Biogr. by A. J. Becher (1847), Rockstro and Wilkens.

Lindblad (lïnt'-blät) **Ad. Fr.,** Löfvingsborg, near Stockholm, 1801—1878; teacher of Jenny Lind; c. excellent Swedish songs and an opera.

Lind'egren, Johan, Ullared, Sweden, Jan. 7, 1842—Stockholm, June 8, 1908; teacher of theory and contrapuntist; from 1884 cantor at the Stockholm Storkyrka; c. and edited church music.

Linden (lïnt'-'n), **Cornelis van der,** Dordrecht, Aug. 24, 1839—Dordrecht, May 28, 1918; prominent Dutch cond.; pupil of Kwast (pf.) and F. Böhme (theory); 1860 cond. Dordrecht; later bandm. the Nat. Guard (1875); cond. Netherland Musicians' Assoc.; c. cantatas with orch., 2 operas, etc.

Linder (lïn'-děr), **Gf.**, Ehingen, July 22, 1842—Stuttgart, Jan. 29, 1918; pupil Stuttgart Cons.; from 1868 teacher there; 1879 professor; c. 2 operas; overture *"Aus nordischer Heldenzeit,"* etc.

Lind'ley, (1) **Robert,** Rotherham, Yorkshire, 1776—London, 1855; 'cellist. (2) **Wm.,** 1802—Manchester, 1869; son of above; 'cellist.

Lindner (lïnt'-něr), (1) **Fr.,** Liegnitz ca. 1540—Nürnberg, 1597; composer. (2) **Adolf,** Lobenstein, 1808—Leipzig, 1867; horn-player. (3) **Ernst Otto Timotheus,** Breslau, 1820—Berlin, 1867; conductor and writer.

Lindpaintner (lïnt'-pïnt-něr), **Peter Jos. von,** Coblenz, Dec. 9, 1791—Nonnenhorn, Aug. 21, 1856; eminent conductor, ct.-conductor and dram. composer.

Lin'ley, (1) **Thos., Sr.,** Wells, 1732—London, 1795; conductor and dram. composer; owner with Sheridan of Drury Lane Th., 1776. (2) **Thos., Jr.,** Bath, 1756—drowned at Grimsthorpe, Lincolnshire, 1778; violinist and composer.

Lipat'ti, Dinu, b. Bucharest, 1919—d. Switz., Dec. 2, 1950; noted pianist.

Lipinski (lĭ-pĭn'-shkĭ), **K. Jos.,** Radzyn, Poland, Nov. 4 (Oct. 30 ?), 1790—Urlow, near Lemberg, Dec. 16, 1861; noted violinist and composer; pupil of Paganini; lived in Dresden, 1839–59.

Lipsius (lĭp'-sĭ-oos), **Marie,** Leipzig, Dec. 30, 1837—near Wurzen, Saxony, March 2, 1927; noted writer on Liszt, Beethoven; edited letters of Liszt, Berlioz, etc.; wrote under pen-name **"La Mara."**

Lischin (lēsh'-ĭn), **Grigory Andreevitch,** 1853—St. Petersburg, June 27, 1888; c. operas, incl. *"Don César de Bazan."*

Lissenko (or **Lysenko**), **Nikolai Vitalie-vich**, Grinjki, March 22, 1842—Kiev, Nov. 11, 1912; popular Little Russian comp.; pupil of Panochiny, Dimitriev and Vilczek; then of Leipzig Cons.; 1868, teacher at Kiev; c. 6 operas; children's opera, and popular songs.

Lissmann (lēs'-män), (1) **H. Fritz**, Berlin, 1847—Hamburg, 1894; barytone; m. the sopr. (2) **Anna Marie Gutzschbach.**

List, Emanuel, b. Vienna; operatic bass; sang as a boy chorister at Theater an der Wien; later toured as mem. of quartet and in solo programmes; came to U. S. from England in 1914 and studied in N. Y. with Josiah Zuro, appearing in feature radio theatre presentations; 1922, returned to Europe, studied with Édouard de Reszke and was engaged for Vienna Volksoper; later for Berlin Municipal Op. and then for State Op. on Unter den Linden, where he remained for ten years; after 1932, mem. Met. Op.; noted for his portrayal of "Baron Ochs" in *"Der Rosenkavalier"* and for Wagnerian impersonations; has sung at Covent Garden, at Bayreuth, and in other leading Eur. op. houses.

Listemann (lǐs'-tĕ-män), (1) **Fritz**, Schlotheim, Thuringia, March 25, 1839—Boston, Dec. 28, 1909; violinist; pupil of his uncle Ullrich, and of David, Leipzig Cons., 1858, chamber-virtuoso to the Prince of Rudolstadt; 1867 lived in New York; 1871, 1st vln. Thomas Orch.; from 1878, 1st vln. Philh. Orch.; 1881–85 Symph. Orch.; taught and toured with "Listemann Concert Co."; c. 2 vln.-concertos, etc. (2) **Bernhard**, Schlotheim, Aug. 28, 1841—Chicago, Feb. 11, 1917; bro. of above; pupil of Ullrich, and David, Vieuxtemps and Joachim. 1859–67, 1st vln. in Rudolstadt ct.-orch.; came to America with his bro., lived in Boston; 1871–74, leader Thomas Orch.; 1874 founded the "Philharm. Club," and toured the country; 1878 founded Boston Philh.-Orch.; cond. till 1881, then 4 yrs. leader of the New "Symph.-Orch."; founded "Listemann Quartet"; 1883–93, dir. of the "Listemann Concert Co."; from 1893, prof. Chicago Coll. of Mus.; pub. a *"Method."* (3) **Paul**, b. Boston, Oct. 24, 1871; son and pupil

of (2); studied also with (1) and was a member of the Quartet and Concert Co., 1890–93; studied with Brodsky and Hilf, Leipzig, and with Joachim, at Berlin; concert m. of the Pittsburgh (Pa.) Orch.; 1896, of the "American Orch.," N. Y.; soloist of the "Redpath Concert Co." (4) **Fz.**, New York, Dec. 17, 1873—Chicago, March 11, 1930; bro. of above; 'cellist; pupil of Fries and Giese at Boston, of Julius Klengel, Leipzig; and Hausmann, Berlin; 1st 'cello Pittsburgh Orch. for a year, then lived in N. Y. as teacher and concert-performer.

Liszt (lǐst), **Franz** (originally **Ferencz**), Raiding, near Oedenburg, Hungary, Oct. 22, 1811—Bayreuth, July 31, 1886; in many ways the most brilliant of all pianists, and a composer whose poorest works are too popular, while he is not granted the credit due his more solid achievements; as great a patron of art, also, as he was creator. Son and pupil of an amateur; at nine played in public, at Oedenburg, Ries' E♭ concerto. A group of Hungarian counts subscribed a 6 years' annuity of 600 florins, and the family moved to Vienna, where **L.** studied with Czerny (pf.), and Salieri (theory) for 18 months. Beethoven hearing him play his trio op. 97, embraced him. At 12 he gave v. succ. concerts in Vienna and his father took him to Paris, where he was refused as a foreigner because of Cherubini's objections to "infant phenomena;" hereafter **L.** was his own teacher, except in comp. which he studied with Paër and Reicha. At 14, his 1-act operetta, *"Don Sancho"* had 5 performances at the Acad. royale de musique. On his father's death in 1827 he supported his mother by teaching, soon becoming the salon-idol he always remained. He was strongly influenced by Chopin, von Weber, Paganini and Berlioz. He had a brilliant series of heart-affairs, beginning with the literary Countess d'Agoult ("Daniel Stern"), with whom he lived in Geneva (1835–39). She bore him a son and three daughters; Cosima, the youngest, became the wife of von Bülow, later of Wagner. 1839, he successfully undertook to earn by concerts money enough for the completion of the

Beethoven monument at Bonn. 1849, ct.-cond. at Weimar, with royal encouragement to aid mus. progress. He made himself the greatest patron among creative artists, aiding Wagner materially by productions of his works at Weimar and by pf.-transcriptions, aiding also Raff, Schumann, and Berlioz, finally resigning before the opposition to, and failure of, an opera by Cornelius (q. v.). 1859-70, he lived chiefly at Rome, where in 1866 the Pope, Pius IX., made him an abbé. 1870 he was reconciled with the Weimar Court. 1875 pres. of the new Acad. of Mus. at Pesth; he spent his last years at Weimar, Pesth, and Rome, followed by a large retinue of disciples and pupils whom he taught free of charge. He died during a Bayreuth Festival. C. 2 SYMPHS.: *"Dante"* (after the "Divina Commedia" with female chorus); *"Eine Faustsymphonie"* ("Faust," "Gretchen," "Mephistopheles," with male chorus); SYMPH. POEMS: *"Ce qu'on entend sur la montagne"* (Victor Hugo); *"Tasso, lamento e trionfo"*; *"Les Préludes"*; *"Orpheus"*; *"Prometheus"*; *"Mazeppa"*; *"Festklänge"*; *"Héroïde funèbre"*; *"Hungaria"*; *"Hamlet"*; *"Hunnenschlacht"*; *"Die Ideale"* (Schiller); and *"Von der Wiege bis zum Grabe"* (Michael Zichy); ALSO FOR ORCH. *"Zwei Episoden aus Lenaus Faust"* (Der nächtliche Zug, 2 Mephisto-wälzer), etc. FOR PIANO: 2 concertos; *"Danse macabre"* with orch.; *"Concerto pathétique"*; 15 *"Rhapsodies hongroises"*; *"Rhapsodie espagnole"*; *"Sonata in B Min."*; *"Fantasia and Fugue on B–A–C–H"*; variations on a theme from Bach's *B-min. mass;* 10 *"Harmonies poétiques et réligieuses"*; *"Années de pèlerinage"*; 3 *"Apparitions,"* 2 ballades; 6 *"Consolations"*; 2 élégies; 2 légendes (*"St. François D'Assise"* and *"St. François de Paul"*); *"Liebesträume"* (Notturnos); *"Études d'éxecution transcendante"*; *"Ab irato, étude de perfectionnement"*; concert-études, *"Waldesrauschen"* and *"Gnomenreigen"*; *"Technische Studien"* (12 books), etc., and many transcriptions of symphs., overtures, 50 songs by Schubert, etc. Vocal comps.: 4 masses, incl. *Missa solennis* (the "Graner" Festival Mass); requiem;

3 oratorios, *"Die Legende von der Heiligen Elisabeth," "Stanislavs,"* and *"Christus"*; Psalms 13th, 18th, etc., with orch. and other church-music; 3 cantatas with orch.; male choruses, 60 songs, etc. Wrote life of Chopin, of Franz, etc. Complete ed. of his writings in 6 vols. Biogr. by L. Ramann, 1880. There is an extensive Liszt literature; among studies of his life and work are those by Göllerich, Kapp, Schrader, Raabe, Corder, Habets, Hervey, Huneker, Newman, Pourtalès, Sitwell, W. Wallace and La Mara; a complete edition of his musical works is being prepared by Breitkopf and Härtel, under the auspices of a committee headed by Raabe. (See article, page 502.)

Litolff (lē'-tôlf), **H. Chas.,** London, Feb. 6, 1818—Paris, Aug. 6, 1891; prominent pianist, conductor, publisher and composer.

Litta (lǐt'-tä), Duca Giulio, Visconte Arese, Milan, 1822—Vedano, near Monza, 1891; dram. composer.

Litvinne (lēt'-vǐn), Felia, St. Petersburg, 1860 (?)—Paris, Oct. 12, 1936; soprano; pupil of Mme. Barth-Banderoli and Maurel, début Th. des Italiens, Paris; 1896-97, sang Wagner at Met. Op., N. Y.; then in St. Petersburg; later res. in Paris; sister-in-law of Éd. de Reszke.

Litzau (lēt'-tsow), Jn. Barend, Rotterdam, 1822—1893; pianist, organist and composer.

Liverati (lē-vĕ-rä'-tē), Giov., Bologna, 1772—after 1817; noted tenor conductor and dram. composer.

Ljungberg (yĕt'-tä-yōōng'-bĕrkh), b. Sundsvall, Sweden, Oct. 4, 1893; soprano; studied in Stockholm; 1924, guest at Covent Garden as "Salome"; sang Met. Op., N. Y., in same rôle, also Wagner operas, and Howard Hanson's *"Merry Mount."*

Lloyd (loid), (1) **Edw.,** London, March 7, 1845—March 31, 1927; noted concert tenor; choir-boy, Westminster Abbey, with Jas. Turle, till 1860; from 1874, first tenor, Leeds Festival; sang at Cincinnati Festival 1888, and had toured the U. S.; gave farewell concert, London, 1900. (2) **Chas. Harford,** Thornbury, Gloucestershire, Engl., Oct. 16, 1849—London, Oct. 16, 1919; 1891, Mus. Doc. Oxford; 1876,

organist Gloucester Cath.; 1892 precentor and mus.-teacher Eton Coll.; founded Oxford Univ. Mus.-Club; 1877–80, cond. Gloucester Festivals; Oxford Symph. Concerts; c. 7 cantatas, mus. to "*Alcestis*" (Oxford, 1887); full cath. service, etc.

Lobe (lō'-bĕ), **Jn. Chr.**, Weimar, May 30, 1797—Leipzig, July 27, 1881; flutist, vla.-player, and dram. composer; wrote important treatises.

Lo'bo (or **Lopez**) (lō'-pĕs) (or **Lupus**), **Duarte**, Portuguese composer at Lisbon, 1600.

Locatel'li, Pietro, Bergamo, 1693—Amsterdam, 1764; vln.-virtuoso, regarded as marvellous for his double-stopping and effects procured by changed accordature (v. D. D.) in which Paganini imitated him; composer.

Locke, Matthew, Exeter, England, 1632 (33 ?)—London, 1677; composer.

Lo'der, (1) Edw. Jas., Bath, 1813—London, 1865; dram. composer. (2) **Kate Fanny (Lady Thompson)** Bath, Aug. 21, 1825—London, Aug. 30, 1904; pianist, cousin of E. J. Loder (q. v.); pupil of the R. A. M., London, winning the King's scholarship, 1839 and 1841; from 1844 Prof. of harmony there; played with great success at Phil. concerts and elsewhere; 1851 married the surgeon Henry Thompson, afterward knighted; c. an opera, overture, violin sonata, etc.

Loeb (lāp), **Jules,** Strassburg, May 13, 1852—Paris, Nov., 1933; pupil of Chevillard, Paris Cons., won 1st prize; solo 'cellist at the Opéra, and the Cons. Concerts; member of the Marsick Quartet, and the "Société pour instrs. à vent et à cordes."

Loeffler (lĕf'-lĕr), **Chas. Martin Tornov,** Mühlhausen, Alsatia, Jan. 30, 1861—Medfield, Mass., May 20, 1935; violinist and notable composer; pupil of Massart, Leonardi, Joachim and Guiraud (comp.); played in Pasdeloup's orch.; later in Prince Dervier's orch.; resigned from the Boston Symph. Orch., 1903, to give his time entirely to composition; c. a fantastic concerto for 'cello and orch. (1894); divertimento for violin and orch. (1897); his symph. poem for 2 viole d'amore "*La Mort des*

Tintagiles" was prod. by the Boston Symph. 1897; he revised it for one viola d'amore and it was prod. 1901, with the composer as the soloist; his "*Divertissement Espagnol*" for saxophone, and orch. was prod. 1901; his 2 symph. poems, "*Avant que tu ne t'en ailles*" (after Verlaine's "*La bonne chanson,*") and "*Villanelle du diable*" (after Rollinat) were prod. 1902; his "*Pagan Poem*" for orch., piano, 3 trumpets and Engl. horn 1907. Other works include (for orch.) "*Les Veillées de l' Ukraine*" (1891), "*Memories of My Childhood,*" both showing impressions gained in early visit to Russia; "*Poem*"; and "*Evocation*" for orch. with choral voices; (for chorus) "*Hora Mystica,*" "*By the Rivers of Babylon,*" "*Canticum Fratris Solis*" (setting of St. Francis' Canticle to the Sun); (chamber works) Music for 4 stringed instruments; 2 Rhapsodies for oboe, viola and piano; "*To the Memory of Victor Chapman*" for string quartet; Sextet for strings; Octet for strings, harp and two clarinets; and important songs.

Loeillet (lwä-yā'), **J. Bap.,** Ghent, 1653—London, 1728; noted virtuoso on flute and harp; composer.

Loewe. Vide LÖWE.

Loewengard (lā'vĕn-gärt), **Max Julius,** Frankfort-on-Main, Oct. 2, 1860—Hamburg, Nov. 19, 1915; writer and composer; pupil of Raff, then teacher at Wiesbaden Cons.; 1904 critic in Hamburg and 1908 teacher at the Cons.; author of text books in theory; c. comic opera "*Die 14 Nothelfer.*"

Logier (lō'-jēr), **Jn. Bd.,** Cassel, 1777—Dublin, 1846; flutist, writer and composer; invented the "chiroplast."

Logroscino (lô-grō-shē'-nō), **Nicolà,** Naples, ca. 1700—1763; professor of cpt.; composer; pupil of Durante; 1747, prof. of cpt. at Palermo, then lived in Naples and prod. some 20 light operas; he was brilliantly successful, and was the first to close acts with an ensemble.

Löhlein (lā'-līn), **Georg Simon,** Neustadt, 1727—Danzig, 1782; pianist and teacher.

Lohmann (lō'-män), **Peter,** Schwelm, Westphalia, April 24, 1833—Leipzig, Jan. 10, 1907, where he had lived since 1856; 1858–61, writer for "*Neue Zeitschrift für Musik*"; wrote treatises and several dramas set to music by Huber, Goetze, etc.

Löhr (lär), (1) **G. Augustus**, Norwich, Engl., 1821—Leicester, 1897; organist and conductor. (2) **Richard H.**, Leicester, Engl., June 13, 1856—St. Leonard's-on-Sea, Jan. 16, 1927; studied R. A. M., won two medals; organist, London; 1882, concert-pianist; c. oratorios; wrote *"Primer of Music,"* etc.

Lohse (lō'-zĕ), **Otto**, Dresden, Sept. 21, 1858—Baden-Baden, May 5, 1925; for years cond. Hamburg City Th., 1895-96, Damrosch Op. Co., in which the prima donna was his wife **Klafsky** (q. v.); cond. Covent Garden, 1901; cond. City Th., Strassburg, 1897—1904; after 1904, in Cologne; 1912-23, dir. of Leipzig Op.; c. succ. opera *"Der Prinz Wider Willen"* (Cologne, 1898).

Lolli (lôl'-lĭ), **Ant.**, Bergamo, ca. 1730 ('40 ?)—Palermo, 1802; violinist and leader; composer and writer.

Lomagne, B. de. Vide SOUBIES.

Lo'makin, Gabriel Joakimovich, St. Petersburg April 6, 1812—Gatschina, May 21, 1885; teacher.

London, George, b. Canada; studied San Francisco; basso; début, Vienna Op., 1949; La Scala; Met Op., 1951.

Long'hurst, (1) **Wm. H.**, Lambeth, Engl., Oct. 6, 1819—Canterbury, 1904; chorister in Canterbury Cath.; later asst.-organist, master of the choristers and lay-clerk; 1873, organist; 1875, Mus. Doc. and mus.-lecturer; c. oratorios, cath. service, etc. (2) **J. Alex**, 1809-1855, singer.

Long'o, Alessandro, Amantea, 1864—Naples, 1946; pianist; ed. D. Scarlatti.

Longy (lôn-zhē), (1) **Gustave Georges Léopold**, Abbéville, Aug. 29, 1868—April 14, 1930; pupil Paris Cons. taking second oboe prize 1885, first prize 1886; oboist with Lamoureux and at Op. Com.; from 1898 first oboist Boston Symph., founding 1900 the Longy Club (flute, oboe, clarinet, horn, bassoon, piano), and giving important concerts; 1890-1913, also cond. of the Orchestral Club, and from 1915 dir. of the MacDowell Orch. In 1916 he founded the notable Longy School of Music, with a faculty incl. many solo players of the Boston Symph. Orch. This institution has had a continued existence until the present day, upholding high standards and

moving its headquarters to Cambridge, Mass., after many years in Boston. (2) **Renée (Longy-Miquelle)**, his daughter, also an able musician, especially known as a teacher of *solfège;* mem. faculty, Curtis Inst. of Music, Philadelphia.

Loo'mis, Harvey Worthington, b. Brooklyn, N. Y., Feb. 5, 1865—Roxbury, Mass., Dec. 25, 1931; composer; pupil of Dvořák at the National Cons., New York, 1892, winning a 3-years' scholarship; lived in New York; c. pantomimes and music to poems; pf.-pcs. and songs.

Lopat'nikoff, Nikolai, b. Reval, March 16, 1903; composer; studied at Petrograd Cons., also with W. Rehberg, Grabner and Toch; after 1920 res. in Karlsruhe, later in Helsingfors; c. modern-style works of originality and strong formal sense, among which a symph. was performed by N. Y. Philh. Orch. under Lange; also chamber music and piano works.

Lopez. Vide LOBO.

Lorenz (lō'-rĕnts), (1) **Fz.**, Stein, Lower Austria, 1805—Vienna, 1883; writer. (2) **Karl Ad.**, Köslin, Pomerania, Aug. 13, 1837—Stettin, March 3, 1923; c. quartets, etc., as a sch.-boy; studied with Dehn, Kiel and Gehrig, Berlin, and at Berlin Univ.; 1861, Dr. Phil.; 1866, Municipal Dir., Stettin, cond. symph. concerts, etc.; teacher in two gymnasiums; founded the "Stettin Musikverein" (for oratorio); 1885, professor; c. 2 succ. operas, overtures, etc. (3) **Julius**, Hanover, Oct. 1, 1862—Glogau, Oct. 1, 1924; from 1884, cond. Singakademie, Glogau; 1895, of the "Arion," New York; c. an opera *"Die Rekruten,"* and overtures. (4) **Max**, b. Düsseldorf, May 19, 1901; tenor; studied with Grenzebach; sang heroic rôles at Dresden Op., and after 1934 at Berlin State Op.; also, beginning 1933, at Bayreuth Fest., ("Parsifal," "Siegfried," "Walther"); was mem. of Met. Op. Co., N. Y., for several seasons.

Lo'ris, Lori'tus. Vide GLAREANUS.

Lortzing (lôrt'-tsĭng), (Gv.), **Albert**, Berlin, Oct. 23, 1801—Jan. 21, 1851; an actor, son of actors, and m. an actress, 1823. Had a few lessons with Rungenhagen; chiefly self-taught; 1826, actor at Detmold; prod. 2 vaudevilles with succ.; 1833-

44, tenor at Leipzig th.; prod. succ. *"Die beiden Schützen"*; 1837 and 1839, *"Czar und Zimmerman"*; 4 others followed, then *"Der Wildschütz,"* 1842; cond. at Leipzig Op., then travelled, producing 6 more operas, incl. *"Undine"* (1845); *"Der Waffenschmied"* (1846); his melodious unction keeps those works mentioned still popular, and his *"Regina"* was posthumously prod. Berlin, 1899.

Los An'geles, Victoria de, b. Spain; won Internat'l Contest, Geneva; Met Op., from 1950; Covent Garden; soprano noted for lyric, coloratura roles; has sung Elsa, Butterfly, Rosina.

Löschhorn (lĕsh'-hôrn), **Albert,** Berlin, June 27, 1819—June 4, 1905; pupil of L. Berger, Kollitschgy, Grell and A. W. Bach at the R. Inst. for Churchmusic; 1851, pf.-teacher there; 1859, professor; noted teacher; writer and composer.

Lossius, Lucas, Vacha, Hesse-Cassel, Oct. 18, 1508—Lüneburg, 1582; rector, theorist and compiler.

Lotti (lôt'-tē), **Ant.,** Venice, ca. 1667—Venice, Jan. 5, 1740; son of the ct.-cond. at Hanover; pupil of Legrenzi; at 16 prod. an opera at Venice; 1697 organist there; prod. 20 operas with general succ.; was noted as an organist, and more famed as a composer of churchmusic.

Lotze (lôt'-tsĕ), **Rudolf Hn.,** Bautzen, 1817—Berlin, 1881; professor and writer.

Louis (loo'-ēs), (1) **Fd.,** Friedrichsfelde, near Berlin, 1772—Saalfeld, 1806; Prince of Russia, nephew of Frederick II.; composer. (2) (loo'-ē) **Rudolf,** Schwetzingen, Jan. 30, 1870—Munich, Nov. 15, 1914; pupil at Geneva and Vienna, where he was made Ph. D., studied conducting with Mottl; theatre-cond. at Landshut and Lübeck; after 1907 writer and theory teacher in Munich; c. symph. fantasie *"Proteus"* (Basel, 1903).

Lowe (lō), **Edw.,** Salisbury, Engl., 1610 (-15?)—Oxford, 1682; organist, professor and composer.

Löwe (lā'-vĕ) **(Jn.) Karl** (Gf.), Löbejün, near Halle, Nov. 30, 1796—Kiel, April 20, 1869; son and pupil of a cantor; studied with Türk on a royal stipend; 1821-66 town mus.-dir. at Stettin; toured Europe singing his own fine "ballades" or dramatic solos; also c. 5 operas, 17 oratorios, etc., wrote a "Selbst-biographie (1870)." His *"Edward"* and *"Erlkönig"* famous.

Löwenstern (lā'-vĕn-shtĕrn) (or **Leuenstern** or **Leonastro**), **Matthaeus Apelles von,** Neustadt, 1594—Bernstadt, 1648; poet and composer; son of a saddler named Löwe; became a privy councillor and was ennobled by Ferdinand II., taking the name of von Loewenstern; c. words and music of *"Frühlings-Morgen"* (30 sacred songs), oratorio *"Judith"* (1646), etc.

Lualdi (loo-äl'-dē), **Adriano,** b. Larino (Campobasso), March 22, 1887; composer of stage works; editor.

Lübeck (lü'-bĕk), (1) **Vincentius,** Paddingbüttel, near Bremen, 1654—Hamburg, Feb. 9, 1740; famous organist. (2) **Jn. H.,** Alphen, Holland, 1799—The Hague, 1865; violinist and ct.-conductor. (3) **Ernst,** The Hague, 1829—Paris, 1876; son of above; pianist. (4) **Louis,** The Hague, 1838—Berlin, March 8, 1904; bro. of above; pupil of Jacquard; 1863-70, 'cello-teacher, Leipzig Cons.; then in Frankfort.

Lü'benau, L. Vide JADASSOHN, S.

Luboshutz (loo'-bō-shoots), **Lea,** b. Odessa, Feb. 22, 1889; studied at Moscow Cons., and with Hrimaly and Ysaye; violinist and soloist with orchs. in Europe and U. S.; teacher, Curtis Inst. of Music, Philadelphia.

Lubrich (loo'-brĭkh), **Fritz,** b. Bärsdorf, July 29, 1862; 1890 cantor at Peilau, Silesia; editor and composer.

Lu'cas, (1) **Chas.,** Salisbury, 1808—London, 1869; 'cellist and composer. (2) **Stanley,** after 1861 secretary to the R. Soc. of Mus.; and 1866-80 of the Philh. Soc. (3) **Clarence,** b. Canada, 1866; studied Paris Cons.; critic; conductor; comp. of operas, etc.

Lucca (look'-kä), **Pauline,** Vienna, April 25, 1841—Feb. 28, 1908; famous soprano; studied with Uschmann and Lewy; in chorus Vienna Op.; 1859 won attention as "First Bridesmaid" in *"Der Freischütz,"* engaged at Olmütz, for leading rôles; Meyerbeer chose her to create "Selika" in *"L'Africaine"* at Berlin, where she was engaged as ct.-singer for life; sang in London annually, and broke her Berlin engagement (1872) to sing in the United States for two years; 1860 m. Baron von

Rhaden (divorced, 1872); m. von Wallhofen in America; lived in Vienna.

Luck'stone, Isidore, Baltimore, Md., Jan. 29, 1861—N. Y., March 12, 1941; pupil of P. Scharwenka; toured as accompanist for many noted artists; after 1897 in N. Y. as teacher of singing, where he headed vocal dept., N. Y. Univ., for a time.

Ludikar (loō'-dĕ-kär), **Pavel,** b. Prague; studied law at Univ. of Prague; also music; his father a cond. of Prague Opera and prof. at Cons. there, his mother an opera singer; début as "Sarastro," Prague, 1906; sang with Boston Op. Co., 1913–14; later mem. Met. Op. Co., N. Y., for several seasons; also sang at La Scala, in Paris and at Baden-Baden Mozart festivals.

Ludwig, (1) **August,** b. Waldheim, Saxony, Jan. 15, 1865; critic and comp.; pupil of Cologne and Munich Cons.; attracted attention by the completion of Schubert's Unfinished symph., with a "*Philosophic scherzo,*" and a "*March of Fate*"; c. also an overture "*Ad Astra,*" songs, etc. (2) **Friedrich,** Potsdam, May 8, 1872 —Göttingen, Oct. 3, 1930; historian of music; docent at Strassburg University; after 1920, prof. musical science, Göttingen; author works on music of 13th and 14th century.

Lugert (loo'-gĕrt), **Josef,** Frohnau, Bohemia, Oct. 30, 1841—Linz, Jan. 17, 1928; teacher; pupil of Prague Organ School, and violinist in German Landestheater there; later piano teacher at Prague Cons.; 1905 Royal Music Inspector; organised orchestra schools, and won fame as a teacher; c. symph., serenades for orch., "*In Memoriam*" for full orch. with English horn solo; also wrote technical books.

Luigini (lwē-zhē'-nē), **Alexandre (Clément L. Jos.)** Lyons, March 9, 1850 —Paris, July 29, 1906; pupil and prize-winner at the Cons.; 1869 leader in Grand Théâtre, Lyons, and founder of the Cons. concerts and prof.; 1897 cond. at Op. Comique, Paris; c. comic operas, "*Les caprices de Margot*" (Lyons, 1877), "*Faublas*" (1881), ballets, etc.

Lully (rightly Lulli) (lül-lē, or lool'-lĭ), (1) **J. Bap. de,** Florence, Nov. 29, 1632—Paris, March 22, 1687. A Franciscan monk taught him the

violin and guitar. His parents were poor; the Chev. de Guise took the boy in 1646 to France to entertain Mlle. de Montpensier, but he was set to work in the scullery, where Count de Nogent heard him play the vln. and placed him in the private band. L., however, set to music a satirical poem on Mlle. de M. and she dismissed him. He studied the harps. and comp. with Métru, Roberday, and Gigault, and became a member of the King's private orchestra; 1652, he became head of the "24 violins"; he organised a second group, "les petits violons," of 16 instrs. and made it the best orchestra in France. 1653, ct.-composer and prod. masques and ballets in which Louis XIV. took part and Lully as "M. Baptiste," danced and acted. 1672, the king held him in such favour that he gave him letters patent for an "Académie royale de musique" (now the Gr. Opéra); a rival theatre was closed by the police (v. CAMPRA). With this opportunity (cf. Wagner's Bayreuth Theatre) the transplanted Italian proceeded to found French opera—idiomatic mus. to texts in the vernacular, and free of the superornamentation of the Italian Sch. He held the vogue till Gluck put him in eclipse. L. was dir., stagemanager, conductor, and even at times machinist, as well as composer. He was fortunate in his librettist, Quinault. He developed the overture, and introduced the brass into the orch. He was famous for his temper and once while cond. furiously struck his own foot with the bâton, producing a fatal abscess. His works, mainly on classical subjects, include "*Les Fêtes de l'Amour et de Bacchus*"; a pastoral pasticcio (1672); "*Cadmus et Hermione*"; "*Alceste*"; "*Thésée*"; "*Le Carnaval,*" opera-ballet; "*Atys,*" "*Isis,*" "*Psyche*"; "*Bellérophon*"; "*Proserpine*"; "*Le Triomphe de L'Amour*"; "*Persée*"; "*Phaëton*"; "*Amadis de Gaule*"; "*Roland*"; "*Armide et Renaud*"; "*Acis et Galatée,*" historic pastoral (1686), etc., also symphs., a mass, etc. (2) **Louis de,** Paris, 1664—after 1713; son of above; dramatic composer.

Lum'bye, (1) **Hans Chr.,** Copenhagen, 1810—1874; conductor and composer of pop. dance-mus. His son and successor (2) **G.**, c. opera "*The Witch's Flute.*"

Lund, John Reinhold, Hamburg, Germany, Oct. 20, 1859—Buffalo, N. Y., Feb. 1, 1925; conductor, composer; studied at Leipzig Cons.; cond. of chorus, Bremen Op., 1880–83; after 1884 asst. cond. to Damrosch with German Op. Co., N. Y.; 1887–1903, cond. Buffalo Orch. and Orpheus Soc.; toured as cond. of Herbert operettas; after 1914 again in Buffalo.

Lunn, (1) **Henry Charles**, London, 1817 —Jan. 23, 1894; editor and author; pupil Royal Acad. of Music, later dir.; 1863–87, edited *The Musical Times*, London. (2) (**Louisa**) **Kirkby,** Manchester, Nov. 8, 1873— London, Feb. 17, 1930; mezzo-soprano; pupil of J. H. Greenwood, then of Visetti, R. A. M., London, gaining a scholarship in 1894. Appeared in a student performance of Schumann's "*Genoveva,*" 1893, with such success that she was engaged by Sir Augustus Harris; 1897–09 contralto of Carl Rosa Company; then married W. J. K. Pearsen; sang in concert; 1901 began engagements at Covent Garden; sang much at festivals; 1902 at Met. Op. House, New York and with Boston Symph. and other orchs., 1907 created "Kundry" in first English performance of "*Parsifal*" by the Henry W. Savage Company.

Luporini (loo-po-rē'-nē), **Gaetano,** b. Lucca, Italy, Dec. 12, 1865; pupil of Primo Quilici, graduating from the Pacini Mus. Inst.; c. opera "*Marcella,*" succ. lyric comedy, "*I Dispetti Amorosi*" (Turin, 1894); v. succ. opera "*La Collana di Pasqua*" (Naples, 1896), etc.; cond. at Lucca.

Lupot (lü-pō), (1) **Nicolas,** Stuttgart, 1758—Paris, 1824; chief of a French family of vln.-makers, incl. his great grandfather (2) **Jean;** his grandfather (3) **Laurent** (b. 1696), his father (4) **François,** his bro. (5) **François** (d. 1837), and his son-in-law, **Chas. Fr. Gand** of **Gand & Bernardel,** Paris.

Lusci'nius (Latin form of **Nachtgall** or **Nachtigall** (näkht'-(ĭ)-gäl), "Nightingale"), **Othmar,** Strassburg, 1487—ca. 1536; organist, theorist and composer.

Lussan (dŭ lüs-säṅ), **Zélie de,** b. New York, 1863; pupil of her mother;

début in concert and stage, 1886; 1889, Carl Rosa Co., London; 1894–5, Met. Op.; Covent Garden, 1895–1902; d. London, Dec. 18, 1949.

Lussy (loos'-sē), **Mathis,** Stans, Switz., April 8, 1828—Montreux, Jan. 21. 1910; pupil of Businger and Nägeli; pf.-teacher, Paris, and writer.

Lustig (loos'-tĭkh), **Jacob Wm.,** Hamburg, Sept. 21, 1706–1796; organist and theorist.

Lüstner (lĭst'-n'r), (1) **Ignaz P.,** Poischwitz, near Jauer, 1793—Breslau, 1873; violin teacher. His four sons were (2) **K.,** Breslau, Nov. 10, 1834—Wiesbaden, April 9, 1906; pianist and 'cellist; after 1872, teacher in Wiesbaden. (3) **Otto,** Breslau, 1839—Barmen, 1889; town mus.-dir. at Barmen. (4) **Louis,** Breslau, June 30, 1840—Wiesbaden, Jan. 24, 1918; violinist, and after 1874, cond. at Wiesbaden. (5) **G.,** 1847—1887; 'cellist; ct.-cond. at Berlin.

Luther (loo'-tĕr), **Martin,** Eisleben, Nov. 10, 1483—Feb. 18, 1546; the great reformer concerned himself also with church-mus., issuing "*Formula missae*" (1523), and a new order for the German mass. He wrote the words of at least 36 chorals, and is generally believed to have c. 13 choral-tunes (incl. the famous "*Ein feste Burg ist unser Gott,*" and "*Jesaia den Propheten das gescha*"), his method being to play them on the flute (which he played well) while his friends and assistants, the cond. Konrad Rupff and cantor Jn. Walther, wrote them out.

Lut'kin, Peter Christian, Thompsonville, Wis., March 27, 1858—Evanston, Ill., Dec. 27, 1931; teacher, conductor and composer; studied at Berlin Hochsch.; with Stepanov, Moszkowski, Leschetizky and others; after 1888 theory teacher, Amer. Cons., Chicago; and following 1891 at the school of music, Northwestern Univ., Evanston, Ill.; there after 1908 he conducted the annual Chicago North Shore Fests.; in 1911 and 1920 was pres. of the Music Teachers' Nat'l Association.

Lutz (loots), **Wm. Meyer,** Kissingen, 1822—West Kensington, Jan. 31, 1903; pianist and dram. composer; from 1848, conductor at London.

Lux (looks), **Fr.,** Ruhla, Thuringia,

1820—Mayence, 1895; conductor, organist, pianist and dram. composer.

Luython (or Luiton) (lī-tôn), Carl, Antwerp (?)—Prague, 1620; important composer of madrigals, masses, fugues, etc.; 1576 court organist to Maximilian II. and to Rudolf II.

Luzzaschi (lood-zäs'-kē), Luzzasco, d. Ferrara, 1607; court organist; pupil of Ciprian de Rore, and teacher of Frescobaldi; c. madrigals, etc.

Luzzi (lood'-zē), Luigi, Olevano di Lomellina, 1828—Stradella, 1870; dram. composer.

Lvoff (or Lwoff) (l'vôf), Alexis, Reval, 1799—on his estate, Govt. of Kovno, 1871; violinist and conductor; c. the Russian national hymn and 4 operas.

Lyra (lē'-rä), Justus W., Osnabrück, 1822—Gehrden, 1882; composer.

Lysberg (lēs-běrkh) (rightly Bovy), Chas. Samuel, Lysberg, near Geneva, 1821—Geneva, 1873; pianist and dram. composer.

Lyssenko, vide LISSENKO.

M

Maas (mäs), (1) Jos., Dartford, 1847—1886; tenor. (2) Louis (Ph. O.), Wiesbaden, 1852 — Boston, 1889; pianist, conductor and composer. (3) Gerald Christopher, b. Mannheim, 1888; 'cellist;' pupil of Paris Cons. and of Julius Klengel; played in Munich Konzertverein orch.; 1912, Berlin Op. orch.; 1914, taught at Hoch Cons., Frankfort; played in Rebner Quartet; after 1916 in U. S., where he was a member of Letz Quartet, 1917–21.

Mabellini (mä-běl-lē'-nē), Teodulo, Pistoia, Italy, 1817—Florence, 1897; ct.-conductor and dram. composer.

Macbeth', (1) Allan, Greenock, Scotland, March 13, 1856—Glasgow, 1910; pupil of Leipzig Cons.; organist in Glasgow; after 1890, principal sch. of mus., Glasgow Athenæum; c. an operetta, 2 cantatas, chamber-mus., etc. (2) Florence, b. Mankato, Minn., 1891; coloratura soprano; studied with Yeatman Griffith; sang in England; op. début, Darmstadt, 1913; after 1914 sang with Chicago Op. Co., also at Ravinia Op. and in concerts.

MacCunn', Hamish, Greenock, Scotland, March 22, 1868—London, Aug. 2, 1916; British composer;

pupil of Parry, R. A. M., having won a scholarship for comp.; at 19, several of his orch.-pcs. were prod. by Manns; at 20 commissioned to c. a cantata for the Glasgow Choral Union; gave concerts at the studio of John Pettie, whose daughter he m., 1889; 1888–94, prof. of harm. R. A. M.; 1898, cond. Carl Rosa Op. Co.; c operas, "Jeanie Deans" (Edinburgh, 1894), "Diarmid and Ghriné" (Covent Garden, 1897); 5 cantatas incl. "The Death of Parry Reed" (male chorus and orch.), overtures "Cior Mhor," "The Land of the Mountain and the Flood"; ballad overture, "The Dowie Dens o' Yarrow"; ballade, "The Ship o' the Fiend," with orch.; 8th Psalm with orch., etc.

MacDow'ell, Edward, New York, Dec. 18, 1861—Jan. 23, 1908; eminent American composer and one of the most original and virile of creators among his countrymen; pupil of J. Buitrago, P Desvernine and Teresa Carreño, N. Y.; 1876, Paris Cons.; 1879, with Heymann (pf.) and Raff (comp.) Frankfort 1881–82, chief pf. teacher at Darmstadt Cons.; at 21, Raff (who was deeply interested in his progress) and Liszt procured the performance of his works at the annual festival of the "Allgemeiner deutscher Musikverein"; lived in Wiesbaden; 1888, Boston, 1896, prof. of mus. in Columbia Univ., New York; Mus. Doc. h. c., Princeton Univ. and 1902, Penn. U. also; he gave frequent pf.-recitals, and played his concertos with the Boston Symph. and other orchs. In Jan. 1904, he resigned his professorship at Columbia University from dissatisfaction with the faculty's attitude toward music as a high art. He was succeeded by Cornelius Rybner (q. v.). He had cond. the Mendelssohn Glee Club for two years. In 1905 he fell a prey to cerebral trouble that ended his beautiful career. Faithfully tended by his wife, he lingered under increasing clouds, till his death, Jan. 23, 1908, at New York. So great was his hold upon the American public that a MacDowell Club with many branches was formed to carry on his ideals of art and to aid the struggling musician: a choral branch under the leadership of Kurt Schindler attained a very high standard, taking the title of "Schola Cantorum" in 1912; a biography of MacDowell was written by Lawrence Gilman, 1905. His widow has been an active force in Amer. music, having founded the MacDowell Colony on the composer's estate at Peterboro, N. H., as a creative centre for young Amer. comps., scholarships there being defrayed by M.-Clubs throughout U. S. ORCHESTRAL COMPOSITIONS: 2 poems "*Hamlet*" and "*Ophelia*"; symph. poems, "*Lancelot and Elaine*," "*Lamia*" and "*Roland*," op. 35, romance for 'cello with orch.; 3 orch. suites incl. "*In October*" and "*Indian Suite.*" FOR PIANO. 4 sonatas "*Tragica*," "*Eroica*" ("*Flos regum Arthurus*"), "*Scandinavian*" and "*Celtic*"; prelude and fugue, modern suite; forest idyls, 3 poems, "*Moon-pictures*," 6 poems after Heine, 4 "*Little Poems*"; technical exercises (3 books), and 12 virtuoso-studies, etc., and many songs of great charm and individuality. (See article, page 503.)

Mace, Thos., ca. 1613—1709; Engl. lutenist, inventor and writer.

Macfar'lane, W. Chas., b. London, Oct. 2, 1870; organist; brought to New York at 4; pupil of his father and of S. P. Warren; c. anthems, etc.

Macfar'ren, (1) Sir **G. Alex.**, London, March 2, 1813—Oct. 31, 1887; notable English composer and scholar; son and pupil of the playwright G. Macfarren; also studied with Ch. Lucas and C. Potter, R. A. M.; 1834, prof. there, even after blindness overtook him; from 1875 prof. at Cambridge Univ. Mus. Doc. there 1876; from 1876, also principal of the R. A. M.; 1883, knighted; c. 13 operas, 9 of them prod.; 4 oratorios, 5 cantatas, 8 symphonies, 7 overtures, incl. "*Chevy Chase*," "*Don Carlos*," "*Hamlet*" and "*Festival*," concertos, sonatas, etc.; wrote textbooks, articles; ed. old texts, etc.; biog. by Banister (London, '91). (2) **Natalia**, Lübeck, 1827—Bakewell, April 9, 1916; wife of above; contralto, translator and writer. (3) **Walter Cecil**, London, Aug. 28, 1826—Sept. 2, 1905; bro. and pupil (in comp.) of (1) studied with Turle, Holmes (pf.) and Potter (comp.); from 1846. pf.-prof. at the R. A. M., of which he was a Fellow; 1873-80.

cond. Acad. Concerts; dir. and treasurer Philharm. Soc.; pianist, lecturer, editor, and composer of a symph., 7 overtures, a cantata "*The Song of the Sunbeam*," services, etc.

Machault (or Machau, Machaud, Machut) (mă-shō), **Guillaume (Gulielmus) de Mascandio,** Machault in the Ardennes, 1300—ca. 1372; troubadour; composer.

Macken'zie, Sir **Alex. Campbell,** Edinburgh, Aug. 22, 1847—London, April 28, 1935; notable British composer; pupil of Ulrich (pf.) and Stein (comp.), Sondershausen Cons.; at 14 a violinist in the Ducal Orch.; 1862, won the King's scholarship, R. A. M., and studied with Sainton, Jewson, and Lucas; from 1865 teacher and cond. Edinburgh; 1888 of Cambridge; 1896 of Edinburgh U.; 1894 knighted; 1888–1924, principal R. A. M. (vice Macfarren); 1892 cond. Philh. Soc.; c. operas, "*Colomba*" (Drury Lane, 1883), "*The Troubadour*" (ibid. 1886), and "*His Majesty, or the Court of Vingotia*" (1897; comic), "*Cricket on the Hearth*" (MS.); oratorios, "*The Rose of Sharon*" (Norwich Festival, 1884), and "*Bethlehem*" (1894); cantatas, "*Jason*" (Bristol Festival, 1882), "*The Bride*," "*The Story of Sayid*" (Leeds Festival, '86), "*The New Covenant*," "*The Dream of Jubal*," "*The Cotter's Saturday Night*," and "*Veni, Creator Spiritus*"; 2 Scottish rhapsodies, a ballad, with orch., "*La belle dame sans merci*"; overtures "*Cervantes*," "*To a comedy*," "*Tempo di ballo*," "*Twelfth Night*," "*Britannia*"; a vln.-concerto, a "*Pibroch*" for vln. and orch.; "*Scottish Concertos*" for pf., etc.

Maclean', (1) Chas. Donald, Cambridge, March 27, 1843—London, June 23, 1916; pupil of Ferdinand Hiller; organist at Oxford, later at Eton and (after 1880) in London; for a time in India; c. oratorios, etc. (2) **Alex. Morvaren,** Eton, July 20, 1872—London, May 18, 1936; active for many years as theatre cond. and comp. of music for plays in London; also orch. and choral works. (3) **Quentin Morvaren,** b. London, May 14, 1896; son of (2); also a prolific comp. of music for the stage; a pupil of Straube, Reger and Krehl.

Maclen'nan, Francis, Bay City, Mich., 1879—Port Washington, N. Y.,

1935; tenor; studied New York, London and Berlin; sang in London, 1902; after 1904 with Savage Op. Co., in U. S.; 1907, Royal Op., Berlin; 1913, Hamburg Op.; 1915–17, Chicago Op. Co., later again in Berlin; m. Florence Easton, soprano; divorced.

MacMill'an, Sir **Ernest Campbell,** b. Mimico, Ontario, Aug. 18, 1893; composer, conductor, organist; studied in Toronto and Edinburgh with Niecks, Hollins and W. B. Ross; Mus. D., Oxford, 1918; Fellow of the R. Coll. of Music, London; 1926, principal, Toronto Cons., and dean of faculty of music, Univ. of Toronto; 1935, knighted by British Gov't.; c. and arr. choruses and songs, c. orch. and chamber music; cond. Toronto Symph. Orchestra.

Macmil'len, Francis, b. Marietta, Ohio, Oct. 14, 1885; violinist; pupil of Listemann, Chicago; at 10, pupil of Markees, Berlin; at 15 of César Thomson at Brussels Cons.; sharing first violin prize 1902 and taking Van Hal prize; played in Brussels, etc.; 1903 London; after 1906 toured U. S.

Macpher'son, (1) **Charles Stewart,** composer; b. Liverpool, March 29, 1865; pupil of R. A. M., London, with a scholarship; gained also the Balfe scholarship and medals; 1887 prof. there; 1892 a fellow; 1903 prof. Royal Normal College for the Blind; c. symph., 2 overtures, a fine mass with orch. (1898); *"Concerto alla fantasia"* for violin, etc.; wrote theoretical text books. (2) **Charles,** Edinburgh, May 10, 1870—May 28, 1927; 1890 pupil R. A. M., winning Lucas prize 1892; later teacher of counterpoint there; 1895, suborganist at St. Paul's, London; c. overture *"Cridhe an Ghaidhil"* (London, 1895); orch. suites, *"Highland"* and *"Hallowe'en"*; *"Psalm 187"* for choir and orch., etc.

Macque (mäk), **Jean de,** Flemish choirmaster in Rome 1576–82; 1610 at Royal Chapel Naples; c. madrigals and motets.

Mad'dy, Joseph Edgar, b. Wellington, Kans., Oct. 14, 1891; conductor, educator; studied with Czerwonky, Ludwig Becker, Arthur Hartmanr; hon. Mus. D., Cincinnati Cons., 1930; mem., Minneapolis Symph., 1909–14; prof. public school music,

Univ. of Mich.; organised and cond. Nat'l High School Orch. after 1926; dir. summer school and camp of this group at Interlochen, Mich.; pres. Music Educators Nat'l Conference, 1936; author of books on instr. technique and teaching.

Mader (mä'-děr), **Raoul (M.),** b. Pressburg, Hungary, June 25, 1856; studied Vienna Cons.; took 1st prize for pf. and comp., and the great silver medal and the Liszt prize as best pianist in the Cons.; 1882–95, 1st "coach" for solo singers, Vienna. ct.-opera, also asst.-cond. From 1895 cond. Royal Opera, Budapest; 1917–19, dir. Vienna, Volksoper; 1921–25, dir. Budapest Op.; c. 2 comic operas, 4 ballets, incl. *"Die Sireneninsel,"* and *"She"* (after Rider Haggard), parody on Mascagni's *"Cavalleria Rusticana"* (Th. an der Wien, 1892); d. (?).

Madeto'ja, Leevi, b. Oulu, Finland, Feb. 17, 1887; composer; studied at Helsingfors Univ. and at Music Institute there under Järnefelt and Sibelius; also in Paris with d'Indy and in Vienna with Fuchs; 1912–14, second cond. of Helsingfors Philh.; 1914–16, cond. Wiborg Orch.; since then teacher of comp. and mem. of directorate at Helsingfors Mus. Inst.; c. opera *"Pohjalatsia";* 3 symphonies; *"Stabat Mater"* for women's chorus; other choral works, chamber music, pf. pcs., songs; d. 1947.

Maganini (mäg-ä-ně'-ně), **Quinto,** b. Fairfield, Cal., Nov. 30, 1897; composer, conductor, flutist; studied with Barrère and Nadia Boulanger; winner of Pulitzer Prize, 1927, and of Guggenheim Fellowship; played as flutist in San Francisco and N. Y. Symph. Orchs.; guest cond. with leading orchs. and also of his own Little Symph.; c. orch., chamber music and vocal works.

Mag(g)ini (mäd-jě'-ně) (or **Magino**), **Giov. Paolo,** Botticini-Marino, Italy, 1580—Brescia, ca. 1640; vln.-maker, rivaling Stradivari and Guarneri; his double-basses particularly good; label, "Gio. Paolo Maggini, Brescia."

Magnard (mīn-yär), **Albéric,** Paris, June 9, 1865—killed by German soldiers while defending his estate at Senlis, Sept. 3, 1914; composer; pupil of the Cons. (winning first harmony prize 1888), then of d'Indy; c. 3 symph., overture, suite in ancient

DICTIONARY OF MUSICIANS 273

style; hymns to *"Justice"* and to *"Venus,"* 1-act opera *"Yolande"* (Brussels, 1892); 3-act *"Guercœur"*; important chamber music, etc.

Mag'nus, Désiré (rightly **Magnus Deutz**), Brussels, 1828—Paris, 1884; teacher, composer and critic.

Mahillon (mä-ē-yôn), **Chas. Victor**, Brussels, March 10, 1841—St. Jean, Cape Ferrat, June 17, 1924; after 1877 custodian of mus. instrs., Brussels Cons.; editor and writer; manager wind-inst. factory of his father.

Mahler (mä'-lĕr), (1) **Gustav**, Kalischt, Bohemia, July 7, 1860—Vienna, May 18, 1911; highly gifted composer and conductor; pupil of the Cons. and Univ. at Prague and Vienna, with Bruckner as one of his teachers; began his career in 1880 as theatre cond. in Hall, Lubjlana and Olmütz; asst. cond., Cassel, 1883; asst. to Angelo Neumann at the Prague German Op., 1885-86; in latter year at Leipzig Op., under Nikisch; at Budapest Royal Op., 1888-91; at the Hamburg City Theatre, 1891-97, and orch. cond. as successor to Bülow. Beginning 1897 he was in Vienna, 1st as cond. at the Court Op., then from 1900 to 1907 its dir. during a most brilliant period. In 1907 he was called to the Met. Op., where he led German operas, and in 1909 was elected cond. of the N. Y. Philh. Orch. at what was then the largest salary ever paid a leader ($30,000 per annum). Partially as a result of a typhoid infection and partly of a nervous breakdown, he gave up his post and returned to Vienna in 1911, where he died the following year. He has had a strongly augmented fame as a comp. in recent years, owing to the championship of various notable conductors, such as Mengelberg, Bruno Walter, etc., and also to the organization of Mahler societies in various countries, of which there is one in the U. S. His output is highly individual, but there is a strong division of opinion as to its ultimate artistic rank. That he was a master of orchestration is generally admitted; he chose subjects of vast scope for his compositions, with programmes drawn from literature, and in several of his symphs. he employs the human voice as an adjunct; he generally uses a large musical apparatus.

His comps. include: 10 symphonies, 1, D major (1891); 2, C minor, with contralto and chorus (1895); 3, D minor, known as *"La Programmatica,"* with contralto soloist, men's and boys' choruses (1896); 4, G major, known as *"The Heavenly Life,"* with soprano soloist (1901); 5, C♯ minor (1904); 6, A minor (1906); 7, E minor (Prague, 1908); 8, E flat major, in 2 sections, known as "the symphony of a thousand" from the large choral, orch. and solo forces employed (Munich, 1910); 9, D major, posthumous, 1st heard in Vienna under Bruno Walter, 1912; and 10, left unfinished but ed. by Franz Mikorey, and prod. under the title *"Sinfonia Engadine"* in Berlin, 1913. His other principal works are: *"Das Lied von der Erde"* for tenor and alto soloists and orch., after old Chinese poems (also a posth. work, first heard 1911, and since often perf. with growing popularity); *"Das Klagende Lied,"* for soloists, chorus and orch.; 4 *"Lieder eines Fahrenden Gesellen,"* 12 songs from *"Des Knaben Wunderhorn"*; songs to poems by Rückert; 5 *"Kindertotenlieder"*; 3 *"Hefte Lieder"*; and other songs from his earlier period; fragments from a youthful opera, *"Die Argonauten"*; a fairy tale opera, *"Rübezahl"* with text by the composer; sketches for an opera based on Weber's *"Die Drei Pintos,"* early chamber music, etc. Studies of Mahler have been written by Specht, Bekker, Stefan, Guido Adler and Arthur Neisser. (2) **Alma Maria** (née Schindler), his wife, a pupil of Labor and Zemlinsky, c. songs; (3) **Fritz**, his nephew, a conductor, active in Germany and (1936) in the U. S.

Mahu (mä'-oo), **Stephan**, b. Germany, ct.-singer and composer, 1538.

Maier (mī'-ĕr), (1) **Julius Jos.**, Freiburg, Baden, 1821—Munich, 1889; teacher and writer. (2) **Guy**, b Buffalo, N. Y., 1892; pianist; studied at New England Cons. with Procto; and Schnabel; début, Boston, 1915; has toured as solo pianist and in two-piano programmes with Lee Pattison; prof. piano, Univ. of Mich.; has given many lecture-recitals for children on lives of composers.

Maikapar (mä'-kä-pär), **Samuel**, b. Chersson, Russia, Dec. 18, 1867;

pianist; pupil of the Cons., and of Leschetizky; settled in Moscow; c. piano pieces.

Maillard (mī-yăr), **Jean,** 16th century French composer; pupil of Deprès; c. important motets and masses, from one of which Palestrina took themes for a mass of his own.

Maillart (mī-yăr), **Louis** (called **Aimé**), Montpellier, Herault, France, 1817—Moulins, Allier, 1871; dram. composer.

Mailly (mī-yē), **Alphonse J. Ernest,** Brussels, Nov. 27, 1833—Jan., 1918; pianist, and organ virtuoso; pupil of Girschner, Brussels Cons.; 1861 pf.-teacher there; 1868 organ-teacher; composer.

Mainardi (mä-ē-när'-dē), **Enrico,** b. Milan, May 19, 1897; 'cellist; studied Verdi Cons., Milan and in Berlin with Hugo Becker; début in Milan, 1909; taught at Rome Acad. after 1933; 1929–31, 1st 'cellist of Berlin State Op. orch.; has made concert appearances in Eur. countries.

Mainzer (mīn'-tsĕr), **Abbé Jos.,** Trier, 1807—Manchester, 1851; singing-teacher, writer and dram. composer.

Maison (mä-sôn'), **René,** b. Trameries, Belgium, Nov. 24, 1895; tenor; studied Antwerp, Brussels and Paris; mem. of Monte Carlo Op., 1922–25; later sang at Paris Op. and Op.-Comique; for several seasons with Chicago Op., and 1935 with Met. Op., N. Y., in Wagnerian and French rôles, also in "Fidelio."

Maitland (māt'-lănd) **J. Alex. Fuller-,** London, April 7, 1856—Canforth, Lancashire, March 30, 1936; 1882, M. A. Trinity Coll., Cambridge; lecturer and critic for various papers; 1889–1911 London Times; ed. the Appendix to Grove's Dict.; pianist at the Bach choir concerts; wrote "Masters of German Music" and many authoritative works. Edited the "Fitzwilliam Virginal Book" with Barclay Squire.

Majo (mä'-yō), **Fran. di** (called **Ciccio di Majo**), Naples, ca. 1740—Rome, 1770; organist and noted composer of operas and church-mus.

Major (mä'-yôr), **Julius J.,** Kaschau, Hungary, Dec. 13, 1859—Budapest, Jan. 30, 1925; pupil of the Landes-Musik Akad. at Budapest; founded a music school and singing societies there: c. a symph., operas, "Lisbeth"

and "Erysika" (Pest, 1901), "Szechi Maria" (Klausenburg, 1906), etc.

Majorano. Vide CAFFARELLI.

Malash'kin, Leonid Dimitrievitch, 1842—Moscow, Feb. 11, 1902; Russian composer of an opera, a symph., songs, etc.

Malder (mäl'-dĕr), **Pierre van,** Brussels, 1724—1768; violinist and composer.

Malherbe (mäl-ărb), **Chas. Théodore,** Paris, April 21, 1853—Oct. 5, 1911; at first a lawyer, then studied with Danhauser, Wormser, and Massenet; also pub. some original comps., and transcriptions; Danhauser's sec.; 1896, asst.-archivist, Gr. Opéra; Officer of the Acad. and of Pub. Instruction; Chev. of various orders. Ed., Le Ménestrel, and prolific writer on Wagner, etc.; owned probably the best private coll. of mus.-autographs in the world; ed. Rameau's complete works.

Malibran (mäl-ĭ-brän), (1) **M. Felicità** (née **Garcia**), Paris, March 24, 1808—Manchester, Sept. 23, 1836 (from singing too soon after being thrown and dragged by a horse). In some respects the greatest of all women vocalists; she had a contralto voice with an additional soprano register and several well-concealed "head tones" between; she improvised frequently on the stage, and also c.; at 5 she played a child's part and one evening broke out singing the chief rôle to the amusement of the audience; at 7 studied with Pauseron; at 15 studied with her father (v. GARCIA); début, London, 1825; sang in opera in New York, 1825–27 with great succ.; she had a personality that compelled extraordinary homage. She m. Malibran; when he became bankrupt she divorced him and 1836 m. De Bériot, ct.-violinist with whom she had lived since 1830. (2) **Alex.,** Paris, 1823—1867; violinist and composer.

Malipiero (mäl-ē-pē-ā'-rō), **Gian Francesco,** b. Venice, March 18, 1882; composer; mem. of a family line of musicians for some generations; pupil of the Liceo in Bologna, studying with Enrico Bossi; after 1913 lived for a time in Paris in touch with modern musical circle incl. Casella; at this time submitted 5 scores to Italian Nat'l Contest and won 4 prizes under different names; this occasion.d criticism when his earlier scores were performed in Italy, where his recognition has been slower than in other countries; after 1920 he came to be recognised as one of the leading creators of his country, a cultivated, intellectual personality, and in his music embodying romantic and poetic qualities, individual color and atmosphere, with an idiom of marked modernity; after 1921 he taught comp. at the Parma Cons.; his productions before 1911 have been disavowed by him as not representative; later works include: (operas) *"Sette Canzoni,"* orig. series of short operatic sketches; *"Pantea";* *"Three Goldoni Comedies";* *"Filomela e l'Infatuato";* *"Orfeo";* *"Il Mistero di Venezia";* *"La Favola di Figlio Cambiato"* (to Pirandello book, which had première in Brunswick, Germany, but on Rome hearing, 1934, was stormily hissed and withdrawn after one perf. owing to satire on royalty and church); *"Giulio Cesare"* (Genoa, 1935–36 with succ.); *"Antonio e Cleopatra,"* Florence, 1938. (Ballets) *"La Baruffe Chiozzotte,"* *"La Mascherata delle Principesse Prigionere";* (orch.) *"Impressioni del Vero"* (2 series); *"Pause del Silenzio";* *"Ditirambo Tragico";* *"Oriente Immaginario";* *"La Cimarosiana";* Symphony; vln. concerto; (chamber music) *"Rispetti e Strambotti"* and *"Stornelli e Ballate"* for string quartet; Sonata à Tre; 'cello sonata; (choral works) *"San Francesco d'Assisi,"* mystery for soloists, chorus and orch. (N. Y., 1921); *"Princess Eulalia,"* for soloists, chorus and orch. (N. Y. Oratorio Soc., 1927); also piano music, songs, etc.

Mal'ling, (1) Jörgen, Copenhagen, 1836—July 12, 1905; Danish composer and teacher; from 1875 in Vienna. His brother (2) **Otto** (**Baldemar**), Copenhagen, June 1, 1848 —Oct. 5, 1915; pupil of Gade and Hartmann at the Cons., later teacher there; organist and founder of concert association; c. symph.; violin fantasie with orch., overture, chamber music, and valuable organ pieces.

Mallinger (mäl'-lǐng-ĕr), **Mathilde** (née Lichtenegger), Agram, Feb. 17, 1847 —Berlin, April 19, 1920; soprano; pupil of Giordigiani and Vogl, Prague Cons., and Lewy, Vienna; début, Munich, 1866; 1868, created

"Eva" in the *"Meistersinger";* m. Baron von Schimmelpfennig; 1890, singing-teacher, Prague Cons.

Malten (mäl'-tĕn), **Therese,** Insterburg, East Prussia, June 21, 1855— Dresden, Jan. 2, 1930; soprano; pupil of Engel (voice), and Kahle (action), Berlin; at 18 début, Dresden as "Pamina," and engaged there for life; created "Kundry" (*"Parsifal"*) at Bayreuth, 1882; 1898, ct.-chamber singer.

Malvezzi (mäl-vĕd'-zē), **Christofano,** Lucca, 1547—Florence, 1597; canon in Florence; and chapel master to the Grand Dukes of Tuscany; collected and composed dramatic intermezzi, 1591, etc.

Mälzel (mĕl'-tsĕl), **Jn. Nepomuk,** Ratisbon, 1772—on a voyage, July 31, 1838; mus.-teacher; inv. "panharmonion" (a sort of orchestrion), an automaton-trumpeter, and an automatic chess-player; while experimenting with his "chronometer," a sort of metronome (v. D. D.), he saw Winkel's invention, adopted its chief features and patented the result as Mälzel's metronome (v. D. D.).

Mana-Zuc'ca (rightly **Zuckerman**), b. New York, 1891; woman composer; studied in U. S. and Europe; toured as pianist, also sang in light opera; has c. works for orch., chamber music, and a large number of highly successful songs.

Man'chester, Arthur Livingston, b. Bass River, N. J., Feb. 9, 1862; organist, editor, educator; pupil of Zeckwer, Gilchrist, Bussmann and Tubbs; dir. of music schools; from 1904–13 at Converse Coll., Spartanburg, S. C.; 1913–18, Southwestern Univ., Georgetown, Tex., and afterward at Hardin Coll.; assoc. ed. *The Étude,* 1893–96; ed. *The Musician* (Boston), 1896–1902; pres. of M. T. N. A., 1900–02, and ed. its pub., *The Messenger.*

Mancinelli (män-chǐ-nĕl'-lǐ), **Luigi,** Orvieto, Papal States, Feb. 5, 1848— Rome, Feb. 2, 1921; intended for commerce, self-taught on the pf., but permitted to study at 14 with Sbolci (Florence, 'cello); at 15, 3rd 'cellist Pergola Th., earning his living the next 8 years; studied with Mabellini (comp.); 1870 in the orchestra of the opera at Rome; 1874, 2nd cond.; 1875, cond.; 1881, dir. Bologna Cons., which he made one of the best in Italy: 1886–88, cond. at Drury Lane, London; 1888–95, Royal Th., Madrid; till 1906 at Covent Garden, London, and, 1894–1902, at Met. Op., N. Y.; in Italy called "il Wagnerista" for his advocacy; c. opera "*Isora di Provenza*" (Bologna, 1884); succ. "*Ero e Leandro*" (Madrid, 1897, New York, 1899); an oratorio, etc.; overture and entr'actemus. to Cossa's "*Cleopatra*."

Mancini (män-chē'-nē), (1) **Fran.**, Naples, 1679—1739 cond. and dram. composer. (2) **Giambattista**, Ascoli, 1716—Vienna, 1800; writer on voice.

Manci'nus, Thomas, Schwerin, 1550—Wolfenbüttel ca. 1620; Dutch composer of "*Passions according to St. Matthew and St. John*"; cond. to Duke of Brunswick.

Mandl (mänt'-'l), **Richard**, Prossnitz, Moravia, 1859—Vienna, April 1, 1918; pianist; pupil Vienna Cons., later of Delibes, Paris, where he settled 1886; c. 1-act opera "*Rencontre Imprévue*" (Rouen, 1889); "*Chanson Provençal*" for voice and orch., orch. scherzo (Lamoureux concerts, 1894); symph. poem, with organ, mezzo-sopr. and female chorus, "*Griselidis*" (Vienna, 1906?); overture "*To a Gascon Knight drama*" (Wiesbaden, 1910), piano pieces, etc.

Mandyczewski (män-dē-chéf'-skĭ), **Eusebius**, Czernovitz, Aug. 18, 1857—Vienna, July 15, 1929; pupil of Fuchs and Nottebohm; from 1897 teacher Vienna Cons.; writer and editor of Schubert's works, for which he was made Ph. D., Leipzig. After 1914 he was comp. teacher at the Vienna Cons.; he trained the Vienna Singakademie chorus from 1887, and was librarian of the Musikfreunde, whose historic archives he kept; also chairman of the Tonkünstlerverein, and a personal friend of Brahms, whose complete works (as well as those of Haydn) he edited.

Manén (mä'-nän) **Joan**, b. Barcelona, March 14, 1883; violinist; composer; travelled as prodigy pianist, then took up violin; pupil of Alard; c. operas "*Giovanni di Napoli*" (Barcelona, 1903), "*Akté*" (do.); "*Der Fackeltanz*" (Frankfort -on - Main 1909); symph. poem "*Nuova Catalonia*," violin concertos, etc.

Manfredini (män-frē-dē'nē), (1) **Francesco**, b. Pistoja, 1688; violinist; 1711

cond. at Monaco; c. oratorios concertos, etc. His son (2) **Vincenzo**, Pistoja, 1737—St. Petersburg, 1799, as court cond., c. sonatas, etc.

Mangeot (män-zhō), **Ed. Jos.**, Nantes, France, 1834--Paris, 1898; pf.-maker and editor; inv. piano "à double clavier renversé."

Mangold (män'-gôlt), (1) **G. M.**, 1776—1835; violinist. (2) (Jn.) **Wm.**, Darmstadt, 1796—1875; conductor and dram. composer. (3) **K. (L. Amand)**, Darmstadt, 1813—Obers'dorf, Algau, 1889; bro. of above, dir., conductor and composer. (4) **K. G.**, 1812—London, 1887; pianist, composer and teacher.

Mann, Arthur Henry, Norwich, Engl., May 16, 1850—Cambridge, Nov. 11, 1929; chorister at the cath. with Dr. Buck; organist various churches; since 1876, King's Coll., Cambridge; 1871, F. C. O., 1882, Mus. Doc., Oxford; Händel scholar; with Prout discovered the original wind-parts of the "*Messiah*"; ed. the *Fitzwilliam Catalogue* with Maitland, etc.; c. "*Ecce Homo*," with orch.; "*Te Deum*," "*Evening Service*," for orch., etc.

Man'ners, (1) **Charles** (rightly Southcote Mansergh), London, Dec. 27, 1857—Dublin, May 3, 1935; bass; pupil Dublin Academy and R. A. M., London, and of Shakespeare; début 1882; 1890 Covent Garden; 1893 toured America; 1896 South Africa; 1897, organised Moody-Manners Opera Co. touring the provinces with three companies, two seasons at Covent Garden. In 1890 he married (2) **Fanny Moody**, b. Redruth, Nov. 23, 1866; soprano; pupil of Mme. Sainton Dolby; début 1887 with Carl Rosa Co., from 1890 sang with her husband; d. 1945.

Mannes (măn'-nĕs), (1) **David**, b. New York, Feb. 16, 1866; violinist, conductor, educator; studied in New York, Berlin and Brussels; played in N. Y. Symph., 1898 concertm.; cond. Symph. Club after 1902; taught at Music School Settlement, N. Y., for some years; beginning 1916, founded and dir. the David Mannes Music School, with his wife (2) **Clara** (née **Damrosch**) as co-dir.; cond. of concert series at Met. Museum of Art beginning 1920; gave concerts for young people and adults in cities near N. Y.; toured in sonata recitals with his wife, an accomplished pianist; ed. *New Songs for New Voices*, with Mrs. Mannes and Louis Untermeyer, 1928. (3) **Leopold Damrosch,** b. New York, Dec. 6, 1899; son of the preceding; composer and pianist; grad. Harvard Univ.; pupil of Guy Maier, Cortot, Scalero and others; Pulitzer Prize for comp.; also Guggenheim Fellowship; teacher of comp. and lecturer at David Mannes Music School; and of theory at Inst. of Mus. Art, N. Y.; c. string quartet, variations for piano, suite for 2 pianos, suite for orch.; introd. and allegro for vln. and piano; songs; incid. music to "*The Tempest,*" etc.

Man'ney, Chas. Fonteyn, b. Brooklyn, 1872; studied with Wm. Arms Fisher and J. Wallace Goodrich, Boston; comp.: d. N.Y., Oct. 31, 1951.

Manns (mäns), Sir **Augustus,** Stolzenburg, near Stettin, March 12, 1825—London, March 2, 1907; noted conductor; son of a glass-blower, who with his sons formed a quintet (vlns., 'cello, horn, and flute); at 15, apprenticed to Urban of Elbing; later 1st clar. of a regimental band, Dantzig; 1848, at Posen. Wieprecht got him a place as 1st vln. in Gungl's orch. at Berlin; 1849–51, cond. Kroll's Garden; regimental bandm. Königsberg and Cologne (1854); joined Crystal Palace band, London, as asst.-cond. to Schallen, who pub. as his own **M.'s** arrangement of certain quadrilles; whereupon **M.** resigned, publicly stating the reason; 1859 he succeeded S., he later made the band a full orch., giving famous and very popular Saturday Concerts till 1900, when the public ceased to support it; he also cond. 7 Triennial Händel Festivals, concerts of the Glasgow Choral Union, 1879–92, etc. He was knighted 1904.

Mannstädt (män'-shtĕt), **Fz.,** Hagen, Westphalia, July 8, 1852—Wiesbaden, Jan. 18, 1932; pupil Stern Cons., Berlin; 1874, cond. at Mayence; 1876, Berlin Symph. Orch.; 1879, pf.-t. Stern Cons.; 1893–97, cond. Berlin Philh.; then returned to Wiesbaden, where he had been a conductor and teacher.

Mantius (män'-tsĭ-oos), **Ed.,** Schwerin, 1806—Bad Ilmenau, 1874; tenor.

Man'uel, Roland (rightly **Levy**), b. Paris, March 22, 1891; composer, critic.

Manzuoli (män-tsoo-ō'-lē), **Giov.,** b. Florence, ca. 1725; famous soprano-musico.

Ma'pleson, Col. **Jas. H.,** London, May 4, 1828—Nov. 14, 1901; famous impresario; studied R. A. M., London; a singer, and vla.-player in an orch.; 1861, managed Italian Opera at the Lyceum; 1862–68, was at H. M.'s Th.; 1869, Drury Lane; 1877, reopened H. M.'s Th.; gave opera at Acad. of Mus., New York, with varying succ. in different seasons.

Mara (mä'-rä), **Gertrud Elisabeth** (née **Schmeling**), Cassel, Feb. 23, 1749—Reval, Jan. 20, 1833; phenomenal soprano, with compass, g–e''' (v. PITCH, D. D.), who reached a high pinnacle of art over difficulties (ranging from rickets to the Moscow fire) not surpassed in the wildest fiction; she m. in 1773, the 'cellist Mara, divorced him 1799; teacher.

Mara, La. Vide LIPSIUS, MARIE.

Marais (mă-rĕ'), (1) **Marin,** Paris, March 31, 1656—Aug. 15, 1728; the greatest viola-da-gambist of his time; c. symphonies, etc. (2) **Roland,** son of above; solo gambist; pub. pcs. for gamba.

Mar'beck, J. (or **Merbecke**), 1523—1585; Engl. organist and composer.

Marcello (mär-chĕl'-lō), **Benedetto,** Venice, July 24, 1686—Brescia, July 24, 1739; noted composer, pupil of Gasparini and Lotti; held gov't positions; pub. satires, and c. 50 psalms, madrigals, operas, oratorios, etc.

Marchand (mär-shäṅ), **Louis,** Lyons, 1669—in poverty, Paris, 1732; an org.-virtuoso whose fame wilted before his failure to meet J. S. Bach in a duel of virtuosity; c. clavecin pcs., etc.

Mar'chant, Arthur Wm., London, Oct. 18, 1850—Sterling, Nov. 23, 1922; organist in English churches; 1880–82, St. John's Cath., Denver, Col.; 1895, organist, Dumfries, Scotland; wrote text-books; c. Psalm 48, with orch.; "*A Morning Service*" and an "*Evening Service,*" etc.

Marchesi (mär-kā'-zē), (1) **Luigi** ("**Marchesi'ni**"), Milan, 1755—Inzago, Dec. 14, 1829; soprano musico. (2) **Salvatore,** Cavaliere **De Castrone** (dä-käs-trō'-nĕ) (Marchese **Della Rajata**), Palermo, Jan. 15, 1822—Paris, Feb. 20, 1908; studied mus. with Raimondi, Lamperti and Fontana; exiled after the Revolution of

1848 and début as barytone, N. Y.; then studied with Garcia, London; a succ. concert-singer; 1852 m. Mathilde Graumann (v. *infra*), and they sang together in opera, later taught together at Vienna Cons., 1865–69, Cologne Cons.; 1869–81, Vienna, then in Paris; pub. a vocal method, translations, etc.; c. songs. (3) **Mathilde** (née **Graumann**), Frankfort-on-M., March 24, 1821—London, Nov. 18, 1913; famous singing-teacher; pupil of Nicolai, Vienna, and Garcia, Paris; sang in concert; wife of above (q. v.); pub. a vocal method, vocalises, and autobiog. *"Marchesi and Music,"* enlarged from *"Aus meinem Leben"* (Düsseldorf, 1887). (4) **Blanche**, Paris, 1863—London, 1940; daughter of (3) and (2); soprano; after 1896 lived in London as singing teacher; later in Paris; author, *"A Singer's Pilgrimage"*; m. Baron André Caccamisi.

Marchetti (mär-kĕt'-tĭ), **Filippo**, Bolognola, Italy, Feb. 26, 1831—Rome, Jan. 18, 1902; pupil of Lillo and Conti, Royal Cons., Naples; at 21 prod. succ. opera, *"Gentile da Varano"* (Turin), *"La Demente"* (1857); singing-teacher, Rome; went to Milan and prod. succ. *"Giulietta e Romeo"* (1865), and *"Ruy-Blas"* (La Scala, 1869). From 1881, dir. R. Accad. di Santa Cecilia, Rome; prod. 3 other operas, symphonies, and church-music.

Marchet'tus of Padua (**Marchetto da Padova**), lived in Cesena, ca. 1270—ca. 1320; learned theorist. (Gerbert.)

Marchisio (mär-kē'sĭ-ō), (1) **Barbara**, Turin, Dec. 12, 1834—Mira near Venice, April 19, 1919; opera singer in Paris and London; sang usually with her sister. (2) **Carlotta**, Turin, 1836—1872.

Marcoux (mär-kōō'), **Vanni**, b. Turin, 1879; barytone; of French-Italian ancestry; studied with Collino and Boyer; after 1899 appeared with succ. in Paris, London and Brussels; came to U. S. and was active with Chicago Op. for a number of seasons; refinement of character portrayal and diction distinguished his perfs. of such rôles as "Boris Godounoff" and "Don Quichotte."

Maréchal (mär-ā-shăl), (1) **Henri**, Paris, Jan. 22, 1842—May 10, 1924; pupil of Cons., 1870, won Grand Prix de Rome; prod. 1-act op.-com. *"Les Amoureux de Cathérine"* (Op.-Com., 1876); also 3-act op.-com. *"La Traverne des Trabans"* (ibid., '81); *"Déidamie"* (Gr. Opéra, '93); *"Calendal"* (Rouen, '94); c. sacred drama *"Le Miracle de Naim"* ('91), etc. (2) **Maurice**, b. Dijon, France, Oct. 3, 1892; 'cellist; pupil of Paris Cons.; 1st prize in 'cello; after 1912 soloist with leading Paris orchs.; played in trio with Thibaud and Cortot; toured U. S. as recitalist.

Marenco (mä-rĕn'-kō), **Romualdo**, Novi Ligure, Italy, March 1, 1841— Milan, Oct. 10, 1907; violinist; then 2d bassoon, Doria Th., Genoa, where he prod. a ballet; studied cpt. with Fenaroli and Mattoi; 1873, dir. of ballet at La Scala, Milan; c. 4 operas, and over 20 ballets.

Marenzio (mä-rĕn'-tsĭ-ō), **Luca**, Coccaglio, near Brescia, ca. 1553—("of love disprized") Rome, Aug. 22, 1599; famous composer of madrigals, also of motets, etc.

Mareš (mä'-rĕsh), **Johann A.**, Chotebor, Bohemia, 1719—St. Petersburg, 1794; invented the Russian "hunting-horn mus.," each horn sounding one tone.

Maretzek (mä-rĕt'-shĕk), **Max**, Brünn, Moravia, June 28, 1821—Pleasant Plains, Staten Island, N. Y., May 14, 1897; well-known impresario; also dram. composer and teacher.

Mariani (mä-rĭ-ä'-nē), **Angelo**, Ravenna, Oct. 11, 1821—Genoa, June 13, 1873; famous conductor.

Marimon (mä-rē-môṅ), **Marie**, b. Liége, 1839; pupil of Duprez; début, 1857; soprano; d. (?).

Marin (mä-răṅ), **M. Martin Marcelle de**, b. Bayonne, France, Sept. 8, 1769; harpist and composer.

Marini (mä-rē'-nē), (1) **Biagio**, Brescia—Padua, ca. 1660; violinist and composer. (2) **Carlo A.**, b. Bergamo; violinist and composer, 1696.

Marinuzzi (mär-ē-nōōd'-sē), **Gino**, b. Palermo, March 24, 1882; conductor and composer; dir. Bologna Liceo, 1915–18; cond. Costanzi Theatre, Rome, and 1919–21 with Chicago Op., where his *"Jacquerie"* was prod., 1921; later res. in San Remo; has also cond. in South America, in Turin, Milan and at Rome with much succ.; c. also operas, *"Il Sogno del Poeta,"* *"Barberina"*; (orch.) *"Suite Siciliano"*; Requiem, etc.; d. Milan, 1945.

Mario (mä'-rĭ-ō), (1) **Giuseppe**, Conte

di Candia, Cagliari, Sardinia, Oct. 17, 1810—Rome, Dec. 11, 1883; eminent tenor; pupil of Bordogni and Poncharde; début, Paris Opéra, 1838; toured Europe and America with greatest success; m. Giulia Grisi. (2) **Queena** (rightly Tillotson), b. Akron, Ohio, August 21, 1896; soprano; studied with Oscar Saenger and Sembrich; mem. of Met. Op. Co., author of a novel; m. Wilfred Pelletier; divorced; d. N. Y., 1951.

Mar'iotte, Antoine, b. Avignon, Dec. 22, 1875; pupil of d'Indy; composer operas, etc.; d. during World War II.

Markevitch (mär-kyä'-vĕch), **Igor,** b. Kiev, Russia, July 27, 1912; composer and pianist; studied with Nadia Boulanger in Paris, where he lived after 1926; also for a time with Vittorio Rieti; commissioned by Diaghileff to write a ballet, but that impresario died before it could be written; 1st came into prominence with perf. of his Concerto Grosso in Paris, 1929, and Piano Concerto, same year in London; his works reveal a polyphonic style of uncompromising harshness, much rhythmic vitality and logical clarity, but an almost total lack of feeling; his music has been called highly original and significant by some, merely sensational by other critics; c. (orch.) Sinfonietta; Concerto Grosso; Piano Concerto; Partita; "*Rebus*"; "*Hymnes*" (an excerpt played by Boston Symph., 1934); (chamber music) Serenade for vln., clar. and bassoon; (choral works) Psalm the last causing a bitter division of opinion between adherents and detractors when played at the I. S. C. M. Fest. in Florence); and a cantata, "*Paradise Lost*" (perf. in London and Paris, 1936).

Markull (mär-kool'), **Fr. Wm.,** Reichenbach, near Elbing, 1816—Danzig, 1887; pianist, critic and dram. composer.

Markwort (märk'-vôrt), **Jn. Chr.,** Riesling, near Brunswick, 1778—Bessungen, 1866; tenor and writer.

Marmontel (mär-môṅ-tĕl), **Ant. Fran.,** Clermont-Ferrand, Puy-de-Dôme, July 18, 1816—Paris, Jan. 15, 1898; pupil Paris Cons., 1848; pf.-teacher there, noted for famous pupils; writer of historic and didactic treatises; composer.

Marpurg (mär'-poorkh), (1) **Fr. Wm.,**

Seehausen, Altmark, Nov. 21, 1718—Berlin, May 22, 1795; important theorist; wrote treatises of great historic and theoretic value, much translated. (2) **Fr.,** Paderborn, 1825—Wiesbaden, 1884; great-grandson of above; violinist, pianist, cond. and dram. composer.

Mar'schalk, Max, b. Berlin, April 7, 1863—on voyage, 1940; c. opera, "*Ju Flammen*" (Gotha, 1896); musical piece "*Aucassin und Nicolette*" (Stuttgart, 1907); incid. music to "*Und Pippa tanzt*" (Berlin, 1906), and to Maeterlinck's "*Sister Beatrice*" (Berlin, 1904); critic of Berlin "*Vossische Zeitung*," 1895–1933.

Marschner (märsh'-nĕr), (1) **H.** (August), Zittau, Saxony, Aug. 16, 1795 (not 1796)—Hanover, Dec. 14, 1861; eminent opera-composer of Weber's school but great modernity, and remarkable brilliance of instrumentation; studied piano from age of 6, sang as a boy, then pupil of Bergt (org.); studied law Leipzig U. 1813, then turned to mus. entirely; pupil of Schicht; the Graf von Amadée became his patron, and he went to Vienna; later taught at Pressburg; c. 3 operas, the last prod. 1820 at Dresden by C. M. von Weber; 1823, he became co.-dir. of opera there with von W. and Morlacchi; 1826, cond. Leipzig Th. and prod. "*Der Vampyr*" (1828) and "*Der Templer und die Jüdin*"; both widely succ. and still heard; 1831–59, ct.-cond. Hanover, when he was pensioned; while ct.-cond. he prod. "*Hans Heiling*" (Berlin, 1833), also very succ. and still alive; he prod. 8 other operas; c. incidental music, choruses, etc. (2) **Fz.,** b. Leitmeritz, Bohemia, March 26, 1855; pupil Prague Cons., and Bruckner, Vienna; after 1886, teacher Female Teachers' Seminary, Vienna; pub. a treatise on piano-touch; d. n. Poggstall, Austria, Aug. 28, 1932.

Marshall, (1) **John Patton,** b. Rockfort, Mass., 1877—Boston, 1941; pupil B. J. Lang, MacDowell, Chadwick, and Norris; 1903 Prof. of Music, Boston University; c. songs and piano pieces. (2) **Charles;** b. Waterville, Me.; tenor; studied with William Whitney, Vannucini and Lombardi; sang in Italian opera houses after début in Florence, 1901; also in Russia, Greece and Turkey; mem. Chicago Op. for a decade after 1921 singing heroic tenor rôles in Italian; d. Lake George, N. Y., May, 1951.

Marsick (mär-sĭk), (1) Martin P. Jos., Jupille, near Liége, Belgium, March 9, 1848—Paris, Oct. 21, 1924; prominent violinist; pupil of Désiré Haynberg, Liége Cons.; at 12 organist of the cath., and a vocalist; pupil of Léonard, Brussels Cons., later of Massenet at Paris Cons. (taking 1st vln. prize); and of Joachim at Berlin; début, Paris, 1873; toured Europe and (1895–96) U. S.; 1892, vln.-prof., Paris Cons.; c. 3 vln.-concertos, etc. **(2) Armand**, b. Liége, 1878; pupil of Ropartz and d'Indy; 1900, teacher and conductor in Athens; composer.

Marteau (mär-tō), Henri, Rheims, March 31, 1874—Lichtenberg, Oct. 3, 1934; excellent violinist; pupil Paris Cons.; 1892, took 1st prize; toured U. S., 1893, 1898; Russia, 1899; then compelled to spend a year in the French army; founded "Marteau Prize for vln.-sonata c. by a native-born American"; 1900 toured America; from 1900 teacher at Geneva Cons.; 1908–15, successor to Joachim at the Royal Hochschule für Musik, Berlin; 1921, Prague; 1926–28, Leipzig Cons.; later Dresden; c. chamber music, vln. works, etc.

Martelli, E. Vide COTTRAU, T.

Martin (mär-tăṅ), (1) Jn. Blaisé, Lyons, 1768—Paris, 1837; barytone. **(2) Sir George Clement**, Lambourne, Berks, Sept. 11, 1844—London, 1916; organist various churches; teacher in R. Coll. of Mus.; c. anthems; knighted, 1889. **(3) Riccardo (Hugh Whitfield)**, b. Hopkinsville, Ky., Nov. 18, 1881; tenor; studied violin; comp. with MacDowell; singing with Escalais, Sbriglia and Lombardi; début as "Faust," Nantes, France, 1904; sang in Verona and Milan; made Amer. début with French Op. Co., New Orleans; sang with Met. Op. Co., 1907–15; Boston Op. Co., 1915–17; at Covent Garden, and after 1920 with Chicago Op., also in concerts; d. N. Y., Aug. 11, 1952.

Martin y Solar (mär-tēn'-ē-sō-lär'), Vicente, Valencia, Spain, 1754—St. Petersburg, March 3, 1806; organist at Alicante; prod. operas in Italy in succ. rivalry with Cimarosa and Paisiello and in Vienna with Mozart; his best work was "*La Cosa Rara*,"

1785; 1788–1801, dir. Italian Op. at St. Petersburg; then teacher; c. 10 operas, ballets, etc.

Martinel'li, Giovanni, b. Montagnana, Italy, Oct. 22, 1885; notable tenor; at first an instrumentalist in Milan; début 1912, Covent Garden in "*La Tosca*" with great success; mem. of Met. Op. Co., N. Y., since 1913, with outstanding rank in wide variety of Italian and French rôles; has sung in South America, in Brussels and in many Italian theatres with eminent succ.; also in concerts.

Martines (mär-tē'-nĕs) (or Martinez) (mär-tē'-nĕth), Marianne di, Vienna, 1744—1812; singer, pianist and composer.

Martini (mär-tē'-nē), (1) Giambattista (or Giov. Bat.) (known as **Padre M.**), Bologna, April 24, 1706—Oct. 4, 1784; son and pupil of a violinist ((2) **Antonio Maria M.**), he studied with Predieri and Riccieri, Zanotti and Perti; took orders 1729; cond. from 1725 at church of San Francisco, Bologna; as a composer of church-mus., a theorist and teacher he won European fame; he also pub. a history of ancient mus., and treatises. **(3)** (rightly **Schwarzendorf**) (shvärts'-ĕn-dôrf), **Jean Paul Egide**, Freistadt, Palatinate, 1741—Paris, 1816; dram. composer. **(4) Nino**, b. Verona, Italy, 1905; tenor; pupil of Giovanni Zenatello; op. début in Italy at 21, in "*I Puritani*"; Amer. début as the "Duke" in "*Rigoletto*" with Phila. Grand Op. Co., 1931; mem. Met. Op. Co., after 1933; also active as concert, radio and film artist.

Martin'u, Bohuslav, b. Policka, Bohemia, Dec. 8, 1890; composer; studied at Prague Cons. (violin), also comp. with Suk and Roussel; c. sacred opera, "*Mysteries of the Virgin Mary*"; many chamber music works in advanced modern manner, among which are several string quartets, quintet, concerto for string quartet and orch., harpsichord concerto; symph. music and accompaniment to films; some of his works perf. in America by Boston Symph. and at Coolidge Fest., Pittsfield, Mass.

Martucci (mär-toot'-chē), Gius., Capua, Jan. 6, 1856—Naples, June 1, 1909; son and pupil of a trumpetplayer; début as pianist Naples, 1867; studied at the Cons.; 1874, prof. there; cond. the orch. and concerts estab. by Prince d'Ardore, and dir. of the Società del Quartetto; from 1875, toured with succ. as pianist; 1886–1902, dir. Bologna Cons.; 1902, Naples; c. 2 symph., pf.-concerto, chamber, choral works, etc.

Marty (măr-tē), **G. Eugène**, Paris, May 16, 1860—Vichy, Oct. 11, 1908; studied at the Cons. 1882; won the Grand Prix de Rome with cantata "*Edith*"; since 1894, prof. for ensemble singing there; 1895–96, chorusm. and cond. of the Concerts de l'Opéra; 1901, dir. concerts of the Cons.; c. several suites for orch., pantomime, "*Le Duc de Ferrare*," 3-act opera (1896), etc.

Marx (märx), (1) **Ad. Bd.**, Halle, May 15, 1795—Berlin, May 17, 1866; eminent theorist; founded with Schlesinger, "*Berliner allgemeine musikalische Zeitung*"; editor, prof. and mus.-dir., 1832; c. opera; wrote v. succ. and important treatises. (2) **Joseph**, b. Graz, Austria, May 11, 1882; composer, educator; studied with Degner, also at Univ., Ph. D.; prof. Vienna Akad., after 1914; succeeded Loewe as dir., 1922–25; 1925–27, also rector of the Hochschule; known for his songs, espec. "*Italienisches Liederbuch*"; also c. orch., chamber and choral music; a symph.; "*Castella Romana*" for piano and orch., etc.

Marxsen (märx'-zĕn), **Eduard**, Nienstädten, near Altona, 1806—Altona, 1887; organist and teacher.

Marzials (mär-tsĭ-äls'), **Theodor**, Brussels, Dec. 21, 1850—Feb., 1920; pupil of M. L. Lawson, London; studied later in Paris and Milan; 1870, supt. mus.-dept. British Museum; barytone and composer of pop. songs.

Marzo (mär'-tsō), **Ed.**, Naples, 1852— June 7, 1929; pupil of Nacciarone, Miceli and Papalardo; 1867, New York, as boy pianist; became opera and concert-cond., and accompanist to Carlotta Patti, Sarasate, etc.; organist at St. Agnes' Church, N. Y.; later at All Saints; 1884, knighted by the King of Italy; 1892, member of the R. Acad. of S. Cecilia; lived in N. Y. as singing teacher; pub. 6 masses (3 with orch.), etc.

Mascagni (mäs-kän'-yē), **Pietro**, b. Leghorn, Dec. 7, 1863—d. Rome, Aug. 2, 1945; baker's son; disliked law

study; secretly studied piano, later at Soffredini's Mus.-Sch.; studied pf., harm., cpt., and comp.; his father, finding him out, locked him in the house, whence he was rescued at 14 by an uncle; upon the uncle's death he was befriended by Count Florestan, while studying with Ponchielli and Saladino, at Milan Cons. He was cond. of various small troupes, finally cond. of the mus.-soc. at Cerignola; he won the prize offered by the mus.-pub. Sonzogno, for a 1-act opera, with "*Cavalleria Rusticana*," which had a sensational succ. (Costanzi Th., Rome, 1890) and has been universally performed; while fiercely assailed by the critics it has produced a school of short operas showing a tendency to excessive realism and strenuousness, yet offering a much-needed relief from the eternal classic, mythologic or costume-play plots and bringing serious opera as close home to real life as comic opera; 1895, dir. of the Rossini Cons. at Pesaro. **M.**'s later operas have not fared so well as his "*Cavalleria Rusticana*"; they include; "*L'Amico Fritz*" (Rome and Berlin, 1891), "*I Rantzau*" (Florence, 1892), fairly succ.; "*Guglielmo Ratcliff*" (Milan, La Scala, 1895), "*Silvano*" (ibid., 1895); 1-act "bozzetto" "*Zanetto*" (Pesaro, 1896); and the fairly succ. "*Iris*" (Rome, 1898; revised La Scala, Milan, 1899); "*Le Maschere*" simultaneously prod. without succ. in 6 cities in Italy, Jan., 1901; he c. also (previously to *Cav. Rust.*) 2-act opera "*Il Filanda*," and Schiller's "*Hymn to Joy*"; also a "*Hymn in Honor of Admiral Dewey, U. S. N.*" (July, 1899), etc. 1902, toured America with his own opera-troupe; he was dir. of Pesaro Cons. until 1903; 1909, cond. at Teatro Costanzi, Rome; c. also "*Amica*" (Monte Carlo, 1905, Cologne, 1907); 1910 he c. opera "*Isabeau*" for the U. S. but not completing it on time became involved in a lawsuit. The opera was prod. at Venice and Milan simultaneously, 1912, with moderate succ. Later operas include "*Parisina*" (Milan, 1913); "*Lodoletta*" (Rome, 1917); operetta, "*Sì*" (Rome, 1919); "*Il Piccolo Marat*" (Rome, 1921, with succ. of short duration); "*Nerone*" (Rome, 1935), an attempt to show Nero as an art-lover and amorist; also symph., choral and other works. **M.** has appeared widely in Italy as a cond. of his works, also in orch. concerts; mem. of Italian Academy.

Maschek (mä-shäk′), (1) **Vincenz,** Zwikovecz, Bohemia, 1755—Prague, 1831; pf. and harmonica-virtuoso; organist and dram. composer. (2) **Paul,** 1761—Vienna, 1826; bro. of above; pianist.

Mascheroni (mäs-kĕ-rō′-nē), **Edoardo,** Milan, 1857—March 4, 1941; cond. and composer; pupil of Boucheron; 1883 theatre cond. at Leghorn, later at Teatro Apollo, Rome; 1893 chosen to cond. Verdi's *"Falstaff"* at La Scala; c. *"Requiem"* for King Victor Emanuel, also by Royal command another *"Requiem"* for the royal chapel; c. operas *"Lorenza"* (Rome, 1901) successful throughout Europe and South America; *"La Perugina,"* etc.

Ma′son, (1) Rev. **Wm.,** Hull, Engl., 1724—Aston, 1797; writer and composer. (2) **Lowell,** Medfield, Mass., Jan. 24, 1792—Orange, N. J., Aug. 11, 1872; pioneer in American comp. and teaching; c. v. succ. and remunerative colls., principally of sacred music. (3) **Wm.,** Boston, Mass., Jan. 24, 1829—New York, July 14, 1908; prominent American teacher and technician; son of above; studied with Henry Schmidt (pf.) in Boston; at 17, début as pianist there; 1849, studied with Moscheles, Hauptmann and Richter, at Leipzig; with Dreyschock at Prague; and Liszt, at Weimar; he played in Weimar, Prague, and Frankfort, London, and 1854-55 in American cities; 1855 lived in New York as teacher; 1872, Mus. Doc. *h. c.,* Yale; pub. *"Touch and Technic, a Method for Artistic Piano playing"*; *"A Method for the Pf."* with E. S. Hoadley (1867); *"System for Beginners"* (1871); *"Mason's Pf.-Technics"* (1878); and *"Memoirs"* (New York, 1901); c. a serenata for 'cello and many pf.-pcs. in classical form. (4) **Luther Whiting,** Turner, Maine, 1828 — Buckfield, Maine, 1896; devised the v. succ. *"National System"* of mus.-charts and books; wrote *"Die neue Gesangschule."* (5) **Daniel Gregory,** b. Brookline, Mass., Nov. 20, 1873—Greenwich, Conn., Dec. 4, 1953; pupil of Johns, Nevin, J. K. Paine, Chadwick, d'Indy

and Goetschius; graduated Harvard, 1895; author of articles and books on musical topics; c. violin and piano sonata, piano variations, quartet in A major; pastorale for violin, clarinet and piano; elegy for piano, symphonies and other orch. works, songs, etc.; prof. of music at Columbia Univ., N. Y. Author, *"From Grieg to Brahms," "Guide to Music," "Beethoven and His Forerunners," "Great Modern Composers," "The Romantic Composers," "Appreciation of Music"* (with T. W. Surette); *"Orchestral Instruments,"* etc.; ed. *"The Art of Music."* (6) **Henry Lowell,** b. Boston, 1864; grandson of Lowell M.; mem. of firm of Mason & Hamlin, piano mfrs. after 1888; pres., 1915; author of histories of piano and reed organ, and stories of operas. (7) **Edith Barnes,** b. St. Louis, Mo., 1892; soprano; studied with Clement and Maurel; mem. Boston Op., 1913; Met. Op. Co., 1915-17, and again after 1935; appeared with Paris Op. and Op. Comique, 1918-21; Chicago Op., 1921-30; also at La Scala, Monte Carlo, Havana, Mexico City and at Ravinia (Chicago), in lyric rôles; m. Giorgio Polacco, conductor.

Massa (mäs′-sä), **Nicolò,** Calice, Ligure, Italy, 1854—Genoa, 1894; c. operas.

Massaini (mäs-sä-ē′-nē), **Tiburzio,** b. Cremona, 16th cent.; Augustine monk; cond. and composer.

Massart (mäs-săr′), (1) **Lambert Jos.,** Liége, July 19, 1811—Paris, Feb. 13, 1892; violinist and prof. Paris Cons. (2) **Louise Aglæ** (née Masson), Paris, 1827—1887; wife of above; pianist and, 1875, teacher at the Cons. (3) **Nestor, H. J.,** Ciney, Belgium, 1849—Ostende, 1899; tenor opera singer; operatic favourite in Europe and America.

Massé (mäs-sä), **Felix M.** (called Victor), Lorient, Mar. 7, 1822—Paris, July 5, 1884; pupil Paris Cons.; won Grand prix de Rome, prof. of cpt. there 1872; c. 18 operas, 13 prod., incl. the still succ. *"Les noces de Jeannette"* (Op. Com. 1853).

Massenet (mäs-nä), **Jules (Émile Fr.),** Montaud, near St. Étienne, France, May 12, 1842—Paris, Aug. 13, 1912 (of cancer); eminent French opera-composer; pupil of Laurent (pf.), Reber (harm.), Savard and Ambr.

Thomas (comp.) at the Cons.; took first prizes for piano and fugue; 1863, the Grand prix de Rome with cantata "*David Rizzio*"; 1878–96 prof. of comp. at the Cons.; 1878, member of the Académie, Commander of the Legion of Honour. C. operas, almost all of them succ. and many still in the repertory of the Paris Opéra and Op. Com., 1-act comic opera "*La Grand Tanta*" (1867); the operas, "*Don César de Bazan*" (1872); "*Le Roi de Lahore*" (1877); "*Hérodiade*" (1884); "*Manon Lescaut*" (one of the greatest successes in the history of the Op.-Com.), "*Le Cid*" (1885); fairy-opera (1889) "*Esclarmonde*"; "*Le Mage*" (1891); "*Werther*" (1892); lyric comedy, "*Thaïs*" (1894); 1-act com.-op. "*Le Portrait de Manon*" (1894); lyric episode, "*La Navarraise*" (London, 1894; Paris, 1895); "*Sapho*" (Op.-Com., 1897); "*Cendrillon*" (Op.-Com., 1899); also 4-act drama "*Marie-Magdeleine*" (Odéon Th., 1873); "*Éve*," a mystery, 1875; oratorio, "*La Vièrge*," 1880; conte lyrique "*Griselidis*" (Op.-Com., 1901); "*Jongleur de Nôtre Dame*," (Monte Carlo, 1902) (sung widely; Covent Garden, 1906, New York Manhattan Opera, 1910); "*Cherubin*" (Op. Com. Paris, 1905); "*Ariane*" (1906); "*Thérèse*" (Monte Carlo, 1907); "*Don Quichotte*" (Paris, 1911); "*Roma*" (Paris, Opéra, 1912); oratorios "*La Terre Promise*" (Paris, 1900); piano concerto (1903); ballets, "*La cigale*" (Paris, 1903), "*Espada*" (Monte Carlo, 1908), "*Bacchus*" (1909), "*Panurge*" (1913), opera "*Cleopâtre*"; orch. suites; overtures incl. "*Phèdre*"; pf.-pcs., songs, etc.

Maszynski (mä-shĭn'-shkĭ), **Peter**, b. Warsaw, 1855; pianist and composer; pupil of Mikhalovski, Roguski and Noszkowski; his "*Chor zniviarzy*" won a prize at Cracow; teacher at the Musical Institute; cond.; c. violin sonata, incid. music, a cantata in honor of the jubilee of Sienkiewicz, etc.; d. (?).

Materna (mä-tĕr'-nä), **Amalie**, St. Georgen, Styria, July 10, 1845—Vienna, Jan. 18, 1918; noted soprano; daughter of a sch.-master; sang in church and concert at Graz; début 1865 in opera as soubrette; m. an actor, K. Friedrich, and sang with him in operetta at the Carl Th.,

Vienna; 1869–90 príma donna, Vienna ct.-opera; toured America 1884 and 1894; she created "Brünnhilde,' at Bayreuth, 1876, and "Kundry" in "*Parsifal*," 1882; after 1900 taught in Vienna.

Math'ews, Wm. Smyth Babcock, New London, N. H., May 8, 1837—Denver, Col., April 8, 1912; prominent teacher and writer; studied at New London; later at Lowell and Boston; 1860–63, pf.-teacher Macon, Ga.; 1867–93, organist Chicago; 1868–72, ed. "*Musical Independent*"; 1878–86, critic of Chicago *Times*, *Morning News*, and *Tribune*; 1891, founded and ed. the magazine *Music*; pub many books of educational value.

Mathias (mä-tē'-äs), **Georges** (Amédée St. Clair), Paris, Oct. 14, 1826—Oct. 14, 1910; pupil of Kalkbrenner and Chopin (pf.) and of Paris Cons.; 1862, pianist and prof. there, c. symph., overtures, etc.

Mathieu (mät-yŭ), (1) **Adolphe Chas. Ghislain**, Mons, Belgium, June 22, 1840—Paris, 1883; custodian of MSS. Brussels Library; writer. (2) **Émile (Louis V.)**, Lille, Oct. 16, 1844—Sept., 1932; studied Louvain Mus. Sch. and Brussels Cons.; won 1st harm. prize, and 1st pf. prize, 1869, and 1871, won 2nd Grand prix de Rome; 1867–73, prof. pf. and harm., Louvain Mus. Sch.; 1881–98, dir. Louvain Mus.-Sch.; 1898, dir. R. Cons. at Ghent; c. 7 operas, mostly comic, a ballet, 5 cantatas and 2 children's cantatas, 3 (text and music) "*Poèmes lyriques et symphoniques*," symph. poems, etc.

Mattei (mät-tā'-ē), (1) Abbate **Stanislao**, Bologna, 1750—1825; professor, conductor and writer. (2) **Tito**, Campobasso, near Naples, May 24, 1841—London, March 30, 1914; pianist to the King of Italy; pupil at 11 and later "Professore," Accad. di Santa Cecilia, Rome; received a gold medal from Pius IX.; toured Europe; 1865–71, cond. at H. M.'s Th., London; c. 3 operas incl. "*Maria, di Gand*" (H. M.'s Th., 1880); ballet, pop. songs, etc.

Matteis (mät-tā'-ēs), (1) **Nicolà**, Italian violinist, 1672, London. (2) **Nicolà**, d. 1749, son of above; teacher.

Matthay', **Tobias Augustus**, b. London, Feb. 19, 1858; pianist; pupil R. A. M.; teacher there; c. "*Hero and Leander*," for chorus and orch., etc. One of most eminent piano masters, with many famous pupils. An Amer. M. Assoc. formed among these which annually awards a scholarship in his memory. Author of important treatises; d. Haslemere, 1945.

Mat(t)heson (mät'-tĕ-zōn), **Jn.**, Hamburg, Sept. 28, 1681—April 17, 1764; versatile diplomat and musician, a singer, composer and player on the org. and harps.; operatic tenor; important in the development of the church cantata afterward advanced by Bach; the first to introduce women into church-service; pub. valuable and controversial treatises; c. 88 works; 1715–28, mus. dir., Hamburg Cath.

Matthison-Hansen (mät'-tĭ-zōn-hän'-zĕn), (1) **Hans**, Flensburg, Denmark, 1807—Roeskilde, 1890; organist and composer. (2) **Godfred**, Roeskilde, Nov. 1, 1832—Copenhagen, Oct. 14, 1909; son of above; 1859, organist German Friedrichskirche, Copenhagen; 1862, won the Ancker scholarship, and studied at Leipzig; 1867, organist at St. John's and organ-teacher Copenhagen Cons.; from 1877, asst.-organist to his father; later organist of Trinity Ch.; c. vln. sonata, 'cello sonata, etc.

Matzenauer (mät'-sĕn-ow-ĕr), **Margarete**, b. Temesvar, Hungary, June 1, 1881; contralto; her father a conductor and mother an opera singer; studied with Mmes. Mielke and Neuendorf and Franz Emerich; début, Strasbourg, 1901; mem. of this co. to 1904; thereafter until 1911 with Munich. Op.; Met. Op., N. Y., 1911–30; also soloist with orchs., and in recital; has taught and appeared in films; m. Edoardo Ferrari-Fontana, tenor; divorced.

Maubourg (mō'-bōōrg), **Jeanne**, b. Namur, 1875; soprano; her teachers included Mmes. Labarre and Jouron-Duvernay; she sang at La Monnaie, Brussels, 1897–1907; at Covent Garden after 1900, and at Met. Op., N. Y., 1909–14; afterward teaching in New York.

Mauduit (mō-dwē), **Jacques**, Paris, Sept. 16, 1557—Aug. 21, 1627; lute player and composer of chansons and a requiem for the poet Ronsard.

Mauke (mow'-kĕ), **Wilhelm**, Hamburg, Feb. 25, 1867—Wiesbaden, Aug. 25, 1930; pupil of Löwe and Huber; then at Munich Akad. der Tonkunst; acted as critic; c. symph poem "*Einsamkeit*" (after Stuck and Nietzsche), operas, songs, etc.

Maurel (mō-rĕl), **Victor**, Marseilles June 17, 1848—New York, Oct. 22 1923; eminent barytone; studied Marseilles and with Vauthrot at the Paris Cons., gaining 1st prizes in singing and opera; début, 1868 at the Gr. Opéra as "de Nevers" in "*Les Huguenots*"; 1870, sang at La Scala, Milan, then in New York, Egypt, Russia with Patti, London, etc.; 1883, co-director Th. Italien, Paris, without succ.; sang in all the capitals as the supreme dramatic artist of his operatic generation, his splendid impersonation and vocal art carrying conviction after his voice lost its youth; he created "Iago" in Verdi's "*Otello*," 1887, and stamped "Don Giovanni" and other rôles with his own personality as a criterion; after 1909 taught in New York.

Maurer (mow'-rĕr), **L. Wm.**, Potsdam, Feb. 8, 1789—St. Petersburg, Oct. 25, 1878; distinguished violinist and dram. composer.

Maurin (mō-răn), **Jean Pierre**, Avignon, 1822—Paris, 1894; violinist and teacher.

May, (1) **Edw. Collett**, Greenwich, 1806—London, 1887; vocal teacher and writer. (2) **Florence**, pianist, London; daughter of above; wrote biography of Brahms, of whom she was a pupil.

Mayer (mī'-ĕr), (1) **Chas.**, Königsberg, 1799—Dresden, 1862; pianist and composer. (2) **Emilie**, Friedland, Mecklenburg, May 14, 1821—Berlin, April 10, 1883; pupil of Löwe, Marx and Wieprecht; lived in Berlin; c. 7 symphonies, 12 overtures, an operetta, "*Die Fischerin*," etc. (3) **Wm.** (pseud. **W. A. Remy**), Prague, 1831—Graz, 1898; excellent teacher of cpt. and comp.; composer. (4) Vide MAYER.

Mayerhoff (mī'-ĕr-hôf), **Fz.**, b. Chemnitz, 1864—1938; studied at Leipzig Cons.; theatre-cond. various cities; from 1885, Chemnitz; 1888, cantor Petrikirche, and cond. Mus. Soc.; 1910, cond. of Lehrergesangverein; 1915, Leipzig Riedel-Verein; 1911, Royal Prof., c. sacred choruses, etc.

May'nor, Dorothy, noted Negro lyric soprano; début, Berkshire Fest., 1939.

Mayr (mīr), (1) **(Jn.) Simon,** Mendorf, Bavaria, June 14, 1763—blind, Bergamo, Dec. 2, 1845; famous teacher and dram. composer; pupil of Lenzi and Bertoni; lived in Venice as church-composer; 1794 prod. v. succ. opera "*Saffo*," followed by 70 more; 1802, cond. Santa Maria Maggiore, Bergamo, and 1805, dir. Mus. Inst.; wrote a life of Haydn, treatises and verse; he is said to have been the first to use the orchestral crescendo in Italy; biog. by Alborghetti and Galli (Bergamo, 1875). (2) **Richard,** Salzburg, Nov. 18, 1877—Vienna, Dec. 1, 1935; bass; studied at Vienna Cons., made début as "Hagen" at Bayreuth Fest., 1902; mem. of Vienna Op., 1902–35, singing wide range of rôles, but especially renowned for his *buffo* characterizations, such as "Baron Ochs" in "*Der Rosenkavalier*"; Covent Garden, 1924; Met. Op., N. Y., 1927 (début as "Pogner" in "*Die Meistersinger*"); also heard in Wagner and Mozart rôles at Salzburg Festivals.

Mayrberger (mīr'-bĕrkh-ĕr), **K.,** Vienna, 1828—Pressburg, 1881; conductor and dram. composer.

Mayseder (mī'-zā-dĕr), **Jos.,** Vienna, Oct. 26, 1789—Nov. 21, 1863; eminent violinist, teacher and composer; 2nd vln. of famous "Schuppanzigh Quartet."

Mazas (mă-zäs), **Jacques Féréol,** Béziers, France, 1782—1849; violinist, writer and dram. composer.

Mazzinghi (mäd-zēn'-gǐ), **Jos.,** of Corsican extraction, London, 1765 —London, 1839; organist, teacher and dram. composer.

Mazzocchi (mäd-zôk'-kǐ), **Dom.,** Civitá Castellana, Rome, ca. 1590— ca. 1650; composer.

Mazzolani (mäd-zō-lä'-nē), **Antonio,** Ruina, Ferrara, Dec. 26, 1819— Ferrara, Jan. 25, 1900; composer of successful operas and choruses.

Mazzucato (mäd-zoo-kät'-tō), **Alberto,** Udine, 1813—Milan, 1877; violinist, teacher, editor and composer.

McConathy, Osbourne, b. Pitts Point, Ky., 1875; educator, conductor; studied with Luther Mason, Karl Schmidt, Percy Goetschius; dir. Louisville Fests., 1900–03; cond. in Boston, choruses, bands, etc., 1904–12; assoc. cond., Evanston, Ill.,

North Shore Fests., 1913–25; teacher of theory and methods at various Amer. univs.; has served as pres., Music Teachers Nat'l Ass'n. and Music Supervisors Nat'l Conference; author and ed. of works on school music; d. 1949.

McCor'mack, John, b. Athlone, 1884; tenor; pupil of Sabatini, Milan; début Covent Garden, 1907, with great success; 1910 sang with Philadelphia Opera Co.; 1911 Chicago Opera Co.; toured Australia, 1912, with the Melba Opera Co. and in concert with immense succ. in U. S. and Europe; created a Papal Knight; d. at his estate near Dublin, 1945.

McEw'en, Sir John Blackwood, b. Hawick, April 13, 1868; Scots composer and pupil R. A. M.; from 1898 prof. there and dir., 1924; knighted, 1934; c. symph., 2 overtures, "*Hellas*" for women's voices and orch. "*The Last Chantey*," chorus and orch. Milton's "*Nativity*," do.; c. vln. and chamber wks., songs; d. London, June 14, 1948.

McKin'ley, Carl, b. Yarmouth, Me., Oct. 9, 1895; composer; grad. Knox Cons., Galesburg, Ill.; also of Harvard Univ.; studied with G. Dethier, Rothwell, R. Goldmark, and Nadia Boulanger; his symph. poem, "*The Blue Flower*," won Flagler Prize, 1921; cond. his "*Masquerade*" at N. Y. Stadium concerts, 1926; won Guggenheim Fellowship, 1927–29; was solo répetiteur at Munich Op., later teacher of organ, theory and history of music at N. E. Cons.

McPhee', Colin, b. Canada, 1901; composer, of modern style works, incl. piano concertos with orch. and also with wind octet; sonatina for two flutes, clar., trumpet and piano; "*Sea Chanty*" suite for barytone and unison male chorus; symph. in one movement, and "*Sarabande*" for orch.; also music for films and songs.

Mederitsch (mā'-dĕ-rǐtsh), **Jn.** (called **Gallus**), b. Nimburg, Bohemia, ca. 1765—died 1835, Lemberg; pianist and composer.

Medt'ner, Nicholas, b. Moscow, Dec. 24, 1879; composer, pianist; studied with Safonoff, at Moscow Cons; won medal there and also Rubinstein prize, Vienna, 1900; prof. Moscow Cons., 1902–3; has toured in many Eur. cities, also America 1929-30 in programs of his works;

these exhibit a more or less classical approach with some descriptive qualities; c. many works for piano, incl. sonatas, *"Dithyramben,"* *"Novellen,"* *"Fairy-Tales,"* *"Tragödie-Fragment"*; also vln. sonata and songs; d. London, Nov. 13, 1951.

Meerens (mā-räṅs), **Chas.**, Bruges, Dec. 26, 1831—near Brusseis, Jan. 14, 1909; 'cellist and acoustician.

Meerts (mārts), **Lambert** (Jos.), Brussels, 1800—1863; violinist, professor and composer.

Mees (māz), **Arthur,** Columbus, Ohio, Feb. 13, 1850—New York, April 26, 1923; pupil of Th. Kullak (pf.), Weitzmann (theory), and H. Dorn (cond.), Berlin; cond. Cincinnati May Fest. Chorus; asst.-cond. various societies in New York, Albany, etc.; 1896, asst.-cond. Thomas Orch., Chicago; 1898—1904, cond. Mendelssohn Glee Club, New York; 1887-96, wrote programme notes for N. Y. Philh. Orch., pf.-studies; pub. *"Choirs and Choral Music."*

Megerlin (mā-gĕr-lăṅ), **Alfred,** b. Antwerp, Belgium, 1880; violinist; pupil Antwerp and Brussels Cons.; after 1914 in U. S. and for a period beginning 1917, concertm. of N. Y. Philh. Orch.

Mehlig (mā'-lĭkh), **Anna,** Stuttgart, July 11, 1846—Berlin, July 16, 1928; pianist, pupil of Lebert and Liszt; m. Antwerp merchant Falk.

Mehrkens (mār'-kĕns), **Fr. Ad.,** Neuenkirchen, near Otterndorf-on-Elbe, April 22, 1840—Hamburg, May 31, 1899; pupil, Leipzig Cons.; lived in Hamburg as pianist, teacher and conductor; from 1871, cond. of the Bach-Gesellschaft; c. a symph., a Te Deum, etc.

Méhul (mā-ül), **Étienne Nicolas,** (Henri), Givet, Ardennes, June 22, 1763—of consumption, Paris, Oct. 18, 1817; one of the great masters of French opera, a student of orch. effects, and a special master of the overture; son of a cook; pupil of an old blind organist; at 10, studied with Wm. Hauser; at 14, his asst.; 1778, taught in Paris and studied with Edelmann (pf. and comp.); Gluck's advice and assistance turned him to dram. comp., after a succ. cantata with orch. (1782). He c. 3 operas, never prod., and now lost, a 4th was accepted but not performed until after the succ. of the op.-com.

"Euphrosyne et Coradin" (Th. Italien, 1790); 15 other operas followed with general succ. incl. *"Stratonice"* (1792), *"Le Congrès des Rois"* (1793) with 11 collaborators; 1705, inspector of the new Cons., and a member of the Academie; 1797, *"Le Jeune Henri"* was hissed off as irreverent toward Henri IV., though the fine overture had been demanded three times; the opera buffa *"L'irato, ou l'emporté"* (1801) made great succ. and lightened the quality of later operas; his best work was *"Joseph"* (1807); for four years he wrote only ballets; he left 6 unprod. operas incl. *"Valentine de Milan,"* completed by Daussoigne-Méhul, and prod. 1822; he c. also inferior symphs. and pf.-sonatas, and very pop. choruses *"Chant du départ,"* *"C. de victoire,"* *"Chant de retour,"* etc. Biogr. by Vieillard, 1859, and A. Pougin, 1889.

Meibom (mī'-bôm) (or **Meibo'mius,** **Marcus,** Tönning, Schleswig, 1626 (?)—Utrecht, 1711; theorist and collector; his great work is a valuable historical coll. of old composers.

Meifred (mĕ-frā), **Jos. J. P. Émile,** Colmars, Basses-Alps, 1791—Paris, 1867; horn-virtuoso, professor and writer.

Meiland (mī'-länt), **Jakob,** Senftenberg, Lower Lusatia, 1542—Celle, 1577; important contrapuntist.

Meinardus (mī-nar'-doos), **L. Siegfried,** Hooksiel, Oldenburg, 1827—Bielefeld, 1896; writer and dram. composer.

Meiners (mī'-nĕrs), **Giov. Bat.,** Milan, 1826—Cortenova, Como, 1897; conductor and dram. composer.

Meisle (mīz'-lē), **Kathryn,** b. Philadelphia; contralto; studied at Phila. Cons., début as soloist with Minneapolis Symph., 1921, and won reputation as a concert singer before entering opera; début in latter field as "Erda," Chicago Op., 1923; also as guest with Cologne Op., and after 1934 with Met. Op. Co.; m. Calvin Franklin, concert manager.

Meister (mī'-shtĕr), **K. Severin,** Königstein (Taunus), 1818—Montabaur, (Westerwald), 1881; teacher and mus. director.

Mel (mĕl), **Rinaldo de,** Flemish musician, 16th cent.

Mela (mā'-lä), (1) **del M.** Vide DEL

MELA. (2) **Vincenzo**, Verona, 1821
—Cologna, Vaneia, 1897; dram.
composer.

Melar'tin, Erkki, Kexholm, Finland,
Feb. 7, 1875—Helsingfors, Feb. 14,
1937; pupil of Wegelius; after 1911
dir. of Helsingfors Cons.; c. orch.
music, songs, etc.

Melba (mĕl'-bä), **Nellie** (rightly **Mitchell**), Melbourne, Australia, May
19, 1861—Feb. 23, 1931; one of the
chief colorature-sopranos of her time,
with a voice of great range, purity
and flexibility; pupil of Mme. Marchesi; début Th. de la Monnaie,
Brussels, 1887, as "Gilda" in "*Rigoletto*," sang in Europe and America
with greatest succ. in both opera and
concert; after 1888 at Covent Garden; the following year in Paris
as "Ophelia"; from 1893 at Met. Op.,
N. Y., where she was one of the
notable luminaries in casts with the
brothers de Reszke; 1906–07 at
Manhattan Op., and in 1917, Chicago Op.; she gave a series of special
perfs. in 1922–23 with the British
Nat'l Op. Co. in London, then
organized her own co. for a season
in Australia; as a reward for her
extensive work in giving benefit
concerts during the war was created
a Dame Commander of the British
Empire; her gala "farewell" at
Covent Garden, when she appeared
in scenes from her favorite operas,
was in 1926; founded Melba Scholarship for women singers in her native
country.

Melcér (mĕl'-tsĕr), **H. von**, Kalish,
Poland, Sept. 21, 1869—killed in
battle, Galicia, 1915; pianist and
composer; 1895 won Rubinstein
prize with Concertstück for pf. and
orch.

Melchior (mĕl'-kĭ-ôr), (1) **Edw. A.**, b.
Rotterdam, Nov. 6, 1860; teacher
and lexicographer. (2) **Lauritz**, b.
Copenhagen, March 20, 1890; tenor;
studied at Cons. in native city,
début Royal Op. there, 1913; afterward a pupil of Beigel, Grenzebach,
Mme. Bahr-Mildenburg and Karl
Kittel; Covent Garden, 1924, same
year at Bayreuth, where his "Parsifal"
roused much admiration; after 1926
mem. of Met. Op. Co., excelling in
Wagnerian rôles; has also sung
"Otello" at Covent Garden and with
San Francisco Op. Co.

Melchiori (mĕl-kĭ-ō'-rē). Ant.. Parma

1827—Milan, 1897· violinist and
composer.

Melgunow (mĕl'-goo-nôf), **Julius von**,
Kostroma, Russia, Sept. 11, 1846—
Moscow, March 31, 1893; pupil of
Henselt and the Rubinsteins; also
of Moscow Cons. and R. Westphal,
whose system he adapted to Bach's;
pub. a coll. of folk-songs.

Mel'is, Carmen, b. Cagliari, Sardinia,
1885; soprano; sang 1909 at Manhattan Op. House, N. Y.; 1911,
Boston Op. Co.; after 1913 for a
time with Met. Op., also appearing
at the Paris Op. and widely in Italy.

Mel'ton, Jas., tenor, b. 1904; Met. '42.

Meltz'er, Charles Henry, London,
June 7, 1853 of Russian parentage—
New York, Jan. 14, 1936; critic;
pupil of the Sorbonne, Paris, later
journalist on various New York
papers; author and translator of
plays and librettos.

Meluzzi (mā-lood'-zē), **Salvatore**,
Rome, July 22, 1813—April 17,
1897; eminent organist, composer
and conductor.

Membrée (män-brā), **Edmond**, Valenciennes, 1820—Château Damont,
near Paris, 1882; dram. composer.

Mendel (mĕn'-dĕl), **Hn.**, Halle, 1834
—Berlin, 1876; writer and lexicographer.

Mendelssohn, (1) **(Jakob Ludwig)
Felix** (rightly **Mendelssohn-Bartholdy)** (mĕn'-d'l-zōn-bär-tôl'-dē),
Hamburg, Feb. 3, 1809—Leipzig,
Nov. 4, 1847; eminent composer of
remarkably early maturity. Greatgrandson of a Jewish sch.-master,
Mendel, who adopted Christianity
and had his children reared in the
Christian faith; grandson of the
prominent philosopher Moses: son of
the banker Abraham M. Pf.-pupil
of his mother, Lea Salomon-Bartholdy, as was also his elder sister
Fanny (v. HENSEL). The family-life
of the Mendelssohns is almost unique
in history for its happiness and
mutual devotion. **M.** studied also
with L. Berger, Zelter (theory),
Hennings (vln.) and Mme. Bigot
(pf.). At 10 he entered the Singakademie, as an alto; the same year
his setting of the 19th Psalm was
performed by the Akademie. Every
Sunday a small orch. performed at
his father's house, and his comps.
were heard here early and often; he
usually cond. these concerts even as

a child. 1825 his father took him to Paris to consult Cherubini, who offered to teach him, but the father preferred to have him at home. At 12 he began the series of 44 vols., in which he kept copies of his comps. This year he c. bet. 50 and 60 pcs., incl. a cantata, a mus. comedy, a pf.-trio, 2 pf.-sonatas, a vln.-sonata, songs, etc. At 9 he had played the pf. in public; at 12 he was a notable improviser (while playing a Bach fugue at Goethe's request he extemporised the Development which he had suddenly forgotten). At 17 he c. the remarkably original, beautiful and (in advance) Wagnerian overture to *"A Midsummer Night's Dream,"* and the superb octet for strings (op. 20). This same year he matriculated at Berlin Univ. with a translation of Terence, said to be the first German attempt to render Terence in his own metres. He also painted, and was proficient in gymnastics and billiards. At 18 he prod. the succ. opera *"Die Hochzeit des Camacho,"* at the Berlin Opera, in which he used the leitmotif (v. D. D.). At 20 he compelled and conducted the first performance since the composer's death of the Bach *"Passion according to St. Matthew"* at the Singakademie. This was the first step in the great crusade he waged, taking Bach out of obsolescence into the pre-eminence he now keeps. 1830, **M.** declined the chair of mus. at the Berlin Univ. The year before he had made the first of nine voyages to England, where he has stood next to Händel in popularity and influence. He cond. his symph. in C minor, at the London Philh., which gave him his first official recognition as a composer. The same year he was invited (in vain) to c. a festival hymn for the anniversary of the emancipation of the natives of Ceylon, and in his letters (in which his sunny nature finds free play) he referred to himself as "Composer to the Island of Ceylon." He appeared also with brilliant succ. as pianist and organist. He now travelled in Scotland, Switzerland, and elsewhere, and returning to London, conducted the *"Hebrides"* overture, played his G min. concerto and B min. Capriccio brillant, and pub. his first 6 "Songs without Words" (c. in Ven-

ice, 1830). His race and his amazing energy and succ. made him much opposition at Berlin, and he was refused the conductorship of the Singakademie in 1833, although he had arranged a series of concerts for the benefit of the Orch. Pension Fund. 1833, he cond. the Lower Rhine Mus. Festival at Düsseldorf, and became Town Mus. Dir. of the ch.-mus., the opera, and two singing-societies, for a salary of 600 thaler (about $450). 1835, he became cond. of the Gewandhaus Orch., Leipzig, which (with Fd. David as leader) he raised to the highest efficiency; the Univ. made him, in 1836, Dr. Phil., *h. c.;* 1836, he cond. his oratorio *"Paulus,"* the Lower Rhine Festival, Düsseldorf, in 1837 also at the Birmingham Festival. 1837, he m. Cécile Charlotte Sophie Jeanrenaud of Frankfort, daughter of a French Protestant clergyman. She bore him five children, Karl, Marie, Paul, Felix, and "Lili" (Elisabeth). In 1841 Friedrich Wilhelm IV. invited him to take charge of the grand orch. and choral concerts at Berlin. The hostility to him was however so general that he wished to resign, but at the King's request organised the cath. mus., later famous as the "Domchor" (cath. choir). He was made R. Gen. Mus. Dir. With Schumann, Hauptmann, David, Becker, and Pohlenz, in the faculty, he organised the since famous Conservatorium of Mus. at Leipzig (since 1876 the "R. Cons."); he again cond. the Gewandhaus Concerts. 1845 he cond. *"Elijah"* at Birmingham. He resigned the Gewandhaus conductorship to Gade, and the piano-dept. to Moscheles, whom he invited from London. Upon hearing the news of the sudden death of his idolised sister, Fanny Hensel, he fell insensible and lived only 6 months. **M.** was kept from opera by inability to find a satisfactory libretto. Besides *"Die Hochzeit des Camacho"* he left an unfinished opera *"Lorelei,"* an operetta *"Son and Stranger,"* and 5 small unpub. operas. He c. 3 oratorios, *"Paulus"* (St. Paul) *"Elias"* (Elijah), and *"Christus"* (unfinished), the symph. cantata *"Lobgesang,"* op. 52; the ballade, with orch. *"Die erste Walpurgis-*

nacht," op. 60; 2 *"Festgesänge,"*
"An die Künstler" (for male chorus
and brass), and *"Zur Säcularfeier
der Buchdruckerkunst"* ("Gutenberg
Cantata"), with orch.; mus. to the
plays *"Antigone"* (op. 55), *"Athalie"*
(op. 74), *"Œdipus in Colonos"*
(op. 93), and *"A Midsummer Night's
Dream"* (op. 61); c. also vocal works
with orch., hymn, *"Tu es Petrus,"*
Psalms 114, 115, and 95, prayer
"Verleih' uns Frieden," and sopr.
concert-aria *"Infelice"* (op. 94).
4 SYMPHONIES, in C min.; A min.
(or *"Scotch"*); A (or *"Italian"*);
D (or *"Reformation"*). OVER-
TURES, *"Sommernachtstraum"* ("A
Midsummer Night's Dream"), op.
21; *"Hebrides," "Die Fingalshöhle"*
(or "Fingal's Cave"), op. 26; *"Meer-
stille und glückliche Fahrt"* ("Calm
Sea and Prosperous Voyage"), *"Die
Schöne Melusine"* ("The lovely
Melusine") (op. 32), *"Ruy Blas"*
(op. 95). *"Trumpet"* overture, and
an overture for wind-band (op. 24);
c. also andante, scherzo, capriccio,
and fugue, for string-orch. (op. 81),
funeral march (op. 103), and march
(op. 108); 2 pf.-concertos, in G. min.
and D. min.; capriccio brillant;
rondo brillant, and serenade and
allegro giocoso, for pf. with orch.;
vln.-concerto in E min. (op. 64); a
string octet, quartets, 2 quintets, a
pf.-sextet, 7 string-quartets, 3 pf.-
quartets, 2 pf.-trios, 2 trios for clar.,
basset horn, and pf.; 2 'cello-sonatas,
a sonata for vln., variations concertantes (op. 17) and *"Lied ohne
Worte"* (op. 109), for 'cello with pf.,
religious and secular choruses, 13
vocal duets, and 83 songs. FOR
PIANO, 3 sonatas; capriccio;
Charakterstücke; rondo capriccioso;
4 fantasias, incl. *"The Last Rose of
Summer"; "Lieder ohne Worte"*
("Songs without Words") in 8 books;
"Sonate écossaise," 6 preludes and
fugues, *"Variations sérieuses,"* etc.;
6 Kinderstücke, 3 preludes and 3
studies, op. 104; *"Albumblatt,"*
"Perpetuum mobile," etc. 4-hand
variations; 4-hand allegro brillant;
duo concertant (with Moscheles),
for 2 pfs. on the march-theme in
Weber's *"Preciosa."* FOR ORGAN,
3 preludes and fugues; 5 sonatas, op.
65; preludes in C min.
Biogr. by his eldest son Karl (1871);
by Hiller (187.); S. Hensel (1870);

Eckardt (1888); an extended article
by Grove (in his Dictionary), etc.
Numerous editions of his letters are
published. Memoirs by Lampadius,
Kaufman, Rockstro, Runciman and
Stratton. (See article, page 504.)
(2) **Arnold,** Ratibor, Dec. 26, 1855—
Darmstadt, Feb. 19, 1933; grand-
nephew of above; studied with
Haupt, Kiel, Grell, Taubert; organist
and teacher in the Univ. at Bonn;
then teacher at Cologne Cons.; then
at Darmstadt, professor; from 1912
taught Hoch Cons., Frankfort-on-
Main; D. Theol., Giessen Univ.,
1917. C. operas *"Elsi"* (Cologne
City Th., 1894), *"Der Bärenhäuter,"*
and *"Die Minneburg"*; also many
choral works of high quality; songs,
etc.
Mendès (män-děs), **Catulle,** Bordeaux
May 22, 1841—Paris, Feb. 8, 1909;
poet; librettist of pop. poems and
operettas.
Mengal (män-găl), **Martin Jos.,**
Ghent, 1784—1851; horn-virtuoso
and dram. composer.
Meng'elberg (1), **Willem,** b. Utrecht,
March 28, 1871—Chur, Switz.,
March 21, 1951; pupil Hol, Wurff
and Petri at Utrecht, then at
Cologne Cons.; 1891, dir. at Lucerne; from 1895 to 1945 Mengelberg
has been the brilliant cond. of the
Amsterdam Concertgebouw Orch.,
an organisation which he shaped into
one of the leading ensembles in
Europe; after 1898 also of the Toonkunst choral society there. Beginning 1903 he served as guest leader
of many Eur. orchs., incl. the London
Philh.; 1905 he visited N. Y. as one
of the conductors of the Philh. Orch.;
1907 led the Frankfort Museum
Concerts and, 1908, the Caecilien-
verein there; in 1921 he returned to
N. Y. as cond. of the short-lived
Nat'l Symph. Orch., and made so
powerful an impression that he
was engaged for the Philh. when the
former orch. was merged with it.
He conducted annually in N. Y.
until 1930 with a pronounced musical following; he also appeared as
guest cond. in the principal Eur.
capitals. Also a proficient pianist,
and a notable champion of the
works of Mahler. (2) **Rudolf,** b.
Crefeld, Germany, Feb. 1, 1892; cousin
of (1); composer and writer; wrote
programme notes for Amsterdam

Concertgebouw, of which after 1925 he was vice-director.

Mengés, Isolde, b. Brighton, Engl., 1894; violinist; studied with her father, who was dir. of Brighton Cons.; then with Leon Sametini and Auer; début, London, 1913; U. S., 1916.

Mengewein (měng'-ě-vīn), **K.,** Zaunroda, Thuringia, Sept. 9, 1052—near Berlin, April 7, 1908; from 1881–86, teacher at Freudenberg's Cons. Wiesbaden; co-founder of a Cons. at Berlin, 1886; c. oratorio, festival cantata, operetta, overture *"Dornröschen,"* etc.

Mengozzi (měn-gôd'-zē), **Bdo.,** Florence, 1758—Paris, March, 1800; tenor, writer and composer of 13 operas.

Menotti, Gian-Cario, b. Milan, 1911; composer; studied Curtis Inst., Phila.; c. one-act opera, *"Amelia Goes to the Ball,"* Met. Op., 1937–8; *"The Island God"* (ibid., 1942); 2-act opera, *"The Medium"*; 3-act, *"The Consul"*; 1-act *"The Telephone"*; ballet *"Sebastian."*

Menter (měn'-těr), (1) **Jos.,** Deutenkofen, Bavaria, 1808—Munich, 1856; 'cellist. (2) **(Menter-Popper) Sophie,** Munich, July 29, 1846—near Munich, Feb. 23, 1918; daughter of above; eminent pianist; pupil of Schönchen, Lebert and Niest; début, 1863; in 1867, studied with Tausig; 1869, with Liszt; 1872, m. the 'cellist Popper (divorced 1886); ct.-pianist to the Emperor of Austria; 1878–87, prof. St. Petersburg Cons.; then lived at her country-seat, Castle Itter, in the Tyrol.

Menuhin (měn'-ōō-hǐn), (1) **Yehudi,** b. New York, Jan. 22, 1917; remarkable for his precocious genius as violinist; res. in San Francisco as child; began vln. study at 4 with Louis Persinger; at 7 début with San Francisco Orch., creating a furore as prodigy; N. Y. recital, following year, roused much interest; was then taken to Paris for study with Enesco; début at 10 in that city with Lamoureux Orch. was triumphal event, closely followed by his appearance as soloist with N. Y. Symph. in Beethoven concerto, then further Eur. conquests incl. remarkable feat of playing Bach, Beethoven and Brahms concertos in one evening with Berlin Symph. under Bruno Walter; at 15, chosen to play Brahms

concerto with N. Y. Philh., showing ripened stylistic authority; has also been a pupil of Adolf Busch, and has appeared in sonata recitals with his young sister (2) **Hephzibah,** pianist, in London, Paris and New York with equal applause; following world tour, incl. Antipodes, 1935–36, he went into temporary retirement of 2 years on his ranch in Cal. for further musical study and recreation.

Merbecke, J. Vide MARBECK.

Mercadante (měr-kä-dän'-tě), **Gius. Saverio,** Altamura, Sept. 17, 1795—Naples, Dec. 17, 1870; pupil of Zingarelli and in 1840 his successor as dir. of Naples Cons.; in 1819 prod. an opera with great succ. and followed it with 60 others, incl. *"Elisa e Claudio"* (Naples, 1866), *"Il Giuramento"* (Milan, 1837); he lived in various cities; 1833 cond. at Novara Cath.; 1862 he went blind; he c. also 2 symphonies, 4 funeral symphonies, 20 masses, etc.

Méreaux (mā-rō), (1) **J. Nicolas Amédée Lefroid de,** Paris, 1745—1797; organist and dram. composer. (2) **Jos. N. L. de,** b. Paris, 1767; son of above; organist, and pianist. (3) **J. A. L. de,** Paris, 1803—Rouen, 1874; son of above; pianist, composer and writer.

Merian (mā'-rǐ-än), **Hans,** Basel, 1857—Leipzig, 1905; writer.

Méric (mā-rǐk). Vide LALANDE.

Mériel (mā-rǐ-ěl), **Paul,** Mondoubleau, 1818—Toulouse, 1897; violinist, cond. and dram. composer; dir. Toulouse Cons.

Merikan'to, Oscar, Helsingfors, Aug. 5, 1868—Feb. 17, 1924; organist and composer; studied Helsingfors, Leipzig and Berlin; organist and cond. at Nat'l Op., Helsingfors; c. (operas) *"The Girl of Pohja"* and *"The Death of Elina"*; works for organ, piano, violin, songs; ed. collection of folk-songs.

Merk (měrk), **Jos.,** Vienna, 1795—Ober-Döbling, 1852; violinist and composer.

Merkel (měr'-kěl), (1) **Gustav (Ad.),** Oberoderwitz, Saxony, Nov. 12, 1827—Dresden, Oct. 30, 1885; org. and composer. (2) **K. L.,** wrote treatises on throat, etc.

Merklin (měr'-klēn), **Jos.,** Oberhausen, Baden, Jan. 17, 1819—Nancy, June

10, 1905; org.-builder at Brussels; son of an org.-builder; took his brother-in-law, F. Schütze, into partnership, as "Merklin-Schütze," 1858; in 1855, est. a branch in Paris.

Mérö, Yolanda, b. Budapest, Aug. 30, 1887; pianist; studied at Cons. there, and made her début as soloist with Dresden Philh., 1907; toured in Eur. cities, also South and Central America, has lived in U. S. for a number of years, where she gave many recitals; c. "*Capriccio Ungharese*" for piano and orch.; m. Hermann Irion, mem. firm of Steinway & Sons.

Merola (mä'-rō-lä), **Gaetano,** b. Naples, Jan. 4, 1881; conductor; studied Naples Cons.; 1899, asst. cond., Met. Op.; later with Savage Op. Co., at Manhattan Op., and for some years gen'l dir. of San Francisco Op.; d. while conducting a concert, San Francisco, Aug. 30, 1953.

Mersenne (mĕr-sĕn), **Marin,** Oize (Maine), France, Sept. 8, 1588—Paris, Sept. 1, 1648; writer of mus. treatises.

Mertens (mär'-tĕns), **Jos.,** Antwerp, Feb. 17, 1834—Brussels, June 30, 1901; 1st vln. at the opera there and teacher at the Cons.; 1878–79, cond. Flemish Opera, Brussels; later, dir. at Royal Th., The Hague; prod. succ. Flemish and French operettas and operas, incl. "*De Zwarte Kapitein*" (The Hague, 1877).

Mertke (mĕrt'-kĕ), **Ed.,** Riga, 1833—Röga, 1895; pianist, violinist, composer and collector.

Mertz (märts), **Jos. K.,** Pressburg, Hungary, 1806—Vienna, 1856; guitar-virtuoso.

Merula (mä-roo'-lä), **Tarquinio,** b. Bergamo; violinist and composer, 1623–40.

Merulo (mä-roo'-lō) (rightly **Merlot'ti**), **Claudio** (called "**Da Coreggio**"), Coreggio, April 8, 1533—Parma, May 4, 1604; eminent organist, dram. composer and famous teacher; pupil of Menon and G. Donati; he was a leader of the Venetian sch. and bordered on the new tonality.

Merz (märts), **K.,** Bensheim, near Frankfort-on-Main, 1836—Wooster, Ohio, 1890; teacher and writer.

Messager (mĕs-sä-zhä), **André (Chas. Prosper),** Montlucon, Allier, France, Dec. 30, 1853—Paris, Feb. 24, 1929; pupil of Niedermeyer School and of

Saint-Saëns; 1874, organist of the choir, St. Sulpice; cond. at Brussels; organist at St.-Paul-Saint-Louis; Paris, cond. at Sainte Marie des Batignolles; 1898–1903, cond. Op. Com.; Chev. of the Legion of Honour; 1901–07, mus.-dir. Covent Garden, London; 1907–19, one of directors of the Opéra at Paris, and from 1908 cond. of the concerts of the Cons.; 1919–20, dir. Op.-Comique; completed Bernicat's unfinished score, "*François les Bas Bleus*" (Folies-Dramatiques, 1883), following it with about 20 other comic operettas and operas, incl. the succ. "*Le Chevalier d' Harmental*" (Op.-Com., 1896); "*La Basoche*" (Op.-Com., 1890, Bremen, 1892, as "*Zwei Konige*"); "*Mirette*" (Savoy, London, 1894); "*Les P'tites Michu*" (Paris, 1894) enormous success; "*Véronique*" (1899); "*Fortunio*" (Op. Com. 1907); "*Beatrice*" (Monte Carlo, 1914); operetta, "*L'Amour Masqué*" (Paris, 1923); mus. comedy, "*Passionnément*" (do., 1926); the ballets, "*Scaramouche*," "*Les Deux Pigeons*", songs, etc.

Messchaert (mä'-shärt), **Johannes,** Hoorn, Holland, 1857—Zurich, 1922; barytone; teacher, cond.; toured.

Messiaén, Olivier, b. Avignon, 1908; comp., organist. (V.Composers' List.)

Mestrino (mäs-trē'-nō), **Niccolò,** Milan, 1748—Paris, 1789; violinist, conductor, and composer.

Metastasio (mä-täs-tä'-zǐ-ō) (rightly **Trapassi,** but changed to **M.,** a pun on **T.** to please his patron Gravina), **P. Ant. Dom. Bonaventura,** Rome, Jan. 13, 1698—Vienna, April 12, 1782; poet and dramatist; wrote librettos set to mus. by Gluck and Mozart.

Methfessel (mät'-fĕs-sĕl), **Albert Gl.,** Stadtilm, Thuringia, 1785—Heckenbeck, 1869; dram. composer.

Métra (mä-trä), **(Jules Louis) Olivier,** Rheims, 1830—Paris, 1889; violinist and double-bass player, conductor and dram. composer.

Mettenleiter (mĕt'-tĕn-lī-tĕr), (1) **Jn. G.,** St. Ulrich, near Ulm, 1812—Ratisbon, 1858; organist and composer. (2) **Dominicus,** Thannhausen, Würtemberg, 1822—Ratisbon, 1868; brother of above; writer and composer.

Metzdorff (mĕts'-dôrf), **Richard,** Danzig, June 28, 1844—Berlin, April

26, 1919; pupil of Fl. Geyer, Dehn, and Kiel, Berlin; cond. at various cities; c. opera *"Rosamunde"* (Weimar, 1875); succ. *"Hagbart und Signe"* (Weimar, 1893); c. also 3 symph. incl. *"Tragic"*; overture *"King Lear"*; *"Frau Alice,"* ballade, with orch., etc.

Meurs, de. Vide MURIS, DE.

Meursius (mŭr'-sĭ-oos), Jns., Loozduinen, near The Hague, 1579—Denmark, 1639; prof. and writer.

Meyer (mī'-ĕr), (1) Ld. von (called "De Meyer"), Baden, near Vienna, 1816—Dresden, 1883; pianist and composer. (2) Jenny, Berlin, 1834—1894; concert-singer; 1865 teacher, 1888 proprietress Stern Cons. Berlin. (3) **Waldemar**, b. Berlin, Feb. 4, 1853; violinist, pupil of Joachim; 1873–81, member of the Berlin ct. orch. (4) **Gustav**, b. Königsberg, Prussia, June 14, 1859; pupil of Leipzig Cons.; cond. various cities; 1895, Leipzig City Th. 1903, Prague; c. 4-act farce, ballet-pantomime, etc. D. Prague, ?.

Meyerbeer (mī'-ĕr-bār), **Giacomo** (rightly Jakob Liebmann Beer; by adding the name "Meyer" he secured a large inheritance from a wealthy relative; he then Italianised "Jacob" as "Giacomo"), Berlin, Sept. 5, 1791—Paris, May 2, 1864; son of a Jewish banker; a precocious and remarkable pianist; pupil of Lauska and Clementi; at 7 played in public; studied with Zelter, Anselm, Weber; 1810, was invited by Abbé Vogler to live in his house as a son and pupil; did so for 2 years, one of his fellow-pupils being his devoted friend C. M. von Weber. Here he c. an oratorio and 2 operas *"Jephthas Gelübde"* (Ct.-Op., Munich, 1813) and *"Alimilek"* (Munich, 1813), the first a failure, the latter accepted for Vienna, whither he went and made a great succ. as pianist though his opera was not a succ. In his discouragement Salieri told him he needed only to understand the voice, and advised an Italian journey. He went to Venice in 1815 and, carried away with Rossini's vogue, c. 6 Italian operas which had succ., especially *"Il Crociato in Egitto"* (Venice, 1824). While writing this last he went to Berlin hoping to prod. 3-act German opera, *"Das Brandenburger Thor"*; though he found no hearing, Weber begged him not to give himself up to Italian influences. In the 6 years of silence that followed, occurred his marriage, his father's death, and the death of his two children. In 1826, he went to Paris to live, and made a profound and exhaustive study of French opera from Lully down, forming his third style, in which acc. to Mendel "he united to the flowing melody of the Italians and the solid harmony of the Germans the pathetic declamation and the varied, piquant rhythm of the French." He made a coalition with the sophisticated librettist, Scribe, and his first French opera, *"Robert le Diable"* (Gr. Opéra, 1831), was an enormous succ., financially establishing the Opéra itself, though **M.** had had to pay the manager Véron a large sum to secure its production. Less pop. succ. at first, but more critical favour attended *"Les Huguenots"* (1836); its prod. at Berlin, 1842, led King Fr. Wm. IV, to call him there as Gen. Mus.-Dir. His opera *"Das Feldlager in Schlesien"* (1843), had only mod. succ. until Jenny Lind sang it in 1844; 1847, he visited Vienna and London; returning to Berlin he prod. Wagner's new work *"Rienzi"*; later he obtained *"The Flying Dutchman"* performance, after its rejection elsewhere. The extent to which he befriended Wagner is matter of bitter controversy, some claiming that he gave only formal assistance while Wagner was obscure, and fought him with underhanded methods and a "press-bureau," when Wagner attained power. At any rate Wagner despised and publicly assailed the music of Meyerbeer. Yet, whether or no Wagner borrowed money from **M.**, he certainly borrowed numberless points of artistic construction from him. In 1849, *"Le Prophète"* (finished 1843) was prod. at the Paris Gr. Opéra (1849) followed by the successes *"L'Étoile du Nord"* (Op.-Com., 1854), some of it taken from his *"Das Feldlager in Schlesien"*; and *"Dinorah, ou le Pardon de Ploërmel"* (Op. Com., 1859). *"L'Africaine"* (worked on with constant and characteristic changes from 1838) was prod. at the Paris Gr. Opéra, 1865, a year after his death. **M.** left by will 10,000 thaler ($7,500) for the foundation of a *Meyerbeer Scholarship*, for which only Germans under 28, and pupils of the Berlin "Hochschule," the Stern Cons., and the Cologne Cons., are eligible. Competitors must submit a vocal fugue *à 8* (for double chorus), an overture for full orch., and a dram. cantata *à 3*, with orch. (text of cantata, and text and theme of fugue being given). The fund gives six months in Italy, six in Paris, and six more in Vienna, Munich and Dresden together. **M. c.** also incid. music to *"Struensee"* (the tragedy by his brother, Michael Beer; Berlin, 1846), choruses to Æschylus' *"Eumenides"*; festival-play *"Das Hoffest von Ferrara"*; monodrama *"Thevelindens Liebe,"* for sopr. solo, chorus with clar. obbligato (Vienna, 1813); cantatas, *"Gutenberg"* and *"Maria und ihr Genius"* (for the silver wedding of Prince and Princess Carl of Prussia); *"Der Genius der Musik am Grabe Beethoven"*; serenade *"Brautgeleite aus der Heimath"* (for the wedding of Princess Louise of Prussia); ode to Rauch (the sculptor), with orch.; 7 sacred odes *a cappella;* *"Festhymnus"* (for the King of Prussia's silver wedding); 3 *"Fackeltänze,"* for wind-band, also scored for orch. (for the weddings of the King of Bavaria, and the Princesses Charlotte and Anna of Prussia); grand march for the Schiller Centenary (1859); overture in march-form (for opening of London Exhibition, 1862); coronation march for King Wilhelm I. (1863); church-music; pf.-pcs., etc. Biog. by A. de Lasalle (1864); H. Blaze de Bury (1865); Ella (1868); H. Mendel (1868), and J. Schucht, 1869. Other memoirs by Pougin, Kohut, J. Weber, Curzon, Eymieu, Dauriac, Hervey, Kapp, etc. (See article, page 505.)

Meyer-Helmund (mī'-ĕr-hĕl-moont), **Erik,** St. Petersburg, April 13 (25 new style), 1861—Berlin, April 4, 1932; pupil of his father and of Kiel and Stockhausen; prod. comic operas, incl. the succ. *"Der Liebeskampf"* (Dresden, 1892); succ. ballet *"Rübezahl"* (or *"Der Berggeist"*) (Leipzig, 1893); 1-act burlesque *"Trischka"* (Riga, 1894); and pop. songs.

Meyer-Olbersleben (mī'-ĕr-ŏl'-bĕrs- lä-bĕn), **Max,** Olbersleben, near Weimar, April 5, 1850—Würzburg, Dec. 31, 1927; pupil of his father, of Müller-Hartung and Liszt, on whose recommendation he was given a stipend by the Duke, and studied with Rheinberger and Wüllner; 1877, teacher of cpt., and comp. R. Cons. of Mus., Würzburg; 1907–20, dir. of same; 1879, cond. the *"Liedertafel"*; 1885, Royal Prof.; 1896, dir. *"Deutscher Sängerbund,"* and co-dir. the Fifth National *Sängerfest,* Stuttgart; c. succ. romantic opera *"Cläre Dettin"* (Würzburg, 1896), and a comic opera *"Der Hauben Krieg"* (Munich Opera); overtures, *"Feierklänge"* and *"Festouvertüre";* fine choruses; chamber-mus., etc.

Mézeray (māz-rĕ'), **L. Chas. Lazare Costard de,** Brunswick, 1810—Asnières, near Paris, April, 1887; barytone and dram. composer.

Miaskowsky (mē-äs-kôf'-skē), **Nicolas,** b. near Warsaw, Apr. 20, 1881—d. Moscow, Aug. 9, 1950; Russian comp.; his father a general in the Russian army, and early trained to follow in the profession of military engineer; 1906, entered St. Petersburg Cons., where he studied with Glière, Liadoff, Witol and Rimsky-Korsakoff; early composed pf. sonata; after serving in Russian armies during war, came into prominence as a symph. comp. in pos-revolutionary period; composed many works in this form, several of which have been played in the U. S.; his music is neo-romantic though with some modern harmonic influence by Scriabin, Prokofieff, Debussy, etc.; but in general he carries on the tradition of Tschaikowsky in Russian music; after 1921, prof. of theory at Moscow Cons.; c. (orch.) 27 symphonies; Sinfonietta; *"The Silence";* *"A Tale";* *"Alastor";* (chamber works) 3 string quartets; also piano music and songs.

Miceli (mē-chā'-lē), **Giorgio,** Reggio di Calabria, 1836—Naples, 1895; c. 6 operas, 2 biblical operas, etc.

Michael (mē'-khä-ĕl), (1) **Rogier,** d. Dresden, 1618; tenor and cond. to the Elector; c. motets. His son (2) **Tobias,** b. Dresden, 1592; church cond. Leipzig; c. church music, etc.

Michaelis (mē-khä'-ā-lēs), **Chr. Fr.,** Leipzig, 1770—1834; writer.

Micheli (mē-kā'-lē), **Romano,** Rome.

ca. 15?5—ca. 1655; conductor, writer and composer of notable canons, etc.
Middelschulte (mid'-děl-shool-tě), **Wilhelm**, Werne, April 3, 1863—May 4, 1943; organist; pupil of the Berlin Inst. for church music; from 1888 organist there; in 1891 settled in Chicago; 1894–1918, org. of the Thomas orch.; c. canons and fugue on "*Our Father in Heaven*"; organ concerto on a theme of Bach's; canonic fantasie on Bach, etc.

Mielck (mēlk), **Ernst**, Wiborg, Oct. 24, 1877—Locarno, Oct. 22, 1899; Finnish composer, who, in spite of his pitifully brief life of 22 years, gained a place of national importance; pupil of Tietse, Radecke and Bruch; c. Finnish symph.; overture "*Macbeth*"; Finnish fantasie for chorus and orch.; Finnish orch. suite, etc.

Miersch (mērsh), (1) **Carl Alex. Johannes**, Dresden, 1865—Cincinnati, O., Sept. 8, 1916; violinist; pupil of the Cons. and of Massart; 1888–90 teacher in Aberdeen, then for a year with the Boston Symph. Orch.; 1894–98 artistic dir. of the Athens Cons. and court violinist; 1902, returned to the U. S.; from 1910 at Cincinnati Coll. of Music. His brother (2) **Paul Fr.**, b. Dresden, Jan. 18, 1868; 'cellist, pupil of Royal Akad., Munich; from 1892 in New York, for five years soloist N. Y. Symph. Orch., 1898, soloist Met. Opera; c. Indian rhapsody, for orch., 'cello and violin concertos, etc.

Mignard (mēn-yǎr), **Alexander Konstantinovich** (rightly **Scheltobrjuchov**), b. Warsaw Aug. 13, 1852; pupil of the Cons. and of Saint-Saëns at the Paris Cons.; lawyer and statesman at Warsaw; c. operas, overtures, 2 symph., etc. D. Moscow, ?.

Migot (mē'-gō), **Georges**, b. Paris, Feb. 27, 1891; composer; studied with Bouval, Ganaye and Widor; won Boulanger, Lepaulle, Halphen and Blumenthal prizes; c. chamber and orch. music; author books on aesthetics (he is also a painter).

Mihalovich (mē-hä'-lō-vĭch), **Edmund von**, Fericsancze, Slavonia, Sept. 13, 1842—Budapest, April 22, 1929; pupil of Hauptmann and von Bülow; 1887–1919, dir. R. Acad. of Mus., Budapest; c. romantic opera "*Hagbarth und Signe*" (Dresden, 1882); succ. opera "*Toldi*" (Pesth, 1893);

ballads for full orch. ("*Das Geister schiff*," "*Hero und Leander*," "*Le ronde du sabbat*," "*Die Nixe*"), a symph., etc.

Mikorey, (1) **Franz**, b. Munich, June 3, 1873; conductor; son of the opera tenor, (2) **Max M.** (1850—1907); pupil of Thuille and Herzogenberg; cond. at Dessau, 1902–18; 1919 in Helsingfors; 1924–28, Braunschweig; c. operas, piano concerto, piano quintet and trio, songs, etc.; arranged Mahler's posth. "*Sinfonia Engadine.*"

Miksch (mēksh), **Jn.** Aloys, Georgenthal, Bohemia, 1765—Dresden, 1845; barytone and celebrated teacher.

Mikuli (mē'-koo-lē), **Karl**, Czernowitz, Bukowina, 1821—Lemberg, 1897; pupil of Chopin and ed. of standard edition of his works, composer.

Milanollo (mī-län-ôl'-lō), (1) **Teresa**, Savigliano, near Turin, Aug. 28, 1827—Paris, Oct. 25, 1904; violinist; studied with Ferrero, Gebbaro, and Mora, at Turin, and played in public at 6; afterwards touring with great succ. Her sister (2) **Maria**, 1832—1848, violinist.

Mil'anov, Zinka, b. Zagreb, pupil of Ternina; sang Prague, Vien., Salzburg under Toscanini; Sop. Met. Op. 1936.

Milde (mēl'-dě), (1) **Hans Feodor von**, Petronell, near Vienna, April 13, 1821—Weimar, Dec. 10, 1899; pupil of Hauser and Manuel Garcia, created "Telramund" in "*Lohengrin*," Weimar, 1850; life-member of the Weimar ct.-opera. (2) **Rosa** (née Agthe), Weimar, June 25, 1827—'an. 26, 1906; wife of above; created "Elsa," sang at Weimar till 1876. (3) **Fz. von**, Weimar, March 4, 1855—Munich, Dec. 6, 1929; son and pupil of (1) and (2); barytone, 1878 at Hanover ct.-th.

Mil'denberg, Albert, Brooklyn Jan. 13, 1878—Raleigh, N. C., 1918; pupil of Joseffy, Bruno Oskar Klein, C. C. Müller; c. orch. suites, operas.

Mildenburg, Anna von (Bahr-), b. Vienna, Nov. 29, 1872; notable dramatic soprano; pupil of Vienna Cons.; 1895, début in Hamburg; 1897, Bayreuth; 1908–17 a leading mem. of the Vienna Ct.-Op.; esp. known for her Wagnerian interpretations; after 1919 teacher of singing at the Munich Akad.; from 1920 also dram. dir. for Wagner works at the Munich Op.; m. Hermann Bahr, poet and playwright, with whom she wrote *"Bayreuth und das Wagner-Theater"* (1912).

Milder-Hauptmann (mĕl'-dĕr-howpt'-män), **Pauline Anna**, Constantinople, 1785—Berlin, 1838; soprano; Beethoven wrote the rôle of "Fidelio" for her

Mildner (mĕlt'-nĕr), **Moritz**, Türnitz, Bohemia, 1812—Prague, 1865; vln.-teacher.

Milhaud (mĕl'-ō), **Darius**, b. Aix-en-Provence, France, Sept. 4, 1892; studied Paris Cons., mem. of former Group of Six, in which (with Honegger) he was most considerable figure; he was a pioneer in the use of jazz in art forms, and leading exponent of polytonal style; was at one time attached to diplomatic post at Brazil, from which he derived some folk inspiration in his pop. piano pieces *"Saudados do Brazil"* (also orch.); many of his post-war ballets and other works were flippant in manner, but he has also given modern neo-classic treatment to Greek myths; visited U.S. in 1923 and 1927, appearing as guest leader with orchs. in N.Y., Phila. and Boston and in chamber concerts of his music elsewhere; also lectured at several Amer. univ. C. (operas) *"La Brebis Égarée," "Protée," "Les Malheurs d'Orphée," "Esther de Carpentras," "Le Pauvre Matelot";* (3 "opéras minuits" forming triptych) *"L'Enlèvement d'Europe," "L'Abandon d'Ariane"* and *"La Délivrance de Thésée"; "Maximilien," "Christophe Colombe"* (Berlin State Op., 1928); (farce) *"Le Bœuf sur le Toit";* (ballets) *"L'Homme et son Désir"* (given by Swedish Ballet in N.Y.), *"La Création du Monde"* (in which jazz themes are artistically employed), *"Salade," "Le Train Bleu," "L'Éventail de Jeanne," "La Bien-Aimée";* a cantata in 5 parts, *"Le Retour de l'Enfant Prodigue"* to a text by André Gide; music for the Orestes and Agamemnon; 6 symphonies, suites, serenade, hymns for orch., *"Catalogues de Fleurs"* and *"Machines Agricoles"* for voice and ensemble; *"Rag Caprices," "Actualities";* vln. concerto; *"Cinema Fantasie,"* for vln. and orch.; 15 str. quartets; *"Suite Provençale"* for orch., etc. Studies of his music have been writ-

ten by Prunières, Coeuroy, Landormy; prof. Mills Coll., Cal., 1941.

Mililotti (mē-lē-lôt'-tē), (1) **Leopoido**, Ravenna, Aug. 6, 1835—Marsiglia, Jan. 28, 1911; studied at Rome and lived there as singing-teacher; pub. songs and wrote. His brother (2) **Giuseppe**, 1833—1883, prod. 2 operettas.

Millard', **Harrison**, Boston, Mass., Nov. 27, 1830—1895; studied in Italy; tenor concert-singer; toured Great Britain; lived in New York from 1856, as singer and teacher; c. an opera, grand mass, and many pop. songs.

Mil'ler, **Edw.**, Norwich, 1731—Doncaster, 1807; organist, composer, and writer.

Millet (mĕl'-yĕt), **Luis**, b. Barcelona, April 18, 1867; pupil of Vidiella and Pedrell; founded and cond. the Orféo Catalá society; c. choruses and orch. fantasies on folk-themes.

Milleville (mĭl-lĕ-vĭl'-lĕ), (1) **Fran.**, b. Ferrara, ca. 1565; conductor and composer; son and pupil of (2) **Alessandro**, organist, and composer to the Ducal Court.

Mil'lico, **Giuseppe**, b. Modena, ca. 1730; male soprano, and dram. composer.

Mil'ligan, **Harold Vincent**, b. Astoria, Ore., Oct. 31, 1888; organist, composer, writer; grad. and post-grad. courses, Guilmant Organ School, N.Y.; studied with T. Tertius Noble and Arthur E. Johnstone; toured U.S. as organ soloist; org. and choir dir. at various N.Y. churches, more recently at Riverside Church; gen'l sec'y, A. G. O.; and was pres. of Nat'l Ass'n of Org.; exec. dir., Nat'l Music League; c. operettas, songs, organ works, incid. music to plays; author, *"Stephen Foster; The First American Composer"; "Pioneer Amer. Composers,"* Vols. I and II; ed. *"Colonial Love Lyrics";* d. N.Y., April 12, 1951.

Mil'ligen, **Simon Van**, Rotterdam, Dec. 14, 1849—Amsterdam, March 11, 1929; organist; pupil of Nicolai, Bargiel, etc.; for many years municipal dir. of Gouda, later in Amsterdam as critic and teacher; c. operas *"Brinio"* and *"Darthula"* (The Hague, 1898), etc.

Millöcker (mĭl'-lĕk-ĕr), **K.**, Vienna, May 29, 1842—Baden near Vienna, Dec. 31, 1899; pupil of the Cons.; 1864, th.-cond. at Graz; 1866, Harmonie-Th., in Vienna; from 1869, Th. an der Wien; c. many graceful and succ. operettas, and comic operas, incl. 2 prod. at 23, *"Der todte Gast"* and *"Die beiden Binder"* (Pesth, 1865); *"Das verwünschene Schloss"* (1878), with songs in Upper Austrian dialect; the widely pop. *"Der Bettelstudent"* (Dec. 6, 1881; in Italian as *"Il Guitarrera,"* in English *"The Beggar Student"*); *"Die sieben Schwaben"* (1887, in Engl. *"The 7 Swabians"*); *"Der arme Jonathan"* (1890, in Engl. *"Poor Jonathan"*); *"Das Sonntagskind"* (1892); *" Nordlicht"* (1897); c. also pf.-pcs.

Mills, Sebastian Bach, Cirencester, England, March 13, 1838—Wiesbaden, Dec. 21, 1898; organist; pf.-teacher, New York.

Milon (mē-lôṅ). Vide TRIAL.

Mil'stein, Nathan, b. Odessa, Dec. 31, 1904; violinist; pupil of Auer and Ysaye; began Russian tours at 19, also appearances with Horowitz, pianist; visited various other Eur. countries and South America; U. S. début, 1929-30; has internat'l reputation as brilliant virtuoso and has appeared with leading orchs. of U. S. and Europe, also as recitalist.

Mil'ton, J., d. 1646(7?); father of the English poet; a scrivener in London, and an excellent musician and composer.

Minc'us, Ludwig, Vienna, 1827—after 1897; violinist and cond. in St. Petersburg; 1872, ballet composer at the Imperial Opera; then retired to Vienna; c. 16 ballets, including *"La Source"* in collaboration with Delibes.

Mingotti (mēn-gôt'-tǐ), **Regina** (née **Valentini**); b. Naples, 1721; soprano.

Minoja (mē-nō'-yä), **Ambrogio,** Ospedaletto, 1752—Milan, 1825; singing-teacher and composer.

Mirande (mē-räṅd), **Hippolyte,** b. Lyons, May 4, 1862; pupil of Dubois and Guiraud, Paris Cons.; 1886-90, prof. Geneva Cons.; 1890, Sec.-Gen. Gr. Th., Lyons, and prof. of mus. history, Lyons Cons.; critic; organist at the synagogue; c. v. succ. ballet, *" Une Fête Directoire"* (Lyons, 1895); overtures, *"Rodogune,"* *"Frithjof,"* *"Macbeth,"* *"Prométhée,"* and *"La mort de Roland,"* etc.

Mirecki (mē-rets'-kē), **Franz,** Cracow, April 1, 1791—May 29, 1862; pupil

of Hummel and Cherubini; after 1838 director of school of opera singing in Cracow; c. operas, ballets, etc.

Mi'rovitch, Alfred, b. St. Petersburg, 1834; pianist; studied law; grad Cons. in native city, pupil of Essipov; won gold medal and Rubinstein prize; début, Berlin, 1911; has toured Europe, Far East and U. S., also teaching in Los Angeles; c. piano works and songs.

Miry (mē'-rē), **Karel,** Ghent, 1823—1889; professor and dram. composer.

Missa (mǐs'-sä), **Edmond Jear Louis,** Rheims, June 12, 1861—Paris, Jan. 29, 1910; pupil of Massenet, Paris Cons.; won Prix Cressent; lived in Paris, as teacher; c. an op. com., *"Juge et Partie"* (Op.-Com., 1886), followed by others, also pantomimes; *" Ninon de Lenclos,"* lyric episode (1895), etc.

Mitro'poulos, Dmitri, b. Athens, 1896; composer, conductor; grad. Athens Cons., 1919; studied piano with Wassenhoven, comp. with Marsick and Busoni, organ with Desmet, Brussels; was répétiteur at Berlin Op. until 1925; later successful orch. cond., in Athens; guest leader London, Paris and Boston Symph. Orchs., 1935; 1937, appointed cond. of the Minneapolis Symph. Orch.; co-conductor with Stokowski, N. Y. Philh., 1949; mus. dir., same, 1950.

Mit'terer, Ignaz Martin, St. Justina, Tyrol, Feb. 2, 1850—Brixen, Aug. 18, 1924, composer and director; pupil of his uncle **Anton M.,** (a choirmaster), and of Father Huber; 1874 became a priest; studied at Regensburg under Jakob, Haberl and Haller; 1880 chaplain in Rome; 1882-85, cathedral cond. at Regensburg, later at Brixen as dir. in the cathedral; his compositions show the influence of Palestrina; c. masses with orch., offertories and a great amount of church music.

Mitterwurzer (mǐt'-těr-voor-tsěr), **Anton,** Sterzing, Tyrol, 1818—Döbling, near Vienna, 1876; barytone.

Mizler (mǐts'-lěr), **Lorenz Chp.** (ennobled as **M. von Kolof**), Heidenheim, Würtemberg, 1711—Warsaw, 1778; writer, editor and composer.

Mlynarski (m'lē-när'-skǐ), **Emil,** Kibarty, Suvalki, July 18, 1870—Warsaw, April 5, 1935; pupil St. Petersburg Cons.; 1893 cond. and teacher at Warsaw; 1894 at Odessa;

from 1899 cond. at Opera House, Warsaw; also cond. Phil. orch.; 1904–07 director of the Cons.; 1910–18, dir. Choral and Orch. Union, Glasgow; 1918–24, dir. Warsaw Op. and Cons.; after 1930 for several seasons in Phila., U. S., as head of orch. dept., Curtis Inst. of Music, also guest cond. with Phila. Orch.; he appeared as cond. in numerous Eur. capitals, incl. London; c. symphony, "*Polonia*," 2 vln. concertos (the 1st winning Paderewski Prize, 1898); a comic opera "*A Summer Night*"; piano works, etc.

Mocquereau (môk-rō), Dom **André**, La Tessouale, France, June 6, 1849 —Solesmes, Jan. 18, 1930; writer; 'cello pupil of Dancla; from 1875 Benedictine monk, teacher of choral singing at the Abbey of Solesmes, later prior; founder and editor of the *Paléographie musicale;* in 1903 on the exile of the order, moved to the Isle of Wight, continuing the publication of his great work; authority on Gregorian chant, on which he wrote "*Rhythmique Grégorienne*" (vol. I, 1908), etc.

Modernus (mō-der′-noos), **Jacobus** (rightly **Jacque Moderne;** called **Grand Jacques,** or **J. M. de Pinguento,** because of his stoutness); cond. at Notre Dame, Lyons; pub. and composer, 1532–67.

Moe′ran, Ernest John, b. Osterley, Dec. 31, 1894—d. Kenmare, Ire., 1950; of Irish extraction; in large part self-taught; but studied at R. Coll. of Music, London, 1913–14; made large collection of folk-songs of Norfolk; c. orch. rhapsody, 4 string quartets, sonata for vln. and piano; toccata and "*Stalham River*," variations, etc., for piano; 2 vln. sonatas, 2 piano trios, serenade-trio for strings; "*Cushinsheean*," symph. impression for orch.; "*Lonely Waters*" for small orch., and many songs and piano pieces, also a symph., 1937.

Mohr (mōr), **Hn.,** Nienstedt, 1830—Philadelphia, 1896; composer.

Möhring (mā′-rǐng), **Fd.,** Alt-Ruppin, 1816—Wiesbaden, 1887; organist, teacher, and dram. composer.

Moir, Frank Lewis, Market Harborough, Engl., April 22, 1852—Deal, Engl., Aug., 1902; studied painting at S. Kensington, also mus.; won scholarship Nat. Training Sch. (1876); c. a comic opera, church-

services, madrigal "*When at Chloe's Eyes I Gaze*" (Madr. Soc. prize, 1881), many pop. songs, etc.

Moiseiwitsch (mō-ǐ-sā′-ǐ-vǐch), **Benno,** b. Odessa, Feb. 22, 1890; pianist; studied with Klimoff at Odessa Acad., winning Rubinstein Stipend, also with Leschetizky, Vienna; made début in England with succ., 1908, followed by orchestral and recital appearances throughout British Empire and on continent, also in U. S.; has particular reputation for Chopin playing, but repertoire incl. classic and modern works.

Mojsisovics (mō-sē′-sō-vǐch), **Roderich von,** b. Graz, May 10, 1877; pupil of Degner, and of the Cologne Cons., and Munich Akad.; 1903 cond. in various cities; 1912–30, dir. Graz Cons.; c. symph. "*In the Alps,*" symph. poem "*Stella,*" "*Chorus Mysticus*" from "*Faust*" for soli, double chorus, organ and orch., etc.

Mol, de. Vide DEMOL.

Molinari (mōl-ē-nä′-rē), **Bernardino,** b. Rome, April 11, 1880; conductor; studied there organ and comp.; at St. Cecilia Liceo with Renzi and Falchi; cond. Augusteo Orch. Rome, beginning 1909 and after 1915 taking this ensemble on tours of Italy, later also to Switzerland, Germany and Czechoslovakia; he has appeared as guest cond. in many world capitals, incl. Antwerp, London, Geneva, Vienna; with New York Philh. and St. Louis Orch., 1928; and in subsequent years also in San Francisco, Los Angeles, Detroit and Phila., again in N. Y., 1930–31; he has transcribed for orch. works by Debussy, Monteverdi, Vivaldi and others; d. Rome, Dec. 25, 1952.

Molique (mōl-ēk′), **Wm. Bd.,** Nürnberg, Oct. 7, 1802—Cannstadt, May 10, 1869; eminent violinist; son and pupil of a town-musician; studied with Rovelli on royal stipend; 1820, successor of R. as leader of Munich orch.; studied with Spohr; 1826, "Musik-direktor" at Stuttgart; 1849–66, London; also toured with great succ.; c. an oratorio, 6 famous vln.-concertos, etc.

Mollenhauer (mōl′-lĕn-how-ĕr), three brothers, b. at Erfurt. (1) **Fr.,** 1818—1885; violinist and composer. (2) **H.,** 1825; 'cellist. (3) **Ed.,** Erfurt, 1827—Owatonna, Minn., 1914; violinist; pupil of Ernst, and of Spohr;

1853, New York, founded a vln.-sch.; one of the originators of the "Conservatory System" in America; c. 2 operas; 3 symphonies, incl. the "*Passion*," string-quartets, vln.-pcs., etc. (4) **Emil**, Brooklyn, N. Y., Aug. 4, 1855—Boston, Dec. 10, 1927; son of (1); violinist at 9, then with Boston Symph. Orch.; 1899 cond. Boston Handel and Haydn Society; 1900, Apollo Club; led Boston Symph. at various expositions.

Moller (or **Möller**) (môl'-lěr, or měl-ler), **Joachim.** Vide BURGK.

Molloy', **Jas. Lyman**, b. Cornolore, Ireland, 1837—Wooleys, Bucks, England, Feb. 4, 1909; c. operettas; pub. Irish melodies with new accompaniments and c. pop. songs.

Mol'ter, **Johann Melchior**, mus. director in Durlach, 1733; amazingly prolific writer; c. 169 symph., 14 overtures, etc.

Momigny (mō-mēn'-yē), **Jérome Jos. de**, Philippeville, 1762—Paris, 1838; theorist and dram. composer.

Mompou (môm'-pōō), **Federico**, b. Barcelona, 1905; composer; studied with Motte Lacroix, but developed own manner of composition which he styles "primitive"; c. piano works, esp. suites.

Monasterio (mō-näs-tā'-rǐ-o), **Gesù**, Potes, Spain, April 18, 1836—Santander, Sept. 28, 1903; violinist; début at 9, then pupil of De Bériot, Brussels Cons.; made v. succ. tours; 1861 founded Quartet Soc., Madrid; ct.-violinist, prof., and (1894) dir. Madrid Cons.; c. pop. vln.-pcs.

Monath (mōn'-ǎth), **Hortense**, American pianist; studied first with her mother, then with Ernest Hutcheson in N. Y., and Schnabel in Berlin; début, Hamburg; gave recitals in Italian cities, appeared with Vienna Philh., Hamburg Philh., and at Salzburg Fest.; returned to U. S. 1934, appearing with Boston Symph. and in solo concerts.

Mondonville (môn-dôn-vē'-yŭ), **J. Jos. Cassanea de** (de M. being his wife's maiden name), Narbonne, 1711—Belleville, near Paris, 1772; violinist, conductor and dram. composer.

Moniuszko (mō-nǐ-oosh'-kō), **Stanislaw**, Ubiel, Lithuania, May 5, 1819—Warsaw, June 4, 1872; pupil of Freyer and Rungenhagen; i. Berlin,

then at Wilna; c. 15 notable Polish operas incl. "*Halka*," a nat'l classic; also masses, songs, etc.; organist, director, professor. Biogr. by A. Walicki (Warsaw, 1873).

Monk, (1) **Edwin G.**, Frome, Engl., December 13, 1819—Radley, Jan. 3, 1900; pupil of G. A. Macfarren; Mus. Doc. Oxon, 1856; 1859-83, organist York Minster; ed. choral books, etc.; c. 2 odes, unison service, etc. (2) **Wm. H.**, London, 1823—Stoke Newington, London, 1889; organist, professor of vocal mus.; editor.

Monn, **Georg Matthias**, Lower Austria, 1717—Vienna, Oct. 3, 1750; organist and comp. of highly important instrumental works, symphonies, etc., marking a transition to the modern style.

Monod (mŭ-nō), **Edmond**, Lyons, Feb. 4, 1871; author and teacher; pupil of Roth, Stepanov and Leschetizky; 1899-1906 teacher in Berlin; 1907 prof. at Geneva Cons.; c. songs.

Monpou (môn-poo) (**Fran. L.**) **Hip.**, Paris, 1804—Orleans, 1841; c. of light operas and songs.

Monsigny (môn-sēn-yē), **P. Alex.**, Fauquembergue, near St.-Omer, Oct. 17, 1729—Paris, Jan. 14, 1817; ill-trained but melodious French comic opera writer of noble birth but left poor on his father's death; became a clerk, later steward to the Duke of Orleans; he had studied the vln. as a child and now studied harm. for 5 months with Gianotti; at 30 prod. a succ. 1-act op., followed by 12 others, the last, "*Félix, ou l'enfant trouvé*" (1777), the greatest succ. of all; immediately m., ceased to write; his stewardship and his royalties had brought him riches, which the Revolution swept away; he was given a pension of 2,400 francs ($480) a year by the Op. Com.; 1800-02, inspector at the Cons.; 1813, member of the Acad.; 1816, Legion of Honour. Biogr. by Alexandre (1819), and Hédouin, 1820.

Montanari (môn-tä-nä'-rē), **Francesco**, Padua (?)—Rome, 1730; violinist at St. Peter's, Rome; c. 12 violin sonatas.

Monte (môn'-tě), **Filippo** (or **Philippus de**) (**Philippe de Mons**) (dǔ-môns), probably at Mons (or Malines). 1521—Prague, July 4, 1603; conductor and celebrated composer.

Montéclair (môn-tā-klăr), **Michel Pignolet de,** Chaumont, 1666—Saint-Denis, n. Paris, Sept., 1737; double-bass player; dram. composer and writer of methods.

Montefiore (môn-tĕ-fĭ-ō'-rē), **Tommaso Mosè,** composer; Livorno, 1855—Rome, March 13, 1933; pupil of Mabellini; critic under the penname of "*Puck*," editor; c. operas "*Un bacio a portatore*" (Florence, 1884), and "*Cecilia*" (Ravenna, 1905).

Montemezzi (môn-tā-měd'-sē), **Italo,** Verona, May 31, 1875—May 15, 1952; studied at Milan Cons.; c. (operas) "*Giovanni Gallurese*" (Turin, 1905, prod. at Met. Op., N. Y., with slight succ. 2 decades later); "*Hellera*" (do., 1009); "*L'Amore dei Tre Re*" (Milan, 1913) won immediate succ. for its tragic action, noble restraint and original adaptation of modern dram. and harmonic idiom to classic theme; Met. Op., following year, with equal succ. and has been periodically restored; "*La Nave*" (Chicago, 1918); "*Principezza Lontana*" (unfinished); "*La Notte di Zoraima*," one-act opera with melodramatic story, which proved disappointing when given in Milan and at Met. Op. in 1931; also cantata, "*Il Cantico dei Cantici*," etc.

Monteux (môn-tü'), **Pierre,** b. Paris, April 4, 1875; conductor; studied Paris Cons.; 1st prize there; after 1894 orch. and opera cond., in Paris, also as guest in London, Berlin, Vienna, Budapest; visited U. S. in 1916 with Diaghileff Ballet Russe; cond. Met. Op., 1917–19; in 1918 called to take charge of Boston Symph. for a time pending arrival of Rabaud; 1919–24 regular leader of that orch.; thereafter active also with Phila. Orch. and at Hollywood Bowl; following period as regular leader of Amsterdam Concertgebouw Orch., he returned to America for summer concerts at Los Angeles and was engaged as permanent leader of San Francisco Symph., beginning 1935; has especial rep. as interpreter of modern scores; leads concerts and opera as guest at Holland Festival and elsewhere in Europe, and also has a course of instruction for young conductors in Maine.

Monteverde (môn-tā-věr'-dĕ) (he signed his name, **Monteverdi**), **Clau-**dio (Giov. A.), Cremona (bapt., May 15), 1567—Venice, Nov. 29, 1643; eminent composer; when young, vla.-player in the orch. of Duke Gonzaga, Mantua, and studied cpt. with Ingegneri. At 17 and at 20 pub. Canzonette à 3, and madrigals, in which appeared (among many unintentional or unbeautiful effects) the harmonic innovations for which he is famous and which led Rockstro to call him "not only the greatest musician of his own age, but the inventor of a system of harmony which has remained in uninterrupted use to the present day." His progressions include the unprepared entrance of dissonances, the dominant seventh and the ninth (v. D. D., CHORD, PROGRESSION, SUSPENSION PREPARATION, etc.). He was bitterly assailed in pamphlets, particularly by Artuso and he replied in kind. The outcome was his complete triumph and the establishment of the new school of song and accompaniment. His victory, while salutary for art in general and dramatic song in particular, was too complete; for the bigoted defenders of polyphonic music dragged down with them in their ruin the splendid edifice of church-mus. built to perfection by Palestrina and others. 1603, M. became his teacher's successor as Maestro to the Duke and c. for the wedding of the Duke's son to Margherita of Savoy the opera "*Arianne*," in which Ariadne's grief moved the audience to tears. In 1608 he prod. his opera "*Orfeo*" with the unheard-of orchestra of 36 pieces (Riemann states that "*Arianne*" was the 2d work and "*Orfeo*" the first). "*Orfeo*" was published in 1609 and in 1615, and the score shows great modernity, Rockstro comparing its preludes with one bass-note sustained throughout to the Introduction to "*Das Rheingold*," and its continual recitative also to that of Wagner.

In 1608 appeared his mythological spectacle "*Ballo delle Ingrate*." Vespers and motets (pub. 1610) gave him such fame that he was in 1613 made Maestro di Cappella at San Marco, Venice, at the unprecedented salary of 300 ducats (the usual salary had been 200), but it was raised to 500 in 1616, and a house and travelling expenses given him. 1621, his

very romantic Requiem was given with effect. In 1624, he intoduced the then startling novelty of an instrumental tremolo (which the musicians at first refused to play) into his dramatic interlude, *"Il Combattimento di Tancredi e Clorinda"*; 1627 he c. 5 dramatic episodes incl. *"Bradamante"* and *"Dido,"* for the court at Parma; 1630, opera *"Proserpina Rapita"*; in 1637 in the first opera-house opened at Venice, the Teatro di S. Cassiano, operas having hitherto been performed at the palaces of the nobility (v. PERI) M. prod. the operas *"Adone"* (Venice, 1639); *"Le Nozze di Enea con Lavinia"* (1641), *"Il Ritorno di Ulisse in Patria"* (1641), and *"L'Incoronazione di Poppea"* (1642). He earned the title of "the father of the art of instrumentation"; was the most popular and influential composer of his time.
In 1636 he joined the priesthood and is heard of no more. C. masses, psalms, hymns, magnificats, motets, madrigals, etc.
There has been a strong revival of interest in his music within recent years. D'Indy arranged *"Poppea"* and *"Orfeo"* for prod. in Paris; and the latter work was also rescored by Respighi and prod. in Rome. A biog. by Prunières was published, 1926.

Moody, Fanny, vide MANNERS (2).

Moor (mōor), (1) **Karel,** b. Belohrad, Hungary, Nov. 26, 1873; composer; pupil of Prague Cons. and that in Vienna; played and taught violin in Prague; after 1902 active in Czech Philh. and theatres in Bohemia, Trieste and Jugoslavia; c. operas, orch. and chamber works. (2) **Emanuel,** Keskemet, Hungary, Feb. 19, 1863—Mt. Pelerin, Vevey, Switzerland, Oct. 21, 1931; pianist, composer; in 1920 invented a novel piano in which several keyboards are connected with couplers and may be played together; m. Winifred Christie, Scottish pianist, who has toured with much succ. as recitalist on this instrument in Europe and U. S.

Moore, (1) **Thos.,** Dublin, 1779—near Devizes, 1852; famous poet; pianist and singer. (2) **Douglas Stuart,** b. Cutchogue, Long Island, N. Y., 1893;

composer; studied Yale Univ. under Parker and D. S. Smith, later in Paris with d'Indy and Nadia Boulanger; formerly dir. of music, Cleveland Museum of Art; 1926, awarded Pulitzer Prize and Guggenheim Fellowship; assoc. prof. of music, Columbia Univ.; c. (orch.) *"Pageant of P. T. Barnum," "Moby Dick," "Museum Pieces," "Symphony of Autumn"*; operas, *"White Wings," "Devil and Daniel Webster."*
(3) **Grace,** b. Jellico, Tenn., Dec. 5, 1901; soprano; studied Ward-Belmont School, Nashville, and Wilson-Greene School, Washington; vocal study in Europe; began singing career in musical comedy and revues in N. Y.; later trained for opera and made début, Met. Op., 1928; also sang at Paris Op.-Comique in following year as "Louise"; after several seasons, left grand opera to star in operetta, *"The Du Barry,"* in N. Y.; then entered musical films with striking succ.; guest appearances as "Mimi" at Covent Garden, 1935, were attended with unusual ovations; d. in airplane disaster, Copenhagen, Jan. 26, 1947.

Moraës (mō-răńs), **Joäo da Silva,** Lisbon, Dec. 27, 1689—ca. 1747; important Portuguese composer of church music; cond. at the Cathedral.

Morales (mō-răl'-ās) **Cristobal,** Seville, 1500—Malaga, 1553; entered Papal chapel ca. 1540; eminent Spanish contrapuntist and composer.

Moralt (mō'-rält), the name of four brothers famous at Munich as a quartet. (1) **Jos.,** Schwetzingen, near Mannheim, 1775—Munich, 1828, 1st violinist. (2) **Jn. Bpt.,** Mannheim, 1777—Munich, 18?5; 2d violinist; composer. (3) **Philipp,** Munich, 1780—1829; 'cellist. (4) **G.,** Munich, 1781—1818; vla.-player.

Moran-Olden (rightly F. Tappenhorn) (mō'-rän-ōl'-děn), **Fanny,** Oldenburg, Sept. 28, 1855—near Berlin, Feb. 13, 1905; pupil of Haas and Götze; début as "Fanny Olden" at the Gewandhaus. 1877; 1878, leading sopr., Frankfort; 1888–89, New York; m. in 1879 the tenor **K. Moran;** 1897, m. Bertram, ct.-singer at Munich.

Morel (mō-rěl), **Auguste Fran.,** Marseilles, 1809—Paris, 1881; dir. of the Marseilles Cons. and dram. composer.

Morelli (mō-rĕl'-lē), (1) **Giacomo,** Venice, 1745—1819; librarian, San Marco. (2) **Giov.,** Italian bass, in London, 1787.

Morelot (môr-lō), **Stephen,** Dijon, Jan. 12, 1820—Beaumont, Oct. 7, 1899; from 1845, co-ed, *Revue de la Musique;* 1847, sent by the Ministry of Pub. Instruction to study church-mus. in Italy; wrote a work on plain-chant, an attempt to revive ancient harmonisation, etc.

Morena (mō-rä'-nä), **Berta,** b. Mannheim, Jan. 27, 1878; pupil of Frau Röhr-Brajnin and Mme. de Sales; 1898-1923 at Munich Court Theatre; and 1908 with Met. Op., N. Y.; also in concert with Boston Symph.; d. Rottach, Oct. 7, 1952.

Mor'gan, (1) **G. Washbourne,** Gloucester, Engl., 1822—Tacoma, U. S., 1892; organist and conductor. (2) **J. Paul,** Oberlin, Ohio, 1841—Oakland, Cal., 1879; organist and composer.

Morini (mō-rē'-nē), **Erica,** b. Vienna, May 26, 1906; violinist; studied with her father, Oscar Marinka, and with Sevcik at Vienna Cons.; début in that city, 1916; 1st visited U. S., 5 years later, when she made a pronounced impression, although only 15, as a spirited and fluent technician; after several years' absence during which she appeared widely in Europe and Australia as orchestral soloist and in recital, she returned to America in 1930 and 1935 as a matured and impressive performer.

Morlacchi (môr-läk'-kē), **Fran.,** Perugia, June 14, 1784—Innsbruck, Oct. 28, 1841; pupil of Zingarelli, Padre Martini, etc., from 1810 cond. of Italian opera, Dresden; c. many succ. operas, also church-music, incl. Tuba Mirum, inspired by Michelangelo's *"Last Judgment"*; biog. by Count Rossi-Scotti (1870).

Mor'ley, (1) **Thos.,** 1557—1603; pupil of Byrd; 1588, Mus. Bac., Oxford; 1592, Gentleman of the Chapel Royal; also Epistler and Gospeller; c. the only contemporary Shakespearean song extant, *"It Was a Lover and His Lass"* from *"As You Like It,"* pub. 1600 in one of his very numerous colls.; he wrote the first English treatise on mus. (1597) still valuable, and ed. (1599) a curious treatise on ensemble playing; some of his madrigals and melodious ballets

are still heard. (2) **Wm.,** d. 1731; Mus. Bac. Oxford, 1713; 1715, Gent. of the Chapel Royal; c. one of the earliest known double-chants, songs, etc.

Mor'nington, Earl of (Garrett C. Wellesley), Dangan, Ireland, July 19, 1735—May 22, 1781; founded Academy of Music, 1757; 1764 Mus. Doc. (Dublin) and Prof.; 1760 created Viscount Wellesley and Earl of M.; c. glees and madrigals; one of his sons was the Duke of Wellington.

Morris, (1) **Robt. O.,** London, 1886—Dec. 15, 1948; studied Royal Coll. of Music, where later taught cpt.; also at Curtis Inst. of Music, Philadelphia. (2) **Harold,** b. San Antonio, Tex., 1890; composer; c. symphony, piano concerto, string quartet, piano quintet, vln. and piano sonata; *"Poem after Tagore's 'Gitanjali'"* for orch.; rhapsody for piano, vln. and 'cello; has appeared as piano soloist in his works with leading Amer. orchestras.

Morse, Chas. H., Bradford, Mass., Jan. 5, 1853—Boston, June 4, 1927; 1873, graduate New Engl. Cons.; studied with Perabo, and Baermann, 1879; 1873, teacher N. E. Cons.; 1875-84, Mus. Dir. Wellesley Coll.; from 1891, organist Plymouth Church, Brooklyn; pub. collections of organ-pieces and composed.

Mor'telmans, Lodevijk, b. Antwerp, Feb. 5, 1868; pupil of the Cons. and Brussels Cons.; c. symph. *"Germania,"* symph. poem *"Wilde Jagd,"* etc.; after 1902, prof. of comp., Antwerp Cons.; d. June 24, 1952.

Mortier de Fontaine (môrt-yā dŭ fôn-tĕn), **H. Louis Stanislas,** Wisniewiec, Russia, 1816—London, 1883: pianist.

Mor'timer, Peter, Putenham, Surrey, 1750—Dresden, 1828; a Moravian brother; writer.

Mosca (môs'-kä), (1) **Giuseppe,** Naples, 1772—Messina, 1839; conductor and dram. composer. (2) **Luigi,** Naples, 1775—1824; bro. of above; prof. of singing.

Moscheles (mô'-shĕ-lĕs), **Ignaz,** Prague, May 30, 1794—Leipzig, March 10, 1870; son of a Jewish merchant; at 10 pupil of Dionys Weber, Prague Cons.; at 14 played publicly a concerto of his own; studied with Albrechtsberger and Salieri while earning his living as a pianist and teacher; at 20 was chosen to prepare the pf.-score of *"Fidelio"* under Beethoven's supervision; as a pianist a succ. rival of Hummel and Meyerbeer; he could not comprehend or play Chopin or Liszt, but had large influence on subsequent technic; after tours, he lived in London 1821–46, when Mendelssohn, who had been his pupil, persuaded him to join the newly founded Leipzig Cons., of which he became one of the pillars; c. 8 pf.-concertos, incl. *"fantastique," "pathétique"* and *"pastoral"; "Sonata"* and *"Sonate symphonique,"* for pf. 4 hands, and *"Sonate caracteristique," "Sonate mélancolique,"* and many standard studies; biog. (1872) by his wife Charlotte (née Embden).

Mosel (mō'-zĕl), (1) **Ignaz Fz.**, Edler von, Vienna, 1772–1844; conductor, writer and dram. composer. (2) **Giovanni Felice**, b. Florence, 1754; violinist; pupil of Nardini and his successor as court cond., 1793; c. violin music, etc.

Mosenthal (mō'-zĕn-täl), **Jos.**, Cassel, Nov. 30, 1834—New York, Jan. 6, 1896; from 1867, cond. Mendelssohn Glee Club, New York, also violinist, organist and composer.

Moser (mō'-zĕr), (1) **K.**, Berlin, 1774–1851; violinist and conductor. (2) **Andreas**, 1859–1925; pupil Joachim; noted vln. teacher in Berlin. (3) **Hans I.**, his son, b. Berlin, 1889; prof., writer.

Mosewius (mō-zā'-vĭ-oos), **Jn. Th.**, Königsberg, 1788 — Schaffhausen, 1858; opera-singer and writer.

Moson'yi (rightly **Michael Brandt**), Boldog-Aszony, Hungary, 1814—Pesth, 1870; pf.-teacher and composer.

Mos'solov, Alex., b. Kiev, Russia, Aug. 10, 1900; one of most individual and accomplished of Soviet composers; came into internat'l prominence for his descriptive works for orch. and chamber ensembles which are based on the rhythms and sounds of labor; esp. *"The Soviet Iron Foundry,"* in radical dissonantal style, which has been played by a number of Amer. orchs.; piano pieces, etc.

Moszkowski (mŏsh-kŏf'-shkĭ), (1) **Moritz**, Breslau, Aug. 23, 1854—Paris, March 4, 1925; son of a wealthy Polish gentleman; pupil of Dresden

Cons., Stern and Kullak Cons.; teacher Stern Cons. for years; later début with succ. as pianist, Berlin, 1873; until 1897 Berlin then Paris; as a composer, prod. succ. opera, *"Boabdil der Maurenkönig"* (Berlin, 1882); symph. poem *"Jeanne d'Arc"; "Phantastischer Zug"* for orch.; 2 orchestral suites and a vln.-concerto; c. many pop. pf.-pcs., incl. *"Aus. allen Herren Länder,"* and *"Spanische Tänze."* (2) **Alex.**, Pilica, Poland, Jan. 15, 1851—Berlin, Sept. 26, 1934; bro. of above; critic, editor and writer at Berlin.

Motta, José Da, vide **Da Motta.**

Mottl (mŏt'-'l), (1) **Felix**, Unter-St. Veit, near Vienna, Aug. 24, 1856—Munich, July 2, 1911; prominent conductor; as a boy-soprano, entered Löwenberg "Konvikt," then studied at the Vienna Cons., graduating with high honours; cond. the Academical Wagnerverein for some time; 1880, ct.-cond. at Carlsruhe, also, until 1892, cond. Philh. Concerts; 1893 the Grand Duke app. him Gen. Mus. Dir.; 1886, cond.-in-chief, Bayreuth; invited to be ct.-cond. but he declined; 1898 declined a similar call to Munich; led succ. concerts London and Paris; 1892, he m. (2) **Henriette Standhartner** (b. Vienna, Dec. 6, 1866, ct. opera singer at Weimar and Carlsruhe). M. came to N. Y., 1903–04, to conduct the first perfs. of *"Parsifal"* outside Bayreuth, but owing to protests of Wagner family did not do so; 1904 he became co-director of the Royal Academy of Music, Munich; he was cond. the United Royal Operas there, when he fell ill of arteriosclerosis and died in July, 1911. Shortly before his death he was divorced from his first wife and married Sdenka Fassbender, of the Munich Opera. He is particularly known for his orch. arrangements of ballet suites by Gluck and Rameau, but also c. succ. operas, *"Agnes Bernauer"* (Weimar, 1880), and the 1-act *"Fürst und Sänger"* (Carlsruhe, 1893); prod. also a "Festspiel," *"Eberstein,"* songs, etc.

Mount-Edg'cumbe, Richard, Earl of, 1764 — Richmond, Surrey, 1839; wrote *"Reminiscences of an Amateur";* c. opera *"Zenobia."*

Mouret (moo-rā), **J. Jos.**, Avignon, 1682—insane asylum, Charenton, 1738; conductor and composer.

Moussorgsky (moo-sôrg'-skē), **Modest Petrovich**, Karevo, Ukraine, March 28, 1835—St. Petersburg, March 28, 1881; one of the most important Russian composers, perhaps the most original of the Nationalistic school of that country and the "father" of the whole modern movement for anti-formalism, and expression by means of folk idioms. He was the son of an impoverished noble family; early learned to play the piano, 1st from his mother, then from a teacher named Herke. He was largely self-instructed in comp. and began to compose songs before he was 20. He entered the Russian army, and as a young officer was introduced by César Cui to Balakireff (with whom he had some fitful instruction in comp.). He had also come to know Dargomizhsky earlier. He lived in St. Petersburg as a minor State official, his life a constant struggle with poverty, depression and drink. One of the bright spots was a journey to South Russia as accompanist to the singer Leonowa in 1879. His death occurred at the age of 46 in the Nikolai Military Hospital at Petersburg.

Largely unappreciated by his contemporaries, but his fame has steadily increased since his death. Especially in his marvellous collection of some 60 songs, most of them grim and somewhat mordant, he has shown an outstanding gift for expression and character portrayal. He is most celebrated for his 2 principal operas, the stupendous nationalistic folk drama, "*Boris Godounoff*," conceived most originally with the people as the main protagonists and the chorus the featured performers, and the lesser but also impressive "*Khovanstchina*," both based on Russian folk and liturgical idioms. The first was originally prod. in St. Petersburg, 1874, but withdrawn after a few perfs. Fifteen years after **M.'s** death it was revised by Rimsky-Korsakoff, who added to it his brilliant orchestration, and smoothed down what he considered its "uncouth" qualities. In this form it made its way over the opera stages of the world and made a profound impression. Only in 1925 was the original version of the work published by the Soviet musical authorities and eagerly performed in Europe and the U. S. (concert hearing under Stokowski, Phila.). Other smaller operatic works are "*The Marriage*" (one-act, based on Gogol's comedy), 1868; and "*The Fair at Sorotchinsi*," partially finished and completed by Tcherepnine. As an orch. composer, **M.** is best known by the symph. poem, "*Night on the Bald Mountain*," much revised by Rimsky-Korsakoff. His famous suite of descriptive pieces for piano, "*Pictures from an Exhibition*," has been orchestrated by Ravel and has enjoyed wide popularity; also c. song cycles, "*Without Sunlight*," "*Songs and Dances of Death*," "*The Children's Room*"; (chorus) "*The Defeat of Sennacherib*," etc. The chief Moussorgsky biographies are by Calvocoressi and Riesemann; a collection of his letters has been published. (See article, page 506.)

Mouton (moo-tôn) (**Jean de Hollingue** (ôl'-lăng) (called "Mouton")), Holling (?), near Metz—St. Quentin, Oct. 30, 1522; important contrapuntist; c. motets, masses, psalms, chansons, etc.

Mouzin (moo-zăn), **P. Nicolas** (called **Édouard**), Metz, July 13, 1822—Paris, 1894; studied at Metz branch of the Paris Cons.; 1842 teacher there, 1854, dir.; 1871, teacher at the Paris Cons.; writer; c. 2 operas, symphs., etc.

Mozart (mō'-tsärt) (originally **Motzert**), (1) (**Jn. G.**) **Ld.**, Augsburg, 1719—Salzburg, 1787; father of W. A. M.; dram. composer. (2) (**Maria**) **Anna** (called "**Nannerl**"), Salzburg, 1751—1829; daughter and pupil of above; pianist; c. org. pcs. (3) **Wolfgang Amadeus** (baptised Jns. Chrysostomus Wolfgangus Theophilus), Salzburg, Jan. 27, 1756—Vienna, Dec. 5, 1791; son of (1), and bro. of (2); one of the major divinities of music. Of unrivalled precocity in performance, composition, and acoustic sensitiveness; at 3 his talent and his discovery of thirds (v. D. D.), led his father to teach him. He began at once to compose little minuets which his father and later he himself noted down. He and his sister made a joint début at Munich, when he was barely 6, though he had appeared as a performer 4 months before in a comedy at the Univ. at Salzburg. He appeared the same year in Vienna, fascinating the court. He now learned the vln. and org. without instruction. At 7 he was in Paris, where his first works were pub., "*II Sonates pour le clavecin.*" The next year he was in London, delighting royalty, winning the honest praise of musicians and coming victoriously out of remarkable tests of his ability as sight-reader and improviser. During his father's illness, while silence was required, he c. his first symph. Here his 6 sonatas for vln. and harps, were pub. and his first symph. performed frequently. He won the friendship of J. Chr. Bach, and was given singing lessons by Manzuoli. Before leaving England he wrote a motet to English words in commemoration of a visit to the British Museum. The family stopped at various cities on the way home, the children playing at courts with constant succ., a concert being given at Amsterdam in 1766, at which all the instrumental music was **M.'s**. At Biberach he competed as organist without result against a boy 2 years older, Sixtus Bachmann. Returning to Salzburg, in 1766, **M.** was set to studying Fux, etc. 1767 he c. an oratorio, 1768, an opera, "*La Finta Semplice*," at the Emperor's request. Its production was postponed by the now jealous musicians till 1769. Meanwhile a German opera "*Bastien und Bastienne*" had been performed, and **M.** made his début as cond. in 1768 (aged 12), with his solemn mass. The Archbishop made him Konzertmeister, with salary, but his father wished him to enjoy study in Italy. His concerts were sensations, the Pope gave him the order of the Golden Spur (also given to Gluck), and at his father's behest he signed a few compositions by his new title Signor Cavaliere Amadeo, but soon dropped this. After tests he was elected a member of the Accademia Filarmonica of Bologna. At 14 he gave a concert at Mantua in which according to the programme he promises to play "a Symphony of his own composition; a Clavichord-concerto, which will be handed to him, and which he will immediately

play at sight; a Sonata handed him in like manner, which he will provide with variations, and afterwards repeat in another key; an Aria, the words for which will be handed to him, and which he will immediately set to music and sing himself, accompanying himself on the clavichord; a Sonata for clavichord on a subject given him by the leader of the violins; a Strict Fugue on a theme to be selected, which he will improvise on the clavichord; a trio, in which he will execute a violin-part *all' improvviso;* and finally, the latest Symphony composed by himself." In Rome, after twice hearing Allegri's famous "*Miserere,*" long kept secret, he correctly wrote out the entire score from memory. At Milan he prod. 3-act opera seria "*Mitridate, re di Ponto*" (1770), which had 20 consecutive performances under his direction. 1771, he brought out a dramatic serenade, "*Ascanio in Alba,*" for the wedding of Archduke Ferdinand. 1772 his friendly protector, the Archbishop of Salzburg, died; his successor, Hieronymous, Count of Colloredo, treated **M.** with the greatest inappreciation, compelling him to sit with the servant (though **M.** was frequently entertained at the houses of the nobility with great distinction); and when **M.** demanded his discharge in 1781, he had him kicked out by a servant. It was for his installation that **M.** had c. the dramatic "*Il Sogno di Scipione*" (1775), "*Lucio Silla*" (1772), and "*La Finta Giardiniera,*" prod. at Milan, under his own direction, 1775; later "*Il Re Pastore*" at Salzburg during Archduke Maximilian's visit. 1778 he went with his mother to Paris, where he won little attention in the struggle between Gluck and Piccini. At length after his mother's death he returned to Salzburg as Konzertmeister, and ct.-organist; but settled in Vienna, after prod. the opera "*Idomeneo*" (Munich, Jan., 1781). On commission for the Emperor he wrote ("*Belmonte und Constance, oder*) *Die Entführung aus dem Serail,*" prod. with great succ., despite the machinations of the theatrical clique, 1782; a month later he m. Constance Weber (the sister of Aloysia, whom he had loved in Mannheim). She bore him six children, four sons and two daughters. The small receipts for compositions and concerts were quickly spent on luxuries beyond their means, and as neither was a good manager of resources, many hardships followed. After two unfinished operas he prod. a mus. comedy, *"Der Schauspieldirektor"* (Schönbrunn, 1786). May 1, in Vienna, his opera buffa *"Le Nozze di Figaro"* ("Marriage of Figaro") was rescued from intrigues into a very great succ. The then famous librettist Da Ponte next wrote the book for *"Don Giovanni"* ("Don Juan"), which made a very great succ. at Prague (1787), and led the Emperor to appoint M. "chamber composer," at 800 gulden ($400) a year (Gluck, just deceased, had 2,000 gulden). 1789 he accompanied Prince Karl Lichnowski to Berlin, playing for the Dresden court, and at the Thomaskirche, Leipzig. King Fr. Wm. II., hearing him at Potsdam, offered him the post of 1st Royal cond. with 3,000 thaler ($2,250) a year, but M. would not abandon his "good Kaiser"; still Fr. Wm. II. ordered three quartets, for which he paid well. Hearing this, the Emperor ordered the opera buffa *"Così fan Tutte"* (Vienna, 1790). Soon after its production the Emperor died; his successor Ld. II. cared little for M., leaving him in greatest hardship. His devoted friend Jos. Haydn now went to London. M. made a tour, pawning his plate to pay the expenses. For the coronation of Leopold II., as King of Bohemia, at Prague, he was invited to write the festival opera *"La Clemenza di Tito,"* performed 1791. He returned to Vienna and c. *"Die Zauberflöte"* ("Magic Flute," Vienna, Sept. 30, 1791), a work in which are exploited the allegories of the Masonry of which M. was a member. It made a decided succ. He was, however, growing weaker and suffering from fainting fits, claiming that he had been poisoned. A mysterious stranger had commissioned him to write a requiem, and M. began it with a superstitious dread that the messenger had come from the other world to announce his death. It has since been learned that he was Leutgeb, the steward of

Count von Walsegg, who gave the work out as his own, not, however, destroying the MS. The work was not quite completed by Mozart, who had his pupil Süssmayer fill out the incomplete portions. Mozart died of malignant typhus. A violent rain-storm coming up in the midst of the funeral, the party turned back leaving the body to be interred in some spot, never after discovered, in the ground allotted to paupers in the St. Mary cemetery. The profits of a Mus. Festival given by the Frankfort "Liederkranz," June 25, 1838, were devoted to founding a Mozart Scholarship, the interest amounting in 1896 to 1500 marks, applied quadrennially to the aid of talented young composers of limited means. At Salzburg the *Mozarteum,* a municipal musical institute founded in his memory, consists of an orch. soc. pledged to perform his church-music in the 14 churches of the town, to give 12 concerts yearly, and to sustain a mus.-sch. in which the musicians of the orch. give instruction.

A complete ed. of M.'s works pub. by Breitkopf & Härtel (1876–86), contains much church-mus. inc. 15 masses, cantatas *"Davidde penitente"* (masonic), *"Maurerfreude"* and *"Kleine Freimaurercantate,"* etc.; stage-works, besides those mentioned, *"Die Schuldigkeit des ersten Gebots"* (only partially his own), *"Apollo et Hyacinthus"* (Latin comedy with mus.); *"Zaïde"* (unfinished); *"Thamos, König in Aegypten"* (choruses and entr'actes; Berlin, 1786); *"Idomeneo, re di Creta, ossia Ilia ed Idamante."* ORCH. WORKS: 41 symph.; 2 symph. movements; 31 divertimenti, serenades, and cassations; 9 marches; 25 dances, *"Masonic Funeral-Music"*; *"A Musical Jest"* for string-orch. and 2 horns; a sonata for bassoon and 'cello; phantasie for Glockenspiel; andante for barrel-organ, etc.; 6 vln.-concertos, bassoon-concerto, a concerto for flute and harp, 2 flute-concertos, horn-concertos, a clarinet-concerto, 25 pf.-concertos, a double concerto for 2 pfs., a triple concerto for 3 pfs. CHAMBER-MUSIC: 7 string-quintets; 26 string-quartets; *"Nachtmusik"* for string-quintet; 42 vln.-sonatas, etc. PF.-MUSIC: for 4 hands; 5 sonatas.

306 DICTIONARY OF MUSICIANS

and an andante with variations; for
2 pfs., a fugue, and a sonata; 17 solo
sonatas; a fantasie and fugue;
3 fantasias; 36 cadenzas to pf.-
concertos; rondos, etc.; 17 organ
sonatas, etc. Vocal Music: 27
arias, and 1 rondo for sopr. with
orch.; German war-song; a comic
duet; 34 songs; a song with chorus
and org.; a 3-part chorus with org.;
a comic terzet with pf.; 20 canons.
His unstageworthy opera *"Idomeneo"* was provided with a new book,
and extensively rescored by Richard
Strauss for the Munich Fest., 1930.
The best of many biographies is
by Otto Jahn (1856–59, 4 volumes
in English, London, 1882), etc.
His letters, ed. by Hans Mersmann,
have also been published and translated in two volumes. One of his
two overtures was found at the Paris
Cons. 1901. Six unpublished sonatas were found in Buckingham
Palace, 1902. A violin concerto (the
"Adelaide"), c. at 10 yrs., was recovered in 1934.
Other memoirs have been issued by
Berlioz, Dent, Holmes, Kerst, Break-
speare and Mersmann. (See article,
page 508.)
(4) **Wolfgang Amadeus**, Vienna,
July 26, 1791—Carlsbad, July 29,
1844; son of above; pianist, teacher
and composer of pf.-concertos, sonatas, etc.
Muck (mook), **Carl**, b. Darmstadt,
Oct. 22, 1859—Stuttgart, March 4,
1940; pupil of Leipzig Cons., cond.
at various cities; 1892, ct.-cond.
Royal Op., Berlin; 1899, cond. German Opera in London; 1903–05 alternated with Mottl as cond. of the
Vienna Phil.; 1906–08 on leave of absence he cond. Boston Symph. during
the winters; appearing also at Paris,
Madrid, etc.; 1901, 2, 4, 6, and 8
cond. *"Parsifal"* at Bayreuth. By
arrangement with the Boston Symph.
he continued his contract, sending
Max Fiedler to conduct in his place
1909–12; and returning 1912. He
made a most brilliant impression as
a musician of the highest order, and
raised the orch. to hitherto unparalleled efficiency. In 1918 he was
accused of anti-Amer. activity and
was interned as an enemy alien during the remainder of the war and
deported, 1919. He was again active in Germany, after 1922. as

leader of the Hamburg Philh. Orch.,
and conducted elsewhere, incl. Bayreuth.
Mu'die, Thos. Molleson, Chelsea, 1809
—London, 1876; teacher, organist
and composer.
Muffat (moof'-fät), (1) **G.**, Schlett-
stadt, ca. 1645—Passau, Feb. 23,
1704; organist, conductor and composer. (2) **Aug. Gottlieb**, Passau,
April, 1690—Vienna, Dec. 10, 1770;
son of above; organist and composer.
Mugellini (moo-gĕl-lē'-nē), **Bruno**, Potenza, Dec. 24, 1871—Bologna,
Jan. 15, 1912; pianist; pupil of
Tofano, Busi and Martucci; 1898
teacher Bologna Lyceum; 1911, dir.;
c. prize symph. poem *"Alle fonte del
Clitumno"*; 'cello sonata, etc.; edited
Bach, Czerny and Clementi.
Mugnone (moon-yō'-nā), **Leopoldo**, b.
Naples, Sept. 29, 1858; noted conductor; pupil of Cons. in native city;
beginning 1885 cond. at Costanzi
Theatre, Rome; led première of
Verdi's *"Falstaff,"* Milan, 1893; esp
known for his Wagnerian perfs.; c
operas, etc.; d. (?).
Mühldörfer (mül'-dĕrf-ĕr), (1) **Wm.**,
1803—Mannheim, 1897; ct.-inspector
of theatres, Mannheim. (2) **Wm.K.**,
Graz, Styria, March 6, 1836—
Cologne, 1919; son of above; studied
at Linz-on-Danube and Mannheim;
actor; 1855, th.-cond., Ulm; 1867–81,
2d cond. at Cologne; c. 4 operas, incl.
successful *"Iolanthe"* (Cologne, 1890),
overtures, etc.
Mühlfeld (mül'-fĕlt), **Richard**, Salzungen, Feb. 28, 1856—Meiningen,
June 1, 1907; clarinettist for whom
Brahms c. a trio and sonata; studied
with Büchner at Meiningen, where he
lived after 1873; 1875–96, 1st clarinet
at Bayreuth.
Mühling (mü'-lǐng), **Aug.**, Raguhn,
1786—Magdeburg, 1847; organist
and composer.
Mukle (moo'-klē), **May Henrietta**, b.
London, May 14, 1880; 'cellist; appeared as child prodigy; later pupil
of R. A. M., and of Hambleton; from
1900 made world tours; played in trio
with Maud Powell, violinist, and her
sister Anna, pianist; visited Australia,
U. S., South Africa, Honolulu, etc.
Mulé (moo-lā'), **Giuseppe**, b. Sicily,
June 28, 1885; composer; studied at
Palermo Cons.; early active as
'cellist; cond. opera and concerts;
after 1922, dir. of Palermo Cons.,

and 1925 succeeded Respighi as dir. of Liceo of Santa Cecilia, Rome; c. (operas) *"La Monacella dell Fontana," "Dafni,"* etc., which have had succ. productions; also oratorio, orch. music; d. Rome, Sept. 10, 1951.
Müller (mül'-lĕr), (1) **Chr.**, org.-builder at Amsterdam, ca. 1720-70. (2) **Wm. Chr.**, Wassungen, Meiningen, 1752—Bremen, 1831; mus. director and writer. (3) **Aug. Eberhard,** Nordheim, Hanover, 1767—Weimar, 1817; son and pupil of an organist; organist, ct.-conductor and dram. composer. (4) **Wenzel,** Tyrnau, Moravia, 1767—Baden, near Vienna, 1835; conductor and composer of 200 operas. (5) **Fr.**, Orlamünde, 1786—Rudolstadt, 1871; clarinettist, conductor and composer. (6) **Ivan (Iwan)**, Reval, 1786—Bückeburg, 1854; inv. of the clarinet with 13 keys, and altclarinet; finally ct.-mus. (7) **Peter,** Kesselstadt, Hanau, 1791 —Langen, 1877; c. operas, and famous *"Jugendlieder,"* etc. (8) Two famous German quartet parties, (a) The bros. **K. Fr.** (1797—1873), **Th. H. Gus.** (1799—1855), **Aug. Th.** (1802—1875), and **Fz. Fd. G.** (1808—1855), sons of (9) **Aegidius Chp. M.** (d. 1841, Hofmus. to Duke of Brunswick), all b. Brunswick, and ...n the orch. there—**K.** as Konzertmeister, **Th.** 1st 'cello, **Gv.** symph.-director, and **G.** conductor. (b) The four sons of the **Karl Fr.** above, who organised 1855 a ct.-quartet. **Hugo,** 2d vln. (1832—1886); **Bd.,** 1825— 1895; viola; **Wm.,** 1834—N. Y., 1897; 'cello; **Karl, Jr.,** 1829—1907; 1st vln. in Stuttgart and Hamburg; m. Elvina Berghaus and took name **Müller-Berghaus,** under which he c. a symph., etc. (10) (Rightly **Schmid**) **Ad. Sr.,** Tolna, Hungary, 1801—Vienna, 1886; singer, conductor and dram. composer. (11) **Ad., Jr.,** Vienna 1839—1901, son of above; 1875, cond. German opera at Rotterdam; prod. 4 operas and 5 operettas, incl. the succ. *"Der Blondin von Namur"* (Vienna, 1898). (12) **Jns.,** Coblenz, 1801—Berlin, 1858; writer. (13) **Fz. K. Fr.,** Weimar, 1806—1876; one of the first to recognise Wagner; pub. treatises on his work. (14) **Aug.,** 1810—1867; eminent double-bass. (15) **K.,** Weissensee, near Erfurt, 1818—Frankfort, 1894; conductor and composer.

(16) **Maria,** b. Prague, Jan. 29, 1898; noted operatic lyric soprano; début as Elsa, Linz, 1920; sang with Linz Op., 1920-21; Prague, 1921-1923; Munich State Op., 1923-24; after latter year until 1935 she was a member of Met. Op. Co., N. Y., also singing at Berlin State Op. after 1926, and at Bayreuth from 1930; her repertoire includes both Italian and German roles.
Mül'ler-Hartung, K. (Wm.), Sulza, May 19, 1834—Charlottenburg, Berlin, June 11, 1908; pupil of Kühmstedt, Eisenach; mus.-dir. and teacher at the Seminary; 1864, prof.; 1869, opera-cond. Weimar; 1872, founder and dir. Gr. Ducal "Orchester-und-Musikschule"; wrote a system of music theory (vol. i. *"Harmonielehre"* appeared in 1879); composer.
Müller-Reuter (roi-tĕr), **Theodor,** Dresden, Sept. 1, 1858—Leipzig, Aug. 16, 1919; pupil of Fr. and Alwin Wieck (pf.); J. Otto and Meinardus (comp.); and the Hoch Cons., Frankfort; 1879-87, teacher Strasbourg Cons.; 1887, cond. at Dresden; 1892, teacher in the Cons.; mus.-dir. at Crefeld, 1893-1918; c. 2 operas, Paternoster, with orch.; *"Hackelberend's Funeral"* for chorus and orchestra (1902), etc.
Munch(münsh), **Charles,** b.Strasbourg, Sept. 26, 1891; son of Ernst Münch, dir. of Choeur St.-Guillaume; studied violin with his father, with Capet, Paris, and Flesch, Berlin; 1919, prof. at Strasbourg Cons. and cond. there; 1926, concertmaster of Gewandhaus Orch., Leipzig; 193?, led concerts of Paris Symph., Lamoureux Orch.; founded Paris Philh. Orch.; 1938, cond. Orch. des Concerts du Conservatoire; Amer. début as guest cond., Boston Symph., 1946; mus.-dir. of same, 1949.
Munck, de. Vide DEMUNCK.
Mun'dy, (1) **William,** d. 1591(?); Gentleman of the Chapel Royal, 1563; c. anthems, etc. His son (2) **John,** d. Windsor, 1630; where he had been organist from 1585; c. madrigals and a fantasia describing the weather.
Munsel', **Patrice,** Amer. coloratura soprano; pupil of William Pierce Herman, N. Y.; won Met. Op. radio auditions at 17; début, Met. Op., 1943, as Philine; also sang Gilda, Lucia, Lakmé, etc.; and in concerts.

Muratore (mü'-rä-tôr), **Lucien,** b. Marseilles, 1878; tenor; grad. of Cons. there, also studied Paris Cons.; began career as actor; début at Paris Op.-Comique, 1902, in Hahn's *"La Carmelite"*; at the Opera as "Rinaldo" in *"Armide,"* 1905; after 1913 he was a pop. mem. of the Chicago Op., singing romantic rôles opposite Mary Garden; he also appeared in Buenos Aires; esp. noted for his "Romeo," "Don José"; d. Paris, July 16, 1954.

Mur'doch, William, b. Bendigo, Victoria, Feb. 10, 1888; pianist; début in London, 1910; thereafter toured Europe, Australia, and after 1914 U. S.; d. Dorking, Eng., Sept. 9, 1942.

Muris (dŭ mü'-rēs), **Jns. de (or de Meurs)** (dŭ mŭrs), eminent theorist; wrote treatise *"Speculum Musicae"* (probably ca. 1325) (Coussemaker).

Mur'phy, Lambert, b. Springfield, Mass., April 15, 1885; tenor; grad. Harvard Univ.; studied with Thomas Cushman, Isadore Luckstone and Herbert Witherspoon; soloist in N. Y. and Boston churches; mem. Met. Op. Co., 1911–15; also active as orch. and fest. soloist and in radio d. Hancock, N. H., July 24, 1954.

Murschhauser (moorsh'-how-zĕr), **Fz. X. Anton,** Zabern, near Strassburg, 1663—Munich, 1738; conductor and theorist.

Murska (moor'-shkä), **Ilma, di,** Croatia, 1836—Munich, Jan. 16, 1889; famous dramatic soprano, with remarkable compass of nearly 3 octaves.

Musard (mü-zăr), (1) **Philippe,** Paris, 1793—1859; c. pop. dances. (2) **Alfred,** 1828—1881; orch.-cond., and composer; son of above.

Musin (moo-zēn), **Bonaventura.** Vide FURLANETTO.

Musin (mü-zăň), **Ovide,** Nandrin, n. Liége, Sept. 22, 1854—Brooklyn, N. Y., Oct. 30, 1929; violinist; pupil of Liége Cons.; at 11 took 1st vln.-prize; studied then at Paris Cons.; at 14 won the gold medal for solo and quartet playing; taught a year at the Cons. then toured Europe with great succ.; later organised a concert-troupe and toured America, then the world; 1897, returned to Liége as vln.-teacher at the Cons.; 1898, vln.-professor; 1908–10, dir. of his own music school in N. Y.

Musiol (moo'-zĭ-ōl), **Robt. Paul Jn.,** Breslau, Jan. 14, 1846—Fraustadt,

Oct. 19, 1903; from 1873–91 teacher and cantor at Röhrsdorf, Posen; pub. mus. lexicons; c. part-songs, etc.

Musorgsky, see MOUSSORGSKY.

Mustel (müs-tĕl), **Victor,** b. Havre, 1815; mfr. and improver of the harmonium.

Müthel (mē'-tĕl), **Johann Gottfried,** Mölln, 1720—Riga, after 1790; organist; c. sonatas and songs.

Muzio (moo'-tsĭ-ō), (1) **Emanuele,** Zibello, near Parma, Aug. 25, 1825—Paris, Nov. 27, 1890; pupil of Provesi and Verdi, and (for pf.) of Verdi's first wife, Margherita Barezzi; 1852, cond. It. Opera, Brussels; later, London, New York (Acad. of Mus.); 1875 noted singing teacher, Paris; c. 4 operas, etc. (2) **Claudia,** Pavia. 1892—Rome, May 24, 1936; notable soprano; daughter of Carlo Muzio, stage director at Covent Garden and at Met. Op., N. Y.; studied harp and piano; singing with Mme. Casaloni; début as "Manon" at Arezzo; sang in a number of Italian opera houses, including La Scala, also at Covent Garden; début Met. Op. as "Tosca," 1918; sang there for several seasons with notable success; after 1922 with Chicago Op. for a decade with eminent popularity; also in Rome, Paris, Buenos Aires, Monte Carlo, Naples, Genoa, Havana, and with San Francisco Op.; returned to Met. Op. for a perf. as "Violetta" in 1933 and as "Santuzza," 1934; created title rôle in Refice's opera, *"Cecilia,"* in Rome and Buenos Aires.

Mysliweczek (mē-slē'-vä-chĕk), **Jos.** (called "Il Boemo," or "Venatorini"), near Prague, March 9, 1737—Rome, Feb. 4, 1781; prod. about 30 pop. operas in Italy; c. symphs., pf.-sonatas praised by Mozart, etc.

Mysz-Gmeiner, vide GMEINER.

N

Naaff (näf), **Anton E. Aug.,** Weitentrebetitsch, Bohemia, Nov. 28, 1850—Vienna, Dec. 27, 1918; mus. editor and poet at Vienna.

Na'bokoff, Nicholas, b. Poland, April 7, 1903; composer; studied at St. Petersburg Imp. Lyceum; at Berlin Hochsch. with Busoni, and in Stuttgart; res. in Paris; visited U. S., 1933; c. (ballets) *"Union Pacific,"* *"Aphrodite,"* *"A Ballet Ode,"* *"Commedie"*; (choral work) *"Job"*; (orch.) Symphonie Lyrique; concerto for piano and orch.; (opera) *"Le Fiancé."*

Nachbaur (näkh'-bowr), **Fz.**, Schloss Giessen, near Friedrichshafen, March 25, 1835—Munich, March 21, 1902; pupil of Pischek; sang at theatres in Prague and other cities; 1866-90, "Kammersänger," Munich.

Náchez (nä'-chĕs) **(Tivadar (Theodor) Naschitz** (nä'-shĭts)), Budapest, May 1, 1859—Lausanne, May 29, 1930; vln.-virtuoso; pupil of Sabatil, Joachim and Leonard; toured the continent; lived in Paris and (1889) London; c. 2 concertos for vln., 2 Hungarian Rhapsodies, requiem mass, with orch., etc.

Nadaud (nä-dō), **Gv.**, Roubaix, France, Feb. 20, 1820—Paris, 1893; celebrated poet, composer of chansons; also c. operettas.

Nadermann (nä'-dĕr-män), **François Jos.**, Paris, 1773—1835; harpist, teacher and composer.

Nagel (nä'-gĕl), **Willibald**, b. Mühlheim, Jan. 12, 1863; writer; pub. *"Geschichte der Musik in England"* (1897); d. Stuttgart, Oct. 17, 1929.

Nägeli (nä'-gĕl-ē), **Jn. Hans G.**, Wetzikon, near Zurich, 1773—1836; mus.-publisher, writer and composer.

Nagiller (nä'-gĭl-lĕr), **Matthäus**, Münster, Tyrol, 1815—Innsbrück, 1874; conductor and dram. composer.

Nanini (nä-nē'-nē) (incorrectly **Nanino**), (1) **Giov. M.**, Tivoli, Italy, 1545—Rome, March 11, 1607; noted Italian composer; pupil of Goudimel; cond. at Vallerano, 1571-75, at Santa Maria Maggiore, Rome (vice Palestrina); 1575 founded a pub. mus.-sch. in which Palestrina was one of the teachers; 1577, papal singer; 1604 cond. Sistine Chapel; his 6-part motet *"Hodie nobis cœlorum rex"* is still sung there every Christmas morning. (2) **Giov. Bernardino**, Vallerano, ca. 1560—Rome, 1623; younger bro. (Riemann says nephew) and pupil of above; conductor and notable composer.

Nantier-Didiée (nänt-yä dēd-yä), **Constance Betsy R.**, Île de la Réunion, 1831—Madrid, 1867; v. succ. mezzo-soprano.

Napo'leão, Arthur, Oporto, March 6, 1843—Rio de Janeiro, May 12, 1925; pianist and cond.; at 9 made a sensation at the courts of Lisbon, London (1852), and Berlin (1854), then studied with Hallé, at Manchester;

toured Europe, and N. and S. America. 1868 (1871 ?) settled in Rio de Janeiro as mus.-seller, etc.

Nápravnik (Náprawnik) (nä-präf'-nēk), **Eduard**, Bejst, near Königgratz, Aug. 24, 1839—St. Petersburg, Nov. 10, 1915; pupil Prague Org.-Sch.; from 1856 teacher Maydl Inst. for Mus., Prague; 1861, cond. to Prince Yussupoff at St. Petersburg; then organist and 2nd cond. Russian Opera; from 1869 1st cond.; 1870-82, cond. the Mus. Soc.; c. 4 operas, incl. the succ. *"Dubroffsky"* (St. P., 1895); symph. poem *"The Demon,"* overtures, incl. *"Vlasta"* (1861), etc.

Nardini (när-dē'-nē), **Pietro**, Fibiana, Tuscany, 1722—Florence, May 7, 1793; noted violinist; pupil of Tartini; ct.-musician at Stuttgart and Florence; composer.

Nares (närz), **Jas.**, Stanwell, Middlesex, 1715—London, Feb. 10, 1783; organist and composer.

Naret-Koning (nä'-rĕt-kō-nĭng), **Jn. Jos. D.**, Amsterdam, Feb. 25, 1838—Frankfort, March 28, 1905; violinist; pupil of David, Leipzig; from 1878 leader City Th., Frankfort; pub. songs, etc.

Nasolini (nä-sō-lē'-nē), **Sebastiano**, Piacenza, ca. 1768—(?); prod. 30 operas in Italy.

Natale (nä-tä'-lĕ), **Pompeo**, choirsinger and composer at S. Maria Maggiore, Rome, 1662.

Na'than, Isaac, Canterbury, 1792—Sydney, Australia, 1864; writer.

Natorp (nä'-tôrp), **Bd. Chr. L.**, Werden-on-Ruhr, Nov. 12, 1774—Münster, Feb. 8, 1846; reformer of church and sch.-mus.; writer.

Nau (na'-oo), **Maria Dolores Benedicte Josefina**, of Spanish parents, New York, March 18, 1818—Paris, Feb. 1891; soprano; pupil of Mme. Damoreau-Cinti, Paris Cons., taking 1st prize in 1834; début at the Opéra, 1836; sang minor rôles there 6 years, etc.; 1844-48 and 1851-53, leading rôles, singing in other cities; retired, 1856.

Naudin (nä'-oo-dēn), **Emilio**, Parma, Oct. 23, 1823—Bologna, May 5, 1890; tenor; pupil of Panizza, Milan; début, Cremona. Meyerbeer in his will requested him to create the rôle of "Vasco" in *"L'Africaine"* (1865), which he did.

Naue (now'-ĕ), **Jn. Fr.**, Halle, 1787—1858; organist and composer.

Nauenburg (now'-ĕn-boorkh), **Gv.**, Halle, May 20, 1803—after 1862; barytone and singing-teacher; writer and composer.

Naumann (now'-män), (1) **Jn. Gl.** (Italianised as **Giov. Amadeo**), Blasewitz, near Dresden, April 17, 1741—Dresden, Oct. 23, 1801; pupil of Tartini and Padre Martini; 1764, ct.-cond., Dresden; 1776, cond.; prod. 23 operas and excellent church-music. (2) **Emil**, Berlin, Sept. 8, 1827 — Dresden, June 23, 1888; grandson of above; court church mus.-dir., Berlin; c. an opera, a famous oratorio *"Christus der Friedensbote"*; pub. many valuable treatises. (3) **K. Ernst**, Freiberg, Saxony, Aug. 15, 1832—Jena, Dec. 15, 1910; grandson of (1), studied with Hauptmann, Richter, Wenzel and Langer, Leipzig (1850), Dr. Philh. at the Univ., 1858; studied with Joh. Schneider (org.) in Dresden; mus.-dir. and organist, Jena; prof., 1877; pub. many valuable revisions of classical works, for the Bach-Gesellschaft; c. the first sonata for vla., much chamber-mus., etc.

Nava (nä'-vä), (1) **Ant. Maria**, Italy, 1775—1826; teacher and composer for guitar. (2) **Gaetano**, Milan, 1802—1875; son and pupil of above; prof. at the Cons. and composer.

Naval (nä-väl'), **Fz.**, b. Laibach, Austria, Oct. 20, 1865—Vienna, (?); tenor; pupil of Gänsbacher; 1903-4, N. Y.

Navrátil (nä-vrä'-tĕl), **Carl**, Prague, April 24, 1867—Dec. 23, 1936; violinist; composer; pupil of Adler and Ondříček; c. symph.; symph. poems, *"Jan Hus," "Zalco,"* etc.; opera *"Salammbô,"* lyric drama, *"Hermann"*; violin concerto, etc.; wrote biog. of Smetana.

Nawratil (nä-vrä'-tĕl), **K.**, Vienna, Oct. 7, 1836—April 6, 1914; pupil of Nottebohm (cpt.); excellent teacher; pub. Psalm XXX with orch., an overture, chamber mus., etc.

Nay'lor, (1) **J.**, b. Stanningly, near Leeds, 1838—at sea, 1897; organist and composer. (2) **Sidney**, London, 1841—1893; organist. (3) **Edward Woodall**, Scarborough, Feb. 9, 1867 —May 7, 1934; composer; pupil of his father, Dr. John N. (q. v.); and at the R. C. M., London; organist at various churches; 1897 made Mus. Doc. by Cambridge University, where he had taken the degrees of B. A., M. A., and Mus. B.; organist from 1897 at Cambridge (Emanuel College); lecturer there from 1902; c. Ricordi prize opera *"The Angelus"* (Covent Garden, 1909); cantata *"Arthur the King"* (Harrogate, 1902), church music, etc.

Ned'bal, **Oscar**, Tabor, Bohemia, March 25, 1874—(suicide) Zagreb, Dec. 24, 1930; vla.-player in the "Bohemian" string-quartet; studied Prague Cons. (comp. with Dvořák); he was dir. Bohemian Phil., Prague 1896-1906; thereafter cond. Vienna Volksoper, also the Tonkünstler orch.; c. ballet *"Der faule Hans"* (Vienna, 1903), scherzo caprice for orch., violin sonata, etc.

Neefe (nā'-fĕ), **Chr. Gl.**, Chemnitz, 1748—Dessau, 1798; mus.-director and conductor.

Nef (nāf), (Dr.) **K.**, b. St. Gall, Aug. 22, 1873—Basle, Feb. 9, 1935; Ph.D.; studied Leipzig Cons. and Univ.; after 1923, prof. of mus. science, Basle Univ.

Neitzel (nīt'-tsĕl), **Otto**, Falkenburg, Pomerania, July 6, 1852—Cologne, March 10, 1920; pupil of Kullak's Acad., Berlin; Dr. Philh., 1875, at the Univ.; toured as pianist; 1879-81, teacher Moscow Cons.; then Cologne Cons.; 1887, also critic; prod. operas: *"Angela"* (Halle, 1887), text and music of, *"Dido"* (Weimar, 1888) and *"Der Alte Dessauer"* (Wiesbaden, 1889), etc.

Nen'na, **Pomponio**, b. Bari, Naples; pub. madrigals, 1585—1631.

Neri (nā'-rē), **Filippo**, Florence, July 21, 1515—Rome, May 26, 1595; preacher in the oratory (It. *oratorio*) of San Girolamo. From the music c. for illustrations by Animuccia and Palestrina arose the term "oratorio."

Neruda (nä-roo'-dä), (1) **Jakob**, d. 1732; violinist. (2) **Jn. Chrysostom**, Rossiez, 1705—1763; violinist; son of above. (3) **Jn. Baptist** **G.**, 1707—Dresden, 1780; composer, son of Jakob. (4) (**Normann-Neruda**) (or **Lady Hallé**) **Wilma Maria Fran.**, Brünn, March 21, 1839—Berlin, April 15, 1911; noted violinist (daughter of (5) **Josef**, an organist); she studied with Jansa; at 7 played in public at Vienna with her sister (6) **Amalie** (a pianist); then toured Germany with her father, sister and bro.; 1864, in Paris, she m. L. Normann; played annually in London:

she m. Hallé (q.v.), 1888, and toured Australia with him, 1890–91; 1899, America. (7) **Franz**, Brünn, Dec. 3, 1843—Copenhagen, March 19, 1915; 'cellist, son of **Josef N.**, and brother of **Normann-N.**, (q.v.) pupil of Royal Chapel at Copenhagen; from 1892 successor of Gade as dir. of the Copenhagen Music Society; also dir. of Stockholm Music Society; 1894, prof., c. "*Slovak*" march, orch. suite "*From the Bohemian Forest,*" 'cello pieces, etc.

Ness'ler, Victor E., Baldenheim, Alsatia, Jan. 28, 1841—Strassburg, May 28, 1890; studied with Th. Stern at Strassburg; 1864, prod. succ. opera, "*Fleurette*"; studied in Leipzig, became cond. of the "Sängerkreis" and chorusm. City Th., where he prod. with general succ. 4 operettas and 4 operas, incl. two still pop. "*Der Rattenfänger von Hameln*" (1879), "*Der Trompeter von Säkkingen*" (1884); c. also "*Der Blumen Rache,*" ballade, with orch.; pop. and comic songs, etc.

Nesvad'ba, Jos., Vyskeř, Bohemia, 1824—Darmstadt, 1876; conductor and dram. composer.

Nešvera (nêsh-vä'-rä), **Jos.**, Proskoles, Bohemia, Oct. 24, 1842—Olmütz, April 4, 1914; cond. Olmütz Cath.; c. succ. opera "*Perdita*" (Prague, 1897); masses, De Profundis, with orch., etc.

Netzer (nět'-tsĕr), **Jos.**, Imst. Tyrol, 1808—Graz, 1864; teacher, conductor and dram. composer.

Neubauer (nä'-oo-bow-ĕr), **Fz. Chr.**, Horzin, Bohemia, 1760—Bückeburg, 1795; violinist, conductor and composer.

Neuendorff (noi'-ĕn-dôrf), **Ad.**, Hamburg, June 13, 1843—New York, Nov. 5, 1897; at 12 taken to America; pianist, concert-violinist, prominent conductor and composer of comic operas.

Neukomm (noi'-kôm), **Sigismund**, Ritter von, Salzburg, 1778—Paris, 1858; organist, conductor and composer.

Neumann (noi'-män), **Angelo**, Vienna, Aug. 18, 1838—Prague, Dec. 20, 1910; studied singing with Stilke-Sessi, début as lyric tenor, 1859; 1862–76, Vienna ct.-opera; 1876–82, Leipzig opera; as manager of a travelling company prod. Wagner operas; 1882–85, manager Bremen opera; then German opera. Prague.

Neumark (noi'-märk), **G.**, Langensalza 1621—Weimar, 1681; composer.

Neupert (noi'-pĕrt), **Edmund**, Christiania, April 1, 1842—New York, June 22, 1888; pianist; pupil of Kullak's Academy and teacher at Stern Cons.; 1861 at Copenhagen cons.; 1888 at Moscow Cons.; from 1883 at New York; c. piano studies, etc.

Neusiedler (noi'-zēt-lĕr) (or **Newsidler**), (1) **Hans**, b. Pressburg—Nürnberg, 1563; lute-maker. (2) (or **Neysidler**) **Melchior**, d. Nürnberg, 1590; lutenist and composer at Augsburg; 2 books of lute mus. (Venice, 1566), etc.

Neuville (nŭ-vē'-yĕ), **Valentin**, b. Rexpoede, French Flanders, 1863; organist; pupil of Brussels Cons.; org. at Lyons and after 1894 in London; c. 2 symph., an oratorio "*Nôtre Dame de Fourvières,*" 6 operas, including "*L'Aveugle*" (1901), and "*Les Willis*" (1902).

Nevada (nĕ-vä'-dä) (rightly **Wixon**), (1) **Emma**, b. Alpha, Cal., 1862; d. Liverpool, June 20, 1940; soprano; pupil of Marchesi in Vienna; début London, 1880; sang in various Italian cities; 1883 and 1898 Paris, Op.-Com.; 1885 sang Opera Festival, Chicago, and again in 1889; 1898, Op.-Com., Paris, 1885 m. Dr. Raymond Palmer; 1900 America. (2) **Mignon**, b. ca. 1887; her daughter; soprano, heard in Europe in opera.

Nevin (nĕv'-ĭn), (1) **Ethelbert** (Woodbridge), Edgeworth, Penn., Nov. 25, 1862—New Haven, Conn., Feb. 17, 1901; prominent American composer; pupil of von der Heide and E. Günther (pf.) at Pittsburgh; of von Böhme (voice), at Dresden, 1877–78; of Pearce (N. Y.), B. J. Lang and Stephen A. Emery (Boston); von Bülow, Klindworth, and K. Bial, Berlin; lived in Florence, Venice, Paris, and New York as teacher and composer; after 1900 at Sewickley, near Pittsburgh, Pa.; c. a pf.-suite; song-cycles "*In Arcady,*" and a posthumous "*The Quest of Heart's Desire*": highly artistic piano pieces and many song albums of well-deserved popularity. His songs are genuinely lyrical, with an exuberance of musical passion, and accompaniments full of colour, individuality and novelty. (2) **Arthur**, b. Vine Acre, Edgeworth, Pa., April 17, 1871;

bro. of above; from 1891 studied with Goetschius, Boston, then at Berlin with Humperdinck, Boise and Klindworth; spent the summers of 1903 and 1904 among the Blackfeet Indians in Montana, collecting material for his Indian opera *"Poia,"* libretto by Randolph Hartley (prod. in concert form by the Pittsburgh Orch. and as an opera at the Royal Opera, Berlin); c. also 1-act opera *"Twilight"*; orch. suites *"Lorna Doone"* (prod. by Karl Muck in Berlin), and *"Love Dreams"* (Pittsburgh Orch.); also songs; 1915-20, taught Univ. of Kansas; d. Sewickley, Penn., July 10, 1943.

New'comb, Ethel, b. Whitney Point, N. Y., 1879; pianist; pupil and later asst. to Leschetizky in Vienna, where she made début 1903; after 1908 toured U. S., England, Germany.

New'man, Ernest, b. Liverpool, Nov. 30, 1868; prominent critic and writer on music; studied at the univ. there; intended for civil service in India, but withdrew because of ill health and entered business in native city; beginning 1903 he took music as his life work, teaching at Midland Inst., Birmingham. In 1905 he lived in Manchester as music critic of the *Guardian;* 1906, Birmingham *Daily Post;* 1919-20, of the London *Observer;* after 1920 of the London *Sunday Times* of which his weekly column is a much-read feature; 1923 also on the ed. staff of the weekly *Glasgow Herald;* in 1924-25, he was guest critic of the New York *Evening Post.* He has been an aggressive upholder of high ideals in interpretation and as a biographer has been no less unsparing in his moral and artistic judgments, esp. in his works on Wagner and Liszt. Author of *"Gluck and the Opera," "A Study of Wagner," "Wagner," "Musical Studies," "Elgar," "Richard Strauss," "Wagner As Man and Artist," "A Musical Motley," "The Piano-Player and Its Music," "A Music Critic's Holiday," "Hugo Wolf," "Stories of the Great Operas," "The Unconscious Beethoven," "Facts and Fiction about Wagner," "The Man Liszt,"* etc. He translated Weingartner's work on conducting, Schweitzer's biography of Bach, and Wagner's music dramas for the Breitkopf and Härtel edition; dir. the collection of the series *"The New Library of Music,"*

and 1912-14 ed. *The Piano-Player Review.*

New'march, Rosa, b. Leamington Spa, Eng., 1857—Worthing, April 9, 1940; writer of music of mod. Russia; translated Deiters' *"Brahms,"* Habet's *"Borodin and Liszt,"* Modeste Tschaikowsky's biography of his brother and d'Indy's *"César Franck"* into Eng.; author, *" Henry J. Wood," "The Russian Opera," "Songs to a Singer," "Jean Sibelius," "The Russian Arts," "Life of Tschaikowsky,"* etc.

Newsidler, Neysidler. Vide NEUSIEDLER.

Ney (nī), **Elly,** b. Düsseldorf, Sept. 27, 1882; pianist; pupil of Cologne Cons., of Leschetizky and Sauer; won Mendelssohn-Ibach Prize; taught at Cologne Cons.; toured Europe and U. S. as recitalist and orch. soloist; a performer of strong temperament, esp. known as interpreter of Brahms; m. Willem van Hoogstraten, conductor; divorced.

Niccolò de Malta. Vide ISOUARD.

Nichelmann (nĭkh'-ĕl-män), **Chp.,** Treuenbrietzen, Brandenburg, 1717 —Berlin, 1762; cembalist and writer.

Nicholl (nĭk'-ôl), **Horace Wadham,** Tipton, near Birmingham, Engl., March 17, 1848—New York, March 10, 1922; son and pupil of a musician, John N.; studied with Samuel Prince; 1867-70 organist at Dudley; 1871 organist at Pittsburgh, Pa., 1878, editor, New York. 1888-95 prof. at Farmington, Conn.; contributed to various periodicals; pub. a book on harmony; c. 12 symphonic preludes and fugues for organ, suite for full orch. (op. 3); a cycle of 4 oratorios with orch.; symph. poem *"Tartarus";* 2 symphonies; a psychic sketch *" Hamlet,"* etc.

Nich'olls, Agnes, b. Cheltenham, July 14, 1877; soprano; pupil of Visetti at the R. C. M., London, with a scholarship; début 1895 in a revival of Purcell's *"Dido and Aeneas";* studied also with John Acton; 1901, and 1904-06 sang at Covent Garden; has sung much in concert and oratorios, and at the Cincinnati Festival, 1904; in which year she married Hamilton Harty (q.v.).

Nick'lass-Kempt'ner, Selma, Breslau, April 2, 1849—Berlin, Dec. 22, 1928; noted coloratura soprano and teacher; studied at Stern Cons.; début, 1867;

sang in Rotterdam 10 years; then
teacher Vienna Cons.; 1893, Berlin.
Nicodé (nē'-kō-dā), **Jean Louis,** Jer-
czik, near Posen, Aug. 12, 1853—
near Dresden, Oct. 5, 1919; pupil of
his father and the organist Hartkäs,
and at Kullak's Acad.; lived in Berlin
as a pianist and teacher; 1878–85
pf.-teacher Dresden Cons.; 1897,
cond. Leipzig "Riedel Verein"; c.
symph. poem *"Maria Stuart"; "Fa-
schingsbilder," "Sinfonische Varia-
tionen,"* op. 27; *"Das Meer,"* symph.
ode, for full orch.; "Erbarmen,"
hymn for alto with orch., etc.
Nicolai (nē'-kō-lī), (1) **Otto,** Königsberg, June 9, 1810—of apoplexy,
Berlin, May 11, 1849; son and pupil
of a singing-teacher; studied with
Zelter and Klein, later with Baini at
Rome, where he was organist at the
embassy chapel; 1837–38 theatre-
cond. at Vienna; again in Rome;
1841–47 ct.-cond. at Vienna and
founded the Phil., 1842; 1847 cond.
of the opera and cath.-choir, Berlin;
prod. 5 v. succ. operas, incl. *"Il
Templario"* (Turin, 1840; known in
Germany as *"Der Templer,"* based
on Scott's *"Ivanhoe"*); and the unc-
tuous and still popular opera *"Die
lustigen Weiber von Windsor,"* based
on and known in English as *"The
Merry Wives of Windsor"* (Berlin,
1849); he c. also a symph., etc.; biog.
by Mendel (Berlin, 1868); his diary
("Tagebücher") was pub. Leipizg,
1893. (2) **Wm. Fr. Gerard,** Leyden,
Nov. 20, 1829—The Hague, April 25,
1896; professor; notable conductor
and composer.
Nicolau (nē'-kō-lä-oo), **Antonio,** Barcelona, June 8, 1858—Feb. 26, 1933;
pupil of Pujol and Balart; cond. of
Catalonian Concert Society in Paris,
then dir. municipal music school at
Barcelona; c. opera, choral works,
etc.
Nicolini (nē-kō-lē'-nē), (1) **Nicolino**
Grimaldi detto, Naples, ca. 1673—
Venice, (?) after 1726; tenor, whom
Addison called "perhaps the greatest
performer in dramatic music that
ever appeared upon a stage"; he was
a contralto in Italy as early as 1694
and was decorated with the Order of
St. Mark; from 1708–1716 in England rousing a furore; created
"Rinaldo" in Handel's opera, 1711;
returned to sing in Italy. (2) **Giuseppe,** Pincenza, Jan. 29, 1762—

Dec. 18, 1842; conductor and operatic composer. (3) **Ernest [Nicholas],**
Tours, France, Feb. 23, 1834—Pau,
Jan. 19, 1898; tenor; 1886, m. Adelina Patti.
Nic'olson, Richard, d. 1639; Engl. organist.
Niecks (nēks), **Frederick (Friedrich),**
Düsseldorf, Feb. 3, 1845—Edin-
burgh, June 29, 1924; lecturer, critic,
etc.; pupil of Langhans, Grünewald,
and Auer (vln.); début at 12; 1868,
organist, Dumfries, Scotland, and
viola-player in a quartet with A. C.
Mackenzie; studied in Leipzig Univ.
(1877), and travelled Italy; critic,
London; 1891, Ried Prof. of Mus.,
Edinburgh Univ.; pub. notable biog.
of *"Frederic Chopin as a Man and a
Musician"* (1888); a *"Dict. of Mus.
Terms,"* etc.
Niedermeyer (nē'-dĕr-mī-ĕr), **Louis,**
Nyon, Switzerland, 1802 — Paris,
1861; dramatic composer and theorist.
Niedt (nēt), **Fr. Erhardt,** d. Copenhagen, 1717; writer.
Nielsen (nēl'-sĕn), (1) **Carl,** Nörre-
Lyndelse, Fünen Island, June 9, 1864
—Copenhagen, Oct. 2, 1931; important Danish composer; pupil of Gade,
member of the Copenhagen court
orch., and from 1904 assistant cond.
succeeding Svendsen; after 1915
assoc. dir., Copenhagen R. Cons.;
c. 6 symph., No. 2 *"The Four
Temperaments";* Violin Concerto;
operas, *"Saul and David"* (1902),
"Masquerade" (1906); chorus with
orch., *"Hymnus amoris";* chamber
music, etc. (2) **Ludolf,** b. Nörre-Tolde,
Zealand, Jan. 29, 1876; pupil Copenhagen and Leipzig Cons.; viola player
in Andersen's Orch.; c. operas, choral,
symph., chamber music, songs, etc. (3)
Alice, b. Nashville, Tenn., 1876;
soprano; sang with Bostonians Light
Op. Co.; later in London; op. début at
Naples, 1903 as "Marguerite"; also
sang at Covent Garden; with Met. Op.
Co., 1910; d. N. Y., March 8, 1943.
Niemann (nē'-män), (1) **Albert,** Erxle-
ben, near Magdeburg, Jan. 15, 1831
—Berlin, Jan. 13, 1917; 1849, with-
out study sang in minor rôles at
Dessau; then studied with F. Schnei-
der, and the bar. Nusch; sang at
Hanover, then studied with Duprez,
Paris; 1860–66, dram. tenor, Han-
over, later at the ct.-opera, Berlin;
Wagner chose him to create "Tann-

häuser" (Paris, 1861), and "Siegmund" (Bayreuth, 1876); he sang at
Met. Op., 1886–88, making deep impression as dram. artist; retired 1889.
(2) **Rudolf (Fr.)**, Wesselburen, Holstein, 1838—Wiesbaden, 1898; pianist and composer. (3) **Walter**, b.
Hamburg, Oct. 10, 1876; son of
(2), composer; d. Nov. 1, 1953.
Nietzsche (nēt'-shě), **Fr.**, Röcken, near
Lützen, Oct. 15, 1844—(insane)
Aug., 1900; prof. at Basel Univ.;
notable, if eccentric, philosopher; as
a partisan of Wagner he pub. *"Die
Geburt der Tragödie aus dem Geiste
der Musik," "Richard Wagner in
Bayreuth"*; while *"Der Fall Wagner,"*
and *"Nietzsche contra Wagner"* at-
tack Wagner as violently as he once
praised him; his philosophical work
"Also sprach Zarathustra" provides
the title of R. Strauss's symph. poem.
Nieviadomski (n'yäv-yä-dôm'shkǐ),
Stanislav, b. Soposzyn, Galicia, Nov.
4, 1859; pupil of Mikuli, Krenn, and
Jadassohn; teacher at Lemberg Cons.,
where he d. 1936; comp.
Niggli (nǐg'-glē), **Arnold**, Aarburg,
Switzerland, Dec. 20, 1843—Zurich,
May 30, 1927; writer.
Nikisch (nǐk'-ǐsh), (1) **Arthur**, Szent
Miklos, Hungary, Oct. 12, 1855—
Leipzig, Jan. 23, 1922; eminent con-
ductor; son of the head-bookkeeper
to Prince Lichtenstein; pupil of
Dessoff (comp.) and Hellmesberger
(vln.), Vienna Cons., graduating at
19 with prizes for vln., and for a
string-sextet; violinist in the ct.-
orch.; then 2nd cond. Leipzig Th.;
1882–89, 1st. cond.; 1889–93, cond.
Boston Symph. Orch., 1893–95, dir.
Royal Opera, Budapest, and cond.
Philh. Concerts; 1895, cond. Gewandhaus Concerts, Leipzig (vice
Reinecke), also Phil. concerts, Berlin;
1902–07, dir. Leipzig Cons.; 1905–06
dir. the Stadttheater; toured widely
with the Berlin Phil., and acted as
guest cond. in many capitals; April,
1912, toured the U. S. as cond. of the
London Phil. with immense success.
He c. a symph., a cantata *"Christ-
nacht,"* orch. fantasie *"Der Trompeter"*; etc. His wife (2) **Amélie**
(née Heuser), b. in Brussels; sang in
Cassel and Leipzig operas, and composed music. (3) **Mitja**, b. Leipzig,
May 21, 1899; son of (1); pianist;
toured U. S.; d. Venice, Aug. 5, 1936.
Nilsson (nēls'-sōn). **Christine**, near

Wexio, Sweden, Aug. 20, 1843—
Stockholm, Nov. 22, 1921; eminent
soprano, compass 2½ octaves (g–d");
pupil of Baroness Leuhausen and
F. Berwald, Stockholm; later, in
Paris, of Wartel; début, 1864, Th.-
Lyrique, Paris, engaged for 3 years
there; 1868–70, Opéra; toured America (1870–74 and 1884) and Europe;
1872, she m. Auguste Rouzaud (d.
1882); 1887, m. Count Casa di
Miranda.
Nin, Joaquin, b. Havana, Sept. 29,
1859—Oct. 24, 1949; composer; studied
piano with Moszkowski and comp.
at Schola Cantorum, Paris, where he
taught, 1906–08; toured as pianist;
he is known esp. as composer and
arranger of Spanish pop. folk music;
mem. of the French Legion of Honour
and the Spanish Academy.
Nini (nē'-nē), **Ales.**, Fano, Romagna,
1805—Bergamo, 1880; cond. and
dram. composer.
Nisard (nē-zǎr), **Théodore** (pen-name
of Abbé **Théodule Eleazar X. Norman**), Quaregnon, near Mons, Jan.
27, 1812—Paris, 1887; chorister at
Cambrai; studied in Douay; 1839,
dir. Enghien Gymnasium, and 1842,
2d *chef de chant* and organist St.-
Germain, Paris; then confined himself to writing valuable treatises on
plain-chant, etc.
Nissen (nǐs'-sěn), (1) **G. Nicolaus von**,
Hadersleben, Denmark, 1765—Salz-
burg, March 24, 1826; councillor of
State; m. the widow of Mozart,
1809, and aided her in preparing his
biog. (1828). (2) (**Nissen-Saloman**)
Henriette, Gothenburg, Sweden,
March 12, 1819—Harzburg, Aug. 27,
1879; great singer and teacher; pupil
of Chopin and Manuel Garcia; début
Paris, 1843; 1850, m. Siegfried Saloman, from 1859 teacher St. Petersburg Cons. (3) **Erica**. Vide LIE.
Nivers (nē-vǎrs), **Guillaume Gabriel**,
Melun, 1617—after 1701; organist,
singer and composer.
Nix'on, (1) **H. G.**, Winchester, 1796—
1849; organist and composer. (2)
Jas. Cassana, 1823—1842; violinist;
son of above. (3) **H. Cotter**, London, 1842—Bromley, 1907; organist
and composer.
No'ack, Sylvain, b. Rotterdam, Aug.
21, 1881; at first a pianist, then violin
pupil of André Spoor, Amsterdam;
at 17 entered the Cons., as a pupil of
Eiderling, winning first prize, 1903,

and becoming a teacher there; 1905 settled in Rotterdam, and toured widely; 1906 concertm. at Aix-la-Chapelle; from 1908 second concertmaster Boston Symph.; after 1919, concertmaster, Los Angeles; d. 1953.

No'ble, Thomas Tertius, b. Bath, May 5, 1867; composer; pupil of the R. C. M., London, winning a scholarship, and later teaching there; org. at Cambridge, Ely Cathedral, and from 1898 at York Minster, founding the York Symphony Orch.; c. church music with orch., cantata *"Gloria Domini,"* music to Aristophanes' *"Wasps,"* etc.; since 1913 in N. Y. as org. and dir. of music, St. Thomas' d. Rockport, Mass., May 5, 1953.

Nohl (nōl), **(K. Fr.) L.,** Iserlohn, 1831—Heidelberg, 1885; 1880, professor and writer; wrote biogs. of Beethoven, Mozart, etc., and published many colls. of the letters of composers.

Nohr (nōr), **Chr. Fr.,** Langensalza, Thuringia, 1800—Meiningen, 1875; violinist and dram. composer.

Norblin (nôr-blăn), (1) **Louis Pierre Martin,** Warsaw, 1781—Chateau Conantre, Marne, 1854; 'cellist and professor. (2) **Émile,** 1821—1880; son of above; 'cellist.

Nor'dica, Lillian (stage-name of **Lillian Norton**), Farmington, Me., 1859—Batavia, Java, May 10, 1914, while on world tour; pupil of John O'Neill and of N. E. Cons., Boston; concert-début, Boston, 1876; 1878, toured Europe with Gilmore's Band; studied opera with San Giovanni, Milan; début at Brescia, 1880; 1881, Gr. Opéra, Paris; 1882, m. Frederick A. Gower; 1885, he made a balloon ascension and never returned; she retired till 1887; sang Covent Garden, London same year; 1888, began appearances at Met. Op., N. Y. as striking and brilliant artist of notable powers; afterward appeared regularly in U. S., England, etc.; 1894 chosen to sing "Elsa" at Bayreuth; In 1910–11 she was with the Boston Op. Co. Throughout her career she was a prominent concert and festival singer. In early years she sang many Italian rôles but later almost wholly Wagner operas; 1896, m. Zoltan F. Doeme, Hungarian singer (divorced 1904) and in 1909, Geo. W. Young, N. Y. financier.

Nordqvist (nôrt'-kwĭst), **Johan Conrad,** Venersborg, April 11, 1840—Stockholm, April 16, 1920; Swedish composer; pupil Stockholm Musikakademie; 1864 military bandmaster, then with state funds studied in Dresden and Paris; from 1875 organist and teacher at Stockholm; 1881 teacher of harmony at the Musikakad.; 1885 court cond.; c. orch. works, etc.

Nor'draak (nôr'-drāk), **Rikard,** Christiania, June 12, 1842—Berlin, March 20, 1866; composer whose early death ended a promising career; pupil of Kiel and Kullak; c. incid. music to Björnson's *"Maria Stuart"* and *"Sigurd Slembe,"* piano pieces, etc.

No'ren, Heinrich Gottlieb, Graz, Jan. 6, 1861—Rottach, June 6, 1928; violinist; pupil of Massart; concertmaster in various countries; from 1896-1902 in Crefeld, where he founded a Cons.; teacher at Stern Cons., in Berlin; later in Dresden; c. orch. variations *"Kaleidoskop"* (Dresden, 1907), serenade for orch., etc.

Noré'na, Eidé, (née **Kaja Hansen**) b. Oslo, Norway; soprano; studied and made début in Scandinavia; sang at La Scala with succ.; at Covent Garden, 1924-25, and at Paris Op.; Amer. début in N. Y. concert, 1926; heard in opera at Baden-Baden Fest. same year; a mem. of Chicago Op., 1926-27, and after 1933 of Met. Op., N. Y.

Norman. Vide NISARD.

Nor'man(n), L., Stockholm, 1831—1885; conductor, professor and composer. Vide NERUDA.

Nor'ris, (1) **Wm.,** d. ca. 1710; English composer. (2) **Thos.,** 1741-1790; English male soprano, organist and composer. (3) **Homer A.,** Wayne, Maine, Oct. 4, 1860—New York, 1920; notable theorist; studied with Marston, Hale, Chadwick and Emery, Boston; lived there as teacher; also studied 4 years in Paris with Dubois, Godard, Gigout and Guilmant; c. overture *"Zoroaster,"* cantata *"Nain"* and songs; pub. "Harmony" and "Counterpoint" on French basis.

Noszkowski (nôsh-kôf'-shkĭ), **Sigismund (Zygismunt von),** Warsaw, May 2, 1846—July 24, 1909; pupil of Warsaw Mus. Inst.; inv. a mus.-notation for the blind, and was sent by the Mus. Soc. to study with Kiel and Raif, Berlin; 1876 cond.; 1881,

dir. of the Mus. Soc., Warsaw, and
(1888) prof. at the Cons.; prod. succ.
opéra *"Livia"* (Lemberg, 1898); c.
symph., overture *"Das Meerauge,"*
etc.

Noszler (nôsh'-lĕr), **K. Eduard,** b.
Reichenbach, Saxony, March 26,
1863; pupil of Leipzig Cons.; 1888—
93, organist Frauenkirche, Bremen;
1887, cond. Male Choral Union;
1893, organist Bremen Cath., and
1896, cond. Neue Singakademie; c.
symph., "Lustspiel-Ouvertüre," etc.

Notker (nôt'-kĕr) (called **Balbulus,**
"the stammerer"), 830–912, monk
at St. Gallen; important writer and
composer of sequences. (V. D. D.)

Nottebohm (nôt'-tĕ-bōm), **Martin Gv.,**
Lüdenscheid, Westphalia, 1817—
Graz, 1882; teacher and writer chiefly
of valuable Beethoven works and
discoveries; also composer.

Nouguès (noo-gĕs), **Jean,** Bordeaux,
1876—Auteuil, Aug. 29, 1932; composer of operas " *Yannha*" (Barcelona, 1897); *"Thamyris"* (Bordeaux,
1904); *"Quo Vadis"* (Paris Gaité,
1910, Berlin Royal Op., 1912);
*"Chiquito," "L'Éclaircie," "La Dan-
seuse de Pompeii"* (Rouen).

Nourrit (noor-rē), (1) **Louis,** Montpellier, 1780—Brunoy, 1831; leading
tenor Gr. Opéra, Paris. (2) **Ad.,**
Paris, 1802—suicide, Naples, 1839;
eminent tenor; son and successor
(1825) of above; pupil of Garcia and
teacher at the Cons.; also composer.

Nováček (nō'-vä-chĕk), **Ottokar,** Fe-
hértemplom, Hungary, May 13, 1866
—New York, Feb. 3, 1900; violinist;
pupil of his father, of Dont, and at
Leipzig Cons., where he won the
Mendelssohn prize, 1889; 1891 member Boston Symph. Orch.; 1892–03
Damrosch Orch., N. Y.; heart-
trouble forced his retirement; c.
chamber music, Bulgarian dances
and other violin pieces.

Novaes (nō-vä'-äs), **Guiomar,** b. São
Paulo, Brazil, Feb. 28, 1895; pianist;
began to study piano at 5 with
Chiafarelli; grad. Paris Cons., pupil
of Philipp, won 1st prize; made début
in Paris, 1907, followed by appearances in Germany, Italy, Switzerland
and Brazil; her début in the U. S.
took place at N. Y., 1915; her playing
won warm applause for its refinement, brilliance and expressiveness;
after a few years' retirement, returned to North America in 1934,

deepening the impression by matured
interpretative powers; m. Octavio
Pinto, composer.

No'vák, Vítězslav, b. Kamenitz, Bohemia, Dec. 5, 1870; important Bohemian composer; pupil of Prague Cons.
under Dvořák, later teacher at
Prague; from 1909 teacher of composition at the Cons.; 1919–22, its
dir.; c. overture *"Maryscha,"* symph
poems *"On the High Tatra,"*
and *"Eternal Longing"; "Slovak"*
Suite; d. n. Prague, July 18, 1949.

Novello (nō-vĕl'-lō), (1) **Vincent,** London, Sept. 6, 1781—Nice, Aug. 9,
1861; son of Italian father and English mother; founded, 1811, the
pub. firm Novello & Co.; notable organist, pianist and composer. (2)
Clara Anastasia, London, Jan. 10,
1818—Rome, March 12, 1908; 4th
daughter of (1); pupil Paris Cons.,
succ. operatic début Padua, 1841,
but made her best succ. in oratorio;
1843, m. Count Gigliucci; ret. 1860.

Noverre (nō-vär), **J. G.,** Paris, April 29,
1727—St. Germain, Nov. 19, 1810;
solo-dancer at Berlin; ballet-master
at the Op.-Com., Paris; inv. the
dramatic ballet.

Novot'na, Jarmila, Czech soprano;
sang Prague Op., Vienna State Op.;
début Met. Op., 1940, as Mimi; also
at Glyndebourne Fest.

Nowakowski (nō-vä-kôf'-shkĭ), **Jozef,**
Mniszck, 1800—Warsaw, 1865; pf.-
teacher, professor and composer.

Nowowiejski (nō-vō-vē'-shkĭ), **Felix,**
b. Wartenburg, 1877—d. Poznan,
1946; composer, pupil Stern Cons., and
Regensburg Church Mus. Sch.;
1902, won Berlin Meyerbeer prize
with oratorio *"Die Rückkehr des
verlorenen Sohnes"*; c. 2 symph.;
opera *"Quo Vadis"* (1907); oratorio
"Die Auffindung des Kreuzes" (Lemberg, 1906). *"Quo Vadis"* was given
as an oratorio New York, **1912.**

O

Oakeley (ōk'-lĭ), Sir **Herbert Stanley,**
Ealing, Middlesex, July 22, 1830—
Eastbourne, Oct. 26, 1903; while at
Oxford, studied with Elvey (harm.),
later at Leipzig Cons., with Schnei-
der, Dresden, and Breidenstein,
Bonn.; 1865–91, Ried Prof. of Mus.,
Edinburgh Univ., developing the
annual Ried Concerts into a 3-days'
Festival; his org.-recitals had a large

influence; knighted 1876; Mus. Doc., Cantab., 1871; Oxon., Dublin, 1887; 1892, Emeritus Professor; composer to the Queen in Scotland, and 1887, Pres., Cheltenham Mus. Festival; pub. a cantata *"Jubilee Lyric," "Suite in the Olden Style," "Pastorale,"* Festival March, and a Funeral March (op. 23) for orch.; pf.-sonata, etc.

O'ber, Margarete, b. Berlin, 1885; contralto; studied with Stolzenberg, then with Arthur Arndt (whom she married); sang at Stettin, and at Berlin Op.; 1913–17, Met. Op., N. Y.; later again active in Berlin.

O'berhoffer, (1) **Heinrich,** Pfalzel, Dec. 9, 1824—Luxembourg, May 30, 1885; organist at Luxembourg, c. church music. (2) **Emil,** Munich, Aug. 10, 1867—San Diego, Cal., May 22, 1933; pupil of Kistler, and I. Philipp; settled in Minneapolis, Minn.; cond. Phil. Club. and 1905–22, Minn. Symph. Orch., with which he toured the U. S., 1912; c. church music, songs, etc.

Oberthür (ō'-bĕr-tür), **K.,** Munich, 1819—London, 1895; harpist, teacher and dramatic composer.

Obrecht, vide HOBRECHT.

O'brist, Aloys., San Remo, March 30, 1867—(suicide) Stuttgart, June 29, 1910; pupil of Müller Hartung at Weimar; cond. in various cities; from 1900 at Weimar; mus. director and coll. of mus. instruments.

O'Car'olan, Turlough, Newton, Meath, 1670—Roscommon, 1738; Irish harpist.

Ochs (ŏkhs), (1) **Traugott,** Altenfeld, Oct. 19, 1854—Berlin, Aug. 27, 1919, where he was dir. of his own school after 1911; pupil of Stade, Erdmannsdörfer, Kiel, and the R. Inst. for Church-mus.; 1899, artistic dir. Mus.-Union and the Mus.-Sch., Brünn; then civic. dir., Bielefeld, and ct.-dir., Sondershausen; c. *"Deutsches Aufgebot"* for male chorus and orch.; requiem, etc. (2) **Siegfried,** Frankfort-on-Main, April 19, 1858—Berlin, Feb. 6, 1929; studied R. Hochschule für Musik, Berlin, later with Kiel and Urban, and von Bülow, who brought into publicity a small choral union, the "Philharmonischer Chor.," of which he was cond., and which is now the largest singing-society in Berlin; also a singing-teacher and writer, 1901, Munich; c. succ. comic

opera (text and music) *"Im Namen des Gesetzes"* (Hamburg, 1888); 2 operettas; many choruses, duets, songs, etc.; ed. some of Bach's cantatas.

Ochsenkuhn (ŏkh'-zān-koon), **Sebastian,** d. Heidelberg, Aug. 20, 1574; lutenist and composer.

O'dington, Walter de ("Monk of Evesham"), b. Odington, Gloucestershire; d. ca. 1330; important theorist. (Coussemaker.)

O'do de Clugny (dŭ klün'-yē) (Saint), became in 927 abbot of Clugny, where he d. 942; writer. (Gerbert.)

Oeglin (ākh'-lēn), **Erhard,** 16th cent. German printer of Augsburg, the first to print figured mus. with types.

Oelschlegel (āl'-shlä-gĕl), **Alfred,** Anscha, Bohemia, Feb. 25, 1847—Leipzig, June 19, 1916; Prague Org.-Sch.; th.-cond. at Hamburg, etc., and Karltheater, Vienna; later bandm. Klagenfurt; c. operettas *"Prinz und Maurer"* (Klagenfurt, 1884); succ. *"Die Raubritter"* (Vienna, 1888); succ. *"Der Landstreicher"* (Magdeburg, 1893).

Oelsner (ĕls'-nĕr), (Fr.) **Bruno,** b. Neudorf, near Annaberg, Saxony, July 29, 1861; pupil of Leipzig Cons.; solo-vla., ct.-orch. Darmstadt; studied with de Haan (comp.); 1882, vln.-teacher Darmstadt Cons., with title Grand Ducal Chamber-mus.; prod. at Darmstadt 1-act operas, incl. succ. *"Der Brautgang"* (1894); also a cantata with orch., etc.

Oesten (ā'-shtĕn), **Theodor,** Berlin, 1813—1870; pianist and composer.

Oesterlein (ā'-shtĕr-līn), **Nikolaus,** 1842 —Vienna, 1898; maker of the coll. known as the *"Wagner Museum."*

Oettingen, Arthur Joachim, 1836—1920; imp. writer and physicist.

Offenbach (ŏf'-fĕn-bäkh), **Jacques,** Cologne, June 21, 1819—Paris, Oct. 5, 1880; eminent writer of light opera; studied 'cello at the Cons., then joined Op.-Com. orch., Paris; c. chansonnettes (parodying La Fontaine), played the 'cello in concerts, and c. 'cello-pcs.; 1849, cond. Th.-Français, prod. unsucc. 1-act operetta *"Pepito"* (Op.-Com., 1853); others followed till 1855–66 he had a theatre for his own work; 1872–76, manager Th. de la Gaité; 1877, toured America; his 102 stage-works include the ballet-pantomime *"Le Papillon"* and the v. succ. operas.

"*Orphée aux Enfers*," 1858; "*La Belle Hélène*," 1864; "*Barbe-Bleu*" and "*La Vie Parisienne*," 1866; "*La Grande Duchesse de Gérolstein*," 1867; "*Madame Favart*," 1879. The grand opera, "*The Tales of Hoffmann*," his masterpiece was prod. posthumously 1881.

Oginski (ō-gēn'-shkǐ), (1) Prince **Michael Cléophas**, Guron, near Warsaw, 1765—Florence, 1833; composer. (2) **Michael Casimir**, Warsaw, 1731—1803; uncle of above; said to have inv. the pedals of the harp.

O'keghem (or **Okekem, Okenghem, Ockegheim, Ock'enheim**), **Jean de** (or **Joannes**), probably Termonde, East Flanders, ca. 1430—Tours, 1495; an eminent contrapuntist; the founder of the Second (or New) Netherland Sch. Chorister, Antwerp cathedral; studied with Dufay; 1454, ct.-cond. and composer to Charles VII. at Paris; 1467, royal cond. to Louis XI.; toured Spain and Flanders on stipend; c. masses, motets, canons, etc.

Oldberg, Arne, b. Youngstown, Ohio, July 12, 1874; began piano studies with his father at 5; at 6 was playing Haydn symphonies in duet form; pupil of Aug. Hyllested, Chicago; 1893–95 of Leschetizky, Vienna; from 1895 in Chicago with Middelschulte (counterpoint); Ad. Koelling (instrumentation) and F. G. Gleason; 1898 with J. Rheinberger, Munich; from 1899 teacher at Northwestern Univ., Ill.; c. 2 symphs. (F minor, winning National Federation prize 1911); overture "*Paola and Francesca*" (played 3 times by Thomas Orch.); Festival Overture, 12 orch. variations, horn concerto, chamber music, piano sonata, etc.

Olib'rio, Flavio Anicio. Vide J. F. AGRICOLA.

Ol'iphant, Thos., Condie, Perthshire, 1799—London, 1873; theorist and collector.

Ollone (dôl-lŭn), **Max d'**, b. Besançon, June 13, 1875; pupil Paris Cons., taking the Prix de Rome, 1897; for a time after 1923, dir., Amer. Cons., Fontainebleau; c. cantata "*Frédégonde*," lyric scene "*Jeanne d' Arc à Domrémy*," etc.

Olsen (ōl'-zĕn), **Ole**, b. Hammerfest, Norway, July 4, 1851—Christiania, Nov. 9, 1927: composer.

Olszewska (ŏl-shĕv'-skä), **Maria**, b. Augsburg, Aug. 8, 1892; contralto; début, Crefeld, Germany; later sang at Hamburg State Theatre, Vienna State Op., Berlin Städtische Op., at Munich Fest., Covent Garden; Amer. début with Chicago Op., 1930–31; after 1932 sang for several seasons with Met. Op. Co., also in various Eur. theatres and in South America; m. Dr. Emil Schipper, basso.

Ondricek (ôn'-drǐ-chĕk), **Fz.**, Prague, April 29, 1859—Milan, April 13, 1922; violinist; pupil of his father, and at 14 member of his small orch. for dance mus.; then studied Prague Cons. and with Massart, Paris Cons., took first prize for vln.-playing; toured Europe and America; after 1907 in Vienna, where prof. at Cons.

Onegin (ôn-yā'-gǐn), **Sigrid** (née **Hoffmann**), b. Stockholm, June 1, 1891; German contralto; pupil of Ress in Frankfort, also of Eugen Rob, and di Ranieri in Milan; after 1912 active as concert singer; studied for opera on advice of Schillings; début at Stuttgart; after 1919 at Munich Op.; Amer. début as soloist with Phila. Orch., 1922; sang at Met. Op. House same season, "Amneris," "Brangäne" and other Wagnerian rôles; one of leading contemporary singers, with great flexibility and range, incl. both soprano and coloratura contralto; has appeared widely in opera and concerts in Europe and Amer., at Salzburg; d. Magliaso, Switz., June 17 (?), 1943.

O'Neill, (1) **Norman**, Kensington, March 14, 1875—London, March 3, 1934; cond., pupil of Somervell and Hoch Cons. at Frankfort; c. incid. music to "*Hamlet*" (1904), "*King Lear*" (1908), "*The Blue Bird*" (1909); overture "*In Autumn*," "*In Springtime*"; fantasy for voices and orch. "*Woldemar*"; Scotch rhapsody; ballade with orch. "*La belle dame sans merci*" (London, 1910), etc.; 1899, he married (2) **Adine Rückert**, pianist; pupil of Clara Schumann and Mme. Clause-Szavardy. He taught R. A. M. after 1924.

Ons'low, G., Clermont-Ferrand, France, 1784—1852; grandson of the first Lord Onslow; amateur 'cellist and pianist; prod. 4 succ. comic operas; 34 string-quintets; 36 quartets; and other chamber-music.

Opienski (ŏp-yĕn'-shkǐ), **Heinrich**, b. Cracow, June 13. 1870: pupil of

Zelénski there, of d'Indy and Urban; critic in Warsaw, then pupil of Riemann in history, and of Nikisch in conducting; from 1907 teacher at history at the Warsaw Music School, and from 1908 cond. of the Opera; 1919, dir. of a music school in Posen; from 1926, lived in Geneva; c. prize cantata in honour of Mickiewicz; opera "*Maria*," symph. poem "*Lilla Weneda*"; d. Morges, Switz., Jan. 22, 1942.

Ordenstein (ôr'-děn-shtīn), **H.**, Worms, Jan. 7, 1856—Carlsruhe, March 22, 1921; pianist; pupil of Leipzig Cons., also in Paris; 1879–81, teacher at Carlsruhe; 1881–82, at Kullak's Acad., Berlin; 1884, founded Carlsruhe Cons.; made prof. by Grand Duke of Baden.

Orefice, dell'. Vide DELL' OREFICE.

Orgeni (ôr-gā'-nē) (**Orgenyi**) (ôr-gān'-yē), **Anna Maria Aglaia**, Tismenice, Galicia, Dec. 17, 1843—Vienna, March 15, 1926; colorature soprano; pupil of Mme. Viardot-Garcia; début, 1865, Berlin Opera; 1886, teacher Dresden Cons.

Orlan'di, Fernando, Parma, 1777—Jan. 5, 1848; 1809–28 singing teacher at Milan Cons.; then at Munich Music School; c. 26 operas.

Orlandini (ôr-län-dē'-nē) **Giuseppe Maria**, Bologna, 1688—Florence, ca. 1750; opera composer, c. 44 operas, 3 oratorios, etc.

Orlando, or **Orlandus**. Vide LASSO.

Or'loff, Nikolai, b. Jeletz, Russia, Feb. 26, 1892; pianist; pupil of Moscow Cons., gold medal; also studied comp. with Taneiev; 1913–15, prof. at Moscow Philharmonie, 1917 at Cons.; after 1921 made concert tours of Europe and U. S., winning prominent position as virtuoso.

Or'mandy, Eugene, b. Budapest, Nov. 18, 1899; studied R. Acad. of Music there, winning diploma in vln., 1914, and professor's dip., 3 years later; pupil of Hubay; toured as violinist; prof. Hungarian State Cons., 1919; came to America and played as concertm. in Capitol Theater, N. Y., 1921; guest cond. with N. Y. Philh. and Phila. Orch. in summer seasons, 1930; succeeded Verbrugghen as cond. Minneapolis Symph., also appeared as guest with other Amer. orchs., Budapest Philh., etc., and in 1936 was appointed as regular cond. Phila. Orch., sharing bâton with Stokowski; 1938, sole conductor.

Orn'stein, Leo, b. Krementchug, Russia, Dec. 11, 1895; composer, pianist; studied St. Petersburg Cons., with Glazounoff and Inst. of Musical Art, N. Y.; début, in latter city, 1911; played as soloist with orchs. in N. Y., Los Angeles, Phila., Boston, St. Louis, Chicago; early attracted prominence for radical style of comp., but later works more conservative; c. piano concerto, vln. sonata, 'cello sonata, piano quintet, string quartet, choral music, songs, and piano music.

Orologio (ôr-ō-lō'-jǐ-ō), (1) and (2), **Alessandro**, two contemporary madrigal composers of the same name, one of them in 1603 became vice-chapelmaster to Emperor Rudolph at Prague; the other vice-chapelmaster to the Electoral Court at Dresden the same year.

Ortigue (ôr-tēg), **Jos. Louis de**, Cavallon, Vaucluse, 1802—Paris, 1866; writer.

Ortiz (ôr-těth), **Diego**, b. Toledo, ca. 1530; from 1558 chapelmaster to Duke of Alva; c. important book of sacred music (pub. Venice, 1565).

Ort'mann, Otto, b. Baltimore, Md., Jan. 25, 1889; pianist, educator; grad. Baltimore City Coll.; also Peabody Cons.; studied piano with Coulson, Boyle, Breitner, Landow; comp. with Blackhead, Boise, Siemann, Strube; after 1913 taught at Peabody Inst., and succeeded the late Harold Randolph as dir.; noted for research in the psychology of music; author, "*The Physical Basis of Piano Touch and Tone*," "*The Physiological Basis of Touch and Tone*," etc.

Orto (ôr'-tō), **Giov. de** (Italian form of Jean Dujardin) (dü-zhär'-dǎn); Latinised as **de Hor'to** (called "Marbriano"); contrapuntist and composer 15th and 16th centuries.

Os'borne, G. Alex., Limerick, Ireland, 1806—London, 1893; composer.

Osiander (ō'-zē- änt-ěr), **Lucas**, Nürnberg, 1534—Stuttgart, 1604; writer and composer.

Ostrčil (ôstr'-chǐl), **Otakar**, Smichov, Feb. 25, 1879—Prague, 1935; composer and conductor; pupil in comp. of Fibich; also of Prague Univ.; 1901, prof. at Prague Acad.; 1909–22, cond. notable orch. of amateur players in that city; 1914, chief cond. at Weinberge Stadttheater, Prague; after 1920 chief cond. at Prague Nat'l Theater; a notable propagandist for the younger generation of Czech composers; c. operas, "*Vlastas Ende*," "*Kunalas Augen*," "*Poupê*," "*Legende von Erin*," also orch., chamber music and choral works, songs, etc.

O'Sul'livan, Denis, San Francisco, April 25, 1868—Columbus, Ohio, Feb. 1, 1908; barytone of Irish descent; pupil of Talbo and Formes; later of Vannucini, Santley and Shakespeare; début 1895 in concert; also in opera with Carl Rosa Co.; 1896 created the title rôle in Stanford's "*Shamus O'Brien*" and sang it in England and America.

Othegraven (ō'-tĕ-grä-vĕn), **August von,** b. Cologne, June 2, 1864; pupil of the Cons. and from 1889 teacher there; c. fairy play "*The Sleeping Beauty*" (Cologne, 1907), songs, etc.

Othmayr (ōt'-mī-ĕr), **Kaspar,** Amberg, 1515—Nürnberg, 1553; composer.

Otho. Vide ODO.

Ott(o) (or **Ottl**), **Hans,** ca. 1533—1550; pub. in Nürnberg.

Ottani (ōt-tä'-nē), **Abbate Bernardino,** Bologna, 1736—Turin, 1827; dram. composer.

Otterstroem (ōt'-tĕr-strŭm), **Thorvald,** b. Copenhagen, July 17, 1868; composer; piano pupil of Sophie Menter, St. Petersburg; from 1892 in Chicago; c. 24 preludes and fugues for piano, chamber music, etc.

Otto (ōt'-tō), (1) Vide OTT. (2) (**Ernst**) **Julius,** Königstein, Saxony, Sept. 1, 1804—Dresden, March 5, 1877; notable composer of cycles for male chorus, songs, operas, etc. (3) **Valerius,** organist at Prague, 1607; c. church music. (4) **Stephan,** b. Freiburg, Saxony, ca. 1594; cantor there and at Schandau; c. church music.

Otto-Alvsleben (ōt'-tō-älf'-slä-bĕn), **Melitta** (née Alvsleben), Dresden, 1842—1893; soprano; married, 1866.

Oudin (oo-dăṅ), **Eugène** (Espérance), New York, 1858—London, 1894; barytone, pianist and composer.

Oudrid y Segura (oo-drēdh' ē sä-goo'-rä), **Cristobal,** Badajoz, 1829—Madrid, March 15, 1877; conductor and dram. composer.

Oulibichef. Vide ULIBISHEV.

Ouse'ley, Sir Fr. Arthur Gore, London, Aug. 12, 1825—Hereford, April 6, 1889; notable theorist and composer; pianist and organist remarkable for fugal improvisation; wrote important

treatises, etc.; c. an opera at 8; M. A. Oxford, 1840, Mus. Doc. there, 1854; also from Durham and Cambridge, 1862; from 1855 Prof. of Music at Oxford, vice Sir H. R. Bishop; c. 2 oratorios incl. "*Hagar*."

P

Pabst (päpst), (1) **Aug.,** Elberfeld, May 30, 1811—Riga, July 21, 1885; director and composer of operas. (2) **Louis,** Königsberg, July 18, 1846 —?; son of above; pianist and composer. From 1899, head pf.-teacher Moscow Philh. Sch. (3) **Paul,** Königsberg, 1854—Moscow, 1897; son of (1); pf.-prof.; director.

Pacchiarotti (päk-kǐ-ä-rōt'-tē), **Gasparo,** Fabriano, Ancona, 1744—Padua, Oct. 28, 1821; one of the greatest and most succ. of 18th cent. singers; soprano-musico.

Pacchioni (päk-kǐ-ō'-nē), **Antonio Maria,** Modena, 1654–1738, priest, court chaplain; c. oratorios, etc.

Pacelli (pä-chĕl'-lē), **Asprilio,** Varciano, ca. 1570—Warsaw, May 3, 1623; Italian choirmaster; 1604, called to Warsaw as chapelmaster to the King; c. motets, etc.

Pache (päkh'-ĕ), (1) **Johannes,** b. Bischofswerda, Dec. 9, 1857—Limbach, Dec. 21, 1897; organist and composer of male choruses, etc. (2) **Joseph,** Friedland, Silesia, June 1, 1861—Baltimore, Dec. 7, 1926; pupil Royal Akad., Munich, and of Scharwenka Cons., and Max Bruch; settled in New York and founded 1903 an oratorio society; from 1904 dir. oratorio society in Baltimore.

Pachelbel (päkh'-ĕl-bĕl), (1) **J.,** Nürnberg, Sept. 1, 1653—March 3, 1706; org.-virtuoso and composer. (2) **Wm. Hieronymus,** b. Erfurt, 1685; son of above; organist and composer.

Pachler-Koschak (päkh'-lĕr-kō'-shäk), **Marie Leopoldine,** Graz, Oct. 2, 1792 —April 10, 1855; pianist and composer; friend of Beethoven.

Pachmann (päkh-män), **Vladimir de,** Odessa, July 27, 1848—Rome, Jan. 8, 1933; notable pianist especially devoted to Chopin's mus.; son and pupil of a prof. at Vienna Univ.; studied also with Dachs, Vienna Cons.; 1869 toured Russia with great succ. that followed him throughout Europe and America; in Denmark he received the Order of the Danebrog from the King; 1916, Beethoven medal of London Philh.; returned to U. S. 1923 after a decade's absence; in final years his playing was marked by many eccentricities. He was more noted for refinement of effects in his playing than for sustained strength of interpretation. Ed. works of Chopin.

Pachulski (pä-khool'-shkĭ), **Henry**, b. Poland, Oct. 4, 1859; pupil Warsaw Cons., 1886–1917, prof. Moscow Cons.; c. pf. pcs.; d (?).

Pac(c)ini (pä-chē'-nē), (1) **Andrea**, b. Italy, ca. 1700; male contralto. (2) **A. Fran. Gaetano Saverio**, Naples, 1778—Paris, 1866; singing-teacher, conductor and composer of comic operas. (3) **Giov.**, Catania, Feb. 17, 1796—Pescia, Dec. 6, 1867; son of a tenor; pupil of Marchesi, Padre Mattei and Furlanetto; 1813–35, prod. 40 operas, the last failing, he established a sch. at Viareggio, later Lucca, wrote treatises, etc.; 1840, the succ. of *"Saffo"* set him to work again, and he turned out 40 more operas, also oratorios, a symph. *"Dante,"* etc. (4) **Emilio**, 1810—Neuilly, near Paris, Dec. 2, 1898; bro. of above; librettist of *"Il Trovatore,"* etc.

Pacius (pä'-tsĭ-oos), **Fr.**, Hamburg, March 19, 1809—Helsingfors, Jan. 9, 1891; violinist; c. the Finnish National Hymn, operas, etc.

Paderewski (päd-ĕ-rĕf'-shkĭ), **Ignace Jan**, b. Kurilovka, Poland, Nov. 18, 1860—N. Y., June 29, 1941; famous pianist; pupil of Raguski (harm. and cpt.) Warsaw Cons., of Urban and Wuerst, Berlin; of Leschetizky, Vienna. 1878–83, pf.-teacher, Warsaw Cons.; has toured Europe and America with unprecedented success. His first wife, who died young, bore him a son. 1899, m. Mme. Gorski. He settled at Morges, Switzerland, continuing to tour the world; 1912, in South Africa; 1909 director Warsaw Cons. During the World War, **P.** gave many concerts to raise funds for his native country. He abandoned music to work for the cause of Polish nat'l independence and was elected Premier of the new Republic in 1919, having taken part in the Peace Conference at Versailles. The following year he retired from polit. life, renewing his interest in the

piano, but did not resume public perf. until 1922. His return to the U. S. in a tour of remarkable interest and succ. in that year was followed by others of like import. In 1935–36 he was again announced to tour America after several years' absence, but this visit was cancelled owing to the pianist's illness. 1896 he set aside $10,000 as the Paderewski fund, the interest to be devoted to triennial prizes "to composers of American birth without distinction as to age or religion;" 1. $500 for best orchestral work in symph. form; 2. $300 for best comp. for solo instr. with orch.; 3. $200 for best chamber-music work. C. succ. opera *"Manru"* (Ct.-Th., Dresden, 1901 also at Met. Op.); opera *"Sakuntala"* (text by C. Mendès), a symphony in memory of the revolution of 1864, (1908; Boston Symph., 1909; Richter, London, 1909); a second symph., an hour and twenty minutes long (1912); piano sonata, variations, and fugue for piano (1907), etc. Polish fantasia for pf. with orch. op. 19, *"Légende No. 2,"* for pf. op. 20, and many original and brilliant pf.-pcs. incl. *"Chants du voyageur,"* a vln. sonata; vars. and fugue on original theme; op. 14, *' Humoresques de concert for pf."* (*Book* 1; *Menuet, Sarabande, Caprice; Book* 2, *Burlesque, Intermezzo polacco, Cracovienne fantastique*); *"Dans le désert, toccata"*; v. pop. Minuet (op. 1); songs, etc.

Padilla y Ramos (pä-dēl'-yä ē rä'-mōs), Murcia, Spain, 1842 — Auteuil, France, Nov. 21, 1906; pupil of Mabellini, Florence; barytone at Messina, Turin, etc., St. Petersburg, Vienna and Berlin; 1869, m. Désirée Artot. (q.v.)

Paër (pä'-ĕr), **Ferdinando**, Parma, June 1, 1771—Paris, May 3, 1839. 1807, ct.-cond. to Napoleon and cond. Op.-Com.; 1812, cond. Th.-Italien (vice Spontini); violinist and c. 43 operas, of which *"Il Maestro di Capella"* is still sung.

Paesiello. Vide PAISIELLO.

Paganini (päg-ä-nē'-nē), **Niccolò**, Genoa, Oct. 27, 1782—Nice, May 27, 1840; pre-eminent violin-virtuoso. Studied with G. Servetto and G. Dosta; at 8 he c. a vln.-sonata; at 9 he played in public with greatest succ.; from 1795 he studied with Ghiretti and Aless. Rolla (though **P.**

denied this), at Parma. 1798, he ran away from his severe father after a concert at Lucca, and played at Pisa and other places. At 15 he was a passionate gambler, and very dissipated. Fits of gambling alternated with periods when he practised 10 hours a day, the result being a ruined constitution. He pawned his violin to pay a gambling debt, but a M. Levron presented him with a Joseph Guarnerius, which P. willed to Genoa. In 1804 he went home, and practised till 1805, when he had extraordinary succ. making a sensation by brilliant performances on the G string alone; soon ct.-soloist at Lucca; then to 1827 he toured Italy, crushing all rivalry with an extraordinary technic; 1827, Pope Leo XII. conferred on him the Order of the Golden Spur; he played at Vienna, receiving from the municipality the great gold medal of St. Salvator; from the Emperor the honorary title of ct.-virtuoso. 1829, Berlin; 1831, Paris; 1831, London. 1833–34, Paris; then retired to his villa at Parma. He lost 50,000 francs on a scheme to establish a gambling house with concert-annex at Paris, the gambling-license being refused. Though his earnings were enormous, he was not generous except spasmodically; he gave Berlioz $4,000 as a compliment for his *"Symphonie Fantastique"* (B. had written *"Harold in Italy"* for P.'s Stradivari viola). He m. the singer Antonia Bianchi, and he left his son Achille $400,000 (£80,000). He died of phthisis of the larynx. His technic was never equalled, and it provoked superstitious dread among his auditors, his ghoulish appearance aiding the impression. He was sometimes the charlatan and some of his effects were due to special tunings (scordatures), but his virtuosity has never been rivalled. C. 24 caprices for violin-solo; of which pf.-transcriptions were made by Schumann and Liszt; 12 sonatas for violin and guitar (op. 2); do. (op. 3); 3 gran quartetti; concerto in E♭ (solo part in D, for a vln. tuned a semitone high); concerto in B min.; *"La Campanella,"* with Rondo à la clochette (op. 7); variations on many themes, *"Le Streghe," "God save the King," "The Carnival of Venice,"*

etc.; concert Allegro *"Moto perpetuo"* (op. 12); a sonata with accomp. of vln., 'cello or pf., and studies, etc. Biog. by Fétis (Paris, 1851; London, 1852); A. Niggli (1882); O. Bruni (Florence, 1873). Other studies by Stratton (1907), Prod'homme (1907), Bonaventura (1911), Kapp (1913), Day (1929), and Codignola (1936).

Page, (1) **J.,** England, ca. 1750—London, 1812; tenor. (2) **Nathaniel Clifford,** b. San Francisco, Oct. 26, 1866; pupil of E. S. Kelley; after 1895 res. in N. Y. as mus. editor; c. an opera *"The First Lieutenant"* (1889); incid. mus. for *"Moonlight Blossom"* (London, 1898), using Japanese themes; orch. suites, piano pieces, songs, etc.

Paine (pān), **J. Knowles,** Portland, Me., Jan. 9, 1839—Cambridge, Mass., April 25, 1906; American composer of importance; pupil of Kotzschmar, at Portland, Haupt (cpt.), Fischer (singing), and Wieprecht (instr.), Berlin; gave org.-concerts in Berlin and American cities, then lived in Boston as organist West Church; 1862, teacher of mus. Harvard Univ., and organist at Appleton Chapel, Cambridge; from 1876, prof. of mus. and organist at Harvard; c. an opera (text and mus.) *"Azara";* oratorio *"St. Peter," "Centennial Hymn,"* with orch. (to open the Philadelphia Exposition, 1876); *"Columbus March and Hymn"* (to open the Columbian Exposition, Chicago, 1893); mus. to Sophokles' *"Œdipus Tyrannus"* for male voices and orch. (prod. at Harvard, 1881); 3 cantatas with orch. *"The Realm of Fancy," "The Nativity," "Song of Promise,"* 2 symphs. op. 23, in C min., and op. 34 in A (*"Spring symph."*); 2 symph. poems, *"The Tempest"* and *"An Island Fantasy";* overture to *"As You Like It";* Domine Salvum with orch.; mass, with orch.; chamber-mus., vln.-sonata, etc.

Paisiello (pä-ē-sĭ-ĕl'-lō) (or **Paesiello**) (pä-ā-sĭ-ĕl'-lō), Taranto, Italy, May 9, 1740—Naples, June 5, 1816. At 5 studied at Jesuit sch. in Taranto with a priest Resta; later studied with Durante, Cotumacci and Abos, Cons. di S. Onofrio, at Naples: teacher there, 1759–61. He c. masses, etc., till a comic intermezzo

(Cons. Theatre, 1763) won him a commission to c. an opera for the Marsigli Th., at Bologna, where his comic opera "*La Pupilla, ossio il Mondo alla Rovescia,*" was prod. 1764. (Grove calls this work 2 operas.) In 12 years he prod. 50 operas mainly succ., though in rivalry with Piccinni and Cimarosa; these include "*Il Marchese di Tulipano*" (Rome, 1766); "*L'Idolo Cinese*" (Naples, 1767) and "*La Serva Padrona*" (Naples, 1769). He was notable also for his jealousy and devotion to intrigue. 1776-84, St. Petersburg, with a splendid salary and on invitation from Empress Catherine. Here he prod. 1776 "*Il Barbiere di Siviglia,*" gaining such succ. that the later and better opera by Rossini was received as a sacrilege with great hostility at first; on his return from Russia he prod. at Vienna one of his best works, "*Il Re Teodoro,*" and 12 symph. for Joseph II. 1784-99, cond. to Ferdinand IV. of Naples; and prod. various works incl. "*L'Olimpiade*" (1786) and "*Nina, o la Pazza per Amore*" (1789), "*La Molinara*" and "*I Zingari in Fiera.*" During the revolution 1799-1801, he won the favour of the Republican govt., also regained the favour of royalty at the Restoration, till Napoleon who had always admired him called him to Paris, 1802-03, as cond. Here P. lived in magnificence, lording it over Cherubini and Méhul. 1803-15, he was in Naples again as ct.-cond. In 1815, on the return of Ferdinand IV., he was reduced to a small salary; soon his wife died, and he shortly after. A composer of great prolificity, melodic grace and simplicity, his works are rarely heard now. He c. 100 operas, a Passion oratorio (Warsaw, 1784); 3 solemn masses, Te Deum for double chorus and 2 orch.; requiem with orch. (performed at his own funeral); 30 masses with orch., 40 motets, 12 symphs., and other things in proportion. Biog. by Le Seuer (1816), Quatremere de Quincy (1817), Schizzi (Milan, 1833), Villarosa (Naples, 1840); other memoirs by Palma (1891), Pupino (1908), Panareo (1910), and Abert (1919).

Paix (pä'-ēx), **Jacob**, Augsburg, 1550—after 1590; organist and composer.

Paladilhe (păl-ä-dēl), **Émile**, Montpellier, June 3, 1844—Paris, Jan. 8, 1926; studied with Marmontel (pf.), Benoit (org.) and Halévy (cpt.), Paris Cons.; won 1st prize for pf. and org., 1857; 1860, Grand prix de Rome, with the cantata "*Le Czar Ivan IV.*" (Opéra, 1860); from Rome, he sent an Italian opera buffa, an overture and a symph.; 1872, prod. the 1-act comic opera "*Le Passant*" (Op.-Com.) followed by 5 operas incl. the still pop. "*Patrie*" (Opéra, 1886; 1889, Hamburg, as "*Vaterland*"; 1895, Milan, as "*Patria*"); and c. also 2 masses, a symph., chamber music, piano pieces, songs, etc.

Palestrina (pä-lĕs-trē'-nä) (rightly **Giovanni Pierluigi Sante**, called **da Palestrina**, from his birthplace), Palestrina, near Rome, probably Dec. 27, 1525 (though date has long been controversial)—Rome, Feb. 2, 1594. One of the most revered names in liturgical music and the foremost composer of the Roman Catholic Church; he was b. of poor parents, little is known of his early life; he is said to have earned his living first as a church-singer; probably studied in Goudimel's sch., 1540, and was, 1544-51, organist at Palestrina, then magister puerorum (master of the boys), in the Cappella Giula, with title "maestro della capella della Basilica Vaticana." He dedicated a book of masses to Pope Julius III., who, Jan., 1554, admitted him to the Pontifical Chapel as a singer, against the rules, P. having a wife and no voice. July 30, 1555, Paul IV. dismissed him with a pension of 6 scudi per month. This blow affected him so deeply (he had 4 children to support) that he suffered nervous prostration. On Oct. 1, however, the Pope appointed him cond. at the Lateran. 1560, he prod. his famous "*Improperia*" (v. D. D.) for Holy Week, with such succ., that the Pope secured them for the Sistine Chapel, where they have been performed on every Good Friday since. 1561, he took the better-salaried post of cond. at Santa Maria Maggiore. The Pope was determined to rid church-mus. of its astonishing secular qualities: first, the use of street-ballads, even when indecent, as *canti fermi*, many of the choir actually singing the words; and second, the riotous counterpoint with which the sacred texts and the secular tunes were overrun. The Council of Trent and a committee of 8 cardinals, considering the matter seriously, decided not to revolutionise church-music entirely, and in 1564 commissioned Palestrina, by this time famous, to write a mass which should reform, without uprooting, ecclesiastical polyphony. He wrote three, all noble, the third, the "*Missa papæ Marcelli*," winning the most profound praise. He was called "the saviour of music," and appointed composer to the Pontifical Chapel. 1571, he became and remained till death maestro of St. Peter's. He also composed for the "Congregazione del Oratorio" (v. NERI); taught in Nanini's sch., and was from 1581 maestro concertatore to Prince Buoncompagni. Pope Sixtus V. wished to appoint him maestro of the Sistine Chapel, but the singers refused to serve under a layman. He was, however, commissioned to revise the Roman Gradual and Antiphonal, by Pope Gregory XIII.; he pub. the "Directorium chori" (1582), the offices of Holy Week (1587), and the *Præfationes* (1588), but on the death of his pupil and assist. Giudetti, he was compelled to leave the work unfinished. A complete ed. of his works is pub. by Breitkopf and Härtel: Vols. i.–vii. contain 262 motets; Vol. viii., 45 hymns; Vol. ix., 68 offertories; Vols. x.–xxiv., 92 Masses; Vol. xxv., 9 Lamentations each in various arrangements in 3, 4, 5, 6, or 8 parts; Vol. xxvi., 17 Litanies, Motets and Psalms in 3–12 parts; Vol. xxvii., 35 Magnificats; Vol. xxviii., about 90 Italian (secular) Madrigals; Vol. xxix., 56 Church-Madrigals (Latin); Vol. xxx. (from cols. of 16th-17th cent.), 12 Cantiones sacræ, 12 Cant. profanæ, and 14 Cant. sacræ; Vol. xxxi. (from archives of the Pontifical Chapel, etc.), 56 miscellaneous numbers, many doubtful, incl. 11, "Esercizi sopra la scala"; Vol. xxxii., 60 miscellaneous comp. incl. 8 Ricercari, Responses, Antiphones, etc.; Vol. xxxiii., Documents, Index, Bibliography, etc. Among his best masses are "*Æterna Christi numera,*" "*Dies*

sanctificatus," "*O sacrum convivium,*" in 8 parts; "*Assumpta est Maria in coelum,*" "*Dilexi quoniam,*" "*Ecce ego Joannes,*" "*Papæ Marcelli*" in 6 parts; "*Tu es Petrus*" in 6 parts; these, the Motet "*Exaudi Domine,*" 3 Lamentations, also selected Madrigals, Canzonets, etc., are pub. separately. Biog. by Baini (Rome, 1828); A. Bartolini (Rome, 1870); Bäumker (1877); Cametti (Milan, 1895). Also further studies by Brenet (1905); Raf. Casimiri (1918); Zoe Kendrick Pyne (1922); P. Wagner, etc. (See article, page 509.)

Pallavicini (päl-lä-vē-chē'-nē), (1) (or **Pallavicino**) **Benedetto,** Cremona —Mantua (?), after 1616; conductor and composer. (2) **Carlo,** Brescia, 1630—Dresden, 1688; conductor and dram. composer.

Palme (päl'-mĕ), **Rudolph,** Barby-on-Elbe, Oct. 23, 1834—Magdeburg, Jan. 8, 1909; pupil of A. G. Ritter; organist; R. Mus. Dir. and organist at Magdeburg; c. concert-fantasias with male chorus, sonatas, etc., for org.

Palm'er, Horatio Richmond, Sherburne, N. Y., April 26, 1834— Yonkers, N. Y., 1907; pupil of his father and sister, and studied in New York, Berlin and Florence; at 18, began composing; at 20 choruscond.; 1857, teacher at Rushford Acad.; after the Civil War, Chicago; ed. *Concordia;* cond. various societies from 1873, cond. New Church Choral Union, giving concerts, sometimes with 4,000 singers; 1877, Dean of the Chautauqua Sch. of Mus.; Mus. Doc. (Chicago Univ. and Alfred Univ.); pub. colls. and treatises.

Palm'gren, Selim, b. Björneborg, Finland, Feb. 16, 1878—d. 1952; studied at Helsingfors Cons., and with Berger, Klathe and Busoni; toured Scandinavia as pianist, 1900; cond. Helsingfors choral society and later the orch. in Abo; c. operas, piano concertos, symphonic poems, piano pieces, choruses and songs, some of these having internat'l hearings; 1923, teacher of comp. at Eastman School of Music, Rochester, N. Y.; m. Maikki Järnefelt, singer.

Paloschi (pä-lôs'-kē), **Giov.,** 1824— 1892, member of the Milan firm of Ricordi.

Palot'ta, Matteo, Palermo, 1680— Vienna, 1758; ct.-composer and writer.

Paminger (pä'-mĭng-ĕr) (or **Pammigerus, Panni'gerus), Leonhardt,** Aschau, Upper Alsatia, 1495—Passau, 1567; composer.

Pancera (pän-chä'-rä), **Ella,** Vienna, Aug. 15, 1875 (of Italian parents) —Bad Ischl, May 10, 1932; pianist; pupil of Epstein and Vockner; début at 13; toured widely.

Panizza (pä-nĭd'-zä), **Ettore,** b. Buenos Aires, Aug. 12, 1875; conductor; pupil of Milan Cons.; after 1899 active as cond. in various Italian theatres; 1907-13, Covent Garden; 1916, La Scala; also in Paris, Buenos Aires; Chicago Op., and after 1934 as chief cond. of Italian works at Met. Op., succeeding Serafin; c. opera "*Il fidanzeto del mare*" (Buenos Aires, 1897); "*Medioevo latino*" (Geneva, 1900); "*Aurora*" (Buenos Aires, 1908); translated Berlioz's treatise on instrumentation (1913).

Pan'ny, Jos., Kolmitzberg. Lower Austria, 1794—Mayence, 1838; violinist, teacher and composer.

Panof'ka, H., Breslau, 1807—Florence, 1887; violinist, writer and composer.

Panseron (pän-sŭ-rôṅ), **Aug. Mathieu,** Paris, 1796—1859; writer of vocal methods, études, etc.; composer.

Panzner (pänts'-nĕr), **K.,** Teplitz, Bohemia, March 2, 1866—Düsseldorf, Dec. 7, 1923; pupil of Nicodé and Dräeseke; cond. at Sondershausen th.; 2 years later at Elberfeld; 1893, 1st cond. Leipzig city th.; 1899, cond. Philh. concerts, Bremen; after 1909, munic. dir. of music, Düsseldorf.

Paolucci (pä-ō-loo'-chē), **Giuseppe,** Siena, May 25, 1726—Assisi, April 26, 1776; Franciscan monk; c. church music.

Pape (pä'-pĕ), **Jn. H.,** Sarstedt, near Hanover, July 1, 1789—Paris, Feb. 2, 1875; distinguished maker and improver of the piano; he inv. a transposing piano, introd. padded hammers, etc.

Papier (pä-pēr'), (1) **Louis,** Leipzig, 1829—1878; organist, singing-teacher and composer. (2) **Rosa,** Baden, near Vienna, 1858—Vienna, Feb. 9, 1932; mezzo-soprano; Imp. Op., Vienna; 1881, m. Dr. Hans Paumgartner.

Papini (pä-pē'-nē), **Guido,** Camagiore, near Florence, Aug. 1, 1847—London, Oct. 20, 1912; violinist; pupil of

Giorgetti; début at 13; toured Europe; composer.

Papperitz (pap'-pē-rēts), **Benj. Robt.,** Pirna, Saxony, Dec. 4, 1826—Leipzig, Sept. 29, 1903; pupil of Hauptmann, Richter and Moscheles, Leipzig Cons., 1851; teacher of harm. and cpt. there; from 1868-69, also organist of Nikolaikirche there; 1882, R. Prof.; composer.

Paque (päk), **Guil.,** Brussels, 1825— London, 1876; 'cello-virtuoso and teacher.

Paradies (or **Paradisi**) (pä-rä-dē'-ĕs, or dē'-sē), **P. Dom.,** Naples, 1710— Venice, 1792; pupil of Porpora; harps.-player and teacher, also dram. composer.

Paradis (pä-rä-dĕs'), **Maria Theresia von,** Vienna, May 15, 1759— Feb. 1, 1824; a skilful blind organist and pianist for whom Mozart wrote a concerto; daughter of an Imperial Councillor; teacher of pf. and voice; c. an opera.

Paray (pär-ä'-ē), **Paul,** b. Tréport, France, May 24, 1886; conductor; pupil of Paris Cons., Prix de Rome winner; after 1921 cond. Lamoureux Concerts, Paris, succeeding Chevillard in 1923 as leader of this orch.; cond. Detroit Symph. after 1952.

Parent (pă-räṅ), **Charlotte Frances Hortense,** London, March 22, 1837— Paris, Jan. 12, 1929; pianist; pupil of Mme. Farreṅc, Paris Cons.; founded "École préparatoire au professorat," Paris; wrote a pf.-method, etc. (2) **Armand,** Liége, Feb. 5, 1863—Paris, Jan. 19, 1934; noted violinist.

Parepa-Rosa (pä-rä'-pä-rō'-zä) (née **Parepa de Boyescu), Euphrosyne,** Edinburgh, May 7, 1836—London, Jan. 21, 1874; daughter and pupil of Elizabeth Seguin, a singer; eminent soprano in opera and oratorio; her strong and sympathetic voice had a compass of 2½ octaves reaching to d''' (v. PITCH, D.D.); début at 16, Malta; 1865 m. Carl Rosa; toured Europe and America.

Par'ish-Al'vars, Elias, Teignmouth, Engl., Feb. 28, 1808—Vienna, Jan. 25, 1849; of Jewish descent; noted harp-virtuoso and composer.

Parisini (pä-rĭ-sē'-nē), **Federico,** Bologna, 1825—Jan. 4, 1891; theorist and dram. composer.

Parke, (1) **J.,** 1745—1829; Engl. oboist and composer. (2) **Wm. Thos.,**

London, 1762—1847; bro. of above; oboist, composer and writer.

Park'er, (1) Jas. Cutler Dunn, Boston, Mass., June 2, 1828—1916; studied Leipzig Cons.; lived in Boston and Brookline; 1862, organist "Parker Club," vocal soc.; 1864-91, organist Trinity Ch., and for years organist Händel and Haydn Soc.; prof. Boston Univ. Coll. of Mus., and Examiner N. E. Cons.; writer and transl.; c. *"Redemption Hymn"* (1877); cantata *"The Blind King"* (1886); *"St. John,"* with orch.; oratorio, *"The Life of Man"*; church-services, etc. (2) **H.,** b. London, Aug. 4, 1845; pupil of Leipzig Cons., and of Lefort, Paris; singing-teacher and cond. London; wrote treatise *"The Voice"*; c. comic opera *"Mignonette"* (London, 1889); *"Jerusalem,"* for bass-solo and chorus (Albert Hall, 1884); gavottes, etc., for orch.; pf.-pcs. (3) **Horatio Wm.,** Auburndale, Mass., Sept. 15, 1863—Cedarhurst, N. Y., Dec. 18, 1919; prominent American composer; pupil of his mother, later of Emery (theory) J. Orth (pf.), and Chadwick (comp.), Boston; organist Dedham and Boston; studied 1882-85 with Rheinberger (org. and comp.) and L. Abel (cond.), Munich; organist and prof. of mus. St. Paul's Sch., Garden City, New York; 1886, organist St. Andrew's, Harlem; 1888, Ch. of the Holy Trinity, N. Y.; 1894, prof. of mus., Yale Univ.; 1899, cond. his notable oratorio *"Hora Novissima"* at Worcester (Engl.) Festival with great succ. (first given at Worcester [U. S. A.] Festival, 1893). Pub. coll. of org.-pcs. In May, 1911, his opera *"Mona,"* libretto by Brian Hooker (b. N. Y. Nov. 2, 1880, a graduate of Yale, 1902, and instructor there 1905-10), won the $10,000 prize offered by the Met. Op. Co. for the best grand opera in English by an American. It was prod. with succ., 1912; his opera *"Fairyland"* (text by Hooker) won prize offered by Nat'l. Fed. of Women's Clubs and was perf. at the fest. of this body at Los Angeles, 1915; Mus. D., Cambridge Univ., 1902; c. oratorios, *"Hora Novissima"* (1893), and *"St. Christopher"* (1896); cantatas *"King Trojan"* (Munich, 1885), *"The Holy Child," "The Kobold"* and *"Harold Harfager,"* prize-cantata, *"Dream King"* (1893);

symph. in C.; concert-overture; heroic-overture *"Regulus"*; overture to *"Count Robert of Paris," "Cohal Mahr,"* for bar.-solo and orch. (1893); *"Commencement Ode,"* Yale Univ. (1895); McCagg prize chorus *a cappella* (1898); *"A Northern Ballad"* for orch. (1899); also many other choruses; string quintet; string quartet; suite for piano trio; violin suite, songs, etc. (4) **Henry Taylor,** Boston, 1867—March 30, 1934; music and dramatic critic; after 1905 until his death, the distinguished critic of the Boston *Transcript*, noted for a highly analytic if somewhat involved literary style.

(Parkina) Park'inson, Elizabeth, Kansas City, Mo., 1882—Colorado Springs, Col., 1922; soprano; pupil of Mrs. Lawton, Kansas City, Miolan Carvalho, de la Nux and Mme. Marchesi; début, Paris, 1902; Covent Garden, 1904-07; also sang at English fests. and concerts; toured Australia.

Par'low, Kathleen, b. Calgary, Canada 1890; violinist; taken to California at 5, and studied there with Conrad and Holmes; début there at 6; at 15 gave a recital in London and appeared with the London Symph. Orch.; then studied with Auer; 1907 began to tour.

Par'ratt, Sir Walter, Huddersfield, Feb. 10, 1841—Windsor, March 27, 1924; at 7 sang in church; at 10 knew Bach's *"Well-tempered Clavichord"* by heart; at 11, organist Armitage Bridge; 1872 Magdalen Coll., Oxford; 1882, St. George's Chapel, Windsor Mus. Bac. Oxon., 1873; 1883, organ-prof. R. C. M.; knighted 1892; 1893, Master of Mus. in Ordinary to the Queen and 1901 to the King; prof. of music, Oxford Univ., 1908-18; wrote articles; c. mus. to *"Agamemnon"* and *"Orestes," "Elegy to Patroclus,"* anthems, org · and pf.-pcs., etc.

Par'ry, (1) J., Ruabon, N. Wales— Wynnstay, Oct. 7, 1782; Welsh bard, harper, and composer. (2) **J.** (called "Bardd Alaw," i e., master of song), Denbigh, Feb. 18, 1776—London, April 8, 1851; clarinettist; cond. of the Eisteddfod for years; critic, teacher and composer in London; pub. colls., etc. (3) **J. Orlando,** London, 1810—E. Molesey, 1879; son of above; pianist, harpist, singer and composer. (4) Jos., Merthyr Tydvil, Wales, May 21, 1841—Penarth, Feb. 17, 1903; the son of a labourer; at 10 worked in a puddling-furnace; 1854 emigrated to America with his family, but returned to Britain, won Eisteddfod prizes for songs; 1868 studied R. A. M. on a fund especially raised by Brinley Richards; 1871, Mus. Bac. Cambr.; prof. of music, Univ. Col., Aberystwith; 1878, Mus. Doc.; 1888, Mus. Lecturer at Cardiff; also Fellow R. A. M. C. 4 operas, cantatas *"The Prodigal Son," "Nebuchadnezzar,"* and *"Cambria"; "Druids' Chorus";* an orchestral ballade, overtures, etc.

(5) Sir **Chas. Hubert Hastings,** Bournemouth, England, Feb. 27, 1848—near Littlehampton, Oct. 7, 1918; eminent English composer; from 1861, while at Eton, pupil of G. Elvy (comp.), was pianist, organist, singer, and composer at the concerts of the Musical Soc. At 18, while still at Eton, he took "Mus. Bac." at Oxford, wrote a cantata, *"O Lord, Thou hast cast us out"*; 1867, Exeter Coll., Oxford; founded "Univ. Mus. Club"; 1874, M. A.; studied with Bennett and Macfarren, and Dannreuther (pf.), and Pierson, Stuttgart. At 26 prod. *"Intermezzo religioso,"* for strings (Gloucester Festival); 1883, Choragus of Oxford and Mus. Doc. Cantab.; do. Oxon, 1884, do. Dublin, 1891; 1894 dir. R. C. M.; 1898, knighted; 1902 made a baronet; active as lecturer and writer of essays and books incl. the notable *"Evolution of the Art of Music"* (1896). C. also 4 symphs.; symph vars.; overtures, *"To an Unwritten Tragedy"* and *"Guillem de Cabestanh"*; oratorios *"Judith," "Job," "King Saul"*; mus. to Aristophanes' *"Birds"* (1883), and *"Frogs"* (1892); and to *"Hypatia"* (1893); the following were prod. at prominent festivals: scenes from Shelley's *"Prometheus Unbound,"* with orch. (Gloucester festival, 1880); *"The Glories of Our Blood and State"; "Suite moderne," "Ode on St. Cecilia's Day," "L'Allegro ed Il Penseroso," "De profundis,"* with 3 choirs and orch.; chamber-mus.; vln.-and pf.-sonatas, songs, etc.; *"Invocation to Music"*; Magnificat, in Latin. In 1908 his health forcd his resignation of the Oxford Professorship; c.

also Processional Music for the coronation of Edward VII (1903); a simfonia sacra for soli, chorus and orch. (Gloucester Festival, 1904); music to Aristophanes' *"Clouds"* (Oxford, 1905); Browning's *"Pied Piper"* with orch. (Norwich Fest., 1905); symph. poem *"The Vision of Life"* (Cardiff Fest., 1907); cantata (Worcester Fest., 1908); revision of 4th symph. (Philharmonic, 1910); wrote important work on Bach; *"The Music of the 17th Century,"* for the Oxford History of Music (1902), etc.

Par'sons, (1) **Robt.,** Exeter, drowned Newark, Engl., 1569; composer. (2) **J.,** d. 1623; probably son of above; organist and composer. (3) Sir **Wm.,** 1746—1817: master of King's Band and teacher. (4) **Albert Ross,** Sandusky, O., Sept. 16, 1847—Mt. Kisco, N. Y., June 14, 1933; noteworthy American teacher; pupil of F. K. Ritter, N. Y., and at Leipzig Cons.; later of Tausig, Kullak, Weitzmann and Würst, Berlin; 1871, New York; organist 1885, Fifth Av. Presb. Ch.; same year taught at Met. Coll. of Music; 1890, pres. Music Teachers' Nat'l. Assoc.; 1893, head of Amer. Coll. of Musicians; translator, editor, and writer of various works; c. vocal quartets. songs, etc.

Pasdeloup (pä-dŭ-loo), **Jules Étienne,** Paris, Sept. 15, 1819—Fontainebleau, Aug. 13, 1887; eminent cond.· pianist; pupil Paris Cons., 1847-50, pf.-teacher, and 1855-68, teacher of ensemble there; 1851, cond. famou concerts (known from 1861 "concerts populaires"); v. succ. till 1884, when they fell before the popularity of Colonne and Lamoureux; a benefit festival brought him 100,000 francs ($20,000).

Pasquali (päs-kwä'-lē), **Nicoló,** Italy—Edinburgh, 1757; writer and composer.

Pasqué (păs-kā'), **Ernst,** Cologne, 1821—Alsbach, 1892; barytone; director and writer.

Pasquini (päs-kwē'-nē), **Bdo.,** Massa di Valdinevole, Tuscany, Dec. 8, 1637—Rome, Nov. 22, 1710; noted organist at San Maria Maggiore; pupil of Vittori and Cesti; teacher and composer of 10 operas, 8 oratorios, cantatas, sonatas, suites, etc.

Pasta (päs'-tä) (née **Negri**), (1) **Giuditta,** Milan, April 9, 1798—villa on

Lake Como, April 1, 1865; a noted Jewish singer; pupil of Asioli; début, 1815, but had no succ.; studied with Scappa, and reappeared with greatest succ. Her powerful voice (range a–d''', v. PITCH, D. D.) had always some irregularities, but her dramatic power was great and she invented embellishments with much skill; m. the tenor (2) **Pasta**, before 1816; she created "La Sonnambula" and "Norma" and earned a fortune.

Pas'ternack, Jos. A., Czentochowa, Poland, 1881—Chicago, April 29, 1940; studied Warsaw Cons.; violist in Met. Op. orch. and asst. cond., 1909–10; cond. Century Op. Co., afterward of Phila. Philh.; Boston "Pops," 1916; mus. dir., Victor Phon. Co. and Stanley Co. of America; after 1927 cond. in radio programmes for Nat'l. Broadcasting Co.

Pa'tey, Janet Monach (née Whytock), London, 1842—Sheffield, 1894; alto.

Pa'ton, Mary Ann (Mrs. Wood), Edinburgh, 1802—Bucliffe Hall, near Wakefield, 1864; prominent soprano; m. tenor Jos. Wood, 1831.

Patti (pät'tē), (1) **Carlotta**, Florence, 1840—Paris, June 27, 1889; eminent concert colorature-soprano; pupil of her father, (2) **Salvatore P.**, a tenor, and her mother, (3) **Caterina** (née Chiesa), a soprano. (4) **Adelina (Adela Juana Maria)**, Madrid, Feb. 10, 1843—Craig-y-Nos, Breconshire, Wales, Sept. 27, 1919; one of the most eminent colorature-singers in history; sister of (1), and like her a pupil of her parents; sang in public as a mere child; then studied with Max Strakosch (husband of her sister Amelia); début, at 16, New York, Nov. 24, 1859, as "Lucia" (under the stage-name "the little Florinda"); 1861, London, Covent Garden; 1862, Paris Th. Italien; 1868, m. the Marquis de Caux. Her career, covering more than 40 years, brought her phenomenal adulation in the principal music centres, although she sang only about 30 rôles and these usually in the older Italian operas. Not a great actress, she relied for her effects upon consummate vocal technique rather than emotional powers. She withdrew from the stage 1906 and, except for a brief tour in the U. S., lived at her castle Craig-y-Nos, in Wales. 1886, m. and toured with the tenor Nicolini (d.

1898); 1899 m. a Swedish nobleman, Baron Cederström. (5) **Carlo**, Madrid, 1842—St. Louis, Mo., March, 1873; bro. of above: violinist.

Pat'tison, (1) **J. Nelson**, Niagara Falls, N. Y., Oct. 22, 1845—New York, 1905; pianist; pupil of Liszt, Thalberg, Henselt and von Bülow (pf.), and Haupt (harm.); toured U. S. as pianist with Parepa Rosa, etc.; c. symph. for orch. and military band "Niagara"; concert overture, etc. (2) **Lee, b.** Grand Rapids, Wis., July 22, 1890; pianist and composer; grad. New England Cons. with honours; studied piano with Baermann and Schnabel; comp. with Chadwick and Juon; début, Boston, 1913; has made many tours in duo-piano recitals with Guy Maier, and in double concertos with leading Amer. orchs.; c. songs and piano works, made many transcriptions for two pianos; dir. of Met. Op. spring season, 1937.

Pauer (pow'-ĕr), (1) **Ernst**, Vienna, Dec. 21, 1826—near Darmstadt, May 9, 1905; noted pianist; son of a prominent Lutheran clergyman; pupil of Th. Dirza, W. A. Mozart, Jr. (pf.), and Sechter (comp.), later of Fr. Lachner, Munich; 1847–51, dir. mus. societies at Mayence; 1851, London; 1859, prof. at the R. A. M.; in 1861, gave historical performances of clavecin and pf.-mus.; 1866, pianist to Austrian Court; 1867, prof. at the Nat. Training Sch.; 1883, R. C. M.; 1870, lecturer; toured U. S.; ed. the classics; pub. mus. primers, colls. of old clavier-works, and many didactic works; c. a quintet, vln. arrangements of symphs., etc. (2) **Max.**, b. London, Oct. 31, 1866; son and pupil of above; then studied with Lachner Carlsruhe; 1887, pf.-prof. Cologne Cons.; 1893, chamber-virtuoso to the Grand Duke of Hesse; 1897, prof. Stuttgart Cons.; 1898, made prof. by the King of Würtemberg; he became dir. of Stuttgart Cons. 1908, succeeding De Lange; 1924, dir. Leipzig Cons.; pub. pf.-pieces.

Pauly, Rose, Hungarian sopr.; sang "Elektra" with striking success, Met. Op., 1937–8.

Paumann (pow'-män), **Konrad, b.** (blind) Nürnberg, ca. 1410—Munich, Jan. 25, 1473; c. the oldest extant book of org.-pcs.

Paumgartner (powm'-gärtnĕr), (1) Dr. **Hans,** 1844—Vienna, May 23, 1893; pianist; critic and composer. (2) **Bernhard,** b. Vienna, Nov. 14, 1887; after 1919 dir. Salzburg Mozarteum.

Paur (powr), (1) **Emil,** Czernowitz, Bukovina, Aug. 29, 1855—Mistek, Moravia, June 7, 1932; noted conductor; pupil of his father; at 8 he played vln. and pf. in public; studied with Dessoff (comp.) and Hellmesberger (vln.) Vienna Cons. (fellow pupil with Nikisch and Mottl); graduated with first prizes; 1870, first vln. and assist.-soloist in ct.-opera orch.; 1876, cond. at Cassel; later Königsberg; 1880, 1st ct.-cond. Mannheim; 1891, cond. Leipzig City Th.; 1893–98, cond. Boston (U. S. A.) symph. Orch. (vice Nikisch); 1898, New York Philh. Concerts (vice Seidl); 1899—1902, dir. of the Nat. Cons., N. Y. (vice Dvořák); 1900, cond. German opera of the Met. Op.; he returned to Europe, 1903; cond. concerts in Madrid; 1904–10, returned to the U. S. as cond. Pittsburgh Symph. Orch.; 1912–13, at Berlin Op.; c. symphony; piano concerto; vln. concerto, string quartet, vln. sonata, pf.-pcs., songs. (2) **Maria** (née **Burger**), Gengenbach, Black Forest, 1862—New York, 1899; wife of above; pianist; pupil Stuttgart Cons., Leschetizky and Essipoff, Vienna. (3) **Kurt,** son of (1) and (2), an accomplished pianist; res. in the U. S.

Pauwels (pow'-vĕls), **Jean Engelbert,** Brussels, 1768—1804; violinist, conductor and dram. composer.

Pavesi (pä-vä'-sē), **Stefano,** Cremona, 1779—Crema, 1850; dram. composer.

Pax'ton, Stephen, d. 1787; Engl. composer.

Payer (pī-ĕr), **Hieronymus,** Meidling, near Vienna, 1787—Wiedburg, near Vienna, 1845; conductor and dram. composer.

Peace, Albert Lister, Huddersfield, Engl., Jan. 26, 1844—Liverpool, March 14, 1912; prominent organist; pupil of Horn and Parratt; 1875, Mus. Doc. Oxon; 1873, organist Glasgow cath.; 1897, of St. George's Hall, Liverpool (vice Best); c. Psalm 138 with orch., org.-music.

Pearce, (1) **Stephen Austen,** London, Nov. 7, 1836—April 9, 1900; pupil of J. L. Hopkins; Mus. Doc. Oxford, 1864, same year U. S. and Canada;

then organist 2 London churches; 1872, vocal-teacher, Columbia Coll., N. Y., and lecturer Peabody Inst. and Johns Hopkins Univ., Baltimore; 1879–85, organist Collegiate Church, N. Y.; writer and composer of a 3-act opera, a children's opera, an oratorio and a church-cantata in strict fugal style (prod. at Oxford), overture, etc. (2) **Chas. Wm.,** Salisbury, England, Dec. 5, 1856—London, Dec. 2, 1928; pupil of Ayluard, Hoyte, Read and Prout; 1881, Mus. Bac., 1884 Mus. Doc., Cambridge. From 1871 organist various London churches. 1882 Prof. of Trinity College; co-editor, organist and choir-master; wrote various text-books, and c. an oratorio.

Pear'sall, Robt. Lucas De, Clifton, Engl., 1795—Schloss Wartensee, Lake of Constance, 1856; writer and composer.

Pearson. Vide PIERSON.

Pedrell (pā'-dhrĕl), **Felipe,** Tortosa, Spain, Feb. 19, 1841—Barcelona, Aug. 19, 1922; composer; 1894, prof. of Mus. History and Æsthetics, Royal Cons., Madrid; editor, critic, lexicographer and writer; c. operas, including "*Quasimodo*" (Barcelona, 1875), a trilogy "*Los Pinneos*" (Barcelona, 1902), "*La Celestina*" (1904), "*La Matinada*" (1905), a Gloria mass with orch.; also wrote and edited important historical works.

Pedrotti (pā-drôt'-tē), **Carlo,** Verona, Nov. 12, 1817—suicide, Oct. 16, 1892; conductor and composer of 16 operas, etc.

Peerce, Jan, Amer. tenor; début Met. Op., 1940.

Pelletier (pĕl'-tē-ā), **Wilfred,** b. Canada; conductor; won Quebec gov't. scholarship, studied in Europe; early tours as accompanist; cond. Met. Op., N. Y., also with Ravinia, Los Angeles and San Francisco Op., and as guest with Canadian orchs.; m. Queena Mario, soprano; divorced. (2) Rose Bampton.

Pembaur (päm'-bowr), (1) **Jos.,** Innsbruck, May 23, 1848—Feb. 19, 1923; studied Vienna Cons., later at Munich R. Sch. of Mus.; 1875, dir. and headmaster, Innsbruck Mus. Sch.; prod. v. succ. opera "*Zigeunerleben*" (1898), choral works with orch.; symph. "*Im Tyrol*," etc. (2) **Jos.,** b. Innsbruck, April 2o,

1875; pianist; son of (1); taught Munich Acad., 1897–1900; Leipzig Cons., 1903–21; c. piano works, songs, etc. D. Munich, Jan. 30, 1937.

Peña y Goni (pän'-yä ē gō'-nē), **Antonio**, San Sebastian, Spain, 1846— Madrid, 1896; critic and composer.

Peñalosa (pĕn-yä-lō'-sä), **Francisco**, Spanish composer, 1470—1535; cond. to Ferdinand the Catholic, then singer in Papal Chapel.

Pénavaire (pä-nä-vār), **Jean Grégoire**, Lesparre, Sept. 15, 1840—Paris, Sept., 1906; composer; theatre-cond. at Nantes; c. overtures *"Tasso,"* *"Cervantes"*; symph. poem with chorus, *"La vision des Croisées,"* comic opera and ballets.

Pen'na, **Lorenzo**, Bologna, 1613— Imola, 1693; conductor and composer.

Pentenrieder (pĕn'-tĕn-rē-dĕr), **Fz. X.**, Kaufbeuren, Bavaria, 1813—Munich, 1867; organist and dram. composer.

Pepusch (pä'-poosh), **John Chr.** (**Jn. Chp.**), Berlin, 1667—London, July 20, 1752; violinist, composer and writer; pupil of Klingenberg and Grosse; held a position at the Prussian Court, but 1697 seeing the king kill an officer without trial he went to London. 1710 founded the famous "Academy of Antient Music"; 1712 organist and composer to Duke of Chandos (succeeded by Händel), dir. Lincoln Inn's Theatre, for which he c. 4 masques, the music to the enormously pop. *"Beggar's Opera,"* etc.; 1730 m. de l'Épire, the singer.

Perabo (pä'-rä-bō), (**Jn.**) **Ernst**, Wiesbaden, Germany, Nov. 14, 1845— Boston, Oct. 29, 1920; at 7 brought to New York; pupil of his father; then of Moscheles and Wenzel (pf.), Papperitz, Richter, and Hauptmann (harm.), and Reinecke (comp.), Leipzig Cons., returned to America, 1865; succ. concert-pianist; lived in Boston as teacher and pianist; c. arrangements, etc.

Pereira (pä-rä'-ē-rä), (1) **Marcos Soares**, Caminha, Portugal—Lisbon, Jan. 7, 1655; c. a mass, etc. (2) **Domingos Nuñes**, Lisbon—Camarate, near Lisbon, 1729; cond. and composer.

Perepelitzin (pä-rĕ-pĕ-lĕt'-shĕn), **Polycarp D.**, Odessa, Dec. 26, 1818— St. Petersburg, June 14, 1887; Russian colonel; pupil of Lipinski (vln.); writer and composer.

Perez (pä'-rĕth), **Davide**, (1) of Spanish parents, Naples, 1711—Lisbon, 1778; cond. at Palermo Cath.; 1752, ct.-cond., Lisbon; rival of Jomelli as c. of operas, incl. *"Demofoonte"*; c. also notable church-mus. (2) **Juan Ginez**, Orihuela, Murcia, Oct. 7, 1548—Orihuela, 1612; royal chaplain and comp. of church music.

Perfall (pĕr'-fäl), **K.**, Freiherr **von**, Munich, Jan. 29, 1824—Jan. 14, 1907; studied mus. with Hauptmann, Leipzig; 1854–64 founded and cond. the still succ. "Oratorio Soc."; in 1864, Intendant ct.-mus.; 1867– 1893, Intendant Ct.-Th.; writer and composer of operas, cantatas, etc.

Perger (pĕr'-gĕr), **Richard von**, Vienna, Jan. 10, 1854—Jan. 11, 1911; pupil of Brahms; 1890–95, dir. and cond. Rotterdam Cons.; 1895–99, cond. *"Gesellschafts-concerte,"* Vienna; 1899– 1907, dir. of Cons. there; prod. (text and mus.) succ. comic opera *"Der Richter von Granada"* (Cologne, 1889), a vaudeville, vln.-concerto, etc.

Pergolesi (pĕr-gō-lā'-sē), **Giov. Bat.**, Jesi, Papal States, Jan. 4, 1710—(of consumption) Pozzuoli, near Naples, March 16, 1736; eminent composer. At 16 entered the Cons. dei Poveri di Gesù Cristo, Naples, and studied with de Matteis (vln.), Greco (cpt.), Durante, and Feo (cpt.). He speedily won attention by novel harmonies and threw off contrapuntal shackles early. His last student-work, the biblical drama *"San Guglielmo D'Aquitania"* (prod. with comic intermezzi at the convent of S. Agnello Maggiore, Naples, 1731), shows the beginnings of vivid and original fancy. He prod. at Naples in 1731 the excellent and novel opera *"Sallustia,"* and the intermezzo *"Amor Fa l' Uomo Cieco,"* which had no succ., while the opera seria *"Ricimero"* was a distinct failure. But he found a patron in the Prince of Stigliano, for whom he wrote 30 terzets for vln. with bass; he was commissioned to compose a solemn mass for Naples, which was performed after the earthquake of 1731, as a votive offering to the patron saint of the city. It brought him immediate fame. After four stage-works, prod. in 1732 the intermezzo *"La Serva Padrona"* (Naples, 1733); won him note as a dramatic composer and has served as a model of comic operas since; it has only 2 characters and the accompaniment is a string-quartet with occasional support of horns. His subsequent 6 operas were received without interest (except for the intermezzo to "*Adriano*" first given as "*Livietta e Tracollo*" and later as "*La Contadina Astuta*"), though after his death they were revived with immense enthusiasm, and their harmonic novelty, sweetness, delicacy and melodic charm were recognised, "*La Serva Padrona*" and "*Il Maestro di Musica*" becoming standards in France. Of the failure of "*L'Olimpiade*," v. DUNI. Irregular habits due to regular disappointments undermined Pergolesi's constitution, and he died of consumption at the baths of Pozzuoli, finishing five days before his death his masterpiece, the celebrated "*Stabat Mater*" for soprano and alto with string orch. and org. He c. also 3 masses with orch.; Dixit for double chorus and orch.; a Kyrie cum gloria; a Miserere, and a Laudate with orch., etc.; an oratorio, "*La Natività*," a cantata "*Orfeo*" for solo voice and orch.; a cantata, "*Giasone*"; 6 cantatas with string-accomp.; 30 trios, etc. Biog. by Blasis (1817); Villarosa (1831). Other memoirs by Boyer, Fracassetti, Schletterer, Faustina-Fasini, Radiciotti, Barchiesi, etc.

Peri (pā'-rē), (1) **Jacopo** (called "**Il Zazzerino**," i.e., the long-haired), Rome, Aug. 20, 1561—Florence, Aug. 12, 1633; pupil of Malvezzi; court-cond. at 3 successive courts; an enthusiast in everything classic, he haunted the salons of Count Bardi and Corsi, where he joined the attempt at revival of Greek musical recitative, with Caccini and Corsi; he set to mus. Rinuccini's text of "*Dafne*"; this was doubtless the first opera ever written; its effort at reproducing the supposed manner of Æschylos, Sophokles, etc., was called "stile rappresentativo"; the opera was given only once, and privately at Bardi's house, but it won Peri a commission to set Rinuccini's text "*Euridice*" for the wedding of Maria de' Medici and Henry IV. of France (1600); an ed. of his works was pub. 1603, incl. madrigals, etc. (2) **Achille**. Reggio d'Emilia, Italy,

1812—1880; conductor and dram. composer.

Perisine. Vide LA RUE.

Perne (pǎrn), **Fran. L.**, Paris, 1772—May 26, 1832; pupil of Abbé d'Haudimont (harm. and cpt.); 1792, chorus-singer at the Opéra; 1799, double-bass player in the orch.; 1801, prod. a grand festival mass; the next year he c. a triple fugue to be sung backwards on reversing the page; 1811, prof. harm. at the Cons.; 1816, Inspector Gen.; 1819, libr., 1822, retired to an estate near Laon; he returned to Paris a few weeks before he died; he was indefatigable in research, and an authority on Greek notation, the troubadours, etc.; writer and composer.

Perosi (pā-rō'-sē), Don **Lorenzo**, b. Tortona, Italy, Dec. 20, 1872; a priest and organist who has composed a large variety of sacred mus.; it aims to use modern resources and ancient principles; pupil of Saladino, Milan Cons.; 1894, of Haberl's Domchorschule, Ratisbon; 1895, cond. at Imola; from 1897, at San Marco, Venice; his sacred trilogy "*La Passione di Cristo*" (a, "*La Cena del Signore*"; b, "*L'Orazione al Monte*"; c, "*La Morte del Redentore*"), Milan, 1897, at the Ital. Congress for Sacred Mus., created a sensation, and has been widely performed; 1898, Pope Leo XIII. made him honorary *maestro* of the Papal Choir; c. also 25 masses; c. also oratorios, "*La Transfigurazione del Nostro Signore Gesù Cristo*" (1898), "*La Risurrezione di Lazaro*" (Venice, July 27, 1898, in La Fenice Th., by special permission), "*Il Natale del Redentore*" (Como, 1899); "*Mosè*" (Rome, 1902); "*Leo the Great*" (1902), "*Il Giudizio Universale*" (The Last Judgment), Rome, 1904; and "*In Patris Memoriam*" (1910); orch. variations (1904), cantatas "*Anima*" (1908), and "*Dies Iste*"; requiem for Leo XIII. (1909), etc. He announced an ambitious undertaking to compose ten symphonies, each named after an Italian city, and had completed those devoted to Rome, Florence, Venice and Bologna when he suffered a nervous breakdown in 1917 and was obliged to forego composition. In 1922 he was reported to be confined in a sanitarium, but the following year was able to prepare a revision of his oratorio, "*The Resurrection*," which was presented at Rome.

Peroti'nus, Magnus, Magister; 12th cent. composer; conductor at Nôtre-Dame, Paris. (Coussemaker.)

Perotti (pä-rôt'-tē), Giov. Ag., Vercelli, 1769—Venice, 1855; writer and composer.

Perrin (pĕr-răṅ), Pierre (called *l'abbé*, though never ordained), Lyons, ca. 1620—Paris, 1675; librettist of the first French operas.

Perron (pĕr'-rōn), Karl, Frankenthal, Jan. 3, 1858—Dresden, July 15, 1928; barytone; studied with Hey and Hasselbeck and Stockhausen; concert-début, 1880; 1884-91, Leipzig City th.; then at Dresden ct.-opera.

Per'ry, (1) G., Norwich, 1793—London, 1862; director and composer. (2) Edw. Baxter, Haverhill, Mass., Feb. 17, 1855—Camden, Me., June 13, 1924; pianist; blind from an early age; pupil of J. W. Hill, Boston; later of Kullak, Clara Schumann, Pruckner and Liszt; played before the German Emperor; in 10 years he gave 1,200 concerts in America; originated the "lecture-recital"; c. fantasia "*Loreley*," "*The Lost Island*," etc., for piano.

Persiani (pĕr-sĭ-ä'-nē), (1) (née Tacchinardi) (täk-kĭ-när'-dē), Fanny, Rome, Oct. 4, 1812—Passy, near Paris, May 3, 1867; daughter and pupil of the tenor-singer Nicolà T.; one of the most noted and succ. colorature-sopranos of the century; lacking in appearance and possessed of a faulty voice, she compelled homage by her perfect technic; in 1830 she m. (2) Giuseppe Persiani (1799—1869), a composer of operas.

Per'singer, Louis, b. Rochester, Ill., Feb. 11, 1888; violinist; pupil of Becker, Ysaye and others; toured in European cities, later active as concertm. of Berlin Philh., and San Francisco Symph., led Chamber Music Soc. of latter city, 1916-28 (afterward known as Persinger Quartet); taught Cleveland Inst. of Music, 1929-30; after latter year faculty member of Juilliard School, N. Y.

Persuis (pĕr-swēs), Louis Luc Loiseau de, Metz, 1769—Paris, 1839; violinist, conductor, prof. and comp.

Perti (pĕr'-tē), Jacopo A., Bologna,

June 6, 1661—April 10, 1756; one of the chief 17th cent. composers of operas; pupil of Padre Franceschini; at 19 prod. a mass; church-conductor and composer of oratorios, etc., also 21 operas.

Pescetti (pä-shĕt'-tē), Giov. Bat., Venice, 1704—(probably) 1766; organist and dram. composer.

Peschka-Leutner (pĕsh'-kä-loit'-nĕr), Minna, Vienna, 1839—Wiesbaden, 1890; soprano.

Pessard (pĕs-săr), Émile Louis Fortuné, Montmartre, Seine, May 28, 1843—Paris, Feb. 10, 1917; pupil of Paris Cons.; won 1st harm. prize; 1866, Grand Prix de Rome, with cantata "*Dalila*" (Opéra, 1867); 1878-80, inspector of singing, Paris schools; 1881, prof. of harm. at the Cons.; dir. of mus. instruction in the Legion of Honour; after 1895, critic; prod. many comic operas and operettas, incl. "*Le Capitaine Fracasse*" (Th. Lyr., 1878); c. also masses, etc.

Peters (pä'-tĕrs), Carl Fr., Leipzig pub. firm, founded 1814 by C. F. Peters; 1893, a large library was opened to the public as the "Bibliothek Peters."

Petersen (pä'-tĕr-zĕn), Peter Nikolaus, Bederkesa, 1761—Hamburg, 1830; player on, improver of, and composer for, the flute.

Petersilea (pä'-tĕr-sē'-lä-ä), Carlyle, Boston, Mass., Jan. 18, 1844—near Los Angeles, Cal., June 11, 1903; pianist and teacher; pupil of his father, and at Leipzig Cons., winning the Helbig prize for pf.-playing; toured Germany with succ.; lived in Boston; est. 1871 "The Petersilea Acad. of Mus."; 1886, teacher New Engl. Cons.; 1884 studied with Liszt at Weimar, and gave a concert at the Singakademie, Berlin; after 1894 res. in Cal.; pub. pf.-studies.

Peterson-Berger (pä'-tĕr-son-bĕrkh-ĕr), Wilhelm, b. Ullanger, Sweden, Feb. 27, 1867; composer; studied in Dresden and in Stockholm where he was critic and régisseur at the opera; c. dramatic work "*Ran*" (Stockholm, 1903), and other operas, orch. pieces, sonatas, etc.; d. Frösön, Dec. 3, 1942.

Petit, Adrien. Vide COCLICUS.

Petrejus (pä-trä'-yoos), Jns., Langendorf, Franconia—Nürnberg, 1550; mus.-printer.

Petrella (pä-trĕl'-lä), Errico, Palermo,

DICTIONARY OF MUSICIANS 333

Dec. 1, 1813—in poverty, Genoa, April 7, 1877; v. succ. Italian composer of operas, rivalling Verdi's popularity, *"Marco Visconti"* and *"La Contessa d'Amalfi"* most succ.; pupil of Saverio del Giudice (vln.) and Naples Conservatorium.

Petri (pā'-trē), (1) **H.**, Zeyst, near Utrecht, April 5, 1856—Dresden, April 7, 1914; violinist; pupil of David; 1882–89 leader Gewandhaus Orch. with Brodsky, then leader Dresden Ct.-orch.; composer. (2) **Egon,** b. Hanover, Germany, March 23, 1881; pianist; son of (1); studied with Carreño, Buchmayer, Busoni; also (comp.) with Draeseke; after 1921 taught at Berlin Hochsch.; one of the most intellectual of present-day pianists and an outstanding virtuoso; concert tours of U. S. and Europe.

Petrini (pā-trē'-nē), **Fz.,** Berlin, 1744 —Paris, 1819; harpist and theorist.

Petrov (pā'-trôf), **Ossip Afanassjevich,** Elisavetgrad, Nov. 15, 1807—St. Petersburg, Mar. 14, 1878; famous Russian barytone-bass, with remarkable compass of nearly four octaves (B-g''); discovered on the stage of a country fair by Lebedev; created "Sussanin" in *"Life for the Czar"*; Glinka wrote *"Ruslan"* for him, and he created rôles in many of the chief Russian operas, singing up to four days before his death in his seventy-first year.

Petrucci (pā-troot'-chē), **Ottaviano dei,** Fossombrone, June 18, 1466 —May 7, 1539, inv. of mus.-printing with movable types; in 1498 received from the Council of the Republic of Venice a 20 years' monopoly of mus.-printing by his method; 1511–23 at Fossombrone with a 15 years' privilege for the Papal States; his method, which required 2 impressions, one of the lines, one of the notes, was beautifully managed and specimens are valuable; he publ. many of the most important comps. of his time and of previous composers.

Pe'trus Platen'sis. Vide LA RUE.

Petsch'nikoff, Alex., b. Jeletz, Russia, Feb. 8, 1873; violinist; pupil Moscow Cons.; at 10 entered Moscow Cons. and took prize; toured Europe with great succ., 1895–96; America, 1899; 1913–21, taught Munich Cons.; later in Buenos Aires, where d. 1949.

Petyrek (pä'-tē-rěk), **Felix, b.** Brünn, Austria, May 14, 1892; composer, pianist; studied at Vienna Univ. and Acad., pupil of Godowsky, Sauer and Schreker; 1919–21, taught at Salzburg Mozarteum; 1921–23, at Berlin Hochsch.; c. chamber music, piano and vocal works in modern style; d. Vienna, Dec. 1, 1951.

Petz'et, Walter, b. Breslau, Oct. 10, 1866; pupil of Kleffel, Rheinberger and von Bülow; 1887–96 piano teacher in America, then at Helsingfors Cons., and 1898 at Karlsruhe Cons.; d. Dresden, Aug. 13, 1941.

Petzold (pět'-tsôlt), **Chr.,** Königstein, 1677—Dresden, 1733: ct.-organist and composer.

Peurl (Bäwerl, Bäurl, or Beurlin), Paul, organist at Steyer; important composer of suites, etc. (1611–20).

Pevernage (pŭ-věr-näzh), **André** (or **Andreas),** Courtray, Belgium, 1543 —Antwerp, 1591; choirm. Nôtre-Dame and composer.

Pezze (pěd'-zě), **Ales.,** b. Milan, 1835; 'cellist; in London from 1857; pupil Merighi; d. London, June, 1914.

Pfannstiehl (pfän'-shtēl), **Bernhard,** b. Schmalkalden, Thuringia, Dec. 18, 1861; blind organist; pupil Leipzig Cons., winning the Mendelssohn prize three times; from 1903 org. at Chemnitz; 1912, Dresden Kreuzkirche; d. Freiburg, Oct. 21, 1940.

Pfeiffer (pfīf'-fěr), **K.,** 1833 (?)—Vienna, 1897; dram. composer. (2) (pfěf-fä), **Georges Jean,** Versailles, Dec. 12, 1835—Paris, Feb. 14, 1908; pianist; pupil of Maleden and Damcke; 1862 début; won Prix Chartier for chamber-mus.; critic; member of the firm of Pleyel, Wolff et Cie., Paris; c. a symph., a symph. poem, *"Jeanne d'Arc"*; pf. concertos, 3 operettas, oratorio *"Hagar,"* etc.

Pfeil (pfīl), **H.,** Leipzig, Dec. 18, 1835— April 17, 1899; 1862, ed. *"Sängerhalle"* (the organ of the Sängerbund); c. male choruses.

Pfitz'ner, Hans, Moscow, May 5, 1869 —Salzburg, May 22, 1949; pupil Hoch Cons., Frankfort; 1892, teacher pf. and theory, Coblenz Cons.; 1894–95, asst.-cond. City Th., Mayence; 1897–1903, teacher in Stern Cons., Berlin; 1903–07, cond. Theater des Westens, Berlin; 1908–18, munic. music dir. and head of Cons. at Munich; 1910–16, also opera dir. in

Strassburg; 1920–26, master class, Berlin Acad. of Arts; 1929–34, prof. Munich Akad. der Tonkunst; a prolific composer in Neo-Romantic style, he produced the operas *"Der Arme Heinrich"* (1893), *"Die Rose vom Liebesgarten"* (1909), *"Pales- trina"* (1917), music drama having a largely male cast; impressive but over-weighty score much sung in Germany; *"Christelflein"* (fairy-tale opera) and *"Das Herz,"* based on medieval legend (1931); also incid. music to plays; cantata, *"Von Deutscher Seele"* (sung in N. Y. by Friends of Music Soc.); other choral works, piano, vln. and 'cello con- certos; much chamber and orch. music, songs, etc.; he ed. and arranged E. T. A. Hoffmann's *"Undine"* and works of Marschner for modern presentation; also c. scherzo for orch.; ballad *"Herr Oluff"* for bar. and orch., pf.-trio.

Pflughaupt (pflookh'-howpt), (1) **Robt.,** Berlin, 1833—Aix-la-Chapelle, 1871; pianist and composer. (2) **Sophie** (née **Stschepin**), Dünaburg, Russia, 1837—Aix-la-Chapelle, 1867; pianist.

Pfohl (pfōl), **Fd.,** b. Elbogen, Bohemia, Oct. 12, 1863; critic; studied mus. at Leipzig; c. orch. music; author of books on Wagner, Nikisch. D., Hamburg-Bergedorf, Dec. 16, 1949.

Pfundt (pfoont), **Ernst Gotthold Benj.,** Dommitzsch, near Torgau, 1806— Leipzig, 1871; tympanist; inv. the "machine-head"; wrote method for kettle-drum.

Phalèse (fä-lĕz'), **P.** (**Petrus Phale'- sius**), b. Louvain, ca. 1510; 1545, est. a mus.-publishing business; 1579 re- moved to Antwerp, as "Pierre Phal- èse et Jean Bellère."

Phelps, Ellsworth C., Middletown, Conn., Aug. 11, 1827—Brooklyn, N. Y., 1913; self-taught; at 19 organist; from 1857, Brooklyn; teacher in pub. schools for 30 years; c. 2 comic operas; symphs. *"Hia- watha,"* and *"Emancipation"*; 4 symphonic poems; Psalm 145, with orch., etc.

Philidor (rightly **Danican**) (fē-lĭ-dôr or dă-nĭ-kän). A famous French family called usually **Danican- Philidor,** the name Philidor being taken from a remark of the King comparing **Jean D.** with his favourite oboist Philidor. There seem to have

been two named **Michel,** (1) **the** first, b. Dauphine—d. Paris, ca. 1650, the oboist whom the King praised; the other (2) **Michel,** d. 1659, ct.-mus. (3) **Jean,** d. Paris, Sept. 8, 1679, in the King's military band. (4) **André D.-P.** (l'aîné), b. Aug. 11, 1730; cromorne-player and composer. He had 16 children. (5) **Jacques** (le cadet), Paris, 1657— Versailles, 1708; bro. of (4), oboist, etc., favourite of Louis XIV.; c. military music, etc.; he had 12 children, four of whom were musi- cians, the best known being (6) **Pierre,** 1681—1731; flutist; c. suites, etc., for flutes. (7) **Anne,** Paris, 1681—1728; eldest son of (4); flute- player, and conductor; before he was 20, prod. operas at court. (8) **Michel,** b. Versailles, 1683, 2nd son of (4); a drummer. (9) **Fran.,** Versailles, 1689—1717(18 ?), 3rd son of (4); oboist and bass-violist; c. flute-pcs. (10) **Fran. André,** Dreux, Sept. 7, 1726—London, Aug. 31, 1795; last and greatest of the family, the youngest son of (4); remarkable chess-player of European fame; mu- sical pupil of Campra. At 30 he sud- denly began to prod. operas with great succ., his best works being the following (among 25 notable for orch. and harm. brilliance): *"Le Diable à quatre"* (Op.-Com., 1756); *"Le Maréchal"* (1761), performed over 200 times; *"Le Sorcier"* and *"Tom Jones"* (only 8 weeks apart, in 1704; the latter containing the then novelty of an unaccompanied quartet); the grand opera, his best work, *"Ernelinde,"* 1767 (revised, 1769, as *"Sandomir"*). Biog. by Allen (Philadelphia, 1863). He had four sons all ct. mus.: (11) **Pierre,** Paris, 1681—1740(?); oboist, flutist and violist; c. suites and prod. a pastorale at court. (12) **Jacques,** 1686—1725, oboist. (13) **François,** 1695—1726, oboist. (14) **Nicolas,** 1699—1769; played the serpent, etc.

Phil'ipp, Isidor (Edmond), b. Buda- pest, Sept. 2, 1863; pianist; a natural- ised French citizen; came to Paris as a child; at 16 pupil of Georges Mathias, at the Cons.; won 1st. pf.- prize, in 1883; studied with Saint- Saëns, Stephen Heller, and Ritter; played with succ. in European cities; est. concerts (with Loeb and Berthelier), producing modern

French chamber-comps.; reorganised the "Société des instr. à vent"; cofounder and pres. of the "Soc. d'Art"; after 1903 prof. at Paris Cons.; also taught at Fontainebleau Amer. Cons.; master classes in Boston and N. Y., 1934–35; pub. a "Suite fantastique," a "Rêverie mélancolique," a "Sérénade humoristique," for orch. In U. S. since 1941.

Philippe, (1) de Caserte. Vide CASERTA. (2) de Mons. Vide MONTE. (3) de Vitry. Vide VITRY.

Phil'ipps, (1) Peters (or Petrus Philip'-pus, Pietro Filip'po), England, ca. 1560—after 1633, organist and composer. (2) **Arthur**, b. 1605, organist at Oxford, prof., and composer. (3) **Henry**, Bristol, 1801—Dalston, 1876; bass-barytone. (4) **Wm.** Lovell, Bristol, 1816—1860; 'cellist and composer. (5) **Adelaide**, Stratford-on-Avon, 1833—Carlsbad, 1882; contralto; pupil of Garcia.

Piastro (pē-äs'-trō), **Mishel**, b. Kertch, Russia, 1900; violinist; conductor.

Piatigorsky (pē-ăt-ē-gôr'-skē), **Gregor**, b. Ekaterinoslaw, Russia, April 20, 1903; 'cellist; studied violin, later 'cello with Glehn in Moscow; 1st 'cellist of Berlin Philh., 1923; began solo appearances with leading continental orchs., also in chamber music concerts; Amer. tours after 1929; has appeared widely in recital and as a first-rank solo performer.

Piatti (pē-ät'-tē), (1) **Alfredo Carlo**, Bergamo, Jan. 8, 1822—Bergamo, July 19, 1901; 'cello-virtuoso (son of a violinist, (2) **Antonio P.**, d. Feb. 27, 1878); pupil of his grand-uncle, Zanetti, and of Merighi, Milan Cons.; début, Milan, 1838; at 7 had played in an orch., 1849, 1st 'cello It. opera, London; from 1859 at Monday and Saturday Pop. Concerts of chamber-mus.; pub. a method for 'cello, 2 'cello-concertos, vocal mus. with 'cello obbligato, etc.

Piccaver (pē'-kä-věr), **Alfred**, b. Lone Sutton, England, Feb. 5, 1887; tenor; in early youth came to America and had vocal instruction in N. Y. and Milan; 1907–12, mem. Prague Landestheatre; after 1912, sang regularly with Vienna State Op., where he enjoyed marked popularity, esp. in Italian rôles; 1923, guest appearances with Chicago Opera.

Piccinni (or **Piccini** or **Picinni**) (pĭt-chǐn'-nē), (1) **Nicolâ**, Bari, Jan. 16, 1728—Passy, near Paris, May 7, 1800; operatic composer, famous as a rival of Gluck. Son of a musician who opposed his tastes. The Bishop of Bari recognising his talent and irrepressible passion for music overcame opposition, and at 14 he entered the Cons. di San Onofrio, Naples, remaining for 12 years, as favourite pupil of Leo and Durante. He entered into competition with the popular Logroscino, and prod. the v. succ. opera-buffa "Le Donne Dispettose" (1754), followed by (1755) "Gelosia per Gelosia" and "Il Curioso del suo proprio Danno," which had the unprecedented run of four years; "Alessandro nelle Indie" (Rome, 1758), and "Cecchina Zitella, o La Buona Figliuola" (Rome, 1760), the most success. work of its kind in Europe, though written in 3 weeks, were hailed as masterworks. His new dramatic fervour and his extended duets and varied finales gave him such prestige that he is said to have c. 133 dramatic works, incl. "Il Re Pastore" (1760); "L'Olimpiade" (1761) previously though less succ. set by Pergolesi, Galuppi and Jomelli; revised 1771; "Bernice" (1764); "La Cecchina Maretata" (1765); "Didone abbandonata" (1767); "Antigone" (1771). 1773, the Roman public favoured his pupil Anfossi, and hissed one of P.'s operas, which prostrated him with grief; on recovering he regained favour with "I Viaggiatori." In response to flattering invitations in 1776 he removed with his family to Paris, spent a whole year learning the tongue and writing his first French opera, "Roland" (Opéra, 1778), which had a succ. said to be due largely to the necessity that the anti-Gluck faction was under to find a rival. The war between the "Gluck-ists" and "Piccinists" was violent and incessant, though P. regretted his position and made a vain effort after Gluck's death to raise a fund for annual concerts in his memory. He had succ. with the following French operas, "Le fat méprisé" (1779), "Atys" (1780), "Didon," "Le dormeur éveillé," and "Le faux Lord" (all 3 in 1783). In 1778, as dir. It. Opéra, whose performances alternated with the French company at the Opera, he produced his best Italian works with succ. The management simultaneously commissioned both Gluck and P. to set the opera *"Iphigénie en Tauride"*; P. had his libretto rewritten by Ginguené, and his version was delayed till after Gluck had made a triumph and left Paris. P.'s opera, though usually called a failure, ran 17 nights in spite of having an intoxicated prima donna on the first night to start the joke *"Iphigénie en Champagne."* Half a dozen others failed or were never performed. A new rival, Sacchini, now appeared. When this second succ. rival died, the large-hearted Piccinni delivered a glowing funeral-eulogy over him. 1784, he was Maître de chant at the new "École royale de musique et déclamation." His last operatic attempts in French were unsucc. At the outbreak of the Revolution he lost his positions, and retired to Naples, on a pension. But his daughter m. a young French radical, and P., suspected of republicanism, was kept a prisoner in his own house for four years, in extreme poverty. 1798, he returned to France, was fêted at the Cons., presented with 5,000 francs and small irregular pension. He was prostrated for some months by paralysis; a sixth inspectorship was created at the Cons. for him, but he soon fell ill and died. (2) **Luigi,** Naples, 1766—Passy, July 31, 1827; son and pupil of above; ct.-cond. at Stockholm and dr. composer. (3) **Louis Alex.,** Paris, 1779—1850; grandson and pupil of (1); conductor and dram.-composer.

Piccolomini (pĭk-kō-lō'-mē-nē), **Maria,** Siena, March 15, 1834—near Florence, Dec. 23, 1899; mezzo-soprano of "hardly one octave and a half-compass" (Chorley), but so excellent an actress, that she became a great rage; pupil of Mazzarelli and Raimondi, Florence; début there 1852, with great succ., sang in Italy, London, Paris and New York (1858); 1863, m. the Marquis Gaetani, and retired from the stage.

Pichel (or **Pichl**) (pĕsh'-'l), **Wenzel,** Bechin, Bohemia, 1741—Vienna, 1805; violinist; c. 700 works.

Picinni. Vide PICCINNI.

Pick-Mangiagalli (pēk-män-jä-gäl'-ē), **Riccardo,** Strakonitz, July 10, 1882—Milan, July 8, 1949; studied at Milan Cons.; c. (ballets) *"Il Salice d'Oro"* (La Scala, 1914); *"Il Carillon Magico"* (given by Met. Op. Co., N. Y.); *"Mahit"* (La Scala, 1923); *"Casanova a Venezia"* (do., 1929); (opera) *"Basi e Bote"* (Rome, 1927); also orch. works, chamber music, vln. and piano pieces, songs.

Piel (pēl), **Peter,** Kessenich, near Bonn, Aug. 12, 1835—Boppard, Aug. 21, 1904; from 1868, teacher Boppard-on-Rhine; 1887, R. Mus.-Dir.; wrote a harm.; c. 8 Magnificats (in the church-modes), etc.

Pieragon, or **Pierchon.** Vide LA RUE.

Pierné (p'yĕr-nä) (**H. Constant**) **Gabriel,** Metz, Aug. 16, 1863—Brittany, July 17, 1937; pupil Marmontel, Franck Massenet; 1st prize (1879), do. for cpt. and fugue (1881), do. for organ (1882) and Grand Prix de Rome (1882); 1890, organist Ste. Clothilde (vice César Franck); 1893, prod. spectacle *"Bouton d'or"*; opera, *"Izéil"* (1894); succ. *"Vendée"* (Lyons, 1897); a hymn to the Russian visitors, *"La Fraternelle,"* 1893; from 1910 he cond. the Colonne concerts Paris; he c. very successful choral work, *"Croisade des Enfants"* (1905), *"La coupe enchantée"* (Paris, 1895; Stuttgart, 1907): opera *"La fille de Tabarin"* (Op. Com., 1901), oratorio *"Les enfants de Bethlehem"* (1907); *"Les Fioretti de St. Francis d'Assise"* (Paris, 1912), etc. P. had shown a wide versatility in writing incid. music for dramas. His ballet, *"Cydalise et le Chèvre-Pied,"* in which his musical style kept abreast of the more recent harmonic innovations, had a pronounced succ. when presented in Paris, 1919. Excerpts from this score have proved pop. on orch. programmes in the U. S. His works also include the opera, *"On ne badine pas avec l'Amour"*; concerto for piano and orch.; concerto for bassoon and orch.; sonata for vln. and piano; sonata da camera; chamber trio; pieces for piano, harp and other instruments; songs, etc.

Pierre (pǐ-ăr'), **Constant,** Passy, Aug. 24, 1855—Paris, Jan., 1918; pupil of Paris Cons.; bassoon-player; assist. sec. at the Cons.; ed. *Le Monde musical;* wrote a history of the Opéra orchestra (for which the

"Soc. des compositeurs" awarded a prize, 1889), etc.

Pier'son, (1) or **Pier'zon.** Vide LA RUE. (2) (rightly **Pearson**), **Henry Hugo** (early pen-name "**Edgar Mansfeldt**"), Oxford, 1816—Leipzig, 1873; prof. of mus.; prod. in Germany 4 operas.

Piéton (pǐ-ā-tôn), **Loyset**, French contrapuntist, 1531.

Pijper (pī'-pĕr), **Willem**, b. Zeist, Holland, 1894—d. n. The Hague, March 19, 1947; composer; pupil of Johan Wagenaar, and Mme. von Luntern (piano); active as music critic; dir. Amsterdam Cons., 1929; c. orch. chamber and choral music.

Pilati (pē-lä'-tē), **Auguste** (rightly **Pilate**), Bouchain, Sept. 29, 1810 —Paris, Aug. 1, 1877; c. operettas under name of A. P. Juliano.

Pilk'ington, Francis, Engl. lutenist and composer, 1595–1614.

Pillois (pēl'-wä), **Jacques,** Paris, 1877 —New York, Jan. 3, 1935; composer; pupil of Vierne and Widor at Paris Cons.; taught music history at Fontainebleau School after 1921; also at N. Y. Univ., 1927–30, and Smith Coll., 1929–30; won Trement, Nicolo and Rousseau Prizes; laureate of French Inst.; res. in America after 1929; c. orch., chamber music and vocal works.

Pilotti (pē-lôt'-tē), **Giuseppe,** Bologna, 1784—1838; son and succ. of an org.-builder; professor, writer and dram. composer.

Pinel'li, Ettore, Rome, Oct. 18, 1843— Sept. 17, 1915; violinist; pupil of Ramaciotti and Joachim; 1866, founded (with Sgambati) soc. for classical chamber-mus.; 1874, the "Società Orchestrale Romana," which he cond.; 1877, in the Liceo Musicale of Santa Cecilia; also cond. ct.-concerts alternately with Sgambati; c. overture "*Rapsodia italiana,*" etc.

Pinel'lo de Gherardi (gä-rär'-dē), **Giov. Bat.,** Genoa, ca. 1540—Prague, 1587; court cond. and composer.

Pinsuti (pǐn-soo'-tē), **Ciro,** Sinalunga, Siena, 1829—Florence, 1888; famous vocal teacher at the R. A. M., London, from 1856; composer of operas and very popular songs.

Pinza (pēnt'-sä), **Ezio,** b. Rome; basso; early trained as civil engineer, but gave up this profession for vocal career: début at Rome R. Op.; later

heard in Turin, Naples, for 3 years at La Scala; after 1926 sang with Met. Op. Co., also at Covent Garden and widely in concerts, incl. tour of Australia.

Pipegrop (pē'-pĕ-grôp) (called **Baryphonus**), **H.,** Wernigerode, 1581— Quedlinburg, 1655; town-cantor and theorist.

Pipelare (pē-pĕ-lä'-rĕ), **Matthæus,** 16th cent. Belgian composer.

Pirani (pē-rä'-nē), **Eugenio,** b. Bologna, 1852—Berlin, 1939; pianist, pupil of Golonelli, Bologna Liceo Musicale, and of Th. Kullak (pf.) and Kiel (comp.); 1870–80 in Kullak's Acad.; lived in Heidelberg till 1895, then Berlin; after 1901 toured U. S.; 1904 estab. music school in Brooklyn, N. Y.; wrote essays; c. symph. poem "*Heidelberg,*" etc.; later in Berlin.

Pir'ro, André, b. St. Dizier, Feb. 12, 1869; organist and historian; from 1896, teacher at the Schola cantorum, Paris; 1904 taught at "École des hautes études sociales"; 1912, director; d. Paris, 1943.

Pisa (pē'-zä), **Agostino,** wrote earliest known treatise on conducting, etc. (2d ed., Rome, 1611.)

Pisari (pē-sä'-rē), **Pasquale,** Rome, 1725—1778; bass-singer and composer, whom Padre Martini called the "Palestrina of the 18th cent."

Pisaroni (pē-sä-rō'-nē), **Benedetta Rosamonda,** Piacenza, 1793—1872; high soprano; after an illness became a contralto.

Pisendel (pē'-zĕnt-ĕl), **Jn. G.,** Karlsburg, 1687—Dresden, 1755; violinist and composer.

Pisk, Paul A., b. Vienna, May 16, 1893; composer; professor, University of Redlands, Cal., 1937.

Pistocchi (pēs-tôk'-kē), **Fran. Ant.,** Palermo, 1659—Bologna, May 13, 1726; founder of famous Sch. of Singing at Bologna; c. operas.

Pis'ton, Walter, b. Rockland, Me., Jan. 20, 1894; composer; early studied at art school, then vln. and piano privately; theory at Harvard Univ., later in Paris with Nadia Boulanger; showed radical tendencies in harmony but strongly logical sense of structure in his works; c. (orch.) Symphonic Piece (Boston Symph., 1928); Orch. Suite (Phila. Orch., 1932); Symphonic poem; (chamber music) string quartet; 3

pieces for flute, clar. and bassoon, etc.; mem. of mus. faculty, Harvard University. (See Composers' List)

Pitoni (pē-tŏ'-nē), **Gius. Ottavîo,** Rieti, Italy, March 18, 1657—Rome, Feb. 1, 1743; an eminent teacher and composer; pupil of Natale and Froggia; from 1677 cond. Coll. of San Marco, Rome; c. a Dixit in 16 parts for 4 choirs, etc.

Pitt, Percy, London, Jan. 4, 1870— Hampstead, Nov. 23, 1932; organist and prominent English composer; pupil of Reinecke, Jadassohn and Rheinberger; 1896 organist Queen's Hall; 1902 adviser and cond. Covent Garden; dir., 1907; 1915-18, Beecham Op. Co.; 1920-24, ass't. dir. British Nat'l. Op. Co.; 1927, mus. dir. British Broadcasting Corp.; c. Sinfonietta (Birmingham Fest., 1906); symphonic prelude "*Le sang des crépuscules,*" ballade for violin and orch.; orch. suites, etc.

Piutti (pē-oot'-tē), (1) **K.,** Elgersburg, Thuringia, April 30, 1846—Leipzig, June 17, 1902; notable organist; pupil, and from 1875, teacher Leipzig Cons.; 1880, also organist Thomaskirche; wrote a harm.; c. 6 fugal fantasias, 8 preludes, "*Wedding Sonata,*" etc., for organ. (2) **Max.,** Luisenhall, near Erfurt, 1852—Jackson, Mich., 1885; brother of above; writer, teacher and composer.

Pixis (pĕx'-ēs), (1) **Fr. Wm.,** Mannheim, 1786—Prague, 1842; violinist and conductor. (2) **Jn. Peter,** Mannheim, 1788—Baden-Baden, 1874; bro. of above; pianist, teacher and dram. composer.

Pizzetti (pēd-sĕt'-ē), **Ildebrando,** b. Parma, Sept. 20, 1880; composer; studied with his father and at Parma Cons., made study of Greek and Gregorian modes, which have influenced his style of comp.; in his operas he has shown original method in which voices are treated in flexible, semi-declamatory manner; a highly sensitive writer for the chorus, which is allotted some of the most important passages in his stage works; he taught comp. at the Istituto Musicale in Florence after 1909, becoming its director in 1918; visited U. S., 1930; c. (operas) "*Fedra*" (1915); "*Debora e Jaele*" (1922); "*Lo Straniero*" (Rome, 1930); "*Fra Gherardo*" (première, La Scala, Milan, May 16, 1928, also

at Met. Op., 1929); "*Orseolc*" (Florence Fest., 1935, repeated in other cities); incid. music to "*Edipo Re*" and "*La Nave*"; "*Lamento*" for tenor and orch.; Requiem in memory of King Humbert: (orch.) "*Overture per una Farsa Tragica,*" "*Sinfonia del Fuoco,*" "*Concerto dell'Estate,*" "*Rondo Veneziano*" (N. Y. Philh. under Toscanini, 1930); 'cello sonata, vln. sonata, piano pieces and songs; has written essay on Greek music, works on contemporary composers and on Bellini; "*Intermezzi Critici,*" also many articles, some under pseudonym "*Ildebrando di Parma*"; after 1936 appointed prof. of comp. at Liceo of Santa Cecilia, Rome, to succeed the late Ottorino Respighi.

Pizzi (pĭd'-zē), **Emilio,** Verona, Feb. 2, 1862—Bergamo, 1931; pupil of Ponchielli and Bazzini, Milan Cons., graduating 1884; took 1st prize Milan, 1885, for 1-act opera "*Lina*"; 1st and 2d prize, Florence, for 2 string quartets; prize of 5,000 francs, Bologna, 1889, for succ. grand opera "*Guglielmo Ratcliff*" (Bologna, 1889); 1897, dir. of mus.-sch. at Bergamo and at church of S. Maria Maggiore; c. also 2 1-act operas "*Gabriella*" and "*Rosalba*" (written for Adelina Patti, 1893-96), etc.

Plaidy (plī'-dē), **Louis,** Hubertusburg, Saxony, Nov. 28, 1810—Grimma, March 3, 1874; eminent pf.-teacher; pupil of Agthe and Haase; at first a violinist; 1843, invited by Mendelssohn to teach at the then new Leipzig Cons., and did so till 1865; wrote text-books.

Plançon (plän-sôn), **Pol Henri,** Fumay, Ardennes, June 12, 1854—Paris, 1914; famous barytone; pupil of Duprez and Sbriglia; début, 1877, at Lyons; 1883-93, at the Paris Opéra; 1891-1904, Covent Garden annually, and 1893-1906, at Met. Op. House, N. Y.

Planquette (plän-kĕt), **(Jean) Robert,** Paris, March 31, 1848—Jan. 28, 1903; studied comp. with Duprato, Paris Cons., c. chansons and "*Saynètes*" for "cafés-concerts"; prod. succ. 1-act operetta "*Paille d'Avoine*" (1874) followed by others incl. the still pop. comic opera, "*Les Cloches de Corneville*" (Folies-Dramatiques, 1877), given over 400 times, consecutively, and widely popular elsewhere (known in Engl.

as "Chimes of Normandy"); later works incl. "*Mam'zelle Quat'sous*" {Gaité, 1897) and for London "*The Old Guard*" (1887), and "*Paul Jones*" (1889).

Plantade (plän-tăd), (1) **Chas. H.**, Pontoise, 1764—Paris, 1839; prof. of singing at Paris Cons.; ct.-conductor and dram. composer. (2) **Chas. Fran.**, Paris, 1787—1870; son of above; composer.

Planté (plän-tā), **Francis**, Orthez, Basses Pyrénees, March 2, 1839— Dax, Dec. 19, 1934; noted pianist; pupil of Marmontel at Paris Cons.; won 1st prize after 7 months' tuition; pupil of Bazin (harm.) then self-taught for 10 years, during which time he studied in seclusion in the Pyrenees; reappeared with succ.; toured widely in Europe, from 1872 until 1900, when he retired except for occasional concerts; c. transcriptions.

Platania (plä-tä'-nĭ-ä), **Pietro**, Catania, April 5, 1828—Naples, April 26, 1907; pupil of P. Raimondi, at the Cons. there; 1863, dir. Palermo Cons.; later cond. Milan, 1885-1902, dir. R. Coll. of Mus. at Naples; wrote a treatise on canon and fugue; c. 5 operas; a symph. "*L'Italia*"; funeral symphony in memory of Pacini, festival symph. with choruses to welcome King Humbert in 1878, etc.

Platel (plä-těl), **Nicolas Jos.**, Versailles, 1777—Brussels, 1835; 'cellist; prof. and composer.

Pla'to, eminent Greek philosopher, 429 —347 B. C.; formulated in his "*Ti-maeus*" a system of harm., interpreted in Th. H. Martin's "*Études sur les Timée de Platon*," etc.

Play'ford, (1) **John**, 1623—1686; London mus.-publisher. (2) **Henry**, his son and successor, 1657—1720.

Pleyel (plī'ĕl, or plĕ'-yĕl), (1) **Ignaz Jos.**, Ruppertsthal, near Vienna, June 1, 1757—at his estate near Paris, Nov. 14, 1831; pianist, ct.-cond.; founded, 1797, at Paris a piano factory later known as Pleyel, Wolff & Co.; c. 29 symphs., sonatas, etc. (2) **Camille**, Strassburg, 1788— Paris, 1855; son, pupil and successor of above; a pianist and composer; his successor in business was August Wolff. (3) **Marie Félicité Denise**, Paris, 1811 — St.-Josse-ten-Noode, 1875; wife of (2); pianist and teacher.

Plüddemann (plüt'-dĕ-män), **Martin,**

Kolberg, 1854—Berlin, 1897; conductor and singing teacher, writer and composer.

Plutarch (Plutar'chos) (ploo'-tärk), Chaeronea, Boeotia, ca. 50 A. D.— 120 (131 ?); the Greek biographer; wrote treatises "*De musica*," containing important data.

Pochhammer (pôkh'-häm-měr), **Adolf**, b. Rheine, Aug. 14, 1864; pupil of Hamburg Cons.; teacher at Wiesbaden Cons.; 1902-28, dir. Cons. in Aachen; c. songs.

Pochon (pôsh'-ôṅ), **Alfred**, b. Yverdon, Switzerland, 1878; violinist, composer; 1st appeared in public at 11; pupil of César Thomson, whose ass't. teacher he was at Brussels Cons. after 1898; played in Thomson Quartet, also in orch. under Ysaye there; 1902 organised Flonzaley Quartet for the Amer. music patron, de Coppet; played 1st as leader, then as 2nd vln. in this group; c. vln. and chamber works and made transcriptions.

Poenitz (pä'-nĭtsh), **Fz.**, Bischofswerda, Aug. 17, 1850—Berlin, March 19, 1913; harpist; studied with Weitzmann, Berlin; after 1861, at the ct. opera; composer.

Poglietti (pōl-yĕt'-tē), **Alessandro**, from 1661 court organist; murdered by the Turks in the siege of Vienna, 1683; c. clavier pieces.

Pohl (pōl), (1) **K. Fd.**, Darmstadt, 1819 —Vienna, 1887; writer. (2) **Richard**, Leipzig, 1826—Baden-Baden, 1896; ed. and writer (pen-name "Hant"). (3) **Bd.** Vide POLLINI.

Pohlenz (pō'-lěnts), **Chr. Aug.**, Saalgast, Niederlausitz, 1790—Leipzig, 1843; organist, conductor and composer.

Pohlig (pō'-lĭkh), **Karl**, Teplitz, Feb. 10, 1864—Brunswick, June 17, 1928; pupil of Liszt; cond. Graz, Hamburg, Covent Garden, etc.; 1907—1912, Phila. Orch.; 1914-24, gen'l. music dir., Brunswick, Germany; c. orch. pieces and songs.

Poirée (pwä'-rā), **Elie Émile Gabriel**, Villeneuve, St. Georges, Oct. 9, 1850 —Paris, May 26, 1925; librarian, author; c. string quartet, etc.

Poise (pwäz), **Jn. Alex. Fd.**, Nîmes, 1828—Paris, 1892; dram. composer.

Poisot (pwä-zō), **Chas. Émile**, Dijon, France, July 8, 1822—March, 1904; pianist; pupil of Paris Cons.; co-founder "Soc. des Compositeurs";

founder and dir. Dijon Cons., also from 1872 cond. Soc. for Sacred and Classical Mus.; dram. composer and writer.

Poiszl (poish'-'l), **Jn. Nepomuk,** Freiherr **von,** Haukenzell, Bavaria, 1783 —Munich, 1865; dram. composer.

Polac'co, Giorgio, b. Venice, April 12, 1875; pupil Milan Cons.; cond. in London, Italy, Spain, South America; 1907, Royal Op., Wiesbaden; 1908, Berlin Royal Op.; 1911–12, cond. H. W. Savage's prod. of *"Girl of the Golden West"*; 1912, engaged for Met. Op., N. Y.; 1913 also at Covent Garden; 1918–31, cond. of Chicago Op.; guest appearances in Europe; c. operas, *"Rahab"* (Budapest), and *"Fortunatus,"* etc.; m. Edith Mason; divorced.

Pölchau (pĕl'-khow), **G.,** Cremon, Livonia, 1773—Berlin, 1836; librarian and collector.

Poldini (pôl-dē'-nē), **Eduard,** b. Pest, June 13, 1869; composer of opera *"Vagabond and Princess"* (Pest, 1903), children's operas and many pop. piano pieces.

Poldowski (pŏl-dŏf'-skē), pen-name of **Lady Dean Paul,** d. London, June 28, 1932; composer; daughter of H. Wieniewski; c. many modern works, chamber, pf. and vocal music.

Pole, Wm., Birmingham, Engl., April 22, 1814—London, Dec. 30, 1900; Mus. Doc. Oxon., 1864; 1876–90, examiner in Mus. London Univ.; writer; c. Psalm 100 in cantata-form, etc.

Polidoro (pō-lĭ-dō'-rō), (1) **Giuseppe,** d. Naples, 1873; singing-teacher, Naples Cons. (2) **Federigo,** Naples, Oct. 22, 1845—near Naples, Aug. 14, 1903; son and pupil of above; studied with Lillo, Conti and d'Arienzo, essayist and historian under pen-name "Acuti."

Polko (pôl'-kō) (née **Vogel**), **Élise,** Leipzig, Jan. 13, 1822—Munich, May 15, 1899; mezzo-soprano and writer of romantic musical essays.

Pol'lak, Egon, Prague, May 3, 1879—June 14, 1933; conductor; was from 1917 to 1931 the gen'l. music dir. of the Hamburg Op., and 1929–30, cond. with the Chicago Opera.

Pollarolo (pôl-lä-rō'-lō), (1) **Carlo Francesco,** Brescia, ca. 1653—Venice, 1722; composer; organist and assistant-cond. at St. Mark's; c. 3 oratorios, 68 operas, etc. His son and pupil (2) **Antonio,** Venice, 1680—

Venice, 1746; 1723, cond. at St. Mark's; c. operas.

Polledro (pôl-lā'-drō), **Giov. Bat.,** Piovà, n. Turin, 1781—1853; violinist, cond. and composer.

Polleri (pôl-lā'-rē), **Giov. Bat.,** Genoa, June 28, 1855—Oct., 1923; organist; from 1887 teacher in the U. S.; 1894, in Genoa; from 1898 dir. of the Cons.; c. organ pieces, etc.

Pollini (pôl-lē'-nē), (1) **Fran.,** Laibach, Carniola, 1763—Milan, Sept. 17, 1846; pianist and pf.-prof., 1809, Milan Cons.; perhaps the first to write pf.-music on 3 staves. (2) **Bd.** (rightly **Pohl**), Cologne, Dec. 16, 1838—Hamburg, Nov. 27, 1897; tenor, later barytone; but more famous as manager; his second wife was Bianca Bianchi. (3) **Cesare,** Cavaliere de, Padua, July 13, 1858—Jan. 26, 1912; studied with Bazzini, Milan; 1883–85 dir. of a Cons. at Padua; resigned to write and compose.

Pollitzer (pôl'-lĭts-ĕr), **Ad.,** Pesth, July 23, 1832—London, Nov. 14, 1900; violinist; pupil of Böhm (vln.) and Preyer (comp.), Vienna; toured Europe, then studied with Alard at Paris; 1851 leader H. M.'s Th., London; later New Philh. Soc.; prof of vln., London Acad. of Mus.; 1890, director.

Ponchard (pôn-shăr), (1) **L. Ant. Éléonore,** Paris, 1787—1866; tenor and prof. at the Cons. (2) **Chas.,** Paris, 1824—1891; son of above; teacher at the Cons.

Ponchielli (pôn-kĭ-ĕl'-lē), **Amilcare,** Paderno Fasolaro, Cremona, Aug. 31, 1834—Milan, Jan. 16, 1886; opera composer; pupil Milan Cons.; organist, then bandmaster, 1881; cond. Piacenza Cath. from 1856; c. 10 operas, incl. *"La Gioconda,"* widely popular; 1902 his son discovered a MS. opera *"I Mori di Valenza"* (composed, 1878–79).

Poniatowski (pō-nĭ-ä-tôf'-shkĭ), **Jozef** (Michal Xawery Franciszek Jan), Prince of Monte Rotondo, Rome, 1816 — Chiselhurst, Engl., 1873; tenor and dram. composer.

Pons (pôns), (1) **Charles,** French composer; from about 1901 active as composer of many operas of lighter nature, including *"L'Epreuve," "Mourette," "La Voile de Bonheur," "Francaise"*; oratorio, *"La Samaritaine"*; music for various plays. ȧ

Mass, and piano works. (2) **Lily,** b. Cannes, France, April 16, 1904; coloratura soprano, of French-Italian parentage; studied piano at Paris Cons. and singing with Alberti De Gorostiaga; in her native country she had fulfilled only minor engagements in various seaside resorts, making operatic début at Mulhouse in *"Louise,"* 1928; became protégée of Maria Gay, who discovered her unusual gifts; wholly unknown in America, she made début with Met. Op. Co., New York, as "Lucia," Jan. 3, 1931, with sensational succ., and immediately became leading mem. of that co.; has sung in opera and concert in Paris, Rome, London and elsewhere as one of leading vocalists of the day; also with wide following in radio programmes and films.

Ponselle (pŏn-sĕl'), (1) **Rosa,** b. Meriden, Conn.; dramatic soprano; of Italian parents; family name, Ponzillo; early heard as church soloist in native town, later as vaudeville singer with her sister; had vocal instruction for opera from William Thorner and Romano Romani; was brought to attention of Caruso, under whose sponsorship she made Met. Op. début as "Leonora" in *"Forza del Destino"* in 1918 with impressive success; until 1936 was a leading mem. of that co., her rôles incl. "Norma," "Donna Anna," the heroine in Spontini's *"La Vestale,"* and many other Italian dramatic works, also *"Carmen"*; in these she has shown outstanding beauty and opulence of voice; has appeared at Covent Garden, making a particular succ. as "Violetta"; also in Italy; widely as a recital and orchestral soloist, and on the radio. (2) **Carmela,** her sister, mezzo-soprano; has sung with Met. Op. and with other Amer. lyric organisations; also in concert and radio.

Ponte, Lorenzo da. Vide DA PONTE.

Pop'ov, Ivan Gegorovich, b. Ekaterinodar, 1859; pupil Moscow Phil. School, from 1900, director of society in Stavropol, Caucasus; c. symph., Armenian rhapsody; symph. poem *"Freedom,"* overture, *"Ivan the Terrible"*; d. (?).

Popp'er (pŏp'-pĕr), **David,** Prague, Dec. 9, 1843—Baden near Vienna, Aug. 7, 1913; prominent 'cellist; pupil of Goltermann, Prague Cons.; a member of Prince von Hechingen's

orch., at Löwenburg; toured Europe with greatest succ.; 1868–73, 1st 'cello, Vienna ct.-orch.; 1872 m. Sophie Menter (divorced, 1886); c. excellent and pop. 'cello-pcs., a concerto, etc.

Porges (pôr'-gĕs), **H.,** Prague, Nov. 25, 1837—Munich, Nov. 17, 1900; pupil of Müller (pf.), Rummel (harm.) and Zwonar (cpt.); 1863 co.-ed. *"Neue Zeitschrift fur Musik"*; friend and champion of Wagner; lived in Vienna; 1867 was called to Munich by King Ludwig II.; pf.-teacher R. Sch. of Mus. and 1871 R. Musikdirector; writer and composer.

Por'pora, Niccolò A. (wrote his name "Niccolà," printed it as here), Naples, Aug. 19, 1686—Feb., 1766; eminent vocal teacher at London, 1729–36; ct.-conductor; as dram. composer, rival of Händel, c. about 50 operas.

Porporino (-rē'-nō). Vide UBERTI.

Porsile (pôr-sē'-lĕ), **Giuseppe,** b. Naples, 1672—Vienna, 1750; court cond.; c. 6 operas, etc.

Porta (pôr'-tä), (1) Padre **Costanzo,** Cremona, ca. 1530—Padua, 1601; writer and composer. (2) **Fran. della,** Milan, ca. 1590—1666; composer. (3) **Giov.,** Venice, ca. 1690—Munich, 1755; ct.-cond. and dram. composer.

Por'ter, (1) **Walter,** d. London, 1659; tenor and composer. (2) **Quincy,** b. New Haven, Conn., 1897; composer; grad. Yale Univ. Sch. of Mus., 1921; studied with Horatio Parker and David Stanley Smith, winning two prizes; also with d'Indy, in Paris, and Ernest Bloch; taught mus. theory, Cleveland Inst. of Mus., 1922–8; then studied three years in Paris on Guggenheim Fellowship; prof. of mus., Vassar College, 1932–8; dean of faculty, New England Cons., from 1938; c. symphony (N. Y. Philh., 1938), 4 string quartets, and other orch., chamber mus.; Yale Univ., 1947. (3) **Cole,** Amer. composer; studied Yale; c. stage shows, incl. *"Kiss Me, Kate."*

Portugal (Portogallo) (pôr-tŭ-gäl' or pôr-tō-gäl'-lo), i.e., "The Portuguese", **Marcos A.** (acc. to Vasconcellos, rightly **"Portugal da Fonseca,"** not **M. A. Simão** as in Fétis), Lisbon, March 24, 1762—of apoplexy, Rio de Janeiro, Feb. 7, 1830; the most eminent of Portuguese composers; studied Italy and prod.

3 operas there; 1790 ct.-cond. Lisbon, also theatre cond. and produced 20 operas; 1810 followed the court to Rio and prod. operas; 1813 dir. of a Cons. at Vera Cruz.

Pothier (pōt-yā), **Dom Jos.,** Bouze-mount, near Saint-Dié, Dec. 7, 1835 —Dec. 8, 1923; 1866, prof. of theology, Solesmes monastery; writer and theorist.

Pott, August, Northeim, Hanover, Nov. 7, 1806—Graz, Aug. 27, 1883; violinist and composer, pupil of Spohr.

Pot'ter, Philip Cipriani Hambly, London, Oct. 2, 1792—Sept. 26, 1871; pianist, writer and composer.

Pottgiesser (pôt'-gēs-sĕr), **Karl,** b. Dortmund, Aug. 8, 1861; pupil of H. Riemann: after 1890 lived in Munich; c. opera "*Heimkehr*" (Cologne, 1903), a Festspiel, choruses, etc.; chapter 1 of *St. Paul's First Epistle*, for voices, organ and orch.; oratorio "*Gott ist der Liebe*"; choruses, etc.

Poueigh, (poo-ā) **(Marie Octave Géraud) Jean,** b. Toulouse, Feb. 24, 1876; studied with the Jesuit fathers at Toulouse; at 19 took up harmony with Hugounant of the Cons., which he entered in 1897, receiving the second harmony prize 1898; he then studied in Paris with Caussade, Lenepveu and Fauré, receiving criticisms from d'Indy. His comps. include sonata for piano and violin (performed by Enesco and Aubert, 1906); orch. suite "*Fünn*" (1906 and 1908 at Lamoureux concerts), poem with orch. "*Sentellière de Rêve*," dramatic poem for solos, choir and orch. "*Les Lointains*"; 5-act lyric drama, "*Le Meneur de Louves*"; "*Le Soir rôde*" (song with orch.), etc.

Pougin, Fran. Aug. Arthur (Paroisse), Châteauroux, Indre, France, Aug. 6, 1834—Paris, Aug. 8, 1921; pupil Paris Cons.; 1856-59, asst.-cond. Folies-Nouvelles; till 1863, violinist at Op.-Com., then important critic, essayist and biographer; ed. the supplement to "*Fétis*" (1878).

Pouishnoff (poo-ēsh'-nôf), **Lev,** b. Russia, Oct. 11, 1891; pianist; studied at St. Petersburg Cons., with Essipov, Rimsky-Korsakoff, Liadoff, Glazounoff, Tcherepnine; 1913 taught at Tiflis Cons.; also led orch. concerts there; toured Russia, Persia and England, living in the latter

country; one of leading piano virtuosi of day.

Poulenc (poo'-lŭnk), **Francis,** b. Paris, Jan. 7, 1889; composer; mem. of former Group of Six; pupil of Viñes and Koechlin; one of most gifted composers in the little circle of insouciant Parisian modernists devoted to lighter phases of music; his works parody folk-songs, military marches, tangos, etc., and he often changes his style within a composition; c. (ballet with voice) "*Les Biches*," prod. with succ. by Diaghileff, Monte Carlo, 1925 (ballet); "*Les Mariés de la Tour Eiffel*" (given in N. Y. by Swedish Ballet); "*Le Bestiaire*" for voice and piano; "*Rhapsodie Nègre*" and other chamber music pieces; two-piano concerto; sonata for 4 hands; sonata for 2 clarinets; various song cycles with small orch., and some pop. piano pieces incl. "*Mouvements perpétuels*," op.-com., "*Mamelles de Thirésias*."

Pow'ell, (1) **Walter,** Oxford, 1697—1744, counter-tenor. (2) **Maud,** Peru, Ill., Aug. 22, 1868—Uniontown, Pa., Jan. 8, 1920; notable American violinist; pupil of Lewis, later in Paris and of Schradieck, Leipzig, and of Joachim; toured widely with success Europe and America; début Berlin Phil., 1885; the same year in America with Theo. Thomas orch.; married H. Godfrey Turner. (3) **John,** b. Richmond, Va., 1882; pianist and composer; pupil of Hahr, Leschetizky and Navratil; début, Vienna, 1907, followed by tours in Germany, France, England; after 1912, heard as soloist with leading Amer. orchs. and as recitalist; c. (orch.) "*Negro Rhapsody*," "*Natchez-on-the Hill*"; piano and vln. concertos, string quartets, 2 vln. sonatas (the "*Virginiesque*" being well known); 3 piano sonatas (subtitled "*Psychologique*," "*Noble*' and "*Teutonica*"); piano suites, "*At the Fair*" and "*In the South*," etc.; active in folk-music festival movement in the South.

Pradher (rightly **Pradère**) (prăd-ā, or prä-dăr), **Louis Barthélemy,** Paris, 1781—Gray, Haute-Saône, 1843; noted teacher at the Cons. and the court; pianist, and dram. composer.

Präger (prä'-gĕr), **Fd. Chr. Wm.,** Leipzig, Jan. 22, 1815—London, Sept. 1, 1891; son of **Aloys P.,** cond.;

'cellist, later pianist and writer; c. symph. poem *"Life and Love, Battle and Victory,"* overture *"Abellino,"* etc.

Prätorius (prä-tō'-rĭ-oos) (Latinised form of **Schulz(e)**), (1) **Gottschalk,** Salzwedel, 1528—Wittenberg, 1573; writer. (2) **Chp.,** b. Bunzlau; pub. a funeral song on Melanchthon (1560). (3) **Hieronymus,** Hamburg, 1560—1629; son of an organist; organist; c. church-mus., etc., with his son (4) **Jakob,** d. 1651, organist; (5) **Bartholomäus,** composer, Berlin, 1616. (6) (or **Praetorius**), **Michael,** Kreuzberg, Thuringia, Feb. 15, 1571—Wolfenbüttel, Feb. 15, 1621; conductor and ct.-organist. Eminent as a composer of church- and dance-mus.; wrote valuable historical "Syntagma musicum."

Pratt, (1) **J.,** Cambridge, Engl., 1772—1855; organist and composer. (2) **Chas. E.,** Hartford, Conn., 1841—New York, 1902; pianist, cond. and composer. (3) **Silas Gamaliel,** Addison, Vt., Aug. 4, 1846—Pittsburgh, Pa., Oct. 31, 1916; prominent American composer for orch.; at 12 thrown on his own resources, became a clerk in mus.-houses; studied with Bendel, and Kullak (pf.), Wuerst and Kiel (comp.); 1871 organised Apollo Club, Chicago; 1875, returned to Berlin, and studied with H. Dorn; prod. *"Anniversary Overture"* there 1876; 1877, Chicago; gave symph. concerts, 1878, and prod. his opera *"Zenobia,"* 1882, 1885, gave concerts of his own comp. Crystal Palace, London; 1890, pf.-prof. N. Y. Metropolitan Cons.; c. lyric opera *"Lucille"* (Chicago, 1887); *"The Last Inca,"* cantata with orch. which ran for three weeks; 2 symphs. (No. 2, *"Prodigal Son"*), *"Magdalena's Lament"* (based on Murillo's picture) for orch.; an excellent symph. suite, *"The Tempest"*; a grotesque suite *"The Brownies"*; cantata *"Columbus."* etc. (4) **Waldo Selden,** b. Philadelphia, Nov. 10, 1857; d. Hartford, July 29, 1939; Mus. D. Syracuse Univ.; prof. music and Hymnology, Hartford Theol. Sem., 1882–1917; later emeritus prof.; taught Inst. of Mus. Art, New York, 1905–20; lecturer, music history and science, Smith Coll., 1895–1908; ed. of *"New Encyclopedia of Music and Musicians"*; author, *"History of Music."*

"Musical Ministries in the Church," *"The Music of the Pilgrims,"* etc.

Predieri (prä-dĭ-ā'-rē), (1) **Giacomo Cesare,** d. after 1743; from 1696 cond. at Bologna Cath.; c. oratorios, motets, etc. (2) **Luca Ant.,** Bologna, 1688—1767; ct.-cond. and dram. composer.

Preindl (prīnt' 'l), **Jos.,** Marbach, Lower Austria, 1756—Vienna, 1823; conductor, writer and collector.

Preitz (prīts), **Fz.,** Zerbst, Aug. 12, 1856 —July 17, 1916; concert-organist; pupil of Leipzig Cons., singing-teacher, Zerbst Gymnasium, and cantor at the ct.-church; pub. a requiem, etc.

Pren'tice, Thos. Ridley, Paslow Hall, Ongar, Essex, 1842—Hampstead, 1895; teacher, pianist and writer.

Pres'sel, Gv Ad., Tübingen, 1827—Berlin, 1890; dram. composer.

Pressen'da, Johannes Franciscus, Lequio-Berria, Jan. 6, 1777—Turin, Sept. 11, 1854; violin maker.

Pres'ser, Theodore, Pittsburgh, Pa., July 3, 1848—Philadelphia, Oct. 27, 1925; publisher; 1883, founded and ed. *The Etude*; 1906, endowed Presser Home for Musicians, Phila.; now administered by Presser Foundation; transl. text-books; c. pf.-pcs., etc.

Prévost (prä-vō), **Eugène Prosper,** Paris, Aug. 23, 1809—New Orleans, Aug. 30, 1872, conductor and singing-teacher; prod. operas in Paris and New Orleans.

Preyer (prī'-ĕr), (1) **Gf.,** Hausbrunn, Lower Austria, March 15, 1807—Vienna, 1901; organist, pupil of Sechter; 1838, prof. of harm. and cpt. at the Cons.; 1844–48, dir.; 1844, also vice ct.-cond.; 1846, ct.-organist; 1853, con. at St. Stephen's; 1876, pensioned as "Vice-Hofkapellmeister"; prod. symphony, masses, etc. (2) **Wm. Thierry,** Manchester, Engl., July 4, 1841—Wiesbaden, July 15, 1807; studied Bonn Univ.; 1869–94 prof. of physiology, Jena; acoustician.

Pribik (prē'-bĭk), **Joseph,** b. Bohemia, 1853; pupil Prague Cons.; director of opera in various cities; from 1894 of Odessa Symph. Orch.; c. suites, operas, etc.; d. (?).

Prihoda (prē-hŏ'-dä), **Vasa,** Vodnany, Bohemia, Aug. 24, 1900; violin virtuoso; a pupil of Marak at Prague Cons.; early showed unusual musical talent; his 1st major succ. came

when he played in an audition for
Toscanini in Milan and made his
début there in concert, 1920; since
that time he has played with marked
succ. in many Eur. cities, also visiting U. S.

Prill (prĭl), K., Berlin, Oct. 22, 1864—
Vienna, Aug. 18, 1931; son and pupil
of a mus.-dir., and pupil of Helmich,
Wirth, and Joachim (at the Hoch-
schule); violinist; 1883–85 leader
Bilse's orch., 1885 at Magdeburg;
from 1891, of the Gewandhaus Orch.,
Leipzig; later at Nürnberg; 1901, at
Schwerin, after 1897, Vienna.

Primavera (prē'-mä-vä'-rä), **Giovanni Leonardo,** b. Barletta; from
1573, concertmaster at Milan.

Prim'rose, Wm., b. Glasgow; violist.

Pri'oris, Johannes, organist at St.
Peter's, Rome, 1490; 1507, cond. to
Louis XII of France; c. motets, etc.

Proch (prōkh), **H.,** Böhmisch-Leipa,
July 22, 1809—Vienna, Dec. 18,
1878; noted vocal teacher and conductor; c. comic opera and famous
vocal variations.

Procházka (prō-khäz'-kä), **Rudolf,
Freiherr von,** Prague, Feb. 23, 1864
—Mar. 23, 1936; pupil of Fibich and
Grünberger; magistrate in Prague;
author of biographies; c. dramatic
tone story. *"Das Glück"* (Vienna,
1898); sacred melody *"Christus,"* etc.

Prod'homme, Jacques Gabriel, b.
Paris, Nov. 28, 1871; writer on
music; pupil of the École des Hautes
Études Sociales; critic on various
Paris papers; 1897-9100 in Munich; author, *"Le Cycle Berlioz," "H. Berlioz,"
"sa Vie et Ses Oeuvres," "Les Symphonies de Beethoven," "La Jeunesse de
Beethoven," "Paganini," "Wagner et
la France," "L'Opéra—1669-1925,"* etc.

Pro'fe, (or Profius) Ambrosius, Breslau, Feb. 12, 1589—Breslau, Dec. 27,
1661; organist; c. church music.

Prokofieff (prō-kō'-fĕ-ĕf), **Serge,** b.
Russia, Apr. 23, 1891—d. March, 1953;
composer, pianist; began study with
Taneieff in Moscow at 10, later with
Gliere; won Rubinstein prize at
Petersburg Cons. where he studied
with Liadoff, Rimsky-Korsakoff and
the elder Tcherepnine; while a
student c. 2 operas, 6 sonatas, many
piano pieces, all unpublished; made
début as comp. at 18, when Petersburg Soc. for Contemp. Music gave
a concert of his works; early pub. a

Sinfonietta, several symph. poems
and his 1st and 2nd piano concertos;
after graduation went to London,
where Diaghileff commissioned a
ballet, which became his "Scythian"
suite for orch.; all his works show
bold harmonic clashes, many are in
a somewhat satiric vein; the majority exploit an original rhythmic
style and spirit of experimentation;
c. (operas) *"The Gambler"* (later
revised); *"The Love of the Three
Oranges"* (Chicago Op., 1922); *"The
Flaming Angel";* (ballets) *"Chout,"
"Le Pas d'Acier," "The Prodigal
Son," "Sur le Borysthene";* (orch.)
6 symphonies, Divertimento, also a
much played *"Classical"* symphony
in Mozartian vein; (piano) 5 concertos, 5 sonatas, various smaller
pieces; two vln. concertos, sonata
for 2 violins unaccompanied, 'cello
concerto, string quartet, ballade for
'cello; mus. fable for reciter and
orch., *"Peter and the Wolf"* (also
arr. as ballet); ballet, *"Cinderella";*
music for film, *"Alex. Nevsky."*

Proksch (prŏksh), (1) **Josef,** Reichenberg, Bohemia, 1794—Prague, 1864;
pianist, writer and composer; founded
a pf.-school; his children and successors were (2) **Theodor,** 1843—
1876; and (3) **Marie,** 1836—1900.

Proske (prŏsh'-kĕ), **K.,** Gröbnig, Upper Silesia, 1794—Ratisbon, 1861:
canon, conductor, publisher, editor
and composer.

Proth'eroe, Daniel, Wales, Nov. 24,
1866—Chicago, Feb. 24, 1934; choral
conductor; after 1894 in Milwaukee,
where he led Arion Chorus beginning
1899; from 1904 in Chicago; taught
Sherwood Music School; Mus. D.

Prout (prowt), (1) **Ebenezer,** Oundle,
Northamptonshire, March 1, 1835—
Hackney near London, Dec. 5, 1909;
prominent theorist and composer.
Save for a few piano lessons as a boy,
and with Chas. Salaman, wholly
self-taught. B.A. London Univ.,
1854; 1859 took up music; 1861–73,
organist Union Chapel, Islington;
1861–85, pf.-prof. at the Crystal
Palace Sch. of Art; from 1876 prof.
of harm. and comp. at the Nat.
Training Sch.; 1879, at the R. A. M.
(Vice A. Sullivan), also cond. 1876-
90, the Hackney Choral Assoc.;
1874 Critic on the *Acad.* 1879,
on the *Athenaeum.* Contributed
53 articles to *"Grove's Dictionary."*

1894, prof. of mus., Dublin Univ.;
1895, Mus. Doc. *h. c.* Dublin and
Edinburg Univ. Pub. many valu-
able and original treatises, incl.
"*Harmony*" (1889, 10 editions);
"*Counterpoint, Strict and Free*"
(1890); "*Double Counterpoint and
Canon*" (1891); "*Fugue*" (1891);
"*Fugal Analysis*" (1892); "*Musical Form*" (1893); "*Applied Forms*"
(1895); "*The Orchestra*" (1898–
1900); c. 4 symphs., 2 overtures,
"*Twelfth Night*" and "*Rokeby*";
suite de ballet for orch.; suite in D;
cantatas; a Magnificat, Evening
Service, Psalm 126 (St. Paul's, 1891);
Psalm 100 "*The Song of Judith*"
(Norwich, 1867), "*Freedom*" (1885),
all with orch., 2 organ-concertos, 2
prize pf.-quartets, etc. (2) **Louis
Beethoven,** b. London, Sept. 14,
1864; son of above; from 1888,
prof. of harm. Crystal Palace Sch. of
Art; pub treatises; c. Psalm 93.

Pruckner (prook'-něr), (1) **Dionys,**
Munich, May 12, 1834—Heidelberg,
Dec. 1, 1896; pianist and teacher.
(2) **Caroline,** Vienna, Nov. 4, 1832—
June 16, 1908; succ. operatic soprano; 1855, suddenly lost her voice;
1870 opened a Sch. of Opera; pub.
a vocal treatise (1872) for which she
was made Prof.

Prudent (prü-däṅ) (**Beunie-Prudent**),
Émile, Angoulême, 1817—Paris,
1863; pianist and composer.

Prume (prüm), (1) **Fran. Hubert,**
Stavelot, near Liége, 1816—1849;
ct.-prof. and composer. (2) **Fz. H.,**
nephew of the above. Vide JEHIN-
PRUME.

Prumier (prüm-yā), (1) **Ant.,** Paris,
1794—1868; harpist; prof. at the
Cons., and composer. (2) **Ange
Conrad,** 1820—Paris, 1884; son,
pupil and successor of above.

Prunières (prün-yěr), **Henry,** b. Paris,
May 24, 1886; critic and writer on
music; pupil of Rolland; Litt. D.;
after 1919 ed. *La Revue Musicale;*
founded modern concerts; noted musicologist; d. Nanterre, Apr. 11, 1942.

Puccini (poot-chē'-nē), (1) **Giacomo,**
b. Italy, 1712; pupil of Padre Martini; organist; c. church-music. (2)
Antonio, b. 1747; son of above; c.
church-music and (acc. to Fétis) operas; m. di capp. to Republic of San
Lucca; his son and successor (3) **Domenico,** 1771—1815; c. church-music
and many comic operas; his son (4)

Michele, 1812—1864; pupil of Mercadante; lived at San Lucca as
church and opera-composer; his son
(5) **Giacomo,** Lucca, Italy, Dec. 23,
1858—Brussels, Nov. 29, 1924; noted
opera composer; pupil of Angeloni at
Lucca; then of A. Ponchielli, Milan
Cons., graduating with a "*Capriccio
sinfonico*"; 1893, prof. of comp.
there; prod. 1-act opera "*Le Villi*"
(Milan, 1884); extended later to
2 acts and prod. at La Scala; succ.
"*Edgar*" (La Scala, Milan, 1889);
succ. lyric drama "*Manon Lescaut*"
(Turin, 1893); widely popular opera
seria "*La Bohême*" (Turin, 1896);
succ. "*La Tosca*" (London, Covent
Garden, 1900); "*Madame Butterfly*"
(La Scala, Milan, 1904) a dire failure
and withdrawn after one perform-
ance; revised and brought out at
Brescia the same year with a success
that has spread all over the world,
being sung throughout America in
English by the Henry W. Savage
Company. It was based on a play
by John Luther Long and David
Belasco. His next opera was also
based on a play of Belasco's, "*The
Girl of the Golden West*" ("*La
Fanciulla del West*"), and first prod.
New York Met. Op., 1910, with
much success and later in Italy,
England, etc. He prod. also "*La
Rondine,*" a lighter work on Viennese
models (Monte Carlo, 1917); his
Trittico or triptych of 1-act operas,
"*Il Tabarro,*" "*Suor Angelica*" and
"*Gianni Schicchi*" (Met. Op., 1918),
the last of which, a sparkling comedy,
has won a place in the repertoire and
has been called his most musicianly
work; and his last opus, "*Turandot,*"
not quite complete at his death,
but with a final scene by Alfano,
after his sketches, prod. at La Scala,
April 25, 1926. A master of fluent
melody, he gave perhaps the most
pop. works to the modern opera
stage, despite his lack in thorough
contrapuntal knowledge; this was
compensated for by skilled sense of
the theatre and an instinct for
creating mood, pathos and atmosphere. He also c. some vocal and
instrumental works not for the stage.
Memoirs by Dry, Specht, etc.

Puchalski (poo-chäl'-shkǐ), **Vladimir
V.,** 1848—Feb. 23, 1933; pupil
at St. Petersburg Cons.; pianist:
1876-1913, director Imperial Music

School in Kiev; c. Little-Russian fantasie for orch., opera, etc.

Puchat (poo'-khät), **Max**, Breslau, 1859—in the Karwendel Mountains, Aug. 12, 1919; pianist, pupil of Kiel, at Berlin; 1884, Mendelssohn prize; c. symph. poems *"Euphorion"* and *"Tragödie eines Künstlers"*; overture; a pf.-concerto, etc.

Pucitta (poo-chĭt'-tä), **V.**, Civitavecchia, 1778—Milan, 1861; cembalist and dram. composer.

Pudor (poo'-dôr), (1) **Jn. Fr.**, Delitzsch, Saxony, 1835—Dresden, 1887; from 1859 proprietor Dresden Cons. (2) **Dr. H.**, b. Dresden, 1865; son and successor of above in the Cons., which he sold 1890 to E. Krantz; wrote many essays.

Puente (poo-ĕn'-tĕ), **Giuseppe del**, Naples, April, 1845—Philadelphia, May 25, 1900; operatic barytone and teacher.

Puget (pü-zhā), **Paul Chas. M.**, b. Nantes, June 25, 1848; pupil of Paris Cons., took Grand Prix de Rome; prod. comic opera *"Le Signal"* (Op. Com., 1886); mod. succ. opera *"Beaucoup de Bruit Pour Rien"* (*"Much Ado about Nothing"*) (ibid., 1899); incid. mus. to *"Lorenzaccio,"* etc.; d. (?).

Pugnani (poon-yä'-nē), **Gaetano**, Turin, Nov. 27, 1731—July 15, 1798; famous violinist, dram. composer and conductor.

Pugni (poon'-yē), **Cesare**, Genoa, 1805—St. Petersburg, 1870; dram. composer.

Pugno (pün-yō), **Raoul**, Montrouge, Seine, France, June 23, 1852—Moscow, Jan. 3, 1914 (while on concert tour); prominent pianist; pupil of Paris Cons.; 1866 took 1st pf.-prize, 1867, 1st. harm.-prize; 1869, 1st org.-prize; organist and cond., Paris; from 1896, prof. of piano at the Cons.; after 1897 toured U. S. with succ.; Officier of the Académie; prod. an oratorio, *"La Resurrection de Lazare"*; comic opera *"Ninetta"*; 2 opéras bouffes; 3 1-act vaudev.-operettas *"La Petite Poucette"* (Berlin, as *"Der Talisman"*); etc.

Pujol (poo'-hôl), **Juan Bautista**, Barcelona, 1836—Dec., 1898; pianist, author of a method; c. piano pieces.

Puliti (poo-lē'-tē), **Leto**, Florence, 1818—1875; composer.

Punto, G. Vide STICH.

Puppo (poop'-pō), **Gius.**, Lucca, June 12, 1749—in poverty, Florence, April 19, 1827; an eccentric violinist, conductor and composer.

Purcell (pŭr'-sĕl), (1) **H.**, d. London, 1664; gentleman of the Chapel Royal, and Master of the Choristers at Westminster Abbey. (2) **Henry** (called "the younger"), London, 1658—of consumption, Dean's Yard, Westminster, Nov. 21, 1695; nephew of (1); one of the most eminent of English composers. Chorister Chapel Royal, and studied with Cooke, Humfrey, and Dr. Blow; at 18 c. mus. for Dryden's tragedy, *"Aurungzebe,"* and Shadwell's comedy *"Epsom Wells"*; pub. a song; at 19 an overture, etc., to Aphra Behn's tragedy, *"Abdelazor,"* and an elegy on Matthew Locke; at 20 c. music to Shadwell's version of *"Timon of Athens"*; 1680, incid. mus., and a short opera *"Dido and Æneas"* written to order for Josias Priest for his "boarding sch. for young gentlewomen"; c. also the *"Ode or Welcome Song for His Royal Highness"* Duke of York, and *"A Song to Welcome Home His Majesty from Windsor."* From 1680 organist Westminster Abbey, where he is buried. 1682, organist Chapel Royal; 1683, composer-in-ordinary to the King. His first pub. chamber-mus. is dated the year 1683. He c. *"Odes"* to King Charles 1684, and to King James in 1685, 28 in all. He c. mus. for 35 dram. works of the time. 1695 he pub. his first real opera, *"Dioclesian."* The Purcell Society (organised, 1876) has issued many of his works in a proposed complete edition (18 vols. had appeared before 1922) and has given frequent performances of them in London. The Mus. Antiq. Soc. has pub. others; his widow pub. in 1697 *"A Collection of Ayres Composed for the Theatre and upon Other Occasions"*; also songs for 1-3 voices, from his theatrical works and odes; and the *"Orpheus Brittanicus"* in 2 parts (Part i, 1698, Part ii, 1702). W. Barclay Squire issued his original works for harpsichord (4 vols.). Playford's *"Theatre of Musick"* (1687), and other colls. contain many of his works; *"Purcell's Sacred Music"* pub. in 6 vols. (Novello). Biographical works on **P.** have been pub. by Arundell, Cummings, H. Dupré, Holland, Runciman, Scholes, Westrup. (See article, page 510.) (3) **Edw.**, 1689—1740; son of above; organist and composer. (4) **Daniel,** London, 1660—Dec. 12, 1717; bro. of above; 1688, organist; 1695, succ. his bro. as dram. composer; c. incid. mus. to ten dramas; odes, incl. funeral ode for his brother, etc.

Putea´nus, Ericius (Latinised form of H. Van de Putte) (poot´-tĕ) (Gallicised to **Dupuy**), Venloo, Holland, 1574—Louvain, 1646; professor and writer.

Pyne (pīn), (1) **Geo.**, 1790—1877, Engl. male alto. (2) **Jas. Kendrick,** 1852—1938; Engl. organist. (3) **Louisa Fanny,** England, 1832—London, March 20, 1904; soprano, daughter of (2); pupil of Sir G. Smart; début, Boulogne, 1849; 1868, m. Frank Bodda, a barytone.

Pythag´oras, Samos, Greece, ca. 582, B. C.—Metapontum, ca. 500 B. C.; famous philosopher and mathematician; developed an elaborate system of musical ratios.

Q

Quadflieg (kvät´-flēkh), **Gerhard Jakob,** Breberen, Aug. 27, 1854—Elberfeld, Feb. 23, 1915; pupil Church Music School, Regensburg; from 1881, teacher; from 1898, rector at Elberfeld; also cond. and organist; c. 7 masses, many motets, etc.

Quadrio (kwä´-drĭ-ō), **Fran. Saverio,** Ponte, Valtellina, 1695—Milan, 1756; theorist.

Quagliati (kwäl-yä´-tē), **Paolo,** d. Rome, ca. 1627; cembalist; c. one of the earliest mus. dramas (1611).

Quantz (kvänts), **Jn. Joachim,** Oberscheden, Hanover, 1697—Potsdam, 1773; noted flutist; inv. the second key and sliding top for tuning the flute; taught Frederick the Great; c. 500 flute pcs.

Quaranta (kwä-rän´-tä), **Fran.,** Naples, 1848—Milan, 1897; singing-teacher and dram. composer.

Quarenghi (kwä-rän´-gē), **Guglielmo,** Casalmaggiore, 1826—Milan, 1882; ´cellist, professor, conductor and dram. composer.

Quarles, Jas. Thos., b. St. Louis, Nov. 7, 1877; organist; pupil of Galloway, Vieh, Ehling and Kroeger; also with Widor in Paris; active for many years in native city, incl. Scottish Rite Cath.; founded Choral Art Soc. there; after 1913 at Cornell Univ., where asst. prof., 1916; prof. of music, Univ. of Missouri, 1923.

Quatremère de Quincey (kăt-rŭ-măr´-dŭ-kăn-sē´), **Ant. Chrysostome,** Paris, 1755—1849; writer.

Queisser (kvīs´-sĕr), **Carl T.,** Döben, 1800—Leipzig, 1846; noted trombonist.

Quercu (kvĕr´-koo), **Simon de** (Latinised from **Van Eycken** or **Du Chesne**), b. in Brabant; theorist and ct.-chapel-singer, Milan, ca. 1500.

Quil´ter, Roger, b. Brighton, Nov. 1, 1877; composer; pupil of Knorr, Frankfort; c. serenade for orch. part songs, and many attractive songs; d. London, Sept. 21, 1953.

Quinault (kē-nō), (1) **Philippe,** Paris, 1635—1688; Lully's librettist. (2) **J. Bap. Maurice,** d. Gien, 1744; singer, actor and composer of ballets, etc.

Quiroga (kē-rō´-gä), **Manuel,** b. Pontavedra, Spain, 1890; violinist; pupil of R. Cons. in Madrid and Paris Cons.; one of leading virtuosi of vln.; has toured Spain, France, England and (1936) U. S. A.

R

Raabe (rä´-bĕ), **Peter,** b. Frankfort-am-Oder, Nov. 27, 1872; pupil of Bargiel; cond. at various theatres; 1899 at the Opera, Amsterdam; 1903, dir. Kaim orch., Munich; 1907-20, court cond. Weimar; c. song and piano pieces; after 1910, curator of Weimar Liszt museum; also writer on this composer and head of a committee to publish his complete works; 1920-34, gen. mus. dir., Aachen; 1935, pres. of Reich Mus. Chamber; d. Frankfort-on-Oder, 1945.

Rabaud (rä´-bō), (1) **Henri,** b. Paris, Nov. 10, 1873—Sept. 12, 1949; pupil of Massenet and Gédalge at Paris Cons.; awarded Prix de Rome, 1894; son of the ´cellist (2) **Hippolyte R.** (who also taught at the Cons.); he served as cond. at the Op.-Comique and after 1908 also at the Opéra; 1914-18, chief cond. at latter house; 1918-19, he succeeded Muck as cond. of Boston Symph. Orch.; after 1920 he was dir. of the Paris Cons. (vice Fauré); c. many works in a witty, modern style of considerable colourfulness and charm, including the operas "*La Fille de Roland*" (Op.-Comique, 1904); "*Le Premier Glaive*" (Béziers Arena, 1908); "*Marouf*" (Paris, 1914, also at Met. Op. and with succ. at Ravinia Op., his most effective stage composition); "*Antoine et Cléopâtre*"; "*L'Appel de la Mer*" (1-act, Op.-Comique, 1924); also the oratorio "*Job*" (1900); 4 Psalms for soloists, chorus and orch.; 2 symphonies; symph. poem, "*La Procession Nocturne*" after Lenau's "*Faust*," a much played work; "*Poème Virgilien*" and "*Divertissement sur des Airs Russes*," both for orch.; string quartet, songs, etc.

Rachmaninoff (räkh-mä'-nē-nôf), **Sergei**, Novgorod, April 1, 1873—Los Angeles, March 28, 1943; pianist, composer; pupil of Siloti (pf.) and Arensky (theory), Moscow Cons.; 1891, took gold medal; c. succ. 1-act opera "*Aleko*" (Moscow, 1893); in 1899 appeared in London as conductor and pianist; from 1903 piano prof. Maryinski Inst. for Girls, Moscow; 1912, appointed chief cond. of the Opera St. Petersburg. He began a series of notable tours of Europe and (after 1905) in the U. S., where from 1917 he made his home, as his estates in Russia had been confiscated by the Soviets. He also passed summers at his villa outside Paris. His fame as a pianist had become world-wide and he had toured each season as one of the most fêted of performers, invariably playing to large audiences. His comps. include 3 symphonies; the tone poem, "*Isle of the Dead*"; 4 piano concertos; and a virtuosic work for piano and orch., "*Rhapsody on a Theme of Paganini*," in which he has toured extensively as soloist; (chamber music) "*Elegiac*" Trio; sonata for 'cello and piano; (choral works) "*The Bells*" (after the poem by Poe); six choruses for women's voices; "*Fate*"; (operas) "*Aleko*" and "*Francesca da Rimini*"; a mass and other church music; also a large number of piano works, incl. several famous Preludes, and songs which have gained a wide popularity. (See article, page 510.)

Radecke (rä'-děk-ĕ), (1) **Rudolf**, Dittmannsdorf, Silesia, 1829—Berlin, 1893; conductor, teacher and composer. (2) (**Albert Martin**), **Robert**, Dittmannsdorf, Oct. 31, 1830—Wernigerode, June 21, 1911; bro. of above; pupil of Leipzig Cons.; 1st vln. in Gewandhaus; then pianist and organist, Berlin; later mus.-dir. ct.-th.; 1871–84, ct.-cond.; 1883–88, artistic dir. Stern Cons.; 1892, dir. R. Inst. for Church-mus., Berlin; c. 1-act "*Liederspiel*," "*Die Mönkguter*" (Berlin, 1874); a symph., 2 overtures, etc. (3) **Ernst**, Berlin, Dec. 8, 1866—Winterthur, Oct. 8, 1920; son of above; Dr. Phil. at Berlin U., 1891; 1893, town mus.-director and teacher, Winterthur, Switzerland.

Radeglia (rä-dāl'-yä), **Vittorio**, b. Constantinople, 1863; composer; c. operas "*Colomba*" (Milan, 1887). "*Amore occulto*" (Constantinople, 1904), etc. C. Turkish National Anthem.

Radicati (rä-dĭ-kä'-tē), **Felice da Maurizio di**, Turin, 1778—Vienna, April 14, 1823; violinist, court composer and 1815 cond. at Bologna; c. operas and important chamber music.

Radoux (rä-doo), (1) **Jean Théodore**, Liége, Nov. 5, 1835—March 21, 1911; pupil at the Cons.; 1856, teacher of bassoon there; 1859, won Prix de Rome with cantata "*Le Juif Errant*"; studied with Halévy, Paris; 1872, dir. Liége Cons.; pub. biog. of Vieuxtemps (1891); prod. 2 comic operas, oratorio "*Cain*," cantata "*La Fille de Jephté*" with orch., 2 symph. tone-pictures, symph. overture, Te Deum, etc. His son (2) **Charles**, b. Liége, 1877; composer: pupil of Cons. in native city; won Prix de Rome, 1907; after 1900 prof. at Liége Conservatory.

Radziwill (rät'-tsē-vĭl), Prince **Anton H.**, Wilna, 1775—Berlin, 1833; singer and composer; patron of Beethoven and Chopin.

Raff (räf), (1) Vide RAAF. (2) **Jos. Joachim**, Lachen, Lake of Zurich, May 27, 1822—Frankfort-on-Main, June 25, 1882; eminent composer, particularly in the field of programmatic romanticism. Son of an organist; too poor to attend a Univ. he became a sch.-teacher; was self-taught in comp. and vln.; 1843 he sent some comps. to Mendelssohn, who recommended them to a publisher. R. accompanied Liszt on a concert-tour as far as Cologne (1846) where he lived for a time, writing reviews; later von Bülow played his "Concertstück"; his opera "König Alfred" was accepted by the ct.-th., but forestalled by the Revolution of 1848; it was prod. in revised form at Weimar by Liszt. He pub. (1854) a pamphlet Die Wagnerfrage. 1854, m. the actress Doris Genast, and obtained vogue at Wiesbaden as a pf.-teacher. 1863, his first symph., "An das Vaterland," won the prize of the Viennese "Gesellschaft der Musikfreunde"; 1870, his comic opera "Dame Kobold," was prod. at Weimar. 1877, dir. Hoch Cons. at Frankfort. He was a very prolific and uneven composer. The Raff Memorial Soc. pub. at Frankfort (1886) a complete list of his works which incl. 11 symphs.: No. 1, "An das Vaterland"; famous No. 3, in F, "Im Walde" (1869); No. 5, op. 177 in E, the noted "Lenore"; No. 6, op. 189 in D min., "Gelebt, gestrebt-gelitten, gestritten-gestorben, umworben"; No. 7, op. 201 in Bb, "In den Alpen"; No. 8, op. 205, A, "Frühlingsklänge"; No. 9, op. 208, E min., "Im Sommer"; No. 11, op. 214, A min., "Der Winter" (posthumous); a Sinfonietta; 4 suites No. 2, "In ungarischer Weise"; No. 3, "Italienisch"; No. 4, "Thüringer"; 9 overtures, the "Jubel-Fest-" and "Concert-ouvertüre"; "Festouverture" for wind; "Ein feste Burg," "Romeo and Juliet," "Othello," "Macbeth," and "The Tempest"; festival cantata "Deutschlands Auferstehung"; "De profundis" in 8 parts, op. 141; "Im Kahn" and "Der Tanz"; for mixed chorus "Morgenlied" and "Einer Entschlafenen"; "Die Tageszeiten"; "Die Jägerbraut und die Hirtin," 2 scenes for solo voice; all with orch; the oratorio "Weltende, Gericht, Neue Welt" (Revelations) (Leeds, 1882); "Die Sterne" and "Dornröschen" (MS.); 4 unperformed operas, "Die Eifersüchtigen" (text and music); "Die Parole," "Benedetto Marcello" and "Samson"; mus. to Genast's "Bernard von Weimar" (1858); "Ode au printemps" for pf. and orch.; "La fête d'Amour" suite for vln. with orch.; 2 'cello-concertos; much chamber-mus., incl. op. 192 (3 nos., "Suite älterer Form," "Die schöne Müllerin." "Suite in canon-

form"); 5 vln. sonatas; 'cello-sonata; 2 pf.-sonatas, suites, sonatinas; "Homage au néo-romantisme," "Messagers du printemps," "Chant d'Ondine" (arpeggio tremolo étude), Ungarische Rhapsodie, Spanische Rhapsodie, 2 études mélodique, op. 130 ("Cavatina," and the famous "La Fileuse"), many paraphrases; many suites, incl. 2 cycles, "Maria Stuart" and "Bonded de Nesle"; 30 male quartets, etc.

Rahlwes (räl'-väs), Alf., b. Wesel, Oct. 23, 1878; pupil Cologne Cons.; conductor; d. Halle, Apr. 20, 1946.

Raida (rī'-dä), Karl Alex., Paris, Oct. 4, 1852—Berlin, Nov. 26, 1923); pupil Stuttgart and Dresden Cons.; theatre-cond. in various cities; 1878–92, in Berlin; from 1895, Munich; c. operettas, ballets, etc.

Raif (rīf), Oscar, The Hague, 1847—Berlin, 1899; pianist, teacher and composer.

Raimondi (rä-ē-môn'-dē), (1) Ignazio, Naples, 1733—1813; violinist and composer. (2) P., Rome, Dec. 20, 1786—Oct. 30, 1853; extraordinary contrapuntist, rivalling the ancient masters in ingenuity; prof. of cpt., and cond. at St. Peter's; prod. 62 operatic works and 21 ballets, 4 masses w. orch. and 5 oratorios, besides the monumental trilogy "Giuseppe" (Joseph) consisting of 3 oratorios ("Potifar," "Giuseppe" "Giacobbe"), performed at Rome, 1852 separately, then all at once by 400 musicians, producing such frantic excitement that the composer fainted away; he c. also an opera buffa and an opera seria performable together; 4 four-voiced fugues which could be combined into one fugue à 16, etc., incl. a fugue for 64 parts in 16 choirs; he wrote essays explaining his methods.

Rains, Leon, b. New York, 1870; basso; pupil of Saenger and Bouhy; 1897–99, sang with Damrosch Op. Co.; at Dresden Op. in latter year; Met. Op., 1908; afterward teacher and lecturer in N. Y. and on Pacific Coast.

Raisa (rä-ē'-zä), Rosa, b. Bielostok, Poland; soprano; studied at Naples Cons. with Marchisio; début, Parma, 1913; was member Chicago Op. for many seasons, singing Italian dram. rôles principally, also "Elisabeth"; a voice of notable size and strong dram. talents; has also appeared at Covent Garden, La Scala (where created title rôle in Puccini's "*Turandot*"), Rome, Buenos Aires, Paris Op., Mexico City, Rio de Janeiro, Los Angeles, Ravinia and Detroit Operas, in Amer. première of Rocca's "*The Dybbuk*" (in English) with last organisation; m. Giacomo Rimini, barytone.

Ramann (rä'-män), **Lina**, Mainstockheim, near Kitzingen, June 24, 1833—Munich, March 30, 1912; pupil of Franz and Frau Brendel, Leipzig; 1858, founded a mus.-seminary for female teachers, 1865–90, a mus.-sch. at Nürnberg; pub. treatises and composed. Author of life of Liszt (3 vols.), 1880–94, a translation of his literary works, and a "*Liszt-Pädagogium*" (5 vols.), his piano works with annotations.

Rameau (rä-mō), (1) **J. Philippe**, Dijon, Sept. 25, 1683—of typhoid, Paris, Sept. 12, 1764; eminent as theorist, composer and organist. At 7 he could play at sight on the clavecin any music given him; from 10 to 14 he attended the Jesuit Coll. at Dijon; but taking no interest in anything but music was dismissed and left to study music by himself. He was sent to Italy, 1701, to break off a love affair, but did not care to study there, and joined a travelling French opera-troupe as violinist. Later he became organist at two churches in Paris, 1717. He studied org. with Louis Marchand, who found his pupil a rival, and in a competition favoured his competitor, Daquin, as organist of St. Paul's; R. went as organist to Lille, later to Clermont (where lived his brother (2) **Claude**, a clever organist, and his father (3) **Jean Fran.**, a gifted but dissipated organist and poet). After 4 years he returned to Paris, and pub. a treatise on harm. which attracted some attention. He became organist Sainte-Croix-de-la-Bretonnerie; and c. songs and dances for pieces by Piron, at the Op.-Com.; 1726, he pub. his epoch-making "*Nouveau système de musique théorique*," based on his own studies of the monochord (v. D. D.); in this work among many things inconsistent, involved and arbitrary (and later modified or discarded) was much of remarkable even sensational

novelty, such as the discovery of the law of chord-inversion. He founded his system on (1) chord-building by thirds; (2) the classification of chords and their inversions to one head each, thus reducing the consonant and dissonant combinations to a fixed number of root-chords; (3) a fundamental bass ("basse fondamentale," not our thorough-bass), an imaginary series of root-tones forming the real bases of all the chord-progressions of a composition. His theories provoked much criticism, but soon won him pupils from far and wide and the pre-eminence as theorist that he enjoyed as organist. He followed his first theoretic treatises with 5 other treatises. He now obtained the libretto "*Samson*" from Voltaire (whom he strikingly resembled in appearance) but the work was rejected on account of its biblical subject. "*Hippolyte et Aricie*," libretto by Abbé Pelegrin, was prod. at the Opéra, 1733, with so little succ. that he was about to renounce the stage, but his friends prevailed and he prod., 1735, the succ. ballet-opera "*Les Indes Galantes*," and at the age of 54 his masterpiece "*Castor et Pollux*," a great succ. as were most of his later works for 23 years, "*Les Fêtes d' Hébé*" (1739), "*Dardanus*" (1739), "*La Princesse de Navarre*," "*Les Fêtes de Polhymnie*," and "*Le Temple de la Gloire*" (1745), "*Les Fêtes de l' Hymen et de l' Amour, ou les Dieux d' Egypte*" (1747), "*Zaïs*" (1748), "*Pygmalion*" (1748), "*Platée ou Junon jalouse*," "*Neïs*" and "*Zoroastre*" (the "*Samson*" music with another libretto) (1749), "*Acanthe et Céphise*," "*La Guirlande*," and "*La Naissance d'Osiris*" (1751), "*Daphnis et Églé*," "*Lycis et Délie*" and "*Le Retour d'Astrée*" (1753), "*Anacréon*," "*Les Surprises de l'Amour*," and "*Les Sybarites*" (1757), "*Les Paladins*" (1760). He c. also others not prod. His mus. is full of richness, novelty and truth, though he wrote only fairly for the voice. He said himself that were he younger he would revolutionise his style along the lines of Pergolesi. 1745 the King made him chamber-composer. His patent of nobility was registered, just before his death. He c. also many books of mus. for clavecin, etc.; of these a complete ed. is pub. by Steingräber, edited by Riemann. In 1895 a complete ed. of his works was begun by Durand, Saint-Saëns and Malherbe, including his cantatas and motets. Biog. by du Charger (1761), Nisard (1867), Griqne (1876). Other memoirs by Chabanon, Maret, Poisot, Pougin, Garraud, Brenet, Laurencie, and Laloy.

Ra'min, Günther, b. Carlsruhe, Germany, Oct. 15, 1898; organist; pupil of St. Thomas School, Leipzig, and Cons. in that city; after 1918 org. at St. Thomas' Church there; later at Dresden Kreuzkirche; also active as choral cond.; has toured widely as organ virtuoso, incl. U. S.

Randegger (rän'-dĕd-jĕr), **Alberto,** Trieste, April 13, 1832—London, Dec. 18, 1911; pupil of Lafont (pf.), and Ricci (comp.); at 20 prod. 2 ballets and an opera, "*Il Lazzarone,*" in collab. with 3 others, at Trieste; then th.-cond. at Fiume, Zara, Sinigagli, Brescia and Venice, where he prod. grand opera "*Bianca Capello*" (1854); ca. 1854, London, as a singing-teacher; 1868 prof. of singing, R. A. M.; later dir. and a member of the Committee of Management; also prof. of singing R. C. M.; 1857 cond. It. Opera, St. James's Th.; 1879–85, Carl Rosa company; and from 1881, the Norwich Triennial Festival. Wrote "*Primer on Singing.*" C. comic opera "*The Rival Beauties*" (London, 1864); the 150th Psalm with orch. and org. (Boston Jubilee, 1872); dram. cantata "*Fridolin*" (1873, Birmingham); 2 dram. scenes "*Medea*" (Leipzig, 1869) and "*Saffo*" (London, 187ɔ); cantata, "*Werther's Shadow*" (Norwich, 1902), etc.

Randhartinger (ränt-härt'-ing-ĕr), **Benedikt,** Ruprechtshofen, Lower Austria, 1802—Vienna, 1893; at 10 soprano; conductor and composer of over 600 works.

Randolph, Harold, Richmond, Va., Oct. 31, 1861—Northeast Harbor, Me., July 6, 1927; pupil of Mrs. Auerbach and Carl Faelten. at Peabody Cons., Baltimore; from 1898 its director; pianist, played with Boston Symph., etc.

Rangström (räng'-strĕm), **Ture,** b. Stockholm, Nov. 30, 1884—May 11, 1947; composer; studied with Julius Hey in Berlin, 1905–07; also for a short time comp. with Johan Lindegren in his native city and with Pfitzner in Berlin; active as music critic of the *Stockholms Dagblad* and as singing teacher for a time; 1922–25, cond. Gothenburg Musikverein symph. concerts; 1919, mem. of R. Acad. of Music, Stockholm; c. (operas) "*Die Kronbraut*" (Stuttgart, 1919), "*Middelalderig*" (Stockholm, 1918); also 3 symphonies, chamber music, choral works, more than 100 songs, etc.

Raoul de Coucy. Vide COUCY.

Rapee (rä'-pā), **Erno,** b. Budapest, June 4, 1891; conductor; grad. with honours from Cons. in native city; early appeared as pianist; came to U. S. as dir. of Hungarian Op. Co., 1913; cond. of leading N. Y. film theatres, incl. the Rialto; later musical dir. of Capitol and Roxy Theatres; for a time dir. of the Capitol in Berlin, where he made guest appearance with Philh., also of orchs. in Vienna and Budapest; later assoc. with Warner Bros. and First Nat'l. Studios, Hollywood, and more recently mus. dir. of Nat'l. Broadcasting Co. and cond. of notable series of concerts by Gen'l. Motors Symph. Orch., Radio City Mus. Dir. 1933–45. d. New York, June, 1945.

Rap'pold, Marie (née **Winteroth**), b. Brooklyn, N. Y., 1880(?); soprano, sang in London at 10; studied with Oscar Saenger and sang in concert; from 1905 Met. O.

Rappoldi (räp-pôl'-dē), (1) **Eduard,** Vienna, Feb. 21, 1831—Dresden, May 16, 1903; pupil at the Cons.; 1854–61, violinist ct.-opera; leader at Rotterdam, then teacher Hochschule, Berlin; then leader opera-orch., Dresden, and 1893 head vln.-teacher at the Cons.; c. chambermus., etc. (2) **Laura Rappoldi-Kahrer** (kä'-rĕr), Mistelbach, near Vienna, Jan. 14, 1853—Dresden, Aug. 1, 1925; wife of above; pianist; pupil of Vienna Cons. and of Liszt.

Rase'lius, Andreas, Hahnbach, upper Palatinate, ca. 1563—Heidelberg, Jan. 6, 1602; court cond. and comp.

Rastrelli (räs-trĕl'-lē), (1) **Jos.,** Dresden, 1799—1842; ct.-conductor and dram. composer; son and pupil of (2) **Vincenzo,** 1760—1839.

Ras(o)umovski (rä-zoo-môi'-shkĭ) Count (from 1815 Prince) **Andreas Kyrillovitch,** Nov. 2. 1752—Sept.

23, 1836; Russian ambassador at Vienna, 1793–1809; to whom Beethoven dedicated the 3 quartets, op. 59.

Ratez (rä-tĕs), **Émile P.**, Besançon, Nov. 5, 1851—Lille, Aug. 25, 1905; pupil of Bazin and Massenet at Paris Cons.; vla.-player, Op.-Com.; chorusm. under Colonne; 1891, dir. the Lille branch of the Paris Cons.; prod. 2 operas *"Ruse d'Amour"* (Besançon, 1885), and succ. *"Lydéric"* (Lille, 1895); c. a symph. poem with soli and chorus, *"Scènes héroïques,"* etc.

Rathaus (rät'-häs), **Karel,** b. Tarnopol, Poland (then Austria), Sept. 16, 1895; composer in radical modern style; pupil of Schreker in Vienna and Berlin; his early orch. works, an overture and *"Tanzstück,"* were heard in Berlin soon after the war; his first opera, *"Der letzte Pierrot,"* prod. at the Berlin State Op., 1927, showed highly original methods; succ. was gained by his opera, *"Fremde Erde,"* at the same theatre in 1931, a morbid study of the fate befalling refugees in America; also c. (operas) *"Sergeant Grischa,"* *"Schweik,"* and *"Uriel Acosta,"* (orch.) 2 symphonies, suite, etc.; (chamber music) 2 string quartets, Serenade for 4 wind instruments and piano; (choral) *"Pastorale und Tanzweise,"* *"Lied ohne Worte,"* prof. Queens Coll., N. Y., 1941.

Rauchenecker (row'-khĕ-nĕk-ēr), **G. Wm.**, Munich, March 8, 1844—Elberfeld, July 17, 1906; pupil of Th. Lachner, Baumgartner and Jos. Walter (vln.); dir. Avignon Cons.; 1873, mus.-dir. at Winterthur; 1874, prod. prize cantata, *"Niklaus von der Flüe"* (Zurich Music Festival); for one year cond. Berlin Philh. Concerts; 1889, mus. dir. at Elberfeld, where he prod. 3 succ. operas, *"Die letzten Tage von Thule"* (1889), *"Ingo"* (1893), and *"Sanna"* (1-act, 1893); c. also *"Le Florentin"* (1910 prod.); a symph., etc.

Rauzzini (rä-ood-zē'-nē), (1) **Venanzio**, Rome, 1747—Bath, Engl., 1810; tenor and dram. composer. (2) **Matteo**, d. 1791; bro. of above; dram. composer.

Ravel (rä-vĕl'), **Maurice**, Ciboure, France, March 7, 1875—Paris, Dec. 28, 1937; one of the most brilliant and resourceful of modern composers,

not slavishly a follower in the tradition of Debussy, but amplifying the impressionistic formulae with an individual quality and virtuosity. His birthplace is in the Pyrenees, and childhood impressions of Spanish music are evident in some of his works. At 12 he took up res. in Paris, where he entered the Cons. in 1899, a pupil of Gédalge. In 1902 he won 2nd Prix de Rome, but in 1905, although he had already composed some of his early piano works, his brilliant string quartet and his song cycle *"Shéhérazade,"* he was excluded from the competition. This summary action resulted in a controversy on the part of his admirers, and as a result the head of the Cons., Théo. Dubois, resigned. Further controversy over the merits of R. was stirred in 1907, when his *"Histoires Naturelles"* for voice and piano were premièred, this opus dividing listeners into two camps on the question whether or not he was an imitator of Debussy. His music steadily gained public following, with the publication of his brilliant *"Rhapsodie Espagnole"* for orch., the piano suite, *"Gaspard de la Nuit,"* and the spirited one-act opera, *"L'Heure Espagnole,"* with its element of satire (Op.-Comique, 1911). The ballet, *"Daphnis et Chloe"* (one of R.'s most inspired works) was prod. by Diaghileff in 1912 to much applause. In recent years almost everything from his pen has been greeted with enthusiasm, perhaps the two outstanding successes in his orch. production being the virtuosic *"La Valse,"* an "apotheosis" of the dance, which uses all the modern wizardry of instrumentation to create a brilliant and kaleidoscopic picture; and the somewhat overrated *"Bolero,"* which develops a monotonous dance theme by a process of repetition until the effect on the hearer is almost hypnotic (created to be danced by Ida Rubinstein). His piano concerto and concerto for the left hand alone (composed for Paul Wittgenstein) show cerebral manipulation of material that in some instances is trite despite its engaging flippancy. His principal works, in addition to those already named, include the charming series of richly coloured nursery pictures for orch., *"Ma Mère L'Oye"*

(French equivalent of Mother Goose); his scintillant orchestration of Moussorgsky's "*Pictures from an Exhibition*"; a nursery opera, "*L'Enfant et les Sortilèges*," in which a naughty child is punished when his toys come to life; his popular Introduction and Allegro for flute and string quartet; chamber works, incl. a trio and a septet, and a large number of much-played piano pieces, some artistic songs and vln. works. A biog. of R. has been written by Roland-Manuel. (See article, pp. 512–16.)

Ra'venscroft, (1) **Thos.**, 1593—London, 1635 (?); prominent early English composer and writer. (2) **John**, d. 1740; violinist, London.

Ravera (rä-vä'-rä), **Niccolò Teresio**, b. Alessandria, Italy, Feb. 24, 1851— (?); pupil Milan Cons.; won first prizes for pf., organ and comp.; cond. Th.-Lyrique de la Galérie-Vivienne, Paris; c. 7 operas.

Ravina (rä-vē'-nä), **J. H.**, Bordeaux, May 20, 1818—Paris, Sept. 30, 1906; pianist; pupil of Zimmermann (pf.) and Laurent (theory) at Paris Cons., won first pf.-prize, 1834; 1st harm.-prize, 1836; asst.-teacher there till 1837, and also studied with Reicha and Leborne; made tours; 1861, Chev. of the Legion of Honour; c. a concerto, etc.

Raway (rä'-vĭ), **Erasme**, Liége, June 2, 1850—Brussels, Oct., 1918; priest, teacher and cathedral cond. at Liége; c. church works, Hindu scenes, a dramatic dialog. "*Freya*," etc.

Raymond (rĕ'-môn), **G. M.**, Chambéry, 1769—1839; acoustician.

Rea (rā), **Wm.**, London, March 25, 1827—Newcastle, March 8, 1903; articled pupil of Josiah Pittmann; at 16, organist; studied with Sterndale Bennett (pf., comp. and instr.) then at Leipzig and Prague; returned to London, and gave chamber-concerts; 1856, founded the Polyhymnian Choir; organist at various churches; c. anthems, etc.

Reading (rĕd'-ĭng), (1) **John**, 1645—Winchester, Engl., 1692; organist and composer of "Dulce domum," etc. (2) **John**, 1677—London, Sept. 2, 1764; son of above; organist and composer; the "*Portuguese Hymn*," "*Adeste Fideles*," is credited to him. (3) **John**, 1674—1720; organist.

Reay (rā). **Samuel**, Hexham, Engl., March 17, 1822—Newark-on-Trent,

July 21, 1905; a pupil of Henshaw and Stimpson; 1841, organist St. Andrew's, Newcastle; song-schoolmaster, Newark Parish Ch. and cond. Philh. Soc.; c. Psalm 102, with string-orch.; Communion Service, etc.

Rebel (rŭ-bĕl), (1) **J. Ferry**, Paris, 1661—1747; conductor and composer. (2) **Fran.**, Paris, 1701—1775; violinist and dram. composer.

Rebello (rä-bĕl'-lō), **João Lourenço** (João Soares), Caminha, 1609—San Amaro, Nov. 16, 1661, eminent Portuguese composer.

Reber (rŭ-bā), **Napoléon H.**, Mühlhausen, Alsatia, Oct. 21, 1807—Paris, Nov. 24, 1880; 1851, prof. of comp., Paris Cons.; pub. one of the best French harm. treatises (1862); c. comic operas, etc.

Rebicek (rä'-bĭ-tsĕk), **Josef**, Prague, Feb. 7, 1844—Berlin, March 24, 1904; violinist; pupil Prague Cons.; 1861, Weimar ct.-orch.; 1863, leader royal th., Wiesbaden; 1875, R. Mus.-Dir.; 1882, leader and op.-dir. Imp. Th. Warsaw; 1891, cond. Nat. Th., Pesth; 1893, at Wiesbaden; 1897, cond. Berlin Philh. Orch.

Rebikov (rĕb'-ĭ'-kôf), **Vladimir Ivanovich**, Krasnojarsk, Siberia, June 1 (N. S.), 1866—Yalta, Crimea, Dec. 1, 1920; pupil Moscow Cons., and in Berlin; 1897–1902 cond. in Kishinev; later in Berlin and Vienna; theorist and composer of originality, as in his piece "*Satan's Diversions*," his "*Melomimik*," lyric scenes in pantomime, 1-act fairy opera, "*Der Christbaum*," etc.

Rebling (rāp'-lĭng), (1) **Gv.**, Barby, Magdeburg, July 10, 1821—Magdeburg, Jan. 9, 1902; pupil of Fr. Schneider at Dessau; 1856, R. Mus.-Dir.; 1858, organist Johanniskirche; 1846, founded and cond. a church choral soc.; 1897, c. Psalms, "*a cappella*," 'cello-sonata, etc. (2) **Fr.**, Barby, Aug. 14, 1835—Leipzig, Oct. 15, 1900; pupil of Leipzig Cons. and of Götz (singing); 1865–78, tenor at various theatres; from 1877, singing-teacher Leipzig Cons.

Red'head, **Richard**, Harrow, Engl., 1820—May, 1901; studied at Magdalen Coll., Oxford; organist of St. Mary Magdalene's Ch., London; ed. colls.; c. masses, etc.

Ree (rā), (1) **Anton**, Aarhus, Jutland, 1820—Copenhagen, 1886; pianist, teacher and writer. (2) **Louis, b.** Edinburgh, 1861; pianist.

Reed, (1) **Thos. German,** Bristol, 1817 —Upper East Sheen, Surrey, 1888; pianist and singer. In 1844 he m. (2) **Priscilla Horton** (1818—1895), a fine actress and contralto. Their entertainments were continued by their son (3) **Alfred German** (d. London, March 10, 1895). (4) **Robt. Hopké,** and (5) **Wm.,** bros. of (1); 'cellists.

Reeve, Wm., London, 1757—1815; c. operettas.

Reeves, (1) **(John) Sims,** Woolwich, Sept. 26, 1818 (acc. to Grove, Shooters Hill, Oct. 21, 1822)— London, Oct. 25, 1900; noted tenor; at 14 organist of North Cray Ch.; learned the vln., 'cello, oboe and bassoon; and studied with J. B. Cramer (pf.) and W. H. Callcott (harm.); début as barytone, 1839, studied with Hobbs and Cooke, and sang minor tenor parts at Drury Lane; then studied with Bordogni, Paris, and Mazzucato, Milan, sang at La Scala, 1846, Drury Lane, 1847, with great succ.; début in Italian opera, 1848, at H. M.'s Th., also in oratorio at the Worcester and Norwich Festivals, the same year; retired in 1891, but on account of reverses, reappeared in 1893; and 1898 made succ. tour of South Africa; pub. "*Life and Recollections*" (London, 1888); he m., 1850, (2) **Emma Lucombe,** opera and concert soprano. (3) **Herbert,** his son and pupil, studied at Milan; concert-début, 1880.

Refice (rā-fē'-chä), **Licinio, b.** Rome, Feb. 12, 1885; composer; a Roman Catholic priest; pupil of Boezi, Falchi and Renzi, at St. Cecilia Liceo; after 1910 taught liturgical music at Pontifical School of Sacred Music; 1911, cond. Capella Liberiana at Church of S. Ma. Maggiore; c. many motets, masses, cantatas, and a sacred opera, "*Cecilia,*" which had marked succ. in Rome and Buenos Aires.

Regan, Anna. Vide SCHIMON-REGAN.

Reger (rā'-gĕr), **Max,** Brand, Bavaria, March 19, 1873—Leipzig, May 11, 1916; pupil of Lindner and H. Riemann; important composer, especially in chamber music and sacred music; 1891–96 he was teacher at Wiesbaden Cons., then took his year of military service. After a severe illness he settled in Munich, 1901,

and married there; 1905 he taught counterpoint at the Royal Academy; 1907–08 taught composition at Munich Cons., and was University music dir.; 1908 was named Royal Prof. and Dr. Phil. by Jena; 1910 Mus. D. Berlin U.; in 1911, he became General Music Dir. at Meiningen, cond. Meiningen orch., continuing to teach one day a week at Leipzig Cons. He toured with the orch., 1912. His compositions are exceedingly numerous, and include a Sinfonietta, op. 90, symph. prologue to a tragedy, op. 108, "*Lustpiel*" overture (1911), violin concerto; a vast amount of chamber music, sonatas for piano, organ, violin, clarinet, 'cello, variations, fugues, canons in all keys, left-hand studies, and transcriptions for piano; much organ music; "*Gesang der Verklärten*" for choir and orch., "*An die Hoffnung*" for contralto and orch. (1912); three orch. pieces "*Nocturne,*" "*Elfenspuk,*" and "*Helios*" (1912); organ fantasie and fugue,B-A-C-H; violin suite op. 103, sonata op. 42, for violin alone; tone-poems for pianos, "*Aus meinem Tagebuch*"; cantatas, male and mixed choruses, and many beautiful sacred and secular songs. His music as a whole is marked by elaborate formal and contrapuntal structure, sometimes developed to the point of pedantry. R., though a strong influence upon German musicians of his time, represents a type of comp. in whom ponderous scientific knowledge and great practical ability are unleavened by a sense of proportion. In the field of organ comp. he holds an honourable place. Biog. also thematic catalogue of his works, by Fritz Stein.

Régis (rā'-zhēs), **Jns.,** Belgian cptist.; contemporary of Okeghem.

Regnal, Fr. Vide FR. D'ERLANGER.

Regnart (or **Regnard**) (rĕkh'-närt), (1) **Jacob,** Netherlands, 1540—Prague, ca. 1600; Innsbruck, cond.; popular composer. His brothers (2) **Fz.,** (3) **K.,** and (4) **Pascasius,** also c. songs.

Rehbaum (rā'-bowm), **Theobald,** Berlin, Aug. 7, 1835—Feb. 2, 1918; pupil of H. Ries (vln.) and Kiel (comp.); c. 7 operas incl. "*Turandot*" (Berlin, 1888), etc.

Rehberg (rā'-bĕrkh), (1) **Willy,** Morges, Switz., 1863—Mannheim, 1937; son and pupil of (2) **Fr. R.** (a mus.-

teacher); later studied at Zurich Mus.-Sch. and Leipzig Cons.; pf.-teacher there till 1890; 1888-90, cond. at Altenburg; 1890, head pf.-teacher Geneva Cons.; 1892, also cond. Geneva Municipal Orch.; 1907, taught Hoch Cons., Frankfort; 1917, dir. Mannheim Hochsch.; 1921-26, dir. Basel Cons.; c. vln.-sonata, pf.-sonata, etc. (3) **Walter, b.** Geneva, 1900; son of (2); pianist.

Rehfeld (rā'-fĕlt), **Fabian, Tuchel,** W. Prussia, Jan. 23, 1842—Berlin, Nov. 11, 1920; violinist; pupil of Zimmermann and Grünwald, Berlin, 1868, royal chamber-mus.; 1873, leader ct.-orch.

Reicha (rī'-khä), (1) (rightly **Rejcha,** rā'-khä), **Jos.,** Prague, 1746—Bonn, 1795; 'cellist, violinist, and cond. at Bonn. (2) **Anton (Jos.),** Prague, Feb. 25, 1770—Paris, May 28, 1836; nephew and pupil of above; flutist, vla.-player, and teacher.

Rehkemper (rā'-kĕmp-ĕr), **Heinr., b.** Schwerte, 1894; barytone; Munich Op., after 1926.

Reichardt (rī'-khärt), (1) **Jn. Fr.,** Königsberg, Nov. 25, 1752—Giebichenstein near Halle, June 27, 1814; cond., editor and dram. composer; pupil of Richter and Veichtner; 1775, ct.-cond. to Frederick the Great, later to Fr. Wm. II. and III., then to Jerome Bonaparte; he prod. many German and Italian operas and influential Singspiele; also c. 7 symphs., a passion, etc., and notable songs. (2) **Luise,** Berlin, 1779—Hamburg, 1826; daughter of above; singing-teacher. (3) **Gv.,** Schmarsow, near Demmin, 1797—Berlin, 1884; conductor; c. pop. songs. (4) **Alex.,** Packs, Hungary, 1825—Boulogne-sur-Mer, 1885; tenor.

Reichel (rī'-khĕl), (1) **Ad. H. Jn.,** Tursznitz, W. Prussia, 1817—Berne, March 4, 1896; pupil of Dehn and L. Berger; Berlin; pf.-teacher, Paris; 1857-67, taught comp. at Dresden Cons.; 1867, municipal mus.-dir. Berne, Switz.; c. pf.-concertos, etc. (2) **Fr.,** Oberoderwitz, Lusatia, 1833 —Dresden, 1889; cantor and org.-composer.

Reicher-Kindermann (rī'-khĕr-kĭn'-dĕr-män), (1) **Hedwig,** Munich, 1853 —Trieste, 1883; soprano; daughter of the barytone, A. Kindermann; m. (2) **Reicher,** an opera singer.

Reichmann (rīkh'-män), **Th.,** Rostock, March 15, 1849—Marbach, May 22, 1903; barytone, pupil of Mantius, Elsler, Ress and Lamperti; 1882-89, ct.-opera Vienna; 1882, created "Amfortas" in "*Parsifal*," Bayreuth; 1889-90, New York; then Vienna.

Reichwein (rīkh'-vīn), **Leopold,** director and composer; b. Breslau, May 16, 1878; cond. 1909 of the Court Opera at Carlsruhe; after 1913 in Vienna; 1921, succeeded Schalk as cond. of Musikfreunde concerts and Singverein there; c. operas "*Vasantasena*" (Breslau, 1903), "*Die Liebenden von Kandahar*" (1907), and music for "*Faust*" (Mannheim, 1909).

Reid (rēd), General **John,** Straloch, Perthshire, 1721(?)—London, 1806; a musical amateur, founded a chair of mus. Edinburgh Univ.

Reijnvaan (or **Reynwaen**) (rĕn'-vän), **Jean Verschuere, LL.D.;** Middleburg, Holland, 1743—Flushing, May 12, 1809; organist and composer.

Reimann (rī'-män), (1) **Mathieu (Matthias Reymannus),** Löwenberg, 1544 —1597; composer. (2) **Ignaz,** Albendorf, Silesia, 1820—Rengersdorf, 1885; composer. (3) **H.,** Rengersdorf, March 14, 1850—Berlin, May 24, 1906; son and pupil of (2); 1887 asst.-libr., R. Library, Berlin; organist to the Philh. Soc.; teacher of organ and theory, Scharwenka-Klindworth Cons., and (1895) organist at the Gnadenkirche; prominent critic and writer; c. sonatas and studies for organ.

Reinagle (rī'-nä-gĕl), (1) **Jos.,** Portsmouth, 1762—Oxford, 1836; son of a German mus., horn-player and composer, 1785. (2) **Hugh,** d. young at Lisbon; bro. of above; 'cellist. (3) **Alex.,** Portsmouth, 1756—Baltimore, Md., 1809; versatile composer, pianist, cond. and theatre manager; his works are among the earliest prod. in America that have definite value and historical interest.

Reinecke (rī'-nĕk-ĕ), (1) **Ld., K.** Dessau, 1774—Güsten, 1820; leader and dram. composer. (2) **K. (H. Carsten),** Altona, June 23, 1824—Leipzig, March 10, 1910; noteworthy pianist and teacher; son and pupil of a music-teacher; at 11, played in public; at 19 toured Denmark and Sweden; at Leipzig advised by Mendelssohn and Schumann; ct.-pianist at Copenhagen; 1851 teacher Cologne Cons.; 1854-59 mus.-dir.

Barmen; 1859–60 mus.-dir. and cond. Singakademie, Breslau; 1860–95 cond. Gewandhaus Concerts, Leipzig; also prof. of pf.-playing and free comp., Leipzig Cons.; 1897 "Studiendirektor" there; Dr. Phil. *h. c.*, Leipzig Univ.; Royal Professor; toured almost annually with great succ., c. 2 masses, 3 symphs., 5 overtures: *"Dame Kobold," "Aladin," "Friedensfeier," "Festouvertüre," "In Memoriam"* (of David), *"Zenobia,"* introd. and fugue with chorus and orch.; funeral march for Emperor William I.; concertos for vln., 'cello and harp.; prod. grand opera *" König Manfred"* (Wiesbaden, 1867); 3 comic operas; fairy opera *"Die Teufelchen auf der Himmelswiese"* (Glarus, 1899); mus. to Schiller's *"Tell"*; oratorio *"Belsazar"*; 2 cantatas *"Hakon Jarl,"* and *"Die Flucht nach Ægypten,"* with orch.; 5 fairy cantatas, 4 concertos, many sonatas; *"Aus der Jugendzeit,"* op. 106; *" Neues Notenbuch fur Kleine Leute,"* op. 107; concert-arias, 20 canons for 3 female voices, and excellent songs for children.

Reiner (rī'-nĕr), (1) **Jacob,** Altdorf, Württemberg, ca. 1560—1606; composer. (2) **Fritz,** b. Budapest, Dec. 19, 1888; conductor; studied Budapest Acad. of Music, comp. with Hans Koessler, piano with Stephen Thoman; cond. Budapest Op.-Comique, 1909; Laibach Op., 1910; Budapest Volksop., 1911–14; Dresden State Op., and symph. concerts, 1914–21; Cincinnati Symph., 1922–31; thereafter headed orch. dept., Curtis Inst. of Music, Phila.; appearances with Phila. Orch.; at Hollywood Bowl and in various other Amer. and Eur. cities; cond. German opera perfs. of Phila. Orch., 1934–35; at Covent Garden, 1936, and San Francisco Op.; 1938 cond. Pittsburgh Symph.; 1948–49, début as cond. Met. Op.; cond. Chicago Symph., 1953.

Rein'hardt, Heinrich, Pressburg, April 13, 1865—Vienna, Jan. 31, 1922; c. operettas for Vienna: *"Das süsse Mädel"* (1901); *"Ein Mädchen für Alles"* (Munich, 1908). *"Die Sprudelfee"* (which had marked succ. in America as *"The Spring Maid"*), etc.; music ed., Vienna *Tageblatt.*

Reinhold (rīn'-hölt), **Th. Christlieb,** d. Dresden, March 24, 1755; cantor, teacher and composer.

Reinke(n) (rīn'-kĕn) (or **Reinicke**), **Jn. Adam,** Deventer, Holland, April 27, 1623—Hamburg, Nov. 24, 1722, noted organist and composer.

Reinsdorf (rīns'-dôrf), **Otto,** Köselitz, 1848—Berlin, 1890; editor.

Reinthaler (rīn'-täl-ĕr), **K. (Martin),** Erfurt, 1822—Bremen, 1896; singing-teacher, organist, conductor and dram. composer.

Reisenauer (rī'-zĕ-now-ĕr), **Alfred,** Königsberg. Nov. 1, 1863—Liebau, Russia, Oct. 3, 1907; pianist; pupil of L. Köhler and Liszt; début, 1881, Rome, with Liszt; toured; composer; taught Leipzig Cons., 1900–06.

Reiser (rī'-zĕr), **Aug. Fr.,** Gammertingen, Württemberg, Jan. 19, 1840—Haigerloch, Oct. 22, 1904; 1880–86, ed. Cologne *Neue Musikzeitung;* c. 2 symphs., choruses, incl. *"Barbarossa,"* for double ch., etc.

Reiset. Vide DE GRANDVAL.

Reiss (rīs), (1) **K. H. Ad.,** Frankfort-on-Main, April 24, 1829—April 5, 1908; pupil of Hauptmann, Leipzig; chorus-master and cond. various theatres; 1854, 1st cond. Mayence; 1856, 2d., later 1st cond. at Cassel (vice Spohr). 1881–86, ct.-th., Wiesbaden; prod. opera, *"Otto der Schütz"* (Mayence, 1856). (2) **Albert,** b. Berlin, 1870—Nice, 1940; tenor; studied law, then became an actor, discovered by Pollini; pupil of Liebau and Stolzenberg; début in opera at Königsberg, later at Posen and Wiesbaden, famous as "Mime" and "David," 1901–17, at Met. Op., N. Y.

Reissiger (rīs'-sīkh-ĕr), (1) **Chr. Gl.,** ca. 1790; comp. (2) **K. Gl.,** Belzig, near Wittenberg, Jan. 31, 1798—Dresden, Nov. 7, 1859; son of above; pupil of Schicht and Winter; singer. pianist and teacher; 1826, on invitation, organised at The Hague the still succ. Cons.; ct.-cond. Dresden (vice Weber); c. 8 operas, 10 masses. (3) **Fr. Aug.,** Belzig, 1809—Frederikshald, 1883; bro. of above; military bandm.; composer.

Reissmann (rīs'-män), **Aug.,** Frankenstein, Silesia, Nov. 14, 1825—Berlin, Dec. 1, 1903; studied there and at Breslau; 1863–80, lectured at Stern Cons., Berlin; then lived in Leipzig (Dr. Phil., 1875), Wiesbaden and Berlin; writer of important historical works, and lexicographer; c. 3 operas, 2 dram. scenes, an oratorio, etc.

Reiter (rī'-tĕr), (1) Ernst, Wertheim, Baden, 1814—Basel, 1875; vln.-prof. and dram. composer. (2) Josef, b. Braunau, Jan. 19, 1862; composer; Viennese composer of operas, including "Der Totentanz" (Dessau, 1908), symph., cantatas, male choruses, etc.; 1908–11, dir., Mozarteum at Salzburg.

Rellstab (rĕl'-shtäp), (1) Jn. K. Fr., Berlin, 1759—1813; son and successor of owner of a printing-establishment; critic, teacher, and composer. (2) (H. Fr.) L., Berlin, 1799—1860; the noted novelist, son of above; wrote biog., libretti and criticisms which got him twice imprisoned; c. part-songs.

Remenyi (rĕm'-ān-yē), Eduard, Heves, Hungary, 1830—on the stage, of apoplexy, San Francisco, Cal., May 15, 1898; noted violinist; pupil of Böhm, Vienna Cons.; banished for his part in Hungarian Revolution; toured America; 1854, solo violinist to Queen Victoria; 1860, pardoned by Austrian Emperor and made ct.-violinist; toured widely, 1866 round the world; c. a vln.-concerto, transcriptions, etc.

Rem'mert, Martha, b. Gross-Schwein, near Glogau, Aug. 4, 1854; pianist; pupil of Kullak, Tausig and Liszt; 1900, founder Liszt Acad. for piano in Berlin; d. (?).

Rémusat (Rémuzat) (rā-mü-zä), Jean, Bordeaux, 1815—Shanghai, 1880; flute-virtuoso; writer and composer.

Remy, W. A. Vide MAYER, WM.

Rénard (rā-nǎr), Marie, b. Graz, Jan. 18, 1863; soprano; début, Graz, 1882; 1885–88, Berlin ct.-opera; 1888–1901, Vienna ct.-opera; m. Count Kinsky and retired from stage.

Renaud (rŭ-nō), (1) Albert, b. Paris, 1855; pupil of Franck and Délibes; organist St. François-Xavier; critic, La Patrie; c. 4-act "féerie," "Aladin" (1891); opéra comique "À la Houzarde" ('91); operetta "Le Soleil de Minuit" (1898); ballets, etc., d. (?). (2) Maurice, 1862—Paris, Oct. 16, 1933; notable bass; pupil of Paris Cons.; 1883–90, at R. Opera, Brussels; 1890–91, Op.-Com., Paris; from 1891–1902, Gr. Opéra; equally fine in comic and serious works; had a repertory of 50 operas; sang with Chicago Op. Co. and at Manhattan Op., N. Y.

Rendano (rĕn-dä'-nō), Alfonso, Carolei, Calabria, April 5, 1853—Rome, Sept. 10, 1931; pianist; pupil of Naples Cons., Thalberg and Leipzig Cons.; toured; c. piano-pcs.

Renié (rŭn-yā'), Henriette, b. Paris, Sept. 18, 1875; harpist, composer; pupil ot Paris Cons.; has appeared with leading French orchs.; c. many works for harp; a noted teacher.

Ren'ner, Josef, Schmatzhausen, Bavaria, 1832—Ratisbon, 1895; editor. Res'nik, Regina, b. Brooklyn, N. Y.; soprano; studied with Rosalie Miller; début, Met. Op., 1944, as Leonora ("Trovatore"); sang "Fidelio," etc.

Respighi (rĕ-spē'-gē), Ottorino, Bologna, July 9, 1879—Rome, April 18, 1936; composer, conductor, pianist; studied Bologna Liceo, vln. with Sarti, comp. with Martucci; also in St. Petersburg, 1902, with Rimsky-Korsakoff; later in Berlin with Bruch; prof. of comp., Bologna Liceo, 1913; after 1924, at Liceo of Santa Cecilia, Rome; appeared as guest cond. and pianist in his works in Europe and America; c. (operas) "Re Enzo," "Semirama," "Maria Vittoria," "Belfagor" (1923), "La Campana Sommersa" (after Hauptmann's drama), heard in several Italian theatres, also at Met. Op., 1928; "La Fiamma" (Rome, Buenos Aires and Chicago Op., 1935, with considerable succ.); (opera-oratorio) "Maria Egiziaca," world première, N. Y. Philh. in staged version, 1932, composer conducting, also later in Paris; another opera, "Lucrezia," completed just before his death; (puppet play) "The Sleeping Princess"; a series of highly succ. symph. poems of colorful descriptive nature, incl. "Fountains of Rome," "Pines of Rome," "Roman Festivals," "Church Windows," "Primavera," "Ballade of the Gnomides"; suite to the "Birds" of Aristophanes; piano concerto, string quartets, and many other works for vln., organ, piano, as well as orch. transcriptions of Bach, etc.

Reszké. Vide DE RESZKE.

Rethberg (rāt'-bĕrkh), Elisabeth (née Sättler), b. Schwarzenberg, Germany, Sept. 22, 1894; soprano; studied piano, later voice, at Dresden Cons.; début, Dresden Op., 1915; sang with this company until 1922; début with Met. Op., N. Y., in latter year as "Aïda" and took leading place as a singer of German and Italian rôles; guest appearances, Covent Garden, La Scala, Rome R. Op., Paris Op., Budapest, Vienna, at Ravinia (Chicago), Los Angeles and San Francisco. Has toured widely as recitalist and soloist with leading orchs. in Europe and U. S.; created rôle of "Helen" in Strauss's "*Aegyptische Helena*" at Dresden, 1928.

Réti (rā'-tē), **Rudolf,** b. Uzize, Serbia, Nov. 27, 1885; composer of modernstyle chamber music, songs, etc.

Reubke (roip'-kĕ), (1) **Ad.,** Halberstadt, 1805—1875; org.-builder at Hausendorf, near Quedlinburg. (2) **Emil,** Hausneindorf, 1836—1885; son and successor of above. (3) **Julius R.,** Hausneindorf, 1834—Pillnitz, 1858; bro. of above; pianist and composer. (4) **Otto R.,** Hausneindorf, Nov. 2, 1842—Halle, May 18, 1913; bro. of above; pupil of Von Bülow and Marx; mus.-teacher and conductor, Halle; 1892, mus.-dir. at .he University.

Reuling (roi'-lĭng), (**L.**) **Wm.,** Darmstadt, 1802—Munich, 1879; conductor and dram. composer.

Reuss (rois), (1) **Eduard,** New York, Sept. 16, 1851—Dresden, Feb. 18, 1911; pupil of Ed. Krüger and of Liszt; 1880, teacher at Carlsruhe; after 1896 in Wiesbaden; dir. Cons. there, 1902; later in Dresden and Berlin as teacher. His wife, (2) **Reuss-Belce** (-bĕl'-tsĕ) **Louise,** b. Vienna, 1863; soprano; pupil of Gänsbacher; début as "Elsa," Carlsruhe, 1884; later at Wiesbaden, and Bayreuth as one of the "Norns" and "Walküre" for years; 1900 sang Wagner in Spain, 1901, Met. Op., N. Y. (3) **H. XXIV.,** Prince of Reuss-Köstritz; Trebschen, Brandenburg, Dec. 8, 1855—Ernstbrunn near Vienna, Oct. 2, 1910; pupil of Herzogenberg and Rust, Leipzig; c. 2 symphs., a mass, etc.

Reuter (roi'-tĕr), **Florizel von,** b. Davenport, Iowa, Jan. 21, 1893; violinist; pupil of Bendix, Chicago, and of Marteau, in Europe; has toured America with popular success; c. operas, orch. and vln. works.

Reutter (roit'-tĕr), (1) **G.** (Senior), Vienna, 1656—Aug., 1738; theorbist, ct.-organist and conductor. (2) (**Jn. Adam**), **G.** (Junior), Vienna, 1708—1772; son and (1738) successor of above as ct.-conductor; c. opera, etc. (3) **Hn.,** b. Stuttgart, 1900; com-

poser; after 1936, dir. Hoch **Cons.,** Frankfurt.

Rey (rĕ), (1) **J. Bap.,** Lauzerte, 1734—Paris, 1810; conductor, professor of harm. and dram. composer. (2) **L. Chas. Jos.,** bro. of above; for 40 years 'cellist, Gr. Opéra. (3) **J. Bap.** (II.), b. Tarascon, ca. 1760; from 1795 till 1822, 'cellist, Gr. Opéra, and theorist. (4) **V. F. S.,** b. Lyons, ca. 1762; theorist. (5) Vide REYER.

Reyer (rĕ-yā) (rightly Rey), **L. Étienne Ernest,** Marseilles, Dec. 1, 1823—near Hyères, Jan. 15, 1909; prominent French composer; studied as a child in the free municipal sch. of mus.; while in the Govt. financial bureau at Algiers, c. a solemn mass and pub. songs; the Revolution of 1848 deprived him of his position and he retired to Paris where he studied with his aunt, Mme. Farrenc; librarian at Opéra (vice Berlioz); 1876, Académie; critic *Journal des Débats;* 1862, Chev. of the Legion of Honour; 1886, Officier. Prod. a symph. ode with choruses "*Le Sélam*" (Th. Italien 1850); 1-act comedy-opera "*Maître Wolfram*" (Th.-Lyrique, 1854), a ballet-pantomime "*Sacountala*" (Opéra, 1858); comedy-opera "*La Statue*" (Th.-Lyr., 1861, revived at the Opéra 1878 without succ.); unsucc. opera "*Erostrate*" (Baden-Baden, 1862); the still pop. opera "*Sigurd*" (Brussels, 1884), and "*Salammbô*" (Brussels, 1890). C. a cantata "*Victoire*" (1859); a hymn, "*L' Union des Arts*" (1862); a dram. scene, "*La Madeleine au Desert*" (1874); male choruses; also some church-mus. Pub. a volume of essays, 1875.

Reznicek (rĕz'-nĭ-chĕk), **Emil Nicolaus, Freiherr von,** b. Vienna, May 4, 1861; studied Leipzig Cons.; th.-conductor various cities; 1896, 1st cond. ct.-th., Mannheim; after 1901 lived in Berlin; 1902, founded orch. concerts there; 1906, taught Scharwenka Cons.; 1907–08, dir., Warsaw Op. and Philh.; 1909–11, cond. Komische Op., Berlin; after 1920 taught at Hochsch. there; prod. at Prague operas "*Die Jungfrau von Orleans*" (1887), "*Satanella*" (1888), "*Emerich Fortunat*" (1889), comic opera (text and music), "*Donna Diana*" (1894), all very succ.; Volks-oper. "*Till Eulenspiegel*" (Berlin, 1903), "*Eros* *und Psyche"* (1917), *"Ritt.·r Blaubart"* (1918), etc. C. also a requiem, a symph. suite, etc.; d. Berlin, 1945.

Rhaw (Rhau) (row), **G.,** Eisfeld, Franconia, 1488—Wittenberg, 1548; mus.-printer and composer.

Rheinberger (rīn'bĕrkh-ĕr), **Jos.** (Gabriel), Vaduz, Lichtenstein, March 17, 1839—(of nerve and lung troubles) Munich, Nov. 25, 1901; eminent teacher and composer. At 5 played the piano; at 7 a good organist; studied R. Sch. of Mus., Munich; 1859, teacher of theory there; also organist at the ct.-church of St. Michael, and cond. Oratorio Soc., 1865–67, *"Repetitor"* ct.-opera; Royal Prof. and Inspector of the Sch. of Mus.; from 1877 ct.-cond. Royal Chapel-Choir; m. Franziska von Hoffnas, a poetess (1822—1892), prod. romantic opera *"Die 7 Raben"* (Munich, 1869); comic opera *"Des Thürmers Töchterlein"* (Munich, 1873); *"Christophorus,"* a mass for double choir (dedicated to Leo XIII.); mass, with orch.; requiem for soldiers of the Franco-Prussian War; 2 Stabat Maters; 4 cantatas with orch.; 2 choral ballades, *"Florentine"* symph.; symph. tone-picture *"Wallenstein"*; a symphonic fantasia; 3 overtures *"Demetrius," "The Taming of the Shrew," "Triumph"*; 2 organ-concertos; pf.-concertos, chamber-music; vln.-sonatas; pf.-sonatas ("symphonique"; op. 47; "romantic," op. 184), etc., notably 18 important org.-sonatas; left unfinished mass in A minor (finished by his pupil L. A. Coerne).

Rhené-Baton (rā-nā bä'-tôn), (rightly **René Baton**), b. Courseulles-sur-Mer Sept. 5, 1879—Paris, Oct., 1940; conductor; also active as composer; studied piano at Paris Cons.; comp. with André Bloch and Gédalge; choral dir., Op.-Comique in early career; later cond. of Soc. des Concerts Populaires in Angers, and St. Cecilia Soc. in Bordeaux; asst. cond., Lamoureux Concerts; after 1916, cond., Pasdeloup Concerts; c. orch. works, songs, etc.

Riccati (rīk-kä'-tē), **Count Giordano,** b. Castelfranco, 1709—Treviso, 1790; theorist.

Ricci (rīt'-chē), (1) **Luigi,** Naples, 1805 —insane, in asylum, Prague, 1859; conductor and dram. composer; m. (2) **Lidia Stoltz,** who bore him two

children, of whom (3) **Adelaide** sang at Th. des It., Paris, 1867, and died soon after. (4) **Federico,** Naples, 1809—Conegliano, 1877; bro. of (1) and collaborator in 4 of his operas; among which *"Crispino e la Comare"* still holds the stage; also himself c. others. (5) **Ruggiero,** b. California, July 24, 1920; violinist; early attracted attention as child prodigy; studied with his father, a band-master; 1st San Francisco recital at 8, following training by Louis Persinger; during 1931 gave concerts in Chicago and N. Y., playing Beethoven Concerto with orch. under baton of his teacher in latter city to sensational ovation; also toured Europe.

Riccitelli (rē-chē-tāl'-lē), **Primo,** b. Cognoli, 1880—Giulianova, 1941; pupil of Mascagni at Pesaro; c. several stage works incl. 1-act opera, *"I Compagnacci,"* prod. at Rome and Met. Op. House.

Riccius (rēk'-tsĭ-oos), (1) **Aug. Fd.,** Bernstadt, Saxony, 1819—Carlsbad, 1886; conductor, critic, singing-teacher and composer. (2) **K. Aug.,** Bernstadt, July 26, 1830—Dresden, July 8, 1893; nephew of above; conductor, violinist and composer of comic operas, etc.

Rice, Fenelon B., Green, Ohio, Jan. 2, 1841—Oberlin, Ohio, Oct. 26, 1901; studied Boston, Mass., later Leipzig; for 3 years organist, Boston; from 1871, dir. Oberlin (Ohio) Cons. of Mus.; Mus. Doc. Hillsdale (Mich.) Coll.

Richafort (rēsh-ä-fôr), **Jean,** important Flemish composer of masses, motets and songs; pupil of Deprès; 1543, choirmaster in Bruges.

Rich'ards, (H.) Brinley, Carmarthen, Wales, Nov. 13, 1817—London, May 1, 1885; pop. composer and pianist.

Richault (rē-shō), (1) **Chas. Simon,** Chartres, 1780—Paris, 1866; mus.-publisher, succeeded by his sons (2) **Guillaume Simon** (1806—1877) and (3) **Léon** (1839—1895).

Riche, A. Le. Vide DIVITIS.

Richter (rĭkh'-tĕr), (1) **Fz. X.,** Holeschau, Moravia, 1709—1789; cond., writer and composer. (2) **Jn. Chr. Chp.,** Neustadt-am-Kulm, 1727—Schwarzenbach - on - Saale, 1779; Father of Jean Paul R.; organist. (3) **Ernst H. Ld.,** Thiergarten, Prussian Silesia. 1805—Steinau -on-Oder, 1876; notable teacher; c.

opera, etc. (4) **Ernst Fr.** (**Eduard**), Gross Schönau, Saxony, Oct. 24, 1808 —Leipzig, April 9, 1879; eminent theorist; pupil of Weinlig, and self-taught; 1843 teacher at Leipzig Cons. newly founded; 1843–47, conductor Singakademie; organist various churches, 1863 mus.-dir. Nikolaikirche, 1868 mus.-dir. and cantor Thomaskirche; Prof.; wrote a standard "*Lehrbuch der Harmonie*" (1853), and "*Lehrbuch der Fuge*"; c. an oratorio, masses, etc. (5) **Alfred,** Leipzig, April 1, 1846 — Berlin, March 1, 1919; son of above; teacher at the Cons., 1872–83; then lived in London; 1897, Leipzig; pub. supplement to his father's "*Harmonie*," and "*Kontrapunkt*"; also "*Das Klavierspiel für Musikstudierende*" (Leipzig, 1898). (6) **Hans,** b. Raab, Hungary, April 4, 1843—Bayreuth, Dec. 5, 1916; eminent conductor; son of the cond. of the local cath.; his mother was a prominent sopr. and later a distinguished teacher; choirboy in the ct.-chapel, Vienna; studied with Sechter (piano-playing), and Kleinecke (the French horn), at the Cons.; horn-player in Kärtnertor Th. orch.; then with Wagner, 1866–67 in Lucerne, making a fair copy of the "*Meistersinger*" score. On W.'s recommendation, 1867, chorusm., Munich Opera. 1868–69 ct.-cond. under von Bülow. Cond. first performance of "*Lohengrin*" (Brussels, 1870); again at Lucerne with Wagner, making fair copy of the score of the "*Nibelungen Ring*"; 1871–75, cond., Pesth National Th.; then cond. of the Imp. Opera, Vienna, 1893, 1st cond., after 1875 also cond. "*Gesellschaft der Musikfreunde*" excepting 1882–83. Selected by Wagner to cond. the "*Ring des Niebelungen*" (Bayreuth, 1876), and alternate cond. with Wagner at the Wagner Concerts, Albert Hall, London, 1877; chief-cond. Bayreuth Festivals, and 1879–97, annually cond. Philh. concerts at London. Cond. several Lower Rhenish Festivals and 1885–1912 the Birmingham Festivals. In 1885, Mus. Doc. *h. c.*, Oxford Univ. In 1898 the freedom of the city of Vienna was given him.

Ricieri (rē-chā′-rĕ), **Giov. A.,** Venice, 1679—Bologna, 1746; male soprano and composer.

Ricordi (rē-kôr′-dē), (1) **Giov.,** Milan,

1785—1853; founder of the mus.-publishing firm in Milan; violinist and conductor; succeeded by his son (2) **Tito** (1811—1888); then by (3) **Giulio** (Milan, Dec. 19, 1840-- June 6, 1912; also ed. of the *Gazetta Musicale.* (4) **Tito** (1865—1933), a grandson, was a librettist. After 1912 the firm was dir. by Dr. Carlo Clausetti (with Renzo Balcarenghi, beginning 1919).

Rider-Kelsey, Corinne, b Le Roy, N. Y., Feb. 24, 1880; soprano; studied with L. A. Torrens, Chicago, Mr. and Mrs. Toedt, N. Y.; sang widely in concert and oratorio; 1908, début in opera at Covent Garden; d. Toledo, O., July 10, 1947.

Riechers (rē′-khĕrs), Aug., Hanover, 1836—Berlin, 1893; maker and repairer of vlns.; writer.

Riedel (rē′-d′l) (1) **Karl,** Kronenberg, Oct. 6, 1827—Leipzig, June 3, 1888, pupil Leipzig Cons.; 1854, founded the noted choral society Riedelverein; pres. Wagnerverein, etc.; pub. colls (2) **Hn.,** Burg, near Magdeburg, Jan. 2, 1847—Brunswick, Oct. 6 1913; pupil Vienna Cons.; ct.-cond Brunswick, composer. (3) **Fürchtegott Ernst Aug.,** Chemnitz, May 22, 1855—Plauen, Feb. 6, 1929; pupil Leipzig Cons.; from 1890, town cantor, Plauen, Saxony, also cond.; c. cantatas, etc.

Riedt (rēt), **Fr. Wm.,** Berlin, 1712—1784; flute-virtuoso; writer and composer.

Riegger (rē′-gĕr), **Wallingford,** b. Albany, Ga., April 29, 1885; composer; grad., Inst. of Mus. Art, N. Y., also studied at Berlin Hochsch.; cond. at Würzburg Op.; at Königsberg and with Blüthner Orch., Berlin; taught at Drake Coll. and Ithaca Cons.; Paderewski Prize, 1922, for piano trio in B minor; Coolidge Prize, 1924, for chamber work, "*La Belle Dame sans Merci*"; c. Rhapsody for Orch. (N. Y. Philh.); "*Study in Sonority*" (Phila. Orch.); "*Frenetic Rhythms*"; (chamber music) Chromatic Quartet; "*Dichotomy*"; canons for woodwinds; Divertissement; suite for flute solo, etc.

Riehl (rēl), **Wm. H. von,** Biebrich, 1823 —Munich, 1897: director, writer and composer.

Riem (rēm), **Fr. Wm.,** Kölleda, Thuringia, 1779—Bremen, 1857; organist, conductor and composer.

Riemann (rē'-män), **Hugo**, Grossmehlra, near Sondershausen, July 18, 1849—Leipzig, July 10, 1919; notable theorist. Son of a farmer who taught him the rudiments of mus., and who had prod. an opera and choral pcs. at Sondershausen, but opposed his son's mus. ambitions; the youth, however, studied theory with Frankenberger, and piano with Barthel and Ratzenberger, at Sondershausen. Studied law, then philosophy and history, at Berlin and Tübingen; after serving in the campaign of 1870–71, entered Leipzig Cons.; 1873, Dr. Phil. Göttingen; wrote dissertation *"Musikalische Logik"*; until 1878, a cond. and teacher at Bielefeld, then lecturer Leipzig Univ.; 1880–81, teacher of mus. at Bromberg; then till 1890, Hamburg Cons., then the Wiesbaden Cons.; 1895, lecturer at Leipzig Univ.; m. in 1876. Notable at times under pseud. **"Hugibert Ries"** as an essayist, writer of theoretical treatises of much originality, also an important historian and lexicographer; mus.-ed. of Meyer's *Konversationslexikon* and ed. a valuable *"Musik-Lexikon"* (1882; Engl. ed. 1893); c. chamber-mus., vln.-sonata, etc.

Riemenschneider (rē'-mĕn-shnī-dĕr), (1) **G.**, Stralsund, April 1, 1848—Breslau, Sept. 14, 1913; pupil of Haupt and Kiel; th.-cond. Lübeck (1875) and Danzig; later cond. Breslau concert-orch.; c. operas *"Mondeszauber"* (Danzig, 1887), and *"Die Eisjungfrau"* (symphonic picture), *"Julinacht,"* etc. (2) **Albert,** b. Berea, O., Aug. 31, 1878; organist, conductor, teacher; pupil of Reinhold, Fuchs, Widor and Guilmant; dir. Baldwin-Wallace Cons., Berea, and cond. of annual Bach fests. there; d. Akron, O., July 20, 1950.

Riepel (rē'-pĕl), **Jos.**, Horschlag, Upper Austria, 1708 — Ratisbon, 1782; chamber-musician, theorist and composer.

Ries (rēs), (1) **Fz.** (der alter), Bonn, 1755—Bremen, 1846; leader, later ct.-mus. dir., Bonn. (2) **Fd.**, Bonn, Nov. 29, 1784—Frankfort-on-Main, Jan. 13, 1838; noted pianist; pupil of Beethoven (of whom he wrote a valuable sketch) and Albrechtsberger; toured, 1813–24, London, m. an English woman; from 1830, l. Frankfort as cond.; c. 8 operas, 6

symphs., etc. (3) **Peter Jos.**, 1790—London, 1882; bro. of above; Royal Prussian Prof. (4) **Hubert,** Bonn, April 1, 1802—Berlin, Sept. 14, 1886; bro. of above; violinist, teacher and composer of valuable method, studies, etc., for vln. (5) **Fz.**, Berlin, April 7, 1846—Naumburg, June 20, 1932; son and pupil of (4); studied with Massart at Paris Cons. and with Kiel (comp.); concert-violinist till 1875 when he retired, and entered mus.-publishing (Ries & Erler, Berlin), c. orch. and chamber-mus., etc.

Riesenfeld (rēs'-ĕn-fĕld), **Hugo, b.** Vienna, 1883; Los Angeles, 1939; played in orch. of Vienna Op. as violinist; came to U. S. and served as concertm. of orch. at Manhattan Op. House, N. Y.; later as cond. in film theatres; former dir. of Rialto, Rivoli and Criterion Theatres, N. Y.; active in Hollywood as mus. dir. of film productions; c. operettas, orch. works, songs, etc.

Rieter-Biedermann (rē'-tĕr-bē'-dĕr-män), **J. Melchior**, 1811—Winterthur, Switz., 1876; founded pub.-house, 1849; 1862, branch at Leipzig.

Rieti (rē-ā'-tē), **Vittorio, b.** Alexandria, Jan. 28, 1898; composer; grad. Bocconi Univ., Milan; pupil in music of Frugatta and Respighi; c. (ballets) *"Arche de Noè," "Barabau"* and *"Le Bal"* (the two latter works prod. by Diaghileff); (opera) *"Orphee";* also concerto for wind and orch., piano concerto, string quartet and other chamber music.

Rietsch (rētsh), **Heinrich**, Falkenau, Sept. 22, 1860—Prague, Dec. 13, 1927; professor and composer; pupil of Krenn, Mandyczewski, and Fuchs; from 1892 teacher in Vienna; from 1900 prof. at the German Univ., Prague; author, and historian; c. opera, chamber music, etc.

Rietz (rēts), (1) **Jn. Fr. R.**, d. Berlin, 1828; vla.-player, royal chamber-mus. (2) **Eduard,** Berlin, 1802—1832; son of above, violinist and tenor; founded the Berlin Philh. Soc., 1826; was its cond. till death. (3) **Julius,** Berlin, Dec. 28, 1812—Dresden, Sept. 12, 1877; son of (1); 'cellist and cond.: pupil of Schmidt, Romberg and Ganz; 1834, asst.-cond. to Mendelssohn, Düsseldorf opera; 1835, his successor; 1847, cond. Singakademie, Leipzig, later also cond. Gewandhaus and prof. of comp. at the Cons.; 1860, ct.-cond. at Dresden; later dir. of the Cons.; editor of scores; c. 4 operas, 3 symphs., various overtures, masses, etc.

Riga (rē'-gä), **Frantz (François)**, Liége, 1831—Schaerbeek, near Brussels, 1892; conductor and composer of male choruses, etc.

Righini (rē-gē'-nē), **V.**, Bologna, Jan. 22, 1756—Aug. 19, 1812; tenor, singing-teacher and court-cond. at Mayence, later Berlin; c. 20 operas, etc., incl. vocalises.

Rimbault (rĭm'-bōlt), (1) **Stephen Francis**, organist and composer, 1773—1837. (2) **Edw. Fran.**, London, June 13, 1816—Sept. 26, 1876; son and pupil of above; organist and noted lecturer, editor, essayist and writer of numerous valuable historical works based on research.

Ri'mini, Giacomo, b. Verona, Italy; Chicago, 1952; barytone; pupil Conti-Forono; début at Desenzano, 1910; mem. of Chicago Op. for a number of years after 1914, and sang at Ravinia Op.; has been heard in Eur. theatres, esp. in Italy, also South America; m. Rosa Raisa, soprano.

Rimsky-Korsakov (rĭm'-shkĭ-kôr'-sä-kôf), **Nikolas Andrejevitch**, Tikhvin, Novgorod, March 18 (new style), 1844 —near St. Petersburg, June 21, 1908; notable Russian composer; studied at the Naval Inst., Petersburg; also took pf.-lessons; 1861, took up mus. as a profession after study with Balakirev; at 21 prod. his first symph.; 1871, prof. of comp. and instr. at Petersb. Cons., also 1873–84 inspector of Marine Bands; 1874–87, dir. Free Sch. of Mus., and until 1881, cond. there; 1883, asst. cond. (to Balakirev) of the Imp. Orch.; from 1886, cond. Russian Symph. Concerts; 1889, cond. 2 Russian concerts at the Trocadero, Paris. He orchestrated Dargomyzsky's "*Commodore*," Moussorgsky's "*Boris Godounoff*" and "*Khovanstchyna*" and Borodin's "*Prince Igor*"; pub. coll. of Russian songs and a harmony. C. operas "*Pskovitjanka*" ("The Girl from Pskov") (St. Petersburg, Imp. Th. 1873); "*A May Night*" (do. 1880); "*Snegorotchka*" ("*The Snow Princess*") (do. 1882); "*Mozart und Salieri*" (Moscow); opera ballet

"*Mlada*" (Petersburg, 1892); opera "*Christmas Eve*" (1895); opera "*Zarskaja Newjesta*" ("*The Tsar's Bride*") (1901), as well as 3 symphs. incl. "*Antar*" (1881), Sinfonietta; "*Russian*" overture; Servian fantasia, mus. tableau "*Sadko*" (1876); pf.-concerto, etc.; symphonic suite, "*Schêhêrazade*" (Boston Symph., 1897), used for the Russian ballets in Paris, 1911, with immense success; in 1901 he ceased to cond. Russian symph.; 1905 he wrote a letter protesting against the use of armed force in the Cons. to repress students' political expression, and he was dismissed; Glazounoff, Liadov, and others at once resigned, public feeling was aroused, and his opera "*Kotschei*" was prod. at the Théâtre du Passage, 1905, with great acclaim; later he was reinstated and Glazounoff chosen director. His opera "*Kitesch*" was prod. the same year, "*Le Coq d'Or*," a satiric comedy of a mythical kingdom (a thinly veiled criticism of Imp. Russia in his day), which was for a time forbidden prod. by the censor, reached the stage 1910. A master of orchestration, he carried on the Liszt tradition of the tone-poem but added his own brilliant finesse of instrumental colouring. His operas include attractive folksong elements. Previously pub. in Russian, his autobiography, "*My Musical Life*," was issued in English tr., 1923. He wrote a treatise on instrumentation, ed. by Steinberg (2 vols., 1913). Memoirs by Yasrobtsiev, Findeisen, Lapshin, Montagu-Nathan, Newmarch. (See article, page 516.)

Rinaldi (rē-näl'-dē), **Giov.**, Reggiolo, Italy, 1840—Genoa, 1895; pianist.

Rinck (rĭnk), **Jn. Chr. H.**, Elgersburg, Thuringia, Feb. 18, 1770—Darmstadt, Aug. 7, 1846, famous organist, writer and composer; pupil of Kittel, etc.; town organist Giesen, then, 1805, at Darmstadt, where he also taught in the seminary; 1813 ct.-organist there; autobiog. (Breslau, 1833).

Ringel, Federico. Vide F. D'ERLANGER.

Rinuccini (rē-noot-chē'-nē), **Ottavio**, Florence, 1562—1621; the librettist of the first opera ever performed, Peri (q. v.) and Caccini's "*Dafne*" (1594), also of Peri's "*Euridice*"

(1600), and Monteverde's *"Arianna a Nasso"* (1608).

Riotte (rĭ-ôt), **Phillip J.,** St. Mendel, Trèves, Aug., 1776—1856; conductor and dram. composer.

Ripa (rē'-pä), **Alberto da** (called Alberto Mantovano), b. Mantua—d. 1551; lutenist and composer.

Rischbieter (rĭsh'-bë-tĕr), **Wm. Albert,** Brunswick, 1834—Dresden, Feb. 10, 1910; pupil of Hauptmann, theory; violinist in Leipzig and other cities; from 1862 teacher harm. and cpt., Dresden Cons., pub. treatises, etc.; c. symph., overtures, etc.

Riseley (rĭz'-lĭ), **George,** Bristol, Aug. 28, 1845—April 12, 1932; organist; pupil of Corfe, his successor at Bristol Cathedral; cond. orch. societies; pensioned, 1898, then cond. London; c. *Jubilee Ode,* 1887, etc.

Risler (rēs'-lĕr), **Edouard,** Baden-Baden, Feb. 23, 1873—July 22, 1929; notable pianist; pupil of Diemer and d'Albert, Stavenhagen, etc.; taught at Paris Cons. after 1907; Chev. of the Legion of Honour.

Ristori (rēs-tō'-rē), **Giov. Alberto,** Bologna, 1692—Dresden, Feb. 7, 1753; organist and conductor; c. 2 of the earliest comic operas, also church-music.

Rit'ter, (1) **G. Wenzel,** Mannheim. April 7, 1748—Berlin, June 16, 1808; bassoonist, Berlin ct.-orch.; composer. (2) **Aug. Gf.,** Erfurt, Aug. 25, 1811—Magdeburg, Aug. 26, 1885; organ-virtuoso, editor and composer. (3) **Alex,** Narva (or Reval), Russia, June 27 (new style), 1833—Munich, April 12, 1896; violinist; c. succ. operettas, etc. (4) **Frédéric Louis,** Strassburg, June 22, 1834—Antwerp, July 22, 1891; prof. of mus. and conductor at Loraine; 1856, Cincinnati (U. S. A.), organist Philh. orch. and Cecilia Soc.; 1861 New York, cond. the Arion; 1867 prof. Vassar Col.; wrote *"Music in England,"* and *"Music in America"* (both N. Y., 1883); and other historical works; c. 3 symphs., etc. (5) **(Raymond-Ritter) Fanny,** b. Philadelphia, 1840; wife of above; writer and translator. (6) (rightly **Bennet) Théodore,** near Paris, 1841—Paris, 1886; pianist and composer. (7) **Hermann,** Wismar, Sept. 16, 1849—Würzburg, Jan. 22, 1926; violinist; studied Berlin with Joachim, etc.; invented and played a viola alta; for 20 yrs. teacher

at Würzburg. (8) **Josef,** Salzburg, Oct. 3, 1859—June 21, 1911; barytone at Vienna.

Ritter-Götze (gĕt-'tsĕ), **Marie,** Berlin, Nov. 2, 1865—London, 1922; mezzosopr.; pupil of Jenny Meyer and Levysohn; début R. Opera, Berlin; later Hamburg for 4 years; sang at Met. Op. and in concert U. S. A., 1890–1902; then Berlin R. Opera.

Rivarde (rē-vär'-dĕ), **Serge Achille,** b. N. Y., Oct. 31, 1865—London, March 31, 1940; violinist; at 11 taken to Europe, pupil of Dancla, Paris Cons.; dividing first prize, 1879, with Ondriček; 1885–90, solo violinist Lamoureux orch., from 1899, prof. R. C. M., London.

Rivé-King (rē'-vā-kĭng), **Julie,** b. Cincinnati, 1857—Indianapolis, 1937; noteworthy pianist; toured the world with great succ.; c. pop. pf.-pcs.; taught Bush Cons., Chicago.

Rivier (rē'-vē-ā), **Jean,** b. Villemeuble, France, 1896; won 1st prize counterpoint and fugue, Paris Cons.; c. orch. works, among which an *"Overture for a Don Quichotte"* has been played by several Amer. orchestras.

Rob'erton, Sir Hugh, b. Glasgow; conductor and composer; has won an important place as a choral leader with his Toynbee House Choir and particularly the Glasgow Orpheus Choir, which made a tour of America; a pioneer in the competitive fest. movement in Scotland; knighted by British gov't. for musical work; c. songs; d. Glasgow, Oct. 17, 1952.

Roberts, John Varley, near Leeds, 1841 —Oxford, 1920; eminent English organist; 1882–1918 succeeded Parratt as org. at Magdalen Coll., Oxford; cond. Univ. Glee and Madrigal Soc.; c. cantatas, organ works, etc.

Robeson, (1) **Lila,** b. Cleveland, O., 1880; contralto; pupil of Burnham, Mrs. Ford, Luckstone and Saenger; sang in concerts after 1905 and in 1912 at Met. Op., New York; later active as a teacher in Cleveland. (2) **Paul,** b. Princeton, N. J., April 9, 1898; Negro bass and actor; grad. of Rutgers Univ. and Columbia; has appeared on dram. stage, incl. *"Othello"* in London, also as song recitalist and in films.

Rob'inson, (1) **Jos.,** Dublin, 1815—1898; famous cond. and composer; his wife, (2) **Fanny Arthur,** 1831—1879, was a pianist and composer.

(3) **Franklin**, b. New York, Jan. 27, 1875; organist, theorist; studied music at Columbia Univ. with MacDowell and Rybner; grad. Coll. of the City of N. Y.; after 1908 taught at Inst. of Mus. Art; devised novel system of teaching harmony through ear-training; author of *"Aural Harmony"*; d. Northeast Harbor, Me., 1946.

Robyn (rō'-bĭn), (1) **Alfred G.**, St. Louis, Mo., April 29, 1860—New York, Oct. 18, 1935; son of (2) **Wm. R.** (who organised the first symph. orch. west of Pittsburgh); at 10 **A.** succeeded his father as organist at St. John's Church; at 16 solo-pianist with Emma Abbott's Co.; prod. comic opera *"Jacinta"*; c. pf.-concerto, etc., also pop. songs (incl. *"Answer"*), etc.

Roc'ca, Lodovico, b. Turin, Nov. 29, 1895; composer; studied Milan Cons.; doctorate, Turin Univ., 1920; won hon. diploma from Parma Cons. operatic competition; also prizes offered by Musica e Musici, Milan, and Italian Music League, N. Y.; c. (opera) *"Il Dibuk"* (after Anski drama), which had a striking succ. at Milan and Rome, and was given in N. Y., Chicago and Detroit (in English tr.) by Civic Op. Co. of last-named city, 1936; also considerable music for orch., among which the suite *"Chiaroscuri"* and the poem *"La Cella Azzurra"* have had frequent hearings; and many chamber music works.

Rochlitz (rōkh'-lĭts), **Jn. Fr.,** Leipzig, Feb. 12, 1769—Dec. 16, 1842; composer, editor and prominent writer of essays, biog. and librettos.

Röckel (rĕk'-ĕl), (1) **Jos. Aug.,** Neumburg-vorm-Wald, Upper Palatine, 1783—Anhalt-Cöthen, 1870; singer, prof. and operatic dir. at Aix; 1829-32, of a German co. at Paris; 1832, London. (2) **Aug.,** Graz, 1814 —Budapest, 1876; joint-conductor at Dresden opera (with Wagner); 1848, abandoned mus. for politics. (3) **Edw.,** Trèves, Nov. 20, 1816—Bath, Nov. 2, 1889; pupil of his uncle, J. N. Hummel; toured as pianist; from 1848 lived Bath, Eng.; c. pf.-pcs. (4) **Jos. (Ld.),** London, April 11, 1838—1923; bro. of above; pupil of Eisenhofer, Götze, and of his father and bro. Eduard (pf.); lived in Bristol, as teacher and pianist; c. cantatas, pf.-pcs., pop. songs, etc.

Rock'stro (rightly **Rackstraw**), **Wm. Smyth,** North Cheam, Surrey, Jan. 5, 1823—London, July 2, 1895; notable historian; pupil Leipzig Cons.; pianist and teacher, London; 1891, lecturer R. A. M. and R. C. M.; wrote treatises, biog. and *"General History of Music"* (1886); c. overture, cantata *"The Good Shepherd,"* etc.

Roda (rō'-dä), **Fd. von,** Rudolstadt, 1815—near Kriwitz, 1876; mus.-dir. and composer.

Rode (rôd), **(Jacques) P. (Jos.),** Bordeaux, Feb. 16, 1774—Château-Bourbon, near Damazon, Nov. 25, 1830; notable violinist; pupil of Fauvel and Viotti; début, Paris, 1790; toured; prof. at the Cons.; 1800, soloist to Napoleon, later to the Czar; c. 13 concertos, famous études, etc.; wrote a method (with Baillot & Kreutzer).

Rode (rō'-dĕ), (1) **Jn. Gf.,** Kirchscheidungen, Feb. 25, 1797—Potsdam, Jan. 8, 1857; horn-virtuoso; c. tone-pictures, etc. (2) **Th.,** Potsdam, 1821—Berlin, 1883; son of above; singing-teacher and writer. (3) **Wilhelm,** b. Hanover, Germany. Feb. 17, 1887; noted barytone and theatre manager; pupil of R. Moest in native city; début in Bremen; sang later in Breslau, Stuttgart, Munich, Vienna and Berlin, also as guest in London; after 1934 he was the manager of the Berlin Deutsches Opernhaus (formerly the Städtische Oper), but also continued his singing career.

Röder (rä'-dĕr), (1) **Jn. Michael,** d. ca. 1740; Berlin org.-builder. (2) **Fructuo'sus,** Simmershausen, March 5, 1747—Naples, 1789; notable organist. (3) **G. V.,** Rammungen, Franconia, ca. 1778—Altötting, Bavaria, 1848; ct.-cond. and composer. (4) **Carl Gl.,** Stötteritz, near Leipzig, 1812—Gohlis, 1883; 1846, founded the largest mus. and engraving establishment in the world; in 1872, his sons-in-law, C. L. H. Wolf and C. E. M. Rentsch, became partners. (5) **Martin,** Berlin, April 7, 1851—Boston, Mass., June 10, 1895; pupil R. Hochschule; conductor and teacher of singing in various cities, incl. Dublin and Boston; critic and writer under pseud. **"Raro Miedtner";** wrote essays, librettos, etc.; c. 3 operas, a symph., 2 symph. poems, etc.

Rodg'ers, Richard, b. N. Y.; studied at Columbia Univ.; c. many successful shows, incl. *"Oklahoma!" "Carousel."*

Rodolphe (rō'-dôlf) (or **Rudolph**), **Jean Jos.,** Strassburg, Oct. 14, 1730—Paris, Aug. 18, 1812; horn-virtuoso and violinist; pub. treatises; prod. operas.

Rodzinski (rŏd-zhēn'-skē), **Artur,** b. Spolato, Dalmatia, 1896; conductor; LL. D., Vienna Univ.; studied Acad. of Music there, under Marx, Schreker, Sauer, Lalewicz and Schalk; cond. Lemberg Op., later Warsaw Op. and Philh.; asst. cond. Phila. Orch., cond. Grand Op. Co. of that city and Curtis Inst. Orch.; 1930, Los Angeles Philh.; 1933, Cleveland Orch.; 1936-37, N. Y. Philh. for part of season; as guest in Hollywood Bowl, San Francisco, Detroit and Rochester, also at Salzburg Fest.

Rogel (rō'-hěl), **José,** Orihuela, Alicante, Dec. 24, 1829—Cartagena, Feb. 25, 1901; conductor and composer of 61 zarzuelas, etc.

Roger (rō-zhā), (1) **Gve. Hip.,** La Chapelle St.-Denis, near Paris, Dec. 17, 1815—Paris, Sept. 12, 1879; noted tenor; created *"Le Prophète"*; 1868, prof. of singing at the Cons. (2) **Victor,** Montpellier, France, July 22, 1853—Paris, Dec. 2, 1903; pupil École Niedermeyer; critic of *La France;* prod. about 20 operettas, etc., incl. *"La Petite Tâche"* (1898); succ. *"Poule Blanche"* (1899); and succ. *"Mlle. Georges"* (1900).

Roger-Ducasse. Vide DUCASSE.

Rogers (rä'-jěrs), (1) **Benj.,** Windsor, 1614—Oxford, 1698; organist at Dublin; later at Windsor; c. the hymn sung annually at 5 A. M., May 1, on the top of Magdalen tower, Oxford. (2) **John,** d. Aldersgate, ca. 1663; lutenist to Chas. II. (3) **Sir John Leman,** 1780—1847; composer; pres. Madrigal Soc. (4) **Clara Kathleen** (née **Barnett**), Cheltenham, Engl., Jan. 14, 1844—Boston, March 8, 1931; daughter and pupil of John Barnett; pupil of Leipzig Cons.; studied also singing with Götze and Sangiovanni, at Milan; début Turin, 1863 (under name **"Clara Doria"**); sang in Italy, then in London concerts; 1871, America with Parepa-Rosa Co.; 1872-73, also with Maretzek Co.; lived in Boston as singer and teacher; 1878, m. a Boston lawyer, Henry M. R.; pub.

"The Philosophy of Singing" (New York, 1893), c. songs, sonata for pf. and vln., etc. (5) **Roland,** West Bromwich, Staffordshire, Nov. 17, 1847—Bangor, July 30, 1927; at 11, organist at St. Peter's there; 1871-91, organist at Bangor Cath. and cond. of the Penrhyn and Arvonic Choirs, teacher in Wales; 1875, Mus. Doc. Oxford; c. cantatas *"Prayer and Praise"* (with orch.), *"The Garden"* (prize, Llandudno, 1896); and *"Florabel";* Psalm 130, for soli, chorus and strings; a symph., etc. (6) **James H.,** Fair Haven, Conn., 1857; at 18 studied in Berlin with Löschhorn, Haupt, Éhrlich and Rohde, and at Paris with Firsot, Guilmant and Widor; after 1883 lived in Cleveland, Ohio, as organist, pianist, critic and composer of notable songs; org. Euclid Ave. Temple; d. Dec., 1940. (7) **Francis,** b. Roxbury, Mass., April 14, 1870; barytone; grad. Harvard Univ.; appeared widely as recitalist; taught singing at Yale Univ. for a time, later privately, and at Juilliard Grad. School of Mus.; chairman, Amer. committee, Fontainebleau Cons.; Chev., Legion of Honour; d. N.Y., 1951;(8) **Bernard,** b. New York, Feb. 4, 1893; composer; studied Inst. of Mus. Art and with Ernest Bloch; Guggenheim Fellowship and Pulitzer Music Award; after 1930 taught comp. at Eastman School of Mus., Rochester, N.Y.; c. (orch.) symphony; *"Adonais";* prelude to *"Hamlet"; "Fairy Tales"* (N. Y. Philh., 1936); (chamber orch.) *"Soliloquy"* for strings; *"Pastorale"; "Nocturne";* (choral work) *"The Raising of Lazarus";* string quartet, opera,*"TheWarrior"*(Met.Op.,1947).

Rognone (rōn-yō'-nĕ), (1) **Riccardo,** a Milanese violinist. His son (2) **Fran.,** pub. a vln. method, 1614, etc.

Roguski (rō-goo'-skĭ), **Gustav,** Warsaw, 1839—April 5, 1921; pupil there and of Marx, Kiel, and Berlioz; from 1865 prof. of composition at the Warsaw Cons.; c. symph., 2 masses, chamber music, etc.

Rohde (rō'-dĕ), **Eduard,** Halle-on-Saale, 1828—Berlin, March 25, 1883; writer of pf.-method; singing teacher and composer.

Röhr (rār), **Hugo,** b. Dresden, Feb. 13, 1866—Munich, 1937; conductor; pupil of the Cons.; 1896-1934, cond. at Munich State Opera; also prof. at

Akad.; c. oratorio *"Ekkehard,"* opera *"Vater unser"* (Munich, 1904), etc.

Rokitansky (rō-kĭ-tän'-shkĭ), **Victor,** Freiherr **von,** Vienna, 1836—1896; pub. treatises on singing.

Rol'la, **Ales.,** Pavia, April 22, 1757— Milan, Sept. 15, 1841; violinist and teacher; prof. of vln. and vla.; Paganini was his pupil.

Rolland (rŭl-län), **Romain,** b. Clamecy, Jan.29,1866—Vezeday,Dec.29,1944; taught at Ecole normale supérieure, Paris; 1900 organised an international congress of music; historian at Paris; author of many historical and critical works, dramatic poems, and the musical romance *"Jean Christophe"* (1905-1908); notable works on Beethoven, Handel, early French music, etc.

Rolle (rôl'-lě), **Jn., H.,** Quedlinburg, Dec. 23, 1718—Magdeburg, Dec. 29, 1785; son and successor of the town mus.-dir. of Magdeburg; 1741–46, vla.-player, Berlin ct.-orch.; c. 4 Passions, 20 oratorios, etc.

Röllig (rěl'-lĭkh), **K. Ld.,** Vienna, 1761 —March 4, 1804; harmonica-player, inv. of the "Orphika" and "Xanorphika" (v. D. D.); wrote treatises on them; c. comic opera.

Rôman, **Johann Helmich,** Stockholm, 1694—near Calmar, 1758, called the father of Swedish music; pupil of Händel in London with a municipal stipend; 1727, court cond. at Stockholm; c. symphonies, etc. (2) **Stella,** Rumanian soprano; studied in Milan; Met. Op., from 1940, *Aida, Leonora, Violetta* and other dram. roles.

Romaniello (rō-män-ĭ-ěl'-lō), (1) **Luigi,** Naples, Oct. 27, 1858—Buenos Aires, Dec., 1916; pianist; pupil of his father, his brother (2) **Vincenzo** (b. Naples, 1858) and at Naples Cons.; graduating with highest honours; dir. of the pf.-dept. there, later member of the Soc. del Quartetto, also pianist Ferni Quartet; instructor in the R. "Educandato di San Marsellino" and critic; Chev. of the Italian Crown; 1896, Buenos Aires; pub. a pf.-method (prize at Naples, 1886); c. 3 operas, symphonic poems *"Corsair"* and *"Manfred,"* 2 symphs., etc.

Romanini (rō-mä-nē'-nē), **Romano,** Parma, 1864—1934; pupil of Mandovani (vln.) and Dacci (comp.) at the Cons.; 1st vln. Teatro Regio; then cond. concert and theatre-orch.

at Savigliano; 1890, prof. of vln.; 1897, director "Istituto Venturi," Brescia; c. succ. opera *"Al Campo"* (Brescia, 1895), symph., etc.

Romano, (1) **Alessandro** (q. v.). (2) **Giulio.** Vide CACCINI.

Romberg (rôm'-běrkh), (1) **Anton (a)** and (2) **H.,** two brothers, lived in Berlin, 1792. (3) **Anton (b),** Westphalia, 1745—1812 (1742—1814, acc. to Riemann); bassoonist. (4) **Gerhard H.,** b. 1748; clarinettist and mus.-dir. at Münster. (5) **Bd.,** Dincklage, near Münster, Nov. 11, 1767—Hamburg, Aug. 13, 1841; the head of the German sch. of 'cellists; prof.; ct.-cond., 1815–19; c. many operas, incid. mus.; 9 excellent concertos. (6) **Andreas (Jakob),** Vechta, near Münster, 1767—Gotha, 1821; vln.-virtuoso; son of (7) **Gerhard H.,** b. 1748; dir. and clarinettist. (8) **Sigmund,** b. Hungary, 1887; composer of popular light operas; a cousin of Alfred Grünfeld, pianist (q. v.); grad. Bucharest Univ.; pupil of Heuberger in Vienna; has long been res. in N. Y.; his extensive list of stage works includes *"The Blue Paradise," "Maytime," "The Student Prince," "The Desert Song,"* and others; d. N. Y., Nov. 8, 1951.

Ron'ald, **Sir Landon,** b. London, June 7, 1873—Aug. 14, 1938; composer; son of Henry Russell, composer, and bro. of the impresario of that name; studied R. Coll. of Music, London, with Parry, Stanford and Parratt; début as pianist; former cond. at Covent Garden and with Augustus Harris Op. Co. on tour; with London Symph., Royal Albert Hall Orch., and at various times with Scottish Orch., Manchester Symph., London and Liverpool Philh. Orchs., also widely as guest in continental cities; prin. Guildhall School of Music, 1910–38; fellow R. Coll. of Music, 1924; c. ballets, orch. and piano music, and songs; served as music critic of various publications; author, *"Variations on a Personal Theme," "Schumann," "Tschaikowsky."*

Ronchetti-Monteviti (rôn-kět'-té môntä-vē'-tē), **Stefano,** Asti, 1814— Casale Monferrato, 1882; pupil of B. Neri, Milan; 1850, prof. of comp. at the Cons.; 1877, dir.; c. an opera, a motet, etc.

Ronconi (rôn-kō'-nē), (1) **Dom.,** Lendinara, Rovigo, July 11, 1772—

Milan, April 13, 1839; singer and famous vocal-teacher; tenor, 1809, dir. of the ct.-opera, Vienna, 1819–29; singing-master to the princess, Munich; 1829, founded a singing-sch. at Milan; pub. vocal exercises. (2) **Giorgio**, Milan, 1810—1890; son of above; barytone; 1863, teacher at Cordova, Spain; from 1867, New York; composer. (3) **Felice**, Venice, 1811—St. Petersburg, 1875; singing-teacher and writer. (4) **Sebastiano**, b. Venice, 1814; barytone, violinist and teacher, Milan.

Röntgen (rĕnt'-gĕn), (1) **Engelbert**, Deventer, Holland, 1829—Leipzig, 1897; violinist. (2) **Julius**, Leipzig, May 9, 1855—Utrecht, Sept. 13, 1932; pianist; son of above; pupil of Hauptmann and E. F. Richter, Plaidy, Reinecke and Fr. Lachner; at 10 began to c.; at 17 pub. a vln.-sonata; début as pianist, 1878; teacher mus.-sch., Amsterdam; 1886–98, cond. to the Soc. for the Promotion of Mus., also Felix Meritis Soc.; co-founder (1885) of the Cons.; dir. after 1913; c. *"Toskanische Rispetti,"* an operetta for voices and pf.; a pf.-concerto, symphony, 'cello concerto, 3 vln. sonatas, 3 'cello sonatas, 2 piano sonatas, piano trio, opera *"Agnete"* (1914), etc.

Root, (1) **G. Ed. Fr.**, Sheffield, Mass., Aug. 30, 1820—Barley's Island, Aug. 6, 1895; teacher of singing and conductor; pupil of Webb, Boston; studied Paris, 1850; c. *"Battle-cry of Freedom," "Tramp, Tramp, Tramp," "Just before the Battle, Mother,"* etc. (2) **Fr. Woodman**, Boston, Mass., June 13, 1846—Chicago, 1916; son and pupil of above; pupil of Blodgett and Mason, New York; organist; 1869-70, studied in Europe; later lecturer, writer and teacher of large vocal classes.

Roo'tham, (1) **Daniel Wilberforce**, Cambridge, Aug. 15, 1837—April, 1922; pupil of Walmesley and Schira; 1865-77, cathedral org.; Bristol; cond. Bristol madrigal society. His son (2) **Cyril Bradley**, Bristol, Oct. 5, 1875—Cambridge, Engl., March 18, 1938; Mus. B. at Cambridge, 1900; from 1901, organist there, St. John's College; pupil also at R. C. M., London; c. overture *"The Spirit of Comedy,"* and vocal works with orch. *"Albert Graeme's Song"; "Andromeda"* (Bristol Festival, 1908),

"Coronach," etc.; after 1912, dir. of Cambridge Univ. Music Soc.

Rooy, van. Vide VAN ROOY.

Ropartz (rō-părs), **J. Guy, b.** Quingamp, France, June 15, 1864; pupil Dubois, Massenet, and César Franck; from 1894, dir. Nancy Cons., and cond. symph. concerts; from 1919, dir. Strasbourg Cons.; c. symph. on a Breton chorale; incid. music to Loti's *"Pêcheur d'Islande";* suite *"Dimanche breton"; Psalm 136* for organ and orch., chamber music, pf.-pcs., songs, etc.

Rore (rō'-rĕ), **Cipriano de**, Mechlin, 1516—Parma, 1565; eminent composer of Venetian sch.; pupil of Willaert, 1550, and his successor, 1563; ct.-conductor.

Rorich (rō'-rǐkh), **Carl, b.** Nürnberg, Feb. 27, 1869; pupil of R. Sch. of Mus., Würzburg; from 1892, teacher Gr. Ducal Sch. of Mus., Weimar; after 1914 dir. of school of music, Nürnberg; c. an overture *"Märchen";* suites, etc.; d. Nürnberg, 1941.

Ro'sa, (1) **Salvato're**, Ranella, Naples, 1615—Rome, 1673; famous painter and poet; wrote a satire on mus., etc.; composer. (2) **Carl** (rightly **Carl Rose**), Hamburg, 1842—Paris, 1889; violinist; 1867, m. Parepa-Rosa, and with her organised an English opera-company; toured with great frequency, especially at head of an Engl. opera syndicate.

Rösch (rĕsh), **Friedrich**, Memmingen, Dec. 12, 1862—Berlin, Oct. 29, 1925; author and conductor of male choruses, etc.; pupil of Wohlmuth and Rheinberger; lived in various cities; from 1898 in Berlin.

Rosé (rō'-zā), **Arnold Josef, b.** Jassy, 1863—d. 1946; pupil of Heissler, Vienna Cons.; 1st vln. Rosé Quartet, since 1881, soloist, Vienna ct.-orch., and 1888, leader Bayreuth Festivals; long prof. at Vienna State Acad. of Mus., and concertm. at the State Opera; 1902, m. a sister of Mahler.

Roseingrave (rōz'-ǐn-grāv), **Thos.**, Dublin—London, 1753 (?); 12 years organist at St. George's; Hanover Square; composer and writer.

Rösel (rä'-zĕl), **Rudolf Arthur**, Münchenbernsdorf, Gera, Aug. 23, 1859—Weimar, April 3, 1934; pupil of Weimar Mus.-Sch., later of Thomson; 1877-79, 1st vln. various cities; from 1888 in the Weimar ct.-orch.; also teacher at Mus.-Sch.; c. fairly succ. "lyric stage-play" "*Halimah*" (Weimar, 1895), symph. poem "*Frühlingsstürme,*" a notturno for horn with orch., a notturno for oboe with orch., etc.

Rosellen (rō-zĕl-läṅ), **H.**, Paris, 1811 —1876; pf.-teacher, writer and composer.

Ro'sen, Max, b. Rumania, 1900; violinist; lived in New York as child; studied there and in Europe; début, Dresden, 1915; after 1918 appeared in U. S. with success.

Ro'senfeld, (1) **Leopold,** Copenhagen, July 21, 1850—July 19, 1909; studied in Germany; critic and teacher in Copenhagen; c. vocal works with orch., "*Henrik og Else,*" "*Liden Helga,*" "*Naar Solen daler,*" songs, etc. (2) **Maurice,** b. Vienna, Dec. 31, 1867—Chicago, Feb. 25, 1939; studied Columbia Univ.; piano with Hyllested and Spanuth; grad. Chicago Mus. Coll.; where later taught and became dir.; in 1916 estab. his own school in Chicago; critic for the *Examiner* and after 1917 for the *News.* (3) **Paul,** American writer; author of books and articles on modern music, incl. *Musical Chronicle, Musical Portraits, An Hour with American Music*; d. N. Y., 1946.

Rosenhain (rō'-zĕn-hīn), **Jacob** (**Jacques**), Mannheim, 1813—Baden-Baden, 1894; pianist and dram. composer.

Rosenmüller (rō'-zĕn-mǐl-lĕr), **Jn.**, 1619 —Wolfenbüttel, 1684; mus.-director and composer.

Rosenthal (rō'-zĕn-täl), (1) **Moriz,** b. Lemberg, Dec. 18, 1862—d. N. Y., 1946; pianist; at 8 his ability won the aid of Mikuli; at 10, pupil of R. Joseffy; at 14, gave a concert Vienna; Royal Pianist; 1876–86, pupil of Liszt; from 1887, toured America and Europe; pub. (with L. Schytte) "*Technical Studies for the Highest Degree of Development.*" (2) **Hedwig Kanner,** his wife, pf. teacher in U. S. (3) **Manuel,** French conductor, composer; cond. Seattle Symph., 1949.

Rosetti (rō-sĕt'-tē), **Fran. Ant.** (**Fz. Anton Rössler,** rĕs-lĕr), Leitmeritz, Bohemia, 1750—Ludwigslust, 1792, ct.-conductor and composer.

Ross, Hugh, b. Langport, England, Aug. 21, 1898; conductor; studied Oxford Univ., R. Coll. of Music; cond. Winnipeg (Can.) Male Choir after 1921; Winnipeg Symph., 1923-

27; beginning latter year, Schola Cantorum, N. Y.

Rossi (rôs'-sē), (1) **Giov. Bat.,** Genoese monk; theorist, ca. 1618. (2) **Abbate Fran.,** b. Bari, Italy, ca. 1645, canon and dram. composer. (3) **Gaetano,** Verona, 1780—1855; librettist. (4) **Luigi Felice,** Brandizzo, Piedmont, 1804—Turin, 1863; essayist and translator. (5) **Lauro,** Macerata, 1810—Cremona, 1885; wrote a harmony and c. operas. (6) **Giov. Gaetano,** Borgo, S. Donino, Parma, 1828—Genoa, 1886; c. 4 operas. (7) **Carlo,** Lemberg, April 4, 1839— Venice, Oct., 1906; pupil of Menzel; from 1851 in Venice; c. symph., etc. (8) **Cesare,** near Mantua, Jan. 20, 1858—Casalmaggiore, July 27, 1930; c. operas "*I fugitivi*" (Trient, 1896) and "*Naďeya*" (Prague, 1903).

Rossini (rôs-sē'-nē), **Gioacchino A.,** Pesaro, Feb. 29, 1792—Ruelle, near Paris, Nov. 13, 1868; eminent Italian opera-composer. His father was inspector of slaughter-houses and also horn-player in strolling troupes in which the mother (a baker's daughter) was *prima donna buffa.* Left in charge of a pork-butcher, R. picked up some knowledge of the harpsichord from a teacher, Prinetti; 1802 studied with Angelo Tesci; this began his tuition; he made rapid progress, and sang in church, and afterwards joined his parents as a singer, horn-player and accompanist in the theatre. At 14 he studied comp. with Padre Mattei, and 'cello with Cavedagni at the Bologna Liceo. At 15 he prod. a cantata "*Il Pianto d'Armonia per la Morte d'Orfeo,*" which won a prize. Mattei soon told him that, though he had not enough cpt. to write church-mus., he knew enough to write operas, and he ceased to study. At 17 he prod. a succ. 1-act opera buffa "*La Cambiale di Matrimonio*" (Venice, 1810); next year, a succ. 2-act opera buffa "*L'Equivoco Stravagante,*" Bologna. He received various commissions, writing 5 operas during 1812. 1813, his "*Tancredi*" (Fenice Th., Venice) was an immense succ. and "*L'Italiana in Algeri,*" an opera buffa (San Benedetto Th.), was also succ. Two failures followed with disheartening effect, but "*Elisabetta*" (its libretto curiously anticipating Scott's "*Kenilworth*") was a succ. (Naples, 1813).

and in it he dropped *recitativo secco.* A failure followed and on the first night of the next work the public resentment at his daring to set to mus. the text of one of Paisiello's operas led to its being hissed. This work *"Almaviva"* (Rome, 1816) was better received the second night and gradually est. itself in its subsequent fame under the title *"Il Barbiere di Siviglia"*; 1815-23 he was under contract to write two operas yearly for Barbaja, manager of La Scala at Milan, the Italian opera, Vienna, and Neapolitan theatres. His salary was 12,000 lire (about $2,400). During these 8 years he c. 20 operas, travelling from town to town and working under highest pressure. 1821 he m. Isabella Colbran (d. 1845), who had sung in his operas. The ill-succ. of his most carefully written *"Semiramide"* (Venice, 1823) and an offer from Benelli, a mgr., led him to London where he was lionised and in 5 months earned £7,000. For 18 months he was mgr. of the Th. Italien at Paris, and prod. several operas with artistic but not financial succ. He was, however, "Premier compositeur du roi" and "Inspector-général du chant en France," sinecures with a salary of 20,000 francs ($4,000). He lost these in the Revolution of 1830, but afterwards on going to law received a pension of 6,000 francs. At the Gr. Opéra he prod. with succ. revisions in French of earlier Italian succs. 1829 he gave there his greatly succ. masterpiece *"Guglielmo Tell."* At the age of 37, having prod. under his direction Meyerbeer's first opera and having heard *"Les Huguenots,"* R. foreswore opera and never wrote again anything more dramatic than his famous *"Stabat Mater"* (1832), not performed entire till 1842; *"Petite messe solennelle,"* with orch.; a cantata for the Exposition of 1867; and pf.-pcs. with burlesque names. He retired to Bologna and Florence, returning to Paris in 1855. 1847 he m. Olympe Pelissier. He c. 35 operas, 16 cantatas, canzonets and arias, *"Gorgheggi e solfeggi per soprano per rendere la voce agile,"* *"Chant des Titans"* for 4 basses with orch.; *"Tantum ergo"* for 3 male voices with orch.; *"Quoniam"* for solo bass with orch.; *"O salutaris"* for solo quartet. etc. Biog. by Stendhal

(1823), Azevedo (1865), H. S. Edwards (London, 1869), Zanolini (1875), Struth (Leipzig), Dr. A. Kohut (Leipzig, 1892). Other memoirs by Carpani, d'Ortigue, Bettoni, Blaze de Bury, Escudier, Mirecourt, Montazio, Pougin, Silvestri, Sittard, Thrane, Checchi, Gandolfi, Dauriae, Corradi, Istel, Curzon, and Francis Toye (1934). (See article, page 517.)

Rost (rôst), (1) **Nicolas**, comp., 1583 —1614. (2) **Fr. Wm. Ehrenfried,** Bautzen, 1768—Leipzig, 1835; writer.

Roswaen'ge, Helge, b. Copenhagen, 1897; tenor.

Roth (rōt), (1) **Ph.,** Tarnowitz, Silesia, 1853—Berlin, 1898; 'cellist. (2) **Bertrand,** b. Degersheim, St. Gallen, Feb. 12, 1855; pianist; pupil of Leipzig Cons. and Liszt; teacher Hoch Cons., Frankfort, co-founder. Raff Cons., 1882; 1885-90, Dresden Cons.; then opened a private mus.-sch. there. (3) **Feri,** b. Zolyon, Hungary, July 18, 1899; violinist; grad. R. Hungarian School of Music, Budapest; played in orch. at Budapest Op. and Berlin Volksop.; in 1922 formed well-known Roth Quartet, and has toured with it in leading Eur. and Amer. cities.

Rothier (rō'-tē-ā), **Léon,** b. Rheims, Dec. 26, 1874; bass; studied Paris Cons., won 1st prizes in 3 years; sang with Paris Op., and after 1910 with Met. Op.; d. N. Y. Dec. 6, 1951.

Rothmühl (rōt'-mül), **Nikolaus,** Warsaw, March 24, 1857—Berlin, May 24, 1926; tenor; pupil of Gänsbacher; début, Dresden ct.-theatre, then Berlin, etc.; toured widely, incl. America; then at Stuttgart ct.-opera; for some years dir. of opera school at Stern Cons., Berlin.

Roth'well, Walter Henry, London, Sept. 22, 1872—Los Angeles, March 11, 1927; conducted the first English performance of *"Parsifal"* in America; pupil Vienna Royal Acad.; cond. in various cities, and at Amsterdam Royal Opera; 1903, America to conduct English productions of *"Parsifal,"* and *"Madame Butterfly"*; 1908-15, cond. St. Paul, Minn., Orch.; 1916, at N. Y. Stadium concerts; 1917-18, guest cond., Cincinnati and Detroit; after 1919 until his death, of the Los Angeles Philh. Orch.

Rotoli (rō-tō'-lē), **Augusto,** Rome, Jan. 17, 1847—Boston, Nov. 26, 1904; pupil of Lucchesi; founded and cond. "Società corale de' concerti sagri," 1876, singing-master to Princess Margherita; 1878, maestro, Capella reale del Sudario; 1885, invited to Boston, Mass., as teacher in the N. E. Cons.; Chev. of the Ital. Crown, etc. C. mass for the funeral of Victor Emmanuel, 1878; "*Salmo elegiaco,*" with orch. (1878), etc.

Rot'tenberg (-bĕrkh), Dr. **Ludwig,** Czernowicz, Oct. 11, 1864—Frankfort-on-Main, May 6, 1932; studied vln. and piano with Fuchs, and theory with Mandyczewski; début as pianist; 1888, director; 1891, cond. at Brünn, then 1st opera cond. at Frankfort; in 1912–13, cond. of Wagner at Covent Garden; c. opera, vln. sonata, songs.

Rotter (rôt'-tĕr), **L.,** Vienna, 1810—1895; pianist, conductor, theorist and composer.

Rottmanner (rôt'-män-nĕr), **Ed.,** Munich, 1809—Speyer, 1843; organist.

Rouget de l'Isle (roo-zhā dŭ-lĕl), **Claude Jos.,** Lons-le-Saulnier, Jura, May 10, 1760—Choisy-le-Roy, June 27, 1836; composer of the "*Marseillaise,*" military engineer, poet, librettist, violinist and singer; wrote "*La Marseillaise,*" picking out the air on his vln.; he called it "*Chant de Guerre,*" but it grew popular first in Marseilles, and was brought to Paris by Marseillaise volunteers in 1792; **R.** was imprisoned for refusing to take an oath against the crown, but was released, and lived in Paris in great poverty.

Rousseau (roos-sō), (1) **Jean Jacques,** Geneva, June 28, 1712—Ermenonville, near Paris, July 3, 1778. The great writer; mainly self-taught in mus., but aiming to reform notation by the substitution of numerals for letters and note-heads, read before the Académie, 1742, a "*Dissertation sur la musique moderne*" (1743); his opera, "*Les Muses Galantes,*" had one private representation (1745); his revision of the intermezzo "*La Reine de Navarre*" (by Voltaire and Rameau) was a failure; but his opera "*Le Devin du Village*" (Gr. Opéra, 1752) was succ. for 60 years. He wrote mus. articles for the "*Encyclopédie,*" which were roughly handled by Rameau and others, but revised and re-pub. as "*Dictionnaire de musique*" (1768). In 1752 he participated in the "Guerre des Bouffons,"

between the partisans of French and Italian opera, **R.** siding with the Italianists and declaring that a French national music was impossible and undesirable; for which the members of the opera burned him in effigy. "*Pygmalion*" (1773) was v. succ. being a novelty—a melodrama, all the dialogue spoken, the orch. furnishing interludes and background. Six new arias for "*Le Devin du Village,*" and a coll. of 100 romances and duets "*Les consolations des misères de ma vie*" (1781), and fragments of an opera, "*Daphnis et Chloé,*" were pub. (1780). (2) **Samuel Alex.,** Neuvemaison, Aisne, June 11, 1853—Paris, Oct. 1, 1904; pupil of Paris Cons., 1878, won the Prix Cressent, and 2d Grand Prix de Rome; prod. 1-act comedy-opera "*Dianorah*" (Op.-Com., 1879); 1891, won the Prize of the City of Paris, with opera "*Merowig*"; 1892, 1st cond. Th. Lyrique; 1898, prod. fairly succ. lyric drama "*La Cloche du Rhin*"; c. also a solemn mass, etc.

Roussel (roos'-sĕl), **Albert,** b. Tourcoing, April 5, 1869—Royan, France, Aug. 23, 1937; composer; a naval student, he made a voyage to China as an ensign; but resigned in 1894 and took up music, studying harmony with Gigout; 1898 entered the Schola Cantorum and studied under d'Indy till 1907; 1902–14, prof. of counterpoint at the Schola Cantorum. His comps. include symph. prelude, "*Résurrection*" (after Tolstoi's novel); symph., sketch, "*Vendanges*"; "*Le poème de la Forêt*" (1904–06); symph. sketches "*Evocations*" (1910–11), poem for orch. "*La Menace*" (1907), etc. Inspired by his visit to the East in 1909–10, **R.** prod. a Hindu ballet, "*Padmavati,*" which had a markedly successful première at the Paris Op., 1923. Other productions include the orch. works, "*Le Festin de l'Araignée*" and "*Pour une Fête de Printemps*"; 4 symphonies; concerto for orch.; concerto for piano and orch.; "*Petite Suite*"; "*Psaume,*" for orch. with employment of choral voices; the ballet, "*Bacchus and Ariadne*"; the opera, "*La Naissance de la Lyre,*" which treats an allegorical theme; 2 sonatas for piano and vln.; trio for flute, viola and 'cello; quintet; sextet; and various piano pieces and smaller vocal compositions. He visited the U. S. and took part in perfs. of his works at the Chicago Chamber Music Fest. under the patronage of Mrs. F. S. Coolidge in 1930.

Roussier (roos-sĭ-ā), Abbé **P. Jos.**, Marseilles, 1716—Écouis, Normandy, ca. 1790; canon and theorist.

Rovel'li, (1) **Giu.**, Bergamo, 1753—Parma, 1806; 'cellist. (2) **P.**, Bergamo, 1793—1838; nephew of above; violinist and composer.

Rovet'ta, Giov., d. Venice, 1668; pupil of Monteverde, and his successor (1644) at San Marco; c. operas, etc.

Row'botham, John F., b. Edinburgh, April 18, 1854; studied Oxford, Berlin, Paris, Vienna, Dresden; wrote numerous histories of mus., biogs., etc.; d. London, 1925.

Roze (rôz), (1) **Marie**, Paris, 1846—June 21, 1926; eminent operatic soprano; pupil of Paris Cons.; long active as singer and teacher in Paris; 1882, London, later U. S. Her son (2) **Raymond**, London, 1875—1920; pupil of Brussels Cons.; 1911, cond. London Op. House; cond. His Majesty's Theatre, and c. incid. music for Beerbohm Tree's prods. of Shakespeare's "*Macbeth*," etc., c. text and music of operas "*Joan of Arc*" (in concert from Queen's Hall, 1911); "*Antony and Cleopatra*"; a symph. poem on the same subject (Queen's Hall, 1911); songs, etc.

Rozkošny (rôz'-kôsh-nē), **Josef Richard**, Prague, Sept. 21, 1833—1913; pianist; pupil of Jiranek, Tomaschek and Kittl; toured, then lived in Prague; prod. there 9 Bohemian operas; c. also overtures, 2 masses, etc.

Różycki (roo-zhēt'-skĭ), **Ludomir von**, b. Warsaw, 1883; pupil of the Cons. and of Humperdinck; from 1908 teacher at the Cons. in Lemberg and cond. at the Opera; then in Warsaw; c. operas "*Boleslas der Kühne*" (Lemberg, 1909); "*Eros and Psyche*" (1917), "*Beatrice Cenci*" (1922), 6 symphonic poems, piano quintet, piano trio, sonatas for vln., for 'cello and piano; songs; d. Jan. 1, 1953.

Rub'bra, Edmund, b. Northampton, Eng., 1901; composer; pupil Wm. Morris, R. C. M.; c. symphs., etc.

Ru'benson, A., Stockholm, 1826—1901; vlnist., comp.; dir. S. Cons. after 1872.

Rubert (roo'-bĕrt), **Johann Martin**, Nuremberg, 1614—Stralsund, 1680; organist and comp.

Rubinel'li, Giovanni Battista, Brescia, ca. 1753—1829; Italian opera singer; début at 18, Stuttgart.

Rubini (roo-bē'-nē), **Giov. Bat.**, Romano, Bergamo, April 7, 1795—at his castle, near Romano, March 2, 1854; famous tenor, said to have been the first to use the vibrato and the sob, both since abused; his range was from E—b' (with a falsetto register to f'. (v. PITCH, D. D.); Bellini wrote many operas for him; toured with Liszt, earning by one concert over $10,000; had one of the largest fortunes ever amassed by a singer.

Rubinstein (roo'-bĭn-shtīn), (1) **Anton Gregorovitch**, of Jewish parents, Wechwotynecz, Bessarabia, Nov. (16) 28, 1829—Peterhof, near St. Petersburg, Nov. 20, 1894; one of the greatest of the world's pianists. Early taken to Moscow, where his father est. a pencil factory, he was at first a pupil of his mother; at 7, of Alex. Villoing, who was his only pf.-teacher. At 9 he made a tour with Villoing as far as Paris, where, in 1840, he played before Chopin and Liszt, who advised him to study in Germany. He toured further and returned to Moscow in 1843. His brother, Nikolai (v. below), was also musical, and in 1844 both were taken to Berlin, where Anton studied comp. with Dehn. Returning to Russia after a tour through Hungary, with the flutist Heindl, he lived in Petersburg under the patronage of the Grand Duchess Helen; he prod. 2 Russian operas; 1854–58, with the assistance of Count Wielhorski and the Grand Duchess, he made a wide tour, finding himself now well known as composer and pianist; 1858, ct.-pianist and cond. of ct.-concerts, Petersburg; 1859, dir. Russian Mus. Soc.; 1862, founded the Imp. Cons. at Petersburg, and was its dir. until 1867; 1865, he m. Vera Tchekuanoff. 1867–70, he toured Europe, with greatest imaginable succ.; 1872–73, he gave in America 215 concerts, from which he earned $40,000 (£8,000); but he could never be induced to cross the ocean again, though offered $125,000 (£25,000) for fifty concerts. 1887–91, again dir. Petersburg Cons., then lived in Berlin; 1891, in Dresden. The Czar bestowed on him the Order of Vladimir carrying with it nobility, and the

title of Imp. Russian State Councillor; he was an officer of the Legion of Honour, a Knight of the Prussian Ordre pour le mérite, etc. He instituted the *Rubinstein prizes* of 5,000 francs each for pf.-playing and composition open every 5 years to men between 20 and 26 of any nationality.
He wrote his *"Memoirs,"* also *"Die Musik und ihre Meister"* (1892), *"Gedankenkorl"* (1892).
As a pianist **R.** is second only to Liszt, whom he perhaps excelled in fire and leonine breadth. He was, however, frequently inaccurate in his performance. He chiefly wished to be remembered as a composer but his music has lost its erstwhile popularity in recent years, save for occasional hearings of his piano works. He placed great hope in the creation of what he called "Sacred Opera" (oratorio to be enacted with costume and scenery). In this "new form" he c. *"The Tower of Babel," "Paradise Lost," "Moses," "Christus."* Besides the noteworthy operas *"Nero"* (Hamburg, 1879), *"The Demon"* (Russian, P., 1875), and *"Die Makkabäer"* (German, Berlin, 1875), he c. 11 other operas, a ballet *"La Vigne"* (*Die Rebe*), and 2 cantatas with orch. C. also 6 symphs. (incl. the famous *"Ocean,"* op. 42, in C, in 7 movements); op. 95, in D min. (*"Dramatic"*); op. 107, in G min. (in memory of Gr. Duch. Helen). "Character-pictures" *"Faust," "Ivan IV.,"* and *"Don Quixote"*; 3 concert-overtures, incl. op. 43 (*"Triomphale"*), and op. 116 (*"Anthony and Cleopatra"*); a Suite in 6 movements, op. 119 (his last work); symph. poem *"La Russie"*; 5 pf.-concertos; fantasia eroica with orch.; vln.-concerto; romance and caprice for vln. with orch.; 2 'cello-concertos; vln.-sonatas; vln.-sonata (arr. for vln. by David), etc. FOR PIANO SOLO: suite; 4 sonatas, 6 preludes, 6 études, 5 barca-rolles; *"Kamenoi-Ostrow"* (*"Isle of Kamenoi"* in the Neva, a series of 24 "pictures"); *"Soirées de St. P.,"* *"Miscellanies," "Le Bal,"* 10 pcs. op. 14; *"Album de Peterhof,"* etc. FOR PF. 4 HANDS, sonata, *"Bal Costumé,"* 6 Charakterbilder, fantasia for 2 pfs.; over 100 songs, 18 duets, choruses, etc.
Autobiog. *"Memoirs"* (St. P., 1880;

Leipzig, 1893). Biogr. by McArthur (London, 1889). Other studies by Baskin, Vogel, Lissowski, Sveriev, Zabel, Soubies, Cavos-Degtarev, Martinov, Rodenberg, Droucker, Findeisen, La Mara, Bernstein and Arthur Hervey.
(2) **Nikolai,** Moscow, June 2, 1835— (of consumption), Paris, March 23, 1881; bro. of above, who declared **N.** to be the better pianist of the two; founder Moscow Mus. Soc.; dir. Moscow Cons. from its foundation, 1864; c. pf.-pcs. etc.   (3) **Jos.,** Staro-Constantinov, Russia, Feb. 8, 1847 —(suicide) Lucerne, Sept. 15, 1884; pianist for rehearsals at Bayreuth; composer. (4) **Jacques,** Russia. 1874 —Paris, 1902; son of (1).   (5) **Arthur,** b. Lodz, Poland, 1886; pianist; pupil of Breithaupt in Berlin; since his 12th year touring in recitals as a prodigy; has been heard as mature artist with much succ. in Europe, Far East and U. S. (6) **Beryl,** b. Athens, Ga., Oct. 26, 1898; pianist, composer; studied with Alexander Lambert, Vianna da Motta and Busoni; début with Met. Op. orch. at 13; played with leading Amer. orchs. and in London (1925); dean (later, dir.) and head of piano dept., Cleveland Inst. of Music; c. opera, orch. wks., pf. pcs.; conductor; d. Cleveland, Dec. 29, 1953. (7) **Ida,** b. Kharkov, Russia, 1893; noted actress and dancer; pupil of the tragedian Lensky; gave series of dance productions in Paris, which incl. creation of D'Annunzio's and Debussy's *"Martyre de St. Sebastien"* (written for her) at Théâtre du Châtelet, 1911; also many other modern ballet scores created for and premièred by her, incl. title rôle in Stravinsky's *"Perséphone,"* which utilises mime-reciter, tenor soloist, chorus and orch.
Rückauf (rïk'-owf), **Anton,** Schloss Alt-Erloa, Prague, March 13, 1855— Sept. 19, 1903; composer; pupil of Proksch, and teacher at his institute, then pupil of Nottebohm and Navratil, at Vienna; c. opera *"Die Rosenthalerin"* (Dresden, 1897), songs, etc.
Ruckers (rook'-ĕrs), family of clavecin-makers at Antwerp, superior to all others. (1) **Hans** (Senior), d. ca. 1640; father of (2) **Fz.,** b. 1776. (3) **Hans** (Junior), b. 1578. (4) **Andries** (Senior), b. 1579. (5) **Anton,**

b. 1581; the last mfr. was (6) Andries (Junior), 1607–67.

Rucsicska. Vide RUZICKA.

Rudersdorff (roo'-dĕrs-dôrf), Hermine, Ivanowsky, Ukraine, Dec. 12, 1822 —Boston, Mass., Feb. 26, 1882; noted soprano and teacher.

Rudhyar (rŭd'-yĕr), Dane, b. Paris, 1895; composer; has lived in U. S. since 1916; won Los Angeles Orch. prize, 1920, for symph. poem, *"Surge of Fire"*; author of book on Debussy; his orch. works incl. also Three Dance Poems, Sinfonietta, *"Desert Chants," "Ouranos"; "Five Stanzas"; "To the Real"*; symphony; *"Hero Chants,"* etc.

Rudnick (root'-nĭk), Wilhelm, Dammerkow, Pomerania, Dec. 30, 1850— Liegnetz, Aug. 7, 1927; pupil of Kullak's Acad., and of Dienel; org. at Liegnitz; c. opera *"Otto der Schütz"* (1887); oratorio *"Judas Iscariot," "Der Verlorene Sohn,"* etc.

Ru'dolph, (1) Jn. J. R., Arch-duke of Austria, Florence, 1788 — Baden, Vienna, 1831; pianist and composer; pupil and intimate friend of Beethoven. (2) Jn. J., 1730—1812, vln. and horn player.

Rudorff (roo'-dôrf), Ernst Fr. K., Berlin, Jan. 18, 1840—Dec. 31, 1916; pupil of Bargiel (pf.) and Leipzig Cons.; private pupil of Hauptmann and Reinecke; 1865, pf.-teacher, Cologne Cons.; 1867 founded the Bach-verein; 1869 head pf.-teacher Berlin Hochschule; 1880–90 cond. Stern Gesangverein; c. symphs., overtures, etc.

Ruegger (rüg'-gĕr), Elsa, b. Lucerne, Dec. 6, 1881; 'cellist; studied with Jacobs and Anna Campowski at the Cons. there, taking 1st prize at 13; toured widely America and Europe; 1908–14, taught Scharwenka Cons., Berlin; later res. in San Francisco, m. Edmund Lichtenstein, violinist.

Rüfer (rü'-fär), (1) Ph. (Barthélémy), Liége, June 7, 1844—Berlin, Sept. 15, 1919; son of a German organist. (2) Philipp R., pupil of Liége Cons.; 1869–71, mus.-dir. at Essen; pf.-teacher Stern's Cons., Kullak's Cons., and from 1881 Scharwenka's, Berlin, c. operas *"Merlin"* (Berlin, 1887); succ. *"Ingo"* (Berlin, 1896); symph. in F.; 3 overtures, etc.

Ruffo (roof'-fō), (1) V., b. Verona; maestro of the Cath.; composer (1550–88). (2) Titta, b. Pisa, June

9, 1877; eminent barytone; pupil of St. Cecilia Cons., Rome; after two years dismissed and advised to give up singing; then Cassini of Milan taught him gratis; he won his first success at Rio Janeiro and throughout South America, then triumphed in Italy, later in Vienna; 1912 a sensation in Paris and engaged for Chi.-Phil. Opera Co., appearing Philadelphia, Nov. 4, 1912; 1922–9, with Met. Op., and widely also in Europe; d. Florence, July 6, 1953.

Ruggeri (Ruggieri) (rood-jä'-rē), a Cremonian family of vln.-makers, (1) Fran., flourished, 1668—1720. (2) Giov. Bat. (1700—1725), and (3) P. (1700—1720), probably his sons. (4) Guido and (5) V., both of Cremona in 18th cent. R. violins resemble Amatis. (6) Giov. M., Venetian composer; prod. operas there 1696—1712.

Ruggi (rood'-jē), Fran., Naples, 1767— 1845; conductor, professor and dram. composer.

Rug'gles, Carl, b. Marion, Mass., 1876; composer; studied Harvard Univ., founded and cond. Winona (Minn.) Symph. for several years; c. orch. and chamber works of highly original harmonic and rhythmic style, incl. *"Portals"* for string orch., *"Men and Angels," "Sun-Treader,"* and *"Men and Mountains,"* also songs with orch.; several of his works perf. at fests. of Internat'l. Soc. for Contemp. Music in Europe.

Rühlmann (rül'-män), (Ad.) Julius, Dresden, 1816—1877; court-trombonist; professor, writer and composer.

Rum'ford, R. Kennerly, b. London, Sept. 2, 1871; concert barytone; studied in Frankfort, Berlin and Paris; m. Clara Butt, 1900.

Rummel (room'-mĕl), (1) Chr. (Fz. L. Fr. Alex.), Brichsenstadt, Bavaria, 1787—Wiesbaden, 1849; clarinettist, and composer. (2) Josephine, Manyares, Spain, 1812 — Wiesbaden, 1877; daughter of above; ct.-pianist. (3) Jos., Wiesbaden, 1818—London, 1880; son and pupil of (1); ct.-pianist and composer. (4) Franziska, Wiesbaden, 1821—Brussels, 1873; ct.-singer; sister of above; m. Peter Schott, the pub. (5) Aug., Wiesbaden, 1824—London, 1886; pianist. (6) Fz., London, Jan. 11, 1853—Berlin, 1901; pianist; son of

(3); pupil of Brassin, Brussels Cons., winning 1st prize, 1872, 1877–78, toured Holland with Ole Bull; toured America 3 times; teacher Stern's Cons., then Kullak's, Berlin; 1897 "Professor" from the Duke of Anhalt. (7) **Walter Morse**, b. Berlin, July 19, 1882; noted pianist; son of (6); pupil of Fabian, Godowsky, Kaun and Debussy; after 1913 toured in Europe; m. Therese Chaigneau, pianist; d. Bordeaux, 1953.

Run'ciman, John F., England, 1866—London, April, 1916; prominent critic. Educated at the science school (now Rutherford College), Newcastle-on-Tyne; organist from childhood; 1887, took position in London; from 1894 musical critic *Saturday Review;* later, until 1898, also acting editor and managing director; also editor of the quarterly *The Chord*, and of the *Musician's Library;* for some years correspondent Boston *Musical Record;* 1901, of New York *Musical Courier;* some of his essays were published as *"Old Scores and New Readings"* (1899); wrote biographical studies of Wagner and of Purcell.

Rung (roongk), **Henrik**, Copenhagen, 1807—1871; conductor and dram. composer.

Runge (roong'-ĕ), **Paul**, Heinrichsfeld, Posen, Jan. 2, 1848—Colmar, July 4, 1911; pupil of Church Music Institute, Berlin, and J. Schneider; from 1873 at Colmar as historian and comp.

Rungenhagen (roong'-ĕn-hä-gĕn), **K. Fr.**, Berlin, 1778—1851; Professor, conductor and dramatic composer.

Rünger (rēng'-ĕr), **Gertrud**; b. Posen, Poland; dramatic soprano (originally contralto); studied in Berlin; sang at Erfurt, Magdeburg, Cologne, then at Vienna State Op. for a number of seasons; in 1935 became member of the Berlin State Op. assuming soprano rôles; guest appearances at Salzburg Fest., Amsterdam, Paris and London; in 1936–37 engaged for Met. Op., New York.

Rupff. Vide LUTHER, M.

Rus'sell, (1) **Wm.**, London, 1777—1813; pianist. (2) **Henry**, Sheerness, 1812—London, Dec. 6, 1900; v. pop. Engl. song-composer. (3) Sir **Henry**, London, 1871—London, Oct. 11, 1937; son of (2); noted English impresario and voice teacher: pupil of

R. C. M., London; 1905, dir. of Covent Garden Op.; 1905 brought his co. to Boston; 1909–14, dir. Boston Op. Co., with which he visited Paris, 1914; bro. of Sir Landon Ronald. (4) **Louis Arthur**, b. Newark, N. J., Feb. 24, 1854—Sept. 5, 1925; pupil of Warren, Bristow, and C. C. Müller, New York; studied, London, 1878–95; organist and choirm., Newark; after 1879, cond. Schubert Vocal Soc.; after 1885, Easton (Pa.) Choral Soc.; 1885, founded the Newark Coll. of Mus., of which he was dir. and teacher; 1893, organised Newark Symph. Orch.; wrote various books; c. cantata with orch., *"A Pastoral Rhapsody,"* etc. (5) **Ella (Countess de Rhigini)**, Cleveland, O., March 30, 1864—Florence, Jan. 16, 1935; soprano; pupil of Cleveland Cons., Mme. de la Grange and Ed. Pluque (acting); début, *"Il Trovatore,"* Prato, Italy, 1882; sang with succ. on Continent; Covent Garden, 1885; later with Carl Rosa Opera Company.

Rust (roost), (1) **Fr. Wm.**, Wörlitz, near Dessau, July 6, 1739—Dessau, Mar. 28, 1796; violinist; bro. and pupil of an amateur violinist in J. S. Bach's orch. at Leipzig; ct.-mus. director; c. stage pieces, etc. (2) **Wm. K.**, 1787—1855; son of above; pupil of Türk; organist and composer. (3) **Wm.**, Dessau, Aug. 15, 1822—Leipzig, May 2, 1892, nephew of above; composer; notable organist and teacher; cond. Berlin Bach-Verein and editor of Bach's text.

Ruta (roo'-tä), **Michele**, Caserta, 1827—Naples, Jan. 24, 1896; theorist and dram. composer.

Rüter (rē'-tĕr), **Hugo**, b. Hamburg, Sept. 7, 1859; pupil of the Cons.; from 1882 singing teacher and cond. at Wandsbeck; 1897, Hamburg; c. symph.; 2 operas, etc.

Ruthardt (root'-härt), (1) **Fr.**, 1800—1862; oboist and composer. (2) **Julius**, Stuttgart, Dec. 13, 1841—Constance, Oct. 13, 1909; son of above; violinist, th.-conductor 1885 at Bremen; c. incid. mus. songs. (3) **Ad.**, Stuttgart, Feb. 9, 1849—Leipzig, Sept. 12, 1934; bro. of above; pupil of the Cons.; 1868–85, teacher in Geneva, then Leipzig Cons.; writer and composer.

Ruzicka (Rucsicska, Rutschitschka,

DICTIONARY OF MUSICIANS 375

ctc.) (root-shētsh'-kä), Wenzel,
Jaumentz, Moravia, 1758—Vienna,
1823; bandm. and dram. composer
and ct.-organist; Schubert was his
pupil.
Ry'an, Thos., Ireland, 1827—New Bedford, Mass., March 25, 1903; at 17
went to the U. S.; studied Boston,
1849; co-founder "Mendelssohn
Quintet Club," with which he toured
America; clarinet and vla.-virtuoso;
c. quintets, quartets, songs, etc.;
wrote "Recollections of an Old Musician" (New York, 1890).
Ryba (rē'-bä), Jakob Jan., Przestitz,
Bohemia, 1765—Roczmittal, 1815; c.
6 comic operas, etc.
Rybakov (rē'-bä-kôf), Sergei Gavrilo-
vich, b. 1867; pupil of St. Petersburg
Cons.; author studies of music in
Russia and Turkestan.
Rybner (rib-ner), (1) Cornelius, Copenhagen, Oct. 26, 1855—N. Y., Jan. 21,
1929; pupil Gade, Reinecke; 1892,
cond. Carlsruhe Philh. Soc.; 1904-19,
he succeeded MacDowell as prof. of
music Columbia University, N. Y.,
c. 3-act dance legend "Prinz Ador"
(Carlsruhe, 1903), etc.; had given
piano recitals, often with his daughter (2) Dagmar, b. 1890; also a
talented pianist, début Carlsruhe,
playing the Schumann concerto
under Mottl; toured the U. S.; c.
songs.
Ryelandt (rē'-länt), Joseph, b. Bruges,
April 7, 1870; composer; pupil of
Tinel; c. choral works with orch.,
"St. Cécile," and "Purgatorium,"
chamber music, etc.

S

Saar (zär), Louis Victor Fz., Rotterdam, Dec. 10, 1868—St. Louis, Nov.
23, 1937; composer; studied with
Rheinberger and Abel, Munich Cons.;
then with Brahms; 1891 took the
Mendelssohn composition prize for a
pf.-suite and songs; 1892-95, opera-
accompanist, New York; 1896-98,
teacher, comp. and cpt., National
Cons., N. Y.; 1898, Coll. of Mus.;
critic and composer for piano; principal of the dept. of theory at Cincinnati College of Music from 1906;
after 1917 at Chicago Mus. Coll.;
prizes for composition; c. string
quartet, piano quartet, sonatas for
vln., for 'cello and for horn; organ,
choral pieces; many songs, etc.

Sabane'iev, Leonid, b. Moscow, Nov.
19, 1881; pianist and writer on music,
also composer; after 1920, dir. of
State Inst. for Musical Science; c.
piano trios and other pieces; author,
"History of Russian Music."
Sabata. Vide DE SABATA.
Sabbatini (säb-bä-tē'-nē), (1) Galeazzo,
b. Pesaro; ct.-maestro and composer
(1627-39). (2) Luigi A., Albano
Liziale, Rome, 1739—Padua, 1809;
maestro, writer and composer.
Sacchi (säk'-kē), Don Giovenale, Bar-
fio, Como, 1726—Milan, 1789; writer.
Sacchini (säk-kē'-nē), A. M. Gasparo,
Pozzuoli, near Naples, June 23, 1734
—Paris, Oct. 8, 1786; eminent Neapolitan opera composer, son of a poor
fisher. Discovered and taught by
Durante and others; 1756, prod. succ.
intermezzo "Fra Donata," followed
by others in Neapolitan dialect;
1762-66, at Rome in a keen rivalry
with Piccinni; 1772-82, London, succ.
as composer but not as financier.
Fled from creditors to Paris where he
had succ. and prod. many works,
incl. "Œdipe à Colone," his best work.
He c. over 60 operas, 6 oratorios, etc.
Sachs (zäkhs), (1) Hans, Nürnberg,
Nov. 5, 1494—Jan. 19, 1576; a
cobbler; chief of the Meistersinger
(v. D. D.) and hero of Wagner's opera
of that name; he wrote over 4,000
poems, 1,700 tales and 200 dramatic
poems; also c. melodies. (2) Julius,
Waldhof, Meiningen, 1830—Frankfort-on-Main, 1888; pianist. (3) Melchior Ernst, Mittelsinn, Lower
Franconia, Feb. 28, 1843—Munich,
May 18, 1917; pupil Munich Cons.
and of Rheinberger; 1868-72, cond.
"Liederkranz"; 1871, teacher of
harm. Sch. of Mus.; founded and long
cond. "Tonkünstlerverein" concerts;
c. opera, ballade with orch., etc.
(4) Curt, b. Berlin, 1881; noted critic
and musicologist, Ph. D., Berlin
Univ.; an authority on instruments,
author of many wks.; taught N.Y.U.
(5) Léo, b. Alsace, 1868; c. operas,
chamber music, songs.
Sachse-Hofmeister (zäkhs'-ĕ-hôf'-mī-
shtĕr), Anna, Gumpoldskirchen, near
Vienna, July 26, 1850—Berlin, Nov.
15, 1904; soprano.
Sacrati (sä-krä-tē), Francesco, d. Modena, May 20, 1650; court cond. and
important early composer of opera.
Saen'ger, (1) Gustav, New York,
May 31, 1865—Dec. 10, 1935; violin-

ist, conductor, editor; played in orch. at Met. Op., with N. Y. Philh. and Symph.; cond. Empire Theatre after 1893; ed. *The Metronome* and *The Musical Observer;* c. instrumental pieces, songs. (2) **Oscar,** Brooklyn, N. Y., Jan. 5, 1868—Washington, D. C., April 20, 1926; barytone, vocal teacher; pupil of Bouhy; taught Nat'l. Cons., N. Y.; sang with Hinrichs Amer. Op. Co.; teacher of many prominent artists.

Saf'onoff, (1) **W.,** Istchory, Caucasus, Feb. 6 (new style), 1852—Kislovodsk, March 13, 1918; pupil of Leschetizky and Zaremba; then of Brassin, Petersburg Cons., taking gold medal, 1881–85, teacher there; 1885, Moscow; 1889, dir. of the Cons. there, and 1890 conductor; in 1906 he visited London and cond. the Phil. Orch.; 1906–09 he cond. the Philh. Orch., New York City, with great success, then returned to Russia. A famous teacher, among his pupils being many eminent Russian musicians. (2) **Maria,** his daughter, is a pianist.

Ságh (säkh), **Jos.,** b. Pesth, March 13, 1852; Hungarian lexicographer; 1885, founder and editor of mus. paper *Zenelap;* d. Vac, Jan. 25, 1922.

Sagitta'rius. Vide SCHÜTZ.

Sahla (zä'-lä), **Richard,** Graz, Sept. 17, 1855—Stadthagen, April 30, 1931; violinist; pupil of David, Leipzig Cons.; début, Gewandhaus, 1873; 1888, ct.-cond. Bückeburg; founded an oratorio-soc. there; c. a Roumanian Rhapsody, etc.

Saint-Amans (săn-tä-män), **L. Jos.,** Marseilles, 1749—Paris, 1820; conductor at Brussels and dram. composer.

Saint-Georges (săn-zhôrzh), (1) ——, Chev. **de,** Guadeloupe, 1745—Paris, 1799 (or 1801); mulatto violinist and composer. (2) **Jules H. Vernoy,** Marquis **de,** Paris, 1801—1875; librettist of many works, especially in collaboration with Halévy.

Saint-Huberty (săn-tü-bĕr-tē), **Antoinette Cécile Clavel** (called **St.-Huberty,** rightly **Clavel),** Toul, ca. 1756—London, 1812, noted soprano, Gr. Opéra, Paris, 1777–89; 1790, m. the Count d'Entraigues; they were assassinated at their country seat, near London, 1812 (probably from political motives).

Saint-Lambert (săn-län-bär), **Michel de,** Parisian harpsichord-teacher; wrote methods (1680–1700).

Saint-Lubin (săn-lü-băn), **Léon de,** Turin, 1805—Berlin, 1850; violinist and dram. composer.

Sainton (săn-tôn), (1) **Prosper (Ph. Catherine),** Toulouse, 1813—London, 1890; violinist and composer. (2) **Sainton-Dolby, Charlotte Helen** (née **Dolby),** London, 1821—1885; contralto-singer.

Saint-Saëns (săn-sän), **Chas. Camille,** Paris, Oct. 9, 1835—Algiers, Dec. 16, 1921; eminent French composer. Began to study the piano before 3; at 5 played a Grétry opera from the score; at 7 entered the Cons., pupil of Stamaty (pf.) Maleden and Halévy (comp.), and Benoist (org.); 1st org.-prize, 1851; at 16, prod. a symph.; 1853, organist Saint-Méry; 1858, the Madeleine; also till 1870 pf.-teacher Niedermeyer Sch.; made frequent tours as pianist and conductor of his works, incl. U. S., 1906 and 1915. He was a writer of unusual gifts. 1894, Commander of the Legion of Honour. C. operas: 1-act *"La Princesse Jaune"* (Op.-Com., 1872); *"Le Timbre d'Argent,"* 4-acts (Th.-Lyr., 1877); the very succ. *"Samson et Dalila"* (Weimar, 1877, often sung as an oratorio); *"Proserpine"* (Op.-Com., 1887); *"Ascanio"* (Opéra, 1890); comic *"Phryne"* (Op.-Com., 1893); *"Parisatis"* (Béziers, 1902); *"Lola"* (1901), *"Les Barbares"* (1901), *"Andromaque"* (1903), *"Hélène"* (Monte Carlo, 1904), *"L'Ancêtre"* (do., 1906), *"Dejanire"* (1911); wrote the last 2 acts of Guiraud's unfinished *"Frédégonde"* (Opéra, 1895). C. ballets, music to *"Antigone"* (Comedie-Française); and Gallet's *"Déjanire"* (Béziers, 1898, with orch. of 250, chorus of 200, and ballet of 60 in open air). C. also a Christmas oratorio; the "Biblical opera" *"Le Déluge";* 2 masses; ode *"La Lyre et la Harpe"* (Birmingham Fest., 1879); cantata *"La feu céléste"* (1900); fantaisie for violin and harp (1907); *"La Muse et le Poète"* for violin and orch., 1909; *"Overture de Fête,"* op. 133, 1909; songs, piano pieces, string quartet, septet, 2 piano trios, 2 vln. sonatas, organ works, *"La jota aragonese"* for orch.; 5 pf.-concertos; 2 vln.-concertos, Introdjction and Rondo Capriccioso. *"Havanaise"* both for vln. and orch.; *"Carneval des Animaux,"* descriptive suite (humorous) for 2 pianos and orch.; 2 'cello-concertos; cantata *"Les Noces de Prométhée"* (1867); Psalm 19, with orch. (London, 1885); 5 symphs., symphonic poems, *"Le rouet d'Omphale," "Phaëton," "Danse macabre," "La jeunesse d' Hercule"*; 2 orch. suites, the first *"Algérienne,"* etc. A highly versatile composer, his works showed refinement, spirit, genial melody and a fine sense of form. He was one of the leading figures in the restoration of French symphonic music. His nature lacked, however, qualities of depth and universality. A thematic catalogue of his works was pub. by Durand, 1897, and revised, 1907. Memoirs by Loanda, Blondel, Bellaigue, Neitzel, Baumann, Bonnerot, Montargis, Hervey, Rolland, Jullien, Séré, etc.

Sala (sä'-lä), **Nicola,** near Benevento, Italy, ca. 1715—Naples, 1800; maestro, theorist and dram. composer.

Sal'aman, Chas. Kensington, London, March 3, 1811—June 23, 1901; pianist; pupil of Rimbault and Chas. Neate; début 1828, then studied with H. Herz, Paris; 1831, teacher in London; 1840, founded a choral soc.; 1858, founded the Mus. Soc. of London; also the Mus. Assoc., 1874; critic and essayist; c. orch. pcs., etc.

Saldoni (säl-dō'-nē), **Don Baltasar,** Barcelona, 1807 — 1890; organist, singing-teacher, writer and dram. composer.

Sale (säl), **Fran.,** Belgian ct.-tenor and composer, 1589.

Saléza (sǎl-ā-zä), **Albert,** Bruges, Béarn, 1867—Paris, 1916; notable tenor; pupil Paris Cons.; 1st prize in singing, 2d. in opera; début Op.-Com., 1888; 1889–91, at Nice; from 1892, engaged at the Opéra, Paris; 1898–1901, Met. Op., New York; after 1911 he taught at the Paris Cons.

Salieri (säl-ĭ-ä'-rē), (1) **Ant.,** Legnano, Verona, Aug. 19, 1750—Vienna, May 7 (12 ?), 1825; noted operatic composer and organist; pupil of his brother (2) **Francesco** (violinist) and of Simoni, Pascetti and Pacini; taken to Vienna by Gassman; his successor as ct.-composer and cond. of Italian opera; he prod. many operas there, then one at Paris under Gluck's

name, G. kindly confessing the ruse when the opera was a succ.; 1788, ct.-cond. Vienna; was a rival of Mozart and unjustly accused of poisoning him; c. 40 operas, 12 oratorios, etc.

Salimbeni (säl-ĭm-bä'-nē), **Felice,** Milan, ca. 1712—Laibach, 1751; soprano-musico.

Salinas (sǎ-lē'-nǎs), **Fran.,** Burgos, Spain, ca. 1512—1590; professor.

Sal'mond, Felix, b. London, Nov. 19, 1888; 'cellist; studied with Whitehouse, R. Coll. of Music, and Edouard Jacobs, Brussels; début, London, 1909; appeared widely in Europe; after 1922 in N. Y., where gained rep. as fine technician; has played with leading orchs. and in chamber music and recital programmes;head of 'cello dept., Juilliard School; d. N. Y., Feb. 19, 1952.

Salò, Gasparo da. Vide GASPARO.

Saloman (zä'-lō-män), **Siegfried,** Tondern, Schleswig, 1816—Stockholm, 1899; violinist, lecturer and dram. composer.

Salomé (sǎl-ō-mā), **Th. César,** Paris, 1834—St. Germain, 1896; composer and organist.

Salomon (zä'-lō-mōn), (1) **Jn. Peter,** Bonn, Jan., 1745—London, Nov. 25, 1815; vln.-virtuoso; from 1781, London; 1786, organised famous Salomon concerts for which Haydn, whom he brought over, c. special works. (2) **Hector,** Strassburg, May 29, 1838—Paris, 1906; pupil of Jonas and Marmontel (pf.), Bazin (harm.) and Halévy (comp.); in 1870, 2d chorusm., later *chef de chant,* Gr. Opéra; c. operas, etc.

Salt'er, Sumner, Burlington, Ia., 1856—N. Y., March 5, 1944; studied at Amherst Coll. and music in Boston; 1900–02, taught at Cornell Univ. and Ithaca Cons.; 1905, mus. dir. at Williams College; active as recitalist, organist and mus. dir.; ed. *The Pianist and Organist,* N. Y.; c. church-mus. (2) **Mary Turner,** Peoria, Ill., 1856—Orangeburg, N. Y., 1938; studied singing with Alfred Arthur, Burlington, Ia.; then pupil of Max Schilling, John O'Neill, and Mme. Rudersdorf, Boston; 1877 succeeded Emma Thursby as soprano of Broadway Tabernacle, N. Y.; 1879, soprano Trinity Church, New Haven, teaching also at Wellesley College; 1881, married Sumner Salter, who was her teacher in composition; 1893 retired from church and concert work, devoting her time to teaching and composition of songs.

Salvayre (săl-văr) (**Gervais Bd.**), **Gaston,** Toulouse, June 24, 1847— May 16, 1916; studied at the cath.-maîtrise, then at Toulouse Cons.; later Paris Cons., taking the Grand Prix de Rome, 1872, with cantata *"Calypso"*; 1877, chorusm. at the Opéra-Populaire; 1894 in Servia; later critic of *"Gil Blas"*; Chev. of the Legion of Honour; c. operas *"Le Bravo"* (1877), *"Richard III."* (Petersburg, 1883), *"Egmont"* (Op.-Com., 1886), *"La Dame de Montsoreau"* (Opéra, 1888), etc.; c. also Biblical symph., *"La Resurrection,"* 113th Psalm with orch., etc.

Salzedo (säl-zä'-dō), **Carlos,** b. Arcachon, France, April 6, 1885; harpist, composer; studied Bordeaux and Paris Cons., 1st prize solfege, piano and harp; toured in Europe as harpist, later with Amer. orchs. and in recital; dir. harp dept., Curtis Inst. of Music, Phila.; founded Salzedo Harp Ensemble; c. works for harp and orch., in which he has appeared as performer or cond.

Samara (sä-mä'-rä), **Spiro,** Corfù, 1861 —Athens, 1917; pupil of Enrico Stancampiano in Athens; later of Délibes, Paris Cons.; prod. succ. opera, *"Flora Mirabilis"* (Milan, 1886); *"Medge"* (Rome, 1888); *"Lionella"* (Milan, 1891); *"La Martire"* (Naples, 1894; Paris, 1898); *"La Furia Domata"* (Milan, 1895); *"Histoire d'amour"* (Paris, 1902), etc.

Samar'off (née Hickenlooper), **Olga,** b. San Antonio, Texas, Aug. 8, 1882 —d. N. Y., May 17, 1948; pianist; at 9 pupil of Von Sternberg, later of Marmontel, Widor, and the Paris Cons.; studied again with Ernest Hutcheson and with Jedliczka; début, N. Y., 1905; 1906, London; toured widely; 1911 married Leopold Stokowski; divorced; she retired from concert work following an injury to her wrist sustained in a fall; for 2 seasons she was guest music critic of the New York *Post;* founder and dir. of the "Laymen's Music Courses," and had made many lecture appearances throughout the country to promote music appreciation; faculty mem. of the Juilliard School of Music, N. Y. C.. and of

the Phila. Cons. of Music; secretary of the Schubert Memorial, Inc.

Samazeuilh (săm-ä-zŭ'-ē), **Gustave,** b. Bordeaux, June 2, 1877; Parisian critic and composer; pupil of Chausson and d'Indy; c. notable orch., chamber and vocal music; secretary of the Société Nationale de Musique and contributor to numerous publications. Wrote life of Paul Dukas (1913).

Samin'sky, Lazare, b. in the Crimea 1883; composer; studied at St. Petersburg Cons., also with Rimsky-Korsakoff, Tcherepnine and Liadoff; 1918, dir. of Tiflis People's Cons.; cond. at Duke of York Theatre, London, 1920; after 1921 lived in N. Y.; mem. of board of directors, League of Composers; dir. of music at Temple Emanu-El; has been active as cond. of modern music programmes; c. (ballets) *"Vision of Ariel,"* *"Lament of Rachel,"* *"Gagliarda of a Merry Plague,"* *"Jephtha's Daughter"*; 5 symphonies with descriptive titles; *"Litanies of Women"* for mez.-sopr. and chamber orch.; piano works, song cycles, etc.

Sammar'co, Mario, Palermo, Sicily, 1873—Milan, Jan. 24, 1930; noted barytone; pupil of Cantelli; after 1894 sang in Milan, later in other Eur. cities; 1905–14 at Covent Garden, 1907–10 with much succ. at Manhattan Op. House, N. Y.; and after 1910 for some seasons with the Chicago Opera Company.

Sammartini (säm-mär-tē'-nē), (1) **Pietro,** ct.-mus. at Florence, etc. (1635–44). (2) **Giov. Bat.** Milan, 1701–1775; organist, conductor and composer. (3) **Giu.,** d. London, 1740; oboist; bro. of above.

Sam'mons, Albert, b. London, Feb. 23, 1886; violinist; studied with his father, with Saunders and Weist-Hill; début, Harrowgate, 1906; has appeared widely as soloist, also as concertm. of Beecham Symph. Orch. and for a time as a mem. of the London String Quartet.

Samuel (säm-wĕl), (1) **Ad.,** Liége, 1824 —Ghent, 1898; theorist and dram. composer. (2) **Harold,** London, May 23, 1879—Jan. 15, 1937; pianist; studied R. C. M. with Stanford and Dannreuther; début London, 1894; had attained internat'l. rank as a Bach performer particularly, but also in other music of classical period; had given Bach cycles of clavier music (played on modern piano but brilliantly suggesting harpsichord), covering a week in both London and N. Y.; toured U. S. after 1925; appearances with leading orchs.; had also lectured and served as examiner for the R. C. M. and R. A. M.

San'born, Pitts, b. Port Huron, Mich., d. N. Y., March 7, 1941; critic; M. A., Harvard, 1902; music ed. N.Y. *Globe*, 1905–25; later with N. Y. *Daily Mail* and continuing on the N.Y. *Telegram* when merged with this paper; also with *World-Telegram* following merger with N. Y. *World;* has written novel in 2 vols., *"Prima Donna,"* also many programme annotations and magazine articles; dir. of Inst. of the Audible Arts.

Sances (sän'-chĕs), **Giovanni Felice,** Rome, 1600—Vienna, Nov. 24, 1679; tenor and court cond. at Vienna; one of the first to write "cantatas"; c. operas, oratorios, etc.

Sanctis, de. Vide DE SANCTIS.

Sandberger (zänt'-bĕrkh-ĕr), **Ad.,** b. Würzburg, Dec. 19, 1864; studied at the R. Sch. of Mus. there, and at Munich, also with Spitta; 1887, Dr. Phil.; mus. libr., Munich Library, and lecturer at the Univ.; 1898 prof. of mus. at Prague Univ.; 1909–29, prof. mus. history, Munich Univ.; ed. Orlando di Lasso's complete works; wrote biog., hist., essays, etc.; c. opera *"Ludwig der Springer"* (Coburg, 1895), etc.; d. Munich, 1943.

Sanders, C. Vide LEUCKART.

San'derson, (1) **Jas.,** Workington, Durham, 1769—ca. 1841; violinist, teacher and composer. (2) **Lillian,** b. Sheboygan, Wis., Oct. 13, 1867; concert mezzo-soprano; pupil of Stockhausen, Frankfort-on-Main; début Berlin, 1890; toured Europe. (3) **Sibyl,** Sacramento, Cal., 1865—Paris, May 16, 1903; soprano, opera-singer; pupil of de la Grange and Massenet, who wrote his *"Thaïs"* and *"Esclarmonde"* for her; succ. début, Op.-Com., 1889; sang there for several years; 1898 in New York Met. Op., and variously in Europe.

Sandoni. Vide CUZZONI.

Sandt (zänt), **Max van de,** Rotterdam, Oct. 18, 1863—Cologne, July 14, 1934; pianist; pupil of his father and Liszt; toured Europe; 1889, pf.-teacher Stern Cons., Berlin; 1896, Cologne Cons.; 1910, Bonn Conservatory

Sangiovanni (sän-jō-vän'-nē), **A.,** Bergamo, 1831—Milan, 1892; prof. of singing.

Santini (sän-tē'-nē), Abbate **Fortunato,** Rome, 1778—1862; coll. a notable mus.-library.

Sant'ley, (1) Sir **Chas.,** Liverpool, Feb. 28, 1834—Hove near London, Sept. 22, 1922; noted operatic and concert barytone; pupil Nava, Milan, Garcia, London; début, 1857; won pre-eminence in England at festivals, etc.; operatic début, Covent Garden, 1859; 1875 with Carl Rosa Co.; 1871 and 1891, America; retired 1900; knighted 1907; also a painter; c. a mass with orch.; a berceuse for orch.; songs (pub. under the pseud. **"Ralph Betterton"**), etc. His wife, (2) **Gertrude Kemble** (Charles Kemble's granddaughter) (d. 1882), was a soprano; their daughter (3) **Edith** was a successful soprano, till her marriage in 1884 with the Hon. R. H. Lyttleton.

Santoliquido (sän-tō-lē-kwē'-dō), **Francesco,** b. Naples, Aug. 6, 1883; composer; grad. St. Cecilia Liceo, Rome; for a time res. in Tunis; a delicate and colourful style is revealed in his chamber music and songs; c. (operas) *"La Favola di Helga," "L'Ignota"* and *"Ferhuda"*; (Mimo-drama) *"La Bajadera dalla Maschera Gialla";* (cantata) *"L'Ultima Visione di Cassandra";* (overture) *"La Morte di Tintagiles";* (symph. poem) *"Nelle Oasi Sahariani";* 2 symphonies; (suites) *"Paesaggi"* and *"Acquerelli,"* piano music and songs; wrote essay on music after Wagner, Debussy and Strauss.

Santucci (sän-toot'-chē), **Marco,** Camajore, 1762—Lucca, 1843; conductor and composer.

Sapell'nikoff, Wassily, b. Odessa, Nov. 2, 1868; pianist; pupil of Fz. Kessler, and then (with a stipend from the city of Odessa) of L. Brassin and Sophie Menter, Petersburg Cons., 1888, début Hamburg; toured; taught Moscow Cons., 1897–99; c. opera and pf.-pieces.

Sap'io, Romualdo, Palermo, 1858—N. Y., Sept. 22, 1943; pupil of Naples Cons.; toured U. S. after 1888 as cond. for Patti, Albani, Nordica; beginning 1892 taught at Nat'l. Cons., N. Y.; later privately; m. Clementine de Vere, soprano.

Saran (zä'-rän), **Aug.** (Fr.). Altenplathow, Province of Saxony, Feb. 28, 1836—Bromberg, Feb. 23, 1922; pupil of Fr. Ehrlich and of R. Franz; teacher, army-chaplain (1873); 1885 cond. of a church-choral soc. at Bromberg; writer and composer.

Sarasate (sä-rä-sä'-tĕ), Pablo (Martin Meliton Sarasate y Navascuez) de, Pamplona, Spain, March 10, 1844—Biarritz, Sept. 20, 1908; eminent violinist; at 10 played before the Queen, who presented him with a Stradivari, after succ. concerts in Spain he studied with Alard (vln.) and Reber (comp.), Paris Cons., taking 1st vln.-prize 1857, and a premier accessit, 1859, in harm.; he made very wide and very succ. tours; 1889, America. For him Lalo c. his 1st vln.-concerto and the "Symph. espagnole"; Bruch, his 2nd concerto and the Scotch Fantasia; A. C. Mackenzie, the "Pibroch" Suite. S. pub. "Zigeunerweisen" for vln. and orch.; Spanish Dances, etc.

Sar'gent, Sir Malcolm, b. Stamford, Engl., Apr. 29, 1895; conductor; début 1921 at Queen's Hall "Proms."; later cond. Liverpool Philh.; knighted 1947.

Sarmiento (sär-mǐ-ĕn'-tō), Salvatore, Palermo, 1817—Naples, 1869; conductor and dram. composer.

Saro (sä'-rō), J. H., Jessen, Saxony, 1827—Berlin, 1891; bandmaster and writer.

Sarrette (sär-rĕt), Bd., Bordeaux, 1765—Paris, 1858; founder and director till 1814 of the Paris Cons. which he gradually developed from a sch. started by the band of the Paris National Guard.

Sarri (sär'-rē), Dom., Trani, Naples, 1678—after 1741; conductor and dram. composer.

Sarti (sär'-tē), Giuseppe (called Il Domenichino) (ĕl dō-mĕn-ĭ-kē-nō), Faenza, Dec. 1, 1729—(of gout) Berlin, July 28, 1802; pupil of either Vallotti or Padre Martini; 1748-50 organist Faenza Cath.; 1751 he prod. at Faenza succ. opera "Pompeo in Armenia," followed by "Il Re Pastore" (Venice, 1753) and others so succ. that at 24 he was called to Copenhagen as dir. Italian opera and court-cond.; he was summarily dismissed for political reasons; 1775-09, dir. Cons. dell' Ospedaletto, Venice; in competition (with Paisiello and others) he won the position of cond. at Milan Cath.: he prod. from 1776—

84, 15 operas; he also prod. grand cantatas and several masses, etc. Catherine II. invited him to Petersburg. As he passed Vienna, he was received by the Emperor, and met Mozart, complaining, however, of the "barbarisms" in M.'s quartets and finding 19 mortal errors in 36 bars. Lived at Petersburg 18 years, excepting a brief period of disgrace, due to Todi, during which exile he founded a fine sch. at Ukraine. 1793 he was restored to the Empress' favour, and placed at the head of a Cons. He raised the Italian opera to high efficiency, inv. a very accurate machine for counting vibrations and was ennobled in 1795. In a Te Deum (on the taking of Otchakow by Potemkin) the music was reinforced by fireworks and cannon. He set the libretto "Hega" by the Empress. He c. 40 operas, masses, some still performed, etc.

Sartorio (sär-tō'-rǐ-ō), A., Venice, ca. 1620—ca. 1681; conductor and dram. composer.

Saslav'sky, Alex., b. Kharkov, Russia, Feb. 9, 1876; violinist; pupil of Gorsky and Gruen; after 1903 concertm. of N. Y. Symph.; 1904-08 of Russian Symph., N. Y.; after 1919 of Los Angeles Philh.; d. San Francisco, Aug. 2, 1924.

Sass (säs) (at first sang under the name Sax), Marie Constance, Ghent, Jan. 26, 1838—Auteuil near Paris, Nov. 8, 1907; a chansonette-singer in a Paris café, found and taught by Mme. Ugalde; début Th.-Lyrique, 1859, as soprano, 1860-71, at the Opéra, then in Italy; 1864, m. the barytone Castelmary, divorced 1867.

Satie (sä'-tē), Erik, Honfleur, France, May 17, 1866—Arcueil, Aug. 5, 1925; composer; early musical training rather irregular, with periods of study at Paris Cons. and Schola Cantorum; research in Gregorian music influenced him; pioneer in forming original style of extreme simplicity, which was innovational in a day of exaggerated romanticism; had marked influence on Debussy, whom he met 1889, and later on a whole generation of modern composers, incl. Group of Six (Honegger, Milhaud, Poulenc, Auric, Durey and Germaine Tailleferre), and even a younger coterie known as the École d'Arcueil (named after village where

DICTIONARY OF MUSICIANS

381

S. was assistant postmaster); he was influenced by classic Greek art, but above all was a satirist of pretences, naming many of his works by absurd titles; c. (opera) *"Paul et Virginie,"* (symph. drama) *"Socrate"*; (ballets) *" Uspud"* and *"Parade"*; many piano pieces, of which *"Ogives," "Gymnopédies"* (several of latter orchestrated by Debussy and widely perf.) antedated and were strikingly like later harmonic style of that composer.

Satter (zät'-tĕr), **Gustav,** Vienna, Feb. 12, 1832—Savannah, Ga., 1879; studied Vienna, Paris; 1854-60 toured the U. S. and Brazil; returned to Paris, where Berlioz warmly praised his compositions; lived in various cities; c. opera *"Olanthe,"* overtures *"Lorelei," "Julius Cesar," "An die Freude,"* 2 symphs., a symph. tone-picture *"Washington,"* etc.

Sauer (zow'-ĕr), (1) **Wm.,** Friedland, Mecklenburg, 1831—Frankfort, 1916; org.-builder from 1857 at Frankfort-on-Oder. (2) Vide LEIDESDORF. (3) **Émil, von,** b. Hamburg, 1862—Vienna, 1942; pianist; pupil of his mother; of N. Rubinstein at Moscow, 1881, and of Liszt at Weimar; from 1882 toured Europe and 1898-99 U. S. with great succ.; 1901-07, and again after 1915, head of pf.-dept. Vienna Cons.; comp.

Sauguet (sō'-gä), **Henri,** b. 1901; c. op. *"Chartreuse de Parme"* (Paris,'40) etc.

Sauret (sō-rä), **Emile,** Dun-le-Roi, Cher, France, May 22, 1852—London, Feb. 12, 1920; notable violinist; pupil of Paris Cons. and of de Bériot, Brussels Cons.; at 8 began succ. European tours; America 1872, and frequently thereafter; 1880-81, t. Kullak's Acad., Berlin; lived in Berlin till 1890, then prof. R. A. M., London; wrote *"Gradus ad Parnassum du violoniste"* (Leipzig, 1894); c. 2 vln.-concertos, etc.

Sauveur (sō-vŭr'), **Jos.,** La Flèche, 1653—Paris, 1716; a deaf-mute, who learned to speak at 7, and became a notable investigator in acoustics (which word in fact he invented); he was the first to calculate absolute vibration-numbers and to explain overtones; pub. many treatises (1700-13).

Sauzay (sō-zĕ'), (**Chas.**) **Eugène,** Paris, July 14, 1809—Jan. 24, 1901; violinist, pupil of Vidal; later of Baillot at

the Cons.; won 1st and 2nd vln.-prize, and prize for fugue; 2nd vln. and afterwards vla. in Baillot's quartet, and m. B.'s daughter (a pianist); 1840 solo violinist to Louis Philippe; later leader of 2nd vlns. Napoleon III.'s orch.; 1860 vln.-prof. at the Cons.; pub. a treatise; c. a string-trio, *"Études harmoniques,"* etc.

Savage, Henry W., New Hampshire, 1860—Boston, Nov. 29, 1927; impresario; graduate of Harvard; as a builder and real estate owner in 1895 took over the Castle Square Theatre, Boston, and organised a stock co. which gave light and serious operas for many years in Boston, New York, etc.; produced many new American operettas as well as plays; made the immensely successful productions of *"Parsifal"* and *"Madame Butterfly"* in English by the touring Savage Opera Company.

Savard (să-vär), (1) **M. Gabriel Aug.,** Paris, 1814—1881; prof. of harm. and thorough-bass at the Cons.; pub. treatises. (2) **M. E. A.,** b. Paris, May 15, 1861; pupil of the Cons., taking the Prix de Rome, 1886; from 1902 dir. Lyons Cons.

Savart (să-vär), **F.,** Mézières, 1791—Paris, 1841; acoustician.

Saw'yer, F. J., Brighton, June 19, 1857—April 29, 1908. Bachelor of music, Oxford, 1877; Mus. Doc., 1884, Fellow R. C. of organists; organist for over 30 years; prof. of singing; c. oratorios, cantatas, etc.

Sax (săx), (1) **Chas. Jos.,** Dinant-sur-Meuse, Belgium, 1791—Paris, 1865; studied flute and clarinet, Brussels Cons.; from 1815 managed an instr.-factory at Brussels, making a specialty of brass instrs.; he made many improvements; 1853 he joined his son Ad. in Paris. (2) (**Ant. Jos.**) **Adolphe,** Dinant, Nov. 6, 1814—Paris, Feb. 4, 1894; son of above; eminent maker and inv. of instrs.; he inv. the family of instrs. called the saxophone (v. D. D.); in Paris he continued to make improvements inventing the saxhorns, saxotromba, etc.; 1857 teacher of the saxophone, Paris Cons. and pub. a saxophone method; he had much litigation over the priority of his inventions, but always won. (3) **Alphonse,** bro. and co-worker of above. (4) **Marie,** Vide SASS.

Sayão (sä-yä-nō), Bidu, Brazilian soprano; sang Met. Op., from 1936-7.
Sbriglia (sbrēl'-yä), Giovanni, b.
Naples, 1840; tenor and famous
teacher; pupil of De Roxas; début
Naples, 1851; sang throughout Italy
and toured America with Patti and
others; became a very successful
teacher in Paris, numbering the De
Reszkés, Plançon, Nordica, Sander-
son, etc., among his pupils. Mem.
French Académie; d. Paris, (?).
Scacchi (skäk'-kē), Marco, b. Rome;
ct.-conductor 1618-48; writer and
composer.
Scalchi (skäl'-kē), Sofia, b. Turin,
Nov. 29, 1850; alto or mezzo-soprano
of unusual range f-b'' (v. PITCH
D. D.); pupil of Boccabadati; début
Mantua (1866); she sang throughout
Europe, often in North and South
America with much succ.; 1875 m.
Count Luigi Lolli; after 1896 retired
from stage and lived at her villa near
Turin; d. circa 1910.
Scalero (skä-lä'-rō), Rosario, b. near
Turin, Dec. 24, 1870; violinist, com-
poser, teacher; pupil of Turin Liceo
and in London and Leipzig; taught
St. Cecilia Liceo, Rome (comp.),
there in 1913 founded Societa del
Quartetto; after 1919 res. in N. Y.,
as comp. teacher; c. orch., chamber
and choral works.
Scaletta (skä-lĕt'-tä), Orazio, Cremona
-Padua, 1630; conductor and com-
poser.
Scandel'li, Ant., Brescia, 1517—Dresden, 1580; conductor and composer.
Scaria (skä'-rĭ-ä), Emil, Graz, 1838—
Blasewitz, 1886; bass; created
"Wotan" at Bayreuth, 1876, and
"Gurnemanz" ("Parsifal"), 1882.
Scarlatti (skär-lät'-tē), (1) Alessandro,
Trapani, Sicily, 1659—Naples, 1725;
founder of the "Neapolitan Sch.";
noted teacher and an important
innovator in opera (he prod. over
115); in 1680 he is first heard of as
conducting his own opera; he introduced the innovation of the orchestral
ritornello, and a partial recitativo
obbligato (v. D. D.); 1684 court-cond.;
1703, 2nd cond. S. Maria Maggiore,
Rome; 1707-09, 1st. cond.; teacher
at 3 conservatories, San Onofrio;
de' Poveri di Gesù Christi, and the
Loreto. (2) Domenico (Girolamo),
Naples, Oct. 26, 1685—1757; son and
pupil of above; studied also with
Gasparini; eminent virtuoso and

composer for harpsichord; founded
modern pf.-technic; devised many
now familiar feats; the first to compose in free style without contrapuntal elaboration and mass; in a
competition with Händel he proved
himself equal as a harpsichordist, but
confessed himself hopelessly defeated
as an organist; he was thereafter a
good friend, almost an idolater, crossing himself when he mentioned
Händel; 1715-19 he was maestro at
St. Peter's, 1720 at London; 1720
court-cembalist Lisbon; his gambling
left his family destitute; from 1710
he prod. operas, incl. the first setting
of "Amleto" (1715). (3) Giuseppe,
Naples, 1712—Vienna, 1777; grandson of (1); dram. composer. (4)
Fran., c. a melodrama in MS. at
Rome. (5) Pietro, c. opera "Cli-
tarro," with intermezzi by Hasse.
Schachner (shäkh'-nĕr), Rudolf Jos.,
Munich, 1816—Reichenhall, 1896;
pianist, teacher and composer.
Schack (Cziak) (shäk or chäk), Benedikt, Mirowitz, Bohemia, 1758—
Munich, 1826; tenor and dram. composer.
Schad (shät), Jos., b. Steinach, Bavaria, 1812—Bordeaux, 1879; pianist
and composer.
Schade (shä'-dĕ), (1) (Schadaus)
Abraham, pub. a valuable coll. of
384 motets (1611-16). (2) Carl,
singing-teacher and writer (1828-31).
Schäffer (shĕf'-fĕr), (1) Aug., Rheinberg, 1814 — Baden-Baden, 1879;
dram. composer. (2) Julius, Cre-
vese, Altmark, Sept. 28, 1823—
Breslau, Feb. 10, 1902; studied with
Dehn, Berlin; 1855 mus. dir. to the
Grand Duke at Schwerin; founded
and conducted the "Schlosskirchen-
chor", 1860 mus.-dir. at the Univ.
and cond. Singakademie, Breslau;
1871, "R. Mus.-Dir."; 1878 prof.;
Dr. Phil. h. c. (Breslau), 1872; wrote
defence of his friend Franz' accompaniments to Bach and Händel;
composer.
Schafhäutl (shäf'-hī-tl), K. Fz. Emil
von, Ingolstadt, 1803—Munich,
1890; professor and theorist.
Schalk (shäl'k), (1) Franz, Vienna,
May 27, 1863—Sept. 2, 1931; pupil
of Bruckner; notable cond., first
at Graz, then 1st cond. at the Prague
Opera and Philh. concerts; 1899
1st cond. ct.-opera, Berlin; 1898 at
Covent Garden, 1899 gave the

DICTIONARY OF MUSICIANS 383

complete Wagner Ring cycle in New York; after 1900, first cond. of the Vienna Op., of which after 1918 he was dir. (with Richard Strauss from 1919, and 1924–28 sole dir.); also led Gesellschafts concerts there until 1921, and dir. a class for conductors at the State Akad. until 1909. His bro. (2) **Josef**, Vienna, 1857—1911; prof. of pf., Vienna Cons.; writer.

Scharfe (shär'-fĕ), **Gustav**, Grimma, Saxony, 1835—Dresden, 1892; barytone, teacher and composer.

Scharfenberg (shär'-fen-bĕrkh), **Wm.**, Cassel, Germany, 1819—Quogue, N. Y., 1895; pianist, teacher and editor.

Scharwenka (shär-vĕn'-kä), (1) (**L.**, **Philipp**, Samter, Posen, Feb. 16, 1847—Bad Nauheim, July 16, 1917; pupil of Würst and Kullak's Acad., Berlin, also of H. Dorn; 1870. teacher of theory and comp. at the Acad.; 1880 founded (with his bro. Xaver) the "Scharwenka Cons."; 1891, accompanied his bro. to New York; returned, 1892, as co-dir. of the Cons., later, 1893, merged in the Klindworth Cons.; also a caricaturist and illustrated a satire by Alex. Moszkowski (Berlin, 1881); 1902, R. Professor; c. "*Herbstfeier*" and "*Sakuntala*," for soli, chorus and orch., 2 symphs., "*Arkadische Suite*" and "*Serenade*" for orch., festival overture, Trio in G, op. 112, etc. (2) (**Fz.**) **Xaver**, Samter, Jan. 6, 1850—Berlin, Dec. 8, 1924; bro. of above; distinguished pianist and composer; pupil of Kullak and Würst, Kullak's Acad.; 1868, teacher there; at 19 gave public concert at the Singakademie, with succ.; for 10 years he gave annually 3 chamber-concerts there (with Sauret and H. Grünfeld); cond. of subscription concerts; 1874, toured Europe and America; 1880, co-founder the "Berlin Scharw. Cons.," dir. till 1891 then founded a Cons. in New York; 1898, Berlin, as dir. Klindworth-Scharwenka Cons.; ct.-pianist to the Emperor of Austria, "Prof." from the King of Prussia; c. succ. opera "*Mataswintha*" (Weimar, 1896); symph., 3 pf.-concertos, etc.

Schebek (shā'-bĕk), **Edmund**, Petersdorf, Moravia, 1819—Prague, 1895; amateur authority on vln.-construction, etc.

Schebest (shā'-bĕst), **Agnes**, Vienna,

1813—Stuttgart, 1869; mezzo-soprano.

Schechner-Waagen (shĕk'-nĕr-vä'-gĕn), **Nanette**, Munich, 1806—1860; noted soprano; 1832, m. Waagen, a painter.

Scheel (shēl), **Fritz**, Lübeck, Germany, Nov. 7, 1852—Philadelphia, March 13, 1907; conductor; son of a long line of musicians; studied with his father and with David at Leipzig; cond. in Bremerhaven, 1869; Schwerin, 1873; Chemnitz, 1884; Hamburg, 1890; Chicago Exp., 1894; founded and cond. San Francisco Symph., 1895–99; 1899, summer concerts in Woodside Park in Phila. met with succ. and led to founding of Phila. Orch., which he led from 1900 to his death; also Orpheus and Eurydice Clubs after 1905.

Scheibe (shī'-bĕ), (1) **Jn.**, d. Leipzig, 1748; celebrated org.-builder. (2) **Jn. Ad.**, Leipzig, 1708—Copenhagen, 1776; son of above; organist, editor and composer.

Scheibler (shī'-blĕr), **Jn. H.**, Montjoie, near Aix-la-Chapelle, 1777—Crefeld, 1837; acoustician and inventor.

Scheidemann (shī'-dĕ-män), (1) **Heinrich**, Hamburg, ca. 1596—1663; organist; pupil and successor of his father (2) **Hans S.**, organist Katherinenkirche.

Scheidemantel (shī-dĕ-män-tĕl), **K.**, Weimar, Jan. 21, 1859—June 26, 1923; pupil of Bodo Borchers; sang at the ct.-th., 1878–86; pupil of Stockhausen; 1885, "Kammersänger"; 1886, Dresden ct.-opera; 1886, sang "Amfortas" in "*Parsifal*" at Bayreuth.

Scheidt (shīt), **Samuel**, Halle-on-Saale, 1587—1654; famous organist and composer; pupil of Sweelinck; organist of Moritzkirche and ct.-conductor; c. notable chorals, etc.

Schein (shīn), **Jn. Hermann**, Grünhain, Saxony, 1586—Leipzig, 1630; soprano; ct.-conductor and composer.

Scheinpflug (shīn'-pflookh), **Paul**, Loschwitz, Dresden, Sept. 10, 1875—Memel, Lithuania, March 12, 1937; pupil of the Cons.; from 1909 cond. at Königsberg; 1914, led Blüthner Orch., Berlin; 1920, city mus. dir. at Duisburg; c. opera "*Das Hofkonzert*" (Berlin, 1922), "*Frühlings Symph.*," chamber music, etc.; overture to a comedy of Shakespeare (based on English melody of 16th century), Boston Symph. Orch., 1909; tone-poems for orch., songs, etc.

Schelble (shĕl'-blĕ), **Jn. Nepomuk,** Hüfingen, Black Forest, 1789—Frankfort-on-Main, 1837; notable cond. and singing-teacher; tenor; c. operas, etc.

Schelle (shĕl'-lĕ), (1) **Jn.,** Geising, Saxony, 1648—Leipzig, 1701; cantor Thomaskirche. (2) **K. Ed.,** Biesenthal, near Berlin, 1816—Vienna, 1882; critic, lecturer and writer.

Schel'ling, Ernest Henry, b. Belvidere, N. J., July 26, 1876—N. Y., Dec. 8, 1939; pianist, composer; 1st appeared as child pianist in Phila.; pupil of Mathias at Paris Cons., and of Moszkowski, Pruckner, Leschetizky, Huber, Barth and Paderewski; has appeared widely as recitalist and soloist with orchs. in Europe and U. S.; in recent years has been esp. prominent as composer and conductor; in latter capacity has led young people's concerts of N. Y. Philh. Orch. annually, also appearing with Los Angeles and other orchs. as lecturer-conductor; guest with Phila. Orch. and Boston Symph.; in 1935–36 appointed cond. of Baltimore Symph. Orch.; c. *"Fantastic Suite"* for piano and orch., in which he appeared as soloist with Amsterdam Concertgebouw, 1907, and with Boston, N. Y., and Chicago Symphs.; also Symphony in C Minor; Orchestral Suite; *"Symphonic Legend"*; violin concerto (played by Kreisler, with Boston Symph., 1916); sonata for vln. and piano; *"A Victory Ball,"* vivid orch. depiction of dance on Armistice Day, after poem by Noyes, given its première in 1923 by N. Y. Philh. and subsequently played; *"Impressions from an Artist's Life"* (Boston Symph., 1915), in form of variations for piano and orch.; *"Divertimento"* for string quartet and piano (Flonzaley Quartet, 1925); tone poem, *"Morocco,"* for orch., premièred by N. Y. Philh., 1927; various other chamber music and piano works.

Schelper (shĕl'-pĕr), **Otto,** Rostock, April 10, 1840—Leipzig, Jan. 10, 1906; an actor, later barytone in opera, at Bremen; 1872–76, Cologne, then sang leading rôles, Leipzig City Theatre.

Schenck (shĕnk), (1) **Jean (Johann),** gamba-player and dram. composer, 1688–93, Amsterdam. (2) **Jn.,** Wiener-Neustadt, Lower Austria, 1761—Vienna, 1836; c. operettas. **Peter Petrovich,** b. St. Petersburg, Feb. 23, 1870; pupil of the Cons., and of Saloviev; librarian and critic; c. operas, 3 symph., etc.

Schenker (shĕnk'-ĕr), **H.,** 1868—Vienna, 1935; pianist, theorist.

Scherchen (shĕr'-khĕn), **Hermann,** b. Berlin, June 21, 1891; conductor; viola player; largely self-taught; played in Berlin Philh. Orch.; cond. of symph. concerts at Riga, 1914; interned during war in Russia; founded and led Neue Musikgesellschaft, Berlin, 1918; Grotrian-Steinweg Orch., Leipzig, 1921–22; after latter year, the Museum Concerts in Frankfort, and cond. as guest in England and other countries; noted as an exponent of contemporary music, appearing at international festivals; ed. *Melos,* Berlin music paper, 1920–21; c. string quartet, piano sonata, songs.

Scherer (shā'-rĕr), **Sebastian Anton,** organist at Ulm Minster and composer, 1664.

Schering (shā'-rĭnk), **Arnold,** b. Breslau, April 2, 1877; violinist and historian, pupil of Joachim and Succo; prof. of music history at Leipzig Univ. after 1915; author and prof. Berlin U.; d. Berlin, 1941.

Scherman, Thos., b. N. Y.; founder and cond., Little Orchestra Soc.

Scherzer (shĕr'-tsĕr), **Otto,** Ansbach, 1821—Stuttgart, 1886; violinist and organist.

Schetky (shĕt'-kē), **Chp.,** Darmstadt, 1740—Edinburgh, 1773; 'cellist and composer.

Schicht (shĭkht), **Jn. Gf.,** Reichenau, Saxony, 1753—Leipzig, 1823; pupil of an uncle (org. and pf.); pianist, conductor and writer; c. 4 oratorios, chorals, etc.

Schick (shĭk) (née **Hamel**), **Margarete Luise,** Mayence, 1773—Berlin, 1809; soprano; pupil of Steffani and Righini; début, Mayence, 1791; from 1794, Royal Opera, Berlin.

Schiedermayer (shē'-dĕr-mī-ĕr), **Johann Baptist,** June 23, 1779—Linz-on Danube, Jan. 6, 1840; cath.-organist; wrote a textbook on chorals and a vln.-method, c. symphs., sacred mus., org.-pcs., etc.

Schiedmayer (shēt'-mī-ĕr) & Söhne, Stuttgart firm of piano-makers, founded in 1806 by Johann Lorenz S. (1786—1860).

Schikaneder (shē'-kä-nä-dĕr), Emanuel Jn., Ratisbon, 1748—Vienna, 1812; the librettist of Mozart's "Zauberflöte" in which he created "Papageno"; a manager, actor and singer.

Schildt (shĭlt), Melchior, Hanover (?), 1592—1667; organist.

Schilling (shĭl-ling), Gv., Schwiegershausen, near Hanover, 1803—Nebraska, U. S. A., 1881; wrote textbooks and treatises, etc.

Schil'lings, Max (von), Düren, April 19, 1868—Berlin, July 24, 1933; notable composer; studied with Brambach and von Königslöw; 1892, stage-manager at Bayreuth; 1890 while studying law, at Munich, c. the opera "Ingwelde" (prod. by Mottl, Carlsruhe, 1894); played in many other cities; c. also opera "Der Pfeifertag" (Schwerin, 1901); 2 symph. fantasias "Meergruss," 1895, and "Seemorgen"; incid. music to plays; "Hexenlied" for reciter, with piano or orch.; successful opera, "Mona Lisa" (Stuttgart, 1915; Met. Op., 1923, and Chicago Op.); and many other works; Royal Prof., 1903; 1908-18, gen. mus. dir., Stuttgart; 1919-25, intendant, Berlin State Op.; and active as guest cond. elsewhere; 1932, pres., Prussian Acad. of Arts; 1933, intendant of Berlin Städtische Op.; he was granted a patent of nobility by the King of Würtemburg; toured the U. S., 1930, as cond. of Wagnerian Op. Co.; m. Barbara Kemp, soprano.

Schimon (shē'-mōn), (1) Ad., Vienna, 1820—Leipzig,1887; singing-teacher, accompanist and dram. composer, etc.; 1872, m. the soprano (2) Anna Regan, Bohemia, 1842—Munich, 1902; pupil of Manuel Garcia and Stockhausen; sang in Italy and Germany; court-singer in Russia; 1874, teacher of singing Leipzig Cons.; 1877-86, R. Sch. of Mus., Munich; again at Leipzig Cons. where his wife taught and was also after death of her husband, singing-teacher at Munich.

Schindelmeisser (shĭn'-dĕl-mīs-sĕr), L., Königsberg, 1811—Darmstadt, 1864; ct.-conductor and dram. composer.

Schindler (shĭnt'-lĕr), (1) Anton, Meedl,

Moravia, 1795—Bockenheim, near Frankfort, 1864; violinist and conductor; friend and biographer of Beethoven. (2) Kurt, Berlin, Feb. 17, 1882—New York, Nov. 16, 1935; conductor, musicologist; studied Berlin and Munich Univ., music with Ansorge, Bussler, Gernsheim and Thuille; cond. Stuttgart Op., 1902; Würzburg, 1903; ass't cond. to Mottl and Zumpe, Munich, and to Strauss at Berlin, 1903-05; same capacity at Met. Op., N. Y., 1905-08; founded MacDowell Chorus, N. Y., 1909, which he developed into one of the city's most important choruses, the Schola Cantorum in 1912; made collections of Russian, Finnish, Spanish folk music.

Schipa (skē'-pä) Tito, b. Lecce, 1889; tenor; Chicago Op., from 1919; Met. Op., 1934.

Schirmer (shēr'-mĕr), (1) Gustav, Königsee, Saxony, 1829—Eisenach, Thuringia, 1893; son and grandson of court piano-makers at Sondershausen; 1837 came to New York; founded pub. firm, Beer & Schirmer, 1866 S. obtained the entire business since known as G. Schirmer; 1893 incorporated under management of (2) Rudolf E. (New York, 1859—Santa Barbara, Cal., 1919) and (3) Gustav (New York, 1864—1907), sons of above. After 1915 the firm pub. the notable Musical Quarterly.

Schjelderup (shĕlt'-ĕr-oop), Gerhard, Christiansand, Norway, Nov. 17, 1859—Benedikt Beuern, July 29, 1933; composer and 'cellist; pupil of Franchomme, Savard and Massenet; c. operas "Norwegische Hochzeit" (Prague, 1900), and "Frühlings Nacht," a symph. and orch. works, "Eine Sommernacht auf dem Fjord," etc.

Schladebach (shlä'-dĕ-bäkh), Julius, Dresden, 1810—Kiel, 1872; wrote treatise on the voice.

Schläger (shlā'-gĕr), Hans, Filskirchen, Upper Austria, 1820—Salzburg, 1885; conductor and dram. composer.

Schleinitz (shlī'-nĭts), H. Conrad, Zschaitz, Saxony, 1802—Leipzig, 1881; dir. Leipzig Cons. (vice Mendelssohn).

Schlesinger (shlā'-zĭng-ĕr), two mus.-pub. firms. (a) at Berlin, founded 1810 by (1) Ad. Martin, from 1851 managed by his son (2) Heinrich

(d. 1870); 1864 under R. Lienau. (b) at Paris, founded 1834 by (3) **Moritz Ad.**, son of (1); under Louis Brandus in 1846. (4) **Sebastian Benson**, Hamburg, Sept. 24, 1837— Paris, 1917; at 13 went to U. S.; studied at Boston with Otto Dresel; for 17 years Imp. German Consul at Boston; then lived in Paris; pub. many pop. songs and piano-pieces.

Schletterer (shlĕt'-tĕr-ĕr), **Hans Michel**, Ansbach, 1824—Augsburg, 1893; mus.-dir., writer and composer.

Schlick (shlĭk), (1) **Arnold**, ct.-organist to the Elector Palatine, and composer, 1511. (2) **Jn. Konrad**, Münster (?), Westphalia, 1759—Gotha, 1825; 'cellist and composer.

Schlimbach (shlĭm'-bäkh), **G. Chr. Fr.**, b. Ohrdrof, Thuringia, 1760, organist, writer on org.-building, etc.

Schlögel (shlā'-gĕl), **Xavier**, b. Brillonville, Belgium, 1854—Ciney, 1889; pupil Liége Cons.; c. mass with orch., chamber music, etc.

Schlösser (shlĕs'-sĕr), (1) **Louis**, Darmstadt 1800—1886; ct.-conductor and dram. composer. (2) **(K. Wm.) Ad.**, Darmstadt, Feb. 1, 1830—near Dorking, Engl., Nov. 10, 1913; son and pupil of above; pianist, début Frankfort, 1847; toured; from 1854, teacher in London; c. pf.-quartet and trio, etc.

Schlottmann (shlŏt'-män), **Louis**, Berlin, Nov. 12, 1826—June 13, 1905; concert-pianist, pupil of Taubert and Dehn; lived in Berlin as teacher; 1875, R. Mus.-Dir.; c. overture to "*Romeo and Juliet*," "*Trauermarsch*" for orch., etc.

Schlusnus (shlōōs'-nōōs), **Heinrich**, b. Braubach, Germany, Aug. 6, 1888; barytone; pupil of Louis Bachner; début, Hamburg Op., 1915; Nuremberg Op., 1915-17; after that year with Berlin State Op., for a season with Chicago Op., and has appeared with prominent orchs. in Europe and U. S.; also a distinguished Lieder singer; d. Frankfort, 1952.

Schmedes (shmä'-dĕs), **Erik**, near Copenhagen, Aug. 27, 1868—Vienna, March 23, 1931; originally a pianist; then studied singing with Rothmühl; sang as barytone in various theatres; studied with Iffert and, 1898-1924, sang tenor rôles at Vienna; 1899 "*Siegfried*" and "*Parsifal*" at Bayreuth; also in N. Y., 1908-09; long one of most eminent heroic tenors.

Schmelzer (shmĕl'-tsĕr), **Jn. H.**, b. ca. 1630—d. June 30, 1680, Vienna; ct.-cond. and composer.

Schmid(t) (shmĭt), (1) **Bd.**, organist at Strassburg, 1560. He was succeeded by (2) **Bd. Schmid**, the younger. (3) **Anton**, Pohl, Bohemia, 1787—1857; mus. libr. Vienna Library; writer.

Schmidt (shmĭt), (1) **Jn. Phil. Samuel**, Königsberg, 1779—Berlin, 1853; Govt. official, critic, writer and dram. composer. (2) **Jos.**, Bückeburg, 1795 —1865; violinist, ct.-conductor and composer. (3) **Hermann**, Berlin, 1810—1845; ballet-conductor and ct.-composer; c. operetta. (4) **Gustav**, Weimar, 1816—Darmstadt, 1882; ct.-conductor and dram. composer. (5) **Arthur P.**, Altona, Ger., April 1, 1846—1921; est. mus.-pub. business, Boston and Leipzig, 1876. (6) **Leopold**, Berlin, Aug. 2, 1860— April 30, 1927; writer on music; Ph. D.; early in life an operetta cond.; from 1897 critic of the Berlin *Tageblatt;* author of studies of Mozart and Haydn, etc.; adapted Offenbach works for modern perfs. (7) **Franz**, b. Pressburg, Hungary, Dec. 22, 1874—Vienna, 1939; comp.; pupil Hellmesberger; 1892-1910, played as solo 'cellist in Vienna Ct.-Op.; from 1910 teacher of advanced piano perf. at the Akad. der Tonkunst there, of which he was dir. after 1925; 1927-30, rector of the Hochsch. für Musik; c. operas, "*Notre Dame*," "*Fredegundis*"; 4 symphonies; 2 string quartets; piano concerto; piano quintet for left hand (written for Paul Wittgenstein); organ works, songs; chor. wk., "*Book of 7 Seals*."

Schmitt (shmĭt), (1) **Jos.**, 1764— Frankfort-on-Main, 1818; writer, violinist and composer. (2) **Nikolaus**, b. Germany; bassoonist and composer; from 1779, *chef de musique* of the French Guards at Paris. (3) **Aloys**, Erlenbach, Bavaria, 1788 —Frankfort-on-Main, 1866; eminent teacher, pianist, writer and dram. composer. (4) **Jacob (Jacques)**, Obernburg, Bavaria, 1803—Hamburg, 1853; bro. and pupil of above; wrote a method and c. (5) **(G.) Aloys**, Hanover, Feb. 2, 1827—Dresden, Oct., 1902; pianist and cond.; son and pupil of (3); pupil Vollweiler (theory), Heidelberg; toured: then th.-cond. at Aix-la-Chapelle, etc.,

1857–92 ct.-cond. at Schwerin;
from 1893, dir. "Dreyssig'sche Singakademie," Dresden. He c. 3 operas,
incl. "*Trilby*" (Frankfort, 1845):
incid. music; overtures, etc. He
arranged the fragments of Mozart's
C minor mass into a complete work;
died of an apoplectic stroke while
conducting his own "*In Memoriam.*".
(6) **Hans**, Koben, Bohemia, Jan. 14.
1835—Vienna, Jan. 14, 1907; pianoteacher and oboist; pf.-pupil of
Dachs, Vienna Cons., taking the
silver medal; later, teacher there;
wrote a vocal method; c. important
instructive pcs., etc. (7) **Florent**,
b. Blâmont, France, Sept. 28, 1870;
studied at Nancy; 1889, entered
Paris Cons. winning second Prix de
Rome 1897; first 1900, with cantata
"*Sémiramis.*" He sent from Rome
a symph. poem "*Combat des Raksasas
et Délivrance de Sita,*" a symph.
étude based on Poe's "*Le Palais
hanté*" and the "*46th Psalm,*" which
was later played with success, 1906,
increasing to furore (1910 and
Colonne Concerts, 1912); his piano
quintet (1909) has won fame; his
"*Tragédie de Salomé*" was danced
by Loie Fuller 1907; his symph.
poem "*Sélamlik*" (1904), chamber
music, piano pieces, and songs have
given him a high place in France.
He was dir. of the Lyons Cons. after
1921, and is a mem. of the exec.
committee of the Société Musicale
Independante and the Société Nationale de Musique. He has participated as pianist in many concerts
of his works, visiting the U. S. in
this capacity under the auspices of
Pro Musica. His comps. also include: the ballet "*Le Petit Elfe
Ferme-l'œil*" (Op.-Comique, 1924);
music for Shakespeare's "*Antony
and Cleopatra*" (Paris, 1921); the
choral works, "*Chansons à Quatre
Voix,*" "*Pendant la Tempête,*"
"*Danse des Devadasis,*" and "*Chant
de Guerre,*" the last for soprano
soloist, male chorus and orch. (Paris,
1928); the orch. works, "*En Été,*"
"*Reflêts d'Allemagne,*" and "*Pu-
pazzi,*" suites, orig. for piano;
"*Musiques de plein-air,*" "*Rapsodie
Viennoise,*" "*Danse d'Abisag,*"
(Paris, 1926); "*Fonctionnaire
MCMXII, Inaction en Musique,*"
an amusing satire (Paris, 1927):
"*Salambo*" (do.); "*Rêves*"; "*Légende*";

"*Dionysiaques*"; "*Keroshal*" for
tenor and orch.; "*Chant du Soir*",
"*Sonata Libre*" and "*Quatre Pièces*"
for vln. and piano; "*Deux Pièces*"
and "*Chant Élégiaque*" for 'cello
and piano; Andante et Scherzo, for
harp and string quartet; Lied et
Scherzo for double wind quartet;
piano works; songs with piano; four-
part songs with orch.; a cappella
choral songs; choruses with orch.;
also orch. versions of piano pieces
by Chopin and Schubert. S. is the
subject of studies published by Séré,
Calvocoressi, Ferroud and Coeuroy.

Schmitz, E. Robert, b. Paris, 1889;
d. San Francisco, 1949; studied Paris
Cons., with Diémer and Chevillard;
1st prize in piano; founded and dir.
A. M. M. A. Choir, Paris, 1911, and
also estab. his own orch.; first Amer.
concert tour, 1919; formed Franco-
Amer. Musical Soc., 1920, devoted
to perf. of French music in N. Y.
and elsewhere; this after 1923 became Pro Musica, Inc., with branches
in many cities, presenting eminent
composers in concerts of their works.

Schmul'ler, Alexander, Mozyr, Russia,
Dec. 5, 1880—Amsterdam, March
29, 1933; noted violinist; pupil of
Sevcik, Hrimaly and Auer; took
up res. in Berlin, 1908, where he
taught at the Stern Cons. until 1914,
when he was called to the Amsterdam Cons.; he made many concert
tours, incl. some with Max Reger.

Schnabel (shnä'-běl), (1) **Jos. Ignaz**,
Naumburg, Silesia, 1767—Breslau,
1831; conductor and composer. (2)
Michael, Naumburg, 1775—Breslau,
1842; bro. of above; founded at
Breslau (1814) a piano factory, carried on by his son (3) **K.** (1809—
1881) pianist and composer. (4)
Artur, b. Lipnik, Carinthia, April 17,
1882—Axenstein, Switz., Aug. 15,
1951; pupil of Leschetizky; played
leading Austrian and German cities;
lived in Berlin, 1901–33, where he
was heard in many sonata recitals
with Flesch; 1925–33, prof. at the
Hochschule there; attracted a wide
following for his Beethoven sonata
programs, giving complete cycles of
these piano works in London, Berlin
and N. Y.; has played as soloist with
leading orchs. in Europe and U. S.,
also prominent as a teacher; c. songs
and piano music, also chamber
works in ultramodern idiom; **m.**

Therese Behr, contralto; ed. Beethoven piano sonatas. (5) Karl Ulrich, son of (4), b. 1909, pianist; pupil of Berlin Hochsch., studied with Leonid Kreutzer; after 1925 appeared widely in Eur. cities; first Amer. tour, 1936–7.

Schneegass (shnä'-gäs) (Snegas'-sius), Cyriak, Busleben, near Gotha, 1546–1597; theorist and composer.

Schneevoigt (shnā'-foikht), Georg, b. Wiborg, Nov. 8, 1872; Finnish conductor and 'cellist; studied with Schröder, Klengel and Jacobs; lived in Helsingfors as teacher in the Cons., 1894–99; cond. Kaim Orch., Munich; 1903–07; Kiev Orch., 1909–10; Riga Orch., 1910–12; Helsingfors Symph., 1912–14; Stockholm Konsertförenigung Orch.. 1914–24, besides also leading summer concerts at Scheveningen, Holland: founded Oslo Philh. Orch., 1919; 1927–29, cond. Los Angeles Philh. Orch.; latter year, gen. dir. Riga Op.; after 1932, cond. in Malmö; mem. French Legion of Honour; d. Malmö, Nov. 28, 1947.

Schneider (shnī'-dĕr), (1) Jn., Lauter near Coburg, 1702–Leipzig, 1787; famous improviser and organist. (2) G. Abraham, Darmstadt, 1770–Berlin, 1839; horn-virtuoso; conductor, composer of masses, etc. (3) Louis, Berlin, 1805–Potsdam, 1878; son of (2); writer. (4) (Jn. G.) Wm., Rathenow, Prussia, 1781–Berlin, 1811; pianist, teacher, composer and writer. (5) Wm., Neudorf, Saxony, 1783–Merseburg, 1843; organist and writer. (6) Jn. Gottlob, 1753–Gernsdorf, 1840; organist. (7) (Jn. Chr.) Fr., Alt-Waltersdorf, Saxony, Jan. 3, 1786–Dessau, Nov. 23, 1853; son and pupil of (6): at 10 c. a symphony; 1821 ct.-conductor at Dessau; wrote textbooks and c. 15 oratorios, incl. famous "Das Weltgericht"; biog. by F. Kempe. (8) Jn. (Gottlob), Alt-Gersdorf, Oct. 28, 1789–Dresden, April 13, 1864; bro. of above; eminent organist and teacher. As a boy a soprano of remarkable range (to f'' acc. to Riemann, v. PITCH, D. D.); later, tenor; 1825 ct.-organist, Dresden, also conductor; made tours; c. fugues, etc., for organ. (9) Jn. Gottlieb, Alt-Gersdorf, 1797–Hirschberg, 1856; bro. of above; organist. (10) Theodor, Dessau, May 14, 1827 —Zittau, June 15, 1909: son and

pupil of (7); pupil of Drechsler ('cello): 1845, 'cellist, Dessau ct.-orch.; 1854 cantor and choir-dir. court and city churches; 1860–96 cantor and mus.-dir. Jakobikirche, Chemnitz; also cond. (11) (Jn.) Julius, Berlin, 1805–1885; pianist, organist and mus.-director; and c. operas; son of (12) Jn. S., pf.-mfr. at Berlin. (13) K., Strehlen, 1822–Cologne, 1882; tenor. (14) K. Ernst, Aschersleben, 1819–Dresden, 1893; writer.

Schnitzer, Germaine, b. Paris, May 28, 1889; pianist; pupil of Paris Cons., grad. at age of 14; also of Pugno and Sauer; after 1904 toured widely, 1906 in U. S., where following her marriage in 1913 to Dr. Leo Bürger of N Y., she has made her home.

Schnorr von Karolsfeld (shnôr fôn kä'-rôls-fĕlt), (1) L., Munich, 1836–Dresden, 1865; noted tenor; created Wagner's "Tristan"; c. opera at Munich (1865), his wife, (2) Malwina (née Garrigues) (d. Carlsruhe, 1904), created "Isolde."

Schnyder von Wartensee (shnē'-dĕr fôn vär'-tĕn-zā), X., Lucerne, 1786–Frankfort-on-Main, 1868; teacher, writer and composer.

Schoberlechner (shō'-bĕr-lĕkh-nĕr), Fz., Vienna, 1797–Berlin, 1843; pianist, conductor and dram. composer.

Schöberlein (shā'-bĕr-līn), L., Kolmberg, Bavaria, 1813–Göttingen, 1881; writer.

Schoeck (shĕk), Othmar, b. Brunnen, Sept. 1, 1886; Swiss composer; pupil of Reger; cond. in Zurich and St. Gallen; c opera, orch., chamber music.

Schoenefeld (shā-'nĕ-fĕlt), H., Milwaukee, Wis., Oct. 4, 1857—Los Angeles, Aug. 4, 1936; son and pupil of a musician; later studied Leipzig Cons.; winning a prize for a chorus with orch. performed at the Gewandhaus; then studied with E. Lassen (comp.), Weimar; toured Germany as a pianist; from 1879, Chicago, as pianist and teacher, also cond. the "Germania Männerchor." After 1904 lived in Los Angeles. where in 1915 he cond. the first Pacific Sängerfest; C. "The Three Indians," ode with orch.; 2 symphs. ("Rural," "Springtime"); 2 overtures, "In the Sunny South" (based on Ethiopian themes) and *"The American Flag"*; vln.-sonata (Henri Marteau prize, 1899), pf.-pcs., etc.

Schöffer (shĕf'-fĕr), **Peter** (the younger), mus.-printer at Mayence and Strassburg, 1530–39.

Schœlcher (shĕl-shär) **Victor,** Paris, 1804—1893; writer, statesman and biographer of Händel.

Scholes (skōls), **Percy A.,** b. Leeds, England, 1877; writer; grad. Oxford Univ.; associate R. Coll. of Music; formerly master of music at Kent Coll., Canterbury; 1901–03, Kings-.ccd Coll., S. Africa; 1904, taught Leeds Munic. School of Music; and inspector for London Board of Education; extension lecturer for Oxford, London and Manchester Univs.; founded Home Music Study Union; after 1915 he visited America several times as lecturer; later lived in Switzerland; author, *"Purcell," "Arthur Bliss," "Crotchets," "Everyman and His Music," "The Columbia History of Music"* (compilation of phonograph records), *"Listener's Guide to Music," "Listener's History of Music," "The Puritans and Music," "An Introduction to British Music";* and with W. Earhart, *"Complete Book of the Great Musicians."*

Scholtz (shôlts), **Hn.,** Breslau, June 9, 1845—Dresden, July 13, 1918; pianist; pupil of Brosig, Liszt, von Bülow and Rheinberger; teacher in Dresden, 1880 chamber virtuoso; c. concerto; edited Chopin's text.

Scholz (shôlts), (1) **F.,** Gernstadt, 1787—Moscow, 1830; in latter city after 1815 as opera cond.; c. ballets, etc. (2) **Bd. E.,** Mayence, March 30, 1835—Munich, Dec. 26, 1916; pupil of Ernst Pauer, Mayence, and of Dehn, Berlin; 1856 teacher R. Sch. of Mus., Munich; 1859–65, ct.-conductor Hanover Th.; 1871–78, cond. Breslau Orch. Soc.; 1883–1908, dir. of the Hoch Cons., Frankfort (vice Raff); Dr. Phil. *h. c.* (Breslau Univ.), "Royal Prussian Professor," etc.; pub. essays *"Wohin treiben wir?"* (Frankfort, 1897); prod. 9 operas incl. succ. *"Ingo"* (Frankfort, 1898). C. *"Das Siegesfest"* and *"Das Lied von der Glocke"* for soli, chorus and orch.; symph. poem *"Malinconia";* symph. overtures *"Iphigenia"* and *"Im Freien,"* etc.

Schönberg (shän'-bĕrkh), **Arnold,** b. Vienna, Sept. 13, 1874—Brentwood.

Cal., Jul. 13, 1951; noted comp.; exercised profound effect on other composers of his period by his pathbreaking system of free harmonic writing; the "father" of atonality, and in his later works the exponent of the theory that any of the tones of the chromatic scale may be combined with equal effectiveness; the form of his works is, however, in the classical tradition. He began quite early to compose chamber music, and studied vln. and 'cello; in theory he evolved his own method, except for a brief period of study in 1894 with his future brother-in-law, Alexander Zemlinsky. He made a piano version of latter's opera, *"Sarema";* an early string quartet from this period has been lost; some songs were heard in Vienna about 1900. From the previous year dates his popular string sextet, *"Verklärte Nacht,"* in a romantic, somewhat Tristanesque idiom, which has had wide currency in its arrangement for string orch. In 1901, following his marriage to Mathilde Zemlinsky, S. took up res. in Berlin; there he produced his symph. poem, *"Pelleas und Melisande."* In 1903 he returned to Vienna and began his important labors as a theory teacher; in the next 4 years he continued his early post-Wagnerian period with his 6 orch. songs, his string quartet, 8 songs (op. 6), 2 ballades (op. 12), his much-played *"Kammersinfonie,"* and the second string quartet with voice; also from 1910–11 dates his *"Gurrelieder"* for soloists, chorus, orch. Later his music began to reveal an abstract, anti-romantic quality; his 3rd and most important manner (which has been called "expressionistic" and said to have parallels with the painting of such a figure as Kokoschka) is heralded by his songs to lyrics of Stefan George, op. 15. The compositions of this period include 3 piano pieces (op. 11), the radical *"Five Orchestral Pieces"* (op. 16), which created a sensational effect when 1st played in Europe and U. S.; the monodrama, *"Erwartung,"* for one woman singer and orch., which portrays the anguish in the mind of one waiting for her lover (one of S's. most original works, 1st staged at Prague in 1924); *"Die Glückliche Hand"*

(The Hand of Fate), a form of opera to the composer's own text. It symbolically narrates the struggle of a man to preserve the joy and dignity of life against the malign effects of an evil incubus, the mysterious menace of the world about him, and the snares of a rich dandy who wins away his wife (prod. Vienna Volksop., 1924; also in N. Y. by Phila. Orch. under Stokowski in stage version, 1930). 1911 marked S's. 2nd removal to Berlin, and the production of his highly original "*Pierrot Lunaire*" (op. 21), settings of a cycle of 21 poems by Albert Giraud, which describe the somewhat decadent and haunted longings of a moonstricken Pierrot for his native Bergamo; this work is called a "melodrama" and introduced to the world of music, in its score for a woman reciter-singer and chamber ensemble, S's. famous device of the "*Sprechstimme*," or voice that half speaks, half sings. 1915-17, he worked on an oratorio, "*Jacob's Ladder*," writing both text and music (not completed); and the following year founded in Vienna a Society for Private Perfs. of Music, which introd. the scores of his immediate circle to a small group of those interested; 1920-21, he lectured on comp. in Amsterdam; 1923, after return to Vienna, he issued some piano pieces, a quintet, and Serenade for barytone and chamber orch. Beginning 1923 he was Busoni's successor as teacher of master class in comp. at Berlin Hochschule, for about a decade; then came to America 1933 and taught comp. in Boston and N. Y.; 1935 faculty mem. of Univ. of Cal. at Los Angeles, occupying chair of comp. Apart from his compositions, his influence has been preëminent in the field of theory, which he may be said to have revolutionised with his publication of a "*Harmonielehre*"; also c. (operas) "*Von Heute auf Morgen*" (1-act attempt at work in more pop. style, not highly successful); "*Moses and Aaron*"; (orch.) theme and variations; suite for strings (in old-time style); 'cello concerto after an early work by Monn; and a reworking for string quartet and orch. of a Händel concerto grosso; in 1936 his Fourth Str. Quartet was prem.

in Los Angeles; c. "*Survivor from Warsaw*" for narrator, male cho., and orch.; "*Ode to Napoleon*," etc. Studies of his music have been published by Wellesz, Erwin Stein and others, besides an essay by Huneker, etc. (See article, page 518.)

Schönberger (shän'-bĕrkh-ĕr), **Benno,** b. Vienna, Sept. 12, 1863; pianist; pupil of Vienna Cons., studied also with Liszt; toured; 1885 teacher, Vienna; later in Sweden (1886), then London; 1894 toured America; d. England, March 9, 1930.

Schorr (shôr), **Friedrich,** b. Nagyvarad, Hungary, Sept. 2, 1888; barytone; studied with Robinson in Vienna; sang at Graz, 1911-16; Prague, 1916-18; Cologne, 1918-23; then Berlin; came to U.S. with Wagnerian Op. Co., 1923; mem. Met. Op. Co. after 1924; has sung widely in Europe and S. America, and at Covent Garden, esp. in Wagnerian roles; d. Farmington, Conn., Aug., 1953.

Schott (shôt), (1) **Bd.,** d. 1817; founded (Mayence, 1773) the mus.-pub. firm of B. Schott, carried on by his sons (2) **Andreas** (1781—1840) and (3) **Jn. Jos.** (1782—1855), under the firm-name of "B. Schott's Söhne"; later managers at Mayence and the London branch were Fz. von Landwehr and Dr. L. Strecker. (4) **Anton,** Schloss Staufeneck, Swabian Alp, June 25, 1846—Stuttgart, Jan. 8, 1913; tenor; 1865-71 an artillery officer in the French campaign; then studied with Frau Schebest-Strauss; 1871, Munich opera; 1872-75 Berlin opera; leading tenor at Schwerin and Hanover, made concert-tours; 1882 in Italy with Neumann's Wagner troupe.

Schradi(e)ck (shrä'-dĕk), **Henry,** Hamburg, April 29, 1846—Brooklyn, N. Y., March 28, 1918; noted violinist; pupil of his father and of Leonard, Brussels Cons., David, Leipzig; 1864-68 teacher Moscow Cons., then leader Philh. Concerts, Hamburg; 1874-82, co-leader, Gewandhaus Orch. and theatre-orch., Leipzig, also teacher for a time at the Cons. 1883-89, prof. of vln., Cincinnati Cons., U. S. A.; returned to Germany as leader of the Hamburg Philh. Soc.; afterward head vln.-prof. Nat. Cons., N. Y., and later Broad St. Cons., Philadelphia; after 1912 also at Amer. Inst. of Applied Mus.,

N. Y.; pub. excellent technical studies for vln.

Schramm (shräm), (1) **Melchior**, German organist and contrapuntist, 1595. (2) **Paul**, b. Vienna, Sept. 22, 1892; pianist and composer; pupil of R. Kaiser and Leschetizky.

Schreck (shrĕk), **Gustav**, Zeulenroda, Sept. 8, 1849—Leipzig, Jan. 22, 1918; pupil of Leipzig Cons.; 1885 teacher of theory and comp., Leipzig Cons.; 1892, mus.-dir. and cantor, and cond. of the "Thomanerchor": prod. concert-cantatas, oratorio, "*Christus der Auferstandene*" (Gewandhaus, 1892), church-music, etc.

Schreker (shrĕk'-ĕr), **Franz**, Monaco, March 23, 1878—Berlin, March 21, 1934; composer; pupil of Fuchs, Vienna; founded and cond. Philh. Chorus, Vienna, 1911; prof. of comp., Vienna Acad., 1912; dir. Berlin Hochsch., 1920–32; master class, Akad. der Künste there, 1931–32; noted for his original music dramas, usually on somewhat Freudian erotic subjects, with musical system based on new and unusual "clang-tints," and using his own texts; c. (operas) "*Der Ferne Klang*" (Frankfort, 1912); "*Das Spielwerk und die Prinzessin*" (Vienna, 1913); "*Die Gezeichneten*" (1918); "*Der Schatzgräber*" (1920); "*Irrelohe*," "*Memnon*," "*Der Schmied von Ghent*"; (pantomime) "*Der Geburtstag der Infantin*" (after Wilde); Sinfonietta, "*Nachtstück*" and prelude to a drama for orch., choral works and songs; his influence as a teacher was considerable; his style excelled in richness of orchestral color and subtlety of detail, but his works for the stage were of such a complicated nature that they have never been produced outside of Germany and Austria. Studies of his music have been written by Kapp and Bekker.

Schrems (shrĕms), **Jos.**, Warmensteinach, Upper Palatinate, 1815—Ratisbon, 1872; conductor, editor and teacher.

Schröder (shrä'-dĕr), (1) **Hermann**, Quedlinburg, July 28, 1843—Berlin, Jan. 31, 1909; violinist, writer and composer; pupil of A. Ritter, Magdeburg; from 1885, teacher R. Inst. for church-mus., Berlin, and at a mus.-sch. of his own. (2) **Karl**,

Quedlinburg, Dec. 18, 1848— Bremen, Sept. 22, 1935; bro. of above; 'cellist and composer; pupil of Drechsler, Dessau and Kiel, Berlin; at 14, 1st 'cello ct.-orch. at Sondershausen, and teacher in the Cons.; 1873, 'cello Brunswick ct.-orch.; 1874, solo 'cellist Gewandhaus Orch., and th.-orch., Leipzig, also teacher at the Cons., and made tours; 1881, ct.-cond., Sondershausen; cond. German Opera at Amsterdam; until 1888, Berlin ct.-opera; till 1890, the Hamburg Opera; returned to Sondershausen as ct.-cond. and dir. Cons.; 1911–24, at Stern Cons.; wrote 'cello-method, catechism on conducting and the 'cello. C. succ. opera "*Aspasia*" (Sondershausen, 1892); a succ. 1-act opera "*Der Asket*" (Leipzig, 1893); succ. operetta "*Malajo*" (Bunzlau, 1887); 1871, founded the "Schröder Quartett," with his brothers (1) **Hermann** (3) **Fz.** and (4) **Alwin**, b. Neuhaldensleben June 15, 1855— Detroit, Nov. 10, 1920; pupil of his father and brother Hermann, André (pf.), and De Ahna (vln.), W. Tappert (theory); self-taught as a 'cellist, as which he has won his fame; 1875, 1st 'cello in Liebig's "Concert-Orchester," later under Fliege and Laube (Hamburg); 1880, Leipzig. as asst. of (1), whom he succeeded, 1881, in the Gewandhaus, theatre and Cons.; 1886, Boston, as first 'cellist Symph. Orch.; member of the Kneisel Quartet; 1903 he resigned from the Boston Symph. Orch., and joined the Kneisel Quartet; 1905–7, teacher at New York Institute of Musical Art; 1907, first 'cello teacher at Hoch Cons., Frankfort-on-Main; 1908, returned to Boston as co-founder of Hess-Schroeder Quartet; 1910, first 'cellist of Boston Symph; resigned 1917 for concert tours; later a mem. of the Margulies Trio and Boston String Quartet until 1919.

Schröder-Devrient (shrä'-dĕr-dā'-frĭ-ĕnt) **Wilhelmine**, Hamburg, 1804— Coburg, 1860; eminent soprano; daughter of Fr. Schröder, barytone, and the actress, Antoinette Sophie Bürger; pupil of Mazatti; début, Vienna, 1821; m. the actor Karl D. (divorced 1828, after bearing him 4 children; married twice afterward); she created the rôle of "Adriano

Colonna" in the "*Rienzi*" of Wagner, whose style she deeply affected.

Schröder-Hanfstängl. Vide HANF-STÄNGL.

Schröter (shrä-tĕr), (1) **Leonhardt,** Torgau, ca. 1540—d. in Magdeburg, 1595; eminent contrapuntist. (2) **Chp. Gl.,** Hohenstein, Saxony, 1699 —Nordhausen, 1782; noted organist; claimed in a pamphlet (1763) to have invented, 1717, the pianoforte, but was forestalled by Cristofori; composer. (3) **Corona (Elisabeth Wilhelmine),** Guben, 1751—Ilmenau, 1802; celebrated soprano; pupil of her father, (4) **Joh. Fr. S.,** chambersinger. (5) **Joh. Samuel,** Warsaw, 1750—London, 1788, son of (4); pianist. (6) **Joh. H.** (b. Warsaw, 1762), son of (4); violinist.

Schubart (shoo'-bärt), (**Chr. Fr.**) **Daniel,** Sontheim, Swabia, 1739—Stuttgart, 1791; poet; organist and composer.

Schubert (shoo'-bĕrt), (1) **Jos.,** Warnsdorf, Bohemia, 1757—Dresden, 1812; violinist, and dram. composer. (2) **Jn. Fr.,** Rudolstadt, 1770—Cologne, 1811; violinist, writer and composer, (3) **Fd.,** Lichtenthal, near Vienna, 1794—Vienna, 1859; elder bro. of the great composer (4) and passionately devoted to him; dir. Normal Sch., Vienna; c. church-mus., a requiem for his brother, etc.
(4) **Franz (Peter),** Lichtenthal, near Vienna, Jan. 31, 1797—of typhus, Vienna, Nov. 19, 1828; one of the most eminent of the world's composers. One of the 14 children of a schoolmaster at Lichtenthal, who taught him the vln.; also studied with Holzer there; at 10, first soprano in the church-choir, and c. songs and little instrumental pcs. 1808, a singer in the Vienna court choir, and also in the "Convict" (the training-sch. for the court singers). He played in the sch.-orchestra, finally as first vln., and studied theory with Ruczicka and Salieri. His earliest extant composition is a 4-hand fantasia of 12 movements written when he was 13. He had a frenzy for writing, and a fellow-pupil, Spaun, generously furnished him with mus.-paper, a luxury beyond the means of Schubert. At 15 he had written much, incl. an overture; at 16 he c. his first symph.; 1813, his voice broke and he left the "Con-

vict," where the unrestrained license allowed him in his compositions accounts for the crudeness of some of his early works and the faults of form that always characterised him, as well as for his immediate and profound individuality; at 17 he c. his first mass. In order to escape military conscription he studied a few months at the Normal Sch. and took the post of elementary teacher in his father's sch. He taught there until 1816, spending his leisure in studying with Salieri, and in comp. particularly of songs, of which he wrote as many as 8 in one day—144 in his 18th year (1815), including "*Der Erlkönig*"; 1814-16, he also c. 2 operettas, 3 Singspiele and 3 incomplete stage-pieces, 4 masses. 1816, he applied, without succ., for the directorship of the new State mus.-sch. at Laybach (salary $100 (£20) a year). From 1817 he lived in Vienna, except two summers (1818 and 1824), spent at Zelész, Hungary, as teacher in Count Esterházy's family. How S. existed is a matter of mystery, except for the help of such friends as Fz. von Schober, who aided him with the utmost generosity. The famous tenor Michael Vogl popularised his songs. By his 21st year (1818) S. had c. six of his symphs. and a great mass of work. His mus. farce "*Die Zwillingsbrüder*" was prod. (Kärnthnerthor Th., 1820, but ran only six nights). 1821, after he had written over 600 compositions, his "*Erlkönig*" was sung at a public concert of the "Musikverein" and elsewhere, with a wide sale that attended most of his subsequent publication of songs and pf.-pcs.; though he was sadly underpaid by his publishers, sometimes receiving only a gulden (20 cents, less than a shilling) for them. In 1822 he declined the post of organist at the court chapel; but could never obtain a salaried position, though many efforts were made. At 31 he gave his first concert of his own works, with good succ. (1828). In 1822, he had finished a grand opera "*Alfonso und Estrel'a*," the libretto bad, the scoring too difficult for the musicians at Graz, where it was put in rehearsal; it was withdrawn, not to be prod. till 1854 under Liszt and in 1881 when Jn. Fuchs rewrote the libretto and prod. it at Carlsruhe with great succ. In 1825 a work, "*Rosamunde*," was prod. at the Th. an-der-Wien, with applause for the music, but it was withdrawn after a second performance. Other works of his had not even productions, his stubborn refusal to alter a note preventing the profitable performance of dram. scenes, etc. His health finally broke under the strain of composition all day on a little food and revelry till late at night. He died of typhus and was buried, at his own request, in the "Ostfriedhof" at Währing, near Beethoven. A complete critical edition of his works is pub. by Breitkopf & Härtel. These incl., besides those mentioned, an opera "*Adrast*" (unfinished), 3-act operettas "*Der Teufels Lustschloss*" and "*Der Spiegelritter*"; SINGSPIELE: "*Der Vierjährige Posten*," "*Fernando*"; "*Claudine von Villabella*" (unfinished); "*Die Freunde von Salamanca*" and "*Der Minnesänger*"; all written 1814–1816; none performed; 3-act melodrama, "*Die Zauberharfe*" (Aug. 19, 1820); 3-act opera, "*Sakuntala*" (not finished or performed); 1-act operetta, "*Die Verschworenen, oder der häusliche Krieg*" (Vienna, 1861); 3-act opera, "*Fierabras*" (Vienna, 1861); "*Die Burgschaft*," 3-act opera (c. 1816; prod. by Fz. Lachner, Pesth, 1827); unprod. operas "*Der Graf von Gleichen*" (1827) and "*Die Salzbergwerke*"; 6 masses; "*Deutsche Messe*"; unfinished oratorio "*Lazarus*," "*Tantum ergo*" (with orch.); 2 "*Stabat Mater*," etc. CHORAL WORKS WITH ORCH., OR INSTRS.: "*Miriams Siegesgesang*"; prayer, "*Vor der Schlacht*"; hymn, "*Herr unser Gott*," "*Hymne an den Heiligen Geist*," "*Morgengesang im Walde*," "*Nachtgesang im Walde*" and "*Nachthelle*," "*Schlachtlied*," "*Glaube, Hoffnung und Liebe*," several cantatas and part-songs. ORCH. AND CHAMBER-MUS.: 10 symphs., No. 8 the "unfinished" in B min., 7 overtures (Nos. 2 and 5 "in the Italian style"); vln.-concerto; rondo for vln. with orch.; octet; pf.-quintet ("*Forellenquintet*," with double bass); string-quintet with 2 'celli; 14 string-quartets; 2 pf.-trios; 2 string-trios; rondo brilliant, phantasie in C, sonata, 3 sonatinas, nocturne for 'cello and pf.; introd. and vars. for flute and pf.: 17 pf.-sonatas (incl. op.

78, fantasia), 3 grand sonatas, posthumous; 8 impromptus, 6 moments musicaux; many variations, many waltzes, incl. "*Valses sentimentales*," "*Homage aux belles Viennoises*," "*Valses nobles*," 12 "*Grätzer Wälzer*," "*Wanderer-Fantasie*"; FOR PF., 4 HANDS: 2 sonatas, "*Divertissement à l'hongroise*," "*Grand rondo*," "*Notre amitié*," rondo in D, "*Lebensstürme*," fugue, polonaises, variations, waltzes, 4 Ländler; marches, incl. "Trauermarsch" and "héroique." SONGS WITH PIANO: "*Erlkönig*," op. 1; "*Gretchen am Spinnrade*," op. 2; "*Heidenröslein*," op. 3; "*Der Wanderer*" and "*Der du von dem Himmel bist*," op. 4; Suleika songs, Mignon's songs, 2 song cycles by Wilhelm Müller, "*Die Schöne Müllerin*" and "*Die Winterreise*," containing 20 and 24 numbers; 7 songs from "*Fräulein vom See*" (Scott's "*Lady of the Lake*"), 9 songs from "*Ossian*"; 6 songs by Heine in the "*Schwanengesang*," etc. (more than 600 in all). As part of the celebration of his death centenary in 1928, the Columbia Phonograph Co. offered a prize for internat'l composers to complete the Unfinished Symph. This aroused so much protest from musicians, however, that the contest was changed to one for a work "in the style of" Schubert, and was won by Kurt Atterberg of Sweden. Biog. by Kreissle von Hellborn (Vienna, 1861, 1865); Reissman, Berlin, 1873); A. Niggli (1880); Barbedette (Paris, 1866); Max Friedländer; other studies by La Mara, Risse, Austin, Frost, H. Ritter, Skalla, Curzon, Zenger, Heuberger, Duncan, Klatte, Bourgault-Ducoudray, Antcliffe, Dahms, Deutsch and Schiebler, Bie, Clutsam, Flower, Kobald and Ewen. His songs are the subject of studies by Capell and Le Massena. His letters and other writings were pub. in English translation (Knopf, 1928). (See article, page 521.)

(5) Fz. Anton, 1768—1824; violinist; R. Konzertmeister. (6) Fz., Dresden, 1808—1878; son and pupil of (5); violinist, Konzertmeister R. orch. and composer. (7) Maschinka, wife of (6) and daughter of G. A. Schneider, 1815—Dresden, 1882; soprano. (8) Georgine, Dresden, 1840—Potsdam, 1878; daughter and pupil

of (7); pupil also of Jenny Lind and
Garcia; sang in many European
cities. (9) **Louis,** Dessau, 1828—
Dresden, 1884; violinist; singing-
teacher and composer.
Schuberth (shoo'-bĕrt), (1) **Gottlob,**
Karsdorf, 1778—Hamburg, 1846;
oboist and clarinettist. (2) **Julius**
(Fd. G.), Magdeburg, 1804—Leipzig,
1875; son of above; founded firm of
"J. Schuberth & Co.," Hamburg,
1826; Leipzig branch, 1832; New
York, 1850. His brother (3) **Fr.**
Wm. (b. 1817), took the Hamburg
house, 1853 (under firm-name "Fritz
Schuberth"); 1872, at Weimar
founded the mus.-library "Liszt-
Schuberth Stiftung"; 1891 succeeded
by Felix Siegel; New York branch
later owned by J. H. F. Meyer.
(4) **L.,** Magdeburg, 1806—St. Petersburg, 1850; son and pupil of (1) and
von Webser; at 16 dir. Stadt Th. at
Magdeburg; conductor Oldenburg,
1845; cond. German opera, St.
Petersburg; c. operas, symphs., etc.
(5) **K.,** Magdeburg, 1811—Zurich,
1863; bro. of above; noted 'cellist;
pupil of Hesse and Dotzauer; toured
widely; soloist to the Czar; ct.-cond.,
dir. at the U.; c. 2 'cello-concertos.
Schubiger (shoo'-bĭkh-ĕr), **Anselm,** Uz-
nach, Canton of St. Gallen, 1815—
1888; important writer.
Schuch (shookh), (1) **Ernst von,** Graz,
Styria, Nov. 23, 1847—Dresden,
May 10, 1914; pupil of E. Stoltz and
O. Dessoff; 1872, cond. Pollini's It.
Op.; from 1873 ct.-cond. Dresden,
then R. Ct.-Councillor and Gen.-
Mus.-Dir. (2) **Clementine Proska,**
Vienna, Feb. 12, 1853—June 11,
1932; wife of above; 1873–1904,
colorature-sopr., Dresden ct.-theatre.
Schucht (shookht), **Jean F.,** Holz-
thalleben, Thuringia, 1822—Leipzig,
1894; critic and composer.
Schücker (shĭk'-ĕr), **Edmund,** Vienna,
1860—Bad Kreuznach, 1911; harp-
ist; pupil of Zamara, Vienna Cons.;
1884, teacher Leipzig Cons., and
harpist Gewandhaus Orch.; 1890,
ct.-harpist to Duke of Saxe-Alten-
burg; 1891, Chicago Orchestra.
Schulhoff (shool'-hóf), (1) **Julius,**
Prague, 1825—Berlin, 1898; notable
pianist; pupil of Kisch, Tedesco and
Tomaschek; début, Dresden, 1842;
lived in Paris as teacher, then Dresden and Berlin; c. pf.-pcs., etc.
(2) Erwin, b. Prague, June 8, 1894;

composer; studied at Cons. there,
also at Leipzig (comp. with Reger),
and at Cologne (cond. with Steinbach); won Mendelssohn Prize in
piano at Berlin Hochsch.; also in
comp.; c. 2 symphonies, with vocal
solos; overtures, orch. variations,
piano concerto, suite for chamber
orch., string quartet, vln. suite, piano
variations, and smaller pieces for
piano, all in advanced modern style,
incl. atonality.
Schultheiss (shoolt'-hīs), **Benedict,** d.
1693; organist and composer, Nürn-
berg.
Schulthesius (shool-tā'-zĭ-oos), **Jn.**
Paul, Fechheim, Saxe-Coburg, 1748—
Leghorn, 1816; theorist and composer.
Schultz-Adaiewski (shoolts-ä-da-yĕf'-
ski), **Ella von,** St. Petersburg,
Feb. 10, 1846—Bonn, July 29, 1926;
pupil of Henselt and the St. Petersburg Cons.; pianist; toured and from
1882 lived at Venice; c. opera *"Die
Morgenröte der Freiheit"*; *"Sonate
grecque"* for clarinet and piano, etc.
Schultze (shoolt'-tsĕ), (1) **Jn.,** organist
and composer, Dannenberg, Bruns-
wick, 1612. (2) **Chp.,** cantor, etc.,
Delitzsch, Saxony (1647 — 1668).
(3) Dr. **Wm. H.,** Celle, Hanover,
1827—Syracuse, N. Y., 1888; violinist and professor. (4) **Ad.,** b. Schwerin, Nov. 3, 1853; pianist; pupil of
Kullak's Acad., Berlin; teacher there;
1886-90 ct.-cond., Sondershausen
and dir. of the Cons.; later in Berlin;
c. a pf.-concerto, etc.
Schulz (shoolts), (1). Vide PRÄTORIUS.
(2) **Jn. Abraham Peter,** Lüneburg,
March 30 (31 ?), 1747—Schwedt,
June 10, 1800; important predecessor
of Schubert as a song-writer; pupil
of Kirnberger, Berlin; teacher there,
1780, ct.-cond. at Rheinsberg; 1787-
94, ct.-cond. Copenhagen; and theorist; c. operas, oratorios, etc. (3) **Jn.**
Ph. Chr., Langensalza, Thuringia,
1773—Leipzig, 1827; cond. and
composer. (4) **Fd.,** Kossar, 1821—
Berlin, 1897; 1856 conductor, mus.-
dir., singing-teacher and composer.
(5) **August,** Brunswick, June 15, 1837
—Feb. 12, 1909; violinist; pupil of
Zinkeisen, Leibrock, and Joachim;
leader of the Ducal Orch. there; c.
pop. male quartets. (6) **Leo,** Posen,
1865—Crescenta, Cal., 1944, cellist; pupil Berlin Hochsch.; soloist
Philh. there; 1890–1931 with N. Y.

Fhilh.; taught at Nat'l Cons.; mem. Margulies Trio, 1904–15.

Schulz-Beuthen (shoolts-boi'-tĕn), **H.,** Beuthen, Upper Silesia, June 19, 1838—Dresden, March 12, 1915; pupil of Leipzig Cons., and of Riedel; 1881, pf.-teacher, Dresden Cons.; 1893, in Vienna; after 1895 again at Dresden Cons.; prof., 1911; a Wagner and Liszt disciple; c. 4 operas, 8 symphonies, "*Haydn*," "*Frühlingsfeier*," E♭, "*Schön Elizabeth*," "*Reformation-S.*" (with organ); "*König Lear*," and a "*Kinder-Sinfonie*"; symph. poem, "*Die Todteninsel*"; 3 overtures, incl. "*Indianischer Kriegstanz*"; cantatas with orch., "*Befreiungsgesang der Verbannten Israels*," and "*Harald*," requiem and Psalms 42, 43, and 125 with orch. Psalm 13, *a cappella* male choruses, etc.

Schulz-Schwerin (shoolts-shvā'-rēn), **K.,** Schwerin, Jan. 3, 1845—Mannheim, May 24, 1913; pianist; pupil of Stern Cons., Berlin; ct.-pianist to Grand Duke of Mecklenburg; 1885–1901, teacher at Stern Cons., Berlin; then in Mannheim; c. a symph., overtures "*Torquato Tasso*," "*Die Braut von Messina*," and "*Triomphale*"; Sanctus, Benedictus, etc., with orch., etc.

Schulze (shoolts'-ĕ), (1) **Jn. Fr.,** Milbitz, Thuringia, 1793—Paulinzelle, 1858; org.-builder with his sons at Mühlhausen. (2) **Ad.,** Mannhagen, near Mölln, April 13, 1835—Jena, April, 1920; concert-bass; pupil of Carl Voigt, Hamburg, and Garcia, London; head-prof. of singing R. Hochschule, Berlin.

Schuman (shoo'män), **Wm.,** b. N. Y., 1910; comp.; grad. Colum. U., pupil Haubiel, Roy Harris; c. symphs., etc.; pres., Juilliard Sch. of Music, N. Y.

Schumann (shoo'-män), (1) **Robert (Alex.),** Zwickau, Saxony, June 8, 1810—insane, Endenich, near Bonn, July 29, 1856; one of the most individual and eminent of composers. Youngest son of a book-seller (of literary taste and author of a biog. gallery to which R. contributed at 14). Pupil of a local organist, Kuntzsch (pf.), who prophesied immortality for him; at 6 he began to compose, at 11, untaught, he c. for chorus and orch. At 17 he set poems of his own to mus. 1820–28, attended Zwickau Gymnasium; then

matriculated at Leipzig Univ. to study law and philosophy. 1829 Heidelberg, where he also studied mus., practising the piano 7 hours a day; played once in public with great succ. 1830, Leipzig, where he lived with Friedrich Wieck, with whom he studied the piano; he also studied comp. with H. Dorn. In trying to acquire independence of the fingers by suspending the fourth finger of the right hand in a sling while practising with the others he crippled this finger and foiled his ambition to be the chief virtuoso of his time. He now made comp. his first ambition. In 1833, his first symph. was performed with little succ., the first movement having been played in public by Wieck's 13-year old daughter, Clara, with whom S. fell in love. The father liked S. as a son, but not as a son-in-law, and put every obstacle in his way, until in 1840, after a year's law-suit, the father was forced to consent and the two lovers, both now distinguished, were united in one of the happiest marriages known in art; she giving his work publicity in her very popular concerts; he devoted to her and dedicating much of his best work to her. 1834 he founded the *Neue Zeitschrift für Musik*, and was its editor till 1844. His essays and criticisms (signed FLORESTAN, EUSEBIUS, MEISTER RARO, 2, 12, 22, ETC., JEANQUIRIT, etc.) are among the noblest works in the history of criticism, particularly in the matter of recognising new genius and heralding it fearlessly and fervently. (Chopin, Berlioz, and Brahms, profited by this quality. Of Wagner he did not altogether approve.) In his writings he constructed an imaginary band of ardent young Davids attacking the Goliath of Philistinism. He called this group the "Davidsbündler." His pen-name "EUSEBIUS," represents the vehement side of his nature, "FLORESTAN," the gentle and poetic side. His paper had some succ., which was not bettered by a removal to Vienna, 1838–39, and a return to Leipzig. 1840, Dr. Phil., Jena. 1840 was mainly devoted to his important song-composition; 1841 to symph. work; 1842 to chamber-mus., incl. his pf.-quintet (op. 44) which gave him European fame.

1843 was choral, "*Das Paradies und Peri*" (from Moore's "Lalla Rookh"), having a great succ.; he also began his choric mus. for "*Faust.*" The same year, on the invitation of his warm personal friend Mendelssohn, he became teacher of pf. and comp., and of playing from score at the newly founded Leipzig Cons.; 1844, after going with his wife on a concert-tour to Russia, he removed to Dresden and resigned the editorship of the *Neue Zeitschrift;* lived at Dresden until 1850 teaching and composing such works as the great C-major symph., 1846, and the opera "*Genoveva*" (1848; prod. 1850 without succ.; its exclusion of recitative displeasing the public). 1847 cond. of the "Liedertafel"; 1848 organised the "Chorgesangverein." 1850, Düsseldorf as town mus.-dir. (vice Fd. Hiller). 1853, signs of insanity, first noted in 1833 and more in 1845, compelled him to retire. 1854 he threw himself into the Rhine, whence he was rescued by some boatmen; he was then taken to an asylum at Endenich near Bonn, where he remained in acute melancholia, varied by intervals of complete lucidity, when he composed as before. A complete ed. of his comps. is edited by Clara Schumann and publ. by Breitkopf & Härtel. It includes, besides the works mentioned, mus. to Byron's "*Manfred,*" Goethe's "*Faust,*" cantatas, "*Der Rose Pilgerfahrt,*" with orch.; "*Adventlied,*" for sopr., chorus and orch.; "*Abschiedslied,*" chorus with wood-wind or pf.; requiem for "*Mignon*"; "*Nachtlied,*" for chorus and orch.; ballades "*Der Königssohn,*" "*Des Sängers Fluch*" (op. 139), "*Vom Pagen und der Königstochter,*" "*Das Glück von Edenhall,*" and "*Neujahrslied*"; Missa sacra, and requiem mass, with orch.; 4 symphs. (No. 3, op. 97, in E♭ the "*Rheinische,*" or "*Cologne,*" symph.); "*Ouvertüre, Scherzo und Finale,*" op. 52; 4 concert overtures "*Die Braut von Messina,*" "*Festouvertüre,*" "*Julius Cæsar*" and "*Hermann und Dorothea*"; pf.-concerto; Concert-stück, and concert-allegro, 'cello-concerto; fantasia for vln. with orch., etc.

Much remarkable CHAMBER MUSIC: incl. pf.-quintet in E♭ op. 44; 3 pf.-trios, etc.; 6 org.-studies in canon-

form, "*Skizzen für den Pedal-flügel*"; 6 org.-fugues on B–A–C–H, op. 60. FOR PF.: Op. 1, Variations on A–B–E–G–G (the name of a young woman); op. 2 "*Papillons*"; op. 3, "*Studies after Paganini's Caprices*"; op. 5, "*Impromptus on theme by Cl. Wieck*"; op. 6, "*Davidsbündlertänze*"; op. 9, "*Carnaval*"; op. 10, "*Studies on Paganini's Caprices*"; op. 15, thirteen "*Kinderscenen*"; op. 16, "*Kreisleriana*"; op. 21, "*Novelletten*" (4 books), 3 sonatas (No. 3 "Concert sans orchestre"), and 3 sonatas for the young; op. 23 "*Nachtstücke*"; op. 26 "*Faschingsschwank aus Wien*"; op. 68, "*Album für die Jugend,*" a canon on "*An Alexis.*" FOR PF. 4 HANDS: Op. 66, "*Bilder aus Osten,*" after Rückert, 12 "*Clavierstücke für kleine und grosse Kinder*"; op. 109, "*Ballscenen.*" Many choruses *a cappella*; many songs and duets, incl. ten *Spanische Liebeslieder*,. with 4-hand accomp., op. 138; Liederkreis (Heine), song-cycle, op. 24, and Liederkreis (12 poems by Eichendorff), op. 39; "*Myrthen,*" op. 25; Lieder und Gesänge, 5 sets; 12 poems (Körner), op. 35; 6 poems (Rückert), in collaboration with his wife, op. 37; "*Frauenliebe und Leben,*" op. 42; "*Dichterliebe,*" op. 48; "*Liederalbum für die Jugend,*" op. 79; 6 songs from Byron's "*Hebrew Melodies,*" op. 95 (with pf. or harp); nine Lieder und Gesänge from "*Wilhelm Meister,*" op. 98a, etc. In 1937 a posth. vln.-concerto in D minor, never perf. but willed by Joachim to the Prussian State Library, was premiered by Yehudi Menuhin.

His writings are pub. in 4 vols., 1854; 4 vols. in English, London, 1875; and his letters ed. by his wife (1885) and (1886) by Jansen.

Biogr. by von Wasielewski (1858), Reissmann (1865), Ambros (1860), L. Mesnard (Paris, 1876), H. Reimann (1887), H. Erler (1887), S. Bagge (1879), Waldersee (1880), and by Ph. Spitta (1882). Other biographical studies by La Mara, Fuller-Maitland, Batka, Abert, Patterson, Schneider and Maréchal, Oldmeadow, Mauclaire, Wolff, Hartog, Steiner, Calvocoressi, Dahms, Von der Pforten, Basche, Bedford, Niecks, Ronald, and Eugenie Schumann, his daughter (in English, 1931). (See article, page 523.)

(2) **Clara** (Josephine), née **Wieck**, Leipzig, Sept. 13, 1819—Frankfort-on-Main, May 20, 1896; eminent pianist; wife of above (q. v.). She played in public at 9; at 11 at the Gewandhaus; toured from 1832; Vienna (1836) received the title of Imp. Chamber-virtuoso. On Sept. 12, 1840, m. Schumann (q. v.). After he died she went with her children to Berlin; 1863 to Wiesbaden, resuming her public career as a concert-pianist; 1878-92 pf.-teacher Hoch Cons., Frankfort. Besides editing Schumann's works, his early letters and finger-exercises from Czerny, she c. pf.-concerto, preludes and fugues, pf.-trio, Vars. on a theme by Schumann, many songs, incl. 3 in Schumann's op. 37 (Nos. 2, 4, and 11). Biog. by Litzmann, 1902. (3) **Georg** (Alfred), b. Königstein, Saxony, Oct. 25, 1866; d. Berlin, 1952; pupil of the city mus.-dir., pupil of his grandfather, a cantor, and of K. A. Fischer, B. Rollfuss, and Fr. Baumfelder, Dresden, then of Leipzig Cons., where he c. 2 symphs., a serenade for orch., a pf.-quintet, a vln.-sonata, etc., taking the Beethoven prize, 1887; lived 2 years in Berlin; 1892-96, cond. at Danzig; 1896-1900, Bremen Philh. Orch. and chorus; after 1900 of Berlin Singakademie, a notable chorus; 1916, hon. Mus. D.; Berlin Univ.; mem. of the Acad. of Arts; after 1913 leader of master class in comp. at the Univ.; c. oratorios, 2 symphonies, and many other works for orch., chamber music, choruses, piano pieces, songs, etc. (4) **Elisabeth**, b. Merseburg, Germany, June 13, 1891; soprano; 1909-15, sang at Hamburg Op.; after 1919 at Vienna State Op., also for a time at Met. Op., and toured U. S. 1921 in programs with Richard Strauss; d. N. Y., Apr. 23, 1952.

Schumann-Heink (shoo'-män-hīnk), **Ernestine** (née **Rössler**), n. Prague, June 15, 1861—Hollywood, Nov. 17, 1936; famous contralto; pupil of Marietta von Leclair, Graz; début Dresden, 1878, in "Il Trovatore"; sang there 4 years; 1883 Hamburg City Th.; 1896, sang "Erda," "Waltraute," and the First Norn at Bayreuth; m Herr Heink, 1883; m. Paul Schumann, 1893; from 1898, in America; 1899-1904 she sang at

Berlin Royal Opera as well as at Met. Op., N. Y.; 1904 she starred in a comic opera, "Love's Lottery"; 1909 she created "Clytemnestra" in Strauss's "Elektra" at Dresden; Paul Schumann, d. 1904; she m. William Rapp, Jr., 1905; divorced him, 1912; she had sung in concert with enormous success in America and in opera abroad; became naturalised American, 1908. In recent years she had been engaged as a radio singer and had played parts in the films, also to some extent active as a teacher.

Schünemann (shü'-nĕ-män), **G.**, b. Berlin, March 13, 1884; musicologist; Ph.D., Leipzig Univ.; taught Berlin Univ.; dir. Prussian State Library, div. of music.

Schuppan (shoop'-pän), **Adolf**, b. Berlin, June 5, 1863; pupil of B. Härtel; c. chamber music.

Schuppanzigh (shoop'-pän-tsĭkh), **Ignaz**, Vienna, 1776—1830; violinist, conductor and teacher.

Schürer (shü'-rĕr), **Jn. G.**, Raudnitz, Bohemia, 1720—Dresden, 1786; dram. composer.

Schuricht (shōō'-rĕkht), **Carl**, b. Danzig, July 3, 1880; conductor; studied at Berlin Hochsch.; with Humperdinck and Rudorff; cond. opera and concerts, Zwickau, Dortmund, Frankfort, and after 1912 at Wiesbaden; has made guest appearances in other countries, incl. London and U. S. (guest cond. St. Louis Symph., 1929).

Schurig (shoo'-rĭkh), (**Volkmar**) **Julius** (**Wm.**), Aue, Saxony, 1802—Dresden, 1899; composer and teacher.

Schuster (shoo'-shtĕr), **Jos.**, Dresden, 1748—1812; ct.-conductor; c. pop. operas, symphs., etc.

Schütt (shüt), **Eduard**, Petersburg, Oct. 22, 1856—near Merano, July 28, 1933; pianist; pupil of Petersen and Stein, Petersb. Cons.; studied at Leipzig Cons.; in 1881 succeeded Mottl as cond. Akademischer Wagnerverein, Vienna; c. succ. comic opera "Signor Formica" (Vienna, 1892); pf.-concerto, etc., but is best known as the composer of many popular small pf.-pieces.

Schütz (shüts), (**Sagitta'rius**) **H.**, "The father of German music," Köstritz, Saxony, Oct. 8, 1585—Dresden, Nov. 6, 1672; in 1607 entered Marburg Univ. to study law, but, 1609, was sent to Venice by Landgrave

Moritz of Hesse-Cassel to study with Giov. Gabrieli; 1612 returned to Cassel as ct.-organist; 1615 cond. to the Elector of Saxony at Dresden; he frequently revisited Italy, whence he brought much to modify and enlarge German mus.; also made long visits to Copenhagen as ct.-cond. 1627, on royal invitation for the wedding of Princess Sophie of Saxony, he c. the first German opera, the libretto being a transl. from the *"Dafne"* of Peri (q. v.); this work is lost, as is also the ballet, *"Orpheus und Eurydice,"* 1638, for the wedding of Jn. Georg II. of Saxony. Carl Riedel revived interest in S. by pub. and producing *"Die 7 Worte Christi am Kreuz,"* and a *"Passion."* A complete ed. of S.'s works is pub. by Breitkopf and Härtel in 16 vols.; they include sacred and secular mus. of great historical importance as the predecessor whom Händel and Bach rather developed than discarded; he was born just a hundred years before them and shows great dramatic force and truth in his choral work, combining with the old polyphonic structure a modern fire that makes many of his works still beautiful. Biog. by Ph. Spitta, and Fr. Spitta (1886), also André Pirro (1913).

Schwalm (shvälm), (1) **Robt.**, Erfurt, Dec. 6, 1845—Königsberg, March 6, 1912; pupil of Pflughaupt and Leipzig Cons.; cond. at Königsberg; c. opera, male choruses with orch. oratorio, etc. (2) **Oscar**, Erfurt, Sept. 11, 1856—Berlin, Feb. 11, 1936; pupil of Leipzig Cons.; 1886-88, proprietor of Kahnt's pub.-house in Leipzig; also critic for the *Tageblatt*, etc.; c. an overture; pf.-pcs., etc.

Schwanenberg (shvän'-ĕn-bĕrkh), **Jn. Gf.**, Wolfenbüttel, 1740—Brunswick, 1804; ct.-conductor and dram. composer.

Schwantzer (shvän'-tsĕr), **Hugo**, Oberglogau, 1829—Berlin, 1886; organist, teacher and composer.

Schwarz (shvärts), (1) **Wm.**, Stuttgart, 1825—Berlin, 1878; singer and teacher. (2) **Max**, Hanover, Dec. 1, 1856—Frankfort-on-Main, July 3, 1923; son of above; pupil of Bendel, Bülow, and Liszt; pianist; 1880-83, teacher Hoch Cons., Frankfort; then co-founder, after Raff's death, of the Raff Cons.: from 1885 its dir.

Schwedler (shvāt'-lĕr), **(Otto) Maximilian**, b. Hirschberg, Silesia, March 31, 1853; flutist; pupil of Fr. Meinel, Dresden; in Leipzig municipal and Gewandhaus Orch.; 1895-1918, 1st flute; after 1908 taught at Leipzig Cons.; inv. the "Schwedler flute"; wrote a pamphlet on it and c. transcriptions; d. Leipzig, 1940.

Schweitzer (shvīt'-tsĕr), (1) **Anton**, Coburg, 1735—Gotha, 1787; conductor and composer. (2) **Albert**, b. Colmar, Alsace, 1875; eminent organist and writer of life of Bach; ed. B.'s organ works.

Schwencke (shvĕnk'-ĕ), (1) **Jn. Gl.**, 1744—1823; bassoonist. (2) **Chr. Fr. Gl.**, Wachenhausen, Harz, 1767—Hamburg, 1822; son of above; cantor and mus.-dir. (3) **Jn. Fr.**, Hamburg, 1792—1852; son and pupil of (2); composer. (4) **K.**, Hamburg, 1797—?; pianist; son of (2). (5) **Fr. Gl.**, Hamburg, 1823—1896; virtuoso on the pf. and organ; composer.

Schwindel (shvĭnt'-l), **Fr.**, d. Carlsruhe, 1786; violinist; c. operettas, symphonies, etc.

Schytte (shēt'-tĕ), **L. (Th.)**, Aarhus, Jutland, April 28, 1848—Berlin, Nov. 10, 1909; druggist, then studied with Ree, Neupert, Gebauer, Gade, Taubert, and Liszt (comp.); 1887-88 teacher Horák's Institute, Vienna; lived in Vienna as concert-pianist and teacher; c. 2 comic operas; pf.-concerto; pantomimes for 4 hands, sonata, etc.

Scontrino (skôn-trē'-nō), **A.**, Trapani, 1850—Florence, Jan. 7, 1922; pupil of Platania, Palermo; lived in Milan as teacher; after 1897 prof. of cpt. at Florence Cons.; c. 5 operas, incl. succ. 1-act *"Gringoire"* (1890), and *"La Cortigiana"* (Milan, 1896); c. *"Sinfonia marinaresca"* (Naples, 1897).

Scott, (1) **Lady John Douglas** (née Alicia Ann Spottiswoode); Spottiswoode, 1810—March 12, 1900; composer of *"Annie Laurie,"* and other songs. (2) **Cyril**, b. Oxton, England, Sept. 27, 1879; composer; studied Hoch Cons., Frankfort, with Ivan Knorr and Uzielli; has c. many attractive modern-style works (esp. in smaller forms), some of them exotic in coloring, incl. 2 symphonies, 4 overtures, 2 passacaglias on Irish themes; piano concerto, various chamber music works; also (opera) *"The*

Alchemist," piano music and songs; author "*The Philosophy of Modernism*"; visited U. S. as perf. in his music, 1920.

Scot'ti, Antonio, Naples, Jan. 25, 1866 —Feb. 26, 1936; notable barytone; début Malta, 1889; sang in various cities; from 1899 at Covent Garden and Met. Op. House, N. Y., regularly; famous as "Don Giovanni," and in later years as "Falstaff," "Scarpia," in "*Tosca,*" and the evil Chinese villain in Franco Leoni's 1-act "thriller," "*L'Oracolo.*" One of the most distinguished dram. artists of his period, he was a regular mem. of the Met. Op. Co. until 1933, his 25th anniversary with this co. being marked by special ceremonies in 1924. His last few years were clouded by ill health and poverty, as his fortune had been lost and his farewell perf. was given as a benefit for him; his death occurred obscurely in Naples.

Scotto (skôt'-tō), (1) **Ottaviano,** and his son (2) **Girolamo,** mus.-printers at Venice, 1536–39, and 1539–73, respectively; the latter was also a composer.

Scriabine (skrē-ä'-bĕn), **Alexander Nicolaievitch,** Moscow, Jan. 10, 1872 —April 14, 1915; eminent composer and pianist; pupil of Moscow Cons., studying with Safonoff (piano) and Taneiev (comp.) also with Arensky; after 1892 he lived in Paris, Brussels and Amsterdam, and also toured in various cities of Europe as a pianist; but returned to Moscow and taught in the Cons., 1898–1903; in 1907 he visited the U. S. and in 1914 England, as performer in his works. He devoted the latter part of his life exclusively to composition, living in other countries until 1910, when he again took up res. in Moscow. In his earliest piano works, he was influenced by Chopin, Liszt and Wagner, but he soon developed a markedly personal style, which also shows traces of folk-song inspiration and the nationalist idiom of the Russian Five. The earliest period includes op. 1 to 25, and numbers the 1st 2 symphonies in E (with chorus) and C minor, the piano sonatas, op. 6, 19 and 23; the études of op. 8, and the preludes, op. 11, 15 and 17. In his 2nd period his creative work took on a new, somewhat mysterious

and ecstatic note, and he developed a highly original harmonic system, while his orch. writings were also individual, as exemplified in his "*Divine Poem*" and "*Poème de l'Extase,*" the intensely poignant style of which bears a resemblance to Wagner's "*Tristan*" but is extended to new vehemence of expression. The 2nd period includes also the 4th piano sonata, op. 30; the "*Poème Satanique,*" the 8 études, op. 42, 5th sonata, op. 53, and many smaller pf. works. His 3rd period saw the development of an entirely original harmony based on a so-called "synthetic chord" composed of 7 tones—C, F sharp, B, E, A, D, G —which S. sometimes called the "mystic chord." His theories at this time turned more and more toward the mystical and semireligious, so that he conceived his music as a sort of rite. The works of the final period include "*Prometheus*" (subtitled "*The Poem of Fire*"), scored for orch., piano, organ, chorus and color-organ, the 5 sonatas, op. 62, 64, 66, 68 and 70; the "*Poème Nocturne,*" "*Guirlande*" and "*Vers la Flamme,*" and many briefer piano numbers. He sought to combine the arts of tone, light, and even—in the "*Mysterium*" on which he was working at his death—various elements of smell by the use of perfumes. Studies of S. and his music have been written by Sabaneiev, Karatygin, Gunst, de Schloezer, Hull, Swan, etc. His letters were ed. by Sabaneiev and pub. in Moscow, 1923.

Scribe (skrēb), **Eugène,** Paris, 1791—1861; most prolific of French dramatists, and wrote over 100 librettos, incl. "*Fra Diavolo,*" "*Prophète,*" "*L'Africaine.*"

Scudo (skoo'-dō), **Paolo,** Venice, 1806 —insane, Blois, 1864; writer.

Sea'shore, Carl Emil, b. Mörlunda, Sweden, Jan. 28, 1866; psychologist; grad. Gustavus Adolphus Coll., U. S. A.; Ph. D., Yale Univ., where he taught until 1902; after latter year at State Univ. of Iowa (dean, Grad. Coll., 1908), where he has carried on important experimentation in musical psychology, esp. to determine bases of musical talent; has invented instruments such as audiometer, tonoscope, chronograph, etc., to measure tonal vibrations and the like; author *"The Psychology of Musical Talent,"* 1917, and many important monographs; d. 1949.

Sebald (zä'-bält), Alex., Pesth, April 29, 1869—Chicago, June 30, 1934; violinist; pupil of Saphir and C. Thomson; member of Gewandhaus orch., Leipzig, and toured with Gewandhaus Quartet; toured widely from 1903; was concertm. Berlin Royal Orch.; 1906 taught in Chicago; 1907 opened a school in Berlin; wrote a method and c. violin pieces, etc.

Sebastiani (sä-bäs-tĭ-ä'-nē), Jn., b. Weimar, 1622; conductor and composer.

Šebor (shä'-bôr), K. (Karel), Brandeis, Bohemia, July 18 (Aug. 13 ?), 1843 —Prague, May 17, 1903; pupil Prague Cons. and of Kittl; 1864–67, cond. Nat. Opera; from 1871 military bandm., Vienna; prod. at Prague 5 Czech operas; c. symphs., overtures, etc.

Sechter (zĕkh'-tĕr), Simon, Friedberg, Bohemia, Oct. 11, 1788—Vienna, Sept. 10, 1867; eminent contrapuntist and teacher, ct.-organist, prof. of harm.; wrote valuable treatises; c. burlesque opera *"Ali Hitch-Hasch."*

Seck'endorff, Karl Siegmund, Freiherr von, Erlangen, Nov. 26, 1744—Ansbach, April 26, 1785; c. a monodrama and songs to Goethe's texts.

Seeg(e)r (sā'-gĕr) (or Segert or Zeckert), Joseph Norbert, Rzepin, Bohemia, March 21, 1716—Prague, April 22, 1782; composer; famous organist and teacher; c. toccatas, masses, etc.

Seeling (zā'-lĭng), Hans (Hanuš), Prague, 1828—1862; piano-virtuoso and composer.

Seghers (sŭ-gärs'), Fran. J. Bap., Brussels, 1801 — Margency, near Paris, 1881; violinist and conductor.

Segond (sŭ-gôn), L. A., a physician at Paris; studied singing with Manuel Garcia, and wrote *"Hygiène du chanteur"* (1846), etc.

Segovia (sĕ-gō-vē'-ä), Andrés, b. Jaén, Spain, 1894; guitarist; most eminent performer of his period, incl. Bach and other classics, Spanish romantic school of 19th cent. and modern composers of his country; has toured Europe and U. S.

Seguro'la, Andres de, b. Barcelona— d. there, Jan. 23, 1953; studied law at Barcelona; then took up singing with success; member of Met. Op.

Co. for a decade, then manager of series of morning musicales in N. Y with distinguished clientèle; in later years a voice teacher in Los Angeles, also making film appearances.

Seguin (sĕg'-wĭn), (1) Albert Edw. S., London, 1809—New York, 1852; bass. (2) Elizabeth, his sister, mother of Parepa Rosa. (3) Ann Childe, wife of (1); operatic singer; début, 1828; retired and lived New York, 1880. (4) Wm. H., 1814—1850; bro. of (1); bass.

Seidel (zī'-dĕl), (1) Fr. L., Treuenbrietzen, Brandenburg, 1765—Charlottenburg, 1831; organist and dram. composer. (2) Jn. Julius, Breslau, 1810—1856; organist and writer. (3) Toscha, b. Odessa, Nov. 17, 1899; violinist; studied Petersburg Cons. with Auer; early attracted attention by precocious gifts as youthful virtuoso; début, Oslo, 1915; toured in leading Eur. cities, later in America with succ. as orch. soloist and recitalist; lived in Los Angeles for years; transcribed many pieces for vln.; founded string trio, and has been heard in radio programs.

Seidl (zīt'-'l), (1) Anton, Pesth, May 7, 1850—New York, March 28, 1898; eminent cond., particularly of Wagnerian mus.; pupil Leipzig Cons.; 1870 chorusm. Vienna opera; 1872-79, assisted Wagner in score of *"Nibelungen Ring";* 1879–83 cond. for Neumann's Wagner-troupe; 1883–85 cond. Bremen opera (m. there the soprano (2) Frl. Krauss); 1885–91 Met. Op., N. Y., also from 1895–97 cond. N. Y. Philh. Orch.; 1886 and 1897 cond. at Bayreuth; 1897 cond. Covent Garden, London. (3) Arthur, b. Munich, June 8, 1863; pupil R. Sch. of Mus. at Ratisbon and of Paul, Stade, Spitta, and Bellermann; Dr. Phil., Leipzig, 1887; critic; lectured at Leipzig Cons., 1904–09; writer.

Seifert (zī'-fĕrt), Uso, Römhild, Thuringia, Feb. 9, 1852—Dresden, June 4, 1912; pupil of Dresden Cons.; teacher there and organist; wrote pf.-method, pf.-pcs., etc.

Seiffert (zīf'-fĕrt), Max, b. Beeskow, Feb. 9, 1868; historian and composer; pupil of Spitta; from 1891 at Berlin as author and 1907 Royal Prof.; 1914, mem. of Prussian Academy of Arts; d. Schleswig, Apr. 13, 1948.

Seifriz (zī-frĭts), Max, Rottweil, Würtemberg, 1827—Stuttgart, 1885; violinist, ct.-cond. and composer.

Seiss (zīs), **Isidor** (**Wm.**), Dresden, Dec. 23, 1840—Cologne, Sept. 25, 1905; pianist; pupil of Leipzig Cons.; 1871 pf.-teacher Cologne Cons.; 1878 Prof.; conductor Musikalische Gesellschaft; c. studies in bravura, etc.

Séjan (sā-zhäṅ), **Nicolas**, Paris, 1745—1819; famous organist; 1772, Notre Dame; 1783, St. Sulpice; 1783, royal chapel; teacher and composer.

Sekles (zĕk'-lĕs), **Bernhard**, Frankfort-on-Main, June 20, 1872—Dec. 15, 1934; pupil of Hoch Cons., 1896 teacher of theory there, and after 1923 its dir.; also serving as theatre cond. at Heidelberg and Mainz from 1893; c. opera, "*Schahrazade*" (1917); ballet, "*Der Zwerg und die Infantin*" after Wilde's story (1913); a burlesque stage work, "*Die Hochzeit des Faun*" (1921); symph. poem, "*Aus den Gärten der Semiramis*"; "*Kleine Suite*" for orch.; "*Die Temperamente*," serenade for 11 instruments; passacaglia and fugue for string quartet; 'cello sonata, men's and women's choruses; a number of songs. Wrote book on music dictation, 1905.

Sel'by, Bertram Luard, Kent, Engl., Feb. 12, 1853—Rochester, England, 1919; organist, Salisbury Cath.; 1900–16, at Rochester Cath.; c. 2 operas; a 1-act operetta ("duologue"), successful "*Weather or No*" (London, 1896), Berlin as "*Das Wetterhäuschen*," 1896; org.-sonatas, etc.

Seligmann (za'-lǐkh-män), **Hippolyte Prosper**, Paris, 1817—Monte Carlo, 1882; 'cellist and composer.

Selle (zĕl'-lĕ), **Thos.**, Zorbig, Saxony, 1599—Hamburg, 1663; cantor and composer.

Sellner (zĕl'-nĕr), **Jos.**, Landau, Bavaria, 1787—Vienna, 1843; oboe-virtuoso, teacher, writer and composer.

Sel'mer, Johann, Christiania, Jan. 20, 1844—Venice, July 21, 1910; Norwegian composer; cond. and author; pupil of A. Thomas, Paris, Richter and Paul, Leipzig; 1883–86 cond. Phil. orch., Christiania; c. Norwegian Festival March, "*Scène funèbre*," Finnish Festival Bells, "*In the Mountains*," "*Carnival in Flanders*," etc., for orch., choral works with orch., songs, etc.

Sembach (zĕm'-bakh), **Johannes**, b. Berlin, March 9, 1881; tenor; sang

Vienna, 1903; Dresden, 1907; Met. Op., 1914–17, and after 1920.

Sembrich (zĕm'-brĭkh), **Marcella** (rightly **Praxede Marcelline Kochanska**, Sembrich being her mother's maiden name), Wisniewszyk, Galicia, Feb. 15, 1858—New York, Jan. 11, 1935; eminent colorature soprano; pupil (later the wife) of Wm. Stengel (piano), Lemberg Cons.; studied with Epstein at Vienna, and singing with Victor Rokitansky and with G. B. Lamperti, Jr., at Milan, début, May, 1877, at Athens; studied German opera at Berlin with Lewy; sang for 18 months Dresden ct.-th.; from June, 1880, London, and, 1883–84, toured Europe and America; 1884, studied with Francesco Lamperti, Sr.; 1898–1909 sang at Met. Op. and in concert in America with greatest succ.; 1900, managed her own opera co. in Germany; in later years she was active as a master teacher at Juilliard School of Music, N. Y., and Curtis Inst. of Music, Philadelphia.

Semet (sŭ-mā), **Théophile** (**Aimé Émile**), Lille, 1824—Corbeil, near Paris, 1888; drummer and dram. composer.

Senaillé (sŭn-ĭ-yā), **Jean Baptiste**, Paris, Nov. 23, 1687—Oct. 8, 1730; famous violinist; at court of Louis XV.; c. violin sonatas, etc.

Senesino (sān-ĕ-sē'-nō), **Bernardi Francesco** (called the Sienese), Siena, 1680—ca. 1750; male contralto or mezzo-sopr.; sang in Händel's operas till 1729, where he quarrelled with H. and went over to Bononcini; made a fortune and returned to Siena.

Senff (zĕnf), **Bartholf**, Friedrichshall, near Coburg, 1815—Badenweiler, 1900; founder Leipzig mus.-pub. house (1850), also editor.

Sen(f)fl (zĕnf'l) (or **Senfel**), **L.**, Zurich (?), ca. 1492—Munich, ca. 1555; eminent contrapuntist, ct.-cond. and composer.

Senger-Bettaque (zĕng'-kĕr-bĕt-täk-vĕ), **Katharina**, b. Berlin, Aug. 2, 1862; soprano; a ballet dancer at the Imperial Opera, Berlin, then studied with Dorn, and 1879 appeared on the same stage in soubrette rôles; sang in various cities, 1888 in Bayreuth as "Eva"; 1895 married the actor Alex. Senger; in later years a teacher.

Senkrah (zān'-krā) (rightly **Hark'ness**), **Arma Leorette**, New York, 1864—

suicide, Weimar, Aug. 4, 1900; violinist; pupil of Arno Hilf, Leipzig; Wieniawski, and Massart, Paris Cons.; toured with succ.

Serafin (sä'-rä-fēn), **Tullio**, b. Rottanova di Cavazzere, Dec. 8, 1878; conductor; studied at Milan Cons.; début at Ferrara; later cond. opera at La Scala, at Rome, Florence, Bologna, Venice, Turin (also symph. concerts), in South America; leading cond. of Italian works at Met. Op. House, for a decade after 1924; thereafter general dir. of Rome Royal Op.; m. Elena Rakowska, soprano.

Serafino (sä-rä-fē'-nō), (1) **Santo**, vln.-maker at Venice, 1730–45; his label is "Sanctus Seraphin Utinensis fecit Venetiis, Anno, 17—". (2) **Gregorio**, his nephew, also was a vln.-maker, label "Georgius Seraphin Sancti nepos fecit Venetiis, 17—."

Serassi (sä-räs'-sē), Italian family of org.-builders at Bergamo. The founder (1) **Giuseppe** (*il vecchio*), Gordano, 1694—Crema, 1760. His son (2) **Andrea Luigi**, 1725—1799. (3) **Giuseppe** (*il giovane*), Bergamo, 1750—1817; succeeded by his sons (4) **Carlo** and (5) **Giuseppe**.

Serato (sä-rä'-tō), **Arrigo**, b. Bologna, Feb. 7, 1877; violinist, son and pupil of a violinist and prof. at the cons.; later pupil of Sarti; played with success in Germany and elsewhere; after 1914 taught at Liceo of Santa Cecilia, Rome; d. 1949.

Ser'kin, Rudolf, b. Eger, Bohemia, March 28, 1903; pianist; his parents were Russian, but became Austrian citizens; pupil of Richard Robert, also in comp. with Marx and Schönberg; at 12 played concerto in Vienna, after 1920 appeared with succ. in Berlin; esp. known for sonata recitals with Adolf Busch, with whom he made Amer. début at Washington Festival.

Sermisy (sĕr-mē-sē), **Claude de** (called **Claudin**, not **Claudin Lejeune**), ca. 1490—1562; French ct.-cond., composer.

Serov (or **Sjeroff, Syeroff** (s'yä-rôf)); **Alex. Nikolajevitch**, Petersburg, Jan. 23, 1820—Feb. 1 (new style), 1871; important Russian composer and critic; a lawyer, studied 'cello with Karl Schuberth; 1863 prod. grand opera (text and mus.) "*Judith*," and the Czar granted him a pension; he was a lecturer on mus. at Moscow and Petersb. Universities and wrote his own librettos; 1865 prod. "*Rogneda*" with succ.; laid aside 2 unfinished operas to finish "*Wrazyiasiela*" but died before it was done. Soloviev finished it and it was prod. with succ.

Serpette (sĕr-pĕt), (**H. Chas. A.**) **Gaston**, Nantes, Nov. 4, 1846—Paris, Nov. 3, 1904; pupil of Thomas, Paris Cons.; 1871, taking 1st Grand prix de Rome, wrote cantata "*Jeanne d'Arc*"; 1874, prod. opera-bouffe "*La Branche Cassée*" (Bouffes-Parisiens), followed by 30 other light works.

Serrão (sĕr-rä'-nō), **Paolo**, Filadelfia, Catanzaro, 1830—Naples, March 17, 1907; pupil of Naples Cons.; political troubles prevented the prod. of his opera "*L'Impostore*" in 1852, and another in 1857, but he prod. "*Pergolesi*" and "*La Duchessa di Guisa*" (1865), and "*Il Figliuol prodigo*" (1868); c. also an oratorio, a requiem, a funeral symph. (for Mercadante), etc.

Serran'o (or **Serrão**), **Emilio**, b. Vitoria, 1850; court pianist at Madrid; prof. at the Cons., and dir. of Royal Opera; c. operas.

Servais (sĕr-vĕ), (1) **Adrien Fran.**, Hal, near Brussels, 1807—1866; eminent 'cellist and teacher; pupil of his father and of Platel, début Paris. 1834; 1848, Prof. Brussels Cons. and soloist to the King; toured widely; c. 3 concertos for 'cello, etc. (2) **Jos.**, Hal, 1850—1885; son and pupil of above; 'cellist and prof. Brussels Cons. (3) **Franz** or **François** (Matthieu), 1844—Asnières, Jan. 14, 1901; cond. at Brussels; c. opera "*L'Appolonide*" or "*Ion*" (Carlsruhe 1899). Son of Adrien Fr. (q. v.).

Sessions (sĕsh'-ŏns), **Roger**, b. Brooklyn, N. Y., Dec. 28, 1896; composer; studied Yale School of Music with Parker, also with Ernest Bloch; taught theory, Cleveland Inst. of Music, 1921–25; awarded Damrosch Fellowship at Amer. Acad. in Rome, 1928; founded (with Aaron Copland) Copland - Sessions Concerts; dir. school of music, N. Y.; c. 2 symphonies (1st played by Boston Symph. and at Internat'l Soc. for Contemp. Music Fest., Geneva); incidental music to Andreyeff's "*Black Maskers*," suite which has been perf. by many Amer. orchs.; vln. concerto; prof. of mus., Princeton U., 1953.

Setaccioli (sā-tä-chē-ōl'-ē), Giacomo, Corneto Tarquinia, Italy, Dec. 8, 1868—Siena, Dec. 5, 1925; composer; studied at Liceo of Santa Cecila, Rome, where his opera, "*La Sorella di Mark*," was given at Costanzi Theatre, 1896; c. (opera) "*Adrienne Lecouvreur*"; theory teacher after 1922 at St. Cecilia Acad., and succeeded Pizzetti as dir. of Cherubini Cons., Florence, 1925.

Ševcik (shěf'-chĭk), Otokar, Horaždiowitz, Bohemia, March 22, 1852—Pisek, Jan. 18, 1934; famous violin teacher; pupil of Prague Cons.; from 1870 concertmaster various cities; 1875 prof. at Kiev; 1892-1906 at Prague Cons.; 1909-19, dir. of master school of vln., Vienna State Cons.; later taught in U. S. and at Pisek; teacher of Kubelik, Kocian, etc.; author of methods; c. Bohemian dances, variations, etc.

Sévérac (sā-vā-răk), Déodat de, Saint Felix, July 20, 1873—Roussillon, March 23, 1921; writer and composer; pupil Toulouse Cons., and the Schola cantorum, Paris; c. 2-act lyric drama "*Le Cœur de Moulin*" (Op. Com. Paris, 1909); lyric tragedy "*Héliogabale*" (Arènes de Beziers, 1910); "*Muguetto*" (1911); "*Hélène de Sparte*" (Paris 1912); symph. poems, "*Nymphes au Crépuscule*" and "*Didon et Enée*"; a piano sonata, etc.

Sevitzky (sē-vēt'-skē), Fabien, b. Vishni Volotchek, Russia, Sept. 30, 1893; (family name, Koussevitzky, nephew of Serge); conductor; studied Petersburg Cons. with Siloti and Liadoff, grad. with gold medal; played with Moscow Imp. Theatre orch.; coming to America, he founded Chamber String Sinfonietta at Phila.; also for a time cond. of Boston People's Symph.; 1937, appointed cond. of Indianapolis Symph.; m. Maria Koussevitzky, singer.

Seyffardt (zīf'-färt), Ernst Hn., b. Crefeld, 1859; pupil of Cologne Cons. and of Kiel; 1892-1924, conductor Neuer Singverein, Stuttgart; c. dram. scene "*Thusnelda*," "*Trauerfeier beim Tode einer Jungfrau*," sonatas, MS. opera "*The Bells of Plurs*," etc.; d. Partenkirchen, 1942.

Seyfried (zī'-frēt), Ignaz X., Ritter von, Vienna, 1776—1841; conductor, writer and dram. composer.

Sey'mour, John Laurence, b. Los An-

geles, 1893; c. 1-act opera, "*In the Pasha's Garden*," Met. Op., 1935.

Sgambati (sgäm-bä'-tē), Giovanni, Rome, May 28, 1843—Dec. 15, 1914; important pianist and conductor; pupil of Aldega, Barbieri and Natalucci, later of Liszt; at 6 played in public, sang in Church and cond. small orchestras; later he toured Italy and Germany; 1877, head-teacher Accad. di S. Cecilia, Rome; 1896, founded "Nuova Società Musicale Romana"; admirer and friend of Wagner; c. requiem with orch. (1896), 2 symphs., overtures, pf.-concerto, an octet, 2 pf.-quintets, a string-quartet (op. 17) and piano pcs., etc.

Shakespeare, Wm., Croydon, Engl., June 16, 1849—Golders Green, Nov. 1, 1931; noted voice teacher; at 13 organist; pupil of Molique (comp.); 1866, won King's scholarship R.A.M., and studied there with Bennett; 1871, took Mendelssohn Scholarship for pf.-playing and comp.; studied with Reinecke, Leipzig; 1872, singing at Milan; from 1875, concert and oratorio-singer; 1878, prof. of singing, R.A.M.; in 1880, 1886, cond. of the concerts there; resigned; won high reputation as a singing-teacher; c. overtures, a symph., pf.-concerto, etc.

Sha'porin, Yuri, b. Glukhov, Chernigovski Province, Russia, 1889; composer; pupil of Leningrad Cons., studying with Sokolov, Tcherepnine and M. Steinberg; c. incidental music for plays, piano sonatas, choral and orch. works; (opera) "*The Decembrists*" (text by A. N. Tolstoy), and a symph. in C minor with chorus, portraying events in Russian revolution of 1917 (perf. in London and U. S.).

Sharp, Cecil James, London, Nov. 22, 1859—Hampstead, England, June 23, 1924; writer and collector of folk music; grad. Cambridge Univ.; assoc. to Chief Justice of So. Australia, 1883-89; principal, Hampstead Cons. of Music, London, 1896-1905; after 1911 dir. of Stratford-on-Avon School of Folk-song; author of valuable collections of British folk-songs, dances, etc.; spent several years in Kentucky Mountains, collecting material.

Sharpe, Herbert Francis, Halifax, Yorkshire, March 1, 1861—London, Oct. 14, 1925; Queen's Scholar, Nat. Training Sch., London; gave pf.-concerts; 1884, prof. R. C. M.; 1890, examiner; wrote "*Pianoforte Sch.*" (with Stanley Lucas); c. comic opera, etc.

Shat'tuck, Arthur, b. Neenah, Wis., April 19, 1881; pianist; pupil of Leschetizky; début as soloist with the Copenhagen Philh.; made many tours; d. N. Y., Oct. 16, 1951.

Sha'vitch, Vladimir, b. Russia; conductor; studied with Godowsky, Busoni, Kaun and Juon; cond. Syracuse (N. Y.) Symph. for several years after 1924; appeared at Moscow State Op., 1929; guest cond. of London Symph., and orchs. in Berlin, Paris, Madrid, Moscow, Leningrad, also in Detroit, San Francisco and Los Angeles; res. in London, where he has promoted a mechanical device to reproduce orch. and chorus in opera, synchronised with actual soloists; d. W. Palm Beach, Fla., 1947.

Shaw, (1) Mary, London, 1814—Hadleigh, Suffolk, 1876; noted contralto and teacher. (2) **Bernard,** b. Dublin, 1856—1950; noted critic, playwright, in his early days a music and dram. critic; author, "*The Perfect Wagnerite,*" etc. (3) **Geoffrey,** b. Clapham, Nov. 14, 1879; studied at St. Paul's Cath. Choir School; at Derby School and at Cambridge with Wood and Stanford; c. church and other music. His bro. (4) **Martin,** b. London, March 9, 1876; composer; studied at R. C. M. with Stanford; organist and dir. of League of Arts; c. church music, a ballad opera, "*Mr. Pepys,*" incidental music to plays, chamber and orch. works, etc.; author, "*Principles of Church Music Comp.*"; ed. "*Songs of Britain,*" etc.

Shed'lock, John South, Reading, Engl., 1843—London, Jan. 9, 1919; graduate, London Univ., 1864; pupil of E. Lübeck (pf.) and Lalo (comp.), Paris; teacher and concert-pianist, London, 1879; critic for the *Athenæum;* also lectured at the R. A. M.; pub. articles, "*The Pianoforte Sonata, Its Origin and Development*" (London, 1895); editor and translator; c. string-quartet, etc.

Shel'ley, Harry Rowe, b. New Haven, Conn., June 8, 1858; pupil of Stoeckel at Yale, Dudley Buck, Vogrich and Dvořák (New York); organist various churches, also teacher of theory and comp. Metropolitan College, N. Y.; c. "*The Inheritance Divine,*"

sacred cantata, 2 symphs. (the first Eb, performed, N. Y., 1897), vln.-concerto (1891), cantata "*Vexilla Regis*" (N. Y., 1894), and suite "*Baden-Baden,*" etc., for orch.; church-mus., pf. and org.-pcs. and songs;d.nearNewHaven,Conn.,1947.

Shep'ard, (1) Thos. Griffin, Madison, Conn., April 23, 1848—Brooklyn, N. Y., 1905; pupil of G. W. and J. P. Morgan; organist various churches in New Haven; instructor, Yale Glee Club and cond. Oratorio Soc., also dir. Apollo Club (male voices); teacher and critic; c. comic opera, Christmas cantata, etc. (2) **Frank Hartson,** Bethel, Conn., Sept. 20, 1863—Orange, N. J., 1913; pupil of Thayer, Boston; organist various towns; 1886-90, studied Leipzig; 1888, organist English Chapel there; 1891, est. a sch. at Orange, N. J.; organist there; writer of text-books and treatises.

Shepherd, Arthur, b. Paris, Idaho, Feb. 19, 1880; 1892, pupil at N. E. Cons. Boston, of Dennée and Faelten (piano), Benj. Cutter (harmony); Goetschius and Chadwick (comp.); graduated 1897, and settled in Salt Lake City as teacher; cond. Salt Lake Symph. Orch.; from 1909, teacher of piano, harmony and cpt. at N. E. Cons.; 1902, won Paderewski prize with "*Ouverture Joyeuse*"; 1909 won two Nat. Fed. prizes with piano sonata, and song, "*The Lost Child*"; c. also barytone solo with chor. and orch., songs and piano pieces; 1920, asst. cond., Cleveland Orch.; prof. of music, Western Reserve Univ. and critic.

Sher'wood, (1) Wm. Hall, Lyons, N. Y., Jan. 31, 1854—Chicago, Jan. 7, 1911; noteworthy pianist and teacher of piano; son and pupil of Rev. L. H. Sherwood, founder of Lyons Mus. Acad.; pupil also of Heimberger, Pychowski and Wm. Mason; studied 5 years under Th. Kullak, Weitzmann, Wuerst and Deppe (Berlin), Richter (Leipzig), K. Doppler and Scotson Clark (Stuttgart) and Liszt (Weimar); début with succ., Berlin; returned 1876 to the U. S., and toured with great succ.; teacher N. E. Cons., Boston, later, New York; 1889. Chicago, as head of the pf.-section of the Cons.; 1897, founded "Sherwood Piano Sch."; 1887 he m. his

pupil, Estella F. Adams, also pianist;
pub. pf.-pcs. (2) **Percy**, b. of English parents, Dresden, May 23, 1866;
pupil of Hermann Scholtz (pf.); later
of Dresden Cons.; concert-pianist
and until 1914, teacher, Dresden
Cons.; later active in London; c.
pf.-pcs.

Shield, Wm., Whickham, Durham,
1748—London, 1829; violinist, writer
and composer.

Shostako'vitch, Dimitri, b. St. Petersburg, Sept. 16, 1906; composer; pupil
of Glazounoff and Steinberg at Cons.;
precocious musician; while still in his
twenties he attracted attention for
an opera, "*The Nose*"; this was followed by other stage works and
orch. music, incl. several symphs.,
chamber music, and piano works; his
symphs. played in America by Stokowski with the Phila. Orch., were
given speedily by other ensembles, as
were subsequent works in this form;
in substance, his music is synthetic,
combining older styles, and marked
by a virtuosic, often flippant and
ironic touch; a consummate orchestrator and a humorist of pungent
variety, S. made an international
furore with his opera, "*Katerina
Ismailova*" (known also as "*Lady
Macbeth of Mzensk*"), which treats a
brutal drama of lust, intrigue and
murder in a bold, realistic manner;
first prod. at Leningrad, it was highly
popular in other Russian theatres
and was prod. in America by the
Cleveland Orch. and Russian singers
under Rodzinski both in its own city
and N. Y. at the Met. Op. House in
1935; this work, heard in concert
form in London also, was later suppressed by the Soviet authorities,
together with his ballet, "*Limpid
Stream*," on the grounds that the
composer was misusing his talents by
cultivating a "formalistic" and sensational style of writing; he was encouraged to hew closer to the classic
line of Russian music by being commissioned to prepare a new ballet;
c. also a piano concerto, a sonata and
smaller works for this instrument;
some of his symphs. (notably that
known as "*May Day*") include programs of revolutionary content.

Shudi. Vide BROADWOOD.

Sibelius (sē-bā'-lē-ōōs), **Jan**, b. Tavastehus, Finland, Dec. 8, 1865; one of
the most important and original

composers of his period, influential
not so much through any outward
modernity of musical speech, as by
the power and freedom with which
he has used traditional material to
gain new expressive results.
As a boy he played piano, improvised
and wrote simple compositions; at 15
began vln. study with a local bandmaster; played in school orch. and in
chamber music groups, but was entered as a student of law at Univ. of
Helsingfors, 1885. Later he gave up
law and in 1889 went to Berlin for
further study, then to Vienna, where
he was a pupil of Carl Goldmark,
Robert Fuchs and others. He married Aino Järnefelt, and returned to
his native country, 1892.
His first composition to attract wide
attention was his orch. work, "*En
Saga*." He taught comp. and vln.
at the Helsingfors Music Inst. for a
brief period, but after 1900 received
a stipend from the Finnish Government to devote himself exclusively to
comp. He visited Paris in 1900 and
led some of his works at the Exposition there with the Helsingfors Orch.
under Kajanus. In the following
year he also conducted at Heidelberg
Fest.
His later career has been one of increasing honours, with esp. esteem
from his countrymen, who celebrated
his 70th birthday anniversary in 1935
with an official fest. at Helsingfors,
when the highest tributes were paid
him. His journeys to other countries included a visit to America in
1914, when he led his symph. poem,
"*Daughters of the Ocean*," at the
Norfolk Fest., and Yale Univ. conferred on him the degree of Mus. D.
His music in the larger forms, incl.
7 monumental symphs., was fairly
slow in making its way into the
repertoires of other countries, but
esp. in England and America has in
recent years been assigned a place
among the most important of the
present day.
In addition, his works include:
(orch.) "*Pohjola's Daughter*"; "*The
Swan of Tuonela*"; "*Karelia*"; "*Tapiola*"; "*Frühlingslied*"; "*Lemminkainen's Homecoming*"; "*The Dryads*"; "*Pelleas und Melisande*";
"*Night Ride and Sunrise*"; "*Pan
and Echo*" (dance intermezzo); 2
orch. suites, called "*Scènes Histo-*

riques"; *"Suite caracteristique"*; 2 Serenades for vln. and orch.; *"The Bard"*; (symph. poem); and the pop. nationalistic tone poem, *"Finlandia"*; (chamber music) *"Voces Intimae"* for string quartet; vln. pieces; (opera) *"Die Jungfrau im Turme"*; incid. music to Ad. Paul's drama, *"King Christian II."*; to Procope's *"Belshazzar,"* and to the morality play, *"Everyman"*; (chorus) Academic Festival Cantata; *"Gesang der Athener"* and *"Die Gefangene Königin,"* both for chorus and orch.; *"Des Fahrmanns Braut"* for barytore and orch.; *"My Land"* for mixed chorus and orch.; *"Jordens Sang"* (Der Erde Lied) for mixed chorus, female solo choir and orch.; *"Maan Virsi,"* cantata for mixed chorus and orch.; (pantomime) *"Scaramouche"* (Copenhagen, 1922); also many male choruses, songs and piano works.

In his larger compositions, S. has shown an original method of construction, developing his themes out of short units which later coalesce into their final form. His inspirations are drawn very largely from Nature, and though his works are "absolute" music in the highest sense, many of them contain picturesque legendary suggestions from the Finnish epics, such as the *"Kalevala."* It is, however, not true that his personality is essentially a gloomy or mystical one, for there are boisterous humor and rude strength in many of his works. S. is the subject of important biographies and studies by Rosa Newmarch, Cecil Gray, Walter Niemann, etc. (See article, page 526.)

Siboni (sē-bō'-nē), (1) **Giu.**, Forli, 1780 — Copenhagen, 1839; tenor. (2) **Erik (Anton Waldemar)**, Copenhagen, 1828—1892; pianist, organist, teacher and dram. composer. (3) **Johanna Frederika** (née Crull), Rostock, Jan. 30, 1839—(?); pianist; pupil of Moscheles; 1866 m. above.

Sichra (sĭkh'-rä), **Andreas Ossipovich**, Wilna, 1772—St. Petersburg, 1861; guitarist and composer.

Sick (sĭk), **Theodor Bernhard**, Copenhagen, Nov. 7, 1827—1893; artillery officer and composer of chamber music.

Sieber (zē'-bĕr), **Fd.**, Vienna, 1822—Berlin, 1895; famous singing-teacher.

Siegel (zē'-gĕl), (1) **E. F. W.**, d. 1869;

founded, 1846, mus.-pub. firm at Leipzig, later owned by R. Linnemann. (2) **F.** Vide SCHUBERTH, J.

Sieveking (zē'-vĕ-kĭng), **Martinus**, b. Amsterdam, March 24, 1867; notable pianist; pupil of his father, of J. Röntgen, Leipzig Cons., and Coenen (harm.); 1890 played in London; made v. succ. tours; 1895 Boston; 1896–97 American tour; from 1915 dir. of a music school in N. Y.; c. a suite (played by Lamoureux, Paris), etc.

Siface (sē-fä'-chĕ) (rightly **Grossi**), **Giov. Fran.**, robbed and murdered in Northern Italy, ca. 1699; sopranomusico; ca. 1675 member Papal Chapel.

Sighicelli (sē-gĭ-chĕl'-lē), family of violinists. (1) **Filippo**, San Cesario, Modena, 1686—Modena, 1773; violinist. (2) **Giu.**, Modena, 1737—·1826; son of above; violinist. (3) **Carlo**, Modena, 1772—1806; son of (2), also attached to court. (4) **A.**, Modena, 1802—1883; son of (3); eminent violinist and conductor. (5) **V.**, Cento, July 30, 1830—Paris, Feb. 15, 1905; son and pupil of (4); pupil of Hellmesberger, Mayseder, and 1849 solo-violinist and 2nd ct.-cond. Modena; from 1855, teacher Paris; c. vln.-fantasias, etc.

Sigismondi (sē-jĭs-môn'-dē), **Giu.**, Naples, 1739—1826; singing-teacher and dram. composer.

Silas (sē'läs), **Éduard**, Amsterdam, Aug. 22, 1827—West Kensington, England, Feb. 8, 1909; pianist; début Amsterdam, 1837; pupil of Neher, Kalkbrenner, etc.; later of Benoist and Halévy, Paris Cons.; winning 1st prize for org. playing, 1849, in competition with Saint-Saëns and Cohen; since 1890 lived in England as organist; 1866 Assemblée général des Catholiques en Belgique awarded him 1st prize (gold medal and 1,000 francs) for a mass; later prof. of harm. Guildhall Sch. and the London Acad. of Mus.; c. oratorio *"Joash"* (Norwich Fest., 1863), Kyrie Eleison with orch., 3 symphs., 3 overtures etc.

Silbermann (zēl'-bĕr-män), (1) **Andreas**, Klein-Bobritzsch, Saxony, 1678 — Strassburg, 1734; org. builder at Strassburg. (2) **Gf.**, Klein-Bobritzsch, 1683 — Dresden, 1753; bro. of above and his apprentice; the first German to manufacture pianofortes, but preceded by Cristo-

tori; inv. *cembal d'amour* (v. D. D.).
(3) **Jn. Andreas**, Strassburg, 1712—
1783; son of (1); org.-builder.
(4) **Jn. Daniel**, 1717—Leipzig, 1766;
son of (1), successor of (2). (5) **Jn.
H.**, Strassburg, 1727—1799; son of
(1); pf.-maker. (6) **Jn. Fr.**, 1762—
1817; son of (5), org.-builder, organist and composer.
Silcher (zĭl'-khĕr), **Fr.**, Schnait,
Württemberg, 1789—Tübingen, 1860;
noted song-composer; pupil of his
father and of Auberlen; teacher at
Stuttgart, 1817; mus.-dir. at Tübingen Univ.; pub. a text-book and
collected and c. chorals, etc.
Siloti (sē'-lō-tē), **Alex.**, b. Charkov,
1863—N.Y., 1945; pianist, pupil
of Zwereff and of N. Rubinstein and
Tchaikovsky, Moscow Cons.; winning a gold medal; début, Moscow,
1880; studied with Liszt 3 years;
1887-90, prof. Moscow Cons.; made
v. succ. tours, 1898-90, America;
1901, appeared as cond. with Philh.
in Moscow; 1904, founded his own
orch. in St. Petersburg for notable
concerts, until 1919; since 1922 he
has lived in N. Y., as faculty mem.,
Juilliard School of Music, and has
made appearances as recitalist and
orch. soloist; c. pf.-pieces.
Silva (zēl'-vä), (1) **Andreas de**, 16th
cent. contrapuntist; c. motets, etc.
(2) **David Poll de**, St. Esprit, near
Bayonne, 1834 — Clermont, Oise,
1875; blind; pupil of his mother who
c. operas, oratorios, etc.; wrote out
his comp. by dictation.
Silver (sĕl-vār), **Chas.**, Paris, April 16,
1868; pupil of Dubois and Massenet
at the Cons.; won Grand prix de
Rome with cantata "*L'Interdit*"; c.
operetta, elegiac poem "*Raïs*"; 4-act
fairy opera "*La Belle au Bois Dormant*" (Paris, 1895), oratorio "*Tobie*"; opera, "*La Mégère Apprivoi-
sée*," 1922, etc.
Simandl (zē'-mänt'l), **Fz.**, Blatna, 1840
—Vienna, 1912; 1st double-bass
Vienna court orch.; 1869 teacher at
the Cons.; pub. method for contrabass.
Simão. Vide PORTUGAL.
Simon (sē'-môn), (1) **Jean Henri**, Antwerp, 1783—1861; violinist. (2) **Anton Yulievich**, France, 1851—?;
composer; pupil of Paris Cons.; 1871
theatre cond. in Moscow; 1891 prof.
at Phil. Society School; c. 6 operas,
symph. poems. etc.

Simons-Candeille. Vide CANDEILLE.
Simp'son (or **Sympson**), (1) **Chp.**, d.
London, ca. 1677; player on the
viola da gamba; pub. text-books.
(2) **Thos.**, b. England; from ca. 1615,
violinist in Germany; composer.
Sim'rock, (1) **Nicolaus**, Bonn, 1752—
1834; founded there 1790 mus.-pub.
house; 1805 Berlin branch founded
by his son (2) **Peter Jos.**; 1870 in
Berlin under (3), **Fritz**, 1841—
Lausanne, Sept., 1901.
Sin'clair (sink'lĕr), **J.**, near Edinburgh, 1791—Margate, 1857; tenor.
Sinding (zĭnt'-ĭng), **Christian**, b.
Kongsberg, Norway, Jan. 11, 1856;
Oslo, Dec. 3, 1941; composer; pupil
Leipzig Cons., later with Royal
Scholarship, studied at Dresden,
Munich, and Berlin; lived in Christiania as organist and teacher; in
1915 he was granted a govt. pension
for life to enable him to give all his
time to comp.; in 1921-22 he accepted a call to the Eastman School,
Rochester, N. Y., as guest teacher of
comp., returning afterward to Norway. In his own country he is
accounted next to Grieg in importance as a nationalistic composer.
His large output includes 3 symphs.;
piano concerto; 3 vln. concertos and
many smaller pieces of this instrument; suite "*Episodes Chevale-
resques*"; "*Rondo Infinito*"; suite in
A minor; "*Legende*" and Romanze
in D, for orch. with vln.; piano
quintet; string quartet; 3 piano trios;
2 serenades for two violins and
piano; vln. suites, variations, etc.;
pf.-sonata, suite, variations, and
many smaller pieces, incl. the pop.
"*Frühlingsräuschen*"; also an opera,
"*Der Heilige Berg*" and more than
200 songs and other vocal works.
Singelée (sănzh-lā), **J. Bap.**, Brussels,
1812—Ostend, 1875; violinist and
composer.
Singer (zĭng'-ĕr), (1) **Peter**, Häfelgehr
(Lechthal), 1810—Salzburg, 1882;
monk; inv. (1839) the "Pansym-
phonikon" (v. D. D.); composer.
(2) **Edmund**, Totis, Hungary, Oct.
14, 1830—Stuttgart, Jan. 23, 1912;
violinist; pupil of Ellinger, at Pesth,
then of Kohne; toured, then studied
with Jos. Böhm, Vienna, and at Paris
Cons.; 1853-61 leader at Weimar,
then leader at Stuttgart, and prof.
at the Cons. (3) **Otto**, Sora, Saxony,
1833—New York, 1894; pianist.

conductor, teacher and composer. (4) **Otto, Jr.,** Dresden, 1863— Leipzig, 1931; violinist; studied under Kiel and Rheinberger; 1899, taught Cologne Cons. and cond.; later in Leipzig. (5) **Richard,** Budapest, 1879—N. Y., 1940; pianist; pupil, Leschetizky and Busoni; toured widely.

Singher (săn-gär'), **Martial,** French barytone; studied at Paris Cons.; sang leading roles at Paris Op., incl. Wotan; début, Met. Op., 1943.

Sin'ico, (1) **Francesco,** Trieste, 1810—1865; conductor and composer. His son (2) **Giuseppe,** Trieste, Feb. 10, 1836—Dec. 31, 1907, c. operas.

Sinigaglia (sē-nĭ-gäl'-yä), **Leone,** b. Turin, Aug. 14, 1868; pupil of the Cons. and of Mandyczewski; c. violin concerto, rhapsody *"Piemontese,"* for violin and orch., string quartet, concert étude for quartet, overture *"Le baruffe chiozzotte,"* etc.; d. 1944.

Sir'men (Syrmen), (1) **Luigi,** violinist and cond. at Bergamo; his wife, (2) **Maddalena Lombardini de,** b. Venice, 1735—d. towards end of cent.; prominent violinist; pupil of Tartini; later singer and composer.

Sistermanns (zĭst'-ĕr-mäns), **Anton,** Herzogenbusch, Holland, Aug. 5, 1865—March 18, 1926; bass; pupil of Stockhausen; 1899, sang "Pogner" at Bayreuth; 1904–15, taught Scharwenka Cons., Berlin, later lived in The Hague.

Sitt (zĭt), **Hans,** Prague, Sept. 21, 1850—Leipzig, March 10, 1922; violinist; studied Prague Cons.; 1867, leader theatre-orch., Breslau; 1869, cond. there, later in Prague, etc.; 1883, teacher of vln. Leipzig Cons. and vla.-player Brodsky Quartet; cond. of various societies; c. 3 vln.-concertos, a vla.-concerto, a 'cello-concerto, etc.

Sittard (sĭt-tär), (1) **Josef,** Aix-la-Chapelle, June 4, 1846—Hamburg, Nov. 23, 1903; pupil, Stuttgart Cons., later teacher of singing and pf. there; lecturer on mus.; 1885, critic; 1891, prof.; writer and composer. (2) **Alfred,** b. Stuttgart, Nov. 4, 1878; organist; son and pupil of (1), also of Armbrust and Koehler, later of Cologne Cons.; won Mendelssohn Prize 1902; 1903, org. of Dresden Kreuzkirche; after 1912 of the new Michaeliskirche in Hamburg and also cond. of choir there.

Sivori (sē-vō'-rē), **Ernesto Camillo,** Genoa, 1815—1894; famous violinist and composer; début at 6; pupil of Costa and Paganini; toured widely.

Sjögren (shäkh'-rĕn), (**Jn. Gv.**) **Emil,** Stockholm, June 16, 1853—March 4, 1918; pupil of the Cons. there; later of Kiel (cpt.) and Haupt (org. at Berlin); 1890, organist Johankirke, Stockholm; c. sonatas, vln. and piano works, songs, etc.

Skil'ton, Charles Sanford, b. Northampton, Mass., 1868—Lawrence, Kan., Mar. 12, 1941; studied Berlin Hochsch. with Bargiel and Boise, also Dudley Buck in N. Y.; prof. organ, theory and history of music, State Univ. of Kansas after 1903; c. orch. and other music, some of it based on Indian themes, which has had repeated hearings.

Skriabine, vide SCRIABINE.

Skroup (or Skraup) (shkroop or shkrä'-oop), (1) **Fz.** (**František**), Vosic, Bohemia, 1801—Rotterdam, 1862; conductor and dram. composer. (2) **Jan Nepomuk,** Vosic, 1811—Prague, 1892; bro. of above; conductor, singing-teacher, writer and dram. composer.

Skuherský (skoo'-hĕr-shkē), **Fz.** (**František**) **Sdenko,** Opocno, Bohemia, 1830—Budweis, 1892; organist, conductor, theorist and composer.

Slaughter (slôt'-ĕr), **A. Walter,** London, 1860—March 2, 1908; chorister at St. Andrew's, Wells St., London; pupil of A. Cellier and Jacobi; cond. Drury Lane and St. James's Th.; prod. comic operas and a succ. mus.-comedy "*The French Maid*" (1897), etc.

Slavik (slä'-vēk), **Jos.,** Jince, Bohemia, 1806—Pesth, 1833; violinist.

Slenczynski (slĕn-chēn'-skē), **Ruth,** b. Sacramento, Cal., Jan. 15, 1925; pianist of remarkable precocity; the daughter of a violinist; had 1st piano lesson at age of 3 and at 4 gave her 1st concert in Oakland, Cal.; at 5, played before audience of 3,500 at San Francisco; she was taken to Berlin for further study, and a year later, in 1931, gave a concert at the Bach Saal there, astonishing an audience of musical authorities by the ease with which she played an extended program of taxing masterpieces; 1932, at 7 made début in Paris with equally amazing results; one of her typical recitals incl. a Bach and Mozart sonata, a Chopin group, Beethoven's theme and variations on "*Nel cor piu mi sento*," and 2 Schubert works; following this she returned to the U. S. and gave concerts to triumphal ovations.

Slezak (slĕt'-säk), (1) Leo, b. Schönberg, 1875—Bavaria, June, 1946; tenor; studied with Robinson in Brünn; later with Jean de Reszke; début as "Lohengrin," Brünn Op., 1896; sang in Berlin and Breslau; after 1909, member of Vienna Op.; Covent Garden, 1909 ("Otello"); Met. Op., N. Y., 1909–13; also in Munich, Dresden, Wiesbaden, Budapest, Paris, Prague and La Scala, singing heroic rôles. (2) Walter, his son, has sung with succ. in operetta in New York.

Slivinski (slĭ-vēn'-shkĭ), Jos. von, Warsaw, Dec. 15, 1865—March 2, 1930; pianist; pupil of Strobl, Leschetizky and Anton Rubinstein; début, 1890; America, 1893; toured with Leipzig Philh. orch.; lived Paris.

Slonim'sky, Nicholas, b. St. Petersburg, April 15, 1894; conductor, pianist; studied at Cons. there; gave concerts in Eur. cities; cond. Chamber Orch. of Boston and also as guest in programs of modern music abroad; has taught and lectured; c. chamber, piano and vocal music.

Slo'per (Edw. Hugh), Lindsay, London, 1826—1887; pianist, teacher, writer and composer.

Smal'lens, Alexander, b. St. Petersburg; conductor; studied at Inst. of Mus. Art, N. Y., and at Paris Cons.; asst. cond., Boston Op., 1911; later with Century Op. Co., on tours with Pavlowa; at Chicago Op., 1919–22 (premières of De Koven and Prokofieff works); Phila. Civic Op., 1923–30; also as asst. cond. with Phila. Orch., and as leader of operas with that ensemble; cond. opera, Lewisohn Stadium summer seasons and elsewhere.

Smareglia (smä-rāl'-yä), A., Pola, Istria, May 5, 1854—Grado, April 15, 1929; studied Vienna and at the Milan Cons., graduating with a symph. work "*Eleanora*"; prod. 6 operas, incl. "*Preziosa*"; (Milan, 1879), "*Bianca da Cervia*" (Milan, La Scala, 1882), "*Il Vassallo di Szigeth*" (Vienna, 1889, as "*Der Vasall von Szigeth*," New York, 1890), and "*La Falena*" (Venice, 1897; "*Oceana*," 1903; "*Notte di S.

Silvestro," 1907; "*L'Abisso*," 1914; 1921, prof. of comp., Trieste Cons.

Smart, (1) Sir G. (Thos.), London, 1776—1867; noted conductor, pupil of Dupuis and Arnold; knighted, 1811; cond. Phil. Soc., 1813–44. (2) Henry, Dublin, 1778—1823; bro. of above; violinist; leader Drury Lane, 1812–21; piano-manufacturer. (3) Henry, London, Oct. 26, 1813—(blind) July 6, 1879, son and pupil of (2); studied with Kearns; organist in London from 1836; c. an opera "*Bertha*" (1855), many cantatas, etc.

Smetana (smä'-tä-nä), Fr. (Bedrich), Leitomischl, Bohemia, 1824—insane, Prague, 1884, noted composer and pianist; pupil of Proksch and Liszt; 1848, organised a sch. at Prague; 1866–74, cond. Nat. Theatre Prague. Partially because of alleged intrigues against him and his growing deafness, he resigned this post in the latter year. The state of his health grew worse and finally his reason gave way. C. a string-quartet, 8 operas, incl. the comic masterpiece "*Prodaná nevěsta*" ("*The Bartered Bride*"), 1866; 9 symph. poems, incl. a cycle of 6 "*Má Vlast*" ("*My Country*"), symph. of "*Triumph*," etc.

Smet'erlin, Jan, b. Bielsko, Poland, 1892; pianist; studied at Vienna Piano Master School, and with Godowsky; has appeared with succ. as piano virtuoso in Paris, London, Vienna, Berlin, Warsaw and other cities, and after 1930 in Amer. cities as orch. soloist and in recitals.

Smith, (1) Bd. (Bd. Schmidt) (called "Father Smith"), Germany, ca. 1630—London, 1708; ct. org.-builder. (2) Robt., Cambridge, 1689—1768; acoustician. (3) J. Christopher (Johann Chr. Schmidt), Ansbach, 1712—Bath, 1795; dram. composer. (4) John Stafford, Gloucester, Engl., ca. 1750—London, 1836; organist and composer. (5) Edw. Woodley, 1775—1849, lay-vicar at Windsor. (6) Geo. Townshend, Windsor, 1813—Hereford, 1877; son of above; composer. (7) Montern, bro. of above; singer. (8) Samuel, b. Eton, 1821; bro. of above; organist. (9) John, Cambridge, 1795—1861; composer and prof. (10) Robt. Archibald, Reading, 1780—1829; composer and violinist. (11) Alice Mary (Mrs. Meadows White), London, 1839—1884; composer. (12) Sydney Dor-

chester, Engl., 1839—London, 1889;
pianist, teacher, writer, etc. (13)
Wilson G., Elyria, Ohio, Aug. 19,
1855—1929; composer; pupil of Otto
Singer, at Cincinnati; at Berlin,
1880–82, of Kiel, the Scharwenkas,
Neumann, Moszkowski and Raif;
after 1882, lived in Cleveland as
teacher of pf., voice and comp.; pub.
numerous graceful pf.-pcs. and songs,
also *"Octave Studies"* and other
valuable technical works. (14) **David
Stanley,** b. Toledo, Ohio, July 6,
1877—New Haven, Conn., Dec. 17,
1949; pupil of Parker at Yale;
grad. 1900, composing Ode for barytone (Herbert Witherspoon), chorus
and orch.; studied then with Thuille
and Widor abroad; 1903 Mus. Bac.
Yale; from 1904 teacher; from 1912
dir. of music dept. (vice Parker) at
Yale; 1909, won Paderewski Prize
with *"The Fallen Star,"* for chorus
and orch. Other comps. include
symphs. in F minor and D; symph.
poem, *"Darkness and Dawn"*; overtures in E flat, *"Joyeuse," "Sérieuse"*
and *"Prince Hal"*; *"Commemoration
March"*; Allegro Giocoso; Symph.
Ballad; *"L'Allegro," "Il Pensieroso"*
and *"Four Impressions"*; prelude,
choral and fugue for organ, and orch.;
fantasy for piano and orch.; string
quartets in E minor and A; piano
trio; and (chorus) *"Commencement
Ode," "The Djinns," "Rhapsody of
St. Bernard"*; anthems and songs.
(15) **Carleton Sprague,** b. N. Y., 1905;
Ph. D., Vienna Univ.; musicologist.
Smolen'ski, Stephan V., Kasan, 1848—
St. Petersburg, Aug. 6, 1909; prof. of
history of Russian church music at
Moscow Cons.; 1901 cond. court
chapel at St. Petersburg; author of
important historical works.
Smyth, Dame **Ethel,** b. London, April
23, 1858—May 8, 1944; daughter of,
general; pupil Leipzig Cons. and
of Herzogenberg. Her string quintet
was played there 1884; her violin
sonata 1887; c. orch. serenade
(London, 1890), overture *"Antony
and Cleopatra"* (do.); *"Mass in D"*
(London, 1893 under Barnby), and
operas *"Fantasio"* (her own libretto,
Weimar 1898, Carlsruhe, 1901);
1-act *"Der Wald"* (her own German
libretto, Dresden, 1901, Covent
Garden, 1902 and 1903, Met. Op.,
N. Y., 1903); 3-act *"Les Naufra-
geurs"* (book by Leforestier), given

at Leipzig, 1906, as *"Strandrecht"*
(Prague, do.); c. also the operas
"The Boatswain's Mate" (1917),
"Fête Galante" (1923), *"Entente
Cordiale,"* 1-act, 1925; string quintet,
sonata for vln. and pf.; pf. sonatas;
choral work, *"The Prison"*; concerto
for vln. and horn with orch., etc.;
author, *"Impressions That Remained"*
(1919), *"Streaks of Life"* (1921); created Dame Commander of Empire,
1920.
Soares, João. Vide REBELLO.
Sodermann (sä'-dĕr-män), **August
Johan,** Stockholm, 1832 — 1876;
theatre-conductor there; pupil of
Hauptmann and Richter; c. Swedish
operetta, a notable mass with orch.,
etc.
So'dero, Cesare, Naples, Aug. 2, 1886
—N. Y., Dec. 16, 1947; conductor;
grad. of Naples Cons.; cond. in U. S.
with Aborn and Savage Opera Cos.;
for some years with NBC in radio
versions of operas; later at Met. Op.
Soffredini (sôf-frĕ-dē'-nē), **Alfredo,**
from 1896, ed.-in-chief, Milan *Gaz-
zetta Musicale;* prod. (text and
mus.) 2-act children's opera *"Il Piccolo Haydn"* (Pavia, 1893), etc.
Sokal'ski, Peter Petrovich, Charkov,
Sept. 26, 1832—Odessa, April 11,
1887; author and composer of operas
and piano pieces.
Sok'oloff, Nikolai, b. Kiev, Russia,
May 28, 1886; conductor; came to
America at early age; studied Yale
School of Music, also vln. with
Loeffler; played in Boston Symph.,
cond. newly organised Cleveland
Orch. from 1918 for a decade and a
half; founded and led N. Y. Orch.
for several seasons; has appeared as
guest with London Symph., orchs.
in Chicago, Cincinnati, Phila., San
Francisco and elsewhere; national
dir. of Fed. Mus. Proj.; 1938–9 cond.
Seattle Symph. Orch.
Sokolov (sō'-kō-lôf), **Nicholas,** Peters-
burg, March 26, 1859—March 27,
1922; pupil at the Cons.; taught
harm. in the Imp. Chapel; c. an elegy
(op. 4), and intermezzo for orch., etc.
Soldat (zōl'-dät), **Marie,** b. Graz,
March 25, 1864; violinist; pupil of
Pleiner and Pott, and of Joachim,
formed string quartet, toured.
Soler, Antonio, Olot, n. Gerona, 1729—
Escorial Monastery, 1783; composer.
Solié (sōl-yā) (rightly **Soulier**), (1) **J.
P.,** Nimes, 1753—Paris, 1812; bary-

tone; c. comic operas, many pop.
(2) **Chas.**, son of above; conductor;
prod. a comic opera (Nice, 1877).
Sol'omon,b. London,1903;familyname
Cutner; pianist; studied with Ma-
thildeVerne; toured widely,incl. U.S.
Soloviev (or **Solowiew**) (sō'-lō-vēf),
Nicolai Theopometovitch, Petrosa-
vodsk, Russia, April 27 (May 9),
1846—St. Petersburg, Dec. 14, 1916;
pupil of N. J. Zaremba (theory),
Imp. Cons. at Petersburg; 1874 prof.
there; also critic, editor and Councillor of State; c. comic opera
"*Vakula, The Smith*" (Petersb.,
1875), and grand opera "*Cordelia*"
(Petersb., 1883, in German, Prague,
1890); finished Seroff's opera "*The
Demon's Power*"; c. symph. picture,
"*Russia and the Mongols*" (Moscow,
1882); cantata, "*Death of Samson*," etc.
Soltys (sôl'-tēs), **Mieczyslaw**, Lemberg,
Feb. 7, 1863—Nov. 12, 1929; pupil of
Krenn and Gigout; director and
teacher Lemberg Cons.; c. operas,
symph., oratorio, etc.
Som'ervell, Sir **Arthur**, Windermere,
1863—London, May 2, 1937; pupil
Berlin Hochschule, Stanford and
Parry, R. C. M.; c. mass, with orch.
(1891), "*A Song of Praise*," "*The
Forsaken Merman*" (Leeds Fest.,
1895), "*The Power of Sound*," elegy
for alto with orch., suite for small
orch. "*In Arcady*," song cycle on
Tennyson's "*Maude*," etc.; writer.
Somis (sō'-mēs), **Giov. Bat.**, Piedmont,
1676—Turin, 1763; violinist, teacher
and conductor.
Sommer (zôm'-měr), Dr. **Hans** (rightly
Hans Fr. Aug. Zincke) (tsĭnk'-ĕ),
Brunswick, July 20, 1837—April 28,
1922; pupil of Meves and J. O.
Grimm; graduate, later prof. at
Göttingen Univ.; from 1888 lived in
Weimar; c. succ. opera "*Lorelei*"
(Brunswick, 1891), 1-act "*Bühnen-
spiel*," "*Saint Foix*" (Munich, 1894),
1-act "*Der Meerman*" (Weimar,
1896), "*Rübezahl*" (1902), etc.
Son'neck, **Oscar Geo. Th.**, Jersey City,
N. J., Oct. 6, 1873—New York,
Oct. 31, 1928; noted editor and
author; at 20 studied at Heidelberg,
Munich and Italy; 1899 returned to
America; music librarian at the Li-
brary of Congress, and after 1902
dir. of music division; 1915, ed. of
The Musical Quarterly; wrote valuable works on early history of music
ir America.

Sonnleithner (zôn'-līt-něr), (1) **Chp. S.**,
Szegedin, 1734—Vienna, 1786; dean
of jurisprudence, Vienna; composer.
(2) **Jos.**, Vienna, 1765—1835; son of
above; 1827, discovered the famous
9th cent. Antiphonary of St. Gallen
in neume-notation. (3) **Ld. von**,
Vienna, 1797—1873; nephew of
above; devoted friend of Schubert.
Sontag (zôn'-täkh), **Henriette** (**Gertrude Walpurgis**), Coblenz, Jan. 3,
1806—of cholera, Mexico, June 17,
1854; famous coloratura-soprano, her
voice taking e''' easily; daughter of
two actors; operatic singer; 1823
created von Weber's "Euryanthe."
Sontheim (zôn'-tīm), **H.**, Jebenhausen,
Feb. 3, 1820—Stuttgart, Aug. 2,
1912; notable tenor; début Carlsruhe, 1839; 1872, pensioned.
Sor (rightly **Sors**) (sôr), **Fdo.**, Barcelona, 1778—Paris, 1839; guitar-
virtuoso and dram. composer.
Sorge (zôr'-gě), **G. Ands.**, Mellenbach,
Schwarzburg, 1703 — Lobenstein,
1778; famous organist and theorist;
ct.-organist and composer.
Soriano, (1) **Fran.** Vide SURIANO.
(2) **Soriano-Fuertes** (sō-rĭ-ä'-nō-foo-
ěr'-těs), Don **Mariano**, Murcia, 1817
—Madrid, 1880; son and pupil of the
dir. royal chamber-mus. (1841);
prod. several zarzuelas, aiming to
estab. national opera; conductor and
writer of historical works.
Sormann (zôr'-män), **Alfred** (**Richard
Gotthilf**), Danzig, May 16, 1861—
Berlin, Sept. 17, 1913; pianist; pupil
of R. Hochschule, Berlin, and of
Liszt; début 1886; 1889, ct.-pianist
to Grand Duke of Mecklenburg-
Strelitz; taught Stern Cons., Berlin;
c. concerto, etc.
Soubies (soo-bĭ-ĕs), **Albert**, Paris,
May 10, 1846—March 19, 1918;
mus.-historiographer and critic; a
lawyer, then pupil of Savard and
Bazin (harm. and comp.) at the
Cons.; 1874 he revived the famous
"*Almanach des spectacles*, *Alm.
Duchesne*"; for this the Académie,
1893, awarded him the Prix Voirac;
1876, critic for *Le Soir*, under
name "*B. de Lomagne*"; officer of
public instruction, and Legion of
Honour, also of the Russian order
Stanislas; writer of valuable historical works, etc.
Soubre (soobr), **Etienne Jos.**, Liége,
1813—1871; director and dram.
comp.

Souhaitty (soo-ĕt-tē'), **J. Jac.**, Franciscan monk at Paris, the first to use figures for popular notation, 1665–78.

Soulier (soo-yä). Vide SOLIE.

Sousa (soo'-sä), **John Philip,** Washington, D. C., Nov. 6, 1856—Reading, Pa., March 6, 1932, while on tour; son of a Spanish trombonist in the U. S. Marine Corps band. Pupil of John Esputa and G. F. Benkert (harm. and comp.); at 17 cond. of travelling theatrical troupes; 1877, violinist in Offenbach's orch. in America; dir. "Philadelphia Churchchoir Pinafore Co."; 1880–92, bandm. U. S. Marine Corps; resigned and organised the military band bearing his own name, which toured America and Europe with greatest succ.; (1900), Paris, Exposition. Compiled, by Govt. order, "*National Patriotic and Typical Airs of All Countries*"; wrote instruction-books for trumpet and drum, and for vln. C. 7 comic operas incl. v. succ. "*El Capitan*," succ. (text and music) "*The Bride Elect*," "*The Charlatan*" and "*Chris and the Wonderful Lamp*," a symph. poem "*The Chariot Race*" (from "*Ben Hur*"); suites, "*The Last Days of Pompeii*," "*Three Quotations*," and "*Sheridan's Ride*"; and many immensely succ. marches popular throughout the world, "*Washington Post*," "*High School Cadets*," "*Stars and Stripes Forever*," "*Imperial Edward*," etc.

Sow'erby, Leo, b. Grand Rapids, Mich., May 1, 1895; composer; grad. of Amer. Cons., Chicago; won fellowship at Amer. Acad. in Rome, 1921; active as org. and teacher of comp. in Chicago; c. symph. works, piano concerto, Ballad for 2 pianos and orch., choral and piano pieces, songs.

Spaeth, Sigmund, b. Philadelphia, April 10, 1885; critic, author, lecturer; grad. Haverford Coll., Ph. D., Princeton, 1910; critic of N. Y. *Evening Mail*, 1914–18; active as writer of musical essays and books, also in radio programmes; exec. of Community Concerts Corp., N. Y.; author,"*The Common Sense of Music*," "*Barber Shop Ballads*," "*Words and Music*," "*Read 'Em and Weep*," "*Weep Some More, My Lady*," "*American Mountain Songs*," "*The Facts of Life in Popular Song*."

Spal'ding, (1) **Albert,** b. Chicago,

Aug. 15, 1888; violinist; studied in New York, Paris and Florence; début in Paris, 1905; first Amer. appearance as soloist with N. Y. Symph.. 1908; took rank as one of foremost performers, both for technical excellence and refined musicianship; has played with leading orchs. in U. S. and Europe; c. works for violin; d. N. Y., May 26, 1953.

(2) **Walter Raymond,** b. Northampton, Mass., May 22, 1865; organist and pedagogue; pupil of Guilmant, Widor, Rheinberger and Thuille; org. in various Boston churches; after 1895 associated with Harvard Univ. as theory teacher, (prof. in 1907), also at Radcliffe Coll; author of books on theory.

Spanuth (spän'-oot), **August,** Brinkum, Hanover, March 15, 1857—Berlin, Jan. 9, 1920; pianist and critic; pupil of Hoch Cons., Frankfort-on-Main; 1886–1893 Chicago as pianist and teacher; then in New York as critic; 1906 returned to Berlin as teacher at Stern Cons.; 1907, ed. periodical *Signale für die Musikalische Welt.*

Spataro (spä-tä'-rō) (or **Spat'arus, Spada'ro, Spada'rius**), **Giov.,** Bologna, ca. 1460—1541; conductor and theorist.

Speaight (spāt), **Joseph,** b. London, Oct. 24, 1868; violinist, composer; pupil of his father and of the Guildhall School of Music, where he taught after 1894; c. 2 symphonies, various other orch. works, chamber music incl. string quartet, piano pieces, choruses, songs, etc.

Speaks, Oley, b. Canal Winchester, O., c. of many popular ballads, incl. "*Sylvia*" and "*The Road to Mandalay*"; res. in N. Y.; mem., board of directors, Amer. Soc. of Composers, Authors and Publishers.

Specht (spĕkht), **Richard,** Vienna, Dec. 7, 1870—March 18, 1932; wellknown critic and writer on music; author, "*Gustav Mahler*," "*Richard Strauss und Sein Werk*," "*Julius Bittner*," "*Reznicek*," "*Brahms*," "*Puccini*," etc.

Speer, (1) **Charlton T.,** Cheltenham, Nov. 21, 1859—London, 1921; pupil R. A. M. London, winning a scholarship; from 1885 prof. of piano there, also organist at various churches; c. 2 operas, "*The Battle of Lake Regillus*," for chorus and orch.; symph. poem, "*King Arthur*," etc. His cousin (2) **William Henry,** b. London, 1863; organist; pupil of Lloyd and the R. C. M.; 1906 Mus. Doc. Cambridge; c. symph., overture, orch., rhapsody, ballad, *"The Jackdaw of Rheims,"* etc.

Speidel (shpī'-děl), **Wm.,** Ulm, 1826— Stuttgart, 1899; pianist, conductor, composer.

Spel'man, Timothy Mather, b. Brooklyn, N. Y., Jan. 21, 1891; composer; pupil of Spalding and Hill (Harvard), also of Courvoisier; for some years res. in Florence.

Spen'cer, Eleanor, b. Chicago, Nov. 30, 1890; pianist; pupil of Leschetizky; début with London Philh., 1912; made N. Y. début following year; has appeared as soloist with orchs. in Europe and U. S., also in recitals.

Spen'diarov, Alexander Afanasovitch, Kachov, Province of Taurien, Russia, Nov. 1, 1871—May, 1928, at Erivan, Armenia, where since 1924 he was dir. of the State Cons.; early in life a lawyer, but later studied with Rimsky-Korsakoff; passed most of his life in the Crimea; c. operas, orch. *"Sketches from the Crimea," "The Three Palm Trees,"* songs, piano works incl. *"Erivan Studies,"* etc.

Spengel (shpěng'-ěl), **Julius H.,** Hamburg, June 12, 1853—April 17, 1936; pupil of Cologne Cons. and Berlin Hochschule, taught in Hamburg, and studied with Gradener and Armbrust; 1878–1927, cond. Cäcilienverein; singing-teacher and organist; c. symph., 'cello-sonata, etc.

Speyer (Speier) (shpī'-ěr), **Wilhelm,** Frankfort, 1790—1878; violinist and composer.

Spicker (shpīk'-ěr), **Max,** Königsberg, Prussia, Aug. 16, 1858—New York, Oct. 16, 1912; pupil of Louis Köhler, then of Leipzig Cons.; theatre conductor various cities; 1882–88, cond. "Beethoven Männerchor," New York; 1888–95 Dir. Brooklyn Cons.: teacher Nat. Cons., New York; arranged operatic scores for pf.; c. orch. suite, cantata with orch., etc.

Spiering (shpē'-rĭng), **Theodor,** St. Louis, Missouri, 1871 — Munich, Aug. 11, 1925; violinist; pupil of H. Schradieck, Cincinnati; then of Joachim, Berlin; founder and 1st vln. "Spiering Quartet," Chicago; taught in his own school there; 1905–06 at Stern Cons., Berlin; 1909, concertm., N. Y., Philh., and

in 1911 cond. as Mahler's substitute; later led Blüthner and Philh. Orchs. in Berlin; toured as cond. with Pavlowa, etc.

Spindler (shpĭnt'-lěr), **Fritz,** Würzbach, near Lobenstein, Nov. 24, 1817— near Dresden, Dec. 26, 1905; pianist; studied mus. with Fr. Schneider at Dessau; from 1841, lived in Dresden as teacher; c. 3 symphs., pf.-concerto, v. pop. salon-pcs., etc.

Spinelli (spĭ-něl'-lĭ), **Nicola,** Turin, 1865—Rome, Oct. 17, 1909; notable opera composer; pupil of Naples Cons.; 1890 took 2nd Sonzogno prize with 1-act opera *"Cobilla,"* Mascagni winning 1st prize; prod. v. succ. 3-act lyric drama *"A Basso Porto"* (1894, New York, 1899).

Spiridio (spē-rē'-dĭ-ō), **Berthold,** monk, organist and composer, Bamberg, 1665–91.

Spirid'ion. Vide XYNDAS.

Spitta (shpĭt'-tä), (**Julius Aug.**) **Philipp,** Wechold, near Hoya, Hanover, Dec. 27, 1841—Berlin, April 13, 1894; wrote noted life of J. S. Bach.

Spivakov'sky, Tossy, b. Odessa, 1907; pupil Serato; violinist; res. in U. S. where toured widely in concerts.

Spof'forth, Reginald, Nottingham. Southwell, 1769—Kensington, 1827; c. glees, etc.

Spohr (shpōr), **Ludwig** (in his autobiography he calls himself **Louis**), Brunswick, April 5, 1784—Cassel, Oct. 22, 1859; eminent violinist and conductor; notable composer and teacher. Son of a physician who removed to Seesen, 1786; pupil of his mother, and at 5 studied with Riemenschneider (vln.) and Dufour; then with Kunisch, Hartung and Maucourt, Brunswick; at 14 he played a concerto of his own at court. He became a member of the Ducal Orch.; 1802 pupil of Fz. Eck, whom he accompanied to St. Petersburg; 1803, returned to the Ducal Orch.; 1804 toured with great succ.; 1805, leader Duke of Gotha's orch.; m. Dorette Scheidler (d. 1834) the harpplayer and toured with her, 1807 and 1809. 1836 he m. the pianist Marianne Pfeiffer (d. 1892); 1812, after brilliant concerts at Vienna, leader at the Th. an der Wien; 1815, toured Italy (playing a concertante of his own with Paganini at Rome); 1817– 19 opera-cond. at Frankfort; prod. here succ. opera *"Faust";* 1820, visited England with his wife, played at Philharm. Concerts, and prod. there two symphs.; introducing into England the habit of conducting with a bâton. Gave concerts at Paris with little succ. From 1822 ct.-cond. at Cassel; 1857, retired for political reasons on a reduced pension. During his period as a cond. he prod. Wagner's *"Fliegende Holländer"* (1842), and *"Tannhäuser"* (1853), but could not overcome the opposition to a production of *"Lohengrin."* He soon recognised Wagner as the greatest living dramatic composer, but did not care for Beethoven or Weber. He is among the first of the second-best composers, his highest attainments being the opera *"Jessonda"* (Cassel, 1823), the oratorio *"Die Letzten Dinge"* (Cassel, 1826; in England as *"The Last Judgment"*); the grand symph. *"Die Weihe der Töne"* (*"The Consecration of Tone,"* 1832) and the classic vln.-concertos. His *"Violin-School"* (1831 in 3 parts), is a standard. He c. 11 operas in all; dram. cantata, *"Das Befreite Deutschland"*; a mass, etc., with orch.; 9 symphs.; No. 4 op. 86 in F (*"Weihe der Töne"*); No. 6 op. 116, G (*"Historical"*; dedicated to the London Philh. Soc.); 7 op. 121, C (*"Irdisches und Göttliches im Menschenleben"*) for 2 orchs.; 8 op. 137, G min. (ded. to the London Philharm.); 9 op. 143, B min. (*"Die Jahreszeiten"*), 8 overtures, and 15 vln.-concertos; No. 8 (op. 47, in A min., *"in modo d'una scena cantante"*) "quartet-concerto" for 2 vlns., vla., and 'cello with orch.; 2 concertantes for 2 vlns. with orch.; grande polonaise for vlns. with orch., 2 clar.-concertos; much chamber-mus. Autobiogr. (Cassel, 1860, 1861, 2 vols.); Biogr. by Malibran (Frankfort, 1860); by H. M. Schletterer (1881).

Spontini (spôn-tē'-nē), **Gasparo** (**Luigi Pacifico**), Majolati, Ancone, Nov. 14, 1774—Jan. 24, 1851; noteworthy cond. and dram. composer. Son of poor peasants who intended him for the church, he ran away, and an uncle, at San Vito, provided him with teaching. At 17 entered the Cons. della Pietà de' Turchini at Naples. 1796, commissioned to write an opera for the Teatro Argentina at Rome, its director having heard some of his church-mus. in Naples, he left the Cons. without permission and prod. succ. opera, *"I Puntigli delle Donne"*; Piccinni secured his reinstatement and gave him valuable advice. He prod. operas with succ. in various cities and in Palermo, where he was cond. to the Neapolitan court which had fled before the French. After having produced 16 light Italian operas, he went to Paris (1803), where three successive failures and a study of Mozart's works led him to change his style. After supporting himself as a singing-teacher he won succ. with his substantial 1-act opera *"Milton"* (Th. Feydeau Nov. 27, 1804); the Empress Josephine, to whom he had dedicated the score, appointed him "chamber-composer." He c. a cantata *"L'eccelsa Gara,"* celebrating the victory of Austerlitz. The Empress's power secured a hearing for his opera *"La Vestale,"* which after three years of delay and polishing, was prod. with greatest succ. 1807; by a unanimous verdict of the judges, Méhul, Gossec and Grétry, Napoleon's prize for the best dram. work of the decade was awarded to it. It was followed with equal succ. by the grand opera *"Fernand Cortez,"* 1809. 1810, dir. It. opera; dismissed for financial irregularity; 1814 Louis XVIII., appointed him ct.-composer. He c. 2 stage-pieces in glorification of the Restoration. The opera *"Olympie"* was prod. 1819 without succ., though when revised and prod. 1826 it prospered. 1820, he became ct.-composer and gen. mus.-dir. at Berlin; he prod. his old operas with succ., and c. the festival play *"Lalla Rukh"* (1821), remodelled as *"Nurmahal"* (1822); *"Alcidor"* (1825) and *"Agnes von Hohenstaufen"* (1829), none of which were widely succ. A period of violent jealousies and quarrels with the Intendant Brühl, and virulent intrigues, culminated after a score of stormy years in his being royally reprimanded, and finally driven out of the theatre by a hostile audience. He retired in 1841 on full pay. He went to Paris, then to Italy. 1844 the Pope gave him the rank and title of "Conte di Sant' Andrea"; he was a knight of the Prussian "Ordre pour le mérite," member of the Berlin Akademie (1839), and Paris

Académie, and Di. Phil., Halle Univ. Biog. by L. de Loménie (1841); Montanari (1851); Raoul-Rochette (1882).

Sporck, Georges, b. Paris, April 9, 1870; pupil of the Cons. and of d'Indy; c. symph. poems, symphonie "Vivaraise," "Esquisses symphoniques," etc.

Spross, Chas. Gilbert, b. Poughkeepsie, N. Y., Jan. 6, 1874; composer, pianist; pupil of X. Scharwenka, Emil Giamm and Carl Lachmund; org. in various cities; accompanist for noted artists; c. choral works, songs, etc.

Squire, (1) Wm. Henry, b. Ross, Herefordshire, Aug. 8, 1871; 'cellist; son and pupil of an amateur violinist; début at 7; won scholarship at the R. C. M., and studied with Powell and Parry; second début, 1891; c. 'cello-concerto. (2) William Barclay, London, Oct. 18, 1855—Jan. 14, 1927; historian and author, educated at Cambridge, 1879, B. A.; 1902, M. A.; critic, librettist and antiquarian; ed. works of Purcell, Byrd and Palestrina, and with Fuller-Maitland, the "Fitzwilliam Virginal Book."

Stabile (stä'-bē-lĕ), Annibale, d. Rome, ca. 1595; conductor and composer.

Stade (shtä'-dĕ), (1) H. Bd., Ettischleben, 1816—Arnstadt, 1882; organist and composer. (?) Fr. Wm., Halle, Aug. 25, 1817—Altenburg, March 24, 1902; organist, pupil of Fr. Schneider, Dessau; mus.-dir. and Dr. Phil. h. c. Jena Univ.; 1860–1891, ct.-organist and cond. at Altenburg; c. 2 symphs.; Festouvertüre, music to "Orestes"; cantatas, with orch.; choral works, vln.-sonata; "Kindersonate" (4 hands), etc. (3) Dr. Fritz (L. Rudolf), Sondershausen, Jan. 8, 1844—Leipzig, June 12, 1928; pupil of Riedl and Richter, Leipzig, and teacher there; pub. an answer to Hanslick's "Vom Musikalisch-Schönen," etc.

Staden (shtä'-dĕn), (1) Jn., Nürnberg, 1581—1634; organist and composer. (2) Sigmund Theopil, 1607–1655, son and successor of above; c. "Seelewig," one of the earliest extant German operas (cf. H. SCHÜTZ' opera "Dafne").

Stadler (shtät'-lĕr), Maximilian, Melk, Lower Austria, 1748—Vienna, 1833; composer and writer.

Stadlmayer (shtät'-'l-mi-ĕ:), Jn.- Frei-

sing, Bavaria, 1560 — Innsbruck, July 12, 1648; conductor, composer.

Stadtfeldt (shtät'-fĕlt), Alex., Wiesbaden, 1826—Brussels, 1853, dram. composer.

Stägemann (shtä'-gĕ-män), (1) Max, Freienwalde-on-Oder, May 10, 1843 —Leipzig, Jan. 29, 1905; pupil of Dresden Cons.; barytone and "chamber-singer" at Hanover; 1877, dir. of Königsberg Th.; later, manager Leipzig City Th.; his daughter, (2) Helene, d. Dresden, Aug. 24, 1923; noted Liedersinger, m. Botho Sigwart (Count Eulenberg).

Stahlknecht (shtäl-k'nĕkht), two brothers, (1) Ad., Warsaw, 1813—Berlin, 1887; violinist and dram. composer. (2) Julius, Posen, 1817—Berlin, 1892; 'cellist royal orchestra.

Stainer (or Steiner) (shtī-nĕr), (1) Jakob, Absam, Tyrol, 1621—1683; inventor and manufacturer of instrs. (2) Markus, his brother, also vln.- and vla.-maker.

Stainer (stä'-nĕr), Sir John, London, June 4, 1840—Verona, Mar. 31, 1901; chorister at St. Paul's; studied with Bayley (harm.) and Steggal (cpt.), and later Cooper (org.); 1854–60, organist various places, then Univ. organist at Oxford; (1859) Bac. Mus., and (1865) Mus. Doc.; 1866, Examiner for mus. degrees; 1872–88, organist of St. Paul's, resigning on account of his eyesight; 1876, prof. of org. and harm. Nat. Training Sch. for Mus.; 1881, principal in R. C. M.; 1883, again at Oxford; 1882, Govt. Inspector of Mus. in the Training-Sch.; 1878, Chev. of the Legion of Honour; knighted, 1888; 1889, prof. of mus. at Oxford Univ.; pub. treatises and (with Barret) a "Dict. of Mus. Terms," 1875; c. oratorio "Gideon," cantatas "The Daughter of Jairus" (Worc. Fest., 1878), "St. Mary Magdalene" (Gloucester, 1883), and "The Crucifixion" (London, 1887), services, etc.

Stamaty (stä-mä-tē), Camille M., Rome, 1811—Paris, 1870; pianist and composer.

Stamitz (shtä'-mĭts), (1) Jn. Wenzel Anton, Deutsch-Brod., Bohemia, 1717—Mannheim, 1757; notable violinist and composer. (2) Anton Thaddäus, Deutsch-Brod., 1721— Altbunzlau, 1768; bro. of above; canon; 'cellist, Mannheim. (3) K.,

Mannheim, 1746—Jena, 1801; violinist and viole d'amour-performer, conductor and composer. (4) **Anton**, Mannheim, 1754—Paris, ca. 1820, bro. of above; violinist and composer.

Stan'ford, Sir **Chas.** Villiers, Dublin, Sept. 30, 1852—London, March 29, 1924; pianist and notable composer; pupil of Sir Robt. Stewart and Arthur O'Leary (comp.), and Ernst Pauer (pf.), London; 1870 won organ scholarship at Queen's Coll., Cambridge; 1873–92, organist of Trinity Coll., Cambridge, also cond. Univ. Mus. Soc. (till 1893); 1875–76, studied comp. with Reinecke at Leipzig, and Kiel, Berlin. M. A., Cantab., 1878; Mus. Doc., Oxford, 1883, Cambridge, 1888; 1883, prof. of comp. and cond., R. C. M.; 1885, cond. Bach Choir; 1887, prof. of Mus. at Cambridge; 1897, cond. Leeds Philh. Soc.; he was knighted, 1901, and made cond. of the Leeds Festival, resigning the Bach Choir, 1904. C. operas, "*The Veiled Prophet of Khorassan*" (Hanover, 1881); "*Savonarola*" (Hamburg, 1884); "*The Canterbury Pilgrims*" (London, Covent Garden, 1884); v. succ. "*Shamus O'Brien*" (London, 1896); "*Much Ado about Nothing*" (Covent Garden, 1901, Leipzig, 1902); incid. mus. to various plays; operas, "*The Critic*," "*Travelling Companion*," oratorio, "*The Resurrection*" (1875); "*The Three Holy Children*" (Birmingham, 1885); Psalm 96 (1877); "*Elegiac Ode*" (Norwich, 1884); "*The Revenge*" (Leeds, 1886); "*Jubilee Ode*" (1887), etc. "*The Bard*" (Cardiff, 1895); "*Phaudrig Crochoore*" (Norwich, 1896); requiem, 3 Morning and Evening Services; a Communion Service, etc.; 6 symphs. "*Elegiac*," in D min. (No. 3); "*Irish*," (No. 4); "*Thro' Youth to Strife, Thro' Death to Life*"; and No. 5 "*L'allegro ed il penseroso*"; 2 overtures, a pf.-concerto; "*Irish Rhapsody*" (1902); motet with orch., "*The Lord of Might*" (1903); symphony No. 6, "*In Memoriam G. F. Watts*," 7th symphony (London Phil., Feb., 1912), "*Stabat Mater*," with orch. (Leeds Fest., 1907); "*Wellington*," for voices and orch., incid. mus. to "*Attila*" (1907), overture "*Ave atque Vale*" (Haydn Centenary, 1909), etc.

Stan'ley, (1) (**Chas.**) **John**, London,

1713–1786; organist and conductor, (2) **Albert Augustus**, Manville, Rhode Island, May 25, 1851—Ann Arbor, Mich., May 19, 1932; studied in Providence, and at Leipzig; organist, Providence; 1888–1922, prof. of mus., Univ. of Michigan; from 1893, cond. important series of Ann Arbor Fests., by Choral Union of that city; c. "*The City of Freedom*," ode, with orch. (Boston, 1883); Psalm 21 (Providence, 1892), and Commemoration Ode "*Chorus triumphalis*," with orch.; symph. "*The Awakening of the Soul*"; symph. poem "*Altis*," etc.

Starczewski (stär-chěf'-skǐ), **Felix**, b. Warsaw, 1868; critic and author; pupil of the Music Institute and of Humperdinck, Fleischer, and d'Indy; taught piano at Warsaw Cons.; c. orchestral pieces, etc.

Stark (shtärk), **L.**, Munich, 1831—Stuttgart, 1884; teacher, editor and composer.

Starke (shtärk'-ĕ) **Fr.**, Elsterwerda, 1774—Döbling, near Vienna, 1835; bana.n., writer and composer.

Stasny (shtäs'-nē), (1) **L.**, Prague, 1823—Frankfort, 1883; conductor and dram. composer. (2) Vide STIASTNY.

Stassof, Vlad., 1824—1906; Russian critic and writer.

Statkov'ski, Roman von, near Kalisch, Jan. 5, 1860—Warsaw, 1926; pupil of Zelenski, and of St. Petersburg Cons.; teacher of instrumentation and history at Warsaw Cons. His opera "*Philaenis*" took an international prize in London and was prod., Warsaw, 1904; c. also opera "*Maria*" (Warsaw, 1906); fantasie and polonaise for orch., piano pieces, etc.

Staudigl (shtow'-dēkh-'l), (1) **Josef**, Wöllersdorf, Lower Austria, 1807—(insane), Michaelbeuerngrund, near Vienna, 1861; bass and ct.-conductor. (2) **Josef**, Vienna, March 18, 1850—Carlsruhe, 1916; son of above; barytone; pupil of Rokitansky at the Cons.; chamber-singer to the Grand Duke at Carlsruhe and a member of the ct.-opera. His wife (3) **Gisela**, singer; pupil of Marchesi, 1899 Wiesbaden ct.-opera.

Stavenhagen (shtä'-fĕn-hä-gĕn), **Bd.**, Greiz, Reuss, Nov. 24, 1862—Geneva, Dec. 26, 1914; pianist; pupil of Kiel, at the Meisterschule, and of Rudorff, at the Hochschule, Berlin; 1880. won the Mendelssohn prize for pf.; pupil of Liszt, 1885; toured Europe with succ. and the U. S. (1894–95); 1890, ct.-pianist and ct.-conductor at Weimar; Knight of the White Falcon order; from 1898 ct.-cond. at Munich; c. pf.-pcs.

Stcherbatcheff (stchĕr'-bät-chĕf), (1) **Nicolas**, St. Petersburg, Aug. 24, 1853—?; prominent figure in the neo-Russian sch.; c. *"Deux idylles pour orchestre"*; *"Féeries et pantomimes," "Mosaïque, album pittoresque,"* etc., for pf.; songs *"Au soir tombant,"* etc. (2) **Vladimir**, b. Warsaw, Jan. 24, 1889; pupil of St. Petersburg Cons.; composer of 2 symphonies, chamber music, piano pieces, songs.

Stearns, Theodore, Berea, O., 1880—Los Angeles, Nov. 1, 1935; composer, grad. Würzburg Univ.; cond. musical comedies in N. Y.; served as music critic on N. Y. *Morning Telegraph* and Chicago *Herald Examiner;* awarded Guggenheim Fellowship, 1927; c. (operas) *"Snowbird"* (Chicago Op. 1922, Dresden State Op. 1927), *"Atlantis,"* both to own librettos, *"Suite Caprese,"* etc.

Ste'ber, Eleanor, American soprano; début, Met. Op., 1940.

Stefan (stä'-fän), **Paul,** b. Brünn, Nov. 25, 1879; music critic and writer; Ph. D.; after 1888 lived in Vienna; ed. *Musikblätter des Anbruch,* publication of Universal Edition; author of studies of Mahler, Schubert, Schönberg; d. N. Y., Nov. 12, 1943.

Stefani (stä'-fä-nē), (1) **Jan,** Prague, 1746—Warsaw, Feb. 24, 1829; Mus. Director; director at Warsaw Cathedral; c. opera *"Die Krakowiter und die Bergvölker,"* 1794, and others, also masses and polonaises. His son (2) **Josef,** Warsaw, April 16, 1800 — (?); pupil of Elsner; c. ballets, operettas, also 10 masses, etc.

Stef'fan, Joseph Anton, Copidino, Bohemia, March 14, 1726—Vienna, 1800; court piano teacher at Vienna, numbering among his pupils Marie Antoinette and Queen Caroline of Naples; c. piano pieces and songs.

Steffani (stĕf-fä'-nē), **Abbate Agostino,** Castelfranco, Venetia, 1654—Frankfort-on-Main, 1728; eminent composer of daring originality and great power both in instrumentation and general construction; ct.- and chamber-musician and ct.-organist; prod. 20 operas.

Steffens (shtĕf'-fĕns), **Julius,** Stargard,

Pomerania, 1831—Wiesbaden, 1882; 'cellist and composer.

Steg'gall, (1) **Chas.,** London, June 3, 1826—June 7, 1905; pupil of Bennett, R. A. M., 1851; prof. of org. and harm. there; Mus. Bac. and Mus. Doc., Cambridge; from 1864, organist Lincoln's Inn Chapel; wrote method for org.; ed. colls., and c. Psalms 105, and 33 with orch.; services, etc. (2) **Reginald,** b. London, April 17, 1867; son and asst.-organist of above, later his successor; pupil R. A. M.; from 1895, prof. of org. there; c. mass with orch. and organ, *"Festival Evening Service"* with orch., a symph., 3 overtures, etc.

Stegmann (stäkh'-män), **K. David,** Dresden, 1751—Bonn, 1826; tenor, cond. and dram. composer.

Stegmayer (shtäkh'-mī-ĕr), **Fd.,** Vienna, 1803 — 1863; conductor, singing-teacher and composer.

Stehle (shtā'-lĕ), **Gv. Ed.,** Steinhausen, Würtemberg, Feb. 17, 1839—St. Gallen, June 21, 1915; cond. at St. Gallen Cath.; c. symph. tone-picture *"Saul,"* for org.

Steibelt (shtī'-bĕlt), **Daniel,** Berlin, 1765—St. Petersburg, 1823; a most unvirtuous virtuoso. Under patronage of the Crown Prince, a pupil of Kirnberger, early début; 1790, favourite pianist, teacher and composer at Paris; prod. v. succ. opera *"Roméo et Juliette"* (1793). He seems to have suffered from kleptomania and general dishonesty, which with his insolence, snobbery, and his debts, forced him to leave Paris in 1797, for London, where he was equally succ.; the *"Storm Rondo"* (or the finale of his 3rd concerto *"L'Orage, précédé d'un rondeau pastoral"*), rivalling the notorious *"Battle of Prague,"* by Koczwara. 1799, he toured Germany, challenging Beethoven at Vienna with disastrous results. He carried Haydn's *"Creation"* back to Paris and prod. it, 1800, with great succ., with himself as cembalist; but had to leave Paris again, remaining in London, until 1805, when he revisited Paris for 3 years; 1808 toured and settled in Petersburg; 1810, Imp. ct.-cond. and cond. of French Opera; here prod. 2 new operas, as well as earlier ones. In spite of his odious personality, his virtuosity was remarkable, and his compositions show much originality in modulation and scoring. He wrote a pop. pf.-method; c. 6 operas, 5 ballets, and much piano-mus., including 50 études, many programme-pcs. of extraordinary vogue.

Stein (shtīn), (1) **Jn. Andreas**, Heidelsheim, Palatinate, 1728—Augsburg, 1792; inv. "German (Viennese) pf.-action"; organist and famous pf.-maker. Succeeded by son (2) **Matthäus Andreas** (Augsburg, 1776—Vienna, 1842), who 1802 set up for himself in Vienna. (3) **Maria Anna** (or **Nanette Streicher**), Augsburg, 1769—Vienna, 1838; daughter of (1); a devoted friend of Beethoven; also a manager of the pf.-factory. Her son (4) **Jn. Bapt.** (b. Vienna, 1795), was her successor. (5) **Fr.**, Augsburg, 1781 — (of consumption) Vienna, 1808; bro. of above; prominent pianist. (6) **Karoline** (née **Haar**), pianist and teacher. (7) **K. Andreas**, Vienna, 1797—1863; son and successor of (2); pupil of Förster, ct.-pf.-maker and composer. (8) **Eduard**, Kleinschirma, Saxony, 1818—Sondershausen, 1864; ct.-conductor and composer. (9) **Theodor**, Altona, 1819—St. Petersburg, March 9, 1893; pianist; début at 12; 1872, pf.-prof. Petersburg Cons. (10) **Fritz**, b. Heidelberg, Dec. 17, 1879; theologian at first, then studied music; 1902, organist and cond. at Heidelberg; 1906, musical dir. of Jena University, cond. academic concerts; 1914, ct.-cond. in Meiningen (vice Reger); 1928–33, prof. of musical science and munic. mus. dir. in Kiel; after 1933, dir. of State Hochschule, Berlin; ed. thematic catalogue of Reger's works and wrote his biography.

Steinbach (shtīn'-bäkh), (1) **Emil**, Lengenrieden, Baden, Nov. 14, 1849—Mayence, Dec. 6, 1919; pupil Leipzig Cons.; 1877, cond. Mayence town-orch.; c. orch. and chamber-mus., etc. (2) **Fritz**, Grünsfeld, Baden, June 17, 1855—Munich, Aug. 13, 1916; bro. and pupil of above; also pupil Leipzig Cons.; won Mozart Scholarship; 1880–86, 2nd cond. at Mayence; 1886 ct.-cond. Meiningen; pub. a septet, 'cello-sonata, songs.

Steinberg, (1) **Maximilian**, Vilna, 1888—d. Dec. 6, 1947; composer and teacher; studied at Petersburg Univ.

and Cons.; teacher latter sch.; comp. (2) **Wm.**, German conductor; 1937, ass't. to Toscanini, NBC Symph.; cond., Buffalo Symph.

Steindel (shtīn'-děl), **Bruno**, b. Zwickau, Saxony, Aug. 29, 1869; 1st 'cello, Berlin Philh.; later in the Chicago Orch.; d. S. Monica, Cal., 1949.

Steiner. Vide STAINER.

Steingräber (shtīn'-gräp-ěr), **Theodor**, Neustadt-on-the-Orla, Jan. 25, 1830—Leipzig, April 5, 1904; founder of Hanover mus.-pub. firm; from 1890 in Leipzig; wrote a pf.-method under the pseud. "**Gustav Damm**."

Stein'way & Sons, firm of pf.-makers, New York and Hamburg; founded by (1) **H. Engelhard Steinweg** (shtīn'-vākh), Wolfshagen, Harz, 1797—New York, 1871; journeyman org.-builder, Seesen, ca. 1820; he worked at night on his first piano, which combined the good points of Old English and recent German instrs.; it made immediate succ.; after the Revolution of 1848, he emigrated to New York in 1850 with four sons, (2) **Chas.**, Seesen, 1829—1865. (3) **H.**, Seesen, 1829—New York, 1865. (4) **Wm.**, Seesen, 1836—New York, 1896; (5) **Albert**, Seesen, 1840—New York, 1877; leaving the business in charge of (6) **Theodor** (Seesen, 1825—Brunswick, 1889). Father and sons worked in different factories till 1853, when they combined as Steinway & Sons. In 1865 Theodor, who had moved to Brunswick, sold the business to the firm Grotrian, Helferich & Schulz, Theodor Steinwegs Nachfolger (i. e. "successors") (v. STEINWEG), and became a partner in the N. Y. firm, now the largest of its kind in the world.

Steinweg, Original form of "Steinway" (q. v. No. 6).

Stelzner (shtělts'-něr), **Alfred**, Hamburg, Dec. 29, 1852—Dresden, July 14, 1906 (suicide); inv. the violotta and cellone, etc. (v. D. D.); they were used in the orch. of his fairy opera "*Rübezahl*" (Dresden, 1902).

Stendhal (stän-däl), pen-name of **Marie Henri Beyle** (běl), Grenoble, Jan. 23, 1783—Paris, March 23, 1842; French consul at Civitavecchia, 1831–42, and author of numerous books on music.

Sten'hammar, (1) **Fredrika**, Wisby, 1836—Stockholm 1880; operatic soprano: born Andrée. (2) **Ulrik,** Stockholm, 1829–1875; composer of oratorio *"Saul,"* etc. His son (3) **Wilhelm,** Stockholm, Feb. 7, 1871— Nov. 20, 1927; pianist; pupil of the Cons., and of H. Barth; from 1898 cond. Phil. Society in Stockholm; from 1900 assistant cond. at the Royal Theatre; 1907–23, cond. of Gothenburg Symph. Orch.; c. symph., *"Prinsessan och Svennen"* for voices and orch., music. dramas *"Tirfing"* (Stockholm, 1898), and *"Das Fest auf Solhaug"* (Stuttgart, 1899), overture *"Excelsior,"* and many songs.

Sterkel (shtĕr'-kĕl), Abbé **Jn. Fz. X.,** Würzburg, 1750—Würzburg, 1817; conductor, organist and composer.

Ster'ling, (1) **Antoinette,** Sterlingville, N. Y., Jan. 23, 1850—Hampstead, Jan. 10, 1904; concert and oratorio contralto, range *e* flat—*f''* (v. PITCH, D. D.); pupil of Mme. Marchesi, Viardot-Garcia and Manuel Garcia; sang for a time in Henry Ward Beecher's Ch., at Brooklyn; from 1873, London; 1875, m. John Mac-Kinlay. (2) **Winthrop S.,** Cincinnati, 1859—1943; pupil Cin. Coll.; Leipzig Cons., also under R. Hoffman (comp.) and Frau Unger-Haupt (voice), later in London under Turpin, Behnke and Shakespeare; organist West London Tabernacle; from 1887, prof. Cincinnati Coll. of Mus.; 1903, founder and dean of Met. Coll. of Mus.; founder, Sigma Alpha Iota.

Stern (shtĕrn), (1) **Julius,** Breslau, 1820 —Berlin, 1883; cond., teacher and composer. (2) **Leo,** Brighton, Engl., 1870—London, Sept. 3, 1904; 'cellist; pupil of Piatti and of Klengel and Davidoff, Leipzig; toured U.S., 1897. (3) **Isaac,** b. Kriminiesz, Russia; stud. San Francisco Cons.; violinist; toured U.S., So. America, Europe, Australia.

Sternberg (stĕrn'-bĕrkh), **Constantin (Ivanovitch),** Edler **von,** St. Petersburg, July 9, 1852—Philadelphia, March 31, 1924; pianist; pupil of Leipzig Cons., Berlin Akademie, and of Liszt; conductor various churches; from 1877, toured widely; 1880, United States; from 1890, dir. "Sternberg Sch. of Mus.," Philadelphia; c. pf.—pieces, etc.

Ste'vens, Risë (rē'-zā), American. Mezzo-Sopr.; Met. Op., 1938.

Ste'venson, (1) Sir **J. Andrew,** Dublin, ca. 1762—1833; Mus. Doc.; c. Irish operas; son of (2) **John** (vio-

linist in the State-Band at Dublin). **Stew'art,** (1) Sir **Robt.** Prescott, Dublin, 1825—1894; organist, professor, conductor and composer. (2) **Humphrey John,** London, May 22, 1856— San Diego, Cal., Dec. 28, 1932; eminent organist; after 1836 in San Francisco; 1915, at San Diego Exp. where he remained to give annual series of several hundred recitals on organ in Balboa Park. (3) **Reginald,** pianist; cond. Baltimore Symph.; dir., Peabody Cons., 1942.

Stiastny (Stastný) (sht'yäst'-nē), (1) **Bd.** Wenzel, Prague, 1760—1835; 'cellist, professor and composer. (2) **Fz. Jn.,** Prague, 1764—Mannheim, ca. 1820; bro. and pupil of above; 'cello-virtuoso and composer.

Stich (stīkh), **Jan Václav** (or **Jn. Wenzel**) (Italianised as **"Giovanni Punto"**), Zchuzicz, Bohemia, 1746— Prague, 1803; eminent horn-virtuoso, writer and composer.

Stiedry (shtē'-drē), **Fritz,** b. Vienna, Oct. 11, 1883; conductor; pupil of Mandyczewski; 1907–08, ass't cond. at Dresden Op.; then in various opera theatres; 1916–23, first cond. at Berlin State Op.; 1924–05, dir., Vienna Volksoper; 1929–33 cond. at Municipal Op., Berlin; 1933–08, gen. mus. dir. of Leningrad Philh. Orch.; 1938, cond. New Friends of Music; also Met. Op., and Covent Garden.

Stierlin (shtēr'-lǐn), **Joh. Gottfr. Adolf.,** b. Adenau, Oct. 14, 1859—Münster, April 26, 1930; bass; pupil of F. Schmidt; 1897 founded a Cons. in Münster.

Still, William Grant, b. Woodville, Miss., 1895; Negro composer; among his works, marked by exotic note and modern use of instrumental color, are: (ballet) *"La Guiablesse,"* perf. in Rochester also by Chicago Op.; works for orch., incl. *"Afro-American"* Symphony (N. Y. Philh.); *"Darker America," "Africa," "From the Black Belt," "Puritan Epic," "Levee Land," "From the Journal of a Wanderer," "Log Cabin Ballads,"* opera,*"Troubled Island"* (N.Y.1949).

Stock, Frederick, b. Dülich, Nov. 11, 1872—Chicago, Oct. 20, 1942; son of military bandmaster; then studied with Humperdinck, Zöllner, Jensen and Wüllner, at the Cologne Cons.; 1891–95 violinist in the City Orch.; then joined the Symph. Orch. in Chicago; 1899 became assistant cond.

to Theodore Thomas, on whose death in 1905 he was chosen as conductor; c. symphonic poems, symph., variations, chamber music, songs, etc.

Stockhausen (shtôk'-how-zĕn), (1) **Fz.**, 1792—1868; harpist and composer. His wife (2) **Margarethe** (née **Schmuck**), Gebweiler, 1803—Colmar, 1877; pupil of Cartruffo, Paris; concert-soprano; toured with her husband. (3) **Julius**, Paris, July 22, 1826—Frankfort, Sept. 22, 1906; barytone and eminent teacher; son of above; pupil of Paris Cons. and of Manuel Garcia; succ. concert-singer; 1862-67, cond. Philh. Concerts and Singakademie, at Hamburg; 1869-70, chamber-singer at Stuttgart; 1878-79 and 1882-98, teacher of singing, Hoch Cons., Frankfort; then private teacher; pub. a Method. (4) **Fz.**, Gebweiler, Jan. 30, 1839—Strassburg, Jan. 4, 1926; pupil of Alkan and of Leipzig Cons.; 1868-79, cond. at Strassburg; from 1871 to 1907, teacher Strassburg Cons.; 1892, R. Prof.

Stoessel (stĕs'-ĕl), **Albert**, b. St. Louis, Oct. 11, 1894—N. Y., May 12, 1943; conductor, violinist; studied at Berlin Hochsch., début in that city as violinist; cond. N. Y. Oratorio Soc., succeeding Damrosch, 1921; also Worcester, Mass., and (formerly) Westchester, N. Y., Fests.; 1924, dir. music faculty, N. Y. Univ.; 1930, dir. of opera dept. and cond. of Orch. at Juilliard School, N. Y.; mus. dir. at Chautauqua, N. Y.; c. orch. works, incl. *"Suite Antique,"* vln. sonata, works for piano, songs and choruses; author, *Technique of the Baton.*

Stojowski (stō-yôf'-shkĭ), **Sigismond**, Strelce, 1870—N. Y., Nov. 5, 1946; pianist; pupil of L. Zelenski at Cracow, and at Paris Cons., winning 1st prizes for pf. and comp.; studied with Paderewski; he has lived in New York since 1905 as piano prof. Musical Art Inst. 1905-11, then till 1917 at Von Ende School; afterwards teaching privately and giving frequent recitals, particularly of his own works. C. symph. (Leipzig, 1898); romance for violin and orch.; chor. with orch. *"Spring"*; Polish Rhapsodie for piano and orch.; violin concerto (1908); 3 piano concertos and many other works for this instrument; variations and fugue for string quartet; 2 vln. sonatas;

'cello sonata; choral work, *"A Prayer for Poland"*; Fantaisie for trombone orch. suite, songs, etc.; m. Luisa Morales-Machado, pianist.

Stokowski (stō-kôf'-skĭ), **Leopold**, b. London, April 18, 1882; of Polish parentage; graduated at Oxford; studied at Paris Cons., acted as cond. there; 1905-08 mus. dir. St. Bartholomew's, N. Y.; 1908, cond. in London; 1909-12, cond. Cincinnati Symph. Orch.; after 1912, cond. Philadelphia Orch., vice Carl Pohlig; 1911, married the pianist Olga Samaroff; divorced; (2) Evangeline Brewster Johnson. One of the most brilliant and individual conductors of his day, distinguished by his Spartan discipline over the orch., his tendency to select unconventional music for his programmes, esp. of modern composers. His musical style excels in great clarity and transparency of musical texture, beauty of tone, and exquisite finish of detail. He has arranged for orch. many remarkable transcriptions of works by Bach. In 1930-31 he was guest cond. of the N. Y. Philh. Orch.; in 1936 he took his own orch. for a transcontinental tour of the U. S. He has been identified also with productions of modern operas and ballets by the Phila. Grand Op. Co., the Phila. Orch. and the League of Composers, N. Y. He left Phila Orch., 1938; appeared in films; and formed Amer. Youth. Orch. for tour of So. Amer.; later led N. Y. City Symph. and Hollywood Bowl Orchs. In 1948-9 he was joint mus. dir., N. Y. Philh. with Dimitri Mitropoulos.

Stoltz, (1) **Rosine** (rightly **Victorine Nöb**) (shtôlts or nāp), Paris, Feb. 13, 1815—July 31, 1903; pupil of Choron's Sch.; mezzo-soprano; 1837-47, Gr. Opéra, Paris; other stage names **"Mme. Ternaux,"** **"Mlle. Héloise,"** **"Rose Niva"**; m. successively a baron and 2 princes; c. songs. (2) **Therese**, Bohemia, 1834—Milan, 1902; soprano; début, La Scala, 1865; created "Aïda" in Italy.

Stolz, Robt., b. Graz, 1880; comp. of operettas and films; res. in U. S.

Stoltzer (shtôlts'-ĕr), **Thos.**, Silesia, ca. 1490—Ofen, 1526; ct.-conductor and composer.

Stölz(e)l (shtĕlts'-ĕl), **Gf. H.**, Grünstädtl, Saxony, 1690—Gotha, 1749; ct.-conductor and dram. composer.

Stolzenberg (shtôl'-tsĕn-bĕrkh), **Benno,** Königsberg, Feb. 25, 1829—Berlin, 1908; tenor; pupil of Mantius and H. Dorn; début, Königsberg, 1852; dir. Danzig City Th.; teacher, Berlin; 1885, Cologne Cons.; from 1896, dir. of a vocal sch. at Berlin.

Stöpel (shtā'-pĕl), **Fz. (David Chp.),** Oberheldrungen, Saxony, 1794— Paris, 1836; theorist.

Stör (shtār), **K.,** Stolberg, Harz, 1814 —Weimar, 1889; violinist, cond. and dram. composer.

Sto'race, (1) **Stephen,** London, 1763 —(of gout) 1796, prod. 18 stage-works; son and pupil of (2) **Stefano S.,** an Italian double-bass-player. (3) **Anna Selina** (1766—1817), famous colorature-soprano; daughter and pupil of (2); sang in public at 8; then début, Florence, 1780; created "Susanna" in Mozart's *"Figaro."*

Stracciari (strä-chä'-rē), **Riccardo; b.** Bologna, June 26, 1875; eminent barytone; pupil of Liceo in native city; début in *"La Bohème"* at birthplace, 1900; later sang with succ. in many cities of Italy, Spain, North and South America; after 1926 taught at the Naples Conservatory.

Stradal (strä'-däl), **August,** Teplitz, 1860—Schönlinde, Bohemia, March 13, 1930; pupil of Door, Bruckner and Liszt; pianist and composer.

Stradella (strä-dĕl'-lä), **Alessandro,** probably Naples or Venice, ca. 1645 —Genoa, after 1681 (the date of his last cantata); important Italian composer, of whom little is actually known, though he is the hero of an extraordinarily melodramatic legend of jealous nobility, paid assassins, and love pursued. In a work by Bonnet-Bourdelot (1715), it is said that his name was Stradel and being engaged to write an opera for Venice, he eloped with the mistress of a nobleman who sent paid *bravi* to assassinate him in Rome. These men were overcome by the beauty of an oratorio of his and warned him of his danger. He fled to Turin with the woman who passed for his wife, and after being followed here and there, and recovering from numerous wounds, was finally slain in Genoa. Flotow made an opera of this story, in which there is much that is incredible. S. was also credited with being a singer and poet, and a wonder-

ful harpist. In any case, 148 of his works exist in MS. in the Modena Library, and others elsewhere, incl. 8 oratorios, many cantatas, madrigals, duets, etc. The church-aria *"Pietà, Signore,"* and the arias *"O del mio dolce ardor"* and *"Se i miei sospiri,"* are probably wrongly attributed to him. Monographs by P. Richard, "A. Stradella" (1866), and Catelane.

Stradivari (Stradivarius) (sträd-ĭ-vä'-rē, or vä'-rĭ-oos), (1) **Antonio,** Cremona, 1644 (1650 ?)—Dec. 17 (18 ?), 1737; maker of vlns., vlas., 'cellos, etc., who established a type and proportion never improved; his tone is also supreme among vlns. (with the possible exception of those of Jos. Guarneri); he probably worked for Niccolò Amati, 1667–79; 1680, he purchased the house in which his workshop thereafter was situated; 1700–25, is his best period, but he worked to 1736; his label reads "Antonius Stradivarius Cremonensis. Fecit Anno . . . (A † S)." Of his eleven children, 2 sons, (2) **Fran.** (1671—1745) and (3) **Omobono** (1679 —1742), were his assistants. Monographs, by Lombardini (1872), Fétis (1856); Wasielewski and Riechers.

Straeten, van der. Vide VANDER-STRAETEN.

Strakosch (shträ'-kôsh), (1) **Moritz,** Lemberg, Galicia, 1825—Paris, Oct. 9, 1887; pianist and impresario; c. operas; teacher of Adelina, and husband of Carlotta, Patti. (2) **Max,** d. New York, 1892; bro. of above and equally famous as impresario.

Stran'sky, Josef, Humpolec, Bohemia, Sept. 9, 1872—New York, March 6, 1936; of German parents; studied medicine at first; and then music while at the universities of Vienna, Leipzig and Prague; début as cond. at Prague Opera, succeeding Muck, later succeeded Mahler at Hamburg; cond. Blüthner orch., Berlin; 1911, succeeded Mahler as cond. N. Y. Philh. Orch., of which he was the successful sole leader until 1923; 1923–24, cond. State Symph. Orch., N. Y., then resigning to become a dealer in paintings.

Straube (strow'-bĕ), **C.,** b. Berlin, Jan. 6, 1873; noted organist; pupil of Riemann, Rüfer, and A. Becker; 1902 organist Thomaskirche (vice C. Piatti); from 1903 he alsr cond.

the Bach Verein there; 1907 organ teacher at Leipzig Cons.; after 1918, Cantor of the Thomaskirche; 1919, merged the B.-Verein with the Gewandhaus Choir; led notable Bach Fests.; d. Leipzig, Apr. 27, 1950.

Straus (shtrows), **Oskar,** b. Vienna, April 6, 1870; pupil of Grädener and Max Bruch; cond. theatres in various cities; c. overture *"Der Traum ein Leben,"* chamber music and many operas, some of them extremely successful, especially *"Ein Walzertraum"* (Vienna, 1906; London and America as *"The Waltz Dream"*); *"Der tapfere Soldat"* (Vienna, 1908), (*"Chocolate Soldier"*); d. Ischl, 1954.

Strauss (shtrows), (1) **Jos.,** Brünn, 1793—Carlsruhe, Dec. 1 (2 ?), 1866; violinist, mus.-director, ct.-conductor; c. operas. (2) **Jn.** (Sr.), Vienna, March 14, 1804—(of scarlet fever) Sept. 25, 1849, "The Father of the Waltz"; son of proprietor of a beer and dance-hall; conductor and composer of 152 waltzes all more or less famous. (3) **Jn.** (Jr.), Vienna, Oct. 25, 1825—June 3, 1899; "The Waltz-King"; son of above, who opposed the mus. tastes of the three sons, for whom the mother secured secret instruction. In 1844 conductor of court-balls and very succ. orch. concerts. He had c. a waltz at 6, and his later comps. eclipsed the success of those of his father, after whose death he united the two orchestras. 1862, he m. the singer Henriette Treffz; (d. 1878); (2) Angelica Dittrich; (3) Marie Strauss; c. 400 pcs. of dance-music; his waltzes *"The beautiful blue Danube,"* *"Künstlerleben,"* *"Wiener Blut,"* *"The 1001 Nights,"* *"Wine, Women and Song,"* etc., are dance-rhapsodies whose verve and colour have deserved and won the highest praise of severe musicians. His light operas rival his waltzes in charm and succ. and incl. the v. succ. *"Die Fledermaus"* ('74). (4) **Jos.,** Vienna, Aug. 22, 1827—July 22, 1870; bro. of above, during whose illness in 1853 he served as cond.; later formed an orch. of his own and learned the vln.; on a tour to Warsaw a brain ailment showed itself (long attributed to a beating by officers); died in the arms of his wife (whom he had m. in 1857); he c. 283 dances. (5) **Eduard,** Vienna, Feb. 14, 1835—

Dec. 28, 1916; bro. and succ. of Johann as cond. of the ct.-balls and orch.; took his orch. to America 1892 and 1900; c. dance-mus. (6) **Ludwig,** Pressburg, March 28, 1836—Cambridge, Engl., 1899; violinist. (7) **Victor von,** Royal opera conductor, Berlin, 1902. (8) **Richard,** b. Munich, June 11, 1864—d. Garmisch, Sept. 8, 1949; early showed brilliant genius; son of (8) Fz. S. (chambermus. and horn-player); studied also with W. Meyer. At 4 he c. a polka. He took a regular Gymnasium course 1874–82, and spent two years at the univ. At 17 his first symph. was prod. by Levi; his *"Serenade"* for 13 wind-instrs. had much succ. with the Meiningen orch. under von Bülow, to whom S. became asst., and (1885) successor as ct.-mus. dir. at Meiningen; 1886, 3rd cond. at Munich; 1889, ct.-cond. at Weimar under Lassen; 1894, cond. at the ct.-opera, Munich, also 1894, cond. Berlin Philh., and from 1898, cond. at Berlin Royal Opera. He m. the soprano, Pauline de Ahna, who created "Freihilde" in his opera *"Guntram"* (Weimar, 1894, Munich, '95). His 1-act opera *"Feuersnoth"* (*"Fire-Famine"*), libretto by Wolzogen, was prod. Dresden, Nov. 21, 1901, with much success. He has also cond. with great succ. in various cities. A Strauss Festival was given in London, 1903, with S. conducting the Amsterdam Orch.; 1904 he was made general musical director of the Berlin Royal Opera. In the same year he cond. in the U. S. C. symph. op. 12; symphonic fantasie *"Aus Italien,"* *"Wanderers Sturmlied"* (Goethe), for 6-part chorus, and full orch.; tone-poems, *"Don Juan,"* op. 20; *"Macbeth,"* op. 23; *"Tod und Verklärung,"* op. 24, the symph. poems *"Also sprach Zarathustra"* (after Nietzsche), *"Ein Heldenleben"* (op. 40), and *"Don Quixote"*; op. 28, Orchester-Rondo *"Till Eulenspiegel's lustige Streiche"*; chamber-mus.; vln.-concerto; 5 *"Stimmungsbilder"* for pf.; concerto for Waldhorn; *"Enoch Arden,"* melodrama for pf. and recitation, and many songs. 16-part *a cappella* chorus *"Der Abend"* (1902), ballad for chorus and orch. *"Taillefer"* (1902); *"Sinfonia Domestica"* (1904); operas *"Salomé"* (1 act after Oscar Wilde, Dresden,

1905, and throughout Europe; prod. at Met. Op., 1907; it was withdrawn after one performance but restored 1934 with succ.); *"Elektra"* (Dresden, 1909, and at Manhattan Op., N. Y., 1910); *"Der Rosenkavalier"* (Dresden, June 26, 1911, and at Met. Op., 1913); *"Ariadne auf Naxos"* (Stuttgart, Oct. 25, 1912, revised 1917); *"Die Frau ohne Schatten"* (1921); *"Intermezzo"* (1924, a work said to be based on a mild marital misunderstanding in his own career); *"Die Aegyptische Helena"* (Dresden, 1928, also at Met. Op. House, without succ.); *"Arabella"* (1933, comedy which uses waltz themes somewhat in manner of *"Rosenkavalier"* but not as strong as that world-conquering work); *"Die Schweigsame Frau"* (1933); the ballets *"Josephslegende"* (1914) and *"Schlagobers"* ("Whipped Cream," allegory of pastry shop, 1923). Also a pf.-concerto for the left hand, *"Parergon zur Sinfonia Domestica und Panathenaeen-zug,"* written for Paul Wittgenstein. His last important orch. work was the rather weak *"Alpensinfonie"* (1915), *"Metamorphosen"* (for 23 string insts.); Oboe Concerto; opera, *"Liebe der Danaë."* His later works have tended to revert to a greater simplicity in scoring, some, like his incidental music to *"Der Bürger als Edelmann,"* have Mozartian influence. His post-war works have displayed a decline in invention, though his scoring wizardry is still in evidence. S. made a notable tour of the U. S. in 1921, when he led a cycle of his works in N. Y. with the Phila. Orch.; cond. in many Eur. cities; 1919–24, dir. with Schalk of the Vienna Op.; 1933–35, he was pres. of the Reich Music Chamber in Germany; in 1938 a 1-act opera, *"Friedenstag,"* was premièred at the Munich State Op.; and *"Daphne,"* at Dresden, 1938; opera, *"Capriccio."* Biographical works by Seidl, Klatte, Hutschenruijter, Brecher, Urban, Bie, Newman, Steinitzer, Finck, Waltershausen, and studies of his comps. by Gilman, Hutcheson, Rose and Pruewer, Schattmann, etc. S. revised and completed Berlioz's treatise on instrumentation. (See article, page 529.)

Stravinsky (strä-vēn'-skē), **Igor**, b. Oranienbaum, Russia, June 17, 1882;

composer; one of most striking technical innovators of his period, a remarkable craftsman and highly influential upon other composers, studied comp. with Rimsky-Korsakoff, in whose memory he wrote a *"Chant Funèbre"* and also his early symph. piece, *"Fireworks,"* for the wedding of the latter's daughter; his first productions were marked by original and highly brilliant impressionistic use of orch. color, exploiting strange timbres and instrumental effects, and drew upon Russian folklore, esp. for his pop. ballets *"L'Oiseau de Feu"* and *"Petrouchka,"* which created much interest when prod. by Diaghileff. With *"Le Sacre du Printemps"* (1913), the strident and bizarre effects that made *"Petrouchka"* a masterpiece of bitter irony were augmented with an unprecedented complexity of rhythm and harsh, grinding dissonances which literally portrayed the earth-beating dances of a prehistoric race in a spring fest.; to this period belongs also his Chinese fairy opera, *"Le Rossignol,"* more delicately dissonant and based on an Andersen story, which was given by the Met. Op. Co., 1926. After *"Les Noces,"* written as a "symphony" but prod. as a ballet which portrays Russian wedding customs of the past with salty gusto, the style of S. became progressively more reticent and also economical of means. His ironic *"Histoire du Soldat"* with a chamber ensemble and narrator, has been danced and also presented in concert form; his *"Renard,"* a sort of animal fable in chamber style with voice and instruments, is also marked by delightful wit; a short opera, *"Mavra,"* oddly echoes (with intent) Glinka and Italian styles. The tendency to compose in the manner of earlier creators asserts itself increasingly in his later works, which has been construed as symptomatic of his attempt to find new paths, but by others as a confession of lack of inspiration. Beginning with his post-war productions, his music is increasingly neo-classic in style. It takes the form of compositions for small instrumental combinations, for various solo instruments with orch. and in concertante form, which embody his strivings after an ideal of "pure music," in which emotion and overemphasis are sternly restricted. Parallel to this, **S.** has shown a fondness for antique subjects and Greek myths, treated in heroic manner and in neo-classic garb: such are his *"Oedipus Rex,"* a dram. cantata for soloists, male chorus, narrator and orch. (prod. in Paris, N. Y. and elsewhere); his *"Symphonie de Psaumes"* for chorus and orch., settings of 3 Hebrew psalms stressing warlike spirit in austere fashion; *"Apollon Musagète"* for orch.; and *"Perséphone,"* a mimetic cantata based on the Greek myth, in which a woman mime-reciter, tenor, chorus and orch. take part (given in concert form by the Boston Symph., under the composer); has also c. (ballets) *"Pulcinella"* (after Pergolesi), *"Baiser de la Fée"* and *"Les Abeilles"*; (orch.) *"Scherzo Fantastique,"* a symphony; suites based upon his most pop. ballet scores; *"Le Rossignol"* (symph. poem); "Symphonie Concertante" and Octuor for wind instruments; Concertino; a Concerto and a Capriccio for piano and orch.; two-piano concerto; vln. concerto; "Duo Concertante" for piano and vln., and many other smaller pieces for piano and other insts.; ballets, *"Card Party,"* *"Orpheus"*; Mass for male voices; many songs. Was guest cond. of various orchs., incl. N.Y. Philh., Phila., Boston, Chicago and elsewhere. Soon after the war he took up res. in U.S. and has become a citizen of that country. He has toured with Samuel Dushkin, violinist, and with his son, Soulima Stravinsky, pianist, in chamber programmes; has visited leading Eur. cities and S. A. as a guest cond.; Eliot Chair of Poetry, Harvard, 1940. **S.** has published a book of reminiscences, as well as various "manifestos" and the like, setting forth his artistic ideals. A biography (in French) by André Schaeffner was pub. 1931. A large number of essays on the composer and his work have been issued, by Van Vechten, Wise, Montagu-Nathan, Boris de Schloezer and others. Edwin Evans has written a study of his *"Firebird"* and *"Petrouchka."* (See article, page 530.)

Streabbog. Vide GOBBAERTS.

Streat'feild, Rich. Alex., Carshalton, 1866—London, 1919; writer; 1898–1912, critic of London *Daily Graphic*; author, *"Masters of Italian Music," "The Opera," "Modern Music and Musicians," "Handel," "Life Stories of Great Composers,"* etc.

Street (shtrāt), **G. Ernest,** of French parents, Vienna, 1854—1908; pupil of Bizet and Damcke, Paris; critic there; 1898, of *L'Éclair;* c. operettas, 1-act mimodrama *"Fides"* (Op.-Com., 1894), 3-act opera *"Mignonette,"* parody of Thomas's *"Mignon"* (1896), ballet, *"Scaramouche"* with Messager, 1891, etc.

Streicher (shtrī'-khĕr), (1) **Jn. Andreas,** Stuttgart, 1761—Vienna, 1833; piano-maker and professor; 1793 inv. the pf.-action which drops the hammer from above; succeeded 1832 by his son (2) **Jn. Bapt.,** 1794–1871, who was succeeded by his son (3) **Emil.**

Strelezki (strĕ-lĕt'-shkĭ), **Anton** (rightly **Burnand**), Croydon, Engl., Dec. 5, 1859—1907; pupil of Leipzig Cons., and of Frau Schumann; c. popular songs, and pf.-pcs.

Strepponi. Vide VERDI.

Striggio (strĭd'-jō), **Ales.,** b. Mantua, ca. 1535; lutenist, composer and conductor.

Strinasacchi (strē-nä-säk'-kē), **Regina,** Ostiglia, near Mantua, 1764—Dresden, 1839; violinist.

String'ham, Edwin John, b. Kenosha, Wis., July 11, 1890; composer, educator; grad. Northwestern Univ.; Ped. Doc., Cincinnati Cons., studied with Respighi at St. Cecilia Acad., Rome; hon. Mus. D., Denver Coll, of Music; dean, College of Music, Denver, 1919–29; mem. faculty of music education, Teachers College, Columbia Univ.; also taught Union Seminary, N. Y.; c. orch. works, incl. symphony, suites, overtures, etc., played by several major Amer. orchestras.

Strong, (1) **Templeton,** N. Y., 1856—Geneva, 1948; pupil Leipzig Cons.; c. symph. *"In den Bergen"*; symph. poem *"Undine"* (op. 14); *"Gestrebt—Gewonnen—Gescheitert"*; f. orch. with vln.-obbligato; choral works with orch.; pf.-pcs., etc. (2) **Susan,** b. Brooklyn, N. Y., 1875; operatic soprano; studied with Korbay; sang in Italy, England and in U. S. with companies under Mapleson and Damrosch; Met. Op., 1899–1900.

Strozzi (strôd'-zē), (1) **Pietro, b.** Florence, 16th cent.; co-founder of the *stile rappresentativo* (v. PERI); set to music Caccini's "*La Mascarada degli Accecati,*" 1595. (2) Abbate **Gregorio,** apostolic protonotary at Naples; composer, 1683.

Strube (shtroo'-bĕ), **Gustav, b.** Ballenstedt, Harz, March 3, 1867; violinist; pupil of his father; at 10 in Ballenstedt orch.; at 16 pupil of Leipzig Cons.; played in the Gewandhaus Orch., later prof. at Mannheim Cons.; 1889, Boston, Mass., in Symph. Orch.; c. symphony in C minor, in B minor; overtures "*The Maid of Orleans*"; "*Fantastic*"; "*Puck*"; symph. poems "*Longing,*" "*Fantastic Dance*"; concertos, violin, 'cello, etc.; 1909 he became a cond. of the Worcester Festivals; 1913 taught Peabody Cons., Baltimore; after 1916 he cond. Symph. Orch. there.

Stueckgold (shtēk'-gôlt), **Grete, b.** London, July 6, 1895; soprano; of English-German parentage; studied voice in Germany with Jacques Stueckgold; operatic début in Nuremberg; engaged for Berlin Städtische Oper, where she sang with succ., incl. leading rôle in Handel's "*Otto and Theophanes*" under Bruno Walter; mem. Met. Op. Co., N. Y., for several seasons after 1929; also a high-ranking concert artist (esp. Lieder singer) and has appeared in radio programmes; m. Gustav Schuetzendorf, barytone.

Stuntz (shtoonts), **Jos. Hartmann,** Arlesheim, near Basel, 1793—Munich, 1859; dram. composer.

Such (zookh), **Percy, b.** June 27, 1878; 'cellist; studied with Robt. Haasmanns; toured widely.

Sucher (zoo'-khĕr), (1) **Josef,** Döbör, Hungary, Nov. 23, 1844—Berlin, April 4, 1908; eminent cond.; studied singing and the vln., Vienna; pupil of Sechter (comp.); vice-cond. of the acad. Gesangverein; coach for solo singers at the ct.-opera; 1876, cond. Leipzig City Th.; 1877, m. the distinguished Wagnerian soprano, (2) **Rosa Hasselbeck,** Velburg, Upper Palatinate, Feb. 23, 1849—Eschweiler, April 16, 1927; 1878–88 they were engaged by Pollini at Hamburg; later as cond. of the Royal

Opera at Berlin (retired 1899), and prima donna (retired 1898). Frau S. was daughter of a musician and sang small rôles at Munich and elsewhere at first, later prominent in Wagner opera which she sang at Bayreuth and in America.

Suk (sook), **Josef,** Křečovic, Bohemia, Jan. 4, 1874—Beneschau, May 29, 1935; composer and violinist; pupil and son-in-law of Dvořák at Prague Cons., 1896, 2nd vln. "Bohemian String-Quartet"; c. a dramatic overture "*Winter's Tale,*" suite for orch. op. 16 "*Ein Märchen,*" 2 symphonies, 2 string quartets, piano quartet and trio, and a choral work, "*Under the Apple Tree,*" etc.

Sul'livan, Sir **Arthur Seymour,** London, May 14, 1842—Nov. 22, 1900; eminent composer of national English comic opera; v. succ. in churchmus. also; at 12 a chorister under Helmore, Chapel Royal; at 13 pub. a song; 1856, the first Mendelssohn Scholar of the R. A. M.; studied also at Leipzig Cons., etc. At 18 cond. his overture "*Lalla Rookh*"; at 20 prod. his mus. to "*The Tempest*" (Crystal Palace); at 22 his notable cantata "*Kenilworth*" (Birmingham festival); cond. of the London Philharm. (1885–87); and from 1880, the Leeds Festivals. 1876–81, principal, and prof. of comp. at the Nat. Training Sch. for Mus.; Mus. Doc. *h.c.*, Cambridge (1876), and Oxford (1879), Chev. of the Legion of Honour, 1878; grand organist to the Freemasons, 1887; knighted, 1883. C. symphony (played at the Gewandhaus, Leipzig, etc.) overtures "*In Memoriam*" (on his father's death), "*Marmion,*" "*Di ballo,*" and "*Sapphire Necklace*"; oratorios and cantatas, incl. "*The Golden Legend*" (1886); "*A Festival Te Deum*" (1872), Ode "*I Wish to Tune my Quivering Lyre,*" with orch., and succ. incid. mus. to 8 of Shakespeare's plays and others; c. much v. succ. church-mus. of all kinds. His operas include the grand opera, "*Ivanhoe*" (1891), the romantic opera, "*Rose of Persia*" (1900), neither a succ.

His chief contribution to music was his brilliant series of truly English comic operas, with the equally brilliant librettos of W. S. Gilbert. Some of these had a world-wide succ., and "*Patience*" was a satire of equal effectiveness with Molière's "*Les Précieuses Ridicules.*" Among 16 comic operas were the following great successes: "*Cox and Box*" (1867), "*Trial by Jury*" (1875), "*H. M. S. Pinafore*" (1878), "*The Pirates of Penzance*" (1880), "*Patience*" (1881), "*Iolanthe*" (1882), "*The Mikado*" (1885), "*Ruddigore*" (1887), "*The Yeomen of the Guard*" (1888), "*The Gondoliers,*" "*Utopia (Limited)*" (1893); "*Contrabandista*" (1867, revised 1894 as "*The Chieftain*"), "*The Emerald Isle*" (1901), finished by Edw. German, libretto by Basil Hood. Among many works on S. and his music are those by Lawrence, Wells, Wyndham, Findon, Goldberg, Bridgeman, Mackenzie, Dunhill, Godwin, and a life (with letters and diaries) by Herbert Sullivan and Newman Flower (1927). (See article, page 533.)

Sulzer (zool'-tsĕr), (1) **Jn. G.**, Winterthur, 1720—Berlin, 1779; writer and professor. (2) **Salomon,** of Jewish parents, Hohenems, Vorarlberg, 1804 —Vienna, 1890; prof. of singing and composer. (3) **Julius,** Vienna, 1834 —1891; son of above; violinist and conductor, and c. operas. His sisters (4) **Marie** and (5) **Henriette,** singers.

Supervia (soo-pĕr-vē'-ä), **Conchita,** Spain, 1899—London, March 30, 1936; coloratura mezzo-soprano; début, Buenos Aires, at 14; sang with Madrid Op., later at La Scala, Paris, Vienna with succ., acquiring rep. for great flexibility of voice and wide range; also with Chicago Op., 1932 as "Carmen" and "Rosina"; at Covent Garden in "*L'Italiana in Algeri*" and "*Cenerentola*"; she was also a popular recitalist, esp. in Spanish music, and esteemed for her beauty and charm of personality.

Suppé, Fz. von (fōn-zoop'-pā), Spalato, Dalmatia, 1819—Vienna, May 21, 1895; very popular operetta composer; pupil of Padua, Cigala, and Ferrari; at first unpaid cond. at the Josephstädter Th.; then at Pressburg and Baden and at Vienna; he c. 2 grand operas, a symph., a Missa Dalmatica, a requiem, "*L'estremo giudizio.*" overtures (incl. the immensely pop. "*Dichter und Bauer,*" pub. for 59 combinations). Of his Singspiele, comediettas, etc., some (like "*Tannenhauser*" and "*Dinorah*") are

parodies, of the others the most succ. are "*Fatinitza*" (Vienna, 1876), and "*Boccaccio*" (1879).

Surette (sū-rĕt'), **Thos. Whitney, b.** Concord, Mass., Sept. 7, 1862— May 19, 1941; graduated Harvard, 1891; pupil there of Arthur Foote (pf.), and J. K. Paine; organist, Baltimore; then University Extension lecturer (Phila.); after 1921, taught at Bryn Mawr Coll., Pa.; wrote treatises, etc.; pub. 2-act operetta "*Priscilla,*" etc.

Suriano (or Soriano) (soo'-[or sō'] rĭ-ä-nō), **Fran.,** Rome, 1549—Jan., 1620; conductor and notable composer; pupil of Nanini and Palestrina; cond. S. Maria Maggiore, and 1603, at St. Peter's, Rome.

Süssmayer (züs'-mī-ĕr), **Fz. X.,** Steyr, Upper Austria, 1766—Vienna, 1803; conductor and dram. composer.

Suter (zoo'-tĕr), **Hermann,** Kaiserstuhl, Switzerland, April 28, 1870— Basel, June 22, 1926; pupil of his father, an organist, and of the Stuttgart and Leipzig Cons.; from 1892, organist and cond. in Zürich, from 1902 in Basel as cond.; c. quartets and choruses.

Sutor (zoo'-tôr), **Wilhelm,** Edelstetten, 1774—Linden, Sept. 7, 1828; court cond. at Hanover; c. operas, etc.

Su'tro, (1) **Rose Laura** (Baltimore, 1870), pianist, and (2) **Ottilie** (Baltimore, 1872), pianist, sisters noted for their two-piano concerts; pupils of Berlin Hochsch.

Svan'holm, Set, Swedish heroic tenor; heard Stockholm Opera; elsewhere Europe; engaged M. O. H. 1946–7; debut as Siegfried.

Svecenski (svä-chĕn'-skĕ), **Louis,** Osijek, Croatia, 1862—New York, June 18, 1926; violinist and violist; pupil of Vienna Cons.; 1885–1903 played in Boston Symph.; 1885– 1917, viola of Kneisel Quartet; taught at Inst. of Mus. Art, N. Y., and later at Curtis Inst., Philadelphia.

Svendsen (svĕnt'-zĕn), (1) **Oluf,** Christiania, 1832—London, 1888; flutist. (2) **Johan (Severin),** Christiania, Sept. 30, 1840—Copenhagen, June 13, 1911; important, though eclectic composer; son of a bandm.; at 11 c. vln.-pcs.; at 15 enlisted in the army and was soon bandm., and played flute, clarinet, and vln.; with a stipend from

Charles XV., he studied v'n.; at 23 he became pupil of David and Hauptmann, Richter, and Reinecke, Leipzig Cons.; toured 1868–69, in Musard's orch.; and at the Odéon, Paris; 1869, Leipzig; 1871, m. an American in New York; 1872–77, and 1880–83, cond. Christiania Mus. Assoc.; 1883–1908, ct.-cond. at Copenhagen; from 1896, cond. Royal Th. there. C. 2 symphonies, overture to Björnson's *"Sigurd Slembe"*; *"Romeo and Juliet,"* funeral march for Charles XV., coronation march (for Oscar II.), wedding-cantata, etc., with orch.; op. 16, *"Carnaval des artistes norvégiens,"* humorous march; 4 *"Norwegian Rhapsodies"* for orch.; vln. and 'cello concertos, chamber-music and songs, etc.

Swar'thout, (1) **Donald Malcolm,** b. Pawpaw, Ill., Aug. 9, 1884; educator; studied in Chicago, at Leipzig Cons., and piano with Philipp; formerly assoc. dir. of music, Oxford Coll., Ohio, and Millikin Univ.; after 1923, prof. of pf. and dean, School of Fine Arts, Univ. of Kansas, where he served as cond. of Lawrence Choral Union and of annual music fests.; sec'y, Music Teachers Nat'l Assoc.; ed. *University Course of Music Study.* (2) **Gladys,** b. Deepwater, Mo., Dec. 25, 1904; mezzo-soprano; studied in Kansas City and at Bush Cons., Chicago; début, 1923, as soloist with Minneapolis Symph.; mem. Chicago Civic Op. Co., 1924–25; Ravinia Op. Co., 1927–29; after latter year mem. Met. Op. Co.; also active as concert, radio and film artist; m. Frank Chapman, barytone.

Sweelinck (or **Swelinck,** the best 2 of the 7 spellings) (svā'-lǐnk), (1) **Jan Pieter** (called **Jan Pieterszoon**), Amsterdam, 1562—Oct. 16, 1621; chief of Dutch organists. Son and (1577–81) successor, probably also pupil, of (2) **Pieter** (d. 1573), who had won pre-eminence as the org.-virtuoso and teacher of his own time. (1) was the first to employ the pedal in a real fugal part, and originated the org.-fugue; c. psalms, motets, etc.

Sweet, Reginald, b. Yonkers, N. Y., Oct. 14, 1885; composer; pupil of Noyes, Eisenberger, Koch and Kaun; taught at Chautauqua and in N. Y.; c. (one-act opera) *"Riders to the Sea,"* chamber music, etc.

Swert, Jules de. Vide DESWERT.

Swieten (svē'tĕn), **Gf.,** Baron **von,** 1734—Vienna, 1803; eminent patron, but unimportant composer, of music; c. 6 symphs.

Swinnerton, Heap. Vide HEAP.

Sympson. Vide SIMPSON.

Szanto (shän'tō), **Theodore,** Vienna, June 3, 1877—Budapest, Jan. 1, 1934; noted pianist; pupil of Koessler at Budapest Acad.; also of Busoni; lived in Budapest, 1914–21 in Switzerland, then in Paris and Helsingfors; composer.

Szarvady. Vide CLAUSZ-SZARVADY.

Székely (shā'-kĕ-lē), **Imre (Emeric),** Matyasfalva, Hungary, May 8, 1823 —Budapest, April 8, 1887; pianist; studied in Budapest; toured 1846; from 1852 teacher Budapest; c. Hungarian fantasias on national airs; pf.-concertos, etc.

Szell (shĕl), **Georg,** b. Budapest, June 7, 1897; conductor, composer; studied with Robert, Mandyczewski and Reger; début with Tonkünstler Orch., Vienna, at 11; asst. cond. R. Opera, Berlin, 1915; cond. Strasbourg, 1917; dir. Düsseldorf Op., 1921; cond. Berlin State Op., 1924–29; dir. Prague Op. after 1929; has appeared with leading orchs. in Europe, incl. London and U. S. (guest cond. St. Louis Symph., 1930–1); cond. Met. Op., 1944; cond. Cleveland Orch., from 1946.

Szenkar (shĕn'-kär), **Eugen,** b. Budapest, April 9, 1891; conductor; pupil of Budapest Acad.; after 1911 active as opera cond.; 1922 in Frankfort; 1923–24, at Berlin Volksop.; 1924–33, in Cologne; after 1934 cond. of Moscow Philh.; later in Brazil.

Szigeti (sē-gĕt'-ē), **Joseph,** b. Budapest, Sept. 2, 1892; violinist; studied with Hubay; performer of high musicianship and purity of style; an outstanding virtuoso; has appeared with important orchs. in Europe and U. S., also as recitalist and chamber music player; particularly noted for his perfs. of Beethoven and Bach; has ed. and transcribed many works for violin.

Szumowska (shoo-mōf'-shkä), **Antoinette,** Lublin, Poland, Feb. 22, 1868 —Rumson, N. J., Aug. 18, 1938; pianist; pupil of Strobel, Michalowski and Paderewski; played with great succ. at London, Paris, New

York, Boston, etc.; m. Joseph Adamowski; lived in Boston.

Szymanowska (shē-mä-nôf'-shkä), **Maria** (née **Wolowska**), Poland, 1790—(of cholera), Petersburg, 1832; pianist; pupil of Field at Moscow; ct.-pianist at Petersburg; Goethe was infatuated with her and she with him; c. 24 mazurkas, etc.

Szymanowski (shē-män-ôf'-skē), **Karol**, Timoshovka, Ukraine, 1883—near Lausanne, March 27, 1937; Polish composer, considered the most important creative figure of his nation since Chopin; early composed piano pieces during study with Noskowski, which have marked individuality; about 1914 his style underwent a change to more complex harmony; the transitional period in his work marked by the music drama, (one act) "*Hagith*," comp. 1912 but not prod. in Warsaw until 1922, which shows a somewhat Straussian style; later his works are increasingly marked by atonality and post-impressionism, also by greater subtlety, refinement of effect, and emotional power; c. (operas) "*Hagith*"; "*King Roger*"; (ballet) "*Harnasie*" (with vocal solcist); (masques) "*Scheherazade*"; "*Tantris the Fool*"; "*Don Juan's Serenade*"; (orch.) 3 symphonies; "*Penthesilea*"; Serenata; Sinfonia Concertante; vln. concerto; (chamber music) string quartet, vln. and piano sonata; (choral works) "*Stabat Mater*," "*Demeter*," "*Agave*"; and many piano works incl. "*Masks*" and "*Myths*," songs, etc.

T

Tacchinardi (täk-kĭ-när'-dē), (1) **Nicola**, Florence, 1772—1859; at 17 a violinist; later a tenor of greatest European popularity, even singing "Don Giovanni" (transposed) with succ., though he was hideous and a hunchback. His daughter (2) **Fanny Tacchinardi-Persiani** (v. PERSIANI). His daughter (3) **Elisa** was a pianist.

Tadolini (tä-dō-lē'-nē), (1) **Giov.**, Bologna, 1793—1872; dram. composer; m. (2) **Eugenia Savorini** (b. Forli, 1809), a singer.

Taffanel (tăf'-fŭ-nĕl), **Claude Paul**, Bordeaux, Sept. 16, 1844—Paris,

Nov. 22, 1908; flutist, pupil of Dorns (flute) and Reber (comp); 3rd cond. Grand Opéra, Paris; 1892, dir. Paris Cons. concerts—resigned, 1901; 1893, prof. of flute there.

Tag (täkh), **Chr. Gotthilf**, Bayerfeld, Saxony, 1735—Niederzwönitz, 1811; composer.

Tagliafico (täl-yä-fē'-kō), **Jos. Dieudonné**, Toulon, Jan. 1, 1821—Nice, Jan. 27, 1900; operatic singer and stage-manager in London.

Tagliana (täl-yä'-nä), **Emilia**, b. Milan, 1854; pupil of the Cons. there, also of Lamperti; coloratura-soprano in various cities; 1873–77, Vienna.

Tagliavini (täl-yä-vē'-nē), **F.**, noted Ital. lyric tenor; M. O. H. 1946–7.

Täglichsbeck (täkh'-lĭkhs-bĕk), **Thos.**, Ansbach, 1799—Baden-Baden, 1867; violinist, conductor and dram. composer.

Taglioni (täl-yō'-nē), **Fdo.**, Naples Sept. 14, 1810—?; son of the famous ballet-master **Salvatore T.** (1790—1868). 1842–49, cond. at Laziano; till 1852, leader San Carlo Th., Naples; editor and conductor; founded a sch. for choral singing; pub pamphlets and sacred songs.

Tailleferre (tī'-fĕr), **Germaine**, b. Pau-St.-Maur near Paris, April 19, 1892; composer, pianist; pupil of Paris Cons.; belonged to "Group of Six"; her works marked by taste and sensitiveness, not radical in manner, but in tradition of Debussy, Fauré, etc.; visited U. S. as guest pianist in her works; c. Ballade for piano and orch.; "*Pastorale*," "*Les Jeux de Plein Air*"; string quartet; (ballet) "*Le Marchand d'Oiseaux*" (Swedish Ballet, Paris, 1923), etc.

Tal'ich, Vaclav, b. Kromentz, Moravia, 1883; conductor; pupil of Prague Cons., of Reger and Nikisch in Leipzig, also studied in Milan; played vln. in Berlin Philh.; later active as cond. in Tiflis, Prague, Laibach, Pilsen, and after 1918 with the Czech Philh. Orch.; toured in other countries; 1936, appointed dir. of Prague National Theatre, succeeding the late Ottakar Ostrcil.

Tal'ley, Marion, b. Nevada, Mo., 1907; coloratura sopraro; early studied piano and vln., then voice with a local instructor; sang in a church choir, and gave public concert in Kansas City; her unusual vocal promise led tc a subscription by

DICTIONARY OF MUSICIANS

429

residents of latter city for further study in N. Y. and Italy; made début with Met. Op. Co., as "Gilda," 1926, an occasion attended by sensational public interest; sang other coloratura rôles with this company during the next few seasons; later appeared at Ravinia Op. and as guest with Chicago Op. Co.; also in concerts, radio and musical films.

Tal(l)ys (or **Tallis**), **Thos.**, ca. (1520–29) —London, Nov. 23, 1585; an early English composer whose remarkable contrapuntal ability and harmonic richness place him close to Palestrina. His training is not known; 1540, he ceased to be organist at Waltham Abbey and joined the Chapel Royal; he was co-organist with Byrd and shared his monopoly of mus.-paper and printing; he c. notable church mus. for both Catholic and English services, also a song in 40 parts, etc.

Tamagno (tä-män'-yō), **Fran.**, Turin, 1851—Varese, Aug. 31, 1903; robust tenor; début, Palermo; sang with great succ. at La Scala, Milan, 1880, throughout Europe and in both Americas. 1887, he created Verdi's "Otello."

Tam'berlik, **Enrico**, Rome, 1820—Paris, 1889; famous tenor; pupil of Borgna and Guglielmi; début, Naples, 1841; he had a powerful high c'''.

Tamburini (täm-boo-rē'-nē), **A.**, Faenza, March 28, 1800—Nice, Nov. 9, 1876. Next to Lablache, perhaps the most succ. of male singers; a lyric bass with compass of 2 octaves; the son and pupil of a bandm. A horn-player first, then pupil of Boni and Asioli; début, Centi, 1818.

Tanaka (tä-nä'-kä), **Shohé**, Japanese theorist; pupil of Spitta; inv. the enharmonium with just intonation.

Tanejew (or **Taneiev**) (tä'-nä-yĕf), (1) **Sergei**, b. near Vladimir, Russia, Nov. 13, 1856—Moscow, June 18, 1915; pupil of N. Rubinstein and Tchaikowsky; prof. of theory and comp. Moscow Cons.; after 1878, dir.; prod. 3-act opera "Oresteia" (St. Petersburg, 1895); a cantata "John of Damascus," 1884; four symphonies, No. 1 pub. 1902, a Russian overture, seven string quartets. His uncle (2) **Alexander Sergeivich**, St. Petersburg, Jan. 5, 1850 —Feb. 7, 1918; statesman and high chancellor; was a pupil of Reichel and later of Rimsky-Korsakov and

Petrov; c. 3 symphs.; symph. poem "Alecha Popovich"; operas, 3 string quartets, etc.

Tans'man, **Alexandre**, b. Lodz, Poland, June 12, 1897; composer; studied at Warsaw Univ., also with Gawronski, Vas and others; one of most talented modern composers and has made tours in leading Eur. countries, also in America after 1927, appearing as guest cond. and pianist with important orchs.; c. (opera) "Nuit Kurde"; (orch.) symphony; "Danse de la Sorcière"; Symphonic Overture; Polish Dances; Sinfonietta; 2 piano concertos, chamber music, etc.

Tansur (tän'-sŭr), **Wm.**, Dunchurch in Warwickshire, 1706—St. Neots, 1783; organist, teacher, writer and composer.

Tappert (täp'-pĕrt), **Wm.**, Ober-Thomaswaldau, Silesia, Feb. 19, 1830 —Berlin, Oct. 27, 1907; important theorist; a schoolmaster; then 1856, studied with Dehn theory; Kullak's Acad.; lived in Berlin from 1866 as a writer, e litor and composer.

Tarchi (tär'-kē), **Angelo**, Naples, 1760 —Paris, 1814; dramatic composer.

Tarditi (tär-dē'-tē), **Orazio**, d. after 1670; from 1648, maestro Faenza Cath.; composer.

Tartini (tär-tē'-nē), **Giuseppe**, Pirano, Istria, April 8, 1692—Padua, Feb. 26, 1770; eminent violinist, composer and scientist; at first he studied for the priesthood at his father's wish; then law, finally mus.; apparently self-taught as a violinist. A charge of abduction, due to his secret marriage with a niece of Cardinal Cornaro, led him to take refuge in the Franciscan monastery at Assisi, where for two years he practiced the vln. and studied comp. After a reconciliation he returned to Padua. Later he heard the violinist Veracini at Venice, and sending his wife to relations, retired to Ancona for further study. 1714, he discovered the combinational tones (v. D. D., "RESULTANT") and utilised them in perfecting intonation; 1721, solo-violinist and cond. at St. Antonio, Padua; 1723–25, chamber-mus. to Count Kinsky, Prague; 1728, founded a vln.-school at Padua; pub. treatises on harm. and acoustics; he published 18 vln.-concertos, 50 sonatas with bass, etc., incl. the famous, posthumous "Il Trillo del

Diavolo," an effort to reproduce a sonata played to him by the devil in a dream. Biog. Fanzago (Padua, 1770); J. A. Hiller (1784), Fayolle (1810).

Tasca (täs'-kä), P. Ant. (Baron), Noto, Sicily, April 1, 1864—May 14, 1934; composer of opera "*A Santa Lucia*," succ. in Germany, 1902; symph., string quartet, etc.

Taskin (täs-kăň), (1) Pascal, Theux (Liége), 1723—Paris, 1793; celebrated instr.-maker in Paris; introd. the piano-pedal worked by the foot instead of the knee; inv. leather tangents for clavichord, the armandine, etc. (2) Jos. Pascal, 1750—1829; nephew of above; keeper of the King's Instruments. (3) H. Jos., Versailles, 1779—Paris, 1852; son of above; organist. (4) (Emile) Alex., Paris, 1853—1897; grandson of (3); barytone.

Tauber (tow'-bĕr), Richard, Linz, May 16, 1892—London, Jan. 8, 1948; opera and concert tenor; studied Hoch Cons., Frankfort, with Carl Beines; début as "Tamino" in "*Magic Flute*," Chemnitz, 1913; mem. Dresden Op., 1914–24; after latter year sang principally at Vienna and Berlin State Ops., also in Paris, Salzburg, Munich, etc.; won wide popularity in the light operas of Lehar, in whose "*Land of Smiles*" he later made London début; 1st Amer. appearances in recitals, 1931.

Taubert (tow'-bĕrt), (1) (K. Gf.) Wm., Berlin, 1811—1891; noted pianist and composer of operas, incid. mus. to Shakespeare, etc.; pupil of Neidthardt, Berger and Klein; ct.-cond. at Berlin. (2) Otto, Naumburg-on-Saale, June 26, 1833—Torgau, Aug. 1, 1903; pupil of O. Claudius and "prefect" of the cath.-choir; 1863, prof., cantor and cond. at Torgau; pub. treatises; composer. (3) Ernst Eduard, Regenwalde, Pomerania, Sept. 25, 1838—Berlin, July, 14, 1934; studied at the Stern Cons., Berlin; Prof., 1898; pub. chamber-mus., etc.

Taubmann (towp'-män), Otto, Hamburg, March 8, 1859—Berlin, July 4, 1929; mus. director; pupil Dresden Cons.; 1886–89 dir. Wiesbaden Cons.; 1891 theatre cond. in St. Petersburg; from 1895 in Berlin as critic; c. mass with orch. (1898), choral drama "*Sängerweihe*" (Elberfeld, 1904), "Psalm 13" with orch., etc.

Taudou (tō-doo), A. (Antonin Barthélémy), Perpignan, France, Aug. 24, 1846—Paris, July 6, 1925; violinist; pupil of Paris Cons., winning Grand prix de Rome, 1889; member of the Opéra-orch.; from 1883, prof. of harm. at the Cons.; c. vln.-concerto, etc.

Tausch (towsh), Fz., Heidelberg, 1762 —Berlin, 1817; clarinettist and composer.

Tausig (tow'-zĭkh), (1) Aloys, 1817—1885; pianist and composer, pupil of Thalberg. (2) Karl, Warsaw, Nov. 4, 1841—(of typhoid fever), Leipzig, July 17, 1871; remarkable piano-virtuoso; son and pupil of above; and of Liszt; début, Berlin, 1858; lived Dresden and Vienna as notable cond.; 1865 founded a sch. at Berlin; c. brilliant exercises, transcriptions, etc.

Tauwitz (tow'-vĭts), Eduard, Glatz, Silesia, 1812—Prague, 1894; conductor; c. more than 1,000 comps. incl. 3 operas.

Tav'erner, (1) John, d. Boston, England; organist and composer at Oxford, 1530. (2) Rev. J., d. Stoke Newington, 1638; organist and composer.

Tayber. Vide TEYBER.

Tay'lor, (1) Edw., Norwich, Engl., 1784—Brentwood, 1863; bass, conductor, critic, lecturer and writer. (2) Franklin, Birmingham, Engl., Feb. 5, 1843—London, 1919; pianist and teacher; pupil of C. Flavell (pf.) and T. Redsmore (org.); also of Leipzig Cons.; 1876–82, prof. Nat. Training Sch., and from 1883, at the R. C. M.; Pres. of Acad. for the Higher Development of pf.-playing; writer and translator. (3) (Joseph) Deems, b. New York, Dec. 22, 1885; composer, critic, editor; grad. N. Y. U., from which also hon. Mus. D., 1927; mem. editorial staff, Nelson Encyclopedia, 1906–07; Encyclopedia Britannica, 1908; assistant Sunday ed., N. Y. *Tribune*, 1916; served as correspondent for *Tribune* in France, 1916–17; associate ed., *Collier's Weekly*, 1917–19; music critic, N. Y. *World*, 1921–25; ed., *Musical America*, 1927–29; mem. producing board, Amer. Op. Co.; advisory board, Encyclopedia Brittanica; member, Nat'l Institute of Arts and Letters, Society for the Publication of American Music, Authors' League of America; c. musical comedy, "*The Echo*," prod. on Broadway, 1910; symph. poem, "*The Siren Song*," awarded National Fed. of Music Clubs prize, 1912; (cantatas) "*The Chambered Nautilus*" and "*The Highwayman*," latter for MacDowell Fest., 1914; suite for orch., "*Through the Looking Glass*"; rhapsody for small orch., "*Portrait of a Lady*"; (pantomime) "*A Kiss in Xanadu*"; symph. poem, "*Jurgen*" commissioned by N. Y. Symph., 1925; suite for jazz orch., "*Circus Day*," 1925, later arranged for symph. orch.; (operas) "*The King's Henchman*" (to libretto by Edna St. Vincent Millay), commissioned by Met. Op. Co., 1927; "*Peter Ibbetson*" (after Du Maurier novel), commissioned by Metropolitan, 1930–31; incid. music to Obey's drama "*Lucrece*" for Katharine Cornell; also choral works and arrangements, songs, piano pieces; has appeared as guest cond. of his works with leading Amer. orch.; opera, "*Ramuntcho*" on Basque theme (Philadelphia Op. Co., 1942); author of many books on music.

Tchaikovsky (or Tschaikowsky, etc.) (tshä-ĕ-kŏf'-shkĭ), Peter Iljitch, Wotkinsk, in the Government of Wiätka, May 7, 1840—(of cholera) Petersburg, Nov. 6, 1893; eminent Russian composer. Studied law, and entered the government civil service; did not take up mus. seriously till 22; then entered the newly founded Petersburg Cons., under Zaremba and A. Rubinstein, 1865, winning a prize medal for Schiller's ode "*An die Freude*" (also used in Beethoven's 9th symph.); 1866–77, instructor of harm. there; then lived Petersburg, Italy, Switzerland, as composer. He visited England and appeared at Phil. Concerts, 1888 and '89; visited New York for the dedication of the new Carnegie Music Hall, and cond. his own compositions. 1893, Mus. Doc. *h. c.*, Cambridge. Writer, and translator of harm. text-books. C. 11 Russian operas, incl. "*The Voyevode*" (Moscow, 1869), "*Opritchnnyk*" (Petersb., 1874); "*Vakula, the Smith*" (Petersb., 1876); "*Jevgenjie Onegin*"; 1879, "*Eugene Onegin*," in German (Hamburg, 1892), and posthumous "*Pique Dame*" (Vienna ct.-th., 1902); 3 ballets, "*Le Lac des Cygnes*" (op. 20), "*La Belle au Bois Dormant*"

(1890), and "*Le Casse-Noisette*" (op. 71); a coronation cantata with orch.; 2 masses; 6 symphs., incl. No. 6 in B minor, the famous "*Pathétique*"; 7 symph. poems, "*The Tempest*," "*Francesca da Rimini*," "*Manfred*," "*Romeo and Juliet*" (a fantasy-overture); "*Hamlet*," "*Fatum*," and "*Le Voyevode*" (symph. ballad); 4 orch. suites incl. "*Mozartiana*;" 3 overtures "*1812*" (op. 49), "*Triomphale*" on the Danish natl. hymn; "*L'Orage*"; "Marche slave," coronation march; 3 pf.-concertos; a pf.-fantasia with orch.; vln.-concerto; capriccio for 'cello with orch.; string-sextet "*Souvenir de Florence*," 3 string-quartets, a pf.-trio, pieces for vln. and 'cello; and pf.-pcs., incl. "*Souvenir de Hapsal*," sonata "*The Seasons*," 12 characteristic pcs., "*Kinder Album*"; 6 duets, Russian songs, etc. Also pub. a harmony; his "*Erinnerungen*" and translations of Gevaert, etc.

Among many biographical works are those in English by Evans, Lee, Newmarch, Ronald, Bowen and Meck; the one by Mrs. Newmarch containing extracts from T's. critical writings and the diary of his 1888 tour. The composer's bro. Modeste pub. a "*Life and Letters of T.*", 1906. (See article, page 537.)

Tebaldini (tä-bäl-dē'-nē), Giovanni, b. Brescia, Sept. 7, 1864; historian; pupil Milan Cons., and in musical history of Amelli, Haberl and Haller; 1889 cond. at St. Mark's, Venice; 1894 at San Antonio, Padua; from 1897, dir. Parma Cons., after 1902 church cond. at Loreto; 1926, in Naples as prof.; wrote historical works, and c. orch., also church music.

Tedesco (tä'-dĕs'-kō), Ignaz (Amadeus), Prague, 1817—Odessa, Nov. 13, 1882; brilliant pianist ("the Hannibal of octaves"); composer.

Telemann (tä'-lĕ-män), (1) G. Philipp, Magdeburg, March 14, 1681—Hamburg, June 25, 1767; mainly self-taught; conductor; 1709, ct.-cond.; he overshadowed J. S. Bach in contemporary esteem and was one of the most prolific and facile composers incl. 40 operas, 44 passions, etc.; autobiog., 1731. (2) G. Michael, Plön, Holstein, 1748—Riga, 1831; grandson of above; cantor, theorist and comp.

Tel'ford. Vide FRANCIS BOOTT.

Tel'lefsen, Thos. Dyke Acland, Trond-
heim, Norway, 1823—Paris, 1874;
pianist and composer.

Telman'yi, Emil, b. Arad, Hungary,
June 22, 1892; violinist; pupil of
Moritz Unger, Hubay, Koessler and
Herzfeld; début in Berlin, 1911,
playing Elgar concerto; toured U. S.
and Europe; m. daughter of Carl
Nielsen, composer; res. in Copen-
hagen.

Tem'pleton, J., Riccarton, Scotland,
1802—New Hampton, near London,
1886; tenor.

Tenaglia (tä-näl'-yä), Anton Fran., b.
Florence; conductor at Rome; c. the
first known opera using an aria da
capo. "Clearco," 1661.

Ten Brink. Vide BRINK, TEN.

Tenducci (ten-doot'-chē), Giusto F.,
b. Siena, 1736; famous male operatic
soprano.

Ten Kate. Vide KATE, TEN.

Ternina (tăr-nē'-nǎ), Milka, Begisše,
Croatia, 1863—Zagreb, 1940; noted
dramatic soprano; studied with Gänsbacher, début Leipzig, 1883; then
sang Graz and Bremen; 1890 Munich,
named "court-singer"; sang in Bayreuth and in America 1899–1904
(Met. Op. Co.).

Terpan'der, b. Antissa, Lesbos, 7th
cent. B. C.; called the "Father of
Greek music."

Terrabugio (tĕr-rä-boo'-jō), Giuseppe,
Primiero, May 13, 1843—Jan. 9,
1933; writer; pupil of Rheinberger,
etc.; from 1883 editor of Musica
Sacra at Milan, and active in the
reform of church music; author of
organ methods; c. overtures, 12
masses, and much church music.

Terradellas (Terradeglias) (tĕr-rä-dĕl'-
läs or däl'-yäs), Domingo (Domenico), Barcelona, Spain (baptised,
Feb. 13, 1711)—Rome, 1751; dram.
composer.

Ter'ry, (1) Sir Richard Runciman,
Ellington, 1865—London, April 18,
1938; organist; 1890–92 at Elston
School, then in Antigua, West Indies,
at St. John's Cathedral; 1896–1901
Downside Abbey; 1901–24 at Westminster Cathedral; active in reviving
early English Catholic music. (2)
Charles Sanford, Newport Pagnell,
Oct. 24, 1864—Aberdeenshire, Nov.
5, 1936; studied Clare Coll., Cambridge; after 1903 prof. at the Univ.
of Aberdeen; honorary Mus. Doc.,
Edinburgh; founded 1st competition

fest. in Scotland, 1909; a specialist
in the music of Bach, of whom he
wrote biog. and many other studies;
also tr. cantata texts into English.

Terschak (tĕr'-shäk), Ad., Prague,
1832—Breslau, 1901; flutist; pupil
of Zierer, Vienna Cons.; toured; c.
flute-pcs.

Ter'tis, Lionel, b. West Hartlepool,
England, Dec. 29, 1876; viola virtuoso; studied at Leipzig and R.
Coll. of Music, London, originally
piano, then vln. and viola; he is the
most eminent British performer on
last instrument and a number of composers have written works for him;
has toured United States.

Terziani (tĕr-tsǐ-ä'-nē), Eugenio, Rome,
1824—1889; prof., conductor and
dram. composer.

Teschner (tĕshǐ-nĕr), Gv. Wm., Magdeburg, 1800—Dresden, 1883; teacher,
composer and editor.

Tesi-Tramontini (tä'-zē-trä-môn-tē'-
nē), Vittoria, Florence, Feb. 13, 1700
—Vienna, 1775; famous contralto.

Tessarin (tĕs'-sä-rēn), Fran., Venice,
Dec. 3, 1820—Rome, June 3c, 1889;
pianist and teacher; pupil of A.
Fanno and G. B. Ferrari; c. opera
"L'Ultimo Abencerragio" (Venice,
1858); a cantata, etc.

Tessarini (tĕs-sä-rē'-nē), Carlo, b.
Rimini, 1690; famous violinist, writer
and composer.

Testoré (tĕs-tō'-rä), (1) Carlo Giu.,
vln.-maker at Milan, ca. 1687—1710,
with his sons (2) Carlo A. and
(3) Pietro A.

Tetrazzini (tĕt-rä-tsē'-nē), Luisa, b.
Florence, 1871—Milan, April 28,
1940; soprano; pupil of Ceccherini,
and her sister Eva, wife of Cleofonte
Campanini; début 1895 as "Inez" in
"L'Africaine," Teatro Pagliano,
Florence; later at Rome and elsewhere, touring widely in Russia
and South America; a favourite in
San Francisco, her fame had not
reached eastward till after a season
of great success at Covent Garden,
1907, she made a sensation at the
Manhattan Opera, N. Y., 1908–10;
Chicago Op., 1913–14; she long held
a foremost position among the
world's sopranos in opera and
concert.

Teyber (or Tayber) (tī'-bĕr), (1) Anton, Vienna, 1754—1822; conductor,
cembalist and composer. (2) Fr.

Vienna, 1756—1810; bro. of above; organist and dram. composer.

Teyte (tāt), **Maggie** (rightly **Tate**), b. Wolverhampton, England, April 17, 1890; soprano; studied R. Coll. of Music and with Jean de Reszke; début as "Zerlina," Monte Carlo, 1907; sang with Paris Op.-Comique, Beecham Op. Co., Chicago Op., 1911–14; Boston Op., 1915–17; Covent Garden, 1923, 1930; has also appeared with orchs. and in recital.

Thadewaldt (tä'-dĕ-vält), **Hermann,** Bodenhagen, Pomerania, April 8, 1827—Berlin, Feb. 11, 1909; 1850–55, bandm. at Düsseldorf; 1893–95, cond. at Dieppe; 1857 at Berlin. Founded (1872) Allgemeine Deutscher Musikverband.

Thalberg (täl'-bĕrkh), (1) **Sigismund,** Geneva, Jan. 7, 1812—Naples, April 27, 1871; famous piano-virtuoso and composer. "Being the son of Prince Dietrichstein, who had many wives without being married, T. had several brothers of different family names" (Grove). His mother was the Baroness von Wetzlar. Both of the parents took the greatest interest in his education. He was intended for a diplomatic career, but after his succ. as a pianist at 14, gave himself up to mus. He had some tuition from Hummel (pf.) and Sechter (comp.), but chiefly from Mittag, a bassoonist. At 16 three florid compositions appeared; at 18 a pf.-concerto. The same year he toured Germany with much succ.; 1834, ct.-pianist at Vienna; 1835, he conquered Paris, and later the rest of Europe. 1843, he m. Mme. Boucher, daughter of Lablache; 1851, his first opera "*Florida*," failed in London, and 1855, "*Cristina di Svezia*" failed in Vienna. He then toured Brazil (1855), and 1856, United States; retiring in 1858 to his villa at Posilippo, near Naples. 1862, Paris and London; 1863, second Brazilian tour; 1864, retired again. He was remarkable for his legato effects and for the singing-tone, Liszt saying "Thalberg is the only artist who can play the violin on the keyboard." He originated the subsequently abused scheme of dividing a central melody between the two thumbs, and enveloping it in arpeggiated ornament. His comps. include many florid transcriptions of opera-tunes,

also a grand concerto, 6 nocturnes, "*La Cadence*," and "*Marche funèbre variée,*" etc. (2) **Marcian,** b. Odessa, 1877; pianist; pupil of Leipzig Cons.; toured in Europe; after 1913 teacher of advanced students at Cincinnati Conservatory.

Thayer (thā'-ĕr), (1) **Alex. Wheelock,** South Natick, Mass., Oct. 22, 1817—Trieste, July 15, 1897; graduated Harvard, 1843; was librarian there for some years; 1849 went to Europe and began materials for life of Beethoven; 1862, America as journalist; 1854 returned to Germany and frequently afterwards as his means permitted; 1862, U. S. consular agent at Vienna; later, till death, consul at Trieste; besides many articles he wrote a great but uncompleted life of Beethoven; though written in English it was first pub. in a German trans. by H. Deiters, in 5 vols. (Berlin, 1866–1908). The English edition, completed by H. E. Krehbiel, was pub. 1921, under the sponsorship of the Beethoven Ass'n, N. Y. (3 vols.). (2) **(Whitney) Eugene,** Mendon, Mass., 1838—Burlington, Vermont, 1889; organist, editor, composer.

Theile (tī'-lĕ), **Jn.,** Naumburg, 1646—1724; conductor and composer.

Thébom, Blanche, Am. mezzo; Met. Op., 1944.

Thern (tärn), (1) **Karl (Karolý),** Iglo, Upper Hungary, 1817—Vienna, 1886; conductor, professor and dram. composer. His sons and pf.-pupils (also pupils of Moscheles and Reinecke), (2) **Willi** (Ofen, June 22, 1847—Vienna, April 7, 1911) and (3) **Louis** (Pesth, Dec. 18, 1848—Vienna, March 12, 1920) were teachers.

Thibaud (tē'-bō), (1) **Jos.,** b. Bordeaux, Jan. 25, 1875; pianist; pupil of L. Diémer, Paris Cons., taking 1st prize for pf.-playing, 1892; 1895–96, accompanied Marsick to America. (2) **Jacques,** b. Bordeaux, Sept. 27, 1880; violinist; pupil of Marsick at Paris Cons., winning first prize at 16; played at the Café Rouge and was engaged for Colonne's orch., became soloist, 1898; toured the world as leading virtuoso; member trio with Casals, Cortot; d. in plane disaster in the French Alps, Sept. 1, 1953.

Thibaut IV. (tē-bō-kǎtr), King of Navarre; Troyes, 1201—Pamplona, 1253; composer.

Thibaut (tē'-bowt), **Anton Fr. Justus,** Hameln, 1774—Heidelberg, 1840; professor and writer.

Thiele (tē'-lĕ), **Jno. Fr. Ludwig,** Harzgerode, near Bernburg, 1816—Berlin, 1848; organist and composer.

Thierfelder (tēr'-fĕlt-ĕr), **Albert (Wm.),** Mühlhausen, April 30, 1846—Rostock, Jan. 5, 1924; pupil of Leipzig Univ. and Dr. Phil.; studied with Hauptmann, Richter and Paul; cond. various cities; from 1887 mus.-dir. and prof. Rostock Univ.; writer of important treatises; prod. 5 operas, incl. succ. "*Der Heirathstein*" (text and music) (Rostock, 1898), "*Zlatorog,*" and "*Frau Holde,*" for soli, chorus, and orch., and 2 symphs., etc.

Thieriot (tē'-rĭ-ō), (1) **Paul Emil,** Leipzig, 1780 — Wiesbaden, 1831; violinist. (2) **Fd.,** Hamburg, April 7, 1838—Aug. 4, 1919; pupil of E. Marxsen, and Rheinberger; mus.-dir. at Hamburg, Leipzig, and Glogau; lived in Hamburg; c. symph. fantasy "*Loch Lomond,*" vln.-concerto, etc.

Thill (tēl), **Georges,** b. Paris, 1899; tenor, studied with de Lucia, Pandolfini, Dupré, and at Paris Cons.; début, Paris Op. 1924; sang at Monte Carlo, Brussels, Covent Garden, La Scala, Buenos Aires, and with Met. Op. Co., 1931–32.

Thillon (tē-yôn), **Anna** (née **Hunt**), London, 1819—Torquay, 1903; very succ. soprano; pupil of Bordogni, Tadolini, and Thillon, marrying the last named at 15; début, Paris, 1838; 1844, Auber's "*Crown Diamonds*" was written for her; 1850–54, in America, the first to produce opera in San Francisco; retired 1867 to Torquay.

Thimus (tē'-moos), **Albert, Freiherr von,** Cologne, 1806—1846; writer.

Thoma (tō'-mä), **Rudolf,** Lesewitz, near Steinau-on-Oder, Feb. 22, 1829 —Breslau, Oct. 20, 1908; pupil of R. Inst. for Church-mus., Berlin; 1857, cantor, Hirschberg, then Breslau, 1870, "R. Music Dir."; founder of a singing-soc., dir. of a sch.; c. 2 operas, 2 oratorios, etc.

Thomas (tō-mäs) (**Chas. Louis**), **Ambroise,** Metz, Aug. 5, 1811—Paris, Feb. 12, 1896; pupil of Paris Cons.; winning 1st pf.-prize, 1829; harm., 1830; Grand prix de Rome (1832),

with cantata "*Hermann et Ketty.*" After 3 years in Italy, returned to Paris, and up to 1843, prod. nine stage-pcs., at the Opéra and Op.-Com. with fair succ. The failure of the last was retrieved after a silence of 5 years by "*Le Cid*" (1849), "*Le Songe d' Une Nuit d' Été*" (1850, both at the Op.-Com.). 1851 elected to the Académie. The next 6 operas were only moderately succ.; but "*Mignon*" (Op.-Com., 1866) made a world-wide succ. and "*Hamlet*" (Opéra, 1868) a lasting succ. in Paris, where it is still sung. "*Gille et Gillotin*" (1874), "*Françoise de Rimini*" (1882), and the ballet, "*La Tempête*" (Opéra, 1889), were his last dram. works; 1871, dir. of the Cons.; 1845, Chev.; 1858, Officier; 1868, Commander of the Legion of Honour. C. also cantatas; messe solennelle (Nôtre-Dame, 1865); many excellent "chœurs orphéoniques" (3-part male choruses), etc.

Thomas (täm'-üs), (1) **J.,** Bridgend, Glamorganshire, March 1, 1826—March 19, 1913; 1861 made "Pencerdd Gwalia," *i.e.*, Chief Bard of Wales; pupil at the R. A. M.; 1851, harpist, R. It. Opera; toured Europe, 1852–62 played at the Gewandhaus, etc. 1862, cond. of the first annual concert of Welsh mus., with a chorus of 400, and 20 harps; 1871, harpist to the Queen; leader in the Eisteddfodau, and harp-prof. R. C. M. C. dram. cantata "*Llewelyn*" (1863); a Welsh scene "*The Bride of Neath Valley*" (1866); patriotic songs, with harp; 2 harp-concertos, etc. (2) **Lewis Wm.,** Bath, April, 1826—London, 1896; concert-bass, editor and critic. (3) **Robert Harold,** Cheltenham, July 8, 1834—London, July 29. 1885; pianist; pupil of Sterndale Bennett, C. Potter, and Blagrove; début 1850; pf.-prof. R. A. M. and Guildhall Sch., London; c. overtures, etc. (4) **Theodor(e),** Esens, East Friesland, Oct. 11, 1835 —Chicago, Jan. 4, 1905; eminent cond., educator and stimulator of mus. taste in America; son and pupil of a violinist, at 6 played in public; at 10 was brought to New York, where he soon entered an orch.; 1851, toured as soloist, later with Jenny Lind, Grisi, etc.; 1855, began the Mason and Thomas Soirées (with DR. WM. MASON); 1864-69 cond.

"Symph. Soirées"; 1869 made concert-tour with an orch. of 54; 1876 at Philadelphia Centennial with ill-succ. leading to disbandment; 1878-80, pres. Cincinnati Coll. of Mus.; 1880, cond. New York, Philh. Orch.; from 1888, dir. Chicago Cons., also cond. Chicago Orch. (5) **Arthur Goring**, Ralton Park, near Eastbourne, Sussex, Nov. 21, 1850— London, March 20, 1892; took up music at 24 and studied with Emile Durand, later with Sullivan and Prout R. A. M., London, winning Lucas Prize, 1879; lived in London, C. 2 operas, v. succ. *"Esmeralda"* (Drury Lane, 1883, New York, 1900); *"Nadeshda"* (1885); *"The Golden Web"* (score finished by Waddington, Liverpool, 1893); a choral ode, *"The Sun Worshippers"* (Norwich, 1881), v. succ. cantata, *"The Swan and the Skylark"* (Birmingham, 1894, instrumented by C. V. Stanford); psalm with orchestra (1878); 3 vocal scenes, *"Hero and Leander"* (1880), etc. (6) **John Charles**, b. Meyersdale, Pa.; notable barytone; early designed for medical career, but while studying in a Baltimore medical coll., won scholarship at Peabody Cons.; pupil of Blanche S. Blackman and Adelin Fermin; début, 1912, in a stage production; sang in operettas in N. Y. where he made début as recitalist, 1921; op. first appearance in Washington, D. C., in *"Aïda"*; sang for several seasons after 1925 with La Monnaie Op., Brussels; 1929, with Phila. Grand Op.; Chicago Op., 1930-31; mem. Met. Op. after 1933; also with San Francisco and Los Angeles Op. Cos.; has wide following as concert singer and in radio.

Thomé (tō-mā), **Francis** (rightly **François Luc. Jos.**), Port Louis, Mauritius, Oct. 18, 1850—Paris, Nov. 16, 1909; pupil of Marmontel (pf.), and Duprato (theory), Paris Cons.; lived in Paris as teacher and critic; c. *"Roméo et Juliette"*; a mystery, *"L'Enfant Jésus"*; symph. ode *"Hymne à la Nuit"* and many pop. songs and pf.-pcs.

Thomp'son, (1) **Randall**, b. New York, April 12, 1899; composer; grad. Harvard Univ.; studied music there and with Ernest Bloch; 1922, awarded Fellowship at American Acad. in Rome; also Guggenheim Fellowship,

1929-31; for a time asst. prof. of music, Wellesley Coll. and lecturer on music at Harvard; 1931-32, cond. Dessoff Choirs, New York; c. 2 symphonies (the second, in E minor, perf. by Rochester Philh. and N. Y. Philh., 1933-34); *"Piper at the Gates of Dawn"* for orch.; *"Seven Odes of Horace"* for chorus, 3 with orch. accompaniment; *"Americana,"* setting of amusing news notes from provincial papers, quoted from *American Mercury,* for chorus; *"The Peaceable Kingdom,"* oratorio (Boston, 1935-36); also piano sonata and suite; important string quartet; songs, piano pieces, etc. (2) **Oscar**; critic, N. Y. *Post,* 1927-34; N. Y. *Sun,* from 1936, vice Henderson; author, *"Debussy,"* *"How to Listen to Music,"* *"Practical Music Criticism"*; d. N. Y. July 2, 1945.

Thomson (täm'-sŭn), (1) **Geo.**, Limekilns, Fife, 1757—Leith, 1851; notable coll. and pub. of Scotch, Welsh and Irish melodies, to which he had special instrumental accompaniments written by Beethoven. Pleyel, etc. (2) **Virgil**, b. Kansas City, Kan., 1896; composer; studied U. S. and Paris; has c. much chamber music of witty and ironic style, attracting particular attention for his opera, *"Four Saints in Three Acts,"* to text by Gertrude Stein, prod. in Hartford, Conn., and N. Y., 1934; also masses for men's and women's voices; *"Saints' Procession"* for male voices and piano; *"Five Phrases from the Song of Solomon"* for soprano and percussion; *"Sonata da Chiesa"*; vln. sonata, *"Oraison Funèbre"* for chamber orch.; *"Three Psalms"* for feminine chorus; smaller works for piano and voice; critic. N. Y. Herald Trib

Thomson (tôn-sôn), **César**, Liége, March 17, 1857—Lugano, Aug. 21, 1931; notable violinist; from 7 pupil of Liége Cons.; at 11, winning the gold medal; then pupil of Vieuxtemps, Léonard, Wieniawski and Massart; 1873-83, chamber-mus. to Baron von Derwies at Lugano, and a member of Bilse's orch., Berlin; 1883-97, teacher at Liége Cons.; 1898, vln.-prof. Brussels Cons. (vice Ysaye); toured widely; after 1894 United States; 1924 taught at Ithaca, N. Y., Cons.

Thooft (toft), **Willem Frans**, Amsterdam, July 10, 1820—Rotterdam,

Aug. 27, 1900; pupil of Dupont, Hauptmann and Richter; founded the German opera at Rotterdam, 1860; c. choral prize symphony, "*Karl V.*" (1861); 3 other symphs., an opera, etc.

Thor'borg, Kerstin; Swedish contralto; esp. noted as a Wagnerian singer; has appeared with succ. in Vienna, Prague and elsewhere on the Continent; 1936, at Salzburg Fest. and at Covent Garden; engaged for Met. Op. Co., 1936–37.

Thorne (thôrn), **Edw. H.,** Cranborne, Dorset, May 9, 1834 — London, Dec. 26, 1916; pianist and org.; chorister under Elvey; organist various churches; from 1891, at St. Anne's, Soho, London; cond. St. Anne's Choral and Orch'l Soc. C. Psalm 57, with orch.; Magnificat and Nunc dimittis with orch. and organ; an overture; "*Sonata elegia*" for pf.

Thrane (trä-ně), **Waldemar,** Christiania, 1790–1828; violinist; c. overtures, etc.

Thuille (too-ē'-lě), **L. (Wm. Ands. M.),** Bozen, Tyrol, Nov. 30, 1861— Munich, Feb. 5, 1907; pupil of Jos. Pembaur (pf., cpt.), at Innsbruck; Baermann (pf.) and Rheinberger (comp.) Munich Mus.-Sch.; from 1883, teacher of pf. and theory there; also cond. "*Liederhort*"; 1891, R. Prof. of Mus.; c. succ. opera "*Theuerdank*" (Munich, 1897, Luitpold Prize), opera "*Lobetanz*" (Carlsruhe and Berlin, 1898); "*Romantic*" overture, sextet for piano and wind, sonatas, etc.

Thurner (toor'-něr), **Fr. Eugen,** Montbeliard, 1785—Amsterdam, 1827; oboe-virtuoso; composer.

Thurs'by, Emma, Brooklyn, N. Y., Nov. 17, 1857—New York, July 4, 1931; famous concert-soprano; pupil of Meyer (Brooklyn), Errani (New York) and Mme. Rudersdorff (Boston), then of Lamperti and San Giovanni, Milan; concert-début, America, Plymouth Church, Brooklyn, 1875; sang in concert and oratorio, and with Gilmore (1875); frequently toured Europe and America with great succ.; compass c'–e''' (v. PITCH, D. D.).

Tib'bett, Lawrence, b. Bakersfield, Cal., Nov. 16, 1896; barytone; studied with Joseph Dupuy, Basil Ruysdael, and Frank La Forge; early

acted on dram. stage; recital début, Los Angeles, 1917; sang in opera at Hollywood Bowl, 1923, and same year made début with Met. Op. Co., where in 1925 he leaped into sudden prominence with his dram. perf. as "Ford" in "*Falstaff*"; he is a singing actor of much resource and a finished vocalist; has since sung leading rôles in Italian, French, German and English works, particularly character parts; created "Col. Ibbetson" in Deems Taylor's "*Peter Ibbetson*" and "Brutus Jones" in Louis Gruenberg's "*Emperor Jones*"; has sung widely in concert and with orchs., also as "Don Juan" in Goossens' opera, Covent Garden, 1937, at Vienna, Prague, etc.

Tichatschek (tēkh.'-ät-shěk), **Jos. Aloys,** Ober-Weckelsdorf, Bohemia, 1807— Dresden, 1886; tenor; created Wagner's "Rienzi" and "Tannhäuser."

Tieffenbrücker. Vide DUIFFOPRUGGAR.

Tiehsen (tē'-zěn), **Otto,** Danzig, 1817 —Berlin, 1849; c. comic opera.

Tiersch (tērsh), **Otto,** Kalbsrieth, Thuringia, 1838—Berlin, 1892; singing teacher and theorist.

Tiersot (tǐ-ěr'-sō), **(J. Bapt. Elisée) Julien,** Bourg-en-Bresse, France, July 5, 1857—Aug., 1936; pupil of Franck, Paris Cons.; from 1883, asst. libr. there; pub. essays, incl. "*Histoire de la chanson populaire en France,*" Bordun Prize, 1885; c. "*Hellas*" for soli, chorus and orch.; rhapsodies on popular airs, etc.

Tiessin (tē'-sěn), **Heinz,** b. Königsberg, Germany, April 10, 1887; composer; pupil of Stern Cons., and of Wilhelm Klatte; critic of Berlin *Allgemeine Zeitung,* 1912–17; asst. cond. at Berlin Op. and Volksbühne, and dir. of Univ. Orch. there; after 1925 taught comp. at Berlin Hochschule; c. (opera) "*Revolutionsdrama*" (Berlin, 1927); (dance drama) "*Salambo*" (Duisburg, 1929); several symphonies, other orch. works, chamber music, piano pieces, songs.

Tietjens (rightly **Titiens**) (tēt'-yěns), **Therese Johanne Alex.,** of Hungarian parents, Hamburg, July 17, 1831—London, Oct. 3, 1877; famous soprano; teachers unknown; début, Hamburg, 1849; from 1858, chiefly in London in grand and comic opera.

Til'borghs, Jos., Nieuwmoer, Sept. 18, 1830—?; theorist; pupil of Lemmens (org.) and Fétis (comp.), Brussels Cons.; from 1882, prof. of org.

Ghent Cons.; and of cpt. Antwerp Mus.-Sch.; comp. organ-pieces and motets.

Till'metz, Rudolf, Munich, April 1, 1847—Jan. 25, 1915; flutist; pupil of Bohm; 1864 soloist in court orch.; 1883 teacher in Royal Musichsch., and cond. to Prince Ludwig Fd.; c. flute works.

Tilman (tēl'-män), **Alfred,** Brussels, 1848—1895; composer and pianist.

Tilmant (tēl'-măn), (1) **Théophile Alex.,** Valenciennes, 1799—Asnières, 1878; conductor. His brother (2) **Alex.,** 1808—Paris, 1880; 'cellist.

Timanoff (tē'-män-ôf), **Vera,** b. Ufa, Russia, Feb. 18, 1855; pianist; pupil of L. Nowitzky, A. Rubinstein, Tausig and Liszt; lived in Petersburg, Prague (1871) and Vienna (1872); d. (?).

Tim'mermans, Armand, b. Antwerp, 1860; pupil of the Cons., and teacher in Antwerp, c. prize winning choral works.

Tinc'toris, Johannes (called **John Tinctor;** or Giov. Del Tintore; rightly **Jean de Vaerwere** (vär'-wā-rĕ), Poperinghe, ca. 1446 (or 35, some say 1450)—Nivelles, 1511; canon; wrote, 1477, the earliest known dict. of mus. (ca. 1475), etc.; composer.

Tinel (tē-nĕl'), **Edgar,** Sinay, Belgium, March 27, 1854—Brussels, Oct. 28, ᵡ912; pianist and composer; son and pupil of a poor school-teacher and organist; pupil also of Brussels Cons.; 1st pf.-prize, 1873, and pub. op. 1, 4 nocturnes for solo-voice with pf.; 1877, won Grand prix de Rome w. cantata "*Klokke Roeland*" (op. 17); 1881, dir. Inst. for Sacred Mus. at Malines; 1888, prod. very succ. oratorio, "*Franciscus*" (op. 36); 1889, inspector State mus. schs.; 1896, prof. of cpt. and fugue, Brussels Cons.; pub. a treatise on Gregorian chant, and prod. a "*Grand Mass of the Holy Virgin of Lourdes*," for 5 parts (op. 41), Te Deum, Alleluia, motets and sacred songs, incid. mus., pf.-pcs., etc.

Tiraboschi (tē-rä-bôs'-kē), **Girolamo,** Bergamo, 1731 — Modena, 1784; writer.

Tirindelli (tē-rĭn-dĕl'-lē), **P. Adolfo,** Conegliano, 1858—Rome, Feb. 6, 1937; pupil Milan Cons., then of Boniforti; cond. at Gorizia 3 years, then studied with Grün and Massart; 1887, vln.-prof. Liceo Benedetto Marcello, Venice; 1893, dir., also cond. "Verdi Orchestra"; made Cavaliere, 1894; played with the Boston Symph. Orch. in 1895; 1896–1922 taught Cincinnati Cons., and led orch. there; afterward in Rome. C. 1-act opera "*L'Atenaide*" (Venice, 1892), etc.

Tischer (tĭsh'-ĕr), **Gerhard,** b. Lübnitz, Nov. 10, 1877; historian, Ph. D., Berlin, 1903; from 1904 teacher of musical history in Cologne; later pub. and editor.

Titelouze (tēt-looz), **Jean,** St. Omer, 1563—Rouen, Oct. 25, 1633; organist; called the "founder of French organ music"; 1585 org. at St. Jean, Rouen, from 1588 at the cathedral there; c. mass, and organ works.

Titov or **Titoff** (tē'-tôf), (1) **Vassili,** 17th century church composer. (2) **Alexei Nikolaievich,** 1769—St. Petersburg, Nov. 2, 1827; Russian cavalry general; c. 13 operas. His brother (3) **Sergei N.,** b. 1770; c. operas and ballets. (4) **Nikolai Alexeivich,** St. Petersburg, May 10, 1800—Dec. 22, 1875; son of (2) called the "grandfather of Russian song"; a lieutenant-general, whose songs were the first to obtain foreign vogue; c. also popular dances and marches.

Toch (tôkh), **Ernst,** b. Vienna, Dec. 7, 1887; composer; pupil of Willi Rehberg in Frankfort (piano); 1913–14, taught comp. at Mannheim Hochsch., later privately; in composition largely self-taught; one of the more original creators in modern musical idiom; visited U. S. as soloist in his piano concerto with Boston Symph., 1933, and estab. residence here as teacher and composer; c. (operas) "*Die Prinzessin auf der Erbse*," "*Der Fächer*"; incid. music to Euripides' "*Bacchantes*"; "*Die Chinesische Flöte*" for soprano soloist and chamber orch.; several string quartets; 2 piano concertos; "*An mein Vaterland*" for org. and orch.; Five Pieces for chamber orch.; "*Bunte*" Suite for small orch.; Dance Suite for chamber orch.; concerto for 'cello and chamber orch.; "*Phantastische Nacht-Musik*" and Fantasy on the Chimes of Westminster for orch.; 2 Divertimenti for string duc· overture,"*Pinocchio*"; pf.works,songs.

Todi (tō'-dē), **Luiza Rosa** (née de Aguiar),** Setubal, Portugal, Jan. 9,

1753—Lisbon, Oct. 1, 1833; famous mezzo-soprano; an actress at 15, then pupil of Perez; sang London, 1712; 1777 v. succ. at Madrid; 1783 provoked a famous rivalry with Mara; 1780 ct.-singer, Berlin.

Todt (tōt), **Joh. Aug. Wilhelm,** Düsterort, July 29, 1833—Stettin, Oct. 26, 1900; organist, cantor and composer.

Toeschi (tō-äs'-kē) (in German tä'-shē), (1) **Carlo Giu.** (rightly **Toesca della Castella-Monte**), Romagna, 1724—Munich, 1788, ct.-mus., director and composer. (2) **Jn. Bapt.,** Mannheim, ca. 1745—Munich, May, 180c; son and successor of above; noted violinist; c. 18 symphs., etc.

Tofano (tō-fä'-nō), **Gustavo,** Naples, Dec. 22, 1844—June 30, 1899; pupil at the Bologna Cons. and prof. there; pianist and composer.

Tofft, Alfred, Copenhagen, Jan. 2, 1865 —Jan. 30, 1931; pupil of Nebelong and Bohlmann; c. opera "*Vifandaka*" (Copenhagen, 1898), songs, etc.

Tofte (tŏf'-tĕ), **Lars Waldemar,** Copenhagen, Oct. 21, 1832—June, 1907; court violinist and teacher at the Cons.

Tokat'yan, Armand, b. Alexandria, 1898; tenor Met. Op. from 1922.

Tolbecque (tŏl'-bĕk), four Belgian brothers. (1) **Isidore Jos.,** Hanzinne, 1794—Vichy, 1871; conductor and composer. (2) **Jean. Bapt. Jos.,** 1797—Paris, 1869; violinist and conductor. (3) **Aug. Jos.,** 1801—Paris, 1869; violinist. (4) **Chas. Jos.,** Paris, 1806—1835; violinist and conductor. (5) **Aug.,** Paris, March 30, 1830—Niorte, March 8, 1919; son of (3); 'cellist: pupil of the Cons., and 1849 took 1st prize; 1865-71, teacher Marseilles Cons.; later 'cellist in the Paris Cons. concerts; pub. "*La Gymnastique du Violoncelle*" (op. 14); prod. succ. 1-act comic opera "*Après la Valse*" (Niort, 1895).

Toll'efsen, (1) **Augusta** (née **Schnabel**), b. Boise, Idaho, 1885; pianist; studied with Käthe Widmann, a pupil of Mme. Clara Schumann; and with Godowsky and Gallico; toured in Europe and U. S., with orchs. in N. Y.; mem. of Tollefsen Trio; m. Carl Tollefsen. (2) **Carl,** b. Hull, Yorkshire, England, 1882 (Scandinavian parents); violinist; pupil of Lichtenberg, Kneisel, Schradieck,

Goetschius and Rubin Goldmark; played in N. Y. Symph.; mem. of Schnabel Trio (afterward Tollefsen Trio); active as teacher.

Tol'lius, Jan. b. Amersfort, 1550 (?)— Copenhagen, 1603; church-cond. in Italian cities; 1601 court-cond. at Copenhagen; c. motets, madrigals, etc.

Tolstoi (tŏl'-stō-ē), **Count Theophil Matveievich,** 1809—St. Petersburg, March 4, 1881; critic under penname "Rostislav" and composer; studied singing with Rubini, comp. with Fuchs, Miller, Raimondi and Hebel; 1832 prod. opera "*Birichino di Parigi*," Naples; 1835 at St. Petersburg, its failure led Nicholas I. to forbid the Italian singers to appear in Russian works. He c. also songs.

Tomaschek, Jn. Wenzel (rightly **Jan Václav Tomášek**) (täm'-ä-shĕk), Skutsch, Bohemia, April 17, 1774— Prague, April 3, 1850; notable pianist, organist; also c. operas and pf. pcs.

Tomasini (tō-mä-sē'-nē), **Luigi (Aloysius),** Pesaro, 1741—Esterház, 1808; violinist and director; he had two daughters who sang in opera at Eisenstadt and 2 sons.

Tombelle (tôn-bĕl), **Fd. de la,** Paris, Aug. 3, 1854 — Castelnau-Feyrac, Aug. 13, 1928; pupil of Guilmant and Dubois, Paris Cons.; his quartet and symph. won 1st prize of the "Société des compositeurs;" Officer of Pub. Instruction, Paris; c. orch. suites, etc.

Tomeoni (tō-mä-ō'-nē), (1) **Florido,** Lucca, 1757—Paris, 1820; teacher and theorist. (2) **Pellegrino,** b. Lucca, ca. 1759; bro. of above; teacher and writer in Florence.

Tom'kins, (1) **Rev. Thos.,** Engl. composer, Gloucester, 1600. His son (2) **J.,** d. 1638; organist and composer. (3) **Thos.,** d. 1656; organist at Worcester cath.; composer; son of (1). (4) **Giles,** d. 1668; bro. and succ. of above. (5) **Robt.,** son of (2); 1641 one of the King's musicians.

Tommasi (tōm-mäs'-sē), **Giu. M.,** Cardinal, Alicante, Sicily, 1649—Rome, 1713; writer.

Tommasini (tŏ-mä-sē'-nē), **Vincenzo,** b. Rome, Sept. 17, 1880; composer. grad. Univ. of Rome; studied piano with Mazzarella, vln. with Pinelli, comp. with Falchi; won Rome Nat'l

Prize, 1912; mem. of St. Cecilia Acad.; c. a ballet, "*The Good-Humoured Ladies*" based on Scarlatti sonatas, which was prod. by Diaghileff; also 2 operas, "*Medée*" and "*Uguale Fortuna*," heard, resp. at Trieste, 1906, and Rome, 1913; (orch.) "*Chiari di Luna*," "*Il Beato Regno*," "*Paesaggi Toscani*," prelude, fanfare and fugue, "*Carnevale di Venezia*"; 2 string quartets, sonata for vln., pf., and songs; d. 1950.

Ton'ning, Gerard, b. Stavanger, Norway, 1860—N. Y., 1940; comp. and teacher; pupil of Munich Cons.; 1887, active in Duluth as choral cond.; also led trio; after 1905 in Seattle; c. opera, "*Leif Erikson*," instrumental works, songs, etc.

Topfer (tĕp'-fĕr), Jn. Gl., Niederrossla, Thuringia, 1791—Weimar, 1870; organist, writer and composer.

Topler (tĕp'-lĕr), Michael, Ullersdorf, Jan. 15, 1804—Brühl, Nov. 12, 1874; teacher and composer of church music.

Torchi (tôr'-kē), Luigi, Mordano, Bologna, Nov. 7, 1858—Sept. 18, 1920; graduate, Bologna Cons., 1876, then studied with Serrao (comp.) at Naples Cons. and at Leipzig Cons. where he c. a symph., an overture, a string quartet; 1885-91, prof. of mus. history, Liceo Rossini, Pesaro; then at Bologna Cons., 1895 also prof. of comp.; began a great 34-vol. coll. of the chief Italian works of the 15–18 centuries, "*L'arte musicale in Italia*" (7 vols. pub.).

Torelli (tō-rĕl'-lē), Giu., Verona, ca. 1660—Ansbach, 1708; violinist and composer; developer of the "concerto grosso."

Tor'rance, Rev. G. Wm., Rathmines, near Dublin, 1835—Kilkenny, Aug. 20, 1907; chorister, Dublin; organist at St. Andrew's, and St. Anne's; studied at Leipzig, 1856; 1866, priest; 1869, Melbourne, Australia; 1895, incumbent at St. John's there; Mus. Doc., *h. c.* Dublin, 1879; he returned to Ireland, 1897, and 1900 became canon at Kilkenny. His madrigal "*Dry be that tear*," won Molyneux prize and London Madrigal Society medal, 1903; c. succ. oratorios, "*Abraham*" (Dublin, 1855), "*The Captivity*" (1864), and "*The Revelation*" (Melbourne, 1882), services, an opera, etc.

Torri (tôr'-rē), Pietro, ca. 1665—

Munich, 1737; court-conductor and dram. composer.

Tor'rington, Fr. Herbert, Dudley, Engl., Oct. 20, 1837—Toronto, 1917; pianist and conductor; articled pupil of Jas. Fitzgerald; at 16 organist at Bewdley; 1856–68, organist, Great St. James's Church, Montreal, Canada; also solo-violinist, cond. and band-master; his orch. represented Canada at the Boston Peace Jubilee, 1869; then teacher New Engl. Cons.; 1st vln. Handel and Haydn, and other socs.; from 1873, organist Metropolitan Ch., Toronto, Canada, and cond. Toronto Philh. Soc.; 1886, organised the first Toronto mus. festival; 1888, founded Toronto Coll. of Mus.; c. services, etc.

Toscanini (tŏs-kä-nē'-nē), Arturo, b. Parma, Italy, March 25, 1867; most eminent conductor of his period; pupil of the Cons. in his native city, where he won a diploma in 'cello playing and comp. in 1885; he had already participated ably in a concert tour as 'cellist the preceding year, incl. appearances at the Exposition in Turin; in the spring of 1886 he was engaged as 'cellist for the opera season in Rio de Janeiro, and his début as conductor occurred on the second night of the season, when he took over the orch. after the batonist of the occasion had been hissed by the public; he at once proved his mettle; and the perf. was a triumph. In 1887 he conducted in Turin the première of Catalani's "*Edmea*." He led many orchestral concerts there, incl. more than 40 programs during the Exposition of 1898, when he gave the first perfs. in Italy of Verdi's 3 sacred works, "*Stabat Mater*," "*Te Deum*" and "*Laudi alla Vergine*." He also appeared in Bologna and Genoa. In 1895 he gave the 1st Italian perfs. of Wagner's "*Götterdämmerung*" at the Regio in Turin. He conducted opera and symph. concerts at La Scala under the management of Gatti-Casazza from 1898 to 1908. When that impresario came to the Met. Op. in the latter year, he engaged Toscanini as conductor. T. remained in N. Y. until 1915, giving a long series of brilliant perfs., incl. the premières of works by Puccini, Dukas, Wolf-Ferrari, Montemezzi and Giordano, and conducting "*Göt-*

terdämmerung" and Gluck's *"Armide."* During this period in N. Y., he also led 2 symphonic concerts in 1913. He left the Met. as a result of a reported dissatisfaction with its artistic policy and returned to Italy in 1915, where he was active during the war as a conductor of concerts for welfare work. He toured the U. S. and Canada with an orch. composed of musicians from La Scala, and also led fests. in Turin and Milan in 1920. In the following year he became the mus. dir. at La Scala, a post which he retained until 1929. During this period he led the world premières of Boito's *"Nerone"* in 1924, of Puccini's posthumous opera *"Turandot"* in 1926. Beginning with the season of 1926–27 he was guest conductor of the N. Y. Philh. Orch. He immediately estab. a reputation as perhaps the most brilliant cond. who had ever appeared in N. Y. After 1928 he became permanent cond. of this orch., and later musical director, sharing the podium with several others during each season. In 1930 he took the orch. for a tour of leading Eur. cities. In summer of 1932 he conducted at the Bayreuth Fest., but severed his connection with Bayreuth later as the result of his disapproval of discriminations made by the Nat'l Socialist régime in that country against musicians of Jewish birth. He was one of a number of prominent musicians who addressed a cablegram of protest to the German govt. He led a few concerts (exchanging the Philh. bâton with Stokowski) at head of the Phila. Orch. in 1930–31. In 1933 he began a series of annual appearances at the Salzburg Fest., but resigned 1938; has also conducted brilliant concerts at London, Vienna and Paris. In 1936 he announced his resignation as cond. of the N. Y. Philh. Orch. because of the strain imposed by a regular post. His special virtues as a cond. consist in his fidelity to the composer's score, the extreme perfection of detail and the lyrical tone with which he endows even the most abstruse modern works. He invariably conducts without a score. He cond. for 17 years (1937–54) the N.B.C. Symph. Orch., N. Y., esp. created by Nat'l Broadcasting Co.

Tosel'li, Enrico, Florence, March 13, 1883—Jan. 15, 1926; composer and pianist; pupil of Sgambati and Martucci; début Monte Carlo, 1896; played in London and America, 1901; he eloped with Princess Louise of Saxony, whom he m.; c. pop. operettas, songs and pf.-pieces; his *"Serenade"* esp. well-known.

Tosi (tō'-zē), **Pier Fran.,** Bologna, 1647 —London, 1727; celebrated contralto musico and singing-teacher.

Tosti (tôs'-tē), **Fran. Paolo,** Ortona, Abruzzi, April 7, 1846—Rome, Dec. 6, 1916; pupil of the R. C. di S. Pietro a Majella, Naples; subteacher there till 1869; then ct.-singing-teacher at Rome; 1875 sang with great succ. London, and lived there as a teacher; 1880, singing-master to the Royal family; 1894, prof. R. A. M.; pub. a coll. of *"Canti popolari abruzzesi"* (Milan), and c. pop. songs.

Tottmann (tôt'-män), **Carl Albert,** Zittau, July 31, 1837—near Leipzig, Feb. 26, 1917; studied Dresden, and with Hauptmann, at Leipzig Cons.; violinist in the Gewandhaus Orch.; teacher of theory and history at Leipzig, also lecturer; 1873, Prof., for compendium of vln.-literature.

Toulmouche (tool-moosh), **Fr.,** Nantes, Aug. 3, 1850—Paris, Feb. 20, 1909; pupil of Victor Massé; 1894, dir. theatre "Menus-Plaisirs"; prod. many operettas.

Tourel', Jennie, French-Can. mezzo-soprano; Met. Op., 1943–5, sang Rosina, Carmen, etc.; also concerts.

Tourjée (toor-zhā), **Eben,** Warwick, Rhode Island, 1834—Boston, 1891; organist, teacher and founder of N. E. Cons.

Tournemire (toorn-mĕr), **Charles Arnould,** b. Bordeaux, Jan. 22, 1870; d. Paris, Oct., 1939; successor of César Franck at Ste. Clothilde; pupil of the Paris Cons. (winning first organ prize 1891); then of d'Indy. The City of Paris prize was awarded to his *"Le Sang de la Sirène,"* for voices and orch. 1904, and it has been given in various cities; c. 8 symphonies, lyric tragedy *"Nittetis,"* chamber music, etc.

Tours (toors), **Berthold,** Rotterdam, Dec. 17, 1838—London, March 11, 1897; violinist, composer and editor; pupil Brussels and Leipzig Conservatory.

Tourte (toort), **Fran.**, Paris, 1747—1835; famous maker of vln.-bows; est. the standard since followed.

To'vey, Sir **Donald Francis**, b. Eton, July 17, 1875—Edinburgh, July 10, 1940; pupil Sophie Weisse (piano), Parratt, Higgs and Parry (comp.); graduated at Oxford, 1898; began to compose at 8; at 19 gave a concert at Windsor with Joachim; from 1900 played in London and on the continent; 1914 succeeded Niecks as prof. at Edinburgh Univ.; 1917 founded Reid Orch. in Edinburgh; 1924, hon. Fellow of R. C. M., London; knighted, 1935; c. 4 pf. trios, pf. quartet, string quartet, pf. sonata and concerto; symphony; 3 vln. sonatas; incid. music to plays, etc.; writer on music.

Traetta (trä-ĕt'-tä) (not **Trajetta**), (1) **Tommaso** (**Michele Fran. Saverio**), Bitonto, Naples, March 30, 1727—Venice, April 6, 1779; pupil of Durante; 1758, maestro to Duke of Parma; 1765, given a life-pension by the Spanish King; 1768, ct.-composer at Petersburg; he prod. 37 operas, many of them v. succ.; c. also an oratorio, masses, etc. (2) **Filippo**, Venice, 1777—Philadelphia, 1854; son of above; from 1799 in America as an exile; wrote a vocal method; c. opera, oratorios, etc.

Trapp (trŏp), **Max**, b. Berlin, Nov. 1, 1887; composer; studied with Juon, also with Dohnanyi at Berlin Hochsch., c. 4 symphonies, vln. and piano concertos, 2 string quartets, 2 piano quartets, a piano quintet, and other orch. works, piano pieces and songs.

Trasuntino (trä-soon-tē'-nō), **Vito**, harps.-maker and inv., Rome, 1555—1606.

Traubel, **Helen**, b. St. Louis, Mo.; soprano; Met. Op., début 1937.

Trebelli (trä-bĕl'-lē), **Zelia** (rightly **Guillebert**), Paris, 1838—Étretât, Aug. 18, 1892; noted mezzo-soprano; pupil of Wartel; début, Madrid, 1859; 1863, m. Bellini; sang in Europe and (1884) U. S. with great succ.

Tre'harne, **Bryceson**, b. Merthyr Tydvil, Wales, May 30, 1879; composer; pupil of Parry, Stanford and Davies at R. Coll. of Music, also in Paris, Milan, Munich; taught at Adelaide (Australia) Univ., 1901–11; after 1912 in Paris where worked with Gordon Craig; interned in Germany during war; later res. in London and Boston; c. several hundred songs and orch. pieces; d. N. Y., Feb. 4, 1948.

Tren'to, **Vittorio**, b. Venice, 1761 (or 1765); d. after 1826; mus.-dir. and dram. composer.

Treu (Italianised **Fedele**) (troi, or fä-dā'-lĕ), **Daniel Gl.**, Stuttgart, 1695—Breslau, 1749; violinist, conductor and dram. composer.

Tréville (trä-vē-yŭ), **Yvonne de** (rightly **Le Gièrce**), b. Galveston, Tex., 1881; of French father and American mother; soprano; pupil of Marchesi; 1901 sang in Spain; 1902, at Paris Opéra Comique; 1911–12, Boston Op., also recitals; d. N. Y., 1954.

Trevisan (trä'-vē-sän), **Vittorio**, b. Venice; operatic bass; sang buffo rôles, of which he was a specialist, for a number of seasons with Chicago and Ravinia Op. Cos.; afterward active as teacher in Chicago.

Trial (trĭ-ăl), (1) **Jean Claude**, Avignon, 1732—Paris, 1771; dir. Paris Opéra and dram. composer. (2) **Antoine**, 1736—suicide, 1795; bro. of above; tenor; his wife (3) **Marie Jeanne** (née Milon) was a coloraturesopr. Their son (4) **Armand Emmanuel**, Paris, 1771—1803; dram. composer.

Triébert (trĭ'-ā-băr'), (1) **Chas. L.**, Paris, 1810—July, 1867; oboist and professor and manufacturer of instrs. (2) **Frédéric**, 1813—1878; bro. and partner of above, and maker of bassoons. (3) **Frédéric**, son of (2); oboist.

Trit'to, **Giacomo**, Altamura, Naples, 1733—Naples, 1824; professor of cpt. and dram. composer.

Tromboncino (trŏm-bôn-chē'-nō), **Bartholomaeus**, c. at Verona, 1504–10.

Tromlitz (trŏm'-lĭts), **Jn. G.**, Gera, 1726—Leipzig, 1805; flute-player, maker and teacher.

Trot'ter, **Thomas Henry Yorke**, Nov. 6, 1854—London, March 11, 1934; writer on music and pedagogue; grad. New College, Oxford; 1892, Mus. Doc.; after 1915 prin. of the Incorp. London Acad. of Music; devised influential new method of teaching, based upon ear training and rhythmic exercise; author *"Constructive Harmony"*; *"Ear-Training and Sight-Reading Gradus"*; *"The Making of Musicians"*; *"Music and Mind."*

Trout'beck, Rev. **J.**, Blencowe, Cumberland, 1832—London, 1899; pub. psalters and transl. libretti.

Tschaikowsky. Vide TCHAIKOVSKY.

Tscherep'nine, (1) Nikolai, St. Petersburg, May 15, 1873—Paris, June 28, 1945; pupil of Cons. in native city, studying with Van Arck and Rimsky-Korsakoff; after 1907 dir. of class for orch. there, and of the Maryinsky Theatre company; 1908, cond. at Paris Op.-Comique of Rimsky-Korsakoff's "Snow Maiden"; 1909–14, cond. of Diaghileff Russian Ballet; 1918–21, dir. of Tiflis Cons.; after 1921 took up residence in Paris; originally much influenced by Rimsky-Korsakoff and Tschaikowsky; his later works have shown modernistic elements, esp. some derived from Debussy and Ravel; there is a strong ingredient of Russian folk-music in his scores; c. (ballets) "Le Pavillon d'Armide," "Narcisse et Echo," "Le Masque de la Mort Rouge" (after Poe), "La Favola della Principessa Ulyba," "Dionysius" (1921), "Favola Russa" (1923), "Romance of a Mummy" (1926); (orch.) Sinfonietta; Overture to "La Princesse Lointaine" of Rostand; "Fantasie Dramatique"; symph. poems, "Dans la Caverne des Sorcières" (after Shakespeare's "Macbeth") and "Das Verzauberte Königsreich"; "Six Impressions" (after Puschkin's "The Gold Fish"); piano concerto, and other pieces for that instrument; "Poème Lyrique" for vln. and orch.; string quartet in A minor; "Songs of Sappho" for soprano, women's chorus and orch.; also liturgical works, other choruses and songs. (2) Alexander, b. St. Petersburg, Jan. 8, 1899; son of Nikolai T.; at 19 completed musical studies in native city and was appointed dir. of Tiflis Op.; after Russian Revolution lived with his family in Paris, where he entered Cons. for further study in piano (Philipp) and comp.; made début with prod. of his first piano concerto at Monte Carlo, 1923; his opera, "Ol-Ol" (based on Andreyev's "The Days of Our Life"), prod. in Weimar, 1928, also in N. Y. by Russian opera troupe in 1934; made a world tour, incl. the U. S.; appeared as guest cond. of his works with Boston Symph., 1931; and later was resident for some time in China; c. also (opera) "Hochzeit der Sobeide"; (ballet) "Ajanta's Frescoes"; (orch.) 2 piano concertos, "Rhapsodie Gor-

gienne," incid. music to plays, etc.; (chamber music) string quartet, concerto da camera, trio; also Three Pieces for chamber orch.; Suite Divertissement for piano and string quartet, etc.

Tscheschichin (chĕsh-ē'-chēn), Vsevolod Ievgrafovich, b. Riga, Feb. 18, 1865; critic and author.

Tschirch (tshĕrkh), Fr. Wm., Lichtenau, 1818—Gera, 1892; ct.-conductor and dram. composer.

Tschudi. Vide BROADWOOD.

Tua (too'-ä),(1) Teresina, b. Turin, April 23, 1866; violinist; pupil of Massart, Paris Cons., took 1st prize 1880; toured Europe, and, 1887, America, with great succ.; 1889, m. Count Franchi-Verney della Valetta (d. 1911); (2) Count Emilio Quadrio; 1915–24, taught Milan Cons., then at Liceo of Santa Cecilia, Rome.

Tucher (too'-khĕr), Gl., Freiherr von, Nürnberg, 1798—1877; writer.

Tuck'erman, Samuel Parkman, Boston, Mass., 1819—Newport, 1890; organist, editor and composer.

Tuczek (toots'-sĕk), Fz., Prague, ca. 1755—Pesth, 1820; tenor; conductor and dram. composer.

Tud'way, Thos., England, ca. 1650—London, 1726; organist and professor, Cambridge, 1704–26; Mus. Doc. there, 1705; made a coll. of contemporary services, also c. services, etc.

Tulou (tü-loo), J. L., Paris, Sept., 1786—Nantes, 1865; chief flutist of his time; at 14 at the Opéra; 1826–56, flute-prof. at the Cons.; composer.

Tuma (too'-mä), Fz., Kostelecz, Bohemia, 1704—Vienna, 1774; gamba-virtuoso and composer.

Tunder (toon'-dĕr), Fz., 1614—Lübeck, 1667; organist Marienkirche, as predecessor of Buxtehude.

Tunsted(e) (tŭn'-stĕd) (or Dunstede), Simon, b. Norwich, d. Bruisyard, Suffolk, 1369; writer. (Coussemaker.)

Turina (too-rē'-nä), Joaquin, b. Seville, Dec. 9, 1882—Madrid, Jan. 14, 1949; composer; one of most pop. recent creative figures of Spain; studied piano with Trago and Moszkowski; comp. with Torres and then with d'Indy at Paris Schola Cantorum; returned to Spain with De Falla; has served as music critic, as cond. of Spanish perfs. by Russian Ballet, and as pianist of Quinteto de

Madrid, which he founded; his music is imbued with folk rhythms and is richly colored in impressionistic style; c. (stage works) *"Margot," "La Adúltera Penitente," "Jardin de Oriente";* (orch.) *"La Procesión del Rocio," "Evangelio de Navidad," "Sinfonia Sevillano," "Danzas Fantasticas";* (chamber music) piano quintet, string quartet, *"Escena Andaluza"* for viola, piano and quartet; *"Poema de una Sanluquena,"* suite for vln. and piano; also many vocal works; ed. encyclopedia of music (2 vols.), and pub. collected articles and criticisms.

Turini (too-rē'-nē). (1) **Gregorio,** Brescia, ca. 1560—Prague, ca. 1600; singer, cornet-player and composer. (2) **Fran.,** Brescia, ca. 1590—1656; son of above; organist and comp.

Türk (türk), **Daniel Gl.,** Claussnitz, Saxony, Aug. 10, 1750—Halle, Aug. 26, 1813; eminent organist and teacher, theorist and composer.

Turle (tŭrl), **Jas.,** Somerton, Engl., 1802—London, 1882; organist, conductor, editor and composer.

Tur'ner, Wm., 1652—1740; English Mus. Doc. Cambridge; composer.

Turnhout (tĭrn'-hoot), (1) **Gerard de** (rightly **Gheert Jacques**), Turnhout, Belgium, ca. 1520—Madrid, 1580; cond. at Antwerp Cath. and to the Court at Spain, 1572; composer. (2) **Jean,** son of above; ct.-conductor and composer, ca. 1595.

Tur'pin, Edmund Hart, Nottingham, May 4, 1835—London, Oct. 25, 1907; concert-organist; lecturer, editor and writer; pupil of Hullah and Pauer, London; organist various London churches; from 1888 at St. Bride's; in 1889 Mus. Doc.; then c. masses, 2 oratorios, cantatas, symph. *"The Monastery,"* overtures, etc.

Turtshaninoff (toort-shä'-nĭ-nôf), **Peter Ivanovitch,** St. Petersburg, 1779—1856; composer.

Tutkov'ski, Nikolai Apollonovich, b. Lipovetz, Feb. 17, 1857; pianist; pupil of Puchalski; from 1881-90 teacher of history at St. Petersburg Cons.; from 1893 dir. of Cons. in Kiev; c. symph. *"Pensée élégiaque"* and *"Bachanale bohémienne"* for orch.; d. (?).

Tye (tī), **Christopher,** d. Westminster, 1572; 1554-61, organist Ely cathedral and composer.

Tyn'dall, J., Leighlin Bridge, Ireland, 1820—Haslemere, Engl., 1893; famous scientist and acoustician.

U

Ubaldus. Vide HUCBALD.

Uber (oo'-bĕr), (1) **Chr. Benj.,** Breslau, 1764—1812; dram. composer. (2) **Chr. Fr. Hermann,** Breslau, 1781—Dresden, 1822; son of above; opera-conductor and composer. (3) **Alex.,** Breslau, 1783—Carolath, Silesia, 1824; bro. of (2); 'cellist, conductor and composer.

Überlée (ü'-bĕr-lā), **Adelbert,** Berlin, June 27, 1837 — Charlottenburg, March 15, 1897; organist and royal director; c. opera, oratorio, etc.

Uberti (oo-bĕr'-tē), (**Hubert**) **A.,** Verona, 1697 (?)—Berlin, 1783; brilliant soprano-musico and teacher of Malibran, Grisi, etc.

Uccellini (oo-chĕl-lē'-nē), **Don Marco,** conductor and composer at Florence, 1673.

Ugbaldus, Uchubaldus. Vide HUCBALD.

Ugalde (ü-găld), **Delphine** (née Beauce), Paris, Dec. 3, 1829—July 18, 1910; soprano at Op.-Com., etc.; 1866, also managed the Bouffes-Parisiens; twice m.; c. an opera.

Ugolini (oo-gō-lē'-nē), **V.,** Perugia, ca. 1570—1626; teacher and important composer; pupil of Nanini; 1620-26 maestro at St. Peter's.

Uhl (ool), **Edmund,** Prague, Oct. 25, 1853—Wiesbaden, March, 1929; pupil of Leipzig Cons. winning Helbig pf.-prize, 1878; after that year teacher at the Freudenberg Cons., Wiesbaden; organist at the Synagogue; and critic; c. Romance for vln. with orch., etc.

Uhlig (oo'-lĭkh), **Th.,** Wurzen, Saxony, 1822—Dresden, 1853; violinist, theorist and composer.

Ujj (oo'-yĭ), **Bela von,** b. Vienna, July 2, 1873; Hungarian composer, blind from his 7th year; c. opera *"Der Bauernfeind"* (Baden, near Vienna, 1897); operettas *"Der Herr Professor"* (Vienna, 1903), *"Kaisermanöver"* (do., 1907), and *"Der Müller und sein Kind"* (Graz, 1907).

Ulibisheff (in French **Oulibischeff**) (oo-lē'-bĭ-shĕf), **Alex. D.,** Dresden, 1794—Nishnij Novgorod, 1858; diplomat and writer of biographies.

Ulrich (ool'-rĭkh), **Hugo** (**Otto**), Oppeln, Silesia, 1827—Berlin, 1872; teacher and dram. composer.

Umbreit (oom'-brīt), **K. Gl.**, Rehstedt, near Gotha, 1763 — 1829; org.-virtuoso and composer.

Umlauf (oom'-lowf), (1) **Ignaz**, Vienna, 1756—Mödling, 1796; music director; asst.-conductor to Salieri. (2) **Michael**, Vienna, 1781—1842; son of above; conductor and dram. composer.

Umlauft (oom'-lowft), **Paul**, Meissen, Oct. 27, 1853—Dresden, June 7, 1934; pupil Leipzig Cons.; with Mozart scholarship 1879–83; c. succ. 1-act opera *"Evanthia"* (Gotha, 1893) (won Duke of Coburg-Gotha's prize); dram. poem *"Agandecca,"* with orch. (1892); *"Mittelhochdeutsches Liederspiel,"* etc.

Unger (oong'-ĕr), (1) **Jn. Fr.**, Brunswick, 1716—1781; inventor. (2) (in Ital. **Ungher) Caroline**, Stuhlweissenburg, Hungary, 1803—at her villa, near Florence, 1877; soprano; 1840, m. Sabatier. (3) **G.**, Leipzig, 1837—1887; tenor.

Up'ton, G. Putnam, Roxburg, Mass., Oct. 25, 1835—Chicago, May 20, 1919; graduate Brown Univ., 1854; 1861–85, on the editorial staff, Chicago *Tribune;* founder (1872) and first pres. Apollo Club; translator and writer of valuable essays, incl. *"Standard Operas"* (1890); *"Standard Oratorios"* (1891); *"Standard Symphs."* (1892), etc.

Urbach (oor'-băkh), **Otto**, Eisenach, Feb. 6, 1871—Dresden, Dec. 14, 1927; composer; pupil of Müller-Hartung, Stavenhagen, Scholz, Knorr and Humperdinck; won the Liszt stipend, 1890, and the Mozart stipend 1896, and studied with Draeseke and Klindworth; from 1898 piano teacher at the Dresden Cons.; c. opera *"Der Müller von Sanssouci"* (Frankfort, 1896).

Urban (oor'-bän), (1) **Chr.**, b. Elbing, 1778; mus.-director, theorist and composer. (2) **H.**, Berlin, Aug. 27, 1837—Nov. 24, 1901; pupil of Ries, Laub, Helman, etc.; violinist and theorist; 1881, teacher at Kullak's Acad.; c. symph. *"Frühling,"* overtures to *"Fiesco"* (Schiller), *"Scheherazade,"* and *"Zu einem Fastnachtsspiel,"* etc. (3) **Fr. Julius**, Berlin, Dec. 23, 1838—July 17, 1918; bro. of above: solo boy-soprano in the Domchor; pupil of H. Ries, and

Helmann (vln.), Grell (theory), Elsner and Mantius (singing); singing-teacher, Berlin; wrote vocal methods and songs.

Urbani. Vide VALENTINI.

Urhan (ür-äṅ), **Chrétien**, Montjoie, 1790—Paris, 1845; eccentric and gifted player on stringed instrs., ancient and modern; organist and composer.

Urich (oo'-rĭkh), **Jean**, Trinidad, 1849–1939; pupil of Gounod; prod. operas *"Der Lootse," "Hermann und Dorothea,"* and 2-act *"Le Carillon"* (Berlin, 1902).

Urio (oo'-rĭ-ō), **Fran. A.**, b. Milan, 1660; writer and composer.

Urlus (ōōr'-lōōs), **Jacques**, Amsterdam, 1868—Noordwyk, June 6, 1935; noted tenor; pupil of Hol, Noltenius, the Amsterdam Cons., making his début in latter city in 1894; after 1900 at Leipzig Stadttheatre; sang also in many other Eur. cities; at Bayreuth from 1911, and in N. Y., 1913–17; one of leading Wagnerian tenors of his day.

Ursillo (oor-sĭl'-lō), **Fabio** (or simply **Fabio**), 18th cent. archlute virtuoso and composer at Rome.

Urso (oor'-sō), (1) **Camilla**, Nantes, France, 1842—New York, Jan. 20, 1902; vln.-virtuoso (daughter of (2) **Salvator**, organist and flutist); pupil of Massart; she played in America with great succ. at 10; toured the world; m. Fr. Luères.

Urspruch (oor'-sprookh), **Anton**, Frankfort-on-Main, Feb. 17, 1850—Jan. 11, 1907; pupil of Ignaz Lachner and M. Wallenstein, Raff and Liszt; pf.-teacher Hoch Cons.; from 1887 at Raff Cons.; c. opera *"Der Sturm"* (based on Shakespeare's *"Tempest,"* Frankfort, 1888), comic opera (text and music) *"Das Unmöglichste von Allem"* (Carlsruhe, 1897), a symph., pf.-concerto, etc.

U(u)tendal (or **Utenthal, Uutendal**) (ü'-tĕn-däl), **Alex.**, d. Innsbruck, May 8, 1581; Flemish conductor and composer.

V

Vaccai (väk-kä'-ē), **Niccolö**, Tolentino, Papal States, 1790—Pesaro, 1848, noted singing-teacher; prof. of comp. Milan Cons.; wrote vocal method; c. an opera, funeral cantata, etc.

Vacqueras (vă-kā'-răs), Beltrame, 1481 singer at St. Peter's, Rome; 1483–1507 papal chapel singer; c. motets, etc.

Vaet (vät), Jacques, d. Vienna, 1567; Flemish conductor and composer.

Valente (vä-lĕn'-tĕ), Vincenzo, Corigliano, near Cosenza, Feb. 21, 1855 —Naples, Sept. 6, 1921; c. operas and songs.

Valentini (vä-lĕn-tē'-nē), (1) Giov., ca. 1615; organist and composer. (2) Giov., Naples, 1779–1788; dram. composer. (3) P. Fran., Rome, ca. 1570—1654; eminent contrapuntist; pupil of Nanini. (4) (Rightly Valentino Urbani) (oor-bä'-nĕ), celebrated contralto-musico; later a tenor; London, 1707. (5) Giu., b. Rome(?), 1681; violinist and composer.

Valentino (văl-än-tē'-nō), Henri Justin Armand Jos., Lille, 1785—Versailles, 1856; conductor Paris Opéra, 1820–31, then at Op. Com. till 1837.

Valet'ta, Ippolito. Vide FRANCHI-VERNEY.

Vallas (väy'-äs), Léon, b. Roanne, May 17, 1879; writer; author of studies of Debussy and Georges Migot.

Vallin (vä'-yăn), Ninon, b. Montalieu-Vercieu, prov. of Dauphiné, France; soprano; studied at Lyons Cons.; début, Paris Op.-Comique in "Carmen"; later sang in opera at Buenos Aires, also at Paris Op., La Scala, Rome R. Op., Madrid, Vienna, Budapest, Barcelona, Stockholm and Constantinople; esp. known as a recitalist of modern French music, incl. Debussy; toured U. S. in concerts.

Valotti (väl-lôt'-tē), Fran. A., Vercelli, June 11, 1697—Padua, Jan. 16, 1780; noted organist, theorist and composer.

Valverde (väl-vär'-dā), (1) Joaquin, d. Madrid, March 19, 1910; c. zarzuelas and songs. (2) Quirino, his son, also c.

Van Bei'num, Eduard, Dutch conductor; led Amsterdam Concertgebouw Orch., 1945; also guest cond. London and elsewhere.

Van den Eeden (ā'-dĕn), (1) Gilles, d. 1792; first teacher of Beethoven; son or nephew of (2) Heinrich; ct.-mus. to the Elector of Cologne.

Van der Straeten (strä'-tĕn), Edmond, Oudenaarden, Belgium, 1826—1895; writer of treatises: c. opera, etc.

Van der Stucken (vän'-dĕr-shtook'-ĕn), Frank (Valentin), Fredericksburg, Gillespie Co., Texas, Oct. 15, 1858—Hamburg, Aug. 18, 1929; son of Belgian father and German mother; notable composer and conductor; at 8 taken by his parents to Antwerp, studied with Benoît, later with Reinecke, Sänger and Grieg; 1881–82, cond. at Breslau City Th.; 1883, in Rudolstadt with Grieg, and in Weimar with Liszt; prod. opera "Vlasda" (Paris, 1883); 1884, called to be mus.-dir. of the "Arion," New York; he was dean of the Cincinnati College of Music 1897–1901; cond. Cincinnati Symph. 1895–1907, when he returned to Germany, retaining the conductorship of the Cincinnati May Festivals; c. symph. prologue "William Ratcliff" (Cincinnati, 1899); orch. episode, "Pagina d'amore," with choruses and songs; "Festival March," for orch., "Pax Triumphans," etc.

Van der Veer', Nevada, b. Springfield Center, N. Y.; contralto; studied with Beigel, Arthur Fagge, and Marie Roze, Paris; has appeared widely as oratorio soloist and with orchs.; later active as teacher at Cleveland Inst. of Music; m. Reed Miller, tenor.

Van Dier'en, Bernard, Holland, Dec. 27, 1884—London, April 24, 1936; composer; of mixed Dutch and French parentage; studied in Rotterdam, Leyden, Berlin and London, first in science, and after 1904 exclusively in music; came to London 1909 as musical corr. for the Nieuwe Rotterdamsche Courant, where he remained; developed complex contrapuntal style, partly influenced by early choral schools of the Netherlands; c. symph. for soloists, chorus and orch., after Chinese text; 4 string quartets, several of which were heard at European modern music fests.; "Diaphonie" for barytone and chamber orch., after 3 Shakespeare sonnets; (opera buffa) "The Tailor" (text by Robert Nicholls); and various other chamber music and vocal works; m. Frida Kindler, pianist.

Van Dres'ser, Marcia, Memphis, 1880—London, 1937; soprano; studied Chicago, Munich and Paris; after 1898 sang in light and grand opera in Europe and, beginning 1914, in United States.

Van Duyze (vän doi'-zĕ), **Florimond,** Ghent, Aug. 4, 1848—May 18, 1910; lawyer and amateur; pupil of Ghent Cons., winning Grand prix de Rome, 1873, with cantata "*Torquato Tasso's Dood*"; prod. 7 operas, Antwerp and Ghent; c. also ode-symphonie "*Die Nacht.*"

Van Dyck (vän dīk), **Ernest (Marie Hubert),** Antwerp, April 2, 1861—Berlaer-les-Lierre (Antwerp), Aug. 31, 1923; noted tenor; studied law, was then a journalist at Paris; studied singing with St. Yves; début Paris, 1887, as "Lohengrin"; 1892 sang "Parsifal" at Bayreuth; 1888 engaged for the Vienna ct.-opera; sang in the chief capitals, London, and 1899–1902, New York; later taught at Antwerp and Brussels conservatories.

Van Gordon, Cyrena, b. Camden, Ohio, Sept. 4, 1896; contralto; name originally Procock; studied Cincinnati Coll. of Music; début, Chicago Op. as "Amneris," 1913; sang many contralto rôles with this co.; for a time with Met. Op. Co.; her repertoire incl. German, Italian and French parts.

Van Hoog'straten, Willem, b. Utrecht, March 18, 1884; conductor; studied Cologne Cons.; début as cond., Hamburg, 1911; he also appeared at Hamburg, Vienna and Salzburg; as cond. N. Y. Philh., 1923–24; of Portland, Ore., Symph., after 1925, regularly at the Lewisohn Stadium concerts in N. Y. following 1921; and as a guest with many Eur. and Amer. ensembles, incl. Bonn Beethoven Fest.; hon. Music D., Univ. of Oregon, 1926; m. Elly Ney, pianist; divorced.

Van Hoose, Ellison, Murfreesboro, Tenn., Aug. 18, 1869—Houston, Tex., March 24, 1936; tenor; studied U. S. and Europe, teachers incl. Jean de Reszke and Cotogni; after 1897, sang with Damrosch-Ellis Op. Co.; at Mayence Op., and 1911–12, Chicago Op. Co.; also in oratorio and concerts; later church mus. dir. in Houston.

Vanneo (vän-nä'-ō), **Stefano,** b. Recanati, Ancona, 1493; monk and writer.

Van Rooy (vän rō'-ĭ), **Anton,** Rotterdam, Jan. 12, 1870—Munich, Nov. 28, 1932; notable barytone; pupil of Stockhausen at Frankfort; sang in oratorio and concerts; later at Bayreuth, 1897; then at Berlin ct.-opera; sang with succ. London (1898), 1898–1908 in New York annually; then at Frankfort Opera; his greatest rôle was "Wotan."

Van Vech'ten, Carl, b. Cedar Rapids, Iowa, 1880; writer; Grad. Univ. of Chicago; on staff of N. Y. *Times,* later N. Y. *Press;* ed. program notes of N. Y. Symph., 1910–11; in later years esp. known as a novelist, but also pub. books on music and art criticism; author, "*Music after the Great War,*" "*Music and Bad Manners,*" "*Interpreters and Interpretations,*" "*The Merry-Go-Round,*" "*The Music of Spain,*" etc.

Van Vliet, Cornelius, b. Rotterdam, Sept. 1, 1886; 'cellist; pupil of Eberle and Mossel; played Concertgebouw Orch. under Mengelberg; 1st 'cellist Leipzig Philh.; Prague Philh.; solo appearances, Munich, Vienna, and Helsingfors, where taught in Cons.; after 1911 in U. S. as recitalist, 'cellist in N. Y. Trio and long first 'cellist of N. Y. Philharmonic.

Van Westerhout (wĕs'-tĕr-howt), **Niccolo** (of Dutch parents), Mola di Bari, 1862—Naples, 1898; dram. composer.

Van Zanten, Cornelie, see **Zanten.**

Varèse (vä-rĕs'), **Edgar,** b. Paris, Dec. 22, 1885; composer; studied at Schola Cantorum with Roussel and d'Indy, at Paris Cons. with Widor; 1907, won Bourse Artistique of City of Paris; 1909, founded Symphonischer Chor., Berlin; after 1916 res. in N. Y., where founded New Symph. Orch., giving modern scores for several years; has c. orch. and chamber wks., incl. "*Hyperprism,*" etc.

Varnay (vär-nī'), **Astrid,** Swed.-Am. soprano; début Met. Op., 1941, as Sieglinde while still in twenties.

Varney (vär-nē), (1) **P. Jos. Alphonse,** Paris, 1811—1879; conductor and composer of operettas. (2) **Louis,** Paris, 1844—Cauterets, 1908; son and pupil of above; prod. over 30 operettas, comic operas, "revues."

Vasconcellos (väs-kōn-sĕl'-lōs), **Joaquim de,** Oporto, Feb. 10, 1849—?; Portuguese lexicographer and historian.

Vasquez y Gomez (väs'-kĕth ē gō'-mĕth), **Marino,** Granada. Feb. 3, 1831—Madrid, June, 1894; concertmaster at Madrid Royal Theatre; c. zarzuelas, etc.

Vasseur (vă̆s-sŭr), **Léon** (**Félix Aug.**
Jos.), Bapaume, Pas-de-Calais, May
28, 1844—Paris, 1917; studied École
Niedermeyer; from 1870 organist Versailles Cath.; cond. Folies-
Bergères and the Concerts de Paris
(1882); prod. over 30 light operas;
c. also masses, etc.

Vassilen'ko, Sergei Nikiforovich, b.
Moscow, March 31, 1872; writer;
pupil of the Cons., winning gold
medal, 1901; c. cantata "*The Legend
of the Sunken City of Kitesch*" (given
as an opera, Moscow, 1903); "*Epic
Poem*" for orch., choral works
"*Nebuchadnezzar*," and "*Daphnis*,"
etc.

Vatielli (vä-tĭ̆-ĕl'-lē), **Francesco,** b.
Pesaro, Jan. 1, 1877; pupil of Liceo
Rossini, 1905 librarian at Bologna,
teacher and writer on history; c.
intermezzi, etc.

Vaucorbeil (vō-kôr-bĕ'), Aug. Emanuel,
Rouen, 1821—Paris, 1884; 1880, dir.
the Opéra; c. comic-opera, etc.

Vaughan-Williams, Ralph; see **Williams, Ralph Vaughan.**

Vavrinecz (vä'-vrē-nĕts), **Mauritius,**
Czegled, Hungary, July 18, 1858—
Budapest, Aug. 5, 1913; studied
Pesth Cons., and with R. Volkmann;
cath. cond. at Pesth; c. 4-act opera
"*Ratcliff*" (Prague, 1895), succ. 1-act
opera "*Rosamunda*" (Frankfort-on-
Main, 1895), oratorio, 5 masses, a
symph., etc.

Vecchi(i) (vĕk'-kē-[ē]), (1) **Orazio,**
Modena, 1550—Feb. 19, 1603; noted
composer; from 1596 maestro Modena cath.; his "mus.-comedy" "*Am-
fiparnasso*," in which the chorus
joined in all the mus., even the
monologues, appeared the same year
as PERI's (q. v.) "*Dafne*"; c. also
madrigals, etc. (2) **Orfeo,** Milan,
1540—ca. 1604; maestro, and composer.

Vecsey (vĕt'-chĕ-ē), **Franz von,** Budapest, March 23, 1893—Rome, April
4, 1935; violinist; at 8, pupil of
Hubay; at 10 accepted by Joachim,
and toured Germany, England and
America with immense success;
toured South America, 1911; reappeared in London, 1912; later
toured as mature artist.

Veit (vīt), **Wenzel H.** (**Václav Jin-
dřich**), Repic, near Leitmeritz,
Bohemia, 1806—Leitmeritz, 1864;
composer.

Velluti (vĕl-loo'-tē), **Giov. Bat.,** Monterone, Ancona, 1781—San Burson,
1861; the last of the great male
soprani.

Venatorini. Vide MYSLIWECZEK.

Venosa, Prince of. Vide GESUALDO.

Venth (vĕnt), **Karl,** Cologne, Feb. 10,
1860—San Antonio, Tex., Jan. 20,
1938; pupil of the Cons. and of
Wieniawski; 1880 in New York as
concertmaster at Met. Op. House,
founded 1888 a cons. in Brooklyn; c.
Schiller's "*Bells*" for chorus and
orch., etc.; after 1908 lived in Texas;
dean of woman's coll. and orch.
cond., Dallas.

Ver'to, (1) **Ivo de,** b. Spain; ct.-
o ,unist at Munich and composer
(1561–91). (2) Lattia, Naples, 1735
—London, 1777; c. operas.

Venturelli (vĕn-too-rĕl'-lē), **V.,** Man-
t 1851—(suicide) 1895; essayist
a. dram. composer.

Ventirini (vĕ i-too-rē'-ne), **Francesco,**
d. never April 18, 1745; from
160 n the Hanoverian court chapel
as cond.: c. concertos, etc.

Venzano (vĕn-tsä'-nō), **Luigi,** Genoa,
ca. 1814—1878; 'cellist and teacher;
c. opera, pop. songs, etc.

Veracini (va i-che -nē), (1) **A.,** violinist at Florence 1696). (2) **Fran.
Maria,** Florence ca. 1685—near
Pisa, ca. 1750; nephew and pupil of
above: notable violinist, the greatest
of his time: composer.

Verbrug'ghen. Henri, Brussels, Aug. 1,
1873—Northfield, Minn., Nov. 12,
1934; conductor, violinist; studied
at Brussels Cons., 1st prize in vln.,
also with Hubay and Ysaye; soloist
with English orchs. and with Lamoureux; 1902, concertm. and asst.
cond., Scottish Orch., Glasgow;
succeeded Coward as cond. of Choral
Union in that city; also org. string
quartet and served as guest leader
in London and Continental cities;
was dir. for 8 years of New South
Wales State Cons., Sydney, and
there founded and led State Orch.;
came to N. Y. after war and was
guest cond. of Russian Symph., 1918;
guest cond. of Minneapolis Symph.,
1922; appointed regular cond. and
served until 1931, when illness
caused him to resign post; he led
this orch. on tour, incl. N. Y., with
eminent succ. and founded and
played 1st vln. in quartet bearing his
name; headed music dept. at Carle-

ton Coll., Northfield, for several years before his death.

Verdelot, (vărd-lō) (Italianised, Verdelot'to), Philippe, d. before 1567; famous Flemish madrigal-composer and singer at San Marco, Venice; between 1530–40 in Florence.

Verdi (věr'-dē), (Fortunio) Giuseppe (Fran.), Le Roncole, near Busseto, Duchy of Parma, Oct. 9, 1813— Milan, Jan. 27, 1901; eminent Italian opera composer. Son of an innkeeper and grocer; pupil, and at 10 successor of the village organist, Baistrocchi, for three years pupil of Provesi at Busseto; 1831 with the aid of his father's friend, Barezzi, he went to Milan, where he was refused admission to the Cons. by Basili, who thought him lacking in mus. talent. He became a pupil of Lavigna, cembalist, at La Scala, 1833, cond. Philh. Soc., and organist at Busseto; 1836 m. Barezzi's daughter Margherita. 1839, his opera "Oberto" was prod. with fair succ. at La Scala, Milan. He was commissioned by Merelli, the manager to write three operas, one every eight months, at 4,000 lire ($800 or £160) apiece, and half the copyright. The first was a comic opera "Un Giorno di Regno," which failed (1840), doubtless in part because his two children and wife had died within three months. V.'s combined distress drove him to rescind his agreement and renounce composition for over a year, when he was persuaded by Merelli to set the opera "Nabucco" ("Nebuchadrezzar"), prod. at La Scala, 1842, with great applause, the chief rôle being taken by Giuseppina Strepponi (1815–97), whom he m. in 1844. "I Lombardi alla prima Crociata" (La Scala, 1843) was still more succ. and is still played in Italy (in Paris as "Jérusalem"). "Ernani" (Venice, 1844) was prod. on 15 different stages in 9 months. 8 unsucc. works followed, incl. "I due Foscari" (Rome, 1844), "Macbeth" (Florence, 1847; revised Paris, 1865), and "I Masnadieri" (after Schiller's "Robbers" London, H. M. Th., 1847). "Luisa Miller" (Naples, 1849) was well received and is still sung in Italy. "Stiffelio" (Trieste, 1850); later as "Guglielmo Welingrode"; also with another libretto as "Arnoldo" (1857), was

three times a failure. "Rigoletto," c. in 40 days (Venice) (also given as "Viscardello"), began a three years' period of universal succ., it was followed by the world-wide successes "Il Trovatore" (Rome, 1853) and "La Traviata" (Venice Th., 1853; also given as "Violetta"), a fiasco at first because of a poor cast; "Les Vêpres Siciliennes" (Paris Opéra, 1855; in Italian "I Vespri Siciliani"; also given as "Giovanna di Guzman") was fairly succ.; "Simon Boccanegra" (Venice, 1857; succ. revised, Milan, 1881), "Un Ballo in Maschera" (Rome, 1859), "La Forza del Destino" (Petersburg, 1862), and "Don Carlos" (Paris, Opéra, 1867), made no deep impression, though they served as a schooling and marked a gradual broadening from mere Italian lyricism to a substantial harmony and orchestration. "Aïda" (written for the Khedive of Egypt) was prod. Cairo, 1871, at La Scala, Milan, 1872, and has had everywhere a great succ. The Khedive gave him £3,000 for it. His "Manzoni Requiem" (1874) made a sensation in Italy; "Otello" (Milan, 1887) was a work worthy of its composer, and in his last opera "Falstaff," written at the age of eighty, he showed not only an unimpaired but a progressive and novel style. He also c. 2 symphs., 6 pf.-concertos, "Inno delle Nazioni," for the London Exhibition (1862), songs, etc.

In 1893 he was offered the title "Marchese di Busseto," but was too democratic to accept it. He lived at his villa Sant' Agata, near Busseto. His funeral brought 100,000 witnesses, though his will ordered that it should be simple and quiet. He left the bulk of his fortune to found a home for aged and outworn musicians in Milan, where there is also a Verdi museum.

Following a period in which V.'s operas were unfavourably compared with Wagner's, there has been a marked tendency to rank him as an even superior musical dramatist in some respects. Particularly in Germany, after 1920, a new interest in his works arose, partly as the result of translations and adaptations made by Franz Werfel, who also pub. a novel based on V.'s life.

Biog. by Gino Monaldi (in German,

trans. by L. Holthof, Leipzig, 1898); Checchi, 1887; Blanche Roosevelt (London, 1887); Crowest (1897); Visetti (1905); Bonavia (1930) and Toye (1931). Other memoirs by Pougin, Hanslick, Prince Valori, Parodi, Perinello, Cavaretta, Basso, Boni, Colonna, Sorge, Voss, Garibaldi, Bragagnolo and Bettazzi, d'Angeli, Bellaigue, Lottici, Righetti, Mackenzie, Chop, Roncaglia, and Neisser. (See article, page 538.)

Verdonck', Cornelius, Turnhout, Belgium, 1563—Antwerp, 1625; composer.

Vere-Sapio (văr-sä'-pǐ-ō), Clementine (Duchêne) de, b. Paris; soprano; daughter of a Belgian nobleman, and an Englishwoman; pupil of Mme. Albertini-Baucarde, Florence; début there at 16, sang at leading theatres, Europe, later in concert, also in the United States; 1896, she returned to opera; 1899, toured U. S. with an opera troupe of which her husband, Romualdo Sapio, was mgr.; 1900–1901 at Metropolitan, N. Y., and Covent Garden; d. N. Y., 1954.

Verhey (věr'-hī), Th. H. H., Rotterdam, 1848—Jan. 28, 1929; pupil of the Royal Music Sch., at The Hague and of Bargiel; teacher at Rotterdam; c. operas, a mass, chamber music, etc.

Verhulst (věr-hoolst'), Jns. (Josephus Herman), The Hague, 1816—1891; cond.; famous composer; pupil of Volcke at the Cons. there, later R. mus.-dir.; cond. many societies, etc.; intimate friend of Schumann; c. symphony, 3 overtures, etc.

Vernier (věrn-yā), Jean Aimé, b. Paris, 1769; harpist and composer.

Véron (vā-rôn), Désiré, Paris, 1798—1867; critic, writer and manager of the Opéra.

Verstovsky (or **Werstowski**), Alexei Nikolaievich, Tambov, Feb. 18 (March 1), 1799—Moscow, Nov. 5 (17), 1862; composer; while studying civil engineering at the Institute in St. Petersburg, he was also a pupil of John Field and Steibelt (piano), Böhm (violin), Tarquini (voice), Brandt and Tseiner (theory); c. a vaudeville at 19, and soon acquired a vogue; at 25 was inspector of the Imp. Opera, Moscow; at 29, c. a succ. opera, "*Pan Tvardovski*," followed by five others, including "*Askold's Tomb*" (1835), which had

enormous success and was revived in 1897; was accepted as a beginning of national opera and had undoubted influence on its development. He c. also cantatas and 29 popular songs.

Vesque von Püttlingen (věsk fōn pǐt'-lǐng-ěn), Jn., Opole, Poland, 1803—Vienna, 1883; pianist of Belgian parentage; c. 6 operas; used pen-name "J. Hoven."

Ves'tris, Lucia E., London, 1797—Fulham, 1856; opera-singer.

Vetter (fět-těr), Nikolaus, Königsee, 1666—Rudolfstadt, 1710; court organist and important choral composer.

Viadana (vē-ä-dä'-nä), Ludovico (da) (rightly L. Grossi), Viadana, near Mantua, 1564 — Gualtieri, 1645; noted church-composer; maestro at Mantua cath.; important early figure in the development of basso continuo (v. D. D.).

Vian'na da Mot'ta, José, see **Da Motta.**

Vianesi (vē-ä-nä'-zē), Auguste Chas. Léonard François, Leghorn, Nov. 2, 1837—New York, Nov. 11, 1908; studied in Paris 1859, cond. Drury Lane, London; then at New York, Moscow and Petersburg; 12 years cond. at Covent Garden; also in other cities; 1887, 1st cond. Gr. Opéra, Paris; cond. New York, 1891–92.

Viardot-Garcia (vǐ-ȧr'-dō-gär-thē'-ä), (1) (Michelle Fde.) Pauline, Paris, July 18, 1821—May 18, 1910; famous mezzo-soprano and teacher; daughter of Manuel Garcia (q.v.), studied pf. with Vega at Mexico Cath., then with Neysenberg and Liszt, and Reicha (harm.); and singing with her father and mother; concert début, Brussels, 1837; opera début, London, 1839, engaged by Viardot, dir. Th. Italien, Paris, and sang there until 1841, when she m. him and made European tours with him. In 1849 she created "Fides" in "*Le Prophète*," Paris, "Sapho" (Gounod's opera), 1851; 1863, retired to Baden-Baden; from 1871 lived in Paris as teacher. Her voice had the remarkable compass of more than 3 octaves from bass c–f'''. Wrote a vocal method and c. 3 operas, 60 songs, and also 6 pcs. for pf. and vln. Biogr. by La Mara. (2) Louise Héritte Viardot, Paris, Dec. 14, 1841 —Heidelberg, Jan., 1918; daughter of above: singing-teacher Hoch

Cons., Frankfort (till 1886); then est. a sch. at Berlin; c. 2 comic operas, a pf.-quartet, etc. (3) Mme. **Chamerot,** and (4) **Marianne V.,** daughters of (1) were concert-singers.

Vicentino (vē-chĕn-tē'-nō), **Nicola,** Vicenza, 1511—Rome, 1572; conductor, theorist and composer; inv. "archiorgano."

Victorio. Vide VITTORIA.

Vidal (vē-dăl, (1) **B.,** d. Paris, 1880; guitar-virtuoso, teacher and composer. (2) **Jean Jos.,** Sòreze, 1789 —Paris, 1867; violinist. (3) **Louis A.,** Rouen, July 10, 1820—Paris, Jan. 7, 1891; 'cellist and writer; pupil of Franchomme; pub. important historical works. (4) **Paul Antonin,** Toulouse, June 16, 1863—Paris, April 9, 1931; pupil of Paris Cons., winning first Grand prix de Rome, 1881; from 1894, taught at the Cons.; 1896, cond. at the Opéra; prod. 3-act lyric fantasy *"Eros"* (1892), a ballet *"La Maladetta"* (1893), 2 1-act operettas; lyric drama *"Guernica"* (Op. Com., 1895); *"La Reine Fiammette"* (1898); *"La Burgonde"* (1898); *"Ramses"* (1908); orch. suite, *"Les mystères d'Eleusis,"* etc.

Vierdank (fēr'-dänk), **Jn.,** organist and composer at Stralsund 1641.

Vierling (fēr'-lǐng), (1) **Jn. Gf.,** Metzels, near Meiningen, 1750—Schmalkalden, 1813; organist and composer. (2) **Jacob V.,** 1796—1867, organist. (3) **Georg,** Frankenthal, Palatinate, Sept. 5, 1820—Wiesbaden, May 1, 1901; son and pupil of above, also of Rinck (org.), Marx (comp.); 1847, organist at Frankfort-on-Oder; 1852-53, cond. Liedertafel, Mayence; then lived in Berlin, founder and for years cond. Bach-verein; prof. and R. Mus.-Dir.; c. notable secular oratorios, *"Der Raub der Sabinerinnen"* (op. 50), *"Alarichs Tod"* and *"Konstantin"*; Psalm 137, with orch.; and other choral works; a symph.; 5 overtures, incl. *"Im Frühling"*; capriccio for pf. with orch., etc.

Vierne, Louis Victor Jules, Poitiers, France, Oct. 8, 1870—at organ, Notre Dame, Paris, June 2, 1937; pupil of Paris Cons. under Franck and Widor, the latter making him his asst. as org. at St. Sulpice in 1892, and in his classes at the Cons.,

1894; after 1900 he was org. at Notre Dame; from 1911 instructor in organ master class at the Schola Cantorum; he gave recitals in many Eur. cities; teacher of Nadia Boulanger, Joseph Bonnet and Marcel Dupré; c. 5 symphonies for organ and other works for this instrument; Missa Solemnis for choir and orch.; various other church comps.; orch., chamber music and piano pieces, etc.

Vieuxtemps (v'yŭ-tän), (1) **Henri,** Verviers, Belgium, Feb. 20, 1820—Mustapha, Algiers, June 6, 1881; eminent violinist and composer; son and pupil of a piano-tuner and instr.-maker, then pupil of Lecloux, with whom he toured at 8; then pupil of de Bériot (vln.), Sechter (harm.), Reicha (comp.); he toured Europe with great succ., and three times America (1844, 1857 and 1870); 1845, m. Josephine Eder, a Vienna pianist; 1846-52, solo-violinist to the Czar and prof. at the Petersburg Cons.; 1871-73, prof. at the Brussels Cons.; then paralysis of his left side stopped his playing. He c. 6 concertos, several concertinos, an overture on the Belgian national hymn (op. 41), fantaisie-caprice, with orch.; fantaisies on Slavic themes, *"Hommage à Paganini,"* caprice, sonata, vars. on *"Yankee Doodle,"* 2 'cello-concertos, a grand solo duo for vln. and 'cello (with Servais), etc. Biog. by Radoux (1891). (2) **Jules Jos. Ernest,** Brussels, March 18, 1832—Belfast, March 20, 1896; bro. of above; solo-'cellist It. Opera, London; also in Hallé's orch. at Manchester. (3) **Jean Joseph Lucien,** Verviers, July 5, 1828—Brussels, Jan. 1901; pianist and composer; pianist, teacher, and c. of piano pieces, brother of Henri and Jules V. (q. v.).

Viganò (vē-gä-nō'), **Salvatore,** Naples, 1769—Milan, 1821; ballet-dancer and succ. composer of ballets.

Vigna (vēn'-yä), **Arturo,** Turin, 1863--Milan, Jan. 5, 1927; cond. Met. Op. House, N. Y., 1903-07; pupil Milan Cons.

Vilbac(k) (vēl-băk), **(Alphonse Chas.) Renaud de,** Montpellier, 1829—Paris, 1884; pianist and organist; c. comic operas.

Villa-Lo'bos, Heitor, b. Rio de Janeiro, March 5, 1881; composer; studied with Franca, Braga and Nyendem-

berg; début as 'cellist at 12; made
tour of Brazil, where has led orchs.
as well as in Europe; attracted
attention for his comps. in chamber
music and other forms, based on
Brazilian folk-music, marked by
unusual pungency and originality
in expression; he is advanced in
modern technical devices, and independent in idiom and personality; c.
sonatas, trios, quintet, sextet, octet,
4 concertos, many symphonic works,
and piano pieces, some of which are
based on characteristic African
dances, and several suites for children; adaptations of native folk-
songs, with Portuguese, French and
Spanish texts.

Villanis (vĕl-lä'-nēs), Luigi Alberto,
San Mauro, near Turin, June 24,
1863—Pesaro, Sept. 27, 1906; LL.D.
Turin Univ., 1887, then pupil of
Thermignon, and Cravero (comp.);
1890 prof. of mus. æsthetics and
history, Turin Univ.; critic and
writer.

Villarosa (vĕl-lä-rō'-sä), Carlantonio
de Rosa, Marchese di, Naples, 1762
—1847; Royal Historiographer, 1823,
and writer on music.

Villars (vē-yărs), Fran. de, Ile Bour-
bon, 1825—Paris, 1879; critic and
historian.

Villebois (vē'-yŭ-bwä), Constantin
Petrovitch, 1817—Warsaw, 1882;
composer.

Vil'loing, Alex, St. Petersburg, 1808—
1878; pf.-teacher; wrote method
and c. pf.-pcs.

Villoteau (vē'-yŏ-tō), Guillaume André, Bellême, 1759—Paris, 1839;
tenor and writer.

Vinay (vē'-nī), Raoul, Chilean tenor;
début Met. Op., 1945, as Don Jose;
sang Otello there and at La Scala.

Vincent (văṅ-säṅ), (1) Alex. Jos. Hy-
culphe, Hesdin, Pas-de-Calais, 1797
—Paris, 1868; pub. treatises claiming that the Greeks used harm., etc.
(fĭn'-tsĕnt), (2) H. Jos., Teilheim,
near Würzburg, Feb. 23, 1819—
Vienna, May 20, 1901; gave up
theology and law and became a tenor
in theatres at Vienna (1849), Halle
and Würzburg; from 1872, singing-
teacher and conductor; lived at
Vienna; pub. treatises; c. operettas.

Vinci (vēn'-chē), (1) Pietro, b. Nicosia,
Sicily, 1540; maestro and composer.
(2) Leonardo; Strongoli, Calabria,

1690—Naples, 1730; maestro and
dram. composer.

Viñes (vēn'-yĕs), Ricardo, b. Lérida,
Spain, Feb. 5, 1875; pianist; pupil
of Pujol at Barcelona Cons., also
of de Bériot, Lavignac and Godard
at Paris Cons.; esp. known as
interpreter of modern French, Russian and Spanish music, and a
pioneer in the playing of Debussy;
lived in Paris; d. Barcelona, 1943.

Viola (vē-ō'-lä), (1) Alfonso della, ct.-
composer at Ferrara, 1541–63 to
Ercole II. (2) Fran., pupil of Willaert; maestro at Ferrara, and composer, 1558–73.

Viole (fē'-ō-lĕ), Rudolf, Schochwitz,
Mansfield, 1825—Berlin, 1867; pianist and composer.

Viotta (fē-ōt'-tä), Henri, Amsterdam,
July 16, 1848—Montreux, Feb. 18,
1933; studied Cologne Cons.; also
a lawyer, 1883; founder and cond.,
Amsterdam Wagner Soc., etc.; 1889,
ed. Maandblad voor Muziek; 1896
—1917, dir. Cons. at The Hague;
1903–17, cond. of Residentie Orkest;
publ. a "Lexicon der Toonkunst."

Viotti (vē-ōt'-tē), Giov. Bat., Fonta-
neto da Pò, Vercelli, Italy, May 23,
1753—London, March 3, 1824; son
of a blacksmith; at first self-
taught, then, under patronage of
Prince della Cisterna, studied with
Pugnani at Turin; soon entered the
ct.-orchestra; 1780 toured with Pugnani, was invited to become ct.-
violinist to Catherine II., but went
to Paris, then London, playing with
greatest succ.; 1783 an inferior
violinist drew a larger audience, and
in disgust he retired from concerts
and became a teacher and accompanist to Marie Antoinette and cond.
to the Prince de Soubise. Failing
to be dir. of the Opera, 1787, he
joined Léonard, the Queen's hair-
dresser, and est. It. Opéra, 1789;
prospering till the Revolution. He
went to London as a violinist and
played with great succ. 1795, mgr.
It. Opéra and dir. Opera Concerts
there; failing he went into the wine-
trade. Later returned to Paris, and
became dir. of the Opera, 1819–22,
then pensioned with 6,000 francs
He pub. 29 vln.-concertos (the first
written in the modern sonata-form,
and supported with broadened orchestration). C. also 2 Concertantes
for 2 vlns., 21 string-quartets, 51 vln.-

duos, 18 sonatas, etc. Biogr. by
Fayolle (Paris, 1810); Baillot (1825),
and Arthur Pougin (1888).

Virdung (fēr'-doongk), **Sebastian,**
priest and organist at Basel, 1511;
writer and composer.

Visetti (vē-sĕt'-tē), **Alberto Ant.,**
Spalato, Dalmatia, May 13, 1846—
London, July 9, 1928; pupil of
Mazzucato, Milan Cons.; concert-
pianist at Nice; then Paris, cond.
to the Empress Eugénie; 1871, on the
fall of the Empire, vocal teacher in the
R. C. M., London; dir. Bath Philh.
Soc., 1878–90; pub. a "*History of the
Art of Singing,*" and translations.

Vitali (vē-tä'-lē), (1) **Filippo,** b. Florence, singer and composer, 1631. (2)
Giov. Bat., Cremona, ca. 1644—
Modena, Oct. 12, 1692; 2d ct.-cond.
and composer of important sonatas,
ballets, etc. (3) **Tomaso,** b. Bologna, middle of 17th cent.; leader
there, and c. a chaconne.

Vitry (vē-trē) **Philippe De (Philippus
di Vitria'co),** b. Vitry, Pas-de-Calais;
d. 1361, as Bishop of Meaux; theorist.

Vittadini (vē-tä-dē'-nē), **Franco,** b.
Pavia, Italy, April, 1884; composer;
pupil of Cons. Verdi, Milan; c.
(operas) "*Anima Allegra*" (Costanzi,
Rome, 1921, also at Met. Op.
House); "*Nazareth*" (based on Selma
Lagerlöf story), (Pavia, 1925); "*La
Sagredo*"; also masses, motets and
organ pieces.

Vittori (vĭt-tō'-rē), **Loreto,** Spoleto,
1604—Rome, 1670; composer.

Vittoria (vĭt-tō'-rĭ-ä), **Tomaso Ludovico da** (rightly **Tomas Luis De
Victoria**), Avila(?), Spain, ca. 1540—
Madrid, Aug. 27, 1611; went to
Rome early; 1573 maestro Collegium
Germanicum; 1575, of S. Apollinaris;
friend and disciple of Palestrina;
1589–1602 vice ct.-conductor, Madrid; c. notable works incl. a requiem
for the Empress Maria, 1605.

Vivaldi (vē-väl'-dē), **Abbate Ant.,**
Venice, ca. 1675–1743; celebrated
violinist; from 1713 dir. Cons. della
Pietà. One of the early masters
of Italian music, **V.** in his remarkable
concerti developed the form created
by Corelli and G. Torelli and thus
was one of the precursors of the
symphony. Sixteen of his concerti
were transcribed by Bach for clavier
or otherwise musically extended,
and the concerto in D minor by
Friedemann Bach for organ is a

transcription of one of his for vln.
He c. some 150 vln. concerti; 18 vln.
sonatas; 12 trios for vlns. and 'cello;
6 quintets for flute, vln., viola, 'cello
and organ-bass; some 40 operas, as
well as many cantatas, arias and
other vocal works.

Vives (vē'-väs), **Amadeo,** Barcelona,
1871—Madrid, Dec. 2, 1932; composer of many Spanish zarzuelas
and other stage works; succeeded
Tomas Breton as teacher of comp.
at Madrid R. Cons. of Music; also
a leading writer on music in Spain.

Vivier (vēv-yā), (1) **Albert Jos.,** Huy,
Belgium, Dec. 15, 1816—Brussels,
Jan. 3, 1903; pupil of Fétis; c. opera
and wrote a harmony. (2) **Eugène
Léon,** Ajaccio, 1821—Nice, Feb. 24,
1900; remarkable horn-virtuoso;
pupil of Gallay, then joined orch.
at Paris Opéra; made many tours
was a favourite of Napoleon III.,
then retired to Nice; a wit and a
composer of excellent songs.

Vix, Géneviève, 1887—Paris, 1940;
soprano; sang at Madrid, Buenos
Aires and (1917–18) with Chicago
Opera Company.

Vizentini (vē-zĕn-te'-nē), **Louis Albert,**
Paris, Nov. 9, 1841—Oct. 1906;
violinist; pupil of the Paris and
Brussels Cons.; critic on the *Figaro;*
cond. in theatres in various cities;
c. operettas, ballets, etc.

Vleeshouwer (flās'-hoo-vĕr), **Albert
de,** b. Antwerp, June 8, 1863; pupil
of Jan Blockx; prod. 2 operas,
"*L'École des Pères*" (1892) and
"*Zryni*" (Antwerp, 1895), symphonic poem, "*De wilde Jäger,*" etc.

Vock'ner, Josef, Ebensee, March 18,
1842—Vienna, Sept. 11, 1906; organ
teacher at the Cons.; c. oratorio,
organ fugues, etc.

Vogel (fō'-gĕl), (1) **Jn. Chr.,** Nürnberg, 1756—Paris, 1788; dram. composer. (2) **L.,** flutist and composer.
Paris, 1792–1798. (3) **Fr. Wm.
Fd.,** Havelberg, Prussia, Sept. 9,
1807—Bergen, 1892; pupil of Birnbach, Berlin; toured as organist;
from 1852, at Bergen, Norway; pub.
a concertino for org. with trombones;
symph., overture, 2 operettas, etc.
(4) **(Chas. Louis) Ad.,** Lille, 1808—
Paris, 1892; violinist and dram.
composer. (5) **(Wm.) Moritz,**
Sorgau, near Freiburg, Silesia, July
9, 1846—Leipzig, Oct. 30, 1922;
pianist; pupil of Leipzig Cons.;

teacher, critic and conductor of choral socs., Leipzig; pub. pf. method, c. rondos, etc. (6) (Ad.) **Bd.**, Plauen, Saxony, 1847—Leipzig, 1898; journalist, writer and composer. (7) **Emil**, Wriezen-on-Oder, Jan. 21, 1859—Berlin, June 18, 1908; Dr. Phil., Berlin, 1887; 1883, sent to Italy by the govt. as Haberl's asst. in studying Palestrina's works; from 1893, lib. Peters Mus. Library, Leipzig; pub. monographs, etc. (8) **Vladimir,** b. Moscow, Feb. 29, 1896; noted modern composer; pupil of Busoni in comp.; in his works strongly influenced by atonal theories of Schönberg; he lived in Berlin 1918–33, after latter year in Strasbourg; a number of his works have been perf. at fests. of the I. S. C. M. c. oratorio, symph., suite, orch. pieces, string quartet, piano works, chorus, etc.

Voggenhuber (fôg'-gĕn-hoo-bĕr), **Vilma von** (Frau **V. Krolop**), Pesth, 1845—Berlin 1888; dram. soprano at Berlin ct.-opera 1868–88.

Vogl (fōkh'-'l), (1) **Jn. Michael**, Steyr, 1768—Vienna, 1840; tenor and conductor (v. FZ. SCHUBERT). (2) **Heinrich,** Au, Munich, Jan. 15, 1845—on the stage, Munich, April 21, 1900; famous tenor; début Munich ct.-opera, 1865; sang there thereafter; eminent in Wagnerian rôles at Bayreuth; prod. an opera *"Der Fremdling"* (Munich, 1899). (3) **Therese** (née **Thoma**), Tutzing, Lake of Starnberg, Nov. 12, 1845—Munich, Sept. 29, 1921; from 1868, wife of above, and like him, eminent in Wagner opera; dram. soprano; pupil of Hauser and Herger, Munich Cons.; 1864, Carlsruhe; 1865–92, Munich, then retired.

Vogler (fōkh'-lĕr), **Georg Jos.** ("Abbé Vogler"), Würzburg, June 15, 1749 —Darmstadt, May 6, 1814; famous organist; theorist and composer; pupil of Padre Martini and Vallotti; took orders at Rome; 1786–99, court-conductor Stockholm; 1807, ct.-cond. at Darmstadt; he was eminent as a teacher of radical methods; toured widely as a concert organist with his "c chestrion"; he wrote many treatises; c. 10 operas, a symphony, etc.

Vogrich (fō'-grĭkh), **Max** (**Wm. Carl**), Szeben (Hermannstadt), Transylvania, Jan. 24, 1852—New York,

June 10, 1916; pianist, at 7 he played in public, then pupil of Leipzig Cons.; 1870–78, toured Europe, Mexico and South America; then U. S. with Wilhelmj; 1882–86, in Australia, where he m.; after 1886, lived in New York; c. 3 grand operas (text and music) incl. *"Wanda"* (Florence, 1875); c. also an oratorio *"The Captivity"* (1884; Met. Op. 1891); 2 cantatas, Missa Solemnis; 2 symphs., vln.-concerto, etc.

Vogt (fōkht), (1) **Gustave**, Strassburg, 1781—Paris, 1870; oboist, professor and composer. (2) **Jn.** (**Jean**), Gross-Tinz, near Liegnitz, 1823— Eberswalde, 1888; pianist and composer. (3) **Augustus Stephen,** Washington, Ont., Aug. 14, 1861 —Toronto, Sept. 17, 1926; pianist, teacher; studied Leipzig Cons.; after 1888 taught in Toronto, 1892 at Cons., of which dir. after 1913; founded and led Mendelssohn Choir there, 1894–1917; Mus. D.

Voigt (foikht), (1) **Jn. G. Hermann,** Osterwieck, Saxony, 1769—1811; organist and composer. (2) **K.,** Hamburg, 1808—1879; conductor. (3) **Henriette** (née **Kunze**), 1808— Oct. 15, 1839; distinguished amateur musician at Leipzig; intimate friend of Schumann.

Volbach (fôl'-bäkh), **Fritz,** b. Wipperfürth, Dec. 17, 1861; organ-virtuoso; pupil of Cologne Cons. for a year; studied philosophy, then took up music again at the Royal Inst. for church mus., Berlin; from 1887 teacher there; 1892 cond. at Mainz; 1907 at Tübingen; after 1919 at Münster Univ.; has written biogs. and edited musical texts; c. symph., symph. poems, *"Ostern"* (Easter), for organ and orch. (Sheffield Fest., 1902); *"Es waren zwei Königskinder," "Alt Heidelberg, du Feine,"* a series of vocal works with orch. he cond. in London; d. Dec. 6, 19⁄1

Volckmar (fôlk'-mär), **Wm.** (**Valentin**), Hersfeld, Cassel, 1812—Homberg, near Cassel, 1887; mus.-teacher, organist, writer and composer.

Volkland (fôlk'-länt), **Alfred,** Brunswick, April 10, 1841—Basel, 1905; pupil Leipzig Cons.; ct.-pianist at Sondershausen; from 1867, ct.-cond. there 1869–75, cond. Leipzig Euterpe, also co-founder the Bach-Verein; after 1875, cond. at Basel; 1889, Dr. Phil. *k. c.* (Basel Univ.).

Volkmann (fôlk'-män), (**Fr.**) **Robt.**, Lommatzsch, Saxony, April 6, 1815 —Budapest, Oct. 30, 1883; notable composer; son and pupil of a cantor; studied with Friebel (vln. and 'cello), Anacker (comp.) and K. F. Becker, at Leipzig; 1839–42, taught mus. at Prague; thereafter lived in Pesth, excepting 1854–58, Vienna; for years prof. of harm. and cpt. at the Nat. Acad. of Mus., Prague; c. 2 symphs.; 3 serenades for strings; 2 overtures, incl. "*Richard III.*"; concerto for 'cello, Concertstück for pf. and orch.; 2 masses with orch.; Christmas Carol of the 12th cent.; old German hymns for double male chorus; 6 duets on old German poems; 2 wedding-songs; alto solo with orch., "*An die Nacht*"; dram.-scene for soprano with orch., "*Sappho*"; pf.-pcs. and songs. Biog. by Vogel (Leipzig, 1875).

Vollerthun (fôl'-ĕr-tōōn), G., b. Fürstenau, Sept. 29, 1876; composer.

Vollhardt (fôl'-härt), **Emil Reinhardt**, Seifersdorf, Saxony, Oct. 16, 1858—Zwickau, Feb. 10, 1926; pupil of Leipzig Cons.; cantor Marienkirche and cond. at Zwickau; c. motets and songs.

Vollweiler (fôl'-vī-lĕr), K., Offenbach, 1813—Heidelberg, 1848; pianoteacher and composer.

Volpe (vôl'-pē), **Arnold**, b. Kovno, Russia, July 9, 1869—Miami, Fla., Feb. 2, 1940; studied at Warsaw Cons., with Auer in St. Petersburg, and comp. with Soloviev; came to America in 1898; 1904, founded Volpe Symph. Orch. in N. Y.; 1916, led Stadium Concerts at College of the City of New York; 1922, dir. of Kansas City Cons.; has since taught at Miami, Fla., Univ., and led orch. concerts there.

Voretzsch (vō'-rĕtsh), **Jns. Felix**, Altkirchen, July 17, 1835—Halle, May 10, 1908; pianist and conductor.

Voss, (1) (Vos'sius) **Gerhard Jn.**, Heidelberg, 1577—Amsterdam, 1649; writer on mus. (2) **Isaak**, Leyden, 1618—Windsor, Engl., 1689; son of above; canon and writer. (3) **Chas.**, Schmarsow, Pomerania, 1815—Verona, 1882; pianist and composer.

Vredemann (frä'-dĕ-män), (1) **Jakob**, teacher and composer, Leuwarden, ca. 1600—1640. (2) **Michael**, teacher and theorist, Arnheim, 1612.

Vreuls (vrŭls), **Victor**, b. Verviers,

Feb. 4, 1876; pupil Liége Cons. and of d'Indy, at whose Schola cantorum he became teacher of harmony; 1906–20, dir. of Luxembourg Cons.; 1903 won the Picard prize of the Belgian Free Academy; c. symphonic poems, "*Triptyque*" for voice and orch., chamber music and songs.

Vroye (vrwä), **Th. Jos. De**, Villers-la-Ville, Belgium, 1804—Liége, 1873; canon and theorist.

Vuillaume (vwē-yôm), **Jean Baptiste**, Mirecourt, Dept. of Vosges, France, Oct. 7, 1798—Paris, March 19, 1875; 1821–25, in partnership with Lete; he was v. succ. and a remarkable imitator of Stradivari; inv. 1851, "octobasse" (v. D.D.); 1855, a larger viola "contre-alto"; in 1867 a mute, the "pedale sourdine," etc.

Vuillermoz, Émile, b. Lyons, 1879: Paris mus. critic; c. songs, etc.

Vulpius (fool'-pĭ-oos), **Melchior**, Wasungen, ca. 1560—Weimar, 1616, cantor and composer.

W

Waack (väk), **Karl**, Lübeck, March 6, 1861—Neuminster, March 7, 1922; pupil of Grand-ducal School, Weimar; cond. in Finland and at Riga; 1890 studied with H. Riemann, returned to Riga as editor, cond. and author; after 1915 led pop. concerts of Musik-Freunde in Lübeck.

Wachtel (väkh'-tĕl), (1) **Theodor**, Hamburg, 1823—Frankfort-on-Main, 1893; noted tenor; son and successor of a livery-stable keeper; studied with Frl. Grandjean. His son (2) **Th.** (d. Dessau, 1875) was for a time a tenor.

Wad'dington, Sidney Peine, b. Lincoln, July 23, 1869; composer; pupil R. C. M., London; later teacher there and pianist to Covent Garden; c. "*John Gilpin*" for chorus and orch. (1894); "*Ode to Music*," do.; violin and 'cello sonatas, etc.

Waelput (väl'-poot), **Hendrik**, Ghent, 1845—1885; cond., professor and dram. composer.

Waelrant (wäl'-ränt), **Hubert**, Tongerloo, Brabant, ca. 1517—Antwerp, 1595; a mus.-pub. and teacher; introduced "Bocedisation" (v. D.D.); c. motets, etc.

Wagenaar (väkh'-ĕ-när), (1) **Johan**, Utrecht, 1862–1941; organist at

DICTIONARY OF MUSICIANS 455

the Cathedral; 1904, dir. of mus. school there; 1919, dir. of Cons. of Music in The Hague; c. "Fritjofs Meerfahrt" and "Saul and David" for orch., overture "Cyrano de Bergerac," etc. (2) **Bernard,** b. Arnhem, Holland, Aug. 18, 1894; composer; studied Utrecht Music School of the Toonkunst Soc., comp. with Johan Wagenaar; came to America in 1925; has taught comp. at Juilliard School of Music, N. Y.; c. (orch.) 2 symphonies, Divertimento, Sinfonietta (chosen to represent U. S. at Liége Fest. of I. S. C. M. 1930); sonata for vln. and piano (prize of Soc. for Pub. of Amer. Music, 1928); also "Three Songs from the Chinese" for voice, flute, harp and piano; his works have been performed by N. Y. Philh., Detroit Symph., and other ensembles.

Wagenseil (vä'-gĕn-zīl), (1) **Jn. Chp.,** Nürnberg, 1633 — Altdorf, 1708; writer. (2) **G. Chp.,** Vienna, 1715—1777; teacher and composer.

Wagner (väkh'-nĕr), (1) **K. Jakob,** Darmstadt, 1772—1822; hornvirtuoso, concert-conductor; c. operas. (2) **Ernst David,** Dramburg, Pomerania, 1806—Berlin, 1883; cantor, organist, mus.-director and composer; pub. essays.

(3) (Wm.) **Richard,** Leipzig, May 22, 1813—Venice, Feb. 13, 1883; eminent opera composer; son of a clerk in the city police-court, who died when W. was six months old; the mother m. an actor and playwright, Ludwig Geyer of Dresden. W. attended the Dresden Kreuzschule until 1827; he transl. 12 books of the Odyssey, and at 14 wrote a bombastic and bloody Shakespearean tragedy; 1827, he studied at the Nikolai Gymnasium, Leipzig, where the family lived while his sister Rosalie was engaged at the City Theatre there. Wagner was impelled music-ward by hearing a Beethoven symph. and took up Logir's "Thoroughbass." He then studied theory with the organist Gottlieb Müller and c. a string-quartet, a sonata and an aria. 1830, after matriculation at Leipzig Univ., he studied six months with Th. Weinlig (comp.) and c. a pf.-sonata, and a 4-hand polonaise. He studied Beethoven's symphs. very thoroughly. At 19 he c. a symph. in 4 movements,

prod. at the Gewandhaus, Leipzig 1833. He wrote the libretto for an opera, "Die Hochzeit," an introduction, septet, and a chorus 1832, but his sister Rosalie thought it immoral and he gave it up; 1833 his brother Albert, stage-manager and singer at the Würzburg Theatre invited him to be chorusm. there. He c. a romantic opera in 3 acts "Die Feen," to his own libretto (after "La Donna serpente," by Gozzi); it was accepted but never performed, by the Leipzig th.-dir. Ringelhardt (given at Munich, 1888). 1834, he became cond. at the Magdeburg Th. Here he c. (text and music) "Das Liebesverbot (after Shakespeare's "Measure for Measure"), performed by a bankrupt troupe, 1836. Th.-cond. at Königsberg, and m. (1835) an actress Wilhelmine Planer, who d. 1866, after they had separated in 1861. He c. an overture "Rule Britannia." 1837 cond. Riga opera. Moved by Meyerbeer's triumphs at the Gr. Opéra at Paris, W. went there, July, 1839, by sea. The voyage lasted 3½ weeks and was very stormy; the experience suggested to him the opera "Flying Dutchman." Meyerbeer gave him letters to musicians and pubs. in Paris; here he suffered poverty and supported himself by songwriting, arranging dances for piano and cornet, preparing the pf.-score of Halévy's "Reine de Chypre," and writing articles. His operas were scornfully rejected and he could get no hearing till the v. succ. "Rienzi" was prod., Dresden, 1842, and "Der Fliegende Holländer," Jan. 2, 1843. The novelties in this work provoked a furious opposition that never ceased. 1843-49 he was cond. of Dresden Opera, also cond. Dresden Liedertafel, for which he wrote a biblical scene, "Das Liebesmahl der Apostel," for 3 choirs, a cappella, later with full orch. "Tannhäuser" was prod., Dresden, 1845, with succ. in spite of bitter opposition. In 1848 "Lohengrin" was finished; but the mgr. of the Opera did not care to risk the work. He now wrote out a little sketch "Die Nibelungen, Weltgeschichte aus der Sage"; a prose study on "Der Niebelungen-Mythus als Entwurf zu einem Drama" (1848), and a 3-act drama with Prologue, written in alliterative verse, "Sieg

fried's Tod," preparations for the great work to follow. A rashly expressed sympathy with the revolutionary cause (1849) made flight necessary; he went to Weimar with Liszt, but had to go on to Paris to escape the order for his arrest. 1849 he proceeded to Zurich, were he wrote a series of remarkable essays: *"Die Kunst und die Revolution"* (1849), *"Das Kunstwerk der Zukunft," "Kunst und Klima," "Das Judenthum in der Musik"* (1850), *"Oper und Drama," "Erinnerungen an Spontini,"* a prose drama *"Wieland der Schmiedt,"* and the 3 poems of the Niebelungen trilogy (privately printed 1853). The music of *"Das Rheingold"* was finished 1854, *"Die Walküre,"* 1856. He cond. orch. concerts with much succ., lectured on the mus. drama, prod. *"Tannhäuser"* (Zurich, 1855); 1855 he cond. 8 concerts of the London Philh. Soc. 1857 he left *"Siegfried"* unfinished and c. *"Tristan und Isolde."* 1860 he gave concerts of his own works, winning many enthusiastic enemies and some valuable friends. The French Emperor ordered *"Tannhäuser"* to be prod. at the Gr. Opéra, March 13, 1861. It provoked such an elaborate and violent opposition (for omitting the ballet) that it was withdrawn after the third performance.
W. was now permitted to return to Germany; *"Tristan"* was accepted at the Vienna ct.-opera, but after 57 rehearsals the singers declared it impossible to learn. In 1863, he pub. text of the *"Nibelung Ring"* despairing of ever completing the mus. When his financial state was most desperate, King Ludwig II. of Bavaria (1864) invited him to Munich and summoned von Bülow as cond. to prod. *"Tristan und Isolde"* (June 10, 1865); but opposition was so bitter that W. settled at Triebschen, Lucerne, and completed the scores of *"Die Meistersinger"* (prod. Munich, 1868) and *"Der Ring des Nibelungen," "Siegfried"* (1869) and *"Götterdämmerung"* (1874).
Though King Ludwig's scheme for a special Wagner Theatre in Munich was given up, there were by now enough Wagner-lovers and societies throughout the world, to subscribe funds for a theatre at Bayreuth, where the corner-stone was laid in

1872, on his 60th birthday. In August, 1876, complete performances of *"Der Ring des Nibelungen"* were given there under most splendid auspices, but with a deficit of $37,500, paid off by a partially succ. festival in London, 1877, and by the setting aside of the royalties from performances at Munich. He now set to work on the *"Bühnenweihfestspiel"* (Stage - consecrating - festival - play) *"Parsifal,"* finished, and prod. in 1882. The same year ill-health sent him to Venice, where he d. suddenly. His writings (extravagantly praised and condemned) are pub. in various eds. There is an English translation in 8 volumes, by Wm. Ashton Ellis.
1870 he m. Cosima, the divorced wife of von Bülow and natural daughter of Liszt (she d. 1930). After his death she had charge of the Bayreuth Festivals for a number of years, but 1909 yielded the direction to her son, Siegfried. Since his death, 1930, his widow, Winifred has been in charge.
In the half century since W.'s death his music has been universally accepted as the corner-stone of modern operatic repertoires. Concerning his personal character there has been much polemical writing, ranging from actual vilification to the most fervid veneration. Particularly about his autobiography, controversy has centred, with some commentators asserting that his life history was altered somewhat after a few privately printed copies of the original edition were struck off. It was therefore of sensational interest when, in 1929, the so-called "Burrell Collection" of Wagneriana, made by an Englishwoman of that name, who wrote a biog. of his earlier years, was discovered in a strongbox in Great Britain after her death. This collection was bought by Mrs. Mary Louise Curtis Bok and now is housed at the Curtis Inst. of Music, Phila. But the "revelations" it was supposed to contain, as thus far made public, only in minor details altered the impressions contained in his book, *"Mein Leben."*
Besides his operas and the other works mentioned he c. a symph. (1832); 6 overtures, incl. *"Konzertouvertüre ziemlich fugirt," "Polo-*

nia," "*Columbus,*" "*Rule Britannia*"; "*New Year's Cantata*"; incid. mus. to Gleich's farce "*Der Berggeist*" (Magdeburg, 1836); "*Huldigungsmarsch*" (1864, finished by Raff); "*Siegfried Idyll*" (1870, for his son then a year old), "*Kaisermarsch*" (1870), "*Festival March*" (for the Centennial Exposition, Philadelphia, 1876), "*Gelegenheits-Cantata*" (for unveiling a statue of King Friedrich, August, 1843), "*Gruss an den König*" (1843, pf.), "*An Weber's Grabe*" (Funeral March for wind-instrs. on motives from Weber's "*Euryanthe,*" and double quartet for voices, 1844). FOR PF.: sonata; polonaise, for four hands; fantaisie, "*Albumsonate, für Frau Mathilde Wesendonck*" (1853); "*Ankunft bei den Schwarzen Schwanen*" (1861); "*Ein Albumblatt für Fürstin Metternich*" (1861), "*Albumblatt für Frau Betty Schott*" (1875). SONGS: "*Carnavalslied*" from "*Das Liebesverbot*" (1835-36); "*Dors, mon enfant,*" "*Mignonne,*" "*Attente*" (1839-40), "*Les deux Grenadiers*" (1839); "*Der Tannenbaum*" (1840); "*Kraftliedchen*" (1871), "*Fünf Gedichte*"; 1, "*Der Engel*"; 2, "*Stehe still*"; 3, "*Im Treibhaus*"; 4, "*Schmerzen*", 5, "*Träume*" (1862).

Biog. by C. F. Glasenapp (1876); F. Hueffer (1881); R. Pohl (1883); W. Tappert (1883); H. v. Wolzogen (1883); Ad. Jullien (1886); H. T. Finck (1893); H. S. Chamberlain (1897); E. Dannreuther, F. Präger (1893); G. Kobbé; Glasenapp and Ellis (1900). There are many treatises on his works. His letters have also been published in various forms. Among the vast number of other studies of his life and music are works by Torchi, Lidgey, Henderson, Kienzl, Newman, Mrs. Burrell, Adler, Buerkner, Koch, Schjelderup, Lichtenberger, E. Schmitz, Hadden, Kapp, Pfohl, Batka, Runciman, Huckel, Aldrich, Becker, Blackburn, Buesst, Heintz, Krehbiel, Lavignac, McSpadden, Neumann, Pourtalès, Shaw, Thompson and Wallace. "*Wagner-Lexikons*" have been published by Tappert and Stein, a "*Wagner-Encyclopedia*" by Glasenapp, while a comprehensive list of more than 10,000 books and essays on his life and music is contained in Oesterlein's "*Katalog einer Wagner-*

Bibliothek." There is also a "*Wagner-Jahrbuch*" and much material has been issued in the "*Bayreuther Blätter,*" ed. by Wolzogen. (See articles, page 538.) (4) **Siegfried**, Triebschen, Lucerne, June 6, 1869—Bayreuth, Aug. 4, 1930; only son of above; attended a polytechnic sch., but took up mus. as pupil of Kniese and Humperdinck; 1893, concert-cond. in Germany, Austria, Italy and England; from 1898 he was teacher in Vienna; 1901 cond. Acad. Singing Society, and Tonkünstler Orch.; 1912, cond. special concert of the London Symph. orch.; from 1896 he cond. at Bayreuth; later co-director with his mother, and 1909 both artistic and mus. dir.; in 1924 he visited the U. S. as cond. to raise funds for resumption of the fests. (discontinued 1914); m. Winifred Klindworth, who since his death has had charge at Bayreuth; c. operas "*Der Kobold*" (Hamburg, 1904), "*Bruder Lustig*" (do., 1905), "*Das Sternengebot*" (do., 1908), "*Banadietrich*" (Elberfeld, 1910) and "*Schwarzschwanenreich*" (Black-swan Country), "*Sonnenflammen,*" "*Der Heidenkönig,*" "*Der Friedensengel,*" also male and female choruses; a symph. poem "*Sehnsucht*" (Schiller), text and music of mod. succ. comicromantic opera "*Der Bärenhäuter*" (Munich Ct. Th., 1899), unsucc., "*Herzog Wildfang*" (1901). (5) **(Jachmann-Wagner), Johanna**, near Hanover, Oct. 13, 1828—Würzburg, Oct. 16, 1894; niece of (1); dram. soprano; created "Elizabeth," 1845; m. a Judge Jachmann.

Waissel (vīs'-sĕl), **(Waisse'lius) Matthias,** b. Bartenstein, Prussia; lutenist and composer at Frankfort, 1573.

Walcker (väl'-kĕr), (1) **Eberhard Fr.,** Cannstadt, 1794—Ludwigsburg, 1872; son of a skilled org.-builder; himself a noted org.-builder; succeeded by his five sons, (2) **H.** (b. Oct. 10, 1828), (3) **Fr.** (b. Sept. 17, 1829), (4) **K.** (b. March 6, 1845), (5) **Paul** (b. May 31, 1846), and (6) **Eberhard** (b. April 8, 1850).

Waldersee (väl'-dĕr-zā), **Paul, Count von,** Potsdam, Sept. 3, 1831—Königsberg, June 14, 1906; a Prussian officer from 1848-71, then took up mus.; editor of Beethoven and Mozart works.

Waldteufel (vält'-toi-fĕl), **Emil,** Strassburg, Dec. 9, 1837—Paris, Feb. 16, 1915; pupil Paris Cons.; pianist to Empress Eugénie; c. immensely succ. waltzes.

Wa'ley, Simon, London, 1827—1875; pianist and composer.

Walker (wôk'-ĕr), (1) **Jos. Casper,** Dublin, 1760—St.-Valéry, France, 1810; writer. (2) **Jos. and Sons,** org.-builders, London. (3) **Edyth,** Hopewell, N. Y., 1870—N. Y., 1950; contralto; studied Dresden Cons. with Orgeni; engaged at the Vienna opera for 4 years as 1st alto; also in concert; Met. Op. Co., 1903–06; then in Berlin, Hamburg and, 1912–17, Munich Op.; after 1933 taught at Amer. Cons., Fontainebleau. (4) **Ernest,** b. Bombay, July 15, 1870; composer; Mus. Bac. Oxford, 1893; Mus. Doc. 1898; from 1900, dir. at Balliol College; mainly self-taught as composer of *"Stabat Mater," "Hymn to Dionysus,"* and *"Ode to Nightingale"* for voices and orch.; overture, chamber music, songs, etc.; d. London, 1948.

Wal'lace, (1) **Wm. Vincent,** Waterford, Ireland, June 1, 1814—Château de Bages, Haute Garonne, Oct. 12, 1865; violinist; wandered over the world; c. very pop. pf.-pcs. and c. 6 operas includ. the very succ. *"Maritana"* (London, 1845); and *"Lurline"* (do. 1860). (2) **William,** b. Greenock, July 3, 1860; at first a surgeon; in 1889 took up music and studied at the R. A. M., London, till 1890; c. symph. *"The Creation"* (New Brighton, 1892); choral symph. *"Koheleth";* 6 symph. poems, *"The Passing of Beatrice"* (Crystal Palace, 1892), *"Amboss oder Hammer"* (do., 1896), *"Sister Helen"* (do. 1899), *"Greeting to the New Century"* (London Phil., 1891), *"Sir William Wallace"* (Queen's Hall, 1905), *"François Villon"* (New Symph., 1909); also by New York Phil., 1910, 1912), overtures, suites, song cycles, 1-act lyric tragedy *"Brassolis,"* etc.; author of *"Threshold of Music";* d. Malmesbury, 1940.

Wallaschek (väl'-lä-shĕk), **Richard,** Brünn, Nov. 16, 1860—Vienna, April 24, 1917; after 1896 docent at Univ. in latter city; pub. 1886, valuable treatise *"Æsthetik der Tonkunst."*

Wallenstein (väl'-lĕn-shtīn), (1) **Mar-**tin, Frankfort-on-Main, 1843—1896; pianist; c. comic opera. (2) **Alfred,** b. Chicago, Oct. 7, 1898; 'cellist and conductor; studied with Julius Klengel; début, Los Angeles, 1912; solo 'cellist in Chicago Symph., afterwards for several seasons with N. Y. Philh., with which he also appeared as soloist; cond. of orch. on the radio, after 1935 mus. dir. Mutual Network; from 1943 also cond. L. A. Philh.

Wallerstein (väl'-lĕr-shtīn), **Anton,** Dresden, 1813—Geneva, 1892; violinist and composer.

Wall'is, J., Ashford, Kent, 1616—London, 1693; acoustician.

Walliser (väl'-lĭ-zĕr), **Chp. Thos.,** Strassburg, 1568—1648; mus.-dir., theorist and composer.

Wallnöfer (väl'-nä-fĕr), **Ad.,** b. Vienna, April 26, 1854; pupil of Waldmüller, Krenn and Dessoff (comp.), Rokitansky (singing); barytone at Vienna; 1882, with Neumann's troupe; 1897–98, N. Y.; after 1908 lived in Munich; for a time active as theatre dir. in Stettin and Neustrelitz; c. succ. op. *"Eddystone"* (Prague); d. (?).

Walmisley (wämz'-lĭ), (1) **Thos. Forbes,** London, 1783—1866; organist and composer. (2) **Thos. Attwood,** London, 1814—Hastings, 1856; son of above; professor and composer.

Walsh, John, d. London, 1736; mus.-publisher.

Walter (väl'-tĕr), (1) **Ignaz,** Radowitz, Bohemia, 1759 — Ratisbon, 1822; tenor and composer. (2) **Juliane** (née **Roberts**), wife of above; a singer. (3) **Aug.,** Stuttgart, 1821 —Basel, Jan. 22, 1896; mus.-director and composer. (4) **Gustav,** Bilin, Bohemia, Feb. 11, 1834—Vienna, Jan. 31, 1910; tenor; pupil of Prague Cons.; début in Brunn; 1856-87, principal lyric tenor at Vienna ct.-opera. (5) **Bruno,** b. Berlin, Sept. 15, 1876; family name Schlesinger; noted conductor; studied at Stern Cons., Berlin, with Radecke, Ehrlich and Bussler; early held bâton posts in both opera and orchestral music at Cologne, Hamburg, Breslau, Pressburg and Riga; 1900-01, Berlin Ct.-Opera; 1901-12, Vienna Ct.-Opera; 1913-22, gen. mus. dir. at Munich, succeeding Mottl; he made visits to the U. S. as guest cond. of the N. Y. Symph. in the next 2 seasons; 1925-29, mus. dir. of Berlin

Städtische Oper: 1929-33, cond. of Gewandhaus Orch., Leipzig; also led annual series with Berlin Philh. Orch.; appeared much in other countries, including Covent Garden, London, at the Salzburg Fest., in Paris, Vienna and Amsterdam; in 1933 he resigned his Berlin posts following accession to political power of the Nat'l Socialists; co-dir. Vienna Op., and Philh. Orch., 1936-38; cond. part of season with N. Y. Philh. Orch. in 1933 and 1934; c. orch. works, chamber music and songs.

Walther von der Vogelweide (väl'-ter fōn dĕr fō'-gĕl-vī-dĕ), in the Tyrol (?), ca. 1160—Würzburg, after 1227; the chief Minnesinger and lyric poet of mediæval Germany.

Walther (väl'-tĕr), (1) Jn., Thuringia, 1496—Torgau, 1570; singer and composer; ct.-conductor. (V. MARTIN LUTHER.) (2) Jn. Jakob, b. Witterda, near Erfurt, 1650; ct.-musician, publisher and composer. (3) Jn. Gf., Erfurt, 1684—Weimar, 1748; organist, writer and composer. (4) Jn. Chp., Weimar, 1715-71; organist and composer.

Wal'thew, Richard H., b. London, Nov. 4, 1872; pupil of the Guildhall and with scholarship at R. C. M. under Parry; 1907 prof. at Queen's College, and opera class at the Guildhall; 1909 cond. at Finsbury, c. "*Pied Piper*" for chorus and orch; piano concerto, two operettas, etc.

Wal'ton, Sir William, born in Oldham, England, March 29, 1902; composer; pupil at 10 at Christ Church Cath., Oxford; later studied music at that Univ. with Sir Hugh Allen and E. J. Dent, but mostly self-trained; he came to the fore while still young with a piano quartet, a string quartet, and esp. successfully with an amusing work called "*Façade*," settings of poems by Edith Sitwell, for reciter and small ensemble, the speaking voice issuing from a megaphone in a backdrop; he also c. "*Portsmouth Point*" overture, "*Dr. Syntax*," a "pedagogical overture"; "*The Passionate Pilgrim*" for tenor and orch.; a viola concerto, and a symph. which was anticipated with so much interest that parts were performed before it was completed (1935); his cantata, "*Belshazzar's Feast*" (1933) first heard at an English fest., later in London, N. Y.

hon. Mus. D., Oxford, Durham and Dublin; knighted, 1951.

Wälzel (vĕl'-tsĕl), Camillo, Magdeburg, 1829—Vienna, 1895; librettist, (pseud. F. Zell).

Wambach (väm'-bäkh), Émile (X.), Arlon, Luxembourg, Nov. 26, 1854—Antwerp, May 6, 1924; pupil of Antwerp Cons.; c. symph. poem, "*Aan de boorden van de Schelde*," orch. fantasias, Flemish drama "*Nathan's Parabel*"; 2 oratorios; a hymn for chorus and orch., etc.

Wangemann (väng'-ĕ-män), Otto, Loitz-on-the-Peene, Jan. 9, 1848—Berlin, Feb. 25, 1914; pupil of G. Flügel, Stettin and Fr. Kiel at Berlin; 1878, organist and singing-teacher Demmin Gymnasium; wrote org. treatise.

Wanhal (Van Hal) (vän'-häl), Jn. Bapt., Neu-Nechanitz, Bohemia, 1739—Vienna, 1813; composer.

Wannenmacher (vän'-nĕn-mäkh-ĕr) (or **Vannius**), **Johannes,** d. Interlaken, ca. 1551; important Swiss church composer and canon; renounced Catholicism, was tortured, and banished.

Wanski (vän'-shkĭ), (1) Jn. Nepomuk, b. ca. 1800 (?); son of (2) Jan (a pop. Polish song-composer); violinist; pupil of Baillot; toured widely, then lived at Aix; wrote a vln. method and c. études, etc.

Ward, J., d. before 1641; English composer.

Ware, Harriet, b. Waupun, Wis., 1877; graduated at Pillsbury Cons. Owatonna, Minn., 1895; pupil of Wm. Mason, N. Y. for 2 years, then of Stojowski (piano and comp.) and Juliana, Paris, later of Hugo Kaun, Berlin; c. "*The Fay Song*"; cantata "*Sir Olaf*" (New York Symph. 1910), piano pieces and many songs.

Warlamoff (vär'-lä-môf), Alex. Jegorovitch, Moscow, 1801—1848; singing-teacher and composer.

"Warlock, Peter", see Heseltine, Philip.

War'ner, H. Waldo, b. Northampton, England, Jan. 4, 1874; composer, violinist; studied Guildhall School of Music, London; laureate, R. A. M., 1895-96; assoc., Guildhall School with gold medal, 1899, fellow, 1924; mem. of London String Quartet 1908-29 as viola player; c. string quartets, orch. music, 3 piano trios, piano quintet, and other works, incl.

"The Pixie Ring," popular with quartets; awarded Coolidge and Cobbett chamber music prizes and that of Phila. Mus. Fund Soc.

War'nery, Edmond, b. Elbeuf, 1876; operatic tenor (originally barytone); pupil of Paris Cons.; 1899—1907, sang at Paris Op.-Comique; after 1910 with Chicago Op.

Warn'ke, Heinrich, b. near Heide, Holstein, 1871; 'cellist; studied at Hamburg and Leipzig Cons.; after 1898 played in Kaim Orch., Munich; mem. of trio with Weingartner and Rettich; from 1905 mem. of Boston Symphony Orchestra.

Warnots (văr-nō), (1) **Jean Arnold,** (1801—1861). (2) **Henri,** Brussels, 1832—1893; opera-tenor; son and pupil of above; c. operetta. His daughter and pupil (3) **Elly,** b Liége, 1862; soprano; début, Brussels, 1879; sang there, then at Florence, Paris Op.-Com., etc.

Warot (vă-rō), (1) **Charles,** Dunkirk, Nov. 14, 1804—Brussels, July 29, 1836; violinist and theatre-cond.; pupil of Fridzeri; c. operas, 3 grand masses, etc. His brother (2) **Victor,** Ghent, 1808—Bois Colombes, 1877; cond. and teacher; c. operettas, a mass, etc. (3) **Victor Alex. Jos.,** Verviers, 1834—Paris, 1906; son of (2); opera tenor, later teacher at Paris Cons.

War'ren, (1) **Jos.,** London, 1804—Kent, 1881; organist, pianist, violinist, composer and writer. (2) **G. Wm.,** Albany, N. Y., Aug. 17, 1828—New York, 1902; self-taught organist; from 1870, organist St. Thomas's Ch., New York; prof. Columbia Univ.; c. church-mus. (3) **Samuel Prowse,** Montreal, Canada, Feb. 18, 1841—New York, Oct. 7, 1915; organist; pupil of Haupt, Gv. Schumann (pf.) and Wieprecht (instr.); 1865-67. organist of All Souls' Ch., New York; later at Trinity Ch.; c. church-mus., org.-pcs., etc. (4) **Richard Henry,** Albany, N. Y., Sept. 17, 1859—South Chatham, Mass., Dec. 3, 1933; son and pupil of (2), also studied abroad; from 1886 org. at St. Bartholomew's, N. Y.; founder and cond. of church choral soc., which gave many important works their 1st hearing; c. choruses, songs, etc. (5) **Leonard,** Amer. barytone; sang Radio City Mus. Hall, won Met. Op. auditions; début 1940.

Wartel (văr-tĕl), (1) **Pierre Fran.,** Versailles, 1806—Paris, 1882; tenor. (2) **Atala Thérèse** (née **Adrien**), Paris, July 2, 1814—Nov. 6, 1865; wife of above; 1831-38, prof. at Paris Cons.; c. pf.-studies, etc. (3) **Emil,** son of above; sang for years Th. Lyrique, then founded a sch.

Wasielewski (vä-zē-lĕf'-shki), **Jos. W. von,** Gross-Leesen, Danzig, 1822—Sondershausen, 1896; violinist, conductor, critic, composer, and important historical writer.

Wassermann (väs'-sĕr-män), **H. Jos.,** Schwarzbach, near Fulda, 1791—Riehen, n. Basel, 1838; violinist and composer.

Wat'son, (1) **Thos.,** Eng. composer, 1590. (2) **Wm. Michael,** Newcastle-on-Tyne, 1840—E. Dulwich, London, 1889; teacher and composer under pen-name **Jules Favre.**

Watts, Wintter, b. Cincinnati, O, March 14, 1886; composer; studied painting and architecture, also singing in Florence, and theory with Goetschius; 1919, won Loeb Prize; c. (orch.) *"Two Etchings";* incid. music to *"Alice in Wonderland,"* ballads and songs, some of them with orch., and the vocal cycles, *"Vignettes of Italy," "Wings of Night," "Like Music on the Water."*

Webb, (1) **Daniel,** Taunton, 1735—Bath, 1815; writer. (2) **G. Jas.,** Rushmore Lodge, near Salisbury, Engl., 1803—Orange, N. J., 1887; organist and editor.

Webbe (wĕb), (1) **Samuel, Sr.,** Minorca, 1740—London, 1816; ed. colls., etc. (2) **Samuel, Jr.,** London, 1770—1843; son of above; writer and composer.

Web'ber, Amherst, b. Cannes, Oct. 25, 1867; studied music at Oxford, then at Dresden with Nicodé and at Paris Cons.; pianist to Covent Garden and Met. Op., N. Y.; c. symph. (Warsaw Phil., 1904, Boston Symph., 1905); 1-act opera *"Fiorella"* (London, 1905), songs, etc.; d. London, July 26, 1946.

Weber (vā'-bĕr), (1) **Fridolin** (b. Zelli, 1733—d. 1764), and his bro. (2) **Fz. Anton** (Freiburg, 1734—Mannheim, 1812), were violinists in the orch. of the Elector K. Theodor. Fz. became cond. of Eutin town orch. His four daughters were (3) **Josepha** (d. 1820), soprano; m. the violinist Hofer, 1789, later m.

& bass, Meyer. For her Mozart c. "The Queen of the Night" in the *"Magic Flute."* (4) **Aloysia,** 1750—Salzburg, 1839. Mozart's first love; she m. an actor, Lange, 1780 and toured as a singer. (5) **Constanze,** Zell, 1763—Salzburg, 1842. Mozart's wife (1782); 1809, m. Nissen. (6) **Sophie,** 1764—Salzburg, 1843; m. the tenor Haibl. (7) **Fr. Aug.,** Heilbronn, 1753—1806; physician and c. (8) **Bd. Anselm,** Mannheim, April 18, 1766—Berlin, March 23, 1821; pianist, conductor and dram. composer. (9) **(Fr.) Dionys.** Welchau, Bohemia, Oct. 9, 1766—Prague, Dec. 25, 1842; 1811, founder and 1st dir. Prague Cons., c. operas, etc. (10) **Gf.,** theorist and composer, Freinsheim, near Mannheim, 1779—Kreuznach, Sept. 12, 1839; amateur pianist, flutist and 'cellist, also cond.; wrote essays and valuable treatises; c. 3 masses, a requiem and a Te Deum with orch. and pf.-sonata. (11) **Fridolin** (II.), b. 1761; son of (2), and step-broth. of (12); pupil of Haydn; singer and mus.-director. (12) **K. Maria (Fr. Ernst), Freiherr von,** Eutin, Oldenburg, Dec. 18, 1786—(of consumption) London, June 5, 1826; son of the second wife of (2) and cousin, by marriage, of Mozart; the founder of German national opera (Wagner shows his influence deeply), and of the Romantic Sch.; perhaps the most widely influential German composer of the cent. He was important not solely as a path-finder, but also showed a striking artistic individuality; he was also a notable pianist (he could stretch a 12th), and a pioneer in modern pianistic composition. At first a pupil of his step-bro. (11). His mother, Genoveva (d. 1798, of consumption), was a dram. singer, and the family led a wandering life. At 10 he became pf.-pupil of J. P. Heuschkel. As a chorister in the cathedral at Salzburg, 1797, he had gratuitous lessons in comp. from Michael Haydn, to whom he dedicated his first published comps., six fughettas (1798). 1798—1800, at Munich, he studied singing with Valesi, and comp. with Kalcher. At 12 he c. an opera (the MS. lost or burned). He also appeared as concert-pianist. He met Aloys Senefelder, the inv. of lithography, and

engraved his own op. 2, 1800, **and** made improvements in the process. At 13 he c. and prod. with succ. the opera *"Das Waldmädchen"* (Freiburg, also played at Chemnitz, Prague, Vienna and St. Petersburg). In 1801, he c. a third opera *"Peter Schmoll und seine Nachbarn"* (Augsburg, 1803?); 1803, in Vienna, he became a pupil of Abbé Vogler. 1804, cond. Breslau City Th.; resigned 1806; supported himself by lessons, then mus.-intendant to Duke Eugen of Würtemberg; 1807, private secretary to Duke Ludwig at Stuttgart, and mus.-master to his children. In a turmoil of intrigue and dissipation he forgot his art, until he became involved in a quarrel leading to his banishment in 1810. This sobered him and awoke his better self. Going to Mannheim, he prod. his first symph.; then rejoined Abbé Vogler, at Darmstadt. His opera *"Silvana"* was prod. (Frankfort-on-Main, 1810), and *"Abu Hassan,"* a comic Singspiel (Munich, 1811). He made a concert-tour to various cities, 1813, cond. of the Landständisches Th. at Prague, where he reorganised the opera, and won such note that in 1816 the King of Saxony called him to Dresden to reorganise the Royal Opera. At 20 he began *"Der Freischütz,"* but gave it up till later (the incid. mus. to Wolff's *"Preciosa"* took 3 weeks). In 1817, he m. the singer Karoline Brandt, a member of his company to whom he had long been engaged. They toured together as pianist and singer. *"Der Freischütz"* was prod. with tremendous succ., Berlin, 1821; its strong nationalism provoking a frenzy of admiration. But *"Euryanthe"* (Vienna, 1823) had much less succ. 1824, he was commissioned to write *"Oberon,"* for Covent Garden, London, but consumption delayed its completion; it was prod. (London, 1826) with much succ. He lived only eight weeks longer; his body was taken to the family vault at Dresden. Dramatic Works: Besides the operas already mentioned he c. *"Rübezahl"* (begun 1804, not completed): *"Die Drei Pintos"* (completed by G. Mahler, written and prod. Leipzig, 1888). Incid. mus. to Schiller's *"Turandot,"* Müllner's *"König Yngurd,"* Gehe's *"Heinrich IV.,"* and Houwald's "*Der Leuchtthurm.*" C. also cantatas, incl. "*Der erste Ton*" (1808); and "*Kampf und Sieg*" (on the battle of Waterloo), with orch. (1815); "*Natur und Liebe,*" 1818; hymn, "*In seiner Ordnung schafft der Herr,*" with orch.; (1812), 2 masses and 2 offertories, with orch.; some very pop. songs, four scenas and arias for soprano with orch.; 2 scenas and arias for tenor, chorus and orch.; 19 part-songs, some very pop.; and children's songs; 6 canons à 3–4; duets (op. 31); 2 symphs. (both in C); Jubel-Ouvertüre; 2 clarinet-concertos; bassoon-concerto; adagio and rondo ungarese for bassoon with orch.; variations for many instrs.; chamber-mus.; 2 pf.-concertos, Concertstück with orch., 10 sonatas, a 4-hand sonata, the famous waltz "*Aufforderung zum Tanze*" ("*Invitation to the Dance*"), op. 65; 12 Allemandes; 6 Ecossaises; 18 "*Valses favorites de l'impératrice de France*"; several sets of Variations, etc. The so-called "*Weber's Last Waltz*" (*Thought or Farewell*) was written by Reissiger; a MS. copy of it being found in W.'s papers. Biog. by Barbedette (Paris, 1862, Leipzig, 1864–68). Jähns (Leipzig, 1873); Carl v. Weber (W.'s grandson) pub. his beautiful letters to his wife (1886); Th. Hell (1828). An almost ideal biog. is that of W.'s son the Baron Max Maria von W. (in 3 vols., 1866–68). Other memoirs by Benedict, Reissmann, Nohl, Skalla, Gehrmann, Höcker, Von der Pfordten, O. Schmidt, etc. Thematic catalogue by Jähns, 1871.

(13) Edmund von, Hildesheim, 1766 —Würzburg, 1828; mus.-director and composer. (14) Ernst H., Wittenberg, June 24, 1795—Leipzig, Jan., 1878, with his brother (15) Wm. Ed. (1804—1891), prof. at Göttingen; writer on acoustics, etc. (16) Fz., Cologne, 1805—1876; organist, conductor and composer. (17) Eduard W., town-musician, Frankenberg. (18) K. H., Frankenberg, Aug. 9, 1834—?; son of above; pupil of Leipzig Cons., 1866–70; from 1877, dir. Imp. Russian Mus. Soc. at Saratov, pub. a pf.-method. (19) G. Victor, Ober-Erlenbach, Upper Hesse, Feb. 25, 1838—Mayence, Sept. 24, 1911; pupil of Schrems, Ratisbon; took orders;

since 1866, cond. at Mayence Cath., expert and writer on org.-building; composer. (20) Gustav, Münchenbuchsee, Switzerland, 1845—Zurich, 1887; organist, conductor and composer. (21) Miroslaw, Prague, Nov. 9, 1854—Munich, Jan. 2, 1906; violinist; pupil of his father; at 10 played before the Austrian Emperor, and toured; pupil of Blazek, Prague; also of the Cons.; Konzertmeister, royal orch. at Wiesbaden, and 2nd cond. at the opera (resigned, 1893); 1889, R. Mus.-Dir. C. incid. mus. to ballet "*Die Rheinnixe*" (Wiesbaden, 1884), 2 string quartets (the 2nd taking prize at Petersburg, 1891), etc.

Webern (vā'-bĕrn), Anton von, b. Vienna, 1883—d. 1945; composer; Ph. D., Vienna Univ., studied theory with Guido Adler and comp. with Schönberg, whose atonal musical system he adopted, but with some individual changes; one of the outstanding members of the Schönberg circle, W. has in recent years developed a highly reticent musical style, writing extremely short pieces, with fragile timbres only employed and with much economy of design; these have an exquisite quality, if rather abstract and aloof; c. (orch.) Passacaglia, Six Pieces, Five Pieces, 5 symphs.; (chamber music) quartet, trio, vln. and 'cello works, choruses, songs, piano pieces, etc.; winner of Vienna State Prize, 1924.

Wecker (vĕk'-ĕr), Georg Kaspar, Nuremberg, 1632—1695; organist, teacher and composer.

Weckerlin (vĕk-ĕr-lăn), Jean Bapt. Th., Gebweiller, Alsatia, Nov. 9, 1821—Trottberg, Alsatia, May 10, 1910; entered his father's business of cotton-dyeing; in 1844, studied singing with Ponchard and compn. with Halévy at the Paris Cons., prod. heroic choral symph. "*Roland,*" 1847; gave mus.-lessons; 1853, prod. succ. 1-act opera, "*L'Organiste dans l'embarras*" (100 performances, Th.-Lyrique), followed by several privately performed operettas, 2 comic operas in Alsatian dialect, 1-act opera "*Après Fontenot*" (Th.-Lyrique, 1877); 1869, asst.-libr. Paris Cons.; 1876, libr.; wrote bibliogr. and other articles and treatises, and ed. valuable colls. C. "*Symphonie de la forêt,*" an oratorio *"Le Jugement Dernier,"* 2 cantatas, incl. *"Paix, Charité, Grandeur"* (Opéra, 1866); the ode-symphonie *"Les Poèmes de la Mer,"* etc.

Weckmann (věk'-män), **Matthias,** Oppershausen, 1621—Hamburg, 1674; organ-virtuoso and comp.

Wedekind (vā'-dě-kĭnt), **Erika,** b. Hanover, Nov. 13, 1869; coloratura soprano; pupil of Orgeni at Dresden Cons.; 1894—1909 at court opera Dresden, then at Berlin Comic Opera.

Weelkes (wěks), **Thos.,** organist Chichester Cathedral; c. notable madrigals, etc.; d. London, Nov. 30, 1623.

Wegeler (vä'-gě-lěr), **Fz. Gerhard,** Bonn, 1765—Koblenz, 1848; physician and biographer of Beethoven.

Wegelius (vä-gä'-lĭ-oos), **Martin,** Helsingfors, Nov. 10, 1846—March 22, 1906; pupil of Bibl, Vienna, and Richter and Paul, Leipzig; 1878, opera cond. and dir. of the Cons. at Helsingfors; pub. text-books; c. overture *"Daniel Hjort"*; a ballade with orch; *"Mignon"* for sopr. with orch., etc.

Wehle (vā'-lě), **K.,** Prague, 1825—Paris, 1883; pianist and composer.

Wehrle (vär'-le), **Hugo,** Donaueschingen, July 19, 1847—Freiburg, March 29, 1919); violinist; pupil of Leipzig Cons. and Paris Cons.; toured and played in Singer's Quartet till nervous trouble lamed his hand; 1898 retired to Freiburg; c. violin pieces.

Weidig (vī'-dĭkh), **Adolf,** Hamburg, Nov. 28, 1867—Hinsdale, Ill., Sept. 24, 1931; pupil of the Cons. and winning Mozart stipend, pupil of Rheinberger; from 1892, teacher in Chicago and co-director of the American Cons.; c. orch. and chamber music.

Weidt (vīt), (1) **K.,** b. Bern, March 7, 1857; 1889 cond. at Klagenfurt; lived in Heidelberg; c. male choruses. (2) **Lucy,** Troppau, 1880—Vienna, 1927; noted opera soprano, 1910–11 at Met. Op., N. Y., also sang at Munich, Milan and in South America.

Weigl (vĭkh'-'l), (1) **Jos.,** Eisenstadt, Hungary, 1766—Vienna, 1846; ct.-conductor and dram. composer. (2) **Taddäus,** Vienna, 1774 (?)—1844; bro. of above; c. operettas.

Weill (vīl), (1) **Kurt,** Dessau, Mar. 2, 1900—N. Y., Apr. 3, 1950; composer; studied at Berlin Hochsch. for a

time; then with Busoni; came into prominence with orch. Fantasy, Passacaglia and Hymn (1923); 1st major succ. with one-act opera, *"Der Protagonist"* (Dresden Op.), has since c. highly versatile and ingenious modern stage works, incl. *"Mahagonny," "Drei-Groschen"* Oper (jazz treatment of Gay's *"Beggar's Opera,"* with new text by Brecht, which had great vogue in Central Europe and was sung in English version in N. Y.); *"Na und?"*; *"Der Czar lässt sich photographieren"*; *"Der Jasager"* (school opera, based on Japanese story, prod. by Neighborhood Music School, N. Y.); *"Royal Palace"* (Berlin Op., work using cinema and in jazz style); *"The Seven Cardinal Sins," "Marie Galante," "A Kingdom for a Cow"*; (orch.) Divertimento; *"Quodlibet"*; *"Lindbergh's Flight"* (with solo male voice); also string quartet, and choral works, *"Recordare"* and *"The New Orpheus,"* latter given in stage version at Berlin Op.; visited America and was present at concert of his works by League of Composers, 1935; he took up res. in U. S. after this year and made marked succ. as composer of musical plays, incl. *"Lady in the Dark," "Street Scene," "Lost in the Stars,"* and folk opera, *"Down in the Valley."* (2) **Hermann,** Germany, 1878—Blue Mt. Lake, N. Y., 1949; barytone; pupil of Mottl and Dippel; début Freiburg, 1900; sang at Bayreuth; Met. Op., in heroic roles, 1911–7; Amfortas, Wotan, Sachs, etc.

Weinberger (vīn'-běrkh-ěr), (1) **K. Fr.,** Wallerstein, 1853—Würzburg, 1908; teacher and cath. cond. at Würzburg. (2) **Karl,** b. Vienna, April 3, 1861; c. 9 succ. operettas, incl. *"Die Ulanen"* (Vienna, 1891), *"Lachende Erben"* (1892), *"Die Blumen-Mary"* (ib., 1897), *"Adam und Eva"* (ib., 1898). (3) **Jaromir,** b. Vinohrady, Bohemia, 1896; composer; pupil of Kricka and Karel Hofmeister; also studied at Leipzig Cons. with Reger; taught at Ithaca Cons., 1923; c. (operas) *"Schwanda the Bagpipe Player"* (Prague, 1927, but later trans. into German and enjoyed enormous vogue for several years in Germany and Austria because of its sprightly Czech folk tunes and modern orch. treatment; also given at Met. Op., 1931); *"The Beloved*

Voice" (Munich Op., 1930); (orch.)
"Overture to a Marionette Play";
"Scherzo Giocoso," "Don Quichote";
(pantomime) *"Die Entführung der
Eveline"*; piano sonata, cham. music;
op., *"Wallenstein,"* Vienna, 1937.

Weiner (vī'-nĕr), **Leo,** b. Budapest,
April 16, 1885; composer; studied
with Koessler at the Prague Acad.,
also in other countries; after 1913,
teacher of theory at Buda-Pest
Acad.; c. orch. works, string quartets, trio, vln. sonata; quartet in F
sharp minor winning Coolidge Prize,
1921; also arr. works of Bach and
others for orchestra.

Weingartner (vīn'-gärt-nĕr), **(Paul)
Felix,** Zara, Dalmatia, June 2, 1863
—Winterthur, May 7, 1942; pupil
W. A. Remy; later of Leipzig Cons.,
winning Mozart prize; friend of Liszt
at Weimar, where his opera *"Sakuntala"* was prod. 1884; until 1889,
theatre cond. at Königsberg, Danzig,
Hamburg; 1889, Mannheim; 1891–97,
was cond. Berlin ct.-opera, also cond.
symph. concerts at the Royal orch.;
from 1898 lived in Munich as cond.
Kaim concerts as well as the R.
Orch. Berlin; in 1908–11, he succeeded Mahler as dir. of the Vienna
Royal Op., also leading concerts of
the Philh. Orch. in that city; in
1912–14, 1st. cond. at the Hamburg
Op.; then ct.-cond. at Darmstadt
and dir. of the Cons. there; he continued to make notable guest appearances in various cities, incl. visits to
America in 1905–06 and 1912–13;
1919–20 he was dir. of the Vienna
Volksoper; 1928–35, dir. of Basel
Cons., and cond. of orch. there; in
1935 he was again called to the
directorship of the Vienna Op., but
resigned in 1936 after differences
with the state officials over artistic
policy; c. operas *"Sakuntala"* (1884),
"Malawika" (Munich, 1886), *"Gene-
sius"* (Berlin, 1893), withdrawn by
the author because of press attacks
and revived with succ. at Mannheim
and elsewhere; *"Orestes"* (Berlin,
June 15, 1902); c. symph. poems
*"König Lear," "Das Gefilde der
Seligen,"* a drama *"Golgotha"* (1908),
3 symph., *"Frühlingsmärchenspiel"*
(Weimar, 1908), music to *"Faust"*
(do., 1908); operas, *"Dame Kobold"*
(to his own libretto), 1916; *"Meister
Andrea"* (1920); *"Terokayn"* (1920);
"Julian the Apostate." He orches-

trated Beethoven's Hammerklavier
pf.-sonata and ed. an unfinished
Schubert symphony (not the famous
one); wrote *" Über das Dirigieren,"
"Die Symphonie nach Beethoven,"*
etc.; m. Marie Juillerat, 1891;
Baroness Feodora de Dreyfus, 1903;
Lucille Marcel, singer, 1912 (she d.
1921); Mme. Kalisch, actress, 1922;
and later Carmen Studer, a talented
conductor.

Weinlig (or **Weinlich**) (vīn'-lĭkh), (1)
Chr. Ehregott, Dresden, 1743—1813;
organist and composer. (2) **(Chr.)
Th.,** Dresden, 1780—Leipzig, 1842;
nephew and pupil of above; cantor,
theorist and composer.

Weinwurm (vīn'-voorm), **Rudolf,**
Schaidldorf-on-the-Thaja, Lower
Austria, April 3, 1835—Vienna, May
25, 1911; chorister, ct.-chapel, Vienna; 1858, studied law and founded
the Univ. Gesangverein; mus.-dir.;
1880 mus.-dir. of the Univ.; pub.
treatises and composer.

Weinzierl (vīn'-tsĕrl), **Max,** Ritter **von,**
Bergstadl, Bohemia, 1841—Mödling,
near Vienna, 1898; conductor and
dram. composer.

Weis (vīs), **Karel,** b. Prague, Feb. 13,
1862—1936; composer of a succ.
2-act opera *"The Polish Jew"* (Berlin, 1902); comic opera *"The Twins"*
(Frankfort, 1903), etc.

Weismann (vīs'-män), **Julius,** b. Freiburg, Dec. 26, 1879; pupil of Royal
Musicschool, Munich, then with
Herzogenberg and Thuille; from
1905 in Freiburg as composer of
choral works, a symph., the operas,
"Traumspiel" (after Strindbergplay),
"Schwanenweiss," "Leonceund Lena,"
etc.; d. Singen, Dec. 22, 1950.

Weiss (vīs), (1) **K.,** Mühlhausen, ca.
1738—London, 1795; composer. (2)
K., b. 1777, son and pupil of above;
writer and composer. (3) **K.,** bro.
of above; prod. the opera *"Twelfth
Night"* (Prague, 1892). (4) **Fz.,**
Silesia, 1778—Vienna, 1830; viola-
virtuoso and composer.

Weissheimer (vīs'-hī-mĕr), **Wendelin,**
Osthofen, Feb. 26, 1828—Nurem-
berg, June 16, 1910; mus. director
and composer; pupil Leipzig Cons.,
teacher and theatre-cond. in various
cities; c. 2 operas, *"Theodor Körner"*
(Munich, 1872), and *"Meister Martin
und seine Gesellen"* (Carlsruhe, 1897),
bass solo with orch., *"Das Grab in
Busento,"* etc.; wrote memoirs.

Weist-Hill, H., London, 1828—1891; violinist; pupil R. A. M.; cond. various concerts with much hospitality to novelties; 1880 principal Guildhall Sch.

Weitzmann (vīts'-män), **K. Fr.,** Berlin, 1808—1880; eminent theorist; c. operas, etc.; wrote valuable treatises,

Welcker von Gontershausen (věl'-kěr fŏn gŏn'-těrs-how-zěn), **H.,** Gontershausen, Hesse, 1811—Darmstadt, 1873; ct.-pf.-maker and writer.

Wel'don, (1) **J.,** Chichester, Engl., 1676—London, 1736; org., comp.

Welitsch (vä'-lēch), Ljuba, Jugoslav sopr.; début Met. Op., 1949, as Salome.

Wellesz (vä'-lěsh), **Egon,** b. Vienna, Oct. 21, 1885; composer, educator; Ph. D., Vienna Univ., 1908, Mus. D., 1909; studied history of music with Guido Adler, comp. with Schönberg, by whose atonal methods he was influenced; prof. of musicology, Vienna Univ., after 1929; vice-pres., Austrian Composers' Soc. and active on juries of I. S. C. M.; c. (operas) *"Die Prinzessin Girnara"* (Frankfort, 1921); *"Alkestis"* (Mannheim, 1924); *"Scherz, List und Rache"* (chamber opera), (Stuttgart, 1928); (ballets) *"Die Nächtlichen"* (Berlin, 1925), *"Persisches"* (1925); *"Opferung des Gefangenen"* (Cologne 1926); *"Achilles auf Skyros"*; string quartets, piano music and songs; has works on music; taught Oxford Univ.

Wels (věls), **Chas.,** Prague, Aug. 24, 1825—New York, 1906; pupil of Tomaschek; 1847, ct.-pianist; 1849, New York as concert-pianist and teacher; c. concert-overture and suite for orch.; a pf.-concerto, etc.

Welsh (1) **Thomas,** Wells, Somerset, 1780—Brighton, 1848; bass and singing-teacher. (2) **Mary Anne** (née **Wilson**), 1802—1867; wife and pupil of above; v. succ. soprano, earning £10,000 ($50,000) the first year of her short career.

Wendel (věn'-děl), **Ernst,** b. Breslau, 1876; violinist and director; pupil of Wirth, Joachim, Lucco and Bargiel; 1896 joined Thomas Orch.. Chicago; 1898 cond. Königsberg Musikverein; 1909 cond. Bremen Phil.; gen. mus. dir., 1921; 1912–15, cond. also of Berlin Musikfreunde concerts; c. choruses; d. Jena, 1938.

Wendling (věnt'-lǐng), (1) **Jn. Bapt.,** from 1754–1800 flutist in Mannheim:

band composer. His wife (2) **Dorothea** (née **Spurni**), Stuttgart, 1737—Munich, 1811, was a singer. (3) **K.,** d. 1794; violinist in Mannheim band. His wife (4) **Auguste Elizabethe,** was a singer. (5) **K.,** Frankenthal, Rhine Palatinate, Nov. 14, 1857—Leipzig, 1918; pianist; pupil Leipzig Cons.; performer on Jankó keyboard; teacher of it from 1887 at Leipzig Cons; ct.-pianist to Prince of Waldeck.

Wenzel (věn'-tsěl), (1) **Ernst Fd.,** Walddorf, near Lobau, 1808—Bad Kösen, 1880; pf.-teacher and writer. (2) **Leopold,** Naples, Jan. 23, 1847 —Paris, Aug., 1925; studied Cons. S. Pietro a Majella; at 13 toured as violinist; 1866 joined Métra's orch. at Marseilles; 1871, conductor; later cond. of the Alcazar, Paris; 1883, London; from 1889 cond. at the Empire Th.; prod. operettas, many ballets, etc.

Wenzel von Gamter (or **Szamotulski**) (shä-mō-tool'-skǐ), Gamter, 1525— Cracow, 1572; Polish composer of church music.

Werbecke, Gaspar van. Vide GASPAR.

Werckmeister (vărk'-mī-shtěr), **Ands.,** Beneckenstein, 1645—Halberstadt, 1706; organist, important theorist and composer.

Wermann (văr'-män), **Fr. Oskar,** Neichen, near Trebsen, Saxony, April 30, 1840—near Dresden, Nov. 22, 1906; pianist and organist; pupil of Leipzig Cons.; 1868, teacher R. Seminary, Dresden; 1876, mus. dir. 3 churches and cantor at the Kreuzschule there; c. *"Reformations-Cantate,"* mass in 8 parts, etc.

Werner (văr'-něr), (1) **Gregorius Jos.,** 1695—Eisenstadt, 1766; conductor and composer. (2) **Jn. Gottlob,** Hoyer, Saxony, 1777—Merseburg, 1822; organist, mus.-director, teacher and composer. (3) **H.,** near Erfurt, 1800—Brunswick, 1833; composer. (4) **Josef,** Würzburg, June 25, 1837 —Munich, Nov. 14, 1922; 'cellist; pupil of the Cons. there; teacher Munich School of Music; pub. a method; c. pcs. for 'cello, etc.

Wer'renrath, Reinald, b. Brooklyn, N. Y., Aug. 7, 1883; barytone; grad. N. Y. U., pupil of Frank King Clark, Carl Dufft, Percy Rector Stephens, Arthur Mees and Victor Maurel; début in N. Y. concert, 1907; appeared widely as a concert and oratorio singer: also with Met. Op.

(début as "Silvio," 1919); 1921, London; made many recital tours; assoc. as vocal counsel with leading radio co., d. Plattsburg, N.Y., Sept. 12, 1953.

Wert (vārt), **Jacob van**, b. Netherlands, 1536—Mantua, 1596; conductor and composer.

Wesembeck. Vide BURBURE DE W.

Wes'ley, (1) **Chas.**, Bristol, Engl., Dec. 11, 1757—London, May 23, 1834; nephew of the evangelist John W.; teacher, organist and composer. (2) **Samuel**, Bristol, Engl., 1766—London, 1837; bro. and pupil of above; organist and composer. (3) **Samuel Sebastian**, London, Aug. 14, 1800—Gloucester, April 19, 1876; son of above; organist.

Wessel (věs'-sěl), **Chr. R.**, Bremen, 1797 — Eastbourne, 1885; mus.-publisher, London.

Wessely (věs'-sě-lē), (1) **Jn.**, Frauenburg, Bohemia, 1762—Ballenstedt, 1814; violinist; c. comic operas. (2) **(K.) Bd.**, Berlin, 1768—Potsdam, 1826; dram. composer. (3) **Hans**, Vienna, Dec. 23, 1862—Innsbruck, Sept. 29, 1926; violinist; pupil of the Cons.; toured with success; from 1889 prof. R. A. M., London, leader of the W. Quartet.

West, J. Ebenezer, South Hackney, London, Dec. 7, 1863—Feb., 1929; concert-organist and pianist; pupil of Bridge and Prout, R. A. M.; 1891, organist S. Hackney Parish Ch.; c. 2 cantatas; Psalm 130; services, etc.

West'brook, Wm. Jos., London, 1831 —Sydenham, 1894; organist, conductor and composer.

West'lake, Fr., Romsey, Hampshire, 1840—London, 1898; composer.

Westmeyer (věsht'-mī-ěr), **Wm.**, Iburg, near Osnabrück, 1832—Bonn, 1880; c. operas.

Westmore'land, J. Jane, Earl of, London, 1784 — Apthorpe House, 1859; dram. composer.

Westphal (věsht'-fäl), **Rudolf (G. Hn.)**, Oberkirchen, Lippe-Schaumburg, 1826—Stadthagen, 1892; writer.

West'rop, H. J., Lavenham, Suffolk, 1812—1879; pianist, violinist, singer, organist and composer.

Wettergren (vět'-těr-grěn), **Gertrud**, b. Esloev, Sweden; contralto; studied at Stockholm Acad. and R. School of Op.; début at R. Op. there, 1922, as "Cherubino"; sang leading rôles with this co.; esp. noted as "Carmen";

début, Met. Op. Co., N. Y., as "Amneris," 1935.

Wetzel (vět'-tsěl), **Hermann**, b. Kyritz, Pomerania, March 11, 1879; teacher at Riemann Cons. 1905–07; then in Potsdam as teacher and author; c. songs, etc.

Wetzler (věts'-lěr), **Hermann Hans**, Frankfort, 1870—N. Y., May 29, 1943; pupil of Frau Schumann (pf.), B. Scholz (comp.), Ivan Knorr (cpt.), H. Heerman (vln.), and Humperdinck (orchestration); 1893, New York, as pianist and teacher; asst.-org. Trinity Ch.; from 1902 cond. his own symphony orch.; 1905, dir. Hamburg Op.; 1908 cond. in Russia, then in various German cities; c. opera "*The Basque Venus*," etc.

Weweler (vā'-vě-lěr), **August**, b. Recke, Westphalia, Oct. 20, 1868; composer; pupil Leipzig Cons.; c. fairy opera "*Dornröschen*" (Kassel, 1903), comic opera "*Der grobe Märker*" (Detmold, 1908), etc.

Weymarn (vī'-märn), **Paul Platonovich**, b. St. Petersburg, 1857; son of a lieut.-general and himself an officer; gave up the army for music; wrote biographies, criticisms, 'cello-pieces, etc.; d. (?).

Weyse (vī'-zě), **Chp. Ernst Fr.**, Altona, 1774—Copenhagen, 1842; dram. composer.

Whelp'ley, Benj. Lincoln, b. Eastport, Maine, Oct. 23, 1864; studied with B. J. Lang, etc., at Boston, 1890 in Paris; lived in Boston as teacher and composer.

White, (1) **Robt.**, d. Westminster, Nov. 7 (11 ?), 1574; organist at Ely Cath. (1562–67); noted in his day as organist and composer. Often confused with (2) **Wm.** (c. fantasias or "fancies" for org., etc.) and (3) Rev. **Matthew**, Mus. Doc. 1629; c. anthems and catches. (4) **Alice Mary, Meadows** (née Smith), 1839—1884; pupil of Bennett, and Macfarren, London; c. symphs., cantatas, etc. (5) **J., W.** Springfield, Mass., March 12, 1855—Bad Neuheim, Germany, July 18, 1902; pupil of Dudley Buck; then of Haupt (org. and cpt.), Rheinberger; gave org.-concerts in various German cities; 1887–96, organist, New York; from 1897 lived in Munich; pub. Missa Solemnis; O salutaris; c. an oratorio "*Alpha and Omega*," etc. (6) **Maude Valérie**, b. of English parents, Dieppe,

June 23, 1855—London, Nov. 2, 1937; pupil of O. May and W. S. Rockstro, and of R. A. M., Mendelssohn Scholar, 1879, also studied in Vienna; lived in London; c. mass; pf.-pcs.; *"Pictures from Abroad"* and pop. songs, etc. (7) **Carolina,** b. Dorchester, Mass., Dec. 23, 1883; pupil of Weldon Hunt; concert début, 1905; 1907 studied with Sebastian at Naples; début at San Carlo Theatre, 1908; sang in Italy, and from 1910 with Chicago Op. Co.; 1911 with Boston Op.

White'hill, Clarence, Marengo, Iowa, Nov. 5, 1871—New York, Dec. 18, 1932; notable bass; début in *"Roméo et Juliette,"* Brussels, 1899; sang Paris Op. Com. and Bayreuth; Met. Op., 1900–31, except during 1911–15, when he sang with Chicago Op.

Whitehouse, William Edward, b. London, May 20, 1859—Jan. 12, 1935; 'cellist; pupil of Pettit and R. A. M., winning prize, 1878; and from 1882 teacher there; later prof., member of Ludwig Quartet and London Trio.

White'man, Paul, b. Denver, Colo., 1891; conductor; son of a supervisor of music in Denver public schools; early studied to be viola player; during World War became cond. of a U. S. Navy Orch., and began experiments in original style of syncopated dance music, for which he acquired internat'l reputation; has toured widely in U. S., also one season in Europe as head of his own orch.; encouraged prod. of symphonic jazz comps. by giving concerts of new works of this form in New York.

Whith'orne, Emerson, b. Cleveland, O., Sept. 6, 1884; composer; studied with James H. Rogers, Leschetizky, Schnabel and Robert Fuchs; lived in London, 1907–14, where was critic of Pall Mall *Gazette,* 1913; served as exec. ed., Art Publication Soc., St. Louis, 1915–20; c. (orch.) symphonies, *"Fata Morgana," " New York Days and Nights"* (Salzburg Fest., 1923); *"Ranga," "The City of Ys," "The Aeroplane";* vln. concerto; *"Saturday's Child"* for mezzosoprano, tenor, and small orch.; string quartets, incl. *"Three Greek Impressions";* (dance satire) *"Sooner or Later"* (prod. in N. Y.); piano quintet, also music to plays incl. O'Neill's *"Marco Millions"; "The Grim Troubadour"* for voice and

string quartet; songs and piano works; *"Sierra Morena"* and *"The Dream Pedlar,"* for orch.

Whi'ting, (1) G. Elbridge, Holliston, Mass., Sept. 14, 1842—Cambridge, Mass., 1923; organist at Worcester when 13; later at Hartford, Conn. (where he founded the Beethoven Soc.); later organist in various Boston churches; studied with G. W. Morgan, New York, and Best, Liverpool; Haupt and Radecke, Berlin; till 1879, teacher at the N. E. Cons.; Boston; till 1882, at the Cincinnati Coll. of Mus.; then again at the N. E. Cons.; c. masses with orch. and organ, cantatas, ballade with orch., *" Henry of Navarre,"* pf.-concerto, etc. (2) **Arthur Battelle,** Cambridge, Mass., June 20, 1861—Beverly, Mass., July 21, 1936; nephew of above; pf.-pupil of W. H. Sherwood; début at 19, Boston; studied with Chadwick and J. C. D. Parker; then with Rheinberger, in Munich; lived in Boston, organist of N. E. Cons. until 1897; organised concerts at Harvard, Yale and Princeton; teacher of pf. and comp.; c. fantasy with orch., concert-overture, concert-étude, church-service, concerto, song cycles, etc.

Whitney, Samuel Brenton, Woodstock Vermont, June 4, 1842—Brattleboro, Vt., 1914; organist; pupil of Chas. Wells and J. K. Paine; 1871, organist, Ch. of the Advent, Boston; conductor of church-choir festivals; org.-prof. and lecturer, Boston U. and N. E. Cons.; c. anthems, org.-sonatas, etc.

Whit'taker, William Gillies, Newcastle-on-Tyne, England, July 23, 1876—1944; composer, cond.; studied with Frederic Austin and G. F. Huntley; hon. Mus. Doc., Durham Univ., 1921; c. orch., chamber, choral and piano music in modern style; author of books on music.

Whyt'horne (or **Whitehorne), Thos.,** b. 1528; Engl. composer.

Wichern (věkh'-ěrn), **Karoline,** Horn, near Hamburg, Sept. 13, 1836—March 19, 1906; soprano; led choruses at the houses of correction for 20 years, then for 15 years taught in Manchester, returning 1896 to her previous task; 1900 cond. at Hamburg a concert of her own orchestral works; c. vocal works.

Wichmann (věkh'-män), **Hermann,**

Berlin, Oct. 24, 1824—Rome, Aug. 27, 1905; studied at R. Akademie; also with Taubert, Mendelssohn and Spohr; then lived in Berlin; c. symphs., sonatas, etc.

Wichtl (vĭkht'-'l), **G.**, Trostberg, Bavaria, 1805—Bunzlau, Silesia, 1877; violinist, conductor and dram. composer.

Wickenhausser (vĭk'-ĕn-hows'-sĕr), **Richard,** Brünn, 1867—Vienna, 1936; pupil of Leipzig Cons.; 1894 was given a stipend on the advice of Brahms and Hanslick; 1895 leader of a singing society in Brünn; 1902 in Graz; 1907 dir. Vienna Singakademie, c. choral works, also 2 piano sonatas, a violin sonata, etc.

Widmann (vēt'-män), (1) **Erasmus,** poet-laureate, organist and conductor at Weikersheim; publisher and composer (1607). (2) **Benedikt,** Bräunlingen, March 5, 1820—Frankfort, 1910; rector at Frankfort; theorist and composer. (3) **Jos. Victor,** Nennowitz, Moravia, Feb. 20, 1842 —Berne, 1912; at 3 taken to Switzerland; wrote librettos and biog. of Brahms.

Widor (vē-dôr), **Chas. (M.),** b. Lyons, Feb. 24, 1845—Paris, March 12, 1937; son of an Alsatian of Hungarian descent (organist at Lyons); studied with Lemmens (org.) and Fétis (comp.), Brussels; at 15 organist at St. François, Lyons, and 1869–1935, organist at St. Sulpice, Paris; 1890, teacher at the Paris Cons.; from 1896 prof. of cpt., fugue and comp.; critic (under pen-name "Aulètes") and dir. of the soc. "La Concordia," c. v. succ. ballet "La Korrigane" (Opéra, 1880); music to "Conte d'Avril" (Odéon, 1885); "Les Jacobites" (Odéon, 1885); unsucc. lyric drama "Maître Ambros" (Op.-Com., May 6, 1896); 3 pantomimes; a mass for 2 choirs and 2 orgs.; Psalm 112, with orch. and org.; "La nuit de Walpurgis," for chorus and orch.; 3 symphs.; 10 org. symphs. incl. "Gotique," a concerto for vln., 'cello, and pf., org.-sonatas, etc.; Chevalier, Legion of Honour; 1910, member of Académie, and after 1913 secretary of this body.

Wieck (vēk), (1) **Fr.,** Pretzsch, near Torgau, 1785—Loschwitz, near Dresden, 1873; est. a pf.-factory and library at Leipzig; eminent pf.-teacher; also singing-teacher and composer;

teacher also of his daughter (2) **Clara.** (Vide SCHUMANN.) (3) **Alwin,** Leipzig, 1821—1885; son of (1); pupil of David; violinist at St. Petersburg; later pf.-teacher at Dresden. (4) **Marie,** Leipzig, Jan. 17, 1832—1916; pianist; daughter of (1); played in public at 8; 1858, ct.-pianist to the Prince of Hohenzollern; toured; est. a sch. in Dresden; 1914, Royal Professor.

Wiedemann (vē'-dĕ-män), **Ernst Jn.,** Hohengiersdorf, Silesia, 1797—Potsdam, 1873; organist, teacher and composer.

Wiederkehr (vē'-dĕr-kār), **Jacob Chr. Michael,** Strassburg, 1739—Paris, 1823; 'cellist, bassoonist, tambourinist and composer.

Wiedermann (vē'-dĕr-män), **K. Fr.,** Görisseiffen, Dec. 25, 1856—Berlin, 1918; organist and Royal Dir., in Berlin; c. overture, songs, etc.

Wiegand (vē'-gänt), **Josef Anton H.,** Fränkisch-Crumbach in the Odenwald, 1842—Frankfort, 1899; bass. b.

Wiehmayer (vē'-mī-ĕr), **Theodor,** b. Marienfeld, Westphalia, Jan. 7, 1870; pianist; pupil Leipzig Cons. and of Krause; début Leipzig, 1890; teacher there; 1902–06 at the Cons.; from 1908 at Stuttgart Cons., 1909 prof.; c. piano pieces and songs.

Wielhorski. Vide WILHORSKI.

Wiemann (vē'-män), **Robert,** b. Frankenhausen, Nov. 4, 1870; pupil Leipzig Cons.; cond. various theatre orchs. and singing societies; from 1899 in Osnabrück; 1910, munic. dir. of music, Stettin; c. orch. works, "Erdenwallen," "Kassandra," etc.; choral works with orch., etc.

Wieniawski (v'yä-nē-äf'-shkĭ), (1) **H.,** Lublin, Poland, July 10, 1835—Moscow, April 12, 1880; eminent violinist and composer; début, at Petersburg, at 13; studied with Clavel and Massart, and Colet (harmony) Paris Cons.; won 1st vln.-prize, 1846; 1860, solo-violinist to Czar, and 1862–67, teacher at the Petersburg Cons.; 1875-77, vln.-prof. Brussels Cons. (vice Vieuxtemps); toured widely, 1872 U. S. with Rubinstein; c. 2 concertos, etc. (2) **Jos.,** Lublin, May 23, 1837—Brussels, Nov. 11, 1912; famous pianist; at 10 pupil of Paris Cons.; at 13 toured with his brother, then studied with Marx at Berlin; 1866, teacher at the Moscow Cons.; est. a pf.-sch. of his own; later teacher in Brussels Cons.; c. 2 overtures, suite romantique for orch., pf.-concerto, etc.

Wieprecht (vē'-prĕkht), **Wm. Fr.**, Aschersleben, 1802—Berlin, 1872; famous trombonist and violinist; inv. the bass tuba (1835).

Wietrowetz (vē'-trō-vĕtz), **Gabriele**, b. Laibach, Carmola, Jan. 13, 1866; violinist; pupil of Joachim, winning Mendelssohn prize at Berlin Hochsch.; début 1885 at Münster; toured and from 1904, teacher at the Berlin Hochsch.; founded quartet.

Wig'man, Mary, b. Hanover, Germany; dancer; studied Berlin, Dresden-Hellerau and Rome; pupil of and asst. to Rudolf von Laban in Munich and elsewhere; after 1919 came forward with her own dance recitals, which exhibited style of notable freedom and force, a feature of which was discarding of all conventional "prettiness" and pirouetting of the classic ballet school; Frl. Wigman, as she has expressed it, danced "man's kinship with the earth and with feet flat on the earth"; although the general tendency was apparent in dance world since Isadora Duncan, the Wigman style developed into an internat'l cult known as the "free dance" and she estab. schools in many German cities, also in other countries incl. U. S. after 1920; has also toured several times in America as soloist and with her girl dance group; one of her tenets is dancing to percussion, with special scores created for her.

Wihan (vē'-hän), **Hans (Hanuš)**, Politz, near Braunau, June 5, 1855—Prague, May 3, 1920; 'cellist; pupil of Prague Cons.; 1873, prof. of 'cello, Mozarteum, Salzburg; 1877-80, chamber-virtuoso to Prince Schwarzburg-Sondershausen; 1880, 1st solo-'cellist Munich ct.-orch.; 1888, prof. at Prague Cons., a member "Bohemian String Quartet."

Wihtol (vē'-tôl) **Jos.**, b. Wolmar, Livonia, 1863; studied at Mitau; then with Johansen (harm.) and Rimsky-Korsakov (comp. and instrumentation) Petersburg Cons.; 1886, prof. of harm. there; 1918, dir. of Riga Opera; 1919, founded New Cons. there; c. "La fête Ligho," symph. picture, "Dramatic" overture, etc

Wilbye (wĭl'-bĭ), **J.**; lutenist and teacher, London, 1598; most brilliant composer of madrigals.

Wild (vēlt), **Fz.**, Niederhollabrunn, Lower Austria, 1792—Oberdöbling, near Vienna, 1860; tenor.

Wilder (vēl-dăr), **Jérome Albert Victor van**, Wettern, near Ghent, 1835—Paris, 1892; writer and translator.

Wilhelm (vēl'-hĕlm), **K.**, Schmalkalden, 1815—1873; "R. Prussian Mus. Dir."; c. "Die Wacht am Rhein," etc.

Wilhelmj (vēl-hĕl'-mē), (1) **Aug. (Emil Daniel Fd.)**, Usingen, Nassau, Sept. 21, 1845—London, Jan. 22, 1908; eminent violinist; pupil of Fischer at Wiesbaden; played in public at 8; at 16 recommended to David by Liszt as a young Paganini; he studied 1861-64, with David (vln.), Hauptmann and Richter, Leipzig Cons.; 1862, the Gewandhaus; 1864, studied with Raff at Frankfort; from 1865, toured the world; 1876, leader of Bayreuth orch.; lived for years at Biebrich-on-Rhine, where he est. (with R. Niemann) a "Hochschule" for vln.; 1886, lived at Blasewitz, near Dresden; 1894, head-prof. Guildhall Sch., London; 1895, he m. the pianist Mariella Mausch; c. "Hochzeits-Cantate" with orch., vln.-pcs., etc. His son (2) **Adolf**, b. 1872, violinist; after 1898 vln.-prof. Belfast Cons.

Wilhem (rightly **Bocquillon**) (vēl-än or bôk-ē-yôn), **Guillaume Louis**, Paris, 1781—1842; dir.-gen. of all Paris schools; founder of the great system of popular singing societies or "Orphéonistes" (v. D. D.); pub. many treatises on his method of "mutual instruction" and a 10-vol. coll. of comps.

Wi(e)lhórski (vēl-hôr'-shkĭ), (1) Count **Matvéi Júrjevitch**, Volhynia, 1787—Petersburg (?), 1863; 'cellist. His brother (2) Count **Michaíl Júrjevitch**, Volhynia, 1788—Moscow, 1856; composer.

Willaert (wĭl'-lärt) (**Wigliar'dus, Vigliar, Vuigliart**), **Adrian** (called **Adriano**), Flanders, ca. 1480—Venice, 1562; eminent composer and teacher; called the founder of the Venetian Sch.; a very prolific composer; pupil of Mouton and Josquin Desprès; 1516 at Rome, later at Ferrara; then mus. to the King of Bohemia; Dec. 12, 1527, maestro at San Marco, Venice, where he organised a famous sch.; c. 5 masses, many motets, psalms, madrigals, etc.; the first to write for two choirs.

Wil'lan, Healey, b. Balham, England, 1880; composer and organist; studied St. Savior's Choral School, Eastham; org. in leading British churches; after 1913 res. in Toronto as theory teacher at Cons., and later vice-pres. and dir.; c. choral and organ works.

Wille (vĭl'-lĕ), **Georg,** b. Greiz, Sept. 20, 1869; 'cellist; from 1899 court-concertmaster at Royal Chapel in Dresden and teacher in the Cons.; pupil of Leipzig Cons.

Willeke (vĕl'-ā-kĕ), **Willem,** b. The Hague, 1878; 'cellist, conductor; studied Hague and Amsterdam Cons., pupil of Hartog; solo 'cellist Leipzig Philh., 1901–03; afterward at Covent Garden and Vienna Op., mem. Kneisel Quartet, 1907–17; founded in latter year the Elshuco Trio and was its 'cellist; life dir. of Berkshire Music Colony; taught at Inst. of Musical Art, N. Y., where cond. orch.; appeared in U. S. as orch. soloist and in recitals.

Willent-Bordogni (vĕ-yäṅ-bôr-dōn-yē), **Jean Bapt. Jos.,** Douai, 1809—Paris, 1852; bassoon-virtuoso, teacher, writer and dram. composer. 1834, m. the daughter of Bordogni.

Williams, (1) **Charles Lee,** Winchester, May 1, 1853—Gloucester, Aug. 29, 1935; organist; pupil of Arnold; 1882–98 org. at Gloucester Cathedral; cond. of festivals; c. cantatas, church music, etc. (2) **Charles Francis Abdy,** Dawlish, July 16, 1855—Milford, Feb. 27, 1933; took music degrees at both Cambridge and Oxford; later pupil Leipzig Cons.; organist at various posts; authority on Greek music and Plain song; c. church music, choruses for *"Alcestis," "Antigone,"* and *"Agamemnon."* (3) **Ralph Vaughan,** b. Down Ampney, England, Oct. 12, 1872; composer; grad. Trinity Coll., Cambridge; Mus. D., Oxford and Cambridge; studied R. Coll. of Music with Moore, Parry, Stanford, Wood, Parratt, Sharpe, Gray, also with Ravel and Bruch; was early active as an organist, and has been extension lecturer at Oxford; it is, however, as a composer that he has estab. a rank among the outstanding musical figures of the day; as a symphonist he has an especial aptitude, and some of his

music has been influenced by English folk-song in which he has been a leading investigator; esp. popular in other countries are his *"London" Symphony,* a programmatic work depicting sights of that metropolis, but welded cleverly into impressive symph. form; and his *"Pastorale" Symphony,* which is exquisitely compounded of English country traditional tunes treated with the hand of a poet and an expert craftsman; his extremely large output includes also stage works and various forms of chamber music, part-songs, choral arrangements of folk-music; in his later music, W. has shown a tendency to depart from descriptive writing into more abstract realms and to court aggressive dissonance; c. (opera) *"Hugh the Drover";* (ballet) *"Old King Cole";* (orch.) *"Three Impressions," "In the Fen Country,"* three *" Norfolk Rhapsodies"; "Bucolic Suite"; "Heroic Elegy"; "Serenade"; "Fantasia on a Theme by Thomas Tallis";* suite for *"The Wasps"* of Aristophanes; Fantasie for piano and orch.; *"Concerto Academico"* for vln. and orch.; *"Studies in English Folk Music"* for vln.; a string quartet, (masque for dancing) *"Job";* Symphony in F (no program or title); 2 piano quintets; (choral works) *"Toward the Unknown Region"; "A Sea Symphony"; "The Garden of Proserpine";* five *"Mystical Songs";* (oratorio) *"Sancta Civitas";* 3 Nocturnes for barytone with orch.; (song cycles) *"The House of Life," "Songs of Travel," "On Wenlock Edge";* arr. Purcell's *"Welcome Songs,"* also many folk-songs, madrigals, etc.; ed. *"The English Hymnal."* (See page 544.)

Wil'liamson, John Finley, b. Canton, O., June 23, 1887; conductor, educator; studied with Bispham and Witherspoon, also Otterbein Coll.; hon. Mus. D., Wooster Univ.; served as dean of Ithaca Cons.; founder and dean of Westminster Choir School, now at Princeton Univ.; and cond. Westminster Choir, with which he toured U. S. and Europe; c. and arr. choral works.

Willing (vĭl'-lĭng), (1) **Jn. L.,** Kühndorf, 1755—Nordhausen, 1805; organist and composer. (2) (wĭl'-lĭng) **Chr. Edwin,** London, Feb. 28, 1830—St. Albans, Dec. 1, 1904; organist various London churches, conductor and teacher.

Wil'lis, (1) **H.,** England, April 27, 1821 —London, Feb. 11, 1901; prominent org.-builder and improver. (2) **Richard Storrs,** Boston, Mass., Feb. 10, 1819—Detroit, May 7, 1900; bro. of N. P. Willis the poet; critic and editor in N. Y., later Detroit; composer.

Will'man, (1) **Magdalena,** d. 1801; famous soprano; her brother, (2) **K.,** violinist.

Willmers (vïl'-mĕrs), **H. Rudolf,** Berlin, 1821—Vienna, 1878; pianist and composer.

Wilm (vïlm). **Nicolai von,** Riga, March 4, 1834—Wiesbaden, Feb. 20, 1911; pianist; studied Leipzig Cons.; 1857, 2nd cond. Riga City Th.; then Petersburg, 1860; teacher of pf. and theory Imp. Nicolai Inst.; 1875, Dresden; 1878, Wiesbaden; c. pop. string-sextet, 'cello and vln.-sonatas, male-choruses, etc.

Wilms (vïlms), **Jan Willem,** Witzhelden, Schwarzburg-Sondershausen, 1772—Amsterdam, 1847; teacher and org.-composer.

Wilsing (vïl'-zïng), **Daniel Fr. Ed.,** Hörde, near Dortmund, Oct. 21, 1809 —Berlin, May 2, 1893; 1829-34, organist in Wesel, then Berlin; c. oratorio *"Jesus Christus,"* in 2 parts (Bonn, 1889); a De profundis à 16 (gold medal for Art, Berlin); pf.-sonata, etc.

Wil'son, (1) **J.,** Faversham, Kent, 1594 —London, 1673; famous lutenist and composer. (2) **J.,** Edinburgh, 1800 —(of cholera) Quebec, 1849; tenor. (3) **Mortimer,** Chariton, Iowa, Aug. 6, 1876—New York, Jan. 27, 1932; composer; studied in Chicago with Jacobsohn, Gleason and Middleschulte; 1901-07, taught theory, Univ. Sch. of Mus., Lincoln, Nebr.; then a pupil of Sitt and Reger in Leipzig; 1911, taught Atlanta Cons.; and cond. symph. orch. there; 1916-18, at Brenau Coll., Gainesville, Ga.; later consultant at Nat'l Acad. of Mus., N. Y.; author of many orch. and other pieces, incl. musical scores for motion pictures.

Wilt (vïlt), **Marie** (née **Liebenthaler),** Vienna, Jan. 30, 1833—(suicide) Sept. 24, 1891; famous operatic soprano; début 1865 at Graz; sang throughout Europe, also popular in concerts. In 1866-67 she sang at

Covent Garden under the name "Vilda," again in 1874-75.

Wiltberger (vïlt'-bĕrkh-ĕr), **Heinrich,** Sobernheim, Aug. 17, 1841—Colmar, 1916; son of an organist; 1872-1906 teacher in Alsace; co-founder of the Cecilia society and composer of church music, and favourite Alsatian composer of male-choruses.

Winderstein (vïn'-dĕr-shtïn), **Hans (Wm. Gv.),** Lüneburg, Oct. 29, 1856 —Hanau, June 23, 1925; violinist; pupil of Leipzig Cons.; also playing in Gewandhaus Orch.; 1880-84, leader in Baron von Derwies' orch. at Nice; till 1887, vln.-teacher at Winterthur (Switzerland) Cons., then cond. at Nürnberg; 1893-96, dir. Philh. Orch., at Munich, and at the Kaim Concerts; 1896, organised and conducted the "Winderstein Orch."; 1898, cond. Leipzig Singakademie; c. Trauermarsch, Valse-Caprice and Ständchen for orch.; orch. suite, etc.

Winding (vïn'-dïng), **Aug. (Henrik),** Taaro (Laaland), Denmark, March 24, 1835—Copenhagen, June 16, 1899; pianist; pupil of Reinecke, Ree, Dreyschock and Gade; dir. and prof. Copenhagen Cons.; c. vln.-concerto, sonatas, etc.

Wing'ham, Thos., London, 1846—1893; organist and composer.

Winkel (vïnk'-ĕl), **Dietrich Nikolaus,** Amsterdam, ca. 1780—1826; a mechanician; inv. the "componium" and "metronome," which later Mälzel (q. v.) appropriated.

Winkelmann (vïnk'-ĕl-män), **Hermann,** Brunswick, March 8, 1849—Mauer (Vienna), Jan. 18, 1912, tenor; pupil of Koch at Hanover; début Sondershausen, 1875; sang at Altenburg, Darmstadt and Hamburg; then at ct.-opera, Vienna, 1882; created "Parsifal" at Bayreuth.

Winkler (vïnk'-lĕr), **Alex. Adolfovich,** Charkov, March 3, 1865—Leningrad, 1935; pianist; studied at Charkov and at Vienna under Leschetizky and Navrátil; teacher at Charkov; from 1896 at St. Petersburg Cons.; c. prize-winning string quartet, op. 7, piano pieces, etc.

Win'ner, Septimus, Philadelphia, 1826 —Nov. 23, 1902; writer of pop. songs and methods; said to have written 200 technical books on instruments and to have c. and arranged over 2,000 pcs. for vln. and piano; also wrote for *Graham's Mag.,* wher

Poe was editor. His songs include "*Listen to the Mocking Bird*," and "*Give us Back our old Commander*"; founder of Musical Fund Soc.

Winogradsky (vē-nō-grät'-shkǐ), **Alex.,** Kiev, Russia, Aug. 3 (new style), 1856—1912; noted cond.; pupil of Soloviev, Petersb. Cons.; 1884–86, dir. Imp. Sch. of Mus. at Saratov; 1888, of Imp. Soc. of Mus. at Kiev; in Paris, 1894, he cond. Russian programmes at the concerts "d'Harcourt" and "Colonne," 1896.

Winter (vǐn'-tĕr), **Peter von,** Mannheim, 1754—Munich, 1825; studied with Abbé Vogler, but mainly self-taught; violinist and ct.-conductor; composer of v. succ. operas, 38 in all; c. 9 symphs. incl. "*Die Schlacht*" and much church-mus.

Winter-Hjelm (vǐn'-tĕr-hyĕlm₁), **Otto,** Christiania, Oct. 8, 1837—Oslo, May 3, 1931; organist; pupil Leipzig Cons. and of Kullak and Wüerst; dir. Phil. concerts; c. 2 symph., 50 Psalms, 46 Norwegian "*Fjeld melodier*" or mountain songs, etc.

Winterberger (vǐn'-tĕr-bĕrkh-ĕr), **Alex.,** Weimar, Aug. 14, 1834—Leipzig, Sept. 23, 1914; pianist; pupil of Leipzig Cons. and of Liszt. 1861, pf.-prof. at Petersburg Cons.; 1872, lived in Leipzig; c. pf.-pcs. and songs.

Winterfeld (vǐn'-tĕr-fĕlt), **K. G. Aug. Vivigens von,** Berlin, 1784—1852; libr. and writer of valuable historical works.

Wippern (vǐp'-pĕrn), **Louise (Harriers-Wippern),** Hildesheim (or Bückeburg), 1835(7)—Görbersdorf, Silesia, 1878; operatic singer.

Wirth (vērt), **Emanuel,** Luditz, Bohemia, Oct. 18, 1842—Berlin, Jan. 5, 1923; violinist; pupil of Prague Cons., 1864–77; teacher at Rotterdam Cons., and orch.-leader; then vla.-player in the Joachim Quartet, Berlin, and vln.-prof. at the Hochschule; Royal Prof.

Wirtz (vērts), **Charles Louis,** The Hague, Sept. 1, 1841—Breda, 1935; pupil of the Cons.; later piano teacher there; c. church music.

Wise, Michael, England, 1648 ?—in a street brawl, Salisbury, 1687; tenor and notable early composer of anthems, etc.

Wis'ke, Mortimer, Troy, N. Y., Jan. 12, 1853—Lewiston, Me., July 9, 1934; long active as cond. and fest. dir. in New York, New Jersey

and elsewhere; from 1872 organist and dir. Brooklyn; c. church and organ music.

Wit (vēt), **Paul de,** Maastricht, Jan. 4, 1852—Leipzig, Dec. 10, 1925; cellist and viola da gambist; coll. of ancient instrs.

Witek (vē'-tĕk), **Anton,** Saaz, Bohemia, 1872—Winchester, Mass., Aug. 19, 1933; noted violinist; pupil of Bennewitz; at Prague Cons.; 1894 concertm. Berlin Philh.; toured in solo recitals and with Vita Gerhardt (whom he later m.); in 1903 with her and Joseph Malkin formed Trio; 1905, played concertos by Beethoven, Paganini and Brahms in one concert; after 1910, concertm. of Boston Symph.; 1918 resigned this post and gave himself to solo work and teaching; in 1926, after the death of his first wife, he m. Alma Rosengron, a former pupil.

With'erspoon, Herbert, Buffalo, N. Y., July 21, 1873—New York, May 10, 1935; notable basso cantante; graduated Yale Univ.; pupil of J. W. Hall, N. Y., and Dubulle, Paris; sang in opera, Castle Square Co., N. Y., and with Boston Symph. and other orchs. throughout U. S.; v. succ. début in recital, N. Y., 1902; coached with Lamperti in Berlin; in 1908 he joined the Met. Op., N. Y., and sang there until 1916 with increasing success, making especially deep impression in the rôles of "Gurnemanz," "King Mark," etc. Gave recitals in London with great success, 1910, and continued his concert and oratorio appearances; he was active in later years as a voice teacher and choral cond. in N. Y. and Chicago; 1925–29, pres. of Chicago Musical Coll.; vice-pres. and artistic dir. of Chicago Civic Op. Co., 1931; dir. Cincinnati Cons., 1932–33; 1935 appointed general manager of Met. Op. Co., N. Y., to succeed Giulio Gatti-Casazza, and had begun intensive work on the repertoire for the following season when he was stricken fatally with a heart attack in his offices at the opera house; he m. (1) Greta Hughes, singer; divorced; (2) Florence Hinkle, soprano (d. 1933); (3) Mrs. Blanche Skeath.

Witkowski (vǐt-kôf'-skǐ), **Georges Martin** (rightly **Martin**), b. Mostagneaux, 1867—died in Paris, during 1943; French comp.; son of a Polish woman and a French military officer; himself trained in the officers' school at St. Cyr; but early showed talent for composition; after producing a 5-act opera and various symph. works, he entered the Paris Schola Cantorum, where he studied under D'Indy; in 1902, when he left the army, he founded in Lyons a mixed chorus and in 1905 the Soc. des Grands Concerts; his earlier style was based on the classical, but in later works he has shown modern tendencies; c. 2 symphs., piano quintet, string quartet, sonata for vln. and piano; choral work, "*Poème de la maison*"; and "*Mon Lac*" for piano and orch., prod. in Paris, 1921.

Witt (vĭt), (1) **Fr.**, Halten-Bergstetten, 1770 — Würzburg, 1837; violinist, conductor and dram. composer. (2) **Theodor de**, Wesel, 1823—(of consumption) Rome, 1855; organist and composer. (3) **Fz.**, Walderbach, Bavaria, 1834—Schatzhofen, 1888; editor and writer.

Witte (vĭt'-tĕ), (1) **Chr. Gl. Fr.**, d. 1873; org.-builder. (2) **G. H.**, Utrecht, Nov. 16, 1843—Essen, 1929; son of above; pupil of R. Mus. Sch. at The Hague, then of Leipzig Cons.; teacher in Leipzig till 1867, then in Alsatia, 1871; cond. at Essen, 1882; R. Mus. Dir.; c. pf.-quartet (prize at Florence), grand Elegy for vln. and orch., etc.

Wittgenstein (vĭt'-gĕn-stīn), **Paul**, b. Vienna, Nov. 5, 1887; pianist; lost one arm in the war, but acquired notable facility in performing works for one hand; among noted composers who wrote works for him were Ravel (concerto for one hand) and Richard Strauss, whose symph. study, "*Panathenaenzug*" (piano and orch.) was given première by W. and Vienna Philh. under Schalk in 1929; toured U. S. with succ., 1935.

Wittich (vĭt'-tĭkh), **Marie**, Giessen, May 27, 1868—Dresden, Sept., 1931; soprano; studied with Frau Otto-Ubridy; sung various cities; 1901 Dresden ct.-opera.

Witting (vĭt'-tĭnk), **Karl**, Jülich, Sept. 8, 1823—Dresden, June 28, 1907; tenor singer; pupil of Reichel in Paris; teacher in various cities; c. 'cello sonata, etc.

Wladigeroff (vlăd-ē-gä'-rŏf), **Pantscho**, b. Zurich, 1899, of Bulgarian parents; composer; studied with Paul Juon

and Georg Schumann; orig. a theatre cond. with Max Reinhardt in Berlin; has c. incid. music to Strindberg's "*Dream Play*," works for orch., piano and violin.

Wohlfahrt (vōl'-färt), **H.**, Kössnitz, near Apolda, 1797—Connewitz, 1883; noted teacher, writer and composer.

Woldemar (vōl-dŭ-măr) (rightly **Michel**), Orléans, 1750—Clermont-Ferrand, 1816; conductor and composer; wrote methods; inv. a mus.-stenography "*Tableau melotachigraphique*," and mus.-correspondence "*Notographie*."

Wolf (vôlf), (1) **Ernst Wm.**, Grossheringen, 1735—Weimar, 1792; ct.-conductor; c. 42 pf.-sonatas. (2) **Fd.**, Vienna, 1796—1866; writer. (3) **L.**, Frankfort-on-Main, 1804—Vienna, 1859; pianist, violinist and composer. (4) **Wm.**, Breslau, April 22, 1838—Berlin, 1913; pupil of Kullak, teacher of mus.-history, Berlin, also writer and composer. (5) **Hugo**, Windischgrätz, Styria, March 13, 1860—Vienna, Feb. 22, 1903; notable composer, esp. famed for his many beautiful songs; began study of vln. and piano with his father at 5; for a time attended the Vienna Cons. but was expelled as "incorrigible." A shy, sensitive figure he was principally self-taught, and held only minor posts, as asst. and chorusmaster at the Salzburg Op., under Muck, 1881–82, and as critic for the Vienna *Salonblatt*, 1884–87. His life was a desperate struggle with poverty and was attended by little recognition; he eked out his income by giving occasional piano and vln. lessons; after 1888 he began writing the series of more than 275 songs which were later to make him immortal. He had ambitions to compose for the stage, and his opera, "*Der Corregidor*," based on a Spanish comedy, Alarcon's "*Three-Cornered Hat*," was prod. in Mannheim, 1896, but despite the praise it received was not given repetitions; he was at work on another opera, "*Manuel Venegas*," when his mind failed. After spending some months in an asylum he was released but had to return in 1898; paralysis set in and he lived for 5 years in a helpless condition. His great genius was discovered only slowly, but today he is generally ranked among the few foremost

Lieder composers, including Schubert, Brahms and Franz. His songs have had a great and growing popularity with recitalists the world over. His comps. include, besides the pop. Spanish and Italian *"Liederbücher,"* the *"Lieder aus der Jugendzeit,"* his Goethe, Mörike and Eichendorff songs; choral works, most pop. being *"Elfenlied"* and *"Feuerreiter"*; also a partially completed symph., *"Italian Serenade"* for small orch., a vln. concerto and other works. His *"Corregidor"* has been cond. by Bruno Walter at the Munich and Salzburg Fests. and in 1936 an official ceremony was held at the latter event. More than a score of unknown songs, some youthful, were discovered in 1936. His literary productions were ed. by Batka and Werner and pub. in 1911. Memoirs have been issued by Decsey, Haberlandt, P. Mueller, E. Schmitz, Newman, Morold, Schur and others. There are W.-Vereins in various Eur. cities.

Wolf-Ferrari (völf-fä-rä'-rē), **Ermanno,** Venice, Jan. 12, 1876—Jan. 21, 1948; composer; b. of German father, Italian mother; studied at the Munich Acad. with Rheinberger; 1902–07, dir. Liceo Benedetto Marcello, Venice; after latter year lived in Neubiberg, Bavaria, for the most part devoting himself to comp.; c. (operas) *"La Sulamita"* (1889); *"Aschenbrödel"* (Venice, 1900); *"Le Donne Curiose"* (Munich, 1903; also sung at Met. Op. House, 1912); *"I Quattri Rusteghi"* (Munich, 1906); *"L'Amore Medico"* (after Molière), (Dresden, 1913); the 3 previous works as well as *"Il Segreto di Susanna"* (1-act, called an "Intermezzo," Munich, 1909), being comic in theme and musically reviving a somewhat Mozartean type of sparkling melody; totally different is *"The Jewels of the Madonna"* (Berlin R. Op., 1911, Chicago, 1912), a melodrama which provides the composer's single attempt to imitate the works of the *veristic* school; later productions include: *"Liebesband der Marchesa"* (Dresden, 1925); *"Das Himmelskleid"* (Munich, 1927); *"Sly"* (La Scala, Milan, 1927); *"La Vedova Scaltra"* (1931) and *"Il Campiello"* (Rome, 1936). He also c. the choral work, *"La Vita Nuova,"* and opuses for orch.

and piano, and for various chamber combinations; a symphony da camera, vln. sonata, piano quartet, etc.

Wolff (völf), (1). Vide WOLF (4). (2) **Edouard,** Warsaw, 1816—Paris. 1880; pianist and composer. (3) **Auguste Désiré Bd.,** Paris, 1821—1887; pianist, pf.-teacher and maker; head of firm "Pleyel-Wolff." (4) **Hermann,** Cologne, 1845—Berlin, 1902; pupil of Fz. Kroll and Würst; editor, concert-agent and mgr. at Berlin; c. pf.-pcs. and songs. (5) **Erich,** Vienna, Dec. 3, 1874—New York, March 20, 1913; notable song composer; pupil of Door, Robert Fuchs and J. N. Fuchs at the Cons. of the Musikfreunde in his native city; he lived there until 1906 and later in Berlin; made many tours as an accompanist for Lieder singers, incl. visits to the U. S.; his death occurred on one of these tours; c. ballet, *"Zlatorog,"* prod. in Prague, 1913; a vln. concerto and a number of Lieder which have won marked popularity since his death; he wrote a study of Schumann's songs in their original and later published forms.

Wölf(f)l (vělf'-'l) (**Woelfel, Woelfle),** Jos., Salzburg, 1772—London, 1812; composer; his enormous hands and great contrapuntal skill made him a pf.-virtuoso whose rivalry with Beethoven divided Vienna into factions; but the rivals had mutual respect and W. dedicated his op. 6 to B.; c. light operas (1795–98).

Wolfram (völ'-främ), (1) **Jn. Chr.,** d. 1828; organist and writer at Goldbach, near Gotha. (2) **Jos. Maria,** Dobrzan, Bohemia, 1789—Teplitz, 1839; conductor and dram. composer.

Wolfrum (völ'-froom), **Philipp,** Schwarzenbach-am-Wald, Bavaria, Dec. 17, 1854—Samaden, May 8, 1919; pupil Munich Sch. of Mus.; mus.-dir. Heidelberg Univ.; Dr. Phil. h. c. (Leipzig, 1891); c. *"Grosses Halleluja,"* and other choruses, pf.-pcs., etc.

Wolkenstein (völ'-kĕn-shtīn), **Oswald von,** Tyrol, ca. 1377—Aug. 2, 1445; a knight, ambassador, and wanderer, "the last of the Minnesinger," c. poems and melodies.

Wollanck (völ'-länk), **Fr.,** Berlin, 1782—1831; amateur composer of an opera.

Wolle (völ'-lĕ), **John Frederick,** Bethlehem, Pa., April 4, 1863—Jan. 12,

1933; founder of a choir with which from 1900 he gave remarkable productions of the works of Bach; in 1901 at a three-day festival the Christmas oratorio, *"Passion According to St. Matthew,"* and Mass in B minor were given entire; 1904, a nine-day festival of Bach's works was given; 1905 prof. University of California and cond. symph. concerts at the Open Air Greek Theatre at Berkeley, Cal.; later again active in Bethlehem until his death.

Wollenhaupt (vŏl'-lĕn-howpt), **H. Ad.**, Schkeuditz, near Leipzig, 1827—New York, 1865; pianist, teacher and composer; from 1845 in New York.

Wollick (vŏl'-lĭk) (**Volli'cius, Bolli'cius**), **Nicolas**, b. Bar-le-Duc; teacher and writer at Metz, 1501–12.

Wol'stenholme, William, Blackburn, Feb. 24, 1865—Hampstead, July 23, 1931; organist, blind from birth; pupil of Dr. Done, Mus. B. Oxford, 1887, from 1888 organist in London; toured the U. S. 1908; c. organ music of all kinds, piano sonata, choral ballad, *"Sir Humphrey Gilbert,"* etc.

Wolzogen (und Neuhaus) (vŏl'-tsō-gĕn oont noi-hows), (1) **K. Aug. Alfred,** Freiherr **von,** Frankfort, 1823—San Remo, 1883; writer. (2) **Hans (Paul),** Freiherr **von,** Potsdam, 1848 —Bayreuth, June 2, 1938; son of above; lived as writer at Potsdam till 1877. Wagner made him editor of the *Baireuther Blätter.* Author of many books on Wagner's music.

Wood, (1) Mrs. **Mary Ann.** Vide PATON. (2) Sir **Henry J.,** London, March 3, 1870—Aug. 19, 1944; cond.; pupil of his father; at 10 an organist; 1883–85, gave org.-recitals; studied at R. A. M. with Prout and others; then cond. societies; 1891–92, Carl Rosa Op. Co.; 1894, Marie Roze Co.; after 1895, Queens Hall Prom. Concerts, London; visited U. S. as cond. of Boston Symph., at Hollywood Bowl, etc. C. oratorio *"Dorothea,"* operettas, masses, songs, etc.; wrote treatise on singing; cond. of the Sheffield Festivals in 1902 and of the Norwich Festivals in 1908. (3) **Charles,** Armagh, June 15, 1866— Cambridge, England, July 11, 1926; pupil of T. O. Marks, and at R. C. M., London, winning the Morley scholarship, later teacher there, and cond. Cambridge U. Musical Society; Mus. Doc. Cambridge, 1894; LL. D.

Leeds, 1904; c. *"Ode to the West Wind,"* voices and orch., incid. music to Greek plays; *"Dirge for Twc Veterans"* (Leeds Fest., 1901), *"Ballad of Dundee"* (do., 1904); symphonic variations on *"Patrick Sarsfield"* (London, 1907), songs, etc.

Wood'forde-Fin'den, Amy, b. Valparaiso, Chile, of British parents; d. London, March 13, 1919; her father British Consul in Valparaiso; composer; studied with Adolph Schlosser, Winter and Amy Horrocks; c. many songs, among which the cycle of *"Indian Love Lyrics"* to verses of Laurence Hope, have had world-wide popularity; m. Col. Woodforde-Finden, officer in Indian Army (retired).

Wood'man, Raymond Huntington, Brooklyn, N. Y., 1861—1943; piano pupil of his father, of Dudley Buck, and César Franck; 1875–79, asst.-organist to his father, at Flushing, L. I.; 1894–97, mus.-editor *N. Y Evangelist;* 1880, organist First Presb. Ch., Brooklyn; 1889, head of org.-dept. Metr. Coll. of Mus., N. Y., etc.; c. pf.- and org.-pcs.

Wool'dridge, H. Ellis, Winchester, March 28, 1845—London, 1917; writer; historian; at first a painter and 1895 Slade Prof. of Fine Arts at Oxford; wrote extensively on mediæval music.

Wooll'ett, Henry, Havre, 1864—1936; noted teacher, composer; dir. of music school in native city.

Wormser (vôrm-zăr), **André (Alphonse Toussaint),** Paris, Nov. 1, 1851— Nov. 4, 1926; pupil of Marmontel (pf.) and Bazin, Paris Cons., taking 1st pf.-prize, 1872; Grand prix de Rome, 1875; lived in Paris; c. the opéras-comique *"Adèle de Ponthieu"* (Aix-les-Bains, 1877), *"Rivoli"* (Paris, 1896); v. succ. pantomime *"L'Enfant Prodigue"* (Paris, 1890, London, 1891, New York, 1893); pantomime *"L'Idéal"* (London, 1896); ballet, *"L'Étoile"* (Paris, 1897), etc.

Worobkiewicz (vôr-ôp-k'-yā'-vĭch), **Isidor,** Czernowitz, 1836—Sept. 18, 1903; priest in the Greek church, and pupil on stipend at Vienna Cons.; later teacher of church music at Czernowitz and author; c. Roumanian sengs, etc.

Wot'quenne, Alfred, b. Lobbes, Hennegau, Jan. 25, 1867; pupil Brussels Cons.; 1894, Librarian; d. 1939.

Wouters (voo'-tărs), (**Fran.**) **Adolphe,** Brussels, May 28, 1849—April 16, 1924; pupil, and 1871–1920, pf.-prof. at the Cons. there; 1886, organist Nôtre-Dame de Finistère, and cond. at Saint-Nicolas; c. 3 masses solen-nelles (under pseud. "**Don Adolfo**"), a grand Te Deum, overture, etc.

Woyrsch (voirsh), **Felix von,** b. Trop-pau, Austrian Silesia, Oct. 8, 1860; studied with A. Chevallier, Ham-burg, but mainly self-taught; after 1895, organist and conductor at Altona; c. 4 comic operas incl. succ. "*Wikingerfahrt*" (Nürnberg, 1896), 4 choral works with orch.; symph.; symph. prologue to "*Divina Comme-dia*," etc.; d. Altona, 1944.

Wranitzky (frä-nēt'-shkĭ), (1) **Paul,** Neureisch, Moravia, 1756—Vienna, 1808; violinist, conductor and dram. composer. (2) **Anton,** Neureisch, 1761—Vienna, 1819; violinist; bro. and pupil of above; conductor and composer.

Wüerst (vü'-ĕrst), **Richard (Fd.),** Ber-lin, 1824—1881; teacher, critic and dram. composer.

Wüllner (vĭl'-nĕr), (1) **Fz.,** Münster, Jan. 28, 1832—Cologne, Sept. 8, 1902; noted conductor; studied Mün-ster, later at Berlin, Brussels, Co-logne, Bremen, Hanover and Leipzig, and gave concerts as pianist; 1854, pf.-teacher Munich Cons.; 1858, town mus.-dir. at Aix-la-Chapelle; 1861, "R. Mus.-Dir." 1864, 1882, 1886 and 1890 he conducted the Lower Rhine Mus. Fest.; cond. the ct.-chapel, Munich; 1867, dir. choral classes in the Sch. of Mus.; in 1869, cond. ct.-opera and the Acad. Con-certs (vice von Bülow), giving Wag-ner's "*Rheingold*" and "*Walküre*" their first hearing. 1870, 1st ct.-cond., R. Prof. 1875; in 1877, ct.-cond. at Dresden, and artistic dir. of the Cons.; 1883–84, cond. Berlin Philh.; 1884, dir. Cologne Cons.; was Dr. Phil. Leipzig U.; c. cantata "*Hein-rich der Finkler,*" with orch. (1st prize, Aix-la-Chapelle "Liedertafel" 1864); new arrangement (with added recitatives) of von Weber's "*Oberon*"; Psalm 125, with orch.; Miserere and Stabat Mater, for double chorus, masses. chamber-mus., etc. (2) **Lud-wig,** Münster, Aug. 19, 1858—Berlin, March 22, 1938; son of above; Dr. phil., then studied Cologne Cons.; 1888. dir. a church choir;

became an actor in spite of a vocal impediment, then a tenor singer in concert, also in opera (as "Tann-häuser," etc.). Eminent as a Lieder singer and reciter; toured widely, incl. United States.

Wunderlich (voon'-dĕr-lĭkh), **Jn. G.,** Bayreuth, 1755—Paris, 1819; flute-virtuoso and prof. Paris Cons.; also composer.

Würfel (vür'-fĕl), **Wm.,** Planian, Bo-hemia, 1791—Vienna, 1852; pianist, prof., conductor and dram. composer.

Wurm (voorm), (1) **Mary J. A.,** b. Southampton, 1860—Munich, 1938; pianist; pupil of Pruckner and Stark, Anna Mehlig, Mary Krebs, Jos. Wieniawski, Raff and Frau Schu-mann; 1884, won the Mendelssohn Scholarship; studied with Stanford, Sullivan, Bridge and Reinecke; played with succ. Leipzig, Berlin, etc.; c. an overture; a pf.-concerto; sonatas, etc. Her sisters (2) **Alice** and (3) **Ma-thilde,** also pianists, the latter known as **Verne** (d. London, June 4, 1936), a notable recitalist and teacher.

Wylde (wĭld), **H.,** Bushy, Hertford-shire, 1822—London, 1890; pianist, organist and teacher.

Wyszkowski. Vide HOFMANN, C.

X

Xylander (rightly **Holtzmann**) (ksĕ'-länt-ĕr or hŏlts'-män), **Wm.,** Augs-burg, 1532—Heidelberg, 1576, writer.

Xyndas (ksĕn'-däs), **Spiridion,** Corfú, 1812—(in poverty) Athens, 1896; Greek composer of succ. ballad-operas.

Y

Yon, Pietro, Settimo Vittone, Italy, 1886 —Huntington, N. Y., 1943; studied with Fumagalli, at Turin Cons. and at Acad. of St. Cecila, Rome, winning honours; after 1907 res. in N. Y., where was mus. dir. and org. at St. Patrick's Cathedral; known as organ recitalist; hon. org. of Bas. of St. Peter's, Rome; c. many masses, an oratorio "*The Triumph of St. Pa-trick*"; and many choral and organ works, and songs.

Yonge (yŭng). Vide YOUNG.

Yost (yŏst), **Michel,** Paris, 1754—1786; celebrated clarinettist and composer.

Young, (1) (or **Yonge**), **Nicholas,** b. Lewis, Sussex; d. 1619; pub. "*Musica*

Transalpina," colls. of Italian madrigals, 1597. (2) J. **Matthew Wilson,** Durham, Engl., 1822—W. Norwood, 1897; organist and composer.

Yradier (ē-rădh'-ĭ-är), **Sebastian,** Sauciego, Spain, Jan. 20, 1809—Vitoria, Dec. 6, 1865; Spanish song-composer.

Yriarte (ē-rĭ-är'-tĕ), Don **Tomas de,** Teneriffe, ca. 1750—Santa Maria, near Cadiz, 1791; writer.

Ysaye (ē-sī'-yŭ), (1) **Eugène,** Liége, July 16, 1858—Brussels, May 13, 1931; prominent violinist, son and pupil of a cond. and violinist, then pupil of Liége Cons., and of Wieniawski and Vieuxtemps; later with govt.-stipend studied in Paris; till 1881, leader in Bilse's orch., Berlin, made v. succ. tours throughout Europe and N. America; from 1886, head prof. of vln. Brussels Cons., and leader "Ysaye Quartet"; 1893, Chev. of the Legion of Honour; 1918–22, cond. Cincinnati Symph. and biennial fest.; later again in Belgium; c. opera, *"Peter the Miner"* (1930); suffered amputation of one leg in 1929 and never fully recovered health; c. vln.-concertos; variations on a theme by Paganini; Poème élégiaque for vln. with orch. (or pf.), etc. (2) **Théopile,** Verviers, 1865—Nice, 1918; bro. of (1); composer, pianist; pupil of Liége Cons. and of Franck; dir. of Brussels Acad. of Music.

Yussupoff (yoos'-soo-pôf), Prince **Nicolai,** Petersburg, 1827—Baden-Baden, 1891; violinist; pupil of Vieuxtemps; writer of treatises, and c. a programme-symph. *"Gonzalvo de Cordova,"* with vln. obbligato; *"Concerto symphonique,"* for vln., etc.

Yzac (ē'-zäk). Vide ISAAC.

Z

Zabalza y Olaso (thä-bǎl'-thä ē ō-lä'-sō), Don **Damaso,** Irurita, Navarre, 1833—Madrid, 1894; pianist and teacher; prof. Madrid Cons.; c. studies.

Zabel (tsä'-bĕl), **Albert,** Berlin, 1835—St. Petersburg, 1910; harpist; pupil Berlin Royal Inst. for church mus.; soloist Berlin Opera; from 1851 at Royal Ballet orch. St. Petersburg; from 1862 prof. at the Cons.; c. harp concertos, etc.

Zacconi (tsäk-kō'-nē), **Ludovico,** b. Pesaro, 1555—1627; monk and important theorist.

Zach (tsäkh), **Johann,** (1) Czelakowicz, 1699—Bruchsal, 1773; director at Mayence and composer of church music. (2) **Max Wilh.,** Lemberg, 1864—St. Louis, 1921; violinist and conductor; pupil of Vienna Cons.; played in Boston Symph., and 1887–97 cond. summer concerts there; 1900, mem. Adamowski Quartet; after 1907, cond. of St. Louis Symphony.

Zachau (tsäkh'-ow), (1) **Peter,** town-musician, Lübeck, composer for viola da gamba, 1693. (2) **Fr. Wm.,** Leipzig, 1663—Halle, 1712; Händel's teacher; organist and composer.

Zahn (tsän), **Johannes,** Espenbach, Franconia, Aug. 1, 1817—Neudettelsau, Feb. 17, 1895; historian of church music, and compiler of hymn books, etc.

Zajczek (zä'-ĭ-tsĕk), **Julius,** Vienna, 1877—1929; composer of opera *"Helmbrecht"* (Graz, 1906).

Zajič (zä'-yēch), **Florian,** Unhoscht, Bohemia, May 4, 1853—Berlin, May 17, 1926; violinist; son of poor parents; on a stipend studied at Prague Cons.; member theatre-orch., Augsburg; 1881, leader at Mannheim and Strassburg; 1889, at Hamburg; 1891, teacher Stern Cons., Berlin; later at Klindworth-Scharwenka Cons.; toured widely and was made chamber-virtuoso 1885 and given Russian order of Stanislas.

Zamara (tsä-mä'-rä), (1) **Antonio,** Milan, June 13, 1829—Hietzing, near Vienna, Nov. 11, 1901; harp-virtuoso, pupil of Sechters; teacher at Vienna Cons.; c. for harp, flute, etc. (2) **Alfred Maria,** b. Vienna, April 28, 1863; c. operettas.

Zamminer (tsäm'-mē-nĕr), **Fr.,** Darmstadt, 1818 (?)—Giessen, 1856; acoustician.

Zanardini (tsä-när-dē'-nē), **Angelo,** Venice, 1820—Milan, 1893; c. opera, also writer and translator of libretti.

Zandonai (tsän-dō-nä'-ē), **Riccardo,** Sacco, 1883—Rome, June 18 (?) 1944; pupil of Gianferrai at Trento; from 1899 at Rossini Cons., Pesaro, in 1902 winning comp. prize with symph. poem for voices and orch.; c. also *"Serenata Mediævale"* for cello, 2 harps, and strings; *"Ave Maria"* for female voices, harp, and strings; *"O Padre Nostro"* (from Dante's Purgatorio), for chorus, orch., and organ; operas, *"Grillo del Focolare*

(Cricket on the Hearth) (Turin, 1908), and with great success elsewhere, and the highly succ. "*Conchita*" (based on Pierre Louy's "*Femme et le Pantin*" (Milan, 1911, Covent Garden, 1912, etc.); "*Melænis*" (Milan, 1912); "*Francesca da Rimini*," to a libretto drawn by Tito Ricordi from the tragedy of D'Annunzio (adjudged his masterpiece), (Teatro Regio, Turin, 1914; Met. Op., 1916); "*La Via della Finestra*," on a comic theme from a play by Scribe, book by Adami (Pesaro, 1919); "*Giulietta e Romeo*," a new version of the original Italian story on this subject, book by Rossato (Rome, Teatro Costanzi, 1921); "*I Cavalieri di Ekebù*," after Selma Lagerlöf's novel, "*Gösta Berling*," book by Rossato (La Scala, Milan, 1925); "*Giuliano*," a mystic legend based on Flaubert's story, with book by Rossato (Naples, 1928); "*La Farsa Amorosa*," based on the Spanish comedy, "*Three-Cornered Hat*," (Rome and Milan, 1935–36); also symph. works, "*Concerto Romantico*" for vln. and orch.; Requiem Mass, and various other vocal compositions.

Zandt, van (fän-tsänt), **Marie,** New York, Oct. 8, 1861—Cannes, Dec. 31, 1919; (daughter of (2) Jeanie van Z., singer formerly in Royal and Carl Rosa Companies); pupil of Lamperti, Milan; début, Turin, 1879; sang in London, then from 1880 at Op.-Com., Paris, with great succ.; 1884, temporary loss of voice due to prostration brought on her such violent criticism that she took a leave of absence and sang with succ. at St. Petersburg, etc.; on her return, 1885, she met the same opposition and sang thereafter in England, etc.; compass *a-f'''*.

Zanella (tsä-něl'-lä), **Amilcare,** b. Monticelli d'Ongina, Sept. 26, 1873; pupil of Parma Cons. and from 1903 director, after years as operatic cond. in South America, etc.; c. a symph. fantasie and fugue for piano and orch., operas, etc.; d. 1949.

Zanettini. Vide GIANETTINI.

Zang (tsäng), **Jn. H.,** Zella St. Blasii 1733—Mainstockheim, 1811; cantor; pianist.

Zange (tsäng'-ě) (**Zang'ius**), **Nicolaus,** d. Berlin, before 1620; conductor and composer.

Zani de Ferranti (dsä'-ně dä fěr-rän-tē), **Marco Aurelio,** Bologna, 1800—Pisa, 1878; guitar-virtuoso.

Zanobi. Vide GAGLIANO.

Zan'ten, Cornelie Van, b. Dordrecht, 1855—d. The Hague, 1946; soprano, pupil of Geul, Schneider, and Fr. Lamperti; début in Turin, sang throughout Europe, and with the "National Opera" in America; then sang at Amsterdam and taught in the Cons.; from 1903 teacher in Berlin.

Zarate (thä-rä'-tě), **Eleodoro Ortiz de,** b. Valparaiso, Dec. 29, 1865; pupil of Collegio di San Luis there; 1885 won 1st govt. prize, and studied Milan Cons. with Saladino; won prize 1886, for opera "*Giovanna la Pazza*"; studied in Italy; 1895, prod. the first Chilean opera, the succ. "*La Fioraia de Lugano*" (Santiago, Chile, Nov. 10).

Zaremba (tsä-räm'-bä), **Nicolai Ivanovitch de,** 1821—Petersburg, 1879; teacher.

Zarembski (tsä-rěmp'-shkǐ), **Jules de,** Shitomir, Russian Poland, 1854—1885; pianist, pf.-prof. and composer.

Zarlino (dsär-lē'-nō), **Gioseffo** (called **Zarlinus Clodiensis**), Chioggia, March 22, 1517—Venice, Feb. 14, 1590; eminent theorist, conductor and composer; a Franciscan monk; pupil of Willaert at Venice; from 1565 cond. at San Marco, also chaplain at San Severo; his comps. are almost all lost; he was commissioned by the Republic to write mus. in celebration of Lepanto, a mass for the plague of 1577 and in welcome of Henri III., 1574, on which occasion he also c. a dram. work "*Orfeo*"; his theoretical ability is shown by the great work "*Instituzioni harmoniche*" (1558).

Zarzycki (zär-zěk'-ē), **Alex,** Lemberg, Austrian Poland, 1834—Warsaw, 1895; pianist, conductor and dram. composer.

Zaytz (dsä'-ěts), **Giovanni von,** Fiume, Jan. 21, 1832—Agram, Dec. 17, 1914; pupil of Lauro Rossi, Milan Cons.; 1870 theatre-conductor and singing-teacher at the Cons. at Agram; c. the first Croatian opera "*Nicola Subic Zrinjski*" (1876), also 20 German Singspiele, masses, etc.

Zeckwer (tsěk'-vär), (1) **Richard,** Stendal, Prussia, April 30, 1850—Philadelphia, Dec. 30, 1922; pianist; pupil Leipzig Cons.; from 1870 organist at

Philadelphia; 1870 teacher Phila. Mus. Acad.; 1876 director, composer. (2) **Camille**, son of (1) b. Phila., 1875 —Aug. 7, 1924; pianist, composer.

Zelenka (zĕ-lĕn'-kä), **Jan Dismas**, Lannowicz, Bohemia, 1679—Dresden, 1745; conductor and composer.

Želenski (zhĕ-lĕn-shkĭ), **Ladislas**, on the family estate Gradkowice, Galicia, July 6, 1837—Cracow, Jan. 23, 1921; pupil of Mirecki at Cracow, Krejči at Prague, and Damcke at Paris; prof. of comp., later dir., Warsaw Cons.; c. a symph., 2 cantatas, etc. for orch.; succ. opera *"Goplana"* (Cracow, 1896), etc.

Zell, F. Vide WÄLZEL.

Zel'ler (tsĕ'-lĕr), **Dr. Karl**, St. Peter-in-der-Au, Lower Austria, July 19, 1842—Baden, near Vienna, Aug. 17, 1898; c. operettas.

Zellner (tsĕl'-nĕr), (1) **Ld. Alex.**, Agram, 1823—Vienna, 1894; son and pupil of an organist; editor, professor, writer and composer. (2) **Julius**, Vienna, 1832—Mürzzuschlag, Styria, 1900; c. 2 symphs., etc.

Zelter (tsĕl'-tĕr), **Karl Fr.**, Berlin, Dec. 11, 1758—May 15, 1832; son of a mason; studied with Kirnberger and Fasch, to whom he was assistant and 1800 successor as cond. of the Singakademie; 1809 he founded the "Liedertafel" from which grew the great "Deutscher Sängerbund" of 50,000 members, for which he c. famous male choruses; 1819, founder and dir. R. Inst. for church-mus.; friend of Goethe, whose songs he set; c. also oratorios, etc.

Zemlin'sky, Alexander von, Vienna, Oct. 4, 1872—Larchmont, N. Y., March 16, 1942; composer, conductor; studied Vienna Cons.; cond. at various theatres, then at the Op. in that city; also at Mannheim, Prague, Berlin and elsewhere; c. (operas) *"Sarema," "Es War Einmal," "Kleider Machen Leute," "Kreidekreis";* orch. and choral works, chamber music, piano pieces, songs; brother-in-law and teacher of Schönberg.

Zenatello (tsĕn-ä-tĕl'-lō), **Giovanni**, b. Verona, Feb. 22, 1879; popular operatic tenor, appearing at Covent Garden 1905, and from 1907 in America; 1907-09 at Manhattan Op., N. Y.; 1909-14, Boston Op. Co.; later active as voice teacher in N. Y. and Europe; m. Maria Gay, contralto; d. N. Y., Feb. 11, 1949.

Zenger (tsĕng'-ĕr), **Max**, Munich, Feb. 2, 1837—Nov. 16, 1911; pupil of Stark, and Leipzig Cons.; 1860, cond. at Ratisbon; 1869 mus.-dir. Munich ct.-opera; 1878-85, Munich Oratorio Soc., etc.; Dr. Phil. *h. c.*, 1897; c. 4 operas; succ. oratorio *"Kain"* (after Byron, Munich, 1867), cantatas with orch., "tragic" symph., chamber music, songs, etc.

Zenta. Vide AUGUSTA HOLMES.

Zerr (tsĕr), **Anna**, Baden-Baden, 1822 —on her estate, near Oberkirch, 1881; singer.

Zerrahn (tsĕr-rän), **K.**, Malchow, Mecklenburg, July 28, 1826—Milton, Mass., Dec. 29, 1909; distinguished conductor; studied with Fr. Weber and at Hanover and Berlin; 1848, America, as a member of Germania Orch.; 1854-95, cond. Handel and Haydn Soc., Boston; also cond. Harvard Symph. Concerts, and prof. of harm., instr. and singing, N. E. Cons

Zeugheer (tsoikh'-här), **Jakob** (known as **J. Z. Hermann**), Zurich, 1805—Liverpool, 1865; violinist and conductor.

Zeuner (tsoi'-nĕr), **K. Traugott**, Dresden, 1775—Paris, 1841; pianist, teacher and composer.

Ziani (dsē-ä'-nē), (1) **P. Andrea**, Venice, ca. 1630—Vienna, 1711; organist and dram. composer. (2) **Marco A.**, Venice, 1653—Vienna, 1715; nephew of above; ct. conductor and dram. composer.

Zichy (tsē'-shē), **Count Géza, Sztára,** Hungary, July 22, 1849—Budapest, Jan. 14, 1924; noted left-handed piano-virtuoso, having at 17 lost his right arm; pupil of Mayrberger, Volkmann and Liszt; holding high legal positions; also made tours for charity. 1890-94, Intendant Nat. Th. and Opera, Pesth. C. succ. operas, *"Aldr"* (Pesth, 1896); *"Meister Roland"* (Pesth, 1899, Magdeburg, 1902), cantata, etc.; pf.-pcs., for the left-hand and studies (with preface by Liszt), etc.

Zieg'ler, Edw., b. Baltimore, March 25, 1870—N. Y., 1947; critic; studied music with F. X. Arens; critic, N. Y. *World*, 1903-08; mus. and dram. critic, *Herald*, 1908-17; *American*, 1920; after 1917 exec. of Met. Op. Co., asst. gen. manager, after 1920.

Ziehn (tsēn) **Bernhard**, Erfurt, Jan.

20, 1845—Chicago, Sept. 8, 1912; theorist; came to Chicago 1868; teacher and organist; author of important works: "*Harmonie und Modulationslehre*" (Berlin, 1888), "Five and Six Part Harmonies" (Milwaukee, 1911), etc.

Ziehrer (tsē'-rĕr), **Carl Michael,** Vienna, May 2, 1843—Nov. 14, 1922; military bandmaster; toured; c. 600 dances and an operetta "*Ein tolles Mädel*" (Nuremberg, 1908).

Zilcher (tsĭlkh'-ĕr), **Hermann,** b. Frankfort-on-Main, Aug. 18, 1881; pupil of the Hoch Cons.; c. concerto for 2 violins with orch., violin concerto, etc.; 1901, won Mozart Prize for comp.; 1905, taught Hoch Cons., Frankfort; 1908, Munich Akad. der Tonkunst; after 1920, dir. of State Cons., Würzburg, and cond. of orch. concerts there; c. operas, choral, orch. mus., etc.; d. Würzburg, 1948.

Zimbalist (tsĭm'-bä-lĭst), **Efrem,** b. Rostov, Russia, May 7, 1889; notable violinist; pupil of his father, a conductor; 1901–07 at St. Petersburg Cons. under Auer, winning gold medal and scholarship; toured Europe and 1911 America, where he has made his home for a number of years; c. Slavic dances, etc., for violin. Dir., Curtis Inst. of Mus., Phila.

Zimmermann (tsĭm'-mĕr-män), (1) **Anton,** Pressburg, 1741—1781; conductor, composer and organist. (2) **Pierre Jos. Guillaume,** Paris, March 19, 1785—Oct. 29, 1853; famous pf.-teacher; pupil, later, 1816–48, prof., at Paris Cons., c. comic opera and many pf.-pcs. (3) **Agnes,** Cologne, July 5, 1845—London, Nov. 14, 1925; pianist; at 9 pupil of London R. A. M., winning King's Scholarship twice, and also silver medal; début, Crystal Palace, 1863; toured with great succ.; ed. scores and c. a pf.-trio, etc.

Zingarelli (tsĭn-gä-rĕl'-lē), **Nicola A.,** Naples, April 4, 1752—Torre del Greco, near Naples, May 5, 1837; violinist, teacher and eminent composer; the succ. of his grand operas throughout Europe was almost equalled by his noble and devout sacred mus.; pupil of Fenarolo and Speranza; his first opera was prod. at 16, and followed by another at 21, but he had no succ. till "*Alsinda*," written in 7 days (La Scala, Milan, 1785); he followed this with many others, incl. his best, "*Giulietta e Romeo*" (ibid., 1796); 1792, cond. at Milan Cath.; 1794, at Loreto; 1804 at St. Peter's, Rome, 1811, imprisoned for refusal to conduct a service in honour of the King of Rome, the son of Napoleon, who took him to Paris, released him, and paid him well for a mass; 1813, dir. Naples Cons.; 1816, cond. at the cath.; he was a notable teacher; c. 34 operas, masses of all kinds in a series "*Annuale di Loreto*" for every day in the year, 80 magnificats, etc.

Zingel (tsĭng'-ĕl), **Rudolf Ewald,** b. Liegnitz, Sept. 5, 1876; pupil Berlin Royal Hochsch.; from 1899 dir. Singakad. at Frankfort-on-Oder; from 1907 at Greifswald; c. operas "*Margot*" (Frankfort-on-Main, 1902), "*Liebeszauber*" (Stralsund, 1908), "*Persepolis*" (Rostock, 1909).

Zinkeisen (tsĭnk'-ī-zĕn), **Konrad L. Dietrich,** Hanover, 1779—Brunswick, 1838; violinist, conductor and composer.

Zipoli (dsē'-pō-lē), **Dom.,** organist, Jesuit Church, Rome; pub. important clavier-sonatas, treatises, etc. (1726).

Zoeller (tsĕl'-lĕr), **Carl,** Berlin, 1840—London, 1889; writer and notable composer.

Zoilo (dsō'-ē-lō), **Annibale,** conductor at Laterano, Rome, 1561–70, 1571, singer, Papal Chapel; c. madrigals, etc.

Zöllner (tsĕl'-nĕr), (1) **K. H.,** Oels, Silesia, 1792 — Wandsbeck, near Hamburg, 1836; org.-virtuoso, writer and dram. composer. (2) **K. Fr.,** Mittelhausen, Thuringia, March 17, 1800—Leipzig, Sept. 25, 1860; famous composer of male choruses; pupil of Schicht, Thomasschule, Leipzig; vocal-teacher there, founded a Liedertafel "Zöllner-verein," other socs. of similar nature, organised 1859 to form a "Z.-band." (3) **H.,** b. Leipzig, July 4, 1854; son of above; pupil Leipzig Cons.; 1878, mus.-dir. Dorpat Univ.; 1885, Cologne Cons. and conductor various vocal socs.; 1889, toured Italy with a male chorus; from 1890, cond. New York "Deutscher Liederkranz"; 1898, mus.-dir. Leipzig University and cond. "Paulinerchor"; critic of *Tageblatt* there; 1907 taught Stern Cons., Berlin; 1908, cond. Antwerp Op., after 1912 in Freiburg; c. 10

operas, 11 choral works with orch., cantata *"Die neue Welt"* (won international prize, Cleveland, Ohio, 1892), a symph., oratorio, male choruses; d. May 8, 1941.

Zopff (tsôpf), **Hermann,** Glogau, 1826 —Leipzig, 1883; editor, writer and dram. composer.

Zschiesche (tshē'-shĕ), **Aug.,** Berlin, 1800—1876; dram. bass.

Zschocher (tshôkh'-ĕr), **Jn.,** Leipzig, 1821—1897; pianist.

Zumpe (tsoom'-pĕ), **Hermann,** Taubenheim, Upper Lusatia, April 9, 1850—Munich, Sept. 4, 1903; grad. Seminary at Bautzen; taught a year at Weigsdorf; from 1871 at Leipzig; also studied with Tottmann; 1873-76, at Bayreuth, as copyist and asst. to Wagner; thereafter th. cond. various cities; 1891, ct.-cond. at Stuttgart; 1895, ct.-cond. Munich; later at Schwerin; 1901, Meiningen; c. 2 operas; v. succ. operettas *"Farinelli"* (Vienna, 1886), *"Karin"* (Hamburg, 1888), and *"Polnische Wirtschaft"* (Berlin, 1891); overture *"Wallenstein's Tod,"* etc.

Zumsteeg (tsoom'-shtäkh), (1) **Jn. Rudolf,** Sachsenflur, Odenwald, 1760 —Stuttgart, 1802; 'cellist and ct.-conductor; c. operas and important "durch-komponirten" ballads, before Löwe (q.v.). His daughter (2) **Emilie,** Stuttgart, 1797—1857, was a pop. song-composer.

Zur Mühlen (tsoor-mü'-lĕn), **Raimund von,** on his father's estate, Livonia, Nov. 10, 1854—Steyning, Sussex, Dec. 9, 1931; concert-tenor; studied at Hochschule, Berlin, with Stock-hausen at Frankfort, and Bussine at Paris; later active as an important voice teacher.

Zur Nieden (tsoor nē'-dĕn), **Albrecht,** Emmerich-on-Rhine, 1819 — Duisburg, 1872; mus.-director, conductor and composer.

Zuschneid (tsoo-shnīt'), **Karl,** Oberglogau, Silesia, May 29, 1854—Weimar, Aug. 18, 1926; pupil Stuttgart Cons.; director of societies in various towns; from 1907 dir. Mannheim Hochschule; c. male choruses with orch., etc.

Zvonař (tsvŏ'-närzh), **Jos. Ld.,** Kublov, near Prague, 1824—Prague, 1865; teacher, theorist and dram. composer.

Zweers (tsvärs), **Bernard,** Amsterdam, May 18, 1854—Dec. 9, 1924; composer of 4 symphs., sonatas, etc.; studied with Jadassohn.

Zweig (tsvīg), **Fritz,** b. Olmütz, Sept. 8, 1893; conductor; pupil of Schönberg in Vienna; after 1912, opera conductor at Mannheim; 1921-3, in Barmen-Elberfeld; 1923-5, at the Berlin Grosse Volksoper; 1925, Municipal Op., Berlin; 1927-33, at Berlin State Op.; 1934, Prague; later in U. S.

Zwintscher (tsvĭnt'-shĕr), **Bruno,** Ziegenhain, Saxony, May 15, 1838—near Dresden, March 4, 1905; pianist; pupil of Julius Otto, then of Leipzig Cons.; 1875-98, teacher there; writer.

Zwyssig (tsvēs'-sĭkh), **P. Alberich,** (rightly **Joseph**), Bauen, Nov. 17, 1808—Mehrerau, Nov. 17, 1854; lived at Cistercian abbey Mehrerau; entered the Cistercian order 1826; c. *"Swiss Psalm,"* etc.

SHORT BIOGRAPHIES OF MUSICIANS

JOHANN SEBASTIAN BACH

By Sir Charles Hubert H. Parry

FOR more than a century before J. S. Bach came upon the scene, a succession of exceptionally gifted and earnest composers had been hard at work developing the methods and style of organ-music. Andrea Gabrieli and his nephew Giovanni Gabrieli and Claudio Merulo in Venice and Ian Pieterzoon Swelinck in Amsterdam had already done much to define its true sphere and style before the era of pure choral-music was ended. The early years of the seventeenth century saw Frescobaldi in the zenith of his fame, and his pupil Froberger following worthily in his footsteps; and throughout the century rapid progress in the accumulation of artistic methods and the development of true instrumental forms was made by such famous organists as Scheidt, Scheidemann, Pachelbel, Muffat, Reinken, and Buxtehude. And when it is considered that this branch of art already enjoyed an advantage over the new secular form of art which began to be cultivated at the end of the sixteenth century, through having its foundation securely laid in the old style of sacred choral-music, it seems natural that by the beginning of the eighteenth century it should appear to be the most mature of all the branches of art then cultivated. ¶These circumstances had profound and far-reaching influence upon J. S. Bach's musical character. In unravelling the secrets of art he was naturally attracted by that branch which possessed methods most fully developed for the formulation of the artistic impulses which were urging him to utterance. But the attraction was enhanced by the fact that organ-music had already become a kind of appanage of German composers, and had proved the one special form of art in which the fervent religion of Teutonic Protestants found the highest artistic expression. ¶Hence it came about that, great as his powers were as a composer of choral-music and of suites and secular instrumental music, he was first and foremost a writer of organ-music, and inasmuch as organ-music was the only branch of art which was even approximately mature in his youthful and most impressionable days, the methods and diction of organ-music permeated and served as the foundation of his style in all branches of art which he attempted. In his earlier years he copied out and studied the works of great composers for the organ, and watched with critical appreciation the performances of great organists such as Reinken and Buxtehude. It is easy to trace in his own work the impression made on him by the interlinked suspensions of Frescobaldi and Froberger and by the vivacity of their fugue subjects; by the treatment of chorale melodies with elaborate figuration of accompanying counterpoint in which Pachelbel excelled, by the copious picturesqueness of detail and the richness and emotional force of the harmonisation of Buxtehude. ¶He brought all such specialities of earlier composers into the sphere of his own operations, and fused them into consistency by the force of his personality, and this assimilation became the foundation of his life's work. Most of his best organ-music, such

i. HANS BACH

at *Wechmar* about 1561

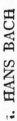
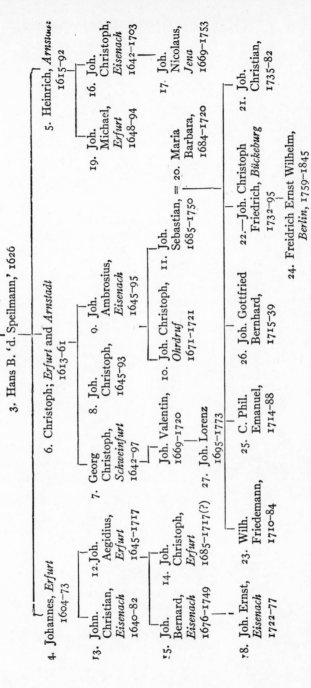

From *Dictionary of Music and Musicians*, by Sir George Grove, edited by J. A. Fuller Maitland, published by The Macmillan Company.

as the sonatas, preludes, fugues, fantasias, canzonas and movements founded
on chorales, and the great passacaglio in C minor, belong to comparatively
early years, and his concentration on this branch of work was only relieved by
the production of a few church cantatas, which showed that he had begun to
consider other forms of art, in which in later years he attained such comprehensive mastery.   After many years spent in several organistships, came the
singular central episode of his life, when the appointment as Capellmeister to
the Prince of Anhalt-Cöthen caused him to apply his mind almost exclusively
for some years to secular instrumental music, mainly of a domestic kind.
¶He sought for his models and types of procedure in the suites and ordres of
the French composers, such as Couperin and Dieupart; and among the examples
of the so-called French overture, which came into prominence in Lulli's operas,
and had found such a brilliant imitator in Muffat.   He studied also the instrumental compositions of the Italians, such as the concertos of Vivaldi, and the
sonatas for stringed instruments of other Italian composers such as Albinoni
and Legrenzi and even German imitations of such works like Reinken's "*Hortus
Musicus*"; and the outcome was a perfect outpouring of suites and partitas for
the domestic keyed instruments, solo sonatas for violin, flute, viole de gamba
and concertos for strings and various combinations of orchestral instruments;
and last and perhaps most notable of all, the collection of the twenty-four preludes and fugues in all keys, which he called—as a sort of manifesto of his belief
in the system of equal temperament, which made all keys equally available for
the purposes of the composer—"*Das Wohltemperirte Clavier.*"   Underlying a
very large proportion of the works of various kinds, even dance tunes or movements for a solo instrument like the violin, fugue principles of procedure are
predominant.   The lightest dance tunes have a contrapuntal texture, and in
the more serious and artistic examples it is so woven as to display beautiful
combinations of ornament and melodic designs, ingenious sophistications of
accent and subtleties of rhythm such as are only possible in the style of instrumental counterpoint which had sprung up in the development of the artistic
requirements of organ fugues.   ¶In the famous collection of preludes and
fugues, which he ultimately increased to forty-eight by the addition of a second
collection, the style of instrumental counterpoint which had been developed for
organ-music found a new but most congenial sphere.   As the works are written
for the domestic keyed instruments such as the tender expressive clavichord,
or the picturesque harpsichord, they necessarily illustrated different artistic
intentions from such as characterised genuine organ-music.   Large scope of
design and powerful effects of tune were obviously out of place, and more subtle
treatment and greater intrinsic interest of detail were inevitable.   ¶Thus the
fugue became much more compact than the organ-fugues, and the treatment
of melodic line and expressive harmony more intimately human.   The composer deals with more variety of style than in his organ-compositions, and many
of the fugues may be taken as studies in human moods, such a playfulness and
gaiety, pathos and melancholy, contemplation and fervour, merriment, dignity,
and confidence.   The adaptation of known principles of artistic procedure to a
purpose, at that time so novel, was characteristic of Bach's attitude toward art;
and this is as true of the preludes as of the fugues.   The genealogy of the preludes may in some cases be traced back as far as the figurate preludes and little
fantasias of such early types as were produced by the Elizabethan composers

of virginal music and their contemporaries in other countries; though the form is enormously enhanced in J. S. Bach's hands by the skilful use of more definite and attractive figures, and a higher balance of organisation in each work. However, the forms of the preludes are extremely various. Some seem to be almost without precedent. As, for instance, the rapturous instrumental song with solo part and accompaniment all combined for one instrument. ¶Among the preludes are also a few of the rare anticipations of complete sonatas of the harmonic kind, movements with distinct contrast of key in the first half, "working out," and modulation in the central part, and a recapitulation of the concrete material of the opening portion to conclude with. These occasional excursions out of what seemed to be his most congenial ground, are often thoroughly successful, but all the same his venture into the Italian manner and the Italian type of form proves rather that he grasped their artistic meaning fully than that he believed in their efficiency as vehicles for the highest aspirations of the composer. In the latter part of his life J. S. Bach dealt more in the grand forms which bring into play the methods and resources of many subordinate forms of art, both instrumental and vocal—such as the noble settings of the Passion, the masses—especially the great one in B minor—the work known as the "*Christmas Oratorio*" and the immense collection of church cantatas written for Sundays and festivals in the churches in Leipzig. In all of these branches of art he had precursors, and the types of various kinds had been explored. The Italian aria-form had been more or less transformed for German purposes before he gave it his own exceptional character and high artistic organisation ¶The peculiar form of expressive recitative, so earnest and deeply emotional, which became a characteristic feature of German music and prefigured much in its latest dramatic manifestations, had found worthy exposition. The treatment of chorales with rich harmonisation and elaborate part-writing and the development of the so-called motet choruses and choral fugues and even the peculiar contrapuntal treatment of the accompanying instruments had all found characteristic German exponents. Moreover, the form of Passion music had engaged the attention of composers for nearly two hundred years and had arrived at a considerable degree of development recently in the hands of Kuhnau, Keiser and Händel himself. But Bach's treatment of the scheme so immeasurably distanced all those who went before him that in later time his settings "*according to St. Matthew*" and "*St. John*" seem to stand almost alone in their pre-eminent glory. The same is the case with his church cantatas. ¶The best work even of such composers as Buxtehude and John Christophe Bach seems singularly bald by the side of the copious variety and the inventive vigour of his work of this kind. True it is that in all such cases, and even in such mighty phenomena as the choruses in the B minor mass, he built upon the foundation his predecessors supplied and with methods they had helped to make available. ¶His peculiar quality was to divine how the resources of art which he found in being could be applied to purposes so grand and comprehensive that it is difficult to realise that the methods were in truth the same as had been used by his forerunners. His artistic powers and insight were at such an immeasurably higher plane than those who preceded him that music seems at once to have stepped out of childishness into maturity at his bidding. ¶In a sense his work is final and isolated. His work stands alone as the summing-up of a long period of preparation; and the summing-up in his characteristically Teutonic direction seemed so complete that nothing remained to be said in the lines which he had illustrated. No composer followed in his footsteps. Those who understood him saw that they could not approach him; and the world in general wanted a more easy-going and accommodating standard of art. So the succeeding generation of composers cultivated the more plausible Italian manner and the easily manipulated Italian form. ¶It was not for a century that his style and methods began to exert influence, and they came back to regenerate the world growing stale with the overpersistency of harmonic forms of the sonata order. ¶Indeed it was the rise of what was called the romantic movement which brought J. S. Bach back into the hearts of men, and made his ways of procedure suggestive of new developments. The foremost prophets of the Romantic movement, Schumann and Chopin, were his most ardent admirers. ¶To the Classicists the style of J. S. Bach had seemed somewhat archaic. But as men began to long for human expression in art and the greater elasticity of form which helps to closer characterisation of mood and feeling, the richness of possibilities and the greater pliancy of the forms Bach used became more and more apparent. At the same time the perfect adaptation of means to ends which his perfect self-containment manifests may serve as a corrective and a counterpoise in the turbulent times which follow the opening of the floodgates of dramatic passion. Those who cherish a constant love of the human art of John Sebastian Bach have still a guiding light which will not betray them. (*See Dictionary entry, page 38.*)

LUDWIG VAN BEETHOVEN

By H. E. KREHBIEL

IN ONE respect Beethoven stands alone in the history of music. The influence of all his fellows, from Bach to Wagner and Brahms, can be determined in matter as well as manner, and set down in plain terms; his full significance is yet to be grounded. Beethoven was a gigantic reservoir into which a hundred proud streams poured their waters; he is a mighty lake out of which a thousand streams have flowed through all the territories which the musical art has peopled, and from which torrents are still pouring to irrigate lands that are still *terrae incognitae*. ¶In some respects his genius is an enigma. Whence came his profound knowledge of the musical art as it existed before him? He was not precocious as Mozart was. He was a diligent pupil, but not an orderly one. Except in childhood he was unruly, and impatient of discipline. The sternness and cruelty of a dissipated father made his earliest studies a suffering and an oppression. In later years he performed his duties toward Albrechtsberger, but refused to yield himself to that teacher's domination as he had already refused to bow to the authority of Haydn—an authority which he felt was too carelessly exercised. Yet the world knows how conscious he was of the potency of the learned forms into which Albrechtsberger strove to induct him, and the charm of romantic expression exemplified in Haydn. ¶He refused to acknowledge these men as his teachers, while they returned the compliment by refusing to own him as their pupil. Haydn condemned his first trios; Albrechtsberger advised his other pupils to have nothing to do with him because, as he said,

"he had never learned anything, and would never do anything in decent style."
Yet Beethoven was proud of his ability in the department of study for which he
had gone to this teacher of counterpoint. In his old age he considered Cherubini the greatest of his living contemporaries, and Händel the greatest of the
great dead. Note the significance: both were masters in the severe forms.
Taking no account of the canons, fugues, and variations which occur incidentally in his symphonies, sonatas, and quartets, we find that Beethoven left an
extraordinarily large number of compositions in these forms behind him—no
less than thirty-five canons, five independent fugues and thirty-two sets of
variations for different instruments. Could there be a more convincing demonstration of his devotion to the scientific side of his art? ¶But he was no
more and no less an iconoclast in these forms than in the romantic. Proof of
another kind I found in an anecdote recorded in Mr. Thayer's note-book as
related to him by the nephew of the observer of the incident. ¶In 1809
Wilhelm Rust sat in a coffee-house in Vienna with Beethoven. A French
officer happening to pass, Beethoven doubled up his fist and exclaimed: "If I
were a general and knew as much about strategy as I know about counterpoint,
being a composer—I'd cut out some work for you fellows." ¶The great
difference between him and his teachers was one of conception touching the
uses to which counterpoint and fugue should be put. To Albrechtsberger the
sciences existed for their own sake; for Beethoven they existed only as a medium
of expression. There was nothing sacrosanct about them. As he himself said,
it was a good thing to learn the rules in order afterward to know what was
contrary to them, and, he might have added, also to know how to violate them
when musical expression could thereby be promoted. ¶Yet Beethoven's
greatest significance as an influence is not as a destroyer of forms and contemner
of rules, as so many would have us believe who justify all manner of lawlessness
to-day and quote Beethoven as an excuse; but as a widener of forms and a creator of rules for the development of expression, which is and must ever remain
the aim of musical art. He was the prototype of Wagner's *Hans Sachs*, who
wished due respect paid to the laws of the poet's craft so that poetical creation
might go on within the lines of beauty, but who also wished spontaneous creative
impulse to have its rights. Where he differed from the pedants who sought to
stem the original flow of his utterance, was in realising better than they that
art-works are the source of rules quite as much as their outcome. He felt, with
Faust, that "In the beginning was the Deed," neither the "Word," nor the
"Thought," nor the "Power," but the "Deed"; from that can be deduced the
other potencies. ¶"Beethoven was not only the embodiment of all that was
before him, but also of that which was yet to come. In his works music returned to its original purpose with its power raised a hundred-fold." I have
said this before and elsewhere, but as I cannot say it better and want it said
again, I say it again, and here. It is easy rhetoric to descant upon the tremendous strides which music has made in the last half century, the transformation
of forms, the augmentation of expressive potencies (rhythmic, melodic, harmonic, instrumental), the widening of the horizon of the things proper to musical
expression and much else; but he has not yet learned his Beethoven who does
not see all that has yet appeared to be essential in these things distinctly foreshadowed in the music of the master who, in a larger, more comprehensive,
more luminous sense than was dreamed of before or since, was priest, king, hero,

and seer. A priest unceasing in his offerings in the Temple Beautiful! A king whose dominion is over the despotic rulers in man's emotional nature! A hero who knew his mission and subordinated to it himself, his longings, his loves, his very life! A seer, as Ruskin says of Imagination, "in the prophetic sense, calling the things that are not as though they were, and forever delighting to dwell on that which is not tangibly present." ¶Like *Faust* he ever heard the dread words ringing in his ears: "*Entbehren sollst du, sollst entbehren.*" His art asked his all; he knew it and gave his all; and then the *Gottheit* which he was wont to invoke, hushed the noises of the material world that he might the better hear the whisperings of the spirit pervading it; and raised a barrier between him and mankind to force him to be a witness and historian of the struggle between the human and the divine reflected in his own soul. All the misanthropy which filled his later years could not shake his devotion to an ideal which had sprung from truest artistic appreciation and been nurtured by enforced introspection. This is the key to Beethoven's music. ¶But it will not serve the purposes of this study merely to generalise. If the contention set forth is to be maintained, there must be some martialling of evidence. Confining ourselves to the cyclical form, the symphony, we note that Beethoven introduced a wider range and a freer use of keys than were employed by his models, Haydn and Mozart; abolished much of what sounds like mere *remplissage* in the connecting portions between themes, substituting therefor phrases developed out of the themes themselves; introduced original episodic matter; extended the free fantasia and coda; developed the old minuet into the scherzo, which could better carry on the psychological story which he wished to tell in the four chapters of his instrumental poem; infused unity into his works, not only by bringing the spiritual bonds between the movements more clearly before our percipience, but also by making the material bonds obvious and incontrovertible. This last achievement has its simplest as well as most eloquent illustrations in the community of rhythms between the first, third, and last movements of the *Fifth Symphony*, and all the movements of the *Seventh;* the recurrence of themes in different movements of the *Fifth* and *Ninth;* the family likenesses, physiognomical resemblances, between the principal melodies of the *Ninth;* finally the programmatic conceit back of the *Sixth.* ¶The acceptance and continuation of the hints contained in these innovations is published in the abolition of pauses between the movements in the "Scotch" symphony of Mendelssohn, the adoption of the same device by Schumann, together with community of theme in the symphony in D minor, the invention of *"l'idée fixe"* by Berlioz for his *"Symphonie Fantastique"* and the successive recapitulation of material already used in the second, third, and fourth movements in the symphony, *"From the New World,"* by Dvořák. ¶It has not been necessary to go far afield for examples; the proofs are surely convincing and come down to our own day. Moreover we find an illustration of the same principle, coupled with an exposition of Beethoven's system of thematic, instead of melodic, development—another form of variation, in brief—in all the symphonic poems of Liszt and his imitators down to Richard Strauss. ¶Beethoven's license may have degenerated into lawlessness, but he pointed a way that has been followed in all the particulars enumerated, and also broke down the barriers between voices and instruments in the symphonic forms to the delight of many successors. His revolutionary proceeding in the Ninth symphony found imitation by Mendelssohn in his *"Hymn of Praise,"* by Berlioz in his *"Romeo and Juliet,"* by Liszt in his *"Faust"* and *"Dante"* symphonies, by Nicodé in *"Das Meer,"* and by Mahler in his symphony with contralto solo. (*See page 51.*)

HECTOR BERLIOZ

By Ernest Newman

Berlioz's early influences were as much literary as musical. His reading was mainly romantic; his musical gods were Beethoven, Weber, and Gluck, whose orchestral works influenced him most. He knew little of Beethoven's piano writings, and did not like Bach. ¶Into the intellectual world of the Beethoven symphony and the operas of Gluck and Weber he breathed the newer, more nervous life of the French Romanticists. Colour and sensation became as important as form and the pure idea. ¶These influences and his literary instincts led him to graft the programme form on the older symphony. All his music aims at something concrete. Instead of the abstract world of the classical symphonists he gives us definite emotions, or paints definite scenes. Colour, passion, and veracity were the prime needs; form had to follow their guidance. Hence both his successes and his failures. His virtue is truth and vivacity of expression; his defect the pursuit of these to the detriment of the musical interest. ¶All modern programmists have built upon him—Liszt, Richard Strauss, and Tschaikowsky. Wagner felt his influence, though he belittled it. ¶His own words, "I have taken up music where Beethoven left it," indicate his position. He is the real beginner of that interpenetration of music and the poetic idea which has transformed modern art. (*See page 59.*)

GEORGES BIZET

By Edward E. Ziegler

As Bizet's last work was his best, it is logical to argue that his untimely death has cheated us of compositions more valuable than *"Carmen"*; but beyond mere conjecture such an estimate can have no value and his rank among opera-composers must be determined by *"Carmen."* That the stage was his real field, is proven clearly by the persistency with which he composed for it, and a study of his different efforts proves the wisdom of his choice, for there are no master-pieces among his songs, or among his piano-compositions, and even his most successful orchestral number is the *"First Suite"* compiled for his incidental music to Daudet's *"L'Arlésienne."* ¶His early letters confess his musical creed: Mozart and Beethoven, Rossini and Meyerbeer; this is catholic, to say the least, but later he acknowledged his preference for the Germans in general and Beethoven as the master of all. But Bizet was a stranger to the larger forms in music—for two years he toiled intermittently at a symphony and produced only the *"Roman Suite"* as a result—and his work shows more tendency to follow Gounod's teaching than that of his high ideals. He was bitterly accused of being a follower of Wagner; Paris, knowing so lamentably little of

Wagner's music, then condemned that of Bizet's, which it did not like or could not understand, by labelling it "Wagnerian," and thus put it hopelessly beyond the possibility of discussion.   As a matter of fact there is no trace of Wagner to be found in Bizet's music, and the only resemblance between the two is that both were innovators who presented their theories about dramatic art in practical forms, proving them by their operas.   ¶Bizet realised the sorry state of the French operatic stage, but contented himself with an effort at reforming the minor stage of the Opéra-Comique, and it is doubtless due in a great measure to the precedent of *"Carmen"* that to-day the Opéra-Comique is on a higher artistic plane than the Opéra.   ¶A direct musical influence it would be difficult to trace to Bizet.   As an orchestral colourist he had been outdone and outdared by even his contemporaries; nor did he bequeath to us a new art-form.   But because he demanded a more sincere libretto than any of those with which that maker of marionette opera-books, Scribe, had conjured all Paris, and because in his music he did not fear contact with throbbing life, he commands our respect.   His work shows a musical sincerity foreign to French composers generally, and he deserved a better fate than a sequence of failures ending with an early death.   (*See Dictionary of Musicians entry, page 64.*)

JOHANNES BRAHMS

By James Huneker

Schumann, in his much-discussed article "New Paths," called Brahms the true successor to Beethoven.   His prediction was verified.   To-day Johannes Brahms stands for the ultra-classic in symphonic music, though singularly enough he is really a hardy romanticist, who has widened and deepened the symphonic form.   The career of Brahms compared to Wagner's was a quiet, scholarly, uneventful one.   A severe student and self-critic, he made his way slowly, for the Wagner furor was at hand, and the modest writer of chamber music, of songs and symphonies, was completely eclipsed by the glory of his so-called rival.   ¶It was Von Bülow's audacious epigram, "The three B's,—Bach, Beethoven, and Brahms," that drew down upon the head of the innocent composer the ire of the Wagner camp.   As a matter of record Brahms never posed as an opponent, much less as a rival of the Bayreuth hero; indeed he was an admirer, and knew his scores as only he could know a score—absolutely.   But he was not in the least affected by Wagner—how could he be, working as he did in such a totally different *genre?*   This *genre*, however, was not the out-worked vein it was so contemptuously christened by the new men.   To-day Brahms is a modern among the moderns—indeed his has also been called the music of the future.   ¶To old forms like the symphony, to the smaller forms, he has brought an abounding invention, a vitality in execution, and a musical intellect the most profound since Beethoven's.   To the complex symphonic structure of Beethoven he had superadded a polyphony almost Bachian in its mastery of intricate voicing and the weaving of a marvellous contrapuntal web.   The dignity of his themes, the depth and sweetness of his *cantilena*, the massiveness of his musical architecture—he is in music the born builder—combined with a fecund fantasy, a grim but elastic humour, and no little susceptibility, mark Brahms as one of the elect, a master among masters. His control of the orchestra is absolute in its eloquence, though he is no painter, no seeker after the unique word, the only colour. ¶He has been reproached for a colour monotone by those critics who are easily moved by brilliant and showy externals. But that reproach falls to earth when the adaptability of the garb to the musical idea is discovered. Brahms never erred in this matter; his taste was impeccable. ¶He had a message and he delivered it in tones that befitted its weight, its importance. He is a symphonist primarily; his themes as if carven from granite are symphonic and not dramatic themes, and in his development of them he is second only to Beethoven. A philosopher, he views his subject from every possible side, and the result is an edifice of tone comparable to a Gothic Cathedral. In his songs he is the sweet-voiced, the tender German lyrist, deep in feeling, capricious, noble and moving as Schumann or Schubert. He will rank with these song writers. In chamber music, in the amiable conjunction of piano and strings, trios, quartettes, quintetts, horn-trio and two clarinet-quintetts, Brahms is supreme. He has written a sterling violin-concerto dedicated to Joachim and played first by him. His two piano-concertos in D minor and B flat major, introduced here by Rafael Joseffy, are masterpieces; though pianists complain of the dearth of display passages, they are sincere in feeling and perfect concertos in the balance of the solo instrument with the orchestra. ¶The Brahms solo piano-music is a new and independent literature. He wrote three sonatas; of these the last is the most popular; its andante and scherzo are beautiful specimens of piano-writing. The solo scherzo in E flat minor, opus 4, was a great favourite with Liszt, who saw in it traces of Chopin. The little pieces written during the closing years of the composer's life are exquisite and poetic gems, conceived by a poet, executed with all the dainty cunning of a lapidary. These miniatures are Brahms in his most genial mood. The forger of thunderbolts was now resting and plotting lovely little gardens of fragrant flowers. ¶His extraordinary technical invention is nowhere better evidenced than in his Paganini variations for the piano, the Ultima Thule of pianists. These variations are paralleled in his St. Anthony variations for orchestra, a noble disproof of the assertion that Brahms had no intimate feeling for the orchestra. His *German Requiem* written in 1868 is tremendous in its scope and elemental power. It is the apotheosis of a nation's grief. ¶He was not uniformly successful—little wonder, for his published works number 130. But if this Titan stumbled, was intermittent in his inspiration, the main body of his work stands out marmoreal, of overwhelming grandeur, truly German, and withal, sounding the big note as no one has sounded it in music since Beethoven. (*See page 77.*)

FRÉDÉRIC FRANÇOIS CHOPIN

By James Huneker

Chopin's home education doubtless preserved in him a certain feminine delicacy which never deserted him. ¶At the age of nine he played a Gyrowetz concerto in public and improvised, but seemed more solicitous about the impression his new collar made on the audience, than for the success of his music. ¶As a composer of nineteen he was remarkable and far in advance of his critics and audiences. The disturbed political atmosphere of Poland coupled with an unsuccessful love affair—he vainly adored the singer Constantia Gladowska— decided him on a residence in Vienna. There his playing did not create any enthusiasm, and in the fall of the year he went to Stuttgart *en route* for Paris. It was in the German city that he heard of the downfall of Warsaw and of his patriotic hopes; for Chopin was a fierce patriot, but because of his slender physique, a non-combatant. He journeyed at once to Paris and settled there. ¶His intimacy with the famous novelist George Sand lasted ten years, and her influence, hurtful according to some, and valuable according to others, was most potent and enduring. His sensitive nature was subject to many rude shocks during his companionship with the coarser-fibred and more intellectual woman. Yet it cannot be denied that from his most ardent pangs, he, artist- like, contrived to wring some of his sweetest and most subtle music. The shock of the separation, a separation that was inevitable, shattered Chopin's bruised spirit, and two years later he died, if not of a broken heart, partially of dis- appointment, chagrin, and spleen. His lungs, always weak, became hopelessly diseased, and after a profitless tour in England and Scotland, where he was really too weak to play, he died of consumption and was buried in Père-Lachaise, near the graves of Cherubini and Bellini. His funeral, an imposing one, called out the representative artistic spirits of the city. Seldom has genius been so accompanied to its last resting-place. ¶During his lifetime Chopin was the centre of a circle of wit, talent, and fashion. Balzac, Delacroix, Liszt, Meyer- beer, Heine, Bellini, Berlioz, Mendelssohn, were a few among his intimate associates. His spiritual and original piano-playing admitted him into the inner circle of aristocracy, and he was sought for persistently until his life was sapped by sorrow and constant social duties. ¶Chopin played but seldom in public, for he was unfitted by nature to cope with the audiences of the larger concert halls. That task he gratefully resigned to Liszt. But in the twilight of the salon among the favoured choice souls, his playing took on almost un- earthly qualities. His touch, light in weight, was exquisite in *timbre;* his tone ranged from *forte* to a feathery *pianissimo*, while his style was absolutely unique. Tender, martial, ironical, capricious, gay, and sad, this young Pole held in bondage the entire emotional gamut. Never had the piano sounded so before, sounded so aërial, so witty, so passionate; and it may be doubted if it has sounded thus since; for, while Liszt, Rubinstein, Tausig, Joseffy, Heyman, DePachmann, Essipoff, Rosenthal, and Paderewski were, and are, remarkable interpreters, yet those who heard Chopin the pianist despair in their efforts to describe his spiritual performances. His light, finely articulated hand explains some of the characteristics of his technics; the wide-spread harmonies, the changeful play of inner voices; the novel figuration; and the lovely melodic life. ¶Chopin is the poet of his instrument, the musical poet of Poland. He caught up and treasured the folk-songs of his country, and gave them to the world in an idealised form. His mazurkas are tiny poems full of caprice, wounded pride, ecstatic moments; his four ballads are epical in scope, containing noble melodies, the form absolutely original; the four scherzos are evidences of Chopin's creative powers, for here the form is again novel; the content startling. Bitterness, frantic and cruel, followed by rapturous outbursts of melody arouse in the listener the most vivid emotions. It is Chopin at the apex of his power. The polonaises are passionate and patriotic, or else fantastic and graceful, but always wonder-breeding. His waltzes are for the salon, and for the soul—like the mazurkas. Of the three sonatas, the one in B flat minor is the most satisfactory. Without organic unity it nevertheless astonishes by its originality and depth. Its slow movement is the funeral march, now a banal concert number. In his four Impromptus Chopin is full of charm, while in the *Barcarolle* and in the *Fantaisie, opus 49* he almost achieves perfection. The nocturnes and *Cradle Song*, now for the most part war-worn from repetition, contain much beautiful music. *The Studies, opus 10* and *25* with the *Preludes, opus 28* are Chopin in all his dazzling invention, his never-failing fancy, poetry, daring harmonic innovations and moving melodic richness. ¶He changed the modern map of music by his subtle and profound experimentings with the possibilities of chromatic harmonies, and for this ranks among the great composers. Within his range he is the most perfect lyrist that ever sang, and the ethereal sonorities of his style, his discreet and original use of the *tempo rubato*, make him a forerunner of all that is free, individual and exotic in latter-day music. ¶Chopin was not happiest in writing for orchestra or for piano in conjunction with violin or violoncello. His two concertos contain charming episodes, but do not cohere, do not make the eloquent appeal of the smallest of his mazurkas. He was not fashioned for the epic, this master of intimate moods. He wrote variations, fantasies, a 'cello-sonata, a piano-trio and bolero, a tarantelle and songs. ¶We have forgotten them; but never so long as the piano remains the piano, will Chopin be forgotten. He is, as Rubinstein said, its soul. (*See page 100.*)

CLAUDE DEBUSSY

By RICHARD ANTHONY LEONARD

A CONTEMPORARY once described Debussy as "a musician of genius, who has the forehead of a Pekinese dog, a horror of his neighbour, a fiery glance and a slightly husky voice." If the portrait is only partly flattering, at least it leaves us assured that Debussy was extraordinary even down to the unimportant externals. He *was* a man of genius—one of the greatest of a century which teemed with geniuses. He was the founder of the so-called school of impressionism in music; he gave it a form, a language, and a spirit, and he endowed it with most of its finest works. To French music in general he provided an impetus that had been lacking for many years; he liberated it from the Germanic influence and bequeathed it a style in harmony with the character of the French. His influence on all modern music has been enormous. The stream of musical thought has taken on new colours and flows to-day in different channels than it would have, had Debussy never lived. ¶If he had a bulging forehead, then it was simply the outward evidence of a powerful intellect, of a mind capable of grappling with some of the most difficult problems that ever confronted any artist, and of solving many of them. If he had a horror of his neighbour, it was merely one of the phases of his solitary and fastidious nature. The obvious and the hackneyed repelled him; he was drawn instead to the internal, intangible side of life, to the reticent and the hidden. There lay the inspiration for his impressionistic art. If he had a fiery glance, so, too, did he have stubborn courage. His was a soul in rebellion and he needed a certain obstinacy and a disdain of his inferiors if he was to achieve his revolutionary ends. ¶Debussy was in revolt even as a youth of sixteen at the Paris Conservatoire, where he shocked his teachers by questioning the classic rules of harmony and counter-point. He was a brilliant enough student to win the coveted Prix de Rome at the age of twenty-two, with his cantata *"L'Enfant Prodigue,"* but he left his studies at the Villa Medici in Rome before the three-year course was completed. In his sky loomed the gigantic figure of Richard Wagner, the great god of all nineteenth-century revolutionists, the man who had broken down the barriers of form in music, given melody a new elasticity and freedom, and let harmony run riot. ¶But Debussy's most potent early influences came from the sister art of painting, where a group of men known as the impressionists were in rebellion against the established canons of the Academy. This famous move-ment grew from the studies by Edouard Manet of the effect of light and atmos-phere on colour. The impressionists sought to interpret not so much the direct or photographic representation of an object as the impression which that object left upon them—the emotions which it conjured up. They were more concerned with light, colour, and atmosphere than with form and structural balance. To this new art, and to its practitioners and champions, Debussy was powerfully drawn. He came to know the work of Manet and Monet, Pissarro, Degas, and Whistler. He sought the company and literary advice of the allied poets and writers—the "Symbolists"—Stéphane Mallarmé, Pierre Louÿs, Paul Verlaine, and André Gide. ¶As early as 1894, when he was but thirty-two, Debussy had already laid the foundations of his refined, subtle, and exquisitely fashioned art. In that year he completed *"L'Après-midi d'un Faune,"* after the famous eclogue of his friend Mallarmé. In this superb score (it remains to-day one of the most perfect of all Debussy's works) his music evokes with sensuous delicacy the dreams and desires of a faun on a hot summer afternoon. It was an instant success. Even the more obtuse critics of his time realised that a new voice of singular impressiveness had spoken. ¶With his next major works, the three *"Nocturnes"* for orchestra *("Nuages," "Fêtes"* and *"Sirènes"),* Debussy's impressionistic methods had become firmly fixed. In these scores all is cloudlike and impalpable; the orchestral colouring is transparent and light as air. The composer uses his instruments with a marvellous economy and yet with a richness of effect that is magical. His harmonic scheme is new and daring, while the old ideas of harmonic progression he discards, until his modu-lations move freely outside the boundaries of a key centre. After the first performances of these works, in 1900, Debussy had definitely arrived as a composer. But his greatness was far from established. It was still to be many years before the more conservative critics and even many musicians of discern-ment could stomach his advanced style. ¶In 1902 came the first performance of his opera, *"Pelléas and Mélisande,"* a work which had absorbed Debussy's creative energies for more than ten years. No opera since *"Tristan and Isolde"* let loose such torrents of controversy. It divided the music world into two warring factions: one side saw the composer reducing the established canons of opera to fragments in a manner straining for novelty and effect; the other looked upon him as the Messiah of a new movement in music, and called *"Pelléas and Mélisande"* the most perfect work for the lyric stage since *"Tristan and Isolde."* Debussy had, in fact, succeeded in carrying out the ideal which Wagner set up but never fully realised himself: i.e., the perfect union of poetic text, dramatic action, and music. In *"Pelléas and Mélisande"* the music moves hand-in-hand with the drama; there are no arias, no set vocal pieces, and no thematic development in the orchestra to hamper the dialogue on the stage. The drama unfolds itself in song of a recitative style, following the inflections of the speaking voice. Under this the orchestra lays a richly decorative pattern of sound, accenting and underlining the text and action but only at rare moments rising in climactic intensity to overshadow all else. ¶Following *"Pelléas and Mélisande"* Debussy's creative powers moved rapidly to their apex. Between 1902 and 1912 he produced some of his finest piano music (including the Preludes, *"L'Isle joyeuse"* and the superb *"Reflets dans l'eau"*) as well as his three great orchestral canvases, *"La Mer," "Iberia,"* and *"Rondes de Printemps."* In *"La Mer"* and *"Iberia"* Debussy reached the highest point in the development of impressionism in music. Here colour and atmosphere are present in unparalleled richness, while the old frameworks of form and contrapuntal development have almost vanished. Debussy is the master of his technique. And he refutes, once for all, the notion that his art is effeminate or essentially small-scaled. ¶Debussy was to produce one more major work of consequence, his *"Le Martyre de Saint-Sebastien"* in 1911, and thereafter his art began to suffer a tragic decline. It grew formularised, mannered, stale. The composer seemed no longer able to rouse himself from the laziness which had always been his besetting sin. The outbreak of the World War affected him profoundly, and in 1915 he began to suffer acutely from the disease which was to cause his death three years later. His work during this period is often the merest shadow of its former greatness. Composition had always been difficult for him; and now, under the pressure of the war horror, the ever-increasing pain of his disease, and a recalcitrant inspiration, the effort of work must have become intolerable. He tried heroically to continue, but in March 1918 he died—this creator of some of the most exquisite sounds in all music—to the noise of "Big Bertha's" shells crashing into the streets of Paris. ¶With the passage of time and the appearance of composers even more revolutionary, much of the strangeness has disappeared from the music of Debussy. His technical discoveries and innovations have been analysed until they are the familiar property of every music student and the common coin of even the modern jazz band arranger. Even so, his contributions to the purely technical side of music are not yet fully appreciated. ¶Debussy is most famous for his unusual harmonies. He began early to use chords which did not belong to the scale or key of the work. Gradually these interlopers assumed greater and greater importance until in his mature works the idea of a key centre almost disappears and it is often impossible to name the key or tonality that predominates at a given moment. Debussy used the chord as an entity in itself, not merely as the support of a melody or the result of the contrapuntal movement of different voices. He mixed completely unrelated chords, and he made great use of chords of the seventh, ninth, and eleventh. From Wagner he learned the subtle aesthetic value of the dissonance and he expanded its use with telling effect. One of his favourite devices was the "gliding" of chords, that is, the parallel movement of the same chord through any of the twelve tones of the scale. This required, of course, the use of parallel or "consecutive" fifths and octaves—once the unforgivable sin of orthodox harmony. ¶Another of Debussy's most valuable innovations was his use of neglected scales, notably the whole-tone scale and the pentatonic, or five-tone scale. The former in particular is used so extensively that it gives its characteristic colouring to a great part of the composer's work. Debussy also employed the medieval modes, for their novel tonal colouring and to gain the effect of a classic or archaic style; and there are uses of the ancient organum of the early Roman Church. ¶Great as was his mastery of harmony, Debussy could never have wrought as he did without equal gifts for melody—melody being in the last analysis the *sine qua non* of all music that endures. For a long time his singular skill in this respect was overlooked, largely because he neither harmonised nor developed his themes in the expected manner. Now, when we may see his work in truer perspective, his melodic material stands out in its proper light— beautifully curviform, full of originality and exquisite charm. ¶Of Debussy's use of the orchestra it is difficult to speak without excess of praise. For his most delicate, most elusive, most enigmatic ideas he seemed always able to find the most richly eloquent orchestral voice. He expanded the entire instrumental palette, inventing a whole new range of prismatic values. Yet his most magical effects are often achieved with a reticence and an economy of means that leave us breathless. (*See Dictionary of Musicians entry, page 119.*)

MANUEL DE FALLA

By Richard Anthony Leonard

THE GREAT NATIONALIST MOVEMENT in music, which began in Russia in the nineteenth century, had its repercussions all over Europe. Composers in Germany, Hungary, France, Italy, and England awoke to the possibilities of native folk music and legend as the source of their inspiration. But Spain lagged behind. For many years the most effective Spanish music was composed by men who were not Spaniards at all, but Frenchmen like Bizet, Chabrier, Debussy and Ravel, and even Russians like Rimsky-Korsakoff. ¶The first important steps toward a truly native Spanish music were taken by Albeniz and Granados; but neither of these men ever gained the stature sufficient to place them in the class of first-rate creators. Both were gifted in manipulating the externals of the Spanish idiom—the characteristic dance rhythms and melodies, the warm, languorous colouring. But for the most part the best contributions of both were in the smaller forms—piano pieces and songs. With the rise of Manuel de Falla, however, Spain has at last produced a composer of unquestioned genius; one who, almost single-handed, has created a genuinely nationalistic music for his country. ¶Falla was born in Cadiz, in Andalusia, in 1876. His first important work was the short opera, "*La Vida Breve*," composed in 1904 and 1905, in which he displays a remarkable maturity of style and technique. Two years later Falla went to Paris, where he met Debussy. That was the most important event in his creative life, for he fell under the spell of the French composer, absorbing the ideas of Impressionism which were to influence all his major works thereafter. ¶The most immediate effect of this new influence was the composition of the three Nocturnes for orchestra and piano, "*Nights in the Gardens of Spain.*" Then followed what is probably Falla's masterpiece, the ballet "*El Amor Brujo*," performed with great success in 1915.

A second ballet, "*The Three Cornered Hat*," produced by Diaghileff in 1919, made the composer internationally famous. Since then Falla's chief works have been a marionette opera, "*The Puppet Show*," and a concerto for harpsichord. It will be noted that Falla's output has been comparatively small; even so, it has been sufficient to bring him world fame and an honoured place among the most important composers of his time. ¶Falla's music represents by far the finest and most effective use that has yet been made of the Spanish idiom. It is infinitely more subtle and truer to the spirit of Spain than any of the attempts made by foreign composers, with the exception of Debussy. For Falla, although steeped in the folk music and popular dance tunes of Spain, never makes direct use of them. In his music the conventional mannerisms of melody, the dance rhythms, the characteristic harmonies and ornamental figures are suggested, insinuated, but rarely referred to directly. For these purposes the impressionistic technique is, of course, invaluable; and Falla's debt to Debussy is undeniably large. His harmonic scheme is thoroughly "modern" in scope and exceptionally rich—not at all bound by the limits of his native material. In the field of orchestration Falla has developed effects of great beauty and originality, sometimes by borrowing the effects belonging to popular Spanish instruments. He works subtly and often with disarming simplicity to achieve his ends. ¶In his finest works, like "*El Amor Brujo*" and "*Nights in the Gardens of Spain*," this composer has made a notable contribution to the music of our time, not only in the quality of the work itself, but by his proof that the Spanish idiom can be made the basis for great music in the larger forms. So completely is he the master of his materials that he is able to give them variety instead of monotony, and a universal rather then a narrow provincial appeal. (*See Dictionary of Musicians entry, page 121.*)

CÉSAR FRANCK

By Richard Anthony Leonard

IT IS NO EXAGGERATION to say that the father of modern French music came perilously close to dying without issue. For César Franck, the man whose work engendered the rebirth of music in France after 1870, lived for almost three quarters of his life in obscurity. It was not until after his fifty-fifth year that he began to produce the series of masterpieces which brought him posthumous fame and a place among the immortals of his art. French music had declined hopelessly after Berlioz; Rosa Newmarch declares that the public taste had "degenerated into a craze for opera of a merely frivolous kind." Then came this shy, painfully modest little organist and pedagogue who was to build, in the twilight of his life, a new and enduring edifice of cathedralesque beauty, one that rested for the most part upon the solid classicism of J. S. Bach. Ambitious young French composers of the eighteen-eighties, who had despaired of the future music of their country, listened to Franck's violin sonata and his string quartet, to his "*Beatitudes*" and the Symphony in D minor—and raised their eyes in wonder. Here at last was a French composer (albeit he was born in Belgium) who by a lifetime of industry and with stainless purity of motive could revive and expand the old classic forms and clothe them with a new aesthetic personality of his own. Thus César Franck became the spiritual father of most of the younger men who were to help him restore French music to its former greatness—of D'Indy, Chausson, Duparc and of Debussy and Ravel. ¶The salient qualities of Franck's music can be explained only by the details of his life and character. Born in Liége in 1822, the son of a banker, he was brought by his father to the Paris Conservatoire at the age of fifteen. He became one of the most brilliant and talented pupils of that venerable institution, and was advised to follow the career of virtuoso. But once he had left the Conservatoire he was hardly ever again to be beyond the pressure of economic necessity. He became a church organist and a teacher of the piano. Vincent D'Indy (his pupil, biographer, and devoted disciple) has left us a picture of his master that is both revealing and pathetic. Every morning for almost fifty years Franck arose at five-thirty and spent two hours at composition. After breakfast he went out to give his piano lessons, hurrying all over Paris to provide the rudiments of music training to recalcitrant young ladies in boarding schools and colleges . . . "invariably in a hurry, invariably absent-minded and making grimaces, running rather than walking, dressed in an overcoat too large and trousers a size too short." In the evening, after a long day of teaching, he still had energy left for a few minutes' work on his scores. When he became organist of the Church of Ste. Clothilde, a post he held for thirty years, he began to satisfy the only other great passion in his life besides composition. He was a great organist and a transcendent improviser. In 1866 Franz Liszt went to Ste. Clothilde and after hearing Franck left "evoking the name of J. S. Bach in inevitable comparison." ¶That was Franck's life for half a century. There is no doubt that under the strain of the teaching routine his music suffered; for most of his earlier work, though competent and sincere, is seldom of first quality. But through perseverance, prodigious industry, and selfless devotion to his ideal he succeeded at last. After he had reached the age of fifty-five he began to produce the great works which finally brought him fame. His quintet for piano and strings, his oratorio, "The Beatitudes," the prelude, chorale and fugue for piano, the symphonic variations; the sonata for violin and piano, the Symphony in D minor, the string quartet, and the three organ chorales are all products of this closing period of his life. ¶Because his music was so much the soul of classic purity, without the slightest acknowledgment to current fads or styles, even Franck's finest works were often slow in achieving deserved recognition. At the first performance of the Symphony in D minor, Gounod pronounced the work "the affirmation of incompetence pushed to dogmatic lengths." But Franck merely said, "Oh, it sounded well, just as I thought it would." He became so used to obscurity and so indifferent to public acclaim that he seemed almost surprised when fame at last overtook him. When his string quartet scored an unexpected success at a performance in Paris in 1890, Franck was utterly bewildered by the ovation. "There, you see," he said, "the public is beginning to understand me." He was then sixty-eight years old and within a few months of his death. ¶For the expression of his musical ideals Franck was fortunate in two aspects of his purely technical equipment: the first was his mastery of the classic forms, the result of a lifetime of study as well as a natural predilection; and the second was his extraordinary resource as a harmonist. Franck's harmonies remain to-day the most characteristic feature of his work. They are richly varied and expressive, full of unexpected chromatic modulations, flooded with colour and light. Franck owed much in this respect to Wagner and to Liszt; but his music is mostly lacking in the sensuous qualities that mirrored the passions of the great Germans. Sensuosity seemed not to exist for Franck. He was a man of almost saint-like modesty, for whom the love of his fellow men was a cardinal life-principle. His piety was utterly sincere, his faith in his religion deep and abiding. This spiritual and mystic nature speaks in almost every bar of his works. His music soars and sings; it is full of the choiring of angelic voices, the perpetual adoration of heavenly hosts. (*See Dictionary of Musicians entry, page 155.*)

GEORGE GERSHWIN

By FERDE GROFÉ

GERSHWIN proved in his own achievements what Paul Whiteman and I had always believed when we were first associated in his band (I as pianist and arranger): that the better elements of jazz could be incorporated into art music and be the basis of a series of symphonic creations typically expressive of our nation. ¶Until Gershwin wrote his "*Rhapsody In Blue*," our serious American orchestral composers had been preponderatingly influenced by their German and French predecessors and contemporaries. Of course, there were essays in adapting the Indian and Negro idioms, but there was nothing that completely represented the particular spirit, atmosphere and voice of our land. Even Dvořák's "*New World*" symphony, themed with tunes of Southern implication, was found by experts to be more Czech than American. ¶Gershwin's early songs showed strong originality in melody, harmony and rhythm, but it was not until he composed the "*Rhapsody*" and the "*Preludes*" for piano, that critics pricked up their ears, promoted him from Broadway, and admitted him into the charmed circle of serious creators. ¶I had done some arranging for Gershwin before he came to me with the piano score of the "*Rhapsody*" in 1923–24. I was astonished at the resource and taste displayed in his newest manuscript. It fired my imagination and inspired me as I had never been before. Naturally I am proud of the orchestration of the "*Rhapsody*." ¶There are those who do not think that Gershwin grew musically after the "*Rhapsody*," but I disagree with them emphatically. I consider his "*Concerto in F*" the most important piano opus in that form ever to come from the pen of an American composer. It is essentially individual and national, with a slow movement of irresistible feeling. The "*Second Rhapsody*" is completely different from the "*Blue*," and yet speaks in novel and convincing utterance. "*An American in Paris*" is a lifelike characterisation of our people, confident, ebullient, mostly gay, and perhaps a bit swaggering. The "*Cuban Overture*" presents delightful persiflage and good-natured satirisation of the rhumba style. "*Porgy and Bess*" frankly puzzled the hidebound critics. It may not be a "grand opera" in the strictest sense of the term, but it surely is a brilliant, warm-blooded, witty and indigenous piece of writing. The picturesquesness and psychology of the famous Southern drama have been set forth with the utmost fidelity. ¶A distinctive Gershwin touch typified all his music, even the rollicking and sentimental songs and other numbers he did for Broadway. Some of them have become classics in their field. I do not imagine, for instance, that *"The Man I Love"* could ever lose its heart-filling appeal, even though *"I Got Rhythm"* might diminish in popularity should newer dance metres come into vogue. ¶Gershwin has left a measure of fame that is not writ in water. (*See Dictionary of Musicians entry, page 168.*)

VICTOR HERBERT

By Deems Taylor

When Theodore Thomas conducted his third Popular Matinee for Young People in Steinway Hall on the afternoon of Saturday, December tenth, his programme included, among other things, Mendelssohn's *"Fingal's Cave"* overture, the prelude to *"Lohengrin,"* and a new *"Concerto for Violoncello and Orchestra"* by the brilliant twenty-eight-year-old first 'cellist of the Metropolitan Opera House orchestra. The composer played the solo part. On the evening of the same day, in the Metropolitan, the young 'cellist again played his new work at the season's second concert of the Philharmonic Society. "The violoncello concerto was introduced in place of the scene from '*Euryanthe,*' '*Wo berg ich mich?*', which was announced for Herr Emil Fischer, but who became hoarse after the public rehearsal on the preceding day." ¶This, from Henry E. Krehbiel's *"Review of the New York Musical Season, 1887–88,"* is the earliest mention of Victor Herbert as a composer that I have been able to find. The young Irishman who spoke English with a brogue that had a bewildering Teutonic flavour (he had been brought up and educated in Germany, where he lived from his fifth to his twenty-fifth year) was known chiefly as a 'cellist, and a good one. In 1886, when his wife, Therese Foerster, of the Stuttgart Opera, had been engaged for the Metropolitan in New York, Herbert came to America with her, where he entered the orchestra of the Metropolitan. Before long he gave up the career of instrumentalist to become, successively, assistant conductor with Thomas and Seidl, bandmaster of the Twenty-Second Regiment Band in New York, and conductor of the Pittsburgh Symphony Orchestra. ¶In later years he organised his own orchestra, which existed as a more or less loosely constructed unit almost to the time of his death; but it is not as a conductor, first-rate leader though he was, that we remember him. In Germany he had composed, aside from the 'cello concerto, a 'cello suite and a suite for strings. These, together with a cantata, *"The Captive,"* written in America, all come under the head of "serious" music, and they possess undeniable charm and—as one would expect of Herbert—great technical fluency; all the work of a young composer concerning whose future one could say nothing more definite than that he possessed great talent. ¶It was not long before the direction in which that talent was to turn became increasingly clear. In 1894 he wrote, and saw produced, a comic opera, *"Prince Ananias."* I know little about it, have not, as a matter of fact, heard any of the score. I do know, however, that it attracted critical attention and was successful enough to procure its composer another commission. This was a starring vehicle for Frank Daniels, a fantastic musical farce written by Harry B. Smith. It was called *"The Wizard of the Nile."* Opening on the evening of November 4, 1895, at the Casino Theatre in New York, it was an instant success, not only in America, but, later, in Mexico, England, and Germany. Herbert had found his calling. ¶The *"Wizard"* was the second in a list of musical comedies, operettas, and extravaganzas that is far too long to enumerate here—even if it were necessary. *"The Gold Bug," "The Serenade," "The Idol's Eye," "The Fortune Teller," "Babes in Toyland," "Mlle. Modiste," "The Red Mill," "Naughty Marietta," "The Princess Pat," "The Madcap Duchess," "Eileen"*—these are a handful of the best known of the forty-odd scores that flowed from Herbert's inexhaustible pen during the forty years between *"Prince Ananias"* and his swan song, *"Orange Blossoms."* Add to his stage works the quantity of overtures, divertimenti, and other short instrumental pieces that he wrote, and the sum of his separate vocal and instrumental numbers comes to well over a thousand. ¶Other composers of light music have equalled this output (Johann Strauss the Younger and Jacques Offenbach probably exceeded it; Sullivan wrote about half as much), but none, in my opinion, has ever maintained its incredibly high average of excellence. To me, Victor Herbert's music, taken on its average, is the finest repertoire of light opera music ever written. Strauss can be gluily sentimental at times; Offenbach can and does write pages whose apparent purpose is merely to keep things going until an idea turns up. Herbert can be sentimental upon occasion, Lord knows; witness *"I'm Falling in Love with Someone"* and *"Ah, Sweet Mystery of Life"* from *"Naughty Marietta."* But even at his worst he generally contrives something—an unexpected melodic leap, a piquant chord progression—that saves him from complete banality. And throughout his scores you will be hard put to it to find a passage that can honestly be called perfunctory, that does not contain some wholly individual turn of phrase of which one says, "That's Herbert." His music is light, superficial, if you like; it was meant to be. But its crystalline charm and glossy perfection of finish contrive to give it a detached, aristocratic flavour that keeps it from ever becoming obvious and cheap. ¶Ordinarily, one would expect the music of a man whose entire education, academic and musical, was German, to reflect the characteristics of his stepmother country. As a matter of fact, except for its consummate workmanship and the Viennese character of his waltz rhythms, I can find nothing at all Teutonic about Herbert's music. It is, if anything, French. Not the adopted French style of Offenbach, but the truly Gallic style of, for example, Bizet. The two seem to me curiously alike in the quality of their talent: unhackneyed but instantly remembered melodies, vocally grateful (the fact that Mrs. Herbert was an opera singer undoubtedly had much to do with that), a tendency to make sudden brief incursions into remote keys, an effective and ingenious sense of rhythm, and an unerring feeling for style and atmosphere. The composer of the *"Card Song"* from *"Carmen"* might well have written the verse of the *"Gypsy Serenade"* from *"The Fortune Teller,"* just as the composer of *"Panamericana"* might have written the Habañera from *"Carmen."* ¶One striking feature of his music is its extraordinary variety. In his own field I know of no one who can equal him in versatility of style. The gypsy music in *"The Fortune Teller"* has a true gypsy flavour; *"In the Toymaker's Workshop"* is a brilliantly successful modern *"Kindersimfonie"*; there is real eighteenth-century atmosphere in much of *"The Madcap Duchess"* score; and the Oriental music of *"Algeria,"* while not perhaps the Orient of Algiers, is at least the Orient of Borodin. He was a master of rhythm; not the rhythm of contemporary jazz—he never mastered that.   On the other hand, unlike the contemporary jazz composer, he had not one but a dozen dance rhythms at his fingertips.   He was particularly happy in writing pieces that called for *tempo rubato* playing.   Trifles like the *"Absinthe Frappé," "Punchinello,"* and *"Badinage"* are little masterpieces of this style of writing.   ¶In neither of his two ventures into the field of grand opera, *"Madeleine"* and *"Natoma,"* was he successful.   There were two reasons for this failure, I think.   One was—and this is the tragedy of Herbert's career—that he never found a librettist who could match him.   All his life he was a genius working with hacks; clever, even brilliant men, expert in the kind of word carpentry that turns out successful musical-comedy books and lyrics, but nonetheless hacks.   Many of Arthur Sullivan's best numbers obviously owe their form to the inspiration of Gilbert's lyrics.   In Herbert's case I always have the feeling that the music pulls the lyrics along, that if Herbert wrote brilliant and charming tunes, he wrote them without help, that the inspiration for them came entirely from within.   No man can set banal and pedestrian words to music for half a lifetime without having his poetic sense blunted.   Herbert's ear for literary English was never very keen—the result, probably, of speaking little but German for twenty years. As he grew older, he seemed at times to be almost incapable of judging good lyrics or a good libretto.   Music came to him so easily that the words became little more than a take-off; so why bother about them?   ¶But grand opera is a different matter.   No composer can write a continuous score, lasting two or three hours, without inevitably reflecting the quality of his libretto; if the music is to have any distinction, the libretto must possess some sort of distinction, either poetic or dramatic, in its own right.   ¶*"Madeleine"* and *"Natoma"* had neither.   The former is a little better poetically, but neither has any real dramatic interest.   As for the words of *"Natoma,"* no critic has ever been cruel enough to do them full justice.   The oft-quoted phrase from the *"Vaquero's Song,"* "See how the bull, upon his knees, Snorts when his neck we tighter squeeze," is one of dozens of similar triumphs of bathos.   In too many places the music of *"Natoma"* sounds trivial, prettily uninteresting, "catchy" in the Broadway sense of the word, rather than the music of a serious lyric drama. How could it be otherwise?   It is an all-too-perfect setting of the words.   For a hint as to what he might have done, had he been given a genuinely poetic and emotionally sincere libretto, listen to the prelude to the third act.   Here, freed momentarily from the necessity of setting refined doggerel to music, he writes broadly and nobly.   ¶Many of Verdi's librettists were hacks, too; but Verdi always managed to whip even the worst written libretto into some sort of dramatic shape, so that if he lacked words that were an inspiration, at least he had a situation.   But this Herbert was helpless to do.   The second reason that his operas failed is that he was not by instinct a dramatic composer.   ¶This seems an odd thing to say of a composer who had spent twenty years in the theatre.   But theatrical music is not necessarily dramatic music.   Particularly is this true of musical comedy, where the score exists primarily for its own sake, rather than to advance or enhance the action.   The order in which the musical numbers occur is determined solely by considerations of *musical* rather than dramatic effectiveness.   But a successful grand opera must be a dramatic unit. The words and music combine to create the drama, and the composer must be prepared to sacrifice or cut short his happiest inspirations if the action requires him to do so.   Herbert had had no experience at this sort of thing.   He had not acquired Verdi's or Puccini's or Bizet's knack of carrying the action along through the medium of—apparently—purely musical numbers.   He could stop the action and burst into song, or he could stop the music and underline dialogue; but he could not combine the two styles of writing, or hide the seams, so to speak, in his musical fabric.   His operatic scores, consequently, sound short-winded and scrappy.   ¶He took their failure much to heart.   But that is his tragedy, not ours.   He was put here to sing, and sing he did—for forty years; and we are still under the spell of the charm and bubbling freshness of what he sang.   There has never been anyone quite like him.   (*See page 204.*)

FRANZ LISZT

By Henry T. Finck

THERE are two great paradoxes in the career of Liszt.   The first is that just as Rossini, the most popular opera composer of his day, ceased writing operas thirty-nine years before his death, so Liszt, the greatest and most adored pianist of all times, ceased playing in public (except for an occasional charitable purpose) about the same number of years before his end came.   He had, with his inimitable art, familiarised concert-goers with nearly all the best compositions for the piano, created by other masters.   He had transcribed for the same instrument a large number of songs, operatic melodies and orchestral works (the number of these transcriptions at his death was 371), thereby vastly increasing their vogue.   He also wrote altogether 160 original compositions for the pianoforte, many of them as new in form as in substance; unique among them being the fifteen Hungarian rhapsodies—collections of Magyar melodies with gypsy ornaments, moulded by him into works of art, after the manner of epic poets.   But—and here lies the second paradox—Liszt, the greatest of all pianists, was not satisfied with the piano.   In many of his pieces for it, he endeavours to impart to it orchestral power and variety of tonal effect; and finally, when he became conductor at Weimar (1849), he transferred his attention chiefly to the orchestra.   ¶Of his thirty-four orchestral works, the most important are the "*Faust*" and "*Dante*" symphonies, and thirteen symphonic poems, in which he deviated from the old symphonic form in a spirit similar to Wagner's operatic reforms—abolishing the mosaic of unconnected movements and allowing the underlying poetic idea (programme) to shape the form of the music.   Of great importance and beauty also are his sixty songs, which represent the climax of the tendency to mirror in the music, not only the general spirit of the poem, but every line and word.   The last period of his life was largely given up to the writing of sacred compositions.   Among these, the most original in substance is the "*Legend of St. Elizabeth*," the most original in form "*Christus*," in which the last remnants of the opera (the aria and recitative) are eliminated from the oratorio, and little remains besides choruses and instrumental numbers.   Liszt's genius in early life was shaped largely by Schubert, Chopin, Berlioz, and Wagner.   His own influence on the pianists and orchestral writers of Germany, France, and Russia, can hardly be overestimated.   (*See page 263.*)

EDWARD MacDOWELL

By Richard Anthony Leonard

THE MUSIC of Edward MacDowell is heard much less frequently these days than it was at the time of his death, in the first decade of the present century; but it will be a long time before our debt to him is paid. For it was MacDowell who proved, once for all, that America was not a musical desert; that it could produce a composer of high rank, gifted with distinction and originality of utterance, whose genius would be recognised not only in his own country but in Europe as well. MacDowell was in fact the first important American composer. He was the pioneer who broke the ground and who, by the potency of his example, gave courage to many an American composer who came after him. ¶MacDowell was born in New York City in 1861 and he displayed such early talent for the piano that at the age of fifteen he was taken by his mother to Europe to study music. When he returned to America in 1888 after twelve years in France and Germany, the state of music in his native country was (and always had been) far from exhilarating. What little serious musical composition there was could only be described in terms of mediocrity. It was the palest of imitations of European models, so devoid of life-blood that it is now practically impossible to name a single work of major proportions which has survived into our time. On his return MacDowell and his early compositions were received with immense acclaim. For once (as more than one critic of that day remarked) a prophet had great honour in his own country. MacDowell's first appearances in New York and Boston as a young composer-pianist were scenes of wildest enthusiasm, almost without parallel in American concert-halls. And in the ensuing decade he received ovations ordinarily reserved for the very greatest European artists. ¶To-day when we are able to view the sum of MacDowell's achievement, that early enthusiasm still seems justified. It is true there was nothing in his technical equipment and little in his inspiration that had not been gained in Europe. His music belongs in the great stream of the Romantic movement, and his musical ancestors were Liszt, Mendelssohn, Wagner, Tchaikovsky, Greig, and his teacher, Raff. He created nothing that could be called "typically American," nor did any "American school" spring from the soil that he broke. But his achievement is none the less valid. He proved that an American could have the strength and stature to grapple with musical composition in its more serious forms; that he could take European models and manipulate them with outstanding ability; that he could give them an accent which is vigorously and singularly his own. ¶The whole of MacDowell's work is not large, for he died, after a tragic mental decline, in his forty-seventh year. Most of it was for the piano, of which instrument he attained a notable mastery. In fact it was only the counter-attraction of composition which prevented him from becoming one of the important piano virtuosos of his day. His best works, as we may judge them to-day, are probably the second *Piano Concerto*, the second *"Indian Suite,"* some of the shorter piano pieces, and the four *Piano Sonatas*—especially the *"Keltic"* sonata, a work of powerful emotion and heroic sweep, undeservedly neglected to-day. He also wrote many songs, several symphonic poems and a number of small choral works. ¶MacDowell was a man of unimpeachable sincerity and deep sensitivity. He worshipped nature, and in a great number of his shorter and best-known pieces he went for his inspiration to the sea, to the New England woods for which he had an abiding love, and to the artless beauty of simple flowers. Poetry was another of the motivating forces of his work—the poetry of Keats, Tennyson, Shakespeare, Dante, Heine and Goethe. His own gift for poetic writing was not inconsequential and he provided the verses for a number of his songs. Coupled with this sentimental strain in MacDowell's make-up was another and equally assertive quality of manly vigour—a full-blooded, sinewy quality. Thus we find in his work a wide emotional range: from the fragile tenderness of some of the piano pieces and songs to the heroic, grandiose style of the *Sonatas*, music of such breadth and spaciousness, of such concentrated power that it often strains the resources of the instrument. ¶Some of the best of these works suffer neglect to-day but it cannot in justice be said that this is wholly the composer's fault. Because he was a part of the great Romantic movement in music which has since been overshadowed by revolutionary new developments, he (like many another Romantic composer who just missed being first-rate) has gone into eclipse. But with the inevitable turn in the cycle of events it is possible that he may yet enjoy a return to favour. Chief among the gifts which work to keep his music alive is the indispensable gift of melody. This MacDowell had in abundance. His melodies are always expressive and often deeply felt; they have staying power, and even when they are so simple as to reach the least exacting of listeners, they seldom descend into the commonplace. MacDowell was not an innovator in any sense, but he did contrive to stamp his music with an individuality that is entirely his own. Sometimes it was by an unusual harmonic progression, or by a character-istic moulding of the melodic line but whatever the effect, it was unmistakably his. Lastly, MacDowell was a natural music-maker. Too much American music both before and after him betrays fatally the conscious effort; it smells of the lamp. But MacDowell's was utterly spontaneous and free. He had a noble imagination, and the wings to follow it far. (*See Biographical Dictionary of Musicians entry, page 270.*)

FELIX MENDELSSOHN–BARTHOLDY

By Vernon Blackburn

Felix Mendelssohn–bartholdy almost rivalled Mozart in the precocity of his genius. Music came to him, as it were, straight out of the skies. He played with it from boyhood, and at the age of nineteen wrote his greatest work. I refer, of course, to the overture to "*A Midsummer Night's Dream.*" It would be difficult to say exactly whence Mendelssohn derived the leading motives of his musical tendency. Mozart, of course, did much for him, but he was a bril-liant, though, I should imagine, a superficial, student of the great John Sebastian and of the train of German and Austrian composers, including Haydn, which succeeded the period of that great master, Beethoven, with whom, of course, he was intimate from his childhood. One remembers the story of his playing one of the symphonies to Goethe; but I doubt if Beethoven had a very serious in fluence over this gay, companionable, brilliant musician to whom music was not so much a spiritual as a pantheistic influence. ¶The external world to him fired his brain, and his delicate genius responded to the influence. His personality was neither commonplace nor profoundly interesting. There is a certain class of German youth which makes a point of exuberance, of high spirits and somewhat boisterous assertiveness of the bright side of life. Such a temperament is usually accompanied by a certain shallowness of spirit, and by a certain naïf outlook which is just a trifle irritating to the serious man. ¶His place in the art of music has not, I should imagine, been quite definitely settled even at this day. While Sir George Grove would place him among the archangels of musical creation, there are others who prefer to rank him as quite in the front rank of the second class. On the whole, my judgment ranges with the latter, although there are times, of course, when he strayed into the really great things of his art, as for example in the *"Watchman,"* from the *"Hymn of Praise,"* or *"How Lovely Are the Messengers,"* from *"St. Paul."* There will be none, however, I imagine, not even Sir George Grove himself, to rank Mendelssohn with Mozart, John Sebastian Bach, and Händel, and that alone may be taken as a test as to whether he really may be placed among the great gods. ¶If I were asked to assign his position, in the flash of a phrase, I should call him the Ganymede, the cupbearer of Jupiter's table. He was in the company of the gods, and he served them, he pleased them well; and his dwelling-place was in the palace of Jove; but he was not of royal rank, though he wore the livery of the great kings of art. And his influence has been confined chiefly to the more elegant song-writers of the time, to the composers of graceful and forgotten oratorios, and to the brilliant comic opera record of Sir Arthur Sullivan. And this, though Mendelssohn, after arriving at man's estate, never wrote a note that indicates him as possessing one flash of genuine humour. The disciple has here indeed outstripped the master. (*See page 287.*)

GIACOMO MEYERBEER

By Irenaeus Prime-Stevenson

Within the last fifty years, especially since the Wagnerian measuring-rule was applied right and left, up and down, to almost all the lyric drama, more in enthusiasm than in good judgment, and also since opera-making has come to be talked of as a sort of exact science—Meyerbeer has been ungraciously handled by a certain school of criticism. This school is rich in Podsnaps. If we can believe these arbiters and observers, Meyerbeer was a feeble charlatan in French opera, or in any kind of opera, a vulgar and bawdy melodist and a commonplace orchestrator. Moreover, we must, by such critics, believe that the public as well as the critics have so thoroughly "found him out," that the popular interest in his works is over; that *"The Huguenots,"* *"L'Africaine,"* and *"Le Prophète"* are works that bore everybody of true musical intelligence—"the souls of them fumed forth, the hearts of them torn out." ¶Unfortunately for these undiscerning prophets, their premises are obviously wrong, and their results are short-sighted. Meyerbeer is a composer full of faults. His inconsistencies are a continual irritation. His shortcomings are plain to the ear.

His superficial, emotional side, too, is indisputable. He was never sure of himself, or rarely so; and that is fatal often to artistic strength. But when all is counted against him, Meyerbeer is still a great composer, an operatic master to be reckoned with for a long operatic time to come; and as for the world in general it is far from setting him aside when his best scores are the question. ¶His splendid subtler mastery of true dramatic effect is, after all, as emphatic as his cheaper method of making a point. He does not, alas! sustain his melodies. He does not work out good themes as they deserve, over and over. He gives-out, he resorts to noise and clap-trap. His favourite rhythm ♫♪♩ is tedious. ¶But notwithstanding all, he is a genius in dramatic, pathetic melody. He is constantly able to move us legitimately by his beautiful art as an orchestral colourist. He writes for the operatic actor as a singer, perfectly and consistently, as well as for the operatic artist as a declaimer. He is a king at great musical phrases, words and music so linked that we cannot think of them as not together. And as a merely French composer Meyerbeer is of the first rank A sincere and learned musician himself, especially influenced by the greatest and even severest German and Italian musicians, he is distinctly a descendant in artistic speech of no less than Gluck. One often finds a Gluck-like nobility of phrase in Meyerbeer's dialogue, a Gluck-like outstart of melody, to atone for all that is savoury of Offenbach or worse. ¶As for Meyerbeer's influence on not only the French opera but in far wider range, that is undeniable. From Halévy to Reyer French opera since his day has never set his monitions aside, and Wagner (heretical as it sounds to say so) never quite drew away from the French principles in dramatic opera that he often most repudiated—exactly as he repudiates his eternal practical debts to Meyerbeer for no vague kindness. ¶Meyerbeer is the Scott, the Jokai, of opera, forever. Just as we forgive technical error or error of sentiment in both here and there, so must we forgive Meyerbeer: and in admiring his best scenes much indeed is to be forgot! ¶Personally, he was a large-souled and a good man as well as a man of finest cultivation and polish. His charities were numberless and his large bequests have continued them. Take him all in all, he was a creator and an influencer of, we may say, permanent dignity and honour in the general gallery of the really great, not merely the pseudo-great, operatic sovereigns. (*See page 293.*)

MODEST PETROVICH MOUSSORGSKY

By Richard Anthony Leonard

It would have amazed the contemporaries of Modest Petrovich Moussorgsky could they have foreseen the homage which is paid the man to-day. Though he was one of the original "Five," that little band of determined men who created the Russian school of music in the nineteenth century, he was the one from whom least was expected and for whom most had to be forgiven. When he died in 1881 at the age of forty-two (a victim of poverty, drink, and broken hopes) his work was so imperfectly understood that his friends, before publishing it, sought to cover up what they thought to be his musical illiteracy. His fellow-member of the "Five," Rimsky-Korsakoff, was a firm believer in Moussorgsky's great talent; so he "rearranged" many of Moussorgsky's works, "touching them up to make them more understandable to the public," remov- ing what he thought to be crudities of theoretical music procedure.   In short, Moussorgsky was looked upon as a bungler—a man of powerful and original talent who, through his failure to master the fundamentals of harmony, counter- point, and form, had left tragically little of enduring quality to the world. ¶But we see him with far different eyes to-day. As a writer of songs he is now ranked with Schubert, Schumann, and Wolf. We call him one of the supreme masters of the music drama, and we name his opera "*Boris Godounoff*" one of the two greatest works for the lyric stage since Wagner. More than that, Moussorgsky is now seen to be the wellspring from which much of the important music of the twentieth century has flowed.   ¶Moussorgsky's musical "illiteracy" was due in part to his early association with Balakireff.   That astonishing young man, who was the original inspiring genius of the "Five," was almost entirely self-taught in harmony, counterpoint, and form; and because he understood by instinct what other men could acquire only by rigorous training, he disparaged the necessity for such training.   Many author- ities have agreed with Moussorgsky's contemporaries in lamenting the influence of Balakireff in this respect.   But it must be remembered that Moussorgsky, a revolutionist and an innovator to the core, would probably have learned the rules only to break them.   He repeatedly defended his unorthodox procedure, on the ground that he was trying to express something in music that had never been done before.   His mistakes and crudities were often the outward evidences of his powerful individuality seeking new forms of expression.   They were the trademarks of his genius.   ¶Absolute or purely formal music interested Mous- sorgsky hardly at all.   Such abstract tone-weaving as writing symphonies, sonatas, or suites was foreign to his purposes.   Instead he devoted most of his creative energies to operas and songs—i.e., to those forms which gave him access to the human heart.   He was profoundly, avidly interested in his fellow- men, and he spent his life searching their minds and characters.   What he discovered in that search and the way he put his findings into music constitute one of the great glories of the tonal art.   ¶He left us hardly more than forty songs, yet they are perfect testaments to his intense and concentrated force, to the wide and daring range of his subject matter, and above all to his deep and touching sympathy with the pitiful human victims of a pitiless world The very titles are indicative: e.g., "*The Orphan Beggar Child*," "*Peasant's Cradle Song*," "*O My Savishna*" (the plaint of the village idiot for love and sympathy), "*The Ragamuffin*," "*The Song of the Flea*," and the song-cycles "*Sunless*," "*In the Nursery*," and "*Songs and Dances of Death*."   In his songs Moussorgsky attempted always to express in tones the very letter and spirit of the text: the picture that the words painted, the inmost thought of the character, the subtlest shades of idea and meaning that could not even be ex- pressed in the words.   In realising this ideal he refused to be bound by the conventional song forms and formulas.   What did it matter if a song began in one key and ended in another?   Or if one chord followed another harshly and gratingly, not properly "prepared"?   Or if a song ended without a cadence? The justification was always in the text.   And the end was often miraculously realised.   ¶Besides the songs, the works upon which most of Moussorgsky's reputation rests to-day are his operas, "*Boris Godounoff*" and "*Khovanstchina*":

the brilliant tone picture, *"A Night on the Bare Mountain,"* which is probably the most satisfactory of Rimsky-Korsakoff's revisions of the composer's music; and his single great work for the piano, *"Pictures at an Exhibition,"* best known to-day in Ravel's superb orchestration. ¶*"Khovanstchina"* was found in a chaotic state after Moussorgsky's death—unfinished, only partly orchestrated, and almost twice too long. Rimsky-Korsakoff orchestrated the entire work, made numerous cuts, and generally "touched up" the harmonies and part-writing. Whether he was justified in his ministrations or whether he was guilty of malpractice is a matter of endless controversy. At any rate, his version remains a work of singular power and beauty. About *"Boris"* there is less question. It is the capstone of Moussorgsky's achievement, and Rimsky-Korsakoff was probably wrong in attempting twice to revise it. True, he did not make nearly as many or as drastic changes as he made in *"Khovanstchina"*; and (to do him complete justice) it was his versions which brought the opera world fame and Moussorgsky a rightful place in the sun. But since 1928, when the Soviet government published the original score, it has become apparent that, aside from certain weaknesses in the orchestration, Moussorgsky had wrought far better than anyone of his time realised. It is possible that the opera may again stand on its own feet, as it did so successfully during the composer's lifetime. ¶No matter which version of *"Boris"* eventually displaces the other, however, certain indisputable facts remain. The intense nationalism of this work, its use of material derived from or imitative of folk-music, its astonishingly modern blending of music and text, have all been the inspiration of numberless composers since Moussorgsky's day. And above all it discloses the composer's unique genius for portraying mankind and his crown of sorrows. Like Macbeth, it is a "tragedy of twilight and the setting in of thick darkness upon a human soul." (*See Dictionary of Musicians entry, page 303.*)

WOLFGANG AMADEUS MOZART

By Vernon Blackburn

John Chrysostom Wolfgang Amadeus Mozart, the son of a tolerably good musician, by name Leopold, from his earliest years displayed the most extraordinary sense of musical precocity. At the age of three years he was able to pick out harmonies on the harpsichord; by the time he was seven, he had already burdened his young soul with the responsibility of various compositions which are more interesting than such compositions might be expected to be. The darling of courts in his childhood (for his father took him early on his travels for purposes of exhibition as a musical prodigy), the intensely industrious youth, the creator of a dramatic art in music, separate and by itself in the world, the greatest master of melody that this earth has ever seen, the writer of innumerable symphonies, innumerable songs, innumerable sonatas, the possessor of a musical memory such as had never been conferred on the son of man before, he was the brilliant artist of high spirits, the man who lived life to the very last drop of the glass. ¶In a word, a genius, in art and in living, of the highest flower. He went down to his grave before he was forty years of age, buried no man knows where, deserted of friends, deserted even in his last journey to the

Vienna cemetery by his wife; abjectly poor, with not a soul to weep for him, not a soul to care what became of these sacred relics. Here was, indeed, a combination of glory and the darkest tragedy which can scarcely be found outside the Attic drama. ¶Yet, from the critical point of view, it can scarcely be said that Mozart was in any sense a revolutionary; he was the glorious link which combined the music of the last century with the music of this. The strictest formalist, the impeccable master of counterpoint, the respecter in every way of traditions, you can see him, as it were, on the tiptoe of the future, bearing on his brilliant soul, and bearing it lightly, all the burdens of the past. ¶But it is as a writer of opera that his fame is like to last longest, for it is here that he brought the brilliant qualities of the consummate musician to combine with the scarcely less brilliant qualities of the dramatist. Many men who might have written music equally noteworthy could not have touched the dramatic significance of it. "Don Giovanni," that glory of our blood and state, "Le Nozze di Figaro," "Cosi Fan Tutte," "Die Zauberflöte," these remain as noble a testimony of his great genius in the musico-dramatic world as the centuries are likely to bring forth. Then consider the G minor symphony—so different in quality from the quality of Beethoven at his best, and therefore not comparable to the great nine, but in its way the very flower of musical genius. Then again, such work as he brought into the Requiem declares him to be, as a master of the emotions, of supernatural terror, unsurpassed; I would almost say unsurpassable. In a word, here was the golden child of music, adding to the simplicity of his childishness the complex wisdom of the serpent. ¶Poor Mozart! Yet, who is ordinary man that he should say "poor" of such an immortal creature? Poor as it seems to us, yet it is not likely that he would have given up one golden moment of his glorious inspiration in exchange for the comforts of a Sultan. He was an artist, every inch of him. (See Dictionary of Musicians entry, page 303.)

GIOVANNI PALESTRINA

By W. J. HENDERSON

PALESTRINA'S work in musical history was bringing order out of chaos in church-music, and setting the model for the loftiest purity of style. The music of the Church had become too complex through the extreme development of rigidly canonic writing. Palestrina, following the lead of some of his predecessors, who had begun to write in free counter-point, showed how this new style could be made to yield the finest possible results in the composition of music for the mass, and other parts of the Roman ritual. By adhering to the ecclesiastical scale and avoiding chromatic progressions, by clinging to purely religious thought and excluding anything like passion, Palestrina produced works which have remained to this day the perfect model of church-music. ¶The contrapuntal skill in his writing is masterly, but it never parades itself. Its most beautiful effects are produced with apparent spontaneity, and frequent chord harmonies of enchanting loveliness seem to be accidental. The Roman school of church-composers was founded by Palestrina, and his influence is even yet perceptible in the music of the Holy City. He has universally been accorded the position of the greatest of all church-composers. (See also page 323.)

HENRY PURCELL

By John F. Runciman

THE early English school reached a magnificent culmination in Purcell. Many influences went to the shaping of him. Behind was the contrapuntal English school, of which Tallis and Byrde were exemplars; more immediately behind was Pelham Humphries, who brought to England all that France knew; and it is as good as certain that he knew what the Italians, with Corelli at their head, had accomplished. That is to say, he must have learned how to handle many parts in a chorus or orchestral movement; learned how to write recitative and expressive song; learned what could be done in the way of chamber-music; and such orchestral colouring as was possible at that day. ¶To these acquired masteries he brought a native ear for miraculous colour in music—as witness his *"Tempest"* music, written for the worst libretto that the world has not listened to; a glorious invention of expressive or picturesque melody, though chiefly picturesque; a fine instinct for the dramatic, and for expressing it in music; and the most noble sense of the splendid effects to be gained by throwing about masses of vocal tone in the manner afterwards appropriated and made entirely his own by Handel. ¶Those who have studied Purcell's scores will be astonished by the extent to which Handel took his themes and modes of using them. In that lies his sole contribution to what must be called the "progress" of music. Later English composers, to their shame, and certainly to their utter confusion, copied Handel instead of developing on Purcell's lines. They profited nothing; and Purcell remains as the last of the tribe of the genuinely creative English musicians before Elgar. He was determined to excel in everything he touched; and he excelled in everything. His forms are at once broad and flexible; his harmonies are as daring as Sebastian Bach's; his themes have a great dignity and vigour; and on everything he wrote there rests an early morning freshness. No music has preserved its freshness better; the dew is still on it. ¶Born just before the Restoration, he felt to the full the anti-Puritan reaction; he shared in the revival of the sheer joy of being alive; and his music is filled with a cheerful health such as one finds in no music written since his day. But he experienced the deeper emotions; and one may find in his works profound utterances of grief and sorrow, of the mystery and terror of all life. He was entirely pagan, and wrote no real religious music —religious as we use the word when we speak of Sweelinck, Palestrina, or Byrde. But power is there, and delicacy, and marvellous beauty; and above all that external freshness and picturesque quality which give his music the character that stamps and marks it off as his own. (*See page 346.*)

SERGEI RACHMANINOFF

By Richard Anthony Leonard

SERGEI RACHMANINOFF is one of those not infrequent composers whose artistic convictions become fixed at an early time in their lives, and who thereafter, despite the pull of a thousand counterattractions, never relinquish those early ties. He was born in Russia in 1873, and by the time he had reached his early twenties the great nationalist movement in Russian music had reached its high tide. In his early compositions Rachmaninoff identified himself with one of the phases of that movement. Since then he had witnessed the whole art of music passing through a vast metamorphosis; nevertheless he had hardly moved from his original position. ¶The figure of Rachmaninoff the concert pianist was a familiar one the world over, and in many ways was revealing of Rachmaninoff the composer. He was tall, powerfully built, commanding, with wrists and fingers of steel; his closely cropped hair, strong nose and deep-set, melancholy eyes all bespoke a nature that was austere, aloof, proudly individualistic. In short, a man of forceful inner convictions that could not easily be shaken. Seeing him made it easy to understand how, at an early age, he might have discovered his own aims and ideals, as well as his limitations, and how he might steadfastly have refused for the rest of his creative life to veer his course, regardless of how the winds of musical fashion might blow. That is why to-day much of Rachmaninoff's music sounds like a voice from the past, speaking the Romantic speech of the eighteen-eighties and nineties. ¶Rachmaninoff is often spoken of as a kind of connecting link between the two main branches of Russian music of the nineteenth century. One group included the arch-Nationalists, led by the famous "Five," who preached that all Russian music should come directly from the native soil; that it should be based on Russian literature, folk songs and legends, and the music of the Russian Church. They were opposed by the so-called Eclectics, composers like Tchaikowsky and Rubinstein, who had studied and were sympathetic with the trends of music in western Europe. While he was still in his teens Rachmaninoff met Tchaikowsky, and the influence of the great Russian Romanticist upon the talented young man was profound and lasting. Nevertheless, Rachmaninoff stands not entirely with either school, but between the two. He has the technical equipment of an Eclectic, a thorough knowledge of the methods and procedure of the French and German schools of the nineteenth century; but his thematic material, the whole colour and feeling of his music, is unmistakably Russian. ¶Rachmaninoff has composed in many forms, but the bulk of his enduring work centres around the piano. His piano solos are among the most famous and popular pieces produced for that instrument in the present century. The composer's own pre-eminence as a concert pianist as well as the ingratiating qualities of the pieces themselves has been responsible for their widespread favour. They are chiefly in the small forms, the preludes predominating, and most of them bear the marks of Chopin's influence. They lack the depth and subtlety of Chopin's greater works, but they are brilliantly pianistic and exemplify the composer's mastery of the technical resources of the instrument. ¶In the larger forms Rachmaninoff's most distinguished works are undoubtedly the piano concertos. He has written four; but the Second, in C minor, is most often performed to-day, in fact it remains one of the most successful concertos produced in the past four decades. It is typically a work of the Romantic era, melodious and expressive, alternating between long-breathing, darkly coloured cantabile phrases and powerfully built climaxes, grandiose and declamatory. The flavour of the work is strongly Russian, and shows the influence of Tchaikowsky. The piano part is in the virtuoso vein throughout. ¶Several of

Rachmaninoff's orchestral works, such as his Second Symphony in E minor, his symphonic poem, *"The Island of the Dead,"* and *"The Bells"* (for chorus, soloists, and orchestra) enjoyed a wide vogue in the early part of the present century, but they are less often heard to-day.   Recently his brilliant *"Rhapsody on a Theme of Paganini,"* for piano and orchestra, and his long-awaited Third Symphony have received genuine acclaim.   All these works give evidence of the composer's masterful command of the orchestra, and his ability to sustain, in the difficult large forms, a lofty inspiration.   ¶Rachmaninoff's songs are for the most part deeply coloured and rich in sentiment, more in the lyrical pattern of Tchaikowsky than in the stark, unadorned style of Moussorgsky.   Several of them, like *"Floods of Spring"* and *"In the Silence of Night,"* have achieved a popularity almost as widespread as the piano preludes.   *(See Dictionary of Musicians entry, page 348.)*

MAURICE RAVEL

By Richard Anthony Leonard

The music of Maurice Ravel suffered for a long time from unjust comparison with that of Claude Debussy.   It used to be the fashion to say that Ravel was a kind of minor Debussy, who was more imitative than original, more clever than profound.   Perhaps such comparisons were inevitable: they were both Frenchmen, they were contemporaries (Ravel being but a dozen years younger than Debussy), and both were leading exemplars of the impressionist movement in music.   They even displayed a curious parallelism in their choice of subjects.   It is true that Debussy had the more original creative gifts.   His impressionism is more subtle and mysterious than Ravel's; his was indeed the deeper and more enigmatic mind.   But Ravel had his gifts, too, not nearly so inconsiderable as his early detractors had surmised.   ¶For one thing Ravel was a scrupulous craftsman.   One might search his music from *"Jeux d'Eau"* to the two piano concertos, and find scarcely a bar that gave evidence of having been set down carelessly, or that, for want of new inspiration, was obviously repetitious of something he had done before.   Furthermore, he was a craftsman not merely in one form but in many.   He wrote a number of exquisite songs; his piano music is brilliant and effective; his string-quartet is one of the best in modern music; his *"L'Heure Espagnole"* is a delicious comic opera; while *"Daphnis and Chloe"* is one of the two or three greatest ballets of our time.   ¶Ravel's indebtedness to Debussy is incontestable, but we can discern now that it was nevertheless limited.   It lay chiefly in the field of harmony— in his use of seventh and ninth chords, parallel chords, polytonality, the twelve-tone scale, the medieval modes, etc.   But we discern, too, that Ravel's music has a rhythmic quality that Debussy's often lacks.   The latter's music is liquid, flowing, sensuous, vague in outline.   Ravel's is more incisive, definite, clean-cut.   And Ravel was far more preoccupied with form than Debussy ever was.   He had a special liking for the formal classicism of the eighteenth-century masters, especially Couperin, Rameau, and Mozart.   He admired their elegance, their perfection of style, their economy of means.   His study of these masters is reflected in a great deal of his work—most obviously in his

Sonatine and "*Tombeau de Couperin*" for the piano, his string-quartet, and the first movement of his Piano Concerto. It has given his work a balance and symmetry, a classic grace that is almost unique in impressionistic music. ¶Debussy was of course a supreme stylist, but so was Ravel—and in a totally different sense. There was one problem of style which Ravel delighted in solving: that of taking the essentials of another musical idiom and translating them into his own impressionistic medium. The above-mentioned works based on the eighteenth-century masters are typical examples; others are his numerous excursions into the Spanish idiom in such works as "*Rhapsody Espagnole*," "*L'Heure Espagnole*," "*Bolero*," and "*Alborado del Gracioso*"; his brilliant study of the Strauss waltz in "*La Valse*"; and his paraphrase of Liszt's Hungarian Rhapsodies in "*Tzigane*," for violin and orchestra. We even find the last movement of his piano-concerto tinctured with American jazz. ¶In the art of orchestration Ravel stood at the summit. Some of his pieces are very nearly études in orchestration; "*Bolero*," for example, is hardly more than an instrumental *tour de force*. But in others he made his orchestration an integral part of his inspiration. "*Daphnis and Chloe*" is a matchless example. Here it is the orchestral garb almost as much as the substance of the music itself which gives this work its exquisite antique flavour, its air of pure Arcadian beauty. And in his orchestral arrangement of Moussorgsky's "*Pictures at an Exhibition*," by precisely the same means Ravel achieves a miraculous affinity with the nineteenth-century Russian composer. Surely the Greece of Longus and the Russia of Moussorgsky stand at the poles; and yet is it not one of the triumphs and one of the mysteries of art that an elegant, urbane, and somewhat ironical Frenchman of the twentieth century can reach out, through music, and touch them both? ¶Many critics have observed Ravel's sly wit, his unexpected irony. More than one has intimated that a coldness in his nature must have found its way into his work, that it too often lacks the warmth of human sympathy. This is partly true. Ravel's music never wrings the heart as, say, Debussy's does in the last act of "*Pelléas and Mélisande*." Ravel abhorred sentimentality even more than Debussy did, more than most Frenchmen. He could no more have been guilty of a sentimental orgy like "*Ein Heldenleben*" than Richard Strauss could have written anything so cold and glittering and cynical as "*La Valse*." But Ravel had his moments, too, a few moments when he exposed—half-ashamedly—an innate tenderness of heart. One of them is in his early "*Pavane pour une Infante defunte*"; others are to be found in his "*Ma Mère L'Oye*." And is not "*Daphnis and Chloe*" a monument to the wild ecstasy of young love, alive in every bar with breathing passion? ¶Ravel's whole life, both personal and artistic, was that of an arch-aristocrat—perfectly ordered, fastidious, withdrawn. He never married, and he had few intimate friends; so that most of his life after the World War was spent at Montfort l'Amaury, near Paris, in surroundings so quiet as to make him practically a recluse. For several years before he died the same terrible black veil that had covered the faces of Schumann and Smetana covered his. ¶We might sum him up to say that he was one of the very greatest of French composers; that whatever he set out to do in music he accomplished by sheer force of craftsmanship and elegance of taste; that his music is "modern" to the core—singularly a product of his time and his country; and that, above all, he shares with Debussy the distinction of having contributed most to the impressionist movement in music. (*See Dictionary of Musicians entry, page 352.*)

RECOLLECTIONS OF MY LAZY CHILDHOOD

By Maurice Ravel

In the last few years of his life Ravel met the most tragic fate that can overtake anyone. He began to lose his mind. What made the disaster even more terrible was the fact that he had intervals of complete lucidity, during which he realised all too well what was happening to him. He died in Paris on the 28th of December, 1937. ¶Shortly before his death, during one of his lucid intervals, the composer wrote an essay that he called *Mes Souvenirs d'Enfant Paresseux* ("Recollections of My Lazy Childhood"), in which he discussed the various influences that shaped his career, gave a partial estimate of his own work, and voiced his own declaration of faith as an artist. The article was published in the French newspaper *Paris-Soir* a week after Ravel's death. It has never been widely read here, was not reprinted. It appears here in my own translation.

Deems Taylor

For me [writes Ravel] there have never been several arts: Only one. Music, painting, and literature differ only as to their means of expression. So there are not various kinds of artists, only various kinds of specialists. The need for specialisation becomes greater and greater as our field of knowledge broadens; for nothing, even in art, can be acquired without hard study. Consequently it has become impossible for us to follow the example of Leonardo da Vinci, who managed to be an amateur of all the arts—even of painting! ¶As for myself, I was certainly born to be a musician; but if I am not a writer, it is simply because of the lack of the *impulse* to be one. I notice, for example, that when I read, my attitude is a professional one, as if I were a writer. The same with painting. I look at a picture, not with the eyes of a picture lover, but with those of a painter. This comes, perhaps, from the fact that as a child I was gifted in many ways; a fact that, needless to say, greatly worried my parents. It worried them all the more because my various artistic leanings were coupled with an extraordinary laziness. I never worked except "taxi" fashion; that is to say, in order to induce me to make the slightest exertion, I had to be bribed. ¶In school, the only study that amused me somewhat was that of mathematics —to the great joy of my father, who was an engineer. My mother, who was a Basque and, like all the people of her country, a musician, would have liked to see me a little more zealous in my piano studies. But they merely bored me. However, the minute I took up the study of composition, everyone realised that my path lay in that direction. It even amused me! Which was not extraordinary, after all, since my interest in mathematics tended to bring me to music. I became interested to such a point that, inveterately lazy as I had been up to then, I began to work nights as well as in the daytime—a habit that, unfortunately for my health, has always persisted. My teacher, Charles René, started me working exercises in composition when I was no more than sixteen or seventeen; but it was not until three or four years later that I devoted myself to serious attempts at composition. I had made others before, but kept them carefully hidden. At the Conservatoire I was enrolled both as a composition student and as a pianist. In the latter capacity I was a member of the class of Camille de Bériot, who soon noticed that while I had definitely the temperament of an artist, I had a minimum amount of zeal as an executant. Meanwhile I plunged ardently into the study of harmony, counterpoint, and fugue, and notwithstanding the fact that up to then I had written very little, I began to feel the itch to compose. ¶It was at that time that I began to make continual discoveries among the works of my favourite authors, feeling, meanwhile, that I had something to say in another direction. The influences that I felt at that time confirm me in my belief that there are *not* various kinds of arts. I did fall under the spell of one musician: Chabrier. Not yet has he been given the rank that he deserves, for modern French music all stems from him. He played, in music, the part that Manet played in painting. And, as a matter of fact, Chabrier owned some of the finest of Manet's paintings. The discovery of Debussy was less of a shock to me, in that I had already surrendered to Chabrier. And if I have been influenced by Debussy I have been so deliberately, and have always felt that I could escape him whenever I chose. In any case, I never completely accepted Debussy's principles, and I believe that that should be obvious to anyone. As a matter of fact, as regards musical technique, my teacher has certainly been Edgar Allan Poe. To me the finest treatise on composition, certainly the one that has influenced me the most, is Poe's essay on the genesis of a poem. Mallarmé to the contrary, when he claims that the essay was written as a joke. I firmly believe that Poe wrote his poem, "The Raven," exactly as he says he did. ¶My passion for discovering new things, in painting, literature, and music, was not merely a phenomenon of my youth. I have always had it, especially about myself. It is this passion for discovery that has always driven me to try to renew my artistic self. ¶I never put down a work until I have made absolutely certain that there is nothing about it that I could not improve. The great thrill comes when I do put it down. After that I have no more interest in it. I have never tried to write in the style of Ravel. If I have found new ways of expressing myself, I leave it to others to discover them. If you want to convict me of inconsistency by hurling my earlier works at my head, well and good. I know that a conscious artist is always right. ¶I say "conscious," rather than "sincere"; for there is something humiliating about the latter term. A true artist *cannot* be sincere. The imaginary, the false, if you please, used to create an illusion, is mankind's one great superiority over the animals, and, when he undertakes to create a work of art, the artist's one point of superiority over the rest of mankind. Anyone who rests his claim on so-called spontaneity alone, is merely babbling. ¶In art, everything that is not significant must be rejected. Massenet, who was so highly gifted, squandered himself through too much sincerity. He wrote down, literally, everything that came into his head; with the result that he spent his career saying the same thing over and over again. What he thought were discoveries were only reminiscences. As a matter of fact, artists seldom exercise enough self-mastery. After all, since we cannot say what we have to say without deliberately exploiting, and so translating, our own emotions, is it not better at least to be conscious of that fact, and realise that great art is simply a supreme form of pretense?

The thing that people sometimes call my own lack of sentiment is simply my scrupulous care to avoid saying the obvious and unimportant. ¶As for the charge they level against me, of writing "only masterpieces" that is, of creating works that leave me nothing more to say in that particular idiom, I can only answer that, if that were true, I should be the first to know it and that there would be nothing left for me to do, except either to stop work, or to die. I say this, despite the example of the Lord, who took a long rest after having created the world . . . and who was so wrong! (*See also page 352.*)

RIMSKY–KORSAKOFF

By Richard Anthony Leonard

OF THE ORIGINAL "Five" who created the Russian school of music in the nineteenth century, four were essentially amateurs. Balakireff was looked upon by his fellows as a professional musician; but Cui was an army officer, an engineer of fortifications; Borodin was a doctor and a teacher of chemistry; Moussorgsky, after his retirement from the army, spent his life as a government clerk. Rimsky-Korsakoff was a naval officer. As a young midshipman he had fallen under the spell of the fascinating Balakireff, and wrote his first symphony before he was twenty-one years old. At that time he was so ignorant of music theory (Balakireff having scorned the necessity for academic training in harmony, counterpoint, form, etc.) that he did not even know the names of the common chords. ¶But Rimsky-Korsakoff was the one member of the famous group who refused to remain an amateur. In fact, he became one of the most skilful musicians of his time, and a consummate master of many aspects of musical technique. He accomplished this through years of unceasing industry. Harmony and counterpoint he learned only after he had accepted a professorship at the St. Petersburg Conservatory! He taught simply by teaching himself first and keeping one jump ahead of his pupils. To understand orchestration more fully he bought many of the instruments and learned how to play them. He succeeded so well that he was later able to write a manual of orchestration which remains a classic to this day. ¶Rimsky-Korsakoff's life was a steady progression, a carefully planned development of a great natural talent. He was a perfectionist, who never ceased polishing not only the brilliant facets of his music but the very tools of his trade as well. He seemed never to be idle; and when he was not adding to his own immense output he was spurring on his friends Borodin and Moussorgsky to similar achievement—helping them with their orchestrating, even completing and editing their works after their deaths. ¶It is curious that for all his methodical mind and well-ordered habits Rimsky-Korsakoff's music is the most fanciful, picturesque, and charmingly extravagant of all the nineteenth-century Russians. It offers a contrast with the music of Moussorgsky, for example, that is almost as great as the gulf between the temperaments of the two men. Moussorgsky's art was that of the natural dramatist, the realistic interpreter of the hearts of men. His music is often shaggy and unkempt; it reeks continually of the Russian soil. Rimsky-Korsakoff's is melodic, lyrical, and essentially pictorial. It is Russian, but with a blend of the exotic East; and its polished technique often covers melodic

ideas that are commonplace. There is no doubt now that Moussorgsky was
the more powerful and original genius, for his music has grown steadily with
the years and a whole generation of modern composers have fed upon it.
Rimsky-Korsakoff's, on the other hand, has declined. ¶Though he composed
in many forms, Rimsky-Korsakoff's operas constitute the great bulk of his
works. He wrote fifteen, nearly all of them based on Russian stories, legends,
or dramas. For a time they were so important a part of the operatic repertoire
in Russia that he seemed destined to become the equivalent in his native country of Wagner in Germany and Verdi in Italy. But in recent years many of
these works have faded and now suffer neglect. Outside of Russia one hears
only the exquisite "*Le Coq d'Or*," and occasionally "*Sadko*" and "*Snyegoo-
rochka*." ¶Far more popular are the purely orchestral works: the "*Capriccio
Espagnol*," the Russian Easter overture, the "*Antar*" Suite, and—inevitably—
"*Scheherezade*." There is still great vitality in these pieces, and they are
likely to represent their composer on symphonic programmes for many years.
They will live because, for one thing, Rimsky-Korsakoff had the gift of lyricism,
and his melodies (though often somewhat obvious) nearly always have charm.
He knew, too, how to hide their defects by his expert use of colourful harmonies.
He was also a past-master of orchestration, by which he gave his music a mar-
vellous clarity of expression, a richness of texture, and a brilliance that is almost
Oriental in its opulent splendour. For his discoveries in the science of instru-
mentation, a host of modern composers—Stravinsky, Ravel, Falla, Respighi,
Prokofieff, etc.—owe him a great debt. ¶Russia owes him a great debt, too.
For at a time when nationalism in music was still on trial in western Europe,
he was her most ardent and successful propagandist. He proved by his own
technical mastery that nationalism need not be synonymous with amateurism.
He made it plain that the literature, legend, folk, and church music of a single
nation might be made the basis for a treasury of musical inspiration. (*See
Dictionary of Musicians entry, page 362.*)

GIOACCHINO ROSSINI

By Irenaeus Prime-Stevenson

It is like a page of goldenest sunshine in the volume of musical personalia
to review the brief, brilliant, artistic story of Rossini's activity or to glance at
his long and happy life. Almost from the first came to him fame, fortune,
and opportunity for that amazing fecundity of mind which was so curiously
sorted with his indolence of body. Few men of genius have lived and worked
and rivalled and succeeded, of whom so little is current that is ungracious or
discreditable. ¶As to Rossini's place in art, albeit a huge fraction of his
operas are empty to our ears, and bore us with their flowery ornamentation
and feeble dramatic substructure, we have no right to predict that thorough
neglect will soon deliver to darkness and dust such scores as "*L'Italiana in
Algeri*," "*Il Barbiere di Seviglia*," "*Guglielmo Tell*,"—and possibly "*Semiramide*," for the world will have lost too completely a natural irresistible
feeling for melody, for restrained elegance of orchestral diction, and above all
for the perfect expression of true comedy in music. Only in one other master,

Mozart, to whom Rossini felt that he owed so much, and to whom he declared himself so far inferior, do we meet equal sincerity, taste, and eloquence as prolifically put into operatic song and orchestration. ¶And as to *"Tell,"* with that noble and serious work, a striking variant from the old Italianistic Rossini, a work by a mature and serious-minded composer of the first order, all the great and the little musical world will long have to reckon. ¶The great influences on Rossini were two: Mozart, whose greatest successor in Italian operatic comedy Rossini certainly is; and a mixture of French form and French dramatic spirit with German importance in every detail of the orchestra. ¶It cannot be said that Rossini founded a school. He "said it all himself," as the phrase goes; and his imitators either gave over copying (often with most happy and significant advantages to great individualities for themselves, as in the instances of Meyerbeer and Donizetti and Verdi), or else they were not of substance in their efforts to eclipse the dazzling master of Pesaro. His effect upon the whole operatic public of Europe was for a time almost demoralising, paralysing to all other music. ¶Immediately after the striking renunciation of his career, at only thirty-seven years of age, came the Wagner movement. (*See Dictionary of Musicians entry, page 368.*)

ARNOLD SCHÖNBERG

By Richard Anthony Leonard

Arnold Schönberg is either music's most hopelessly misguided fanatic or her supreme martyr. He occupies the "last and lofty station" of a St. Simeon Stylites, for his is an ideal which few beside himself have had the temerity even to acknowledge but which he pursues with the demoniac intensity of a zealot. Schönberg is the most advanced of all ultra-modernists, and (if we may change our metaphor) no one can yet see whether his explorations along the course of music's stream are pointing the way to the future, or whether he has drawn himself off into the shallows of a stagnant backwater. No composer since Wagner has been exposed to such merciless critical diatribes. No composer's music has drawn from audiences such unrestrained resentment, ridicule, and even hatred. "Empty ingenuity and ingenious pedantry" . . . "the fanciful imaginings of a lunatic" . . . "the drunken gesture of a learned professor" . . . these are but samples of the criticism that Schönberg's music has met unfailingly for three decades. ¶There is a revealing sentence in Egon Wellesz's sympathetic study of this composer and his works. Speaking of a performance of a group of Schönberg's early songs, in Vienna in 1900, Dr. Wellesz writes, "When the performance was over there was a mild 'scene' in the hall. 'And from that time,' said Schönberg with a smile one day when he was telling me about it, 'the scandal has never ceased.'" Indeed it has not, as those who heard the first New York performance of Schönberg's *"Variations for Orchestra"* twenty-nine years later can testify. ¶Yet there can be no question that Schönberg's mastery of the purely technical side of music might well be the envy of any musician of our time. The same is true of his unswerving sincerity and his intellectual strength. This man, it must be remembered, was practically self-taught in an art whose mechanics have been compared, for their complexity, to those of astronomy. At twenty-six he composed the *"Gurre-Lieder,"* a work of gargantuan size, on a par for sheer physical bulk with Mahler's *"Symphony of One Thousand."* As a teacher he is probably without a peer. His pupils (some of the foremost German composers of to-day) revere him as the most inspiring of pedagogues and prophets. His books and essays on music, notably his great treatise on harmony, are unrivalled in their contributions to the aesthetics of this art. In the face of such accomplishment only the bigoted or the ignorant could fail to accord Schönberg the fullest measure of tolerance in his strivings toward a new frontier in music. ¶This supreme ultra-modernist began his career in the nineties as a post-romanticist, steeped in the music of Richard Wagner. His early songs, his sextet, *"Verklärte Nacht,"* and the *"Gurre-Lieder"* all bear the inevitable marks of *"Tristan and Isolde."* The *"Gurre-Lieder"* is, in fact, a huge over-expansion of the Wagnerian style and method, a grandiose enlargement of already-stale nineteenth-century romanticism. It is a remarkable achievement for a young man of twenty-six but it suffers from having been born too late. All through his early work Schönberg displays a prodigious mastery of the technical side of his art. His symphonic poem, *"Pelleas and Melisande,"* is of a contrapuntal density almost without parallel, while in the two early string quartets there is a superb handling of the thematic material and of the part writing. Nevertheless, the composer leaves the impression that he is unsatisfied by the facility which he has achieved so quickly in the existing styles and that he is struggling toward new concepts of beauty and form. Moreover, facility is not by any means the whole of accomplishment, and it is disturbing to find in much of this early work a lack of first-rate creative ideas. ¶With the completion in 1909 of his famous Opus 11, the *"Three Piano Pieces,"* Schönberg arrived at the point of his "complete break with the past." Here was the beginning of a journey which he was to travel with a fixed and unshakable purpose for the remainder of his creative life. These three small pieces are Schönberg's first complete expression of his new atonal style. Atonality is not the only feature of Schönberg's music, from this point on, which is to be looked upon as revolutionary and even bizarre. His work abounds in innovation. (There are, for example, the use of the *"Sprechgesang,"* or song speech, the elaborate synchronisation of music and stage lighting in his opera, *"Die Glückliche Hand,"* and his highly individual uses of orchestration.) But all else is of secondary importance when compared with the far-reaching effect of atonality. In the public mind at least it is his use of atonality which is the kernel of Schönberg's art, and the fundamental cause for which ultimately he is to be canonised or damned. ¶Atonality is a new word, coined to express the antithesis of tonality, i.e., *without tonality.* To Schönberg the idea of a single key or tonal centre was a limitation; so he turned to atonality in which all twelve tones of the scale are given equal importance and complete independence. In atonality the old laws of harmony and tonality are no longer obeyed. Schönberg even refused the compromise of a mixture, purposely banning all consonant chords of orthodox procedure from his scheme. Coexisting with atonality in the Schönbergian method is the new type of counterpoint which he evolved to accompany it. As every music student knows, orthodox counterpoint required in melodic writing the copious use of scale lines, alternating with skips and leaps. Schönberg's melodies consist largely of wide leaps of every possible interval, often extending (even in the vocal parts) beyond the limits of an octave. These melodies, though angular and eccentric in the extreme, are always subjected religiously to the basic principles of unity and variety; chief themes as well as secondary themes and accompaniment material are derived from the same basic musical germs. ¶This so-called dissonant counterpoint became the basis of all Schönberg's work after 1909. His scores are thick, labyrinthine masses of contrapuntal development in which he displays an almost superhuman facility in the manipulation of the traditional devices. His music abounds in imitation, fugue, canon, inverted canon, and even the crab-canon, or "cancrizans," in which the melody progresses to a certain point and then reverses itself until the entire part is played, note for note, backward to the beginning. Lest the unwary might imagine that dissonant counterpoint, being released from the strict laws of orthodox harmony, might be a relatively simple matter, it must be pointed out that Schönberg in his scheme is guided by an entirely new set of rules which are even more stern and unrelenting than the old ones. They are rules of his own devising, an outgrowth of his inner convictions about the course which the music of the future must take. Often they seem strained and pedantic to the point of sheer perversity, suggesting that Schönberg, in his struggle to free music from her traditional fetters, had succeeded only to forge an entirely new set himself. ¶The net result of these methods is one of the most curious, if not utterly bewildering, developments in the history of music. To the eye, there is no doubt that Schönberg's music is based upon the logical application of sound aesthetic principles. We may clearly see in his scores the use of time-tested principles as foundation stones for his innovations. But to the ear it is the new, the startling, and even the downright ugly which predominate. Dissonance follows dissonance until all semblance of a connection with the past seems to disappear, and the ear longs for the eventual appearance of a consonance or even the suggestion of a tonality. For many listeners this is a development which has tortured the art of music out of shape to suit an arbitrary and self-imposed discipline, an experiment in beauty which destroys beauty and leaves only a shell of ugliness and frustration. For them it is significant that the most effective of all Schönberg's works is his "*Pierrot Lunaire.*" This melodrama consists of twenty-one songs scored for eight instruments and a "sprechstimme"—that is, a soloist who half speaks, half sings. The poems upon which the songs are based relate the never-ending struggle between idealism and materialism. Pierrot, the embodiment of idealistic youth, passes from spirituality to the depths of degradation and sin, then back to regeneration and idealism. It is a decadent idea, sicklied o'er and staled by a thousand different uses. Schönberg's is precisely the setting that it deserves. He distills into his weird score the essence of a decayed romanticism. His music is perverse and morbid, heavy with the scent of sickening perfume; it is ironic and sinister, full of malicious humour that seems always on the point of breaking into the cackling laughter of sheer insanity. ¶Significant, too, is the fact that the only work, not merely of Schönberg's but of any of his close followers, which has as yet received a genuine and widespread acclaim is the opera "*Wozzeck,*" by his distinguished pupil, Alban Berg. Here is a score of singular originality, the most powerful contribution of our time to the operatic stage. Its story is one that chills and repells the listener—a welter of human misery and suffering, of perversion, murder, and suicide

The lyric muse walks into the charnel house and the psychopathic ward, and the music follows, suiting itself perfectly to its surroundings. In other words, it is to conceptions of the morbid and the decadent that the Schönbergian art has so far found its most successful application. ¶There is another pertinent observation to be made here. In *"Wozzeck"* Berg uses with consummate skill all of Schönberg's complicated atonal and contrapuntal technique—but his work has a power and a colour and an inner vitality that are lacking in the work of his master. *"Wozzeck"* may be monstrous, but at least it walks. Too much of Schönberg, on the other hand, is inert and static. Too often we are amazed at his immense resource, only to be disappointed that his inspiration remains still-born. It is possible, of course, that Schönberg is another Cézanne, an artist misunderstood and despised during his lifetime, only to be canonised after his death. But at present it would seem that his influence, not his work, is to cast the longer shadow. (*See Dictionary of Musicians entry, page 389.*)

FRANZ SCHUBERT

By H. A. Scott

FRANZ SCHUBERT was very nearly the greatest of all composers. If he had lived longer, been more carefully trained when young, and received greater appreciation in his lifetime—three very reasonable "might-have-beens"— who shall set limits to the heights which he might have won? He died at thirty-one. If others of the masters had been cut off at this age what treasures the world would have lost!—in the case, say of Händel, every one of his oratorios; in that of Beethoven, his seven greatest symphonies; in that of Wagner, all his operas after *"Tannhäuser"* and *"Lohengrin"*; in that of Brahms, the *"German Requiem"* and all his symphonies. ¶It does not follow that Schubert would necessarily have developed in any like manner. But at least there are reasons for thinking that he might have done so. We know that in the last year of his life he contemplated taking lessons in counterpoint, that on his death-bed he spoke of "entirely new harmonies and rhythms" running through his head, and that he had the loftiest of ambitions. As it was, and taking his works as they stand, certain weaknesses distinguish them which there is no overlooking. That fabulous fertility which could beget six of the *"Winterreise"* songs at a single sitting, three of the pianoforte sonatas in as many weeks, and eight operas in a year, was not counterbalanced by a like faculty in the matter of self-criticism and concentration. Too many of his bigger works lack form and proportion. He did not trouble sufficiently to work out and make the most of the inspired thoughts which came to him in such unparalleled abundance. He was a stupendous genius, it might almost be said, with an infinite capacity for *not* taking pains—whose "profuse strains of unpremeditated art" were at once too profuse and too unpremeditated. ¶But even so only one or two of the very greatest names can stand before his in music's history. He occupies a position only one degree short of the very highest. In the actual quality of his inspiration indeed perhaps there is not one who could be ranked before him. No composer in the whole history of music was more wondrously endowed by nature, whether one considers either the surpassing beauty of his ideas or the profusion of their supply. ¶In Schubert's music at its best there is a haunting and unutterable loveliness, an exquisite blending of tenderness, sweetness, and purity, with strength, nobility, and grandeur, to which, for the true Schubertian, there is perhaps no equivalent in the works of all the other masters put together. And this applies, it should be said, not less to his instrumental pieces than to his songs. ¶The notion that Schubert is great only in his songs is one of those stock judgments which, once accepted, it seems almost impossible to eradicate. In point of fact nothing could be wider of the mark than this belief. Schubert left imperishable works in nearly every branch of music. His songs comprise no doubt his most characteristic and distinctive achievements, inasmuch as nothing like them had ever been so much as attempted before. But so far as concerns the specific quality of their music, they were equalled, if not surpassed, by such works as the symphonies, his chamber compositions, and those exquisite one-movement pieces for the pianoforte, the *"Impromptus"* and *"Moments Musicals,"* which in their way, be it said, were only a degree less epoch-making than the songs. ¶What then is the distinctive place in music of this divinely gifted tone-poet? His distinction is twofold: he created the song as we know it, and more than any other composer he influenced the development of the romantic movement. As the greatest of all song-writers, Schubert's position is assured. It seems safe to say that his noblest achievements under this head will never be surpassed. The Schubert song, of which the text throughout is mirrored in the accompaniment, in which every bar of the music is conditioned by the words, thoughts, and dramatic or emotional content of the poem illustrated, was a distinctive creation in its way not one whit less wonderful than, say, the Beethoven symphony or the Wagnerian music-drama. Such songs as *"Der Erlkönig," "Die junge Nonne," "Der Tod und das Mädchen," "Der Atlas," "Der Doppelgänger,"* or *"Gruppe aus dem Tartarus,"* to name but half-a-dozen almost at random from his more descriptive examples, were a totally new thing in music, the influence of which upon all succeeding composers, not only of songs but of every kind of dramatic or illustrative music, not excluding opera, it would be hard to over-esteem. ¶And more remarkable still perhaps is the fact that this superb emotional and dramatic expressiveness was attained without the smallest sacrifice of qualities specifically musical—nay, took shape in music of the greatest beauty, richness, variety and charm, as music alone and without reference to the text. Schubert's creation of the song in truth partakes almost of the miraculous, for he not only invented an absolutely new kind of song, but developed its utmost possibilities, one might almost say, at a blow —in a word did this new thing at the first time of asking and did it supremely well. ¶Schubert's influence as song-writer it would be hardly possible to exaggerate. It was truly not a reform which he introduced but a revolution. As to his influence on the composers of the romantic school one has only to consider in general the whole character of his music with its all-pervading poetry and emotional expressiveness, and in particular such works as those already named, his *"Impromptus"* and *"Moments Musicals"* to wit, to realise the character of the connection. Here also, in these last-named works, he did that which no one before him had attempted, inventing new forms for the expression of moods too delicate, too intimate, and too personal for treatment in the larger movements of established type, and once again left behind him creations of an entirely novel kind, which later composers have striven in vain to improve upon. ¶Perhaps in the whole range of pianoforte music there are no passages more ravishingly beautiful—more enchanting to the ear, regarded from the purely sensuous standpoint—than some to be found in these inspired works. Had Schubert left nothing further than this slender volume of "*Impromptus*" and "*Moments Musicals*" for the pianoforte his name would live forever in the records of the art. ¶If Schubert's essays in the larger forms—the symphony and the sonata—are to a certain extent impaired by the qualities alluded to, this is by no means to deny their enormous significance and importance. Schubert in these larger works may have been diffuse at times, may not always have developed to the full the wondrous ideas which came to him in such abundance, his works may sometimes lack proportion; but what qualities are theirs by way of comparison!—what wealth of melody! what intoxicating harmonies! what irresistible rhythms! what magical modulations! Recall such creations as the C major and the B minor symphonies, the quintet in C major, the D minor, A minor, and G major quartets, and the sonatas in A minor, B flat, and G among his larger piano works, and of what account seem the dry-as-dusts' and analysts' strictures in the face of such imperishable compositions as these? Nor should it be overlooked that in these larger works also Schubert's methods, if he kept within the recognised forms, were all his own, and as such were full of influence upon his successors. Apart from such technical matters as his harmonies, modulations, instrumentation, and the like, under all of which heads he made striking advances, he breathed into these established forms also a spirit of romance, a yearning, wistful, personal note of lyric tenderness and fervour whereby they are distinguished from all earlier compositions of their kind. ¶Well might it be said by Grove of Schubert that "there never has been one like him and there never will be another"; by Liszt that he was "le musicien le plus poète que jamais"; and by the inscription on his tomb that "Die Tonkunst begrub hier einen reichen Besitz aber noch viel schönere Hoffnungen." (*See Dictionary of Musicians entry, page 392.*)

ROBERT SCHUMANN

By Richard Aldrich

Schumann's music falls into three groups or periods as easily as Beethoven's. There is, first, the product of his early, exuberant style, those wonderful series of short piano pieces, slight in form, but soaring into imaginative power; saying little, but vaguely hinting at much. The second period is one of more self-centred activity, of greater poise, of more conservative methods; his ideal had expanded, and was leading him to compose in a larger mould, with a broader sweep of imagination, and with a greater regard for form as itself an element of beauty. And, in his last period, we must group those of his works that show the failing powers, the exhausted imagination of an intellect already overshadowed by its approaching doom. ¶Schumann's beginnings in music were as nearly the spontaneous outpourings of himself as can well be thought of. It is difficult to derive the sources of even his first attempts from the music of his predecessors. He studied some of Hummel's works, and greatly admired Moscheles, and, the critics say, that the *"Abegg"* variations, *Opus 1*, are in the Hummel-Moscheles style. He was devoted to Schubert from his early years, and played his little piano pieces, especially the dances, with great love; perhaps the traces of this may be found in the *Papillons, Opus 2*. But even here, the influence, if there be any, related more to the concise and sententious form, the poetic content, than to the fibre of the music itself. It is not the kind of resemblance that you will find to Mozart and Haydn all through the earliest works of Beethoven. Bach, too, formed a part of young Schumann's musical daily bread; we may perhaps discern that influence in the instinctive feeling for contrapuntal movement—though of a very free, and, as it were, untechnical sort—in those earliest piano pieces; but here again comparison of the specifically musical style reveals nothing. ¶There is one influence, however, that cannot be overlooked in computing the forces bearing on Schumann's formative period; that is Jean Paul Richter. All readers of Schumann's letters know how steeped he was in the spirit of this singular German fantastic, this overwrought romantic symbolist, a story-teller, philosopher, and poet in one. He was all in all to Schumann; not only the young man's literary style—he was already a copious writer—but his very ideals in music, were moulded on Jean Paul's, and thickly overlaid with his mannerisms. For in these early years of Schumann's life music and poetry seem to meet on common ground, and to take their impulse from one and the same starting-point. In Jean Paul, all that charming crew of *"Davidites,"* with *"Florestan"* and *"Eusebius"* as their forefront, have their prototypes; and their appearance in the early *Zeitschrift* articles is no more characteristic of this influence than their appearance in the *"Carnéval"* and the *"Davidsbündlertänze."* ¶With his attainment of his heart's desire in his marriage with Clara Wieck, in 1840, there seems to have come a mellowing, a ripening force in Schumann's musical inspiration—if you will, a conservative force that led him to see the significance and value of those musical forms to which he had at first been indifferent. Some of his ardent companions in the revolutionary parties of the earlier years saw in this a backsliding from his professions. But the fact that he parted company with *"Florestan"* and *"Eusebius,"* and erased their names from the reissues of musical works once signed by them, can be for us naught but an indication of intellectual growth. We enjoy those romantic and engaging figures, but we see greater things than they were concerned with in the symphonies, the piano-quintette, the string-quartettes, the piano-concerto, the third part of *"Faust,"* and *"Paradise and the Peri."* ¶The contributions of Schumann to the development of the art are important and permanent. What he did to develop the expressive power of the pianoforte is all his own. He wrote for the instrument in a new way, calling for new and elaborate advances in technique—not the brilliant finger-dexterity of Chopin and Liszt, but a deeper underlying potency of expression through interlacing parts, skilfully disposed harmonies, the inner voices of chords, and through new demands as to variety of tone quality, contrasts of colour and the enrichment of the whole through pedal effects. It has been called a crabbed style, but it is no less idiomatic of the piano than the more open and brilliant manner that was developed at the same period by the virtuoso-school of pianoforte-playing and composition. ¶Schumann's use of short pieces, in connected series, as an exposition of what is really a single poetic idea running through them all, is his own creation, and one that succeeding composers have made the most of. So is his idealised form of programme-music—music, that is, expressing some definite, concrete, external idea. But his wise judgment on music of this kind must always be kept in mind, that it must always be beautiful and intelligible as music without the need of explanation through titles, in which he saw only an aid or stimulus to the hearer's imagination. Space is lacking to discuss his later experiments in modifying or developing the classical or sonata form to increase its unity and its emotional potency, such as are to be found in the D-minor and C-major symphonies, and the piano-quintette. Schumann added something peculiarly his own to the Lied, in his enhancement of the accompaniment's significance, increasing its power of expression in co-operation, sometimes almost on equal terms with the voice, and, in many instances, giving its ritournelles or instrumental postludes an independent elaboration and meaning of their own. ¶Schumann came of a well-to-do family, and his early general education and social surroundings had been far beyond those of most musicians. The fact that he was not only well read, but a writer himself of peculiar charm and individuality, a critic of quickening insight and generous discernment, reacted, as it needs must, on his music. Though he was, early in his youth, of a lively character, he was always disposed toward moodiness; and by the time he reached manhood he had fallen into a state of remarkable taciturnity and introspection. Wrapped in his own thoughts, he would, when in the company of friends or fellow-musicians, sit silent hour after hour, with his head leaning on his hand, often with an incipient smile upon his face, and with his lips pursed, as though to whistle. His letters show him to have been of a sweet and affectionate nature toward his family and intimates; kindly and generous in his estimate and treatment of others, yet roused to anger by a wrong, and capable of deep and glowing resentment. ¶Schumann's place in modern music was slowly won, both in his native land and elsewhere, but there is little sign yet of its being shaken. His symphonies suffer unduly, through their unskilful orchestration, in the estimation of a generation to whom fine feeling for orchestral colour is essential, but the magnificent elegance of the two great overtures (to "*Manfred*" and "*Genoveva*") is little discounted in this way; the string-quartettes and the piano-quintette and quartette seem to lose none of their beauty as they recede in historical perspective; the piano concertos and a great number of the songs are heard repeatedly, every year, with unremitted joy. His solo piano-pieces appeal less and less to the taste of the latterday piano-virtuoso who cannot utilise music calling so little for nimbleness of finger and brilliancy of effect; but it is impossible to deny that these pieces are still competent, as few others are, to serve deep and sincere music lovers "for the enjoyment of god at home." Schumann will always have a commanding hold, a commanding place in the nineteenth century, the century of evolution, the century that struck off the academic bonds from art. In the noble band of romantic adventurers into new and unexplored realms of music, Schumann was a leader, but he never failed in his bold and chivalrous championship of the rectitude of his art. (*See also page 395.*)

JEAN SIBELIUS

BY RICHARD ANTHONY LEONARD

THE MUSIC of Jean Sibelius stood before the world for more than three decades before this composer began to receive his just dues.   On the stage of modern music he was for years a powerful but never a dominating figure; he remained aloof and in the half-light, never in the centre of the stage.   Had Sibelius died as recently as 1925 it might have been with the belief that much of his finest work was destined for oblivion.   But now at last he stands forth in his true stature as one of the two or three greatest composers of our time, while for many critical admirers he is the master spirit of all twentieth-century musicians. ¶No mystery surrounds this long-delayed recognition, for two often-encountered factors had been at work.   The first is the inherently difficult, almost forbidding quality of Sibelius' greatest work, a quality which makes early appreciation well-nigh impossible.   The second was the appearance, at the moment when Sibelius began his first serious work of composition, of new and startling trends in modern music—first the impressionism of Debussy, then the ultramodernism of Stravinsky, and finally the atonality of Schönberg—a small revolution which was to absorb the attention of the music world for more than thirty years, during which time Sibelius and his works had to wait, alone and neglected, in the ante-room.   Still a third factor should be mentioned; it was accidental but neverthe-less potent.   Sibelius was unfortunate in that several of his early minor works (notably "*Finlandia*" and "*Valse triste*") achieved a widespread and super-ficial popularity.   For many years musicians (even symphony conductors of otherwise discerning taste) thought of Sibelius in terms of these competent but essentially second-rate scores—to the great detriment of his other vastly more important works.   ¶There is special interest in the fact that Sibelius was born in 1865, for it indicates that he is a contemporary of Debussy (born 1862) and of Richard Strauss (born 1864).   The contrast in the creative careers of these three men is curiously revealing.   Debussy died in 1918, and for six years before that the flame of his inspiration had tragically drooped.   Strauss has survived into old age, but the genius who composed "*Der Rosenkavalier*" and "*Till Eulenspiegel*" has been dead these many years.   Sibelius, alone of the three, grew old without suffering a serious decline in his creative powers.   During the first decade of the twentieth century, when the other two men had already reached their zenith, Sibelius' star was rising in a steady curve; in the second decade, when they had passed their peak, he had just entered the great creative period of his life.   ¶It should be noted, too, that all three men began their im-portant work in the nineties, at the time when the tremendous tide of Wagner-ism was moving toward its flood.   The most vital single consideration in Sibelius' early life is the fact that he was not—and never did become—a Wagner-ite.   Sibelius has always disliked Wagner's music.   So many composers, like Strauss, had succumbed to the Wagnerian magic and spent their lives largely in imitation of him.   But Sibelius turned completely away from Wagner, and therein lay the ultimate salvation of his creative soul.   In his finest work we find instead a definite kinship with Brahms.   To-day indeed it becomes in-creasingly evident that the Sibelius symphonies are the most powerful essays in that form since the death of Brahms.   An English protagonist of Sibelius, Cecil Gray, goes even further, declaring that for Sibelius' equal as a symphonist we must actually name the All-Highest—Beethoven himself.   ¶The whole body of Sibelius' work comprises an enormous quantity of music in a great variety of forms.   Besides the seven symphonies there are more than fifty orchestral and choral works, large and small; incidental music to a number of plays, a violin concerto, a string quartet, dozens of piano pieces, more than one hundred songs, and a number of miscellaneous works of every type—many of which have never been published.   In such a wealth of material it is inevitable that there should be a wide variation in quality.   But the general level is uncommonly high.   The greater works fall mainly into two categories—the tone poems and the symphonies.   The latter are the more likely to prove the supreme examples of the composer's genius, but it was the former which first established him and which even to-day remain in the public consciousness as his most characteristic creations.   ¶The Sibelius of the tone poems is closely akin to nature and they are an unmistakable product of his Northern environment. He himself has written, "It is true I am a dreamer and a poet of nature.   I love the sounds of the field and forest, water and mountains."   He is profoundly moved, too, by the legends of the North, especially by the Finnish mythology. From these two wellsprings of inspiration have come many of his best works. "*The Oceanides*," for example, is an impressionistic tone picture with the myriad aspects of the sea as its background.   The stupendous "*Tapiola*" (one of Sibelius' masterpieces) takes its name from Tapio, the Finnish forest god. "*En Saga*," the first work of Sibelius to become widely known outside of Finland, is a symphonic poem based on an unnamed legend.   Most potent of all sources of material for this composer has been the "*Kalevala*," the great national epic of the Finns.   From its runes he has drawn the brilliant "*Pohjola's Daughter*," a tonal painting of the maiden of Pohjola sitting upon a rainbow, spinning. Also "*The Origin of Fire*," for barytone solo, male chorus and orchestra, in which Ukko, the Zeus of the Finnish mythology, restores sunlight and warmth to a world plunged in darkness.   The story of the Creation as told in the "*Kalevala*" is set forth in "*Lunnotar*," for soprano solo and orchestra.   Other runes of the same work are the basis for "*The Song of Vaino*," for chorus and orchestra; the "*Legend*" for orchestra, "*The Return of Lemminkainen*" and its companion piece, the famous "*Swan of Tuonela*."   In the Finnish mythology Tuonela is the Hell, or land of death.   ¶In dominating such tremendous material—the painting of vast, icy Northern spaces, of mighty half-barbaric legends—Sibelius displays complete mastery.   He brings to his task a prodigious technical equipment, an Olympian style, and a sovereign imagination. The result is music of truly epic quality.   "It is blood-brother to the wind and silence," writes Paul Rosenfeld; "to the lowering cliffs and the spray, to harsh crying of sea-birds and the breath of fog.   . . .   The orchestral compositions of Sibelius seem to have passed over black torrents and desolate moorlands, through pallid sunlight and grim primeval forests, and become drenched with them.   The instrumentation is all wet grays and blacks, relieved only by bits of brightness wan and elusive as the Northern summer, frostily green as the polar lights.   The works are full of gnawing of bassoons and the bleakness of the English horn, full of shattering trombones and screaming violins, full of the sinister rolling of drums, the menacing reverberation of cymbals, the icy glittering of harps. The musical ideas of those of the compositions that are finally realised recall the ruggedness and hardiness and starkness of things that persist in the Finnish winter. The rhythms seem to approach the wild, unnumbered rhythms of the forest and the wind and the flickering sunlight." ¶In spite of these qualities in the music of Sibelius it cannot be said that he has ever evolved a special or characteristic "style." We may speak of Debussy's typical harmonies, or Stravinsky's rhythms, or Schönberg's atonality; but no such ready epithetic qualities associate themselves with the work of the great Finn. For that reason there are no Sibelius imitators, and there probably never will be. There never has been a Sibelius school or a Sibelius cult—no swarm of gadfly imitators such as flitted around Stravinsky and Schönberg. The music of Sibelius contains little that is revolutionary or startlingly new, little upon which the facile imitator may seize. His development as an artist has been a slow, steady growth, based solidly on the foundations of his great predecessors and coloured only by his strong Northern personality. His mastery is all-embracing: his melodies are aggressive and strong, full of salt and savour; his harmonies are richly expressive or acrid and harsh, depending upon his specific aims; while his superb command of modern orchestration is exercised only for the most legitimate purposes, never for mere virtuosity for its own sake. ¶In the seven Sibelius symphonies all these qualities are present in superabundance. The First Symphony, written in 1899 when the composer was thirty-four, is largely orthodox in form. It contains strong reminders of Grieg, Tchaikowski, and Dvořák, but its melodies are distinctive and unhackneyed, its orchestration brilliantly effective. Even to-day, when so much of the music of the late nineteenth century has faded and grown stale, this work retains its vital freshness. The Second Symphony is closely akin to the First; it contains a finale of the type beloved by late Victorians. Yet it gives strong evidence of the composer's growth and its inner construction contains acorns that were later to produce some of his greatest oaks. For his Third Symphony Sibelius uses a process of reduction. The form is scaled down to three movements, the orchestration is restrained, while the imposing, dramatic dignity of the thematic material of the preceding symphonies is discarded for simple, straightforward melodies. The prevailing mood of the work is sunny and bright. ¶In his Fourth Symphony Sibelius produced not only the crown of his own endeavour, but one of the most astonishing works in all modern music. Early performances left its hearers baffled and unsatisfied, while most conductors thought it so harsh and ungrateful that it lay neglected for almost twenty years. The reasons are not far to seek. It is a remote, solitary, deeply introspective work, saturated with the darkest gloom. Its themes sound bare and elementary, and often so sparsely developed that at first hearing they seem not to be developed at all. "The Fourth Symphony," writes Cecil Gray, "is the outcome of a process of sheer starvation, of a fakirlike asceticism and self-denial. It is gaunt, spectral, emaciated almost; the question is no longer one of superfluous flesh, but of any flesh at all—the very bones protrude." When the outward strangeness of this extraordinary work wears off we begin to feel the workings of the powerful and original creative mind beneath it, and the desperate suffering which must have brought it to fruition. No other music of our time is such a distilled essence of intolerable pain. ¶Sibelius returns to something nearer serenity in his Fifth Symphony. Here is a far more conventional work than the Fourth, but every

bar contains the stamp of its creator.   The last movement is a notable success—
a stirring, triumphant finale that nevertheless contrives to be unhackneyed.
For many critics Sibelius' Sixth Symphony represents something of a falling off
in creative interest.   It is a restrained, carefully poised work, lacking the
intensity of the Fourth and the brilliance of the Fifth.   But with the Seventh
Symphony we come again upon an undisputed masterpiece.   This symphony
is in one gigantic movement, a vast massing of the composer's creative forces
for a single stunning attack.   It has no counterpart in the music of our time.
(*See Dictionary of Musicians entry, page 405.*)

RICHARD STRAUSS

By James Huneker

That Richard Strauss was the son of the famous horn-player may explain
his predilection for the beautiful instrument.   ¶At Meiningen he met Alexander Ritter, a pupil of Wagner, and this friendship, with Von Bülow's daily
coaching, decided Richard Strauss's tendency in art.   He became a composer
of the future, a man of the new school.   He travelled much—he went to Greece,
Italy, and Egypt for incipient lung-trouble—and on "guesting" tours, on which
he was received with enthusiasm; he was a modern conductor in all the implications of the phrase.   A man of good physique, Scandinavian in appearance,
Strauss was widely cultured and well read in classic and modern literature.
¶In music he was a true descendant of Berlioz, Liszt, Wagner, though early
in his career he showed marked traces of a devotion to Brahms.   This is
more noticeable in his piano and orchestra *Burleske in D minor*, in the solo
sonata and in the *"Wanderer's Sturmlied," opus 14*, for six-voiced chorus
and orchestra.   ¶He has in his symphonic forms pushed to the verge of the
sublime—or the ridiculous—or both—the poetic programme (Vide D. D.,
"programme music").   His *"Don Juan," "Macbeth," "Death and Transfigura-
tion," "Till Eulenspiegel's Merry Pranks," "Thus Spake Zarathustra," "Don
Quixote,"* and *"Ein Heldenleben"* are tokens of labours almost Balzacian in
their intensity.   An emotional strenuousness, a marvellous mastery of the
orchestral apparatus, an abnormal colour and rhythmic sense, combined with
poetic feeling, bizarre, even grotesque methods of utterance, an utter defiance
of formalism either classic or romantic, and a thematic invention not commen-
surate with his other gifts—all these qualities jumbled in amazing juxtaposition
and flavoured by a powerful individuality, easily made Richard Strauss the
leader of the New German School and a formidable figure in the musical arena.
¶As a song-writer his various collections have met with the greatest success,
for he has a happy method of welding music and poem into a perfect, if somewhat startling, whole.   Form he abandons utterly, striving to capture the idea
as he perceives it, in its full bloom.   *Opera* 10, 15, 17, 127, 29, 32, are favourites;
the later songs are difficult and almost cryptic in sentiment and execution.
Strauss was the greatest master of the orchestra of his day.   (*See page 422.*)

IGOR STRAVINSKY

By Richard Anthony Leonard

WHATEVER the future may think of him, Igor Stravinsky has achieved during his lifetime a place in modern music so far attained by no other composer of the twentieth century. One almost uses the word "notorious" in connection with Stravinsky. Specifically he is responsible for that most infamous of all scores, "*Le Sacre du Printemps.*" When Diaghileff first produced this ballet in Paris in 1913, with choreography by Nijinsky, much of the music was drowned out by the hissing, stamping, and yelling of the enraged audience. They heard a tonal picture of the coming of Spring in pagan Russia, and it assaulted their ears and their emotions with a ferocity that knew no bounds. It was cacophonous, complex, intense—it was sadistic, frenzied, horrifying. After its first concert performance in England in 1921 outraged citizens took arms in typical British fashion and wrote letters of protest to the newspapers. Lawrence Gilman relates that one man, shaken to his emotional roots, insisted that the score "stood for all the unnamable horrors of revolution, murder, and rapine." In 1924, when New York first heard the concert version of the work, indignant members of the old school walked out in droves, unwilling to listen to the "blasphemous destruction of music as an art"; while to later performances sensation-seekers flocked as they would to a gangster's funeral. ¶The cause of all this pother was a small-sized, slight-figured Russian, with the full lips and slanting eyes of a Tartar—a cold little man with the calculating interest of an experimenter in music, an iconoclast and a hater of all sentiment. This is the man around whom the entire ultra-modernist movement in music revolved. For almost twenty years, following the outbreak of the Great War, Stravinsky bestrode the narrow world of music like a Colossus. His every score was accorded instant recognition wherever important music is played. Imitators and disciples sprang up everywhere, until effeminate Frenchmen. staid young Englishmen, and talented American Jews were all slavishly imitating the bitter polytonality and shocking rhythms of this ultra-modern primitiv ist Russian. The concert halls of Europe and America rang with a new and strange music. The rich, sensuous styles of Wagner and Strauss began to disappear; their smooth-flowing, long-breathing melodic line gave way to hard, angular rhythms and short, metallic utterance. Atonality became the reigning fashion; notes without benefit of a key centre were juxtaposed in counterpoint that shrieked. ¶Stravinsky was not by any means the sole moving force in this revolution which swept the art of music; for more than a decade before the war the currents had been moving swiftly toward this climax. But he, more than any other composer, epitomises the upheaval that finally took place. His music reflected, more than any other, the profound changes wrought in every phase of man's activity and thought during the second and third decades of the twentieth century. It reflected a cold, hard cynicism, a disdain of sentiment, a preoccupation with pure, steely mechanics, mixed with occasional outbursts of an almost frenzied despair—in brief, all the characteristics of a race of men whose faiths, traditions, and sentiments, whose moorings to a nostalgic past were all blasted away in the shell-shock of a monstrous war. ¶Possibly the future will look with bewilderment upon the huge clouds of controversial dust which Stravinsky's music raised when it burst upon an unprepared world. Much of its strangeness has already vanished; atonality, polytonality, poly-harmony, and all the other devices of ultra-modern composition no longer raise even a critical eyebrow. But a span of years must still pass before any final critical estimate can be made of Stravinsky's fundamental importance. The composer himself has complicated the issues and rendered final judgment difficult by refusing to remain in the categories which musicians and critics, in their disturbed attempts to classify, have tried to create for him. Several times in the course of his development he has changed his style, advanced new and often disquieting theories, or taken unto himself strange and incongruous gods to worship. Few composers have been more completely unpredictable. ¶As with so many revolutionists, Stravinsky's beginnings were orthodox. His early works, after a period of study with Rimsky-Korsakoff, include a set of piano études, a song cycle, a symphony after the manner of Tchaikowsky, and several short orchestral pieces. One of these, "Fireworks," was composed as a wedding present for Rimsky's daughter, and is a deftly orchestrated, exceed-ingly clever mimicry of fire and light. Another, "Scherzo fantastique," though a work of less originality, brought about the most important single happening in Stravinsky's early life. It was heard by Serge Diaghileff, who promptly commissioned the young composer to write for his Russian ballet. Between 1909 and 1914 Stravinsky composed "L'Oiseau de Feu," "Petrouchka," and "Le Sacre du Printemps," all in collaboration with Diaghileff, who produced them first in Paris. All three were landmarks in the history of the ballet and in the course of modern music. Moreover, in the short space of those four years the composer had traversed an astonishing span of creative development and achieved a climax which, for many critics, he has never again approached. With "L'Oiseau de Feu" he stepped with one stride out of the class of the talented but still uncertain amateur to an assured and immensely gifted mas-tery. Much of this work is plainly derived from Stravinsky's Russian prede-cessors; nevertheless it is full of originality and charm and it exhibits a use of the orchestra that is both exquisite and brilliant. "Petrouchka" represents another stride forward—a huge stride. Here Stravinsky discloses a genius not only for scene painting in music but also for the far more difficult art of character delineation. With incredible vividness and speed he draws for us a picture of the Russian peasant fair—a marvellous phantasmagoria of gypsies, dancers, organ-grinders, drunkards, animals—in a whirl of merry-making and noise. Against this background are mimed the four main characters—the Charlatan and his three puppets, the Blackamoor, the Ballerina, and Petrouch-ka. Stravinsky exposes their cruelty and vulgarity, their gaiety and charm, their morbid, violent passions, and their pathetic struggling for a transient happiness. Petrouchka, "a child-like soul crying in a withered hell," is an especial masterpiece of musical characterisation. ¶Of "Le Sacre du Printemps" and its first impressions we have already spoken. It is no longer the terrifying monument that it was in 1913, but it still remains a solitary and profoundly disturbing one. Stravinsky achieved these "Pictures of Pagan Russia" by a combination of effects which were violently new and startling at that time, and which were to leave indelible marks on all the music of the next two decades. Dissonance, atonality, and polyharmony abound in the score, with hardly a bar of orthodox harmony to be found anywhere. The orchestra employed is vast, but its immense frame is often strained to the utmost by the explosive fury of the music. By far the most extraordinary feature of the score is Stravinsky's use of rhythms. They are violent in the extreme, running a huge gamut of intensities and cadences, and often so complex that the time signatures change with almost every bar. It has been rightly said that in this work Stravinsky uses rhythm as a separate entity, much as Debussy had used the chord—divorced from melody and employed purely for its own sake. Rhythm —brutal, stark, realistic rhythm—now became the hallmark of Stravinsky's work. ¶After "*Le Sacre du Printemps*" a change came over the composer—a change about which there still remains certain elements of mystery. Up to this time his work had been unmistakably Russian, as well as pictorial and emotional. Now he sought to develop a new style. His life in Paris suddenly made him aware of the eighteenth century in music, of its abstract purity, its lack of a pronounced nationalism. He announced that he wanted to become "a classicist, an objectivist, a constructive artist." He scaled down his huge orchestral forces and wrote more intimate works like the chamber operas, "*Renard*" and "*L'Histoire du Soldat*," and the cantata with dances, "*Les Noces*." Then he became completely enamoured of the neoclassic style and composed "*Pulcinella*," a "ballet with song," based on airs of Pergolesi, a "*Symphony for Wind Instruments*," an "Octuor," also for wind instruments, a Concerto for piano, wind instruments and percussion, and a Piano Sonata. These works, according to the composer, were "in the style of the eighteenth century viewed from the standpoint of to-day." The view could not have been very good, for often the results were simply an odd mixture of old counterpoint and new atonality. In the later "*Capriccio*" for piano and orchestra and the Concerto for violin it appears that Stravinsky was chiefly influenced by Bach and—*mirabile dictu*—modern jazz. ¶Even though this neoclassic phase was to dominate the composer's work for more than a decade, and although he spoke a great deal in its defense, for the general music public it was a disappointing anti-climax. The world had expected tremendous things from the composer of "*Le Sacre du Printemps*" and "*Petrouchka*"; it felt unexpectedly let down when he produced instead these abstruse cerebral exercises, deliberately drained of the emotional force and the brilliant colouring that had characterized his most potent work. ¶Later, neoclassicism itself was to be supplanted. The seeds of the newest phase are to be found in the opera bouffe, "*Mavra*," which appeared in 1922. It is based on a book of Pushkin's and is an admitted attempt to imitate the style of the early nineteenth-century opera composers. Stravinsky dedicated it to the memory of Pushkin, Glinka, and Tchaikowsky. Later he publicly declared his admiration for Tchaikowsky, to the utter bewilderment of many of his ultra-modernist followers who had already relegated the Russian arch-romanticist to a waxworks of long-forgotten horrors. In 1927 Stravinsky finished "*Oedipus Rex*," an "opera-oratorio," based on a Latin translation of Jean Cocteau's French version of the Greek drama by Sophocles. This dark and sombre score (for orchestra, male chorus, and soloists) Stravinsky declared to be "the largest of all his works," in which his style "had reached the utmost simplification and the greatest similarity with the ideal style to be found in Glinka's '*Life of the Tsar*.'" When, in 1930, he composed his "*Symphony of the Psalms*" for chorus and orchestra, based on verses from three of the Psalms, his purposes began to emerge more clearly. It seemed likely that his cycle of development had turned at last to the neo-romantic stage, and that now the nineteenth century was to be "viewed from the standpoint of to-day." ¶It cannot be denied that Stravinsky no longer enjoys the undisputed eminence and the immense prestige that he did for almost two decades after 1914. His phase of neoclassicism in particular brought about a strong critical revulsion. He has often been termed an opportunist in music, a shrewd observer of fads and fashions, an innovator who used the surface brilliance of his art to buy popular recognition and fame during his lifetime. His shortcomings—notably his weakness in melodic invention—have been proclaimed again and again. None of these factors, however, is likely to mar the enduring reputations of his three great ballets, produced between 1909 and 1914. This was the time when his natural impulses and his Russian heritage of strong, primitive emotionalism were given free rein. As soon as he sought to restrain these impulses and instead apply his tremendous technical skill to the abstract and the unemotional, his work suffered in consequence. ¶The inevitable fact remains that Stravinsky had reached with "*Petrouchka*" and "*Le Sacre du Printemps*" such a peak of creative intensity that almost any work which followed was bound to disappoint. Moreover, we may now discern that "*Le Sacre du Printemps*" was not the beginning of a genuine new phase in modern music, but the ending of one. It is clearly a work of impressionism—an application of Stravinsky's brutal, angular, hard-surfaced technique to the impressionist style. In spite of its primitivist outlines it is highly sophisticated, decadent; it represents the impressionist movement developed finally to overripeness. With its completion Stravinsky was left no course but to seek other modes of expression. (*See Dictionary of Musicians entry, page 423.*)

ARTHUR SEYMOUR SULLIVAN

By Eric Hodgins

AFTER the death of Henry Purcell, it took England some one hundred and fifty years to produce a native composer worthy of any critical notice whatever. She finally succeeded in 1842, when Arthur Seymour Sullivan was born in London. ¶This second son of an Irish clarinetist was marked for music from the first. In an autobiographical moment he once assured a listener that from the age of five onward music was the only thing in his life which meant anything to him. After his father rose sufficiently in the musical world to become bandmaster in the Royal Military College, Sullivan quickly learned to play all the band's instruments. It is recorded by Hesketh Pearson that he composed his first anthem at the age of eight. ¶After this achievement had been followed by a career as a choirboy, as Mendelssohn Scholar at the Royal Academy of Music, and as a brilliant student at the Leipzig Conservatoire, Sullivan settled down in England with the avowed intention of becoming a composer. This was an odd ambition for a young Englishman of the period (it is interesting to remember that Sullivan was roughly the contemporary of Johann Strauss the Younger, and of Johannes Brahms); it was also somewhat eccentric of Sullivan to be such

an energetic enthusiast for the music of Schubert and Schumann, when Mendelssohn was the one composer whom the English regarded as possessing true
merit. But Sullivan was an ingratiating young man, as his personality triumphed over these peculiarities. Soon he was professor of pianoforte and
ballad singing at the Crystal Palace School of Art, and hard at work completing
a work begun in Leipzig: music to Shakespeare's *"Tempest."* Its performance
in 1862, when he was just twenty, instantly made his reputation. ¶It was not,
however, for five years that Sullivan was to begin venturing with the art form
in which his genius was to make him famous, wealthy, and unhappy. Between
1862 and 1867 the official record of Sullivan's productivity lists dozens upon
dozens of oratorios, sacred songs, hymns, cantatas, anthems, and "secular
works." But in 1867 Sullivan joined hands with F. C. Burnand (a humorist
later to become editor of *Punch*), and between them they wrote libretto and
music for a minor theatrical tidbit called *"Cox and Box."* It was well but
mildly regarded. Dabbling thus in the theatre it was inevitable that Sullivan
should sooner or later meet William Schwenck Gilbert, who, while Sullivan was
producing his endless series of religious works, had been turning out heaps of
serious and semi-serious theatrical rubbish sometimes accompanied by music.
The two men were introduced in 1870 by Frederic Clay, a composer who had
been Gilbert's occasional previous collaborator. There thus began one of the
most notable collaborations in the history of the English-speaking theatre. It
opened inauspiciously with the production of *"Thespis, or The Gods Grown
Old"* in 1871, a "comic opera" which withered after a brief run. It took successful root in 1875 with a curtain raiser, *"Trial by Jury,"* originally written to
fill out an evening made not quite long enough (in one sense) by Offenbach's
"La Perichole." It was once and for all confirmed by the unparalleled success
(after an uncertain beginning) of *"Pinafore"* in 1878. Thereafter the Gilbert
and Sullivan collaboration, with one or two small exceptions, swept everything
before it. It was thrice broken off by its partners, who were never able to like
or respect one another, and who never met as friends. But between the date
of the first successful full-length comic opera (*"Pinafore"*) and the last (*"The
Gondoliers,"* produced in 1889) there elapsed eleven years of national acclaim
for librettist and composer alike. The closing years of the collaboration, which
finally ceased in 1896, were marred by increasing quarrels, one semi-failure
(*"Utopia, Limited,"*) and one final effort (*"The Grand Duke"*) which was, by
unanimous testimony, so intolerably bad that it was all but unrecognisable
as a product of the famous partnership. ¶In the course of their quarrels the
partners had frequent recourse to other collaborators. Yet neither was ever
able to write a successful work without the other. Sullivan's significant operas,
therefore, are limited to those for which Gilbert provided the libretti. The
passage of half a century has not dimmed their popularity. Throughout the
English-speaking world they have been heard, year in, year out, almost continuously since their first production. The following is a condensed record:

Opera	Première	No. of Performances at First Production
Thespis, or The Gods Grown Old	December 23, 1871	
Trial by Jury	March 25, 1875	294
The Sorcerer	November 17, 1877	175

H.M.S. Pinafore, or The Lass that Loved a Sailor	May 25, 1878	563
The Pirates of Penzance, or The Slave of Duty	April 3, 1880	366
Patience, or Bunthorne's Bride	April 23, 1881	578
Iolanthe, or The Peer and the Peri ⎱	November 25, 1882	400
Princess Ida, or Castle Adamant	January 5, 1884	147
The Mikado, or The Town of Titipu	March 14, 1885	672
Ruddigore, or The Witch's Curse	January 22, 1887	288
The Yeomen of the Guard, or The Merryman and His Maid	October 3, 1888	423
The Gondoliers, or The King of Barataria	December 7, 1889	559
Utopia, Limited, or The Flowers of Progress	October 7, 1893	245
The Grand Duke, or The Statutory Duel	March 7, 1896	123

¶For his services to the cause of English music, Sullivan was knighted by Queen Victoria in 1883—a distinction not conferred upon his collaborator (of whom the Queen disapproved) until Edward VII redressed the balance in 1907. But the acclaim and honours with which Sullivan was surrounded were disfigured for him by the feeling—fostered by many of his acquaintances—that his talents were being squandered upon the trivialities of Mr. Gilbert's topsy-turvy imagination. The suggestion was even borne to him that the Queen would be pleased to have him compose an opera to which the adjective "grand" could be properly applied. The eventual result of this was *"Ivanhoe,"* composed by Sullivan to a libretto by Julian Sturgis and produced in 1891. ¶The result was not happy. By all accounts, *"Ivanhoe"* contained much good music. Incontestably, however, *"Ivanhoe"* contained no music that would live. In this, it illustrates the anomaly of Sullivan's entire career: the music by which he himself set the greatest store, and on which he laboured hardest, was either stillborn or died in infancy; the music he composed in a fuming fret at the limitations of Gilbert's libretti is the only music that has lived—and it has lived as "light" music never lived before or has since. The *"Kenilworth Cantata"* (1864), *"The Light of the World"* (1873), *"The Martyr of Antioch"* (1880), *"The Golden Legend"* (1886)—every one of these noble efforts is as dead as any music could possibly be. Aside from the Gilbert and Sullivan operas, the pieces of music by Sullivan of which the present-day world has any first-hand knowledge are only two: the rousing *"Onward, Christian Soldiers"* and the lugubrious *"Lost Chord"*—both composed before *"Pinafore"* sealed his fate. ¶But the music for these operas should be monument enough for any composer. Sullivan's supreme gift was the gift of melodic invention—without which music, whatever its pretentions, reduces itself to the status of ear noises. He scored for a small orchestra (two flutes, one oboe, two clarinets, two bassoons, two horns, two cornets, two trombones, percussion and strings) and by the standards of the present some of the instrumentation sounds thin. The traditionalism with which the D'Oyly Carte Opera Company, holders of the performing rights to the operas, carry out their presentations, accounts for the fact that no modernised orchestrations have been made—and anyone who would like to study the full scores of the operas will discover that they are jealously and secretly guarded by the holders of the performing rights and are not made available to anyone else. But Sullivan's orchestrations, if slightly dated to the modern ear, are almost invariably perfect models of deftness, taste, and ingenuity. Cecil Forsyth, in his great work *Orchestration*, sums up his opinion of Sullivan's gifts in instrumentation by pointing to "*Were I Thy Bride*" in "*The Yeomen of the Guard*" and urging his students to observe "not only the notes which Sullivan has written, but the many other notes he might have written and didn't." ¶Two other qualities of Sullivan's musicianship are to be noted. The first is his ability—so painfully and inexplicably rare—to express humour in music. The second—and one of the most significant qualities in the success of the operas— is his uncanny ability, while managing his melody and performing those prodigies of rhythmical skill which Gilbert's lyrics demanded of him, to provide settings for the words which were not only appropriate but which helped rather than hindered the audience's ability to hear what was being sung. One hold of Gilbert and Sullivan operas upon their early audiences lay in the joy those audiences felt that here at last was a native product in an art form which, they had come to think, could never be successfully transplanted from the Continent. Now, however, they heard English words clearly set to tunes which were also their own; they had had no such experience before, and were enchanted. ¶Probably part of Sullivan's unique ability to set Gilbert's words with such sympathy lay in his method of work. On receiving a set of Gilbert's verses, Sullivan's first studies were always directed toward the problems of rhythm; it was only after he had interpreted the words in a system of dots and dashes that he undertook to set his melodic line. Thereafter the operas grew organically. Sullivan would present roughly sketched parts to the singers and supply an approximation of the accompaniment for the piano. From these beginnings, the finished instrumentation grew. ¶Like that of all other composers, Sullivan's level of inspiration varied notably, not only from opera to opera, but often from song to song. He could be banal and tedious. One of his greatest strengths— and weaknesses—was his inexhaustible facility. Many of his loveliest effects he achieved without half trying; effort was unnecessary. Thus if the best solution of some troublesome problem escaped him, he was not apt to agonise to find it—a second or third best solution was already waiting to be set down on paper. There was never a less slovenly composer; but there have been composers who have needed a higher threshold of self-criticism than Sullivan ever felt called upon to apply to himself in the operas he wrote with Gilbert. ¶Any ranking list of the operas in terms of musical excellence means little more than an expression of personal preference. Sullivan did not become greater as the operas progressed; he became only surer. (He also became increasingly repetitive.) The emptiness of "*The Grand Duke*" is unanimously acknowledged. The merits of "*Utopia, Limited*," have never been tested by a D'Oyly Carte revival. "*Thespis*" is as dead as a cantata. "*The Sorcerer*" and "*Princess Ida*" are near the bottom of the list in popularity among the operas still heard. "*Ruddigore*" (originally titled "*Ruddygore*" to the shocked amazement of a people to whom the word *bloody* was once a prime obscenity) was a comparative failure in its first production, but when it was finally revived in 1920 it met a surprising success. For the rest, every opera has its own group of particular enthusiasts. In the United States, "*The Mikado*" seems to enjoy a unique esteem which, in England, is reserved to "*The Gondoliers*." Musically it is hard for some enthusiasts to regard "*The Pirates of Penzance*" as the full equal of most of its brothers. "*Pinafore*," perhaps because of the delirious joy with which an earlier generation regarded it, seems a trifle more faded than most.

"*The Yeomen of the Guard*," seldom performed in this country in the 20th century until the triumphal tour of the D'Oyly Carte players in 1934–35 (repeated in all its enthusiasm in 1936–37), is now certainly regarded as one of Sullivan's major triumphs. But a census of Sullivan's most studious admirers, whether in the United States or England, would probably reveal "*Iolanthe*" in first place as the finest creation of England's most distinguished musician of the 19th century. From the opening woodwind notes of the overture to the rollicking dance tune that concludes the last act, this opera never falters in the beauty and drama of its music or the perfection with which the words and action are carried forth by Sullivan's skill. Of the thrilling moment in Act I when the entrance of the Peers begins, Thomas Dunhill, a balanced and scholarly commentator on Sullivan, has written: "There are, perhaps, only two processional operatic scenes which can be said to compare with this for musical grandeur—one is in '*Aïda*,' and the other is in the last act of '*Die Meistersinger*.'" ¶Sullivan died of heart failure on November 22, 1900. He was buried in St. Paul's Cathedral, his funeral the occasion of national mourning. The successful operas which he composed with Gilbert have survived his own death, the death of Gilbert, the death of three successive British monarchs, and the World War. None of the profound changes in musical taste which have occurred in the four decades since his death have lessened the popularity of the works which he himself regarded so lightly by comparison with the pretentious efforts which were dead long before his time, if not before theirs. (*See also page 425.*)

PETER IYLITCH TSCHAIKOWSKY

By Ernest Newman

Half French in his ancestry, Tschaikowsky's prenatal influences were a blend of East and West. While Westerns regard him as typically Russian, his compatriots think him less "native" than other Russian composers. Like most Slavs, he drew sustenance more from France than Germany. Brahms he thought dull; Wagner he never really understood. He loved music, he said, that came from the heart, that expressed "a deep humanity," like Grieg's. To the delicate brain and nerves of the modern man he added the long-accumulated eruptive passions of his race. He took the language made by the great Germans, and used it to express the complex pessimism of another culture. The colour of life in his music ranges from pale grey to intense black, with here and there a note of angry scarlet tearing through the mass of cloud. Almost all his work, like Tourgenieff's, lies within the one scale of emotions; but from relatively few elements he evokes an infinite variety and complexity. In his songs, for example, though melancholy is the dominant note of nine out of ten, each paints a different shade of the generic mood. ¶More interested in personal, dramatic emotion than in music of abstract beauty, he worked his way through and beyond the ordinary symphonic form, to the symphony with a human significance or the symphonic poem pure and simple. His phrases, scoring his general conceptions, are vital, emotional, intimate. Music, he held, must always interest in the first place; and so he avoided the cold displays of technical artifice which Brahms, for example, so often produced, preferring rather to repeat the old matter with variations of ornamentation. ¶His real contribution to the history of music, apart from the general beauty and expressiveness of his work, was the modification of the symphonic form in obedience to a poetic idea. He took up the suggestions bequeathed by Berlioz and Liszt, and turned them into accomplished realities. (*See also page 431.*)

GIUSEPPE VERDI

By W. J. HENDERSON

VERDI has been the representative Italian opera composer of his time and his personal development in art is that of his country, which has followed his dominating influence. He began to write in the prevalent style of the old Italian school, but even in his early works, which had striking resemblances to those of Donizetti and Bellini, he showed a rude vigour not possessed by either of them. ¶This vigour came conspicuously into notice in his "*Ernani*," though the most familiar example of his style in this period of his development is "*Rigoletto*." The early works show fecundity of melodic invention, but a close adherence to the elementary dance rhythms used by the Neapolitan school. The dramatic element and the virile power of the man, however, continually pressed toward the front till in "*Aïda*," in which the Egyptian subject lured him away from conventions into originality of colour, he entered upon a new field and established himself as a new individuality in music. He idealised the old aria, employed all the resources of modern instrumentation in the orchestral part, and sought for truthful dramatic expression as none of his predecessors had. "*Aïda*" has been the model of the younger Italian school and its influence can be traced through the works of such writers as Mascagni, Leoncavallo, and Puccini. ¶In "*Otello*" Verdi left the old Italian patterns still further behind him, yet without ceasing to be Italian in style or individual in ideas. The voice parts are dominant and essentially melodious at all times, but the determination of the composer to be faithful to the spirit of the text is more manifest than ever before. The work is a monument of genius. In his "*Falstaff*" Verdi produced a comic opera which stands next to Mozart's "*Nozze di Figaro*" and Wagner's "*Die Meistersinger*." The freshness and spontaneity of the score, the marvellous eloquence of the orchestral details and the infinite significance of the recitative make this work one of the masterpieces of modern times. The advance of Verdi from the "drum and trumpet" operas of his youth to the highly organised, subtly significant and opulent scores of his old age, is the feature of his artistic career, and where he has led, Italy has followed. He was the master and the moulder of Italian musical thought for half a century. (*See Dictionary of Musicians entry, page 448.*)

RICHARD WAGNER

By HENRY T. FINCK

WHEN Richard Wagner was living as a political refugee in Switzerland, at the age of thirty-six, he elaborated his theory of the "art-work of the future" in a long essay. Reduced to one sentence, this theory was, that music. poetry, painting, sculpture, and architecture had run their course as separate arts, and that the art-work of the future was to be a combination of them. At a later period he tried to make Beethoven responsible for this theory, so far at least as the union of poetry and music is concerned. Beethoven, he argued, wrote his first eight symphonies for instruments alone, but when he composed the Ninth, the greatest of them all, he reached a point in the last movement where the orchestra no longer sufficed for his purposes, so he called in the aid of the human voice and poetry—Schiller's "*Ode to Joy*." This symphony thus became "the gospel of the art-work of the future"; and beyond it, Wagner maintained, progress was possible only in the direction of the genuine music-drama; "the key to which was thus forged by Beethoven." And when the corner-stone for the Bayreuth Theatre—in which the "art-work of the future" was to be presented to the world—was laid, Wagner significantly made it the occasion for the performance of this epoch-making *Ninth Symphony*. ¶Undoubtedly it was a stroke of genius on the part of Wagner thus to turn the tables on his enemies—who had decried him as a heretic and a foe to music—by claiming their very idol as the sire of his new doctrine. In truth, however, it is not at all probable that Beethoven had in mind any such purpose as Wagner imputes to him. There is no reference to anything of the kind among the biographic documents, whereas, it is known, on the other hand, that Beethoven had been intending nearly all his life to set to music Schiller's "*Ode to Joy*." According to Czerny, he subsequently even pronounced this experiment of incorporating the Ode in his symphony a mistake (*Missgriff*). The voice, in truth, was never congenial to him. "Songs I do not like to write," he said to Rochlitz, in 1822, the very time when he was at work on the "*Ninth Symphony*." In both this work and the "*Missa Solemnis*," of the same period, Beethoven, moreover, uses the human voice like an instrument, and it is probable that in each case his object in employing it was not so much to secure an alliance with poetry as to increase the power of his musical forces, and to enlarge the variety of tone-colours by adding to the orchestra the human voice, alone, concerted, and in massive choral combination. ¶Wagner's musical pedigree must therefore be sought elsewhere. His ancestry might be traced back as far as Peri and the other originators of Italian opera who (strange as it may seem to us who know only the later Italian opera which Wagner reviled) represented a protest in favour of poetry against the tyranny of music in the marriage of these arts. Wagner's whole art was such a protest, and his more immediate progenitor in this respect was Gluck, who found that Italian opera had gradually become ridiculous through the "vanity of singers and the unwise compliance of composers"; and who, therefore, endeavoured to reduce operatic music to its proper function; that of seconding the poetry and deepening the feeling it arouses. Gluck's idea that the relation of poetry to music was much the same as that of a sketch to the colour, "which animates their figures without altering their outlines" was cordially endorsed and adopted by Wagner. ¶The next step in the evolution of Wagnerism is represented by Weber, his indebtedness to whom Wagner frankly acknowledged in several places. He declared that the last scenes in Weber's "*Euryanthe*" realised the ideal of musico-dramatic art, as here the orchestra "interpenetrates the recitatives as the blood does the veins of the body." What Weber himself wrote about this opera: "'*Euryanthe*' is a purely dramatic work, which depends for its success solely on the co-operation of the sister arts, and is certain to lose its effect if deprived of their assistance," shows that his ideal was the same as Wagner's. Had he lived longer, and had he possessed Wagner's pugnacity and iron will, he might have been the man to annihilate the old-fashioned opera and triumphantly establish the modern music-drama. He even made use of leading motives [vide D. D.]. His early opera *"Abu Hassan"* has a melody which is afterwards repeated in a reminiscent way. The *"Freyschütz"* has eleven recurring melodies, and *"Euryanthe"* has eight. ¶While the germs and main principles of Wagnerism may thus be found in Peri, Monteverde, Gluck, and Weber, it remained for Wagner's genius to develop and apply them. Gluck's operas were still far from being perfect works of art. To cite Wagner's own words: "In Gluck's operas we find the aria, the recitative, the ballet still placed side by side with-out any connection"; while opera in general remained after him, as before, a mere variety show, with here a pretty tune, there a graceful skip of a dancer or a brilliant feat of vocalisation, here a dazzling scenic effect, there a volcanic outburst of the orchestra, and the whole without artistic coherence. If a painter put on a canvas a number of human figures and diverse objects totally unrelated to each other, no one would call it a work of art, however well done each figure might be in itself. The opera before Wagner was such a canvas. He was the first who made a genuine picture of it—an art-work organically united in all its parts. He did this by means of the leading motives—the typical melodies and characteristic harmonies which accompany each of the *dramatis personæ* throughout the score, just as their social and moral character ac-companies them, with such modifications as the situation calls for. Weber had used leading motives as we have seen, but only in an elementary way. It remained for Wagner to make them the very framework of the music-drama. He thus taught music to speak a definite language, so that we can almost tell by listening to the orchestra alone what is going on on the stage. ¶His whole aim and desire was to make the drama impressive and intelligible. For this reason he discarded the tuneful style of vocalism in vogue in Italian opera and developed a new vocal style—a sort of melodious declamation or "speech-song." This led to the ridiculous accusation that there was "no melody" in his operas, whereas the orchestral score usually bubbles over with melodies—often two or more at a time. After the singers had begun to master the new vocal style, it was found, moreover, that an artist like Lilli Lehmann or Jean de Reszké could make this speech-song sound smooth, and melodious, too—as smooth and melodious as the bel canto of Rossini and Mozart. And after the singers had learned how to act, and to enunciate distinctly, opera-goers learned that Wagner had written stage-works which were quite as impressive poetically as they were musically. He had an immense advantage over all other com-posers in being able to write his own poems. His best ten operas—*"The Flying Dutchman," "Tannhäuser," "Lohengrin," "Rheingold," "Walküre," "Siegfried," "Götterdämmerung," "Tristan," "Meistersinger,"* and *"Parsifal"* —apart from the music, rank among the best plays ever written in Germany; though to be sure they must not be judged apart from the music any more than the music must be judged apart from the poems. The ludicrous opinions on these works formerly expressed by so many professional musicians and critics were due chiefly to the fact that they did not bear this in mind, though Wagner protested on every possible occasion that he must not be judged from the standpoint of the separate arts, but of the combined arts.   The greatest defects in the present-day performances of his operas is owing to this, that few stage-managers have yet learned that he expects them to be artistic, too, familiar with every detail of the work, so that they can show how every incident on the stage is mirrored and emphasised in the orchestral score.   There is much delightful pantomimic music in these operas, the meaning of which is lost if the stage-manager is a bungler, and the singers poor actors.   ¶With all these reforms and innovations, Wagner never could have become the most commanding figure in the modern music-world had he not been endowed at the same time with the faculty for creating an extraordinary abundance of ideas, melodic and harmonic.   Wilhelm Tappert has truly observed that there is more melody in Wagner's *"Meistersinger"* than in all the operas of the melodious Mozart.   In the field of harmony and modulation Wagner was an innovator of unprecedented originality.   There can be no tragic expression without discord, and he was the greatest of all masters of discord—the musical tragedian par excellence.   In orchestration, too—the art of clothing his ideas in beautiful garbs of various colours—he was without a rival.   ¶As Schubert influenced all song-writers after him, Chopin all the pianoforte-composers, and Beethoven all the symphonists, so Wagner has cast his spell on every writer for the stage. "Wagner is the oxygen, the atmosphere which modern opera breathes," writes Ferdinand Pfohl; and he hardly exaggerates when he adds that "modern opera, apart from Wagner's art, is an empty word, a phantom.   It does not exist." The minor composers of all countries have been indulging for more than half a century in a very bacchanal of plagiarism at his expense, while even the greatest of masters—Dvořák, Grieg, Saint-Saëns, Richard Strauss—have honestly profited by his example in various branches of music.   Rubinstein committed suicide by trying to swim against the current.   The German school of opera, the French, and even the Italian have followed Wagner in abandoning coloratura song and elaborate arias, in giving greater coherence to their scores, and in showing a decent regard for their texts.   In these respects even Verdi, greatest of the Italians, in his last period, paid homage to Wagner's genius.

WAGNER THE MONSTER*

By Deems Taylor

HE WAS AN UNDERSIZED little man, with a head too big for his body—a sickly little man.   His nerves were bad.   He had skin trouble.   It was agony for him to wear anything next to his skin coarser than silk.   And he had delusions of grandeur.   ¶He was a monster of conceit.   Never for one minute did he look at the world or at people except in relation to himself.   He was only the most important person in the world, to himself; in his own eyes he was the only person who existed.   He believed himself to be one of the greatest dramatists in the world, one of the greatest thinkers, and one of the greatest composers.   To

*The reader will be interested to know that other essays by Deems Taylor on a variety of musical subjects appear in *"Of Men and Music"* from which this essay was reprinted through the kind permission of Simon & Schuster, publishers.

hear him talk, he was Shakespeare, and Beethoven, and Plato rolled into one. And you would have had no difficulty in hearing him talk.   He was one of the most exhausting conversationalists that ever lived.   An evening with him was an evening spent in listening to a monologue.   Sometimes he was brilliant; sometimes he was maddeningly tiresome.   But whether he was being brilliant or dull, he had one sole topic of conversation: himself.   What *he* thought and what *he* did.   ¶He had a mania for being in the right.   The slightest hint of disagreement, from anyone, on the most trivial point, was enough to set him off on a harangue that might last for hours, in which he proved himself right in so many ways, and with such exhausting volubility, that in the end his hearer, stunned and deafened, would agree with him, for the sake of peace.   ¶It never occurred to him that he and his doings were not of the most intense and fascinating interest to anyone with whom he came in contact.   He had theories about almost any subject under the sun, including vegetarianism, the drama, politics, and music; and in support of these theories he wrote pamphlets, letters, books . . . thousands upon thousands of words, hundreds and hundreds of pages. He not only wrote these things, and published them—usually at somebody else's expense—but he would sit and read them aloud, for hours, to his friends and his family.   ¶He wrote operas; and no sooner did he have the synopsis of a story, but he would invite—or rather summon—a crowd of his friends to his house and read it aloud to them.   Not for criticism.   For applause.   When the complete poem was written, the friends had to come again, and hear *that* read aloud. Then he would publish the poem, sometimes years before the music that went with it was written.   He played the piano like a composer, in the worst sense of what that implies, and he would sit down at the piano before parties that included some of the finest pianists of his time, and play for them, by the hour, his own music, needless to say.   He had a composer's voice.   And he would invite eminent vocalists to his house, and sing them his operas, taking all the parts.   ¶He had the emotional stability of a six-year-old child.   When he felt out of sorts, he would rave and stamp, or sink into suicidal gloom and talk darkly of going to the East to end his days as a Buddhist monk.   Ten minutes later, when something pleased him, he would rush out of doors and run around the garden, or jump up and down on the sofa, or stand on his head.   He could be grief-stricken over the death of a pet dog, and he could be callous and heartless to a degree that would have made a Roman emperor shudder.   ¶He was almost innocent of any sense of responsibility.   Not only did he seem incapable of supporting himself, but it never occurred to him that he was under any obligation to do so.   He was convinced that the world owed him a living.   In support of this belief, he borrowed money from everybody who was good for a loan— men, women, friends or strangers.   He wrote begging letters by the score, sometimes grovelling without shame, at others loftily offering his intended benefactor the privilege of contributing to his support, and being mortally offended if the recipient declined the honour.   I have found no record of his ever paying or repaying money to anyone who did not have a legal claim upon it.   ¶What money he could lay his hands on he spent like an Indian rajah.   The mere prospect of a performance of one of his operas was enough to set him to running up bills amounting to ten times the amount of his prospective royalties.   On an income that would reduce a more scrupulous man to doing his own laundry, he would keep two servants.   Without enough money in his pocket to pay his rent, he would have the walls and ceiling of his study lined with pink silk.   No one will ever know—certainly he never knew—how much money he owed.   We do know that his greatest benefactor gave him $6,000 to pay the most pressing of his debts in one city, and a year later had to give him $16,000 to enable him to live in another city without being thrown into jail for debt.   ¶He was equally unscrupulous in other ways.   An endless procession of women marches through his life.   His first wife spent twenty years enduring and forgiving his infidelities.   His second wife had been the wife of his most devoted friend and admirer, from whom he stole her.   And even while he was trying to persuade her to leave her first husband he was writing to a friend to enquire whether he could suggest some wealthy woman—*any* wealthy woman—whom he could marry for her money.   ¶He was completely selfish in his other personal relationships.   His liking for his friends was measured solely by the completeness of their devotion to him, or by their usefulness to him, whether financial or artistic.   The minute they failed him—even by so much as refusing a dinner invitation—or began to lessen in usefulness, he cast them off without a second thought.   At the end of his life he had exactly one friend whom he had known even in middle age.   ¶He had a genius for making enemies.   He would insult a man who disagreed with him about the weather.   He would pull endless wires in order to meet some man who admired his work, and was able and anxious to be of use to him—and would proceed to make a mortal enemy of him with some idiotic and wholly uncalled-for exhibition of arrogance and bad manners.   A character in one of his operas was a caricature of one of the most powerful music critics of his day.   Not content with burlesquing him, he invited the critic to his house and read him the libretto aloud in front of his friends.   ¶The name of this monster was Richard Wagner.   Everything that I have said about him you can find on record—in newspapers, in police reports, in the testimony of people who knew him, in his own letters, between the lines of his autobiography.   And the curious thing about this record is that it doesn't matter in the least.   ¶Because this undersized, sickly, disagreeable, fascinating little man was right all the time. The joke was on us.   He *was* one of the world's great dramatists; he *was* a great thinker; he *was* one of the most stupendous musical geniuses that, up to now, the world has ever seen.   The world did owe him a living.   People couldn't know those things at the time, I suppose; and yet to us, who know his music, it does seem as though they should have known.   What if he did talk about himself all the time?   If he had talked about himself twenty-four hours every day for the span of his life he would not have uttered half the number of words that other men have spoken and written about him since his death.   ¶When you consider what he wrote—thirteen operas and music dramas, eleven of them still holding the stage, eight of them unquestionably worth ranking among the world's great musico-dramatic masterpieces—when you listen to what he wrote, the debts and heartaches that people had to endure from him don't seem much of a price.   Eduard Hanslick, the critic whom he caricatured in *"Die Meistersinger"* and who hated him ever after, now lives only because he was caricatured in *"Die Meistersinger."*   The women whose hearts he broke are long since dead; and the man who could never love anyone but himself has made them deathless atonement, I think, with *"Tristan und Isolde."*   Think of the luxury with which for a time, at least, fate rewarded Napoleon, the man who ruined France and looted Europe; and then perhaps you will agree that a few thousand dollars' worth of debts were not too heavy a price to pay for the "*Ring*" trilogy. ¶What if he was faithless to his friends and to his wives? He had one mistress to whom he was faithful to the day of his death: Music. Not for a single moment did he ever compromise with what he believed, with what he dreamed. There is not a line of his music that could have been conceived by a little mind. Even when he is dull, or downright bad, he is dull in the grand manner. There is greatness about his worst mistakes. Listening to his music, one does not forgive him for what he may or may not have been. It is not a matter of forgiveness. It is a matter of being dumb with wonder that his poor brain and body didn't burst under the torment of the demon of creative energy that lived inside him, struggling, clawing, scratching to be released; tearing, shrieking at him to write the music that was in him. The miracle is that what he did in the little space of seventy years could have been done at all, even by a great genius. Is it any wonder that he had no time to be a man? (*See also page 455.*)

VAUGHAN WILLIAMS

By Richard Anthony Leonard

Vaughan Williams is one of the foremost of that little group of valiant Englishmen who are making the music of their native land bloom again after a barrenness of more than two hundred years. The Germans (and before them the Italians) have dominated the art of music for so long that we are apt to forget the extraordinary efflorescence of musical genius which England produced in the sixteenth and seventeenth centuries. Byrd, Morley and Tallis, Wilbye, Weelkes, Gibbons and Henry Purcell composed some of the finest music of their time, and were worthy of mention even with the incomparable Palestrina. But after the death of Purcell, in 1695, English music suffered a serious decline. Later the influence of Händel was devastating, from the standpoint of its effect upon native English genius, for the German set up an ideal which made English composers servile imitators of the Teutonic art for almost two centuries. ¶The present blooming of English music had its origins, of course, in the spectacular rise of Russian music in the nineteenth century and the ensuing spread of nationalism. The famous Five (Moussorgsky, Balakireff, Borodin, Cui, and Rimsky-Korsakoff) revolted against the Germanic tradition and tapped instead as their source of inspiration the marvellously colourful, half-barbaric folk-songs of their native land, and the equally characteristic music of the Russian church. For their literary bases they went to the folk-lore and to the history of Russia. Their immense success created a wave of nationalistic feeling that swept every country in Europe. England was no exception. The renascence of the art of music in England has been one of the most striking developments in twentieth-century music. Men like Bax and Delius, Holst and Vaughan Williams have not wrought with the lasting magnificence of the greater Russians, but they have wrought ably and with important implications for the future. ¶Without attempting any comparative estimate of the work of these Englishmen, it may be said that the one whose contributions have been most typically English is probably Vaughan Williams. This is true even though a great part of his work is clearly impressionistic. owing an immense debt of gratitude to Claude Debussy. His "*London Symphony*," for example, is a panorama of the vast English macrocosm, with many of its typically British aspects; but musically it speaks the impressionistic language of the Frenchman. Impressionism, however, is simply a technique, and when we dig deeper into the music of Vaughan Williams we come upon qualities which only an Englishman could have produced. First of all we find music that is nurtured in the rich soil of English folk-music. All his life Vaughan Williams has collected and studied and used English folk-tunes. Not only is much of his work based directly upon this native material, but many of his original themes are so closely patterned after this original that it is often difficult to tell the old from the new. ¶It is important to note that in English folk-music Vaughan Williams did not have at hand material as brilliantly effective as the Russians had. The popular melodies which the Five and their successors used were heavy with a rich and sensuous beauty; they flashed across the music of nineteenth-century Europe with the startling splendour of the aurora borealis across the night sky. Their characteristic colour and form are instantly evident whenever they are used by modern Russian composers. English folk-music, on the other hand, has few such readily effective attributes. It is a refined and delicately modelled product of a sober people. Vaughan Williams has used it as only an Englishman could—with sobriety and good taste, with moderation and unfailing rectitude. He has used, too, with equal inspiration, the patterns left by his great English predecessors, the Elizabethans who first made English music glorious. The most noted example of his devotion to their art is his "*Fantasia on a Theme by Thomas Tallis*"—an exquisite paraphrase in terms of the modern string orchestra of the work of the great sixteenth-century contrapuntist. ¶After his interest in folk-music the strongest impulse in Vaughan Williams' creative life has come from his love of nature, particularly of the quiet, incomparably beautiful English countryside. Here again is a quality typical of the English, but one too subtle to be translated easily into terms of music. Nevertheless, it has been the inspiration for some of Vaughan Williams' finest scores, including "*The Lark Ascending*," for violin and orchestra; "*On Wenlock Edge*," a song cycle based on "*A Shropshire Lad*"; his first symphony, called "*A Sea Symphony*," in which soprano, barytone, and chorus intone Walt Whitman's rhapsodic invocation to the sea; and above all his "*Pastoral Symphony*"—probably the greatest orchestral work produced in modern England, and certainly this composer's masterpiece. There is nothing photographic about this last work, despite its title; no imitations in music of the sounds of nature. Instead it presents a serene and quiet contemplation, a mood of gentle reverie, of melancholy, and yet a thrilling sense of spaciousness and light. Every listener may find in this music his own images of meadow and plain, of winding river. and the wide, wind-swept sky. Or he may, if he choose, find none of these; but only the intensely personal recital of the composer's inmost confidences, told with a reticence and a delicate charm that has seldom been equalled in modern music. (*See Dictionary of Musicians entry, page 470.*)

A PRONOUNCING & DEFINING DICTIONARY
OF MUSICAL TERMS, INSTRUMENTS, &c.

A

A (*G.* ä; *F. I.* & *Sp.* lä.). 1. A musical pitch (435 vibrations per second, according to the standard adopted in France 1879 and at Vienna 1887, and called diapason normal). 2. Any octave of this pitch. 3. This tone designated in Absolute Pitch (q.v.) as *a'* is invariable on the oboe, and is accordingly used as the tone to which the whole orchestra is attuned. It is hence called the normal tone. 4. The major key with three sharps. 5. The minor key relative to C major.

a, a or **ab**, *L., I., F.* By, from, for, to, at, in, etc.[1]

ab (äp), *G.* "Off." Used of stops.

ab'acus harmon'icus, *L.* 1. A table of notes. 2. The arrangement of the keys and pedals of an instrument.

abanera (ă-bä-nä'-rä), *Sp.* Vide HABANERA.

abandon (ă-bän-dôn), *F.* Lack of all restraint in emotion.

abbadare (äb-bä-dä'-rĕ), *I.* To take care.

abbandonar'si, abbandonatamen'te, abbando'ne, abbando'no, *I.* With abandon.

abbassamen'to, *I.* Lowering. **A. di mano,** (a) down-beat; (b) the carrying of one hand below the other in piano playing. **A. di voce** (vō-chĕ), *I.* Lowering of the voice. Diminution.

abbatimen'to, *I.* Down-beat.

abbellare (äb-bel-lä'-rĕ), *I.* To ornament. **abbelitura(e)** (too'-rä), **a-bellimen'to(i).** Embellishment(s).

abbetont (äp'-bā-tōnt), *G.* With final emphasis.

a-b-c-d-i(e)ren (ä-bä-tsä-dē'rĕn), *G.* To sing the notes by their letter names.

Abend (ä'-bĕnt), *G.* Evening. **-glocke.** Curfew. **-lied** (lēt). Even song. **-musik** (moo-zēk'). Evening music.

[1] Phrases beginning with these and other prepositions will be found under their principal words.

abenteuerlich (ä'-bĕn-toi-ĕr-lĭkh), *G.* Venturesome.

ab'fallen, *G.* To deteriorate. **-gebrochen** (äp'-gĕ-brôkh-ĕn). Interrupted. Vide RADENCE. **Abgesang** (äp'-gĕ-zängk). Refrain. It followed the two *Stollen* in the songs of the Meistersänger. **-gestossen** (äp'-gĕ-shtôs-sĕn). Staccato. **-gleiten** (äp'-glī-tĕn). To slide the finger from a black key to the next white key. **Abkürzung** (äp'-kür-tsoongk). Abbreviation. **-leiten** (äp'-lī-tĕn). To derive from. **-lösen** (äp'-lä-zĕn). To change fingers on a sustained tone. **-nehmend** (äp'-nā-mĕnt). Diminuendo.

abrégés (äb-rā-zhā), *F.* Trackers.

abreichen (äp'-rī-khĕn), *G.* On the violin, to extend the little, or draw back the first, finger.

Abreissung (äp'-rīs-soongk), *G.* Sudden pause.

abrup'tio, *L.* An abrupt halt.

Absatz (äp'-zäts), *G.* 1. Cadence. 2. A phrase.

Abschnitt (äp'-shnĭt), *G.* Section.

abschwellen (äp'-schvĕl-len), *G.* Diminuendo.

absetzen (äp'-zĕt-zĕn), *G.* To strike two keys successively with the same finger.

absolute. Used of music that is self-derived and complete in its own form, meaning, and beauty, as opposed to operatic or programme music.

abstammen (äp'-shtäm-men), *G.* To be derived from.

Abstand (äp'-shtänt), *G.* Interval.

ab'stossen, *G.* To play staccato. **Ab'stosszeichen** (tsī-khĕn). Staccato mark(s).

Abstrak'ten, *G.* Trackers.

Abstufung (äp'-shtoo-foongk), *G.* Shading.

abtönen (äp'-tā-nĕn), *G.* To err from the key.

ab(h)ub (ä'-boob). A Hebrew horn.

abun'dans, *L.* Augmented.

abwechselnd (äp'-vĕkhs-ĕlnt), *G.* Alternating.

Abweichung (äp'-vīkh-oongk), *G.* A variant.

Abyssinian flute. A beak flute.

Abzug (äp'-tsookh). 1. Lifting of a finger or a bow. 2. The sliding of the finger from one key to the next.

académie spirituelle (ăk-ăd-ā-mē spĭr-ēt-wĕl), *F.* A sacred concert.

acathis'tus, *Gr.* Ancient Greek Church hymn in honour of the Virgin.

accademia (ak-käd-ā-mē'-ä), *I.* 1. An Academy. 2. A concert.

accarezzevole (äk-kä-rĕd-zā'vō-lĕ), *I.* Caressing. **accarezzevolmen'te.** Pleadingly.

accell., acceldo. Abbr. of accelerando.

accelerando (ät-chā-lĕ-rän'-dō), *I.* Accelerating (the velocity). **acceleratemen'te.** Swiftly. **accelerato** (rä'-tō). Swift.

accent (in *F.,* ăk-säṅ). **accento** (ät-chĕn'-to), *I.* 1. Emphasis, force, on a tone, a chord, a beat. 2. An accent mark (q.v.). The first beat of every measure receives a *primary accent.* In 4–4 time, the third beat receives a lighter or *secondary* or *subaccent.* 3. In 6–8 or 6–4 time the fourth beat takes a *secondary* accent. In 9–8 time the fourth beat has a *secondary a.*, and the seventh a *tertiary a.* still lighter. The regular skeletonic accent of the standard measure is called the *grammatical, metrical, natural* or *regular a.;* this is modified by the *rhythmical* and the *aesthetic, emotional, pathetic, poetical* or *rhetorical* accent.

accent-mark. One of the numerous signs of stress; as > sforzando or < (strictly tenuto); 'or,, used (a) to indicate *pitch* (q.v.) as c'' and C'' = c² and C₂; (b) as an abbreviation of *foot* (q.v.) as 8' = 8-foot.

accent'or. Leader of a chorus.

accentuare (too-ä'-rĕ), *I.* **accentui(e)-ren** (ak-tsĕn-too-ē'-rĕn), *G.* To accent. To accentuate. **accentua'to.** With marked accent.

accentuation. The act or art of properly distributing emphasis.

accen'tus, *L.* Portion(s) of the ritual song of the Church, chanted by the priest at the altar; in contradistinction to the Concentus, sung by the assistants or choir. **A. ecclesiastici,** *L.* Melodic formulae used in the Church in reciting, the collects, etc. They correspond with the comma, semicolon, interrogation, etc., of ordinary writing, and are of seven kinds, called *immutab'ilis,* monotone; *me'dius,* a minor third; *grav'is,* a fifth; *acu'tus,* sol mi mi sol; *modera'tus,* rising a second and returning; *interr゙gati'vus,* falling a second and returning; *finai'is,* sol la sol fa mi re—thus closing in the Dorian key.

Accessis'ten, *G.* Unpaid choristers.

accessory notes. The subordinate notes of an ornament. **accessory tones.** Overtones.

acciaccato (ät-chä-kä'-tō), *I.* Violent.

Acciaccatur (ät-tsĭ-äk-kä-toor'), *G.* The doubling of the 6–4 chord on the dominant, the right hand alone resolving it.

acciaccatura (ät-chäk-kä-too'-rä), *I.* A short appoggiatura, usually a grace-note, struck at the same time with its principal, but instantly released.

accidentals, *E.* **accidenti** (ät-tshĭ-dĕn'-tē), *I.* **accidents** (äk-sĭ-dän), *F.* Sharps, flats, and naturals, foreign to the key-signature.

accolade (ăk-kô-lăd), *F.* Brace.

accompagnamento (äk-kom-pän-ya-mĕn'-to), *I.* Accompaniment; figured bass. **accompagnare** (yä'-rĕ). To accompany. **accompagnato** (yä'-tō). Accompanied.

accommodare (dä'-rĕ), *I.* To tune.

accompagner (ăk-kôm-pīn-yā), *F.* To accompany. **accompagné** (ăk-kôm-pīn-yā). Accompanied. **accompagnement** (äk-kôm-pīn-yŭ-mäṅ). Accompaniment.

accompaniment. A part or parts added to other principal parts. **a. ad libitum.** Optional accompaniment. **a. obbligato.** Accompaniment essential. **accompanist.** One who plays accompaniments.

accoppiato (äk-kôp-pĭ-ä'-tō), *I.* Tied.

accord, *E.* (in *F.,* ăk-kôr), 1. Consonance. 2. A chord; à l'ouvert, on the open strings; natural, a fundamental chord; parfait, a triad; renversé, inverted; de sixte ajoutée, chord of the added sixth. Vide ALTERED. **accordant** (äk-kôr-däṅ), *F.* In concord. **accorder** (äk-kôr-dā). To tune. **accordeur** (dŭr). 1. A tuner. 2. a set of 12 tuning forks giving the tempered scale. 3. Monochord. **accordoir** (äk-kôr-dwär). A tuning-key, hammer, or cone.

accordamen'to, accordanza (dän'-tsä), *I.* Consonance.

accor'dance, accor'dature, *E.* accordatura (too'rä), *I.* The system of tuning the strings of an instrument; thus, the a. of a violin is g-d-a-e.

accordare (dä-rĕ), *I.* To tune. **accordan'do.** Tuning; in tune.

accor'deon. A free-reed instr. inv. by Damian of Vienna, 1829. The tone is produced by a double set of bellows acting upon metallic tongues. The right hand presses buttons or keys giving an incomplete chromatic scale; the left hand has a few bass tones.

accor'do, *I.* 1. A chord. 2. An old Italian instrument of twelve or more strings.

accoupler (ăk-koo-plä), *F.* To couple. **accouplez** (ăk-koo-plä). "Draw the coupler."

accrescendo (ak-krĕs-shĕn'-do). *I.* Crescen'do. **accrescimento** (ac-crä-shē-mĕn'-tō). Augmentation as of a fugal theme. **punto d'a.,** the dot placed after a note to prolong it. **accresciuto** (shoo'-tō), *I.* Augmented.

acetab'ulum, *L.* An ancient instr. of percussion. Earthen vessels beaten as drums or clashed as cymbals.

achromat'ic. Lacking accidentals and modulations.

acht (äkht), *G.* Eight. **Achtfusston** (äkht'-foos-tōn) or **8-füssig** (füs-sĭkh). Eight-foot tone. **8-stimmig** (shtĭm-mĭkh). For eight voices or instruments.

Achtel (äkhtl), **Achtelnote,** *G.* Eighth note; quaver. **Achtelpause,** *G.* Eighth-rest.

A Chula (ä choo'-lä), *Port.* A dance like the fandango.

ac'ocotl. A Mexican plant from whose stalk an aboriginal wind-instr. of the same name was made.

acolyth'ia, *Gr.* The order of service in the Greek Church.

acous'tics (ä-kow'-stix, or ä-koo'stix), *E.,* **acoustique** (ä-koos-tēk), *F.* The science of sounds. (See article, page 718.)

act-tune. Music between the acts of a play.

acuité (ăk-wē-tĕ), *F.* Acuteness.

acustica (ä-koos'-tĭ-kä), *I.,* **Acustik** (ä-koos-tĕk'), *G.* Acoustics. **acustisch** (tĭsh), *G.* Acoustical.

acuta (ä-koo'-tä), *I.* 1. Acute, shrill. 2. A shrill 2-ft. mixture-stop.

acu'tæ clav'es, *L.* The name given by Guido to the tones from a to g.

acute. High in pitch, shrill.

acutus, *L.* Vide ACCENTUS.

ad, *L.* To, for, at.

adagio (ä-dä'-jo), *I.* 1. Slow, slower than andante, not so slow as lento. 2. A slow movement or division of a symphony or sonata. **adagietto** (ä-dä-jĕt'-tō). A little faster than adagio. **adagissimo** (jĭs-sĭ-mo). Extremely slow.

adaptation, *E.,* **adattazione** (ä-dät-tä-tsĭ-ō'-nĕ), *I.* An arrangement or transcription.

adasio (ä-dä'-sĭ-ō), *I.* Adagio.

added lines. Leger lines. **added sixth.** Vide SIXTH.

additato (äd-dĭ-tä-tō), *I.* Fingered.

additional keys. Those above f''' on the piano. **additional accompaniments.** Accompaniments or parts added to a work by another hand than that of the composer.

addolorato (äd-dō-lō-rä'-tō), *I.* Melancholy.

Adel (ä'-dĕl), *G.* Majesty.

Adi'aphone. Vide GABELKLAVIER.

Adi'aphonon, *G.* A piano of permanent tune, inv. in 1820 by Schuster. The tone was produced by metal bars.

adirato (ä-dĭ-rä'-tō), *I.* Angry. **adiramen'te.** Angrily.

adjunct notes. Unaccented auxiliary notes.

Adjuvant (ät'-yoo-fänt), *G.* Assistant to a chorister.

Adler (ät'-lĕr), *G.* A rarely used organ-stop.

ado'nia. An ancient musical feast.

adornamen'to (pl.-i), *I.* An embellishment.

adoucir (ä-doo-sēr), *F.* To soften, to flatten.

adquis'ta or **adsuma'ta vox,** *L.* The extreme low tone.

adufe (ä-dhoo'-fĕ), *Sp.* Tambou-ine. **adufero** (fä'-rō). Player of it.

A-dur (ä-door), *G.* The key of A major.

æ'rophone. A kind of harmonium.

ængstlich (ĕnkst-lĭkh), *G.* Anxiously.

æol'harmon'ica. A kind of seraphine.

Æo'lian. 1. Vide MODES. 2. The fifth of the authentic Gregorian modes. 3. An automatic reed instrument in which the performer controls the time, the stops, and the expression.

Æo'lian Harp or **Lyre.** An instr. inv. by Kircher in the 17th century It is usually a box set in a window and fitted with 6 or more strings of silk or gut, tuned in unison, passing over bridges about ¾-inch high. The strings are so arranged that the air causes vibration among them. The varying humours of the wind produce a strangely sweet and various harmony, the different overtones being audible in a shifting concord of eerie beauty.

Æolian mute. A combination of the pitch-pipe and mute.

Æolian pianoforte. A piano inv. by T. Gilbert about 1850, and provided with free reeds and a bellows for giving the piano a sustaining power.

æoli′na. 1. A small free-reed mouth instr., inv. by Wheatstone, 1829. 2. An organ-stop.

æolo′dicon or **æolo′dion,** *Gr.* A keyed instr. in which the tone is produced by steel springs, put in vibration by bellows.

æolomelo′dicon. The same instrument with brass tubes to reinforce the springs.

æolopan′talon. An æolodicon combined with a piano.

Æolsharfe (ā-ôls-här′-fĕ), *G.* Aeolian harp.

Æolsklavier (ā-ôls-klä-fēr), *G.* A keyboard wind instr., inv. 1825, by Schortmann, with reeds of wood instead of metal.

Æota′na, *Gr.* A small mouth instr. of short metallic reeds.

Æqual (ā-kwäl), *G.*, from Lat., signifying "8-ft." Vide STOP.

æquiso′nus, *L.* Unison. **æquiso′nans.** Concordant.

æquiva′gans, *L.* Simultaneously syncopated or varied in all the parts.

Æquivoken (ā′-kwĭ-fō-kĕn), *G.* Meistersinger airs of the same name.

ære recurvo., *L.* Bucena.

æ rophone. A French melodeon.

aevia (ē′-vĭ-ä), *L.* Abbr. (the vowels only) of Alleluia.

affabile (äf-fä′-bĭ-lĕ), *I.* Affable. **affabilità** (bē-lĭ-tä′). Cordiality. **affabilmen′te.** Affably.

affanna′to, affano′so, *I.* Tormented, distressed.

affectiert (äf-fĕk-tērt′), *G.* With affectation.

affectueux (äf-fĕk-tü-ŭ′), *F.* Affectionate.

affettazione (tä-tsĭ-ō′-nĕ), *I.* Affectation. **affettatamen′te.** Affectedly.

affet′to, *I.* Affection. **affettuoso.** Affectionate. **affettuosamente.** Affectionately. **affettivo** (tē′-vo). Affecting.

affilar′, *I.* Vide FILAR.

affinity. Close relation (as of keys).

afflizione (äf-flē-tsĭ-ō′-nĕ). Sorrow. **aflit′to.** Sorrowful.

affrettan′do, affrettate (tä′-tĕ). Hurrying. **affretto′so.** Hurried.

afofa′. Portuguese fandango.

after-beat. Two notes used as ending a trill. **after note.** A small unaccented note taking its time from the preceding.

agevole (ä-ja′-vō-lĕ), *I.* Agile. **agevolmen′te.** Nimbly. **agevolezza** (ä-jä-vō-lĕd′-zä). Agility.

aggiustato (äd-joos-tä′-tō), *I.* Adjusted, arranged, adapted. **aggiustatamen′te.** In strict time.

aggraver la fugue (ăg-grä-vä lä füg), *F.* To augment the (subject of a) fugue.

agiatamente (ä-jät-ä-mĕn′-tĕ). Easily.

agilità (ä-jēl-ĭ-tä′), *I.* Agility. **agilmen′te.** Nimbly.

agitato (ä-jĭ-tä′-tō), *I.* Agitated, hurried. **agitamen′to, agitazione** (ä-jē-tä′-tsĭ-ō′-nĕ). Agitation.

agité (ä-zhē-tä), *F.* Agitated.

agli (äl′-yē), *I.* Vide AL.

Ag′nus De′i. *L.* "Lamb of God." Vide MASS.

ago′ge, *Gr.* 1. The order of intervals of melodic progression. 2. Rhythmical order of accents and duration. 3. Expression. **Ago′gik,** *G.* The art of expression by rubato, acceleration, &c. **ago′gic accent.** Expression mark.

agraffe (ä-gräff), *F.* A small pin ᴛᴏ check the vibration of a piano string.

agréments (ä-grä-män), *F.* 1. Embellishments. 2. Incidental music and dancing.

ai (ä′-ē), *I.* To the. Vide AL.

aigre (ĕgr), *F.* Harsh, sharp. **aigrement** (ĕgr-män). Sharply.

aigu (ä-gü), *F.* Acute, shrill.

air, *E.* and *F.* A melody, or tune; an aria. **a. à boire** (bwär). A drinking song. **a. à reprises** (rü-prēz). Catch. **a. chantant** (shän-tän). A lyric. **a. détaché** (dä-tă-shä). A single air detached from a larger work. **a. rapide** (rä-pēd). A flourish. **a. varié** (vă-rĭ-ā). Theme with variations.

Ais (ä-ĭs), *G.* The note or key "A" sharp.

aisé (ĕ-zä), *F.* Easy. **aisément** (ĕ-zä-män). Easily, freely.

aiuton (ĭ′-ū-tän), *Gr.* An organ made of tuning-forks, inv. by Charles Clagget and guaranteed never to require retuning.

ajakli-keman (a-yäk′-le-kä-män). A Turkish violin.

Akkord (äk-kôrt'), *G.* A chord. **A.-passage.** An arpeggio. **A.-zither.** 1. The auto-harp. 2. A set of instruments.

Akromat (ä-krō-mät'), *G.* A musician. **akromatiscl.** (ä-krŏ-mä'-tĭsh), *G.* Achromatic.

Akustik (ä-koos'-tēk), *G.* Acoustics.

à la, au, aux, al, all', alla, alle, allo, agli, ai, *F.* and *I.* Varying combinations of the different genders of the article "the" with the preposition "to," meaning "in the manner of," as *à la grecque,* and *alla cappella.*

a'lamoth, *Heb.* Obscure and disputed musical term in Psalm LXVIII, 25.

alar'um, *L.* all' armi, *I.* A call to arms.

albada (äl-bä'-dhä), *Sp.* A morning serenade.

Alberti Bass. A bass consisting of monotonous simple broken chords. So called after its alleged inventor. Vide B.D.

albogue (äl-bō-gä'), *Sp.* An instr. of the flute species.

Albumblatt (äl'-boom-blät). Album-leaf. Plural, **A.-blätter** (blĕt-ter).

alcuna (äl-koo'-na), *I.* Some; as **con a. licenza,** with some licence.

aleluya, *Sp.* Hallelujah.

alemana (äl-ĕ-mä'-nä), *Sp.* Old Spanish dance.

Alexandre organ. Vide AMERICAN ORGAN.

aliquot. Used of the parts into which a vibrating string is subdivided in producing overtones. **Aliquotflügel,** *G.* A piano inv. by Blüthner with a sympathetic octave string for each note. **Aliquottheorie** (äl'-ĭ-kwôt-tä-ō-rē), *G.* The theory of overtones.

al'la. Vide AL.

allargan'do, *I.* Gradually slower and broader.

all' ova. Vide OTTAVA.

alle (äl'lĕ), *G.* All: alle Instrumente. All the instruments; *tutti.*

allegrativo (al-lä-grä-te'-vō); **allegramen'te, allegran'te,** *I.*; **allégrement** (äl-lä-grŭ-mäṅ), *F.* Gayly and quickly.

allegrettino (äl-lä-grĕt-tē'-nō), *I.* A little slower than allegretto.

allegret'to, *I.* Slower than allegro, but blithe and cheery.

allegrezza (äl-lä-grĕd'-za); **allegria** (grē'-ä), *I.* Joy, cheer.

allegro (äl-lä'-grō), *I.* Very fast, though slower than Presto; it usually indicates a high rate of speed. This may be modified by additional phrases as *allegro ma non troppo.* **allegri di bravura** (äl-lä-grē dē brä-voora), *I.* Compositions to display virtuosity. **allegrissimamen'te, allegris'simo,** *i.* Extremely fast. **allegro con moto,** *I.* **a. di molto.** Very fast. **a. moderato, a. non molto, a. non troppo,** *I.* Moderately fast. **a. giusto** (joos'-to), *I.* Fast; but exactly in time.

allein (äl-līn'), *G.* Alone, single. **A.-sang.** Solo. **A.-sänger, or-spieler.** Solo-singer (or player).

alleluia, allelujah (äl-lä-loo'-yä), *Heb.* "Praise the Lord;" Hallelujah.

Allemande (äl-mänd), *F.* 1. A German national or peasant dance in 3-4 or 3-8 time; in some places 2-4 time. 2. A French imitation of this dance. 3. A movement in the classic Suite of Bach, etc.; in 4-4 time, *andantino,* with a short note on the up-take.

allentato (tä'-tō), **allentamen'to, allentan'do,** *I.* Retarding.

allgemeiner Bass (äl-khĕ-mī'-nĕr bäs), *G.* Thorough bass.

allied. Accessory.

allmählich, allmählig (äl'-mä-lĭkh), *G.* Gradually.

allonger l'archet (äl-lôṅ-zhä lär-shä), *F.* To prolong the bow stroke.

allo'ra, *I.* Then.

Almain, Alman, Almand. Allemande.

Alma Redemp'toris, *L.* Hymn to the Virgin.

al'penhorn, alp'horn. A horn used by the Alpine herdsmen; it is made of strips of firwood from 3 to 8 feet long. It has a limited range.

alphabet. The 7 letters used in music, A-G.

alt (ält), *I.* High. In alt is applied to tones in the first octave above the treble staff, as b''; in altissimo refers to tones in the second octave above the treble staff, as d'''.

al'ta, *I.,* **alt,** *G.* High, or alto; as **Althorn. octava alta.** An octave above.

al'ta, *Sp.* An old Spanish dance.

alterata (ä'-tä), *I.* Scales with notes foreign to the Church modes.

altera'tio, *L.* The doubling of the time value.

alterato (äl-tĕ-rä'-tō), *I.,* **altéré** (äl-tä-rä), *F.,* **altered,** *E.* Changed chromatically, especially applied to certain inverted chords.

alterezza (äl-tĕ-rĕd'-zä), *I.* Haughtiness.

DICTIONARY OF TERMS 551

alternamen'te, alternan'do, *I.* Alternating.

alternations. Tunes for bells.

alternativo (tē'-vō), *I.* 1. Alternative; a choice of methods. 2. A short trio.

Altgeige (ält'-gī-khe), *G.* The viola.

Althorn. Vide SAXHORN.

altieramente (tĭ-ä'-rä), *I.* Haughtily.

alti naturali. Male altos, or counter-tenors, as opposed to castrati.

altisonan'te, altiso'no. Sonorous.

altis'onous. High-sounding, used of the highest male voice.

altis'simo, *L.* Vide ALT.

altist, altista (äl-tēs'-tä), *I.*, **altiste** (äl-tēst), *F.* An alto singer.

Alt'klausel (ält'-klow-zĕl), *G.* The progression of the alto part in a cadence.

alto (äl'-tō), *I.* 1. High; originally applied to the high range of the artificial or falsetto tenors (*castrati, alti naturali, tenori acuti, falsetti,* counter-tenors). Thence the term has been applied to the lower range of women's or boys' voices, ordinarily extending from g below the treble staff to c" (an octave above middle C). 2. Viola, also alto viola. **a. primo,** *I.* The higher alto. **a. secondo,** *T.* The lower alto. **a. tenore,** *I.* The higher tenor.

ai'to-basso, *I.* An obs. dulcimer with a few gut strings, struck with a stick in the left hand, while the performer held a flageolet in the right hand.

alt'ottava, *I.* Vide ALTA.

Altposaune (ält'-pō-zow-nĕ), *G.* Alto-trombone.

al'tra, al'tro, *I.* Another. **altra volta.** Encore. **altro modo.** alternate manner.

Altsänger (ält'-zĕng-er), *G.* Alto, or counter-tenor.

Altschlüssel (ält-shlüs'-sĕl), *G.* The alto clef.

Altviole, *G.* The viola.

al'tus, *L.* Alto or counter-tenor.

alzamento (äl-tsä-mĕn'-to), *I.* An elevating, as of the voice. **a. di mano.** Up-beat.

alzando (äl-tsan'do), *I.* Raising.

amabile (ä-mä'-bĭ-lĕ), *I.* Amiable. **amabilmen'te.** Amiably. **amabilità** (bē-lĭ-tä'). Tenderness.

amarezza (ä-mä-rĕd'-zä), *I.* Bitterness. **amaro** (ä-mä'-rō). Bitter. **amarissimamen'te,** **amarissimo.** Very bitter(ly).

amateur (ăm-ä-tŭr'), *F.* A "lover" of an art, who does not make it his profession; makes it rather an avocation than a vocation.

Amati. A violin made by the brothers Amati. Vide B. D.

am'bira. An African wooden drum with vibrating tongues of wood or iron.

am'bitus, *L.* Compass or range.

am'bo or ambon. The platform where canons were sung in the mediæval Eastern Church.

Ambro'sian, Ambrosia'nus. Introduced by Ambrose. Vide B. D. **A Hymn.** The "Te Deum" doubtfully credited to him.

ambuba'ja (äm-boo-bä'-yä), *L.* A strolling flute-player from Syria. Vide ANBUBA.

ambulant (äṅ-bü-läṅ), *F.* Vagabond musician.

âme (äm), *F.* Soundpost.

amen (ä-mĕn'), *Heb.* "So be it."

American fingering. That system of fingering in which x indicates the thumb; in foreign fingering, the thumb is called the first finger and marked 1.

American organ. Originally called "Melodeon" or "Melodie." A free-reed instrument differing from the older harmonium (q.v.) in that the air is drawn through the reeds by suction, instead of forced outward through them; this gives a superior control and shading; inv. by Jeremiah Carhart. Its superiority, recognised in Europe more than at home, is also due to the better voicing of the reeds and the resonant air-chambers developed by Mason & Hamlin. The stops are many, and imitate various instruments.

amore (ä-mō'-rĕ), *I.* Love; affection. **amorevole** (rä'-vō-lĕ), **amorevolmen'te, amoro'so, amorosamente,** Loving(ly).

amphichord. Lira barberina (q.v.).

A'morschall (ä'-môr-shäll), **Amorsklang,** *G.* An imperfectly valved French horn, inv. by Kölbel, 1760.

ampho'ter, *Gr.* A series of tones common to two registers.

ampollo'so, ampollosamen'te, *I.* ampoulé (äṅ-poo-lä'), *F.* Pompous(ly).

amusement (ä-müz-mäṅ), *F.* A light composition.

an (än), *G.* On (of an organ-stop); "draw."

anab'asis, *Gr.* A series of ascending tones.

anabath'mi, *Gr.* Certain antiphons in the Greek Church.

anacru'sis, anakrusis, *Gr.* 1. The up-beat. 2. The up-take, or accented part of a measure beginning a theme or air.

anafil (ä-nä-fēl'), *Sp.* A Moorish pipe. **anafilero** (fē-lä-rō). A player of it.

anagaza (ä-nä-gä'-thä), *Sp.* A bird-call.

anakamp'sis, anakamp'tos, *Gr.* A series of descending tones.

anaka'ra, *Gr.* Ancient kettle-drum. **anakaris'ta,** *Gr.* Kettle-drummer.

analisi (ä-na-lē'-zē), *I.*, **analyse** (ăn-ä-lēz), *F.* Analysis.

anbu'ba (ya). Syrian flute.

anche (äṅsh), *F.* A reed. **libre.** Free-reed. **jeu d'a.,** or **a. d'orgue.** A reed-stop.

ancia (äṅ-chē'ä), *I.* A reed.

anco'ra, *I.* Once more; yet; still, as **ancor più mosso.** Still more quickly.

Andácht (än'-däkht), *G.* Devotion. **andächtig** (än-děkh'-tǐkh). Devotional.

andamen'to, *I.* 1. Rate of speed. 2. An episode as in a fugue. 3. A fugal theme.

andante (än-dän'-tě), *I.* Literally—"going"; moderately slow, reposeful. Often much qualified by other words, as *con moto, largo, maestoso, più tosto allegretto* = (nearly *allegretto*).

andantino, *I.* Literally, slower than Andante; but usually considered to mean slightly faster.

andare (än-dä'-rä), *I.* To move; as **a diritto,** go straight on; **a. a tempo,** keep strict time.

anem'ochord or **anim'ocorde.** An instr. inv. by Schnell, 1789, aiming to imitate the Æolian harp by means of keys pressing bellows and forcing air against strings.

anemom'eter. Wind-gauge.

ane'sis, *Gr.* 1. Descent from a higher to a lower tone. 2. The lowering of the pitch of strings. Reverse of **epitasis.**

Anfang (än'-fängk), *G.* Beginning. **vom A.,** = *Da capo.* **Anfänger** (än'-fěng-ěr). A beginner. **Anfangsgründe.** Rudiments. **Anfangsritornell.** Prelude.

Anführer (än'-fü-rěr), *G.* Conductor, leader.

angeben (än'gä-běn), *G.* To give. **den Ton a.,** to give the pitch.

Angelica (än-jä'-lǐ-kä), *G.* **angélique** (äṅ-zhä-lēk), **angélot** (äṅ-zhǔ-lō), *F.*

1. An organ-stop. Vide vox. 2. A 17th century keyboard instr. with 17 strings.

angel'ophone. Early form of harmonium.

angemes'sen, *G.* Appropriate.

angenehm (än'-khě-näm), *G.* Pleasing.

angkloung (änk'-loong). A Javanese xylophone.

anglaise (äṅ-glěz), *F.*, **anglico** (än-gle'-kō), *I.* 1. In the "English" style. 2. An English country dance, ballad or hornpipe. 3. A sprightly French dance in 3-4 time.

ango're (än-gō'-rě), **angoscia** (än-gō'-shä), *I.* Anguish.

angoscevole (än-go-shä'-vō-lě), **angosciamen'te, angosciosamen'te, ango-scio'so,** *I.* With anguish or anxiety.

ängstlich (ěngsht'lǐkh), *G.* Anxious(ly).

anhaltend (än'-häl-těnt), *G.* Continuous. **a. Cadenz.** A pedal point or prolonged cadence.

Anhang (än'-hängk), *G.* Coda.

am'ma, *I.* Soul spirit.

animan'do, animato (ä'-to), *I.*, **animé** (än-ǐ-mä), *F.* Animated. **animazione** (ä-nǐ-mä-tsǐ-ō'-ně), *I.* Animation.

animo (än'-ǐ-mō), *I.* Spirit. **animo'so, animosamen'te,** *I.* Boldly.

animocorde. Vide ANEMOCHORD.

An'klang, *G.* Harmony.

Anlage (än'-lä-khě), *G.* Outline.

anlaufen (än'-low-fen), *G.* To increase; to swell.

Anleitung (än'-lī-toongk), *G.* Introduction; instruction.

Anmuth (än'moot), *G.* Sweetness, grace. **anmuthig** (an'moo-tǐkh). Sweetly. **anmuthvoll** (fôl). Full of grace.

anom'aly. Deviation from exactitude due to temperament (q.v.). **anomalous.** As a chord; characterised by a much tempered interval.

anonner (ă-nǔn-nä), *F.* To hesitate, blunder.

anpfeifen (än'-pfī-fen), *G.* To whistle at; to hiss.

An'sa. In Hindu music the note corresponding to our tonic.

Ansatz (än'-zäts), *G.* 1. Embouchure. 2. Attack.

Anschlag (än'-shläkh), *G.* 1. Touch. 2. A short double appoggiatura.

anschwellen (än'-shvěl-lěn), *G.* To increase; swell.

an'singen, *G.* To greet with song.

ansio'so. ansiosamen'te, *I.* Anxiously.

anspielen (än'-shpē-lĕn), *G.* To play first.

Ansprache (än'-spräkh-ĕ), *G.* "Speaking" or intonation.

ansprechen, anstimmen, *G.* To speak; sound.

Anstimmung (än'-shtĭm-moongk), *G.* Intonation.

answer. Vide FUGUE.

antelu'dium, *L.* A prelude.

antece'dent. 1. A subject. 2. Vide FUGUE.

anthem. In the Anglican Church service, a sacred vocal work with or without accompaniment. "There are five species of anthems. 1. **Verse and chorus a.**, consisting of verse and chorus, but beginning in chorus. 2. **Verse a.**, containing verse (i. e., solo) and chorus, but beginning in verse. 3. **Full a.**, consisting wholly of chorus. 4. **Solo a.**, consisting of solos and choruses, but without verse, and 5. **Instrumental a.**" [*Busby.*]

anthe'ma. Greek dance with song.

Anthologie (än-tō-lō-zhē'), **Antholo'- gium,** *F.* and *G.* The collection of hymns, prayers, and lections of the Greek Church.

an'thropoglossa, *Gr.* The vox humana; a stop.

anticipation, anticipamento (än-tē-chē-pä-men'-to), or **anticipazione** (än-tē-chē-pä'-tsĭ-ō'-nĕ), *I.* The sounding of one or more parts of a harmony before the natural and expected place.

antico (än-tē'-kō), *I.* Ancient. **all' a.** in the ancient style.

antienne (äṅs-yĕn), *F.,* **antifona** (än-tē'-fō-nä), *I.* Anthem; antiphon.

atifona'rio, *I.,* **atifonero** (än-tĭ-fō-nä'-rō), *Sp.* A precentor; anthem singer.

antifonal', *Sp.* A book of anthems.

an'tiphon, an'tiphone, antipho'non, antiph'ony. 1. In Greek music, accompaniments in the octave. 2. Responsive singing by parts of a divided choir, or congregation. 3. A short scriptural sentence sung before and after the Psalms or Canticles. The chant or alternate singing in churches and cathedrals.

antiphona, *Gr.* An anthem.

antiphonal, antiphonaire (äṅtĭ-fō-nằr), *F.,* **antiphona'rium,** *L.,* **an'ti'- phonary.** A collection of Catholic antiphons.

Antiphonel. Vide PLANCHETTE.

an'tiphonic. Not in unision: made up of 2 or more parts.

antistro'fa. An ancient Spanish dance.

antith'esis. 1. Contrast. 2. Counter-subject. 3. In fugues applied to the *answer.*

anto'de, *Gr.* Responsive singing.

Antwort (änt'-vôrt), *G.* Answer.

anwachsend (än'väkh-zĕnt), *G.* Crescendo.

aoi'dos, *Gr.* Singer.

aper'to, *I.* 1. Open, broad. 2. In piano music, "use the damper pedal."

aper'tus, *L.* Open; as diapason, canon, pipes.

Apfelregal (äp'fĕl-räkh-ăl), *G.* "Apple-register," an obsolete reed-stop.

aph'ony, aphonie (ă-fō-nē), *F.* Dumbness. **aph'onous.** Without voice.

apoggiatura. Vide APPOGGIATURA.

apolli'no, *Gr.* An invention combining the qualities of several instruments.

apol'lo, apol'lon. A 20-stringed lute inv. in 1678, by Prompt, of Paris.

apollo lyra. An improvement made by Schmidt in 1832, on the Psalm-melodicon (q.v.).

apollo'nicon. A gigantic orchestrion exhibited in 1817, by Flight & Robson, and containing 5 manuals, 45 stops, 1,900 pipes, and kettle-drums. It could be played automatically or by five performers at once.

apollo'nion. An instr. inv. by Voller in 1800; a piano with double key-board, organ-pipes and automatic performer.

apos'trophe. In singing, used to mark a breathing-place.

apot'ome, *Gr.* A major semitone, in Greek music.

appassionato (äp-päs'-sĭ-ō-nä'-tō), **ap-passionatamente,** *I.* Passionate(ly).

appeau (ăp-pō), *F.* Bird-like tone.

Appel (äp-pĕl'), *F.* & *G.* Drum call; assembly.

appenato (ap-pä-nä'-tō), *I.* Distressed.

application (ăp-plĭ-kăs-yôṅ), *F.,* **applicatura** (äp-plĭ-kä-too'-ra), *I.,* **Applikatur** (toor'), *G.* Fingering.

appoggiando (äp-pôd-jän'-dō), **appoggiato** (jä'-tō), *I.* Leaning upon, as a tone that slides into the next *legato.*

appoggiatura (äp-pôd-jä-too'-rä), pl.**e,** *I.* "Leaning note." 1. The short or lesser **a.**, or grace note, is written small with a line through its hook, it receives the accent, but has the minimum of duration; the double, or compound **a.**, contains more than one note and follows the same rule, the first note taking the stress; the unaccented **a.** (*Nachschlag*) follows its principal, is connected with it by a slur, and like other grace notes borrows its time from the principal, but unlike them has no accent. 2. The long **a.** was written small in old music but played at its full value. It is now written large as an unprepared suspension. Almost any dissonantial note can be introduced unprepared as an **a.** 3. A superior **a.** is one placed above its principal; an inferior **a.** one below. Vide GRACE.

apprestare (äp-prä-stä′-rĕ), *I.*, **appreti(e)ren** (äp-prĕ-tē′-rĕn), *G.* To prepare, as an instrument.

Appretur (äp-prĕ-toor′), *G.* The proper set-up of an instrument.

âpre (äpr), *F.* Harsh. **âprement** (äpr-mäṅ). Harshly. **âpreté** (äp-rŭ-tā). Harshness.

Ar (är), *Port.* All.

Arabeske (är-ä-bĕs′-kĕ), *G.*, **arabesque** (är-ä-bĕsk), *F.* 1. An embellishment. 2. A light and graceful form of music, resembling the rondo.

arbit′rio. Pleasure. *A suo a.=ad lib.*

arbit′rii (trĭ-ĭ). Embellishments improvised at pleasure while singing.

arc, *I.* The bow; an abbr. of arco

arcata (är-kä′-tä). Use of the bow.

arca′to. Played with the bow.

Arche (är-kĕ̆), *G.* Sounding-board.

arch-, *E.* & *F.*, **archi-,** *L.*, **arci-** *I.* A prefix, meaning "chief, principal"; of instruments "the greatest."

archeggiare (är-kĕd-jä′-rĕ), *I.* To use the bow, to fiddle.

archet (är-shā), *F.*, **archetto** (är-ket′-to), *I.* Violin bow.

archlute, archiluth, (är-shĭ-lüt), *F.*, **arciliuto** (är-chēl-yoo-tō), *I.* A theorbo in which the bass strings were doubled with an octave and the small strings with a unison.

arcicembalo (är-chĭ-chäm′-bä-lō), *I.* A harpsichord inv. by Vincentino in the 16th century with 6 key-boards and a diatonic, chromatic, and enharmonic scale. He also inv. the so-called arci-organ.

arco (är′-kō), *I.* The bow. **a pun′ta** or **colla punta d'arco.** With the point of the bow. **coll' arco,** or simply **arco** after pizzicato. "Resume the bow." **a. in giù** (joo). Down-bow. **a. in su** (soo). Up-bow. **contr'arco.** Bowing against the rule.

arden′te, ardentemen′te, ardentis′-simo, *I.* Ardent(ly).

arditezza (ar-di-tĕd′-za), *I.* Boldness. **ardito, arditamen′te.** Bold(ly).

Aretin′ian. Concerning Guido D'Arez-

zo or Aretinus, as the **A. syllables.** Vide SOLMISATION (and GUIDO in the B. D.).

argentin (är-zhäṅ-tăṅ), *F.* Silvery.

arghool′. An Egyptian cane pipe with reed mouthpiece.

aria (ä′-rĭ-ä) (pl. **e**), *I.* A song; a melodic composition for a solo voice with instrumental accompaniment. It is usually elaborate. The **a. da capo** with two parts (the first repeated after the second) was the first important form, though the rondo and even the sonata idea have been used. Various sorts of aria are **a. buffa** (boof′-fä), humorous; **cantabile,** lyrical; **concertante** (côn-chĕr-tän′-tĕ) or **da concerto,** for concert use, elaborately accompanied **d'abilità** (dä-bē-lē-tä), for a display of virtuosity; **d'entrata** (dĕn-trä′-tä, or **sortita** (sôr-tē′-tä), for the first appearance or entrance of an operatic character; **di bravura,** highly florid; **da chiesa,** for church with accompaniments of full orchestra; **fuga′ta parlan′te,** declamatory; **tedes′ca,** with closely related accompaniment. **A. d'ostinazione** (dôs-tĭ-nä′-tsĭ-ō′-nĕ), *I.* An aria with a *basso ostinato.* **aggiunte.** One introduced into an opera. **ariettina** (tē′-na), **ariet′ta,** *I.* A short air or melody.

ariette (är-ĭ-ĕt), *F.* Literally "a short aria," actually a grand aria.

arigot (ă-rĭ-gō), *F.* A fife.

ario′sa (or-o), *I.* Melodious(ly), cantabile. **ariose cantate** (ä-rĭ-ō′sĕ kän-tä′tĕ), *I.* Airs in a style between a song and recitative, introducing frequent changes in time and manner. **ario′so.** In the style of an air; between an aria and a recitation. A rather melodious declamation.

arm. Iron end-piece in an organ-roller.

Armandine (ăr-mäṅ-dēn) *F.* A grand piano with gut-strings and no key-board, invented by Pascal Taskin, and named after the singer Mlle. Armand.

arma′rius, *L.* Precentor.

armer la clef (ăr-mä lä klä), *F.* To mark the signature on the clef.

Armgeige (ärm′-gī-khĕ), *G.* Viola da braccia.

armoneggiare (är-mō-nĕd-jä′-rĕ), *I.* To harmonise.

armonia (är-mō-nē′-ä), *I.* Harmony; union. **a. militare.** Military band. **armonia′co** (ä′-kō), **armonia′le. ar-**

monia'to, armo'nico, armonio'so, armoniosamen'te, *I.* Harmonised; harmonious(ly).

armo'nica, *I.* 1. Early form of the accordeon. 2. Musical glasses. Vide HARMONICA. **armonica guida** (gwē-dä). Text-book in harmony.

armure (är-mür), *F.* 1. The key signature. 2. Action, mechanism.

ar'pa (pl. e), *I.* Harp. **a. d'eolo.** Æolian harp. **a. doppia.** 1. Formerly a harp with double strings for each tone. 2. Now a double-action. **arpanet'ta, arpinel'la.** A small harp or lute. Vide SPITZHARFE.

arpège (är-pĕzh), **arpègement** (är-pĕzh-mäṅ), *F.* Arpeggio. **arpèger** (är-pĕ-zhä). To arpeggiate.

arpeggi (är-pĕd'-jē), *I.* Pl. of Arpeggio.

arpeggiare (är-pĕd-jä'rĕ), *I.* 1. To play the harp. 2. To play chords in harp-manner, i. e., waved, broken. **arpeggiamento** (är-pĕd-jä-mĕn'-tō), **arpeggian'do** (pĕd-jän'-dō), **arpeggiato** (jä'-to). Played arpeggio, in imitation of the harp.

arpeggiatura (too'-rä), *I.* A series of arpeggi.

arpeggio (är-pĕd'-jō), *I.* 1. The playing of the notes of a chord quickly, one after another, in the harp style, ripplingly. 2. Such a chord written out.

arpeggione (jō'-nĕ). A small 6-stringed 'cello tuned like a guitar, inv. by Stauffer in 1823.

arpicor'do, *I.* Harpsichord.

arpo'ne, *I.* A harp with horizontal strings, inv. in the 18th century by Barbieri.

arranger (är-räṅ-zhä), *F.* **arrangiren** (är-rän-zhēr'en), *G.* To arrange.

ar'sis, *Gr.* A raising as opposed to thesis. In accent it means the stress; in metre it means the up-beat, and therefore the unaccented part. It is musically most common in the latter sense.

Art (ärt), *G.* Species, quality, as **Tonart,** key.

articolare (är-tē-kō-lä'-rĕ), **I. articuler** (är-tē-kü-lä), *F.,* **artikuliren** (är-tē-koo-lē'-rĕn), *G.* To articulate. **articolato** (lä'tō), *I.* Articulated. **articolazione** (lä'-tsĭ-ō'-nĕ), *I.* Exact and distinct pronunciation; articulation.

artiglich (är'tĭkh-lĭkh), *G.* Neat(ly).

As (äs), *G.* The note A flat. **Asas,** or **Ases.** The note A double flat.

ascaulos or **askau'los,** *Gr.* A bagpipe.

As-dur (äs-door), *G.* The key of A flat major.

Ashantee trumpet. One made of the tusk of an elephant.

asheor (ä-'shĕ-ôr). Hebrew instr. of 10 strings.

As-moll (äs-mŏll), *G.* The key of A flat minor.

aspirare (äs-pĭ-rä'-rĕ), *I.* To breathe audibly.

aspira'tion. 1. The dot indicating *Spiccato.* 2. An obsolete grace note having the effect of a beat in a sustained tone.

asprezza (äs-prĕd'-zä), *I.* Harshness.

assai (äs-sä'-ē), *I.* Very; as **allegro a.,** very fast.

assemblage (äs-säṅ-bläzh), *F.* Double tonguing; rapid execution.

assembly. A rallying call for troops.

assez (äs-sā), *F.* Enough; rather.

assoluto (loo'-to), *I.* Absolute; alone; of a chief singer.

as'sonant, *E.,* **assonan'te,** *I.* Having resemblance in sounds, concordant. **Assonanz** (äs-sō-nänts'), *G.,* **assonanza** (äs-sō-nän'-tsa). *I.* Consonance.

assourdir (ăs-soor-dēr), *F.* To muffle; to deafen. **assourdissant** (dĭs-säṅ). Deafening.

at-abal. A large Moorish drum.

Athem (ä'tām), *G.* Breath, **a.-los.** Breathless. **A.-zug** (tsookh). Respiration.

athmen (ät'-män), *G.* To blow softly.

atonality. A quality possessed by music which employs all 12 tones of the chromatic scale freely, as related only to one another, with no one predominate. Such music has no definite key centre or tonic, to which other tones are related.

attacca (ät-täk'-kä), *I.,* **attaquer** (ăt-tă-kä), *F.* To attack. **attacca subito,** *I.* Attack or begin what follows immediately. **attacca-Ansatz,** *G.* The attack-touch, a quick stroke from near the keys.

attacco, *I.,* **attaque** (ăt-tăk), *F.* 1. A brief fugue theme. 2. A subject for imitation in fugue.

attack. The manner or act of beginning a tone, a phrase or a movement.

atto (ät'-tō), *I.* An act. **a. di cadenza.** Point where a cadence may occur.

au (ō), *F.* "To the; in the style of the." Vide AL, etc.

aubade (ō-băd), *F.* Morning music; a day-break serenade.

audace (ä-oo-dät'-che), *I.* Audacious.

auf (owf), *G.* On, upon, in, at, etc. **-blassen.** To blow upon. **-fassung.** Conception; interpretation. **-führung** (fü-roongk). Performance. **-geregt** (-ge-räkht). Agitated. **-geweckt** (-gĕ-vĕkt). Lively. **-gewecktheil** (tīl). Cheer.

aufhalten, *G.* To retard, to suspend. **Aufhaltung** (owf'-häl-toongk), *G.* A suspension. Vorhalt.

Auflage (owf'-lä-khĕ), *G.* Edition.

auflösen (owf-lä'-zĕn). To resolve. **Auflösung** (owf'-lä-zoongk). 1. Resolution. 2. The solution of a riddle canon. 3. A natural (♮) sign.

Aufsatz (owf'-zäts), *G.* Tube (of a reed-pipe).

Aufschlag (owf'-shläkh), *G.* Up-beat.

Aufschnitt (owf'-shnĭtt), *G.* Mouth (of a pipe).

aufsteigende (owf-shtī'-khĕn-dĕ), *G.* Ascending.

Aufstrich (owf'-shtrĭkh), *G.* An up-bow.

Auf'takt, *G.* Anacrusis; up-take.

Auf'tritt, *G.* A scene.

Aufzug (ow'-ftzookh), *G.* An act.

augmentant, en (ä-nōg-mäṅ-täṅ), *F.* Crescendo.

augmenta'tio, *L.,* **augmenta'tion** (in *F.* ōg-mäṅ-täs'-yôṅ). Increase. 1. Of interval (q.v.) a semitone larger than major, as an **augmented** fifth. 2. Of note-values, as in counterpoint, where a theme may appear with quarter notes changed to half, etc.

augmented, *E.,* **augmenté** (ōg-mäṅ-tä), *F.* Used of 1. Intervals a semitone greater than major. 2. Chords containing such intervals. Vide ALTERED CHORDS.

aul'os, *Gr.* Most important Greek instrument, probably a flute, possibly like the oboe. **aul'etes.** Flute-player.

aulozo'num, *Gr.* The tuning-wire of reeds.

aus (ows), *G.* From, out of. **-arbeitung** (-är-bī-toongk). Elaboration. **-dehnung** (-dä-noongk). Development. **-druck** (-drook). Expression. **-drucksvoll.** Full of expression. **-führung** (fü-roongk). Performance; exposition. **-füllung.** The middle parts. **-gabe** (-gä-bĕ). Edition

-gang. Exit; conclusion. **-gehalten.** Sostenuto. **-gelassen.** Wild; ungovernable. **Aus'gelassenheit** (hīt). Extravagance; wantonness. **-halten.** To sustain. **Aus'haltung.** Sustaining. **Aushaltungszeichen** (tsī-khĕn). The fermata. **-lösung** (-lä-zoongk). The device that releases the hammer of a piano. **äusserste Stimmen** (īs'-sĕr-stĕ shtĭm-mĕn), *G.* Extreme parts.

ausweichen (ows-vikh'n), *G.* To modulate. **Ausweichung** (vī-khoongk), *G.* Modulation; transition.

authentic, *E.,* **autentico** (ä-oo-tĕn'-tī-kō), *I.,* **authentisch** (ow-ten'-tĭsh), *G.* That part of a scale between the tonic and the dominant above; the part between the tonic and the dominant below being called *Plagal.* Vide MODES. **a. cadence.** Vide CADENCE. **a. melody.** One whose range covers the octave above its tonic or final.

au'toharp. A zither whose strings are stopped by a series of dampers so arranged that pressing one down, leaves free certain strings. When these are swept with the plectrum a chord results.

au'tophon. A barrel-organ, whose music is cut in heavy pasteboard.

autos sacramentale (ä'-oo-tos säk-rä-mĕn-tä'-lĕ), *Sp.* Oratorio, or passion music.

auxiliary. Said of tones one degree above or below the true harmonic tone, particularly in a grace; of scales belonging to auxiliary or related keys.

avanera. Vide HABANERA.

ave (ä'vä), *L.* "Hail." **Ave Maria.** "Hail Mary," the salutation of the angel at the Annunciation. which, with the words of Elizabeth (Luke i, 42) and a concluding hymn, has formed a favourite text for music since the 7th century. **Ave maris stella,** *L.* "Hail, star of the sea." A Catholic hymn.

avec (ä-vĕk), *F.* With.

ave'na, *L.* A reed; a pipe.

avicin'ium. A bird-like organ-stop.

avoided. Prepared and then omitted, as a cadence (q.v.).

avoir du retentissement (ä-vwär-dŭ rŭ-täṅ-tēs-mäṅ), *F.* To be repeated and echoed.

azione sacra (ä'-tsī-ō-nĕ sä'-krä). Oratorio; passion music.

DICTIONARY OF TERMS

B

B. 1. A musical pitch, one whole step higher than A, and its octaves. In France and Italy called "si." In Germany B natural is called H (hä), and the term B (bā) confined to B flat. 2. The major key having five sharps; the minor key relative to D major. In old works (and modern German) **square B** (or **B quadratum** or **quadrum** or **durum,** in F. **Bé carré**) stands both for B natural and for the natural sigh (♮) itself. **B rotundum** (or **molle,** in F, **bémol**) stands for B flat, and for the flat sign itself (♭), the tone B having been the first to be chromatically lowered. **B cancellatum** stands for the sharp sign (♯) first formed by crossing the flat (♭) and originally equivalent merely to nullifying or naturalising the flat. In old solmisation B flat was *B fa;* B natural, *B mi.* As abbr. B—*basso;* c. b.—*col basso;* C. B. — *Contrabasso.* Mus. B. — *Bachelor of music.*

baas (bäs) or **base dance.** A dance resembling the minuet.

baazas (bä-zä), *F.* A kind of guitar.

babara (bä-bä'-rä), *Sp.* A Spanish country dance.

baborack'a, bab'orak. Bohemian dances of eccentric rhythm.

baccalaureus musicæ, *L.,* **bachelier** (bǎsh-ǔl-yā), *F.* Bachelor of Music. A degree granted to those who have proved a certain standard of proficiency. Inferior to Doctor of Music.

bacchanale (nǎl), *F.* A Bacchic revel. **bacchanalian songs.** Drinking songs.

bacchia. A Kamschatkan dance in 2-4 time.

bacciocolo (bät-tchĭ-ō-kō'-lō), *I.* A Tuscan guitar.

bachelor. Vide BACCALAUREUS.

back-block. Wrest-block.

badinage (bǎ-dĭ-näzh), *F.* Banter.

back. The under side of a violin.

back-fall. 1. An obsolete sign and the grace note it indicated. Vide GRACES. 2. A lever in the organ.

back-turn. Vide TURN.

baga'na. 10-stringed Abyssinian lyre.

bagatelle (bǎg-à-tĕl), *F.* A trifle.

bagpipe(s). An instr. of great antiquity and wide favour, consisting of a series of pipes furnished with wind from a bag in the player's mouth or a bellows under his arm, or both. It has usually one *chanter* or melody pipe with a reed, and 6 or 8 holes, played with the fingers; 3 *drone pipes* sounding continuously an octave and a fifth.

baguette (bǎ-gĕt), *F.* 1. A drumstick. 2. Bow.

baile (bä-ē'-lĕ), *Sp.* National Spanish dances.

baisser (bēs-sā), *F.* To lower, as the pitch.

bal'afo. A Senegambian xylophone.

balalaika (bä-lä-lī'-kä). A rude Russian or Gipsy guitar with 2 to 4 strings.

balancement (bǎl-äns-män), *F.* A tremolo (as of a violinist's finger).

balance-rail. The wooden strip on which piano keys are balanced.

Bal(c)ken (bäl'-ken), *G.* 1. Bass-bar 2. The heavy lines connecting the stems of a series of small notes.

Balg (bälkh), *G.* Bellows. **B.-zug.** Bellows-stop.

ballabile (bäl-lä'-bĭ-lĕ), *I.* In a dance manner.

bal'lad, Ballade (bǎl-lǎd), *F.* (bäl-lä'-dĕ), *G.* **ballata** (bäl-lä'-tä), *I.* Originally a dance tune (from ballare, to dance); it now means a simple song of popular tone. In instrumental work, it may be as elaborate as "Chopin's Ballades," but it still has an idea of directness and melodiousness, if not narrative. **balladenmässig** (mĕs-sĭkh), *G.* Ballad style. **ballad of ballads.** Solomon's song. **ballad opera.** Light tuneful opera. **alla ballata.** In ballad style. **ballatella, ballatetta.** A short ballata.

ballet (bǎl-lā), *F.,* **Ballett** (bäl-lĕt'), *G.,* **ballet'to,** *I.* 1. An elaborate dance by professionals, often spectacular and narrative. 2. A light glee of the 16th cent. Vide FA-LA. 3. **balletto** was used by Bach for an allegretto in common time.

bal'lo (pl-ī), *I.* A dance, or dance tune, as **b. della stira,** Styrian dance like the waltz; **b. ungaresi,** a syncopated 2-4 Hungarian dance; **da ballo,** in dance style.

ballonchio (bäl-lôn'kĭ-ō), *I.* A country dance.

band. A group of instrumentalists, usually a military band, sometimes an orchestra; oftener a part of the orchestra, as the string-band. **bandmaster.** The leader of a band.

Band (bänt), *G.* A volume.

ban'da, *I.* 1. The brass and the drums of a theatre-orchestra. 2. An orchestra on the stage.

Bande (bän'-dĕ, *G.*, bäṅd, *F.*). 1. The 24 court-violins. 2. A strolling band.

bando'la, bandolon. bandalo're, bandelo're. bando'ra, bandura (ban-doo'ra), *I.* Instrs. of the lute kind, played with a plectrum.

bando'nion. A concertina named after the Heinrich Band, invented by Uhlig, 1830.

bandurria (bän-door'-rĭ-a), *Sp.* A wire-strung guitar.

ban'ia, ban'ja. African instrs. from which the banjo may have been derived.

banjo. A long-necked stringed instrument with a broad, round body, covered with a tight skin, which gives the five to nine strings a quaint sound.

Bänkelsänger (bĕnk'el-zĕng-er), *G.* "Bench-singer(s)," vagabond musician(s).

bar. 1. A vertical line drawn across the stave just before the major accent of each measure; since the bar separates the measures, the word is incorrectly used to denote the measure itself. In psalmody used to mark the end of lines and phrases. 2. A general division of the song of the Meistersänger; it included 2 Stollen and an Abgesang. 3. Vide BARRER.

bar'baro, *I.* Barbarous(ly).

barbarism. Crudeness of progression or combination.

barbet', bar'biton, bar'bitos. 1. Ancient Greek lyre. 2. In 16th cent. a violin.

barcaro'la, barcaruola (bär-kä-roo-ō'-lä), **barca'ta,** *I.*, **barcarolle** (bär-kä-rôl), *F.* 1. An air sung by gondoliers, or boatmen. 2. Hence, a lyrical instrumental composition usually in 6–8 time (Chopin's are in 12–8).

bard. A Celtic minstrel.

bardd alan (bärd-ä'-lăn). A Welsh prof. of music.

Bardiet, Bardit (bär-dēt'), *G.* Ancient German war-song.

bardo'ne, *I.* Vide BARYTONE.

bare. Open; parallel, as **bare fifths.**

Barem (bä'-räm), *G.* Obs. soft organ-stop.

Bärentanz (bär'-ĕn-tänts), *G.* Bear-dance.

bargaret, bargeret, barginet. Vide BERGERET.

baribas'so. A deep barytone.

bariolage (bär-ĭ-ō-läzh), *F.* 1. A med-

ley. 2. A rapid passage showing a distinct design, or "waist-coat pattern."

bar'itenor. The deeper tenor voice.

bariton(e). Vide BARYTON.

baroc'co, *I.*, **barock'**, *G.*, **baroque** (bă-rôk), *F.* Eccentric; uncouth.

Bärpfeife (bär'-pfī-fĕ), *G.* Bear-pipe, an old growling organ-stop.

barquade (bär-kăd), *F.* Old form of barcarolle.

bar'ra, *I.* Bar.

barrage (bär-räzh), *F.* Vide BARRER.

barre (băr), *F.* 1. A bar; also ♭. de **mesure; b.** de répétition, repetition mark. 2. A bridge.

barré (bär-rā), *F.* Vide BARRER.

barred C. The mark for common time. C with a bar through it; a mark of *alla breve.*

barrel. The body of a bell.

barrel chime. Portion of a mechanism ringing a chime of bells.

barrel organ. 1. An instrument, commonly portable, in which the bellows are worked, the pipes blown and the tune automatically played by a crank turning a cylinder set with pegs, so arranged as to open valves in melodic and harmonic order. 2. The same principle is used in street-pianos, the pegs releasing hammers which strike wires.

barrer (băr-rā), *F.* To bar. Pressing the strings of a guitar or lute with the forefinger of the left hand to raise their pitch; **great,** *or* **grand b.,** pressing all the strings; **small b.,** pressing 2 or 3 strings; hence **barré** and **barrage.**

Bart, *G.* Ear, as of an organ-pipe.

bar'yton(e), *E.*, **baryton** (bär-ĭ-tôṅ), **Baryton** (bär-rĭ-tôn'), *G.*, **barito'no.** *I.* 1. The male voice, between bass and tenor, with a compass between low G and g (vide PITCH). If low in quality it is **bass-baryton,** if high, **tenor-baryton.** 2. A brass valved instr. (vide SAX-HORN). 3. The **viola di bordone** (*or* bardone). An obsolete 18th cent. instr. resembling the viola da gamba; its 6 gut-strings being re-enforced by the sympathetic vibration of from 8 to 27 wires. 4. An epithet for any instr. between bass and tenor, as b. clarinet. 5. **b. clef.** The obsolete F clef on the 3d line.

barz (bärz), *Welsh.* A Welsh bard.

bas (bä), *F.* Low. **bas-dessus** (dĕs-sü). Mezzo-soprano.

base, bass, *E.*, Bass (bäs), *G.*, basse (bǎs), *F.*, basso (bäs'-sō), *I.* 1. The base or lowest part of a chord, progression, chorus, etc. 2. An epithet denoting the deepest instr. of a class, as bass clarinet. The double-bass, q.v. 3. Formerly an instr. of 5 or 6 strings between 'cello and double-bass. 4. Affixed to the name of an organ-pipe or stop, it restricts it to the pedal. 5. The lowest male voice, ranging usually from low F to mid. C; basse chantante (shäṅ-täṅt), basso cantan'te, a flexible "lyric" bass voice; basse-contre (kôṅtr), basso profundo (pro-foon'-do), a very low voice; basse taille (tī-yŭ), a high bass; basso buffo, bass comedian. 6. Thorough bass, continued bass, figured bass, Generalbass (gā-nĕ-räl'-bäs), bezifferte Bass, basse chiffrée (shǐf-frä), basse continue (kôṅ-tǎṅ-ü), basse figurée (fĕ-gü-rä), basso contin'uo, basso figura'to, basso numera'to—a species of musical shorthand in which only the bass-part is written with Arabic and Roman numerals indicating the chords (vide CHORD). 7. Fundamentalbass, basse fondamentale, basso fondamentalo, vide FUNDAMENTAL. 8. Ground-bass, drone-bass, basse contrainte (kôṅ-trǎṅt), basso construtto, basso ostinato, basso tenuto, a bass phrase or figure obstinately repeated. 9. basse-contre, a very deep voice; also the double-bass; b. de cremo(r)ne, or, de cromorne or d'hautbois or de flûte traversière, old names for the bassoon; b. de cornet, the serpent; b. d'harmonie, the ophicleide; b. guerrière, a bass clarinet; bass orgue, an instr. inv. in 1812 by Sautermuiter. 10. Bassflöte, an obsolete bassoon; an 8-foot organ-stop on the pedal. Bassgeige, 'cello; grosse Bassgeige, double-bass. Bass-schlüssel, or -zeichen—F clef. 11. basso concertante, the principal bass in recitatives, etc.; also florid music for the lower strings; basso obbligato, a necessary bass-part; b. ottava, an octave lower; b. ripieno, vide RIPIENO; b. rivoltato, inverted bass. 12. bass clef, the F clef. Alberti bass, vide ALBERTI. given bass, a bass on which harmony is to be built. supposed bass, a bass tone not the root of the chord. murky bass, vide MURKY. bassa-

nello, an obsolete instr. bass-bar, bass-bram, in violins, etc., a strip of wood glued inside the belly near the bass string.
basset horn. An obsolete clarinet.
Bassett', bassett'l, Bass'l, *G.* 1. Old name for 'cello. 2. As a prefix= tenor. 3. A 4-ft. flute-stop on the pedal.
basset'to, *I.* The little bass. 2. An obsolete instr. with 4 strings. 3. An 8 or 16 ft. reed-stop. 4. The lowest voice when the bass is silent.
Bassklausel (bäs'-klow-zēl). The progression of the bass in a cadence.
Basslade (bäs'-lä-dĕ), *G.* Soundboard.
basson (bǎs-sôṅ), *F.* Bassoon. b. quart (kǎr). One whose tones are a fourth lower. b. quinte (kǎnt). One whose tones are a fifth higher.
bassoon. The bass voice of the wood-wind. A 9-foot conical tube doubled on itself, with a long double-reed mouth-piece. Its original was the long bombardon, from which it was derived in 1539. It is the bass of the oboes; its natural scale is G major; its music is written in the F clef, save for higher notes which use the tenor clef. All keys are available by means of cross fingering, and it is capable of considerable brilliance. It has three registers, the lowest being very reedy, the highest resembling partly a 'cello and partly a tenor voice, the medium is rather colourless. The compass B'♭-c'' (sometimes to f'').
basta, bastante, *I.* "Enough! stop!"
bastardilla (bäs-tär-dēl'-yä), *Sp.* A kind of flute.
bath'yphon, *Gr.* An obsolete clarinet inv. 1829.
batil'lus, *L.* An Armenian instr. used in the place of bells; a board struck with a hammer.
battant(e) (bǎt-tǎn(t)), *F.* Beating.
bâton de mesure (bǎ-tôṅ dŭ mŭ-zür), *F.* 1. Stick used in beating time. 2. A conductor's manner. 3. A rest of 2 or more measures. 4. baton, The thick line of a measure-rest. b. de reprise. Repeat.
battement (bǎt'-mäṅ), *F.* battimen'to, *I.* Beat.
battere (bät'-tĕ-rĕ), *I.* The down stroke.
batterie (bǎt-rē), *F.* 1. The roll of the drum. 2. Smiting the guitar strings. 3. Broken chords on string

instrs. 4. The group of percussion instruments.

battery. A harpsichord effect amounting to a quick sharp repetition of a chord.

battre (bătr), *F.* To beat.

battuta (bät-too'-tä), *I.* 1. A beat; so **a b.**, with the beat, strictly *a tempo.* 2. A measure. 3. A progression from the 10th on an up-beat to the octave on the down, forbidden in old counterpoint.

Bau (bow), *G.* Construction.

bäuerisch (bī'-ĕr-ĭsh), *G.* Rustic; coarse.

Bauernflöte (bow'-ĕrn-flā-tĕ), **Bauernpfeife, Bäuerlein,** *G.* 1. Rustic flute. 2. A stopped register in old organs.

Bauernlied (bow'-ĕrn-lēt), *G.* A rustic ballad.

baxoncillo (bäx-ōn-thēl'-yō), *Sp.* 1. Small bassoon. 2. Open diapason stop.

bayla, bayle (bä'-ē-lä), *Sp.* A dance.

b b (bā-bä), *G.* Double flat.

B-cancellatum. Vide B.

B-dur (bā-door), *G.* **B. durum,** *L.* The key of B flat major.

bearbeitet (bĕ-är'-bī-tĕt), *G.* Arranged. **Bearbeitung** (bī'-toongk). Adaptation.

beards. Small projections on the side of, or beneath, the mouth of a pipe, to improve the speech; hence, cross-and side-beards.

bearings. The tones and intervals first established by a tuner as a basis.

beat, beating. 1. The hand-motions of a conductor. 2. That part of a measure marked by one beat. 3. One pulsation of a trill. 4. An old ornament consisting of a short preliminary trill with the next note below. Vide GRACES. 5. The throb produced by the interference of two tones of slightly different pitch. Vide ACOUSTICS.

bebisation. Vide SOLMISATION.

Bebung (bā'-boongk), *G.* 1. A tremolo; on the clavichord, a tremolo made by vibrating the finger upon the key. 2. Also, German organ-stop.

bec (bĕk), *F.,* **bec'co,** *I.* The mouthpiece, as of a clarinet. **becco polacco.** A large bagpipe.

bécarre (bā-kăr), *F.* The natural sign (♮).

Becher (bĕkh'-ĕr), *G.* 1. The cup or bell of a wind-instr. 2. The tube of a reed-pipe.

Becken (bĕk-n), *G.* Cymbals.

bedeckt', *G.* Covered; stopped.

bedon (bŭ-dôň), *F.* Old name for drum. **b. de Biscaye.** A tambourine.

Be (bā), *G.* B flat. **Be-be.** B double flat.

beffroi (bŭf-frwä), *F.* 1. Belfry. 2. Tocsin.

befilzen (bĕ-fēl'-tsĕn), *G.* To put felt on. **Befilzung.** Felt.

Begeisterung (bĕ-gīs'-tĕr-oongk), *G.* Enthusiasm.

begleiten (bĕ-glī'-tĕn), *G.* To accompany. **Begleitung.** Accompaniment. **Begleitstimmen.** The accompanying parts. **beglei'tete Fu'ge.** A fugue with free parts.

beide (bī'-dĕ), *G.* Both, usually **die Beiden.**

Beispiel (bī'-shpēl), *G.* Example.

Beisser (bīs'sĕr), *G.* A mordent.

Beitöne (bī'-tä-nĕ), *G.* Accessory tones; harmonics.

Beizeichen (bī'-tsī-khĕn), *G.* Accidentals.

bekielen (bĕ-kē'-lĕn), *G.* To fit with quills.

beklemmt', *G.* Oppressed.

bel (bĕl), *I.* Beautiful, perfect, as **il bel canto.** The perfect (art of) song.

belebend (bĕ-lā'-bĕnt), *G.* Accelerating. **belebt** (bĕ-läpt). Lively. **Belebtheit** (hīt). **Belebung.** Vivacity

beledern (bĕ-lā'-dĕrn), *G.* To cover with leather or felt. **Belederung.** Felt.

belegt (bĕ-lākht'), *G.* Hoarse; veiled.

belieben (bĕ-lē'-bĕn), *G.* Pleasure; at pleasure.

beliebig (bĕ-lē'-bǐkh), *G.* At pleasure.

bell. 1. A hollow metallic instrument set in vibration by a clapper, or ball, within, or by hammers from outside. 2. The wide opening of horns, etc. 3. **B. diapason.** A diapason stop with flaring pipes. **b.-gamba.** A stop whose pipes are topped with a bell. **b.-sharp.** An old form of harp which was swung when played. **b.-metronome.** A met. with a bell-indicator. **b.-scale.** A diapason for testing bells. **b.-piano.** Vide GLOCKENSPIEL.

bellezza (bĕl-lĕd'zä), *I.* Beauty.

bellico'so, bellicosamen'te, *I.* Bellicose(ly).

bello'nion. An automatic instr. inv. in 1812, consisting of 24 trumpets and 2 drums.

bellows. A pneumatic device for supplying air to various instruments.

belly. A soundboard of an instr., violin or piano, over which strings are stretched.

bemerk'bar, *G.* Marked.

bémol (bă-mŭl), *F.*, **bemolle** (bä-môl-lĕ), *I.* The mark called a flat (♭). **bémoliser** (bä-mô-lĭ-zā), *F.*, **bemollizzare** (bä-môl-lĭd-zä'rĕ), *I.* To mark with a flat. **bémolisée**(zä). Flatted.

ben (bän), **bene** (bā'-nĕ), *I.* Well, good; as **ben tenuto,** well-sustained. **a bene placito,** at the good pleasure.

Benedic'ite, Omnia Opera. "All ye works (of the Lord) praise Him," *L.* A canticle for morning prayer.

"Benedictus, Domine," Blessed be Thou, O Lord. A canticle. **Benedic'tus Qui Venit,** *L.* "Blessed is He that cometh," vide MASS.

bequadro (bä-kwä'drō), *I.* The natural sign (♮).

berceuse (bĕr-sŭz), *F.* A cradle-song; hence, an instrumental piece in that spirit.

bergamask, *E.*, **bergamas'ca,** *I.*, **bergamasque** (măsk), *F.* A rustic dance, imitating the clumsy peasants of Bergamask in Italy.

bergeret (bĕr-zhĕ-rä), *F.* A rustic song or dance.

Bergkreiyen, Bergreigen (bărkh-rī'-khen), *G.* Mountain melodies.

berlingozza (bĕr-lĭn-gôd'zä), *I.* A rustic dance.

Bes (bäs), *G.* The note B double flat.

besaiten (bĕ-zī'-tĕn), *G.* To string.

beschleunigend (bĕ-shloi'-nĭ-gĕnt), *G.* Accelerating.

befiedern (bĕ-fē'-dĕrn), *G.* To quill.

bestimmt (bĕ-shtĭmt), *G.* Distinct. **B.-heit** (hīt), *G.* Precision.

betonend, betont (bĕ-tōnt), *G.* Accented. **Betonung.** Accentuation.

betrübt (bĕ-trüpt'), *G.* Troubled.

Bet'tlerleier (lī-ĕr), *G.* Hurdy-gurdy; **Bettleroper.** "Beggar's opera."

bewegen (bĕ-vä'-khĕn), *G.* To agitate. **bewegt** (väkht). Agitated. **Bewegung.** Motion, emotion. **Bewegungsart.** Tempo, a movement.

beziffert (bĕ-tsĭf'-fĕrt), *G.* Figured. Vide BASS.

Bezug (bĕ-tsookh'), *G.* The set of strings for an instrument.

bhat. A Hindu bard.

bianca (bĭ-än'-kä), *I.* A "white" or half note.

bibi (bē-bē), *F.* A pianette.

Bible-regal. A regal that folded up into the size of a tome.

bichord, *L.* An instr. (a) having two strings. (b) Having two strings to each note.

bicin'ium. A 2-part composition.

bien (b'yăn), *F.* Well.

bifara (bē'-fä-rä), **bif'fara, bif'ra,** *I.* A stop with paired pipes slightly out of tune, so as to produce a tremolo.

biju'ga. The two-necked cither.

bina. Vide VINA.

bimmolle (bĭm-môl'-lĕ), *I.* B flat: the flat mark.

bin'ary. Two-fold; two-part. **b. form.** A movement with 2 chief themes or sections. **b. measure.** Common time with its two accents.

bind. A line, usually curved, binding two notes into a sustained tone; or the brace binding staves.

Bindebogen (bĭn'-dĕ-bō-khĕn), *G.* A slur.

bin'den, *G.* To bind; to perform *legato.*

Bindung. A slur; hence, a suspension or syncopation; the legato manner. **Bindungszeichen.** The slur.

biquadro (bē-kwä'-dro), *I.* The natural sign.

bird-organ. A small organ for teaching tunes to birds.

Birn(e) (bĕr'nĕ), *G.* The socket of a mouthpiece.

bis (bēs), *L.* 1. Twice, **bis unca,** 16th note. 2. Used by the French instead of our pseudo-French "encore!" meaning "please repeat."

biscan'to, *I.* A duet.

bischero (bēs'-kä-rō), *I.* A peg or pin.

biscroma (bēs-kro'-ma), *I.*, **biscrome** (bēs-krôm), *F.* A 16th note.

bisdiapa'son, *L.* A double octave, or fifteenth.

biseau (bē-sō), *F.* Stopper of a pipe.

bisin'ium, *L.* A duet.

bisogna (bē-sōn'-yä), *I.* "It is necessary."

bisqua'dro (kwä'-drō), *I.* A natural sign.

bissare (bīs-sä'-rĕ), *I.*, **bisser** (bēs-sā), *F.* To encore.

bis'sex, *L.* A 12-stringed guitar.

bit. A small tube to supplement a crook.

Bit'terkeit (kīt), *G.* Bitterness.

bizzarria (bĭd-zär-rē'-ä), *I.* Eccentricity. **bizzar'ro.** Curious. **bizzarramen'te.** Oddly.

blanche (blänsh), *F.* A "white" or half-note.

Blasebalg (blä'-zĕ-bälkh), *G.* Bellows.
blasen (blä'-zĕn), *G.* To blow. **Bla'-ser.** A blower; an instrument for blowing. **Blasemusik.** Music for wind instrs. **Blas'instrument.** A wind-instrument.
Blatt (blät), *G.* A leaf; a reed.
Blechinstrumente (blĕkh'-ĭn-stroo-mĕn-tĕ), *G.* The brass instruments.
blind (blĭnt), *G.* "Blind," simulated, as a dummy pipe.
Blockflöte (blŏk'-flä-tĕ), *G.* 1. A stop, of large-scale pipes. 2. A 16th century flute.
b-mol (bē-mŏl), *F.* The flat mark ♭. Vide BEMOL.
B-moll (bä-mŏl), *G.* The key of B flat minor.
blocks. Supporting strips in violins, etc.
boat-songs. Water-music, vocal or instrumental.
bob. The changes to which a set of bells can be rung; 6 bells give **bob minor**; 8, **b. major**; 10, **b. royal**; 12, **b. maximus**.
bo'bisation, bocedisation. Vide SOL-MISATION.
bocal (bŏ-kăl), *F.*, **boc'ca**, *I.* Mouth-piece; mouth. **bocca ridente.** "Smiling mouth," believed to aid the production of pure tone. **con bocca chiusa** (kĭ-oo'-zä). With mouth closed, humming. **bocchino** (kē'-no), *I.* Mouthpiece.
bocina (bō-thē'-nä), *Sp.* A large trumpet.
Bockpfeife (bŏk'-pfī-fĕ), *G.* A bag-pipe.
Bockstriller (bŏks'-trĭl-lĕr), *G.* A goatish bleat.
Boden (bō'-dĕn), *G.* The back (of violins, etc.).
Boehm Flöte (bām flä'-tĕ). An improved flute inv. 1834 by Boehm, in which a series of keys simplify the fingering and intonation; the system is also fitted to oboes and clarinets. Vide the B. D.
Bogen (bō'-khĕn), *G.* 1. A bow. 2. A slur, as *Haltebogen*. **Bogenführung.** Bowing. **Bogenstrich.** A stroke of the bow. **Bogeninstrumente.** Stringed instruments. **Bogenflügel, -hammerklavier,** or **-klavier.** Piano-violin.
bois (bwä), *F.* Wood. **les** (lä) **bois.** The wood-wind.
boîte (bwät). Box; swell box. **ouvrez (fermez) la b.** Open (close) the swell.

bolero (bō-lä'-rō), *Sp.* A lively Spanish dance, in 3-4 time, with castanets. See chart of dance-rhythms.
bom'bard, *E.*, **bombarde** (bôn-bărd), *F.*, **bombar'do,** *I.* 1. A very long obsolete shawm, the original of the bassoon (q.v.). 2. A powerful reed-stop of 16-ft. tone.
bombar'don, *E.* (in *F.* bôn-băr-dôn; in *G.* bôm-băr-dōn'). 1. A large, valved bass trumpet. 2. The bass saxhorn. 3. A 16-ft. reed-stop.
bom'bix, *Gr.* Ancient Greek reed instrument.
Bom'bart, bom'mert, *G.* Bombard.
bom'bo, *I.* A figure in repeated tones.
bon (bôn), *F.* Good. **bon temps de la mesure,** *F.* The accented part of a measure.
bonang. A Javanese series of gongs.
bones. Castanets made of bone.
Bonn's bridge. A violin bridge inv. by Bonn of London with a foot under each string, aiming at more resonance for the interior strings.
boot. The foot of a reed-pipe.
bo'ra. A tin trumpet used by the Turkish.
bordone (bôr-do'-nĕ), *I.*, **Bordun** (bôr'-doon), *G.* 1. A covered 16-ft. or 32-ft. stop; the French have 4 and 8 foot bourdons. 2. The lowest string of 'cello and double bass; the free string of a hurdy-gurdy. 3. A great-bell. 4. A drone bass. **B. Flöte,** *G.* A stop. **bourdon de cornemuse** (-kôrn-müz), or **bourdon de musette,** *F.* The drone of a bagpipe.
bouché (boo-shä), *F.* 1. Stopped (of horn, etc., tones). 2. Covered (of pipes).
bouche fermée (boosh fĕr-mā), *F.* With closed mouth; humming.
bouffe (boof), *F.* A buffoon. **opera b.** Comic opera.
boulon. A Senegambian harp.
bour'don, *E.* (in *F.*, boor-dôn). Vide BORDONE.
bourrée (boor-rā), *F.* A lively old Spanish or French dance in 4-4 or 2-4 time. The second and fourth quarters of the measure divided. Used as an alla breve movt. in old suites. See chart of dance-rhythms.
boutade (boo-tăd), *F.* 1. An instrumental spectacular fantasia. 2. An old French dance. 3. A short ballet, impromptu.
bow. An elastic wooden rod with horsehairs (in recent cases, gut-thread) stretched from the bent head or *point*

DICTIONARY OF TERMS 563

to a movable *nut;* the hair being drawn over strings sets them in vibration. **bowhair.** Hair used in making the bows. **bowhand.** The right hand. **bowing.** 1. The art of using the bow. 2. The sign for bowing. The direction in which the bow is drawn is indicated by *down-bow* (marked ⌐) from nut to point; or *up-bow* (marked V or ∧) from point to nut. The back of the bow is sometimes used, and indicated by *sul* or *col legno,* "with the wood." The bow may be allowed to bounce on the strings (the *bounding* or *springing* bow), the *spiccato* (marked by dots over the notes) being played with a loose wrist near the middle of the bow; the *saltato* being with higher leaps. **bow instruments.** String instruments played with a bow. **bow guitar.** A violin shaped like a guitar; vide also PIANO-VIOLIN, and BOW-ZITHER.

boyau (bwä-yō), *F.* Gut-strings. **boyaudier** (bwä-yōd-yā). A maker of them.

bozzetto (bōd-zĕt'-tō), *I.* Sketch.

B-quadratum, B-quadrum, *L.* 1. Vide B. 2. B-natural.

brabançonne (brä-bäṅ-sŭn). The Belgian or Brabantine national hymn.

braccio (brät'-shō), *I.* "Arm." A term applied to instruments held up to the neck, as **viola da b.,** an armcello. Vide VIOLA.

brace. 1. A character used to connect staves. 2. Leather slides on drum-cords.

branches. Parts of a trumpet that conduct the air.

bran de inglaterra (brän dĕ ēn-glätĕr'-ra), *Sp.* An old Spanish dance; the English Brawl.

bran(s)le (bräṅ'-lŭ), *F.* A lively old dance, 4-4 time, led in turn by couples.

brass. General term for the instrs. made of brass (or **brass-wind).** **brass-band.** A military band of only brass instruments.

Bratsche (brät'-shĕ) (pl. -en), *G.* Viola.

Brautlied (browt'lēt), *G.* A wedding-song. **Brautmesse.** Music before the wedding.

Bravour (brä-foor'), *G.* Bravura. **Bravour-arie** or **-stück,** *G.* A florid song or piece.

bravura (brä-voo'rä), *I.,* **bravoure** (brä-voor), *F.* Dexterity, dash. **aria**

di b. A show-piece. **con b.** With brilliancy. **b. mezza.** Medium difficulty.

brawl(e). An old dance in a circle.

break. 1. The point at which one register ends and another begins. 2. Slips of various kinds in tone production. 3. In a stop, the abrupt return to an octave lower, due to insufficient pipes. 4. In compound-stops, a point where the relative pitch changes.

breakdown. An hilarious negro clog.

breit (brīt), *G.* Broad, slow.

Brettgeige (brĕt'-gī-gĕ), *G.* A pocket fiddle.

breve (*E.,* brēv—in *I.,* brā've). **breve** (brĕv), *F.* 1. Formerly the shortest note, now the longest, equal to two whole notes. 2. In o'd music—one-half the longa. **alla breve.** To the breve, i. e., a half note to each beat, formerly four minims to the measure, and in quick time; it is indicated by a common-time signature, with a vertical bar through it; also called **alla cappella,** or **tempo maggiore.**

bre'viary. A book of matins, lauds, and vespers.

Bre'vis, *L.* and *G.* A breve.

bridge. 1. A piece of wood on which strings rest; itself rests on the resonance box or board, to which it transmits vibrations.

brief. 1. A bass-viol bridge. 2. Breve.

brillant(e) (brē-yäṅ(t) in *F.,* in *I.* brĭllän'tĕ). Brilliant.

Brillenbässe (brĭl'-lĕn-bĕs-sĕ), *G.* "Spectacle basses," on account of its resemblance to a pair of spectacles; a name for the abbreviated form of a bass tremolo, two half-notes with thick connecting bar.

brindisi (brĭn'-dē-zē), *I.* A drinking-song.

brio (brē'ō), *I.* Vigour; fire. **con brio,** or **brio'so.** With spirit; vivacity.

brisé (brē-zā), *F.* Broken, as chords. **cadence b.** A trilling grace.

broach. An old instr. played with a crank.

broderies (brôd-rē), *F.* Ornaments.

broken. Vide (interrupted) CADENCE; of chords whose notes are not taken simultaneously, but in arpeggio; so **broken octaves.**

brok'king. Quavering.

B-rotundum, *L.* 1. Flat sign, ♭. 2. The note B flat.

Brummeisen (broom'mī-zĕn), *G.* Jew's harp.

brummen (broom′mĕn), *G.* To hum, drum. **Brummer.** Drone. **Brummton.** Drone. **Brummstimmen.** Humming voices.

bruscamen′te, *I.*, **brusquement** (brüskmäṅ), *F.* Brusquely.

Brust (broost), *G.* The breast or chest, hence **B.-ton** or **-stimme.** Chest voice. **Brust′werk.** The middle pipes of an organ.

buca (boo′-ka), *I.* Sound-hole.

buce′na, *L.*, **buccina** (boot-chĕ′-na), *I.* An ancient curved trumpet.

Büchse (bükh′-sĕ), *G.* Boot (q.v.).

Buch′stabentonschrift, *G.* Alphabetical notation.

bucol′ic, *E.*, **buccol′ica,** *I.*, **bucolique** (bü-kŏ-lēk), *F.* Pastoral.

buffa (boof′fä), or (-o), *I.* Comic; a comic singer. **buffo carica′to.** Comic character. **aria buffa.** Comic aria. **opera buffa.** Comic opera. **buffo′ne.** Comic singer. **buffonesco, -amente.** Burlesque(ly).

buffet. Organ case. **buffet organ.** A small organ.

bugle. 1. A hunting and military horn in 3 or more keys (B♭, C, E♭) having 7 harmonic tones. 2. The key-bugle with 6 keys (inv. in 1815 by Halliday, and named by him after the Duke of Kent) has a chromatic compass b-c‴. 3. Valve-bugle. Vide SAX-HORN.

bugle horn. A hunting-horn.

Bühnenweihfestspiel (bü′-nĕn-vī-fĕsht-shpēl), *G.* "Stage-consecrating-festival-piece." Wagner's name for his opera "*Parsifal.*"

Bund (boont), *G.* Fret. **bundfrei.** Fret free. Vide CLAVICHORD.

Bunge (boong′-ĕ), *G.* A kettle-drum.

bungen (boong′-ĕn), *G.* To drum.

buonaccordo (boo-ŏn-äk-kŏr′-dō), *I.* A child's spinet.

buono(-a) (boo-ō-nō(ä)), *I.* Good. **b. nota.** An accented note. **b. mano.** A skilful hand.

buras′ca, *I.* A comp. descriptive of a storm.

bur′den. 1. A regular refrain. 2. The bass. 3. The drone.

burla (boor′-la), *I.* A quip. **burlan′do, burles′co, burlescamen′te.** Facetious(ly). **burles′ca,** *I.*, **burlesque** (bür-lĕsk), *F.* A travesty. **burlet′ta,** *I.* A light farcical work.

burre (bür), *F.* A dance melody.

bur′then. Burden.

busain (bü-säṅ), *F.*, **Busaun** (boo-

zown′), *G.* A 16-ft. reed-stop on the pedal.

busna (boos′na), *I.* A species of trumpet.

bussone (boos-sō′-nĕ), *I.* Obs. instr. of bassoon type.

button. 1. The knob on a violin-base, etc. 2. An accordeon-key. 3. A leather-disk on the wire of a tracker.

bux′ea tibia, bux′us, *L.* Ancient 3-holed flute.

bys′synge songes. Early English lullabies.

C

(For German words not found here look under **K.**)

C (*G.*, **C** (tsä), *F.*, **ut**; *I.*, **do.**). 1. A musical pitch (mid-C or c′ has 256 vibrations, "philosophical pitch"; c″, 522, international pitch). c′ called **middle-c** from its position on the piano key-board, is the tonic or key-note of the normal major scale. 2. All the octaves of this pitch. 3. The major key having neither flats nor sharps; the minor key relative to E flat major. **C reversed,** an old sign indicating a decrease of one half of the note-values. 4. Vide TIME and NOTATION.

cabalet′ta, *I.* "A little horse." Hence a song (usually a rondo with variations) with an accompaniment in triplets suggesting hoof-beats.

cabinet d'orgue (käb-i-nä dŏrg), *F.* Organ-case.

cabinet organ. A small reed-organ.

cabinet pianoforte. An upright piano.

cabis′cola, *L.* Precentor.

caccia (kät′chä), *I.* A hunt. **alla c.** In hunting style.

cachée (kä-shä), *F.* Hidden (as fifths).

cachucha (kä-choo′-chä), *Sp.* A dance like the bolero.

cacofonia (kä-kō-fō-nē′-ä), *I.*, **cacophonie** (käk-ŏ-fō-nē), *F.*, **cacoph′ony,** *E.* Discord. **cacofon′ico,** *I.* Discordant.

ca′dence, *E.* (in *F.* kä-däṅs), **ca′-dens,** *L.*, **cadenza** (kä-dĕn-tsä), *I.*, **Kadenz** (kä-dĕnts′), *G.* 1. Literally "a fall," hence the subsidence of a melody or harmony to a point of rest; thence any concluding strain, rising or falling. Harmonic cadences are of the following sorts: (a) When the chord of the dominant is followed by the chord of the tonic, with the roots of both chords in the bass and the root of the second chord doubled in the highest voice, it is called a **perfect authentic cadence;** when the first chord has other than the root in the bass, or when the highest voice does not take the tonic in the last chord (takes the third for instance), this cadence is called an **imperfect authentic cadence.** Other names for the **authentic cadence** are, **whole, perfect, full** or **complete cadence; cadence parfaite** (pär-fĕt), *F.* **voll'kommene,** or **eigentliche** (ī'-khĕnt-lĭkh-ĕ) **Kadenz,** *G.* (b) When the cadence is formed by a subdominant chord followed with a tonic, the cadence is called **plagal** (popularly **church** or **amen cadence); cadence plagale** (plä-găl), *F.;* **Plagal'kadenz,** *G.* (c) When a sub-dominant chord is followed by a dominant and a tonic, it is called a **mixed** cadence. (d) When the mediant is prominent the c. is called a **medial** cadence. (e) When the tonic or some other chord is followed by the dominant the cadence is called a **half-cadence, semi-cadence, imperfect cadence, half-close;** c. **imparfaite** (ăn-pär-fĕt) or c. **sur la dominante** or c. **irrégulière** (ēr-räg-ül-yăr), *F.;* **unvollkommene** or **Mittel Kadenz,** *G.* (f) When the chord of the dominant apparently preparing a close, is followed by other than the tonic harmony the progression is called a **deceptive, avoided, broken, interrupted, irregular** or **surprise cadence; cadence évitée** (ā-vī-tä) or **interrompue** (ăn-tĕr-rôn-pü), or **rompue,** *F.;* **cadenza d'ingann'o,** c. **sfuggita** (sfood-jē'-tä) or **fin'ta,** *I.;* **Trug'kadenz** or **-schluss,** or **ab'gebrochene K.,** *G.* (g) When various modulations are introduced between the dominant and its tonic, the cadence is said to be **suspended;** or **sospesa** (sôs-pä'-zä), *I.* (h) When any dissonant harmony is followed by a consonance the French call this a **cadence pleine** (plĕn). (i) A cadence of any kind in which the chords have their roots in the bass is called a **radical** cadence. 2. When the cadence is highly ornate it is called **fioritu'ra** or **fiorita** (fē-ō-rē'-tä). So the word **cadenza** has in English and Italian, and the word **Kadenz** in German, a wide use for designating the florid passage preceding the actual cadence. This may

be vocal or instrumental, may go up as well as down, and may be written out by the composer or some other musician or left to the skill of the performer. This cadenza usually follows a sustained chord in the second inversion (a 6-4 chord) with a fermata or hold-mark over it (in *F. pointe d'orgue*). The Germans accordingly call this an **auf'gehaltene Kadenz,** the *F.* call it a **pointe d'orgue.** 3. The French use **cadence** of a brief trilling ornament as c. **brillante,** or c. **perlée;** c. **pleine** is a trill. 4. Cadence is used of rhythm and velocity also as the "cadence" of double-time in a military sense, is 180 steps to the minute.

ca'dent. An old ornament like a short anticipation.

c(a)esu'ra, *E., I.,* and *L.* **caesure** (sĕ-zür), *F.* 1. A minor rhythmic pause dividing a line or period; hence, 2. The last accented note preceding a **caesura.** c. **tedesca.** A 10-stringed zither.

caisse (kĕs), *F.* A drum. c. **plate** (plăt). A shallow side-drum. **grosse** (grôs) c. The bass drum. c. **roulante** (-roo-länt). The side-drum, of wood. **caisses claires** (kĕs-klăr). The drums.

cal'amus, c. **pastoralis,** or **tibialis,** *L.* A reed used by shepherds.

calan'do, *I.* Diminishing and retarding.

calandro'ne, *I.* A small clarinet.

calascione (kä-lä-shi-ō'-nĕ), *I.* A 2-stringed guitar of lower Italy.

calata (kä-lä'-tä), *I.* A lively dance in 2-4 time.

calcando (kal-kän'-do), *I.* Hurrying.

Calcant (käl'-känt), *G.* Bellows-treader.

Calli'ope. 1. The Greek muse of heroic verse. 2. An instr. played by an engine that fills its metal pipes with steam instead of air.

callithump'ian. Vide SHIVAREE.

calma (käl-mä), *I.* Calm. **calma'to.** With calm.

calore (kä-lō'-rĕ), *I.* Warmth. **Caloro'so.** Animated.

cambiare (käm-bĭ-ä'rĕ), *I.* To change. **nota cambia'ta.** Changing note.

cam'era, *I.* Chamber, used in distinction from a large auditorium, as *musica di c., sonata di c., alla c.*

camminan'do, *I.* Andante.

campana (käm-pä'-nä), *I.* A bell. **campanel'la (or o),** *I.* A little bell.

campanile (nē'-lĕ), *I.* A belfrey.
campanol'ogy. The art of ringing or making bells. campano'ne, *I.* A great bell. campana'rum concer'tus, or modula'tio, *L.* Chimes. campanarum pulsa'tor, *L.* A ringer of bells.

canarder (kă-năr-dā), *F.* To imitate a duck; to *couac.*

canarie (kă-nă-rē), *F.*, cana'ry, cana'ries, *E.*, canario (kä-nä'-rĭ-ō), *I.* A lively old dance in 3-8, 6-8 or 12-8 time. Named from the Canary Islands.

cancan (käṅ-käṅ). A boisterous French dance.

cancel. The natural sign, ♮. cancellatum, *L.* Vide B.

Cancellen (kän'-tsel-lĕn), *G.* Grooves in an organ.

can'crizans, cancrica'nus, *L.*, cancrizzante (kän'-krĭd-zän'-tĕ), *I.* Retrograde. Vide CANON.

canere (ka'-nĕ-rĕ), *L.* To sing; to play.

cangiare (kän-jä'-rĕ), *I.* To change; to alter.

can'na, *I.* A reed, or pipe. c. d'anima. Flue-pipe. c. a lingua. Reedpipe.

cannon-drum. East Indian tomtom.

can'on (in *F.*, kă-nôṅ), canone (känō'-nĕ), *I.*, *G.* Canon or Kanon (kä'-nōn). The most rigid form of imitation, a subject (antecedent) being followed accurately by an answer (consequent); once the playground of musical ingenuity, all forms of complication being indulged in. A canon written out completely was full or aper'to. Often only the antecedent (or canon) was written out, the consequent (now called fuga or consequenza) being left to the performer's skill; this was called close or chiuso (kĭ-oo'-zo). If the entrances of the other parts were indicated by cabalistic signs, it was a riddle-canon (Räthsel-Kanon), or enigmatical or enigmatico. Canons were named by the interval between answer and antecedent and by the general treatment as in Imitation (q.v.).

,canonic hours. Vide HORÆ.

cano'nici, *L.* The Pythagoreans, who developed musical science from the abstract mathematics of intervals; opposed to Aristoxenos and the harmonici, who developed it from the actual practice of music.

cantabile (kän-tä'-bĭ-lĕ), *I.* Lyrical.

cantajuolo (kän-tä-yoo-ō'-lō), cantamban'co, *I.* A street singer. cantamen'to, *I.* Air; cantilena.

cantan'do (kän-tän'-dō), *I.* In a melodious, singing style.

can'tans, *L.* Singing.

cantan'te, *I.* A singer; also a vocal part. c. ariose. A form of melody transitional between air and recitative.

cantare (tä'-rĕ), *I.* To sing. c. di maniera (män-yä'-rä) or maniera'ta. To sing with mannerism. c. a orecchio (o-rĕk'-kĭ-ō). To sing by ear. c. a aria. To sing with improvised cadenzas.

cantarina (rē'-nä), *Sp.* A womansinger.

cantata (kän-tä'-tä), *I.*, cantate (käṅtät), *F.*, Cantate (kän-tä'-tĕ), *G.* 1. Originally, something sung, in distinction to something played (*sonata*). 2. Now a work for chorus and solo, often with orchestral accompaniment; a short oratorio of a narrative style; a short opera not meant for the theatre. c. amoro'sa, *I.* A cantata having love for its subject. c. mora'le or spiritua'le. A *sacred* cantata designed for the church. cantatil'la, cantatille (tē'-yŭ), cantati'na. A short cantata; an air preceded by a recitative.

canta'tor, *L.* A singer; a chanter.

cantato're, *I.* A male singer. cantatrice (trē-chĕ). A female singer. c. buffa. A woman who sings in comic opera.

cantato'rium, *L.* The Roman Catholic book containing the music of the Antiphonary and Gradual.

Canterei (kän'-tĕ-rī), *G.* 1. The dwelling-house of the cantor. 2. A class of choristers.

canterellare (kän-tĕ-rĕl-lä'-rĕ), *I.* To sing softly. canterellan'do. Singing softly.

canti carnascialeschi (cär-nä-shä-lĕs'-kĕ), canti carnevali (kär-nĕ-vä'-lĕ), *I.* Songs of the carnival week.

can'ticles, *E.*, can'tico, *I.*, cantiquc (käṅ-tēk), *F.*, can'ticum, *L.* 1. Biblical lyrics, the Song of Songs (canticum canticorum). 2. A sacred chant with scriptural text. 3. The cantica majora include the Magnificat, Benedictus and Nunc dimittis. The cantica minora are seven texts from the Old Testament.

can'tillate, *E.* To recite with occasional musical tones; hence, **cantillation.**

cantilena (kän-tĭ-lā′-nä), *I.* The melody; air.

cantilla′tio, *L.* A singing style of declamation.

cantino (tē′-nō), *I.* The smallest string on a violin.

can′to, *I.* 1. A song; a melody; the voice. **col canto.** "With" (i. e., adopting the time and expression of) the voice or melody. 2. The art of singing, as **il bel canto,** the old art of allegedly perfect production. 3. The highest part in concert music. 4. The soprano voice. 5. The highest string of an instrument. **c. a cappella.** Vocal music without accompaniment. **c. ambrosiano.** Ambrosian chant (Vide CANTUS). **c. armonico.** A part song. **c. clef.** The C clef on the first line. **c. concertante** (kón-chĕr-tän′-tĕ). The treble of the principal concerting parts. **c. cromat′ico.** Chromatic melody. **c. fermo.** 1. A chant or melody. 2. Choral unison. 3. Cantus firmus. **c. figurato.** A figured melody instead of figured bass (q.v.). **c. fiorito.** A much ornamented air. **c. fune′bre.** Funeral song. **c. grego′riano.** The Gregorian chant. **c. plana.** Plain chant. **c. necessa′rio.** A principal part. **c. primo.** The first treble or soprano. **c. recitativo.** Recitative. **c. ripie′no.** Vide RIPIENO. **c. rivolta′to.** The treble inverted. **c. secondo.** The second treble. **c. semplice.** A simple song.

cantolla′no, *Sp.* Precentor.

cantor, *L.* Singer. **c. choralis.** Precentor. **cantori** are the singers that sit near the cantor, on the left side; opposite to **decani,** those on the dean's side.

can′tus, *L.* 1. A song; a melody. 2. The treble or soprano part. **c. Ambrosia′nus.** The four chants introduced by St. Ambrose, in the fourth century, supposed to be derived from Greek melodies. **c. figura′lis** (or **figuratus**). Mensurable music; melody with figurate embellishment. **c. fir′mus.** (a) The melody originally given to the tenors, later to the sopranos; (b) plain song; (c) a theme or air chosen for counterpoint; this air remains the same, i.e., "firm," as the different voices take it, while the accompanying voices always change;

in distinction to the **c. f.** they are called the *counterpoint* (q.v.). **c. coronatus.** A *c. fractus* when accompanied by a fa-burden. **c. durus.** A song modulating into a key with one or more sharps, almost the same as "major key." **c. ecclesiasticus.** Church-music, particularly plain song; also the singing of the liturgy. **c. fractus.** Broken melody. **c. Gregorianus.** A melody introduced by St. Gregory. **c. planus.** Plain song. **c. mensurabilis.** Regular, or measured, melody. Vide MENSURABLE MUSIC. **c. mollis.** Song in the minor.

ca′nun, *Tur.* A Turkish zither.

canzona, canzone (kän-tsō′-nĕ), *I.* 1. A folk-song. 2. A part-song. 3. An instrumental work, in two or three parts, with passages in imitation, somewhat like the madrigal. **canzonaccia** (nät′-chä). A low song. **canzoncina** (chē′-nä). A short canzone, or song. **c. sacra.** A sacred song, **canzonet, canzonnet′ta, canzonina.** A short canzone. **canzoniere** (tsōn-ya′-rĕ). A song-book.

caoine, caoineadh (kŭ-ēn′-ē-ŭ), *Irish.* A funeral song.

capis′col. A precentor.

capis′trum. A face bandage worn by ancient trumpeters.

capo (kä′-pō), *I.* The head or beginning. **da capo** (return and play again), from the beginning. **capo d'opera, capo-lavoro.** Master-piece, chief work. **c. violino.** The first violin. **capo-dastro, c. di tasto.** Vide CAPOTASTO. **c. d'instrumenti.** Leader. **c. d'orchestra.** The conductor.

capodastre (kăp-ô-dăstr), *F.* Capotasto.

capo′na. A Spanish dance.

capotasto (kä-pō-täs′-to), *I.* 1. The nut of a fingerboard. 2. A strip fastened across a fretted fingerboard and serving as a movable nut to raise the pitch of all the strings at once.

cappel′la, *I.* 1. A chapel, or church. 2. A band of musicians. **A c. or alla c.** (a) Without instrumental accompaniment. (b) Alla breve. **da c.** In solemn church style.

cappello chinese (kē-nä′-zĕ), *I.* Vide CHAPEAU.

caprice, *E.* and *F.,* **capriccio** (kä-prēt′-chō), *I.* A whimsical work of irregular form. **capriccietto** (chĕt′-tō),

I. A short caprice, **capricciosamen'-te**, **capriccio'so**, *I.*, **capricieuse-ment** (kă-prēs-yŭz'-män), **capricieux** (kă-prēs-yŭ), *F.* Capricious(ly).

captan'dum, ad, *L.* Takingly, brilliantly.

caput scho'lae, *L.* Precentor.

caractères de musique (kăr-ăk-tăr dŭ mü-zēk), *F.* Musical symbols.

caramillo (kä-rä-mēl'yō), *Sp.* A flageolet.

carattere (kä-rät'-tä-rĕ), *I.* Character, dignity.

caressant (kă-rĕs-säṅ'), *F.*, **carezzando** (kä-rĕd-zän'-dō), **carezzevole** (zä'-vō-lĕ), *I.* Caressing; tender.

carica'to (kä'-tō), *I.* Exaggerated.

carillon (kä-rē-yôṅ), *F.* 1. A set of fixed bells on which tunes may be played by hand or mechanism. 2. A composition suggesting or using bells. 3. The simultaneous clashing of many large bells. 4. A bell-like stop. **c. à clavier,** *F.* A set of keys and pedals, acting on bells. **carillonner** (kä-rē-yô-nā'), *F.* To ring bells. **carillonneur** (nŭr), *F.* A bell-ringer.

carità (kä-rē-tä'), *I.* Tenderness.

Carmagnole (kăr-mĭn-yôl), *F.* A famous French revolutionary song. It derived its name from the town Carmagnola.

carmen, *L.* A song. **c. natalitium.** A carol of the Nativity.

carol. 1. A song of joy and devotion. 2. Ballads for Christmas and Easter. 3. An old circling dance.

caro'la, *I.* A circling dance, resembling the Carmagnole. **carolet'ta.** A little dance.

carrée (kăr-rā), *F.* A breve.

carrure des phrases (kăr-rür-dä fräz), *F.* The balance of the phrases.

cart'el, *E.*, **cartelle** (kăr-tĕl), *F.* 1. The first draft of a score. 2. A sheet of hide or varnished cloth on which music could be sketched and erased.

cartellone (lō'-nĕ), *I.* A catalogue of operas to be performed.

cas'sa, *I.* The drum. **c. grande, c. militare.** The great drum. **c. armonica.** The body (as of a 'cello).

cassa'tio, *L.*, **cassazione** (käs-sä'-tsĭ-ō'-nĕ), *I.* 1. The final number. 2. A serenade consisting of instrumental pieces.

castagnetta (käs-tän-yĕt'tä), *I.*, **castagnettes** (kăs-tĭn-yĕt), *F.*, **castagnole** (käs-tän-yō'-lĕ), **castañetas** (kăs-tän-yä'tăs), **castanuelas** (kăs-tän-voo-ä'-lăs). *Sp.*, **castanheta**

(käs-tänyä'-tä), *Port.*, **castanets,** *E.* Small, concave shells of ivory or hard wood, carried in the hand and rhythmically snapped by dancers in Spain and other countries.

castrato (käs-trä'-tŏ), *I.* An artificial male soprano or alto; a eunuch.

catch. A round in which the singers catch up their lines at the cue; usually with humorous and ambiguous effect.

catena di trilli (kä-tä'-nä), *I.* A chain of trills.

catgut. A small string for violins, made of the intestines of sheep and lambs, rarely of cats.

catling. A lute-string of smallest size.

cattivo (kät-te'-vō), *I.* "Bad." **c. tempo.** The weak beat.

catzoze'rath. Hebrew trumpet.

cauda, *L.* The tail of a note.

cavallet'to, *I.* 1. A cabaletta. 2. A small bridge. 3. The break in the registers.

cavata (kä-vä'-tä), *I.* 1. Tone-production. 2. A recitative; a cavatina.

cavatina (kä-vä-tē'nä), *I.*, **cavatine** (kăv-ă-tēn), *F.* A melody of one strain only.

c-barré (üt-băr-rä), *F.* Vide BARRED C.

c-clef. The tenor clef; wherever it stands it indicates middle C.

C-dur (tsä-door), *G.* The key of C major.

cebell'. A theme in common time with variations and alternation of high and low notes. A sort of English gavotte.

cecilium (sŭ-sē'-lĭ-ŭṅ), *F.* A key-board reed instr. the size and shape of a 'cello, the left hand playing keys, the right working bellows.

cedez (sā-dā), *F.* Decrease!

celamustel (sä-lä-mü-stĕl), *F.* A harmonium with unusual imitative stops.

celere (chä'-lä-rĕ), *I.* Rapid. **celerità** (rĭ-tä'). Rapidity.

céleste (sā-lĕst), *F.* Celestial, applied to stops of soft, sweet tone, and to a piano pedal of the same effect.

celestina (chä-lĕs-tē'nä), *I.* 1. A 4-ft. stop. 2. A tremolo stop in reed organs.

cell. Vide ELLIS (B. D.).

'cello (chĕl'lō). Abbr. and common name of *violoncello.* **cello'ne.** A 'cello inv. by Stelzner gaining increased sonority by its method of stringing.

cembalo (chäm'bä-lō), **cembolo** (chäm'-

ḃō-lō), *I.*, cembal (sän-băl), *F.* 1.
A harpsichord. 2. A cymbal.
cembalista, *I.* A player on either.
cembal d'amour, *F.* A very large
harpsichord. tutto il c., *I.* Loud
pedal. c. onnicordo, *I.* Proteus.
cembalist, *E.* A player on the
harpsichord.
cembanel'la, cennamel'la, *I.* A
flute.
cent, *E.* The hundredth part of an
equal semitone. Vide ELLIS (B. D.).
cento (chān'-tō), cento'ne, *I.*, centon
(sän-tôn), *F.* 1. The Gregorian antiphonary. 2. A patchwork or medley.
cercare (chār-kä'-rĕ), *I.* To search.
c. la nota. A common effect in singing where a note taken by skip is
lightly anticipated with a short grace.
cer'valet, cervelat. An obsolete clarinet.
Ces (tsĕs), *G.* The note C flat. Ceses.
C double flat.
cesura, cesure. Vide CÆSURA.
cetera (chā'-tĕ-rä), *I.* A cittern.
c. f. Abbr. of *Cantus firmus.*
cha chi (chä-chē), *Chinese.* A chromatic kin.
chacona (chä-kō'-nä), *Sp.*, chaconne
(shă-kŭn), *F.*, ciaccona (chäk-kō'-
nä), *I.* A slow dance probably Spanish in origin; in 3-4 time with a
groundbass; almost always in major,
in contrast with the *passacaglia;* and
generally in form of variations.
chair organ. Vide CHOIR ORGAN.
chalameau, *E.*, chalumeau (shăl-ŭ-mō),
F., Chalämau, Chalämaus (shäl'-ä-
mows), *G.* 1. An ancient pipe blown
through a calamus, or reed. 2. The
low register of the clarinet; as a
direction it means "an octave lower,"
being cancelled by *clar.* or *clarinet.*
3. The chanter of a bag-pipe.
chalil (kä-lel), *Heb.* Hebrew pipe or
flute.
chalotte (shă-lôt'). A tube to receive
a reed.
chamber music. Music composed for
a small auditorium, as a string quartet or a pianoforte trio.
chamber-organ. A cabinet organ.
chang. A Persian harp.
change. 1. A tune rung on a chime.
2. Vide MODULATION. 3. Mutation.
4. (a) changing-note. A note foreign to the immediate harmony and
entering (unlike the passing-note) on
a strong beat; when two or more appear simultaneously they make a

changing-chord. (b) In old counterpoint, a passing discord entering unaccented and then skipping.
changeable. Used of chants that may
be sung either in the major or minor
mode.
changer de jeu (shän-zhā dŭ zhŭ), *F.*
To change the stops.
chanson (shän-sôn), *F.* A song; a
ballad. c. bachique (bă-shēk). A
drinking-song. c. des rues (dā-rü).
A street-song; a vaudeville. chan-
sonnette (nĕt). A little or short
song. chansonnier (sŭn-yā). A
song-writer; a book of songs.
chant. 1. Originally a song, and still
so meant in the French word (vide
below), since the Gregorian time used
of vocal music marked by the recitation of many syllables on one tone,
and employed for prose texts such as
the Canticles and Psalms. There
are two sorts of chant, the Gregorian
and the Anglican. (a) The Gregorian is a short tune to be repeated in
successive sections of prose; it has 8
tones and is in four parts; the *intonation* (or *inchoatio*) or opening
notes; the *first reciting note* (or *dominant*); the *mediation;* the *second
reciting note* (or *dominant*); the *termination* (ending or cadence). (b)
The Anglican omits the *intonation*
and differs in the rhythm and mode
but has the same monotone recitation
with modulations in the middle (mediation) and end (termination). The
Anglican has two parts of 3 and 4
measures, 7 in all; this is the *single
chant,* there are also *double, triple,*
and *quadruple* forms of proportionate
length. In chanting, the fitting of
the unequal phrases to the music is
called *pointing,* and consists of reciting them strictly within the duration
of the notes except those of the 1st
and 4th measures which are enlarged
to fit the words. Words to be sung
to the cadence are cut off from those
to be sung to the reciting-note, by a
vertical line called the *cadence-mark.*
2. Any recitation of chant-like
character. 3. A tone. 4. A *cantus
firmus.* 5. Vide PLAIN-CHANT. 6.
Vide CHANGEABLE. 7. **Free-chant.**
A form in which the hemistichs consist of only 2 measures. 8. Roman
Chant-Gregorian. 9. **Phrygian
chant.** One intended to provoke
wrath.
chant (shän), *F.* Song; tune; vocal

part. **c. amoureux.** Love song.
c. d'église, or **grégorien.** Gregorian
chant. **c. égal, c. en ison.** Chant
on one tone, or with one interval of
two tones. **c. figuré.** Figured counterpoint. **c. funèbre.** Funeral song.
c. royal. A sacred song; or a prayer
for the monarch; the mode in which
such prayer was sung. **c. sur le
livre,** i. e., "on the book," vocal
counterpoint extemporized on a
printed *cantus firmus.*
chanter, *E.* 1. One who chants.
arch-c. The leader of the chants.
2. The tenor or melodic pipe of a
bag-pipe.
chanter (shän-tā), *F.* To sing. **c.
à livre ouvert** (ä lēv-roovĕr). To
sing at sight. **chantant(e).** Lyric.
basse c. Vide BASS. **café c.** (kä-
fā-chän-täń). A music hall. **chan-
té(e)** (shän-tā). Sung. **chanteur
(euse).** A male (female) singer.
chantonner. Canterellare.
chanterelle (shänt-ŭ-rĕl), *F.* The highest and smallest string of an instrument.
chanterie (shän-trē). *F.* **chantry,** *E.*
A chapel endowed for daily mass.
chanterres (shän-tĕr), *F.* 10th century ballad-singers.
chan'tor, *E.* A singer in a cathedral
choir.
chantre (shäńtr), *F.* Choir-leader.
grand c. Precentor. **second c.** A
chorister.
chapeau (shă-pō), *F.* A "hat"; a tie.
c. chinois (shēn-wä). A set of small
bells arranged on a frame like a Chinese hat. Cf. CRESCENT.
chapel. Musicians in the retinue of a
great personage.
chapelle (shă-pĕl), *F.* Cappella.
characteristic. Strongly individual in
character, or mood, used of a composition (as **Charakterstück,** *G.*).
c. note or **tone.** The leading-tone or
any tone peculiar to a key. **c. chord.**
The principal chord. **Charakter-
stimme,** *G.* A solo-stop.
charivari (shă-rĭ-vä'-rĭ), *F.* Vide SHI-
VAREE.
chasse (shăs), *F.* The hunt. **à la c.**
In hunting style.
chatsoteroth. A Hebrew trumpet.
che (kā), *I.* Than, that, which.
che chi (kā-kē). One of the eight
species of Chinese music.
chef (shĕf), *F.* Leader, chief. **chef-
d'attaque** (dăt-tăk). 1. The leader,
or first violin. 2. Leader of a chorus.

chef-d'oeuvre (shä-dŭvr). Masterpiece. **chef-d'orchestre** (shĕf-dôr-
kĕstr). The leader. **ch. du chant.**
Leader of an opera chorus.
cheipour. A Persian trumpet.
chel'idonizing. Singing a spring or
"swallow song."
chel'ys. 1. Vide LYRE. 2. Old name
for viol.
cheng (chĕng). A Chinese mouth-
organ, a gourd with many free reeds;
it suggested the invention of the harmonium.
cheng chi (chĕng-chē). One of the
eight species of Chinese music.
cherub'ical hymn. The Trisagion.
chest of viols. A group or set of viols,
two basses, two tenors, and two
trebles.
chest tone, chest voice. The lowest
register of the voice.
chevalet (shĕv-ä-lā), *F.* Bridge.
cheville (shĕ-vē'-yĕ), *F.* Peg.
chevroter (shĕv-rŏ-tā), *F.* To bleat
like a goat, hence, **chevrotement**
(shĕ-vrŏt-mŏń). A tremor or shake
in singing.
chiarenta'na, *I.* An Italian country
dance.
chiarina (kē-ä-rē'-nä), *I.* A clarion.
chiaro (kē-ä'-rō), *I.* Clear, pure. **chia-
ramen'te.** Brightly, purely. **chia-
rezza** (rĕd'-zä). Clearness. **di c.**
Clearly.
chiave (kē-ä'-vĕ), *I.* 1. A clef. 2.
Key. 3. Tuning-key. 4. A failure.
5. **c. maestro.** The fundamental
key or note.
chiavette (vĕt'-tĕ), *I. pl.* Transposing
clefs of the 16th century; of which
the high **c.** indicated that its line was
to be read a third higher, the low **c.,**
a third lower. Thus the C clef might
indicate e or eb; or a, or ab.
chickera (kē'-kĕ-rä) or **chikarah.** A
Hindu bow instrument.
chiesa (kē-ä'-zä), *I.* A church. **da c.**
For the church, or in sacred style, as
sonata or *concerto da chiesa.*
chiffre (shĭfr), *F.* A figure in thorough
bass. **basse chiffrée** (shĭf-frā). Figured bass.
chifonie (shē-fō-nē'), *F.* Old name for
hurdy-gurdy.
chime. A set of bells tuned to a scale.
chime-barrel. Portion of the mechanism for ringing a chime.
chimney. A tube in the cap of a
stopped pipe.
Chinese flute. Bamboo flute.
Chinese hat. Vide CHAPEAU.

Chinese scale. Five notes without semitones; the music is written on five perpendicular lines, the pitch is indicated by distinctive names.

chinnor, chinor. Vide KINNOR.

chirimia (chē-rē-mē'ä), *Sp.* The oboe; clarion.

chirogym'nast. A mechanical contrivance for exercising the fingers.

chi-roplast (ki'rō). A device of gloves and bars, inv. 1814 by Logier, to keep the hands and fingers of piano-players in the right position.

chitarra (kē-tär'-rä), *I.* 1. A guitar, a cithara. **c. coll' arco.** A violin with guitar-shaped body. **chitarris'ta.** One who plays on the guitar. **chittarrina** (rē'-nä). Small Neapolitan guitar. **chitarro'ne.** A double guitar.

chiterna (kē-tĕr'-nä), *I.* Quinterna.

chiuso (kē-oo'-zō), *I.* Closed. Vide CANON and BOCCA. **chiuden'do.** Closing.

Chladni's figures. Vide NODAL FIGURES.

choeur (kŭr), *F.* Choir, chorus. **à grand c.** For full chorus.

choice note. An alternative note.

choir. 1. A body of singers usually in a church. 2. Their place in the church. 3. A subdivision of a chorus or orchestra. **c. organ.** Vide ORGAN. **grand c.** The combination of all the reed-stops.

Chor (kôr), *G.* Same as Choir 1, 2, 3; also on the piano, or organ, a unison, i. e., all the strings or pipes belonging to one digital or pipe; hence a piano with 3 strings to each tone is **drei-chörig.**

chora'gus, chore'gus (kō). The donor of a choral or dramatic work. At Oxford the director of Church music.

cho'ral. Pertaining to a choir or chorus. **choral service.** A service in which the entire liturgy is intoned or chanted.

cho'rale, Choral (kō-räl'), *G.* 1. Choral psalm or hymn. 2. Early German-Protestant hymn.

chora'leon. Vide ÆOLOMELODICON.

choraliter (kō-räl'-ĭ-tĕr), **choralmässig** (mĕs-sikh), *G.* In choral style.

Choramt (kôr'-ämt), *G.* Choral service.

choraul'es. A Greek flutist.

chord. 1. A string. 2. Vide VOCAL C. 3. A combination of three or more tones, whether pleasant or discordant.

The chords which are the building-material of all our music are made up of thirds laid brick-wise one upon another. A single third is not counted a chord, two thirds (for instance the two intervals, g-b-d) make up a **triad;** another third (d to f) makes a chord, called a **seventh** (g-b-d-f) because the interval (q.v.) from g to f is a seventh; adding another third gives a **chord of the ninth** or a **ninth chord** (g-b-d-f-a), two other additions give the **chords of the eleventh** and **thirteenth** (g-b-d-f-a-c-e) (these last are usually cacophonous, and their existence as special chords is denied by some theorists). To add another third brings us back, on the tempered scale, to g, from which the chord grew and which is known as the **fundamental** or **root** of the chord. Chords are distinguished in mode, as **major** or **minor,** from the majority or minority of their intervals, a **minor** triad differing from a **major** in having a minor third, the fifth being **perfect** in both cases. When the chord has been constructed as above (g-b-d-f) it is said to be in the **first** or **root** or **fundamental** or **perfect position;** it may re-appear with any of its notes as the lowest (though g always remains the **root**). When the 3d (b) is in the bass, it is said to be in the 2d position; when the fifth (d), it is in its 3d position. With any of its notes other than the root in the bass the chord is said to be **inverted.** The names of these **inversions** have been cumbrously taken from the intervals between the lowest note and the others, no interval being stated in terms of over an octave, the greatest interval being named first, and some of the intervals being unmentioned, especially those of doubled notes: thus the intervals in that inversion of a seventh chord in which the seventh is in the bass might be, counting upward, 11 (-4), 16 (-2), 20 (-6), but it would be called, for short, a 4-2 chord, or chord of the second and fourth.

A line or dash through any Arabic numeral as ♯ means that the note it represents is sharpened; it may be also preceded by a natural or flat. A sharp or flat standing over a bass r te means that the *third* of the c rd is to be sharpened or flattened;

In the following table the names of all the inversions are given. In thorough-bass these inversions are indicated by Arabic numerals above the bass notes.

A triad in the root or fundamental position is marked—3 or $\frac{5}{3}$ or $\frac{8}{5}$.

A triad in the 1st inversion is called **a chord of the 6th** and marked $\frac{3}{6}$.

A triad in the 2d inversion is called **a chord of the 4th and 6th** or a **six-four** chord and marked $\frac{6}{4}$.

A 7th chord in the root or fundamental position is marked 7 or $\frac{7}{5}$.

A 7th chord in the 1st inversion is called **a chord of the 5th and 6th** or a **six-five** chord, and marked $\frac{6}{5}$ or $\frac{6}{5}$. [with a 3 above]

A 7th chord in the 2d inversion is called **a chord of the 3d, 4th and 6th,** or a **four-three** chord and marked $\frac{3}{4}$ or $\frac{6}{4}$.

A 7th chord in the 3d inversion is called **a chord of the 2d and 4th** or a **four-two** chord and marked 2 or $\frac{4}{2}$ [6 above]. [marked 2 or $\frac{4}{6}$]

A 9th chord in the root or fundamental position is marked 9 or $\frac{9}{7}$ $\frac{9}{5}$ [with 2 / 3 / 3] according as the 5th or 7th is omitted.

a dash or horizontal line following a numeral continues its tone in the next chord.

The character (but not the inversion) of chords may be indicated by Roman numerals indicating the degree of the scale on which they are founded, the scale being noted by a large letter for major (as C), and a small for minor (as c). Thus IV means a triad on the fourth degree with a major third and perfect fifth; iv. a triad on the fourth degree with minor 3d and perfect fifth. An accent after the numeral indicates an augmented fifth, as IV'; a small cipher indicates a diminished fifth, as VII°; a small 7 indicates a chord of the seventh. These devices are an heirloom from an age of little modulation and formal counterpoint; they were shorthand then, but to our music they are handcuffs. They have only a dry text-book career, and alert theorists are rapidly denying them the right even to this existence. Other kinds of chords are characteristic, the leading chord; chromatic, containing a chromatic tone; common, a triad; accidental, produced by anticipation or suspension; altered, having some tone chromatically changed with modulatory .fect (one of the bugaboos of the the(sts),

vide ALTERED; anomalous, vide ANOMALY; augmented, having an augmented fifth; broken, vide BROKEN; derivative, formed by inversion; diatonic, a triad; diminished, having an imperfect 5th and diminished 7th; dominant, the triad or 7th chord on the dominant; doubtful, equivocal, resolvable in many ways, as the diminished 7th; imperfect, having an imperfect fifth, or having some tone omitted; leading, the dominant chord; related or relative, containing a tone in common; solid, opposed to broken; threefold, a triad; transient, modulatory. (See article, *Altered Chords*, page 720.)

chord'a, *L.* A string; a note. c. characteristica. The leading note, c. dominant septima. The dominant chord of the seventh; nc'na, the ninth. chordæ essentia'les. The tonic, third and fifth. chordæ voca'les. Vocal chords.

chordaulo'dian, chordomelo'd:on. A large automatic barrel organ, inv. by Kaufmann, 1812.

Chordienst (kôr'-dēnst), *G.* Choral service. Chordirektor. A director who trains a chorus at the opera house.

chordom'eter. A gauge for measuring strings.

Chöre (kär'ĕ), *G. plural.* Choirs, cho ruses.

Chorist', *G.*, choriste (kô-rēst), *F.*, chorister, *E.* 1. A leader of a choir. 2. A choral singer. Chorsänger, C.-schüler, C.-knabe (kôr'-knä-bĕ), *G.* Choir-boy.

Chorstimme (kôr-shtĭm-mĕ), *G.* Chorus part.

Chorton (kôr-tōn), *G.* "Choir-pitch." 1. The pitch at which choruses formerly sang in Germany. 2. Choral tune.

chorus. 1. A company of singers; especially in opera, etc., the supporting body of vocalists who do not sing solos. 2. A composition for a chorus, usually in 4 parts—a "double chorus" requires 8 parts. 3. A refrain. 4. The compound stops. 5. The bagpipe, or drone-pipe. 7. Marine trumpet. 8. The free-staves of the crwth. chorusmaster. The chief singer in a chorus.

choutarah. Vide TAMBOURA.

Chris'te eleison (ā-lā'ē-sōn), *Gr.* "Christ have mercy"; part of the Kyrie.

Christmesse, Christmette (krēst'-mĕt-tĕ), *G.* Christmas matins.

chro'ma, *Gr.* 1. A chromatic modification of the Greek tetrachord. 2. A sharp or a flat. c. duplex. A double sharp. 3. c. diesis. A semitone. 4. (Or c. simplex.) An eighth note. c. duplex. A 16th note.

chromam'eter. A tuning-fork.

chromat'ic, chromatique (tēk), *F.*, chromatisch (mä'-tĭsh), *G.*, cromat'ico, *I.* 1. Literally, "coloured" and implying a foreign or added tinge, specifically that given to the sober diatonic notes natural to a key, by an unrelated sharp, flat or natural that is not of modulatory effect. A whole scale may be chromatic (i. e., progress by semitones); a chord, an interval or a progression altered by a flat or sharp is called chromatic, and the process of so modifying it is called c. alteration; an instr. playing semitones is called c., and the signs themselves that sharpen or flatten a tone are called c. signs, or chromatics. 2. Vide MODES.

chronom'eter. Metronome, particularly Godfrey Weber's.

chronomètre (krŏn-ô-mĕtr), *F.* A form of monochord inv. 1827, by Raller, to teach piano-tuning.

chrotta (krot'ta). Vide CROWD.

church cadence. The plagal cadence.

church modes. Vide MODES.

chute (shüt), *F.* An obsolete sliding embellishment.

ciaconne. Vide CHACONNE.

ciaramella (chä-rä-mĕl'-lä), *I.* A bag-pipe.

cicogna (chē-cōn-yä), *I.* Mouthpiece.

cicu'ta, *L.* A Pan's pipe.

cicutrenna (chē-koo-trĕn'-na), *I.* A pipe.

cifrato (chē-frä'-to), *I.* Figured.

cimbalo (chēm'-bä-lŏ), *I.* 1. Cymbal. 2. Tambourine. 3. Harpsichord or dulcimer.

cimbalon. Vide CZIMBALON.

Cimbel (tsĭm'-bĕl), *G.* A high mixture stop. Cimbelstern. A group of star-shaped cymbals attached to old organs.

cinelli (chē-nĕl'-lē), *I.*, Cinellen (tsē-nĕl'-lĕn), *G.* Cymbals.

Cink (tsĭnk), *G.* 1. A small reed-stop. 2. Vide ZINK.

cinq (sănk), *F.*, cinque (chēn'kwĕ), *I.* Five; the fifth voice or part in a quintet. a c.—in 5 parts. cinque-pace (sănk-păs). Old French dance in quintuple time.

cin'yra. Old name for harp.

ciphering. The sounding of organ pipes, when the keys are not touched, due to leakage. cipher system. An old notation using numerals instead of letters.

circle of fifths. A method of modulation by dominants. Vide TEMPERAMENT and preliminary essay, INTRODUCTION TO MUSIC.

circular canon. A canon going through the major keys.

circular scale. The curved row of tuning-pins.

Cis (tsēs), *G.* The note C sharp. Cis-is. C double sharp. Cis-dur. C ♯ major. Cis-moll. C ♯ minor.

cistel'la, *L.* A dulcimer.

cistre (sēstr), *F.* Cither.

cistrum, *L.* Vide SISTRUM.

citara (chē-tä'-rä), *I.* Cither.

citaredo (thē-tä-rā'-dhō), *Sp.*, citarista (chē-tä-rēs'-tä), *I.* A minstrel, a player upon the harp or cittern.

citerna (chē-tĕr'-nä), *I.* Quinterna.

cith'ara, *L.* The large lyre from which the guitar and zither are derived. c. biju'ga. A 2-necked c. c. hispanica. The Spanish guitar. keyed c. The clavicitherium. cith'aris. The theorbo. citharoe'dus. A singing lutenist.

**cith'er, cithera, cithern, cittern, cyth-
orn.** An old guitar-like instr., strung
with wire and played with a plectrum; sometimes with a bow, or
by means of keys.

cito'le. A dulcimer.

cit'tam. Ancient English guitar.

civetteria (chē-vĕt-tĕ-rē'-ä), *I.* Co-
quetry.

clair (klăr), *F.* Clear, shrill, loud.

claircylindre (klăr-si-lăṅdr), *F.* Vide
CLAVICYLINDER.

clairon (klăr-ôṅ), *F.* 1. Trumpet. 2.
Reed-stop. 3. Vide CLARINET. 4.
A bugler.

clang. 1. A bell-tone. 2. In acoustics a fundamental tone with its
group of over and under-tones, their
completeness giving the **clang-colour**
or **clang-tint,** Tyndall's word.

clang-key, *E.,* **Klangschlüssel,** *G.* Riemann's word for his system of chord
designation intended to supplant
thorough-bass as a better method of
describing a combination by its
qualities. Intervals are reckoned,
not from the bass, but from the
principal tone of each chord. He
uses Arabian figures for major,
Roman for minor chords, the former
indicating an interval upwards from
a tone, the latter an interval below,
as follows: 1 (I). Principal tone.
2 (II). Major 2d. 3 (III). Major
3d. 4 (IV). Perfect 4th. 5 (V).
Perfect 5th. 6 (VI). Major 6th.
7 (VII). Minor 7th. 8 (VIII).
Octave. 9 (IX). Major 9th. 10
(X). Major 10th. < indicates
raising a tone by a semitone. >
Lowering it a semitone; "tones
doubly raised or lowered being in-
conceivable musically." The major
chord (or upper-clang) is abbreviated
+ (for 5-3-1), the minor chord (or
under-clang) is abbr. ° (for I-III-V)
—thus a+ or a°. Feeling that, for
instance, the tone C in the major
triad a♭-c-e♭ has a different meaning
from the tone c in the minor triad
a-c-e, he has coined for this "**substitution of clangs**" the word **Klang-
vertretung** (kläng'-fĕr-trä'-toongk).

clang-succession is a chord-progression with regard to its **clang-
meaning,** that is, a tonality which
does not consider every chord in its
proper absolute key but in its relation to some other chord to which
it plays the part of **principal** or **related clang.** Fuller particulars of

this interesting philosophy must be
sought in Riemann's Dictionary of
Music, and other of his writings.

claquebois (klăk-bwä), *F.* A xylophone.

clar. Abbr. of *Clarinet.*

clarabel'la, *L.* A soft-voiced wood
organ-stop.

claribel flute. 1. A flute. 2. A 4-ft.
clarabella.

clar'ichord, clarico'lo, clar'igold. An
old harp, or a clavichord.

Clarin (klä-rēn', *G.* In *F.* klăr-ăṅ).
1. A clarion. 2. A 4-ft. reed-stop.
Clarinblasen. Soft notes of the
trumpet.

clar'inet, clarinette (nĕt), *F.,* **clarinetto,** *I.* An important wood-wind
instr. with a single beating reed,
cylindrical tube and bell. It is in
effect a stopped pipe (q.v.) and
sounds an octave lower than other
wood-wind of its length; it has only
the odd-numbered partials in the
overtone-scale, and requires a different fingering from the oboe, etc. It
has 18 holes, including 13 with keys,
by means of which it has a range of
3 octaves and a sixth, which range
is sharply divided into four distinct
qualities of tone: 1. The **highest,** or
superacute, being (in the normal
soprano clarinet in C) d'''-c''''.
2. The **high** or **clarinetto** or **clarion**
register (whence the instr. took its
name) b'-c'''. 3. The **medium,**
f'-b'♭. 4. The **chalumeau** (shăl'-ü-
mō) or **Schalmei** (shäl-mī) g-e';
the qualities being respectively.
1. Shrill. 2. Liquid and clear. 3.
Veiled and feeble. 4. Rich and
sonorous like a contralto voice.

The clarinet is a transposing instr.
written in the C clef; it is made in
many sizes to adapt it to different
keys; the **large soprano** in C, B♭
(often called simply "clarinet in B")
and A; the **small soprano** in D, E, F,
A♭; the **alto** or **barytone** in F and
E♭, the **bass** (an octave lower than
the sopranos) in C, B♭ and A. The
soprano in B♭ is the most brilliant;
the soprano in A is very tender in
tone. The small sopranos are too
shrill for use except in military bands
in which the clarinet group serves the
substantial purpose served by the
strings in the orchestra.

The clarinet is an improvement
(made by Denner of Nürnberg, 1700)
upon the old **chalumeau** or **Schalmei,**

whose name still persists in the low register of the clarinet. The **ch.** had a single, beating reed, a cylindrical tube and nine holes, each of which produced a tone giving a compass of these natural tones, f-a'. By placing a hole and a key at a nodal point dividing the tube into 3 equal parts, overblowing became possible in the twelfth, i. e., the 3d partials (vide ACOUSTICS). This new register was called *clarinetto* or *clarion* for its clarity of tone, and from this word came the present name of the instr., all of whose gaps have been filled by means of the Böhm key-mechanism, etc., though the fingering is still difficult and a slip gives a squawk called the "goose" or *couac.* 2. A soft 8-ft. reed-stop. **clarinet flute.** A flue-stop with holes in the cover.

clarino (klä-rē'-nō), *I.*, **clarion,** *E.* (in *F.* klär-yôṅ). 1. A small trumpet. 2. A 4-foot organ reed-stop, an octave above the trumpet. 3. The trumpet parts in score. **c. harmonique.** A reed-stop.

clarionet. Obsolescent spelling of clarinet.

clarionet-flute. A stop.

clarone (klä-rō'-nĕ), *I.* A clarinet.

clàrseach (klär'-säkh), **clarseth** (klär'-sĕ). The old Irish harp.

claus'ula, *L.* A dance.

clavecin (klăv-săṅ), *F.* 1. The harpsichord. 2. The keys a bell-ringer plays on. **c. acoustique.** An instr. of the 18th cent. imitating various instruments.

Claviatur (klä-fĭ-ä-toor'), *G.* The key-board.

clav'ichord. Prototype of the piano, the strings being set in vibration not by hammers, but by small brass wedges (called tangents) on the ends of the keys; these set only one section of the string in vibration.

clavicyl'inder. An instr. inv. by Chladni, about 1800, consisting of cylinders of glass attuned.

clavicymbalum, *L.*, **clavicem'balo,** *I.* The harpsichord.

clavicythe'rium, *L.* An upright harp-sichord of the 13th century.

Clavier (klăv-yā, *F.*, in *G.* klä-fēr'). 1. The key-board. 2. An old name for the clavichord. 3. **c. de récit.** The swell manual. 4. In French use, the gamut included in the stave. 5. Vide KLAVIER.

clav'is, *L.* and *G.* 1. A key. 2. A clef. 3. A note. 4. Handle of a bellows.

clé (klā), **clef** (klā), *F.* (In English pron. "klĕf.") A florid form of a letter, used as a symbol with a fixed note-meaning, from which it takes its name, as the so-called "c" clef denoting that whichever line it grips is middle C (c'). The most common clefs are the "G" (or **treble c.** or **clef sol,** or **clef descant,** or **violin c.**) which is always seen now on the 2d line; the F. (or **bass** or **c. de fay**). (These two are those used in piano music.) The C (or **clef d'ut**) is used movably and is called the **soprano** (or **German soprano**) or **discant c.**; or the **alto**; or the **tenor** (or **mean** or **counter-tenor**) clef, according as it is placed on the first, the 3d or the 4th line, in each of which cases it marks middle C. The C clef is found in various forms and is still used in music for the 'cello and other instruments and in contrapuntal writing.

The obsolete clefs are the F on the 3d line (the **barytone clef**), the C on the 2d line (the **mezzo soprano**), the G on the 1st line (the **French violin,** or **French treble clef.**)

clear flute. Organ-stop.

clef d'accordeur (dăk-kôr-dŭr), *F.* Tuning-hammer.

cloc'ca, *L.*, **cloche** (klôsh), *F.* A bell. **clochette.** A hand-bell.

clock. To swing the clapper of a stationary bell.

clog, *Irish.* A shuffling dance.

cloro'ne, *I.* Alto clarinet.

close (klōz). A cadence.

close harmony or **position.** That in which the chords spread over little space; when a chord extends beyond an octave it is said to be in **open position.**

close play. Lute-playing in which the fingers remain on the strings.

close score. That with more than one voice on a stave.

C-moll (tsä-môl), *G.* The key of C minor.

c. o. Abbr. of *choir-organ.*

coalotino (kō-ä-lŏt-tē'-nō), *I.* Concertino.

cocchina (kôk-kē'-na), *I.* An Italian country-dance.

co'da, *I.* "Tail." 1. An additional termination to the body of a composition, ranging from a few chords to a long passage. 2. The stem of a note.

codet'ta. 1. A short coda. 2. A short passage in fugue, between the end of the subject and the entry of the answer.

co'don, *Gr.* 1. A little bell. 2. The bell of a trumpet.

coelesti'no (or -a). A name formerly applied to various keyed instruments.

coffre (kôfr), *F.* The frame of an instrument.

cogli (kōl'-yē), coi (kō'-e), col, coll', colla, collo, *I.* Forms of the preposition "con," and the definite article meaning "with the."

colachon (kō-lă-shôñ), *F.* An instr. like a lute with longer neck.

colascione. Vide CALASCIONE.

collet (kôl-lā), *F.* The neck, as of a violin.

collinet (kôl-lǐ-nā). A flageolet, named from a famous virtuoso on it.

colofo'nia, *I.*, colophane (kôl-ō-făn), *F.*, Colophonium (kô-lô-fō'-nǐ-oom), *G.*, col'ophony, *E.* Resin.

colorato (kō-lō-rä'-to), *I.* Florid.

coloratura (kō-lō-rä-too'-rà) (pl. e), *I.*, Coloraturen (kô-lô-rä-too'-rĕn), *G.* Ornaments and ornamental passages, in vocal or instrumental music; brilliant vocalization.

coloris (kô-lō-rē'), *F.*, Colorit (rēt'), *G.* The "colour"-scheme of a work.

colour. 1. Vide NOTATION. 2. Timbre. 3. Literally colour; to some minds each tone, or each key, has a distinctive actual colour, as C is red to some, C♯ scarlet, C♮ blood red, C♭ darker, etc. The Editor has even met a painter who claimed the ability to play any picture or paint any composition.

colpo, di, *I.* "At a blow," abruptly.

combinational tones. Vide RESULTANT TONES.

combination mode. The ambiguous mode resulting from resolving a dominant chord in a minor key to the tonic major.

combination pedals. Vide COMPOSITION PEDALS.

come (kō'mĕ), *I.* As, like, the same as. c. prima. As before, as at first. c. sopra. As above. c. sta. Exactly as it stands.

co'mes, *L.* 1. In fugue, the companion or answer, to the dux (leader), or subject. 2. In canon, the consequent.

comiquement (kō-mēk-mäñ), *F.* Comically.

com'ma. 1. A breathing-mark. 2. A theoretical term indicating the minute difference between two tones nearly identical. (a) The comma syntonum, or c. of Didymus, is that between a major and a minor tone 80:81. (b) The comma ditonicum, or c. of Pythagoras, is that by which six whole notes with the ratio 9:8 exceed the octave, or $531 + : 524 +$.

com(m)odamen'te, com'(m)odo, *I.* With ease.

common. Vide CHORD and TURN. c. measure or time. 4-4 time.

compass. Range of a voice or instr.

compiacevole (kôm-pǐä-chā'-vō-lĕ), compiacevolmen'te, *I.* Pleasantly).

complainte (kôñ-plănt), *F.* A religious ballad.

com'plement. That quantity or interval which fills up an octave, as a fourth is c. to a fifth.

complementary part. In fugue, the part added to the subject and counter-subject.

complete. Vide CADENCE.

completo'rium, *L.*, com'pletory, *E.* 1. An Ambrosian anthem supplementary to the antiphon. 2. A compline.

complin(e), *L.* Vide HORÆ CANONICÆ.

componis'ta, *I.* A composer.

compo'num. A machine inv. by Winkel to present a given theme in endless variety of forms.

composition, *I.* The act, art or science of writing original music.

composition pedals. Pedals inv. by J. C. Bishop, connected with a mechanism for bringing into use several stops simultaneously.

composizione di tavolino (kôm-pō-zē-tsǐ-ō'-nĕ dē tä-vō-lē'-nō), *I.* Table-music.

compos'to, *I.* Composed, quiet.

compound. Of intervals, those exceeding the octave. c. stop. One having more than one rank of pipes. c. measures or times. Those which contain more than one principal accent, as 6-4, 9-8, etc.

compressed score. Close score.

comprimaria (kôm-prē-mä'-rǐ-ä), *I.* The next in rank to a *prima donna.*

con (kōn), *I.* "With"; it is often combined with the article "the," vide COGLI, etc. *con.* 8va, vide OTTAVA.

concave pedals. Radiating pedals.

concealed. Vide HIDDEN.
concento (kŏn-chĕn'-to), *I.* 1. Concord. 2. Non-arpeggiation.
concen'tus, *L.* 1. Concord, vide AC-
CENTUS.
concert (in *F.* kŏṅ-săr'). 1. A public
performance. 2. c. spirituel. Sacred concert. Dutch c. An improvised chorus of little regularity and
much hilarity. 3. A concerto. 4. A
set of instrs. of different size, vide
CHEST OF VIOLS.
concertante (kŏn-chĕr-tän'-tĕ), *I.* 1.
A piece in which each part is alternately principal, as a *duo concertante.*
2. A concerto for two or more instrs.,
with orchestral accomp. c. style. In
brilliant concert style. c. parts.
Parts for solo instrs. in an orchestral
work.
concertato (tä'-to), *I.,* concerted, *E.*
Used of music for several voices or
instruments.
concert-grand. The largest size of the
piano.
concertina (kŏn-sĕr-tē'-nä). Chas.
Wheatstone's improved accordeon
(q.v.) inv. 1829. It is double-
action, producing tone on being
drawn out or compressed. Its 2 key-
boards are hexagonal, and the *English treble c.* (much superior to the
German) has a range of four octaves
from g below middle C with all the
chromatic tones. The c is to be
had also in *alto, tenor, bass* and
double-bass ranges.
concertino (kŏn-chĕr-tē'-nō), *I.* 1. A
small concerto. 2. Principal as opposed to *ripieno,* e. g., violino c.,
principal violin. 3. The first-violin
part.
concertis'ta, *I.* Virtuoso.
Concertmeister (kŏn-tsĕrt-mīshtĕr), *G.*
1. The leader. 2. The first of the
first-violins.
concerto (kŏn-chĕr'-tō), *I.* 1. A concert. 2. A composition for one—
two (*double*) three (*triple*)—or more
solo instruments with orchestral
accompaniment. It is usually in
sonata form with modifications to
allow of virtuosity, notably the
cadenzas played by the performer of
the solo part just before the concluding tutti of the first and last movement. Formerly the word was applied to concertante. Torelli is credited with the modern form. The c.
without orchestral accompaniment
(c. a solo) is very rare. c. da ca-

mera. Chamber concerto, opposed
to *grosso.* c. da chiesa (kĭ-ā'-zä)
or c. ecclesiastico. (a) In Viadana's
work, merely motets with accomp.
for organ. (b) A concerto for church
use. c. doppio. a c. for two or
more instruments. c. gros'so. A
composition for full orchestra. c.
spirituale. Sacred concert.
concert pitch. Vide A, of which the
French standard is now generally
adopted. By this all the tones are
regulated. In England c. p. refers
to a pitch almost half a tone higher
than the international pitch.
Concertspieler (kŏn-tsĕrt'-shpē-lĕr), *G.*
A solo or concerto player. Concert'stück (shtük). 1. A concert-
piece. 2. A concerto.
concitato (kŏn-chĭ-tä'-tō), *I.* Agitated.
conclusione (kloo-zĭ-ō'-nĕ), *I.* Conclusion.
concord. An harmonious combination. concordant. 1. Harmonious.
2. In French use (pron. kŏn-kôr-
däṅ), a barytone.
con-dissonant. Used of a triad which
is consonant with each of two
mutually dissonant triads.
Conducten (dook'-tĕn), *G.* Wind-
tubes.
conductor. The time-beater and director of a chorus or orchestra. (See
article, page 723.)
conduct'us, *L.* That form of discant
in the 12th century in which not only
the improvised counterpoint of the
singers was original, but the central
melody (or *cantus firmus*) also.
conduit (kŏṅ-dwē), *F.* 1. A wind-
trunk. 2. Conductus.
cone-gamba. The bell-gamba.
confinal. Vide FINAL.
conjoint, or conjunct, *E.,* congiunto
(joon'-to), *I.* 1. Used of notes lying
immediately next to each other; of
motion or *succession* proceeding regularly by single degrees. 2. Applied
by the Greeks to tetrachords, in
which the highest note of the lower,
was also the lowest note of the upper,
tetrachord.
connecting note. One common to
successive chords.
consecutive. Following in immediate
succession. Chiefly applied to progressions of intervals such as perfect
fifths and octaves, strictly forbidden
in most cases.
conseguente (gwĕn'-tĕ), *I.,* con'se-

quent, *E.* In fugue or canon, the imitation or answer of the subject.

conservatoire (kôn-sĕr-vä-twär), *F.,* **conservato'rio,** *I.,* **Conservatorium** (oom), *G.,* **conservatory,** *E.* A school of music.

consolan'te, *I.* Consoling. **consolatamen'te.** Cheeringly.

con'sonance, *E.,* **consonanza** (nän'-tsä), *I.* An accord of sounds, not only agreeable but restful, cf. DISSONANCE. **imperfect c.** A major or minor third or sixth. **perfect c.** An octave, fifth or fourth. **consonant.** Harmonious. **c. chord.** One without a dissonant interval.

consort. 1. To be in accord. 2. A set, as of viols, cf. CHEST.

constit'uents. Partial tones.

cont. Abbr. of *contano.*

contadines'co, *I.* Rustic.

contano, *I.* "They count," of instrs. which "rest."

continua'to (tĭn-oo-ä'-tō), *I.* Sustained.

continued bass. Vide BASS (6).

continuo, *I.* Vide BASS (6)

con'tra. Against or under. As a prefix to names of instruments, or of organ-stops, it indicates a pitch an octave lower than the standard, as **Contraposaune, contra-octave.** (Vide PITCH.) **contra-acro.** Bowing against the rule. **contra-tempo.** Syncopation. **contrabass** (kôn-trä-bäs). The double-bass. **contrabombarde.** A 32-ft. stop in the pedal.

contraddanza (kôn-träd-dän'tsä), *I.* A country-dance.

contralto (kôn-träl'-tō), *I.* The deepest female voice. The term means lower than the *alto* (high), the former name ot male soprano.

contrappunto (poon'-tō), *I.* Counterpoint. **contrappuntista.** One skilled in cpt. **c. alla decima.** Double counterpoint in the tenth. **c. alla mente.** Improvised cpt. **alla zoppa,** or **syncopata.** Syncopated cpt. **c. doppio.** Double cpt. **c. doppio alla duo decima.** Double cpt. in the twelfth. **c. sciolto** (shôl'-tō). Free cpt. **c. sopra** (sotto) **il soggetto** (sôd-jĕt'-to). Cpt. above (below) the subject.

contrapunct'us, *L.* Counterpoint. **c. flo'ridum,** *L.* Florid cpt. **c. in decima gradi.** Double cpt. in which the parts move in tenths or thirds below the subject. **c. simplex.** Simple cpt.

con'trapuntal. Relating to counterpoint. **contrapunt'ist.** One skilled in counterpoint.

contrario (trä'-rĭ-ō), *I.* Contrary. Vide MOTION. **contrary bow.** A reversed stroke.

contrasogetto (sôd-jĕt'-to), *I.* Counter-subject.

contratenor. Vide COUNTER-TENOR.

Contratöne (kôn'trä-tä-nĕ), *G.* The deeper bass tones.

contraviolo'ne, *I.* Double-bass.

contre (kôntr), *F.* Contra, or counter, as **contrebasse.** Double-bass. **c. éclisse.** Lining. **c. partie.** A part contrasted with another, as bass and soprano. **contrepoint** (kôntr-pwăṅ). Counterpoint. **contresujet.** Counter-subject. **contre-temps.** Syncopation.

contredanse (kôn-trŭ-däṅs), *F.* A country-dance, in which the dancers stand in opposite ranks.

conver'sio, *L.* Inversion.

coper'to, *I.* 1. Covered (as fifths). 2. Muffled (as drums).

cop'ula, *I.* 1. A coupler. 2. A stop requiring a coupler.

cor. Abbr. of *cornet.*

cor (kôr), *F.* Horn. **cor-alt.** Alto horn. **cor-basse.** Bass-horn. **c.-anglais.** "English horn," in reality an alto oboe (q.v.). **c. de basset.** Basset-horn. **c. de chasse** (shäs). Hunting-horn; the French horn. **c. de postillon.** Postilion's horn. **c. de signal.** A bugle. **c. de nuit.** The Cremona stop. **c. de vaches.** Cow-horn. **c. omnitonique.** A Sax-horn.

corale (kō-rä'lĕ), *I.* Chora.

coranto (kō-rän'-tō), *I.* Vide COURANTE.

corda (kôr'-dä), *I.* A string; *una corda,* one string, i. e., the soft pedal; *due* (two) or *tre* (three) or *tutte* (all) *le corde* (the strings), "release the soft pedal!" In violin-playing, *due-corde* means "play the same note on 2 strings simultaneously"; *1ma, 2da, 3za,* or *4ta corda,* means that the passage is all to be played on the string indicated.

cordatura (too'-ra), *I.* Vide ACCORD (3).

corde (kôrd), *F.* A. A string. **c. à boyau.** Catgut. **c. à jour** (zhoor). **c. à vide** (vēd). Open string. **c. de luth.** A lute-string. **c. fausse** (fōs). A false string. **c. sourde.** (soord). A mute-string.

cordier (kôrd-yā), *F.* **cordiera** (kôr-dĭ-ā-rä′), *I.* Tail-piece.

cordomètre (kôr-dō-mĕtr), *F.* String-gauge.

corifeo (kō-rĭ-fā′-ō), *I.* Leader of a ballet. **corimagistro** (mä-jēs′-trō). Leader of a chorus.

corista (kō-rēs′-tä), *I.* 1. Chorister. 2. Tuning-fork or pitch-pipe.

cormorne. 1. A soft-toned horn. 2. A reed-stop.

corn (kôrn). *Welsh.* Horn.

cornamusa (kôr-nä-moo′-zä), *I.,* **cornemuse** (kôrn-müz), *F.* Bagpipe.

cor′net (not cornet′), *E.* (in *F.* kôr-nā), **Cornett′,** *G.* 1. Loosely used of the *cornet à pistons* (q. v.). 2. An obsolete wind instr. of the 15th cent. made *straight* (*diritto* or *muto*) and *bent* (*curvo* or *torto*); the latter was also called **cornon** or **cornetto basso** and was the original of the serpent. 3. Various reed-stops as **echo c.,** **mounted c., grand c., c. de récit, C. dreifach** (or 3-ranked).

corneta (kôr-nä′-tä), **cornet′to,** *I.* A 16-ft. reed-stop.

cornet à bouquin (boo-kăň), *F.* Bugle-horn.

cornet à pistons (kôr-nā tä pēs-tôň), *F.* A 3-valved chromatic brass instrument of the trumpet family. It has a plebeian voice of great agility. It is a transposing instr. written in the G clef. It is usually in B♭, and has crooks (A, A♭, G). It has a chromatic compass, f♯ -c′ ′ ′.

cor′no, *I.* Horn. **c. alto.** A horn of high pitch. **c. basso.** A bass-horn. **c. di basset′to.** 1. The basset-horn. 2. A soft-reed stop. **c. di caccia** (kät′-chä). The hunting or French horn. **c. dolce** (dōl′chĕ). An organ-stop. **c. in B basso.** A low B horn. **c. inglese** (ēn-glā′-zĕ). The English horn (vide OBOE). **c. ventile** (vĕn-tē′-lĕ). Chromatic horn. **c. sor′do.** A horn with dampers.

cornope′an. 1. Cornet à pistons. 2. An 8-ft. reed-stop.

co′ro, *I.* and *Sp.* Chorus. **c. della chiesa,** *I.* Church-choir. **c. primo.** The first chorus.

coro′na, *I.* A pause or fermate (⌒).

coronach (kôr′-ō-näkh). A Gaelic dirge.

corps (kôr), *F.* Body (as of an instrument). **c. de ballet** (băl-lā). All the dancers in a ballet. **c. d'harmonie** (dăr-mō-r.ē). A fundamental

chord. **c. de musique.** A band. **c. de réchange.** The crook of a horn. **c. de voix.** Body or range of a voice.

corren′te, *I.* Vide COURANTE.

Coryphaeus, *G.* 1. The conductor of the chorus. 2. At Oxford, a special instructor in music.

coryphée (kō-rĭ-fā), *F.* 1. The leader of dancers. 2. A ballet-dancer.

cosaque (kō-săk), *F.* The Cossack dance.

cotillon (kō-tē-yôň), *F.* "Petticoat." An elaborate ceremonial dance of many couples, not unlike the German.

couac (kwăk), *F.* Vide GOOSE.

couched harp. Spinet.

coulé (koo-lā), *F.* 1. Slurred. 2. A grace note consisting of two or three sliding notes, indicated by a dash between the notes.

coulisse (koo-lēs), *F.* 1. Slide (vide TROMBONE). 2. Side-scene, wing (of a theatre).

count. A beat. To *count time,* to measure the beats audibly or mentally.

counter-. A prefix indicating contrast, as *counter-tenor* (once a name for the alto voice), is higher than the usual tenor; often falsetto or artificial tenor; *counter-bass* is lower than the usual bass; *counter-tenor clef,* vide CLEF; *counter-subject,* vide FUGUE.

counterpoint. Originally notes were called "points"; the literal meaning of counterpoint is therefore "note against (or in accompaniment with) note"; it is loosely used of the combination of independent voices as in a quartet. It is more strictly used (a) of the art of writing simultaneous melodies or (b) of the melodic part added to a given part called the *cantus firmus* (q.v.). The contrapuntal style differs from the harmonic in that while the latter consists of melody accompanied by chords, the former is a combination of melodic parts. The supreme contrapuntal forms are Canon and Fugue. Of counterpoint there are five *species:* 1. Note against note—a semibreve against a semibreve. 2. Two notes against one. 3. Four notes against one. 4. Syncopation. 5. Florid counterpoint—a mixture of the preceding species. Counterpoint is also *Simple* and *Double.* In the latter, the parts are invertible, i. e., may be transposed an octave, or ninth, tenth, twelfth, etc., above or below one another. Counterpoint is *triple* (or *quadruple*) when 3 or 4 parts are mutually invertible. (See article, page 727.)

counterynge ye songe (kown'-tĕr-ing the sŏng) (old *E.*). Descant.

country-dance. Whatever the etymology, a country-dance is a contradance (in duple or triple time) in which partners are ranged opposite each other.

coup (koo), *F.* Blow. **c. d'archet** (dăr-shā). A stroke of the bow. **c. de glotte** (glŏt). A snappy vocal attack. **double c. de langue.** Double-tonguing. **c. de baguette** (bă-gĕt). Beat of the drum. **c. de cloche** (klŏsh). Stroke of a bell.

couper le sujet (koo-pā lŭ soo-zhā), *F.* To cut or contract the subject.

coup'ler. An organ mechanism connecting 2 manuals, or manuals with pedals.

couplet. Two notes occupying the time of a triplet.

courante (koo-ränt), *F.* "Running," an old dance in 3-2 and 6-4 time. Hence an instrumental piece in the same style. Vide SUITE. The second part of the suite, usually in passage work.

couronne (koo-rŭn), *F.* A hold.

course. A group of strings sounding in unison.

courtal (koor-tăl), **courtaud** (koor-tō), **courtaut** (koor-tō), *F.* An old short bassoon.

couvre-feu (koovr-fŭ), *F.* Curfew.

covered. 1. Hidden, used of progressions (q.v.). 2. Used of pipes and stops (q.v.). 3. Used of strings wrapped with fine wire.

c. p. Abbr. of *colla parte*, or *counterpoint*.

cr., cres., cresc. Abbr. of *crescendo*.

crackle. In lute-playing, to play chords brokenly.

cracoviak, *Pol.*, **cracovienne** (krä-kō'-vĭ-ĕn), *F.* A Polish dance in syncopated 2-4 time.

creanluidh (krän'-loo-ē). Vide PI-BROCH.

Cre'do, *L.* "I believe." Vide MASS.

crem'balum, *L.* Jew's harp.

Cremona (krā-mō'-nä), *I.* 1. A town in Italy, hence an instr. made there by the Stradivari, the Amati, or Guarnerius. 2. A corrupt form of crom-horn.

cremorn. Vide CROM-HORN.

crepitac'ulum or **crepun'dia,** *L.* Ancient frictional castanets.

crescendo (krĕ-shĕn'-dō), *I.* "Increasing," i. e., in loudness. **c. il tempo.** Increasing in speed. **C-zug,** *G.* The swell-box, or crescendo pedal.

cres'cent. A Turkish instr. of crescent-shaped metal plates hung on a pavilion; or small bells on an inverted crescent.

criard(e) (krē-ăr(d)), *F.* Bawling.

crib'rum, *L.* Sound-board.

croche (krŏsh), *F.* An eighth note. **c. double.** Sixteenth note. **c. quadruple.** A sixty-fourth note. **c. triple.** 32d note.

crochet (krō-shā), *F.* The hook of a note. **croche'ta,** *L.* A quarter note.

croisement (kwäz-män), *F.* Crossing (as of parts).

croma (krō'-mä) (pl. e), *I.* An eighth note. "**crome**" written under notes of larger value indicates that they are to be played as eighth notes.

cromat'ica, *I.* Chromatic.

crom'-horn. 1. A melancholy double-reed wood-wind instr. of the 16th cent. 2. A 4, 8 or 16-ft. reed-stop.

crom'mo, *I.* A choral dirge.

cromor'na, *I.*, **cromorne** (krō-mŏrn), *F.* Crom-horn.

cronach. Same as **coronach.**

crook. 1. A curved tube inserted in horns, etc., altering the length of the tube, therefore the key. 2. The mouth-piece of a bassoon. 3. A device in old harps for raising a string a half tone.

crooked flute. An Egyptian instrument.

crooked horn or **trumpet.** Buccina.

crope'zia, *Gr.* Wooden clogs worn by the Greeks in beating time.

croque-note (krŏk-nŏt), *F.* An unintelligent virtuoso.

cross. 1. The head of a lute. 2. Vide FINGERING.

cross-beards. Vide BEARDS.

cross-fingering. A method of playing old flutes.

cross flute. A transverse flute.

cross-relation. Vide FALSE.

crotale (krō-tăl), *F.*, **crota'lo,** *I.*. **cro'talum,** *L.* An ancient small cymbal or castanet.

crot'chet. A quarter note. **crot'chet rest.** A quarter rest.

crowd. The crwth (q.v.).

crowie. Old English instr. of the bassoon type.

Crucifix'us, *L.* "Crucified," part of the Credo. Vide MASS.

cruit (krū'ĭt), *Irish.* Old Irish Crwth.

crush-note. Acciaccatura.

crutch'etam. Name originally given to the crotchet.

crwth (krooth), *Welsh.* An old instr. of Welsh or Irish crigin; it was somewhat lyre-shaped, had six strings, and was the first European instr. played with a bow.

c. s. Abbr. of *Con sordino.*

csárdás (tsär-däsh), *Magyar.* A Hungarian (Magyar) dance in 2-4 or 4-4 time. Triple time is very exceptional, and not true to the national character. The Csardas (from csarda, "inn on the heath") is often preceded by a moderate movement called **lassu** (from *lassan,* slow). The quick movement is called **fris** or **friska** (cf. the German *frisch,* fresh, brisk, lively).

C-Schlüssel (tsä'-shlüs-sĕl), *G.* C clef (vide CLEF).

cto. Abbr. of *Concerto.*

cue. Notes from another part inserted as a guide.

cuivre (kwēvr), *F.* **les cuivres.** The brasses. *faire cuivrer* (făr kwēv-rā). To half-stop a French horn with clangorous effect.

Cum sancto spiritu, *L.* "With the Holy Ghost." Part of the Gloria. Vide MASS.

cupo (koo'-po), *I.* Dark, reserved.

Currenda'ner, Curren'de, *G.* Young carol-singers.

cushion dance. An old English round dance in triple time, each dancer placing before another of his or her choice a cushion on which both kneel and kiss.

custo (koos'-tō), *I.,* **custos,** *L.* A direct.

cuvette (kü-vĕt), *F.* Pedestal of a harp.

cycle. A complete set (as of songs). **cyclical forms** (*G.* **cyclische Formen**). Those made up of a set or cycle of movements, as the sonata, suite or symphony.

Cyl'inder, *G.* Ventil piston.

cym'bals, *E.,* **cymbales** (săṅ-bǎl), *F.* 1. Circular metal plates, clashed together. 2. A steel triangle with a number of rings. 3. A high-pitched mixture-stop.

cymbalum, *L.* 1. Cymbal. 2. A mediæval series of eight drums to a scale.

czakan (tshäk'-än). A Bohemian bamboo flute.

czardas (tshär'-däsh). Vide CSÁRDÁS.

czimken (tschĭm'-kĕn). A Polish country-dance.

czymbalom (tshĭm'-bä-lôm). The Hungarian dulcimer.

D

D. In *G.* pron. dä, *F.* ré (rā), *I.* re (rā). 1. A musical pitch, the next full step above C in all its octaves. 2. The major key having two sharps; the minor key relative to F major. 3. Abbr. **d** = *discantus,* or *dessus,* in *da capo, dal segno, main droit, mano drit.o,* **d'** abbr. of *de* before a vowel.

da (dä), *L.* By, from, for, through, in the style of, etc.

dabbuda (däb-boo'-da), *I.* A psaltery.

da capo (dä kä'-pō), *I.* "From the beginning." A sign of repetition.

Dach (däkh), *G.* "Roof." The belly of a violin, etc.

Dachschweller (däkh'-shvĕl-ler), *G.* Swell-box.

dactyi'ion, *Gr.* An apparatus of 10 rings hung from steel springs above the key-board, used to strengthen the fingers; inv. by Herz, 1835.

dada. A term in drum music—the left hand.

daddy-mammy. A colloquial term for a roll on the side-drum.

dagli (däl-yē), **dai** (dä-ē), **dal, dall', dal'le, dal'lo, dalla.** *I.* Combinations of the prep. **da** with the article "the."

daina (dä-ē'-nä), **dainos.** A tender Lithuanian folk-song.

daire (dä-ē'-rā), *I.* The tambourine.

dal, *I.* Vide DAGLI.

dalzimr. An Egyptian reed instrument.

damenisa'tion. Vide SOLMISATION.

damper. 1. In pianos a cushion which when raised by the touch of the key or the use of the *damper pedal* (often called the "loud pedal") permits the vibration of strings; when released it silences the vibration. 2. A mute for brass instruments.

dämpfen (dĕmp'-fen), *G.* To muffle. **Dämp'fer.** A mute or damper. **Dämp'fung.** Damping mechanism.

Danklied (dänk'-lēt), *G.* A thanksgiving song.

danse (däṅs), *F.* A dance, or dancetune. **contre d.** (kôṅtr). A country-dance, a quadrille. **d. de matelot** (mǎt-lō). A horn-pipe. **danseries** (däṅs-rē). Dance-tunes.

Chart of Dance-Rhythms.

BOLERO. { Spanish national dance. A pantomime in honor of Cupid, accompanied with castanets.

Theme. ♩ = 88.

Accomp. or

BOURRÉE. { French or Spanish. The periods commence on the fourth and end on the third beat.

Allegro. or

CHACON(N)E. { Moorish, Spanish, or Italian. Begins on the second beat; contains a basso ostinato.

Moderato. or

CRACOVIENNE. { Polish. Full of syncopations and unexpected accent.

Allegro.

CZARDAS. { Hungarian national dance, beginning with a slow, sad Lassan, followed by a fiercely rapid Friska. The rhythm is too varied to plot, but this germ usually appears:

FANDANGO. { Spanish dance with guitar and castanets, performed between verses.

Allegro.

GAVOTTE. { Old French. Periods begin on the third and end upon the second beat. It is generally combined with a Musette.

or

HABANERA. { Cuban national dance. Accompaniment of marked rhythm, theme greatly varied and syncopated.

Theme. or or

Accomp.

LAENDLER. Slow Tyrolese waltz.

MAZURKA. { Polish national dance of stately character, with varied accents.

MINUET. { Old French, of stately character. The third beat is slightly accented.

Moderato.

MUSETTE. { Old French dance, now usually part of the Gavotte. Its bag-pipe origin gives it a drone-bass. See Gavotte.

POLKA. { Bohemian (not Polish) rapid round dance.

Allegro.

POLONAISE. { Polish dance, formerly very stately. It commences with a strong accent and closes on the last beat, thus:

Moderato. Close.

SALTARELLO. { Italian and Spanish dance of leaping and bounding style.

Allegro. or

SARABANDE. { Spanish or Moorish dance of much solemnity.

Andante. or

TARANTELLA. { Old Italian dance of great violence, said either to be the result of, or an antidote for, the tarantula bite. Also said to be of Tarentine origin.

Presto. and

WALTZ. { A dance of uncertain origin and varied speed.

Vienna, or Quick Waltz.

German, or Slow Waltz.

Two Step. or

danza (dän'-tsä), *I.* A dance or dance-tune. **danzet'ta.** A little dance.

daraboo'ka or **darabuk'keh.** A small Arabian drum.

dar la voce (där lä vō-chĕ), *I.* Give the key-note.

Darmsaite (därm'-zī-tĕ) (pl. **en**), *G.* Gut-string.

Darsteller (där'-shtĕl-ler), *G.* A performer. **Darstellung.** Performance.

dash. 1. A staccato mark. 2. Vide CHORD. 3. Vide COULÉ.

Da'sian-notierung, *G.* Hucbald's notation, using forms of the letter F for 14 tones.

Dauer (dow-ĕr), *G.* Duration.

Daumen (dow'-mĕn), *G.* The thumb. **D.-aufsatz.** Thumb-position. **D.-klapper.** Castanet.

D. C. Abbr. of *da capo.*

D-dur (dä-door), *G.* D major.

de (dŭ), *F.* Of, in, from, by. *De plus en plus vite.* More and more quickly.

dead march. Funeral march.

debile, debole (dā'-bō-lä), *I.* Feeble.

dec'achord, decachor'don, decacor'do, *L.* An ancient harp or guitar with ten strings.

dec'ad. Vide ELLIS (B. D.).

dé'cani, *L. pl.* Vide CANTORI.

Decem (dā-tsĕm), *G.* Vide DECIMA (2).

deceptive. Vide CADENCE.

déchant (dā-shäṅ), *F.* Discant.

décidé (dā-sē-dā), **décidément** (dā-sē-dā-mäṅ), *F.* Decisive(ly).

decima (de-rima'), *L.* 1. A tenth. 2. An organ-stop sounding the tenth. **d. plena de tonis.** A major tenth. **d. non plena de tonis.** A minor tenth. **d. tertia, quarta, quinta.** Intervals of the 13th, 14th, 15th.

Dé'cime (dā-sēm), *F.* (dā-tsēm'), *G.* A tenth.

decimo'le. A group of ten equal notes.

dé'cisif (dā-sē-sēf), **décisivement** (sēv-mäṅ), *F.* Decisive(ly).

decisione (dā-chē'-zĭ-ō'nĕ), *I.* Decision. **decisivo** (dā-chĭ-sē'vō). **deciso** (dā-chē'-zō). In a bold manner, decisively.

Decke (dĕk'ĕ), *G.* 1. Sound-board. 2. Belly. 3. Cover or top for organ-stops.

declaman'do (dā-clä-män'-dō), *I.* With declamatory expression.

declamation, declamazione (dā-klä-mä-tsī-ō'-nĕ), *I.* Singing in declamatory style.

déclaver (dā-klă-vä), *F.* To change the key.

décomposé (dā-kôṅ-pō-zä), *F.* Disconnected.

décompter (dā-kôṅ-tä), *F.* To use the portamento.

décoration (dā-kō-răs-yôṅ), *F.* The signature.

decorative notes. Notes of embellishment.

découplez (dā-koo-plä), *F.* Uncouple.

décousu(e) (dā-koo-sü), *F.* Disjointed.

decr., decres. Abbr. of *decrescendo.*

decrescendo (dā-krĕsh-ĕn'-dō), *I.* Diminishing in loudness.

dec'uplet. A group of ten equal notes.

dedicato (dā-dĭ-kä'tō), *I.,* **dédié** (dād-yä), *F.* Dedicated.

deduct'io, *L.* 1. Resolution. 2. In Guido d'Arezzo's hexachords, the ascending series.

deficiendo (dā-fē-chĕn'-dō), *I.* Dying away.

degli (dāl'-yē), **dei** (dā-ē), **del, dell',** **del'la, del'le, del'lo,** *I.* Of the; than the.

degré (dŭ-grä), *F.,* **degree,** *E.* 1. Line or space on the staff. 2. One of the diatonic tones of a scale.

dehnen (dā'-nĕn), *G.* To extend. **gedehnt** (gĕ-dānt). Prolonged, slow. **Dehnung.** Prolongation. **Dehnungsstrich.** 1. The line or dot in vocal music holding one syllable over several notes. 2. A long bow-stroke.

délassement (dā-läs-mäṅ), *F.* A light piece.

deliberato (dā-lē-bĕ-rä'-to), **deliberatamen'te,** *I.* Deliberate(ly).

délicatesse (dā-lĭ-kä-tĕs), *F.,* **delicatezza** (dā-lĭ-kä-tĕd'-zä), *I.* Delicacy.

delicato (dā-lĭ-kä'-tō), **delicatamen'te,** *I.* Delicate(ly). **delicatissimamen'te, delicatis'simo.** Most delicate(ly).

délié (dāl-yä), *F.* Light, easy.

delir'io, *I.* Frenzy, excitement.

delizio'so or **-amente,** *I.* Delicious(ly).

dem (dām), *G.* "To the." Dative of "the."

démancher (dā-mäṅ-shä), *F.* To change or cross hands; to shift on the 'cello or violin; hence **démanché, démanchement** (dā-mäṅsh-mäṅ).

demande (dŭ-mänd), *F.* The "question," subject of a fugue.

demi (dŭ-mē), *F.* Half. **d.-baton** (bă-tôṅ). A semibreve; or 2-measure rest. **d.-cadence** (kä-däṅs). A half cadence. **d.-croche** A 16th note.

d.-jeu. With half power, *mf*. d.-mesure. Half measure. d.-staccato. Lightly staccato. d.-pause. A half rest. d.-quart de soupir. A 32d rest. d.-soupir. An 8th rest. d.-temps. A half beat. d.-ton. A half tone.

demi-dit'onus, *L*. A minor 3d.

demi-quaver. A 16th note, or semiquaver.

dem'isemiquaver. A 32d note.

dem'itone. A semitone.

demoiselle (dĕm-wä-zĕl), *F*. Tracker.

Denis d'or (dŭn-ē-dôr). A piano with pedals and many qualities of sound, inv. 1762 by Procopius Divis.

depen'dent. Used of a chord requiring resolution.

depres'sio, *I*. Lowering, as of the hand in time-beating; or of a tone chromatically.

De profun'dis, *L*. "From the depths." One of the penitential psalms.

der (dĕr), *G*. 1. The. 2. Of the.

deriv'ative. 1. The root of a chord. 2. An inversion.

dérivé (dā-rē-vā), *F*. 1. Derivative. 2. An inversion. 3. Inverted.

dernière (dĕrn-yăr), *F*. Last. d. fois. The last time.

Des (dĕs), *G*. 1. The note D♭. 2. From the; of the.

désaccorder (dā-zăk-kôr-dā), *F*. To untune. désaccordé. Untuned.

des'cant. Vide DISCANT.

descend. To pass from higher to lower pitch. descent. Such a passing.

descendere (dā-shĕn'-dĕ-rĕ), *I*., descendre (dŭ-säṅdr), *F*. To descend. d. d'un ton. To descend a step. descendant (dŭ-säṅ-däṅ). Descending.

deschant (dŭ-shäṅ), *F*. Discant.

Desdes (dāsdās) or Deses (dāsās), *G*. D double flat.

Des-dur (dās'-door), *G*. D♭ major.

desiderio (dā-sē-dā'-rĭ-ō), *I*. Desire, passion.

desinvolturato (vōl-too-rä'-to), *I*., avec désinvolture (ă-vĕk dā-säṅ-vôl-tür), *F*. Free, easy.

Des-moll (dās-môl), *G*. D♭ minor.

desperazione. Vide DISPERAZIONE.

Dessauer Marsch (dĕs'-sow-er märsh), *G*. One of the national march-songs of Germany.

dessin (dus-säṅ), *F*. Sign.

dessus (dŭs-sü), *F*. 1. Treble or upper part. 2. Old name for violin.

desto (dās'-tō), *I*. Brisk, sprightly

desterità (tā-rĕ-tä'), *I*. Dexterity.

destra (dās'-trä), *I*. Right. d. mano. Right hand. colla d. With the right hand.

détaché (dā-tă-shā), *F*. Detached; with separate bow movements, but not staccato. grand d. With a whole bow-stroke to each note.

determinazione (dā-tĕr-mĭ-nä-tsĭ-ō'-nĕ), *I*. Determination. determinato (nä'-tō). Determined, resolute.

detoni(e)ren (dā-tō-nē'-rĕn), *G*., détonner (dā-tŭn-nā), *F*. To sing or play off the key; hence détonnation (dā-tun-näs'-yôṅ).

detto (dĕt'-tō), *I*. The same; ditto.

deut'erus. Vide MODES.

deutlich (doit'-lĭkh), *G*. Distinctly.

Deutsch (doitsh), *G*. "German." deutsche Flöte. The German or transverse flute. deutscher Bass. An obsolete 5 or 6 stringed double-bass. deutsche Tabulatur. Vide TABLATURE. deutsche Tänze. Old slow waltzes.

deux (dŭ), *F*. Two. à deuxhuit (dŭz-wēt). In 2-8 time. à d. mains. For 2 hands. d.-quatre. 2-4 time. d.-temps. The two-step, or a fast waltz with two measures to the beat, also called *Valse à d. t.* deux fois. twice.

deuxième (dŭz-yĕm), *F*. Second. d. position (pō-zēs-yôṅ). 1. The second fret. 2. The second position or half-shift.

development. Working out; free fantasy. Vide FORM.

devo'to, *I*. Devout. devozione (dā-vō-tsĭ-ō'-nĕ). Devotion.

dex'tra, *L*., dextre (dĕxtr), *F*. 1. Right; the right hand. 2. Vide TIBIA.

Dezem (dā-tsām'), *G*. Vide DECIMA.

Dezime (dā'-tsē-mĕ), *G*. A tenth.

di (dē), *I*. Of, with, for, from, by, etc. di molto. Extremely, as *allegro di molto*.

di'a, *Gr*. Through.

diacon'icon, *Gr*. Collects in the Greek Church.

di'adrom, *Gr*. Vibration.

diagonal bellows. The old form with slanting flap.

diagram'ma, *Gr*. Diagram. 1. The Greek scale. 2. The staff. 3. A score.

dialogo (dē-ä-lō'-gō), *I*., dialogue (dē-ä-lôg), *F*. Dialogue. a duet.

diamond-shaped notes. Vide HARMONICS.

diana (dē-ä'-r.ä), *I.*, **Diane** (dĭ-ăn), *F.* The reveille.

diap. Abbr. of *diapason*.

diapa'son, *Gr.* pron., in *E.* (dī-ä-pā'-sŏn; in *F.*, dē-ăp-ä-sôn). 1. An octave. **d. (cum) diapente.** An octave with the fifth—a twelfth. **d. con diatesseron.** An octave with the fourth—an eleventh. 2. Range. 3. Absolute pitch, as **d. normal,** international pitch, vide A (1). 4. In the organ, the sonorous chief foundation-stops, one of 8 and one of 16-foot pitch on the manual, on the pedal, 16-foot; the *open d.* has metal pipes open at the top, the *stopped d.* has wooden pipes closed at the top. In other countries they are called *principal*.

diapen'te, *Gr.* A perfect fifth; vide DIAPASON (4). **d. col dito'no.** A major 7th. **d. col semidito'no.** A minor 7th. **d. cum semito'nio.** A minor 6th. **d. cum tono.** A major 6th.

diapentisa're, *Mediœval L.* 1. To discant at the interval of a 5th. 2. To proceed by 5ths. 3. To tune by 5ths. 4. In French usage, discant at the intervals of the 2d, 3d, 6th, and 7th.

diaphonics. The science of refracted sounds.

diaph'ony. 1. In Greek music, dissonance. 2. In the middle ages, the earliest form of 2-voiced counterpoint.

diapla'sion. Vide VIS-À-VIS.

diaschis'ma or **diaskhisma,** *Gr.* Vide SCHISMA and ELLIS (B. D.).

dias'tema, *Gr.* An interval.

diastolic(s), *Gr.* Diastolik (ĭĕk'), *G.* Art of phrasing.

diates'seron, *Gr.* Interval of a fourth.

diaton'ic, *E.*, **diato'nico,** *I.*, **diatonique** (dē-ä-tôn-ēk), *F.*, **diatonisch** (dē-ä-tōn'-ĭsh), *G.* 1. Going through, or confined to, the tones of any one key, with no flats, sharps, or naturals belonging to another key—opposed to *chromatic;* hence a *d. scale* is the regular scale of any predominant key; a *d. interval, chord,* or *progression* is an unaltered interval, chord, or progression containing no tones foreign to the key; a *d. melody* or *harmony* clings to one scale; a *d. instrument* sounds only the tones of the one key from which it takes its name; a *d. modulation* goes to the nearest related key. 2. One of the three

genera in Greek music. Vide MODES.

diaul'os, *Gr.* A double flute with 2 tubes, 1 mouthpiece.

diazeux'is, *Gr.* The separation of two tetrachords by a tone; the tone separating them; hence the adjective **diazeuc'tic.** Vide MODES.

di'chord. An instrument (a) with 2 strings; (b) with 2 strings to each note.

dicta'tion, dictée musicale (dēk-tä mü-zĭ-kăl), *F.* The performance of musical phrases to be written on paper by the listener(s).

die (dē), *G.* The.

die, *E.* A steel punch for engraving music.

diecetto (dē-ā-chĕt'tō), *I.* A composition for 10 instruments.

diesare (dē-ā-sä'-rĕ), *I.*, **diéser** (dē-ā-zä), *F.* To sharpen a tone or note.

dièse or **dièze** (dē-ĕz), *F.* Sharp (♯).

Di'es i'rae, *L.* "Day of wrath," second movement of the Requiem.

diesis (dē-ā'-sĭs), *Gr.* and *I.*, **diésis** (dĭ-ä'sē), *F.* 1. The sharp (♯). 2. The *enharmonic d.* is the difference between a diatonic and a chromatic semitone (ratio 128 : 125), or between 3 major thirds and one octave. 3. A quarter tone, the unit of tone-division in Aristotle's system. 4. The Pythagorean semitone or limma.

diezeug'menon, *Gr.* Disjunct. Vide MODES.

dif'ference tones. Vide RESULTANT TONES.

differen'tiale or **distinct'io tonorum,** *L.* **Differenzen** (ĕn'-tsĕn), *G.* The different cadences available for the saeculorum amen of each psalm-tone.

difficile (dĭf-fē'-chē-lä), *I.* (dĭf-fĭ-sēl), *F.* Difficult.

dig'ital. A key to be pressed by a finger (as opposed to *pedal* = foot-key).

digito'rium. A dumb instr. with five keys for exercising the fingers.

dignità (dēn-yĭ-tä'), **dignita'de, dignitate** (tä'-tĕ), *I.* Dignity.

digressio'ne, *I.* Deviation.

dilettant(e) (dē-lĕt-tän(t)), *I.* An amateur.

dilettosamen'te, *I.* Pleasantly.

dilicato (de-lĭ-kä'-tō), **dilicatamen'te,** *I.* Delicate(ly). **dilicatezza** (tĕd'-zä). Delicateness. **dilicatis'simo.** Most delicate.

diligenza (dē-lĭ-jĕn'-tsä), *I.* Diligence, care.

dilu'dium, *L.* An interlude.

diluendo (dē-loo-en'dō), *I.* Fading away.

dim., dimin. Abbr. of *diminuendo.*

diminished. 1. Used of intervals which are a semitone smaller than the minor intervals; used also of chords containing such intervals. Fourths, fifths and octaves, however, being called "perfect" instead of "major," are, when contracted a semitone, said to be, not "minor," but *diminished.* When inverted, *d. intervals* become *augmented* and vice versa. A *d. triad* contains a minor 3d and an imperfect (or diminished) fifth. The *chord of the d. seventh* is the 7th chord built on the leading tone of a minor key. *d. imitation, subject* or *theme,* is used when the answer reappears in notes of lessened time-value.

diminuendo (dē-mē-noo-ĕn'-dō), *I.* Diminishing gradually in loudness. **d. molto.** With extreme diminution of power.

diminuer (dĭ-mē-nü-ā), *F.* To diminish. **diminué** (dĭ-mēn-ü-ā). Diminished. **en diminuant beaucoup.** Diminuendo molto.

diminu'tion, *E.* (in *F.* dē-mē-nüs-yôn), **diminuzione** (dē-mĭ-noo-tsĭ-ō'-nĕ), *I.* In cpt., the repetition or imitation of a theme, in notes of shorter duration; opposed to *augmentation.*

diox'ia, *Gr.* Diapente.

dip. The extent to which a key or pedal may be depressed.

dipho'nium. A vocal duet.

direct'. 1. A mark placed at the end of a staff (a) to indicate the position of the note next following (м/); (b) = &c. 2. Vide TURN. 3. To conduct. **d. motion.** Similar or parallel motion.

directeur (dĭ-rĕk-tŭr), *F.,* **diretto're,** *I.* Director; conductor.

diriger (dē-rē-zhā), *F.,* **dirigiren** (dē-rē-jē'-rĕn), *G.* To conduct.

dirit'to(a), dritto, *I.* Direct. **alla d.** Straight on.

Dis (dēs), *G.* The note D sharp.

disaccentato (ät-chĕn-tä'-tō), *I.* Unaccented.

disarmo'nico, *I.* Discordant. **disarmonia** (nē'-ä). Discord.

dis'cant, *E.,* **discant'us,** *L.* "Diverse song." 1. The early form of cpt., the addition, usually by improvisation, of one or more parts to a given melody. Contrary motion was much

used and elaborate rules made. *Double, triple, quadruple d.* refer to the number of parts. 2. The highest part, voice or register; the highest of a family of instrs. **d. clef.** The soprano clef.

discendere (dē-shān'-dĕ-rĕ), *I.* To descend.

disciolto (dĕ-shôl'-tō), *I.* Skilful, dexterous.

discord, *E.,* **discorde** (dēs-kôrd), *F.,* **discor'dia,** *L.,* **discordanza** (dän'-tsä), *I.* 1. Ugliness of sound; an inharmonious combination of tones. 2. Loosely used for DISSONANCE (q.v.). **discordan'te, discordantemen'te,** *I.* Discordant(ly).

discreto (dĭs-krā'-tō), *I.* Discreet **discrezione** (dĭs-krā-tsĭ-ō'nĕ). Discretion.

disdiapa'son. In mediæval music, a double octave, a 15th.

Dis-dis (dēs-dēs), *G.* D double sharp.

Dis-dur (dēs-door), *G.* D ♯ major.

Disharmonie (dēs-här-mō-nē'), *G.* Discord. **disharmo'nisch** (nĭsh). Discordant.

disinvol'to, disinvolturato (vōl-too-rä'-tō), *I.* Easy. **disinvoltura** (too'-rä). Ease.

Disis (dēs-ēs), *G.* D double sharp.

disjunct'. Disjoined. A te'm applied by the Greeks to tetrachords where the lowest sound of the upper was one degree higher than the highest sound of the lower. Vide MODES.

disjunct succession. A succession of skips.

Diskant (dēs-känt'), *G.* Discant 1. and 2. **D.-schlüssel.** The soprano clef. **D.-geige.** The soprano of the strings, i. e., the violin. **Diskan'tist, D.-sänger.** Treble singer. **D.-register, D.-stimme.** Half-stops. **D.-saite.** The highest string.

Dis-moll (dēs-môl), *G.* D♯ minor.

dispar'te, *I.* Aside.

dispera'to (ä'-tō), *I.* Desperate. **disperazione** (dĭs-pĕ-rä-tsĭ-ō'-nĕ), *I.* Despair.

dispersed. Used of chords or harmonies whose elements are at wide intervals.

disposition. 1. Arrangement of parts of a score, chorus, or orchestra. 2. Estimate as to make-up and cost of an organ.

dissonance, *E.* (*F.* dĭs-sō-näns). **Dissonanz** (dēs-sō-nänts'), *G.,* **dissonanza** (dĭs-sō-nän'-tsä), *I.* 1. Loosely used for discord. 2. In acoustics

DICTIONARY OF TERMS

587

used of combinations producing beats. 3. In composition used of tones or combinations (irrespective of their pleasantness or unpleasantness of effect) that do not give a sense of rest, but demand motion and resolution in some other tone or chord.

dis'sonant, *E.* (*F.* dĭs-sō-näṅ), **dissonan'te**, *I.* Dissonant.

dissonare (dĭs-sō-nä'-rĕ), *I.*, **dissoner** (dēs-sō-nā), *F.*, **dissoniren** (dĭs-sō-nē'-rĕn), *G.* To form dissonance.

distance. Interval.

distanza (dēs-tän'-tsä), *I.* Interval, distance. **in d.** In the distance.

distinct'io. 1. Vide DIFFERENTIALE. 2. A pause in Gregorian vocal music.

distin'to, **distintamen'te**, *I.* Distinct(ly).

distonare (tō-nä'-rĕ), *I.*, **distoniren** (dēs-tō-nē'-rĕn), *G.* To be out of tune.

distro'pha. In plain-song, a double square note of lesser stress than the tristropha.

di'tal. A key raising the string of a lute or guitar a semitone. **d. harp.** A chromatic lute with a dital to each of its 12 to 18 strings; inv. by Light, 1778.

diteggiatura (dē-tĕd-jä-too'-rä), *I.* Fingering.

dith'yramb, *E.*, **dithyrambe** (dē-tĭ-rämb), *F.*, **Dithyrambe** (dē-tĭ-räm'-bĕ), *G.*, **ditirambo** (dē-tē-räm'-bō), *I.* A rhapsody in honour of Bacchus; a wine-rapture.

dito (dē'tō), *I.* Finger. **d. grosso.** The thumb.

di'tone, *E.*, **diton** (dē-tôṅ), *F.*, **ditono** (dē-tō'-nō), *I.*, **dito'nus**, *L.* A Pythagorean major third greater by a comma than our major third.

ditty. A naïve little song.

div. Abbr. of *divisi.*

diver'bia, *L.*, **diver'bio**, *I.* A musical dialogue.

divertimen'to, *I.*, **divertissement** (dĭ-vĕr'-tēs-mäṅ), *F.* 1. A musical diversion; a potpourri, a series of songs or dances inserted in operas and plays; a short ballet, in one or several movements. 2. In fugue, an episode.

divide. Vide DIVISION.

divisi (dē-vē'-zē), *I.* Divided. When 2 parts are written on one stave, to ensure their not being played as double-stops by one instr. they are marked "*divisi.*" When a single

note is to be played by two instrs. the sign is *a due*, separated.

divisio modi, *L.* A point formerly serving the purpose of the present bar.

division. 1. A variation. 2. A long note divided into short notes. 3. A series of notes sung to one syllable. To "divide" or "run a division" is to execute such a series. **d.-viol.** The viola da gamba. **division-mark.** A figure and a slur binding a number of notes of foreign rhythm, as a triplet or quintole.

division (dĕ-vēz'-yôṅ), *F.* A double bar.

divo'to, **divotamen'te**, *I.* Devout(ly).

divozione (dē-vō-tsĭ-ō'-nĕ). Devotion.

dixième (dēz-yĕm), *F.* A tenth.

d. m. Abbr. of *destra mano.*

D-moll (dä-môl), *G.* D minor.

do (dō), *I.* 1. A syllable applied to the first note of a scale in solmisation. In the "*fixed do*" system, the name **do** is always applied to C. In the "*movable do*" system, **do** is always the tonic or key-note; it has displaced the original syllable *ut.* Vide SOLMISATION. 2. In France and Italy, the name for C.

Dock'e (dôk'-ĕ), *G.* A wooden jack.

dodecaphonic, "twelve-toned." Atonal; i.e., written according to the principles of Arnold Schönberg, repeating a "tone-row" of 12 different notes.

dodecachor'don, *Gr.* 1. The bissex. 2. Vide GLAREANUS in the B. D.

dodec'upla di cro'me, *I.* 12-8 time. **d. di semicrome.** 12-16 time.

dodec'uplet. A group of 12 equal notes.

doglia (dōl'yä), *I.* Grief.

doh (dō). Vide TONIC-SOL-FA.

doigt (dwä), *F.* Finger. **doigté** (dwä-tā).** Fingered, or fingering. **doigter** (dwä-tā). To finger; the art of fingering any instrument. **doigtés fourchus** (dwä-tā foor-shü). Cross-fingerings.

dol. Abbr. of *dolce.*

dolce (dōl'-chĕ), *I.* Sweet, soft. **dolcezza** (dōl-chĕd'-zä). Sweetness. **dolcemen'te.** Softly. **dolcis'simo.** 1. With extreme sweetness. 2. A very soft flute-stop.

Dolcian (dôl-tsĭ-än'), *G.*, **dolciana** (o) (dōl-chĕ-ä'-nä), **dolcino** (dol-chē-no), *I.* 1. An obsolete small bassoon. 2. A reed-stop.

dolciato (dol-chä'-tō), *I.* Softened.

dolciss. Abbr of *dolcissimo.*

dolemment (do-lĕm-mäṅ), *F.* Dolefully.

dolen'do, dolente, *I.* Sad. **dolentemen'te.** Sadly.

dolent (dō-läṅ), *F.* Sorrowful, mournful.

dolore (dō-lō'rĕ), *I.* Grief, sorrow. **dolorc'so, dolorosamen'te.** Sorrowful(ly).

Dolzflöte (dôlts'-flä-tĕ), *G.* 1. An obsolete flute. 2. A flute-stop.

Dom (dôm) or **Domkirche** (kēr'-khĕ), *G.* A cathedral. **Domchor** (kōr). The cathedral choir.

dom'inant, *E.,* **dominante** (dôm-ĭ-nänt), *F.,* **Dominante** (dō-mĭ-nän'-tĕ), *G.* & *I.* 1. The fifth tone of a scale, so called because it is the principal tone after the tonic and its chord or harmony indicates the key and demands resolution in the tonic; hence **d. chord,** the triad or the 7th chord built on the dominant. 2. The key whose tonic is the dominant of the principal key; hence the expression, "to modulate to the dominant," thus the key of G is the dominant to the key of C. In the sonata formula the dominant key is the one usually chosen for the contrasting second subject, after which the tonic key is re-established; hence the *dominant section.* 3. Vide CHANT (1) a.

Domine, salvum fac, *L.* "Lord, make him hale," first words of a Catholic prayer for the health of the sovereign.

Domin'icali Psalmi, *L.* Psalms in the Vespers.

Do'na no'bis pa'cem, *L.* "Grant us Thy peace." Vide MASS.

donna, *I.* Lady. **prima donna.** Leading lady in opera.

do'po, *I.* After.

doppel (dôp'l), *G.* Double. **doppel-B** or **doppel-Be** (dôp''l-bä). The double flat (♭♭). **D.-blatt.** Double reed. **D.-chor.** Double chorus. **D.-fagott.** Double bassoon. **D.-flöte.** 1. Double flute. 2. A stop-pipe with two mouths. **D.-fuge.** Double fugue. **D.-flügel.** 1. Vide VIS-À-VIS. 2. Vide PIANO À CLAVIERS RENVERSÉS. *D.*-gedeckt. Double-stopped diapason. **D.-geige.** An organ-stop. **D.-griff.** Double stop on the violin, etc.; paired notes on other instruments. **D.-kanon.** Canon with two subjects. **D.-kreuz** (kroits). The double sharp. **D.-okta've.** Double

octave. **D.-punkt.** Double dot after a note. **D.-quintpommer.** A large bombard. **D.-schlag.** A double beat, a turn. **D.-schritt.** A quick march. **D.-zunge.** Double tonguing.

doppelt (dôp'plt), *G.* Doubled. **d. Trillerlauf.** Double cadence. **doppeltgestrichene Note.** A 16th note. **doppelte Noten.** Double notes.

dop'pio (or **a**), *I.* Double; sometimes used to mean "play also the octave"; with names of instrs. it means larger and deeper. **d. movimento** or **d. tempo.** Twice as fast. **d. pedale.** Playing the pedals in octaves. **d. lyra.** A double lyre.

do-re-mi. Vide SOLMISATION.

Dorian, Doric, *E.,* **dorien** (dō-rĭ-äṅ), *F.* Vide MODES.

dossologia (dôs-sō-lō-jä), *I.* Doxology.

dot. 1. A point placed after a note to increase its duration one half. **double dot.** Two dots placed after a note to increase its duration three fourths. 2. A point placed above or below a note to indicate that it is to be played staccato; if slurred, mezzo-staccato. 3. A series of dots above a note indicate that it is to be divided into that number of small notes. 4. Vide REPEAT.

double. *As a noun.* 1. A repetition. 2. A variation. 3. Any 16-foot stop. 4. A change rung on 5 bells. *As a verb.* 1. To add the superior or inferior octave to the written tones of any part. 2. To give the same tones to different instrs. *As an adjective.* 1. Doubled, paired, as the 2-mouthed d. flageolet. 2. Repeated in the octave or in other instrs. 3. Vide PITCH, concerning **double C, double octave, d. chant,** vide CHANT 1b. **d. drum.** One beaten at both ends. **d. reed.** The combination of 2 reeds in the mouthpiece of one instr. **d. flute.** (a) A flute capable of producing two tones at once. (b) An organ-stop. **d. grand pianoforte.** An instr. inv. by James Pierson, of New York, with a set of keys at either end. **d. action harp.** Vide HARP. **d. lyre.** A double lyre. **d. demisemiquaver.** A 64th note. **double flat.** A symbol of two flats (♭♭) lowering its note two semitones. **double sharp.** A symbol (✕) raising a note two semitones. **d. note.** A breve. **d. time.** (a) 2-4 time. (b)

In the army a running step or cadence of 180 to the minute. **d. concerto** or **sonata.** A concerto or sonata for two solo instrs., as violin and piano. **d. octave.** An interval of a 15th or 2 octaves. **d. quartet.** Eight singers. **d. chorus.** Two choirs. **d. afternote.** 2 after-notes. **d. beat.** A beat repeated. **d. shake** or **trill.** Two notes (3ds or 6ths) shaken together. **d. backfall.** An old grace. **d. relish,** vide RELISH. **d. suspension.** The suspension of two notes of a chord. **d. triplet.** A sextole. **d. pedal.** Pedal-point on 2 notes. **double bar.** Two thin or thick lines vertically cleaving the stave to show the end of a major part, or of the whole composition. "**doubled**" is used of notes repeated in the octave or in other instruments, as "the 'cellos are *d.* by the bassoons."

Concerning the **double letters** (AA, BB, etc., or D.A, D.B, etc.), vide PITCH. In England **d.** is applied to the tones from G to F inclusive. 4. Deeper by an octave. **d. bassoon.** An instr. an octave lower than the bassoon. Its compass extends from B,,b to F. **d. bourdon.** A 32-ft. stop. **d. diapason.** A stop an octave below diapason, 16-ft. on the manuals, 32-ft. on the pedals. **d. dulciana.** A 16-ft. dulciana. **d. hautboy.** A 16-ft. stop. 5. **double counterpoint** and **d. descant** refer to parts so written that they may be inverted. Vide COUNTERPOINT. **d. fugue.** A fugue with 2 subjects. 6. **double stopping.** The playing of two or more notes at once on a stringed instr. **d.-stopped diapason.** A double diapason with covered pipes. **double tonguing** or **d. tonguing.** In flute and trumpet playing, the production of rapid staccato tones by striking the upper teeth and the hard palate alternately with the tongue. **double trouble.** A quick shuffle of the feet in The breakdown. **double trava'le.** The trill of a tambourine m^de by drawing the wet thumb across it. **d. twelfth.** A stop sounding the fifth above the foundation-stops. The **double-bass** got its name from an obsolete higher instr., the *bass* of the stringed instrs., and of the orchestra. Its compass is from E, or G, to *a*, its 3 strings

being tuned by the Italian and French system, G,-D-A, by the English, A,-D-G. With 4 strings it is tuned E,-A,-D,-G. Its music is written an octave higher than it sounds.

double (doo-bl), *F.* 1. Repetition with variations, pl. **doubles.** Obsolete. 2. In the minuet, a short trio with the main harmonies of the first subject retained. *As an adjective.* Double, **d.-barre.** Double bar. **D.-bémol.** Double flat. **d.-corde.** (a) Double stopping. (b) Playing the same note on 2 strings simultaneously. **d. coup de langue** (koo-dŭ läng). Double tonguing. **d. croche.** A 16th note. **d. dièse.** Double sharp. **d. main.** An octave-coupler. **d. octave.** Double octave. **d. touche** (toosh). In harmoniums, etc., a key-fall adjustable at two heights to regulate the volume of tone. **d. triple.** 3-2 time.

doublé (doo-blā), *F.* 1. A turn. 2. Doubled.

doublette' (ĕt), *F.* 1. A 2-ft. stop. 2. A stop with 2 ranks of pipes. Vide FIFTEENTH.

doublophone. A combination of euphonium and trombone inv. by Besson, Paris, 1891.

doubtful. Vide EQUIVOCAL.

douleur (doo-lŭr), *F.* Grief. **douloureux** (doo-loo-rü'). Sad. **douloureusement** (doo-loor-ŭz-män). Sadly.

doux (doo), **douce** (doos), *F.* Soft, sweet. **doucement** (doos-män). Softly.

douzième (dooz-yĕm), *F.* A twelfth.

downbeat. 1. The fall of the hand in time-beating, marking the major accent of the measure. 2. The accent itself, or thesis.

downbow. Vide BOW.

doxolo'gia, *L.,* **doxologie** (dŏx-ŏl'ō-zhē), *F.,* **doxol'ogy,** *E.* A sacred hymn of praise; strictly, the *Greater* (or *major* or *magna*) D. is the gloria in excelsis. The *Lesser* (or *minor* or *parva*) D. is the gloria Patri.

drag. 1. A retardation. 2. In lute-music, a portamento downward.

Drahtsaite (drät'-zī-tĕ), *G.* Wire string.

dramma lir'ico or **per musica** (moo'-zĭ-kä), *I.* An opera or musical drama.

drammat'ico, *I.* Dramatic. **drammaticamen'te.** Dramatically.

590 DICTIONARY OF TERMS

drängend (dreng'-ĕnt), *G.* Hurrying.

drawknob or **drawstop.** In the organ a knob which when pulled admits the wind to a stop, or couples certain stops. **d. s. action.** The mechanism of stops.

Dreher (drā'-ĕr), *G.* An obsolete Austrian waltz like the Ländler.

Drehorgel (drā'-ôrg-ĕl), *G.* Barrel-organ.

Drehsessel (drā'-zĕs-sĕl), **Drehstuhl** (drā-shtool), *G.* A music-stool.

drei (drī), *G.* Three. **Dreiachteltakt** (drī-äkht'-ĕl-täkt). 3-8 time. **-händig** (hĕn-dĭkh). For three hands. **-angel** (drī'-äng-ēl). Triangle. **-chörig** (kär-ĭkh). Three-choired. Applied to (a) pianos having three strings to each note. (b) Compositions for three choirs. **-gesang** (drī'ge-zäng). Trio. **-gestrichen.** 3-lined; vide PITCH. **-klang.** A triad. **-mal** (drī'-mäl). Thrice. **-spiel** (drī'shpēl). A trio. **-stimmig.** Three-voiced. **Dreivierteltakt** (drī-fĕr'tĕl-täkt). 3-4 time. **Dreizweiteltakt** (drī-tsvī'-tel-täkt). 3-2 time.

dreist (drīsht), *G.* Brave, confident. **Dreistigkeit** (drīsh'tĭkh-kīt). Boldness.

drem'la, *Pol.* A Jew's harp.

dringend (drĭng'ĕnt), *G.* Hastening.

Dritte (drĭt'-tĕ), *G.* Third.

drit'to, *I.* Right. **mano d.** Right hand.

dri'ving note. A syncopated note.

droit (dwä), **droite** (dwät), *F.* Right. **main droite.** Right hand.

Drommete (drôm-mā'tĕ), *G.* A trumpet.

drone or **drone-pipe.** Vide BAGPIPE.

drone-bass. A form of monotonous pedal-point suggesting a bagpipe. Vide MUSETTE.

drönen (drā'nĕn), *G.* To drone.

Drucker (drook'er), *G.* 1. A tour-de-force in performance. 2. Sticker.

Druckwerk (vĕrk), *G.* In an organ, an action exerted through stickers. **Druckbalg** (drook-bälkh). A concussion bellows.

drum. An instr. of percussion, of great antiquity and variety; it consists of one or two membranes stretched taut over the ends of a hollowed chamber of wood or metal. The tightness of this membrane regulates the pitch of the one tone of which it is capable. Many drums do not produce a musical tone, but are merely of rhythmic value; besides the savage forms, there are (a) the small, shrill **side drum** (or **tenor-drum**) with two heads, the upper only being beaten with two wooden sticks; this is capable of a sharp rattling roll, which may be emphasized by drawing strings (or snares) of gut across the lower head; the drum is then called a **snaredrum;** (b) the **tambourine;** (c) the big deep-booming **bass-drum** beaten on both sides or on one, with padded sticks. The musical drum is the **kettle-drum** (q.v.). **drum-major.** The officer conducting a band on the march.

dru'ma, *Irish.* A drum.

drum-bass. The monotonous giving out of the tonic and dominant in double-bass music.

D. S. Abbr. of *Dal Segno.*

duc'tus, *L.* Melodic progression. 1. **d. rectus.** Ascending. 2. **d. reversus** or **revertens.** Descending; or 3. **d. circumcurrens.** Ascending and descending.

Dudeler (doo'dĕl-er), *G.* A wretched singer or player.

Du'delkasten, *G.* Barrel-organ.

Dudelsack (doo'd'l-zäk), **Dudelkastensack,** *G.* A bagpipe.

due (doo'-ĕ), *I.* Two; in two parts. Vide DIVISI. **d. corde.** Vide CORDA. **d. cori.** Two choirs or choruses. **d. pedali,** *I.* Both pedals to be used. **due volte.** Twice. *A due,* vide DIVISI.

duet, Duett (doo-et'), *G.,* **duet'to,** *I.* A composition for two singers, or instrumentalists; a 2-hand piece for two manuals of an organ. **duettino** (tē'no), *I.* A short duet.

dulçâina (dool-sä-ē'na), *Port.* A beak flute. Also doçaina.

dulcet. A stop.

dulcian. 1. Vide DOLCIAN. 2. An organ-stop.

dulciana stop, dolcan, dolcin, dulcan, or **dulzain.** 1. An 8-ft. stop of soft sweet quality. **d. principal.** A 4-ft. stop. 2. A dolcian.

dulcimer. A very ancient instr. with a wooden frame, a sound-board with sound-holes, two bridges, and wire strings. It is played upon with two padded hammers; compass g to d." The czimbalom is a very familiar form.

dulzaina (dool-thä-ē'-nä), *Sp.* A small trumpet.

dumb piano, dumb spinet. A keyboard without strings or hammers meant for silent practice.

dummy pipes. Ornamental organ pipes that make no sound.

dump. An obsolete slow dance in 4-4 time.

dumpf (doompf), **dumpfig** (doomp'-fĭkh), *G.* Dull, muffled. **Dumpfigkeit** (kīt). Dulness.

duo (doo' ō), *I.* Two; in two parts; a duet, especially of 2 voices or instrs. of the same kind. **d. concertante.** A duo in which each part is alternately principal.

duodecima (doo-ō-dā'chĭ-mä), *I.* The twelfth; a stop, a twelfth above the diapasons. **d. acuta,** *L.* A twelfth above. **d. gravi,** *L.* A twelfth below.

duodecimole, *I.* A group of twelve equal notes.

duode'nal, duodena'rium, duodena'-tion. See A. J. ELLIS in the B. D.

duodram'ma, *I.* A dramatic piece for 2 actors or singers.

duoi (doo-ō'e), *I.* Two.

duole, *G.* Vide COUPLET.

duolo (doo-ō'lō), *I.* Sorrow, grief.

duomo (doo-ō'mō), *I.* A cathedral.

dupla (doo'-plä), *L.* Double. Vide NOTATION.

duple time. Double time; 2 beats to the measure. Vide TIME.

duplex longa. Vide NOTATION.

duplication. Doubling.

duplo (doo-plō), *I.* Double.

dur (door), *G.* Major, as A-dur.

dur (dür), *F.* 1. Hard, harsh of tone. 2. Major.

duramen'te (doo-rä-mĕn'-tĕ), *I.* Sternly.

durchaus (doorkh-ows), *G.* Throughout.

durchdringend (doorkh'-drĭng-ĕnt), *G.* Penetrating, shrill.

Durch'führung (für-oongk), *G.* Development; working out. Vide FORM.

Durchgang (gäng), *G.* Passage. **Durch'gangston.** Passing note, or changing note, called *regelmässig,* when on a weak beat; *unregelmässig,* on a strong beat (or *schwerer Durch'-gang*).

durchgehend (doorkh'gä-ĕnt), *G.* 1. Passing, transitional. 2. Complete. **d. Stimmen.** Complete organ-stops.

durch'komponert (nērt), *G.* "Composed through," used of a song whose every stanza has individual treatment. Through-composed.

durchschlagende (shläkh-ĕnt-ĕ), *G.* Free (of a reed).

durchstechen (stĕkh-ĕn), *G.* Vide RUN (2). **D.-stecher.** Notes made by running.

durée (dü-rā), *F.* Length, duration.

durezza (doo-rĕd'-zä), *I.* Hardness, harshness.

dur-moll Tonart (door'-môl-tōn'-ärt), *G.* Major-minor-mode. Vide COMBINATION MODE.

duro(a) (dooro), *I.* Rude, harsh.

durus, *L.* 1. Major, as *cantus d.* 2. Natural, as *b. durum.*

Dutch concert. Vide CONCERT.

Dütchen (düt'-khĕn), *G.* A small cornet.

duten (doo'-ten), *G.* To toot.

dux, *L.* "Leader, guide"; the subject of a fugue (q.v.)

dy'ad. A concord of two tones.

dynam'ics. The theory of the different degrees of power applied to notes.

Dystonie (des-to-nē'), *G.* and *Gr.* Bad intonation.

E

E. Pron. ā in *G.*; in *F.* and *I.* called *mi* (mē). 1. A musical pitch, two full steps above C. 2. All its octaves. 3. The major scale having four sharps; the minor scale relative to G major.

e (ā), *I.* And; written *ed* before vowels.

ear. 1. A projecting metal plate on either side of the mouth of organ-pipes. 2. A musical sense of pitch, interval, etc.; the capability of distinguishing between tone-qualities.

ebollizione (ā-bôl-lēt tsĭ-ō'-nĕ), *I.* Ebullition, overflow of emotion. **ebollimen'to.** Ebullient(ly).

écart (ā-kăr), *F.* A long stretch on the piano.

ec'bole, *Gr.* The sharpening of a tone.

eccedente (ĕt-chĕ-dĕn'-tĕ), *I.* Augmented.

ecclesia (ĕk-klā'zĭ-ä), *L.* and *I.* Church. **ecclesiastical modes.** Vide MODES. **ecclesiastico,** *I.* Ecclesiastic.

ecco (ĕk'-ko). 1. Behold. 2. Echo.

échappement (ā-shăp-män), *F.* Release. **double é.** Repeating-mechanism.

echeggiare (ā-kĕd-jä'-rĕ), *I.* To echo.

echei'on (pl. a), *Gr.* 1. A drum or gong. 2. A sound-screen. 3. Resonance-box of a lyre.

échelette (āsh-lĕt), *F.* Xylophone.
échelle (ā-shĕl), *F.* The scale or gamut.
échelon (āsh-lôṅ), *F.* A degree.
ech'o (in *F.* ā-ko). 1. An imitation of an echo. 2. An echo-stop. 3. A harpsichord-stop. e. cornet, e. dulciana. Organ-stops. e. organ. A set of pipes inside a box or at a distance giving an echo effect.
ech'ometer. A device for measuring the power of an echo.
éclisses (ā-klēs), *F.* Ribs (of a violin, etc.).
ec'logue. A pastoral.
ec'lysis, *Gr.* The flattening of a tone.
eco (ā-ko), *I.* Echo.
école (ā-kŭl), *F.* School, method.
écossais (ā-kôs-sā), écossaise (ā-kôs-sĕz), *F.*, Ecossäse (ā-kôs-sā'zĕ), *G.* "Scotch." 1. A grave old dance, in 3-2 or 3-4 time. 2. A lively country-dance in 2-4 time.
écu (ā-kü), *F.* A shield on the face of mandolins, etc.
ed (ĕd), *I.* And.
edel (ā'dl), *G.* Noble.
E-dur (ā-door), *G.* E major.
Effekt', *G.*, effet (ĕf-fä), *F.*, effet'to, *I.* Effect. Effekt-piano, G. The effect marked "fp" (forte piano).
effort (ĕf-fôr), *F.* A guttural vocal attack.
également (ā-găl-mäṅ), *F.* Equally, evenly. égalité (ā-găl-ĭ-tā), *F.* Equality, evenness.
egloga (āl'yō-ga), *I.*, églogue (āg-lôg), *F.* A pastoral.
eguale (ā-goo-ä'lĕ), *I.* 1. Equal, even. 2. Applied to a composition for voices or instrs. of one kind, as female voices only. egualezza (lĕd'zä), egualanza (än'-tsä). Evenness. egualmen'te. Evenly, alike.
ei'domusikon. A melograph.
eifrig (īf'-rĭkh), *G.* Ardent.
eigentlich (īkh'-ĕnt-lĭkh), *G.* Right, strict, in perfect time. e. Fuge. A strict fugue. e. Kadenz. Perfect cadence.
Eigenton (ī'-khĕn-tōn), *G.* The tone natural to a wind or other instr., its "own tone."
eight or 8. The octave. con 8va. With the octave below or above. Vide OTTAVA.
eighteenth. A double octave plus a fourth.
eight-foot. 8-ft. Vide FOOT.
eighth. 1. An octave. 2. An eighth note. eighth note. A quaver, of half

the value of a quarter note. eighth rest. A rest of an eighth-note duration.
eilen (ī'lĕn), *G.* To hurry. eilend (lĕnt). Accelerating. eilig (ī'-lĭkh). Swift.
ein (īn), eine (ī'nĕ), eins (īns), *G.* One, once. einchörig (kā'-rĭkh). Used, 1. Of an instr. which has but one string to each note. 2. Of a comp. for one choir. eingestrichen (īn-ghĕ-strĭkh'-ĕn). Once-accented. Vide PITCH.
einfach (īn-fäkh), *G.* Simple, plain. einfache Kontrapunkt. Simple counterpoint. Einfalt. Simplicity.
Eingang (īn'-gäng), *G.* Introduction Eingang der Messe. The Introit. Eingang'schlüssel. Introductory key.
eingreifen (īn'-grī-fĕn), *G.* (a) To strike (of strings). (b) To interlace (of the fingers in piano-playing)
Einheit (īn'-hīt), *G.* Unity. einhelfen. To prompt. Einhelfer. Prompter. einige(n) (ī'nĭkh-ĕn). Some, any Einigkeit (kīt). Unity, harmony. Einklang (īn'kläng). Unison. Einlage (īn-läkh-ĕ). A short interpolation. Einleitung (īn'lī-toongk). Introduction. Einleitungssatz (zäts) or spiel. Overture, prelude. einmal (īn-mäl). Once. Einmüthigkeit (īn-müt'-ĭkh-kīt). Unanimity. Einsaiter (zī'-ter). The monochord. Einsang. A solo. Einsatz. (a) Attack. (b) Entrance. Einsatzstück. Crook. Einsatzzeichen (īn'zätz-tsīkh'n). 1. The sign the leader gives the performers to commence. 2. In a canon the mark indicating the entrance of the imitating voice. einschlagen. To strike in. einschlafend. Dying away. einschmeichelnd (shmīkh-ĕlnt). Insinuating. Einschnitt (shnĭt). A phrase. einsetzen. To enter, attack. einsetzender Hornist. A horn-player, whose thick lips must surround, instead of press the mouthpiece. einsingen. (a) To learn singing by practice. (b) To lull to sleep. einspielen. (a) To get an instr. in good working order. (b) To attain command of a piece. einstimmen. To tune. einstimmig. For one part. Einstimmigkeit. Literally, one-voiced-ness. eintönig. Monotonous. Eintracht. Accord. einträchtig (trĕkh-tĭkh). Concordant. eintretend (trā-tĕnt). Enter-

ing. **Eintritt.** Entrance, entry, beginning. **Einverständniss** (fershtĕnt-nĭs). Agreement.

Eïs (ā'-ēs), *G.* E sharp. **Eïsis.** E double sharp.

Eisenvioline (ī'-zĕn), *G.* A nail-fiddle.

Eisteddfod (ēs'-tĕd-fôd), *Welsh.* An assemblage of Welsh bards and musicians; first held in 1078.

Eklog(u)e (āk'-lôkh-ĕ), *G.* Eclogue.

éla. Name of the highest tone in the Aretinian scale; e''.

electric organ. One having electric connections in place of trackers.

electric piano. A piano inv. 1851, and unsuccessfully attempted often since, till Dr. Eisenmann of Berlin in 1891 succeeded in obtaining an instr. capable of swelling on a sustained tone, and securing many beautiful effects.

élégamment (āl-ā-găm-män̄), *F.,* **elegantemen'te,** *I.* Elegantly, gracefully. **elegante** (āl-ĕ-gän'tĕ), *I.* Elegant. **eleganza** (āl-ĕ-gän'tsä), *I.* Elegance, grace.

elegia (ā-lä-jē'-ä), *I.,* **élégie** (á-lä-zhē), *F.,* **Elegie** (ĕl-ä-jē'), *G.,* **elegy,** *E.* A mournful composition or dirge. **elegiaco** (jäk'-ō), *I.,* **élégiaque** (ā-lä-zhăk), *F.* **elegiac.**

él'ément (ā-lä-män̄), *F.* One of the series of tones in a scale. **é. métrique.** A measure-note.

elevamen'to, elevatezza (āl-ā-vätĕd'-zä), *I.,* **elevazione** (vä-tsĭ-ō'nĕ). Elevation. **elevato** (vä'to). Elevated. exalted, sublime.

eleva'tio, *L.,* **elevation.** 1. The upbeat. 2. The rising of a melody beyond the compass of a mode. 3. A motet or other comp. performed during the elevation of the Host.

eleventh. An octave plus a fourth.

Elfte (ĕlf'te), *G.* Eleventh.

Ellenlänge (ĕllĕn-lĕng-ĕ), *G.* An ell (in pipe-measuring).

Ellis's system. See A. J. ELLIS in the B. D.

embellir (än̄-bĕl-lēr), *F.* To embellish. **embellissement** (lēs-män̄), *F.* Embellishment.

embellishment. Ornament, decoration. Vide GRACE.

embouchure (än̄-boo-shür), *F.* 1. The mouthpiece of a wind instr. 2. The position the mouth assumes in playing the instrument.

E-moll (ā-môl), *G.* E minor.

emmelei'a, *Gr.* 1. Consonance. 2. A tragic dance.

emozione (ā-mō-tsĭ-ō'-nĕ), *I.* Emotion.

empâter les sons (än-pä-tä lä sòṅ), *F.* To produce a legato. **exécution** or **voix empatée.** A blurred style.

Empfindung (ĕmp-fĭnt'-oongk), *G.* Feeling, emotion. **e. svoll.** Full of feeling.

Emphase (*G.* ĕm-fä'-zĕ, *F.* än̄-făz). Emphasis. **emphasis.** Stress or accent.

emphatique (än̄-fă-tēk), *F.* **emphatisch** (ĕm-fä'-tĭsh), *G.* Emphatic. **emphatiquement** (tēk-män̄), *F.* Emphatically.

empito (ĕm'-pē-tō), *I.* Impetuosity. **empituosamen'te.** Impetuously.

emporté (än-pôr-tā), *F.* Passionate, hurried. **emportement** (pôrt-män̄). Passion, transport.

empressé (än-prĕs-sā), *F.* Hurried. **empressement** (prĕs-män̄), *F.* Zeal.

en (än̄), *F.* In; often used with the participle, as *en descendant,* descending; *en badinant* scherzando.

enarmo'nico, *I.* Enharmonic.

enclavure du manche (än̄-klă-vür dü män̄sh). Space for the insertion of the neck (of a violin) into the belly.

encore (än̄-kôr), *F.* Again; a recall. Used by the English to demand a repetition; the French use "*bis.*"

Ende (ĕnt'ĕ), *G.* End, conclusion.

end-man. One of the chief negro minstrels who sits at either end of their semicircle.

energia (ĕn-ĕr-jē'ä), *I.,* **energie** (ĕn-ĕr-zhē), *F.* Energy. **energico** (ĕn-ār'jĭ-kō), **energicamen'te,** *I.* Energetic(ally). **energique** (ĕn-ĕr-zhēk), *F.,* **energisch** (ĕn-ăr'zhĭsh), *G.* Energetic. **energiquement** (zhēk-män̄), *F.* Energetically.

enfasi (ĕn-fä'zē), *I.* Emphasis. **enfat'ico, enfaticamen'te,** *I.* Emphatic(ally).

enfiatamente (ĕn-fē-ä'-tä-mĕn'-tĕ), *I.* Proudly.

enfler (än̄-flā), *F.* To swell, increase.

eng (ĕngk), *G.* Close, compressed; applied, (a) to the stretto in fugue, (b) to narrow straight organ-pipes. **enge Harmonie** (or **Lage**). Close harmony.

Engelstimme (ĕng'ĕl-shtĭm-mĕ), *G.* "Angel voice." Angelica; a stop.

Engführung (ĕng'-für-oongk), *G.* Stretto.

englisch (ĕng'lĭsh), *G.* English. **e. Horn.** English horn. **e. Mechanik,** in pianos, the English action. **e. Tanz.** Vide ANGLAISE. **e. Viollet**

(vē-ō-lĕt'). (a) An old way of tuning the violin—e-a-e'-a'. (b) An obsolete *viola a'amore* with 14 sympathetic strings beneath the others.

English fingering. Same as American fingering.

English horn. A species of oboe (q.v.).

enguichure (äṅ-gē-shür), *F.* Embouchure.

enharmonic, enharmon'icus, *L.,* **enharmonique** (ĕn-ăr-môn-ēk), *F.,* **enharmonisch** (ĕn-här-mō'-nīsh), *G.* 1. Differing in name or notation, but not in sound, as c sharp and d flat. Mathematically and actually c ♯ and d ♭ differ by an appreciable interval, but for convenience sake and in the name of *temperament* (q.v.) they are the same tone on the keyboard instruments and, by contagion, have become so in singing and the playing of stringed and wind instruments. Tones that are identical in our present artificial scale, but not in actuality or acoustics, are called **enharmonic**; hence *chords and intervals* written differently and sounding alike are called **enharmonic,** and the change of the key by such chords is called **enharmonic modulation;** the writing of the same chord in 2 notations is **e. change.** Instruments have been frequently invented making a distinction between such tones as c sharp and d flat, and giving them separate digitals. These instrs. are called **enharmonic.** The **e. scale** is, strictly, a scale with more than the twelve semitones of our usual scale; the term is loosely applied to scales as c sharp and d flat, having the same sound. 2. Vide MODES. 3. Vide DIESIS.

enigmatical. Vide CANON.

énoncer (ā-nôṅ-sā), *F.* To enunciate. **énonciation** (ā-nôṅ-siăs-yôṅ). Enunciation.

eno'plia, *Gr.* Spartan war-music.

ensemble (än-säṅ'bl), *F.* 1. Together; the whole; all the factors considered as a unit. 2. The quality of their co-operation. **morceau d'e.** A number requiring more than one performer.

entgegen (ĕnt-gā'khĕn), **e.-gesetzt,** *G.* Contrary, opposite.

entr'acte (än-träkt), *F.* Music played between the acts, or of such character.

entran'te, entrata (ĕn-trä'-tä), *I.,* **entrada** (ĕn-trä'-dhá), *Sp.,* **entrée** (äṅ-trā), *F.* 1. Entrance; introduction, or music of such character, as in a ballet. 2. An old polonaise-like dance in 4-4 time.

entre-chats (äṅt-rŭ-shä), *F.* The entering bounds of a dancer.

entremese (ĕn-trĕ-mä'-sä), *Sp.* A burlesque interlude.

entremets (äṅt-rŭ-mä), *F.* Slight interlude.

entry (obs.). An act.

Entscheidung (ĕnt'-shī-doongk), *G.* Decision. **entschieden** (ĕnt-shē'-dĕn), *G.* Decided.

entschlafen (ĕnt-shlä'fĕn), *G.* To die away (lit. to fall asleep).

Entschliessung (ĕnt'-shlēs-soongk), *G.* Resolution.

entschlossen (ĕnt-shlôs'sĕn), *G.* Resolute. **Entschluss** (ĕnt'-shloos), *G.* Resolution.

Entwurf (ĕnt'-voorf), *G.* Sketch, outline.

enunciato (ā-noon-chĭ-ä'-tō), *I.* Enunciated. **enunciazione** (ä'-tsĭ-ō'-nĕ), *I.* Enunciation.

en'voy. Postscript, or ending, of a ballad.

Eolia (ē-ō'lĭ-ä), **Eolian** (ē-ō'lĭ-än), *I* Vide ÆOLIAN.

epicède (ĕp-i-sĕd), *F.,* **epicedio** (ĕp-ĭ-chä'dĭ-ō), *I.,* **epice'dium,** *L.* An elegy, dirge, funeral-song, or ode.

epigo'nion, *Gr.,* **epigo'nium,** *L.* An ancient Greek lyre, with 40 strings, named from Epignon.

epile'nia, *Gr.* Vineyard songs.

epinic'ion, *Gr.* 1. A triumphal song. 2. The Triumphal Sanctus in the Greek Church.

epio'dion, *Gr.* A dirge.

episode, épisode (ā-pē-sôd), *F.,* **episo'dio,** *I.* All incidental portions of composition. Vide FUGUE. **episodisch** (ĕp-ĭ-zō-dĭsh), *G.* Episodic.

epistle side. The left or south side of the altar; the right or north is the gospel side.

epis'trophe, *Gr.* A refrain.

epitalamio (ĕp-ĭ-tä-lä'mĭ-ō), *I.,* **epith'alme** (ĕp-ĭ-tălm), *F.,* **epithalami'on,** *Gr.,* **epithalamium,** **epithal'amy,** *L.* and *E.* Wedding-ode.

epit'asis, *Gr.* Vide ANESIS.

epito'nion, *Gr.* 1. A pitch-pipe. 2. A tuning-wrench.

ep'ode, *Gr.* After-song. 1. A refrain. 2. The conclusion of an ode. 3. A retraction.

ep'tacorde (ĕp-tä-kôrd), *F.*, eptacor'-do, *I.* 1. A heptachord. 2. A seventh. 3. A scale of seven notes.

equabile (ā-kwä'bĭ-lā), *I.* Equal, alike. equabilmen'te. Smoothly.

equal. 1. Of counterpoint, consisting of notes of equal duration. 2. Vide TEMPERAMENT. 3. Of voices, alike (all male, for instance); not mixed.

e'quisonance, equisonnance (ā-kē-sŭn-näns), *F.* Unison, as of octaves. e'quisonant. Of like sound; in unison. In guitar music used of different ways of stopping the same note.

equiso'no (ā-kwē'sō-nō), *I.* In the unison or octave.

equiv'ocal. Used of chords which may by slight change in notation belong to more than one key.

Erard action. Vide HARP.

erbeb, *Arab.* Rebec.

erfreulich (ĕr-froi'-lĭkh), *G.* Joyous.

ergrif'fen, *G.* Stirred, affected. E-heit (hīt). Agitation.

erhaben (ĕr-hä'-bĕn), *G.* Exalted, sublime. Erhabenheit (hīt). Sublimity.

erheben (ĕr-hā'bĕn), *G.* To raise, to elevate; as the hand, in beating time.

erhöhen (ĕr-hā'ĕn), *G.* To raise. Erhöhung (ĕr-hā'oongk), *G.* Raising, sharpening. E.-zeichen. Sharps, double sharps, or naturals following flats.

ermattet (ĕr-mät'-tĕt), *G.* Exhausted.

Erniedrigung (ĕr-nē'-drĭkh-oongk), *G.* Depression by means of a flat or natural. E.-szeichen. A sign for lowering a note.

ernst (ĕrnsht), ernsthaft (ĕrnst'häft), *G.* Earnest. Ernsthaftigkeit (ĕrnst'häf-tĭkh-kīt), Ernstlichkeit (lĭkh-kīt). Earnestness.

Erntelied (ĕrn'tĕ-lēt), *G.* Harvest-song.

Eröffnung (ĕr-ĕf'noongk), *G.* Opening, beginning. E.-sstück. Overture.

eroico (ā-ro'ĭ-kō or -a), *I.* Heroic. "*Sinfonia eroica,*" Beethoven's 3d symphony.

erot'ico, *I.*, érotique (ā-rô-tēk), *F.*, erot'ic. 1. Amorous. 2. An amorous composition.

erst (ĕrsht), *G.* First. erste Mal. First time.

ersterben, *G.* To die away.

ertönen (ĕr-tä'-nĕn), *G.* To sound.

Erweckung (ĕr-vĕk'oongk), *G.* Animation.

erweitern (ĕr-vī'-tĕrn), *G.* To develop, expand. erweitert. Expanded, as

erweiterte Harmonie. Open harmony. erweiterter Satz. A movement fully developed thematically. Erweiterung. The widening of an interval in a fugal theme.

Erzähler (ĕr-tsä'lĕr), *G.* The narrator in Passion music.

Erzlaüte (ĕrts'-low-tĕ), *G.* The archlute.

Es (ĕs), *G.* The note E flat.

esacordo (ā-sä-kôr'do), *I.* 1. Hexachord. 2. A sixth.

esat'to, *I.* Exact, strict.

Es-dur (ĕs-door), *G.* E flat major.

esecuzione (ās-ĕ-koot-sĭ-ō'nĕ), *I.* Execution. esecuto're. Performer.

eseguire (ā-sā-goo-ē'-rĕ). To execute.

esem'pio, *I.* Example.

esercizio (ā-sĕr-chē'tsĭ-ō) (pl. i), *I.* An exercise.

Es-es (ĕs-ĕs), *G.* E double flat.

esitamento (ā-sē-ta-mĕn'tō), esitazione (ā-sē-tä-tsĭ-ō'nĕ), *I.* Hesitation.

Es-mol (ĕs-môl), *G.* E flat minor.

espace (ŭs-păs), *F.* A space in the staff.

espagnol (ĕs-pän-yôl), *F.*, espagnuolo (ĕs-pän-yoo-ō'lō), *I.* "Spanish"; in Spanish style.

esper'to, *I.* Expert.

espiran'do, *I.* Dying.

espr., espress. Abbr. of *Espressivo*.

espressione (sĭ-ō'nĕ), *I.* Expression, feeling. espressivo (sē'vo), *I.* Expressive.

espringale (ĕs-prĭn-gä'-lĕ), *I.* Spring-dance.

essem'pio, *I.* Example.

essen'tial. (a) Of *harmonies*, the three chief harmonies in any key, *viz.*, the tonic, dominant, and subdominant. (b) Of *notes*, those that make up a chord, in distinction from ornamental, and other foreign notes. e seventh. (a) The leading note. (b) The 7th chord in the dominant.

estemporale (rä'lĕ), estemporaneo (rä'-nĕ-ō), *I.* Extemporaneous.

estinguendo (ĕs-tĭn-goo-ĕn'dō), *I.* Dying away.

estinto (ĕs-tēn'-tō) (or a), *I.* Extinguished, almost inaudible.

estravaganza (ĕs-trä-vä-gän'tsä), *I.* Extravaganza.

estremamente (ĕs-trā-mä-men'-tĕ), *I.* Extremely.

estribilho (ĕs-trĭ-bēl'-yō). A familiar Portuguese air.

estrinciendo (ĕs-trēn-chän'do), *I.* Playing incisively

estriniendo (ĕs-trēn-yän'do), *I.* Very legato.

es'tro, *I.* Poetic fire.

et, *L.* And.

et (ā), *F.* And.

étalon (ā-tă-lôn), *F.* Vide SCALE 3.

éteinte (ā-tănt), *F.* Almost inaudible.

étendre (ā-tändr), *F.* To extend, spread. **étendue** (ā-tän-dü). Compass.

Et Incarna'tus, *L.* "And He was born," etc. Part of the Credo.

étoffé (ā-tôf-fā), *F.* Having "body," as a voice.

étouffer (ā-toof-fā), *F.* To deaden the tone. **étouffé** (ā-toof-fā). Stifled, muffled; in harp-playing a deadening of the tones by touching the strings. **étouffoir** (ā-toof-wär). Damper.

etre en répétition (ĕt'răñ rā-pā-tēs-yôn), *F.* To be in rehearsal.

Et Res'urrexit, *L.* "And rose again." A part of the Credo.

-et'to (or **a**), *I.* Little; an Italian suffix, as *trombetta.* A little trumpet.

et'tacordo, *I.* Instr. with 7 strings.

étude (ā-tüd), *F.* A study. A comp. outwardly intended for practice and facility in some special difficulty of technic; often marked with much art, and in the **é. de concert** (dŭ-kôn-săr), concert-study, intended for public display. **étudier** (ā-tüd-yā). To study, to practise. Vide STUDY.

Et Vi'tam, *L.* "And life everlasting." Part of the Credo.

etwas (ĕt'väs), *G.* Some, somewhat. **e. langsamer.** A little slower.

eufonia (ā-oo-fō-nē'ä), *I.* Euphony. **eufo'nico.** Harmonious.

euharmon'ic (ū). Producing harmony or concordant sounds. Well-harmonied, not tempered. **e. organ.** An instr. of American origin, inv. by H. W. Poole, 1848, and containing the untempered intervals. Vide ENHARMONIC.

euouae. The vowels in the words "Seculorum, Amen," at the end of the "Gloria Patri"; (a) the trope of the Gregorian Lesser Doxology; (b) any trope (q.v.).

Euphon (yoo-fôn). A glass harmonica (compass from c to f′′′) inv. by Chladni, about 1790; the tone produced by rubbing with wet fingers strips of glass, connected with metal rods; also called **eupho'nium.**

eupho'niad. An instr. of American origin, containing thirty keys, and

tones of the organ, horn, bassoon, clarinet, and violin.

euphonic-horn, eupho'nion. Sommerophone.

eupho'nious. Harmonious.

eupho'nium. A bass brass instr. used in military bands. It has two tubes, played from a single mouthpiece.

Euter'pe, *G.* The seventh muse, patroness of flute-music and song.

evacua'tio, *L.* In old notation, the reduction by one-half of a solid note's value by writing only its outline.

Evakuant (ā-väk-oo-änt'), *G.* The exhaust-pallet; also **evacuant,** *E.*

éveillé (ā-vā-yā), *F.* Gay, sprightly.

evening, or **even, song.** Evening service in the Anglican Church.

ever'sio, *L.* In cpt., inversion.

evirato (ā-vē-rä'-tō), *I.* A eunuch with a soprano or alto voice.

evolu'tio, *L.* In cpt., inversion.

evovae. Vide EUOUAE.

exécutant (ĕx-ā-kü-tän), *F.* A performer.

exe'quiae, *L.,* **Exequien** (ĕx-ā'kwĬ-ĕn), *G.* Obsequies; requiems.

exercice (ĕx-ĕr-sēs), *F.,* **Exercit'ium** (ĕx-ĕr-tsē'tsĬ-oom), *G.,* **exercise.** A practice piece; a problem in composition, or technic.

exhaust pallet or **valve.** A stop opening a valve which exhausts the bellows of an organ.

exposi'tion. Development; the working out of a theme. Vide FORM and FUGUE.

expressif (ĕx-prŭs-ēf), *F.* Expressive.

expres'sion (in *F.* ĕx-prŭs-yôn). The psychological and spiritual elements of music, its message and eloquence. The delivery of a composition with fidelity to its meaning. Hence an **expression-mark** is any sign that will aid in the interpretation of a composition. In French the word e. is also used specifically of the vibrato effect. **expression-stop.** An harmonium-stop giving the pedals close control of the expression.

expressive-organ, Expressivorgel (sĕf-ôr-khĕl), *G.,* **orgue expressif,** *F.* The harmonium.

extempora'neous. Without premeditation. **extem'pore,** *L.* Improvised; off-hand. **extemporize.** To improvise. **extemporizing machine.** A melograph for recording extemporization.

extended. 1. Dispersed, as a chord. 2. Enlarged, as a development. **e**

phrase. One with three measures instead of the usual two, etc. **e. section.** One containing from 5 to 8 measures.

extension (ĕz-täns-yôṅ), *F.* Stretch, or compass on the violin; the extension of the forefinger or little finger of the left hand. **extension pedal.** Loud pedal.

extra'neous. Foreign to the key. **e. modulation.** Transition to an unrelated key.

extravaganza (ĕx-trä-vä-gän'tsä), *I.* 1. An ornament in bad taste. 2. A musical burlesque, usually spectacular.

extreme, extrême (ĕx-trĕm), *F.* 1. The highest and lowest parts. 2. Augmented. **chord of the e. sixth.** An altered chord. (Vide ALTERED.)

F

ƒ. *E.* and *G.*; in *F.* and *I.* called **fà** (fä). 1. A musical pitch, a perfect fourth above C in all its octaves. 2. The major key having one flat; the minor key relative to A flat major. **F clef, F Schlüssel,** *G.* The bass clef gripping the line *F.* **f. holes** (in *G.* **F. Löcher** (ĕf-lĕkh-ĕr); in *F.* **les F.** (lä-zĕf). The f-shaped sound-holes in the belly of violins, etc. **f, ff, fff,** etc. Abbr. of *forte* and *fortissimo.*

ƒa (fä), *I.* 1. The fourth of the syllables of solmisation (q.v.). 2. Name of F. in France and Italy, **fa-feint** (fäṅ), *F.,* **fa fint'o,** *I.,* **fa fict'um,** *L.* Obsolete term for any flatted note. **fa mi.** Formerly the descent of half a tone from F to E; now any such descent. **fa bémol,** F flat. **fa dièse.** F sharp. **faburden.** 1. A counterpoint of thirds and sixths added by ear to a *cantus firmus.* 2. Later any improvised accompaniment. 3. A burden. 4. A drone-bass. 5. Intonation of the Psalms.

fabliau (fåb-lĭ-ō), *F.* An old narrative poem. **fablier** (lĭ-ä). A trouvère.

faces d'un accord (fäs d'ŭn ăk-kôr), *F.* The positions of a chord; a triad has 3, a seventh 4, etc.

fach (fäkh), *G.* (lit. -fold). Ranked; as **dreifach.** Three-ranked (of pipes).

fächerförmiges Pedal (fĕkh'-ĕr-fĕr-mĭkh-ĕs pä-däl), *G.* A fan-shaped pedal-board.

facile (fă-sēl), *F.,* **facile** (fä'-chē-lĕ). Light, easy. **facilità** (fä-chē-lĭ-tä'), *I.,* **facilité** (fä-sēl-ĭ-tä), *F* 1. Facil-

ity. 2. An easier arrangement of a piece or passage. **facilement** (fä-sēl-mäṅ), *F.,* **facilmente** (fä-chēl-mĕn'-tä), *I.* Easily.

Fackeltanz (fäk'ĕl-tänts), *G.* Dance with flambeaux in a minuet form, 4-4 time.

facture (fäk-tür), *F.,* **Faktur** (fäktoor'), *G.* 1. Scheme or construction, workmanship. 2. The scale of pipes.

-fädig (fä-dĭkh), *G.* Threaded (of violin-strings), as **vierfädig.** 4-threaded.

fading (fåd'-ĭng), *Irish.* A dance; a refrain.

fag. Abbr. of *fagotti.*

fag'ot, *E.,* **Fagott** (fä-gôt'), *G.,* **fagot'-to,** *I.* 1. A bassoon. 2. A reed-stop (also **Fagottzug**). **fagottino** (tē'no), *I.* A small bassoon. **Fagottist** (fä-gôt-test'), *G.* **fagottista** (tēs'-tä), *I.* A performer on the bassoon. **fagotto contro,** *I.* A bassoon, an octave, a fifth, or a fourth lower. **fagotto'ne.** A large obs. bassoon, an octave lower.

fah. Fa in Tonic sol-fa.

Fähnenmarsch (fä'-nĕn-märsh), *G.* The march played when the colours are lodged.

faible (fĕb'l) F. Weak. **temps f.** Weak-beat.

faire (făr), *F.* To do, make. **f. des fredons.** A trill. **faites bien sentir la mélodie** (fĕt-bǐ-äṅ-sän-tēr lä mä-lō-dē), *F.* Keep the melody very distinct.

fa-la. 1. An old refrain. 2. A song with such refrain or a dance. **falalel'la,** *I.* A nonsense song.

fall. 1. A cadence. 2. Vide FLY.

falo'tico, *I.* Fantastic.

falsa (fäl'-sä) (or o), *I.* **false,** *E.,* **falsch** (fälsh), *G.* False, wrong, out of tune. **false accent.** Accent removed from the first to the second or fourth beat. **f. bordone.** (a) Faburden. (b) The reciting-notes. **f. cadence.** An imperfect or interrupted cadence. **f. fifth.** An im perfect fifth. **f. relation.** (a) The appearance simultaneously or consecutively in different voices of the same notes chromatically altered, as C sharp and C flat, implying a disagreement or incompatibility. (b) The appearance of the tritone (q.v.) in different voices. Though strictly forbidden in the text-books, late composers ignore the rule.

altogether. **f. string.** An ill-made string giving a bad tone. **f. triad.** The diminished triad having a false fifth.

Falsett (fäl-zĕt'), *G.*, **falset'to,** *I.* 1. The top or artificial register of the voice, having an unnatural or effeminate sound. 2. One who uses this register. **fan'cy.** 1. A slight tune. 2. A fantasy.

fandan'go, *Sp.* A popular Spanish dance in triple time accompanied with castanets (or tambourine) and guitar, the dance being interpolated between vocal couplets.

fanfare, *E.* (pron. in *F.* fän-fär), **fanfara** (fän-fä'-rä), *I.* 1. A trumpet-flourish. 2. A brass-band.

fantaisie (fän-tĕ-zē), *F.*, **fantasia** (fän-tä-zē'ä), *I.*, **Fantasie** (fän-tä-zē'), *G.* 1. Fantasy, caprice, a composition free in spirit and form. 2. An arpeggiated prelude. 3. A potpourri. 4. An improvisation. 5. Formerly a work, vocal or instrumental, full of free imitation. **free fantasia** or **fantasy,** same as Development. Vide FORM. **fantasio'so,** *I.* Fantastic. **fantasiren** (zē'rĕn), *G.* To improvise.

fantas'tico, **fantasticamen'te,** *I.*, **fantastique** (fän-täs-tēk), *F.*, **fantastisch** (fän-täs'-tĭsh), *G.* Capricious.

faran'dola, *I.*, **farandole** (fär-äṅ-dôl), **farandoule** (fär-äṅ-dool), *F.* A circle dance in 6-8 time.

farneticamen'te, *I.* Deliriously.

farsa in musica (moo'zi-ka), *I.* A burletta.

farsia (fär'sĭ-ä), *I.* A canticle in Italian and Latin sung at Catholic festivals.

fascia (fä'-shä), *I.* 1. A tie. 2. A rib.

fasto'so, **fastosamen'te,** *I.* Pompous(ly).

fattura (fät-too'-rä), *I.* Vide FACTURE.

faucette (fō-sĕt), **fausset** (fō-sä), *F.*, Falsetto.

faux (fō) or **fausse** (fōs), *F.* False, out of tune. **f. accord** (fō zăk-kôr). A dissonance. **f. bourdon** (fō-boor-dôṅ). Vide FABURDEN. **f. quinte.** Imperfect fifth. **F. clef.** The bass-clef. Vide CLEF.

F-dur (ĕf-door), *G.* F major.

feathering. The bowing of swift staccato.

Federklavier (fä-dĕr-klä-fēr'), *G.* Spinet.

feeders. Small bellows to supply large.

Feier (fī'ĕr), *G.* Festival, celebration. **F.-gesang.** Anthem **feierlich.** Festive, solemn. **F.-keit.** Solemnity.

feigned voice. Falsetto voice.

feilen (fī-lĕn), *G.* To polish.

fein (fīn), *G.* Fine, refined.

feint. In drum music, a figure.

feinte (fĕnt), *F.* Old name for semitone, accidental.

Feld (fĕlt), *G.* Field. **F. flöte.** A peasant flute. **F. Kunstpfeifer** (koonst'pfī-fĕr). A military musician. **Feldmusik** (fĕlt-moo-zēk'). Military music. **Feldrohr** (rōr), *G.* A rural pipe. **F.-stück.** A cavalry call. **F.-ton.** The key-note of a military wind instr. **F.-trompete.** Military trumpet.

fe'rial. Non-festal, secular.

fer'ma, *I.* Firm. **fermamen'te,** *I.* Firmly.

fermare il tuono. Vide MESSA DI VOCE.

fer'mate, *E.* (in *G.* fĕr-mä'-tĕ), **fermata** (fĕr-mä'-tä), *I.* 1. A symbol ⌒ or ⌣ above or below a note, rest or bar indicating a long pause upon it; *f. ad libitum,* often occurring before a cadenza. 2. A stop, on the violin.

fermato (mä'-tō), *I.* Firmly, **fermezza** (fĕr-mĕd'-zä). Firmness. **fermo** (fĕr'mo). Firm. Vide CANTUS FIRMUS.

fermement (fĕrm-mäṅ), *F.* Firmly.

Ferne (fĕr'nĕ), *G.* Distance. **wie aus der F.** (vĕ-ows-dĕr). As if from the distance. **Fern-flöte.** A covered 8-ft. stop. **Fern-werk.** Echo-organ.

feroce (fä-rō'-chĕ), **ferocemen'te,** *I.* Fierce(ly). **ferocità** (fä-rō-chĭ-tä). Fierceness.

fertig (fĕr-tĭkh), *G.* Ready, nimble. **F.-keit** (kīt). Dexterity.

fervemment (făr-vĕ-mäṅ), *F.* Fervently.

ferven'te, **fer'vido,** *I.* Fervent. **ferventemen'te,** **fervidamen'te.** Vehemently.

Fes (fĕs), *G.* The note Fb. **Feses** (fĕs'ĕs). F double flat.

Fest (fĕsht), *G.* 1. Feast, festival. 2. Firm, steady. **Festigkeit** (fĕs-tĭkh-kīt). Firmness, steadiness. **festlich** (fĕst-lĭkh). Festive, solemn **Festlichkeit.** Solemnity. **Festlied.** A festive-song. **Festouvertüre.** A brilliant overture. **Festzeit** (tsīt). Festival-time.

festivo (fĕs-tē'vō), **festivamen'te**, *I.* Gay(ly). **festività** (fĕs-tē-vĭ-tä). Festivity, gayety.

festo'so, *I.* Merry, cheerful, gay.

Feuer (foi'ĕr), *G.* Fire, ardour, passion. **feurig** (rĭkh). Ardent, passionate.

fff. Abbr. of *Fortissimo.*

F holes. Vide F.

fiacco (fĭ-äk'kō), *I.* Feeble, languishing.

fiasco (fĭ-äs'-kō), *I.* A failure; not so used in Italy.

fiato (fĭ-ä'-tō), *I.* Breath; voice.

fictus(a)-(um), *L.* "Feigned." 1. Vide FA. 2. **musica ficta.** Former name for music transposed.

fiddle. Violin. **iron f.** An arrangement of nails or rods played with a bow, inv. by Jn. Wilde, 18th cent. **fiddler.** Violinist, commonly a poor player. **fiddlestick.** Violin-bow.

Fidel (fē'-dĕl), *G.* Violin.

fi'des, *L.* 1. A string. 2. A stringed instr. **fid'icen.** One who plays a stringed instr. **fidicina.** A woman-player.

fidic'ula, *L.* A small lute.

fiducia (fĭ-doo'-chä), *I.* Confidence.

Fiedel (fē'-dl), *G.* A violin. **Strohfidel.** Xylophone. **F.-bogen** (bōkh'-ĕn). A violin-bow. **F.-brett** (brĕt). A squeaky violin. **Fiedler** (fēt'-lĕr). A fiddler.

fiel. An old name for violin.

field-music. Martial music.

fier (fē-ăr), **fière** (fĭ-ăr), *F.* Proud, lofty, fierce. **fièrement** (fĭ-ăr-mäṅ). Fiercely. **fièrté** (f'yăr-tä'). Fierceness.

fiero (fe-ä'-rō), **fieramen'te**, *I.* Fierce-(ly). **fierezza** (rĕd'-zä). Fierceness.

fife. 1. A 6-holed octave cross-flute, usually in the key of F or Bb, chiefly used in military music, differing from the piccolo in lacking keys; compass d'-d'''. 2. A 2-foot stop.

fif'faro, *I.* Fife.

fifre (fēfr), *F.* 1. A fife. 2. A fifer. 3. An harmonium-stop.

fifteenth. 1. An interval of two octaves. 2. A 2-ft. stop, two octaves above the diapasons.

fifth. 1. The fifth tone of a scale, the dominant. 2. An interval containing five tones, the extremes included. as C-G (the ratio being 2 : 3). The tonic and the dominant of a key constitute a *perfect* (or less strictly, *major*) *fifth.* To widen the interval by lowering the lower (or raising the

upper) tone a half-step results in an *augmented* (or *superfluous, extreme, sharp* or *pluperfect*) *fifth*, as c-g♯, or cb-g; to narrow the interval a semitone by raising the lower or lowering the upper tone a half-step results in a *diminished* (or *imperfect, false, flat, minor* or *defective*) *fifth.* Two parts or voices according to the rules may not progress by perfect fifths either in *conse̬utive* or *parallel* manner, whether the fifths are *open* or (*covered, concealed*) *hidden* (q.v.). Though this rule is the very ABC of harmonic law, it is not justified by science, by history, or by latest practice. **Circle of fifths.** Vide TEMPERAMENT. **fifthy.** With the second partial (a fifth) noticeably marked.

Figur (fē-goor'), *G.* A figure, or numeral.

figura (fē-goo'-rä), *L.* and *I.* Vide FIGURE. **f. liga'ta.** A ligature. **f. muta** (moo-ta). A rest. **f. obli'qua.** In old music, an oblique symbol indicating that two superimposed notes (as g-b) were to be sung obliquely (thus g-b-b-g).

figural, *E.* (in G. fē-goo-räl'). Figurate. **F.-gesang.** Cantus figuratus, counterpoint.

figuration. 1. The use of figures or ornamented passages in the variation of a theme. 2. The writing or the filling out of figured bass. 3. In cpt. the interpolation of figures, changing notes, etc.

figurato (fē-goo-rä'-tō), *I.*, **figuré** (fē-gü-rä), *F.* **figurate,** or **figured.** 1. Ornamented with figures, hence florid, free. 2. Provided with numerals, as **figured bass.** Vide BASS 6, and CHORD.

figure, *E.* (in *F.* pron. fĭ-gür). 1. A pattern or design in grouped notes which may be repeated variously. 2. A numeral, **f. of diminution.** A number diminishing the duration of a note.

fil (fēl), *F.* Thread (of a string).

filar il tuono or **la voce** (fē-lär ēl too-ō'-nō or lä vō'-chĕ), *I.*, **filer un son** or **la voix** (fē-lä rŭṅ sóṅ or lä vwä), *F.* To draw the tone out to a thread of sound.

filarmo'nico, *I.* Music-loving.

filet de voix (fē-lä dŭ vwä), *F.* A mere thread of tone.

filling-up. 1. Of parts, those of harmonic but not melodic use. 2. Of stops, mutation.

filo (fē'-lō), *I.* Thread. **f. di voce.** Softest possible tone.

filpen (fēl'-pĕn), *G.* Vide FISTULIREN.

fi'lum, *L.* Stem, of a note.

fin (făn), *F.* The end; fine. **f. à qui** (fă nä kē). End here.

fi'nal. The note of rest in church-modes corresponding to our Tonic; in authentic modes the *F.* is on the first degree; in plagal, on the 4th. These are called *regular finals.* Others occur frequently and are *irregular* or *confinals.* Vide MODES. **f. close.** A finishing cadence.

finale (fē-nä'-lĕ, *I.; in F.* fĭ-năl). 1. The conclusion, usually elaborate, as the closing chorus of an act in opera; in sonatas, symphonies, an independent movement. 2. A final.

final'is, *L.* Vide ACCENTUS ECCLESIASTICI.

fine (fē'-nĕ), *I.* The end; it may appear sometimes before a *da capo* sign, in which case the movement is to be played to the repeat-bar and then repeated to the Fine, where it ends.

Finger (In *E.* fĭng'-gĕr; in *G.* fĭng'-ĕr). Finger. **F.-bildner, finger-developer.** A device for keeping the last joint of the fingers up; inv. by Seeber. **F.-brett.** Finger-board. **F.-fertigkeit.** Agility. **F.-leiter** (līt'-ĕr). The chiroplast. **F.-satz, F.-setzung.** Fingering. **Enger** or **gedehnter, Fingersatz.** Close (or stretched) fingering. **F.-wechsel** (vĕkhs'l). Change of fingers. **fingerboard.** In a stringed instr. the neck on which the strings are stopped. **finger-cymbals.** Tiny cymbals fixed on the fingers. **finger-holes.** The holes on wind-instrs. by which the pitch is regulated.

fingering. 1. The manner of using the fingers on instrs. 2. The symbols indicating a fingering. In the *German F.* the thumb is marked 1, the fingers 2, 3, 4, 5; in an older German method the thumb was marked by a circle O; in the *English,* or *American F.* the thumb is marked with a cross, the fingers, 1, 2, 3, 4.

finire il tuono, *I.* Vide MESSA DI VOCE.

fi'nite. Of a canon, not repeated, ending with the finish of the theme; not "infinite."

finito(a) (fĭ-nē'-tō), *I.* Finished.

fino (fē'-nō), *I.* To, as far as, till.

finto(a) (fēn'-tō), *I.* Feigned. **ca-**

denza f. Vide CADENCE (f). **fa finto.** Vide FA.

fioco(a) (fĭ-ô'-kō), *I.* Hoarse, faint. **fiochetto.** Rather hoarse. **fiochezza** (fē-ō-kĕd'-zä). Hoarseness.

fiore (fĭ-ō'-rĕ), *I.* Flower. **a f. di labbre.** Lightly on the lip.

fioreggiare (fē-ō-rĕd-jä'-rĕ), *I.* To add figures to.

fioret'to, *I.* A little ornament.

fioriscente (fē-ō-rĭ-shĕn'-tĕ), *I.,* **fiorito** (fē-ō-rē'-tō). Florid. **fioritezza** (fē-ō-rĭ-tĕd'-zä). Embellishment.

fioritura (fē-ō-rĭ-too'rä) (pl. **e**), *I.* Florid ornament.

first. 1. The highest voice-part or string; the lowest line or space. 2 A unison or prime.

Fis (fēs), *G.* The note F♯. **Fis-dur** (fēs-door). F♯ major. **Fis-f.s.** The note F double sharp. **Fis-moll.** F♯ minor.

Fistel (fĭsh-tel), *G.* Falsetto (also **F.-stimme**).

Fistola (fēs'-tō-lä), *I.,* **fis'tula,** *L.* A reed, a pipe. **f. dulcis.** The *flûte à bec.* **f. germanica.** German flute. **f. panis** or **f. pastoralis.** The Pandean pipes. **f. pastorica.** An oaten pipe used in Roman theatres to express disapprobation. **fistulator,** *L.,* a piper. **fistuliren** (fĭs-too-lē'rĕn), *G.* 1. To sing falsetto. 2. Of organ-pipes, to overblow.

fith'ele. Old English name for fiddle.

fixed-Do. That system of solmisation in which the syllables are fixed, i. e., **do** is given always to C (sharp, flat. or natural), **re** to D, etc.

fixed tone or **intonation.** Used of the piano and instrs. in which the player cannot change the pitch of a tone, as on the violin, etc.

Flachflöte (fläkh'flā-tĕ), *G.* 1. Flageolet. 2. An organ-stop.

flag. 1. Abbr. for *flageolet,* or *flageolet tones.* 2. A hook.

flageolet'. E. (*F.* flăzh-ō-lā), **Flageolett** (flä-jĕ-ō-lĕt'), *G.,* **flagioletta** (flä-jō-lĕt'ta), *I.* 1. A small flute played at the end, compass g'-b''' flat. **double f.** An instr. with 2 different-sized flageolets meeting in one mouthpiece, inv. by Bainbridge, 1800. 2. **flageo'let** or **flageolet-tones** or **Töne.** Vide HARMONICS. 3. A 1- or 2-ft. stop.

flam. In drum music a grace note, *close f.,* as short as possible; *open f.,* with a brief interval.

Fla′mmenorgel, *G* Pyrophone.

Flaschinett (fläsh′ĭ-nĕt′), *G.* The flageolet.

flat. 1. A symbol (♭) lowering the note before which it is placed one semitone; placed in the signature it affects every note occurring on its line or space. The **double flat** (♭♭), formerly a *great flat*, lowers the note two semitones. **flat fifth.** Vide FIFTH. **flat tuning.** Of a lute tuned to the former lower French pitch. 2. *As a verb*, to lower a note a semitone; preferably to **flatten.**

flatter la corde (flăt-tä lä′ kôrd), *F.* To flatter or caress the string.

flautando (flä-oo-tän′dō), **flautato** (tä′to), *I.* 1. Drawing the bow gently across the strings near the bridge, producing a "fluty" tone. 2. Producing harmonics.

flauto (fla′oo-tō), *I.* Flute. **flautis′- ta.** Performer on the flute. **flautino** (tē′-no). 1. A small octave-flute. 2. A piccolo. 3. Same as *flautando.* **f. piccolo.** The shrill octave-flute. **f. a bec′co.** Beak-flute. **f. alto.** A tenor-flute used in bands. **f. amabile.** An organ-stop. **f. amoroso.** A 4-foot organ-stop. **f. dolce.** 1. A beak-flute. 2. An organ-stop. **flauto′ne.** A large bass-flute. **f. tedesco, transverso, traverso.** 1. The German or transverse flute. 2. An organ-stop.

flebile (flā′-bĭ-lĕ), **flebilmen′te,** *I.* Sad(ly), doleful(ly).

flessibile (flĕs-sē′-bĭ-lā), *I.* Flexible. **flessibilità** (lĭ-tä′), *I.* Flexibility.

Flick′opera, *G.* An opera with new words to old tunes.

fling. A Scotch Highland dance in 4-4 time.

F-Löcher, *G.* F holes. Vide F.

flon-flon (flôṅ-flôṅ), *F.* A refrain to old vaudevilles; hence, trash.

flor′id. Ornamental, embellished.

Flöte (flā′tĕ), *G.* Flute. **flötchen** (flĕt′- khĕn). A little flute. **F.-bass.** A bass-flute. **flöten.** To play the flute. **F.-spieler.** A flute-player. **F.-stimme, F.-zug.** A flute-stop. **Flötenwerk.** A small organ with only flue-pipes. **F. traverso.** 1. The transverse flute. 2. An organ-stop. **Flötist** (flā′-tēst). A flute-player.

flour′ish. 1. A trumpet-fanfare. 2. An embellishment.

flüchtig (flükh′tĭkh), *G.* Light(ly). **Flüchtigkeit** (kīt). Fleetness.

flue-pipe-stop-work. Vide PIPE.

Flügel (flü′-gĕl), *G.* "Wing," hence, 1. A wing-shaped instr.; or the modern grand piano. 2. The ear of a pipe. **F.-harfe.** A small table-harp with upright sound-board. **F.-horn.** 1. A bugle. 2. A keyed bugle or other keyed brass instrument.

flute, *E.,* **flu′ta,** *L.,* **flûte** (flüt), *F.* 1. Now generally used of the *transverse* (or *cross*, or *German*) *flute.* The *beak-* (or *direct*) *flute* (in various sizes) is obsolete. This latter was blown at one end. The *cross-flute* is blown through a hole in the side near the larger end. It is a long tube (formerly slightly conical) with the larger end closed. Usually made of wood, it is sometimes of silver or other metals. The principle is that of the flue-pipe (vide PIPE), and the tone is clear, pure, and especially rich in the lower range, which is too little used. A very ancient instrument (appearing often with two tubes and one mouthpiece as the *double-flute*, one tube furnishing probably a mere drone-bass); its modern form owes much to the improvements of Boehm, and controls with its keys fourteen orifices, with an extreme range of b-c′′′′♯. It is made in six sizes (including the *piccolo*, or *octave*-flute) and sounds as written, is non-transposing. The normal flute is the *C*; there are two others in D flat and E flat. The *piccolo* is in the same keys but the lower octave is not used; it is written an octave lower than it sounds. A *fourth* (or *quart*) flute sounds a fourth higher than the normal flute. 2. An organ-stop. **flute-work.** Vide STOP. **harmonic f.** or **f. armonique.** An organ-stop. **octave-f.** The piccolo. **pastoral** or **shepherd's f.** A short beak-flute. **f. à bec** (ä bĕk), *F.,* **Schnabel-flöte** (shnä-bĕl), *G.* Beak-flute. **f. allemande** (ăl-mänd), *F.* The cross-flute. **f. conique** (kôn-ēk), *F.* 1. Conical flute. 2. An organ-stop. **f. d'amour** (dä′-moor). 1. An obsolete flute in A or in B flat. 2. A 4- or 8-ft. stop. **f. d'Angleterre** (däṅ-glŭ-tăr). The flageolet. **f. du Poitou** (dŭ pwä-too). The bag-pipe. **f. douce** (doos). The beak-flute. **f. minor** (mē-nôr). A 2- or 4-foot stop. **f. octaviante** (ôk-tä-vĭ-änt). Octave-flute; an organ-stop. **f. ouverte** (oo-vărt). An open stop. f. **traversière** (trä-vĕr-sĭ-är). The cross-flute.

flûte, *F. As a direction*—"use harmonics." **flûtée** (tā). Fluty.

fly. The lid covering a key-board.

F-moll (ĕf-môl), *G.* F minor.

fo'co, *I.* Fire, passion. **focosamen'-te.** Ardently. **focosis'simo.** Very ardent. **focoso.** Passionate.

foglietto (fōl-yĕt'-to), *I.* A part which contains all the obbligato passages, used often by conductors instead of a score.

foire des enfants (fwär-dä-zäṅ-fäṅ), *F.* "Children's fair." Toy symphony.

fois (fwä), *F.* Time **première f.** (prŭm-yär). The first time. **deuxième f.** (dŭz-yĕm). The second time. **deux f.** (dŭ-fwä). Twice. **dernière f.** The last time.

ˮolia (fō-lē'-ä), *Sp.*, **follia(e) di spagna** (spän-yä), *I.*, **folies d'espagne** (fô-lë-dĕs-spīn), *F.* 1. A slow Spanish solo-dance in 3-4 time. 2. A species of air with variations.

ˮolia'ted. Ornamented.

folk-music. The body of folk-songs, dances, etc.

folk-song. A strongly racial popular song that has become a tradition. (See article, page 731.)

folk-tone. The folk-song manner or spirit (cf. **Volkston**).

fondamental(e), (fôṅ-dă-mäṅ-tăl) *F.*, **fondamentale** (tä'lĕ), *I.* Fundamental, **son f.** Root. **basse,** or **basso, f.** Vide BASS 6.

fondamen'to, *I.* Fundamental bass.

fonds d'orgue (fôṅ dôrg), *F.* The foundation-stops.

foot. 1. The unit of metre, a distinct rhythmic unit of two or more syllables. 2. Of a pipe, the part below the mouth. 3. Old term for a refrain, or a drone-bass. 4. A unit for the designation of the pitch of pipes and instrs. arrived at as follows. Sound travels 1056 feet per second, the tone $C_{,,}$ has 33 vibrations a second; $1056 \div 33 = 32$ feet, the length of one sound-wave; a 32-foot pipe will therefore sound $C_{,,}$. The pipe giving C (two octaves below middle C) is about 8 feet long. This is taken as the normal length, and while the pipes that make up a so-called 8-foot stop (q.v.) decrease in length as they ascend the scale, they are considered as belonging to the 8-foot tone and they sound as written or played, i. e., when an 8-foot stop is on and the key of mid. C is depressed, mid. C sounds, etc. If this key is depressed when a 4-foot stop is on, the tone an octave higher sounds; when a 32-foot is on, a tone two octaves lower sounds; the 2-foot and 1-foot stops produce tones respectively two and three octaves higher than the key depressed. A stop then is named from the length of its longest pipe and lowest tone. From this use arises the designation of instruments by *foot-measure*, or *foot-tone;* an instr. sounding *as written* (e. g., the flute) is called an 8-foot instr., one sounding an octave higher (e. g., the piccolo-flute) is called a 4-foot instr. Furthermore, this designation is used of octaves; the letters in the great octave (vide PITCH) are known as 8-foot (as 8-ft. C, D, etc.), those in the small octave, as 4-ft. *c, d,* etc.; those in the once-accented as 2-foot, and those in the twice-accented as 1-foot. The word *foot* is sometimes abbreviated by an (′) as 8′, 16′.

The metrical system has been applied with much inaccuracy; 8-feet $= \frac{5}{2}$ metre; 4-feet $= \frac{5}{4}$ m.; 2-feet $= \frac{5}{8}$ m.; 16-ft. $= 5$ m.; 32-ft. $= 10$ m.;

Quinte ($10 \frac{2}{3}, 5 \frac{1}{3}, 2 \frac{2}{3}, 1 \frac{1}{3}$ and $\frac{2}{3}$ feet) $= \frac{10}{3}, \frac{5}{3}, \frac{5}{6}, \frac{5}{12}$ and $\frac{5}{24}$ metres respectively.

Tierce ($6 \frac{2}{5}, 3 \frac{1}{5}, 1 \frac{3}{5}$ and $\frac{4}{5}$ feet) $= \frac{10}{5}$ (or 2), $\frac{5}{5}$ (or 1), $\frac{5}{10}$ ($\frac{1}{2}$), and $\frac{5}{20}$ ($\frac{1}{4}$) metres respectively.

foot-key. Pedal-key.

forbidden. Contrary to musical grammar. Vide HARMONY.

foreign. Alien to the given key, or tonality.

forlana (för-lä'-nä), *I.*, **forlane** (fôr-län), *F.* A lively Venetian dance in 6-8 or 6-4 time.

form. See article, page 733.

formare il tuono. Vide MESSA DI VOCE.

formula. A word respectfully submitted by the editor to obviate the loose use of "sonata-form," which is employed both of a movement and a group of movements—both for the part and the whole; by speaking of the dual-theme movement as written in the *sonata formula* and the group of formulæ, largo, rondo, etc., as in the sonata-*form* much ambiguity will be avoided.

fort, *G.* Off (of an organ-stop).

fort (fôr), **forte** (fôrt), *F.* 1. Loud. 2. **Temps f.** Strong beat.

fortbien (fôrb-yăn), *F.* A modification of the old fortepiano, by Friederici, 1758.

forte (fôr'-tĕ), *I.* 1. Loud. (abbr. f.) **f. possibile.** As loud as possible. **più f.** Louder. **poco f.** Rather loud. **f. piano.** (Abbr. fp.) Loud, then immediately soft. **fortamen'te.** Loudly.

fortement (fôrt-män), *F.* Loudly.

forte-piano. 1. Vide PIANOFORTE. 2. Loud! then soft!

fortezza (fôr'-tĕd'-zä). Force.

fortiss. Abbr. of *fortissimo.*

fortissimo (fôr-tēs'-sĭ-mo), *I.* Very loud. **fortissis'simo.** Double superlative of *forte.* **f. quanto possibile** (kwän'-to pös-sē'-bĭ-lĕ). As loud as possible.

Fortrücken (fôrt'-rükĕn), *G.* The advance of the hand (as in ascending figuration) with the same fingering.

Fortschreitung (fôrt'-shrī-toongk), *G.* Progression. **F. einer Dissonanz.** Resolution. **fortschreiten.** To progress.

Fortsetzung (fôrt'-zĕt-zoongk), *G.* Continuation, development.

forza (fôr'-tsä), *I.* Force, power. **forzan'do, forzato** (fôr-tsä'-tō). Forced, sharply emphasized (marked ∨ ∧ >). **forzare** (fôr-tsä'-rĕ). To strengthen. **f. la voce** (lä vō'chĕ). To force the voice.

foundation-stop. Vide STOP.

fourchette tonique (foor-shĕt tôn-ēk), *F.* Tuning-fork.

fourniture (foor-nĭ-tür), *F.* A mixture-stop.

four-part. Written for four parts.

fourth. 1. The fourth tone of a scale, the subdominant. 2. An interval containing four tones, the extremes included, as d-g, the ratio being 3 : 4. Fourths are *perfect* and *imperfect* rather than *major* or *minor.* An *augmented* (*superfluous, extreme, sharp* or *pluperfect*) *fourth* is one whose upper tone has been raised a half-step, or its lower lowered. A *diminished* (*imperfect, false, minor* or *defective*) *fourth* one whose upper tone has been lowered half a step or its lower raised (cf. FIFTH). **Chord of**

the second and fourth, chord of the 3d, 4th, and 6th, chord of the 4th and 6th. Vide CHORD. **four-three, four-two.** Vide CHORD. **f. flute, f. shift.** Vide FLUTE and SHIFT.

fp. Abbr. Vide FORTE (2).

français (frän-sĕ'), **française** (frän-sĕz), *F.* 1. French. 2. A country-dance in 3-4 time.

francamen'te, *I.* Frankly, boldly.

franchezza (frän-kĕd'-zä), *I.*, **franchise** (frän-shēz), *F.* Boldness, frankness.

franzese (frän-tsä'-zĕ), *I.*, **französisch** (frän-tsä-zĭsh), *G.* "French"; in French style. **Franzton** (fräntstōn), *G.* French pitch.

frappe (frăp), *F.* A manner of beating time with force. **frappé** (frăp-pā). The down-beat.

frapper (frăp-pā), *F.* To strike; to beat time.

frase (frä'-zĕ) (pl. i), *I.* A phrase. **fr. larga.** With broad phrasing. **fraseggiare** (frä-zĕd-jär'rĕ). To phrase.

Frauenstimme (frow'-ĕn-shtĭm'mĕ), *G.* Female voice.

freddo (frĕd'-dō), **freddamen'te,** *I.* Cold(ly). **freddezza** (frĕd-dĕd'zä). Coldness.

fredon (frŭ-dôn), *F.* A trill, or other ornament. **fredonnement** (frŭ-dŭn-män). Humming, trilling. **fredonner** (frŭ-dŭn-nä). To trill, also to hum.

free. Unrestrained, not according to strict rule, as *f. composition,* or *style.* **f. fugue.** Vide FUGUE. **f. reed.** Vide REED. **f. part.** An independent part added to fill up the harmony of canon or fugue. **f. chant.** A form of reciting the Psalms or Canticles using a group of two chords for each hemistich. Vide FRET-FREE.

freemen's songs. Little compositions for three or four voices, in use about 1600.

fregiare (frā-jä'rĕ), *I.* To adorn. **fregiatura** (too'rä). An ornament.

frei (frī), *G.* Free. **Freiheit** (frī-hīt). License. **f. Schreibart** (shrīp'-ärt). Free composition.

French horn. Vide HORN. **French sixth.** Vide ALTERED.

French treble clef. The G on the lowest line of the staff.

fresco (frĕs'-ko), *I.*, **frescamen'te.** Fresh(ly).

fret. One of the thin projecting ridges across the neck of stringed instrs. to divide the strings into different lengths, thus producing different pitches, on pressure. **fretted** and **fret-free.** In the early precursors of the piano, there were fewer strings than keys, each string serving for several notes, through the action of tangents acting as frets. These were called *tied* or *fretted* or *gebunden*. Later instruments were given a string to each note, and these were called *bundfrei*, or *ungebunden* or *free* or *fret-free*.

freteau, fretian, frestel, fretel (frŭ-tĕl), **fretèle, fretetel.** A Pan's pipe.

fret'ta, *I.* Haste.

Freude (froi'-dĕ), *G.* Joy, rejoicing. **Freudengesang.** Song of joy. **freudig** (froi'dĭkh). Joyfully. **Freudigkeit** (kīt). Joyfulness.

fricassée (frē-kăs-sā), *F.* A dance with pantomime in the 18th cent. In the 16th cent. a part-song, each part having different words.

Fries (frēs), *G.* The ornamented inlay on the border of a violin.

frisch (frĭsh), *G.* Fresh, lively.

fris'ka (frĭsh'-kä). The quick movement in the Czardas, and the Hungarian Rhapsody.

frivolo (frē'vō-lo), *I.* Trifling, trashy.

fröhlich (frā-lĭkh), *G.* Joyous, gay. **F.-keit** (kīt). Gayety. **Frohgesang** (frō-khĕ-zäng). Song of joy.

Frohnamt (frōn'ämt), *G.* High Mass.

Frosch (frôsh), *G.* Nut (of a bow).

frottola (frôt'-tō-lä), *I.* A 16th century ballad.

Frühlingslied (frü'lings-lēt), *G.* Spring-song.

Frühmesse (frü'mĕs-sĕ), **Frühstück** (trü'shtük), *G.* Matins.

F-Schlüssel (ĕf-shlüs'ĕl), *G.* The F-clef.

fuga (foo'-gä), *L.* and *I.* "A flight." Vide FUGUE. **f. ad quintam** (octavam). Fugue (also canon) at the 5th (octave). **f. aequalis motus** (or recta). In similar motion, the answer conforming to the ascent and descent of the subject. **f. al contrario** (or riverso or roves'cio) or **fuga contraria** (or per motum contrarium). One whose answer is the subject inverted. **f. authentica.** A fugue with an ascending subject. **f. canonica** (or inconseguenza or perpetua or totalis). A canon. **f. composita** (or inaequalis). One whose subject moves by degrees, not by leaps, as does **f. incomposita. f. del**

tuono, *I.* A tonal fugue, opposed to **f. reale,** a real fugue. **f. doppia,** *I.* A double fugue. **f. homopho'na.** One whose answer is at the unison. **f. impro'pria** (or **irregularis** or **sciolta o. soluta).** An irregular free fugue. **f. in contrario tempo** (or per ar'sin et the'sin). One in which the accented notes of the subject are the unaccented of the answer, and vice versa. **f. in nomine.** A fugue "in name only," i. e., a free fugue. **f. inversa.** One in double counterpoint and contrary motion. **f. libera.** One with free episodes, opposed to **f. ligata** (or **obbligata),** whose episodes are entirely derived. **f. mixta.** One whose answer is varied by augmentation, etc. **f. partialis** (or **periodica).** One without full and perpetual canonic imitation, the usual fugue. **f. per augmentationem** (or **diminutionem).** One whose answer is by augmentation (diminution). **f. per imitationem interruptam.** One whose answer is broken by rests, etc. **f. plagalis.** One with subjects descending below the keynote. **f. propria** (or **regularis).** One in regular form. **f. reddita** or **redita.** One in which canonic progression occurs at the middle or end. **f. retrograda.** One whose answer is in *retrograde* progression. **f. retrograda per motum contrarium.** One whose answer is in contrary motion as well as retrograde progression. **f. ricercata** (rēt-chĕr-kä'-tä). A fugue of the highest development.

fugara (foo-gä'-rä), *I.* A 4- or 8-ft. organ-stop.

fugato (foo-gä'-to), *I.* 1. Freely in the manner of fugue. 2. A passage in such manner.

Fuge (foo'-khĕ), *G.* Fugue. **F. galante** (gä-län'tĕ), *G.* A free fugue in chamber-music style.

fuggire la cadenza (food-jē-rĕ), *I.* To write a deceptive cadence.

fughetta (foo'gĕt'-tä), *I.* A short fugue.

fugirt (foo-gērt'), *G.* In fugue style; also used of the ranks of a mixture-stop.

fugue (*E.* fūg, in *F.* füg). See page 736. **counter f.** One whose subjects move in contrary directions. **double f.** A fugue on two subjects. **f. renversée** (rän-vĕr-sā), *F.* An inverted fugue. **strict f.** One in which the fugal form and its laws are strictly observed. **perpetual f.** A canon. **f. simple,** *F.* A fugue containing but a single subject. **fugued** (fūgd) or **fuguing.** In fugue form, or loosely in fugue manner. **fuguist.** A composer or performer of fugues. Also see FUGA; and article, page 736.

Führer (fü-rĕr), *G.* 1. Conductor. 2. Subject of a fugue.

Füll- (fĭl), *G.* Filling. **F.-flöte.** "Filling flute," a 4-ft. stop. **F.-pfeife** (pfĭ'fĕ). A dummy pipe. **F.-quinte.** A shrill quint-stop useful only in combination. **F.-stelle.** Padding. **F.-stimme.** 1. A part used to fill out harmony. 2. A mutation-stop a 3d or 5th above normal pitch. 3. A part doubling another in the octave or unison.

full. For the voices or instrs. complete. **f. anthem.** Vide ANTHEM. **f. band.** A complete band or orchestra. **f. cadence** or **close.** Vide CADENCE. **f. chord.** A complete chord; in part-music, one in which all the parts join. **f. score.** Vide SCORE. **f. stop** (on the lute). A chord using all the fingers; full chord followed by a pause. **full choir** (or **great** or **swell**). "Draw all the stops of the choir (or great or swell) organ." **full organ.** "Draw all the stops and couplers." **f. service.** 1. One for the whole choir. 2. An office using music as far as permissible. **f. orchestra.** One in which all the instrs. are employed.

fundamental. 1. The root of a chord. 2. The generator of a series of partials. **f. position.** Vide POSITION. **f. tone.** 1. A generator of partials. 2. One of the three principal tones, tonic, dominant or subdominant. **f. bass.** Vide BASE.

Fundamentalbass (foon-dä-mĕn-täl'-bäs), *G.* Vide BASE. **F.-ton.** Fundamental tone.

funèbre (fü-nĕbr), *F.*, **funebre** (foo-nā-brĕ), *I.*, **funerale** (foo-nĕ-rä'-lĕ), *I.*, **funereo** (foo-nā'-rĕ-ō), *I.* Funereal; mournful. *marcia f.* Funeral march.

fünf (fĭnf), *G.* Five. **f.-fach.** Five-fold, in five ranks, of pipes. **f.-stimmig.** For five voices. **f.-stufige.** Pentatonic. **Fünfte** (fĭnf'-tĕ). Fifth. **Fünfzehnte** (fĭnf'tsän-tĕ). Fifteenth.

funzioni (foon tsĭ-ō'nĕ), *I.* (pl.) Masses, and other sacred music in the R. C. Church.

fuoco (fo-ô'kō), *I.* Fire, energy, passion. **fuoco'so.** Fiery.

für (für), *G., preposition.* For.

fureur (fü-rŭr), *F.*, **furia** (foo'-rĭ-ä), *I.* Fury, passion. **Furiant** (foo'rĭ-änt), *G.*, **furie** (foo-rē), *F.* A quick Bohemian dance with irregular rhythm and accent. **furibon'do, furioso,** *I.* Furious, mad. **furieusement** (für-yŭz-män), *F.*, **furiosamen'te,** *I.* Furiously, madly.

furlando (foor-län'-dō), **furlano** (foor-lä'-nō), *I.* Forlana.

furniture stop. Vide STOP.

furore (foo-rō'-rĕ), *I.* Rage; a great success.

fu'sa, *L.*, **fuse** (füz), *F.*, **Fusel** (foo-zĕl'), *G.* An eighth note.

fusée (fü-zā), *F.* A roulade or rapid passage, a skip or slide.

fusel'la, *L.* A 32d note. **fusel'lala.** A 64th note.

Fuss (foos), pl. **Füsse** (fĭs-se), *G.* Foot (q.v.). **Fussklavier.** The pedals of an organ. **füssig** (füs-sikh), *G.* Foot, as 8-*füssig,* 8-foot. **Fusston** (foos-tōn). Foot-tone, as *Achtfusston,* 8-foot tone.

fut (füt), *F.* Barrel (of a drum).

Fütterung (füt'-tĕr-oongk), *G.* Linings.

Future, music of the. Vide ZUKUNFTSMUSIK.

fz. Abbr. of *Forzando.*

G

G. Pron. in *G.* gä; in *F.* and *I.* sol (sŭl in *F.*, sôl in *I.*). 1. A musical pitch, a perfect fifth above C; all its octaves. 2. The major key having one sharp; the minor key relative to B flat major. **G clef.** The treble clef.

g. Abbr. for *main gauche,* left hand, or *grand orgue,* full, or great-organ.

Gabel (gä'bĕl), *G.* A fork. **G.-ton.** The fork-tone, a' used for tuning. **G.-grif'fe.** Cross-fingering. **Stimmg.** Tuning-fork. **G.-klavier** (gä'b'l-klä-fer). A key-board instr. with a scale of tuning-forks, and a sympathetic fork an octave higher for each tone; inv. by Fischer & Fritzsch, Leipzig, 1882.

gagliarda (gäl-yär'dä), *I.*, **Gagliarde** (gäl-yär'-dĕ), *G.* A galliard. **gagliardo** (gäl-yär'-do), **gagliardamen'te,** *I.* Gayly.

gaillarde (gī-yärd), *F.* 1. Merry. 2. A galliard. **gaillardement** (gī-yärd-män). Merrily.

gaio (gä′ĭ-ō), *I.* Gay.

gaita (gä-ē-tä′), *Sp.* 1. Bagpipe. 2. A flageolet. **gaitero** (gä-ē-tä′-ro). A player on the street-organ.

gajo (gä′-yō), *I.* Gay. **gajamen′te.** Gayly.

gala (gä′la), *I.* Gala. *di g.* Gayly. **galamment** (gǎl-ä-män), *F.*, **galante-mente** (tĕ-men-tĕ′), *I.* Graciously. **galant(e)** (gǎ-läṅ(t)), *F.*, **galante** (gä-läṅ′-tĕ), *I.* Graceful, gallant. **galantemen′te,** *I.* Gallantly. **galantria** (gä-län-trē′-ä), *I.* Gallantry.

galant (gä-länt′), *G.* Free. **G. Stil** (or **Schreibart).** The free (as opp. to the *gebundener* or strictly contrapuntal) style of harpsichord composition in the 18th century. **Galanterien** (gä-län-tärē′-ĕn). Ornaments in old harpsichord music. **Galanteriestück** (gä-län-tĕ-rē′stük). A piece in the ornamental style.

galliard (gǎl-yärd), *E.* An old dance similar to the Pavan.

gal′op, *E.* (in *F.* gǎl-ō), **galopade** (gǎl-ō-pǎd), *F.*, **Galopp** (gä-lôp′), *G.*, **galop′po,** *I.* A hopping round-dance in 2-4 time.

galoubé (gä-loo-bā), **galoubet** (gä-loo-bā′), *F.* A small fife with three holes and range of 17 notes, found in Provence.

ɤamba (gäm′-bä), *I.*, **gambe** (gämb), *F.*, **Gambe** (gäm′-bĕ), *G.* 1. Leg; hence, viol di g. Vide VIOLA. 2. An organ-stop; the whole family of stops named after stringed instrs. **Gambenstimme.** A gamba-stop. **Gambenwerk.** A piano-violin. **Gambabass.** A 16-ft. stop on the pedals. **G. major.** A 16-ft. stop. **Gambette** (gäm-bĕt′-tĕ), *G.* An octave gamba-stop. **Gambist′.** A player on the G. **Gambviole** (gämp-fē-ō′lĕ), *G.* Viol di gamba.

gambeta (gäm-bä′-tä), *Sp.* An ancient dance, a caper.

gam′ma, *Gr.*, **gamme** (gǎm), *F.* The Greek G. (Γ). 1. The lowest note (G) of the Aretinian scale. 2. The name of that scale. 3. Scale generally. 4. Compass. 5. A clef for the scale of G. **g. chromatique (descendante, montante).** Chromatic (descending, ascending) scale. **gammes** (gǎm). Scale-exercises.

Gamma ut or Γ ut. G, in the old sol-misation.

gamut. (From gamma ut.) 1. The scale of any key. 2. The staff.

3. In old English church-music, the key of G. **gamut G.** The G on the first line of the bass staff. **Guido′s g.** The scale of two octaves and a sixth introduced by Guido of Arezzo: the tones called by name, ut, re, mi, fa, sol, la, and written in the first octave Γ (gamma) (the lowest tone) A, B to G, in the second g-g; and in the upper sixth gg-dd.

ganascione (gä-nä-shō′nĕ), *I.* A lute.

Gang (gäng), *G.* 1. Rate of movement. 2. A passage.

ganz (gänts), *G.* Whole, all, very. **Ganzinstrumente.** Those brass instrs. of such width that they speak the lowest sound natural to the tube; i. e., they reach the depth of an open organ-pipe of equal length. Narrower instrs. speak only the octave above this natural tone and are called **Halbinstrumente. ganz langsam.** Very slowly. **ganze Note** (gän′tsĕ nō′tĕ). A whole note. **ganzer Ton** (gän′-tser-tōn). **Ganzton.** A whole tone. Vide SECOND. **ganzes Werk.** The full organ. **Ganzschluss.** Final cadence. **ganzverhallend** (fĕr-häl′lent). Dying away entirely.

garbo (gär′-bo), *I.* Grace, elegance. **garbato** (bä′-tō), **garbatamen′te.** Graceful(ly).

garibo (gä-rē′-bō), *I.* Dance, ball.

gariglione (gä-rēl-yō′nĕ), *I.* Chime.

garnir (gär-nēr), *F.* To string a violin.

garrire (gär-rē′rĕ), *I.* To chirp, warble.

Gassenhauer (gäs′-sĕn-hower), *G.* Street-song, trash. **Gassenhauerlin** (lēn). Popular songs of the 16th century.

Gastrollen (gäst′rōl-lĕn), *G.* To go "guesting," i. e., "starring."

gathering note. A pause on a final note of recitation to give time for the chorus to gather.

gauche (gōsh), *F.* Left. **main g.** (mǎṅ). The left hand.

gaudente (gä-oo-dĕn′-tĕ), **gaudio′so, gaudentemen′te,** *I.* Joyful(ly).

Gaumenton (gow′-mĕn-tōṅ), *G.* Guttural tone.

gavot′, *E.*, **gavot′ta,** *I.*, **gavotte** (gä-vôt), *F.* An old French dance (named probably from the people of Gap, called Gavots). It is in 4-4 time, strongly marked; begins on the weak half of a measure and ends on the accented; no notes smaller than eighth notes occur.

gazel'. A piece with a brief constant refrain.

gazzarra (gäd-zär'-rä), *I.* A fête with music and cannon.

G clef. The treble clef.

G-dur (gä-door), *G.* G major.

Gebläse (gĕ-blä'-zĕ), *G.* Bellows.

gebrochen (gĕ-brô'-khĕn), *G.* Broken.

gebunden (gĕ-boon'dĕn), *G.* 1. Tied. g. Dissonanz. A prepared (and tied) dissonance. g. Spiel. Legato-playing. g. Stil. Strict, connected style. 2. Vide FRETTED.

Geburtslied (gĕ-boorts'lēt), *G.* Birth-day-song.

gedackt (gĕ-däkt'), gedeckt (ge-dĕkt'), *G.* Stopped, of pipes. Gedackt-stimmen. Stops with covered pipes. G.-flöte. Stopped flute, in an organ.

gedämpft (gĕ-dĕmpft), *G.* Muffled, muted.

gedehnt (ge-dänt'), *G.* Lengthened, slow.

Gefährte (gĕ-fär'-tē), *G.* Answer (in fugue).

Gefallen (gĕ-fäl'lĕn). Pleasure. nach G. Ad libitum.

gefällig (gĕ-fäl'lĭkh), *G.* Pleasing(ly), agreeably.

Gefiedel (gĕ-fē'dĕl), *G.* Fiddling.

Gefühl (gĕ-fül'), *G.* Feeling, expression. mit G. or gefühlvoll. With feeling.

gegen (gä'-khĕn), *G.* Against, contrary, contrasted with. G.-bewe-gung (be-vākh'-oongk). Contrary motion. G.-fuge. A fugue whose answer is an inversion of the subject. G.-gesang. Antiphony. G.-hall, G.-schall. Resonance, echo. G.-harmonie. Counter-subject in fugue. Gegenpunkt (poonkt). Counter-point. G.-satz. 1. Contrast. 2. A movement. G.-stimme. 1. Counter-tenor or alto. 2. Counter-subject. 3. Any contrapuntal part. g.-stimmig. Dissonant. G.-subjekt. Counter-subject, in a fugue.

gegit'tertes B. B. cancellatum, vide B.

gehend (gä'-ĕnt), *G.* Andante.

Gehörlehre (gĕ-här'-lā-rĕ), *G.* Acoustics. gehörspielen. To play by ear.

Geige (gī'-khĕ) (pl. en), *G.* Violin. geigen (gī'-khen). To play on the violin. G.-blatt. Finger-board of a violin. G.-bogen (bō'khn). Bow. G.-clavicymbel or G.-klavier. Bow-piano. G., *E.*, G.-futter (foot'-ter). Case for a violin. G.-hals. The neck of a violin. G.-harz (härts). Resin. G.-holz (hôlts), *G.* Wood used in

making violins. G.-macher (mäkh-'ĕr). A violin-maker. G.-principal. A diapason stop. G.-saite. Violin-string. G.-sattel, G.-steg (stäkh). Bridge of a violin. G.-schule. A violin method. G.-strich (strĭkh). A stroke of the bow. G.-stück. A comp. for the violin. G.-werk. 1. Piano-violin. 2. A 4-ft. organ-stop. G.-wirbel (vēr'-bel). A violin-peg. G.-zettel (tsĕt'-tĕl). The violin-maker's label. G.-zug. A violin-stop. Geiger (gī'khĕr). Violin-player.

Geist (gīst), *Gr.* Spirit, soul, mind, genius. g.-reich (rīkh), g.-voll (fôl). Spiritual. Geisterharfe. Æolian harp. geistlich. Ecclesiastical, sacred. G.-gesänge. Psalms, hymns.

Geklingel (gĕ-klĭng'ĕl), *G.* Tinkling.

gekneipt (gĕ-knīpt'), *G.* Pizzicato.

gelassen (gĕ-läs'-sen), *G.* Calm, quietly. G.-heit (hīt). Tranquillity.

geläufig (gĕ-lī'fĭkh), *G.* Easy, rapid. G.-keit (kīt). Fluency, ease.

Geläut (gĕ-līt), *G.* A peal.

gelinde (gĕ-lĭn'-de), *G.* Soft, gentle. Gelindigkeit. Sweetness.

gellen (gĕl'lĕn), *G.* To sound loudly. G.-flöte, *G.* Clarinet.

Geltung (gĕl'-toongk), *G.* Value, proportion (of a note).

gemächlich (gĕ-mĕkh'-lĭkh), gemach-sam (gĕ-mäkh'zäm), *G.* Quiet(ly), calm, slow.

gemählig (gĕ-mä'lĭkh), *G.* Gradually.

gemässigt (gĕ-mĕs-sĭkht), *G.* Moderato. gemes'sen. Measured, moderato.

Gemisch (gĕ-mĭsh'), *G.* Mixture (of stops).

Gemshorn (gĕms'-hôrn), *G.* 1. A pipe made of a chamois horn. 2. A stop with tapering pipes, 2, 4, 8-ft. on the manuals, 16-ft. on the pedals. G.-quinte. A quint-stop of this class.

Gemüt(h) (gĕ-müt), *G.* Mind, soul. gemütlich (lĭkh). Expressive.

genera, plural of genus (q.v.).

general (gä-nĕ-räl'), *G.* General. G.-bass (gä-nĕ-räl'-bäs). Thorough-bass. G.-b.-schrift. Thorough-bass notation. G.-pause (pow-ze). A rest or pause for all the instrs. G.-probe. A general rehearsal.

gen'erator, *E.*, générateur (zhä-nä-rä-tür), *F.* Root, fundamental.

genere (jä'-nĕ-rĕ), *I.* 1. A mode or key. 2. A genus.

genero'so (jä-nĕ-rō'sō), *I.* Noble, dignified.

genial'ia, *L.* Cymbals.

génie (zhä-nē), *F.*, **Genie** (gä'-nē), *G.*, **genio** (jä'-nĭ-ō), *I.* Genius, talent, spirit.

genouillère (zhŭn-wĭ-yăr), *F.* Kneelever.

genre (zhäṅr), *F.* 1. Style. g. expressif. The expressive style. 2. Genus, as g. chromatique, g. diatonique, g. enharmonique.

gentil(le) (zhäṅ-tē(l)), *F.*, gentile (jĕn-tē'-lĕ), *I.* Graceful, elegant. **gentilezza** (lĕd'-zä), *I.* Refinement of style. **gentilmen'te.** Gracefully.

ge'nus, pl. **genera,** *L.* 1. Greek classification of tetrachords. Vide MODES. 2. A scale or mode. 3. Class. g. inflatile. Wind instrs. g. percussibile. Instrs. of percussion. ʒ. tensile. Stringed instruments.

gerade (gĕ-rä'-dĕ), *G.* Straight, regular. G.-bewegung (be-va'khoong). Similar motion. G.-taktart or gerader Takt. Common time.

German. Vide FINGERING, FLUTE. G. pedals. Pedal key-board. G. scale. A, H, C, D, E, F, G. (Vide H.) G. sixth. Vide ALTERED CHORDS. G. soprano clef. Vide CLEF.

Ges (gĕs), *G.* The note G flat. **Geses** (gĕs'-ĕs), G double flat.

Gesang (gĕ-zäng'), pl. **Gesänge** (zĕng'ĕ), *G.* Song, melody, air. G.-buch (bookh). Song-book. G.-kunst. Art of song. G.-(s)mässig (mĕs-sĭkh). Adapted for or congenial to the voice. G.-sgruppe (groop-pe). Song-group; the second subject of a sonata formula, which should be lyrical in nature. g.-sweise (vī-ze). In the style of song. G.-verein (fĕr-īn). A choral society.

Geschlecht (gĕ-shlĕkht'), *G.* Genus.

geschleift (gĕ-shlīft'). *G.* Slurred, legato.

Geschmack (gĕ-shmäk), *G.* Taste. g.-voll. Tasteful.

geschwänzte Noten (gĕ-shvĕnts'tĕ no'-tĕn), *G.* Notes with tails.

geschwind (gĕ-shvīnt'), *G.* Quick, rapid. G.-igkeit (kīt). Rapidity. Geschwindmarsch. A quick-step.

Ges-dur (gĕs-door), *Gb* Major. **Geses** (gĕs-ĕs), *G.* G double flat.

Gesicht (ge-zīkht'), *G.* Face, front (of an organ). G.-spfeifen. Front pipes.

Gesinge (gĕ-sĭng'ĕ), *G.* Bad singing, sing-song.

gesponnen (gĕ-shpôn'-nĕn), *G.* Spun. **gesponnene saite.** Covered string. **gesponnener Ton.** A tone drawn out to a mere thread.

gesteigert (gĕ-shtī'-khĕrt), *G.* Crescendo.

gestossen (gĕ-shtôs'sĕn), *G.* Separated, detached.

gestrichen (gĕ-strĭkh'ĕn), *G.* 1. Having hooks (as notes). 2. Having lines or accents. *Oktave,* one-lined octave. Vide PITCH. 3. Crossed, as a numeral, raising the interval a half-tone. Vide CHORD. 4. Cut, as a movement or scene.

get'ern, get'ron. The cittern.

get(h)eilt (gĕ-tīlt'), *G.* Divided. Vide DIVISI. g. Stimmen. Partial stops.

Getön (gĕ-tän), *G.* Clamour.

getragen (gĕ-trä'khĕn), *G.* Sustained.

getrost (gĕ-trôst'), *G.* Confident.

gewichtig (ge-vĭkh'-tĭkh), *G.* Heavy.

gewidmet (gĕ-vēt'-mĕt, *G.* Dedicated.

Gewirbel (gĕ-vēr'bĕl), *G.* Roll of drums.

gewiss (gĕ-vĭs'), *G.* Firm, sure. G.-heit (hīt). Firmness.

geworfener Strich (gĕ-vôrf'-ĕn-ĕr strĭkh), *G.* A springing bow-stroke. Vide BOW.

geziert (gĕ-tsērt'), *G.* Affected, prim.

geyta'rah. Eastern guitar.

ghazel', *Arab.* A piece with simple recurrent theme.

ghiribizzi (gĕ-rĭ-bēd'-zĭ), *I.* Unexpected intervals, fantastic passages. **ghiribizzo'so.** Fantastic.

ghironda (gē-rôn'-dä), *I.* Hurdy-gurdy.

ghit'tern. Old name for cittern.

gicheroso (jē-kĕ-rō'-sō), *I.* Merry.

giga (jē'-gä), *I.*, **gigue** (zhēg), *F.*, **Gigue** (jē'gĕ), *G.* 1. Jig. 2. Old form of viol. **gighardo** (jē-gär'-dō), *I.* A jig.

gigelira (jē-gĕ-lī'rä), *I.* Xylophone.

ging'larus, ging'ras, or **gingri'na.** A small Phœnician flute.

gioco (jô'-kō), *I.* A joke, merriment. **giocoso, giocosamen'te.** Jocose(ly). **giochevole** (jō-kä'vō-lĕ). Merry. **giocolarmen'te.** Merrily.

giocondo (jō-kôn'-dō), **giocoudamen'te,** *I.* Cheerful(ly).

gioja (jō'-yä), *I.* Joy. **giojan'te, giojo'so, giojosamen'te.** Joyful(ly).

gioviale (jō-vĭ-ä'lĕ), *I.* Jovial. **giovialità** (ĭ-tä). Gayety.

giraffe (jĭ-räf'). An upright spinet.

giro (jē'-rō), *I.* A turn.

Gis (gēs), *G.* G sharp. Gisis (gēs-ēs). G double sharp. Gis-moll, G-sharp minor.

gitana (he-tä'-nä), *Sp.* A gipsy.

gittana (jĭt-tä'-na), *I.* A Spanish dance.

git'tern, git'teron, git'tron. Cittern.

gitteth (jĭt'tĕth), *Heb.* An instr. of the harp kind.

giubilazione (joo-bĭ-lä-tsĭ-ō'nĕ), giubilio (joo-bĭ-lē'-ō), giubilo (joo'bĭ-lō), *I.* Jubilation. giubbilo'so. Jubilant.

giucante (joo-kän'-tĕ), giuchevole (joo-kä'-vō-lĕ), *I.* Merry, joyful.

giulivo (joo-lē'vō), giulivamen'te, *I.* Joyful(ly).

giuoco (joo-ô'kō), *I.* 1. A joke, sport. 2. A stop. giuoco'so, giuocan'te. Playful.

giusto (joos'to), *I.* Exact, precise, proper. tempo g. Strict time. allegro g. Rather fast. giustamen'te. Strictly.

given bass. A figured bass.

glais (glĕ), *F.* The passing-bell. g. funèbre. A knell.

glänzend (glen'-tsĕnt), *G.* Brilliant.

glapissant (glä-pĭs-sän), *F.* Shrill.

Glas'harmonika, *G.* Vide HARMONICA.

glasses, musical. Goblets tuned by partial filling with water and played by rubbing their edges evenly with a wet finger.

glatt (glät), *G.* Smooth, even. Glätte (glĕt'tĕ). Smoothness.

glee. An unaccompanied secular comp. for three or more voices; its mood may be grave or gay, its counterpoint is not usually elaborate.

gleich (glīkh), *G.* Equal, alike consonant. gleicher Klang. Consonance, unison. gleicher Kontrapunkt. Equal cpt. gleichschwebende Temperatur (shvä'-bĕn-dĕ). Equal temperament. gleiche Stimmen. Voices of the same sort, as *male.* gleichstimmig (shtĭm-mĭkh). Harmonious.

gleiten (glī'tĕn), *G.* To glide the fingers.

gli (lē), *I.* Pl. The.

glicibarifona (glē-chē-bä-rĭ-fō'-nä), *I.* A wind-instr. inv. by Catterini, 1827; a small expressive organ.

glide. Portamento; glissando.

Glied (glēt), *G.* Link.

glissade (glĭs-säd), *F.,* glissan'do, glissato (glĭs-sä'tō), glissican'do, glissicato (kä'tō), *I.,* glissement (glēs-mäñ), *F.* Gliding, i. e., by sliding

the finger quickly along the keys or the strings; in piano-playing it is done with the finger-nail usually. glisser (glĭs-sä), *F.,* glitschen (glĭt'shĕn), *G.* 1. To glide. 2. An embellishment executed by glissando. glissez la pouce (glĭs-sä lä-poos), *F.* Slide the thumb.

Glocke (glôk'ĕ), *G.* A bell. Glockengeläute (glô'kĕn-gĕ-lī-tĕ). The ringing or chiming of bells. Glock'enist. Bell-ringer. G.-klang. The sound of bells. G.-spiel. 1. Chimes. 2. A stop imitating bells, or causing them to tinkle. 3. An orchestral instr. of bells or tuned steel rods struck with a hammer. Glöckchen (glĕk'khĕn). A little bell. glöckeln (glĕk'-ĕln). To ring little bells. Glockner (glôk'ner). Bell-ringer. Glockleinton (glôk'-līn-tōn). An organ-stop of very small scale and wide measure.

Glo'ria or Gloria in excel'sis Deo, *L.* "Glory to God in the highest." Vide MASS and DOXOLOGY.

Glo'ria Pa'tri, *L.* "Glory to the Father." Vide DOXOLOGY.

glotte (glôt), *F.* The glottis. coup de g. (koo dŭ). A short snappy attack sought by some vocal teachers, but generally believed to be pernicious.

glottis (glät'tis). 1. The upper part of the wind-pip˄, an aperture in the larynx controlling vocal production. 2. A reed used by ancient flutists.

glühend (glü'ĕnt). *G.* Ardent, glowing.

G-moll (gä-môl). G minor.

gnaccare (näk-kä'-rä), *I.* Castanets.

gnacchera (näk-kä'rä), *I.* A tambourine, kettle-drum.

gnomo (nō'-mō). In neumatic notation, a long bar used to indicate a sustained note.

goathorn. Vide GEMSHORN.

gola (gō'lä), *I.* 1. Throat. 2. A guttural voice.

goll trompo. Trumpet used by Danes, Normans, etc.

Gondellied (gôn'dĕl-lēt), *G.,* gondoliera (gôn-dōl-yā'rä), *I.* gondoliersong. Song composed and sung by the Venetian gondoliers; barcarolle. 2. Music in the same style.

gon'dolin. An instr. of the zither-class with four octaves of strings and one octave of piano-keys above them. The pressure of one key submits one tone in all its octaves to the sweep of the plectrum. Chords can thus be played in different positions.

gong. A Chinese instr., a circular plate of metal struck with a padded stick. Also called tam-tam.

goose. A squawk accidentally occurring in the tone of an oboe or other reed instrument.

gorgheggiare (gôr-gĕd-jä'-rĕ), *I.* To trill, shake. **gorgheggiamen'to** Trilling; the art of florid song. **gorgheggio** (gĕd'jō). A trill, a shake. **gorgheggi.** Rapid vocalises.

gos'ba. An Arabian flute.

gospel side. Vide EPISTLE SIDE.

go'to. Japanese dulcimer.

Gottesdienst (gôt'tĕs-dēnst), *G.* Divine service.

gout (goo), *F.* Taste, judgment.

governing key. Principal key.

Grabgesang (gräp'-gĕ-zäng) *G.* **grablied** (lēt), *G.* Dirge.

grace. See article, page 737.

Grad (grät), *G.* Step, degree.

gradare (dä're), *I.* To descend by degrees.

grada'tion. A series of diatonic chords ascending or descending.

gradation (gră-dăs-yôn), *F.*, **gradazione** (grä-dä-tsĭ-ō'nĕ), *I.* A gradual increase or diminution of speed or volume.

gradevole (grä-dā'-vō-lĕ), **gradevolemen'te**, *I.* Graceful(ly). **graditamen'te, graditis'simo.** Very sweetly.

gradire (grä-dē'-rĕ), *I.* To ascend by degrees.

Gradleiter (grät'-lī-tĕr), *G.* A scale.

grado (grä'-do), *I.* A degree, single step. **g. ascendente** (or **descendente**). Ascending (or descending) degree. **di grado.** Moving by step, opposed to **di salto,** moving by skip.

grad'ual, *E.*, **gradua'le,** *L.* 1. Part of the R. C. service sung between the Epistle and Gospel, anciently sung on the altar-steps. 2. A book containing the gradual and other antiphons. The Roman G or **Graduale Romanum.** A celebrated ancient volume of ritual music of the 16th century. 3. **gradual modulation.** That in which the principal modulating chord is reached by others.

gradualmen'te, graduatamen'te, *I.*, **graduellement** (grad-ü-ĕl-män), *F.* By degrees.

graduare (grä-doo-ä'rĕ), *I.* To divide into degrees. **graduazione,** *I.* Vide GRADAZIONE. **gradweise** (grät-vī-ze), *G.* Gradually, by degrees.

gra'dus ad Parnas'sum, *L.* "The road to Parnassus." Name applied by Fux to his text-book in counterpoint; by Clementi to his book of études; hence, any text-book.

graha (grä'-hä), *Hindu.* The opening tone of a song.

grail (grāl). *Early E.* The Roman gradual.

graillement (grĕ-yŭ-män), *F.* A hoarse sound.

grammar. Rules of composition.

grammatical accent. Vide ACCENT.

gramophone. See phonograph music, page 794.

gran (grän), *I.* Great, grand. **g. cassa** or **tamburo.** The great, or bass-drum. **g. prova.** Final rehearsal.

grand. Abbr. of *Grand piano.* Vide PIANO. **g. action.** The action of a grand piano. **grand opera.** Serious opera in which there is no spoken dialogue. **g. stave.** Vide STAFF. **g. choir.** Union of all the reed-stops. **g. cornet.** 16-ft. reed-stop. **g. sonata.** An extended sonata.

grand(e) (grän(d)), *F.*, **grande** (grän'-dĕ), *I.* Grand, great. **g. barré,** *F.* Vide BARRÉ. **g. bourdon.** A 32-ft. stop on the pedal. **g. chantre** (shäntr). Precentor. **g. chœur** (kŭr). Full organ, all the stops, **g. orgue** (grän-dorg). 1. Great organ. 2. Full organ. **g. jeu.** 1. Full organ. 2. A stop bringing all the stops of an harmonium into play. **g. messe.** High Mass. **g. mesure à deux temps.** Duple time. **g. orchestre** (grän-dôr-kĕstr). Full orchestra.

grandeur (grän-dŭr), *F.* 1. Grandeur. 2. Width (of intervals).

grandezza (grän-dēd'-zä), *I.* Grandeur.

grandio'so, *I.* Noble. **grandisonan'te.** Sonorous.

grandsire. Changes on 5 bells. Vide DOUBLE (4).

granulato (grä-noo-lä'-tò), *I.* Slightly staccato.

grappa (gräp'pa), *I.* Brace.

grasseyer (gräs-sŭ-yä), *F.* To pronounce the *r* or *l* thickly; hence, **grasseyement** (gräs-yŭ-män), such pronunciation.

Gra'tias ag'imus, *L.* "We give thanks to Thee." Vide MASS.

gratioso (grä'-tsi-ō'so), *I.* Gracious.

grave (grä'vĕ in *I.*; in *F.* gräv). 1. Grave, deep, slow. 2. A slow movement. **grave harmonics.** Combinatiorial tones. **gravement** (grăv-män), *F.* **gravemente** (grä-vĕ-mĕn'tĕ), *I.* Gravely. **gravezza** (gra-vĕd'-zä), *I.* Gravity.

gravicembalo (grä-vē-chäm'-bä-lō), *I.*, **gravicem'bolo**, *I.*, **gravecem'balum**, *L.* Harpsichord.

gra'vis, *L.* Heavv. Vide ACCENTUS ECCLESIASTICI.

gravisonan'te, *I.* Loud-sounding.

gravità (grä-vĭ-tä'), *I.*, **Gravität** (grä-fē-tät'), *G.*, **gravité** (grä-vĭ-tä), *F.* 1. Solemnity. 2. Relative depth of a tone.

grayle (grāl). *Early E.* The "Roman gradual."

grazia (gräts'-yä), *I.*, **grazie** (gräts-yä), *G.* Grace, elegance. **graziös** (grä-tsĭ-äs), *G.*, **grazio'so**, *I.* Graceful. **graziosamen'te.** Gracefully.

greater. Major (of a scale, sixth, or third). **great octave.** Vide PITCH. **great organ.** Vide ORGAN. **great sixth.** A 6-5 chord with perfect 5th and major 6th.

grec (grĕk), *F.* Greek. *Chorus à la G.* A chorus at the end of an act, as in Greek tragedy.

Greek Modes and Music. See page 762.

Grego'rian, gregorianisch (grĕ-gō-rĭ-än'-ĭsh), *G.*, **grégori'ano** (grä-gō-rĭ-ä'no), *I.*, **grégorien** (grä-gō-rĭ-äñ), *F.* Introduced or regulated by Pope Gregory I. in the sixth century (vide his name in the B. D.). Chiefly used as a synonym for plain-chant. Gevaert in his "Les origines du chant lyrique," 1890, has shown how little reason there is for continuing the traditional view of St. Gregory as a great innovator; he may have been a codifier of music. Much credit belonging to St. Ambrose has been given to him; he did not originate the notation by letters (a-g), sometimes called the *Gregorian letters.* The so-called *Gregorian chant* or *song* is diatonic, without definite rhythm (the words dictating the metre) and keeping to the Church modes. Of *Gregorian chant, modes, tones, etc.* Vide PLAIN-CHANT, and MODES.

greifen (grī'-fĕn), *G.* To take, to finger, to play; to stop (of violin-playing); to stretch.

grel (grĕl), *G.* Shrill. **G.-heit** (hīt). Sharpness.

grelot (grü-lō), *F.* A small bell.

Griff (grĭf), *G.* Touch, manipulation, fingering, stretch. **G.-brett.** Fingerboard. **G.-loch** (lôkh). Hole (as of a flute). **G.-saite** (zī-te). A

stopped, or melody, string as opposed to a sympathetic string.

grillig (grĭl'-lĭkh), *G.* Capricious.

gringotter (grăñ-gô-tä), *F.* To hum.

grisoller (grē-sô-lä), *F.* To warble.

grob (grôp), *G.* Coarse, deep, broad. As a prefix (of organ-pipes); "of broad scale." **G.-gedackt.** A stopped diapason of full, rough tone.

grop'po, groppet'to. Vide GRUPPO, GRUPPETTO.

gros (grō), *F.* Great. **g. tambour.** Great drum.

gros-fa (grō-fä). The old square notation.

gross (grôs), *G.*, **grosse** (grôs), *F.* Great, major. **grosse caisse** (grôs kĕs), *F.* The great drum. **Grossenazard**, *G.* A stop a fifth above the diapasons. **grosse Oktave.** The great octave. Vide PITCH. **grosse Quinte, grosses Quintenbass.** A stop in the pedals, a fifth or twelfth to the great bass. **grosse Sonate.** Grand sonata. **grosses Principal.** A 32-ft. stop. **grosses Terz.** Major third. **grosse Tierce.** Stop producing the third or tenth above the foundation-stops. **grosse Trommel.** The great drum. **grossgedackt** (gĕdäkt). Double-stopped 16-ft. diapason.

grosso (grôs'-sō), *I.* Full, great, grand.

Grossvatertanz (grôs'fä-tĕr-tänts), *G.* "Grandfather's dance"; an old-fashioned dance.

grottes'co, *I.* Grotesque.

ground bass. Vide BASE (8).

group. 1. A series of short notes tied, or sung to one syllable. 2. A division or run. 3. A set of instruments, as *the brass.* 4. The arrangement of parts in score.

Grund (groont), *G.* Ground, foundation. **G.-akkord.** An uninverted chord. **G.-bass.** Fundamental bass. **G.-lage.** Fundamental position. **G.-ton.** Root; tonic. Fundamental of a compound tone. **G.-tonart.** The prevailing key. **G.-stimme.** The bass part.

gruppo (groop'pō), *I.* A group, formerly a trill, shake, or turn. **gruppet'to.** 1. A small group. 2. A turn.

G-Schlüssel (gä'-shlüs-sĕl), *G.* The G clef. Vide CLEF.

guaracha (gwa-rä'-chä), *Sp.* A Spanish dance, with one part in triple and one in 2-4 time, the dancer often accompanying himself on the guitar

guaranita (gwä-rä-nē'-tä), *Sp.* A small guitar.

Guarnerius. Vide the B. D.

guddok (goo-dôk), *Rus.* A 3-stringed violin.

gue. An obsolete Shetland violin with 2 horsehair strings played 'cello-fashion.

guerriero (goo-ĕr-rĭ-ā'-rō), *I.* Martial.

guet (gĕ), *F.* A trumpet flourish.

guia (gē'-ä), *Sp.* Fugue; conductor; leader.

guida (goo-ē'-dä), *I.* (a) Guide 1, 2, 3. (b) Vide PRESA. (c) Also, a tone through which the voice glides in singing an interval legato.

guide. 1. Subject, of fugue. 2. Antecedent of imitation. 3. A direct.

guide (gēd), *F.* Guide 1, 2. **guide-main** (măṅ). A chiroplast, inv. by Kalkbrenner.

guidon (gē-dôṅ), *F.* A direct.

Guido'nian. Relating to Guido d'Arezzo. (Vide B. D.) **G. hand.** A diagram on an outstretched left hand of the *Aretenian syllables.* Vide SOLMISATION.

guil'tern (gĭl'-tern). Cither.

guimbard, guimbarde (găṅ-băr(d)), *F.* A jew's harp.

guion (gē'ōn), *Sp.* A repeat sign.

guitar, *E.,* **guitare** (gĭ-tăr), *F.,* **guitarra** (gē-tär'rä), *Sp.,* **Guitarre** (gĭ-tär'rĕ). *G.* A modern form of the lute, long-necked with frets; six-stringed; compass E-a'' (plus an octave of harmonics) The accordature is E-A-d-g-b-e' (or E-B-e-g-b-e'). Its music is written an octave higher than it sounds. **g. d'amour.** Vide ARPEGGIONE. **g. lyre.** A French six-stringed instr. of lyre-shape.

guiterne (gē-tĕrn), *F.* Ancient guitar.

gu'nibry. A 2-stringed guitar.

Gunst (goonst), *G.* Grace, tenderness.

guracho (goo-rä'-chō), *Sp.* Vide GUARACHA.

gusla (goosh'-la). Servian 1-stringed instr. with skin sound-board.

gusli, gussel. A Russian zither.

gusto (goos-to), *I.* Taste, expression. **gran g.** The grand manner. **gustoso** (goos-to'so), **gustosamente** Tasteful(ly).

G-ut. Vide GAMMA UT.

gut. Strings made of entrails of sheep. **gut** (goot). *G.* Good. **gutdünken** (dünk'ĕn). At pleasure. **guter Takteil.** Strong beat.

gutturale (goot-too-rä'lĕ), **gutturalmen'te,** *I.* Gutteral(ly).

gyta'rah. Nubian guitar. **barbarych.** The Berber guitar.

H

H (In *G.* pron. hä). German name for *B-natural;* B being reserved for B *flat.*

h. Abbr. for *horn, heel. hand.*

Habanera (ä-bä-nä'-räj, *Sp.* A dance popular in Havana; it is in 2-4 time with the first eighth note dotted; syncopation and caprice play a large part. Vide DANCE-RHYTHMS.

Haberrohr (hä'-bĕr-rōr), *G.* Shepherd's flute.

Hackbrett (häk'-brĕt), *G.* Dulcimer.

halb (hälp), *G.* Half, lesser. **halbe Applikatur.** Half-shift. **Halb-bass, -cello,** or **violine.** A small double-bass, 'cello or violin. **H.-violon.** A small double-bass. **halbgedackt** (gĕ-däkt). Half covered (of stops) **H.-instrumente.** Vide GANZINSTRUMENTE. **H.-kadenz** or **-schluss.** Half-cadence. **H.-mond.** Crescent. **H.-note.** Half-note, or **H.-taktnote.** Hand-note; in horn-playing, a stopped note. **H.-orgel,** or **-werk.** An organ with no stops lower than 8-ft pitch. **H.-prinzipal.** An obsolete 4-ft. stop. **H.-rüdenhorn.** Vide HIEFHORN. **h.-stark.** Mezzoforte **H.-stimme.** A half or partial stop **H.-ton,** or **halber Ton.** Semitone **half-cadence** or **half-close.** Vide CADENCE. **half-note.** A minim. **half-note rest.** A pause equal to a half-note. **half-shift.** Vide SHIFT **half-step.** The smallest interval used. **half-stop.** Vide STOP.

hal'il. Vide KHALIL.

Hall (häl), *G.* Sound, clang. **hallen** (häl'lĕn). To sound, to clang. **Hall-drommete** (drôm-mä-te) or **-trompete.** A powerful trumpet.

hallelujah (häl-lĕ-loo'yä), *Heb.* Alleluia.

hal'ling. Norwegian country-dance.

Halmpfeife (pfi'fĕ), *G.* Shepherd's pipe.

Hals (häls), *G.* 1. Neck (of a violin, etc.). 2. Throat. 3. Stem.

Halt (hält), *G.* A pause, a hold.

Hammer (pron. in *G* häm'mĕr). 1. That part of the mechanism of a piano which strikes the strings and produces the tone. 2. Mallet for playing the dulcimer. 3. The striker of a bell. **tuning h.** An instr. for tightening the pegs of a piano or harp. **Hammerklavier** (klä-fēr'), *G.* The modern piano.

hanacca (hä-näk'-kä), *I.*, **hanaise** (ă-něz), *F.*, **Hanakisch** (hä-nä'-kĭsh), *G.* A rapid polonaise-like Moravian dance in 3-4 time.

Hand, harmonic. Vide GUIDONIAN. **hand-guide.** Chiroplast. **h.-harmonic.** Accordeon. **h.-horn.** One without valves or pistons. **h.-organ.** A portable barrel organ (q.v.). **h.-note.** In horn-playing, a stopped note. **Hand** (hänt), pl. **Hände** (hĕnt'ĕ), *G.* Hand. **H.-bassl.** An obsolete instr. between viola and 'cello. **H.-bildner** (or **-leiter**). A chiroplast. **H.-lage.** Position of the hand. **H.-stücke.** Finger-exercises. **H.-trommel.** Tambourine.

handle-piano. Vide BARREL ORGAN 2. **Harfe** (här'-fĕ), *G.* A harp. **Harfen bass** (här'fĕn-bàss). A bass of broken chords. **Harfensaite.** Harpstring. **Harfenspieler.** Harpist. **Harfenett.** Vide SPITZHARFE. **Harfeninstrumente.** Instrs. whose strings are plucked. **H.-laute.** Vide DITAL.

Harke (här'-ke), *G.* Fork for ruling staves.

Harmo'nia, *L.* Daughter of Mars and Venus; music in general.

Harmonic. *As an adjective.* Musical, concordant; relating to harmony (i. e., to chords, etc. as opposed to melody) and to the theory of music. **h. chord.** A generator and its harmonics. (Vide below.) **h. curve.** The figure described by a string in vibration. **h. figuration.** Broken chords, often with passing notes. **h. hand.** Vide GUIDONIAN. **h. mark.** A small circle over a note to be played as an harmonic. **h. note, tone,** vide the noun HARMONIC. **h. scale.** The series of partials (vide ACOUSTICS, page 718). **h. stop.** A flute or reed stop having its pipes pierced midway, so that the harmonics predominate over the fundamental tone, hence **h. flute** and **h. reed. h. triad.** Major triad. **h. trumpet.** The sackbut. *As a noun* (frequently used in the plural). 1. One of the many partial tones that go to make up the compound vibration we call tone, this compound being called by the name of its generator. (Vide ACOUSTICS.)

2. A vibrating string when lightly touched at a nodal point (as that of a half, 3d, 4th, or 5th, etc., of the string's length) will vibrate in divisions (2, 3, 4, or 5, etc.), each division sounding the same tone respectively an octave, a 12th, 15th or 17th, etc., higher than the string. These produce a choir-like unison of exquisite sweetness whose flutiness has given them the name **flageolet-tones.** These harmonics if produced from an open string are called **natural;** from a stopped string, **artificial.** Harmonics are called for by the word **flageolet** or its abbr. *fl.*; or the words *flautando, flautato,* or *flûte,* or by a small circle (o) called the **harmonic-mark** over the note to be touched, or by writing a black note indicating the open string, a diamond-headed note above it showing where the string is to be touched, and a small note above to indicate the actual sound. **Grave Harmonics.** Combinational tones. "Properly speaking, the harmonics of any compound tone are other compound tones of which the primes are partials of the original compound tone of which they are said to be harmonics."

—A. J. ELLIS.

(See article *Harmonic Warnings For Composers,* page 748.)

Harmon'ica. 1. An arrangement by Benj. Franklin of musical glasses in a scale, on a spindle turned by a treadle. The glasses were moistened in a trough, and as they revolved melodies and chords could be played. F. called his device **armonica.** 2. The **mouth-harmonica** or **harmonicon** is a reed mouth-instr. producing different tones when the breath is inhaled and exhaled. 3. A delicate stop. **Harmonica-ätherisch** (ä'-tĕr-ĭsh), *G.* A delicate mixture-stop. **harmonichord.** Vide PIANO-VIOLIN.

harmonicello (chĕl'-lō). A 'cello-like instr. with 15 strings (5 of them wire) inv. by J. K. Bischoff, Nürnberg, 18th century.

harmonici. Vide CANONICI.

harmon'icon. 1. Vide HARMONICA. 2. A keyed harmonica with flue-stop, inv. by W. C. Müller. 3. An orchestrion.

harmoni-cor, *F.* A wind-instr. with harmonium-like reeds in a clarinet-like tube, inv. by Jaulin, Paris.

harmo'nicum. An improved bando-nion; virtually an accordeon worked with treadles, inv. by Brendl and Klosser, Saxony, 1893.

Harmonie (här-mō-nē'), *G.* 1. Harmony. 2. A chord. 3. (a) The wind-instruments collectively, or (b) music for them. h.-eigen, Chordal; appropriate or native to the harmony; opposed to h.-fremd, foreign. H.-lehre (lä-rĕ). Theory of music. H.-musik. Vide HARMONIE 3. H.-trompete. A trumpet employing stopped tones with success. H.-verständiger (fĕr-shtĕn'-dĭkh'-r). A harmonist. harmoniren (här-mō-nē'-rĕn). To harmonise. harmo'-nisch. Harmonious.

harmonist. One versed in the laws of music.

harmonie (är-mō-nē), *F.* 1. Harmony. 2. Harmonics. harmonieux (är-mōn-yŭ'). Harmonious. harmonieusement (yŭz-mäṅ). Harmoniously.

Harmo'nika, *G.* 1. Accordeon. 2. Concertina. H.-tone. Vide HARMONICS.

Harmo'niker, *G.* Harmonici.

harmoniphon. An instr. with keyboard, inv. 1837, by Panis, of Paris, to supply the place of oboes in orchestras. The sounds are produced from reeds acted upon by currents of air.

harmonique (är-mō-nēk), *F.* Harmonic, applied to pipes of double length.

harmoniquement (är-mō-nēk-mäṅ), *F.* Harmonically.

harmo'nium. Vide REED-ORGAN.

har'monise. To combine two or more parts in accordance with the laws of music; to add accompanying chords to a melody.

harmonom'eter. A monochord.

harmony, chromatic (or diatonic). That characterised by chromatic (or diatonic) progression. close h. That in which the 3 highest parts do not cover more than an octave; opposed to open, dispersed, or extended h. compound h. That in which some of the tones are doubled; opposed to simple h. essential h. (a) The fundamental chords of a key. (b) The harmonic outline stripped of embellishment. figured h. That in which the chord progressions are embellished variously; opposed to plain

or natural h., the common triad. forbidden h. A chord whose construction or approach is contrary to the rules of Harmony suspended h. That in which one or more notes are suspended. pure h. (as of a string-quintet). Opposed to tempered h., as of a piano. Vide TEMPERAMENT. strict h. That which is rigidly obedient to the rules; opposed to free h. Two-part (etc.) h. That in which two (or more) parts appear. (See articles *Harmony In Practice*, page 744, and *Modern Harmony*, page 758.)

harp, *E.*, harpe (ärp), *F.* A stringed triangular instr. of great antiquity and variety. The gut-strings which are plucked with both hands are necessarily diatonic. In the old single-action harp (key of E flat, compass F'-d' ' ' ') the notes could be raised a half-tone by the use of pedals. Thanks to the ingenuity of Sebastian Erard, who in 1820 perfected the "double-action harp," all keys are obtainable on the modern harp in fairly quick succession, by the manipulation of seven pedals each raising a string and all its octaves a half or a whole tone. Thus by sharpening or flattening the proper tones, any key may be obtained. The natural scale is C♭, and the more sharps in the key the less the sonority; double flats and sharps are impossible, and remote modulation difficult. There are 46 (or 47) strings, compass C' flat-f' ' ' ' (or g' ' ' ' flat). double h. One with 2 rows of differently tuned strings. triple h. (such as the Welsh). One with 3 rows. Æolian h., h. éolienne. Vide ÆOLIAN. couched h. The spinet. pointed h. Vide SPITZHARFE. chromatic h. Inv. by Pfranger; it has, however, too many strings. jew's harp. A small instr. with metal tongue, played upon by placing it between the teeth, and striking with the tongue and the finger; the breath determines the tone; known in the trade as "Irish harp." h. instruments. Those whose strings are not bowed.

harpechorde (ärp-kôrd), *F.*, harpicordo (är-pĭ-kôr'-dō), *I.* The harpsichord.

harpeggiren (här-pĕd-jē'rĕn), *G.* Vide ARPEGGIATE.

harpe-lute. Vide DITAL. harp-pedal. The soft pedal of a piano.

harpo-lyre. A 3-necked, 21-stringed guitar, inv. by Salomon, 1829.

harp'secol. Vide HARPSICHORD.

harp'sichord. A precursor of the modern piano, whose strings were set in vibration by jacks carrying quills or bits of hard leather (instead of tangents, as in the clavichord). Sometimes it had more than one key-board as in the **vis-à-vis** (vē-zä-vē), which had a key-board at each end. The **double h.** had 2 unison strings and an octave for each tone; and stops for varying the use of these. The **harmonica h.** is an harmonica with key-board.

harp-style. Arpeggio style.

harp-way tuning. Early English accordatures of the viol da gamba facilitating arpeggios.

harsur or **hasur** (hä'-zoor), *Heb.* A Hebrew instr. of 10 strings.

hart, *G.* Major; hard; unprepared. **h. verminderter Dreiklang.** A triad with major 3d and diminished 5th.

hartklingend. Harsh-sounding.

hâte (ät), *F.* Haste, speed.

haubois (ō-bwä), *F.* An oboe.

Haupt (howpt), *G.* Head, principal. **H.-accent.** Principal accent. **H.-akkord.** Fundamental triad. **H.-gesang, H.-melodie.** Principal melody. **H.-kadenz.** Full cadence. **H.-kirche.** Cathedral. **H.-manual.** The great manual; the great organ. **H.-note.** 1. The principal note in a shake, turn or trill. 2. The chord-note. 3. Accented note. 4. Melody-note. **H.-periode.** Principal period. **H.-probe.** The final rehearsal. **H.-satz.** Principal theme, subject or idea. **H.-schluss.** Final cadence. **H.-septime.** Dominant 7th. **H.-stimme.** Principal part. **H.-thema.** Principal theme. **H.-ton.** 1. Fundamental or principal tone. 2. The tonic. 3. The 5th in a minor triad. **H.-tonart.** The principal key. **H.-werk.** Great organ.

hausse (ōs), *F.* Nut of a bow.

hausser (ōs-sā), *F.* To raise the pitch.

haut (ō), **haute** (ōte), *F.* Acute, shrill, high. **haute-contre** (ōt-kôñtr). High tenor. **haute-dessus** (ōt-děs-sü). High treble, soprano. **hautement** (ōt-mäñ). Haughtily. **haute-taille** (ōt-tä-ē). High tenor.

hautb. Abbr. of *Hautboy.*

hautbois (ō-bwä), *F.,* **hautboy** (ho'-boy), *E.* 1. The oboe. 2. An 8-ft. reed-stop. **h.-d'amour.** An organ-stop. Vide OBOE. **hautboy-clarion.** Vide OCTAVE HAUTBOY.

H.-bes (hä-běs), *G.* B double flat. **H.-dur** (hä-door). B major.

head. 1. The part of the note which marks its position on the staff. 2. Point of a bow. 3. Membrane of a drum. 4. The part above the neck of violins, etc., containing the pegs. **head voice.** The upper or highest register of the voice.

heel. The wooden brace fastening the neck of violins, etc., to the body.

Heerhorn (här'-hôrn), *G.* A military trumpet. **Heerpauke** (här'pow-ke), *G.* Old kettle-drum, tymbal. **Heerpauker.** Kettle-drummer.

heftig (hěf'-tǐkh), *G.* Boisterous, passionate. **Heftigkeit** (kīt). Vehemence.

heimlich (hīm'-lǐkh), *G.* Secret, stealthy, mysterious.

heiss (hīs), *G.* Hot, ardent.

heiter (hī'těr), *G.* Serene, glad.

Heldenlied (hěl'děn-lēt), *G.* Hero-song. **heldenmüthig** (mü-tǐkh). Heroic. **Heldentenor.** Dramatic tenor.

hel'icon, *E.,* **Hel'ikon,** *G.* 1. A military bass brass wind-instr., carried over the shoulder; scales, F, E flat, C and B flat (the lowest tone of the bass of which is B,,). 2. Ancient 9-stringed device showing the theory of intervals.

hell (hěl), *G.* Clear, bright.

helper. An octave-pipe set beside one of 8-ft. pitch to add to its brilliance.

hem'i, *G.* Half. **hemidemisemiquaver** (-rest). A 64th note (or rest). **hemidiapen'te.** Diminished fifth. **hemidit'onos,** *Gr.* Minor third.

hemio'la, hemio'lia, *Gr.* 1. The ratio 3:2. 2. Quintuple time. 3. Interval of a 5th. 4. A triplet. 5. Vide NOTATION (COLOUR).

hemiope, *Gr.* An ancient three-holed flute.

hemiphrase. One bar of a phrase.

hemito'nium, *Gr.* A semitone in Greek music (ratio 256:243).

heptachord. 1. Interval of a seventh. 2. A 7-stringed inst. 3. A Greek series of 7 tones with half-tone step between the 3d and 4th.

heptade (hěp'-tǎd), **hep'tadechord,** *E.* Vide ELLIS.

heptam'eris, *Gr.* A seventh part of a meris.

Herabstrich (här'-äp'strĭkh), *G.*
Down-bow. Heraufstrich (här'-owf-
strĭkh). Up-bow.

heraufgehen (här-owf'gäĕn), *G.* To
ascend.

hero'ic, *E.*, heroisch (här'-ō-ĭsh), *G.*,
héroïque (ā-rō-ēk), *F.* Bold, brave.
Vide EROICA.

Herstrich (här-strĭkh), *G.* Down-bow
(on 'cello and double-bass). Herun-
terstrich, *G.* Down-bow (on the
violin, etc.).

hervorgehoben (här-fôr'ghĕ-hō'ben),
hervorhebend (hā'bĕnt), hervortre-
tend (trä-tĕnt), *G.* With emphasis.

Herz (hĕrts), *G.* "Heart." Vide TAS-
SEAU.

herzig (hĕrts-ikh), herzlich (lĭkh), *G.*
Tender.

Hes (hĕs), *G.* B flat when directly
derived from B natural (or H).
Heses, B double flat.

heulen (hoi'-lĕn), *G.* To cipher.

hexachord, *Gr.*, hexachorde (ĕx-ä-
kôrd), *F.* 1. A scale, or system, of
six sounds. 2. A sixth. 3. A six-
stringed lyre.

hexam'eron, *Gr.* Group of six pieces.

hex'aphonic. Composed of six voices.

hey de guise (ĕ-dŭ-gēze), *F.* A
country-dance.

hia'tus. A gap.

hidden. 1. Obscured, covered, yet
implied; thus in the skip, say, from
e to *g*, the tone *f* is implied though
not struck or dwelt on; it could be
called hidden. But the term is used
rather of intervals similarly implied,
thus in the progression, say from e–c
to g–d, the tone *f* is passed over,
and as *f* makes with *c* the same interval as *g* with *d*, that is, a perfect
fifth, the progression becomes a hidden or implied fifth, and is put under
the same ban by stricter theorists,
though sanctioned by free practice.
Similarly a progression, as of g–b'
to c–c' contains hidden octaves.
2. h. canon. Close canon.

Hief (hēf), Hiefstoss (shtôss), *G.*
Sound of the hunting-horn. Hiefhorn, Hifthorn (hĭft), Hüfthorn
(hĭft). A wooden hunt-horn with
2 or 3 notes, and 3 pitches: H.-
zinke (tsĭnk-kĕ). High. Rüdenhorn (rüd'-n). Low. Halb-rüden-
horn. Medium.

hierophon (hēr'-ō-fōn), *Gr.* Singer of
hymns.

higgai'on se'lah, *Heb.* A term, per-

haps calling for stringed instr. and
trumpets.

high. 1. Acute in pitch. 2. Upper,
or first, as h. *soprano.* high bass.
A barytone. higher rhythm. A
rhythm composed of smaller ones.
High mass. Vide MASS. h. tenor.
Counter-tenor. h. treble clef. The
G clef on the first line.

hilfs–. Same as hülfs–.

Hinaufstrich (hĭn-owf'strĭkh), *G.* Up-
bow on the violin, etc. Hinstrich
(hĭn'strĭkh), *G.* Up-bow on 'cello
and double-bass.

Hintersatz, *G.* An old mixture-stop,
re-enforcing the open diapason.

Hirtenflöte (hĭrt'-ĕn-flā'-tĕ), *G.* Shepherd's flute. Hirtengedicht (gĕ-
dĭkht). Pastoral poem. H.-lied
(lēt). Pastoral song. H.-pfeife
(pfī-fe). Pastoral pipe. hirtlich
(hĭrt'-lĭkh). Pastoral, rural.

His (hĭs), *G.* B♯. hisis (hĭs'ĭs), *G.* B
double sharp.

H.-moll (hä'môl), *G.* B minor.

Hoboe (hō-bō'-ĕ), Hoboy (hō-bōē), *G.*
Oboe. Hobo'ist, *G.* Oboist.

hoch (hôkh), *G.* High, sharp, very.
Hochamt (hôkh'ämt). High Mass.
h. feierlich (fī'-ĕr-likh). Very solemn. H.-gesang, H.-lied (lēt)
Ode, hymn. H.-horn. Oboe. H.-
muth (moot). Elevation, pride.
Hochzeitsgedicht (tsīts), Hochzeitslied. Wedding-song. Hochzeits-
marsch. Wedding-march. höchsten
(hĕkh'-shtĕn), *G.* Highest.

hock'et, hocqu'etus. 1. An abrupt
rest. 2. Old English part-music full
of rests and abruptness.

Hof (hôf), *G.* Court; hence, H.-kapelle
(Konzert). Court orchestra (con-
cert). H.-musikant (moo-zi-kant).
Court musician. H.-organist
Court organist.

höflich (hĕf'lĭkʰ), *G.* Graceful. Höf-
lichkeit (kīt). Grace.

Höhe (hä'ĕ), *G.* Height, acuteness;
upper register of; as *Oboen-höhe.*

hoheit (hō'hīt), *G.* Dignity, loftiness.

Hohlflöte (hōl'flā-tĕ), *G.* "Hollow-
toned flute." Open flue-stop of various pitches; in the smaller called
Hohlpfeifen. The mutation-stop in
the fifth is called Hohlquinte.

hok'et, hock'et. A quint-stop.

hold (hōlt'), *G.* Pleasing, sweet.

hold. The fermate. holding-note. A
note sustained while others are in
motion.

hold'ing. *Old E.* Burden.

Holzbläser (hôlts′blä-zĕr), *G.* Player(s) on Holz′blasinstrumente, or wood-wind instruments.

hölzernes Gelächter (hĕlts′-ĕr-nĕs gĕlĕkh′-tĕr), *G.* Xylophone.

Holzflöte (hôlts′flä-tĕ), *G.* "Wood-flute"; a stop.

Holz′harmonika, *G.* Xylophone.

hom′ophone. A letter or character denoting the same sound as another; thus a♯ and b♭ are homophones.

homophon′ic, homoph′onous. 1. Noncontrapuntal, lyric, marked by one melody in predominance. Vide POLYPHONIC. 2. In unison. Vide ANTIPHONIC. h o m o p h ′ o n y, *E.* homophonie (ôm-ôf-ôn-ē), *F.* Music that is homophonic 1 or 2.

hook. The stroke added to the stem of notes smaller than ¼ notes.

hop′per. In piano action, the escapement-lever.

Hop′ser, Hops-tanz (tänts), *G.* Country-dance. Hopswalzer (hôps′ vältsĕr), *G.* Quick waltzes.

hoq′uetus. Hocket.

hora (pl. horae), *L.* Hour(s). horae canonicae. Canonic hours, those at which services are held: lauds. sunrise. prime. First hour (6 a. m.). tierce (or terce). 3d (9 a. m.). Sext. 6th (noon). nones. 9th (3 p. m.). vespers. Evening. compline. Final. Services during the night are called nocturns; the word matins includes both nocturns and lauds. horae regulares. Chant sung at regular hours.

horn (*G.* pl. Hörner) (hĕrn′ĕr), *E.* & *G.* General name for all metal wind-instruments. Specifically, the French horn, a brass conical tube variously curved, with a flaring bell at one end, and a cupped mouthpiece at the other; the shape of this mouthpiece, and the ratio of the width to the length of the tube determining the quality of the instr. The old *natural horn* was diatonic, producing only the tones of its natural scale, some intermediate tones being obtained by putting the hand in the bell, or "stopping" the tone. The key of the horn was changed by taking out one section of its tube (a *crook*), and inserting a section longer or shorter, thus lowering or raising the key. The tone series was thus incomplete, and the *stopped tones* were inaccurate. The natural tones depend on the

amount of wind-pressure (or in F, embouchure, lipping) which must vary with each note according to the natural scale (see ACOUSTICS).

The horn of this century has gradually displaced the natural horn. It is provided with valves (or auxiliary tubes), which practically lengthen or shorten the tube instantaneously. The tone is produced by embouchure combined with valve-manipulation until a complete chromatic scale is obtainable. *Stopped tones* are now not necessary, though available for special effects; they are called for by the sign +, by the word "stopped," or by "son bouché" (sôṅ boo-shā), and are weirdly tragic or romantic.

The range of the horn depends upon its key, the scale of each consisting of a fundamental tone, and the natural series of partials (vide ACOUSTICS), the intermediate tones between the 3d and the 16th partial being obtained by valves or stopping. The horn in C thus sounds C *c*, *g–c′′*, from *g* to *c′′* being nearly complete chromatically, the upper notes being risky. The other horns are lower by the interval between their key and C; they are B flat, A, A flat, G, F, E, E flat, D, C *basso*, B flat *basso*. The keys F♯ (G flat), C♯ (D flat), B and A *basso* are obtained not by changing crooks, but by drawing out a special slide which lowers the key a semitone. In valve-horns the F horn is by far most common. Music for horns is now always written in the G clef, the F clef being used for the low notes, which are always written an octave lower than they sound. For convenience of embouchure, the notes are written as if the horn were always in C, and the player so plays it; but the crook used governs the tone, and a C on the staff sounds as the F below on an F horn, as A flat on the A flat horn, etc. Alpine h. A wooden horn 8 ft. long. basset h. Vide BASSET. hunting-h. The primitive *natural* or *French horn.* hornband. A band of trumpeters. A *Russian H-B.* is one in which each hunting-horn plays but one note horning. Vide SHIVAREE. Hornmusik′, *G.* Music for the brass. Hornquinten, *G.* The hidden fifths prevalent in music for two horns. Hornsordin′, *G.* A conical or pear-shaped mute inserted in the bell.

hornpipe. An old E. shawm with a bell of horn; hence, an old E. dance of great vivacity, in 3-4 or 4-4 time.

Hosan'na, Hosian'na, *Heb.* "Save, I pray," an interjection in prayer, hence part of the Sanctus. Vide MASS.

Hose (hô'-zĕ), *G.* Boot of a pipe.

houl (howl). A Persian military drum.

hours. Vide HORÆ.

hreol (wrā'ôl). A Danish peasant-dance.

H. S. Abbr. for *Hauptsatz.*

huehuetl, huehuitl (wā-wāt'-'l). An Aztec drum 3 feet high with a membrane that could be tightened at will, changing the pitch and furnishing an harmonic bass.

Hüfthorn (hĭft-hôrn), *G.* Bugle-horn.

hug'gab, *Heb.* 1. An organ. 2. Pan's pipes.

huitpied (wēt-pĭ-ā), *F.* Eight feet (of stops). **huitpieds.** An organ with no stops larger than 8 ft.

Huldigungsmarsch (hool-dĭ-goongks-märsh), *G.* A solemn march for reviews.

Hülfs- (hĭlfs), *G.* Auxiliary. **Hülfslinien** (lē'-nĭ-ĕn). Leger-lines. **H.-note. H.-ton.** Auxiliary, accessory note. **H.-stimme** (shtĭm'mĕ). A mutation-stop.

Hummel (hoom'mel), **Hümmelchen** (hĭm'mĕl-khĕn), *G.* 1. A bagpipe. 2. In organs the thorough-bass drone. 3. The Balalaika because it had a sympathetic or drone-string. 4. The drones in a hurdy-gurdy.

hummen (hoom'mĕn), *G.* To hum.

Humor (hoo'-mor), *G.* Humour, whim.

Humoreske (hoo'mo-rĕs'ke), *G.,* **humoresque** (ü-môr-ĕsk), *F.* A humorous or whimsical composition.

hunting-horn. A bugle or French horn. **hunting-song.** Song in praise of the chase. **hunt's-up.** A boisterous morning-song.

hurdy-gurdy. An old instr. with four strings, acted on by a wheel rubbed in resin. Two of the strings are stopped by certain keys the others act as a drone-bass; compass *g–g'* '.

hurry. Premonitory roll of drum or tremolo of strings in stage-music.

hurtig (hoor'tĭkh), *G.* Quick, allegro. **H.-keit** (kīt). Agility.

hydraul'icon, hydraulic organ. An instr. older than the wind-organ, inv. 180 B.C., by Ktesibios of Alexandria, the wind-pressure being regulated by water.

hymn, *F.,* **hymne** (ēmn), *F.,* **Hymne** (hēm'nĕ), *G.* A sacred or patriotic song. **h. vesper.** A hymn sung in the R. C. Vesper service. **hymnal, hymn-book.** A collection of hymns. **hymnology, hymnologie** (ēm-nŏl-ō-zhē). See page 749.

hymnus, *L.* A hymn. **h. Ambrosianus.** The Ambrosian chant.

hy'pate, *Gr.* The uppermost lyre-string but the lowest in tone. **hypaton.** Lowest tetrachord. See page 762.

hypatho'ides. The lower tones in the Greek scale.

hyper (hī'-per), *Gr.* Over, above, of intervals, "super," or "upper" (as **hyperdiapa'son,** the octave above; **h.-diapen'te,** the 5th above; **h.-dito'nos,** the 3d above, etc.); of the Greek transposition scales and ecclesiastical octave species, "a fourth higher"; the Greek octave species "a fifth higher," or "a fourth lower." Vide MODES for such words as **hyperæolian,** etc.

hypo, *Gr.* Below, under; of intervals, "sub," or "lower." **hypodiapa'son.** The lower octave. **h-diapen'te** The fifth below. **h-dito'nos.** The third below. For the names of the Greek transposition scales and ecclesiastical modes, as **hypoæo'lian,** etc., see page 762.

Hzbl. Abbr. oi **Holzbläser** (q. v.).

I

I (ē) *I.,* pl. "The." Also the letter is used by Kirnberger, to indicate a major seventh, as b♮ in place of b♭ in the 7th chord on c. Tartini used *u.*

Ias'tian, *Gr.* The Ionian mode.

ic'tus, *Gr.* Stress, accent, emphasis.

idea. A theme, subject, figure, or motive.

idée fixe (ē-dā fēx), *F.* Berlioz's name for a recurring theme or motive.

idyl, idillio (ē-dēl'lĭ-ō), *I.,* **idylle** (ē-dē-yŭ in *F.,* in *G.* ē-dĭl'lĕ). A pastoral.

il (ēl), *I.* The. **il più** (ēl pē-oo'). The most, e. g., *il più forte possibile.* As loud as possible.

ilarità (ē-lä-rĭ-tä'), *I.* Hilarity.

imboccatura (ĭm-bôk-kä-too'rä), *I.* 1. Mouthpiece. 2. Embouchure.

imbroglio (ĭm-brŏl'yō), *I* "Confusion," a passage of complicated rhythms.

imitando (Ĭm-Ĭ-tän'dō), *I.* Imitating.
i. la voce (vō-chĕ). Imitating the voice.

imitation (pron. in *F.* Ĭm-Ĭ-tăs-yôǹ), **imitatio** (ēm-Ĭ-tä'tsĬ-ō), *I.* The repetition by a second voice (the consequent or answer) of a figure, subject or theme first announced by another (the antecedent or subject). If this repetition be exact, interval for interval, note-value for note-value, the imitation is *strict* or *canonic*, vide CANON; otherwise *free.* **i. at the 5th, octave, etc.** That in which the answer follows the subject at the interval of a 5th, octave, etc. **i. augmented** or **i. by augmentation.** That in which the answer is in notes of greater value than those of the subject. **diminished i.** or **i. by diminution.** A style of imitation in which the answer is given in notes of less value than those of the subject. **freely inverted i.** That in which the order of successive notes is not strictly retained. **i. in contrary motion.** That in which the rising intervals of the subject descend in the answer and vice versa. **i. in different divisions.** That in which the subject is answered in a different division of a measure; for instance, beginning on the accented is answered on the unaccented. **i. in similar motion.** That in which the answer retains the order of notes of the subject. **retrograde i.** (or **i. per recte e retro**), **cancrizans,** or **cancrizante.** That in which the subject is taken backwards in the answer. **reversed retrograde i.** That in which the subject is taken backwards and also in contrary motion in the answer. **strictly inverted i.** That in which note-values are precisely answered in contrary motion. **tonal i.** That which does not alter the key.

imitation pipes and draw-knobs are dummies of more beauty than use.

imitative music. That aiming to mimic the operations of nature, as water-falls, thunder, etc.

imitato (Ĭm-Ĭ-tä'tō), *I.* Imitated. **imitazione** (tä-tsĬ-ō'nĕ). Imitation.

immer (Ĭm'mĕr), *G.* Always, ever, constantly.

immutab'ilis, *L.* Vide ACCENTUS ECCLESIASTICI.

imparfait (ăǹ-păr-fĕ'), *F.* Imperfect.

impaziente (Ĭm-pät-sĬ-ĕn'-tĕ), *I.* Impatient. **impazientemen'te.** Hurriedly.

imperfect. Not perfect or complete. Vide CADENCE and INTERVAL. **i. concords, consonances.** Thirds and sixths, so called because they change from major to minor, still remaining consonant. **i. measure.** Old term for two-fold measure. **i. time.** Old term for common time. **i. triad.** The chord of the third, fifth and eighth, on the seventh degree; it consists of two minor thirds.

imperfection. 1. Vide LIGATURE. 2. Vide NOTATION.

imperfet'to, *I.* Imperfect.

imperioso (Ĭm-pā-rĬ-o'-so), *I.* Pompous. **imperiosamen'te.** Imperiously.

imperturbabile (Ĭm-pĕr-toor-bä'bĬ-lĕ), *I.* Quiet.

impeto (im'-pĕ-tō). **impetuosità** (im-pä-too-ō-zĬ-tä'), *I.* Impetuosity, vehemence. **impetuo'so, impetuosamen'te.** Impetuous(ly).

imponente (nĕn'tĕ), *I.* Imposingly.

implied discord. A concord contained in a dissonant chord as a major third in an augmented 5th (as f-a-c♯).

implied interval. One not specifically indicated by its numeral but implied by another numeral. Vide HIDDEN.

impresario (Ĭm-prĕ-sä'-rĬ-ō), *I.* Manager of opera, concerts, etc.

impromp'tu (in *F.* ăǹ-prôǹ-tü). An extemporaneous comp., or one having a spirit of informality and caprice.

impropre'ria, *L.* "Reproaches." In R. C. ritual, a series of antiphons and responses for Good Friday morning. In Rome sung to old *Faux bourdons* arranged by Palestrina; elsewhere to plain-song from the Graduale Romanum.

impropri'etas. Vide LIGATURE.

im'provise, impro(v)visare (zä'rĕ), *I.*, **improviser** (ăǹ-prô-vē-zä), *F.* To sing or play without premeditation.

improvisateur (ăǹ-prô-vē-zä-tŭr'), **improvisatrice** (trēs), *F.*, **Improvisatoi** (Ĭm-prō-fī-zä'-tôr), *G.*, **Improvvisato're,** *I.* An improviser.

im'provisation. Extemporaneous performance. **Improvisier maschine** (Ĭm-prō-fĬ-zēr' mä-shē'-nĕ), *G.* A melograph. **improvvisata** (zä'tä), *I.* An extempore composition. **improvviso** (Ĭm-prôv-vē'-zō), **improvvisamen'te,** *I.* Extemporaneous(ly).

in (ēn), *I., G.* and *L.* In, into, in the.

inacutire (in-ä-koo-tē'-rĕ), *I.* To sharpen.

in'betont, *G.* With medial emphasis.

Inbrunst (ĭn'broonst), *G.* Fervour. **inbrünstig** (ĭn-brĭn'shtĭkh). Ardent.

incalzando (ĭn-käl-tsän'dō), *I.* Hastening.

Incarna'tus, *L.* "Was born" (of the Virgin Mary). Part of the Credo. Vide MASS.

inch (of wind). In an organ, wind-pressure is gauged by a graduated *U* tube in which water rises, the mean pressure being 3 inches.

inchoa'tio, *L.* Vide CHANT.

incisore (ĭn-chĭ-sōl-rĕ), *I.* Engraver of music.

inconsola'to (lä'-tō), *I.* Mournful.

incordare (dä'-rĕ), *I.* To string.

incrociamen'to (krō-chä), *I.* Crossing.

indeciso (ĭn-dĕ-chē'-zō), *I.* Undecided (implying slight changes of time, a somewhat capricious tempo).

indegnato (ĭn-dän-yä'-tō), **indegnata-men'te,** *I.* Wrathful(ly).

independent. Used of non-dissonant harmony requiring no resolution.

index. 1. A direct. 2. Forefinger.

indifferen'te (rĕn'-tĕ), **indifferente-men'te,** *I.* Indifferent(ly). **in-differenza** (rĕn'-tsä), *I.* Indifference.

infantile (ĭn-fän-tē'lĕ), *I.* Child-like (of the quality of upper notes of some voices).

infe'rior, *L.* Lower.

infernale (ĭn-fĕr-nä'lē), *I.* Infernal.

infervorato (rä'-tō), *I.* Fervent.

infiammatamen'te, *I.* Ardently.

in'finite, *E.,* **infinito** (ĭn-fĭ-nē'-tō), *I.* Used of canon which can be continued indefinitely unless given a special cadence.

inflatil'ia, *L.* Instrs. of inflation; wind-instruments.

inflection. 1. Modification in the pitch of the voice. 2. In chanting a change from the monotone.

in'fra, *L.* Beneath. **Infrabass,** *G.* Sub-bass.

infuriante (ĭn-foo-rĭ-än'tĕ), **infuriato** (ä'-tō), *I.* Furious.

inganno (ĭn-gän'nō), *I.* "Deception"; applied to a deceptive cadence; also to unexpected resolutions or modulations. **d'inganno.** Unexpected.

in gemination. Old term for repetition of words.

ingressa. Vide INTROIT.

Inhalt (ĭn'hält), *G.* Contents; idea.

inharmonic relation. Vide FALSE RELATION.

inner. 1. Used of the alto or tenor part as distinguished from the bass and soprano. 2. Used of a pedal point on an inner part.

innig, inniglich (ĭn'-nĭkh-lĭkh), *G.* Sincere, tender, heartfelt. **Innigkeit** (kīt). Deep feeling.

inno (ĭn'-nō), *I.* A hymn, canticle, ode.

innocente (ĭn-no-chĕn'tĕ), **innocent-emen'te,** *I.* Innocent(ly), artless (ly). **innocenza** (ĭn-nō-chĕn'-tsä). Innocence.

inquieto (ĭn-kwĭ-ä'-tō), *I.* Restless.

insensible (ĭn-sĕn-sē'bĭ-lĕ), **insensi-bilmen'te,** *I.* Imperceptibly, by small degrees.

insisten'do, *I.* Urgent. **insistenza** (tĕn'-tsä). Insistence.

inständig (ĭn-shtĕn'dĭkh), *G.* Urgent, pressing.

instante (ĭn-stän'tĕ), **instantemen'te.** *I.* Vehement(ly), urgent(ly).

in'strument (in *F.* ăn-strü-män). A sonorous body constructed for the production of musical sounds. **i. à cordes** (ä-kôrd). A stringed instr. **i. à l'archet** (ä-lär-shä). Instr. played with a bow. **i. à percussion** (ä pär-küs-yôn). Instr. of percussion. **i. à vent** (ä vän). Wind-instrument.

instrumental, *E.,* **instrumentale** (ĭn-stroo-mĕn-tä'lĕ), *I.* Of music for instrs. as opposed to vocal music.

instrumentare (tä'rĕ), *I.* To compose instrumental music.

in'strumenta'tion (in *F.* ăn-strü-män-täs'yôn), **instrumentazione** (tä-tsĭ-ō'nĕ), *I.,* **Instrumenti(e)rung** (ĭn-stroo-mĕn-tē'-roongk), *G.* The art or act of writing or arranging a composition for instrs., particularly the orchestra (vide article on THE ORCHESTRA AND ORCHESTRATION); sometimes used of piano-playing that produces the effect of other instrs. **Instru-mentenmacher** (mäkh'ĕr), *G.* An instr.-maker.

instrumen'to, *I.,* An instrument. **i. d'arco** (or **a corda**) (där'-kō). A stringed instrument. **i. da campa-nel'la.** Glockenspiel. **i. da fiato** (fĭ-ä'-tō). Wind-instr. **i. du quil'la.** A spinet.

intavolare (ĭn-tä-vō-lä'-rĕ), *I.* To write out or copy music. **intavola-tura** (lä-too'-rä). 1. Notation. 2. Figured bass. 3. Tablature.

integer valor (notarum), *L.* "The integral value" (of notes), i. e., their average duration at a moderate movement. Michael Pretorius set the i. v. of the brevis at about $\frac{1}{10}$ of a minute.

intendant (ăṅ-täṅ-däṅ), *F.*, **intenden'te**. *I.* Director, conductor.

intenzionato (ĭn-tĕn-tsĭ-ō-nä'-tō). Emphatic.

in'terlude. 1. A piece, usually short, played between acts, movements, stanzas, or portions of service. 2. A short operetta.

interlu'dium, *L.*, **intermède** (ăṅ-tĕr-mĕd), *F.*, **intermedio** (ĭn-tĕr-mä'dĭ-ō), **intermezzo** (ĭn-tĕr-mĕd'-zō), *I.* An interlude.

interme'diate. 1. Accidental. 2. Transitional.

intermedietto (ĭn-tĕr-mä'dĭ-ĕt-tō), *I.* A short interlude.

interrogati'vus. Vide ACCENTUS ECCL.

interrotto (rôt'-tō), *I.* Interrupted.

interrupted. Vide CADENCE.

interruzione (root-sĭ-ō'nĕ), *I.* Interruption.

interval, Intervall (ĭn-tĕr-fäl'), *G.*, **intervale** (ăṅ-tĕr-väl), *F.*, **intervallo** (väl'lō), *I.*, **interval'lum**, *L.* The distance, or difference in pitch, between tones, reckoned upwards (unless specially stated). The intervals are, the *first* or *prime* (which is identity, *C* for instance being its own prime); the *second* (as c-d); the *third* or *tierce* (as c-e); the *fourth* or *quart* (as c-f); the *fifth* or *quint* (as c-g); the *sixth* or *sext* (as c-a); the *seventh* or *sept* (as c-b); the *eighth* or *octave* (as c-c'); the *ninth* (as c-d'), etc. Those within the octave are called *simple;* those over the octave, *compound,* since a *tenth* is an octave plus a third, etc.

Intervals are qualified also by their mode; those in the major key of their lower tone (as a-c♯) being called *major*, those a semitone greater than major are *augmented* or *extreme*, *superfluous*, *redundant* or *sharp;* those a semitone less than major are *minor* (as a-c); those a semitone less than minor are *diminished* or *flat* (as a-c♭). The first, fourth, fifth and octave are called *perfect* instead of major, because they do not change their quality as do the others on inversion (q.v.). Other names for intervals are *chromatic*, containing a note foreign to the key, opposed to

diatonic, *dissonant*, needing resolution; opposed to *consonant*, *enharmonic* (q.v.); *harmonic* when struck simultaneously instead of separately, hence opposed to *melodic*. *Forbidden*. Contrary to the rules of Harmony (q.v.). *Consecutive* (q.v.). A *natural* interval is that between two tones of a major scale. The ratios of the vibrations of diatonic intervals are prime, 1 : 1 ; second, 8 : 9 ; third, 4 : 5 ; fourth, 3 : 4 ; fifth, 2 : 3 ; sixth, 3 : 5 ; seventh, 8 : 15 ; octave, 1 : 2.

intervening. Intermediate (of a fugue subject).

intimo (ĭn'-tĭ-mō), *I.* Intimate, expressive. **intimis'simo**. Most expressive.

intonare (ĭn-tō-nä'rĕ), *I.* To intone.

intona'tion. 1. The production of sound by voice or instr., as regards quality and pitch. **false i.** That which is untrue to the key or pitch. 2. The initial phrase of the antiphon. 3. Method of singing plain-chant. 4. Vide CHANT. **fixed i.** Vide FIXED TONE.

intonato (ĭn-tō-nä'-tō), *I.* Tuned, set to music.

in'tonator. Monochord.

intonatura (ĭn-tō-nä-too'rä), **intonazione** (ĭn-tō-nä-tsĭ-ō'nĕ), *I.* Intonation.

intoni(e)ren (ĭn-tō-nē'rĕn), *G.* 1. To intone. 2. To voice, as pipes. 3. The voicing.

Intonireisen (nēr'-ī-zĕn), *G.* A knife used in trimming and tuning pipes.

Intrade (ĭn-trä'-dĕ), *G.* A prelude or entrance-music.

intreccio (ĭn-trĕt'-chō), *I.* "Intrigue." A short dramatic work.

intrepidezza (ĭn-trä-pĭ-dĕd'-zä), *I.* Intrepidity. **intrepido** (ĭn-trä'-pĕ-dō), **intrepidamen'te**. Bold(ly).

introduc'tion, *E.*, **introducimen'to** (doo-chĭ), **introduzione** (doo-tsĭ-ō'nĕ), *I.* The preliminary measures, or movement preparatory for the main subject.

intro'it (in *F.* ăṅ-trwä), **introito** (ĭn-trō-ē'-tō), *I.*, **intro'itus**, *L.* "Entrance"; a hymn or antiphon sung in R. C. service while the priest goes to the altar; in the Anglican Church Communion, when the minister goes to the table. In the Ambrosian ritual called *Ingressa*.

intuonare (in-too-ō-nä'-rĕ), *I.* To intone.

622 DICTIONARY OF TERMS

inven'tion (in *F.* ăn-väns-yôn), in-
venzione (ĭn-věn-tsĭ-ō'-ně), *I.* A
short informal contrapuntal study
with one theme.
Inventions (horn) (ĭn-věn'tsĭ-ōns), *F.*
A Waldhorn fitted with crooks by
Werner, 1760.
inver'sio, *L.,* inver'sion, *E.* The
transposition of the elements of (a),
chords, (b) intervals, (c) themes, (d)
parts. (a) The triad is "inverted"
from its fundamental position with
the root in the bass, to the *first inversion* with the 3d in the bass, and
the *second i.* when the fifth is in the
bass (a 6-4 chord), etc., vide CHORD.
(b) The inversion of intervals is the
lowering of the upper tone an octave,
thus bringing the lower note above,
and the upper below; for example,
to invert a major 6th, *e'b–c',* we lower
c' an octave, securing *c–e'b,* a minor
3d. The new product of an inversion is always the difference between
the first interval and the number 9,
e. g., a 6th inverted becomes a 3d,
a 5th inverted becomes a 4th, etc.
The result of inversion is to change
major intervals to minor, and vice
versa; and augmented to diminish,
and vice versa; but perfect remain
perfect. (c) A theme is inverted by
being repeated backwards, hence,
retrograde inversion, or inversio
cancrizans, "crab-like." (d) Two
parts are inverted when the lower is
raised by an octave (inversio in octavam acutam), or by a fifth, tenth,
twelfth, etc., or when the higher is
lowered by an octave (inversio in
octavam gravem, or inferiorem),
a fifth, tenth, twelfth, etc. (vide
COUNTERPOINT).
invert, inverted. Vide INVERSION.
A *pedal-point* in any part other than
the lowest is called *inverted.* A *turn*
commencing with the lowest note is
inverted.
invi'tatory, *E.,* invitato'rio, *Sp.,* invitato'rium, *L.* 1. An antiphon in
the R. C. Matins. 2. In the Anglican
Church, the versicle "Praise ye the
Lord," and the response sung at
matins. 3. In the Greek Church the
"O come let us worship" sung thrice
before the psalms at the canonical
hours.
invocazione (kä-tsĭ-ō'-ně), *I.* Invocation.
Io'nian, Ion'ic. See page 762.
ira (ē'-rä), *I.* Anger, wrath. irato

(ē-rä'-tō), iratamen'te. Passion-
ate(ly).
Irish harp. 1. An ancient instr. having
more strings than the lyre. 2. Trade
name for "Jew's harp."
irlandais (ēr-län-dě'), *F.,* irländisch
(ēr'-lěnt-ĭsh), *G.* An air or dance in
the Irish style.
iron harp. A semicircular arrangement of tuned iron rods which vibrate sympathetically when a violin
is played.
ironico (ē-rō'-nĭ-kō), *I.,* ironicamen'-
te. Ironical(ly).
irregular, *E.,* irregolare (ēr-rā-gō-
lä'rě), *I.* Not according to strict
rule or practice. Vide CADENCE.
irresoluto (ēr-rā-zō-loo'-tō), *I.* Irres-
olute.
isdegno (ēs-dān'-yō), *I.* Indignation.
i'sochronal, *Gr.,* isoch'ronous. Uniform in time.
i'son. In Greek Church chant, the
movable tonic.
isoton'ic. Used of a system of intervals in which all concords are tempered alike, and contain twelve equal
semitones.
istes'so, *I.* The same. il tempo. The
same time (as before).
istrepito (ēs-trā-pē'-tō), *I.* Noise, blus-
ter.
istrionica (ēs-trĭ-ō'nĭ-kä), *I.* Histri-
onic.
istrumentale (ēs-troo-měn-tä'lě), *I.*
Instrumental. istrumentazione (tä-
tsĭ-ō'në). Instrumentation. istru-
men'to. An instrument.
Italian mordent. Shake or trill of a
tone with the next above. Italian
sixth. Vide ALTERED CHORDS.
Italian strings. Catgut strings
largely made in Rome.
italiano (ē-tä-lĭ-ä'-nō), *I.,* italienisch
(ē-tä-lĭ-ä'-nĭsh), *G.,* italien(ne) (ē-täl-
yän [or yěn]), *F.* Italian.
i'te, mis'sa est (ecclesia), *L.* "Depart, the congregation is dismissed." \
Vide MASS; from the word *missa* the
word mass is derived.

J

Jack, *I.* 1. An upright slip of wood
on the back end of a key-lever,
carrying a crow-quill or piece of
hard leather which projected at
right angles (in the harpsichord), or
a metal tangent (in the clavichord),
and which struck and set in motion
a string. The quill or the leathe-

served as a plectrum. 2. The "hopper."

Jagd (yäkht), *G.* Hunt, hunting. **Jagdhorn, Jagdzink** (tsĭnk). Hunting-horn, bugle-horn. **Jagdruf** (roof). Sound of the horn. **J-lied** (lēt). Hunting-song. **J-sinfonie** (sĭn-fō-nē'). A symphony of the hunt. **J-stück.** A hunting-piece.

Jägerchor (jä'-khĕr-kôr), *G.* Chorus of hunters. **Jägerhorn.** Hunting-horn.

jailtage (yāl'-tāj). The sole musical instr. of Tartary, a slender box of fir, about 4 ft. long, over which six wire strings are stretched. It is played with both hands.

jaleo (hä-lā'-ō), *Sp.* A Spanish dance in 3-8 time, moderato, for one person.

Jalousieschweller (yäl-oo-zē'-shvĕl-lĕr), *G.* "Venetian-blind" swell.

Janitscharenmusik (yä-nĭt-shä'rĕn-moo-zēk'), *G.*, **jan'izary music.** Military music for cymbals, triangles, etc.

Jankó. Vide KEY-BOARD.

jazz. See history of, page 750.

jeu (zhŭ) pl. **jeux** (zhŭ), *F.* 1. Play; style of playing on an instr. 2. A stop on the organ, harmonium, etc. 3. The organ-power, as **grand j.** (gräṅ), or **plain j.** (plăṅ). Full organ. **demi-j.** Half-power. **j. à bouche** (ä boosh). Flue-stop. **j. céleste** (sä-lĕst). Vide CELESTE. **j. d'anche** (dänsh). Reed-stop. **j. d'anges** (dänzh). Vox angelica. **j. d'échos** (dā'-kō). Echo-stop. **j. de flûtes** (flüt). Flute-stop. **j. de mutation** (mü-tăs-yôṅ). Mutation, or a mixture-stop. **j. de timbres** (tăṅbr). Glockenspiel. **j. de violes** (vē-ôl). Consort of viols. **j. de voix humaine** (vwä ü-mĕn). Vox humana. **j. d'orgues** (dôrg). Register, or row of pipes. **jeux forts** (fôr). Loud stops.

Jew's harp or **jewstrump.** Vide HARP.

jig. A light, brisk dance in 6-8 or 12-8 time. Vide SUITE.

jingles. The disks of metal on a tambourine.

jobel (yō'-bĕl), *Heb.* Trumpets or horns.

joc'ulator. A jongleur.

Jodler (yōt'-lĕr), *G.* A style of singing affected by the Tyrolese, falsetto alternating rapidly with chest-regis-

ter. **jodeln** (yō'dĕln). To sing in such style.

jongleur (zhôṅ-glŭr), *F.* A hired or strolling musician. Vide TROUBADOUR.

jota (hō-tä), *Sp.* A Spanish dance in rapid 3-8 time.

jouer de (zhoo-ā-dŭ), *F.* To play upon (as an instr.).

jour (zhoor), *F.* "Day." **corde à j.** Open string.

ju'ba. Part of the breakdown dance of the American negro.

Jubal (yoo'-bäl), *G.* A 2- or 4-ft. stop. **Jubelflöte** (yoo-bĕl-flä'-tĕ), *G.* A stop. **Jubelgesang, Jubellied** (lēt). Song of jubilee. **Jubelhorn.** Key-bugle. **jubelnd** (yoo'-bĕlnt), *G.* Rejoicing. **Jubila'te,** *L.* "Be joyful." The name for the 10th Psalm in the Anglican Church.

jubila'tio, *L.* The cadence on the last syllable of "Alleluia" in R. C. music.

jubiloso (yoo-bĭ-lō'-sō), *I.* Jubilant.

ju'bilus, *L.* 1. An elaborate passage sung to one vowel. 2. Jubilatio.

Judenharfe (yoo'-dĕn), *G.* Jew's harp.

Jula (yoo'-la), *G.* An old 5 ⅓-ft. stop.

jump. 1. A progression by a skip. 2. Vide DUMP.

Jungfernregal (yoonk-fărn-rä'-gäl) or **J-stimme,** *G.* Vox angelica.

Jupiter symphony. Mozart's 49th, in C major.

just. Used of consonant intervals, voices, strings, pipes, etc., that speak or sound with exactness.

juste (zhüst), *F.* Accurate, perfect (of intervals). **justesse** (zhüs-tĕs'). Exactness of intonation.

K

[*NOTE.—Many German words are spelt either with "C" or "K," preferably the latter.*]

Kabaro (kä-bä'-rō). A small Egyptian drum.

Kadenz (kä-dents'), *G.* 1. Cadence (q.v.). 2. Cadenza.

kalamaika (kăl-ä-mä'-kä). A lively Hungarian dance in 2-4 time.

Kalkant (käl-känt'), *G.* Bellows-treader. **K.-glocker.** Signal-bell to the blower.

Kammer (kăm'-mĕr), *G.* Chamber (q.v.). **K.-kantate** (kän-tä'-tĕ). Chamber-cantata. **K. komponist.** Court-composer. **K. konzert.** Chamber-concert, or concerto. **K. duet,**

C. duet. **K. musik, K. spiel** (shpēl). Chamber-music. **K. musikus** (moo'-zĭ-koos). Member of a prince's private band. **K. sänger** (zĕng-ĕr)。 Court-singer. **K. stil** (shtēl). Style of chamber-music. **K. suiten.** Chamber-suites. Vide SUITE. **K. ton.** International pitch. **K. virtuosen.** Court-virtuoso.

kampoul (käm-pool'). A Malay gong.

kandele (kän-dā'-lĕ). 1. Ancient Finnish harp. 2. A dulcimer.

Kanon (kä'-nōn), *G.* "A rule." 1. A canon. 2. A monochord with movable bridge; sometimes it had a second string in unison. **kanonik** (känō'-nēk). Canonic.

kanoon', kanun'. Turkish instr. of the dulcimer variety; the canun.

Kantate (kän-tä'-tĕ), *G.* Cantata.

Kan'tor, *G.* Cantor.

Kanzelle (kän-tsĕl'-lĕ), *G.* Groove in a wind-chest.

Kanzellied (lēt), *G.* Hymn before the sermon.

Kanzone (kän-tsō'-nĕ). *G.* Canzone.

Kapelle (kä-pĕl'-lĕ), *G.* A chapel. 1. A musical establishment, a choir or a band connected with a church or court. 2. Any orchestra. **Kapell-knabe(n)** (knä'-bĕ(n). Choir-boy(s). **Kapellmeister** (kä-pĕl'-mīsh-ter), *G.* 1. Conductor. 2. Chapel-master. **Kapellmeister-musik.** Music full of such strains as must sound reminiscent to the conductor. **K. stil** (kä-pĕl'-shtēl), *G.* Same as *A cappella,* i. e., unaccompanied.

Kapodas'ter, *G.* Capotasto.

Karfreitag (kär-frī'-täkh), *G.* Good Friday.

Kassation (käs-sä'-tsĭ-ōn), *G.* Cassation.

Kastagnetten (käs-tän-yĕt'-tĕn), *G.* Castanets.

Kat'zenmusik (moo-zēk'), *G.* "Cat-music." Charivari.

Kavatine (käv-ä-tē'-nĕ), *G.* Cavatina.

kazoo'. A tube with a vibrating string which gives the voice an amusing quality when spoken or sung through.

keck (kĕk), *G.* Fresh, bold. **Keckheit** (kĕk'-hīt). Boldness, vigour.

keen'ers. Irish paid mourners.

Kehle (kā'-lĕ), *G.* The voice, the throat. **K.-fertigkeit** (fĕr-tĭkh-kīt). Vocal agility. **K.-kopf.** Larynx. **K.-schlag** (shläkh). Coup de glotte. **K.-laut** (lowt). A guttural sound.

Kehrab (kār'-äp), **Kehraus** (ows) *G.*

Colloquial term for the final dance of a ball.

kemangeh (kĕ-män-gäh'). A Turkish stringed instrument.

kenet (kĕn'-ĕt). Abyssinian trumpet.

Ken'ner, *G.* A connoisseur. "one who knows."

Kent bugle (*G.,* **Kenthorn**). Vide BUGLE. So named in honour of the Duke of Kent.

kerana (kĕ-rä'-nä). A Persian horn sounded at sunset and midnight.

ker'anim. Vide KEREN.

ke'ras, *Gr.* A horn.

Keraulophon (kĕ-row'-lŏ-fōn), *G.* An 8-ft. stop, a small round hole bored in the pipe near the top promoting the overtones; inv. by Gray and Davidson.

keren (kĕr'-ĕn), pl. **keranim,** *Heb.* A horn. **keren-Jebel** (ya-bel). Jubilee horn.

Kern (kărn), *G.* The languid (q.v.). **K. stimmen.** The fundamental stops.

kerrena (kĕr-rä'-nä). The kerana.

Kes'sel, *G.* Cup (of a mouthpiece). **Kesselpauke** (pow-kĕ). Kettledrum.

ketch. Old name for catch.

Ket'tentriller, *G.* Chain of trills.

ket'tledrum. A brass or copper kettle over the top of which is stretched a head of vellum, tightened by a ring and tuned by screws, or by cords and braces. **Kettledrums** are usually played in pairs with sticks having flexible handles and soft knobs. Each has a compass of a fifth; the lower may be tuned to any note from F to c, and the higher B flat to f.

key. 1. A family of chords and a chain of tones (i. e., a scale) finding their centre and point of rest in a certain tone (the tonic) from which the key takes its name. All keys conform to the standard for major keys, or to that for minor keys. The signature in which the number of sharps or flats of a major key is written serves as the signature for its *related minor* key, the tonic of which is a minor third below. The key of C has neither sharps nor flats, the key a fifth above (G) has one sharp, the key a fifth below (F) has one flat, and so the progression continues, forming (in a tempered instrument. Vide TEMPERAMENT) what is called the *circle of fifths,* as F♯ and G♭ are enharmonic keys traversing the same tones. The following ingenious chart from Riemann's Dictionary tabulates the keys and their signatures concisely, the flats and sharps appearing in the same order on the signatures as here:

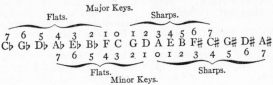

Major Keys.

Flats.   Sharps.

7 6 5 4 3 2 1 0 1 2 3 4 5 6 7
Cb Gb Db Ab Eb Bb F C G D A E B F# C# G# D# A#
7 6 5 4 3 2 1 0 1 2 3 4 5 6 7

Flats.   Sharps.
Minor Keys.

attendant, or related k. Vide RELATED. **chromatic k.** One with sharps or flats, opposed to natural k. **extreme k.** A remote, unrelated k. **parallel k.** a. Related. b. Used of a major and a minor key with the same tonic but different signatures. 2. Old name for clef. 3. A mechanical lever for controlling tone, whether digital or foot-key. 4. One of such keys as those on the outside of a flute covering certain holes. 5. A tuning-hammer. 6. A lever controlling organ-pallets.

key-action. The entire mechanism of a keyed instr.

key-board. The series of digitals or pedals of a piano, organ or such instr. The idea of having a key-board so arranged that each digital can be struck in 3 different places seems to have occurred first to Paul von Jankó, who in 1882 inv. the **Janko keyboard**, which has the look of six contiguous key-boards on a rising plane. The advantages are that all scales are fingered alike and that the reach of the hand is greatly increased, so that a good hand can cover 14 digitals. The consequent simplification and enrichment of piano-resources are inestimably valuable. It may be applied to any key-board and is sometimes called a **chromatic keyboard.**

key-bugle. Vide BUGLE.

key-chord. The triad on the tonic.

keyed. Furnished with keys, as a flute, or piano. **keyed violin.** Piano violin.

key-stop violin. One having a finger-board fitted with thirty-three keys acting as stops perpendicularly upon the strings.

key-harp. An adjustment of tuning-forks over cavities of sonorous metal,

with piano-key action, inv. by Dietz and Second, 1819.

key-note, key-tone. The tonic. **keyship.** Tonality.

key-trumpet. One with keys or valves.

khal'il. Hebrew flute or oboe.

khasan (khä'zän), *Heb.* Chief singer in a synagogue.

Kicks, *G.* Vide GOOSE.

Kielflügel (kēl'-flü-khĕl), *G.* Wing-shaped harpsichord.

kin chi (kĭn chē). A Chinese dulcimer with 5 to 25 silk strings.

Kinderscenen (kĭnt'-ĕr-zā-nĕn), *G.* Childhood scenes. **Kinderstück** (shtük). An easy piece.

king chi (kĭng chē). A Chinese instr. with sixteen pendent stones graduated and struck with a hammer.

kinnor (kĭn'-nôr), *Heb.* A small harp, or lyre.

kin'tal. Small Indian cymbals.

Kirche (kēr'-khĕ), *G.* (in compounds **Kirchen**). Church. **K. kantate** (kän-tä'-tĕ). A cantata for church service. **K. komponist'.** Composer of church music. **K. dienst** (dēnst). Church service. **K. fest** (fĕsht). Church festival. **K. gesang** (gĕ-zäng), **K. lied** (lēt). Canticle, psalm, or hymn. **K. musik** (moo-zēk'). Church music. **K. schluss** (shloos). Plagal cadence. **K. stil** (shtēl). "Church style"; in an ecclesiastical mode. **K. töne** (tän'-ĕ). The church modes.

kis'sar. 5-stringed Nubian lyre.

kit. A small pocket violin, with 3 strings, *c'-g'-d''*.

kitra (kĭ-trä'). A guitar-like instr. of the Arabs.

kitha'ra, *Gr.* Greek lyre.

Klage (klä'-khĕ), *G.* Lamentation. **K.-gedicht** (gĕ-dĭkht), **K.-lied** (lēt). Elegy. **K.-ton** (tōn). Plaintive tune, or melody. **klagend** (klä'-khĕnt). Plaintive.

Klang (kläng), pl. **Klänge** (klĕng'-ĕ), *G.* 1. Sound, ringing. 2. Vide CLANG. **K.-boden.** Sound-board. **K.-far'-be.** Sound-colour, clang-tint. **K.-geschlecht** (gĕ-shlĕkht). A genus, or mode. **K.-lehre** (lä-rĕ). Acoustics. **K.-folge** (fôl-khĕ). A chord-progression in point of tonality. **K.-figuren** (fĭ-goo′-rĕn). Nodal figures. **K.-leiter** (lī-tĕr). A scale. **K.-saal** (zäl). Concert-room. **K.-schlüssel**, **K.-vertretung.** Vide KLANG-KEY. **klanglos** (kläng′lōs), *G.* Soundless.

Klappe (kläp′pĕ), *G.* Valve (of a wind-instr.). **Klappenflügelhorn** (flü′-gĕl), *G.* Keyed bugle. **Klappenhorn.** Keyed horn. **Klapptrompete.** A keyed trumpet.

klar (klär), *G.* Clear, bright. **Klarheit** (klär′-hīt). Clearness, plainness, **klärlich** (klĕr-lĭkh), *G.* Clearly, distinctly.

Klarinette (klä-rĭ-nĕt′-tĕ), *G.* Clarinet. **klassisch** (kläs′sĭsh), *G.* Classical.

Klausel (klow′-zĕl), *G.* A cadence. **Bassklausel.** The progression of the bass in a final cadence from dominant to tonic.

Klaviatur (klä-fĭ-ä-toor′), *G.* Keyboard. **K. harfe** (or **Klavier-harfe**). A harp inv. by Lutz, Vienna, 1893, in which the strings are plucked by plectra manipulated by a key-board. The same man in the same year inv. the **K.-zither**, a small piano with single strings, plucked by means of a key-board.

Klavier (klä-fēr′). 1. Key-board. 2. Key-board instr., especially the clavichord (formerly the piano). **Klavierauszug** (ows-tzookh). Arrangement for piano. **K.-harfe.** Vide KLAVIATUR-HARFE. **K.-harmonium.** An harmonium shaped like a grand piano, inv. by Woroniecki, 1893. **K.-hoboe.** The harmoniphon. **K.-mässig** (mĕs-sĭkh). Suitable for, in the style of the piano. **K.-satz.** Piano-music, or manner. **K.-sonate** (klä-fēr′-sō-nä-tĕ). Piano-sonata. **K.-spieler** (shpē′-lĕr), *G.* Piano-player. **K.-violoncello.** A 'cello in a frame with a key-board arrangement for the left hand, of special advantages; inv. by de Vlaminck, Brussels, 1893. **K.-viola.** A viola with key-board attachment.

klein (klīn), *G.* Small, minor. **K.-bass** (klīn-bäs), **K.-bassgeige** (gi′-khĕ), *G.* Violoncello. **Kleinegedacht.** A flute-stop. **kleinlaut** (lowt), *G.* Small or low in tone of voice.

klingbar (klĭng′-bär), *G.* Resonant. **Klingel** (klĭng′-ĕl). A bell. **klingeln**

(klĭng′-ĕln). To jingle. **klingend** (klĭng-ĕnt). Ringing. **klingende Stimme.** Speaking (as opposed to dummy) pipes. **Klingklang** (klĭng-kläng). Tinkling, bad music.

Klutter (kloot′-tĕr), *G.* A bird-call. **Knabenstimme** (knä′-bĕn-shtĭm-mĕ), *G.* "Boy's voice," counter-tenor.

knee-stop. A lever worked by the knee, and (a) controlling the wind, (b) opening the swell-box, (c) drawing all the stops.

knell. The tolling of a bell.

Knie (knē, not nē). Knee. **K.-guitarre.** Guitarre d'amour. **K.-zug** (tsookh). Knee-stop. **K.-geige** (knē-gī′-khĕ), *G.* Viol da gamba. **K.-rohre** (rō-rĕ), *G.* A mitred pipe.

Knopfregal (knôpf-rä′-gäl), *G.* An obs. reed-stop.

Knote (knō′-tĕ), *G.* Node. **K.-punkt.** Nodal point.

kobsa (kôb′-shä), *Rus.* A crude lute-like instrument.

Kollectivzug (kôl-lĕk-tēf′-tsookh), or **Kombinationspedale** (kôm-bĭ-nä-tsĭ-ōns-pĕ-dä′-lĕ), *G.* Combination pedal.

Kollo (kôl′-lō), *Jap.* A Japanese harp. **kol′lern**, *G.* To sing in a thin reedy voice.

Kolophon′. Resin. **Kombinationstöne** (kôm-bĭ-nä-tsĭ′ōns′-tä-nĕ). Resultant tones. Vide also KOLLEKTIVZUG.

Komiker (kō′-mĭ-kĕr), *G.* A writer of burlettas; comic performer. **komisch** (kō′-mĭsh), *G.* Comical. **Komma** (kôm′-mä), *G.* Comma. **komponi(e)ren** (kôm-pō-nē′-rĕn), *G.* To compose. **komponi(e)rt.** Composed. **Komponist′.** A composer. **Komposition** (kôm-pō-zē′-tsĭ-ōn), *G.* A composition. **Kompositionslehre** (lä-rĕ). The art of composition. **Konservatorium** (tō′-rĭ-oom), *G.* A conservatory. **kon′tra**, *G.* Contra. **Kontrabass.** Double-bass. **K.-fagott.** Double-bassoon. **K.-oktave.** Contra-octave. **K.-punkt.** Counterpoint. **K.-subjekt.** Counter-subject. **K.-töne** (tä-nĕ). The deepest tones of a bass voice.

Konzert (kôn-tsärt′). Concert; concerto. **K.-meister** (mī-shtĕr). First violin; leader. **K.-oper.** Concert opera. **K.-stück** (shtük). A free concerto in one movement, or any short concert-solo.

koous. A Persian brass drum.

Kopfstimme (kŏpf'-shtĭm-mĕ), *G.* Falsetto.
Koppel (kŏp'-pel), *G.* Coupler, coupling-stop. **K. ab** (or **an**). "Coupler off (or on)."
Kornett (kôr-nĕt'), *G.* Cornet.
koryphæ'us, *Gr.* Chief, or leader of the dances.
kos (kōz), *Hun.* A Hungarian dance.
Kosake (kō-sä'-kĕ). A national dance of the Cossacks in 2-4 time.
ko'to. Japanese zither with 13 silk strings, compass 2 octaves.
Kraft (kräft), *G.* Power, energy. **kräftig** (krĕf'-tĭkh). Powerful, vigorous.
Kragen (krä'-khĕn), *G.* Lute peg-box.
Kräusel (kroi'-zel), *G.* Mordent.
Krakoviak (krä-kō'-vĭ-äk), **Krakovienne** (krä-kō-vĭ-ĕn), *F.* The cracovienne.
krebsgängig (kräps'-geng-ĭkh), *G.* "Crab-going"; retrograde imitation. **Krebskanon.** Canon cancrizans.
kreischend (krī'-shĕnt), *G.* Shrieking.
Kreisfuge (krīs'-foo-khĕ), *G.* A canon.
Kreisleriana (krīs'-lä-rĭ-ä'-nä), *G.* A series of piano pieces by Schumann, named after an eccentric conductor called Kreisler, in one of Hoffman's novels.
Kreistanz (krīs'-tänts), *G.* Dance in a circle.
kreol (krä'-ôl). A Danish reel.
Kreuz (kroits), *G.* A sharp. **doppelt K.** A double sharp. **K.-saitig** (zī-tĭkh). Overstrung. **K.-tonart.** Sharp key.
Kriegsgesang (krēkhs'-gĕ-zäng), **Kriegslied** (lēt), *G.* A war-song. **K.-spieler** (shpē'-ler). A military musician.
kriegerisch (krē'-khĕr-ĭsh). Martial.
Krome (krō'-mĕ), *G.* Vide CHROMA.
kro'talon, *Gr.* Crotalum.
krumm (kroom), *G.* Crooked, curved, bent. **K.-bogen** (bō'-khĕn). A crook. **K.-horn.** Crooked horn. 1. An obs. wind-instr. resembling a small cornet; it had a range of nine notes, and was made in several sizes; its plaintive tone has led to its imitation in (2) an organ-stop of 4 and 8 ft. pitch (and in the **Krummhorn-bass,** of 16 ft.). Same as **cromhorn.**
krustische Instrumente (kroos'-tĭsh-ĕ), *G.* Instr. of percussion.
kuhn (koon), *G.* Bold, decided.
Kuhhorn (koo-hôrn), *G.* Swiss "cow-horn."
Kuh-kuk (koo'-kook), *G.* The cuckoo used in toy symphonies.

Kuhreigen (koo'-rī-khĕn), *G.* "Cow-round-up." Vide RANZ DES VACHES.
kuit'-ra. Kitra.
Kunst (koonst), *G.* Art, skill. **K.-fuge** (foo-khe), *fuga ricercata.* Vide FUGUE. **Künstler** (kĭnst'-lr). Artist. **K.-lied** (lēt). An art (as opp. to a folk) song. **K.-pfeifer** (pfī'-fĕr). Street musician. **Kunstwerk der Zukunft** (koonst'-vărk dĕr tsoo'-koonft). "Art work of the future." A term given by Richard Wagner to his theory of music.
ku'rum. Curved trumpet of the Western Nile.
kurz (koorts), *G.* Short, detached, staccato. **kürzen.** To abridge. **kurzer Mordent.** Short mordent. **kurze Oktave.** Short-octave. **kurzer Singesatz.** Cavatina. **Kürzung** (kür'-tsoongk). Abbreviation. **Kürzungszeichen** (tsī'-khen). Sign of abbreviation.
kussir (küs-sēr), *F.* Turkish instrument.
Kyrie eleison (kē'-rĭ-ä ä-lä'-ĕ-sōn), *Gr.* "Lord, have mercy (upon us)." Vide MASS.
kyrielle (kē-rĕ-ĕl), *F.* Litany.
kyr'riole. Old E. for Carol.

L

L. Abbr. for *Left* (*G.*, Links). **l. h.,** *left hand.* **l',** abbr. for *le* or *la,* "the."
la. 1. Vide SOLMISATION. 2. The note A (*F.* and *I*). **la bemol,** or **bemolle,** a♭; **la dièse** (lä dĭ-ĕz), *F.*, a♯.
la (lä), *I.* and *F.* The.
labecedisa'tion. Vide SOLMISATION.
la'bial. Lipped (of flue-pipes). **Labialstimme** (lä-bĭ-äl'-shtĭm-mĕ), or **pfeife** (pfī'-fĕ), *G.* Flue-stops.
labisa'tion. Vide SOLMISATION.
Labien (lä'-bĭ-ĕn), pl., *G.* Pipes.
Labium (la'-bĭ-oom), *L.* and *G.* The lip of a pipe.
lacrimando (lä-krĭ-män'-do), **lacrimo'so,** *I.* Mournful.
Lacrimosa (lä-krĭ-mō'-sä), *L.* "Weeping." An occasional part of the Requiem.
Lade (lä'-dĕ), *G.* Wind-chest of an organ.
Lage (lä'-khĕ), *G.* Position. 1. Of a chord. 2. Of the hand in violin shifts. **eng'e L.** Close harmony, opposed to **weite** (vī'-tĕ), open.
Lagenwechsel (vĕkhs-ĕl), *G.* Shifting.
lagnoso (län-yō'-sō), *I.* Plaintive, doleful.

lagrimando (lä-grĭ-män'-dō), **lagri-mo'so**, *I.* Weeping.

lah. Vide TONIC SOL-FA.

lai (lĕ), *F.* Lay, ditty.

lament'. Old name for harp music or songs of pathos.

lamentabile (lä-mĕn-tä'-bĭ-lĕ), **lamentabilmen'te**, *I.* Mournful(ly). **lamentan'do**, **lamentevole** (lä-mĕn-tä'-vō-lĕ), **lamento'so.** Plaintive.

Lamenta'tions. Words from Jeremiah sung at Vespers in Passion week.

lampon (läṅ-pôṅ), *F.* Drinking-song.

lan'cers, *E.*, **lanciers** (läṅs-yā), *F.* A set of quadrilles.

Länderer (lĕn'-dĕ-rĕr), **Ländler** (lĕnt'-lĕr), *G.* Slow German or Austrian waltz in 3-4 or 3-8 time, the last notes of each measure a dotted 8th and a 16th note.

länderisch (lĕn'-dĕr-ĭsh), *G.* In the Ländler style.

ländlich (lĕnt'-lĭkh), *G.* Rural.

Landlied (länt'-lēt), *G.* Rustic-song.

landu (län'-doo), *Port.* A Portuguese dance in duple time.

landums (län'-dooms), *Port.* Portuguese music of sentimental tone.

lang (läng), *G.* Long.

langsam (läng'-zäm), *G.* Slow(ly), largo. **langsamer** (läng'-zäm-ĕr). Slower.

language, languid. In a flue-pipe a horizontal strip of metal or wood just inside the mouth.

languendo (län'-gwĕn-dō), **languen'te, languido** (län-gwē'-dō), *I.* Languishing. **languemen'te.** Languishingly.

languette (läṅ-gĕt), *F.* 1. The tongue of reed-pipes. 2. Pallet. 3. Key on a wind-instr. 4. Tongue carrying the quill of a jack.

lan'guid. Vide LANGUAGE.

lan'tum. A large hurdygurdy with rotary bellows and reeds played by buttons.

lapid'eon. A scale of flint-stones played with hammers; inv. by Baudry.

largamente (lär-gä-mĕn'-tĕ). Broadly, nobly. Vide LARGO.

largando (lär-gän'-dō), *I.* Broadening becoming largo (q.v.).

large. The longest note in ancient music equal to four breves (eight of our whole notes). Vide NOTATION.

large (lärzh), *F.* Broad, largo. **largement** (lärzh-mäṅ). Broadly.

larghetto (lär-gĕt'-tō), *I.* Not quite so slow as largo.

larghezza (lär-gĕd'-zä), *I.* Breadth, slowness. **larghissimo** (lär-gĭs'-sĭ-mō). Very slow.

largo (lär'-gō), *I.* Slow, noble, broad, usually taken as slower than lento. **l. assai** (äs-sä'-ē), **l. di molto** (dē-mōl'-to). Very slow. **l. ma non troppo.** Slow, but not too slow. **l. un poco** (oon pō'-kō). Rather slow.

larigot (lär-ĭ-gō), *F.* 1. Shepherd's pipe. 2. A very shrill 1⅓-ft. stop.

laringe (lä-rēn'-jĕ), *I.* Larynx.

larmoyant (lärm-wä-yäṅ), *F.* Weeping.

lar'ynx. Upper part of the trachea or wind-pipe; a human reed-pipe varying at will the tones of the voice.

laud (lä-oodh), *Sp.* Lute.

laud, lauda (lä'-oo-dä), *I.* and *L.*, *I.* pl. *laude*, *L.* pl. *laudes.* 1. Hymn(s) of praise. 2. Vide HORA.

Lau'da Si'on, Salvato'rem. "Zion, praise the Saviour"; a sequence sung at the High Mass of Corpus Christi.

laudis'ti, *L.* Psalm-singers.

Lauda'mus Te, *L.* "We praise Thee." Part of the Gloria. Vide MASS.

Lauf (lowf), *G.* 1. Peg-box. 2. A run, a trill. **Lauftanz** (lowf'-tänts). A running dance, corante. **Läufe** (lī'-fĕ). Rapid divisions. **Läufer** (lī'-fĕr). A run, trill, or shake.

Launenstück (low'-nĕn-shtük), *G.* A voluntary.

launig (low'-nĭkh). Humorous.

lauréate (lō-rä-ät), *F.* A winner of the Grand Prix de Rome (q.v.).

laut (lowt), *G.* 1. Loud. 2. A sound. **lautlos** (lowt-lōs). Soundless, mute.

Laute (lowt'-ĕ), *G.* The lute. **Lautenist', Lautenschläger** (shlä'-khĕr), or **spieler** (shpē-lĕr), *G.* Lutenist. **Lautenfutter** (foot-ter), **lautenkasten.** Lute-case. **Lauteninstrumente.** Instrs. whose strings are plucked. **L.-geige.** Viol. **L.-zug.** Lute compass. **L.-macher** (mä'-khĕr). Lute-maker.

läuten (lī'-tĕn). To toll, to sound.

lavol'ta. Old Italian waltz.

lay. Song.

le (lŭ), *F.*, **le** (lä), *I.*, pl. The.

lead (lēd). 1. The announcement by one part of a theme to reappear in others. 2. A sign giving the cue for the entry of the various parts of a canon, etc.

leader. 1. Conductor, director. In older times the first violinist was the actual conductor and is still called "leader" though he has lost his function as conductor. 2. The first

cornet (in bands). 3. The first so-
pranc (in chorus).
leading. 1. *As a noun.* A melodic
progression or tendency. 2. *As an
adjective.* Guiding, compelling, characteristic, predominant. **l.-chord.**
The dominant. **l.-tone,** or **note.**
The 7th degree of a scale (because it
leads in and demands the tonic).
l.-melody. The chief melody.
leading-motive. A musical phrase or
figure (as those in Wagner's operas),
used as a sort of autograph or trade-
mark of a certain character, mood or
sentiment, and recurring whenever
that character or mood is to appear
or is remembered. (See article, page
756.)
lean'ing note. Appoggiatura.
leap. 1. Skip. 2. In piano-playing a
long jump for the hand. 3. A distance composed of several intermediate intervals.
Leben (lā'-bĕn), *G.* Life, vivacity. **le-
bendig** (lā'-bĕn-dĭkh), **lebhaft** (lāp'-
häft). Lively. **Lebhaftigkeit** (kīt).
Vivacity.
leçon (lŭ-sôn), *F.* Lesson, exercise.
ledger line, leger line. A short additional line above or below the staff,
for notes too high or too low to
be written on the staff. **l. l.** are
counted away from the staff, the
nearest being the first. **ledger space.**
The space between two **l. l.**
leere Saiten (lā-rĕ zī'-ten), *G.* Open
strings.
legabile (lĕ-gä'-bĭ-lĕ), **legan'do,** *I.*
Legato.
legare (le-ga-re). To bind, or tie.
legato (lĕ-gä'-tō), *I.* "Bound." In
a smooth, connected manner, opposed
to staccato, and indicated by a slur, or
legato-mark (*G.,* **legato-bogen**)
thus, ⁀. **L. touch.** A touch pro-
longing the tone, till it exactly connects with the next. **legatis'simo.**
Exceedingly legato.
legatura (lā-gä-too'-rä), *I.* 1. A slur.
2. Syncopation. **l. di voce.** Vide
LIGATURE (2).
legend, légende (lā-zhänd), *F.,* **Legende** (lā-gĕn'-dĕ), *G.* A composition in romantic or narrative style.
im Le'gendenton, *G.* In the romance manner.
leger. Vide LEDGER.
leger (lā-zhā), **legère** (lā-zhăr), *F.*
Light, nimble. **legèrement** (män).
Lightly. **legèreté** (lā-zhăr-tā). Agility.

leggenda (lĕd-jĕn'-dä), *I.* A legend.
leggeramente (lĕd-jĕr-ä-mĕn'-te), **leg-
germen'te,** *I.* Lightly. **leggeran-
za** (lĕd-jĕr-än'-tsä). **leggerezza** (lĕd-
jĕr-ĕd'-zä). Lightness.
leggiadro (lĕd-jä'-drō), **leggiadra-
men'te,** *I.* Graceful(ly).
leggiere (lĕd-jä'-rĕ), **leggiero, leg-
gieramen'te, leggiermen'te,** *I.*
Light(ly). **leggierezza** (lĕd-jĕ-rĕd'-
zä). Delicacy.
leggieruco'lo. Rather light.
legno (lān'-yō), *I.* Wood. **col. l.**
To be played with the back or wood
of the bow.
Lehrer (lā'-rĕr), feminine **Lehrerin,** *G.*
Teacher, master.
Leich (līkh), *G.* A lay. A funeral.
Leichenmusik (lī'-khĕn-moo-zēk'), *G.*
Funeral-music. **Leichenton** (tōn).
A lugubrious sound.
leicht (līkht), *G.* Light, easy, facile.
L. bewegt (bĕ-vākht), (a) delicately
swift. (b) agitatedly. **Leichtheit**
(hīt), **Leichtigkeit** (līkh'-tĭkh-kīt).
Lightness, facility. **leichtfertig** (fĕr-
tĭkh). Light(ly), careless(ly).
Leidenschaft (lī'-dĕn-shäft), *G.* Passion. **leidenschaftlich** (līkh). Passionate.
Leier (lī'-er), *G.* A lyre. **L.-kasten**
(käst'en). A hurdygurdy. **Leier-
mädchen** (māt'-khĕn). A girl who
plays on a hurdygurdy. **Leiermann**
(män). A male player of a hurdygurdy. **Leierorgel** (lī'-ĕr-ôrkh-ĕl).
Hand-organ. **Leierspieler** (shpē-lĕr).
One who plays on a lyre.
Leine (lī'-nĕ), *G.* A line on the staff.
leise (lī'-zĕ), *G.* Low, soft, gentle. **l.
wie für sich** (vē für zĭkh). Softly, as
if to one's self.
Leitakkord (līt'-äk-kôrd), *G.* A harmony progressing naturally to another, as the dominant. **Leitmotiv**
(līt'-mō-tĕf). Leading-motive (q.v.).
Leitton (līt'-tōn). The leading note.
Leiter (lī'-tĕr), *G.* 1. Leader. 2.
"Ladder," the scale of any key.
leitereigen (lī-tĕr-īkh'-n). Proper and
peculiar to a key, opposed to foreign
notes which are **l.-fremd** (frĕmt).
lene. Old term for a note sustained,
while other parts move.
leno (lā'-no), *I.* Weak, feeble, faint.
lenezza (lā-nĕd'-zä). Gentleness.
lent (län), *F.* Slow. **lentement** (läänt-
män), *F.* Slowly. **lenteur** (län-
tŭr'). Slowness, delay.
lentando (lĕn-tän'-dō), *I.* Retarding.
lento (lĕn'-tō), *I.* Slow; usually con-

sidered between andante and largo.
l. assai, l. di molto (dē mōl'-tō), l.
lento. Very slow. lentis'simo.
Extremely slow. lentamen'te, len-
temen'te. Slowly. lentezza (lĕn-
tĕd'-zä). Slowness.
lesser. Minor, as the l. third. l.
appoggiatura. Vide APPOGG. l.
barbiton. The kit. l. comma. The
diaschisma.
lesson. A piece of two or three movements for the harpsichord or pianoforte, often combined into a suite.
lesto (lĕs'-tō), I. Lively. lestissimo.
Very quick. lestezza (lĕs-tĕd'-zä),
I. Agility.
letterale (lĕt-tĕ-rä'-lĕ), letteralmen'-
te, I. Literal(ly). Exactly as written.
letter-name. A letter designating a
tone, key, etc., as a, b, c. Letter-
notation is old as the Greeks.
leuto (lä-oo'-tō), I. Lute.
leva (lä'-vä), I. Lift, release, si leva
il sordino, "lift the mute"; si levano
i sordini, "release the dampers."
levé (lŭ-vā'), F. Up-beat.
levet. A blast of a trumpet; reveille.
levezza (lĕ-vĕd'-zä), I. Lightness.
levier pneumatique (lĕv-ĭ-ā'-nŭ-mă-
tēk'), F. The pneumatic lever.
leziosamen'te (lā-tsĭ-ō), I. Affectedly.
lezzioni (lĕd-zĭ-ō'-nē), I., pl. Lessons.
Leyer (lī'-ĕr), G. Lyre.
L. H. Abbr. for "left hand."
liaison (lē-ĕz'-ôṅ), F. 1. A bind or
tie. 2. Vide LIGATURE, 2. 3. l. d'harmonie (dăr-mô-nē). Syncopation.
l. de chant (dŭ-shäṅ). Sostenuto
singing.
libero (lē'-bĕ-rō), liberamen'te, I.
Free(ly), unrestrained(ly).
libitum, L. Pleasure, will. ad libitum.
At the pleasure of the performer,
who may decide tempo, expression,
etc., or even omit the section so
marked.
librement (lēbr-mäṅ), F. Freely.
libret'to. The text of an opera, oratorio, etc. libret'tist. A writer of
such texts.
li'cence (in F. lē-säṅs), licenza (lē-
chĕn'-tsä), I. A deviation from the
rules. con' alcuna (äl-koo'-nä) licenza. With some freedom.
liceo (lē-chā'-ō), I. Lyceum; academy.
-lich- (lĭkh), G. Suffix, equivalent to
"-like," or "-ly."
lich'anos, Gr. Vide LYRE.
lié (lē-ā'), F. Smooth(ly), legato. lié
coulant (koo-laṅ). Slurred but flowing.

Liebeslied (lē'-bĕs-lēt). Love-song.
Liebestod. Love's death. Liebes-
flöte. A flute-stop. Liebhaber
(lēp'-hä-bĕr). Amateur. lieblich
(lēp'-lĭkh). Lovely, charming.
Lieb'lichgedacht (gĕ-däkht). A
stopped-diapason organ register.
Lied (lēt), pl. Lieder (lē'-dĕr), G.
Loosely, any song; technically, a
song (as opposed to the ballad or
Strophenlied), in which the text
predominates over merely melodic
rights, and the music interprets,
rather than disregards, the words.
Such a song in which each stanza has
special music is often called durch-
komponi(e)rtes (doorkh-kôm-pō-
nēr'-tĕs), or one "composed all
through." LIED (or LIEDER) ohne
Worte (ō'-nĕ vôr'-tĕ), G. Song (or
songs) without words. Lied form
(fôrm). The form, or theme of a
song. Liedchen (lēt'-khĕn). A short
song. Liederbuch (bookh). A song
or hymn-book. L.-bund (boont).
A society of singers. L.-cyclus (tsē'-
kloos). A cycle of songs. L.-dichter
(dĭkh'-tĕr). A song-writer. L.-kranz
(kränts). Glee-club. L.-kreis (krīs).
A "wreath" of songs. L.-sammlung
(zäm'-loongk). Collection of songs.
L.-sänger (zĕng'-ĕr). A ballad-
singer. L.-spiel (shpēl). An operetta. L.-sprache (sprä'-khĕ). Words
adapted to songs. L.-tafel (tä'-fĕl).
"Song-table"; a glee-club of male
voices. L.-täfler (tĕf'-lĕr). Glee-
singers. L.-tanz (tänts). A dance
with songs.
ligare (lĭ-gä'-rĕ), ligato (lē-gä'-tō).
Vide LEGARE, LEGATO.
Ligatur (lē-gä-toor'), G., ligatura
(lē-gä-too'-rä), I., lig'ature, E.
(pron. in F. lē-gä-tür'). 1. A succession of notes sung to one syllable
or in one breath, or played with one
stroke of the bow. 2. A tie. 3. A
syncopation. 4. In old music a
succession of notes sung to one
syllable. Vide NOTATION.
ligne (lēn'-yu), F. A line. l. addition-
nelle (ăd-dēs-yŭ-nĕl), or ajouté
(ä-zhoo-tā'), or postiche (pôs-tēsh),
or supplémentaire (sü₂-plä-mäṅ-
tär'). A ledger line.
lig'neum psalte'rium, L. Xylophone.
limite (lē'-mĭ-tĕ), I. Limit.
lim'ma, Gr. An interval in Greek
music, less by a comma than a major
semitone.
linea (lē'-nĕ-ä), I. A line of the staff.

line. One of the five lines making up the ｔaff (q.v.). **added, or ledger line.** Vide LEDGER.

lingua (lǐn'-gwä), *I.* 1. The tongue in a reed. 2. The reed itself.

Lingualpfeife (lēn-goo-äl'-pfī-fě), *G.* A reed-pipe.

lin'gula, *L.* Glottis.

Linie (lē'-nē), pl. **Linien,** *G.* Line(s). **Liniensystem** (lē'-nǐ-ěn-zēs-täm). The staff.

lining-out. The old practice of reading out one or two lines of a hymn before singing them.

li'nings. The supporting strips glued to the ribs of violins, etc.

link (lǐnk), **links** (lǐnks), *G.* Left. **linke Hand** (hänt). The left hand.

li'nos, *Gr.* 1. A rustic air. 2. A dirge.

lip, *E.,* **Lippe** (lǐp'-pě), *G.* 1. The flat surface above or below the mouth of a flue-pipe. 2. Vide EMBOUCHURE. **Lippenpfeife.** A flue-pipe.

lira (lē'-rä), *I.* 1. The Greek lyre. 2. In 16th–18th cent. a viol, hence, l. **barberi'na.** A small viol inv. by Doni in 17 century. **l. da braccio** (dä brät'-shō). Obsolete instr. like the tenor viol, with seven strings. **l. da gam'ba.** An instr. held between the knees and having 12 to 16 strings. **l. dop'pia.** Double lyre. **l. grande** (grän'-dě). A viol with six strings, formerly used in Germany. **l. pagana** (pä-gä'-nä), **l. rustica** (roos'-tǐ-kä), **l. tedesca** (tä-děs'-kä). A hurdygurdy.

lire (lēr), *F.* To read.

liressa (lē-rěs'-sä). A bad lyre.

lirico (lē'-rǐ-kō), *I.* Lyric.

lirone (lē-rō'-ně), *I.* The large bass viol with 24 strings.

liscio (lē'-shō), *I.* Smooth.

lispelnd (lǐs'-pělnt), *G.* Lisping.

l'istesso (lēs-těs'-sō), *I.* The same.

litanei'a, *Gr.,* **litania** (lē-tä-nē'-ä), *L.* and *I.,* **litanie** (lǐ-tǎ-nē'), *F.,* **Litanei** (lē-tä-nī'), *G.,* **lit'any,** *E.* A solemn form of supplication, the minister offering prayers, to which the congregation add "Lord have mercy." *kyrie eleison* is the lesser l.

lit'terae significa'tivae, *L.* Letters of doubtful meaning, used in neumatic notation.

lit'uus, *L.* A kind of trumpet.

liuto (lē-oo'-tō), *I.* A lute.

livre (lèvr), *F.* A book; **à l' ouvert** (oo-vǎr). At first sight.

livret (lē'-vrä), *F.* A libretto.

lo (lō), *I* The.

Lobgesang (lōp'-gě-zäng), **Loblied** (lōp'-lēt), *G.* A hymn of praise.

Loch (lôkh) **in der Stimme,** *G.* "Hole in the voice," used of that part of a register where certain tones are weak or wanting.

loco (lō'-kō), *I.* "Place." 1. A word nullifying *8va* or *all ottava,* and meaning that the notes are to be played as written, not an octave higher or lower as before. 2. A sign for a violinist to return to his original position, form or shift.

Locrian (lo'-krǐ-än), **lokrisch** (lō'-krǐsch), *G.* See MODES, page 762.

lo'geum, *L.* 1. A stage. 2. A motet

Logier'ian system. The system of instruction of John Bernard Logier, including class-work, harmony, etc., and use of the chiroplast.

lombar'do. A dance of Lombardy.

long, longa, *L.* An obsolete note half the length of the *large,* or equal to four of our whole notes. **long double.** An old character equal to four breves. *As an adjective,* **long appoggiatura.** An accented app. of a single note forming part of the theme, and borrowing half the length of the next note. **l. drum.** The bass-drum of military bands. **l. mordent.** of four notes. **l. roll.** A drumbeat to arms. **l. spiel.** An ancient long and narrow Icelandic bow instrument.

longue pause (lông'-pōz), *F.* A long pause.

lontano (lôn-tä'-nō), *I.* Distant, remote. **da l.** At a distance. **lontananza** (lôn-tä-nän'-tsá). Distance.

loop. 1. The vibrating part between 2 nodes. 2. The chord binding the tail-pieces of violins, etc., to the button.

Lösung, fortschreitende (fôrt-shrī-těn-dě-lä'-zoongk), *G.* Resolution.

loud pedal. Vide DAMPER.

lourde (loord), *F.* Heavy. **lourdement** (mäṅ). Heavily.

loure (loor), *F.* 1. An old F. bagpipe; thence; 2. A slow dance in 6-4 time. strongly accented.

louré (loo-rä'), *F.* Smooth(ly), legato.

louvre (loovr), *F.* Applied to an air, called "L'Amiable Vainqueur," a favourite of Louis XIV.; thence a dance.

lu'dus, *L.* Play. **ludi moderator.** Organist. **ludi spirituali.** Miracle-plays.

lugubre (loo-goo'-brě), *I.* Lugubrious, sad.

luinig. A plaintive song of the Hebrides sung by the women at work.

lul'laby. A cradle-song.

lu-lu. The Chinese official laws of music.

lundu (loon'-doo), *Port.* A Portuguese dance in duple time.

lunga (loon'-gä), pl. **lunghe** (loon-ge). *I.* Long, prolonged.

luogo (loo-ô-gō), *I.* Same as LOCO.

lur (loor), *Dan.* 1. A birch-bark instr. similar to the alp-horn. 2. A prehistoric curved and conical bronze instr. 5 to 7 feet long, with cupped mouthpiece, and, instead of a bell, a circular flat plate, ornamented with bosses and bronze tassels.

lusing. An abbr. of lusingato.

lusingando (loo-sēn-gän'-dō), **lusingan'te, lusingato** (gä'-to), **lusinghevole** (gä'-vō-lĕ), *I.*, **lusinghiere** or o (gĭ-ā'-rĕ). Coaxing lusinghevol-men'te. Insinuatingly, persuasively.

lustig (loos'-tĭkh), *G.* Merry, cheerful.

Lustlied (loost'-lēt), *G.* A gay song.

lute (lūt, not loot), *E.*, **lut** or **luth** (lüt), *F.* A very ancient string instr. now obsolete except in the small form of the mandolin and the modified form of the guitar. It was pear-shaped, and had a neck with fretted finger-board. The stringing was various; the largest form having paired strings tuned in unisons, and, besides, a series of strings that did not cross the finger-board but were played upon as a bass. This form required a double neck and was called a theorbo, arch-lute, or chitarrone. The strings, sometimes as many as 13 pairs, were played as in the guitar. Lute-music was written in tablature. Lute-players were called lutists, luters, lutanists, lutenists, or lutinists. A lute-maker was a luthier (lüt-yā), a name also given then, and now, to violin-makers. The trade and its product are called lutherie (lüt-rē'). lutina. A small lute, or mandolin.

luttuoso (loot-too-ō'-sō), **luttuosa-men'te,** *I.* Mournful(ly).

Lyd'ian, *E.*, **lydisch** (lēt'-ĭsh), *G.* Vide MODES, p. 762. **Lydian chant.** A chant of a sorrowful, melancholy style.

Lyon catlins. Thick bass-strings.

lyre (līr in *E.*; in *F.* lēr), **lyra** (lē'-rä), *L.*, *I.*, and *G.* 1. A most ancient instr. consisting of a sound-box or board with 2 long curved arms carrying a cross-bar from which descended, across a bridge, the 3 to 10 strings, struck with a plectrum. On the 8-stringed lyre, the strings were thus named, beginning nearest the body: **hy'pate** (hī'-pä-tĕ) (the lowest in tone), **parhy'pate, lich'anos, me'se, par'amese, trite** (trē'-tĕ), **paranete, nete** (nä'-tĕ). The largest lyre was the **cithara,** the treble was the **chelys.** A large 20-stringed instr. on which octaves were played was the **magadis.** 2. The modern **lyra** is a rebec, and various bow-instrs. have been called lyres, or **lyre-viols,** since the 14th cent.; some have a double neck or bijuga like the theorbo (Vide LUTE), including the **lyra di braccio** (brät'-chō) or arm-viol and **archeviole di l.,** or **l. doppia.** The **l. di gamba** is a leg-viol. **l. barbarina.** An old instr. resembling the guitar, but played with the bow. **l. hex'achordis,** *Gr.* A six-stringed lyre. **l. mendico'rum,** *L.* "Beggar's lyre," a hurdygurdy.

Lyra-sänger (zĕng'-ĕr), or **-spieler** (shpē'-lĕr), *G.* Performer on the lyre. 3. The modern Stahlspiel.

lyr'ic, lyr'ical, lyrisch (lĭr'-ĭsh), *G.* "Fitted to be sung to the lyre," hence used of subjective moods, usually brief and enthusiastic as opposed to narrative, dramatic, or epic. **lyric drama** is opera. **lyric tragedy.** A tragic opera. **l. comedy.** Comic opera. **l. opera.** A ballad opera.

M

M. Abbr. of *Mezzo, Metronome, Mano, Main;* m. f., for *Mezzo-forte*; m. p., *Mezzo-piano;* m. v., *Mezzo-voce.*

M. M. Abbr. for Maelzel's Metronome (q.v.).

ma (mä), *I.* But; as *allegro ma non troppo,* quick, but not too much so.

machalath (mä'-kä-läth), *Heb.* A term employed in the Psalms, supposed by some to mean a flute, but by others to indicate familiar tunes.

machête (mä-shĕ'-tĕ). *Port.* A small guitar with 4 strings, tuned *d'-g'-b'-e''.*

mach-icotage (mäsh-ĭ-kô-täzh), *F.,* **macicota'ticum,** *L.* Embellishment added to the *cantus firmus* of plainchant, customary in France in the 18th cent. The clergy alone sang the embellished or **machicotée** (mäsh-ĭ-kō-tä) plain-song, and were called **machicots** (măsh-ĭ-kō) or **ma-cicico'nici**. The choir sang the *cantus firmus* without embellishment (**si'ne macicota'tico**).

machine-head. A rack and pinion appliance to be used in place of ordinary tuning-pegs.

machol (mä'-kōl), *Heb.* Instr. supposed to be either string or pulsatile.

Madre, alla (äl'-lä mäd'-rĕ). "To the Mother." Used of hymns to the Virgin.

madriale (mä-drĭ-ä'-lĕ), *I.* Madrigal. **madrialet'to.** A short madrigal.

madrigal (in *F.* măd-rĭ-găl; in *G.* mä-drĭ-häl'), **madrigale** (mäd-rĭ-gäl'-ĕ), *I.* 1. Loosely, a short amorous or pastoral lyric. 2. Strictly an unaccompanied chorus in from 2 to 8 parts, based on a *cantus firmus*, and written with elaborate counterpoint. Beginning in Italy in the 15th cent. ıt spread all over Europe. **madrigales'co**, *I.* Pertaining to the madrigal.

maësta (mä-äs-tä'), **maëstade** (mä-äs-tä'-dĕ), **maëstate** (tä'-t), *I.* Majesty, grandeur. **maëstevole** (tä'-vō-lĕ), **maëstevolmen'te**, **maësto'so**, **maëstosamen'te**. Majestic(ally), noble (nobly).

maëstria (mä-äs-trē'-ä), *I.* Mastery, skill.

maestro (mä-äs'-trō), fem., **maestra** (mä-äs'-trä), *I.* Master. **m. al cembale.** A conductor, since he formerly sat at the harpsichord. **m. al piano.** Pianist of an orchestra. **m. del coro.** Master of the choir. **m. di camera.** Conductor of chamber-music. **m. di canto.** A singing-master. **m. di cappella** (dē käp-pĕl'-lä). 1. Chapel-master. 2. Conductor.

mag'adis, *Gr.* 1. Vide LYRE. 2. 16th cent. name for monochord.

mag'adizing. A vocal performance in octaves.

mag'as, *Gr.* 1. Bridge. 2. Fret. 3. Vide MAGADIS, 2.

Magazinbalg (mäkh-ä-tsēn'-bälkh), *G.* Reservoir-bellows.

maggiolata (mäd-jō-lä'-tä), *I.* A song in praise of May.

maggiore (mäd-jō'-re), *I.* "Greater," major.

maggot. An impromptu fantasy.

magistrale (mä-jĭs-trä'-lĕ), *I.* Vide MAESTRALE.

Magnif'icat, *L.* A part of the Vespers from "Magnificat anima mea Dominum," My soul magnifies the Lord.

main (mäṅ), *F.* The hand. **m. droite** (drwät). Right hand. **m. gauche** (gōsh). Left hand. **m. harmonique** (mä-när-mŭn-ēk). Harmonic hand.

maître (mĕtr), *F.* A master, a director. **m. de chappelle** (shä-pĕl). Chapelmaster; conductor; director of a choir. **m. de musique** (dŭ mü-zēk'). Musical director, or teacher.

maîtrise (mĕt-rēz), *F.* A music-school connected with a cathedral.

majestà (mä-yäs-tä'), *I.*, **majesté** (mä-zhĕs-tä), *F.* Majesty. **majestueux** (mä-zhĕst-yŭ'). Majestic. **majestätisch** (mä-yĕs-tä'-tĭsh), *G.* Majestic.

ma'jor, *E.*, **majeur** (mä-zhŭr), *F.* "Greater," as opp. to minor ("less"), and used of intervals greater by a semitone than the minor (though less by a semitone than the augmented); hence, those major chords and major scales and keys in which major intervals predominate. **m. triad.** One with a major 3d and perfect 5th. **m. cadence.** One ending on a **m. triad.**

Mal (mäl), *G.* Time, as **zum ersten M.**, for the first time.

malagueña (mä-lä-gän'-yä), *Sp.* A fandango.

malanconia (mä-län-kō-nē'-ä), **malinconi'a**, *I.* Melancholy. **malenco'nico**, **malincol'ico**, **malinco'nico**, **malinconio'so**, **malincono'so**, **malinconicamen'te**, *I.* In a melancholy style.

mama (mä'-mä), *I.* In drum-music the right hand.

manca (män'-kä), *I.* The left.

mancando (män-kän'-dō), *I.* Decreasing and retarding.

manche (mäṅsh), *F.* Neck (of a violin, etc.).

mandolin(e) (măn'-dō-lĭn), *E.*, **mandolino** (män-dō-lē'-nō), *I.* A small lute with fretted neck, and paired strings played with a plectrum. The compass g-g''''. The Neapolitan (*mandolino napolita'no*) has 4 pairs tuned g-d'-a'-e''; the Milanese (*m. lombardo*) has five or six pairs tuned g-c'-a'-d''-e'', or g-b-e'-a'-d''-e''. **mandolinata** (ä'-tä). To be played with mandolin-like effect. **mando'la, mando'ra, mando're.** A large mandolin.

mangeot (mäṅ-zhō), *F.* A piano *à claviers renversé*.

manico (mä'-nĭ-kō), *I.* Neck (of violin, etc.).

man'ichord, *E.*, manichord'ium, *L.*, manichord'on, *Gr.* An old term for various string instrs. Manichordiendraht (drät), *G.* Wire for the manichord.

maniera (mä-nĭ-ä'-rä), *I.*, manière (măn-yăr), *F.* Manner, style. m. affettata (äf-fĕt-tä'-tä), *I.* Affected delivery. m. languida (län'gwĭ-dä), *I.* A languid style.

Manier (mä-nēr'), pl. Manieren (mä-nē'-rĕn), *G.* Grace(s), embellishment(s).

man'ifold fugue. One with two or more subjects.

Männerchor (mĕn-nĕr-kōr), *G.* Male chorus. Männergesangverein (gĕ-zäng'-fĕr-īn). A male choral society. Män'nerstimmen. Male voices.

mano (mä'-nō), *I.* The hand. m. destra (dās'-trä), m. dritta (dĭ-rĭt'-tä), or dritta (drĭt'-tä). The right hand. m. sinistra (sĭ-nēs'-trä). The left hand.

man'ual, *E.*, Manual (mä-noo-äl'), *G.*, manuale (mä-noo-ä'-lĕ), *I.* and *L.* 1. Key-board of an organ. 2. A digital, especially man'ual-key. manual'-iter. Without pedals, "on the manuals alone." M.-koppel, *G.* A coupler connecting one manual with another. m.-mente (mä-noo-äl-mĕn'-tĕ), *I.* Manually. M.-untersatz (oon-tĕr-zäts), *G.* A 32-ft. stop.

manubrio (mä-noo'-brĭ-ō), *I.*, Manubrien (mä-noo'-brĭ-ĕn), pl., *G.* The handle(s) by which a stop is drawn. M. koppel. A draw-stop collar.

marcan'do, marcato (mär-kä'-tō), *I.* Marked, accented. marcatis'simo. Very strongly marked.

march. A composition to accompany marching. There are two kinds, the *quick m.* or *quickstep*, and the solemn processional, *funeral* or *dead m.* Usually in 4-4 time, the m. may be in 2-4, 3-4 or 6-8 time. The march usually includes a second part, or trio, and a repetition of the first subject. The second part is often lyrical rather than rhythmic. The cadence for the quickstep in the American army is 120 to the minute.

marche (märsh), *F.* 1. A march. 2. A progression, as m. harmonique (är-mŭn-ēk).

marcia (mär'-chä), *I.* A march. m. funèbre (foo-nä'-brĕ). Funeral-march. marcia'le, or marziale (mär-tsĭ-ä'-lĕ), or alla m. In march-style. marciata (mär-chä'-tä). A march.

marked. Accented.

mark. A sign. cadence-m. Vide CHANT. harmonic-m. Vide HARMONIC. metronomic-m. Vide METRONOME. expression-m. Vide EXPRESSION. tempo-m. Vide TEMPO.

markiren (mär-kē'-ren), *G.*, marquer (mär-kā), *F.* To mark, emphasise. markirt (mär-kērt'), *G.*, marqué (märkä'), *F.* Well marked. marquez un peu la mélodie (mär-kä'zŭń pŭ lä mä'-lô-dē'), *F.* "Emphasise the melody slightly."

Marsch (märsh), pl. märsche (mär'-shĕ), *G.* March(es). märschartig (märsh'-är-tĭkh). In the style of a march.

Marseillaise, la (lä mär-sĕ-yĕz), *F.* The French national anthem, written and composed by Capt. Rouget de Lisle, April 24, 1792, and called by him "Chant de guerre de l'armée du Rhin," but first popularised by, and always named after, the soldiers from Marseilles.

marteau (mär-tō), *F.* 1. Hammer, in piano-action. 2. Tuning-key.

martelé (mär-tŭ-lä'), *F.*, martellato (mär-tĕl-lä'-tō), martellan'do, *I.* Strongly marking the notes, as if hammering.

martellement (mär-tĕl-mäń), *F.* 1 Played with the acciaccatura. 2. In old music a mordent.

marziale (mär-tsĭ-ä'-lĕ), *I.* Vide MARCIA.

mascherata (mä-skĕ-rä'-tä). Masquerade.

maschera (mä'-skä-rä), *I.* A mask.

Maschinen (mä-shē'-nĕn), *G.* Pistons. Vide VALVE. M.-pauken. Kettle-drums with a mechanical adjuster of pitch.

mask, *E.*, masque (măsk), *F.*, Maskenspiel (mäs'-kĕn-shpēl), *G.* A spectacular entertainment usually allegorical and dramatic, with music. Very elaborately done in Elizabethan times.

mass. In the R. C. service, that portion accompanying the consecration of the Host. Before this service, those not permitted to take part are dismissed with the words, "Ite missa est" (vide ITE)—hence, by corruption, the name "mass." The service up to the dismissal was called "Mass of the catechumens," that after it, "Mass of the faithful" (*Missa fidelum*). A mass without music is low m.; with music high

m. The musical service is as follows: 1. The **kyrie,** (a) Kyrie Eleison, (b) Christe Eleison, (c) Kyrie Eleison. 2. The **gloria,** or **doxology,** (a) Gratias agimus, (b) Qui tollis, (c) Quoniam, (d) Cum sancto spiritu. 3. The **credo,** (a) Et incarnatus, (b) Crucifixus, (c) Et resurrexit. 4. The **sanctus.** Benedictus and Hosanna. 5. The **agnus dei,** and Dona Nobis. These divisions are named from the first words of their text (which will be found translated under the separate heads). The **short m.** is that of the Protestant Church, which uses only the **kyrie** or the **gloria.**

Masses have been written in all elaborations from simple unison to fullest counterpoint and to choral works in from 8 to 32 parts with orchestral accompaniment. (Vide PALESTRINA in the B. D.)

Mass (mäs), *G.* Measure, time.

mässig (měs'-sikh), *G.* 1. Moderato, moderate(ly). 2. As a suffix, "appropriate to," as *klaviermässig,* etc.

massima (mäs'-sǐ-mä), *I.* The "greatest." 1. A whole note. 2. Augmented intervals. 3. A maxim. Vide NOTATION.

master chord. The dominant. **m. fugue.** An elaborate **fuga ricercata. m. note.** The leading-tone. **m.-singer.** Vide MEISTERSINGER.

Masure (mä-zoo'-rě), *G.,* **Masure(c)k** (mä-zoo'-rěk), *Pol.,* **Masurka** (mä-zoor'-kä), *G.* See MAZOURK.

matachin (mǎ-tǎ-chēn'), *Sp.* A grotesque Merry Andrew dance.

mat'alan. A small Indian flute.

matassins (mǎ-tǎs-sǎn), *F.* 1. Matachin. 2. The dancers of it.

matelotte (mǎt-lôt), *F.* Sailor's hornpipe.

matinare (mä-tǐ-nä'-rě), *I.* To sing matins.

matinata (mä-tǐ-nä'-tä), *I.* Morning serenade.

mat'ins. The first morning service in the R. C. Church. Vide HORÆ.

Maultrommel (mowl'-trôm-měl), *G.* A Jew's harp. **M.-t.-klavier.** Melodicon.

max'im(a), *L.* Vide NOTATION.

Mazourk (mä-tsoork'). **Maz(o)urka** (mä-tsoor'-kä), **mazur** (ma-tsoor'), **Mazur'ca, Mazurek** (mä-tsoo'-rěk), **Mazurka** (mä-tsoor'-kä; pl. **Mazurke,** mä-tsoor'-kě), *G.* **mazurka,** *E.* (mä-zoor'-kä). A Polish national dance

of whimsical mood; in triple time with the 3d beat variously treated.

m. d. Abbr. of Main Droite, right hand.

me. Vide TONIC-SOL-FA.

mean. Inner, as tenor, or alto (of voices); as the *d* or *a* strings (of a violin). **mean clef.** Tenor clef. **mean-tone system.** Vide TEMPERAMENT.

measurable. Vide MENSURABLE.

meas'ure. 1. The unit of rhythm, corresponding to the metrical foot and including the notes between two bars; each measure has one and only one major accent. Vide TIME. 2. Loosely for tempo. 3. A stately dance as the **passy m.,** a cinque-pace. **measure-note,** the typical standard note of a measure as the 8th note in 3-8 time. **measure-rest.** Vide REST.

mécanisme (mä-kǎn-ēzm), *F.* Technic.

Mechanik (mě-kä'-nēk), *G.* 1. Action. 2. Machine-head. 3. The mechanism of fingering and wrist-action. 4. Technic.

mech'anism. 1. Action. 2. Finger and wrist action.

medesimo (mě-dä'-sǐ-mō), **medes'mo,** *I.* The same. **m. tempo.** The same time, as before.

me'dial. 1. Concerning the Mediant. 2. Intermediate or secondary (of accent). Vide CADENCE.

me'diant, médiante (mä'-dǐ-änt), *F.,* **mediante** (mä-dǐ-än'-tě), *G.* and *I.* 1. The third note of the scale. 2. One of the 3 pivotal tones of a mode, midway between final and dominant.

mediation. Vide CHANT.

medius. Vide ACCENTUS ECCL.

medley. A conglomerate of unrelated and usually familiar tunes.

Meertrompete (mär-trôm-pā'-tě), **Meerhorn,** *G.* Sea-trumpet.

mehr (mär), *G.* More. **m. chörig** (kä-rikh). For several choruses. **mehrfach** (mär-fäkh). Manifold, of an interval, a canon, or a compound stop. **mehrstimmig** (shtǐm'-mǐkh). For several voices. **Mehrstimmigkeit durch Brechung** (kīt-doorkh-brěkh-oongk). Polyphony that consists only of broken chords.

Meister (mī'-stěr), *G.* Master. **M. fuge** (foo'-ge). A ricercata fugue. **M.-gesang** (gě-zäng'). Minstrelsong. **M.-sänger** (zěng-ěr), or **singer** (zǐng-ěr). A member of the singing guild founded at Mainz in the 14th cent. and lasting till 1839 at Ulm. Wagner's opera describes their strict and elaborate rules or **Tabulatur.** (Vide Stories of the Operas, *"Die Meistersinger."*) **Meisterstück** (shtük). Masterpiece.

melancolia (mä-län-kō-lē'-ä), *I.*, **mélancolie** (mä-lăṅ-kô-lē'), *F.* Melancholy.

mélange (mä-läṅzh), *F.* A medley.

melis'ma, *Gr.* 1. A vocal embellishment or run. 2. **melismat'ic song.** That in which one syllable is sung to many notes, opposed to **syllabic song.**

melode (mä-lō'-dĕ), or **melodia** (mä-lō-dē'-ä), *I.* 1. Melody. 2. A stop much like the clarabella.

melo'deon. Vide AMERICAN ORGAN.

melod'ic interval, or **step.** One in which the tones are taken in succession, as opposed to **harmonic,** in which they are simultaneously taken.

melo'dica. A tiny pipe-organ with compass of 3½ octaves, inv. 1770, by Stein, of Augsburg.

melodico (mä-lō'-dĭ-kō). Cantando.

melod'icon. A key-board instr., inv. by Riffel, in Copenhagen, the tones produced from tuning-forks.

melod'ics. Theory of melody.

mélodie (mä-lô-dē), *F.* Melody, air. **m. bien sentie** (bĭ-ăṅ säṅ-tē'). The melody well accented.

mélodieuse (mä-lōd-yŭz). Melodious. **mélodieusement** (mäṅ). Melodiously.

Melodik (mĕ-lō'-dēk), *G.* Vide MELODICS.

melo'diograph. Melograph.

melo'dion. A key-board instr. with range of 6 octaves inv. by Dietz, of Emmerich, the tone produced by tuned steel bars pressed by a rotating cylinder.

melodio'so (mĕ-lō-dĭ-ō'-so), *I.*, **melodisch** (mĕ-lō'-dĭsh), *G.* Melodious.

melodista (mä-lō-dēs'-tä), *I.*, **mélodiste** (mä-lō'-dēst), *F.* Melodist.

Melodistik (mĕ-lō-dēs'-tēk), *G.* Melodics.

melo'dium. 1. American organ. 2. Alexandre organ.

mel'odrama, *E.*, **Melodram** (mä'-lō-dräm), *G.*, **mélodrame** (mä-lō-dräm), *F.*, **melodramma** (mä-lō-dräm'-mä), *I.* 1. Originally opera. 2. Spoken drama accompanied with instr. music, hence the music accompanying action. 3. A play of sensational nature.

mel'ody. 1. A tune. 2. A succession of tones, rhythmically and symmetrically arranged, as opposed to harmony, a combination of simultaneous tones. 3. The leading part. **leading m.** A principal melody.

me'lograph. A piano inv. 1827, which recorded what was improvised. Many attempts of this sort have been made, the most successful an electric m., *the Phonaut'ograph,* by Fenby, of England, recording after the manner of telegraphy. This record cut into cardboard is run through a key-board attachment, the *melotrope,* to reproduce the music.

mel'ologue. Recitative and music.

mel'oman, *Gr.*, **mélomane** (mä'-lō-măn), *F.*, **Melômániàc,** *E.* A passionate lover of music. **me'lomanie** (mä-lō-mă-nē), *F.*, **mel'omany.** Music mania.

melopea (mä-lō-pā'-ä), *I.*, **mélopée** (mä-lō-pā), *F.* The art of melody.

mel'ophare. A lantern with oiled music paper sides for use in serenades.

mel'opiano. A device inv. 1870 by Caldera, of Turin, for giving the piano power to increase the volume of a sustained tone. A treadle works small hammers acting rapidly on the strings.

mel'oplaste (mĕl'-ō-plăst). Pierre Galius's simplified method of teaching the rudiments by singing popular airs and pointing the place of the notes on the staff, and by using two metronomes for beats and measures.

melopoea (mĕ-lō-pē'-ä), *Gr.* Art of Composition.

Melos (mä'-lōs). Melody. Used by Wagner for the melody, also the entire implied harmony, the musical idea. Vide RECITATIVE.

mel'otrope. Vide MELOGRAPH.

même (mĕm), *F.* The same. **à la m. tempo.** In the original tempo.

men (män), *I.* Abbr. of meno before a vowel. **men allegro.** Less quick.

menéstrel (mŭ-näs-trĕl'), *F.* Minstrel. Vide TROUBADOUR.

mené'trier (mŭ'nä-trĭ-ā), *F.* A minstrel or rustic musician. Vide TROUBADOUR.

meno (mä'-nō), *I.* Less; not so fast. **m. mosso.** Less speed.

Mensur (mĕn-zoor'), *G.* Measure, of time, intervals, scale of pipes, and sizes of instr. strings, etc.

men'sura, *L.* Measure, time.

men'surable, *E.*, mensural (měn-zoo-räl'), *G.* The original plain-chant was in notes of equal duration; in the 12th cent. the old square notes were modified and given a "measurable" value. The first **mensurable** notes were the *maxima, longa, brevis* and *semibrevis;* in 1300, the *minima* and *semiminima* were added. In the 15th cent. white notes displaced the black, which were chiefly used for smaller values. The music so written, or **mensurable music**, was governed by many complicated laws. Vide NOTATION.

mente (měn'-tě). Mind. alla m. Improvised.

menuet (mŭ-noo-ā'), *F.*, Menuett (měn-oo-ĕt'), *G.*, menuetto (mā-noo-ĕt'-tō), *I.* Minuet.

mer'ula, *L.* A set of pipes in water producing a warbling tone.

me'ris, *Gr.* The 6th part of an octave.

mesau'lion, *Gr.* Symphony, ritornello.

mès'cal. A Turkish instr. of twenty-three cane pipes, each giving three different sounds.

mescolanza (měs-kō-län'-tsä), *I.* A medley.

me'se, me'son, *Gr.* Vide CHART OF GREEK MODES, p. 764, and LYRE.

me'sotonic. 1. Mean-tone. Vide TEMPERAMENT. 2. Vide LYRE.

mes'sa. *I.* A mass.

messa di voce (měs'-sa dǐ vō'-chě), *I.* The gradual swelling and diminishing of a tone; to attack and swell is for-mare il tuono (fŏr-mä'-rě ēl too-ō'-nō); to sustain loudly is fermare il t. (fěr-mä'-rě); to diminish is finire (fē-nē'-rě) il t.

messanza (měs-sän'-tsä), *I.* Quodlibet (q.v.).

messe (měs), *F.*, Messe (měs'-sě), *G.* A mass.

mes'sel, *Arab.* "Measure." The Arabian method of reckoning intervals, the lower notes receiving greater values than the higher because the vibrating portion of the string which produces them is longer.

mesto (mäs'-to), *I.* Melancholy. mesto'so. Sad.

mesure (mŭ-zür'), *F.* Measure. à la m. In time. m. à deux temps (dŭ täṅ). Common time. m. à. trois temps (trwä täṅ). Triple time. m. demi (d'mē). Half measure.

met. Abbr. of Metronome.

metal (mä-tăl'), *Sp.* Strength. compass of the voice

metallico (mě-täl'-lǐ-kō). *I.* (Of a voice) "metallic" in a good sense, clear, ringing, hence ⁓etal'lo, "metal."

metamor'phoses. Variations.

meter, or metre, *E.*, metre (mětr), *F.* In music as in verse, the arrangement of rhythmic units, or measures. The m. of hymns is classified by the number of syllables to a line, the metrical foot and the number of lines to a stanza. In Iambic m. or common m. (C. M.), 4 lines alternately 8 and 6 syllables long; common particular, or hallelujah m. (C. P. M.), 886886; long m. (L. M.), 4 lines of 8 syllables; long particular m. (L. P. M.), or long m. six lines, 6 lines of 8; short m. (S. M.), 6686; short particular m. (S. P. M.), 668668; stanzas of 8 lines are called double (C. M. D.; L. M. D.; S. M. D.). Other line-lengths are sevens and sixes (7676), tens (four 10's), hallelujah (666688, or 66664444). In trochaic m. are sixes (four 6's), sixes and fives (6565), sevens (four 7's), eights and sevens (8787). In Dactylic m. are eights, eights, sevens and fours, etc.; elevens (four 11's), and elevens and tens (11, 10, 11, 10), etc. Classic and French metres depend on *quantity* or length of syllables, instead of on their stress or accentuation as with us. Vide FOOT.

method, *E.*, méthode (mā-tôd), *F.*, metodo (mā'-tō-dō), *I.* A course of instruction; classification; system.

Metrik (mät'-rěk), *G.* Metrical art metrisch (mět'-rǐsh). Metrical.

metro (mā'-tro), *I.* and *Sp.* Metre.

Metrometer (mě-trō-mā'-těr), *G.*, métrometre (mā-trō-mětr), *F.*, metrometro (mā-trō-mā'-trō), *I.* Metronome.

met'ronome, *E.*, Metronom (mā-trō-nôm'), *G.*, métronome (mā-trô-nŭm), *F.*, metronomo (mā-trō-nō'-mō), *I.* A pendulum worked by clock-work, and weighted below; provided with a movable slide, and so graduated that its rate of vibration per minute can be fixed by the slider; with the slider at 60 it beats 60 times a minute, etc. It moves with an audible click; the bell-metronome has also a bell which rings every third or fourth, etc., beat. Perfected by Winkel it was put on the market by Maelzel (vide B. D.), and is called Maelzel's metronome (abbr. M. M.). It is useful as a composer's indication of the standard time of a composition; hence the **metronome-mark,** thus M. M. ♩-90, means a rate for quarter notes equal to 90 per minute, as indicated by the slider set at 90. It is used also to beat time for students. It is made also in watch-form as a **pocket m.**

met′rum, *L.* Metre.

Mette (mĕt′-tĕ), *G.* Matins.

metter la voce, *I.* Same as messa di voce.

mettere in musica (mĕt′-tĕ-rĕ ĭn moo′-zĭ-kä), *I.* To set to music.

mettez (mĕt-tā), *F.* "Draw (a stop)."

mettre d'accord (mĕtr dăk-kôr), *F.* To tune. **m. en musique** (äṅ-mü-zĕk). To set to music. **m. en répétition** (rā-pā-tēs′-yôṅ). To put in rehearsal.

met′zilloth, metzilltheim, *Heb.* Cymbals.

mez. Abbr. of Mezzo.

mezzo (mĕd′-zō), *I.* Medium, half. **m. aria.** Vide ARIA PARLANTE. **m. bravura.** Moderate difficulty. **m. forza** (fôr′-tsä). Moderately loud. **m. manica** (mä′-nĭ-kä). The half-shift. **mezzana** (mĕd-zä′-nä). Middle string of a lute. **m. orchestra.** Half the string-band. **m. voce** (vō′-chĕ), *I.* Half the voice, with moderate tone. **m. forte** (fôr′-tĕ). Moderately loud. **m. piano** (pĭ-ä′-nō), *I.* Rather soft. **m. soprano.** A voice lower than soprano, higher than contralto. **mezzo soprano clef.** The C clef on the second line, in old church-music or madrigals. The treble, or soprano, clef now supplies its place. **m. staccato.** A little detached. **m. teno′re.** A low tenor voice, nearly barytone. **m. tuono** (too-ō′-nō), *I.* A semi-tone.

m. f. Abbr. of mezzo forte.

m. g. Abbr. of main gauche (left hand).

mi (mē), *I.* and *F.* 1. The note E. **mi bémol** (bā′-môl). E flat. **mi dièse** (dĭ-ĕz). The note E sharp. 2. Vide SOLMISATION. 3. The 3d of the scale. *mi contra fa est diabolus in musica,* "mi against fa is the devil in music," was the mediæval objurgation against the tritone (q. v.), mi being B natural in the hard hexachord, fa being F in the natural hexachord. **mi-re-ut.** Vide OCTAVE.

mi′crophone. An instr. for the magnifying of sounds.

mid-c., or **middle c.** *c'* (vide PITCH), because it is in the centre of the piano and between the treble and bass staves.

middle voices. Tenor and alto.

mignon (mēn-yôṅ), *F.* 1. Favourite, pet. 2. Delicate.

militaire (mĭl-ĭ-tăr), *F.,* **militare** (mē-lĭ-tä′-rĕ), *I.,* **militairement** (mĭl-ĭ-tăr′-mäṅ), *F.,* **militarmen′te,** *I.* Martial(ly).

Militärmusik (mē-lĭ-tär′-moo-zēk′). Military band or music.

military band. An orchestra for out-of-doors, substituting for stringed instrs. additional and more powerful clarinets, and using saxophones, cornets, etc., freely.

milote (mē-lō′-tĕ), *Sp.* An Indian dance.

mi′modrama, *E.,* **mimodrame** (mē-mô-drăm′), *F.* Pantomime.

minacciando (mē-nät-chän′-dō), **min-accievole** (chä′-vō-lĕ), **minaccio′so, minaccie′volmente, minaccio′samente.** Threatening(ly).

minagnghinim (mĭ-nängd′-gĭ-nĭm), *Heb.* A table over which was stretched an iron chain and a hempen cord through balls of wood or brass; striking against the table they made a ringing sound.

minder (mĭnt′-ĕr), *G.* Minor, less.

mineur (mē-nŭr′), *F.* Minor.

min′im, minima (mē′-nĭ-mä), *I.,* **minime** (mĭn-ēm′), *F.* A half-note. Vide NOTATION.

Minnedichter (mĭn′-nĕ-dĭkh′-tĕr), **M.-sänger** (zĕng-ĕr), **M.-singer** (zĭng-ĕr), *G.* From the 12th to the 14th century a German troubadour of noble birth celebrating pure love in song (**Minne-gesang**). The singers wrote both words and music, singing and playing on the arpanetta or the viol. Their festivals of contest are reproduced in Wagner's "*Tannhäuser.*" They were less formulaic than their successor the "*Meistersinger.*" In the opera of the latter name, Wagner (vide Stories of the Operas in this book) shows Walter the **Minnesinger** in conflict with the dogmas of the Meistersinger.

mi′nor, *E.,* **minore** (mē-nō′-rĕ), *I.* "Smaller," of intervals, etc., as opposed to **major.** Vide INTERVAL, MAJOR, MODE, SCALE. **m. tone.** The lesser whole tone, 10:9. **m.**

tríad. One with minor 3d and perfect 5th.

mⁱn'strels. Singers, usually of a servile or vagabond class, sometimes acting as attendants on the trouvères and troubadours (q.v.), and generally playing the rebec. **negro m.** One who gives an imitation (usually remote) of the songs, dances, etc., of the American negro.

minue (mē-noo-ä'), *Sp.* A minuet.

minuet (mĭn-ū-ĕt'), *É.*, **minuetto** (mē-noo-ĕt'-tō), *I.* A stately and deliberate dance (originating probably in Poitou in the 17th century) in triple time, with gallant and amorous spirit. As one of the most important music-forms, it contains usually a principal subject and a trio each in contrasted sections. Appearing first as a movement in the suite and partita it became a part of the sonata and symphony, Beethoven substituting for it the Scherzo, and Tchaikovsky, in one case, a Viennese waltz. **minuettina** (tē'-nä), *I.* A little minuet.

miracle, miracle-play. Vide MYSTERY.

mi-re-ut. Vide OCTAVE.

miscel'la, *L.* Mixture-stop.

mise de voix (mēz-dŭ-vwä). Vide MESSA DI VOCE.

miserere (mē-zĕ-rä'-rĕ), *L.* First word of Psalm LI. beginning miserere mei, domine, "Pity me, Lord." Hence a setting of this Psalm sung in the R. C. service for the dead, and during Holy Week.

misericordia (mē'-zä-rĭ-kôr'-dĭ-ä), *L.* A miserere.

misk'in. A little bagpipe.

mis'sa, *L.* and *I.* A mass (q.v.). **m. brevis.** Short mass. **m. can'onica.** A canonical mass. **m. canta'ta.** Chanted mass. **m. pro defunc'tis.** "Mass for the dead." Requiem. **m. solen'nis.** High mass.

mis'sal, *E.*, **missa'le,** *L.*, **Missel** (mĭs'-sĕl), *G.* The mass-book containing the forms of the year.

misshällig, or **misshellig** (mĭs-hĕl'-lĭkh), *G.* Discordant. **Misshalligkeit** (kīt). Dissonance. **Missklang** (kläng). Discord. **missklingen** (mĭs'-klĭng-ĕn), **misslauten** (low-tĕn). To be discordant. **Misslaut** (lowt). Discordant sound. **Misslautend** (low :ĕnt). Dissonant, discordant. **misstimmen** (shtĭm'-mĕn). To put out of tune.

misterio (mĭs-tä'-rĭ-o), **mistero** (mĭs-tä'-rō), *I.* Mystery. **misterio'so, misteriosamen'te.** Mysterious(ly).

mistichanza (mēs-tĭ-kän'-tsä), *I.* Quodlibet (q.v.).

mis'to, *Gr.* Mixed. Vide MODES.

misura (mē-soo'-rä), *I.* Measure. **misurato** (mē-soo-rä'-tō), *I.* In strict time.

mit (mĭt), *G.* With, by.

Mitklang (mĭt'-kläng), *G.* Resonance. **mitklingende Töne** (mĭt'-klĭng-ĕnt-ĕ tä'-nĕ). Overtones.

Mitlaut (mĭt'-lowt), *G.*, **Mitlauter** (mĭt'-low-ter). Concord, consonance. **mitlauten.** To sound with.

mitleidsvoll (mĭt'-līts-fôl), *G.* Compassionate.

Mittel (mĭt'-tĕl), *G.* Middle, half. **mittel c.** (tsä). Middle C. **Mittelkadenz** (kä-dĕnts'). A half-cadence. Vide CADENCE. **Mittel-laut** (lowt). Middle sound. **mittelmässig.** Indifferent. **M.-stimme** (shtĭm'-mĕ). Inner part.

mixed. Vide CADENCE. **m. canon.** Vide CANON. **m. chorus,** etc. One with both male and female voices. **m. in organ,** the mixture-stops.

mix'olydian. See MODES, p. 764.

mixt'ure, *E.*, **mixtu'ra,** *L.*, **Mixtur** (mēx-toor'), *G.* A compound fluestop consisting of 2 to 6 ranks of pipes, giving 2 to 6 harmonics of any tone. The m. is auxiliary only, usually sounding only the octave and the fifth, and aiming to brighten the foundation-stops. Ancient m.'s had from 8 to 24 ranks, the result doubtless being atrocious discord.

mobile (mō-bĭ-lĕ), *I.* Facile, impulsive, fickle.

moderato (mō-dĕ-rä'-tō), *I.* Moderate, in time. **moderatis'simo,** or m. **assai** (äs-sä'-ē). In very moderate time. **moderamen'te.** Moderately. **moderanza** (rän'-tsä), **moderazione** (rä-tsĭ-ō'-nĕ). Moderation. **moderna, alla** (äl'-lä mō-dĕr'-nä), *I.* In the modern style.

modesto (mō-däs'-tō), **modestamente.** Modest(ly).

mod'ification. Temperament (q.v.). **modificazioni** (mō-dē-fĭ-kä-tsĭ-ō'-nē), *I.*, pl. Slight alterations.

modinha (mō-dēn'-ä), *Port.* A short song.

mod. Abbr. of Moderato.

modo (mō'-dō), *I.* and *Sp.* Mode, scale, style. (See article, page 762.)

modto. Abbr. of Moderato.

modolare (mō-dō-lä′-rĕ), **modulare** (mō-doo-lä′rĕ), *I.* To modulate.

modolan′te. Modulating.

mod′ulate, *E.*, **moduler** (mȯd-ü-lā), *F.* To effect a modulation.

modula′tion. 1. Change of key, tonality, or mode (usually to a related key by means of chords on the dominant of the new major, or on the leading-tone of the new minor key). The **m.** may be **transient, transitory,** or **passing,** when it leads to still a third key or back to the first; it may be **final** when it establishes a new tonality. **enharmonic m.** is that by means of enharmonic (q.v.) changes of notation. 2. *Obsolete.* Melodic, or rhythmic measurement, inflection.

modula′tor. Vide TONIC-SOL-FA.

modulatore (mō-doo-lä-tō′-rĕ), *I.* 1. Singer. 2. Tuner.

modulazione (mō-doo-lä-tsɪ̄-ō′-nĕ), *I.* Modulation.

moduliren (mȯ-doo-lē′-rĕn), *G.* To modulate.

mo′dus, *L.* Key, mode, scale.

möglich (mākh′-lĭkh), *G.* Possible. **so rasch wie m.** (zō-räsh-vē). As fast as possible.

mohinda (mō-ēn′-dä). A short Portuguese love-song.

Mohrentanz (mō-rĕn-tänts), *G.* Morisco.

moins (mwăn), *F.* Less.

moll (mȯl), *G.* Minor. **Mollakkord,** or **Molldreiklang.** Minor chord or triad, etc.

molla (mȯl′-lä), *I.* A key (of the flute), etc.

mol′le, *L.* Soft. 1. Vide "B." 2. Used of the hexachord f–d in which b flat was substituted for the older b natural. 3. Minor.

molle (mȯl), *F.* Soft, delicate.

mollemente (mȯl-lĕ-mĕn′tĕ), *I.* Softly, gently.

mol′lis, *L.* Vide MOLLE.

Molltonart (mȯl′-tōn-ärt), *G.* Minor key. **Molltonleiter** (lɪ̄-tĕr). Minor scale.

moltisonante (mȯl-tē-sō-nän′-tĕ), *I.* Resounding, very sonorous.

molto (mȯl′-tō), *I.* Much, very. **di m.** Extremely. **m. adagio.** Very slow. **m. allegro.** Very quick, etc.

momen′tulum, *L.* A 16th rest.

momen′tum, *L.* An 8th rest.

monau′los, *Gr.* An ancient beak-flute.

monocordo (mō′-nō-kȯr′-dō), *I.*, **mon′-ȯchord,** *E.*, **monochorde** (mȯn-ō-kȯrd), *F.* 1. An instr. of one string with a movable bridge, for determining intervals and pitch. 2. Marine trumpet. 3. A clavichord. 4. A German 1-stringed zither with fretted finger-board and resonance-box. 5. **a monocordo** = "on one string," i. e., with the soft (or monochord) pedal down.

monferina (mȯn-fĕ-rē′-nä), *I.* Lively dance in 6-8 time.

monodia (mō-nō-dē′-ä), *I.* **Monodie** (mȯn-ō-dē′), *F.* and *G.* Monody.

monod′ic. For one voice; or with one voice predominant.

monodra′ma, monodrame (drăm). A musical drama with only one actor.

mon′ody. Homophony.

monophon′ic. Homophonic.

monoph′onous. Producing but one tone, as the drum.

mon′otone. 1. Uniformity of sound. 2. Recitation on one tone.

Monotonie (mō-nȯ-tō-nē′), *G.* Monotony.

monot′onous. Monophonous; lacking variety.

montant (mȯn-tän), *F.* Ascending

monter (mȯn-tä), *F.* 1. To string. 2. To tune. 3. To put an instr. together. 4. To ascend.

montre (mȯntr), *F.* The pipes (usually the diapason) erected and "shown" at the front of the organ.

Moor′ish drum. A tambourine.

Moralitäten (mōräl-ɪ̄-tä′-tĕn), *G.*, **moralités** (mȯ-răl-ɪ̄-tä′), *F.*, **moralities,** *E.* Allegorical moral plays of the middle ages, a later form of the mysteries.

morbidezza (mȯr-bĭ-dĕd′-zä), *I.* Luxurious delicacy.

morceau (mȯr-sō), *F.* A "piece." 1. A short composition. 2. A phrase. **m. d'ensemble** (dän-sänbl). A piece harmonised for voices. **m. de genre** (dŭ zhänr). Characteristic piece.

mordant (mȯr-dän), *F.* A trilled grace (q.v.).

mor′dent, *E.*, **Mordent′,** *G.*, **mordente** (mȯr-dĕn′-tĕ), *I.* A grace (q.v.), *long, short,* or *inverted.*

moren′do, moriente (mō-rɪ̄-ĕn′-tĕ), *I.* Dying away; diminishing in volume and speed.

moresca (mō-rĕs′-kä), *I.*, **moresque** (mȯ-rĕsk), *F.* Moorish dance with jingling anklets and clashing swords.

Morgengesang (mȯr′gen-gĕ-zäng), *M.-* **lied** (lēt), *G.* Morning song. **M.-**

ständchen (shtĕnt'-khĕn). Morning serenade.

morisco (mō-rēs'-kō), I. Moorish. Vide MORESCA.

mo'risk. Morris-dance.

mormoramen'to, I. A murmur. mormorando (rän'-dō), mormorevole (rä'-vō-lĕ), mormoro'so. Gently murmuring.

morrice-dance, morris-dance, morriske-dance. An English country-dance of supposedly Moorish origin in 4-4 time, the dancers wearing ankle-bells and grotesque costumes.

mort (in F. môr). A tune at "the death" of the game.

mosso (môs'-sō), I. "Moved," rapid. molto m. Very fast. meno m. Less fast, etc.

mostra (mōs'-trä), I. A direct.

mot (mō), F. A note or strain on the bugle.

motet(t), E., Motette (mō-tĕt'-tĕ), G., motet (mō-tä), F., motet'to, I. 1. An almost always unaccompanied vocal composition contrapuntally developed, and using biblical text; a sacred madrigal. 2. Loosely, an anthem.

mote'tus, L. 1. A motet. 2. An obscure mediæval term.

motif (mō-tēf'), F. Motive, subject.

motion. Progression. 1. Of a single part by degrees (conjunct m.), or by skip (disjunct m.). 2. Of two parts relatively considered; contrary or opposite if one ascends as the other descends; oblique, if one is stationary while the other progresses; parallel or consecutive, if both move in the same direction by the same interval; similar, if both move in the same direction by unequal intervals (the latter terms are loosely used as synonymous); mixed, if, in the case of several parts, two of the above motions occur simultaneously between different parts. 3. perpetual m. Vide PERPETUAL. 4. pulse-motion. That in which the prevailing tone-length is that of the standard note of the measure, as ½ notes predominating in 3-2 time; half-pulse, that in which the prevailing motion is in notes of half the pulse-value, as ¼ notes in 3-2 time, etc. 5. eighth-note motion. That in which the prevailing entrances of tones fall uniformly on eighth notes.

motive, E., Motiv (mō-tēf'), G., motivo (mō-tē'-vō). I. 1. Theme, subject, a brief phrase or figure. 2. Vide LEADING-MOTIVE. 3. In Form, a measure. measure-m. One whose accent is that of the measure.

moto (mō'-tō), I. 1. Motion (q.v.). 2. Speed. con moto. With motion, rather fast. m. contrario (kôn-trä'-rĭ-ō). Contrary motion. m. mis'to. Mixed motion. m. obliquo (ôb-lē'-kwō). Oblique motion. m. ret'to. Parallel motion. m. perpet'uo. Vide PERPETUAL. m. precidente (prä-chĭ-dĕn'-tĕ). The same time as the preceding movement. m. primo (prē'mō). The same time as the first.

motteggiando (môt-tĕd-jän'-dō), I. Mocking(ly), jocose(ly).

mottetto (môt-tĕt'-tō), I. Motet.

mo'tus, L. 1. Motion (q. v.). 2. Movement. m. contrarius. Contrary motion. m. obliquus. Oblique motion.

mouth. The opening in the front of a pipe. m.-harmonica, or m. organ. 1. Vide HARMONICA. 2. Pan's pipes.

mouth'piece. The part of a wind-instr. applied to the lips.

mouvement (moov-mäṅ), F., movimen'to, I. 1. Motion. 2. Movement. m. de l'archet (dŭ-lär'-shä), F. Bowing. bien mouvementé (b'yăṅ moov-mäṅ-tä). Rhythmically elegant; well regulated.

movement. 1. Rate of speed. 2. Style of rhythm, as waltz-m. 3. A major division of a composition, having a certain integrity in itself, as the slow or the 2d m. of a symphony, etc.

m. p. Abbr. of Mezzo-piano.

m. s. Abbr. of Mano Sinistra (left hand).

nuance (mü-äṅs), F. A change or variation of note. Vide MUTATION (2).

mue (mü), F. See MUTATION.

muet (mü-ā), F. Mute.

Mund (moont), G. Mouth. M. harmo'nika. Mouth-harmonica. Vide HARMONICA. M.-loch (lôkh). Mouth of a pipe. M. stück (shtük). Mouthpiece.

muñeira (moon-yā-ē'-rä), Sp. A moderately fast Galician dance, in 2-4 time, beginning on the unaccented beat, with the strong beat in castanet-rhythm.

munter (moon'-tĕr), G. Lively, sprightly. Munterkeit (kīt). Vivacity.

murk'y. Used of a harpsichord comp.

having a bass in broken octaves (called **murky-bass**).

murmeln (moor'-mĕln), *G.* To murmur. **murmelnd** (moor'-melṅt). Murmuring.

Mus. Bac. Abbr. of Bachelor (q.v.) of Music.

Mus. Doc. Abbr. of Doctor (q.v.) of Music.

muse (mūz). 1. One of the nine goddesses of art. 2. The muzzle or tube of a bagpipe.

musetta (moo-zĕt'-tä), *I.*, **musette** (in *E.* mū-zet', in *F.* mü-zĕt). 1. A small, imperfect oboe. 2. A bagpipe with bellows. 3. Hence, a short pastoral dance-tune (often part of the Gavotte) in duple or triple time with a drone-bass. 4. A reed-stop.

musica (moo'-zĭ-kä), *L.* and *I.* Music. **m. da camera** (dä kä'-mĕ-rä). Chamber-music. **m. da teatro** (tä-ä'-trō). Dramatic music. **m. di gat'tì.** "Cat-music." Vide CHARIVARI. **m. plana.** Plain-chant.

musicale (moo-zĭ-kä'-lĕ), **musicalmen'te**, *I.* Musical(ly).

musicale (mū'-zĭ-kăl). An "at home" concert.

music-box. A box containing an automatic musical instr. The *Swiss* **m. b.** has a steel comb of graduated teeth set in vibration by small pegs in a revolving cylinder.

music-drama. An opera (particularly of the Wagnerian school) in which the text and the action determine the music, and are not interrupted by set arias, duets, etc.

musicien (mü-zēs'-yäṅ), *F.* Musician.

musicista (moo-zĭ-chē'-stä), *I.* Musician.

musico (moo'-zĭ-kō), *I.* 1. Musician. 2. A male soprano, particularly a eunuch.

musicone (moo-zĭ-kō'-nĕ), *I.* A great musician.

music-pen. 1. A 5-pointed pen for ruling the staff. 2. A broad-pointed pen for writing music.

music-recorder. A melograph.

music-timekeeper. An English instr. enabling a performer to keep time.

Musik (moo-zēk'), *G.* Music. **Musiker** (moo'-zĭ-kĕr). **Musikus** (koos'). A musician. **Musikalien** (käl'-ĭ-ĕn). Trade name of compositions. **Musikant** (moo-zĭ-känt'). A vagabond musician. **M.-fest.** A musical festival. **Musik'bande,** or **Musikantenbande** (bän-de). A band of strolling musicians. **Musik'diktät** (dĕk-tät). Vide DICTATION. **M.-direktor.** Conductor. **M.-lehrer.** (lä'-rĕr). Music-teacher. **M.-meister** (mī-shtĕr). Bandmaster. **M.-probe** (prō'-bĕ). Rehearsal. **M.-verein** (fĕ-rīn). A musical society. **M.-zeitung** (tsī-toongk). A musical periodical.

musique (mü-zēk'), *F.*, Music. **m. d'église** (dā-glēz). Church-music.

musiquette (mü-zĭ-kĕt). 1. A short composition. 2. Light music.

muta (moo'-ta). "Change!" A direction in scores to change the crooks or tuning of an instr. in preparation for a change of key.

muta'tion, *E.* (in *F.* mü-täs'-yōṅ), **mutazione** (moo-tä-tsĭ-ō'-nĕ), *I.* 1. The transformation of the male voice at puberty (in *F.* **mue** (mü)). 2. Vide SOLMISATION. 3. Shifting. 4. *As prefix,* used of all tierce, quint, etc., **stops** not producing the unison or octave of the foundation-stop.

mute. A device for muffling tone; in string-instrs. a clamp of brass, wood or ivory placed on the bridge and deadening the resonance; in wind-instrs. a pear-shaped leather pad, a cylinder of perforated wood or a pasteboard cone introduced into the bell.

mut(h)ig (moo'-tĭkh), *G.* Courageous, spirited.

muthwillig (moot'-vĭl-likh), *G.* Mischievous.

Muterung (moo'-tĕ-roongk), *G.* Mutation, 1.

mystères (mĭs-tăr), *F.*, **Mysterien** (mē-stä'-rĭ-ĕn), *G.*, **mysteries,** *E.* Mediæval sacred dramas dealing with the Last Judgment and other mysteries, as the **moralities** dealt with allegorical virtues and vices, and **miracle-plays** with the miracles of Christ. The idea persists in the Passion Play dealing with Christ's sufferings. In these dramas, often accompanied with music, oratorio had its beginning.

N

Nabla (nä'-blä), *Heb.* The nebel.

nacaire (nä-kăr), *F.*, **nacara** (nä-kä'-rä), *I.* An obs. kettledrum.

naccara (näk-kä'-ra), **nacchera** (näk-kä'-rä), *I.* Kettledrum.

nach (näkh), *G.* After; according to. **Nach'ahmung** (ä-moongk). Imitation nach Belieben (bĕ-lēb'n). Ad libitum. **Nachdruck** (drook). Emphasis, accent. **nachdrücklich** (drük-lĭkh), **nachdrucksvoll** (drooks'fôl). Emphatic. **nachgi(e)biger** (gē-'bĭkh-ĕr). More slow and sustained. **Nachhall** (häl), **Nachklang** (kläng). Resonance, echo. **nachklingen** (klĭng-ĕn), **nachlassend** (läs'-sĕnt). Slackening in time. **nachlässig** (lĕs-sĭkh). Carelessly. **Nachruf** (roof). A farewell. **Nachsatz** (zäts). The second part of a period, following the **Vordersatz**. **Nachslag** (shläkh). (a) An after-note, an appoggiatura following its principal note (the opposite of *Vorschlag*). (b) An auxiliary note at the end of a shake, also **Nachschliefe** (shlē-fe). **Nachspiel** (shpēl). Postlude. **nach und nach** (oont). By degrees. **Nachtanz** (tänts), *F*. Second movement of a dance.

nächtsverwandte Töne (nĕkhst'fĕr-vänt'-tĕ-tä'-nĕ), *G*. The nearest relative keys.

Nacht (näkht). Night. **N.-horn, N.-schall.** An 8-ft. flue-stop. **N.-hornbass.** The same stop on the pedal. **N.-musikständchen, N.-stück** (shtük). Nocturne, serenade.

Nachtschläger (nakht'-shläkher), **Nachtigall** (näkht'-ĭ-gäl), *G*. Nightingale; an imitative instrument.

nae'nia, *Gr.* A dirge.

nafie (nä'-fē). A Persian trumpet.

nafiri (nä-fē'-rē). An Indian trumpet.

nagârah (nä-gä'-rä), **nagaret'**, **nagareet'.** Oriental kettledrums.

nag'uar. An Indian drum.

Nagelgeige (näkh'ĕl-gī-khĕ), **nailfiddle.** Vide FIDDLE (Iron).

naïf (nä-ēf), *F.*, fem. **naïve** (nä-ēv), *F*. **naïv** (nä-ēf'), *G*. Artless, natural. **naïvement** (nä-ēv-män). Naturally. **naïveté** (nä-ēv-tä). Artlessness, simplicity.

naked. Of intervals, as fourths or fifths lacking the third or other accompaniment.

na'ker, nakeres. *Old E.* Small metal drum(s).

nakokus (nä-kō'-kŭs), *Egypt.* Two brass plates suspended and struck.

nan'ga. Negro harp.

Nänien (nä-nĭ-ĕn), *G*. Dirges.

narrante (när-rän'-tĕ), *I*. In narrative style.

narra'tor. The chief performer in an oratorio or Passion Play.

Narrentanz (när'-rĕn-tänts), *G*. Fool's dance.

nasard (nä-zär), *F.*, **Nas(s)at'** (näs-zät'). *G.*, **nazard'.** An old name for a stop tuned a twelfth above the diapasons. **nasar'do,** *I*. and *Sp.*, **nasarde** (nä-zärd), *F.*, **nassart** (näs'-särt), **na'-sillard.** A 2⅔-foot stop. The **Grosnasard** (grō-nä-zär), *F.*, or **Grossnasat** (grōs-nä-zät'), *G.*, is a quint-stop on manual or pedal. **petit-nasard** (p'tē), or **larigot,** is a 1⅓-ft. stop.

na'son. A 4-ft. flute-stop.

Nationallied (nä-tsĭ-ō-näl'lēt), *G*. National song.

Natur (nä-toor'), *G*. Nature. **N. horn.** A valveless Waldhorn. **N.-scala.** Natural scale. **N.-töne.** Vide NATURAL TONE. **N. trompete.** Valveless trumpet. **natürliche** (nä-tür'-lĭkh-ĕ). Natural. **Naturalist'.** A self-taught singer. **naturalistisch** (ĭst'-ĭsh). Untrained.

nat'ural. 1. The sign ♮ nullifying a sharp or flat. 2. A white digital. **n. harmonics.** Those on an open string. **n. hexachord.** That based on C. **n. modes.** The authentic church modes. **n. modulation.** That to a nearly related key. **n. key,** or **scale.** That of C major. **n. pitch.** That of a pipe not overblown. **n. tones.** Those producible on a wind-instr., as the horn, without altering the length of the tube with valves, keys, etc., hence **natural horn,** etc., one producing tones without valves or keys.

naturale (nä-too-rä'-lĕ), *I*. Natural. **naturali suoni** (soo-ō'-nē). Sounds in the compass of the voice. **naturalmen'te.** Naturally.

natural'is, *L*. Natural; *Cantus* **n.,** music in the *hexachordum* **N.** (the hexachord based on C).

naturel(le) (nät-ü-rĕl), *F*. Natural.

naublum (nō'-bloom), *Heb.* Vide NEBEL.

nay (nā). A Turkish flute.

Neapolitan sixth. Vide ALTERED CHORDS.

nebel (nä-bĕl), **nebel nassor** (nä-bĕl-näs'-sôr), *Heb.* Ten-stringed harp.

neben (nä'-bĕn), *G*. Accessory. **N.-dominant.** The dominant of the dominant. **N.-dreiklang.** Secondary triad. **N.-gedanke.** Subsidiary theme, or idea. **N.-klang.** Accessory tone. **N.-note.** Auxiliary note. **N.-register, N.-züge** (tsü-khĕ). Accessory stops. **N.-septimenakkorde.** Secondary sevenths. **N.-stimme.** Subordinate voice or part. **N.-werk.** Choir-organ.

necessario (nā-chĕs-sä'-rĭ-ō), *I.* Necessary.

nechiloth (nĕk'-ĭ-lôt), **neg(h)inoth** (nĕ'-gĭ-nôt), *Heb.* A wind-instrument.

neck. That part of an instr. which carries the finger-board.

ne'fer. Egyptian guitar.

negligente (nāl-yē-jĕn'-tĕ), **negligentemen'te,** *I.* Negligent(ly). **negligenza** (jĕn'-tsä). Carelessness.

negli (nāl'-yē), **nei** (nā'-ē), *I.,* pl. In the.

nei (nā'-ē), *Tur.* A flute made of cane.

nekeb (nā'-kĕb), *Heb.* A wind-instr. formed of a single tube.

nel, nella, nelle, nello, nell', *I.* In the, at the.

nenia. Vide NAENIA.

neo-German. Used of the programmatic school.

nero (nā'-rō), *I.* "Black." A quarter note.

nete (nā'-tĕ), *G.* Vide LYRE and MODE.

net (nĕt) **nette** (nĕt), *F.,* **nett** (nĕt), *G* nei to, *I.* Neat, clear. **netteté** (nĕt tŭ-tā), *F.* **Nettheit** (nĕt-hīt), **Nettigkeit** (nĕt'-tīkh-kīt), *G.* Neatness, distinctness. **nettamen'te,** *I.* Crisply.

neu (noi), *G.* New. **n.-deutsche Schule** (doit-shĕ shool'-ĕ). Vide NEO-GERMAN SCHOOL.

neu'ma, neume (nūm). 1. One of the characters in the early notation by points, commas, hooks, etc. Lines were introduced later, but they were always rather an aid to memory than a notation. 2. Melisma. 3. A slur. The neumes somewhat resembled modern shorthand and served somewhat the same function. The earlier forms before lines are quite indecipherable. A single note was called *Virga, virgula, punctus,* or *punctum;* a rising inflection sign, *pes,* or *podatus;* a falling inflection, *clinis* or *flexa;* various nuances of performance and special note values were the *ancus, bivirga, cephalicus, distropha, epiphonus, gnomo, oriscus, plica* (tror), *quilisma* (shake), *semivocalis, sinuosa, strophicus, tramea, tremula, trivirga,* etc.

neun (noin), *G.* Nine. **Neunachteltakt** (äkh'-tel-täkt), *G.* Nine-eighth time. **Neunte** (noin'-tĕ). A ninth. **Neunzehnte** (tsän-tĕ). Nineteenth.

neuvième (nŭv-yĕm'), *F.* A ninth.

nex'us, *L.* A binding together.

nicht (nĭkht), *G.* Not.

nicolo (nē'-kō-lō). A 17th cent. bombardon.

nieder (nē'dĕr). *G.* Down. **N.-schlag.** Down-beat, or accented part. **N.-strich.** The down bow.

niedrig (nē'-drĭkh), *G.* Deep, in voice.

nina (nē'nä), *I.* Lullaby (or, **ninnananna**). **ninnare** (nĭn-nä'-rĕ). To sing a lullaby.

nine-eighth. Vide TIME.

nineteenth. 1. An interval of two octaves and a fifth. 2. A stop tuned a nineteenth above the diapasons Vide LARIGOT.

ninth. 1. An interval of an octave and a second. 2. Vide CHORD.

nobile (nō'-bĭ-lĕ), **nobilmente,** *I.,* **noble** (nôbl), **noblement** (nô-blŭ-män), *F.* Noble (nobly). **nobilità** (nō-bē-lĭ-tä'), *I.* Nobility.

noch (nôkh), *G.* Still, yet; as **noch schneller** (shnĕl'-ler). Still quicker.

nocturn(e), *E.,* **nocturne** (nôk-türn), *F.,* **notturno** (nôt-toor'-nō), *I.* 1. Term first used by John Field for a composition of dreamy, night-like mood. 2. Vide HORÆ CANONICÆ.

node, nodalpoint, no'do, *I.* One of the axis-like points or lines in a vibrating body, where there is no vibration (cf. LOOP). **nodal figures.** The chart of vibration produced by sand strewn upon a flat vibrating plate; discovered by Chladni.

no'dus, *L.* "A knot," an enigmatical canon.

noël (nō-ĕl'), *F.* A Christmas carol, Vide NOWELL.

noeud (nŭ), *F.* 1. A turn. 2. A node.

no'fer. Vide NEFER.

noire (nwăr), *F.* "Black," a quarter note.

noise. Early *E.* 1. Music. 2. A band.

no'lae, *L.* Tintinnabulæ.

nomes (nōmz), *Gr.* 1. Airs anciently sung to Cybele, Pan, and other divinities. 2. Compositions regulated by inviolable rules, as canon. 3. A canon. Vide NOMOS.

nomine, in (in nō'-mĭ-nä), *L.* 1. "In the name" (of the Lord). A motet. 2. Vide FUGA.

no'mos, pl. **nomoi,** *Gr.* Law(s). Greek songs fulfilling all the rules.

non (nōn), *I.* Not, no.

nona (nō'-nä), *I.*, None (nō'-nĕ), *G.* A ninth (interval). Nonachord'-o, *I.*, No'nenakkord, *G.* A ninth. Vide CHORD.

nones. Vide HORÆ CANONICÆ.

nonet(t)', *E.*, Nonett', *G.*, nonet'to, *I.* Music for 9 parts.

Non'nengeige (gī-khĕ). "Nun's-fiddle." Vide MARINE TRUMPET.

Nonole (nō-nō'-lĕ), *G.* Nonuplet.

nonny hey nonny. An old *E.* refrain.

non'uplet. A group of nine equal notes.

nor'mal (in *G.* nôr-mäl'). Normal, standard. Normalton (tōn), *G.* The tone A. Normaltonleiter (lī-tĕr), *G.* The natural scale (of C).

nota (nō'-tä), *I.* and *L.* Note. n. bianca. "White" or half-note, etc. n. buona (boo-ō'-nä). Accented note. n. cambiata (käm-bĭ-ä'-tä), or cam'bita, *I.* 1. A changing note. 2. Resolution by skip. n. caratteris'tica. Leading-note. n. cattiva (kät-tē'-vä). Unaccented note. nota contra notam. "Note against note." Vide COUNTERPOINT. n. corona'ta. A note marked with a hold. n. d'abbellimen'to. A note of embellishment. n. di passaggio (dē päs-säd'-jō). A passing note. n. di piacere (dē-pĭ-ä-chā'-rĕ). An optional embellishment. n. falsa. A changing note. n. principale (prēn-chĭ-pä'-lĕ). Principal note. n. quadra'ta. A plain-song note. n. roma'na. A neume. n. sciolta (shōl'-ta). Staccato. n. sensibile (sĕn-sē'-bĭ-lĕ), *I.*, sensi'bilis, *L.* The leading-note. n. digna'ta, *L.* A note marked with a sign. n. sostenuta (sōs-tĕ-noo'-tä). A sustained note.

nota'tion (in *F.* nō-tăs'-yôǹ), notazione (nō-tä'-tsi-ō-nĕ), *I.* Notation. (See article, page 767.)

note. A character representing a musical tone; by its shape indicating the duration, by its position on the staff, the pitch, of the tone. connecting note. A note common to two chords.

note (nôt), *F* Note. n. d'agrément (d'ă-grā-mäǹ). Ornamental note. n. de passage (dŭ păs-säzh). Passing note. n. dièsée (dĭ-ĕ-zā), *F.* Note marked with a sharp. notes coulées (koo-lā). Slurred notes. n. de goût (dŭ-goo). Note of embellishment. n. sensible (säǹ-sēbl'). Leading note. n. surabondantes (sür-ä-bôǹ-dänt). Such incommen-

surate groups as triplets, quintoles, etc. n. liée (lē-ā). Tied note. n. syncopées (săǹ-kô-pä). Syncopated notes.

Noten (nō'-tĕn), *G.*, pl. Notes. Notenblatt (blät). A sheet of music. N.-buch (bookh). Music-book. N.-fresser. "Note-gobbler," one who has facility but no taste. N.-schrift (shrĭft). Musical manuscript. N.-system (zēs-täm). The staff.

noter (nō-tā), *F.* To write out a tune.

no'tograph. Melograph.

notturno (nôt-toor'-nō), *I.* A nocturne.

no'tula, *L.* Note used in ligature.

nourrir le son (noor-rēr lŭ sôǹ), *F.* To attack a note forcibly, and sustain it. un son nourri (noor-rē). A sustained tone.

nourrisson (noor-rēs-sôǹ), *F.* Bard.

nour'singh. A straight Indian trumpet.

no'va, *I.* A small flute.

Novelette (nôf-ĕ-lĕt'), *G.* From *F.*, a short musical romance. Name first given by Schumann to pieces containing considerable freedom of form, treatment, and idea.

novemole (nō-vĕ-mō'-lĕ), *I.* A group of nine equal notes.

no'well. Old *E.* "Good news." 1. A refrain of Christmas carols, hence 2. Carol. Cf. NOËL.

nuances (nü-äǹs), *F.*, pl. 1. Lights and shades of expression; variety. 2. A notation.

null. 1. A cipher. Vide o. 2. Vide TASTO SOLO.

number. 1. An integral portion of an opera, symphony, or programme, etc. 2. A favourite method of designating compositions, as Chopin's "5th" waltz.

numer'ical notation. A scheme introduced by Rousseau, to substitute numerals as names of tones. A similar notation in Massachusetts was called Day's & Beal's "One-line system."

nu'merus, *L.* 1. Number. 2. Rhythm.

Nunc dimit'tis, *L.* "Now dismiss (us)." The text, Luke II. 10–12, often used as a final number.

nun's-fiddle. Marine trumpet.

nuovo (noo-ō'-vō), *I.* New. di nuovo. Again.

nut. 1. The small bridge at the upper end of the finger-board of violins, etc. 2. The movable fastening of the hair of a bow. 3. The "lowest nut," the ridge between tail-piece and tail-pin.

646 DICTIONARY OF TERMS

O

O. A small circle, or cipher, means: 1. An open string. 2. Harmonic. 3. Diminished fifth (or a chord containing one). 4. Tasto solo. 5. To be played with the thumb. 6. Tempus perfectum. Vide NOTATION. 7. Harmonium-stops are marked with a numeral in a circle. 8. In neume-notation, the fourth church mode.

O (ō), **od** (ōd), *I* Or, as, either.

O (ŏ), *L.* Exclamation. *les* **O** *de Noël* (lā-zō dŭ nō-ël), *F.* The Christmas antiphons to the Magnificat, all beginning with "O!"

oaten-pipe. A simple straw cut to form a reed-pipe.

ob. Abbr. for oboe(s).

ob'bligato (ŏb-blĭ-gä'-¨ō), *I.*, **obligé** (ŏb-lĭ-zhā), *F.*, **Obligat** (ŏp-lĭ-gät'), *G.* "Indispensable," of a part which cannot be omitted without injury to completeness; though latterly the term has come almost to mean "optional," as in songs "with violin obb." in which the violin part is frequently omitted.

ob(b)liquo (ŏb-blē'-kwō), *I.* Oblique. Vide MOTION.

ober (ō'-bĕr), *G.* Upper, higher. **O.-dominante.** Dominant. **O.-labium.** Upper lip (of a pipe). **O.-manual.** The upper manual. **O.-stimme.** Upper part. **O.-taste** (täs'-tĕ). Black key. **O.-theil** (tīl). The upper part. **O.-ton.** Harmonic. **phonischer O.-ton.** The 15th partial. **O.-werk.** In an organ with 2 manuals, the choir-organ; with 3, the swell; with 4, the solo.

oblique, obli'quus, *L.* Vide MOTION.

oblique pf. An upright pf. with diagonal strings.

oboe (ō'bō; in *G.* ō-bō'-ĕ), **oboè** (ō-bō-ā'), *I. Plurals:* **oboes,** *E.*, **Oboen,** *G.*, **oboi** (ō-bō'-ē), *I.* 1. A double-reed instr. with conical wooden tube, and 9 to 14 keys; extreme compass *b♭–f'''*. It is non-transposing (except in the case of the B♭ and E♭ oboes for military bands), and is fingered somewhat like a flute. Its tone is reedy and quaint, almost homely; it gives a pastoral atmosphere, or is capable of great melancholy, but rarely of much floridity. The alto of the oboe is the so-called **cor anglais** (kôr äṅ-glĕ'), *F.*, **corno inglese** (kôr-nō-ēn-glä'-zĕ), *I.*, **eng-**

lisches Horn (ĕng'lĭsh-ĕs not ĕng-glĭsh-ĕs), *G.*, or **English horn.** An oboe with a double long tube, and a pitch a fifth lower, extreme compass *g♭–b.''* This is now written as an instr. transposing a fifth. It is even more sombre than the treble oboe—indeed it is the most mournful and inconsolable of instruments. It is a development from the old **oboe da caccia** (dä kät'-shä), in F. or E♭ written in the alto clef. The **o. d'amore** (dä-mō'-rĕ), **o. basso,** and **o. lungo** (loon'-gō) were lower by a minor third than the modern treble oboe, which was formerly called **o. piccolo.** 2. A reed-stop of 4 and 8 ft. pitch, also called **orchestral oboe.**

obois'ta, *I.* Oboist.

Obw. Abbr. for **Oberwerk.**

ocarina (ō-kä-rē'-nä). A terra-cotta bird-shaped instr. of fluty tone.

occhiali (ŏk-kĭ-ä'-lē). 1. White notes. 2. Brillenbasse.

occhetto (ŏk-kĕt'-tō), *I.*, **oche'tus,** *L.* Hocket.

oct'achord. 1. An 8-stringed instr. 2. A series of 8 tones.

oct'aphonic. Eight-voiced.

oc'tave (in *F.* ŏk-tăv, in *G.* ŏk-tä'-fĕ) 1. A consecutive series of eight diatonic tones as from *c'–c''*. 2. The interval of an eighth. 3. A tone an 8th above (or below) another. 4. **large octave, once-marked** or **lined o.,** etc. Vide PITCH. 5. The diapason of the Greek system 6. The eight days following a Church festival. 7. A stop sounding an octave higher than the digital pressed, as **octave-flute** (also used for the *piccolo* (q.v.). **consecutive covered, broken,** etc., **octaves,** vide the adjectives. **rule of the o.** A 17th century system of harmonising the scale giving a bass scale with the normal chords and inversions to accompany it. **short o.** The lowest octave in an organ, where the scale is incomplete or compressed, also called *mi–re–ut.* **o.-scale.** Vide MODES. **o.-coupler.** Vide COUPLER. **o.-staff.** A notation introduced by Adams, of New Jersey, three groups of lines combined in three octaves, dispensing with the flats and sharps, and giving each tone its own place. **octave stop.** 1. A 4-ft. stop. 2. The position of fingers stopping an octave on the finger-board. 3. A mechanical stop in reed-organs, coupling the octave above.

octaviana (ŏk-tä-vĭ-ä′-nä), octavina (ŏk-tä-vē′-nä), *I.*, octavin (ŏk-tä-văṅ), *F.* 1. An octave-spinet. 2. The piccolo. 3. A harpsichord octave-stop. 4. A 2-ft. organ-stop.

Octavin (ŏk-tä-fēn′), *G.* A single reed, conical wood-wind instr. fingered like the oboe; compass c′-c″″, keys B♭ and C. Inv. by O. Adler.

octa′vo attachment. Vide PEDAL (octave).

octet(t)′, octet′to, *I.* A composition for eight parts.

octipho′nium, *L.* Octet.

oc′tobass, *E.*, octobasse (bäs), *F.* A double-bass of huge size, about 12-ft. high. Inv. by Vuillaume. The 3 strings are stopped by means of keys and pedals.

oc′tochord, *L.* 8-stringed lute.

Octole (ŏk-tō′-lĕ), *G.* Octuplet.

oc′tuplet. A group of eight equal notes.

octuor (ŏk-twôr), *F.* Octet.

od (ŏd), *I.* Or.

ode (ŏd). An elaborate lyric, almost a cantata. odische (ō′-dĭsh-ĕ) Musik, *G.* Music for an ode.

Odem (ō′-däm), *G.* Breath.

Odeon (ō-dä′-ŏn), *Gr.*, ode′um, *L.* A public building for music.

oder (ō′-dĕr), *G.* Or, or else.

ode-symphonie (ŏd-säṅ-fō-nē), *F.* A symphony with chorus.

œuvre (ŭvr), *F.* Work, composition.

off. 1. A direction to push in an organ-stop or coupler. 2. False.

offen (ŏf′-fĕn), *G.*, of′fenbar. 1. Open. 2. Parallel. Offenflöte (flä′-te). An open flute-stop.

offertoire (ŏf′-fĕr-twär), *F.*, offerto′rio, *I.* and *Sp.*, offerto′rium, *L.*, of′fertory. The part of the Mass or service, the motet or instrumental piece, performed during the taking of the collection.

offic′ium, *L.* A service. o. defunc-to′rum. Funeral service. o. diur′-num. Daily s. o. matuti′num (nocturn′um) morning (evening) s. o. vesperti′num. Vespers.

oficleida (ō-fĭ-klä′-ĭ-dä), pl. e., *I.* Ophicleide.

ohne (ō′-nĕ), *G.* Without.

oioueae. The vowels of "World without end, Amen." Cf. EVOVAE.

Oktave (ŏk-tä′-fĕ), *G.* Octave (q.v.). oktavi(e)ren (fē′-rĕn). To produce the octave by overblowing. Ok-

tävchen (ŏk-täf′-khĕn), Oktavflöte (flä′-tĕ), or -flötlein (līn). Piccolo. Oktavengattungen (gät-toong-ĕn). Octave-scales. Oktav-folgen (fŏl-khĕn), or -parallelen, or Oktavenverdoppelungen (fĕr-dŏp-pĕl-oong-ĕn). Parallel, or consecutive octaves.

Oktavwaldhorn. A Waldhorn inv. by Eichborn & Heidrich.

Oktavin, *G.* Vide OCTAVIN.

ole, el (ĕl ō′-lĕ), *Sp.* Slow 3-4 dance with castanets.

ol′iphant. A horn made of a tusk.

o′lio. A miscellany.

olivettes (ō-lĭ-vĕt), *F.* Provençal dance after the olives are gathered.

olla podrida (ŏl′-lä pō-drē′-dhä). Medley.

om′bi. An African harp.

om′bra, *L.* Shade; nuance.

om′nes, omnia, *L.* All. Vide TUTTI.

om′nitonic, omnitonique (ŏm-nĭ-tŏ-nēk), *F.* Having all the tones of the chromatic scale, as a horn.

once-accented, or once-marked octave. Vide PITCH.

ondeggiamen′to (ŏn-dĕd-jä-mĕn′-tō). Undulation. ondeggian′te, *I.* ondulé (ŏṅ-dü-lä), *F.* Waving, undulating, trembling. onduliren (ŏn-doo-lē-rĕn), *G.* To make a tremulous tone.

one-lined. Vide PITCH.

ongarese (ŏn-gä-rä′-zĕ) ongherese (ŏn-gĕ-rä′-zĕ), *I.* Hungarian.

onzième (ŏṅz-yĕm), *F.* Eleventh.

op. Abbr. of Opus.

open. 1. Of pipes, open at the top. 2. Of chords, not in *close* position. 3. Of strings, not stopped. 4. Of tone, (a) produced by an open string or by a wind-instr. not stopped, (b) not prod. by valve or key. 5. Of scores, in which a stave is given to each part or instrument.

Oper (ō′-pĕr), *G.*, op′era, *E.* (in *I.* ō′-pĕ-rä), *I.*, opéra (ō-pä-rä), *F.* Drama set to music. o.-bouffe (boof), or buffon (büf-fôṅ), *F.*, o.-buffa (boof′-fä), *I.* Farcical, or low-comedy opera, what we call comic opera. opéra comique (kō-mēk), *F.* Literally "comic opera," but generally used only to indicate that the dialogue is spoken, not sung. The plot may be as serious as **grand opera, opera seria** (sā′-rĭ-ä), *I.*, opera sérieux (sä-rĭ-ŭ), *F.*, in which all dialogue is in recitative and the ensembles are more elaborate. o. di

camera (kä'-mĕ-rä). Opera for a small auditorium. **o. lyrique** (lē-rēk), **ballad-opera.** One in which lyricism has the preference over dramatic action. **o.-drammat'ica,** *I.* Romantic opera. **O.-haus** (hows). Opera-house. **O.-sänger.** Operatic singer. (See article, page 769. Also Opera synopses, page 819 to page 865.)

operet'ta, *I.*, **Operette** (ŏp-ĕ-rĕt'-tĕ), *G.* A small light opera, cf. SING-SPIELE. **Op'erist.** An operatic singer.

Operndichter (ō'-pärn-dĭkh-tĕr), *G.* Libretto writer.

ophicleide (ŏf'-ĭ-klīd). 1. An obsolescent brass instr. the bass of the key-bugle family. The **bass o.** in C, B♭ and A♭ (compass A♭–a'♮) the **alto o.** in F and E♭ (compass 2½ octaves); the **contrabass o.** same compass as the **alt. o.** but an octave lower. The bass tuba (q.v.) has a richer tone and has displaced it. 2. A powerful 4 or 8 ft. reed-stop.

opp. Abbr. of **oppure.**

opposite. Contrary (of motion, q. v.).

oppure (ŏp-poo'-rĕ), *I.* Or, or else.

opus (ō'-poos), *L.* Work, composition; as, Op. 10, the 10th composition, or, more commonly, the 10th publication of a composer. **opus'culum.** A little work. **opus post'humum.** A work published after the death of the composer.

orage (ō-räzh), *F.* "Storm." 1. An imitative composition. 2. A stop.

O'ra pro no'bis, *L.* "Pray for us!" A response to a litany in R. C. service.

oratoire (ŏr-ä-twär), *F.*, **orato'rio,** *I.* and *E.*, **orato'rium,** *L.* (in *G.* ō'-rä-tō'-rĭ-oom). A sacred work constructed like an opera, but performed now without action, costume, or scenery. (See article, page 776.)

orchésographie (ŏr-kā'-zō-grä-fē), *F.* The science and explanation of dancing. **orchésique** (tēk), *F.* Relating to dancing **Orchestik** (ŏr-kĕs-tēk'), *G.* Art of dancing.

or'chestra, *E.* (in *I.* or-kĕs-tra), **Orchester** (ŏr-kĕs'-ter), *G.*, **orchestre** (ŏr-kĕstr), *F.* Literally "dancing-place," that used in front of the stage in Greek tragedy for the chorus; the name was given by the first opera-writers (see PERI, B. D.) to the place occupied by the musicians, thence to the musicians themselves. The word now means the place and

its occupants, and the instrs. in general. The modern **o.** may be (a) **large, full, grand, symphony;** (b) **small.** Parts of the orchestra may be designated, as *string orches-tra*, etc. **Orchesterverein** (fĕr-īn). An orchestral society. **O-stimmen.** Orchestral parts. **orchestral flute** or **oboe.** A stop. **or'chestra'tion.** The art or act of arranging music for orchestra. **or'chestrate,** *E.*, **orches-trare** (ŏr-kĕs-trä'-rĕ), *I.*, **orches-tri(e)ren** (trē'-rĕn), *G.*, **orchestrer** (ŏr-kĕs-trā), *F.* To write for orchestra. (See the *Story of Orchestra and Band Instruments*, page 811; *Orchestras In America*, page 787; *Orchestration of Theatre and Dance Music*, page 780, and *The Orchestra and Orchestration*, page 778.)

orchestrina (trē'-nä), **di ca'mera,** *I.* A small free-reed key-board instr., imitating some orchestral instr. Inv. by W. E. Evans, 1860.

orchestrino (trē'-nō), *I.* A piano violin, inv. by Pouleau, 1808.

orches'trion. 1. A large automatic barrel-organ with many imitative stops. 2. A chamber-organ devised and used on his tours by Abb' Vogler.

ordinario (ŏr-dĭ-nä'-rĭ-ō), *I.* Ordinary, usual, common. **tempo o.** 1. The usual time. 2. 4-4 time.

ordre (ŏrdr), *F.* A suite.

orecchio (ō-rĕk'-kĭ-ō), *I.* Ear. **orec-chiante** (ō-rĕk-kĭ-än'-tĕ). Singing by ear.

oreille (ō-rā'-yŭ), *F.* Ear.

organ, *E.*, **organo** (ŏr-gä'-nō), *I.*, **or-gane** (ŏr-gän), *F.* (See article, page 728.)

organ-bellows. A machine for supplying wind. **o.-blower.** One who works the bellows. **o.-loft.** The part of the church where the organ is placed. **o. metal.** A tin and lead mixture used in pipes. **o. tablature.** Vide TABLATURE. **o. point.** Vide PEDAL POINT. **o. tone.** A tone sustained with uniform power. **buffet o.** Very small organ. **enharmonic, enharmonic organ.** An American instr. giving three or four times the usual sounds within an octave, furnishing the precise intervals for every key, the scale of each key being produced by pressing a pedal. **full organ.** All the power of the organ. **hand-organ** or **barrel-o.** A cylinder turned by hand and acting on keys to produce set tunes. **harmonium o.** A reed instr. voiced to imitate organ-stops. **organet'to,** *I.* A small organ. **organier** (ôr-găn-yä), *F.* Organ-builder. **organique** (ôr-găn-ēk), *F.* Relating to the organ. **organista** (ôr-gä-nēs'-tä), *I.* and *Sp.* 1. An organ-player. 2. Formerly a composer. See p. 728. **organic.** Old term for instrumental. **orga'nicen,** *L.* Organ-player. **organis'trum,** *L.* A hurdygurdy of about 1100 A. D. **organo** (ör-gä'-nō), *I.* Organ (q.v.). **o. di campan'a.** Organ with bells. **o. di legno** (län-yō). Xylophone. **o. pieno** (pĭ-ä'-nō), or **pleno** (plä'-no). Full organ. **o. portatile** (pôr-tä-tē'-lĕ). Portable organ. **organi vocali** (ôr-gä'-nē-vō-kä'-lĕ), *I.,* pl. The vocal organs. **organo, in,** *L.* Vide ORGANUM. **orga'nochor'dium.** A combination of pf. and pipe-organ inv. by Abbé Vogler. **organophon'ic.** Name adopted by a band of Polish performers imitating various instrs. vocally. **organographie** (grä-fē), *F.* The description of an organ. **organologie** (zhē). The science of building and playing the organ. **or'ganum,** *L.,* **or'ganon,** *Gr.* 1. Any instrument, thence the organ. 2. The earliest polyphonic music, a continual progression of two parts in fourths or fifths (also called *diaphony*); later it developed into 3 parts (*tripho'nia*), the third part called *triplum,* hence our term **treble;** then into 4 parts (*tetrapho'nia*). 3. The part rdded to another in 2 part organum. **in organo.** *Old term for* in more than two parts. **o. hydraul'icum.** Hydraulic o. **o. pneumaticum.** The ordinary wind o. **o. simplex,** *L.* A mediæval term probably meaning the unisonal accompaniment of a single voice. **Orgell** (ôr'-gĕl), *G.* An organ. **O.-bälge** (bĕlkh-ĕ). Organ-bellows. **O.-bank** (bänk). Organist's seat. **O.-bauer** (bow-ĕr). Organ-builder. **O.-bühne** (bü-nĕ), or **-chor** (kōr), or **-platz** (pläts). Organ-loft. **O.-gehäuse** (gĕ-hī'-zĕ). Organ-case. **O.-kasten** (käs'tĕn). 1. Cabinet organ. 2. Organ-case. **O.-klang.** Tone of an organ. **O.-kunst** (koonst). The art of playing, or constructing an organ. **O.-metall**

(mä-täl'). Organ-metal. **O.-pfeife** (pfī'-fĕ). Organ-pipe. **O.-punkt** (poonkt). Pedal-point. **O.-register** (rĕ-gēs'-tĕr). Organ-stop. **O.-schule** (shoo'le). Organ-school or method. **O.-spiel** (shpēl). Playing the organ; or the piece played. **O.-spieler** (shpē-lĕr). Organ-player. **O.-stein** (shtīn). Pan's pipes. **O.-stimmen** (shtĭmmĕn). Row of organ-pipes. **O.-stücke** (shtü'-kĕ). Organ-pieces. **O.-treter** (trä'-tĕr). Organ-treader, bellows-blower. **O.-virtuose** (fēr-too-ō'-zĕ). Organ-virtuoso. **O.-wolf** (vôlf). Ciphering. **O.-zug** (tsookh). Organ-stop or row of pipes. **orgeln** (ôr'-gĕln). To play on the organ. **orgue** (ôrg), *F.* Organ. **o. de salon** (dŭ să-lôn), **orgue expressif.** (a) The harmonium. (b) The swell organ. **o. hydraulique** (ē-drō-lēk). Hydraulic organ. **o. à percussion** (pĕr-küs'-yôn). A reed **o.** made by De Provins & Alexandre, Paris. **o. plein** (plăn). Full organ. **o. portatif** (pôr-tä-tēf). A portable organ. **o. de barbarie** (dŭ băr-bä-rē). A barrel-organ, hurdygurdy. **o. positif** (pô-zī-tēf). 1. The choir-organ. 2. A small fixed organ. **orguinette** (ôr-gĭ-nĕt), *F.* A small reed-organ played with a crank, the music being perforated to admit air to the reeds. **orificcio** (ôr-ĭ-fĭt'-chō), *I.* Orifice (of a pipe). **oris'cus.** Vide NEUME. **or'nament,** *E.,* **ornamen'to,** *I.,* **ornement** (ôrn-män), *F.* An embellishment, as the turn grace (q.v.), etc. **ornamental note.** An accessory note. **ornato** (ôr-nä'-tō), **ornamen'te,** *I.* Ornate(ly). **orpha'rion, orphéor(e)on** (ôr-fä-ō-rôn), *F.* A kind of cither. **Orphéon** (ôr-fä-ôn). 1. A piano-violin. 2. A popular male singing society of enormous proportions in France (in 1881 it had 60,000 members). **orphéoniste** (nēst). A member of such society. **Orpheus** (ôrf'-yūs, or ôr'-fĕ-ŭs). Fabled Greek lyre-player and singer of supernatural power. **O.-harmo'nika,** *G.* Pan harmonikon. **orthog'raphy.** Spelling and grammar are as necessary in music as in any other written language Bad spelling occurs in music where, for instance, a chord is written in sharps when the key-relationship shows it to belong in the enharmonic flat notes. Sometimes, however, a note is mis-written intentionally for the sake of easier reading.

os'cillation, E. Oszillation (ŏs-tsĭl-lä-tsĭ-ōn'), G. Beating, vibration.

osia (ō'-sē-ä), ossia (ŏs'-sĭ-ä), I. Or, otherwise, or else. o. più facile (pĭ-oo' fä'-chĭ-lĕ). Or else this more easy way.

osservanza (vän'-tsä), I. Observation, strictness. osservato (vä'-tō). Strict, exact.

ostinato (ŏs-tĭ-nä'-tō), I. 1. Obstinate, continuous. 2. A ground-bass, sometimes basso o.

otez (ō-tā), F. "Off!" (of a stop).

ottava (ŏt-tä'-vä), I. Octave, eighth. o. alta (äl'-tä). The octave above; an octave higher (abbreviated 8va); o. bassa (bäs'-sä). The octave below (abbreviated 8va. bassa). o. supra (soo'-prä). The octave above. coll' o. To be played with the octave added.

ottavino (ŏt-tä-vē'-nō), I. The piccolo.

ottemole (ŏt-tĕ-mō'-lĕ). A group of eight equal notes.

ottet'to, I. Octet.

ou (oo), F. Or, or else.

ougab (oo'-gäb), Heb. Ancient reed-instrument.

ouïe (oo-ē), F. Soundhole.

outer voices. The highest and lowest voices.

ouvert (oo-văr'), F. Open. Vide LIVRE.

ouverture (oo-văr-tür), F., Ouvertüre (oo'-fĕr-tü-rĕ), G., overtura (ō-vĕr-too'-rä), I., overture (ō'-vĕr-tūr, not toor). An elaborate prelude to an opera, oratorio or play, often based (in the concert o.) on the sonata formula; often (in the opera o.) a mere medley of airs; sometimes an independent composition. o. di ballo (dē bäl'-lō), I. An overture introducing dance melodies. Also sinfonia, suite, or prelude to suite.

overblow. 1. To blow with enough force to produce harmonics on a wind-instr. Vide ACOUSTICS and HORN. This feat is constantly necessary in playing many wind-instrs. 2. Of defective pipes, to sound a partial instead of the fundamental.

overchord. Vide PHONE.

overspun. Used of covered strings.

overstrung. Of a piano in which the strings of two or more of the lowest octaves are stretched diagonally under other strings, the object being to economise space.

ovvero (ŏv-vā'-rō), I. Or.

O. W. Abbr. for Oberwerk.

oxypyc'ni. Church modes with a pyknon high in the tetrachord.

P

P. Abbr. of pedale; piano; più, as più forte (pf.); poco, as p. a. p., poco a poco; parte (as colla p.); pointe, F. (toe); and positif (choir-organ).

pad. Vide PIANOFORTE.

padiglione (pä-dēl-yō'-nĕ), I. The bell (of a wind-instr.).

Padovano (pä-do-vä'-nō), Padava'ne, or, Paduane (pä-doo-ä'-nĕ), I. "From Padua." An Italian dance in ternary rhythm. Perhaps the same as Pavan.

paean (pē'-än), Gr. Hymn of invocation, usually to Apollo.

pair of organs. An organ with a complete set of pipes.

paired notes. Thirds, sixths, etc., in pf.-playing.

paisana (pä-ĭ-zä'-nä), Sp. A country-dance.

palalaika. Vide BALALAIKA.

palco (päl'-kō), I. Stage of a theatre; box.

Palestrinastil (shtēl), G. The style of Palestrina (vide B. D.), i. e., a cappella.

palettes (päl-ĕt'), F. The white keys.

pal'let. A spring valve in the wind chest of an organ.

palmadilla (păl-mä-dēl'-yä), Sp. A dance.

pam'be. Small Indian drum.

panathe'næa, Gr. An Athenian festival at which musical contests were held.

Pan'dean pipes, Pan's pipes. A primitive group of reeds or tubes of different lengths, fastened together and tuned, named for the god Pan.

pando'ran, Gr., Pandore (pän-dō'-rĕ), G., pando'ra, pandoura, pandura (pän-doo'-rä), I., pandure (pän̄dür), F. Vide BANDORA.

Panflöte (pän'-flä'-tĕ), G. Pandean pipes.

panharmo'nicon. A kind of orchestrion inv. by Maelzel.

panmelo'deon. A key-board instr. of

wheels impinging on metal rods, inv. 1810, by Leppich.

panorgue (ôrg), *F.* A little reed-organ to be attached to a pf. inv. by J. Jaulin.

pan'sympho'nikon. An orchestrion inv. by Peter Singer, 1839.

pantaleone (pän-tä-lĕ-ō'-nĕ), **pantalon.** An instr. inv. by Pantaleon Hebenstreit, in the 18th century. It was 9 ft. long, 4 ft. wide, and had 186 gut strings, played on with two small sticks. **P.-zug,** *G.* A harpsichord-stop.

pantalon (pän-tä-lôṅ), *F.* First movement of the quadrille.

Papagenoflöte (pä'-pä-gä-nō-flä'-tĕ), *G.* Pan's pipes, from Mozart's *Papageno* (vide "*Magic Flute*" in *Stories of the Operas*).

papillons (pàp-ē-yôṅ), *F.* "Butter-flies." A frail and flitting composition.

parallel. Of intervals, consecutive; of keys, related. Of motion, the progression of two voices in the same direction at a fixed interval. It requires care in handling. **Parallelen** (pä-räl-lä'-lĕn), *G.* 1. Sliders. 2. Consecutives. **Parallelbewegung** (bĕ-vākh'-oongk), *G.* Similar or parallel motion. **Parallel-tonarten** (tōn-är-tĕn), *G.* Related keys.

parame'se, parane'te. Vide LYRE.

par'aphrase. Free or florid transcription.

parhy'pate. Vide LYRE.

Parnas'sus. A mountain in Greece, sacred to Apollo, the Muses, and inspiration generally. *Gradus ad Parnas'sum.* Vide METHOD.

parole(s) (pă-rôl'), *F.* Word(s).

part, *E.* and *G.* 1. The music of an individual voice or instr. 2. A division.

part-book. 1. The music of any one voice or instr. 2. In the 15th-16th cent. a book with separate parts on facing pages.

part-song. A song for three or more voices.

part-writing. Counterpoint.

parte (pär'-tĕ), pl. **i,** *I.* Part(s). **colla p.** With the part, i. e., adopting the tempo of the singer or soloist. **p. cantan'te.** The vocal part, the leading voice. **parti di ripieno** (rē-pĭ-

a'-nō). Supplementary parts. **a p. equale.** With more than one voice of leading importance.

partial. 1. An harmonic. Vide ACOUSTICS. 2. Vide STOP. 3. Vide TURN.

partic'ipating. Accessory. **participa'tum syste'ma,** *L.* Equal temperament.

Partie (pär-tē'), *G.* 1. Variations. 2. Vide SUITE.

partie(s) (pär-tē), *F.* Parts. **p. de remplissage** (dŭ räṅ-plĭ-säzh), *F.* Accessory parts.

partimen'to, *I.* 1. An exercise. 2. Figured bass.

partita (pär-tē'-tä), *I.* 1. Variations. 2. Vide SUITE.

partitino (tē'-no). A small supplementary score.

partition, *E.* (in *F.* pär-tēs-yôṅ), **Partitur** (pär-tĭ-toor'), *G.,* **partitura** (pär-tĭ-too'-rä), **partizione** (pär-tē-tsĭ-ō'-nĕ), *I.* A full score for voices or instrs. **p. cancella'ta.** A set of staves with vertical lines for the bass. **Partiturspiel** (toor'-shpēl), *G.* Playing from the score.

partito (par-tē'-tō), *I.* Scored, divided.

pas (pä), *F.* 1. Step, dance. **p. ordinaire** (pä-zôr-dĭ-năr). March time. **p. de charge** (dŭ shärzh). Double time. **p. seul** (sŭl). A dance for one performer; **p. de deux** (dŭ dŭ). For two, etc. **p. redoublé** (pä-rŭ-doo-blä'). A quick-step. 2. Not, as **pas trop vite** (pä trō vēt). Not too fast.

paspié (päs'-pĭ-ā), *Sp.* A kind of dance.

pas'py. Vide PASSEPIED.

passacaglia (päs-sä-käl'-yä), *I., passacaille* (päs-sä-kī'-yŭ), *F.,* **passacol'le,** *Sp.,* **passagall'o,** *I.* A chaconne with a ground-bass in 3-4 time, always in minor.

passage (in *F.* päs-säzh). 1. A phrase or section. 2. A figure. 3. A run **notes de p.** Grace notes. **passageboards.** Boards on which an organ-tuner may walk.

passaggio (päs-säd'-jō), *I.* 1. A passage. 2. Modulation.

passamezzo (päs-sä-mĕd'-zō). A slow Italian dance, in 2-4 time, resembling the Pavan.

passant (päs-säṅ), *F.* Slide (of a bow).

passepied (päs-pĭ-ā), *F.* A lively old French dance in 3-4, 3-8, or 6-8 time, a quick minuet with three or more reprises, the first of eight bars.

passe-rue (păs-rü). Passacaglio.

passing. Unessential, as a **passing modulation.** A transient modulation. **passing tone,** or note, a brief dissonance on the weak beat, leading from one consonant tone to another; it does not need to be prepared.

Passion, Passion-music. Oratorio, or play. A dramatic or musical setting of the "Passion" (suffering) of Christ. It differs from the oratorio (q.v.) in history and form only in the facts of its being always concerned with the one subject, and in the introduction usually of spiritual reflections.

passionata or **-o** (päs-sĭ-ō-nä'-tä), **passionatamen'te,** *I.* Passionate(ly).

passione (päs-sĭ-ō'-nĕ).   1. Passion, feeling.   2. Vide PASSION.

Passionsmusik (päs-sĭ-ōns-moo-zēk'), *G.* Vide PASSION.

pas'so, *I.* Step.

pas'sy-measure. Old *E.* Passamezzo.

Pastete (päs-tā'-tĕ), *G.* Pasticcio.

pasticcio (päs-tē'-chō), *I.,* **pastiche** (păs-tēsh), *F.*   1. An opera, or other work in which old airs are used to new words.   2. A medley.

pas'toral, pastorale (päs-tō-rä'-lĕ in *I.;* in *F.* păs-tō-rȧl'). An opera, cantata, song or instrumental composition of rustic nature or subject. **p. flute.** Shepherd's pipe. **p. organ point.** Vide PEDAL-POINT.   **pasto rel'la,** *I.,* **pastorelle** (rĕl), *F.* A little pastoral.

pastorita (ē'-tä).   1. A shepherd's pipe. 2. A stop, the Nachthorn.

pastourelle (păs-too-rĕl), *F.*   1. A 6-8 movement of a quadrille.   2. A troubadour lyric.

patetica or **-o** (pä-tā'-tĭ-kä), *I.,* **pathétique** (pä-tā-tēk), *F.,* **pathetisch** (pä-tā'-tĭsh), *G.* Pathetic; a piano sonata in C minor by Beethoven is so-called; and a symphony by Tchaikovski.   **pateticamen'te,** *I.* Pathetically.

patimen'to, *I.* Grief, suffering.

patouille (pät-oo-ē'-yŭ), *F.* Xylophone.

patte (păt), *F.*   1. A special clarinet key.   2. A music-pen.

Pauke(n) (pow'-kĕ(n)), *G.* Kettledrum(s).

pause, *E.,* **pausa** (pä'-oo-zä), *I.,* **pause** (pōz), *F.*   1. A rest of variable length; if very protracted called **lunga** (or long) **pausa.**   2. A fermate. 3. *F.* and *G.* A whole rest. **demipause** (dĕ-mē'-pōz), *F.* A half-rest.

pavan', *E.,* **pavana** (pä-vä'-nä), *I.,* **pavane** (pă-văn'), *F.* A grave stately dance in 3-4 time, generally in three strains, each repeated; once supposed to be derived from *pavo,* peacock, now from *Paduna* (q.v.).

paventato (pä-vĕn-tä'-tō), **pavento'so,** *I.* Fearful, timid.

pavillon (pä-vē'-yôṅ), *F.* The bell of a wind-instr. **p. en l'air** (äṅ lăr). "The bell upwards" (direction to horn-players). **flûte à p.** A stop with flaring pipes. **p. chinois** (shēn-wä). Chinese hat, crescent.

peal.   1. A chime.   2. A change, of bells.

pean. A pæan.

pearly (of runs, etc.). Bright, distinct.

ped. Abbr. of Pedal.

ped'al, *E.* (in *G.* pä-däl'), **pédale** (pä-dăl), *F.,* **pedale** (pä-dä'-lĕ), *I* 1. Abbr. of Pedal-point (q.v.).   2. A foot lever of various musical uses. The piano has usually two pedals: (a) The **damper (openol oud,** or **extension) pedal,** which raises all the dampers from the strings, allowing the tones struck to be sustained and broadened by sympathetic (q.v.) vibration. The use of the damperpedal is indicated by Ped., and its cessation by the mark ✳ or Ⓟ. Wm.

H. Sherwood (vide B. D.) has introduced a more accurate system of continuous lines ⌐⌐ to indicate just when this pedal is to be pressed, how long held and when released. (b) The **soft pedal (pétite** (pä-tēt), **pédale)** in some cases merely lets a cloth fall over the strings, but usually shifts the action so that the hammers strike only one of the two or three strings allotted each tone. Hence its use is indicated by **una corda** (oo'-na kôr'-dă, one string), or **Verschiebung** (fĕr-shē'-boongk), and its discontinuance by **"tre corde"** (trä kôr'-dä, "3 strings"). In the upright pf. this pedal simply moves the hammers nearer the strings. Some pianos are fitted with a (c) **sustaining,** or **prolongation pedal.** A damper-pedal holding the dampers from only those strings struck at the moment, until the pedal is released, thus permitting the sustention of a chord or tone while the hands are busy elsewhere. (d) A. B. Chase has inv. an **octavepedal,** or **octavo-attachment,** sounding also the higher octave. Both pedals (a and b) may be pressed together; this is indicated by **pedale doppio,** or **doppelte.**

The harp (q.v.) has 8 pedals, one opening or closing a panel in the sounding-case with loud or soft effect. Reed-organs, etc., have double pedals or treadles for working the bellows. In the pipe-organ (and in the **pedalier,** q.v.) the pedals are of great variety. There is a pedal key-board, **Pedalklaviatur** (pā-dälʹ-klä-fī-ä-toorʹ), or **Pedalklavier,** *G.,* **clavier des pédales** (dā pā-dălʹ), *F.,* **pedaliera,** *I.,* with a compass of C–f, or, counting stops, from C͵͵ up. This is played by the feet (∨ over a note indicating the right toe; under it, the left: ○ similarly marking the heel). To this part of the organ, called the **pedal-organ,** many stops are often allotted: hence **pedal-pipe, stop-soundboard,** etc.; it is locked from sounding by a **pedal-check** (worked by a stop-knob), a bar running beneath it. The pedal-stops may be made to sound with any of the manuals by means of mechanism, called **pedal-couplers, coupler-pedals,** or **reversible-pedal.**

The word pedal is also given to the organ, to such foot-levers as the **combination,** or **composition pedals (pédales de combinaison),** which if **single-acting** draw out certain new, or push in certain old, stops; if **double-acting** produce certain combinations regardless of the previous registration. The **forte-pedal** draws out all the stops of its key-board; the **mezzo-p.** the chief 4-8 ft. stops; the **piano-pedal** leaving only the softest on; the **crescendo-p.** draws out the full power gradually, the **diminuendo** withdraws it; the **sforzando** produces a sudden fulness. Vide also CELESTE.

The **swell-pedal** works the shutters of the swell-box; if it remains at rest where left, it is called a **balance swell-pedal.**

Pedalflügel (flüʹ-ghĕl), *G.* Pedalier.

Pedalharfe (pĕ-dälʹ-härfĕ), *G.,* **pedal-harp.** A double-action harp.

pedalier (pĕd-ä-lērʹ), *E.,* **pédalier** (pá-dăl-yäʹ), *F.,* **pedalʹion.** A pedal key-board attachable to a piano and playing the bass-strings.

pedal-note, or **tone.** A tone sustained by the pedal or some voice, usually the bass, while the other parts move

independently. As the word "point" originally meant "note," **pedal-point** (abbr. to **pedal**) is synonymous with pedal-note, but is now used rather of the phrase in which the pedal-note occurs. It is displacing the word **organ-point,** derived not from organ, but from *organum* (q.v.) and referring to the long notes of the *cantus firmus* against which the other voices moved, these notes being called *organici puncti,* or *organum notes.* Pedal-point is then a phrase in which one tone is sustained through independent harmonies. The tonic or the dominant is usually the tone sustained. If both are used at once it is called **pastoral.** If the **pedal-pt.** occurs in other voices than the bass it is **inverted.** It is sometimes **exterior,** or **interior.** It may be figurated, trilled, or florid.

peg. A tuning-pin; in the violin, etc., it is set in the head, in a space called the **peg-box.**

pegli (pālʹ-yē), *I.* For the (from *per gli*).

pekʹtis, *Gr.* A Greek lute.

pel, pelʹlo, *I.* For the (from *per il, per lo*).

penilʹlion. A Welsh improvisation of verses.

pennant. Hook.

pennata (pĕn-näʹ-tä), *I.* Quilled (of the spinet, etc.).

penorçon (pŭ-nôrʹ-sôṅ), *F.,* from **penorʹkon,** *Gr.* An ancient guitar.

pensieroso (pĕn-sē-ā-rōʹ-sō), **pensoʹso,** *I.* Pensive, thoughtful.

pentachium, *Gr.* A composition in 5 parts.

penʹtachord. 1. A series of 5 diatonic tones. 2. An instr. with 5 strings.

penʹtatone, *E.,* **penʹtaton,** *Gr.* 1. An interval of 5 whole tones, an augmented sixth. **pentatonʹic.** Having five whole tones. **pentatonic scale.** A five-toned scale, the same as the usual major scale, with the fourth and seventh tones skipped; called also the Scotch scale. The black keys of the piano represent a pentatonic scale.

per, *L.* and *I.* For, by, through, in, from.

percusʹsion, *E.,* **percussione** (pĕr-koos-sĕ-ōʹ-nĕ), *I.* 1. The actual sounding of a tone or chord (as opposed to its preparation or resolution). 2. Instrs. of percussion are those in which the tone is secured by striking, particularly the drums, cymbals, and triangle, also the piano, and so forth. **percussion-stop.** One in which the reed is struck just as it is blown, to emphasise its tone. **percussive.** An instr. of percussion. **perden'do, perden'dosi,** *I.* Dying away in both speed and power. **perdu'na.** Bourdon.

perfect, *E.*, **perfet'to,** *L.* 1. Vide IN-TERVAL, CADENCE, CHORD. 2. An obsolete name for triple time. **perfection.** Vide NOTATION and LIGA-TURE.

Périgourdine (pā-rĭ-goor-dēn), *F.* Cheerful old French dance, in triple time, so called from the province of Perigord.

period, période (pā-rĭ-ôd), *F.*, **periodo** (pā-rĭ-ō'-dō), *I.* A passage containing two or more sections and some form of cadence. Vide FORM. **Periodenbau** (pā'-rĭ-ōd-ĕn-bow), *G.* The building of periods, or composition.

perpetual, perpetuo (pĕr-pā'-too-ō), *I.* 1. Vide CANON. 2. **Perpetual motion,** or **perpet'uum mo'bile,** *L.* A piece of great rapidity and no pause till the end.

pes, *L.* Foot. A ground-bass to a round.

pesante (pā-sän'-tĕ), **pesantemen'te,** *I.* Heavy(ly), impressive(ly), forcibly.

peso, di (dē pā'-sō), *I.* At once.

petit (pŭ-tē'), **petite** (pŭ-tēt), *F.* Small. **choeur p.** A three-part chorus. **p. flute.** Piccolo. **p. mesure à deux temps.** 2-4 time. **petits notes** (pŭ-tē' nôt). Grace notes. **p. pedale.** Soft pedal.

pet'to, *I.* The chest. **voce de p.** Chest voice. **di p.** From the chest.

peu (pŭ), *F.* Little. **un p.** A little. **p. à p.** Little by little.

pezzo (pĕd'-zō), pl. **i,** *I.* A piece or number. **pezzi concertanti.** Concerted numbers.

pf. Abbr. of, 1. Pianoforte. 2. Poco forte.

Pfeife (pfī'-fĕ), *G.* 1. A fife. 2. A pipe, as of an organ. **Pfeifendeckel,** The covering of a pipe. **P.-werk.** The pipe-work. **Pfei'fer.** A fifer.

Phantasie (fän-tä-zē'), *G.* Fantasy, or fantasia. **P.-bilder,** **P.-stücke.** Fanciful pieces of no strict form. **phantasieren** (zē'-rĕn). To improvise. **Phantasier'-maschine.** A melograph. **phantasi(e)rte** (zēr'-tĕ). Improvised.

phil'harmon'ic. Music-loving. **philomèle** (fē-lō-mĕl). Vide ZITHER.

phonas'cus, *L.*, from *Gr.* Singing-teacher.

phisharmon'ica. An octagonal accordeon.

phonaut'ograph. 1. A name given first to a melograph, inv. by Abbé Moigno, a pencil fitted to a vibrating membrane. 2. An electric melograph for key-board instrs. inv. by Fenby. (See article, page 794.)

phone, *Gr.* 1. Voice or tone. 2. Sound, a term appropriated by Dr. Th. Baker, to represent Riemann's term "clang" (q. v.), hence **homophone, under phone, contro-phone,** and **phonic.**

phonet'ics, pho'nics. The science of sounds.

pho'nikon. A metal wind-instr. with globular bell inv. by Czerveny, 1848.

phonom'eter, *E.*, **phonometre** (fôn-ō-mĕtr), *F.* A device for measuring vibration.

phor'minx, *Gr.* An ancient lyre-like instrument.

pho'tinx, *Gr.* An ancient crooked flute.

phrase, *E.* (in *F.* frăz, in *G.* frä'-zĕ). 1. A musical clause. Vide FORM. 2. A short passage or figure. **phrasemark.** A long curve covering a phrase; or any musical punctuation-mark. **phrasi(e)ren** (zē'-rĕn), *G.* To phrase. **phrasé** (frä-zā), *F.*, **phrasing,** *E.*, **Phrasierung** (zē'-roongk), *G.* (a) The act or art of delivering music with due regard to its melodic and rhythmic punctuation, relation and contrast. (b) Signs for such phrasing.

Phrygian (frĭ'-jän), *E.*, from *Gr.* **phrygische** (frē'-jĭsh-ĕ), *G.* Vide MODES.

physharmo'nica. 1. A small reed and bellows attachment to a piano keyboard for sustaining and colouring tones; inv. by Häckel, Vienna, 1818; the forerunner of the harmonium. 2. A free-reed-stop.

piacere, a (ä pĭ-ä-chā'-re), **a piacimen'to,** *I.* At pleasure. **piacevole** (pĭ-ä-chā'-vō-lĕ), **piacevolmen'te.** Pleasant(ly). **piacevolezza** (lĕd'-zä). Suavity.

piagendo (pĭ-ä-jĕn'-dō) *I.* Plaintive. **piagnevole** (pĭ-än-yä'-vō-lĕ), *I.* Sad, mournful.

pianar'tist, *G.* A mechanical attachment for playing the piano.

pianente (pĭ-ä-nĕn'-tĕ), *I.* Gently, softly. **pianet'to.** Very soft.

pianette (nĕt'). A small piano.

piangevole pǐ-än-jä'-vō-lĕ), **piange-volmen'te**, *I.* Doleful(ly).

pianino (nē'-nō), *I.* An upright piano.

pianis'simo, *I.* Very soft. **pianis-sis'simo**. Extremely soft.

pianist (pǐ-än'-ĭst, not pē'-ăn-ĭst), *E.* A piano-player.

pianista (nē'-stä), *I.* 1. A pianist. 2. A mechanical piano.

pianiste (pǐ-än-ēst'), *F.* Pianist of either sex.

piano (pǐ-ä'-nō), *I.* 1. Soft, softly, abbr. (*p*), hence **piano-pedal.** 2. The common form of the word pianoforte (q.v.); this shorter form is altogether used in France, and commonly elsewhere. Many terms are used to indicate sizes and forms of the piano, as the **concert grand** and **par'lour grand** or **piano à queue** (ä-kŭ'), the **semi-grand** or **boudoir** or **p. à queue écourtée** (ä-koor-tä), or **baby-grand.** Smaller form. The **square** or **carré** (căr-rā); **p. à tavolins; the upright** or **cabinet,** or **p. à sécretaire** (sä-krŭ-tăr), or **droit** (drwä), **oblique,** or **à pilastres,** or **vertical,** and still smaller sizes such as the **cottage,** or the **piccolo,** inv. by Wornum, of London, 1829. For practice there are the **dumb p.,** or **p. muet** (mü), and the **Virgil practice-clavier,** etc. **electric p.** One employing electro-magnets in place of hammers. **p-quatuor,** or **p. à archet** (ä är-shä). Vide PIANO-VIOLIN. **p. éolien.** Vide AMEMO-CHORD. The **p. harmon'icorde.** A combination with an harmonium, inv. by Debain. **the p. à claviers renversés** (ä-klăv-yä rän-vĕr-sä). One with 2 key-boards, one above the other, the scale of the upper ascending from right to left. **p. méchanique** (mä-kă-nēk). A mechanical or automatic piano. **p. organisé** (ôr-gă-nǐ-zä). One with physharmonica attached. (See p. 800.)

pianoforte (pǐ-ä'-nō-fôr-tĕ, or commonly pǐ-ä'-nō-fôrt), *E.* and *I.* **piano-forté** (fôr-tä), *F.*

piano score. An arrangement of vocal or orchestral music for piano.

pian'ograph. A melograph, inv. by Guérin.

pianoharp. Vide KLAVIER HARFE.

piano'la. A detachable pneumatic attachment by which a piano may be played mechanically, the performer controlling the speed, the force, and, in a remarkable degree, also the ex-

pression; inv. by E. S. Votey of New York, in 1897. It has 65 felt-covered fingers brought into play by air-power forced through perforated music by treadle action.

piano-organ. Vide BARREL-ORGAN (2).

piano'tist. A mechanical attachment for playing the piano.

piano quatuor (kât-ü-ôr), *F.* Piano-violin.

piano-violin. A numerous group of instrs. endeavouring to combine the fulness and range of the piano with the violin's expression and power of increasing the volume of a sustained tone. In 1610 Hans Heydn of Nürnberg inv. the **Gambenwerk,** in which catgut strings were pressed by resined parchment rollers actuated by a wheel (other authorities say that Heydn's instr. was called **Geigenwerk,** and had wire strings; and that the **Gambenwerk,** or **Klaviergamba,** was inv. by Reich or Gleichmann of Ilmenau, about 1750, and had gut strings). In 1754 Hohlfeld inv. the **Bogenflügel** or **Bogenklavier,** with a horse-hair bow; von Meyer in 1794 provided each string with a bow. In 1800 Hübner devised the **clavecin harmonique,** which Pouleau developed into the **orchestrin.** Other instrs. of the same general idea were the **gambe-clavier,** inv. by Le Voirs, Paris, 1741; the **Bogenklavier** of Garbrecht, Königsberg, 1710; the **Xänorphika** of Röllig, Vienna, 1797; the **Bogenhammerklavier** of Karl Greiner, 1779; the **harmonichord** of Kaufman, 1785; the **piano-violino,** 1837. The most successful is the **piano-quatuor** or **piano-violin,** inv. 1865 by H. C. Baudin, of Paris, consisting of thick single strings to each of which is attached at a nodal point a projecting piece of stiff catgut, which on the pressure of the key is brought in contact with a linen roller turned by pedals, the communicated vibration causing the string to sound; the general principle of these instrs. resembles that of the hurdygurdy.

pian piano (pǐ-än' pǐ-ä'-nō), *I.* Very softly.

piatti (pǐ-ät'-tē), *I.*, pl. Cymbals.

pib (pēb), **pibcorn.** A Welsh pipe.

pibroch (pē'-brôkh), *Scotch.* A war-like composition for the bagpipes, consisting of three or four variations on a theme called the **urlar**; they are of increasing speed and close with a quick movement called the **crean-luidh.**

piccanteria (pĭk-kän-tĕr-ē'-ä), *I.* Piquancy.

picchetta'to, or **picchiettato** (pĭk-kĭ-ĕt-tä'-tō), *I.* Staccato, in violin playing made with a bounding bow, and indicated by slur over dots.

picciolo (pĭt-chō'-lō), *I.* Small.

piccolo (pĭk'-kō-lō), *I.* 1. Small. Vide PIANO. 2. The octave flute (q.v.). 3. A 2-ft. stop. **piccolino** (lē'-no). Very small.

pic'co, picco pipe. A small whistle with 3 holes; it was named after a blind Sardinian peasant who played it in London (1856) with great brilliancy, securing a compass of 3 octaves.

pick. 1. A plectrum. 2. To pluck (of strings).

Pic'kelflöte, *G.* The octave flute.

piece. 1. A composition. 2. An instrument (generally used in pl.).

pièce (pĭ-ĕs'), *F.* 1. A piece; a composition. 2. An opera, or dramatic work. **suite de pièces** (swēt dǔ pĭ-ĕs). A set of pieces.

pieno (pĭ-ā'-nŏ), *I.* Full. **p. coro,** or **p. organo.** Full chorus, or full organ. **pienamen'te.** Fully.

pied (pĭ-ā'), *F.* Foot. **avec les pieds** (lä pĭ-ā). With the feet (on an organ).

pietà (pĭ-ā-tä'), *I.* Pity. **pieto'so, pietosamen'te.** Tender(ly).

pierced gamba. Keraulophon.

pifara (pĭ-fä'-rä), *I.* A fife.

pifferare (rä'-rĕ), *I.* To play the fife. **pif'fero.** 1. A fife. 2. A primitive oboe. 3. A stop, the bifara. **piffera'ro.** A player on the fife.

pikieren (pĭ-kē'-rĕn), *G.* Vide PIQUER.

pilea'ta, *L.* "Capped" (of a covered pipe).

pincé (păṅ-sā), or **pincement** (păṅs-mäṅ), *F.* "Pinched." 1. Plucked (as strings). 2. Pizzicato. 3. A mordent. **p. étouffé.** Acciaccatura. **p. renversé.** Inverted mordent. **instruments à cordes pincées.** Instrs. to be plucked, as guitar, etc., hence **pincer** (păṅ-sā). To play such an instrument. **pincé bemolisé** (or **dièsé**). Trill with a flattened (or sharpened) note.

pipe. A tone-producing tube of reed, wood or metal. 1. One of the earliest musical-instrs., a simple straw. 2. The tone-producing tubes of an organ. (a) **flue-pipe,** or **lip-pipe.** One in which the column of air produces tone by being forced through a small opening with a sharp edge. The **lip-pipe** may be compared to a great flute standing on end (the flute is in fact a lip-pipe). The **foot** rests on the **pipe-rack;** the lower part of the **body** is the **throat;** just above it is an opening called the **mouth,** with an upper and lower **lip;** the **upper lip** is bevelled to an edge called the **leaf.** An **ear** projects on each side of the **mouth;** inside the mouth is a projection called the **block** (if it is very thin it is called the **language**). The passage between lower lip and block is the **windway;** through this the air is driven against the **leaf,** which, vibrating, produces a tone from the air column that fills the upper part or body of the pipe. **flue-pipes** may be **open** at the top, or **covered** (stopped or plugged), the **stopped-p.** sounding an octave lower than the same pipe open. **flue-pipes** are tuned, or voiced, if metal, by flaps at the top called **tuners;** if wood, by small adjustable boards. (b) **reed-pipe.** One depending upon a reed for its tone, the body governing the quality of the tone only. The lowest part of the **reed-p.** is the **boot;** it contains a sheet of metal called the **block,** which contains two apertures, one holding an adjustable **tuning-wire,** the other a **reed,** or **conical tube** (called a **shallot**) with an opening giving play to a vibrating **tongue.** 3. **bent-pipe.** A rectangular bent tube connecting the bellows with the wind-trunk; also a secondary channel from the wind-chest to the wind-trunk. *Speaking pipes* may be *bent* without altering their tone, to fit them into smaller space. **pipe-metal.** That of which organpipes are made, usually an alloy of lead and tin.

pipe-organ. Vide ORGAN.

pique (pēk), *F.* Peg of a 'cello.

piqué (pē-kā'), *F.* Same as picchietato. **piquer** (pē-kā), *F.,* **piquiren** (pē-kē'-rĕn), *G.* To play in such a manner.

pirolino (pē-rō-lē'-nō), *I.* Button.

piston(s). Vide VALVE and CORNET-A PISTONS. **piston-solo,** *G.* Solo for cornet-à-pistons.

pitch. The height or depth of a tone *relatively* to others, or its *absolute* position on the complete scale adopted as the standard and divided into octaves definitely named (see the CHART OF PITCH). The vibration-number of a tone also gives it an **absolute** pitch according to the particular pitch accepted as the standard. The opinion of the civilised races, with the chief exception of England, has settled on the **International** (low or French) pitch adopted in France in 1859, and at the Vienna Congress in 1887. This gives the tone *a'* 435 vibrations a second and *c''* 522 vibrations. An older pitch was the **classical** or **mean** pitch, in which *a'* lay between 415 and 429 vibrations (apparently about the same as the most ancient standards). The desire to secure a more and more brilliant tone led instrument-makers to raise the pitch to outrageous heights. A congress of physicists adopted in 1834 the **Stuttgart Pitch** with *a'* at 440. The **high** or **concert** or **English** pitch gives *a'* about 450, which is a severe and needless strain and distortion. For convenience of calculation a theoretical middle *c'* has been given 256 vibrations, the number being a high power of 2; this so-called **philosophical pitch** gives *a'* about 427 vibrations. The subject of **Pitch-relationships** is too abstruse for explanation here—though important in the tuning and temperament of instruments. The old Pythagorean theorists did not consider the third (as *c* to *e*) to be a legitimate interval; they reached it by four steps of a fifth (ignoring octaves) thus, *c–g, g–d, d–a, a–e*. This gives it the ratio of 64 : 81. But we now accept both the third and the fifth as intervals, and the ratio of a third is 4 : 5, or in larger terms 64 : 80. The note *e* may then be considered a *quint-tone* if reached by steps of a fifth; or a *tierce-tone* if reached by a step of a third. But 64 : 80 differs from 64 : 81 by the ratio of 80 : 81, which is called the *comma syntonum*. Starting from *c'* any tone may be reached by quint or tierce steps up or down. Every tierce step up is $\frac{80}{81}$ less than a quint step and the letter name of a tone reached by a tierce step may be marked with a line under it for every tierce step upward, or a line over it for every tierce step downward, required to reach it.

These lines therefore indicate the number of *commas* by which it is lower or higher than the same tone reached by quint steps.
Relative pitches may also be expressed in (a) fractions showing the relative string lengths required to produce them; (b) in decimals showing relative vibrations; and (c) in logarithms showing comparatively the interval-ratios.
pitch-fork. A tuning-fork.
pitch-pipe. Small reed-pipe of fixed pitch.
più (pē-oo'), *I.* More; as **p. mosso.** More speed; **più tosto.** Rather, as **p. t. allegro.** Rather faster.
piva (pē'-vä), *I.* 1. A bag-pipe. 2. A composition in bag-pipe manner.
pizzican'do, pizzicato (pĭd-zĭ-kä'-tō), *I.* "Pinched," indicating that the strings are not to be bowed, but plucked with the fingers.
placido (plä'-chē-dō), **placidamen'te,** *I.* Placid(ly).
placito (plä'-chē-tō), *I.* Pleasure. A **bene p.** At pleasure, same as **ad libitum.**
pla'gal, *E.,* **pla'galis,** *L.,* **plagalisch** (plä-gä'-lĭsh), *G.* Used of those modes accessory to the authentic (vide MODES), and formed from them by taking the fourth below as the new tonic. Vide also CADENCE.
plagiau'los, *Gr.* Cross-flute.
plain-chant (in French pron. plăñ-shäñ), **plain-song.** The old Gregorian Church-music, so-called from its smooth progress in notes of equal length. It employs 8 modes (q.v.), and is written on four-line staves, employing 3 notes, the long, the breve and semibreve, and two clefs. It is still employed in the R. C. cantillation of priests at the altar, and is the basis of the Episcopal Church service.
plainte (plăñt), *F.* A lament. **plaintif** (plăñ-tēf). Plaintive.
plaisant (plĕz-äñ), *F.* Pleasant.
plaisanterie (plĕz-äñ-tŭ-rē), *F.,* **pleas'anterie.** A cheerful harpsichord piece.
plana (plä'-nä), *L.* and *I.* Plain. *musica P.* plain = chant.
planchette (pläñ-shĕt), *F.* 1. A mechanical piano. 2. A part of its mechanism, a board fitted with pegs.
planta'tion. The manner in which the pipes of a stop are arranged on the sound-board.

planx'ty. Literally, "lament," though sometimes applied to lively melodies used by Welsh harpers.

plaqué (plă-kā), *F.* Played simultaneously (as a chord); opposed to "broken."

play-house tune. Old name for entr'act music.

plec'toral, plec'tron, plec'trum. A small bit of ivory, metal or shell for plucking the strings of mandolins, etc.

plec'traphone. A piano attachment imitating the mandolin.

plein-jeu (plăn-zhŭ), *F.* 1. Full-organ. 2. A mixture-stop.

ple'no orga'no, *L.* Full-organ.

plet'tro, *I.* 1. Bow. 2. Plectrum.

pli'ca, *L.* "Fold." A neume, used as a concluding ornament, indicated by a stroke up or down on the last note of a ligature.

plu'res ex u'na, *L.* "Many from one." Old name for canon.

plus (plü), *F.* More.

pneuma (nū'-mä), *Gr.* "Breath." 1. Neume. 2. The exhausting vocalisation of the closing syllable of the early Christian Alleluia. 3. A jubilation.

pneumat'ic. 1. Used of all wind-instrs. 2. **p. action,** or **lever.** A bellows attachment for lightening the touch of an organ, inv. 1832, by Barker. 3. **p. organ.** The modern wind-organ, so called originally in distinction to the hydraulic.

pocetta (pō-chet'-tä), *I.*, **poche** (pôsh), **pochette** (pŏ-shĕt), *F.* Pocket-fiddle.

pochessimo (pō-kĕs'-sĭ-mō), *I.* As little as possible. **pochettino** (pō-kĕt-tē'-nō), **pochet'to, pochino** (pō-kē'-nō), *I.* Just a little.

poco (pō'-kō), *I.* A little; rather; somewhat. **poco a poco.** Little by little.

poggiato (pôd-jä'-tō), *I.* "Leant" on, dwelt upon.

poi (pō'-ē), *I.* Then, afterwards, as **piano poi forte.** Soft then loud. **poi segue,** then follows; **poi a poi.** By degrees.

point. 1. Old name for note. Vide NOTATION. 2. A dot. 3. Staccato-mark. 4. Head of a bow. 5. The entrance of an important theme. 6. To divide words for chanting, hence **pointing.** 7. **organ-point.** Vide PEDAL-POINT. 8. Vide SIGNS. (In French pronounced pwăn.) A dot. **p. détaché** (dā-tä-shā). Staccato-mark. **p. sur tête** (sür-tĕt). Dot above or below a note. **p. d'arrêt** (dăr-rĕ'), or **p. de repos** (dŭ rŭ-pō). A hold. **p. d'augmentation** (dōg-măn-tăs-yôn). A dot of augmentation. **p. final** (fī-năl'). Final pause. **p. d'orgue** (dôrg). 1. A hold, hence also a cadenza or flourish. 2. Pedal-point.

pointe (pwănt), *F.* 1. Toe, in organ-playing.

pointé (pwän-tā), *F.* Dotted, from **pointer** (pwăn-tā). To dot, or play staccato.

polacca (pō-läk'-kä), *I.* Polonaise. **alla p.** In the style of a polonaise.

polichinelle (pōl - ĭ - shĭ - nĕl'), *F.* "Punch." A clown-dance.

pol'ka. A round dance in lively 2-4 time, originated in Bohemia about 1830. **p. mazurka.** A slower dance in triple time with accent on the last beat. **p. redowa.** Is faster than the **p. m.,** with accent on first beat

polonaise (pôl-ō-nĕz'), *F.,* **Polonäse** (pôl-ō-nä'-zĕ), *G.* A Polish dance in moderate 3-4 time; strictly a march-past. Its rhythm resembles t'.at of the bolero; it begins with a sharply accented 8th note followed by two 16th notes, and four 8th notes; its closing measure is an 8th and two 16th notes; a sharply accented quarter note, an 8th note, and an 8th rest. Also spelt **polonoise** (pôl-ôn-wäz). Vide CHART OF DANCE RHYTHMS.

polska (pôls'ka), *Swedish.* A dance in 3-4 time, usually in the minor.

poly-. A Greek prefix, meaning "many." **polychord.** An instr. inv. by Fr. Hillmer, of Berlin, resembling a double-bass with 10 gut-strings and movable finger-board. **polymorphous.** Used of counterpoint, with a widely varied theme. **polyphon'ic,** or **polyph'onous.** 1. Used of compositions in which more than one theme at a time is given individuality; loosely used of compositions of many parts, but to be sharply distinguished from a mere melody with an accompanying harmony. 2. Used of instrs. that can produce more than one tone at a time (compare homophonic, and homophonous), hence **polyphony** (pŏl-ĭ-fō'-nĭ or pō-lĭf'-ō-nĭ). The treatment of simultaneous parts each independently, i. e., counterpoint. **polytonality.** A quality possessed by music the parts of which are written in several keys simultaneously.

Pommer (pŏm'-mĕr), *G.* Vide BOMBARD.

pompös (pŏm'-pās), *G.*, **pompo'so**, **pomposamen'te**, *I.* Pompous(ly). Majestic(ally).

ponctuation (pônkt-ü-ăs-yôn), *F.* Phrasing, from **ponctuer** (pônk-tü-ā). To phrase.

pondero'so, *I.* Ponderous, heavily marked.

ponticello (pôn-tĭ-chĕl'-lō), *I.* 1. Bridge. **sul. p.** A direction for bow instrs., "play near the bridge." (Abbr. **s. pont.**) 2. The break in the voice.

pont-neuf (pôn-nŭf), *F.* A bridge in Paris, hence a street ballad.

poo'gye. Hindoo nose-flute.

popolare (pō-pō-lä'-rĕ), *I.* Popular.

porrec'tus. Gnomo. Vide NEUME.

port (pôr), *F.* 1. Portamento. 2. Vide CHUTE.

portamen'to. The passage across an interval by means of gliding with imperceptible gradations through all the intermediate tones in one continuous sound (such an effect as is gained by sliding the finger along a string while the bow presses it). Hence a legato style; so a singer is said to have a true **portamento**.

portan'do, *I.* Carrying across, i. e., producing the *portamento* effect; from **portare** (pôr-tä'-rĕ). To carry.

portar (pôr-tär'), *I.* Carry! **p. la battuta.** Follow the beat. **p. la voce.** Sustain the tone. Pl. **portate.**

portata (pôr-tä'-tä), *I.* Staff.

portatif, *F.*, **portativ**, *G.* (pôr-tä-tēf), **por'tative.** A portable organ.

portato (pôr-tä'-tō), *I.* Sustained.

portée (pôr-tā'), *F.* Staff.

porter (pôr-tā), *F.* To carry. **p. la voix.** Produce the portamento.

por'tunal flute. A flue-stop with widetop pipes.

Portunen (pôr-too'-nĕn), *G.* Bourdon.

Pos. Abbr. for **Posaune.**

posato (pō-zä'-tō), *I.* Sedate.

Posaune (pō-zow'-nĕ), pl. **-en**, *G.* 1. Trombone. 2. A trumpet. Hence, **Posauner.** A trombonist. 3. A reedstop. **Posaunzug** (tsookh). Sackbut.

Poschette (pō-shĕt'-tĕ), *G.* Pocketviolin.

posé'ment (pō-zä-mäṅ), *F.* Sedately.

poser (pō-zā), *F.* To poise. **p. la voix.** To attack a tone exactly.

positif, *F.*, **positiv**, *G.* (pō-zē-tēf'), **pos'itive.** Stationary organ; in French choir-organ.

posi'tion, *E.* (pron. in *F.* pō-zēs'-yôṅ), **posizione** (pō-zē-tsĭ-ō'-nĕ), *I.* 1. Vide CHORD. 2. Vide CLOSE. 3. The place of the first finger of the left hand on the finger-board of violins, etc. The **first position** is that in which the fore-finger presses the first semi-tone or tone of the open string; the **half position** that in which the second finger presses the first semitone of the open string. By making a **shift**, the hand reaches the **second position**, that in which the first finger presses at the place occupied by the second finger in the first position; in the **third position** the first finger occupies the place held by the third finger in the first position; and so on.

possibile (pôs-sē'-bĭ-lĕ), *I.* Possible, as *presto p.*, as fast as possible.

posthorn. 1. A straight valveless bugle. 2. A piece or passage imitating a postman's call.

posta, di (dē pōs'-tä), *I* At once.

posthume (pôs-tüm), *F.* Posthumous, pub. after the composer's death.

postlu'deum, *L.* A concluding phrase, composition, or church voluntary.

potenza (pō-tĕn'-tsä), *I.* 1. Old name for musical note or sign. 2. The sound any instr. produces.

pot-pourri (pō-poor'-rē), *F.* Medley.

pouce (poos), *F.* Thumb. In guitar music a direction to sweep the strings with the thumb.

poule, la (lä pool), *F.* "The hen." A quadrille figure; the third.

pour (poor), *F.* For, in order to, as *p. finir,* in order to close.

poussé (poos-sā'), *F.* "Pushed." The up-bow.

pp. Abbr. of **pianissimo.**

prächtig (prĕkh'-tĭkh), *G.* Pompous. **Prachtvoll** (präkht'-fōl), *G.* Full of grandeur.

präcis (prā-tsēs'), *G.* Precise.

praecen'tor, *L.* Choir-leader.

praeam'bulum, *L.* Prelude.

praefa'tio, *L.* The prayers said or sung in the Mass before the Transubstantiation.

praefec'tus cho'ri, *L.* Chorus-leader. **Prall'triller**, *G.* Inverted mordent Vide GRACE.

präludiren (prā-loo-dē'-rĕn), *G.* T preludise.

Prästant (prä′-shtänt), *G.* Principal 4-ft. stop.

precent′or. Choir-director in the Anglican Church.

préchantre (prä-shäntr), *F.* Choir-director.

precipitare (prä-chĕ-pĭ-tä′-rĕ), *I.* To hurry precipitately, hence **precipitato** (tä′-tō). Precipitan′do, precipito′so. Hurried. **precipitamen′te.** Hurriedly. **precipitazione** (tä-tsĭ-ō′-nĕ). Haste.

precisione (prä-chĕ-zĭ-ō′-nĕ), *I.* Precision. **preciso** (prä-chĕ′-sō). Exact.

preghiera (prä-gĭ-ā′-rä), *I.* Prayer.

prelude (prē′-lūd or prĕl′-ūd), *E.*, **prélude** (prä-lüd). *F.*, **preludio** (prä-loo′-dĭ-ō), *I.* 1. An introductory phrase, section, or composition. Hence, a composition of an improvised manner, and brief length. 2. *As a verb,* to improvise such an introductory piece.

premier (prŭm-yä), **première** (prŭm-yăr), *F.* First, as **premier dessus** (dĕs-sü). First treble or soprano. **première fois** (fwä). First time. **à première vue** (vü). At first sight. As a noun, **première** is used of a first production.

prepara′tion, préparation (prä-pă-răs-yôn), *F.*, **preparazione** (prä-pä-rä-tsĭ-ō′-nĕ), *I.* A musical device for softening a discord by preparing the mind for it through the introduction of the dissonant note in a previous chord in which it is consonant. Vide HARMONY. Custom has greatly changed from the early period in which no unprepared dissonance was permitted, for now in free writing almost any dissonance can appear without warning.

prepar′ative note. Appoggiatura.

prepared. 1. Used of a note which had preparation (q.v.). 2. Used of a shake or trill which had two or more introductory notes.

près de (prĕ dŭ), *F.* Near.

presa (prä′-sä), *I.* Vide LEAD (2).

pressant (prĕs-sän), *F.*, **pressante** (prĕs-sänt), *F.*, **pressan′do,** *I.*, **pressirend** (prĕs-sē′-rĕnt), *G.* "Pressing," accelerating.

pressez (prĕs-sā), *F.* Accelerate.

pressure note or tone. One marked thus ⌒, and to be attacked softly and suddenly increased in volume.

prestamen′te, *I.* Very rapidly.

prestant (prŭ-stän), *F.* Principal, 4-ft. open stop.

prestezza, (prĕs-tĕd′-zä), *I.* Rapidity.

presto (präs′-tō), *I.* 1. Fast, faster than allegro, the fastest rate in music except its own superlatives as **prestis′simo** and **prestis′samente.** 2. A movement in very rapid time.

prick. 1. *As a noun,* the head of a note, hence 2. *as a verb,* to write music. **prick-song.** The first written music, in contrast with improvised music. 3. The counterpoint written to a *cantus firmus.*

prière (prĭ-ăr′), *F.* Prayer.

prima (prē′-mä), *I.* First, principal. **da p.** From the beginning. **p. buffa.** Leading woman in comic opera. **prima donna.** "Leading lady" in opera, chief soprano. **p. vista.** First sight. **p. volta.** The first time (abbr. **1ma.** Volta), and used to mark measures to be played before a repetition, and to be skipped after that repetition for the measures marked **seconda volta (2da. volta).**

pri′mary. 1. Used of an accent beginning a measure. 2. Of a triad or chord which constitutes one of the three fundamental triads of a key, viz., those on the tonic, dominant, and the subdominant.

prime (prīm), *E.* (in *G.* and *F.* prēm) 1. The first tone of a scale, the tonic. 2. Used of that interval which is indicated by two notes on the same line or space, but separated by a chromatic distinction. Used also of two notes in unison. Vide INTERVAL. 3. Vide HORÆ.

Primgeiger (prēm′-gī-gĕr), *G.* First violin, leader.

primo (prē′-mō), *I.* First, principal. **tempo p.** At the original tempo. **p. buffo.** Leading man in a comic opera. **p. uomo** (oo-ō′-mō). Old term for first male soprano or tenor. **primo** as a noun, is used of the leading part of a duet.

Primtöne (prēm′-tä-nĕ), *G.* Fundamental tones. **Primzither.** Treble zither.

primice′rio (prē′-mĭ-chä′-rĭ-ō), *I.* **primicerius,** *L.* Cantor.

prin′cipal, *E.* (pron. in *G.* prēn-tsĭ-päl′, in *F.* prăn-sĭ-păl′). 1. In France and Germany used of the open diapason; in England used of an open flue-stop of 4-ft. pitch, on the manual (8 ft. on the pedal) an octave higher than the open diapason. 2. Old name for fugue subject. 3. Old name for trumpet.

As an adjective. 1. Vide PRIMARY. 2. **principal key.** The predominant key of the composition. 3. The **p.** voices are the soprano and bass. 4. **p. close** or **cadence.** One in the principal key. 5. **p. subject** or **theme,** one to which others are subordinate. **principal-bass.** An open diapason stop on the pedals. **principal-work.** The flue-pipes of diapason quality. Vide STOP.

principale (prēn-chǐ-pä'-lĕ), *I.* 1. Diapason-stop. 2. Principal or leading, as an adjective. 3. Old name for the trumpet. **principalino.** 8-ft. stop.

principio (prǐn-chē'-pǐ-ō), *I.* Beginning.

prise, or **p. du sujet** (prēz dǔ sü-zhä), *F.* Entry of the subject.

Probe (prō'-bĕ), *G.* Rehearsal. **Generalprobe.** Final rehearsal.

procéder (prō-sā-dā), *F.* To progress.

procella (prō-chĕl'-lä), *I.* Storm.

pro'em. Ancient heroic song with cithara accompaniment.

programme, *F.,* **program** (prō'-grăm' not prō'-grŭm), *E.,* **program'ma,** *I.,* **Programm** (prō-gräm'), *G.* A list of compositions to be performed. **program - music, Programm - musik** (prō-gräm' moo-zēk'), *G.* Music with a programme, i. e., with a more or less definite description of events of moods. It usually aims to present a suggestion (rarely in decent music an imitation) of some music of nature as a brook, bird-improvisations, forest-sounds, or of some narrative, though its main effort is to deploy the emotions arising from such scenes and thoughts. Beethoven's ideal is expressed in his famous characterisation of his Pastoral Symphony as *mehr Ausdruck als Malerei,* "more an expression than a painting." So long as the "descriptive" element is a mere suggestion, music is capable of most felicitous hints, and programme-music has most ancient and venerable authority, traceable farther back even than Bach (who wrote a musical suggestion of a postilion), to Jannequin, and others. When programme-music stoops to imitation direct it either grows ludicrously incompetent or ceases to be music and becomes noise.

programmist. A devotee of programme-music.

progrès (prō-grĕ), *F.* Progression.

progres'sion, *E.,* **progressione** (sǐ-ō'-nĕ), *I.* 1. **melodic progression.** The advance of the melody from one tone to another. 2. **harmonic p.** The advance of the harmony from one chord to another. These two processes, particularly the latter, are hedged round with continual difficulties and restrictions, some of them based on human nature and acoustics, others deriving no sustenance from either, but depending for their existence in the text-books entirely on tradition, history, conservatism, fashion, or a sense of being rendered artificial by long pedantry. The science of progressions constitutes the greater part of the Theory of Music, and of harmony and counterpoint (q.v.).

progres'sio harmo'nica, *I.* A mixture-stop.

Progressions-schweller (prō-grĕs-sǐ-ōns'-shvĕl-lĕr), *G.* A device inv. by Abbé Vogler, for gradually calling in play, then gradually closing off, the stops of an organ, to produce a crescendo, then a diminuendo.

progressive. 1. Of a stop in which the number of ranks increases with the pitch. 2. Through-composed.

prola'tion, *E.,* **prola'tio,** *L.,* **prolazione** (prō-lä-tsǐ-ō'-nĕ), *I.* 1. The classification of the relative value of the notes in mensurable (q.v.) music, almost corresponding in its four classes to our musical metre. 2. The measurement of the semibreve, **prolatio major,** indicating that it is to be divided into three minims; **p. minor,** indicating two minims; Vide NOTATION.

prolongement (prō-lôṅzh-mäṅ) *F.* 1. A pedal, inv. by Debain, for holding down harmonium keys. 2. That part of the piano action which holds the hammer from its place of rest; a sustaining pedal.

promptement (prôṅt-mäṅ), *F.,* **prontamen'te,** *I.* Promptly, quickly.

pron'to, *I.* Prompt, quick.

pronunziato (prō-noon-tsǐ-ä'-tō), *I.* Enunciated, marked.

proper-chant. Old name for the key of C major.

propor'tio, *L.,* **propor'tion,** *E.* 1. The determination of time in mensurable music by means of fractions. Vide NOTATION. 2. The second part of 16th cent. dance-tunes. Vide SALTARELLA.

propos'ta, *I.* Subject of a fugue.

prosa'rium, *L.* A book of prosae, the prosa being the Sequence (q.v.), sung between the gradual and the Gospel in the R. C. Service.

propri'etas, *L.* A ligature whose first note is a breve. opposita p. One in which the first two notes are semibreves. sine proprietate. Improprietas. Vide NOTATION.

proslambanom'enos. Vide MODES.

Prospekt', *G.* Organ front, hence P.-pfeife(n). Display pipe(s).

pro'teus. A key-board stringed inst. inv. 1650 by Nigetti.

pro'tus. Middle-age term for the first church mode.

pro'va, *I.* Proof, rehearsal. p. generale (jān-ā-rä'-lě), or p. grande. Final rehearsal.

Provençales (proō-väṅ-sǎl'). Troubadours from Provence.

prycke. In Merbecke's notation of 1550 a minim. Vide PRICK.

psallette (sǎl-lět), *F.* A maîtrise.

psalm (in *E.* säm, in *G.* psäl-'m), psaume (psōn), *F.* From a Greek word meaning to pluck a string, hence a harp-song, taken from Jewish religion by the Christian and highly developed, in various manners. Psalmbuch, *G.* A Psalter. Psalmgesang, *G.* Psalmody. P.-lied (lēt). Psalm. P.-sänger, *G.* Psalmsinger. psalm'ody, *E.*, psalmodie (psǎl-mō-dē), *F.* The art or practice of psalm-singing. psalm'ista. An order of clergy.

psalm-melo'dicon. An instr. inv. by Weinrich, in 1828, with eight fingerholes and 25 keys, giving it a compass of 4 octaves, and the power of producing chords of 6 tones.

psalter (säl'-těr, in *G.* psäl'-těr), psautier (psōt-yä), *F.* A book of psalms.

Psalter (psäl'-těr), *G.*, psaltérion (psǎl-tā'-rĭ-ôṅ), *F.*, psalte'rium, *L.*, psaltery (säl'-tě-rĭ), *E.* An ancient stringed instr. with a sound-board, the strings being plucked with the fingers or a plectrum.

psalte'riæ, *L.* Women who played and sang during a feast.

psaume. Vide PSALM.

pulcha (pool'-chä), *Rus.*, pul'ka, *Bohemian.* Polka.

pulpit'ium. 1. A stage. 2. Motet.

pul'satile. Used of instrs. of percussion.

pulsa'tor organo'rum, *L.* Organ-player.

punct'us, *L.* 1. A note, hence punctus contra punctum. "Note against note," i. e., counterpoint. 2. A dot.

Punkt (poonkt), *G.*, punto (poon'-tō), *I.* Dot, punktiert (tērt'), *G.*, puntato (tä'-tō), *I.* Dotted, staccato.

punta (poon'-tä) *I.* Point (of a bow). p. d'organo (dôr-gä'-nō). Pedalpoint. p. per p. Note for note. p. coronato. Fermate.

pupitre (pü-pētr), *F.* Music-desk. p.-improvisateur (pü-pēt'-ráṅ-prō-vē'-zä-tŭr'). A melograph inv. by F. A. E. Keller, 1835.

purf'ling. The ornamental border of violins, etc.

put'ti (poot'-tē), *I.* Choir-boys.

pyk'na, *Gr.* 1. Half and quarter tone progressions, in Greek music. 2. Close notes (q.v.). 3. A semitone.

pyram'idon. A 16 or 32 ft. stop, with top 4 times as wide as the mouth.

py'rophon, *Gr.* "Organ of flames." An instr. inv. by Fr. Kastner, 1875. A key-board with electric attachment, producing gas flames in tubes tuned to the compass C–c''.

Pyr'rhic, Pyrrich'ius. A Greek dance.

Pyth'ian. Games in honour of Apollo, including musical contests.

Pythagore'an. 1. Used of the mathematical investigations in music made by Pythagoras. 2. Used of a lyre, said to have been inv. by him.

Q

Q. This letter inverted in 'cello music indicates that the thumb is to be laid across the strings as a nut.

Quadrat (kvä-drät'), *G.*, quad'rate, *E.*, quadra'tum, *L.* "A square." 1. A natural sign (♮), in *L.* B. quadratum. 2. In mensurable music a breve, hence Quadramusik (moozěk'), *G.* Old music in square notes.

quad'rible. Quatrible.

quadricin'ium, *L.* A 4-voiced composition.

quadriglio (kwä-drēl'-yō), *I.*, quadrille (in *E.* kwä-drĭl', in *F.* kǎd-rē'-yŭ). A square dance in 6-8 and 2-4 time, in five different figures: le pantalon. "Pantaloon." l'été (lā-tā). "Summer." la poule. "The hen." la pastourelle, or la trenise; and la finale.

quadripar'tite. A four-voices composition.

quad'ro, *I.*, quad'rum, *L.* 1. A natural sign (♮). 2. Tableau.

quad'ruple. Four-fold. 1. Vide

COUNTERPOINT. 2. Used of a quaver with four tails, a 64th note. 3. Of rhythm, that with four beats to the measure

quad'ruplet. A group of four equal notes.

quad'riplum, L. Vide TRIPLUM.

quan'tity. The duration of a note or syllable.

quart (in E. kwärt, in F. kăr), quar'ta, L. and I. 1. The interval of a fourth. 2. A fourth. quart de mesure. A quarter rest. quart de soupir (soo-pēr'). A sixteenth rest. quart de son, or ton. A quarter tone. quarta modi, or toni. The subdominant.

quart- (kvärt), G. A prefix indicating that an inst. is a fourth higher (as Quart-flöte, -geige, etc.), or a fourth lower (as Q.-fagott, or -posaune, etc.), than the normal instr.

Quartsext'akkord, G. A 6-4 chord. Vide CHORD.

Quarte (in F. kărt, in G. kvär'-tě). The interval of a fourth. q. de nazard (dŭ nä-zăr'), F. A 15th, also a 2-ft. organ-stop. q. de ton, F. The subdominant. Quartenfolgen, or parallelen, G. Consecutive fourths.

quarter, or quarter note. A crotchet, half of a half-note. quarter rest. A rest of a quarter note's duration.

quarter tone. An interval less than a semi-tone, the difference for example between D sharp and E flat on the violin.

quartet', Quartett', G., quartet'to, I. 1. A composition for 4 voices or instrs. 2. A 4-part composition in sonata form, as a string-quartet.

quar'to, I. Fourth. q. d'aspet'to. A 16th rest. q. di tuono (too-ō'-nō). Quarter tone.

quasi (kwä'-sē), L. and I. As if; almost; somewhat like. andante q. lento = andante, nearly lento. q. sonata. Almost (but not strictly) in sonata form.

quatre (kătr), F. Four.

quatorzième (kă-tôrz'-yĕm), F. A fourteenth.

quat'rible. In old music a progression in parallel fourths, a quinible, being in parallel fifths.

quatricin'ium. Four-part composition.

quattricro'ma, I. 64th note.

quat'tro, I. Four.

quatuor (kăt-ü-ôr), F. Quartet.

qua'ver. An 8th note.

quer- (kvär), G. Prefix meaning cross or transverse, as Q.-flöte. The transverse flute. Q.-pfeife. Swiss fife, with 6 holes and with a compass of two octaves. Q.-stand (shtänt). Cross or false relation. Q.-strich. 1. Ledger line. 2. The single thick tail for a group of notes.

questo or -a (kwäs'-to), I. This; or that.

queue (kŭ), F. Tail. 1. Of notes. 2. Tail-piece of vlns., and so forth. piano à q. Grand piano.

quick-step. A rapid march.

quieto (kwē-ā'-tō), quietamen'te, I. Calm(ly), serene(ly).

quilis'ma. Vide NEUME.

quindecima (kwēn-dä'-chē-mä), I. A 15th. 1. Interval. 2. Organ-stop. a la q., or 15ma. = 2 octaves higher or lower.

Quindezime (kvēn-dä'-tsē-mě), G. A 15th.

quin'ible. Vide QUATRIBLE.

quin'quegrade. Pentatonic.

quint (in E. kwĭnt; in G. kvēnt). 1. A 5th. 2. A 5⅓-ft. stop, sounding a fifth higher than the normal. 3. The e string of the violin. q. stride. Progression of a fifth. Q.-absatz, or abschluss, G. Imperfect cadence. Q.-fagott, G. A bassoon pitched a fifth higher than the normal. Q.-gedackt or Q.-stimme, G. Same as 2. Q.-bass, G. A stop on the pedal sounding a fifth above the double diapason. Q.-fuge (foo'-gě). A fugue with the answer a fifth above the subject. Q.-saite. A treble string. Q.-töne. Quint tone Vide PITCH. Q.-viola. 1. Quinton. 2. A stop a fifth above the gamba.

quin'ta, L. and I. A fifth; vide also QUINTUS. q. decima. Quindecima. q. ed una or quintadena. Vide QUINTATON. q. falsa. The diminished fifth formerly prohibited. q. modi or toni. The dominant. alla q. At the fifth.

Quintaton (kvēn'-tä-tōn), G. A covered 8-, 16-, or 32-ft. flue-stop sounding the 12th as well as the fundamental.

quinte (in F. kănt, in G. kvēn'-tě). Vide QUINT 1, 2, 3. q. octaviante (ŏk-tăv-ĭ-ănt), F. The 12th. Quinten-folgen, or -parallelen, G. Parallel fifths. Quinten-zirkel (tsēr'-

kĕl), *G.* Circle of fifths. Vide TEM-
PERAMENT. **quinten-rein** (rīn), *G.*
"Pure in fifths," used of bow instrs.
quinter (kăṅ-tā), *F.* To sing in quinible.
quinter'na, *I.*, **quin'terne**, *E.* Old
Italian lute with 3 or 5 pairs of gut-
strings, sometimes also 2 single
strings covered with wire.
quinti(e)ren (kvēn-tē'-rĕn), *G.* To
overblow and sound the twelfth.
quintoier, or **quintoyer** (kwēn-twä-yā),
F. 1. To sing in quinible. 2. To
overblow and sound the 12th.
quintet', *E.*, **Quintett'**, *G.*, **quintette** (kwēn-tĕt), *F.*, **quinta'to**, *I.* A
five-part composition.
Quintole (in *E.* quĭn'-tōl; in *G.* kvēn-
tō'-lĕ). Quintuplet.
quinton (kwēn-tôṅ), *F.* 1. The 5-
stringed treble viol. 2. The tenor
viol.
quintuor (kwēn-tü-ôr), *F.* Quintet.
quintu'plum, *L.* Vide TRIPLUM.
quin'tuple. Five-fold.
quin'tuplet. A group of five equal
notes.
quin'tus, *L.*, or **quin'ta.** A fifth part
in compositions; as it occasionally
wandered from one voice to another
it was called q. **vagans.**
quinzième (kăṅz-yĕm), *F.* Fifteenth.
quire. Choir. **qui'rister.** Chorister.
Qui tollis, *L.* "Who takest away (the
sins of the world)." Vide GLORIA.
quitter (kĭt-tā), *F.* To leave.
quodlibet, or **quotlibet**, *L.* "What
(or "as many as") you please." 1.
A comic medley, without connecting
links. 2. A charivari.
Quo'niam tu so'lus, *L.* "For Thou
only (art Holy)." Part of the Gloria.

R

R. Abbr. for 1. *Right*, as *r. h.*, right
hand. 2. *Responsorium* (*r. g.=r.
Graduale*) in Catholic music. 3.
Ripieno. 4. *Clavier de récit* (swell-
manual). In organ music.
raban', **raban'na.** Hindu tambourine.
rabbia (räb-bē'-ä). Mad rage, fury.
rabé (rä-bā'), **rabel'**, *Sp.* Rebec.
raccontan'do, *I.* As if relating or describing.
Rackett', **Rankett'**, *G.* 1. An obsolete
bombard with many curves in its
tube, and a weak voice. Made in
five sizes, it was simplified as the **R.
fagott** by Denner. 2. A reed-stop,
obsolete.

raccourcir (răk-koor-sēr'), *F.* To
abridge.
racler (ră-klä'), *F.* To saw, and
scratch, hence **racleur** (ră-klŭr). A
bad fiddler.
raddolcen'do, **raddolcente** (räd-dól-
chĕn'-tĕ). Growing softer and sweet-
er. **raddolcito** (chē'-tō). Pacified.
raddoppiamen'to, *I.* 1. Doubling, as
the notes of a chord. 2. Multiplying
copies. **raddoppiato** (pĭ-ä'-tō).
Doubled.
Radel (rä'-dĕl), *G.* A solo with chorus.
radia'ting. Used of a fan-shaped
pedal key-board.
rad'ical. Fundamental. See CADENCE.
radio. See article, page 802.
Radleier (rät'-lī-ĕr), *G.* Hurdygurdy.
Radlmaschine (rätl-mä-shē'-nĕ). Valve
mechanism.
rag. The clog dance of the American
negro, perhaps related to the Spanish
verb *raer*, to scrape. The music has
some resemblance to the Abanera
in spirit and syncopation, but is in
4-4 time and of an hilarious char
acter, hence the verb to **rag**, and
rag-time music in this style.
raggione (räd-jŏ'-nĕ), *I.* Proportion.
rago'ke. Small Russian horn.
rake. A 5-pointed device for ruling
off staves.
rall. Abbr. of **rallentando.**
rallentare (tä'-rĕ). To become slower,
hence **rallentan'do** (abbr. *rall*). With
gradually reduced speed. **rallenta-
men'to.** Retardation. **rallentato**
(tä'-tō). Retarded. **rallenta'te.** Retard!
rang (räṅ), *F.* Rank.
range. Compass, as of a voice.
rank. A row of pipes belonging to one
stop.
rant. An old country-dance; a reel.
ranz des vaches (räṅ-dä-väsh), *F.*
"Calling of the cows." A Swiss tune
sung or played on long horns by
herdsmen.
rapido (rä'-pē-dō), **rapidamen'te**, *I.*
Rapid(ly). **rapidità** (rä-pē-dĭ-tä').
Rapidity.
rapsodie (răp-sō-dē), *F.* Rhapsody.
rappel', *F.* A military call.
rasch (räsh), *G.* Fast. **rascher.** Faster.
rasend (rä'-zĕnt), *G.* Raging, hence
Rasegesang, and **Raselied** (rä'-zĕ-
lēt). Dithyramb.
rasgado (räs-gä'-dhō), *Sp.* "Scrap-
ing," hence in guitar playing, sweeping the strings with the thumb to
produce an arpeggio.

rast'ral, ras'trum. Vide RAKE.

Räthselkanon (rät'-zĕl-kä-nōn), G. Vide CANON.

ra'tio. Used of the relative value of vibration-numbers.

rattenen'do, rattenuto (noo'-tō), I. Restraining, or restrained, i. e., retarded.

rattezza (rät-tĕd'-zä), I. Speed.

rauco (rä'-oo-kō), I., rauh (rŏw), G., rauque (rōk), F. Harsh, hoarse, rough. raucedine (rä-oo-chĕ-dē'-nĕ), I. Harshness.

Rauscher (row'-shĕr), G. The rapid repetition of a note.

rausch- (rowsh), G. Prefix denoting a stop of 2 ranks sounding the twelfth and fifteenth, or fifteenth and octave twelfth; hence Rauschflöte, -pfeife, -quinte, -werk; and also Ruszpipe (roos'-pē-pē).

ravanas'tron. A primitive violin with one or two strings, claimed by the Ceylonese as the invention of a king who reigned about 5000 B. C. It is still used by the Buddhists.

rav(v)ivare (vä'-rĕ), I. To accelerate, hence, ravivan'do. Accelerating. ravivato (vä'-tō). Accelerated.

ray. Name for re, in the Tonic-Sol-fa.

re (rā), I., ré (rā), F. 1. Vide SOLMISATION. 2. In France and Italy, the note D.

rebab, Arab. Rebec.

re'bec(k), rebec'ca, re'bet, rebed, rebibe, re'bible. Old E. An early violin with 3 gut-strings. Its origin has been credited to the Moors, who are said to have brought it into Spain; it has been claimed that the Spanish gave it to the Moors; it has been also derived from the British Chrotta, or crwth.

re'al. Vide FUGUE.

récension (rā-săns-yôn), F. An analytical editing.

rechange (rŭ-shänzh). "Change." Hence, corps (kôr) or tons (tôn) de r. Crooks.

recheat'. A hunting recall.

recht(e) (rĕkht(ĕ)), G. Right, as r. Hand.

récit (rā-sē), F. 1. Recitative. 2. A solo part. 3. The chief of several parts. clavier de r. (klăv-yā dŭ). Swell manual on the organ.

recitado (rā-thē-tä'-dhō), Sp. Recitative.

reci'tal. A musical performance given entirely by one performer, or from one composer's works. Said to have been initiated by Liszt in 1840.

recitan'do, recitan'te, recitato (rā-chē-tä'-tō). In recitative style.

récitant (rā-sē-tän), Recitante (rā'-tsē-tänt), F. A man (or woman) soloist.

recitative (rĕs-ĭ-tä-tēv'), E., recitatif (rā-sē-tä-tēf'), F., Recitativ (rā-tsē-tä-tēf'), G., recitativo (rā-chē-tä-tē'-vō), I. Musical declamation or recitation, as opposed to strict melody. It usually aims to be a sort of musical colloquialism. In modern form it began in the first operatic works of Peri (vide B. D.), and the others; it was more or less a singsong declamation with an accompaniment consisting of occasional chords to keep the singer on the key; it was well-called "dry," or recitativo secco, or parlante, and the accompaniment was indicated merely by figured bass. This accompaniment was gradually elaborated into the recitativo stromentato. "Instrumented," or accompagnato, or con accompagnamento or obbligato (in F. accompagné, or obligé). In later opera, particularly Wagner's, the whole musical structure is inclined to be in recitative with a descriptive and complicated orchestral background. Recitative is usually delivered at the singer's pleasure except when specially marked a tempo.

réciter (rā-sē-tā), F. To perform a récit, or solo.

reci'ting note. That tone of a church-mode on which most of the chanting is done, usually the dominant.

rec'ord. Old E. To play the record'er. An obsolete flageolet with 9 holes, one of them covered with gold beater's skin, compass 2 octaves f'–f'''.

recorded music. See PHONOGRAPH MUSIC, page 794.

recreation, récréation (rā-krā-ăs-yôn), F. A light composition.

rec'te et re'tro, L. Forward and backward. Vide CANON.

rec'tus, L. Similar (of motion).

reddi'ta, redita (rā-dē'-tä), I., redite (rŭ-dēt), F. A repeat.

redondilla (rā-dôn-dĕl'-yä), Sp. Roundelay.

redoub'led. Compound (of an interval).

redoublement (rŭ-doob-lŭ-män), F. Doubling.

red'owa, redowak', redowazka (rä-dō-väts'-kä), *Bohemian.* A dance in lively 3-4 time; in the Bohemian form 2-4 time is also employed.

redublicato (rä'-doob-lǐ-kä'-tō), *I.* Redoubled.

reduciren, reduzieren (rä-doo-tsē'-rěn), *G.,* réduire (rä-dwēr), *F.* To arrange or transcribe a composition in a smaller form. Hence, such condensation is called reduction, *E.,* réduction (rä-düks-yôṅ), *F.,* Reduktion (rě-dook'-tsǐ-ōn), *G.,* riduzione (re-doo-tsǐ-ō'-ně), *I.*

reduc'tio, *L.* Reduction (of a mode to its original key).

red-note. See article, p. 767.

reed. Originally a thin and elastic strip of cane, now made of other fibres and of metal. It is fixed in an opening by one end; its free end is set in motion by the breath or by a current of air, and transmits this vibration with musical effect to the column of air in the main tube, to which it serves as a sort of quivering valve. The human larynx has a membranous reed, and the lips of horn-players serve the same purpose, the tone being determined by the tension of the lips and the length of the instrument. Vide EMBOUCHURE. free-reeds vibrate without striking the edges of their sockets. Those which strike the edges are called beating (impinging, percussion, or striking) reeds. They are used in the organ for brass effects. Some instrs., as the oboe and bassoon, have 2 reeds which strike each other, and are called double. Reeds are usually tuned by a sliding *wire* by which the vibrating portion is shortened or lengthened.

reed-instruments. A general name for those employing the reed mechanism, particularly the oboe and clarinet groups of the orchestra.

reed-pipe, r. stop, r. work. Refer to the pipes and stops of an organ which employ reeds.

reed-organ. Originally, a small portable organ called the regal, or a pair of regals (if it had 2 pipes for each digital). This small instr. which could sometimes be folded up like a book or Bible [hence Bibel-regall (bē'-běl-rä'-gäl)], employed beating reeds, in the pipes. In 1810 Grénié inv. what he called the orgue expressif, because he could swell and

diminish the tone. In 1843, Debain developed the *Harmonium*, which possessed several stops. The air pressure is usually applied by pedals worked by treadles; with levers, worked by the knees, to produce a swell. The *American Organ* (q.v.) employed a suction mechanism. The *Vocalion* returns to the harmonium style with elaborate improvements. There are many other instrs. which differ chiefly in name from the typical reed-organ.

reel. A lively dance usually in 4-4 (sometimes 6-8) time, perhaps of Scandinavian origin, but chiefly popular in Scotland. It is danced by 2 couples. The Virginia reel of America is danced by 2 long facing lines, the men on one side, and the women on the other.

refrain'. A burden, or stanza, repeated at the end of each new stanza of a song.

Re'gal (in *G.* rä'-gäl), régale (rä-gäl), *F.* 1. Vide REED-ORGAN. 2. An old suffix indicating a reed-stop. 3. An obsolete xylophone.

Regel (rä'-gěl), *G.* Rule.

re'genschori, *L.* Choirmaster.

Regi'na cœ'li, *L.* "Queen of Heaven." A hymn to the Virgin.

Register (rēj'-ǐs-těr in *E.;* in *G.* rä-jēs'-těr). 1. The handle or draw-knob which bears the name of a stop. Hence, 2. A complete stop, or the set of pipes controlled by a single draw-knob. Accordingly register-ing and registration are the act or art of bringing into play and combination the different stops of an organ. Regis'ter-knopf (knôpf), *G.* Draw-knob. R.-stange (shtäng-ě). Stop-lever. R.-zug (tsookh). The mechanism of the draw-stop. Speaking stops (R.-stimmen, or tönende R.) are distinguished from mechanical stops. stumme (shtoom'-mě) R. 3. A frame through which trackers run. 4. A distinct section of the tone-quality of a voice or instr. Vide VOICE.

registre (rŭ-zhēst'r), *F.,* registro (rä-jēs'-trō), *I.* 1. A stop-knob. 2. Vide REGISTER (4).

registri(e)ren (rä-jēs-trē'-rěn), *G.* To register. Registri(e)ung (trē'-roongk). Registration.

règle (rěgl), *F.,* regola (rä'-gō-lä), *I* Rule.

reg'ula, *L.* 1. Register. 2. Rule.

reg'ular. 1. Strict (of fugue). 2. Similar (of motion).

regula'tion. Adjustment of touch.

Reigen (rī'-gĕn), or **Reihen** (rī'ĕn), *G.* A circular dance.

rein (rīn), *G.* Pure, perfect (of intervals), exact, hence **reingreifen** (grī-fĕn). To play accurately.

Reiselied (rī'-zĕ-lēt), *G.* Traveller's or pilgrim's song.

Reitertrompete (rī'-tĕr-trôm-pā'-tĕ), *G.* A clarion, obsolete straight trumpet 30 inches long.

rela'ted. Vide RELATION.

rela'tion (in *F.* rŭ-lăs-yôṅ), **rela'tio,** *L.,* **relazione** (rā-läts-ĭ-ō'-nĕ), *I.* The affinity of keys based upon the similarity or identity of certain chords. Upon key-relationship the whole subject of harmony and modern counterpoint is largely based, and upon this split hair more great theorists jostle than there were angels dancing upon the needle-point of the old monkish dogmatists. In a liberal sense all keys are closely related. For purposes of distinction those keys are said to be *related* (*attendant, accessory,* or *auxiliary*) which have one or more chords in common. The most nearly related (at least *remote*) keys to any key are those founded on its dominant and subdominant (as the keys of G and F are most nearly related to the key of C), also the absolute and relative major and minor (as *c* minor is the absolute minor of C major while the relative minor to C major is *a* minor, which has the same signature). **false-relation,** or **rela'tio non harmon'ica.** Vide FALSE.

rel'ative key, *E.,* **mode-relatif** (mŏd-rŭl-ä-tēf'), *F.,* **tono relativo** (tē'-vō), *I.* 1. The relative key to a major is the minor key whose tonic is a minor third below. The relative major of a minor key has its tonic a minor third above. Vide RELATION.

religio'so (rā-lē-jĭ-ō'-sō), *I.,* **religi-osamen'te.** Solemn(ly), devout(ly).

rel'ish. An old grace (q.v.).

remote'. Unrelated. Vide RELATION.

remo'tus,-a, *L.* Remote; open (as harmony).

templissage (räṅ-plĭs-säzh), *F.* 1. "Filling," as the inner parts of a harmony. 2. Padding. 3. Cadenzas, and bravura passages.

rentrée (räṅ-trä), *F.* Re-entrance (of a part).

renverser (räṅ-vĕr-sā), *F.* To invert, hence **renversé** (räṅ-vĕr-sā). Inverted. **renversement** (vĕrs-mäṅ) Inversion.

renvoi (räṅ-vwä), *F.* A repeat; a sign of repetition.

repeat. A sign indicating the repetition of certain measures—marked by two or more dots in the spaces between the lines, before (or after) the double bar, which indicates the end (or beginning) of the portion to be repeated.

repeating. 1. Of action in which the hammer rebounds quickly enough to permit a rapid reiteration of the tone. 2. Of mixed stops whose overtones do not keep always the same height above the pitch, but sound an octave lower, as the pitch rises.

repercus'sa (*vox*), *L.* A "repeated tone." 1. In neumes the notes called *bi-, di-,* or *tri.* 2. In Gregorian music, the principal note of a mode. **repercus'sion, repercus'sio,** *L.* 1. Repetition, of a chord or note. 2. The reappearance of the subject of the fugue after the exposition. 3. The dominant of a church-mode.

repeti(e)ren (rā-pā-tē'-rĕn), *G.* 1. Vide to BREAK (3). Hence **repeti(e)ren-de Stimme.** A mixture-stop with a break. 2. To repeat.

Repeti'tion (in *G.* rä-pā-tē'-tsĭ-ōn) 1. The rapid repeating of a note or chord. 2. (In *G.* **Repetions'mecha'nik**). Vide REPEATING (1). 3. Vide BREAK (3).

répétition (rā-pā-tēs-yôṅ), *F.* 1. Rehearsal. 2. Repetition.

répétiteur (rā'-pā'-tē-tŭr'), *F.,* **repetitore** (rā-pā-tē-tō'-rĕ), *I.* Trainer of an opera chorus; the rehearser.

repetizione (rā-pā-tē-tsĭ-ō'-nĕ), **re-petimen'to,** *I.* Repetition.

replica (rā'-plē-kä), *I.* A repeat; repetition, hence **replicato** (kä'-tō). Repeated; doubled.

rep'licate. The octave of a tone.

Replik (rā-plēk'), *G.* Complementary interval.

réplique (rā-plēk), *F.* 1. The octave of a tone. 2. The answer of a fugue. 3. Complementary interval. 4. Cue.

reply. Answer (of a fugue).

répons (rā-pôṅ), *F.* Response (1).

réponse (rā-pôṅs), *F.* Answer.

report. Answer.

repos (rŭ-pō), *F.* Point of repose, following a cadence.

reprise (rē-prīz′), *E.* The reappearance of the first theme of a sonata or symphony after the development.

reprise (rŭ-prēz), *F.* 1. Repetition. 2. Vide REPRISE. 3. Reappearance of a theme. 4. Vide BREAK (3). 5. Revival of a work.

reprendre (rŭ-prän̈dr), *F.* To resume.

Requiem (rā′-kwĭ-ĕm), *L.* The first word and title of the Mass for the Dead (*missa pro defunctis*). Beginning "*Requiem æternam dona eis, domine*" "rest eternal, grant them, Lord." The requiem is divided into the introit, kyrie, gradual (with tractus, "*Absolve*," and sequence "*dies iræ*"). Offertory, "*Domine Jesu Christe*"; Sanctus, and Benedictus; Agnus Dei; and Communion "*Lux æterna.*"

research′. An improvisation used as a prelude to a composition and made up of its chief theme.

res′ervoir. The portion of a bellows in which wind is stored.

resin (rĕz′-ĭn). A refined gum applied to the hair of the bow to improve its grip on the strings.

resolu′tion, résolution (rā-zō-lüs-yôn̈), *F.*, **resolu′tio,** *L.*, **resoluzione** (rā-zō-loo-tsĭ-ō′-ně), *I.* 1. Firmness, determination. 2. The dissolving of dissonance into concord; the satisfaction of the mental demand for that partial repose found only in consonance. Dissonant tones are generally resolved by progressing half a tone or a whole tone down or up.

res′onance, *E.*, **Resonanz** (rā-zō-nänts′), *G.* The sympathetic response of a vibrating body to its own particular tone or tones, under the impulsion of vibrations received from another vibrating body sounding the same tone or tones. Thus if one sounds the note a′ on a violin, a tuning fork of the same pitch will give forth the same tone spontaneously, as also will a piano with the damper pedal down; a pane of glass or a loose plate of metal of the proper nature will also reply; furthermore each partial tone will be affected similarly. This acoustic fact is used for the reinforcing of tones; as cavities of air and sheets of wood have this same property of resonance to all the tones and partials which they themselves contain. The violin, etc., employ a hollow space called the **resonance box,** or **Resonanzkasten,**

G. Certain old instrs. used a *sympathetic string* or **Resonanzsaite,** *G.* The piano, etc., use a **resonance board,** or *sound-board,* **Resonanz′-boden,** *G.*

respiro (rā-spē′-rô), *I.* "A breath"; a sixteenth rest.

respond′. A psalm (or part of one) sung between lessons at canonical hours.

response′, *E.*, **respon′sum,** *L.*, **responsio′ne, respon′so,** *I.* 1. The reply of choir or congregation to a phrase read or chanted by a priest or officiant. in R. C. and Episcopal churches. 2. Responsory. 3. The answer in fugue.

Respon′sory, *E.*, **responso′rium,** *L.* 1. The psalm or portion of one sung between Missal lessons. 2. The graduale. 3. A respond.

responsivo (rā-spôn-sē′-vô), *I.* Responsive(ly).

resserrement (rŭs-sĕr-män̈), *F.* Stretto.

ressort (rŭs-sôr′), *F.* Bass-bar.

rest. 1. A period of rhythmic silence, the tempo continuing to be counted passively. 2. A symbol indicating such rest. The rests are usually named according to the portion of a measure they occupy, as 16*th rest;* sometimes being called after the note which has the same duration, as *quarter-note rest, breve rest.* They may be augmented by dots and may extend beyond the limits of one measure, as the *four-measure rest.* See SIGNS AND SYMBOLS. **large-rest, long-rest.** See p. 767.

restric′tio, *L.* Stretto.

result′ant. Used of secondary tones formed by the combined vibration of two independent tones. Vide ACOUSTICS. When sounded together they produce a *difference tone* or *differential tone* whose vibration equals the difference between theirs; also a *summational tone* whose vibration is the sum of theirs.

Resurrex′it, *L.* "And rose again." Part of the Credo. Vide MASS.

retard′. 1. To diminish the velocity. 2. To suspend and then resolve upwards, hence **retarded progression,** or **retarda′tion, retarda′tio,** *L.* 1. A suspension resolving upwards. 2. A decrease in velocity.

retraite (rŭ-trĕt′), *F.* Retreat, tattoo.

ret′ro. *L.* Backwards. Vide CANON.

ret'rograde, retrogra'dus, *L.*, retrogrado (rä-trō-grä'-dō), *I.* Vide IMITATION.

ret'to, *I.* Direct, similar. Vide MOTION.

réveil (rä-vĕ'), *F.*, reveille (rŭ-vā'-yŭ, in *E.* rĕ-vĕl'-yĕ. In the American army rĕv-ĕ-lē', in *G.* rä-fĭl'-lĕ). "Awakening," the first morning military signal. In old *E.* reveil', or revel'ly.

rev'erie. A contemplative composition.

reversed. Contrary (of motion). rever'sion. Retrograde imitation.

revoice. To tune an organ-pipe.

rf., rfz. Abbr. for Rinforzando.

r. h. Abbr. for right hand.

rhapsodie (răp-sō-dē'), *F.* and *G.*, rhap'sody, *E.* "A song of patches." In ancient music a fragment of an epic poem, sung by a minstrel or rhapsode, or rhapsodist. In modern music a brilliant composition which combines the idea of a medley with the acquired idea of great joy or ecstasy.

rhythm, *E.*, rhyth'mus, *L.* (in *G.* rēt'-moos), rhythme (rēdhm), *F.* The "flow" and undulation of progression, marked by the rise and fall of stress and duration. The arrangement of accented and unaccented, and of long and short sounds. Rhythm usually follows some pattern which is repeated with more or less variation through an entire movement or composition. Rhythm might be called the melody of monotone. It is distinct from melodic or harmonic progression, and can be vividly shown on such an instr. as the drum, and it can be written on a single line without reference to pitch. The rhythm sometimes is so complicated that it is not completed in less than a musical period, vide FORM; but it is usually based upon a fundamental series of pulsations that can be expressed within the limits of three or four or nine beats. These are accordingly taken as a unit and grouped within the limits of a *measure*, and cut off by two bars; the first bar being placed before the strongest accent of the group, the second after the weakest. Time may be expressed by the regular swing of a bâton; rhythm embellishes this bâton pulsation, and usually coincides with it in accentuation. except in a syncopated rhythm.

rhythmique (rēdh-mēk), *F.*, rhythmisch (rēt'-mĭsh), *G.* Rhythmical.

ribattuta (rē-băt-too'-tä), *I.* "Restriking." The slow beginning of a trill.

ribe'ba, ribeca (rē-bä'-kä), *I.* Rebeck.

ribbechino (kē'-nō). Small Rebeck.

ribs. The sides connecting back and belly of violins, etc.

ricerca're, ricercata (rē-chĕr-kä'-tä), *I.*, ricercar (rē-tsĕr-kär'), *G.* "Searched out," cf. *récherché*. Used of compositions or passages, usually of fugal form, and employing all the resources and learning of the composer. Vide FUGUE.

richiamare (rē-kĭ-ä-mä'-rĕ), *I.* To imitate the Richia'mo or bird-call.

ricordanza (rē-kôr-dän'-tsä), *I.* Recollection.

riddo'ne, *I.* A roundelay.

ridevolmente (rē-dä'-vōl-mĕn'-tĕ), *I.* Laughingly.

ridicolosamen'te, *I.* Ridiculously.

rid'dle-canon. Vide CANON.

ridot'to, *I.* 1. Reduced (cf. reduciren). 2. A reduction.

riduzione (rē-doo-tsĭ-ō'-nĕ), *I.* Arrangement, reduction.

Riesenharfe (rē'-zĕn-här-fĕ), *G.* Æolian harp.

rifiormento (rē-fĭ-ôr-mĕn'-tō), *I.* Ornament.

riga (rē'-gä), *I.* Staff.

rigabel'lo, *I.*, rigabel'lum, *L.* Regal.

rigadoon', *E.*, rigaudon, rigodon (rē-gō-dôn), *F.* A lively and humorous dance of Provençal origin, and consisting of three or four reprises, the third in a lower position. The time is usually 4-4, with an uptake of a quarter note.

rigals, rigol(e)s. Regals.

rigore (rē-gō'-rĕ), *I.* Rigour, exactness of tempo. rigoro'so. Exact.

rilasciando (rē-lä-shän'-dō), *I.* Relaxing the speed. rilascian'te. With reduced speed.

rikk. Egyptian tambourine.

rilch (rĭlsh), ril'ka. Russian lute.

rimett. Abbr. for rimettendo, *I.* Retarding.

rinforzare (rĭn-fôr-tsä'-rĕ), *I.* To reinforce, emphasise. rinforzamen'to, rinforzo (fôr'-tsō). Reinforcement. rinforzan'do, -a'to. Suddenly emphasised and accented.

Ringelpauke (rĭng'-ĕl-pow-kĕ), *G.* A rattle with rings on bars.

Ringeltanz (rĭng'-ĕl-tänts), *G.* Circular dance.

ripercussio'ne, *I.* Repercussion.

ripetizione (rē-pā-tē-tsĭ-ō'-nē), ripetitura (too'-rä), *I.* 1. Repetition. 2. Refrain.

ripieno, pl. -i (rē-pē-ā'-nō[ē]), *I.* "Filling." 1. Used of a part or an instr. which merely strengthens and rounds out the harmony, as opposed to *solo* or *concertante.* 2. Used in scores to indicate the entrance of the full band. One who plays a ripieno (in *G.* Ripienstimme, rē-pĭ-ānshtĭm-mĕ) is called Ripienist, or ripienis'ta. 3. A mixture-stop called ripieno *di due, tre, quattro* or *cinque,* according as it has 2, 3, 4, or 5 ranks.

ripienino (nē'-nō). 4-ft. stop.

ripigliare (rē-pēl-yä'-rĕ), ripren'dere (prĕn'-dĕ-rĕ), *I.* To resume, hence, ripiglan'do, riprenden'do. Resuming. ripiglio (rē-pēl'-yō). Reprise.

ripo'so, *I.* Repose, hence riposa'to (zä'-tō), reposatamen'te. Reposeful(ly).

ripresa (rē-prā'-zä), *I.* 1. Reprise. 2. Repeat. 3. The repeat mark.

risentito (rē-sĕn-tē'-tō), *I.* With energetic expression.

risoluzione (rē-zō-loo-tsĭ-ō'-nĕ), *I.* Resolution, 1 and 2. risoluto (loo'-tō), risolutamen'te. Decided(ly), energetic(ally).

risonanza, risuonanza (rē-soo-o-nän'-tsä), *I.* Resonance.

risposta (rēs-spō'-stä), *I.* 1. Consequent. 2. Answer in fugue.

Riss, *G.* "Gap," between registers.

ristret'to, *I.* Stretto.

risvegliato (rēs-vāl-yä'-tō), *I.* Animated.

rit, ritard. Abbr. for ritardando (rētär-dän'-dō). Retarding gradually. ritardato (dä'-to). Retarded. ritar'do, -azio'ne. Retardation.

riten. Abbr. for ritenuto (rē-tā-noo'-tō), *I.* Immediately slower, to be distinguished from ritardando and rallentando as well as from ritenendo, and ritenen'te, which refer to gradual retardation.

ritmo (rēt'-mō), *I.* Rhythm. r. di due (tre) battute (dē doo-ā-bät-too'-tä). Rhythm in 2 (or 3) *measures* to the beat, not in duple or triple time, which means 2 (or 3) beats to the measure. ritmico. Rhythmic.

ritornare (rē-tôr-nä'-rĕ), *I.* To return. ritornan'do. Returning. ritornato (ä'-tō). Reverted.

ritornel', ritornel'lo, *I.,* ritournelle (rē-toor-nĕl'), *F.* 1. A burden or repeated portion, such

as the instrumental prelude, inter- and post-lude of a song, sometimes called the symphony. 2. The tutti parts in a concerto. 3. A repeat. 4. A burden, or refrain.

river'so, riverscio (rē-vĕr'-shō), *I.* 1. Reversed. 2. Retrograde.

rivoglimento (rē-vōl-yĭ-mĕn'-tō), *I.* Inversion or transposition, in counterpoint. rivoltato (rē-vôl-tä'-tō), rivolto (rē-vôl'-tō). Inversion.

robusto (rō-boos'-tō), *I.* Robust. Vide TENOR. robustamen'te. Firmly.

roccoco, rococo (rō-kō'-kō), *I.* Old-fashioned, eccentric.

rock-harmon'icon. A graduated series of rock crystals played with hammers.

Roger de Coverley. Vide SIR R. DE C.

Rohr (rōr), pl. Röhre (rā'-rĕ), *G.* 1. Tube. 2. Reed, usually R.-blatt, reed of oboe, bassoon and clarinet. R.-flöte. "Reed-flute" a half-covered 4, 8 or 16 ft. flue-stop. R.-schelle (shĕl-lĕ). The same stop in 1 or 2 ft. pitch. Doppeirohrflöte. One with double mouth. R.-quint. One sounding a fifth above. Rohrwerk. The reed-stops.

roll (rōl), *E.,* rollo (rôl'-lō), *I.* 1. The trill on drum or tambourine, produced on the kettle-drum by rapid taps with the two sticks; on the side-drum with two taps with the left stick, then two with the right; on the tambourine with the knuckles. 2. long r. (a) Battle or rally signal for troops. (b) Swift arpeggio on the organ. rollan'do. Rolling.

Rolle (rôl'-lĕ), *G.* Rapid up-and-down passages of one figure.

roller. 1. A 2-armed wooden bar on gudgeons connecting two trackers, one to a draw-stop, one to a valve, usually roller-board. 2. Cylinder of music-box or carillon.

Roman. 1. Used of the school of Rome from Goudimel and Palestrina to the 19th century. 2. Of strings made in Italy.

romance (in *F.* rō-mäṅs), romanza (rō-män'-tsä), *I.,* Romanze (rō-män'-tsĕ), *G.,* romaunt, Old *E.* 1. A composition of romantic character, as *r. sans paroles,* a story without words. 2. In *F.* a love-song.

romanesca (rō-mä-nās'-kä), *I.,* romanesque (rō-män-ĕsk'). The galliard.

roman'tic, romantique (rō-mäṅ-tĕk), romanzesco (tsäs'-kō). A term much fought for and much evaded. In general, it means the striving after individuality, novelty, and personality of musical expression as opposed to the repetition of classic forms—the reaction of the molten against the mold. As every generation tries to modify, assimilate and re-spin the art of the preceding, and always meets an opposition from the schoolmen and conservatives, the word really means little more than "modern."

Rome, prix de (prē dŭ rôm), *F.* 1. A stipend granting four years' study in Rome, annually awarded by the French government to competing pupils of the Paris Conservatoire. This is the **grand prix** (gräṅ prē), the **second** (sŭ-kôṅ) being a gold medal. 2. Stipend awarded every other year by the Brussels Cons.

romera (rō-mä'-rä). A Turkish dance.

Romanusbuchstaben (rō-mä'-noosbookh'-shtä-bĕn), *G.* "Letters of Romanus." Vide LITTERÆ SIGNIFICATÆ.

ro'mischer Gesang', *G.* "Roman" Catholic plain-song.

ron'da, *I.* Round.

ronde (rôṅd), *F.* A whole note.

rondeau (rôṅ-dō), *F.*, **ron'do** (rôṅ'-dō), *I.* and *E.* 1. A form originally based on a dance with alternating solos (couplets), and chorus (rondeaux); the form is characterised by a cheerful humour. 2. In classic music a principal subject preceding and interweaving two episodes, with much variation of key and many bridge-passages. 3. The more modern form consists of three themes with the first recurrent, thus A–B–A–C–A–B and coda. The second theme appears in the dominant at first, finally in the tonic, giving the Rondo a close relation with the sonata formula. Vide FORM. A small or easy rondo is called variously, **r. mignon** (mēn-yôṅ), *F.*, **rondilet'ta**, **rondinet'to**, **rondino** (rôṅ-dē'-nō), **rondolet'to**.

rondel'lus. An early form of strict imitation.

rondeña (rôṅ-dän'-yä), *Sp.* Fandango.

root. Fundamental tone of a chord.

rosalia (rō-zä'-lĭ-ä), **Rosalie** (rō-zä-lē'), *G.* 1. A sequence (q.v.) advancing a whole tone each time. 2. Music consisting of cheap and trite sequences and harmonies.

rose (in *G.* rō'-zĕ), **rosa** (rō'-zä), *I.*, **rosette** (rō-zĕt'), *F.* The orna-

mental border of the sound-hole of guitars, etc.

rosin (räz'-ĭn). Resin.

Rostral (rôs'-träl), *G.* A music-pen.

rote, *E.*, **ro'ta**, **rot'ta**, *I.*, **Rot'te**, *G.* "Wheel." 1. Canon, round. 2. Rondeau. 3. Hurdy-gurdy.

rotondo (rō-tôn'-dō), *I.* Round, full.

rot'to, *I.* Broken, interrupted.

ro'tula. A small round or carol.

roulade (roo-lăd), *F.* A florid passage, division, a grace.

roulement (rool-mäṅ), *F.* A roll.

round. 1. Popular form of canon in the unison or octave, without coda, and with a frequent harmonic support or *pes.* 2. A circle-dance. **round o.** A rondo.

round'el, roun'delay. A ballad of the fourteenth century with a recurrent refrain. Also a ring-dance.

roveciamento (rō-vä-shä-mĕn'-tō), *I.*, 1. Reversion. 2. Inversion.

rovescio (rō-vä'-shō), *I.* 1. Retrograde. 2. Inverted. Hence, **al r.** In inversion.

rua'na. Hindu violin.

rubato (roo-bä'-tō), *I.* "Robbed," borrowed, used of a tempo whose strict values are to be disregarded at caprice, the long notes stealing time from the short, etc. It should not depart so far from the tempo as to destroy the sense of rhythm.

Rückfall (rük'-fäl), *G.* Back-fall. **Rück-positiv'.** Vide POSITIVE. **Rück'gang.** Return of the leading theme.

Rückung (rük'-oongk), *G.* 1. Syncopation. 2. Change.

Rüdenhorn (rü'-dĕn-hôrn). Vide HIEFHORN.

Ruhepunkt (roo'-ĕ-poonkt), *G.* Rest. **R. steele, -zeichen.** A pause, a rest.

ruhig (roo'-ĭkh), *G.* Calm, gentle.

Rührtrommel (rür'-). An old-fashioned drum.

Rührung (rü'-roongk), *G.* Emotion.

rule. 1. Old name for line. 2. In music, as in science, not an edict by an authority, but a recorded observation by more or less qualified judges of what has happened with some regularity before. It need not necessarily happen always again. Vide OCTAVE.

rullan'do, rullante (rool-län'-tĕ), *I.* Rolling. **tamburo r.** Side-drum.

run. 1. A rapid flight of notes usually in scales, used in singing on one syllable. 2. Of air in an organ, to leak from the wind-chest into a groove, where it causes certain pipes to give a faint sound called running.

Rundgedicht (roont'-gĕ-dĭkht), *G.* 1. Rondo. 2. Solo with chorus. Also R.-gesang.

russe (rüs), *F.* Russian. à la r. In Russian style.

Russpfeife, Ruszpfeife (roos'-pfī-fĕ), *G.,* ruispipe (rois'-pē-pĕ), *Dutch.* Vide RAUSCHQUINTE.

Rus'sian bassoon. A deep-toned military instrument.

Russian horn band. One in which each horn plays but one tone.

rustico (roos'-tĭ-kŏ), *I.* Rural, rustic.

Rutscher (root'-shĕr), *G.* A galop.

ruvido (roo'-vĭ-dŏ), ruvidamĕn'te, *I.* Rough(ly).

ry'mour. Old *E.* Minstrel.

rythme, rythmé, *F.* Same as *rhythm(é).*

S

S. Abbr. (*dal*) *segno; senza* (*pedale*); *sinistra; solo; sordino;* (*volti*) *subito.*

sab(b)'eca. Hebrew harp.

sabot (să'-bō), *F.* 1. A disk turned by one of the pedals of a double-action harp and carrying two studs which engage and shorten the vibrating portion of a string. 2. A cheap fiddle.

saccade (săk-kăd), *F.* A firm pressure of the bow against two or more strings.

sack'but, sag'but. 1. An old instr. resembling the trombone. 2. Translation of sabeca.

Sackpfeife (săk'-pfī-fĕ), *G.* A bagpipe.

sacque-boute (săk-boot), *F.* Sackbut.

sa'cring-bell. Small bell marking the divisions of the Mass.

sac'rist. Music librarian, and copyist of a church.

sa'cred music. Religious music.

Saite (zī'-tĕ), pl. Saiten, *G.* String(s). Sai'teninstrument. A stringed instrument. S.-chor. A group of strings tuned in unison. S.-fessel, or -halter. Tailpiece. S.-harmo'-nika. A key-board instr. with diminuendo device, inv. by Stein, 1788. S.-orgel. A trichord piano with a fourth string for each note. This string is fanned by a reed of the same pitch, with leather head, thus obtaining a sustained tone, capable of swell and decrease. Treadles and bellows control this part of the instr., which may serve as piano, or organ, or both, or part of either. This instr. was inv. by a Prussian, Karl Gümbel, 1890. S.-klang, or -ton. The sound of a string. S.-spieler. Player on a stringed instr. saitig (zī'-tĭkh). Stringed.

saint's bell. Vide SACRING-BELL.

sal'amie. Oriental flute.

salcional (săl-sĭ-ō-năl). salicet (sä-lĭ-sä). sali'cionell, salicional (sä-lē'-sĭ-ō-năl), *F.* A reed-stop of stringy tone.

Salm (sälm), *G.,* salmo (säl'-mō), pl. i, *I.* A psalm.

salmi (säl'-mē), *F.* Quodlibet.

Salon'flügel, *G.* Parlour grand piano. Salonmusik or -stück. Music for the drawing-room.

sal'pinx. Ancient Greek trumpet.

saltando (säl-tän'-dō), *I.* 1. Proceeding by skips. 2. With bounding bow.

saltarella or (o) (säl-tä-rĕl'-lō), *I.* 1. A very quick dance, in 2-4, 6-8, or 6-4 measure with wide skips. 2. The triple-timed, second part of a 16th century dance in duple time (also called *Hop'peltanz* (tänts). *Nachtanz, G., proportio, L., tourdion, F.* 3. A jack. 4. A *cantus firmus* with accompaniment of sextuplets.

saltato (säl-tä'-tō), *I.* Springing. Vide SALTANDO.

salteret'to, *I.* 1. A rhythmic figure in 6-8 time, the first and fourth quavers dotted.

salter(i)'o (säl-tä-rĭ-ō), *I.,* Salteire (zäl-tī'-rĕ), Saltirsanch (zäl-tērs'-änkh), *G.* ɔ. Psaltery. s. tedesco. Dulcimer.

salto (säl'-tō), *I.* 1. Leap, skip. 2. Dance. di s. By skip.

salvar'(e) (säl-vä'-rĕ), *I.* To resolve.

salvation (săl-văs-yôṅ), *F.* Resolution.

Sal've Regi'na, *L.* "Hail Queen"; R. C. hymn to the Virgin Mary.

sambuca (säm-boo'-kä), *I.,* Sambat', Sambiut (zäm'-bĭ-oot), *G.* Word used variously and ambiguously for various mediæval instrs., bagpipe, hurdygurdy, etc. sambuc'is'tria. One who plays such an instrument.

Sammlung (zäm'-loongk), *G.* Collection.

sampogna (säm-pōn'-yä), sampo'nia, sampu'nia, *I.* 1. A flageolet. 2 Sambuca.

san'cho. A Negro guitar.

Sanct'us, *L.* "Holy." 1. Fourth movement of the Mass. 2. Vide SACRING.

sanft (zänft), *G.* Soft, mild. **S.-gedackt.** A soft-toned stopped pipe. **S.-heit.** Softness, smoothness, gentleness. **sänftig** (zĕnf'-tĭkh), **sanft'-mütig.** Soft, gentle. **S.-mut, S.-mütigkeit** (mü-tĭkh-kĭt). Softness.

Sang (zäng), *G.* Song.

Sänger (zĕng'-ĕr), *G.* Singer(s). **S.-bund** (boont). A society or convention of singers. **S.-verein** (fĕr-īn). Singers' union.

sanglot (säṅ-glō), *F.* "Sob." An old grace in singing, an interjection.

sans (säṅ), *F.* Without.

san'toral, *Sp.* Choir-book.

santur'. A Turkish instr., the psaltery.

saquebute (săk-büt), *F.* Sackbut.

saraband (săr'-ä-bănd), *E.*, **sarabanda** (sär-ä-bän'-dä), *I.*, **sarabande** (sär-ä-bănd in *F.*; in *G.* zä-rä-bän'-dĕ). A stately Spanish dance, perhaps derived from the Saracens, and danced with castanets; it is in slow 3-4 or 3-2 time, with the second note usually prolonged through the second and third beats of the measure.

sarrus'ophone. A double-reed instr., inv. by Sarrus, Paris, 1863. It is made in 6 sizes besides a sopranino and a contra-bass in E♭, and resembles a bassoon in appearance, a trombone in tone.

sartarella (or **-o**), *I.* A tarantella-like dance in 6-8 time.

Sattel (zät'-t'l), *G.* Nut. **S.-machen.** To use the thumb as a nut for producing harmonics on the 'cello. **S.-lage.** Half-position.

Satz (zäts), *G.* 1. Theme or subject. 2. Phrase, half a period, the former half being the **Vordersatz,** the second, the **Nachsatz.** 3. Section of a movement. 4. Movement. 5. A composition. 6. Style, school, as **reiner S.** Pure, strict style.

saun. Burmese harp.

saut (sō), *F.* Skip. **sauter** (sō-tä). To overblow. **sautereau** (sō-tĕ-rō). Jack. **sau'terie,** Old *E.* Psaltery.

sautillé (sō-tē'-yä), *F.* Springing bow.

sauver (sō-vä). To resolve. **sauvement** (sōv-mäṅ). Resolution.

saw'try. Psaltery.

Sax (zäx). A prefix for the numerous inventions or improvements of Adolphe Sax, the Christopher Columbus of metallic instruments, whose impor-

tance lies largely in the application of a valve-mechanism to old *natural* keyed instruments. **saxhorn.** An improvement in various sizes on the key-bugle and ophicleide, used chiefly in military bands except the tuba (q.v.). Saxhorns are made in the following seven principal sizes (variously named), and are also made a semitone lower than each of the following, the compass of each being given in brackets: *Bugles à Pistons:* 1. Sopranino saxhorn (petit saxhorn, petit bugle à pistons, piccolo in *Es.* or e♭ [range a–b'' flat]). 2. Soprano saxhorn (contralto saxhorn, bugle-tenor, Flügelhorn in *B* or B flat) [g–b'' flat]. 3. Alto saxhorn (Althorn in *Es.*) E flat [A–e'']. 4. Tenor saxhorn (baryton en *si♭*, Tenorhorn in *B*, Bassflügelhorn), in B flat [E–b' flat]. *Tubas or bombardons:* 1. Bass saxhorn (tuba-basse en *si♭*, Basstuba, Euphonium, Baryton, Tenorbass in *B*) in B flat [G,–b' flat], also made in C. 2. Low bass saxhorn (bombardon en *mi♭*) in E flat [G, flat–e' flat], also made in F . 3. Contrabass saxhorn (bombardon en *si♭* grave, Kontrabasstuba) in B flat [E flat–b flat], also in C. **sax'ophone.** A keyed brass instr. single-reeded and mouthed like a clarinet and combining in its tone that of the 'cello, cor anglais and clarinet. It is a transposing instr. written in the G clef, made in six sizes with two keys to each, the compass being nearly three octaves: 1. Sopranino or piccolo or aigu in *F* and *E♭*. 2. Soprano in *C* and *B♭*. 3. Contralto in *F* and *E♭*. 4. Tenor in *C* and *B♭*. 5. Barytone in *F* and *E♭*. 6. Bass in *C* and *B♭*. Also **saxofo'nia,** *I.* **sax'otromba.** An instr. in seven sizes standing in tone between the key-bugles, or saxhorns, and the horns. **sax-tuba.** Vide SAXHORNS (*Tubas*).

saynete (sä-ē-nā'-tĕ), *Sp.*, **saynete** (sĕ-nĕt), *F.* Comedietta for two singers.

sbalzo (sbäl'-tsō), *I.* Skip. **sbalzato** (tsä'-tō). Dashing.

sbar'ra, *I.* Bar. **s. doppia.** Double-bar.

scagnello (skän-yĕl'-lō), *I.* Bridge.

scala (skä'-lä), *I.* Scale, gamut.

scald. Scandinavian poet-musician.

scale. From the Latin *scala,* "a ladder," applied to the Aretinian syllables, ut, re, mi. fa, sol, la. In modern usage: 1. The tones of any key (q.v.) taken in succession up or down according to pitch; according to Riemann a chord of the tonic with passing notes, as *c, d, e, f, g, a, b,* and *c,* those passing notes being chosen which lead most inevitably to the next chord-note. **chromatic, diatonic, enharmonic, major, minor, pentatonic,** etc., **scales,** vide the adjectives. See page 762. The so-called German **s.** is a–h–c–d–e–f–g; "b," being reserved for b♭. Vide **H. natural** or **normals.** That of the key of C, which has no chromatics. 2. A series of semitones in successive order. 3. The series of tones belonging to any instr. as a natural horn, **harmonic** or **natural s.** The series of over-tones (vide ACOUSTICS). 4. A compass or range. 5. Dimensions and proportions, as the **s.** of organ-pipes, determined by the ratio of diameter to height, a **broad s.** giving a broad, smooth tone, a **narrow s.** giving a thin, sharp tone.

scannet′to, scanel′la (skä-něl′-lä), *I.* Bridge.

scemando (shě-män′-dō), *I.* Diminishing.

scena (shā′-nä), *I.,* **scène** (sěn), *F.,* **scene** (sēn), *E.* The portion between the entrances of different actors, hence a dramatic recitative usually followed by an aria, often **s. d'entrata** or **d'entrée** (dän-trä). Entry-song. **scenic music.** Dramatic music.

Schablonen (shäp-lō′-něn), *G.* Stencil-patterns, hence **S.-musik.** Trite and formal music. **S.-haft** (häft). Academic.

Schäfer (shä′-fěr), *G.* Shepherd. **S.-lied** (lēt). Pastoral song. **S.-pfeife.** Shepherd's pipe. **S.-tanz.** Rustic dance.

schalkhaft (shälk′-häft), *G.* Sportive, roguish.

Schall (shäl), *G.* Sound, ringing, resonance. **S.-becher, S.-horn, S.-stück,** or **S.-trichter.** Bell (of an instr.). **S.-becken,** *G.* Cymbals. **S.-loch.** Sound-hole. f.-hole. **S.-stab** (shtäp). Triangle.

Schalmay, Schalmei (shäl′-mī), *G.* 1. Shawm. 2. Chalumeau. 3. A reed-stop.

Schanzune (shän-tsoo′-ně), *G.* Chanson.

scharf (shärf), *G.* 1. Sharp. 2. Acute, of a stop.

schaurig (show′-rǐkh), *G.* Weird, ghastly.

Schauspiel (show′-shpēl), *G.* Dramatic piece. **Schauspieler.** Actor.

Scheitholt (shīt-hólt), *G.* Marine trumpet.

Schellen (shěl′-lěn), *G.* Bells, jingles. **S.-baum** (bowm). "Jingle-tree"; Crescent.

Scherz (shěrts), pl. **en,** *G.,* **scherzo** (skěr′-tsō), pl. **i,** *I.* "Jest." 1. A style of instrumental composition in which humour prevails (though those of Chopin are merely moody and whimsical). Those of Beethoven, the greatest master of this style, are often hilariously funny and provoke audible laughter. 2. A form developed from the Minuet and by Beethoven and his successors generally substituted as the 3d (or 2d) movement of the sonata (q.v.) or symphony. The structure varies greatly, but the time is usually triple. **scherzan′do, scherzan′te, scherzevole** (tsā-vō-lě), **scherzo′so,** *I.,* **scherzhaft** (shěrts′-häft), *G.* Sportive, mirthful. **scherzosamen′te,** *I.* Gaily.

schietto (skǐ-ět′-tō), **schiettamen′te,** *I.* Simp(ly). **schietezza** (těd′-zä), neatness.

schisma (skiz′-ma′), *Gr.* A minute difference between intervals. In ancient music, equal to the half of a comma, or the 18th of a tone; in modern acoustics, the 11th of a syntonic comma (the difference between the 3d tierce of the 8th quint and the octave of a given tone). Vide TEMPERAMENT, QUINT, and TIERCE.

Schlachtgesang (shläkht′-gě-zang), *G.* War-song.

Schlag (shläkh), *G.* 1. Stroke, blow. 2. Beat, impulse. **schlagen.** To beat. **Schlagfeder** (fā′-děr). Plectrum. **S.-instrument.** Instr. of percussion. **S.-mani(e)′ren.** The strokes in down-beating. **S.-zither.** The common zither as opposed to the bow-zither.

Schlägel (shlä′-khěl), *G.* Drumstick; hammer.

schlecht (shlěkht), *G.* Faulty, weak. **Schlechter taktt(h)eil** (shlěkh-těr-täkt-tīl), *G.* The unaccented part of a measure.

schleifen (shlī′-f'n), *G.* To slide, slur. **Schleifbogen** (bō-gěn). Slur. **Schleifer** (shlī′-fěr). 1. Slurred note.

2. Slow waltz. **Schleifzeichen.** Slur.

schleppen (shlĕp'-pĕn), *G.* To drag.

schleppend. Dragging.

Schlummer-lied (shloom'-mĕr-lēt), *G.* Slumber-song.

Schluss (shloos), *G.* 1. The end. 2. Cadence, also **S.-fall, S.-kadenz** (or note). Final cadence or note. **S.-satz.** A closing passage or movement. **S.-striche.** Double bar. **S.-zeichen.** 1. A firmate. 2. Double bar. **S.-reim** (rīm). Refrain.

Schlüssel (shlüs'-sĕl), *G.* A clef. **S.-fiedel.** Nail-fiddle. **S. G.** The note *g'* occupied by the G clef.

schmachtend (shmäkh'-tĕnt), *G.* Languishing.

schmeichelnd (shmī'-khĕlnt), *G.* Coaxing, caressing.

schmelzend (shmĕl'-tsĕnt), *G.* Melting.

Schmerz (shmĕrts), *G.* Grief, sorrow. **s.-haft, s.-lich.** Sorrowful.

Schnabel (shnä'-bĕl), *G.* "Beak," mouthpiece. **S.-flöte.** Vide FLUTE.

schnarr (shnär), *G.* Rattle. **S.-pfeifen,** or **-werk.** 1. Reed-pipes, reed-work. 2. Regal. **S.-töne.** A series of rough under-tones exactly paralleling and drowning the overtones as in a tuning-fork vibrating loosely on a box.

Schnecke (shnĕk'-ĕ), *G.* "Snail," scroll.

schnell (shnĕl), *G.* Quick, rapidly. **Schnel'le, Schnelligkeit** (shnĕl'-lĭkh-kīt). Rapidity. **schnel'ler,** *G.* 1. Quicker. 2. Inverted mordent. **Schnell'walzer.** Quick waltz.

Schollrohr (shôl'-rōr), *G.* Brass wind-instrument.

Schottisch (shôt'-tĭsh), *G.,* **schottische** (*E.* and *F.,* shŏt'-tĭsh). "Scottish," rather slow 2-4 time round dance.

schräg (shräkh), *G.* Oblique.

Schreibart (shrīp'-ärt), *G.* Style. **Schreiber.** Music copyist.

schreiend (shrī'-ĕnt), *G.* Screaming, acute. **Schreiwerk.** Acute (mixture-stop). **Schrei'erpfeife.** A sharp 3-rank mixture-stop in octaves.

schrittmäs'sig (shrĭt'-mĕs-sĭkh), *G.* Andante.

Schryari (shrē'-ä-rē), *G.* 1. An obsolete wind-instr. 2. Schreierpfeife.

schub (shoop), *G.* Slide (of a bow).

Schuh (shooh), *G.* "Shoe"; bridge of a marine trumpet. **S.-plattltanz.** An Austrian clog-dance.

schuiftrommpet (shwīf'-trôm-pĕt), *Dutch.* Sackbut.

Schule (shoo'-lĕ), *G.* A school or method. **schulgerecht** (ghĕ-rĕkht). Academic.

Schultergeige (shool-tĕr-gī'-khe), *G.* Shoulder-violin.

Schusterfleck (shoos'-tĕr-flĕk), *G.* Rosalia.

schwach (shväkh), *G.* Weak. **schwacher Taktteil.** Weak beat. **schwächer** (shvĕ'-khĕr). Softer.

Schwärmer (shwĕr'-mĕr), *G.* Rauscher.

Schwebung (shvä'-boongk), *G.* Waving. 1. Tremulant. 2. Beat (of vibration).

Schwegel (shvä'-khĕl). 1. A wind-instr. 2. A flue-pipe. **S.-pfeife.** A 4 or 8 ft. stop with tapering pipes.

Schweige (shvī'-khĕ), *G.* A rest. **S.-zeichen.** Rest-mark.

Schweinskopf (shvīns'-kôpf), *G.* "Pig's head." Used of the profile of a grand piano.

Schweizerflöte (shvī'-tsĕr-flä-tĕ). "Swiss flute." 1. Fife. 2. 8-ft. metal flue-stop. **S.-bass.** The 16-ft. stop on the pedal. **Schweizerpfeife.** 1. 4-ft. stop. 2. Old name of cross flute.

schwellen (shvĕl'-lĕn), *G.* To swell, increase. **Schweller.** The swell. **Schwellwerk.** Swell-organ. **Schwellton.** Messa di voce.

schwer (shvär), *G.* 1. Heavy, ponderous. 2. Difficult. **S.-mütig.** Melancholy.

Schwiegel (shvē'-gĕl), *G.* See SCHWEGEL.

Schwindend (shvĭn'-dĕnt). Dying away.

Schwingung (shvĭng'-oongk), *G.* Vibration.

scialumo (shäl-oo-mō'), *I.* Chalumeau.

scintillant(e) (sǎn-tē-yän(t) in *F.;* shēn-tĭl-län'-tĕ in *I.*). Brilliant.

scioltezza (shôl-tĕd'-zä), *I.* Ease. **sciolto** (shôl'-tō). 1. Light. 2. Free (of fugue). **scioltamen'te.** Easily.

scivolando (shē'-vō-län-dō), *I.* Glissando.

scolia (skō'-lĭ-ä), *Gr.* Festive lyrics.

scordato (skôr-dä'-tō), *I.* 1. Out of tune. 2. Tuned in an unmusical accordature. **scordatura** (too'-rä), *I.,* **scord'ature,** *E.* The unusual tuning of an instr. for special effects, as a violin b-d'-a'-e'' (Paganini).

score. 1. An arrangement of the parts of a composition with bars drawn (or "scored") across all the parts to connect the simultaneous measures. **full** or **orchestral s.** One with a stave to each part, voice or instr. **close, compressed,** or **short s.** (*a*.) One with more than one part on a single stave. (*b*.) An abridged score or sketch. **piano s.** A compression of score to two staves for the instruments with two additional staves for the voice, also **vocal s.** The **organ s.** has a 3d stave for the pedal. **supplementary s.** Staves pasted on when the parts are too numerous for the page. 2. *As a verb*, to arrange for instrs., hence scoring is instrumentation; **score-reading** or **playing**, the mental transposition of the different keys and clefs of a full score into one key.

corren'do, scorrevole (rä'-vō-lĕ), *I.* Gliding, flowing.

Scotch scale. Vide PENTATONIC.

Scotch catch, or **snap.** A rhythmic peculiarity in tunes; as the placing of an accented 16th note before a dotted eighth note with a snapping electric effect. It is a characteristic of Scotch music and also of American negro tunes.

scozzese (skŏd-zā'-sĕ), *I.* Scotch. **alla s.** In Scotch style.

scriva (skrē'-vä), *I.* Written. **si s.** As written.

scroll. The curved head of violins, etc.

sdegno (sdān'-yō), *I.* Disdain, wrath. **sdegnan'te.** Angry. **sdegno'so.** Disdainful.

sdrucciolare (sdroot-chō-lä'-rĕ), *I.* To slide the fingers along the strings or the keys of an instr., hence the noun **sdrucciolamen'to,** and the adjective, **sdrucciolado** (ä'-tō).

se (sä), *I.* If, as, etc. **se bisogna** (bē-sōn'-yä). If necessary. **se piace** (pĭ-ä'-chĕ). If it please (you).

sea-trumpet. Marine trumpet.

sec (sĕk), *F.*, **secco** (sĕk'-kō), *I.* Dry, unornamented, cold, sharp. Vide RECITATIVO. **à table sec** (ä tăb'l sĕk). Without accompaniment.

seccarara (sĕk-kä-rä'-rä), *I.* Neapolitan dance.

sechs (zĕkhs). Six. **S.-achteltakt.** 6-8 time. **S.-vierteltakt.** 6-4 time.

Sechs'er, sechstaktiger (täk-tĭkh-ĕr), **Satz,** *G.* A passage or period in 6 measures. **sechstheilig** (tī'-lĭkh). Six-fold, e. g., in 6 parts.

sechszehn (zĕkhs'-tsän), *G.* Sixteen. **S.-tel.** 16th note. **S.-telpause**

(pow-zĕ). 16th rest. **S.-füssig** (füs-sĭkh). 16-ft. pipe.

second(e) (in *F.* sŭ-kôn(d)), **seconda** or **o** (sā-kôn'-dä), *I.*, **Secunde** (zä-koon'-dĕ), *G.* 1. *As a noun,* (a) The interval (q.v.) between a tone and the next above or below. (b) Alto voice or part. (c) **secondo.** 2d part or player in a duet. (d) **chord of the second** (Secund'akkord). 6-4-2 chord. 2. *As an adjective,* (a) Lower in pitch, as 2d string. (b) Of lower rank or importance, as 2d violin. **seconde dessus.** 2d soprano, **secon'da don'na,** etc. (c) Higher, as the 2d space of a stave. (d) Second in order, as **seconde fois,** subject, etc. **secondan'do.** Following.

secondaire, temps (tän-sŭ-kôn-dăr'), *F.* Weak beat.

sec'ondary. Subordinate (of chords or themes), related (of keys).

sec'tio can'onis, *L.* "The section of the canon." The mathematical division of a string, upon a monochord.

sec'tion. Portion of a composition, variously used as (a) Half a phrase, (b) what is often called a phrase, (c) a group of periods with a distinct completeness. See FORM, p. 733.

sec'ular music. Music that is not sacred.

Secun'de, *G.* Vide SECOND.

secun'dum ar'tem, *L.* According to art or rule.

sedecima (sā-dā'-chē-mä), *I.* and *L.* Sixteenth. 1. Interval. 2. Stop.

Seele (zā'-lĕ), *G.* 1. Soul, feeling. 2. Sound-post. **Seelenamt** (sā'-lĕn-ämt) or **-mes'se.** Requiem.

seer. Bard or rhapsodist.

segno (sān'-yō), *I.* A sign :S:. **al s.** (return), "to the sign." **dal s.** (repeat) "from the sign," to the *Fine.*

segue (sā'-gwĕ), *I.* 1. Follows now follows, as *s. la finale.*—The finale now follows. 2. In a similar manner, to that which precedes. 3. Go on; *s. senza rit,* go on without retarding.

seguendo (sĕ-gwĕn'-dō), **seguen'te,** *I.* Following next. **seguenza** (sā-gwĕn'-tsä). A sequence.

seguidilla (sā-gwē-dēl'-yä), *Sp.* Spanish dance in 3-4 time, usually slow and in minor, with vocal and castanet or guitar accompaniment.

seguite (sĕ-gwē'-tä), *I.* Plural of segue.

seguito (sĕ-gwē'-tō), *I.* Followed, imitated.

sehnlich (zān'-lĭkh), *G.* Longing(ly).

Sehnsucht (zān'-zookht), *G.* Desire, longing. s.-svoll. Full of longing. sehnsüchtig (zān'-zükh-tĭkh). Longingly.

sehr (zār), *G.* Very much.

sei (sā'ē), *I.* Six.

Seitenbewegung (zeit'-ĕn-bĕ-vā'-goongk), *G.* "Side-wise," i. e., oblique motion (q.v.). Seitensatz (zäts). A "side-piece"; episode, or second subject.

seizième (sĕz-yĕm), *F.* Sixteenth.

Sekunde (zĕ-koon'-dĕ), *G.* Second. sekundi(e)ren (dē'-rĕn). To play a second part.

selah (sā'-lä), *Heb.* A term used perhaps to mark a pause or a place for the priests to blow the trumpets.

sem(e)iog'raphy. Notation by signs or notes.

semeiomelodicon (zā-mī'-ō-mĕ-lōd'-ĭ-kōn). A device inv. by Fruh, 1820, for aiding beginners; it consists of a series of note-heads which the finger presses, producing the corresponding tone.

semi (sĕm'-ĭ), *L.* and *I.* Half. s. biscroma. 32d note. semibreve rest. Whole rest. s. chorus. A chorus to be sung by half of the voices. s. cro'ma. A 16th note. semidemisemiquaver (rest). 64th note (or rest). s. diapa'son, diapen'te, diates'seron, di'tonus (or di'tone). Diminished or minor octave, fifth, fourth, third. semidi'tas. The diminution due to a stroke through the time-signature. semidi'tone, semifusa, or semiquaver. 16th note. semigrand. Small grand piano. s. min'im(a). Quarter note. semipausa (pä'-oozä). Whole rest. semiserio (sā'-rĭ-ō). Serio-comic. s. sus'pirium. Quarter rest. s. trillo. Inverted mordent.

sem'itone, *E.*, semito'nium, *L.*, semituono (sĕ-mĭ-too-ō'-nō), *I.* A half-tone, smallest interval written.

semi'tonique (tô-nēk'), *F.* Chromatic. semito'nium mo'di. The leading note. s. fic'tum (naturale). A chromatic (diatonic) half-tone.

semplice (sĕm'-plĭ-chĕ), *I.* Simple. semplicità (sĕm-plē-chĭ-tä'). Simplicity. semplicemen'te. Plainly, without ornament. semplicis'simo. With utmost simplicity.

sempre (sĕm'-prĕ), *I.* Always, continually, throughout.

sen'net. Old *E.* Repeating a note seven times.

sensibile (sĕn-sē'-bĭ-lĕ), *I.* Sensitive, expressive. nota s. Leading note. sensibilità (bē-lĭ-tä'). Feeling. sensibilmen'te. Expressively.

sensible (in *F.* säñ-sēbl). Leading note usually note s.

sen'tence. 1. An interlude strain in the Anglican Church service. 2. Short anthem. 3. Passage, or phrase.

sentimen'to, *I.* Feeling, sentiment.

senza (sĕn'-tsä), *I.* Without, sometimes followed by the infinitive with or without di, as *s. (di) rallentare*, without retarding.

separa'tion. 1. A device for keeping the great organ-stops from speaking. 2. A passing note in a tierce.

sept-chord. Chord of the 7th.

Septdezime (zĕpt-dā'-tsē-mĕ), *G.* A 17th.

septet (sĕp-tĕt'), *E.*, septet'to, *I.*, Septett (zĕp-tĕt'), *G.* Composition for seven voices or instruments.

septième (sĕt-yĕm), *F.*, Septime (zĕp'-tē-mĕ), *G.* Interval of a seventh. Sep'timenakkord. Chord of the seventh.

septimole (mō'-lĕ), septio'le, septo'le, sep'tuplet, *L.* and *I.* A group of seven equal notes.

septuor (sĕp-tü-ôr), *F.* Septet.

sequence (in *F.* sā-käñs), Sequenz (zā-kvĕnts'), *G.*, sequenza (sĕ-kwĕn'-tsä), *I.* 1. The repetition at least three times in succession of a musical pattern, a *melodic* or *harmonic* design, it may proceed chromatically or by whole tones. Vide ROSALIA. 2. A R. C. Church poem (Pro'sa) of the 9th century adopted to the long coda (or sequentia) of vocalising on the vowels of the Hallelujah. In 1568 Pope Pius V abolished all but these five: Victimae paschali laudes; Veni Sancte Spiritus; Lauda sion Salvatorem; Stabat Mater; Dies irae. These are still in use (vide also the separate titles).

ser'aphine (or -a). An early harmonium.

serenade, *E.*, sérénade (sā-rā-năd), *F.*, serenata (sā-rĕ-nä'-tä), *I.* "Evening music." 1. An open-air concert under the window of the person addressed. 2. An instrumental piece of like character. 3. A dramatic cantata of the 18th cent. 4. A composition in chamber-style of several movements.

sereno (sĕ-rä′-nō), *I.* Serene.

sérieusement (sä-rĭ-ŭz′-män), *F.* Seriously.

serinette (sŭr-ĭ-nĕt′), *F.* A bird-organ used for training birds to sing tunes.

seringhi (sĕ-rēn′-gē), *Hin.* Hindu violin.

serio (-a) (sä′-ri-ō), **serio′so,** *I.* Serious, grave.

ser′pent, serpente (sĕr-pĕn′-tĕ), **serpento′no,** *I.* 1. Long curved wood-instr. of coarse tone and compass of 2 octaves. It is practically obsolete, having yielded to the tuba. The **serpentcleide** is wooden but much like the ophicleide. The **contraserpent,** descended to E♭. 2. A reed-stop.

serv′ice. The music for a complete set of the solo and chorus numbers used in the Anglican Church ritual for morning and evening prayer and communion: Venite exultemus, Te Deum, Benedicite, Benedictus dominus, Jubilate, Kyrie, Credo, Sanctus, Agnus Dei, Benedictus fui venit, Gloria magnificat, Cantate Domino, Nunc dimittis, Deus misereatur (vide the separate titles).

sesqui (sĕs′-kwĭ), *L.* Latin prefix "a whole, and a half" joined with **al′tera, ter′tia, quar′ta,** etc., it expresses a kind of ratio. **sesquialtera** (sĕs-kwĭ-äl′-tĕ-rä). 1. The ratio of a perfect fifth which includes one and a half to one (3:2). 2. A 2 to 5 rank mixture-stop producing the 3d, 4th, and 5th partials. **sesquino′na.** Lesser, whole tone (ratio 9:10). **s.-octa′va.** Greater whole tone (8:9). **s.-ter′tia.** Perfect 4th (3:4). **s.-quar′ta.** Major 3d (4:5). **s.-quin′ta,** or **s.-tone.** Minor 3d (5:6).

sesto (sĕs′-tō), *I.* Interval of a sixth.

sestet (sĕs-tĕt′), *E.,* **sestet′to,** *I.* Sextet.

sestina (sĕs-tē′-nä), **sesto′la,** *I.* A sextole.

sette (sĕt′-tĕ), *I.* Seven.

settimo (sĕt′-tĭ-mō), *I.* Interval of a seventh. **settimo′la.** A septimole.

Setzart (zĕts′-ärt), *G.* Style of composition. **Setzkunst** (koonst). Art of composition. **Setzstück.** Crook.

seul(e) (sŭl), *F.* "Alone," solo.

seventeenth′. 1. Two octaves plus a tierce. 2. A tierce-stop.

sev′enth. Vide INTERVAL, CHORD.

severamente (sĕ-vär-ä-mĕn′-tĕ), *I.* Strictly. **severità** (sĕ-vä-rĭ-tä′). Exactness, strictness.

sext. 1. Interval of a 6th. 2. Vide HORAE. 3. A compound stop with 2 ranks a 6th apart.

sex′ta, *L.* Sixth; interval of a 6th.

Sexte (zĕx′-tĕ), *G.* 1. Sixth. 2. A stop with two ranks.

sexquial′tera. Vide SESQUI.

sextet′, *E.,* **Sextett′,** *G.,* **sextuor** (sĕx-tü-ôr), *F.* A composition for six voice-parts, or instrs. Usually a composition in sonata form for six instruments.

sext′ole, sex′tolet, sex′tuplet, *L.* A group of six equal notes. The false s. is a double triplet.

sex′tuple measure. Compound double measure.

sex′tus, *L.* Sixth.

sf. Abbr. of Sforzando.

sfogato (sfō-gä′-tō), *I.* "Exhaled." A lightly executed note. **soprano s.** A high voice.

sforza (sfôr′-tsä), *I.* Force. **sforzan′do, sforzato** (ä′-tō). "Forced," of a particular chord or note to be struck with immediate emphasis. If followed by a softer tone, it is **sfp.,** or **fzp. sforzare la voce.** To overstrain the voice. **sforzatamen′te.** Energetically.

sfuggito (sfood-jē′-tō), *I.* Avoided. Vide CADENCE.

sfumato (sfoo-mä′-tō), *I.* Exhausted (of breath).

sgallinacciare (sgäl-lĭ-nä-chä′-rĕ), *I.* To sing like a rooster (galinaccio).

shade. 1. To place anything near enough to the tip of a pipe to affect its vibration. 2. To observe gradations of force in executing music.

shake. 1. Trill. **double s.** Simultaneous shakes as on sixths or thirds **passing s.** A short trill. **prepared s.** A shake preceded by introductory notes. **shaked graces.** The beat, backfall, cadent, elevation, and double Relish. See GRACE, p. 737.

shalm. Shawm.

sharp. 1. A character (♯) raising the following note a half-tone; if in the signature, raising every note on the line or space it occupies. The **double s.** (×) marks an elevation of two half-steps. 2. *As an adj.* (a) Too high in pitch. (b) Augmented or major (of intervals). (c) With sharps in the key-signature. (d) Shrill (of stops). (e) A black

piano-digital; also any white digital regarded as a semitone above another. **to sharpen,** or **sharp.** To raise the pitch a semitone.
shawm. 1. Ancient Hebrew wind-instr., supposed to be of the reed class. 2. An early form of the oboe with double reeds in a mouthpiece; it still persists in the chanter of the bagpipe. 3. Vide CHALUMEAU.
shem'inith, *Heb.* 1. A stringed instr. 2. Species of music. 3. Section.
shepherd's flute. A short flute, blown through a lip-piece at the end.
shift. 1. A change of the left hand's position on the violin, etc. (vide POSITION), **half-shift** being the 2d position, **whole s.** the 3d, the **double s.** the 4th. 2. Any position except the first, hence **"on the shift"** and **shifting.**
shiv'aree. Corruption, probably of charivari; a grotesque discordant serenade with an orchestra of tin pans, cat-calls, etc., to bridal couples or to other objects of general ridicule. Philip Hale quotes from Gabriel Peignot's "Histoire morale, civile, politique, et littéraire sur Charivari, depuis son origine vers le ive siècle," the exact make-up of such an orchestra for a town of 15,000 or 20,000 inhabitants; "12 copper kettles, 10 saucepans, 4 big boilers, 3 dripping-pans, 12 shovels, and 12 tongs, 12 dish covers for cymbals, 6 frying-pans and pipkins, 4 warming-pans, 8 basins, 6 watering-pots, 10 handbells and mule bells, 4 strings of bells, 2 tambourines, 1 gong, 1 or 2 empty casks, 3 cornets-à-bouquins, 3 big hunting horns, 3 little trumpets, 4 clarinets (badly keyed), 2 oboes, ditto, 2 whistles (these will be enough), 1 musette, 4 wretched violins to scrape, 2 hurdygurdies, 1 marine-trumpet (if you can find one), 4 rattles, 10 screeching voices, 8 howling voices, 3 sucking pigs, 4 dogs to be well whipped. This is all that is necessary. I can assure you that when all this is vigorously set a-going at the same time, the ear will experience all desirable joy."
sho'far. A Heb. trumpet.
short. Vide METER, MORDENT, APPOGGIATURA, SCORE, SHAKE, OCTAVE.
shut'ter. One of the blinds of a swell-box. Vide ORGAN.
si (sē), *F.* and *I.* 1. The note or key of B. 2. Vide SOLMISATION. 3. One

(cf. French **on**), almost equal to **"you,"** as **si leva.** One lifts, you lift. **si piace.** One pleases, if you please, etc.
sib'ilus, *L.* A little flute.
Siciliana (sē-chē-lǐ-ä'-nä), or -**o,** *I.,* **Sicilienne** (sē-sēl-yěn), *F.* A Sicilian peasant dance of slow pastoral nature in 6-8 or 12-8 time. **alla s.** In Siciliana style.
side-drum. Vide DRUM.
side-beards. Vide BEARD.
Sieb (zēp), *G.* Sound-board.
sieben (zē'-běn), *G.* Seven. **S.-pfeife.** Pan's pipes. **S.-klang.** Heptachord. **Siebente** (zē'-běn'-tě). Seventh **Siebenzehnte** (zē'-běn-tsän-tě), *G.* Seventeenth.
Siegesgesang (zēkh'-ěs-gě-zäng), or **Siegeslied** (lēt), *G.* Triumphal song. **Sieges marsch.** A triumphal march.
si(e)fflöte (zēf'-flā-tě), *G.* A 1 or 2 ft. stop of the Hohlflöte species.
siffler (sǐf-flā), *F.* To whistle. **sifflet** (sǐf-flā). 1. A whistle. **s. de pan.** (päṅ). Pan's pipes. **s. diapa'son.** 1. Pitchpipe. 2. A cat-call.
Signalhorn (zēkh-näl'-hôrn), *G.* A bugle. **Signalist** (lēst). Trumpeter.
sign, musical. One of the numerous devices for expressing music visually. Vide chart, SIGNS AND SYMBOLS.
signatur (zēkh'-nä-toor), pl. -**en,** *G.,* **sig'nature,** *E.* 1. The tabulation at the beginning of a composition section or stave, showing (a) the key of the piece (*key-signature*), with such tones as are to be sharpened or flattened unless otherwise marked. (b) The governing time or rhythm (*time-signature*). 2. In Germany a figured bass sign.
signe (sēn'-yǔ), *F.* Sign, as **s. accidental.** An accidental. **s. de silence** (dǔ sē-läṅs). 1. A rest. 2. Vide SEGNO.
sig'net. Sennet.
sig'num, *L.* Sign.
siguidilla (sē-gwē-dēl'-yä), *Sp.* Seguidilla.
Silbendehnung (zēl'-běn-dä-noongk), *G.* Singing a syllable to more than one note.
silence (sē-läṅs), *F.,* **silenzio** (sē-lěn'-tsǐ-ō), *I.* A rest.
sillet (sē-yā), *F.* Nut. **petit s.** The nut at the neck of violins, etc. **grand s.** That at the tailpiece.
silver trumpet. Chatsoteroth. Many instrs. and strings are made of silver.
sim'icon, *Gr.* 35-stringed harp.

SIGNS AND SYMBOLS

(See also GRACES *and* NOTATION,)

NUMERALS AND ACCENTS.

1, 2, 3, etc. See CHORD, METRONOME, FINGERING, TEMPO and REST.

8, 8va. See OTTAVA.

2′, 4′, 8′, 16′. See FOOT.

①, ②, etc. See HARMONIUM.

2/4, 3/4, 6/8, etc. See TEMPO.

⌢³⌢, ⌢⁵⌢, or
..³.., ..⁵.., } See TRIPLET, QUARTOLE. etc.

a′, A′, b″, B″, etc.
or
a¹, b², a⁸, C₁, C₂, etc. } See PITCH.
a̲, a̲̅, etc.

4-tette, 5-tette, etc. Quartette, Quintette, etc.

1-ma, 2-da, etc. Prima (Seconda, etc.) volta.

Man. 1. The Great Organ.

Man. 2. The Choir Organ.

¢, ¢/, etc.
I, II, II₇, VII⁰, etc. } See CHORD.

O. 1. Open string. 2. See HARMONIC. 3. Tasto solo. 4. The heel, in organ-playing. See below.

DOTS, COMMAS, CURVES, LINES, ETC.

• See DOT and NOTATION.

• Staccato.

⌢… Slightly staccato.

⋯⋯ Slightly staccato and marcato.

❘ ❘ Very staccato. Martellato.

▬♪▬ Forte tenuto.

▬▬▬ or ⋯ ⋯⋯ Placed under notes sung to one syllable; in Tonic Sol-fa, placed under the letters.

⌢ Fermate.

÷ or ∥ Abbreviation indicating a repetition of the figure preceding, or of the previous measure(s) or part of a measure.

•S• ⦂S⦂ Presa.

𝄋 ⦂S⦂ ⊕ ⸮ Segno.

▦▦▦▦ Repeat.

× or + Thumb (pfte.-music).

♯ ♭ ♮ Sharp, Flat, Natural,

× Double-sharp.

ʾ or // // or ɣ ɣ Breathing-place.

— Tenuto. Pesante.

⌒ Mezzo legato.

⌒ Bind. Slur. Tie.

≋ Sign of a measure where no bar is required.

> ∧ ∨ < 1. Forte-piano (*fp*). 2. Rinforzando. 3. Sforzato (*sf*).

∧ ∨ or o ∧ or ⌣ ∨ Heel and toe ; in organ-playing placed above the notes for the right foot ; below, for the left.

∧ ⌣ ∧ Slide the toe to the next note.

∨ — ∧ Change toes on the same note.

∨ ∨ 1. Up-bow. 2. Breathing place.

∧ Down-bow in 'cello music.

⊔ ⊓ Down-bow on the violin.

⊓ ⊔ 1. In organ music, alternately heel and toe f the same foot. ˙. Bind.

⌜⌞ Notes thus connected are to be played with the same finger or hand; or to be sung *divisi*.

▭ Pesante.

⟨ Brace.

⌣ or ⌢ Notes so connected are to be played with the same hand, or continue a melody or a resolution from one staff to another.

〰〰 Sign of the continuation of a TRILL (q.v.) or of ALL' OTTAVA (q.v.).

⟨ Arpeggio. A chord preceded by this mark is to be played broken.

ⱽ ⱱ or ⱱ Direct.

ⱱ Inverted Mordent.

Ⱳ Mordent.

tr ⱳⱳ etc. Trill.

∾ Turn.

✳ ⊕ + Release damper-pedal.

└─┐ or └─┘ A recent improved sign marking exactly the points where the pedal is to be pressed and released.

♭ Thumb-position on the 'cello.

< Crescendo.

> Diminuendo.

NOTES. RESTS, AND SIGNATURES.

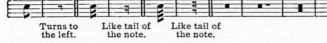

| | BREVE. | | | WHOLE. | | HALF- | | QUARTER- |
| Note. or | or | Rest. | Note. | Rest. | Note. | Rest. | Note. | Rest. or or |

Below the 4th line. Above or upon the 3rd line. Turns to the right.

| EIGHTH. | | SIXTEENTH. | | THIRTY-SECOND. | | Rests of more than one measure. |
| Note. Rest. | | Note. Rest. | | Note. Rest. Two. | | Three. Four. Four. Six. |

Turns to the left. Like tail of the note. Like tail of the note.

KEY SIGNATURES,—Capital letters indicate Major keys; small letters, the relative Minor keys which use the same signatures. White notes indicate the tonics of Major keys; black notes, the tonics of Minor keys.

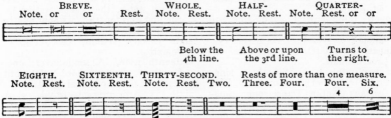

| C | G | D | A | E | B | F sharp | C sharp |
| a | e | b | f sharp | c sharp | g sharp | d sharp | a sharp |

| F | B flat | E flat | A flat | D flat | G flat | C flat |
| d | g | c | f | b flat | e flat | a flat |

sim'ilar. Vide MOTION.

simile (sēm'ĭ-lĕ), *I.*, **simil'iter,** *L.* Similarly. An indication that a certain manner of pedalling or playing is to be continued till otherwise indicated.

simp'la, low, *L.* Quarter note.

simple, *E.* (in *F.* säṅ-pl). 1. Not compound (of intervals). Vide COUNTERPOINT, IMITATION, RHYTHM, etc. 2. Plain, easy. 3. Without valves. **simplement** (säṅ-plŭ-mäṅ). Simply.

sin (sĭn), *I.* As far as. Vide SINO, **sin al.** As far as the.

sincopa (sĭn'-kō-pä), or **-e,** *I.* Syncopation.

sinfonia (sĭn-fō-nē'-ä), *I.*, **Sinfonie** (in *G.* zēn-fō-nē'; in *F.* säṅ-fō-nē). 1. Symphony. 2. In early operas, overture. **s. pittor'ica.** Descriptive symphony. **s. concertan'te, concerta'ta, concertate** (tä'-tĕ). Concerto for many instrs., a concerto symphony. **s. da cam'era.** Chamber quartet.

singen (zĭng'-ĕn), *G.* To sing, to chant. **Singakademie** (ä-kä-dĕ-mē'), **-anstalt** or **-verein.** Vocal society. **Singart** (zĭng'-ärt). Vocal art. **S. chor.** Choir.

singbar (zĭng'-bär). Singable. **singend** (zĭng'-ĕnt). Cantabile. **Sing (e)-tanz** (tänts). Dance-song. **Singfuge.** Vocal fugue. **Singmärchen** (mär'-khĕn). A ballad. **Singmani(e)ren** (mä-nē'-rĕn). Vocal embellishment. **Singschauspiel** (show-shpēl). Drama with songs. **Singschule** (shoo-lĕ). Vocal school or method. **Singspiel** (shpēl). 1. The original form of German opera in the 18th cent. Simple tunes were given to peasants, etc., florid songs to the aristocracy. (Vide J. A. HILLER in the B. D.) **Singstimme.** Voice, vocal part. **Singstück, Singweise.** Air, melody.

singhiozzando (sĭn-gĭ-ôd-zän'-dō), *I.* Sobbing.

sin'gle-action. Vide HARP.

single-chant. A simple melody to one verse of a psalm.

siniestra (sē-nĭ-äs'-trä), *Sp.*, **sinistra** (sĭn'-ĭs-trä), *L.* (in *I.* sē-nēs'-trä). Left (hand). **colla sinistra** (mano). With the left hand. **sinis'trae,** *L.* Vide TIBIA.

sink'apace. A five-step dance. Cinquepace.

sino (sē'-nō), *I.* To, as far as; usually **sin'al.**

si'ren, *E.*, **Sirene** (zē-rä'-nĕ), *G.*, **sirène** (sē-rĕn'), *F.* 1. A mythological being whose vocal powers captivated the human beings on whom she preyed; hence, a prima donna. 2. An instr. for counting vibrations.

Sir Roger de Coverley. An imaginary gentleman of the old school described by Addison; hence an English country-dance in 9-4 time.

sirventes (sēr-vänt), *F.* Troubadour songs of homage.

sistema (sēs-tä'-mä), *I.* Staff.

Sister (zēs-tĕr), *G.* Old 7-stringed guitar.

sis'trum, *L.* An ancient instr., consisting of an iron frame with a number of movable rings; when shaken or struck it sounded.

sit'ar. Hindu guitar.

sito'le. Citole.

Sitz (zĭts), *G.* Position, place.

six (in *F.* sēs). Six. Vide METER, 6-8 time, that in which there are six-eighth notes, the accent resting on the first and fourth. **six pour quatre** (poor kätr). Sextuplet.

sixte (sēkst), **sixième** (sēz-yĕm), *F.* A sixth.

sixteenth note. A semiquaver; one-fourth of a quarter note. **sixteenth rest.** A pause of equal duration.

sixth. 1. An interval (q.v.). 2. A chord. **chord of the s.** or **s. chord.** The first inversion of a chord (q.v.), chord of the **added s. (de la s. ajoutée).** Subdominant triad, with sixth added as f-a-c-d. Vide ALTERED. **little sharp s.** The 2d inversion of the seventh on the second degree. **extreme s.** Vide EXTREME and ALTERED. **six-four, six-five,** etc. Vide CHORD.

sixtine (sēx-tēn'), *F.* Sextuplet.

sixty-fourth (note). A hemidemisemiquaver. **s. rest.** A pause of equal duration.

Skalde (skäl'-dĕ), *G.* Vide SCALD.

skim'mington. A shivaree described in Hardy's novel "The Mayor of Casterbridge."

skip. A progression exceeding a whole step.

Skizze (skĭts'-zĕ), *G.* Sketch, a short piece.

slancio (slän'-chō), *I.* Vehemence.

slargando (slär-gän'-dō), **slargando'si.** *I.* Enlarging, gradually slower.

slentar'do, *I.* Becoming slower.

slide. 1. A movable tube in the shape of a U, used in the **slide-trumpet,**

slide-horn, and the **trombone** (q.v.).
2. A grace of two or more notes
moving diatonically. 3. A portamento. 4. A sliding lath strip which
cuts off a rank of pipes from the wind,
also **slider.** 5. **tuning-s.** A sliding
pitch-pipe sounding thirteen semitones. **sliding-relish.** 6. An old
grace, a slide (2).
slo'gan. Highland war-cry or rallying
word.
slur. 1. A curved line above or beneath two or more notes, which are,
(a) to be played legato, (b) to be
sung to one syllable, hence **slurred**
as opposed to *syllabic* melody.
small octave. Vide PITCH.
smaniante (smä-nĭ-än'-tĕ), **smaniato**
(ä'-tō), **smanio'so,** *I.* Frantic.
sminuendo (smē-noo-ĕn'-dō). Diminishing. **sminuito** (smē-noo-ē'-tō).
Softer.
smoran'do, *I.* Dying away.
smorfioso (smôr-fĭ-ō'-zō), *I.* Affected.
smorz. Abbr. of **smorzando** (smôr-
tsän'-dō), *I.* Dying away. Extinguished.
snap. Vide SCOTCH.
snare-drum. Side-drum. Vide DRUM.
snuff-box. 1. A musical box combined with a snuff-box. 2. A famous waltz written for it.
soave (sō-ä'-vĕ), **soavemen'te,** *I.*
Suave(ly), sweet(ly).
sobb. Damping (on the lute).
sock'et. The round joint which holds
the mouthpiece of a clarinet.
soggetto (sôd-jĕt'-tō), *I.* Subject,
theme, motive. **s. invariato** (ä'-tō).
The invariable subject. **s. variato**
(vä-rĭ-ä'-tō), *I.* Variable subject of
a counterpoint.
sognando (sōn-yän'-dō), *I.* Dreamy.
soh. Tonic Sol-fa, for Sol.
sol (sōl). 1. Vide SOLMISATION. 2.
The note G in France and Italy.
sola (sō'-lä), *I.* Alone, solo.
solem'nis, *L.* Solemn.
solenne (sō-lĕn'-nĕ), **solennemen'te,** *I.*
Solemn(ly). **solennità** (ĭ-tä'). Solemnity.
solfà (sōl-fä'), *I.* 1. Gamut; scale.
2. A bâton. 3. Time, **a bat'tere la
s.,** to beat time.
solfa, *E.* 1. Solmisation (q. v.). 2.
Solfeggio. 3. To sing in solmisation
or solfeggio. 4. Vide TONIC SOL-FA.
solfège (sŭl-fĕzh), *F.,* **solfeggio** (sōl-
fĕd'-jō), *I.* Exercise for the voice in
solmisation or on one syllable. **sol-
feggiare** (sōl-fĕd-jä'-rĕ), *I.,* **solfeg-**

gi(e)ren (zōl-fĕd-jē'-rĕn), *G.,* **solfier**
(sŭl-fĭ-ā), *F.* To sing a solfeggio.
soli (sō-lē), *I.* 1. Plural of solo. 2. A
passage played by one performer to
each part.
sol'id. Of a chord not *broken* (q.v.).
so'list. Soloist, solo-player.
solito (sō-lē'-tō), *I.* Usual. **al s.** As
usual.
sollecito (sōl-lā'-chē'-tō), *I.* Careful,
exact.
solmisation. "The singing of the syllables *do, re,* sol, mi, etc." A venerable method of teaching and singing
scales and intervals ascribed to Guido
D'Arezzo (or Aretinus). It is a convenient crutch for those who are not
going far; but must soon be discarded.
Greek music (Vide MODES) divided
the complete scale into groups of
four consecutive degrees or *tetrachords.* Guido or a disciple divided it
into groups of six degrees, or *hexachords.* It happened that the initial
syllables of the six phrases of a certain familiar hymn to St. John
formed the ascending scale of one of
these hexachords (the one called
naturale). The device was hit upon
(as an aid for weak memories) of
using these syllables as names of the
notes; hence the notes of this hexachord began to be called ut, re, mi,
fa, sol, la. (The hymn ran as follows: "*Ut* queant laxis, *Re*sonare
fibris *Mi*ra gestorum *Fa*muli tuorum
*Sol*ve polluti *La*bii reatum, Sancte
Johannes.") It was later found
convenient to use these syllables for
other hexachords, the *ut* being
movable. A crude form of modulation was developed called *mutation.*
When the modern scale came into
play early in the 17th cent. it
brought into use the heptachord or
scale of seven degrees. A new
syllable *si* was therefore devised
and the so-called *Aretinian syllables,*
used for singing in all the keys; *ut,*
being always the tonic, *sol,* the dominant, etc. The syllables have persisted for primary use and for vocal
exercises ever since. In many countries they have been since used as the
definite names of the notes of the
scale of C, except that the syllable
do (being more easily sung) has displaced *ut* except in France, since its
first use (perhaps by Bononcini), in
1673. This is the only change that

has been accepted among the many that have been advocated, such as the *bocedisation*, or *bodisation* (bo, ce, di, ga, lo, ma, ni) of Waelraut, 1550 (Pedro d'Urenna in 1620 proposing ñi for si), and the *bebisation*, or *labecidation* (la, be, ce, de, me, fe, ge)—satirically called *labisation*—of Hitzler in 1628. The *damenisation* (da, me, ni, po, tu, la, be) of Graun, 1750, was not for solmisation but for use in place of words in vocalising.

solo (sō'lō), *I.* 1. As adjective, "alone." 2. A passage or composition for a single voice or instr. **violino solo** may mean either "violin only"; or the solo (i. e., leading) vln. **solo-organ.** A manual of the organ (q.v.). **solo pitch.** A scordature (q.v.) used by a soloist. **solo quartet.** A group of four soloists; a composition for such a group; a solo with 3-part accompaniment. **solo-stop.** Vide STOP. The word is used in compounds of various languages, as **Solo-sänger,** *G.* Solo-singer, etc.

solomanie (sō-lō-mä-nē'). A Turkish flute, without reed.

sombrer (sòn-brä), *F.* To give a sombre, veiled tone.

somma (sòm'mä), *I.* Greatest, highest, extreme.

Sommer'ophone. A bombardon-like instr. inv. by Sommer of Weimar, 1843 (also called *euphonion, euphonic horn*).

son (sòn), *F.*, **son** (sōn), *Sp.* Sound. **s. harmonique** (sō-nǎr-mō-nēk). Harmonic.

sonabile (sō-nä'-bĭ-lĕ), **sonante** (nän'-tĕ), *I.* Sounding, sonorous.

sonare (sō-nä'-rĕ), *I.* To sound; to ring; to play. **s. alla mente.** To improvise.

sonata (sō-nä'-tä), *I.*, **Sonate** (in *F.* sō-nǎt, in *G.* zō-nä'-tĕ). Music "sounded or played" as opposed to music sung (*cantata*). Originally any instrumental piece, as **s. da chiesa.** For church. **s. da camera.** For the salon. Later the term was applied to a group of three to five dance-tunes of varied rhythms. The treatment came to be less and less lyrical and more and more thematic (q.v.). Such were Bach's organ and violin sonatas. The very human Haydn added a lyric interest as contrast in the form both of counter-themes to the principal

theme and of separate movements of melodious character. Mozart made no formal change but added more human interest and warmth. The sonata now consisted of 3 or 4 movements; first an allegro written on what is confusedly called the sonata-form (the editor suggests "sonata-formula" (q.v.) as a substitute term for describing the structure of this one movement, retaining the word "sonata-form" for the entire group of movements); second, a slow movement; third a minuet; fourth, a rondo, or finale on the same formula as the first movement. Beethoven substituted for the minuet a light and witty scherzo (q.v.); other composers have made other substitutions. This general group of varied movements and moods is applied to many form notably the symphony, the classic overture, the concerto, the string quartet, and chamber-music generally, which are hence said to be "in sonata-form." The **sonata-formula, sonata-piece,** or **Sonatasatz** (zäts), the structure of the first movement, marks the highest period of classic formalism. See article on FORM, p. 733. The word is qualified in many ways as *grand,* a highly elaborate form, *double,* for two solo instrs. A short easy composition with few movements and little development is called **sonatina** (sōn-ä-tē-nä). **sonatil'la,** *I.*, **Sonatine** (zō-nä-tē-nĕ), *G.*

sonatore (tō'-rĕ), feminine **sonatrice** (trē'-chĕ), *I.* A man (or woman) instrumentalist.

sonevole (sō-nä'-vo-lĕ), *I.* Resounding.

sonetto (sō-nĕt'-tō), *I.* A composition based on a poetic sonnet.

song. 1. A melody for voice. 2. Lyric piece for any instr.

song-form. A structure of 3 chief sections, (a) a first theme, (b) a contrasting second theme, (c) a return of the first theme. In poems of many stanzas, the same air is commonly used for all the stanzas regardless of changed language and emphasis. This *strophic* treatment is discarded by more conscientious composers for a treatment in which each stanza is individually set to music with intelligent deference to its meaning. This is the *through-composed* or *durchkomponi(e)rt* (doorkh-kôm-pō-nērt') style.

song without words. A lyric instrumental piece.

sonnante (sòn-nänt), *F.* A scale of hanging steel bars struck with a hammer.

sonner (sŭn-nā), *F.* To sound. **s. le tambour** (lŭ tän-boor). To sound the drum, used of a jarring G string in the 'cello.

sonnerie (sŭn-rē), *F.* 1. Chime. 2. Military call.

sono (sō-nō'), *I.* Sound, tone.

sonomètre (sō-nō-mĕtr), *F.*, **sonome'-ter.** 1. A monochord inv. by Loulis to aid piano-tuners. 2. A sounding-board with two strings for acoustic experiments.

sonore (sō-nôr), *F.*, **sonoro** (sō-nō'-rō), *I.*, **sonoramen'te.** Sonorous(ly). **sonoridad** (sō-nō-rĭ-dädh'), *Sp.*, **sonorità** (sō-nō-rĭ-tä'), *I.*, **sonorité** (sō-nō-rĭ-tā), *F.* Sonority.

sonor'ophone. A form of bombardon.

sonorous (sō-nō'-rous). Capable of musical sound; sounding.

so'nus, *L.* Sound, tone.

so'pra, *I.* Over, above, upon, before. **com'e s.** As above. **di s.** Above. **s. u'na cor'da.** On one string. **par'te di s.** Higher part. **s. dominante.** The dominant. **s. quinta.** Upper dominant. **s. to'nica.** Supertonic.

soprano (sō-prä'-nō), *I.* (pl. -i), **Sopran** (zō-prän'), *G.* 1. The highest kind of human voice, differing from the alto in lying chiefly in the "head-register"; this voice is typically a woman's voice, but is also found in boys. It occurs naturally in some men (called *falsetti, alti naturali,* or *tenorini*), but was obtained artificially in others (called *evirati, castrati*), particularly in the last century when the eunuch "artificial" sopranos achieved marvellous power and agility. The soprano voice has an average range from c'–a'' (Vide PITCH), the tones from f' up being head-tones. The voice occasionally reaches lower, and often higher than this normal range, c''', being not unusual. A voice that reaches f''' or g''' is phenomenal (Agujari sang c'''' three octaves above mid-C). (Vide also MEZZO-SOPRANO.) Soprano voices are divided into the more powerful or *dramatic* (*drammat'ico*), and the flexible, and light or *lyric* (*leggiero*) (lĕd-jä'-rō) or *légier* (lä-zhā). 2. The part sung by the

highest voice or the highest instrument. 3. The instr. which is the *highest* of its class (sometimes an extra high instr. is called **sopranino**). 4. The possessor of a soprano voice. **soprana chorda** (kôr-dä). The E string of a violin. **sopran'ist.** A male soprano. **soprano clef.** The C clef on the first line of the staff; sometimes used of the G clef.

sordo (sôr'-dō), *I.* Muffled, veiled tone. **sordamen'te.** Soft(ly).

sordellina (lē'-nä), *I.* A small 4-piped bagpipe.

sor'dine, *E.*, **Sordino** (sôr-dē'-nō, pl. -i, German pl. -en), *I.* 1. A small tone-softening device, damper or mute to set against piano-strings, in the mouth of a trumpet, or on the bridge of a violin. 2. A kit. **con s.** In piano-playing "use the soft pedal"; in playing violin, horn, etc., "use the mute." **senza** (sĕn'-tsä), **s.** or **s. levato** (lĕ-vä'-tō). "Remove the mute or damper."

sordo'no, *I.*, **sordone** (sôr-dŭn), *r.*, **Sordun** (zôr-doon'), *G.* 1. Obs. bombard of 5 sizes, and 12 ventages. 2. An old stop. 3. In *G.* a trumpet-mute.

sorgfältig (zôrkh'-fĕl-tĭkh), *G.* Careful(ly).

sortita (sôr-tē'-tä), *I.* 1. Entrance aria. 2. Voluntary for close of service.

sospensione (sĭ-ō'-nĕ), *I.* Suspension. **sospensivamen'te.** Doubtfully.

sospiran'do, sospirante (rän -tĕ), **sospirevole** (rä'-vō-lĕ), **sospiro'so,** *I.* 1. Sighing, doleful. 2. A sobbing catch in the breath.

sostenen'do, sostenen'te, *I.* Sustaining the tone.

sostenuto (sōs-tĕ-noo'-tō), *I.* 1. Sustained, prolonged, retarded. 2 Gradually retarded. 3. Andante.

sostinen'te, *I.* Used of instrs. with special device for sustaining tones.

sotto (sôt'-tō), *I.* Under, below. **s. voce** (vō'-chĕ). In an undertone. **s. dominan'te.** Sub-dominant.

soubass (soo-bäs), *F.* Sub-bass.

souf'farah. Oriental reedless wind-instrs. in general.

soum. Burmese harp.

soufflerie (soof-flĕ-rē), *F.* The bellows action. **soufflet** (soof-flä). Bellows. **souffler** (soof-flä). To blow. **souffleur** (flŭr), fem. **souffleuse** (flŭz). 1. Organ-blower. 2. Prompter.

sound. Vide ACOUSTICS.

sound-board, sounding-board. 1. A thin resonant board which by sympathetic vibrations enlarges, enriches and prolongs the tone of the strings stretched across it (as in pianos, the belly of violins, etc.). 2. The cover of the wind-chest, **sound-body** or **box**, a resonance box; s. **bow**, the rim of a bell; s. **hole**, a hole in the resonance box to give communication from the resonance chamber to the air. s. **post.** Vide VIOLIN. s. **register.** A sound-recorder inv. in Paris, 1858. s. **waves.** The alternate condensation and rarefaction of air in vibration (q.v.).

soupape (soo-păp), *F.* Valve.

soupir (soo-pēr), *F.* A quarter rest. **demi-s.** 8th rest. **quart de s.** 16th rest. **huitième** (or **demi quart**) **de s.** 32d rest. **seizième.** 64th rest.

sourdeline (soor-dĕ-lēn), *F.* Sordellina.

sourdement (soord-män), *F.* In a subdued manner.

sourdine (soor-dēn), *F.* 1. Sordino. 2. A soft harmonium-stop. 3. Céleste pedal. 4. An old spinet.

sous (soo), *F.* Under, below. s.-**chantre** (shäntr). Subcantor. s.-**dominante.** Sub-dominant. s.-**médiante.** Sub-mediante. s.-**tonique.** Leading note.

soutenir (soo-tĕ-nēr), *F.* To sustain.

souvenir (soo-vĕ-nēr), *F.* Reminiscence.

Sp. Abbr. of Spitz.

space. The interval between 2 lines of the staff, or between 2 ledger lines.

spagnuola (spän-yoo-ō'-lä), *I.* The guitar.

spalla (späl'-lä), *I.* Vide VIOL.

spanisch (spän-ĭsh), *G.*, **spagnolesco** (spän-yō-lĕs'-kō), *I.* Spanish. **spanischer Reiter** (rī'-ter), *G.* Tones made by *running.* **spanisches Kreuz** (kroits), *G.* Double sharp.

spar'ta, spartita (spär-tē'-tä), or -o, *I.*, **Sparte** (spär'-tĕ), *G.* Partitura.

spartire (tē'-rĕ), *I.* To score; particularly to rescore an old work.

spassapensiero (pĕn-sĭ-ā'-rŏ), *I.* Jew's harp.

spasshaft (späss'-häft), *G.* Sportive(ly). S.-**tigkeit** (tĭkh-kīt). Sportiveness, playfulness.

spa'tium, *L.*, **spazio** (spä'-tsĭ-ō), *I.* A space.

spe'cies. Kind. Vide COUNTERPOINT.

Sperrventil, *G.* Vide VENTIL 2.

spezzato (spĕd-zä'-tō), *I.* Divided.

spianato (spĭ-ä-nä'-tō). 1. Legato. 2. Calm.

spiccato (spĭk-kä'-tō), *I.* Separated. Pointed. Vide BOW.

Spiel (shpēl), *G.* Playing; style of playing. S.-**art.** 1. Style of performance. 2. Touch. s.-**bar.** Playable. S.-**leute** (loi-tĕ). 1. The drummer and fifers of a band. 2. Strolling players. S.-**manieren** (mä-nē'-rĕn). Ornaments, graces. S.-**oper.** Light opera. S.-**tenor,** etc. Light opera tenor, etc.

Spillflöte, *G.* Spitzflöte.

spina (spē'nä), *L.* "Thorn," jack-quill of a spinet (q.v.).

Spin'delflöte, *G.* Spitzflöte.

spinet (spĭn'-ĕt or spĭ-nĕt'), *E.*, **Spinett** (spĭ-nĕt'), *G.*, **spinet'ta,** *I.* Obsolete and small square form of harpsichord, originally called the couched harp, later called spinet, from its quills, or spinae.

spirito (spē'-rĭ-tō), *I.* Spirit, energy. **spirituo'so, spirito'so, spiritosamen'-te.** Spirited(ly).

spirituale (spē-rĭ-too-ä'-lĕ), *I.*, **spirituel** (spĭr-ĭ-too-ĕl'), *F.* Spiritual.

spis'si gravis'simi, *L.* Hypatoides — the deep sounds of the Greek system. **spis'sus,** *L.* "Thick"; full (of intervals).

Spitz (shpĭts), *G.* Point (of bow); toe (of foot). S.-**flöte** (flā-tĕ). A soft stop with pointed pipes. S.-**quint.** Its quint. S.-**harfe** (här'-fĕ). Pointed harp. A small harp with strings on each side of its sounding board.

spondau'lium. Greek hymn with flute.

spread. Open.

spressione (ĭ-ō'-nĕ), *I.* Expression.

springing bow. Vide BOW.

Sprung (sproongk), *G.* A skip. s. **weise** (vī-zĕ). By skip.

square. Vide ORGAN. **square B.** Vide B. **square piano.** Vide PIANO.

squil'la, *I.* A little bell. **squillan'te.** Tinkling.

srou'tis. The 22 degrees of the Hindu scale.

sta (stä), *I.* "Let it stand"; i. e., to be played just as it stands.

Stab'at Ma'ter Do'loro'sa, *L.* "The grieving Mother stood," a hymn on the Crucifixion, written by Jacoponus, 14th cent. Vide SEQUENCE.

stabile (stä'-bĭ-lĕ), *I.* Firm.

stac. Abbr. of Staccato.

staccare (stäk-kä'-rĕ), *I.* To play staccato.

staccato (stäk-kä'-tō), *I.* "Detached," used of short, non-legato notes or a touch which leaves the key or string immediately. This crispness is marked over the notes by round dots called **staccato marks**; it may be modified by a slur over the dots, or emphasised by small wedge-like dots. **staccatis'simo.** As staccato as possible.

Stadt (shtät), *G.* Town, city; used of a salaried municipal musician, as **S.-musikus, -pfeifer,** etc.

staff, stave. The five horizontal parallel lines on, between, above and below which the notes are placed, the pitch of the note being determined by the key-signature and the clef, from which the **s.** takes its name. The usual arrangement is a **bass s.** (with F clef) under a **treble s.** (with G clef); they form a continuous notation except for the middle C, which is sometimes given a line, making the **11-line** or **great s. s. notation** is opp. to alphabetical notation. The **Gregorian s.** had 4 lines.

Stahlharmo'nika (shtäl), *G.* Steel bars played (a) with a bow, inv. by Nobe, 1796, (b) with a hammer; more commonly **Stahlspiel** (shtäl-shpēl).

Stamentienpfeife (shtä-mĕn'-tĭ-ĕn-pfī'-fĕ), *G.* Vide SCHWEGEL.

Stamm (shtäm), *G.* Stem, trunk. **S.-akkord.** A chord in root position, unaltered and uninverted. **S.-ton.** Natural tone. **S.-tonleiter.** Key of C major.

stampita (stäm-pē'-tä), *I.* A song.

Ständchen (shtĕnt'-khĕn), *G.* Serenade.

Standhaftigkeit (shtänt'-häf-tĭkh-kīt), *G.* Firmness.

stanghetta (stän-gĕt'-tä), *I.* A bar.

sta'ple. The tube which holds the oboe's reed.

stark (shtärk), *G.* Strong, loud. **stärker** (shtĕr'-kĕr). Louder.

stave. Staff.

steam-organ. Calliope.

stec'ca, *I.* A choked and strained tone-production.

Stecher (stĕkh'-ĕr), *G.* Sticker. Vide ORGAN.

Steg (stäkh), *G.* Bridge.

Stellung (shtĕl'-loongk), *G.* Position.

stem. The thin stroke attached to the head of a note.

stentan'do, *I.* Retarding. **stentato** (tä'-tō). Slow and forced.

step. A progression to the adjoining note or tone, hence **whole-step,** and **half-step** or **chromatic-step; a** diatonic-step is a progression to the next note of the key.

sterbend (shtĕr'-bĕnt), *G.* Dying away. **Sterbelied** (shtĕr'-bĕ-lēt). Death-song.

steso (stā'-sō), *I.* Extended, prolonged, slow.

stes'so, *I.* The same. **s. tempo.** Same time.

sthénocire (stä-nō-sēr), *F.* A finger-strengthener.

stibbacchiato (stĭb-bäk-kĭ-ä'-tō), *I.* Retarded.

sticca'do, sticcato (stĭk-kä'-tō), *I.* Xylophone.

stick'er. Vide ORGAN.

Stiefel (shtē'-fĕl), *G.* Boot (of a pipe).

Stiel (shtēl), *G.* 1. Stem. 2. Neck.

Stift (shtĭft), *G.* Jack (of violin).

Stil (shtēl), *G.,* **stile** (stē'-lĕ), **stilo** (stē'-lō), *I.,* **sti'lus,** *L.* Style. **s. rigoro'so,** or **osservato** (vä'-tō). Strict style. **s. rappresentativo** (tē'-vō). See OPERA.

still (shtĭl), *G.* Calm, quietly. **S.-gedackt.** A stopped diapason.

Stimme (shtĭm'-mĕ), pl. **-en,** *G.* 1. The voice. 2. Part. **mit der S.** Colla parte. 3. Organ-stop. 4. Sound-post. **Stim'menssatz.** Vocal attack. **Stimm'bänder** (bĕnt-ĕr). Vocal cords. **S.-bildung.** Voice-building. **S.-bruch** (brookh). Change of voice. Vide MUTATION. **S.-buch.** Part-book. **Stimmer.** Tuner; drone. **stimmen.** To tune, or voice. **Stimmflöte,** or **-pfeife.** Pitch-pipe. **S.-führer.** Chorus-leader. **S.-mittel.** Vocal capacity. **S.-ritze** (rĭt-zĕ). Glottis. **S.-holz** (hōlts), or **-hölzchen** (hĕlts'-khĕn), or **-stock.** Sound-post; wrestplank. **S.-werkzeuge** (vĕrk'-tsoi-khĕ). Vocal organs. **S.-führung** (fü-roongk). Part-progression. **S.-gabel** (gä-bĕl). Tuning-fork. **S.-hammer** (häm-mĕr). Tuning-hammer. **S.-horn.** Tuning-cone. **S.-keil.** Tuning-wedge. **S.-krücke.** Tuning-wire. **S.-zange.** Tuning-tongs. **S.-umfang, S.-weite** (vī-tĕ). Compass.

Stimmung (shtĭm'-moongk), *G.* 1. Tune. 2. Accordature. 3. Pitch. 4. Mood. **S. halten.** To keep the key. **S.-bild.** Tone-picture.

stinguendo (stĭn-gwĕn'-dō), *I.* Dying away.

stiracchiato (stē-räk-kĭ-ä'-tō), **stirato** (stē-rä'-tō), *I.* Retarded.

sti'va, *L.* See NEUMA.

Stock (shtôk), *G.* Bundle of 30 strings. **S.-fagott.** Rackett. **S.-flöte.** 1. Bamboo flute. 2. A flute in a walking-stick. **Stöckchen** (shtĕk'-khĕn). Heel (of violin, etc.). (See article on musical instruments, page 811.)

stolz (shtôlts), *G.* Proud.

stonante (nän'-tĕ), *I.* Dissonant.

stone-harmon'ica. See LAPIDEON.

stop. 1. Loosely used for (a) draw-knob and stop-knob and draw-stop, which only carry the label and, by admitting wind, bring into play the stop proper. (b) A mechanical stop, which does not sound or speak, but acts as a coupler, a bell-signal, a tremulant, etc. Strictly, the **sounding,** or **speaking stop** is a complete graduated series of organ-pipes of uniform quality. It is this quality which gives the stop its individual name (as *dulciana, cremona,* etc.). Stops are divided into two chief classes, (a) those with flue-pipes, **flue-work,** or **flue-stops,** and (b) those with reed-pipes (q.v.), **reed-work,** or **reed-stops.** **flue-work** is again divided, according to the character of the pipes, into (a) the cylindrical open pipes that give the **diapason,** or typical organ-quality, also called **principal-stops,** or **-work;** (b) covered, plugged, or stopped pipes (without chimneys), **gedacktwork;** (c) pipes too broad or too narrow of scale to give diapason tone, 3 or 4 sided wooden pipes, and stopped pipes with chimneys.

stops are further grouped according to the length of their pipes as 2-ft., 4-ft., 8-ft., etc., the standard being the 8-ft., or **foundation-stops,** which are the basis of the organ, and to which the other stops are tuned (vide FOOT).

stops which do not produce the unison or the octave of the key-board, but sound the third (tierce), fifth (quint) and such of their octaves as the tenth (double tierce), fifteenth, etc., are called **mutation-stops.**

furniture, mixture, or **compound stops** are composed of 2 or more ranks of pipes and produce the octave of the key depressed and also one or more of its other overtones. A **stop may have its pipes** *divided* between two draw-knobs. If it has a pipe for every key of the key-board, it is *complete;* otherwise it is an *imperfect, incomplete, partial* or *half-stop.*

Some stops are given only to the *pedal;* or to only one of the manuals: these are said to be *on* the pedal, *on* the swell, etc. A **solo-stop** is one complete enough in itself to sound a melody. **stopped.** Vide PIPE.

stop. 2. A fret, or similar position on an unfretted instr. 3. The pressure of the finger at a nodal point of a string. **double stop.** The stopping, hence sounding, of two or more notes at once on the violin, etc. 4. On a wind-instr. the closing with key or finger of a ventage. 5. On horns, etc., the inserting of the hand in the bell to produce a raised tone of muffled quality. Such a tone is said to be **stopped,** as opposed to open or natural.

stop'fen, *G.* To stop (of trumpet, etc.). **stopftöne** (shtôpf'-tä-nĕ). Stopped tones.

stop-knob. Vide STOP.

stor'ta, *I.* A serpent. **stortina** (tē'-nä). A small serpent.

Stosszeichen (shtôs'-tsī-khĕn), *G.* Staccato mark.

str. Abbr. for String(s).

straccicalando (strät-chí-kä-län'-dō), *I.* Prattling.

straccinato (strä-chĭ-nä'-tō), *I.* Retarded.

Strad., Stradivari, Stradivarius, etc. A violin made by Stradivari (vide B. D.), A. D. 1650.

strain. Section, motive, theme, air.

strascicando (strä-shĭ-kän'-dō), **strascinan'do,** *I.* Dragging, playing slowly. **s. l'arco.** Keeping the bow of the violin close to the strings to slur the notes. **strascinato** (ä'-tō). Slow. **strascino** (strä-shē'-nō). A drag, a slurring race, in slow vocal music.

strath'spey. A lively Scotch dance, in common time, employing the Scotch snap freely.

stravagante (gän'-tĕ), *I.* Extravagant, odd. **stravaganza** (gän'-tsä), *I.* Eccentricity.

straw-fiddle. Xylophone. because its bars are often laid on straw cords.

straziante (strä-tsĭ-än'-tĕ), *I.* Mocking.

street-organ. Hand-organ.

Streich (strīkh), G. Stroke (as of a bow), hence S.-instrumente. Stringed instrs. S.-quartett. String quartet. S.-orchester. The strings of the orch. S.-zither. Bow-zither. streichen. 1. To draw the bow. 2. To cut (as a scène). streichend. "Stringy" (of the violin quality of certain stops). Strei'cher. Bow-instr. players.

strene. A breve.

streng (shtrĕng), G. Firm(ly), strict(ly).

strepito (strā'-pĭ-tō), I. Noise. strepito'so, strepitosamen'te. Boisterous(ly).

stretch. The interval covered by the fingers of one hand.

stretta (strĕt'-tä), I. A concluding passage, cr finale, in an opera, taken in quicker time to enhance the effect.

stret'to, sometimes stretta, I., strette (strĕt), F. 1. "Compressed." In fugue a closing treatment in which subject and answer are so compressed as to overlap. s. maëstrale, or majestrale. A strictly canonic stretto. alla s. In stretto-style. andante s. A slow agitato. 2. "Hastened." A closing movement at increased speed.

Strich (strīkh), G. Stroke. 1. A dash. 2. A cut. Strich'art. Manner of bowing.

strict. Used of a composition following the most rigid and severe rules. Vide CANON, FUGUE, etc.

strident (strē-däṅ), F., striden'te, stridevole (dā'-vō-lĕ), I. Sharp, shrill.

striking reed. Vide REED.

string. A sonorous cord made of various materials, the strings of violins, etc., being of gut, or cat-gut (so-called, although made of the entrails of sheep). Guitar, etc., strings are of brass, copper, or a core of steel wire or silk, sometimes covered (wound round with silver or other wire); piano strings are of drawn cast steel. Strings are measured in thickness by a string-gauge. "The strings" is a general term for the stringed instruments of an orchestra (also string-band, etc., or string orchestra). s. pendulum. A Weber chronometer. s. quartet. 1. A group of four instrs. of the violin species, 1st and 2d violin, a viola, and 'cello. 2. All the instrs. of these kinds in the orchestra. 3. A composition for these 4 instrs. s.

quintet, sextet, etc., (a) the string-quartet with addition of some other stringed instr. (as double-bass), or more of the same kind (as an extra violin). The strings of an instr. are numbered beginning with the highest (or soprano or chanterelle). stringy is used of tone (such as that of an organ-stop), which resembles a bow and string instr.). open strings are those which are not pressed with the finger, or stopped. string-organ. Vide SAITENORGEL.

stringendo (jĕn'-dō), I. Accelerating.

Stroh- (shtrō), G. Straw. S.-bass. The husky lower tones of a bass voice. S.-fiedel (fē-dĕl). Xylophone.

stroke. 1. Vide SIGNS. 2. The rise and fall of a pedal.

strombazzata (strôm-bäd-zä'-tä), strombettata (bĕt-tä'-tä), I. Sound of a trumpet. strombettare (tä'-rĕ). To play on the trumpet. strombettiere (tĭ-ä'-rĕ). Trumpeter.

stromentato (tä'-tō), I. Instrumented. Vide RECITATIVE.

stromen'to, strumen'to (pl. -i), I. Instrument(s). s. da fiato (dä fĭ-ä'-tō), or s. di ven'to. Wind-instr. s. d'arco (där'-kō). Bow-instr. s. da cor'da. String-instr. s. da tasto. Key-board instr. s. di legno (di metallo). Wooden (metal) instr. s. di rinforzo (fôr'-tsō). An instr. used to support or strengthen an effect.

Stuben-orgel (shtoo'-bĕn-ôr-gĕl), G. Chamber-organ.

Stück (shtük), pl. Stücke (shtük-ĕ), G. Piece. S.-chen (khĕn). Little tune.

Studie (stoo'-dē), pl. -ien (ĭ-ĕn), G.. studio (stoo'-dĭ-ō), I., stu'dium, L stud'y, E. Vide ÉTUDE and PIANO STUDIES.

Stufe (stoo'-fĕ), pl. en, G. Step, degree. stufenweise (vī-zĕ). By degrees.

stumm (shtoom), G. Dumb. S.-regis'ter. Mechanical stop.

stürmisch (shtür'-mĭsh), G. Stormy. Stürze (shtür'-tsĕ), G. Bell (of horns, etc.). S. in der Höhe (hä'-ĕ). "The bell turned upwards."

Stutt'gart pitch. Vide PITCH.

Stuzflügel (shtoots'-flü-gĕl), G. "Baby" grand piano.

Styl (shtēl), G. Style.

su (soo), I. Above, upon. arco in su. Up-bow.

suabe-flute. A soft stop.

suave (soo-ä'-vĕ), *I.,* **suave** (swăv), *F.* Suave. **suavità** (soo-ä-vĭ-tä'), *I.* Suavity.

sub, *L.* Under, below, beneath.

Subbass (soop'-bäs), *G.,* **subbour'don.** A double-stopped 16 or 32 ft. stop.

subcan'tor. Assistant cantor.

subdiapen'te. The 5th below.

subdom'inant. The fourth tone of a scale or key.

Subflöte, *G.* Sifflöte.

subito (soo-bĭ-tō), *I.,* **subitamen'te.** Sudden(ly), immediate(ly). **volti s.** Turn quickly. **piano subito.** A soft touch immediately after a loud.

sub'ject, *E.,* **Subjekt** (soop'-yĕkht), *G.* A motive or theme for development usually followed by an answer, or second (*secondary* or *subsidiary*) subject, or counter-subject. See article, page 733.

subme'diant. The sixth tone of a scale or key.

suboct'ave. 1. The octave below. 2. Coupler producing the octave below.

subor'dinate. Not principal or fundamental, used of chords on the 2d, 3d, 6th, and 7th degrees of a scale, and of all 7th chords except that on the 5th degree.

subprin'cipal. Below the pedal diapason, a double open bass 32-ft. stop.

subsemifu'sa. *L.* A 32d note.

subsem'itone, subsemito'nium mo'di, *L.* Leading note.

substitu'tion. The resolution of a dissonance in some other part an octave removed.

substitution (süb-stĭ-tüs-yôn̄), *F.* Change of fingers.

subton'ic. Leading note.

succen'tor, *L.* 1. Subcantor. 2. Bass-singer.

succes'sion. 1. Sequence. 2. Progression.

Sufflöte (soof-flä-tĕ), *G.* Sifflöte.

sudden modulation. Modulation to a remote key without intermediate harmony.

suffocato (soof-fō-kä'-tō), *I.* "Suffocated," muffled.

sugli (sool-yē), **sui** (soo-ē), *I.* Vide SUL.

suite (swēt), *F.,* or **suite de pièces** (dŭ pĭ-ĕs'). A set or series of pieces. Originally a group of dances, the s. has followed the line deserted by the sonata. Strictly it is a cycle series of classic dance-forms in one key. The number varies from three to five,

often with a prelude. The dance-forms are chosen from the following: allemande, courante, sarabande, bourée, gigue, gavotte, minuet, passepied, loure, anglaise, polonaise, pavane. The allemande is usually first, the gigue last; the first dances named were the regular constituents, the others being called *intermezzi.* The modern suite aims chiefly at lightness even when extended to the orchestra, and great liberty is now taken with keys and forms.

suivez (swē-vā), *F.* "Follow" (the soloist); continue similarly.

sujet (sü-zhā), *F.* Subject.

sul (sool), **sull',** **sulla** (sool'-lä), *I.* On the, near the, as **sul a.** On the *a* string. **sulla tastiera.** Near the finger-board (of bowing). **sul ponticel'lo.** Near the bridge.

suma'ra. A two-piped Turkish flute.

summa'tional tones. Vide RESULTANT.

sumpun'jah, *Heb.* Sambuca.

sumsen (zoom'-zĕn), *G.* To hum.

suonare (soo-o-nä'-rĕ), *I.* To play, sound, ring. **suonata** (soo-o-nä'-tä). Sonata. **suonatina** (tĕ'-nä). Sonatina.

suono (soo-ō'-nō), *I.* Sound. **suo'ni armonichi** (är-mō'-nĭ-kē). Harmonics.

su'per, *L.* Over, above.

superano (soo-pĕr-ä'-nō), *Sp.* Soprano.

superdom'inant. The 6th tone in the scale.

super'fluous, *E.,* **superflu** (sü-pĕr-flü). *F.* Augmented.

supe'rius, *L.* Higher, i. e., the highest part.

superoc'tave. 1. The octave above. 2. A stop two octaves above the diapasons. 3. Coupler producing the octave above.

superton'ic, *E.,* **supertonique** (sü-pĕr-tôn-ēk'), *F.* The second tone of a scale.

supplican'do, supplichevole (soop-plĭ-kä'-vō-lĕ), **supplichevolmen'te,** *I.* Pleading(ly), appealing(ly).

support'. Accompaniment, reinforcement.

supposed bass. The lowest note of an inverted chord (q.v.).

sur (soor), *I.,* **sur** (sür), *F.* On, upon, over. **sur une corde.** On one string.

surabondant(es) (sür-ä-bôn̄-dän̄(t)), *F.* Used of triplets, quintoles, etc.

suraigu (sür-ĕ-gü), *F.* Over-acute.

surdelina (soor-dä-lē'-nä), *I.* Small bagpipe.

surprise. 1. Vide CADENCE. 2. Name of Haydn's 6th symphony with an unexpected crash breaking in on a long, soft movement.

susdominante (sü-), *F.* Superdominant.

suspended cadence. 1. Vide CADENCE. 2. Vide SUSPENSION.

suspen'sion. 1. The holding back of one note of a chord with the result that it causes, with the following chord, a clash that earnestly demands its progress to the destined note in which it will find resolution (q.v.). 2. The note so suspended. A s. may be *unprepared*, that is, it may be the only note of a group that is not proper to a sudden chord. s. may be *double* or *triple*, by occurring in more than one note of a group at once.

suspir'ium, *L.* 1. A quarter rest. 2. More anciently, a half-rest.

süss (züs), *G.* Sweet(ly). **Süssflöte.** A soft flute-stop.

su(s)surrando (soo(s)-soo-rän'-dō), su(s)surrante (rän'-tě), *I.* Whispering, murmur. **susurra'tion,** *E.* A soft murmur.

sustain. To hold a note during its full time-value; to perform in legato manner, vide also PEDAL-POINT. Vide PEDAL.

svegliato (svāl-yä'-tō), *I.* Lively.

svelto (svěl'-tō), *I.* Light, easy.

sw. Abbr. of Swell-organ.

swell. 1. Gradual increase (and decrease) of sound. 2. The device for increasing and diminishing a sustained tone on an organ, hence **swell-organ,** and **swell key-board.** Part of an organ (the **swell-organ**) is surrounded by a **swell-box,** the front of which is filled with **Venetian swell-blinds** (Jalousie, *G.*), opened or closed by a lever worked by a **swell-pedal.** In old organs, there was but one shutter (**nag's-head swell**); in harpsichords the cover moved.

Swing. See article, page 818.

Sylbe (zěl'-bě), *G.* Syllable.

syllab'ic, *E.,* **syllabisch** (zěl-läp'-ĭsh), *G.,* **syllabique** (sěl-lăb-ēk), *F.* Of an air in which each syllable has its own note.

syllable-names. Do, re, mi, etc., as opposed to *letter-names*, C, d, e, etc. Vide SOLMISATION.

sym'bal. Cymbal.

sympathet'ic. Of strings, etc., which

are made to sound by sympathetic vibration (q.v.), and strengthen some other tone by unison or by sounding some overtone.

symphone'ta, *L.* Polyphony.

sympho'nia, *Gr.* 1. Agreement. 2. Hurdygurdy. 3. A symphony.

symphon'ic, *E.,* **symphonique** (săn-fō-nēk), *F.,* **symphonisch** (zēm-fō'-nĭsh), *G.* Pertaining to or relating to the symphony. **symphonic poem, poème s.** (pō-ěm' săn-fō-nēk), *F.,* **sympho'nische Dichtung** (dĭkh-toongk), *G.* A composition of symphonic demands on orchestra and intelligence, but not built on the sonata form and rather descriptive than thematic. The name was first given by Liszt to some of his best works.

Symphonie (săn-fō-nē in *F.,* in *G.* zēm-fō-nē'). 1. Symphony. 2. Concord. 3. Instrumental accompaniment. 4. String-band. 5. Orchestra. **Symphonie-Ode** (ō-'dě), *G.* Choral symphony.

sympho'nion. 1. A combination of flute-stop with piano, inv. by Kaufmann. 2. A music-box with interchangeable disk in place of a cylinder.

sym'phonist, symphoniste (săn'-fō-nēst'), *F.,* **Sympho'niker, symphonienseser** (zēm-fō'-nĭ-ěn-zā'-zěr), *G.* A composer of symphonies; in *F.* also a church-composer, or member of an orchestra.

sympho'nious. Harmonious.

sym'phony, Symphonie (in *F.* săn-fō-nē', in *G.* zēm-fō-nē'). 1. A sonata for orchestra with all the elaboration and extension permitted by the larger resources. Beethoven (and followers of him) even added a chorus, hence *choral symphony*. Historically founded on the overture. Haydn, the father of the sonata (q.v.), established the form, which has survived with minor substitutions (as in the sonata) till now. 2. In *E.* and elsewhere the instrumental pre-, inter-, and post-ludes, of vocal composition. 3. Old name for hurdygurdy, etc.

sympo'sia. Convivial compositions.

syn'copate. To perform syncopation.

syncopato (sĭn-kō-pä'-tō), *I.,* Syncopated.

syn'copation, *E.,* **syncopa'tio,** *L.,* **syncope** (săn-kôp in *F.,* in *G.* zēn'-kō-pě). A pleasantly confusing rhythmic "intersection" caused by suppressing a natural accent or strong-beat, or moving it from its natural place to a weak beat, usually by means of tying over a note on a weak beat across the time belonging to a strong beat. The note so prolonged is said to be syncopated. In piano-music, only one hand usually has the syncopation.

Synkope (zĕn'-kō-pĕ), *G.* Syncopation. **synkopi(e)ren** (pē'-rĕn). To syncopate.

synnem'menon. (See article, page 762.)

synonyme (sē-nō-nēm), *F.* Homophone.

synton'ic. Vide COMMA.

syntonolyd'ian. Hypolydian.

sy'ren. Siren.

syr'inx, *Gr.,* **syringe** (sē-rănzh), *F.* 1. Pandean pipes. 2. A portion of a hymn to Apollo sung by candidates for Pythian prizes.

sys'tem (in *G.* zēs'-tām). 1. A group of staves. 2. In *G.* a staff.

syste'ma, *Gr.* 1. A tetrachord, or other interval. 2. In *L.* Staff. 3. Hexachord series. (See MODES, p. 762.)

système (sēs-tĕm), *F.* 1. All musical tones. 2. Compass.

syzygi'a, *Gr.* and *L.* A chord. **s. perfecta,** or **simplex.** Triad. **s. composita.** Triad with a tone doubled. **s. propin'qua** (*remo'ta*). Close (open) chord.

szopelka (shō-pĕl'-kä). Russian oboe with brass mouthpiece.

T

T. Abbr. of *Talon, Tasto, Tempo, Tenor, Toe, Tre, Tutti.*

tabal'lo, *I.* A kettle-drum.

tabar (tä-bär'), *I.,* **tab'arde, tab'arte,** Old *E.* A tabor.

tabl. Egyptian drum.

tablatura (täb-lä-too'-rä), *I.,* **tablature** (tă-blä-tür'), *F.,* **tablature** (täb'-lä-tūr), *E.,* **Tabulatur** (tä-boo-lä-toor'), *G.* 1. The Tonic Sol-fa notation. 2. The rules of poetic and musical composition established by the Meistersinger. Vide 'Stories of the Operas." 3. An early form of notation from which our present system got its vertical character, the bar and the tails of its notes. Old tablature had many forms. In lute-tablature the French and English used letters, the Italians, numerals, designating the frets to be touched on the lute. These were written on

a staff with as many lines as the instr. written for hard strings; beneath were stems with tails, indicating the time-value of the notes; these tails represent our modern values except that our whole note (their semibreve) had a stem like that of our half-note; our half-note (their minima) had the tail of an eighth note; our $\frac{1}{4}$ note (semiminima) a double-hooked-stem, our $\frac{1}{8}$ note (fusa) three hooks, our $\frac{1}{16}$ note (semifusa) the tail of a 64th note. The hooks of consecutive notes were often run together in thick lines as in our music. **organ** (or German) **t.** was used for key-board instrs., and employed the letter-names of the notes, the melody being marked on a staff with chord-accompaniment in vertical rows of letters beneath.

table d'harmonie (tăbl dăr-mō-nē), *F.* 1. A table of chords, intervals, etc. 2. Sound-board.

table d'instrument (tăbl dăn-strü-män), *F.* Belly.

ta'ble-music. 1. Part-songs. 2. Music printed so that singers at opposite sides of a table could read it.

ta'bor, taboret', *E.,* **tabourin** (tă-boo-răn), *F.,* **tab'ret.** A small drum; a tambourine without jingles.

ta'cet, pl. **ta'cent,** *L.,* **tace** (tä'-chĕ) pl. **taci** (tä'-chē), **taciasi** (tä-chī-ä'-sĭ), *I.* "Be silent!" as *oboe tacet,* let the oboe be silent.

tac'tus, *L.* The stroke of the hand or bâton in conducting.

Tafel (tä'-fĕl), *G.* Table. **T.-förmiges** (fĕr-mĭkh-ĕs), **klavier,** or **T.-klavier.** Square piano. **T.-musik** (moo-zēk'). 1. Music sung at a banquet. 2. Vide TABLE-MUSIC.

tail. Stem. **tail-piece.** The wooden brace which holds the strings of violins etc., below the bridge.

taille (tī'-yŭ), *F.* 1. Tenor. 2. Viola, also **t. de violin, t. de basson.** Oboe da caccia.

takigo'to. 1. Japanese dulcimer.

Takt (täkt), *G.* 1. Time. 2. Measure. 3. Beat. **im T.** In time. **ein T. wie vorher zwei.** Double the former time. **T.-accent.** Primary accent **T.-art.** Species of time, as duple or triple. **T.-erstickung** (ĕr-shtĭk-oongk). Syncopation. **T.-fach** (fäkh). Space. **T.-fest.** Steady in keeping time. **T.-glied** (glēt). Measure-note. **T.-führer** (fü'-rĕr). Conductor: leader. **T.-halten.** To keep time. takti(e)ren (täk-tēr'-ĕn) or t.-schlagen. To beat time. T.-linie (lĭn'-ē), T.-strich (strĭkh). Barline. t.-mässig (mĕs-sĭkh). In time. T.-messer. Metronome. T.-note. Whole note. T.-pause. Whole rest. T.-stock. Bâton. guter T.-teil. Strong beat. schlechter T.-teil. Weak beat. T.-vorzeichnung, or Taktzeichen (tsī-khĕn). Signature.

talabalac'co, *I.* Moorish drum.

ta'lan. Hindu cymbals.

talon (tä-lôn), *F.* Heel. 1. Of a bow. 2. Of the foot.

tambour (tän-boor), *F.* 1. Drum. 2. Drummer. t. de basque (dŭ bäsk). Tambourine. t. chromatique. Timbalarion. t. roulante (roo-länt). Long drum. t. major (mä-zhôr). Drum-major.

tamb(o)u'ra. An ancient instr., used in the East, like a guitar, struck with a plectrum.

tambouret (tän-boo-rā), *F.*, tambourine (tăm'-boo-rēn), *E.*, Tambourin (tämboo-rēn'), *G.* 1. A small drum, with little bells (called *jingles*) pivoted in the rim. Notes with waved stems indicate a *roll;* notes with vertical lines above, call for the *jingles.* tambourineur (nŭr'), *F.* Tambourine-player.

tambourin (tän-boo-răn), *F.* 1. A tambourine without jingles. 2. A lively dance in 2-4 time with t. accompaniment.

tamburaccio (täm-boo-rät'-chō), *I.* A large drum. tamburel'lo, tamburet'to, *I.* 1. Tabor. 2. Drummer.

tamburino (täm-boo-rē'-nō), *I.* 1. Drummer. 2. Tambourine.

tamburo (täm-boo'-rō), *I.* Side-drum.

tamburone (täm-boo-rō'-nē), *I.* The great drum.

tamis (tă-mē'), *F.* Pipe-rack.

tam'tam'. 1. Indian drum. 2. Gong.

Tanbur (tän-boor'), *G.* Tamburo.

tändelnd (tĕn'-dĕlnt), *G.* Playful, trifling.

tan'gent, *E.*, Tangente (tän-jĕn'-tĕ), *G.* Vide CLAVICHORD. Tangentenflügel. A "wing-shaped" clavichord.

tantino (tän-tē'-nō), *I.* A little.

tanto (tän'-tō), *I.* So much; as much; but allegro non t. Not too quick. allegro t. possibile. As fast as possible.

Tan'tum er'go, *L.* "So much therefore." A hymn sung at the Benediction in the R. C. service.

Tanz (tänts), *G.*, pl. Tänze (tĕn'-tsĕ). A dance. Tänzer (tĕn'-tsĕr). A dancer. Tänzerin (tĕn'-tsĕ-rĭn). A female dancer. T.-lied (lēt). Dancesong. T.-musik, or T.-stück (shtük) Dance-tune.

tap. A single note on the drum. taps. The last military signal at night. It is also used at the funeral of a soldier.

tapada (tä-pädh'-ä), *Sp.* Stop. tapadillo (dhēl'-yō). Baxoncillo.

ta'rabouk. Instr. used by Turks, a parchment over the bottom of a large earthen vessel.

tarantella (tä-rän-tĕl'-lä), tarentelle (tăr-än-tĕl'), *F.* Perhaps of Tarentine origin, but claimed to be derived from the tarantula, two explanations being given, one that the bite of the spider incites a mania for dancing; a more probable one that the fatal effects of the poison find an antidote in violent exercise. The dance is a wild presto in 3-8 or 6-8 time, with increasing frenzy and alternatingly major and minor.

tarau, theyau thro. Burmese violin with 3 silk strings.

tar'do, tardato (tär-dä'-tō), tardan'-do, tardamen'te, *I.* Slow (ly).

Tartini's tones. Resultant tones, first observed by Tartini. (Vide B. D.).

Taschengeige (täsh'-ĕn-gī-khĕ), *G.* Kit.

tasseau (tăs-sō), *F.* The mould on which violins are built.

tastame (täs-tä'-mĕ), *I.*, Tastatur (täs-tä-toor'), *G.*, tastatura (täs-tä-too'-rä), *I.*, tastiera (täs-tĭ-ā'-rä), *I.* Key-board; finger-board. sulla tastiera. Near the finger-board (of a vln.).

Taste (täs'-tĕ), *G.* The touch, hence a key. Tas'tenbreit. Key-board. Tastenstäbchen (stĕp-khĕn). Fret. Tastenschwanz (shvänts). Extremity of key-board. Tastenwerk. A keyed instrument.

tasto (täs'-tō), *I.* 1. Touch. 2. Key. 3. Fret. 4. Finger-board. sul t. "Near the finger-board." t. solo. "One key alone," a note to be played without other harmony than the octaves.

tatto (tät'-tō), *I.* Touch.

tattoo'. The drum-beat at night recalling soldiers to quarters for sleep It precedes taps (q.v.).

tche (chē). A Chinese stringed instrument.

te. Tonic Sol-fa name for the 7th tone *si*.

té (tā). *F.* C sharp.

technic(s) (těkh'-nĭk(s)), *E.*, **Technik** (těkh-nēk'), *G.*, **technique** (těk-nēk), *F.* The mechanical side of musical performance, including dexterity, velocity, distinctness, shading as opposed to the poetical or interpretative side. The means, not the end, of a properly balanced musical ambition.

tech'nicon. A device for training the fingers, inv. by J. Brotherhood, 1889.

tech'niphone. First name of the Virgil Practice-Clavier.

technisch (těkh'-nĭsh), *G.* Technical, used to indicate proficiency.

tedesco (-a) (tě-děs'-kō), *I.* German. **alla t.** In the German style, in waltz-rhythm. **lira t.** Hurdygurdy.

Ʈe De'um Lauda'mus, *L.* "Thee, Lord, we praise," a hymn attributed to St. Ambrosius. Vide MASS.

Ʈeil (tīl), *G.* Vide THEIL.

ʈel'ephone-harp. An instr. for transmitting music by telephone.

tell'tale. An indicator of wind-pressure.

tema (tā'-mä), *I.* Theme; subject; melody.

tem'perament, *E.*, **tempérament** (tän-pä-rä-män), *F.*, **temperamen'-to,** *I.* A method of tuning, representing the triumph of practice over theory; of art over science. It is a system of compromise, whereby, for practical musical purposes, the octave is divided into twelve intervals, none of which is quite true. In the present piano, and similar instrs. the tones *c♯* and *d♭*, for example, are identical, and are given the same string and digital. As a matter of acoustical fact there is a difference between them. If they were given different digitals and tuned exactly, the present freedom of modulation from one key to another would be impossible without some elaborate device, and the piano, organ, etc., would need a greatly increased finger-board, with 53 digitals to the octave instead of 12 as now. The present tuning was not reached without a war of the bitterest sort; but since the 18th century began, only 12 degrees have been given to the octave. The earliest method was **unequal temperament**, the key of C major being tuned true, and the

other tones forced to conform. In the **twelve-semitone system,** the octave was divided into twelve equal parts, no interval being quite true. The **mean-tone** system had the major thirds tuned true, the intermediate space being divided into two equal intervals; this system produced much discord called the *wolf*. **equal temperament** is now generally employed; it is the practice of tuning by fifths. A series of twelve fifths beginning with c lacks only 74/73 of forming a perfect seven octaves; by dividing this slight discrepancy equally among the 12 fifths, the *circle of fifths* is tempered and made perfect; thus in major C–G–D–A–E–B–F♯–(or G♭)–D♭–A♭–E♭–B♭ F– C (B♯); in minor a–e–b–f♯–c♯–g♯–d♯ (or e♭)–b♭–f–c–g–d–a; and one can modulate by means of dominant harmony (chords on the fifths) through the whole succession of keys with almost imperceptible acoustic falsehood. It is this great convenience and simplicity of Equal Temperament that has prevented thus far the acceptance of any of the many instruments invented with the rival method of **just intonation.** Nevertheless the music we know and enjoy has no perfect intervals except the octave; the fifths are a 12th of a *comma* flat; the fourths a 12th of a *comma* sharp; the major thirds ⅛th of a *comma* sharp, etc.

Temperatur (tām-pě-rä-toor'), *G.* Temperament.

tempesto'so, tempestosamen'te. Tempestuous(ly), furious(ly).

tempête (tän-pět), *F.* "Tempest." A boisterous quadrille in 2-4 time.

tem'po, *I.* "Time." 1. Rate of speed, ranging from the slowest to the fastest, thus Grave, largo, lento, adagio, andante, moderato, allegro, presto, prestissimo. 2. Rhythm, measure. 3. Beat. **a tempo.** In exact time (usually appearing after retardation). **t. primo** (or 1mo), or **primiero.** Original speed. **t. alla breve** (brā'-vě). Vide BREVE. **t. a. piacere,** or **senza t.** The time at pleasure. **t. bina'rio** (terna'rio). Duple (triple) time. **t. como'do.** Convenient, moderate time. **t. debole** (dā'-bō-lě). Weak beat. **t. di bal'lo.** Dance-time. **t. di bole'ro, gavot'ta, mar'cia,** etc. In the time of a bolero, gavotte, march, etc. **t. di cappel'la.** In the Church-time.

Vide BREVE. **t. di pri′ma par′te.**
In the same time as the first part.
t. for′te. Strong beat. **t. giusto**
(joos′-tō). In strict time. **l′istesso**
(or **lo stesso**), **t.** Continue at "the
same speed." **t. maggiore** (mäd-
jō′-rĕ). Vide BREVE. **t. mino′re,**
or **t. ordina′rio.** 1. Common time,
4 beats to the measure. 2. The
original time of the piece. **t. perdu′to.**
"Lost," unsteady time. **t. reggiato**
(rĕd-jä′-tō), same as colla parte.
t. rubato. Vide RUBATO. **T. wie
vorher** (vē fôr-här), *G.* Same time
as before.

tempo-mark, Tempo-Bezeichnung (bĕ-
tsīkh′-noongk), *G.* A word or phrase
indicating the standard or unit of
time for a composition, as *andante;*
or indicating some deviation from
this unit, as *meno mosso.*

temporiser (täṅ-pôr-ĭ-zä), *F.* In an
accompaniment, to follow the soloist's
time.

temps (täṅ), *F.* 1. Time. 2. Beat.
t. faible (fĕbl), or **levé** (lŭ-vä).
Weak beat. **t. fort** (fôr), **frappé**
(frăp-pä′). Strong beat.

tem′pus, *L.* Time, i. e., of the breve.
t. perfec′tum (marked O). That in
which the breve equalled 3 semibreves **t. im′perfectum** (marked
( ). That in which it equalled 2
semibreves. **t. bina′rium** (or **terna′-
rium**). Duple or triple time. Vide
NOTATION.

tenete (tĕ-nä′-tĕ), *I.* Hold.

Ten′ebræ, *L.* "Shadows, Darkness";
R. C. Evening Service, during Holy
Week, in commemoration of the
Crucifixion, the candles being extin-
guished one by one.

tenen′do, *I.* Sustaining (as the melody).

tenero (tä′-nĕ-rō), **tenero′so, tenera-
men′te,** *I.* Tender(ly). **tenerezza**
(tä-nĕ-rĕd′-zä). Tenderness.

teneur (tŭ-nŭr), *F. Cantus firmus* of
a hymn.

tenor (in *G.* tä-nôr′), **ténor** (tä-nôr), *F.*
tenore (tä-nō′-rĕ), *I.* 1. The highest male voice produced "in the
chest." Vide SOPRANO. (a) The
more powerful tenor is almost a
barytone and is called **dramatic
(Heldentenor′), teno′re robus′to,** or
di mezzo carattere (dē mĕd′-zō kä-
răt′-tä-rĕ), or **di forza** (dē fôr′-tsä).
Compass c–b′ (♭). The more light
and flexile tenor is called **lyric,
lyrischer** (lēr-ĭsh-ĕr). **Tenore leg-**

giero (lĕd-jä-rō), **légier** (lä-zhä), or **di
grazia** (dē gräts′-yä). Compass
d–c″, sometimes higher. 2. The
part corresponding to the tenor voice
in compass. 3. The highest of a
chime of bells. 4. The viola, as
tenor violin. 5. As a prefix for
instrs. of tenor range; e. g., tenor
trombone (*Tenorposaune*), etc. 6.
tenor C is an octave below mid-c.
7. **tenor-clef, Tenor-schlüssel** or
-zeichen, the C clef on the fourth
line. 8. The lowest string of the
viola. 9. In Gregorian music, the
principal melody taken by a medium
male voice, above which sang the
counter- or **contra-tenor,** or the
altus or *alto.* 10. In mediæval music,
(a) fermate, (b) ambitus, (c) tone of a
mode of the *evovae.* **tenorino** (tä-nō-
rē′-nō), *I.* Falsetto or **castrato** tenor.
Tenorist (tĕn-ō-rēst′), *G.,* **tenorista**
(tän-ō-rēs′-tä), *I.,* **ténoriste** (tä-nō-
rēst′), *F.* A tenor-singer.

tenoroon′. 1. Old tenor oboe, compass
downward to tenor C. 2. A stop
that does not go below E.

ten′sile. Applied to stringed instruments.

tenth. 1. An interval of an octave
and a third. 2. A stop a tenth above
the diapasons. 3. Decima.

tenu(e) (tŭ-nü), *F.,* **tenuto** (tä-noo′-tō),
I. "Held." 1. Sustained. 2. A
sustained note or pedal-point. 3.
Legato. 4. Constantly, as **forte t.**
Pl. **tenute** (note).

téorbe (tä-ôrb), *F.* Theorbo.

teoretico (tä-ō-rä′-tĭ-kō), *I.* Theoretical.

teoria (tä-ō-rē′-ä), *I.* Theory.

tepidità (tä-pē-dĭ′-tä′), *I.* Indifference,
lukewarmth. **tepidamen′te.** Calmly.

teponaz′tli. An Aztec drum still used
in Central America; a log about a
yard long, hollowed from below, then
cut through till two tongues of wood
are left. These sound an interval
when struck with padded sticks.

ter (tĕr), *L.* Thrice, three times (of a
passage to be repeated twice). **ter
un′ca.** "Three-hooked"; 16th note.
ter sanctus. "Thrice holy," referring to the "Holy, holy, holy," of
the Te Deum.

terce. 1. Tierce. 2. Vide HORÆ
CANONICÆ.

tercet (tĕr-sä), *F.* Triplet.

ternaire (tĕr-när), *F.,* **ternario** (tĕr-
nä′-rĭ-ō), *I.,* **ter′nary,** *E.* Triple,
three-fold. **ternary form.** Rondo-

form. **ternary measure.** Triple
time.

terpo′dion. 1. An instr. inv. 1816 by
Buschmann, resembling the harmonium, the tone being produced from
sticks of wood. 2. An 8-ft. stop.

Terpsichore (tĕrp-sĭk′-ō-rĕ). The muse
of dance and song.

ter′tia, *L.,* **Terzia** (tĕr′-tsĭ-ä), *G.* 1.
Third, tierce. **tertia modi.** The
3d degree. 2. A stop sounding a
third or tenth above.

tertian Zweifach (tĕr-tsĭ-än tsvī′-fäkh),
G. A stop combining tierce and
larigot.

Terz (tĕrts) (pl. **en**), *G.,* **terzo(-a)** (tĕr′-
tsō), *I.* 1. Third, (a) the interval,
(b) in number. 2. Tierce, **terzo
mano.** Octave-coupler. **terzadec-
ima, Terzde′zime.** A 13th. **Terz-
quart′akkord,** or **Terzquartsext′-
akkord,** 6–4–3 chord. (Vide CHORD.)
Terzquintsext′akkord, 6–5–3 chord.
(Vide CHORD.) **Terztöne.** Tierce-
tones. **Terzflöte.** 1. Small flute,
a minor third above. 2. A stop.

Terzdecimole (dä-tsĭ-mō′-lĕ). A group
of thirteen equal notes.

Terzett (tĕr-tsĕt′), *G.,* **terzetto** (tĕr-
tsĕt′-tō), *I.* A trio.

terzina (tĕr-tsē′-nä), *I.* A triplet.

tessitura (tĕs-sĭ-too′-rä), *I.,* **tessiture**
(tĕs′-sĭ-tūr), *E.* "The web." The
general "lie" of a song or phrase—
its average pitch, whether high or
low.

tes′ta, *I.* Head. **di t.** In the head
as the voice.

testo (tĕs′-tō), *I.* "Text." 1. Subject,
or theme. 2. The words of a song.

testu′do, *L.* "Tortoise." The lyre.

tête (tĕt not tāt), *F.* Head, of a note;
of a vln., etc.

tet′rachord, *E.,* **tetrachorde** (tĕt-rä-
kôrd), *F.,* **tetracor′do,** *I.* 1. A 4-
stringed instr. 2. The interval of a
fourth. 3. The 4 diatonic tones of
a perfect fourth. (Vide MODES.)
tetrachordal system. Original form
of Tonic Sol-fa.

tetrachor′don, *Gr.* A small piano-like
instr. with a rubber cylinder, impinging on strings.

tet′rad. Chord of the seventh.

tet′radiapa′son. Interval of 4 octaves.

tet′raphone. Tetratone.

tetrapho′nia. Organum in 4 parts.

tetrato′non, *Gr.,* **tet′ratone.** An interval of four whole tones.

T(h)eil (tĭl), *G.* Part. **T.-ton.** Partial
tone.

the′ma, *Gr.,* **Thema** (tā′-mä), *G.,*
thème (tĕm), *F.,* **theme,** *E.* Loosely,
the general idea of a composition.
Strictly, the structural molecule, of
which motive or subject and answer
are the component atoms. The
theme of a "theme with variations,"
tema con variazioni, is an extended
air. Such a work as a sonata has
contrasting themes which are developed. **themat′ic treatment** refers
to the contrapuntal handling of a
musical design as opposed to a lyric
treatment, though the theme itself
may be lyric in nature.

Theorbe (tĕ-ôr′-bĕ), *G.,* **théorbe** (tā-
ôrb), *F.,* **theorbo** (thē-ôr′-bō), *E.*
A large bass lute with two necks,
the longer carrying a set of bass
strings.

Theoretiker (tĕ-ō-rā′-tĭ-kĕr), *G.,*
théoricien (tā-ō-rēs-yän), *F.* A
theorist.

theoria, *Gr.* and *L.,* **théorie** (tā-ō-rē),
F., **theory** (thē′ō-rĭ), *E.* The
science of music, particularly of its
composition.

the′sis, *Gr.* The accented downbeat,
Vide ARSIS.

Theur′gic hymns. Songs performed
in Greek mysteries.

theyau. Vide TARAU.

thin. Used of chords and harmonies
that lack support and fulness.

thior′bo. Theorbo.

third. 1. Vide INTERVAL. 2. The mediant. **third-flute.** Vide TERZFLÖTE.
third-tones. Vide QUINT-TONES.

thirteenth. An octave and a sixth.

thirty-second note. A demisemiquaver. **32d rest.** A rest of equal
duration.

thorough-bass. Vide BASS.

thorough-composed. Vide SONG.

three-eighth time. That in which
each measure contains three eighth
notes.

threefold. Used of triads.

three-lined. Vide PITCH.

three-time. Triple time.

threno′dia, *L.* and *Gr.* A song.
thren′ody. Lamentation.

thrice-marked, or **lined.** Vide PITCH.

thro. Vide TARA.

through-composed. Vide SONG.

thumb-position. On the 'cello, a high
position where the thumb quits the
neck.

thumb-string. Banjo melody-string.

Thürmer (tür′ mĕr), *G.* Town-musician.

DICTIONARY OF TERMS 697

tib'ia (pl. **tib'iae**), *L.* "Shin-bone." 1
Ancient name of all wind-instrs. with
holes, such as the flute, pipe and fife,
originally made from the human leg-
bone. **tibiae pa'res**, *L.*, pl. Two
flutes of the same length. **t. impares.**
Unequal flutes, one for the right hand
and the other for the left, which were
played on by the same performer;
those for the right hand, **t. dextrae**,
being perhaps of higher pitch than
those for the left (**sinistrae**). **t. obli'qua**, or **vas'ca.** Cross-flute. 2.
Name of various flute-stops, as **t.
major**, a 16-ft. covered stop. 3. **t.
utric'ularis.** The bagpipe.

tib'icen (pl. **tibic'ines**, feminine **tibi-
ci'na**), *L.* Flute-player. **tibicin'ium.**
Piping.

tie. A slur; a curved line placed over
notes on the same degree which are
to be sustained as one tone. Vide
SIGNS. **tied-notes.** 1. Those thus
tied. 2. A series of notes (16th
notes, etc.) with a single tail.

tief (tēf), *G.* Deep, low. **tiefer** (tē'-
fĕr). Lower. **8va tiefer.** Octave
below. **tieftönend** (tēf-tä'-nĕnt).
Deep-toned.

dier (tēr). Rank (of pipes).

tierce (tērs), *E.* 1. A third, hence
tierce-tones, those reached by skips
of major thirds. Vide PITCH. 2. The
4th in a series of harmonics. 3. A
mutation stop 2⅓ octaves above diapason. 4. Vide HORÆ CANONICÆ.

tierce (tĭ-ĕrs'), *F.* 1. A third. 2. Vide
HORÆ CANONICÆ. **t. de Picardie**
(dŭ pē-kăr-dē), *F.* Tierce of Picardy;
a major third introduced in the last
chord of a composition in minor;
supposed to have originated in Picardy. **t. coulée** (koo-lā). A sliding
grace in thirds. Vide GRACE.

timbala'rion. A series of 8 drums
chromatically tuned and fitted with
pedals.

timbale (tăṅ-băl), *F.*, **timbal'lo**, *I* A
kettle-drum. **timbalier** (tăṅ-băl-yā),
F. A kettle-drummer.

timbre (täṅ-br), *F.*, **tim'bro**, *I.* 1.
Quality and colour of tone. 2. A ball
struck with a hammer. **jeux de
timbres** (zhŭ-dŭ-tänbr). A chromatic series of small bells or metal
bars. 3. The snare of a drum.

tim'brel. Hebrew tambourine.

time. A word used loosely and inter-
changeably with its Italian equivalent *tempo*, to indicate: 1. Rate of
movement, or speed. 2. Rhythm.

Speed is indicated in various ways by
descriptive words, such as slow, *andante, langsam*, etc., or by the metronome mark.
Rhythm is generally indicated by a
fraction, as 2-4 or 3-8 set at the beginning of the composition or movement. The denominator indicates
the unit of note-value; the numerator
fixes the number of those unit-notes
in each measure. Thus 2-4 means
that the quarter-note is the standard
of value, and that each measure contains two quarter notes or their
equivalents.
With the exception of such rare
rhythms as the 5-8 time, all musical
time-patterns are divisible by 2 or 3,
and are called *duple* or *triple*. Thus
in 2-4 time there are two beats to
the measure, in 3-4 time there are
three. In more elaborate times the
beats may themselves be divided by
twos or threes. These are called
compound duple or *compound triple*
times.
The chart gives the various times in
various languages. (See also Accent
and Tempo.)

timido (tē'-mĭ-dō), *I.* Timid. **timi-
dezza** (tē-mĭ-dĕd'-zä). Timidity.

timoro'so, timorosamen'te, *I.* Tim-
id(ly). **timore** (tĭ-mō'-rĕ). Fear.

timpano (tĭm'-pä-nō) (Pl. **-i**), *I.* Kettle-drum. **t. coper'to.** Muffled
drum. **timpanis'to.** Drummer.

tin'termell. An old dance.

tintinnab'ulum, *L.*, **tintinnabolo**, *I.*
(tĭn-tĭn-nä'-bō-lō), **tintinna'bulo**
(boo-lō). 1. A little bell. 2. A
small rattle of bells.

tintinnamen'to, tintinnio (nē'-ō),
tintin'no, *I.* Tinkling.

tin'to, *I.* Shading.

tiorba (tē-ôr'-bä), *I.* Theorbo.

tipping. Vide DOUBLE-TONGUING.

tirade (tē-răd), *F.* A slide across an
interval.

tiran'na, *Sp.* A national air with
guitar.

tirant (tē-räṅ), *F.* Stop-knob. **t. à
coupler** (ä'-koo-plā). 1. Coupler.
2. Button. 3. Drum-cord.

tirarsi, da (dä tē-rär'-sē), *I.* "With a
slide," as **tromba da t.**

tirasse (tĭ-răs), *F.* 1. A pedal-coupler.
2. A pedal key-board acting only on
the manual pipes.

tirata (tē-rä'-tä), *I.* A group of equal
notes, moving in joint degrees

1. Duple, or Common Time. (mesures à deux ou quatre temps, F. gerader Takt, G. tempi pari, I.)

A. Simple. (binaire, F. einfacher, G. semplice. I.)

Signatures	No. of beats to a meas.	English	French	German	Italian
¢ or 2/2	2	Two-two (alla breve).	Deux-deux.	Zweizweiteltakt.	A cappella (alla breve).
2/4	2	Two-four.	Deux-quatre.	Zweivier "	Due-quarti (quarttro-due).
2/8	2	Two-eight.	Deux-huit.	Zweiach "	Due-ottavi (otto-due).
4/2	4	Four-two.	Quatre-deux.	Vierzwei "	Quattro-mezzi (due-quattro).
C or 4/4	4	Four-four. (common).	Quatre-quatre.	Viervier "	Quattro-quarti (quattro-quattro, binario, ordinario).
4/8	4	Four-eight.	Quatre-huit.	Viverach "	Quattro-ottavi (otto-quattro).
4/16	4	Four-sixteen.	Quatre-seize.	Viersechzehn "	Quattro-sedicesimi (sedici-quattro).
8/8	8	Eight-eight.	Huit-huit.	Achtach "	Otto-ottavi (otto-otto).

B. Compound. (ternaire, F. zusammengesetzer, G. composti, I.)

Signatures	No. of beats to a meas.	English	French	German	Italian
6/2	2	Six-two.	Six-deux.	Sechszweiteltakt.	Sei-mezzi (due-sei).
6/4	2	Six-four.	Six-quatre.	Sechsvier "	Sei-quarti (quattro-sei).
6/8	2	Six-eight.	Six-huit.	Sechsach "	Sei-ottavi (otto-sei).
6/16	2	Six-sixteen.	Six-seize.	Sechssechzehn "	Sei-sedicesimi (sedici-sei).
12/4	4	Twelve-four.	Douze-quatre.	Zwölfvier "	Dodici-quarti (quattro-dodici).
12/8	4	Twelve-eight.	Douze-huit.	Zwölfach "	Dodici-ottavi (otto-dodici).
12/16	4	Twelve-sixteen.	Douze-seize.	Zwölfsechzehn "	Dodici-sedicesimi (sedici-dodici).
24/16	8	Twenty-four-sixteen.	Vingt-quatre-seize.	Vierundzwanzigsechzehn "	Ventiquattro-sedici.

2. Triple time. (mesures à trois temps, F. ungerader, or Tripel Takt, G. tempi dispari, I.)

A. Simple.

Signatures	No. of beats to a meas.	English	French	German	Italian
3 or 3/1	3	Three-one.	Mesure à trois-un.	Dreieinteltakt.	Uno-tre.
3/2	3	Three-two.	à trois-deux.	Dreizwei "	Tre-mezzi (due-tre).
3/4	3	Three-four.	à trois-quatre.	Dreivier "	Tre-quarti (quattro-tre).
3/8	3	Three-eight.	à trois-huit.	Dreiach "	Tre-ottavi (otto-tre).

B. Compound.

Signatures	No. of beats to a meas.	English	French	German	Italian
9/4	3	Nine-four.	à neuf-quatre.	Neunvierteltakt.	Nove-quarti (quattro-nove).
9/8	3	Nine-eight.	à neuf-huit.	Neunach "	Nove-ottavi (otto-nove).
9/16	3	Nine-sixteen.	à neuf-seize.	Neunsechzehn "	Nove-sedicesimi (sedici-nove).
5/4	5	Five-four.	à cinq-quatre.	Fünfvier "	Cinque-quarti (quattro-cinque).
5/8	5	Five-eight.	à cinq-huit.	Fünfach "	Cinque-ottavi (otto-cinque).

NOTE.—Some English writers classify times also as *quadruple* and *octuple*, and indicate compound times by the signatures of the corresponding simple times with a dot added after the denominator.

tirato (tē-rä'-tō), *I.* 1. Down-bow.
2. Pedal-coupler.
tira tutto (tē-rä toot'-tō), *I.* A pedal
mechanism controlling the full power
of an organ.
tiré (tē-rä), *F.* Drawn, pulled; a
down-bow. **tirez** (tē-rä). "Use the
down-bow."
Tischharfe (tĭsh'-här-fĕ), *G.* "Dish
harp," an autoharp.
tit'ty. Hindu bagpipe.
tirolienne. Tyrolienne.
tlap'anhuehue'tl. Huehuetl.
toccata (tôk-kä'-tä), *I.* From **toc-
care**, to touch, to play. In its 16th
century form, a prelude made up of
runs and arpeggios. The modern
toccata develops with great thematic
hilarity and contrapuntal informality
a brilliant, swift and showy improvisation. **toccatina** (tē'-nä), **tocca-
tel'la.** Short toccata.
toccato (tôk-kä'-tō), *I.* A fourth-
trumpet part in place of kettle-drums.
toc'sin. An alarm-bell.
To(d)tesgesang (tōt'-ĕs-gĕ-zäng).
To(d)teslied (lēt), *G.* A dirge.
To(d)tenglöckchen (glĕk'-khĕn).
Funeral-bell. **To(d)tenmarsch**
(märsh). Funeral ("dead") march.
tombeau (tôń-bō), *F.* "Tomb." Dramatic elegy.
tomb'estere. Old *E.* A dancer with
tambourine.
tom'tom. Hindu drums.
Ton (tōn), pl. **Töne** (tä'-nĕ), *G.* 1.
Tone. **T.-bestimmung,** or **-mes-
sung.** Calculation of tones. **Ton-
gattung** (gät'-toongk). The division
of the octave. The selection of tones.
Hence, mode. **T.-rein.** True in
pitch. **T.-bildung.** Tone-production; voice-training. **T.-bühne.**
Orchestra. **T.-dichter.** Tone-poet,
composer (also **T.-setzer**). **T.-
dichtung** (dĭkh-toongk) or **satz.**
Composition. **T.-farbe** (fär-be).
Tone-colour, timbre. **T.-folge.** Series
of tones. **T.-führung.** Melodic
progression, modulation. **T.-fuss,
T.-fall** (or **-schluss**). Cadence.
T.-setzung, or **-verhalt.** Rhythm,
measure. **T.-gang.** Melody. **T.-
gebung.** Intonation. **T.-kunde.**
Science of music. **T.-kunst** (koonst),
Music; the art of music. **Tonkunst-
schule.** School of music. **Ton-
lehre** (tōn'-lā-rĕ). Acoustics. **Ton-
leiter** (lī-tĕr). Scale. **T.-loch.**
Ventage. **T.-malerei.** "Tone-
painting," programme music. **T.-

messer.** Monochord, siren, sono-
meter. **Tonschlüssel** (shlüs'-sĕl).
Key-note. **T.-runge.** Fugue. **T.-
setzkunst.** Art of composition. **T.-
sprache.** Music. **T.-stück** or
-werk. Piece of music. **T.-schrift.**
Musical notes. **T.-verwandschaft.**
Relation of tones. **T.-verziehung.**
Tempo rubato. **T.-veränderung.**
Modulation. **T.-werkzeug.** Instrument (including the voice). **T.-
system,** or **wissenschaft.** Theory
of music. **T.-zeichen.** Note or
other musical sign.
2. Pitch. **den T. angaben** (hal-
ten). To give (keep) the pitch. **T.-
höhe.** Pitch. **T.-lage.** Register.
3. Key, octave-scale, mode, usually
Tonart (tōn'-ärt). **T.-anverwand-
schaft** (fĕr-vänt'-shäft). Key-relationship. **T.-geschlecht** (gĕ-
shlĕkht'). Mode (i. e., major or
minor). **Tonabstand** (äp-shtänt).
Interval. **T.-achtel.** Eighth note.
T.-stufe. Degree. **T.-umfang.**
Compass.
ton (tôń), *F.* 1. Tone. **t. bouché**
(boo-shā). Stopped tone of a horn.
t. entier (äń-tĭ-ā). Whole tone. **t.
feint** (făń). Old term for flatted
tone. **t. ouvert** (oo-văr). Open tone,
of a wind-instr. **t. générateur** (zhā-
nä-rä-tŭr). Fundamental. 2. Pitch,
donner le t. Give the pitch. 3. Key,
scale, mode. **t. majeur** (mineur).
Major (minor) key. **t. relatif.** Related key. **t. de l'église** (dŭ lā-
glēz). Church-mode. 4. Crook of a
horn. **t. de réchange,** or **du cor.**
Tuning-fork.
tonadica (tō-nä-dē'-kä), **tonadilla**
(dēl'-yä), *Sp.* Cheerful song with
guitar.
to'næ fic'ti, *L.* Transposed church-
modes.
to'nal. Relating to a tone, a key,
mode, etc. Vide FUGUE, and IMITA-
TION.
Tonalität (tōn-äl-ĭ-tät'), *G.*, **tonalité**
(tôn-äl-ĭ-tä), *F.*, **tonal'ity,** *E.* The
unity in key-relationship of a phrase
or composition. It may pass out
of the predominant key, but so long
as it does not stray beyond the limits
of easy return and constant relationship with this key, the composition
has not overstepped its general
tonality.
ton'do, *I.* Round, full (of tone).
tone. 1. A sound of musical quality
and regular vibration as opposed to

noise. 2. A sound, (a) of definite pitch, (b) of a definite quality. 3. A full interval of two semitones. 4. A mode. 5. Of *aliquot, combinational, differential, partial, resultant, summational,* etc., tones or *difference-tones, overtones,* etc. Vide those words, also ACOUSTICS. Of *fifth-tones, quint-tones, third tones.* Vide QUINT-TONES. **bridge-tone.** Vide TONIC SOL-FA. **tone-colour.** The distinctive quality or timbre of a tone. **tone-painting.** Description by music. **tone-poem.** A musical expression of sentiment. **determination of t.** The investigation of vibrations, or tone-values, tone-relationship, etc. **tone-relationship.** Tones which concur in a major or minor chord are said to be of the first degree of relationship; c is so related to g, f, e, a♭, a, and e♭, etc.

tönen (tä'-něn), *G.* To sound. **tö'nend.** Sounding.

tongue. 1. Reed, or the vibrating metal slip of a reed; hence, **tongue-pipes.** 2. *As a verb,* to use the tongue in playing wind-instr.; called **tonguing.** Vide DOUBLE-TONGUING. *Triple-tonguing* is the rapid iteration by tongue-thrust with the consonants, t-k-t, t-k-t, etc.

ton'ic, *E.,* tonica (tō'-nē-kä), *I.,* To'-nika, *G.,* tonique (tō-nēk), *F.* 1. The key-note of a key, that on which the scale begins and ends, the tone from which a key takes its name as C. 2. The **tonic-chord,** the diatonic chord built on the key-note. **t.-pedal.** Pedal-point on the key-note. **t. section.** One which closes with a cadence to the tonic of the chief key of the movement.

Tonic Sol-fa. A system of teaching singing, inv. by Sarah Ann Glover, of Norwich, and improved by Rev. John Curwen, and his son John Spencer Curwen. It consists, first, in analysis with constant reference to key-relations, or "tones in key"; the second element is a notation modified from solmisation (q.v.), and consisting of doh for do, ray for re, me for mi, fah for fa, soh for sol, lah for la, te for si. These take the place of notes and are written on one line by their initials, d, r, m, etc., an accent being affixed below or above the letter to indicate an octave lower or higher as d' r'. Sharps are sung dē, rē, etc., flats dä, rä, etc. In

modulation, *bridge-tones* are indicated by the new key-value of the tone large with its old key value small as ᵃd. In notation, rhythm is expressed by time-spaces, the number varying according to the beats or pulses in the bar; a thick bar before a letter marks a strong accent; a colon a weak accent; a dot and a comma mark half and quarter beats, a dash indicates prolongation of tone, a rest is marked by a vacant space.

to'no, *I.* 1. Tone. 2. Key.

to'nos, *Gr.,* to'nus, *L.* 1. A whole tone. **t. grav'is, tris'tis, mys'ticus, harmon'icus, laet'us, devo'tus, angel'icus, perfect'us,** respectively the 1st, 2d, 3d, 4th, 5th, 6th, 7th, and 8th tones in church-music. **t. cur'rens.** Reciting note. **t. peregri'nus.** Foreign tone. 2. Mode.

toquet (tō-kā). **touquet,** *F.* Toccato

toomour'ah. Hindu tambourine.

too'rooree'. Brahmin trumpet.

toph (tōf), *Heb.* Hebrew tambourine.

torcelli (tôr-chĕl'-lē), *I.* Organs.

tosto (tôs'-tō). Quick, rapid.   più tosto. Rather; sooner.

touch. 1. Act or style of pressing the keys of a key-board instr. 2. The response or resistance of the action.

touche (toosh), *F.* 1. Touch. 2. A digital. 3. A fret. 4. A finger-board.

toucher (too-shä), *F.* 1. *As a noun,* touch. 2. *As a verb,* to touch, play.

touchette (too-shĕt'), *F.* Fret.

toujours (too-zhoor), *F.* Always. Vide SEMPRE.

touquet (too-kā), *F.* Toccato.

tourdion (toor-dĭ-ôn), *F.* See SALTA-RELLA 2.

tourmenté (toor-män-tä), *F.* Over-elaborated.

tourne-boute (toorn-boot), *F.* An instr. like a flute.

tour de force (toor dŭ fôrs), *F.* Bravura passage, etc.

tourniquet (toor-nĭ-kā), *F.* Plug, cap.

touta'ri. Hindu bagpipe.

tout (too), pl. touts (too), or toutes (toot), *F.* All. **t. ensemble** (too-tän-sän' bl). All; the whole together; the general effect.

toy. A trivial air or dance. **toy symphony.** A comic work, particularly one by Haydn employing toy cuckoo, trumpet, etc.

tp. Abbr. of Timpani.

tr. Abbr. for trumpet or trill

track'ers, *E.*, **Tractur** (träk-toor'), *G.* Vide ORGAN.

tract, *E.*, **trac'tus,** *L.* Solemn melodies sung from the Psalms during Lent in the Requiem Mass. The words are taken from the Psalms.

tradolce (trä-dōl'-chĕ), *I.* Very sweet.

tradotto (trä-dôt'-tō), *I.* Translated, arranged.

Tra'gen'der Stim'me, *G.* Portamento.

traîné (trĕ-nä), *F.* 1. Slurred. 2. A slow waltz.

trait (trĕ), *F.* 1. Passage as **t. de chant.** Vocal run. 2. A phrase, progression. **t. d'harmonie.** Sequence. 3. Rule. **t. d'octave.** Rate of the octave.

traité (trĕ-tä), *F.* A treatise.

Traktur (träk-toor'), *G.* Trackers. Vide ORGAN.

tranquillezza (trän-kwĭl-lĕd'-zä), **tranquillità** (trän-kwĭl-lĭ-tä'), *I.* Tranquillity. **tranquil'lo, tranquillamen'te.** Calm(ly).

transcription (in *F.* trän-skrēps-yôṅ). A rearrangement of a composition for a different instr. or instrs. **t. uniforme.** The notation, common in French bands, of writing all the transposing instrs. in the G clef.

tran'sient. Used of notes, chords and modulations that are merely passing and secondary, the means, not the end.

tran'sito, *L.*, **transit'ion** (in *F.* tränses-yôṅ). 1. A modulation of transient value; so also in Tonic Sol-fa.

tran'situs, *L.* A passing note (usually **t. re'gularis**). **t. irre'gularis.** Changing note.

transponi(e)ren (pō-nē'-rĕn), *G.* To transpose. **transponi'rende In'strumente.** Transposing instrs.

transpose, *E.*, **transposer** (trän-spô-zä), *F.* To change the pitch of a composition to a key higher or lower. Thus the tonic is replaced by the tonic of the new key, the old dominant by the new, etc.

transposing. 1. Used of **instruments,** which are not written as they sound, but always in the key of C major. This is done so that the player's ease and accuracy may be insured, by keeping the fingering, etc., the same in all keys, the key of the instr. being changed by changing the instr. entirely or merely changing a crook. The extent of this transposition is the interval between the key of the instr. and the key of C major. So an instr.

in B, sounds a half-tone lower than written; an instr. in E♭ sounds a major 6th below or a minor 3d above the actual note. 2. **t. piano,** etc., one in which, by a mechanism, the action is shifted to higher or lower pitch. **t.-scale.** Vide MODES.

transpositeur (träṅs-pō-zĭ-tŭr'), *F.* 1. One who transposes. 2. A single-valve inv. by Gautrot as a substitute for the series usually used. 3. A key-board instr., **piano t.,** inv. by A. Wolff, 1873.

transposition (in *G.* träns-pō-zē'-tsĭ-ōn). The changing of the key of a composition. **T.-skalen.** Transposing Scales. Vide MODES.

transverse flute. Vide FLUTE.

traquenard (träk-när), *F.* A brisk dance.

trascinando (trä-shĭ-nän'-dō), *I.* Dragging, retarding.

trascrit'to, *I.* Copied, transcribed.

trasportato (trä-spôr-tä'-tō), *I.* Transposed. **chiavi trasportati.** Vide CHIAVETTE.

tratt. Abbr. of **trattenuto.**

trattato (trät-tä'-tō), *I.* Treatise.

trattenuto (noo'-tō), *I.* Retarded.

Trauergesang (trow'-ĕr-gĕ-zäng), *G.* Dirge. **Trauermarsch** (märsh). Funeral-march. **trauervoll.** Sad. **traurig** (trow'-rĭkh). Heavy, sad.

travailler (trä-vī-yā), *F.* To work; to lead, play solo part. **travaillé** (vī-yā). Worked up elaborately.

Travers'flöte. 1. A cross-flute. 2. A 4-ft. stop.

traversiere (trä-vĕrs-yăr), *F.*, **traverso** (trä-vĕr'-sō). Vide FLUTE.

tre (trā), *I.* Three. **a tre.** For three voices or instrs. **tre cor'de.** Loud-pedal. Vide PIANO. **tre volte.** Three times.

treble. 1. The highest voice, soprano (from *triplum,* q.v.). 2. Highest part of a comp. 3. Highest register. 4. The highest of a group of instrs. **t. clef.** The G clef. **t. forte stop.** A stop for cabinet organs, increasing the treble at will, while the bass remains soft. **t. staff.** The staff on which the treble clef is placed.

Tredezime (trä-dā'-tsē-mĕ), *G.* Thirteenth.

treibend (trī'-bĕnt), *G.* Hurrying, accelerating.

treizième (trĕz-yĕm), *F.* Thirteenth.

tremblant (träṅ-bläṅ), *F.*, **tremen'do,** *I.* Shaking, **trembler** (blä), *F.* To trill. Vide TREMULANT. **trem-**

blement (trän-bl-mäṅ), *F.* A trill, shake.

tremolando (träm-ō-län'-dō), **tremolate** (lä'-tĕ), **tremolo** (trä'-mō-lō), **tremulo** (trä'-moo-lō), *I.* Trembling, trilling, quivering, reiterated with great rapidity.

trem'olant, trem'ulant. A stop which gives to the tone a waving or trembling effect.

tremore (trä-mō'-rĕ), **tremoro'so**, *I.* Tremor(ous).

tremuli(e)ren (trä-moo-lē'-rĕn), *G.* To trill.

trench'more. An old English dance in triple or compound duple time.

trenise (trä-nēz), *F.* Vide QUADRILLE.

trenodia (trä-nō'-dĭ-ä), *I.* A funeral-dirge.

très (trĕ), *F.* Very.

tres'ca, trescone (trĕs-kō'-nĕ), *I.* A country-dance.

Treter (trä'-tĕr), *G.* Bellows treader.

tri'ad, *E.*, **triade** (in *F.* trē-ăd; in *I.* trē-ä'-dĕ). A chord of three tones. Vide CHORD. **harmonic t.** Major triad.

tri'angle, *E.* (in *F.* trē-äṅgl), **Triangel** (trē'-äng-ĕl), *G.*, **triangolo** (trē-än'-gō-lō), *I.*, **triangulo** (trē-än'-goo-lō), *Sp.*, **triang'ulus**, *L.* A small steel rod bent into a triangle and tapped with a straight rod, for emphasising rhythm. **Triangular harp.** Vide HARP.

tri'as, *L.* Triad. **t. defic'iens.** Imperfect chord. **t. harmo'nica.** Perfect chord.

tri'chord. The three-stringed lyre. **t. piano.** One with three strings tuned in unison for each note. **trichord'-on.** 3-stringed colachon.

Trichter (trĭkh'-tĕr), *G.* 1. Tube of a reed-pipe. 2. Bell of horn, etc.

tricin'ium, *L.* An unaccompanied trio.

tricorde (trē-kôr'-dĕ), *I.* 3-stringed.

tridiapa'son, *Gr.* A triple octave.

tri'gon, trigo'num. A 3-stringed lyre-like instrument.

trihemito'nium, *Gr.* Minor third.

trill, trille (trē'-yŭ), *F.*, **Triller** (trĭl'-lĕr), *G.*, **trillo** (trĭl'-lō), *I.* The rapid alternation of a principal note with an auxiliary, usually the major or minor second above (a small chromatic sign being set above the note when its auxiliary is not to be diatonic). The trill begins on the auxiliary note only when the auxiliary is written as a grace note before the principal, in this case the trill

ends on the principal; normally it ends on the auxiliary. A trill is *long* or *short* (**trillette** (trë-yĕt), *F.*, **trillet'ta, trillet'to**, *I.*) according to the duration of the principal, the short trill sometimes amounting only to a mordent. A series of trills on different notes is a **chain of trills** (**Trillerket'te**). A mere rough rattle on one note instead of two notes crisply trilled is called **goat-trill, Bockstriller, chèvrotement**, or **trillo caprino.** **trillettino** (tē'-nō), *I.* A soft trill. **imperfect t.** One without a turn at the close. In Caccini's Method, 1601, the **trillo** was the reiteration of a single note, our trill being called **gruppo. trillando** (trĕl-län'-dō), *I.* 1. Trilling. 2. A succession, or chain, or shakes on different notes. **trillern** (trĭl'-lĕrn), *G* To trill. Vide GRACES and SIGNS.

trine (trēn). A triad, with 2 major thirds.

Trinkgesang (trĭnk'-gĕ-zäng), **T.-lied** (lēt), *G.* Drinking-song.

trino'na. Open 8-ft. stop.

trio (trē'-ō), *I.* 1. A composition for three instrs. or voices, often in sonata form. **pianoforte trio.** pf., vln., and 'cello. **string trio** (vln., viola (or 2d vln.), and 'cello). (The name was formerly used for 3 instrs., accompanied by a fourth playing basso continuo.) **organ trio.** A strongly contrasted work for 2 manuals and pedal or for 3 manuals. 2. In the dance-form, the contrastingly quiet or lyrical second division. Gaining its name from being once written in 3 parts, the word should now be laid aside as meaningless and confusing, and the phrase second part, or second subject used instead.

Triole (trĭ-ō'-lĕ), *G.*, **triolet** (in *F.* trĕ-ō-lä). A triplet.

triomphale (trē-ôṅ-făl), *F.*, **trionfale** (trē-ōn-fä'-lĕ), *I.* Triumphal. **triomphant** (trē-ôṅ-fäṅ), *F.*, **trionfante** (trē-ôn-fän'tĕ), *I.* Triumphant.

tripar'tite. In three parts.

tripel (trē'-pĕl), *G.* Triple, as **T. fuge,** triple fugue. **T.-konzert.** Triple concerto. **T.-takt.** Triple time. **T.-zunge.** Triple-tonguing.

triph'ony. Three sounds heard at once. **tripho'nia.** Organum in 3 parts. **triphonisch** (trē-fō'-nĭsh), *G.* Triphonic, 3-voiced.

tripla (trē'-plä), *I.* Triple time. **t. de min'ima.** 1. 3-2 time. 2. Triplet.

triple (in *F.* trêp'-l). Threefold. Vide TIME, COUNTERPOINT, etc. **t.-croche** (krôsh). 32d note.

trip'let. A group of three equal notes. **doublet.** A sextole.

trip'lum, *L.* The third part in organum, hence the highest; in 4-part next to the highest, the 4th being called quadruplum; if there is a 5th it is called quintuplum, etc.

tripola (trē'-pö-lä), *I.* Tripla.

Trisa'gion, *Gr.*, **Trisa'gium,** *L.* "Thrice Holy," the Sanctus.

trisemito'nium, *L.* Minor third.

tristezza (trĭs-tĕd'-zä), *I.* Sadness.

tristro'pha, *Gr.* Triple square note of the greater stress.

triton (trē-tôṅ), *F.*, **tritone** (trī'-tōn), *E.*, **tritono** (trē-tō'-nō), *I.*, **tri'tonus,** *L.* (in *G.* trē-tō-noos'). An augmented fourth; long a forbidden interval in strict writing, since it was augmented and was said to be hard to sing. **mi chord of the t.** Third inversion of the dominant seventh, which contains the tritone. Vide MI.

tri'ton a'vis, *L.* "3-toned bird," a West-Indian bird, capable of singing a note, and its twelfth and seventeenth, all at the same time.

Tritt (trĭt), *G.* Treadle, pedal. **Tritt'-schuh** (shoo). Place for the foot on bellows. **Tritt'harfe.** Pedal-harp. **Tritt'bret** or **T.-holz.** The board on which the bellows-treader steps.

tri'tus, *L.* Lydian Church-mode.

triumphirend (trē-oom-fē'-rĕnt), *G.* Triumphant. **Triumphlied** (lēt). Song of triumph.

trois (trwä), *F.* Three. *mesure à trois-deux* (trwä dŭ). 3-2 time. A *trois-huit* (trwä zwēt). 3-8 time. *trois-quatre* (trwä kătr). 3-4 time.

troll. 1. Round or catch. 2. *As a verb,* to sing a catch.

tromba (trōm'-bä), *I.* 1. A trumpet. 2. 8-ft. reed-stop. **t. croma'tica,** *I.* Valve trumpet. **t.-bas'sa,** or **di bas'so,** or **spezzata** (spĕd-zä-tä). The bass trumpet. **t. da tirar'si.** Old slide trumpet, perhaps a soprano trombone. **t.-marina** (ma-rē'-nä), *I.* Marine trumpet. **spezzata** (spĕd-zä'-tä), *I.* An obsolete name for the bass trombone. **t. sor'da.** Muted trumpet. **trombadore** (dō'-rĕ), **trombacelloclyde.** A B♭ ophicleide. **trombet'ta, trombettino** (tē'-no), **trombettatto're** or **-iere** (ĭ-ā'-rĕ). 1. Trumpet. 2. A small trumpet.

trombone (in *E.* träm'-bōn; in *I.*

trôm-bō'-nĕ; in *F.* trôṅ-bŭn), *I.,* pl. **-i.** 1. A trumpet-like instr. with valves; or more anciently, with a tube that may be lengthened or shortened by means of a U-shaped portion to be pushed in or drawn out. This *slide* moving by semitones has seven positions, each of which, virtually, makes a separate instr. of it with a distinct key, the partial tones of this being obtained by variations of pressure (vide EMBOUCHURE). The tone of the instr., though suffering from misuse in bad hands, is of the utmost richness, dignity and humanity. Berlioz calls it "epic." It is a non-transposing instr. in four sizes, the tenor being most used; the tenor and alto are written on the C clef, the bass and contrabass on the F clef, compasses, *tenor,* chromatic E–b'♭ (with *pedaltones* G,–B'♭, and difficult tones b'–d''), *alto,* A–e''♭; bass B,–f'. 2. A powerful 8, 16 or 32 ft. stop.

Trommel (trôm'-mĕl), *G.* Drum. **gros'se T.** Bass drum. **Militär-t.,** or **Wirbel-t.** Side drum. **Roll-t.** Tenor drum. **T.-bass.** A bass note thumped drum-wise. **T.-boden** (bō'-den). Bottom of a drum. **T.-kas'ten.** The body of a drum. **T.-klöpfel** (klĕp-fĕl), or **T.-schlägel** (shlä-gĕl). Drumsticks. **T.-schläger.** Drummer. **trom'meln.** To drum; drumming.

Trommelstück (trôm-mĕl-shtük), *G.* Tambourine, tabor.

trompe (trôṅp), *F.* 1. Hunt-horn. 2. Reed-stop. **t. de Béarn** (dŭ bā-ärn), or **à laquais** (ä lăk-ĕ'). Jew's harp.

Trompete (trôm-pā'-tĕ), *G.* 1. Trumpet. 2. A reed-stop. **Trompetengeige.** Marine trumpet. **Trompetenzug** (tsookh). Trumpet-stop.

Trompeter (trôm-pā'-tĕr), **trompéteur** (trôṅ-pā-tŭr), *F.* Trumpeter.

trompette (trôṅ-pĕt), *F.* 1. A trumpet. 2. Trumpeter. 3. A reed-stop. **t. à coulisse** (ä koo-lēs). Slide-trumpet. **t. à clefs** (ä klā). The trumpet with keys. **t. à pistons** (ä pēs-tôṅ). Valve trumpet. **t. d'harmonie** (dăr-mŭ-nē). Orchestral t. **t. harmonieuse** (ăr-môn-yŭz). Trombone. **t. marine.** Marine trumpet. **t. harmonique** (ăr-mŭn-ēk). A reed-stop.

troop. 1. A quick march for trooping the colours. 2. The 2d drum-beat as a march-signal.

trope, tro'pus. 1. A Gregorian formula for the close of the lesser doxology. 2. Mode.

troppo (tróp'-pō), *I.* Too, too much, *lento ma non* t. Slow, but not too slow.

troubadour (troo-bä-door), *F.*, **trovador** (trō-vă-dhôr), *Sp.*, **trovatore** (trō-vä-tō'-rĕ), *I.* A poet musician, usually of noble rank, skilled in singing, chiefly of love. The cult arising in Southern France, flourished widely from the 11th Century. The t. sometimes had hired minstrels (ménestrels, ménétriers, or jongleurs) in attendance on him. **trouvères** (troovăr), *F.* A cult of poet-musicians contemporary with and often confused with the troubadours, but more characteristic of the north of France, and singing songs rather of war and epic struggle than of love.

trüb(e) (trüp or trü'-bĕ), *G.* Sad.

Trug (trookh), *G.* Deception. **T.-fortschreitung.** Progression of a dissonance, not to its resolution, but to another dissonance. **T.-kadenz,** or **-schluss.** Vide CADENCE.

Trumbscheit (troomp'-shīt), *G.* Marine trumpet.

trump. 1. Trumpet. 2. Jew's harp.

trump'et. 1. A metal wind-instr. with a tube half as long as that of the horn, but bent in longer folds, and with a smaller bell. The tube is narrow and cylindrical till near the bell; the mouthpiece is hemispherical and cupped. It is a transposing instr. written in the G clef (almost always), and in the key of C. Its pitch is an octave higher than that of the horn, and it is used in fewer keys. It is the most commanding of all brass instrs., but its stopped tones are unpleasant. It should be written for in a distinctly vocal manner. It is fitted with crooks to give it any key, the tone being produced by embouchure (q.v.) except in the **valve,** or **chromatic, trumpet;** which is displacing the older form. Its extreme compass is d–b''♭. In England the **slide trumpet** is used, working like a trombone but with shorter slide. Trumpets of the same key but sounding an octave apart are called *alto* (high), and *basso* (low). 2. An 8-ft. reed-stop.

marine trumpet. An old instr. once used for signalling in the English navy, hence its name; also used in convents. whence it was called

"nun's fiddle." It was played chiefly in harmonics, and had one thick gut string, sometimes an octave string, and one or more drone-strings. The box was long and thin with short neck and flat belly; one foot of the bridge rested loosely producing a powerful resonance. **harmonic t.** A sackbut. **reed-t.** A trumpet with 36 brass-reeded pipes inclosed, arranged in a circle, so that each pipe was brought in turn between the mouthpiece and the bell.

Trumscheit (troom'-shīt), *G.* Marine trumpet.

t. s. Abbr. of Tasto Solo.

tscheng (chĕng). Cheng.

tschung (choong). Chinese gong.

tuba (too'-bä), *I.* 1. The lowest of the saxhorns (q.v.), an enormous brass horn with four pistons, a trombonelike mouthpiece, and a compass of 4 octaves. It is a non-transposing instr. (except in the case of a tenor-tuba in B♭, and a bass-tuba in F so written by Wagner), and is written in the G clef. It is usually made of 3 sizes, the **bass** or the **euphonium,** in B flat (compass available B,♭–f'), or in E,♭; the **bombardon,** a fifth lower; and the **contrabass tuba** (or **bombardon**) in B♭ an octave lower than the euphonium. 2. The straight Roman trumpet, or **t. communis;** the **t. duc'-tilis,** being curved. 3. **t. curva.** A limited natural French trumpet of the 18th Century. 4. A powerful 8-ft. reed-stop. **t. major, t. mirab'ilis, t. clarion.** A 4-ft. stop.

tu'bicen, *L.* A trumpeter.

tuck'et. A flourish of trumpets.

tuiau (twē-ō), *F.* Tuyau.

tumultuoso (too-mool-too-ō'-sō), *I.* Agitated.

tun. Ancient Yucatan drum.

tune. An air or melody, usually short and simple.

tu'ner. 1. One who tunes instruments. 2. The flap or cut in the top of a pipe by which it is tuned. 3. Tuning-cone.

tu'ning. 1. The correction of the tone-production of an instr. 2. Accordature. **t.-cone** or **horn.** A cone of horn or metal which can be inserted in the top of an organ-pipe; by "coning out" or increasing its flare and raising its pitch; by "coning in" or pressing it, point upwards. over the top of a pipe, it decreases the flare and lowers the pitch. **t.-**

DICTIONARY OF TERMS

2 705

crook. Vide CROOK. t.-fork. A small steel instr. with two prongs which upon being struck sounds a certain fixed tone. t.-hammer or key. A hand-wrench. t. slide. 1. An English instr. for producing thirteen semitones. 2. An adjustable U-shaped portion of the tube of certain brass instrs. t. wire. Vide REED and PIPE.

tuono (too-ō'-nō), *I.* 1. Mode, as t. ecclesias'tico. Church-mode. 2. Tone.

tuorbe (twôrb), *F.* Theorbo.

tur'ba, pl. -æ, *L.* "Crowd, multitude." The heathen or Jewish chorus in Passion music.

turbinoso (toor-bĭ-nō'-so), *I.* Tempestuous.

turbo (toor' bō), *Gr.* A seashell trumpet.

turco (toor'-kō), *I.* Turkish. alla turca. In the style of Turkish music.

turdion (toor'-dĭ-ōn), *Sp.*, turchesco (toor-kä'-skō), *I.* An old dance.

cürkish (tür'-kĭsh), *G.* Turkish. Turkisch-muzik. Janizary music.

turn. An embellishment consisting of a principal tone (struck twice) and one higher and one lower auxiliary a diatonic second removed, unless a chromatic sign accompanies the symbol; if a sharp or flat is placed above the turn-mark, it alters the higher auxiliary; if below, the lower. The common, direct, or regular turn usually begins on the upper auxiliary; the back or inverted t. begins with the lower; the rebounding or trilled t. begins with a passing shake; the double t. affects two notes at once. Vide GRACES.

turr. 3-stringed Burmese violin.

Tusch (toosh), *G.* A triple flourish of trumpets and drums.

Tute (too'-tĕ), *G.* Cornet.

tutta (toot'-tä), tutto, pl. tutte (toot'-tĕ), or tutti (toot'-tē), *I.* All; the entire band or chorus; in a solo or concerto it means that the full orchestra is to come in. tutte corde (kôr'-dĕ). "All the strings"; i. e., release the soft pedal. tutti. Full band or chorus—the entire force.

tutto ar'co. With the whole bow.

tuyau (twe'-yō), *F.* 1. Tube, as of a horn. 2. Pipe. t. à anche. Reedpipe. t. à bouche. Flue-pipe.

twelfth. 1. An interval of an octave plus a fifth. 2. A stop twelve tones above the diapasons.

twenty-second. A triple octave.

twice-marked, or -accented. Vide PITCH.

two-lined. Vide PITCH. two-time. Duple time. two-step. A dance in 6-8 time, somewhat resembling the waltz, but in duple accent.

tymb'estere. Vide TOMBESTERE.

tym'pan. 1. Timbrel. 2. Drum. 3. Irish instr., perhaps the crowd.

tympani (tĭm'-pä-nē), *I.*, pl. Kettledrums. tympanis'ta. Kettledrummer.

tympanischi'za. Marine trumpet.

tympan'on (tĕm-pä-nôn), *F.* 1. Dulcimer. 2. Kettle-drum.

tym'panum, *L.* 1. Ancient drum resembling the kettle-drum. 2. Kettle-drum. 3. The water-wheel in old hydraulic organs.

ty'pophone. A piano-like instr., with steel wands instead of strings, compass c'-c'''''.

tyrolienne (tē-rōl-yĕn), *F.* 1. Song, or dance peculiar to the Tyrolese; and characterised by the jodel. 2. Round dance in 3-4 time.

tzeltze'lim, *Heb.* Cymbals.

tzet'ze. Abyssinian guitar.

tzi'ti. Hindu bagpipe.

U

Übelklang (ü'-bĕl-kläng) or -laut (lowt), *G.* Discord. üben (ü'-bĕn), *G.* To practise.

über (ü'-bĕr), *G.* Over, above. Ü.-einstimmung (īn-shtĭm-moongk). Harmony. ü.-geführt (gĕ-fürt). Divided (of stops). ü.-greifen (grī-fĕn). (a) To cross the hands; (b) to lift the thumb from the neck of a 'cello. ü.-greifendes System (zĕs'-tām). Hauptmann's plan of forming a new key-system by adding to the group of triads of one key, a triad in its dominant or sub-dominant key. Ü.-blasen (blä-zĕn). Overblowing, to overblow. Ü.-gang (gäng). Transition, modulation. Ü.-leitung (lī-toongk). Transition passage. ü.-mässig (mĕs-sĭkh). Augmented. ü.-schlagen (shlä'-gĕn). (a) To cross over (the hands). (b) To overblow. (c) To break. ü.-setzen (zĕt'-zĕn). To pass a finger over the thumb; or one foot over the other. ü.-steigen (shtī'-gĕn). For a part to soar temporarily higher than the part normally above it.

Übung (ü-boongk), *G.* (pl. -en). Exercise; a study. **Übungsabend.** Pupils' concert.

ugab (oo'-gäb), *Heb.* An organ.

uguale (oo-gwä'-lĕ), *I.* Equal, like. **ugualità** (lĭ-tä'). Equality. **ugualmen'te.** Equality, alike.

umana (oo-mä'-nä), *I.* Human. **voce u.** (vō'-chĕ). 1. The human voice. 2. A stop.

Umfang (oom'-fäng), *G.* Compass.

umgekehrt (oom-gĕ-kärt'), *G.* Reversed, inverted.

Umkehrung (oom-kā'-roongk), *G.* Inversion.

umore (oo-mō'-rĕ), *I.* Humour.

um (oom), *G. Prefix* about, around.

umschlagen (slä'-gĕn). 1. To break, to make a pronounced change of register. 2. To overblow. 3. To make the goose. **Um'stimmung** (shtĭm-moongk). (a) Change. (b) Cordature, pitch or key.

un. Abbr. of Unison.

un (ŭṅ), *F.*, **un** (oon), **una** (oo'-nä), **uno** (oo'-nō), *I.* A, an, one.

unaccented. Vide PITCH.

unaccompanied. Without instrumental accompaniment.

unacknowledged. Used of passing or unessential notes.

un'ca, *L.* "Hooked"; quarter note. **bis unca.** 16th note.

uncoupled. With coupler released.

und (oont), *G.* And.

un'da ma'ris, *L.* "Wave of the sea." A stop tuned sharp or flat and producing an undulating effect by means of beats; sometimes a pipe with two mouths, one higher than the other.

undecima (oon-dä-chē'-mä), *L.* and *I.* An eleventh.

undecimole (oon-dä-chĭ-mō'-lĕ), *I.* A group of eleven equal notes.

underchord. The minor triad.

underpart. That beneath, or subordinate to others.

undersong. A burden.

undertone. A lower partial sometimes produced by the simultaneous sounding of two higher tones. (Vide ACOUSTICS.)

Undezime (oon-dā'-tsē-mĕ), *G.* An eleventh. **Unde'zimo'le.** Undecimole.

undula'tion, *E.*, **undulazione** (oon-doo-lä-tsĭ-ō'-nĕ), *I.* Vibrato effect on bow instruments.

une (ün), *F.* A, an, one.

uneigentliche (oon-ī'-gĕnt-lĭkh-ĕ). Irregular (of fugue).

unendlich(er) (oon-ĕnt'-lĭkh-(ĕr)), *G.* Endless (of canon).

unequal. 1. Vide TEMPERAMENT. 2. Of voices = mixed.

unessen'tial. Used of passing and grace notes, etc.

unfret'ted. Vide FRETTED.

ungar (oon'-gär), **ungarisch** (oon-gä'-rĭsh), *G.* Hungarian.

ungebunden (oon-gĕ-boont'-ĕn), *G.* 1. Vide FRETTED. 2. Unconstrained.

ungeduldig (oon-gĕ-dool'-dĭkh), *G.* Impatient.

ungerade Takt (oon-gĕ-rä'-dĕ täkt), *G.* Triple time.

ungestrichen (oon-gĕ-strĭkh'-ĕn). Unaccented. Vide PITCH.

ungestüm (oon'-gĕ-shtüm), *G.* Impetuous.

ungezwungen (oon-gĕ-tsvoong'-ĕn), *G.* Easy.

ungleich (oon'-glīkh). Unequal. Vide COUNTERPOINT. **ungleichschwebende.** (shvä-bĕn-dĕ). Unequal, of temperament (q.v.).

unharmo'nischer Querstand (kwär'-shtänt) or **umstand** (oom'-shtänt). False relation.

u'nichord, *E.,* **unichor'dum,** *L.* 1. Monochord. 2. Marine trumpet.

union (ün-yôṅ), *F.* Union. **u. des régistres** (dä rä-zhĕstr). Blending of registers.

unione (oo-nĭ-ō'-nĕ), *I.* Coupler.

u'nison (in *G.,* oo-nĭ-zōn'), **uniso'nus,** *L.,* **unisono** (oo-nē-sō'-nō), *I.*; **unisson** (ü-nĭs-sôṅ, *F.* 1. Identity of pitch. 2. Any octave of a pitch. 3. A tone of the same or octave pitch. 4. A prime, hence **augmented unison.** 5. A group of 2 or 3 strings tuned in the piano to one note. **all' unisono, à l'unisson,** in unison, or progressing in the unison or the octave.

unis'onant, unis'onous. In unison or octave.

unito (oo-nē'-tō), **unitamen'te,** *I.* United(ly). **uniti** cancels **divisi** (q.v.).

unmeasured. Without definite measure.

uno (oo'-nō), **una** (oo'-nä), *I.* One; A, an. **uno a uno.** One by one; one after another.

unrein (oon'-rīn'), *G.* Impure; out of tune.

unruhig (oon-roo'-ĭkh), *G.* Restless; uneasy.

unschuldig (oon-shool'-dĭkh), *G.* Innocent.

unsingbar (oon-zĭng'-bär), G. Not singable.

unstrung. Of strings (a) relaxed in tension, (b) removed entirely.

unter (oon'-tĕr), G. Under, below, sub. U.-bass (bäs). Double bass. U.-brechung (brĕkh'-oongk). Interruption. u.-brochen (brôkh-ĕn). Interrupted. U.-dominante (dō-mĭnän'-tĕ). Subdominant. U.-halbton (hälp-tōn). Half-step below. U.-haltungsstück (häl-toongs-shtük). Divertissement. U.-leitton (līt-tōn). Dominant seventh. U.-mediante (mä-dĭ-änt'-ĕ). Submediant. U.-satz (zäts). Supporter; a 32-ft. stop on the pedal. u.-setzen (zĕt'-zĕn). To pass the thumb under a finger; or one foot under another. U.-stimme. Lowest voice, or part. U.-tasten (täs-tĕn). The white keys of the piano or organ. U.-töne (tä-nĕ). Untertönreihe (rī-ĕ). Vide UNDERTONES.

unverziert (oon-fĕr-tsērt'), G. Unornamented.

unvolkommen (oon'-fôl-kôm-mĕn), G. Incomplete.

uomo (oo-ō'-mō), I. A man. Vide PRIMO.

up-beat. 1. The raising of the hand or bâton, hence 2. An unaccented part of a measure.

up-bow. Vide BOW.

upright. Vide PIANO.

ura'nion. An instrument like the harpsichord or piano.

uhr-heen. Chinese violin.

upper-clang. Vide CLANG.

uscir di tuono (oo'-shĕr dē too-ō'-nó), I. To get out of tune.

u'sus, L. 1. The rules of music. 2. Old synonym for neumes and the neume system.

ut (üt in F.; in I. and L. oot). 1. In France the key and note C, so used also in indicating pitch, as ut 2. 2. Vide SOLMISATION. 3. In Latin, as, like that. ut supra. As above, as before.

Ut que'ant lax'is, L. Vide SOLMISATION.

V

V. Abbr. for vide = see; violin(s); volti; voce.

va (vä), I. Go on. va crescendo (krĕ-shĕn'-dō), I. Go on increasing the volume.

vacilando (vät-chĭ-län'-dō), vaci-

lante (län'-tĕ), I. Wavering, irregular.

va'gans, L. Vague. Vide QUINTUS.

vago (vä'-gō), I. Vague, rambling.

valce (väl'-chĕ), I. Waltz.

valeur (vă-lŭr), F., val'or, L., valore (vä-lō'-rĕ), I. Duration (of a note).

valse (väls), F. Waltz; used in E. rather of a concert-piece (v. de salon), than of a strict dance-tune. v. chantée (shän-tä), vocal waltz. v. à deux temps (dŭ täṅ). A quick waltz, with two steps in each measure.

value. Duration of a note or rest.

valve, valvola (väl'-vō-lä), I. 1. The device inv. by Claggett, 1790, and Blühmel, 1813, by which natural brass instrs. are made chromatic. A natural horn produces the fundamental tone naturally made by a column of air of its exact length; it can be made to produce a series of partials of this tone by the method of blowing. Vide EMBOUCHURE and ACOUSTICS. The key of the horn can be changed by substituting for one section of its tube a longer or shorter section called a crook, which alters the length of the horn, and the column of air, and alters therefore its fundamental key and gives it a new series of partials. Until the valve-mechanism was invented a horn could therefore play only in one key at a time. Valve instrs. have auxiliary tubes fitted to the main tube; they are, in fact, merely stationary crooks. The pressure of a certain valve acts as an instantaneous change of crook by shutting off the air in one crook and turning it into another of different length. This device permits the sounding of a complete chromatic scale along the instrument's whole range. The valves are usually three in number, the first lowering the pitch a semitone, the second a tone, the third three semitones, thus giving a command of all keys (cf. HARP), (a) the piston, or piston-valve, is a plunger in an air-tight cylinder; by means of two holes the plunger at rest carries the air through the main tube; when pressed it shuts off the main tube and opens a side-tube, thus changing the key; a spiral spring restores it after pressure to the natural position. (b) the rotary valve is a stop-cock with four holes which produce the same effect. 2. organ-valves are (a) suction-valves, or

suckers, which admit the wind to the bellows and retain it there; (b) **joint-valves** which regulate the air-density in the wind channels. (c) **key-valves** or **pallets,** which are worked by a draw-stop; and (d) the **waste-pallet** relieving the bellows of surplus air.

valzer (väl-tsär), *I.* Waltz. **v. a due passi.** Two-step.

vamp. 1. To improvise an accompaniment or prelude. 2. Such an accompaniment or prelude.

variamento (vä-rĭ-ä-měn'-tō), *I.* Variation, difference. **variamen'te.** Varied, freely.

Varia'tion, *E.* (in *G.* fä-rĭ-ä-tsĭ-ōn', pl. **-en;** in *F.* vär-ĭ-äs-yŏn), **variazione** (vä-rĭ-ä-tsĭ-ō'-ně, pl. **-i),** *I.* The manipulation of a given theme or air. In the old sense (called **doubles),** and in cheap modern usage such as "Home, sweet Home with variations," the air is simply smothered in ornaments, arpeggios, etc.; in the better sense **(character variations)** the theme is subjected to as much remodelling, inversion, change of note-value, etc., as is possible without losing entire sight of its original meaning; sometimes merely the chord-relations are preserved. **variato** (vä-rĭ-ä'-tō), *I.*, **varié** (vă-rĭ-ä), *F.* Treated with variation.

varsoviana (ä'-nä), *I.,* **varsovienne** (vĭ-ěn), *F.* "Warsaw dance." Slow Polish dance in 3-4 time with an up-take of a quarter note, and an accented down-beat in every other measure.

vaudeville (vōd-věl), *F.* 1. A country ballad or roundelay, usually satirical. 2. Operatic or musical comedy.

vc., vcello. Abbr. for violoncello.

veemente (vä-ä-měn'-tě), *I.* Vehement. **veemenza** (měn'-tsä). Force.

veiled, velato (vä-lä'-tō), *I.* Marked by a desirable softening of the metallic quality of a tone; usually acquired by a slight escape of breath.

vellutato (věl-loo-tä'-tō), *I.* Velvety, smooth.

veloce (vě-lō'-chě), **velocemen'te,** *I.* Swift(ly). **velocis'simo.** With extreme rapidity. **velocità** (chē-tä'). Rapidity.

veneziana (vě-nä-tsĭ-ä'-nä), *I.* Venetian.

vent'age. A hole in flutes, etc., to be stopped with finger or key.

Ventil (in *G.* fěn'-tĭl), **ventile** (věn-

tē'-lě), *I.* 1. Valve, hence **Ventilhorn** or **-kornett.** 2. Organ-valve.

venusto (vä-noos'-tō), *I.* Beautiful. charming.

vêpres (věpr), *F.* Vespers.

Veränderungen (fěr-ěn'-děr-oong-ěn), *G.,* pl. Variations.

Verbindung (fěr-bĭn'-doongk), *G.* Binding, combination. **V.-szeichen** (tsĭ-khěn), *G.* Tie.

verdeckt (fěr-děkt'), *G.* Hidden.

verdoppelt (fěr-dôp'-pělt), *G.* Doubled. **Verdop'pelung** (oongk). Doubling.

Verengung (fěr-ěng'-oongk), *G.* Diminution of value or interval.

vergellen (fěr-gěl'-lěn), *G.* To diminish.

vergliedern (fěr-glē'-děrn), *G.* To articulate.

vergnügt (fěr-gnükht), *G.* Cheerful.

Vergrösserung (fěr-grěs'-sĕr-oongk), *G.* Augmentation.

Verhältniss (fěr-hělt'-nĭs), *G.* Ratio or proportion.

verhallend (fěr-häl'-lěnt), *G.* Dying away.

ver'ilay. Vaudeville.

Verkehrung (fěr-kä'-roongk), *G.* Imitation in contrary motion.

Verkleinerung (fěr-klī'-něr-oongk), *G.* Diminution.

Verkürzung (fěr-kür'-tsoongk), *G.* Diminution of value.

Verlängerungszeichen (fěr-lěng'-ěr-oongs-tsī'-khěn), *G.* Dot of prolongation.

verlöschend (fěr-lěsh'-ěnt), *G.* Dying away.

vermindert (fěr-mĭn'-děrt), *G.* Diminished.

Vermittelungssatz (fer-mĭt'-těl-oongks-zäts), *G.* Episode.

verrillon (věr-ē-yŏn), *F.* Mouth-harmonica.

Verschiebung (fěr-shē'-boongk). *G.* "Shift," soft pedal. **ohne V.** Without soft pedal. **mit V.** With soft pedal.

verschwindend (fěr-shvĭn'-děnt), *G.* Dying away.

verse. 1. Portion of an anthem or service to be sung by a soloist to each part, and not by the full chorus; hence **Verse-anthem,** and **Verse-service** for solo voices. 2. Line. 3. Stanza.

verset' (in *F.* věr-sä), **versetto** (věr-sět'-tō), *I.,* **Versette** (fěr-sět'-tě), *G.* 1. Short piece for the organ. 2. Versicle. **versetzen** (fěr-zět'-sěn), *G.* To transpose. **Verset'zung**

(zoongk). Transposition. **Verset'-zungszeichen** (tsī'-khĕn). The sharp, flat, and natural.

ver'sicle, *E.*, **Versikel** (fĕr'-sĭk-ĕl), *G.* A short phrase or line, combining with the response to form one sentence.

versila're, *L.* To sing antiphonally.

verso (vĕr'-sō), *I.* 1. Verse. 2. Air.

Verspätung (fĕr-shpā'-toongk), *G.* Retardation.

verstärkt (fĕr-shtĕrkt'), *G.* Sforzando.

verstimmt (fĕr-shtĭmt'), *G.* 1. Out of tune. 2. Depressed.

ver'tatur, ver'te, *L.* Turn over. **v. subito.** Turn quickly.

ver'tical. Of piano-strings, in one plane; opposed to overstrung.

vertönen (fĕr-tä'-nĕn), *G.* To die away.

verve (vĕrv), *F.* Spirit, energy.

verwandt (fĕr-vänt'). *G.* Related, relative. **V.-schaft** (shäft). Relationship.

Verwechselung (fĕr-vĕkh'-sĕl-oongk), *G.* Change, mutation, of key, etc.

verweilend (fĕr-vī'-lĕnt), *G.* Retarding.

Verwerfung (fĕr-vĕrf'-oongk), *G.* Transposing.

verzi(e)rt (fĕr-tsērt'), *G.* Embellished. **Verzi(e)rung** (tsē'-roongk). Ornament. **Verzögerung** (fĕr-tsākh'-ĕ-roongk), *G.* Retardation.

verzweiflungsvoll (fĕr-tsvī'-floongs-fôl), *G.* Full of despair.

Vesper (fĕs'-pĕr), *G.*, **vespero** (vĕs'-pĕ-rō), **vespro** (vĕs'-prō), *I.*, **ves'-peræ**, *L.* Vespers. Vide HORÆ.

vesperti'ni psal'mi, *I.*, pl. Evening psalms.

vezzoso (vĕd-zō'-sō), *I.*, **vezzosamen'-te**, *I.* Graceful(ly), tender(ly).

vi. Abbr. for violini.

vibrante (vē-brän'-tĕ), *I.* Vibrating, quivering.

vibrato (vē-brä'-tō), *I.* 1. Vibrating, resonant. 2. A strongly tremulous tone of distinct vibrations.

vibra'tion (in *F.* vĕ-brās-yôṅ). The regular oscillation of an elastic body, as a string, sounding-board, etc., contributing rapid periodic changes in the density of the air, which conveys the motion in sound-waves to the ear (without the air the vibrations are not conveyed to the air as sound; in a vacuum, a bell, for example, is not audible). The strength of the tone varies according to the *amplitude* or breadth of vibrations (travelling-distance of the elastic body back and forth); the pitch of the tone varies directly with the *rapidity* of the vibrations. The vibration-numbers of sounds vary in inverse ratio with the length of their sound-wave. A single vibration is from the point of rest to one extreme of motion, but is often calculated from one extreme to the opposite. A double vibration is measured from one extreme to the opposite and back again. **sympathetic v.** is that which is set up in an object (as a string, tuning-fork or even a plate) when the tone to whick it vibrates naturally is sounded by some other instrument. Thus press the loud pedal of a piano, to remove the dampers, and sing or play on a violin any note. This note will be heard at once sounding on the piano-string. Furthermore, its partials will be similarly heard.

vic'ar-choral. Lay vicar of a cathedral choir.

vicenda (vē-chĕn'-dä), *I.* Change. **vicendevole** (dā'vō-lĕ). Vacillating.

Vic'timæ pas'chali lau'des, *L.* "Praise the paschal offering." Vide SEQUENCE.

vi'de, vi'di, *L.* See. **vi-** is often put at the beginning of a passage to be cut, and **-de** at the end.

vide (vēd), *F.* "Empty"; open, of strings, as **corde à v.** opp. to **corde à jouer**, a string to be stopped.

Videl (fē-dĕl), *G.* Fiddle.

viel (fēl), *G.* Much, many. **v.-chörig** (kä-rĭkh). For several choruses. **v.-facher** (fäkh-ĕr). Polymorphous. **v.-stimmig** (shtĭm-mĭkh). Polyphonic.

viel(l)e (vĭ-ĕl), *F.*, **viella** (vĭ-ĕl'-lä), *I.* 1. Hurdygurdy. 2. Old viol. **vielleur** (vĭ-ĕl-lŭr), *F.* Player of the viol.

vier (fĕr), *G.* Four. **V.-achteltakt.** 4-8 time. **v.-doppelt.** Quadruple. **v.-fach** (fĕr'-fäkh). With four ranks of pipes, etc. **v.-füssig** (fēr'-füs-sĭkh). Four-foot (of pipes). **V.-gesang.** 4-part song. **v.-gestrichene Note.** 32d note. **v.-gestrichene Oktave.** Four-marked. Vide PITCH. **v.-händig** (hĕn-dĭkh). For four hands. **V.-klang** (fēr'-kläng). Chord of four tones; a seventh chord **v.-mässig** (fĕr-mĕs-sĭkh). Containing four measures. **v.-saitig.** Four-stringed. **v.-stimmig.** In four-parts.

V.-stück. Quartet. **vierte** (fēr'-tĕ). Fourth. **viertel** or **viertelnote.** Quarter note. **Viertelpause.** Quarter rest. **Viertelton.** Quarter note. **Vierundsechzigstel** (fēr-oont-zĕkhs'-ĭkh-shtĕl). 64th note. **Viervierteltakt** (fēr-fēr'-tĕl-täkt). 4-4 time. **vierzehn** (fēr'-tsān). Fourteen. **vierzehnte.** Fourteenth. **Vierzweiteltact** (fēr-zvī'-tĕl-täkt). 4-2 time.

vietato (vē-ā-tä'-tō), *I.* Forbidden.

vif (vēf), *F.* Brisk, quick.

vigoroso (vē-gō-rō'-sō), **vigorosamen'-te,** *I.* Bold(ly).

viguela (vē-goo-ā'-lä), **vihuela** (vē-hoo-ā'-lä), *Sp.* A primitive guitar.

villageois (vē-lă-zhwä), **villageoise** (zhwäz), *F.* Rustic.

villancico (vēl-yän'-thē-kō), **villancio** (vēl-yän'-thĭ-ō), *Sp.* 1. A church festival anthem. 2. A beginning and ending with chorus.

villanella (vēl-lä-nĕl'-lä), *I.*, **villanelle** (vē-yä-nĕl), *F.* "Village song," 15th cent. Italian folk-song of rustic tone and artless grace.

villanesco (nĕs'-kō), **villareccio** (vēl-lä-rĕt'-chō), *I.* Rustic.

villot'to, *I.* Secular song; cf. VILLA-NELLA.

7i'na. Ancient fretted 7-stringed Hindu instr. with body of bamboo, and two gourds for resonance.

vinata (vē-nä'-tä), *I.* A vintage-song. **vinet'ta.** Little vinata.

vi'ol, viola (vē-ō'-lä), *I.*, **viole** (in *F.* vē'-ōl; in *G.* fē-ō'-lĕ). 1. The **viola** in modern usage is the tenor or alto violin, a little larger in size than the normal violin, and tuned a fifth lower c–g–d'–a'. It is written on the C clef (except high notes, which are written in the G clef). Its tone is more sombre (very richly melancholy and elegiac indeed), and its harmonics are more limited. 2. The prototype of the violin. A fretted bow-instr. with 6 strings (sometimes 5 to 8); flat and tapering back; belly usually flat; sound-holes circular; bridge low to facilitate chords; tuned in fourths with one midway third. In 4 sizes *treble* (*alta*), *alto* (*alt* or *tenore*), *bass* (*bassa*), *contrabass* (*violone*). The **bass-viol** still persists in England. **v. di bardone** (bär-dō'-nĕ), *I.* A barytone viol, of the size of the 'cello, with 6 or 7 gut strings, and a number of wire resonance strings lying along the belly and

tuned diatonically. **v. bastarda** (bäs-tär'-dä), *I.* "Bastard viol." Large viol da gamba. **v. da braccio** (dä brät'-chō). "Arm-viol" as opposed to **v. da gamba,** "Leg-viol." **v. da spalla.** "Shoulder-viol," a larger arm-viol. **viola d'amore** (dä-mō'-rĕ), *I.*, **viole d'amour** (dä-moōr'), *F.* 1. Richly beautiful, but obsolete instr., larger than the viola, furnished with frets and more strings, some above, and some below the finger-board. 2. A stop. **v. pic'-cola** or **marina** (mä-rē'-nä). An instr. resembling the **v. d'amore.** **v. pomposa** (pôm-pō'-sä). A large viol of the compass of the 'cello, but with a fifth string. Inv. by J. S. Bach. **viol da gamba** (dä gäm'-bä), **viol di** (dē) **gamba.** "Leg-viol." A small obsolete violoncello, with frets and five or six strings. **viola alta** An enlarged viola inv. by Hermann Ritter of Wismar, Germany, 1877.

violento (vē-ō-lĕn'-tō), **violentemente** (lĕn-tĕ-mĕn'-tĕ), *I.* Violently. **violenza** (lĕn'-tsä). Fury.

vi'olin', *E.*, **Violine** (fē-ō-lē'-nĕ), *G.*, **violino** (vē-ō-lē'-nō), *I.*, **violon** (vē-ō-lôn), *F.* 1. "Small viol." A universally popular 4-stringed bow-instr. Developed possibly from the Viol, it has also been traced to the *lira da braccio;* it passed through many changes from about 1480–1530, when it assumed a shape little varied since. Though the name usually applies to one size, it may also be stretched to include the whole string quartet (which is the harmonic basis of the modern orchestra): the violin (or treble), the tenor violin or viola, the violoncello and the double bass. The violin proper has four gut or metal strings with the accordature, g–d'–a'–e''. Its tone is capable of great variety, sentiment and brilliance, its range extending from g to the highest note in the orchestra, e''''. It is rich in harmonics, but its resources in chords are limited and must be handled with great care for the fingering. Instrs. of the violin family consist of a curved *body*, or *resonance-box*, whose upper surface or *belly* is joined to a vaulted *back* by *ribs;* the body is curved in at the *waist*, the incurving being accented by *bouts*, whose *corners* are braced with *triangular blocks;* the belly (on which the *bridge* rests between slits called *sound-holes,* or from their shape *f-holes*) is braced with a thin strip (under the G string) called the *bass-bar*. A round prop or *soundpost* beneath the treble foot of the bridge connects the back and the belly. The *finger-board* is on the *neck*, which terminates in a *head* ornamented with a *scroll* and containing a *peg-box*, in which are four movable *pegs* from each of which a string passes across a ridge called the *nut*, along the finger-board and over the bridge to the flat *tail-piece* which is fastened by a *loop* of gut to a *button* in the lower end of the body. 2. A 2, 4, and 8 ft. stop. Violinbo̱gen (fē-ō-lēn'-bō-khĕn), *G.* A vln.-bow. Violin-clef, Violinschlüssel or -zeichen, *G.* The G clef. violinier (lĭn-ĭ-ā), violiniste (nēst), *F.*, violinista (nēs'-tä), *I.*, Violinspieler, *G.* A violin-player. violino alto, *I.* A small tenor viol. violino picciolo (pĭt'-chō-lō), pic'colo, pochetto (kĕt'-tō), *I.* A small vln. tuned a fifth higher. v. pompo'so, *I.* A viola with an additional higher string. violin-principal. A 4 or 8 ft. stop. Violinsaite. Violin-string. Violin-steg (stäkh). Violin-bridge. Violinstimme. Violin-part. Violin-tenor. A vln. of low tone. violon de fer (dŭ fĕr). Iron fiddle. violinata. A piece for violin, or in violin style. violinzo'li. 8-ft. stop on the swell. Violon (fē-ō-lōn'), *G.* The double-bass.

violier (vē-ôl-yā), violiste (lēst'), *F.* Viola-player.

violonar (vē-ō-lō-nǎr'), *F.* Double-bass. violonaro (nǎr'-ō). Octo-bass.

Violoncell (fē-ō-lōn-tsĕl'), *G.*, violoncelle (vē-ō-lôṅ-sĕl), *F.*, violoncello (vē-ō-lōn-chĕl'-lō), *I.* "Little violone." Commonly abbr. 'cello. Large 4-stringed instr. of vln.-family (vide VIOLIN) held between the knees and resting on a *standard* or *peg.* It is tuned an octave below the viola, C, G, d, a. Its music is written chiefly in the C clef, save high notes in the G clef, and low in the F clef (formerly it was all written in the G clef, an octave higher than it sounded). Chords and harmonics are little used, except in solos. The 'cello is one of the most important of orchestral instrs., and one of the most expressive, especially of the graver or more yearning emotions, its gayety being rather sardonic.

violone (vē-ō-lō'-nĕ), violono (lō'-nō), *I.* "Large viol." 1. Double-bass. 2. Pedal-stop.

violot'ta. A large viola devised by Stelzner, Dresden, 1895, and tuned G, d, a, e'.

vir'elay. Vaudeville (also from the town of Vaux de Vire).

vir'gil, *L.* A neume.

Virgil practice-clavier. A mechanical piano inv. by A. K. Virgil, 1883, for practice-purposes, the heaviness of touch being adjustable in 6 gradations; a click answering the depression of a key, and another click its release.

vir'ginal(s). A small spinet-like instr. popular in the time of Queen Elizabeth and placed upon a table.

Virtuos (fēr-too-ōz'), *G.*, virtuoso (vēr-too-ō'-sō), *I.*, virtuose (vĭr-tü-ôz), *F.* A performer of marked skill. Virtuosität (ō-zĭ-tät'), *G.* Virtuosity. Remarkable execution.

vis-à-vis (vē-zä-vē'), *F.* "Face to face." A large double piano with 2 opposite key-boards.

vista (vēs'-tä), *I.* Sight. a prima v. At (first) sight.

visto (vēs'-tō), vito (vē'-tō), vi(s)tamen'te, *I.* Swift(ly).

vite (vēt), vitement (vēt-mäṅ), *F.* Quick(ly).

vitesse (vē-tĕs), *F.* Swiftness.

vivace (vē-vä'-chĕ), *I.* Lively, faster than *Allegro.* vivacemen'te. Briskly, quickly. vivacet'to (chĕt'-tō). Rather lively. vivacezza (chĕd'-zä), vivacità (vē-vä-chĭ-tä'). Vivacity. vivacis'simo. Very fast. vivamen'te. Briskly.

vive (vēv), *F.* Brisk, quick.

viven'dum, ad., *L.* "To live" i. e., for permanence. Written, as opposed to improvised, counterpoint.

vivente (vē-vĕn'-tĕ), vivido (vē'-vĭ-dō), vivo (vē'-vō), *I.* Animated. vivezza (vē-vĕd'-zä). Liveliness.

vla. Abbr. for viola.

vo'cal, vocale (vō-kä'-lĕ in *I.*; in *F.* vō-kǎl'), voca'lis, *L.* Relating or appropriate to the human voice. vocal chords. The two membranes in the larynx whose tensity is regulated at will to produce desired pitches. Vide GLOTTIS. rima vocalis. The opening between the vocal chords.

vocalezzo (vō-kä-lĕd'-zō), *I.* A vocal exercise.

voca'lion. Vide REED-ORGAN.

vocali'ses (in *F.* vō-kä-lēz'). Solfeggio exercises for the voice.

vocaliser (vō-kȧl-ĭ-zā), *F.*, **vocalizzare** (vō-kä-lĭd-zä'-rĕ), *I.*, **vo'calize,** *E.* To practise exercises for the voice without words.

vocalisa'tion (in *F.* vō-kä-lĕ-zȧs-yȯṅ). 1. The practice of exercises for the voice. 2. Display of vocal agility.

vocalizzo (lĭd'-zō, pl. -i), *I.* Vocal exercise.

voce (vō-chĕ), *I.* Voice. **colla v.** "With the voice," i. e., adopting the tempo of the solo part. **v. angelica** (än-jä'-lĭ-kä). "Angel voice." Delicate reed-stop. **v. di bianca** (dē bĭ-än'-kä), *I.* "White voice." Applied to pale and colourless tones, such as the voices of young women, children and poorly trained adults. **v. di ca'mera.** A small voice for the chamber. **v. di go'la.** A guttural, throaty voice. **v. di pet'to.** The chest voice. **v. di tes'ta.** Head voice, the falsetto, upper register. **v. granità** (grä-nē-tä'). A "granite" or massive voice. **mezza voce** (mĕd'-zä). Half the power of the voice; a moderate tone. **v. pasto'sa.** A soft, flexible voice. **v. principale** (prēn-chĭ-pä'-lĕ). Principal voice. **v. rauca** (ra'-oo-kä). A hoarse, rough voice. **v. so'la.** The voice alone. **v. spianata** (spē-ä-nä'-tä). Drawn out; smooth, sustained voice. **v. spiccata** (spĭk-kä'-tä). A clear, distinct voice; well articulated. **v. umana** (oo-mä'-nä). The human voice. Vide VOX HUMANA. **vociaccia** (vō-chĭ-ät'-chä). A bad, disagreeable voice. **vocina** (vō-chē'-nä). Thin little voice.

voces, *L.*, pl. of **vox. v. aequa'les.** Voices of the same kind.

Vogar (fō'-gär), *G.* Fugara.

Vogel (fō'-gĕl), *G.* Bird. **V.-flöte** or **pfeife.** A bird-whistle. **V.-gesang.** "Singing of birds"; stop in old German organs, of small pipes standing in water, through which the wind passes; a merula.

voglia (vōl'-yä), *I.* Ardour.

voice. 1. The sound produced by the larynx of human beings or animals. 2. Part (for any instr.), often voice-part. 3. The tuning and tone of organ-pipes. Of the human voice, these are the following divisions: *basso, tenor, counter-tenor, contralto* or *alto, mezzo-soprano, soprano* (Vide each of these

words). Each voice is also divided into registers (or groups of tones of a uniform quality), the transition from one to another register being sometimes distinct enough to be called a *break;* there are usually two breaks in a male, and three in the female voice. The registers are chest, head and falsetto (q.v.).

voicing. The adjustment of the pitch and quality of a pipe.

voilée (vwä-lä), *F.* Veiled.

voix (vwä), *F.* 1. Voice(s). 2. Part(s). **v. angélique** (vwä-zäṅ-jä-lēk). Vox angelica. **v. céleste** (sä-lĕst), *F.* "Celestial voice," a stop formed of two dulcianas, one slightly sharp, thus giving a vibrato. **v. de poitrine** (dŭ pwä-trēn), *F.* Chest voice. **v. de tête** (dŭ tĕt). Head voice, falsetto voice. **v. glapissante** (glä-pē-säṅt). A shrill voice. **v. grêle** (vwä grĕl). A sharp, thin voice. **v. humaine** (ü-mĕn). Vox humana.

vokal (fō-käl'), *G.* Vocal. **V.-stil** (shtēl). Vocal style.

volante (vō-län'-tĕ), *I.* "Flying," light, swift.

volata (vo-lä'-tä), *I.*, **Volate** (vō-lä'-te) *G.*, **volatine** (vō-lä-tēn), *F.* "Flight," run, rapid series of notes. **volatina** (vō-lä-tē'-nä), *I.* A little volata.

volée (vō-lā), *F.* A volata.

Volk (fōlk), *G.* Folk; of the common people. **V. gesang** (fōlk' gĕ-zäng). **V. s-lied** (slēt), **V. stückchen** (stük'-kh'n), **V.sweise.** Folk-song or folk-music. **im Volkston'** or **Volksweise.** In folk-tone or style. **volkst(h)ümliches** (tüm-lĭkh-ĕs). Lied. Popular folk-song.

voll (fōl), *G.* 1. Full; *mit vollem Werk,* Chore, Orchester,* with the full organ, chorus or orchestra. **völler** (fĕl'-lĕr). Fuller, louder. **volles Werk** (fōl'-lĕs värk). Full organ. **Vollgesang.** Chorus. **vollgriffig** (grif-fĭkh). "Full-handed," with full chords. **volkom'men.** Perfect, complete. **vollstimmig.** Full-toned, full-voiced. **Vollstimmigkeit.** Fullness of tone. **volltönend,** *G.* Sonorous. 2. As a suffix = full, as **gedankenvoll.** Thoughtful.

volonté (vō-lŏṅ-tā), *F.* Will, pleasure. **à v.** At will.

volta (vōl'-tä), *I.* 1. Time. 2. A kind of galliard. **prima v.** (prē'-mä). First time. **una v.** One. **due volte.** Twice.

voltare (vōl-tä'-rĕ), *I* To turn, to turn over.

volte (vōl'-tĕ, *I;* in *F.* vōlt). 1. An obsolete bounding dance in 3-4 time resembling the galliard. 2. Pl. of VOLTA.

volteggiando (vōl-tĕd-jän'-dō), *I.* Crossing the hands. volteggiare. To cross hands.

volti (vōl'-tĕ), *I.* Turn over. v. subito. Turn quickly.

volubilità (vō-loo-bē-lĭ-tä'), *I.* Volubility. volubilmen'te. Fluently.

vol'ume. Quality of tone.

vol'untary. 1. An introductory organpiece often extemporaneous. 2. An introductory anthem. 3. A species of toccata in two or three movements.

volver a la misma cancion (vōl-vär ä lä mēs'-mä kän'-thĭ-ōn), *Sp.* To return to the same (original) air.

vom (fōm), *G.* = *von dem.* From the.

vom Anfang. From the beginning.

vom Blatte (blät'-tĕ). "From the page," i. e., at first sight.

von (fōn), *G.* By, of, from, on.

vor (fōr), *G.* Before, pre-.

Vorausnahme (fōr-ows'-nä-mĕ), Vorgreifung (fōr-grī'-foongk), Vorgriff (fōr'-grĭf), *G.* Anticipation. Vorbereitung (fōr'-bĕ-rī-toongk). Preparation. Vorberei'tungsunterricht (soon'-tĕr-rĭkht). Preparatory instruction.

Vor'dersatz (zäts), *G.* First subject.

Vor'geiger (gī-khĕr), *G.* First violin, leader.

Vorhalt (fōr'-hält), *G.* 1. Suspension. Vorhaltslösung (lä-zoongk). Its resolution. 2. Syncopation.

vorher (fōr-hār), *G.* Before. tempo wie vorher, *G.* The time as before.

vorig (fō'-rĭkh), *G.* Former, preceding. voriges Zeitmass. In the original tempo.

Vorsang (fōr'-zäng), *G.* Act of beginning a song. Vorsänger (fōr'-zĕngĕr). Precentor.

Vorschlag (fōr'-shläkh). Accentuated, appoggiatura.

Vorsetzzei'chen, *G.* Chromatic sign.

Vorspiel (fōr'-shpĕl), *G.* Prelude; overture. Vor'spieler (shpē-lĕr). Leader, principal performer. Vortänzer. Chief dancer. Vorsteller. Performer.

Vortrag (fōr'-träkh), *G.* Execution, interpretation. Vortragsbezeichnung (bĕ-tsīkh-noongk). Expression

mark. vortragsstück. Concertpiece.

vorwärts (fōr'-värts), *G.* "Forward," i. e., faster.

Vorzeichnung (tsīkh'-noongk). 1. Signature. 2. Outline of a composition.

vox (vōx), *L.* Voice. v. acu'ta. 1. A shrill voice. 2. In ancient music, the highest note in the bisdiapason. v. ange'lica, *L.* "Angelic voice," a 4-foot stop of sweet tone, also v. virgin'ea. "Girlish voice." v. antece'dens. The antecedent. v. con'sequens. The consequent. v. grav'is. Low voice. v. huma'na. "Human voice," 8-foot reed-stop usually with tremulous effect. v. retu'sa. 8-foot stop. Plural vo'ces. v. aequales. Voices of the same kind, as male voices. v. areti'niæ. Aretinian syllables. v. bel'gicæ. The syllables of bocedisatio *.*

v. s. Abbr. of Volti subito.

vue (vü), *F.* Sight. à premier v. (ä prŭm-yä vü). At first sight.

vulgans (tibia), *L.* A flute-stop.

vuide (vwēd), *F.* Open (of a string).

vuoto (voo-ō'-tō), *I.* 1. Open (of a string). 2. Empty (of a stage).

v. v. Abbr. for violini.

W

W. 1. In *F.* = v. v., i. e., Violins. 2. Vide the letter i.

Wachtel (väkht'-ĕl), *G.* "Quail." A toy pipe.

wahnsinnig (vän'-zĭn-nĭkh), *G.* Frantic.

waits, *E.* 1. Hautboys. 2. Players on the hautboys. 3. Night-watchmen. 4. Christmas carollers.

Wald (vält), *G.* Forest. Waldflöte, *G.,* or -pfeife. Forest-flute. W.-quinte. A stop. W.-flötenquinte. A stop a fifth higher. Waldhorn (vält'-hôrn), *G.* "Foresthorn"; a winding-horn. (Vide HORN.)

walnika (väl-rē'-kä). Russian bagpipe.

wals (wäls), *Dutch.* A waltz.

waltz, *E.,* Walzer (väl'-tsĕr), *G.* 1. A popular modern round dance in 3-4 time, perhaps of Bohemian origin. The speed and rhythm vary, the Ländler, or German, being slow; the Vienna, or Schleif-walzer being quicker; the Zweitritt, deux-temps, or two-step, having but two steps to the measure. 2. A concert-piece in triple time, usually brilliant.

walynka (vä-lĕn'-kä). Russian bagpipe.

Walze (väl'-tsĕ), *G.* "Roller." An undulating figuration.

wankend (vän'-kĕnt), *G.* Wavering, hesitating.

war'ble. A bagpipe grace.

Wärme (vĕr'-mĕ), *G.* Warmth.

Washington Post. In England a dance (so called from J. P. Sousa's march of that name) in which the man dances behind the woman.

was'sail. A convivial song.

Wasserorgel (väs'-sĕr-ôr-khĕl), *G.* Hydraulic organ.

waste-pallet. Vide VALVE.

water music. Handel's name for certain airs, performed on the water, for the King.

water-organ. Hydraulic organ.

wayghtes. Old *E.* Waits.

Web'er chronom'eter. Metronome, inv. by Weber. A cord divided into five inch-spaces, with a weight at the lower end. Abbr. **Web. Chron.**

Wechsel (vĕkh'-sĕl), *G.* Change. **W.-chor** (kōr). Alternate choir. **W.-gesang.** Antiphonal song. **W.-note** (nō'-tĕ). Changing note.

Wehmuth (vä'-moot), *G.* Sadness. **wehmüthig** (vä'-mü-tǐkh). Sad, sorrowful.

Weiberstimme (vī'-bĕr-shtǐm'-mĕ), *G.* A female voice.

weich (vīkh), *G.* 1. Soft. 2. Minor.

weight of wind. Vide INCH.

Weihnachtslied (vī'-näkhts-lēt), *G.* Christmas hymn.

weinend (vī'-nĕnt), *G.* Weeping.

Weise (vī'-zĕ), *G.* 1. Melody. 2. Manner; as a suffix = -wise.

weisse Note (vīs'-sĕ nō'-tĕ), *G.* "White" note; half or whole note.

weit (vīt), *G.* Dispersed, open (of harmony).

Welle (vĕl'-lĕ), *G.* Roller of an organ. **Wellatur** (toor'). Roller-system. **Wel'lenbrett.** Roller-board.

well-tempered. In equal temperament, as in Bach's "*Well-tempered Clavichord*," a series of clavichord pieces ranging through all the keys. Vide TEMPERAMENT.

Welsh-harp. Vide HARP.

weltlich (vĕlt'-lǐkh), *G.* Secular.

wenig (vä'-nǐkh), *G.* Little. **ein wenig.** A little, rather.

Werk (vĕrk), *G.* 1. Work. 2. Movement. 3. Action. Vide HAUPTWERK

and OBERWERK. 4. A stop. 5. The set of stops belonging to one keyboard.

Wert(h) (vĕrt), *G.* Value, duration.

wesentlich (vä'-zĕnt-lǐkh), *G.* Essential. **wesentliche Dissonanz.** A dissonant chord-tone, opposed to passing-note. **wesentliche Septime.** Dominant seventh.

Wetter-harfe (vĕt'-tĕr-här-fĕ), *G.* "Weather-harp." Æolian harp.

Wettgesang (vĕt'-gĕ-zäng), *G.* A singing-match.

wheel. Refrain, burden.

whiffler. A fifer.

whipping bow. A swift and violent violin attack.

whistle. A small, shrill wind-instr. blown at the end, like an old English flute.

whole note, rest, shift, step, tone, etc. Vide the NOUNS.

wie (vē), *G.* As. **wie aus der Ferne.** As from a distance. **wie oben.** Again as above. **wie vorher** (fōr-här). As before.

wieder (vē'-dĕr), *G.* Again. **W.-gabe** (gä'-bĕ). Performance. **W.-herstellungszeichen** (tsī'-khĕn). The natural sign (♮). **w.-anfangen.** To begin again. **W.-holung** (hō-loongk) Repetition. **W.-holungszeichen.** Sign of repetition. **W.-klang** (kläng), **W.-schall** (shäl). Echo.

Wiegenlied (vē'-gĕn-lēt), *G.* Cradlesong.

wild (vēlt), *G.* Wild.

wind (wīnd). To blow, as a horn.

Wind (in *G.* vǐnt). Air. **w. band.** 1. A band of wind-instrs. 2. The instrs. or the music for them. **windchest.** Vide ORGAN. **w. instruments.** A general name for all instrs. whose tone is produced by the breath or by bellows. **windtrunk.** A passage conveying air from the bellows to the wind-chest. **Windmesser** (mĕs-sĕr), *G.*, **windgauge.** Vide INCH. **W.-harfe**, *G.* Æolian harp. **Windlade** (lä-dĕ), *G.* Wind-chest. Vide ORGAN. **Windstock** (shtôk), *G.* Cover of organpipes. **Windzunge** (tsoong-ĕ), *G.* Tongue of a pipe. **W.-harmo'nika,** *G.* Æolodion.

winselig (vǐn'-zĕ-lǐkh), *G.* Plaintive. **Winselstimme.** Plaintive voice.

Wirbel (vĕr'-bĕl), *G.* 1. Peg (of a violin). **Wirbelkasten.** Peg-box. 2. Stopper of a pipe. 3. Drum-

stick. 4. Roll (on a drum). **Wir-beltanz** (tänts). A whirling dance.
wogend (vō′-gĕnt), *G.* Waving.
wohl (vōl), *G.* Well. **Wohlklang** (vōl′-kläng), **Wohllaut** (lowt). Harmony. **wohlklingend.** Harmonious. **wohltemperi(e)rt** (vōl-tĕm-pĕ-rērt′), *G.* "Well-tempered" (q.v.).
Wolf (in *G.* vôlf). 1. The disagreeable snarling of two pipes not quite in perfect tune. 2. Vide TEMPERAMENT. 3. In bow-instr. the roughness of certain tones due to faulty workmanship. 4. Vide ORGELWOLF. 5. The 12th and most troublesome of the circle of fifths. Vide TEMPERAMENT.
wood-wind. 1. The whole group of wooden instrs. in the orchestra. 2. Organ-stops of wood.
working-out. Development. Vide FORM.
Wortklang (vôrt′-kläng), *G.* Accent, tone.
wrest. A tuning-hammer. **wrestpins.** In a piano movable pins round which one end of the string is wound; by turning this the instr. is tuned.
wrestplank. A plank of several layers of wood in which the wrestpins are driven.
wristguide. Vide CHIROPLAST.
wuchtig (vookh′tĭkh). Weighty, emphatic.
Würde (vür′-dĕ), *G.* Dignity. **würdevoll, würdig** (vür′-dĭkh). Dignified.
Wut(h) (voot), *G.* Madness. **wüthend** (vü′-tĕnt), **wüthig** (tĭkh). Furious.

X

Xænorphika (ksän′-ôr-fĭ-kä), *G.* A piano-violin with a bow to each string, inv. by Röllig, 1797; he also inv. the somewhat similar *orphika.*
xylharmo′nica or **-con,** *Gr.* Utro's improvement in 1810 upon his **xylosiston,** inv. 1807; a euphonion with wooden, instead of glass, rods.
Xylorganon (ksĕl-ôr′-gä-nōn), *Gr.* Xylophone.
xylophone (zĭl′-ō-fōn). A graduated series of bars of wood upon bands of straw or cord, played with wooden mallets, compass 2 octaves.

Y

Yabal (yä′-bäl), *Heb.* Trumpet blast.
yang kin. A Chinese dulcimer with brass strings.

yo. Indian flute.
yo′del, yod′ler. Vide JODEL, JODLER
yue′kin. Chinese guitar.

Z

Za (zä). Formerly applied by the French to B♭ to distinguish it from B♮ or *Si.*
zahlen (tsä′-lĕn), *G.* To count. **zahle.** "Count!" **Zahlzeit** (tsīt). A count.
zaleo (thä-lä′-ō), *Sp.* Vide JALEO.
zampogna (tsäm-pōn′-yä), **zampugna** (poon′-ya), *I.* 1. Ancient bagpipe. 2. A shawm. Vide CORNAMUSA and CHALUMEAU. **zampognare** (pōn-yä′-rĕ). To play the pipes. **zampo-gnato′re.** A piper. **zampognet′ta** or **-ina** (pōn-yē′-nä). A small bagpipe.
za′ner. Egyptian bassoon.
zanze. Vide AMBIRA.
zapateado (thä-pä-tä′-ä-dhō), *Sp.* A dance whose rhythm is emphasised by stamping the heel.
Zapfenstreich (tsä′-pfĕn-strīkh), *G.* The tattoo.
zarabanda (thä-rä-bän′-dhä), *Sp.* Saraband.
zaramel′la (tsä-rä-), *I.* Rustic double-reed pipe with bell-mouth.
Zargen (tsär′-khĕn), *G.,* pl. Sides of violin, etc.
zart (tsärt), *G.,* **zärtlich** (tsärt-likh). Tender, delicate. *mit zarten Stimmen,* with delicate stops. **Zartflöte.** A very soft 4-foot flute-stop.
zarzuela (thär-thoo-ā′-lä), *Sp.* A 2-act drama with music, something like the vaudeville; originating in the 17th century at the royal castle Zarzuela.
Zauber (tsow′-bĕr), *G.* Magic. **Z.-lied** (lēt). Magic song.
zeffiro′so (tsĕf), *I.* Zephyr-like.
zehn (tsān) *G.* Ten. **Zehnte** (tsän′-tĕ). Tenth.
Zeichen (tsī′-khĕn), *G.* Sign(s).
Zeit (tsīt), *G.* Time. **Z.-mass** (tsīt′-mäs), *G.* Tempo. **Zeitmes′ser.** Metronome. **Z.-werth.** Time value.
zèle (zĕl), *F.,* **zelo** (tsä′-lō), *I.* Zeal, ardour. **zelo′so, zelosamen′te.** Zealous(ly).
zeng (tsĕng). Persian cymbals.
Zergliederung (tsĕr-glēt′-ĕr-oongk), *G.* Dissection, or analysis of a subject.
zerstreut (tsĕr-stroit′), *G.* Dispersed.
ze′ze. An African guitar.
Ziehharmo′nica (tsē), *G.* The accordion.

ziemlicn ⟨tsēm'-lĭkh⟩, *G.* Rather; mod:rately.

Zierathen (tsē-rä'-tĕn), *G.*, pl. Ornaments.

zierlich (tsēr-lĭkh), *G.* Neat, graceful.

Ziffer (tsĭf'-fĕr), *G.* Figure, Arabic numeral.

ziganka (chĭ-gän'-kä), *Russian.* Country-dance.

Zigeunerartig (tsē-goin'-ĕr-är-tĭkh), *G.* In gypsy style. **Z.-musik** (moo-zēk'). Gipsy music.

zikrs. Dances of Egyptian dervishes.

zillo (tsĭl'-lō), *I.* Chirp, chirping.

zimbalon. Vide CZIMBALON.

Zimbel (tsēm'-bĕl), *G.* Cymbal. **Z.-stern.** A star hung with small bells in front of an organ and sounded by a current of air.

zingana (chēn-gä'-nä). Bohemian song.

zingarese (tsēn-gä-rā'-zĕ), *I.* Gipsy. **zingaresca** (rĕs'-kä). In the style of gipsies. **zingaro** (tsēn'-gä-rō). Gipsy.

Zinke (tsĭnk'-ĕ), pl. -en, *G.* Cornetto, ancient or modern. **Zinkbläser** (tsĭnk'-blä-zĕr), *G.* Cornet-player.

zith'er (in *G.* tsĭt'-ĕr). 1. The modern (or **Schlagzither**) is a flat, shallow resonance-box without a neck, with about thirty-six strings of various material—wire and gut—some overspun. Under some of the strings at one side lies a fretted finger-board; on these the melody is stopped out with the left hand. These strings, tuned a', a', d', g, c, are plucked with a plectrum attached to the right thumb; the rest of the strings are tuned in fourths, and plucked with the other fingers of the right hand. It is made usually in 3 sizes, the Treble or **Prim** (prēm) -z; the **concert**; and **elegie** (ĕl-ĕ-jē') (or **Alt** or **Lieder**) -z, which is tuned a fourth lower. 2. **bow-zither** or **Streichzither** (strĭkh), *G.* Was originally heart-shaped, but the **philomèle** now resembles a more pointed viola with shallow bouts (the **viola-zither** having a still closer resemblance). The **bow-z.** has a peg in the head, which is rested upon a table, the body being held in the lap. It has four metal strings, g, d, a', e''. 3. A cither. 4. An old German instr. with a sound-box, a neck, a fretted finger-board, and eight or more strings tuned in unison two and two and plucked with a quill. **Z.-harfe.** A

form of keyed auto-harp. **Zitherspieler** (shpē'-lĕr), **Zitherschläger** (shlä-khĕr), *G.* Guitar-player. **zittera** (tsĭt'-tĕ-rä), *I.* Zither.

zitternd (tsĭt'-tĕrnt), *G.* Trembling.

zittino (tsĭt-tē'-nō), *I.* Silence.

zögernd (tsä'-gĕrnt), *G.* Retarding.

zolfà (tsōl-fä'), *I.* Vide SOLFA.

zoppa (tsŏp'-pä), or -o, *I.* Lame, limping. **alla z.** Syncopated; used also of a jerky Magyar rhythm.

zornig (tsŏr'-nĭkh), *G.* Angry.

zoulou (zoo-loo), *F.* "Zulu." A pianette.

zour'na. Oriental oboe.

zu (tsoo), *G.* To, at, by, in, unto.

Zufällig (tsoo'-fĕl-lĭkh), *G.* Accidental (sharp, flat, or natural).

zufolo (tsoo'-fō-lō), *I.* Flageolet, small bird-flute. **zufolone** (lō'-nĕ). A large whistle.

Zug (tsookh), pl. **Züge** (tsü'-khĕ). 1. Draw-stop or register. 2. Slide. **Zugtrompete** (trŏm-pā'-tĕ), *G.* Slide-trumpet; the trombone. **Zugwerke** (vĕr'-kĕ). Tracker-mechanism. **Zügeglöckchen** (glĕk-khĕn), *G.* The passing bell; a knell.

Zuklang (tsoo'-kläng), *G.* Concord.

Zukunftsmusik (tsoo-koonfts'-moozēk'), *G.* "Music of the future." A term applied satirically to Wagner's work by L. F. C. Bischoff, 1850; but later adopted as a watchword by the Wagnerians.

zum (tsoom), *G.* = *zu dem.* To the.

zumma'rah. An Egyptian reed instr. like a bassoon.

zunehmend (tsoo-nä'-mĕnt), *G.* Increasing.

Zunge (tsoong'-ĕ), *G.* 1. Tongue **Dop'pelzunge.** Vide TONGUING. 2. **Z.-pfeife.** Reed-pipe. **Z.-blatt.** Clarinet reed. **Z.-stimme.** Reed-stop. **Z.-werk.** The reed-stops collectively. **auf-** (or **durch-**) **schlagende Z.** Beating (or free) reed.

zur'na. Turkish oboe.

zurück (tsoo-rük'), *G.* Back. **z.-gehend** (gä'-ĕnt), *G.* Returning to the original tempo. **z.-halten.** To retard. **z.-haltend.** Retarding. **Z.-haltung** (häl-toongk) Retardation. **z.-tönen** (tā-nen) or **z.-treiben** (trī-bĕn). To reverberate. **Z.-schlag.** Vide RIBATTUTA.

zusammen (tsoo-zäm'-mĕn), *G.* Together. **z.-gesetzt.** Combined, compound (of time). **Z.-klang, Z.-laut** (lowt). Harmony. **Z.-schlag.**

Vide ACCIACCATURA. z.-streichen.
To slur. Z.-streichung (strī-khoongk). Slurring.
zutraulich (tsoo-trow'-lĭkh), G. Confident(ly).
Zuversicht (tsoo'-fĕr-zĭkht), G. Confidence.
zwanzig (tsvän'-tsĭkh), G. Twenty.
Zwanzigste (tsvän'-tsĭkh-stĕ). Twentieth.
zwei (tsvī), G. Two. z.-chörig (khā-rĭkh). Two-choired. z.-fach (fäkh), z.-fältig (fĕl-tĭkh). 1. In two ranks (organ-pipes). 2. Compound (of intervals). 3. Double (of counterpoint). z.-füssig. Two-foot. Vide PIPE and PITCH. Z.-gesang. A duet. z.-gestrichen. Twice-marked. Vide PITCH. Z.-glied (glēt). Sequence of two chords. Z.-halbertakt. 2-2 time. z.-händige (hĕnt'-ĭkh-ĕ). For two hands. Z.-klang. A chord of two tones. z.-mal (tsvī-mäl). Twice. z.-stimmig. For two parts. Z.-spiel (shpēl). A duet. Zweite (tsvī'-tĕ). Second. Zweitel (-note). Half-note. Z.-tritt. Vide WALTZ.

Z.-unddreissigstel (oont-drī-zĭkh-shtĕl). 32d note. Z.-viertelnote (fēr'-tĕl-nō-tĕ). Half-note. Z.-viertelpause (pow-zĕ). A half rest. Z.-vierteltakt. 2-4 time. Z.-zählighertakt (tsā-lĭkh-ĕr-takt). Duple time. Z.-zweiteltakt (tsvī-tsvī-tĕl-takt). 2-2 time.
zwerchflöte (tsvĕrkh-) or pfeife, G. Transverse flute.
zwischen (tsvĭsh'-ĕn), G. Between. Z.-akt. Intermezzo. Z.-gesang, Z.-handlung, Z.-harmonie, Z.-satz. The episode (in fugue). Z.-raum (-rowm). Space between the lines. Z.-spiel. Interlude. Z.-stille (shtĭl'-lĕ). Pause. Z.-stimme (shtĭm-mĕ). Middle voice. Z.-ton. Intermediate tone.
Zwitscherharfe (tsvĭtsh-ĕr), G. Vide SPITZHARFE.
zwölf (tsvĕlf), G. Twelve. Z.-achteltakt (äkh-tĕl-täkt). 12-8 time. Z.-saiter (zī-tĕr). "12-stringed" bissex.
zymbel (tsēm'-bĕl), G. Vide CYMBAL.
zzxjoanw (shaw). Maori. 1. Drum. 2. Fife. 3. Conclusion.

SPECIAL ARTICLES ON PARTICULAR PHASES OF MUSIC

ACOUSTICS

By J. S. Shedlock

THE TERM Acoustics is derived from a Greek verb signifying to hear, and the science of acoustics tells us about the production and propagation, also the comparison, of sounds. When a pianoforte string is struck by a hammer or a violin string by a bow, it trembles, sways to and fro and thus sets the surrounding air into successive condensation and rarefaction, producing a wave as a light breeze sets a corn-field waving; so we speak of waving air, or waves of air. These waves strike the ear and their motion is passed on to the brain and becomes what is called sound; but by what wonderful process one changes into the other does not concern us here. ¶When the swaying to and fro of the particles of an elastic body is steady and sufficiently rapid, a musical sound results, otherwise, only noise. The word *sound* indeed is generally understood to mean a musical one, hence sound is contrasted with noise. We speak of the noise of thunder or of battle, but of the sound of an instrument or of the human voice. Nature frequently offers a mixture of sound and noise, as in a waterfall, in which sometimes the one, sometimes the other, predominates. ¶*Vibration* is the name given to the swaying to and fro of the particles of an elastic body, and of this motion the clock pendulum gives a clear and simple idea. The particles only sway but the motion is passed on. When a glass ball is pushed against one end of a row of glass balls touching one another, the ball at the other end flies off. The motion of the first ball has been passed on from ball to ball until it has reached the extreme one. Vibrations when steady and sufficiently rapid produce sounds which may be higher or lower, and the higher the sound the greater the number of swayings to and fro, or vibrations, within a given time. There are two special instruments by means of which air-vibrations can be easily counted: one is Savart's toothed wheel, the other the Siren. When one sound is higher than another, it is said to be of higher pitch; when lower, of lower pitch. The shorter a string, the higher its pitch. If a violinist, setting one of the strings of his instrument in motion by means of the bow, slides his finger along that string toward the bridge, the sound will become continually of higher pitch: for the string is gradually shortened, the ever-increasing portion behind the finger being cut off from the vibratory movement caused by the bow. There is, therefore, a topsy-turvy connection between the number of vibrations produced by a string, and the length of that string. ¶Vibration can be felt if a glass jar over which a bow has been drawn is touched lightly with the finger. Vibration can be seen when the string of a piano or violin is struck by a hammer or bow. Vibration can be shown by attaching a strip of sheet copper tapering to a point to one of the prongs of a tuning-fork. If the latter be set in motion, and the copper point be placed on a piece of smoked glass, it will give the exact record of the exact swaying to and fro of the fork. ¶Strings such as are used in the pianoforte and violin when set in motion would of themselves create very faint sound-waves. The sound has to be strengthened. In the pianoforte the motion is not communicated directly to the air, but first to a massive sound-board. In a violin the little sound-post plays an important part in passing on the vibrations from the string to the back of the instrument. The strengthening of tone by such means is apt to be overlooked. ¶Particles of air when set in motion by a vibrating body first move from their point of rest to a certain distance and then back through the point of rest to a similar distance in an opposite direction; the distance between these extreme points is the extent, or as it is named, the *amplitude* of the vibration. As the vibrating body returns to a state of rest, that distance gradually diminishes and finally vanishes, just as it does when, the chain giving out, the clock pendulum slows down and finally stops. The degree of loudness or softness of a sound depends on the extent or amplitude of the vibration, the wider the one the louder the other. Sound travels at freezing temperature at the rate of 1090 feet per second; with increase of temperature there is increase of velocity, for the air thus becomes more elastic. Sound travels faster in water than in air because the former is more elastic. The degree of closeness of the particles of the medium, air, water, gases of different kinds, through which sound travels has also an influence on velocity. ¶Sound diminishes in intensity according to the distance. Throw a stone into a pond and see how the expanding waves become feebler and feebler in proportion as they are distant from the spot which generated them. So it is with sound-waves. Intensity varies inversely as the square of the distance, *i.e.*, if a sound is heard twenty feet away from the instrument producing it, at forty feet, twice the distance, it will only be a quarter as loud: the square of $2 = 4$, and the relationship of the two sounds is as one to four, or $\frac{1}{4}$. This is of course theory; in practice sound is mostly intensified in various ways so that it does not lose its strength at this exact rate. ¶A string set in motion, that is into a state of vibration, produces a note higher or lower according to its length. That note, however, is not a simple sound, but one made up of many sounds. For in addition to the whole string vibrating, it divides into two, three, four, and indeed into many portions, all of which vibrate in themselves at the same time that the whole string is vibrating. And these portions being shorter give out higher sounds than that of the whole string, and they bear themselves the self-evident name of *overtones*. They are also called *upper partials* because they are higher sounds produced by parts of the string. The swaying to and fro of these parts is not so great as that of the whole string, therefore the sounds they produce are fainter. The halves give a louder sound than the thirds, the thirds than the quarters and so on. All these

 sounds mix so thoroughly together as to give the impression of one simple sound, and it is upon their order and number, which differ in different instruments, that quality of tone depends. Here are the first eleven notes of such a compound sound—they can be heard and analysed by pressing the "loud" pedal of a pianoforte, striking the low c indicated and listening intently and long. Out of the overtones which are repeated we secure easily

 the simplest of all chords in harmony. ¶If the key of the low

est note 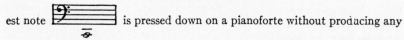 is pressed down on a pianoforte without producing any

sound, and so held, then if the above chord is struck sharply, the fingers after the blow being instantly removed from the keys, then that chord will continue to sound, although the strings which produced it have ceased to vibrate. Portions of the string of the lowest note have been set swaying to and fro, for the key pressed down removing the damper from its string left it free to vibrate. These portions vibrate by what is called *sympathetic attraction.* Repeat the experiment, but immediately after the chord has been struck, raise the key of the lowest note, and the chord is no longer heard. ¶It has already been stated that by means of certain instruments the numbers of vibrations of sounds can be counted, and they can therefore also be compared. Of any two notes an octave apart the upper one has twice as many vibrations as the lower. Of any two notes a perfect fifth apart the relationship between upper and lower is as 3 to 2. Of any two notes a major third apart as 5 to 4, and a minor third as 6 to 5. We see then that the perfect consonances, the 8th, 5th, and 4th, have the simplest relationship, 2 to 1, 3 to 2, 4 to 3. Next in order come the imperfect consonances, the major and minor thirds, 5 to 4, and 6 to 5; in no case is a higher figure than 6 required. From these relationships the major diatonic scale can easily be constructed, and then if the relationships between each note of the scale and the succeeding one be taken, it will be found that the intervals between c and d, f and g, a and b are equal, that d to e and g to a are slightly smaller and that e to f and b to c are alike. The former are called tones, either major or minor, and the last two semitones. (*See Dictionary entry, page 548.*)

ALTERED CHORDS

By Charles W. Pearce

A chord originally formed by a combination of notes belonging to the Diatonic Scale of any key can be chromatically altered by the addition of an accidental ♯, ♭, or ♮, to one or more of its intervals. A chord ceases to be chromatic when it induces modulation: being then a diatonic chord in the new key. In modern harmony, the combinational tendency of the Diatonic Scale is to arrange itself

Fig. 1—The small black notes indicate those intervals above the Dominant which are most susceptible of chromatic alteration.

in a perpendicular series of thirds above the 5th degree or dominant of the scale, according to this formula: ¶Reckoned from the lower note (or root) the intervals are: 1. Major 3d; 2. Perfect 5th; 3. Minor 7th; 4. Major (or minor) 9th; 5. Eleventh (compound 4th); 6. Major (or minor) 13th (compound 6th). ¶Thus the first sign of chromatic alteration is the interchangeability of the major and minor 3d and 6th of the scale. The harmonic

formula shown in Fig. 1 can be built up on the dominant notes of the two adjacent keys (viz.: those keys having one sharp or one flat more or less than the signature of the tonic key). And as these additional formulæ can be used in the tonic key without modulation to either of its adjacent keys, their roots are conveniently called supertonic and tonic to show their relationship to the scale of the tonic. ¶The supertonic root is dominant of the next sharp key. ¶The tonic root is dominant of the next flat key. ¶In the supertonic formula the necessary major 3d of the root (1 of the series) is an invariable chromatic alteration. The interchangeability of the major and minor 3d of the scale (4 of the series) is a confirmation of No. 6 of the Dominant formula (Fig. 1). The interchangeability of the major and minor 7th of the scale (6 of the series) is the characteristic chromatic alter-

FIG. 2—Supertonic Formula.

ation of the supertonic formula. ¶In the tonic formula the necessary minor 7th of the root (3 of the series) is an invariable chromatic alteration. The

FIG. 3—Tonic Formula.

interchangeability of the major and minor 6th of the scale (6 of the series) is a confirmation of No. 4 of the Dominant formula (Fig. 1). The interchangeability of the major and minor 2d of the scale (4 of the series) is the character-istic chromatic alteration of the tonic formula. ¶From the harmonic formulæ shown in Figs. 1, 2, 3, the chromatic scale is derived. This chromatic scale is the same for both major and minor keys having the same tonic; but the difference of key signature induces changes in the number of accidentals used. Compare Figs. 4 and 5. ¶With the introduction of the

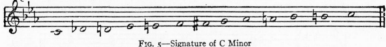

FIG. 4—Signature of C Major

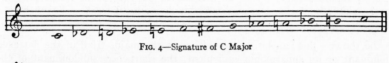

FIG. 5—Signature of C Minor

chromatic element into harmony, the absolute distinction of major and minor disappears, and the key tonality becomes one. ¶To facilitate the notational convenience of the chromatic element in harmony, the enharmonic equivalents of several degrees of the chromatic scale are freely admitted. ¶Chromatic al-teration is chiefly observable in triads and in chords of the seventh with their inversions. ¶Fig. 6 shows the triads on the seven degrees of the diatonic scale. Fig. 7 shows how these triads may be chromatically altered in the same key

I II III IV V VI VII

FIG. 6

FIG. 7

without necessitating modulation to any other key. ¶Of these Nos. 1, 4, 18, 19, and 28, show an enharmonic substitution of C sharp for D flat; Nos. 4, 5, 11, 22, and 25 have G sharp instead of A flat; Nos. 10, 21, 25, and 34 have D sharp for E flat; Nos. 3 and 15 have G flat for F sharp; and No. 30 has C flat for B. It may also be remarked that Nos. 30 and 15 are the only triads of the series which have all three of their notes altered from the notation of the diatonic scale of C; but it will be observed that in No. 30 two of these altered notes (A flat and E flat) are the notes shown in Fig. 1 to be those first susceptible of chromatic alteration in the key of E; and in No. 15 two of the altered notes belong to the supertonic formula shown in Fig. 2. A glance at Fig. 7 is sufficient to show that "enharmonic substitution" is only made use of in modern music in order to throw the altered chords into an easily recognisable harmonic shape such as triads or sevenths (or their inversions). ¶Distinguishing names of a purely fanciful character have been given to the first inversions of several of the chords in Fig. 7 (see Fig. 8). ¶One other triad containing three altered notes remains

Neapolitan Sixth.   Italian Sixths.

1st inversion of   1st inversion of 1st inversion of 1st inversion of 1st inversion of
No. 8, Fig. 7   No. 10, Fig. 7   No. 20, Fig. 7   No. 86. Fig. 7

FIG. 8

to be shown—this can be written either as the major triad of the flattened dominant or its enharmonic equivalent, the sharpened subdominant of the key, as in Fig. 9. ¶Fig. 9 exemplifies also the ordinary treatment of chro-

FIG. 9

matically altered triads, viz.: they are usually followed by some form of dominant harmony. ¶The chords of the seventh built on the seven degrees of the diatonic scale (see Fig. 10) may (like the triads in Fig. 6) undergo chromatic alteration. ¶A chromatic alteration of Fig. 10, I, III, V, VII, has already

I   II   III   IV   V   VI   VII
FIG. 10

been shown in Fig. 3 by the flattening of the leading note of the scale; and similar alterations of Fig. 10, II, and IV, have been observed in Fig. 2 by the sharpening of the subdominant of the scale (see Fig. 11). ¶Fig. 11 shows

I   III   V   VII   II   IV
FIG. 11

that a chord of the seventh may consist of the following different series of intervals from the bass: ¶I, and II, Major 3d: Perfect 5th: Minor 7th; III, and IV, Minor 3d: Dim. 5th: Minor 7th; V, Minor 3d: Perfect 5th: Minor 7th; VII, Major 3d: Perfect 5th: Major 7th. ¶A further reference to Figs. 1, 2, and 3, shows that the harmonic superposition of three minor 3ds one above the other—that familiar combination of notes known as the chord of the Diminished 7th—is possible over every note of the unaltered Diatonic Scale by chromatic or enharmonic alteration without necessitating modulation. ¶Accordingly

I   II   III   IV   V   VI   VII   I   II   IV   V   VI

FIG. 12

each note of the Diatonic Scale may bear the chromatic alteration of its own chord of the 7th as shown in Fig. 13. ¶And with the chromatic alteration

FIG. 13

(Fig. 14) of the root itself the permutations are almost endless. ¶It only remains to give the distinguishing names which have been fancifully applied to one or two of the chromatically altered chords of the 7th in an inverted shape.

French Sixth.   *German Sixth.*

(1)   (2)   (3)   (4)   (5)   (6)

FIG. 14

¶Of these (1) is the second inversion of VII in Fig. 10, with the sixth of its bass chromatically raised.   (2) is the second inversion of II in Fig. 11 with its bass chromatically lowered   (3) is the second inversion of V in Fig. 10, with its bass chromatically lowered.   (4) is the first inversion of II in Fig. 10 with its root chromatically raised.   (5) and (6) are respectively chromatic alterations of the first inversions of IV in Fig. 11, and VII in Fig. 12.   ¶It will be observed that the distinguishing feature of the chords in Fig. 14 is the interval of the *Augmented 6th*.   In the usual resolution of such chords, care should be taken to let the two notes forming the Augmented 6th proceed outwardly, each by step of a semitone.

THE CONDUCTOR AND HIS ART

By DEEMS TAYLOR

THE SYMPHONY CONDUCTOR, as we know him, is a comparatively modern invention.   In the seventeenth and eighteenth centuries he was little more than a time-beater, dividing his time between filling in the harmony at the narpsichord and keeping the players together by waving a roll of music or a violin bow, or pounding on the floor with a cane. Even as late as Beethoven's time he did little more than indicate entrances and mark the tempo. A contemporary performance of a Beethoven symphony must have been distinguished by the almost complete absence of two of the qualities that we of to-day expect as a matter of course to find in a satisfactory orchestral performance: dynamics and variations in instrumental tone colour. ¶Even in our times there have been serious attempts to do without him. Only ten years ago a group of New York instrumentalists organised an orchestra, rehearsed, and gave a concert without any conductor at all. The attitude of the average lay listener seems to vacillate between worshipping him as the creator and sole source of the music and regarding him tolerantly as a more or less superfluous ornament, someone placed on the podium to entertain the audience with a display of calisthenic agility. It is, therefore, decidedly worth while discussing just what his functions are. He certainly did not write the music that the orchestra is playing, and he is certainly not playing it. Just what does he do? What qualities must he possess, what are his duties, and what are his responsibilities? ¶There is one quality that he must possess, first of all. He may possess it without being a good conductor, but he will never be a good conductor if he does not possess it. And that is the intangible thing that we call leadership, the faculty of being able to impress other people with his authority and knowledge, and to induce their minds and bodies to obey his will. He must not only know his business, but he must be able to make the members of the orchestra believe that he does. If he cannot do that, no orchestra will ever play well for him. For on his relations with the players depend the morale, the *esprit de corps*, the team-work of the orchestra as a whole. ¶Second, he must know the technique of conducting. No two conductors beat time exactly alike, but all conductors do describe certain definite patterns in the air with their hands or bâtons, do make certain gestures indicating shades of expression or entrance cues. These patterns and gestures must be sufficiently clear that any one of his players, reading notes with one eye and watching the conductor with the other, knows when he is to come in, when a bar begins, and when it ends. These signals of the conductor's, like the motions one makes when driving a car, must be so habitual and automatic that he doesn't have to think about them, and can leave his mind fiee to concentrate on the music. ¶Besides conducting technique, he must have enormous theoretical technique. He must be able to take a new orchestral score that he has never heard and by studying it analyse its structure, identify its themes and trace their development; determine the instrumental balance at any given moment; and determine the important instrumental entrances . . . all with the ease and surety with which a skilled architect or builder reads the blue-prints of a building that has not yet been erected. This score-reading must be done, of course, before rehearsals begin; for the players come in the expectation that he will tell them what to do. ¶He must not only be able to read new scores; he must be thoroughly familiar with the old ones. Just as there are traditional performances of the classic rôles in the drama, so there are traditional interpretations of the standard works in the orchestral repertoire. Take, for example, Beethoven's *Fifth Symphony*. During the 130 years that have elapsed since that work was first heard, there has grown up what might be called a "standard" performance of it. Generations of conductors have agreed that the various movements should be played at a certain speed, that certain passages be played a little louder or a little softer than they are marked, that certain other passages be hastened or retarded. Needless to say, virtually every conductor departs at times from that traditional performance (in fact, that is one of the reasons why we can tell them apart); but it is expected of any first-rate conductor that he be perfectly familiar with the traditional interpretation before he ventures to try out any different ideas of his own.   The Beethoven *Fifth* is one of perhaps a hundred works with whose traditions he is expected to be familiar.   ¶Our conductor must not only be a leader. He must be prepared to follow, as well, on occasion. . . .   In other words, he must be a good accompanist. It is hard work to make an orchestra accompany any soloist.   Only a player-piano or a record ever gives two identical performances of the same piece, and no matter how carefully a concerto or an aria may have been rehearsed, at the actual performance the conductor must have the alertness to anticipate the slightest variation in the soloist's playing or singing, and the skill to convey that variation instantly to a hundred men, most of whom can neither see nor hear the soloist.   ¶He has many other duties and responsibilities. For one thing he is largely responsible for making up the programmes of his orchestra.   Not only must the conductor determine the order of events on any musical programme, but he must determine the balance and proportion of his series as a whole. He must see to it that the season's programmes contain a sufficient number of the classics; otherwise half his audience will call him a wild-eyed radical: he must also play enough modern music to keep the other half from calling him a hide-bound conservative; and he must play enough new music to keep the critics from calling him a lazy-minded reactionary.   It is this planning, by the way, that keeps conductors from having time heavy on their hands during the summer months.   ¶In the actual performance of his programmes he is responsible for a number of things that we take for granted.   He is at least one-half responsible for the quality of tone that his players produce.   Naturally, if he has poor material he can do little about it; he can't make men play better than they can.   But the fact that he has a superb body of instrumentalists at his command does not mean that they will invariably give their best unless he knows enough to ask for it.   A wind instrument may play a fraction of a tone flat or sharp; and the player, with his ears full of the sound of the other instruments beside him, may be totally unconscious of the fact.   It is the conductor who must hear the sour note and correct it.   His string section has an infinite variety of tone colour at its command; but it is the conductor who must decide with what quality of string tone any given passage is to be played.   ¶Aside from trying to make his orchestra play as beautifully as it can, the conductor has certain responsibilities that are fairly obvious to anyone, in other words, for the details of performance that we call the interpretation of a work.   He must determine tempi and rhythms, the speed at which any portion of the work is to be taken, and the degree to which its rhythms are to be accentuated.   Incidentally, it is in speed that conductors tend to vary most widely.   Superficially their performances may sound alike, but a difference in speed amounting to only a small fraction of a second in any one measure may assume rather impressive proportions in a work that is four or five hundred measures long.   I have known two great conductors to vary as much as six or seven minutes in their playing of the same symphony. Also, I have heard a semi-amateur orchestra, under not quite so great a conductor, take an hour and eight minutes to play Dvořák's *"From the New World"* symphony, the regulation playing time of which is some forty-odd minutes. ¶Dynamics are another great responsibility of the conductor, and dynamics, not just in the simple sense of playing loudly or softly—the players could manage that by themselves fairly well if they watched the markings on the music—but in the sense of *how* loudly and *how* softly at any given moment. One of the things that distinguishes a great conductor is his sense of climax, his power of leading the music up to one high peak of volume and then drawing gradually away from it. Now in his performance of any given work you would probably find, if you had a machine for measuring and recording volume of sound, that there is one point at which the intensity of the sound of the orchestra is greater than at any other. There is a legend that in one of Schumann's symphonies there is a passage marked *"forte possibile"* . . . *"as loudly as possible"*; and that four bars later the composer has written *"crescendo"* . . . "louder." Now I've never tracked that passage down, and it may not exist; but it does illustrate a situation in which any conductor may find himself if he is not careful . . . that of having fired off all his orchestral ammunition on one climax, only to find that another, greater climax, is expected of him later on. Therefore, in general, even though a work may contain five passages for full orchestra, all labelled, *"fortissimo,"* the skilful conductor generally selects one *fortissimo* to be louder than any of the others. To be able to do this he must be tremendously sensitive to slight variations in tonal volume. He must carry in his mind a sound-picture, so to speak, of the climax that he wants long before he gets to it; in addition he must manage to get the orchestra to give him plenty of volume in the lesser climaxes, and still keep the players from getting overenthusiastic and anticipating his effect. The same problem, naturally, is involved in the playing of quiet passages. It all sounds complicated, and it *is* complicated; and only a first-rate conductor can do it. ¶Having determined at least some of the things for which a conductor must be responsible, I have still to answer one fundamental question: Is the conductor essential at an actual performance? He is, of course. The orchestra may have mastered the minutest details of the performance at the rehearsals. Nevertheless, when they come out on the platform, the players are still dependent upon the conductor in many ways. To begin with, somebody has to start and stop them; and the conductor is the logical man to do that. In the second place, they depend on him for the important entrance cues. The first oboe may be perfectly capable, theoretically, of counting thirty-seven bars' rest and then coming in, on the precise beat of the bar, with a difficult solo. But it's one thing to be *able* to do that, unassisted, and quite another to *have* to do it, knowing that a false entry may ruin the whole performance. It makes a very real difference in the quality of any player's performance to know that he can rely upon the conductor to give him the nod or gesture that will bring him in at the proper time, leaving his mind free to concentrate on his playing, without having to worry about bars. Furthermore, no matter how great the orchestra, or how thoroughly it has been rehearsed, it is impossible for the players to memorise every detail of any one performance. The number of concerts in a season is so great, the orchestral literature is so enormous, that the instrumentalists are bound to forget almost as speedily as they learn. They must be reminded of what they know.   The gestures that you see the conductor make when he stands on the platform are those that he made at the rehearsals; they serve, as I say, as a reminder to the players of what he has taught them. Without him, the orchestra might play the notes; but it would fail to give you a thousand subtleties that the conductor, and the conductor alone, can evoke. ¶Incidentally, one of the qualities of a conductor to which the audience is likely to pay great attention is of no importance at all; and that is the grace or awkwardness of his gestures, the way he handles his body; in general, what are known as his platform mannerisms.   Only the audience cares about those. All the orchestra asks is, "Is his beat clear, and does he know how to get what he wants?"   Unfortunately, this being something less than a perfect world, a certain number out of any audience are likely to watch the conductor instead of listening to him, to judge a performance on the merits of the conductor's back instead of on the playing of his men.   As a matter of fact, it is difficult *not* to do so.   There have been times when I, too, have been fooled by an authoritative pair of scapulae!   (*See Dictionary of Terms entry, page 577.*)

COUNTERPOINT

By Homer A. Norris

THE ART of combining melodies is called counterpoint.   When a pianist "plays 'Old Hundred' in one hand, and 'Yankee Doodle' in the other" he illustrates the contrapuntal idea.   Weingartner's arrangement of Weber's

Inversion of above example

"Invitation to the Dance" represents most ingenious counterpoint. In *strict* (plain, simple) counterpoint, no combination of notes representing more than three sounds is allowed; no dissonances except passing notes; no chromatics. ¶Counterpoint is *double* when it may be correctly used either as an upper, or a lower part; *i.e.*, when it admits of double employment. Double counterpoint may be so written as to invert in the 8th, 9th, 12th, or any other interval. The foregoing is an example of double counterpoint. ¶Within the confines of strict counterpoint ecclesiastical music reached its loftiest expression through Palestrina, in about 1600. ¶In modern harmony chords may be built up of three, four, five, and even more different sounds. When the contrapuntal idea is applied to modern harmony, the result is called *free* counterpoint. Free counterpoint is simply a contrapuntal manipulation of modern harmony, as opposed to strict counterpoint which is limited to chords of three sounds. Bach re-established the counterpoint of Palestrina on the modern harmonic bass. In his fugues the contrapuntal, or polyphonic, idea is found in its most perfect form. ¶The very essence of Wagner's music is counterpoint. When the melodies of *"Die Meistersinger"* are brought together in the overture it is modern counterpoint; not an end in itself, but as a means to direct, emotional expression. ¶So from out this old counterpoint has come a new, which to-day permeates all music. Neither Brahms nor Richard Strauss could exist but for the industry of those early *savants*, who, piling notes upon notes, laid a foundation for the cathedral of music which has risen majestically under Bach, Handel, Mozart, Beethoven, Brahms, and Wagner. It is modern counterpoint, counterpoint with a soul in it, which distinguishes all great work to-day and stamps it for posterity. (*See Dictionary of Terms entry, page 579.*)

THE ELECTRIC ORGAN

By Rudolph Ganz

The electric organ, invented by Laurens Hammond, is a striking example of contemporary improvement upon an instrument of great antiquity, and of decided value in the progress of music as an art. It furnishes an individual flavour to the modern ensemble, and it is gradually replacing, for home use and as an orchestral voice, and in many churches, its staid and orthodox predecessor, because it is an instrument instead of a structure, and can be installed with comparative ease and economy. ¶As to the peculiar facility of tone which enables the electric organ to take its place in the modern orchestra as a distinctive voice of undeniable beauty, I can say with the authority of long experience that I believe it has come to stay. ¶Let us look into the past of the organ, that we may understand why the electric organ is an adaptation, rather than an ultimate expression, of the original instrument. In the first place, let us disregard at once a vague but popular idea that the organ was first conceived as an orchestra and choir compressed within a single unit. This idea, of course, is absurd. ¶"The first instrument used in art music," says W. J. Henderson in *The Story of Music*, "was the organ." He explains that, as it was first employed in the church, "it came under the consideration of the only musical scholars of the Middle Ages. ¶"The best organist of our time would not know what to do with one of those early cathedral thunderers. According to the historian Wulstan, who wrote in 951, an organ built in Winchester Cathedral had 400 pipes and thirteen pairs of bellows, requiring seventy blowers. ¶"This instrument sounded but ten tones and was built simply to make as big a noise as possible. Only one note at a time was played on these organs, and that had to be pressed down with the fist or elbow. As long as only a plain chant was required, this system answered well enough; but when harmony was invented, the cumbersome organ could not double the newly-arranged voice parts. The mechanism of the organ, therefore, began to improve in answer to the demands of the music of the church." ¶These crudities of an early beginning evidently had given way to a vast improvement by the time of Bach, for the organ was the instrument upon which Bach performed some of his greatest works. Dr. Spitta gives the following account of Bach's organ at Arnstadt: ¶"The organ was splendidly constructed, all the diapasons being seven-ounce tin, the gedackt also being of metal, instead of wood, as was more usual. The character of the 'Brust-Positiv' must, indeed, have been somewhat shrill, owing to the preponderance of four-foot stops; and it was only by using all the stops in combination that even a moderately good effect could be produced; nor was there on the pedals any deep stop of moderate strength, still the 'Hauptwerk' was well arranged." ¶The *Oberwerk*, or upper manual, had twelve stops; the *Brust-Positiv*, or choir, seven; and the pedals, five; in addition to the coupler. This organ existed until 1863. A new one was then erected as a memorial to Bach, but as many of the old stops as were available were retained. ¶The origin of the organ, second only to the reed instruments in antiquity, supposedly was Roman. The ancient antecedent of the organ apparently was that group of loosely related reeds known as the Pipes of Pan, consisting of a series of hollow reeds of different lengths fastened together, and played by blowing each tube separately. ¶"Of the many Roman instruments," writes Marion Bauer, "the organ, because of its importance in later Christian music, interests us more than all the others. ¶"There had been evidence of the water-aulos (hydraulos) in the writings of Philo of Alexandria (200 B.C.) who credited Ctesibus, engineer, with the invention; of Vetruvius, writer on architecture in Augustus' reign and of Hero of Alexandria. This evidence was not substantiated until 1885, when a pottery model made by Possessor in 100 A.D. was found. A complete description of this organ is given in Stanford & Forsythe's *A History of Music*. ¶"The Romans, however, had a pneumatic as well as a water organ. Primitive types persisted until our own era. They used them in portable forms for their revels and coarse and gaudy circuses. For this reason, the early Christians and many later Christian societies banned the organ, as well as other instruments, as pagan and profane." ¶Keys were first introduced into the organ toward the end of the eleventh century; at first 16, later 22. The large keys were so stiff and clumsy that they had to be pressed down with the fist. The addition of foot-pedals added materially to the musical resources of the organ. The addition of stops to imitate various orchestral instruments, and the invention of the *swell* to increase or diminish the sound, came in the seventeenth century. The first American-built organ was erected in Trinity Church, New York, in 1737. ¶My purpose in thus alluding to the past of the organ is to bring forward a proper consideration of the electric organ as a new instrument; "adapted" from the organ itself, yet possessing certain definite powers which must be regarded as individual and capable of further development. ¶The musical world is indebted to Laurens Hammond for a pioneer effort in the direction of the electric organ, adopting a principle of electric vibration hitherto ignored in the production of pitched tone. ¶The Hammond organ is designed specifically for the home, and amateur use; for the orchestra, and professional use. It has a greater tonal range than most cathedral organs, is instantaneous in action, perfect in pitch—all in a space smaller than a baby grand piano. ¶The tonal pitch of this instrument cannot vary; humidity and temperature do not affect it; it consumes current at the average rate of one cent an hour; and I am told more than 253,000,000 tones are available; its volume is unlimited. ¶Creation of tone depends upon amplification of electrical impulses into sound waves. The impulse is generated by tone-wheels about the size of a silver dollar, which revolve at constant speed close to small magnets, each with a coil wound at one end. They are, in effect, tiny rotating electric generators. ¶On the rim of each tone-wheel is a series of protrusions, regularly spaced, similar to teeth in a gear As the wheel rotates, these *high spots* regularly disturb the magnetic field and a tiny electric current is induced in the coil. ¶For instance, one tone-wheel is so constructed that the ridges on the rim pass the magnet and coil at the rate of 440 per second. When the electric impulse created by the wheel is amplified and made audible the result is a simple tone with a frequency of 440 vibrations, Middle A in International Pitch. There is a separate tone-wheel for every frequency used. ¶Tone-wheels are geared together and are driven by a single constant-speed synchronous motor; each tone-wheel must revolve at its predetermined uniform speed. ¶As the entire process is electrical, the response to the depression of a key is instantaneous. In the traditional organ there is a noticeable *lag* of tone behind each key depression. For this reason music of rapid tempo, formerly impractical for the organ, can be played as readily as on a piano. ¶Variation of tone in this instrument is purely a matter of physics. The harmonic principle of the third and fifth of a single note vibrating in unison with the note itself forms a basic rule of construction for the Hammond. ¶Every complex musical tone consists of a fundamental tone plus a series of harmonic overtones of certain strengths relative to the fundamental. When the harmonics and their relative strengths are specified, the quality or timbre of the tone is specified. A change in the strength of any overtone will alter the quality of the whole tone. ¶The Hammond organ, instead of supplying pipes or reeds with fixed tones, supplies the simple tones which constitute the fixed tones, and the means for combining them. This is done through a series of nine draw-bars of eight strengths each, located above the top manual. Each draw-bar is a small strip on which are marked eight graduations or strengths, the full-closed bar giving a ninth position. One of these draw-bars governs the fundamental tone, and the other eight the overtones. ¶The degree to which each bar is pulled out determines the volume in which the overtone it governs is present in the tone produced when a key on the manual is depressed. Thus an almost inexhaustible variety of tone colours can be produced at the will of the player simply by varying the extent to which the bars are pulled out in relation to each other. Tone colours frequently used, such as the flute, French horn, diapason, full organ and others, can be set permanently on the organ and are brought into use simply by depressing a single *pre-set* key of which there are 11 located at the extreme left of the keyboard of each manual. Thus the organist has instantly available 22 *ready mixed* tones in addition to the facilities provided for creating new tone colours. ¶In considering the musical future of this instrument, one must realise that composers in the past usually utilised musical instruments offered on the market by the manufacturer, as Mr. Joseph Schillinger pointed out in a recent address before the League of Composers. "Richard Wagner had a desire to create new instruments," said Mr. Schillinger, "and they proved impractical. The parts he wrote for these instruments are seldom played to-day on the instruments that were specially constructed for them under his direction (contra-bass trombone and tenor tuba). ¶"The education of composers will not be complete," he added, "without the study of the physics of sound in relation to musical composition. . . . There has been a great deal of disappointment in the electrical instruments among the musicians and composers because they have always been trying to compare these instruments with the ones that are constructed on an entirely different principle and offer an entirely different group of characteristics." ¶But the electric organ is still in its infancy, employing entirely new principles and offering new opportunities which we can only realise by earnest application and sympathetic study. A myriad of effects are available to a performer of musical intelligence, one who is willing to study patiently the proper touch, attack and release, and bring into play the unending combinations of properly balanced tone for legitimate musical expression. As with all musical instruments, when degraded by misuse, this organ may be made ridiculous. However, when used in good taste by a competent and interested person, the instrument proves itself an artistic creation of distinction and dignity. ¶The Hammond organ, as it is now constituted, has great possibilities for outdoor use, in performance of the greater choral and orchestral works. Composers are realising its potential grandeur; conductors, myself included, are glad to use it as a sensitive and superior instrument, particularly as the organist is able to respond instantly to the indications of the bâton. I look forward to a time when the electric organ will have attained a state of development which will make it as necessary a part of contemporary musical life as the piano. (*See The Organ, page 792.*)

FOLK–SONG

By H. E. KREHBIEL

THE BEARING which Folk-music (*i.e.*, Folk-song and Folk-dance) has on national schools of composition gives propriety to an attempt at accurate definition of the subject to which this article is devoted. Folk-song is not popular song in the sense in which the word is most frequently used, but the song of the folk; not only the song admired of the people but, in a strict sense, the song created by the people. It is a body of poetry and music which has come into existence without the influence of conscious art, as a spontaneous utterance, filled with characteristic expression of the feelings of a people. Such songs are marked by certain peculiarities of rhythm, form, and melody which are traceable, more or less clearly, to racial (or national) temperament, modes of life, climatic and political conditions, geographical environment and language. Some of these elements, the spiritual, are elusive, but others can be determined

and classified.   Peoples living in northern climates for instance, are predisposed
to the minor mode, which has melancholy for its most marked characteristic.
Here the influence is generally climatic and geographical.   But peoples living
in cheerful and salubrious climes may also be dominated by gloom if they have
long suffered under oppressive political and social conditions.   ¶Both propo-
sitions are illustrated in the case of Russian Folk-song, which is overwhelmingly
minor in spite of the fact that the Czar's empire extended over nearly thirty
degrees of latitude and had a mean temperature varying from thirty-two degrees
Fahrenheit at Archangel, to fifty-eight degrees in the Caucasus.   It would seem
to be a paradox, moreover, that heavy-hearted song should be paired almost
universally with singularly boisterous and energetic dances; but the reason of
this becomes plain when it is remembered that a measured and decorous mode
of popular amusement is the general expression of equable popular life, while
wild and desperate gayety is frequently the sign of reaction from suffering.
There is a gayety of despair as well as of contentment and happiness.   ¶Inter-
vallic peculiarities are more difficult to explain than rhythmic, and may be said
to be survivals of primitive artistic conditions.   The modern scale was an
evolution, not an inspiration, and the study of savage music discloses many
rudimentary forms of it.   The most idiomatic music of the Finns is confined to
the first five tones of the minor scale, which was the compass of the ancient
Finnish harp—the *kantele*.   Old Irish and Scotch songs share the pentatonic
scale (*i.e.*, the modern diatonic scale omitting the fourth and seventh steps) with
the popular music of China, Japan, and Siam.   In the songs of the negro slaves
of America, I have found the same scale, a major scale with a flat seventh and a
minor scale with a raised sixth, to be predominant.   César Cui mentions the
prevalence in Russia of two major scales, one without the fourth, the other
without the third and seventh.   Hungarian melodies make frequent use of the
interval called the augmented second, which compasses three semitones and is
common to Oriental music.   There is a hint in this of the origin of the Magyars,
who are not Slavs, as is so commonly supposed, but Scythians; they belong to
the Finno-Ungrian stock, and are more nearly related to the Turks than to their
neighbours, the Poles and Russians.   The profusion of ornament which char-
acterises Hungarian music is an importation from the Orient by the Gypsies
who, while the national musicians of Hungary, are nevertheless a Hindu people.
¶These facts, gathered at random from the vast but as yet unexplored storehouse of Folk-music, indicate the possibility of using the study as an aid in the
determination of many things in ethnology and ethnography; for Folk-song
elements have a marvellous tenacity of life.   In the study of Folk-music, however, the purpose of the student should be primarily to discover and, if possible,
account for the elements which differentiate the creations of one race, people,
or tribe from those of another.   This done it will be possible to explain and
describe the distinguishing characteristics of the national schools of composition
based upon Folk-song idioms, such as the Scandinavian, Russian, Polish,
Bohemian and Hungarian. (*See Dictionary of Terms entry, page 602.*)

FORM

By John F. Runciman

A DEFINITION of Form would have this disadvantage: that it would convey absolutely nothing save to those who understood perfectly what the meaning is; and, further, it would occupy much more space than is here available. So instead of trying to reach a perfect definition, let us try what is a much better plan from the lay point of view—let us trace the growth of the mass of principles and their methods of application which are included in this one comprehensive term Form. ¶In the beginning, we may assume, music was without Form, though not always quite void. The savage tootled his melody, caring nothing about repeating phrases, nothing about middle sections, nothing about development. But in the earliest traditional melodies that come down to us we find the germ of all that is now known as Form. ¶In any collection of popular songs the reader will find examples built on the following plan:— first a strain is delivered; then another strain, in another key, is delivered; and finally the first strain is repeated, bringing the whole thing to a satisfactory close. Let us consider for a moment the inwardness of this arrangement. No one wants to sing only one strain and be done with it. To sing a second strain in the same key would prove tiresome, so a feeling of relief, of variety is produced when the thing is lengthened by the addition of a second strain in a new key. But to end in the new key would be quite unsatisfactory: it would be like breaking off in the middle of a sentence. So the first key is re-introduced and the whole song rounded off and made to end with a sense of perfect completeness by a repetition of the first strain in the first key. ¶From this simple example, then, we may infer the whole object of Form: it is to secure, whether in songs or in instrumental movements or in choruses, a piece of music sufficiently long and combining variety with unity. ¶Length, variety, and unity— to attain these is, so far as instrumental music, music without words, is concerned, the whole aim and object of Form. When once music is used in association with words, other than the simplest lyrics, other considerations enter. These we will touch upon later; let us for the present try to get as far as the first instrumental music written in anything approaching regular Form. Naturally this grew out of the polyphonic vocal music, which came before it. If we examine the old music, in a great deal of it we find nothing corresponding to Form as we understand the word to-day. A phrase is delivered by one voice. Let us call that phrase A; it may be two, four, or six bars, or indeed any length. After the first voice has sung it a second voice takes it up, while the first voice proceeds to a second theme or strain which we will call B—a third voice enters with A, the second takes up B, while the first proceeds to yet another new strain, C. Roughly, this is the way in which whole movements are spun out. The modulations are more or less haphazard and dictated entirely by the composer's desire to achieve expression: there is nothing done in obedience to any rule. The first instrumental pieces are built after this plan. ¶These pieces may be compared to the harmless amœba, the tiny speck of protoplasm which swims about, sans eyes, ears, mouth or limbs: simply a shapeless bit of life capable of existing, so long as it remains small. But even the older composers were not content to let their musical creations remain small. They wanted to display their skill in weaving a longer web of music; some of them had something to say, something which demanded length; most of them had the architectonical instinct which forces man to build out of any material he can lay his hands on. Now a long movement, a too long movement, spun on the old plan necessarily becomes tedious, monotonous and difficult to follow—it is at best like a very long sentence or paragraph with never a comma or a period. Moreover, if the music is all the same, if it is homogeneous, it is obvious that one of the principal methods of getting expression, contrast, is ruled out. Last, no musical architecture is possible with a mere series of musical phrases that can only be compared with a lot of strips of wood more or less carelessly nailed together. So gradually the principle of the popular song already referred to was adopted, probably, nay, certainly, quite unconsciously, and there was evolved a very simple and useful Form, one which has been vastly used by all composers and will doubtless be used constantly in the future, however music may develop. ¶In place of the one strain of the simple song one section consisting of many strains was introduced. Following that, in a new key, for the sake of variety, came a second section, also consisting of many strains. Finally the first section was repeated in the original key, bringing the whole movement to a satisfying conclusion. Of this form there are hundreds of examples in the shorter movements of Haydn, Mozart and Beethoven. When a more modern composer uses it, however, he by no means sticks to a couple of keys. Our sense of tonality has grown, we perceive relations between keys, which our forefathers were totally unable to perceive; and the first and second sections may both pass through many keys. But the general principle remains the same. Now this very excellent Form is also very primitive. In Haydn's time, and before it, the instinct to build, to crystallise, music was still at work; more than ever composers wanted to express something; and more than ever it was necessary to secure contrast. ¶So what is commonly called *sonata form* came to be invented. In the simplest examples of this a first theme—corresponding to the first strain of a popular song, as aforesaid—is announced. Then comes the second theme in a fresh key. But after that, instead of a repetition of the first section, there is what is called a *development* or *working-out section*, in which both first and second themes are treated with all the skill and fancy the composer possesses and shown in a dozen or more unsuspected lights. Only after that does the first theme return, and then the second theme. This is called the *Reprise*. But the second theme, if repeated in the key in which it first appeared, would of course end the work inconclusively: wherefore it is placed, on its last appearance, in the key of the first theme. ¶The ingenious reader will observe that if variety is obtained only by change of key then there would be no more variety from the beginning of what is called the reprise. Nor, for that matter, is the mere change from the original key to that of the dominant enough to produce any great variety. The second theme therefore is made as unlike the first in every respect as possible: if the first is bold and rugged, the second may be gentle and soothing; if the first moves rapidly, the second may be long drawn out; if rhythm is strongly marked in the first, the second is in a more subtle and elusive rhythm—in fact contrast is secured by any of the thousand ways open to the composer, and quite easily understood when heard, though anything but easy to describe. ¶Now if we take a symphonic movement of Mozart we find a first theme of marked character; after its delivery (and perhaps brief expansion) all the orchestra goes to work at a cadence in a hammer-and-tongs fashion and lets you know unmistakably that you have reached the end of a section. Then the second theme is announced, clearly. Then we have "development" in which the old tunes are turned into new ones as unlike the old as possible, yet obviously growing out of them. Finally we have the reprise, and then the *coda*, a few bars in the case of Haydn and Mozart stuck on to make an effective conclusion. ¶This is simple sonata form. There was an enormous lot of waste in it: those thumping conventional series of chords at the end of each section, for example, never mean and never did mean anything. At the time they were written the tendency to formulate music, to get conscious control of the material of music, was at its strongest; one of the most powerful desires of Mozart and Haydn was to make their form as clear and distinct as possible; and to that everything else was, in an emergency, sacrificed. In fact, composers of that time seem to have felt as keen a pleasure in the mere regularity and balance of the various parts of movements as in the poetic and sheer musical quality of the parts, even when the balance was secured by the introduction of conventional padding altogether at war with beauty and expression, quite destructive of both. ¶With Beethoven came a change. His music must at first have been very difficult to understand, for instead of the trumpet and drum passages marking the close of the different sections, one section leads straight into another by means of passages of as high musical and poetic quality as any other portions of his movements. Further, he went in for third themes following the second (the second and third being so proportioned as to balance the first), and he mightily extended the coda. Instead of a few noisy bars to end up each movement he started out and developed his theme in new ways, thus adding a fourth main section to the three existing before his time—the first, in which the themes are announced; the second, in which they are developed; the third, in which they are repeated. This was an inevitable corollary of the enormous increase he made in the size of the forms he used. After such huge themes, such lengthy developments, a few chords were not sufficient to wind up; a tail was needed by the symphonic movement before it could be felt to be satisfactory, just as much as a tail is needed by a kite before it will ascend. ¶Let us pause for a moment to sum up. In the early days music had form as a flower or a blade of grass has form; each piece grew more or less by haphazard into some shape, starting from its one theme. The utmost that could be done in that way was done by Bach in his fugues. But the fugue itself was the result of the tendency to formulate music, to press it into the bonds of strict rule, to get a conscious mastery of the material. That tendency, together with the desire to express more complex emotions and the natural instinct of man to build, resulted in certain clearly defined forms, with hard outlines, so to speak. Beethoven came and softened the outlines, hiding the bones of music, as it were, under a beautiful expressive veil of tone. The form is there just the same, and can easily be grasped by anyone who takes the trouble to listen carefully. The fact that for the sake of expression, he prodigiously varied his themes on their repetition, does not alter the fact that they are repeated in a satisfying way. The reader who can follow the form of say the first movement of the Eroica symphony (a symphony being only an orchestral sonata) understands not only the abstract principles of form but the manner of applying those principles to the concrete. ¶The results of these applications are various forms—the Rondo, the Minuet and so on: all are based on one of the two plans; in short pieces one theme is used, set forth and finished with; in longer pieces variety and unity are secured by two or three (or even more) themes of different character placed in different keys. The mere setting of themes one after another can always secure variety of a kind; but whether there is at the same time unity depends entirely upon whether the composer is or is not an artist. There is no rule for that: only genius can solve the problem. So much then for pure music. ¶The application of the principles may be widened in a thousand ways; ten themes may be used instead of two or three or four, the order and relation of the keys used may be altered and added to; but the principles remain the same. ¶But when music ceases to be pure music, when words are added to it, or it is intended to tell a story, then these principles can no longer be applied—or rather, there is no longer any need to apply them. Instead of following the architectonical faculty, the composer must follow the dictates of the dramatic or lyrical faculty. The number, character, mode of development, etc., of the themes is derived from the thing to be conveyed to the listener; and then we get what is called Programme music. But just as in a fine novel the writer reveals architectonical sense, so in a really fine piece of Programme it is revealed. There is very little difference in form, for example—at any rate no essential difference—between a Bach fugue and the Valkyries' Ride of Wagner; the themes are stated and developed in a certain order, and all one's faculties are satisfied—the emotions, the sense of pure beauty in melody and harmony, the architectonical sense, the intellectual appreciation of right handling of the material. ¶Whether music is pure music or Programme music, it must satisfy all these. And though, in the future, we may use quarters and eighths of tones, and though we may arrive at complexities unknown to-day and be able to express subtleties of feelings as yet never felt, the principles by which our feelings are expressed in noble and beautiful Form cannot but remain the same.

FUGUE

By Homer A. Norris

A FUGUE is a composition in which a theme, called the *subject*, is announced by one voice and imitated by other voices. The word comes from the Latin *fuga* (a flight), suggesting the thought of one part starting alone after which the others enter in pursuit. A fugue may be written for any number of voices, but we shall here discuss a four-voiced fugue. ¶The subject is usually short and of such marked character as to fix itself readily on the mind, and is usually so constructed as to admit of overlapping; *i.e.*, so that a second voice may enter without musical friction before the first voice has completed the phrase. This overlapping process is called *stretto*. ¶The subject may be announced by any voice. At its completion there comes a very short passage called *codetta*, after which a second voice sings the subject-matter in another key. This is called the *answer*. ¶In the majority of fugues the answer is a transposition of the subject into the key a perfect fifth above the subject, so that subject and answer correspond to the keys of tonic and dominant. Certain subjects instead of being reproduced literally are changed. Subjects which are changed are known as *tonal* subjects; subjects which remain unchanged are known as *real* subjects. ¶While the second voice is singing the answer, the first voice accompanies it, and usually in one of the forms of double counterpoint. It is then intended for subsequent use. Such an accompanying part is called *counter-subject*. ¶The answer is followed by another codetta, leading back to the original key, where a third voice sings the subject, but in a different octave than that in which the first voice announced it. The other voices continue with contrapuntal accompaniment. Another codetta follows, leading to a fourth voice which sings the answer in the dominant. The part of the fugue that we have discussed is called the *exposition*. The exposition closes the first of the three big divisions of the fugue. ¶The exposition is followed by the first *episode*. In the episode the composer has more freedom than in any other portion of the fugue. New material may be presented; brief modulations to related keys introduced, together with free imitation. ¶After the first episode comes the *middle section*. ¶Here the four voices again present the subject-matter in somewhat the same order as in the first section but in other keys. The principal keys are altogether avoided or only incidentally touched. In this group often occur variations of the subject; it may be shortened or lengthened; the answer may be presented in contrary motion, etc. ¶In the third, and (usually) *final* section a return is made to the original keys. Here the subject and answer are generally combined in stretto. ¶A *strict fugue* is one in which there are either no episodes, or in which the episodic material is drawn entirely from the subject or counter-subject. Nearly all the fugues in Bach's "Das Wohltemperirte Clavier" are strict fugues. ¶In a *free fugue* the episodes are constructed of new material. ¶In a *fugato* passage one voice announces a theme, after which other voices enter in free imitation. ¶A *fughetta* is to a fugue what a sonatina is to a sonata: *i.e.*, it is a little fugue. ¶An academic fugue is the most elaborate, artificial, and purely intellectual expression of musical art. (*See Dictionary of Terms entry, page 604.*)

GRACE

By Rupert Hughes

ONE of the innumerable decorative details of melodic progression. Grace notes are musical parasites borrowing their entire sustenance and duration from the note to which they are tied by a slur. They are consequently vitally affected by the rapidity of the tempo. They are almost invariably written small, and are frequently abbreviated, or indicated by some form of musical shorthand. It is to be noted in playing old music that the appoggiatura was written small merely as a bit of academic hypocrisy to smuggle in thus an unprepared suspension. Though written small it was given one-half (sometimes only a third) the value of the note it was bound to, and two-thirds of the value if the note were dotted. ¶The Chart gives first the modern graces, as written and executed, then a series of old graces made up from Bach's own list, and from those of Couperin and Rameau. ¶Composers who desire to escape the wide diversity of interpretation put on all grace-abbreviations are coming, more and more, to write their ornaments out in full, a procedure for which there is every reason but the one of laziness.

Modern Graces.

Acciacatura, or Short Appoggiatura, I. and E. Kurzer Vorschlag or Zusammenschlag G. Pincé étouffé, F. (Sometimes struck simultaneously and instantly released.)

Long Appoggiatura. Langer Vorschlag or Vorhalt. (Written small but taking its full value.)

Written.

etc.

Played.

Double Appoggiatura, or Slide, E. Anschlag, or Schleifer, or Schneller. G.

Unaccented Appoggiatura, or After-beat. Nachschlag or Nachschleifer. (Also double N.)

Written.

Played.

Shake, or Trill, E. Trillo, I. Trille, F. Triller, G. [Old abbreviations, *t*, +, (*w*, (*w*, *w*, etc.] (The length of the trill varies with the length of the note and the tempo.)

Written.

Begun on the principal.   Begun on the auxiliary.   With After-beat.   With a chromatic sign.

Played.

Chain of Trills, E. Catena di trilli, I. Trillerkette, G.. (May be with or without the afterbeat, at discretion.)

Written.

Played. *a* or *b*

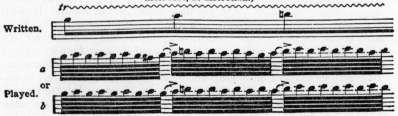

Old Graces.

(Those used in Bach's works from his own explanation.)

From Couperin's List (1713).

Additional Graces (*Obsolete*).

HARMONY IN PRACTICE

By A. J. Goodrich

[Note.—Many of the terms touched upon here will be found treated in more detail under their names—*Ed.*]

In its broader sense Harmony embraces the origin and classification of chords, their rearrangement, inversion, and progression; modulation, resolution, transition, false relation, sequence, suspension, chromatic harmonisation and other topics too numerous to mention here. Yet the fundamental principles of harmony may be easily explained and readily understood. ¶We begin with concords because they are most euphonious and not subject to the somewhat complex theories of resolution. A concord or consonant triad consists of a normal ("perfect") 5th and a major or minor 3d from the root. When the intervals stand in this order the lowest note is the root, or the name-note of the chord. It would thus appear to the eye *all upon lines or all upon spaces;* thus *G b d* form the chord of *G* major. *G, b flat, and d,* would form the chord of *G* minor. ¶Every major key bears six concords, the imperfect triad on the leading note not being a concord. ¶The reader may now sound upon a piano or organ these six concords, each in its first or root position. After sounding the first chord and before proceeding to the next, ascertain the gender,— that is, whether it is masculine (major) or feminine (minor). These distinctions should be determined by the auricular sense, and also by the visual sense. Practice and theory should be thus combined. ¶From the theory of scales and keys and intervals [vide these terms] the reader is supposed to know whether a given chord represents a major or a minor key. The 1st, 3d, and 5th, of every major scale form a major concord: the same numbers in a minor key yield a minor concord. But it is still more important that the ear shall be trained to distinguish between these genders, because music appeals most directly to the auricular faculties.

Concords Classified

When all the concords have been sounded and their characteristics recognised, they should be classified. How many major? How many minor? Which degrees of the scale bear major and which minor concords? ¶Technical terms may be then applied: chord of the tonic, 1; chord of the sub-dominant, 4; chord of the dominant, 5; chord of the super-dominant (relative minor of the tonic), 6; chord of the super-tonic, 2; chord of the mediant, 3. In other words we have as elemental material, the chords of the tonic, sub-dominant, and dominant (always major in a major key) and the relative minors [vide RELATIVE] of these. This process should be repeated in all the major keys.

Concords Rearranged

A chord has as many close positions as it has letters. In the first position the root is lowest. In the second position the root is highest. while the third is below. In the third position the root is in the middle, the 5th being below and the 3d above. ¶At first the different positions are to be effected by rearranging the letters thus: *C, e, g*, root position of the *C* chord. Place the *C* last (an octave higher), and the second position will result *e, g, C.* Now place the *e* last (an octave higher), and the third position will appear,—*g, C, e.* Since no new element has been introduced it is evident that the chord still remains and that *C* is the root. The capital letter serves to indicate to the eye whether the theoretical root is below, in the middle, or at the top. (A distinction is to be made between these simple rearrangements of concords and the actual *inversion* of chords. Inversion comes much later.) Every concord in the key is to be rearranged by means of letters, as indicated, and the different positions are to be numbered in regular order 1, 2, 3. ¶The six concords are now to be rearranged on the key-board, using the letter schemes as a preliminary guide. After the six chords have thus been played in their three close positions the process should be continued in other keys without the aid of letters or written notes. ¶Care must be exercised not to add any new element to the tones of a given chord while its rearrangements are being played. For instance, in the second position of the *F* chord pupils sometimes produce the *A* minor triad by playing *a, C, e,* instead of *a, c, F.* Sound all the concords in their three close positions in every major key. (See Ex. 1.) ¶Also it is desirable to play the rearrangements in this manner descending, as well as ascending. (Interesting examples in this style may be invented.)

EXAMPLE I

PRELIMINARY HARMONISATION

The six rearranged chords in any given key are now selected as a guide. These must appear in notation. Every tone in the major scale of *C* is to be harmonised with as many concords as contain the note to be illustrated. This is to be accomplished at the instrument. 1. Select *c″* (an octave above middle *c*). This is a stationary tone representing, for instance, a soprano part. 2. How many of the six concords in this key contain *c?* (Examine the chart of rearranged chords in *C*, always beginning with the first chord, and ascertain how many contain *c*,—whether above or below is immaterial.) 3. What is the first chord that contains a *c?* What position has *c* at the top? 4. Play this. 5. What is the next chord containing *c?* 6. What position has *c* uppermost? 7. Play this, keeping the same finger (5) upon 3d space *c″*. 8. What is the third chord containing *c?* In what position is *c* uppermost? 9. Play this, the *c* being still in the soprano part, highest. If this much has been correctly executed the following results will appear: The *C* chord will be in its second position, the *F* chord in its first position, and the *A* minor chord in its third position, *e, A, c.* Each chord is to be sounded simultaneously, the letters which represent notes are read from below, upward, therefore *e, g, C,* indicate that the chord of *C* is to be struck, *C* being uppermost. Repeat the process at the piano: *C* chord, 2. *F* chord, 1. *A* minor chord, 3. The fingering should be

5 5 5
2 3 3. (See Ex. 2.) ¶The second chord of the scale is now selected, and this
1 1 1

EXAMPLE II

2 1 3   2 1   3 2 1 etc.

is to be harmonically illustrated in the same manner.   1. How many concords in the key of *C* contain *d?*   (Do not use the imperfect triad in any of these elementary exercises.)   2. What is the first chord containing *d?*   3. What position has *d* at the top?   4. Play this.   5. What is the other chord having a *d?*   (Mention the letter-name of the chord and say whether it be masculine or feminine.)   6. What position of the *G* chord has *d* at the top?   7. Play it, then repeat.   In this manner every tone in the key of *C* should be harmonically illustrated.   Only the six concords in this key are to be used, though each one may be played in any of its three close positions, according to circumstances. Transpose to other major keys.

SIMPLE THEORY OF STRICT CHORD PROGRESSION

Any tone which occurs in any two different chords is called a *connecting tone* Every connecting tone is played by the same finger in both chords or sung by the same voice.   When there are two notes in common between two chords in progression, the connecting tones are retained, or remain stationary—tied or played by the same finger.   (The previous elementary progressions agree with this theory.)   ¶Now arrange a score of four staves, the bass staff below and three treble staves above.   On the first treble staff write the progression *C*, *F*, *A* minor, keeping the connecting notes stationary.   On the second treble staff write the *C* chord in its next position above, *g*, *C*, *e*.   Then write the *F* chord (with *c* in the middle) and the *A* minor chord with *a* and *c* tied from the preceding.   On the third or highest treble staff write the *C* chord in its first position and proceed to make the same progression, *i. e.*, *C* to *F*, and *F* to *A*.   It is to be understood that the progressions on the two upper staves are similar to those on the lowest treble staff, 2 and 3 being rearrangements of 1.   In each instance the same principles are to be applied.   For instance in progressing from the *C* to the *F* the connecting note (*c*) will appear alternately in the soprano, mezzo-

EXAMPLE III

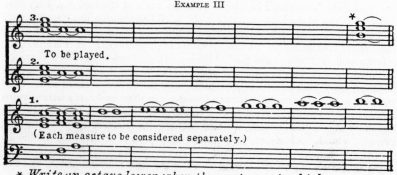

3.

To be played.

2.

1.

(Each measure to be considered separately.)

✻ *Write an octave lower when the parts run too high.*

soprano, and contralto parts.   When the first measure is completed in the three
treble parts, vertically, add the roots in the bass staff immediately beneath the
treble chords.   The bass part moves fundamentally, from root to root, while the
treble parts progress melodically, that is without skipping.   Do not skip the
bass part up or down *more than a 5th.*   ¶Proceed to harmonise *d* with the two
concords which accompany it: then write two rearrangements.   Observe
strictly the connecting-note principle.   When the second measure is completed
in the treble parts add the roots in the bass as before.   Every tone in the scale
is to be treated similarly—2, 4 and 7 having but two chords each as accompanying harmonies.   (See Ex. 3.)   ¶After this scheme has been worked out on
paper, choose another key and proceed to make a similar example at the key-
board, without the aid of notes except perhaps the rearranged chords, which
may be used as a chart.   Continue this process in several other major keys, until
the progressions can be played readily and correctly.

MELODIC SKIPS OF A 3D

When the melody skips up or down a 3d the accompanying harmony remains
the same.   In other words the melody skip may be accompanied by any chord
in the key which contains both notes of the melodic interval.   This has been
partially illustrated in the rearrangement of concords.   Therefore *c* and *e* may
be accompanied by the *C* chord or the *A* minor chord, but *not by both chords.*
When the melody skips, the bass remains stationary as a connecting note.
Consequently there is always a connecting note either above or below in the
present examples.   A skipping theme is given and this should be harmonised
at the piano and on paper.   (See Ex. 4.)

EXAMPLE IV

(Continuous)

SKIPS OF A 4TH

These are harmonised by the same principle, though a skip of a fourth admits
but one chord as accompaniment: that chord which contains both notes of the
skip furnishes the solution.   During the skip the bass remains, and acts as a
connecting note.   Example 5 is to be harmonised practically and theoretically,
as explained.   (*See definition of harmony, Dictionary of Terms, page 614.*)

EXAMPLE V

(8- measure theme)

HARMONIC WARNINGS FOR COMPOSERS

By A. J. Goodrich

Note: These are some of the traditional rules, but are often broken.

1. Don't use any intervals in parallel movement *except* these:

(*a*) Unisons, and octaves when the latter are above or below, with no harmony between the octaves.

(*b*) Major or minor thirds, ascending or descending diatonically.

(*c*) Minor thirds ascending or descending chromatically.

(*d*) Major thirds ascending or descending chromatically. (These were formerly forbidden, but modern composers use them freely for certain purposes. They are, however, rather harsh and incisive.)

(*e*) Major or minor sixths ascending or descending diatonically—like the thirds.

(*f*) Major sixths up or down chromatically.

(*g*) Minor sixths up or down chromatically. (These are inversions of the major thirds, and therefore the same remarks apply.)

(*h*) Augmented fourths may ascend or descend chromatically where they form parts of diminished chords in succession. (The exigencies of notation will require that the imperfect fifth—which is an harmonic equivalent of the augmented fourth—shall appear occasionally in place of the latter. Thus, *c* and *f* sharp may be followed by *b* and *f* natural. Practically the two intervals are identical and interchangeable.)

(*i*) Descending augmented fourths may occur in a series of dominant seventh chords proceeding according to the dominant relation—up a fourth or down a fifth.

2. Don't use *any* of these intervals in parallel movement:

(*a*) Major or minor seconds, ascending or descending.

(*b*) Normal or "perfect" fifths, especially between bass and soprano, or contralto and soprano. The imperfect may follow the perfect fifth. But the reverse of this is rather rough and generally ineffective.

(*c*) [Normal fourths, when they are accompanied by diatonic thirds, above or below, have been frequently employed. A succession of triads in their second or third close positions necessarily involves parallel fourths, as in the Finale to Beethoven's op. 2, *II*.] Parallel fourths ought to be excluded from strict two-part counterpoint, as they are too much inclined to vacuousness.

(*d*) Major or minor sevenths are not to be used in parallel succession. Diminished sevenths sound like major sixths. Therefore these two intervals may succeed each other alternately.

(*e*) Parallel octaves have always been forbidden, and usually their effect is awkward or confusing. Yet hundreds of instances might be quoted from the masters. A simple illustration is the little Romance from Schumann usually coupled with his "Träumerei"—the theme above is doubled by a solo bass part below.

(*f*) Cross relation or false relation is another pitfall into which the young composer is likely to stumble. The effect is sometimes very unpleasant and at other times perfectly satisfactory. ¶The student should avoid at all times all interdicted or suspicious progressions, even though the "evil" be more fancied than real. If he becomes a creative artist he must eventually act on his own responsibility, free and independent of all prescription and formula.

HYMNOLOGY

By H. E. Krehbiel

Hymns, in the sense in which we apply the term, as an adjunct of Christian worship, appear to have been used from the earliest days of the Church. The early Christians naturally borrowed their music from their forefathers in Judea, Greece, and Rome, and the Church thus was quite lacking in any uniformity in this element of worship. Not till the various branches of the Church in the Roman Empire were united under a Christian Emperor, Constantine, is there evidence of attempts to form a system. The first result of this was the Ambrosian chant, and later, the Gregorian, at first congregational, later confined exclusively to the priest. Famous Latin hymns, like the "Te Deum," "Magnificat," "Benedictus," etc., were in use from very early days of the Church, being sung to plain-chant melodies. In the period of the great Church composers—Josquin des Prés, Palestrina, Orlando di Lasso, and others, these hymn-tunes were often used as *canti fermi* for masses and motets; and Palestrina also used them as the basis for a set of "Hymns for the Entire Year," one of the most important of his works. ¶In the meantime a more popular development of hymnal music had been going on in the Mysteries and Miracle-plays, outside the immediate supervision of the Church, that were so conspicuous a feature of popular life and worship in the Middle Ages. In the Church itself the music had been entirely in the hands of the priests and the regular choirs. At the time of the Reformation, however, Luther introduced a great change in this respect, for which the ground was already prepared by the popular development of hymn-singing just mentioned. The chief note of the Reformation was individuality in worship, the transfer of its chief features from the priest to the congregation; and in line with this principle Luther laid great stress on the reintroduction of congregational singing, which had been abandoned since the early days of the Church. Luther produced a great number of hymns, the words of which he fitted to popular melodies of the day. The first Lutheran hymn-book was published in 1524; it was in the vernacular and its popularity in Germany soon became enormous, leading to the speedy issue of innumerable other works of the same kind. Luther not only used the melodies of folk-songs for these hymns, but caused new tunes to be written, and some of them—notably the most famous, "Ein' feste Burg ist unser Gott,"—he is said to have composed himself. It ought to be said, however, that his authorship of the music of this "Battle Hymn of the Reformation" has been disputed. They were all broad choral tunes simply harmonised, such as remain to-day in constant use in Germany, and formed the model for the hymns of the whole Protestant Church. In France the metrical psalms of Marot and Beza were as enthusiastically received by the Protestants as Luther's hymns in Germany; they were originally sung to popular tunes of the day as contained in a psalter published in 1542, by Calvin, in Geneva. Thereafter numerous other collections were published, notably one by Claude Goudimel, in 1565. ¶In England the general cultivation of part-singing in the madrigals made the acceptance of popular hymnody as a part of the new religious movement facile and speedy. Here, as in France, the first hymns were metrical versions of the Psalms in English, and numerous collections of them were published in the last half of the sixteenth century, at first for one part only. "The Whole Psalmes in foure parts," harmonised in the simplest manner possible, published in 1563, was the first harmonised collection of English hymn-tunes. Numerous collections of such tunes were issued thereafter, the most notable being Ravenscroft's, in 1621, and Playford's, in 1671. ¶With the composition of hymns by Wesley and his followers in the eighteenth century came a new poetic material of which musicians were not slow to avail themselves, and which resulted in new hymn-tunes of greater warmth of feeling, differing entirely from the older school of hymns in both melody and harmony. These have had a great, if not always beneficial, influence on the modern development of hymnal music. ¶Hymnology has held a notable place in the history of American music. The stern piety of the Puritan immigrants in New England developed a great activity in this branch of musical art, after it had been freed from the shackles that at first confined it, and the number of early American hymn-tune composers was large. Among these were William Billings (who in 1770 published "The American Psalm Singer: or American Chorister," containing hymns of his own composition), Samuel Holyoke, Andrew Law, Jacob Kimball, Oliver Holden, and others. In the earlier years of the nineteenth century Thomas Hastings, Lowell Mason—whose influence in a secular way on the development of music and musical taste in America was marked—and Nathaniel Gould were the most prominent. (*See Dictionary entry, page 618.*)

JAZZ

By Robert C. Bagar

MANY and confusing are the theories concerning the origin of jazz. The most selfless of investigators would be hard put to it to avoid favouring this appealing probability or that. And to add to the dismay the word jazz itself is also of extremely uncertain derivation. If, perhaps, the jazz idiom had, in a manner of speaking, risen suddenly, and as suddenly achieved the highest plane of musical speech there to rub friendly elbows with its proud confreres of the classics, there would, naturally, be no mystery. The facts attendant on the rise and the making of the grade would then be before us in systematic array. ¶It is not jazz's obscure beginning that is remarkable, but rather that it should be so in a manifestation—to call it that—comparatively recent as jazz. And that takes into account its predecessor, ragtime, and ragtime's predecessors in turn, all of which have been links in a chain of existence spanning no more than four decades or a little over, including, of course, the years of swing, which are now upon us. The legendary births of a galaxy of musical speeches we accept calmly. The remote past is the remote past, hence legend becoming fact and fact legend—a not infrequent phenomenon in either case, as the incessant explorations show—brings about no undue quickening of the pulse, save for a flickering instant at most. The dust is on the ages, and there it reposes is the reasonable attitude. Yet such is not the resignation that would apply to a contemporary product. The desire to know all is the keener because of nearness. And the inevitable answer to that desire is mystery. However, it is generally agreed that jazz came out of New Orleans, all speculation as to how it got there aside for the moment. ¶In all of jazz's serio-comic saga there is, perhaps, nothing as amusing as the proposals respecting the emergence of the word jazz. For instance, one contention has it that it was first known in the Creole argot. It meant "to speed up." Another is that it was born in ugly circumstances in the dance halls of the old West. Still another offers darkest Africa as its spawning ground, and that the spelling was variously jas, jass, jasz, iazz, and so on ad infinitum. But the prize is the one that points to the abbreviation of the name Charles to Chaz as its catapulter into the scheme. The Chaz in the case was a drummer named Charles Washington, who flourished in the city of Vicksburg, Mississippi, around the turn of the century. He was a star percussionist; in fact, the bright, shining light of a small combination. Whenever things lagged during a musical session the leader of the band would call on that worthy to liven them up with the provocative phrase, "Now, Chaz. Now, Chaz." Thus it can be seen how Chaz could easily have become jazz. ¶The days of the minstrel show had an important part in the paving of the way for jazz. The minstrels took spirituals and work songs, distorted them in an elaborate manner unknown up to that time, and they called their concoction "ragging." A mild syncopation—as compared to the present-day complicated expression—ragging, prepared the foundation, nevertheless, for ragtime and, through it, jazz. In 1897 a composer, Kerry Mills by name, turned out a piece titled *Georgia Camp-Meeting.* It was a great success. And this, probably, was the first to be recognised as a ragtime number. Bert Williams' *"O I Don't Know, You're Not So Warm"* had the distinction to be the first printed song whose front cover carried the designation "ragtime." ¶In these items, as in many others of their period, the feature which specifically set them apart as ragtime consisted of a steady, four-beat bass accompaniment to syncopated filips in the melody. The compositions in this sphere fairly gushed forth from the inventive geniuses of the day, *"My Gal's a High-Born Lady,"* for example, was another of the current favourites. ¶In the meantime the orchestral side of the story was undergoing its own development. In 1895 or thereabouts a blind Negro newsboy, who answered to the surprising name of Stale Bread, hawked his papers in a novel manner. He had picked up a fiddle somehow, and his specialty was to attract buyers through the playing of wailing tunes. Soon he was joined by others of his calling and, as a result, a group of four or five newsboys formed a band, which became known as Stale Bread's Spasm Band. Five years later another ensemble made its bow, Razz's Band, which like its forerunner served the fickle goddess of ragtime-metamorphosing-into-jazz. Records being unavailable, it is safe to say that many such organisations must have split the New Orleans air with their odd-assorted screechings. The elementary instrumentation, of course, had something to do with the blatant cacophony. But jazz was imminent, which was sufficient justification. ¶At about the time when America was seeing herself slowly drawn into a world war, a four-piece combination. Brown's Band, made its way up to Chicago for an engagement at Lamb's Café. For the sake of geographical accuracy the group's name was elaborated to Brown's Band from Dixieland. The musicians belonging to this outfit were Raymond Lopez, cornet player; Tom Brown, trombonist; Gus Miller, clarinetist, and William Lambert, drummer. It is significant to note that the patrons of Lamb's emporium did not know what to make of this new music, for by this time, it can be well assumed, the style of playing had already grown to the free-for-all improvisation point, although still in a formative stage. Those hardy members of that first audience, however, were not long holding out. Encouraged by the proprietor of the place to step out on the floor, the patrons soon took to the innovation (for Chicago) with a will. ¶Bert Kelly, a Chicago dance-band manager, had been using the word jazz as an adjective in designating his many ensembles, all collectively called Bert Kelly's Jazz Bands. So that to Mr. Kelly are due the honours for applying that word first in the title of a band. This is of particular importance, for when in 1916 Gus Miller, clarinetist of the Brown Band from Dixieland, severed his connection with the latter organisation he joined the Kelly forces. He was sent out to play an engagement at the Booster's Club in White City. The band remained there a year. But the guests had become converted to this type of orchestra, so the manager, in order to please, obtained another group from New Orleans. When the players arrived they were immediately given the name of the Original Dixieland Band, and the manager, who had liked the sound of the word jazz as communicated to him by the Gus Miller quintet, appropriated the word so that the name now became the Original Dixieland Jazz Band. ¶That was the beginning of an era. Not only did the Original Dixieland Jazz Band take the country by storm, make innumerable recordings, but thereupon every ambitious tyro, as a consequence, got together a combination of five and lorded it in the dance halls, at school hops and so on, contributing to the confusion and, at the same time, doing something for the propagation of the jazz gospel. ¶Advanced as is the present-day swing, it owes its very existence to the "hot" idiom of the Dixieland orchestras. Usually consisting of clarinet, saxophone, banjo, piano and drums, these apostolic delegations featured improvisation to the heart's content and, needless to add, to the dancing feet's exhaustion. There was nothing "straight" about the playing of Dixieland bands, taking straight to mean unembellished melody. But what opportunities hot playing gave to the imaginative performer! Hot music became the expression of the hour. Improvisation by one musician over a steadily flowing groundwork of rhythm was one thing, but two and even three players improvising at the same time was something else again. What has been lately called a new musical form—swing, to be exact—has its roots deeply imbedded in that early mass extemporising. ¶The composer was as nothing compared to the stature of the hot performer. Any simple tune could be treated in the vogue idiom. In truth, the only part of a song retained was the harmonic structure, the melody being made free with and put through innumerable variations in free polyphonic style. One of the most famous leaders of the day was Ted Lewis, whose arpeggiated clarinet runs have been preserved for posterity through his phonograph recordings. But with all this to-do about hot playing there was also the undownable conservative element in jazz concerned with glorifying the melody as well as the harmony of a tune. There was rhythm, of course, as a prime feature of straight playing, but a fluidly moving rhythm, not over-stressed to the neglect of the melody. Even to-day we are aware of the same condition. We have "swing" bands and "sweet" bands, which correspond, respectively, to the hot and straight of the jazz age. ¶Such bands as Paul Whiteman's Orchestra, Isham Jones' Orchestra, Vincent Lopez' Orchestra, which came directly on the heels of the Dixieland ensembles, have retained to this day their essentially sweet or straight characteristics, although if the occasion arises there are musicians in any of these outfits that can sail blithely into split-second "licks," or peculiarly accented figures. The words "corny" and "McGee" came to signify phrasing that was definitely of an elementary order in hot playing. Corny, with its Corn-Belt connotations, meant either farm or small-town expression, not urban, as it were. McGee is of obscure origin. The fox-trot was becoming more and more perfected. Darius Milhaud, the French composer, took up the idiom with great zest. So did Igor Stravinsky. ¶While the craze for hot music was at its height Paul Whiteman, who had been leading an orchestra at the Hotel Alexandria, Los Angeles, in 1920, where he was devoting himself to the purification of jazz music, hit upon the idea of writing out parts for his musicians. Up to that time the playing was all to the unorganised side. A group of players would get the melody from the pianist and then fall into line with melodies, counter-melodies, and harmonies on the way. All very uncertain and lacking system. Ferde Grofé, Whiteman's arranger and pianist, rose quickly to fame through his ingenious orchestrations. A trained musician, possessing a talent far beyond the average, he was responsible in great measure for the sudden return to the "legitimate" (sweet or straight) kind of playing, but this time it was symphonic, orderly, following, as closely as jazz could, the well-intentioned rules of orchestration. ¶Paul Whiteman and his orchestra came East. They appeared nightly at the Palais Royal in New York. The new style with its extremely clever arrangements caught on solidly. But Whiteman was nurturing a secret ambition. Schooled in classical music spheres, he had given up his orthodox career in favour of the sirenish beckoning of jazz which promised much in the way of financial success and, logically enough, glory. Yet he had not freed himself completely from the shackles of his musical education. Symphonic music was still to him the highest form of tonal expression. The extraordinary talent he had surrounded himself with, and with the ever-growing reputation of a young composer, George Gershwin, to urge him on, he commissioned the latter to write a work for his orchestra. The composition was to be a jazz creation, but fitting within the frame of one of the serious music forms. The result was the "*Rhapsody in Blue.*" On February 12, 1924, it was given its world première performance at Aeolian Hall by the Whiteman orchestra. George Gershwin and Zez Confrey were the solo pianists. The work was an immediate success. It was acclaimed by critics and public alike as a fine example of American jazz elevated to concert pitch. There were subsequent concerts, again at Aeolian Hall, and at Carnegie Hall. Thus were Whiteman, Gershwin, and Grofé, who orchestrated the piece, propelled into world prominence. There were tours in this country and in Europe. Everywhere Whiteman and Gershwin were received as visiting potentates. ¶A most illuminating sidelight on the importance achieved by Whiteman is the fact that almost all of his musicians have since climbed to the top as leaders, star performers, or composers. Ferde Grofé, particularly, a respected composer, has a number of successful works to his credit, notably, the *"Grand Canyon"* and *"Hollywood"* suites, *"Mississippi,"* *"Three Shades of Blue,"* and others. ¶Perhaps, because the *"Rhapsody in Blue"* was the first of Tin-Pan Alley's brain children to scale the heights, it will remain for many a year to come the prime favourite of all jazzists, a category that seems to be growing with leaps and bounds to the point of including some of the most noted composers of our time. Of these Darius Milhaud and Igor Stravinsky have already been mentioned. There are others; Aaron Copland, Louis Gruenberg, John Alden Carpenter, Leo Sowerby, Emerson Whithorne, Kurt Weill. Ravel, in his salad days, had not disdained investigating the "blues." An Italian, Sonsogno, had a work of his, *"Il Jazzista Romantico,"* played in Carnegie Hall by the Philharmonic-Symphony Orchestra under the direction of Arturo Toscanini ¶Gershwin had not stopped with his *"Rhapsody."* Its success could only be a great incentive to carry on. And carry on he did, as witness his production of several other works also in the high-plane jazz manner. His Concerto in F, which was introduced to a Carnegie Hall audience by Walter Damrosch, who had commissioned him to write the piece, was one of them. *"An American in Paris"* was another. Then there were several piano preludes (subsequently orchestrated by Roy Bargy, Paul Whiteman's present pianist) and a Rhumba composition. And, of course, the folk opera *"Porgy and Bess."* Nor had he lessened his activities in composing music for Broadway shows and, latterly, films. ¶But the other American composers, referring particularly to those out of Tin-Pan Alley, worked on with a supreme nonchalance, perhaps a little surprised at all the attention the world was giving their creations. Among these we find Rube Bloom, Thomas Griselle, Dana Suesse, John W. Green, Harold Arlen, Zez Confrey, Matt Malneck, Frank Signorelli, Eastwood Lane, Duke Ellington, slaving away at a beloved task, striving for new ideas, constantly keeping pace with every new trend. In this category, too, but several notches above because of more ambitious efforts fit William Grant Still, Ferde Grofé, and Robert Russell Bennett. ¶While all credit is due the jazz performers for infinite progress made in the direction of extending the scope of the idiom, the song writers whose tunes inspired the players to greater heights are deserving of a full measure of attention. Among these the casual survey reveals Irving Berlin, who graduated from singing waiter in a Bowery saloon, Nigger Mike's, to the tremendous hit writer he is to-day; Jerome Kern, a well-trained musician, provider of many of Broadway's successful shows; Richard Rodgers, who together with his partner, Lorenz Hart, has written some of the nation's cleverest songs; Vincent Youmans; Ray Henderson, of the famous trio De Sylva (Buddy), Brown (Lew), and Henderson; George M. Cohan, Walter Donaldson, Lew Pollack, Nathaniel Shilkret, Abel Baer, Abner Silver, Vincent Rose, and, reaching further back, Harry von Tilzer, Charles K. Harris, and so on. If some of the oldsters have been included in what is really a very sketchy outline, it is because the jazz musicians—and, in like manner, the swing musicians—have tootled, pounded, sawed and slapped their hot coloratura to everything and anything that ever came out of a popular composer's creative mind ¶Irving Berlin wrote *"Alexander's Ragtime Band"* in 1912. But time can do nothing to age that classic It is as fresh and invigorating to-day as it ever was, perhaps more, considering the superb orchestral garb that can be given it now. Hits from the Berlin pen have been numerous and each has been a finely wrought piece of writing, both musically and as to text. Consider some of his famous songs: "*When I Lost You*," "*All Alone*," "*What'll I Do?*," "*Remember*," "*Always*," "*Say It Isn't So*," not to omit his innumerable show tunes, his movie tunes. It would be a tremendous task to find another popular composer whose hits could equal, let alone outnumber, Berlin's. ¶Some of the pieces turned out by the other song writers give an extraordinary insight into the variety of expression that has found favour with the American public. Mentioned at random they might be "*Birth of the Blues*," "*That's Why Darkies Were Born*," "*Over There*," "*You're Driving Me Crazy*," "*Charmaine*," "*Jeannine*," "*Farewell to Arms*," "*Whispering*," "*Avalon*," "*Linger a While*," "*Tea for Two*" and "*After the Ball Was Over.*" ¶The bands that made these numbers famous have been part of a fragment of American life that is not to be duplicated in any other side of it. For instance, the records show Paul Whiteman, Isham Jones, Vincent Lopez, Ted Lewis, Rudy Vallee, Fred Waring, Guy Lombardo, Ben Bernie, Wayne King, George Olsen, Ben Pollack, Jean Goldkette and others. ¶No picture of the jazz era would be complete without inclusion of blues songs and their originator, the coloured composer, William C. Handy. Briefly, Handy took the simple darky songs of his time and gave them something of his own which something, specifically, called for the introduction of a minor third into any tune in a major key. The frequent insertion of the minor third or blue note made the piece what was called a "mean" blues. It made the song wail and moan. At the beginning of this century Handy concocted a campaign song for a political candidate who had little chance of victory. It was played with such regularity and affection that it helped put the office seeker into the desired place, besides which the song became a local favourite Having obtained his end, Handy gave the number a new title, "*Memphis Blues.*" It was sent to many publishers and was rejected by all. But Handy, undaunted, printed the tune himself, and a very unfruitful venture that turned out to be. Nobody would buy it. Finally he sold his rights to it for one hundred dollars, which, as is often the case, was the signal for it to become one of the big money earners of that period. In rapid sequence Handy wrote the "*St. Louis Blues*" and the "*Beale Street Blues*," thereby bringing into existence three pieces that have withstood nobly the ravages of time. ¶Since it is to the musicians themselves, the men who played in the bands, that we owe the real development of jazz (witness the continuance of this phenomenon in the world of swing) it would be an omission of huge proportions to neglect naming some of the most prominent in the field, some of whom are busily engaged in the very task to-day. Leon "Bix" Beiderbecke, born 1903–died 1931, was one of the greatest jazz artists known. A disciple of Louis Armstrong, the gifted Negro trumpet player, Beiderbecke, also a trumpet player, is held as the example of what the perfect hot player should be like. He had an extraordinary tone, impeccable taste, flaming imagination, and a technic that few can equal now or could equal then. Also a talented composer, Beiderbecke played the piano almost as well as the trumpet. One composition of his (he wrote several pieces) "*In a Mist*" is, perhaps, a perfect example of the best jazz writing of the period. Beiderbecke was for a time a member of the Paul Whiteman Orchestra. ¶Tommy Dorsey, a trombonist, who is now the leader of his own band, is another of the top-flight performers. There are also Jack Teagarden, trombonist; Benny Goodman, clarinetist, now a band leader; Fletcher Henderson, Claude Hopkins, Fats Waller, all coloured pianists; Red Norvo, xylophonist; these a handful of musicians who had their beginnings in the jazz era and have moved lock, stock and barrel into the current sphere of swing, all of them tremendous influences in the moulding of the idiom from the one to the other. ¶During jazz's most flourishing period, in the years immediately following the Great War, the struggle between the sweet and hot adherents continued unabated. The peculiar and even comical phase of the situation was that those who held out for sweet were usually incapable of playing hot and vice versa. It would seem that the contest is to be a permanent one, for both sides have their constituents, and they are legion. And perhaps more than the musicians the listeners fight on indefatigably for their espoused causes. Whatever the result—and apparently only crossed swords will bring it about—the very combat has, undoubtedly, given greater impetus to the promulgation of jazz. ¶If asked the question, "What is jazz?" the answer might be any one of a hundred loose definitions, each having something to do with the meaning, and not all of them combined capable of expressing it fully. But there must be some working basis, some common ground on which minds may meet to discuss the subject intelligently. The temptation to retort, "What has intelligence to do with it?" might prove too strong, but there would still be the necessity to reach a happy medium of communication through the employment of words. And one might respond that, roughly, jazz, either sweet or hot, is a musical form in which there is an established rhythmic figure in the bass while the original melody is made to fit an improvisatory scheme, second to the purposes of the moment. Loosely, but very loosely, this definition takes care of both sweet jazz and hot jazz. In the case of the former the "improvisatory scheme" is an elementary one; in the case of the latter a complicated one. Even in the playing of the simplest tunes, for instance, the jazz pianist pays little attention to the score; that is, the pianist performing for his own or his friends' enjoyment. Syncopation, spontaneous and pertinent to the harmonic and melodic manifestations, is of the essence, however. ¶Something of the same applies equally to orchestral performance, except that here the improvisation has been scored in great part. Wherever the orchestrator has purposely left a sequence unwritten for some solo instrument is the place for that instrument to take a lick or a "break," which terms have to do with spontaneous improvisation in the nature of some specially accented figure. ¶The variations of this procedure are many and intricate even in jazz playing. Despite the many attempts of commentators to supply definitive tracts on jazz, the fact remains that it can only be played and not talked.

LEADING–MOTIVES

By Gustave Kobbé

OTHER COMPOSERS before Wagner used typical phrases to express some personal characteristic or idea, and repeated them in a manner which suggests what is now termed a leading-motive. Such is the "*Idée fixe*" in Berlioz's "Fantastique" symphony; or the phrase in Weber's "Euryanthe" which occasionally even is spoken of as the "Tomb Motive." I, however, have always considered that Beethoven in the use he made of the opening theme of his Fifth Symphony more nearly approached the leading-motive than any of Wagner's predecessors. The theme recurs with great variety of effect throughout the symphony, the second movement excepted. It is found as a mysterious threatening figure accompanying the second theme of the first movement, while in the Allegro, the scherzo of the symphony, it partakes of a joyous character, to reappear as a disturbing element in the finale. It has the plasticity of a leading-motive, but it may be questioned whether

Beethoven intended to use it for any other than a purely musical effect. In fact any suggestions Wagner may have received from other composers were so slight that the leading-motive in the modern sense may unhesitatingly be said to be his invention. ¶It is easier to say what a leading-motive is not, than to give it a fixed definition. The first idea to disabuse one's self of is that a leading-motive is anything like a label. The "Walhalla" motive in the "Ring of the Nibelung" is not a guide-post which reads "Walhalla to the right—3 miles"— nor does it even represent Walhalla as a pile of masonry. It expresses, in its simple yet lofty measures, the rulership of *Wotan*, the hegemonia of the gods. A leading-motive is a musical searchlight or X-ray which illuminates and enables us to look deep into every character, thought, mood, purpose, idea, and impulse in the drama. Even conscience itself does not escape Wagner. Witness how he lays it bare with his scalpel of leading-motives in the first meeting of *Siegfried* and *Hagen* in "Goetterdaemmerung" with the Curse Motive, which hints at *Hagen's* fell purpose, darkening the noble Siegfried Motive. The use of the Curse in this episode clearly foreshadows the death of the Volsung hero at *Hagen's* hand and lays the gloom of impending tragedy heavily upon the hearer's soul. ¶How plastic a leading-motive may be, how closely welded to the ever-changing phases of the drama and how clearly it expresses them, the wonderful variants of the motive of Siegfried the Fearless—the call *Siegfried* sounds on his silver horn—will show. Joyous and buoyant in its simplest form, it becomes when he takes leave of *Brünnhilde* to sally forth in quest of adventure, heroically grand, and in the Death Music, that strain of triumphant mourning which thrills every hearer and stamps the episode as the greatest climax ever achieved in a musical work for the stage. Indeed, the whole scene is a triumph for the leading-motive idea, since here, as *Siegfried's* lifeless body is borne up on the

mountain crest, the orchestra gives a musical epitome of his career by voicing successively the motives most intimately relating to him which have been heard in the cycle of music-dramas. ¶But Wagner's use of leading-motives singly and in complex combinations according to the trend of the drama however interesting analytically would wholly have failed were not the motives themselves musically valuable. They are enunciated chiefly by the orchestra (which thus forms a constant commentary upon the proceedings of the stage) and they are considered by those who are in the van of musical opinion to have resulted in the most eloquent and sublime—if at times the most tedious—scores ever penned. To appreciate what a genius Wagner really was, it is only necessary to listen to the works of some of his imitators. ¶Liszt in his Symphonic Poems adapted the leading-motive to instrumental music, in which respect Richard Strauss followed him. (*See Dictionary of Terms entry, page 629.*)

MODERN HARMONY

By Quincy Porter

Before undertaking a discussion of some of the important trends of modern harmony, it is essential to consider what came before. It is amazing to contemplate the wealth of music which conformed itself to the classic, tonal system of harmony. That it could have satisfied so well the needs of so noble an array of musical geniuses, men as strikingly contrasted as Bach and Schubert, Mozart and Wagner, Händel and Beethoven, testifies to the richness of its resources, but at the same time demonstrates conclusively that harmony is only one of the constructive elements of music, by no means explaining all that is often asked of it. The genius of Beethoven, for example, manifests itself to a far greater extent in his subtle use of rhythm, the curiously expressive accent of his melody, his dynamic power, than in his harmonic practises, which were fairly conventional. ¶We must review briefly a few of the resources of this system, which many still consider unexhausted. The elimination of modes which did not lend themselves to tonic, dominant, and subdominant relationships, left the listener with only two scales, the major and minor, asymmetrical in their construction, and hence capable of easy definition. Great opportunity was created for modulation, tonal contrast, a feeling of inevitability in harmonic progression based on surprisingly simple acoustical relationships. (Schönberg eloquently explains the simplicity of these relationships in the first part of his book, *Harmonielehre*.) The well-defined and contrasting characteristics of the major and minor scales offered in *themselves* a wealth of resource; the unification of a complicated work about a single tonal centre gave increased power to musical speech. The mass of associations which develop when any language becomes familiar gave the possibility of increasing freedom in the treatment of dissonance, new ways in which to use chromatics, interesting omissions of what could be taken for granted, but the fundamental structure of the system remained the same for over three hundred years. ¶Beethoven himself made a rather unsuccessful attempt to free himself from the bondage of this system, when he wrote the slow movement of his string quartet in A minor, in the Lydian mode, but it was not until the latter part of the nineteenth century that the older modes began to assert a real influence on art music. Men like Moussorgsky and Grieg found new freshness in their native, modal folk music; others, like Franck and d'Indy, more inspired by the modal music which had successfully survived in the church, made some interesting departures from the conventions of the old system by a curious mixing of the modal with the chromatic. ¶Reaction against the conventions of the classic system became widespread. Experiment after experiment was made, using new scales, some oriental in origin, some especially manufactured, but all tending toward a newer and freer conception of harmony. ¶These new departures may be roughly and somewhat arbitrarily classified as: (1) those which can be explained as further extensions of simple, acoustical relationships; (2) those which seem more artificial in character. ¶It is well to state at the outset that those which fit in the second category are not necessarily of less artistic value than those in the first. In the evolution of all arts there is a tendency away from the more natural and simple toward the more artful; away from the spontaneous toward the more carefully reasoned. The mere placing side by side of two sets of four notes to make a mode was already a long step in the direction of the artificial. The major triad fits perfectly into the chord of nature; the minor triad is already an artificial imitation. The major scale, though an artificial arrangement of notes, has many natural relationships, more than any other scale yet found, and lends itself to the use of chords which fit fairly well into the chord of nature. ¶Under the first category let us consider, to begin with, the discovery of new, consonant-sounding chords. Although Debussy may have thought his highly sensitive ear was at fault when he noticed that a major triad with the minor 7th or the major 9th or both added to it sounded to him quite consonant, actually he was beginning to expand the possibilities of reposeful harmonic colour. Soon the augmented 11th was found to fit agreeably. These new chords were built by simply adding more partials (the 7th, 9th and 11th, respectively) to the fundamental. There had been a lapse of seven or eight centuries since any such extension of consonant resources had been made. Since the time of Debussy many other similar chords have been discovered, and whether their innovators evolved them in consideration of acoustical principles or merely by acute listening may well remain their ow..

secret. ¶When two different notes are played, not only the fundamentals but also the partials of both actually sound. Composers have discovered that by actually writing these partials into their chords they can achieve a great variety of clear, well-defined colours, ranging from very consonant to extremely dissonant. Striking effects may be obtained by varying the position of the upper notes of major triads built on two fundamentals separated by the interval of a major 2nd, or a perfect 4th, or a minor 6th. To separate two fundamentals thus reinforced, contemporary composers frequently employ the interval of a major 7th (witness the combination in Stravinsky's *"Sacre"* of the 1st, 3rd, 5th, and 7th partials of E flat, above the 1st, 3rd, and 5th partials of F flat, in the rhythmically repeated chords just after the introduction). Another favourite interval is that of the augmented 4th (see the superposition of the major triad on F sharp above that on C during a long passage in the same composer's *"Petrouchka"*). ¶At another point in the *"Sacre"* Stravinsky has reinforced by adding the more artificial minor triad to fundamentals separated by a major 7th and a minor 9th, giving a darker though similarly conceived effect of colour. There is not space to deal with more intricate combinations which have recently extended the harmonic palette of music, but merely to call attention to a curious quality which some of them possess. Though they may be extremely complicated in their make-up, the various dissonances seem to neutralise one another, producing a state of equilibrium which gives an almost paradoxical effect of consonance. Since all the notes disagree more or less similarly, there is no clear tendency implied; one does not feel the necessity for any one or more of them to move in order to make it less dissonant. These equilibrium chords are accepted as reposeful, and have made satisfactory conclusions for certain types of modern works. ¶In their use of colour-chords, modern composers have frequently gone back to the principles of the old "organum." Instead of limiting themselves to 4ths or 5ths and 8ves in the reinforcing of a melodic line, they have been using some of these colourful, harmonic combinations, such as triads, chords of the major 9th, major 7ths, or minor 2nds. The use of such chords or intervals to strengthen a line is not far removed from the practise of giving a single melodic line to an instrument of a striking colour, to make it stand out from its background with clarity. ¶Coming to the second category, the realm of the more artificial, let us consider chords and scales which are evenly spaced. Although the most important relationships in the tonal system, as in the other arts, are asymmetrical, composers seem unable to resist the lure of perfect symmetry. Like blocks which can be easily fitted together in many different ways, symmetrical chords and scales offer amusing possibilities. The symmetrical diminished 7th chord was worked to death by the romantic composers. Any of the three combinations of sounds that make it can be written so as to relate to any of the 24 major and minor keys. Bach and Beethoven used them freely, but preserved a tonal background that enabled one to keep one's relative position. Liszt often left the listener bewildered, wondering where he was. Nevertheless, the symmetrical has its uses, for it is sometimes temporarily desirable to blindfold the listener. ¶Modern composers have used all varieties of equi-spaced chords and scales. Spacing by perfect 5ths produces an equilibrium chord, whose colour varies chiefly with the number of 5ths that are added. The effect is, of course, particularly brilliant with stringed instruments which are themselves tuned in 5ths. ¶Spacing by perfect

4ths creates a quite different colour. Scriabine and Satie often varied the chord from the perfect by the addition of one augmented fourth, achieving a slight effect of asymmetry. Scriabine, in his effort to expand the possibilities of his system, built of superimposed 4ths as a substitute for the 3rds of the classic system, came to include diminished 4ths as well, and frequently arrived in territory that had already been discovered. ¶Little use has recently been made of the augmented triad, which divides the scale into three equal intervals. It is one of the few chords which harmonise the whole-tone scale, but its possibilities for giving a nebulous, undefined quality to harmony were fairly well exhausted many years ago, more recent and varied ways of giving similar effects having tended to eradicate its use. ¶The diminished 7th chord, to which reference has already been made, is decidedly artificial in its construction. Its colour has become perfectly familiar, however, and it is now used frequently in combination with other chords. Ernest Bloch often combines it with other diminished 7th chords. At the beginning of his sonata for violin and piano, for example, he maintains one of them in the middle register while he presents successively in the bass the notes of a diminished 7th chord a half tone lower. ¶The possibilities of the whole-tone scale were nobly exploited by Debussy, and this is one of the less natural of his discoveries. New uses for it have been found by Hindemith and others, but since only two whole-tone scales exist, its possibilities are very limited. New uses may be discovered, in combination with other, more diatonic factors. ¶During the entire period in which tonal harmony held sway, the chromatic scale was employed frequently, and with growing freedom. Wagner effected an amazing variety of colours by using it on a background of tonal harmony. Without a stabilising factor, this rather artificial spacing of intervals (both unnatural melodically if repeated contiguously, and remote from the simpler harmonic relationships in the chord of nature) may create music which lacks definition. Other methods are being discovered, however, of stabilising chromatic materials by relating them to other modes and scales. The architecture of Schönberg's "Twelved-tone" music depends almost entirely upon the structure and use of its melodic motives. In order to create a feeling of atonality, it meticulously avoids harmonic or melodic emphasis on any one, more than on any other, of the 12 chromatic notes. While experimentation is necessary for the expansion of musical resources, it may also result in rather one-sided emphasis, and there is a growing feeling that present efforts at innovation along the line of symmetry forego much that is of value in the asymmetrical tonal system. ¶Finally we come to a consideration of quarter-tones, whose only justification seems to be their relation to the familiar semi-tone, which, as we have remarked, is in itself quite an arbitrary interval. Ernest Bloch has used them in a piano quintet, but the more faithfully they are executed the more certain is the average audience that the players have produced false notes. They have some melodic value, particularly as passing notes, but little harmonic value. Any step toward increasing the present number of possible tones should give access to consonant intervals, such as the 7th and 11th partials, which we cannot now use. Since they accomplish no other harmonic service, it is the opinion of the writer that they constitute a uselessly long step in the direction of the artificial. ¶No discussion of modern tendencies can omit mention of certain elements which do not properly fall within the scope of the title of this article. Considerations of rhythm, line

and melody, for example, are of foremost importance. Much of the most striking music of the present owes its effectiveness less to harmony than to vitality
of line and forward motion of rhythm, which in themselves create plausible and
artistically justified harmonies. Just as the earlier composers set off their
melodic ideas against one another contrapuntally by the use of instruments with
contrasting colours, so the modern composer sets off his melodic ideas by putting
them in contrasting, non-blending tonalities. In traditional counterpoint, only
rhythmic and directional independence existed between the different voices; in
polytonal counterpoint, harmonic independence is also achieved. The music of
Hindemith is perhaps more understandable from this point of view than from
the harmonic one which he himself exposes. ¶Whether or not the vast experimentation of the past fifty years has yet given rise to works of first magnitude,
it is certain that the goddess Euterpe is no person upon whom to inflict limitations. She has sung most eloquently for many years on a basis of tonal harmony. In the future she will sing new melodies on new harmonies, but some
of the characteristics of the music which has stood the test of time will doubtless
remain. Great art will continue to be at bottom simple, but with its enormously increased resources music will become increasingly universal in its ability
to reflect the infinitely varied phases of human experience and feeling.

MODES

By Rupert Hughes

Perhaps the most graphic definition of modes to the modern mind would be:—
overlapping portions of the C major scale: or successive octave-stretches along
the white keys of the pianoforte. *Ecclesiastical modes* were the Middle Age
perversion of the *Greek modes*. While overthrown by Nineteenth Century
scales and tonality, traces of their influence persevere, and many of the old
chants still in use in the Roman Catholic and Anglican services are more or
less exact specimens of the capabilities of the modes. The Twenty-first
Century will probably qualify and develop our own system of keys out of
shape and recognition. The complete overthrow of the ideas of tonality and
modulation of the earlier part of the Twentieth Century is indeed even now
beginning. We are already over the doorsill of the nullitonic or omnitonic
harmonies, and the multitude of accidental sharps and flats and naturals required to notate the highly chromatic music of our day renders inevitable some
radical change in the system of keys; meanwhile, the obsolete modal systems
have at least a keen historical interest and importance. There is place here for
only an allusion to a few of the salient points. Full statement of the details
and the controversies on them would fill a large library. ¶Though the Greeks
properly gave music a very high place in their educational system, they were too
much engrossed in theories, rules, and restrictions to build up large material.
Their musical resources were of the slenderest. While their noble tragedies
were exactly Wagner's idea of opera, the music to which they were set seems to
have been of the most limited range and variety; and furthermore, absolutely
lacking in harmony even in the Middle Age sense. ¶The Greek system differs
from ours in being all of a minor tendency, in having the notes named down-

wards, and in paying attention only to melody and not at all to chords. The white piano keys from e′ (just above middle C) to the E an octave below, represent their oldest and central mode, the Dorian. By remembering that all these steps are whole tones except the two semitones from c′ to b and F to E, and by representing a whole step by a (+) and a half step by a (—), it will be seen that this Dorian mode descends by the following steps, + + — + + —. These make two similar groups of three steps or four notes, which were called *tetrachords*. The word chord with them meant "string" not "harmony," for their whole music took its rise from their lyre, a stiff and limited, unfretted instrument of many poetical associations but stinted in practical possibilities. The pattern of tetrachord (+ + —) into which this Dorian mode divided was called the Dorian tetrachord. They superimposed on the top note e′ a similar tetrachord of the tones a′, g′, f′, e, and added below another e, d, c, B. To these they added the low A as a supplementary (in Greek *proslambanomenos*). The outer couples of tetrachords overlap. Between the middle two is an imaginary line of separation (*diazeuxis*). Each of these was therefore a "disjunct" (*diazengmenon*) tetrachord. The "complete system" (*systema teleion*) of two octaves (a′ down to A) was divided thus into four tetrachords, each of them given the name which (with its English translation) is shown in the chart herewith. For purposes of modulation they laid across the middle of this system an overlapping or "conjunct" (*synemmenon*) tetrachord in which the b was flattened, d′, c′, bb, a (+ + —). ¶The octave from e′ down to E was, as already stated, called the *Dorian mode*. Other portions of the systema were given other names, d to D being called the *Phrygian*, c′ to C the *Lydian*, and b to B the *Mixo-Lydian*. ¶They conceived a way of extending these octaves by duplicating one of the tetrachords below (in Greek "*hypo*"). Thus, if the upper tetrachord (e′ to a) of the Dorian mode be transferred an octave below, and fastened to the lower tetrachord, we shall no longer have e′, d′, c′, b, a, g, f, e, (+ + — + + —) but a, g, f, e, d, c, B, A, which also is + + — + + —, with the added step + (*proslambanomenos*). This is called the *Hypo-Dorian mode*. ¶The Phrygian, Lydian, and Mixo-Lydian modes do not descend by the same whole and half steps as the Dorian, but as follows: Phrygian (+ — + + + — +), Lydian (— + + — + + —), Mixo-Lydian (+ + + — + + —). It will be found, however, that these modes are capable of the same *hypo*-treatment, thus making two more modes, *Hypo-Phrygian* and *Hypo-Lydian*,— for the Mixo-Lydian (b to B) being too low to add a tetrachord beneath, it is added above, giving e′ to e, which is identical with the Dorian. The principal note (*tonic*) of the regular modes was the top note. Each hypo-mode kept for its chief note the chief note of the original (or its octave). The names and ranges of these seven modes with two others added later are shown in the chart, which shows also the names (and their translations) given each note and each tetrachord. ¶With this system as a foundation and with the use of the conjunct tetrachord and its b flat as an entering wedge, the Greeks gradually added several notes above and below their systema, and inserted half steps between the full steps until they acquired a complete chromatic scale on which they transposed their scales with much melodic freedom. Harmony, of course, they did not have. These transposed scales were not named like the original modes from their chief notes, but were given the name of the scale whose steps they resembled. By making use of the + and —, or other signs for indicating half or

Chart of the Greek Modes.

NOTE. { *Nete* = highest.
Paranete = next highest.
Trite = third.
Paramese = next the middle.
Mese = middle. }

Tetrachordon Hyperboleon.
("Highest Tetrachord.")

Tetrachordon Diezeugmenon.
("Disjoined Tetrachord.")

Tetrachordon Synemmenon.
("Conjoined Tetrachord.")

Tetrachordon Meson.
("Middle Tetrachord.")

Tetrachordon Hypaton.
("Lowest Tetrachord.")

NOTE. { *Lichanos* = forefinger-tone.
Parhypate = next to the lowest.
Hypate = lowest. }

Proslambanomenos ("The Added Tone.")

Nete. Paranete. Trite. Nete. Paranete. Trite. Paramese.
Bb............ Mese. Lichanos. Parhypate. Hypate. Lichanos. Parhypate. Hypate.

$a^1 + g^1 + f^1 - e^1 + d^1 + c^1 + b$ ✚ $a + g + f - e + d + c - B$ ✚ A

✚ + + − + + −   + 6. Hyper-phrygian (or Locrian) a^1-a.

✚ + − + + −   + + 7. Hypo-phrygian (or Ionian) g^1-g.

+ − + + −   + +✚ 8. Hyper-lydian (g^1-g).

− + + −   + + +✚ 9. Hypo-lydian (f^1-f).

1. Dorian (e^1-e) (= Hypo-mixo-lydian). + + − ✚ + + + +

2. Phrygian (d^1-d). + − + + + + + −

3. Lydian (c^1-c). − + + + ✚ + +

4. Mixo-lydian (b-B). ✚ + + + + + −

5. (Æolian or) Hypo-dorian (a-A). + + − + + − +✚

The whole steps are indicated by + ; *the half-steps by* — ; *the Diazeuxis is indicated by* ✚

whole steps, it is easy to plot out the steps of any scale and find its prototype and its name in the original modes. ¶The Greek notation was by letters and symbols. It is too complicated to explain here. ¶A method of manipulating their scale melodically may be mentioned. The tetrachords as described were called diatonic, but in the Dorian e, d, c, b, if the d were omitted, the tetrachord became e — c, b, and was called the *older enharmonic*. A later plan was to keep the d, but lower it by half a tone (that is, to tune the d string to c sharp), making the four strings e, c♯, c, b. This was the *chromatic* genus. A still later plan, called the *newer enharmonic*, was to tune the d to a pure third with the e, making the tetrachord e, c, c, b; the two c strings differing slightly in tone (see the word COMMA). ¶This group of three tones, c, c, b, or c♯, c, b, was the *pyknon* (plural *pykna*). Other variations in the treatment were called *chroai* (colourings). Definite melodies were given definite names, a melody being a *nomos* (*i. e.*, arrangement, order, or setting). ¶Upon this false, but elaborate, system, enormous ingenuity was spent, and appalling complexity and scholarship of a kind were made possible, to the delight of the typical theorist. In respect of melody the Greek modes offered far more freedom than the church modes, which, however, possessed the modern invention of harmony.

ECCLESIASTICAL MODES

Music, along with all the other early Christian arts, borrowed largely from the Greeks, but rejected their warmth and ornate sophistication for a stark rigidity. ¶Early church musicians took the Greek modes as best they could understand them, making as many mistakes as was usual in the degenerate classicism of those times. The Byzantine school perverted Greek music and passed it along, as it had done with painting and architecture. The range and the chromatic graces of later Greek melody were deserted for a heavy march through one octave of one key. Furthermore, the scale was considered now as ascending, instead of descending. ¶St. Ambrose is traditionally credited with establishing four modes for church music. From these St. Gregory was believed to have derived four new modes. The original four are called *Authentic, i. e.,* "governing," or "chief." The latter four are called *Plagal, i. e.,* "oblique" or "inferior." To these were added other modes, some of them being denied a right to exist. As with all the old Greek modes, all the church modes are to be found on the white keys of the piano; no chromatic was allowed except, finally, b flat, which was admitted to avoid the forbidden tritone and the diminished fifth. A melody that did not stray out of its octave mode was called *perfect;* one that did not use all of its range was *imperfect;* one that overstepped its octave was *superfluous;* one that used up both a mode and its plagal was in a *mixed mode.* ¶Greek names were used for the church modes, but with many differences from the old nomenclature. ¶An authentic mode is based on its *Final* or lowest note; the next most important note, usually a fifth or a third above, is its *dominant.* A plagal mode is found a fourth below its authentic, and the *final* of the authentic serves also for the plagal. The dominant of a plagal is a third below that of its authentic (save where it falls on b, in which case c is used). ¶Curiously enough, the two modern keys which we think of as white keys, c major and a minor, were not added until the sixteenth century, and then as the Ionian and Æolian modes. ¶Besides many impressive hymns

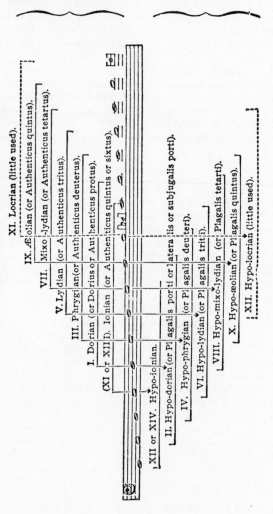

Chart of the Church Modes.

AUTHENTIC MODES,
OR
MODI AUTHENTICI.

Each authentic mode is connected with its plagal by a line through the keynote or finalis of both.

PLAGAL MODES,
OR
MODI PLAGALES.

XI. Locrian (little used).

IX. Æolian (or Authenticus quintus).

VII. Mixo-lydian (or Authenticus tetartus).

V. Lydian (or Authenticus tritus).

III. Phrygian (or Authenticus deuterus).

I. Dorian (or Dorius or Authenticus protus).

(XI or XII). Ionian (or Authenticus quintus or sixtus).

XII or XIV. Hypo-ionian.

II. Hypo-dorian (or Plagalis porti or lateralis or subjugalis porti).

IV. Hypo-phrygian (or Plagalis deuteri).

VI. Hypo-lydian (or Plagalis triti).

VIII. Hypo-mixo-lydian (or Plagalis tetarti).

X. Hypo-æolian (or Plagalis quintus).

XII. Hypo-locrian (little used).

the church modes have been unconsciously allowed to fit many popular modern tunes. It is not hard to test the mode-ship of any air. First, if necessary, bring the melody into a range requiring no key-signature. If it now contains any accidentals save b flat, it is not in any of the modes. Otherwise note the tone on which the air ends. This will be the *final* of its mode. If this is the lowest, or almost the lowest note used, and if the melody does not soar higher than an octave above it, the air is in an *authentic* mode. If the final is in approximately the centre of the melodic range, and if the range does not exceed the fifth above, or the fourth below, it is in a *plagal* mode, or it may be in a *mixed mode*. *The name of the final indicates the mode*. The airs "God save the King" (or "America") and the "Blue Bells of Scotland" are *authentic* melodies. The "Old 100th" and "Eileen Aroon" are *plagal*. "Jock o' Hazeldean" is in a *mixed mode*. ¶Much of the music in the old church modes is as shocking to the modern sense of tonality as our modern music would seem anarchistic to an old master. Superb treasures were given to immortality in those stiff and arbitrary forms. Yet, after all, the modes deserve their eternal obsoleteness. They were unsatisfactory and arbitrary in their own day. They are hopelessly inappropriate to the modern musical ideas and ideals. The majestic beauties of some of their results are but as the impressive fossils of earlier evolution. Their fate should warn us against stolid satisfaction with our own musical system.

NOTATION

By Rupert Hughes

The musical parallel of writing and printing as the means of expressing in universal and permanent symbols the ideas, emotions, and memories of the mind. ¶The Greeks, having only unharmonised melodies to record, made use of the letters of the alphabet in positions and combinations of a most complex yet definitive variety. These letters had reference to tetrachords and transpositions of the most subtle sort (see MODES). The business-like Romans swept away a mass of detail by giving each letter a definite position on the whole scale without reference to tetrachord relations. These letters were written on a straight line over the text to be sung. In the Eighth Century this *alphabetical notation* had given way before a system of symbols looking much like the hooks and curves of modern shorthand. These were called *neumæ* (q. v.) and were of numberless sorts and names. Thus a short single note was a *punctum;* two or three of these in a group were *bipunctum* or *tripunctum;* the standard long note was the *virga* which could be grouped as *bivirga* or *trivirga*. Other terms were *podatus* (a low note joined to a higher), and its reverse called *clivis, clinis,* or *flexa; the scandicus* (three ascending notes) and its reverse, *climacus; the quilisma* (a repeated note), the *gnomo, ancus, distropha* and many others. These neumæ were written over the text and were set higher or lower in a rough form of melodic contour. They were only an aid to the memory and frequently defy decipherment. In time, a few letters were added as abbreviations of speed or force. ¶But about the year 900 a genius (who in his way was almost as great as the inventor of the wheel) hit upon the inspiration of ruling above the text a thin red line and calling it "F." Every neuma on this line stood positively for the tone F, and those above or below the lines were of higher or lower pitch. The genius was soon followed by a man of talent who ruled a yellow line a little higher and called it "C." The ornamental letters set at the head of these lines soon took the forms known to-day as the *clefs*. Not long after, the monk Hucbald erected a series of lines and used the spaces between them to indicate definite pitches, writing at the beginning *T* for a whole step and *S* for a semitone. The hymn to be sung was written in these spaces, each syllable being placed on its proper space. (This gave the verse a stepladder effect resembling the refrains of certain modern humorous poems.) Spaces were added above or below as the melody needed them and each voice had its own set of shelves. ¶This awkward plan suggested the use of the lines instead of the spaces, for notes instead of syllables. Each line was given a definite pitch marked by a letter. ¶Recurrence was now made to the two-line system and somebody (Guido of Arezzo was usually credited with the scheme) added two black lines and made a 4-line staff in which both lines and spaces had fixed pitch values. It only needed the later addition of one more line to give the five-lined staff we still use to-day. ¶The neumæ gradually exchanged their scraggly outlines for the square black heads of the *choral note* (the *nota quadrata* or *quadriquarta*). ¶It now being possible to express the relative pitch of notes, an effort was made to express their relative duration, for the old Plain Song with its notes all of the same length could not satisfy many human musical needs. The modern division into measures of equal length by means of bars was a long time coming. There were two centuries of clumsy *mensurable* (*i. e.*, measurable) *music*. Notes to be sung to the same syllable were grouped together by *ligatures;* they were either set so close together as to touch, or were, if ascending, placed one above the other like a chord; if descending, they were merged in a thick black slanting line (*figura obliqua*). When white or open notes came into use the thick line became an open rectangle sloping in the desired direction. When the first note of the ligature was a breve, it was said to be "*cum proprietate*"; if the first note were a long, it was *sine proprietate;* if a semibreve, it was *cum opposita proprietate;* if the last note were a breve it was *imperfecta;* it was a *ligatura perfecta* when the last note was a long. ¶The method of expressing rhythm was, as said, very cumbersome. Rhythm was classified under three ratios: mode (*modus*), time-value (*tempus*), prolation. ¶The *Modus major* or "Great Mode" concerned the division of the large into longs, being *perfect*(*us*) if there were three longs to a large, and *imperfect*(*us*) if there were two. *Modus minor* or the "Lesser Mode" concerned the division of the long into breves, with the same classes *perfect* or *imperfect*. ¶The division of the breves into semibreves was the *tempus* and was similarly called *perfect*(*um*) or *imperfect*(*um*), a circle indicating perfect time and a semicircle, imperfect. ¶The relation of semibreve to minims was called *prolatio*(*n*), being major or minor (greater or lesser) prolation as the semibreve equalled 3 or 2 minims. The former was indicated by a dot in the time signature. ¶The *position* of the notes also indicated their proportion; a long or a breve followed by a note of its own value was *perfect by position;* a note accompanied by another of less value was imperfect. ¶*Colour* played a part; the red (*notula rubra*) or white (*alba*) or black (*nigra*) note among others of a different colour marked a change from perfection to imperfection. There was later the *proportio hemiol(i)a*, or 2 : 3, indicated by grouped black notes among white.   ¶Speed was open to slackening (*augmentatio*) or acceleration (*diminutio*), the latter being marked by a bar through the time-signature, or by the use of numerals or fractions, called signs of proportion, a term referring to the rhythm of simultaneous voices.   ¶The value of a note was open to *alteratio(n)* by position or by use of the *dot* (*punctum augmentationis, alterationis, (im)perfectionis* or *divisionis*).   ¶Expression marks appeared, along with many other symbols, in the Seventeenth Century; the bar was brought over from lute-tablature, and *mensurable music* disappeared before the convenient complexities of our own era.

THE OPERA

By Robert E. Brady

Opera as we know it to-day is an art form whose origins extend back only to the end of the sixteenth century.   It is true that music in some form played an important part in the representations of the dramas of the ancient Greek tragic poets.   There is evidence that the verses of Sophocles and Aeschylus were declaimed to the accompaniment of stringed and wind-instruments, and that the chorus sang or chanted its comment on the action and progress of the drama. Music was also employed in more or less dramatic fashion by the religious and secular composers of the thirteenth, fourteenth, and fifteenth centuries, by the trouvères in France, and by the players in the mystery and miracle plays which were common throughout Western Europe in the Middle Ages.   ¶But this music was of a type that gave little opportunity for the expression of strong emotion or for the delineation of character.   The need of a new form better suited to dramatic representations was felt by a group of Florentine scholars in the last decade of the sixteenth century.   Enthusiastic devotees of the Revival of Learning, they worshipped the art of ancient Greece with all the fervour characteristic of the period.   What finer contribution to the cause of music could be made, they asked, than to rediscover and recreate the ancient modes which had been of such service to the great tragic poets of the antique world?   ¶Such a task was, of course, impossible of achievement, since little was known of the music of two thousand years ago.   But, undisturbed by the difficulties which were in their way, the little band of scholars set to work to evolve some new system which they believed might at least approximate that employed by the Greek dramatists.   The result of their labours was a revolution in musical theories which contained the germs of modern music drama. ¶Three members of this coterie which habitually met at the palace of one Giovanni Bardi, Conte di Vernio, a patron of the arts, were Jacopo Peri, Vincenzo Galilei (father of the famous astronomer), and Giulio Caccini.   The year 1597 saw the first fruits of their efforts.   "*Dafne*," a dramatic work by Peri in the new style of accompanied recitative, was received with enthusiasm at a private performance in the palace of a Florentine nobleman.   ¶So successful was this first experiment that it was followed, in 1600, by another work by the same composer, "*Euridice*," which was performed at the wedding festivities of King Henry IV of France and Maria de' Medici.   Acclaimed with the same enthusiasm that had greeted its predecessor, it became the model for a series of dramatic pieces on classical subjects by other composers. Opera thus became recognised as a legitimate art form, at first patronised exclusively by the nobility, but destined soon to achieve a place in the lives of the people. ¶Monteverdi's famous opera *"Orfeo"* (1607) marked a further advance in the development of the new genre. Unlike Peri and Caccini, Monteverdi was a musician of distinguished attainments in other forms of composition, especially the madrigal; and he brought to opera all the technical resources of a skilled craftsman. He had already composed an opera *"Arianna,"* which had made a deep impression; but *"Orfeo,"* in the richness of its instrumental accompaniment—more than thirty instruments were employed—and by virtue of its emotional quality, far surpassed previous works of its kind. ¶So widespread was the interest aroused in the new type of entertainment that soon there was a demand for public performances. The first opera house was opened in Venice in 1637. Numerous composers, including Monteverdi, wrote a long list of works which firmly established the vogue of opera in the North. Between 1637 and 1699 eleven theatres were built in Venice, which became the leading city of opera in all Italy. But soon lyric theatres sprang up in all the principal towns. During this period opera itself was undergoing certain changes. The austere classicism of the founders gave way to a freer use of melody and rhythm. The beginnings of the aria were already discernible. Despite opposition of the conservatives, who held to the original pseudo-Greek ideal, opera was taking on the characteristic patterns which foreshadowed the modern Italian school ¶Alessandro Scarlatti did more than any other composer to further this development. A past master in the art of composition, he boldly swept aside the rigid rules which to a great extent had stemmed the tide of creative impulse, and introduced many innovations which added immeasurably to effectiveness of opera both from the musical and dramatic standpoint. Chief among these departures were a more eloquent type of recitative and a richer instrumentation, together with an elaboration of the prelude. Gifted disciples of Scarlatti turned out scores of pieces every year, until opera became the most popular entertainment of the day. This democratisation, indeed, began to sow the seeds of decay. The public was already becoming more interested in lavish spectacle, huge choruses, and favourite singers than in musical worth. But in dignity, passionate sincerity, and technical virtuosity Scarlatti set an example that inspired the best of his successors for more than a century. ¶Meanwhile there were arising in France and Germany, more or less independently, types of lyrical drama that were essentially national in spirit. The roots of French opera are found in the music of the thirteenth-century trouvères, as in Adam de la Halle's *"Le jeu de Robin et de Marion,"* which has come down to us intact. It was the ballet, however, dating from the latter half of the sixteenth century, which was the immediate forebear of seventeenth-century opera in France. ¶Jean Baptiste Lully (1639–1687) was the most famous composer for French ballet in its later development. A talented and resourceful musician, he brought it to a state of perfection that soon won it the favour of the populace as well as the nobility. It thus passed from the court to the theatre. Lully is regarded as the first composer of true French opera. His *"Les Fêtes de l'Amour et de Bacchus,"* produced in 1672, was the forerunner of a long series of similar pieces, both grave and gay. Lully's most distinguished successor was Rameau

(1683-1764), a musician in many respects of greater originality than Lully, but who never attained the latter's popularity. This was partly due to the inferior quality of his libretti. But his music has a freshness, charm, and variety not to be found in the work of his many contemporaries. ¶The rise of opera in England is associated with the name of Henry Purcell (c.1658-1695) His "*Dido and Aeneas*," composed between the years 1688 and 1690, was a work of astonishing originality and beauty. Purcell was to some extent influenced by French and Italian masters, but his art is strongly national. The origin of opera in England is commonly ascribed to the masque, and this is partly true. But another, and perhaps a more direct source of opera lies in the numerous plays for which popular composers of the day provided incidental music. Purcell had been active in this field. He left no successor, the only purely English development which followed being the Ballad Opera, of which John Gay's "*Beggar's Opera*" is the most famous example. But this form eventually disappeared with the introduction of the French and Italian schools. Balfe's "*Bohemian Girl*" and Wallace's "*Maritana*," to be sure, may be regarded as nineteenth-century survivals. The fact that "*Dido and Aeneas*" is Purcell's sole contribution to the operatic literature of his time in England may be explained by the circumstances of its production. It was performed by "young gentlewomen" at the private school of a Mr. Josias Priest at Chelsea. The composer was thus relieved of the necessity of catering to the fashionable public taste of the moment. ¶In Germany, as elsewhere, secular and religious plays of the Middle Ages prepared the soil for the development of opera. But the introduction of Italian works marked the real beginning of German operatic history. Vienna, Munich, and many provincial cities saw productions of the favourite Italian composers. But it was in the North, especially at Hamburg, that German national opera had its inception. ¶The first German opera house was opened in Hamburg in 1678, for the purpose of giving works in the vernacular. Here was produced the first truly German opera, Johann Theile's "*Adam und Eva*." It seems to have been a pretentious, pietistic, and generally dull piece, as were many of its successors, both religious and secular. But with the coming of Reinhardt Keiser in 1694 there was a distinct advance. During the first half of the eighteenth century he composed numerous works, thoroughly German, melodious, and well designed for character delineation. Though they have not survived they exerted an enormous influence in Germany and abroad. ¶One of Keiser's associates in Hamburg was the youthful George Frederic Handel (1685-1759). This man who was to become the greatest composer of his day wrote four operas on classic subjects during his Hamburg days. They showed the talent of the composer but were overshadowed by the brilliant operas with which he dazzled London audiences some years later. ¶"*Rinaldo*," an opera fashioned after the Italian models, was produced in lavish style in London in 1711. It created a sensation, the beauty of its arias winning instant response from a charmed and delighted public. From this time up to 1737 Handel produced a long series of operas along the same lines. The influence of various Italian masters, notably Scarlatti, appears in the suavity and grace of the vocal writing. Indeed, it was as a vocal and choral composer that Handel from the first excelled. ¶Handel's contemporaries included Johann Hasse, of Dresden, born in 1699, who left more than one hundred operas. They were second-rate, however, and depended for their success largely on the extraordinary singing of his wife, Faustina Bordoni. Hasse himself was a singer of the Italian school, and he was one of the first of those opera composers in Germany who worshipped vocalism for its own sake, and played into the hands of favoured singers. Domenico Scarlatti and Buononcini were other leading contemporaries of Hasse. ¶The rise of opera buffa in Italy was an important development during the middle of the eighteenth century. This genre, which had its prototype in France and Germany, was an outgrowth of the comic interludes and intermezzi which were interpolated between the acts of serious works. The opera buffa introduced some innovations that influenced serious opera—a more naturalistic style and greater freedom from convention. The earliest example of this form which has survived is Pergolesi's *"La Serva Padrona"* (1733). Other later examples are Paisiello's *"Barbiere,"* Cimarosa's *"Il matrimonio segreto,"* Mozart's *"Cosi fan tutte,"* Rossini's *"Barber of Seville,"* and Donizetti's *"Don Pasquale."* ¶The first French piece modelled on Italian opera buffa was Jean Jacques Rousseau's *"Le Devin du Village"* (1752), which was inspired by *"La Serva Padrona."* ¶Despite the trend toward naturalism in opera buffa, the serious forms were slow in shaking off classic conventions. Arias were formal, and must follow a definite pattern. A certain number of arias must be allotted to each singer. There must be no trios or quartets. Naturally, all this was fatal to a free development of the drama. Librettists and composers alike were handicapped. Moreover, the voice parts, instead of reflecting the thoughts and feelings of the character, were often mere show-pieces. Great composers like Handel could in a measure surmount such difficulties, but the rank and file were content to abide by the rules and let all truth and dramatic verity go by the boards. ¶Such was the state of opera when Christoph Wilibald Gluck began to compose. His first attempts proved to his satisfaction that he could not succeed by following the antiquated formulas. For years he pondered over new methods whereby he could make music serve the cause of drama as it was originally intended to do. The fruit of his speculations was *"Orfeo"* (1762), a masterpiece that brought about a revolution in opera that was comparable to the political and social upheaval that was to come some years later. ¶In *"Orfeo,"* Gluck swept aside all the fustian of the old forms. Elaborate but meaningless arias overburdened with ornamentation gave place to broad, majestic melodies of profound emotional significance. The opera met with the qualified approval of a public which was not altogether ready to transfer its allegiance from Hasse and his school. Five years later Gluck produced *"Alceste."* In a preface to the published work he outlined his artistic credo. It was his purpose, he wrote, to strip the aria of outworn conventions; to provide an orchestral prelude which should apprise the spectator of the action to be represented, to reduce the disparity between recitative and the aria; and finally to achieve "a grand simplicity." ¶Gluck decided to go to France, since he was dissatisfied with the reception of these two works in Vienna. In Paris, under the patronage of his former pupil, Marie Antoinette, he brought out his *"Iphigénie en Aulide,"* in French, in 1774. Its success was immediate, though there was a powerful faction of reactionaries who championed the Italian school represented by Piccinni. But with his next opera, *"Iphigénie en Tauride,"* Gluck's triumph was complete. A new era in French opera had dawned, which was to have a lasting influence. Gluck to-day is recognised as the first great exponent of modern music drama. ¶But Gluck's reforms, far-reaching as they were, did not divorce opera from an artificial world wholly removed from reality. His was essentially an aristocratic art, in the narrowest sense, which was concerned with the thoughts and feelings of characters having little in common with life and actuality. With the spread of the humanistic cult of naturalism the time was ripe for a composer to interpret the new and restless spirit of the day. ¶One of the great musical geniuses of all time was destined to accomplish this mission: Wolfgang Amadeus Mozart. Only in his first opera, *"Idomeneo"* did Mozart pay homage to Gluck. With *"Die Entfuehring aus dem Serail"* he forsook the Never-never land of pseudoclassical antiquity for a world peopled by human personalities. In *"The Marriage of Figaro"* and *"Don Giovanni"* he portrays human aspirations, follies, and sorrows with masterly insight, by means of music of incomparable beauty. Like Gluck he avoids extravagant vocal ornamentation except in arias like that of the Queen in *"The Magic Flute,"* where it is used for definite dramatic effect. Though Italian influences are apparent in his work, Mozart is essentially a German. To be sure, he used Italian in three of his operas as a language better suited to his purpose. ¶With the spread of the Romantic Movement at the turn of the nineteenth century there came a body of work which marked the transition between eighteenth-century classicism and the new romanticism. The most celebrated opera of this period was Beethoven's *"Fidelio,"* which combines the old classic forms with the new revolutionary spirit. Beethoven had no special urge toward the stage, but after he accepted a commission from the Vienna Theater-an-der-Wien to write an opera he undertook the task with ardour. He chose for his libretto a story of wifely devotion which had already been utilised by Ferdinando Paer, and by Pierre Gaveaux. *"Fidelio"* is an example of the Singspiel in that spoken dialogue alternates with arias, duets, and concerted numbers. Beethoven made many revisions of his original score—he wrote four overtures—and several versions of the work were presented after its initial performance in Vienna in 1805. ¶*"Fidelio,"* despite certain faults, remains the finest example of German opera between Mozart and Wagner; a work of intense dramatic power and musical beauty. Other composers of this transitional period include Cherubini, whose work was greatly admired by Beethoven, and Spontini, whose *"La Vestale"* was revived at the Metropolitan Opera House in 1925. ¶The Romantic Movement was in full flower when Weber's *"Der Freischuetz"* was produced in Dresden in 1822. National feeling in Germany was running high. The public had tired of the tragic and heroic subjects favoured by the Franco-Italian Spontini, and the time was propitious for a work deriving from German folklore. *"Der Freischuetz"* fulfilled in brilliant fashion this desire. It was acclaimed with the wildest enthusiasm, and its author, a picturesque, Byronic figure, became the hero of the day. His great gift for popular melody, his skill in choral writing, and the imaginative treatment of the supernatural made *"Der Freischuetz"* the most beloved opera ever written in Germany. Its extraordinary popularity soon spread to other countries, as witness the story of the choleric English gentleman who advertised for a valet who couldn't whistle a tune from *"Freischuetz."* Unfortunately Weber's later operas were less successful. The best known are *"Euryanthe"* and *"Oberon."* ¶Meanwhile Rossini was infusing new life into Italian opera which, at the beginning of the nineteenth century, had fallen on evil days. He was not a reformer like Gluck, but he determined to substitute for the old clichés of his immediate predecessors a new spirit, at the same time conforming to the prevailing taste of the day. This he accomplished by virtue of his amazing facility, his sparkling brilliancy, and his robust comic gifts. These qualities made him for years the most popular composer in Europe. His serious works are dramatically ineffective, though they contain a wealth of ingratiating melody. "*The Barber of Seville*" (1816) is perhaps the greatest opera buffa ever written. Rossini's style was florid, and he loved vocal display. The same may be said of his chief contemporaries, Bellini and Donizetti. While not of a particularly high order their music is uniformly tuneful and appealing. ¶The popularity of Rossini was partially eclipsed for a time by the advent of Meyerbeer, a German whose career was largely confined to Paris. His grandiose operas created a sensation. "*Robert le Diable*," "*Les Huguenots*," "*L'Africaine*," and "*Le Prophète*" are said to have made the fortune of the Paris Opera. Wagner's caustic indictment of Meyerbeer as a "miserable music maker" is hardly deserved. He possessed undeniable gifts, which would have carried him to greater heights had he not chosen to seek the applause of a fashionable, uncritical Parisian audience. Meyerbeer left no disciples, though his chief contemporary was Halévy, whose "*La Juive*" retains its popularity to-day ¶Giuseppe Verdi (1813–1901) was in many respects the greatest Italian composer of the nineteenth century. His early works reveal no radical departures from accepted conventions, though he introduced a dramatic and virile spirit not to be found in the sweet and graceful operas of Bellini and Donizetti. The works of his middle period like "*Il Trovatore*," "*La Traviata*," "*The Masked Ball*," and "*Rigoletto*" are perhaps his most characteristic and popular operas though by no means the best. In the operas of his third period, "*Aïda*," for example, the set aria is already disappearing and the orchestra plays a more prominent part. In his old age Verdi produced two masterpieces, "*Otello*" (1887) and "*Falstaff*" (1893), which exhibit to an astonishing degree a new spirit and a new technique in Italian opera. Set arias are few, and the orchestra is infinitely more complex than in his earlier works. The characters of Iago and Falstaff are portrayed with a penetrating insight almost Shakespearian. Verdi was fortunate in having the distinguished singing actor, Victor Maurel, as the interpreter of these rôles. ¶The operatic Titan of this same period in Germany was, of course, Richard Wagner whose stupendous genius produced works of such revolutionary character and sustained grandeur as have never been remotely approached by any of his successors. The four operas of the "*Ring*"; "*Tristan and Isolde*," perhaps the greatest love tragedy of all time; "*Die Meistersinger*," a comic opera of epic proportions; and "*Parsifal*," the great religious festival drama—these monuments of a unique genius tower above all the other musical works of the nineteenth century. In these masterpieces of his maturity Wagner developed the leitmotif system to a state of perfection never equalled. ¶Among the composers of the latter half of the century whose work was significant were Arrigo Boito, whose "*Mefistofele*" may have influenced Verdi; Gounod, whose "*Faust*" is perhaps the most popular opera ever written; Bizet, whose "*Carmen*" ranks as the outstanding French opera of the period; Ponchielli and his successor Puccini, whose "*Tosca*," "*La Bohème*," and "*Butterfly*" are in the repertory of opera companies the world over. In the last decade of the century Mascagni, with "*Cavalleria Rusticana*" and Leoncavallo, with "*Pagliacci*" achieved an enormous popularity which has continued ever since. Giordano, Wolf-Ferrari, and Charpentier are among the host of popular composers of a somewhat later date. ¶The name of Puccini stands out as that of the most popular Italian composer of his day. His first work, "*Le Villi*" (1884), was successful. "*Manon Lescaut*" (1893) made up in part for an earlier failure "*Edgar*" (1889); but it was "*Bohème*" (1896) that firmly established Puccini's fame. This was enhanced with "*Tosca*" (1900) and "*Madame Butterfly*" (1904). Of his later works, in which he attempts a more modern idiom with qualified success, "*La Fanciulla del West*" ("*Girl of the Golden West,*") which had its world première at the Metropolitan in 1910, and "*Turandot*," produced in 1924 after the composer's death, are best known. Puccini had a flair for the theatre unequalled by any of his contemporaries, and his music has a lyrical intensity admirably suited to dramatic expression. ¶Not long after Germany threw off the shackles of foreign domination with "*Der Freischuetz*" a national opera also began to emerge in Russia. Glinka was the creator of a new school with his "*Life for the Tsar*." The music is native in origin, fashioned and adapted in a manner to make it acceptable to Western ears. Suggestions of the Orient provide piquant contrasts to the Russian themes. The same holds true with Borodin's "*Prince Igor*," set to an epic poem comparable to the Arthurian romances. Borodin's music abounds in melody, impassioned and richly coloured. Moussorgsky was preëminently realistic in his treatment of the national material he employs. His writing for voice and chorus is superior to his orchestration, which is often stark and bare. His masterpiece, "*Boris Godounoff*," contains superb choral passages and a profoundly tragic and realistic death scene reminiscent of *Macbeth*. Rimsky-Korsakov excelled his predecessors in technical skill. All his works, with one exception, are based on national themes. The most popular of his operas are "*The Snow Maiden*," "*Sadko*," and "*Le Coq d'Or*." ¶The Czech composer Smetana was also the creator of a national opera. His works for the most part are little known outside Central Europe, with the exception of "*The Bartered Bride*," one of the loveliest of modern comic operas. ¶The present century has seen the production of scores of new works by composers of varying importance; but whatever the verdict of posterity may be concerning their merit the fact remains that few of them have achieved a permanent place in the standard repertory. Only a scant half dozen have won sufficient favour to justify frequent performance. ¶The first of these was Debussy's lyrical drama "*Pelléas et Mélisande*," written to a poetic play by Maeterlinck. This unique work, first performed at the Opéra Comique in Paris in 1902, is a landmark in the history of opera. It founded no school, and by reason of the special nature of its book and music it is unlikely to become universally popular. But it remains the finest example of impressionism in modern operatic music; elusive, delicately atmospheric, filled with a wan and wistful beauty wholly indescribable. ¶An opera not unlike "*Pelléas*" in subject matter, but wholly unlike it in other respects, is Italo Montemezzi's "*Love of Three Kings*." It was first produced in Milan in 1913 and one year later, under Toscanini's direction, at the Metropolitan Opera House. Though the composer was virtually unknown and the opera unheralded, it achieved an instantaneous success. The libretto was the work of Sem Benelli, the Italian poet and playwright. The excellence of the book no doubt contributed to the success of the opera; but Montemezzi's music received the highest praise from press and public. It is truly original, owing nothing to Puccini and very little to Verdi or Wagner. The vocal line is graceful and finely melodic. The music is continuous and free, with few recurrent themes. Of external realism there are only some fugitive touches. ¶The third operatic work by a living composer which belongs to the present century is *"Der Rosenkavalier"* by Richard Strauss. It marks a complete change of style from the turgid, neurotic, and melodramatic *"Salomé"* and *"Elektra."* The opera is a *tour de force* of brilliant orchestration which weaves a glittering web of tone fashioned out of Viennese waltz tunes and Mozartean melody. The full modern orchestra is employed with masterly skill to invest these naïve and fragmentary themes with a sophisticated and pungent quality wholly captivating. The trio of women's voices is a reminder of the *"Meistersinger"* quintet, and the monologue of the Marschallin is another high spot in a score that is matched perhaps only by Wagner's comic masterpiece. ¶*"Salomé"* and *"Elektra"* were performed in the United States not long after their European premières. But despite the notable impersonations of such artists as Fremstad, Mazarin, and Mary Garden the public did not take kindly to the hectic and cacophonous music and the lurid books. In recent years, notably in the season of 1937–1938, they were revived at the Metropolitan with conspicuous success. ¶Post-war composers whose contributions to opera have attracted favourable notice from the more critical and, in some cases, substantial support from the general public include Francesco Malipiero (*"Pantea," "Sette Canzoni," "Le Baruffe Chiozzotte," "Orfeo"*); Louis Gruenberg (*"Emperor Jones"*); Deems Taylor (*"The King's Henchman," "Peter Ibbetson"*); Alban Berg (*"Wozzeck," "Lulu"*); Darius Milhaud (*"Christophe Colombe," "Le Pauvre Matelot," "Minute-Operas," "Juarez et Maximilien"*); Paul Hindemith (three one-act operas, *"Cardillac," "Neues vom Tage," "Mathis der Maler"*); Mario Castelnuovo-Tedesco (*"Mandragola"*); Jaromir Weinberger (*"Schwanda"*); Ernst Krenek (*"Die Zwingburg," "Der Sprung ueber den Schatten," "Orpheus," "Jonny Spielt Auf,"* two one-act operas, *"Orest," "Das Leben Karls V"*); Kurt Weill (*"Mahoganny," "Dreigroschenoper," "Der Jasager," "Die Burgschaft," "Der Silbersee"*); Dmitri Shostakovitch (*"Lady Macbeth of Mzensk"*). (*For synopses of many of the operas mentioned see the Opera section, page 819*).

THE ORATORIO

By H. E. KREHBIEL

AN ORATORIO is a musical composition for chorus and solo voices, with orchestral accompaniment, to a poem on a religious or sacred subject, generally in narrative form, though often with dramatic episodes, but without scenery, action, or costume. The origin of the oratorio is to be found in the so-called mysteries and miracle-plays of the thirteenth and fourteenth centuries, which enacted an important part in the life of the common people. These were sung and acted, and though, on account of abuses that crept into them they were frowned upon by the Church, their popularity was never destroyed. The oratorio was brought into existence upon the model of these religious plays by St. Philip of Neri (1515–95), who recognised in them a means of opposing the influence of the Reformation upon the common people. In his chapel or oratory (whence the name oratorio) in Rome he had spiritual songs sung after sermons and other devotions, to "allure young people to pious offices." St. Philip induced capable Italian poets to write the words, and the best composers to furnish the music. By degrees the spiritual songs gave place to musical settings of sacred stories sometimes in dialogue form. The invention of dramatic recitative at the end of the sixteenth century had a marked influence on oratorio. The first to use it was Emilio Cavaliere, whose allegory, "The Soul and the Body," performed in a Roman Church, was the first oratorio corresponding to the modern form. It was, however, intended to be acted in costume, and only gradually did this feature fall into disuse. The later Italian composers, Carissimi, Stradella, Cesti and Alessandro Scarlatti, first developed the new form on the lines in which it has come down to us. Carissimi greatly improved the recitative, giving it more character and musical expressiveness than his predecessors had done, and ventured more boldly into the field of broad choral writing. Cesti and Stradella cultivated still further the natural resources of the chorus at a time when the general tendency in Italy was toward the more obvious and pleasing forms of solo song. Alessandro Scarlatti, who was one of the chief forces in this direction, also contributed to the development of the oratorio by the increased stress he put upon the solo arias in it. But on the whole, as Dr. Parry has remarked, the oratorio had to wait for representatives of more strenuous nations for its ultimate development. ¶That development was destined to come in Germany. While oratorio had thus been taking shape in Italy, there was an important movement going on in Germany by which the Passion was brought into existence. This came about, after a long line of tentative and experimental efforts, through the works of Heinrich Schütz, who had received his training in Italy and carried thence to his native land some of the new ideals of music. His first Passion was produced in 1645. The various attempts that followed this culminated in the settings by J. S. Bach. These works were intended for performance in church in Passion Week, as a religious service partly narrative, partly dramatic and partly reflective in character. The narrative was put into the mouth of the Evangelist, usually the principal tenor, who related the Passion of Christ; the personages in the story spoke for themselves. The chorus was often treated dramatically, representing the emotions of the onlookers, while the solo airs were of a piously reflective character. There was a plentiful interspersion of chorales in which the congregation joined. In the middle there was an intermission for the sermon. The Passion music was also an outgrowth of the mediæval miracle-plays, but it soon fell into disuse and displayed no vitality after the great creations of Bach, the "Passions according to St. Matthew" and "St. John," respectively, composed in the first quarter of the eighteenth century. German art was thenceforward turned into the channels of the oratorio as it was developed in Italy; and the form was brought to its highest perfection by George Frederick Handel. As thus perfected it was not, like the Passions, a part of religious exercises, nor a direct expression of devotional feeling, but epic or narrative, with certain quasi-dramatic traits and sometimes with the use of vivid local colour; but always with the most impressive use of the chorus as the most important medium of expression. Handel's first oratorio "Esther" was written in 1720 and performed first in England in 1732, oratorio being then quite unknown in that country. The long line of masterpieces he produced thereafter gave the final and definite character to the oratorio form which has remained to this day. The greatest of them are "The Messiah," "Judas Maccabæus," "Israel in Egypt," and "Samson." Handel's strength lay chiefly in broad choral writing, and it was natural that the oratorio should develop mainly on this line, as affording a vehicle for more descriptive and characteristic music, thus making up for a lack of pantomime, costume, and scenery. ¶For a considerable period after Handel's death, little of importance in the field of oratorio was produced. Haydn's "Creation" and "The Seasons," written in 1795 and 1801 respectively, still retain some of their vitality and freshness. Beethoven's "Mount of Olives" does not. Oratorios by Spohr and Schneider attained a great but transient popularity, but the next really important works in this form were Mendelssohn's "St. Paul," performed first in 1836, and "Elijah," in 1846. In both of these the dramatic element is foremost, and the musical characterisation of the various persons presented is perhaps more vivid than any previous attempts in this line. Works like Liszt's "St. Elizabeth" and Rubinstein's "Moses" are conceived as operas in which descriptive directions take the place of scenery, costume, and incident. (*See Dictionary of Terms entry, page 648.*)

THE ORCHESTRA AND ORCHESTRATION

BY W. J. HENDERSON

THE MODERN ORCHESTRA dates from the early part of the seventeenth century. Previous to that no attempts at a systematic combination of instruments can be found. The original use of the orchestra was in the accompaniments of operas, and even here the earliest combinations were fortuitous and without special purpose. The earliest writer who seemed to have distinct ideas as to instrumental effects was Claudio Monteverde (1568–1643). His orchestra was the first in which a considerable body of strings, including two violins, figured. He invented some special instrumental effects, and led the way toward the establishment of the string quartet as the foundation of the orchestra. Alessandro Scarlatti (born 1659) wrote for a string quartet similar to that employed in the present orchestra, and used oboes and flutes as his principal wind-instruments. ¶Handel (1658–1759) used all the ordinary instruments of the present orchestra except the clarinet, but not in the same combinations as those of to-day. The orchestra of his time contained a much larger number of oboes and bassoons than ours, because these instruments then were much less powerful. In the early part of the eighteenth century, when the seeds of symphonic music were just beginning to sprout, the orchestra consisted of the same body of strings as now used, but the violoncello was not yet appreciated at its true value, trumpets and tympani being added when brilliancy was needed. Clarinets had not entered the orchestra, but flutes were common. The trombone was employed only in the opera, where alone also the harp was heard. ¶Joseph Haydn (1732–1809) wrote his first symphony in 1759 for first and second violins, violas and basses. two oboes and two horns. Mozart (1756–

ⲟⲅ) introduced clarinets and Haydn learned their use from him, so that his D major symphony, written in 1795, is scored for 2 flutes, 2 oboes, 2 clarinets, 2 horns, 2 kettle-drums, violins, violas, 'cellos and basses, adding in the first movement 2 bassoons and 2 trumpets. In the "Eroica" Beethoven introduced a third horn, and in the fifth symphony a piccolo, a contra-bassoon and three trombones. Four horns were used in the Ninth symphony, and this work contains the entire modern orchestra, except such instruments as have since been introduced for special effects. The operatic writers in their search after dramatic colouring led the way in such introductions, and the romantic composers of symphonic music, building up their great colour schemes, were not slow to accept every suggestion. ¶Nevertheless the orchestra as now constituted is practically that of Beethoven. As ordinarily distributed it is composed of a piccolo, 2 flutes, 2 oboes, 2 clarinets, 2 bassoons, 4 horns, 2 trumpets, 3 trombones, 2 kettle-drums, first and second violins, violas, 'cellos, and basses. The wood-wind instruments are now frequently used in triplets instead of pairs, and the whole wind choir is extended at will by the use of the English horn, the bass clarinet, the tuba, the saxophone or other less common instruments. The harp is also employed at times. ¶ORCHESTRATION, the art of writing for orchestra, has developed rapidly in recent years, yet the fundamental principles are those which guided Mozart and Beethoven. The modern efforts have been in the direction of increased sonority and richness of colour. These ends are obtained by writing for a larger number of instruments and by dividing the old ones into a greater number of parts. The orchestra naturally separates itself into three groups of melodic instruments and one of merely rhythmic ones. The first three groups are the wood-wind, the brass, and the strings, and the other is the "battery," as the group of percussive instruments is called. In this last group only the kettle-drums have musical pitch, except when bells are employed. ¶The wood-wind is divided into flutes, which have no reed mouthpieces; oboes and bassoons, which have mouthpieces with two vibrating reeds; and clarinets, which have mouthpieces with one reed. Flutes used in triplets are capable of independent harmony, but all of a high pitch. Bassoons are the basses of the oboe family, and hence with two oboes and two bassoons, composers can write in full four-part harmony for this class of reed instruments, and let them play by themselves when their peculiar thin, reedy quality is desired. The English horn, the alto of the oboe, can be used as another part. Clarinets have a compass extending through the alto and soprano ranges of the human voice, while the bass clarinet covers the tenor and the bass. Here again the composer can get a full harmony in one family of wood. Thus the wood alone offers three distinct orchestral tints. But the instruments of the different families combine to make new tints. Flutes go well with clarinets or oboes, and clarinets combine admirably with bassoons. Furthermore, the whole wood-band can be used at once with fine effect. The older composers had conventional methods of writing for these instruments, almost always allotting the same parts of the harmony to the same instruments. The moderns have learned to vary this practice with excellent results. All the wood-wind instruments can be used profitably as solo voices. ¶The brass offers three groups, horns, trumpets and trombones, each of which is capable of independent harmony, while each may be combined with the other, or with any part of another to make variety of effects. All are useful for solo effects, the horn being especially good for this purpose. The brass can also be used in many combinations with the wood-wind. Horns, clarinets, and bassoons, for example, are frequently combined. The foundation of the orchestra, however, is the string quartet, as it is called, though it is really a quintet. Violins supply the soprano and alto parts of the harmony, violas part of the alto and all of the tenor; 'cellos run from bass up to low soprano, and basses give the deepest notes. The older composers made but poor use of the viola and the 'cello, but the moderns take every advantage of their compass and their individuality of timbre. Furthermore, the moderns subdivide the strings very often, writing at times for first and second violins in as many as six parts, for violas in two parts, and 'cellos in the same way. In this way the harmony becomes many-voiced and extremely rich. ¶The essential requirements of good orchestration are solidity, balance of tone, contrast and variety. Solidity is obtained by a proper distribution, among the instruments, of the notes of each chord, so that the proper sounds are made the more prominent. The foundation of solidity is good writing for the strings, the mainstay of the orchestra. Balance of tone also depends on a proper dispersal of the harmony, so that the instruments which are providing the harmonic support will not drown out the voices of those which are singing the melody. A perfect understanding of the relative powers of the various instruments is necessary to success in these two matters. Especially must the middle voices be skilfully treated to obtain solidity. If they are too loud, the effect is "muddy"; if they are too weak, the orchestra is "all top and bottom," as the musicians say. ¶Contrast is obtained by transferring the melodic ideas frequently from one of the three divisions of the orchestra to another, while variety is the result of mixing the tints. A theme is never confined to the strings, but is often handed over to the brass, or the wood-wind. But even this would not be sufficient. Consequently the various effects of mingling the voices of the different instruments, flutes and horns, or clarinets and 'cellos, or oboes and violas, are employed. The composer must, of course, know his orchestral colours thoroughly before endeavouring to mix them. Students of orchestral music will find the simplest and most solid colour schemes in the scores of the classic symphonists, while in the modern operas and symphonic works he will hear all the results of the most complex treatment of orchestral tinting. (*See also "Orchestration of Theatre and Dance Music" below; "Orchestra and Band Instruments," page 811; "Orchestras In America," page 787; and Dictionary of Terms entry, page 648*).

ORCHESTRATION OF THEATRE AND DANCE MUSIC

By Robert Russell Bennett

MORE PROGRESS is seen in the orchestral treatment of light music than in any other feature of this type of entertainment, not excluding the melodic and harmonic substance of the pieces themselves. Music designed for immediate popular approval must, of course, work in the direction of the obvious, therefore it can add not more than one experimental feature to what is already well planted in the public ear, and composers do best when they can avoid even that *one* and still be fresh and appealing. ¶Instrumentation is not so limited;

in fact great inventiveness is often shown. Its more imaginative flights are protected from popular failure by the success of the tune and the almost barbaric simplicity of the underlying rhythm, and the arranger finds himself free to borrow at will from all the striking orchestral effects of the masters with no necessity for the hearer to "analyse and understand" him. With the development of recorded music and broadcasting, orchestration assumes greater and greater importance. Robbed of one of its primary ingredients, namely the personal magnetism of the performers, music must look to so-called orchestral colour for a great portion of its individuality, if any is to be achieved. This point is hardly controversial, but if anyone questions it let him make a list of the human imperfections of playing freely pardoned and often enjoyed in the concert-hall, yet simply unpleasant when recorded or transmitted by mechanical instruments. ¶In other words, the spread of radio and phonograph over the world has tended largely to reduce ensemble playing to a chemical mixture whose component parts must be as pure as possible. (For the purposes of this article, the term *music* will refer to what is known as "popular," "light," "commercial," etc., and is not to be confused with the great art of music for musicians and cultured listeners, who might pardonably wonder why we spend time on the details of the scherzo—so to speak—without taking up the profounder movements of life's symphony.) ¶The vast majority of this music is first introduced in the form of songs. Every arrangement for orchestra of these songs falls into one or another formula, depending on the nature of performance intended. This formula changes and develops in each branch as new combinations are successfully tried, but there is never any very revolutionary novelty introduced with success—as a deep study of every new development will reveal. The introduction of greater or smaller combinations, the addition of unusual instruments, the sudden discovery of new playing tricks of instruments and groups of instruments already in use, and the use of the voice or voices with the orchestra to present the words of the song; all these "innovations" are made to cling desperately to the original tune or the semi-barbaric rhythms already mentioned, or both, and the result will not go down as revolutionary.

Theatre Orchestras

With no attempt to go deeply into its history one can say that theatre music has always been composed of songs, dances, and incidental music. For many, many years the formula for the orchestral score of a "number" for the theatre was something as follows: ¶In general, a transcription for orchestra of the piano copy as printed and sold. More specifically, an introduction, vamp, verse, and chorus. The chorus was marked to repeat, with certain instruments playing the second time only, and certain others playing an octave higher on the repeat. This repeat version served either for an accompaniment to the ensemble on the stage, singing *fortissimo*, or for dancing, either by the chorus or by the "principals" (actors or actresses who went into their dance after singing the song through). ¶This loud refrain, or chorus—both of which terms are avoided as confusing in the music of Jerome Kern, where the word "burthen" supplants them—merits a little deeper study, as it has long remained the basis of all arrangements for the purposes enumerated above. Examining briefly the instruments and their treatment, we find something like this:

¶*Flute* or *Flutes:* portions of the melody and little variations at frequent inter-vals, all placed an octave higher than the soprano voice would be on the melody. ¶*Oboe:* the melody, in the register of the soprano voice, with certain allowances for breathing. ¶*Clarinets* (2): the second and third voices of the flute part. ¶*Bassoon:* a mixture of 'cello and bass parts, with sometimes both bass notes and afterbeats. ¶*Horns* (2): mostly afterbeats with an occasional sustained note or a doubling of the counter-melody of the 'cello for a few measures. ¶*Trumpets* (2): the melody and an accompanying line in thirds, sixths, or other pleasant-sounding harmony notes for the second trumpet. These parts were marked "second time only." ¶*Trombone:* bass notes, occasionally the melody and occasionally the counter-melody of the 'cello, also marked "second time only." ¶*Drums:* "oom-pahs" in the loud version—that is—bass-drum and attached cymbal on the bass beats and snare-drum on the afterbeats. Some-times the strain was written out, with bells (glockenspiel) playing the first time through, principally on the melody, and drums for the repeat. ¶*First Violin* or *Violins:* the melody, marked "8 va 2nd time." ¶*Second Violin,* afterbeats, arranged so as to form a full chord with the viola, for the most part by means of double stops, the lower note of which was usually lower than the higher note of the: ¶*Viola,* which served as a "big second fiddle" and com-pleted the harmony of the afterbeats. ¶*'Cello:* a counter-melody, or low har-mony note under the melody of the first violin. This counter was preferably on the A string and was sustained in character especially if the tune of the composition was not. ¶*Bass:* the bass notes, *arco* or *pizzicato.* It is to be borne in mind that this whole strain served, played softly and as marked, for a vocal accompaniment to soli voices on the stage the first time through. All instruments marked "2nd time only" joined in during the "1st Ending" (or "First Time Bars," as they call it in England) and proceeded with the repeat version, *ff* as just described. This briefly detailed résumé is given, not to indicate that it was the first orchestral make-up of a popular refrain, nor that it continued in vogue for a longer period than some other way has or will in the future, but chiefly because it assumes importance as the starting point for all that has followed. ¶It is well to avoid individual names in a study of this kind, but two names, one well known and the other quite obscure, are in-dispensable. These names are Victor Herbert and Frank Saddler. The former influenced theatre orchestration tremendously by enriching the pattern described above in several details; the latter by the introduction of combina-tions of colours and flights of imagination that lead to practically all the sub-sequent styles employed by the countless band arrangers of our era. Victor Herbert was a great musician in every sense of the word—his knowledge of the classics was such that he conducted symphony orchestras for many seasons without reference to scores during rehearsal or concert, and his feeling for the structure of a sound orchestration was infallible. His only concern in the arrangement of his operettas was the simplest, most effective method of pre-senting his charming melodies, and his technical contributions to our formula were the result of no search for unusual sounds, but merely of his desire to make his music sound as beautiful as possible. Frank Saddler, however, was not at home with the broader beauties of a Victor Herbert style of arrangement. He was a champion of small orchestras, filling up his refrain with charming tricks of muted brass, unexpected bass progressions, *pizzicato* effects, duets for two violins against the melody in the lower instruments and many other devices. The main addition of Victor Herbert was the dividing of the violins into three or more expressive parts, the high vibrant 'cello just beneath the melody, and the dramatic, full-sounding brass choir at the climaxes. He detested the usual variations of the flutes and clarinets and kept them low, simple and sonorous. ¶Frank Saddler wrote no operettas of his own. He was an *orchestrator*, versatile and inventive, with a fine ear for every novel effect of the great writers of symphonic music and a genius for adapting their tricks to the current musical-comedy tunes. His arrangements fairly sparkled and a melody of no distinction whatsoever became alluring in his interpretation. No subsequent arranging has done more for the tunes themselves than Saddler's although much has been added to his technique. It is not too much to say that he established once and for all the position of the orchestrator as a personality quite apart from the composer of the songs. He is responsible for the fact that even composers who can make creditable arrangements for the orchestra decline to do so in view of the great advantage to their melodies of having new and equally inspired brains create the orchestrations. ¶Continuing a bit on the technical side, one feature that both of these men struggled for was not fully realised until after their death. Both had visions of emancipating the second violins and violas so that they might play *cantabile*—with the first violins and 'celli— instead of incessant short afterbeats. Saddler eliminated second violins or rather included them with the firsts, and left the rhythm to two or more divided violas. (See the opening bars of Mozart's *G Minor Symphony* for a perfect example of this distribution.) Herbert at times left the rhythm to the harp, often used in metropolitan theatres, whilst his second fiddles soared away with the firsts. After both of these gifted men had passed away a new style of guitar playing came into being and, with a piano or two and a very much refined and softened pulse of drums, solved the oom-pah problem completely and left all other instruments free to indulge in counterpoint or their particular rendition of the melody. Not all music will admit of such an accompaniment but the majority will and the seconds and violas have gone free! ¶Theatre orchestration was undoubtedly the main source of ideas for dance orchestras, at first in its effect on the printed arrangements from which all dance bands played and, later, as the bands elaborated on these printed arrangements, in its more imaginative combinations. However, the use of saxophones, which dates back much farther than one might think, added great possibilities to the dance combinations, and eventually the saxes, plus the rhythm combination of piano (or pianos) and guitar, invaded the theatre and coloured its music. Saxophones are of great value because they are easy to play and can almost be "sung" on without great concern over technical difficulties such as beset flutes, oboes, bassoons, and even clarinets. This does not mean that anyone with a good ear can play them, but a good clarinetist, for example, feels he is on a vacation when playing alto or tenor saxophone. ¶Naturally their development has taken a turn not purely technical. They have grown in warmth of tone and lip and tongue effects, and they are the last answer (up to this writing) to an arranger's prayer when he deals with small bands. They can play loud enough not to be drowned out by trumpets and trombones, and in the softer bits, their peculiar timbre seems to combine low strings, horn, bassoon, and human voice tone, so that (always remembering the simple chord structure of the type of music we are concerned with) the sensitive ear of the sincere musician must acknowledge the live, vibrant pulse they add to an orchestra with inadequate strings, horns and low winds. ¶This becomes even more important where rhythm is the prime factor, since it is almost axiomatic that the smaller the group the better and cleaner the rhythm. ¶In the theatre as one sits in the back rows of a crowded house with a "legitimate" (*i.e.*, saxless) orchestra, the impression is that there are two moods in the orchestration—with brass, and without brass. With saxophones added one is distinctly conscious of three colours: one with predominating brass, and one with wood-wind and saxes. This leaves the "without brass" mood still to be used for the tenderer, more delicate moments and we have actually gained one whole colour. This is of course speaking very broadly of the effect when seeing the show for the first time, and wasting no time listening consciously to the orchestra. ¶It would be silly to say that theatre music cannot do without saxophones. Many productions are so conceived that the tone would be entirely out of place—vulgar and blasphemous. Their great value to the majority of shows is nevertheless incontestable.

This is not meant to be a lesson in theatre arrangements for orchestrators, yet a few of the problems of this most limited of all orchestration jobs will be interesting to all music-lovers. ¶In the first place the general rule to observe is that we are not arranging for the concert stage but for the orchestra pit, and the broad brush of the opera composer is more our pattern than the more precious pastels of symphonists. Not at any time during the performance are we given the undivided attention of the audience. Even overtures, entr'actes and outmarches are accompaniments to a babble of the audience's own conversation and movement, and the orchestra must either be so garish as to stop momentarily the flow of talk or resign itself to the enhancing of a general mood of enjoyment while being practically ignored. The latter is by far the safer plan. ¶In accompanying singers of the musical-comedy stage, a great problem was presented when the popular fancy turned away from big voices to little, thin ones of personal appeal but no vocal power. This necessitated for years the presence of the melody strongly played in the orchestra, since the singer would leave some doubt as to just what the melody was if left to his or her own devices in the matter. Not until the use of microphones, which transform a "croon" into a full vocal tone, was it thought possible to make the orchestration into a pure accompaniment. Somehow a wave of such orchestration followed the radio and motion-picture boom. High sustained violins (divided), piano, guitars, and *pizzicato* bass for rhythm, low sustained wood-wind (maybe sax, *pianissimo*) or a harmless counter-melody in low unison clarinets, with trumpets and trombones chirping out the moment the voice pauses for breath—that became the accepted architecture of song orchestration when voices were "miked." ¶It is also used where no loud-speaker system is present. The reason is vague but somehow the hammering of the public ear by "miked" music has caused voices to grow fuller and more penetrating when left unaided. ¶When the full chorus comes on and the dance begins the orchestra comes nearer to being the feature than at any other time in the show. As suggested above, before the use of saxophones the full brass was indispensable throughout the whole dance except on rare occasions when a delicate four-measure phrase came as a surprise (and "got by" the producer of the show). After the development of the sax it was possible to carry a few measures on the winds for variety, giving the brass a short rest for higher and louder doings later. ¶If we take up the cinema as a part of theatre orchestration we are concerned not so much with music as with sound. In recording, a solo muted violin can be made to drown out a full orchestra playing *fff* by means of a small dial. This may bring up many different possibilities in the facile mind, but the final condition is something like this: The limit of effect is merely the limit of the orchestrator's imagination. There is practically nothing ineffective, there are no boundaries of safe combination of instruments, there is no art in doubling or reinforcing in different sections of the orchestra. All this is theoretically true because of the curious feature known as sound-mixing. However, a sound, well-balanced orchestration renders the task of recording, both by the conductor of the orchestra and by the sound-mixer, very much easier. Although it harnesses the mind of the orchestrator very much as the original art of theatre orchestration has, it makes possible a much simpler system of microphones, and brings a consequent saving in terms of a great deal of time and money for the studios. At least one of the film industry's best musical directors prefers to play the music all into one "mike" and of course the orchestration must in this case be practically as well made as for the concert platform. The orchestras used are in most cases larger than for theatres and an experienced arranger knows that the larger the band the easier his task. As one fine orchestrator, Stephen O. Jones, once said when told of a great orchestration someone had made for a fifty-piece band, "Who *can't* make a good one for that sized bunch?"

DANCE ORCHESTRAS

Years ago when trumpets were more than hazardous in their upper tones, a coloured band had a star player who, after many attempts at a high C sounding B flat, finally resigned himself to missing it and substituting the major second lower which comes out with the same fingering and less effort of the lips (for the studious reader, he sounded the seventh tone of the harmonic series—rather false in intonation—instead of the eighth, for which he was striving). Who shall say that this resultant seventh was not the sire of the W. C. Handy-George Gershwin-Darius Milhad line of "blues" chords that found such a vogue? ¶Likewise in the heart of Kansas there was (also years ago) a small orchestra with no 'cello player. One harness maker had an E flat alto saxophone and one day he discovered that he could read the 'cello part. Looking at a 'cello part one sees at once that all he had to do was use a little imagination in the key signature and read it in the G (treble) clef, and the missing 'cello was missed no more. Who will take the trouble to go farther in a search for the birth of the sax choir in our dance bands? The treatment of this choir by the best dance-arrangers lends credence to the theory at least. This of course ceases to apply when the saxes are doubling on other instruments, a practice that has grown universal since they were introduced. ¶The art of doubling, an art so advanced that many an arrangement for the modern dance orchestra has the names of persons in place of the names of instruments in the wood-wind section, has carried the matter of colouring to an almost fantastic point. Instead of the accustomed "1st Clarinet in B♭" we see on the score

"Elmer," followed by the first measure of his part over which appears "Flute in G" or "Oboe" or "B♭ Tenor" or whatever other instrument Elmer owns and the orchestrator needs. A wood-wind section of six players will give you at various intervals all the tone combinations of a full symphony orchestra's wood-wind, plus beautifully-played saxophones, plus a light-hearted and enthusiastic quality to whatever phrase is played, making up for the lack of virtuosity with spirit and a feeling for ensemble not always obtainable in the larger orchestras. ¶Dance orchestration has long since taken its place as the most imaginative and productive of all arranging. Bands that remain together for long periods develop what is known by the over-worked name of "style" to a degree not possible in any other group. Very much as the old glee clubs and minstrels used to do, the modern dance band discovers its most striking effects in rehearsal and playing. Usually the arranger is one of the band himself and he is thus "in" at the inception of any new twist the players discover. To make the point clearer, a trombonist may arrive at a rehearsal and, in warming his instrument up, play some phrase with a certain personal amplification—some slur with lips instead of the slide, a "rip" which is a series of grace notes up to a high tone, made possible by the harmonic series, playable with no change of slide or valve position, or a hundred other little variations on the usual. Another player hears it or he calls the other's attention to it, they gather in one or two more players and a new find in orchestration is realised. If the effect is sufficiently appealing it sweeps the land; if not it is tried and soon discarded. ¶A glossary of terms such as "rip," "flare," "lick," "break," "release," "redow," etc., provocative as they are, would be of little value because they are out-moded so quickly that a student who took the trouble to learn them would risk that most damning of all stigmas—"corny" (originally "corn-fed," the jazz-player's translation of the French "rococo"). ¶Each of these terms and a great many others may be safely assumed to have grown up in the course of rehearsal and playing by individual instrumentalists, as already described. Not all of the names were originated with the players who discovered the tricks, in fact the majority of the names spring from the picturesque vernacular of the Negro bands. These Negro bands, incidentally, are in a class by themselves as to rhythm, a fact probably due to a simpler set of vibrations in the bodies themselves, but that would be for a student of something besides music to say. In many ways they are pioneers in dance music and a number of them can boast of splendid musicians as their arrangers. They have influenced enormously all popular music, which is not surprising if we consider that the American contribution to popular music is the direct offspring of the "Coon Song." Were it not for the Viennese and English ingredients in our finest operettas we could merely say, "The Negroes continue to set the pace in light music." ¶The "Coon Song" got a new name in Ragtime. Ragtime was later christened Jazz. Jazz became trite as a name before the music did, so its name was again changed to Swing Music. Swing Music became rococo—corny if you like—as a title, but hearts still beat oom-pah, oom-pah, and so do dancing feet; and all nature, bisected, according to Emerson, by an inevitable dualism, continues under different names to go oom-pah, oom-pah, oom-pah, oom-pah. (See "Orchestras and Orchestration," page 778; "Orchestra and Band Instruments," page 811; "Orchestras in America," page 787; and Dictionary of Terms entry, page 648.)

ORCHESTRAS IN AMERICA

By Leonard Liebling

SYMPHONY ORCHESTRAS in the best sense are a comparatively recent development in America, which did not become generally interested in such organisations until about three hundred and fifty years after its discovery. Previously there had been many small and sporadic instrumental ensembles, but it was not until about the middle of the nineteenth century that symphonic bodies came into existence which approximated those then flourishing in Europe. ¶Singing, largely psalmodic, constituted almost the sole tonal utterance of the early settlers and found its greatest practise in New England after the 162c landing at Plymouth Rock. Instrumental music was banned not only in church but also in the homes, the good Pilgrim Fathers basing their ban on the Bible passage in *Amos*, v. 23, "I will not hear the melody of thy viols." Four-part hymns represented the ultimate in harmony until well into the eighteenth century. ¶While the New England Puritans were making up their minds whether it was impious even to sing and not merely read the psalms, Palestrina, Vittoria, and Lassus had already composed monumental choral music; oratorios and lyrical and sacred music dramas (soon to blossom into opera) were winning popularity abroad; and soon after, Purcell, Bach, Handel, the Scarlattis, and others grandly gifted, perfected great forms for pure instrumental music. ¶Beethoven was born in the same year that saw the Boston tanner, William Billings, publish his first crude composition, "The New England Psalm-Singer or American Chorister." In 1713 the first organ came to Boston from England. Other instruments imported by the early colonists were the harpsichord, pianoforte, violin, bass viol ('cello), flute, clarinet, and bassoon. Accompaniments for the choir, after instruments slipped into the church, usually consisted of a flute, bassoon, and bass viol. Frequently only the last-named supported the voices. In 1786 the Stoughton, Mass., Musical Society was organised and performed excerpts from oratorios, accompanied by small groups of instruments. In 1798 Gottlieb Graupner, a German who played in Haydn's orchestra in London (1791–92), went to Boston where he put together the nucleus of the first meagre combination which could at all be considered an orchestra. Then in 1810, with mostly amateurs, he founded a "Philharmonic Society," which met socially and practised Haydn's symphonies. Subsequently, public concerts were held, the last one in 1824, with an orchestra of sixteen—violins, a viola, 'cello, double-bass, flute, clarinet, bassoon, French horn, trumpet, tympani. ¶In 1839 Boston had its Academy Orchestra, started by Henry Schmidt, who at the eight concerts in 1841 introduced the city to Beethoven's *First* and *Fifth* symphonies. When the group disbanded in 1847, Boston had made favourites of six of the nine Beethoven symphonies, as well as Mendelssohn's "*Scotch*," Haydn's "*Militaire*," and Mozart's "*Jupiter*." From twenty-four to forty players performed those works. The society's annual report for 1843 mentions that the season brought for the first time a conductor (Professor Webb) who used a bâton and did not play in the orchestra himself. ¶Succeeding the Academy, came the Musical Fund (1852) with about sixty players, and lasting a number of years. Other aggregations were formed on and off, the only one having a tolerably long life being the Orchestra Society with concerts under the auspices and management of the Harvard Musical Association, born in 1837 at a meeting of the Pierian Sodality composed of alumni of Harvard College. The Harvard Musical Association also had its own orchestra from 1865 to 1882, and prepared the way for the Boston Symphony Orchestra, whose outstanding activity began in 1881 through the generosity of Colonel Henry Lee Higginson, Boston banker, for the next thirty-seven years the sole guarantor of the operating funds. George Henschel was the initial conductor and remained for three years. In 1884–85 he was succeeded by Wilhelm Gericke who improved the orchestra by importing players from Europe. After five years came Artur Nikisch, and for the next four seasons the orchestra rose to a peak of excellence which has never declined since. Emil Paur followed Nikisch for five years. In 1898 Gericke was recalled and stayed until 1905–06 when Karl Muck came from Berlin for two years. Max Fiedler reigned from 1908 to 1912. Then Muck was again the leader until 1918, followed by Henri Rabaud for a single season, Pierre Monteux for five, and some guest conductors until Serge Koussevitzky, the present incumbent, took the bâton in 1924. In 1918 the orchestra was incorporated, and is sponsored financially by a board of directors, fortified by a $1,000,000 endowment fund left by Colonel Higginson. The orchestra's home concerts are held in its own auditorium, Symphony Hall. ¶New York started its orchestral cultivation with a wind band in 1773. Small mixed ensembles appeared there during the next score of years but had a hard time of it. Some of them, as told in the records, were cat-called, vegetable-pelted, and rotten-egged when they tried to introduce Haydn symphonies. Auditors shouted for "Yankee Doodle" and other patriotic tunes. In the 1820s a philharmonic society existed which gave two concerts each year "for the aid of widows and orphans of deceased members." However progressive as New York and Boston tried to be, those future great cities were shamed by Upper Marlborough, Md., where in 1752 an orchestra was employed at a performance of Gay's "The Beggar's Opera." It should be remembered, too, that the first mention of French horns in America came from Benjamin Franklin, who wrote of the fine music in the church at Bethlehem, Pa., where flutes, oboes, French horns and trumpets were accompanied by the organ. ¶Until 1842, the Euterpean Society and the Musical Fund ("Funds" of that period were bodies that provided old-age pensions and insurance for their members) functioned as the leading orchestras of New York. The Fund, all professionals, gave a concert in 1836 with thirty-eight players (two clarinets played the oboe parts) conducted by Alfred Boucher, a 'cellist. The programme included Beethoven's "Eroica" symphony, arranged as a septet. Another commendable project was the Concordia led by Daniel Schlesinger which met in a private room at Delmonico's restaurant. ¶Ureli C. Hill, a New York violinist, studied with Spohr at Cassel, Germany, in 1836, and after his return to his native city felt that it should have an orchestra like the London Philharmonic Society. He kept on doggedly with his idea until he persuaded other New York musicians to join in it. They held a meeting at the Apollo Rooms, April 2, 1842, and organised the Philharmonic Society, with many of the Euterpeans as members. Weekly rehearsals followed until the first concert, December 7, 1842, given at Apollo Hall, a ballroom on Broadway near Canal Street. Four of the members acted as ushers, wearing white kid gloves and carrying long white wands provided by the society. The whole orchestra, except the 'cellists, stood while performing. The players numbered fifty-two. Three concerts were given in the first season, four the next year. By 1854 the membership had increased to sixty-seven, and in 1867 there were ninety-nine. The orchestra was coöperative, appointed its own manager and conductor, and profits went pro rata to the players. After the first season each one received a dividend of $25. In 1855 the amount had increased to $65. ¶Conductors of the first seven seasons of the Philharmonic were U. C. Hill, H. C. Timm, W. Alpers, G. Loder, L. Wiegers, D. G. Etienne, A. Boucher. In 1849 Theodor Eisfeld was chosen sole conductor and after 1854 alternated with Carl Bergmann until the former resigned in 1865–66. Bergmann continued to function until he was succeeded by Dr. Leopold Damrosch in 1876. The next season Theodore Thomas was appointed, Adolf Neuendorff replaced him a year later, and in 1879 Thomas returned, who directed until 1891, when the bâton fell to Anton Seidl. Emil Paur held the leader's stand up to 1902. Walter Damrosch won a single season, 1903, after which the guest-conductor system obtained during 1904–05–06 with a long list of distinguished leaders. Wassili Safonoff headed the orchestra 1906–09; Gustav Mahler 1909–11; Josef Stransky 1911–23 (the final two seasons in conjunction with Willem Mengelberg); Mengelberg, half seasons, the rest of the periods filled by Artur Bodanzky, Henry Hadley (American programmes), Willem van Hoogstraten, Ernest Schelling (children's concerts), Igor Stravinsky, Arturo Toscanini (guest, 1926), Wilhelm Furtwaengler; until in 1927–28, Toscanini began his regular connection, after which he was chief to 1935–36, with associates Mengelberg, Beecham, Molinari, Richard Strauss, Ossip Gabrilowitsch, Erich Kleiber, Bruno Walter, Issay Dobrowen, Hans Lange, Werner Janssen, Otto Klemperer, Artur Rodzinski. In 1936–37 John Barbirolli became the regular conductor, with Rodzinski, Carlos Chavez, Georges Enesco, Igor Stravinsky as associates. ¶In 1912 Joseph Pulitzer, proprietor of the New York *World*, bequeathed $500,000 to the Philharmonic, an endowment later said to be doubled. From 1917 the Philharmonic finances have been guaranteed by a board of directors. In 1930 the Philharmonic made a highly successful European tour with Toscanini. ¶During the course of its existence the Philharmonic has absorbed the National Symphony, City Symphony, American Orchestral Society and New York Symphony, and its concerts were held successively in Apollo Hall, Broadway Tabernacle, Assembly Rooms, Apollo Salon, Niblo's Concert Salon, Metropolitan Hall, Niblo's Garden, Academy of Music, Irving Hall, Steinway Hall, Metropolitan Opera House, and Carnegie Hall, the present location of the Philharmonic when it is not appearing in the summer at the Stadium of the College of the City of New York. ¶In 1878 Dr. Leopold Damrosch founded the New York Symphony Society in competition with Theodore Thomas' own orchestra, and the rivalry of the two groups did much to acquaint New York with the classical masterpieces and the newest creations of Europe. Damrosch and Thomas were the leading musical personalities and educators of their time, as Hill and Bergmann had been before them. After Damrosch's death, in 1885, his son Walter took over the Symphony Society and was its sole conductor until he invited Felix Weingartner as co-leader for the season of 1905–06. Thereafter the younger Damrosch resumed entire charge until he associated himself with radio activities in 1928 when his enterprise was merged with the

Philharmonic whose official title became Philharmonic-Symphony Orchestra. In 1920 the New York Symphony made a European tour financed by H. H. Flagler, who for ten years generously acted as the sole guarantor of the orchestra, in the amount of about $100,000 annually. Walter Damrosch's further creditable contributions to American musical development were his founding of symphony concerts for children, his devotion to the works of Wagner (when that composer still needed championing in the New World), and his prevailing upon Andrew Carnegie to build the great concert-hall named after him, for whose opening festivities Tchaikovsky was brought from Russia to conduct several programmes. ¶Theodore Thomas' personal series commenced in 1864. In 1866 he started his summer concerts at Terrace Garden; in 1877 he moved to Central Park Gardens. During the winters, Thomas toured the country with his orchestra from 1869 to 1878. Just before the turn of the century he gave several winter seasons of Sunday-evening concerts at Lenox Lyceum. ¶America had early visits from European orchestras, notably those of Joseph Gungl (1849) from Berlin, and Louis Julien (1853) from Paris, whose solo double-bass player was the celebrated Bottesini. Julien carried ninety-seven players, the largest aggregation of symphonists the United States had then experienced. He introduced the one-composer programme, devoted to Beethoven, Mozart, Mendelssohn, et al. A number of the men imported by Gungl and Julien remained in this country and joined native orchestras thereby raising their proficiency. Many other highly competent players emigrated here after the 1848 political troubles in Europe. An American travelling orchestra was the Germania, led by the estimable Carl Bergmann. All those touring bands awakened a large part of America to orchestral appreciation and undoubtedly inspired many cities to think seriously of possessing symphonic organisations of their own. ¶During the present century New York had, aside from the orchestras mentioned, the Young Men's Symphony (conductor, Arnold Volpe), Amicitia (amateur), Russian, Symphony (Modest Altschuler), Manhattan (Henry Hadley), Seidl (Anton Seidl), which gave concerts at Brighton Beach, National (Stransky and Bodanzky), Friends of Music (Bodanzky), and numerous lesser intermittent projects of symphonic and chamber-music size. European visitors were the London Symphony (Nikisch), Paris Conservatoire (Messager), La Scala (Toscanini). Orchestras from other cities that have appeared in the metropolis for guest concerts are those of Chicago, Minneapolis, Cincinnati, Elizabeth, N. J. Philadelphia and Boston send their orchestras for regular annual series. There are also courses by the National Orchestral Association (a training medium for young professionals) led by Leon Barzin, and the Women's Symphony Orchestra under Antonia Brico. Several other major cities, too, have female orchestras. ¶The example of Boston and New York spurred their sister cities to emulation and despite high costs, groups of interested sponsors raised funds for orchestras in their own communities or arranged for visits from touring orchestras. Philadelphia had its Musical Fund Society, 1820–57, and Chicago its Philharmonic Society, 1860–68. Milwaukee supported its Musik Verein, organised in 1849–50. Cincinnati had an orchestra as early as 1856; St. Louis in 1838; reorganised in 1859. As late as 1890. however, Boston and New York boasted the only recognised permanent orchestras in the United States. ¶This running review shall not attempt to outline all the pioneer attempts to create orchestras throughout the land but must content itself with the mention of only the chief ones now existing. Chicago's eminent orchestra was founded 1891 by Theodore Thomas, with a guarantee fund raised by popular subscription. Later through the same agency and the help of wealthy Chicagoans, Orchestra Hall was built as a permanent home for the orchestra. Philadelphia's famous orchestra dates from 1890 and was incorporated in 1903. Fritz Scheel led the initial seasons. The present conductors are Leopold Stokowski and Eugene Ormandy. Cincinnati's orchestra was started 1895 (by the Ladies' Musical Club) under Michael Brand. Some later conductors were Theodore Thomas, Frank van der Stucken, Ernst Kunwald, Eugene Ysaye, Leopold Stokowski, Fritz Reiner. At present, Eugene Goossens is the director, in the orchestra's own Music Hall. St. Louis's orchestra, founded 1880, grew out of the local choral society. In 1900 it became an independent organisation. Now its head is Vladimir Golschmann. Kansas City has a Philharmonic dating from 1933 under Karl Krueger. Omaha entered the field importantly in 1924; San Francisco in 1911, with Henry Hadley and later, Alfred Hertz; present conductor, Pierre Monteux. San Francisco's was the first major symphonic body to admit women to its playing membership. Los Angeles, 1919, called Walter Rothwell to take charge of its new Philharmonic Orchestra. Present conductor, Otto Klemperer. Minneapolis entered the symphonic lists in 1903, with Emil Oberhoffer, and he led until his retirement, being succeeded by Henri Verbrugghen. Present conductor, Dimitri Mitropoulos. Washington, D. C., had abortive orchestras (one under Reginald De Koven) until 1931, when the National Symphony came under Hans Kindler, at present still its leader. Baltimore was another city early interested in orchestral practise, but a permanent body did not eventuate until 1915. Present conductor of its Symphony Orchestra is Werner Janssen. Rochester, N. Y., has two orchestras; one connected with the Eastman School of Music and under Howard Hanson; the other, the Philharmonic, founded by George Eastman in 1922. In 1936 Jose Iturbi was appointed permanent conductor with Guy Fraser Harrison as associate. Cleveland's larger orchestra began in 1918 under the auspices of the Fine Arts Association. Nikolai Sokoloff conducted for fifteen years, to be succeeded by Artur Rodzinski. The orchestra has its own home, Severance Hall, one of the finest concert auditoriums in America. ¶Others of the larger orchestras and their leaders are: Birmingham, Ala., Dorsey Whittington; Denver, Horace E. Tureman; Hartford, Conn., Jacques Gordon; Jacksonville, Fla., Clarence Carter; Atlanta, Ga., George F. Lindner; Indianapolis, Ind., Fabien Sevitzky; Des Moines, Ia., William A. Moore; New Orleans, La., Arthur Zack; Fall River, Mass., Ray Groff; Worcester, Mass., Walter Howe; Detroit, Mich., Franco Ghione and Victor Kolar; Grand Rapids, Mich., Karl Wecker; Duluth, Minn., Paul Lemay; Elizabeth, N. J., August May; Newark, N. J., Essex County Symphony, Alexander Smallens; Trenton, N. J., Guglielmo Sabatini; Buffalo, N. Y., Franco Autori; Syracuse, N. Y., André Polah; Albany, N. Y., William Penny Hacker; Columbus, O., Earle Hopkins; Dayton, O., Paul Katz; Toledo, O, Joseph Sainton; Youngstown, O., Michael and Carmine Ficcocelli; Oklahoma City, Okla., Ralph Rose; Seattle, Wash., Nikolai Sokoloff; Erie, Pa., John R. Metcalf; Pittsburgh, Pa., Fritz Reiner; Reading, Pa., Dr. Hans Kindler; Scranton, Pa., Dr. Felix M. Gatz; Providence, R. I., Dr. Wassily Leps; Dallas, Tex., Jacques Singer; Fort Worth, Tex., Brooks Morris; Houston, Tex., Ernst Hoffman.

San Antonio, Tex., Walter Dunham; Norfolk, Va., Henry C. Whitehead; Richmond, Va., Dr. Laird Waller; Tacoma, Wash., Eugene Linden; Milwaukee, Wis., Dr. Sigfrid Parger. ¶American interest in orchestral concerts is wide and growing constantly (helped by the sale of phonograph records and radio performances), only a few large cities being without permanent orchestras supported by private guarantors or municipal funds. The number of orchestras has increased considerably during the past several years, through the activities of the Federal Music Project, in the endeavour to furnish occupation for unemployed musicians. ¶The cost of maintaining a first-class symphony orchestra is high, having risen gradually because of the players' fees demanded by their unions. According to figures revealed at a recent St. Louis meeting of orchestral managers, the total annual expenditure of thirteen major orchestras was $4,346,500. Their earned income amounted to $2,782,100, leaving a deficit of $1,564,400, met by maintenance funds, endowment income and special gifts. The largest single deficit was $178,000, and the least, $57,000. To-day some of the first-desk players receive as much as $200 per week—contrasted with the $25 for a whole season which the members got individually from the New York Philharmonic in 1842. ¶This article omits mention of orchestral developments in the fields of radio (where the National Broadcasting Company established its dignified air-orchestra under the aegis of Toscanini, December 25 1937) and grand and light opera, subjects treated elsewhere in these pages. However, attention is called to the excellent symphony orchestras in some of the leading moving-picture theatres, the best example being Radio City Music Hall in New York, where Erno Rapee functions as chief conductor and daily lists at least one symphonic composition, frequently a movement or two from a symphony. It is estimated that nearly 4,000,000 persons constitute the annual audiences at Music Hall. ¶Add the audiences which crowd the winter concert-halls and the summer series at the New York Stadium, Boston Symphony Hall, Philadelphia Dell, Hollywood Bowl and other outdoor places, and it will be seen that an enormous proportion of the population in America is regularly devoted to the best symphonic communion. ¶In concluding review, let it be repeated that the orchestras which have done most for American musical advancement are those of Boston and New York; and that the conductors similarly to be credited are Ureli Hill, Carl Bergmann, Theodore Thomas, Wilhelm Gericke, Artur Nikisch, the two Damroschs, Anton Seidl, and Arturo Toscanini. *(See "Orchestras and Orchestrations," page 778; "Orchestra and Band Instruments," page 811; "Orchestration of Theatre and Dance Music," page 780; Dictionary of Terms entry, page 648.)*

ORGAN*

By Rupert Hughes

THOUGH MANY INSTRUMENTS are loosely called *organs* (such as the mouth-organ, hand-organ, etc.), the word is generally given to the *pipe-organ*, a microcosmic

---

*A comment on the old organ is included here since so many organs over the country, still in use, were installed before the invention of electrical manuals and blowers.

wind-instrument which contains in its forest of resources almost all the powers
and qualities of almost all other instruments. In the course of time while its
powers have grown ever greater, their control has become always easier and
more centralised. ¶The HISTORY of the organ is, in any completeness, beyond
the space of this work. Its prototypes are the primeval Pan's pipes and the
bagpipe. The 2d century B.C. finds it with a key-board, and pipes supplied by
bellows with air compressed by water. Ctesibius (170 B.C.) invented this
water-organ (Organon hydraulicon) which his pupil Heron described in Greek.
There are many accounts and representations of organs from that point on.
The mediæval monks used organs abundantly, the pipes being 8 to 15 in number
and of no greater than 4-ft. length, the range being usually one octave from
middle *c'* downward, the key-board consisting of lettered plates to be pressed.
In the 10th century there was at Winchester, England, an organ with 2 manuals
for 2 performers, 20 digitals each, and 10 pipes to each digital, 400 in all. In
the 12th century the pipes began to be divided into registers or stops (q. v.).
For two centuries the action became so clumsy that keys were struck with fists
or elbows. Pedals were invented about 1325. Till the 15th century, reed
pipes were unknown. Since that time the resources have been vastly increased,
the variety of tone rendered almost illimitable, and the introduction of water,
steam or electric aid to work the bellows has displaced the need of a man to
serve as organ-pumper or bellows-treader. Electricity has also been called into
play for bringing remote parts of the organ into convenient control, till the per
former with his draw-knobs has almost as easy command as the conductor with
his bâton. ¶The CONSTRUCTION of the manual organ [as distinguished from
the newer type, whose operation, both as to stops and wind-supply, is largely
electrical] is too complicated for detail, but many of the terms following will be
found more fully explained under their separate heads. When looking at a
manual organ, in a church for example, the eye is first caught by the great array
of pipes. These ornamental or *display-pipes* (some of which may be only for
show, *dummy-pipes*) conceal many plain pipes of wood or metal, which are of
various shapes and sizes, according to the quality and pitch of the tone of the
pipe (q. v.). These pipes are grouped together into *registers* or *stops* (q. v.),
each being of uniform quality of tone and furnishing a complete or partially
complete scale (or series of pipes of graduated lengths). Though these pipes
are merely colossal flutes, oboes, trumpets, etc. (each pipe, however, sounding
only one tone), they are too large to be blown by human lungs, and an elaborate
mechanism is used. This is concealed from the eye, which sees only the series
of key-boards for the hands and feet, and the multitude of little *draw-knobs*
grouped within easy reach. ¶Of these key-boards the numbers vary, those for
the hands, the *manuals*, being from 1 to 5 in number and appearing in the following order counting from below, and giving both English and foreign names:

ENGLISH		GERMAN		FRENCH		ITALIAN
Great (Gt.) organ manual		Hauptwerk (Manual	I)	Grand-orgue	(1er clavier)	Principale.
Choir	"	Unterwerk (	" II)	Positierif	(2e ")	Organo di coro.
Swell (Sw.)	"	Schwellwerk (	" III)	Clav. de récit	(3e ")	"d'espressione.
Solo	"	Soloklavier (	" IV)	" des bombardes	(4e ")	" d'assolo.
Echo	"	Echoklavier (	" V)	" d'écho	(5e ")	" d'eco.

Each of these key-boards may be said to control a separate instrument or *partial
organ;* and one often speaks of the *choir-organ, swell organ,* etc. ¶The *pedal-*

key-board, Pedalklaviatur (pā-däl'-klä-fi-ä-toor'), *G.*, or *clavier des pédale:* (klāv-yā-dā-pā-däl') *Fr.*, or *pedallera* (pā-däl-lā'-rä), *I.*, is worked by the feet and is also a separate instrument with stops of its own (vide PEDAL). ¶By means of *couplers*, any two of these key-boards (manuals or pedals) may be connected; or they may all be combined into the *full-organ*. The *coupling-action* is worked by draw-knobs. ¶The organ as a whole, then, is divided into three chief parts: (1) The *action* (key-boards and stops). (2) The *pipe-work*. (3) The *wind-supply*. The *action* we have examined. The pipes (vide PIPE and STOP) are set upright above the wind-chest, the cover of which is called the *sound-board;* the lower part of the pipe, passing through an *upper-board*, which grips its *nose*, sets its *foot* in the *pipe-rack;* below this is a *slider* (worked by a draw-knob), a thin strip of wood with a hole for each pipe of its particular stop. ¶(4) The *wind* is collected from the outer air by *bellows* and led by *feeders* into a *storage-bellows*, where it is compressed by heavy weights; it is next led by a wooden channel or *wind-trunk* into a wooden reservoir, or *wind-chest*, the top of which (the *sound-board*) is pierced by *grooves* closed by valves or *pallets*, and separated by *bars*. ¶To play the organ, we first pull out a *draw-knob*, which drags along a *slider* until its holes are beneath the feet of the pipes of its stop. This stop is now said to be *on* (before being brought into play it was *off*). Having also pulled out a draw-knob setting the wind-supply to work, we next press down one of the digitals on the key-board whose stop we have drawn. In pressing down this digital lever we raise its opposite end, which lifts an up-right rod (a *sticker*), this in turn raising the front end of a horizontal lever (or *back-fall*) whose rear end is thus depressed and pulls down a thin upright strip of wood (a *tracker*) which in turn pulls a wire (a *pull-down* or *pallet-wire*) fastened to a valve (or *pallet*) which opens and lets the air (which was waiting in the groove from the wind-chest) rush up through the slider into the pipe to make it sound or speak. (*Squares* and *roller-boards* sometimes intervene between the stickers and trackers, while *pneumatic* or *electric* actions give still more direct connection between digital and pallet.) This is the mechanism by which each tone is secured. By means of a multitude of stops and couplers, what would be a simple tone or chord on another instrument may become a vast group of tones of various pitches and colours. ¶By means of the *swell* (q. v.) the volume of sound may be gradually increased or diminished while it is sustained. (*See also "The Electric Organ," page 728.*)

PHONOGRAPH MUSIC

By R. D. Darrell

PHONOGRAPH (literally sound-writer) and GRAMOPHONE are currently synony-mous terms—favoured in American and British usage respectively—for an in-strument to record and reproduce sound. Commonly the word phonograph de-notes a sound-reproducing instrument only, used in conjunction with records, flat discs—usually ten or twelve inches in diameter—in the grooves of which sound tracks have been engraved. To-day the instrument is usually operated elec-trically, often in conjunction with a radio with which it shares an amplifying circuit and loudspeaker. For phonographic purposes the combination instrument switches out the detector circuit of the radio (employed to catch broadcast electrical impulses) and switches on a pick-up circuit in which the initial impulses are provided by a needle moving in an electrical field and actuated by the needle point tracing the sound tracks in the grooves of a record spinning on a motor-driven turntable.

HISTORY

The problem of storing up sound—that of the human voice in particular—and releasing it at will occupied man's imagination many years before Thomas Edison's tinfoil phonograph squawked its epochal "Mary had a little lamb" in 1877. But it remained in the world of fantasy (as exemplified by the frozen horn blast in one of Baron Munchausen's tall tales) or found form only in the creation of vocal automatons and music boxes, until Leon Scott's *phonautograph* of 1857 revealed a seminal principle—the ability of a diaphragm to translate sound waves into vibrations of an attached tracing stylus. (The phonautograph, improved by Blake, also gave Bell his first definite conception of the speaking telephone.) A French poet, Charles Cros, was the first to realise the potential reversability of the phonautograph, but no working model of his projected *paleophone* had been built when Edison's original talking machine indented sound tracks on tinfoil and actually played them back. ¶Appropriating the name phonograph (originally coined by an Englishman, Fenby, for a primitive sort of player-piano roll, and first used in its present sense by a friend of Cros, Abbé Lenoir), Edison created a natural sensation and had a lively box-office attraction when he put his machine on public exhibition around 1879. Other experimenters, who had been working along similar lines, followed him into the field in the next decade, most notably Alexander Graham Bell, Charles Sumner Tainter, and Emile Berliner. The first two, working together, produced the *graphophone* (utilising a stylus that cut rather than indented sound tracks, wax instead of tinfoil for the impressible surface, and an improved diaphragm—the mica type used for many years later); Berliner invented the *gramophone*, employing a disc rather than a cylinder record, and followed the phonautograph in tracing the sound track *laterally* (in a sinuous course like the windings of a level road, the width of the oscillations corresponding to the frequencies of the tones recorded) instead of *vertically* (in a series of hills and dales, the depth corresponding to the frequencies of the tones recorded—the system used by both Edison and the Bell-Tainter team). Berliner was also the first to conquer the most serious obstacle to mass production—unlimited and accurate duplication—of records. By 1892 he had evolved a satisfactory process of stamping duplicate discs from a "master" record and of manufacturing discs from a synthetic compound of shellac and mineral earths—substantially the same process and material used for nearly all records to-day. ¶With the twentieth century came a long period of technical refinements and commercial exploitation of two rival systems: (1) Vertically cut cylinders (later vertically cut discs) manufactured mainly by Edison, the early Columbia Company, and Pathé Frères in France: (2) Laterally cut discs manufactured mainly by the Victor Company (purchaser of the Berliner patents), the Gramophone Company in England, and the Columbia Company after 1908. There were affiliated companies, and as the basic patents expired many more were formed, but almost without exception the new concerns identified themselves with the second (Berliner) system. Technical developments were confined largely to minor improvements: quieter record surfaces, more effective diaphragms and amplifying horns, and the like. ¶But the introduction of the Maxfield-Harrison system of electrical recording and reproduction, in 1925, was revolutionary. Stemming from the invention of vacuum tubes and amplifying circuits first brought to public attention in the radio, the new system took over the microphone, amplifiers, and loudspeaker, and replaced the old diaphragm sound-box with an electrical pick-up. In both recording and reproduction the available frequency range became so much wider, the dynamic range was so markedly increased, and tonal fidelity was so greatly enhanced that the old acoustic (or mechanical) recording process was quickly abandoned and the old-style reproducing machine was doomed (almost the only examples produced to-day are low-price portable instruments). And since electrical recording was or seemed more easily adapted to the lateral-cut disc, the rival vertical-cut system quickly faded out of use. Edison made a few attempts at manufacturing electrical recordings, even some with lateral-cut discs, but they were half-hearted and in 1929—within two years of his own death—he gave up his recording activities entirely. (Later, however, his vertical—"hill and dale"—system was successfully adapted to electrical recording by the Bell Telephone Laboratories, but as yet no attempt has been made to exploit the vertically cut "ERPI" records commercially.)

Recorded Music

The phonograph was conceived primarily as a *talking* machine, but once the astonishing novelty of hearing the human voice emerge from a mechanical contrivance had worn off, that function dwindled to minor importance. The *Dictaphone* and similar instruments took over the application of recorded sound for business purposes, and while recent years have seen a revival of interest in "diction" records (*i.e.*, recorded speeches, plays, poems, examples of dialects, etc.), such discs form but a small part of the recorded repertory. Even before 1900 it had become obvious that the phonographic art was to be dedicated substantially to musical entertainment. What type of entertainment was long indicated by Edison's statement of 1891: "Through the faculty with which it [the phonograph] stores up and reproduces music of all sorts, or whistling and recitations, it can be employed to furnish constant amusements to invalids, or to social assemblies, at receptions, dinners, etc." This prophecy formulated his own policy for the next decades' exploitation of his phonograph and cylinders. Sentimental and sacred songs, band and salon orchestral novelties, dance music, whistling solos, comic recitations, and a like order of vaudeville entertainment made up Edison's (and the bulk of other) catalogues for many years. The phonograph was not so much in disrepute as a musical instrument as it was never considered a truly musical medium. It was the tonal equivalent of the comic strip, and pandered to the same mob tastes that turn to-day for satisfaction to a certain and necessarily popular type of broadcast programme. ¶But soon gaudy scarlet-and-gold "celebrity" records began to appear, eventually to enjoy nearly equal popularity. These were the recorded voices of famous singers, and the so-called golden era of this type of record corresponds approximately with the recording career of the brightest in its galaxy of stars: 1902–

1921, the years of Caruso's first records and his death. But right up to the advent of the radio and much-exaggerated "death" of the phonograph it was almost exclusively a medium for popular music and famous voices—the latter esteemed of course by the degree of their celebrity rather than by what they actually sang. ¶At the same time, however, a few pioneers realised the potentialities of recorded fare of a more substantial sort. Several complete operas were attempted, and large sections of Wagnerian music dramas. The Odeon-Parlophone Company was the first to present a complete set of Beethoven symphonies on discs, Columbia experimented with chamber music and subsidised the recording of contemporary British composers, Polydor employed Richard Strauss to direct many of his larger works for the phonograph and even ventured to record the enormous "*Resurrection*" symphony of Mahler. A strange cult was formed of "gramophiles" or "phonomanes"; some banded together in societies to share their treasured discs; a journal, *The Gramophone*, was established at London by Compton Mackenzie in 1923, and three years later Axel B. Johnson started *The Phonograph Monthly Review* at Boston. The cult flourished largely abroad; the American "phonophile" searched the domestic lists for an occasional significant morsel, but was forced to import most of his major recorded works from Europe; and when Mr. Mackenzie compared the repertory available in the United States with that in England, one could hardly blame him for flinging one of America's own topical songs in its face, "You may be fast, but your Mama's gonna slow you down!" ¶The combined upheaval in the wake of the radio and electrical recording seemed to spell the doom of the phonograph in general as well as Edison's own instrument and records. At one stroke every existing record was antiquated and the whole repertory— the good along with the bad—was consigned with the family tintype album to the attic or junk pile. The manufacturers had a marvellous new instrument, but the public was buying radios. The new electrical records were superb, but the vocal stars were mostly dead or dimmed: that market was lost, and the market for tonal vaudeville entertainment and dance music had been preëmpted by the broadcasters. Only the gramophiles were faithful, but they were comparatively few in number and exceedingly particular in their tastes. After the stock market reached the peak of its skyrocket flight and dropped like a plummet, the Edison recording activities were brought to a close with the repeated assertion that recorded operatic and symphonic music did not represent a sound commercial proposition in America, and a melancholy prophecy (that did not seem too far-fetched in those days) that Victor, too, would soon abandon the field. ¶But these were birth and not death pangs. The phonograph was smothered in the rough embrace of radio's Gargantua, but in dying it drew on the very life blood of its conqueror to fashion a young electronic Hercules that would emerge from its sickly childhood to take an honoured place in the world beside—rather than opposed to—its father. The cultists were right and Edison was wrong. Armed with its new powers, and forced by the loss of its old markets, the phonograph turned to serious music and suddenly discovered that the combination of faithful, realistic reproduction and significant musical fare had shattered many an old prejudice. The term "canned music" lost its derogatory force (indeed it has almost been forgotten). It was sufficient that a once-derided mechanistic contraption was an Open Sesame to the world of great music. ¶The new public for recorded music was drawn in part from the old gramophiles, more extensively from musicians and concert-goers, and to no small degree from the newly music-conscious public developed by the better type of broadcasts. And it mushroomed by its own momentum. Almost without exception every musical artist of note was called upon to make records. The recorded repertory grew phenomonally, quickly encompassed the standard symphonic and concert repertories, and was driven by sheer weight of expansive force to seek relatively unfamiliar material, music previously known only to specialists: modern works, the works of Bach, his contemporaries and predecessors. From 1931 this trend gained impetus by the publication of many limited or "society" editions (the complete piano sonatas of Beethoven, *Lieder* by Wolf, Mozart operas, Bach's *Wohltemperirte Klavier* and organ works, etc.), and the establishment of independent recording organisations specialising in rare music (notably *L'Anthologie Sonore, Lumen,* and *L'Oyseau-Lyre* in Paris; *Musicraft, Gamut,* and *Timely* in the United States). ¶With the growth of important material came a growing appreciation of the artistic significance and potentialities of recorded music long obscured by the contemptuous attitude of many professional musicians, the commercial approach of most manufacturers, the lack of consistently planned direction and expert criticism. Led by *The Gramophone* the specialised journals have grown in number and influence; from around 1930 many leading newspapers and magazines throughout the world have published regular record reviews. The Carnegie Foundation established a fund to provide elaborate record libraries and excellent reproducing equipment for schools and colleges, and in addition to these sets many records were purchased by various educational institutions themselves. A number of public libraries (led by the Fifty-Eighth Street branch of the New York Library) established record collections. In 1936 the chaotic and uncharted jungle of multilingual, often inaccurate and inadequate manufacturers' listings of their records were comprehensively surveyed in the monumental *Gramophone Shop Encyclopedia of Recorded Music,* compiled by R. D. Darrell, foreword by Lawrence Gilman. Here for the first time the enormous world output of serious recorded music was listed under one cover, and systematically arranged. Its scope is indicated by the fact that nearly seven hundred composers of note are represented; the "discography" of Wagner alone runs to over twenty-seven pages.

IMPLICATIONS

The individual whose literature is restricted to the daily newspaper may be satisfied musically by the radio alone, but for him whose cultural life is not complete without books, the theatre, and the concert hall, the phonograph is essential. A favourite symphony heard first in concert or on a symphonic broadcast is given permanent domicile and frequent repetition. The advertising slogan "The music you want when you want it" is soundly based on the powerful appeal of the phonograph's salient and unique characteristic—the ability to bring music directly home to one, enabling one to choose and repeat it at will, to listen alone and undisturbed, or in informal, congenial company and surroundings. Nothing can ever take the place of making music oneself, of knowing it as it can only be known through one's own fingers or throat, but individual opportunities and executant skill are limited. (Even here the recent "Spiel mit" and "Accompo" records promise a new method of personal participation—by the help of the phonograph—in music making.) But either as an augmentation of direct participation or as an unavoidable substitute for it, recorded music opens up new and unsurmised horizons. And it may mean far more than *faut de mieux* substitution or escape. The shellac discs are *sounded* scores intelligible to everyone with ears and a mind, breathing life into the intricate hieroglyphics of notation that have had meaning only to the technically expert. The giant works of music may become one's daily bread. ¶The potential repercussions are just beginning to be felt. New artists, discovered on limited or imported records, attain a public long before they have become highly publicised concert figures. A concert in the smallest town is sure to number among its audience men and women who are not only familiar with most of the works to be played, but very likely know them through recorded performances of the world's finest artists. The professional musician must be prepared to meet a new and higher standard of ability and taste. The time is coming when his public is no longer going to be satisfied with the repertory that has served him so well for perhaps a quarter of a century; when his readings are going to be judged in comparison with those of a Schnabel, Heifetz, Szigeti, or Flagstad. Audiences will no longer be satisfied to hear the standard "masterpieces" given casual and routine performances year after year; they will demand fewer and far more carefully prepared performances of the standard works and a radical change in programme-making to embrace a more catholic and vastly expanded repertory. The success of a concert series like that of the New Friends of Music in New York City (that only a few years ago would have been damned as quixotic and highbrow), and its coöperation with a record manufacturer in making available recordings of its principal works is surely prophetic of the new musical trend of the times. ¶New music will lose much of its terrors and instinctive opposition. Heard, reheard, and studied on records, the mysterious screen of new and forbidding idioms can no longer conceal the stature of our contemporary composers; familiarity will reveal them in true perspective, whether they are pygmies or giants. At the other end of the expanding repertory the greatness of Bach and his incalculable scope is just beginning to become apparent to the musical layman. And there were giants before him, many of them scarcely more than names even to specialists, but their music lives in suspended animation, waiting only to be heard, music comparable in craftsmanship and wealth of invention even to that of Bach. The phonograph makes a wide breach in the great ice wall that has separated us from a lost musical Atlantis, opening up a strange and rich tonal world as alien to contemporary concert-goers as the civilisations of Babylonia, Egypt, and Maya, but unlike those preserved in their original ruggedness and colour—a world to be reconquered by anyone who sets the proper record spinning on a turntable. ¶Brave new and old worlds lie at the feet of the phonographic explorer. And this is the supreme irony of the instrument that began with "Mary had a little lamb" and "Cohen on the Telephone" and has not ended by bringing a Toscanini or Beecham into one's own home: that a musical world giving lip service to catholicity, snarling against the rape of the muse by the machine, should dogmatically dictate that certain works of the eighteenth, nineteenth, and twentieth centuries are all we need to know; while a derided mechanistic contrivance of wires, condensers, and vacuum tubes should be an iconoclast and the resurrector of the purest and richest tonal tradition the world has ever known.

The phonograph and recorded music have committed many sins of omission and commission, but for atonement they restore our lost heritage: the music of the Gregorian Chant, of Victoria, Byrd, Sweelinck, Lassus and many another titan, as well as countless unfamiliar works of Bach, Handel, Haydn, and Mozart—works possessing a poignance and profundity of feeling now rarely to be found in the pitifully limited concert repertory which we have drained and trampled to an exhaustion rapidly approaching complete sterility. ¶The quintessence of the meaning of the phonograph and recorded music for the individual was summed up long before the invention of the modern instrument and its coming of age by the author of *The Magic Mountain*, and in the quotation from Thomas Mann that served as text for the *Encyclopedia of Recorded Music* lies the secret of the phonograph's significance and sorcery: ¶". . . And what he felt, understood, and enjoyed, sitting there with folded hands, looking into the black slats of the jalousies whence it all issued, was the triumphant idealism of the music, of art, of the human spirit. . . . Hans Castorp's thoughts or rather his prophetic half-thoughts soared high, as he sat there in night and silence before his truncated sarcophagus of music. They soared higher than his understanding, they were alchemistically enhanced."

PIANOFORTE

By Rupert Hughes

PIANOFORTE (in G. usually restricted to the square piano). The most used and most abused of instruments—a combination of the strings of the harp with a key-board system derived from the organ (in the 14th cent. there is mention of a "stringed instrument of the organ family: the *Exaquir, Sp., Eschiquier d' Angleterre*" i.e., "English chessboard," *F.* or *Esquakiel, G.*). ¶Its HISTORY is obscure and owes much possibly to the monochord and elaborations from it. In the monochord, the hurdygurdy, or organistrum, etc., a single string produced various tones by means of a movable bridge. So the early forms of the piano show a few strings serving for many digitals. The word *monochord* was kept even after the strings were increased in number, but was finally changed to *clavichord* (*clavis* = key) or *clavier;* the movable bridge was displaced by *tangents* which served both to divide the strings as with frets and to sound them. ¶Simultaneously with the fretted clavichord, in which each string served for several tones (as a guitar-string does), prospered a development from the dulcimer, a key-board dulcimer, or *clavicymbal* (from cymbal meaning dulcimer), called in France, *clavecin;* in Italy, *clavi-cembalo* or *arpicordo;* in England, *harpsichord;* in Germany, *Flügel, Kielflügel, Steertstück* or *Schweinskopf*. Small forms of this were the *Virginal(s)*, the *couched harp* or *spinet* (from *spina* = quill), etc. In this variety there was a string for each tone, and the string was sharply plucked with a quill carried at the end of a wooden *jack*. In time the clavichord was also given a string to each tone and was now said to be "fret-free" (*bundfrei*) instead of "fretted" (*gebunden*). The tone was capable of a beautiful trembling effect (*Bebung*) and considerable virtuosity, but there was little possibility of shading from loud to soft. The appearance of the elaborate dulcimer the *Pantaleon* seems to have set the clavi chordists to thinking, and Cristofori, in 1711, invented the hammer-mechanism, which he called, from its power to sound loudly or softly, *piano forte*, literally "loud-and-soft" (this name had been used as early as 1598). In Germany, Silbermann, the organ-builder, won Bach's approval for a *Hammer-klavier* of the same general idea. This idea, with many improvements in detail but little fundamental change, persists to-day in the magnificent instrument on which great gymnasts combine brute-force with legerdemain. ¶The CONSTRUCTION of the piano of our time shows the triumph of ingenuity over a total string-tension of twelve to twenty tons. A powerful cast-iron *frame*, usually cast in one piece and braced with *trusses* and *cross-bars*, braces the wooden *sound-board* below, on which is a raised *bridge* of hard wood, over which are stretched the *strings*. The strings are of steel wire, the bass strings being covered with a finely-wound copper wire. The lowest octave of the bass has one string to each tone, the next octave or more has two strings to each tone, the rest of the instrument has three strings tuned exactly alike as *unisons* for each note. Some of the strings are generally carried back across the others to save space; his is called *overstringing*. The hammer of each tone strikes all three strings at once, except when the soft pedal by shifting lets it strike only one string hence "tre corde" and "una corda"). ¶The ACTION of the piano consists of a key-board of finger-levers or digitals (loosely called keys), the *white* digitals forming the scale of C major, the *black* digitals furnishing the necessary semi-tones to give the piano (by means of temperament, q. v.) a command of all the major and minor keys—the fingering differing for each key except with the Jankó (q. v.) key-board. The pressure of a digital does not, as in the old clavichord or harpsichord, immediately affect the string, but reaches it by a complicated series of levers which bring the hammer into position for a new stroke instantly, so that a tone can, in a proper action, be repeated as rapidly as the fingers can strike the digital. (This is called the *repetition* or *double escapement*—the *double échappement* of Erard being the origin of the many forms of escapement.) The digital carries at the inner end a vertical *pilot* which supports a nearly horizontal *carrier*, at about a right angle to which is the rod called the *hopper*, which fits against the *hammer* by a notch or pro-jection. As soon as the hopper has forced the hammer against the string, it slips loose from the hammer and is brought instantly back (by devices hard to describe briefly) into position so that the hammer on rebounding from the strings finds the hopper ready for an immediate new stroke. The *hammer* is hinged at the *butt*; at the other end of its *shank* is the hammer-shaped *head* with a *pad* of *felt* (or leather). The action which throws the hammer against the strings, and makes it rebound instantly, lifts away from the strings the little *damper*, which muffles the strings when not in use; this damper remains off the strings as long as the digital is held down. ¶By means of the *damper-pedal* (commonly called the "loud pedal") all the dampers may be lifted from all the strings, thus permitting sustained tones and sympathetic vibrations while the hands play other chords. Some pianos have also a *sustaining* as well as a *piano*, or soft pedal (see PEDAL). ¶The piano has a complete chromatic scale with a compass of about seven octaves A͵͵–a''''. It is capable of a rapidity and clarity of utterance of which the organ is incapable; and no other instrument but the organ approaches its resources in chords, range, and brilliance. Except the organ, it is the only self-supporting instrument; it can furnish absorbing employment for the four hands of two performers. The chief lack is the in-ability to swell a sustained tone, and some method of adding this final touch of human interest will doubtless be devised in time by some of the many minds engaged upon the problem.

PIANO STUDIES

By James Huneker

MORE THAN A CENTURY of experience in piano pedagogy has not been fruitless; skilled masters of the instrument no longer burden their pupils with futile finger exercises, and the precious morning hours instead of being devoted to mere digital tortures are now utilised for the memorising of a *répertoire* and the study of especial difficulties in a composition. Since Karl Tausig, the vast and useless étude literature has been sent to Limbo; for in the music itself may be studied the precise technical difficulty to be overcome. ¶After the independence of the fingers, the scales in single and double notes, arpeggios and octaves have been thoroughly mastered, the following studies are generally employed for style, for endurance and the musical development of the scholar; Cramer—edited by Von Bülow; Clementi—edited by Tausig; Kessler—a judicious selection; Kullak's octave school; and the Chopin Etudes, opus 10 and opus 25. After these latter the studies of Liszt and Rubinstein, and Schumann's Symphonic Etudes may be essayed. Of special studies, the Toccata of Czerny, the Schumann Toccata, the Rubinstein Staccato study in C, and Thalberg's study in A minor, opus 45, repeated notes, are recommended. For beginners, Heller's studies in phrasing and later Czerny's finishing studies may be tried. But the Czerny school—with the exception of his excellent special studies for the left hand—is obsolete. ¶For the quick grasp of the Brahms technique, study his fifty-one exercises. Isidor Philipp, taking his cue from Tausig, has given us the marrow of Chopin's technique in a volume of Daily Exercises. For pure polyphony, nothing is better than Bach. For daily gymnastics, use Tausig's studies, but in frugal manner.

RADIO MUSIC

By Lawrence Abbott

MUSICAL HISTORY has been profoundly affected by the development of radio broadcasting, and no survey of contemporary music would be complete without a consideration of radio's effect upon it.

MUSIC BROADCASTING IN ITS INFANCY

Radio, or the wireless transmission of sound, was born in 1895 at Bologna, Italy, when Guglielmo Marconi first succeeded in sending wireless signals on his father's estate. This event marked the origin of practical radiotelegraphy.

Marconi's spark transmitter, however, was incapable of accomplishing the transmission of music and speech, known technically as radiotelephony—without which modern broadcasting would be nonexistent. Eleven years elapsed before Lee De Forest invented the audion, a three-element vacuum tube, and, in an experiment conducted on December 31, 1906, transmitted speech by radio for the first time. In 1907 phonograph music was radioed from Dr. De Forest's laboratory for a distance of 12 miles. The information as to what music was broadcast is unobtainable; but the following year German engineers of the Telefunken Company, during experimental broadcasts between Sandy Hook and Bedloe's Island in New York Harbour, for the benefit of the U. S. Signal Corps, transmitted a phonograph recording of the Anvil Chorus from Verdi's "*Il Trovatore.*" This may well have been the first operatic, or even classical music to be heard by radio. The first "live" music broadcast took place in 1909, at Lee De Forest's laboratory in New York City, when Marguerite Mazarin of Hammerstein's Manhattan Opera Company sang an aria from "*Carmen.*" In the following January, under De Forest's auspices, a far more remarkable event in radio history occurred: in an experimental broadcast from the Metropolitan Opera House in New York, Enrico Caruso sang the rôle of "Turiddu" in "*Cavalleria Rusticana*" and was heard by listeners in various parts of the city as well as by at least one wireless operator at sea. During the next ten years radio remained in an experimental phase; its potential value was considered chiefly as a supplement to the telegraph and telephone, while its possibilities as a purveyor of mass entertainment remained unrecognised.

MUSIC BROADCASTING IN THE UNITED STATES, 1920–1938

Broadcasting in the modern sense—*i.e.*, the daily transmission of speech and music to a widespread public audience in accordance with a regular published schedule—originated in Pittsburgh, Pennsylvania, when station KDKA, owned by the Westinghouse Electric & Manufacturing Company, began operation. Other stations quickly came into existence. At first they were little concerned with serious music, devoting their time chiefly to news bulletins, sporting events, and novelties. Musical broadcasts were limited almost entirely to dance music, popular songs, and salon pieces; this is understandable, since the mass audience to which radio broadcasts necessarily must be directed were at first totally unfamiliar with concert music and unwilling to listen to it. Only gradually did they become educated to its capacity for giving them enjoyment, and so only gradually did radio come to occupy an important position in the field of serious music. ¶In November, 1922, listeners heard the first pick-up of an opera performance originating outside a broadcasting studio (Verdi's "*Aïda,*" performed at Kingsbridge Armoury, New York), and later in that same month the first major symphonic broadcast took place (a concert by the New York Philharmonic Orchestra, in the Hall of the College of the City of New York). The following October, Walter Damrosch pointed the way to the invaluable service radio could perform in the field of music education when a lecture recital of his on Beethoven was broadcast from Carnegie Hall, New York. Two seasons later—in January, 1926—John McCormack and Lucrezia Bori made their radio débuts in a broadcast that inspired other eminent artists to go on the air. In the autumn of 1926 Dr. Damrosch again lent his prestige to the infant radio industry by inaugurating a series of weekly radio symphonic concerts which he continued for six winter seasons. The following January a nation-wide audience heard its first broadcast of a complete opera performed in an opera house (*"Faust,"* broadcast from the Chicago Civic Opera Auditorium). Not quite two years later a still more important milestone occurred: Dr. Damrosch's first music appreciation broadcast in October, 1928. Known the first year as the RCA Educational Hour, and since then as the NBC Music Appreciation Hour, these broadcasts have continued uninterruptedly for more than ten years, have become part of the required curriculum in many thousands of schools, and have brought musical enlightenment and understanding to untold millions of school children and adults. ¶During the last decade (1928–1938), the history of broadcast music has been less a succession of sporadic "firsts" than it has a steady increase in both the volume and quality of serious music broadcasts. During this period network broadcasting rose to its present dominating position and made possible the fullest achievement of radio's potentialities for mass entertainment and education: its ability, for example, to transmit a single memorable musical performance to a world-wide audience. The National Broadcasting Company was formed in 1926, the Columbia Broadcasting System in 1927, and the Mutual Broadcasting System in 1934. To-day broadcasting in the United States consists of these three nation-wide networks plus a number of smaller, regional networks, and many independent stations with no network affiliations. By the late 1920s, also, the American system of broadcasting had become firmly established. Under this system broadcasting is financed by the sale of time to advertisers. Programmes are either commercial (*i.e.*, produced and paid for by firms which wish to advertise their products thereby), or sustaining (furnished by broadcasting stations or networks at their own expense in order to attract listeners and create good will). During the entire history of radio, more than two thirds of all broadcast hours have been sustaining. On the whole, commercial programmes are devoted to mass entertainment of a light nature; most cultural programmes, from which listeners derive aesthetic enjoyment, are sustaining programmes. ¶In October, 1930, the Columbia Broadcasting System brought symphonic music into new prominence when it began its weekly winter-season broadcasts of the Sunday afternoon New York Philharmonic-Symphony concerts—two-hour broadcasts which have continued each season to the present time. Two years later the National Broadcasting Company began a regular series of two-hour broadcasts by the Boston Symphony Orchestra. To-day every important symphony orchestra in the country is heard by radio listeners at some time during the year. ¶In March, 1933, radio pioneered in establishing a new field of orchestral music when Frank Black, conducting what has become known as the NBC String Symphony, inaugurated a series of broadcast concerts devoted exclusively to music for strings alone. Never before had such a series been presented either on the radio or in the concert hall. Since then other string orchestras have been established for broadcast purposes, and in at least one instance (the 1937 Saratoga Spa Music Festival concerts, conducted by F. Charles Adler) the concert hall has followed in radio's footsteps. ¶In November, 1937, another important development took place when the NBC Symphony Orchestra made its début as a full-size, permanent symphony orchestra; this was the first such organisation of major calibre to be established and maintained by an American broadcasting corporation exclusively for studio broadcasts of symphonic music. During the eleven weeks when Arturo Toscanini conducted this orchestra in the winter season of 1937–38 music critics broke a long-standing precedent by treating the concerts in their reviews on a basis of equality with those of the leading symphony societies. ¶Opera became regularly accessible to radio audiences with the first complete opera broadcast from the Metropolitan Opera House ("*Hänsel und Gretel*," December 25, 1931). With the development of international short-wave re-broadcasting, the best European orchestras and opera companies began to be heard in the United States (the first of such broadcasts: London, Symphony Orchestra, 1930; Dresden Opera House, 1930). Chamber music received scant attention until October, 1934, when the National Broadcasting Company's NBC Music Guild inaugurated the hitherto unheard-of procedure of broadcasting four programmes of chamber music weekly, making no concessions to musical illiterates, and employing the leading string quartets of the United States and Europe. Present-day radio programme schedules include a due proportion of chamber music. ¶Among notable recent developments in educational music broadcasts are the lecture recitals of Abram Chasins, devoted to critical analysis of piano compositions illustrated by the performance first of fragments and then of compositions in their entirety (a procedure which cannot be duplicated as successfully either in the large concert hall or by means of the printed page); the NBC Home Symphony, which encourages amateur music making by broadcasting actual rehearsals in which listeners may take part, each instrumentalist adding his own part to the music of a studio orchestra which emanates from his loudspeaker; and various "schools of the air," one broadcast nationally by CBS, others on a state-wide or city-wide basis under the auspices of boards of education. ¶A recent phenomenon is the extensive broadcasting of music, serious as well as light, by "electrical transcription" (either standard phonograph records or recordings made specially for broadcast purposes). This technique has enabled small stations to broadcast many hours of symphonic and operatic music at little expense; its future, however, is somewhat clouded because of uncertainty as to the extent to which recording artists and phonograph companies can legally exercise control over the use to which records are put. ¶The extensive volume in which music of aesthetic value, both instrumental and vocal, is available to the radio public of to-day (omitting from consideration broadcasts of phonograph records) may be gauged by the fact that during 1937 the three principal networks broadcast 3,420 hours of such music—on an average, more than nine hours of it each day.

MUSIC BROADCASTING IN FOREIGN COUNTRIES

On the whole, the development of music broadcasting in other parts of the world has paralleled that of the United States. Chelmsford, England, shares with Pittsburgh, Pennsylvania, the honours of originating scheduled broadcasts. Foreign programmes of serious music to-day compare favourably with those in this country. In virtually every other nation broadcasting is operated or controlled by the government, and is usually supported by taxation. Partly as a consequence, receiving sets are found in a smaller percentage of homes; no other country equals the estimated 82 per cent of American homes which possess radio receivers.

BROADCASTING TECHNIQUE

In order that a musical performance may be transmitted to radio listeners, it must first be picked up by a microphone, which transforms the complex sound waves that reach it into electrical waves; these feeble waves must then be amplified, after which they must travel by cable to the radio station's transmitting tower or antenna; they are then sent through the ether in the form of radio waves, are picked up by the aerial of some distant receiving set, transformed again into electrical waves, amplified once more to proper volume, and through electrical vibrations set up in a sensitive loudspeaker are restored to an approximation of their original form as sound waves. The different steps of this process call for great engineering skill and constant expert supervision in order to prevent the "approximation" from being an extremely inaccurate and distorted one. ¶Various types of microphones are used. The most common one in music broadcasts is the velocity, or ribbon, microphone. It is directional—that is, it responds unequally to sounds approaching it at different angles. Unlike a camera, which "sees" its entire image with equal clarity, the velocity microphone "hears" with greatest volume the sounds that travel to it from points directly in front and with decreasing intensity the sounds which originate at points on either side. The usual type of velocity microphone is bi-directional—that is, it responds equally to sounds in front of it or behind it. One microphone is sufficient to reproduce the sound of a large orchestra or chorus; in fact, it usually does so more successfully than a battery of two or more microphones, the reason for this being that when sound waves reach two different microphones at slightly different times (as will all sound waves except those which emanate from a point equidistant from both microphones), and when the electrical waves thus formed are blended into a single circuit, "wave interference" is produced which mars, theoretically at least, the fidelity of the reproduction. These as well as other factors must be taken into consideration by the director of the broadcast in placing musicians and microphones in the correct relative positions. ¶Acoustical problems also beset the director. The music which we hear in a concert hall consists of sound waves which travel straight from the source of the music to our ears, plus other waves which reach us only after being reflected from the floor, walls, and ceiling. Reflected sound produces reverberation or room resonance. This is disconcerting when excessive; yet without it music would sound strangely flat and lifeless. Resonance within a broadcasting studio is controlled largely by the use of sound-absorbent material in the construction of walls and ceiling, and by adjustable fabric hangings. It can also be increased or decreased, however, by changing the angle at which the microphone is tilted. It is noticeably affected, incidentally, by the presence or absence of a studio audience. In the past, studio broadcasts usually permitted too little reflected sound to be heard; to-day, however, room resonance is more frequently given its due. ¶In arranging the placement of ensembles and orchestras, instruments which are least powerful in tone and highest in pitch must be placed nearest the microphone. In a string quartet the first violin must be slightly nearer and the 'cello slightly further away than the other two players. In a symphony orchestra the violins should be nearest, while it is necessary to place the brass and percussion instruments not only furthest away, but to one side. Sometimes trumpeters are directed to point the bells of their instruments away from the microphone in order to lessen the apparent volume. The placement of horns is especially important; since their bells project backwards, they must not be seated directly in front either of a highly reflecting or of a completely sound-absorbing surface. Often chamber music performers and soloists with piano accompaniment are placed on both sides of a bi-directional microphone. ¶Broadcasting experience has shown that theoretical principles can be relied upon only up to a certain point; the final arbiter must be the ear, provided it is a well-trained musical ear. Hence critical listening, during rehearsals, to the loudspeaker in the soundproof "control room" adjoining the studio is often the most important factor in the supervision of a broadcast. When a broadcast is in progress a final, flexible control over volume of tone is exercised by the studio engineer. This is necessary, since an excessive volume of sound (caused, for instance, by a sudden *fortissimo* roll on the kettledrum) can overload delicate transmission equipment to a point where damage to it will put the broadcast off the air. Under ideal conditions the studio engineer leaves his "gain-control" dials untouched during a concert broadcast, so that variations in dynamics are transmitted with perfect fidelity; when this is not possible, good broadcasting technic requires that alterations in the volume of amplification be made so gradually as to be imperceptible.

Tonal Quality of Broadcast Music

The fidelity with which musical tones are transmitted and received in modern radio broadcasting is a subject of extreme importance. On it depends, to a large extent, the value of radio as a satisfactory medium for the presentation of music. ¶Musical tones and overtones may be scientifically described as sound waves which vibrate at frequencies, or rates of vibration which can be expressed in cycles per second. The lowest tone on the piano, for instance, vibrates at the rate of about 27 cycles per second while the highest vibrates at about 4,000 cycles per second. The oboe's A, from which orchestral musicians tune their instruments, is 440 cycles. In a symphony orchestra, the lowest frequency usually heard is the fundamental tone of the open E string of the double bass, about 40 cycles. The highest clearly audible tones are the upper harmonics of the violins and oboes, about 16,000 cycles. When music is mechanically reproduced, a considerable portion of the extremely low and high frequencies is generally lost in transmission. The omission of low frequencies is most clearly perceptible, since important bass tones are eliminated. The omission of the two upper octaves of high frequencies (4,000 to 16,000 cycles) is not so readily noticeable, since this eliminates only certain overtones; yet these overtones are what give orchestral instruments their characteristic tone quality, and their omission results in a distortion of tonal values. This simplified explanation of scientific principles may help to explain why reproduced music falls short of being an exact replica of the original performance. ¶The old-fashioned phonograph and the first radio receiving sets had an upper limit of about 2,000 cycles, while the tones under 200 cycles reproduced by it were no more than shadows of their original selves. The tone quality of such instruments was consequently far from satisfying. The last fifteen years has witnessed great strides in fidelity of reproduction, but actual results obtainable on most modern receiving sets are still far short of the ideal. The reasons are two-fold, being due to deficiencies both in transmission and in reception. Radio stations are now licensed to transmit at a specified "carrier" frequency, through a "channel" or wave band which is usually 10,000 cycles in width—in other words, extending 5,000 cycles on either side of the frequency allotted. Such a channel can accommodate musical tones which have frequencies up to 5,000 cycles. Few stations transmit frequencies much higher, and these—in theory, at least—overlap into neighbouring channels, causing, under certain conditions, a possibility of interference. In a very few instances, stations have been allocated "high-fidelity" channels of double this width; these can transmit interference-free tones up to 10,000 cycles. As yet, however, receiving sets (with a certain few exceptions) are not designed to reproduce the full range of tones now being transmitted by modern broadcasting stations. The average receiver is not noticeably responsive to frequencies below 100 cycles (G on the bottom line of the bass staff) or above 3,500 (A in the fourth octave above middle C). Midget-size receivers are, of course, limited to an even less extensive range. At present writing, engineering science is capable of building and operating both transmitters and receivers of far greater fidelity. That it is not doing so at present is partly due to public apathy towards faithfulness in the reception of broadcast music, and partly to the fact that high-fidelity transmission cannot be accomplished without a complete re-allocation of station wave lengths and a reduction in the total number of stations licensed to broadcast—steps which the public at large has at present shown no desire to take, and which, in the second instance, would involve losses as well as gains. ¶Another factor which causes radio music to sound differently from music heard in a concert hall is its lack of dimension or perspective. Technically speaking, it is *monaural*. This term may be best explained by a comparison with vision. We see with two eyes, and in so doing we see two slightly different images. These images, when combined by the brain, give us a sense of distance and direction. Ordinary pictures lack perspective, are two-dimensional; pictures seen through a stereoscope are extraordinarily lifelike simply because each eye is permitted to see each picture from its own particular viewpoint. Similarly, our two ears enable us to recognise the precise direction from which any given sound comes; this quality of hearing is known technically as "aural perspective." Whenever we listen to an orchestra in the concert hall our ears, as well as our eyes, give "dimension" to the orchestra. If, however, a sound-proof wall were erected halfway between us and the orchestra, having in it a single small aperture, the sounds reaching our ears would have to travel through this one point and our sense of aural perspective would be lost. This is what takes place in the transmission of radio music. All sounds are transmitted from one point (the microphone) and, again, are reproduced at one point (the loudspeaker). Successful experiments have been conducted with the *binaural* transmission and reproduction of music. Many obstacles, however, would have to be overcome before "binaural broadcasting" could become commercially practicable. Its successful operation would require two microphones, two independent sets of broadcasting equipment, two separate broadcasting channels, and two receiving sets with properly placed loudspeakers in every home which wished to enjoy its advantages.

SIGNIFICANCE OF RADIO MUSIC

Radio must be considered, not as a form of art, but as a means of conveying art to the multitudes. When so considered, its invention may be counted as being as important to music as the invention of printing was to literature. ¶Before the development of radio, art music—like painting, sculpture, and the drama—was the aristocratic property of an infinitesimally small fraction of the country's total population. Symphony orchestras existed in only a handful of American cities; only a tiny proportion of the residents of these cities subscribed to symphony concerts or listened to them at all regularly; even those fortunate persons heard, in most cases, not more than twenty hours of symphonic music a year, and waited, in many instances, several seasons before hearing a repetition of a favourite symphony or tone poem. Other types of vocal and instrumental music were heard by similarly limited audiences. ¶To-day music has become virtually a universal art. This revolutionary change has been wrought primarily by radio, though to some extent other technical developments—the player piano, phonograph, and motion picture—have assisted the transformation. Some indications of the almost-overnight growth of a nation-wide musical public can be observed in the following facts: Since 1928 the number of major symphony orchestras in America has risen from 10 to 17. In the same period the total number of orchestras (according to listings in Pierre Key's Music Yearbook) has increased from 60 to 286; most medium-sized cities now have their own symphony orchestras. Music courses in the public schools, almost unknown in 1920, are now not only widespread but of high calibre. The number of school orchestras in the country has grown prodigiously; it is now estimated at more than 30,000; in addition, there are more than 20,000 school bands. The business of booking concerts and recitals, as reported by leading concert bureaus, surpassed, in 1937, that of any year since 1912 (including even the prosperous year of 1929). Sales of new pianos in 1937 (exclusive of player pianos or reproducing pianos) exceeded those of 1929, as well as of the intervening years. ¶When radio first ceased to be a novelty, musicians began to fear that radio music would prove to be exceedingly harmful, both economically (by ruining the sale of musical instruments and of concert admissions), and artistically (by producing a nation of passive listeners devoid of musical intelligence and unwilling to create music themselves either as performers or composers). When Walter Damrosch first undertook to conduct symphonic broadcasts, he was begged by noted musicians not to do so; they firmly believed that if radio obtained a foothold in the realm of serious music their concert careers would be doomed. The reverse, however, has proved to be true. Radio has produced thousands of new listeners who have become acquainted with symphonies, operas, *lieder*, etc., and have subsequently come to the conclusion that actual performances of music by living artists provide sources of enjoyment which cannot be duplicated by reproduced music. It seems now definitely established that a permanent place exists for both radio broadcasting and the concert hall—that they are supplementary rather than competitive. ¶Radio has, as yet, developed no striking new musical techniques. A few works have been composed especially for radio performance. These include three radio operas: *"The Willow Tree"* by Charles Wakefield

Cadman (NBC, 1932); *"Green Mansions"* by Louis Gruenberg (CBS, 1937); and *"The Old Maid and the Thief"* by Gian-Carlo Menotti (NBC, 1938). Hans Spialek's orchestral suite, *"Manhattan Water Colors"* (1937), contains continuity to be read by an announcer over a musical background. In other instances radio has been found to be an especially successful medium for music composed as background to spoken narration; a noteworthy example is Frank Black's musical setting of Arthur Guiterman's poem, *"Ode to Memorial Day."* ¶To radio may be attributed the growing public demand for less hackneyed, more unfamiliar music. Since the advent of broadcasting, concert audiences have grown thoroughly familiar with the principal works in the literature of music, so that conductors and recitalists find it necessary to delve more and more into the works of lesser-known composers, as well as into the lesser-known compositions of the acknowledged masters, in order to avoid too-frequent repetitions of the so-called standard works. To radio may also be attributed a partial breakdown of the barrier between popular and classical music. Commercial variety programmes frequently feature famous concert artists in performances of serious music side by side with the most popular types of vaudeville entertainers. Even more significant is radio's effect upon the public's standards of performance. By acquainting audiences everywhere with the supreme artistry of such musicians as Toscanini, Heifetz, Flagstad, etc., radio has raised the public's critical standards immeasurably; as a result, mediocre musicians are no longer tolerated, young artists are experiencing increasingly keen competition, while, on the other hand, top-ranking musicians are enjoying greater success than ever before. ¶One curious aspect of modern radio deserves mention: a handicap created by the very abundance of good music which radio provides. In years gone by, when an opera performance or symphony concert was a rare treat, to be enjoyed only after the expenditure of effort and money, it was approached in a mood of keen anticipation and heard with undivided attention. Now, with similar music available at the flick of a dial, many listeners pay but scant attention to what they hear, being chiefly preoccupied with housework, card playing, or reading. Like easily won riches, music broadcasts are often grossly undervalued and unwittingly squandered. ¶Radio, as a purveyor of music, has certainly not reached its ultimate goal. Yet it has travelled amazingly far in its few years of existence. Complaints are voiced that opportunities to hear serious music on the air are too infrequent, and, conversely, that too many hours are devoted to music devoid of artistic value. Yet the proportion of concert music to light, inconsequential music on the air to-day is probably considerably greater than the proportion of good current literature to the cheap output of tabloid newspapers and pulp magazines. Under the American system of broadcasting, government authorities have no voice in the type or quantity of music broadcast to the public; their jurisdiction is limited to the technical phases of broadcasting and to the elimination of programmes that exceed limits of decency or contain fraudulent advertising. Broadcasting in the United States is based on the democratic principle that the public itself shall choose and judge. This it can do by the turn of a dial, selecting between programmes offered simultaneously by two or more competitive stations. Surveys, polls, and, to some extent, fan letters provide broadcasters with a fairly accurate means of estimating programme popularity. If, under this system, serious music occupies only a minor fraction of the time allotted to music on the air, the reason can be traced to the fact that only a small minority of the radio audience actually prefers such music. Broadcasters maintain a scrupulous regard for the rights of small minorities. It is solely because of this that they allot network time to the presentation of music of extremely limited appeal, such as Bach's complete "*Kunst der Fuge*" or atonal chamber music compositions by little-known contemporary composers. It can be assumed that broadcasters will continue to adjust their programmes in the future, as they have in the past, to conform to changing public tastes, and that they will increase the hours of serious music broadcasts as rapidly as the demand for them grows in volume and insistence.

THE STORY OF ORCHESTRA AND BAND INSTRUMENTS

By H. W. Schwartz

Music is as old as history but the orchestra is a modern development, barely 300 years old. The germ of the orchestra was originated by Italian opera writers in the latter sixteenth and in the seventeenth centuries. Their so-called orchestras contained lutes, lyres, harpsichord, viols, flageolets, zinken, and other strange instruments now obsolete. Even the great Bach and Handel were not equal to the task of deciding what instruments were worthy of membership in the symphony orchestra. ¶Haydn is called the "Father of the Symphony" because he cleaned out these old instruments and established the classical symphony orchestra, about 1760. Other instruments were added from time to time and the modern orchestra was developed. ¶Haydn's orchestra was a small one. He built it around a well-disciplined group of strings consisting of 6 first violins, 6 second violins, 3 violas, and 3 string basses. Note that the 'cello was not admitted. To this group he added 2 trumpets and 2 tympani. The trumpets were really bugles and had no valves, because valves were not invented until 1815. He also added 2 hunting horns. These of course had no valves either. Among the wood-winds were two boxwood or coccuswood flutes with from 3 to 6 brass keys, 2 boxwood or coccuswood oboes with 3 to 6 keys. The famous Boehm system key mechanism for wood-winds was not invented until 1832. Two bassoons completed the wood-winds while the wind bass of the orchestra was furnished by the odd-looking instrument called the serpent. ¶In Haydn's day the orchestra was conducted from the harpsichord. Here the conductor sat and played along with the orchestra, nodding his head and occasionally waving his hand to give the beat and maintain the tempo. The harpsichord was the father of the piano, which was invented in 1709 by Cristofori of Italy but which was not used very generally for nearly a hundred years. Such an orchestra gave a performance which was simple and clear in harmonic structure but lacked solidity, variety, and colour. ¶Mozart was a pupil of Haydn but he taught the old master and all other musicians how to use the clarinets in the symphony orchestra. These instruments were made of boxwood and had about a half-dozen brass keys. It is true that Haydn used clarinets in the opera but Mozart was the first to admit them into the more exclusive ranks of the symphony orchestra. Otherwise the orchestra was the same as the Haydn orchestra. As yet there was no con-ductor to stand in front of the orchestra and beat time. The conductor still sat at the harpsichord. ¶Beethoven as a youth studied with the old master, Haydn, but he was too radical in his views and soon left Haydn to pursue his own ideas. Nevertheless, in his first four symphonies he used substantially the same orchestra as that used by Haydn and Mozart. However, in his cele-brated *Fifth Symphony*, composed in 1808, he found the old classical orchestra inadequate for his musical thought. During the first three movements of this symphony he remained classical but in the fourth movement he worked himself up to such a romantic pitch that he broke the bonds of conventional instrumen-tation and in the statement of the opening theme he introduced 2 trombones. Haydn and Mozart had used trombones in the opera but this was the first time they had ever been used in the symphony. At the same time he wrote for the piccolo, really a high soprano flute. The piccolo had been used by Gluck, the opera writer, even before Haydn's day, but this was the début of the piccolo in the symphony. ¶The string section was also augmented by 4 'cellos. Haydn was really the first to use the 'cello in the orchestra. This he finally consented to do in 1795 in his *Symphony in D*, when he was sixty-three years old. The 'cello's place in the orchestra, however, was not secure until Beethoven's time. Even Beethoven did not always use it. In some of his symphonies he scored for it and in some of them he omitted it. But by the time Beethoven died, the 'cello had become accepted as a regular member of the symphony, and the string quartet gave way to the string quintet. Beethoven not only added new instruments but used more of the old instruments known to Haydn and Mozart. The string section was also increased in number of players. And as for the conductor we still find him behind the harpsichord or piano. The Beethoven orchestra added greater solidity and variety but still lacked definite colour treatment. ¶Wagner was a writer of opera but Wagner's opera music is superb orchestration and is played by the symphony orchestra more than any other music. Wagner composed but three symphonies and only one of these is ever heard and that one only seldom. ¶Beethoven wrote his music on 12 staffs but Wagner increased the musical parts to such an extent that 22 staffs were necessary. He added the bass trombone, made possible by an invention of Sax about 1840. This invention consisted of a thumb valve and tubing which bridged the gap in the tenor trombone from E to B♭ below the staff. He wrote for bass clarinets, first used by Meyerbeer in 1836 in his *"Huguenots"* opera. The English horn, first used by Rossini in his *"William Tell"* opera, in 1828, was included in Wagner's score. ¶In 1832 Boehm invented his great mechanism for flute and this mechanism was adapted to the clarinet in 1843 by Klose. Several features of the system were also incorporated on the oboe, especially the ring keys. Therefore Wagner availed himself of the greater facilities of the new and improved wood-winds, and the old flutes, oboes, and clarinets were replaced by the modern instruments. ¶In 1815 Blumel invented the piston-valve and ten years later the rotary valve. Although these improved instruments were not immediately accepted, they had replaced to a large extent the simple trumpets and hunting horns by the time of Wagner. Instead of the bugle type of trumpet he used the improved piston-valve trumpet such as we use to-day. And instead of the old hunting horn he used the rotary valve

French horn with which we are familiar. He seldom used less than 4 of these and often used 6 or 8. He added the bass tuba and threw out the old serpent. Serpents appear for the last time in his *"Rienzi"* overture in 1842. The German bandmaster, Wieprecht, invented the bass tuba in 1829 and it was perfected by Sax in 1842. Wagner is noted for his treatment of the brass but much of his improved handling is due to the new resources of the instruments made possible by the addition of the valves. ¶The percussion section of Wagner's orchestra is also improved. As early as 1760 the opera composer, Gluck, had, used snare-drum, bass-drum, cymbals, and triangle, and they were also used in opera by Haydn and Mozart, but it was Wagner who established these instruments in the symphony. He also was the first to establish the use of the third tympano, although Weber had used the third tympano as early as 1807. At this time, also, the hand-tuned tympani gave way to the more efficient machine, or pedal, tympani. ¶Besides adding a variety of tonal colouring, Wagner also added to the size of the orchestra, increasing the number of stringed instruments as well as of wind-instruments. ¶With such a superb orchestra Wagner was able to paint a musical picture of which even Beethoven scarcely dreamed. He employed a full choir of wood-winds, a full choir of brass, a full choir of strings, and a large and varied percussion section. He divided these choirs into many separate parts, giving a closely integrated harmony, a wide tonal spectrum, and a great variety of orchestral effects. When his music was first heard it was called barbarous and inharmonic. This was because it was new and the ears of the time were not used to this type of music. It has since been accepted as the greatest music of its kind ever written and is probably the most popular music played by the symphony orchestra to-day. ¶By Wagner's time both the harpsichord and piano had been discarded for the bâton and conductor's podium. This custom of directing with the bâton had been made popular by Berlioz and Mendelssohn and has been common now for over a century. Adolph Sax, a Belgian instrument-maker working in Paris, invented the saxophone in 1840. It was early accepted by such French composers as Berlioz and Meyerbeer and by a few of the German composers. To-day most modern composers score for the saxophones. The saxophones serve to blend the wood-winds and the brasses together. ¶Some additional instruments used by moderns are the vibraphone and tubular chimes. The latter take the place of the giant bells of the carillon. Some ancient percussion instruments to earn their place in the symphony orchestra are the Spanish castanets and oriental tambourine. The moderns are colourists and require a wealth of tonal tints in their musical palette. ¶To-day's bands are an outgrowth of the Elizabethan bands of Shakespeare's time. They were composed of oboes, cornettos, flageolets, bugles, serpents, and other wind-instruments. After Sax invented his family of saxhorns, in 1842, the wind band was primarily of brass. There were sopranos, altos, tenors, barytones, and basses—all cup-mouthpiece instruments. This is still the typical wind band of Italy, Germany, and other European countries. ¶America has developed a new type of band although this development is recent. In Civil War days the band was substantially like the bands of Europe and Canada. Later wood-winds were used more prominently. To-day the Band is patterned in general after the symphony orchestra, clarinets and other wood-winds taking the place of the string section. There is less brass and more wood-winds. ¶An important phase of this development is the use of complete choirs of each family. We have, for instance, soprano clarinets, alto clarinets, bass clarinets, and contrabass clarinets, giving a complete range of clarinet colouring. We also have the soprano oboe, the alto oboe, or English horn, the bass oboe, or bassoon, and the contrabass oboe, or contrabass bassoon. The saxophone family is also complete throughout the entire range of the band. Only the flute family is incomplete although there has been some use of the alto and bass flute. ¶1. *The Violin Family*. The ancestor of the violin is the Greek kithara, the first instrument to have a sound chest with top and back separated by straight ribs. The viols developed from this instrument and were well known in the Middle Ages The viols developed into the violin in the late fifteenth century. One Caspar Tieffenbrucker, of Italian Tyrol, is credited with making the first true violin in 1467, twenty-five years before Columbus discovered America. ¶The making of violins early centred at Brescia, a little town in Lombardy, Italy, fifty miles from the Tyrol border, about 1520. This group of craftsmen flourished for one hundred years. The most famous school, however, was the Cremona school, located about forty miles from Brescia. Here the Amati family began attracting attention about the middle of the sixteenth century. A pupil of Niccolo Amati was Antonius Stradivarius who became the most famous maker of them all. During his long lifetime (1645-1737) he made about 950 violins, besides 150 violas and 'cellos. ¶2. *The Flute*. The oldest wind-instrument is the flute. The most primitive is the syrinx or pipes of Pan. It is found in ancient Egyptian tombs and was a favourite instrument with the Greeks. The flute developed along two lines: those blown from the end and those blown from the side. The side-blown flute, commonly called the German flute, nosed out the end-blown flute in Europe in the fourteenth century. But the end-blown flute was popular in England until about 1700. ¶The first key ever used on a wind-instrument was invented in 1677, inventor unknown. Used to bridge the gap in the diatonic scale at the bottom where cross fingering was impossible. The second key was invented in 1726 by Quantz, flute teacher to Frederick the Great. It was used to overcome enharmonic differences but it turned out to be useless. Keys were added from time to time until Boehm's day, about one hundred years later, when the flute had 8 keys. ¶To correct the imperfections of the current flute, Boehm invented his new flute in 1832. It had 14 holes, but how could he cover these 14 holes with 9 fingers? The ring key system was Boehm's solution. This made the flute playable in all keys and revolutionised the instrument. In 1847 he came out with his cylindrical-bore flute, made of metal. This was a still further improvement, having 15 holes and 23 keys. Other improvements were the clutch and Buffet's needle springs. All flutes to-day are close copies of the Boehm flute, although many improvements have been added to the mechanism. ¶3. *Double Reeds*. The Crusaders brought the first oboes to Europe from the Orient nearly a thousand years ago. Even then they were extremely ancient instruments, having been known to the Egyptians for over fifty centuries. It was not until the orchestra began to bud in Italy in the late sixteenth century that they came to be used as a musical instrument. Bach was the first to use all three voices of the oboe family—the soprano oboe, the alto English horn, and the bass bassoon. This he did in his "*Passion*" music, composed in 1723. His English horn, however, was really the early form of alto known as the oboe *da caccia*, which was later crowded out by the superior English horn, invented in 1760 by Ferlandis of Bergamo. The bassoon is an extremely old instrument, its shape having been invented in 1540 by Alfranio, a Catholic priest. ¶The sarrusophone, a sort of metal bassoon, was invented by the French bandmaster Sarrus in 1856. Although built in a complete family, like the saxophone, only contrabass in Eb is used in America. ¶4. *The Single Reeds.* Whereas the range of all other wind-instruments was about two octaves, the chalumeau (primitive clarinet) could play only an octave. Denner in 1690 discovered the beauty in this instrument and made the clarinet a useful instrument. He found that although the chalumeau would not overblow to the octave, as did the flute and oboe, it would overblow to the twelfth when a small hole was bored into the tube up near the mouthpiece. He then added keys to bridge the gap between the first octave and the twelfth and gave the instrument a chromatic scale of over two octaves. In its key development it followed the trend of the flute and oboe. After the Boehm system was invented, Klose, a great clarinet-player of his day, had a clarinet made for his own use incorporating the Boehm system. This was in 1843 and marks the beginning of the true greatness of the clarinet, for this key system made it playable in all keys. ¶The alto clarinet was invented by Horn of Passau in Bavaria in 1770. He called it the basset horn and its key was F. Beethoven and Mendelssohn wrote for the old basset horn but after the middle of the nineteenth century its mechanism became Boehm, its pitch was changed to Eb, and it was called simply the alto clarinet. ¶The bass clarinet is generally credited to Gresner of Dresden. It was invented in 1793 but apparently nobody used it much until after Sax improved the mechanism about 1840. ¶5. *Trumpet, Fluegelhorn, and Cornet.* The trumpet with its cylindrical bore is as old as history. The ancestor of the fluegelhorn is the ancient bugle which had a conical bore. In the thirteenth century the cornetto, ancestor of to-day's cornet, made its appearance. It had a bore which was midway between the cylindrical bore of the trumpet and the conical bore of the bugle. It was a crude instrument made of wood and covered with leather. ¶All three of these instruments were used in the early orchestras but all three had musical limitations because of the gaps in their natural scale. This defect was not remedied until Blumel invented the piston valve in 1815. To-day the trumpet is the principal soprano of the brass choir in the orchestra, while the cornet is the principal soprano of the brass choir in the band. The fluegelhorn is an important instrument in the band and is used to bridge the tonal gap between the cornets and the horns. ¶6. *The Trombone.* For centuries the trombone was nothing but a big trumpet. But in the fourteenth century some genius in northern Italy discovered when working with the tuning slide of his trumpet that moving the slide changed the pitch of the instrument. He saw clearly that this presented a method of bridging the gaps in the natural scale. At first the slide was long enough to add only 4 semitones but before the middle of the sixteenth century the slide was lengthened to add the 6 semitones found on to-day's slide trombone. ¶The early composers called for the trombone, or sackbut, as it was called. They often scored for 5 trombones—2 altos, 2 tenors, and 1 bass. It was Gluck, the opera composer who first made intelligent use of the trombone. He established the style of writing for the trombone in three parts, a style adhered to ever since. Bach, Handel, Haydn, and Mozart used the trombone in oratorios and operas but they refused to use them in the symphony. Beethoven followed their lead in his first four symphonies. But in his great *Fifth Symphony*, composed in 1808, he introduced the trombones because no other instrument could express his musical thought. ¶Shortly after Blumel's invention of the piston valve, valves were added to the trombone. Strangely enough, however, the valve trombone found no wide popularity except in Italy, the birthplace of the slide. It was Sax who added the thumb valve to the bass trombone which bridged the gap between the first and second partial, making it chromatic throughout. This he did before 1850. ¶7. *The French Horn.* Oldest type of horn is the Hebrew *shofar*, made from ram's horn. Our French horn came from the horn used in the chase by French kings. French horns were introduced into the orchestra by Lully in 1664. In Germany the old "waldhorn," or forest horn, made its début in the orchestra in 1705, when Keiser wrote for a pair of horns in his opera *"Octavia."* In 1715 Handel introduced the horns into England, in his *"Water Music."* Six years later Bach called for two horns in his first *"Brandenburg"* concerto, and the place of the horns became assured. ¶Hampl, a Dresden horn-player, invented his famous "machine horn" in 1753. This invention permitted the insertion of the crooks not in the mouthpipe but in the body of the horn and improved intonation. Hampl seven years later discovered that by stopping the horn with the hand the pitch could be raised a semitone and a full tone. This gave a whole new series of notes without the use of slides. The hand-horn became the standard horn and survived until a long time after valves were invented. ¶In 1815 Blumel invented the piston valve. In 1827 he followed this with a rotary valve which has survived on the French horn. In spite of the superiority of the valve horn over the hand-horn, it was twenty years before it was generally called for by composers; and even then, the hand-horn was usually called for for the first and third horn parts, the second and fourth being given to the valve horn. It was not until Wagner's time that the hand-horn gave way to the valve horn, along toward the middle of the nineteenth century. ¶8. *The Tuba Family.* In 1590 Guillaume of Auxerre invented the serpent, a queer-looking instrument about eight feet long, made of wood and covered with leather. It flourished for two hundred years as an important bass instrument, but it is chiefly known for its many and varied progeny. Among these are the ophicleides, a family of six. ¶It was from this family of ophicleides that Sax got his idea for the saxhorns, a family of cup-mouthpiece instruments with piston valves and a conical bore, invented in 1842. Not satisfied with this conical bore, Sax a few years later made another complete family of instruments which he called the saxtrombas. These were very similar to the saxhorns except that the bore was not so conical, being more nearly cylindrical. Although these instruments did not find favour in Europe and quickly died out, our own tubas are really saxtrombas. Whereas the tone of the saxhorns was round and mellow, the tone of the saxtrombas and of our tubas is more solid and on the brilliant side. Since the saxhorns and saxtrombas were not invented until the middle of the nineteenth century, Wagner, Berlioz, and their contemporaries were the first composers to profit by their use. ¶All upright cup-mouthpiece instruments are tubas. These include the alto tuba, the tenor tuba, the barytone tuba, the euphonium, the E♭ bass tuba, and the BB♭ bass tuba; but it is customary in America to use the word tuba for only the bass tubas. The Wagnerian *tuben* do not really belong to this family, although they are cup-mouthpiece instruments and they are in the shape of the upright tubas. They are essentially French horns built in tenor and barytone voices. ¶C. G. Conn made the first sousaphone in 1897, expressly for John Philip Sousa's band. This instrument had the upright bell and Sousa refused to use any other to the end of his days. In 1908 Conn built the first bell-front sousaphone which has superseded the original bell-up model. ¶9. *The Saxophones.* The saxophone was invented by Adolph Sax, a Belgian instrument-maker working in Paris, in 1840. He got his idea while trying to fit a clarinet mouthpiece to the ophicleide, an old cup-mouthpiece instrument. He liked the strange blending of the brass tone of the ophicleide with the reedy tone of the clarinet. He worked over the key mechanism of the ophicleide and this modification of the ophicleide key mechanism became the saxophone mechanism. ¶His family of saxophones included the high Eb soprano, the Bb soprano, the Eb alto, the Bb tenor, the Eb barytone, and the Bb bass. Other members which have since been added are the C soprano, the C tenor or melody, and the F mezzo soprano. Occasionally one sees the contrabass in Eb. C. G. Conn built the first saxophone ever constructed in America, in 1888. ¶10. *Percussion Instruments.* In this family are the instruments struck in various manners to produce sound. They are the most primitive and the oldest of all musical instruments. Divided into two classes: (1) those without musical pitch, such as drums, tomtoms, cymbals, castanets, and (2) those with musical pitch, such as tympani, chimes, bells, vibraphone. ¶The Moors brought kettle-drums to Europe in 711 A.D. Virdung, German historian of music writing, in 1511 describes the kettle-drums of his day, as does Praetorius about a hundred years later. First used in opera by Lully in seventeenth century. Bach and Handel used kettle-drums as did almost all subsequent composers. Weber first to use 3 tympani, in 1807, although Berlioz claims this distinction. Pfund, tympanist for Mendelssohn, invented the machine tympani about 1840. ¶Wagner was most prominent early user of chimes, as in *"Parsifal."* Also used orchestra bells, as in *"Die Walküre."* Saint-Saëns used xylophone to good effect in his *"Danse Macabre."* Tschaikowsky introduced the celesta in the symphony, in his *"Casse-Noisette."* Gluck introduced the drums into the orchestra about 1760. Mozart used bass-drum, cymbal, and triangle a few years later. Origin of snare-drum came from Scotch practice of whipping drum with leather thongs. Tambourine known to Greeks, Assyrians, etc. One of first uses was by Weber, in *"Precosia."* Castanets (word means chestnut wood) are of Spanish origin. One of most famous uses is in Bizet's *"Carmen."* Tamtams are a form of large gong, while tomtoms are small drums with thick leather heads. Cymbals are of Turkish origin and are popular in producing oriental effects. Haydn started the use of "effects" in his *"Seasons."* He started with such sounds as thunder, quail call, and gunshot. Hundreds of effects have been added since his time. *(See "Orchestras and Orchestration," page 778; "Orchestras in America," page 787; "Orchestration of Theatre and Dance Music," page 780; and Dictionary of Terms entry, page 648.)*

SWING MUSIC

By James A. Poling

Swing is a form of music indigenous to America. Its history is vague but it is conventionally believed that swing music originated in the deep South around the first decade of this century. Certainly the first recognised great swing musician was Buddy Balden, a black New Orleans cornetist, and, musically speaking, the grandfather of Louis Armstrong, recognised to-day as one of the greatest swing artists of all time. ¶Swing music made its first important bid for popular approval in 1916, with the appearance at Reisenweber's restaurant in New York of The Original Dixieland Jazz Band. Ted Lewis and Paul Whiteman helped spread its popularity and they in turn were followed by Red Nichols and countless other bands until the popularity of swing became international. Swing music's popularity was climaxed in 1938 with the appearance at Carnegie Hall of Benny Goodman (the greatest clarinetist of his time) and his band in an all-swing concert. ¶Swing differs from other music in that in other musical forms the orchestra re-creates the composer's musical ideas just as the composer conceived them. The performer is in a secondary rôle. In swing the performer appears in a more creative rôle. Through improvisation (*the soul and heartblood of swing*) the performer transforms the composer's fundamental melodic idea into his own conception of the theme. In other words, the swing musician does not simply convey to the listener what was original with the composer; he himself *creates* the musical substance his auditors hear. Hugh Panassie in his book *Hot Jazz* says, "To ignore the talent of the orchestra in jazz (swing) is like ignoring the talent of the composer in classical music." ¶Swing is characterised by a musical idiom and attitude, rather than by a tempo. It is generally polyphonic music composed of melodies that support one another, as contrasted to homophonic music in which the melody is supported by chords. *Ad lib* variations on a simple theme; counterpoint, particularly of the fourth or syncopated variety; involved harmonies; and syncopation, in which the accent is shifted to the unstressed part of a beat or measure—these are fundamental to swing. ¶Whether or not swing is a transient musical form is a subject of considerable debate. The answer generally given by swing addicts is the now classic statement of Louis Armstrong, greatest cornetist of them all, "Folks, take it from me—we couldn't live without a little *swing* now and then, mostly then."

SYNOPSES OF NINETY OPERAS CURRENT IN PRESENT-DAY REPERTOIRES

The operas are arranged alphabetically according to title, and where there is an accepted English title it is used in preference to the original.

AFRICAINE, L'

Composer: GIACOMO MEYERBEER

Book by EUGÈNE SCRIBE

First performance: *Opéra, Paris, April 28, 1865*

5 acts.

VASCO DA GAMA, who is pledged to marry Inez, daughter of a Portuguese admiral, returns with information about a new land and two natives to prove it: Selika, an Indian queen, and Nelusko, attendant. Don Diego, father of Inez, has tried to get her to marry Don Pedro, who now throws Vasco in jail. Selika comes there to protect him from the murderous intent of the jealous Nelusko, and to tell him of her love. Don Pedro decides to find the new land for himself and takes Inez with him, also taking Selika and Nelusko as guides. The latter plans to destroy the ship—a plan which Vasco knows about. He pursues the party in a second ship to warn them. Don Pedro pays no heed and the crew is killed. Vasco's life is spared when Selika informs the natives that he is her husband. However, when Vasco finds that Inez was not killed in the massacre he leaves Selika for his old love. The Indian Queen in despair kills herself, as the faithful Nelusko does likewise, by breathing the poisonous scent of the manchineel tree.

AÏDA

Composer: GIUSEPPE VERDI

Book by ANTONIO GHISLANZONI and composer from Camille du Locle's work, and a sketch by the Egyptologist Mariette

First performance: *Opera, Cairo, December 24, 1871*

4 acts.

AÏDA, living as a slave to Amneris in the Pharaoh's palace at Memphis, is actually the daughter of King Amonasro, invading Ethiopian. Aïda loves Radames who has been selected to defend Egypt against King Amonasro's forces. Amneris, Aïda's mistress, is the daughter of the Pharaoh. She also loves Radames. He returns successful from the Wars and brings with him among the prisoners Amonasro. Aïda goes to her father's arms but does not reveal his rank. Radames asks that all prisoners be set free. All are, except Amonasro. On the banks of the Nile, at night, Radames is waiting to see Aïda one last time before he must marry Amneris. Amonasro persuades Aïda to get Radames to flee with her, also to give information that will help the rearming Ethiopians. She persuades Radames but in getting the information is overheard by Amneris who had gone to spend the night before her marriage in the temple of Isis in prayer. Amonasro and Aïda escape but Radames is caught and sentenced to death by suffocation for treason. Radames spurns freedom at the cost of marrying Amneris and prepares to die. In the tomb Aïda has concealed herself and dies with him.

AMORE DEI TRE RE, L'
(*The Love of the Three Kings*)

Composer: ITALO MONTEMEZZI

Book by SEM BENELLI

First performance: *La Scala, Milan, April 20, 1913*

3 acts.

A TALE of the early days when Huns still invaded Italy. Archibaldo, a Germanic, is conqueror of Altura. Fiora, beautiful native daughter, is married to Manfredo, the conqueror's son, against her own wishes, for she loves Avito, an Alturan prince. Flaminio, aid to Archibaldo, helps this romance as Avito visits the castle often during Manfredo's absences. The affair is assisted by the fact that Archibaldo is blind. Archibaldo is convinced that someone visits Fiora but though he accuses her she will tell him nothing. Manfredo leaves Fiora after a very moving scene in which she almost falls in love with him. But Avito comes immediately after Manfredo leaves and Fiora knows her heart is his. Archibaldo overhears them, Flaminio barely restraining Avito from killing the blind old man. Archibaldo questions her and when she won't tell the name of her lover, kills her. Manfredo, on his return, is overcome with grief but Archibaldo vows he will find the man who made Fiora unfaithful. He puts Fiora's body in a crypt and smears poison on her lips. Avito comes to kiss her farewell and dies, telling Manfredo, who has entered, that Fiora loved him. At this Manfredo wishes only death and kisses Fiora. When Archibaldo enters to identify the victim of his trap he realises in horror that he has destroyed the one most dear to him, his son.

ARIADNE AND BLUEBEARD
(*Ariane et Barbe-Bleue*)

Composer: PAUL DUKAS
Book by MAURICE MAETERLINCK
First performance: *Opéra comique, Paris, May 10, 1907*
3 acts.

ARIADNE is the most recent of Bluebeard's wives. She has come to his castle
in spite of the warnings of the peasantry. Given six silver keys which she may
use and one gold one which she may not, she takes but a cursory glance at the
jewel-filled rooms which the former open and immediately uses the gold key.
She hears the cries of distress of the five earlier wives of Bluebeard. She brings
them out into the light, gives them the jewels and then smiles sardonically,
when Bluebeard returns to his castle, bound and wounded by his enraged
peasantry, for the five wives immediately serve him with new attachment.
Ariadne leaves, never to return.

BARBER OF SEVILLE, THE
(*Il Barbiere di Sivigla*)

Composer: GIOACCHINO ROSSINI
Book by CESARE STERBINI, from Beaumarchais' comedy *Le Barbier de
Seville*
First performance: *Teatro di Torre Argentina, Rome, February 20, 1816*
2 acts.

COUNT ALMAVIVA, disguised as Lindoro, wishes to marry Rosina, ward of Dr.
Bartolo who himself wants to marry her. Figaro, the barber, is asked to help
the count. Don Basilio, the music teacher, protects Rosina for Dr. Bartolo
but she contrives to let the Count know by note that she returns his love.
Balked in his attempt to enter the house as a drunken soldier, the Count later
arrives in the disguise of Don Basilio, who is supposedly indisposed. Figaro
steals the key to the balcony as he shaves the doctor. Don Basilio who arrives
is hushed up and sent off with a bribe. Later he returns to tell Dr. Bartolo,
who is outraged. While the doctor is getting a notary to marry him to Rosina
(who believes now that the Count is untrue to her) Basilio returns with the
notary after Figaro and the Count have arrived. The Count throws off his
disguise to clear himself with Rosina and the two are married by the notary
Basilio had fetched for Dr. Bartolo. This worthy is appeased when the Count
signs Rosina's dowry over to him.

BARTERED BRIDE, THE

Composer: BEDŘICH SMETANA

Book by KAREL SABINA

First performance: *National Theatre, Prague, May 30, 1866*

3 acts.

HANS, recently arrived in the Bohemian village, is in love with Marie whose wealthy parents want her to marry a half-idiot, Wenzel, son of another wealthy family. Marie returns Hans' love but it is impossible to get her parents' consent. Marie absolutely refuses to marry Wenzel and finally a marriage broker is called in. Kezal, the broker, does what he can to persuade Hans to retire, even offering him money. At this point Hans agrees to three hundred crowns if the words "Marie shall marry only Micha's son" are in the contract. Kezal is delighted, and Marie is unhappy because Hans appears to have sold her out. But it develops that Hans is a son by Micha's earlier marriage. Marie and he can be married and can also keep the three hundred crowns as a wedding present.

BOHÈME, LA
(Bohemia)

Composer: GIACOMO PUCCINI

Book by GIUSEPPE GIACOSA and LUIGI ILLICA, from Henri Murger's novel, *Scènes de la vie de Bohème*

First performance: *Teatro Regio, Turin, February 1, 1896*

4 acts.

RODOLFO, poet, Marcello, painter, Schaunard, musician, and Colline, philosopher, are starving in a Paris attic when one of them gets sufficient money for a real meal to which all save Rodolfo repair immediately. He stays to write an article and thereby meets Mimi, an upstairs neighbour who has stumbled into his room in a faint. He revives her and takes her to the restaurant where the others are eating. An old love of Marcello's, Musetta, arrives with an elderly admirer and immediately dispatches him in favour of Marcello. Months later these two are running a wine shop while the romance of Mimi and Rodolfo has been killed by his terrific jealousy. Mimi, who is ill, returns for one last sight of her lover. Later she is taken in by the quartet who are having another extemporaneous feast because of a sudden small windfall. Sick, she is put to bed while medicine is procured through Musetta's gift of her earrings. Mimi dies as Rodolfo realises her love for him. Musetta and Marcello, who have quarrelled, are reunited by the scene.

BORIS GODUNOFF

Composer: MODEST MOUSSORGSKY

Book by the composer, from the play by Alexander Pushkin

First performance: *Imperial Opera House, St. Petersburg, January 24, 1874*

3 acts.

THE SCENE of this opera is laid in Russia where Boris Godunoff has murdered the Czarevitch Dimitri and has himself taken the throne of the country. Enraged by this action a novitiate of a monastery impersonates Dimitri and proceeds toward Moscow. A young Polish girl of rank, Marina, wants to marry Dimitri and ascend the throne with him. Rumours of the masquerader have reached Boris who is already repenting the murder of the Czarevitch. When the would-be Dimitri arrives in Moscow, the aroused public condemns him to death. Boris dies of remorse, leaving the throne to his son.

CARMEN

Composer: GEORGES BIZET

Book by HENRI MEILHAC and LUDOVIC HALÉVY, based on Prosper Mérimée's story

First performance: *Opéra comique, Paris, March 3, 1875*

4 acts.

CARMEN, a Spanish coquette, is arrested for fighting in the cigarette factory of Seville. José, the sergeant put in charge of her, is overcome by her beauty and offers of love. He allows her to escape. For this he is imprisoned. When he regains his freedom he joins a smuggling ring to which Carmen belongs. José is called away to his mother's death bed and on returning finds Carmen has given her affections to Escamillo, a bullfighter. José pleads with her to return to him but she scorns him. Insane with love and jealousy, he stabs her to death

CAVALLERIA RUSTICANA
(*Rustic Chivalry*)

Composer: PIETRO MASCAGNI

Book by G. TARGIONI-TOZZETTI and G. MENASCI, from a story by Giovanni Verga

First performance: *Teatro Costanzi, Rome, May 17, 1890*

1 act.

SANTUZZA has been loved and deserted by Turiddu, local Don Juan. He now loves Lola who is married to Alfio. When Santuzza pleads with him on Easter morning to marry her to protect her from the scandal that must be he knocks her down. As Lola and Turiddu go into Mass they laugh at her. This is too much for Santuzza who finds Alfio and tells him that Lola and Turiddu are carrying on together and are at the moment in the church. Alfio picks a fight with Turiddu and they go off to duel. Mama Lucia, Santuzza's mother, stays with her to hear the result. When the crowd comes running back crying that Alfio has killed Turiddu, Santuzza swoons into her mother's arms.

CONTES D'HOFFMANN, LES

See The Tales of Hoffmann

COQ D'OR, LE
(*The Golden Cock*)

Composer: NIKOLAI RIMSKY-KORSAKOV

Book by VLADIMIR BIELSKY, from a poem by Alexander Pushkin

First performance: *Zimin's Private Theatre, Moscow, May, 1910*

3 acts.

A GOLDEN COCK has been set up in the council chambers of the mythical King, Dodon. The astrologer who put it there claims unusual powers for it. When the cock crows after the King has retired he discovers that the King's son has taken an army and gone out to fight. The King follows. Though he finds his son and the army dead he is relieved of suffering by the sight of the Queen of Shemaka, beautiful beyond words. She accepts his offer of marriage and back they go to his palace. The Astrologer wants to be paid for the Golden Cock and asks the Queen as his price. The King kills the Astrologer whereupon the Golden Cock attacks the King and kills him with his beak. In a dreadful storm that ensues the Queen and the bird disappear. When morning arrives the people mourn the loss of King Dodon. The Astrologer, revived, tells the audience not to worry about the situation since he and the Queen are the only people alive in the kingdom of Dodon anyhow.

COSÌ FAN TUTTE
(*They All Do It*)

Composer: WOLFGANG AMADEUS MOZART

Book by LORENZO DA PONTE

First performance: *Burgtheater, Vienna, January 26, 1790*

2 acts.

DON ALFONSO bets two young officer friends that if they leave their wives for a time, no matter how much the wives love their husbands, the ladies will be unfaithful.   The husbands leave and return masquerading as merchants.   At first neither wife will give in to the ardent advances of the attractive strangers, but finally each does.   In the end the whole matter is cleared up happily, not without some skillful maneuvering by Don Alfonso's helper, Despina, the maid.

CYRANO

Composer: WALTER DAMROSCH

Book by W. J. HENDERSON, from Edmond Rostand's play *Cyrano de Bergerac*

First performance: *Metropolitan Opera House, New York, February 27, 1913*

4 acts.

THE LEADER of the Gascony cadets, Cyrano, loves Roxane, who in turn loves Christian de Neuvillette, a somewhat inarticulate friend of Cyrano's.   Cyrano supplies the words for Christian's famous balcony wooing of Roxane as he (Cyrano) hides in the bushes while Christian seems to speak as one inspired. After Roxane and Christian are married she rushes to the battlefield of Arras to see her husband and perhaps die with him.   The love letters from Christian to Roxane had been written, of course, by Cyrano and Christian accuses Cyrano of having pled his own rather than Christian's case in love.   Rushing into the battle he is quickly brought back dead.   Roxane enters a convent and it isn't until years later that she discovers the fact, even though Cyrano denies it, that Cyrano has loved her always.

DON GIOVANNI

Composer: WOLFGANG AMADEUS MOZART

Book by LORENZO DA PONTE

First performance: *National Theatre, Prague, October 28, 1787*

2 acts.

PATTERNED AFTER the career of the legendary Don Juan this is the story of Don Giovanni who, with his servant, Leporello, enter the house of the Commendatore of Seville to get his daughter, Donna Anna, with whom the Don for the moment is enamoured.   She screams for help and in escaping the Don kills the Commendatore.   As he leaves he is intercepted by Donna Elvira, a woman he has wronged.   As the Don dashes away Leporello shocks her with a listing of the Don's endless affairs.   Don Giovanni, meanwhile, has fallen in love with Zerlina, peasant fiancée of Masetto, and has broken up her wedding party in his attempt to seduce her.   But even the party he gives at his home for peasantry and gentry alike is not successful.   Donna Elvira protects the girl.   Later, after asking the statue of the dead Commendatore to dine with him, he is warned by Donna Elvira, still faithful to him, of dangers about to beset him. Leporello arrives screaming that the statue of the Commendatore is about to enter the room. The Don does not flee but grasps the hand of the statue and is hurled into Hell which opens at the Commendatore's feet.

DONNE CURIOSE, LE
(*The Inquisitive Ladies*)

Composer: ERMANNO WOLF-FERRARI

Book by LUIGI SUGANA, from a play by Carlo Goldini.

First performance: *Residenztheater, Munich, November 27, 1903*

3 acts.

A LIGHT COMEDY in which two lady's maids and their mistresses are anxious to know what goes on in a men's club where women are not permitted. After several trials they arrive inside to find husbands and friends dining well. When the ladies have been forgiven their invasion, the party grows gay with dancing. Rosaura and Florindo provide the only particular love interest.

ELEKTRA
(*Electra*)

Composer: RICHARD STRAUSS

Book by HUGO VON HOFMANNSTHAL, from Sophocles

First performance: *Hofoper, Dresden, January 25, 1909*

1 act.

NEAR THE SERVANTS' QUARTERS of the palace at Mycenae, beside the grave of King Agamemnon, is the scene of this opera. Electra, daughter of Agamemnon wants to avenge her father's murder at the hands of her mother, Clytemnestra, now married to Aegisthus. This pair have reduced Electra and her sister, Chrysothemis, to the status of servants. Their brother Orestes has escaped Clytemnestra is obsessed with superstitions and asks Electra to foretell her days. When Electra does so Clytemnestra screams but is comforted by news from another source that Orestes, who is fated to kill her, is dead. Electra does not believe that he is. She tries to get Chrysothemis to kill Clytemnestra but Chrysothemis is not able. Orestes appears and at first does not recognise his sister Electra. When he does he goes into the palace and kills Clytemnestra. Later he also kills Aegisthus. Wild with joy Electra dances on her father's grave while Chrysothemis screams for Orestes. There is no answer.

EMPEROR JONES, THE

Composer: LOUIS GRUENBERG

Book by the composer from Eugene O'Neill's play

First performance: *Metropolitan Opera House, New York, January 7, 1933*

2 acts (prologue, interlude, and 6 scenes).

BRUTUS JONES, self-termed "emperor" of the Negroes of a West Indian island, has learned from a white trader, Smithers, that the natives intend to kill him. Jones, a former Pullman porter, has risen to his rank on the island by his crafty methods. Taking five lead cartridges and one silver one (for himself, if necessary), Jones plunges into the jungle. He is beset by the visions of men he has tortured, and finally by horrible shapes conjured up by voodoo and witch doctors. He uses his five bullets and finally fires the silver sixth bullet at a Crocodile God, brought to existence by a witch doctor. In the morning he finds he has fled in a wide circle and is back at the edge of the jungle where he is easily captured.

FALSTAFF

Composer: GIUSEPPE VERDI

Book by ARRIGO BOITO, from Shakespeare

First performance: *La Scala, Milan, February 9, 1893*

3 acts.

SIR JOHN FALSTAFF, plotting affairs with both Mrs. Page and Mrs. Ford, wishes to make them pay out financially. The ladies themselves, however, are in on the plot, thanks to Dame Quickly, and are attempting a counterplot. Anne Page, who is in love with the threadbare Fenton, it is hoped by her parents will marry much better. Sir John accepts the invitations to a tête-à-tête sent him by Mrs. Ford and Mrs. Page. Ford himself, dressed as a man named Fontana, delivers the invitations. Sir John attired in his best wooing garments goes to the Fords' house as Fontana (Ford) follows. There, to save Sir John from discovery, after a variety of horseplay, he is tumbled out the window into the Thames. Ford's anger is eased by seeing Sir John's humiliating situation. Wine revives Sir John, however, and he is ready to fall into another trap when Mrs. Ford again invites him to a rendezvous in Windsor Forest. He is to come disguised as a hunter. He arrives and this time elaborate preparations have been made to receive him. Mrs. Ford goes as the Queen of Fairies, Mrs. Page as a nymph, Dame Quickly as a witch, and scores of children as sprites and elves. Sir John, in the moonlit forest scene, is chased and hounded by all until he admits that he has been bested. All unmask for a last chorus together, not before, however, Anne has taken part in a mock marriage ceremony with Fenton, which, it develops, was no mockery but real.

FAUST

Composer: CHARLES GOUNOD

Book by JULES BARBIER and MICHEL CARRÉ, from *Faust* by Goethe

First performance: *Théâtre Lyrique, Paris, March 19, 1850*

5 acts.

FAUST is about to kill himself with poison when Mephistopheles appears in his study and offers him youth in exchange for his soul. Faust accepts after Marguerite is revealed to him at her spinning wheel. Faust and Marguerite fall in love, after which Valentin, her brother, returns from the wars and fights a duel with Faust in which Valentin is killed. Faust and Mephistopheles visit Marguerite in prison where she is waiting death because she killed the child Faust has fathered. Marguerite will not go with them and she is redeemed by her appeals to Heaven. Faust and Mephistopheles disappear.

FIDELIO

Composer: LUDWIG VON BEETHOVEN

Book by JOSEPH SONNLEITHNER and GEORG FRIEDRICH TREITSCHKE from a play by Jean Nicolas Bouilly

First performance: *Theater an der Wien, Vienna, November 20, 1805*

2 acts.

FLORESTAN is the political prisoner of Don Pizarro and is slowly being starved to death in the deepest dungeon of the prison. Leonore, his devoted wife, is unable to explain his sudden disappearance, and finally disguised as a man (Fidelio) goes to the prison and becomes the assistant of the friendly jailor, Rocco. Marcelline, daughter of Rocco, becomes enamoured of Fidelio and invites the jealousy of Jacquino, turnkey who loves her. By encouraging this affair between herself and Marcelline, Leonore (Fidelio) is able to discover that a mysterious prisoner is being given a slow death in the dungeon. Don Pizarro, frightened by a letter from his superior, indicating a visit to the prison, instructs the watch to give a trumpet blast when Don Fernando, his superior, is sighted. He tries to bribe Rocco to kill Florestan in order to get him out of sight but Rocco will only agree to dig the grave. Rocco takes Fidelio with him into the depths of the prison to dig it. There Leonore (Fidelio) reveals herself to Florestan, and draws a pistol on Don Pizarro who arrives to murder Florestan. Don Fernando is announced by the trumpet call and Don Pizarro is lighted up to the surface where he is relieved of his position and Florestan and Leonore are happily reunited.

FLYING DUTCHMAN, THE
(*Der Fliegende Holländer*)

Composer: RICHARD WAGNER

Book by the composer

First performance: *Hoftheater, Dresden, January 2, 1843*

3 acts.

BASED ON THE LEGEND of the Flying Dutchman, this is the history of Vander·
decken who vowed he could sail around the Cape of Good Hope in spite of bad
weather. As payment for such a rash oath he was doomed to sail until he could
find a woman who would be eternally true to him. Vanderdecken meets a
Norwegian sea captain, Daland. He tells Daland about the rich cargo he is
carrying and offers to pay well to stay at Daland's home which is not far from
the port in which they meet. In the Daland household, meantime, Senta, the
daughter, gazes at a picture of the Flying Dutchman. To her amazement his
reincarnation appears in the doorway with her father. Erik, who loves her,
has been in despair because of her obsession with the picture and her desire to
free the man from his endless pilgrimage on the sea. After Vanderdecken and
Senta are alone together she quickly accepts his offer of marriage. Later, however, Vanderdecken sees Senta pursued by Erik and decides if she would give
up one man she might another. Without any warning he therefore boards his
ship and sails away. Senta, rushing to the top of a cliff, screams that she has
been faithful unto death and leaps into the sea. At this the ship sinks and in
the background the pair can be seen mounting heavenward together.

FREISCHÜTZ, DER
(*The Free-Shooter*)

Composer: CARL MARIA VON WEBER

Book by JOHANN FRIEDRICH KIND, from a story in the Gespensterbuch

First performance: *Schauspielhaus, Berlin, June 8, 1821*

3 acts.

THE DEMON ZAMIEL has persuaded Kaspar, devotee of Prince Ottokar of Bohemia, to bargain his soul for a set of magic bullets. Agathe, daughter of
Kuno, the Prince's chief huntsman, loves Max and wants to marry him. Kaspar and Zamiel conspire to make Max a poor shot in the first round of competition for Kuno's position (that worthy is retiring). Max is encouraged to meet
Kaspar and Zamiel where he will receive the magic bullets . . . *i.e.*, Kaspar
will be relieved of the burden of them, and Zamiel will accept Max as his new
ward. Agathe receives a magic wreath from a holy hermit. At the next contest. Max shoots perfectly six times with six of the magic bullets which will do

his will, but the seventh must do Zamiel's. The demon forces Max to shoot Agathe, whose magic wreath, however, saves her life, deflecting the bullet so that it kills Kaspar. Max and Agathe can now wed.

FRIEDENSTAG, DER
(*The Day of Peace*)

Composer: RICHARD STRAUSS

Book by JOSEPH GREGOR

First performance: *National Theatre, Munich, July 24, 1938*

1 act.

DURING THE THIRTY YEARS' WAR a besieged town is being held by a Commander and his Catholic adherents who would rather die than give up. Outside, the besieging troops, led by Holsteiner, are pressing the town hard. A letter from the Emperor, sent by special messenger, orders the town held at all costs. The messenger sings a song of peace which instantly brings cries from the populace who want bread. They plead with the Commander to give in but he will not. The Commander tells the people that they will receive a sign before noon, at which time the gates will be opened. Intending to quiet them while he can make his preparations, the Commander goes ahead with his plan to blow up the town and kill everyone, himself as well. His wife, Maria, hears the preparations in the vaults under the city, and comes to plead with her husband. He is adamant. The enemy is sighted approaching with obvious banners of peace. The Commander cannot believe that this is other than a hoax. Finally, however, Maria, on her knees before her Commander-husband, persuades him to take the proffered hand of the enemy leader, Holsteiner. The populace breaks out into a hymn of peace.

GIANNI SCHICCHI

Composer: GIACOMO PUCCINI

Book by GIOACCHINO FORZANO

First performance: *Metropolitan Opera House, New York, December 14, 1918*

1 act.

THE ESTATE of Buoso Donati has been left not to his immediate relatives, but to charity. The relatives, gathered at his bedside after his death, are in a quandary to find a method of breaking the will. One member of the family, Runuccio, suggests that his prospective father-in-law, Gianni Schicchi, a gentleman of considerable guile and cleverness, be called in. He presents the only possible solution for the situation which is instantly put into action. Since no one except those in the death chamber know of Donati's demise, the body is removed and Gianni Schicchi impersonates Donati. The doctor calls and is delighted to find his patient still alive (he does not recognise the substitution). Gianni Schicchi then calls for legal support and dictates a new will. When the relieved relatives read the will they discover to their horror that he has willed the major part of the estate to Gianni Schicchi! And no one can contest it since each has been a part of the first criminal action.

GIOCONDA, LA
(*The Smiling One*)

Composer: AMILCARE PONCHIELLI

Book by TOBIA GORRIO (Arrigo Boito) from Victor Hugo's play *Angelo, tyran de Padoue*

First performance: *La Scala, Milan, April 8, 1876*

4 acts.

ENZO GRIMALDO, a pirate in the Adriatic, loves Laura Adorno who is married to Alvise Badoero, an inquisitor. La Gioconda is in love with Enzo even though she is a street singer, and he of noble birth. She supports her blind mother, La Cieca. Barnaba, a spy, wants to possess La Gioconda. In a wild scene before the Doges' Palace in Venice Barnaba arranges for Enzo and Laura to meet on an island. He advises Alvise that the meeting will take place. La Gioconda also learns of this rendezvous. Previously, La Cieca has been accused of witchcraft and would have been killed had it not been for the intervention of Laura to whom La Cieca gave her rosary. On the island Enzo and Barnaba arrive, as do shortly Laura and, finally, La Gioconda. The latter is about to stab Laura when she sees her mother's rosary and desists. Alvise is about to arrive on a vessel when Laura and Gioconda leave the island while Enzo burns his ship. Back in Venice Alvise is bent on avenging his honour and arranges to have Laura drink poison. La Gioconda substitutes a sleeping potion so that later at a ball when Alvise draws aside a curtain he reveals a sleeping, though apparently dead, Laura. Enzo is arrested for denouncing Barnaba and, in the general mêlée, La Cieca is taken off by Barnaba. La Gioconda cries that she will give herself to Barnaba if he will but spare Enzo's life. In the last act Enzo comes to La Gioconda and tells her that he only wants to die on Laura's bier. La Gioconda then tells him that Laura, who has been brought in still apparently dead, is only sleeping. She awakens and attests her love for Enzo. La Gioconda helps the two depart in safety to Illyria while she waits to stab herself as Barnaba enters to collect on the bargain they made to free Enzo. To partially avenge himself in losing La Gioconda, Barnaba screams that he has killed La Cieca, but La Gioconda does not hear. She is dead.

GIOIELLI DELLA MADONNA, I
See The Jewels of the Madonna

GIRL OF THE GOLDEN WEST, THE
(*La Fanciulla Del West*)

Composer: GIACOMO PUCCINI

Book by GUELFO CIVINI and CARLO ZANGARINI from David Belasco's play of the same name

First performance: *Metropolitan Opera House, New York, December 10, 1910*

3 acts.

IN THE CALIFORNIA of 1849 Minnie owns a saloon to which Sheriff Rance comes repeatedly to propose marriage. She is not interested but is attracted to a newcomer, Dick Johnson. When the Sheriff and men leave as a posse to search for the outlaw, Ramerrez, Minnie invites Johnson to her cabin for a tête-à-tête. During their love scene the Sheriff knocks and enters, not before Johnson has been hidden above the rafters, however. When Rance has left Johnson admits he is the outlaw, and Minnie tells him to leave. He is later wounded and returns. She repents, hides him again, and almost convinces Rance who has returned that Johnson (Ramerrez) is not there. But blood dropping from the rafters gives Johnson away and Minnie plays poker for his life: Johnson to go free if she wins, and she herself to marry Rance if she loses. She cheats and wins. In the final scene Johnson has been captured and is about to be hung but Minnie intercedes, and the crowd gives him up to her so that the pair can go off to begin a new life together.

GÖTTERDÄMMERUNG

See Ring of the Nibelung

GUILLAUME TELL

See William Tell

HÄNSEL UND GRETEL

Composer: ENGELBERT HUMPERDINCK

Book by ADELHEID WETTE, from a fairy tale by the Brothers Grimm.

First performance: *Hoftheater, Weimar, Germany, December 23, 1893*

3 scenes.

HÄNSEL AND GRETEL are sent into the woods to pick berries. They get lost, and when they are sleepy lie down to rest. Angels come down to protect them, and they spend a peaceful night only to be caught in the morning by the Witch of the forest who loves to eat children. The alert children contrive to lock her in the oven that has been prepared for them. Her death brings to life all the children who have been lost before. The parents of Hänsel and Gretel arrive to take the children home.

HÉRODIADE
(*Herodias*)

Composer: JULES MASSENET

Book by PAUL MILLIET and HENRI GRÉMONT (Italian version by A. Zanardini)

First performance: *Théâtre de la Monnaie, Brussels, December 19, 1881*

4 acts.

IN JERUSALEM of 30 A.D. Salome is searching for the prophet John who once was kind to her. She does not know that Herodias is her mother. Herod is madly in love with Salome. His wife, Herodias, demands that John lose his head because he cursed her. Herod is afraid to issue this order since the people believe in John. Salome offers John her love but he tells her to seek God. Herodias, in consulting Phanuel, a soothsayer, discovers that Salome is her own child. When Herod finds that Salome loves John, he orders the prophet beheaded. Salome immediately assumes this to be the work of Herodias, and draws a dagger to kill her. Herodias stays the girl's hand when she cries that she (Herodias) is Salome's mother. Salome, aghast at this revelation, stabs herself.

HEURE ESPAGNOLE, L'
(*Spanish Time*)

Composer: MAURICE RAVEL

Book by FRANC NOHAIN

First performance: *Opéra comique, Paris, May 19, 1911*

1 act.

IN TOLEDO during the eighteenth century lived Concepcion, beautiful but inconstant wife of Torquemada, clock-maker. She has come upon the happy method of hiding her lovers by putting them in grandfather's-clock cases. Ramiro, a giant henchman, lugs these from room to room, and up and downstairs to suit Concepcion's taste and requirements. However, she becomes so interested in the engaging muscles of the mighty Ramiro that she invites him to her rooms, and forgets about the poet in one clock case and the banker in another. Torquemada returns and humanely releases them, also selling each a clock! Finally, with Concepcion and Ramiro, they all sing an engaging quintet.

HUGUENOTS, LES

Composer: GIACOMO MEYERBEER
Book by EUGÈNE SCRIBE and ÉMILE DESCHAMPS
First performance: *Opéra, Paris, February 29, 1836*
5 acts.

RAOUL DE NANGIS, popular Huguenot, is requested by Marguerite, Queen of Navarre, to come blindfolded to meet the woman she wishes him to marry, Valentine. This beautiful young lady is one Raoul had fallen in love with years before and earlier in this same evening had seen with her affianced, De Nevers, a man from whom she was trying to escape. When the Queen reveals Valentine, Raoul assumes the meeting he chanced to see with De Nevers was an assignation, and cries that he wouldn't think of marrying Valentine. Marguerite later prevents open warfare between the Huguenots and Catholics over this slight. Raoul, still in love with Valentine, watches her step aboard the wedding barge De Nevers has provided. He appears in her room later, and learns the truth as someone enters. Hiding behind a curtain he overhears the whole plan for the St. Bartholomew's Day massacre. When he emerges, Raoul and Valentine sing a passionate love song. In the Italian version it is at this point that they are shot down from offstage and the opera ends. In the fifth act ending, Valentine and Raoul, both Huguenots now, are shot by her father's soldiers not before they have been married, however.

INQUISITIVE WOMEN, THE

See Le Donne Curiose

JEWELS OF THE MADONNA, THE
(*I Gioielli della Madonna*)

Composer: ERMANNO WOLF-FERRARI
Book by the composer, verses by Carlo Zangarini and Enrico Golisciani
First performance: *Kurfürstenoper, Berlin, December 2, 1911*
3 acts.

MALIELLA is a girl free with her favours, whose foster parent, Carmela, has a son Gennaro who is very much in love with her. She loves Rafaele, a lad of rash statements but cool actions. When he offers to steal the jewels of the Madonna for Maliella she is delighted at the shocking bravery of even a suggestion of such action. When Gennaro is taunted by Maliella, the young man takes her seriously, goes out into the moonlight to bring back the jewels. Maliella, once she sees them, is so struck with their beauty that she gives herself to him, and happily dons the precious gems.   To a meeting of Camorrists at the edge of Naples Maliella comes dressed in clothes held close about her.   When she mentions Gennaro's name Rafaele is enraged and hurls her to the floor whereupon her shawl falls open, and reveals the jewels.   Rushing off to the sea the hysterical Maliella disappears, as do all the Camorrists who are afraid of being accused of the theft.   Gennaro has in the meantime arrived.   He asks the Holy Virgin's forgiveness, and stabs himself as the Camorrists return to punish him.

JUGGLER OF NOTRE DAME, THE
(Le Jongleur de Nôtre-dame)

Composer: JULES MASSENET

Book by MAURICE LÉNA, from Anatole France's story

First performance: *Théâtre Monte Carlo, February 18, 1902*

3 acts.

A CROWD is making fun of Jean, a poor juggler, whose bag of tricks the crowd ridicules.   The Prior of the abbey in front of which this action has taken place clears the square, and reproves Jean for his profession.   He does, however, invite him into the abbey.   There Jean finds the monks extolling their various arts, and trying to win him to one of them.   Jean is unhappy because of his own lack of learning but the cook, Boniface, later points out that it is not necessary to be a scholar to worship.   This pleases Jean who goes into the chapel in his juggler outfit, and does his pitiful routine as a humble offering to the Virgin. Just when the enraged Prior and monks are about to throw him out, the Virgin raises her hands in benediction over the boy as he dies.

JUIVE, LA
(The Jewess)

Composer: FROMENTAL HALÉVY

Book by EUGÈNE SCRIBE

First performance: *Opéra, Paris, February 23, 1835*

5 acts.

IN 1414 IN CONSTANCE, Rachel, the supposed daughter of the wealthy Jewish merchant, Eleazar, is loved by Prince Leopold, a man she knows only as Samuel, an artist.   When she discovers that Samuel is not only Prince Leopold but has a wife, Eudoxia, as well, she is overwhelmed, and accuses him publicly.   Cardinal Brogni imprisons all three, also excommunicating the Prince.   Rachel finally recalls her accusation at the behest of Princess Eudoxia, whereupon Eleazer and Rachel are accused of plotting against a Christian. Before they are to die in boiling oil, Eleazar points out that Rachel is not his daughter but the Cardinal's, a child he had saved from the Cardinal's palace when it burned.

KING'S HENCHMAN, THE

Composer DEEMS TAYLOR

Book by EDNA ST. VINCENT MILLAY

First performance: *Metropolitan Opera House, New York, February 17, 1927*

3 acts.

ENGLAND in the tenth century is the scene of this opera in which King Eadgar declares his intention of marrying Aelfrida, rumoured as the extremely beautiful daughter of a thane of Devon. Aethelwold, best friend of the King, is asked to go and present the King's invitation of marriage. Aethelwold has no interest in the ladies but as an act of friendship agrees to do so. In a misty forest of Devonshire on Allhallow Eve Aethelwold lies asleep when Aelfrida approaches reciting an invocation which is to find her a true lover. As though by divine intervention the mist rises, and reveals Aethelwold to Aelfrida. They immediately fall in love. Aethelwold discovers that Aelfrida is the woman he has been sent to find, and departs in order to put temptation behind him. But he returns when she calls him. Without telling her of the King's invitation to marriage, Aethelwold sends word back to King Eadgar that Aelfrida is too homely for a King, and begs leave to marry her himself. They live happily for months until the King sends word that he is coming to visit his faithful servant, and meet his wife. When Aelfrida hears of Aethelwold's duplicity she first agrees to make herself homely, but when the King arrives she appears looking her most beautiful. Aelthelwold kills himself as the King mourns his best friend.

KÖNIGSKINDER, DIE
(*The King's Children*)

Composer: ENGELBERT HUMPERDINCK

Book by ERNST ROSMER (Elsa Bernstein)

First performance (operatic version): *Metropolitan Opera House, New York, December 28, 1910*

3 acts.

THE KING'S SON on seeing a Goose Girl realises he has found the woman who will be his Queen. She, unfortunately, is under a spell from which he cannot free her. When the people of Hellabrunn, who have been expecting their own King, see the King's Son (a lackey at the Inn) bow before the Goose Girl as she comes into the market place they will have nothing to do with the pair as royalty, and drive them out of the city, along with the Fiddler who has accompanied the Goose Girl. One child, alone, believes that they truly are royal. Wandering in the snow the pair come to the Witch's house. She is dead and the Fiddler lives there, though he is out hunting for them. The King's Son is given, in error, a poison loaf left by the Witch. He innocently gives it to the Goose Girl as well as eating of it himself. The children of Hellabrunn find them dead . . . the royal pair that the world has not recognised.

LAKMÉ

Composer: LÉO DELIBES

Book by EDMOND GOUDINET and PHILIPPE GILLE, based on *Le Mariage de Loti* by Goudinet

First performance: *Opéra comique, Paris, April 14, 1883*

3 acts.

LAKMÉ is the daughter of Nilakantha, a fanatic hater of foreigners. She meets Gerald in the temple grounds, trespassing upon which means death for infidels. When the Hindu priest, Nilakantha, sees footprints he demands the man's name of Lakmé, but she will not reveal it. At a village square meeting he has Lakmé sing the Bell Song, and his cunning is rewarded for Gerald reveals himself. Nilakantha instantly stabs him. Lakmé has him spirited off to the forest where she cures him. She leaves to make a love potion for the love which has blossomed between them. When she returns Gerald is leaving, having been urged by a friend to return to his duties as an officer. Lakmé drinks poison, and dies in Gerald's arms.

LOHENGRIN

Composer: RICHARD WAGNER

Book by the composer

First performance: *Hoftheater, Weimar, Germany, August 28, 1850*

3 acts.

AT ANTWERP, Gottfried, the young Duke of Brabant, has disappeared. Count Telramund accuses Elsa, Gottfried's sister, of murdering him. King Henry calls Elsa beneath the oak of justice. Elsa tells of a dream she has had of a knight who will come to protect her, and marry her. Elsa prays, and the boat drawn by a swan appears with the Knight in the prow. He declares himself

Elsa's champion on the condition that she never ask his name or origin. He bests Telramund in battle, but spares his life. Telramund and his heathen wife, Ortrud, plan vengeance. As Elsa is entering the church about to marry the Knight Ortrud tells Elsa she should know her husband's name. After the ceremony in the bridal chamber Elsa, her curiosity aroused, asks her husband's name. Telramund enters with drawn sword, and is killed by the Knight. Because of Elsa's question her husband now leaves her, and, before King Henry, he tells his story and that his name is Lohengrin. He kneels to pray, and the swan leading his boat sinks, Gottfried appearing in his place. A dove pilots Lohengrin's boat down the river out of sight as Elsa falls dead in her brother's arms.

LOUISE

Composer: GUSTAVE CHARPENTIER

Book by the composer

First performance: *Opéra comique, Paris, February 2, 1900*

4 acts.

THE DRESSMAKER, Louise, has become enamoured of an artist, Julien. She wants to marry him, but her father will not give his consent because he believes all artists to be wasters. Disgusted with the restrictions her parents place upon her Louise elopes with Julien, and goes to live with the Bohemians in Montmartre. At a special occasion when Louise is to be honoured as Queen of the Quarter, she is asked to come home because her father is dying. If this is not a trick, then it is fortunate that she goes, for the father recovers almost instantly upon her arrival. Louise refuses to stay, and announces that she is going back to Julien and the Quarter. Louise dodges a chair which her father hurls at her in his anger, and leaves. Her father curses Paris.

LUCIA DI LAMMERMOOR

Composer: GAETANO DONIZETTI

Book by SALVATORE CAMMARANO, from Sir Walter Scott's novel *The Bride of Lammermoor*

First performance: *Teatro San Carlo, September 26, 1835*

3 acts.

EDGAR of Ravenswood (Edgardo) is leaving for France, and renews his vows of love for Lucy Ashton (Lucia) though the two houses have maintained a feud for years. Henry Ashton (Enrico), Lucy's brother, arranges a marriage between his friend Arthur Bucklaw (Arturo) and Lucy by tricking her into believ-

ing Edgar has been untrue. On the marriage night she murders Arthur, and
dies with the last note of her famous "Mad Scene." Edgar, who returned
at the time of the marriage to curse Lucy for faithlessness, now sees the tragic
duplicity that has taken Lucy from him, and stabs himself.

LUSTIGEN WEIBER VON WINDSOR, DIE

See The Merry Wives of Windsor

MADAME BUTTERFLY
(*Madama Butterfly*)

Composer: GIACOMO PUCCINI

Book by GIUSEPPE GIACOSA and LUIGI ILLICA, from the play by David
    Belasco and John Luther Long (itself from Long's *Madam Butterfly*)

First performance: *La Scala, Milan, February 17, 1904*

3 acts.

IN JAPAN, Pinkerton, an officer in the United States navy, finds a young Japanese girl, Cio-Cio-San, attractive to him, and takes her for his wife. She bears
him a son while he is away. The American consul, Sharpless, has become a
good friend to Cio-Cio-San, and when Pinkerton returns with his legitimate wife
from America Sharpless informs him of the existence of a son. Mrs. Pinkerton
wants to adopt the child but Cio-Cio-San will not permit it, and asks Pinkerton
to return a few minutes later for the child. She then blindfolds the child, and
commits hari-kari.

MAGIC FLUTE, THE
(*Die Zauberflöte*)

Composer: WOLFGANG AMADEUS MOZART

Book by EMANUEL SCHIKANEDER

First performance: *Theater auf der Wieden, Vienna, September 30, 1791*

2 acts.

IN A HYPOTHETICAL EGYPT of antiquity, the daughter of an evil Queen has been
taken from her mother by the high priest of Isis, Sarastro. Tamino attempts
to return Pamina, the daughter, to her mother in gratitude for the debt he owes
her since her handladies saved him from a snake. Papageno, the bird-catcher,
accompanies Pamina. Sarastro fascinates Tamino, and instead of freeing the
daughter of the Queen he studies to become a disciple of Sarastro. Finally
however, he is married to Pamina and the evil Queen of the Night is thwarted

MANON

Composer: JULES MASSENET

Book by HENRI MEILHAC and PHILIPPE GILLE based on *L'Histoire de Manon Lescaut* by Abbé Prévost

First performance: *Opéra comique, Paris, January 19, 1884*

5 acts.

ON HER WAY to a convent Manon meets Chevalier des Grieux whom she instantly loves. In Paris where they go to live together the Chevalier is not successful in getting his father's consent to marriage. He is kidnapped by his father after De Bretigny has asked Manon to go with him and be his mistress. After Des Grieux's disappearance she lives with De Bretigny until she finds that the Chevalier is about to take holy orders. She rushes to St. Sulpice and convinces him that he should depart with her. Later, in a gambling house, the Chevalier and Manon are both arrested for cheating at cards. He is freed through his father's influence, but Manon is to be deported to America with others of her sisterhood. Des Grieux and Lescaut, her cousin, had planned to rescue her, but when she appears in the procession to the ship she is ill and spent. She dies in the Chevalier's arms.

MANON LESCAUT

Composer: GIACOMO PUCCINI

Book by DOMENICO OLIVA, MARCO PRAGA, GIUSEPPE GIÀCOSA, LUIGI ILLICA, and GIULIO RICORDI, from Abbé Prévost's *L'Histoire de Manon Lescaut*

First performance: *Teatro Regio, Turin, February 1, 1893*

4 acts.

THE FIRST MEETING and elopement of Manon and Des Grieux is essentially the same as in Massenet's opera (produced in 1884). In the succeeding act Manon is the expensive mistress of Géronte de Ravoir in Paris. Des Grieux finds her, and they are about to run away for the second time when they are halted by Géronte. Manon catches up her jewels only to be arrested as a thief. Later Manon is sentenced to exile in Louisiana and is leaving on a ship filled with others of her kind. Des Grieux accompanies the boat as a member of the crew. Manon dies near New Orleans with the faithful Des Grieux at her side.

MAN WITHOUT A COUNTRY, THE

Composer: WALTER DAMROSCH

Book adapted by the composer from Edward Everett Hale's famous novel; done in verse by Arthur Guiterman

First performance: *Metropolitan Opera House, New York, May 12, 1937*

2 acts (5 scenes).

WHEN AARON BURR tried to form a new republic in the Southwest he drew into his conspiracy Philip Nolan. The opera opens on the island of Blennerhassett where the Ohio joins the Mississippi. Mary Rutledge is present at a party to which Philip Nolan comes to declare his love. When Burr and his party have left for Natchez (he fears arrest) Nolan lingers behind to say good-bye to Mary, and is captured by United States soldiers. Tried at Charleston he is sentenced to never see, or touch foot on, his native soil because, desperate after being plagued with so many questions, he screamed: "Damn, damn the United States! I never wish to hear the cursed name again." Aboard the frigate *Guerrière* Nolan has spent months and years while Mary works for a pardon in Washington. She goes to Gibraltar and comes aboard his ship. He is over-joyed to see her, but asks her to leave since the frigate will shortly pursue pirates. He pleads to be allowed to fight with the *Guerrière* men against the pirates. Mary succeeds in getting the permission, and he dies after killing the Admiral of the enemy ships. Commodore Decatur drawing his own sword lays it in Nolan's arms.

MÂROUF, SAVETIER DU CAIRE
(*Mârouf, The Cobbler of Cairo*)

Composer: HENRI RABAUD

Book by LUCIEN NEPOTY, from the *Arabian Nights*

First performance: *Opéra comique, Paris, May 15, 1914*

5 acts.

TO KHAÏTAN, MÂROUF, the cobbler of Cairo, has come to change his luck, having grown tired of his nagging wife. Mârouf follows the advice of Ali, and creates a fictitious caravan boasting of its early arrival in the city. This talk interests the Sultan and Vizier who overhear him. He is invited to the palace, and finally offered the hand of the Sultan's daughter in marriage. The treasury is opened to Mârouf who gives freely to the people. When the daughter is unveiled Marouf discovers that he loves her, and that she loves him. But the caravan fails to arrive and the Vizier grows suspicious. To the Sultan's ques-tions Mârouf is evasive, but he breaks down and tells the Sultan's daughter about his true state. She suggests that they flee the city which they do

They come upon a man ploughing in a field, and ask him for food.   While he is gone to get it Mârouf ploughs, and unearths a ring which marks the opening of a treasure cave.   The Princess rubs the ring whereupon the workman reappears as a Djinn.   Mârouf instantly wishes for his caravan, and none too soon, for the Sultan and Vizier arrive, and propose to execute Mârouf.   In the nick of time an endless caravan arrives, and Mârouf and his bride are borne off triumphant while Vizier is given a beating for his pessimism.

MARRIAGE OF FIGARO, THE
(*Le Nozze di Figaro*)

Composer: WOLFGANG AMADEUS MOZART

Book by LORENZO DA PONTE, from Beaumarchais' comedy *Le Mariage de Figaro*

First performance: *Burgtheater, Vienna, May 1, 1786*

2 acts.

FIGARO, valet to Count Almaviva, is to marry Susanna, maid to the Countess. Cherubino, a page, is in love with the Countess.   When Cherubino asks Susanna's help the Count arrives to pay her court, and Cherubino hides behind a chair, only to be quickly succeeded there by the Count himself when the music master, Don Basilio, arrives.   The knowledge of intended infidelity of each on the part of another keeps both silent.   The Countess, mildly unhappy about the Count's unfaithfulness, is aided by Susanna, Figaro, and Cherubino in an attempt to mend his ways.   Cherubino is to dress as Susanna.   This is not accomplished before the Count is heard arriving, and Cherubino hides in a closet.   The Count hears him, goes for something with which to pry open the door, only to find Susanna in the closet, Cherubino having leaped out the window.   Marcellina, a duenna, arrives with a promise made by Figaro to marry her daughter in payment of an old debt.   This to the Count eliminates Figaro, and makes the winning of Susanna easy.   But Marcellina turns out to be Figaro's mother.   In a new intrigue, the Countess and Susanna exchange costumes.   In the final resolution the Count and the Countess are reunited, and Figaro and Susanna will be married, at last.

MARTHA

Composer: FRIEDRICH VON FLOTOW

Book by W. FRIEDRICH

First performance: *Kärnthnerthor Theatre, Vienna, November 25, 1847*

5 acts.

IN ENGLAND, during the rule of Queen Anne, Lady Harriet and her friend Nancy, in a spirit of fun, take jobs as maids to two farmers, Lionel and Plunkett.

The men immediately fall in love with the maids who have assumed the names Martha and Julia. The two women quickly tire of their jaunt, and escape by means of Sir Tristram, cousin of Lady Harriet. However, it develops that Lionel is actually the heir to the Earl of Derby's title. A ring left by the man who had masqueraded as Lionel's father proves the young man's rightful heritage. Lady Harriet, who had had him thrown in prison when he threw himself at her feet during the royal hunt, now suddenly ceases to scorn him, and marries him.

MEFISTOFELE
(Mephistofeles)

Composer: ARRIGO BOITO

Book by composer, based on Goethe's *Faust*

First performance: *La Scala, Milan, March 5, 1868*

Prologue, 4 acts, and epilogue.

MEPHISTOPHELES, having made a defiant boast to God that he can break a soul, pursues the young student Faust and, in exchange for supernatural aid, receives Faust's agreement to go with him. Faust makes love to Marguerite as Mephistopheles pays attention to her mother, Martha. Marguerite is visited in prison by Faust where she is to be executed for the murder of her child. She will not flee with him, and is redeemed by her penitence. Faust is then taken by Mephistopheles to ancient Thessaly where he meets Helen of Troy and hears her story. She permits herself to be attracted to Faust. Finally, in the epilogue, Faust has grown ancient, and seems to have lost interest in the world Mephistopheles has provided for him. Though the Evil One conjures up new enticements, Faust dies with the Bible in his hands.

MEISTERSINGER, DIE
(The Master-Singers)

Composer: RICHARD WAGNER

Book by the composer

First performance: *Hof-und-National-Theater, Munich, June 21, 1868*

3 acts.

VEIT POGNER, a rich goldsmith, has promised to give the hand of his daughter, Eva, to the winner of the singing contest on St. John's day. Walther von Stolzing, a knight, has seen Eva in church, and fallen in love with her. Walther applies to the Mastersingers to compete in the contest. Beckmesser, a writer, and rival for Eva's hand, tries to discredit Walther by marking down all his mistakes at the tryout. Walther stays at the house of Hans Sachs, and Eva contrives to see him, betraying their love to the kind old cobbler. Walther, while sleeping, dreams of a prize song, and the next day sings it to Sachs who writes it down. Beckmesser enters the shop and steals the song. Just before the competition Walther composes another verse. At the contest Beckmesser sings the song he has stolen very poorly, and is laughed down. When he tells them Hans Sachs wrote it Hans denies it, and asks Walther to sing. Walther sings all the verses of his song, and is acclaimed by the Guild. Walther receives the hand of Eva as his reward.

MERRY WIVES OF WINDSOR, THE
(*Die Lustigen Weiber Von Windsor*)

Composer: OTTO NICOLAI

Book by SALOMON HERMANN VON MOSENTHAL, from Shakespeare

First performance: *Hofoper, Berlin, March 9, 1849*

3 acts.

SIR JOHN FALSTAFF, who has been writing love letters to Mrs. Ford and Mrs. Page, is drawn into a trap set by the ladies to catch him. He leaps into a clotheshamper to hide when, invited to a tête-à-tête with Mrs. Ford, her husband returns. Later, of course, he is dumped into the river with the dirty clothes. As a secondary theme, the attempt to marry Anne, the daughter of the Pages, offers amusing action. In the end Anne runs away to marry a poor poet, Fenton.

MIGNON

Composer: AMBROISE THOMAS

Book by MICHEL CARRÉ and JULES BARBIER, from Goethe's *Wilhelm Meister*

First performance: *Opéra comique, Paris, November 17, 1866*

3 acts.

IN A GERMAN INN, Lothario, an insane singer, searches for his lost daughter. Mignon, a member of a gypsy tribe entertaining the guests, refuses to dance. Giarno, the gypsy chief, is about to beat her when Wilhelm Meister, a wealthy young man, offers to buy her from him. Giarno accepts and Mignon, dressed as a page, accompanies Wilhelm to a castle where Filina, an actress, is to play "Titania." Wilhelm tells Mignon she must leave his service to protect her reputation. Again a gypsy and in love with Wilhelm, Mignon contemplates suicide. Seeing Wilhelm with Filina, she wishes the castle struck by lightning. Mad Lothario overhears, and sets the castle on fire. Mignon rushes into the building to retrieve a bouquet given to Filina by Wilhelm. Wilhelm saves her, and realises he is in love with her. Lothario regains his sanity on finding Mignon is his lost daughter. Mignon and Wilhelm avow their love for each other.

NATOMA

Composer: VICTOR HERBERT

Book by JOSEPH D. REDDING

First performance: *Metropolitan Opera House, Philadelphia, February 25, 1911*

3 acts.

IN THE EARLY DAYS of California when it was controlled by Mexico, Barbara, the daughter of wealthy rancher Don Francisco, is eagerly awaited by her father. She is returning from school. Paul Merrill is visiting the Don and falls instantly in love with Barbara, being himself devotedly loved by Natoma, an Indian girl. Alvarado, cousin to Barbara, wishes to marry her, and decides to take her away with or without permission. At the fiesta in the village Barbara begs off when asked to dance the pañuela with Alvarado. Castro then asks anyone to dance the dance with him, and Natoma accepts. This is a design of Alvarado's to get the crowd's attention on the dance so that he can abduct Barbara. However, Natoma sees Alvarado throw his serape over Barbara's head, and sidesteps Castro to stab Alvarado. She is given sanctuary by the priest of the mission. She asks to become a nun and is granted the privilege. It is assumed that Barbara will be Paul's.

NORMA

Composer: VINCENZO BELLINI

Book by GIUSEPPE FELICE ROMANI, based on a story by Alexander Soumet and Louis Belmontet

First performance: *La Scala, Milan, December 26, 1831*

2 acts.

NORMA, high priestess of the Druids, secretly loves and has had two children by Pollione, a proconsul of the invading Romans. Because of her love for Pollione she persuades the Druids not to fight the Romans. Pollione, meanwhile, has become enamoured of Adalgisa, a young, virgin priestess, and wants her to return to Rome with him. Adalgisa confesses her love for Pollione to Norma who reveals her own passion for him. They join in denouncing him. Because of Norma's suffering, Adalgisa pleads with Pollione to return to her. He refuses and, instead, plans to abduct Adalgisa. Norma, learning this, sounds the call of War on the Romans. Norma gives him the choice of death or exile. He refuses both and Norma, angered, calls the Druids, and tells them a virgin priestess has broken her vows, and must die by fire as punishment. Pollione, thinking she means Adalgisa, begs her not to do it. But instead of condemning Adalgisa Norma tells the Druids it is she, herself, who has transgressed. Pollione, realising the greatness of Norma, ascends the funeral pyre with her.

NOZZE DI FIGARO, LE

See The Marriage of Figaro

ORPHEUS AND EURYDICE
(*Orfeo Ed Euridice*)

Composer: CHRISTOPH WILLIBALD VON GLUCK

Book by RANIERI DI CALZABIGI, from a Greek legend

First performance: *Hofburgtheater, Vienna, October 5, 1762*

4 acts.

ORPHEUS, who has mourned the loss of Eurydice, wishes to go into the underworld to look for her. He is warned that he must not look back at her. He finds her at last in the Elysian Fields, after having passed safely through Hades. He leads her back, but she pleads him not to look at her. Accidentally he turns to her, and she disappears, returning to the Elysian Fields. Orpheus is in despair until Amor assures him that the gods have relented, and Eurydice will rejoin him again. They meet in the Temple of Love.

OTELLO

Composer: GIUSEPPE VERDI

Book by ARRIGO BOITO, after Shakespeare

First performance: *La Scala, Milan, February 5, 1887*

4 acts.

OTHELLO arrives at Cyprus, and announces that the Turkish fleet has been annihilated. Iago begins to plot against Othello because the latter has promoted Cassio over Iago's head. Roderigo is in love with Desdemona, recently married to Othello. Cassio wounds Montano in a brawl incited by Iago. Othello relieves Cassio of his commission. Desdemona is prevailed upon by Cassio to intercede for him. She accidentally drops a handkerchief which Iago's wife, Emilia, picks up. Iago builds Othello's jealousy of Cassio by showing Othello the handkerchief. Othello, infuriated, decides to poison Desdemona, but Iago counsels smothering her. He himself will take care of Cassio. Othello promotes Iago. The head of the Venetian embassy appears to read an order removing Othello, and placing Cassio in his place. Desdemona who has interceded before this for Cassio is insulted by Othello. Later Othello enters Desdemona's bedroom and strangles her. Before she is quite dead Emilia arrives saying that Roderigo has killed Cassio. Though Desdemona says with her last breath that she died by her own hand, Othello maintains he killed her because she was mistress to Cassio. Emilia then explains the whole handkerchief business, and as she does Montano comes in to report that Roderigo in dying has told of Iago's plot. Iago escapes and Othello, seeing how he has wronged Desdemona, stabs himself.

PAGLIACCI
(*Punchinello*)

Composer: RUGGIERO LEONCAVALLO

Book by the composer

First performance: *Teatro dal Verme, Milan, May 21, 1892*

2 acts.

IN THE FAMOUS PROLOGUE Tonio tells the villagers that actors are but human. A small company of strolling players have arrived in Calabria, and set up their booth. Nedda, wife of Canio who loves her madly, is carrying on an affair with a villager, Silvio. She is also desired by Tonio, the clown, but him she will not tolerate. In revenge Tonio leads Canio to the place where Silvio and Nedda are trysting. Canio tries to kill Silvio but he escapes. Canio then turns on Nedda but she is protected by members of the troupe. That night the actors present a play from their stage, and its action is essentially the drama of the lives of Canio, Silvio, and Nedda. Desperate, Canio finally drops his part in the play and demands of Nedda her lover's name. When she won't tell him he stabs her. Silvio leaps to the stage to protect her, and is in turn killed. Canio turns to the audience and speaks: "The comedy is ended."

PARSIFAL

Composer: RICHARD WAGNER

Book by the composer

First performance: *Festspielhaus, Bayreuth, July 26, 1882*

3 acts.

THE ACTION which has taken place before the play concerns the Spanish Pyrenees where the Knights of the Holy Grail live, guarding two sacred relics: the Spear with which the side of Christ was pierced, and the Cup of the Last Supper which also caught the blood from His side. They have refused Klingsor entry to their order. In a garden which he has created to tempt the Knights he contrives to ensnare Amfortas, King of the Grail, through the agencies of the fascinating Kundry. Amfortas is wounded by the Spear and can find no way to heal his wound. He must find an Innocent Fool, a man who can resist all temptation, and win back the Spear with which to cure Amfortas. He, then, will become the new King. The opera action opens at this point. Parsifal, a boy of the forest, is captured by the Knights for killing a swan. Gurnemanz believes this innocent lad may be the Fool for whom they are waiting. He shows no understanding of the service of the Eucharist which further convinces Gurnemanz. In the castle of Klingsor, Kundry is called to practice her wiles on Parsifal. He resists all temptations and finally, when Klingsor in anger hurls the Spear at him, Parsifal makes the sign of the Cross which protects himself, and destroys the garden. He wanders for some time until he gets back to the castle of the Holy Grail where he is received by Kundry who has repented and is now a servant of the Grail. With the Spear he heals Amfortas' wound. As Amfortas kneels before the new King, Kundry dies. Parsifal has become the Saviour of the Order of the Holy Grail.

PELLÉAS AND MÉLISANDE
(Pelléas et Mélisande)

Composer: CLAUDE DEBUSSY

Poem by MAURICE MAETERLINCK

First performance: Opéra comique, Paris, April 30, 1902

5 acts (12 scenes).

MÉLISANDE is met in the forest by Golaud who has gone there to hunt. He wishes her for his bride, and asks his half-brother, Pelléas, to make the intricate arrangements necessary to please his grandfather, King Arkel of Allemonde. Pelléas is immediately attracted to Mélisande. Golaud is jealous, particularly when the wedding ring, which she has lost in a pool, becomes the centre of suspicion. He spies upon Pelléas and Mélisande, even to holding his child up to see what the pair are doing in her room. Once when she leans out the window to speak to Pelléas her hair falls about his head, and he caresses it as Golaud enters. Finally, his suspicions having driven him mad, he kills Pelléas. When Mélisande lies dying in childbirth, she tells him that she loved Pelléas, but innocently. She dies, leaving him still tormented by doubts.

PETER IBBETSON

Composer: DEEMS TAYLOR

Book by composer and CONSTANCE COLLIER, after her play version of Du Maurier's novel

First performance: Metropolitan Opera House, New York, February 7, 1931

3 acts.

YOUNG PETER IBBETSON, nephew and ward of pompous Colonel Ibbetson, meets Mary, Duchess of Towers, at a London gathering. He doesn't realise that she is the sweetheart of his youth. Peter angers his uncle and leaves to visit France where he spent his childhood. He falls asleep at an inn and dreams of a quarrel between his mother and his uncle. He awakens to find Mary at the inn. They recognise each other and find they are still in love. Mary tells him they must not meet again. Peter returns to London and, in a heated dispute with his uncle, kills him. Sentenced to life imprisonment he is consoled by a message from Mary that they will always be together in their dreams. Forty years later Peter, an old man, hears of Mary's death and sees her in a dream beckoning to him. He dies to meet her in Eternity.

PRINCE IGOR

Composer: ALEXANDER BORODIN

Book by the composer and VLADIMIR STASSOV from the Russian tale *The Epic of the Army of Igor*

First performance: *Imperial Opera House, St. Petersburg, October 23, 1890*

Prologue and 4 acts.

PRINCE IGOR of Severski, in the twelfth century, gives his wife, Yaruslovna, into the keeping of his brother-in-law, Prince Galitsky, and leaves to fight the Polovtses, enemy tribes from the East. He is accompanied by his son, Vladimir. While Prince Igor is away Prince Galitsky seizes the government. His moral will to do so is strengthened by a report that Prince Igor and Vladimir have been captured by the Polovtses. In the meantime, Prince Igor and Vladimir are enjoying the hospitality of Khan Konchak who treats his prisoners like gentlemen. Vladimir refuses to escape when the means is provided by Ovlour, a native convert to Christianity, because he has fallen in love with the Khan's daughter, Konchakovna. He regrets that he didn't take the offer later, for the Polovtsians have pillaged his own native city, and returned with their loot. Vladimir, Igor and Ovlour escape, and return in time to oust Prince Galitsky. Vladimir, recaptured, is saved from execution by Konchakovna.

PROPHETE, LE

Composer: GIACOMO MEYERBEER

Book by EUGÈNE SCRIBE

First performance: *Opéra, Paris, April 26, 1849*

5 acts.

JOHN, an Anabaptist of Germany, wishes to marry Bertha, vassal of Count Oberthal who will not give his consent because she is so beautiful. Bertha, seeking concealment from the Count, is finally given as a hostage to spare the life of Fidès, John's mother, whom the Count holds captive, and will kill if Bertha is not relinquished. John then gives in to the Anabaptists who have wanted him for their leader, and leads a revolt, disguised as the Prophet. Fidès, now a beggar, tells Bertha that John is dead. Bertha assumes that the Prophet has killed him. Fidès is imprisoned as an imposter when she recognises her son as the Prophet. Afraid of advancing enemy forces, the Anabaptists decide to give up John, as Bertha enters to avenge the supposed death of John by killing the Prophet. When she sees that the Prophet is John she kills herself instead. John and his mother are burned in the flames of the palace.

RIENZI, THE LAST OF THE TRIBUNES
(*Rienzi, Der Letzte der Tribunen*)

Composer: RICHARD WAGNER

Book by the composer from Bulwer-Lytton's novel of the same name

First performance: *Hoftheater, Dresden, October 20, 1842*

5 acts.

BASED on the character of Rienzi, the Roman tribune of the fourteenth century, this is the story of the abduction of Irene, sister of Cola di Rienzi. Paolo Orsini, a noble, has captured her. His right to her is contested by Steffano Colonna. Adriano, Colonna's son, protects Irene from the warring factions. When Rienzi decides to overthrow the nobles and save the people, Adriano gives him his support. When this is an accomplished fact the nobles come to the Capitol to submit to his rule. Adriano is convinced that foul work is afoot, and warns Rienzi who prepares himself so that, when Orsini leaps upon him with a dagger, hidden armour protects him. Adriano's pleas for the release of his father, after all the nobles have been condemned to death, leads Rienzi to free them all. The nobles immediately betray their pardon, and battle the people. They are defeated, but Adriano's father, Colonna, is killed. Adriano serves warrant on Rienzi that the death must be avenged. Rienzi is Coronated and, almost immediately, it is rumoured that he is a partisan of the Emperor's. Adriano tries to assassinate him and, unsuccessful, goes to Irene and tells her of the danger Rienzi is in. He asks her to flee with him but she won't. She goes to the Capitol, and finds Rienzi in prayer. He pleads with her to leave with Adriano. She will not go, but stays with her brother in the Capitol, perishing with him. Adriano, who wants to be with her, dies in the flames trying to get to her.

RIGOLETTO

Composer: GIUSEPPE VERDI

Book by FRANCESCO MARIO PIAVE, from Victor Hugo's *Le Roi s'amuse*

First performance: *Teatro la Fenice, Venice, March 11, 1851*

4 acts.

RIGOLETTO, the hump-backed court jester of the Prince of Mantua, laughs at the noblemen of the court for allowing the Prince to be attentive to their wives.

They plot vengeance on him, and Count Monterone curses him. The Prince disguised as a student has been courting Gilda, Rigoletto's daughter, at church. The noblemen abduct her thinking she is Rigoletto's mistress. Rigoletto finds Gilda at the palace with the Prince. He admits she is his daughter, and takes her away. Rigoletto goes to an inn where the Prince is staying, and plans his death with the aid of Sparafucile, a bandit. Maddalena, Sparafucile's sister, begs him not to kill the Prince. Sparafucile promises not to if another comes to the inn before midnight. Gilda overhears this and, dressed as a man, enters the inn. Rigoletto comes at midnight, and is given a body tied in a bag. He is about to throw the bag in the river when he hears the Prince singing in the inn. In a frenzy he unties the bag, and finds Gilda who with her dying breath says she is happy to die for her lover. Rigoletto realises that the curse of Count Monterone has been fulfilled.

Ring of the Nibelung
RHEINGOLD, DAS
(The Rhinegold)

Composer: RICHARD WAGNER

Book by the composer

First performance: *Hof-und-National-Theater, Munich, September 22, 1869*

4 scenes.

THE RHINE MAIDENS, Woglinde, Wellgunde, and Flosshilde guard the Rhinegold in the depths of the Rhine. After telling Alberich, a Nibelung, that anyone able to forge a ring from the gold will possess the world and all its power, he steals the gold from them. Wotan, King of the Gods, and Fricka, his wife, are sleeping before the Valhalla, new home of the Gods, built by the Giants Fafner and Fasolt in return for Freia, the Goddess of Youth and Love. Loge, the God of Fire, tells Wotan of the ring Alberich has made from the Rhinegold. The Giants and Wotan both want the ring, and the Giants take Freia away saying that they will release her if Wotan gets them the gold and the ring before evening. The Gods lose their youth when Freia departs. Wotan and Loge descend beneath the earth, and by trickery obtain the Nibelung treasure, the ring and the Tarnhelm (a magic helmet which enables the wearer to make himself invisible or change his form). Wotan refuses the Giants the ring but gives it up when Erda, the Goddess of Earthly Wisdom, warns him against it, and predicts the fall of the Gods. The curse of the ring is wrought on Fasolt, the first wearer, who is killed by Fafner in a quarrel over it. Wotan leads the Gods to Valhalla over a rainbow bridge which appeared when Donner struck away the clouds.

WALKÜRE, DIE
(*The Valkyr*)

Composer: RICHARD WAGNER

Book by the composer

First performance: *Hof-und-National-Theater, Munich, June 26, 1870*

3 acts.

WOTAN, King of the Gods, begets Siegmund and Sieglinde in a union with a
mortal woman.   Separated at birth Sieglinde is unhappily married to Hunding,
a savage fighter.   She gives a stranger shelter in her house.   Suspecting him
to be Siegmund, her lost brother, she secretly tells him of a sword, Nothung,
Wotan their father placed in a tree for Siegmund to use in his hour of need.   The
stranger pulls the sword from the tree, proving himself her brother.   They
embrace in love and flee to the forest, Hunding pursuing.   Wotan tells Brünnhilde, one of the nine Walküre Maidens he created by a union with Erda the
Earth Goddess, to protect Siegmund against Hunding.   Fricka, his wife and
Goddess of Marriage, makes Wotan reverse his order and protect Hunding,
punishing Siegmund for uniting with Sieglinde in love.   Brünnhilde disobeys
and protects Siegmund.   Fricka forces Wotan to interfere on Hunding's behalf,
and he breaks Siegmund's sword, Nothung, with his spear.   Hunding slays
Siegmund, and for this Wotan kills him in return.   Brünnhilde sends Sieglinde
to the forest to bear the child of her lover.   Wotan, angry at Brünnhilde's dis-
obedience, punishes her by putting her to sleep on a rock surrounded by fire
which only a fearless hero can penetrate, and who only with a kiss can awaken
her.

SIEGFRIED

Composer: RICHARD WAGNER

Book by the composer

First performance: *Festspielhaus, Bayreuth, August 16, 1876*

3 acts.

SIEGFRIED, son of Siegmund and Sieglinde, has grown to manhood in the forest.
His mother, who died at his birth, had given him the broken sword, Nothung.
Mime, the brother of Alberich, who cares for him, tries to forge the sword together but fails.   Siegfried succeeds and, led by Mime, goes to the cave where
Fafner, in the form of a dragon, guards the Rhinegold.   Siegfried kills Fafner
with his sword, and accidentally tastes the dragon's blood which enables him to
understand the birds.   They tell him of the ring, the Rhinegold, and the Tarnhelm in the cave.   He obtains these, and kills Mime who tries to make him
drink a poison potion.   The birds then tell him of Brünnhilde, sleeping on a
rock surrounded by fire.   Siegfried sets out for her, and is stopped by Wotan,

disguised as a wanderer. Siegfried breaks Wotan's spear with his sword, Nothung, thereby demonstrating that man had broken the might of the Gods. He advances to the rock, surmounts the fiery wall, and wakes Brünnhilde with a kiss.

GÖTTERDÄMMERUNG
(*Dusk of the Gods*)

Composer: RICHARD WAGNER

Book by the composer

First performance: *Festspielhaus, Bayreuth, August 17, 1876*

Prologue and 3 acts.

THE THREE NORNS (Fates of Northern mythology) break the golden rope of destiny as they pass it to one another. The Gods, seeing in this their doom, go down into the earth to their mother Erda. Brünnhilde sends Siegfried forth on a journey to the Rhine. Before he leaves he places the ring on her finger to give her strength. By the Rhine is the family of the Gibichungs, Gunther, head of the tribe, Gutrune, his sister, and Hagen, their half-brother. Hagen plans to unite Gunther and Brünnhilde, and Gutrune and Siegfried in marriage. Siegfried enters and, after drinking a potion which blots out his memory of Brünnhilde, he marries Gutrune, and sets out to bring Brünnhilde for Gunther. Brünnhilde refuses to give up Siegfried's ring to Wotan to save the Gods from destruction. Siegfried, disguised as Gunther, comes and takes the ring from Brünnhilde, and tells her she must be his wife. Siegfried returns to Gutrune, and they begin to celebrate a wedding feast. Gunther enters with Brünnhilde who is wild with anger when she sees Siegfried married to Gutrune. She and Hagen plan Siegfried's death and enlist Gunther's aid. She tells Hagen of the vulnerable spot in Siegfried's back. On a hunt Siegfried passes the Rhine, and the Maidens ask for his ring. When he refuses they predict his death. When the potion wears off and Siegfried regains his memory, he relates the story of his life and his love for Brünnhilde. Hagen stabs him in the back, and they bring him to Gutrune. Hagen and Gunther fight over the ring, and Gunther is killed. When Hagen tries to wrench it from Siegfried's finger the dead man raises his hand in warning. Brünnhilde enters, and takes the ring saying it will be restored to the Rhine Maidens after it has been purified by the fire that will burn Siegfried and herself. She lights the funeral pyre of Siegfried and mounted on her horse, Grane, rides into the flames. The Rhine overflows and extinguishes the fire. The Rhine Maidens catch the ring when Brünnhilde flings it to them. Hagen drowns in the waters, and in the distance the Valhalla burns destroying the Gods.

ROMEO AND JULIET
(*Roméo et Juliette*)

Composer: CHARLES GOUNOD
Book by JULES BARBIER and MICHEL CARRÉ, from Shakespeare's play
First performance: *Théâtre Lyrique, Paris, April 27, 1867*
5 acts.

JULIET, of the house of Capulet, meets Romeo at a masked ball given in her home.   In spite of the age-old feud between the houses of Capulet and Montagu (of which Romeo is a member), they are married in Friar Lawrence's cell. Romeo is banished by the Duke for having killed Tybalt who had previously killed Mercutio.   Juliet, after being secretly visited by Romeo in the night, is approached by Capulet who says she must marry Count Paris.   Friar Lawrence gives Juliet a potion to drink which will make her appear dead, though she is only asleep.   When Romeo hears of her supposed death he buys poison for himself, and comes to the tomb to die beside her.   He meets Count Paris, and kills him.   Romeo then drinks the poison, and dies himself.   When Friar Lawrence comes to awaken Juliet he finds swords and blood.   He therefore tries to induce Juliet to flee but she will not.   She stabs herself, and dies beside her husband.

RONDINE, LA
(*The Swallow*)

Composer: GIACOMO PUCCINI
Book by GIUSEPPE ADAMI
First performance: *Monte Carlo, March 27, 1917*
3 acts.

IN THE SALON of Magda, mistress of Rambaldo, a young poet, Prunière voices the opinion that love and marriage are coming back into favour.   He is laughed at but Magda considers seriously what he has said.   Later in the evening, Ruggero, a young, innocent country lad, is introduced.   When he expresses an interest in seeing night life Rambaldo offers to show him.   Magda and her maid follow the men to the Bal Bullier.   There she falls in love with him, and leaves Rambaldo.   In their villa retreat in Antibes Magda is happy with him but Ruggero wants to marry her.   He writes for his mother's consent and she gives it, provided the girl's past is immaculate.   Magda philosophically leaves Ruggero to a safe girl of his mother's choice, and returns to Paris and Rambaldo.

ROSENKAVALIER, DER
(*The Knight of the Rose*)

Composer: RICHARD STRAUSS

Book by HUGO VON HOFMANNSTHAL

First performance: *Hofoper, Dresden, January 26, 1911*

3 acts.

OCTAVIAN, lover of the Princess von Werdenberg, is embracing her in her boudoir when she thinks she hears her husband returning. Octavian quickly disguises himself as a lady's maid only to have the Baron Ochs, a cousin of the Princess, come in to ask her advice about getting a token of love to Sophie, the girl of his choice, daughter of wealthy Faninal. In the course of this arrangement, however, he contrives to make a date with the maid (Octavian). When all are gone except Octavian the Princess becomes blue about the possible fading of her beauty, and when he fails to kiss her good-bye she calls him back to be the messenger with the rose for the Baron. Octavian delivers the rose, and both he and Sophie instantly fall in love. Her father will have no nonsense about her marrying Octavian, particularly after the boy picks a quarrel with the dignified Baron. Sophie must marry the Baron or become a nun. Octavian again assumes his maid's disguise, and keeps his date with the Baron at a country tavern. Here the Baron is subjected to all sorts of indignities and foolishness. When a woman comes in to claim him as her husband, Sophie has her father's permission not to marry the Baron. The Princess arrives to end the trouble, and Sophie leaves with Octavian, not before Octavian has given the Princess one last affectionate look as a token of their past love.

ROSSIGNOL, LE
(*The Nightingale*)

Composer: IGOR STRAVINSKY

Book by the composer and S. MITOUSOV, from a story by Hans Christian Andersen

First performance: *Opéra, Paris, May 26, 1914*

3 acts.

THE EMPEROR OF CHINA is so disheartened that his life is despaired of. Finally a nightingale is brought to him. It sings so sweetly that the Emperor is completely restored, and grants the bird any wish. The nightingale considers itself sufficiently repaid by the Emperor's humility, and asks no more. A mechanical nightingale is then delivered to the Emperor as a gift from the Emperor of Japan. The live nightingale is so outraged at the singing of this imitation that it flies away in disgust. The Emperor immediately grows ill, and curses the live nightingale for leaving him. Finally, the live nightingale takes pity, and returns to bring the Emperor back to health.

SADKO

Composer: NIKOLAI RIMSKY-KORSAKOV

Book by the composer

First performance: *Private Opera House, Moscow, January 6, 1898*

7 acts.

SADKO is a travelling musician who plays upon the gusle. Princess Volkhova, daughter of the Ocean King, is so pleased with him that Sadko is enabled to rise quickly in wealth and position, and shortly he builds a dazzling estate of white stone. At sea one day the water becomes so perturbed that Sadko finally descends to the bottom to play for the Ocean King. The King and his court begin to dance, the whole affair becoming successful to a fault for the Ocean King falls dead from exhaustion. When peace and quiet have finally settled, Sadko, with the Princess, rise to the surface, and spend a happy life in Sadko's white palace.

SALOME

Composer: RICHARD STRAUSS

Poem by OSCAR WILDE (adapted in German by Hedwig Lachmann)

First performance: *Hofoper, Dresden, December 9, 1905*

1 act.

THE SCENE is outside the banquet hall of the palace of the Tetrarch, Herod Antipas. The captain of the guard, Narraboth, watches Salome with fascination as she sits in the great hall. In a cistern can be heard the voice of Jokanaan (John the Baptist) prophesying the coming of the Lord. Salome comes out of the banquet hall and, on hearing Jokanaan's voice, asks that he be brought up so that she can speak to him. When he emerges, tawny and strong, he denounces Herodias, wife of Herod and mother of Salome. Salome, fascinated by this strange man, wants to kiss him. Narraboth, horrified, stabs himself. Jokanaan, uttering a curse, returns to the cistern. Herod and Herodias come into the court from the banquet hall and are annoyed by the presence of the blood of Narraboth. Herod, restless, finally asks Salome to dance for him. She won't until Herod promises to give her what she asks. He promises, and she dances the dance of the seven veils at the conclusion of which she asks for Jokanaan's head on a silver plate. Herod pleads for anything else, but finally consents as Herodias approves the girl's request. When the head is brought from the cistern, Salome takes the plate, and kisses the mouth of Jokanaan. Herod, revolted, orders his soldiers to kill her.

SCHWANDA DER DUDELSACKPFEIFER
(*Schwanda the Bagpiper*)

Composer: JAROMIR WEINBERGER

Book by MILOS KARES

First performance: *National Theatre, Prague, April 27, 1927*

2 acts.

IN CZECHOSLOVAKIA, Schwanda is a famous bagpiper to whose home comes the famous bandit, Babinsky. He falls in love with Dorota, Schwanda's wife. He tries to interest Schwanda in the court of Queen Ice-Heart to which Schwanda decides to go with Babinsky. They go, leaving Dorota in the house. At the court the Queen is so pleased with Schwanda's playing that she wants to marry him, but when Dorota bursts in to announce that he is hers, Queen Ice-Heart orders him executed. Schwanda's bagpipes cannot be found when he asks to play them just before his execution, an event which never takes place since Babinsky has substituted a broom for the headman's axe. The pipes are finally found and Schwanda plays everyone into a good humour. Babinsky makes Schwanda utter a curse which sends him to Hell. Babinsky now assumes his way clear to marry Dorota but she wants only Schwanda and, finally, Babinsky has to go to Hell and play cards with the Devil to win Schwanda back, which he does. Returned to earth Schwanda discovers he has been gone twenty minutes instead of twenty years as it had seemed.

SECRET OF SUZANNE, THE
(*Il Segreto di Susanna*)

Composer: ERMANNO WOLF-FERRARI

Book by ENRICO GOLISCIANI

First performance: *Hofoper, Munich, November 4, 1909*

1 act.

COUNT GIL returns home to discover the faint odour of tobacco in his home. The Countess Gil, beautiful and twenty, will not give him a satisfactory answer, and his jealousy quickly rises. The Count grows enraged, puts on a scene, breaks up furniture and is finally calmed, and sent off to the club by Countess Gil. She then summons the servant, Sante, who never speaks a word in the piece, and asks him to bring her cigarettes. The Count who has been spying at the window discovers the innocent vice his wife is trying to cover, and returns to make peace.

SIEGFRIED

See Ring of the Nibelung

SIMON BOCCANEGRA

Composer: GIUSEPPE VERDI

Book by FRANCESCO MARIA PIAVE (revised by Arrigo Boito) from a play by Antonio Garcia Gutierrez

First performance: *Teatro la Fenice, Venice, March 12, 1857*

Prologue and 3 acts.

BY POPULAR ACCLAIM of workmen Simon Boccanegra is elevated to the estate of a Doge from his position as corsair. Among those who assist in this fourteenth-century conspiracy are Paolo and Pietro. Simon happens upon the house of Grimaldi and discovers that Amelia Grimaldi is in reality his own lost daughter. She is to marry Gabriele Adorno, of Genoa. Paolo, by reason of his assistance to Simon, asks her hand in marriage and is refused. Paolo and Pietro decide to avenge themselves by unseating Simon. They begin by having Amelia kidnapped. Simon is accused of this act by Amelia's tutor, Andrea, and Gabriele. Gabriele tries to stab Simon on his coronation day but Amelia stays him. Andrea and Gabriele are imprisoned. Pietro and Paolo are not successful in persuading them to kill Simon. [One of the several inconsistencies of the libretto.] Gabriele overhears a conversation between Simon and Amelia whereupon he again tries to stab her father. Again she averts the tragedy. When Gabriele finds who Simon is he asks his pardon, and swears to be his defender. But his defense cannot save Simon from the poison that Paolo has given the Doge. Simon dies as he blesses Amelia and Gabriele before their wedding feast.

SNEGOUROTCHKA
(*The Snow Maiden*)

Composer: NIKOLAI RIMSKY-KORSAKOV

Book by ALEXANDER OSTROVSKY, from a Russian folk tale

First performance: *Moscow, January 29, 1882*

Prologue and 4 acts.

MIZGYR, a young Tartar, has fallen in love with the Snow Maiden, lovely daughter of King Winter and Spring. Mizgyr jilts his fiancée, Koupava, in favour of Snegourotchka whereupon the loser, Koupava, appeals to the Czar. He decrees that since the Snow Maiden seems pure, who shall ever be able to win her heart by morning shall have her. Snegourotchka immediately appeals to her mother for the right to love as humans do.   Granted, she discovers that she loves Mizgyr.   But even as she discovers the fact the sun comes out to melt her.   Mizgyr, overwhelmed with grief, commits suicide.

SONNAMBULA, LA
(*The Sleep-walker*)

Composer: VINCENZO BELLINI

Book by GIUSEPPE FELICE ROMANI

First performance: *Teatro Carcano, Milan, March 6, 1831*

2 acts.

ÌMINA, who will shortly marry Elvino, a wealthy countryman, is addicted to sleepwalking and one night in her sleep walks into the chambers of Rodolfo, who is staying at the inn, and enjoying at the moment Amina arrives the attentions of Lisa, the inn's mistress.   Rodolfo, observing Amina's condition, courteously leaves the room to her as she lies down in his bed.   Lisa, who has been the loser in the competition for Elvino, spreads the news that Amina has been indiscreet with Rodolfo.   A highly curious group, including an incredulous Elvino, come to the inn to see her sleeping in Rodolfo's bed.   All is resolved in the end when a handkerchief of Liza's is found in Rodolfo's room, and when the somnambulism is dramatically proved real as Amino walks a dangerous plank across the mill wheel, and is awakened by Elvino himself as he takes her in his arms.

SPANISH HOUR, THE
See L'Heure Espagnole

TALES OF HOFFMANN, THE
(*Les Contes D'Hoffmann*)

Composer: JACQUES OFFENBACH

Book by JULES BARBIER and MICHEL CARRÉ from three tales by E. T. A. Hoffmann

First performance: *Opéra Comique, Paris, February 10, 1881*

Prologue, 3 acts, and an epilogue.

HOFFMANN is telling his drinking companions, particularly his friend Nicklausse, in Luther's Inn about his three disillusioning love affairs.   In the first instance he fell in love with Olympia, a beautiful doll, created by Dr. Spalanzani. By equipping Hoffmann with special glasses the doctor has duped him into believing she is real. She sings and dances with Hoffmann though she does not answer his pleas to marry him. When Olympia's inner mechanism begins to play out she dances out of the ballroom leaving Hoffmann the butt of laughter. Outside a crash is heard as Dr. Coppelius smashes Olympia because Spalanzani had given him a worthless check for his share in the doll. Next Hoffmann is disillusioned in Venice where he falls in love with Giulietta, beauty of renown. Compelled to fight a duel with Giulietta's lover, Schlemihl, Hoffmann kills the man only to have Giulietta run off with another lover. Hoffmann is barely saved from arrest by the faithful Nicklausse. In the final instance Hoffmann has fallen in love with Antonia, the daughter of Crespel, a musician whose wife had died mysteriously years before. Antonia has a beautiful voice, but because of bad health has been instructed not to sing. Dr. Miracle, bent on killing Antonia as he did her mother, contrives finally to make Antonia sing herself to death. Dr. Miracle disappears, and Hoffmann is accused of killing the girl. Returning to Luther's Inn, Nicklausse consols Hoffmann as two characters, Stella and Lindorf, are introduced to little more than extend the opera.

TANNHÄUSER

Composer: RICHARD WAGNER

Book by the composer

First performance: *Hoftheater, Dresden, October 19, 1845*

3 acts.

TANNHÄUSER, a minstrel and singer, has deserted Wartburg, his native village. for Venusberg, on a near-by hill where the Goddess Venus holds him with her charms. When his desires are satisfied he longs to return to his home. He breaks Venus' hold on him when he mentions the Virgin Mary. He is found on the road by the singers of Wartburg, and his friend Wolfram tells him that Elizabeth, pious niece of Herrmann the Landgrave, loves him. He returns with them to Wartburg to sing in the prize contest. Elizabeth is to grant any wish of the winner. Wolfram sings of ideal love which incenses Tannhäuser who has known the sensual love of Venus. He answers with a hymn to Venus. The others uphold Wolfram, and draw swords on Tannhäuser, but Elizabeth protects him. Her father tells him to join the Pilgrimage to Rome to obtain forgiveness from the Pope. When the Pilgrims return Elizabeth asks for Tannhäuser but he isn't among them. Wolfram realises she is about to die. Tannhäuser comes back without the forgiveness of the Pope and calls for Venus. She appears but Wolfram shows him the funeral train of Elizabeth, and Tannhäuser, overcome, throws himself upon her bier. Messengers arrive from Rome to tell of the Pope's forgiveness. and Tannhäuser dies beside Elizabeth, saved from damnation.

THAÏS

Composer: JULES MASSENET

Book by LOUIS GALLET, from the novel by Anatole France

First performance: *Opéra, Paris, March 16, 1894*

3 acts.

ATHANAËL, a young monk in a desert fasting place, has a vision of Thaïs, whom he is convinced he must save. She is a popular courtesan of Alexandria to which city he goes to save her soul. She is attracted to this handsome young man, and is gradually won over to confession. Athanaël takes her to Albine, another desert holy soul, mother of the White Sisterhood. However, he has begun to fall in love with Thaïs who has now turned aside from fleshly love. Athanaël, in his desert fasting place, has a vision of her dying, and hurries to the convent when in anguish he hears her last words as she cries that she has seen the Holy One.

TOSCA

Composer: GIACOMO PUCCINI

Book by GIUSEPPE GIACOSA and LUIGI ILLICA, from Victorien Sardou's play *La Tosca*

First performance: *Teatro Costanzi, Rome, January 4, 1900*

3 acts.

TOSCA, a beautiful singer, is the jealous lover of Mario Cavaradossi, a religious artist. Angelotti, an escaped prisoner, hides in the church in which Mario is painting. Mario helps him escape. Scarpia, chief of Roman police, enters the church and, not finding Angelotti, arrests Mario as an accomplice, and orders him shot. Desiring Tosca for himself, Scarpia promises her lover's liberty in return for her favours. Tosca agrees and Scarpia orders a fake execution of Mario. When Scarpia returns to claim her she stabs him. At dawn the pretended execution of Mario takes place. Tosca hurries to the prone figure of her lover, after the firing, to find he is dead. Hearing noise of approaching soldiers, she realises her murder of Scarpia has been discovered. Climbing the prison wall she leaps to her death.

TRAVIATA, LA
(*The Lost One*)

Composer: GIUSEPPE VERDI

Book by FRANCESCO MARIA PIAVE, from Alexandre Dumas' *La Dame aux Camélias*

First performance: *Teatro la Fenice, Venice, March 6, 1853*

3 acts.

ALFREDO GERMONT has fallen in love with Violetta Valéry (Camille), a beautiful courtesan who has only a short time to live and wishes to make the most of it.   She refuses Alfredo's offer of marriage because she wants to spend the short months remaining to her in gaiety.   Finally she goes to live with Alfredo but his father pleads with her to give him up since their liaison is creating a scandal that makes it hard for Alfredo's sister to marry.   Violetta agrees.   In a gambling house Alfredo sees her, and suspects in his unhappiness that she has left him for an old lover, Baron Douphol.   Seizing this as the easiest way out, Violetta lies in admitting it.   Alfredo wins at the tables and throws his winnings at her in disgust.   His father pleads with him not to behave thus with any woman.   In the end as Violetta dies the father has become reconciled, and Alfredo knows that Violetta loved him.

TRISTAN AND ISOLDE

Composer: RICHARD WAGNER

Book by the composer

First performance: *Hof-und-National-Theater, Munich, June 10, 1865*

3 acts.

ON A SHIP Isolde is being brought from Ireland to Cornwall by Tristan to be the bride of King Mark.   Isolde plans to poison Tristan because he once killed her lover in battle.   Instead of a poison her maid, Brangäne, prepares a love potion.   Both Tristan and Isolde drink of it, and fall into each other's arms. At the King's castle Mark has gone hunting.   Tristan and Isolde meet secretly, but are betrayed to King Mark by a traitor, Melot.   Tristan is mortally wounded in fighting Melot.   He is taken to his castle in Brittany by Kurwenal. When Tristan is dying Kurwenal sends for Isolde hoping she will help him. When she arrives Tristan rips off his bandages, and tries to go to her.   He calls her by name, and falls back dead in her arms.   Isolde, overcome with grief, dies beside him.   King Mark, who has followed the pair to give them his blessing, prays beside their bodies.

TROVATORE, IL
(*The Troubadour*)

Composer: GIUSEPPE VERDI

Book by SALVATORE CAMMARANO, from a play by Antonio Garcia Gutierrez

First performance: *Teatro Apollo, Rome, January 19, 1853*

4 acts.

IN THE FIFTEENTH CENTURY in Aragon the Count di Luna has burned a woman at the stake for bewitching one of his sons. Azucena, the gypsy's daughter, wishes to avenge her mother by killing the Count's son, but kills her own in error. She kidnaps the Count's boy, and takes him to raise as her own. The young Count di Luna, years after these events, is in love with Leonora and jealous of Manrico, a troubadour whom Leonora loves. Leonora is informed falsely that Manrico is dead and decides to become a nun. Manrico snatches her from the altar, a kidnapping that Count di Luna intended to do but Manrico's men beat off those of the Count. Near Castellor, where Manrico has taken Leonora, the Count's guard capture Azucena, and she is condemned to be burned at the stake. Manrico rushes to his mother's rescue. Manrico is captured, and is to be executed with his mother. Leonora offers herself to the Count if he will let Manrico free. She takes a slow poison when this offer is accepted. Azucena is enraged because her mother's death will go unavenged. Leonora dies saying farewell to Manrico, and the Count, breaking his promise, sends Manrico to be executed. Azucena then has her revenge by pointing out to the Count that he has just killed his brother.

TURANDOT

Composer: GIACOMO PUCCINI

Book by GIUSEPPE ADAMI and RENATO SIMONI

First performance: *La Scala, Milan, April 25, 1926*

3 acts.

TURANDOT, in Peking, is a coldly beautiful Princess who offers to marry anyone who can answer three questions she asks. If unsuccessful the young man must lose his head. A young Persian is about to be executed when the unidentified Prince, Calaf, comes into the square and recognises his old father, a Tartar King. Timur, the father, has fallen in the dust and Liù, his servant girl, has stayed with him for years because she once fell in love with Calaf. The beautiful Princess is beseeched to free the young Persian but she is adamant. Then

Calaf shouts that he will try to answer the questions, and, to the Princess' dismay, does so successfully. She then wishes to go back on her bargain but her father insists she marry Calaf. Calaf relents, and will require nothing of her if she can learn his identity by dawn. Overjoyed, the Princess gives an order that everyone must spend the night learning his name, or the whole populace will be executed. Liù stabs herself rather than tell. Finally Calaf himself reveals the truth. Turandot suddenly realises that she has finally truly fallen in love, and goes to his arms.

WERTHER

Composer: JULES MASSENET

Book by ÉDOUARD BLAU, PAUL MILLIET, and GEORGES HARTMAN, from Goethe's novel *The Sorrows of Werther*

First performance: *Hofoper, Vienna, February 16, 1892*

4 acts.

THE DAUGHTER of the bailiff has taken care of her brothers and sisters since her mother's death. She is waiting to go to the ball with Albert, a young man to whom she has become engaged at her mother's wish. Charlotte loves Werther rather than Albert, but marries as her mother wished her to. Months later Werther, having been sent away, returns to retell his love for Charlotte. Her affection has not died either, but she insists he must leave because nothing can ever change her present married status. Werther then says he is going on a long journey and asks to borrow Albert's pistols. Albert complies without questioning, but Charlotte, when she hears of it, is frightened, and hurries to find him only to arrive too late. He dies in her arms.

WILLIAM TELL
(*Guillaume Tell*)

Composer: GIOACCHINO ROSSINI

Book by ÉTIENNE DE JOUY and HIPPOLYTE BIS, from Schiller's play

First performance: *Opéra, Paris, August 3, 1829*

4 acts.

NEAR LAKE LUCERNE in the fourteenth century the Swiss hate their Governor, Gessler, for his killing of Melchtal because Leuthold had killed one of Gessler's men for insulting Leuthold's daughter. Gessler's son, Arnold, joins William Tell and Leuthold, whom Tell has helped to escape. Arnold loves Mathilde, an Austrian Princess, who may someday rule him and his people. Tell organises the Swiss against Gessler a man who has forced indignities on the people which Tell won't stand. Tell's punishment is to shoot an apple off his son's head which he does. When a second arrow falls out of his shirt Tell boldly tells Gessler it was for the Governor's heart if he (Tell) had hit the child. Tell and son are imprisoned but Tell escapes over a wild sea, and kills Gessler. Arnold and Mathilde are united.

WOZZECK

Composer: ALBAN BERG

Book by the composer from Georg Büchner's play

First performance: *Staatsoper, Berlin, December 14, 1925*

3 acts (15 scenes).

WOZZECK, a downtrodden soldier of Germany, imposed upon by all and respected by few, is particularly the object of contempt of his Captain. Wozzeck's mistress, Marie, who has given him a son, is something of a toast of the regiment, and has offered her charms to many beside Wozzeck. The beginning of the action, after these points are well established, is an affair between the handsome Drum Major and Marie. Wozzeck is whipped by the Drum Major in a fight, and begins to see more clearly his lowly place among his fellows, as well as in Marie's esteem. Wozzeck, having slowly fanned his flame of vengeance, stabs Marie to death near a pond into which his weapon falls. In trying to retrieve it he is drowned. An ironic twist concludes the opera—the son of Wozzeck rides his hobbyhorse onto the scene.

SUPPLEMENTARY LIST
OF MODERN COMPOSERS

(Owing to the great increase in numbers of creative figures within recent decades, particularly in the United States, the following additional department has been added to the Music Lovers' Encyclopedia. An effort has been made to give data on composers whose works are being heard in America, rather than to attempt to give an exhaustive list of worldwide scope. See also the main biographical listing for other names.)

Ad'dinsell, Richard, b. London, 1904; studied law at Oxford, later music at the R. C. M., London; composer of incidental music for plays, incl. *"Alice in Wonderland"* (N. Y. prod. by Eva Le Gallienne); and films incl. *"Dangerous Moonlight"* from which the *"Warsaw"* Concerto (pf. and orch.) heard in concert.

Aguirre (ä-g$\overline{oo}$-ē-rà), **Julian,** Buenos Aires, 1868—1924; studied Madrid Cons.; later taught at Buenos Aires Cons.; has been called "the Argentinian Grieg"; esp. known for piano works in smaller forms, such as *"Aires Criollos," "Tristes";* c. suite, *"De Mi Pais"* (perf. Buenos Aires, under Alberto Williams, 1910); etc.

Allende (ä-yän'-dä), **Pedro Humberto,** b. Santiago, Chile, 1885; composer of national leanings; c. *"La Voz de les Calles,"* symph. poem based on streetpedlars' cries (Santiago, 1921); Concerto for 'cello and orch., etc.

Almand', Claude, b. Winnsboro, La., 1915; c. symphony, *"The Waste Land"* (Rochester, N. Y., Civic Orch., 1940); *"John Gilbert"* (A Steamboat Overture), based on popular songs heard on Mississippi River boat of that name (commissioned and perf. under Robert Whitney by Louisville, Ky., Philh. Orch., 1949); Piano Concerto (ibid., 1949); etc.

Alnaes (äl-nä'-äs), **Eyvind,** b. Fredriksstad, Norway, April 29, 1872; studied in Christiania, Leipzig, and Berlin; organist, choir director; best known for his songs and folk ballads; also c. symph. in C minor; symph. variations, piano wks., etc.; d. 1932.

Ardévol, José, b. Barcelona, Spain, 1911; of Catalonian-Cuban ancestry; c. *"Study in Form of a Prelude and Fugue"* for 37 percussion, friction and sibilation instruments; Suite for the same (Mills Coll., Oakland, Cal., 1940), etc.

Arnell, Richard, b. London, 1917; c. overture, *"Highgate Hill"* (Nat'l. Orch. Ass'n., N. Y., 1941); overture, *"1940"*; Sinfonia, Quasi Variazioni; Fantasia for orch.; music for film, *"The Land";* studied with John Ireland at R. C. M., London.

Avshal'amoff, Aaron, b. in Nikolaievsk, Siberia, 1894; c. ballet, *"Dream of Wei Lien"* (Shanghai, 1936); *"Peiping Hutungs"* for symph. orch., based on street cries of Chinese city (Phila. Orch., under Stokowski, 1935; San Francisco Symph., 1949), 2 symphs (No. 2, Cinc. Symph., 1949).

Aya'la, Daniel, b. Pueblo de Abala, Yucatan, 1908; Mexican of Indian extraction; his works based on music of native Indian idiom; c. *"Tribu"* (The Tribe), suite for symph. orch. (Mexican Symph. Orch., under Chavez, 1935), etc.

Babin', Victor, b. Moscow, 1908; studied at Riga Cons. and Berlin Hochsch., piano with Schnabel, comp. with Schreker; after 1933, member of 2-piano team with Vitya Vronsky, whom he m.; U. S. début, 1937, took up residence here; c. Concerto for 2 pfs. and orch.; Sonata-Fantaisie for 'cello and pf.; *"Variations on Theme by Purcell"* (cello and pf.); *"Six Etudes"* for 2 pfs.; *"Strains from Far-off Lands,"* suite for 2 pfs.; str. quartets, songs, etc.

Bacon, Ernst, b. Chicago, 1898; studied there and in Vienna; pupil of Ernest Bloch and Eugene Goossens; c. operas, *"A Tree on the Plains"* and *"A Drumlin Legend"* (both commissioned by Alice M. Ditson Fund and prod. at Columbia Univ., N. Y.); also Symphonies; *"Ford Theatre"* Suite for orch., chamber works, songs.

Bal'ogh, Ernö, b. Budapest, 1897; studied with Bartok and Kodaly at Cons. there; pianist-composer, res.

SUPPLEMENTARY LIST OF MODERN COMPOSERS 867

.n U. S. after 1924; c. *"Pastorale and Capriccio"* (piano, flute, clarinet and strings, commissioned by Station WQXR, 1943); *"Portrait of a City,"* suite for strings and piano (broadcast, in part, over WQXR); piano pieces, etc.

Barlow, Wayne, b. Elyria, O., 1912; grad. (Ph. D.), Eastman Sch. of Music; taught there; won Lillian Fairchild Award, 1935; c. *"The Winter's Passed,"* for oboe and strings, based on two folksongs; *"Lyrical Piece"* for clarinet and pf. (or strings); *"Madrigal for a May Morning"*; *"Sarabande"* for orch.; *"23rd Psalm"* for tenor, mixed chor., and organ (or orch.), etc.

Barber, Samuel. (See also page 44.) Mus. D., *hon. causa,* Curtis Inst. of Music, 1945; member, Nat'l. Inst. of Arts and Letters; first composer to win Pulitzer Prize twice; after service in World War II, awarded postservice fellowship by Guggenheim Foundation; c. also 2 *"Essays for Orch."* (No. 2 by N. Y. Philh.-Symph., under Bruno Walter, 1942); 2 symphs. (No. 2 by Boston Symph. in 1944); overture to *"The School for Scandal"*; *"Capricorn"* Concerto for sm. orch., etc.

Bate, Stanley, b. Plymouth, England, 1912; lives in U. S.; awarded Guggenheim Fellowship; c. sinfonietta for orch.; music for ballets, chamber music; studied with Nadia Boulanger.

Beach, John, b. Gloversville, N. Y., 1877; studied in U. S. and Europe; grad. New England Cons., pupil of Chadwick and Loeffler; c. *"The Asolani,"* suite after Bembo (Minneapolis Symph. under Verbrugghen, 1926); *"Mardi Gras"* for barytone voice and small orch. (New Orleans under Henri Wehrman, William Broussard soloist, 1926); *"New Orleans Street Cries at Dawn"* (Phila. Orch. under Stokowski, 1927); ballet, *"The Phantom Satyr"* (in ballet form at Asolo, Italy, under Francesco de Guarnieri, 1925; concert form by Rochester Little Symph. under Hanson, 1926); *"Pippa's Holiday"* scena for sopr. and orch.; *"Jornida and Jornidel"* (opera, 2-act).

Beck, Conrad, b. Lohn, Switzerland, 1901; c. ballet, *"The Bear"*; cantata in chamber style (text by Louise Labé); oratorio with text by Silesius; other chamber works, songs, etc.

Benatz'ky, Ralph, b. Moravske Budejovice, Austria, 1887; pupil of Veit, Klinger and Mottl; esp. known as composer of operettas, many of which were successfully prod. in Vienna and Berlin; has written nearly 100 scores for the stage, incl. many waltz hits; in U. S. since 1938; best known for operetta *"White Horse Inn,"* prod. in London and U. S.; other works staged in English incl. *"Meet My Sister"*; *"The Apaches"*; *"Cocktail"* and *"Casanova"*; has also c. music for films.

Ber'ger, Arthur V., b. New York, 1912; M. A., N. Y. Univ.; studied also with Milhaud, Piston, Nadia Boulanger, and Vincent Jones; taught at Mills Coll., Texas State Coll., and Brooklyn Coll.; served as music critic of Boston *Transcript,* later of N. Y. *Herald Trib.*; c. Quartet for Woodwinds; Serenade for chamber orch.; 3 Pieces for string orch.; *"Psalm 92"* for chorus; Duo for violin and piano; many pf. pieces, incl. Partita; etc.

Bergs'ma, William, b. Oakland, Cal., 1921; grad. Eastman Sch. of Music; Guggenheim Fellowship, Bearns Prize; c. ballet, *"Gold and the Señor Commandante"* (Rochester, 1942); *"Music on a Quiet Theme"* for orch.; *"Paul Bunyan"* Suite (San Francisco Symph., 1939); *"Variations on a Sea Chanty"* for orch., etc.; won $1000 Amer. Acad. of Arts and Letters Award; Soc. for Pub. of Amer. Music Award; commission, Koussevitzky Foundation.

Berkeley, Lennox, b. near Oxford, Eng., 1903; studied in Paris with Nadia Boulanger; c. ballet, *"The Judgement of Paris"* (Sadler's Wells Ballet, London, 1938); orch. work *"Mont Juic"* (in collaboration with Benjamin Britten); oratorio, *"Jonah"* (Leeds Fest., 1937); chamber music and many piano works.

Bing'ham, Seth, b. Bloomfield, N. J., 1882; grad. Yale Univ.; pupil of Parker and D'Indy; prof. of music, Columbia Univ.; c. *"Pioneer America"* for orch.; choral music, etc.

Blacher (bläkh'-ĕr), **Boris,** b. Jan. 3, 1903, in China, of German parents; later lived in Berlin; c. operas, *"Romeo und Juliet"* (Salzburg Fest., 1950, also in N. Y. in concert version, 1949); *"Preussisches Maerchen"* (1950, Berlin); one-act works, *"Die Flut"* and *"Nachtschwalbe"*; symph.; orch.

suites, chamber music, pf. pieces, etc.

Bowles, Paul, b. New York, 1911; studied with Aaron Copland and Virgil Thomson; c. ballets, *"Yankee Clipper"* (Ballet Caravan and Phila. Orch. under Smallens, 1937) and *"Pastorela";* Suite for sm. orch.; cantata, songs; incid. music for plays, etc.

Brant, Henry, b. Montreal, Can., 1913; studied in U. S. with Rubin Goldmark and George Antheil; won Loeb, Coolidge and Seligman Prizes; c. ballets, *"City Portrait"* and *"The Great American Goof"* (Ballet Theatre, 1940); *"Music for a Five and Ten Cent Store";* Ballad for orch. (WOR Little Symph.), etc.

Brit'ten, Benjamin. (See also page 80.) B. formed the English Opera Group, for perfs. of his works on tour; organized the Aldeburgh Music Fest.; he toured U. S. and Canada with Peter Pears, tenor, in 1949–50, giving joint recitals of his music.; c. also *"Let's Make an Opera,"* opera for children; new version of the *"Beggar's Opera";* and in 1950 was at work on an opera based on Herman Melville's *"Billy Budd,"* with libretto by E. M. Forster; c. *"Soirées Musicales"* (suite after Rossini) (BBC Orch., London, 1937); *"Sinfonia da Requiem"* (N. Y. Philh.-Symph. under Barbirolli, 1941); Sinfonietta (London, 1933); *"Variations on a Theme of Frank Bridge"* for str. orch. (Boyd Neel Orch., Salzburg Fest., 1937); Concerto in D major for pf. and orch. (BBC Orch. under Wood, composer soloist, 1938); *"Diversions on a Theme"* for solo pf. (one hand) and orch. (Phila. Orch., under Ormandy, Paul Wittgenstein, for whom it was written, soloist, 1942); Concerto in D minor for violin and orch. (N. Y. Philh.-Symph. under Barbirolli, Antonio Brosa, soloist, 1940); *"Les Illuminations,"* cycle for tenor and small ensemble, based on Rimbaud poems, etc.

Bruns'wick, Mark, b. New York, 1902; studied with Rubin Goldmark, Ernest Bloch, Roger Sessions and in Paris with Nadia Boulanger; c. Symph. for chorus and orch.; String Quartet; Fantasia for viola solo; motet, *"Fragment of Sappho";* ballet suite on Aristophanes' Lysistrata, etc.; in 1948–9 he was pres. of the Amer. section, ISCM.

Burk'hard, Willy, b. Evillard sur Bienne, Switzerland, 1900; taught piano and composition at Berne Cons.; c. opera, *"The Black Spider,"* on medieval morality play (Lucerne, 1949); cantatas; Violin Concerto; piano works, etc.

Bush, Alan, b. London, Dec. 22, 1900; composer; studied at R. C. M. for a few years, then comp. with Ireland, piano with Schnabel and Moiseiwitsch; musicology at Univ. of Berlin, 1929–31; prof. of comp., at R. A. M., also active as conductor, pianist, lecturer; organised concerts for working class groups; c. 2 Symphs. (No. 2 commissioned for 400th anniv. of City of Nottingham); suite, *"Piers Plowman's Day";* Concerto for pf. and orch. with male chor.; *"Dance"* and *"Resolution"* Overtures; *"English Suite"* for str. orch.; *"Lyric Interlude"* for vln. and pf.; *"Meditation on a German Song of 1848,"* for vln. and pf.; *"Concert Piece"* for cello and pf.; *"Dialectic"* for str. quartet; *"The Winter Journey,"* cantata for mixed chor., strgs. and harp; *"The Press Gang,"* children's opera; also opera on Wat Tyler, etc.

Cage, John, b. Los Angeles, 1912; studied with Schönberg, Cowell, Weiss; c. works for perc. insts. and "prepared" piano, with small objects between strs. to produce novel effects; c. *"Imaginary Landscape"* for percussion orch.; scores for ballets; *"Construction I,"* and *"Construction II"* for percussion insts., etc.

Canteloube (kănt-lōōb), **Joseph,** b. 1879 at Annonay, France; pupil of D'Indy; c. opera *"Le Mas"* (Paris Opéra); arr. folksongs of the Auvergne; c. symph., piano works, songs, etc.

Car'ter, Elliott, b. New York, 1908; studied at Harvard Univ. with Hill and Piston; in Paris with Nadia Boulanger; c. ballet, *"Pocohontas"* (commissioned by Ballet Caravan, 1939); Symphony; works for chorus, songs, etc.

Cas'tro, Juan José, b. Buenos Aires, 1895; after 1930, conductor for opera and orch. concerts at Teatro Colon there; c. opera, *"La Zapatera Prodigiosa"; "Dans le Jardin des Morts"* for orch. (1st prize, Munic. of Buenos Aires, 1924); 3 *"Trozos Sinfonicos"* (ISCM Fest., London, 1931); Sinfonia, etc.

Caturla (kä-tōōr′-lä), **Alejandro Garcia,** Remedios, Cuba, 1906—1940; pupil of Nadia Boulanger in Paris; c. *"Cuban Suite"* for 8 wind insts. and pf.; *"Tres Danzas Cubanas"* (Havana Philh., 1928); chamber music, songs, etc.

Caz′den, Norman, b. New York, 1914; studied Juilliard Grad. Sch.; c. *"Preamble"* and *"3 Dances"* for orch.; Concerto for 10 insts. (Juilliard Grad. Sch., under Bernard Wagenaar, 1937); *"On the Death of a Spanish Child"* (orig. title *"Elegy before Dawn"*) for symph. band, also for chamber orch.; songs, etc.

Chan′ler, Theodore, b. Newport, R. I., 1902; studied with Arthur Shepherd, Percy Goetschius, Ernest Bloch; at Oxford Univ. and with Nadia Boulanger in Paris; c. Sonata for violin and piano; Mass for two women′s voices; *"8 Epitaphs,"* song cycle; *"5 Short Colloquies"* for piano; song cycles; Sonatina for chamber ensemble, etc.

Cimara (chē-mä′-rä), **Pietro,** b. Rome, 1887; studied at Rome Cons., and with Respighi; 1916, début as cond. at Costanzi Theat. in Rome; after 1934, ass′t. cond. at Met. Op.; c. *"Triptych"* for voice and orch.; songs, etc.

Cit′kowitz, Israel, b. in Russia, 1909; brought to U. S. as a child; studied with Copland and Sessions, and in Paris with Nadia Boulanger; taught at Dalcroze Sch., N. Y.; c. choral, orch., chamber works, etc.

Cohn, Arthur, b. Philadelphia, 1910; studied at Juilliard Sch.; dir. of mus. div., Free Library of that city; dir. of Edwin A. Fleisher Music Collection; c. *"Four Symph. Documents"* (Nat′l Symph. Orch. under Kindler, 1941); *"Retrospections"* for str. orch. (Phila. Chamber Orch. under Isadore Freed, in part, 1935); *"Histrionics"* (for str. quartet, later for str. orch.) (N. Y., Stringart Quartet, 1935); 4 Preludes (Greenwich Orch., N. Y., under composer, 1937); *"Nature Pieces,"* suite for orch., etc.; won $500 prize of Soc. for Ancient Insts., for his *"Music for Ancient Insts.,"* 1938.

Contreras (kôn-trä′-räs), **Salvador,** b. Gueramaro, Mexico, 1912; c. Suite for Chamber Orch. (Mexico City, composer conducting, 1941); Music for Symph. Orch.; Three Symphonic Movements, etc.

Cole, Ulric, b. New York, 1905; studied with Homer Grunn in Los Angeles, Goetschius in N. Y.; at Juilliard Sch.; with Boulanger in Paris; c. *"Two Sketches"* for string orch. (orig. two movements from String Quartet No. 1), (Mutual Broadcasting String Symph., under Wallenstein, 1938); Concerto for Piano and Orch.; 2 Sonatas for vln. and pf.; Divertimento for str. orch. and 2 pfs., etc.

Cools, Eugène, Paris, 1877—1936; pupil and later assistant (1907-23) to Gédalge at Paris Cons.; studied with Fauré and Widor; c. Symph. in C minor, which won Prix Cressent in 1906; operas, music to plays, chamber and piano works, songs, etc.; music critic of Le Monde Musicale.

Craw′ford, Ruth, b. East Liverpool, Ohio, 1901; studied in Chicago, also in Paris and Berlin on Guggenheim Fellowship; c. *"Three Songs"* (Amsterdam Fest. of the Intern. Soc. for Contemporary Music, 1933), etc.

Dallapiccola (dä-lä-pē′-kō-lä), **Luigi,** b. Pisino, Italy, 1904; pupil of Florence Cons., and taught there after 1934; atonalist; c. operas, *"Vol de Nuit,"* and *"Il Prigioniero;"* a Partita for orch.; chamber works, etc.

Dela′ney, Robert, b. Baltimore, 1903; studied with Boulanger and Honegger; c. *"Going to Town,"* orch. suite; suite of music for *"The Constant Couple,"* play by Farquhar (Rochester Philh., under Hanson, 1928); *"Symphonic Piece No. 1"* (ibid., 1936); *"Work No. 22,"* scherzo for orch. (Harvard Univ. Orch. under Malcolm Holmes, 1939); choral symph., *"John Brown′s Body"*; 3 Str. Quartets; Vln. Sonata; *"Blake Cycle,"* etc.

Delannoy (dŭ-län-wä′), **Marcel,** b. Ferté-Alais, Isle de France, 1898; studied in Paris with Honegger and Cools; c. ballet-opera, *"Le Fou de la Dame"*; ballet, *"La Pantoufle de Vair"*; Symphony; String Quartet; piano works, songs, etc.

Delgadil′lo, Luis, b. Managua, Nicaragua, 1887; c. *"Ballet Infantil"* for orch. (based on cartoon of Felix the Cat and Mickey Mouse); *"Diciembre"* (Suite Colonial); *"Sinfonia Incaica"*; *"Tectihuacan"* (Suite Mexicana), etc.

Dello Joi′o, Norman, b. New York, 1913; studied at Inst. of Mus. Art, with Gaston Dethier in pf. and org.;

his Piano Trio won Coolidge Award; 1939, awarded fellowship at Juilliard Grad. School, where he studied comp. with Bernard Wagenaar; 1940–1 awarded scholarships at Berkshire Mus. Centre, where he studied with Paul Hindemith, and with the latter also at Yale Univ.; 1942, his Magnificat won N. Y. Town Hall award for composition; 1946, he rec'd. $1,000 grant from Amer. Acad. of Arts and Letters; 1945 and 1946 won Guggenheim Fellowships; c. *"Variations, Chaconne and Finale"* (Pittsburgh Symph. under Reiner, 1948; also by N. Y. Philh.-Symph. under Walter; Boston and Cincinnati Symphs., Nat'l Symph., Washington); *"Serenade"* for orch. (Cleveland Orch. under Szell, 1949); *"New York Profiles,"* suite for sm. orch. commissioned by Nikolai Sokoloff, for Mus. Arts Soc., La Jolla, Cal.; Concertante for clarinet and orch. (written for Artie Shaw and prem. by him with Chautauqua, N. Y., Symph., 1949); Concerto for harp and orch.; Trio for flute, cello and pf.; in 1949 he was a teacher of comp. at Sarah Lawrence Coll.

Delvincourt (děl-věṅ-kōōr'), **Claude,** b. Paris, Jan. 12, 1888; pupil of Widor at Paris Cons.; won Prix de Rome, 1913; wounded and lost sight of one eye in World War I; dir. of Paris Cons. in 1945; c. ballet-opera, *"Lucifer"* (Paris Op., 1948–9); arr. 18th century popular airs; d. in motor acc., Grosseto, Italy, 1954.

Di'amond, David, b. Rochester, N. Y., 1915; studied at Eastman School of Music with Bernard Rogers; also with Roger Sessions; won Guggenheim Fellowships, 1938, 1941; studied at Fontainebleau, with Nadia Boulanger; awarded American Acad. in Rome Prize; c. symphs.; *"Rounds"* for str. orch.; Sonata for vln. and piano; string quartets; incid. music for *"Romeo and Juliet"*; Overture to *"The Tempest"*; Music for Double String Orch.; Psalm for orch. (Juilliard Pub. Award) (after Carl Sandburg) (won Elfrida Whiteman Fellowship, 1935); 2 Symphs. (No. 1 played by N. Y. Philh., under Mitropoulos, 1941); *"Elegy"* (to Memory of Ravel) (Eastman School Fest., 1934); *"The Enormous Room"* (after Cummings) (Cincinnati Symph., 1949) etc.

Don'ovan, Richard, b. New Haven, Conn., 1891; studied at Music School of Yale Univ.; at Inst. of Mus. Art, N. Y., and with Widor in Paris; member, Yale School of Mus. faculty; c. *"Smoke and Steel,"* symph. poem, after poem by Carl Sandburg; Symph. for Chamber Orch. (Yaddo Fest., 1937, composer conducting); *"Ricercare"* for oboe and strings (Eastman Sch. Little Symph., 1939), etc.

Dop'per, Cornelis, Stadskanaal, Friesland, 1870—Amsterdam, 1939; chiefly self-taught, but studied at Leipzig Cons., 1887–90; pupil of Wendling, Reinecke and others; active as choral and operatic conductor, and after 1908 ass't. cond. with the Amsterdam Concertgebouw Orch.; c. 4 operas, incl. *"Het Eerekruis"* (Amsterd., 1894) and *"William Ratcliffe"* (Weimar, 1912); 8 symphs., incl. No. 5 (with chorus) based on Book I of the Iliad (1916); and No. 7 (*"Zuyderzee"*) (1919); *"Paris,"* rhapsodie for orch.; Cello Concerto; Overtures; a popular *"Ciaconna Gothica"* for orch.; Str. Quartet, which won a prize in 1914; Sonatas for vln. and pf., cello and pf.; choral works, piano pieces, and many songs.

Dres'den, Sem, b. Amsterdam, 1881; pupil of Bernard Zweers in that city and of Pfitzner in Berlin; after 1907 teacher of composition at Amsterdam Cons.; founded a madrigal society in 1914; with Daniel Ruyneman and Henri Zagwijn formed Soc. of Modern Dutch Composers; c. Piano Sonata; Sonata for vln. and pf.; 3 Sextets for wind and piano; Trio for 2 oboes and English horn; Praeludium, Scherzo and Finale for 2 pianos; Sonata for Harp and Flute; Sonata for Cello and Pf.; Variations and Suite, both for orch.; String Sextet; a capella choruses, songs, etc.

Duke, John, b. Cumberland, Md., 1899; studied at Peabody Cons.; also with Boulanger and Schnabel; prof. mus., Smith College; c. Overture in D minor for str. orch. (Smith Coll. Symph. Orch. under composer, 1928); Concerto in A major for piano and str. orch. (Springfield, Mass., Fed. Orch., composer soloist, Milton Aronson, cond., 1939); chamber wks., songs, etc.

Ei'nem, Gottfried von, b. Austria, 1918; pupil of Boris Blacher; c. opera, *"Dantons Tod"* (after drama by

Georg Büchner), Salzburg Fest., 1947; song cycles, etc.; in 1949–50 he was reported at work on an opera based on a story by Franz Kafka.

El'well, Herbert, b. Minneapolis, 1898; studied at Univ. of Minnesota; in New York with Ernest Bloch; 1922, went to Europe for study with Nadia Boulanger; 1926, awarded Fellowship at Amer. Acad. in Rome; after 1932 mus. critic for Cleveland *Plain Dealer;* won Eastman School Publication Award; Paderewski Prize, 1946, for his *"Lincoln, Requiem Aeternam";* also c. ballet, *"The Happy Hypocrite";* Orchestral Sketches; Cantata; *"Pastorale"* for sopr. and orch., setting of Song of Songs; Quintet for strings and pf.; Sonata for vln. and pf.; *"Divertimento"* for str. quartet; Sonata and other works for pf.; choruses, songs, etc.

En'gel, Lehman, b. Jackson, Miss., Sept. 14, 1910; studied at Cincinnati Coll. of Mus. and Conservatory, also with Rubin Goldmark and Roger Sessions at Juilliard Grad. Sch.; was cond. and founder, Madrigal Singers; taught at Neighborhood Playhouse Sch., N. Y.; c. operas, *"Medea"* (1-act), *"Pierrot of the Minute";* ballet, *"Phobias"; "Jungle Dance," "Introduction and Allegretto," "Scientific Creation,"* for orch.; choral wks.; incid. music for *"Murder in the Cathedral," "Within the Gates," "Birds"* (Aristophanes), and other dramas; cond. first U. S. perf. of Kurt Weill's opera, *"Der Jasager"* and score for Paul Green's *"Johnny Johnson"* on Broadway, also other theatr. prods.

Ep'pert, Carl, b. Carbon, Ind., 1882; studied in Europe with Hugo Kaun, Nikisch, Kunwald; founded Milwaukee Civic Orch., 1921; c. *"A Symphony of the City,"* symph. cycle in 4 parts, incl. I. *"Traffic"* (second prize in NBC competition, 1932, perf. NBC Orch. under Goossens, and same year by Hollywood Bowl Orch. under Stock); II. *"City Shadows";* III. *"Speed";* IV. *"City Nights"* (latter 3 by Rochester Philh. under Hanson, 1935); *"Escapade,"* mus. satire (Indianapolis Symph. under Sevitzky, 1941); Symphonic Suites I and II (perf., resp., by Chicago and Detroit Symphs., 1941 and 1942); *"Timber,"* for orch. (Juilliard Pub. Award); *"A Cameo Symph.";*

"Symph. of the Land"; opera, *"Kaintuckee,"* etc.

Fernan'dez, Oscar, Rio de Janeiro, Brazil, 1897—1948; founder and for some years dir. of Brazilian Cons. of Mus.; c. opera, *"Malazarte,"* from which the Negro dance, *"Batuque,"* has been widely heard; and *"Imbapara,"* Indian poem for orch., also perf. as a ballet; *"Suite Brasileiro," "Suite Sinfonica sobre Tres Themas Populaires,"* both for orch.; *"Piano Trio Brasileiro,"* etc.

Finney, Ross Lee, b. Wells, Minn., 1906; studied in U. S. with Hill and Sessions, in Europe with Boulanger and Berg; won Pulitzer Scholarship and Guggenheim Fellowship; member of Smith Coll. music faculty; c. dance drama, *"Masse Mensch"; "Barber Shop Ballad"* (based on folksong *"The Dark-eyed Canaler"*), orch. work (commissioned by CBS and premiered under Herrmann, 1940); *"Overture for a Drama"* (Eastman Symph. under Hanson, 1941); *"Slow Piece"* (orch. of movement from 'cello and pf. sonata), (Minneapolis Symph. under Mitropoulos), etc.

Fiorillo (fē-ōr-ĭl'-lō), **Dante,** b. New York, 1905; c. Prelude and Fugue for string orch. (former perf. by Chamber Orch. of Phila., Isadore Freed conducting, 1934; both by N. Y. Civic Orch., 1935); also Concerto; Introduction and Passcaglia; Partita (on theme by an 18th Century Fiorillo)—all for orch.; chamber music, songs, etc.

Forst, Rudolf, b. New York, 1900; violinist; studied comp. with Mason at Columbia Univ.; c. *"Music for Strings"* (orig. a str. quartet, and as such won $250 prize of NBC Music Guild, 1936; played over NBC by Gordon String Quartet, 1937); *"Aubade Mexicaine,"* based on old Spanish songs of Calif. (Greenwich Orch., under Maganini, 1938); Divertimento for chamber orch. (from which, Pastorale and Tempo di Valse given at Yaddo Fest., 1938, and Toccata-Prelude by WOR Symphonietta.

Fort'ner, Wolfgang, b. Leipzig, 1907; studied with Grabner, Kroyer; after 1931 taught comp., Heidelberg; c. ballet, *"Die Weise Rose,"* chm. wks., etc.

Foss, Lukas (name originally Fuchs), b. Berlin, 1922; studied in Berlin and Paris; came to U. S. with parents in

1937; studied at Curtis Inst. of Music, Phila.; served as pianist of Boston Symph. Orch.; c. cantata, *"The Prairie"* (perf. by N. Y. Philh.-Symph. Orch. and vocalists, 1945); *"Recordare"* (to memory of Gandhi), (Boston Symph., 1948–9 under Koussevitzky); ballet, *"Song of Solomon"* (choreographed by Charles Weidman, 1949), etc.

Fran'co, Johan, b. Zaandam, Holland, 1908; studied under Pijper; later res. in U. S.; c. First Symph. (Rotterdam Philh. under Flipse, 1934); Symphony No. 2 (*"George Washington"*), last movement orig. titled Introduction e Scherzo, for clarinet and chamber orch.; *"Serenata Concertante"* for pf. and chamber orch. (Orchestrette Classique under Frederique Petrides, N. Y., William Masselos soloist, 1940); *"Symphony Concertante"* for pf. and orch. (Nat'l Orch. Ass'n., N. Y., under Barzin, Masselos soloist, 1941); *"Concerto Lirico"* for vln. and orch., etc.

Freed, Isadore, b. in Russia, 1900; taken to Philadelphia in the U. S. while quite young; grad. of Univ. of Penna. and medallist of Phila. Cons.; studied with Ernest Bloch; with D'Indy, at Schola Cantorum, Paris; taught at Curtis Inst., Phila.; c. Symph.; Triptych; *"Jeux de Timbres"*; *"Pastorales"* (9 pieces), (Nat'l. Symph., Washington, 1938), all for orch.; chamber works, songs; ballet *"Vibrations"*; one-act opera, *"Homo Sum"*; choral music; opera, *"The Princess and the Vagabond"* (commissioned by Hartt Opera Guild, Hartford, Conn., and prod. there, 1948), etc.

Fuleihan (fōō-lā'-hän), **Anis,** b. Kyrenia, Isle of Cyprus, 1900; came to U. S. in 1915; studied with Alberto Jonas (piano), and made début as pianist; later won Guggenheim Fellowship; c. Symph. No. 1 (N. Y. Philh.-Symph., under Barbirolli, 1936); *"Mediterranean,"* suite for orch. (Cincinnati Symph., under Goossens, 1935); *"Fiesta"* and *"Invocation"* (commissioned and perf. by Indianapolis Symph. under Sevitzky, 1939 and 1941, resp.); Concerto No. 1 for pf. and str. orch. (Saratoga Spa Fest., under F. Charles Adler; composer, soloist, 1937); *"Epithalamium"* (variations for pf. and str. orch.) (Phila. Str. Simfonietta, under Se-

vitzky, composer soloist, 1941), etc.

Gaito (gä-ē'-tō), **Constantine,** b. Buenos Aires, 1878; son of Caystano G., violinist; early showed mus. gifts and was sent for study with Platania in Naples; made concert tour of Italy; 1900, returned to Buenos Aires, founded school; c. operas, *"Strapas"* (1-act); *"Doria"* (3-act); *"Cajo Petronio"* (3-act); Overture; Suite for Orch.; symph. poem, *"El Ombú"* (awarded first municipal prize of Buenos Aires, 1924); songs, etc.

Galin'do, Blas, b. San Gabriel, Jalisco, Mexico, 1911; folk-style composer; grad. and later dir. of Mexican Nat'l Cons.; c. *"Preludios"* for orch.; *"Danza de las Fuerzas Nuevas"* (Mexican ballet suite), chamber works, etc.

Gavazzeni (gä-vä-tsä'-nē), **Gianandrea,** b. Bergamo, 1909; c. *"Preludio Sinfonico"* and *"Concerto Bergamesco"* for orch.; sonatas for vln. and cello; Piano Trio; ballets and melodramas; *"Chants of the Lombard Laborers"* (Venice Mod. Mus. Fest., 1937), etc.

Ghedini (gä-dē'-nē), **Giorgio Federico,** b. Cuneo, Italy, 1892; studied at Verdi Cons., Turin (where he later was prof.) and grad. of Bologna Cons., 1911; cellist, pianist, organist, conductor; c. operas, *"The Bacchantes"* (La Scala, 1948); *"L'Intrusa"* (1-act); Partita and Suite for orch.; *"Marinaresca e Baccanale"* (Chicago Symph., under De Sabata, 1949); *"Dramatic Overture,"* Concerto Grosso; oratorios, masses; Concerto for organ and orch.

Gianneo (hē-än-ā'-ō), **Luis,** b. Buenos Aires, 1897; c. *"Obertura para una Comedia Infantil"* (for chamber orch. of winds and percussion) (NBC Symphony, N. Y., under Juan José Castro, 1941); Violin Concerto, etc.

Gil'lis, Don, b. Cameron, Mo., 1912; B. M., Texas Christian Univ.; M. M., North Texas Teachers Coll.; staff arranger in radio station, Ft. Worth, Tex., for a time; later for a Chicago network, and then mus. dir. of prod., NBC Symph.; c. 5 symphs.; suite, *"The Panhandle,"* *"Portrait of a Frontier Town,"* *"The Raven,"* *"To an Unknown Soldier,"* *"Citizen Tom Paine,"* *"Intermission—10 Minutes,"* *"Symphony Five and a Half"* (cond. by Toscanini with NBC Symph.), *"Prairie Poem,"* *"The Alamo,"* *"Short Overture to an Un-*

written Opera," "Perpetual Emotion," all for orch.; *"Rhapsody"* for harp and orch.; cantata for radio, *"The Crucifixion"*; *"Music for Tonight,"* five str. quartets, pf. quintet, etc.

Ginastera (hē-näs-tä'-rä), **Alberto,** b. Buenos Aires, 1916; c. *"Concierto Argentino"* for pf. and orch. (SODRE Orch., Montevideo, 1941, under Lamberto Baldi, Hugo Balzo soloist) *"Panambi"* (choreographic legend), etc.

Gould, Morton, b. Richmond Hill, N. Y., 1913; stud. at Inst. of Mus. Art, N. Y.; cond. on radio and arranger; grad., N. Y. Univ. at age of 15; precocious in music and early active as pianist; c. *"Chorale and Fugue in Jazz"* (Phila. Orch. Youth Concerts, under Stokowski, 1936); 3 *"American Symphonettes," "Latin American Symphonette,""Spirituals"* (str. choir, orch.) (N. Y. Philh.-Symph.); *"Foster Gallery," "Lincoln Legend,"* *"Cowboy Rhapsody"* for orch.; Piano, Concerto, 3 Sonatas, a Sonatina (all pf.); ballets, *"Interplay"* and *"Fall River Legend"*; band wks., music for plays.

Grif'fis, Elliot, b. Boston, 1893; studied at Ithaca, N. Y., and New England Cons., at Yale Sch. of Mus., and Mannes School, N. Y.; won Pulitzer Fellowship; Mus. D., N. Y. Coll. of Mus.; c. *"Montevallo,"* concerto for strings, piano and organ (based on Southern Mountain tunes); *"Colossus"* (symph. poem, based on legend of Paul Bunyan); *"Fantastic Pursuit"* (symph. for str. orch.); songs, etc.

Guarnieri (gōō-är-nē-ä'-rē), **Camargo,** b. Tiete, São Paulo, Brazil, 1907; conductor; toured U. S. as guest in concerts of his music; inspired by native Brazilian themes; advanced modern style; c. Symphs.; Concerto for Piano and Orch. (Rio de Janeiro, Orquestra do Theatro Municipal, under composer's baton, with Lidia Simoes as soloist, 1949); *"Prologo e Fuga"* for orch.; *"Abertura Concertante," "Danza Brasileira"* and *"Danza Selvagem"* (São Paulo Munic. Orch. under composer's direction); *"Flor de Tremembé"* (Rio de Janeiro, ensemble of the Escuola Nacional de Musica, with Guarnieri directing), etc.

Guion (gī'-ŏn), **David,** b. Ballinger,

Tex., 1895; studied with Godowsky at Vienna Cons.; c. *"Western Ballet,"* based on folk tunes; *"Shingandi,"* African ballet suite; *"Alley Tunes"*; *"Arkansas Traveler"*; *"Turkey in the Straw"*; *"Sheep and Goat Walkin' to the Pasture"*; *"Mother Goose"* suite, for orch.; some 100 songs.

Haieff (hī-ĕf), **Alexei,** b. Russia, 1914; after 1932 in U.S., studied Juilliard School; also in Paris; c. orch. wks.

Halff'ter, Rodolfo, b. Madrid, 1900; bro. of Ernesto H.; a follower of Schoenberg's atonal theories of comp., he lived in Latin America after 1938; c. *"Natures Mortes"* for piano; *"Piezas"* for str. quartet; Suite for Orch.; *"Obertura Concertante"* for piano and orch., etc.

Ham'erik, Ebbe, b. Copenhagen, 1898; son of Asger H.; pupil of his father and Frank Van der Stucken; 1919, made début as conductor in native city; 1919–22 at Royal Theat. in that city as ass't. cond.; appeared in Vienna, Berlin, etc., as orch. cond.; c. opera *"Stepan"* (Mainz, 1924); Symph.; Str. Quartet; *"Sommer"* for barytone and orch.; org. wks.; songs, etc.

Har'rison, Lou, b. Portland, Ore., 1917; c. works for percussion ensemble, incl. *"Canticle," "Fifth Simfony"*; Concerto for Flute, etc.

Hauf'recht, Herbert, b. New York, 1909; studied Juilliard Sch. of Music; c. *"Overture for an Amer. Mural"* (WNYC Concert Orch., composer conducting, 1939); *"Three Fantastic Sketches"* (NBC Symph. Orch. Frank Black, 1941); Suite for str. orch. (Juilliard Grad. Sch. Str. Orch., under Edgar Schenkman, 1934); choruses, songs, etc.

Hel'fer, Walter, b. Lawrence, Mass., 1896; grad. of Harvard Univ.; won Fellowship at Amer. Acad. in Rome; studied with Mason and Respighi; chm. faculty of mus., Hunter Coll., N. Y.; c. Str. Quartet; *"Symphony on Canadian Airs"*; *"Fantasie on Children's Tunes"*; Prelude to *"A Midsummer Night's Dream"* (Paderewski Prize of $1,000, 1938), etc.

Herr'mann, Bernard, b. New York, 1911; studied at Juilliard Grad. School; after 1938 with Columbia Broadcasting System as cond. of orch. programs; led the New Chamber Orch. as guest, also Hallé Orch. in Manchester, Eng.; c. ballet,

"Skating Rink"; Sinfonietta for str. orch.; Nocturne and Scherzo; *"Currier & Ives"* Suite; tone poem, *"The City of Brass"*; Variations on *"Deep River"* and *"Water Boy"*; Symph.; Violin Concerto; *"Moby Dick,"* dram. cantata for soloists, speakers and male chorus (N. Y. Philh.-Symph. Orch.); film scores, etc.

Howe, Mary, b. Richmond, Va., 1882; studied piano with Hutcheson, Harold Randolph; and Burmeister in Germany; comp. with Gustav Strube, and with Nadia Boulanger in Paris; grad. Peabody Cons.; later lived in Washington; c. ballet *"Cards"*; orch. wks., *"Dirge," "Sand," "Stars"*; *"Poema"*; *"Coulennes"*; *"Mists"*; Violin Sonata; Quintet Suite; *"Habañera"* for 2 pfs.; choruses, songs, etc.

Inch, Herbert, b. Missoula, Mont., 1904; grad. Eastman School of Music, Rochester, N. Y.; won Fellowship at Amer. Acad. in Rome; Ernest Bloch Award; Univ. of Rochester Trav. Fellowship; Ph. D., Montana State Univ.; c. *"Serenade"* for string orch. (heard in part at Eastman Sch. Symposium, Rochester Civic Orch., under Hanson, 1939); Symph. No. 1 (Rochester Philh. Orch., under Hanson, 1932); *"Three Pieces"* for small orch. (ibid., 1930); *"Variations on a Modal Theme"* (ibid., 1927) etc.

Ja'cob, Gordon (See also entry in biograph. section); b. Norwood, n. London, 1895; composer; studied at Dulwich Coll., later at R.C.M. with Stanford and Charles Wood; prof. of comp., harmony and orchestration at latter school; c. 2 Symphs.; 3 Suites for Orch.; Concertos for Oboe and Bassoon with Strs.; Rhapsody for Cor Anglais and Strs.; *"Variations on an Original Theme," "Passacaglia on a Well-known Theme"*; *"Fantasie on the Alleluia Hymn"* and *"Festal March,"* all for orch.; Clarinet Quintet; Oboe Quartet; *"Prelude, Passacaglia and Fugue"* for vln. and vla.; *"Three Inventions"* for flute and oboe; choral and pf. music, songs; also ballet *"Uncle Remus,"* etc.; arr. works of older composers, incl. an *"Orlando Gibbons"* Suite and Handel's Overture to *"Theodora"*; author of treatise on instrumentation; D. Mus., London, 1935.

Jemnitz (yām'-nēts), **Alexander,** b. Budapest, 1890; studied with Koessler at Mus. Akad. there, and in

Leipzig with Reger and Straube; was ass't. cond. at Bremen Opera; later in Berlin and then Budapest as teacher and critic; c. orch., chamber mus., ballets; Str. Quartet; Sonatas for vln. and pf.; flute and oboe trios, etc.

Jirak (yē'-räk), **Karl Boleslav,** b. Prague, 1891; studied with Novak and J. B. Foerster; cond. at Hamburg Op., later in Bruenn and cond. of the Hlahol Chorus in Prague; after 1920 taught comp. at Prague Cons.; later as teacher in Chicago; c. 2 Symph.; *"Overture to a Comedy"*; Str. Sextet; Sonatas for vln. and vla.; Pf. Suites and smaller pieces; *"Tragikomoedien,"* song cycle with orch., etc.

John'son, Hunter, b. Benson, N. C., 1906; grad. Eastman Sch. of Music; taught at Univ. of Mich.; awarded Guggenheim Fellowship, 1941; previously had won Fellowship at Amer. Acad. in Rome and studied in Europe, 1933–5; c. Symph.; Concerto for Piano and Small Orch. (Greenwich Concert Orch., N. Y., under Lehman Engel, Harry Cumpson soloist, 1937), etc.

Jolivet (zhô-lē-vā'), **André,** b. Paris, 1905; pupil of Le Flem and Varèse; opponent of neo-classicism, flouting tonality; c. Concerto for Ondes Martenot (electronic inst.) and Orch. (Boston Symph. under Munch, 1949, with Ginette Martenot as soloist); *"Trois Chansons de Ménestrels"* and *"Poèmes Intimes"* for voice and pf.; *"Memories of a Soldier"*; wks. for pf. and org., etc.

Jones, Charles, b. Tamworth, Ontario, Can., 1912; mem. of faculty at Mills Coll., in California; studied and was active as teacher in the U. S., c. Symphs.; Concerto for sm. orch.; Suite for string orch., chamber wks., songs, etc.

Kanitz (kä'-nēts), **Ernst,** b. Vienna, 1894; studied harmony with Heuberger, counterpoint and composition with Schreker; prof. of musical theory at the New Vienna Cons. for some years; later res. as teacher and composer in U. S.; member music faculty, Univ. of Southern California; c. Str. Quartet; Concert Overture; Songs for high voice; Three Songs for medium voice (Salzburg Intern. Chamber Mus. Fest.); *"Das Hohe Lied"* (setting of the Song of Songs) for soloists, chor. and orch.

(perf. by Vienna Philh. Chorus and Vienna Singakademie, under Szell, 1921); Sonata for vln. and pf., etc.

Kau'der, Hugo, b. Tobitschau, Moravia, 1888; went to Vienna in 1905; studied at Vienna Univ.; largely self-taught in mus.; played violin and viola in the Konzertverein Orch. there; 1925, violist of Baltz Quartet; c. Symph. (Vienna, 1924); 'Cello Concerto; 2 Str. Quartets; Divertimento for vln. and vla.; Passacaglia for org.; about 100 songs, etc.

Kay, Ulysses, b. Tucson, Arizona, 1917; grad. Eastman Sch. of Music; won $1000 Alice M. Ditson Fellowship; also $700 prize, American Composers Alliance, sponsored by Broadcast Music, Inc.; c. Sinfonietta (in part by Rochester Civic Orch., under Hanson, 1939); "*Danse Calinda*" (ballet with story by Ridgely Torrence) (ibid., 1941); "*Five Mosaics*" for orch.; Oboe Concerto (ibid., 1940, Sprenkel soloist); "*Of New Horizons*" ($500 1st prize, Fellowship of Amer. Composers and AMC); "*A Short Overture*" (joint award of $1000, Gershwin Memorial Contest, 1947); Piano Sonata (Phi Mu Alpha Award, 1940), etc.; awarded Fellowship, Amer. Acad. in Rome, 1949.

Ken'nan, Kent, b. Milwaukee, Wis., 1913; grad. Eastman Sch. of Music; won Fellowship at Amer. Acad. in Rome; c. Nocturne for viola and small orch.; "*Air de Ballet*" (Detroit Symph. under Kolar, 1941, later part of a Suite, given by Eastman Sch. Little Symph., 1943); "*Lament*" (NBC Symph. Orch. under Black, 1941); "*Night Soliloquy*," for flute, pf. and strings; "*Promenade*" (Santa Cecilia Orch., Rome, 1938, also later part of Suite for Orch.); "*Concertino for an American Going to War*"; Andante for solo oboe and small orch. (Roch. Civic Orch., 1941), etc.

Kerr, Harrison, b. Cleveland, O., 1899; his works heard at Yaddo Fest., Saratoga, N. Y.; taught at Univ. of Oklahoma; member of the Civil Affairs Division, Dept. of the Army; and member of the Intern. Music Council of UNESCO; c. Symph. in D Minor; "*Dance Suite*" (Rochester Symph. under Hanson, 1942); "*Dance Sonata*" for 2 pfs. and percussion (Bennington Coll. Fest., 1938); etc.

Klein'singer, George, b. San Bernar-

dino, Cal., 1914; B. A. in Mus. from N. Y. Univ.; awarded fellowship in comp. at Juilliard Grad. Sch., 1938–40; c. opera, "*Life in a Day of a Secretary*" (1st prize, Nat'l. New Theatre League Contest, 1939); cantata, "*I Hear America Singing*" (St. Louis Symph.; NBC Symph.; Southern Symph.; Springfield Symph.); Fantasy for vln. and orch. (Nat'l. Orch. Ass'n. with Barzin); "*Street Corner*" Concerto for harmonica and orch. (Cleveland Orch.; Boston Pops; Kansas City Philh.); "*Tubby the Tuba*" (N. Y. Philh. under Stokowski; Phila. Orch.; Cincinnati Symph.; Columbus Symph.; Pittsburgh Symph.; Chicago Symph.); "*Overture on American Folk Themes*" (Boston Pops Orch.); "*Pan the Piper*" (Cincinnati Symph. under Thor Johnson); "*Western Rhapsody*" (Buffalo Symph.; Boston Civic Orch.); "*Peewee the Piccolo*" (Phila., Cincinnati and Pittsburgh Symphs.); "*Celeste*" (N. Y. Philh., Phila., Cincinnati, Denver Symph.); String Quartet (WQXR and NBC Quartets); Sonatina for flute, cello and pf. (Sagul Trio); Cello Concerto (Nat'l Orch. Ass'n., 1950); Quintet for Clarinet and Strings (Musicians' Guild; Kroll String Quartet), etc.

Kout'zen, Boris, b. Uman, Russia, 1901; in U. S. after 1924; violinist; in Philadelphia Orch. for a time; studied comp. with Gliere; Mus. D.; c. Symph. in C.; "*Solitude*," nocturne (Phila. Orch., under composer, 1927); "*Valley Forge*," symph. poem (won Juilliard Pub. Prize, perf. by Nat'l. Orch. Ass'n., N. Y., under Barzin, 1940); Concerto for 5 solo insts. and str. orch. (ibid., 1935); "*Mouvement Symphonique*" for vln. and piano, etc.; headed violin dept. at Phila. Cons. of Music; his Str. Quartet No. 2 rec'd award of Soc. for Pub. of Amer. Music.

Kra'sa, Hans, b. Prague, 1895; of German-Czechish extraction; studied with Zemlinsky; his style influenced by Stravinsky and other moderns; esp. known for his Songs with orch., to texts of Christian Morgenstern; c. also opera, "*Betrothal in a Dream*" (won Czech State Prize, 1933) oratorio, "*Die Erde ist des Herrn*"; Symph. for sm. orch. (in U. S. by Koussevitzky and Boston Symph.), Str. Quartet; songs, etc.

Kreutz (kroits), **Arthur,** b. La Crosse, Wis., 1906; won Amer. Prix de Rome and Guggenheim Fellowship; studied Univ. of Wis.; Brussels Cons.; M. A., Columbia Univ.; c. *"Music for Symph. Orch."* (NBC Symph., under Frank Black, 1940); *"Paul Bunyan,"* dance poem (won Nat'l Ass'n. for Amer. Composers and Conductors' Prize); *"Symphonic Sketch on 3 Amer. Folk Tunes"* (ISCM Fest., Berkeley, Cal., 1942); *"American Dances"* (WOR Sinfonietta under Katims, 1941); ballet, *"Long May Our Land Be Bright"* (commissioned by Martha Graham; first c. for pf., then suite for orch., latter cond. by composer, Univ. Symph., Austin, Tex., 1944); Violin Concerto, etc.

Ku'bik, Gail, b. South Coffeyville, Okla., 1914; grad. Eastman Sch. of Music; won Guggenheim and MacDowell Colony Fellowships; award of Soc. for Pub. of Amer. Music; active as comp. for Army films, 1943; c. Concerto in D for Violin and Orch. (awarded 1st prize of $1,000 by Jascha Heifetz in competition held by the publisher, Carl Fischer, Inc.); *"Men and Ships,"* symph. piece; Scherzo from a Symphony (dedicated to the Chicago Symph. on its 50th anniversary); *"Whoopee-Ti-Yi-Yo"* for small orch., based on cowboy tunes (commissioned by CBS whose Concert Orch. perf. it under Bernard Herrmann, 1941); *"American Caprice"* for piano and small orch.; *"Puck"* for chamber orch.; choruses, songs, etc.; won Sinfonia Nat'l Award; Chicago Golden Jubilee Award, and Citation, Nat'l. Ass'n. of Composers and Conductors.

Lap'ham, Claude, b. Ft. Scott, Kan., 1890; composer influenced by Japanese idioms and basing much of his music on an adaptation of them, with Western symphonic technique; c. *"Miharayama"* tone poem for orch., descriptive of Japanese volcano in which unhappy lovers seek death (Tokyo Symph. under Klaus Pringsheim, 1935); Japanese Concerto for Piano and Orch.; song cycles, etc.

La Violette', Wesley, b. St. James, Minn., 1894; studied and lived in Chicago; grad. Northwestern Univ.; Mus. D., Chic. Mus. Coll.; c. First Symph. (Rochester Civic Orch. under Hanson, 1938); *"Tom Thumb"*

Symph. (Chicago, 1942, under Rudolph Ganz); *"The Spook Hour,"* scherzino for orch. (Nat'l Chamber Orch., N. Y., under Ganz, 1931); *"Nocturne"* (ibid., in Aurora, Ill., Ganz conducting); *"San Francisco"* Overture (commissioned by Pierre Monteux, and cond. by composer with San Fran. Symph., 1941); *"Collegiana,"* fest. rhapsody for orch. (Chicago Philh. under Czerwonky, 1936); *"Chorale"* (Amer. Concert Orch., Chicago, under composer, 1936); opera, *"Shylock"* (won David Bispham Memorial Award); etc.

Lecuona (lā-kōō-ō'-nä), **Ernesto,** b. Guanabacoa, Cuba, Aug. 7, 1896; comp., cond., pianist; recitals in Paris and S. Amer.; c. works based on rhumba and other dance rhythms, incl. *"Andalucia," "Malagueña," "Siboney"; "Poem"* for orch.; Pf. Concerto; film scores, etc.

Lee, Dai-Keong, b. Honolulu, 1915; won Guggenheim Fellowship; studied with Roger Sessions; Frederick Jacobi, at Juilliard Grad. Sch.; and Aaron Copland; c. *"Prelude and Hula,"* perf. widely by Amer. orchs.; 2 Symphs., *"Hawaiian Fest. Overture," "Golden Gate"* Overture; *"Pacific Prayer,"* etc.

Lesur (lŭ-sür'), **Daniel,** b. Paris, 1908; studied with Tournemire, Caussade and A. Ferté; 1938, prof. at Schola Cantorum; member of group "Le Jeune France" with Messiaen, Jolivet and Yves Baudrier; c. *"Suite Française"* for orch., his best-known work; *"Passacaille"* for pf. and orch.; *"Trois Lieder"* after Heine, for voice and str. quartet; *"Les Carillons,"* suite for piano; *"La Vie Intérieure"* for organ; songs, etc.

Lévy, Ernst, b. Basel, 1895; pupil of Hans Huber and Egon Petri in that city and Raoul Pugno in Paris; pianist; 1916–21, taught at Basel Cons.; after 1922 in Paris; c. 8 Symphs.; Piano Quintet; 2 String Quartets; Organ Sonata; piano pieces, songs, etc.

Lock'wood, Normand, b. New York, 1906; won Fellowship at Amer. Acad. in Rome, 1929; studied with Respighi and Nadia Boulanger; 1934, won Swift Orch. Prize; taught Oberlin Coll.; c. 6 Str. Quartets; *"Fragments from Sappho"* (girls' voices); *"Drum Taps"* (chor. and orch.); *"Requiem"* for chor., tenor and orch.; *"Dirge for*

Two Veterans" (mixed chor., a cappella), etc.

Lothar (lō'-tär), **Mark,** b. Berlin, 1902; pupil of J. H. Wetzel; early active as pianist; after 1934 conductor at the State Theater in Berlin; c. operas, of popular folk character, incl *"Schneider Wibbel"* (Berlin Op.); *"Tyll"* and *"Lord Spleen"* (both prod. in Weimar); *"Münchausen"* (Dresden Op.); Serenade for Chamber Orch.; music for plays; piano pieces, songs; arr. score of Haydn's opera, *"Lie Welt im Monde"* (N. Y. in Ital., 1949).

Lourié (lōō-rē-ā'), **Arthur,** b. St. Petersburg, 1892; studied at Cons. there; early was influenced by musical "futurism" and experiments in form; left Russia in 1922 and settled in Paris; c. *"Concerto Spirituale"* for chorus, piano and double-basses (Schola Cantorum, N. Y., 1930); *"Sinfonia Dialectica"* (Philadelphia Orch., 1931); short opera, *"Feast during the Plague"*; Str. Quartets, etc.; wrote biog. of Koussevitzky.

Luening, Otto, b. Milwaukee, Wis., 1900; won Guggenheim Fellowship; studied Munich Akad., also with Busoni, Andreae and Jarnach; member of mus. faculty at Columbia Univ.; active as conductor; c. opera, *"Evangeline"* (commissioned by Alice M. Ditson Fund and prod. at Columbia Univ., 1947); *"Prelude to a Hymn Tune by Billings"* (N. Y. Philh.-Symph., with composer conducting, 1937); *"Two Symphonic Sketches"* (ibid., under Hans Lange, 1936); Suite for str. orch. (Saratoga Spa Fest., under F. Charles Adler, 1937); Concertino for flute with strings, harp and celesta (Phila. Chamber Orch. under Isadore Freed, composer soloist, 1935), etc.

Martin (mär-tĕn'), **Frank,** b. Geneva, 1890; studied there with Josef Lauber; lived for a time in Paris, then founded a school at Geneva and taught at the Mus. Inst. there; critic, *"Tribune de Genève"*; c. secular oratorio, *"Le Vin Herbé,"* on Tristram legend, sung widely in Europe; stage works, *"Oedipe Roi," "Romeo et Juliette," "La Nique à Satan"; "Les Dithyrambes"* for chorus; *"Trois Poèmes Païens"* for barytone and orch.; Orch. Suite; Sonata for Vln. and Pf.; Piano Quintet; *"Esquisse"* for sm. orch.; *"Pavane"* for str. orch., *"Fox Trot"* for sm. orch. (Boston Pops Orch.

under Fiedler); oratorio, *"Golgotha"*, Petite Sinfonie Concertante, etc.

McBride, Robert, b. Tucson, Ariz., 1911; taught at the Univ. of Arizona, later at Bennington (Vt.) College; c. works with strong folk ingredient, also jazz influences in some of them; his compositions include *"Mexican Rhapsody"* for orch.; *"Fugato on a Well Known Theme"* (Univ. Chamber Orch., Tucson, 1935); *"Prelude to a Tragedy"* (N. Y. Philh.-Symph., under Hans Lange, 1935); ballet *"Show Piece"* (commissioned by Ballet Caravan, 1937; orch. suite from same played by Philadelphia Orch. under Stokowski, 1937); *"Workout"* for oboe and piano (composer has appeared as oboe soloist in this score in N. Y.), etc.

McDonald, Harl, b. near Boulder, Colo., 1899; largely self-taught, but studied comp. in U. S. and Germany; has served for some years as business mgr. of the Philadelphia Orch., which gave premieres of the following of his works: *"Festival of the Workers,"* suite (1933-4, under Stokowski); Symph. No. 1 (*"Santa Fe Trail"*) (ibid., 1934); Symph. No. 2 (*"Reflections on Era of Turmoil"*) (ibid., 1935); Concerto for 2 Pianos and Orch. (ibid., 1937, Jeanne Behrend and Alex. Kelberine soloists); Suite (*"From Childhood"*) for harp and orch. (ibid., 1941, Ormandy cond., Edna Phillips soloist); Symph. No. 4 (ibid., 1938); *"Three Poems on Aramaic Themes"* (ibid., 1936); *"Rhumba"* Symph.; also *"San Juan Capistrano,"* 2 nocturnes for orch. (Boston Symph. under Koussevitzky, 1939); *"Legend of Arkansas Traveler,"* humoresque for orch. (Ford Orch., Detroit, under Ormandy, on CBS, 1940); *"Miniature Suite"* (Boston Pops Orch., under Fiedler, 1939), etc.

McKay, George Frederick, b. Harrington, Wash., 1899; grad. Eastman Sch. of Music; won first prize for Organ Sonata, Amer. Guild of Organists; hon. mention, for Violin Concerto, Jascha Heifetz Contest; c. Sinfonietta (*"From a Mountain Town"*), (People's Symph., Boston, under Sevitzky, 1934); *"To a Liberator,"* symph. poem (commissioned and perf. by Indianapolis Symph., under Sevitzky, 1940); *"Pioneer Epic"* (Oakland, Cal., Symph.,

1942); *"A Prairie Portrait"* (San Francisco Symph., under Lemay, over MBS, 1941); *"A Lanier Pastorale"* for orch.; *"Fantasy on a Western Folk Song"* for chamber orch. (Seattle Symph., with composer cond., 1935); *"Sonatine for Clarinet and Str. Orch."*; Quintet for woodwinds (hon. mention, NBC chamber music competition), etc.

Menasce, de (dŭ mä-näsh'), Jacques, b. Bad Ischl, Austria, 1905; a Hungarian Baron, but now U. S. citizen; studied at Vienna State Acad. with Marx, Berg, Pisk; pf. with Sauer; début as pianist at Salzburg Fest., 1933; came to U. S., 1941; toured in concerts with Angel Reyes in Europe and America; c. 2 Piano Concertos (No. 2, over CBS); 3 Piano Sonatinas; chamber wks., etc.

Men'nin, Peter, b. Erie, Pa., May 17, 1923; began music study at age of 7; attended Oberlin Cons. before service in World War II; grad. Eastman Sch. of Music (Ph. D.), where taught also for a time on fellowship; studied conducting with Koussevitzky at Berkshire Music Centre; 1947, teacher of comp. at Juilliard Sch. of Music; won $1,000 award of Amer. Acad. of Arts and Letters; Guggenheim Award; Bearns Prize of Columbia Univ.; first George Gershwin Memorial Award, 1945; c. 4 Symphs. (No. 3 commissioned by N. Y. Philh.-Symph. and perf. 1947; No. 4, *"The Cycle,"* for chorus and orch.; New York, 1949); other commissions from League of Composers, Juilliard Musical Foundation, Dallas Symph. Orch., Koussevitzky Music Foundation, the Collegiate Chorale, NBC, and Protestant Radio Commission; c. also *"Folk Overture"*; Fantasia for str. orch.; Sinfonia for chamber orch.; 2 Str. Quartets; Concertino for flute, strings and percussion; Divertimento and Partita, both for pf.; cantata, *"The Christmas Story"*; A Cappella Choruses on Chinese Texts; 2 Choruses for women's voices and pf., etc.

Messiaen (mĕs-ē-än'), Olivier (see also p. 291). M. visited the U. S. in 1949 and taught on faculty of the Berkshire Music Centre; his *"L'Ascension,"* Four Symph. Meditations, perf. at Berkshire Fest. same year; *"Trois Petites Liturgies"* (N. Y. Philh., 1949).

Mignone (mēg-nō'-nä), Francisco, b. São Paulo, Brazil, 1897; active as a conductor of his works, and as such visited the U. S.; c. operas *"El Contratista de Diamantes"* and *"El Innocente"*; oratorio, *"Alegrias de Nossa Senhora"*; *"Congada"* (Afro-Brazilian Dance) (São Paulo Symph. under composer, 1922; Vienna Philh. under Richard Strauss, 1923); *"Festa des Igrejas"* (São Paulo Symph., under composer, 1942); *"Sonho de um Menino Travesso"* (*"Bad Boy's Dream"*) (Rio de Janeiro Munic. Orch., under Villa-Lobos, 1936); *"Suite Brasileira"* (Rio Philh. Orch., under Burle Marx, 1933); 2 *"Fantasias Brasileiras"* for pf. and orch., etc.

Mihalovici (mē-häl-ō-vēt'-sē), Marcel, b. Bucharest, Rumania, 1898; pupil in Paris of D'Indy; c. opera, 1-act, *"L'Intransigeant Pluton,"* from which orch. excerpt, *"Cortège des Divinités Infernales"* has been perf. in U. S.; ballets, *"Karaguez"* and *"Divertissement"* (latter, Paris, 1925); orch. works, *"Notturno,"* *"Introduction au Mouvement Symphonique"* and *"Fantasia"* (last at ISCM Fest., Liege, 1930); chamber works, etc.

Mo'haupt, Richard, b. Breslau, Germany, 1904; studied with Rudolf Bilke and Julius Pruewer; was theatre cond. in Aachen, Breslau and Weimar, also made tours as symph. cond. in other countries; lived after 1932 in Berlin, where won success as opera comp.; but took up res. in U. S. before World War II; c. Piano and Violin Concertos; *"Town Piper Music"* for orch., etc.

Moross', Jerome, b. Brooklyn, N. Y., 1913; c. ballets, *"American Pattern,"* *"Amer. Saga,"* *"Frankie and Johnny"* (Ruth Page, choreographer, 1938); Symph. (3rd movement also heard as sep. work under title, *"Ramble on a Hobo Tune"*) (in entirety by Seattle Symph., under Beecham, 1943); *"Paeans"* (Chamber Symph. Orch., N. Y., under Herrmann, 1932); *"A Tall Story"* (commissioned by CBS and perf. by CBS Orch. under Barlow, 1938); *"Biguine"* (heard over CBS, under Green, 1934); incid. mus. for plays; *"Paul Bunyan,"* ballet suite for orch.; Suite for chamber orch., etc.

Mortari (môr-tä'-rē), Virgilio, b. near Milan, 1902; studied with Rossi and

Pizzetti, influenced by latter's methods in setting vocal music; c. Concertino for piano, violin, clarinet, trumpet and bassoon; Concerto for str. quartet, horns, harp and kettledrums; Rhapsody for timpani, percussion, harp and strings (ISCM Fest. in London, Alfredo Casella conducting, 1931), etc.

Nagin'ski, Charles, Cairo, Egypt, 1909 —Lenox, Mass., 1940; brought to U. S. in early youth; won Walter Damrosch Fellowship at Amer. Acad. in Rome; c. Symph.; "*1936*" for orch.; Sinfonietta (CBS Concert Orch., under Victor Bay, 1938); "*Five Pieces from a Children's Suite*" (Boston Pops Orch. under Fiedler, 1940); ballet suite, "*The Minotaur*"; "*Nocturne and Pantomime*"; Suite for sm. orch. (Greenwich Sinfonietta, N. Y., under Charles Lichter, 1935); Divertimenti for woodwind and for brass; songs; etc.

Nor'doff, Paul, b. Philadelphia, 1909; studied Juilliard Sch. of Mus , N. Y.; won Bearns Prize of Columbia Univ.; awarded Guggenheim Fellowship; taught at Phila. Cons. of Mus.; c. Prelude and Three Small Fugues (last fugue perf. by Phila. Orch. under Stokowski, 1937; complete by Penna. Symph. Orch. under Sabatini, 1940); Suite (St. Louis Symph. under Golschmann, 1940); "*Variations on a Bavarian Dance Theme*"; Piano Concerto (Nat'l. Symph., Washington, under Kindler, composer soloist, 1939); Violin Concerto; songs; etc.; arr. Gluck themes for ballet, "*Tally-Ho*" (Agnes de Mille); c. scores for Martha Graham.

Orff, Carl, b. Munich, 1895; grad. of Akad. der Tonkunst there; served as ass't. cond. in Munich, Mannheim and Darmstadt theatres; 1921-2 pupil of Heinrich Kaminski; he withdrew his comps. for stage, orch., chorus and songs written before then, and in his later works showed a style of aggressive modernism; c. operas, "*Die Kluge*," widely heard in Germany;"*Die Bernauerin*";"*Der Mond*"; "*Antigone*" (Salzburg Fest., 1949); "*Des Turmes Auferstehung*," cantata for solo, chor. and orch. after Werfel; dance play, "*Der Feuerfarbene*," etc.

Palm'er, Robert M., b. Syracuse, N. Y., 1915; grad. Eastman School of Music; awarded $1000 grant of Amer. Acad. of Arts and Letters;

MacDowell Colony Fellowship; has received commissions from Columbia Broadcasting System, 1940; from Koussevitzky Music Foundation, and from Dimitri Mitropoulos; c. Symph.; "*Poem*" for violin and sm. orch. (Rochester Civic Orch., under Hanson, John Celantano, soloist, 1938), chamber works, songs, etc.

Peragallo (pā-rä-gäl'-ō), Mario, b. Rome, 1910; c. opera, "*Ginevra*," prod. with succ., 1937; his first scores marked by post-Puccinian style; later became interested in "twelve-tone" manner; c. "*La Collina*," a "scenic madrigal" based on "*Spoon River Anthology*" by Edgar Lee Masters (prod. at Venice Fest., 1948, and in stage prod. at La Scala, 1950); Music for double str. quartet, etc.; pres., Italian section, ISCM.

Persichetti (pĕr-sē-kä'-tē), Vincent, b. Philadelphia, 1915; at 16 organist and dir. of music, Arch St. Presb. Church there; studied at Combs Coll. of Mus., Curtis Inst. of Mus. and Phila. Cons. of Mus.; grad. (Mus. D.) from latter, where he headed comp. dept. after 1942; also studied comp. with Roy Harris at Colorado Coll.; now member of comp. dept., Juilliard Sch. of Mus.; c. "*Dance Overture*" (won Juilliard Pub. Award, 1943); 3 Piano Sonatas (No. 3, 1st prize, Colorado Coll. Fine Arts Fest.); 2 String Quartets (No. 2, Blue Network chamber mus. prize, 1945); 3 Symphs.; "*The Hollow Men*" for trumpet and str. orch.; Concertino for pf. and orch.; wks. for pf., and other chamber scores, etc.

Petrassi (pā-trä-zē), Goffredo, b. Zagarolo, Italy, 1904; studied at Naples Cons. and with Busoni; in early life he was a music dealer; c. opera, 1-act, "*Il Cordovano*" (La Scala, 1949); Introduction and Allegro, for violin concertante and 11 insts. (perf. at Santa Cecilia Acad., Rome, under Mario Rossi, 1934); Concerto for Orch.; Partita for orch.; works for chor. and orch.; songs, pf. pieces, etc.

Phil'lips, Burrill, b. Omaha, Nebr., 1907; grad. of Eastman Sch. of Music; later taught there; won Guggenheim Fellowship, 1942-3; Amer. Acad. of Arts and Letters Award, 1944; c. ballet, "*Play Ball*" (Eastman Sch. Fest., under Hanson, with Rochester Civic Orch., 1938); "*Selections from McGuffey's Readers*," suite

(Rochester Philh. under Hanson, 1934); *"Three Satiric Fragments"* (Roch. Civic Orch. under same cond., 1941);*"Symphony Concertante"* (Eastman Sch. Little Symph., under Van Hoesen, 1935); *"Dance"* Overture (Roch. Civic Orch., Hanson, 1940); *"Music for Strings"* (ibid., 1939); *"Concert Piece"* for bassoon and str. orch. (Eastman Fest., 1940); *"Scena"* for sm. orch ;*"Declaratives"* (women's voices and sm. orch.); 3 Divertimenti for pf., etc.

Piston, Walter. (See also page 338). C. Concerto for Orch. (Boston Symph., Cambridge concerts, 1934, composer conducting); Prelude and Fugue (Cleveland Orch., under Rodzinski, 1936); Sinfonietta (Zighera Chamber Orch., Boston, Bernard Zighera conducting, 1941); Suite No. 1 for Orch. (Boston Symph. Orch., 1930, composer conducting); ballet, *"The Incredible Flutist"* (Jan Veen and dancers with Boston Pops Orch. under Arthur Fiedler, 1938; symph. suite from same, Pittsburgh Symph. under Reiner, 1940); Suite No. 2 for Orch. (Boston Symph. Orch. under Munch, 1949), etc.

Ponce (pon-sä), **Manuel M.,** Mexico City, 1886—1948; composer influenced by folk music and working mostly in popular smaller forms; studied in Berlin; taught at Mexico City Cons.; decorated by Mexican Govt., 1947; c. *"Chapultepec,"* 2 symph. sketches (Mexican Symph. Orch., under Chavez, 1934); Concerto for Guitar and Orch. (written for Andres Segovia and played by him in Mexico City and in Europe); *"Poema Elegiaco"* for orch.; *"Instantaneas Mexicanas"* (Mexican Snapshots), 7-part suite for chamber orch.; *"Estampas Nocturnas,"* orch. suite; and many songs incl. the pop. *"Estrellita,"* etc.

Poot, Marcel, b. Vilvoorde near Brussels, 1901; studied at Amsterdam Cons. and with Paul Gilson; served as music critic in Brussels; c. *"Jazz Music for Orch."* (Brussels, Defauw Concerts, 1932, also in U. S.); Symphs.; orch. poems, works for stage; pf. pieces and chamber music; dir., Brussels Cons., 1949.

Porrino (pô-rē'-nō), **Ennio,** b. Cagliari, Sardinia, 1910; studied at Accademia di Santa Cecilia in Rome under Respighi and Mule; c. overture,

"Tartarin de Tarascon" (won Prize of Rome Augusteo Orch.); *"Sardegna,"* orch. poem based on Sardinian folksongs (N. Y. Philh.-Symph. under Stokowski, 1949); *"La Visione di Ezechiele"*; *"Sinfonia per una Fiabe"*; *"Saltarella"* all for orch.; *"Tre Canzoni Italiane"* for sm. orch., etc.

Raw'sthorne, Alan, b. Haslingden, Eng., 1905; in his 20's entered R. C. M. (Manchester); 1927, studied pf. in Europe with Petri; taught at Dartington Hall in Eng.; after 1935 in London; c. *"Theme and Variations"* for 2 violins (ISCM Fest., London, 1938); *"Symphonic Studies"* (ibid., Warsaw, 1939); *"Cortèges"* (ibid., London, 1946); *"Street Corner"* Overture; Piano Concerto (London Proms., Kentner soloist); music for films, *"The Captive Heart"* (from which *"Prisoners' March"* heard in concert) and *"School for Secrets,"* Vln. Concerto; *"Bagatelles"* for pf., etc.

Read, Gardner, b. Evanston, Ill., 1913; grad. Eastman Sch. of Music; won fellowship, Berkshire Music Centre; $2000 Cromwell Travelling Fellowship for European study; Juilliard Pub. Prizes, 1938, 1941; MacDowell Fellowship; c. Symph. No. 1 (N. Y. Philh.-Symph., under Barbirolli, 1937—won $1000 first prize of this organization, 1936); Symph. No. 2 (Boston Symph., 1943, comp. conducting; won 1st prize of $1,000 in Paderewski Fund. comp., same year); *"Sketches of the City,"* suite after Carl Sandburg (won Juilliard Pub. Award, 1938; Rochester Civic Orch. under Hanson, 1934); Passacaglia and Fugue (commissioned by Ravinia Fest. Ass'n., 1938, played under Rodzinski at Ravinia, same year); *"Night Flight"* (Eastman Orch. under Hanson, 1944), etc.

Reiser (rī'-zĕr), **Alois,** b. Prague, 1887; pupil of Dvorak; came to U. S. and lived on Pacific Coast; c. *"Summer Evening"* (Prague Philh., 1911); *"Slavic Rhapsody"* (Los Angeles Philh., composer conducting, 1931); *"Erewhon"* (after Samuel Butler) (Los Angeles Fed. Orch., under composer, 1936); Concerto for Cello and Orch. (Los Angeles Philh. under Rodzinski, with Ilya Bronson soloist, 1933), etc.

Revueltas (rä-voo-āl'täs), **Silvestre,** Papasquiero, Mexico, 1899—Mexico City, 1940; composer of folk inspiration, and modern, partly satiric, descriptive style; c. *"Redes"* (Waves), score for film (1934), shown in U. S.; *"Sensemaya"* (Song with Which to Kill a Snake) (N. Y. City Symph., 1948, and N. Y. Philh.-Symph under Stokowski, 1949); Toccata (without Fugue); *"Alcancías"* (Penny Banks); *"Cuauhmahuac"*; *"Esquinas"* (Corners); *"Musica para Charler"* (Conversation Music); *" Homage a Garcia Lorca"*; *"Eight on the Radio"*; *"Pianas"* (Planes); Three Sonnets, etc.

Rold'an, Amadeo, Paris, 1900—Havana, 1939; composer of works influenced by native dances of Cuba; c. ballet, *"La Rebambaramba"* (Havana Philh. under composer played excerpt, 1928); *"Ritmico V and VI,"* pieces for percussion orch. (heard at Cornish Sch., Seattle, Wash., with John Cage conducting); *"Overture on Popular Cuban Themes,"* etc.

Ro'senberg, Hilding, b. Bosjäkloster, Sweden, 1892; studied at Stockholm Cons. and in Dresden; his style has been called "expressionistic"; c. Symph.; *"3 Phantasie Pieces"*; Piano Concerto; Variations and Passacaglia; Sonata for Solo Violin; Trio for flute, vln. and vla.; Suite, *"Orpheus in Town,"* for orch.; Str. Quartet; songs, etc.

Royce, Edward, b. Cambridge, Mass., 1886; member faculty, Eastman Sch. of Music; c. *"Far Ocean,"* tone poem for orch. (Eastman Pub. Award, Roch. Philh., under Howard Hanson, 1929); *"The Fire-Bringers"* (ibid., 1926); songs, etc.

Sae'verud, Harald, b. Bergen, Norway, 1897; studied with Holmsen in Bergen and at the Berlin Hochschule; c. 3 Symphs. (No. 1, 1924, Christiania); Piano Sonata; symph. poems, pf. works, songs, etc.; c. music for Ibsen's *"Peer Gynt"* (1948), etc.

San'ders, Robert, b. Chicago, 1906, studied at Bush Cons., Chicago; won Fellowship at Amer. Acad. in Rome; studied in Paris and in Italy; ass't cond., Chicago Civic Orch., 1933–8; c. Little Symph. in G (won half of award, N. Y. Philh. Prize, 1937–8); Suite for large orch. (Augusteo Orch., Rome, composer conducting, 1929); *"The Tragic Muse"* (Chicago Symph.

under DeLamarter, 1936); songs, etc.

Sanjuan (sän-hōō-än'), **Pedro,** b. San Sebastian, Spain, 1886; lived in Cuba as cond. of Havana Philh. Orch.; more recently in U. S., cond. of Spartanburg, S. C., Fest. and Symph. Orch.; c. *"Rondo Fantastico"* on Basque theme (awarded Nat'l Prize, Spain, 1934; Havana Philh., composer cond., 1926); *"Castilla"* (ibid., 1927); *"Liturgia Negra,"* etc.

Schil'linger, Joseph, Kharkov, Russia, 1895—New York, 1943; c. *"North Russian"* Symph. (commissioned for radio by RCA, N. Y., 1930); *"Orient"* March (Leningrad Philh., 1926, under Malko), etc.; S. is best known as the deviser of a system of composition by means of scientific formulae, the results of which are pub. in *"The Schillinger Method"*; he taught a number of well-known composers and arrangers.

Searle (sĕrl), **Humphrey,** b. Oxford, Eng., 1915; composer; studied at Univ. there and at R. C. M., pupil of Ireland, Jacob and Morris; awarded Octavia Trav. Scholarship and lived in Vienna, 1937–8; studied there with Webern; Secretary of International ISCM; wrote book on Liszt; c. *"Gold Coast Customs,"* setting of lengthy Edith Sitwell poem, for speaker, male chorus, 2 pfs., chamber orch. and percussion (London, 1949, Contemporary Music Centre); *"Overture to a Drama"* (London "Proms," 1949); 2 Suites for Strs; *"Night Music"* for chamber orch.; Piano Concerto; *"Fuga Giocosa"* for orch.; Quintet for bassoon and strs.; Quartet for vln., vla., clar., and bassoon; piano pieces, songs, etc.

Ser'ly, Tibor, b. Losonc, Hungary, 1900; res. in U. S.; arr. Mozart's Fantasia and Fugue (composed for organ in clock) (Budapest Philh., 1935, Serly cond.); arr. for orch. excerpts from Bartok's piano collection, *"Mikrokosmos"* (St. Louis Symph., under Golschmann, in part); also completed Bartok's last Piano Concerto, and Viola Concerto (post.).

Shape'ro, Harold, b. Lynn, Mass., April 29, 1920; studied with Boulanger, Hindemith, Krenek, Slonimsky, Stravinsky, Piston, and Copland; awarded Naumburg Fellowship, Paine Fellowship, Prix de Rome,

Bearns Prize, Gershwin Memorial Award, Guggenheim Fellowship; commissioned by Koussevitzky Music Foundation, for which c. *"Symphony for Classical Orch."* (Boston Symph. Orch., under Leonard Bernstein, 1948); c. also overture, *"The Travellers,"* chamber wks., pf. pieces, etc.

Sieg'meister, Elie, b. New York, 1909; studied with Riegger, Stoessel, Bernard Wagenaar and Nadia Boulanger; grad. Columbia Univ.; won Juilliard Grad. School Fellowship; cond. of the Manhattan Chorus; taught at Brooklyn Coll.; c. Rhapsody for orch.; *"Dance Trilogy"* for 7 insts.; String Quartet; Quintet for wind insts.; *"Walt Whitman"* Overture; *"Amer. Holiday"* for chamber orch.; Theme and Variations for piano; arr. 3 Negro folksongs and other wks. for chorus; songs; *"Ozark Suite"* (ballet version choreographed by Hanya Holm), etc.

Smith, Julia, b. Denton, Tex., 1911; studied Juilliard Sch. of Mus. under Rubin Goldmark and Frederick Jacobi; c. operas, *"Cynthia Parker"* (Tex. State Coll. prod.), *"The Stranger of Manzano"* and *"The Gooseherd and the Goblin,"* work for children (commissioned by Hartt Opera Guild, Hartford, Conn., and prod. there, 1949); *"Liza Jane"* (CBS commission, 1940); suites for orch., chamber works, songs, etc. 2 Pieces for vla. and pf.

Spialek (spē'-ä-lĕk), **Hans,** b. Vienna, 1894; studied Vienna and Moscow Cons.; c. *"The Tall City,"* suite (written for the NBC Symph. under Frank Black, 1933; rev. version, Rochester Philh. under Hanson, 1934); Sinfonietta (NBC Symph. under Black, 1936); Piano Concerto; *"To a Ballerina"* for orch.; in U. S. after 1924; active as arranger for many Broadway musical shows.

Stein'ert, Alexander, b. Boston, 1900; grad. Harvard Univ.; studied in Paris with Loeffler, D'Indy, Gédalge and Koechlin; awarded fellowship at Amer. Acad. in Rome, where studied 3 years; has appeared as pianist and cond.; later res. on Pacific Coast; c. *"Nuit Méridionale"* (Boston Symph. under Koussevitzky, 1926); *"Concerto Sinfonico"* for piano and orch. (ibid., 1935, with composer as soloist), etc.

Strang, Gerald, b. Claresholm, Canada,

1908; c. Symph. (one movement by Fed. Symph., Los Angeles, composer conducting, 1937); *"Percussion Music for Three Players"* (perf. in Seattle, Wash., John Cage conducting, 1938); piano works, etc.

Sutermeis'ter, Heinrich, b. Aug. 12, 1910; Swiss composer and pianist; c. succ. operas, *"Romeo et Juliette,"* also *"Raskolnikov"* (based on Dostoievsky's *"Crime and Punishment"*) (La Scala, 1950) which feature return to melody and strong rhythms, rather than Romanticism and impressionism; chamber music, songs, pf. works, etc.

Terrasse (tĕr-äs'), **Claude,** L'Arbresle, near Lyons, France, 1867—Paris, 1923; studied at Niedermeyer Sch.; first active as organist, then c. some 20 operettas, of which *"La Petite Femme de Loth,"* *"Les Travails de Hercule,"* *"Le Sire de Vergy"* and *"Le Mariage de Télemaque"* are best known, the last his masterpiece.

Thom'son, Virgil. (See also p. 435.) C. opera, *"The Mother of Us All"* (text by Gertrude Stein, commissioned by Alice M. Ditson Fund and prod. at Columbia Univ., 1948); ballet *"Filling Station"* (Ballet Caravan, 1938); scores for documentary films, *"The Plough That Broke the Plains"* and *"The River"*; *"Seine at Night"* for orch.; Cello Concerto, etc.

Tip'pett, Michael, b. London, 1905; studied at R. C. M. there; c. oratorio, *"Child of Our Time"*; cantata for tenor and pf., *"Boyhood End"*; Concerto for double str. orch.; Concerto for Piano and Orch.; 2 String Quartets; Pf. Sonata, etc.

Tocchi (tô'-kē), **Gianluca** (jē-än'-loo-kä), b. Perugia, Italy, 1901; studied in Rome with Respighi; won prizes for comp.; c. orch., *"Rhapsodia Romantico"*; *"Quadro Sonoro"*; *"Record"* (Impressions for Orch.); Concerto for Jazz Orch.; *"Film,"* orch. suite; chamber wks., songs, etc.

Tomasi (tô-mä'-sē), **Henri,** b. Marseilles, 1901; c. *"Don Juan de Mañara,"* suite for orch. (Lamoureux Orch. under Bigot, 1937); *"Deux Danses Cambodgiennes"* (Paris Orchestre National, composer cond., 1935); *"Petite Suite Medievale"* (broadcast, Paris Radiodif. Orch., under composer, 1937); also chamber music, songs, etc.

Trunk (troonk), **Richard,** b. Baden, Germany, 1879; studied at Hoch

Cons., Frankfort, and Munich Mus. Sch.; 1912-14, cond., Arion Soc., New York; 1914-25, choral cond. and critic, Munich; 1925-34, dir. of Cons. in Cologne; after 1934, dir. Akad. der Tonkunst, Munich; c. choral works; Piano Quintet; *"Walpurgisnacht"* for orch.; operetta, *"Herzdame"* (Munich, 1917); and esp. more than 100 songs, incl. cycle after Verlaine.

Uribe (oo-rē'-bä), **Guillermo,** b. Bogota, Colombia, 1880; studied at Academia Nacional de Musica there, and after 1910 was dir. of Nat'l Cons. in same city; studied in Paris under D'Indy (Schola Cantorum) and vln. with Armand Parent, César Thomson and others; founder and cond. of Concert Soc. of Cons. in Bogota; c. Symph. *"del Terruño"* (awarded nat'l prize, 1924); *"Te Deum"*; many chamber works, pf. pieces, etc., of modern trend.

Van Vac'tor, David, b. Plymouth, Indiana, 1906; conductor of Knoxville, Tenn., Symph. Orch.; has toured South America, etc.; c. Symph. in D (1st prize, N. Y. Philh.-Symph Competition, 1937-8, perf. by same, composer cond., 1939); Symph. Suite (commissioned for Ravinia Fest., perf. there 1939, composer cond.); Divertimento for sm. orch. (ibid., under composer); *"Five Little Pieces"* for orch. (Chicago Symph., under DeLamarter, 1931); *"Masque of the Red Death"* (after Poe), for orch.; 2 *"Ouvertures to a Comedy"* (No. 2 by Indianapolis Symph. under Sevitzky, 1941); *"Gothic Impressions"* (Chicago Symph. under composer, 1942), etc.

Vardell', Charles, b. Salisbury, N. C., 1893; grad. (Ph. D.), Eastman Sch. of Music; c. *"Joe Clark Steps Out,"* descriptive piece with jazz influence (Rochester Philh. under Hanson, 1937); latter also given as ballet at Eastman Fest.; *"Saturday Night"* for orch., etc.; received Eastman Pub. Award, 1937.

Veret'ti, Antonio, b. Verona, Italy, 1900; pupil of Alfano; c. opera, *"Il Favorita del Re"* (La Scala, 1932); *"Sinfonia Italiano"* for orch.; suites, overtures, chamber wks., pf. pieces, songs, etc.

Verrall, John, b. Britt, Iowa, 1908; studied with Copland, Jacobi and Kodaly; awarded Guggenheim Fellowship, 1946; member of music faculty, Univ. of Washington; c. 4 String Quartets; Sonata for viola and piano; Serenade for 5 insts., and other chamber music works which show influence of Bartok; *"Concert Piece"* for strings and horn (revised version by N. Y. Philh.-Symph. under Mitropoulos, 1941); *"Portrait of Man"* for orch., etc.

Vomack'a, Boleslav, b. Mlada Boleslav, Czechoslovakia, 1887; studied at Prague Cons. under Novak and others; a govt. official, later a music critic in Prague; early influenced by Schoenberg; c. symph. poem, *"Youth"*; Sonata for vln. and pf.; Piano Sonata; *"The Search,"* suite for pf.; *"1914,"* song cycle; and many choruses.

Wag'ner, Joseph, b. Springfield, Mass., 1900; studied in U. S. and Europe; cond. of Boston Civic Orch. for two decades after 1925, with which he introduced many Amer. wks.; later cond. of Duluth Symphony; c. ballet, *"Hudson River Legend"* (Boston Civic Orch. with Jan Veen Dancers, Arthur Fiedler, cond., 1944); *"Rhapsody for Orch."* (ibid., composer cond., 1925); *"Four Miniatures"* (NBC Symph., under Black, 1941); Concerto for Piano and Orch.; *"Fugal Triptych"* for piano, percussion and str. orch., etc.

Wald, Max, b. Litchfield, Ill., 1889; studied in Chicago and with d'Indy; c. *"The Dancer Dead,"* poem for orch. (awarded $2500 first prize in contest by NBC and perf. by NBC Symph. under Goossens, 1932); *"Retrospectives,"* 2 orch. pieces (Chicago Symph. under Stock, 1926); *"The Streets of Spring,"* overture, etc.

Ward, Robert, b. Cleveland, 1917; grad. Eastman Sch. of Music; won Columbia Univ. Fellowship; MacDowell Fellowship; c. Symph. No. 1 (Juilliard Pub. Award, 1942; perf. by Juilliard Sch. Orch., 1941, under composer); *"A Yankee Overture"*; *"Slow Music for Orch.,"* movement from a Symph., in E minor (Rochester Civic Orch., under Hanson, 1938); 2 Symphs.; Andante and Scherzo for strings, etc.; won Amer. Acad. of Arts and Letters Award, 1946.

Weber, Ben, b. St. Louis, Mo., 1916; studied De Paul Univ., Chicago; uses 12-tone system in his works; c. Concerto for piano solo, cello obbligato and wind insts.; Sonata for cello and pf.; Fantasia for pf.; etc.

Wein'zweig, John, b. Toronto, 1913; staff composer for the Canadian Broadcasting Corp.; c. *"The Enchanted Hill"* (after poem by Walter de la Mare) and Suite, both for small orch. (Rochester Civic Orch., under Hanson, 1938); *"Spectre"* for str. orch. and 4 timpani (broadcast over CBC, Alexander Chuhaldin cond., 1939); *"A Tale of Tuamotu"* for orch. and solo bassoon; choruses, songs.

Weisgall (vīs-gäl), **Hugo,** b. Eibenschütz, Czechoslovakia, 1912; later res. in U. S.; c. ballet, *"Quest"* for Baltimore Ballet Co. \orch. suite from this perf. by N. Y. Philh.-Symph. under Barbirolli, 1942); chamber works, songs, etc.

Weiss, Adolph, b. Baltimore, Md., 1891; bassoonist in N. Y. Philh.; studied with Schönberg; c. *"American Life,"* jazz scherzo for orch. (Conductorless Orch., N. Y., 1930); *"I Segreti,"* tone poem after Goethe (Rochester Philh., under Hanson, 1925); chamber works in modern idiom, vocal scores, etc.

Wes'sel, Mark, b. Coldwater, Mich., 1894; grad. Northwestern Univ.; studied with Schönberg; won Guggenheim and Pulitzer Fellowships; c. *"Ballade"* for violin, oboe and str. orch. (Eastman Sch. Orch. under Belov, 1932); *"Holiday"* and *"Song and Dance"* (Eastman Sch. Fest. under Hanson, 1934); *"Scherzo Burlesque"* for piano and strings (Rochester Little Symph. under Hanson, with composer soloist, 1926); etc.; 1938, prof. of pf. and comp. at Univ. of Colorado.

White, Paul, b. Bangor, Me., 1895; grad. and member of faculty, Eastman Sch. of Music; Mus. Doc., *hon. causa,* Univ. of Maine, 1939; c. *"Five Miniatures"* (Rochester Civic Orch., composer cond., 1934); *"Boston Sketches,"* (*Four Spokes from the Hub*) (Boston Pops Orch. under Fiedler, 1938); Symph. in E minor (Rochester Philh., under Hanson, 1934); *"Lake Spray"* for orch. (ibid., Iturbi cond., 1939); *"Voyage of the Mayflower,"* for chor. and orch.; *"Sea Chanty Quintet"*; Sinfonietta for strings, etc.

Wil'liams, Alberto, b. Buenos Aires, 1862; studied at Paris Cons. with Guirard, Franck, Godard, etc.; 1893, founded Buenos Aires Cons., and was its dir. until 1949; also active as cond.; c. Overtures; *"Poem of the Bells"* for orch.; *"Milongas"* (5 Dances); 9 Symphs.; chamber, piano works and songs; d. 1952.

Wolpe (vol'-pā), **Stefan,** b. Berlin, Aug. 25, 1902; studied at State Acad. of Music there and with Webern; 1934-8, taught theory and comp. at Palestine Cons.; came to the U. S. late in 1928 and was head of theory dept. at Settlement Music School, Philadelphia, 1939-44; in 1946-7 was head of the Department of Comp. at the Brooklyn Free Musical Society; after 1948 dir. of the Contemporary Music Sch., N. Y., and head of its dept. of theory; from 1949, also head of theory and comp. dept., Phila. Musical Acad.; his *"Palestinian Songs"* heard at ISCM Fest., N. Y.; c. operas, *"Schoene Geschichten"* and *"Zeus and Elida"* (both 1927); ballet *"The Man from Midian"* (1942) and 2 orch. suites from same; Concerto for 2 Pianos and 3 Wind Players; for orch., *"5 Pieces,"* Passacaglia, Dances, Concerto, etc.; for chorus, oratorio, *"Passion of Man"* (text by Renn); cantata, *"Let Him Go"* (Becher); *"2 Chinese Epitaphs,"* mixed chor. and drums; cantata, *"Unnamed Lands"* (Whitman); canta *"Yigdal"* (Maimonides) for barytone, chor., and orch.; *"Lament for Ignacio Sanches Mejias"* (Lorca), cantata for sopr., barytone, and sm. orch. (1945, rev. 1949); *"14 Palestinian Songs"* for alto and pf.; for pf., *"4 Studies,"* *"Zemach"* Suite, Toccata, and *"Battle Pieces"*; *"Music for flute, vla. and cello"*; Duo for oboe and clar.; Sonata for oboe and pf.; Concerto for flute, clar., bassoon, horn, trump., tromb., vln., cello and pf.; Trio for clar., vln. and cello; 2 Sonatas for vln. and pf.; songs, etc.

Wolf'mann, Frederick, b. Flushing, N. Y., 1908; grad. of Eastman Sch. of Music; studied there with Hanson and Rogers; 1937, awarded Juilliard Fellowship at Amer. Acad. in Rome; c. *"Songs for Autumn"* (barytone, soprano and orch.); *"Poem"* for flute and orch.; Rhapsody for horn and orch.; *"Song of the Forest Dweller,"* *"Dance of the Torch Bearers,"* *"Songs from a Chinese Lute,"* and *"Pool of Pegasus,"* all for orch.; Scherzo for 8 wind insts.; etc.; 1937, commissioned to comp. orch. work by Mitropoulos for Minneapolis Symph.

Za'dor, Eugen, b. Bataszek, Hungary, 1894; after 1920 lived in Vienna; studied with Heuberger, Reger, Abert and Schering; taught New Cons. there; 1939 in Hollywood as film composer. c. *"Bank-Ban,"* symph. poem; *"Hannele,"* symph. prelude; *"Romantic"* Symph.; operas, 1-act, *"Diana"* (Budapest, 1923); *"Die Insel der Toten"* (Budapest, 1927; Carlsruhe, 1928); opera, *"Christopher Columbus"* (broadcast NBC network, 1939); suite from ballet, *"Machine Men"* (Minneapolis Symph. under Ormandy); *"Variations on a Hungarian Song"* for orch.; his works perf. also under Stokowski, Monteux, Szell, Stock, Barbirolli, etc.; c. and arr. music for films.

Zem'achson, Arnold, b. Vilna, Russia, 1892; res. in U. S.; c. Chorale and Fugue in D minor (Philadelphia Orch. under Stokowski, 1930); Concerto Grosso in E minor (Chicago Symph. under Stock, 1934); Suite in F (WOR Sinfonietta under Wallenstein over Mutual network, 1941). etc.

A TABLE OF
PRONUNCIATIONS

Giving the Code of Symbols used in this Book;
and also a Guide to the Pronunciations of sixteen
Languages, arranged in a novel Tabular Form
by Letters

	A	**B**	**C**
This top row gives the phonetic meaning of the letters and symbols AS USED IN THIS BOOK.	as used in this book : ă as in father ; ā as in fate ; ă as in fat ; ăñ and ăñ, see Note 1.	as in bob.	see *ch*, at end of the alphabet
ARABIAN : very difficult even for sojourners among the people.	as in fat ; before *r* as in far.	as in bob.	as in English ; *ch* like G man, *ch*, see Note 3.
BOHEMIAN : See Note 4. In diphthongs the vowels are pronounced separately, as in Italian.	as *u* in fun ; *á* as in father.	as in bob.	*c* like *ts*, or German *s* like *ch* in child.
DANISH : doubled vowels are simply prolonged.	as in father ; *aa* as *a* in fall.	as in bob.	like Swedish *c*.
DUTCH : *e* in be and ge ; *i* before *k*, *g* and *ng* : and *ij* in the suffix lijk are silent.	when short as in half ; also before *ch* ; when open as in father : *aa*, *aai* (see *ai*), prolonged as in father.	beginning a syllable, as in bet ; ending, as *p* in trap.	only in foreign words ; *s* before *e*, *i* and *y* ; *k*, otherwise.
FLEMISH : dead as a literary language, but of great historic importance.	*a* or *â*, as in father or mica ; *aa* or *ae*, the same prolonged.	as in bob.	like *k* ; *ch* like German
FRENCH : a silent final consonant is usually sounded with the following word when that begins with a vowel. This is called liaison. French syllables have duration rather than accent ; the tendency is, to give a slight stress to the final syllable. In this book accent is rarely marked.	as in făt ; *â* as in father ; see *ai*, *au*, and Note 1.	as in bob.	as *s* before *e*, *i* and *y* ; otherwise, except that always *s*. See *ch*.
GERMAN : long words usually accent the first syllable most strongly, and give a lesser accent to one or more of the others.	as in father ; *â*, see Note 2 ; *ä* is sometimes spelled *ae* ; *ai* = *i* in bite ; for *äu* and *aeu*, see *au*.	beginning a syllable, as in bet ; ending a syllable, as *p* in trap.	like *ts* in hats before *e* and *ä* ; like *k* before and *u* ; *ch*. See Note
HUNGARIAN : long and short vowels are so rather in duration than in sound. There are no silent letters and no accents.	as in what ; *á* is prolonged, as in father.	as in bob.	*cs* = *ch* in church ; *cz* = as in hats.
ITALIAN : doubled consonants are distinctly pronounced, as fred-do. Doubled vowels are also separately pronounced.	as in father and mica ; *â* as in far.	as in bob.	before *e* and *i* as *ch* chime ; *cc* before *e* an = *tch*, as wretched ; = *k*.
NORWEGIAN :	*a* as in father ; *aa* as *o* in no ; *au* as *o* in no.	as in bob.	only in foreign words ; before *e*, *i* and *y* ; a otherwise.
POLISH : consonants strongly sounded are accented thus : *b̓*, *ź ʒ́ ṕ ŕ ś ƚ* *e̓*, *f̓, m̓, n̓, p̓, s̓, w̓, z̓.*	as in father ; *g* as in ball.	as in bob.	*c* = *ts*, as in hats ; *ch* German *ch* ; *cz* = *ch* church.
PORTUGUESE : a very difficult language ; placed usually just back of the teeth. The nasal vowels are also unique. Note 5.	as in father ; when two as *a* occur in a word the first is more like *a* in fat ; *â*, see Note 5.	nearly as in bob ; but softer.	like *s* before *e*, *i* and *y* ; *k* otherwise ; *ç* always *s* ; in *cc* the first *c* is like the second is determi by the following letter
RUSSIAN : has 36 letters, including 12 vowels. It is usually written phonetically in German pronunciation as follows :	when accented, as in father ; unaccented, as in bat ; at the beginning, as *ya* in yacht ; if unaccented, as in yank.	this letter resembling our *f* is pronounced *v*, as in vane, or *f*, as in foe ; the equivalent of our *b* sounds as *b* or *p* in bet or trap.	as in cent or zone ; *ch* German *ch* at the end the beginning, as in *ch*
SPANISH : a language of ideal regularity and precision ; all vowels are separately pronounced.	as in father or in hat ; *â* as in father.	like *v* in very.	before *e* or *i*, as *th* in thi otherwise as *k* ; *ch* as church ; *cu* as *qu* in qu
SWEDISH :	as in father or in mica ; *â* as *o* in go, when long ; when short, as *a* in what ; *ä* as in hare.	as in bob.	before *e*, *i* or *y*, as in ce otherwise as in cash ; = *k*, except in fore words.
WELSH : all vowel combinations are separately pronounced ; the letter w = oo in moon.	as in fat ; *â* as in dare.	as in bob.	always like *k* ; *ch* = G man *ch*, see Note 3.

888

D	E	F	G
in deed ; dh as th in these : dj as in adjoin.	ē as in bean ; ĕ as in pet—at the end of words almost like ŭ.	as in fife.	as in gig.
t like Italian d.	as in prey ; ĕ as in pet.	as in fife.	as in gig.
in deed. For d', dĕ and 'i, see Note 4.	as in pet ; ė as in ere ; ĕ = ya, as in beatitude. See also Note 4.	as in fife.	as in gig.
ginning a syllable as in date ; ending as th in bathe ; after l, n, and r, silent ; ds = ss in hiss.	as in prey and there ; ej like i in bite.	as in fife.	as in gig ; after e or ö like'y in yoke ; between vowels often mute.
the beginning of syllables as in date ; at the end as 'in hot.	when short as in met ; when open as in prey ; ee simply prolongs the sound ; see also eu.	as in fife ; fl as in flow ; fr as in fresh.	like German g ; ng as in looking.
German d and dt.	e or ė as in pet ; eu like French eu; e after a vowel usually simply prolongs it ; ee = a in fate or as in seen ; see eu.	as in fife.	as German g, very guttural.
the beginning or in the middle as d in deadlock ; usually silent at the end of the word ; in liaison it becomes t.	as e in father or u in cut ; as a final syllable generally silent ; é as in prey when it has stress, otherwise as in pet ; è as ai in fair ; ê as in pet ; see ei, d, s, t, z, r.	as in fife, not silent at the ends of words, except in clef ; in liaison it becomes v.	as in gate except before e, i and y, then as s in pleasure (marked here as zh) ; silent when final, becoming k in liaison ; gn as ni in minion.
ginning a syllable as in date ; ending a syllable as in hat ; dt = t in hat.	when long as in prey ; when short as in pet ; ei = i in right ; see eu.	as in fife.	at the beginning of a syllable as in gate, but softer ; at the end, see Note 3 ; ng when final vanishes in a faint k sound as sang = zangk.
in deed ; dj same as 'gy ; djs = j in judge.	before m or a sharp consonant as in fat ; otherwise as e in ten ; é as in prey.	as in fife.	as in gig ; gy = d in due (not doo) ; ggy = gygy or d' d'.
in deed, but softer and more palatal.	as in prey when long ; when short as in pet ; è as in pet.	as in fife.	before e and i as in gem ; gg as dj in adjoin ; gli = ly' like ll in million, gn = ny' or ni in pinion : gu = gw ; gui = wē.
in deed.	as in prey ; but when final as e in father.	as in fife.	as in gig, but before j and y as y in yoke.
in deed ; dz as in adze ; dž as, dge in judge.	e as in met ; ę = French in, see Note 1 ; é = a as in pate.	as in fife.	as in gig.
in deed.	e and é usually as in prey ; ē has a curious closed sound.	'as in fife.	as in gate ; but before e, i and y as in gem.
in deed.	at the beginning of words = yo in yolk if accented ; if unaccented as ye in yesterday ; otherwise as e in pet.	usually represented by the German v or w.	at the beginning usually as in go ; sometimes at the beginning, always at the end as German ch ; see Note 2.
uch like th in those (marked in this book by dh) ; when two ds occur in a word, only the second has this sound, the first as in date.	as in prey when long ; when short as in pet ; é as in prey or pet.	as in fife.	as in gate ; but before e and i, as a very harsh h in hate ; gue = ga as in gate ; gui = ge as in gear ; gn as in ignite ; gl as in glow.
in deed, but silent in ndn and nds and before j or t.	as in film when long ; when short as in pet ; er as ar in bare.	as in fit at the beginning of syllables or after a short vowel ; at end of syllable like v in slave ; before v silent.	as in gate ; before d, e, i, ö, y and after l and r, like y in yoke ; silent before j ; gn = ng in sing.
in date ; dd as th in these.	as in pet ; ē as in bean.	like v in revive ; ff like f in off.	as in gate ; ng as in wrong.

Phonetic meaning of the letters and symbols AS USED IN THIS BOOK.	**H** as in hate.	**I** ī as in fight ; ĭ as in pin.	**J** as in jug.	**K** as in kick ; kh = German ch or g; Note 3.
ARABIAN :	strongly aspirated at end or beginning of a word.	as in pin ; i as in bird.	as in jug.	strongly guttural.
BOHEMIAN :	as in hate.	as in pin ; í as in machine.	like y in yes; after vowels it prolongs their sounds somewhat as y in day, whey, etc.	as in kick.
DANISH :	as in hate but silent before j and v.	as in machine ; after a, e, o, ö, and u like y in yoke.	even with vowels aj, ej, like y in yoke.	as in kick.
DUTCH :	as in hate.	when short as in pin ; when open as e in rely ; ie prolongs the open sound only before r, otherwise as e in rely ; ij same as ei.	as y in yoke.	as in kick ; ks = x fix ; kw = qu quart.
FLEMISH :	as in hate.	i or í as in pin ; ü or ie the same prolonged ; ieu sounds like ē-ü.	as y in yoke.	as in kick ; ks = x in
FRENCH :	always silent.	as in pin, see ei, oi ; í as i in machine, but see ai.	as s in measure (marked in this book as zh).	as in kick.
GERMAN :	as in hate.	as in machine ; ie as in believe.	as y in yoke.	as in kick.
HUNGARIAN :	as in hate.	as the quick e in rely ; í as in machine.	as y in yoke ; jj as y in paying.	as in kick.
ITALIAN :	silent ; after c or g it has simply a hardening effect.	as in machine, but when short as in pin ; at the beginning of words like y in yoke.	same as i ; at the beginning of words like y in yoke ; as a vowel like i in machine.	....
NORWEGIAN :	as in hate.	as in machine ; at the beginning as y in yoke.	as in yoke.	as in kick ; before i a y like h ; kv = qu quarter.
POLISH :	as in hate ; see c, l and n.	i as in machine ; after a consonant it has the effect of the imaginary y in due (not doo) ; iu = u in gun.	as y in yoke.	as in kick.
PORTUGUESE :	silent.	as in machine.	as in jug.	only in foreign words, in kick.
RUSSIAN :	used only in a few native words, and in foreign derivations.	as in machine, but well back in the throat ; after labials (b, f, m, p and v) as i in pin.	as y in yet.	as in kick ; before k and ch softly as German ch.
SPANISH :	usually silent or very slight ; see c.	as in machine when long ; when short as in pin ; í as in machine.	as a very harsh h in hate ; almost like German ch.	....
SWEDISH :	as in hate ; silent before j or v.	as in machine.	as y in yoke.	as in kick but before e, i, ö and y in the same syllable like c
WELSH :	as in hate.	as in machine.	....	as in kick.

890

L	M	N	O	P
as in lull.	as in mum.	as in nun; ñ, see Note 1.	ŏ as in note; oi as in noise; oo as in moon or foot; ô as in wrong; ow as in cow; ôñ, see Note 1.	as in pop.
a lull.	as in mum.	as in nun.	as in note; ö = German ö, see Note 2.	as in pop.
a lull.	as in mum.	as in nun; ñ as in cañon.	as in note; ô as in wrong.	as in pop.
a lull.	as in mum.	as in nun.	when open as in bother; when closed as in move; φ = French eu closed as in peu; ö = the same open as in coeur; see Note 2.	as in pop.
a lull, but when followed by another consonant a short e interpolated, as if k were spelt elek.	as in mum.	as in nun.	as in bother when short, when long as in over; oo = o in over; ooi = o in over followed by i in pin; see oe.	as in pop; ph = f.
a lull.	as in mum.	as in nun.	o as in note or not; oo or oe usually the same prolonged, sometimes like wa in was, oei or oey as ō-ē.	as in pop.
a lily, t sometimes l called "l mouillé") liquid, as y in yoke or paying.	at the beginning, as in mate. See Note 1.	at the beginning, as in name. See Note 1.	as in not; often almost as ŭ in nut; ô as in note; see oi.	at the beginning and middle, as in paper; pui = almost pwe; ph = f; silent when final.
a lull.	as in mum.	as in nun.	as in wrong; ö see Note 2; ô is sometimes spelled oe.	as in pop.
a late; ll or ly = y a paying.	as in mum.	as in nun; ny = n as in new (not noo); nny = nyny, or n' n'.	o as in note; ô is prolonged as in slow; ö = French eu; ö or ô = German long ô.	as in pop.
a lull; see g.	as in mum.	as in nun; see g.	as in note; ô as in wrong.	as in pop.
a lull.	as in mum.	as in nun.	as u in full, but often as o in note or not; oe = a in sale; ö like French eu long or short.	as in pop.
a lull; t is sounded by closing the teeth on the tip of the tongue as l is pronounced.	as in mum.	as in nun.	o as in note; ô is between note and move.	as in pop.
a lull; lh like lli in million.	as in meet, but at end of syllables or after e, like French nasal n. See Note 1.	as in note; but at end of syllables or after e, like French nasal n, see Note 1; nh = ni in minion.	as in note or in not; ô see Note 5.	as in pop; ph = f.
a lull; before a or o, s ll in collar.	as in mum.	as in nun.	as in not.	as in pop.
a look; ll like lli in billiards.	as in mum.	as in nun; ñ divides into ny as ni in minion, thus cañon = canyon.	when long as in note; when short o as in not; ô as in note.	as in pop; silent before s. n and t.
in lull: but usually silent before j.	as in mum.	as in nun; gn = ng in sing.	as in move or not, according to complex rules; ö = German ô.	as in pop.
n look; ll has a curious mingling of th and l	as in mum.	as in nun.	as in gone: ô as in bone; the sound oo is represented by w.	as in pop; ph = f.

Phonetic meaning of the letters and symbols AS USED IN THIS BOOK.	Q	R as in roar.	S as in sense.	T as in tot ; *th* as in think.
ARABIAN :	....	as in roar.	as in sis ; *ss* strongly hissed ; *sh* as in show.	strongly palatal.
BOHEMIAN :	as *qu* in quart.	as in roar ; ř = *rzh* or *rsh* as in "for sure," thus Dvořák is dvôr-zhäk.	*s* as in sis ; š as *sh* in show.	as in tot ; see also Note 4.
DANISH :	*qv* = *qu* in quart.	as in roar.	as in sense ; *ski* or *sky* as in skim.	as in tot.
DUTCH :	*qu* as in quart.	as in hurry.	sharply as in sense ; *sj* = *sh* in show ; see *sch*.	after a hard vowel it is soft in note, otherwise as in
FLEMISH :	*qu* as in quart.	as in roar.	as in suppose.	as in tot ; *dt* as *t* in hat.
FRENCH :	*qu* always as *k* in kick ; *cq* as *k*.	commonly rolled on the back of the tongue ; in Paris almost like *w* in bower ; as a final letter it is sounded except after *e* ; *er* = *a* in sale.	as in suppose ; when final it is silent except in proper names ; in liaison it becomes *z*.	as *t* in tub ; like *s* in such fixes as -tion ; almost ways silent when final = *a* in sale.
GERMAN :	*qu* as *kv* ; thus q u a r t = k'värt.	usually rolled and always strongly sounded.	beginning a syllable before a vowel usually as *z* in zone ; as the end of a syllable as in this ; *sp* and *st* = *shp* and *sht*; *sch* = *sh*.	as in tot ; *th* = *t* in hat.
HUNGARIAN :	....	always trilled.	as *sh* in show ; *sz* = *sh*.	as in tot , *ty* strongly as tube ; *tty* = *ty' ty'* or *t' ts* = *ch*.
ITALIAN :	*qu* as in quart.	usually trilled.	as in suppose ; *sce* = *shā* ; *sci* = *shē* ; *sch* = *sk*.	as in tot ; *ti* usually = *tsi*
NORWEGIAN :	*qu* as in quart.	as in hurry.	as in sis ; *ski* = *sh* in show.	as in tot
POLISH :	....	as in roar *rz* = French *j* or *s* in measure.	as in sense ; *sz* = *sh* in show.	as in tot.
PORTUGUESE :	*qua* as in quart ; before *e* or *i*, *qu* is like *k*.	as in roar and hurry.	as in suppose ; having the *z* sound between vowels.	as in tot.
RUSSIAN :	....	with a burr as *rr* in worry.	as in sense ; *sh* as in show ; *ski* = *shk* ; *sz* = *sh*.	as in tot ; *ts* beginning or e ing as in hats ; *tsch* as *sh* in wa*sht-ch*urn.
SPANISH ·	*qu* as *k* in kick.	as in roar.	as in sense.	as in tot.
SWEDISH :	*qv* = *k* in kin.	as in hurry.	as in sense ; *sk*, *sj*, and *stj* all = *sh* in show.	as in tot ; *tj* = *ch* in chur but if followed by *a* or *e* *ts* in hats ; *th* = *t* in tot.
WELSH :	....	as in roar.	as in sense.	as in tot ; *th* as in think.

U	V	W	X	Y
ways with the sound of ou ; *ŭ*, see Note 2.	as in revive.	as in will.	as in fix.	as in yoke.
n full.	as in revive.	as in will.	....	as in why.
n full; *ŭ* or *ŭ*, as in rule.	as in revive.	as in will ; *w* is silent before *z* and another consonant, as *wzd*.	as in fix.	as *ĭ* in pin; *ý* as *ĭ* in machine.
n rule or full.	as in revive ; silent after *l* and *r*.	only in foreign words.	as in xebec.	like *u* in fur.
en short, as in cut ; when ug, as in rule ; *uu* as *oo* n moon.	at the beginning, as in vote ; at the end, as *f* in off.	as in will.	as in fix.	as in why.
a short German *ŭ*, see ote 2 ; *uu* or *ue*, the ame prolonged ; see *ui*. Note 2.	as in revive.	as in will.	as in fix.	like *i* in machine ; sometimes nasal like French *in*, see Note 1 ; see *ai*.
	as in revive.	in foreign words only, and sounded like *v* in vote ; *wh* sounded as *w* in was.	as in fix or exile ; silent when final ; becoming *z* in liaison.	when alone or when a consonant precedes or follows it, as *e* in bean. When it lies between two vowels it may be said to be divided into two sounds. After an *a* or *e* it is sounded like *ĕ* in pet followed by *y* in yoke (thus rayon becomes ré-yôn) ; with an *o* it sounds like *wă* in was followed by *y*, as in yoke (thus joyeux becomes zhwä-yŭ) ; with *u* it becomes *ē* — *y'* (thus appuyant becomes ăp-pwē-yän).
oo in moon or foot ; *ŭ* sometimes spelled *ue*), ee Note 2.	like *f* in fife.	like *v* in revive, but with a soft trace also of the *w* in was.	as in fix, even at the beginning of a syllable.	as *e* in bean, sometimes like *ŭ* ; see Note 2.
s in pull ; *ŭ* as in rule ; *ŭ* = French *u* ; *ŭ* or *ŭ* the ame prolonged.	as in revive.	....	....	see *g, l, n* and *t*.
in rule ; *ŭ* as in full.	as in revive.	....	....	....
in rule.	as in revive ; *kv* = *qu* in quart.	....	as in fix.	like French *u*.
in rule ; preceded by *i* it s the French *u*.	....	as *v* in revive.	as in fix.	*yj* = *e* in bean.
in rule ; *ŭ*, see Note 5.	as in revive.	....	after *e*, as in vex ; otherwise as *sh* in show.	as *i* in machine.
in due, or as *oo* in moon ; xcept in words of French r German origin. then as French *u*.	as *f* in far or off.	as *f* in far or off.	....	same as Russian *i*.
in rule, when long ; when hort, as in full ; *ŭ* as in ule or full ; *ue* = *wa* in wait.	as in revive.	....	as in fix ; even at the beginning ; in some proper names as *h* in hate.	as *i* in machine.
in rule ; or in full.	as in revive.	like *v* in revive.	....	like French *u* ; see Note 2.
little broader than *i* in this ; *ŭ* = *ee* in seen.	....	sounded like *oo* in moon.	....	as *u* in turn ; at the end of a syllable as in pretty.

Phonetic meaning of the letters and symbols AS USED IN THIS BOOK.	Z as in zone and buzz.	Æ	AI	AU	EUA
ARABIAN :	as in zone.	....	....	....	....
BOHEMIAN :	as in zone ; ž as in azure.	....	....	....	....
DANISH :	only in foreign words, then like s in sis.	like ai both in sail and in said.	like i in bite.	as ow in cow.	....
DUTCH :	as in zone.	....	aai combines a in father with a quick e in meet, almost like y in why.	combines a in fat with oo in moon ; sharper than ow in cow.	....
FLEMISH :	as in zone ; often used interchangeable with s.	same as aa = a prolonged ; aei or aey = ai prolonged.	ai and ay as ai in said ; aei or aey the same prolonged.	....	....
FRENCH :	as in zone.	....	ai, at, ay as e in pet.	as o in zone.	as o in zone
GERMAN :	like ts in hats, even at the beginning of a syllable.	only another spelling of ä. See Note 2.	like i in bite.	as ow in cow ; äu almost like i in bite (actually ah—ē).	....
HUNGARIAN :	as in zone ; ss, see d.	....	....	....	....
ITALIAN :	z as ts in hats ; zz as ds in Windsor.	in vowel combinations the vowels are always separately pronounced in Italian.	....	....	....
NORWEGIAN :	like ts in hats.	....	....	like o in note.	....
POLISH :	as in zone ; ż as s in measure ; zg = g preceded by a buzz.	....	....	....	....
PORTUGUESE :	as in zone ; but at the end of syllables like s in this.	....	....	....	....
RUSSIAN :	as German z = ts ; or as French z = g in menagerie.	same	as	German	diphthongs.
SPANISH :	as th in think.	....	....	....	....
SWEDISH :	like s in sis.	....	....	....	....
WELSH :	....	....	....	....	....

EI	EU	IE	OE	OI as in noise.	OU
....	....	....	....	....	....
....	....	....	....	....	....
....	....	....	....	....	....
bines e in met ith i in pin; the suffix eid = a in te.	same as German short ŏ, see Note 2; eeu = a in fate, with a whispered v after it.	see i; ieu = a in fate, with a soft w after it.	same as oo in moon; oei = oo followed by a short ĭ.	....	combines o in not with u in rule; softer than, but often confused with, au.
....	same as French eu; eeu the same prolonged.	....	as oo in moon; sometimes a simple prolonged ō; or like wa in was; oei or oey = we.	....	....
in pet.	like e in father when short; when long, the same sound prolonged; it lies between e in pet and u in cut, and resembles German ŏ. See Note 2.	....	oe = wa in was; oeu like eu.	oi or oy = wa in was; oin = w followed by the nasal in. See Note 1.	ou = oo in boot; see oi and Note 1.
i in bite.	almost like i in bite with a hint of oi in noise.	as in believe.	only another spelling of ŏ. See Note 2.	....	....
....	....	....	....	....	....
....	....	....	....	....	....
....	....	....	like a in sale.	....	....
....	....	....	....	....	....
....	....	....	....	....	almost as o in note.
ne	as	the	German	diph-	thongs.
....	....	....	....	....	....
....	....	....	....	....	....
....	....	....	....	....	....

Phonetic meaning of the letters and symbols AS USED IN THIS BOOK.	UE	UI	CH as in church ; German *ch* is represented by *kh*, see Note 3.	SCH	SP
ARABIAN :	....	....	like German *ch*.	....	....
BOHEMIAN :	....	....	....	....	....
DANISH :	....	....	as *k*, except in foreign words.	....	....
DUTCH :	....	almost *y* in why; but verging on the French *eu*.	like German *ch*, but more palatal at the beginning of foreign words ; as *sh* in show.	beginning a syllable, as *stch* ; at the end, as simple *s* in this.	as in span.
FLEMISH :	same as a prolonged *u*.	*ui* and *uy* like German *eu*.	like German *ch*. See Note 3.	....	....
FRENCH :	*uei* like *eu*.	....	as *sh* before a vowel ; before a consonant as *k*.	....	....
GERMAN :	only another spelling of *ü*. See Note 2.	....	see Note 3.	like *sh* in show.	like *shp* in d pan.
HUNGARIAN :	....	....	....	....	....
ITALIAN :	....	....	as *k* in kin.	as *sk* in skip.	as in span.
NORWEGIAN :	....	....	....	....	....
POLISH :	....	....	like German *ch*, see Note 3.	....	....
PORTUGUESE :	....	....	....	....	....
RUSSIAN :	....	....	....	....	....
SPANISH :	....	....	as in church.	....	....
SWEDISH :	....	....	....	....	....
WELSH .	....	....	like German *ch*, see Note 3.	....	....

ST	TH
	as in thing ; the *th* in those is represented by *dh*.

....	....
....	....
1 stone.	....
....	....
....	....
sht in ashtub.	like *t* in tot.
....	....
n stone.	....
....	....
....	....
....	....
....	....
....	like *t* in tot.
....	....

No. 1.—The French nasal sounds are easily obtained :
(1) Though spelled with an *m* or *n* (and indicated in this book by an *ñ*) they have really no *n* sound in them, much less the *ng* sound that some foreigners give them. Though variously spelled they are reducible to four vowel sounds pronounced, as we say, "through the nose," though actually with closed nasal passages. If one will pronounce or rather snort the word "wrong" without producing the final *g* at all, one will have exactly the French *on* (1) ; the word "thank" similarly sounded without the *k* will give the French *in* (2) ; the word "trunk" without the *k* gives the French *un* (3) ; the word "donkey" (not pronounced like monkey) contains the French *en* (4). These four are indicated in this book by (1) *ŏñ* ; (2) *ăñ* ; (3) *ŭñ* ; (4) *ăñ*.

The French nasals may be grouped as follows : Those pronounced like (1) are *om, on,* and *eon* after *g ;* like (2) *im, in, aim, ain, ein* and also *en* as an ending ; like (3) *ŭm, un* and *evn ;* like (4) *am, an, ean, aen, aon* and *en* at the beginning of words.

These letters *m* and *n,* however, lose their nasal quality when doubled or when preceding a vowel ; *onne* is pronounced as *one* in done, *ome* or *omme* as in come, *eme* as in *em* in them, etc.

No. 2.—French *u* (which is the same as the German *ü* when long) is easily pronounced if one will pucker his lips to say *oo,* as in moon ; and keeping them strongly puckered, say *e* as in bean. Those who have eaten green persimmons, or had their lips distended with peach fuzz, have the correct position for this *e* sound. There is really no *oo* sound in the French *u* at all, and if one cannot say the *u* correctly he will come much nearer the truth if he uses a plain English long *e,* as in bean, rather than the sound of *u,* as the spelling might suggest.

The German *ü* when short is formed by keeping the lips puckered and saying *i* as in fit, instead of *e* in serene.

The other German modified (or umlauted) vowels are (2) *ä,* pronounced, when long, almost like *a* in sale, but verging on *a* in care (it is marked here simply as *ā*) ; when short much like *e* in pet ; (3) *ö* when long can be secured by puckering the lips for a round, full *o,* as in note and then saying *a* as in sale (it is marked in this book simply as *ā* to avoid the danger of saying a plain *o*) ; when it is short the lips should be puckered for the round *o,* and a short *e* as in pet then pronounced. The caution must be emphasised that in the experiments the lips must be firmly kept in the first, or puckered position, in spite of the temptation to alter it.

No. 3.—German *ch* is not difficult, once caught. Our sound *th* as in think will be found if prolonged to be produced by the simple device of holding the tip of the tongue lightly between the teeth and then breathing. The German *ch* results from pressing the two sides of the tongue firmly against the bicuspid teeth (the two upper teeth on each side back of the canine or eye teeth) and leaving the tip of the tongue free, then breathing the necessary vowel as in *ach, ich,* etc. German *g* is much the same but even softer. Both are indicated in this book by *kh.*

No. 4.—Certain Bohemian letters and combinations insert the sound *y* closely allied to a consonant, as in the French *diable* and *tien,* or the English "How d' ye do?" or "I've caught*ye.*" Bohemian *d, n* and *t* are given this *d'y* and *t'y* sound when followed by *ĕ* or *i* or by an apostrophe as *d', ñ* or *t'.*

Many Bohemian combinations of consonants seem unspeakable because they are spelt with no vowels between. They are no harder to say, however, than such words of ours as "twelfths." Among such consonant chains are *drn, kb, kd, krl, prst, skrz, sr, wl* and *zr.* They must be run together as smoothly as possible.

No. 5.—Portuguese diphthongs are of three sorts ; the first two cannot be distinguished here, they are simply combinations of vowels (sometimes of three vowels or triphthongs) in which each vowel is sounded independently ; in the first class the first vowel takes the accent, in the second class the second vowel is accented. The third class contains a nasal vowel marked *ã, õ* or *ũ,* and pronounced with a strong nasal twang.

No. 6.—In vowel combinations other than those specially mentioned here, the vowels are pronounced separately, each in its own way.

No. 7.—Combinations of consonants other than those mentioned here will be found under their first letter.

No. 8.—As Greek and Latin pronunciations are matters of controversy and personal taste, no system is attempted here. Chinese, Japanese, Hebrew, Hindu, and various other languages are usually spelled phonetically, but on such different national or personal standards that they can hardly be generalised.

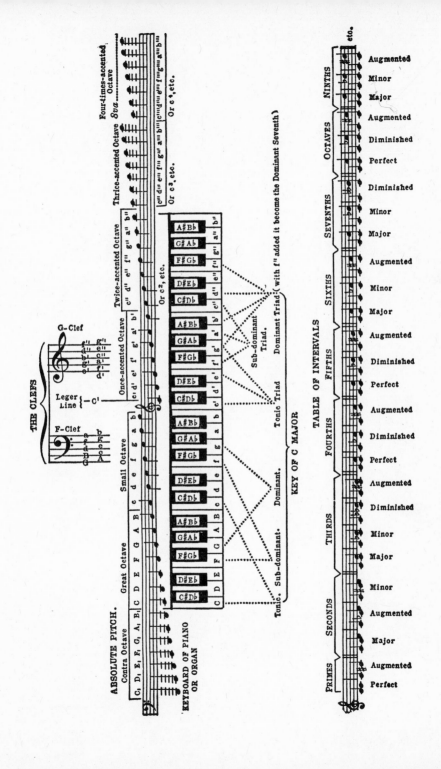

ere by all continuous lines.

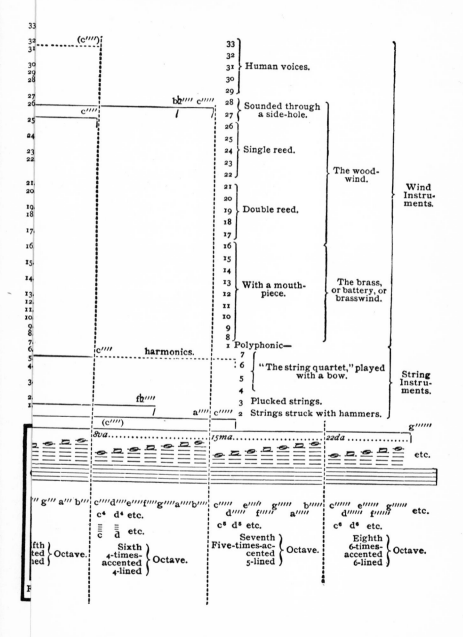